# Photoshop Web Magic, Volume 1

MW01013175

Stanger
Stet · Fortuna · Domus

# Photoshop Web Magic, Volume 1

Ted Schulman, Renée LeWinter,
and Tom Emmanuelides

Hayden
Books

## Photoshop Web Magic, Volume 1

©1996 Ted Schulman and Renée LeWinter

All rights reserved. Printed in the United States of America. No part of this book may be used or reproduced in any form or by any means, or stored in a database or retrieval system, without prior written permission of the publisher except in the case of brief quotations embodied in critical articles and reviews. Making copies of any part of this book for any purpose other than your own personal use is a violation of United States copyright laws. For information, address Hayden Books, 201 W. 103rd Street, Indianapolis, Indiana 46290.

Library of Congress Catalog Number: 96-77851
ISBN: 1-56830-314-9

Copyright © 1996 Hayden Books

Printed in the United States of America 3 4 5 6 7 8 9 0

## Warning and Disclaimer

This book is sold as is, without warranty of any kind, either express or implied. While every precaution has been taken in the preparation of this book, the authors and Hayden Books assume no responsibility for errors or omissions. Neither is any liability assumed for damages resulting from the use of the information or instructions contained herein. It is further stated that the publisher and authors are not responsible for any damage or loss to your data or your equipment that results directly or indirectly from your use of this book.

# The Photoshop Web Magic Team

**Publisher**
Jordan Gold

**Executive Editor**
Beth Millett

**Copy/Production Editor**
Kevin Laseau

**Technical Editor**
Susan Aronoff

**Cover Designer**
Karen Ruggles

**Book Designers**
Renée LeWinter
Gary Adair

**Production Team Supervisors**
Laurie Casey, Joe Millay, Gina Rexrode

**Production Team**
Trina Brown, Daniel Caparo, Maureen Hanrahan, Aleata Howard, Linda Knose, Christopher Morris, Scott Tullis, Megan Wade, Pamela Woolf

Composed in *Goudy* and *Syntax*
Some thumbtab imagery provided by CMCD, Digital Stock, D'Pix, FotoSets, Image Club Graphics, and PhotoDisc, 1995.

# About the Authors

Ted Schulman has 20 plus years of experience as an award-winning producer, director, and developer of over 250 multi-media, video, and film projects. His clients have included leading Fortune 500 companies.

Since 1992, Ted has combined his background in social anthropology with Internet development. He focuses on the creation of community-based Web sites to help bring advanced communications to underserved communities.

Ted can be found on the Web at TSPI.com (email address ts@tspi).

Renée LeWinter is an artist, print, and multimedia designer and computer imaging consultant. For more than 20 years she has worked with software developers to foster the evolution of the digital studio.

Renée's articles have appeared in leading trade publications where she writes about the creative style, business, and technology trends that impact artists and designers.

Renée is represented on the World Wide Web by the 911 Gallery `http://www.911Gallery.org/911/`.

Tom Emmanuelides founded THAT Agency, an interactive new media company, where for the last 7 years he has served as president and creative director.

Based in New York City, Tom has applied his multidisciplinary skills to interface design, programming interactive titles, and advanced multimedia Web development. Tom also does consulting for local and international companies addressing the Internet market.

Tom can be reached at THATAGENCY.com.

# Trademark Acknowledgments

All terms mentioned in this book that are known to be trademarks or services marks have been appropriately capitalized. Hayden Books cannot attest to the accuracy of this information. Use of a term in this book should not be regarded as affecting the validity of any trademark or service mark. Apple, Mac, Macintosh, and Power Macintosh are registered trademarks and Apple Script is a trademark of Apple Computer, Inc. Microsoft and Windows are registered trademarks and Windows NT is a trademark of Microsoft Corporation in the USA and other countries.

# Dedication

*For Meril, Julia, and Peter for their support and patience—Ted*

*For my mother—Renée*

*My Mother and Father, in memory of Richard L. Heinrich, Viola S. Goodsir and Mark M. Monolides—Tom*

# Acknowledgments

**Special Contributors**

Carrie Notte

Robert Desbiens

**Special Thanks to:**

Cynthia Baron, Robert DeBenedictis, Betty Gerisch, Laurence LeWinter, Douglas Mitchell, Michael Nolan, Chris Schiavo, Marian Schiavo and Greg Simsic

We would like to thank our team at Hayden Books—Melanie Rigney, Beth Millett, Kevin Laseau, Susan Aronoff, and the Macmillan design group.

# Hayden Books

The staff of Hayden Books is committed to bringing you the best computer books. What our readers think of Hayden is important to our ability to serve our customers. If you have any comments, no matter how great or how small, we'd appreciate your taking the time to send us a note.

You can reach Hayden Books at the following:

Macmillan Computer Publishing
Web Design and Graphics
201 West 103rd Street
Indianapolis, IN 46290
317-581-3833

Visit our Web site at `http://www.mcp.com`

# Contents at a Glance

# Contents

# Introduction

Photoshop has become an indispensable tool for Web page design. Search through the Web and in site after site, there are examples of dynamic Web graphics created with Photoshop.

*Photoshop Web Magic, Volume 1* presents easy to use recipes for creating those Web page graphics. Use the colorful thumbtabs to browse through the book to find techniques, hints, and tips for designing custom backgrounds, buttons, titles, menus bars, rules, icons, and animations that can enhance and improve your Web site.

Whether you are a designer or a programmer, interested in creating Web pages for your business or for personal expression, *Photoshop Web Magic, Volume 1* shows you how to add a professional flair to your Web site. Don't forget to check out Appendix A, where we have included some of our favorite bookmarks locating design resources and downloadable shareware graphics collections.

Hope to see you on the Web!

Ted Schulman

Renée LeWinter

Tom Emmanuelides

# Before You Start

## Welcome

This book was not meant to be an introductory guide to Photoshop or the World Wide Web. Even if you are new to Photoshop or the Web, you will still be able to find lots of useful information. Regardless of your level of experience, this book will help you to build dynamic Web graphics with easy-to-follow instructions. If you possess a general understanding of Photoshop but may need the occasional reminder, Photoshop Basics will help refresh your memory on fundamental tasks without slowing you down.

## System Setup

Adobe recommends 32MB of RAM for Power Macintosh and Windows 3.1, Windows 95, or Windows NT. If you are running a 68030-based Macintosh, Adobe recommends 24MB of RAM, but we suggest that you add extra memory if you can afford it. The new Photoshop 4.0 filters and other third-party software will push your system to its limits. If you plan to do Web design and development professionally, then consider this yardstick. You will be using your system software + Photoshop + HTML editor + word processor + Web navigator + fonts + email +... all open at the same time. Add all these together and you will have a barometer of your memory needs.

Photoshop 4.0 is shipping exclusively on CD-ROM, so it is important that you have a CD-ROM drive. Have lots of storage and consider purchasing at least a two gigabyte hard drive and an alternative external removable drive for back-up. You will be building a large library of pictures and graphics.

We also recommend using Photoshop 4.0 or later because we used many of the new 4.0 features such as the Actions palette to write this book. If you are still working with 3.05 or an earlier version, check out the Photoshop Basics section before using this book. Adobe made changes in the Photoshop 4.0 interface including the toolbar and we followed the new interface in our instructions. Keep in mind that if you are duplicating our examples with an earlier version of Photoshop, your results may not exactly match ours.



## Adobe Photoshop 4.0

Adobe Photoshop 4.0 for Apple Macintosh and Microsoft Windows platforms introduced several key new features. These include the Actions palette; Adjustment Layers; Free Transform; a new Navigator palette; Guides and Grids; 48 artistic filters, and custom, multicolor Gradients. Also of particular interest to Web designers are the following new features.

**Copyright Protection** Adobe introduces digital watermarking, using Imagemarc software developed by Digimarc Corporation. This feature enables creative professionals who plan to post their images on the Web, to protect the copyright by embedding an imperceptible, digital watermark in each image. This watermark, not apparent to the human eye, is still readable even after an image has been edited, or printed and rescanned. Adobe Photoshop will recognize the watermarked file when it is opened and will verify that the image is held under copyright.

**New Web File Formats** Adobe Photoshop 4.0 introduces support for three new Web file formats.

- Portable Network Graphics (PNG)—A new RGB file format
- Progressive JPEG—Including new user controls over JPEG settings
- Portable Document Format (PDF)—The Adobe Acrobat format

These new formats are in addition to version 3.0 support for transparent, interlaced GIF files with the GIF 89a plug-in. These new formats are explained in detail in the Adobe manual and at the Adobe Web site.

**Web Access to Adobe** Remember to check out Adobe's Web site on the World Wide Web. Their address is `http://www.adobe.com`. The site is updated frequently, and we find it useful for locating information about Adobe products, user groups, and software demos and updates. Abode also provides a calendar of special events and conferences that they sponsor.

## Conventions



### Resolution and Color

To create graphics in Photoshop for the Web you will want to work in RGB mode and set the file resolution to 72 dpi. Unless otherwise noted all files were created with white backgrounds as a default setting. Because we had to prepare our examples for printing on paper, we set our file resolution to 150 dpi for the variations and 300 dpi for the thumbtabs. Our colors may not match exactly what you are seeing on-screen since we converted our RGB files to CMYK. Our colors are noted in the book in RGB (0, 0, 0).

### File Size and Download Times

The smaller the file size the faster the download time. Remember that one Web page may contain several graphic elements and each must download before your Web page is completed. Also, do not assume that Web surfers have fast modems. The average Web surfer is still using a 14.4 modem and not the faster 28.8. If you can manage, make your files 30K or smaller and take advantage of Netscape's and Microsoft's support of layering in their browsers. Layering enables you to build more complex graphics by overlapping several graphic files on top of each other when you download a page. This way you can avoid blank screens.

The Adobe Photoshop 4.0 manual has a detailed chapter on Saving and Exporting Images. Check out our bookmarks list in Appendix A for online resources for finding the most up-to-date information. The Web is a perpetually moving target where technical specifications are concerned. Microsoft, Netscape, and other browser developers are continuing to update and change their software. Look for more Java applets and third-party plug-ins for animation, video, and sound.

## The Toolbox

Occasionally in this book we have used a third-party filter or a specially prepared preset file. Any of these extra tools that are not included standard with Photoshop 4.0 are listed in the Toolbox in the lower-left corner of the first page of each technique. The Toolbox lists everything you'll need to create each effect and any of its variations. The CD-ROM that comes with this book contains all of the files needed to perform all of the basic techniques. For information on accessing these files, turn to Appendix C, "What's on the CD-ROM."

## The Steps

**The Blue Type** As you work through the steps you will see phrases that are colored a light blue. The same phrases are listed in alphabetical order in the Photoshop Basics section. If the phrase in blue asks you to perform a task that you are unfamiliar with, then you can find that phrase in the Photoshop Basics section, followed by instructions on how to perform that task. Advanced users may simply perform the task as normal.

**Menu Commands** You will also see instructions that look like this:

Filter→Blur→Gaussian Blur (2 pixels)

This example asks you to apply the Gaussian Blur filter. To perform this command, click the Filter menu at the top of the screen and drag down to Blur. When Blur is highlighted, a new menu will open to the right from which you can choose Gaussian Blur.

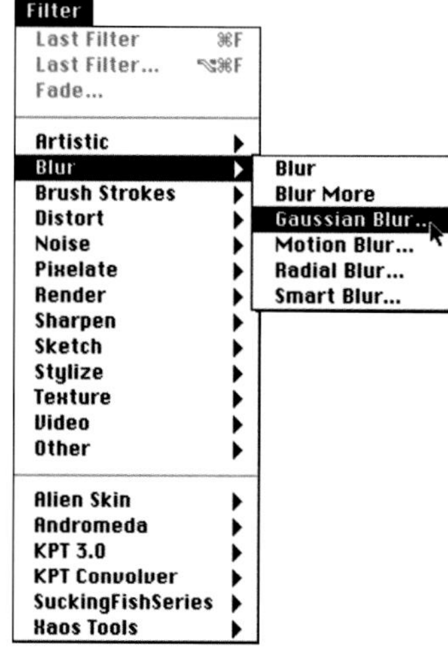


In this example, a dialog box appears that asks you for more information. All of the settings needed to perform each task appear in the text of the instruction step. The example above is telling you to enter 2 pixels as the Radius.

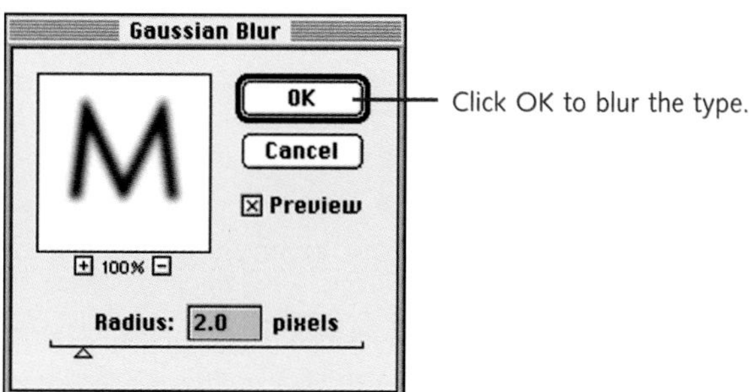


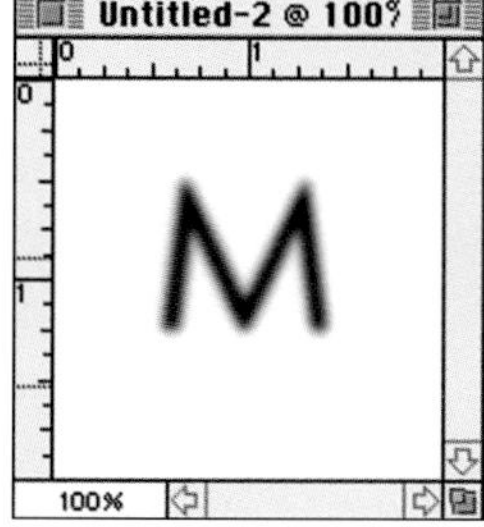


**Settings** Following each action in the steps are settings for you to use with that feature. These settings are meant to act as guides; the best settings for your Web graphic may vary. For starters, begin with the settings that you see in the figures as you proceed through the technique. Although we tried to use settings that would work for 72 dpi screen resolution, we were constrained by the needs of print reproduction. As a rule of thumb, if it looks good on your monitor it will probably work. If you do need to adjust your monitor, set your settings lower. The following two images demonstrate the importance of adjusting for resolution differences. A 5-pixel Radius Gaussian Blur was applied to both images.

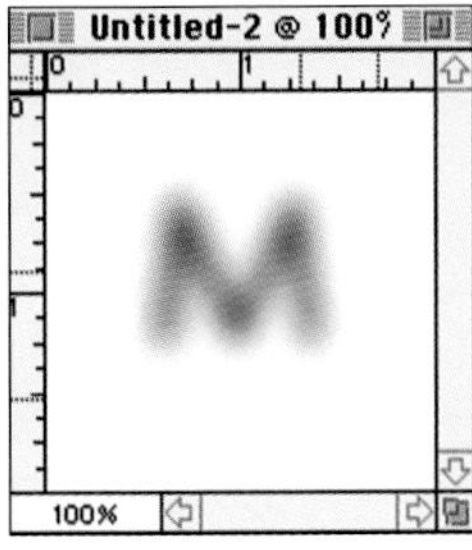


150 DPI

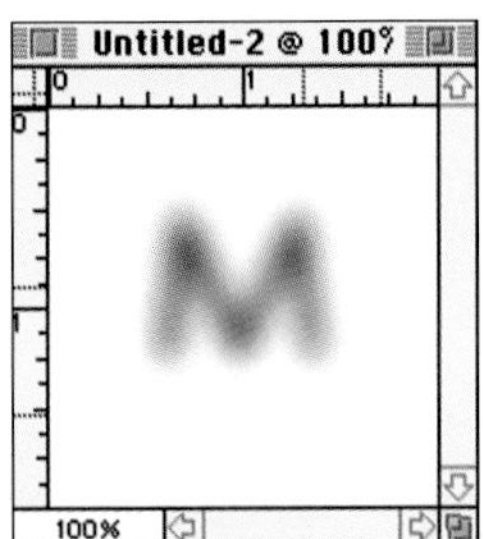


300 DPI

Tips Occasionally in this book you'll also see some paragraphs of text that have been separated out to create Tips. Tips are additional bits of information that can help you render a better effect by providing more information beyond the basic steps of each lesson.

# Photoshop Basics

## How to Use This Section

This part of the book is intended to help new and novice users of Photoshop with the simple, basic tasks required to do the Web graphics we have created. Each of these tasks corresponds to the text highlighted in blue, so users can easily find the instructions they need in this chapter.

This chapter proceeds on two assumptions: that you're creating our Web graphics in Photoshop 4.0, and that you're keeping the Tool and Layer/Channel/Path palettes open. If one or both of the Tool and Layer/Channel/Path palettes are closed when you refer to this chapter, you can reopen them by name using the Window menu at the top of the screen. If you're using an earlier version of Photoshop, you can refer to the Photoshop manual for instructions on how to perform these tasks—also keep in mind that Photoshop 2.5 does not offer the ability to work in layers.

Please note that keyboard shortcuts for Adobe Photoshop for Windows appear between brackets [].

## The Tools Palette

If you're not familiar with Photoshop's Tool palette, there's no reason to panic. With a bit of experimentation, it doesn't take long to learn each tool's individual functions. To help the beginning Photoshop user along the way, here is a representation of the toolbars from both Photoshop 3.0 and 4.0. This will also help advanced users find the rearranged tools.

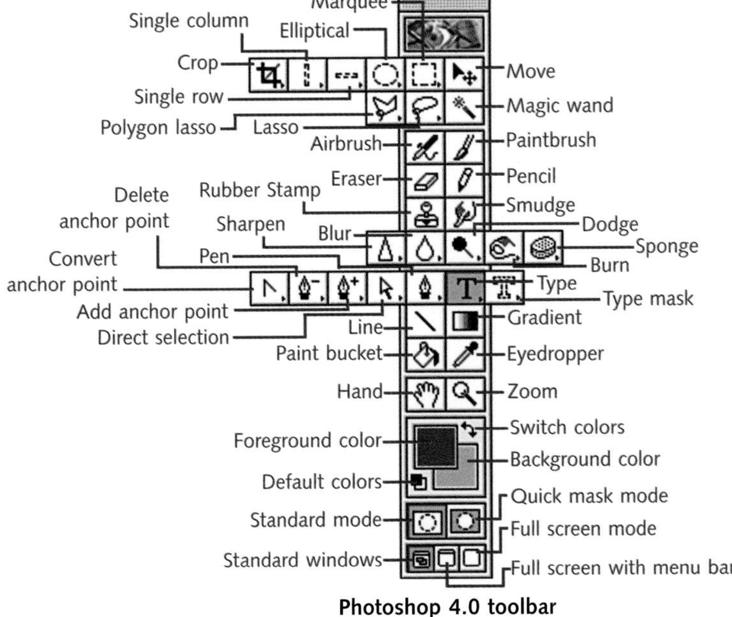


**Photoshop 4.0 toolbar**

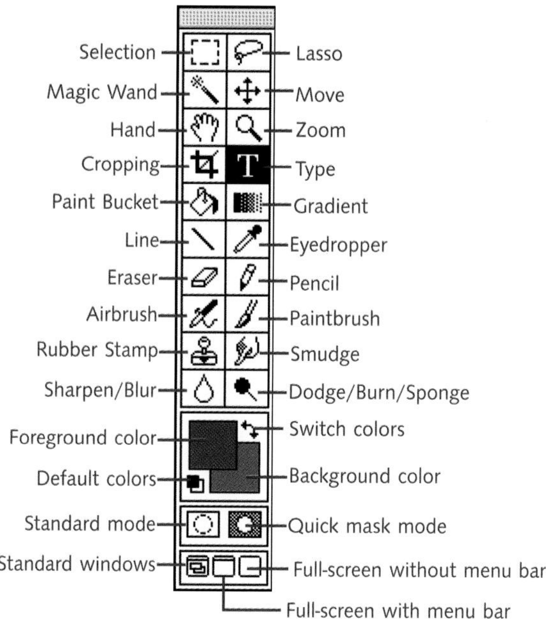


**Photoshop 3.0 toolbar**

## Basic Photoshop Tasks

### Add a Vertical/Horizontal Guide

Shortcut: Press Command-; [Control-;] to Show Guides and press Command-R [Control-R] to Show Rulers.

To add a vertical or horizontal guide, choose View=›Show Guides and View=›Show Rulers.

With any tool selected, drag a guide from either the horizontal or vertical ruler. To align the guide with a ruler position, hold down the Shift key as you drag the guide.

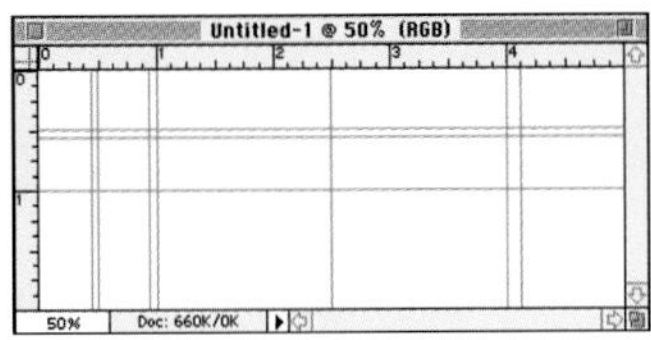


**TIP** **As you drag the guide, hold down the Option [Alt] key to switch between horizontal or vertical guides, or vice versa.**

## Choose a Foreground or Background Color

**Shortcuts**: Press D to change the colors to their defaults (black for the foreground, white for the background).

Press X to switch the foreground and background colors.

To change the foreground or background color click the Foreground or Background icon.

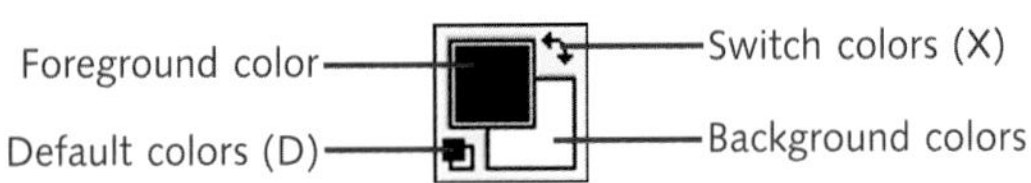


The Color Picker dialog box appears, enabling you to choose a new foreground or background color by moving and clicking the cursor (now a circle) along the spectrum box, or by changing specific RGB, CMYK, or other percentage values. Note that the Foreground and Background icons on the Tool palette now reflect your color choices.

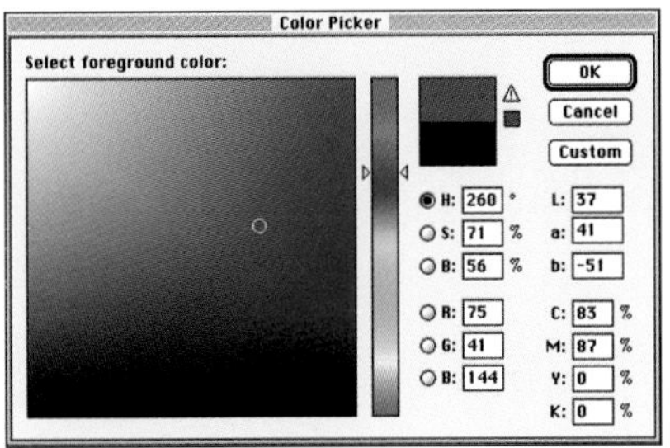


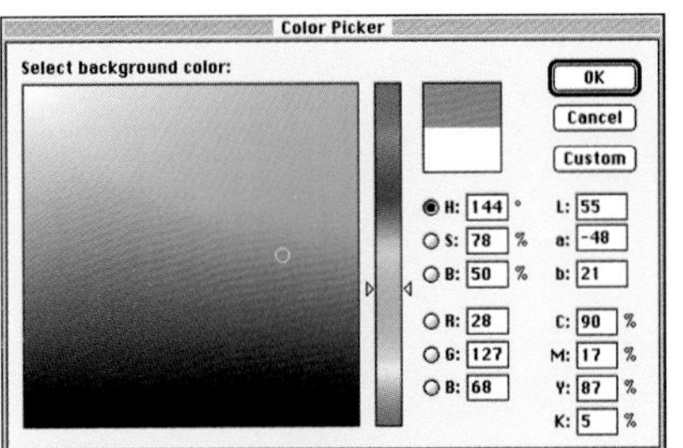


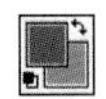

## Convert to a New Mode

To convert from one color mode to another color mode, click on the Image menu at the top of the screen and scroll down to the Mode selection, then scroll down to select your mode of preference. For example, if you wanted to switch from CMYK mode to RGB mode, you would choose Image➡Mode➡RGB. The check mark to the left of CMYK will move up to RGB, indicating you are now in RGB mode.

TIP **Remember, there is a different range of colors available for each color mode. For example, no matter what color mode the file is in on screen, your printer (if it prints in color) is going to print your work in CMYK. Since the color ranges for RGB and CMYK are different, you should convert your RGB image to CMYK before printing. Otherwise, you may be in for a big surprise when your bright green prints as a dull tan.**

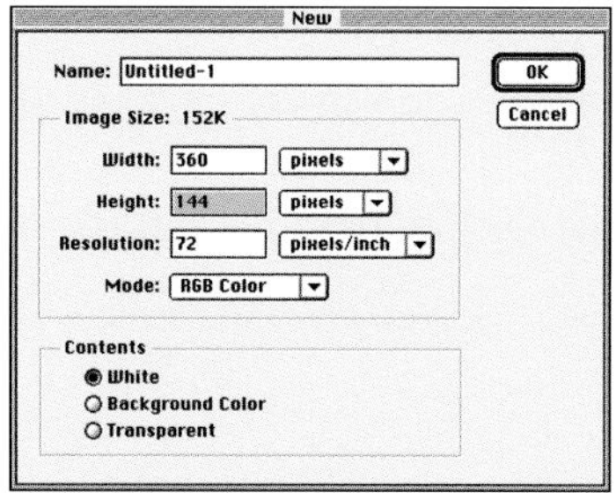


## Create/Edit a Grid

To create or edit a grid, choose File➡Preferences➡Guides and Grids, and use the dialog box to set your preferences.

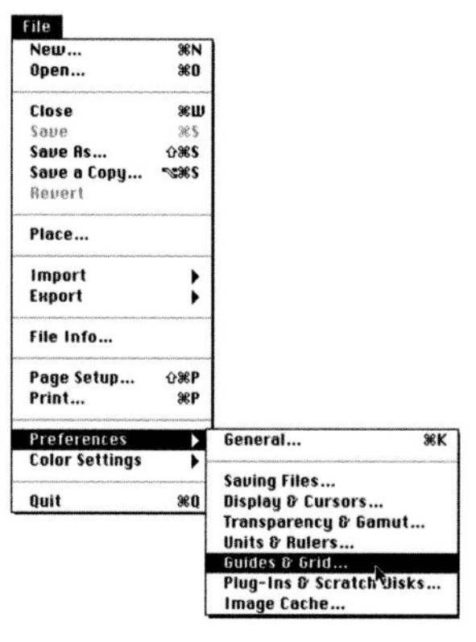


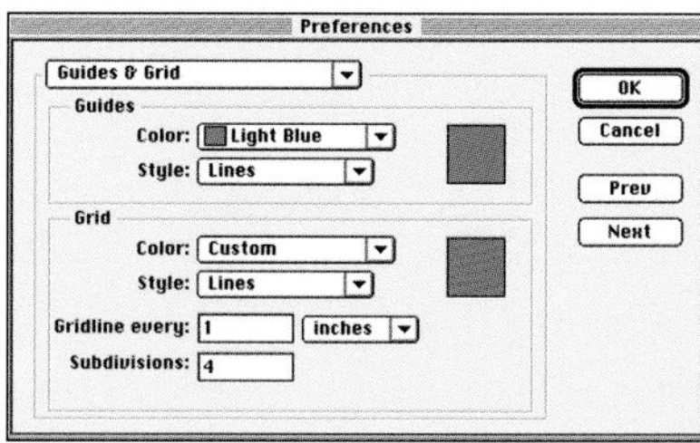

## Create a Layer Mask

To create a layer mask, choose Layer⇒Add Layer Mask, and choose either Reveal All (white) or Hide All (black). For the purposes of the effects in this book, always choose Reveal All. A layer mask is used to mask out, or hide, specified parts of a layer.

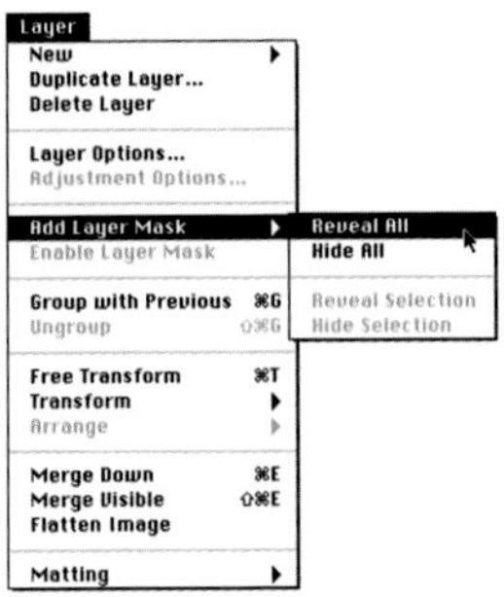


## Create an Adjustment Layer

**Shortcuts:** Command-click [Control-click] the new layer icon on the Layers palette.

This is a new feature available only in Photoshop 4.0. To create an adjustment layer, choose Layer⇒New⇒Adjustment Layer. If you want to confine the effects of the color and tonal adjustments to a selected area, make a selection before creating the layer.

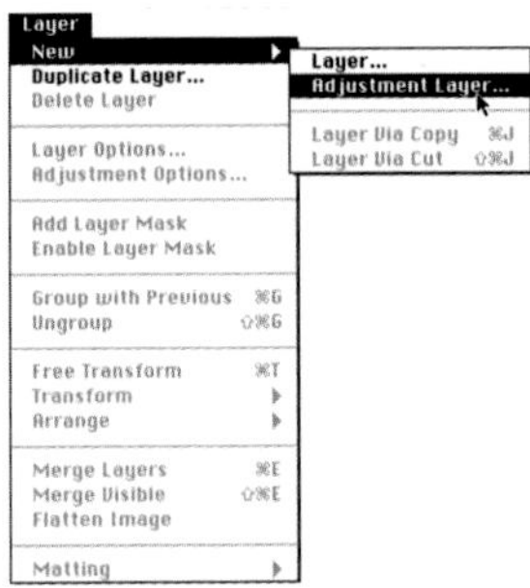


Use the New Adjustment Layer dialog box to establish your adjustment options and settings.

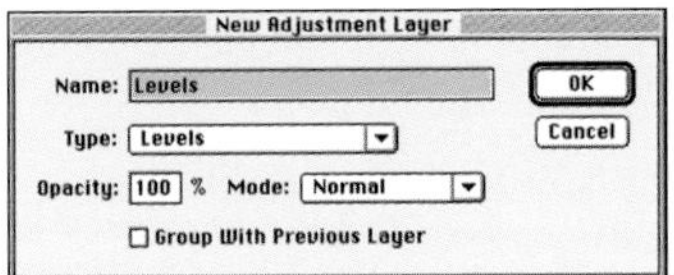


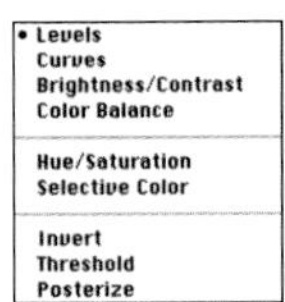

### Create a New Channel

**Shortcuts:** Click the new channel icon on the Channels palette.

To create a new channel, choose New Channel from the Channels palette pop-up menu.

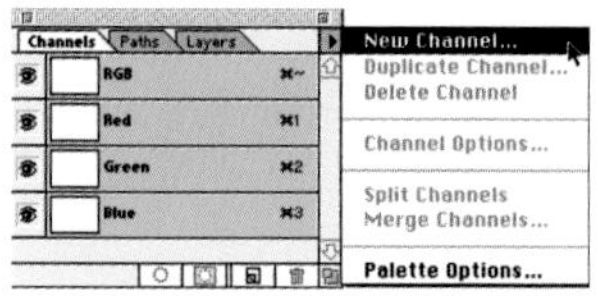


Use the Channel Options dialog box to establish your settings. Unless otherwise noted, we have always used Photoshop's defaults when creating a new channel. This figure shows Photoshop's default settings.

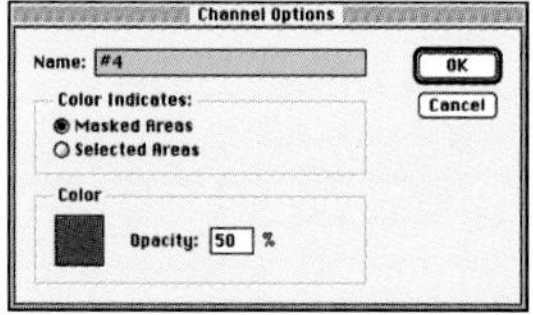


### Create a New File

**Shortcuts:** Press Command-N [Control-N].

To create a new file, choose File➛New. The New dialog box appears, where you can name your new file and establish other settings. See "Before You Start," for information on the conventions we used when creating new files for the Web graphic examples in this book.



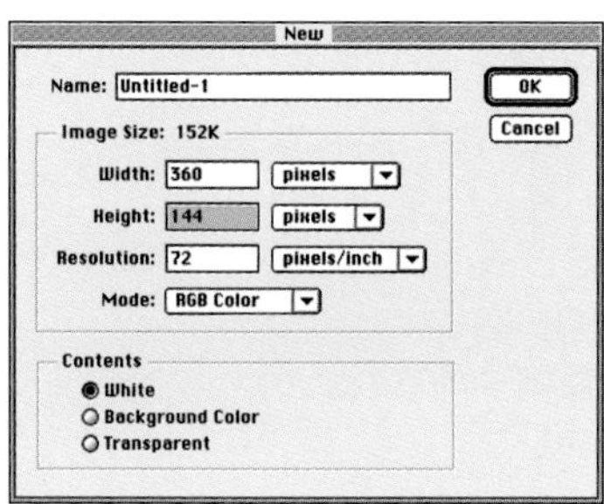


### Create a New Layer

**Shortcuts:** Click the New Layer icon on the Layers palette.

To create a new layer, choose New Layer from the Layer palette pop-up menu, or choose Layer➛New➛Layer.

The New Layer dialog box opens, enabling you to name the new layer and establish other settings.

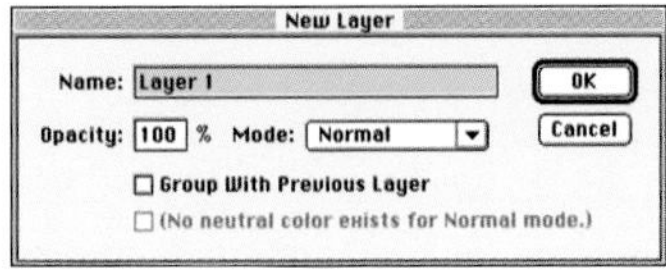


## Delete a Channel

To delete a channel, go to the Channels palette, select the channel you want to delete, and drag it to the Trash icon at the lower-right corner—just like you would get rid of a document on the desktop by dragging it to the Trash. You can also select the channel you want to delete and choose Delete channel from the Channels palette pop-up menu.

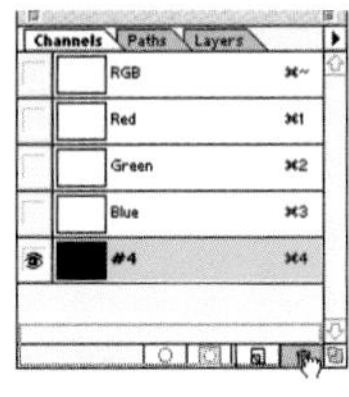


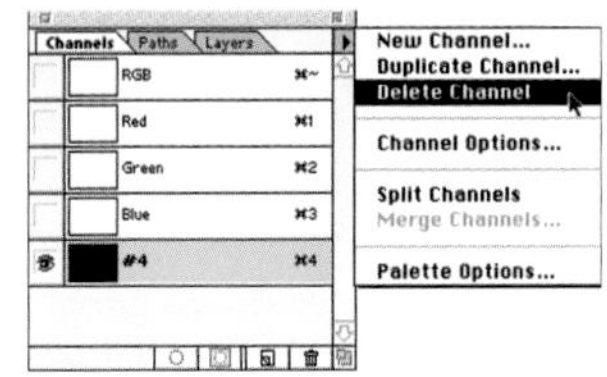


## Deselect a Selection

**Shortcut:** Press Command-D [Control-D].

To deselect a selection, choose Select→None. The marquee disappears. Switching selection tools will also deselect a selection.

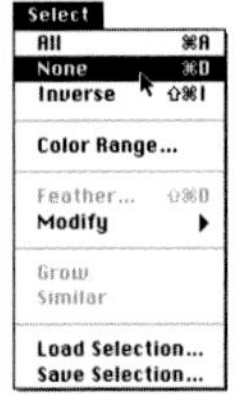

## Duplicate a Channel

**Shortcut:** Click the channel you want to duplicate, and drag it on top of the new channel icon.

To create a duplicate of a channel, make the channel active, then select Duplicate Channel from the Channels palette pop-up menu.

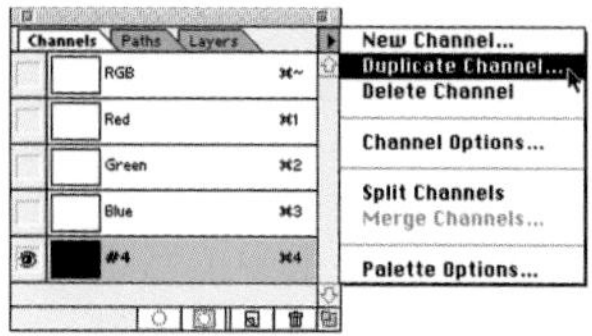


This creates a new copy of the channel you selected for duplication and causes the Duplicate Channel dialog box to appear.

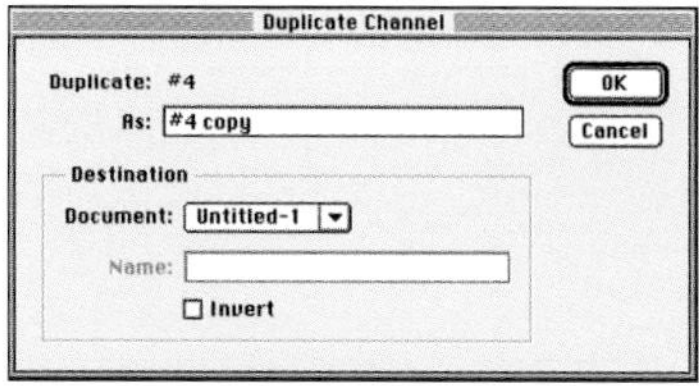


## Enter/Exit Quick Mask

**Shortcuts:** Press Q to enter and exit Quick Mask mode.

Click the Quick Mask icon to switch to Quick Mask mode and the Standard mode icon to return to Standard mode.

Essentially a Quick Mask is a temporary channel. When you're in Quick Mask mode you can use any of Photoshop's tools and functions to change the selection without changing the image. When you switch back to Standard mode you'll have a new selection.

## Enter the Text

There are two type tools in Photoshop 4.0—the standard Type tool and the Type Mask tool. Each effect in this book specifies which type tool to use.

Before entering the text using the standard Type tool, make sure the foreground color is set to the color you want the text to be. If you are entering text into a layer, then the standard Type tool creates a new layer for the type.

The Type Mask tool creates selection outlines of the text you enter without filling them with a new color and without creating a new layer.

To enter the text, select the type tool you want to use, and then click anywhere in the image to open the Type Tool dialog box. Type the text in the large box at the bottom of the dialog box, and make your attribute choices from the options above. Unless noted otherwise in the instructions, always make sure you have the Anti-Aliased box checked.

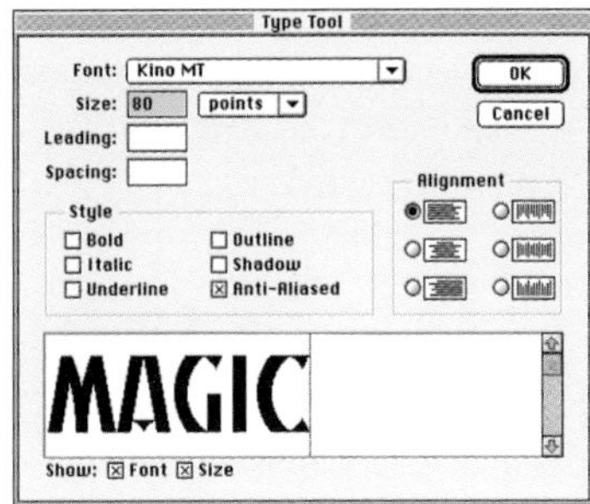


After clicking OK, move the type into position with the Marquee (Type Mask tool) tool.

## Export to GIF Format

To export to a GIF format, choose File➙Export➙GIF89a Export. Use the GIF89a format for graphics with transparent areas. In the dialog box choose either the Exact, Adaptive or System Palette (GIF supports a maximum of 256 colors). If you created a custom palette, click Load to locate and select your custom palette. Consult your Photoshop manual or *Designing Web Graphics* by Lynda Weinman for a more detailed discussion of color palette options versus file sizes.

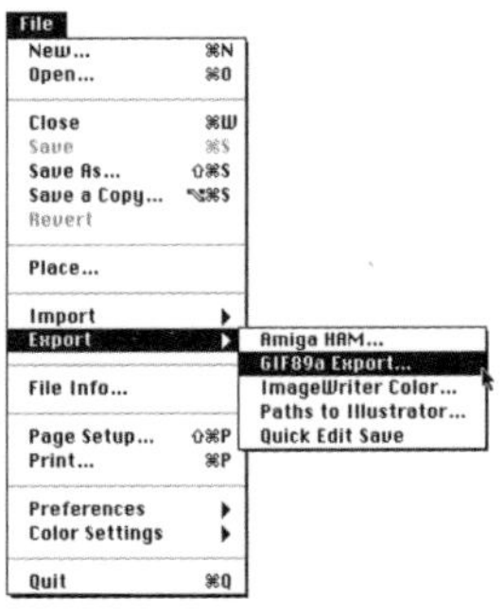


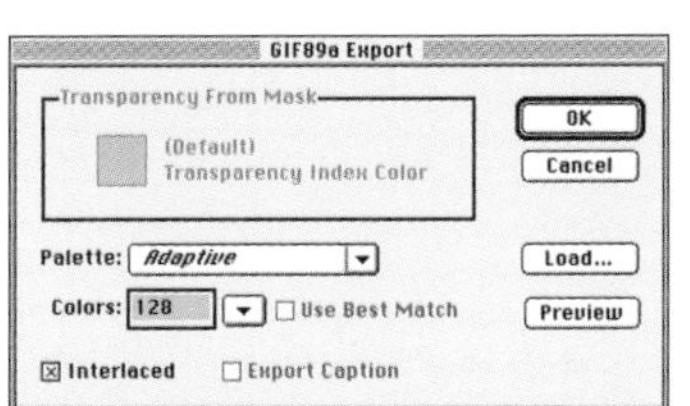


8
16
32
64
✓128
255
256

The adaptive palette displays the best results for continuous tone images. Here are two examples (shown in the GIF89a preview window) where the adaptive palette was limited to 128 colors and 16 colors.

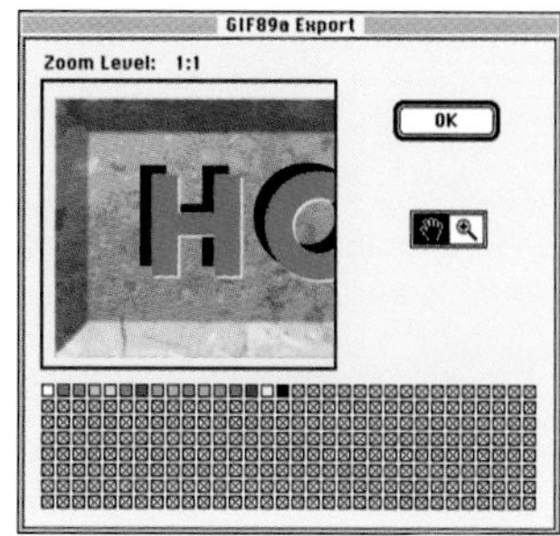


**TIP** **A new alternative to the GIF format is the PNG format. Unlike GIF, PNG keeps all color information in an image, uses a lossless compression scheme, supports alpha channels, and enables you to specify how transparent areas will look. Choose File➸Save as➸PNG.**

### Fill a Selection with Foreground or Background Color

First, select the foreground or background color you wish to use (see page 2 in this section for instructions). Keep the selection active and press Option-Delete to fill the selection with the foreground color. If you are in the Background layer or any layer that has the Preserve Transparency option turned on, then you can press Delete to fill in the selection with the background color.

You can also fill in your selections by choosing Edit➸Fill.

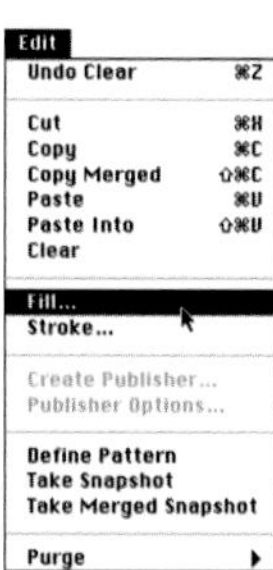

This causes the Fill dialog box to appear, enabling you to establish the Contents option you wish to use, the Opacity, and the blending Mode.

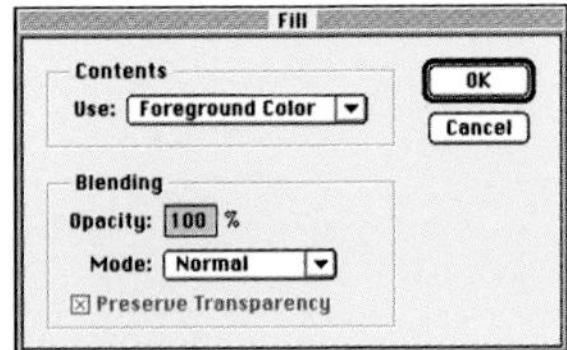


**TIP** **If a selection is empty (a transparent area of a layer) and the Preserve Transparency option is turned on for that layer, you will not be able to fill the selection. To fill the selection, simply turn off the Preserve Transparency option before filling it.**

## Flatten an Image

To flatten an image (merge all the layers into a single layer), choose Flatten Image from the Layers palette arrow menu, or choose Layer⇒Flatten Image.

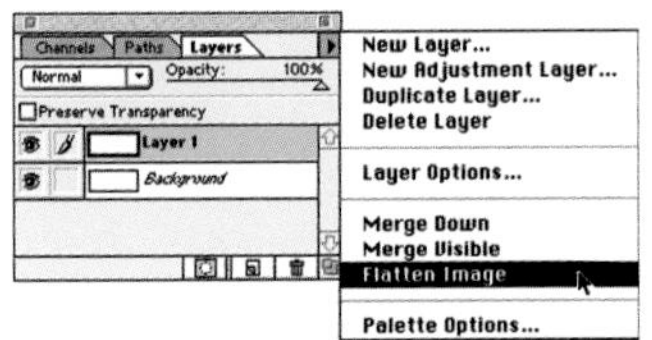

## Load a Selection

**Shortcut:** Hold down the Command [Control] key and click the channel (on the Channels palette) containing the selection you want to load.

To load a selection, choose Select⇒Load Selection. This brings up the Load Selection dialog box, where you can establish document, channel, and operation variables.

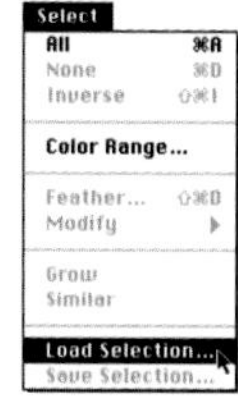


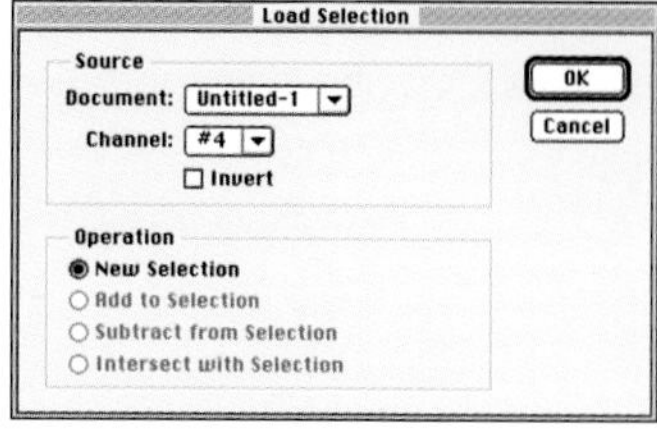


### Load a Transparency as a Selection Mask (of a Layer)

To load a layer transparency as a selection mask, hold down the Command [Control] key and click on the thumbnail (on the Layers palette) containing the transparency as a selection mask you want to load.

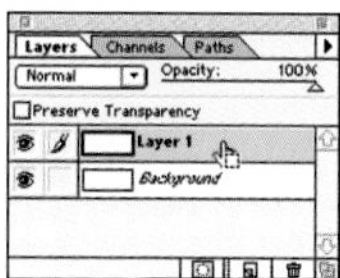


### Make a Channel Active

To make a channel active for editing or modification, click on its thumbnail or title in the Channels palette.

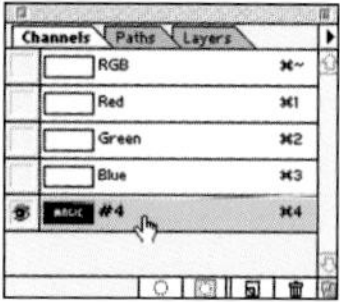


You can tell the channel is active if it is highlighted with a color and its title text becomes bold.

### Make a Layer Active

To make a layer active, click on its thumbnail or title in the Layers palette.

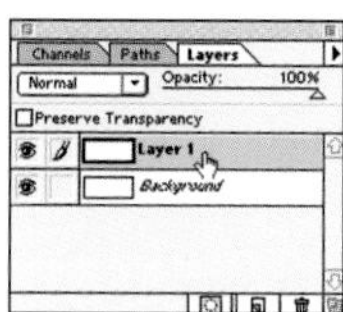


You can tell the layer is active if it is highlighted with a color and its title text becomes bold.

### Make a Layer Visible/Invisible

To make a Layer visible, click in the leftmost column in the Layers palette. If an eye appears, then the layer is visible. If the column is empty, then that layer is hidden (invisible).

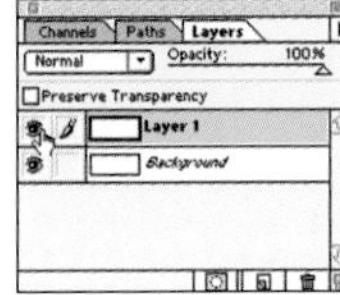


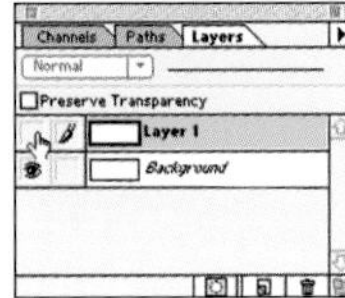


### Merge Layer Down

**Shortcut:** Press Command-E [Control-E].

To merge a Layer down, select the layer and then choose Layer➞Merge Down. Remember to check that the layer you wish to merge down into is visible.

### Merge Visible Layers

**Shortcut:** Press Shift + Command-E [Shift + Control-E].

To merge visible layers, choose Layer➞Merge Visible. See heading Make a layer visible/invisible for a review of how to select layers for merging.

### Move a Layer

To move a Layer, click on the layer you want to move in the Layers palette and drag it up or down along the list of layers to the place you want to move it. As you drag the layer, the lines between the layers will darken indicating where the layer will fall if you let go.

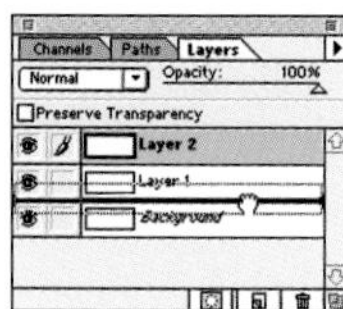

The layer you have moved will appear between layers, numerically "out of order."

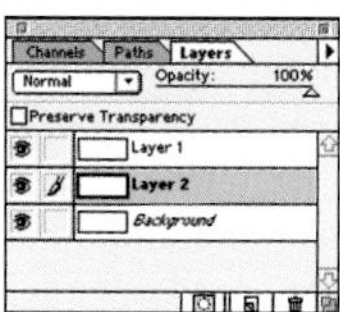

### Return to the Composite Channel

**Shortcut:** Press Command-~ [Control-~].

If you want to return to the composite channel, click on its thumbnail or title (RGB, CMYK, Lab). The composite channel will always be the one with the Command-~ [Control-~] after its title.

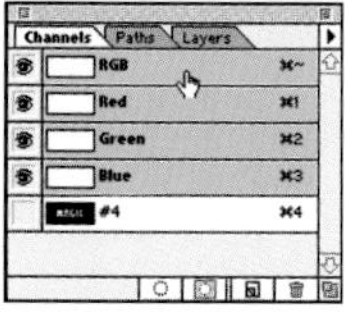

If you are in an RGB file, then channels 0 through 3 should now be active because each of the R, G, and B channels are individual parts of the RGB channel.

## Save a File

To save new a file, choose File⇒Save. This will bring up the Save dialog box, where you should name your untitled new file and choose a format in which to save it.

To save as another file, choose File⇒Save As. This will bring up the Save As dialog box, where you should rename your file and choose a format in which to save it. If a file format which you would like to use is not an option, then use the save a copy command instead.

File format selection is going to depend on what you have in your file, what you want to keep when you save it, and what you're going to do with it afterward. Consult a detailed Web site design book, such as *Creating Killer Web Sites* by David Siegel or *Designing Web Graphics* by Lynda Weinman, for more guidance on which file format is best for your needs.

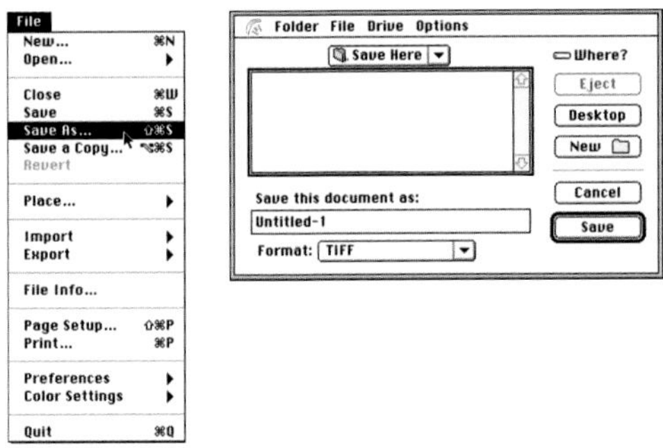


## Save as JPEG

To save as a JPEG file format follow the instructions in Save as a file. In the JPEG dialog box, experiment with the JPEG settings to find the best result for each photograph. Set the options to maximize image quality while keeping the file size as small as possible.

JPEG (Joint Photographic Experts Group) has become the standard for displaying photographs and other continuous tone images on the Web. The JPEG is a lossy compression routine that reduces file sizes without reducing color depth (JPEG supports millions of colors). Because JPEG is a lossy technique, don't resave a JPEG format again as a JPEG. The image will deteriorate.

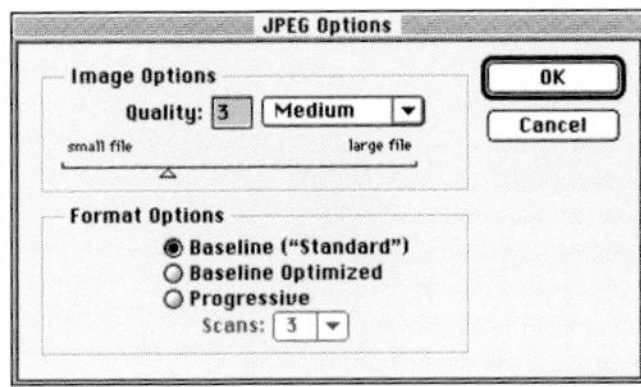

## Save a Selection

**Shortcut:** Click on the save selection icon on the Channels palette.

To save a selection, choose Select➡Save Selection.

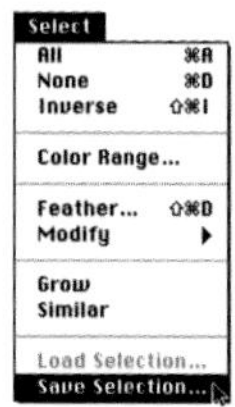


The Save Selection dialog will open. Choose your desired options and click OK to save the selection.

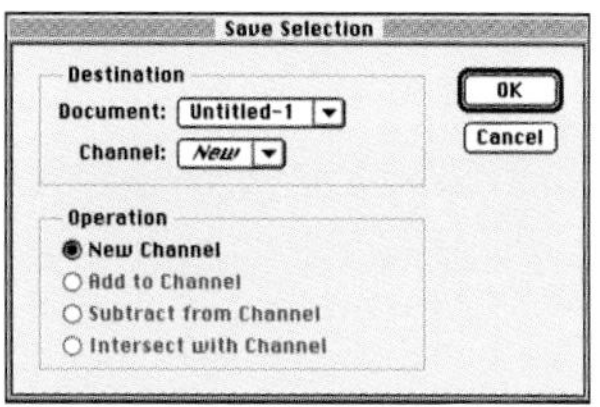


## Switch Foreground/Background Colors

**Shortcut:** Press X to switch the foreground and background colors.

To switch the foreground and background colors, click on the Switch Colors icon. This flips the two colors shown in this icon only, and does not affect the image.

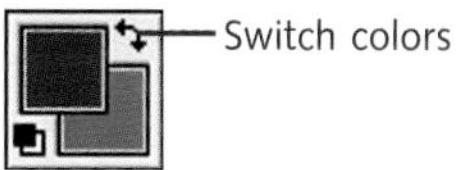


## Switch to Default Colors

**Shortcut:** Press D to switch to the default foreground and background colors.

To change the foreground and background colors to black and white respectively, click on the Default Colors icon.

# PART I

## Backgrounds

The background's "look and feel" sets the stylistic foundation for your Web site. You can select either a solid color or a texture for a background. Solid colors are assigned as hex color values using the body color command in HTML. For textured backgrounds, GIFs or JPEGs can be used. On a Web page, the browser tiles the background image. To create faster download times, make your tiles small—about 96×96 pixels.

There is, of course, no 100 percent performance guarantee when downloading any file from the Web. When assigning textured backgrounds to your Web pages, also choose a background color for your default that is the dominant color in your texture. If there is a technical glitch and the textured look does not download correctly, then your default background color is visible. The Web site design still looks great.

When writing the HTML body background command, make sure that the color command comes first before assigning the JPEG or GIF background texture file. Whatever is assigned last is the look the browser will display.

Patterns on Web page background tiles can be matched on all sides creating a totally seamless background image. By using Photoshop's offset filter you can make your own patterns tile seamlessly.

**1** Create a new file. It can be any size, but should be square. Later you will reduce it to the actual size of the tile.

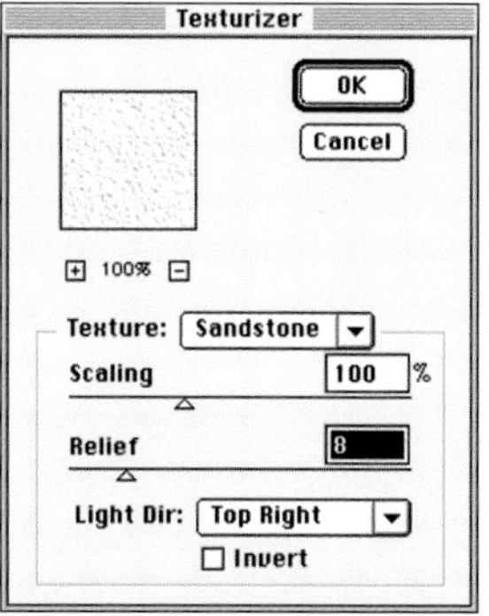


**2** Choose Filter⇢Texture⇢Texturizer (Sandstone, Scaling: 100%, Relief: 8%). This filter makes it a snap to create basic textures (brick, burlap, canvas, and sandstone) for your backgrounds.

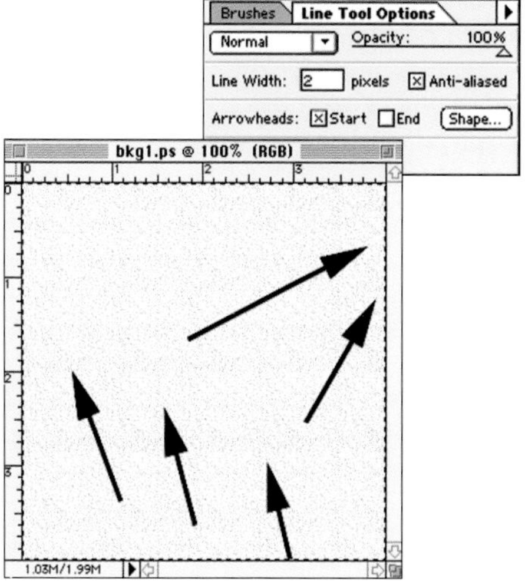


**3** Create a new layer (Layer 1). Double-click the Line tool icon on the Toolbox to view the Line tool palette (Opacity: 100%, Line Width: 2, Anti-aliased on, Arrowheads: At Start). Draw a few lines to create a random pattern. Keep the lines toward the right side and bottom of the image so the offset filter will work.

**4** Select➺All. Choose Filter➺Other➺Offset (Horizontal: 80 pixels right, Vertical: 80 pixels down, Undefined Areas: Wrap Around). This filter wraps one side of the image around to the opposite side.

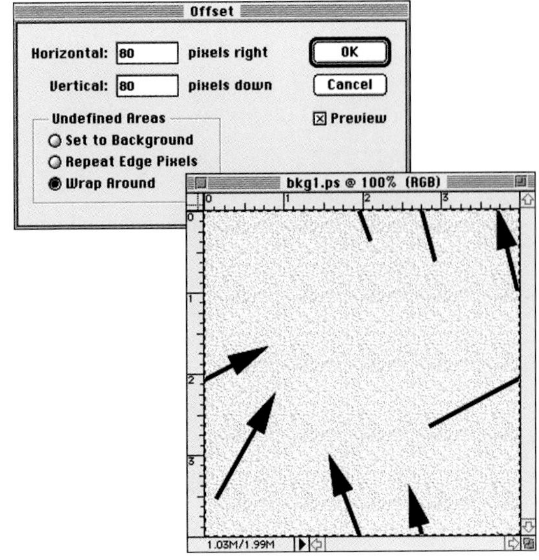


**5** With the Line tool, fill in the empty spaces.

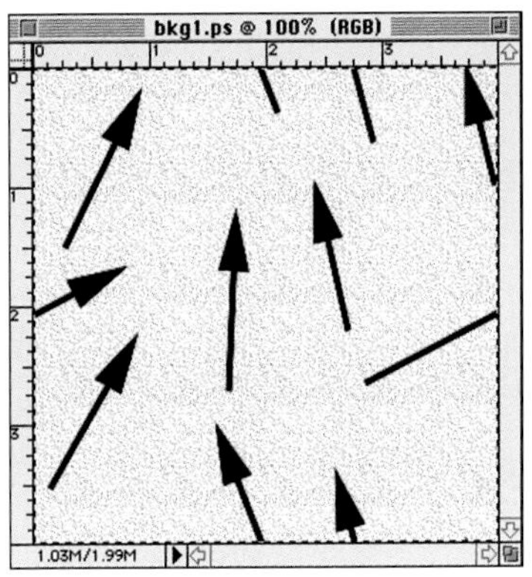


**6** Adjust the opacity of Layer 1 to 20%, using the slider on the Layers palette.

**For best results adjust the opacity to a low setting so that your pattern does not interfere with the legibility of the text on your Web page.**

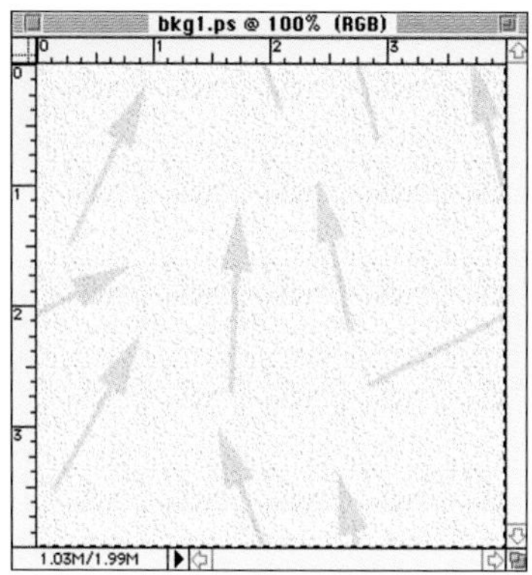


**7** Choose Image➸Image Size➸Pixel Dimensions (Width: 72, Height: 72).

TIP **To preview your tiled image, select the entire tile and choose Edit➸Define Pattern. Then create a new, larger file, and Edit➸Fill (Pattern).**

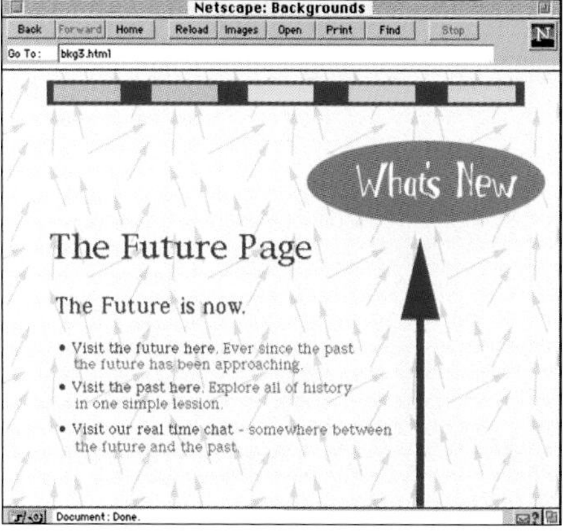


**8** Export to GIF format.

## VARIATIONS

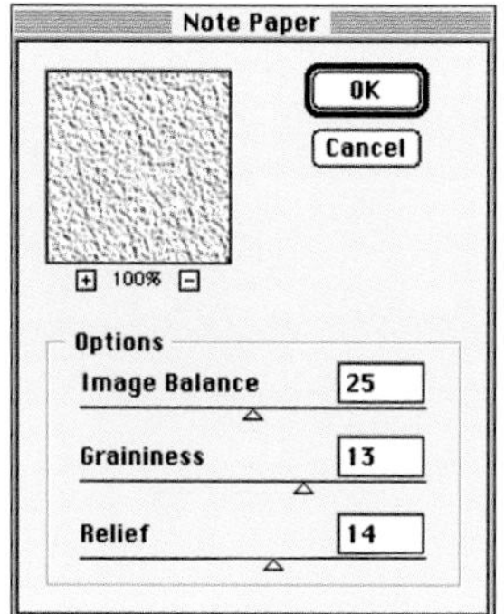


**1** Instead of the Texturizer filter, we used Photoshop 4.0's Note Paper filter, Filter➸Sketch➸Note Paper (Image Balance: 25, Graininess: 13, Relief: 14).

**2** Synstelien Design's Dreamtime dingbat font adds the graphic elements.

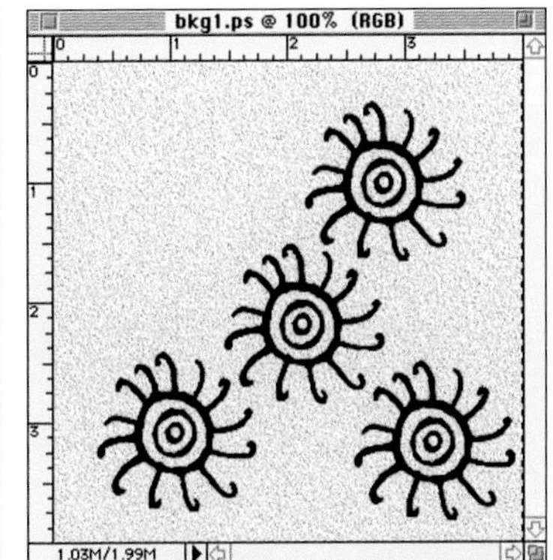


**3** The Offset filter moves the dingbats 144 pixels (50% of the image size) to the right and down.

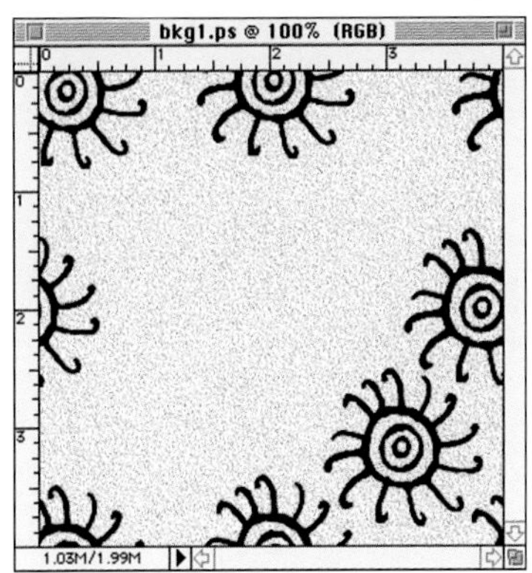


**4** We filled in the center of the tile with more dingbats.

**5** We flattened the image, chose a foreground color and filled it with (Foreground Color, Opacity: 100%, Mode: Soft Light)

**6** Export to GIF format. ■

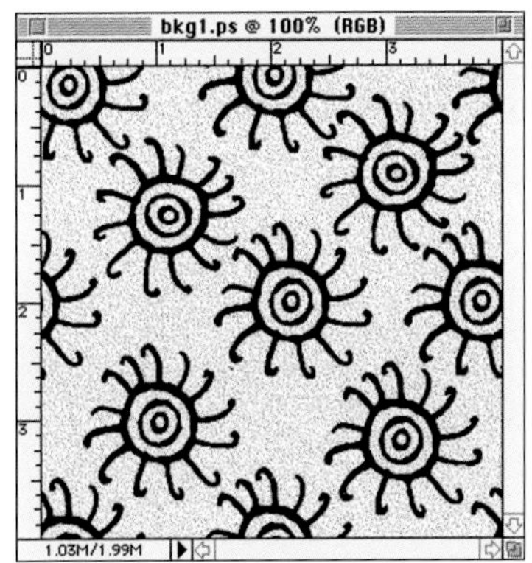

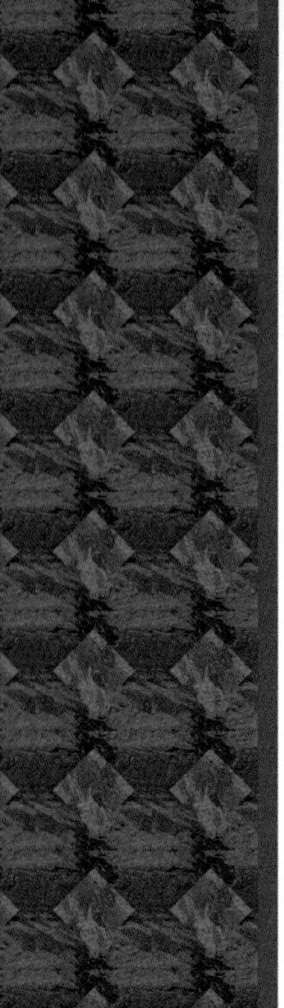

## Parquet Tiles

You can create interesting and varied parquet effects by rotating and placing tiles within tiles.

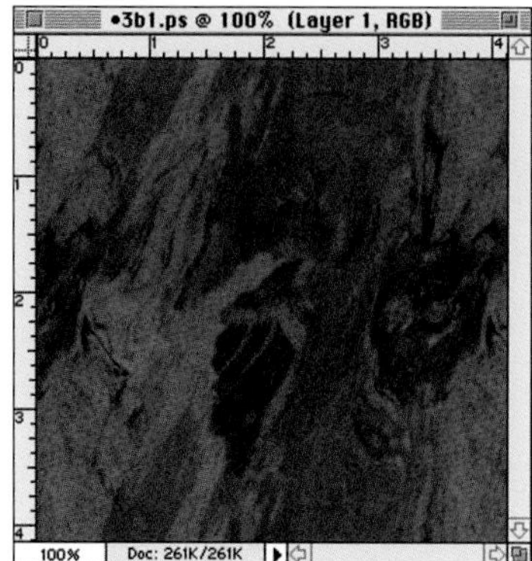


**1** Open a file containing a texture of your choice or use the granite texture file from the CD (in the textures folder or directory). In this exercise we worked with a 4"×4" file at 72 dpi.

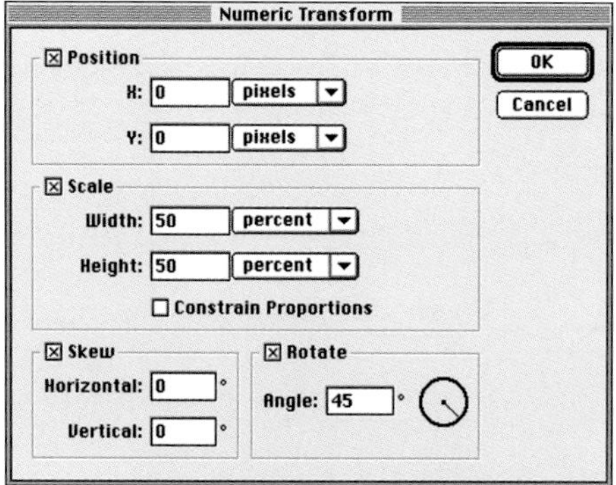


**2** Select→All and copy and paste the image. Choose Layer→Transform→Numeric (Scale: Width: 50%, Height: 50%, Rotate: 45°).

**3** Choose Filter→Stylize→Emboss (Angle: 135, Height: 2 pixels, Amount 50%).



**TOOLBOX**

Alien Skin's Swirl

Alien Skin's Drop Shadow

**4** Choose Image=›Adjust=›Brightness/Contrast (Brightness: 10, Contrast: -5). This makes the inset tile more prominent.

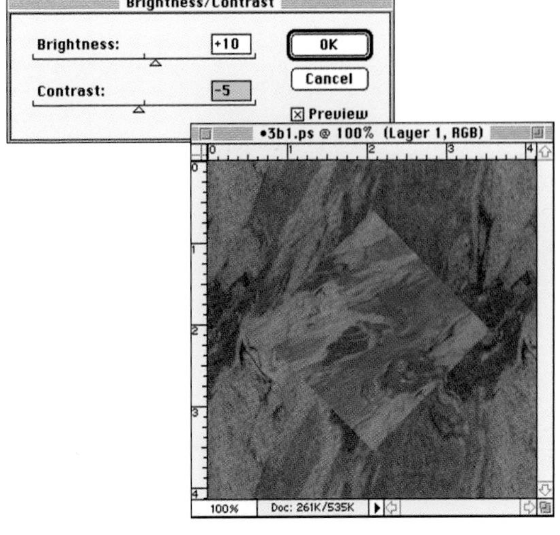


**5** Make the Background layer active. To add color to the Background, choose Image=›Adjust=›Variations. We chose to add more yellow.

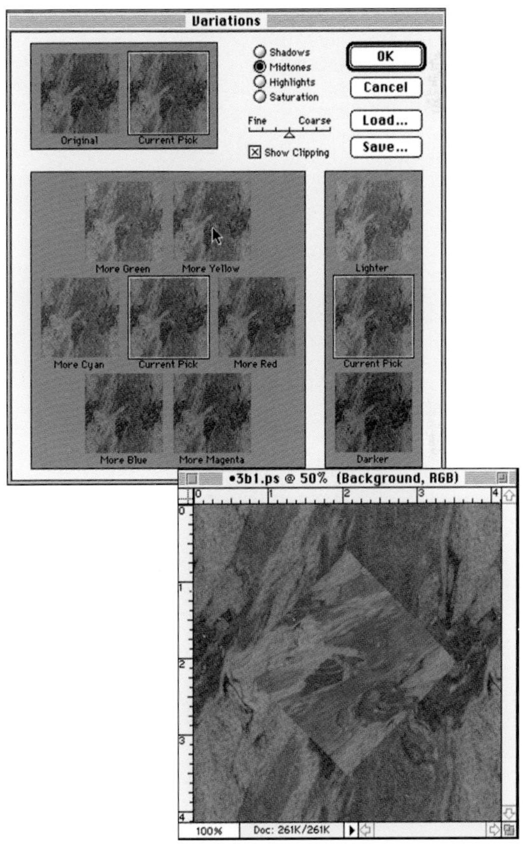

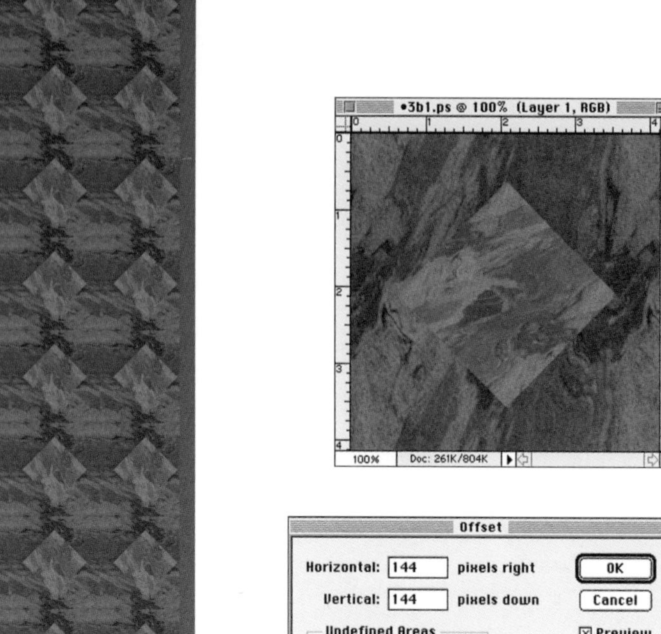


**6** Make Layer 1 active. Choose Image⇒Adjust⇒Variations. Drag the Saturation slider up one notch toward Coarse and add yellow.

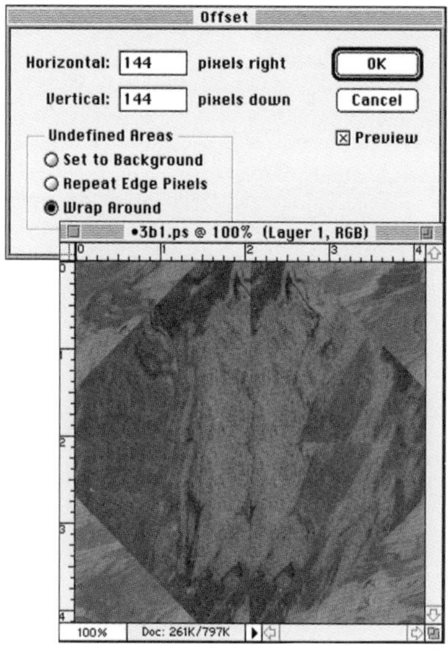


**7** Flatten image. Select⇒All. Choose Filter⇒Other⇒Offset (Horizontal: 144, Vertical: 144, Undefined Areas: Wrap Around). The dimensions entered in the Horizontal and Vertical text entry boxes should be 50% of the size of your image, otherwise your image will not wrap correctly.

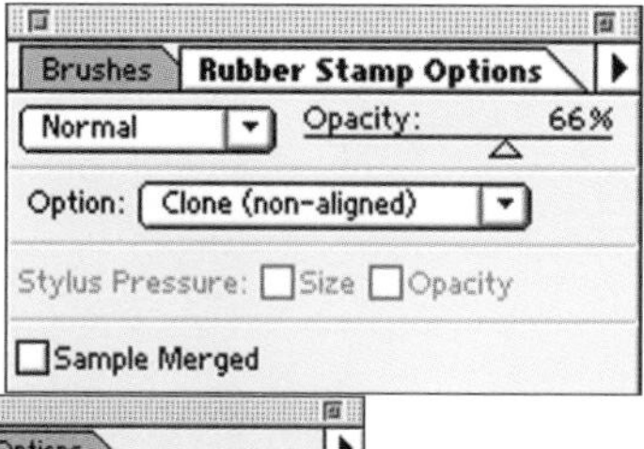


**8** To touch up any hard seams use the Rubber Stamp tool (Opacity: 66%, Clone (non-aligned)). Choose a small- to medium-size soft brush and stroke in the direction of the pattern.

**9** Choose Window⇒Navigator palette. Use the Navigator palette to zoom into the image for precise cloning. Photoshop 4.0's new Navigator palette enables you to zoom into specific areas using a zoom slider or typing in numeric percentages.

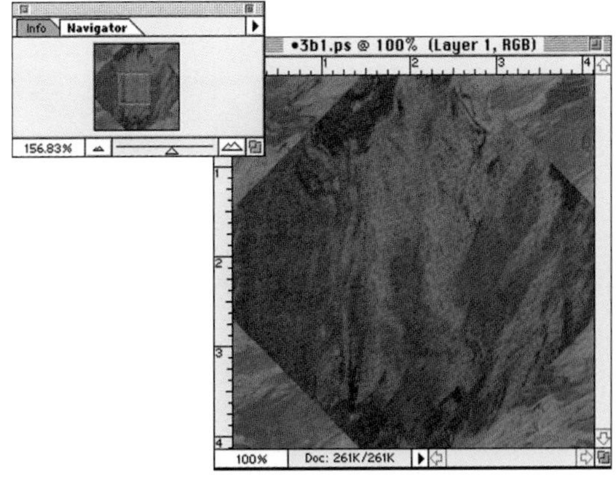


TIP **You can also zoom into your image by typing in a new percentage in the lower-left side of your image window.**

**10** Select Image⇒Image Size (Print Size: 50% or smaller, Contains Proportions: On). This resizes the image to create the final tile.

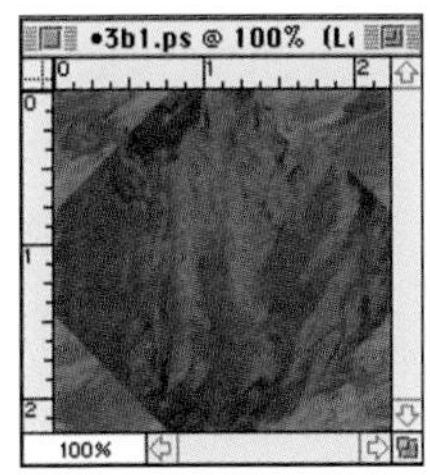


To finish this Web page we made buttons using Alien Skin's Swirl filter and added a drop shadow to define and add depth to the page.

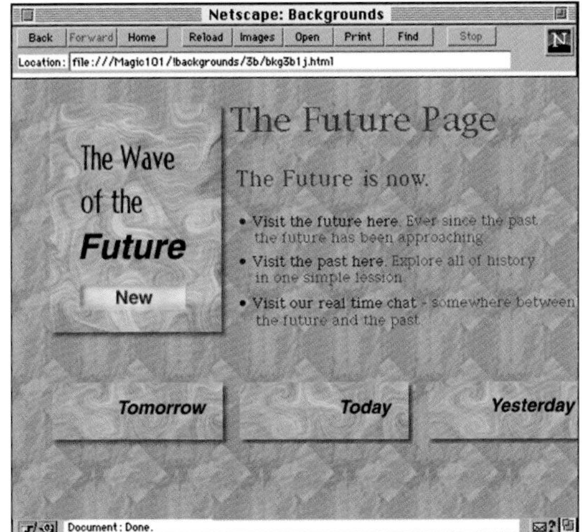

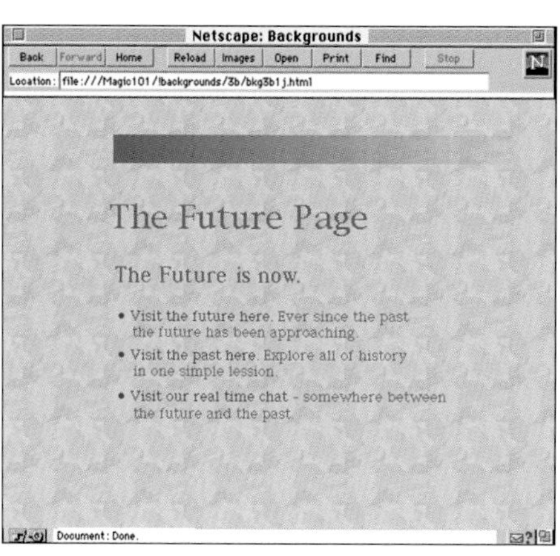


## VARIATIONS

After Step 2, we copied and pasted Layer 1, then rotated it another 45° to create the star pattern. ■

## Wave Backgrounds

The ancient art of weaving can be updated for Web pages using Photoshop's Wave filter as a digital loom. With the Wave filter's random function, no two backgrounds are ever quite the same.

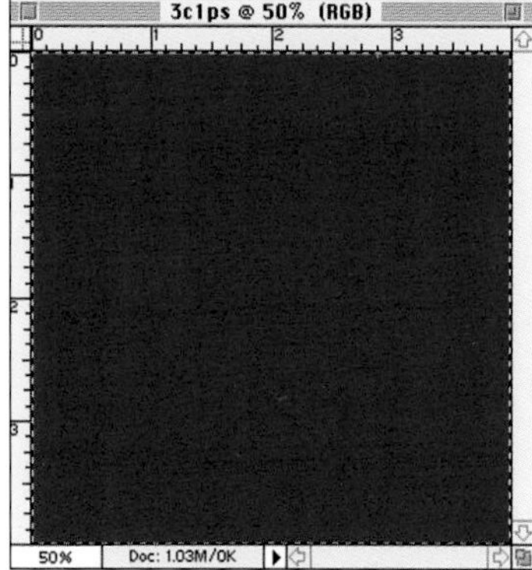


**1** Create a new file. Choose white as the foreground color and a dark color for the background color. We used a dark blue in this example. Select➜All and press the Delete key to fill the image with the background color.

**2** Choose Filter➜Render➜Difference Clouds.

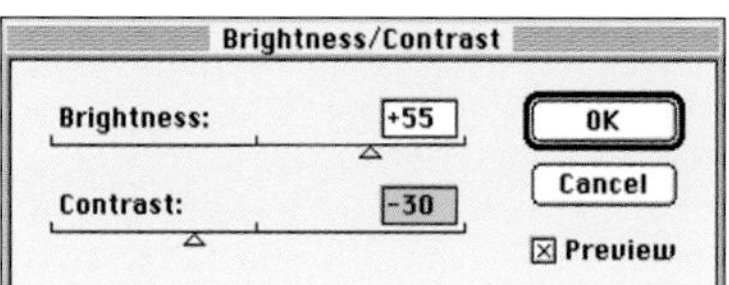


**3** Choose Image➜Adjust➜Brightness/Contrast. Move the Brightness slider up to around +55, and the Contrast slider down to around -30. This creates a more even image with less contrast.

**TIP** **The Brightness/Contrast filter can be used on almost any image to lower the contrast so that the pattern does not interfere with the legibility of type on the Web page.**

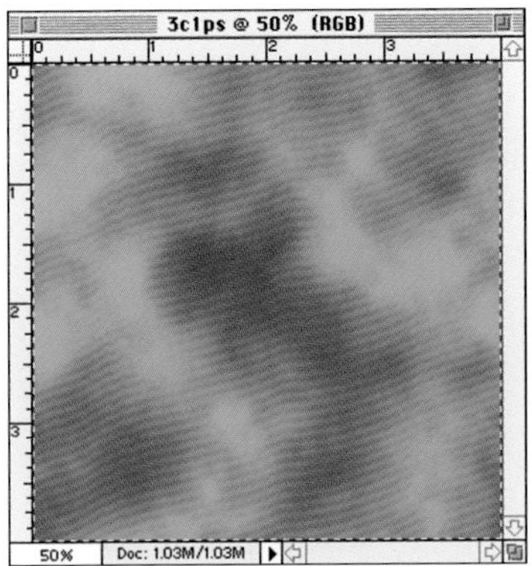


**4** Choose Filter⇒Distort⇒Wave. We used the following settings: Number of Generators: 2; Type: Square; Wavelength: Min: 10, Max: 120; Amplitude: 22: 140; Undefined Areas: Repeat Edge Pixels. Because this filter uses a Randomize function, no two patterns are ever identical. Click the Randomize button until you find a pattern you like.

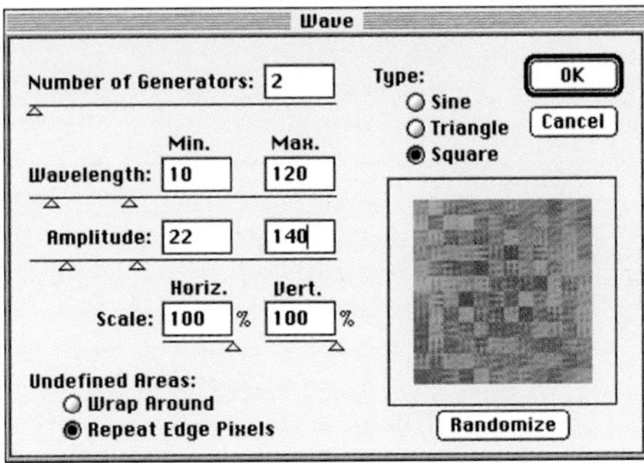


**5** Select an area of the image that is evenly blended. This will become the tile.

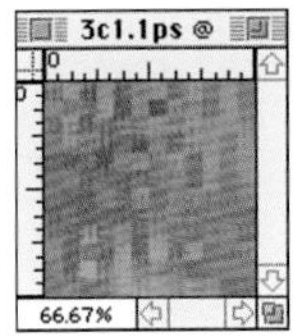


**6** Copy your selection and paste into a new file, then export to GIF format.

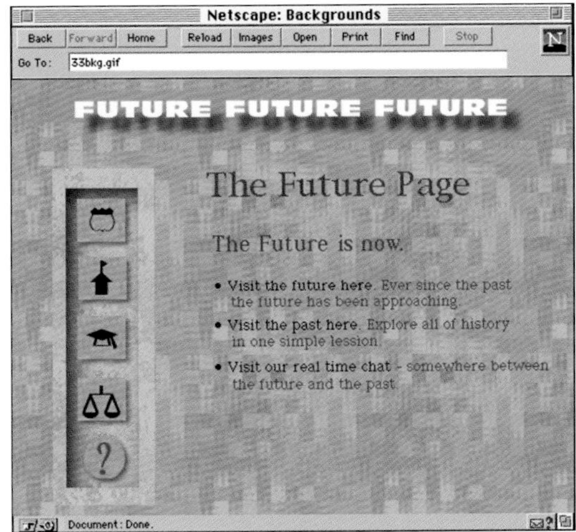

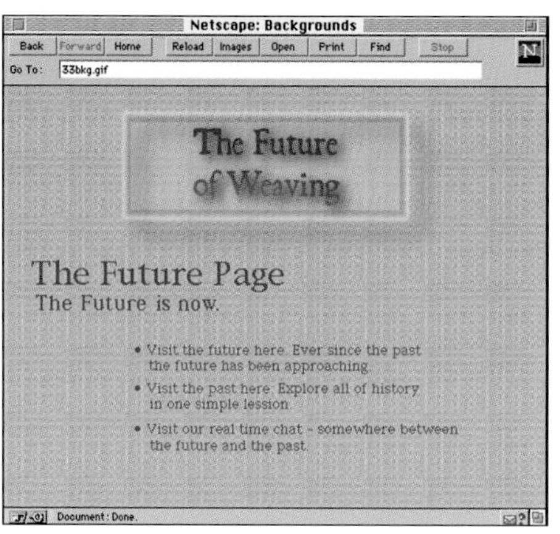

## VARIATIONS

You can create unlimited patterns by choosing different background colors and randomizing the Wave filter. We kept all other settings the same for this example.

Changing the Number of Generators from 2 to 1 creates larger patterns.

## Tiles on Tiles

Photoshop's filters can be used to create quick and easy tiles that are composed of smaller tiles.

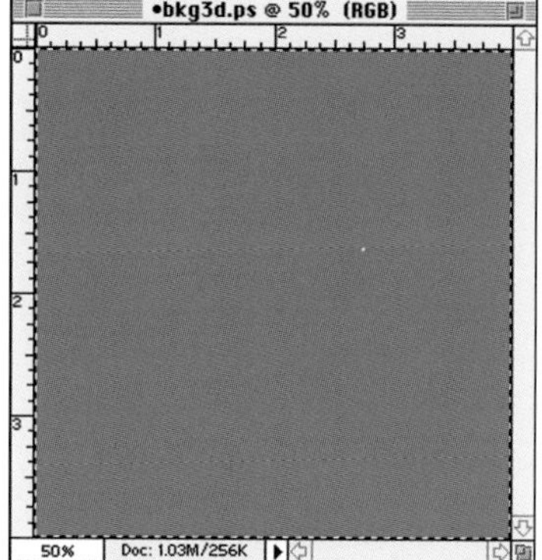


**1** Create a new file, choose a background color, and fill the selection with the background color.

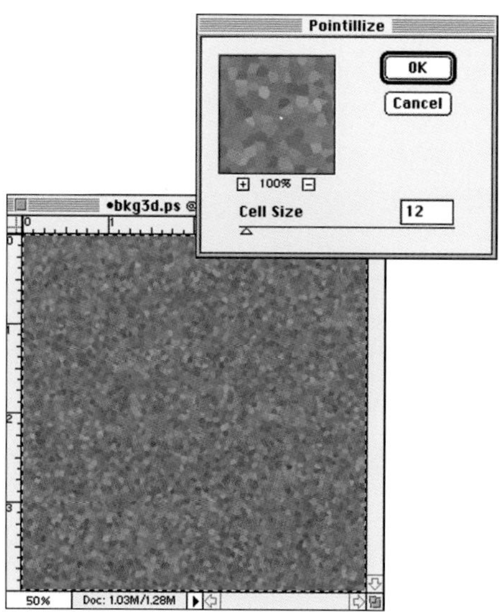


**2** Choose Filter→Pixelate→Pointillize (Cell Size: 12).

**3** Next, apply Filter➞Stylize➞ Extrude (Type: Pyramids, Size: 20 Pixels, Depth: 8, Random). A smaller size creates smaller tiles.

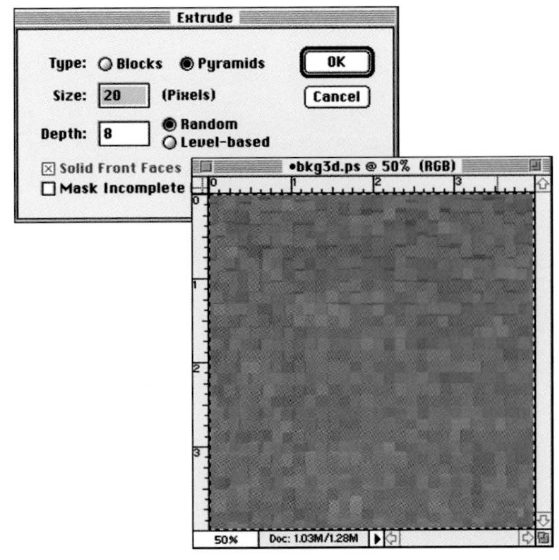


**4** Select an area of the image that is fully randomized. Copy and paste the selection to a new file. Save as a JPEG.

We have found that for this image, JPEG files are smaller than GIFs.

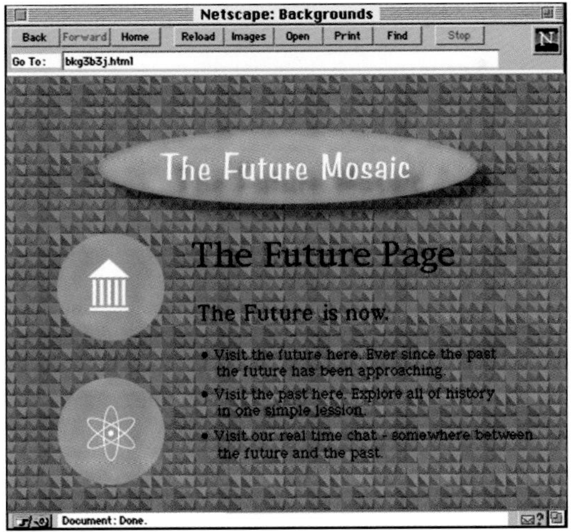

# VARIATIONS

For this variation, first we removed the color with Image⇒Adjust⇒Desaturate. The tiles can now be retinted with Image⇒Adjust⇒Hue Saturation. Click the Colorize checkbox and lower the Saturation to around 50% before selecting your color.

### Blocks

For this variation we chose a turquoise color and selected Blocks instead of Pyramids and Solid Front Faces in the Extrude dialog box.

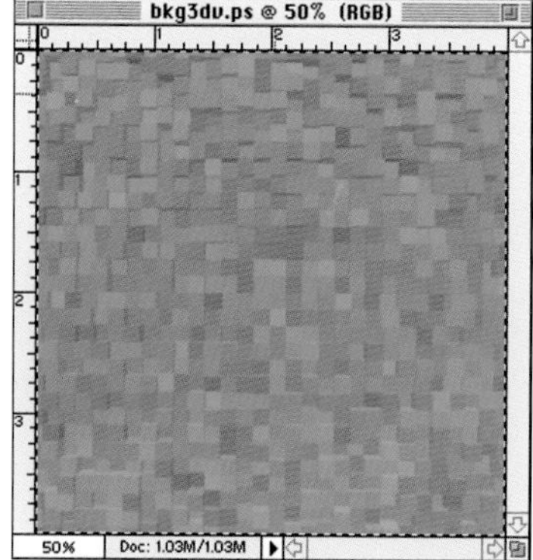


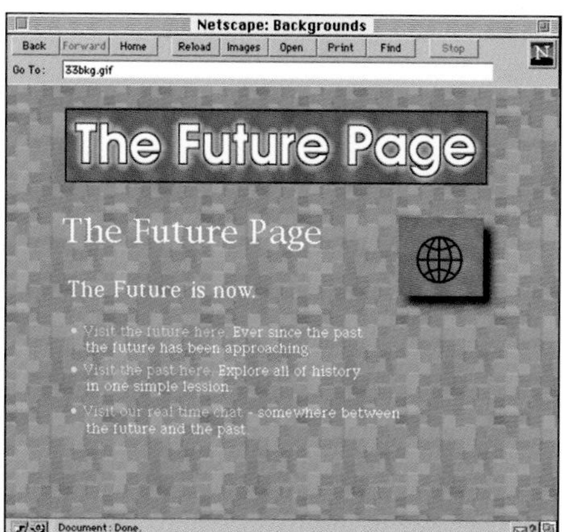

### Patchwork

An alternative to the Extrude filter is the Patchwork filter, which creates more uniform squares than the Extrude filter. After Step 2, we applied Filter➟Texture➟Patchwork (Tile Size: 2, Relief: 1).

**For more variations with tiles, try applying additional filters such as Texturizer, Glowing Edges, or Diffuse.** ■

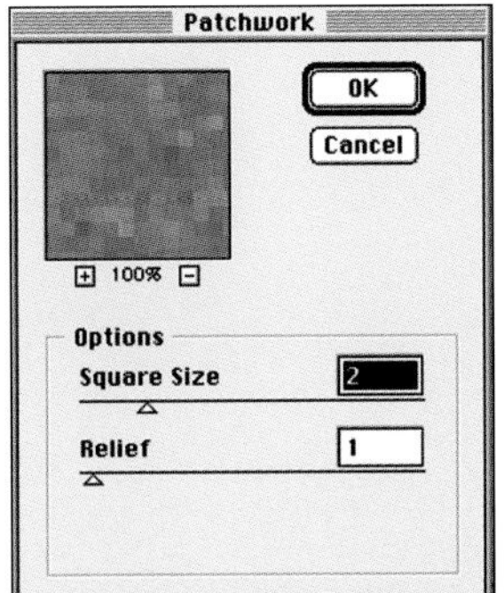


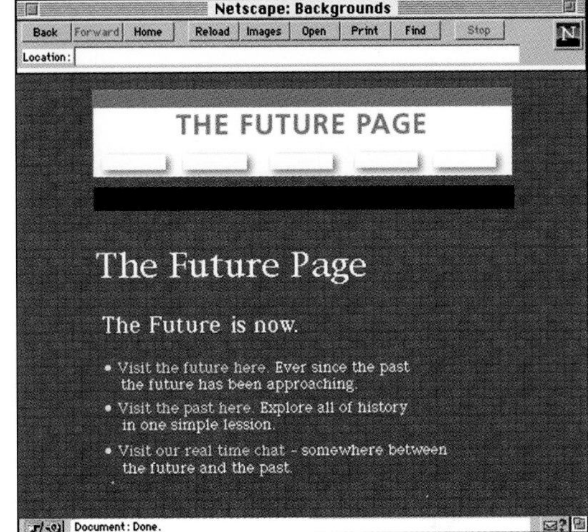

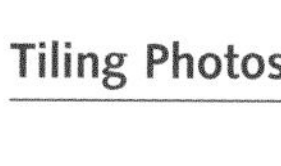

## Tiling Photos

Backgrounds made from photographic patterns are a great way to liven up a Web page. Although you might not want to use a photographic background on every page in a site, they can help to identify a page as unique topic or section placemarkers.

**1** Open the image for your background tile. The best images for tiles contain repeating or random patterns. We used an image from Photo 24 in this exercise. (This image can be found in the WebMagic folder on the CD.)

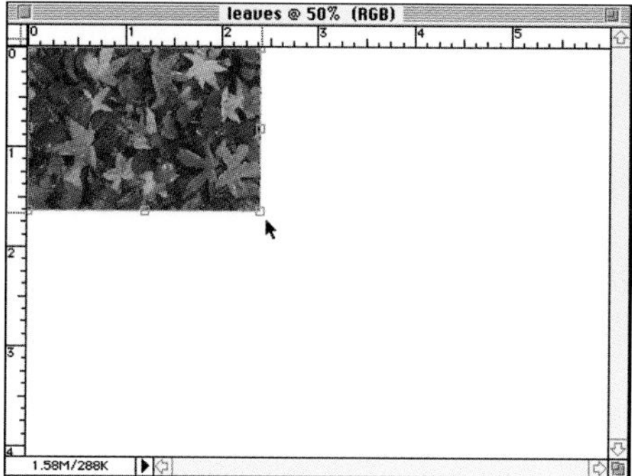


**2** Select➻All, then use Layer➻Transform➻Scale to shrink the image to the size you want. Press the Shift key while scaling the image to keep the proportions from changing.

**3** Crop the final selection to size by selecting Image➻Crop. After changing an image size or cropping, to sharpen the image always choose Filter➻Sharpen➻Unsharp Mask (we used: Amount: 50, Radius: 1, Threshold: 1). These settings will vary depending upon the image.

**4** Choose Image➛Adjust➛Brightness/Contrast to adjust the contrast. For this photograph we set Brightness to +70 and Contrast to -70.

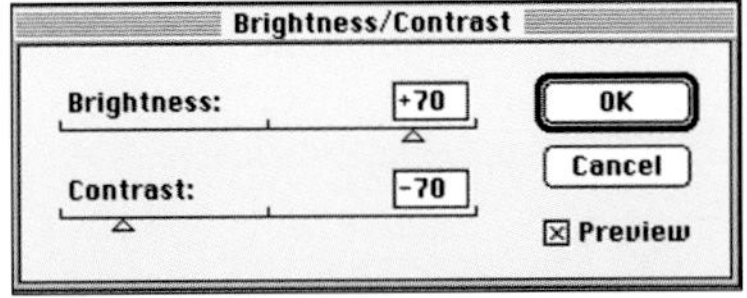


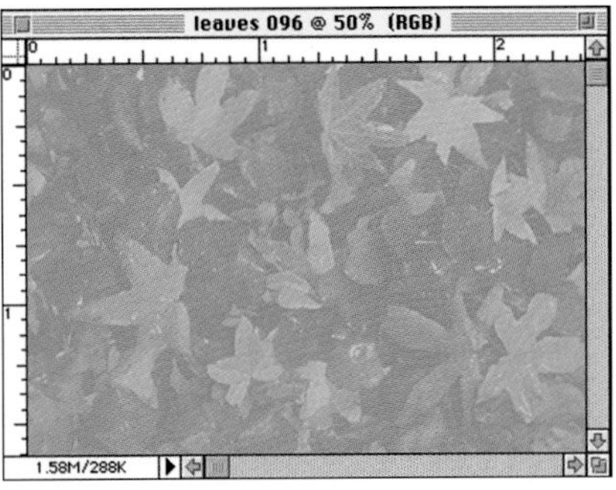


**5** Save as JPEG. This file is only 3K when saved as a JPEG; the same GIF file is 16K—a very substantial difference.

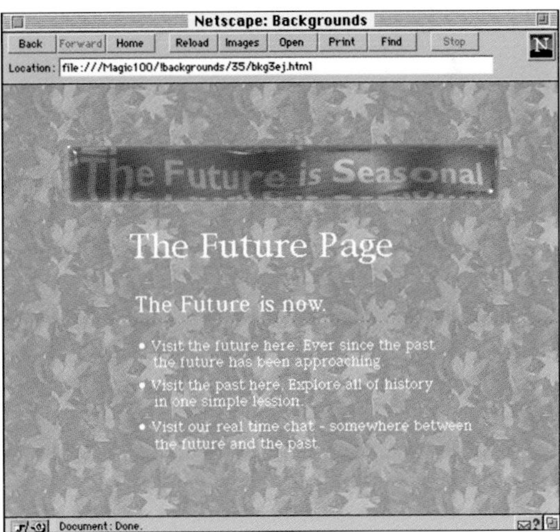

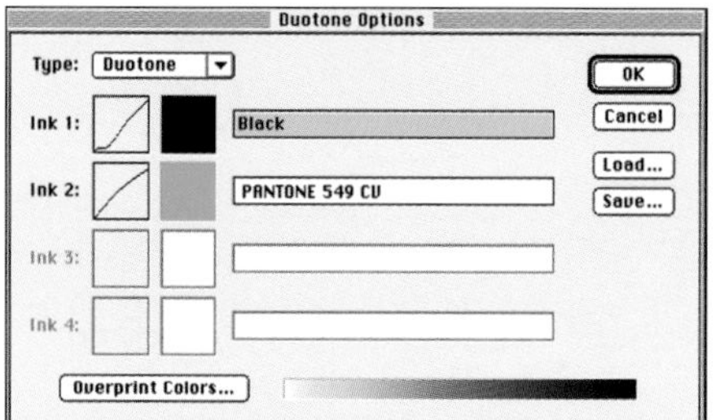


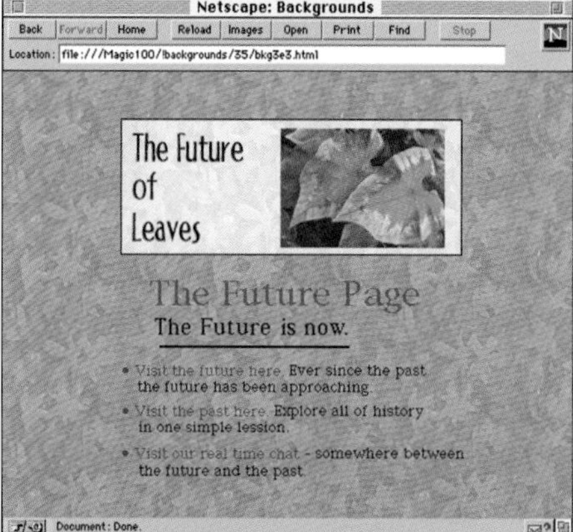

## VARIATIONS

To make this background more subtle, we removed the color with Image⇒Mode⇒Grayscale. Then we converted the image to duotone using Image⇒Mode⇒Duotone. We used black as our first color and green for our second color.

Light-colored type on dark backgrounds can be very effective.

**1** Open a file containing a small random pattern, such as this image of coffee beans on a platter.

**2** Zoom in to the image and select an area that is random, without any distinguishing characteristics.

**3** Choose Image➜Crop to crop the image to the selection. Then choose Filter➜Other➜Offset about 50% of the image size. In this case we used Horizontal: 47 pixels right, Vertical: 49 pixels down.

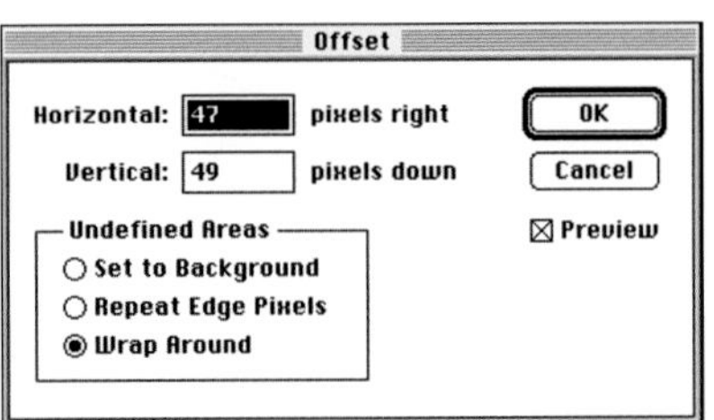


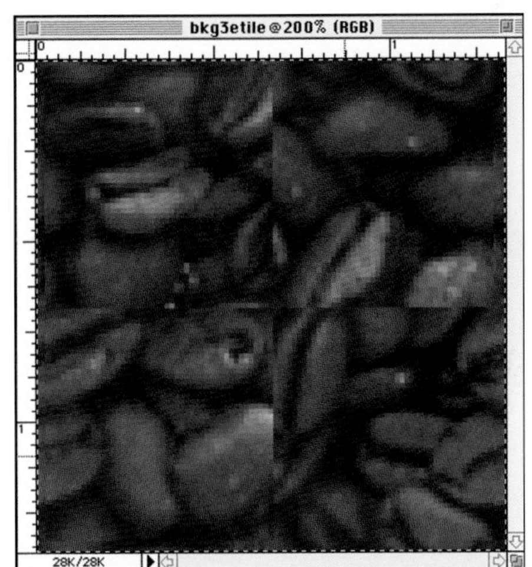

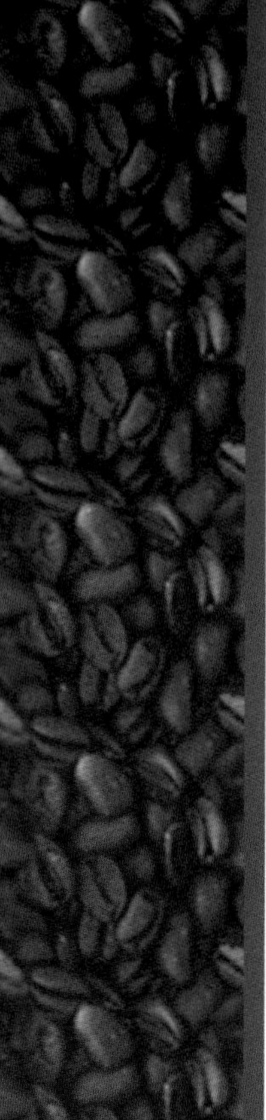

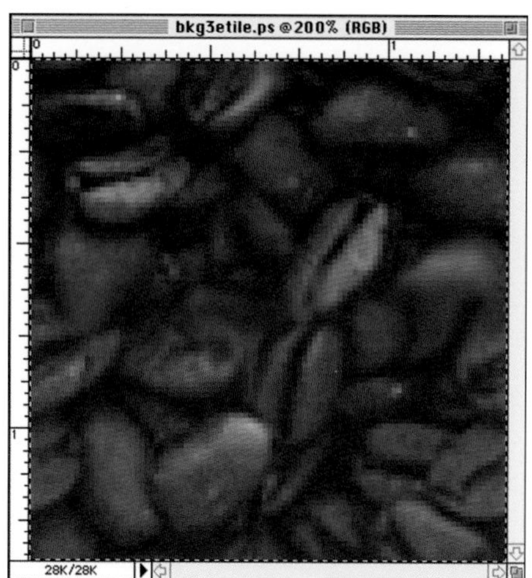


4 Double-click the Smudge tool icon. Set the Smudge tool Pressure to around 70% and select a small soft brush to work with. Zoom into the image again if you need to and carefully smudge the image across the seam. Use short strokes and follow the direction of the pattern.

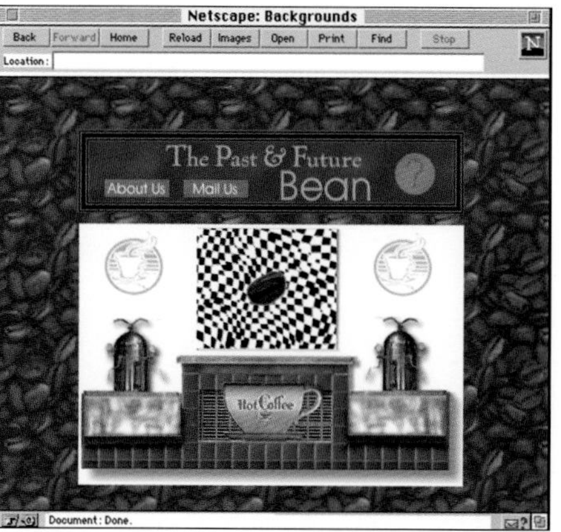


**5** Save as a JPEG file.

**6** Here we choose Image➛Adjust➛Brightness/Contrast (Brightness: -20, Contrast: -75) to make help make Web page type more legible. ■

Repeating type as a background wallpaper is a common technique used in television news broadcasts and corporate presentations. If you really want to stress the name of the company, Web site, or product, this technique might be just what the doctor ordered.

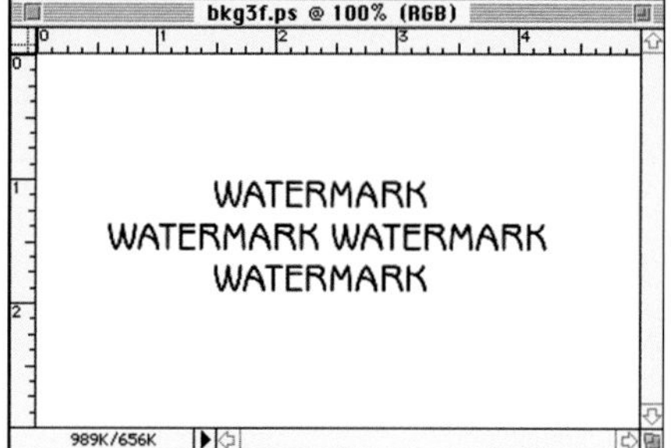


**1** Create a new file and create a new layer. With the Type tool enter the text. Repeat the same word on three lines, once on the first and third lines, twice on the center line, leaving a space between the two words on the center line. Set Text Alignment to Center.

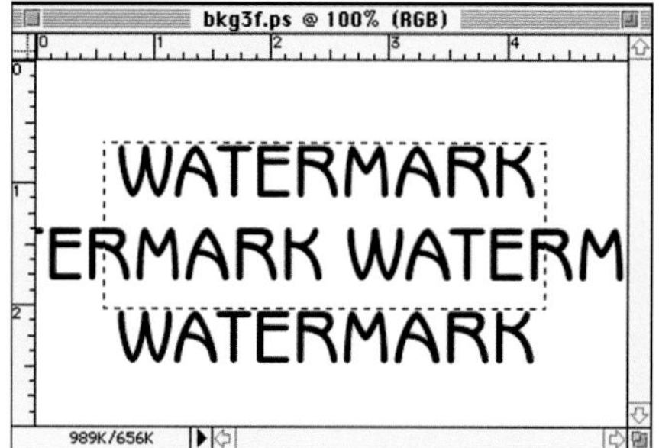


**2** This step requires some accuracy. Use the marquee tool to select the top two lines of text (the bottom line of text is used only as a guide for spacing). Begin the selection directly above the bottom line and extend the selection to the top edge of the first line. Letters can be cut through at the ends of the selection as long as both ends of the selection cut through the same letter at the same place.

**This exercise is easier to set-up if you use all upper case letters with a font like Helvetica Black or another heavy, sans serif font. When making the marquee selection, leave a small space in front and behind the top word, to insure that the words do not run together when the pattern is applied.**

3 Save the selection as a new channel (Channel #4) and choose Edit➡Define Pattern.

4 To test if your selection will work as a tile, create a new file and choose Edit➡Fill (Use: Pattern, Opacity: 100%, Mode: Normal).

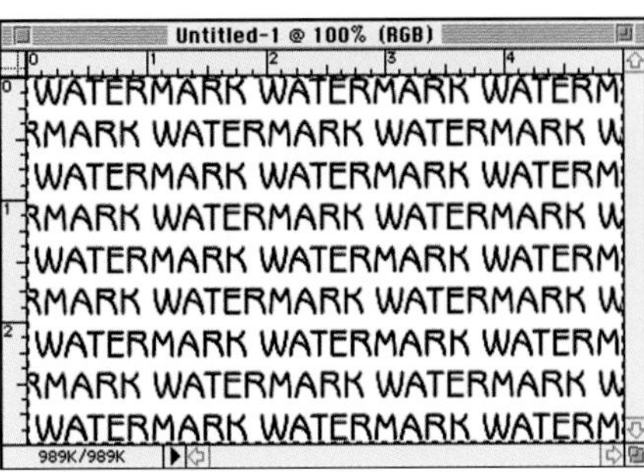

5 Return to the original file. With the type layer selected, set the Opacity slider bar on the Layer palette to 10%. Load the selection Channel #4 Image➡Crop, and use the Unsharp mask Filter➡Sharpen➡Unsharp Mask to resharpen the image (the unsharp mask settings will vary depending upon your image and the amount of resizing you have done).

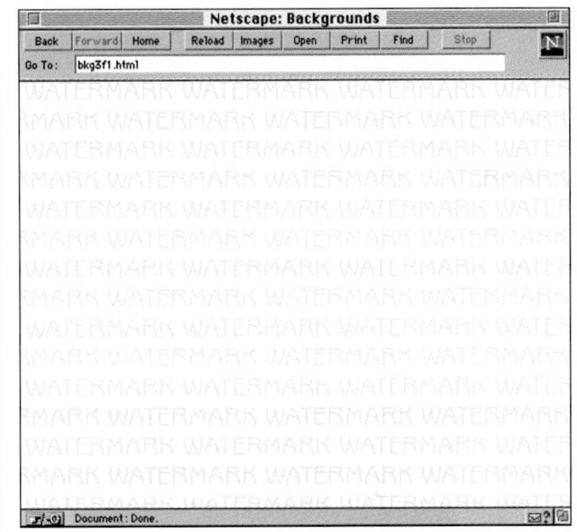

6 Export to GIF format.

## VARIATIONS

In this example, after Step 2, save the text selection (Channel #4). Select➡All, and fill with the color of your choice. Load the selection Channel #4. Finally, use Image➡Adjust➡Brightness/Contrast to brighten the selection by setting Saturation to +10%.

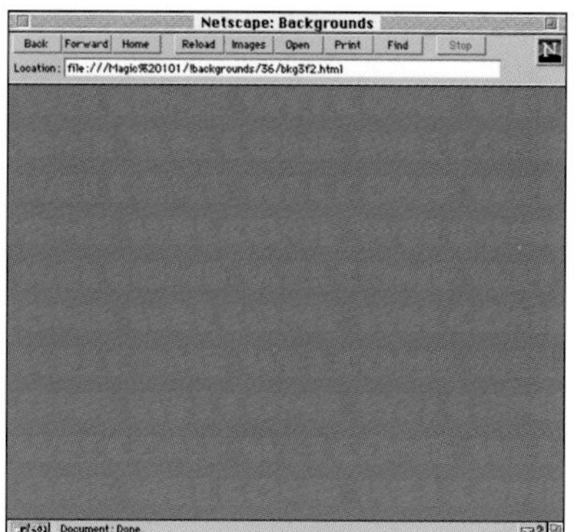


**TIP** **To hide the marquee while working use Command-H [Control-H]. This toggles the marquee between visible and invisible while still keeping it active.**

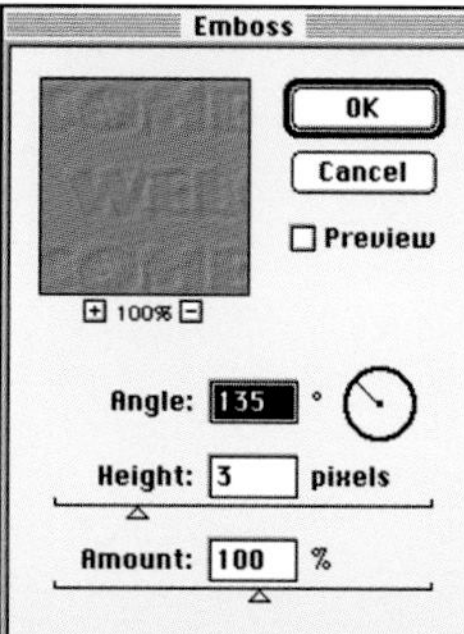


After Step 2, merge layers. Select➛All, then choose Filter➛Stylize➛Emboss (Height 5 pixels, Amount: 100%). Color can be added using Edit➛Fill (Soft Light, 100%). ■

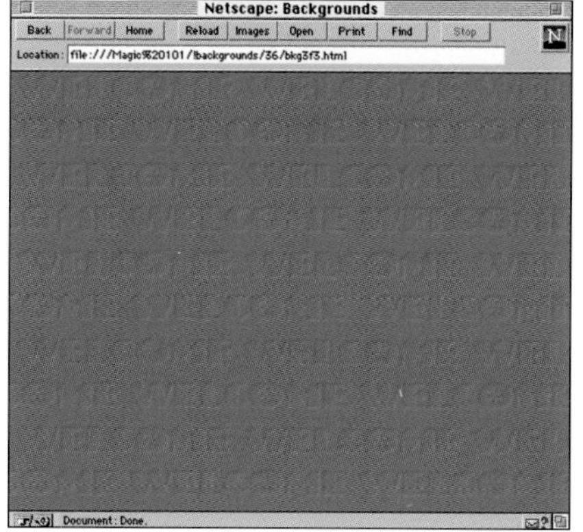

## PostScript Patterns

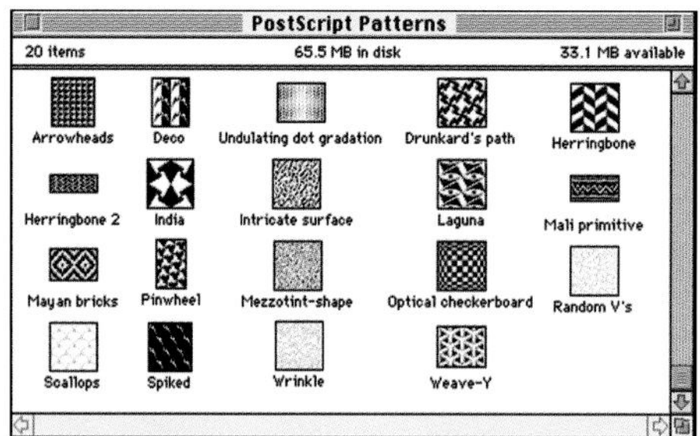


Included with Photoshop is a collection of PostScript Patterns that you can easily use as background tiles in your Web pages. The PostScript Pattern folder is located in the Goodies folder supplied with Photoshop. Our favorite patterns include Deco, Drunkard's path, Laguna, and Optical checkerboard.

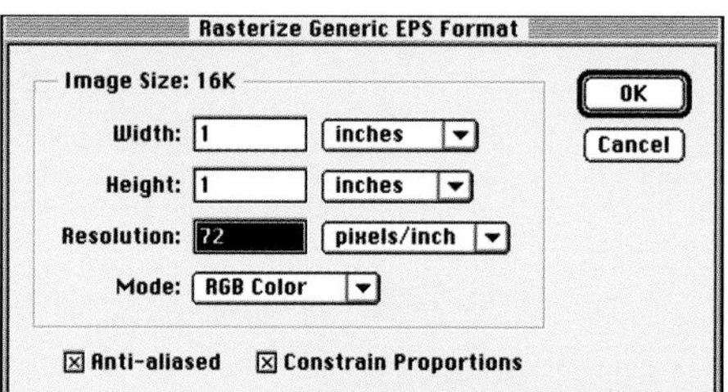


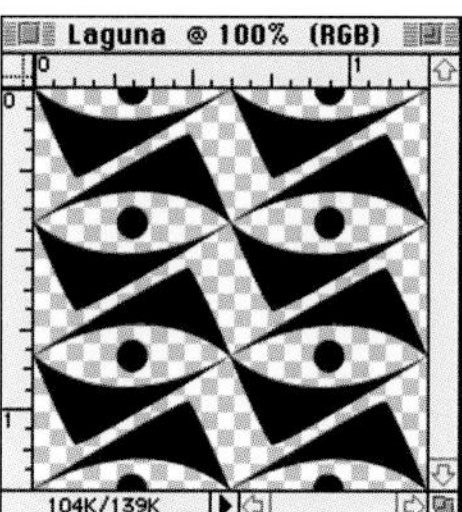


**1** Open a pattern from the PostScript Patterns folder: Choose File➞Open (Photoshop/ Goodies/Brushes & Patterns/ PostScript Patterns).The postscript patterns will open in Grayscale mode, convert mode to RGB. Note: The Postscript patterns in the Goodies folder are in Adobe Illustrator format—for more information on working with Illustrator files in Photoshop refer to the Photoshop manual.

TIP **Illustrator files can be opened at larger sizes or higher resolutions because they are vector-based and therefore resolution independent. Increase the dimensions of the image to create larger tiles.**

**2** Choose Select➵Color Range (Select: Highlights, Selection Preview: Black Matte, Selection Radio Button chosen). Save the selection (Channel #4)

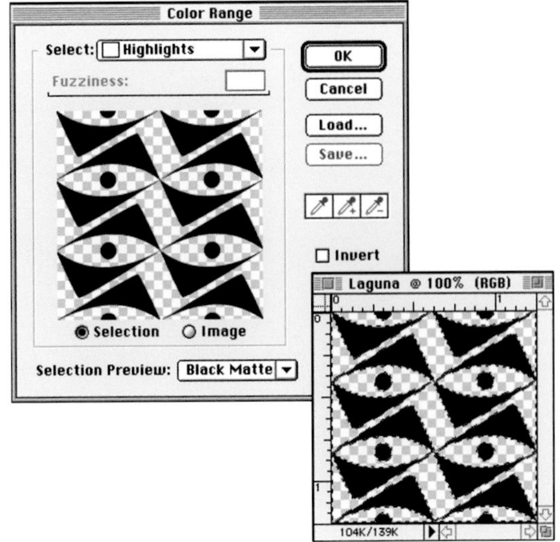


**3** Choose Image: Mode (RGB). Choose a foreground color. Select➵All, then choose Edit➵Fill (Use: Foreground Color). (We used RGB values 204, 153, 204). Next, load Channel #4 and fill it with a complementary color.

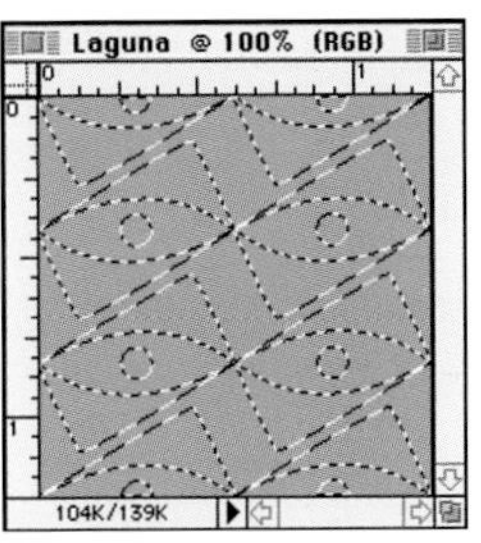


**4** Export to GIF format. Because this file uses only two colors, it reduces to around 1K as a GIF.

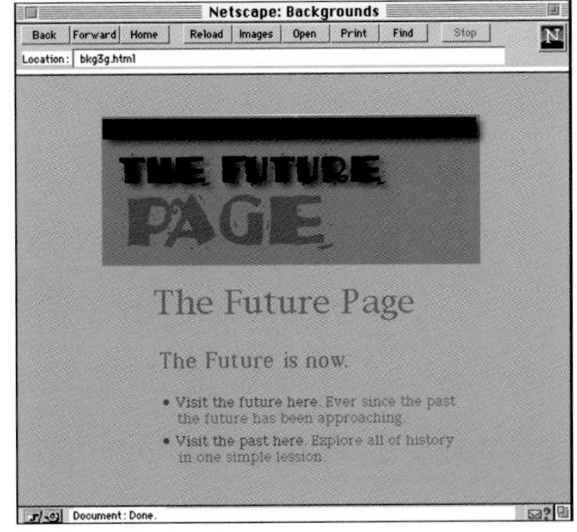

# VARIATIONS

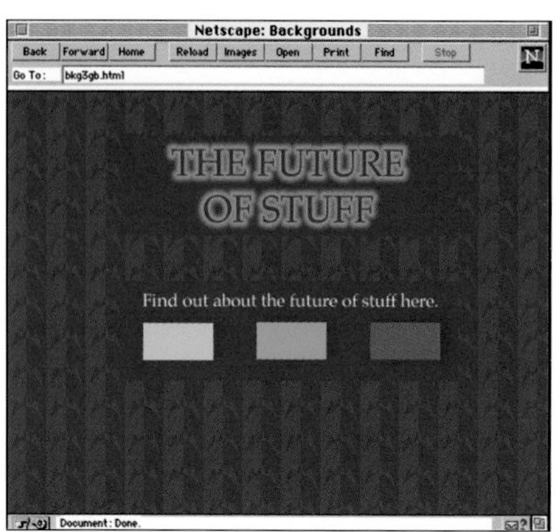


An example of the Deco pattern: Note how contrast has been kept low so that the background does not interfere with legibility of type on the Web page.

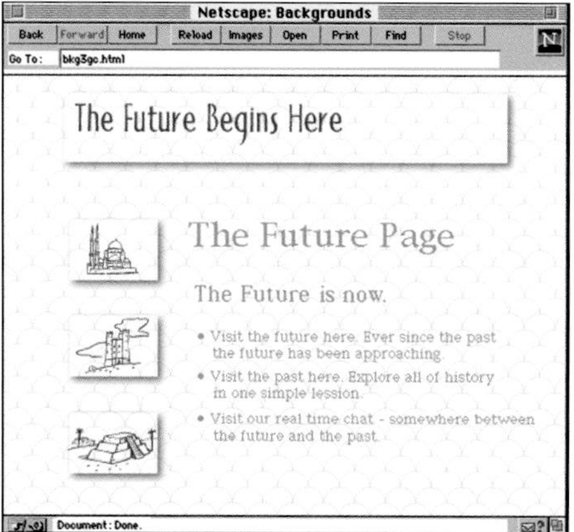


To create just a hint of the Scallops pattern on this page we used Filter➞Brightness/Contrast (Brightness: +30, Contrast: -70).

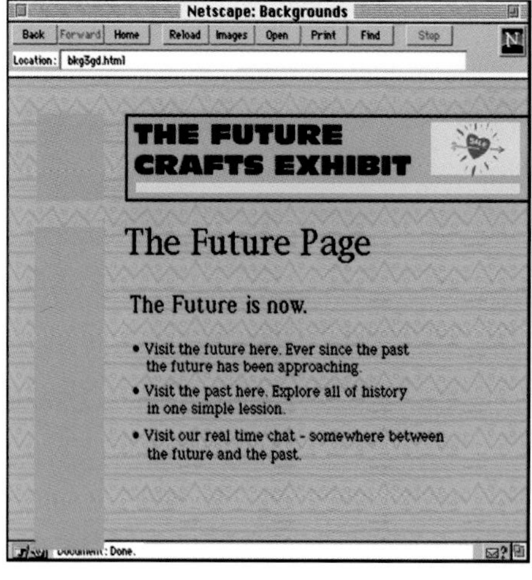


To colorize the Mali primitive we chose Image➞Mode (RGB), selected all, and then filled it with soft light, Edit➞Fill (Use: Foreground Color, Opacity: 100%, Mode: Soft Light). ■

## Diagonal Backgrounds

Diagonals work nicely as backgrounds for Web pages because they seem to defy the horizontal and vertical tiling of background patterns and they can create interesting effects, (especially wide diagonals) when you are scrolling the page.

**1** Create a new file, and then double-click the Line tool icon on the Toolbox to open the Line tool Options dialog box. Set the line width to 10 pixels and turn anti-aliasing off. Switch to the default colors and draw a black line across the image. Choose a new foreground color, then draw the second line a few pixels away from the first line. Use the Magic Wand tool to select the second line.

**2** Zoom into the page to enlarge the image, and with the line selected choose the Move tool and use the arrow key to move the line so they both touch. Then use the rectangular Marquee tool to select a portion of both lines from top to bottom.

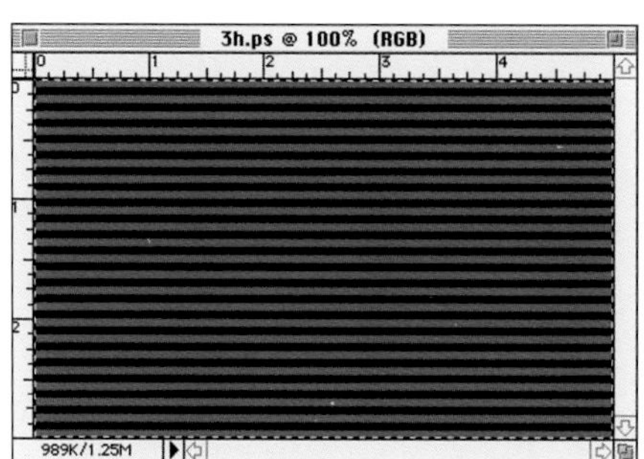


**3** Choose Edit➞Define Pattern. Select all and choose Edit➞Fill (Pattern, 100%, Normal).

**TIP** **For color consistency across platforms use the non-dithering 216 color palette for fill colors in your backgrounds.**

**4** With the image still selected, choose Image➛Rotate Canvas➛ Arbitrary (Angle: 45% CCW).

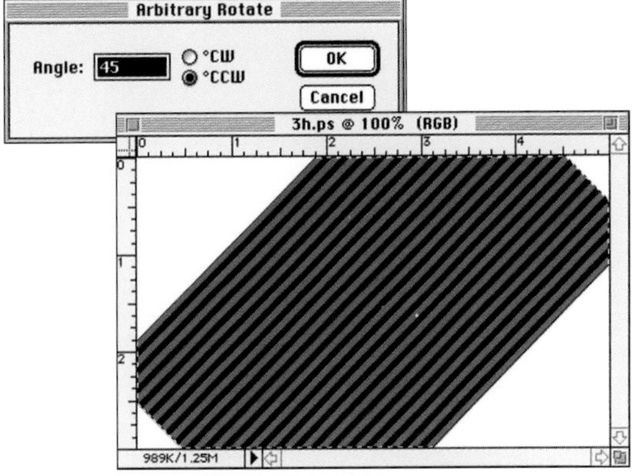


**5** Zoom into the image again to make the selection for the tile. Choose an even number of stripes, begin with the top left corner on a black stripe and end with the bottom right corner just touching a black line. Keep the selection square by holding down the Shift key while dragging. Save the selection (Channel #4).

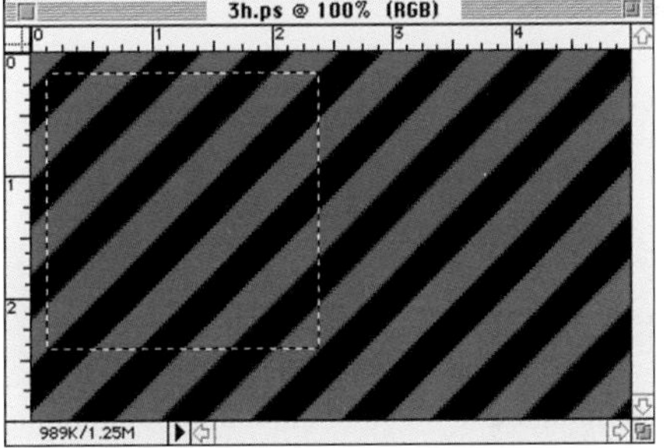


**6** Copy and paste the selection into a new file and export to GIF format.

# VARIATIONS

**1** After Step 5, choose Select➔Color Range (Select: Sampled Colors, Fuzziness: 80, Selection Preview: None, and choose Selection). Press the cursor on a black line and then click OK. All the black in your image should now be selected. Save this selection (Channel #5).

**2** To create subtle lines first select all and press Delete. Load the selection Channel #5 and choose Image➔Adjust➔Brightness/Contrast (Brightness: +10, Contrast: 0)

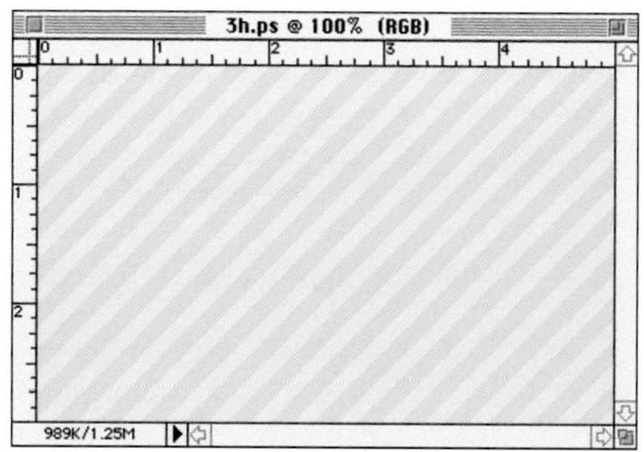


**3** Choose Select➔Inverse then Select➔Feather (Radius: 3 pixels) and then Image➔Brightness/Contrast (Brightness: -60, Contrast: 0). This adds some dimension to the stripes.

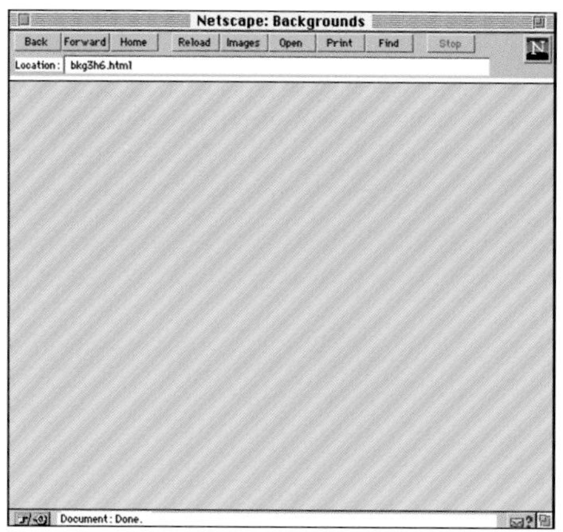

## Fabric Textures

The Glowing Edges filter was applied next to create this fabric-like texture. Select Filter➜Stylize➜Glowing Edges (Edge Width: 4, Edge Brightness: 6, Smoothness: 1). ■

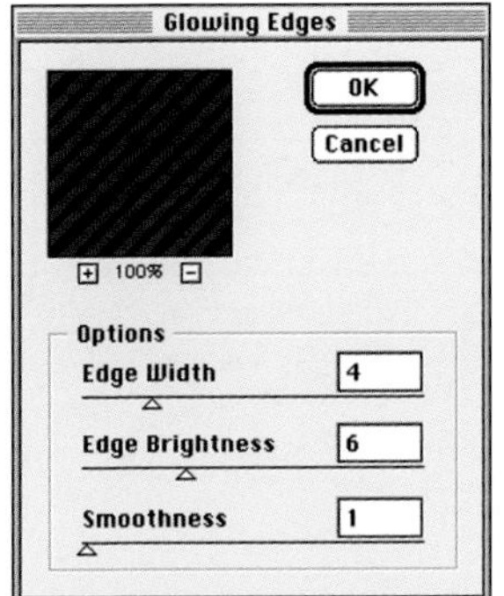

BORDERS

## Borders

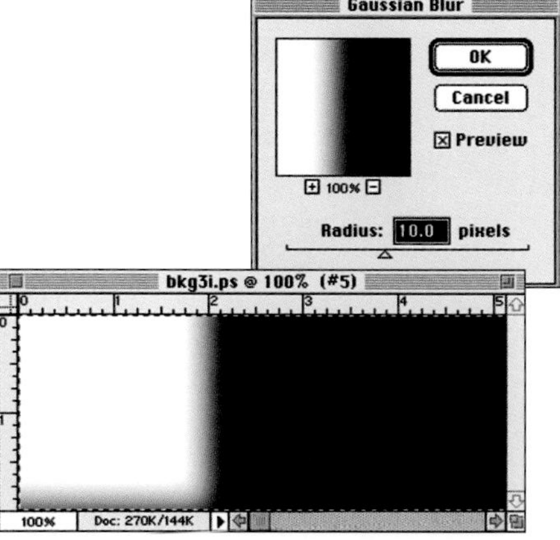


**1** Create a new file at least 640 pixels wide—the minimum width of a standard computer monitor. When creating background graphics with a border, note that the tile should run the full width of the screen. Choose View➛Show Grid and select an area about 2 inches wide on the left side of the image, save the selection (Channel #4), and then fill it with the color of your choice. Choose View➛ Hide Grid.

**2** To make a drop shadow on the border, duplicate Channel #4 (Channel #5). Then make Channel #5 visible. Choose Filter➛Blur➛ Gaussian Blur (Radius: 10.0 pixels). Leaving Channel #5 selected, hold down the Option [Alt] key and press the right arrow key twice. The result will extend the drop shadow by 2 pixels.

**TIP** **Sometimes when creating channel selections that have had a Gaussian Blur applied, the following may appear in a dialog box: "Warning: No pixels are more than 50% selected. The selection edges will not be visible." This is not a problem. Click OK.**

**3** Return to the composite channel. Load the selection Channel #5, then load the selection Channel #4, but use subtract from selection. Select Edit➞Fill (Use: Black, Opacity 80%).

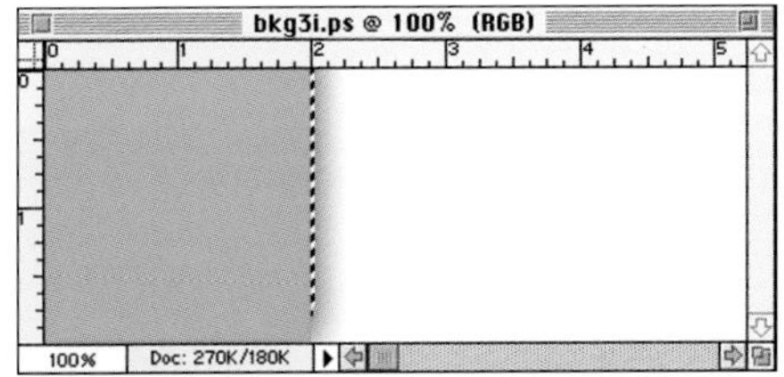


**4** Select an area that is the full width of the image and about 1/2 inch in height. Copy and paste the selection into a new file. Choose Layers➞Flatten Image. Export to GIF format.

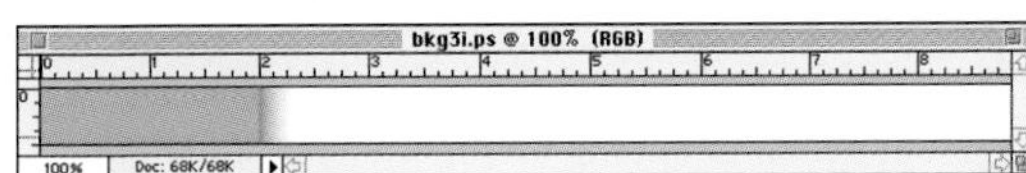


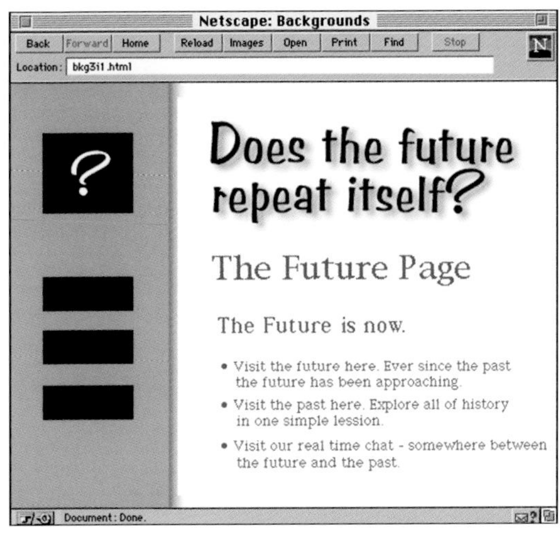

**Large areas of white or a single color do not substantially add to the size of GIF files.**

# VARIATIONS

To make a background look like note paper, draw two vertical lines for the border and one horizontal line across the image. The height of your selection will equal the line spacing on the background.

**1** Create a new file 640 pixels wide. Photoshop 4.0's new Guides feature is especially helpful when creating artwork that requires accuracy. Add vertical guides at 1 inch and 1 1/4 inches and five horizontal guides 1/2 inch apart.

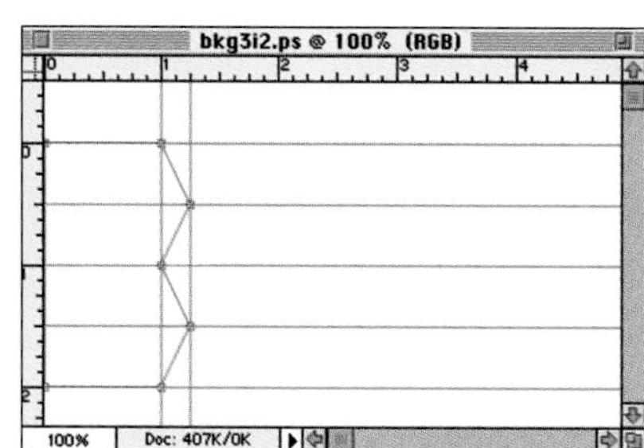


**2** Using the Pen tool, draw a path with three hinge points on the left side and two hinge points on the right side. Place the right top, center, and bottom hinge points at 1 inch and place the other two hinge points at 1 1/4 inch.

**3** Select the Convert Anchor Point tool from under the Pen tool in the Toolbox. Click the hinge point at 1 1/4 inch and drag down vertically 1/4 inch to create a curve point.

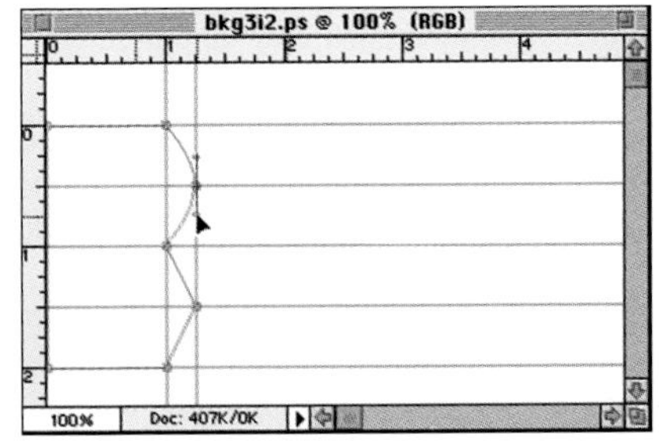


**4** Repeat the above step on the second hinge point at 1 1/4 inch. Then double-click the Work Path in the Paths palette to save the path as a selection.

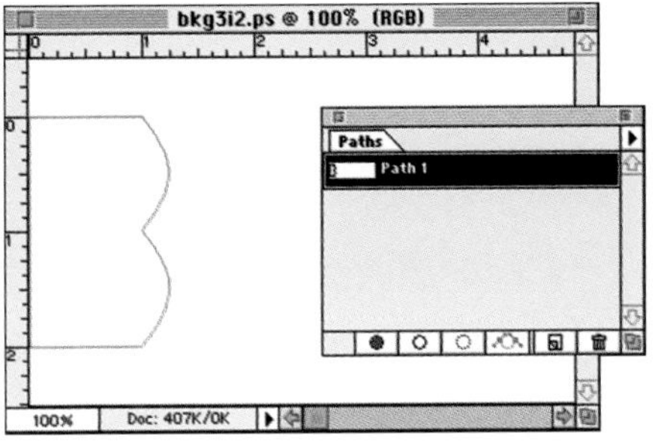


**5** Choose a foreground color. From the Paths pop-up menu choose Fill→Path (Use: Foreground Color). Then use the rectangular Marquee tool to make a selection that includes only one curve in the scallop and is the full width of the image (640 pixels).

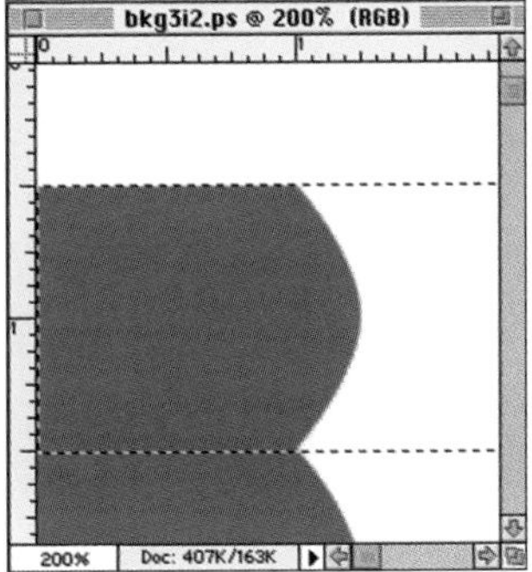

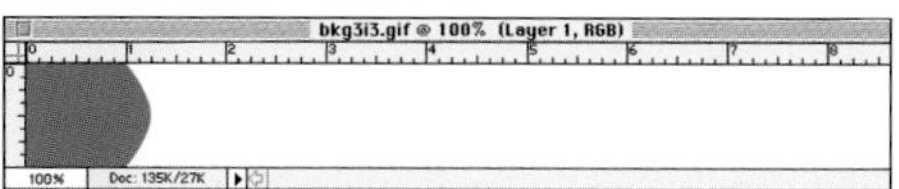


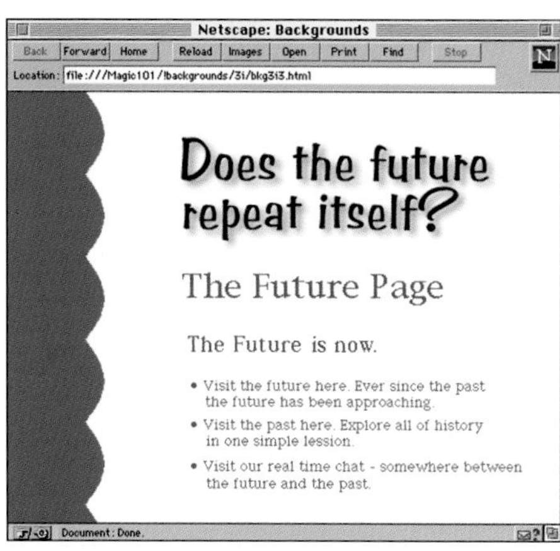


**6** Copy and paste the selection into a new file and export to GIF format. ■

### Terazzo

Terazzo is a commercial program by Xaos Tools specifically designed to make tile patterns. Select an image (for this example we choose a stock photo from Photo24 Texture Resource) and move Terrazzo's selection tile around to get instant tileable artwork!

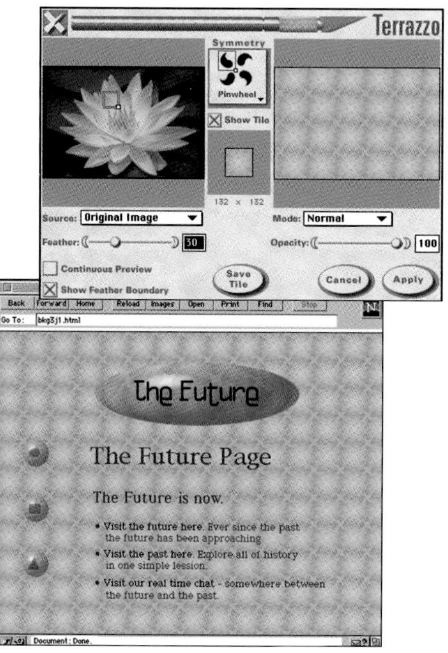


Dragging or resizing the tile creates new patterns.

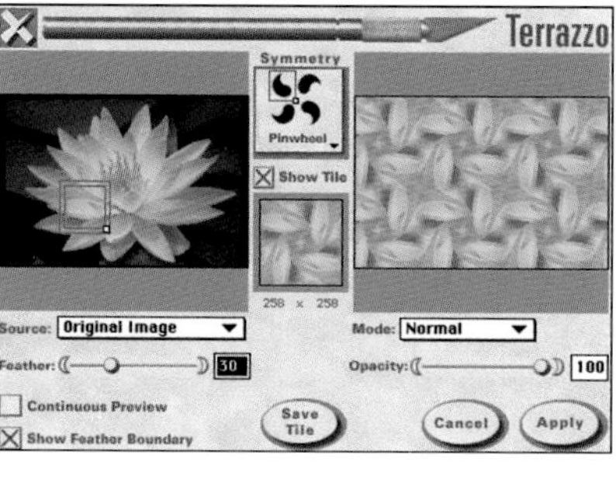


Terrazo offers 18 different symmetries for creating all kinds of patterns. This is an example of Primrose Path symmetry.

### Kai's Power Tools

Kai's Power Tools by MetaTools is one of the most useful and innovative collections of filters made for Photoshop. Texture Explorer is one of the most useful tools you can find for creating new textures from scratch.

If you don't have Texture Explorer, don't fret. You can find a sampling of background tiles made with KPT at the KPT Backgrounds Archive Web page:

http://the-tech.mit.edu/cgibin/KPT_bgs2.pl?Original1. ■

# Part II

## Titling

If there is one thing that can truly define the visual style and identity of a Web site, it is the application of typography. The choice of font styles, the size and color of the text, and the organization of type on the page create the dominant graphic identity of the site.

Unlike print, the Web page is a dynamic medium. Successfully combining decorative bitmapped type created in Photoshop with HTML-generated fonts requires an understanding and acceptance that the viewer is now your partner in the design process. Your Web page design can and will be modified by the viewer's browser, selected browser preferences, operating system, and hardware configuration.

Large ornamental type is used sparingly as a substitute for photographic images or illustrations. Any type on a Web page that is not HTML-generated text is bitmapped and viewed at screen resolution, either at 72 or 100 dpi. To maximize text readability use a solid-colored, anti-aliased typeface.

When you select the 216-color safe palette (also called a non-dithering palette), your smaller text will not lose legibility when viewed across different computer platforms. The safe palette works well because the colors are not dithered. Dithered colors don't work because they are visual simulations of color, just like a pointillist painting. A dithered color, built by selecting pixels from the available colors in a palette, is a random pattern your eye optically reads as a solid color. Filling text with a dithered color pattern adds visual noise to the font. This noise causes the thin strokes of the characters and smaller-sized text to lose image clarity.

## Shadows for Buttons

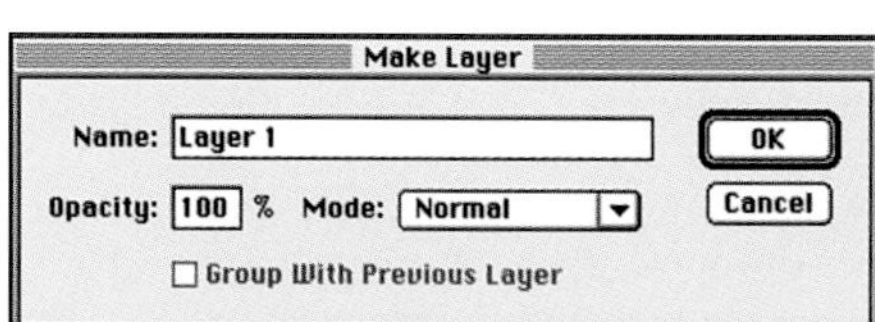

Shadowed text works well in buttons with textures by helping to demarcate the text from the button. Adding a black shadow to the text helps to sharpen the edge of the letters, making them easier to read.

**1** Create a new file with mode set to RGB and background transparent, or open a file containing the selected button style. We are using Bevel button on page 126.

**2** In layers dialog box, double-click background to open make layer dialog box. Rename background: Layer 1. Choose a foreground color for your label, maximizing contrast of foreground to background.

TIP **If you open a file that has been flattened, there will only be a Background. Renaming the background as Layer 1 creates a transparent background.**

**3** Enter the text. We selected Futura Bold, center alignment, anti-aliased on, spacing: 3. Use the move tool to position the text. This is Layer 2.

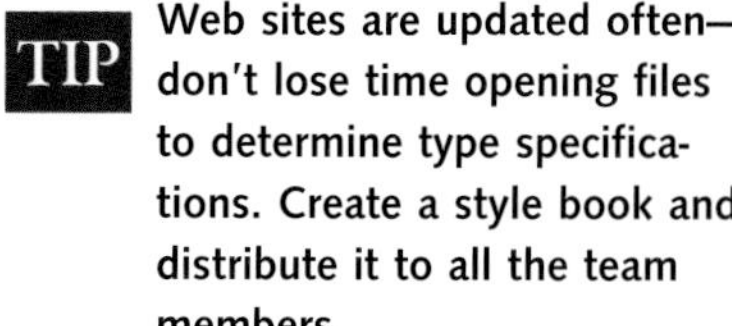

TIP **Web sites are updated often—don't lose time opening files to determine type specifications. Create a style book and distribute it to all the team members.**

4 Duplicate Layer 2 and name it Layer 3. Move Layer 3 below Layer 2. Make the Layer 2 invisible. Select Layer 3 shadow text. Choose Edit⇒Fill (Use Black).

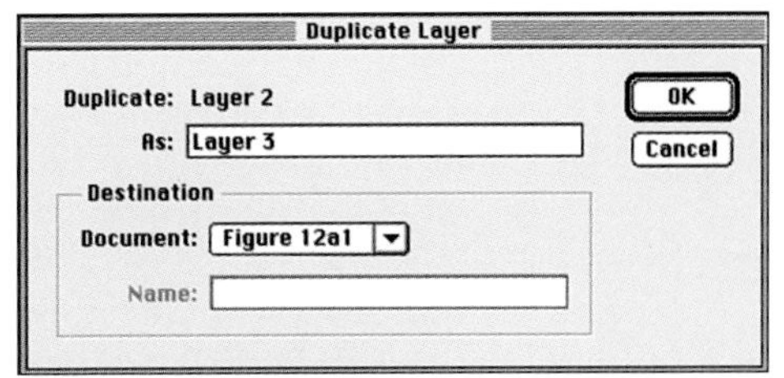


5 Choose Filter⇒Gaussian Blur (1 pixel). A slight blur makes the shadow appear to be part of the button's surface.

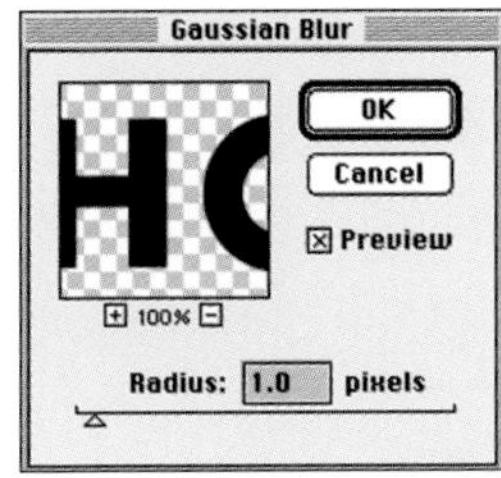


6 Select the Move tool. Using the arrow keys, move the shadow 4 pixels to the left and 4 pixels up. The Shadow should not appear to be touching the next character in Layer 2 text.

7 Layer 2 visible again and keep the Layer 3 active. Check for legibility of text. Adjust the postioning of shadow to foreground text as needed. Deselect the shadow.

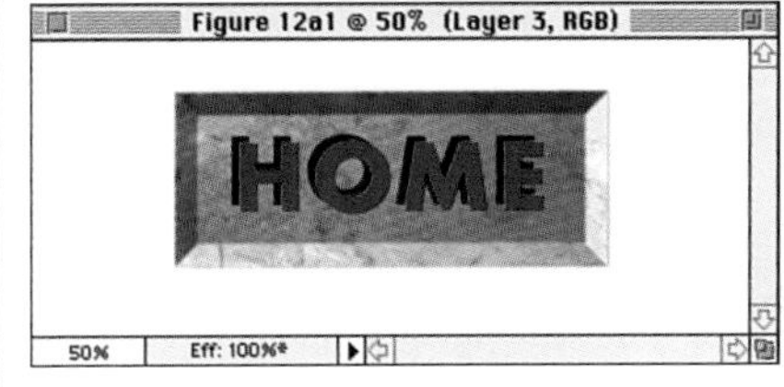


8 Export GIF format.

## VARIATION

You can create the effect of light hitting the text and creating the shadow. Using the Eyedropper tool, choose a light foreground color from the button texture to color match text highlight to the button color palette. Repeat Steps 4 and 5. Rename the layer as Layer 4. Move Layer 4 below Layer 2, but above the Shadow. Move the highlight text one pixel horizontally, and vertically one pixel to the side opposite the drop shadow. ■

## Object Shadows

Use drop shadows in your Web pages to help identify graphics and artwork that function as clickable links. This helps people to visually identify and separate the different elements of the page.

Here we used a variety of third-party plug-in filters to create different kinds of shadow effects. Check out the demos and sample catalog on the CD-ROM. (An optional Photoshop filter to use instead will appear between brackets.)

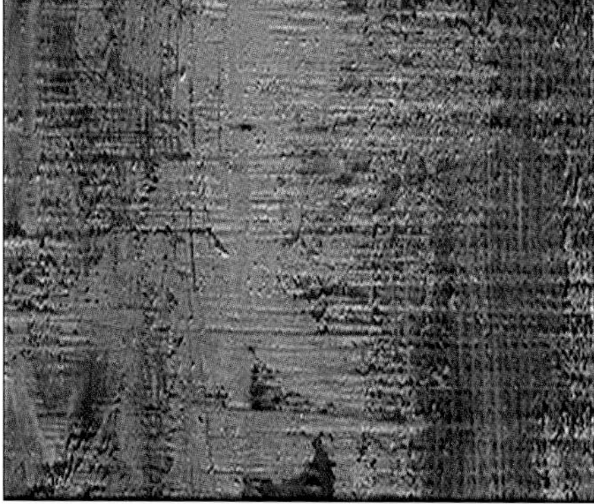

©PhotoSpin 1995

**1** Open a file containing the image or texture you want to use. Select one from the MetaTools Power Photos Series sampler collection included on the CD-ROM.

**2** Create a new file.

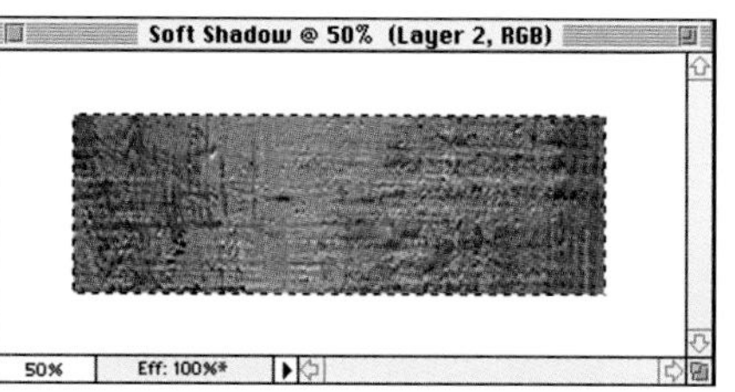


**3** Select a rectangular area with the Marquee tool large enough to fit your text with a shadow. Edit➛Paste into Paste your previously copied image into the selection, creating a new layer with a layer mask.

**4** In Layer 2, use the Marquee tool to select the rectangle selection that you pasted into. To soften the wood grain texture, choose Filter➛Blur➛KPT Gaussian Blur Weave [Angled Strokes].



### TOOLBOX

Alien Skin's
Drop Shadow
Motion Trail
Carve

KPT Gaussian
Blur Weave
Electricity

**5** Remove the layer mask by dragging the Layer Mask icon into the Trash icon on the Layers palette. Press the Apply button when the Warning dialog box appears.

**When you drag the Layer Mask into the Trash, a dialog box appears giving you the option to discard or apply the mask. If you apply the mask all unused areas of the image hidden by the Mask are removed.**

**6** Using the rectangular Marquee tool, select the textured rectangle and add an Alien Skin Black Box Drop Shadow (X and Y shadow Offset 32 pixels, Blur 25, Opacity 60%, Shadow Color black).

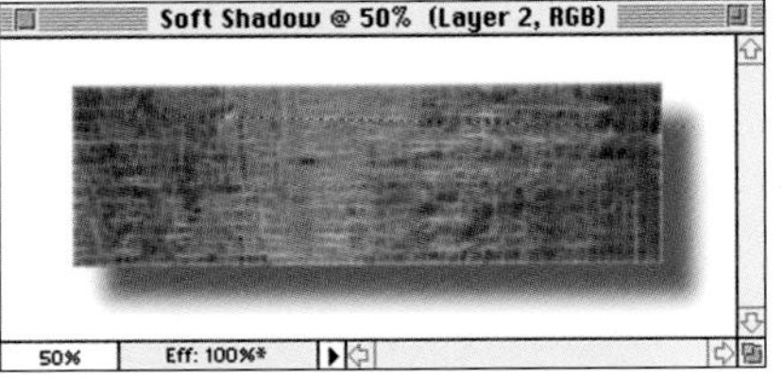


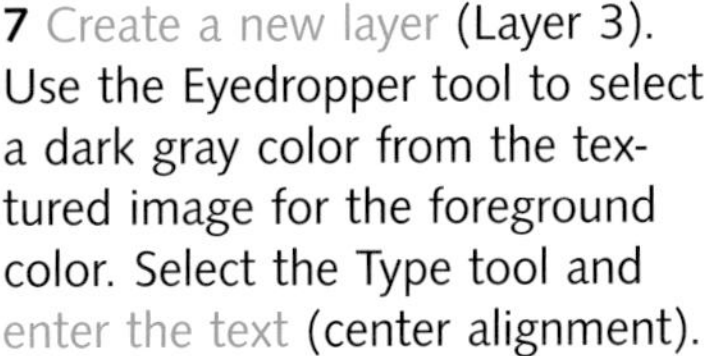

**7** Create a new layer (Layer 3). Use the Eyedropper tool to select a dark gray color from the textured image for the foreground color. Select the Type tool and enter the text (center alignment).

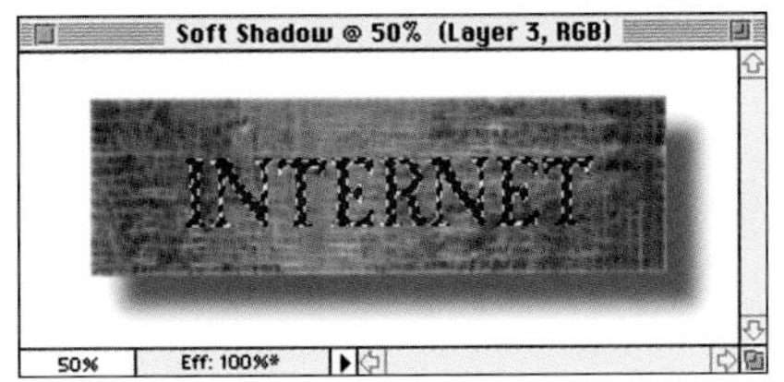


**8** Duplicate Layer 3 twice (changing the name to Layer 4 and Layer 5). Make Layer 3 active and make Layers 4 and 5 invisible.

**9** Use the Magic Wand tool to select Layer 3 text. Choose Filter➞Blur➞KPT Gaussian Electrify [Gaussian Blur]. Select the Move tool and use the arrow keys to move the text 7 pixels right and 7 pixels down. Deselect text.

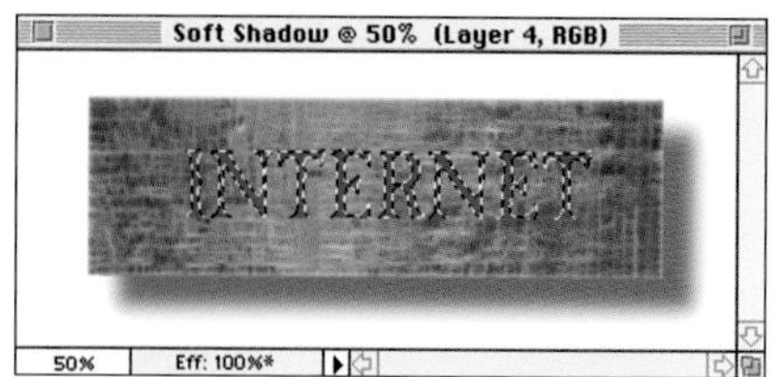


**10** Make Layer 4 visible and active. Make Layer 3 invisible. With the Magic Wand tool and Shift key, select the text on Layer 4. Fill the selection with a new foreground color. We used a medium blue, (15, 72, 149) for this example.

**11** Choose Filter➛Alien Skin➛ Motion Trail (length 24 pixels, opacity 80%, direction 315°, with Just Smear Edges activated) [Wind].

**12** Make Layer 5 visible. Choose a foreground color (we used 231, 213, 214) With the Magic Wand tool, select the text and fill with the light beige color.

**13** Export the image to GIF format.

**The Paste into command adds layers. To keep file sizes manageable, merge down layers wherever possible.** ■

## Filling Type with an Image

Pasting an image into a heading maximizes use of screen area. By combining pictures with text, the enhanced effect adds both decorative value and visual meaning to the words. This technique can be particularly useful for Web sites targeting an international, multilinguistic audience.

**1** Open the PhotoDisc image file or another stock photograph that complements your Web page design.

© PhotoDisc, Inc. 1996

**2** Choose Image➙Image Size and totally resize the image to fit the design layout (in our example, 3.5 inches by 3.5 inches, 72 dpi). Choose Filter➙Sharpen➙Unsharp Mask.

Image Size

Pixel Dimensions: 298K (was 10.1M)
Width: 282 pixels
Height: 360 pixels

OK
Cancel
Auto...

Print Size:
Width: 3.921 inches
Height: 5 inches
Resolution: 72 pixels/inch

☒ Constrain Proportions
☒ Resample Image Bicubic

**TIP** **Avoid converting a high resolution 300 dpi image directly to 72 dpi. It is better to make the transition in several steps using 300, 266, 200 and 72 dpi. (These numbers and steps may vary: Factor in image content and detail. Test**

**different settings and compare results. Save the settings for future reference.)**

**Apply the Unsharp Mask to the final file. However, remember when applying unsharp mask settings, what you see onscreen is what you will want to use in your Web page. Begin with a threshold setting of five for images with skin tones.**

**3** Create a new file. Enter the text using the Type Mask tool. We selected Franklin Gothic Heavy (center alignment).

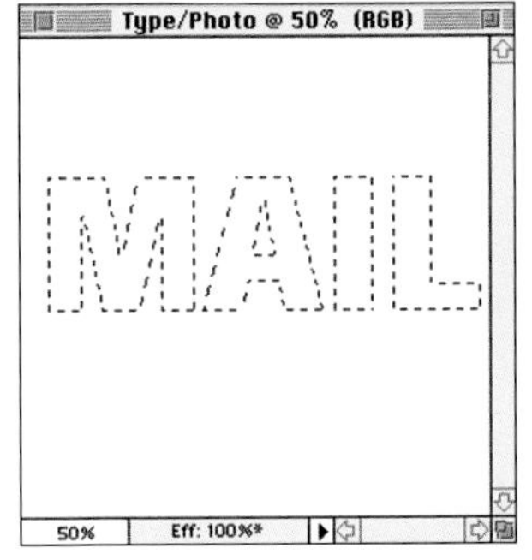


**4** Copy the resampled image and Edit➻Paste Into the type selection and enable the layer mask. Apply, then remove, the layer mask. This masks out unused portions of the image.

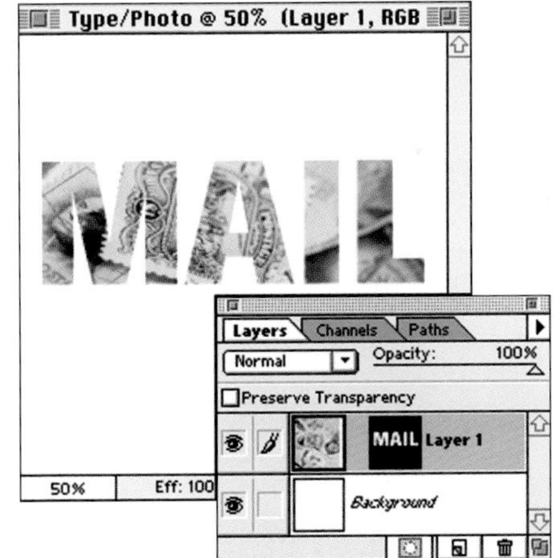

5 Create a drop shadow with the Alien Skin Black Box filter. Filter settings are x shadow offset: 7 pixels, y shadow offset: 9 pixels, blur: 61, opacity: 88% and shadow color: black. If you don't have the Alien Skin filter, see Shadows (page 70) for an alternative method. Deselect the text. Fill the background with a color. Save.

## VARIATIONS

### Adding a Selection

© PhotoDisc, Inc. 1996

1 Open another PhotoDisc image—an envelope, located in the PhotoDisc folder on the CD-ROM. Repeat Step 2. Use the Pen tool to select the envelope. This creates a Work Path in the Paths palette.

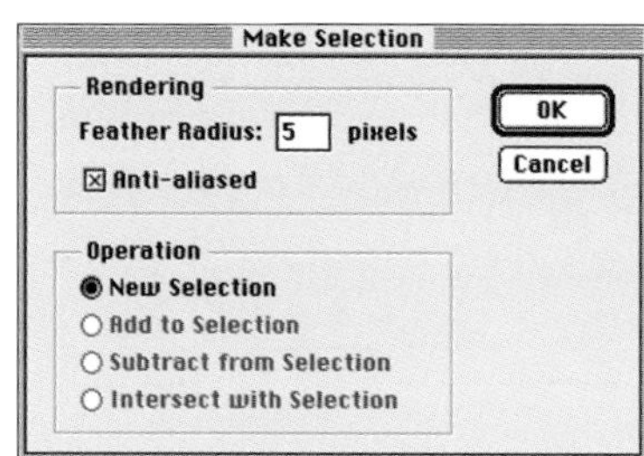


2 In the Path palette pop-up menu, choose Make Selection (Feather: 5 pixels).

3 Copy and Paste the selected envelope into the new file with the text and background. Move Layer 2 below Layer 1.

**4** Select Layer 1. Use the Move tool to reposition the text to the bottom of the window. Save as a new file.

**5** Export to GIF format. ■

For text heavy sites, translating a 2D header or label into three-dimensional letters can easily bring a distinctive, one-of-a-kind look to your Web page. Animated 3D "flying logos," like those seen in the opening titling sequence of a TV program, can add visual interest and create an easy to remember identity for your Web site or corporate banner. If you are interested in animating your 3D type, check out our Animation section beginning on page 205.

If you would like to add 3D type or icons to your Web page, but you don't know how to do 3D graphics—here is an alternative. Using the Photoshop Type Mask tool, one-color decorative fonts can be filled with different colors, tones, and textures to create a simulated 3D effect.

**1** Create a new file or open a file containing the selected button style. We are using Bevel Button on page 126.

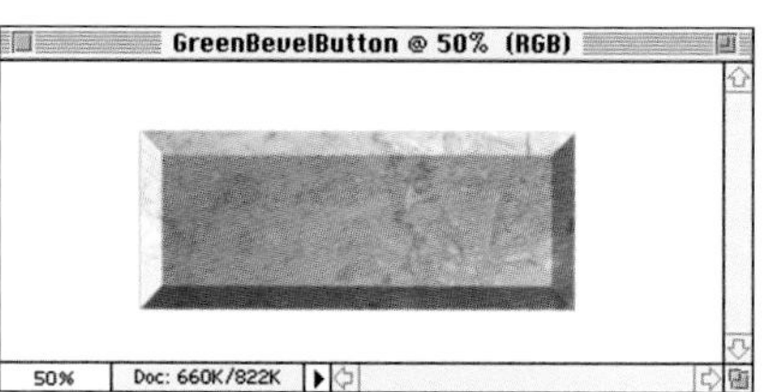


**2** Choose Image➙Rotate Canvas➙180°. Rotating the canvas will make the button's light source match the shadow pattern on the text.

**3** Choose Image➛Adjust➛ Hue/Saturation. Adjust the hue slider bar to +85 to create a green button.

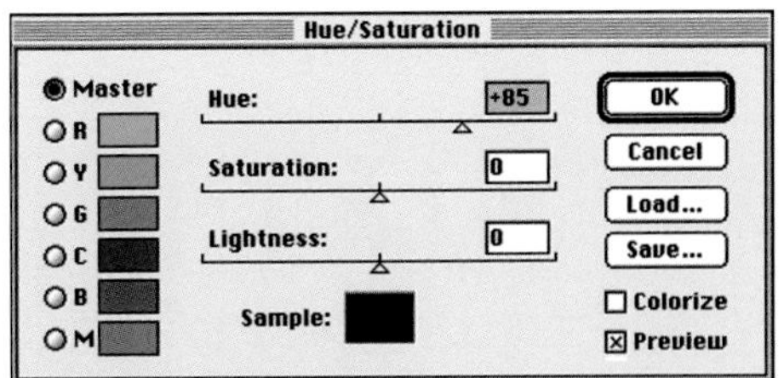


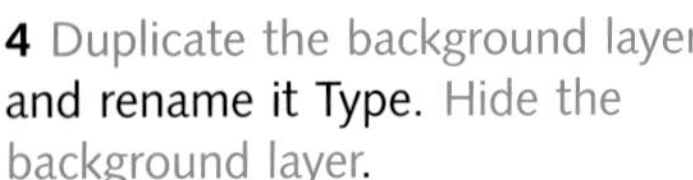

**4** Duplicate the background layer and rename it Type. Hide the background layer.

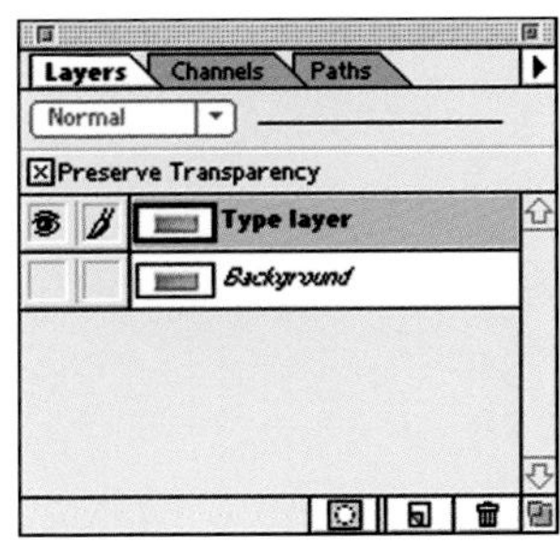


**5** Make the Type layer active and use the Type Mask tool to enter the text. We selected BuxomD (center alignment and Spacing: 3). If you don't have BuxomD, we provide a file, 3Dtype, with the word HOME typeset in the CD-ROM folder named WebMagic. You can use the file to create a mask.

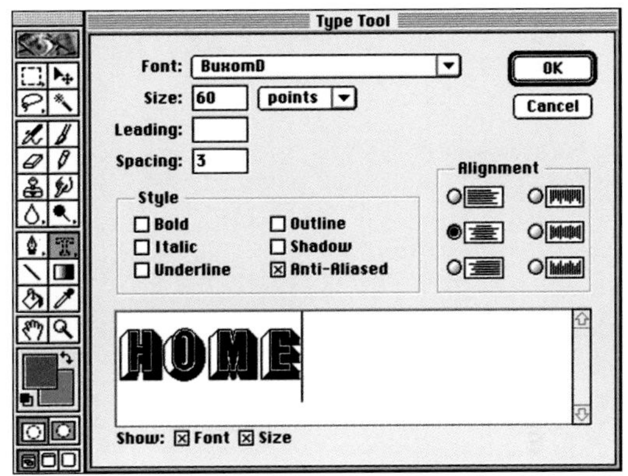


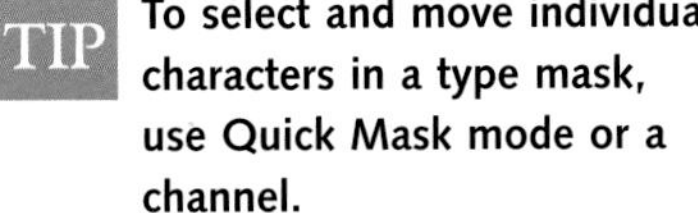

TIP **To select and move individual characters in a type mask, use Quick Mask mode or a channel.**

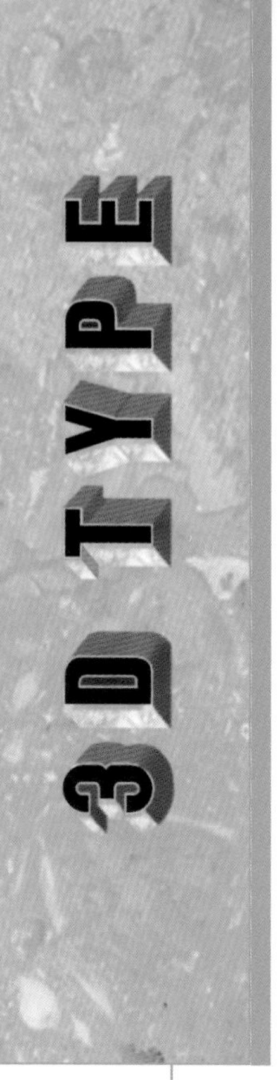


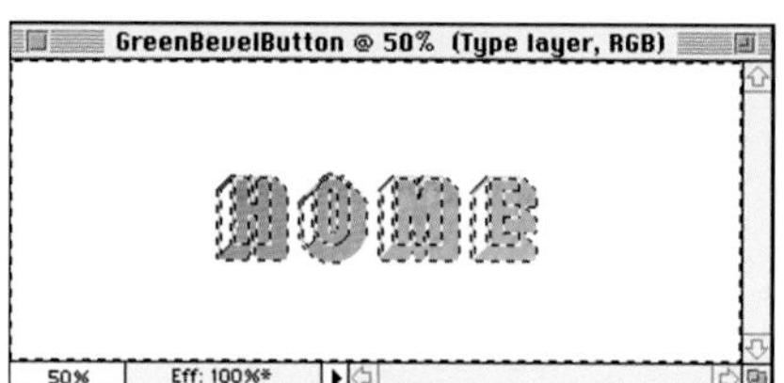


6 Invert the type mask. Choose Select➔Inverse and delete. The Type layer displays filled text with a transparent background.

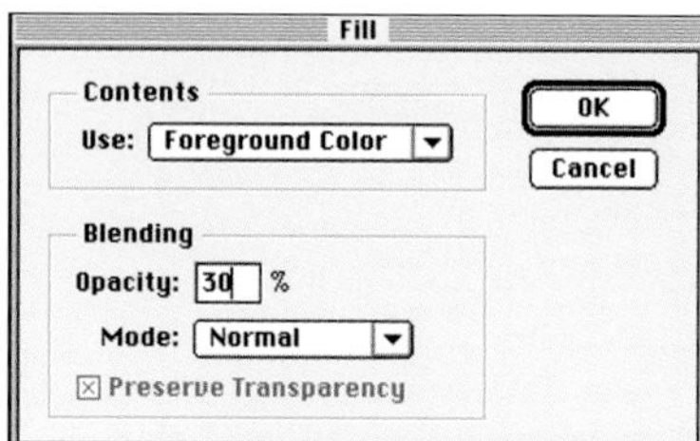


7 Choose Select➔Inverse. Keep the type mask active. Edit➔Fill (Use: Black, Opacity: 30%). This darkens the textured text to match the button's right side bevel.

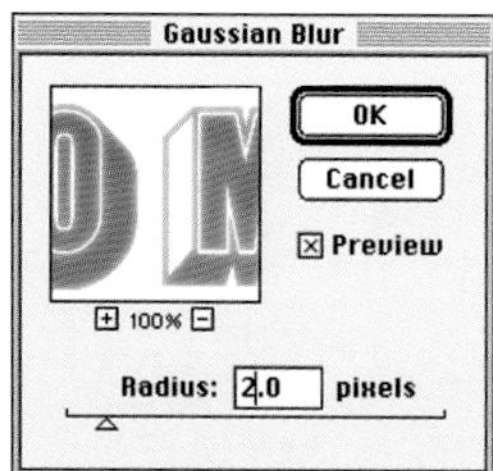


8 Choose Filter➔Gaussian Blur (2 pixels). Make the background color visible. The type and button now appear to be molded together. Deselect the text.

9 Make the background layer active. Use the Marquee tool to select the left button bevel. Choose Edit➔Copy. We are copying the button's left bevel to paste into the left side of each letter.

10 Select the Type layer. Use the Magic Wand tool to select the left side of each letter one at a time. Choose Edit➔Paste Into, pasting in the section of the bevel you copied in Step 9. Paste into creates a layer mask. Remove the layer mask by dragging the Layer Mask icon into the Trash icon on the Layers palette. Deselect the text.

**11** Use the Magic Wand tool and the shift key to select the top face of each letter. Fill the selection with the foreground color. (We used the RGB values 39, 17, 46.) Deselect the text.

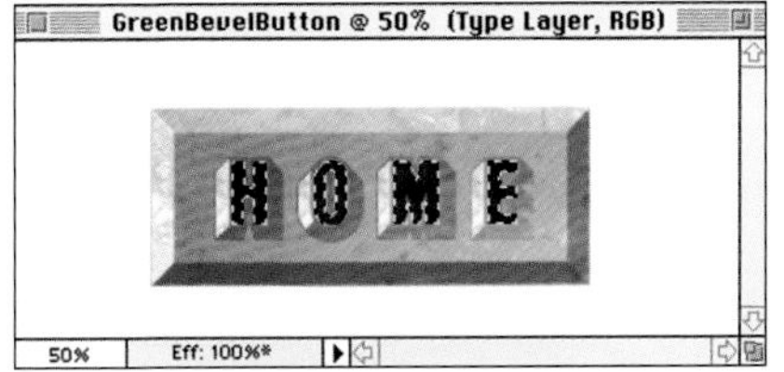


**12** Use the Magic Wand tool and the Shift key to select the shadow in each letter. Choose Select➛Inverse. Enter Quick Mask. Edit the mask to deselect all areas except lower portions of letters and the base of letter E's three horizontal cross-strokes. Exit Quick Mask.

**13** Choose Edit➛Fill. (Use: Black, Opacity: 30%) to fill the selection with black.

**14** Export to GIF format. ■

## Outlined Caps

When pictures are not appropriate, substitute large numbers as decorative elements on a Web page. Numbers can help organize information and they also serve as imagemaps to "hot link" to other pages or Web sites.

**1** Create a new file. Keep file dimensions (height and width) to a minimum. Set margins as narrow as possible to keep files small for faster file download times.

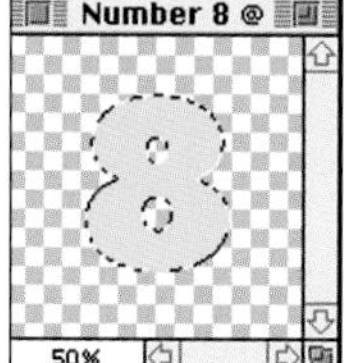


**2** Choose a foreground color to be the outline color. We picked a bright yellow (RGB 251, 243, 5). Enter the text. We used Futura Extra Black (center alignment). With the Magic Wand tool, select number 8. Use the Move tool to move it into position. Keep the text selected.

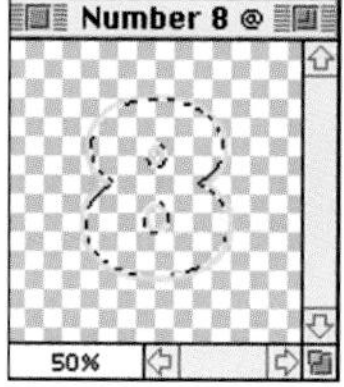


**3** Turn off the Preserve Transparency Option. Choose Edit➞Stroke (8 pixels) to convert the text to outline font. The text has a yellow stroke and a yellow fill. Press Delete to remove the yellow fill.

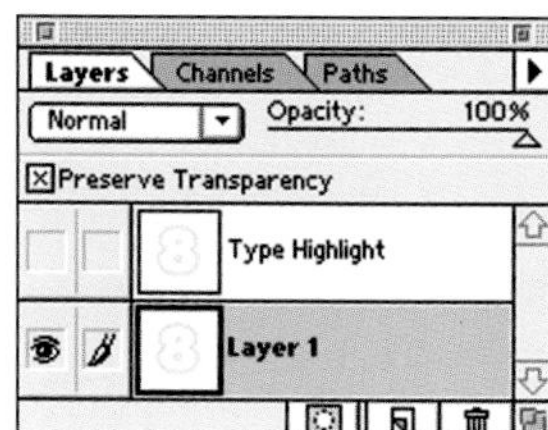


**4** Duplicate Layer 1 twice. Rename Layer 1 copies: Layer 2 and Layer 3. Hide Layer 3. Make Layer 2 active. Because we will apply a Gaussian blur to the yellow outline, we created this second duplicate layer to keep a copy of the colored line at full intensity and sharpness.

**TOOLBOX**

KPT Texture Explorer

**5** Choose Filter➝Gaussian Blur (2 pixels).

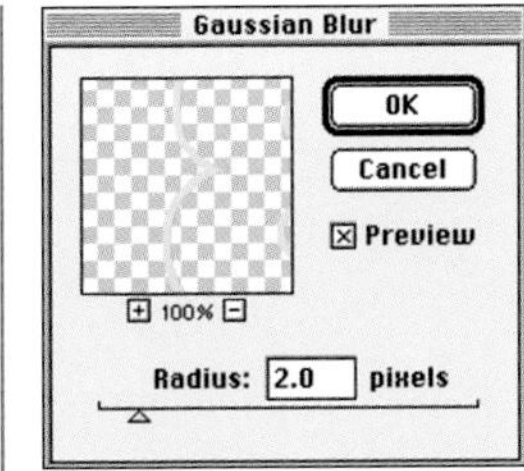


**TIP** **If you want a larger glow around your letter, try Filter➝Stylize➝Glowing Edges or the Alien Skin Black Box filter Glow.**

**6** Select Layer 1. Use the magic wand tool to select the interior space between the outlines of the unblurred number 8 on Layer 1. Turn off the preserve transparency option. Choose a foreground color, a vivid green (RGB 18, 140, 53). Fill the selected center area of the letter.

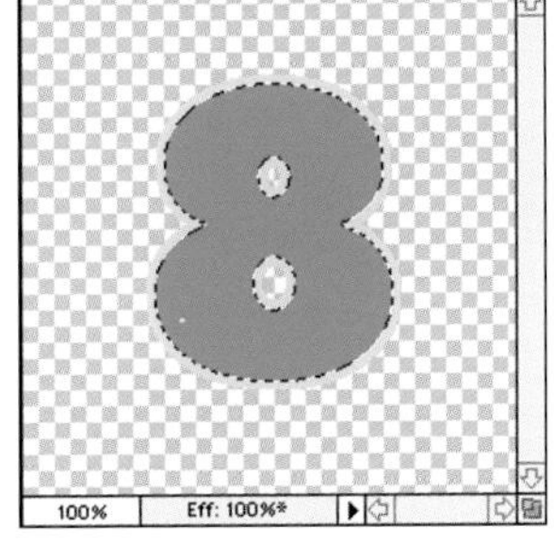


**7** With the center of the letter still selected, choose Filter➝Noise➝Add Noise (80 pixels, Distribution Uniform)

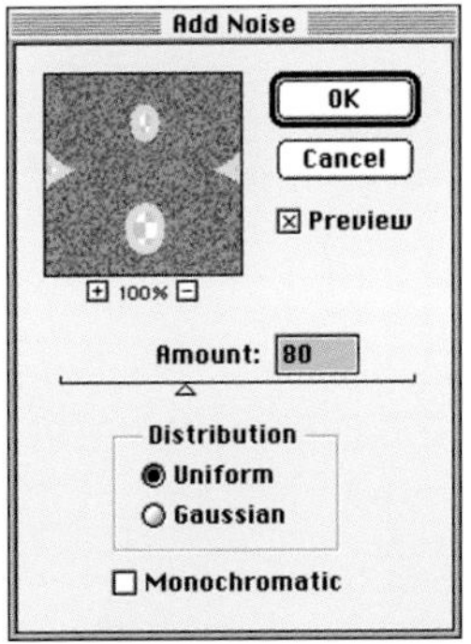


**8** Make the Layer 3 visible. Flatten the image. Export to GIF format.

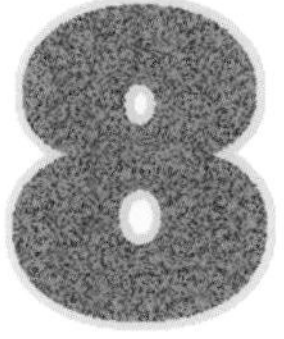

## VARIATIONS

Another alternative is to fill the text with a texture and then crystallize the filled area. Repeat steps 1-6, but apply a texture with a filter instead. (We used Filter➛KPT Texture Explorer 2.1➛Effects textures➛Egyptian Green.) After the text is filled, select Filter➛Pixelate➛Crystallize. Set Cell Size to 10. ■

## Initial Caps

KPT Gradient Designer offers a wide assortment of patterns to create backdrops for initial letters. When reducing file sizes for faster downloads, some gradients may band when used with a limited color palette. As an alternative, an additional filter can be applied to create a hand-drawn effect before the file is exported to GIF or saved as a JPEG file.

The typeface is ITC Rennie Mackintosh Ornaments for each of the following five examples. We provide these five ornaments filled with gradients as preset files on the CD-ROM, in the WebMagic folder. If you would like to try other gradients, check out the KPT Gradient Designer demo on the CD-ROM or select the Photoshop 4.0 Gradient tool.

### Ornament A

Open the file CRM1. Select Ornament A. Use Filter➸Blur to remove jaggies. Apply Filter➸Texture➸ Mosaic Tiles

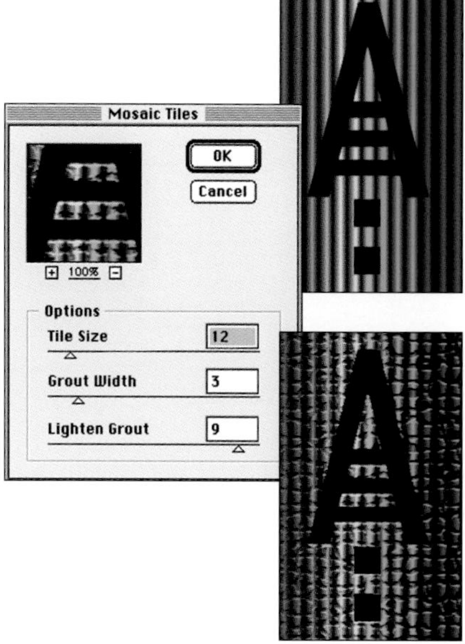

**TOOLBOX**

KPT Gradient Designer

Xaos Tools Paint Alchemy

### Ornament B

Open the file CRM2. Select Ornament B. Apply Filter➛Brush Strokes➛Spatter. Use the default settings.

### Ornament C

Open the file CRM3. Select Ornament C. Apply Filter➛Texture➛Stained Glass (Change size: 5).

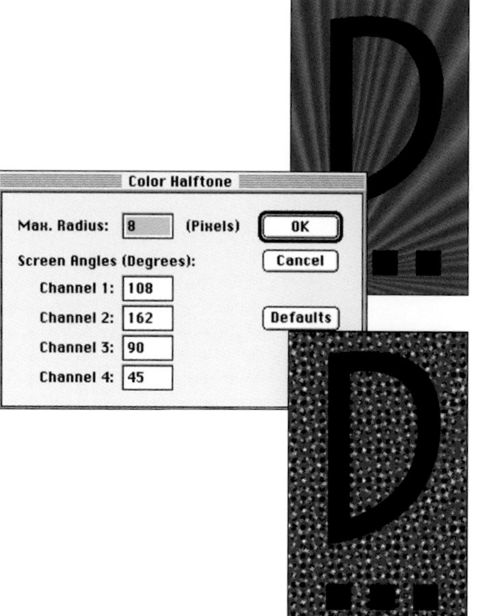


## Ornament D

Open the file CRM4. Select Ornament D. Choose Filter➛Pixelate➛Color Halftone Use default settings.

## Ornament E

Open the file CRM5. Select Ornament E. Apply Filter➛Xaos Tools➛Paint Alchemy, with the settings in the dialog box to the left. The Paint Alchemy demo is on the CD-ROM. ■

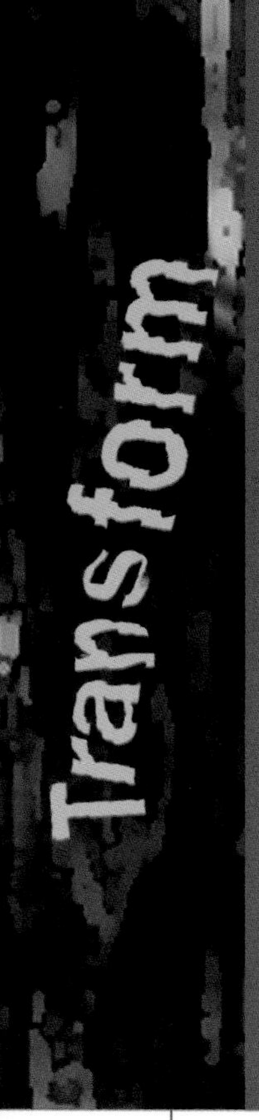


## Free Transform

Adobe has updated the Transform features in Photoshop 4.0. Here we combine Transform—numeric entry with the new Free Transform feature and the Radial Blur and Ripple filters to create warped text on a painterly background.

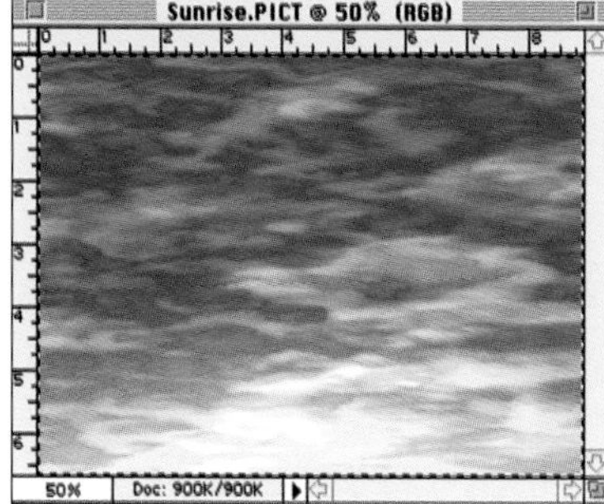


1 Create a new file, or open a file containing a textured background. There are samples in the Adobe folder on the CD-ROM. For this example, we picked Sunrise, created with Adobe TextureMaker.

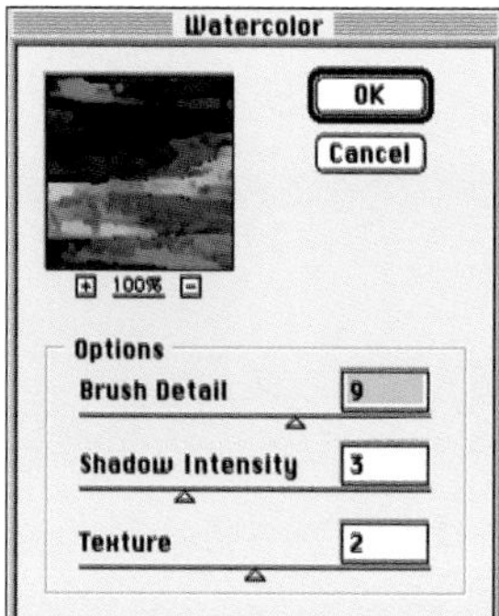


2 Choose Filter➛Artistic➛Watercolor. (Shadow Intensity: 3, Texture: 2). This filter creates a more painterly and irregular textured effect.

**TIP** **Photoshop 4.0 incorporates the Gallery Effects artistic effects filters that were separate plug-ins for 3.0. They can convert an over used stock photograph into a fresh new look. Experiment with the settings and set-up a library of pre-sets. It will save production time later.**

3 Create a new file. Make the stock photo texture file active. Check the pixel dimensions of the file you created in Step 1. In the Marquee Options palette choose Style⇛Fixed Size. Enter the pixel dimensions of the Step 1 file. Drag the marquee selection from the stock photo file to the new file. The new file now has the photographic texture as a background on Layer 1.

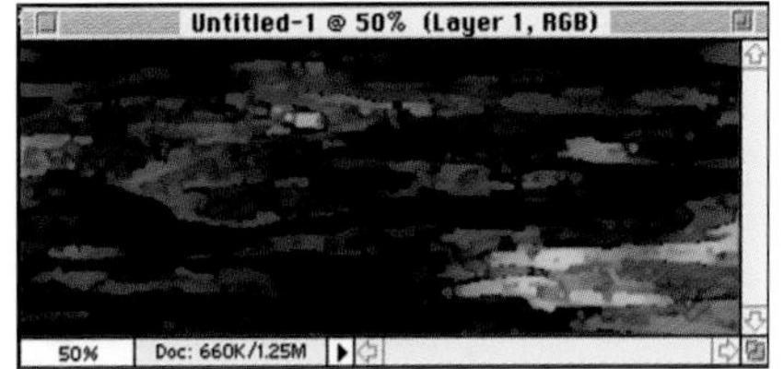


4 Use the Eyedropper tool to choose a foreground color from the background texture. Enter the text. We selected Helvetica Bold, center alignment, anti-aliased on, spacing: 0. Use the Move tool to position the text. This creates Layer 2.

5 Select the cap "F". Choose Layer⇛Transform⇛Numeric (Shift-Command-T) [Shift-Control-T] Set Scale to Width: 90%, Height: 100%, Skew to Horizontal and Vertical: -5°.

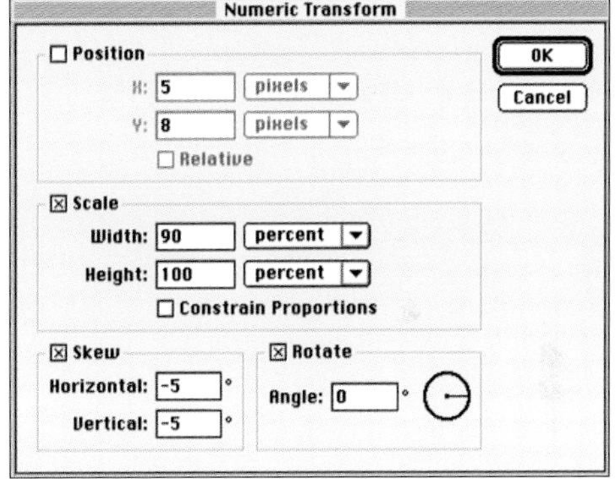

6 Repeat the procedure for the lower case "r", and the two "e"s. For each letter we increased the numeric value for scale by 5% for both the height and the width, skew by 2° horizontally and vertically, plus or minus and rotate by 10°. The important factor is to create a fluid visual flow as your eye moves from one letter to another.

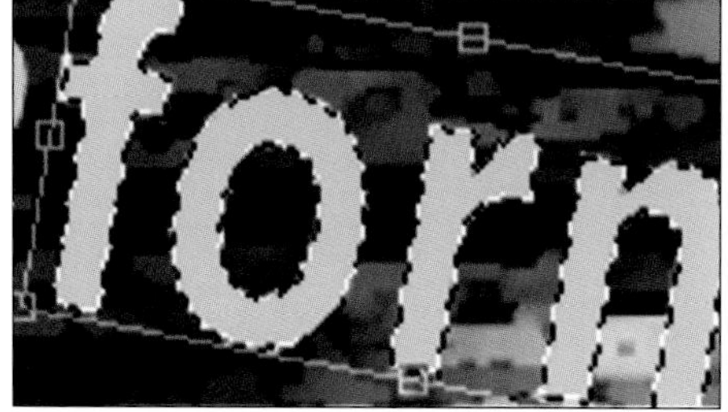


7 Select the letters "form". While selected choose Layer⇛Free Transform (Command-T) [Control-T]. A selection box with handles will appear. Move the cursor so that it is outside the selection box and rotate the selection clockwise. Use the Escape key to cancel any changes you are not satisfied with.

TIP **If the cursor shows a straight line with arrows at each end, you can scale the height or width by moving in a straight line. Moving at a 45° angle to the corner changes both height and width at the same time. If the arrows on the cursor are at an angle to each other, then you will be rotating the selection.**

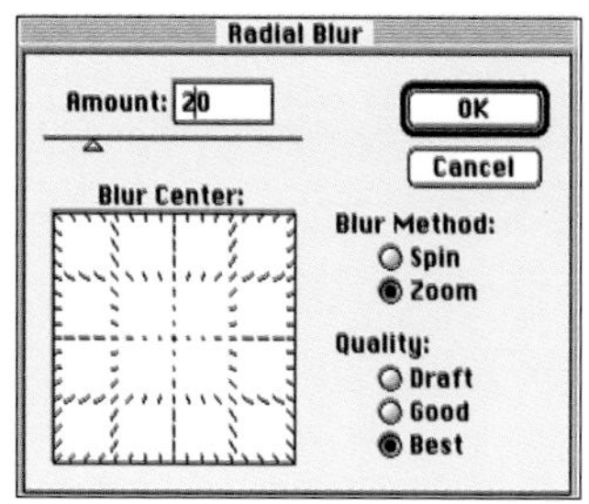


8 Deselect the floating selection and duplicate Layer 2 Hide Layer 2 copy. Select the text on Layer 2. Choose Edit⇛Fill (Use: Black). This will be the shadow text. Apply Filter⇛Blur⇛Radial Blur. Try settings in figure. The blur filter creates a sensation of shimmering motion.

**9** While the text on Layer 2 is selected, choose Layer➨Transform➨Numeric (Shift-Command-T) [Shift-Control-T] and rotate all the text clockwise an additional 15°. This makes the shadow more visible behind the foreground text.

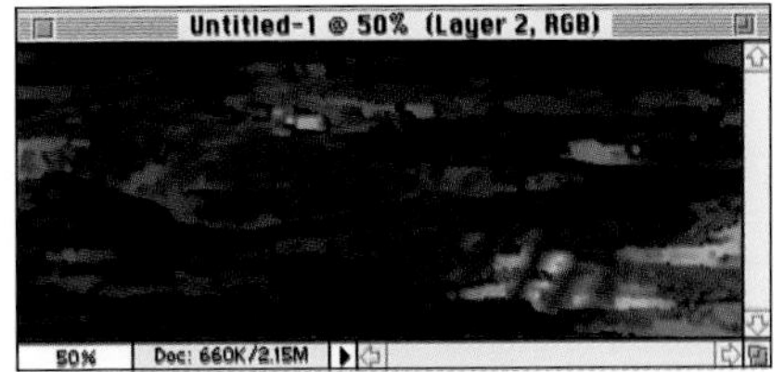


**10** Make Layer 2 copy visible, and active. Choose the first three letters and apply Filter➨Distort➨Ripple (Amount: 100%, Size: Medium).

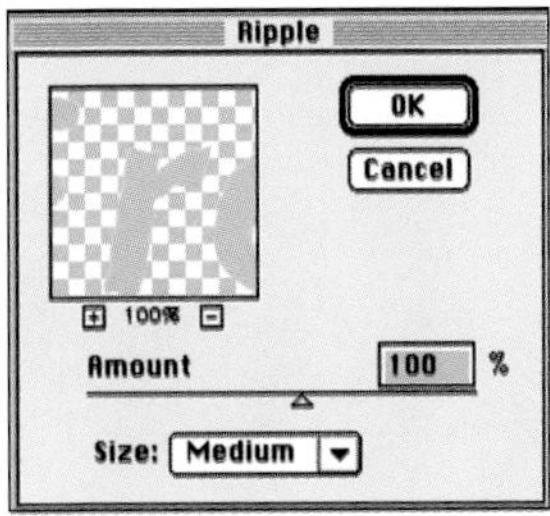


**11** Deselect first three letters. Select the remaining five letters. Apply the Ripple filter again, but change the size to large.

**12** Export to GIF format. ■

# Part III

## Icons

Icons and pictographs are popular on Web pages because they transcend language barriers and international borders. Icons quickly identify key elements and links on a Web page.

As informational devices within a site, icons should represent a common visual style and clearly reinforce the literal meaning of the link or page identity, such as "mail" or "home page." You can use icons on buttons to serve as placemarkers that help the site visitor find information. The same icon can then be used as an identifier in a page header to brand that page or section.

Just like fonts, icons are available as collections in a wide variety of themes and styles. Use Photoshop filters, such as Bas Relief or Neon Glow and Photoshop color editing techniques, to customize these icons to fit your personal design style.

A word of caution—before using any stock art collection or trademark, read the small print on the package. Some collections are for print use only, and their licensing agreements forbid distribution via electronic media. Find out what a company's policy is before using its trademarks. Written permission may be required.

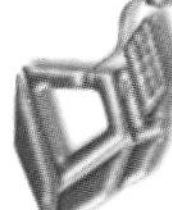
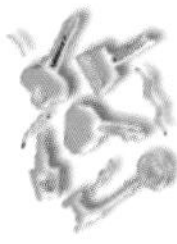

## 2D Clip Art

Creating a dramatic menu bar from 2D clip art is fast and easy with Photoshop 4.0. By enhancing and modifying Dingbat fonts you can quickly create a site worthy of a Fortune 500 company.

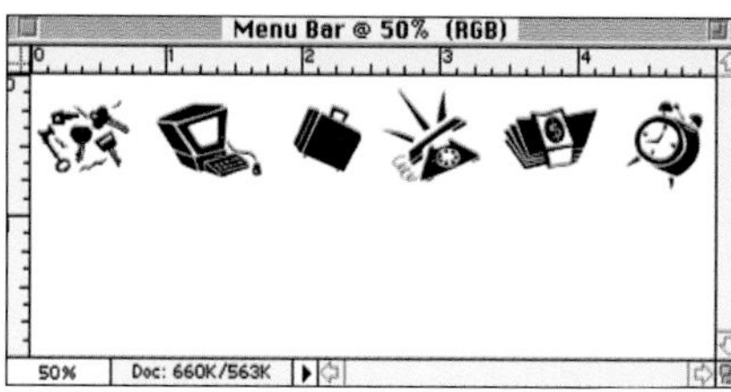


**1** Create a new file. Type your images using a dingbat font or import 2D clip art into your new file. Save the selection (Channel #4). We used the DF Commercials font for this example.

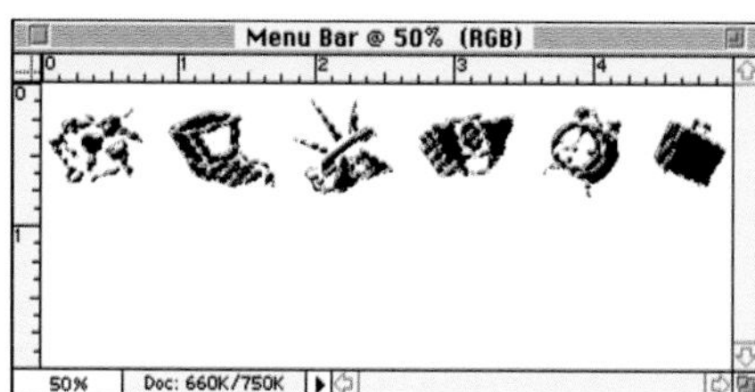


**2** Choose foreground and background colors. We chose royal blue for the foreground and white for the background. A white background gives the best results.

**TIP** **You can complement the use of Dingbat and Ornaments fonts in menu bars by also using them as a subtle background pattern. Use pale colors or light gray for background patterns.**

**3** Select⇢None. Choose Filter⇢Sketch⇢Bas Relief.

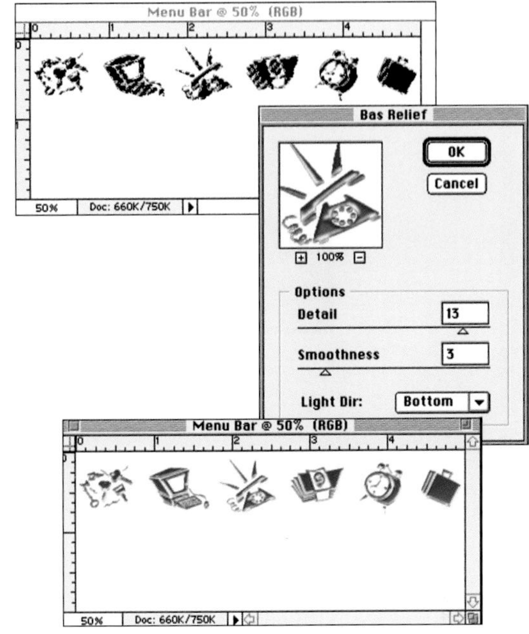


**4** Add more dimension to your button bar by implementing the drop shadow technique. See Shadows, page 70, for detailed instructions.

**5** With the Type tool, enter the text for each button.

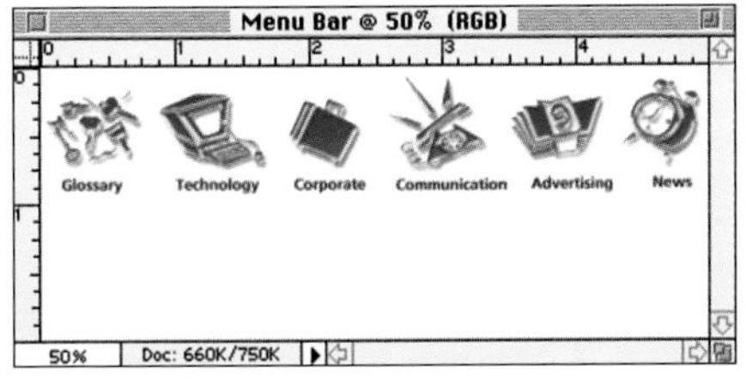


**6** With the Crop tool, crop your final image as close as possible to ensure fast download. Export to GIF format.

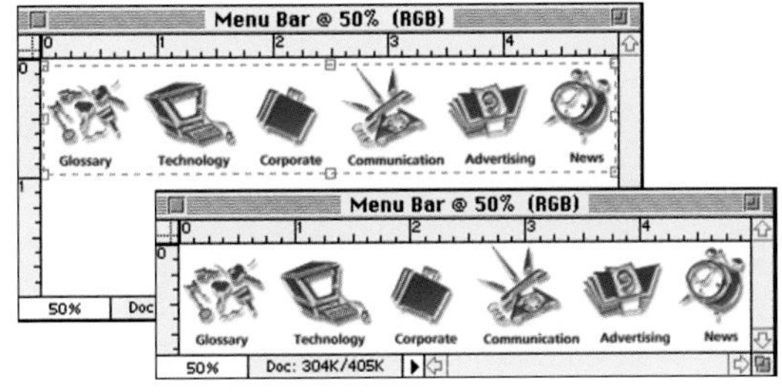

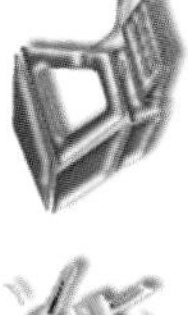

# VARIATIONS

Adjusting the brightness and contrast creates a subtle, washed-out effect. Load the selection Channel #4 and choose Image➛Adjust➛ Brightness/Contrast (Brightness: +100, Contrast: -27). Try different settings until you find ones that suit your colors and art.

You can also select each clip art icon and vary the Color Balance to create a variety of colors in your menu bar. ■

## Neon

Just as in real life, a neon sign on a Web page can attract attention to the site.

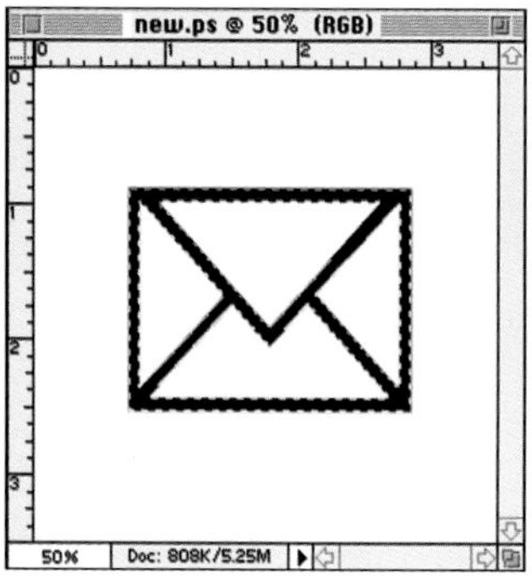

**1** Open a file containing black-and-white line art. For this exercise we used an outline of a typical mail icon. (The icon can be found in the WebMagic folder on the CD). If the image you choose is in gray tone mode, convert mode to RGB.

**2** Select the black area of the icon from the original image with the Magic Wand tool. Create a new document 20 pixels larger than the size of the icon. Using the Move tool, drag a copy into the new document. Save the selection (Channel #4). Select→All and fill the background with black.

**3** On the new layer (Layer 1), load a channel selection (Channel #4). Choose Edit→Fill (Use: White).

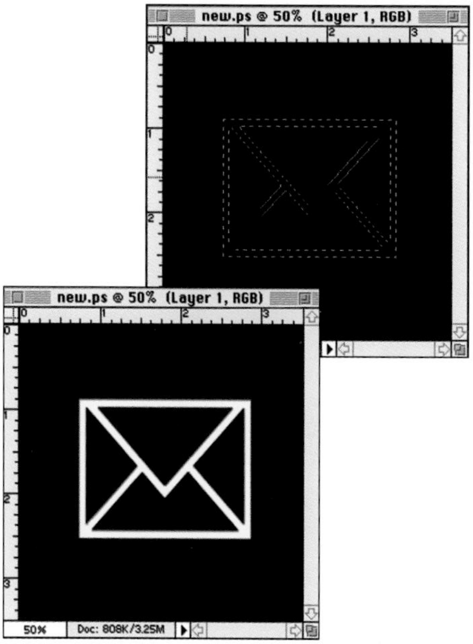

**4** Choose new foreground and background colors. Use bright colors with different tonal values that will work well together (one light and one dark) making the darker one the background color. In this example we used Pantone 1788 and Pantone 257 respectively. Create a new layer (Layer 2). Select⇒Load Selection (#4). Edit⇒Fill (Use: Background Color).

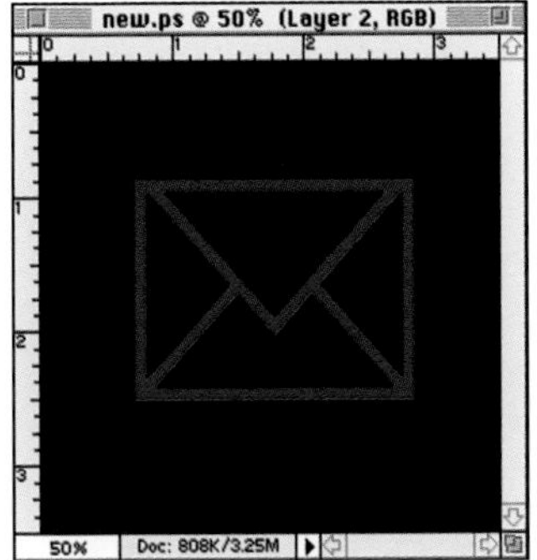


**5** Create a new layer (Layer 3), (the selection from Step 2 is now active on the new layer). Edit⇒Fill⇒(Use: Foreground color).

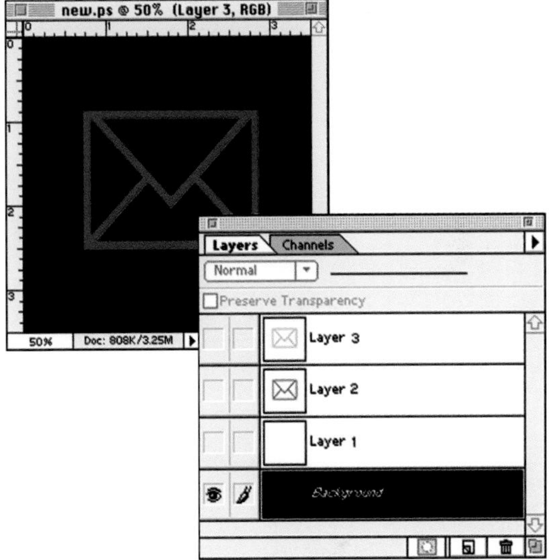


**6** Hide Layer 3 and make Layer 2 active and Load the selection Channel #4. Select⇒Modify⇒Contract (Width 3 pixels). Delete the selection. The deleted area makes part of Layer 1 visible.

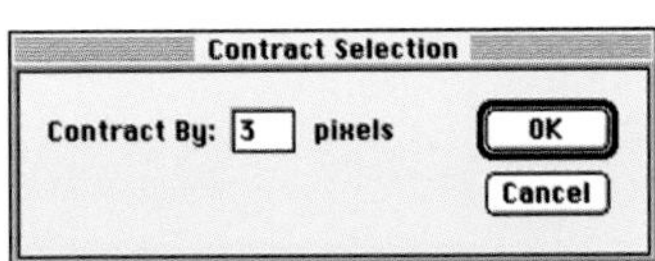


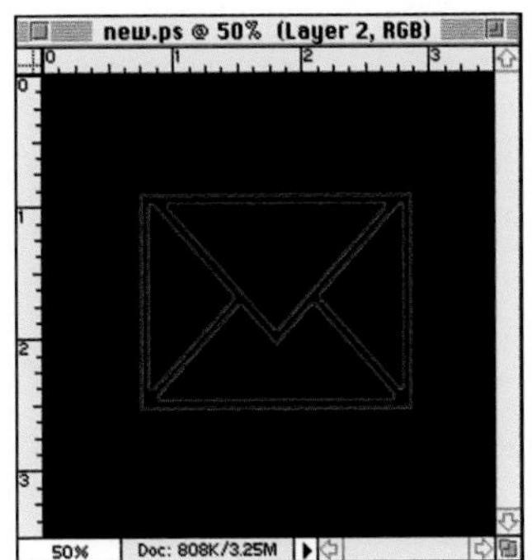

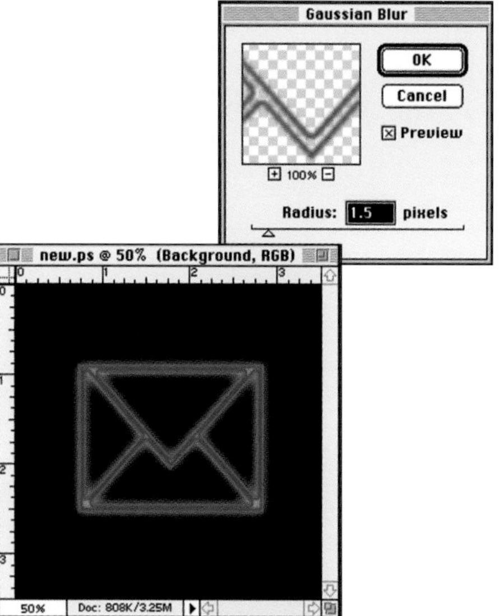


**7** Make Layer 3 active and load the selection Channel #4. Select➜Modify➜Contract (width 2 pixels) and delete the selection.

**8** Make Layer 1 active. Choose Filter➜Blur➜Gaussian Blur (5 pixels). Repeat the process for Layer 2 (3 pixels) and Layer 3 (1.5 pixels.)

**9** Make all layers visible and Save the file as neon1.ps (Photoshop document). Export as a GIF with the name neon1.gif. This will give you the final glowing neon icon.

**10** To add a flashing effect to this image, Revert to neon.ps. Hide Layer #1 (white) and export as a GIF.

TIP The exported GIFs from your image (neon1.gif and neon2.gif) can be built into an animated GIF image using a GIF animation program, and added to an HTML page for a flashing neon sign effect. ■

# PART IV

## Rules

Rules are both decorative and functional elements for organizing Web sites and pages. Rules define columns and page divisions within the compositional grid and highlight areas of content and activity.

On Web pages with large amounts of HTML text, rules act as visual markers helping readers keep their place. Rules, in combination with icons or text links, also serve as navigation options for returning to the top of a page or to other locations in the site.

When selecting a rule style, color, and weight, consider how the rule works with both the HTML text and other graphic devices. Keep things in balance—rules are added detail, not the first thing you notice when looking at a Web page.

Photoshop offers an infinite series of possibilities for creating a library of rules. In the following techniques, we show you how to build rules by customizing brushes or applying filters to Zapf Dingbats. Mix and match. Have fun!

## Using Custom Brushes

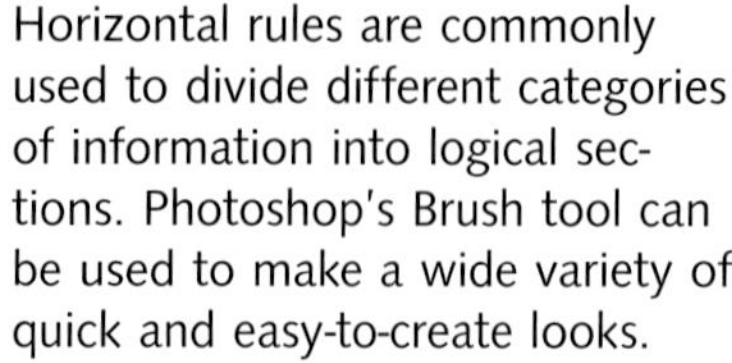

Horizontal rules are commonly used to divide different categories of information into logical sections. Photoshop's Brush tool can be used to make a wide variety of quick and easy-to-create looks.

1 Create a new file wider than the Web page you are working on. Double-click the Paintbrush tool and select the Brushes tab. Using the palette's pop-up menu, Load Brushes from the Photoshop application's Goodies folder. We loaded the Assorted and the Square brushes.

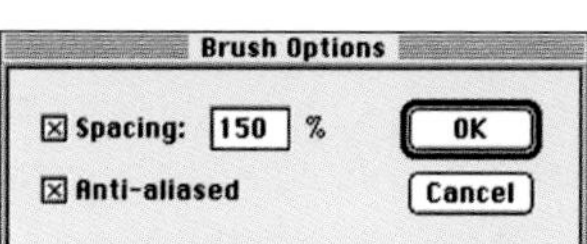


2 Select the brush shown in the figure. Double-click its icon to access the Brush Options dialog box. Set the Spacing to 150%.

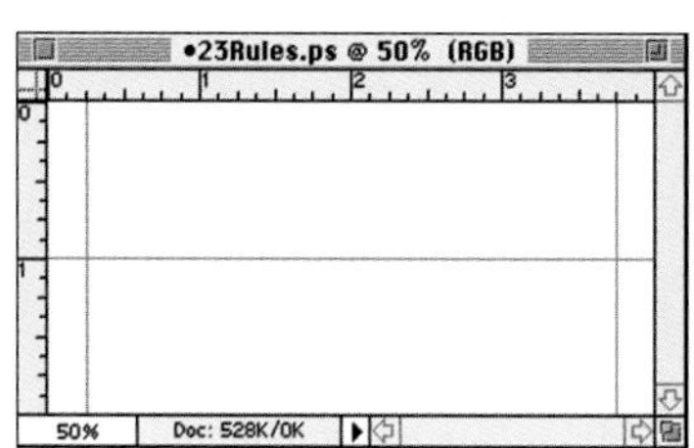


3 Choose a foreground color. Add two vertical guides to define the width of your Web page. Add one horizontal guide as a placement guide.

**4** Click at the intersection of the guides on the left side of the image area. Hold the Shift key down and click at the intersection of the guides on the right side of the image area. This draws a line with your paintbrush.

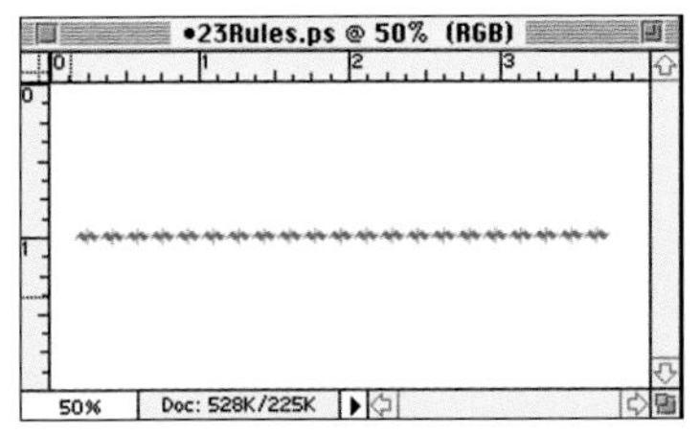


**5** As a finishing touch we added a drop shadow. First we used the Magic Wand tool to select the background, inverted the selection, and applied an Alien Skin Drop Shadow. See the Soft Shadow section on page 72 if you don't have the Alien Skin package.

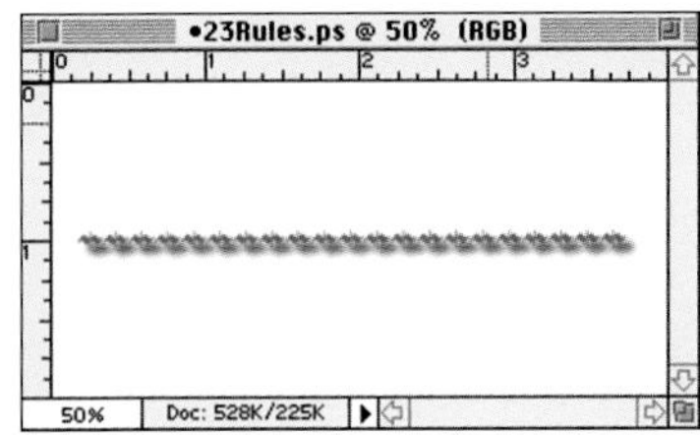


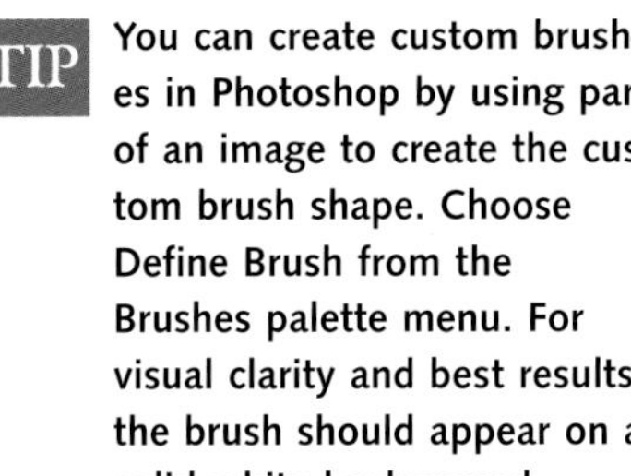

TIP

**You can create custom brushes in Photoshop by using part of an image to create the custom brush shape. Choose Define Brush from the Brushes palette menu. For visual clarity and best results the brush should appear on a solid white background.**

## VARIATIONS

This variation uses square brushes. The red rule was made with the largest brush, with the spacing unaltered at 25%. We set the spacing of the blue rule to 250% and the spacing of the yellow rule to 150%.

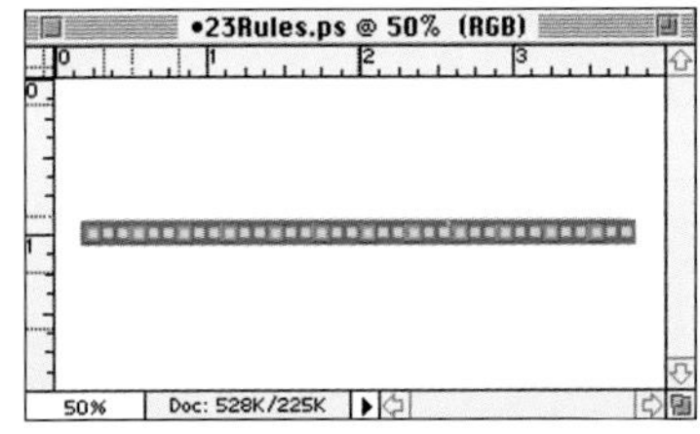

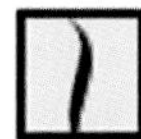

For this variation we combined two brushes to create a mock moiré pattern. The first brush was spaced at 20%; the second at 90%. ■

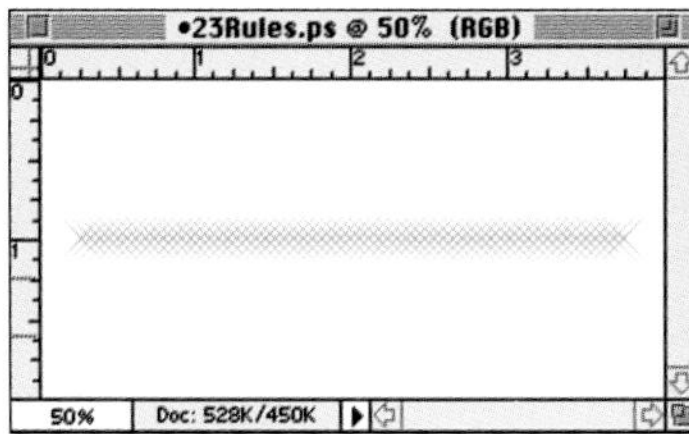


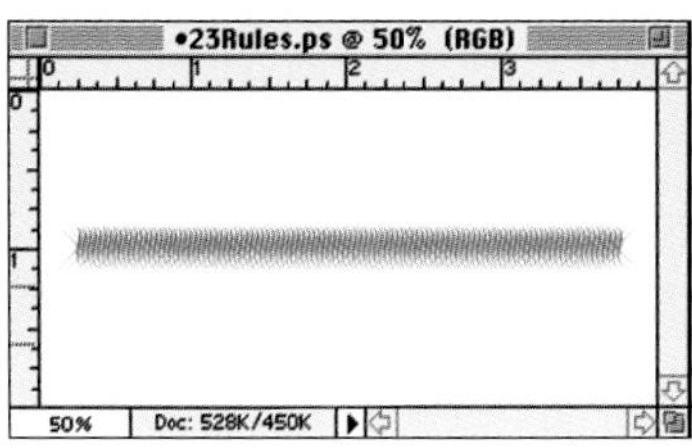

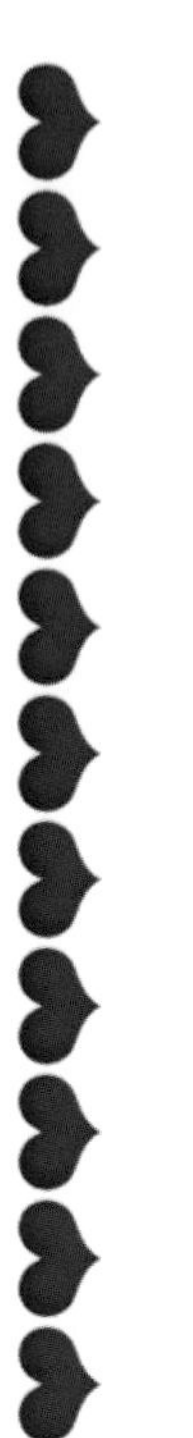

## Using Decorative Fonts

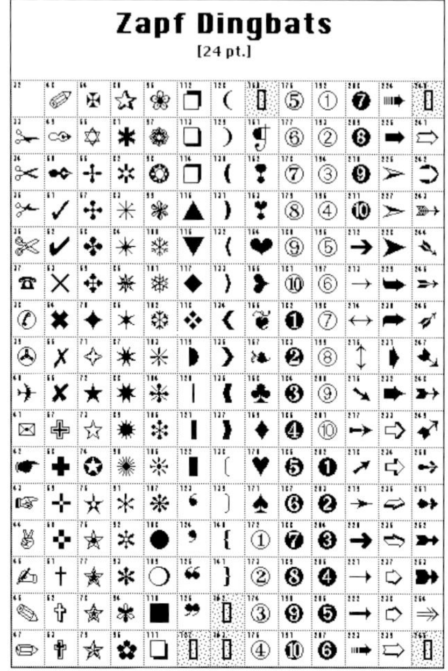


Ornamental and dingbat fonts can be used as a quick and easy way to create original and decorative rules. There are literally thousands of pictograms and embellishments suitable for use in creating rules. In this exercise we used Zapf Dingbats, which is universally available and comes with most computers and many font collections.

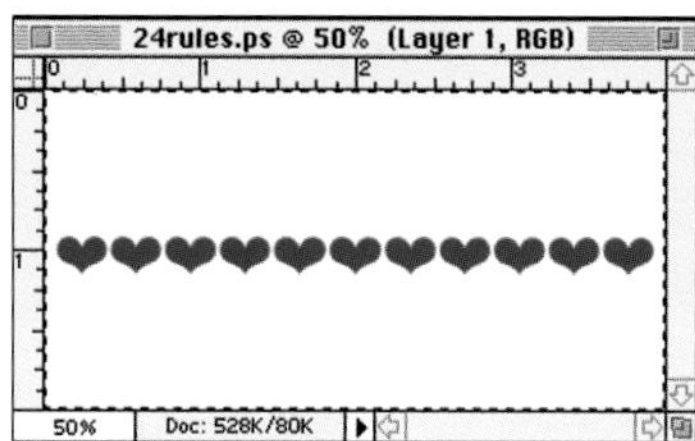


**1** Create a new file that is longer than the width of the Web page you are working on. Choose a foreground color. With the Type tool create a row of dingbats (Layer 1). We chose a heart for this rule.

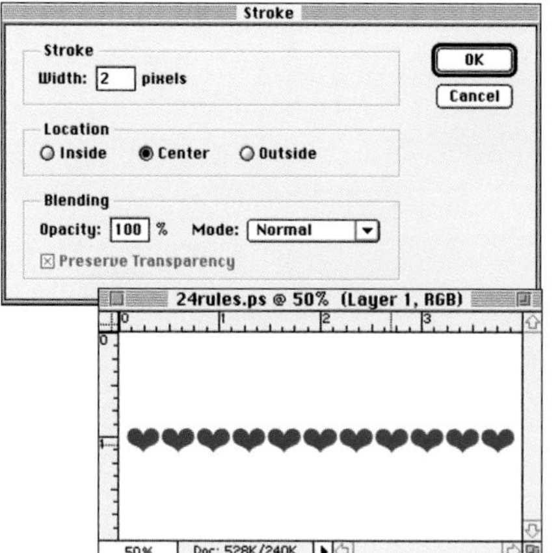


**2** Choose a new foreground color (red) and choose Edit➛Stroke (2 pixels, center). This creates a little more visual interest for the rule.



TOOLBOX

Alien Skin's Cutout

**3** As a finishing touch we added a cut-out effect. Duplicate Layer 1 and hide that created layer, Layer 1 copy. Make Layer 1 active and use the Magic Wand to select the white background. Choose Select➔Inverse then choose Filter➔Alien Skin➔Cutout (X Offset: 2 pixels, Y Offset: 2 pixels, Blur: 4 pixel, Opacity: 60%, Shadow: Black, Fill: Transparent). Select the Move tool and use the arrow keys to offset Layer 1. Make Layer 1 copy visible.

**TIP** **When you use a graphic more than once in a Web page, the graphic is still downloaded only once. Rules can be used multiple times throughout a Web page without affecting the download time.**

## VARIATIONS

Here we created a colored rectangle as the primary rule and then used the Type Mask tool to add the Zapf iron cross dingbats (Shift-2) with four spaces between each. After adding the dingbats choose white as the background color and press Delete.

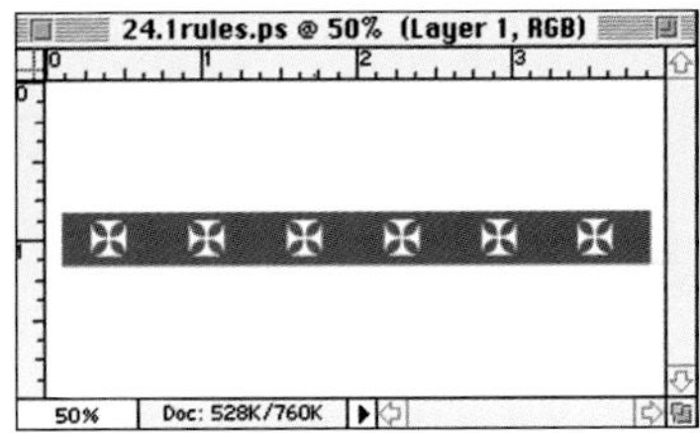


Rules can also be navigational elements. We used the Type Mask tool to create a line of circles (L in Zapf Dingbats) and used the Gradient tool to apply a gradient (foreground to background). We then added a single arrow (Option-Shift-; in Zapf Dingbats) at the end as a pointer.

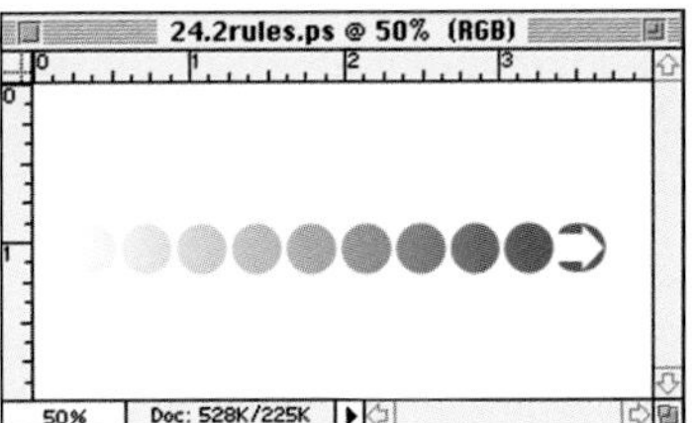

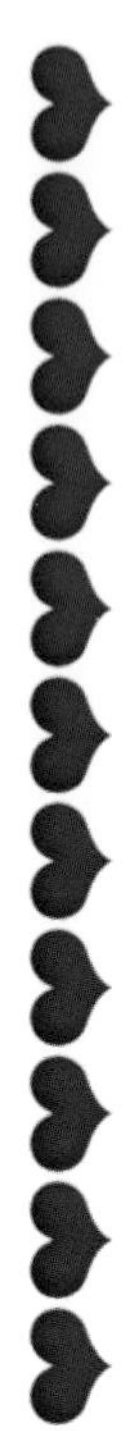

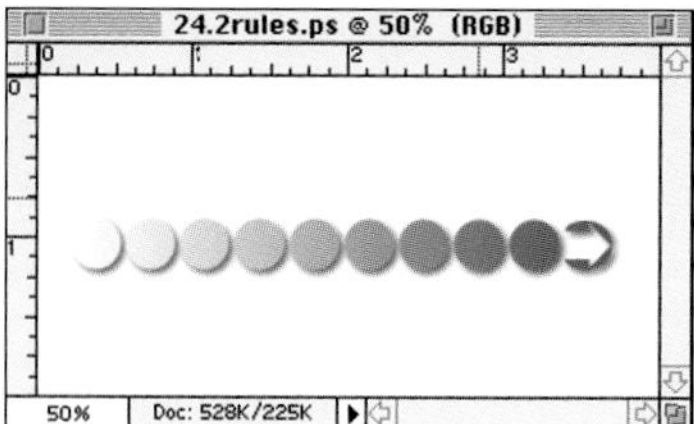


To finish the rule we added a drop shadow using Alien Skin drop shadow filter (X offset: 4, Y offset: 4 Blur: 8 Opacity: 65). ■

# PART V

## Buttons and Bullets

Buttons and bullets are place markers that help readers navigate through a Web site. The 'look' and 'feel' of a Web page is often dominated by buttons and bullets. While they are certainly not necessary on every Web page, buttons and bullets are important for helping visitors understand where they are, where they were, and where they could go next.

When used correctly buttons and bullets facilitate finding information quickly. But remember, too many buttons or bullets on a page can be as confusing as understanding the front panel of a VCR. Finding the right balance is key to supporting a successful interactive experience for Web site visitors.

A button should identify itself as an object meant to be pressed. Adding drop shadows to create a simulated 3D effect encourages visitors to interact with the button. Other techniques, such as an animated GIF (see pages 205 through 238), can be used to highlight special events, promotions, and other key information.

## Basic Gradients

Gradients can be used to create a variety of effects for your buttons. This example gives your button a metallic or chrome effect.

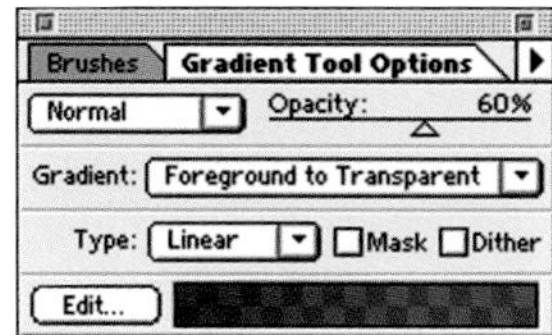


**1** Create a new file. Double-click the Gradient tool and set the options to Mode: Normal, Opacity: 60%, Gradient: Foreground to Transparent (foreground is set to black), Type: Linear, Mask: on, and Dither: off (keeping dithering off helps keep the file size smaller when converted to GIF format).

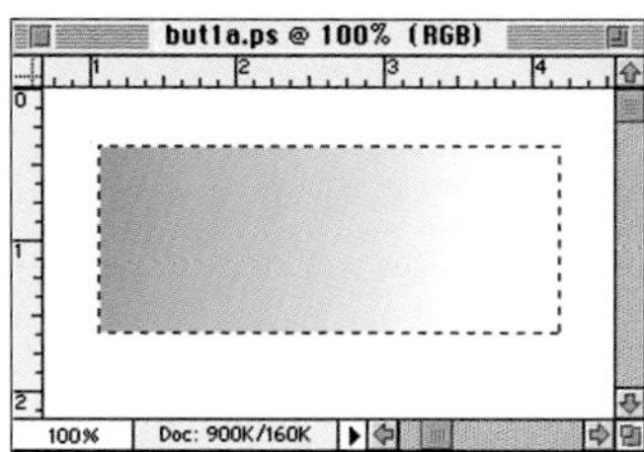


**2** Make a selection for the button (the selection can be larger than the final button size—you can always shrink it later) and save the selection (Channel #4). With the Gradient tool, start outside the selection and click and drag across approximately 80% of the selection. Dragging on a diagonal angle will tilt the gradient for more visual interest.

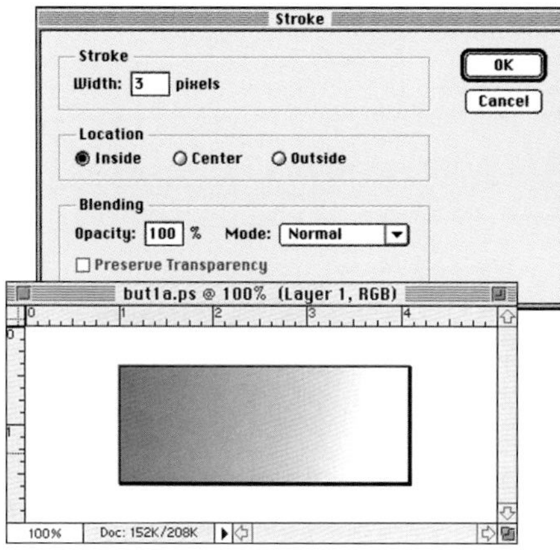


**3** Choose Edit➔Stroke (Width: 3 pixels, Location: Inside, Mode: Normal). This creates a border around the button. The width can be any size, but be sure to set the Location radio button to Inside. This keeps the border inside the selection you saved as Channel #4.

# Variations

## Rainbow Gradient

This alternative to a plain border adds a sense of dimension to the button.

**1** After Step 2, choose Select➙Modify➙Border (Width: 6 pixels). Make the border twice as thick as you want the final version to be. Edit➙Fill (Foreground Color).

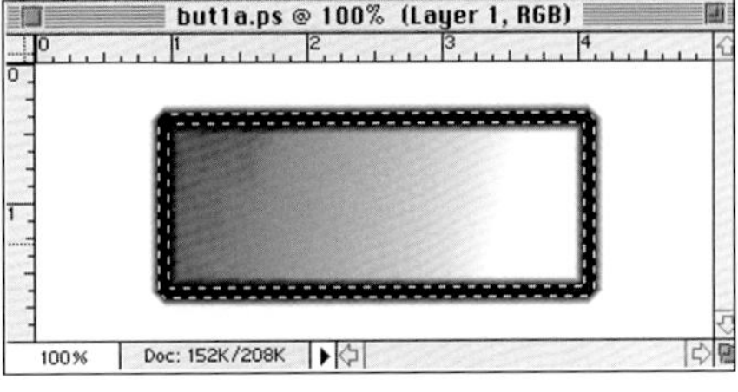


**2** Load the selection Channel #4, Select➙Inverse, and press Delete. This fills the area around the button with the background color and gives the button sharp edges. Notice how the corners of the button have a mitered effect.

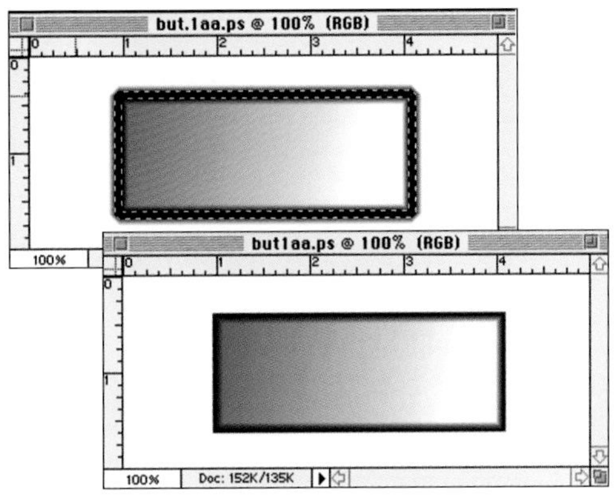


**3** For this button, we set the Gradient tool to Spectrum (Opacity: 50%).

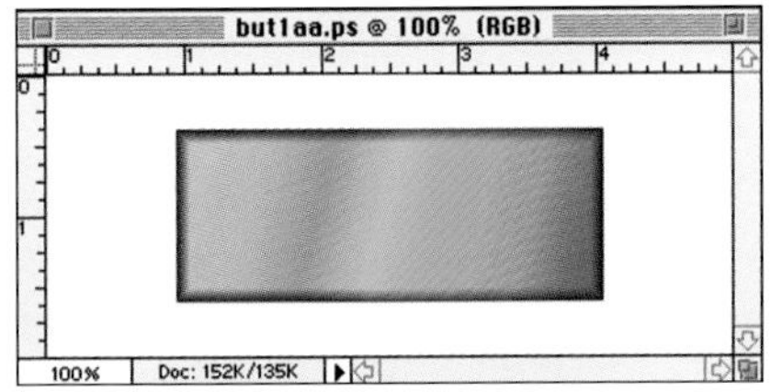

## Metallic Gradient

Gradients on the vertical axis can be used to create metallic effects when they begin darker at the top and bottom and lighten towards the center. For this effect your foreground color should be black and your background color should be white.

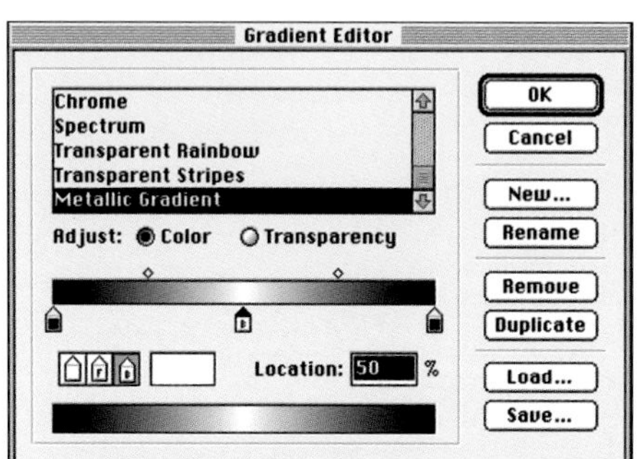


**1** Set the Gradient tool to Mode: Normal; Opacity: 65%; Gradient: Foreground to Transparent; Type: Linear; Mask: off; and Dither: off. Click the Edit button to access the Gradient Editor.

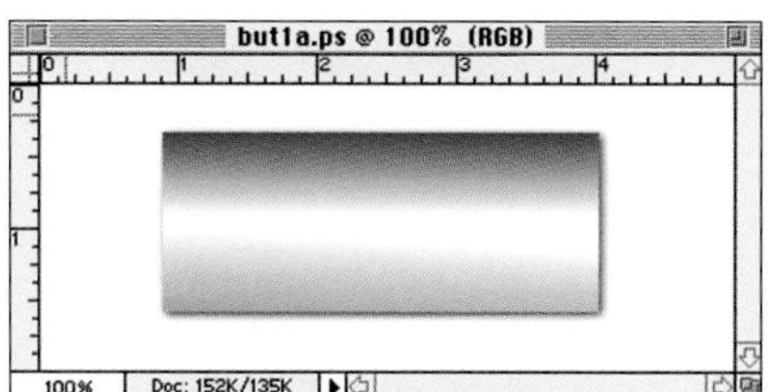


Click New to create a custom gradient. To add a new color click below the midpoint of the gradient bar. A new color icon appears where you clicked. Click the color icon with the B in it to change the color. The new color is your background color (in this case, white).

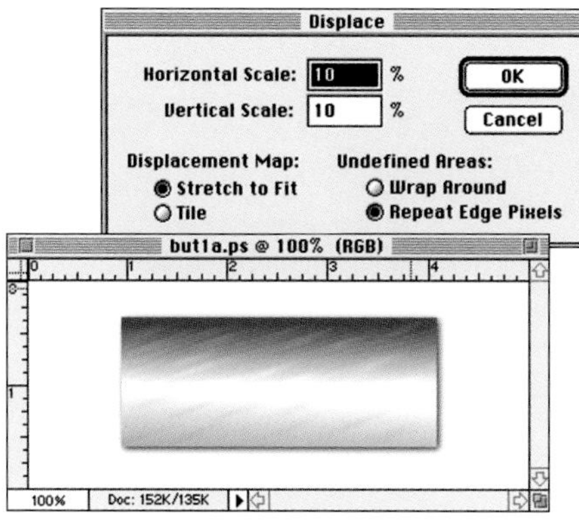


**2** Choose Filter➞Distort➞Displace and use the default settings. A dialog box appears requesting that you choose a displacement map.

The Displacement Map function uses patterns that can be applied as dmaps (displacement maps). The maps are located inside the Photoshop Plug-ins folder. For this effect we chose Schnable Effect, a swirly line pattern. Locate the file Schnable Effect and click Open.

## Crossing Gradients

Choose colors for the foreground and background and Load the selection Channel #4. Set the Gradient tool for Foreground to Background and drag the Gradient tool horizontally across the button. Choose Select→Modify→Contract (16 pixels). (The frame size of the button is determined by the number of pixels you contract the selection.) Drag the Gradient tool across this selection in the opposite direction to create the second gradient.

**In addition to being able to create your own gradients with multiple colors and blendings, each gradient contains a transparency mask to control the opacity of the gradient fill at different locations on the gradient bar. Click the Transparency radio button on the Gradient Editor to replace the transparency adjustment squares with the color adjustment squares.** ■

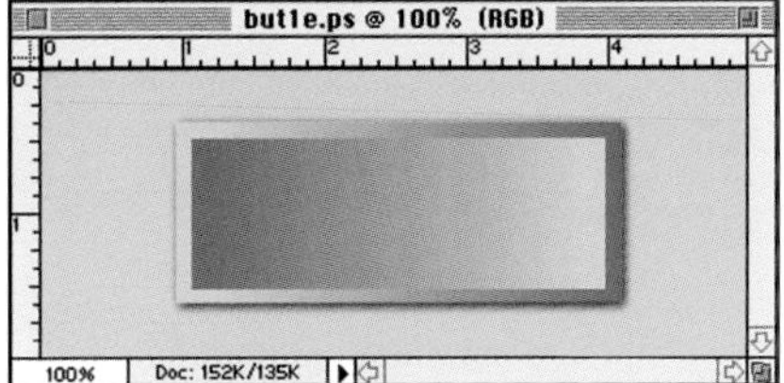

## Radial Gradients

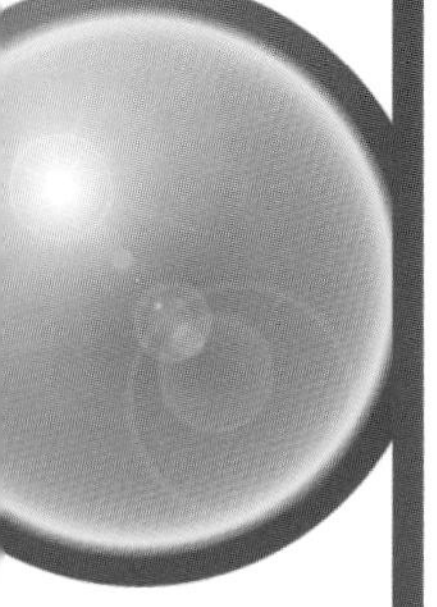

With Photoshop 4.0's new Gradient tool, simple and complex radial gradients can be applied to create an infinite range of stylized, decorative, and dimensional buttons.

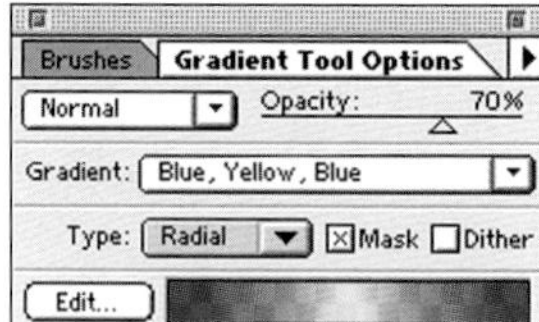


**1** Create a new file. Choose View➙Show Grid. With the Elliptical Marquee tool, make a round selection for your button.

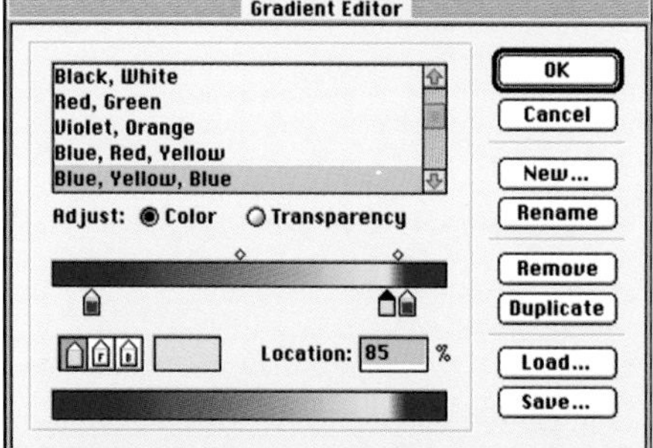


**2** Double-click the Gradient tool icon. (Opacity: 70%; Gradient: Blue, Yellow, Blue; Type: Radial; Dither: off). Click Edit. Select the yellow color square and type 85 in the Location entry box. Select the left-most diamond above the gradient bar and type 80 in the Location entry box.

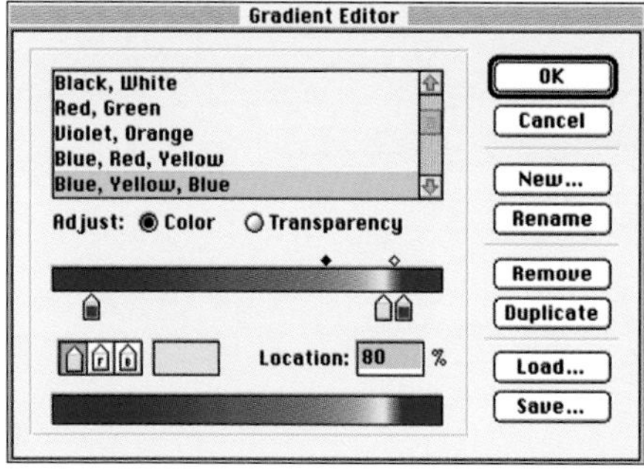


**TIP** **Gradients can be gradual or sharply defined. A sharply defined gradient can create an edge effect within your button while the gradual use of gradients creates a sense of depth. Adjusting the diamonds above the gradient bar will control the transition of the gradient.**

TOOLBOX

Alien Skin's Drop Shadow

**3** Use the grid to locate the center of the selection and drag the Gradient tool from the center to the edge of your selection. Choose View➛Hide Grid.

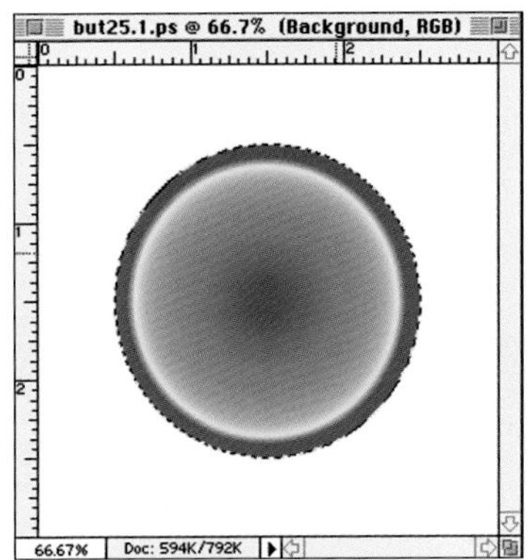


**4** Choose Filter➛Render➛Lens Flare. (Brightness: 150%, Type: 105mm prime). The lens flare creates a highlight on the button.

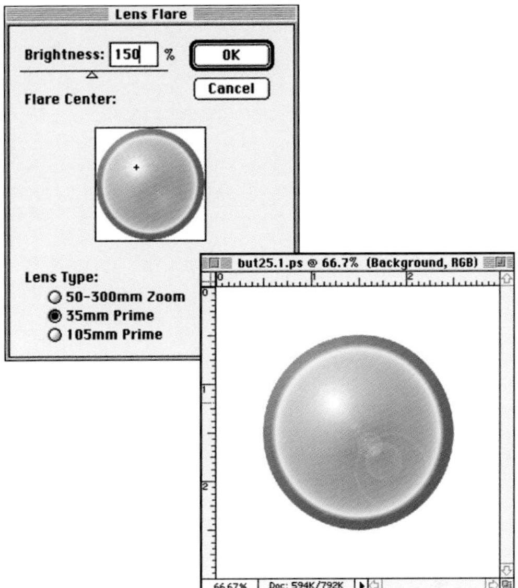

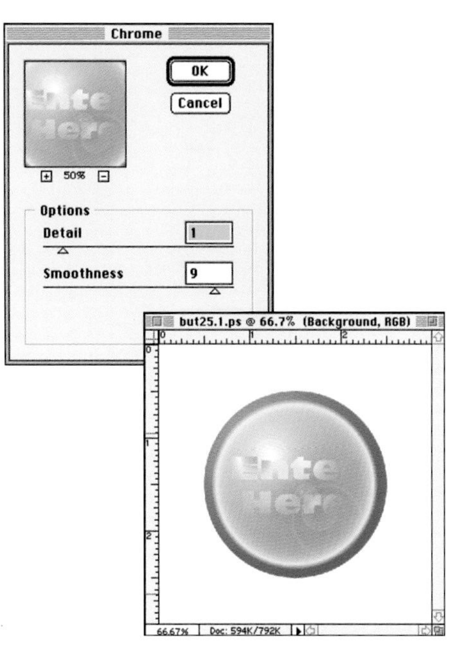


**5** With the Type Mask tool, enter your text. Choose Filter➞Sketch➞Chrome (Detail: 1, Smoothness: 9). Keep detail low so the filter doesn't interfere with the legibility of type. Save the selection (Channel #4).

**6** To finish the button, we applied a drop shadow with the Alien Skin Drop Shadow filter and then brightened the text to improve readability. You can also apply a soft shadow (see page 72).

## Variations

### Linear Gradient

This button has a linear gradient instead of radial. We also changed the bright yellow to an orange.

## Spectrum Gradient

For this variation we chose Spectrum instead of Blue, Yellow, Blue from the Gradient Tool dialog box in Step 1. We also adjusted the opacity of the gradient to 50%.

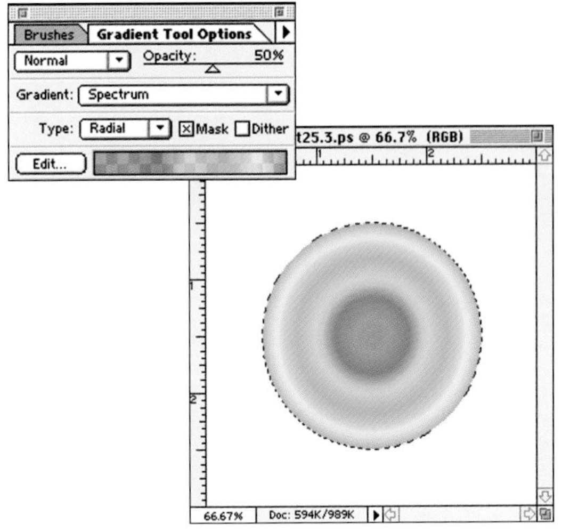


After we applied the gradient we chose Filter➝Brush Strokes➝ Spatter (Spray Radius: 18, Smoothness: 11) to break up the gradient for a more organic feel.

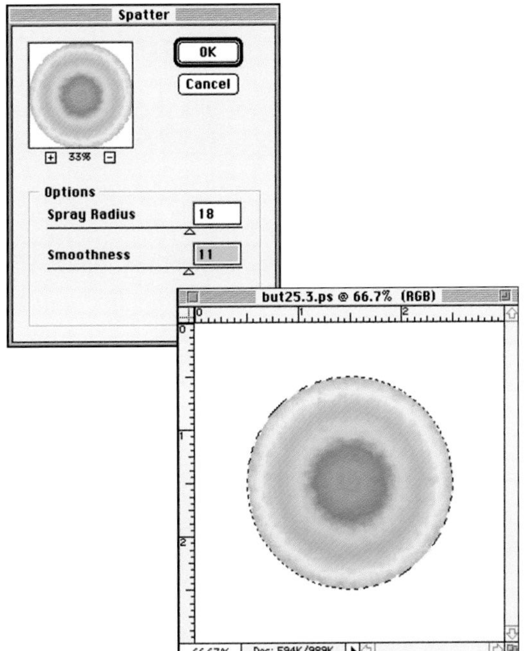

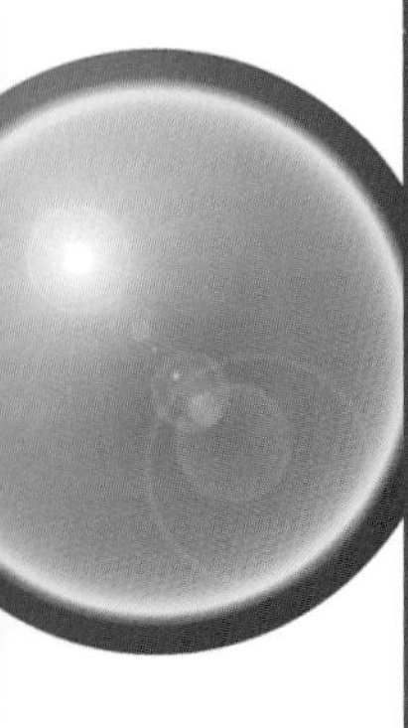

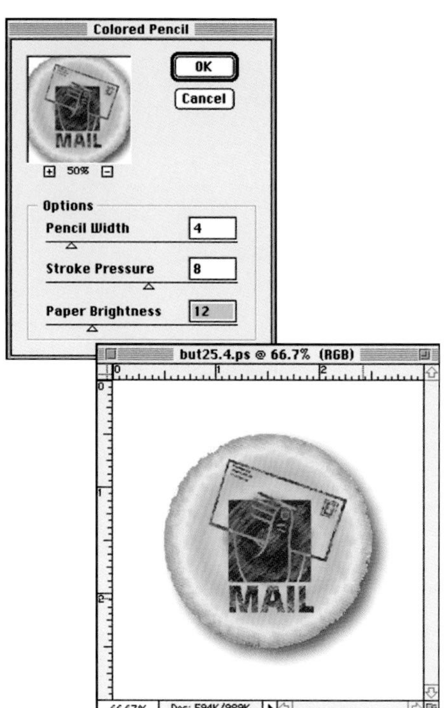


Finally, we added an icon and applied Filter➻Artistic➻Colored Pencil (Pencil Width: 4, Stroke Pressure: 8, Paper Brightness: 12). ■

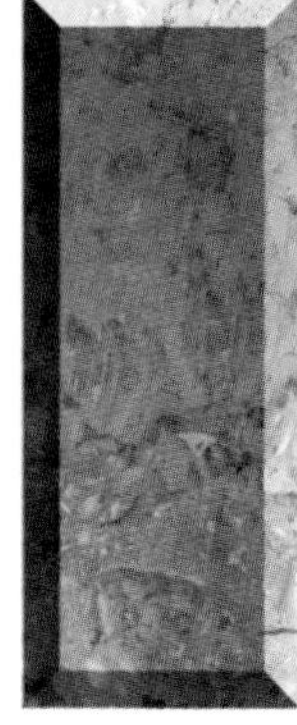

## Bevel

Bevels have long been used as architecture and wood working details. They accent otherwise plain edges and add a finishing touch. On a Web page they can add dimension and depth to buttons. Photoshop's Lighting Effects filter is the primary tool for creating customized bevels.

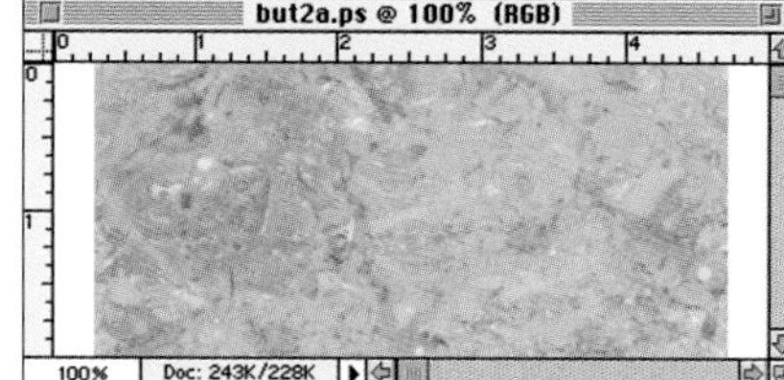


**1** Open a file with a texture for your button. (There is a texture folder on the CD with a variety of textures.) Make a selection for your button and save the selection (Channel #4).

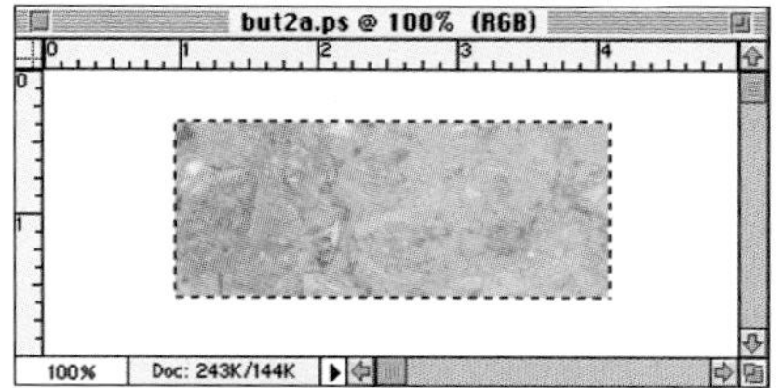


**2** Choose Select➛Inverse and press Delete to fill the area surrounding the button with the background color.

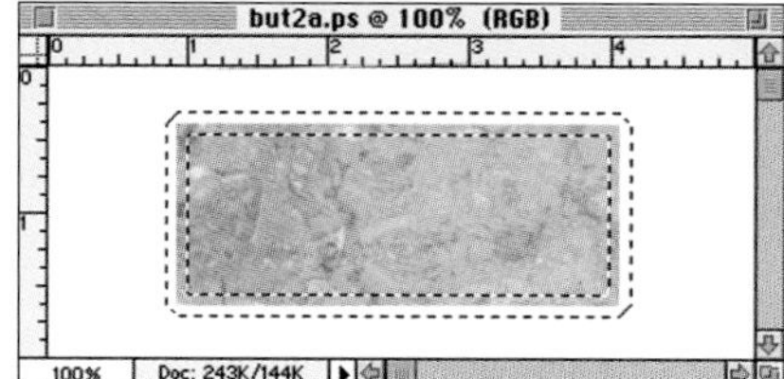


**3** Select➛Inverse again to reselect the button. Choose Select➛Modify➛Border (8 pixels). This defines the width of the bevel. Save the selection as a new channel (Channel #5).

**TIP** **To make the bevel even more defined, load the selection Channel #5 and make it the active channel. Fill the selection with white. Select➛All and apply Filter➛Blur➛Gaussian Blur (3 pixels). Increasing the number of pixels for the blur increases the softness of the bevel even more.**

**TOOLBOX**

Alien Skin's
Inner Bevel
Outer Bevel

SuckingFish
DekoBoko
Frame Curtain

4 Load Channel #4 and choose Filter➛Render➛Lighting Effects. Use 2 o'clock Spotlight from the from the style presets. Choose Texture Channel: #5, and set the Height slider to 50%. To position the light on your object move the small circle in the center, to move the light futher or closer from the object expand or contract the outer circle.

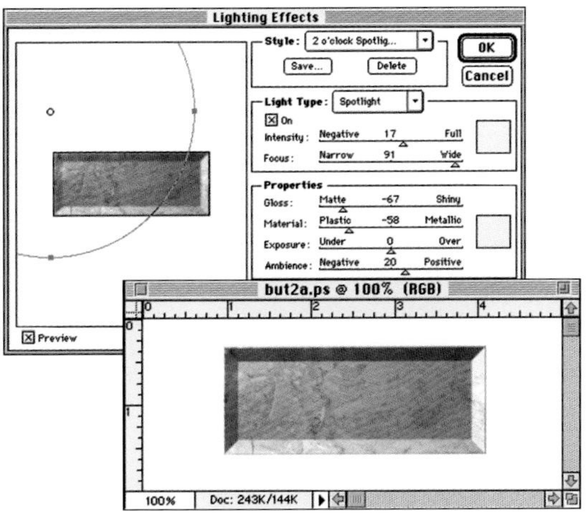


## VARIATION

### Alien Skin Filters

The Alien Skin commercial filter package contains two filters that make creating bevels a snap. The Inner Bevel filter applies the bevel inside of the selected area. Sliders give you control of bevel width, shadows, highlights, and light direction. The filter also contains a half-dozen preset bevels to choose from.

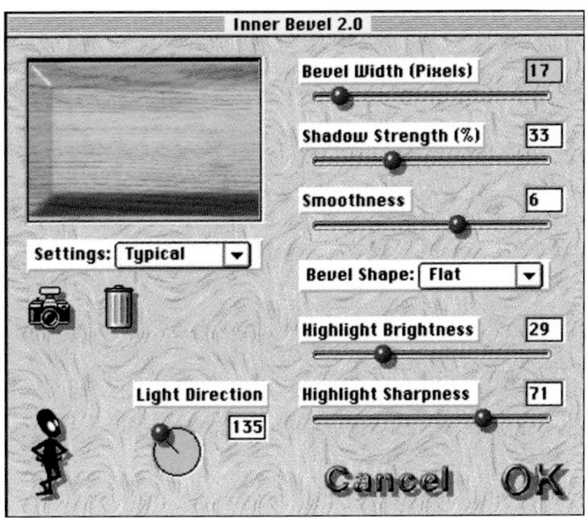


The filter even adds subtle detail to the bevel—note the highlight on the top-left corner.

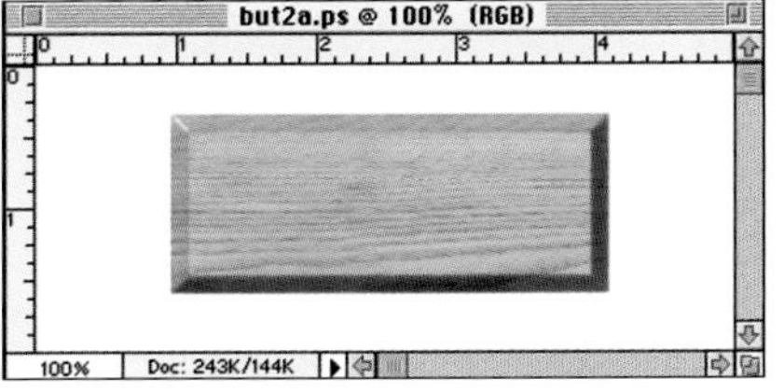

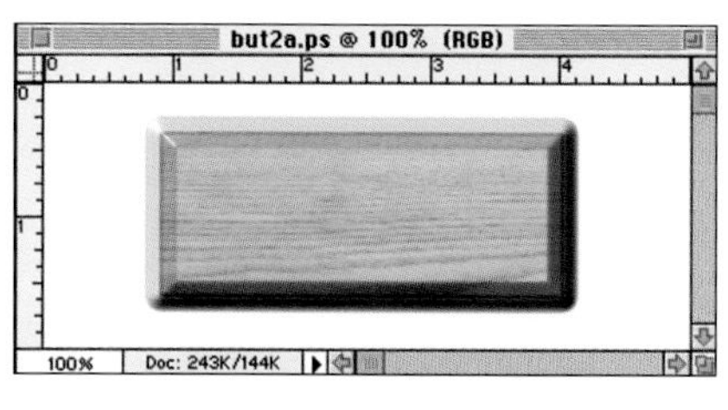


The Outer Bevel filter applies a bevel to the area outside of the selection. This is a great feature for making buttons look as if they are encased in the background.

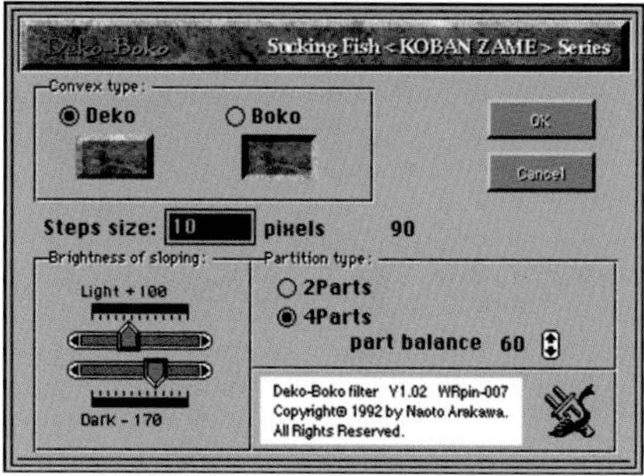


## SuckingFish Filters

A mailware (the author Naoto Arakawa in Japan simply requests an email if you like his filters) filter package with a bevel filter is the SuckingFish Series of filters. Not quite as feature-rich as the Alien Skin bevel filters, the DekoBoko filter creates one-step bevels and includes an inverse option that can be used to create depressed buttons.

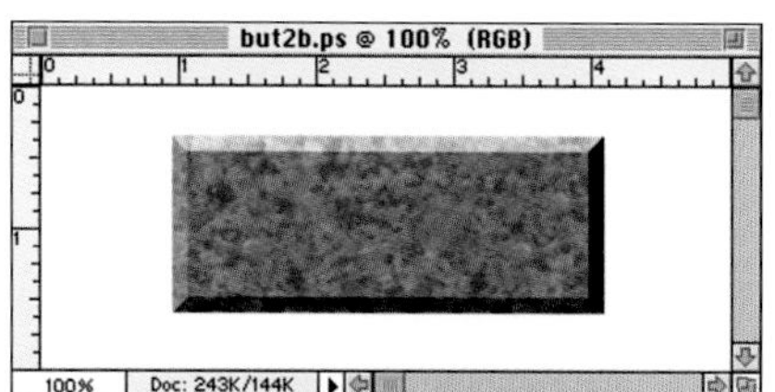


The SuckingFish filters are for the Macintosh only and are on the Photoshop Web Magic CD-ROM.

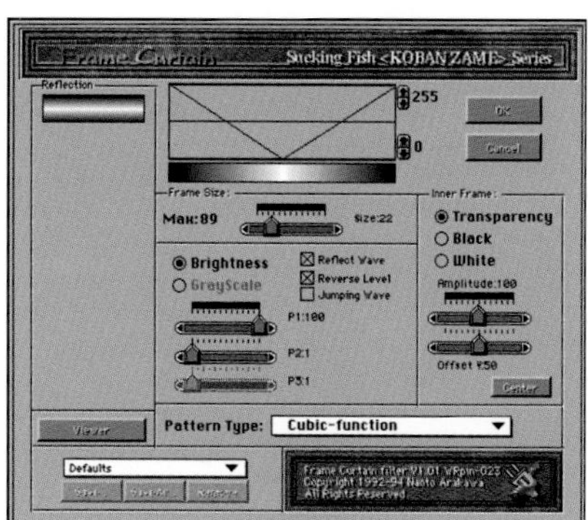


Included in the SuckingFish Series is the Frame Curtain filter, which converts waveforms into grayscale frames for objects. It comes with over 30 preset frames and offers options for creating an unlimited number of variations. ■

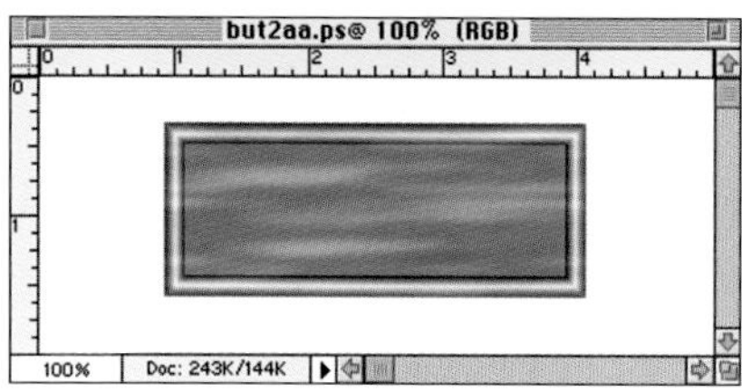

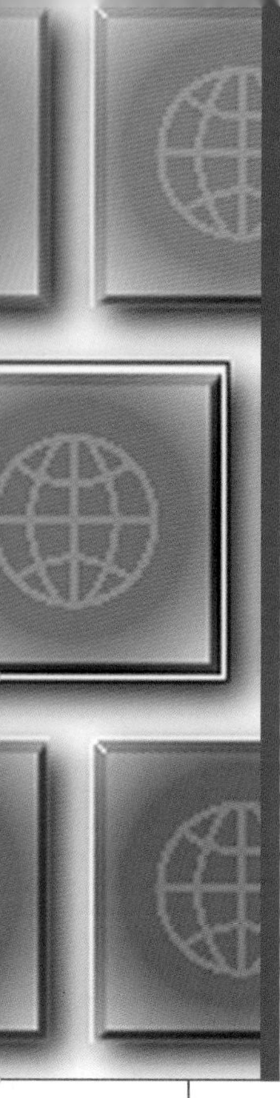

## Multicolored Variations

Color-coding Web sites can assist visitors in finding their way around the site or help identify where they are. The Photoshop Variations filter can be used to create an entire site's worth of color-coded buttons at once.

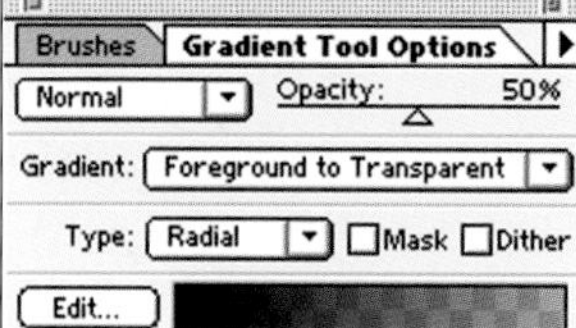


**1** Create a new file, then make a selection for the button and save the selection as a new channel (Channel #4). Double-click the Gradient tool icon to access the Gradient Options palette (Mode: Normal, Opacity: 50%, Gradient: Foreground to Transparent, Type: Radial, Mask: on, Dither: off).

**2** Click OK and drag to create a gradient, beginning in the center of the image and ending slightly outside one of the selection's corners.

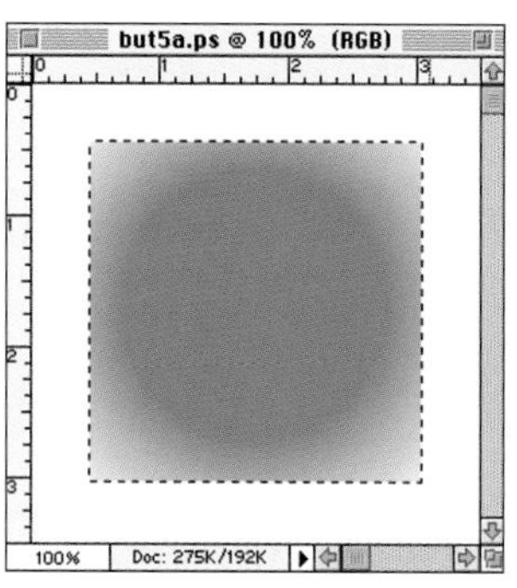

**TOOLBOX**

Alien Skin's Inner Bevel

**3** Apply a bevel using Alien Skin Inner Bevel. If you don't have the Alien Skin filter, follow the steps in the Bevel Button section (pages 126-129) to create the bevel or skip this step.

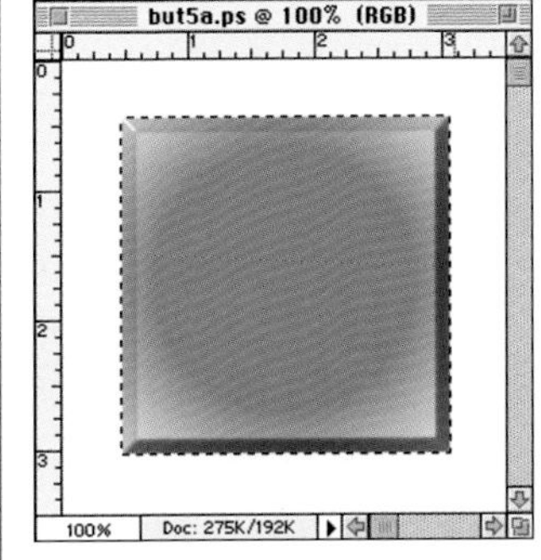


**4** To create a consistent look across the site we used a globe from the Carta font at 150 points. With the Type Mask tool, enter your dingbat text.

**5** With the selection active on the background, choose Image=›Adjust=›Brightness/Contrast (Brightness: +70). If you prefer to use an icon from another source, pasting the icon into the file will automatically create a new layer. You can then adjust the brightness/contrast of the layer by adding an adjustment layer Layer=›New=›Adjustment Layer: Brightness/Contrast.

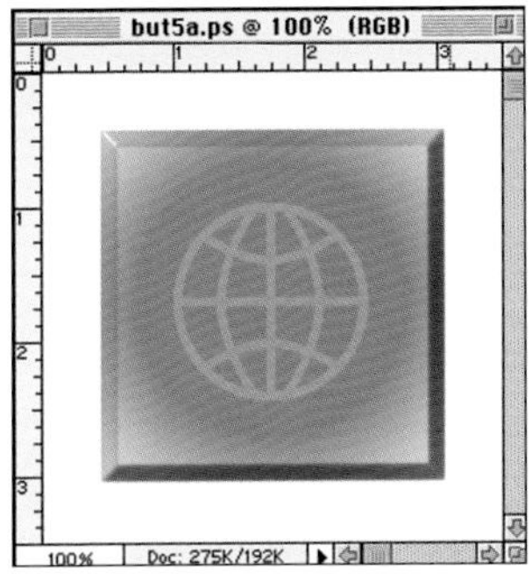


**6** Load the selection Channel #4 and choose Image=›Adjust=›Variations. You have six color-coded buttons surrounding your original gray button in the center.

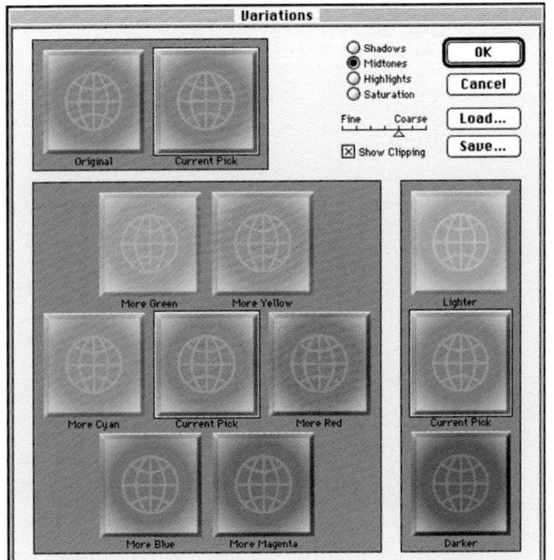

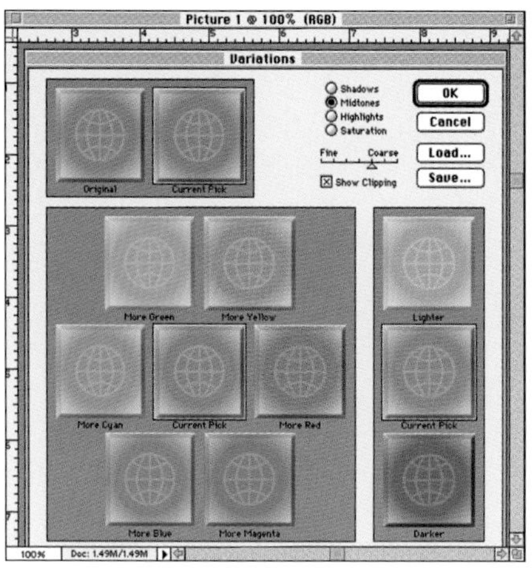

**7** To use this image you will have to take a screen-snapshot of it. On a Mac (Command-Shift-3) you will hear what sounds like a camera click. The file is saved as a PICT file named Picture 1 on your start-up disk. On Windows use F13 (Print Screen on some keyboards). The file is sent to the Clipboard and can be pasted into a new file.

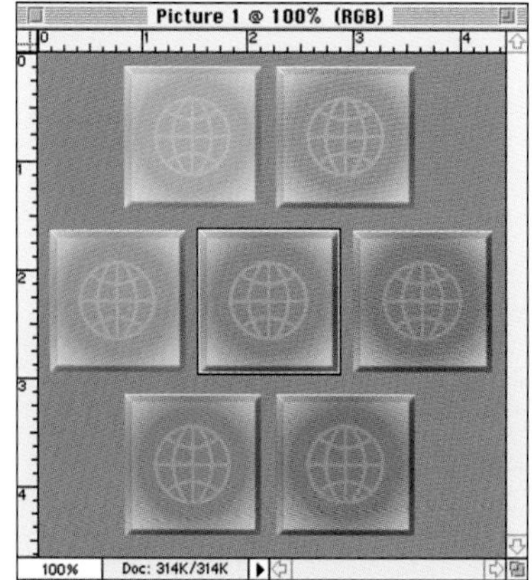

**8** On a Mac Open Picture 1. [On Windows create a new file and paste the clipboard into the file.] Crop the image to select the box containing the colored buttons. Select the Eyedropper tool. Hold down the option key while picking up the background gray from the image to assign it as your background color. Remove the type labels by marqueeing around the type and pressing delete.

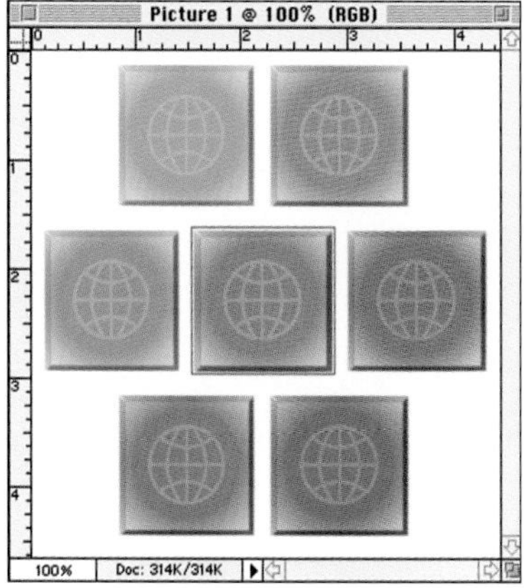

**9** Choose a new background color (we used white). Use the Magic Wand tool (Tolerance: 2) to select the gray background and press Delete to fill the background with your selected color.

**10** Choose Select➛Inverse. Save the selection (Channel #4). This channel can be used to apply a drop shadow or glow effect to the buttons. You can save the entire image as a GIF to be used as an imagemap on your Web pages. Or crop, copy, and paste each button to a new file for use as separate buttons.

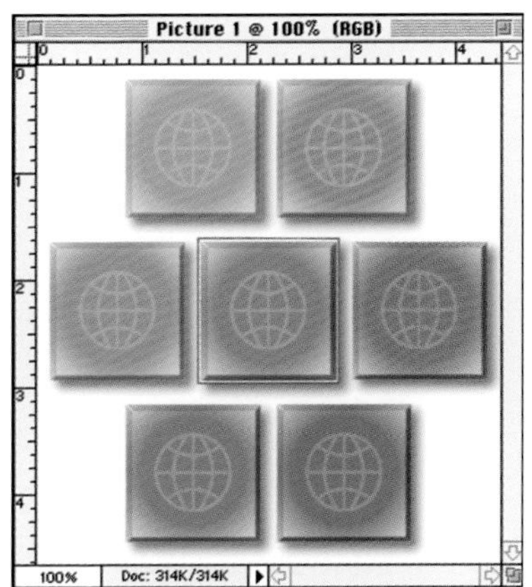


## VARIATION

This variation creates rectangular buttons and easy to do, one step edge effects.

**1** Create a new file, make a selection for the button, and save the selection (Channel #4). To create a basic background texture choose Filter➛Sketch➛Note Paper (Image Balance: 25, Graininess: 12, Relief: 11.)

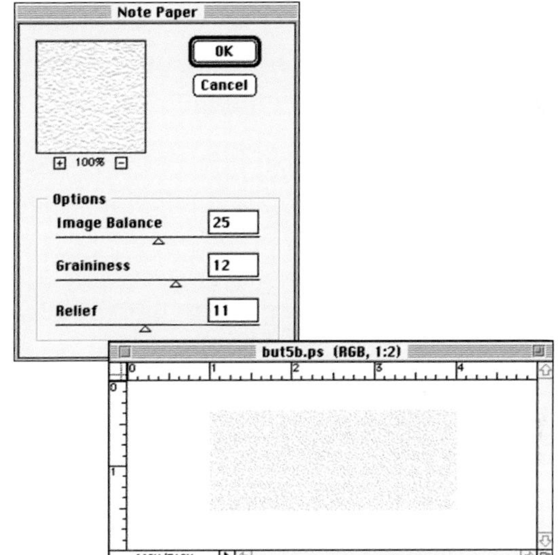


**2** Choose Image➛Adjust➛Variations and follow Steps 6 through 9.

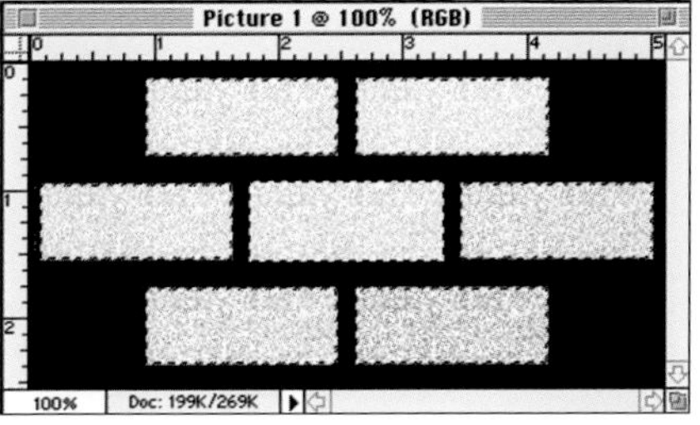

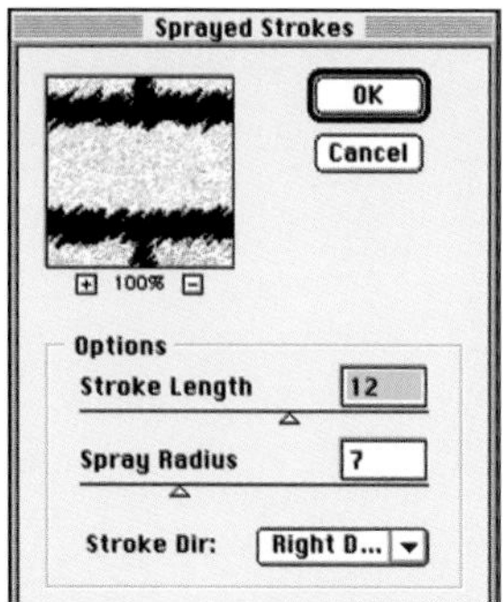


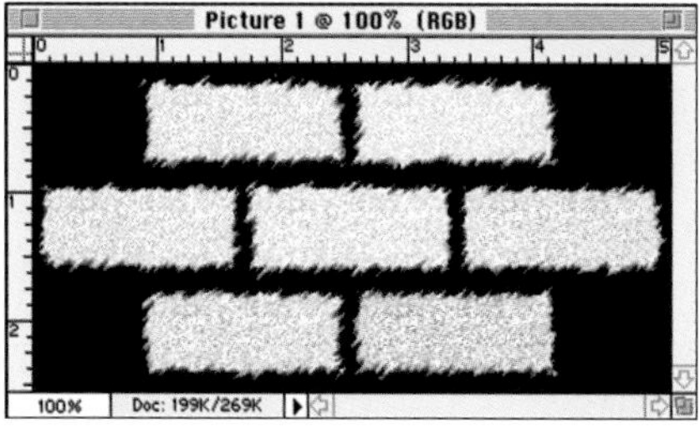


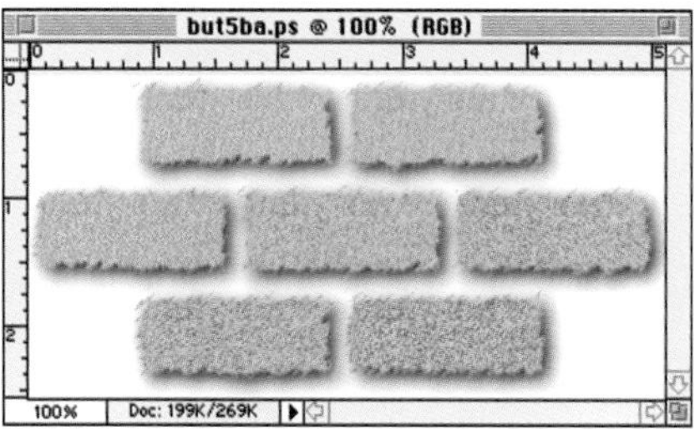


**3** With the buttons selected choose Select➞Modify➞Contract (8 pixels), then choose Select➞Inverse. Choose Filter➞Brush Strokes➞Sprayed Strokes (Stroke Length: 12, Spray Radius: 7, Stroke Direction: Right Diagonal).

**4** You can now use the Eyedropper tool to select the background as in Step 9. ■

## Globe Buttons

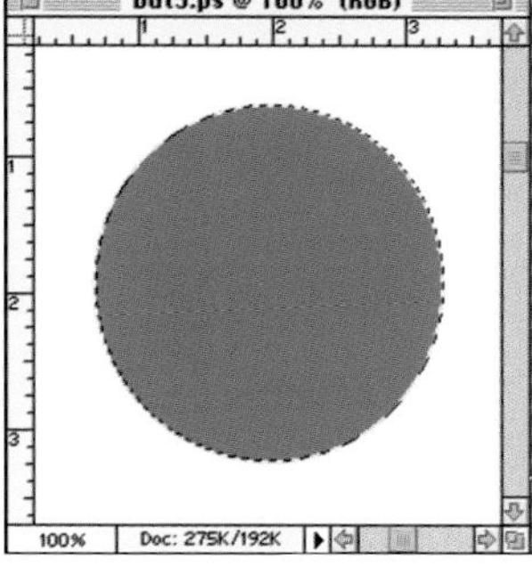


The three-dimensional aspect of spheres and globes is created by the way light hits an object and creates highlights and shadows. Photoshop's Lighting Effects filter helps to bring these aspects of 3D to flat illustration.

**1** Create a new file (Contents: White). Make a round selection and save the selection as a new channel (Channel #4). Select a color of your choice for the background color. Press Delete to fill your selection with color. Leave the sphere selected.

TIP **Work with the background color you intend to use for your final Web page. By keeping the colors consistent the anti-aliased pixels around the edges of your object will blend cleanly with your background.**

**2** To create a sphere with soft reflective qualities choose Filter➔Render➔Lighting Effects. Match the settings shown in the figure. You'll need to expand the light's area and change the light's center. Once you are pleased with the effect save the settings as a new Style named Soft Sphere for future use.

To tweak the light, adjust the size of the circle in the Preview box and vary the Intensity and Focus settings. Once you are pleased with the settings, save them. Click OK and you have a sphere.

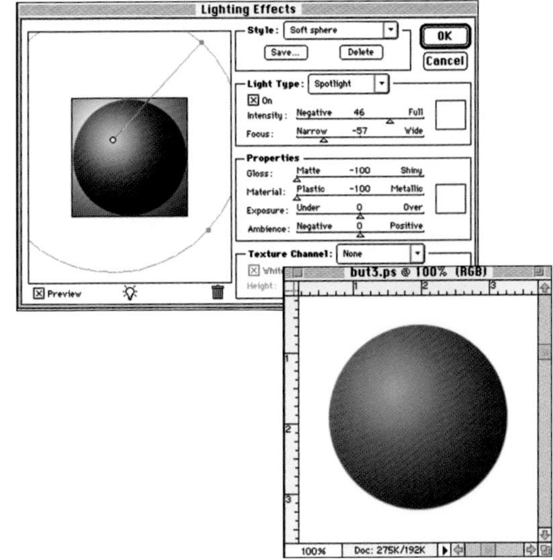


# VARIATIONS

## Metallic Reflection

To create a sphere with more reflective highlights use the settings shown in the figure. By increasing the Gloss settings the highlight in the center of the light will be brighter, increasing the overall brightness of the image.

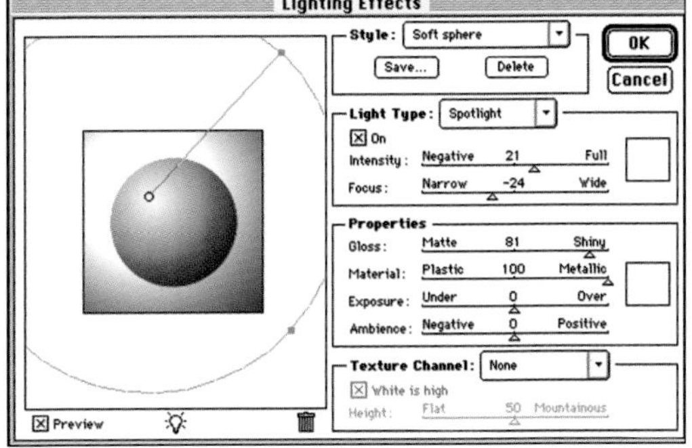


**TIP** **Light has a gray tint when it reflects off metal objects; light reflecting off of plastic retains more of the original hue of the object.**

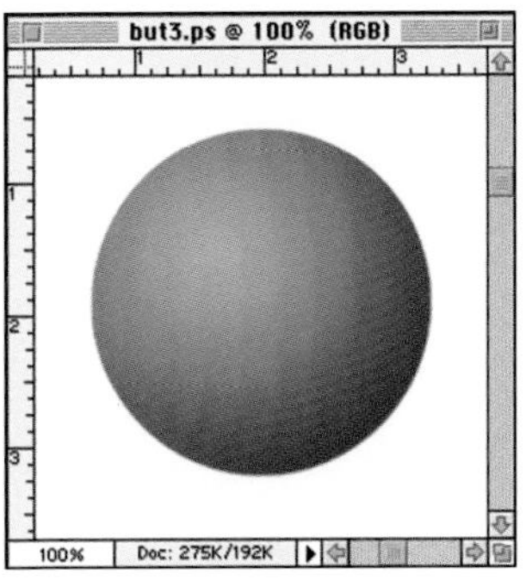

## Indented Sphere

In this example we created an indent in the center of the button to add a feeling of depth.

**1** After creating the initial sphere choose Select➙Modify➙Contract (16 pixels).

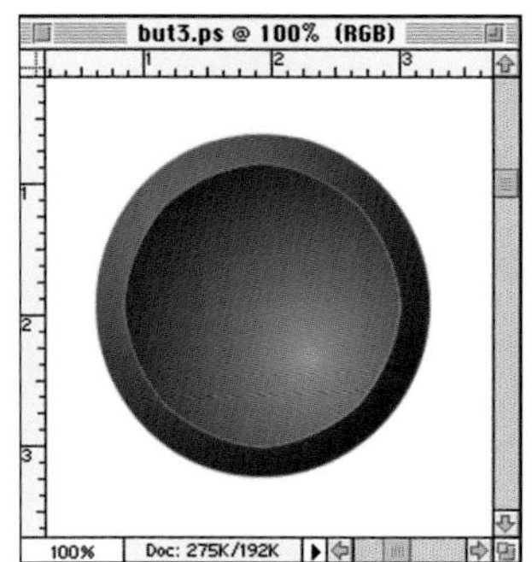


**2** Choose Layer➙Transform➙ Rotate (90°CW). The globe appears to be inverted and receding into the button.

## Feathered Indent

For this button we feathered the selection by 4 pixels (Select➙ Feather) before rotating the center section.

## Beveled Globe

**1** After creating the initial sphere, choose Select⇒Modify⇒Contract (16 pixels), then save as a new selection (Channel #5). Next, Select⇒Load Selection (Channel #4, New Selection); and Select⇒Load Selection (Channel #5, Subtract from Selection). Save as a new channel (Channel #6).

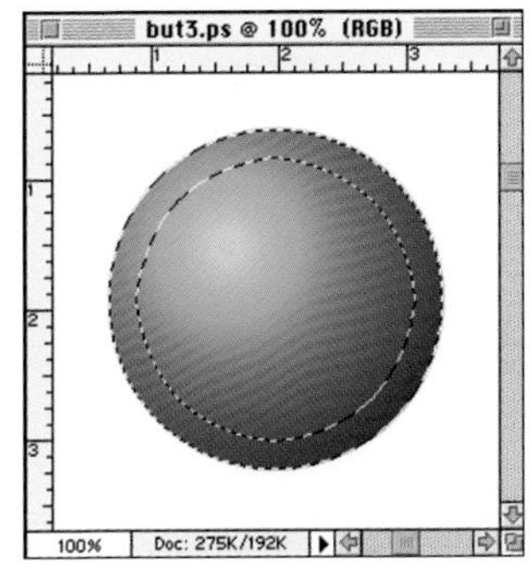


**2** Load the selection Channel #4. Make Channel #6 visible. Choose Filter⇒Blur⇒Gaussian Blur (3 pixels) to soften the edge of the bevel.

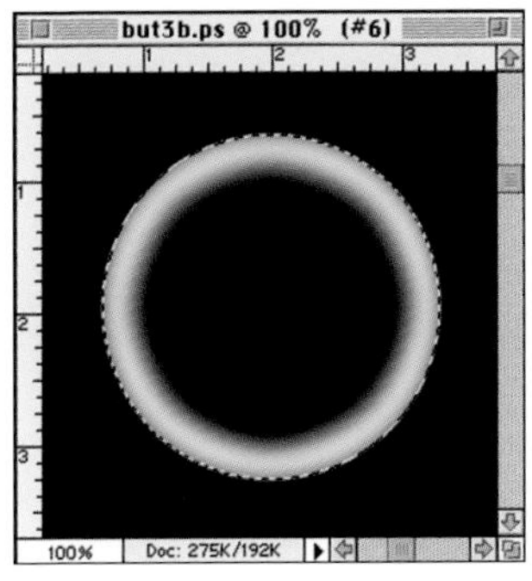


**3** With Channel #4 still selected, return to the composite channel, and choose Filter⇒Render⇒ Lighting Effects. In the Lighting Effects dialog box, set the Texture Channel to Channel #6 and rotate the light source to be opposite the globe's original light source.

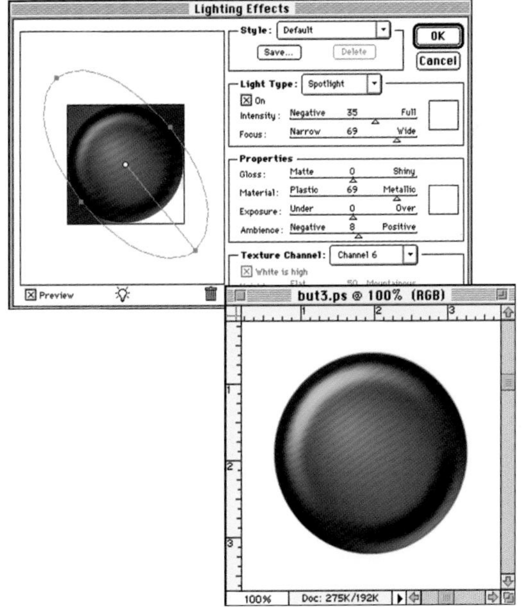

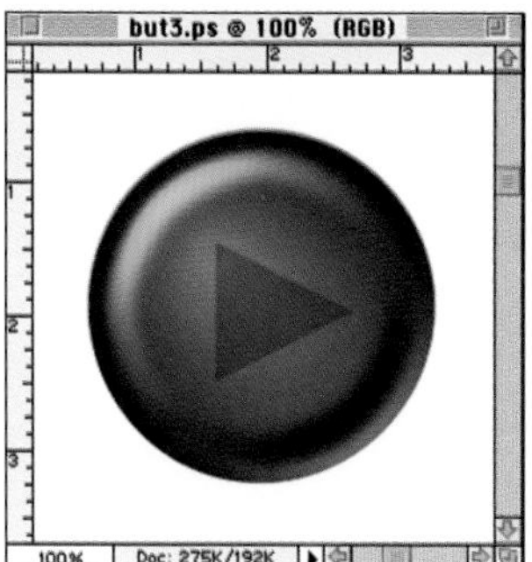


**4** To finish the button we added a triangle-shaped dingbat as a directional arrow. The dingbat was selected and saved as Channel #7. The layer was then hidden and the background made active. With the selection on the background layer, choose Image➝Adjust➝Brightness/Contrast (Brightness: -20%). ■

## Spherized Photos

Photographs can be given a convincing 3D effect, appearing to wrap around a globe, by using both the Spherize and Lighting Effects filters. In this example we used a photograph from VisualSoftware's Textures for Professionals CD-ROM.

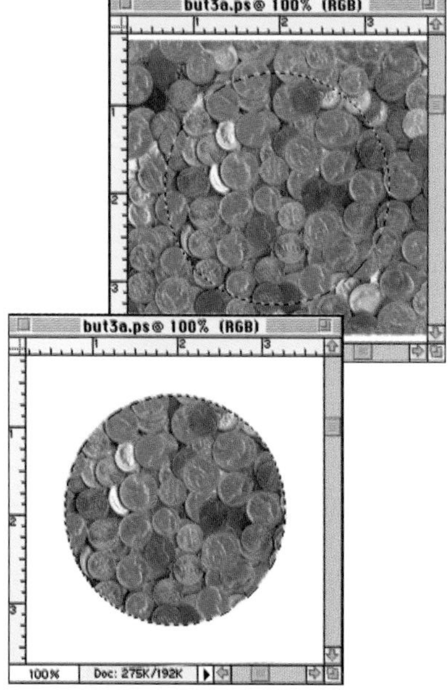


**1** Open a file containing a photograph of your choice. Make a round selection and save the selection as a new channel (Channel #4). Select a background color of your choice. Choose Select➛Inverse then press delete to fill with the background color.

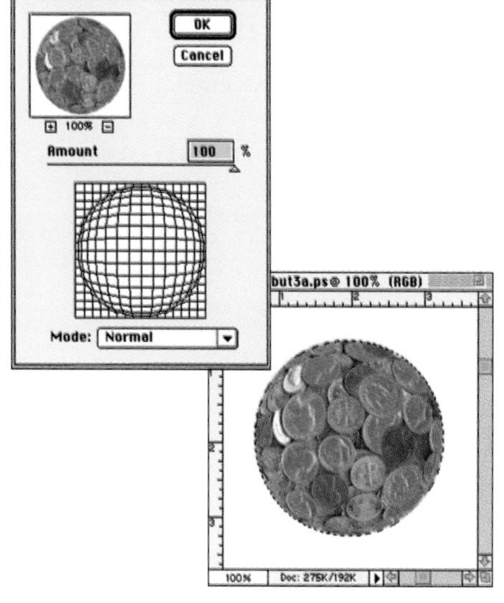


**2** Invert the selection again (or load selection Channel #4) and choose Filter➛Distort➛Spherize (Amount: 100%, Mode: normal). If parts of your image distort too heavily, try lower settings.

**TOOLBOX**

Alien Skin's Outer Bevel

**3** Choose Filter➾Render➾Lighting Effects. Select 2 o'clock Spotlight from the Style menu. You may need to experiment to find settings that work best with your photograph.

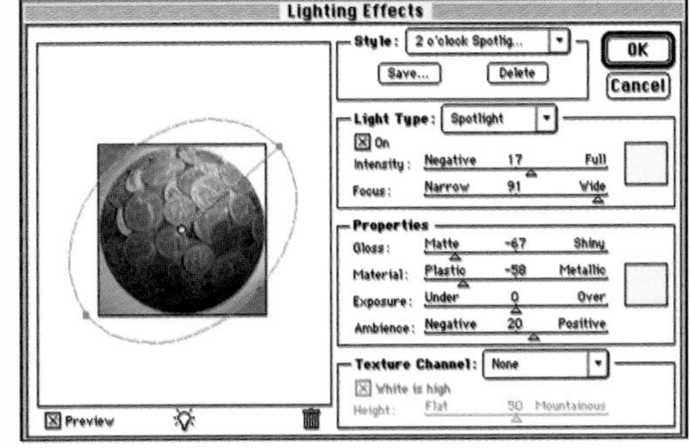


**TIP** **For the most realistic 3D effect, match the direction of the light with the direction of the primary light source in the photograph.**

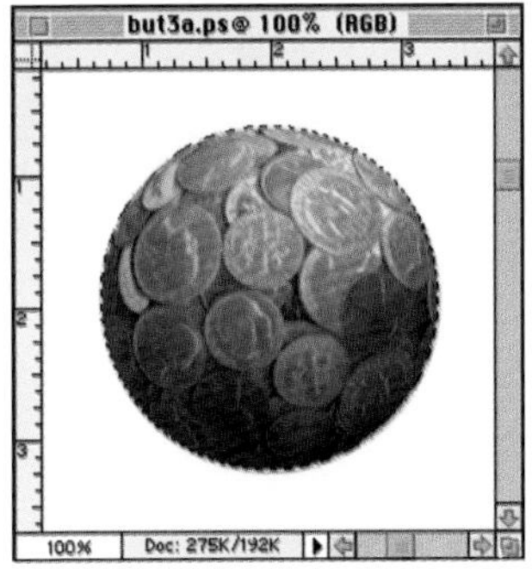


**4** Use the Type Mask tool to enter the text. Save text as a new channel (Channel #5) and then hide the new layer. Make Channel #5 active (Command-5) [Control-5]. Select➾All and choose Filter➾Distort➾Spherize (100%, Normal).

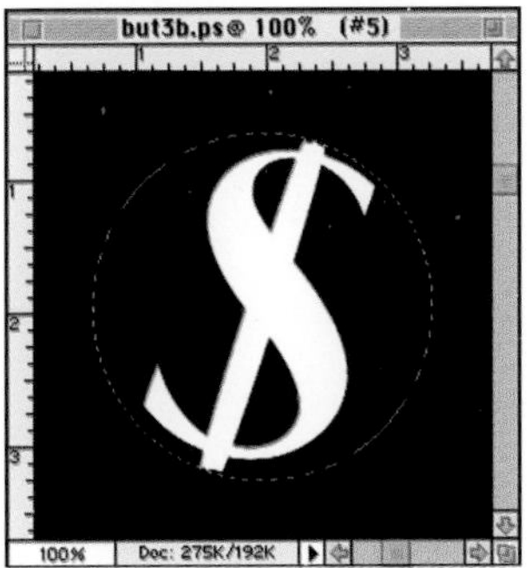

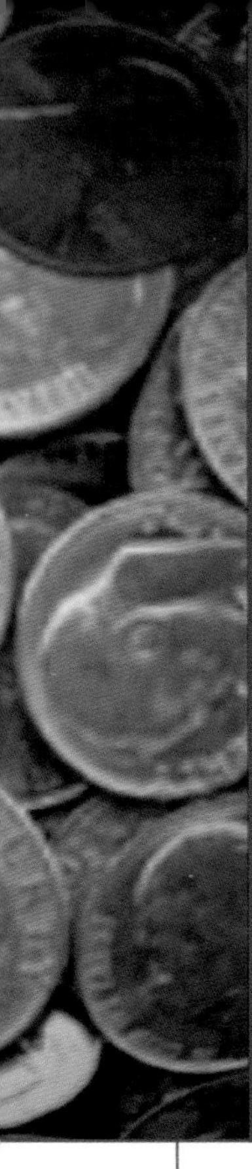

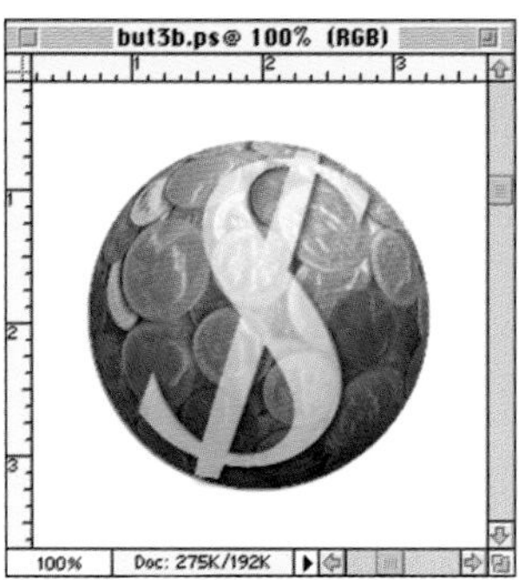

**5** Return to the Composite channel (Command-~ [Control-~]. Load the Channel #5 selection to make the type selection active. Choose Image→Adjust→Brightness/Contrast (Brightness: +50, Contrast: -10).

**6** The final step is to apply a drop shadow. We used the Alien Skin Drop Shadow filter (x and y offset 3 pixels, Blur 5 pixels, and Opacity 50%). Export to GIF format and make the background color transparent when saving as a GIF.

## VARIATION

To make the curved button appear as if it is recessed into a console with a frame we used the Alien Skin Outer Bevel filter with Settings: Button. ■

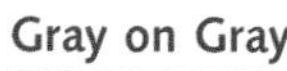

## Gray on Gray

The default background color for Netscape Navigator, Internet Explorer, and most other browsers is gray. Because it is so neutral, gray works well in Web sites where utility and function are the primary focus. Many of Photoshop's filters can be used to create textures to make attractive buttons in the gray range.

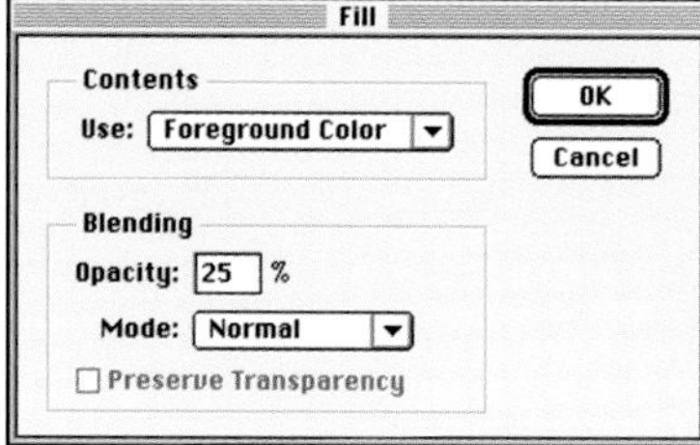


**1** Create a new file. Choose Edit➞Fill (Use Black, Opacity: 25%). This will create a 25% gray screen—the same as browser default gray (the hexadecimal value of default gray on a Web page is C3C3C3—place this value in the Body command to keep a gray page gray even if a user has defined a different default background color).

Halftone Pattern
OK
Cancel
100%
Options
Size 1
Contrast 0
Pattern Type: Line

**2** Create a rectangular selection for the button and save the selection (Channel #4). Choose Filter➞Sketch➞Halftone Pattern (Size: 1, Screen Type: Line, Contrast: 0). You can create larger lines by increasing the Size setting.

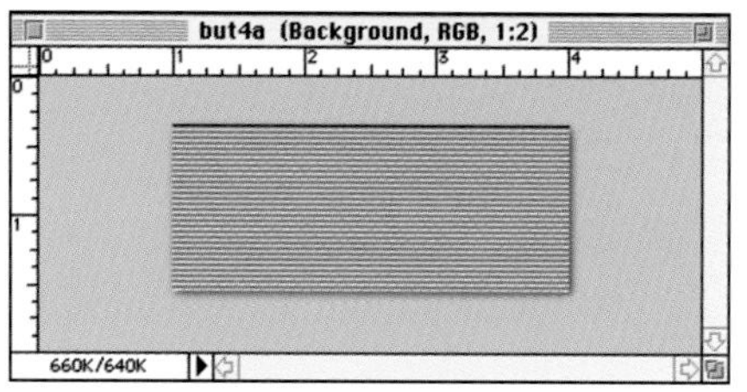
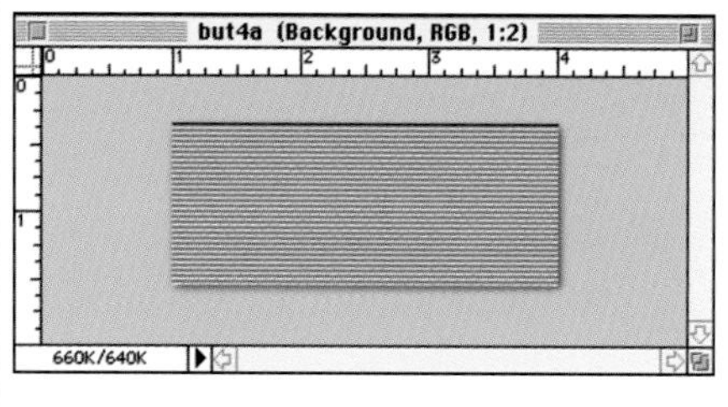


**3** Create a drop shadow using Alien Skin Drop Shadow filter (x, y offset: 3 pixels, blur: 6 pixels, and opacity: 70%) or follow the Soft Shadow exercise on page 72.

**TOOLBOX**

Alien Skin's
Drop Shadow
Inner Bevel
Patchwork

KPT Page Curl

**4** Select all and choose Filter➾Distort➾Wave. The Wave filter is capable of a multitude of effects and distortions. For this effect we chose Number of Generators: 1; Type: Sine Wavelength: Min: 10; Max: 166, Amplitude: Min: 5; Max: 35. Undefined Areas: Repeat edge pixels. The settings you use can vary as you explore the various Wave functions. Keep Number of Generators set to one while adjusting the Wavelength and Amplitude sliders for a wide range of effects and distortions. Click the Randomize button for different wave effects.

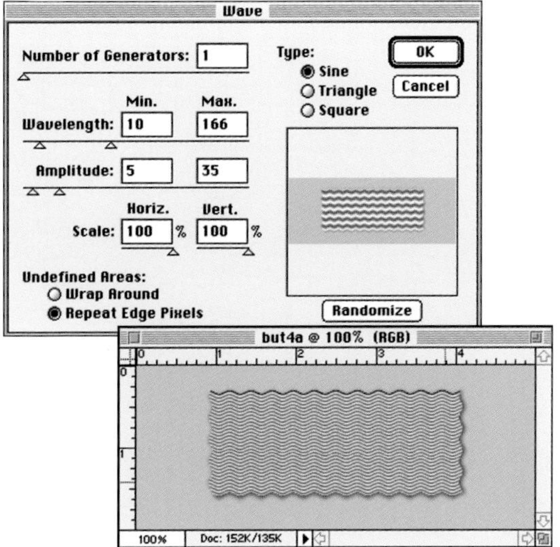


**TIP** **Any of the buttons in this exercise, or in this book, can be colorized by using the Hue/Saturation function from the Image menu. Check the Colorize box on the Hue/Saturation dialog box. Your image will turn a bright red. Lower the saturation to around 50% and then select a new color for your button with the Hue slider.**

## VARIATIONS

Photoshop 4.0's extended selection of filters makes it easy to create an almost limitless number patterns and textures for buttons.

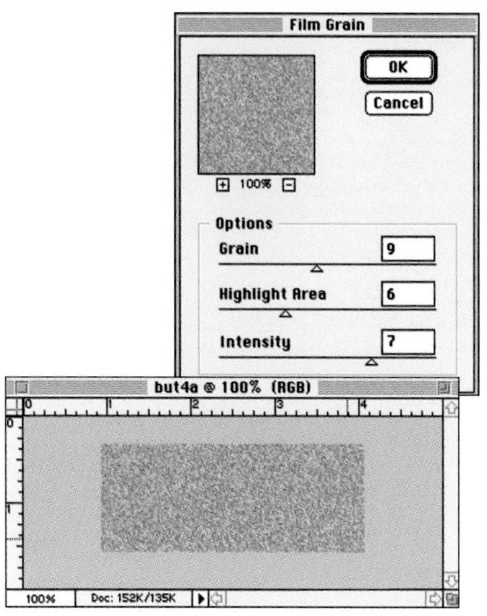


## Crosshatch Button

**1** Follow Step 1 to create a 25% gray background and make a selection for your button. Choose Filter➛Artistic➛Film Grain (Grain: 9, Highlight Area: 6, Highlight Intensity: 7). To try variations on the slider settings click Preview and press apply when you have a texture you like.

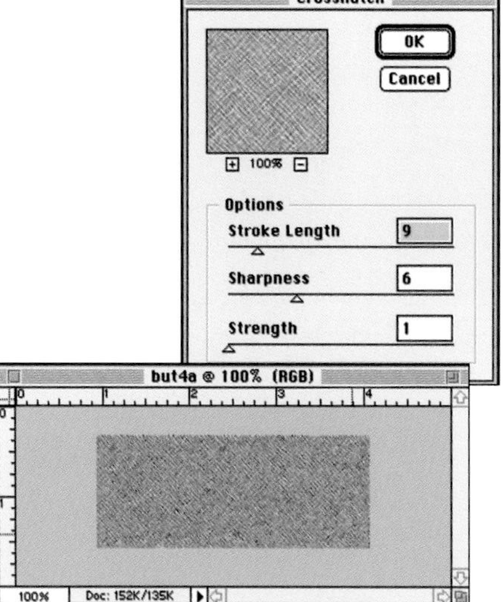


**2** Choose Filter➛Brush Strokes➛ Crosshatch (Stroke Length: 9, Sharpness: 6, Strength: 1). Keeping the Sharpness and Strength settings low produces a diffused effect that won't interfere with the legibility of the type on the button.

**3** For the type treatment on this button we stuck with gray tones using a 25% gray (same as the background color) for the first word and 75% gray for the second word, "Here."

## Background Bevels

Beveled buttons that are the same color as the background have a very neat look and create the appearance of being fully integrated into the Web page.

**1** Follow Step 1 to create a 25% gray background and make a selection for your button. We then applied the Alien Skin Inner Bevel filter (Low Flat). If you do not have this filter, you can create a bevel by following Steps 3 and 4 in the Beveled Button exercise (page 126).

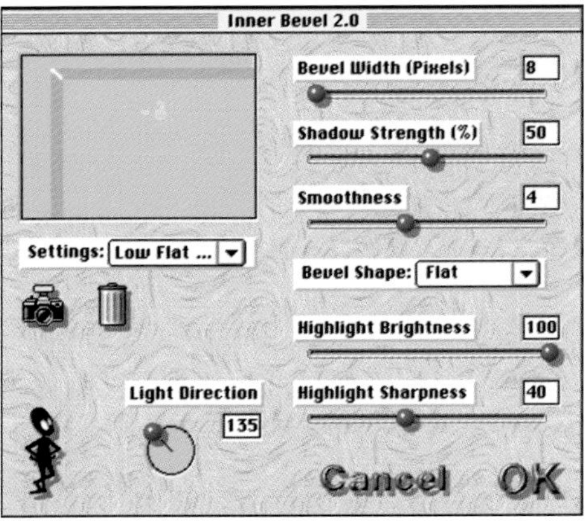


**2** Make a rectangular selection containing about 80% of the area inside the button. Choose Image➞Adjust➞Brightness/Contrast (Brightness: +25, Contrast: 0).

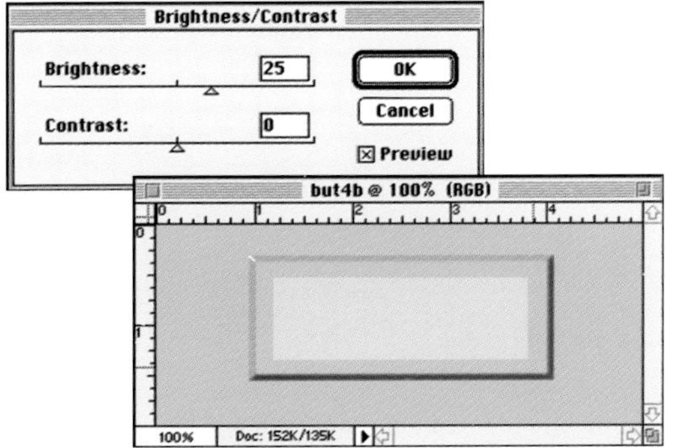

## Velcro

This combination of Photoshop 4.0 filters can make buttons look like fabric labels or even strips of velcro.

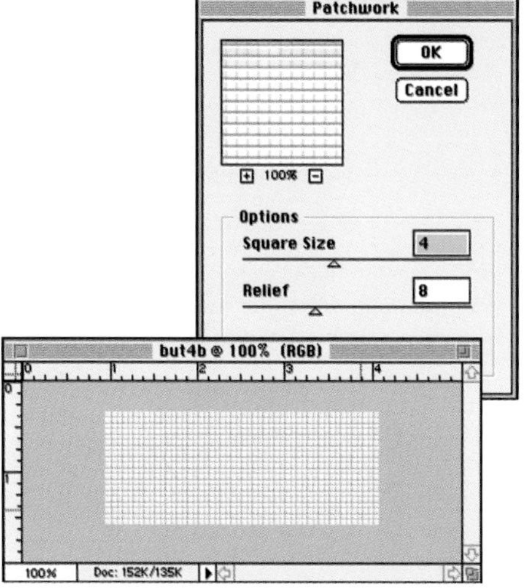


**1** Follow Step 1 to create a 25% gray background and make a selection for your button. Choose Filter➡Texture➡Patchwork (Square Size: 4, Relief: 8).

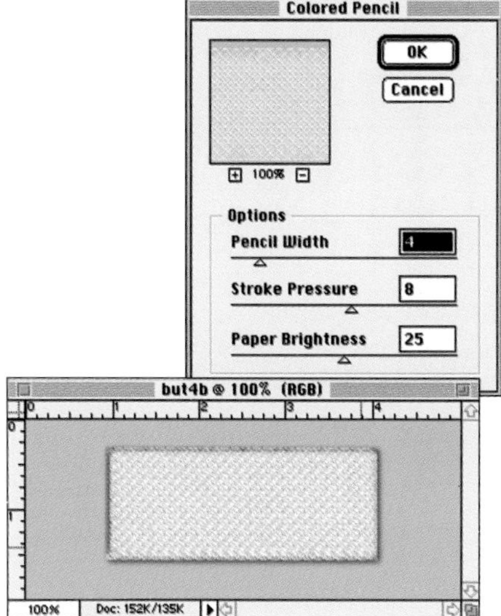


**2** With the button still selected, choose Filter➡Artistic➡Colored Pencil (Pencil Width: 4; Stroke Pressure: 8, Paper Brightness: 25). Notice how this filter creates what appears to be a border around the button. Export to GIF format.

**3** We used MetaTools KPT Page Curl filter and finished the button by adding a drop shadow.

This filter enables you to adjust the direction and degree of curl by clicking and dragging. When used sparingly on Web pages, the Curl filter adds an interesting 3-D focal point for important buttons or information. ■

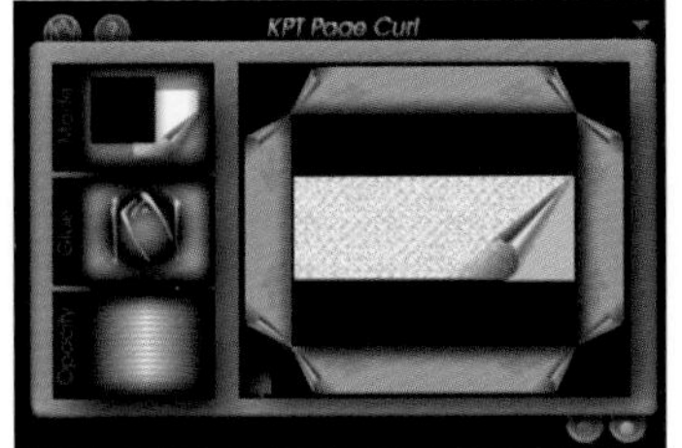


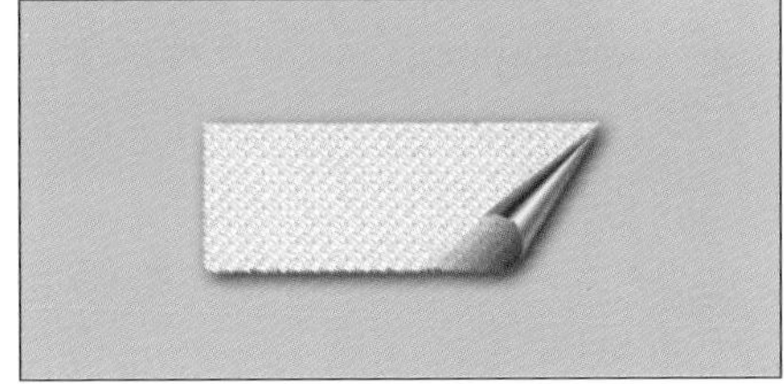

## Pill Shaped

Pill-shaped buttons—not quite rectangles and not quite ovals—can be used to add a distinctive look to Web pages.

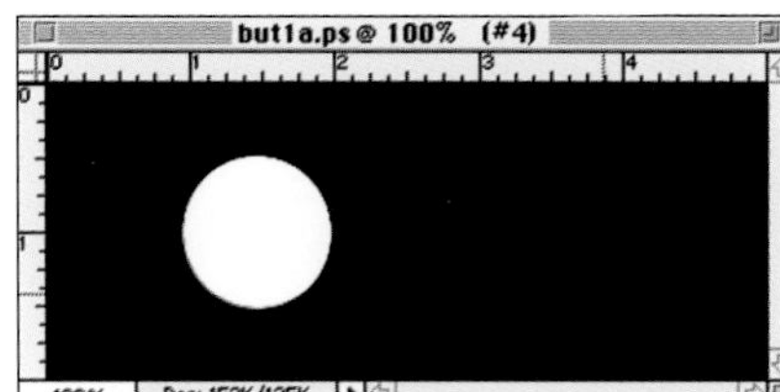


1 Create a new file. Double-click the Marquee icon and select the elliptical Marquee tool. Hold down the Shift key while using the Marquee tool to make a round selection for the button. Save the selection (Channel #4). Make Channel #4 visible.

2 Select the rectangular Marquee tool. Carefully draw a rectangular selection cutting through the center, even with the top and bottom of the circle, and extending about 1/2 of the width of your intended button. You might want to zoom in to make the image as large as possible.

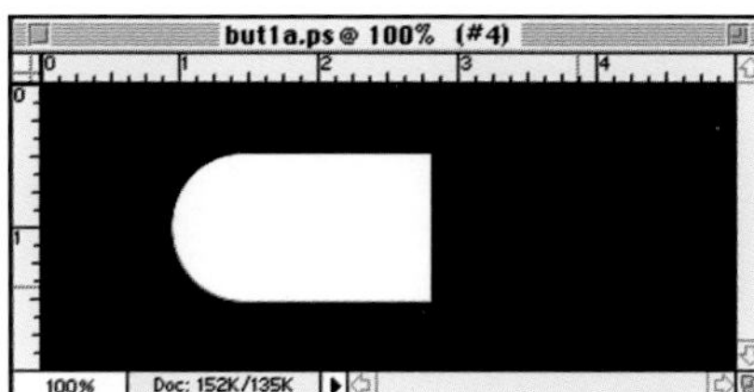


3 Choose Edit→Fill (Use: White, Opacity: 100%, Mode: Normal). Load the selection Channel #4.

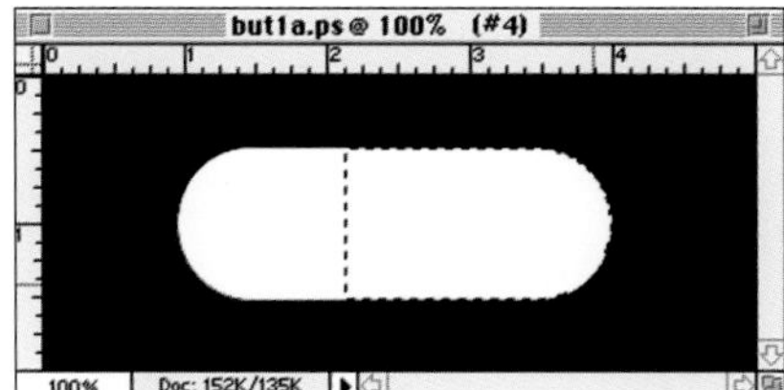


4 Copy and paste your selection to create a floating selection. Choose Layer→Transform→Flip→Horizontal. Place the flipped selection to complete the other side of the pill. Adjust the width of the pill by overlapping the selection, if you want.

**5** Duplicate Channel #4 (Channel #5). Set the Marquee tool to elliptical. Make Channel #5 active and make a long elliptical selection across the bottom half of the button. Next we'll add some highlight to the selection.

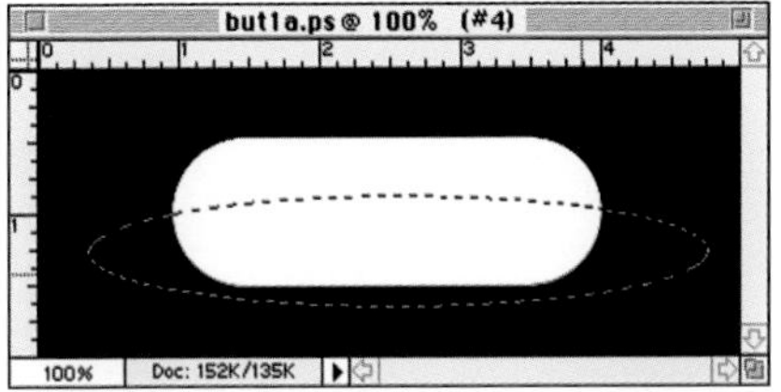


**6** Choose Edit➔Fill (Use: Black, Opacity: 100%, Mode: Normal) Deselect. Soften the edges with Filter➔Blur➔Gaussian Blur (6 pixels). More blur will create a softer highlight, less blur a sharper, more defined highlight.

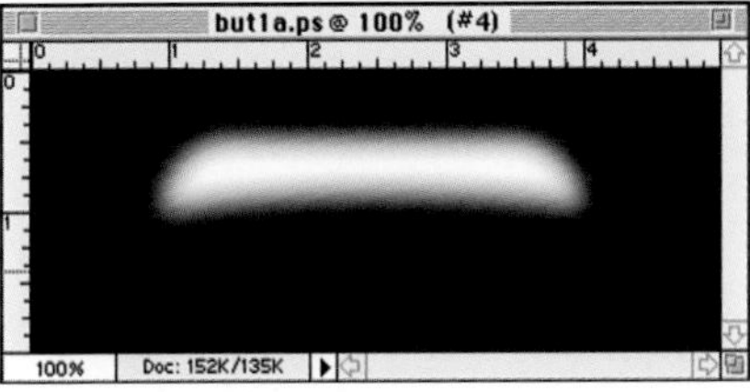


**7** Return to the composite channel. Load the selection Channel #4, and fill the selection with a color of your choice. We used the RGB values 94, 208, 255 in this example. Then, with Channel #4 still selected, load the selection Channel #5 (Subtract from Selection).

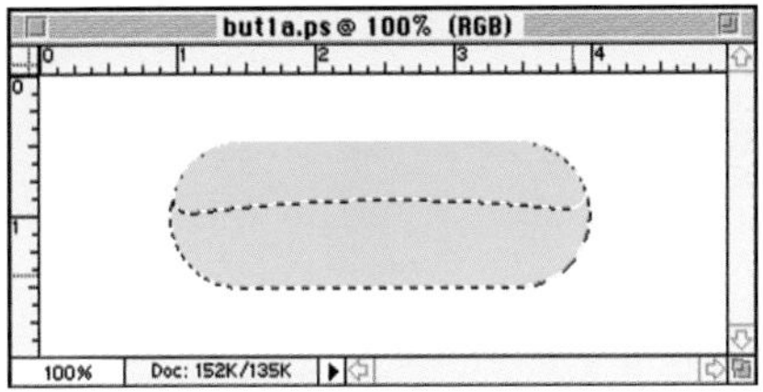


**8** Choose Image➔Adjust➔ Brightness/Contast (Brightness: -50, Contrast: 0). The top half of the button should appear lighter, as if it is a curved cylinder with a light source shining from above.

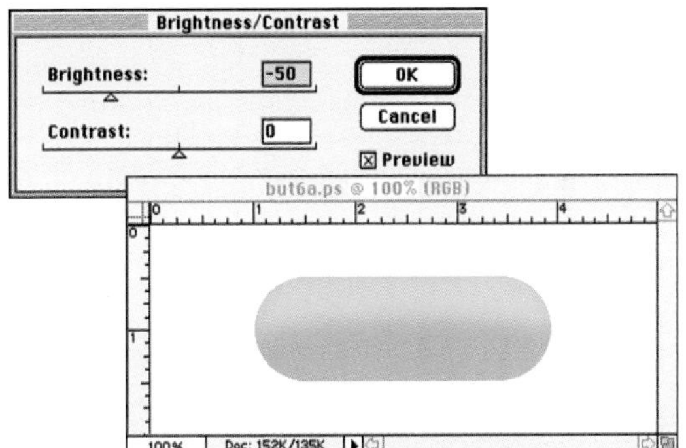

**9** To add some subtle highlights to the button use Filters→Artistic→Plastic Wrap (Highlight Strength: 6, Detail: 12, Smoothness: 13). This filter produces different effects depending upon the size of the selection and color and variations in the image. Try the above settings as a starting point and experiment from there.

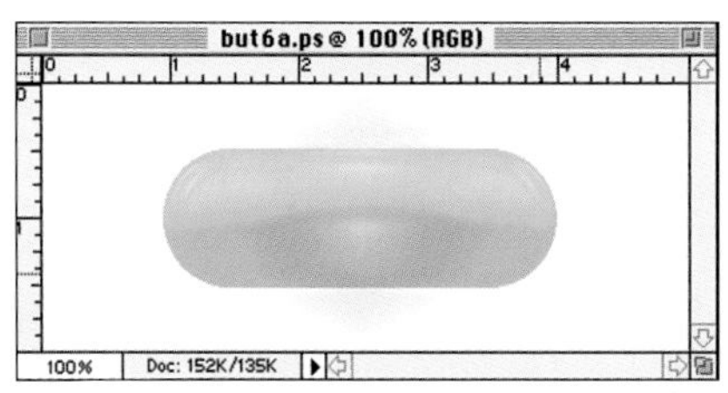


**10** To increase the illusion of light hitting the button from above, with the button still selected, choose Filter→Render→Lighting Effects. Choose the preset Style: Parallel Directional. This style setting defaults to a blue light tint (like placing a colored gel over a light). Adjust the tint to a hue similar but darker than the color of your button.

**TIP** **After you become comfortable using the Lighting Effects filter, try different combinations of color for Light Type and Properties. You will find that "painting with light" will add considerable realism and subtlety to your art.**

**11** To finish the button we used a funky typeface named Dogs on Mars. To enhance the carved look of the lettering we used the Alien Skin Carve filter with a Bevel Width set to 3 pixels. Finally, export as a GIF.

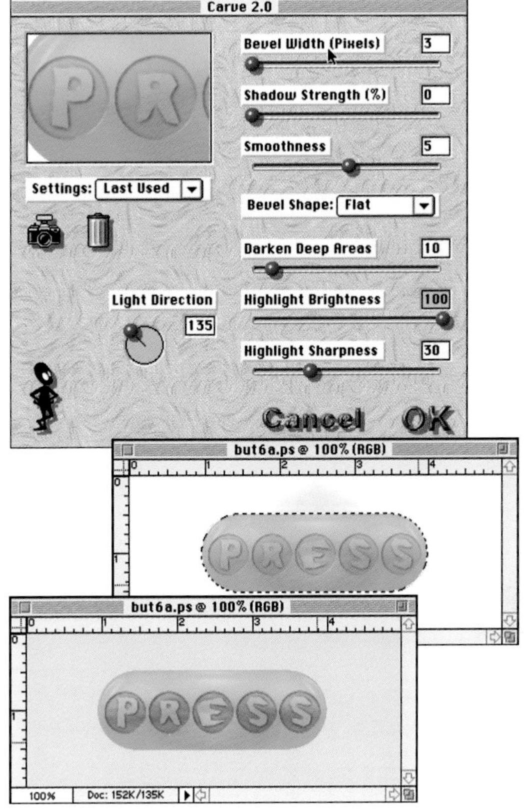


# VARIATION

To create this silver bullet we used the lighting effects texture channel with high metallic properties.

Following Step 6 we returned to the composite channel, loaded the selection, and (Channel #4) chose Edit➛Stroke (Width: 3 pixels, Location: Inside, Opacity: 100%, Mode: Normal) to create a solid black border around the button.

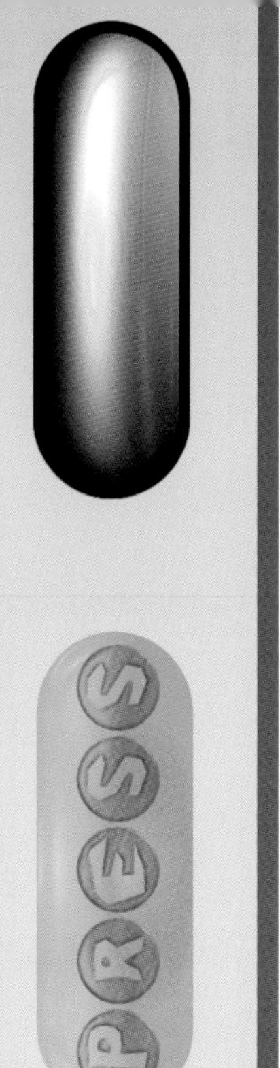


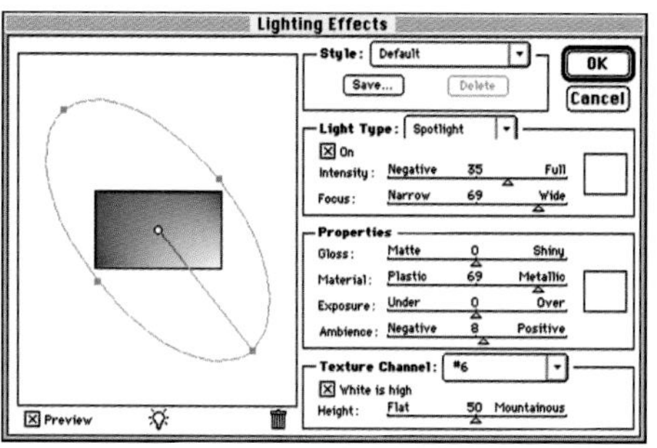


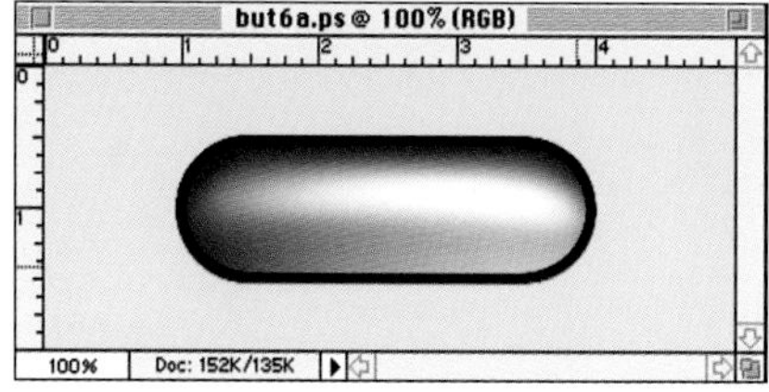


We chose Filter➵Render➵Lighting Effects (Style: Default) and assigned Channel #5 as the Texture Channel. The results were a bit too contrasting and harsh. We used the undo key and tried it again. To compensate, we made a second copy of Channel #5 (Channel #6) and applied an additional Gaussian Blur of 6 pixels to the channel. We then tried the Lighting Effects filter again using Channel #6 for this result. ■

## Glass

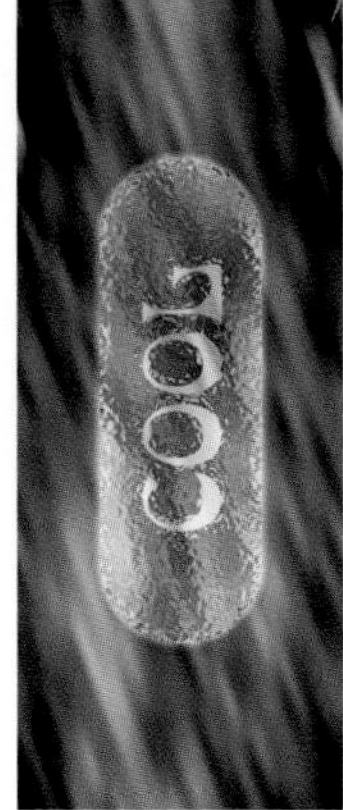


In the past, creating glass effects required a fairly complicated series of processes including creating multiple channels, calculation adjustments, and smudging to replicate the unique reflective and refractive qualities of glass. In Photoshop 4.0 that process has been made much easier with the introduction of the Glass filter.

**1** Open a file containing a texture of your choice (Sample textures can be found on the CD in the Web Magic folder) or create a new file and create a texture. For this example we used MetaTools KPT Texture Explorer and chose a preset texture. Make a selection for your button and save the selection (Channel #4). For this exercise we used the pill shape mask (from Technique #32), but you can use any shape you choose.

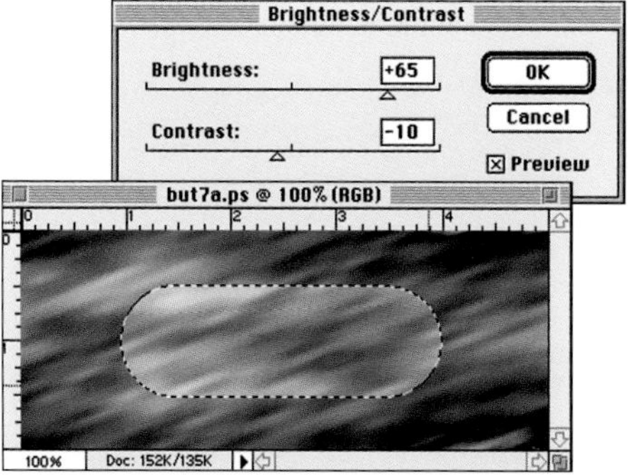


**2** Choose Image➛Adjust➛Brightness/Contrast (Brightness: +65, Contrast: -10). Increasing the brightness and lowering the contrast adds a subtle gray glass-like haze to the image.

**3** Choose Select➛Modify➛Border (3 pixels), then choose Image➛Adjust➛Brightness/Contrast (Brightness: +60, Contrast: 0). This creates the light glow around the object. Use the Type Mask tool to enter the type. Save the type selection (Channel #5).

**4** Choose Image➵Adjust➵ Brightness/Contrast (Brightness: +60, Contrast: 0). This makes the text appear transparent and gives it the same degree of brightness as the button's border. As an optional step we applied a drop shadow using Alien Skin 2.0 with an x and y offset of 3 pixels, a 12 pixel blur, and opacity of 40%. Or, refer to page 70, "Shadows for Buttons."

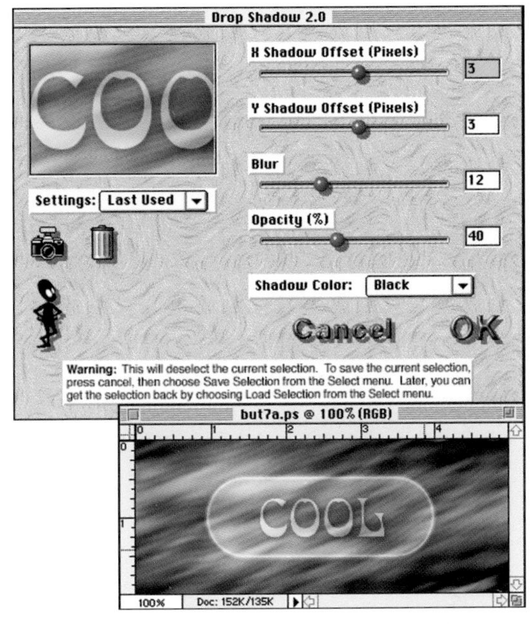


**5** Load the selection Channel #4, then load the selection Channel #5 (Subtract from Selection).

**6** Choose Filter➵Glass (Frosted, Scaling: 30% 100%). Adjust the Effect Controls to your liking. We used Distortion at 5 and Smoothness at 3. Use the Preview button to fine tune your settings and apply. Finally, export as a GIF.

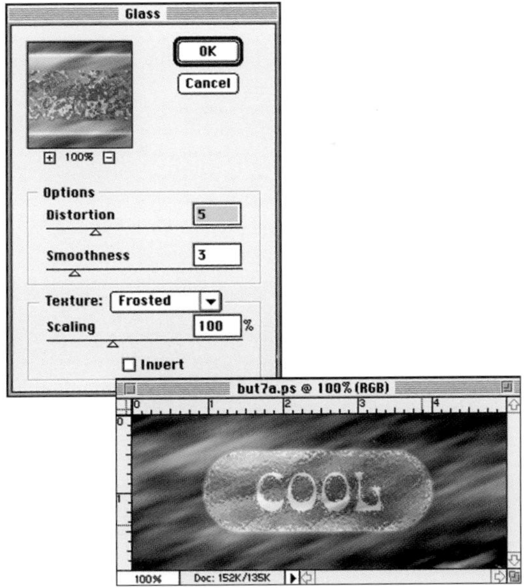

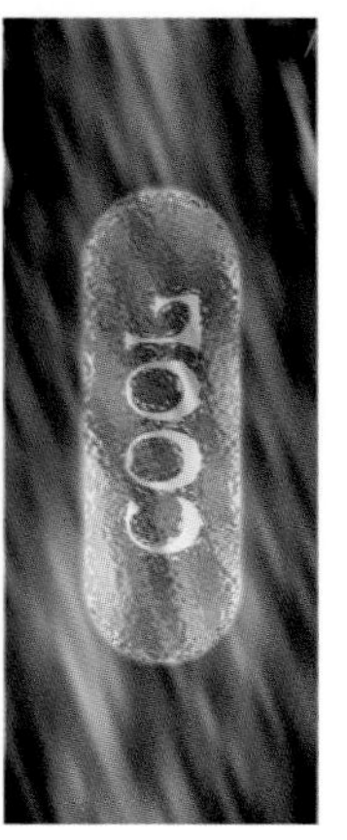

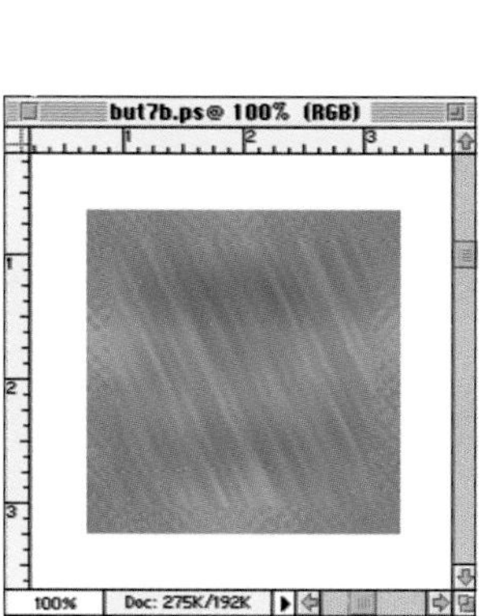


**TIP** **The Glass Surface Controls dialog box contains 4 different textures: frosted, blocks, canvas, and tiny lens, but you can also import a custom PICT file as a texture. Try using them in combination for glass on glass effects. (Frosted glass buttons on a stained glass title plaque, for example.)**

## VARIATION

For this variation on glass buttons we created a glass border with a stained glass insert in the center.

First we chose a different texture from MetaTools KPT Texture Explorer and filled our button selection with it. Save the selection (Channel #4). We choose Selection➼Modify➼Contract (16 pixels) and saved the result as a new channel (Channel #5).

Loading the selection Channel #4, then loading the selection Channel #5 (Subtract from Selection) created the border selection that was saved as a new channel (Channel #6).

With Channel #6 selected we applied the Glass filter with tiny lens chosen as the texture.

A glow was applied around the center box as described in Step 3.

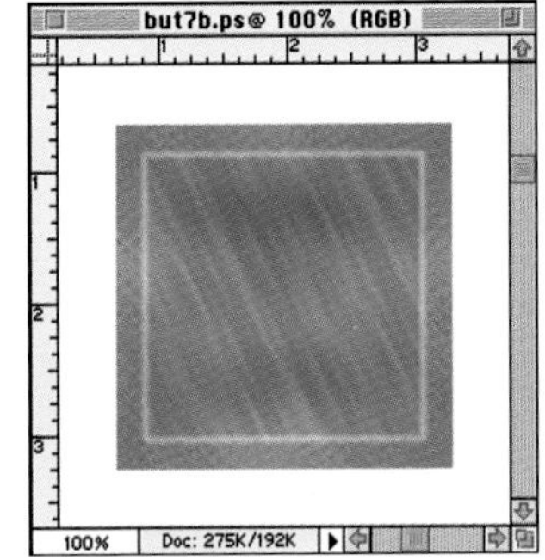


With Channel #5 selected, we chose Filter➛Stained Glass (Cell Size: 10, Border Thickness: 4, Light Intensity: 3). You can almost feel the light shining through the window. ■

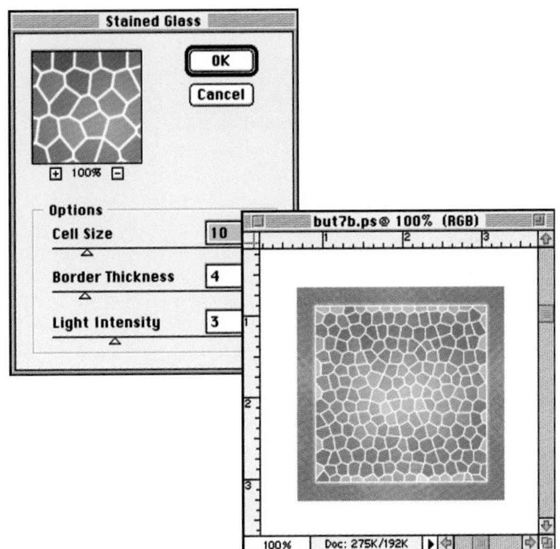

## Concentric Circles

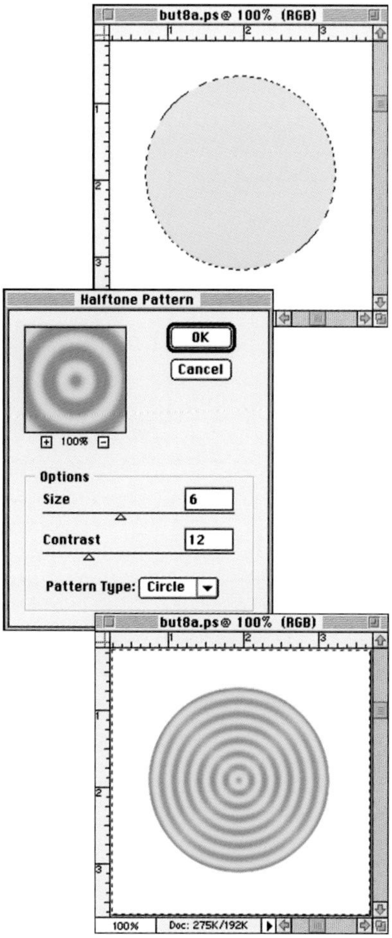

Besides creating halftone dots, Photoshop 4.0's new Halftone Screen filter can create concentric circles—when someone clicks a bulls-eye button they know they are going someplace important.

**1** Create a new file. Double-click the Marquee tool and select Elliptical from the Shape pop-up menu that appears. With the Marquee tool selected, hold down the Shift key to make a circular selection.

**2** Choose the foreground and background colors. In this case we chose yellow (RGB: 200, 213, 34) for the foreground and aqua (RGB: 89, 150, 157) for the background. Choose Filter➔Halftone Pattern (Size: 6, Contrast: 12, Screen Type: Circle). The Size slider adjusts the width of the circles.

**3** Select→All and choose Filter→Distort→Spherize (Amount: 100%, Mode: Horizontal). This will stretch the button along the horizontal axis to create a shape that is not quite an ellipse but more like a rounded rectangle.

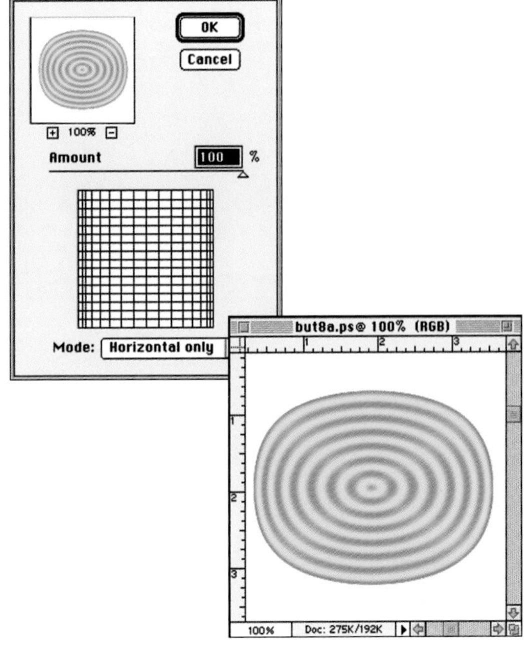


**4** To select the new button shape, double-click the Magic Wand icon and set the options (Tolerance to 2, Anti-aliased: on). Click the white area surrounding the button. Choose Select→Inverse, and save the selection as a new channel (Channel #4).

**5** Choose Filter→Reticulation (Density: 20, Black Level: 31, White Level: 20). This adds some texture to mimic the rough surface of a cork dart board.

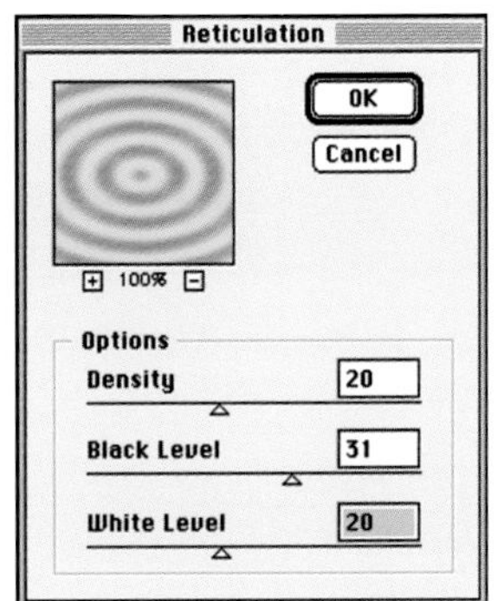

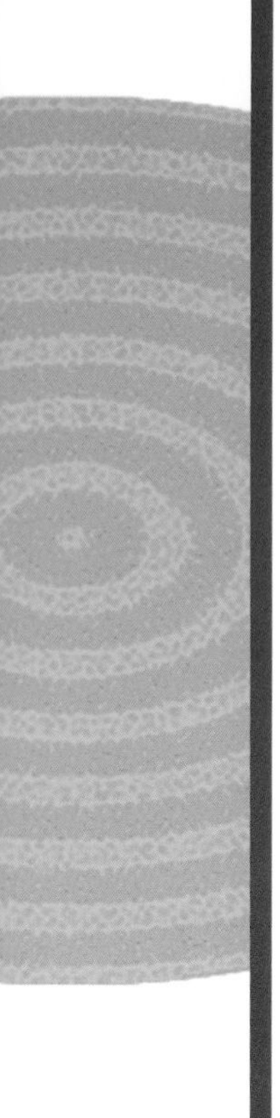

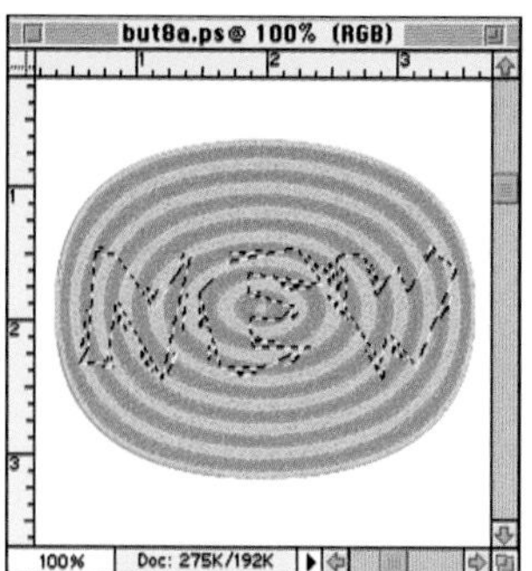


**6** To add transparent type to the button, choose the Type Mask tool, enter the text and save the type selection as a new channel (Channel #5).

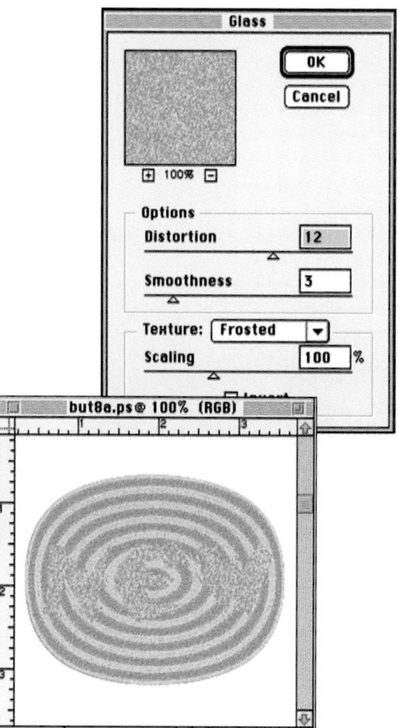


**7** With the type outline selected on the background layer, choose Filter→Glass (Distortion: 12, Smoothness: 3, Texture: Frosted, Scaling 100%).

**8** To define the type from the background choose Image➔Adjust➔Hue/Saturation. We used a Hue setting of -160, Saturation 0, and Lightness -35. You may want to adjust these settings to find the ones that work best with your color scheme.

Hue/Saturation
Master
R
Y
G
C
B
M
Hue: -160
Saturation: 0
Lightness: -35
Sample:
OK
Cancel
Load...
Save...
Colorize
Preview

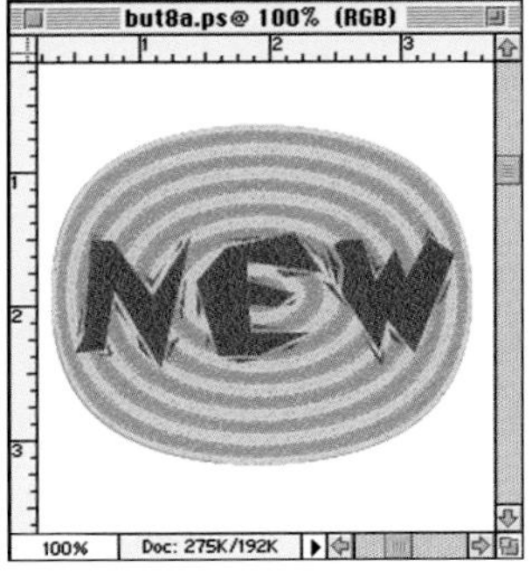


**9** To make a rectangular button, use the rectangular Marquee tool to make a selection, and choose Select➔Inverse. Switch to the default colors and press the Delete key to fill the selection with white. Select➔Inverse. Add a drop shadow. For the drop shadow we used the Alien Skin Drop Shadow 2.0 filter.

TIP **Many of Photoshop 4.0's new filters enable you to save your settings. This makes it easier and faster to repeat your favorite looks.**

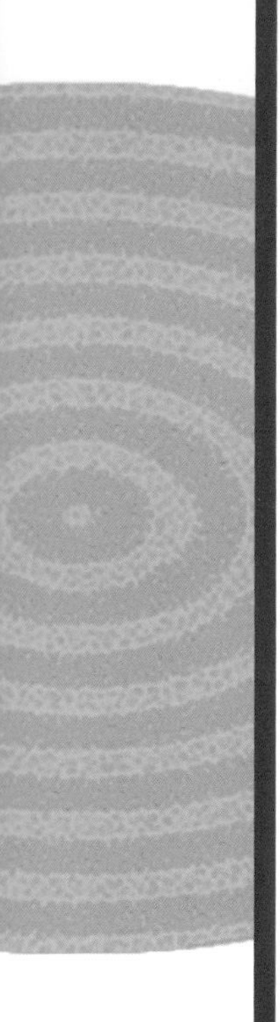

## Swirled Ripples

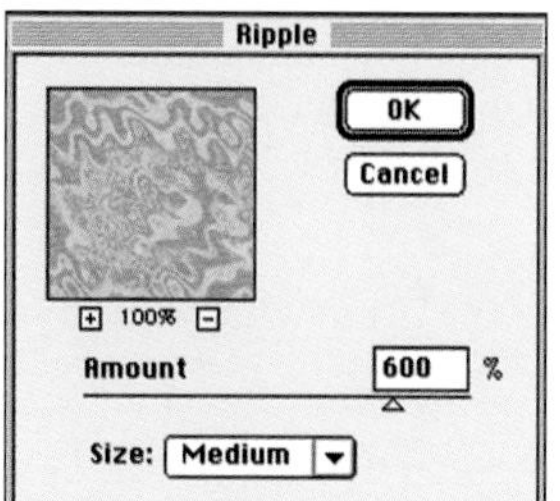


To create this somewhat beat-up looking button, do steps 1 and 2, then choose Filters➛Distort➛ Ripple (Amount: 600, Size: Medium).

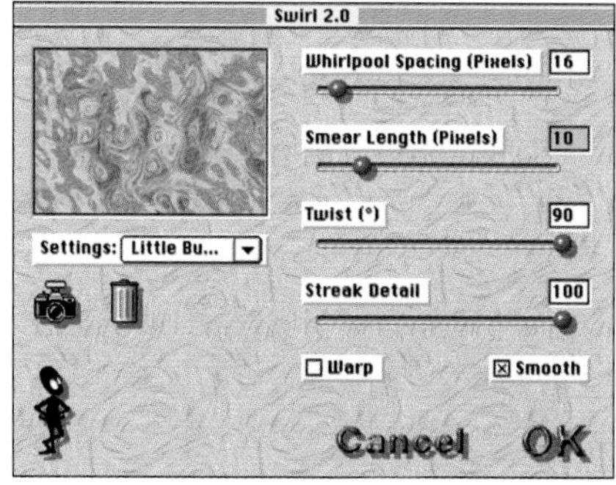


Instead of using the Glass filter in Step 6 we used Alien Skin's Swirl filter with Little Bubbles selected from the filter's preset pop-up menu.

Finally we chose the Alien Skin Glow filter to add a white glow around the type and added a drop shadow to the button.

### Twirled Halftone

On this variation we set the halftone screen filter at its smallest setting (Size: 1, Screen Type: Circle, Contrast: 5).

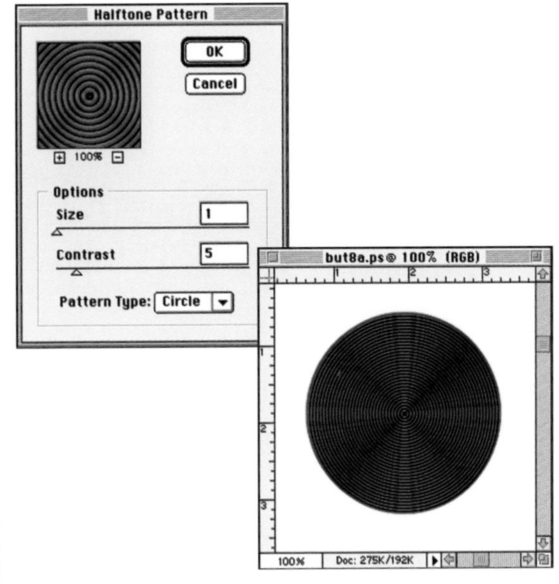


To generate a moiré pattern, we then reapplied the halftone pattern with the Screen Type set to dot (Size: 3, Contrast 5, Screen Type: Dot).

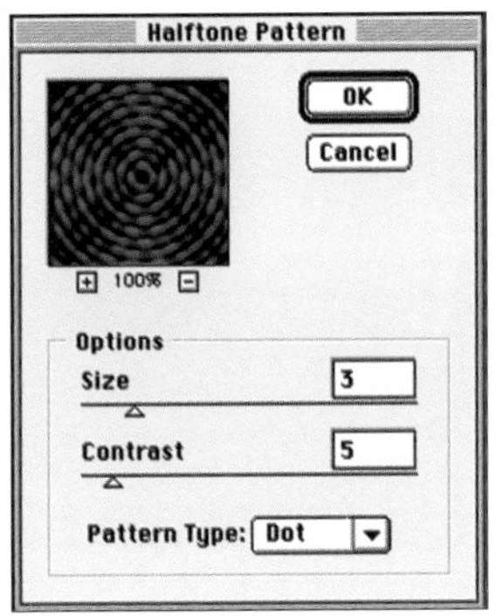

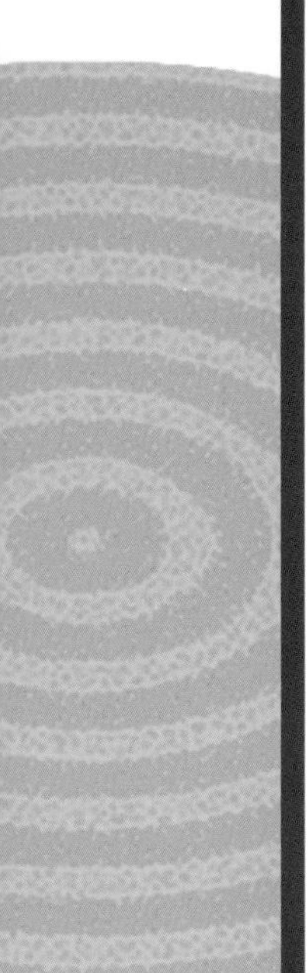

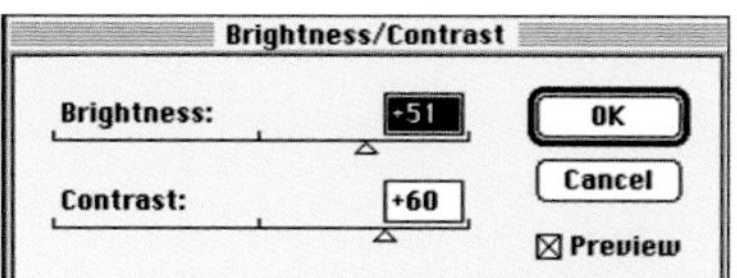


Depending on what colors you chose, the combination of the two filters might make the image appear very dark. To adjust for this we chose Image➛Adjust➛Brightness/Contrast (Brightness: +51, Contrast: +60)

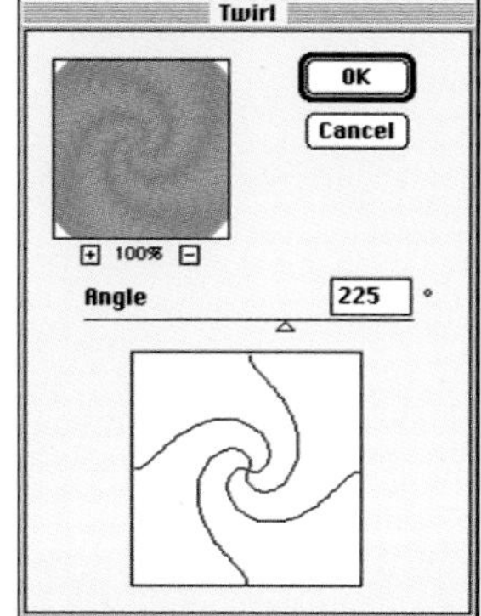


Finally, to add a sense of motion to the button we applied Filter➛Distort➛Twirl (Angle: 225). ■

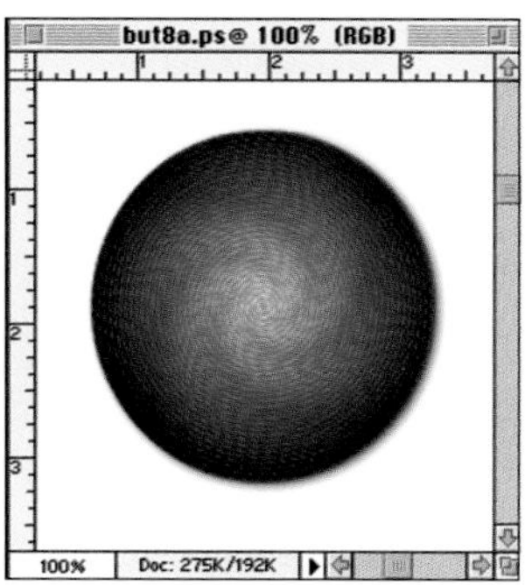

## Directional Buttons

Buttons are intended to take you places; this button helps stress that point.

**1** Create a new file. Create a square selection for your button (hold down the Shift key while creating the selection to keep it square) and save the selection (Channel #4). Choose foreground and background colors and press Delete to fill the selection with your background color. Select➞None.

**2** Double-click the Marquee tool and select Elliptical from the Shape pop-up menu in the options palette. Hold down the Shift key to make a circular selection inside the square selection as shown in the figure. Save the selection (Channel #5).

**3** Load the selection Channel #4. Choose Filter➞Render➞Lighting effects (Texture Channel: Channel #5, White is high, Height: 50). Adjust the points on the circle in the lighting preview box to match the figure. To tweak the light, adjust the light's position and focus by moving the circles in the preview box. Save your changes to this panel.

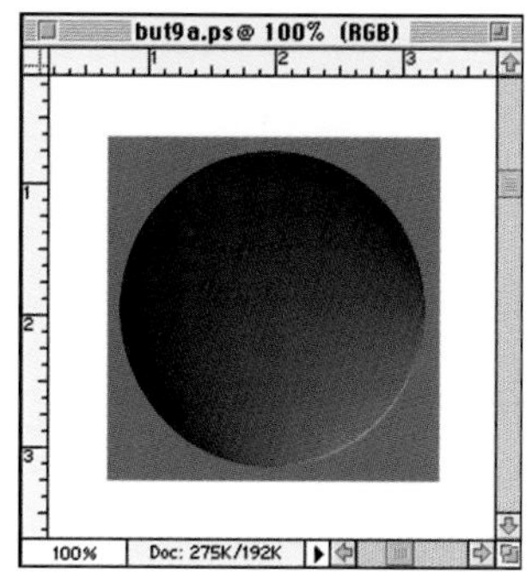

**4** With Channel #4 still selected, load the selection Channel #5 (Subtract from Selection). Save the new selection (Channel #6).

**5** Choose Selection➛Modify➛Contract Selection (Contract By: 8 pixels). Save the new selection, choosing Channel #6 instead of New to overwrite the existing Channel #6, which is not needed again.

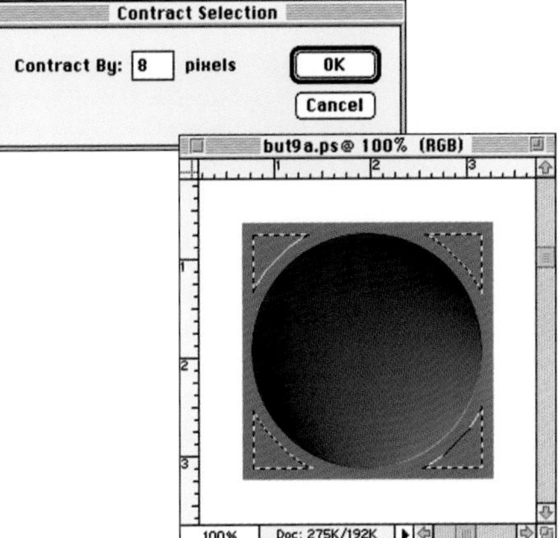


**6** Load the selection Channel #5 (Add to Selection). Save as a new selection (Channel #7).

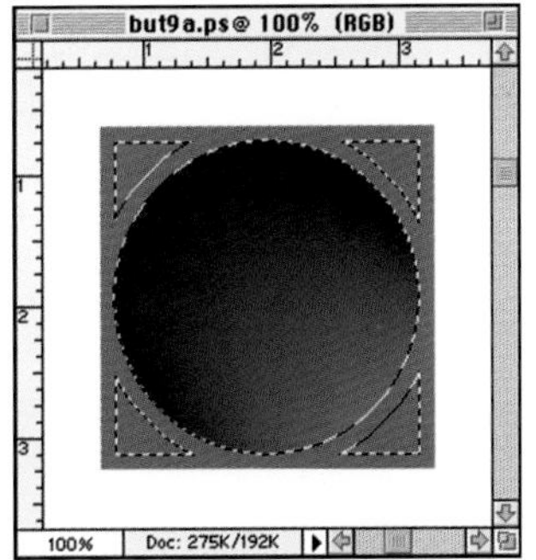

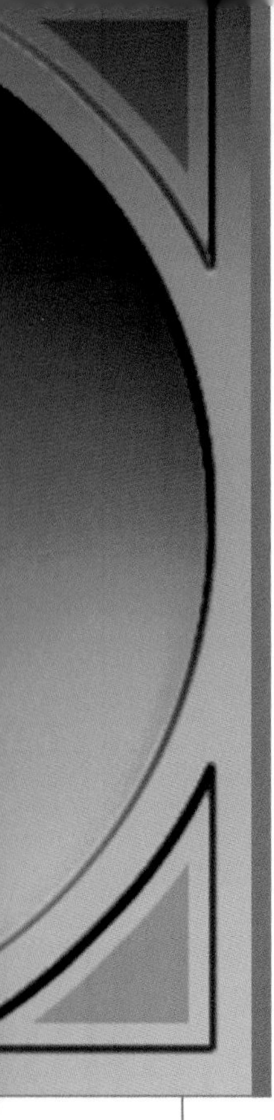

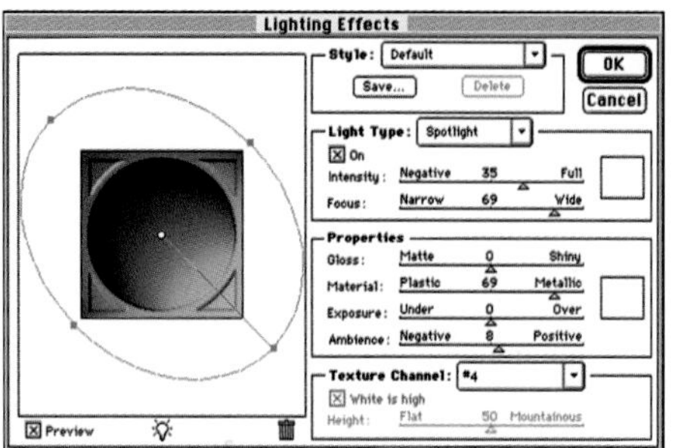


**7** Load the selection Channel #4 and then choose Filter➛Render➛ Lighting Effects. Select Channel #7 as the Texture Channel. Adjust the points on the circle in the lighting preview box to match the figure.

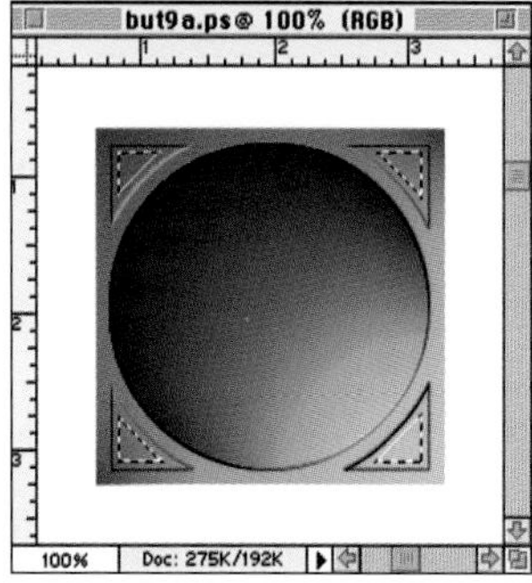


**8** Load the selection Channel #6 and then choose Select➛Modify➛ Contract Selection (3 pixels).

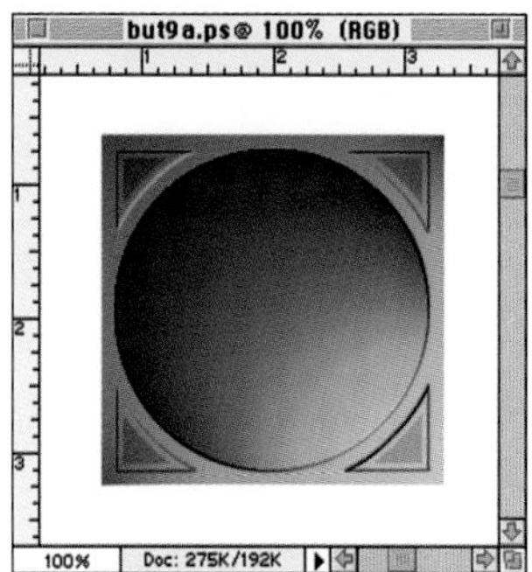


**9** Choose Image➛Brightness/ Contrast (Brightness: -30, Contrast: 0). This creates a darker accent triangle in each corner.

**10** To finish the button, we added transparent type. Enter the text using the Type Mask tool, and save the type selection as a new channel (Channel #8).

**11** To brighten the text, Choose Image➛Adjust➛Brightness/Contrast (Brightness: +50, Contrast: 0). We added a drop shadow using Alien Skin's Drop Shadow 2.0 filter with a 2 pixel X and Y Offset, a 4 pixel Blur, and Opacity set to 50%.

## VARIATIONS

To make this button point to compass directions, follow the directions through Step 9, then switch to default colors. Load the selection Channel #4, and choose Layer➛Transform➛Numeric...➛ Rotate (Angle 45 degrees).

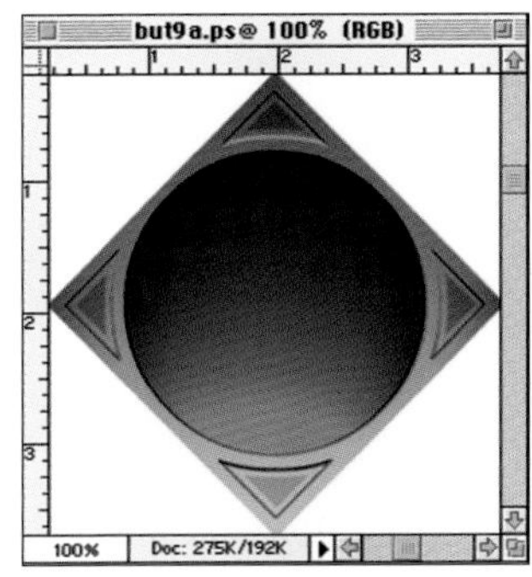


This multi-directional button was created by selecting a color for the background before rotating the selection 45 degrees.

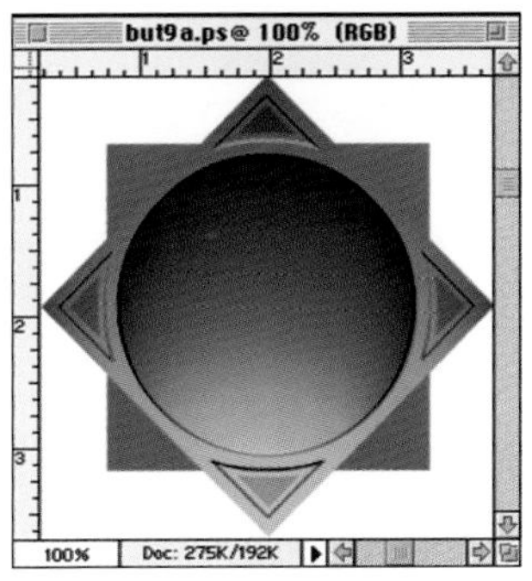


We applied a bevel effect here by loading Channel #5, contracting the selection by 8 pixels, and feathering it by 2 pixels. We then rotated the contracted selection 180 degrees (Layer➛Transform➛ Rotate 180°). ■

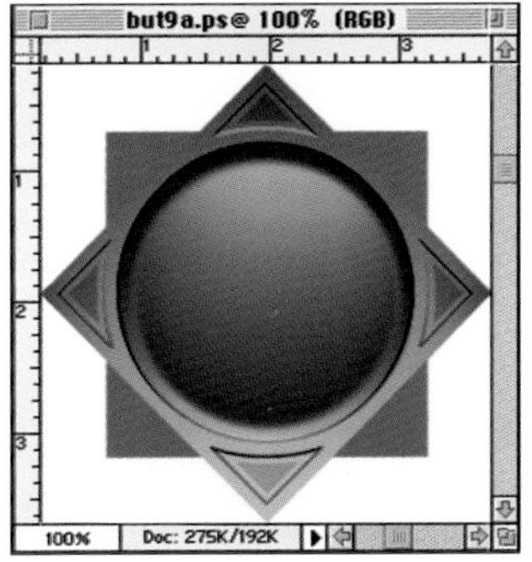

## Objects on Buttons

Photoshop's path tool is used to turn photographic images into decorative buttons and icons. Image processing filters such as Ink Outline and Watercolor are used to create a wide range of illustrative effects.

**1** Open the file containing the image you will be using for your button (the crafts stand photo can be found on the CD in the Web Magic folder).

**2** Zoom in to fill your screen with the image detail that you are going to crop. Choose the Pen tool from the toolbox. Define the outline of the object, placing anchor points where needed.

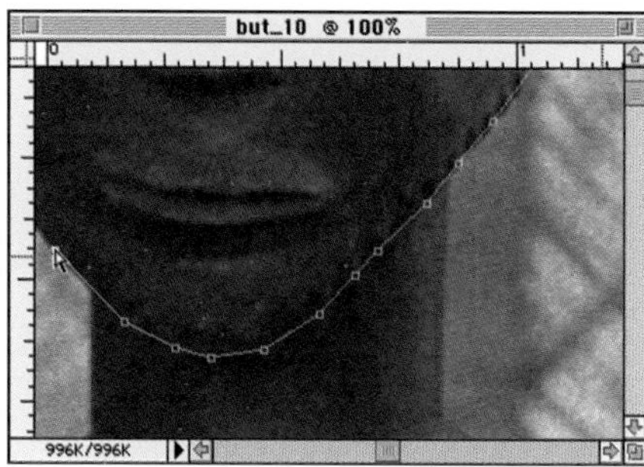


**TIP** **You can adjust the portion of the image you are viewing without deselecting the Path tool. When you move your cursor to the window's scroll-bars, the pointer returns.**

**3** After you have finished outlining your selection, choose Make Selection from the Paths palette pop-up menu. Save the selection (Channel #4). Return to the Paths palette pop-up menu and Turn off Path (Paths palette pop-up menu).

**4** Choose Selection➸Inverse. Press the Delete key to get rid of the photograph outside of your selection.

**5** To create a background pattern for this object we chose Filter➸Render➸Clouds. A single pass of the Clouds filter is very subtle and light, so we applied the filter a second time.

**6** Load channel selection #4. We used Alien Skin Glow filter with Settings: Diffuse to add a light white glow around the object. Then we added the Alien Skin Drop Shadow filter with an X and Y Offset of 8 pixels, Blur: 10 pixels, and Opacity: 90%.

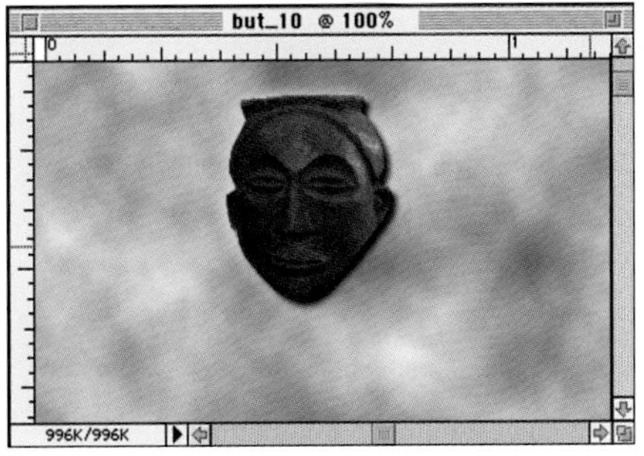


**7** Make a rectangular selection around the object to define the button (leave room to add the type), and save as a new selection (Channel #5).

**8** Choose Select➸Modify➸Border (6 pixels) and then choose Image➸Adjust➸Brightness/Contrast (Brightness: +32, Contrast: 0).

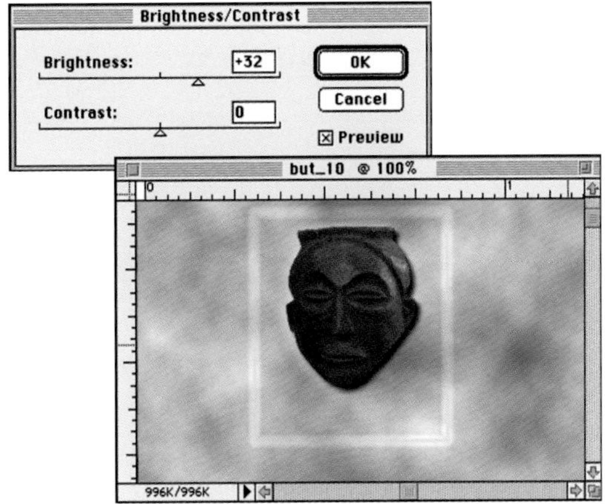

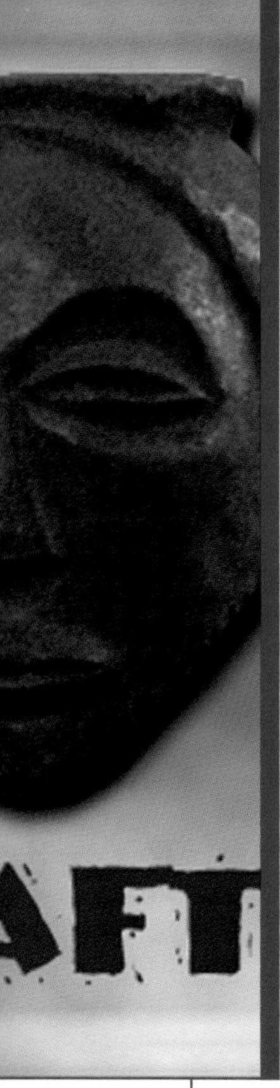

**9** Add type to the button. Choose Select➝Load Selection (Channel #5), then crop the file: Image➝Crop. Save as a JPEG.

**TIP** **JPEG files retain the full color depth of the file and can look substantially different on different color depth displays. You should view your final JPEGs at 256 colors as well as millions of colors to see how they are affected by the viewer's screen.**

## VARIATIONS

### Weathered Bronze

We were able change the texture of the African icon to a weathered bronze look by using the Ink Outlines filter. With the mask selected (Channel #4), choose Filter➝Brush Strokes➝Ink Outlines (Stroke Length: 4, Dark Intensity: 20, Light Intensity: 10).

Ink Outlines
OK
Cancel
200%
Options
Stroke Length 4
Dark Intensity 20
Light Intensity 10

This filter lowered the contrast and overall made the image much darker. To adjust for this, choose Image➝Adjust➝Brightness/Contrast (Brightness: +26, Contrast: +70).

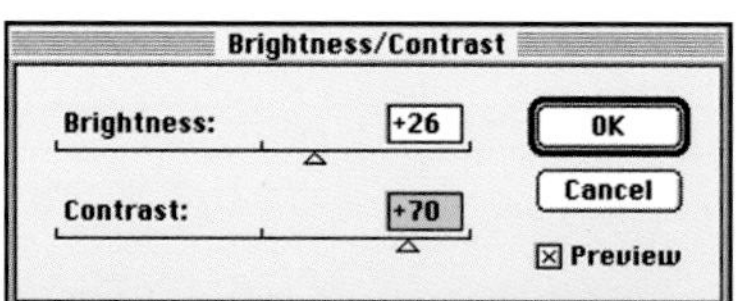

We created a copper-like effect on the mask with the Watercolor filter. With the mask selected (Channel #4), choose Filter➛Artistic➛Watercolor (Brush Detail: 13, Shadow Intensity: 1, Texture: 1).

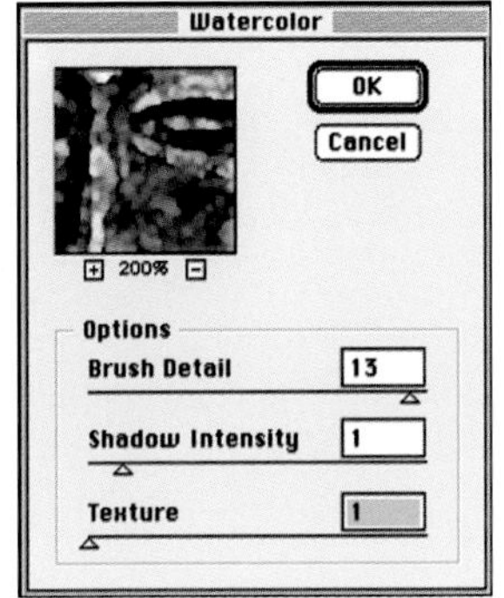


After applying this filter we adjusted brightness and contrast. Choose Image➛Adjust➛Brightness/Contrast (Brightness: +20, Contrast: +72). ■

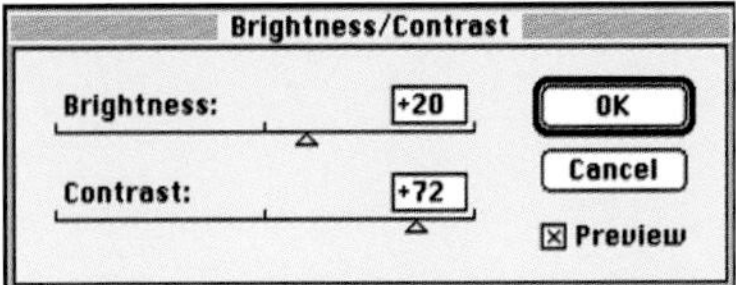

# PART VI

## Menu Bars

Menu bars are the keystone of a Web site's navigational system. They are the third level of user interface after the site visitors' computer operating systems and their browsers or interconnect systems.

The menu bar defines the architecture of your Web site's interface by displaying discrete, consistent information through all levels of interactivity. The menu prioritizes information and sets the main topics, headings, and locations within the site.

A typical menu bar for a site will contain links to areas such as:

- The home page
- The main index or table of contents page
- The about us or our product page
- Frequently Asked Questions (FAQs)
- Forums or chat rooms
- A contact page for getting in touch via email or for linking to sales and service support groups

In the following exercises, we demonstrate how to use Photoshop to build a variety of menu bar styles, including folder tabs. We recommend testing any menu bar—depending upon the overall organization and style of your Web page design, some menu bars styles will work better than others.

This exercise uses HTML's 0 margin and borderless frames functionality that has been developed for 3.0 browsers. The final effect will have the appearance of multiple file folder tabs across the top of the Web page, but it will really be one image that we cut apart and import in segments.

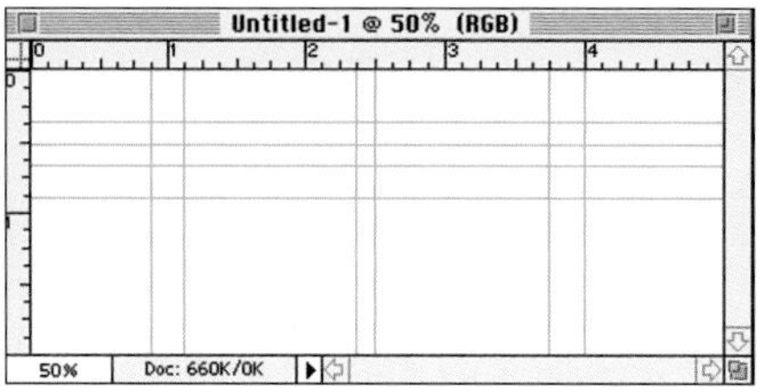

**1** Create a new file and save it as a Photoshop document (38a.ps). The tabs are 1¼ inches wide, with ⅛ inch between them.

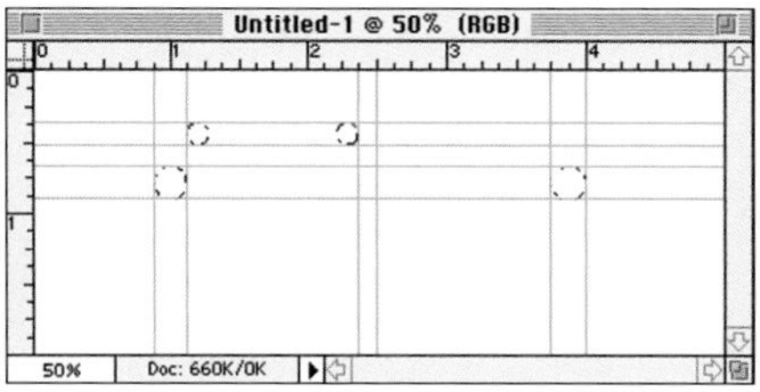

**2** With the Elliptical Marquee tool, select circular areas inside the guidelines at the top of the tab and sides of the folders, as shown in the figure. Hold down the Shift key to add to the selection.

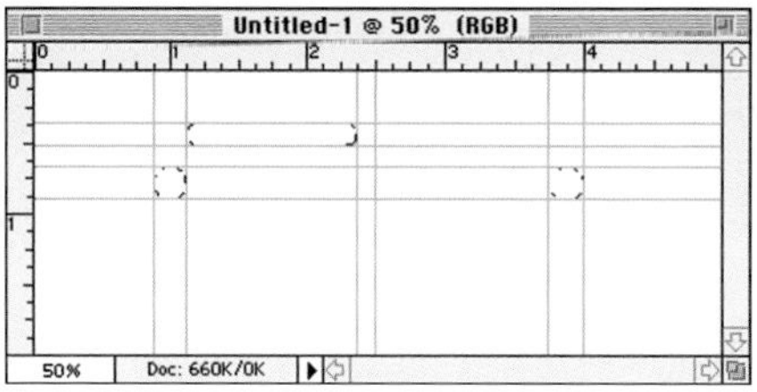

**3** With the Rectangular Marquee tool, hold down the Shift key to add to the previous selection and select the space between the top two circles.

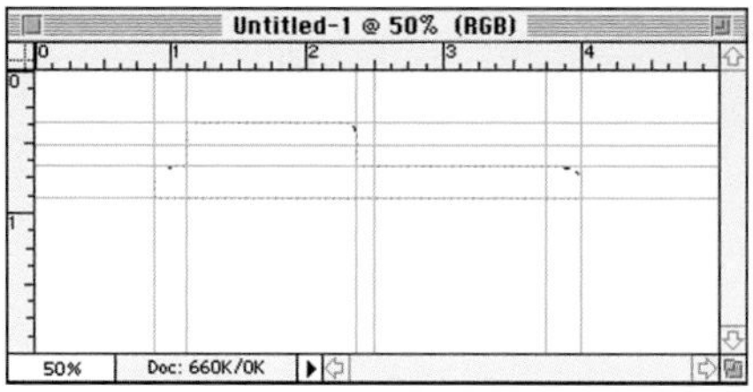

**4** Continue to add to the selection, connecting all the circles incorporating them into one selection. For the bottom left and right corners, you will need to drag out the selection to the corners of the guidelines to make them square. Save the selection (Channel #4).

**5** Click the New Channel icon in the Channels palette to make a new empty channel (Channel #5). With the Channels palette still active, load channel selection #4 into Channel #5. Choose Layer➛Transform➛Flip Horizontal. Fill the selection with the foreground color (white).

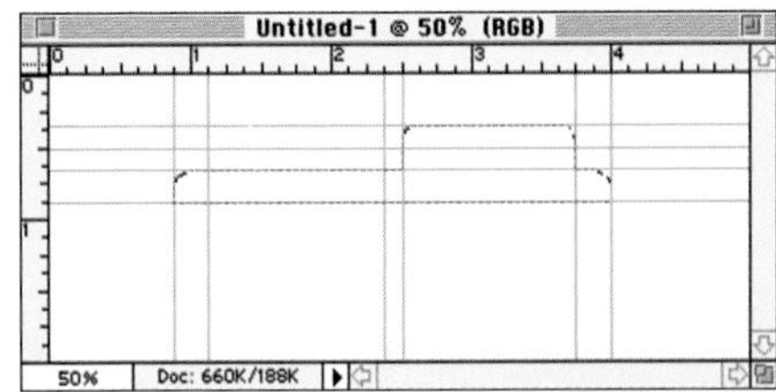


**6** Return to the composite channel. Fill the background with a color. Create a new layer (dropshadow 1) and load the left tab selection (Channel #4). Choose Select➛Feather (5 pixels).

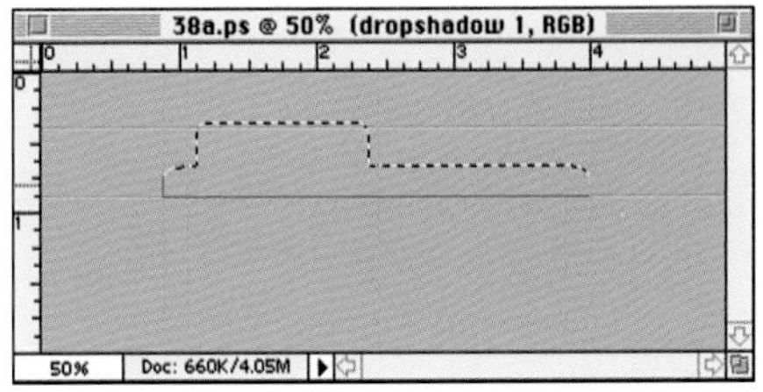


**7** Fill the selection with black.

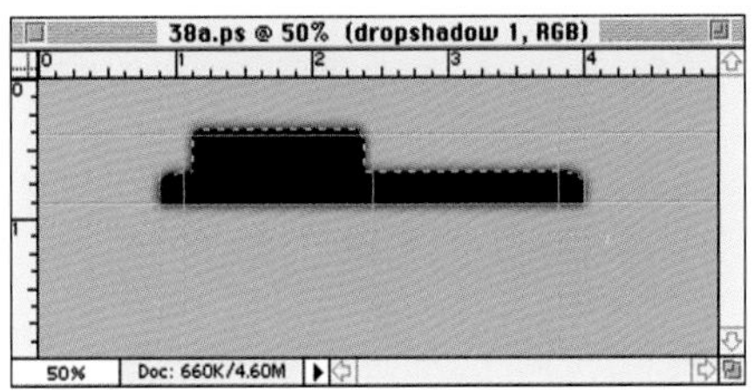


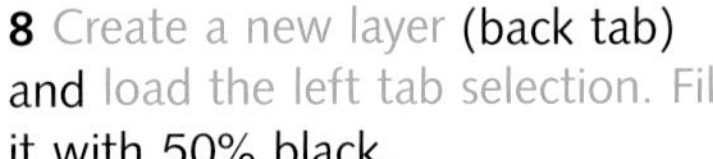

**8** Create a new layer (back tab) and load the left tab selection. Fill it with 50% black.

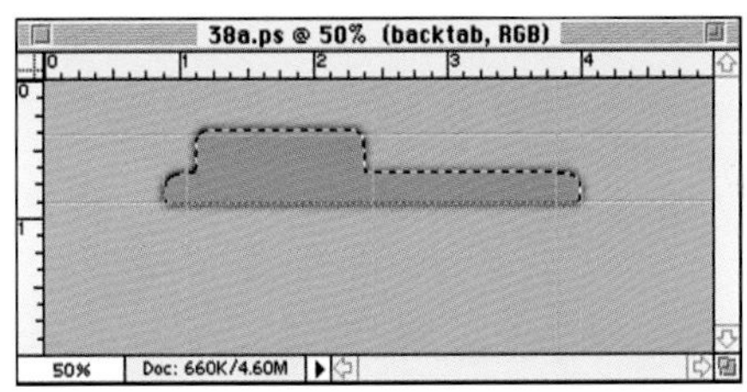


**9** Create a new layer (Type Layer 1). Enter the text.

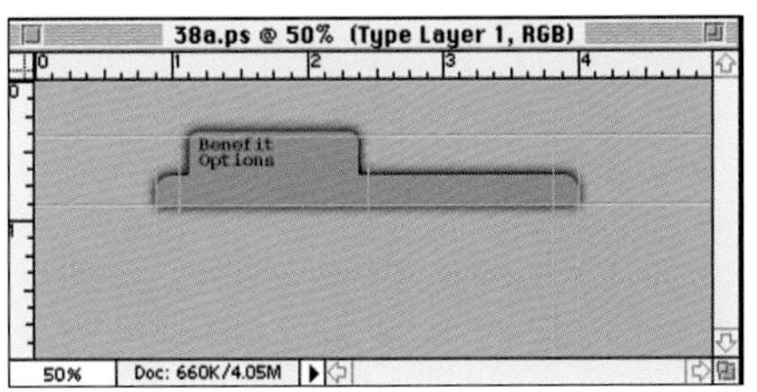

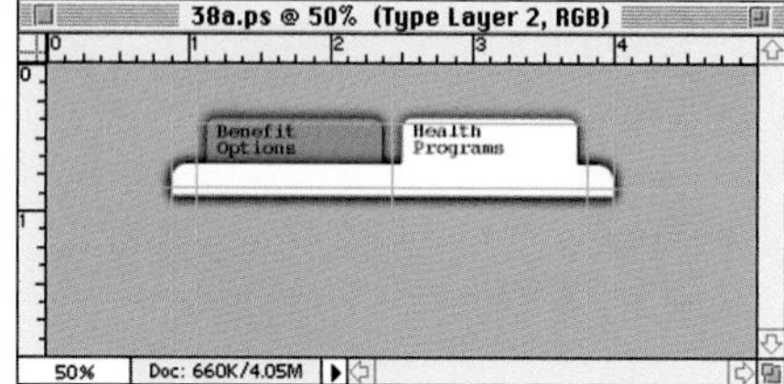


**10** Repeat Steps 6 through 9 naming the layers dropshadow 2, front tab, and type layer 2. Feather and fill the drop shadow layer as in Steps 5 and 6 with black. Fill the Front Tab layer selection with white and enter the type on Type Layer 2.

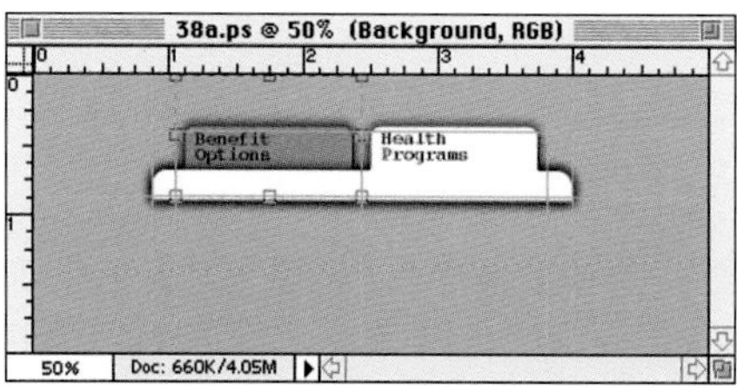


**11** Move the bottom guideline up slightly by clicking it and dragging, enough to cut off the bottom drop shadow when you crop it. Save the image.

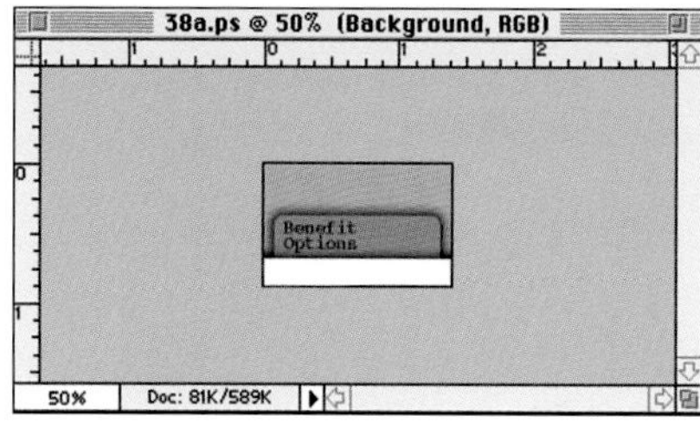


**12** With the Crop tool, drag your pointer across the image within the guidelines that define the left tab.

**13** Double-click the image to crop it. Export to GIF format.

**14** Revert to the original image (38a.ps). With the Crop tool, select the area defining the right tab. Double-click to crop it. Export to GIF format.

**15** Revert to the original image (38a.ps). With the Crop tool, select the area defining the left side. Double-click to crop it. Export to GIF format.

**16** Revert one more time and select the right side, crop, and export. Repeat this process for as many buttons as you need.

**17** Create two versions for each button, one in back and one in front. Place the GIFs in a table in your HTML code, specifying <topmargin=0> and <leftmargin=0> to get the images to butt right up to the outside of the browser window.

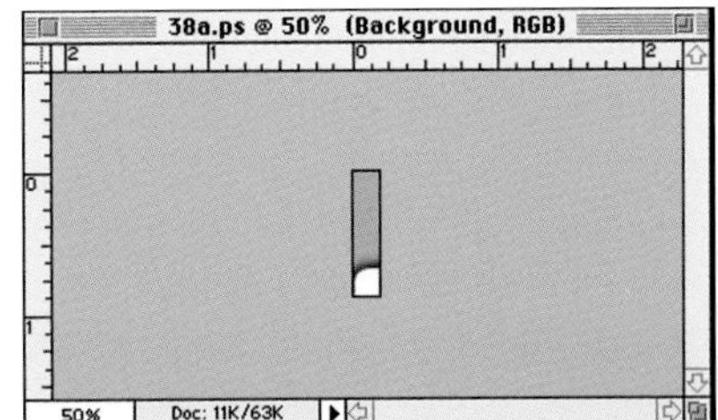


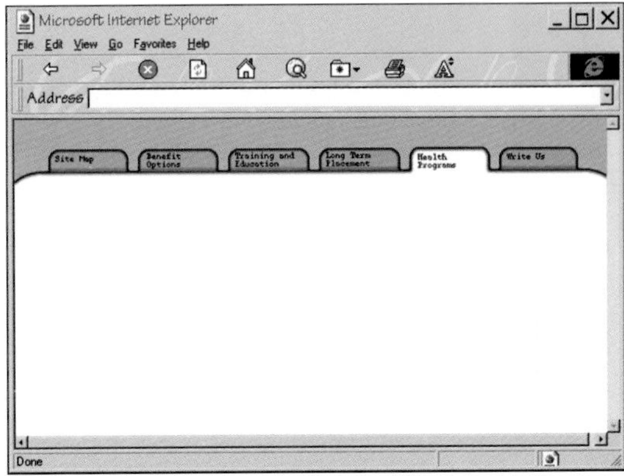

## Buttons on Image

Incorporating navigational buttons into a photograph or existing artwork can transform almost any image into a useful interface. By combining Gaussian Blur with Brightness/Contrast adjustments, almost any part of the image can become a button.

Fig1_ @ 50% (RGB)

50%
Doc: 1.06M/1.06M

© Photo 24

**1** Open your selected image. We used a photo from the Photo 24 Flowers and Leaves series. You could also use a custom texture.

Preferences

Guides & Grid
Guides
Color: Green
Style: Lines
Grid
Color: Custom
Style: Lines
Gridline every: 1 inches
Subdivisions: 3
OK
Cancel
Prev
Next

**2** Choose File➡Preferences➡Guides & Grid (Gridline every 1", Subdivisions 3"). This gives you gridlines to create the buttons.

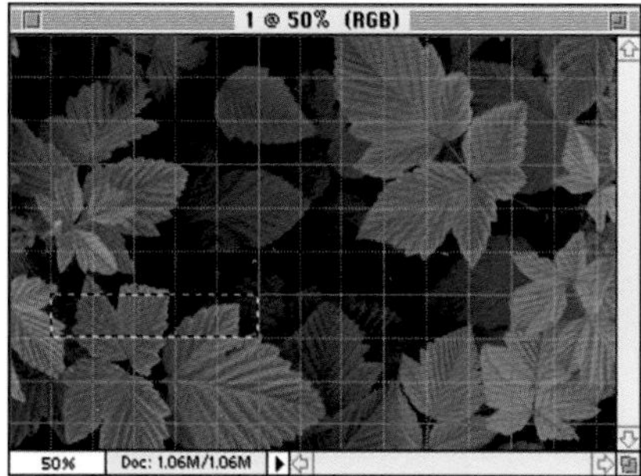


**3** With the Marquee tool, select the area for your button. Save the selection (Channel #4).

**4** Make Channel #4 active. Copy and paste the selection into the grid to create as many buttons as you want.

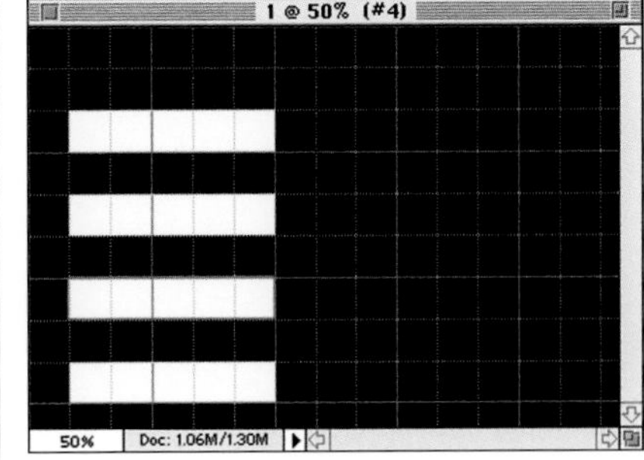


**5** Return to the composite channel. Load the selection Channel #4.

**6** Choose Filter➔Blur➔Gaussian Blur (5.8 pixels). You can adjust the slider until you get the desired effect.

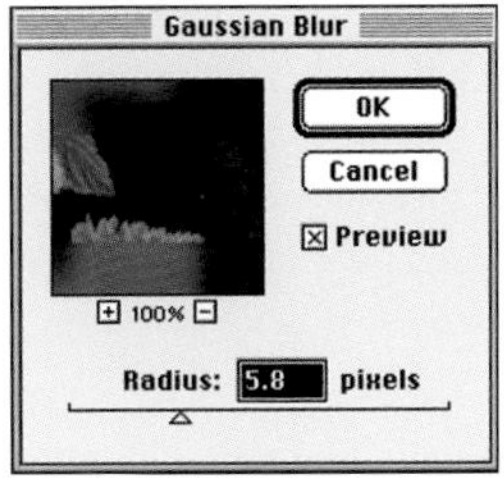


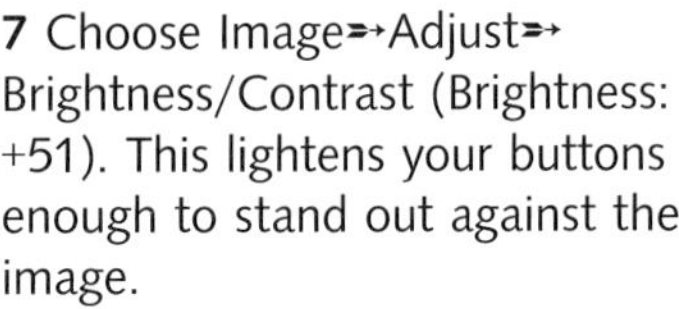

**7** Choose Image➔Adjust➔Brightness/Contrast (Brightness: +51). This lightens your buttons enough to stand out against the image.

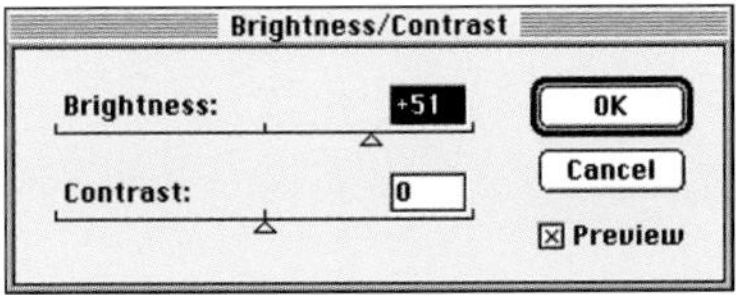


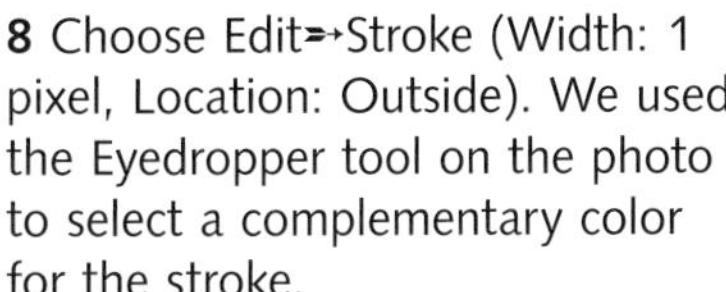

**8** Choose Edit➔Stroke (Width: 1 pixel, Location: Outside). We used the Eyedropper tool on the photo to select a complementary color for the stroke.

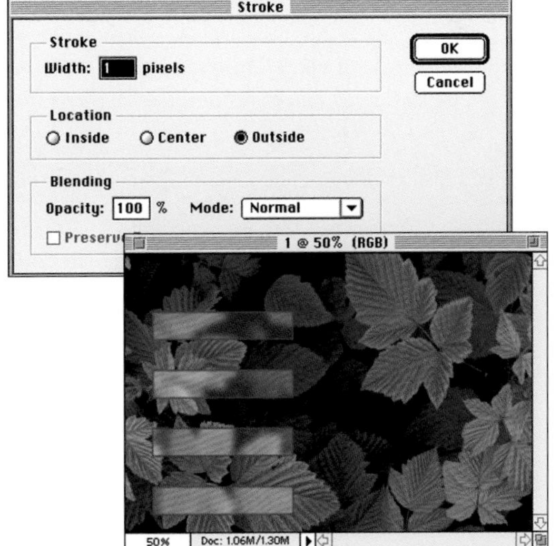

**9** To finish the image, we added a drop shadow to the buttons (see Soft Shadows, page 72), and used Filter➔Blur➔Motion Blur (Angle: 45°, Distance: 60 pixels) as a variation to the Gaussian Blur filter. ■

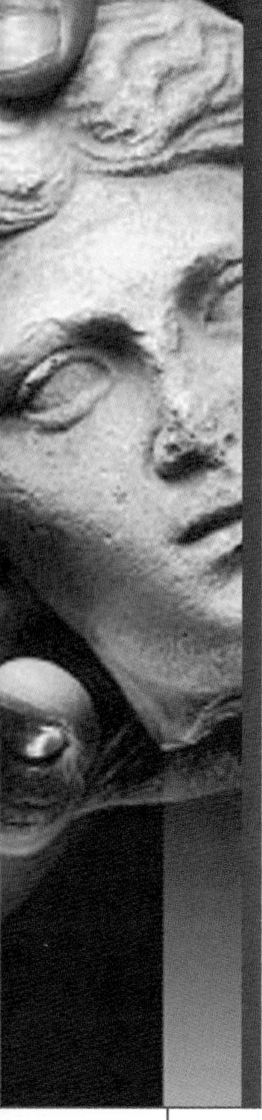

## Gradient Stripes

Matching image color precisely with background colors on your Web page is an important design consideration. One way of doing this is to use a 216-color no-dither palette optimized for the Web. Another way is to use a Color Picker utility to find a color's hexidecimal value for placement in your HTML document. After selecting a color, the Gradient tool offers a way to merge your graphics into a Web page's background.

Using several gradients across an image will blend the image into the background of your page, integrating the graphics into the Web page. It's important that you match the image color precisely with your background color—use a 216-color, non-dithering palette or a color picker utility to match colors. These tools can be found in the WebTools folder on the CD.

**1** Choose an image to place over a color that will match the color of the background in your Web page. Select all and copy the image.

2 Create a new file that is larger than the image will be on the Web page (the New Image dialog box will reflect the current size of the image you have just copied. Add about an inch to the width and the height of the new image.) Paste the image. (This creates Layer 1.)

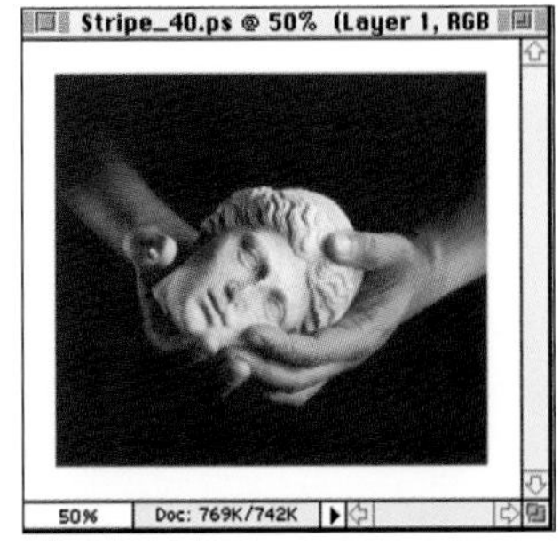


3 Choose a background color from the 216-color non-dithering palette a Color Picker utility (included on the CD in the WebTools folder) to define the hexadecimal values of the color. Fill the Background layer with the background color.

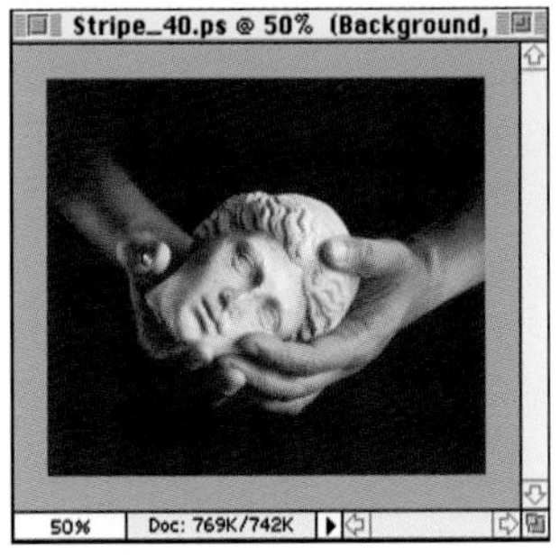


4 Choose View➸Show Grid. It's best if you either trim your photo with the Selection tool or edit your grid to fit the photo evenly. We used the grid default setting for this example.

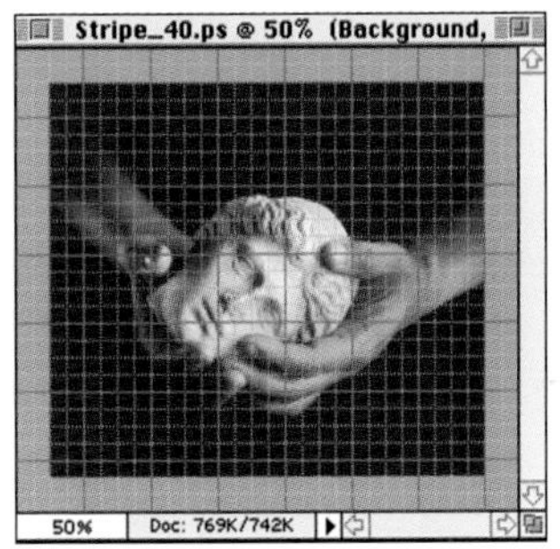


5 Use the Rectangular Marquee tool to make a vertical selection for the first gradient stripe. Continue to add horizontal selections by holding down the Shift key. Save the selection (Channel #4) in case you want to use it later. Choose View➸Hide grid.

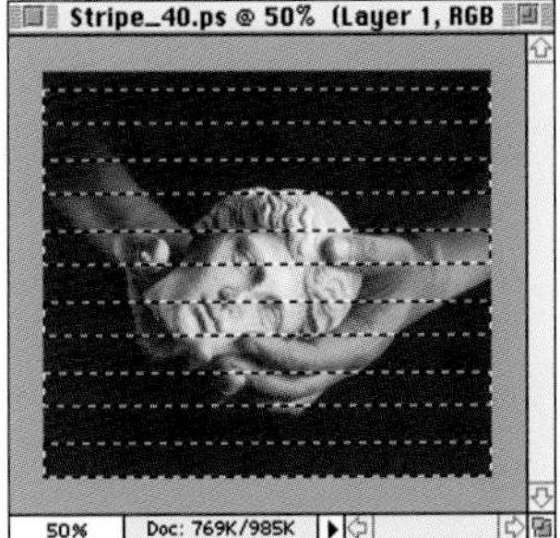

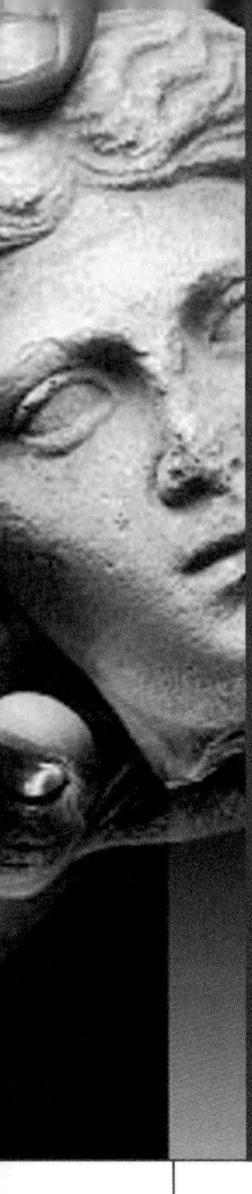

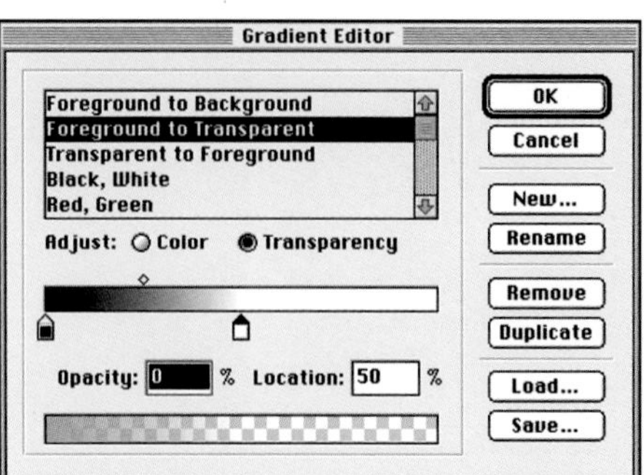


**6** Switch Foreground/Background colors. Double-click the Gradient tool (Opacity: 100%, Gradient: Foreground to Transparent, Dither: off). Click the Edit Gradient button. Select the Transparency radio button and slide the Transparency icon (the right box) to Location: 50%.

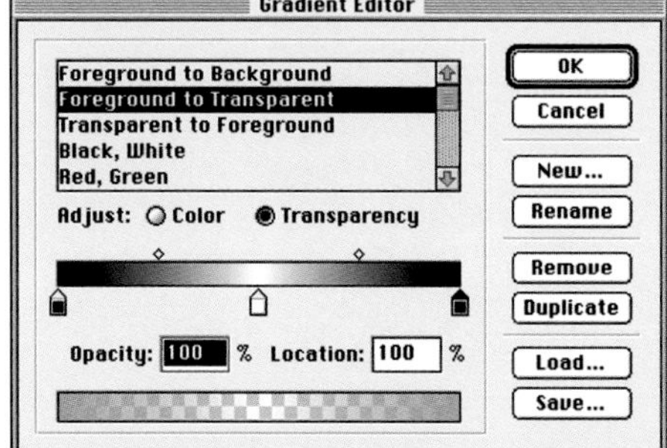


**7** Click directly under the far right end of the Transparency bar to add a color box at Location: 100%.

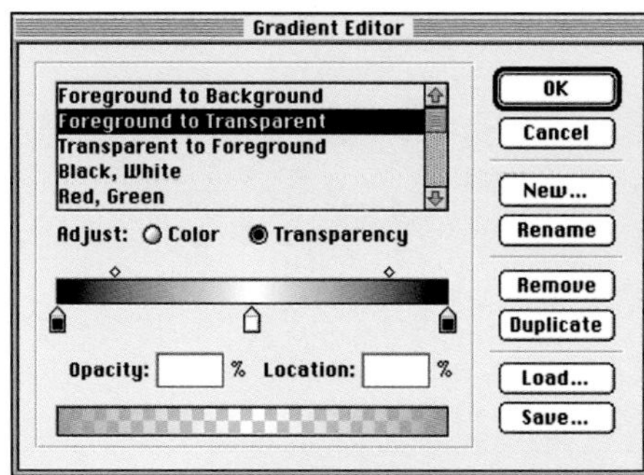


**8** Drag the left diamond over the Transparency bar to Location: 30%. To expand the transparent area of the gradient, drag the right diamond to Location: 70%.

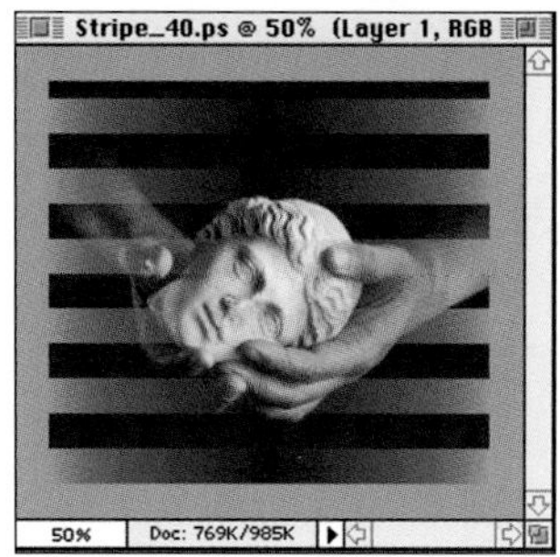

## VARIATIONS

Here we added gradients to only one side of the image and added text to use the gradients as buttons.

**The possibilities of gradients are endless. Create your own library of gradients by saving new ones as Gradient presets and revising or deleting the ones you are not interested in.** ■

## White on White

Matching the color of the menu bar or text heading to the background has become a popular design style. The 3D effect is built by varying the hue and value in the shadow. Here we combine the Stroke feature with the Neon Glow filter to create a white-on-white menu bar.

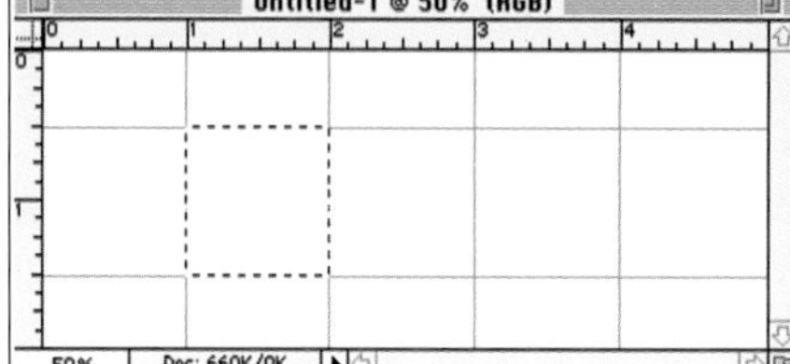


**1** Create a new file (Width: 5 inches, Height 2 inches). Add vertical and horizontal guides. We placed vertical guides at each inch mark, and two horizontal guides a half inch from the top and bottom edges of the image area. With the Marquee tool select a rectangle corresponding to meeting points of the horizontal and vertical guides.

Stroke
Stroke
Width: 16 pixels
Location
Inside Center Outside
Blending
Opacity: 100 % Mode: Overlay
Preserve Transparency
OK
Cancel

**2** Create a new layer (Layer 1). Set the foreground color to white. Choose Edit➛Stroke (Width: 16 pixels, Location: Inside, Mode: Overlay). Because the Background is white, the effect will not be visible until the Neon Glow filter is applied.

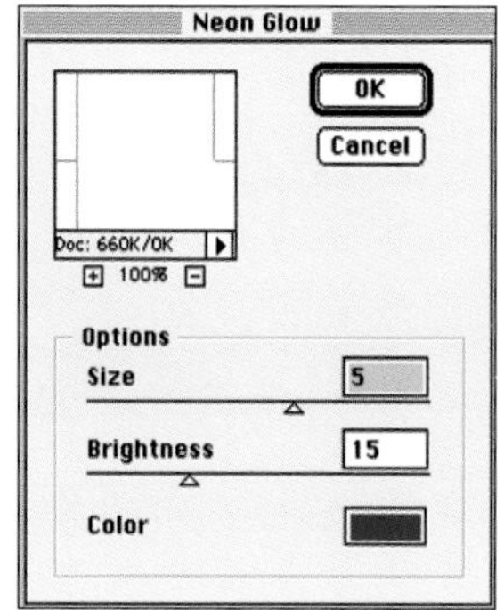


**3** Apply Filter➛Artistic➛Neon Glow. Choose the Move tool, hold down the Option [Alt] key and drag out four copies of the square.

**4** After completing the five squares, use Steps 1 through 3 to create the upper and lower horizontal bars, but set the stroke width to 8 pixels.

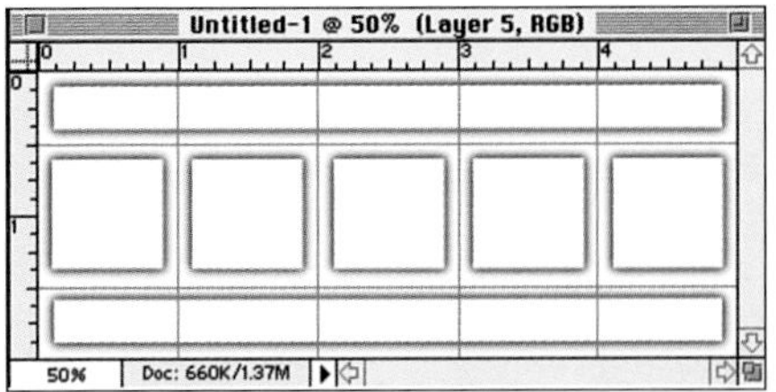


**5** With the Type Mask tool, enter the text. We used Syntax Heavy, center alignment, anti-aliased on, spacing: 0. Use the Move tool to position the text. Add text to each of the buttons. Apply the same stroke as in Step 4 and the same neon glow as in Step 3.

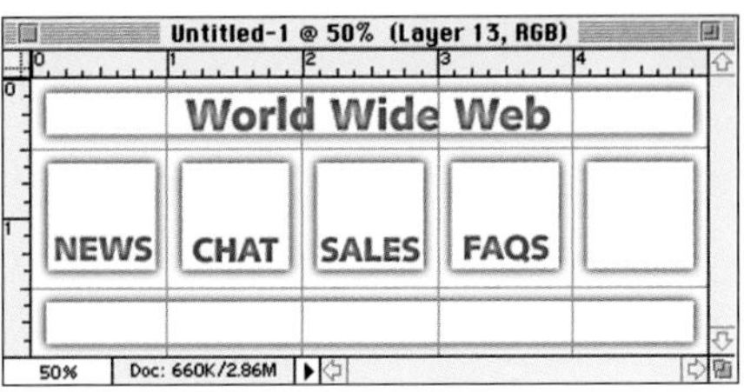


**6** The word DEMO is too long for the box width. Choose Layer➛Free Transform. Scale the text by moving tabs with cursor until it fits the box shape. Keep the same text height.

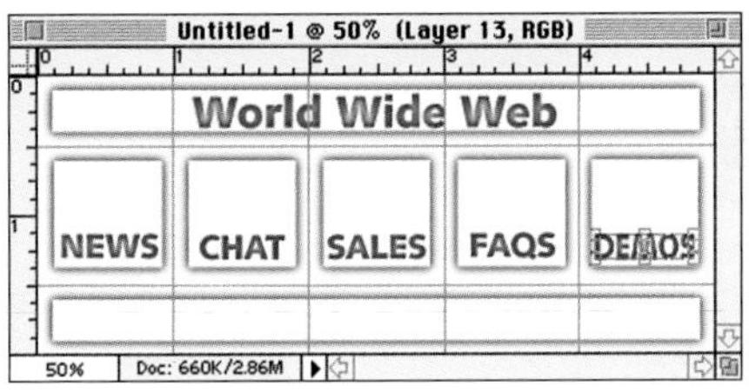


**7** Repeat Step 5 to add text to the bottom bar. Flatten image. Export to GIF format.

## VARIATIONS

Changing the background to gray creates another possibility. After placing all text, merge all layers except the Background. Because the neon effect expands the width of the rectangular menu bars, there is no transparent space open except in the center of the shapes. When you change the background to gray, the new color will only fill the interior of the rectangular menu bars. Add additional text, such as numerals. ■

## Cut Outs

While drop shadows are used to reinforce the visual illusion that objects are floating above the Web page, cutouts are the visual opposite, causing parts of the image to appear to recede into the page. Cutouts work well with objects that have drop shadows to further highlight and add interest to them.

**1** Open a file containing the texture you plan to use. In this example we used a marbleized texture, which you can find in the Web Magic folder on the CD-ROM. Choose View➞Show Grid. Use the guides to make a selection for your first button.

**2** Save the selection (Channel #4). Make Channel #4 active. With the selection still active, copy and paste the new button selection. Repeat cut and paste until you have created all of your button selections, using the guidelines to align them. Return to the composite channel. Choose View➞Hide Grid.

**3** Select➞All and copy the selection. Paste the selection, which will create a new layer (Layer 1). Load the selection Channel #4 and delete.

**4** With Channel #4 still active make the background layer active. Choose Filter➝Gaussian Blur (2.0 pixels). Then choose Image➝Adjust➝Brightness/Contrast (Brightness: +40, Contrast: -10).

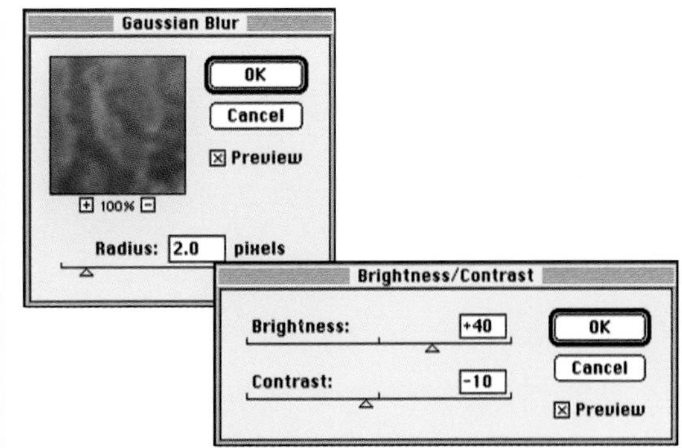


**5** Choose Select➝None, then create a new layer (Layer 2) and fill it with black. Load the selection Channel #4 and delete.

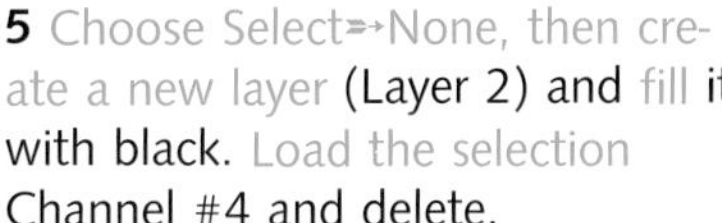

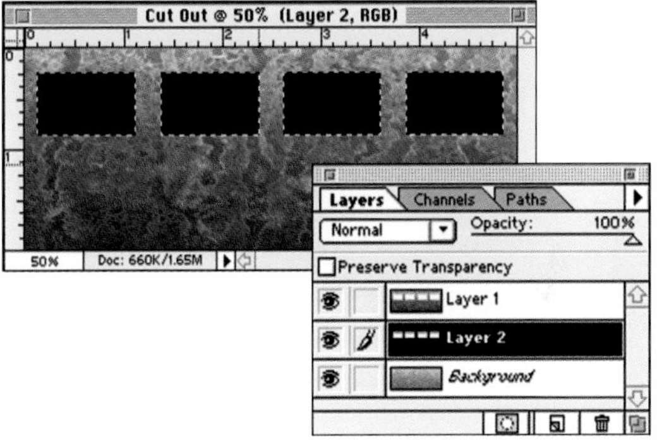


**6** Select➝All and choose Filter➝Gaussian Blur (6.0 pixels). With the Move tool, offset Layer 2 down and to the right to position the shadow in the upper-left edges of the buttons.

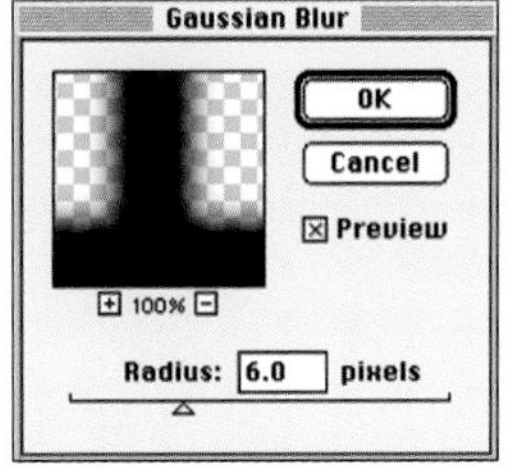


**7** Create a new layer (Layer 3) and use the Type Mask tool to enter the text, then fill it with black. In this example we used the font Allise. Choose Image➝Adjust➝Brightness/Contrast (Brightness: -85, Contrast: +10).

**8** Flatten the image and export to GIF format.

## VARIATIONS

The cutout technique works great with type also. In Step 1, enter text with the Type Mask tool to make a selection. Save the selection (Channel #4) and continue with Steps 2 through 6. Flatten the image and export to GIF format.

Here we used a solid color for the cutout effect and added a beveled edge. Using the same color as the background of your Web page creates the illusion of the menu bar emerging from your background. ■

## Duotones

Working with black-and-white photos on the Web, where everything is usually in full living color, can be a bit of a challenge. Changing an image to a duotone and using pattern filters jazzes up an otherwise dull photo. The final output for this exercise will be four separate images to be used as navigational buttons. Each image must match the others perfectly, so we'll make use of Photoshop 4.0's new guideline feature.

©Digital Stock Inc. 1996.

**1** Open the image you will be using for this exercise. We used an image from Digital Stock, Inc.

**2** We created four separate sections in the image by adding three horizontal guidelines over the image about 5/8 of an inch apart, and one vertical guideline to ensure proper text alignment. If the rulers are not visible choose View➙Show Rulers.

**3** Choose a foreground color and Enter your text using the solid Type tool.

**4** To help define the text we added a drop shadow following the technique in Object Shadows. (See page 72).

**5** Save the file as a Photoshop document(duotone.ps). Choose Image➨Mode➨Duotone (black and Pantone Red 032 CV).

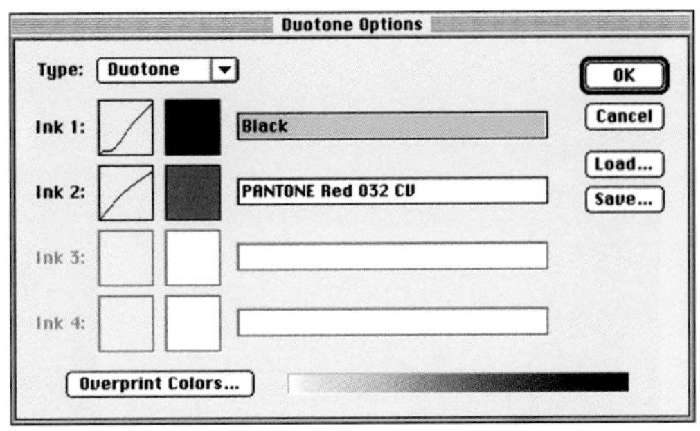


**6** Work in Full Screen mode. With the Marquee tool, starting outside the image area, drag the marquee over the top section of the image and allow the selection to snap to the top horizontal guide. Make sure you have the "snap to guides" selected in the View drop-down menu.

**7** Choose Image➨Edit➨Crop. This cuts away all but the top section of the image, which will be used as your first button. Choose Image➨Mode➨RGB, this will convert the image to RGB color allowing it to be exported to GIF89 format (name the file duotone1.gif).

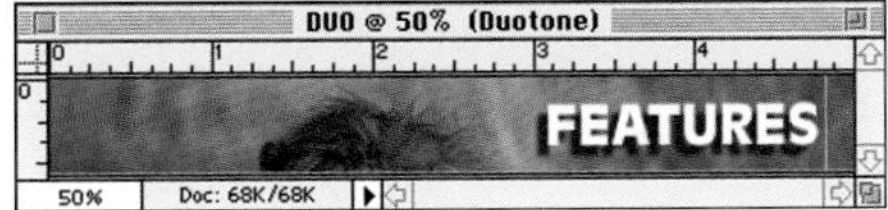


**8** Revert to the original image (duotone.ps) and repeat Steps 3 and 4 with the new type. Choose Image➨Mode➨Duotone and select a different color combination. We used black and a blue with RGB values 6, 6, 125.

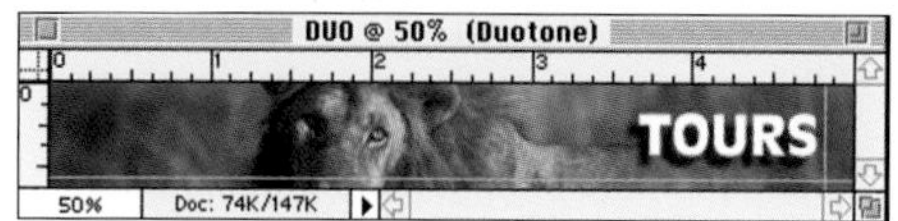


**9** Select the area between the second and third guidelines and let it snap to the guides. Choose Image➸Crop and export to GIF format (duotone2.gif) creating the second button for your Web site.

**10** Repeat Step 3 through 7 for as many buttons as you'd like. We made four.

# Variations

## Duotone and Mezzotint

Working with the filters in Photoshop 4.0 can give you some interesting and varied effects. In our variation we used a combination of duotone and Mezzotint filters to create Web page buttons, which each have two versions. One to show an active link and one to show an inactive link. This variation actually works with two separate images that are cut and combined in different configurations inside the HTML document.

**1** Choose: Pixelate➸Mezzotint➸Small dots on the Grayscale image and save it as a new Photoshop document.

**2** For the second image we created a duotone as described in Step 5 and saved that as a new Photoshop document.

**3** We added type and different drop shadow effects to jazz up the image, then cut and saved the separate pieces of each image for use in the HTML document as buttons.

**4** Use the different images to show which link you've connected to by highlighting that button and graying back the rest of the image. ■

# PART VII

## Animation

Animation is becoming an increasingly important aspect of Web page design. Seen as a welcome relief from pages of static HTML text, animation brings a fresh new energy to the conventional Web site.

Animation can be used to enhance pages or content themes. With greater frequency, companies are animating their Web advertising banners. The animation serves as the visual lure, enticing visitors to click the link to view the corporate message.

Animations do not need to be complex. Some of the best animations on the Web are small, discrete, and load quickly. Composed using a flip book technique, the animations are built with as few as two or three frames that may play once or loop continuously.

This series of individual frames can be created in Photoshop using the layers and actions palettes and the GIF89a format. When completed, the frames are then exported to software programs, such as GIF Builder or GIF Construction Set, for animating. In the following pages we demonstrate how to create some basic animation effects.

## Rotate Animation

Rotating an object has always been fairly easy in Photoshop. Photoshop 4.0's Actions feature helps automate the process by allowing you to assign a single function key to a series of steps.

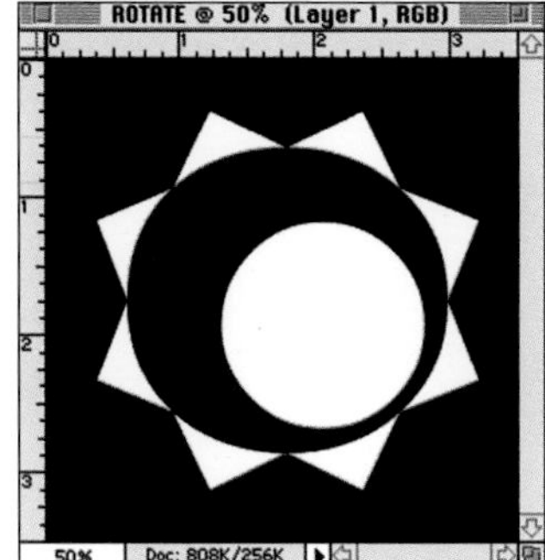


**1** Create a new file or open an existing file containing a graphic for the animation. We used a stylized "O" from the decorative Crystal Balzac font in this example (included on the CD). If you are using an existing image, select the graphic. If you are creating a new image using text for this exercise when you create text with the Type tool, you are adding a layer to your document. The text appears on that new layer filled with the foreground color. Choose Layers➙Preserve Transparency.

**2** Select the Gradient tool and set the tool options to Opacity: 100%; Gradient: Blue, Red, Yellow; Type: linear.

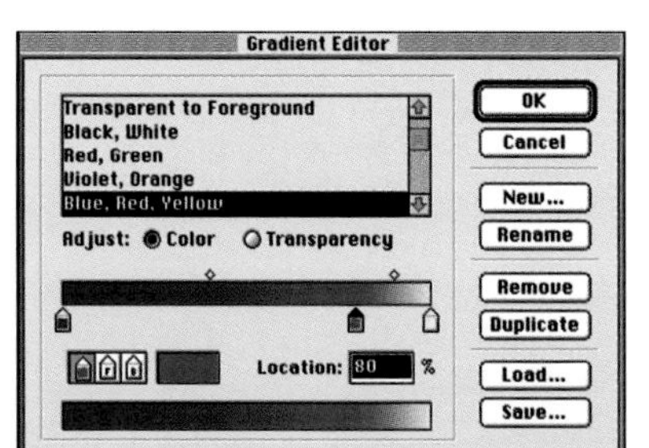


Click the Edit button in the tool options panel and set the Red slider to 80%. You may want to save new gradient variations for the future by renaming them. Click and drag across your selection to define direction and length of gradation as shown in the figure.

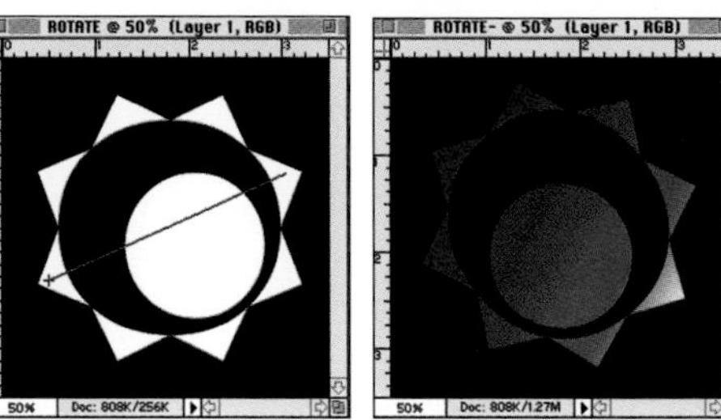

**3** Choose Windows➵Show Actions. Create a new action from the Actions Palette pop-up menu and name the action Rotate/Export. Assign a function key and a color and click the record button. From this point on all actions will be recorded to help automate the animation process.

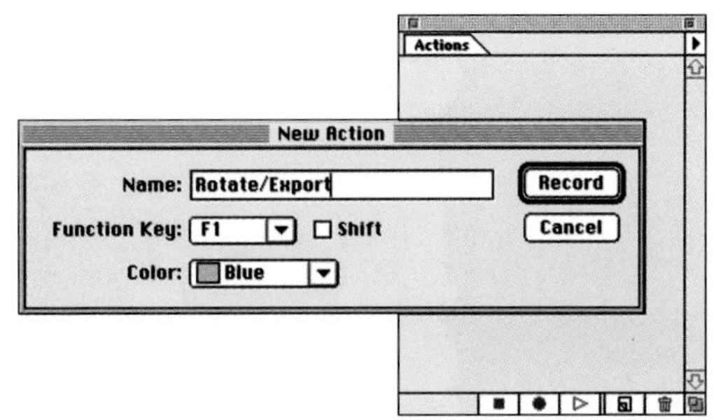


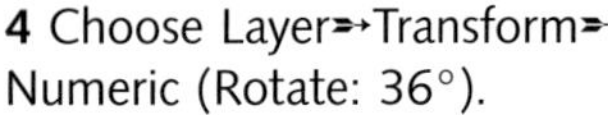

**4** Choose Layer➵Transform➵ Numeric (Rotate: 36°).

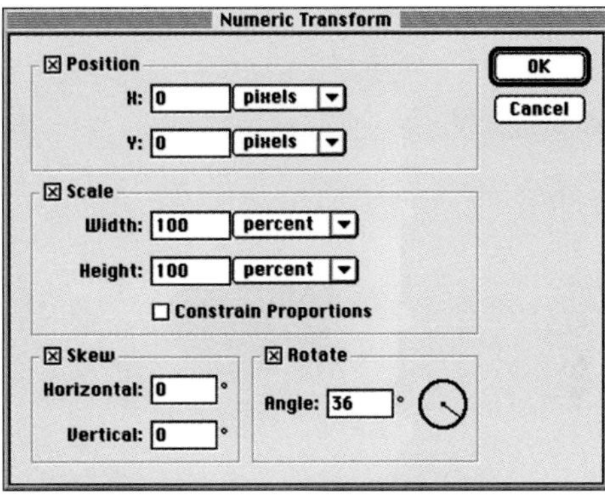


**5** Export to GIF89a format and save the file.

**TIP** **By using the function key assigned to these steps, you create a series of files. When naming these files, give them sequential names (rotate1.gif, rotate2.gif, rotate3.gif and so on).**

**6** Return to the Actions dialog box and stop recording the Action (in the Actions Palette pop-up menu).

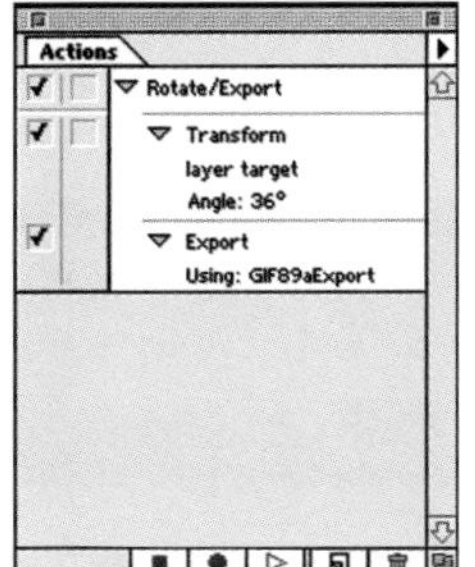

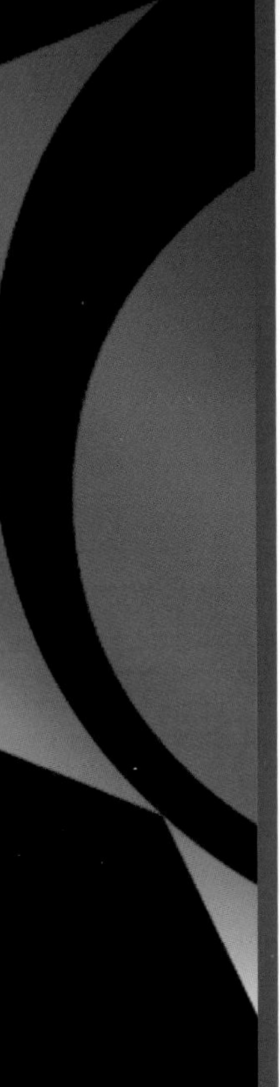

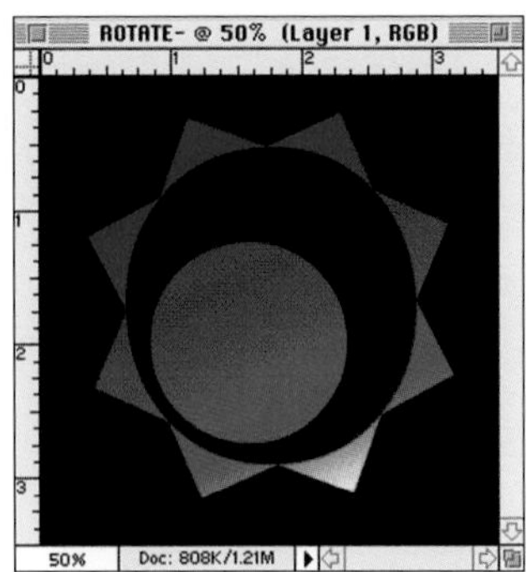


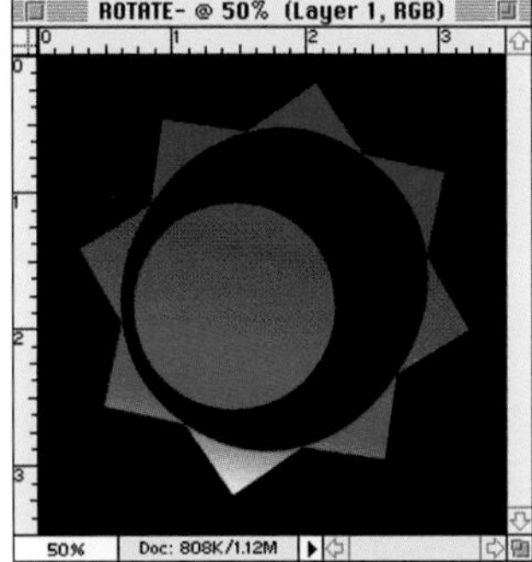


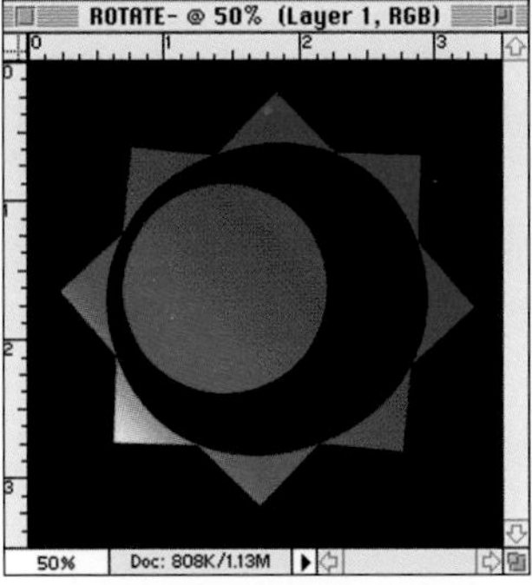


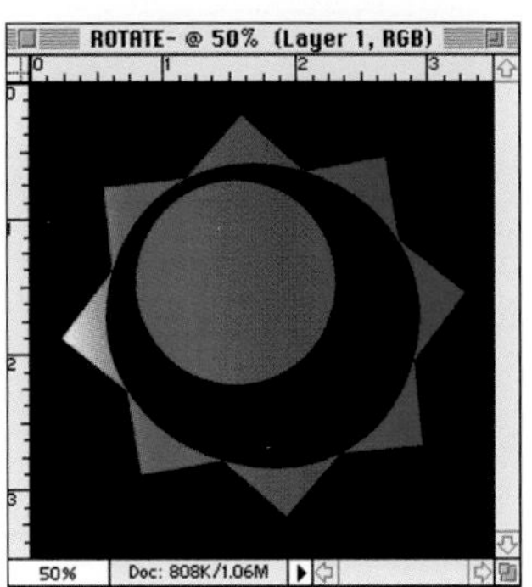


**7** Use the function key you designated to create the rest of the GIFs for the animation.

Save the entire sequence in its own folder as you export it. This makes opening and importing into your animation program easier.

After you have all the individual files for your rotation, you are ready to import them into GifBuilder (Macintosh), Gif Construction Set (Windows), or another animation program.

## VARIATIONS

In this example we rotate only the beveled edge of this button. The bevel rotation requires only four steps and creates a good-looking rotating button effect. Instead of rotating the image 36° as in the previous exercise, this button requires only four 90° rotations. The text was pasted into the center of each image after it was rotated. ■

## Fade On/Off Animation

The Gaussian Blur filter can be used repeatedly on images to create an excellent fade effect. Each time the Gaussian Blur is applied, the image spreads and appears lighter. This process is used to make objects appear to disappear or (if placed in reverse order in an animation program) to fade-up and appear.

**1** Create a new file or open an existing file containing the image you are using for the animation. Remember to allow enough space (approximately 1/2 inch or more) around the entire image for the fade to spread as it gets lighter. Choose Select➜All.

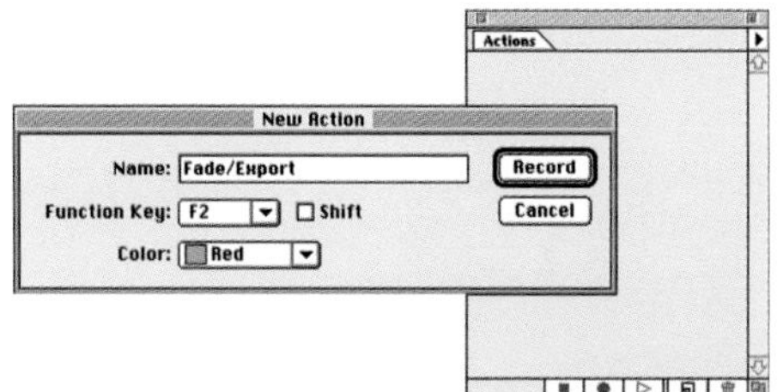


**2** Create a new action called Fade/Export. Choose a function key for your new action. Click the record button.

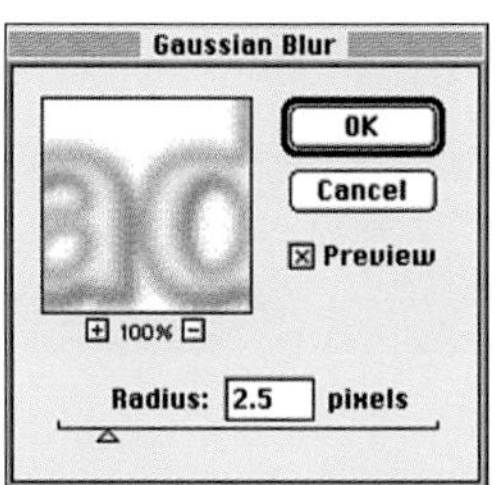


**3** Choose Filter➜Blur➜Gaussian Blur (2.5 pixels). A higher blur number will require fewer animation steps.

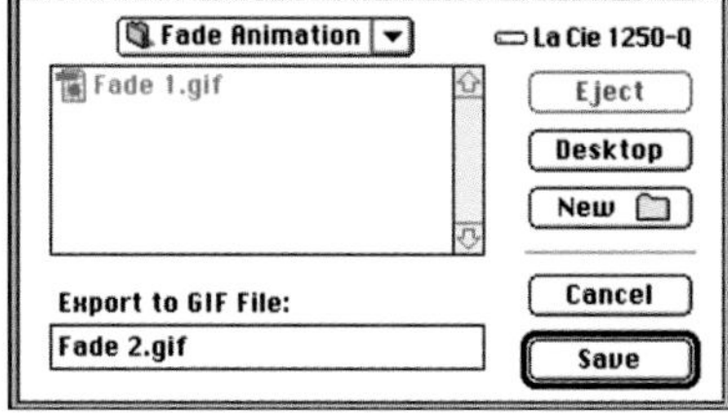


**4** Export to GIF format. Name the GIFs sequentially (fade1.gif, fade 2.gif, fade3.gif and so on) and save them in their own folder as you export it. The example in this exercise requires seven steps to fully fade. The number of steps required varies depending on the image and the setting you choose for the Gaussian Blur.

**5** Return to the Action dialog box and stop recording the Action (In the Actions Palette pop-up menu).

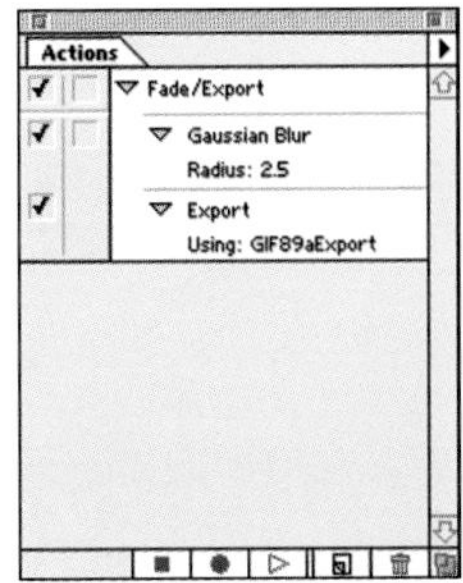


The action has now been recorded and you can use the function key you designated to create the rest of the GIFs for the animation. (If you have a keyboard without function keys, you can highlight the action in the palette and press play at the bottom of the palette or use the Action palette's pop-up menu to view the palette in Button mode.

**6** When you play this action a Gaussian blur is automatically applied to your image, the GIF89a Export dialog box appears, and, when you click OK, a Save dialog box appears where you can name your new GIF. Successive blurs produce a full fade effect. Continue this process until you have faded your image as desired.

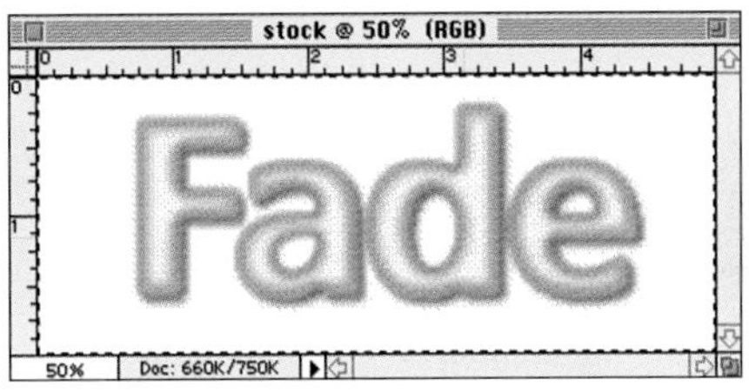


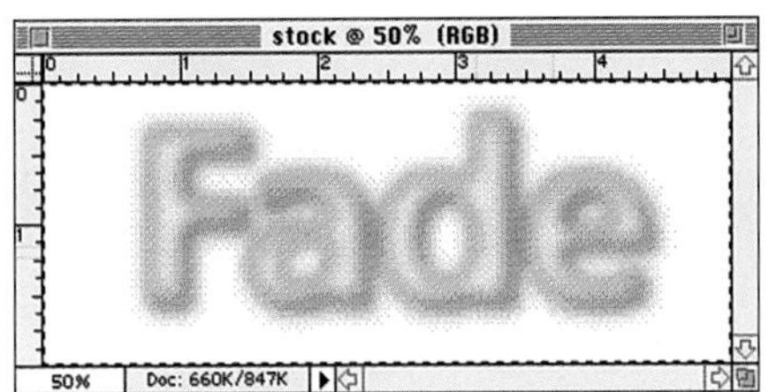


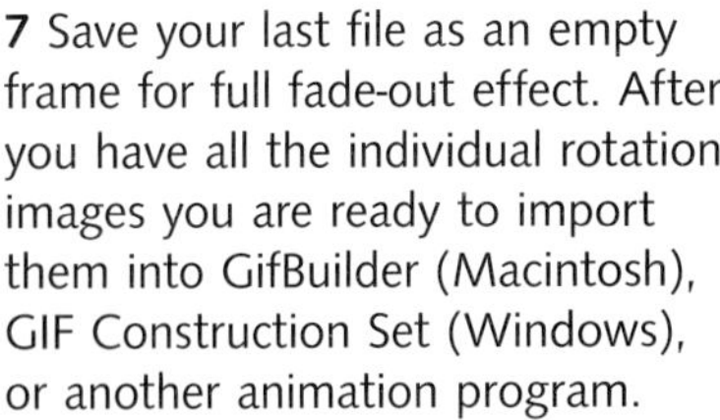

**7** Save your last file as an empty frame for full fade-out effect. After you have all the individual rotation images you are ready to import them into GifBuilder (Macintosh), GIF Construction Set (Windows), or another animation program.

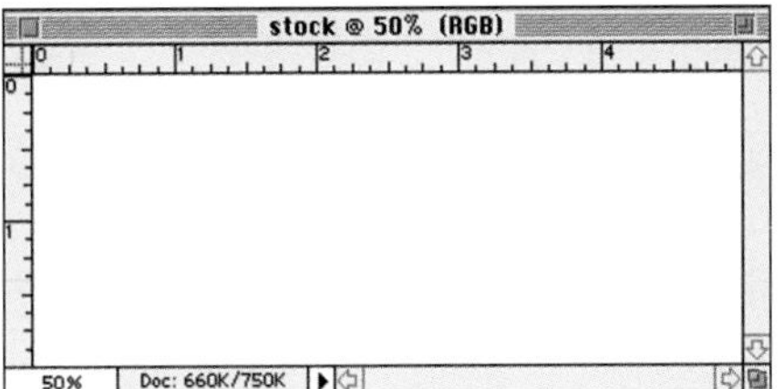

TIP As you create the different steps of an animation, you might want to alter the pace of the motion (in the preceding example, for example, you might want to increase the rate of fade). To do this, select the step of the action you want to change, then choose Record Again in the Action options pop-up menu. The Record Again command reflects the option you selected (in our example the palette command is Record "Gaussian Blur" Again). At this point you can add a custom setting.

## Write-On Animation

This exercise illustrates an animation that writes a word one letter at a time from left to right. This simple technique requires the creation of sequential images with a new letter added to each one. The final effect is similar to type applied by a typewriter.

**1** Open a copy of an existing file containing the type for the animation. For this exercise we used the Jasper type face with a chrome effect.

**Animation programs such as GifBuilder, Gif Construction Set, and others offer many features for image manipulation and animation such as image offset, interframe delay, and palette control. Some Web-based animation programs even contain more advanced functions such as morphing.**

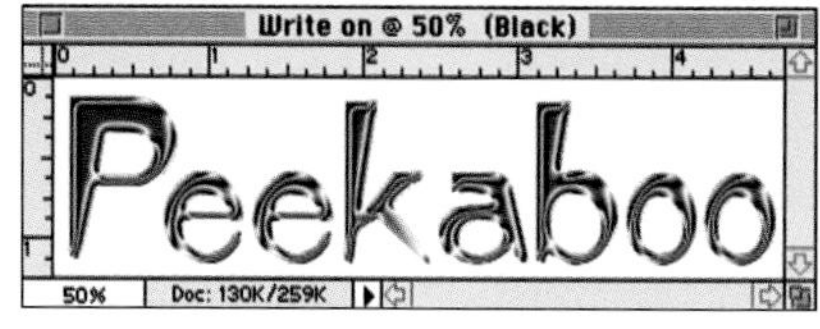


**2** Use the Crop tool from the Marquee pop-up menu to drag a selection around the image. When you are satisfied with the selection, press Return/Enter to crop. This keeps the file sizes small. Note: For illustration purposes we did not crop our artwork tightly.

**3** Create a new layer (Layer 1) and use the Marquee tool (or lasso) to select the portion of the image that will *not* appear in the first frame of the animation. Choose Edit➞Fill➞ (Use: White, Opacity: 100%, Mode: Normal). Save a copy of this image as a protection just in case you make a mistake and write over the original file.

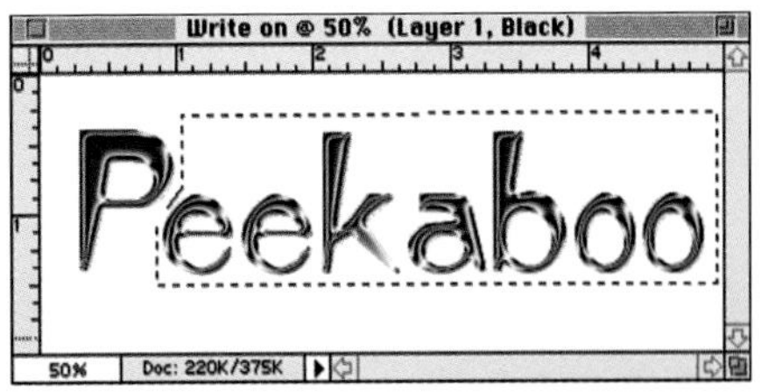


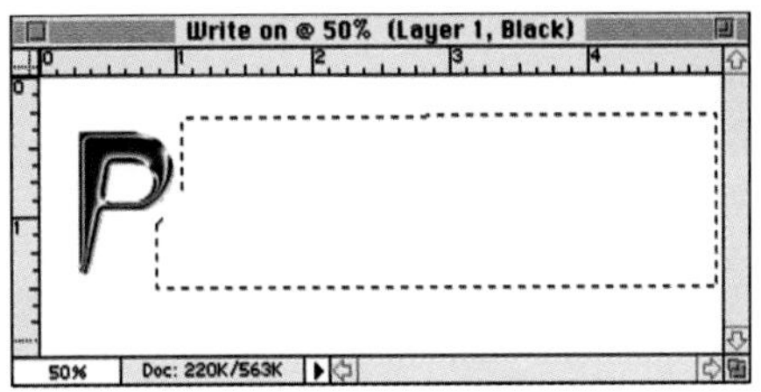


**4** Export as a GIF. Give the GIF a sequential name such as letter1.gif, letter2.gif, letter3.gif, and so on.

**5** Make Layer 1 active. Use the Move tool to drag the white box on Layer 1 to reveal the characters that appear in the second frame of the animation. Hold the Shift key down to constrain the motion horizontally. Export as a GIF.

**6** Repeat Step 5 until you have exported a GIF for each letter.

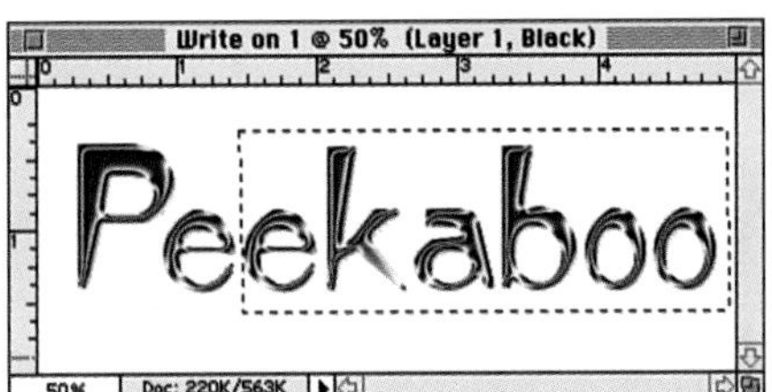


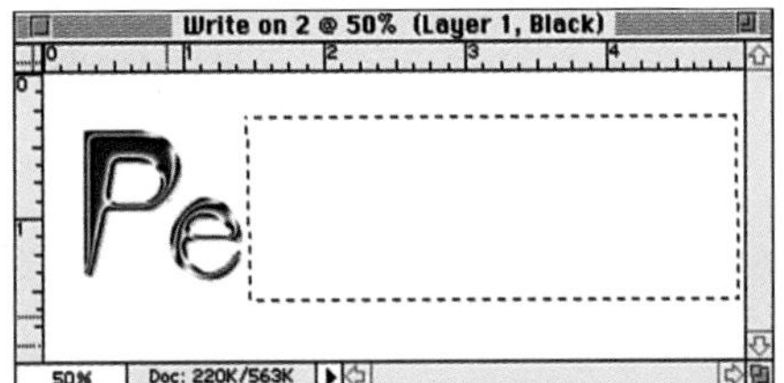

## VARIATIONS

You don't have to use letters as the units for this effect. Here we used circular selections to create a different effect.

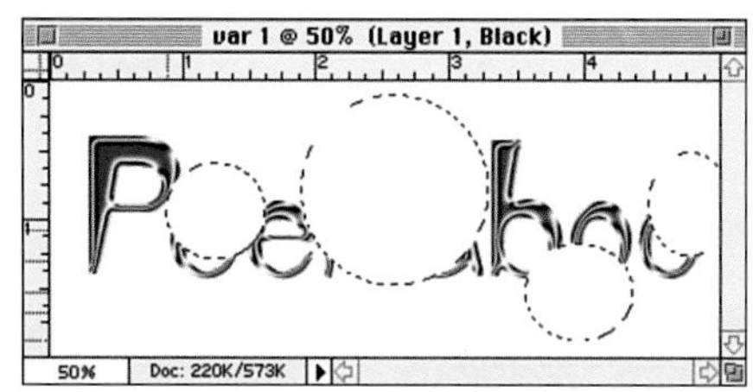


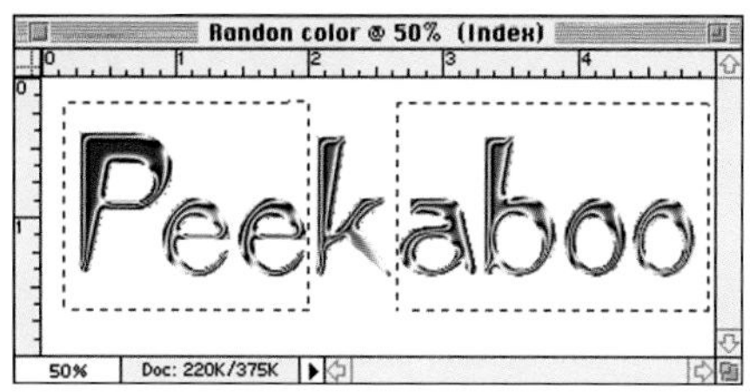


We created this colorful variation by using Image➵Adjust➵Color Balance and changing the settings for each frame. ■

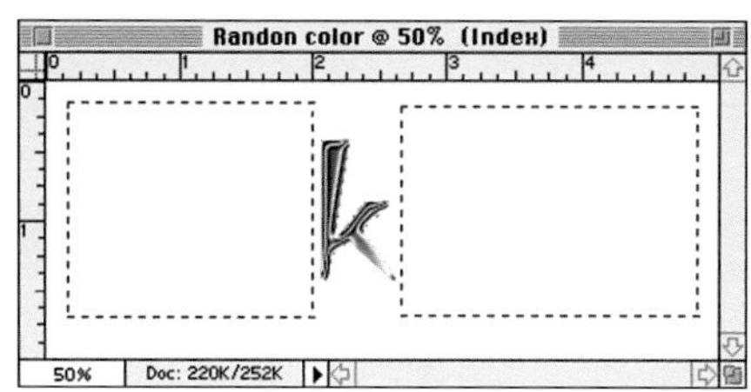

## Three Step Marquee

Chaser lights flashing around movie marquees, in carnivals, and other entertainment venues have been used traditionally to add flash and fanfare. The marquee effect of flashing lights framing an image can be achieved with only three frames of animation giving that exciting carnival effect of moving lights.

**1** Create a new file. Select a round brush and open the Brush Options dialog box and set the Spacing to 130%. Using Photoshop's brush options you can set any brush to create uniform lines of shapes.

TIP **Any setting over 100% will separate the brush strokes and enable you to use it as a repeating pattern line. A round brush will create a line of bullets.**

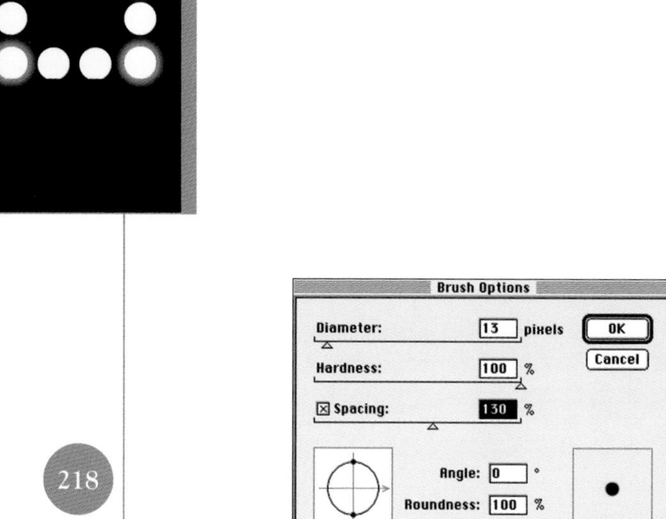


**2** Use the modified brush with the Paintbrush tool to draw a horizontal line creating a line of bullet points. With the Marquee tool select three bullet points. Keep the selection tight to the bullets.

TIP **Press the Command key to access the Move tool when another tool is active. Holding down the Option key when you drag a selection with the Move tool will create a copy of the selection. Holding down the Shift key as you drag constrains the drag horizontally, vertically or 45° diagonally.**

**3** Choose Edit➔Define Pattern. Then create a new file (we chose 250 pixels high×450 pixels wide for this example). Choose Edit➜Fill➜Pattern. You will wind up with broken bullets along some of the edges, Don't worry, just delete any broken bullets first to clean up the edges of your image.

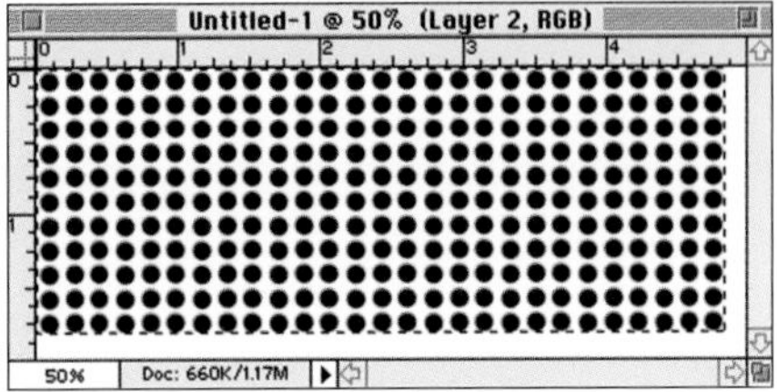


**4** After any broken bullets are deleted, you will have a clean edge of solid bullets around the parameter of your image. You want to end up with a rectangular box defined by a single line of solid bullet points. You'll need to place your Marquee tool just inside the first outside row of bullets. Select all the bullets inside the outer row of bullets except those on the outer edges, as shown in the figure.

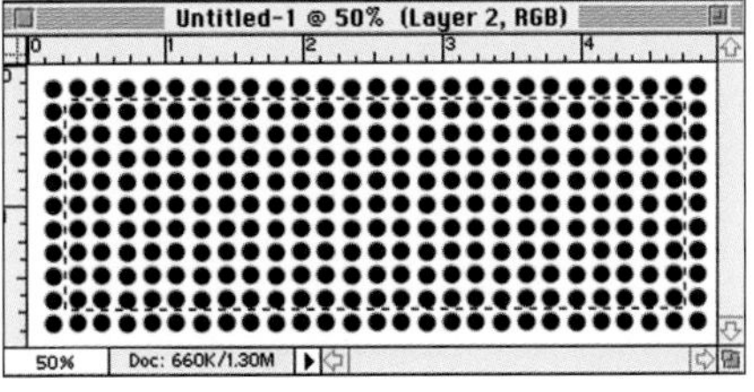


**5** Delete the selection. You're left with an even border of bullets that will be the base for your marquee. With the Magic Wand tool select one of the black bullets and choose Select➜Similar. Save the selection. After the selection is saved, select All, Edit➜Fill➜Black, creating a black background.

**When you save a selection, you are creating a channel. Every time you save a selection an additional channel is added. If you are working in RGB, the first selection saved is named Channel #4. If you are working in CMYK, the first selection you save is named Channel #5. Just as you can customize the names of layers, you can also change the names of channels. If you are saving multiple selections, it will make life a lot easier if you give specific names to**

**channels. Also bear in mind that every time you save a selection you are adding another 8-bit brightness channel to your document and the size of your document will increase accordingly. It is a good idea to delete unnecessary channels.**

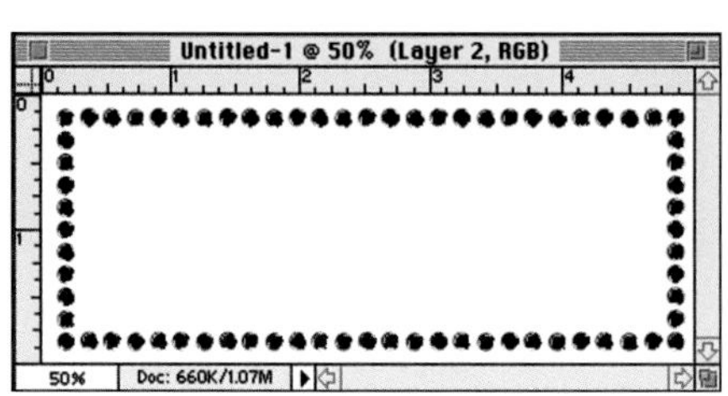


**6** Create a new layer (Layer 1) and load selection (#4). Choose Select➞Modify➞Expand (2 pixels). From the Window Menu choose show swatches, place your pointer over the yellow square in the first row of color swatches and click on it. Choose Edit➞Fill➞Foreground color. Duplicate the new layer 2 times. You will now have 3 layers and the *Background*.

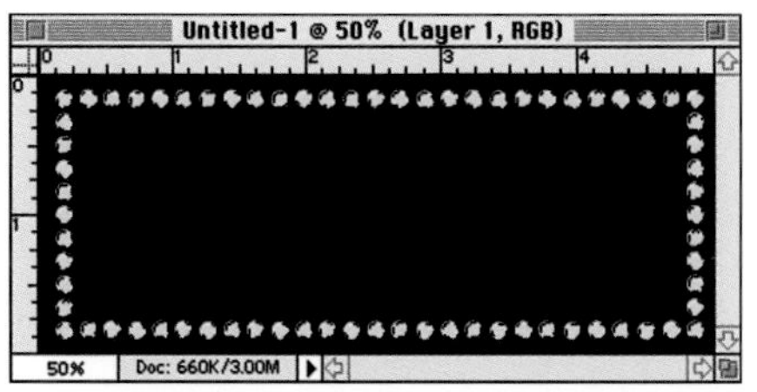


**7** Create a new layer (Layer 4), load the selection. Choose Edit➞Fill (Use: White).

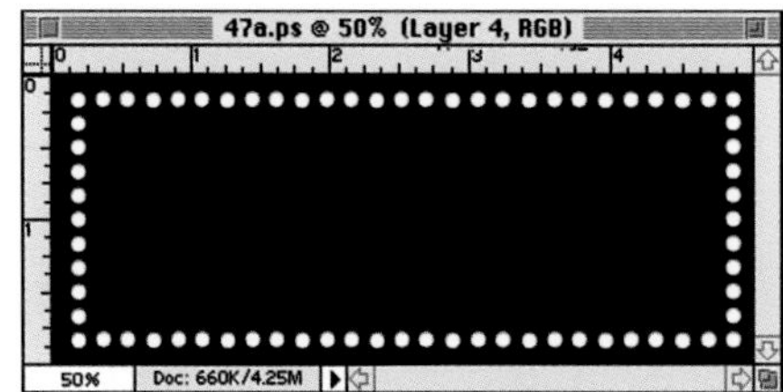


**8** To create the glowing light effect around the light, Make Layer 1 active, Option-click on the eye icon to hide the other layers, and use the Magic Wand tool and the Shift key to select every third bullet. Choose Select➞Inverse and delete. Then Press Command-A (select all) and choose Filter➞Gaussian Blur (5 pixels).

**Option-clicking the eye icon toggles between showing and hiding layers. If you Option-click a layer that is NOT visible, that layer becomes visible and the other layers**

**are hidden. You still, however, need to click the layer name in the palette to make it active.**

**9** Make Layer 2 active and repeat Step 8 moving one bullet to the right from the one place you started on Layer 1. Make sure you're always selecting the bullet to the right of the one you deleted on Layer 1. Repeat this process with Layer 3.

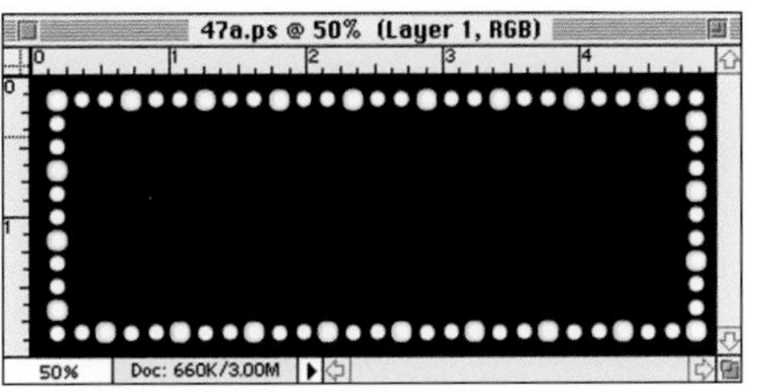


**10** Create a new layer (Layer 5) and place any type or other images that need to be present in the marquee. If you are creating type in this document, do NOT make a new layer. Simply select the Type tool and create the text—in Photoshop 4.0, text created with the Type tool comes in on a new layer. In this example we added the word Marquee.... Using Layer 5 keeps the versions you save consistent so that only the "lights" of the marquee appear to be moving.

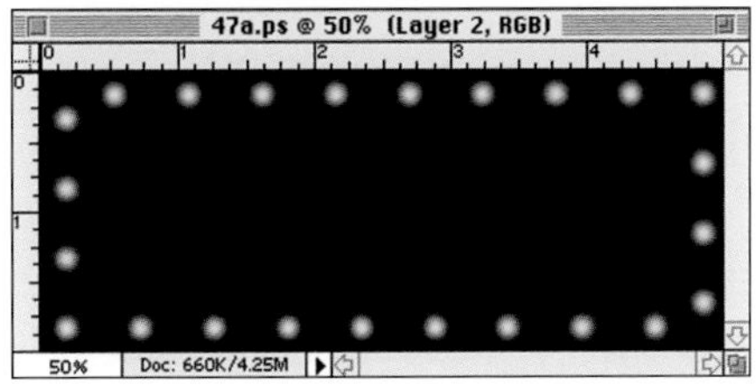


**11** Make the background, Layer 1, Layer 4, and Layer 5 visible and export to GIF format.

**12** Make Layers 2, 4 and 5 visible and export to GIF format.

Repeat Step 12 one more time, this time using Layers 3, 4, and 5, creating a total of three GIFs.

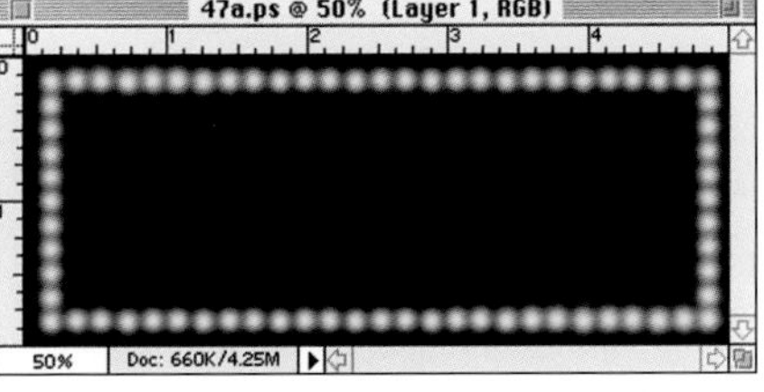


TIP **You can now import the files into GifBuilder (Macintosh), GIF Construction Set (Windows) or another animation program to create the final animation.**

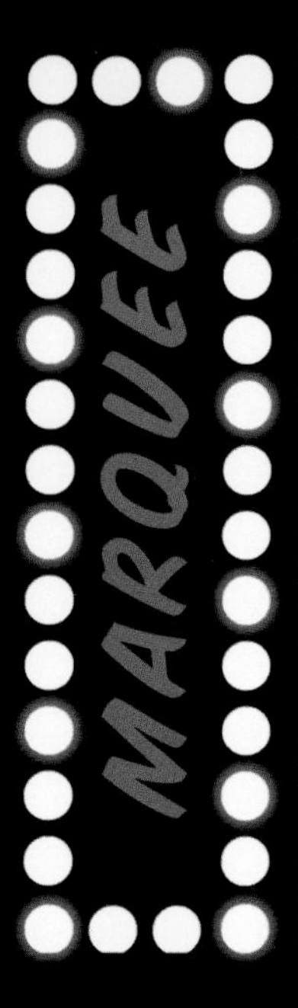


## Variation

This variation makes the lights chase around the frame, pause, flash on and off, and then go back to chasing.

**1** Open your original Photoshop document and make all three layers of the blurred yellow bullets visible, hiding the text layer (Layer 5) and the layer with the white bullets (Layer 4). Export to GIF format.

**2** Return to the original document and make the background, Layer 4, and Layer 5 visible. Export to GIF format.

**3** In your GIF animation program, insert the GIF from Step 2 after the original three GIFs. Insert the GIF from Step 1, followed by the GIF from Step 2 again, and then repeat the series of the first three GIFs in reverse order. ■

## Twirl Animation

Twisted or twirled animation effects are easier to do with Photoshop 4.0 and its new Actions palette because you can record every step of a sequential action and save it. In this exercise we combined the Twirl filter with Transform to create an animation that spins and shrinks at the same time.

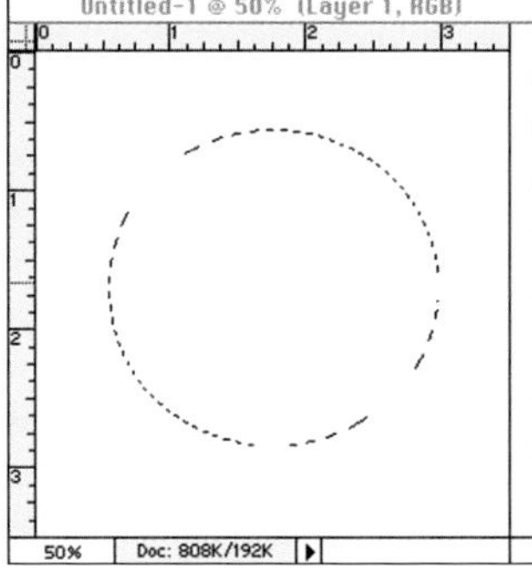
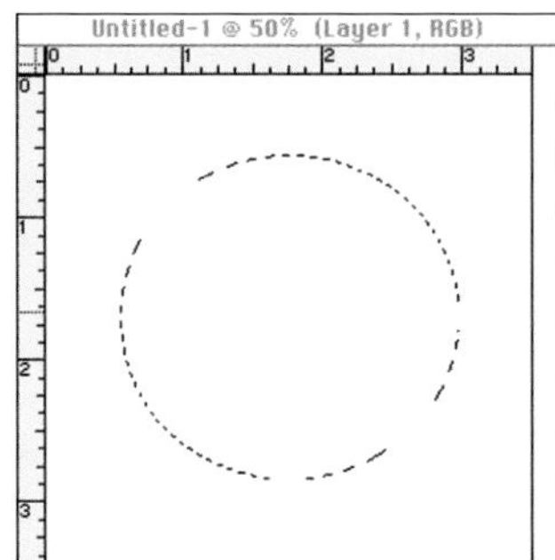


**1** Create a new file (Background: white) and select the Ellipse marquee tool. Select a circular area.

**TIP** **Keep animated GIFs fairly small. As you design your animation, keep in mind that because it is a local file, the animation runs as fast as your computer can play it. When it is viewed the final animation plays only as fast as the animation file loads on a Web page (usually 14.4 or 28.8 Kbs). It is only after the file is finished loading that it will run as fast as it is programmed to run.**

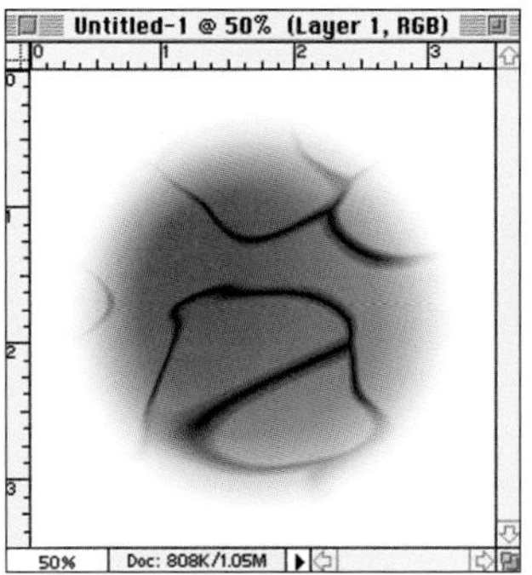


**2** Choose Selection Menu➛Feather (15 pixels). Fill with your pattern or texture. We used a texture from MetaTools KPT Texture Explorer for this example. You can also use an existing texture file: Open the file containing the texture you want to use. Select all and choose Edit➛Define Pattern. Return to the original file and with the feathered selection still selected choose Edit➛Fill➛(Use: Pattern).

**3** For the button in the center of the twirl, create a new layer (Layer #1). Select a rectangular area and Edit➔Fill➔Foreground (White, Opacity: 80%).

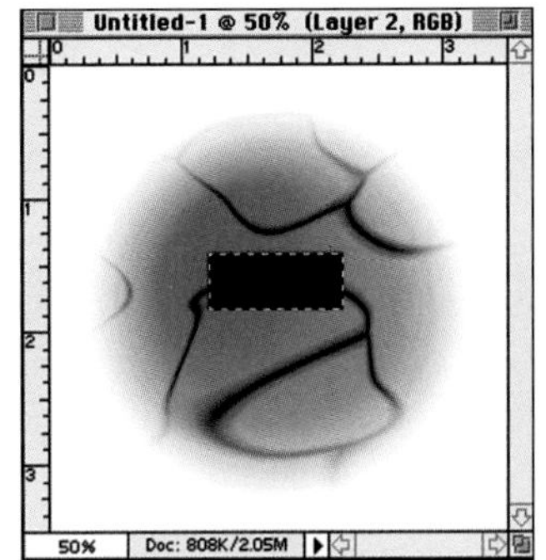


**4** With the rectangle still selected, create a new layer (Layer 2). Choose a foreground color for the button and fill a selection with the foreground color. We then added a bevel using the Alien Skin Inner Bevel filter. Return to Layer 1, select the Move tool, and use the arrow keys to move it down and to the right to create a drop shadow.

**5** Use the Type tool to add type to the button. This creates a new Layer (Layer 3). Choose a Foreground color for the type.

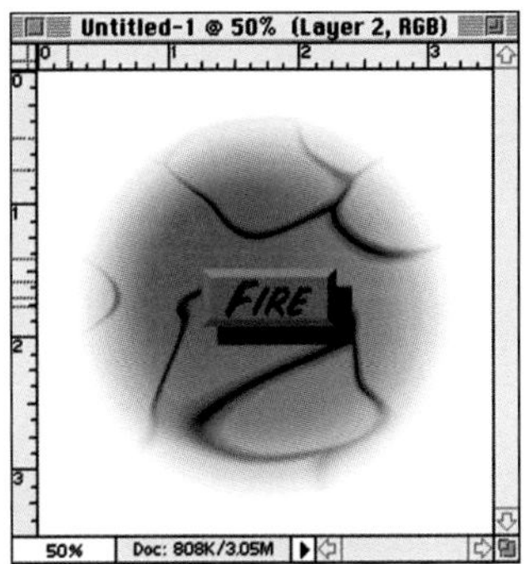

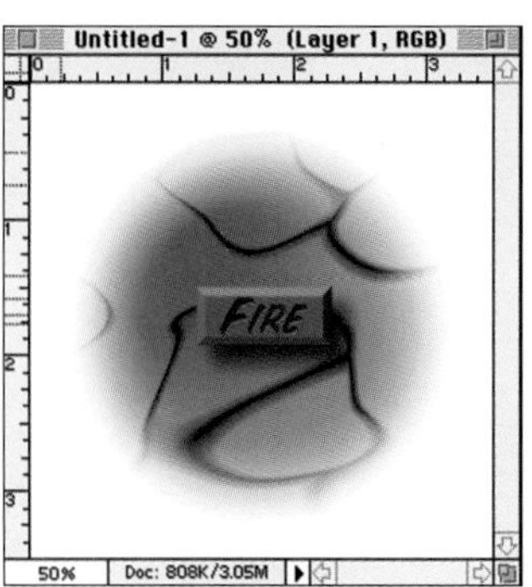


6 To soften the drop shadow, keep Layer 1 active and apply Filter➾Blur➾Gaussian Blur (3 pixels). Save the file as a Photoshop document, naming it "base.gif" and export it as a GIF89a.

New Action

| Name: | Untitled-1 | Record |
|---|---|---|
| Function Key: | None ☐ Shift | Cancel |
| Color: | None | |

7 Now we'll apply the twirl effect. Open the Actions palette and choose Window➾Show Actions. Create a new action. Name the action and assign a function key and color for the button. Click Record. Every action you take will be recorded and saved for future use.

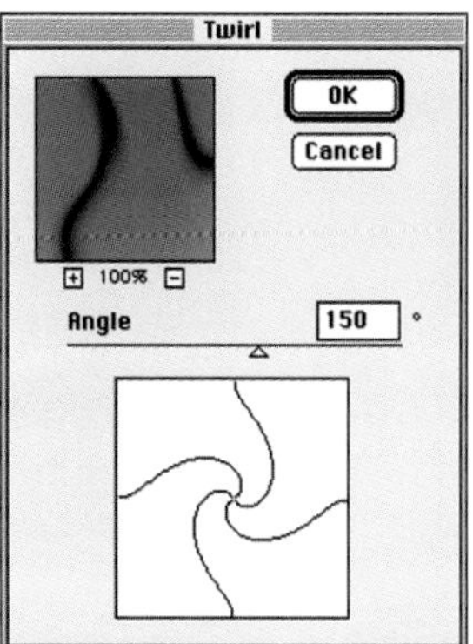


8 Select➾All, make the background layer active, and then choose Filter➾Distort➾Twirl (150°).

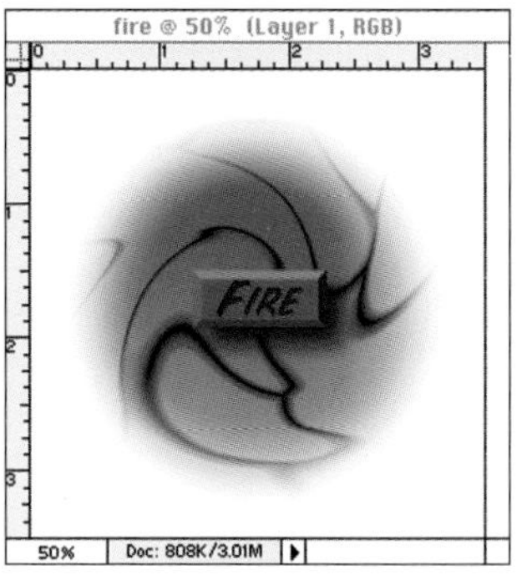


9 Export the image as a GIF89a file. Name it twirl1.gif.

**10** Click the stop button on the Actions palette.

**11** Click Play on your Actions palette. The image is rotated an additional 150°. When the export dialog box appears, name the image twirl2.gif and save it in the same folder as the rest of your images.

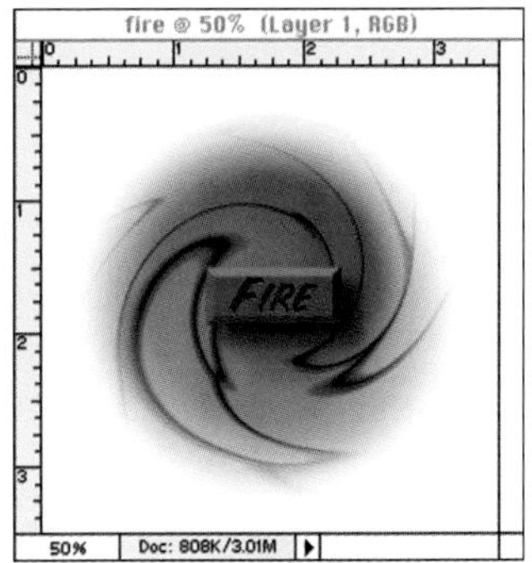


**12** Repeat Step 11 two more times, naming the GIFs sequentially (twirl3.gif, twirl4.gif).

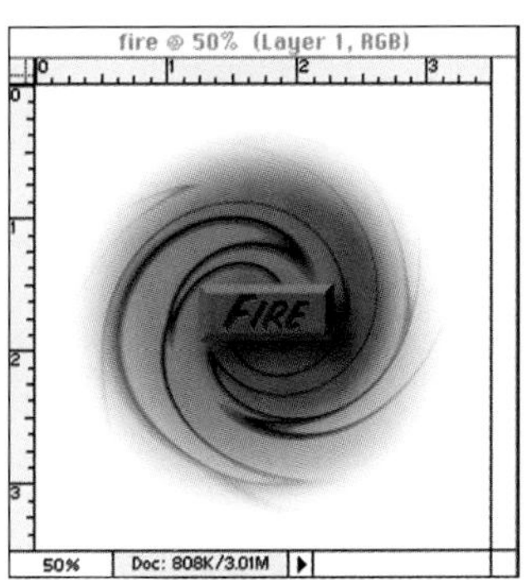


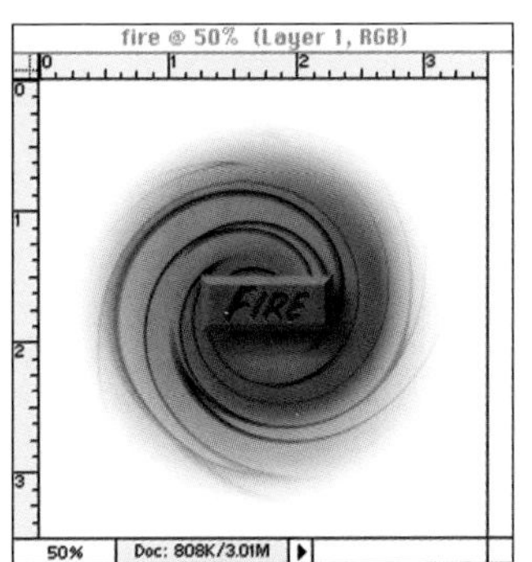

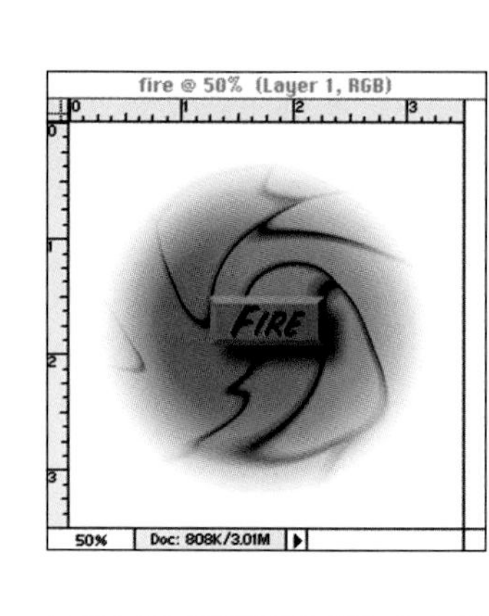

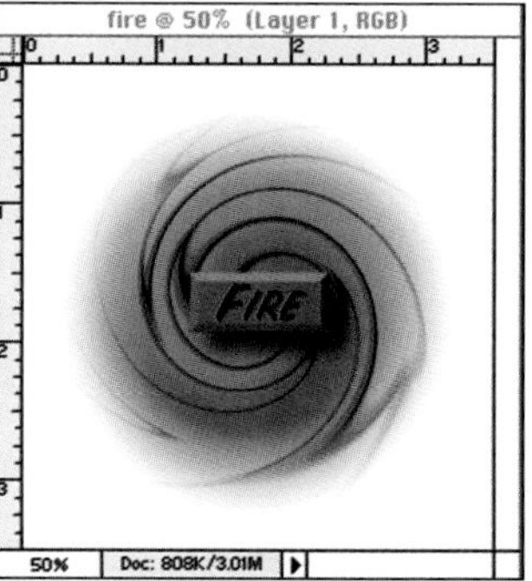


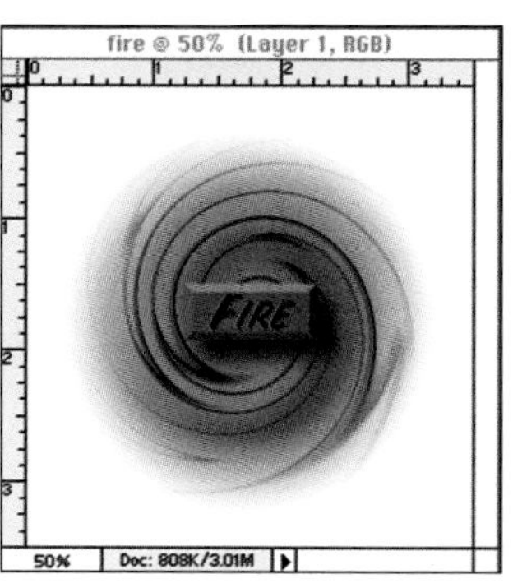


**13** Creating the twirl in the opposite direction follows the same process, entering a negative number in the Twirl dialog box. Revert to the file saved in Step 5. On the Actions palette select the Twirl action. From the Actions palette's pop-up menu choose Record Twirl Again. Enter -150° in the Twirl dialog box. Export the file to GIF format (twirl5.gif).

**14** The action is now modified to twirl in the opposite direction. Repeat the action 3 more times, as above in Step 12, to create the additional GIFs.

**15** You are now ready to bring the GIF sequence into an animation program such as GifBuilder or Gif Construction Set. Arrange the GIFs in the following order: base, twirl1.gif, twirl2.gif, twirl3.gif, twirl4.gif, twirl3.gif, twirl2.gif, twirl1.gif, base.gif, twirl5.gif, twirl6.gif, twirl7.gif, twirl8.gif, twirl7.gif, twirl6.gif, twirl5.gif. Set the animation to loop forever and you will have an animation that twirls to the right and unwinds, then to the left and unwinds.

# VARIATION

### Shrinking Twirl

This variation combines two Photoshop effects, twirl and numeric transform, into each Action step, creating an effect that shrinks and grows as it twirls.

In this exercise we added two additional steps to the action: Numeric Transform to shrink the graphic and a Revert command to bring you back to the original file (The Revert is necessary to make the Numeric Transform work smoothly). Because we are reverting after each step, you have to enter the values manually into the Twirl and Transform dialog boxes.

**1** Follow Steps 1-5 to create the base image for the animation. In this example we made an open frame instead of a solid button.

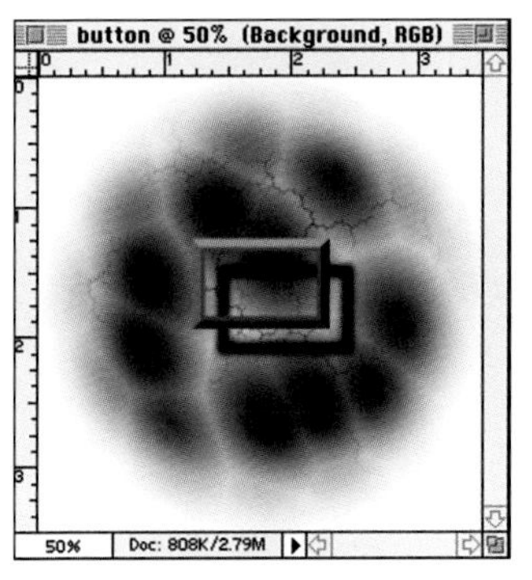


**2** Make the background layer active and Select➛All. Create a new action. Name the action, make a function key assignment, and select a color for the action button. Press Record on the Actions palette to begin recording. Choose Filter➛Distort➛Twirl (100°), then choose Layers➛Transform➛Numeric (Scale: Horiz: 90, Vert: 90). Next, choose

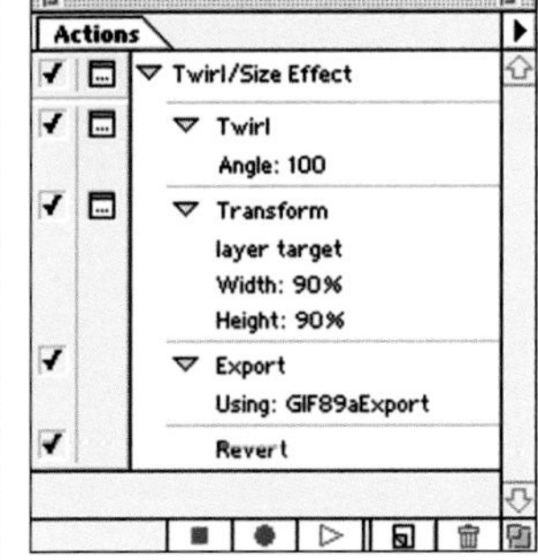

File➛Export as GIF89a, name the GIF, and choose File➛Revert.

**3** To the left of the action commands on the Actions palette are break point check boxes (containing an icon of a dialog box). Select the boxes next to your actions. The Toggle option causes the action to pause at the dialog box of each element of your action, waiting for input.

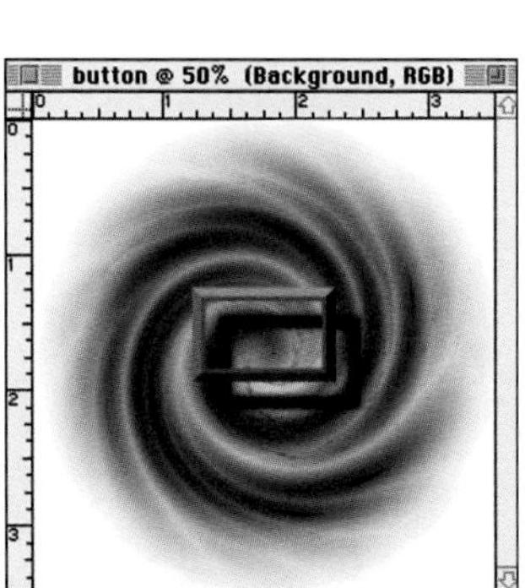


**4** With each execution of the action, increase the Twirl value by 100° and reduce the Numeric Transform tool Scale by 10%.

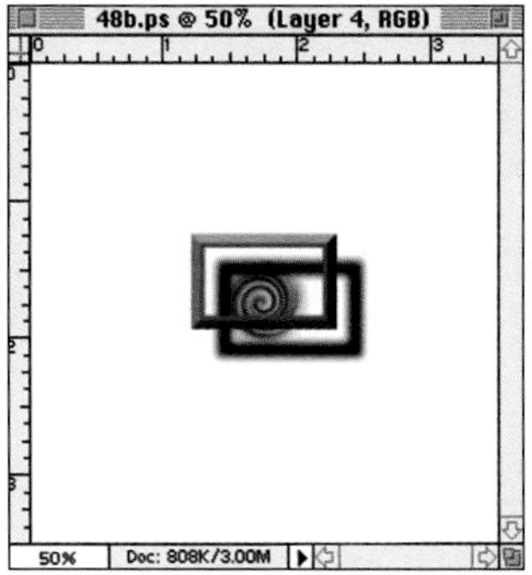


**5** Repeat the process until the textured twirl almost disappears behind the button, this should take eight or nine steps. ■

## Using GifBuilder

GifBuilder is a Mac-only freeware utility from Yves Piguet designed for creating animated GIF files. You can use an existing animated GIF, a group of PICT, GIF and TIFF files, or a QuickTime movie. GifBuilder will output these file formats as a GIF89a file with multiple pages, creating an animation that you can use on the Web.

GifBuilder is a user-friendly program which provides many options. These include interlacing, color palettes, pixel depth, dithering, image size, background color, looping, transparency, frame offset, interframe delay, disposal method and saving options.

This exercise will demonstrate only the basics of GifBuilder touching upon looping, and interframe delay. You can find the program in the Web Tools folder. For further information on how GifBuilder works refer to the documentation provided with the program.

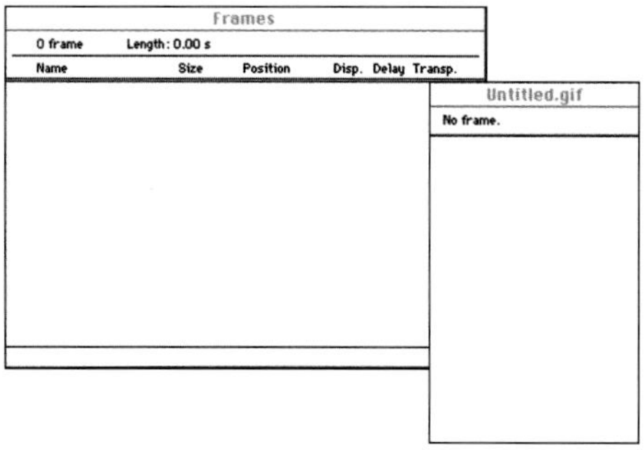

**1** Open GifBuilder.

**2** Choose File➛Add Frame (Command-K) and add each GIF file for the animation.

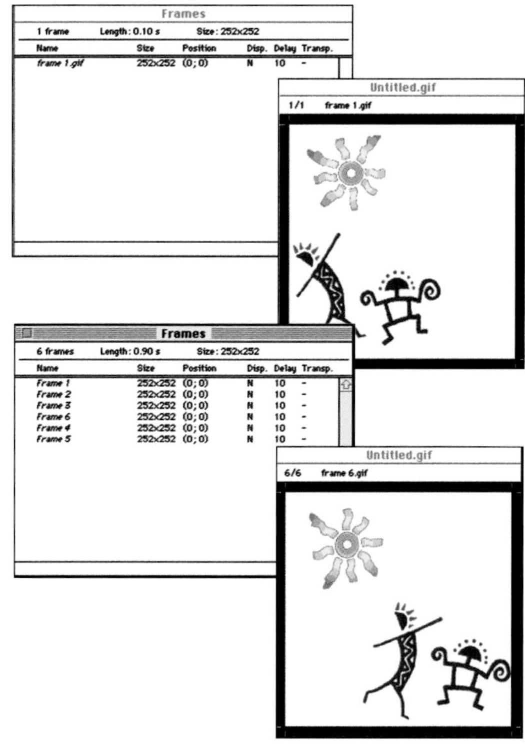


**TIP** **Always save your original animation files in alphabetical or numerical order, that is, 1ani.gif, 2ani.gif, and so on. GifBuilder will then open and place the frames in the correct order.**

**3** Choose Animation➛Start (Command-R) to play your animation. If you want to rearrange your frames, select the frame. As you drag the frame, a guideline will appear. Place the guideline where you would like the frame placed.

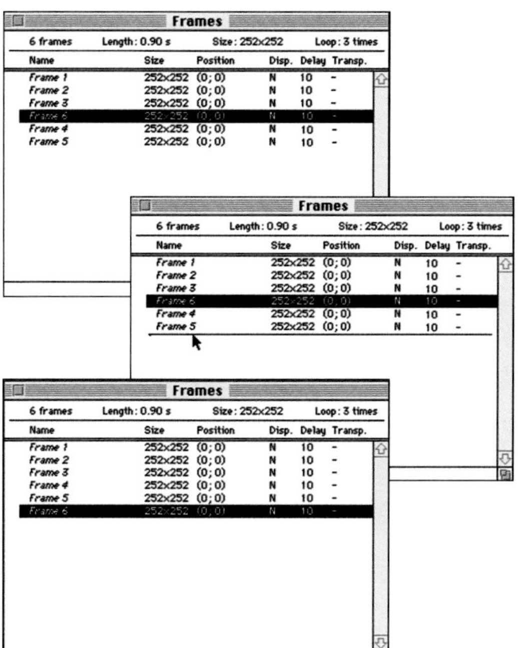

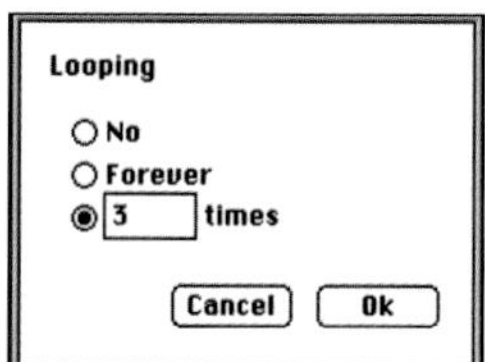


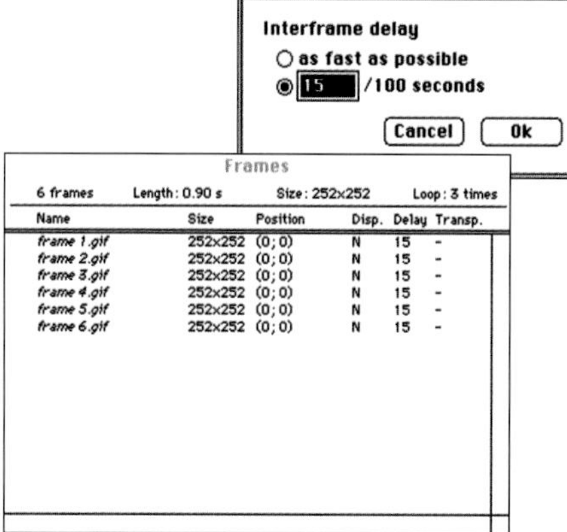


**4** Choose Options➛Loop. Using the looping dialog box loop your graphic as desired. You can set the animation to play once, any number of times, or forever. For this exercise we looped it 3 times.

**5** To adjust timing between frames, choose Options➛Interframe delay (or double-click the number display in the Delay column on the Frames window). Set the time for each frame. For this exercise we chose 15. The delay time can vary from frame to frame for special effects.

**6** Choose File➛Save as. You can now place the finished GIF animation on a Web page as you would any other GIF. To view this animation open gb1.gif (in the Animation Examples folder on the CD-ROM) in GifBuilder or a Web browser.

## Variations

### Looping Animations

By duplicating selected frames, we created a smooth looping effect.

Select all frames except the first and last. Use Command-D to duplicate the selected frames, then arrange the duplicated frames in reverse order. This will create a smooth continuous loop effect.

To view this animation open gb2.gif (in the Animation Examples folder on the CD-ROM) in GifBuilder or a Web browser.

## Delaying and Duplicating Frames

This variation demonstrates inter-frame delay and duplicate frame effects. Changing the delay to 20 and duplicating frames 3 and 4 creates a pause and dancing effect with the figures in mid-animations.

To view this animation open gb3.gif (in the Animation Examples folder on the CD-ROM) in GifBuilder or a Web browser. ■

## GIF Construction Set

To create animations for the Web you need an animation program. The GIF Construction Set from Alchemy Mindworks is a simple to use shareware program for Windows that can be downloaded from www.mindworkshop.com. You work with dialog boxes that takes you step by step through the process for creating animated GIFs for the Web.

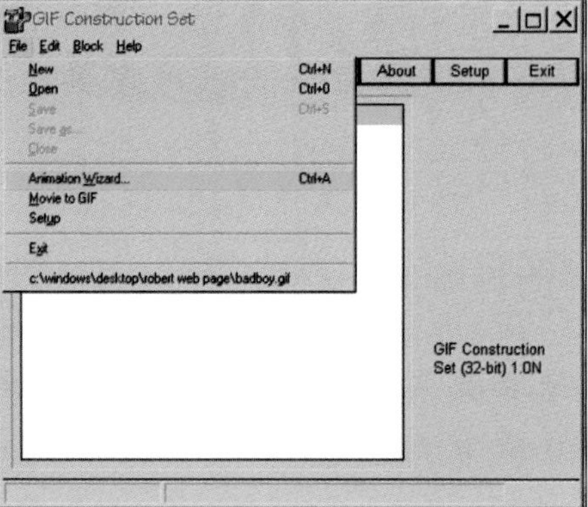


**1** Open the program and select the Animation Wizard from the File menu to start the automation process.

**2** Follow the instructions on the different dialog boxes and the program will take you through each step, asking you several questions about the type of animation you want to create. Make sure you select the option "For use on the World Wide Web".

**3** Next the program requests that you enter delay time between screens measured in hundredths of seconds.

**4** Locate the GIF files included in the animation. The program compiles an animated GIF file including the images in your sequence.

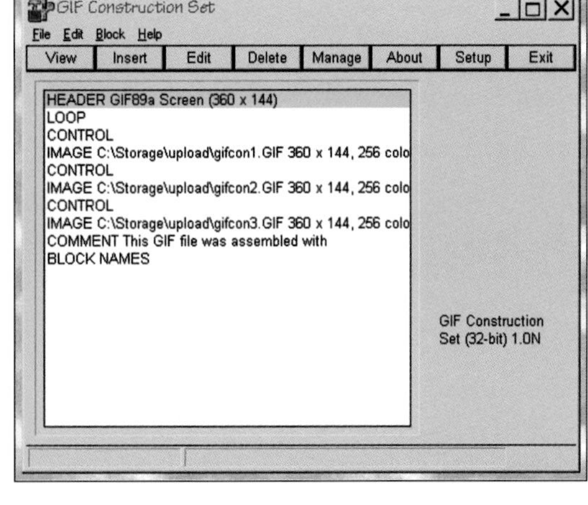


**5** Click View to see the animation in action. You can change or edit the animation with GIF Construction Set's easy-to-use buttons bar. You can alter the speed, looping effects, and even insert or reorder frames.

**6** When you are pleased with the way the animation works, save it as a GIF file. Place the animated GIF into your Web page just like a standard GIF file:

```
<IMG SCR="xx.gif" WIDTH="xx"
HEIGHT="xx" ALT="animated
gif"> ■
```

# Appendix A

## Web Resources Links

HTML pages containing these links can be found in the WebMagic folder on the CD.

### Information SuperLibrary

`http://www.mcp.com`

Viacom's Information SuperLibrary contains the complete text of The Internet Starter Kit (both Windows and Mac versions). Overall the site contains the depth of information you would expect from the world's largest publisher of computer books.

### Dodd's Magic Locator

`http://www.netdepot.com/~gargoyle/magic/links.html`

Photoshop Web Magic's favorite link to magic on the Web. A great gateway site to magicians, magazines, organizations, retailers, news, and just about anything else on magic.

### Photoshop Resources

#### Adobe

`http://www.adobe.com`

The Adobe site contains continuing product support information, Photoshop and design tips, updates, plug-ins and other up to date information.

#### Adobe Plug-In Source Catalog

`http://www.imageclub.com/aps/`

The Adobe Plug-in Source is a comprehensive software catalog that brings the power of plug-ins to your workstation.

#### The KPT Photoshop Forum

`http://the-tech.mit.edu/cgi-bin/HyperNews/get/KPT/pshop.html`

This ongoing forum is for any questions or discussion about using Adobe Photoshop and any of its third party add-ins.

216 Colors of Netscape

http://www.connect.hawaii.com/hc/webmasters/Netscape.colors.html

This is the place to learn about using the 216-color Safe Palette on the Web.

Metatools—KPT Plug-ins

http://www.metatools.com

The developers of Kai Power Tools and other very cool graphics software.

PNG (Portable Network Graphics) Home Page

http://quest.jpl.nasa.gov/PNG/"

Find out more about the PNG graphic format here.

Pantone: What's New

http://www.pantone.com/whatsnew.html

A great place for color resources, information, and software.

## Design Resources

Designers Guide to the Net

http://www.zender.com/designers-guide-net

This site, and the book it is based on, attempts to raise the right questions, and propose answers that will help designers in the information future.

Pursuing Page Publishing

http://www.links.net/webpub/

Tips on "Publish yo' self" at this site. Includes a guide to designing with HTML and links to many other Web resources.

Cybergrrl

http://www.cybergrrl.com

Author of Designing Web Graphics, Lynda Weinman's Cybergrrl site can help guide you through getting started on the Web, offer HTML instruction, link you to important Web sites, and lots more.

Web Wonk—Tips for Writers and Designers

http://www.dsiegel.com/tips/index.html

Web Wonk by David Siegel, author of *Building Killer Web Sites*, will help you to build better Web pages, use email, and offers great tips on Web site graphic design.

### Tom's Tips for Web Designers

`http://www.the-tech.mit.edu/KPT/Toms/index.html`

Find all kinds of Photoshop tips here including: Web design, using filters, and links to other resources.

### Ventana: Photoshop f/x

`http://www.vmedia.com/vvc/onlcomp/phshpfx/`

This site is based on the book Photoshop f/x, lots of design tips, and links to Photoshop resources.

### Yahoo Design and Layout

`http://www.yahoo.com/Computers_and_Internet/Internet/World_Wide_Web/Page_`
`➥Design_and_Layout`

This Yahoo category is as up to date and comprehensive as it gets. It includes links to Animated GIFs, Backgrounds, Color Information, Commercial Books, Commercial Web Page, Designers, HTML, Icons, Imagemaps, Programming, Transparent Images, and Validation/Check.

## Backgrounds

### Texture Land—Abnormal Textures Index

`http://www.meat.com/textures/aindex.html`

This site offers one of the largest selections of backgrounds on the Web.

### KALEIDESCAPE

`http://www.steveconley.com/kaleid.htm`

This site claims to offer "hundreds of the snazziest textures in the universe."

### Textures Unlimited!

`http://www.smoky.org/~bzhuk/texture/f-1.html`

Click on a texture at this site and it automatically shows you what the tile looks like when applied to a Web page. There are some flashy textures here and music clips to download.

Greg's Texture Tiles Page

http://mars.ark.com/~gschorno/tiles/

Find lots of tiles here in a simple table-based layout.

The Background Sampler

http://www.netscape.com/assist/net_sites/bg/backgrounds.html

Netscape's collection of backgrounds. Lots of basic textures and standard patterns here.

The Wallpaper Machine

http://www.cacr.caltech.edu/cgi-bin/wallpaper.pl

This interactive page makes funky random background patterns each time you click reload.

Netscape—Color Backgrounds

http://home.netscape.com/assist/net_sites/bg/

Netscape's instruction page on using background color with HTML3.

InfiNet's background colors list

http://www.infi.net/wwwimages/colorindex.html

Information on setting and using hex color for Web page backgrounds and text.

## Type on the Web

TypoGraphic



http://www.razorfish.com/bluedot/typo/

"This site is meant to illustrate the beauty, poetry, complexity, and history of type, while raising relevant questions about how typography is treated in the digital media, specifically online."

DesktopPublishing.com

http://desktoppublishing.com/

Lots of fonts, images, and links to a wide range of design and programming resources.

Type Directors Club

http://members.aol.com/typeclub/index.html

An organization dedicated to the appreciation and understanding of letterforms and calligraphy.

### BitStream Fonts

http://www2.digitalriver.com/bit/index.html

Over 1,000 fonts for sale online.

### Letraset

http://www.letraset.com/letraset/

Download a free sample font, review new fonts, plus clip art and stock photography.

### Coolfont

http://members.aol.com/fontdude/coolfont.htm

If you are into grunge and other trendy types of fonts Fontdude's site offers a great collection for a modest fee.

## Buttons On the Web

### Welcome to the WebTools Home Page

http://www.artbeatswebtools.com/frdoor.html

Artbeats WebTools is a CD-ROM containing hundreds of Web page elements: buttons, headings, rules, and so on. Download sample images here.

### Download Free Clipart

http://www.sausage.com/clipart.htm

The folks at Sausage Software, makers of the Hot Dog Pro HTML editor, offer some very nice textures, clip art, and buttons for your pages.



### Button World

http://www.demon.co.uk/Tangent/buttons.html

Button World is a collection of blank buttons, each one is optimized for rapid transmission over the Internet. Add text to these buttons and use them on your web pages.

## Clip Art on the Web

### Doubleexposure Homepage Starter Kit

http://www.doubleexposure.com

Icons, buttons, clip art—order collections from this site or download and use some of the sample images they offer.

### Metatools - Metatoys

http://metatoys.metatools.com

Search through over 2,200 images from the Power Photos and MetaPhotos collections online, then purchase and download just the images you want for immediate use.

### Publishers Depot

http://www.publishersdepot.com/

This site calls itself a one-stop site for digital photography, fonts, video, and audio. It pretty much lives up to its claim with thousands of images and resources to choose from.

### Photodisc

http://www.photodisc.com/

Simply the largest collection of royalty free, digital stock photography on the Internet.

## Animation Resources

### Gallery of GIF Animation

http://www.reiworld.com/royalef/galframe.htm

This is one of the best starting points for information on GIF animation resources, samples, and technical information.



### Java Resources

http://studwww.rug.ac.be/~vwillems/JAVA/

Java samples, animations, and lots of links and resources.

## The Web Getting Started

### CERN—Where the Web was Developed

http://www.cern.ch/

CERN, European Laboratory for Particle Physics, this is where the Web was developed. CERN's Expert support: The WWW Support Team runs the main WWW server at CERN and gives general support to WWW information.

### The World Wide Web Consortium

http://www.w3.org/hypertext/WWW/

W3C is an industry consortium which develops common standards for the evolution of the Web by producing specifications and reference software.

### InterNIC Domain Registration Services

http://www.internic.net

The InterNIC is the primary source for domain registration. You can do a search here for names that aren't already taken.

### The List (Internet Service Providers)

http://www.thelist.com/

Get information on over 3,000 ISPs, Internet Service Providers. Listed geographically and by area code.

### c/net Guide to ISPs

http://www.cnet.com/Content/Reviews/Compare/ISP/

Tips on how to choose an ISP along with vital statistics on national and local ISPs. Find out which ISPs live up to their claims, and which you should be wary of until they clean up their act.

### WPD—Magazine Rack

http://www.littleblue.com/webpro/magazinerack.html

The Web Professionals' Digest—Magazine Rack links you to over 75 Web based, Web focused magazines.



### A Beginners Guide to URLs

http://shemp.ncsa.uiuc.edu/NCSA/Staff/SDG/TESTER/Experimental/demoweb/url-primer.html"

What is a URL? A URL is a Uniform Resource Locator. This beginner's guide offers a quick walk through of some of the more common URL types and how to use them.

### Beginners Guide to HTML

http://www.ncsa.uiuc.edu/General/Internet/WWW/HTMLPrimer.html

This is the most requested page on the National Center for Supercomputing Applications (NCSA) Web site. If you are interested in learning HTML this is the starting point.

### Glenn's Cheat Sheet on HTML Style

`http://info.med.yale.edu/caim/StyleManual_Top.HTML`

Learn HTML directly from Yale's Center for Advanced Instructional Media. This site contains concise HTML instructions and tips.

### Submit It

`http://submit-it.permalink.com/submit-it/`

Once you have your site up on the Web you will need to get it listed on search engines, and so on. One of the best places to do this is at Submit it.

## Web Resources

### Shareware.com

`http://www.shareware.com`

If it's shareware you can find it here. Over 200,000 searchable, downloadable software files.

### Bandwidth Conservation Society

`http://www.infohiway.com/faster`

This site is a resource to help Web page designers with an interest in optimizing performance, but still maintaining an appropriate graphic standard. Information on file formats, links to Java applets, and more.

### BrowserWatch

`http://browserwatch.iworld.com`



Go to this site to keep up on the latest news on browsers, plug-ins, and other Web resources.

### Web trends

`http://www.interse.com/webtrends/`

Keep track of which browsers are being used on the Web. This site tracks and graphs browser usage.

### EFF—The Electronic Frontier Foundation

`http://www.eff.org/`

The EFF is an important organization helping to keep the Web free from censorship.

### JavaWorld—Java Jumps

`http://www.javaworld.com/common/jw-jumps.html`

JavaWorlds—Java Jumps this is a comprehensive collection of links to Java resources, collections, tools, and so on.

### The VRML Repository

`http://sdsc.edu/vrml`

The VRML Repository is an impartial, comprehensive, community resource for the dissemination of information relating to VRML. Maintained by the San Diego Supercomputer Center (SDSC).

### The Perl Language Home Page

`http://www.perl.com/perl/index.html`

Learn about Perl a common CGI language, with over 5,000 Perl resources and CGI's.

### CGI Test Cases

`http://hoohoo.ncsa.uiuc.edu/cgi/examples.html`

A collection of CGI's to add forms, animation, functionality, and more to your Web pages.

# Appendix B

## Contributors Listing

For more information on the software, filters, fonts, stock photography, and textures we used to create our Web graphics, please contact the following companies.

### Fonts

International Typeface Corporation

228 East 45th Street - 12th floor

New York, New York 10017

voice: 212/949-8072

fax: 212/949-8485

itc@esselte.com or typeface@aol.com

### Software and Filters

Adobe Systems, Inc.

345 Park Avenue

San Jose, CA 95110-2704

voice: 408/536-6000

800/833-6687

fax: 408/537-6000

http://www.adobe.com

Alien Skin Software

1100 Wake Forest Rd., Suite 101

Raleigh, NC 27604

voice: 919/832-4124

fax: 919/832-4065

alien-skin@alienskin.com

Equilibrium

Three Harbor Drive - Suite 111

Sausalito, CA 94965

voice: 415/332-4343

800/524-8651

fax: 415/332-4433

http://www.equilibrium.com

Equilibrium DeBabelizer® Lite LE $59.00 value—Free!

Yves Piguet

http://iawww.epfl.ch/Staff/Yves.Piguet/

mailto:piguet@ia.epfl.ch

MetaTools

6303 Carpinteria Avenue

Carpinteria, CA 93013

voice: 805/566-6200

800/472-9025

fax: 805/566-6385

KPTSupport@aol.com

Naoto Arakawa

GCA00443@niftyserve.or.jp



Specular International

7 Pomeroy Lane

Amherst, MA 01002

voice: 413/253-3100

fax: 413/253-0540

http://www.specular.com

Xaos Tools Inc.

600 Townsend St. - Suite 270 East

San Francisco, CA 94103

voice: 415/487-7000

800/289-9267

fax: 415/558-9886

macinfo@xaostools.com

## Stock Imagery & Textures

Digital Stock

400 South Sierra Avenue - Suite 100

Solana Beach, CA 92075-2262

voice: 619/794-4040

800/545-4514

fax: 619/794-4041

http://www.digitalstock.com

D'Pix

A Division of Amber Productions, Inc.

414 West Fourth Avenue

PO Box 572

Columbus, OH 43216-0572

voice: 614/299-7192

fax: 614/294-0002

email:amber@infinet.com

Image Club Graphics

A Division of Adobe Systems Inc.

729 Twenty-Fourth Ave. SE

Calgary, AB CANADA

T2G 5K8

voice: 403/262-8008

800/661-9410

fax: 403/261-7013

`http://www.imageclub.com`

Used with express permission. Adobe® and Image Club Graphics™ are trademarks of Adobe Systems Incorporated.

Jawai Interactive

401 East Fourth St. #443

Austin, TX 78701-3745

voice: 512/469-0502

fax: 512/469-7850

`http://www.jawai.com` or sales @jawai.com

PHOTO 24 Texture Resource

7948 Faust Avenue

West Hills, CA 91304

voice: 818/999-4184

800/582-9492 outside CA

fax: 818/999-5704

`http://www.photo24.com` (effective 1/1/97)

PhotoDisc, Inc.

2013 Fourth Avenue - 4th floor

Seattle, WA 98121

voice: 206/441-9355

800/528-3472

fax: 206/441-9379

http://www.photodisc.com

## Production Note

During this book project we used an EPSON Stylus ProXL color ink jet printer and an EPSON ES-1200C scanner.

Some images provided by Digital Stock, D'Pix, Image Club Graphics, Meta Tools, PHOTO 24 and PhotoDisc, 1996.

Some fonts provided by ITC and URW, 1996.

# Appendix C

## What's on the CD-ROM

The CD-ROM that comes with this book is both Macintosh and Windows compatible. Please note: There are several demos and tryouts available for Macintosh users that are not available for Windows users, and vice versa. This means one of two things: either the product has not been created for that platform, or a version of the product is being created but is not yet completed.

We suggest that you refer to the READ ME and other information files included in the demo software program's folder. Also, visit the corporate Web sites; the URLs are noted in the Contributors Listing (Appendix B). There are often demos of new software available for downloading and tryout.

### Contents

The CD-ROM is divided into seven folders:

**WebMagic** This is a collection of ready-to-use files which we created for use with the tutorials. Open this folder, when you need to refer to these files to complete an exercise. Inside the WebMagic folder are several folders. You can use the links.html file to set up our Bookmarks list on your computer for easy Web browsing.

**WebTools** This is a collection of programs that will help you to be more productive when you build your Web graphics.

**Effects** You can use this collection of effects for manipulating images in Photoshop. Featured are a backgrounds and border sampler from ITC (International Typeface Corporation) and an Acrobat PDF file describing the new products from Auto F/X.

**Filters** Within this folder are freeware, some shareware and some commercial demos of popular filters. You can use these filters to modify and change your images into totally new looks. Experiment, have fun. This is where Photoshop helps you to release your creative potential.

**Fonts** Here we have a sample of fonts from ITC, a recognized leader in typeface design and innovation.

**Images** We include a collection of 72 dpi images from leading digital stock photography companies. There are textures for backgrounds and photos for combining with type or building menu bars, icons or buttons.

**Software** Contained in this folder are demos and working copies of commercial software. Included are demos from Adobe and MetaTools, and for Macintosh users Equilibrium DeBabelizer. There are also software demos in the WebTools folder.

### Contents

For detailed instructions on how to install and use the resources located in the CD-ROM folders, please consult the READ ME, ABOUT or START HERE files in the individual company folders. General installation information is as follows:

**WebMagic Files** Copy these files to a folder of your choice on your hard drive.

**Filters** Filters are copied into the Photoshop Plug-ins folder, which is located in the same folder as your Adobe Photoshop application. After copying, restart your computer and then relaunch Photoshop. Select Filter from the menu. These third-party filters will appear at the end of the Adobe standard filters list.

**Fonts** Fonts are placed into the Fonts Folder, which is located in your System Folder. Open the Font folder on the CD-ROM. Drag the font you would like to try out to your closed System Folder. A message will appear stating that the fonts will be moved to Fonts folder. In the case of Type 1 fonts, you will need to drag both the bitmap and printer files to your closed System Folder. Relaunch Photoshop to use the fonts.

**Images and Textures** Refer to the READ ME files accompanying each of these collections for instructions about installation. If there are no special instructions, then you can open these files from within Photoshop. Copy those files to the hard drive that you want to access quickly.



### A Note about Shareware

Please register and support the shareware concept. Follow the guidelines set forth by the author, including, if required, forwarding a modest shareware payment. Your purchase of this book and accompanying CD-ROM does not release you from this obligation. Refer to the READ ME and other information files which accompany each of the programs for additional information.

# Gallery

## Backgrounds

Random Tiles, *page 24*

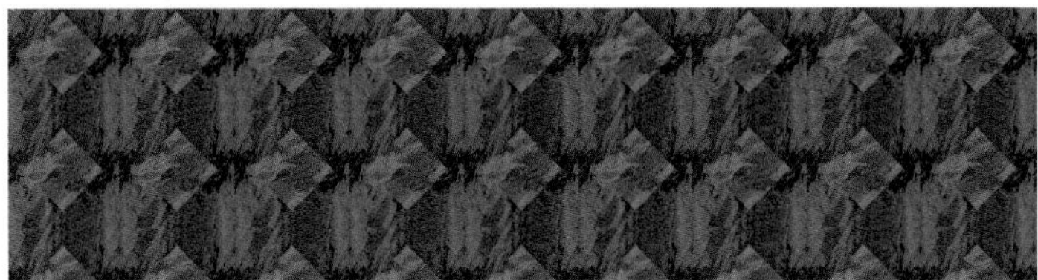

Parquet Tiles, *page 28*

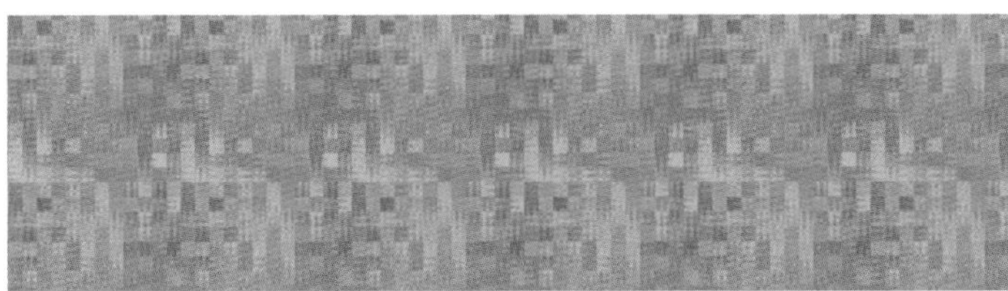

Wave Backgrounds, *page 34*

Tiles on Tiles, *page 38*

Tiling Photos, *page 42*

Type Wallpaper, *page 48*

PostScript Patterns, *page 52*

Diagonal Backgrounds, *page 56*

Borders, *page 60*

Tile Machines

Tile Machines, *page 66*

## Titling

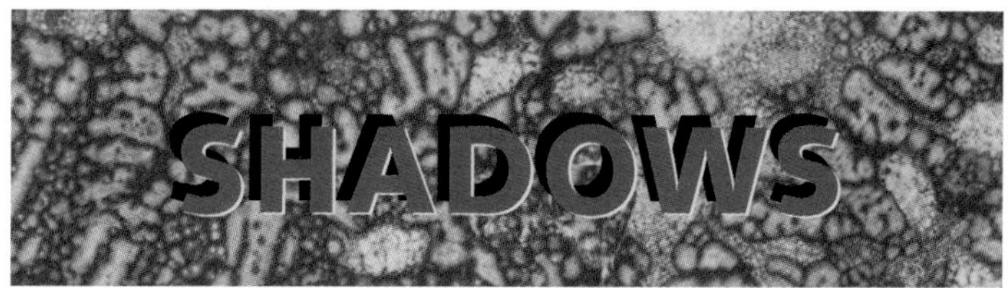


Shadows for Buttons, *page 70*

Object Shadows, *page 72*

Filling Type with an Image, *page 76*

3D Type, *page 80*

OUTLINE CAPS

Outlined Caps, *page 84*

Initial Caps, *page 88*

Free Transform, *page 92*

## Icons

2D Clip Art, *page 98*

Neon, *page 102*

## Rules

Using Custom Brushes, *page 108*

Using Decorative Fonts, *page 112*

## Buttons and Bullets

Basic Gradient, *page 116*

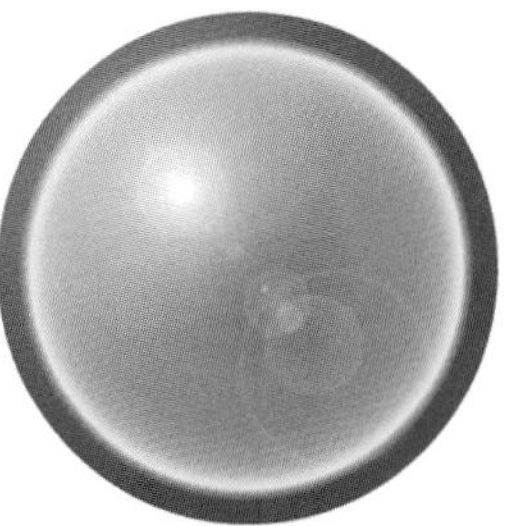

Radial Gradients, *page 120*

Bevel, *page 126*

Multicolored Variations, *page 130*

Globe Buttons, *page 136*

Spherized Photos, *page 142*

Gray on Gray, *page 146*

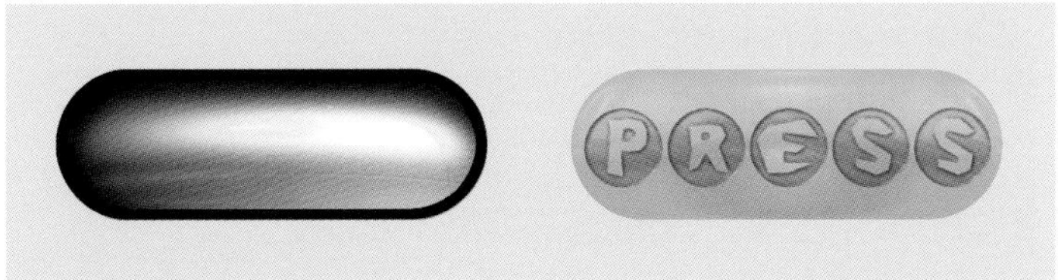


Pill Shaped, *page 152*

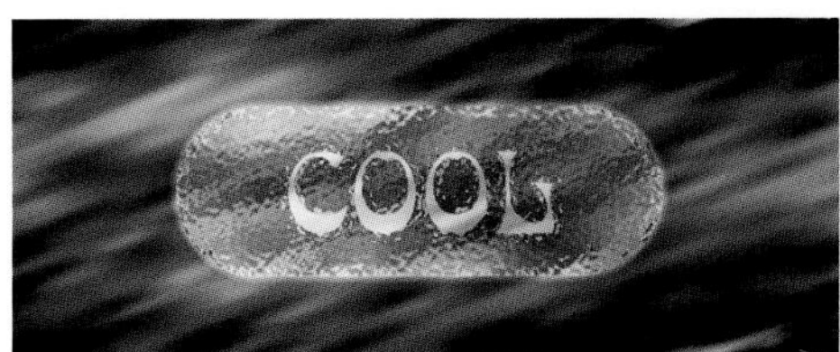


Glass, *page 158*

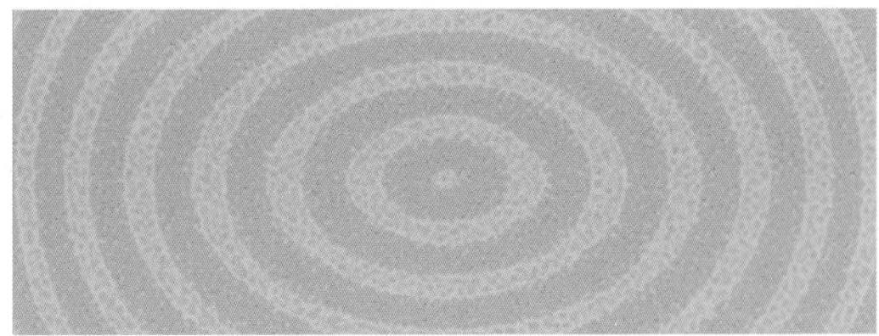

Concentric Circles, *page 162*

Directional Buttons, *page 170*

Objects on Buttons, *page 174*

## Menu Bars

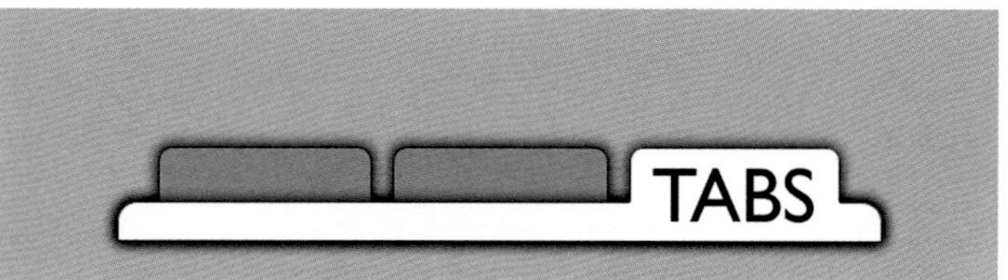


Tabs, *page 180*

Buttons on Image, *page 184*

Gradient Stripes, *page 188*

WHITE ON WHITE

White on White, *page 192*

Cut Outs, *page 196*

Duotones, *page 200*

## Animation

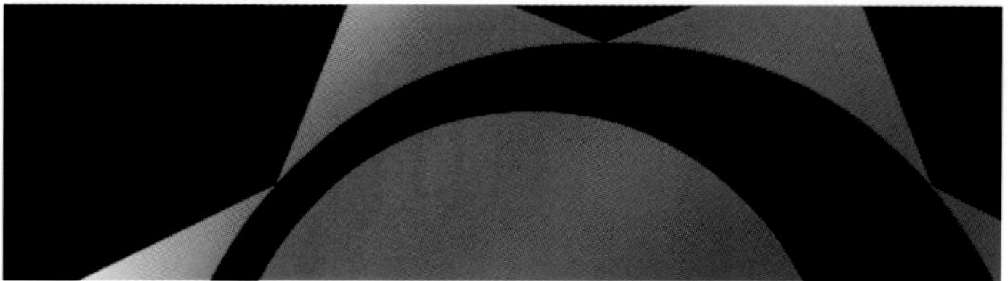

Rotate Animation, *page 206*

Fade Animation

Fade On/Off Animation, *page 210*

Write-On Animation, *page 214*

Three Step Marquee Animation, *page 218*

Twirl Animation, *page 224*

GifBuilder

GifBuilder, *page 232*

GIF Construction Set

GIF Construction Set, *page 236*

# Other DESIGN/GRAPHICS Titles

**Photoshop 4 Studio Skills**
Photoshop 4 Studio Skills is the fast, fun, easy way to learn the features of this powerful graphics program.

- Explore the ins and outs of the newest features of Photoshop 4
- Find out how to create Photoshop images for the web
- Learn how to effectively work in layers and grayscale
- Discover the best methods for working with color

*Steven Moniz*
1-56830-356-4 ■ $35.00 USA/$49.95 CDN
352 pp., 7 3/8 x 9 1/8, Covers PC and Macintosh
*Available Now*

**Adobe FAQ**
1-56830-372-6 ■ $50.00 USA/$71.00 CDN
*Available Now*

**Photoshop Textures Magic**
1-56830-368-8 ■ $39.99 USA/$56.95 CDN
*Available Now*

**Classroom in a Book: Adobe Illustrator**
1-56830-371-8 ■ $45.00 USA/$63.95 CDN
*Available Now*

**Classroom in a Book: Adobe PageMaker**
1-56830-370-x ■ $45.00 USA/$61.95 CDN
*Available Now*

**Classroom in a Book: Adobe Photoshop**
1-56830-317-3 ■ $45.00 USA/$63.95 CDN
*Available Now*

**Illustrator Type Magic**
1-56830-334-3 ■ $39.99 USA/$56.95 CDN
*Available Now*

**Photoshop Magic: Expert Edition**
1-56830-416-1 ■ $55.00 USA/$77.95 CDN
*Available November 1997*

**Illustrator 7 Complete**
1-56830-364-5 ■ $45.00 USA/$63.95 CDN
*Available Now*

**Digital Type Design Guide**
1-56830-190-1 ■ $45.00 USA/$61.95 CDN
*Available Now*

**Digital Prepress Complete**
1-56830-328-9 ■ $55.00 USA/$77.95 CDN
*Available Now*

**Photoshop Type Magic**
1-56830-220-7 ■ $35.00 USA/$47.95 CDN
*Available Now*

**Photoshop Type Magic 2**
1-56830-329-7 ■ $39.99 USA/$56.95 CDN
*Available Now*

**Photoshop 4 Complete**
1-56830-323-8 ■ $45.00 USA/$61.95 CDN
*Available Now*

**PageMaker 6.5 Complete**
1-56830-331-9 ■ $45.00 USA/$61.95 CDN
*Available Now*

**Stop Stealing Sheep & find out how type works**
0-672-48543-5 ■ $19.95 USA/$26.99 CDN
*Available Now*

Copyright © 1997, Macmillan Computer Publishing USA. A Simon & Schuster Company.
The Publishing Operation of Viacom, Inc.

**Visit your fine local bookstore, or for more information visit us at http://www.mcp.com**

# Other Adobe Titles

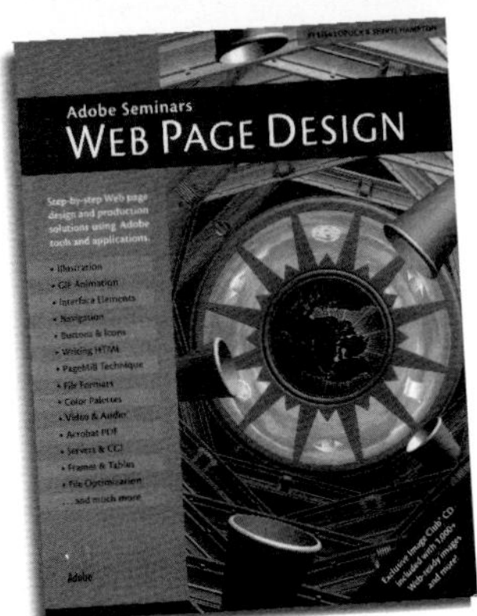


## Adobe Seminars: Web Page Design

All the elements of serving a Web page have been isolated and broken down into accessible components. From buttons to sample CGI scripts, each Web page component is then rebuilt using popular Adobe applications to simulate how Web pages are actually created. The result is a reference book of clear, simple explanations and effective design and production techniques that are reusable page after Web page.

*Lisa Lopuck and Sheryl Hampton*
1-56830-426-9 ■ $40.00 USA/$57.00 CAN
241 PP
*Available Now*

**Adobe Persuasion: Classroom in a Book**
1-56830-316-5 ■ $40.00 US/$56.95 CAN
*Available Now*

**Adobe Premiere for Macintosh: Classroom in a Book, 2E**
1-56830-119-7 ■ $49.95 US/$65.95 CAN
*Available Now*

**Adobe Premiere for Windows: Classroom in a Book, 2E**
1-56830-172-3 ■ $50.00 US/$68.95 CAN
*Available Now*

**Adobe Pagemill 2.0: Classroom in a Book**
1-56830-319-X ■ $40.00 US/$57.00 CAN
*Available Now*

**Adobe After Effects: Classroom in a Book**
1-56830-369-6 ■ $45.00 US/$59.00 CAN
*Available Now*

**Interactivity by Design**
1-56830-221-5 ■ $40.00 US/$54.95 CAN
*Available Now*

**Internet Publishing with Acrobat**
1-56830-300-9 ■ $40.00 US/$54.95 CAN
*Available Now*

**Adobe Illustrator: Classroom in a Book**
1-56830-371-8 ■ $45.00 US/$59.00 CAN
*Available Now*

**Adobe Pagemaker: Classroom in a Book**
1-56830-370-X ■ $45.00 US/$64.00 CAN
*Available Now*

**Adobe Photoshop: Classroom in a Book**
1-56830-371-3 ■ $45.00 US/$59.00 CAN
*Available Now*

**Branding with Type**
1-56830-248-7 ■ $18.00 US/$25.00 CAN
*Available Now*

**Adobe Framemaker: Classroom in a Book**
1-56830-399-8 ■ $45.00 US/$63.95 CAN
*Available Now*

**Design Essentials, 2E**
1-56830-093-X ■ $40.00 US/$54.95 CAN
*Available Now*

**Adobe Designing Business**
1-56830-282-7 ■ $60.00 US/$81.95 CAN
*Available Now*

**Stop Stealing Sheep & Find Out How Type Works**
0-672-48543-5 ■ $19.95 US/$26.99 CAN
*Available Now*

Copyright © 1998, Macmillan Computer Publishing USA. A Simon & Schuster Company.
The Publishing Operation of Viacom, Inc.

# Turn to the *Authoritative* Encyclopedia of Computing

You'll find over 150 full text books online, hundreds of shareware/freeware applications, online computing classes and 10 computing resource centers full of expert advice from the editors and publishers of:

- Adobe Press
- BradyGAMES
- Cisco Press
- Hayden Books
- Lycos Press
- New Riders
- Que
- Que Education & Training
- Sams Publishing
- Waite Group Press
- Ziff-Davis Press

When you're looking for computing information, consult the authority. The Authoritative Encyclopedia of Computing at mcp.com.

## Get the best information and learn about latest developments in:

- Design
- Graphics and Multimedia
- Enterprise Computing and DBMS
- General Internet Information
- Operating Systems
- Networking and Hardware
- PC and Video Gaming
- Productivity Applications
- Programming
- Web Programming and Administration
- Web Publishing

# Technical Support

If you need assistance with the information provided by Macmillan Computer Publishing, please access the information available on our web site at **http://www.mcp.com/feedback.** Our most Frequently Asked Questions are answered there. If you do not find the answers to your questions on our web site, you may contact Macmillan User Services at **(317) 581-3833** or email us at **support@mcp.com**.

# REGISTRATION CARD

## Photoshop Web Magic, Volume 1

Name ______________________ Title ______________

Company______________________ Type of business ______________

Address ______________________

City/State/ZIP ______________________

Have you used these types of books before? ☐ yes ☐ no

If yes, which ones? ______________________

______________________

How many computer books do you purchase each year? ☐ 1–5 ☐ 6 or more

How did you learn about this book? ______________________

☐ recommended by a friend
☐ recommended by store personnel
☐ saw in catalog
☐ received ad in mail
☐ read book review
☐ saw on bookshelf

Where did you purchase this book? ______________________

Which applications do you currently use? ______________________

Which computer magazines do you subscribe to? ______________________

What trade shows do you attend? ______________________

Please number the top three factors which most influenced your decision for this book purchase.

☐ cover
☐ approach to content
☐ logo
☐ layout/design
☐ price
☐ author's reputation
☐ publisher's reputation
☐ other ______________

Would you like to be placed on our preferred mailing list? ☐ yes ☐ no e-mail address ______________

☐ **I would like to see my name in print!** You may use my name and quote me in future Hayden products and promotions. My daytime phone number is: ______________________

Comments ______________________

______________________

______________________

**Hayden Books** Attn: Product Marketing ◆ 201 West 103rd Street ◆ Indianapolis, Indiana 46290 USA

Visit our Web Page **http://WWW.MCP.com**

Fold Here

NO POSTAGE
NECESSARY
IF MAILED
IN THE
UNITED STATES

POSTAGE WILL BE PAID BY THE ADDRESSEE

HAYDEN BOOKS
Attn: Product Marketing
201 W 103RD ST
INDIANAPOLIS IN 46290-9058

# Photoshop Type Magic 2

Stanger
Stet · Fortuna · Domus

# Photoshop Type Magic 2

BY GREG SIMSIC

# Photoshop Type Magic 2

©1996 Hayden Books

All rights reserved. Printed in the United States of America. No part of this book may be used or reproduced in any form or by any means, or stored in a database or retrieval system, without prior written permission of the publisher except in the case of brief quotations embodied in critical articles and reviews. Making copies of any part of this book for any purpose other than your own personal use is a violation of United States copyright laws. For information, address Hayden Books, 201 W. 103rd Street, Indianapolis, Indiana 46290.

Library of Congress Catalog Number: 96-77856
ISBN: 1-56830-329-7

Copyright © 1996 Hayden Books

Printed in the United States of America 3 4 5 6 7 8 9 0

## Warning and Disclaimer

This book is sold as is, without warranty of any kind, either express or implied. While every precaution has been taken in the preparation of this book, the author and Hayden Books assume no responsibility for errors or omissions. Neither is any liability assumed for damages resulting from the use of the information or instructions contained herein. It is further stated that the publisher and author are not responsible for any damage or loss to your data or your equipment that results directly or indirectly from your use of this book.

**President of Developer, Technical and Graphics Group**
Richard Swadley

**Associate Publisher**
John Pierce

**Publishing Manager**
Melanie Rigney

**Managing Editor**
Lisa Wilson

**Marketing Manager**
Stacey Oldham

**Acquisitions and Development Editor**
Beth Millett

**Production Editor**
Kevin Laseau

**Technical Editor**
Gary Adair

**Publishing Coordinator**
Rachel Byers

**Cover Designer**
Aren Howell

**Book Designer**
Gary Adair

**Manufacturing Coordinator**
Brook Farling

**Production Team Supervisors**
Joe Millay
Regina Rexrode

**Production Team**
Trina Brown, Dan Caparo, Aleata Howard, Linda Knose, Christopher Morris, Scott Tullis, Pamela Woolf

## About the Author

**Greg Simsic**

*Photoshop Type Magic 2* is Greg's second book, following his coauthorship of the successful *Photoshop Type Magic*. He has done freelance design work for the likes of BradyGAMES Publishing and DayDream, Inc. Greg holds a degree in the liberal arts from Ball State University and is currently a student of sculpture at Herron School of Art in Indianapolis. While not staring lovingly into his magic crystal computer monitor, Greg roams across the midwestern landscape looking for loose change.

## Trademark Acknowledgments

All terms mentioned in this book that are known to be trademarks or service marks have been appropriately capitalized. Hayden Books cannot attest to the accuracy of this information. Use of a term in this book should not be regarded as affecting the validity of any trademark or service mark.

Apple, Mac, Macintosh, and Power Macintosh are registered trademarks and AppleScript is a trademark of Apple Computer, Inc. Microsoft and Windows are registered trademarks and Windows NT is a trademark of Microsoft Corporation in the USA and other countries.

## Dedication

This book is dedicated to the flowers next to my computer.

- Greg

## Special Thanks to...

David, Becky, Michael, Rich, and Gary for making the first volume of *Photoshop Type Magic* a success and making this second volume possible.

Beth and the rest of the Hayden team for making the making of this book so easy.

Adobe for creating an application that allows my wandering mind a way to earn a living.

## Hayden Books

The staff of Hayden Books is committed to bringing you the best computer books. What our readers think of Hayden is important to our ability to serve our customers. If you have any comments, no matter how great or how small, we'd appreciate your taking the time to send us a note.

You can reach Hayden Books at the following address:

Hayden Books
201 West 103rd Street
Indianapolis, IN 46290
317-581-3833

Email addresses:

America Online: Hayden Bks
Internet: hayden@hayden.com

Visit the Hayden Books Web site at `http://www.hayden.com`

# Contents at a Glance

# Contents

# Introduction

I just couldn't stop. I was fooling around on my Mac again, and out popped a few more type effects to keep you busy.

Perhaps you peeked in to see what's new. Unfortunately, there is nothing new. It's the same old, boring thing—great type that's easy to make. If you're just getting started with Photoshop, then do not fear—the special blue type radiates a magical field of power that will transform you into...no, no, no. The blue type refers you to special instructions in the Photoshop Basics section of the book. If you know your way around Photoshop then you can zip right through the uncluttered—but informative—steps that take you through techniques that will spur your own creative and technical forces into action.

Don't forget to check out all the stuff on the CD, keep brushing your teeth, and experiment, experiment, experiment! Oh, wait...toothpaste type. Hmmm... There's work to do. Gotta go. Happy typing.

Greg Simsic

# Before You Start

## Welcome

Welcome to this second volume of special type techniques for Adobe Photoshop users. More than a how-to manual—this book is a what-to guide. The steps in this book tell you exactly what you need to do in order to create exactly what you want. Flip through the alphabetized thumbtabs to find the type effect you want to create and follow the concise, explanatory steps. If you need a little extra help, flip to the "Photoshop Basics" section. But, before you jump into the type treatments, let me tell you a little about how this book works. A quick read now will maximize your time later.

## System Setup

Here are the system recommendations for creating these type treatments.

Mac users: The Adobe Photoshop 4.0 Info box suggests a memory allocation of 21 megabytes (MB) of RAM to run Photoshop. And your system software may need as much as 10MB of RAM. That's a full bowl of soup, but if you've got the memory, then I would recommend setting the Preferred memory size even higher than 21MB. If you don't have 21MB to spare, then just quit all other applications and give it everything you've got. Generally, I give Photoshop 40MB of RAM.

PC users: Adobe suggests 32MB of RAM for Photoshop on any 386 or faster processor running Windows 3.1, Windows 95, or Windows NT, but 40MB is better. Quit any application you can before starting Photoshop to maximize the running of the application. Photoshop runs 32-bit native on both Windows 95 and Windows NT operating systems.

It is not crucial, but it will help if you have a CD-ROM drive. A number of the effects in this book use files that are contained on the CD that comes with this book. (See Appendix B, "What's on the CD-ROM," for information on accessing those files.) However, even if you don't have a CD-ROM drive, you still can perform all of the effects described in the book.



## Adobe Photoshop 4.0

All of the techniques in this book were created with Adobe Photoshop 4.0, and that's the version I recommend you use. If you're attempting to duplicate these techniques using an earlier version of Photoshop, your results may differ slightly or significantly. If you're working with version 3.0, then you still will be able to create all of the effects in the book. However, keep in mind you will need to adjust the instructions for the differences between the two versions. You will see that even some of the old Photoshop features work differently in Photoshop 4.0. Most of the effects in this book use features that were not available in earlier versions of Photoshop.

## Conventions

Every image in this book was created initially as a RGB file. You can make your effects in any appropriate color mode, but you should be aware of the variations this will cause as you proceed through the steps. For example, the first new channel created in an RGB file is automatically named Channel #4. But the first new channel created in a CMYK file is named Channel #5. You also should be aware of the differences in the color ranges of the various color modes. Some colors that look great in RGB mode may look like mud after you convert the file color mode to CMYK. **Note:** Quite a few techniques in this book use the Lighting Effects filter. This filter will not work in a CMYK or Grayscale file.

If you would like more detailed information about the different color modes, refer to a good general book such as *Adobe Photoshop Classroom in a Book*, or to your user manuals.

Also, every type image (except Fur) was created as a 5-inch by 2-inch, 150-dpi resolution file. (The thumbtab images were created as 300 dpi files.) If you are going to work in a resolution other than 150 dpi, remember that some of the filters and commands will require different settings than the settings I used. Because there are fewer pixels in a 72 dpi image, a Gaussian Blur radius of 5 pixels will blur the image more than if it were a 150 dpi image. Just keep an eye on the figures next to the steps and match the outcome as close as you can.

## The Toolbox

For some of the effects, I used a third-party filter or a specially prepared preset file. Any of these extras tools that are not included with the standard Photoshop software are listed in the Toolbox in the lower-left corner of the first page of each technique. The Toolbox lists everything that you will need to create each type effect and any of its variations. The CD-ROM that comes with this book contains all the files needed to perform all of the basic techniques. For information on accessing these files, turn to Appendix B, "What's on the CD-ROM."



## The Steps

### The Blue Type

As you work through the steps, you will see phrases that are colored a light blue. These same phrases are listed in alphabetical order in the "Photoshop Basics" section. If the phrase in blue asks you to perform a task that you are unfamiliar with, then you can find that phrase in the "Photoshop Basics" section and follow the instructions on how to perform that task. Advanced users can perform the task as they normally would.

## Menu Commands

You also will see instructions that look like this:

Filter➛Blur➛Gaussian Blur (2 pixels)
This example asks you to apply the Gaussian Blur filter. To perform this command, click on the Filter menu at the top of the screen and drag down to Blur. When Blur is highlighted a new menu opens to the right, from which you can choose Gaussian Blur.

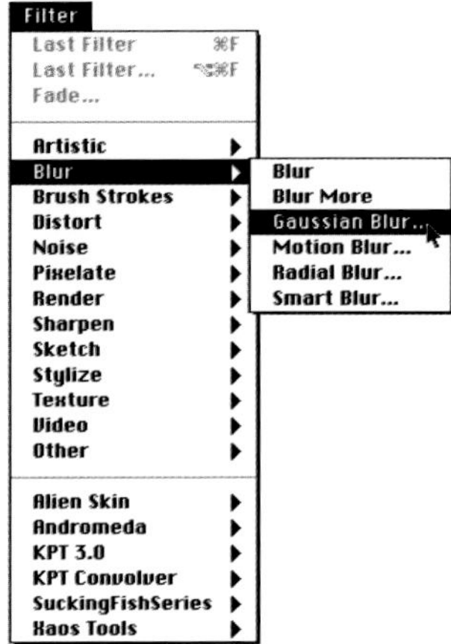


In this example, a dialog box appears asking you for more information. All of the settings that you need to perform each task appear in the text of the step. The previous example tells you to enter 2 pixels as the Radius.

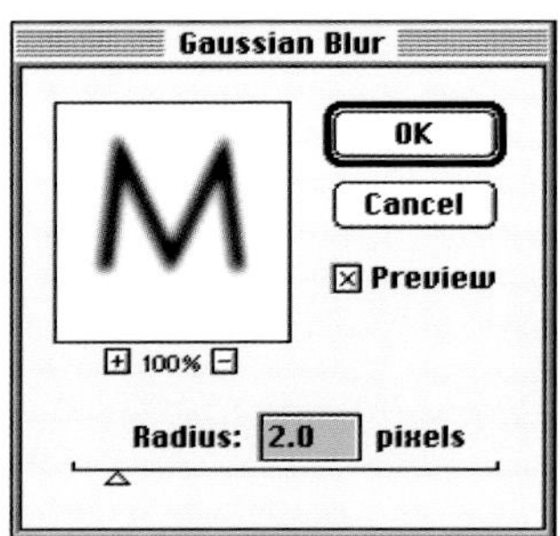


Click OK to blur the type.

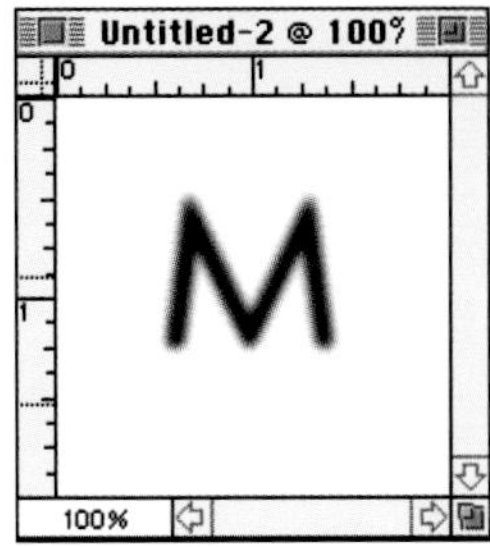


### Settings

Following each action in the steps, you will find the settings for that feature. These recommended settings are meant to act as guides; the best settings for your type effect may vary. As a rule of thumb, it is best to match the outcome that you see in the figures as you progress through the technique. The greatest differences occur when the resolution of your file or the point size of your type are significantly different from what I used. The following two images demonstrate the importance of adjusting for resolution differences. A 6-pixel Radius Gaussian Blur was applied to both images.

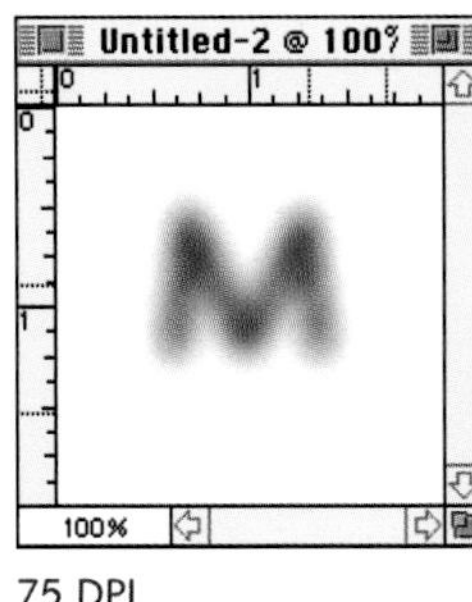


75 DPI

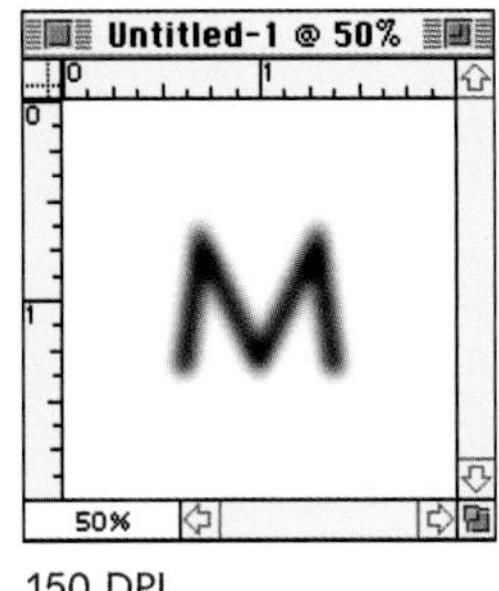


150 DPI



### Tips

Throughout the book, you will find additional bits of information to help you render a better type effect. These tips provide information beyond the basic steps of each lesson. ■

# Photoshop Basics

The goal of this section is to help new and novice users of Photoshop with the simple, basic tasks required to create the type effects described and illustrated in this book. Each of the basic tasks described in this section corresponds to the blue highlighted text in the chapters that follow. Here, users can easily find the instructions they need for performing a particular Photoshop task.

This chapter proceeds on two assumptions: that you're creating our type effects in Photoshop 4.0; and that you're keeping the Tool and Layer/Channel/Path palettes open. If one or both of the Tool and Layer/Channel/Path palettes are closed when you refer to this chapter, you can reopen them by name by using the Window menu at the top of the screen. If you're using an earlier version of Photoshop, you can refer to the Photoshop manual for instructions on how to perform these tasks. Also keep in mind that Photoshop 2.5 does not offer the capability to work in layers.

## The Tools Palette

If you're not familiar with Photoshop's Tool palette, there's no reason to panic. With a bit of experimentation, it doesn't take long to learn each tool's individual functions. To help the beginning Photoshop user along the way, here is a representation of the toolbars from both Photoshop 3.0 and 4.0. This will also help advanced users find the rearranged tools.

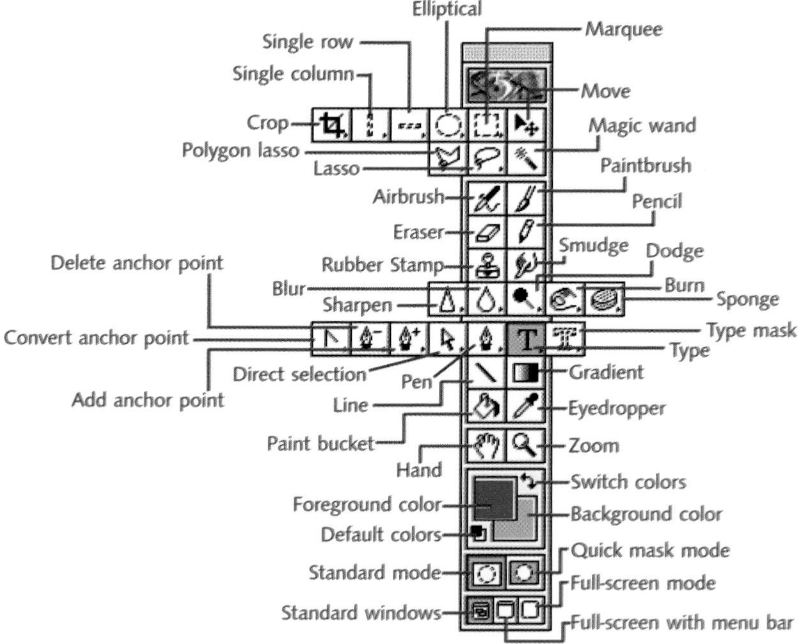


**Photoshop 4.0 toolbar**

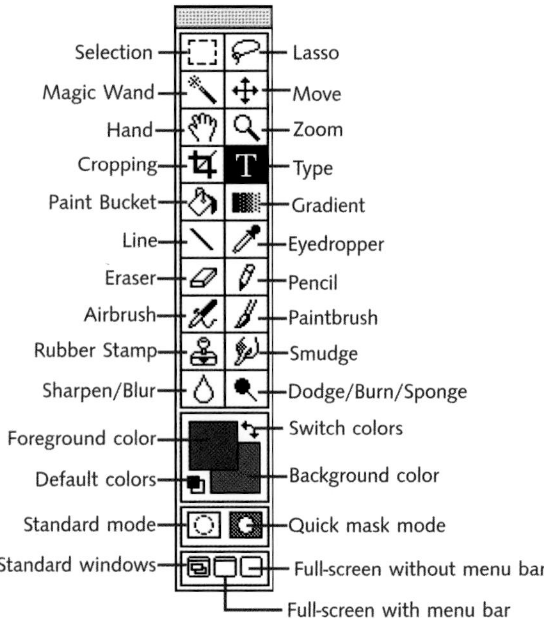


**Photoshop 3.0 toolbar**

## Basic Photoshop Tasks

### Choose a Foreground or Background Color

**Shortcuts:** Press D to change colors to their defaults: black for the Foreground, and white for the Background.

Press X to switch the Foreground color with the Background color.

To change the Foreground or Background color click on either the Foreground icon or the Background icon.

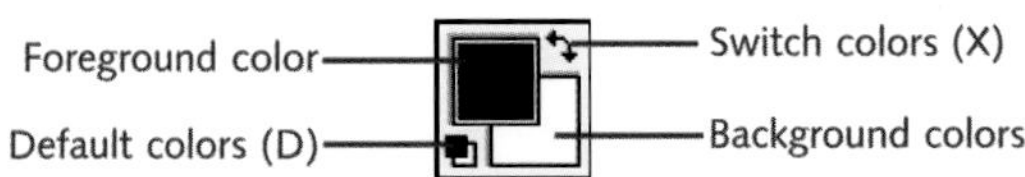


The Color Picker dialog box appears, which enables you to choose a new Foreground or Background color by moving and clicking the cursor (now a circle) along the spectrum box, or by changing specific RGB, CMYK, or other percentage values. Note that the Foreground and Background icons on the Tool palette now reflect your color choices.

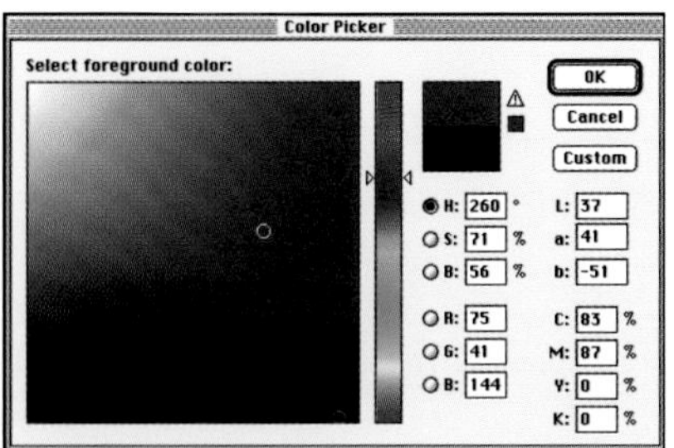


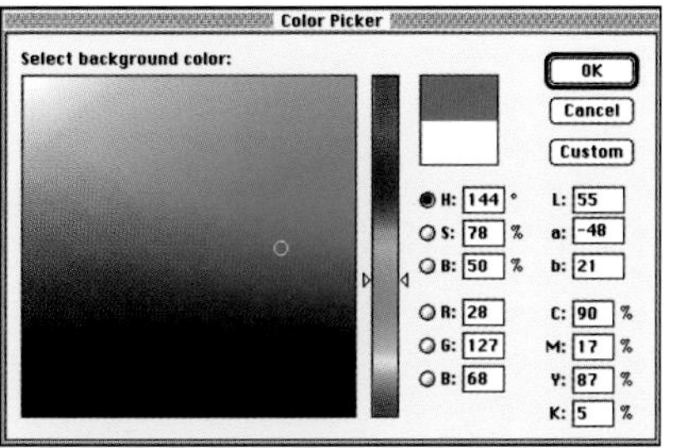

## Convert to a New Mode

To convert from one color mode to another, click on the Image menu at the top of the screen and scroll down to the Mode selection. You then can scroll down to select the mode of your preference. For example, if you want to switch from CMYK mode to Multichannel mode, you choose Image→Mode→Multichannel. The checkmark to the left of CMYK will move down to Multichannel, indicating that you are now in Multichannel mode.

**TIP** **Remember that there is a different range of colors available for each color mode. No matter what color mode the file is in onscreen, your printer (if it prints in color) is going to print your work in CMYK. Because the color ranges for RGB and CMYK are different, you should convert your RGB image to CMYK before printing. Otherwise, you may be in for a big surprise when your bright green prints as a dull tan.**

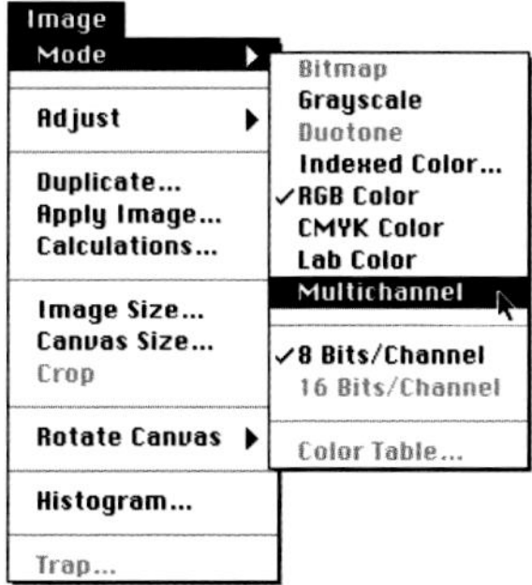


## Create a Layer Mask

To create a layer mask, choose Layer→Add Layer Mask, and choose either Reveal All (white) or Hide All (black). For the purposes of the effects in this book, always choose Reveal All. A layer mask is used to mask out (or hide) specified parts of a layer.

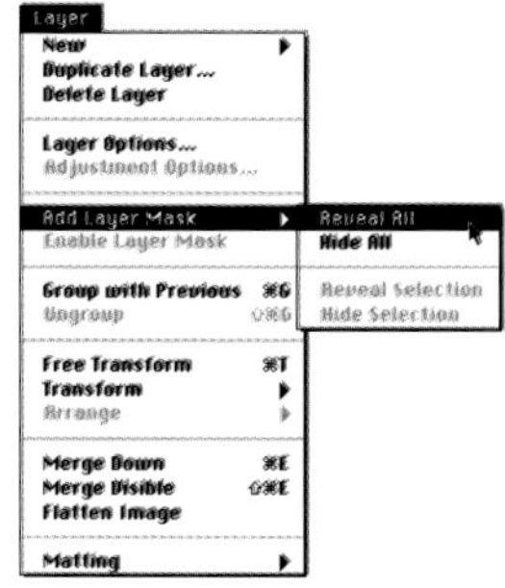


## Create a New Channel

**Shortcuts:** Click the New Channel icon on the Channels palette.

To create a new channel, choose New Channel from the Channels palette pop-up menu.

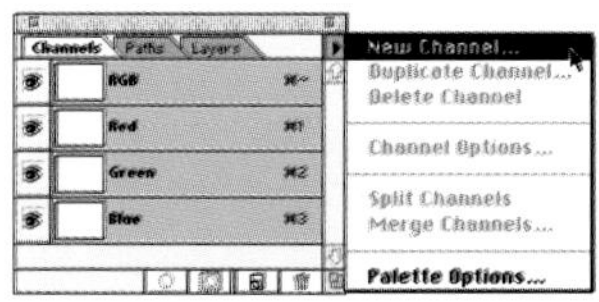


Use the Channel Options dialog box to establish your settings. Unless noted otherwise, we used the default settings when creating a new channel. This figure shows Photoshop's default settings.

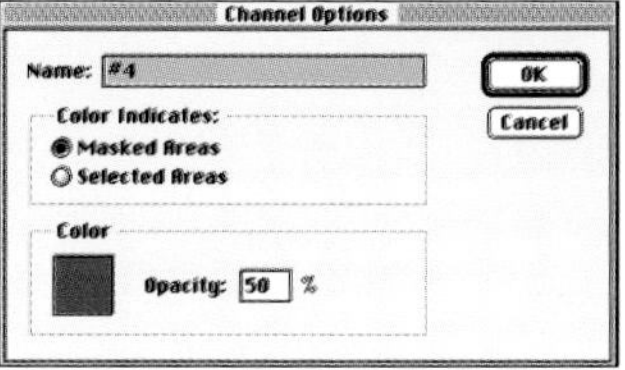


## Create a New File

**Shortcuts:** Press Command-N [Control-N].

To create a new file, choose File➞New. The New dialog box appears, which is where you name your new file and establish other settings. See Part I, "About this Book," for information on the conventions that were used when creating new files for the type effects in this book.

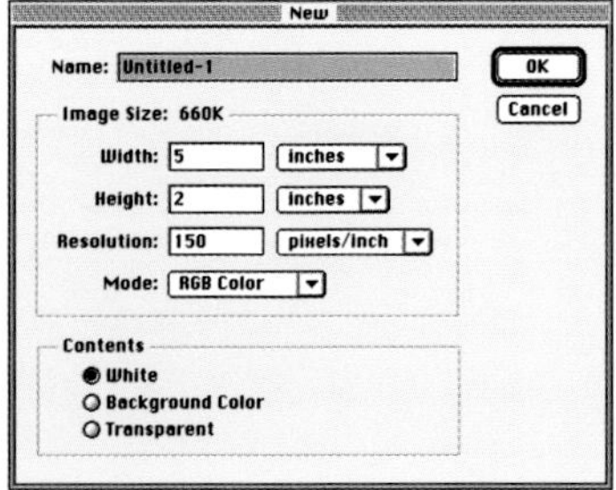


## Create a New Layer

**Shortcuts:** Click the New Layer icon on the Layers palette.

To create a new layer, choose New Layer from the Layer palette pop-up menu, or choose Layer➛New➛Layer.

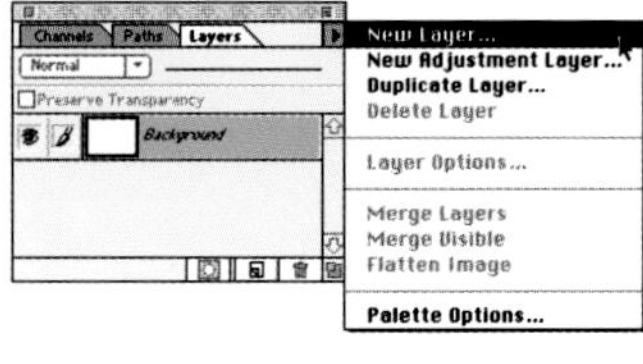


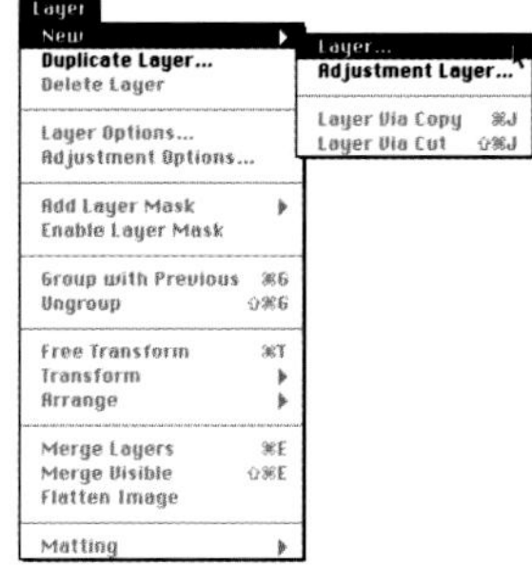


The New Layer dialog box opens, which is where you name the new layer and establish other settings.

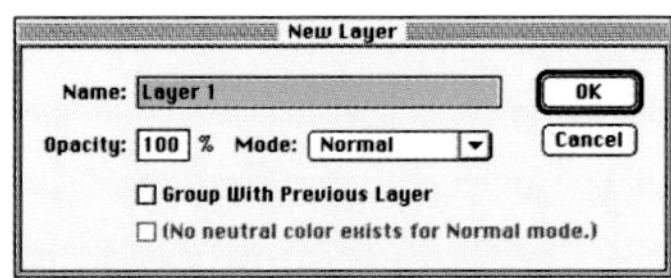


## Delete a Channel

To delete a channel, go to the Channels palette and select the channel you want to delete; drag it to the Trash icon at the lower-right corner (just like you would to get rid of a document on the Desktop). You also can select the channel you want to delete, and choose Delete Channel from the Channels palette arrow menu.

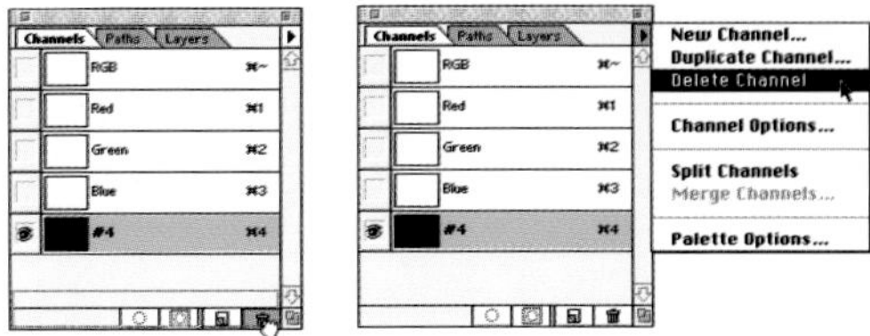


## Deselect a Selection

**Shortcut:** Press Command [Control]-D.

To deselect a selection, choose Select➾None. The marquee disappears.

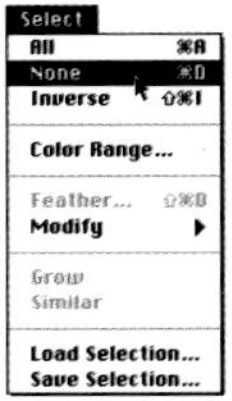


## Duplicate a Channel

**Shortcut:** Click the channel you want to duplicate, and drag it on top of the New Channel icon.

To create a duplicate of a channel, make the channel active and then select Duplicate Channel from the Channels palette pop-up menu.

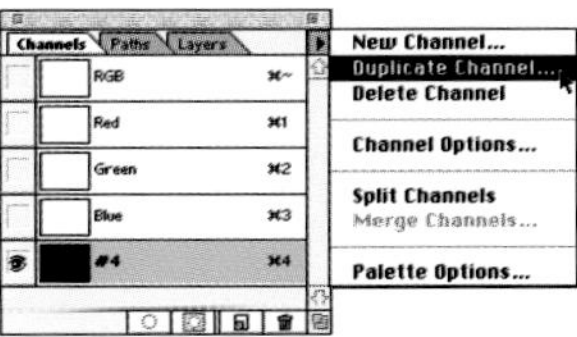


A new copy of the channel you selected for duplication is created automatically, and the Duplicate Channel dialog box appears.

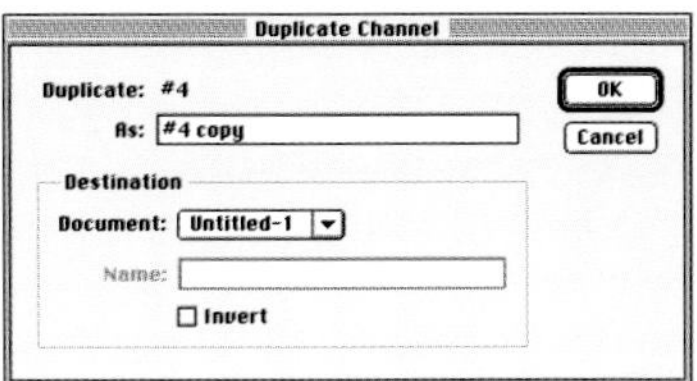

### Enter/Exit Quick Mask

**Shortcuts:** Press Q to enter and exit the Quick Mask mode.

Click the Quick Mask icon to switch to Quick Mask mode; conversely, click the Standard mode icon to return to Standard mode.

Essentially a Quick Mask is a temporary channel. When you're in Quick Mask mode you can use any of the Photoshop tools and functions to change the selection without changing the image. When you switch back to Standard mode you'll have a new selection.

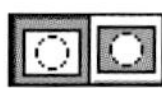

### Enter the Text

There are two Type tools in Photoshop 4.0; the standard Type tool and the Type Mask tool. Each effect in this book specifies which type tool to use.

Before entering the text using the standard Type tool, make sure that the foreground color is set to your desired text color. Often, the instructions in this book ask you to enter text into a channel. Unless noted otherwise, it is assumed that you are entering white text onto the black background of the channel. If you are entering text into a layer, then the standard Type tool will create a new layer for the type.

The Type Mask tool creates selection outlines of the text you enter without filling the outlines with a new color, and without creating a new layer.

To enter the text, select the type tool that you want to use, and then click anywhere in the image to open the Type Tool dialog box. Type the text in the large box at the bottom of the dialog box, and make your attribute choices from the options (listed previously). Unless noted otherwise in the instructions, always make sure that you have the Anti-Aliased box checked.



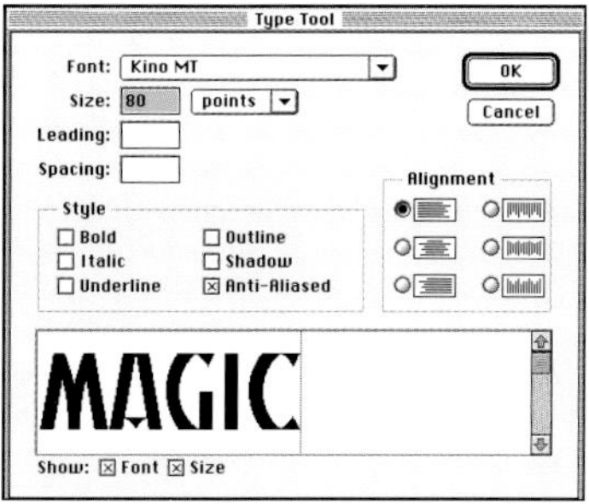


After clicking OK, move the type into position with the Move (standard Type tool) or Marquee (Type Mask tool) tool.

### Fill a Selection with Foreground or Background Color

First, select the Foreground or Background color you wish to use (see page 6 in this section for instructions). Keep the selection active and press the Option-Delete keys to fill the selection with the Foreground color. If you are in the Background layer or any layer that has the Preserve Transparency option turned on, then you can press Delete to fill in the selection with the Background color.

You also can fill in your selections by choosing Edit➙Fill.

This causes the Fill dialog box to appear, allowing you to establish the Contents option you wish to use, the Opacity, and the blending Mode.

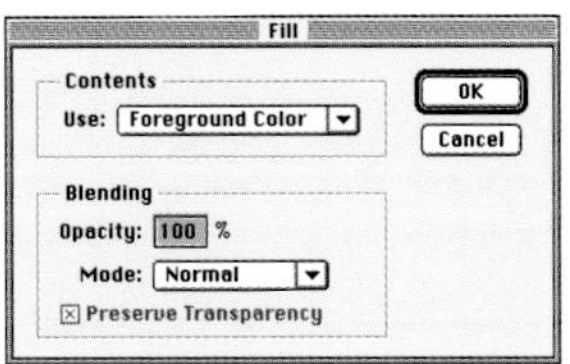


**TIP** **If a selection is empty (a transparent area of a layer) and the Preserve Transparency option is turned on for that layer, then you will not be able to fill the selection. To fill the selection, simply turn off the Preserve Transparency option before filling it.**

### Flatten an Image

To flatten an image (merge all the layers into a single layer), choose Flatten Image from the Layers palette arrow menu, or choose Layer➙Flatten Image.

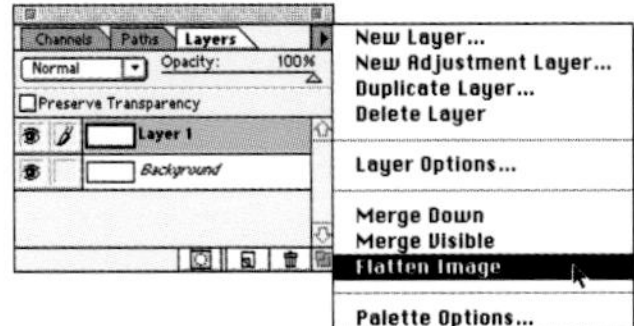

## Load a Selection

**Shortcut:** Hold down the Command key and click on the channel (on the Channels palette) that contains the selection you want to load.

To load a selection, choose Select➡Load Selection. This brings up the Load Selection dialog box, where you can establish document, channel, and operation variables.

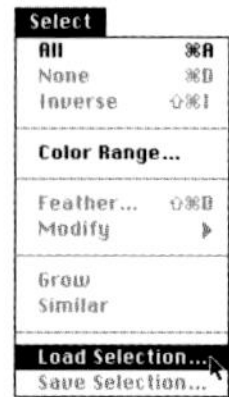


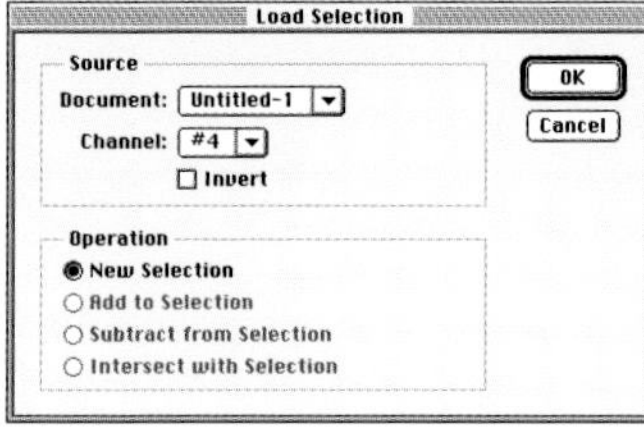


## Load the Transparency Selection (of a Layer)

To load the transparency selection of a layer, hold down the Command key and click on the layer (on the Layers palette) that contains the transparency selection you want to load.

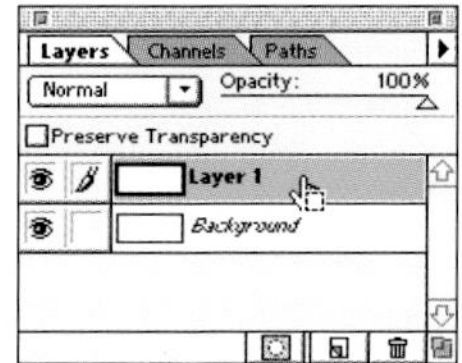


## Make a Channel Active

To make a channel active for editing or modification, click on its thumbnail or title on the Channels palette.

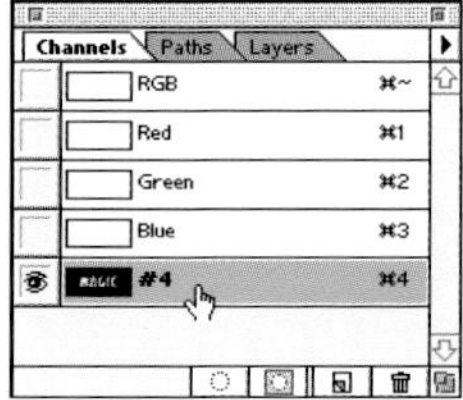


You can tell the channel is active if it is highlighted with a color.

### Make a Layer Active

To make a layer active, click on its thumbnail or title in the Layers palette.

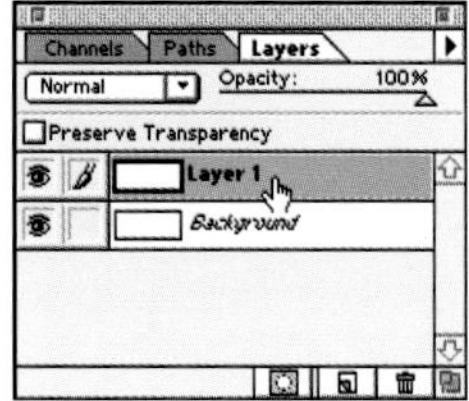

You can tell the layer is active if it is highlighted with a color.

### Make a Layer Visible/Invisible

To make a Layer visible, click in the left-most column in the Layers palette. If an eye appears, then the layer is visible. If the column is empty, then that layer is hidden (invisible).

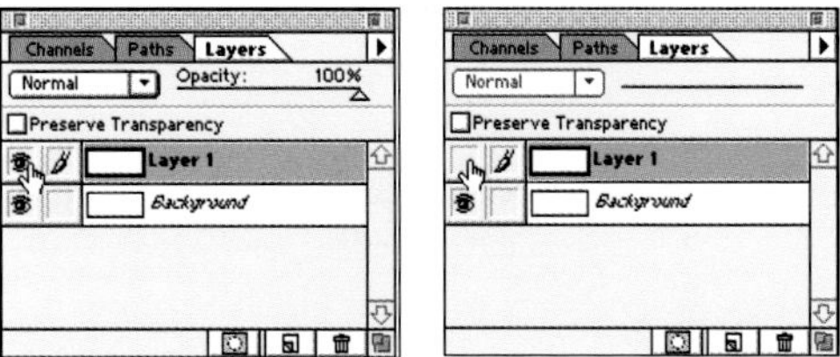

### Move a Layer

To move a Layer, click on the layer you want to move in the Layers palette and drag it up or down the list of layers to the place you want to move it. As you drag the layer, the lines between the layers will darken to indicate where the layer will fall if you let go.

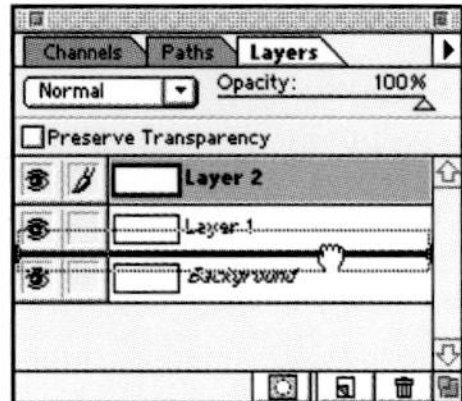

The layer you moved will appear numerically out of order.

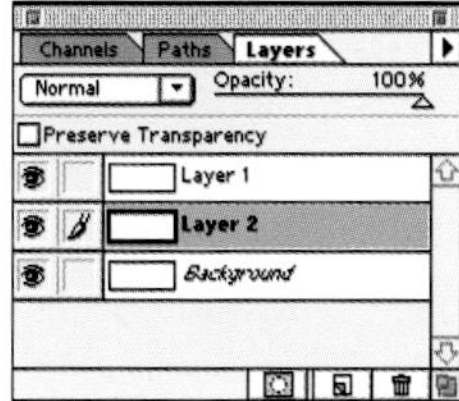


## Return to the Composite Channel

**Shortcut:** Press Command-`.

If you want to return to the composite channel, click on its thumbnail or title (RGB, CMYK, Lab). The composite channel always will be the one with (Command-~) [Control-~] after its title.

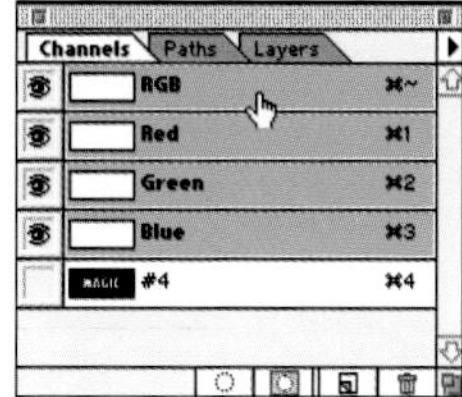


If you are in an RGB file, the first four channels should now be active because each of the R, G, and B channels are individual parts of the RGB channel.

## Save a File

To save a file, choose File➡Save As. This displays the Save As dialog box, where you name your new file and choose a format in which to save it.

File format selection depends on what you have in your file, what you want to keep when you save it, and what you're going to do with the file after it is saved. Consult a detailed Photoshop book, such as *Adobe Photoshop Classroom in a Book*, for more guidance on which file format is best for your needs.

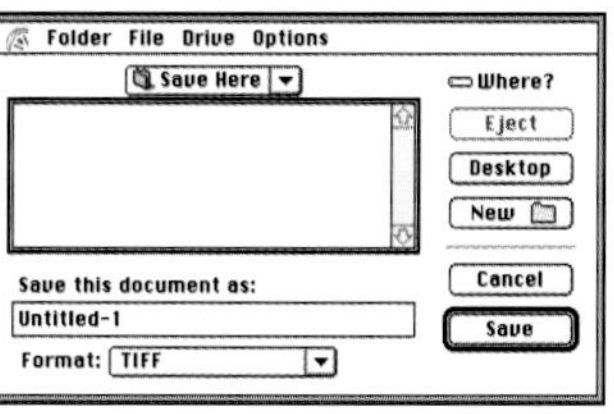

## Save a Selection

**Shortcut:** Click the Save Selection icon on the Channels palette.

To save a selection, choose Select➔Save Selection.

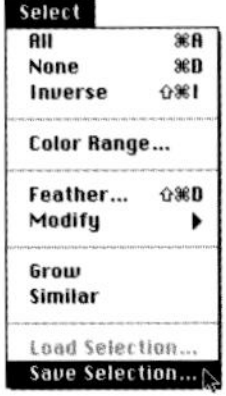


The Save Selection dialog box opens. Choose your options and click OK to save the selection.

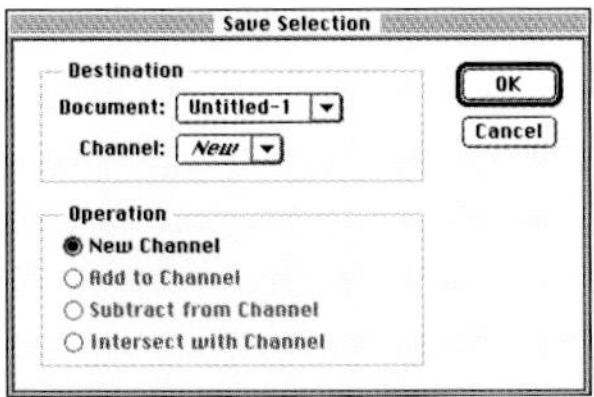


## Switch Foreground/Background Colors

**Shortcut:** Press X to switch the Foreground and Background colors.

To switch the foreground and background colors, click on the Switch Colors icon. This flips the two colors shown in this icon only, and does not affect the rest of the image.

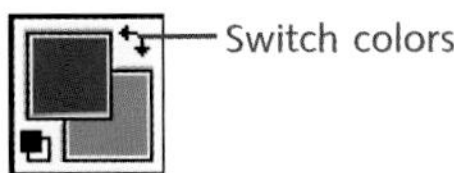


## Switch to Default Colors

**Shortcut:** Press D to switch to the default foreground and background colors.

To change the foreground and background colors to black and white respectively, click on the Default Colors icon.

## Turn On/Off Preserve Transparency

To turn on or off the Preserve Transparency option for a particular layer, first make that layer the active layer. Then, click the Preserve Transparency checkbox on the Layers palette. This option is not available for the Background layer. ■

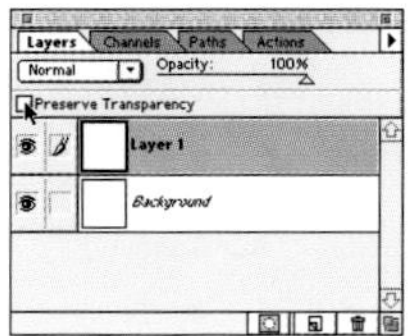

Follow the bouncing balls, or rather the numbered steps, to create a shaded sphere onto which you can lay type.

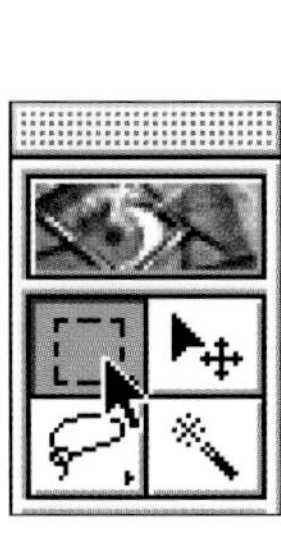

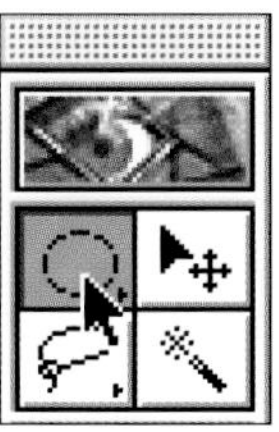

1 Create a new file. Click the Marquee tool on the Tools floating palette to select it. You can scroll through the different Marquee tools by holding down the Option [Alt] key and clicking on the current Marquee tool. Find the Elliptical Marquee.

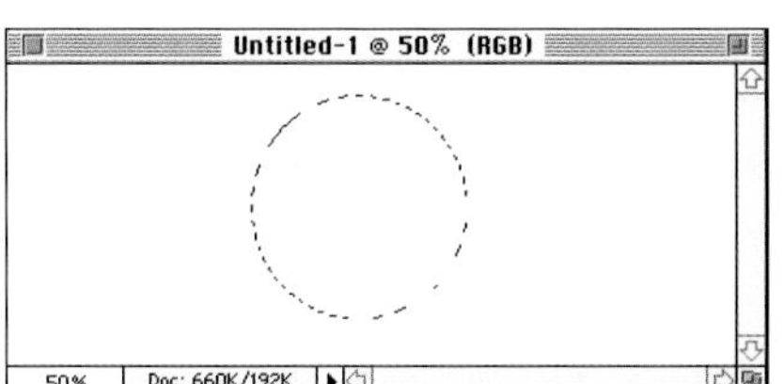


2 With the Marquee tool, draw a circle. If you hold down the Shift key while dragging the Marquee, the selection will be constrained to a perfect circle.

3 Change the foreground color to a color for the ball, and the background color to the color for the shadow. You can use white for the ball but I wanted to add a little color, so I used the CMYK values 4, 1, 51, 0, for the ball and black for the shadow.

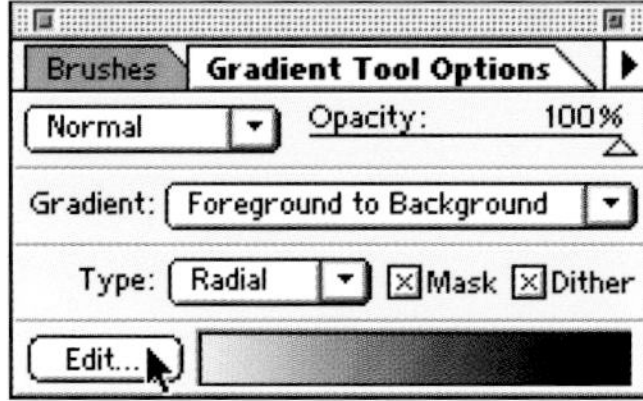


4 Double-click the Gradient tool to select it and to display the Gradient Tool Options floating palette.

**5** Fine-tune the gradient for the ball. First, click the Type pop-up menu and change the Type to Radial. Also, make sure that the Gradient is set to Foreground to Background.

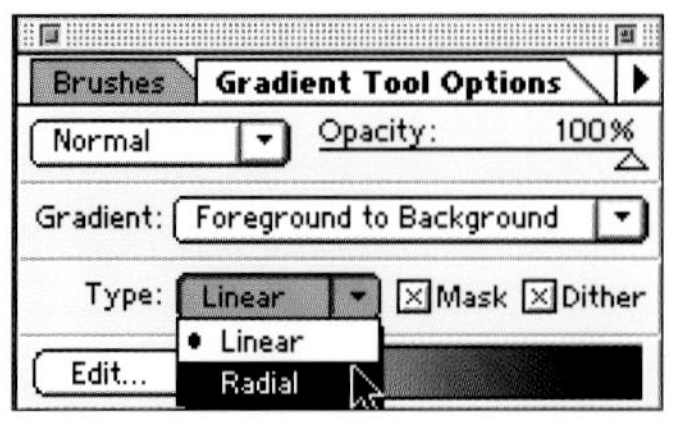


Then click the Edit button (as shown in the previous figure). A new dialog box will appear. Click the tab in the lower left that has an "F" inside it. Then click the pointer just below the colored gradient above. Drag the new "F" marker until the Location box reads 22%.

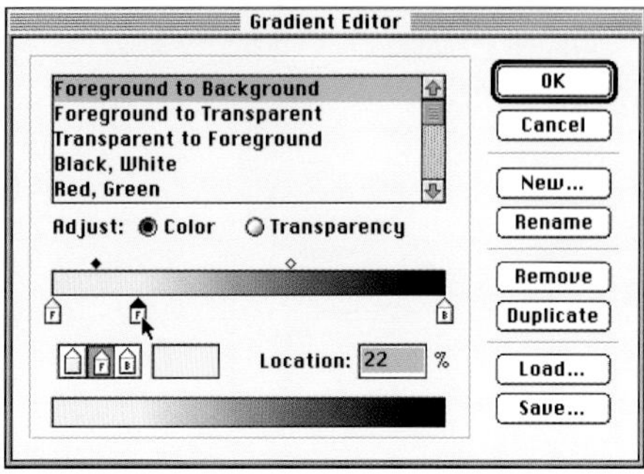


Grab the diamond above the colored gradient, which is to the right of the marker you just placed. Drag it to the right until the Location box reads 62%. Click OK.

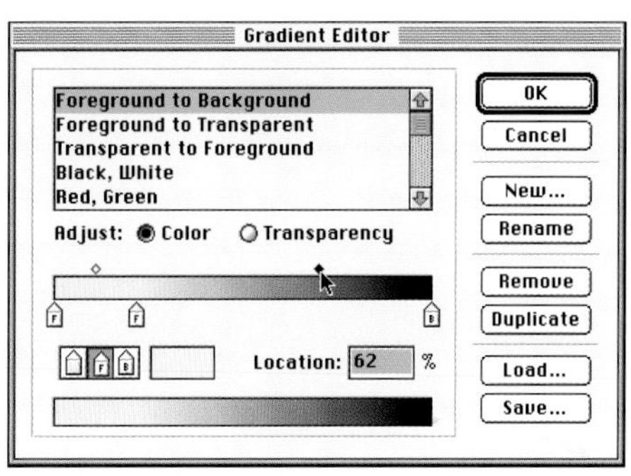


**6** Now, back to the circle selection. Click and drag the Gradient tool from the upper left part of the active selection to the lower right part of the selection as shown here.

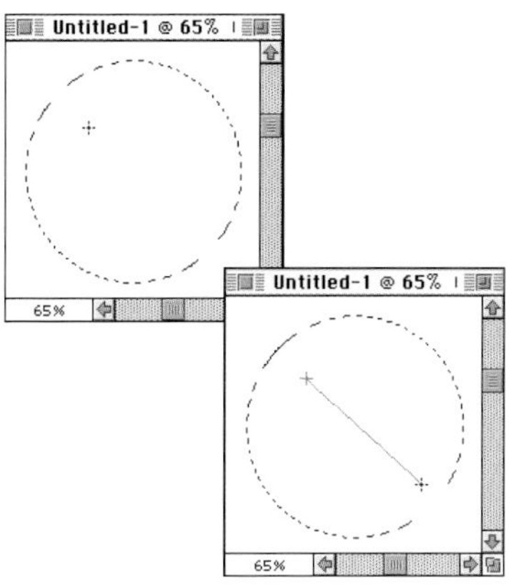

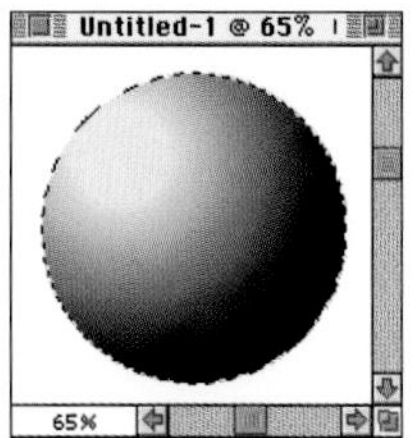


Here's what I got. If you don't like what you get, press Command-Z [Control-Z] and repeat this step.

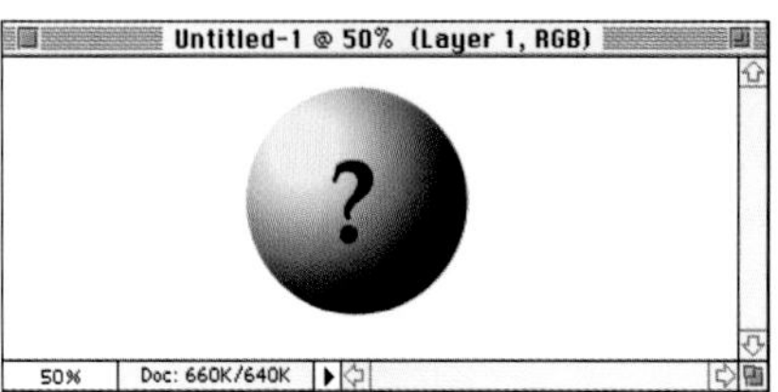


**7** Change the foreground color to a color for the type. I used black. Then use the Type tool to enter the letter for the ball. I used 55 point Palatino. The type will drop automatically into a new layer (Layer 1). Position it in the center of the sphere, and deselect the type.

**8** Get the elliptical Marquee tool and draw a perfect circle around the number that is smaller than the ball behind it. Something similar to this will do. Turn off the Preserve Transparency option for layer 1.

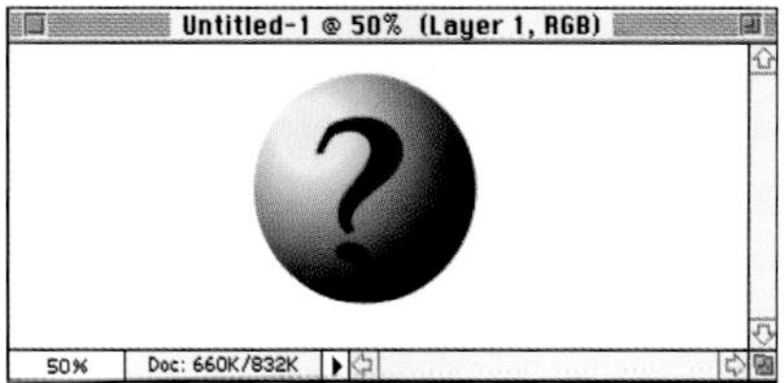


**9** Next, choose Filter➛Distort➛Spherize (Normal), and slide the amount to the maximum. I applied the filter a second time (Command-F) [Control-F]. Flatten the image and you're finished.

## Variations

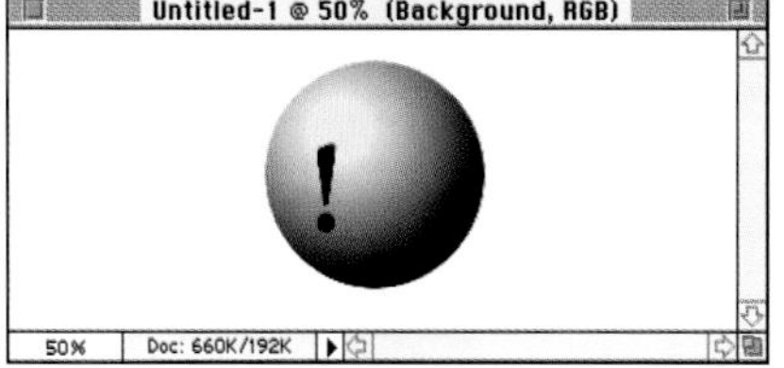


### Off-Center

You don't have to keep the letter in the middle of the ball. After you type it in, just drag it to the spot where you want it and continue with the steps described earlier.

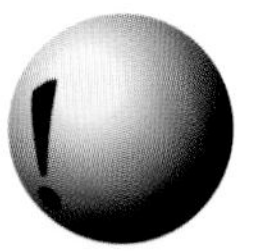

### Highlights

After flattening the layers, you can add a highlight that will blend the letter onto the ball better. Change the Foreground color to white. Double-click the Gradient tool and use the settings that you see here.

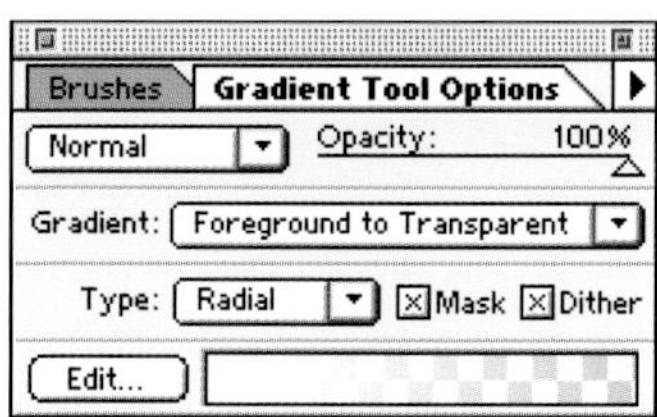


This is what you get.

Here's another way to make glossier balls. Perform Steps 1 through 3, except in Step 3 make the Foreground color white and the Background color black. You can do this by pressing D, and then X. The ball selection should still be active. Do Steps 4, 5, and 6, and make a new layer and name it Color. Keep the selection active. Change the foreground color to a color for the ball, and press the Option-Delete keys to fill the selection. The gradation disappears. From the pop-up menu on the Layers palette change the mode to Color. There is your shiny ball. Complete Steps 7 through 9 to add the text.

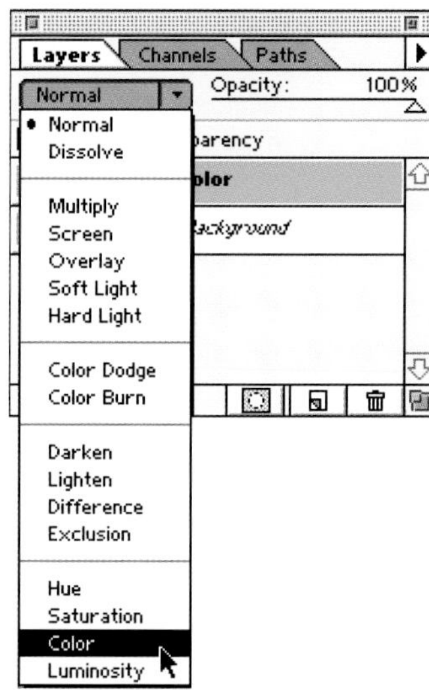

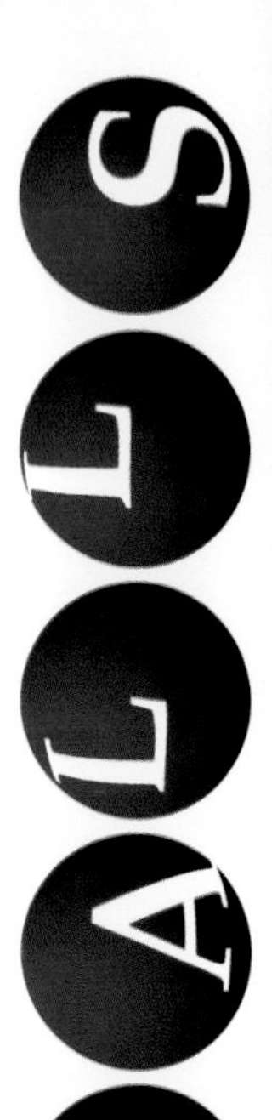


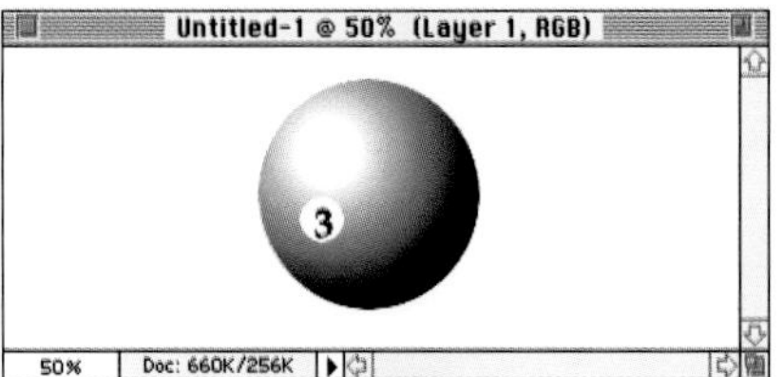

### Billiards

Now turn that ball into a billiards ball. I used Method 2 for this variation. After finishing Step 6, make a new Layer and select the Elliptical Marquee tool again. Click and drag a perfect circle on top of the ball. Change the foreground color to white and fill the selection.

Do Steps 7 through 9. In Step 8, I drew the Marquee selection to match the outline of the ball. Here is how the type turned out. ■

How retro! First we will make a guide for the type with large letters, then build the letters one at a time.

1 Create a new file. Use the Type tool to enter the text. Use a basic, sans serif, hard-edged font like Helvetica for this type that will serve as the guide for the individual letters. I used Impact at 90 points. The type will drop automatically into a new layer (Layer 1).

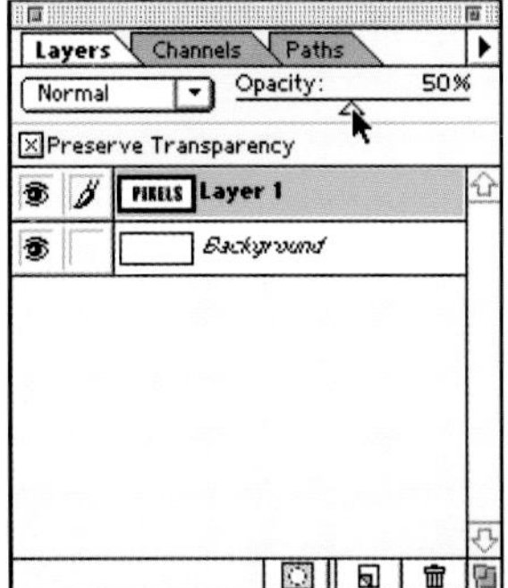


2 Use the Opacity slider on the Layers palette to lower the opacity of Layer 1 to 50%.

3 Make a new layer (Layer 2). Then make the Background layer and Layer 1 invisible.

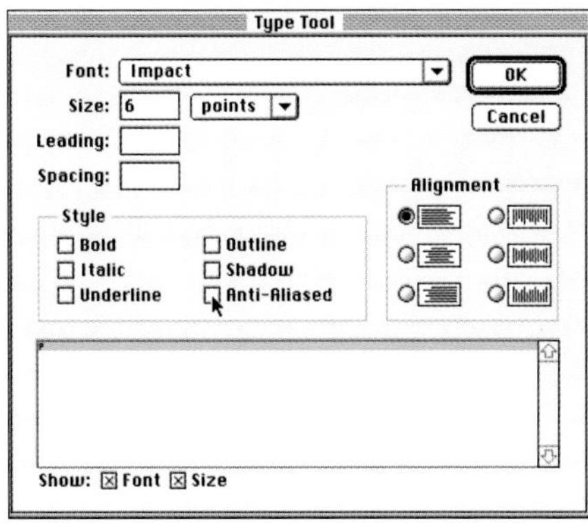


4 Use the Type tool to enter the first letter of the word you typed in Step 1. Make the type about 15 times smaller than the type you chose in Step 1. The letters probably will be so small (6 points in my case) that you will want to turn off Anti-Aliasing. However, be careful that the letters remain intact, because turning off Anti-Aliasing can trim them down.

**5** Select a box around the letter with the Marquee tool. Leave just a little room around the letter, like this.

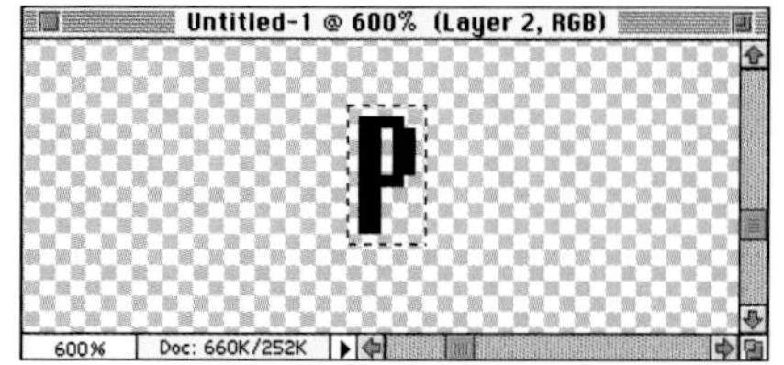


**TIP** **When working with type this small, it helps to zoom in. Use the Zoom tool to enlarge the image. (In this example, I have zoomed in to 600% in order to make a more accurate selection.)**

**6** Choose Edit➛Define Pattern to define the selected letter as a pattern. Press Delete to get rid of the letter.

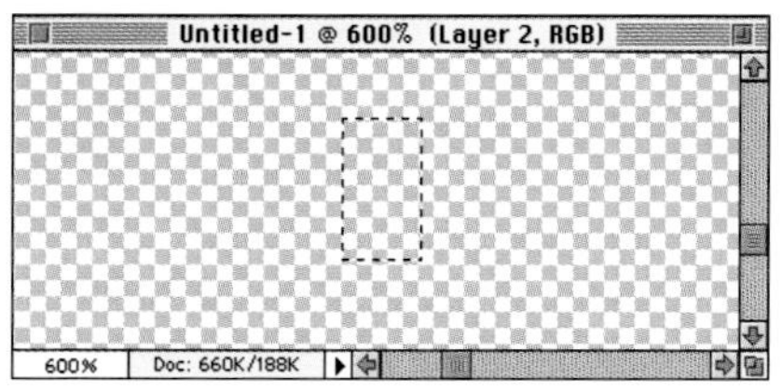


**7** Make Layer 1 visible again. Hold the Command [Control] key and click on the Layer 1 preview on the Layers palette to load the type selection.

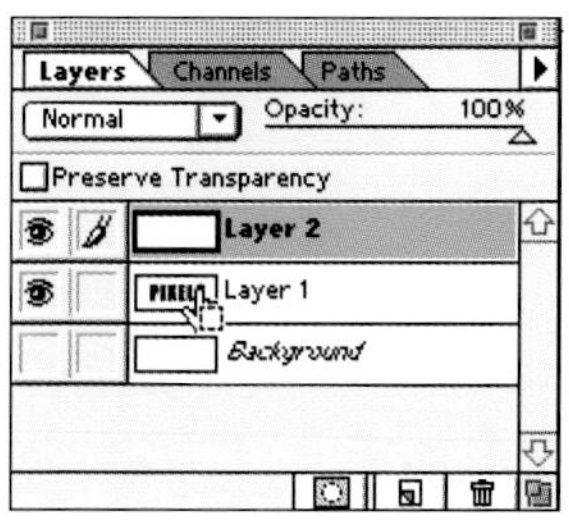


**8** Change the foreground color to black. Make Layer 2 active, and choose Edit➛Fill. Click on the Contents pop-up menu and choose Pattern. Keep the Opacity set at 100%, and the Mode set at Normal.

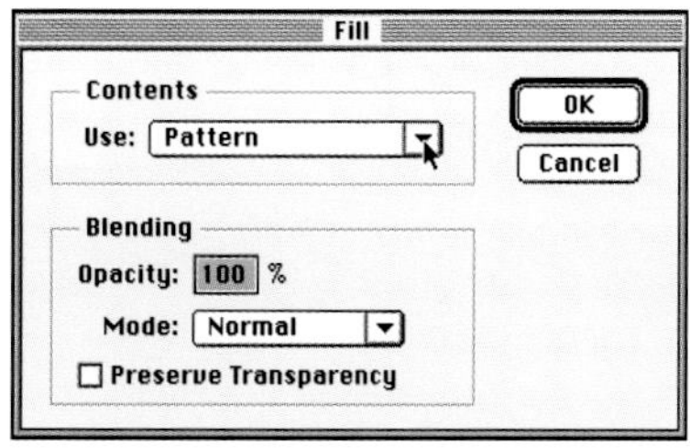


Now you can see how the small type size you chose in Step 3 works inside the type you entered in Step 1.

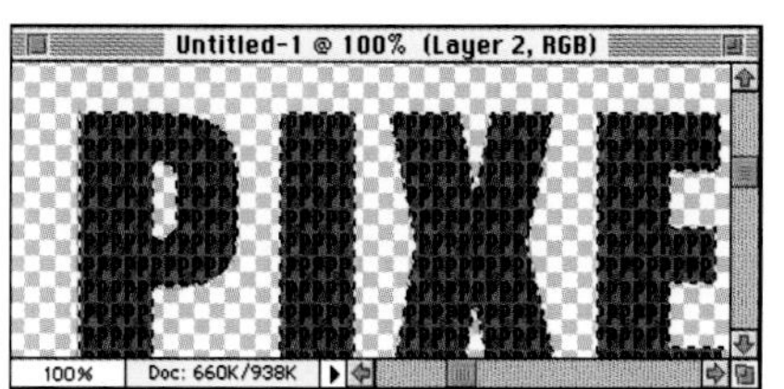

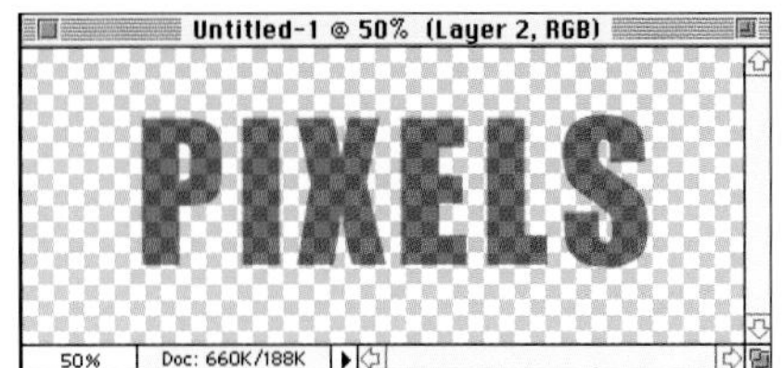


**9** Press Command-Z [Control-Z] to undo the fill. If the small type size does not look right inside the larger type, then go back and enter the text again in Step 3. If the space between the letters is too much, then you probably selected too much area around the type in Step 4. Go back to Step 3 and try it again.

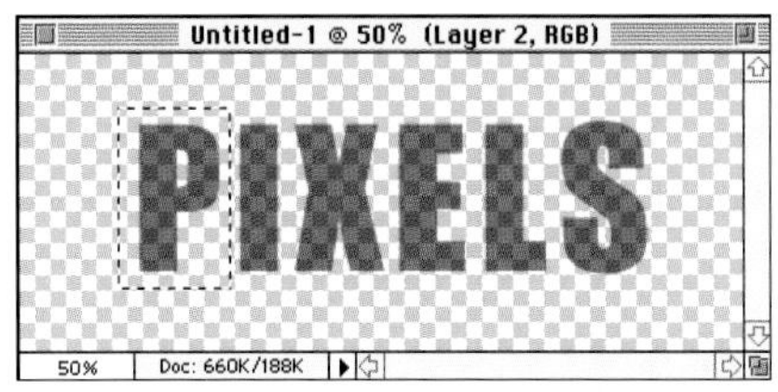


**10** After you have established the right size and spacing for the letters, then select the Marquee tool. Drag a rectangle around the first letter like this.

**11** Choose Edit→Fill and use the same settings you used in Step 8.

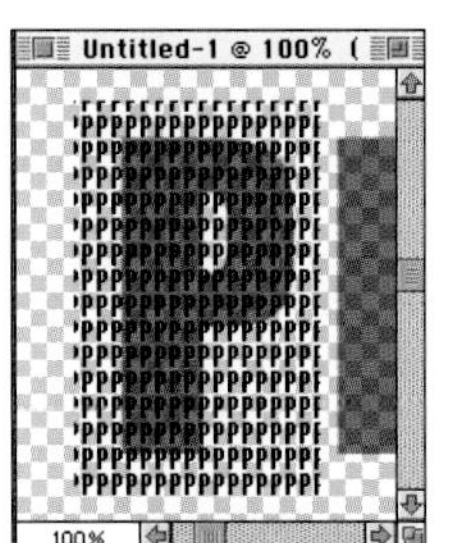


**12** Select the Move tool and use the arrow keys to move the letters into a convenient location (so they fit nicely, or as nicely as you can get them) over the Layer 1 type.

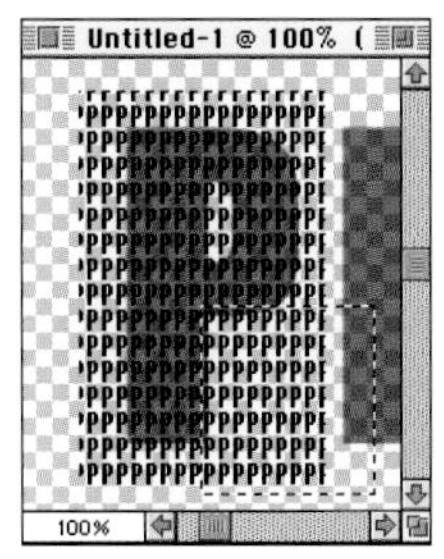


**13** When satisfied, deselect the type. With the Marquee tool drag rectangles around the letters that you want to take away, like this:

After making several selections and deleting their contents, you should end up with something like this.

**TIP** **You will probably have to make some judgment calls about which letters to delete and which to keep. The best rule is to be consistent with all the letters.**

**14** Deselect the letters. Make Layer 1 invisible again. Use the Type tool to enter the next letter at the same point size in an undefined area of Layer 2.

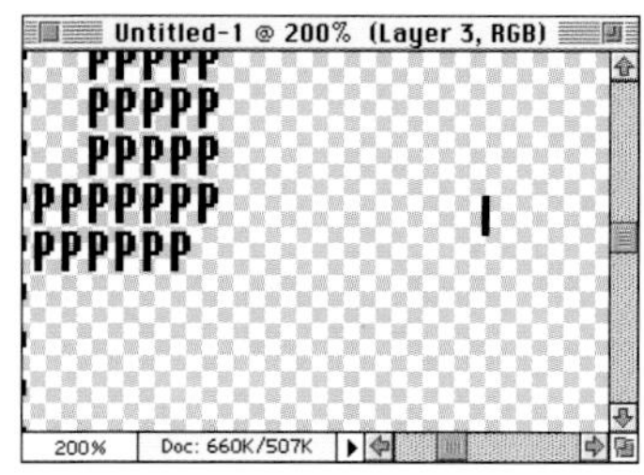


**15** Perform Steps 5, 6, and 7. Make Layer 1 visible again. Then do Steps 11 through 14.

**16** Continue this routine until all of the letters are complete. Remove Layer 1 when you are finished. Then flatten the image.

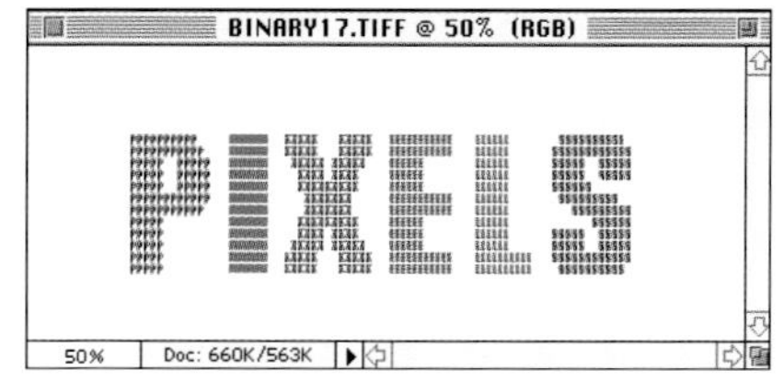


## VARIATIONS

After removing Layer 1 in Step 16, hold the Command [Control] key and click the Layer 2 preview on the Layers palette to select all the letters of all the letters. Then choose Filter➛Noise➛Add Noise (Amount: 100; Distribution: Gaussian). Applying this filter adds the colored noise that you see in the thumbtab image. ■

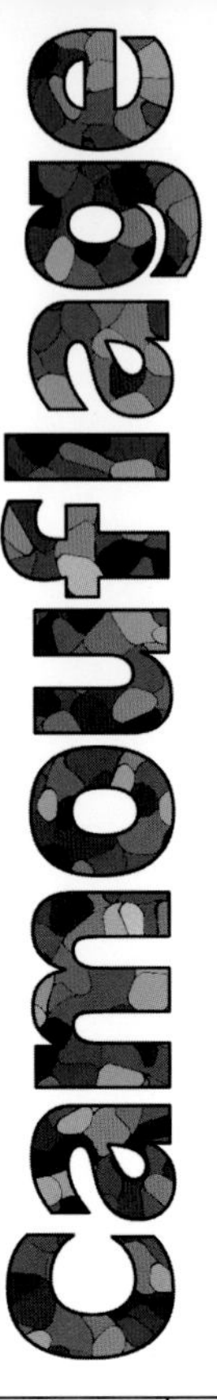


In this effect, the Crystallize and Median filters work together to separate the text into flat areas of color—just what the camouflage needs.

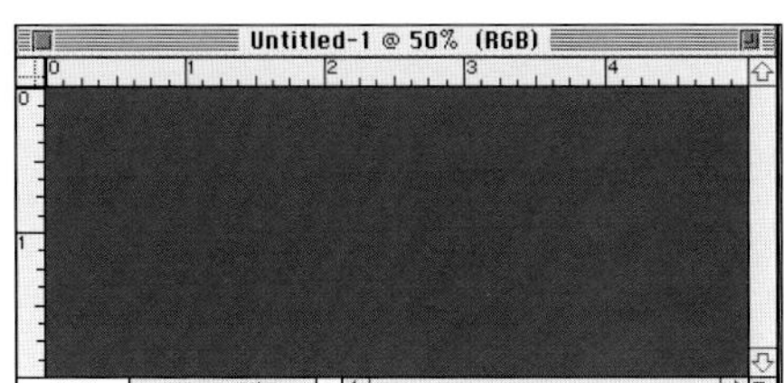


**1** Create a new file. Change the foreground color to these CMYK values: 81, 31, 100, 16. Fill the image with this color.

**2** Choose Filter→Noise→Add Noise. Turn on the Monochromatic option and keep the Amount low. (I set the Amount at 50.)

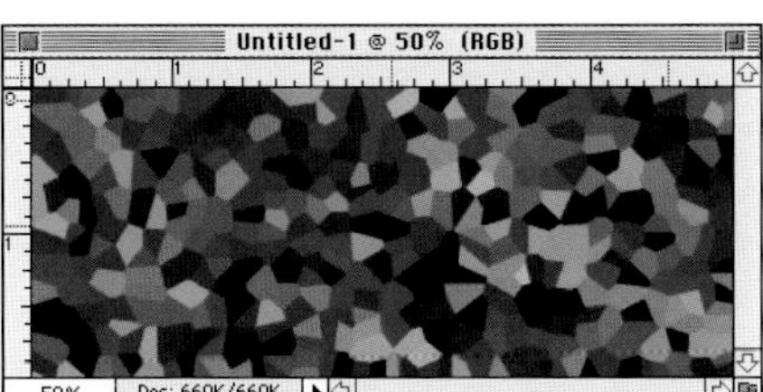


**3** Choose Filter→Pixelate→Crystallize. This filter divides the text into flat color areas. (I used a Cell Size of 30.)

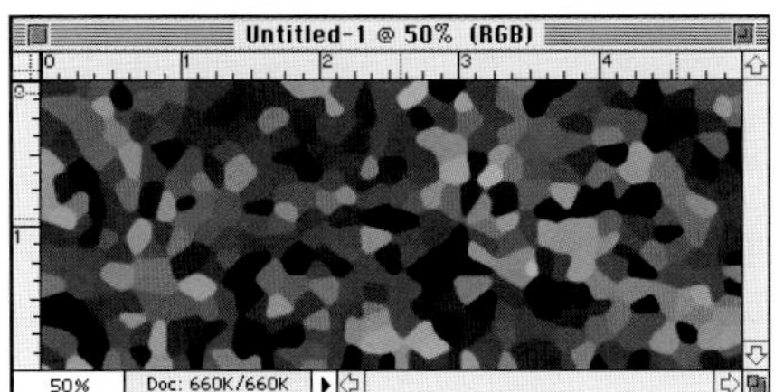


**4** To finish creating the color shapes, choose Filter→Noise→Median. Use a low setting, such as 5, which is what was used here.

**5** Next, use the Type Mask tool to enter the text. This font is Incised Black at 90 points.

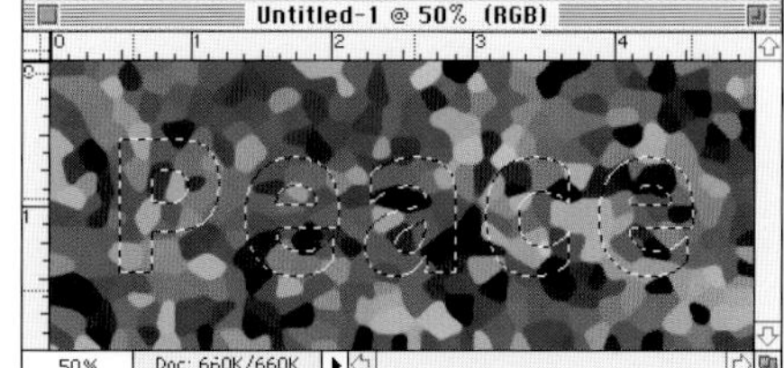


**6** Choose Select➛Inverse. Then press Delete to fill everything with white, except the type.

**7** Choose Select➛Inverse again. Then press Command [Control]-J to copy the type into a new layer (Layer 1).

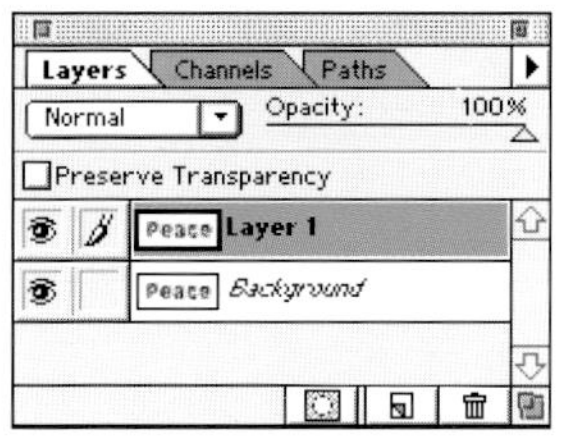


**8** Choose Filter➛Stylize➛Find Edges.

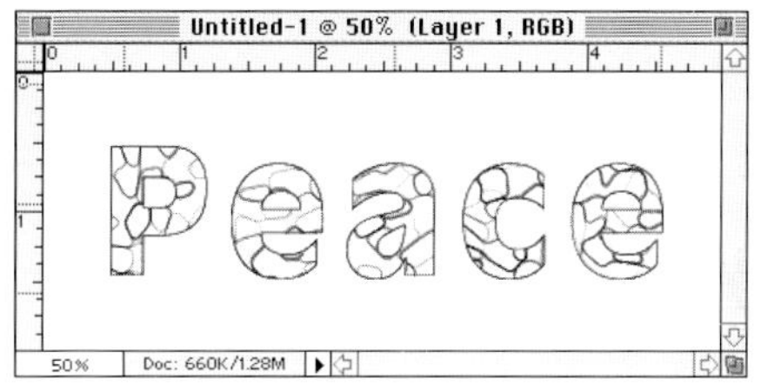


**9** Then choose Image➛Adjust➛Threshold. Slide the marker all the way to the right, until the Level reads 255.

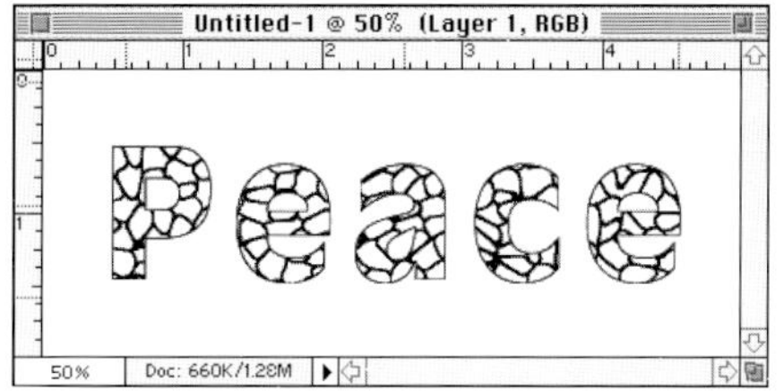

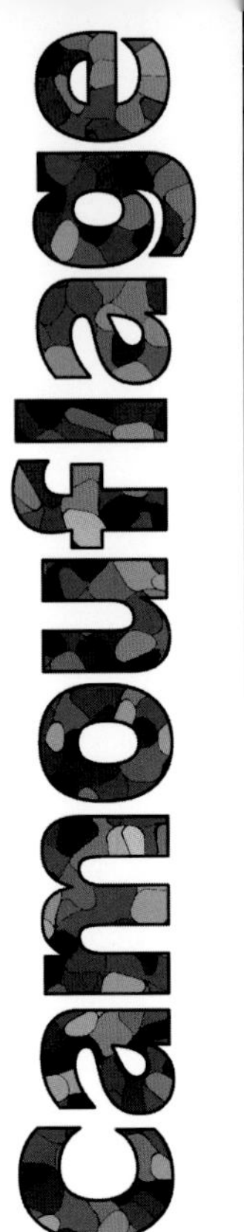


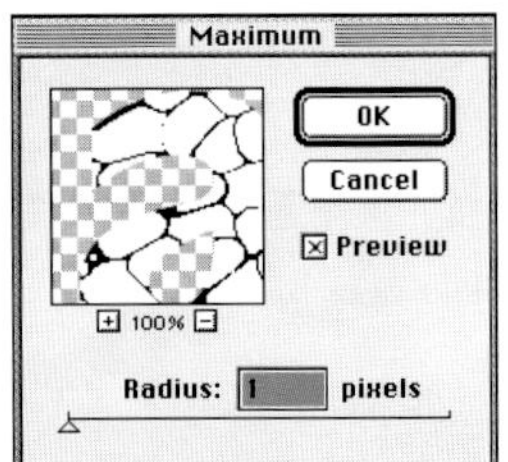


**10** Choose Filter➝Other➝ Maximum. This filter thins down the black lines. Use the minimum setting, 1 pixel.

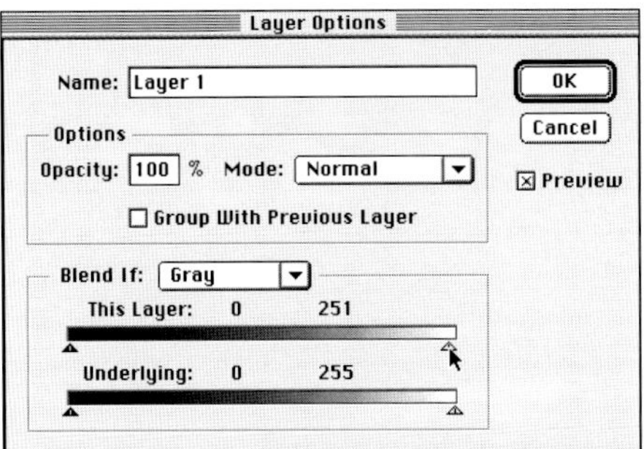


**11** Next, choose Layer➝Layer Options. Inside the Blend If box, grab the white This Layer slider and drag it to the left just a little—until the indicator above lowers to about 251.

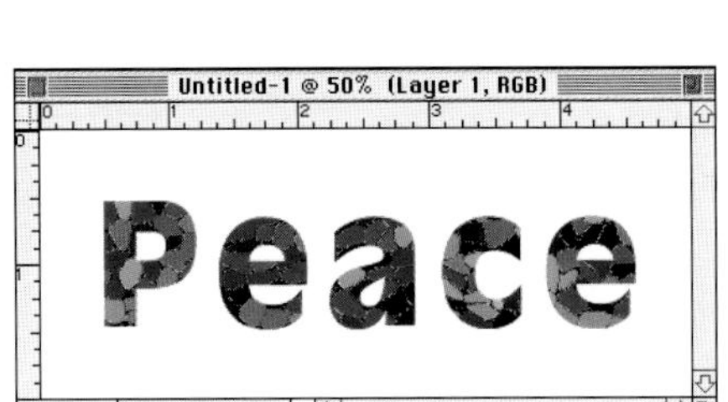


Click OK and your type should now look like this. ■

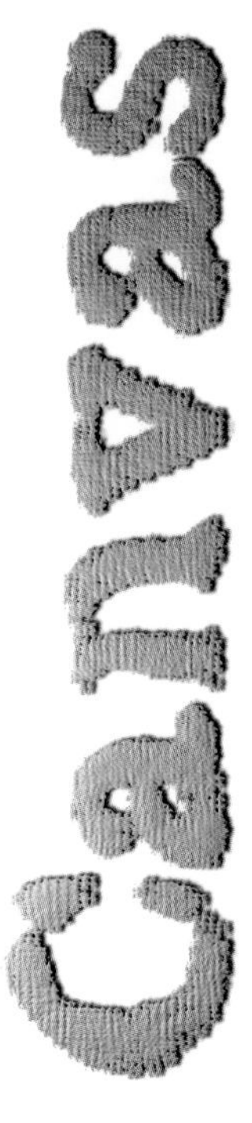


What's great about this canvas type is that you can use the same technique to create many different textures. And, it's all done with the Paintbrush tool—and some help from the Lighting Effects filter.

**1** Create a new file, and a new channel (#4).

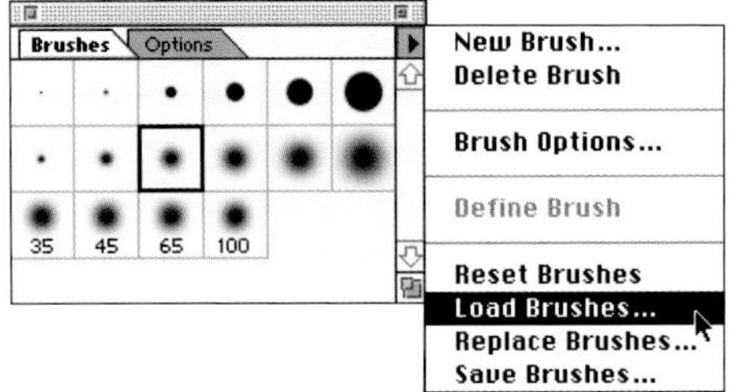


**2** Double-click the Paintbrush tool to select it, and to bring forward the Paintbrush Options dialog box. Click the Brushes tab to bring the brushes to the front. Then, click the Brushes arrow menu and choose Load Brushes.

**3** A dialog box opens so that you can find the brushes file that you want to use. Just for you, I have made a special brush to help create this texture. Actually, I modified one of Photoshop's Assorted Brushes. Follow this path to open the Magic Brushes file: Photoshop Type Magic 2➵Type Magic Presets➵Magic Brush. Open the file.

**4** The Brushes palette now should include a new brush. Select the new brush.

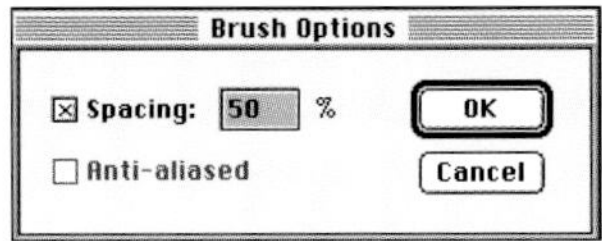


**5** Double-click the new brush to open the Brush Options dialog box. Change the Spacing to 50%.

**TOOLBOX**

Canvas (Lighting Style Preset)

KPT Gradient Designers

**6** Change the foreground color to white. Click in the image area and drag the brush.

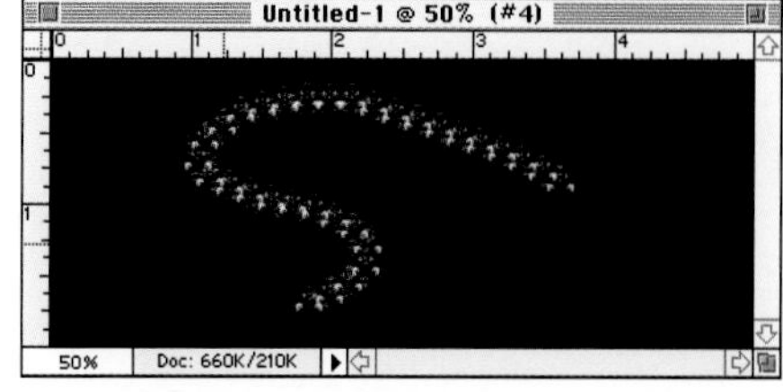


**7** Go crazy rubbing the brush all over the image. Keep in mind that you are creating a texture—don't obliterate the black. I used a circular motion when creating this texture, seen here in a close-up.

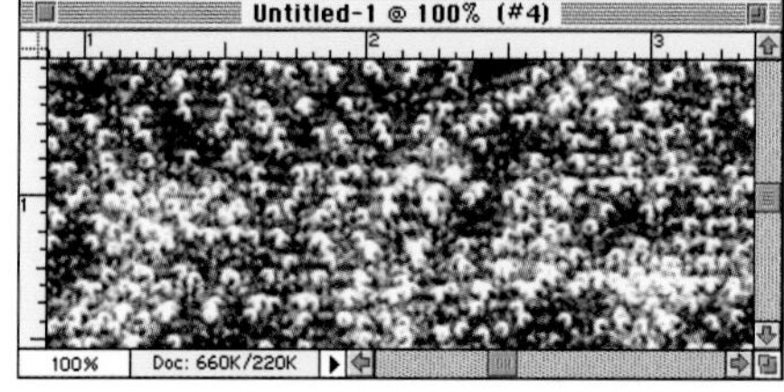


**8** To finish the texture, choose Filter➛Pixelate➛Fragment.

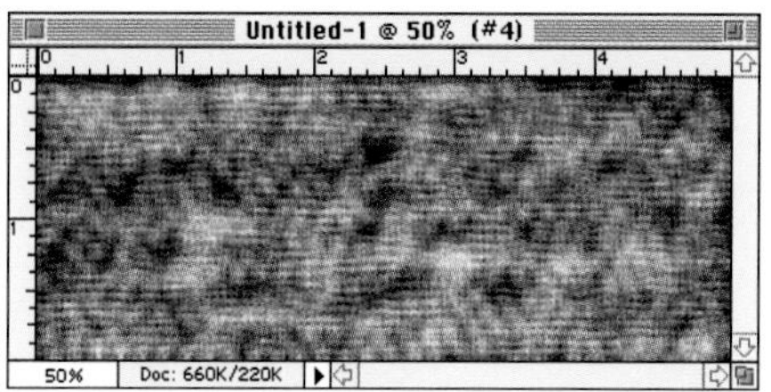


**9** Return to the composite channel and make the Background layer active. Use the Type Mask tool to enter the text. I used Attic at 85 points.

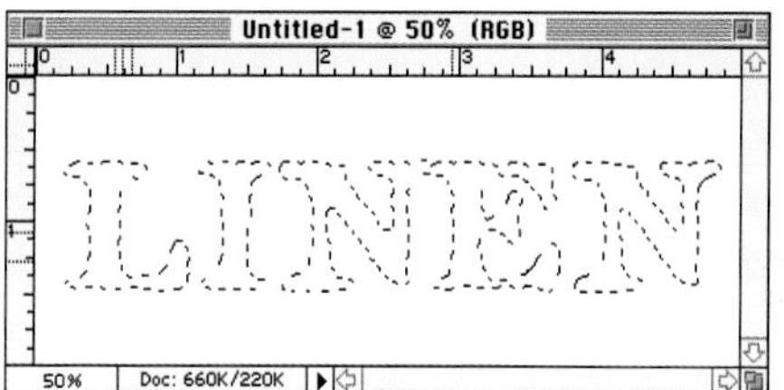

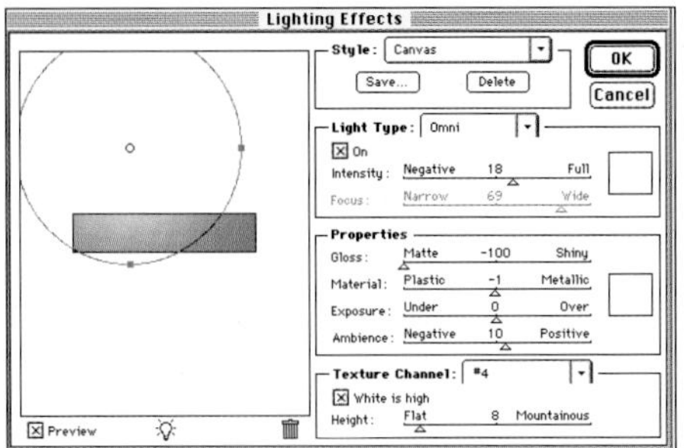


10 Choose Filter➛Render➛Lighting Effects. If you have loaded the Lighting Style presets from the CD, you can select Canvas from the Style pop-up menu or match the settings you see here.

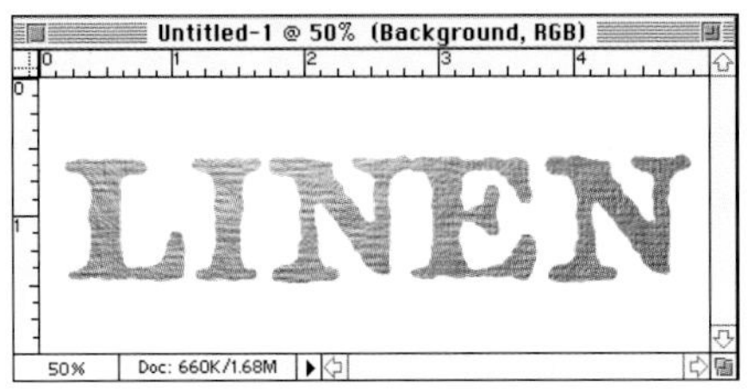


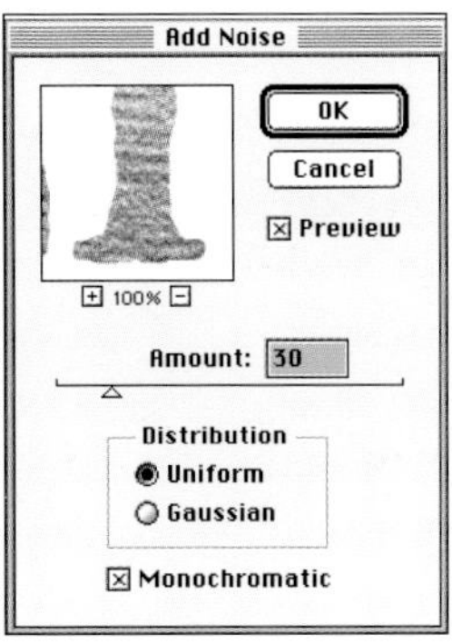


11 Choose Filter➛Noise➛Add Noise. Turn on the Monochromatic option, but don't overdo the noise. I set the Amount to 30. The texture may have looked a little plastic, adding noise will give the texture a more natural look.

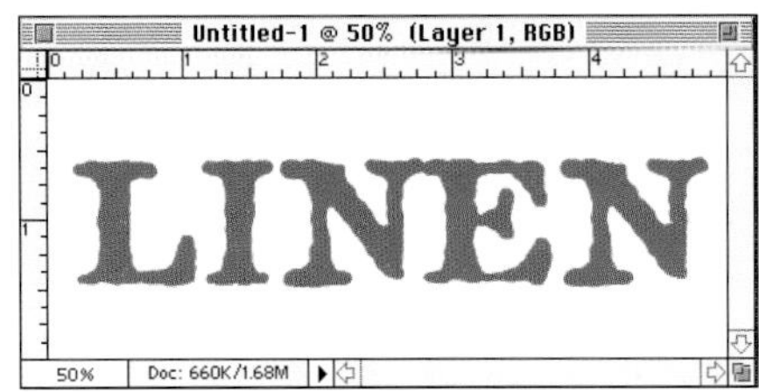


12 Keep the selection active and make a new layer (Layer 1). Change the foreground color to a color for the type, and fill the selection in Layer 1.

**13** Convert the Layer 1 blending mode to Color.

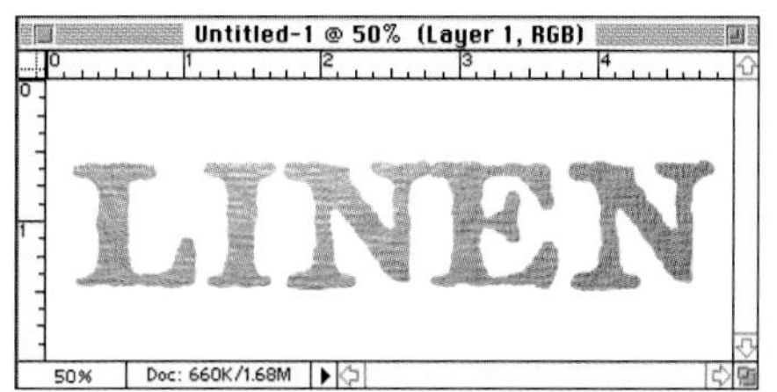


## VARIATIONS

Instead of filling the Layer 1 selection with a flat color in Step 11, I used the KPT Gradient Designer. I chose the Multi Color nonlinear preset gradient. Now do Step 12.

How do you create the rough edges as seen on the thumbtab? Follow the steps described below.

After Step 1, use the Type tool to enter the text into Channel #4. Deselect the text.

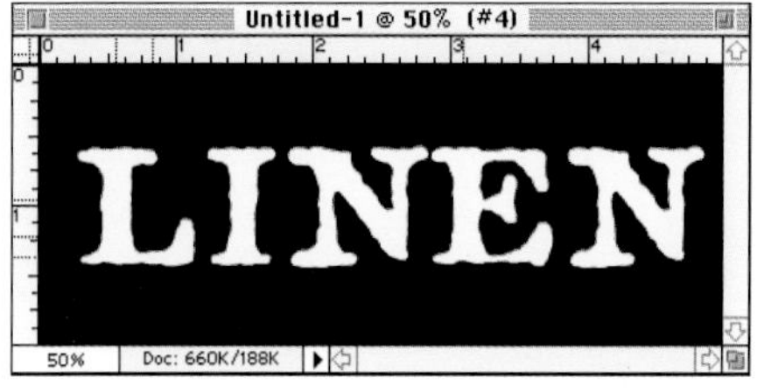


Then create a new channel (#5). Keep Channel #5 as the active channel, but make Channel #4 visible as well.

Change the foreground color to white. Then, select the same brush shown in Step 4 above. Paint over the letters. Be sloppy, but not too sloppy. You want something like this:

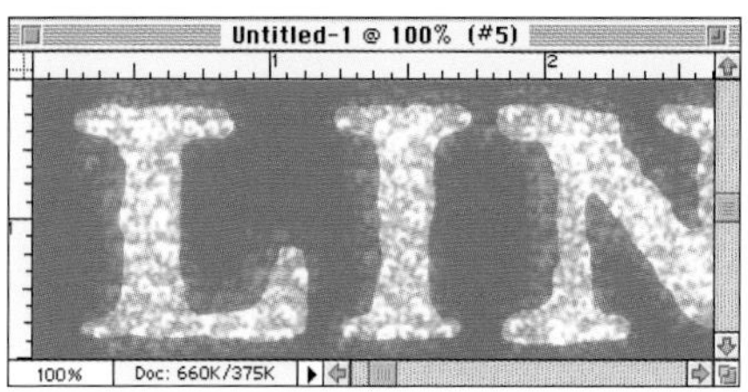

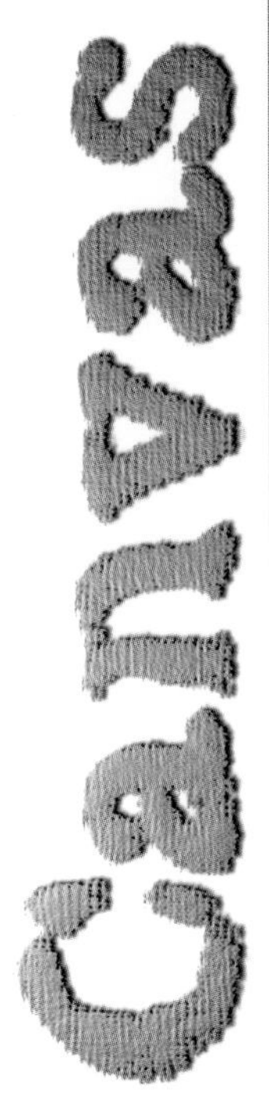

Follow the instructions in Step 8, and then duplicate Channel #5 to create Channel #5 copy.

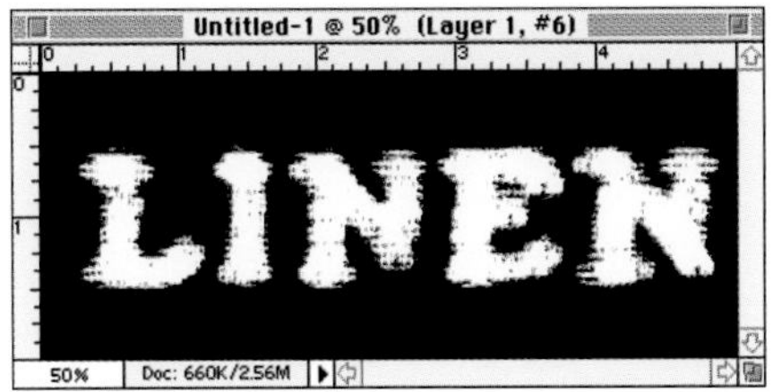


Choose Image➝Adjust➝Threshold. Use the slider to set the Level close to 80. The shape of the white area will be the shape of the type.

Return to the composite channel, and load the selection Channel #5 copy. In the Lighting Effects dialog box, in Step 10, change the Texture channel to Channel #5. Do Steps 11 and 12. ■

# CARPET

This quick effect takes advantage of the Accented Edges filter—one of the new Brush Strokes filters in Photoshop 4.0. Using the right settings in this filter is the key to creating the carpet texture.

**1** Create a new file. Use the Type Mask tool to enter the text. Benguiat Bold at 120 points was used for this example.

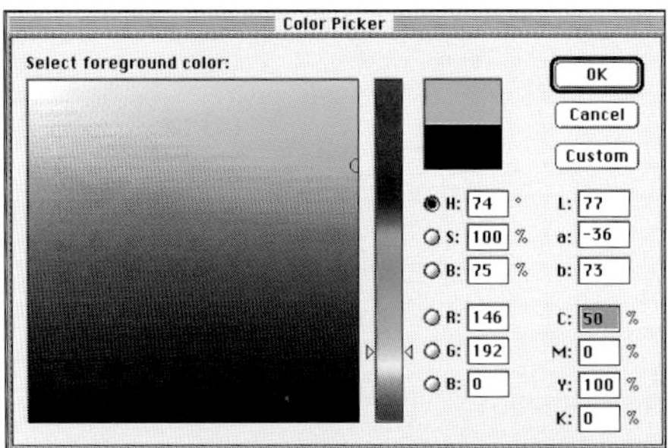


**2** Change the foreground color to a color for the carpet. I used these CMYK values: 50, 0, 100, 0. Fill the selection with this color.

**3** Save the type selection to create Channel #4.

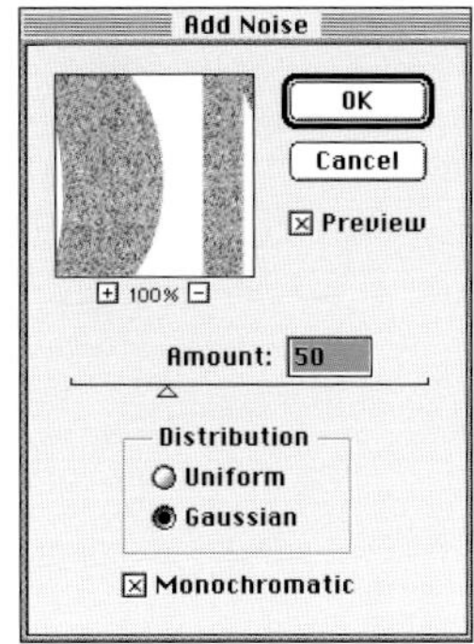


**4** While keeping the selection active, choose Filter➛Noise➛Add Noise. Set the Amount at a value just under the point at which white pixels show up in the preview. I set the Amount at 50. (Gaussian, Monochromatic). Deselect the text.

**5** Next, choose Filter➛Brush Strokes➛Accented Edges. This filter can create many varied effects, but to create the carpet texture match the setting as seen here (Edge Width: 1, Edge Brightness: 22, Smoothness: 2).

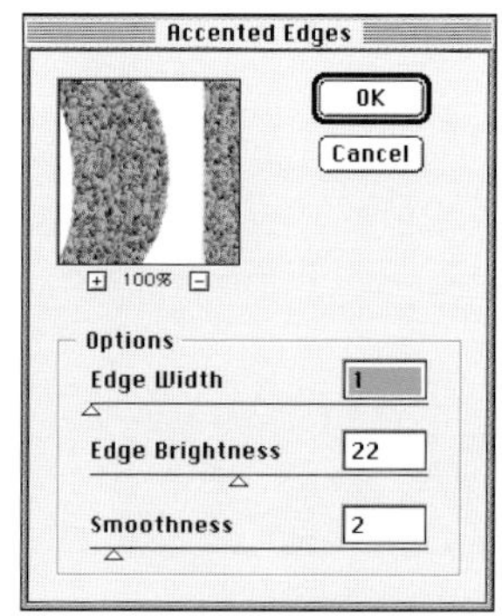


Your type will have a texture like this:

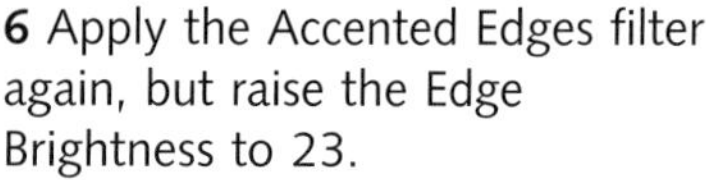

**6** Apply the Accented Edges filter again, but raise the Edge Brightness to 23.

**7** Load the selection you saved in Step 3 (Channel #4). Then choose Select➛Modify➛Contract. Contract the type selection 1 pixel.

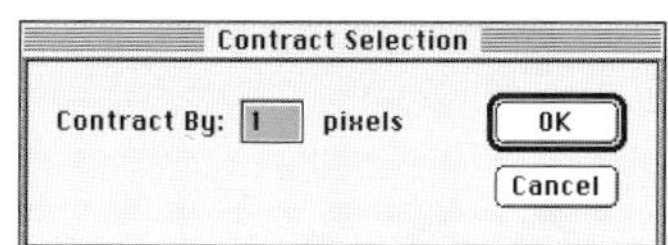


**8** Finally, choose Filter➛Pixelate➛Fragment. Here's a detail of the texture...

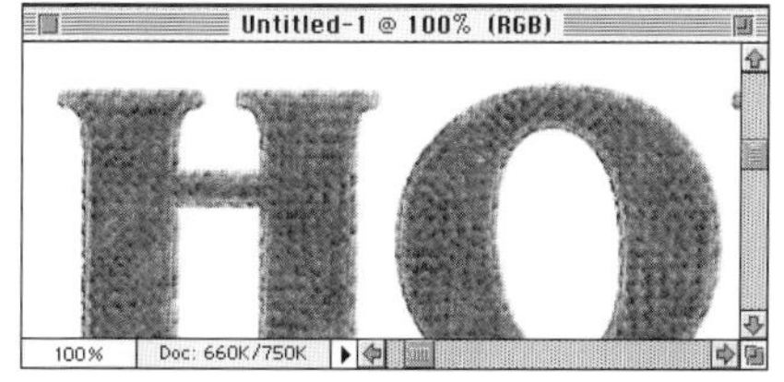


...and here is the final type. ■

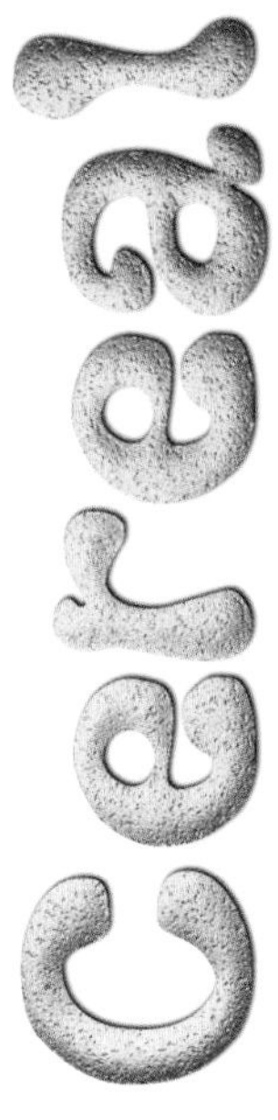


The unlikely Ocean Ripple filter works with the Lighting Effects filter to round out these crunchy letters.

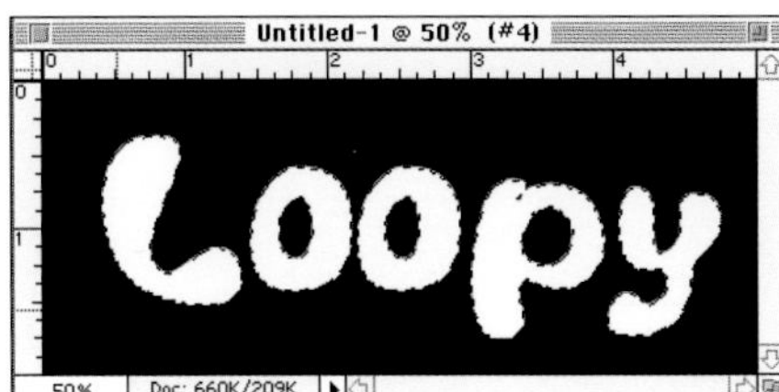


**1** Create a new file, and a new channel (#4). Use the Type tool to enter the text. Font choice for this effect is important. I used Thickhead (100 points) because the shapes of the letters look like bulbous Cheerios.

**2** Save the selection to create Channel #5. Keep the text selection active.

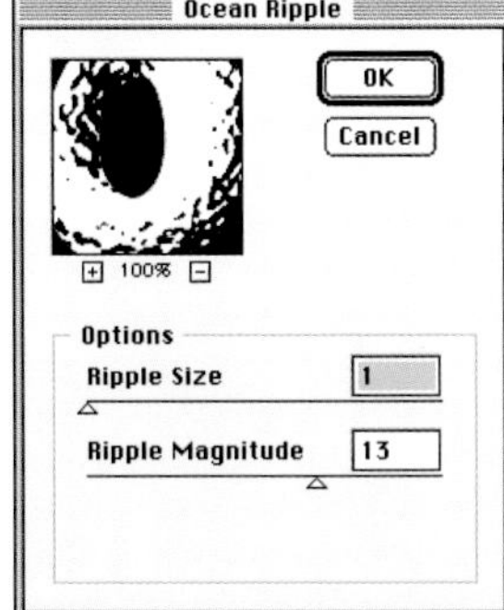


**3** Choose Filter➛Distort➛Ocean Ripple. This is one of the new filters from Photoshop 4.0. Try these settings to distort just parts of the type: Ripple Size: 1; Ripple Magnitude: 13.

**TIP** **If the word you typed is too long, the Ocean Ripple filter may distort some of the letters too much. If this happens, try selecting only a few of the letters at a time, and apply the filter. Continue until the Ocean Ripple filter has been applied to all the letters. Then load the selection Channel #5 to select all the letters again.**

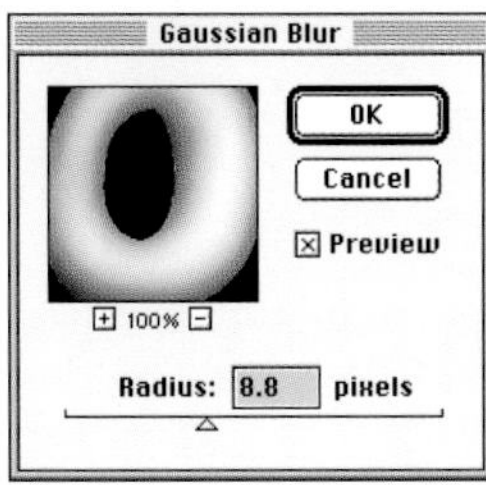


**4** Next, choose Filter➛Blur➛Gaussian Blur. Blur the text enough to smooth out the distortion created by the Ocean Ripple filter. I set the Radius at 8.8.

## TOOLBOX

Cereal (Lighting Style Preset)

**5** Create a new channel (#6). The selection should still be active. Choose Filter➛Pixelate➛ Mezzotint. Select the Coarse Dots option from the pop-up menu.

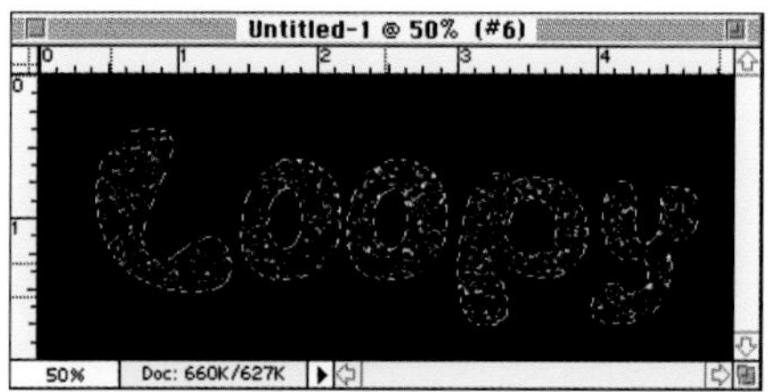


**6** Make Channel #4 active, then load the selection Channel #6.

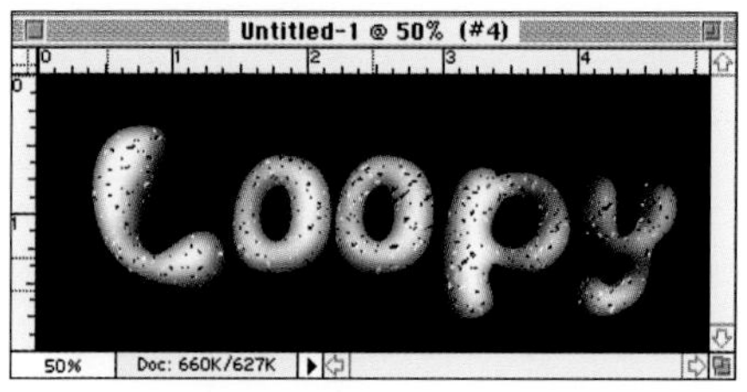


**7** Choose Image➛Adjust➛ Brightness/Contrast. Lower the Brightness value to about -35. Deselect the selection.

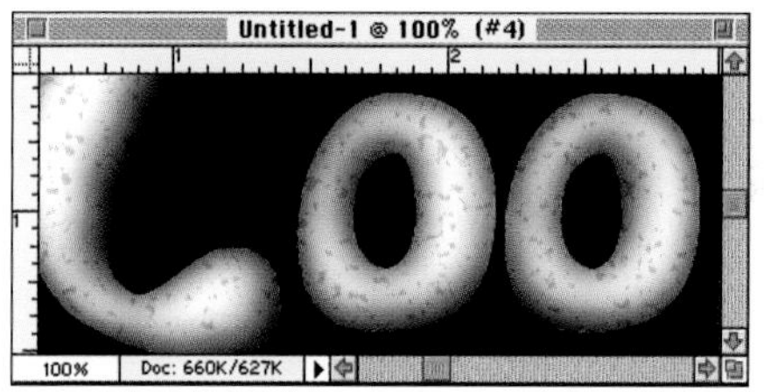


**8** Load the selection Channel #5. Choose Filter➛Noise➛Add Noise (Gaussian). Set the Amount to around 4. The noise helps create some shallower bumps in the cereal letters, but keep it low.

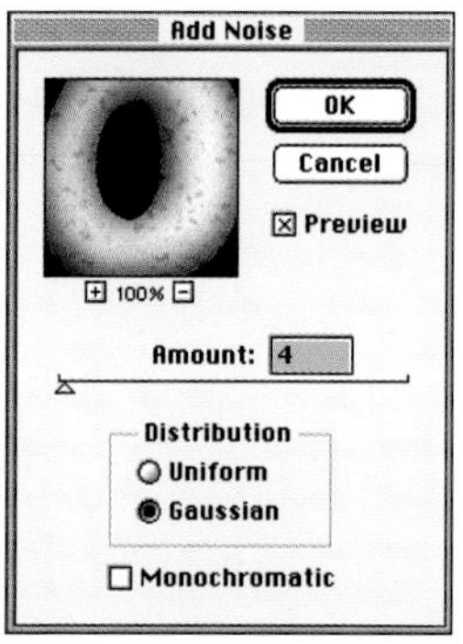


**9** Return to the composite channel. Keep the selection active.

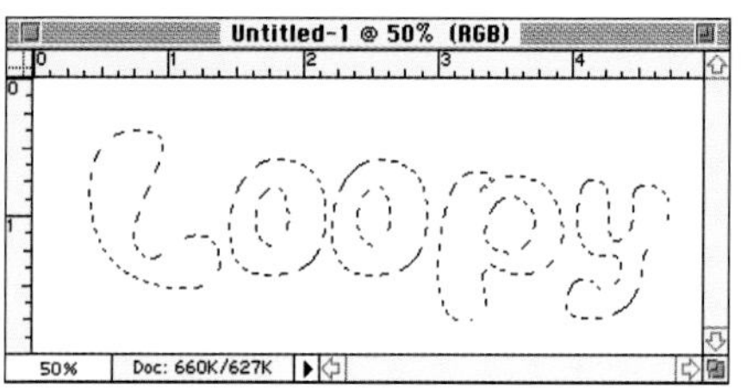

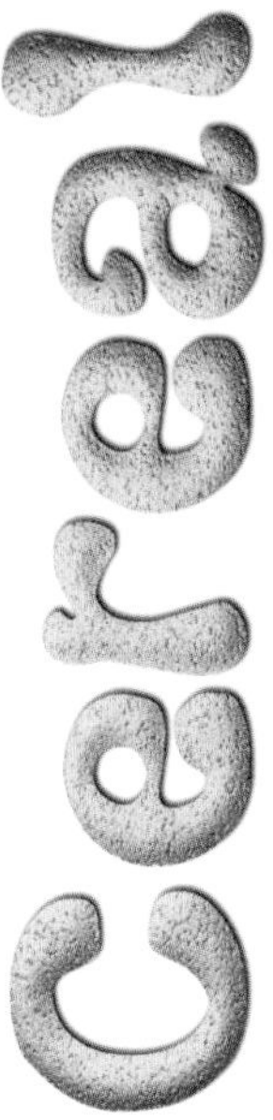


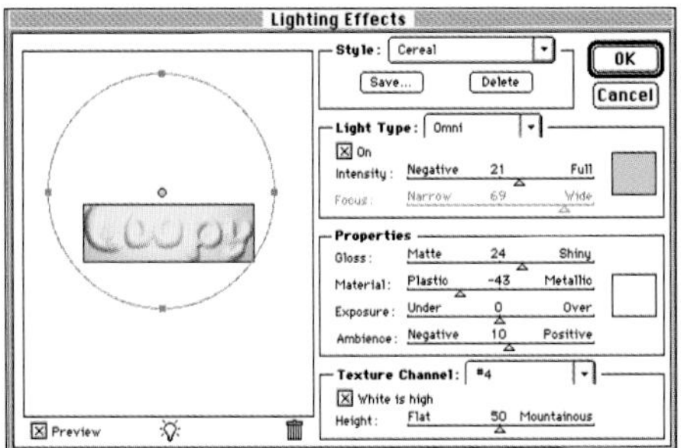


10 Choose Filter➛Render➛ Lighting Effects. Choose the Cereal preset from the Style pop-up menu, or match the settings in this figure. Use the Texture Channel Height to adjust the fullness of the letters.

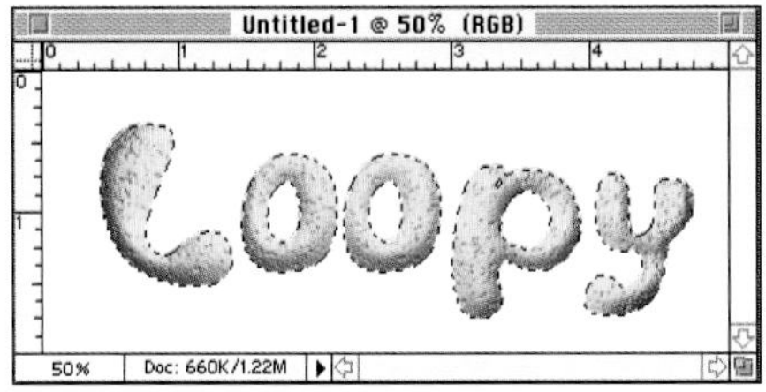


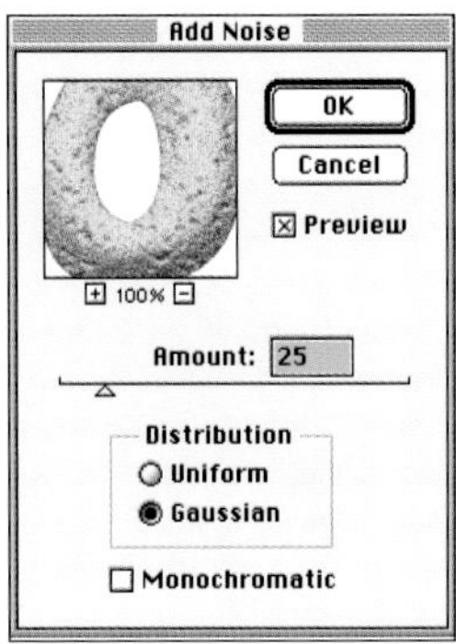


11 As a final touch, I chose Filter➛Noise➛Add Noise and lowered the Amount to 25. This noise will give the cereal texture a little graininess, and we all know how important grain is to our diets.

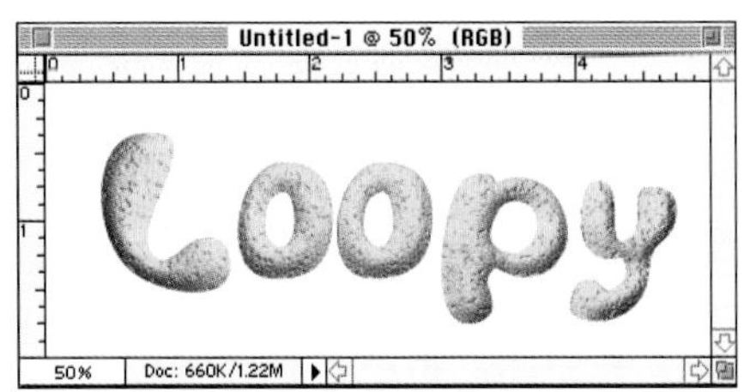

## Variations

I just couldn't resist adding this milky background and a shadow.

If you have a hard-edged font that you want to round off for this effect, follow these steps.

In Step 1, use the Type Mask tool instead of the Type tool. This font is Impact at 100 points.

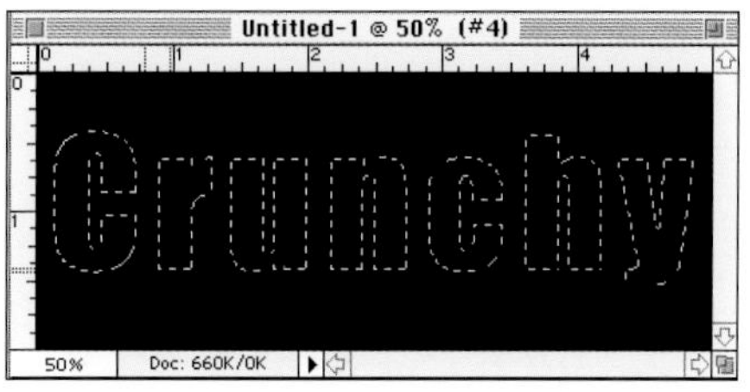


Then choose Select➛Modify➛Smooth. You may have to try different settings before you get the one you want. I smoothed the selection 10 pixels.

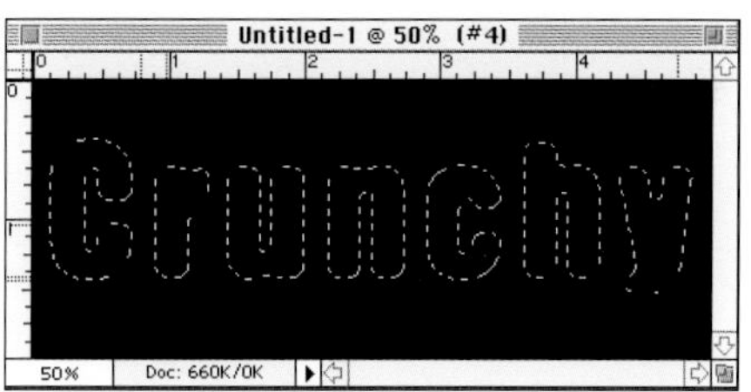


Fill the selection with white and finish the steps above (Steps 2 through 11).

If you're looking for a change from your everyday breakfast type, try Waffles (page 206). ■

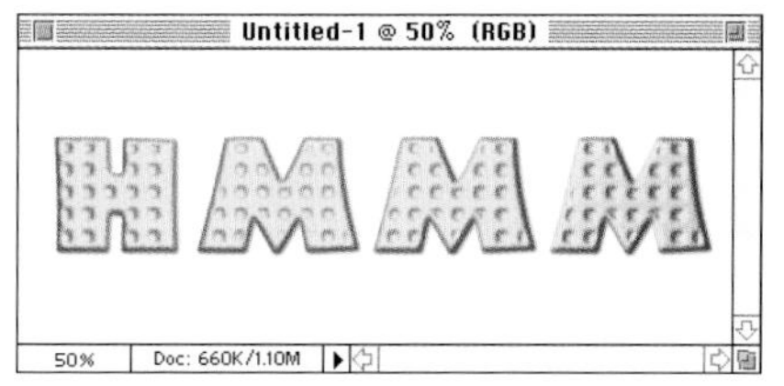

Making a checkered pattern takes only a few steps. Once you've got that down, you can use Photoshop's filters to make some unique alterations.

**1** Create a new file, and a new layer (Layer 1). Change the Foreground color to one of the colors you want to use for the checkers, and fill the entire layer with the color. I used the CMYK values 24, 24, 98, and 16.

**2** Double-click the Marquee tool to select it and to bring the Marquee Options floating palette to the front. Change the style to Fixed Size, and set the Width and Height to 10 pixels. These dimensions determine the size of the squares in the checkered pattern. Adjust it to your liking, but make sure you always keep the Width and Height the same.

**3** Next, click in the image area once with the Marquee tool. A square selection appears. Change the Foreground color to the second color for the checkers. I used the CMYK values 99, 70, 7, and 1. Fill the selection with this color.

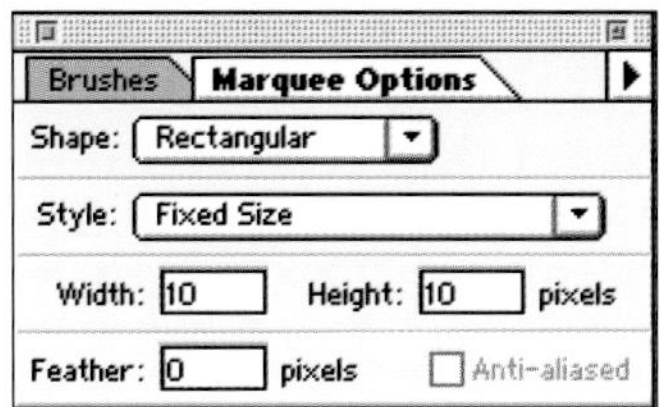


**4** Use the Marquee tool to move the selection so that the upper-left corner of the selection meets the lower-right corner of the colored square that you created in Step 3. Fill this selection with the same color that you used in Step 3.

**5** Find the Marquee Options floating palette again, and double the Width and Height sizes (20 pixels for me).

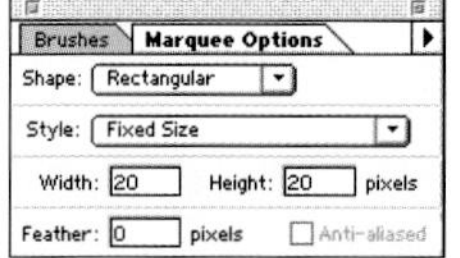


**6** Use the Marquee tool to click in the image area. Drag the new, larger, square selection so that it includes both of the colored squares.

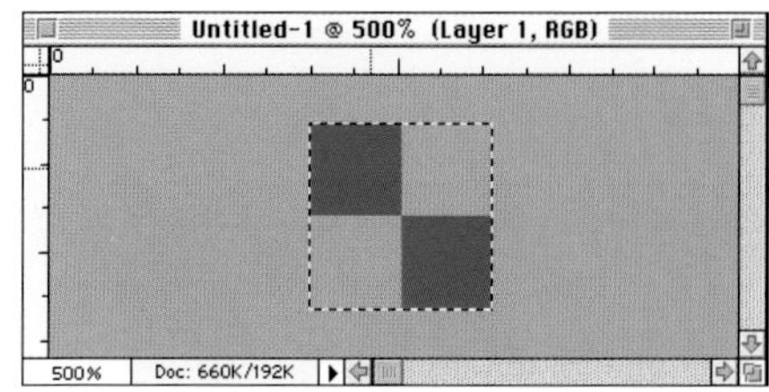


**7** Choose Edit➛Define pattern and then choose Select➛All. Press Delete to clear the image window. Deselect the selection.

**8** Use the Type Mask tool to enter the text. I used Frutiger Ultra Black at 90 points.

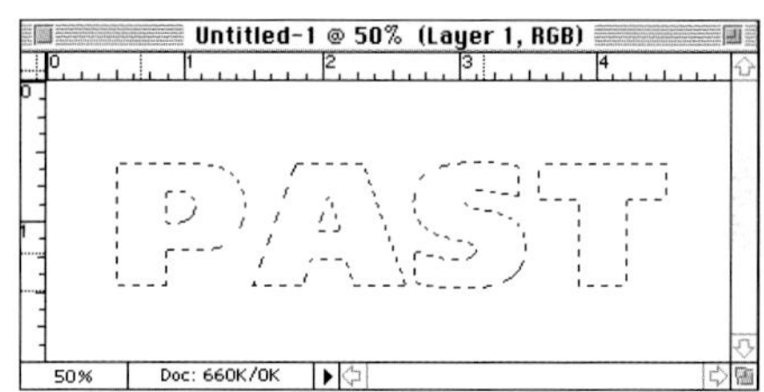


**9** Choose Edit➛Fill. In the dialog box, change the Contents option to Pattern. Click OK, and you've got checkers.

## Diagonal Checks

Do Steps 1 though 6 above, and then choose Layer➛Transform➛Numeric. The only setting you need to change is the angle. Change it to 45°.

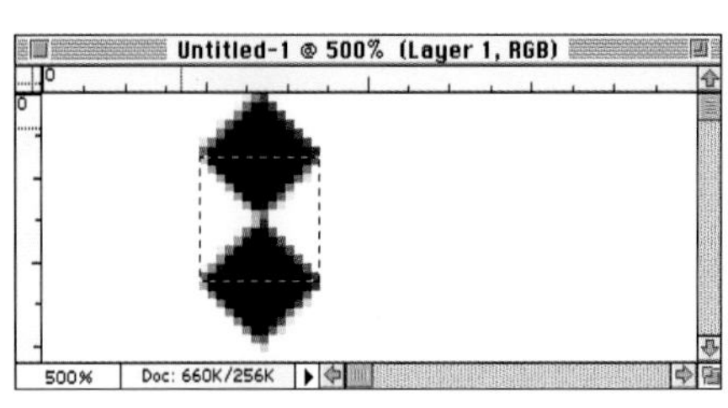


Again, find the Marquee Options floating palette. Change the style to Constrain Aspect Ratio and make sure that the Width and Height settings are changed to 1. This option keeps the selection a perfect square. Drag the Marquee to make a selection like this:

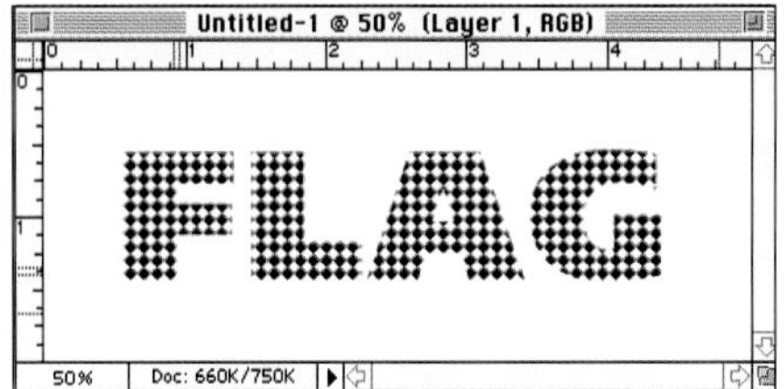


When you finish Steps 7 through 9, your type should look like this.

## VARIATIONS

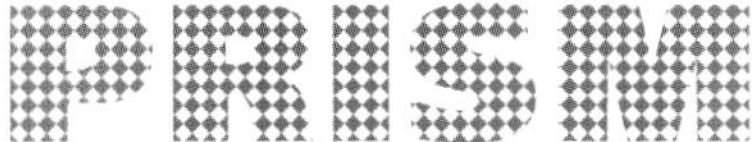


Keep the type selection active after Step 9, and make a new layer (Layer 2). Use the Gradient tool to fill the type selection with the Yellow, Violet, Orange, Blue preset gradient. Then change the Layer 2 mode to Color.

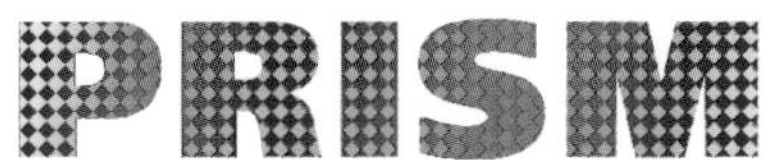


Or, change the layer mode to Difference.

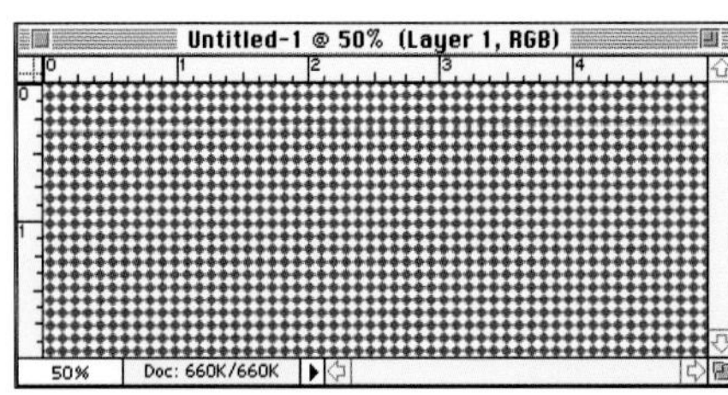


Skip Step 8 above, and follow the instructions in Step 9. The entire layer (Layer 1) should fill with checkers.

Then choose Filter➙Brush Strokes➙Crosshatch and use these settings: Stroke Length, 3; Sharpness, 9; Strength, 3.

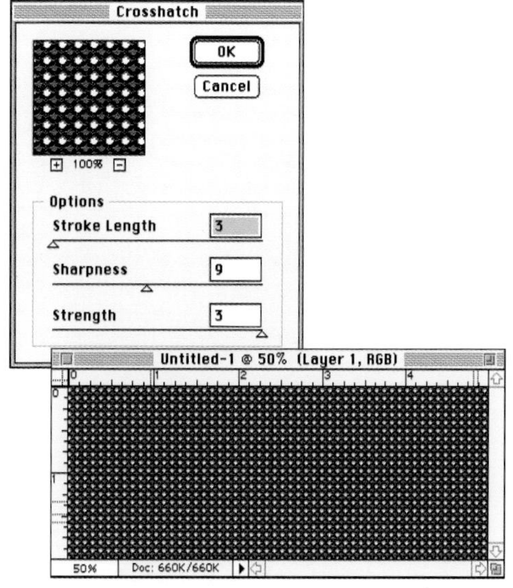


Now do Step 8. Choose Select➙Inverse and press Delete.

NAPKIN

Try these settings for the Crosshatch filter for a different effect: Stroke Length, 13; Sharpness, 20; Strength, 3.

SOCKS

To make plaid text that is a little different from the technique on page 144, use these settings in the Crosshatch filter: Stroke Length, 9; Sharpness, 5; Strength, 3.

TIE

Try applying the same filter again, but this time use the original settings: Stroke Length, 3; Sharpness, 9; Strength, 3.

BOXERS

For these variations, first I made the checkered type in channels. You can do this by creating a new file, and a channel (#4). Then start with Step 2 above. In Steps 3 and 4, fill the selections with white. Skip Step 8, so the entire

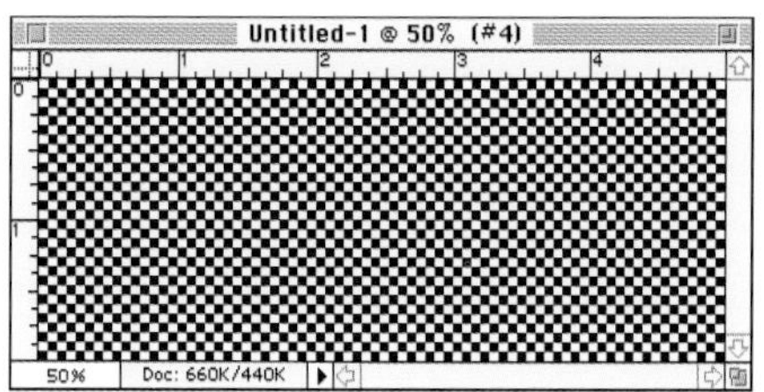

channel fills with the checks. I started by making these two channels. Channel #4:

and Channel #5.

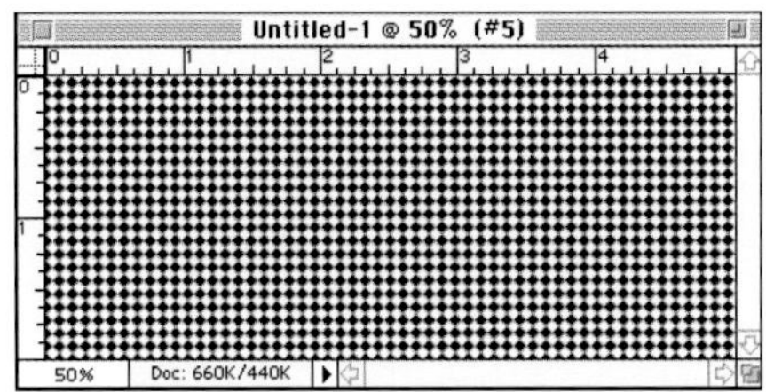


Return to the composite channel and load the selection Channel #5. Choose a foreground color and fill the selection.

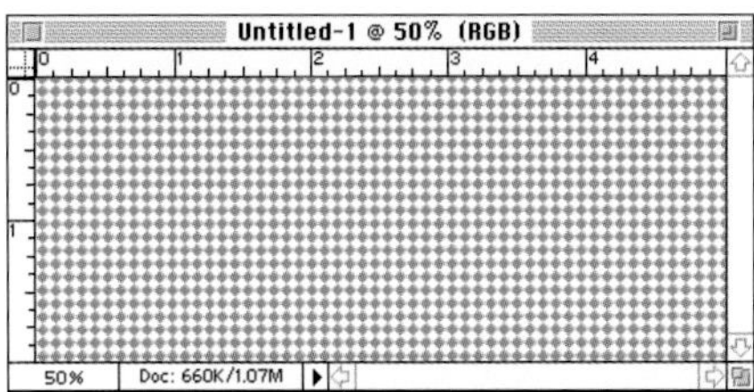


Choose Select➛Inverse. Choose another foreground color and fill the selection.

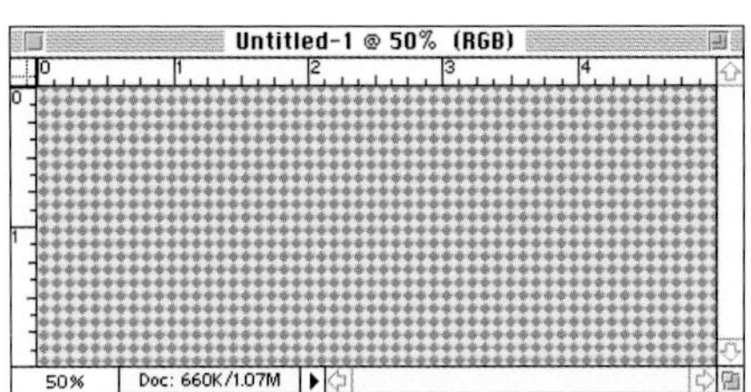


Then load the selection Channel #4 and choose Filter➛Blur➛ Gaussian Blur. I set the Radius at 2.3 pixels, but you can use this setting to create a variety of different patterns. Find something you like and move on.

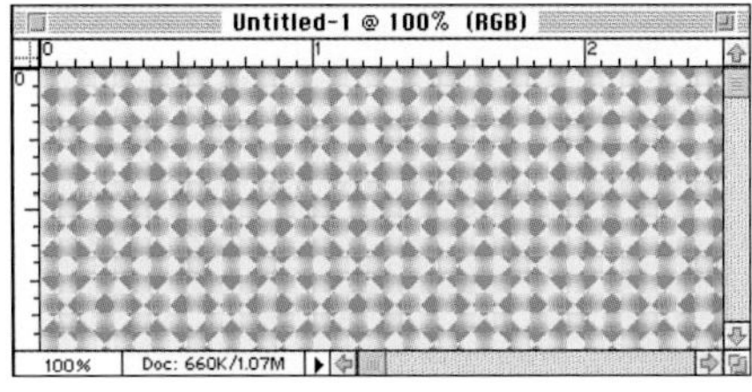


That is an interesting effect by itself. Try changing the foreground color again and choosing Filter➛ Render➛Difference Clouds.

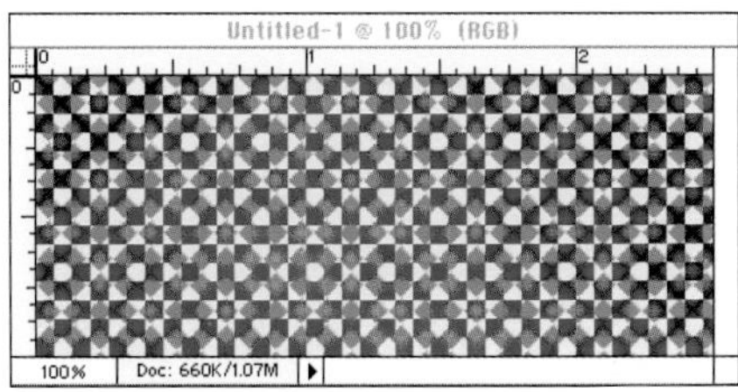

You can repeat the last step as many times as you want.

Then do Step 8 on page 45. Choose Select➔Inverse and press Delete. ■

Airbrushed chrome is one of the old standby type effects. It is quick and easy to create, but Photoshop 4.0 has made it even easier to create with its new custom gradients feature.

1 Create a new file, and a new channel (#4). Use the Type tool to enter the text into this new channel. For this effect, I used Poplar-Laudatio at 110 points.

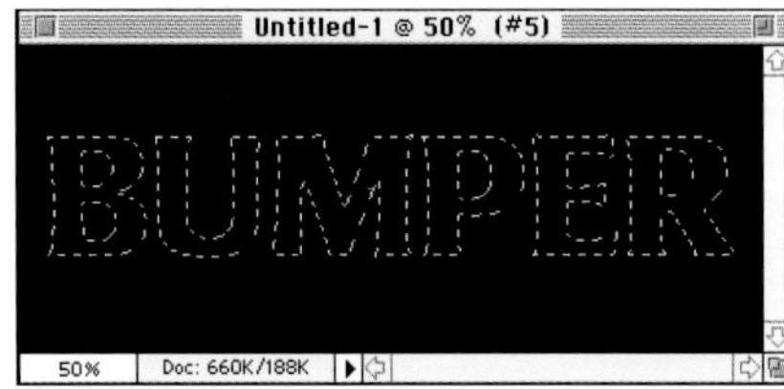


2 Create another new channel (#5). The selection should still be active.

Expand Selection

Expand By: 6 pixels

OK

Cancel

3 Choose Select➸Modify➸Expand. The number you enter here determines the width of the metallic border. I expanded the selection 6 pixels.

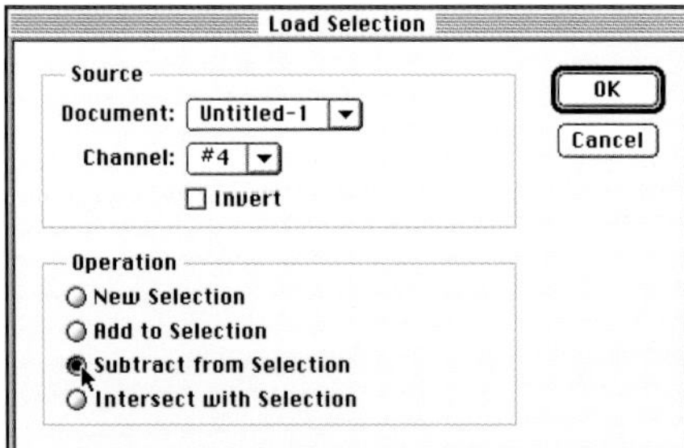


4 Next, load the selection Channel #4, with the Subtract from Selection option turned on.

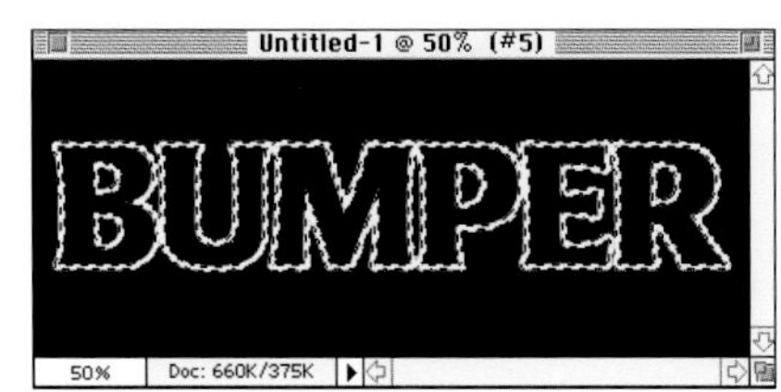


5 Fill the selection with white.

TOOLBOX

Chrome (Lighting Style Preset)

**6** Return to the composite channel. The thin border selection should be active. Again, choose Select➛Modify➛Expand (2 pixels).

**7** Choose Filter➛Render➛Lighting Effects. This filter raises the border slightly. Choose Chrome from the Style pop-up menu or match the settings in this figure, which are not much different from the default values.

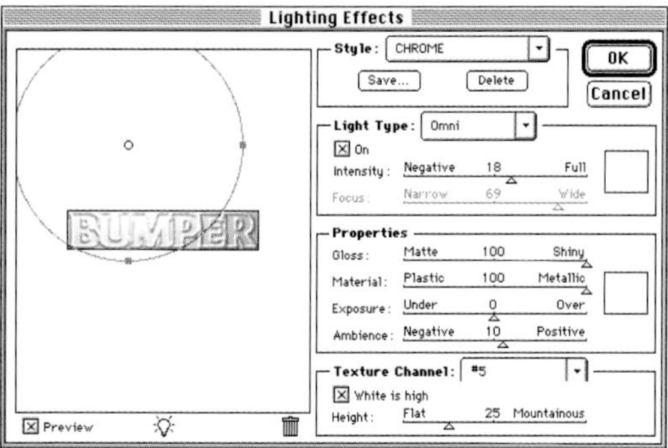


The type should now look like this.

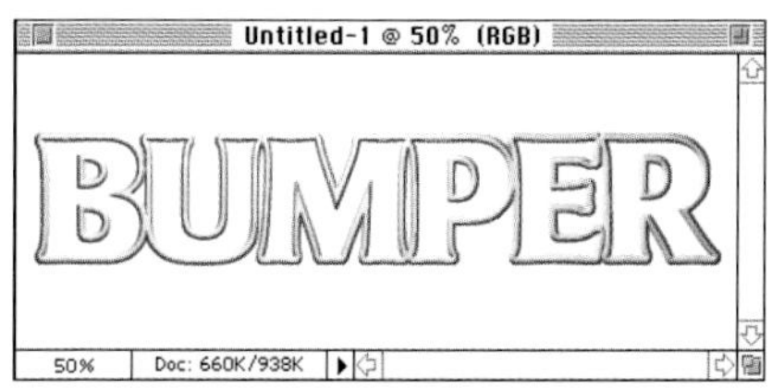


**8** Load the selection Channel #4. Double-click the Gradient Tool icon to display the Gradient Tool Options floating palette. As mentioned earlier, one of the great new features of Photoshop 4.0 is that you can define your own gradients. For those of you familiar with making custom gradients in Adobe Illustrator, Photoshop's custom gradient feature is very similar.

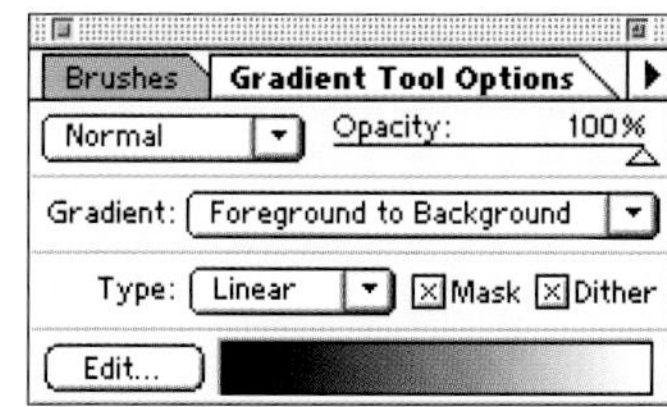

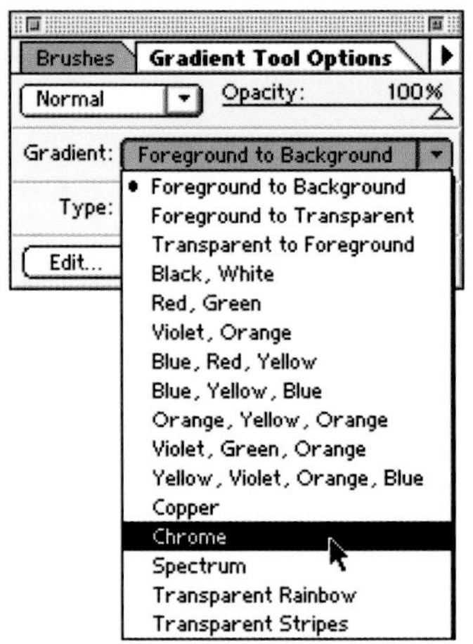


Click the Gradient pop-up menu and choose—you guessed it—Chrome. This is your lucky day. Adobe Photoshop includes a preset Chrome gradient.

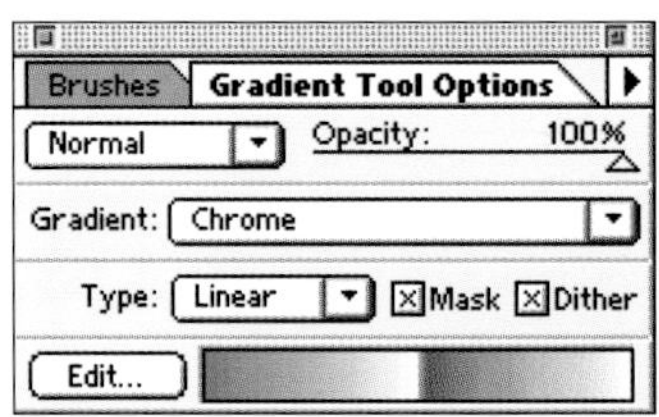


Match the rest of the settings to what you see in this figure.

**9** Hold down the Shift key and click the Gradient tool inside the type, near the top of one of the letters. Then drag straight down (holding the Shift key forces the line to remain straight) to the bottom of the letters.

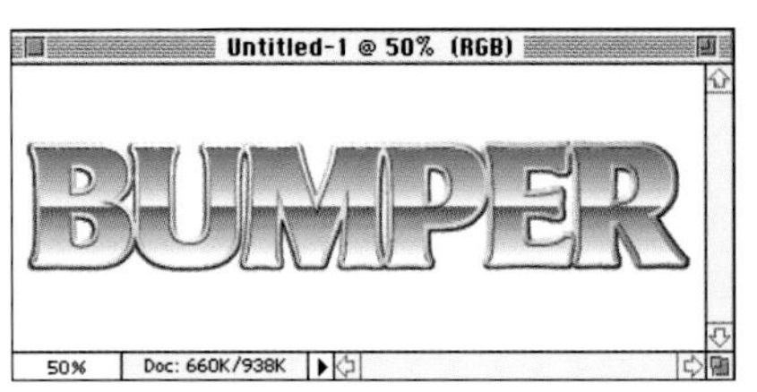


Now that was easy.

## VARIATIONS

You can adjust the preset Chrome gradient if it's not quite right for your effect. Drag the middle markers to change where the two gradients meet; or click one of the markers to highlight it. Then click the color box below and choose a new color for the blend. I changed the Chrome gradient as you can see in this figure...

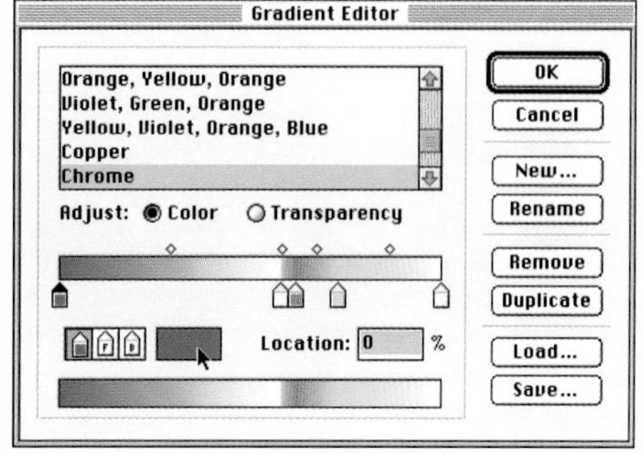


...and got this.

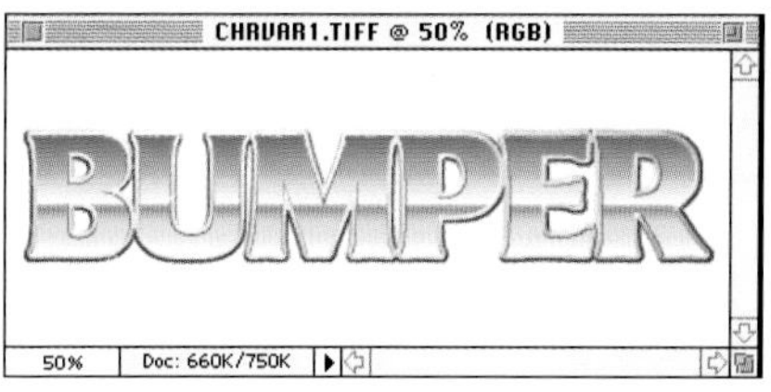


This effect is just begging for some highlight sparkles. Flip to page 102 to learn an easy way to put them on your type. ■

For this effect you will create a texture channel to be used by the Lighting Effects filter.

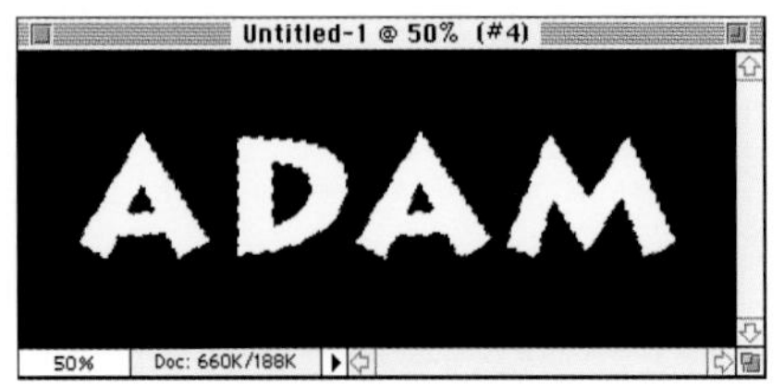


**1** Create a new file, and a new channel (#4). Use the Type tool to enter the text. The type in this example is Lithos Black at 80 points.

**2** Save the selection to create Channel #5. Deselect the type.

**3** Then choose Filter➵Render➵ Difference Clouds to fill the channel (#4).

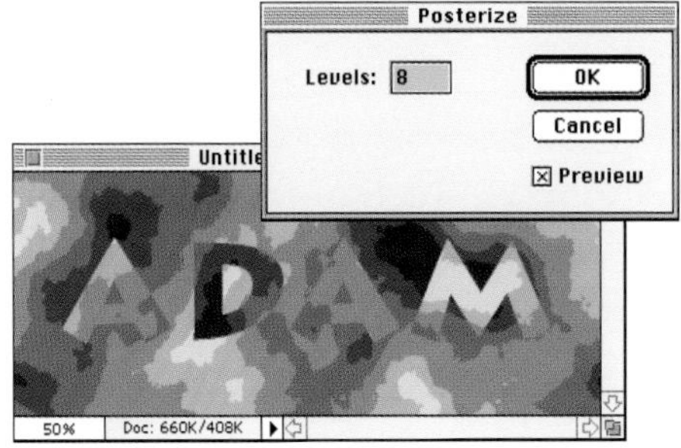


**4** Choose Image➵Adjust➵ Posterize. Keep the setting low. I used 8 levels. This step flattens the cloud gradation into flat areas that look like scraped clay.

**TOOLBOX**

Clay (Lighting Style Preset)

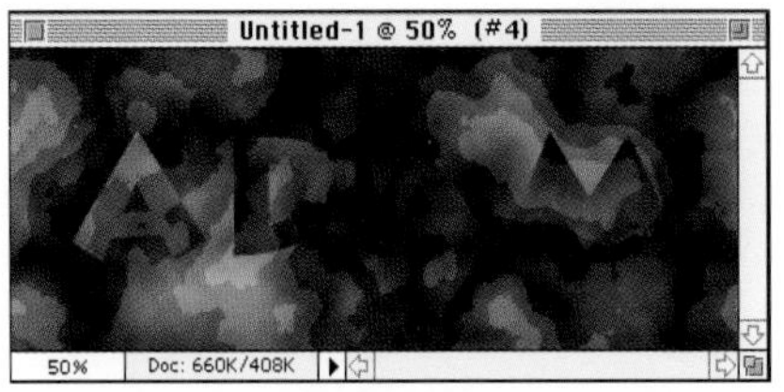


**5** Then choose Filter➵Render➵ Difference Clouds, again. This is the channel that will be used for the clay texture.

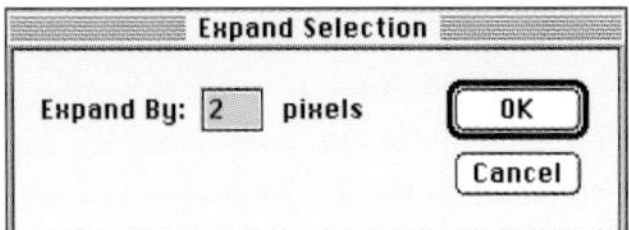


**6** Return to the composite channel, and load the selection Channel #5. Choose Select➵ Modify➵Expand (2 pixels). Expanding the selection eventually gives the type its lip.

**7** Choose Filter➔Render➔Lighting Effects. You can choose Clay from the Style menu or match the settings in this figure.

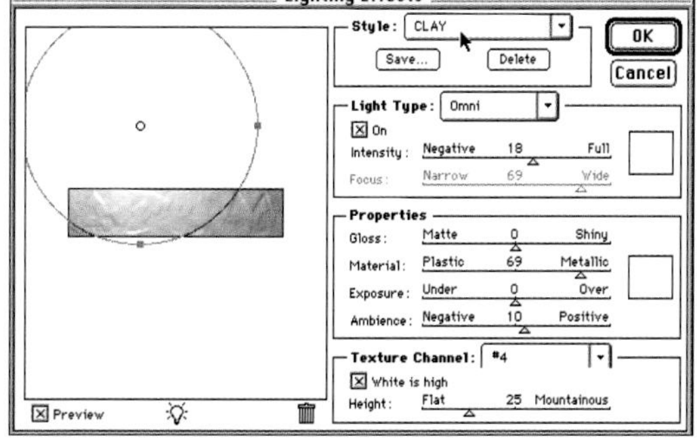


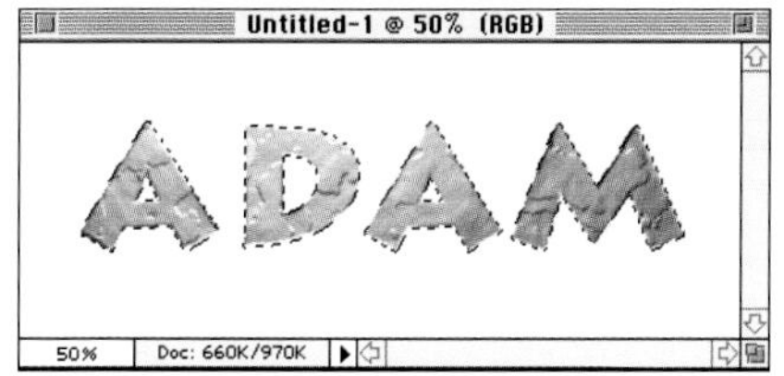


**8** Keep the selection active and choose Image➔Adjust➔Auto Levels.

**9** Then choose Image➔Adjust➔ Hue/Saturation. Check the Colorize box and try these settings:

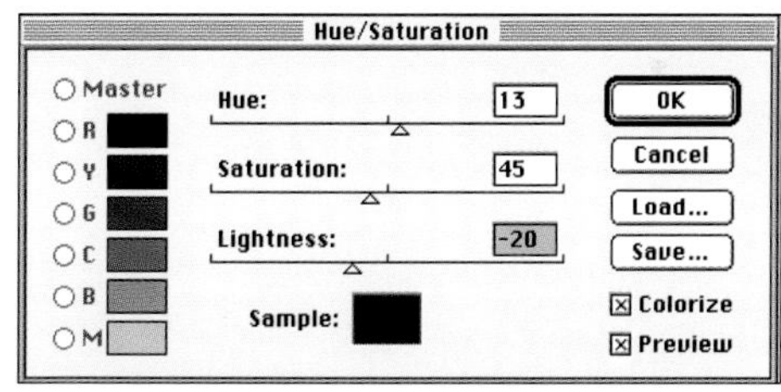


Deselect the text.

# VARIATIONS

## Adding Cracks

To add cracks, follow the previous steps with these exceptions:

After Step 5:

**5(a)** Create a new channel (#6). Choose Filter➔Render➔Clouds. Then choose Image➔Adjust➔Posterize (8 levels), and Filter➔Render➔Difference Clouds. Look familiar?

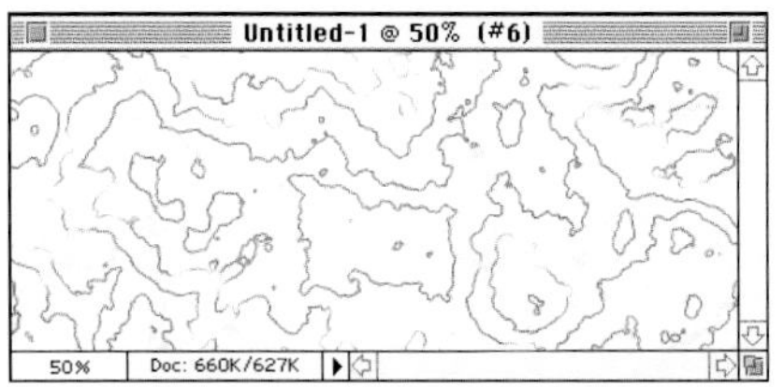


**5(b)** Next, choose Filter➔Stylize➔Find Edges.

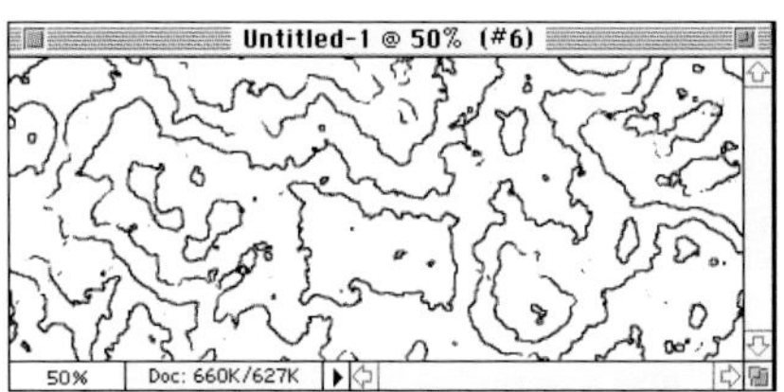


**5(c)** Then choose Image➔Adjust➔Threshold. The slider can be used to control the heaviness of the clay cracks. The threshold level for this example was set at 223.

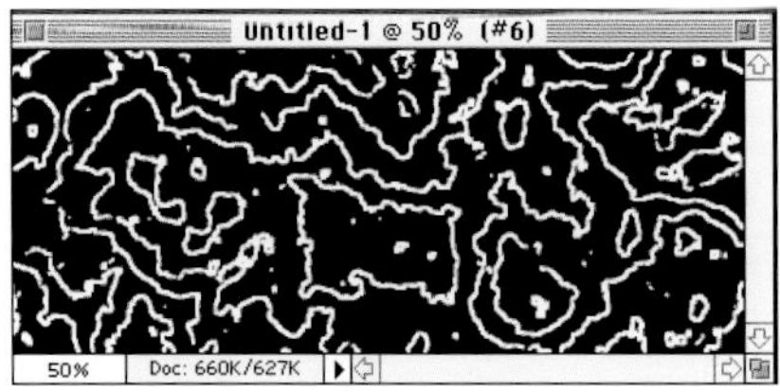


**5(d)** Press Command-I [Control-I] to invert the channel. Then choose Filter➔Other➔Maximum (1) to widen the white lines.

**5(e)** Make Channel #4 the active channel and load the selection Channel #6, with the cracks you just made. Fill the selection with black.

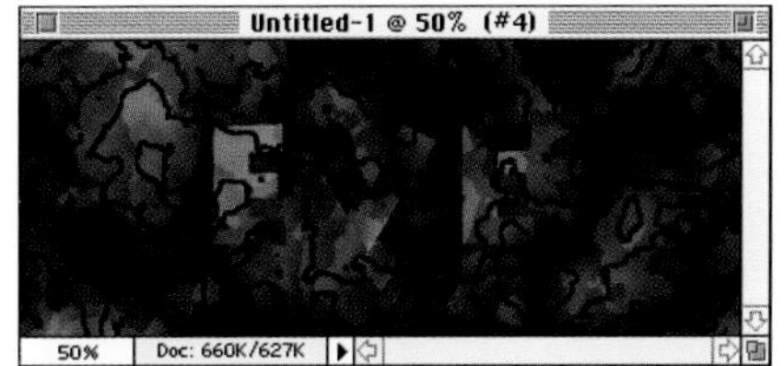


**6(a)** Do Step 6, then load the selection Channel #6 and check the Subtract from Selection option in the Load Selection dialog box. You should have a selection like this.

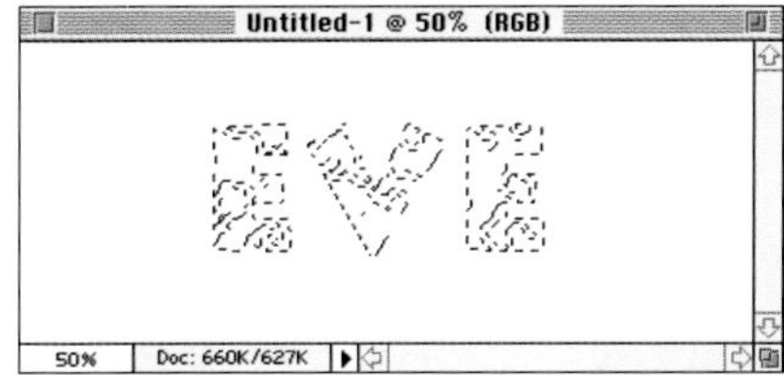


Complete the rest of the steps, and you should end up with an effect that looks something like this. ■

The Noise and Crystallize filters team up to do most of the work for this effect.

**1** Create a new file. Use the Type Mask tool to enter the text. I used the Birch font at 90 points. Choose black for the foreground color and fill the text selection.

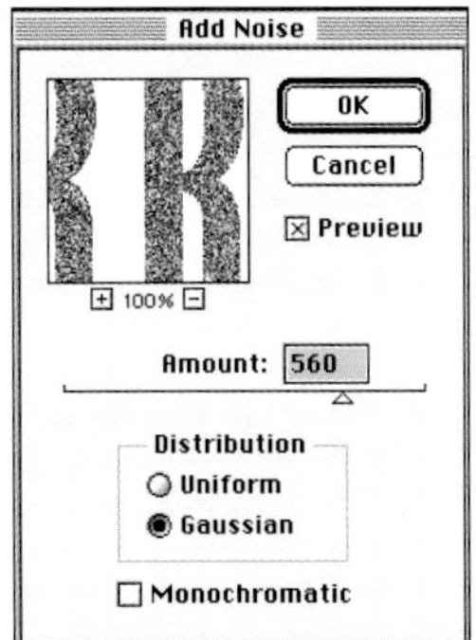


**2** Choose Filter➜Noise➜Add Noise. Slide the marker to the right until most of the black pixels are replaced by colored pixels. For the desired effect in this example, the marker was moved until the amount hit 560. Deselect the text.

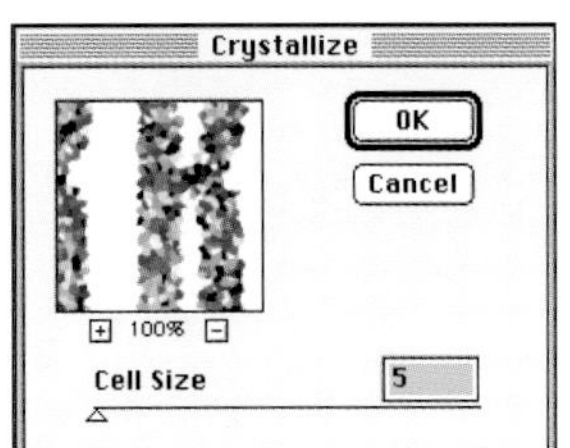


**3** Then choose Filter➜Pixelate➜Crystallize. In the preview you will see the noise pixels turn into flakes (the greater the Cell Size, the larger the flakes). Just make sure that you still can read the text. Here's how the text looks with a Cell Size of 5.

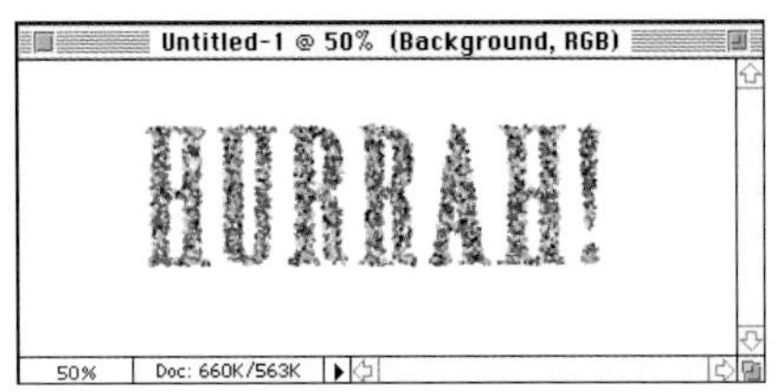

**4** Now, we need to get rid of all the blacks and grays. Choose Image➸Adjust➸Selective Color. From the Colors pop-up menu choose Blacks. Then slide the black marker all the way to the left (-100%). Do the same for the Neutrals and Whites categories. You will see all the blacks and grays disappear from your text.

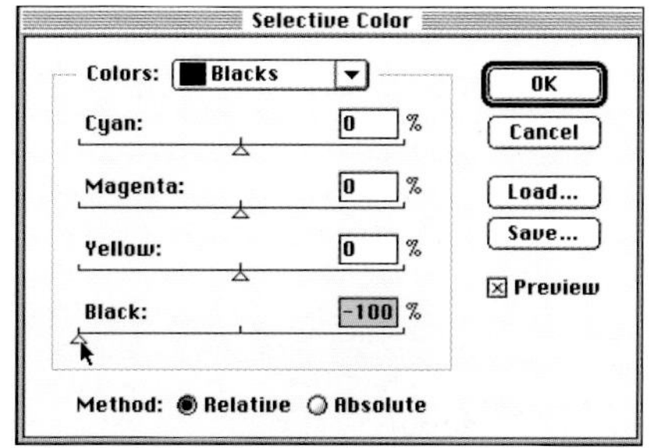


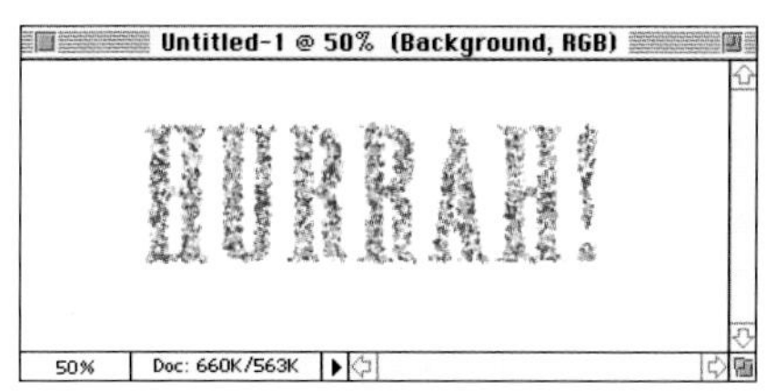


**5** Now to control that glaring color, choose Image➸Adjust➸Replace Color. Oh no—so many controls! Just relax and play. Use the Eyedropper to click on a color in the image window. All similar colors will be selected. The Fuzziness slider control allows you to expand the selection to include more similar colors. With the Hue, Saturation, and Lightness sliders you can change the color you selected. When you are satisfied with the first color change click OK. Then repeat this step to change the next color. ■

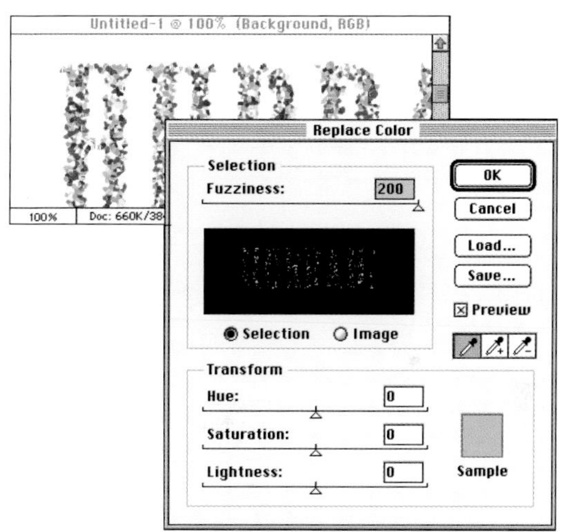


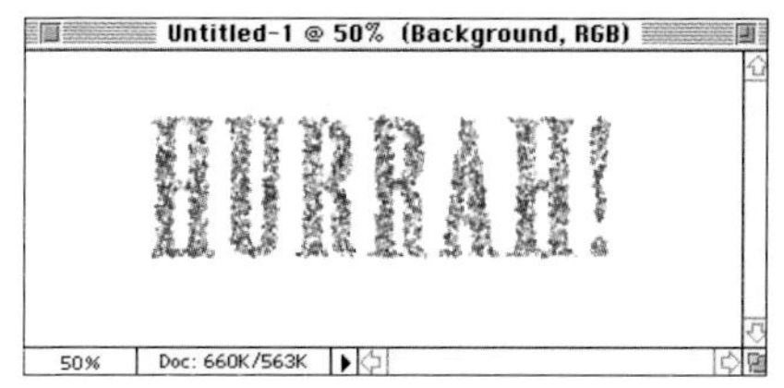

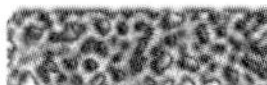
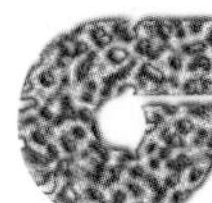
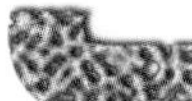

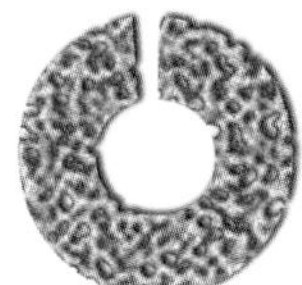

One of the new Sketch filters in Photoshop 4.0, Reticulation, allows you to create this coral effect. This filter produces just the right texture that you can coax into becoming coral.

**1** Create a new file, and a new channel (#4).

**2** Choose Filter→Sketch→Reticulation. The settings in this filter do not have to be precise. Just to make it easy though, I entered 20 for all three variables.

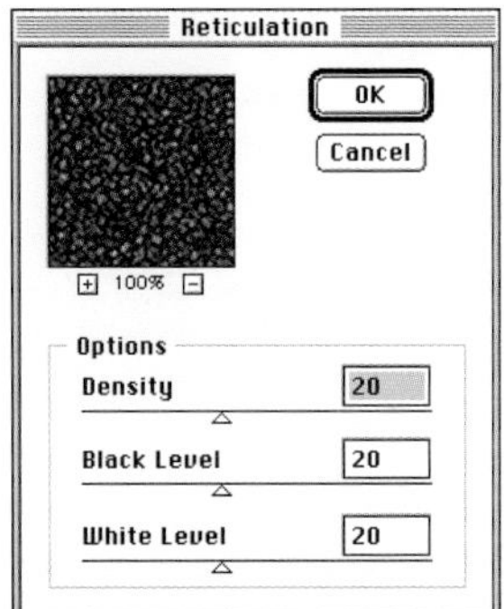


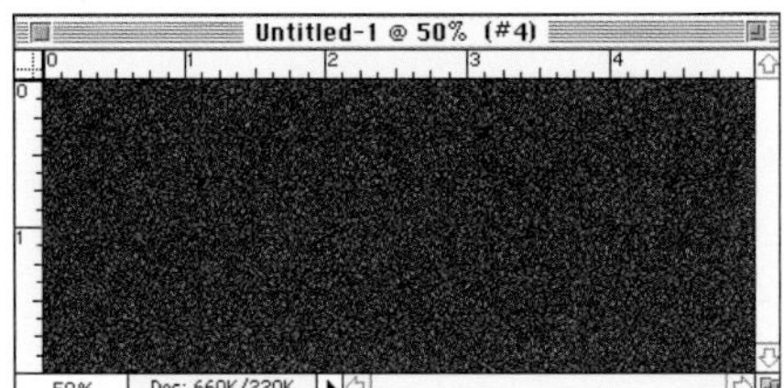


**3** Choose Image→Adjust→Invert. Now you can see the beginning of the coral pattern.

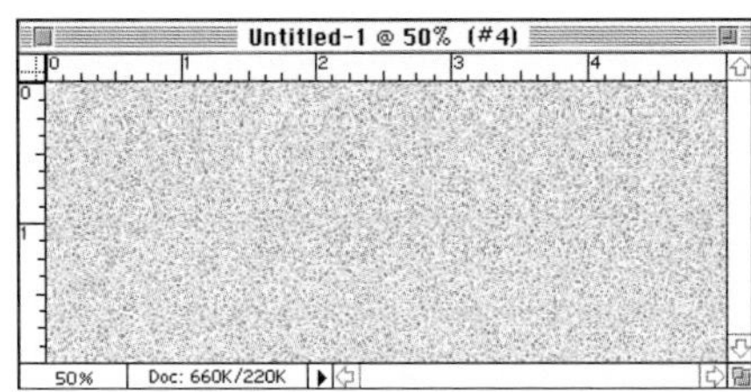

**4** You may need to enlarge the pattern for your type. To do this, select the rectangular Marquee tool and drag a selection, like this:

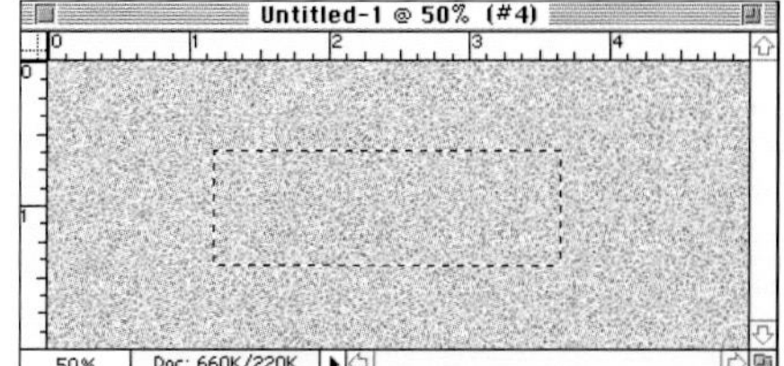


**5** Then choose Layer⇒Free Transform. Grab the corners of the box and drag them toward the corners of the image window.

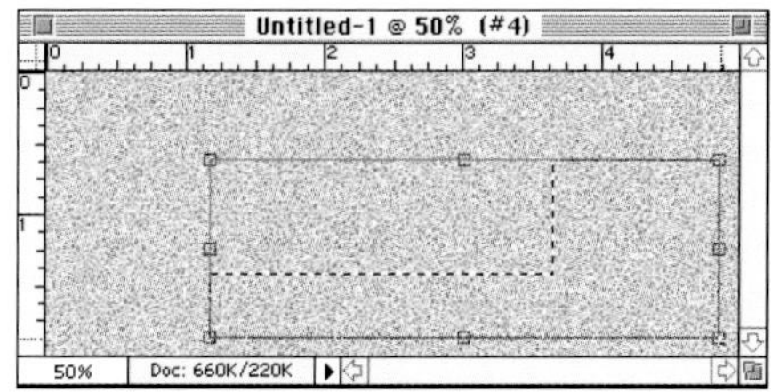


Press the Return [Enter] key to accept the changes.

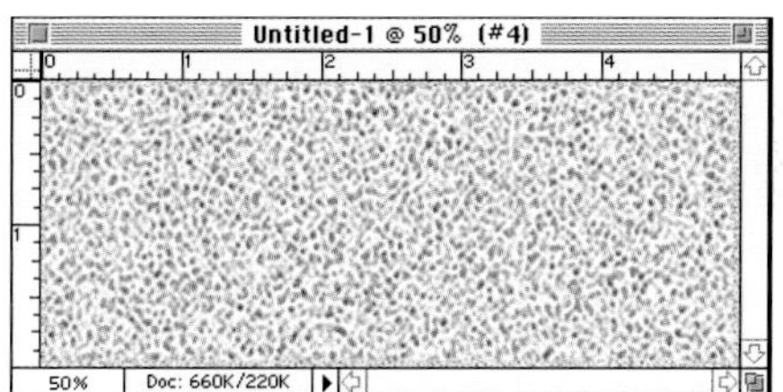


**6** Choose Image⇒Adjust⇒Levels. The graph in the Levels dialog box shows a large mound piled up on the right side. Grab the left (black) marker and slide it to the right until it is under the beginning of this mound.

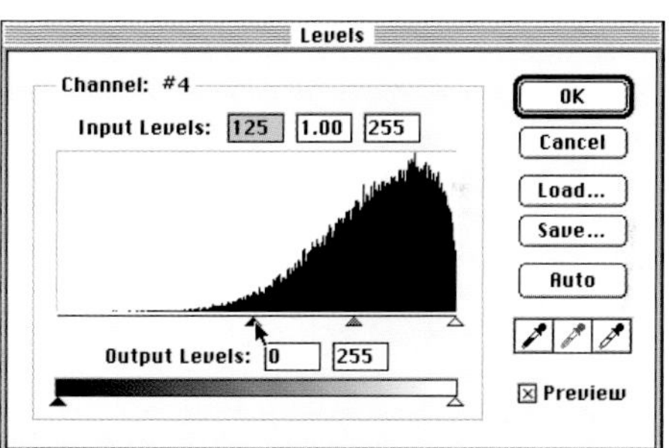


You are looking for something like this:

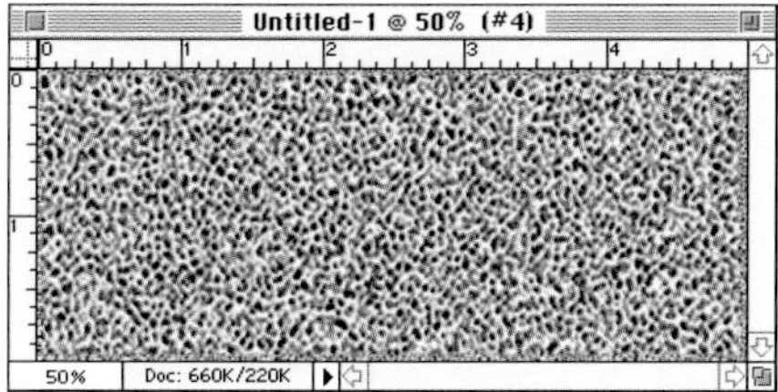

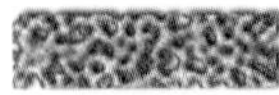
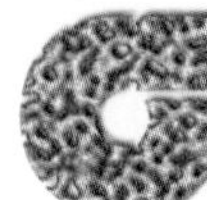
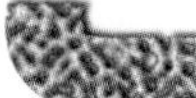
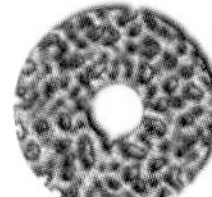
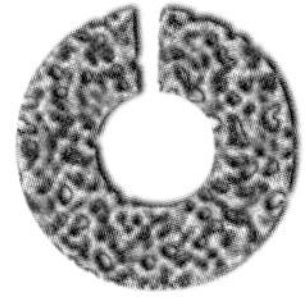

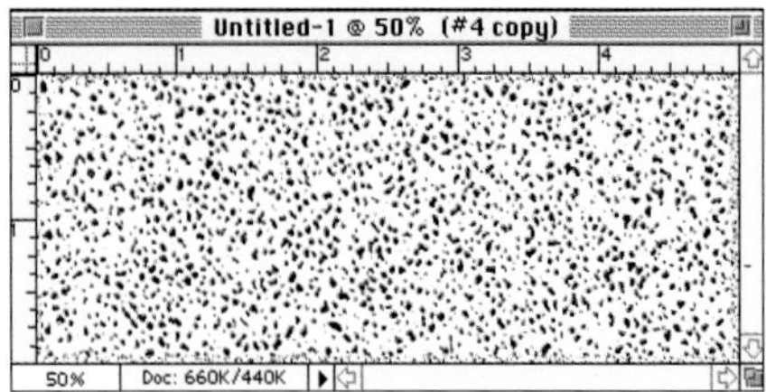


**7** Duplicate Channel #4 to create Channel #4 copy. Then choose Image➝Adjust➝Threshold. Set the Threshold Level near 76. This channel, along with Channel #6 (created in Step 9), will be used to set the outlines of the wriggling coral.

**8** Return to the composite channel and make a new layer (Layer 1). Then use the Type Mask tool to enter the text. I used the Bauhaus font at 120 points.

**9** Save the selection to create Channel #6.

**10** Then load the selection Channel #4, with the Intersect with Selection option turned on.

**11** Change the foreground color to white and fill the selection. You won't see any change on the screen because the Background layer is visible and is filled with white.

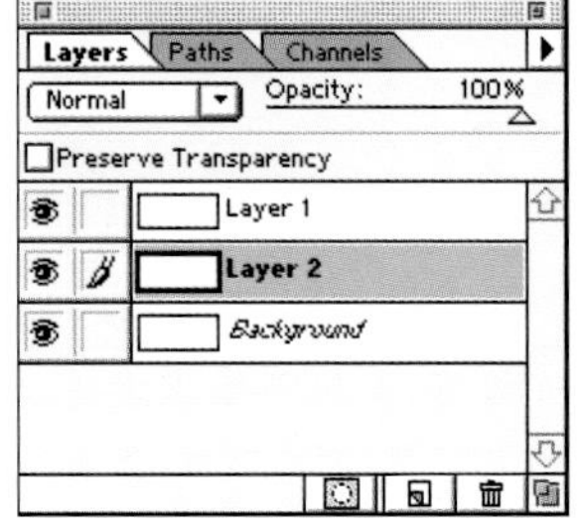


**12** Make another new layer (Layer 2), and move the new layer below Layer 1.

**13** Now load the selection Channel #6 (the channel that contains the type selection). Then load the selection Channel #4 copy with the Intersect with Selection option turned on.

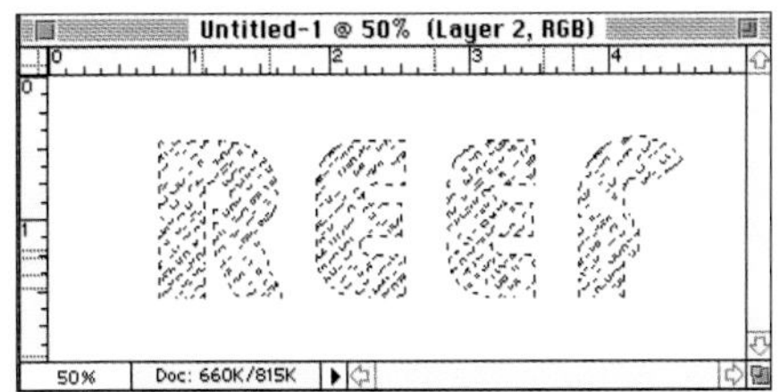


**14** Change the foreground color to black and fill the selection.

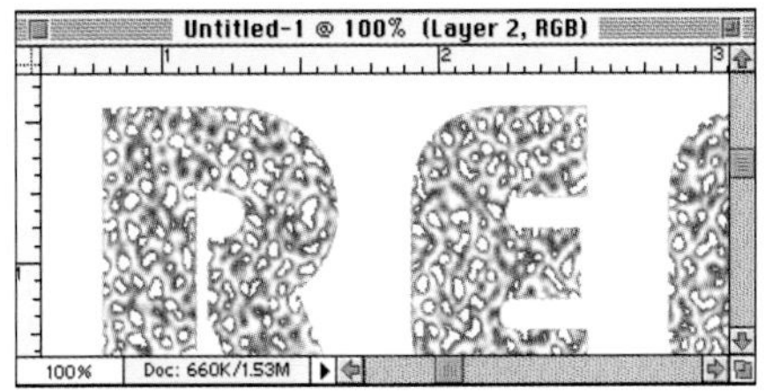


**15** Make a duplicate of Layer 2 to create Layer 2 copy. Then move Layer 2 copy above Layer 1.

**16** Change the blending mode for Layer 2 copy to Color. It will appear as though the black has disappeared.

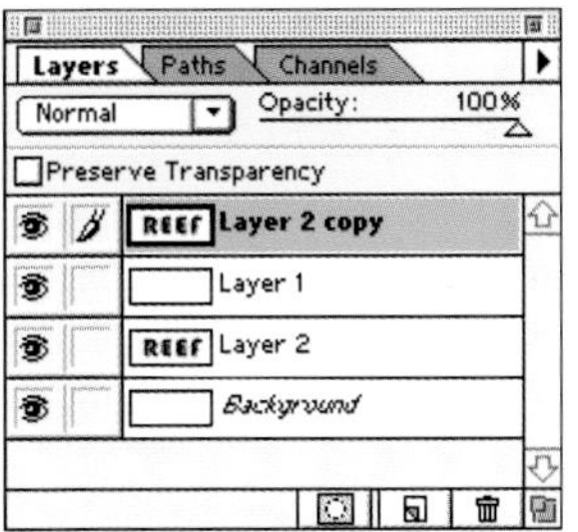


**17** Choose Image➛Adjust➛Hue/Saturation. Turn on the Colorize option. Raise the Lightness and use the Hue and Saturation markers to choose a color for your coral type.

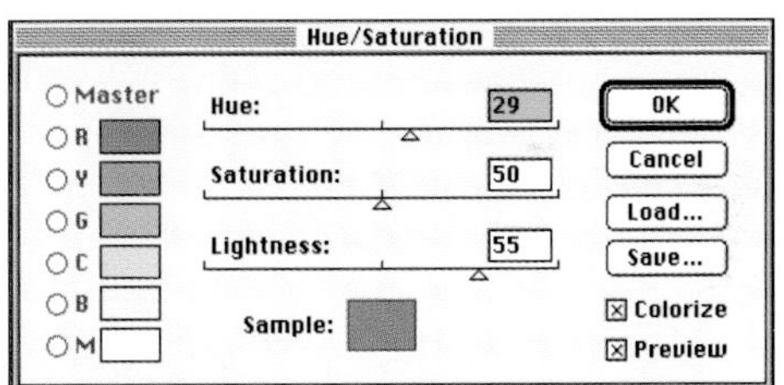


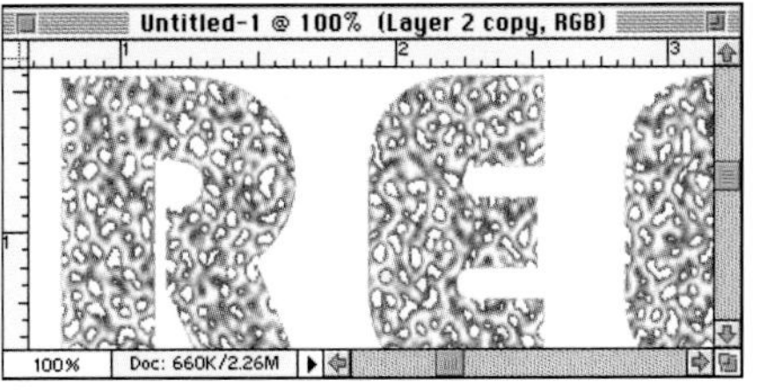

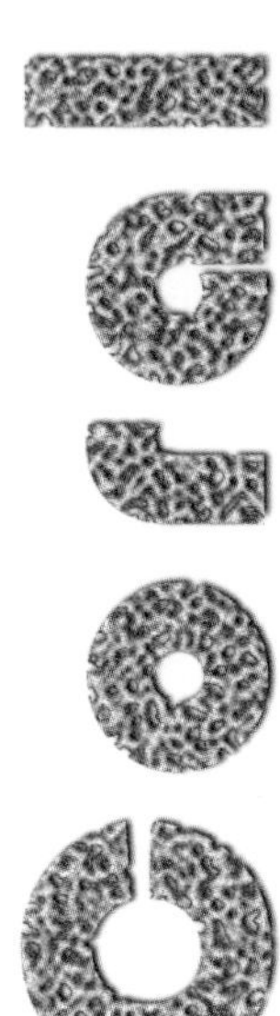


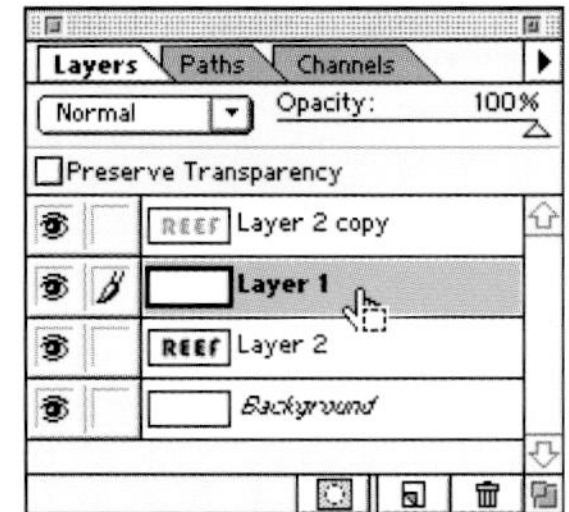


**18** To work on the texture, make Layer 1 the active layer, and load the transparency selection of Layer 1.

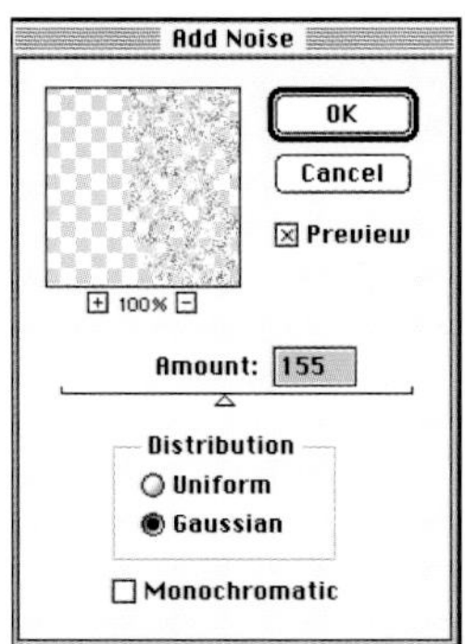


**19** Choose Filter➞Noise➞Add Noise. I kept the Monochromatic option unchecked. Choose Gaussian and set the Amount at 155. Try other settings to produce slightly different textures.

Click OK and you're finished. ■

This effect involves a little channel work to create some fancy selections that will fluff up your type.

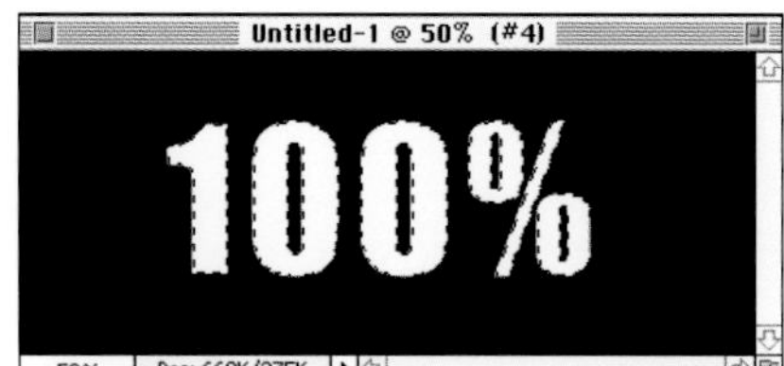


**1** Create a new file, and a new channel (#4). Use the Type tool to enter the text. I used Impact at 90 points. Save the selection to create Channel #5.

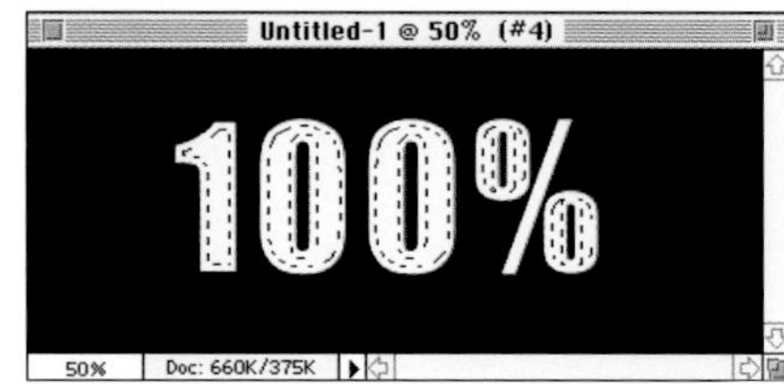


**2** Choose Select→Modify→Contract. Contract the selection so that it shrinks to about one-third of its width. I chose 6 pixels. Save the selection to create Channel #6.

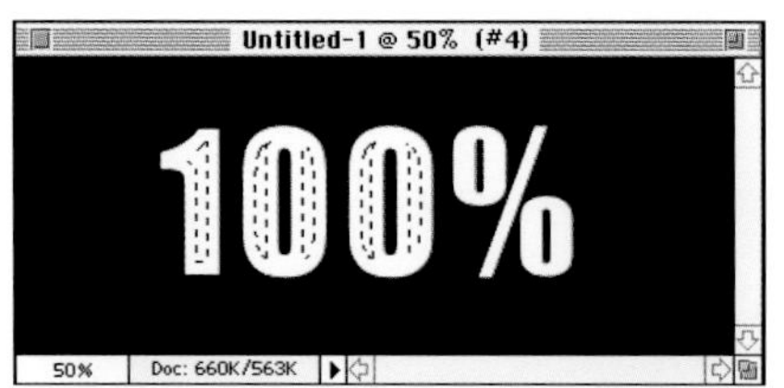


**3** Again, choose Select→Modify→Contract. Contract the selection to the same amount as in Step 2. Save the selection to create Channel #7.

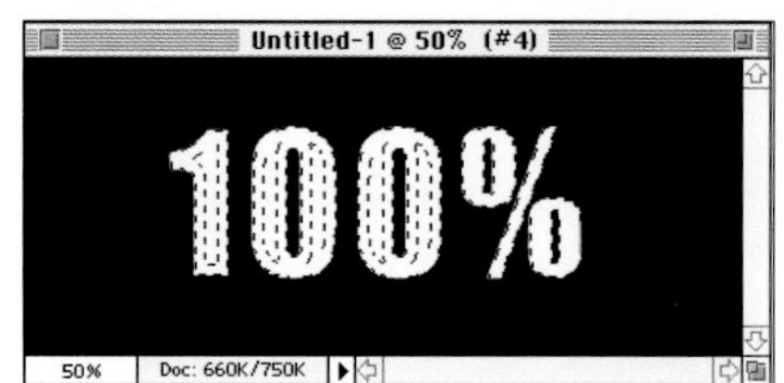


**4** Load the selection Channel #5, and then load the selection Channel #7 with the Subtract from Selection option turned on.

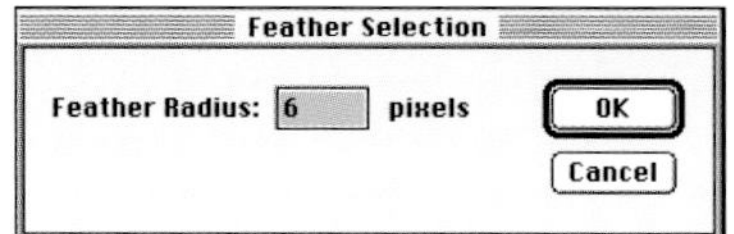


**5** Choose Select→Feather. Feather the selection to about the same amount as you contracted it in Step 2. All of the feathering you do in this technique helps to make sure that the texture is soft.

**6** Choose Filter➸Noise➸Add Noise (Gaussian). Add a low to medium amount of noise. Just make sure that you add less noise in Step 8. I set the Amount at 140 pixels.

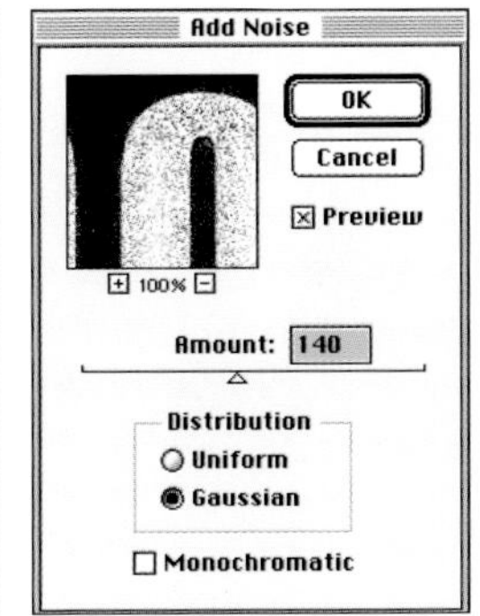


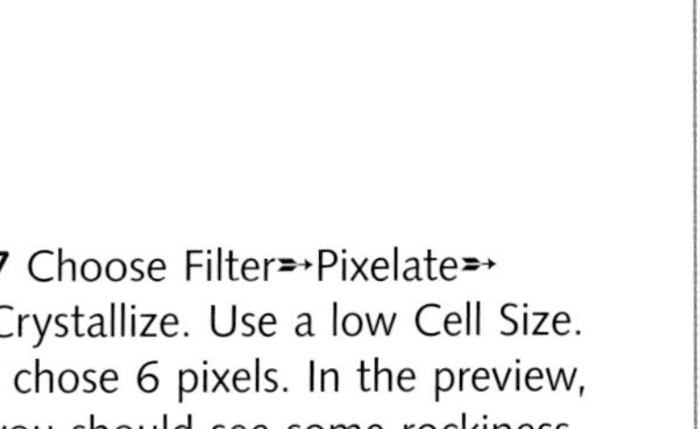

**7** Choose Filter➸Pixelate➸Crystallize. Use a low Cell Size. I chose 6 pixels. In the preview, you should see some rockiness appear among the noise. Keep the rocks small.

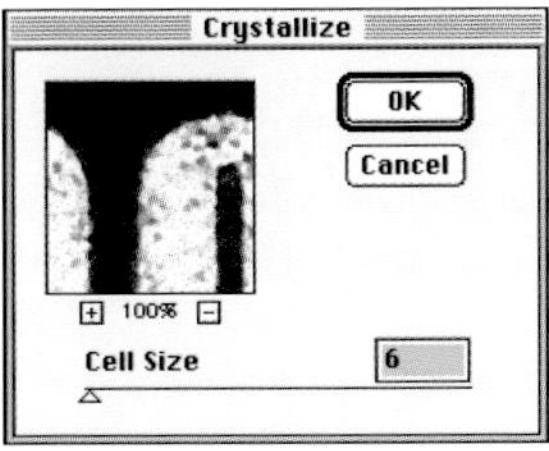


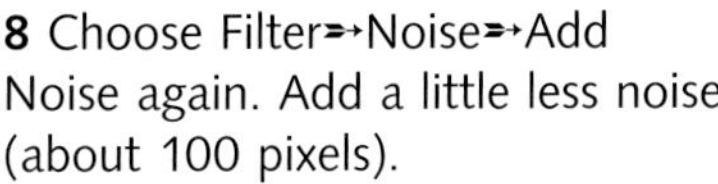

**8** Choose Filter➸Noise➸Add Noise again. Add a little less noise (about 100 pixels).

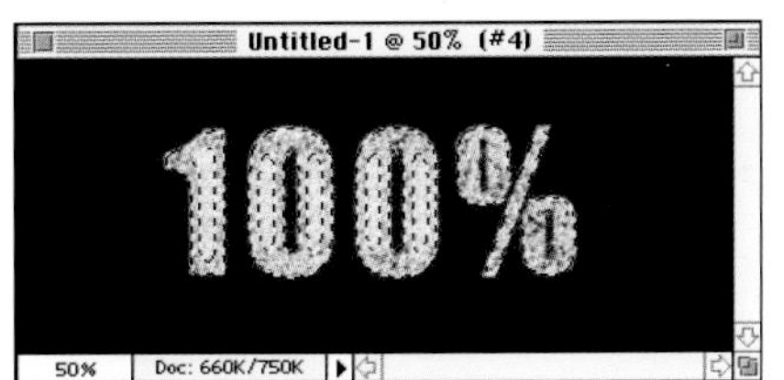


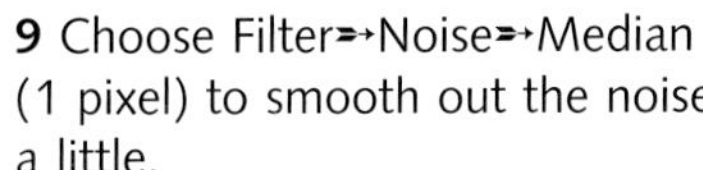

**9** Choose Filter➸Noise➸Median (1 pixel) to smooth out the noise a little.

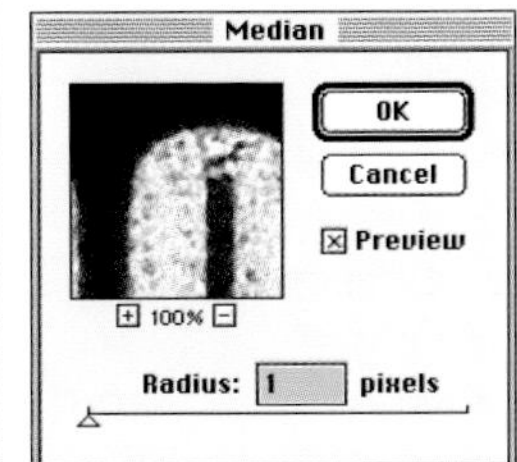

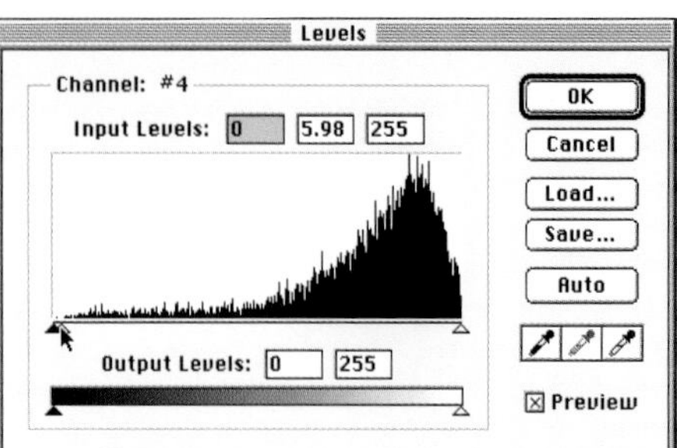


**10** Choose Image➝Adjust➝Levels, and grab the middle (gray) marker and slide it all the way to the left.

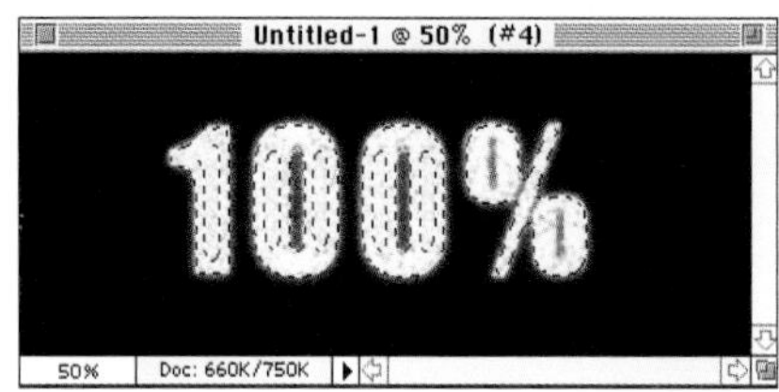


You now are about halfway through this effect and your type should look something like this.

**11** Now let's run through this same routine one more time. Load the selection Channel #5, then load the selection Channel #6 with the Subtract from Selection option turned on. Choose Select➝Feather and feather the selection about half as much as you did in Step 5.

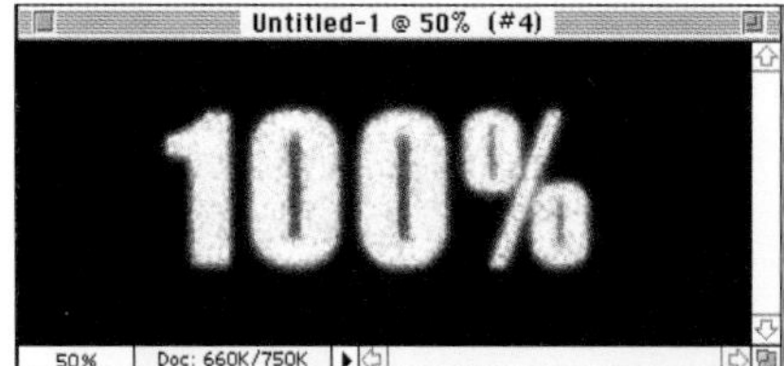


**12** Do Steps 7 through 9 with this new selection.

**13** Load the selection Channel #4 (the same channel that you should be in).

**14** Choose Image➛Adjust➛Levels, grab the middle (gray) marker and slide it all the way to the left. (This is the same thing you did in Step 10.)

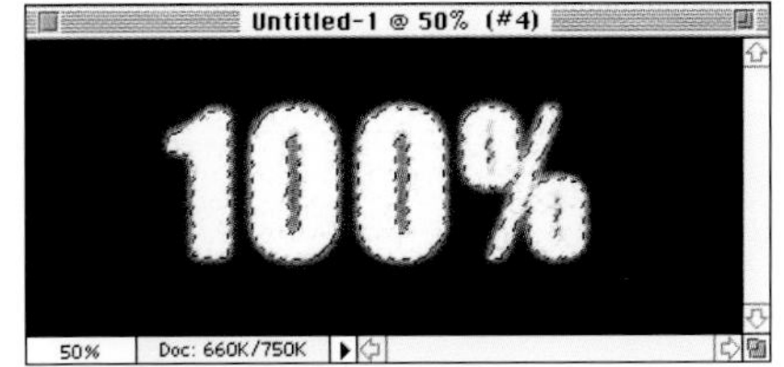


**15** Return to the composite channel. Make a new layer (Layer 1), then make another new layer (Layer 2).

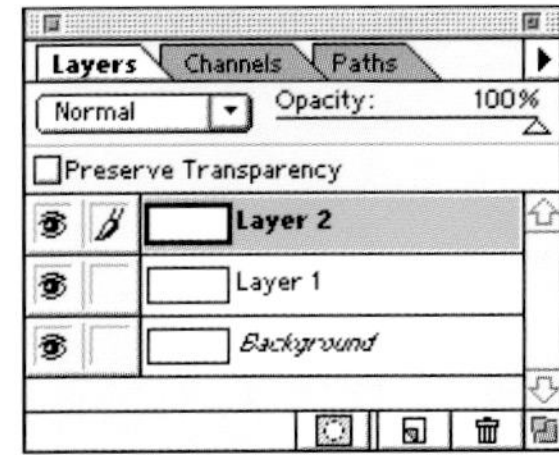


**16** Change the foreground color to white and load the selection Channel #4. Fill the selection with white. Nothing will happen in the image window because you just filled white on white. But you will see the effect in a few steps.

**17** Make Layer 1 the active layer. Change the foreground color to black. Fill the selection.

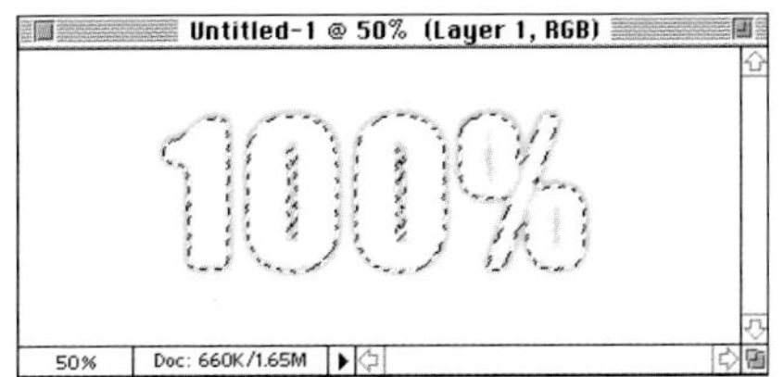


**18** Select the Move tool and use the keyboard arrow keys to move the shadow (Layer 1) two keystrokes to the right, and two keystrokes down.

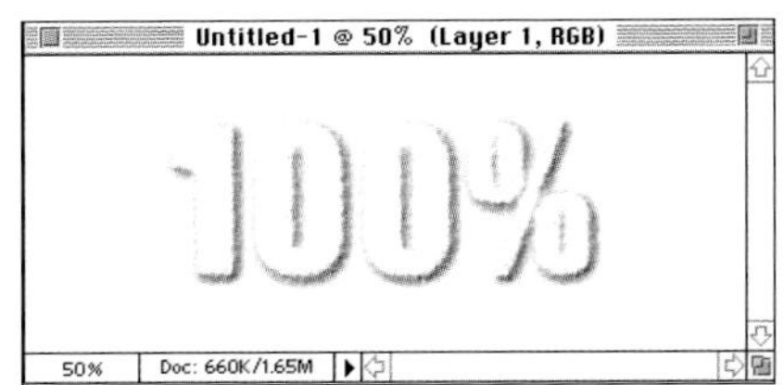

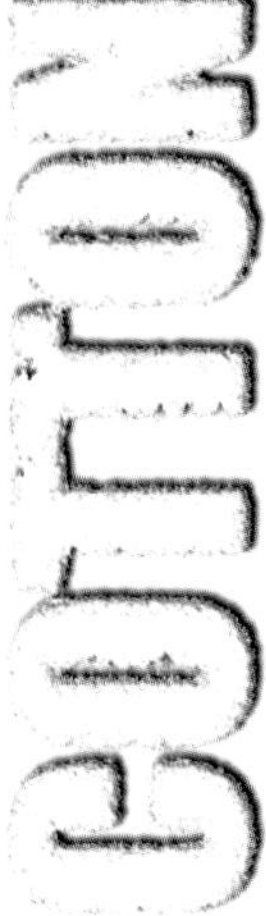

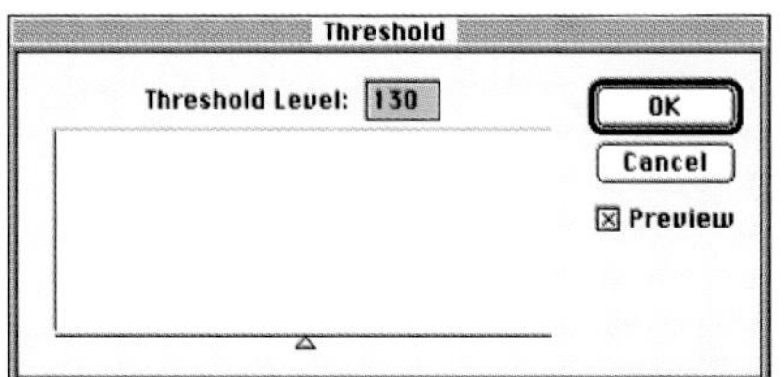


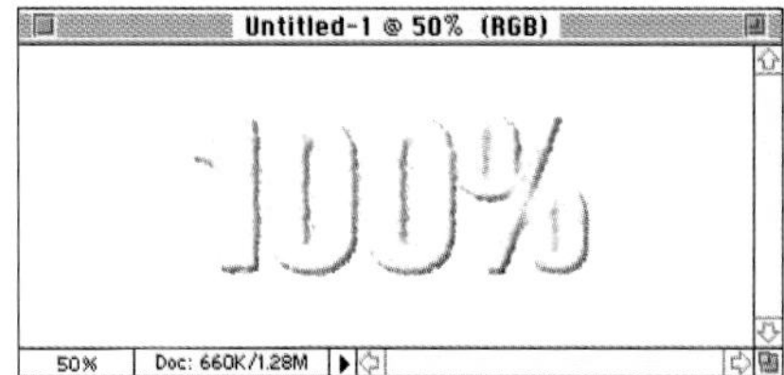


**19** Deselect the text. Choose Image⇒Adjust⇒Threshold. Slide the marker to the left, watching the preview until you get something that looks like this. Flatten the image and you're finished. ■

For this effect, you first need to break up the edges of the type, and then use the Lighting Effects filter to raise the interior of the type.

**1** Create a new file, and a new channel (#4). Use the Type tool to enter the text into the new channel. A font with serifs (prey for our decaying techniques) works well. I used Sabon at 120 points for this example.

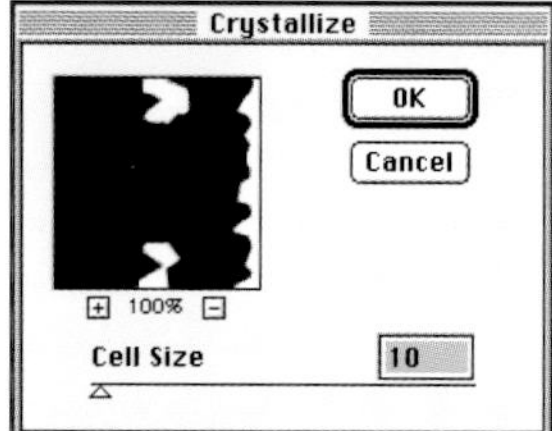


**2** Deselect the type, then choose Filter➛Pixelate➛Crystallize. This filter will roughen the edges. Keep the Cell Size small so that the interiors of the letters remain intact. For this example, I set the Cell Size to 10.

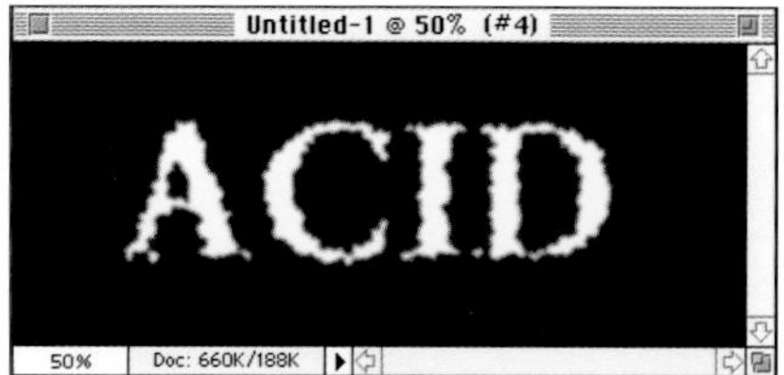


**3** Choose Filter➛Blur➛Gaussian Blur, and blur the type just a little. I chose a Radius of 2.

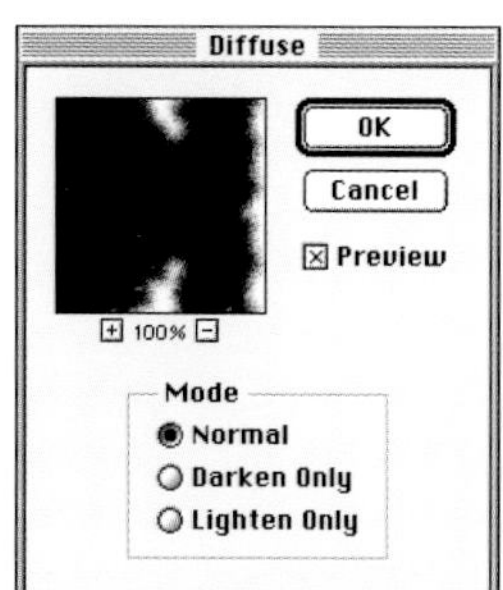


**TIP** **With smaller type, the blurring may not be necessary.**

**4** Next, choose Filter➛Stylize➛Diffuse (Normal).

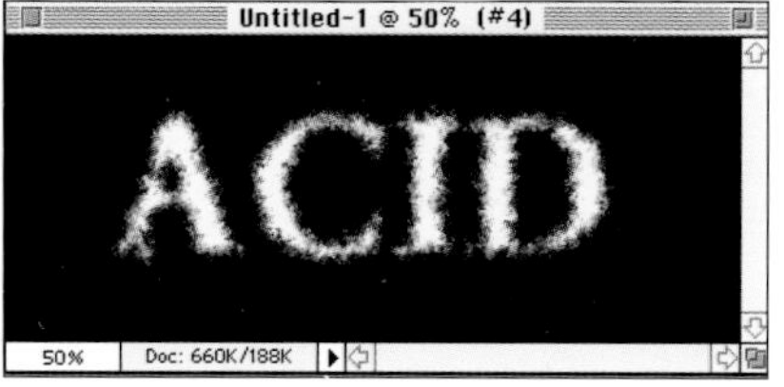


**5** The decaying has begun. The more times you apply this filter, the more the type will break up. The larger the type, the more applications it will take to break it up. After the filter was applied 20 times, the text channel looked like this:



**TOOLBOX**

Decay (Lighting Style Preset)

**TIP** **If you want to reapply the last filter that you used with the same settings, press Command-F [Control-F].**

**6** Return to the composite channel, and load the selection you just created (Channel #4).

**7** Change the foreground color to a color for your type. I used the CMYK values 16, 8, 69, 2. Fill the selection with the color.

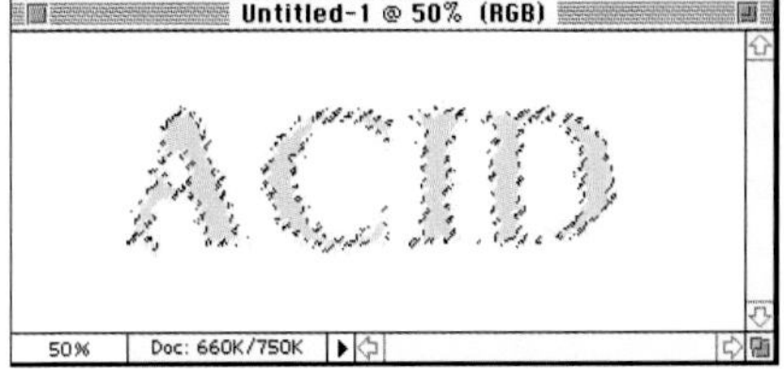


**8** Choose Filter➛Render➛Lighting Effects. In the Lighting Effects dialog box you can click the Style menu and find the Decay preset or just match the settings seen in this figure.

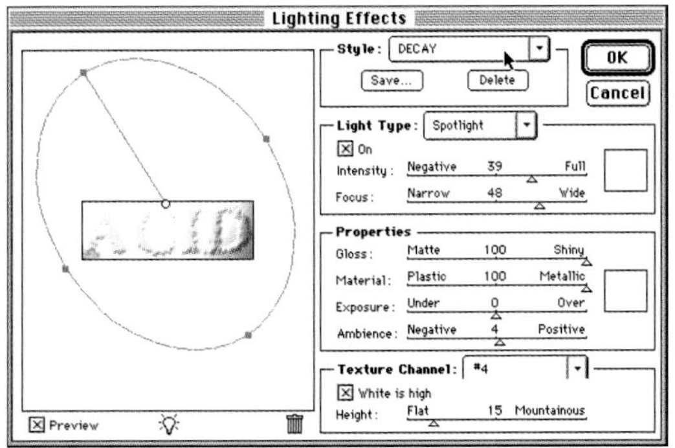


**9** Deselect the type, and you're finished. ■

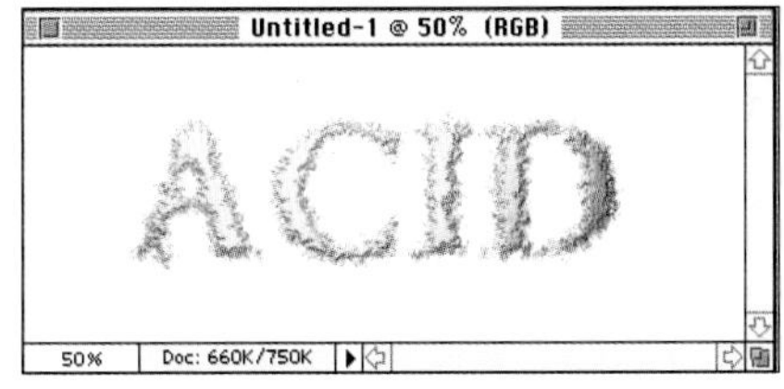

This effect runs through a number of filters, but the Clouds filter gives this effect the realistic touch it needs.

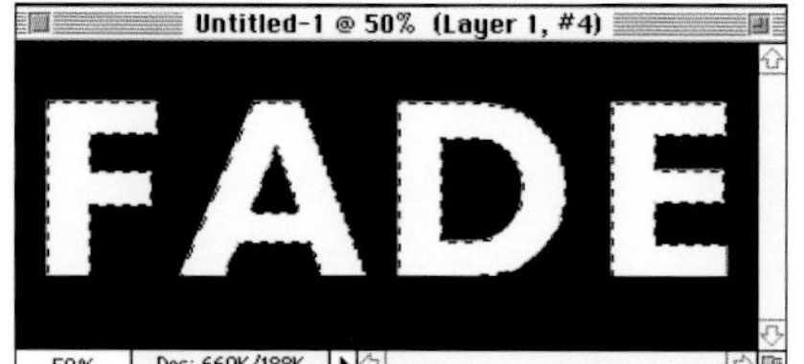


**1** Create a new file, a new layer (Layer 1), and a new channel (#4). Use the Type tool to enter the text in the channel. It is helpful to use a thick font that can disappear in places and still be readable. In this example, I used Humanst at 120 points.

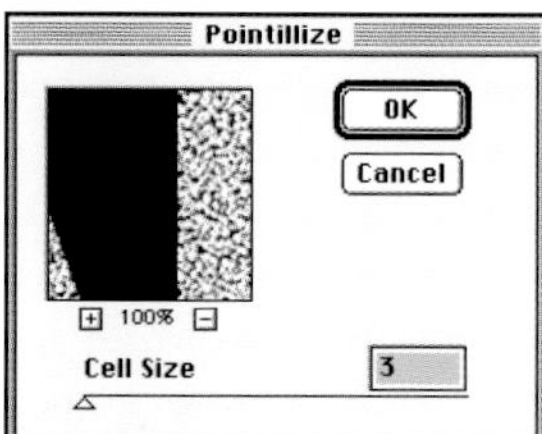


**2** Next, choose Filter➝Pixelate➝Pointillize and select the smallest possible Cell Size: 3.

**3** Choose Filter➝Pixelate➝Fragment.

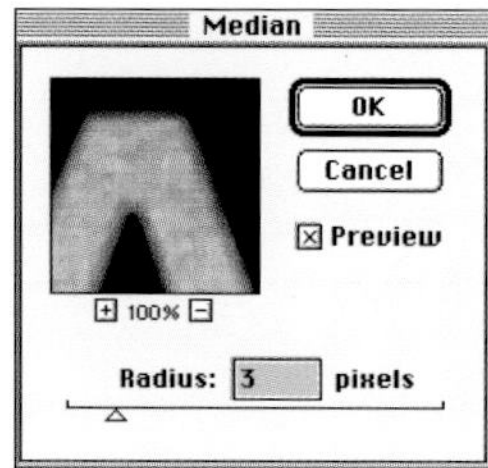


**4** Deselect the text, and choose Filter➝Noise➝Median. In this example, I used a Radius of 3 pixels.

**5** To increase the contrast in this channel, choose Image⇒Adjust⇒ Levels. Look at the figure here to see the settings that were used.

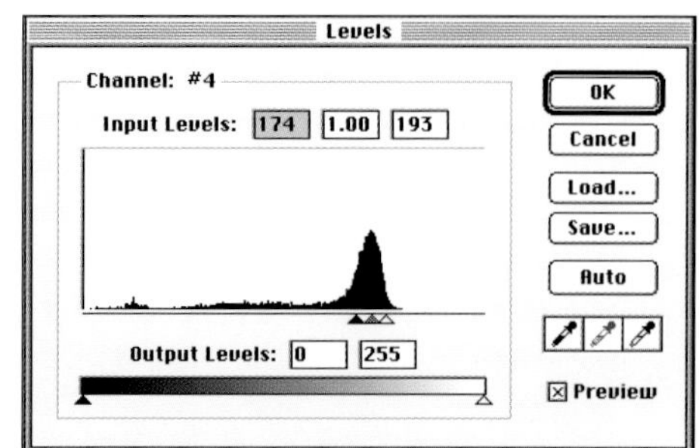


You can vary the settings, but watch the preview to make sure you get something similar to what you see in this figure.

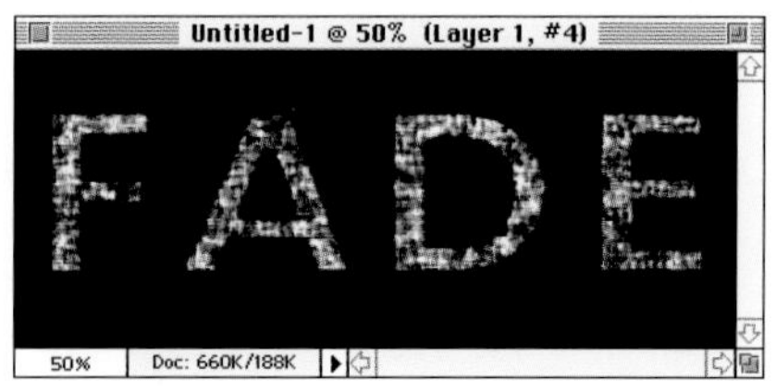


**6** Next, choose Filter⇒Sharpen⇒ Sharpen.

**7** Make a copy of Channel #4 to create Channel #5. In Channel #5, choose Image⇒Adjust⇒Levels. Slide the middle Input triangle all the way to the left. Don't touch the others.

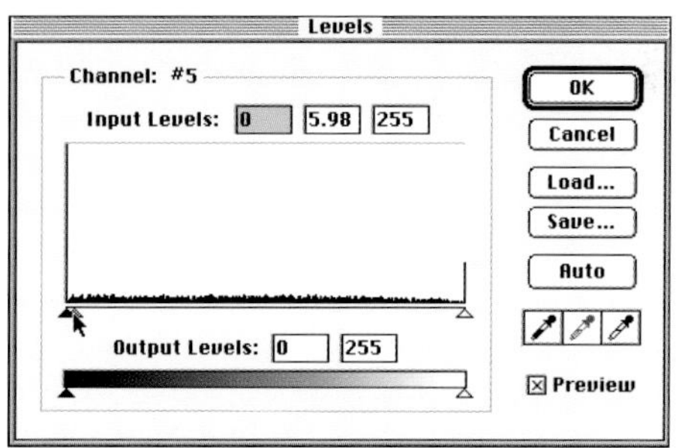


The channel should look like this:

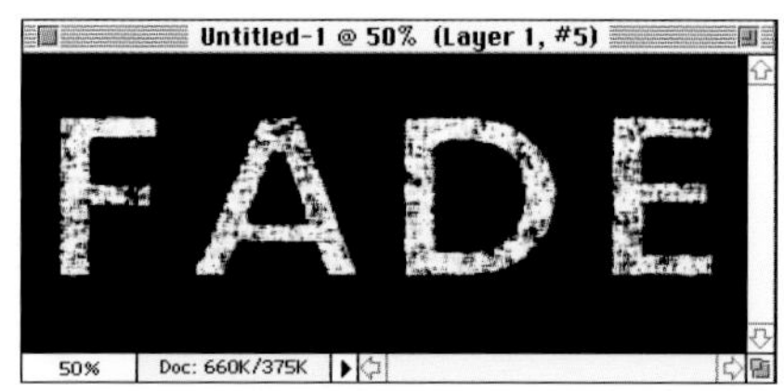


**8** Return to the composite channel, and make Layer 1 the active layer. Load the selection Channel #5. Change the foreground color to a color for the type, and fill the selection. I used the CMYK values 17, 98, 100, and 4, in this example.

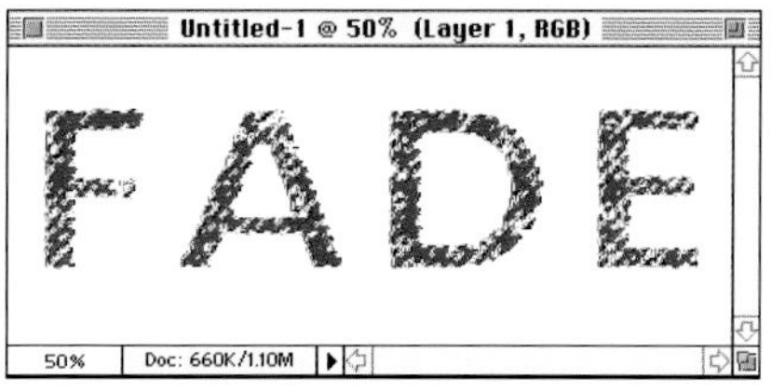

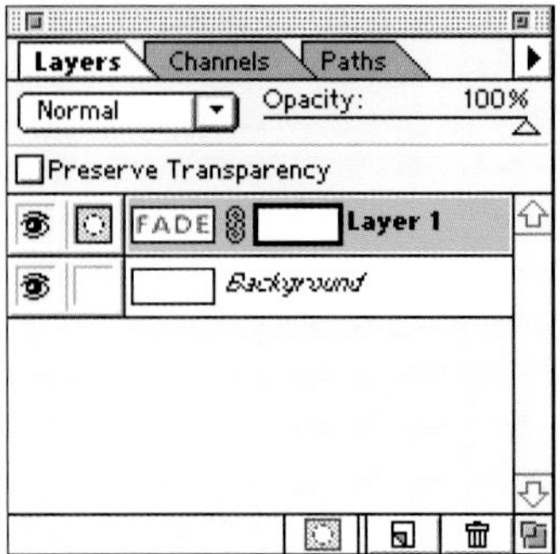


**9** Choose Layer➞Add Layer Mask➞Reveal All to add a clear Layer mask to Layer 1. The Layers palette should look like this:

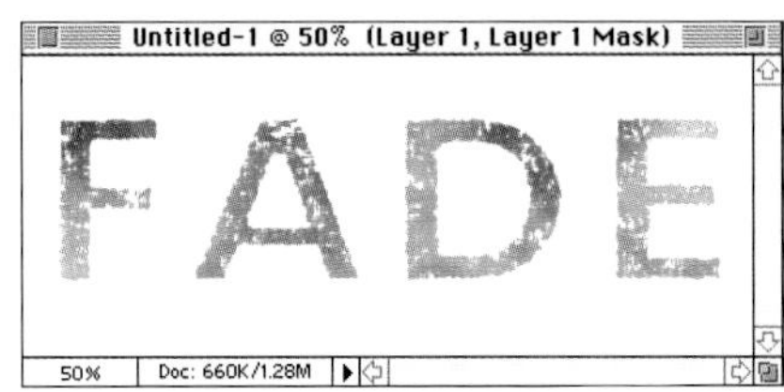


**10** The heavy black border around the preview of the Layer mask means that it is the active area. Also, the selection still should be active. Choose Filter➞Render➞ Clouds. The red type will dim.

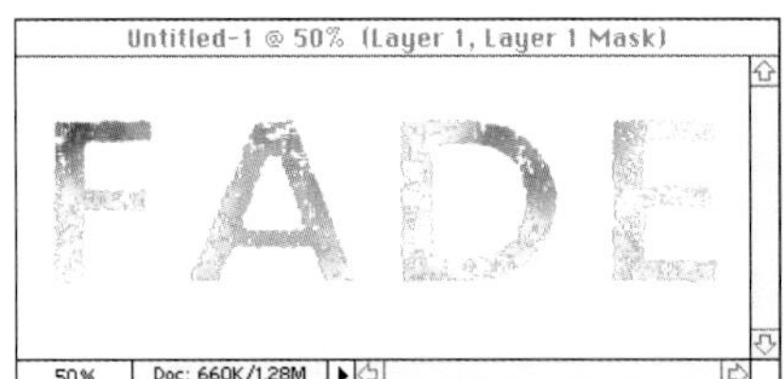


**11** Next, choose Image➞Adjust➞ Levels. Slide the black marker to the right until most of—but not all—the type fades away. The image preview should look something like this:

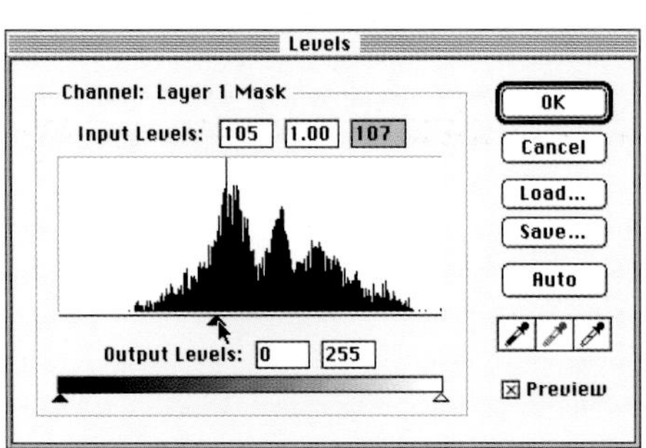


Then grab the right (white) marker and slide it to the left until all three markers line up on top of each other, like this:

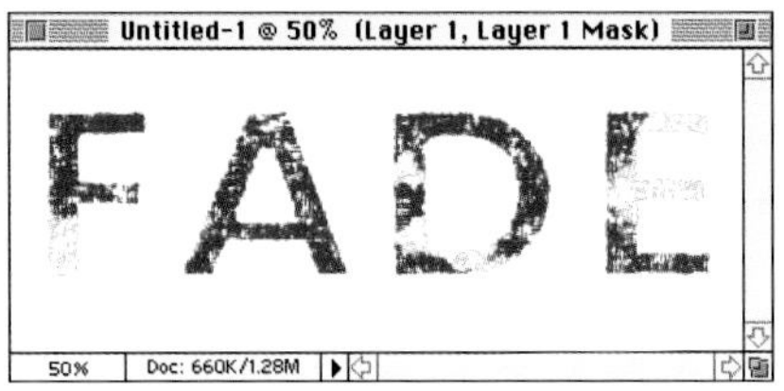


Your type should now look similar to this:

**12** Click on the Layer 1 preview to make it active. The black box will switch from the Layer mask to the Layer preview.

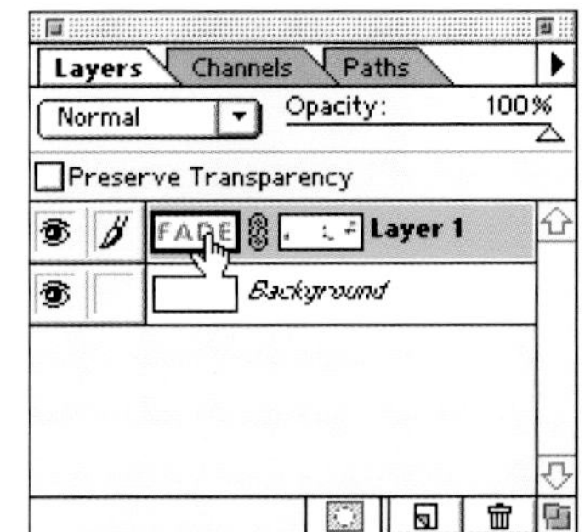


**13** Finally, load the selection Channel #4 and choose Image➛Adjust➛Hue/Saturation. Click on the Colorize checkbox and use the sliders to add depth to the color. Here are the settings used for this example.

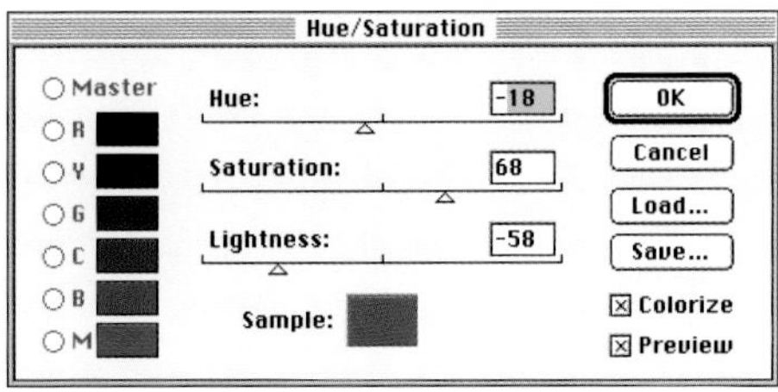


That's all there is to it.

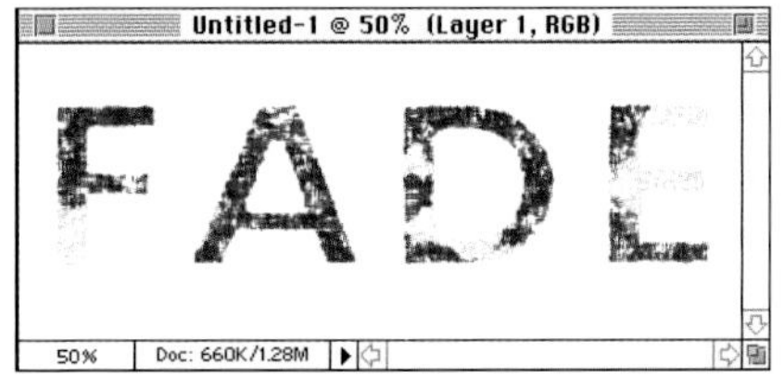


# VARIATIONS

## A Quick Method

Create a new file. Change the foreground color to white, and use the Type tool to enter the text. It will be placed into a new layer (Layer 1), but you won't see anything until you do the next step (since you have put white text on a white background). Perform Steps 2 through 6, then use the Hue/Saturation dialog box as described in Step 13 above. ■

Among the many new filters Adobe has included with Photoshop 4.0 is the Ocean Ripple distortion filter. It comes in handy here for creating this messy type.

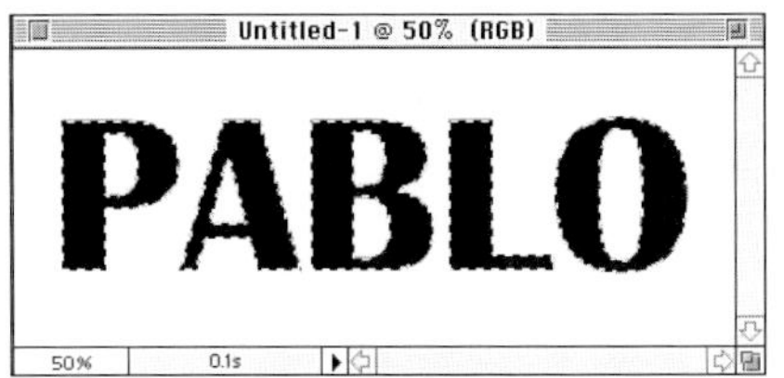


1 Create a new file. Use the Type Mask tool to enter the text. This font is Britannic Bold at 110 points. Fill the text with black.

2 With the type selection still active, choose Filter➞Noise➞Add Noise. Raise the Amount to approximately 400.

Add Noise
OK
Cancel
Preview
100%
Amount: 400
Distribution
Uniform
Gaussian
Monochromatic

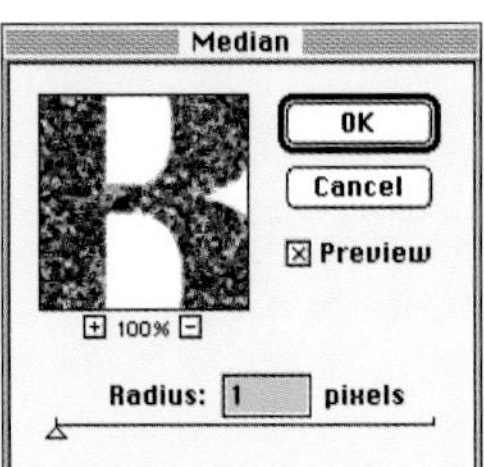


3 Deselect the type. Choose Filter➞Noise➞Median (1 pixel).

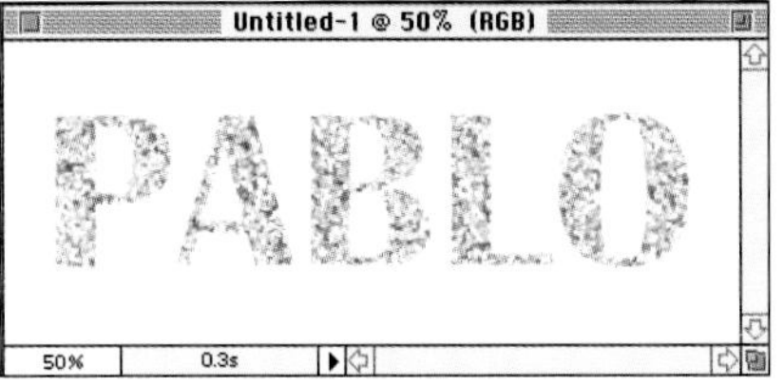


4 Then choose Filter➞Other➞Maximum (2 pixels). You should have something that looks like this:

**5** Choose Image➵Adjust➵Hue/Saturation and turn on the Colorize option. Then use the Hue slider to find a color for your type. I set the Hue slider at 38.

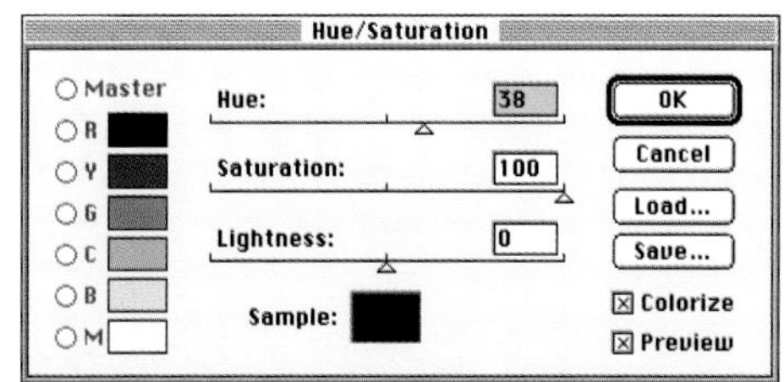


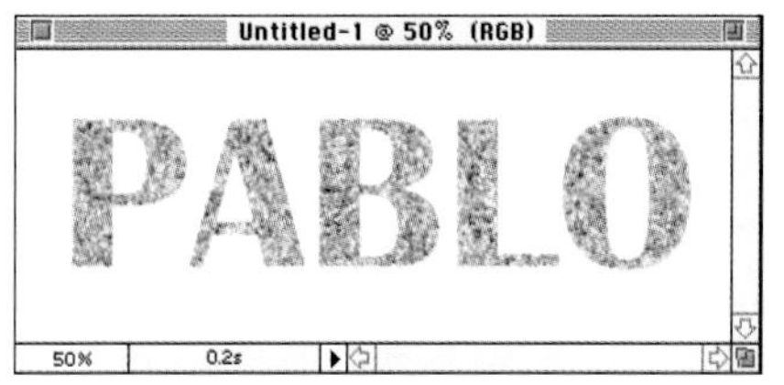


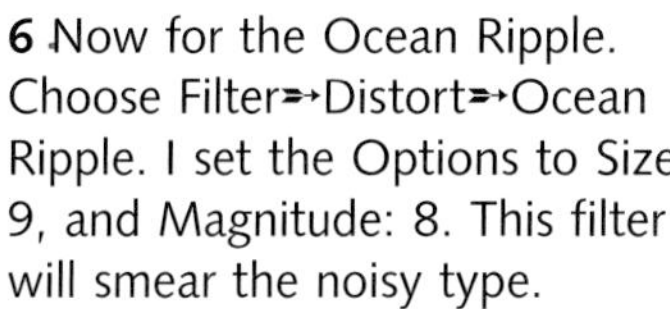

**6** Now for the Ocean Ripple. Choose Filter➵Distort➵Ocean Ripple. I set the Options to Size: 9, and Magnitude: 8. This filter will smear the noisy type.

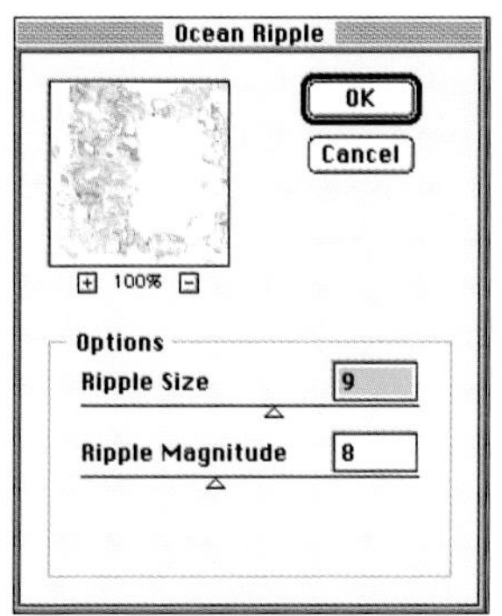


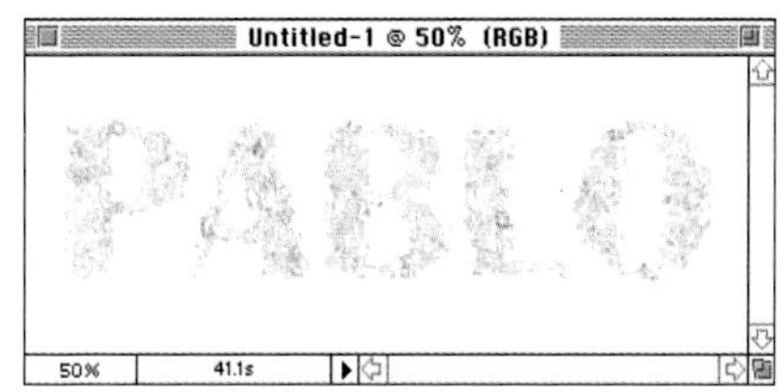

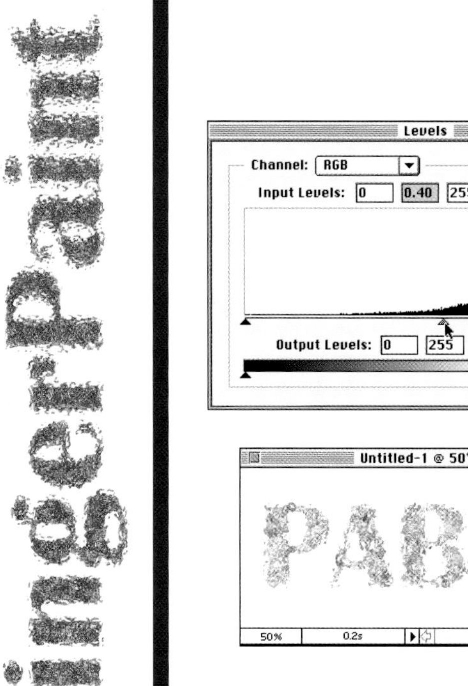


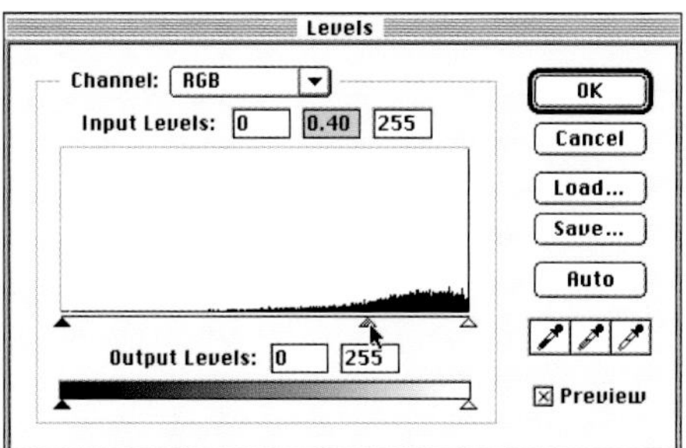


**7** You may want to raise the contrast or add some darker colors to the type. Choose Image➛Adjust➛Levels and slide the middle (gray) marker to the right.

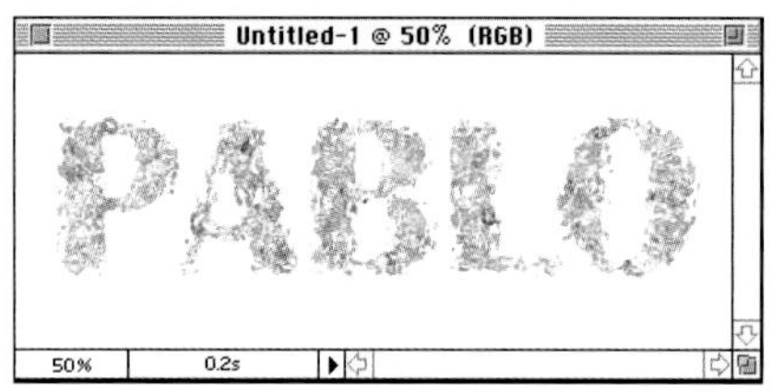


## VARIATIONS

While in the Levels dialog box in Step 7, slide the black marker to the right—until the Input indicators look like this:

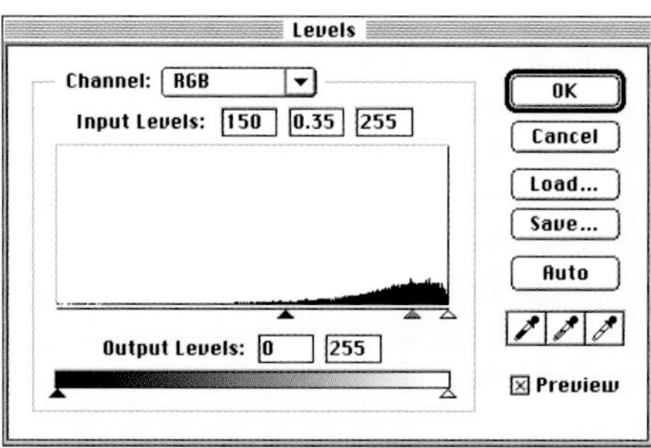

I call this "cheese pizza" type.

Who would fingerpaint in monochrome type? Follow these steps to add color(s) to the type.

**1** Follow the steps above to create the first color. Before deselecting the type in Step 3, save the selection to create Channel #4.

**2** Make a new layer, and fill the layer with white. Load the selection Channel #4, and fill it with black.

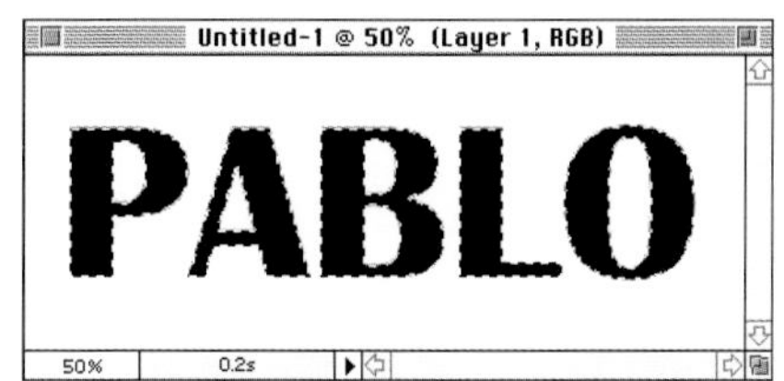


**3** Complete Steps 2 through 7 as described above.

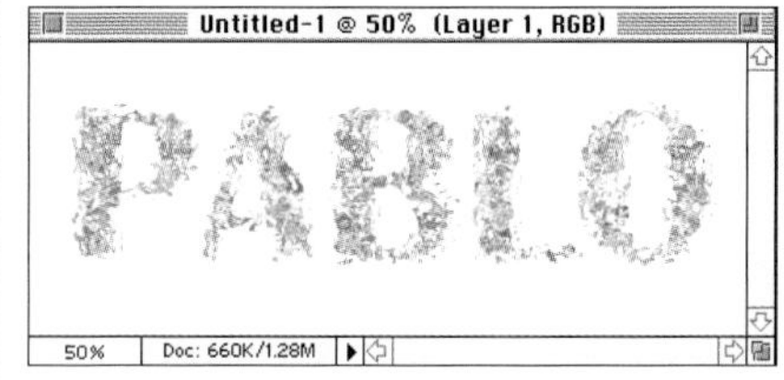


**4** While the new layer is active, choose Layer➾Layer Options. Hold the Option [Alt] key and grab the left half of the white slider that is below the This Layer gradation. The triangle will split in half. Drag the left half to the left to about 150.

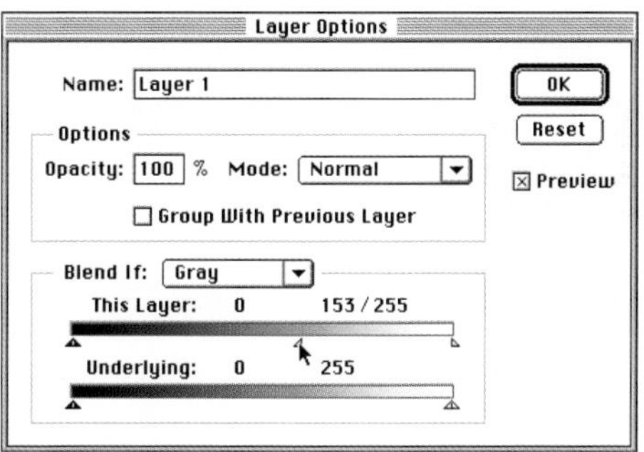


**5** Do the same for the Underlying Layer slider.

Layer Options
Name: Layer 1
OK
Reset
Options
Opacity: 100 % Mode: Normal
Preview
Group With Previous Layer
Blend If: Gray
This Layer: 0 153 / 255
Underlying: 0 237 / 255

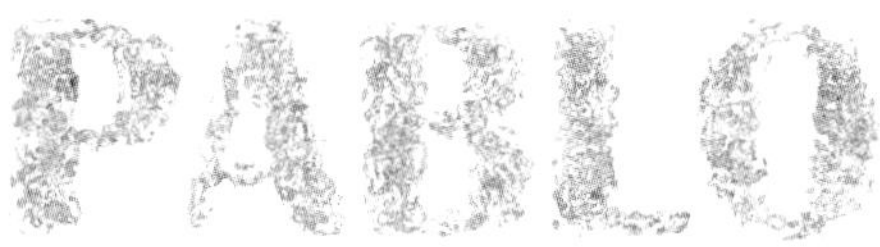

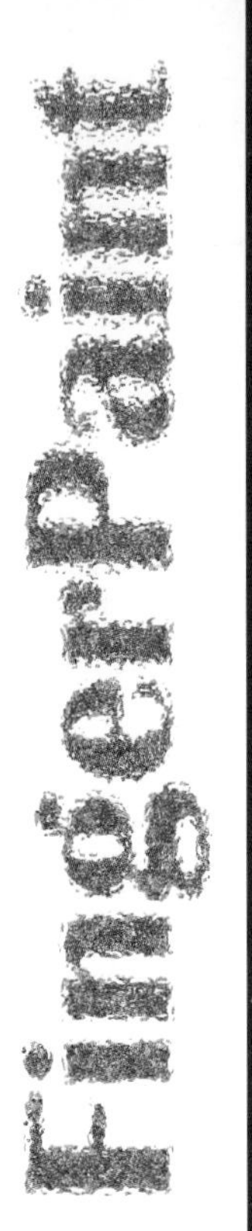

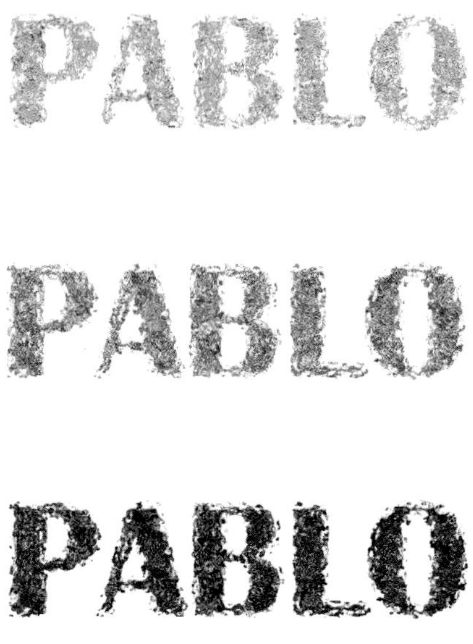

You can add as many colors as you want. Just keep repeating the last four steps. This image has four colors.

The layers' blending modes were changed to come up with these two variations. ■

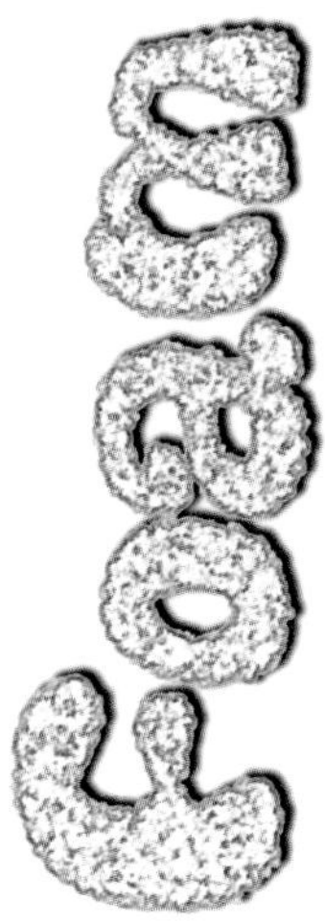


Here's the companion to the Tiles effect (page 190). To make it happen, two selection channels were made with basic filters.

**1** Create a new file, and a new channel (#4). Use the Type tool to enter the text. I used Thickhead at 100 points. Add some spacing so the foam has room to lather. I set the spacing at 5.

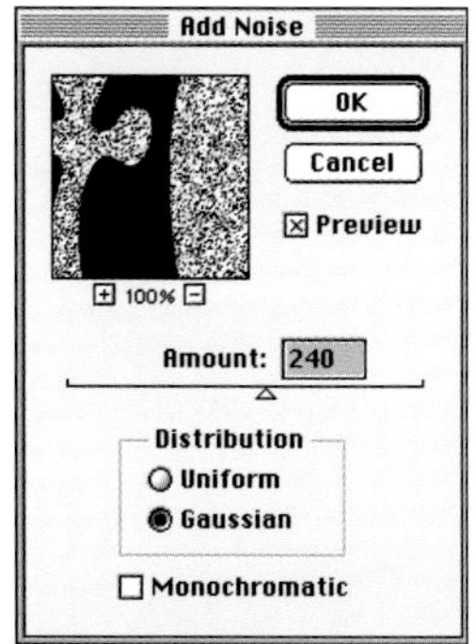


**2** Keep the selection active, and choose Filter➾Noise➾Add Noise. Add a medium amount of noise to break up the interior of the text. I set the Amount at 240.

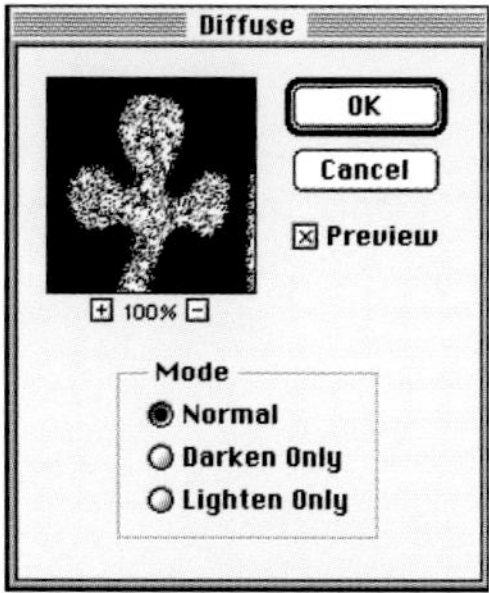


**3** Deselect the type, and choose Filter➾Stylize➾Diffuse. This filter starts spreading out the type.

**4** Reapply the same filter to your heart's content, and watch the type squirm as it sprays pixels into the black. I applied the Diffuse filter eight times.

5 Duplicate this channel to create Channel #4 copy.

6 Choose Filter➛Blur➛Gaussian Blur. All you want is a slight fuzziness. I blurred the channel with a Radius of 0.5.

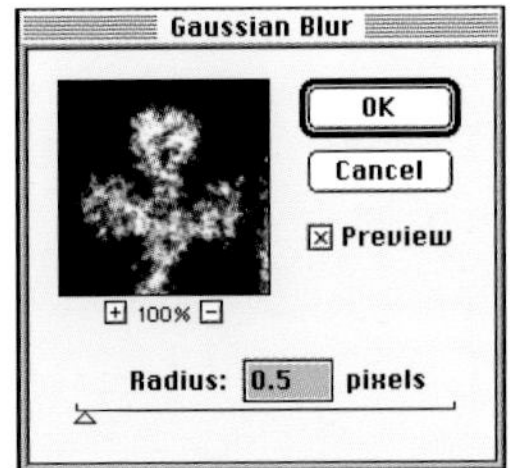


7 Return to the composite channel, and load the selection Channel #4.

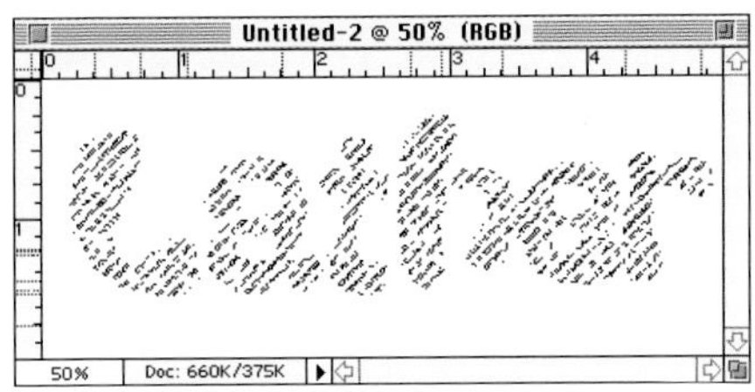


8 Choose Select➛Feather. Again, just a small amount. I chose 1 pixel.

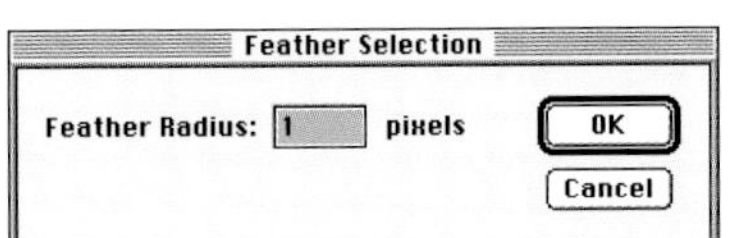


9 Change the foreground color to a color for the foam. The foam will end up white, but this color will be the tint that you see in the Foam example. I used the CMYK values 100, 75, 0, 40.

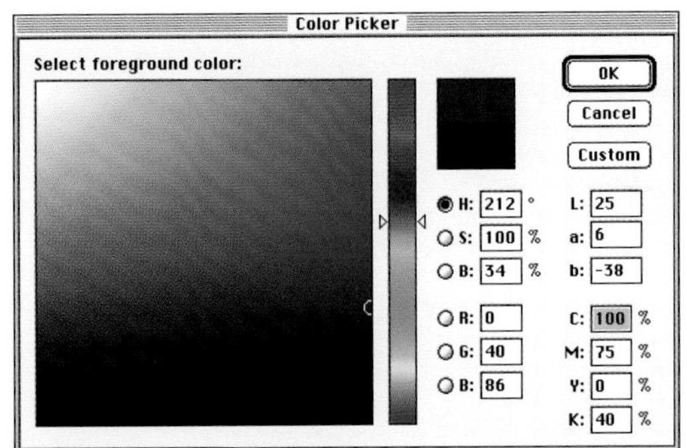

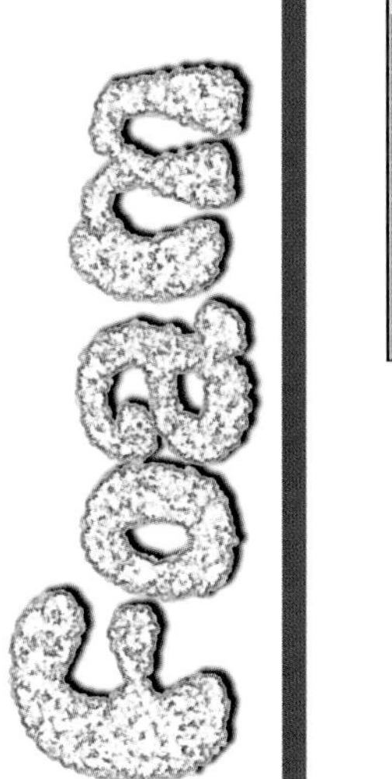


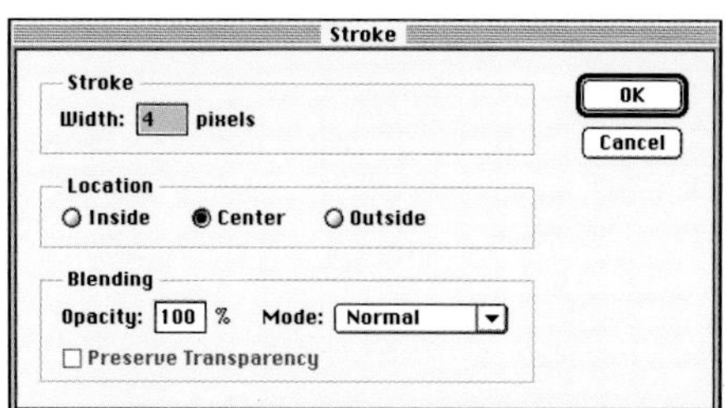


**10** Choose Edit➼Stroke. Match these settings...

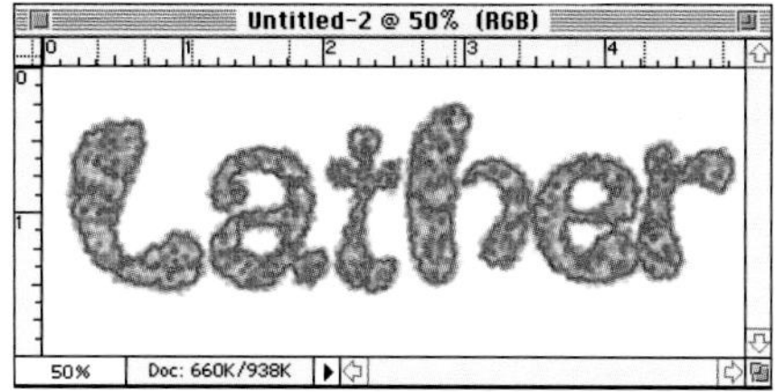


...and click OK.

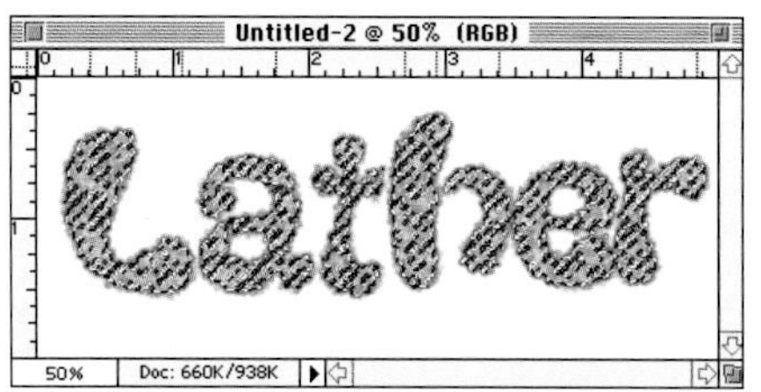


**11** Next, load the other selection Channel #4 copy.

**12** Change the foreground color to white and fill the selection.

## VARIATIONS

If you want a whiter interior, then keep the selection active after Step 12, and choose Image➼Adjust➼Brightness/Contrast. Raise the Brightness to +100.

To add a little more color, keep the selection active after Step 12 and make a new layer (Layer 1). Choose a foreground color and fill the selection.

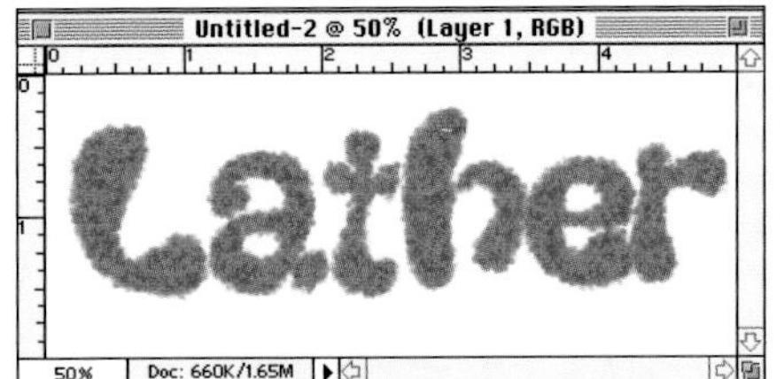


Then change the Layer 1 mode to Color.

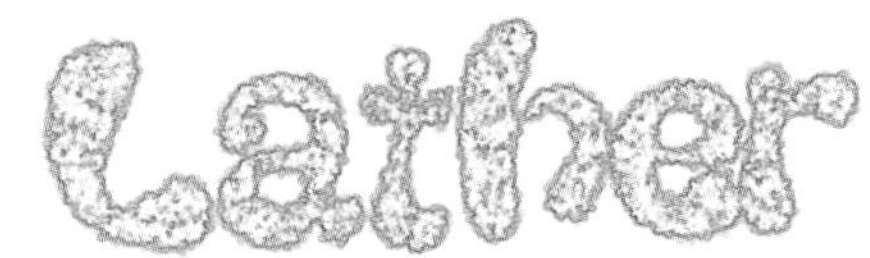

Try the other modes, too. This one has the same color, but I changed the Layer 1 mode to Hard Light and lowered the Opacity to 25%.

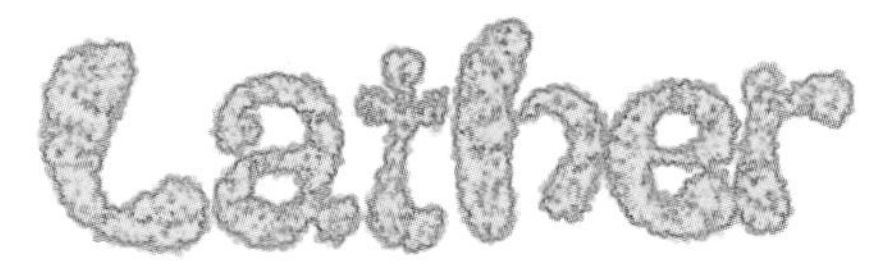

Now, try Color Dodge (Opacity: 50%).

If you want more contrast, then deselect the type and choose Image➸Adjust➸Levels. Drag the left (black) Input marker to the right. You should get something like this. ■

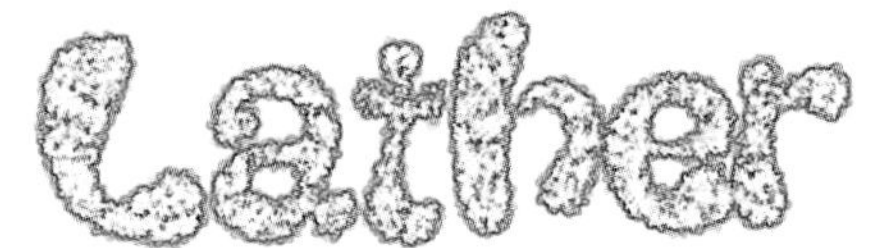

This effect might be the quickest in the book, thanks to the Lighting Effects filter.

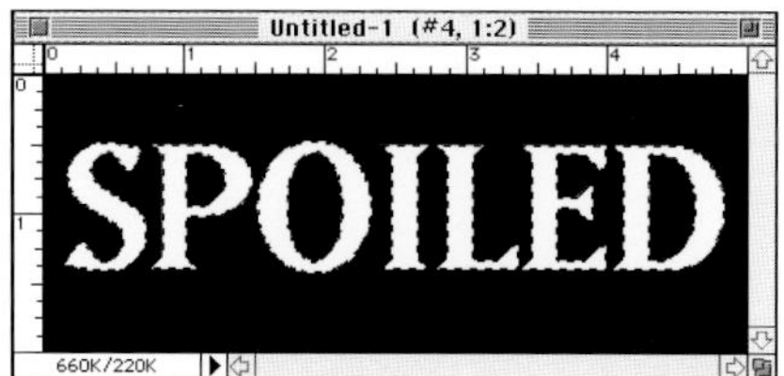


**1** Create a new file, and a new channel (#4). Use the Type tool to enter the text. For this effect, I used 110-point Matrix.

**2** Keep the selection active and fill it with clouds by choosing Filter➛Render➛Clouds.

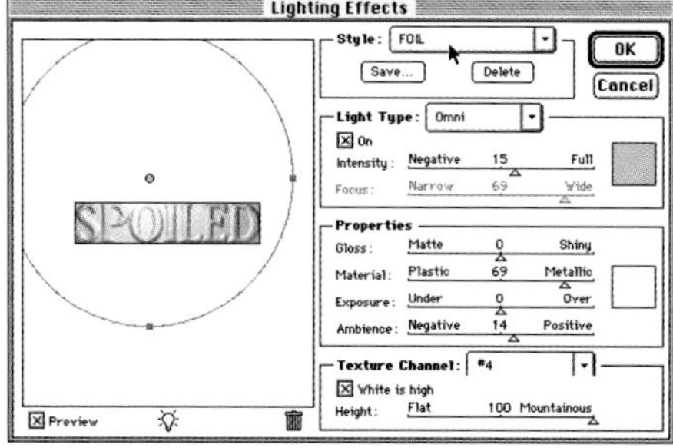


**3** Return to the composite channel. Keep the type selection active, and choose Filter➛Render➛Lighting Effects. If you have loaded the Lighting Styles presets from the CD, you can choose Foil from the pop-up Style menu. Otherwise, match the settings seen in this figure.

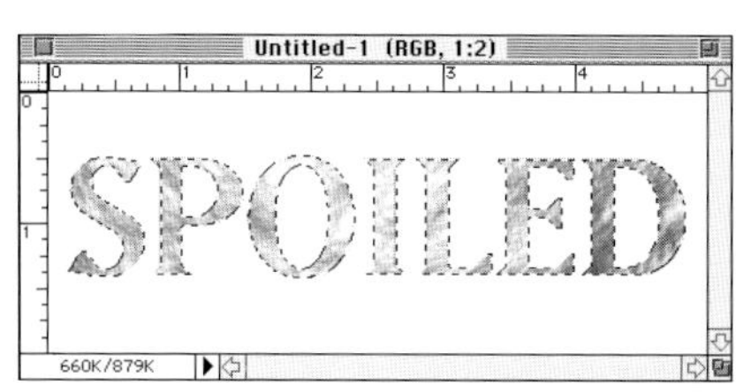


**4** To brighten the foil, choose Image➛Adjust➛Brightness/Contrast and slide the Contrast marker to +40.

## TOOLBOX

Foil (Lighting Style Preset)

Gold (Lighting Style Preset)

**5** Ready for wrapping.

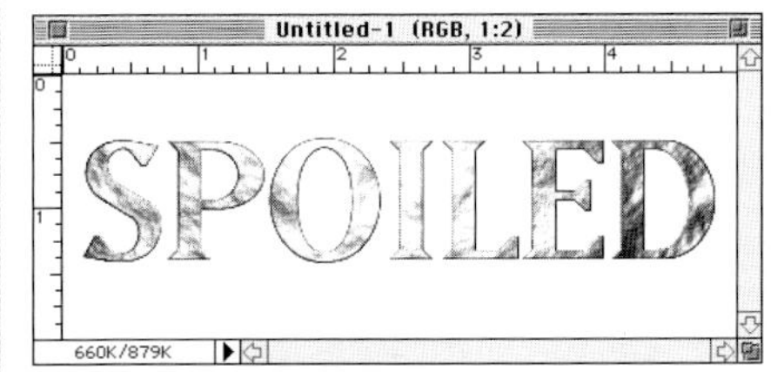


**6** You also can use the new Polygon Lasso tool to draw a jagged selection.

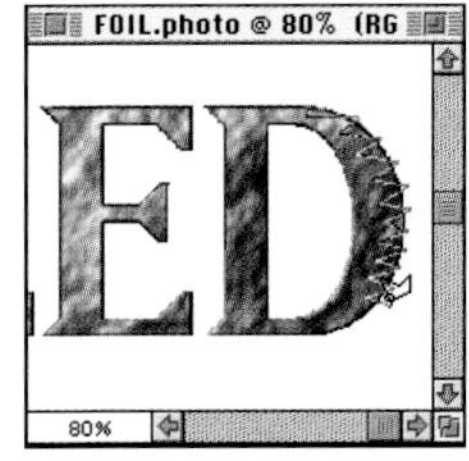


Press Delete to give your type some teeth.

SPOILED

## VARIATIONS

It's easy to turn this foil into gold leaf. In the Lighting Effects dialog box, just click on the color square in the Light Type box, and change the CMYK values to 25, 16, 71, 6 (or simply choose Gold from the Style menu).

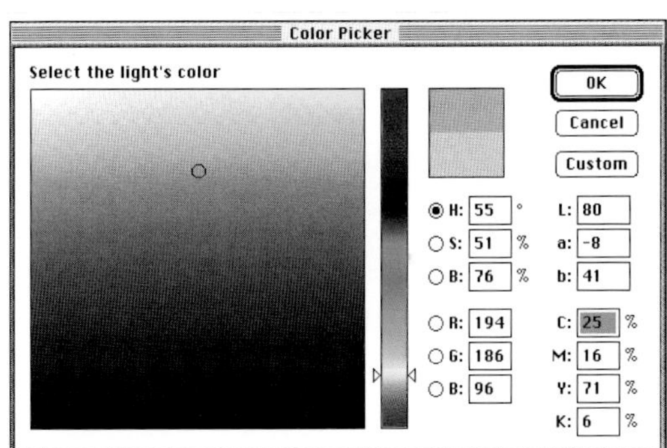


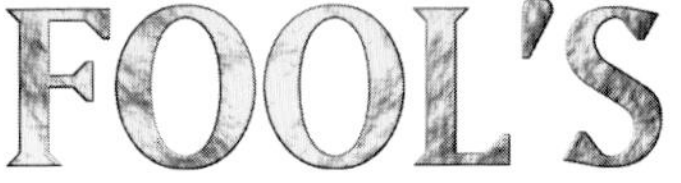

Here are a few simple ways to quickly transform basic fonts into something unique.

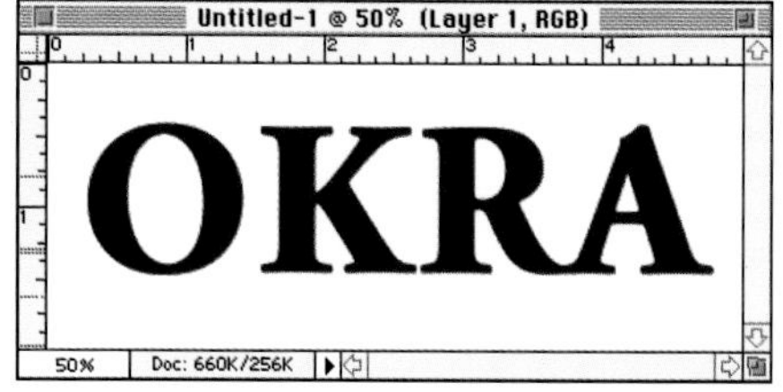


**1** To begin each of the variations below, create a new file and use the Type Mask tool to enter the text. The type you end up with largely depends on the type you start with. This effect was started with 90-point Agaramond Bold. Change the foreground color to a color for the text, and fill the type selection.

## The Maximum Filter

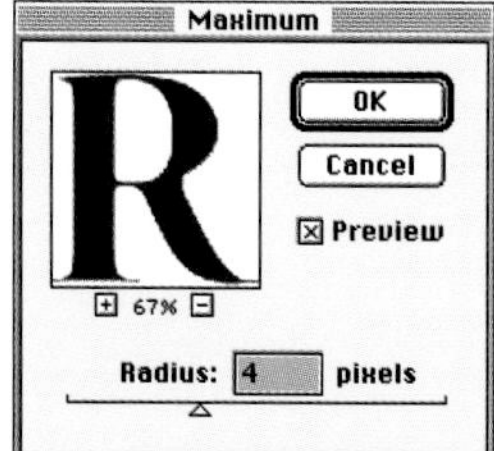


Slim the type down with the Maximum filter. Deselect the type, then choose Filter➛Other➛ Maximum. As you increase the Radius in the dialog box the type shrinks more and more. Try a Radius of 4.

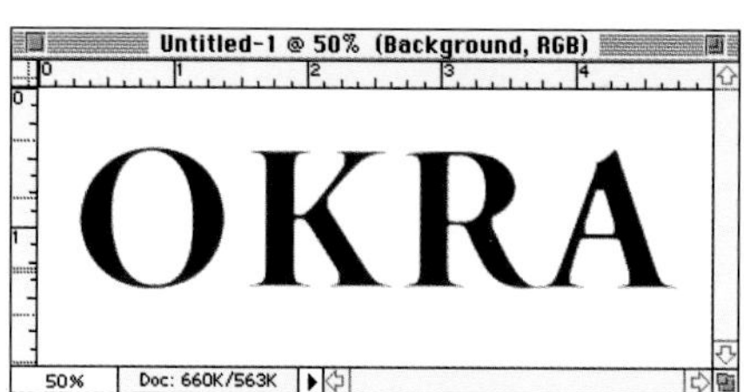


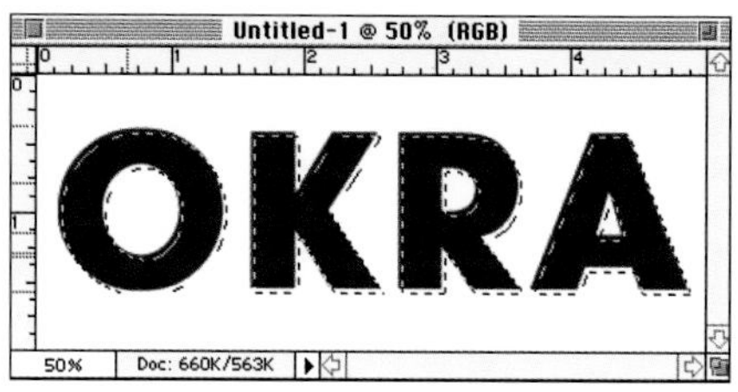


Here's another one you can make with the Maximum filter. I used Avant Garde Bold at 90 points in Step 1. Select the Marquee tool and move the selection (not the type) two keystrokes to the right and two keystrokes down.

Then choose Filter→Other→ Maximum (6 pixels).

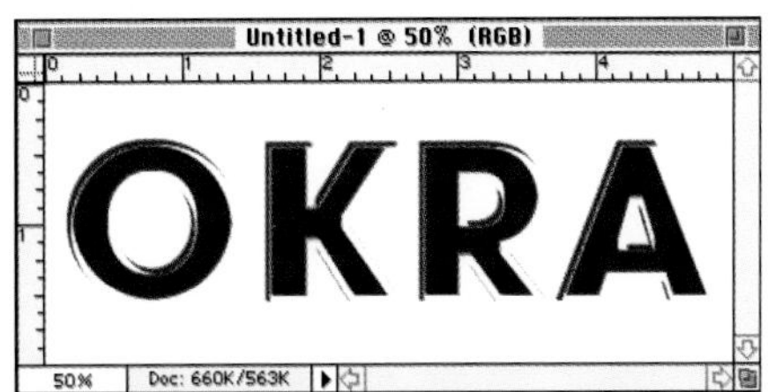


Follow the instructions in Step 1 (using Humanst521 Bold at 85 points), then choose Select→ Modify→Contract (4 pixels).

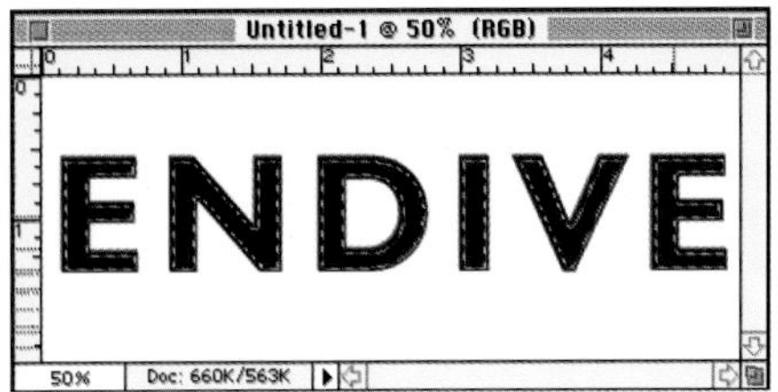


Select the Move tool and use the arrow keys to move the inside of the type. I moved the selection one keystroke down and two keystrokes left.

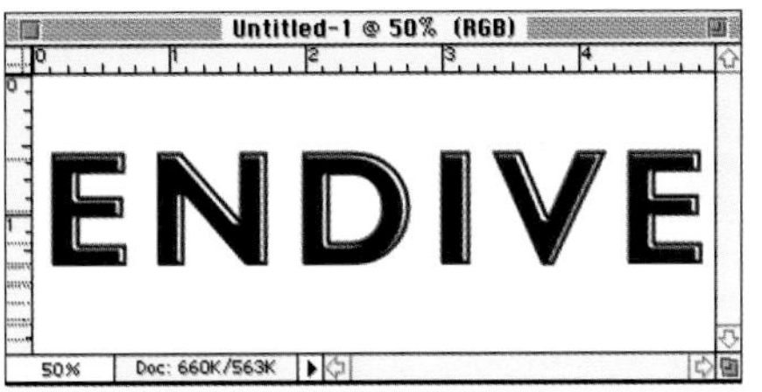


You can continue to alter this effect. I selected the Marquee tool and moved the selection back to its original place. Then I selected the Move tool and moved the selection contents again in the same direction.

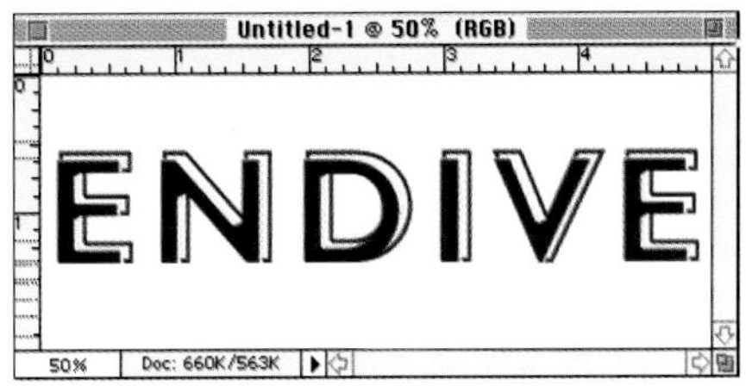


And again.

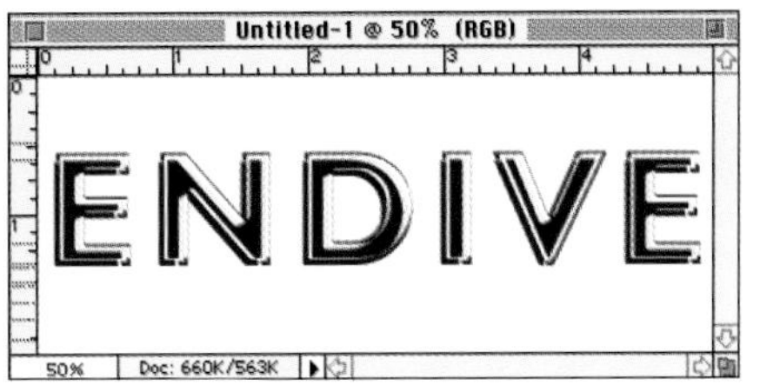

## Displace

Follow the instructions in Step 1 (using Helvetica Condensed Black at 120 points). Deselect the type.

Now choose Filter➢Distort➢Displace. I used 10% for both the Horizontal and Vertical Scales. Select Stretch to Fit.

When asked to find a displacement map, follow this path: Adobe Photoshop 4.0➢Plug-ins➢Displacement Maps. Choose the 12-sided file for some minor edge tweaking.

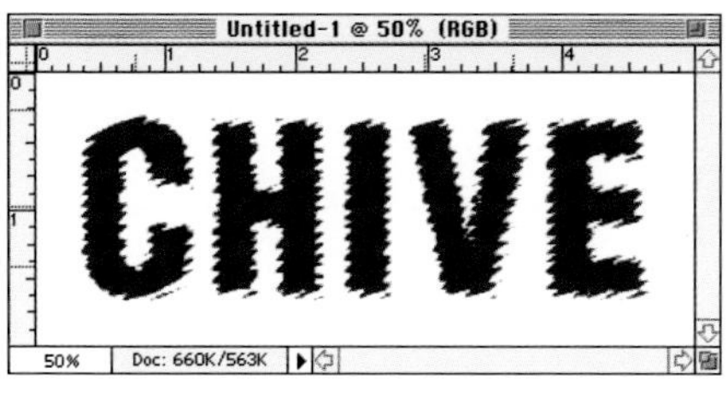


Several of the other Displacement maps have a similar effect on the type. For something different, change the Horizontal and Vertical Scale settings to 5, and choose the Fragment Layers file as the displacement map.

## Posterize

Do Step 1 (using Bremen Bold at 85 points), and deselect the type. Then blur it by choosing Filter⇒Blur⇒Gaussian Blur (Radius: 8).

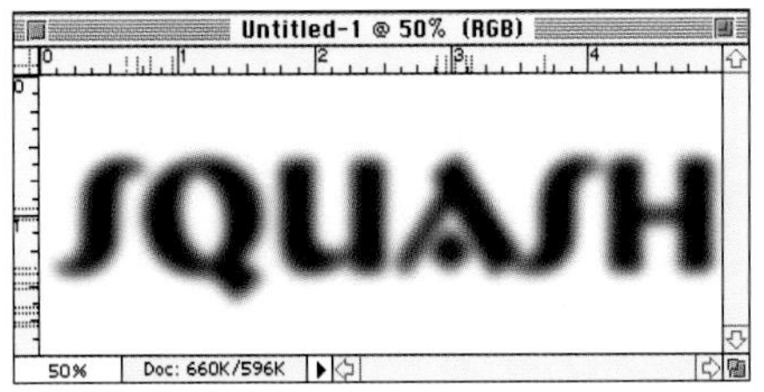


Then choose Image⇒Adjust⇒Posterize (3 levels) to divide the type into three flat areas of color.

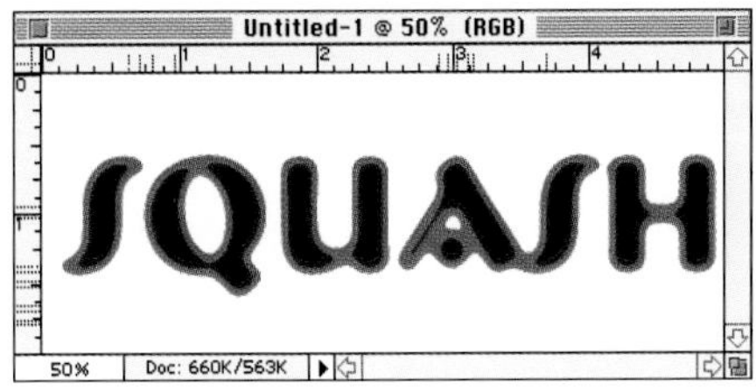


You can add one more step by choosing Filter⇒Stylize⇒Find Edges to get this outlined type.

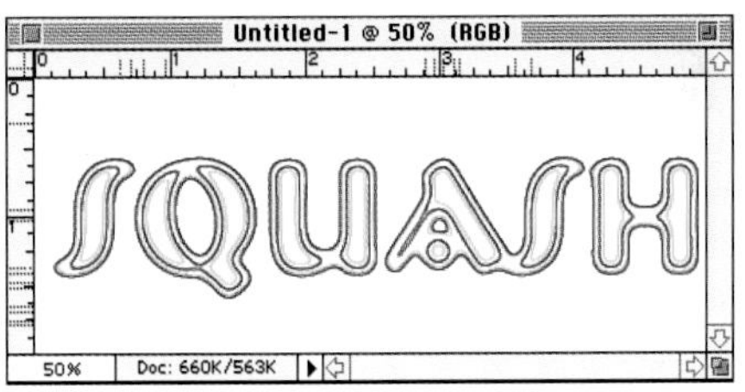


## More quick alterations…

Do Step 1 again (using Agaramond Bold at 90 points). Keep the type selected and choose Filter⇒Blur⇒Gaussian Blur (about 6 pixels). Deselect the type and choose Image⇒Adjust⇒Threshold. Set the Threshold Level to reduce and smooth your type. I set it at 120.

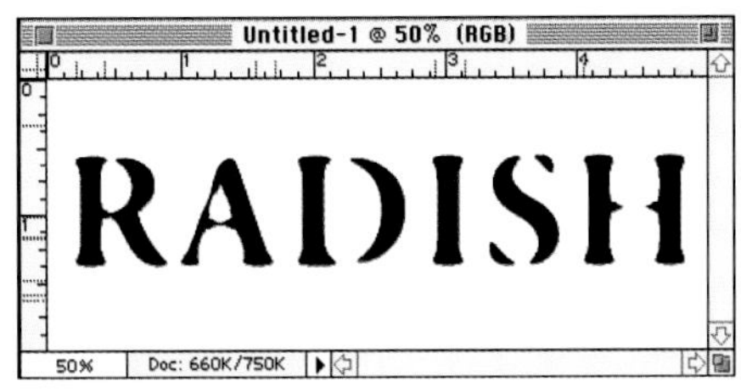


Before deselecting the type above, save the selection to create Channel #4. After using the Threshold feature, load the selection Channel #4, and choose Filter⇒Stylize⇒Wind (Blast, From the Left).

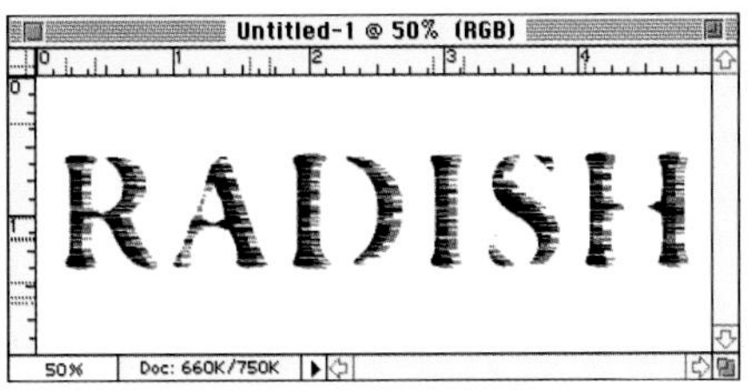

Follow the instructions in Step 1 (using Bodega Sans Black at 100 points). Deselect the type. Choose Filter➛Pixelate➛Fragment, and then choose Filter➛Noise➛ Median (9).

After creating the previous effect, apply Filter➛Stylize➛Trace Contour (Upper, 125).

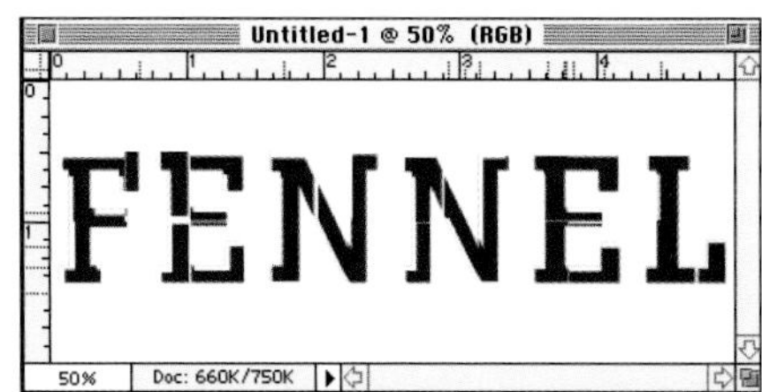


Perform Step 1 and use City Medium at 95 points. Then, choose Filter➛Stylize➛Tiles (Number of Tiles: 2; Maximum Offset: 10%).

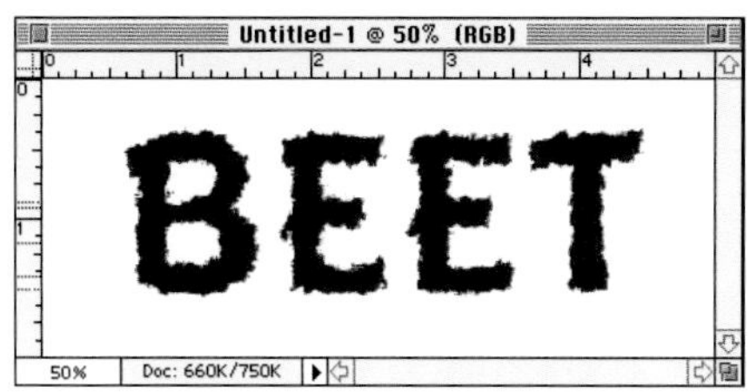


Do Step 1 (using Badger Bold at 120 points). Deselect the type, and try one of the Brush Strokes filters, for example Spatter: Filter➛Brush Strokes➛Spatter (Spray Radius: 16; Smoothness: 9). ■

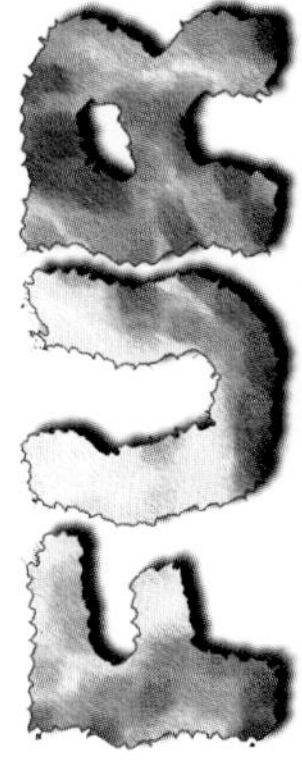

A combination of filters sets up the Motion Blur filter to make a short-haired type effect.

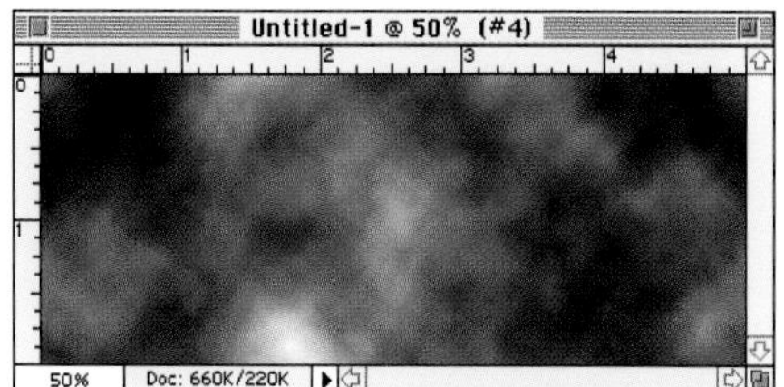


1 Create a new file, and a new channel (#4). Choose Filter➸Render➸Clouds to fill the channel with clouds to start the texture.

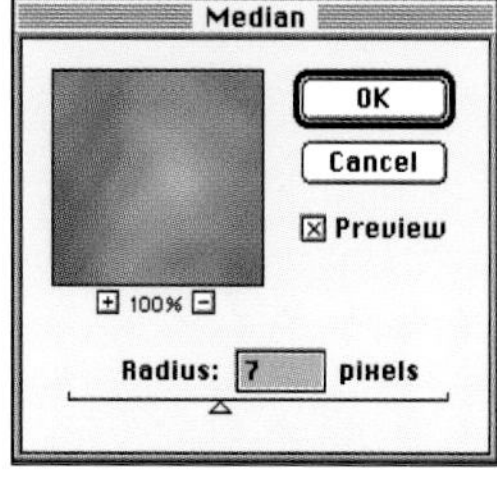


2 Choose Filter➸Noise➸Median (7 pixels) to smooth the clouds.

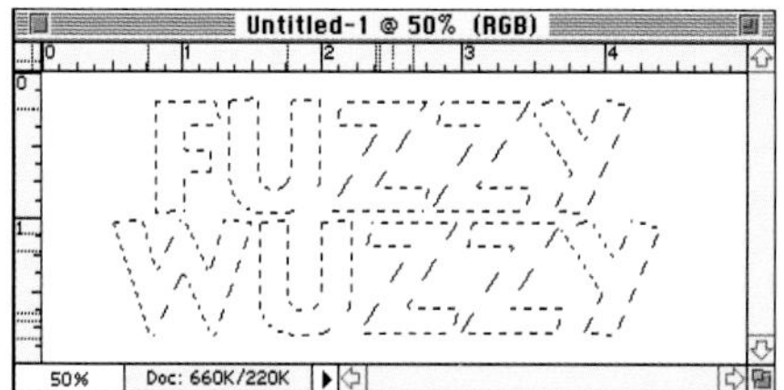


3 Return to the composite channel, and use the Type Mask tool to enter the text. I used 80-point Kabel.

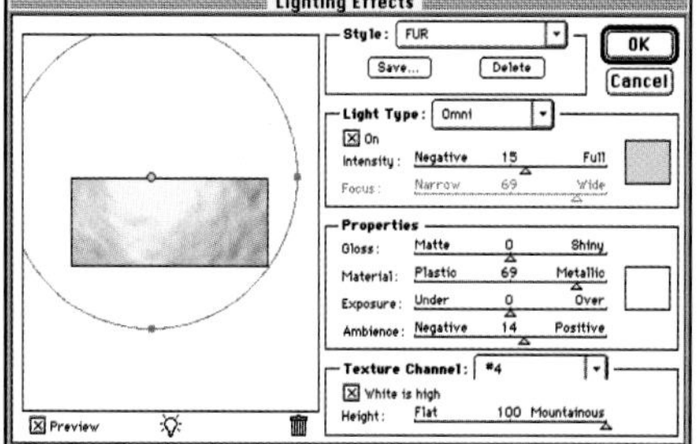


4 Choose Filter➸Render➸Lighting Effects. Use the settings as shown in this figure. If you loaded the preset files from the CD, then you can choose Fur from the Style pop-up menu. The light color in the Light Type box is going to determine the color of the fur. If you want something different from what I used, then change it now.

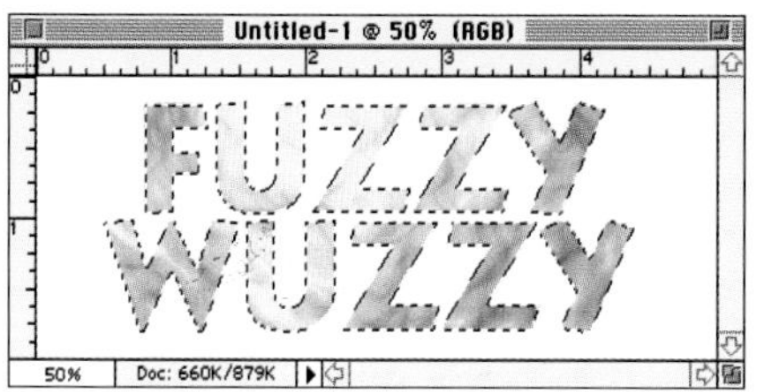

TOOLBOX

Fur (Lighting Style Preset)

5 Keep the selection active, and choose Filter➾Other➾Minimum (7 pixels). The Minimum filter adds some contrast and helps create some spots in the texture.

6 To read just the middle values, choose Image➾Adjust➾Levels. Grab the middle (gray) slider and drag it to the right, until the center Input Levels hits .60. Then slide the white marker to the left, just a little, to about 240.

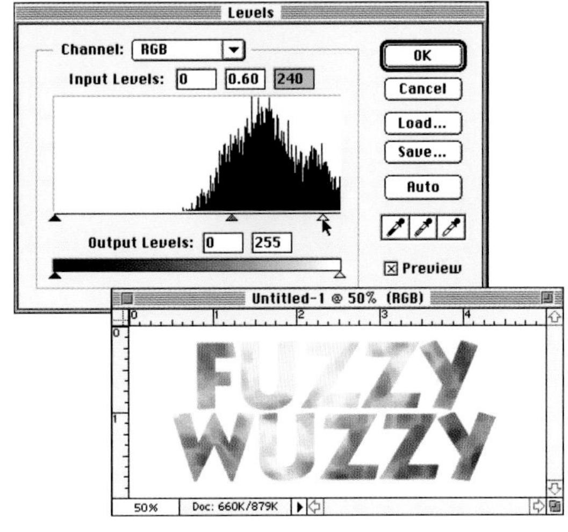


7 Now, add a little noise: Filter➾Noise➾Add Noise (12 pixels). Make sure the Monochromatic box is checked.

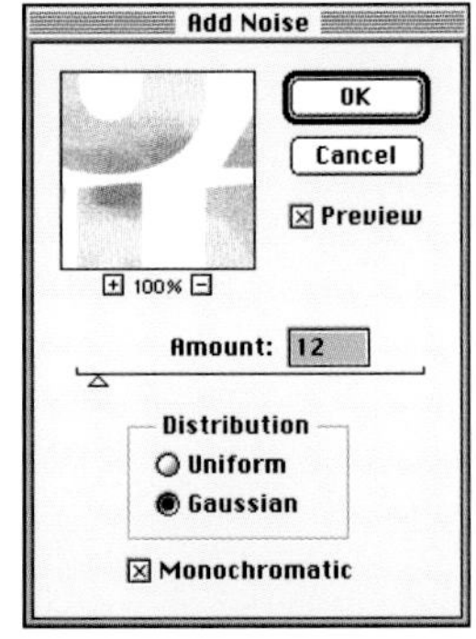


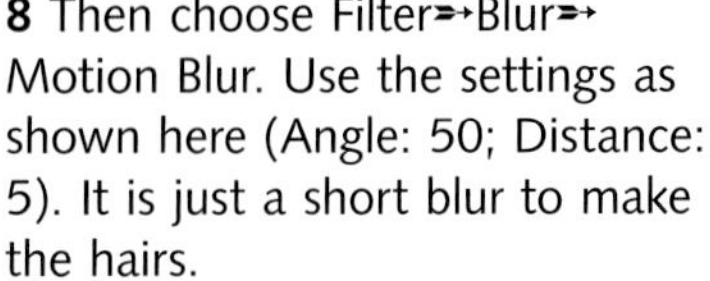

8 Then choose Filter➾Blur➾Motion Blur. Use the settings as shown here (Angle: 50; Distance: 5). It is just a short blur to make the hairs.

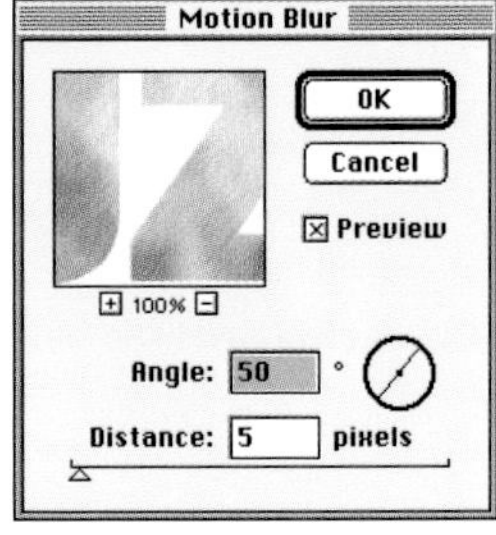

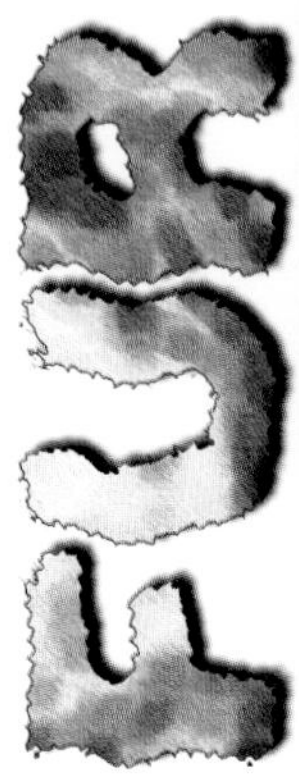


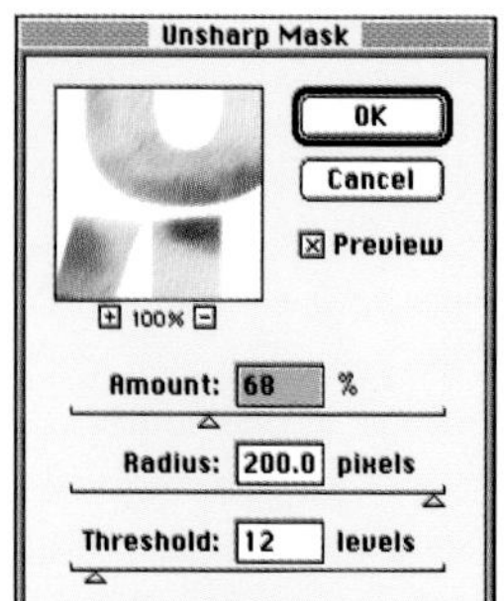


**9** Choose Filter➾Sharpen➾ Unsharp Mask. Try these settings: Amount: 68%, Radius: 200 pixels, and Threshold: 12.

**10** A black stroke helps this type stand out from the background. Choose Edit➾Stroke (2 pixels; Center: 100%, and Normal). ■

# GOLD

These steps are similar to the Foil effect, but the effect is created by using the same commands in a different order. If you want to make gold leaf, then flip to the Foil section on page 89.

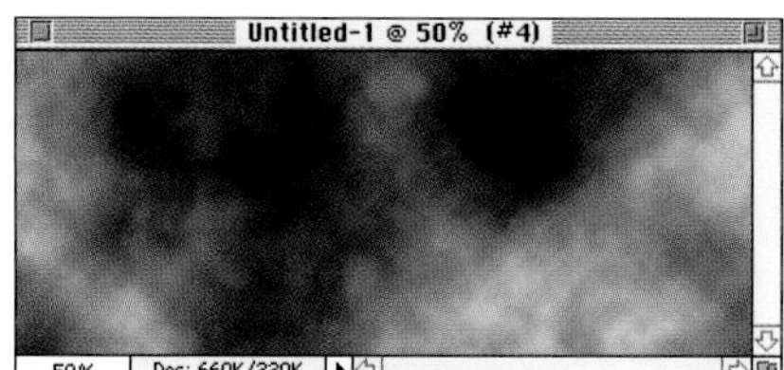


**1** Create a new file, and a new channel (#4). Fill the channel with clouds by choosing Filter➛Render➛Clouds.

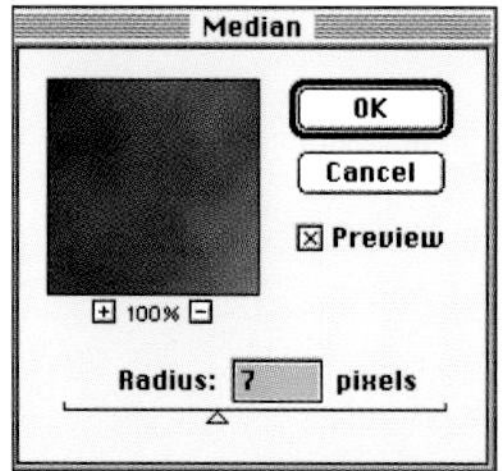


**2** Choose Filter➛Noise➛Median. I chose 7 pixels. You will not see much effect on the clouds; however, this filter will meld the field of clouds into like areas.

**3** Return to the composite channel. Use the Type Mask tool to enter the text. I used Matrix at 130 points for this effect.

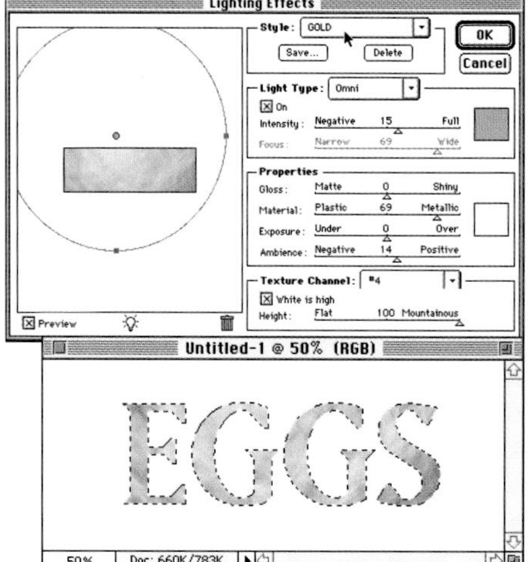


**4** Keep the type selection active, and choose Filter➛Render➛Lighting Effects. If you have loaded the files from the CD, then choose Gold from the Style pop-up menu; otherwise match the settings seen here.



**TOOLBOX**

Gold (Lighting Style Preset)

**5** Keep the selection active and choose Filter➛Other➛Minimum (7 pixels).

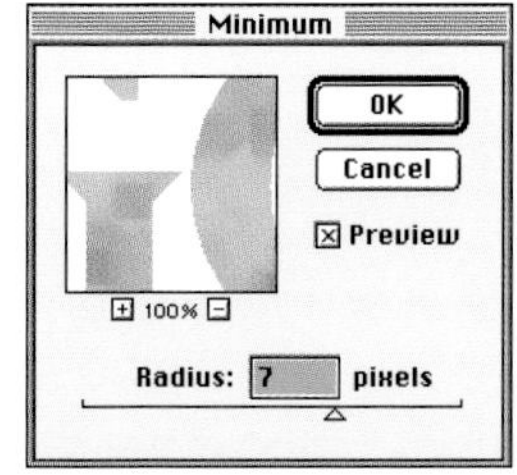


**6** Then Choose Image➛Adjust➛ Brightness/Contrast and slide the Contrast marker up until your type looks like my final image here. I set the Contrast to +40. Deselect the text.

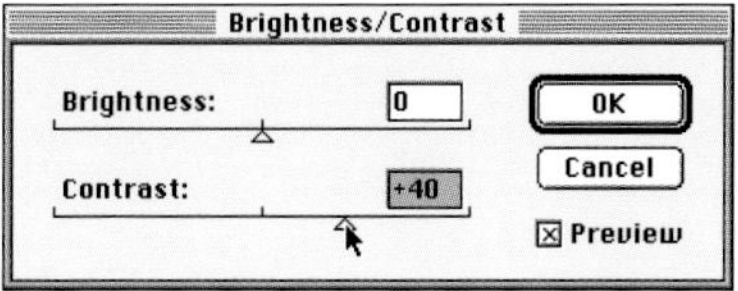


That's it.

## VARIATIONS

To change the golden eggs to copper, keep the selection active and make a new layer. Double-click the Gradient tool to select it and bring to the front the Gradient Tool Options floating palette. Choose the Copper custom gradient from the Gradient pop-up menu. Click and drag the Gradient tool across the type selection in any direction. Then from the Layers palette menu change the Layer 1 mode to Hue. ■

# Highlights

## TOOLBOX

Andromeda's Star Filter

Here are three quick ways to add a sparkle to your type—plus a fourth method, courtesy of Andromeda's Star filter.

## The Custom Paintbrush

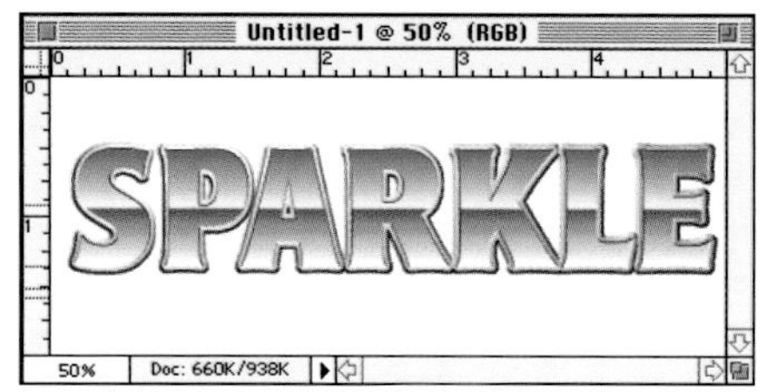


**1** Open the file containing the type you want to add highlights to. This type was created with the Chrome (Airbrushed) effect on page 50.

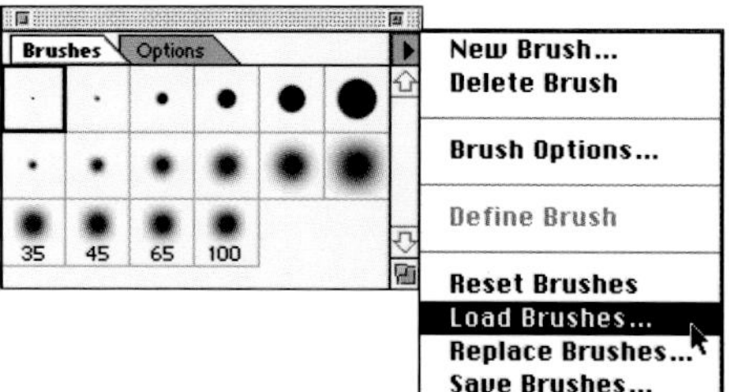


**2** Double-click the Paintbrush tool to select it and to bring the Paintbrush Options floating palette to the front. Click on the Brushes tab to make the brushes palette active. Then choose Load Brushes from the arrow menu.

**3** Follow this path to open the Assorted Brushes file: Adobe Photoshop 4.0➛Goodies➛Brushes & Patterns➛Assorted Brushes. A range of new brushes will appear in the Brushes palette.

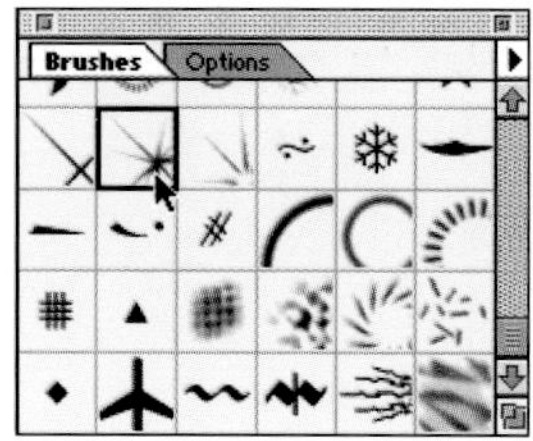


**4** Scroll to the bottom of the palette and select this brush:

**TIP** **You can use the brushes on either side of the brush I recommended for slightly different sparkles.**

**5** Choose white for the foreground color.

**6** To add sparkles to the type, use the Paintbrush tool to click on the type where you want the sparkle. Don't drag the brush or you will smear the sparkle.

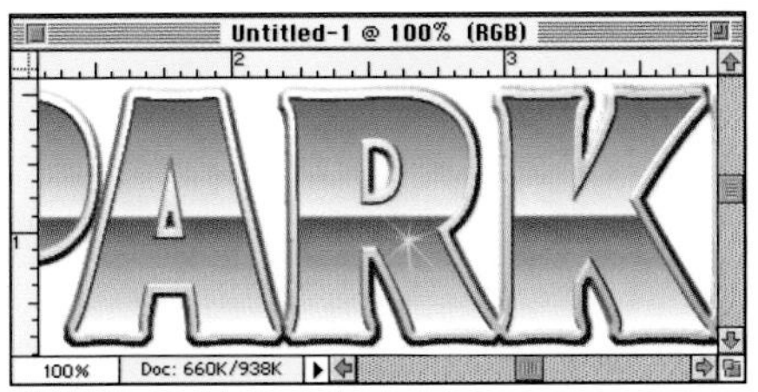


Sparkles, sparkles, sparkles.

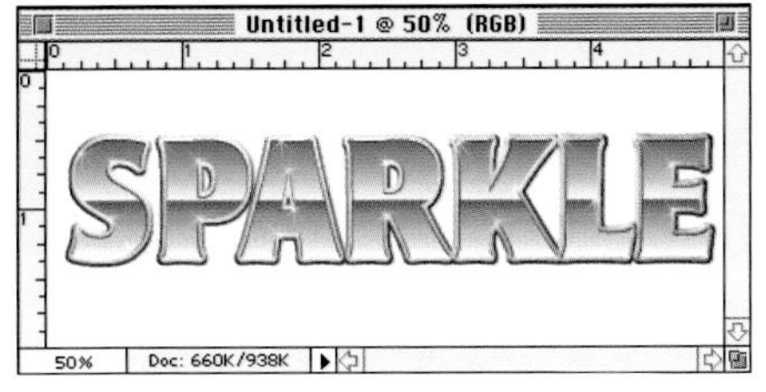

**To intensify a sparkle, click twice on the same spot.**

## The Lens Flare

**1** For this method, I started with this type created using the Reflector effect (page 148).

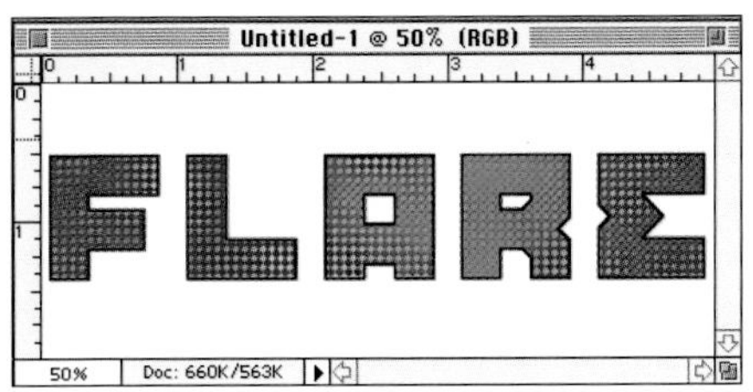


**2** Choose Filter→Render→Lens Flare. In the dialog box preview, drag the flare to a spot on the type. I set the Brightness at 151%. Just make sure that the Brightness percentage is not so high that you have all highlight and no type.

Click OK and you're finished.

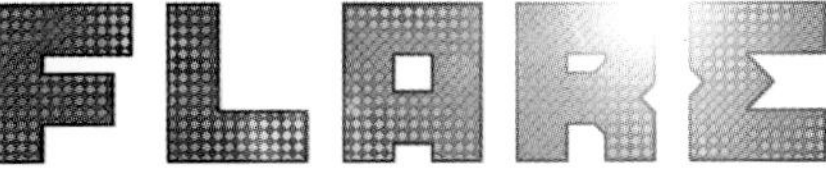

## The Gradient Highlight

1 This type was created using the Balls effect on page 18.

2 Choose white for the foreground color, or another color for the highlight.

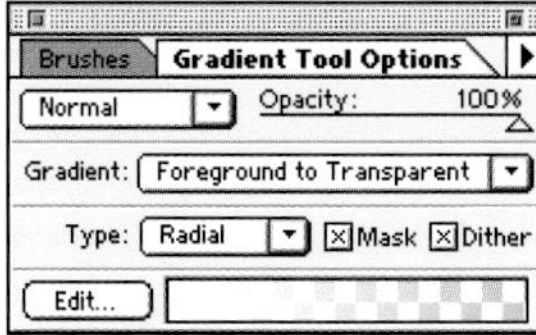


3 Double-click the Gradient tool to select it and to bring the Gradient Tool Options floating palette forward. Change the Gradient to Foreground to Transparent and the Type to Radial.

4 Click on the Edit button, then click on the Transparency button. Grab the black marker and slide it to the right a little. Then grab the diamond on top and slide it to the left a little. Click OK.

5 Click and drag with the Gradient tool from the point for the center of the highlight. Drag the Gradient line until it reaches as far as you want the highlight to spread.

## Andromeda's Star filter

If you have Andromeda's Star filter, then you've got one more way to add a highlight to your type. There is a demo version of this filter on the CD. See page 230 to find out how to access it.

**1** I made some Stained Glass type for this filter (page 172).

**2** Choose Filter➛Andromeda➛Star. The dialog box enables you to control every aspect of the star. Try the settings shown in the figure. ■

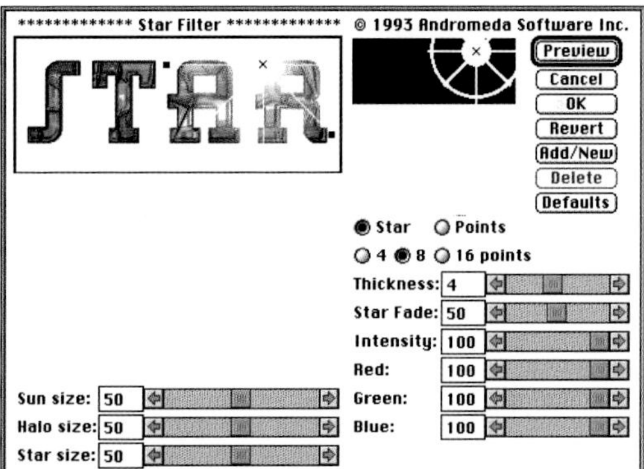


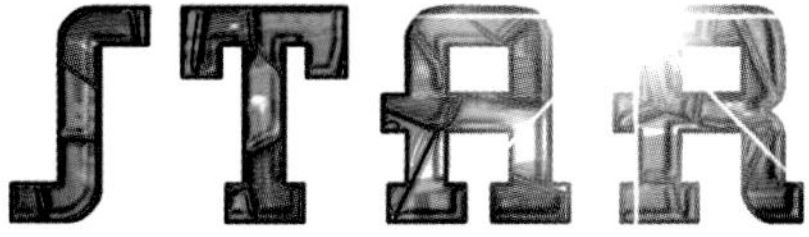

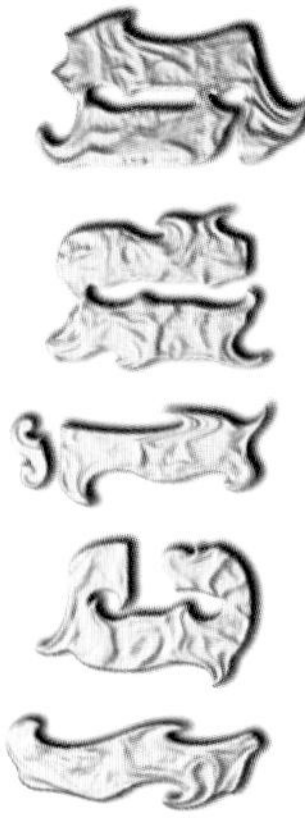

The Difference Clouds and Find Edges filters create this sticky texture and the Twirl filter pulls out the swirls to make this sweet effect.

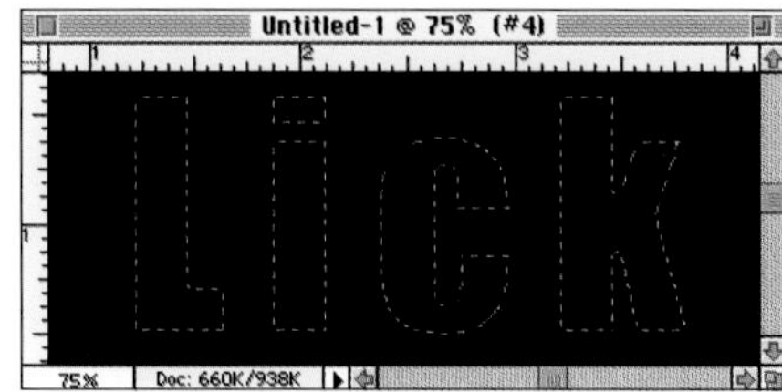


1 Create a new file, and a new channel (#4). Use the Type Mask tool to enter the text. Any font will work with this effect, but I prefer something thick to give the filters enough room to work. I chose Impact at 100 points. You may want to add some spacing to make room for the swirls.

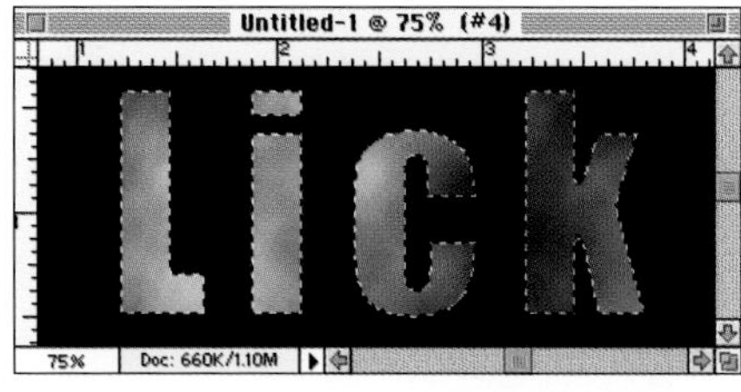


2 Choose Filter➞Render➞Difference Clouds to start creating the texture.

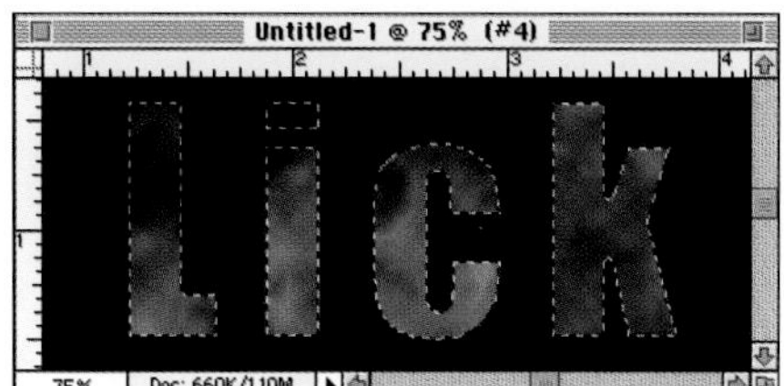


3 The patterns in the clouds will become the swirling texture of the icing. To produce more variety, apply the Difference Clouds filter again. (I applied the filter four more times.) You can skip this step if you want.

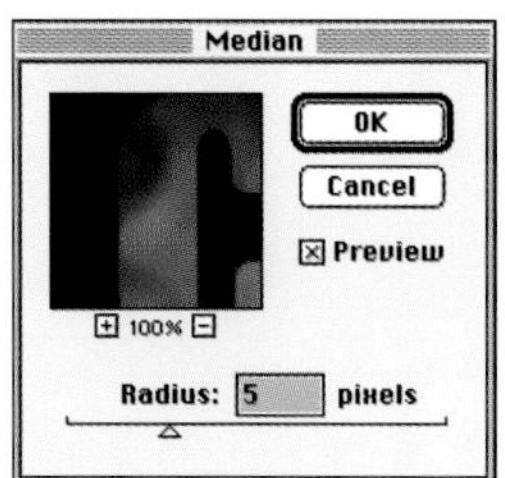


4 Next, choose Filter➞Noise➞Median. The higher the Radius, the fewer the swirls that will appear inside the type. I set the Radius at 5. You will not, however, see the results of this filter until Step 6. The clouds should be little blurry now.

## TOOLBOX

Icing (Lighting Style Preset)

**5** Choose Filter➵Stylize➵Find Edges.

**6** Choose Image➵Adjust➵Invert. Now you should see faint white swirls—very faint.

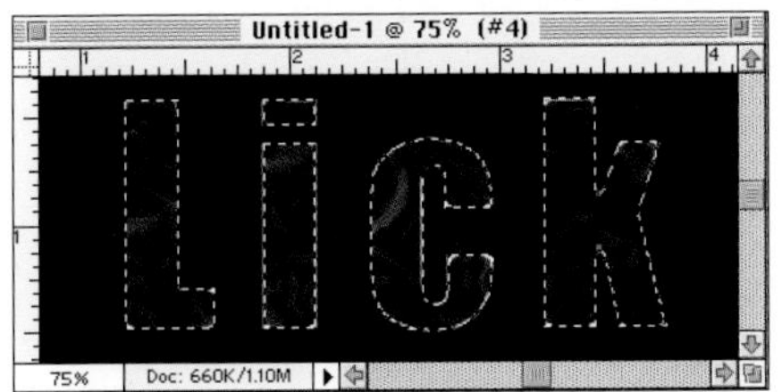


**7** Choose Image➵Adjust➵Levels. Slide the white (right) Input marker way over to the left. Then nudge the gray (middle) Input marker to the right—just a touch.

You want to get something like this:

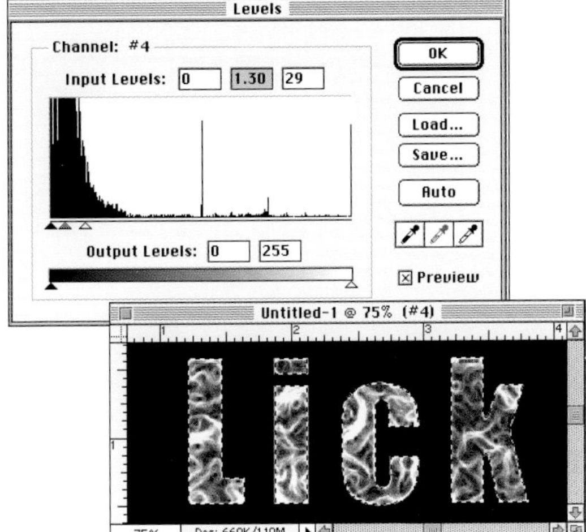


**8** To get rid of the white border, choose Select➵Modify➵Contract. Contract the selection enough so that it no longer includes the white border. This selection is contracted 2 pixels.

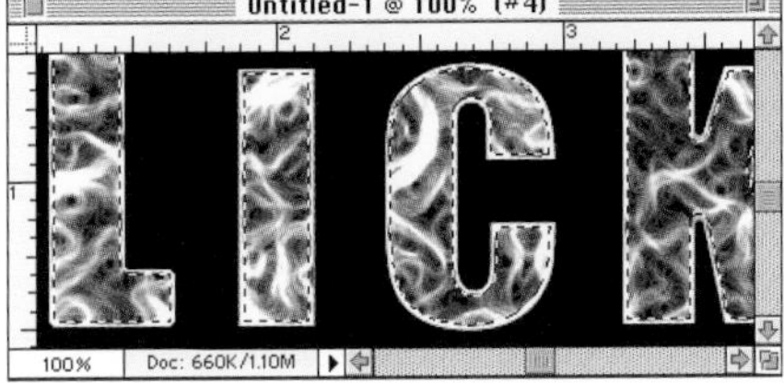

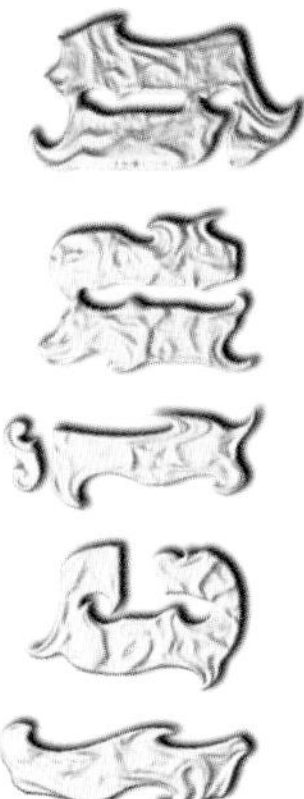

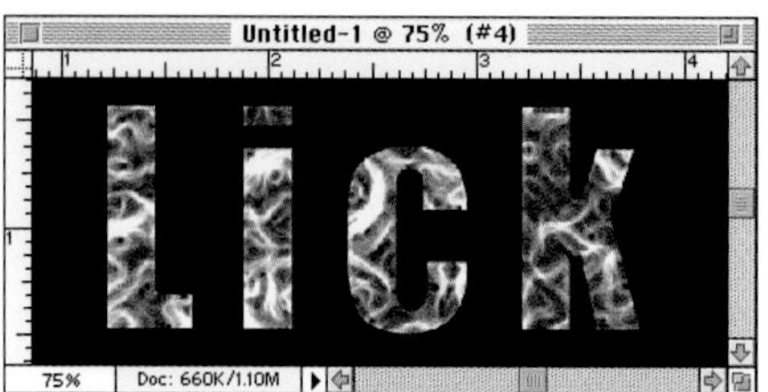


**9** Choose Select→Inverse, and press Delete to fill the selection with black.

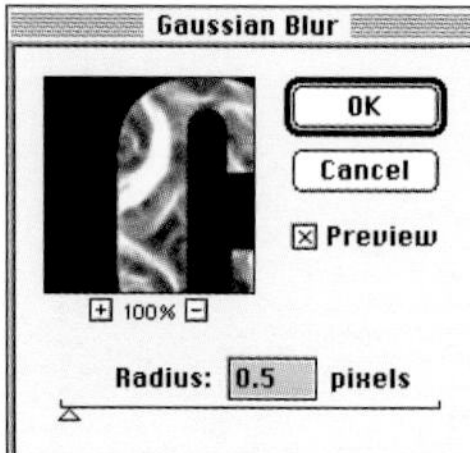


**10** Choose Select→Inverse. Now blur the swirls a little by choosing Filter→Blur→Gaussian Blur (Radius: 0.5). Deselect the text.

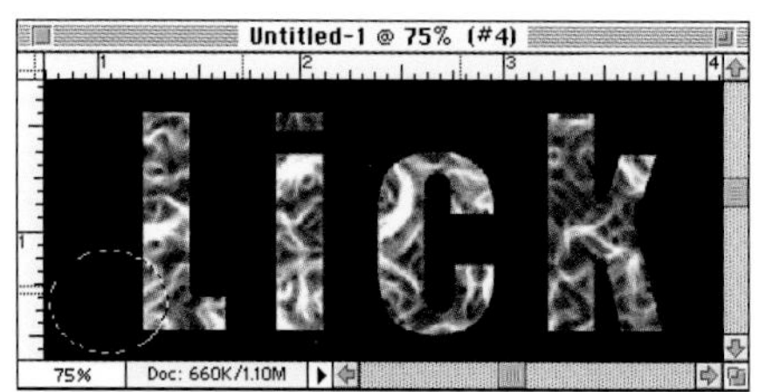


**11** To get the swirls to extend past the hard edges, use the Twirl filter. First, select the Elliptical Marquee tool and make a selection like this.

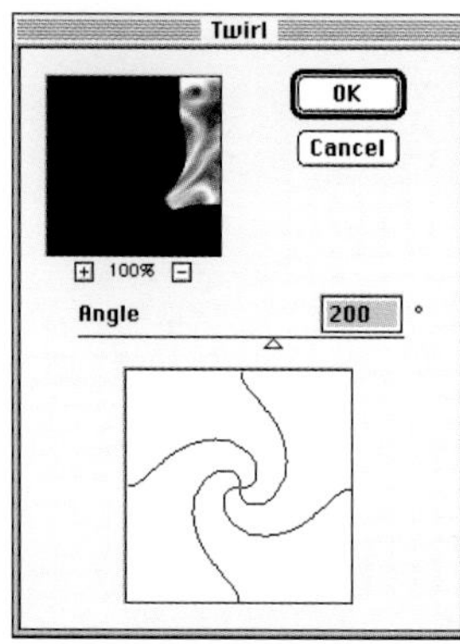


**12** Then choose Filter→Distort→Twirl. Watch the preview, and set the Angle so that a hook forms in the selection.

**13** Keep making selections and applying the Twirl filter. I set the Twirl angle at 200, and pressed Command-F [Control-F] to reapply the Twirl filter with the same settings. To create more dramatic swirls, apply the filter to the same selection several times.

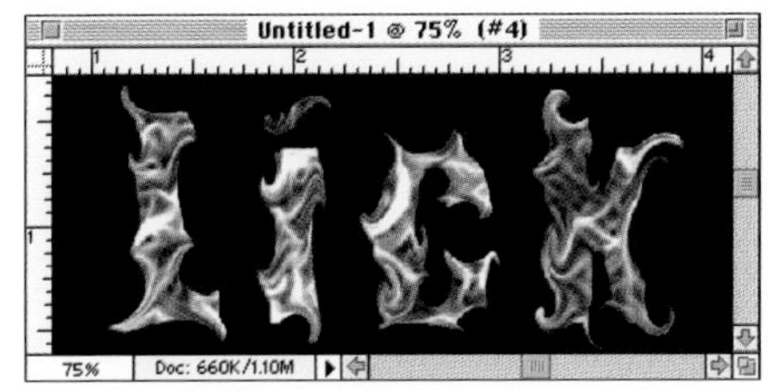


**14** Double-click the Wand tool to select it and bring the Wand Options floating palette to the front. Set the Tolerance to 10, and click the Wand in a black area outside of the type. If you have letters with holes in them (such as o's and p's), then hold the Shift key down and click inside the holes as well. Choose Select→Inverse to select the swirled texture.

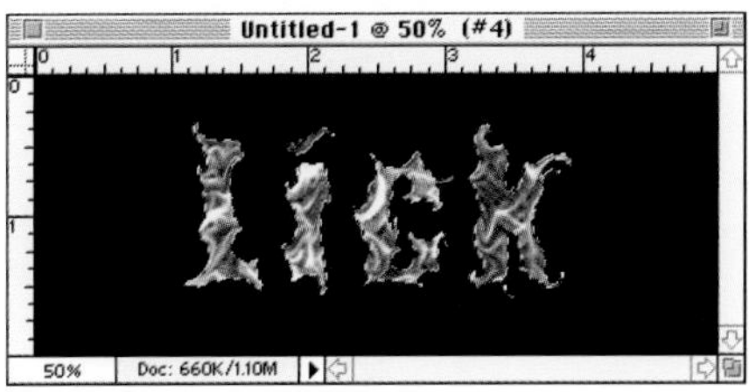


**15** If your text has too much contrast (like mine), then choose Image→Adjust→Brightness→Contrast. Raise the Brightness (+40) and lower the Contrast (-30).

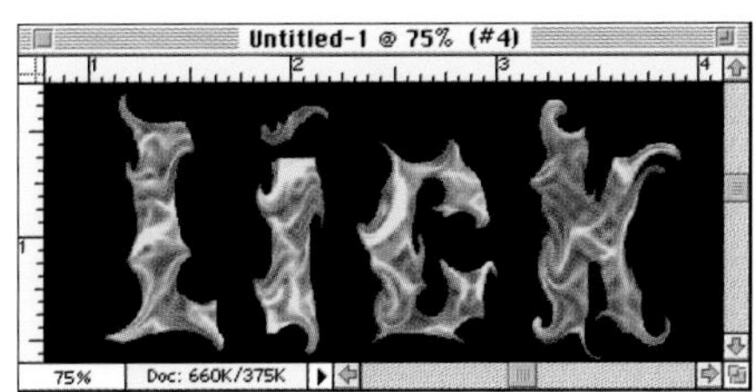


**16** Finally, blur the text a little more by choosing Filter→Blur→Gaussian Blur (Radius: 1).

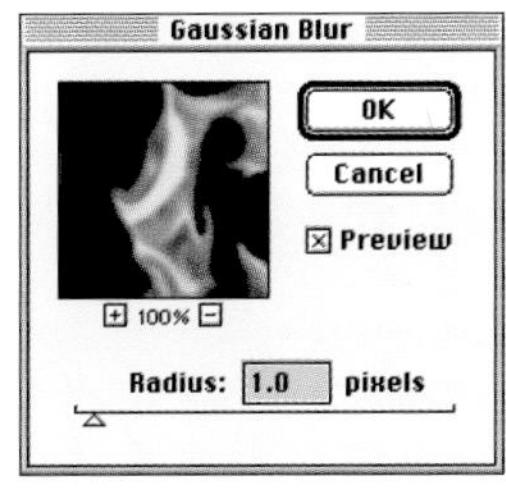


**17** Return to the composite channel. The selection should still be active.

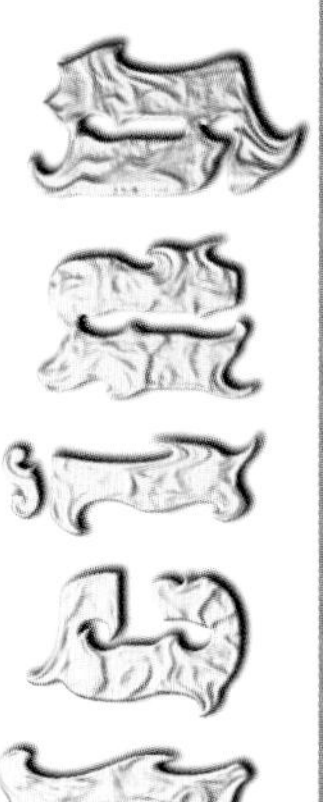

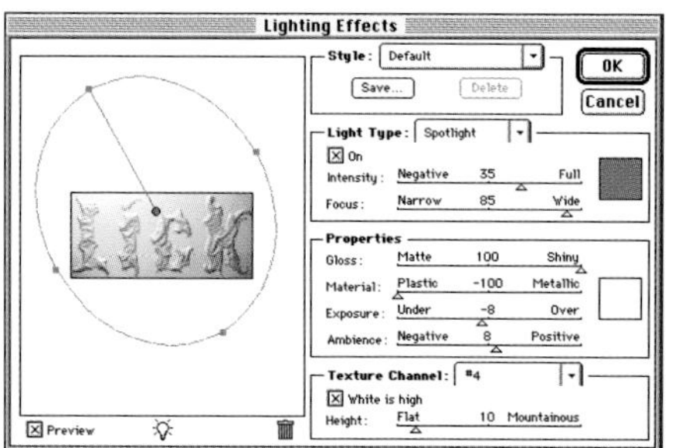


18 Choose Filter➛Render➛Lighting Effects. Match the settings you see in this figure, or select the Icing preset from the pop-up menu. The Light Type color becomes the color of the icing. The CMYK values for this color are 35, 67, 5, 3.

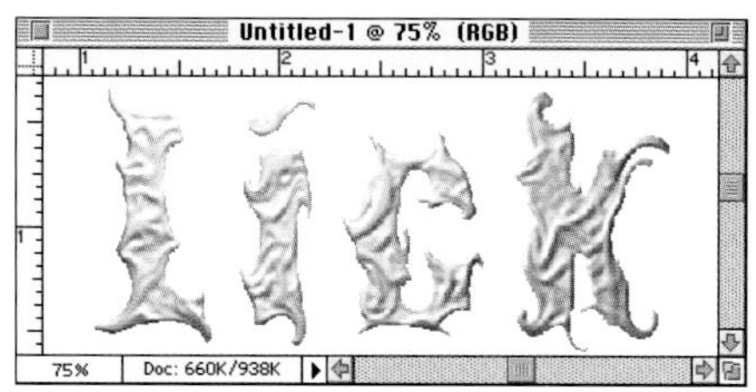


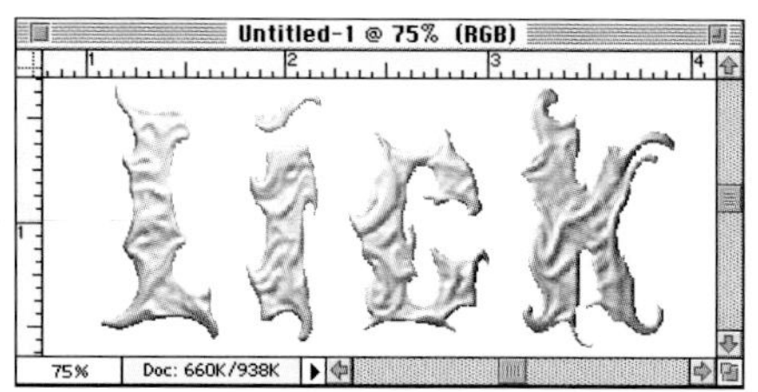


19 As a final touch I chose Select➛Modify➛Border (5 pixels) to select only the border. Then, I chose Filter➛Sharpen➛Sharpen Edges to harden the edges of the type.

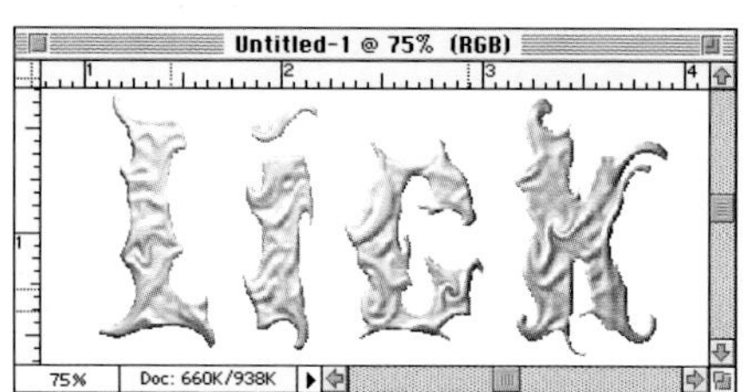


20 You can continue to do some swirling after you have applied the Lighting Effect filter, but your effect will look best if you keep the selection inside the type. ■

# LICENSE PLATE

A little blurring and the Lighting Effects filter let you bang out this effect in no time.

**1** Create a new file, and a new channel (#4). Use the Type tool to enter the text. Helvetica Condensed has that "license plate" look (70 points).

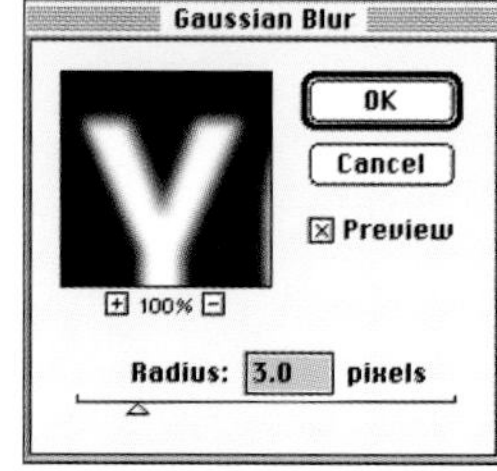


**2** Deselect the text, and make a copy of this channel to create Channel #4 copy. Then choose Filter➞Blur➞Gaussian Blur (Radius: 3).

**3** Load the selection Channel #4 copy (the same channel that is active).

**4** Press Command-Option-F [Control-Option-F] to bring back the Gaussian Blur dialog box. Slide the Radius marker up until dark patches begin to appear at the ends of the letters. I set the Radius at 9 pixels for this example. Your text should look something like this.

**5** With the selection still active, press Command-I [Control-I] to invert the interior of the type.

**TOOLBOX**

License Plate (Lighting Style Preset)

6 Then choose Image➛Adjust➛Brightness/Contrast and slide the Brightness marker up until your type looks something like what you see in the figure. Bring back almost all of the brightness. For me, this meant that I raised the Brightness all the way to +100, then chose Image➛Adjust➛Brightness/Contrast again and raised the Brightness to +50.

7 Return to the composite channel. Load the original type selection (Channel #4). Choose Select➛Modify➛Contract (1 pixel), and Select➛Modify➛Smooth (2 pixels), then Select➛Feather (1 pixel).

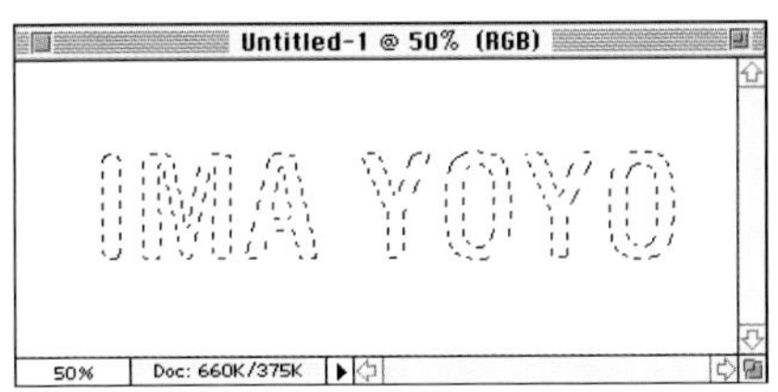


8 Change the foreground color to a color for the type. I used the CMYK values 0, 100, 100, 40. Fill the selection with the color.

9 If you know license plates, then you probably have noticed how the ink is never quite centered on the raised metal. Deselect the type. Select the Move tool and use the arrow keys to move the type a little.

10 Choose Filter➛Render➛Lighting Effects. Click on the Styles pop-up menu and select License Plate. If you have not loaded the presets from the CD, then match the settings as seen in this figure. ■

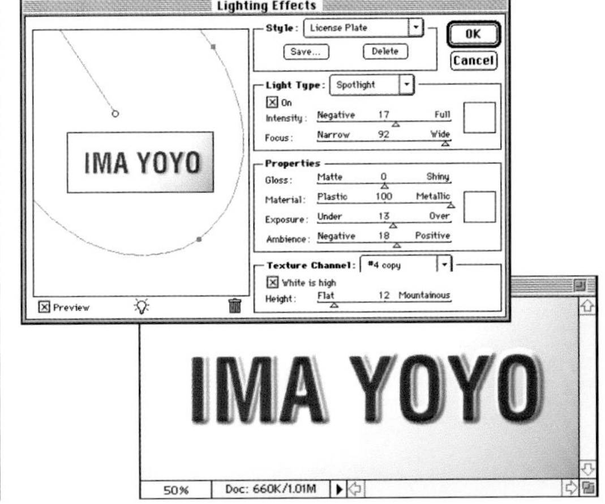

# LIGHTS

This simple effect creates lighted type that does not need a dark background. You also can create a snap with a variation of this technique.

**1** Create a new file. Make a new layer (Layer 1), and change the foreground color to black.

**2** Next, use the Type tool to enter the text. This is Anna at 110 points.

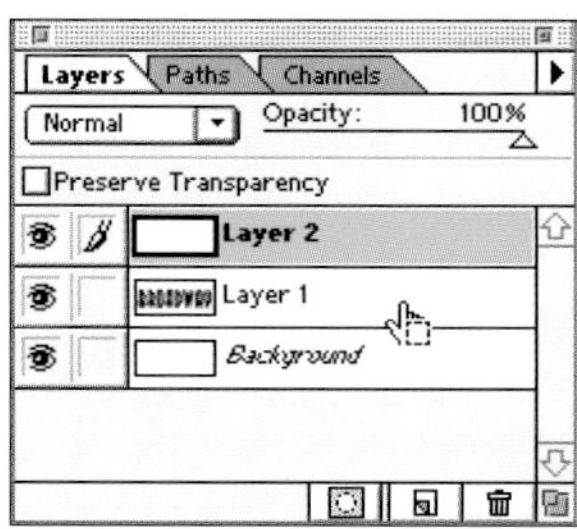


**3** Make another new layer (Layer 2), and load the transparency selection of Layer 1.

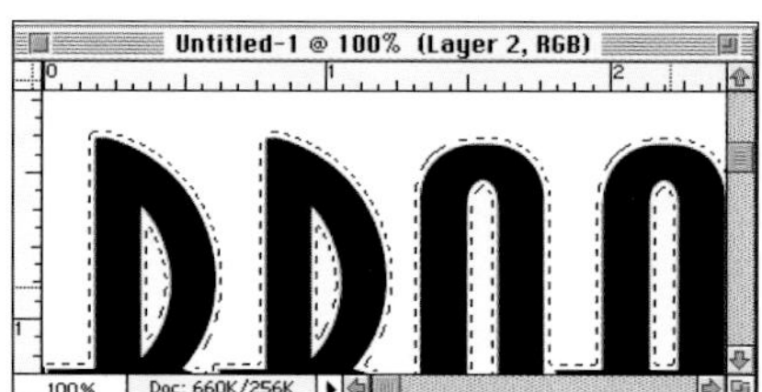


**4** Choose Select➛Modify➛Expand. Expand the selection so that you see a thin strip of white around the type. (I expanded this type selection 3 pixels.)

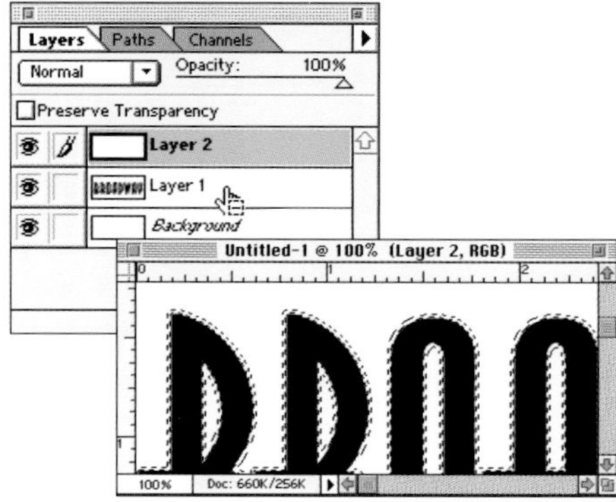


**5** Hold the Command and Option [Control and Alt] keys and click the Layer 1 preview to subtract the transparency selection of Layer 1 from the current selection. You will see a minus sign appear inside of the box on the back of the hand pointer. The thin white strip created in Step 4 should now be selected.

**6** Fill the selection with 50% gray.

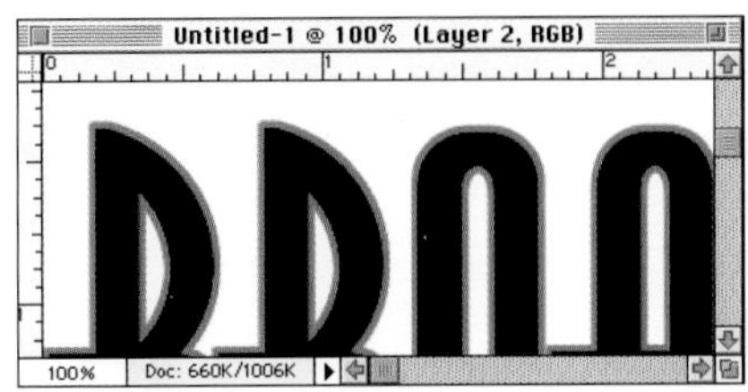


**7** Create a new channel (#4), and fill the selection with white. Choose Filter➛Stylize➛Emboss and use these settings: Angle: 160°; Height: 1 pixel; Amount: 168%. Your settings may vary, but make sure that you see some contrast in the thin lines. The color should be a flat gray or white.

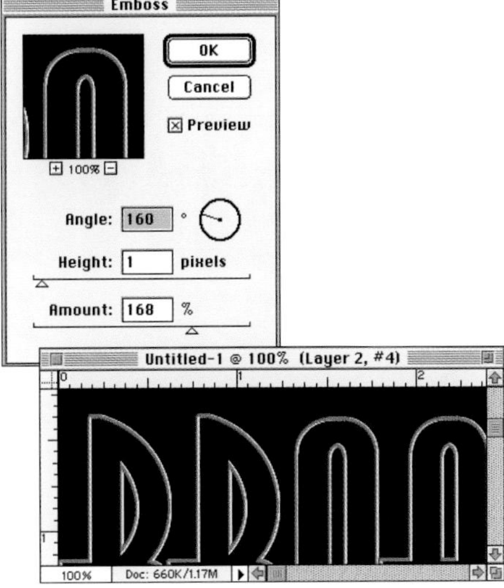


**8** Return to the Composite channel. The selection should still be active, and Layer 2 should be the active layer.

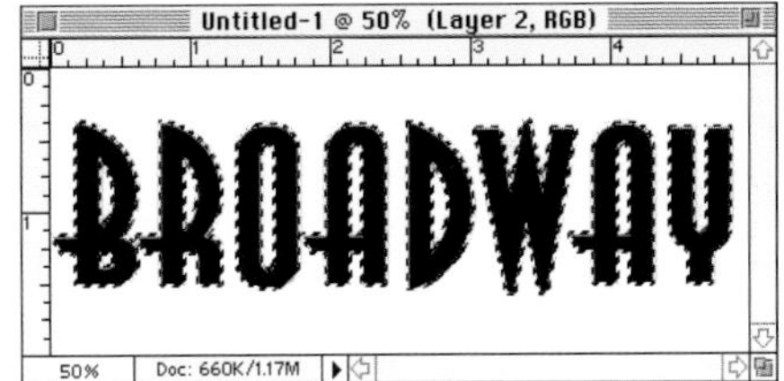

**9** Choose Filter➛Render➛Lighting Effects. Match these settings or select Outlines from the Styles pop-up menu.

**10** Make a new layer (Layer 3), and load the transparency selection of Layer 1 (the original type selection).

**11** Choose Select➛Feather. The amount that you feather the selection will depend on the point size of your type and the resolution of the file. You want to feather the selection enough so that it expands over the trim. (I feathered this type selection 5 pixels.)

**12** Change the foreground color to a color for the light, and fill the selection to flip on the light switch. I used the CMYK values 0, 0, 94, 0.

## Variations

You also can make each light a different color. After loading the Layer 1 transparency selection in Step 10, select the rectangular Marquee tool. Then hold down the Option and Shift [Alt and Shift] keys while dragging the Marque tool to create a selection around only the letter that you want, like this:

Proceed with Steps 11 and 12 to light up that letter.

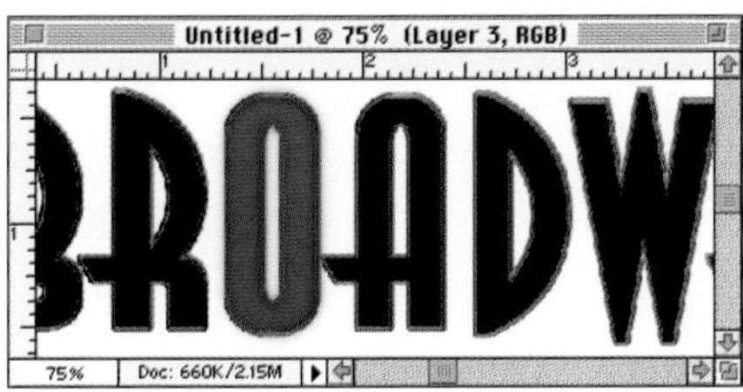


Repeat the process for each letter in the word.

You can always add the dark background by filling the background layer with black. I also loaded the Layer 1 transparency selection; I feathered (Select➡Feather) it 6 pixels, and filled it with white.

This snap type was made using a similar technique that started with the Paintbrush tool.

**1** Create a new file, and a new layer (Layer 1). Double-click the Paintbrush tool to select it and to bring forward the Paintbrush Options floating palette. Then click the Brushes tab to bring the Brushes palette to the front.

**2** From the arrow menu on the Brushes palette, choose Reset Brushes to make sure that the default brushes are loaded. Click OK in the dialog box that opens.

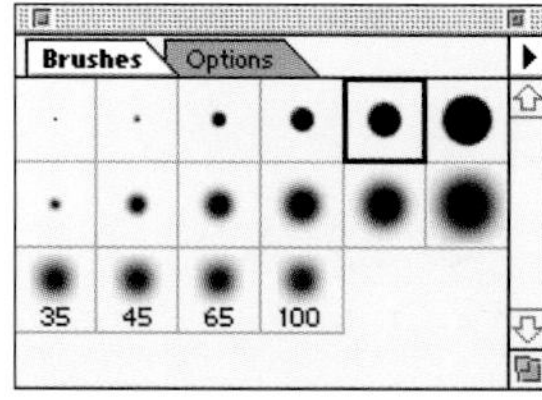


**3** Select any of the hard brushes, and change the Foreground color to black.

**4** Use the brush and click one circle at a time to build your type.

**Turn on the Grid (View➞Show Grid) and the Snap to Grid (View➞Snap to Grid) options to keep your circles in line.**

**5** Follow the instructions in Steps 3 through 12 starting on page 114. In Step 4, expand the selection only 2 pixels, and in Step 11, feather the selection 1 pixel.

**6** Make the Background layer active, and load the transparency selection of Layer 2. Then load the transparency selection of Layer 3 while holding down the Shift key to add this selection to the existing selection. Choose Select➸Feather (1 pixel), and fill the selection with black. Deselect the selection; select the Move tool, and nudge the selection to the right. ■

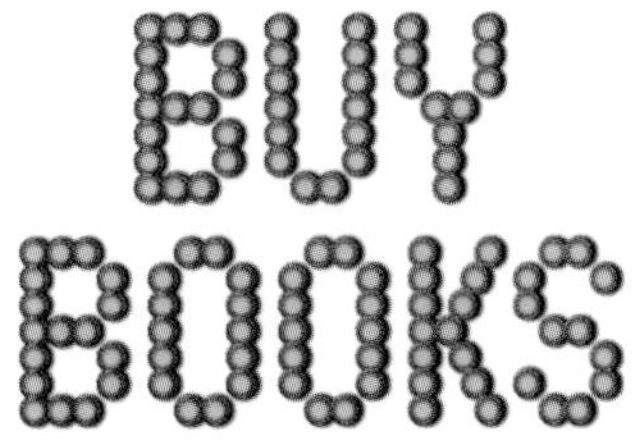

The Clouds filter helps create this realistic marble from scratch.

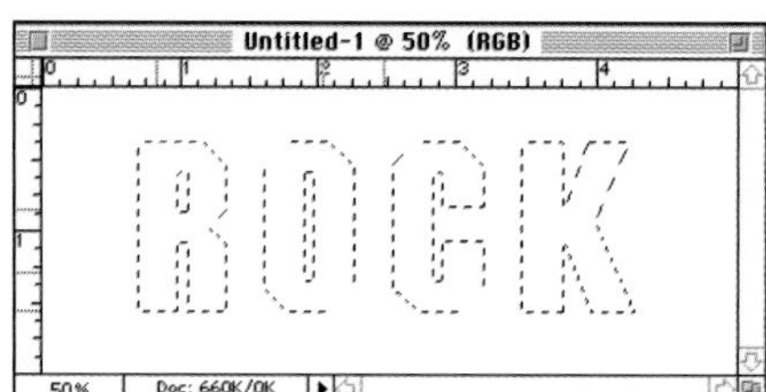

1 Create a new file. Use the Type Mask tool to enter the text. Marble looks good in a blocky font such as Machine (120 points).

2 Keep the selection active, and choose Filter→Render→Difference Clouds.

3 Reapply this filter a few times. The more times you apply the filter, the more the veins of the marble break up. I applied the Difference Clouds filter two times. Here is what my type looked like:

4 Choose Filter→Stylize→Find Edges. This filter pulls the veins out of the clouds.

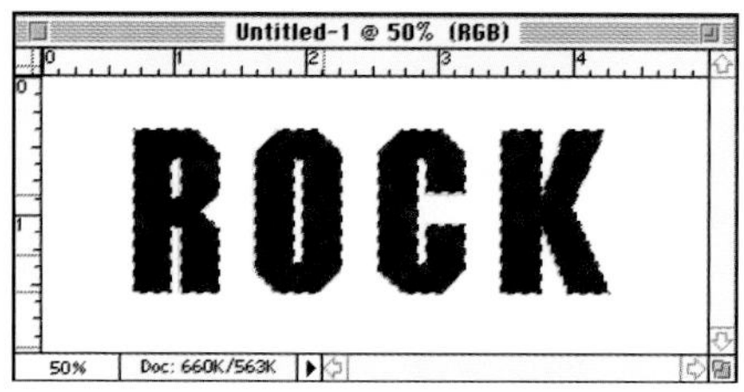

5 Choose Image→Adjust→Invert.

6 Next, choose Image→Adjust→ Levels. Grab the right (white) Input marker and slide it to the left until it sits under the beginning of the steep slope in the graph (shown in the figure). Then nudge the middle (gray) input marker to the right.

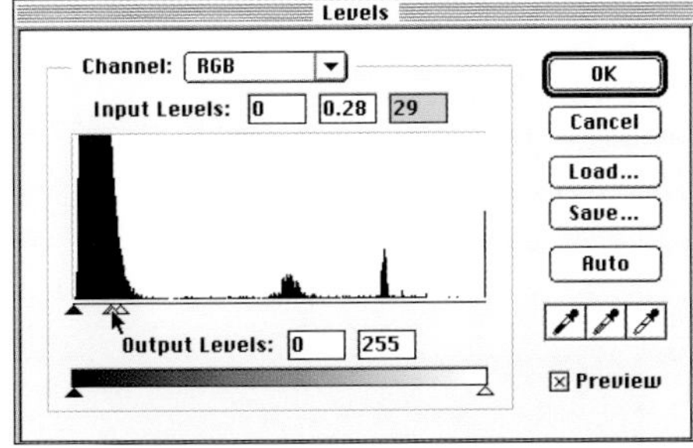


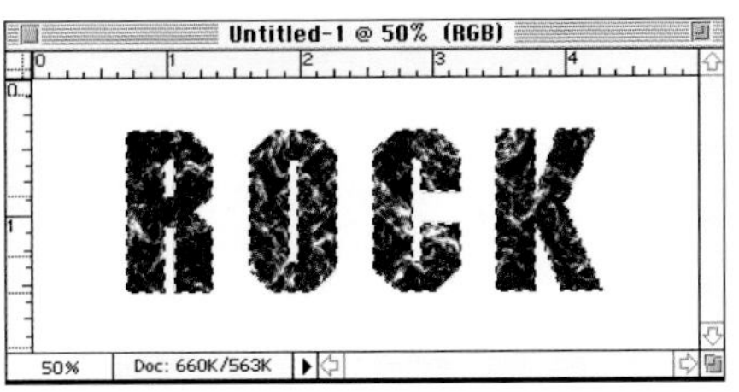


7 Choose Image→Adjust→ Hue/Saturation. Turn on the Colorize option. Then slide the Saturation marker down so that the color isn't too bright. I set the Saturation at 0. Use the Hue slider to find a color for the marble. For more color, nudge the Lightness up just a little.

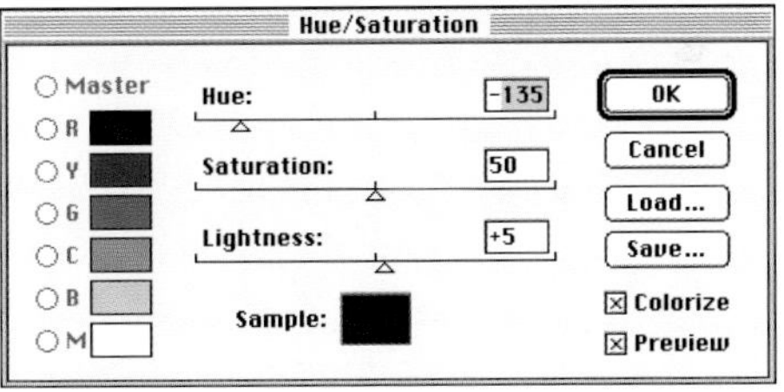


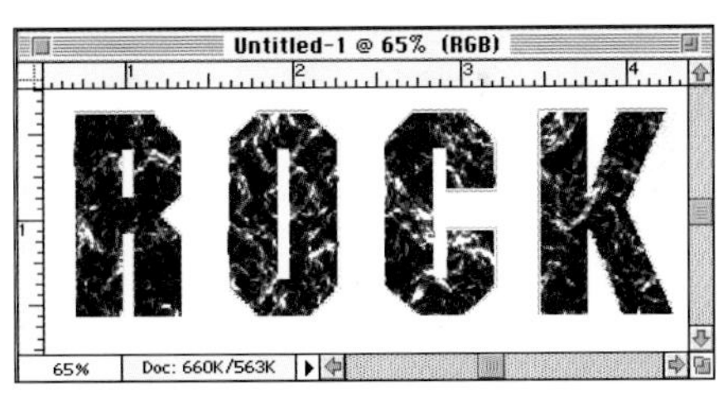


8 The Find Edges filter leaves a funny edge on the type. Choose Select→Modify→Contract. Contract the selection 1 or 2 pixels—just enough so that the selection is inside the marble. I chose 2 pixels. Choose Select→Inverse and press Delete to fill the background with white. ■

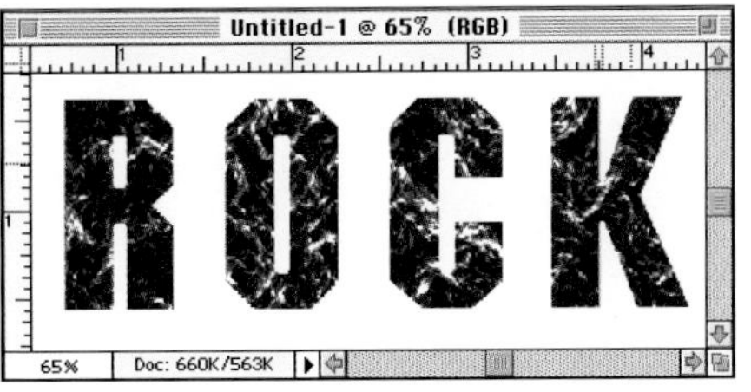

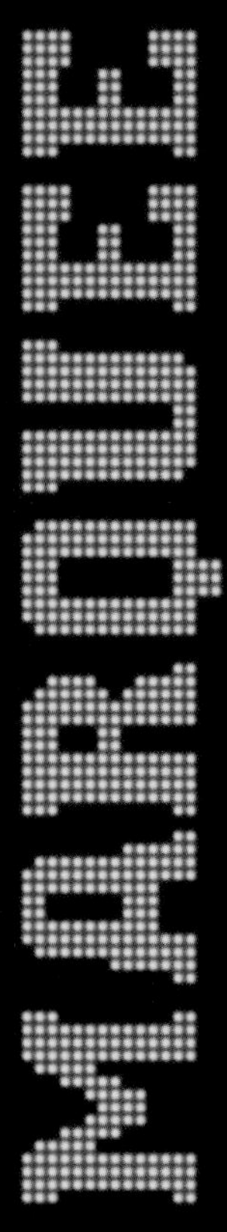

Put your name in lights. The time-consuming part of this effect is building an even grid of lights; however, the new Guides and Grid feature in Adobe Photoshop 4.0 makes it a lot easier.

**1** Create a new file. Change the foreground color to black (or another dark color) to contrast with the shining lights. Fill the Background layer with black.

**2** Change the foreground color to white. Use the Type tool to enter the text. The type will drop automatically into a new layer (Layer 1). This type will serve as a guide for building the lights. Use a good fat font that can hold plenty of lights. I used City Bold at 60 points in this example. Move the type into place.

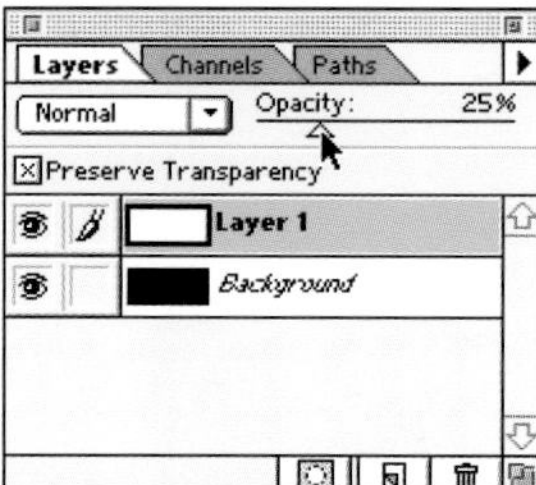


**3** Use the Opacity slider on the Layers palette to lower the opacity of Layer 1 to 25%.

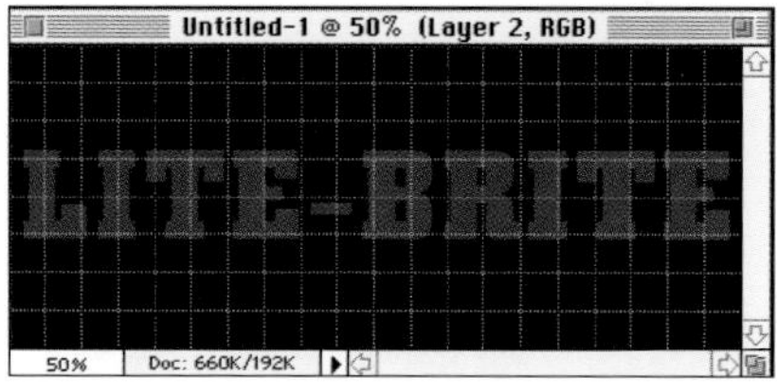


**4** Make a new layer (Layer 2). Choose View➝Show Grid to turn on the grids.

5 Zoom in on the type so you can see one letter well. I zoomed in to 150%.

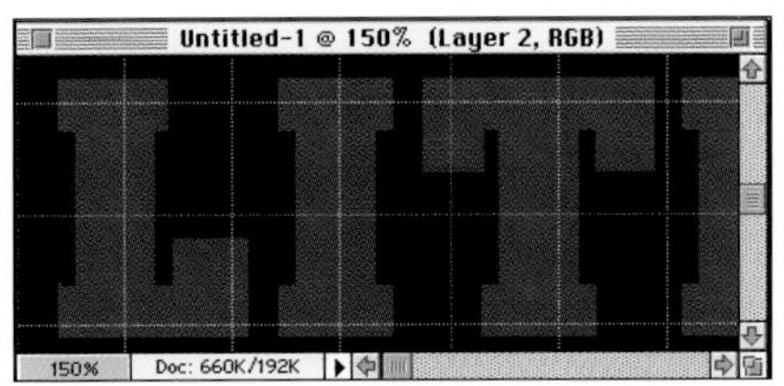


6 Choose File➸Preferences➸Guides & Grid. The gridline distance determines how large the lights are relative to the type. As you change the Gridline distance setting, watch the image window to see how well the grid fits your type. Each grid square will become one light in your type. For this example, I set the Gridline every setting to 8 pixels, and kept the Subdivisions at 1.

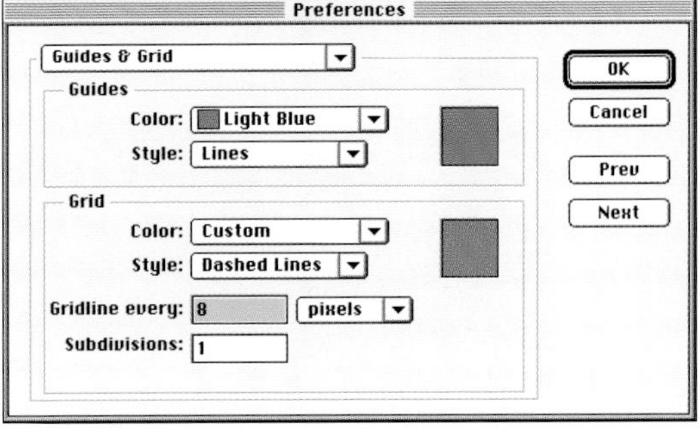


The image window is filled with lines.

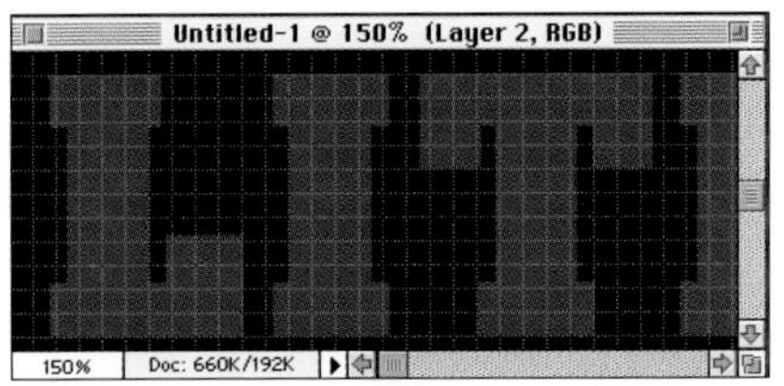


7 Make Layer 1 the active layer and select the Move tool. Move the faded type into alignment with the grid. It does not have to be perfect since this type only serves as a guide for choosing where to place the lights. If it doesn't fit well, then change either the Grid or the type size.

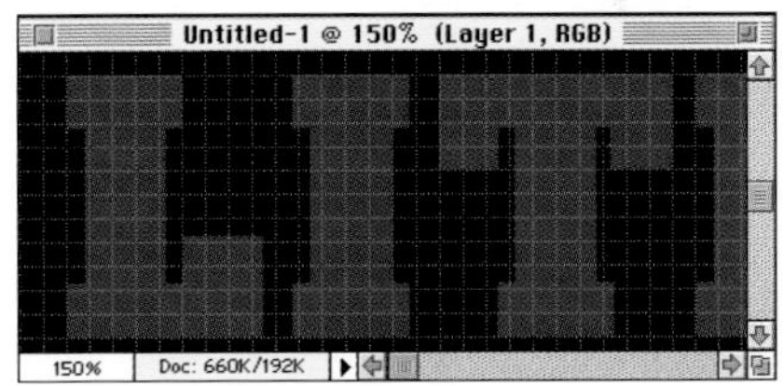


8 Make Layer 2 the active layer again. Double-click the Marquee tool. Choose the Elliptical Marquee and set the style to fixed size. I set the fixed size to one-half the Gridline distance selected in Step 6. Make sure that you turn off Anti-Aliasing.

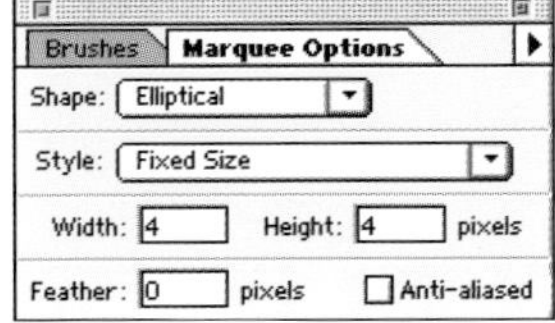

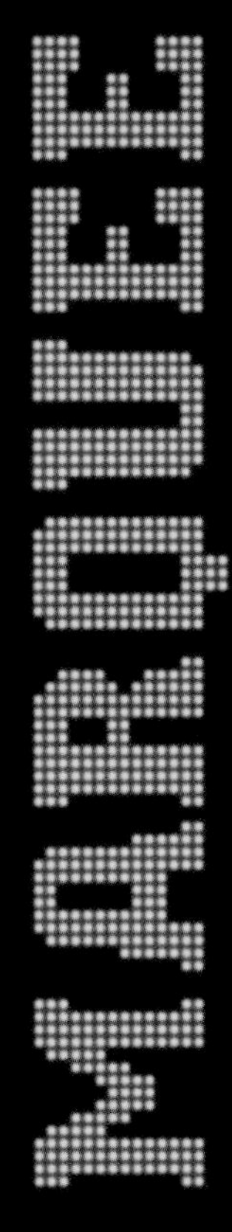


9 Also make sure that the View➛Snap to Guides option is turned on (it will have a check mark next to it). With the Marquee tool, click in the upper-left corner of the first grid box that you want to contain a light. The grid snap should align the fixed selection right into the corner.

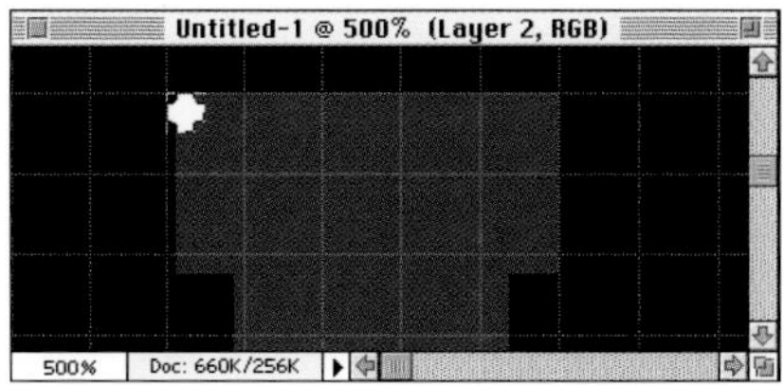


10 Fill the selection with white.

11 Keep clicking and filling, using the grid lines and the underlying type as guides. Here is the type after filling in all the lights.

Load Selection

Source
Document: Untitled-1
Channel: *Layer 2 Transparency*
☐ Invert

Operation
◉ New Selection
○ Add to Selection
○ Subtract from Selection
○ Intersect with Selection

OK
Cancel

12 Load the transparency selection of Layer 2. Then make a new layer (Layer 3), and make Layers 1 and 2 invisible.

13 Choose Select➛Feather (2 pixels) to soften the selection. Then fill the selection with white.

**14** Change the foreground color to a color for the type. I used a bright yellow from Photoshop's default swatches.

**15** Load the transparency selection of Layer 2 again. Choose Select→Feather. Feather the selection just 1 pixel this time. Fill it with the foreground color. ■

In this effect I will show you how to take an image and crack it into little pieces of color using the Crystallize filter.

**1** Open a file that contains an image you can use for the mosaic tiles. Select the portion you want to use, copy it, and close the file. For this example I used the Fruit image from Photoshop's Tutorial file (Adobe Photoshop 4.0➡Tutorial➡Fruit).

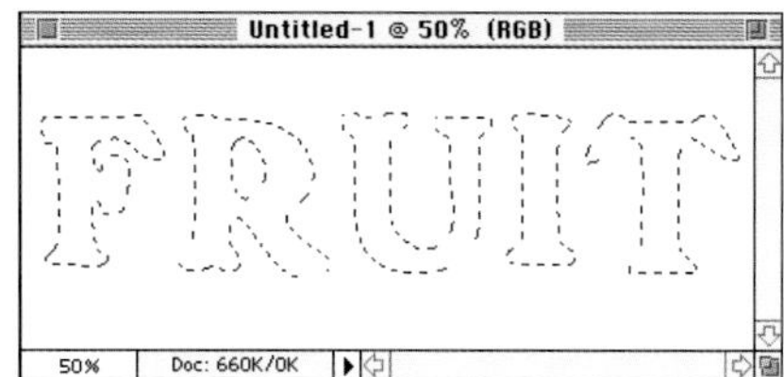


**2** Create a new file, and use the Type Mask tool to enter the text. I used Frankenfont at 100 points. Keep the selection active.

**3** Choose Edit➡Paste Into. The image you copied for your mosaic is pasted into the selected text. Choose Layer➡Merge Down to bring everything back to the Background layer.

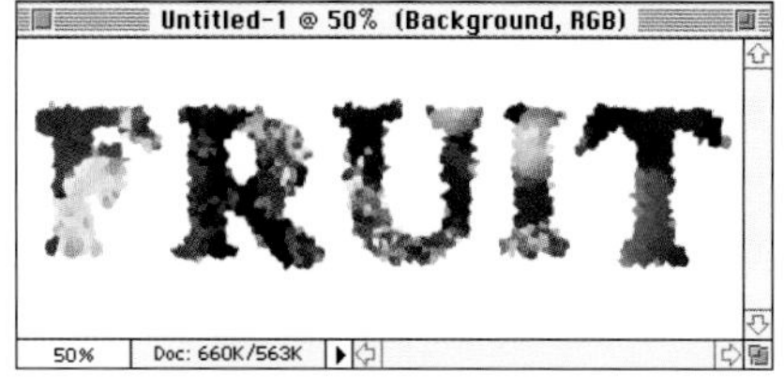


**4** Choose Filter➡Pixelate➡Crystallize, and type in a Cell (tile) Size (10).

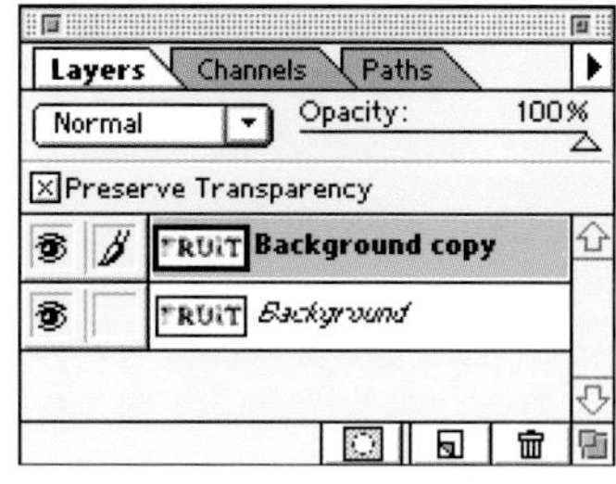


**5** It's a good start, but we need some grout. Make a copy of this layer to create the Background layer copy.



TOOLBOX

Mosaic (Lighting Style Preset)

**6** To create the lines for the grout, choose Filter➙Stylize➙Find Edges.

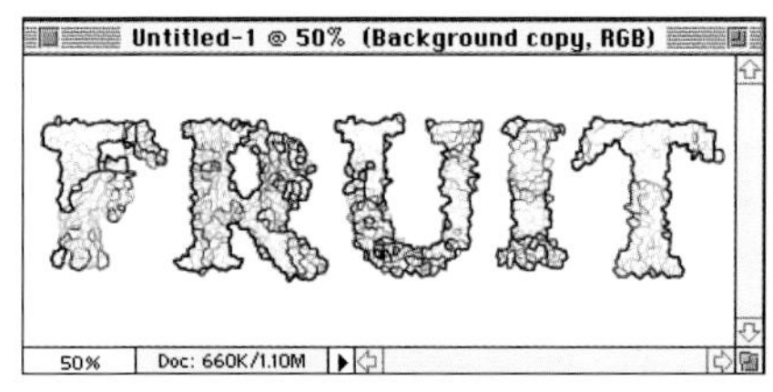


**7** To clean up the lines do the following commands: Image➙Adjust➙Threshold (255), and Filter➙Other➙Maximum (Radius: 1). Your image should transform like this:

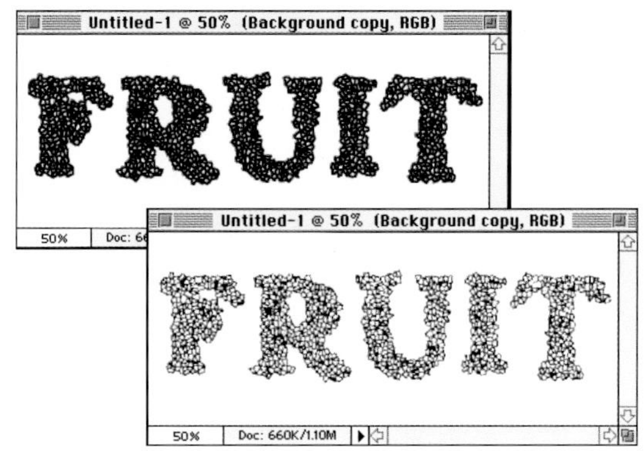


**8** Select the Magic Wand tool and be very careful to click on a white area inside your text in the Background layer copy. Then choose Select➙Similar. All the white in this layer will be selected. Press Delete, and deselect the selection. Presto, mosaic type.

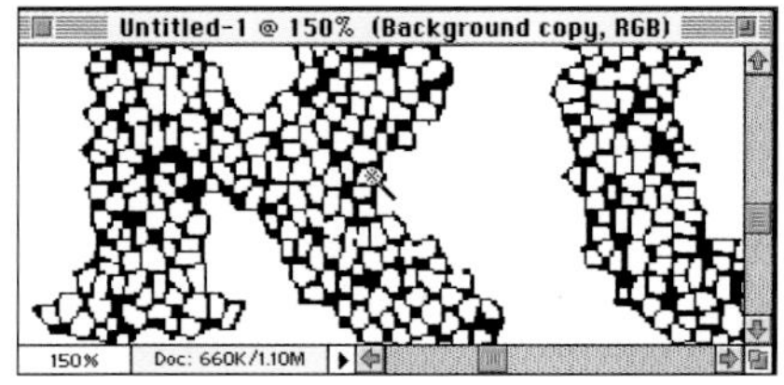

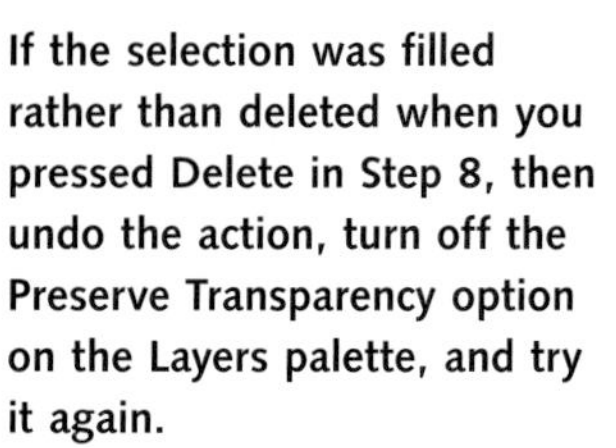

**TIP** **If the selection was filled rather than deleted when you pressed Delete in Step 8, then undo the action, turn off the Preserve Transparency option on the Layers palette, and try it again.**

## VARIATIONS

This method is similar to the previous one; however, a few extra steps will improve the appearance of the grout.

**1** Perform Step 1. (For this variation, I used the same image that was used in the previous steps.)

**2** Then create a new channel (#4), and use the Type tool to enter the text. (Again, I used Frankenfont at 100 points.) Deselect the text.

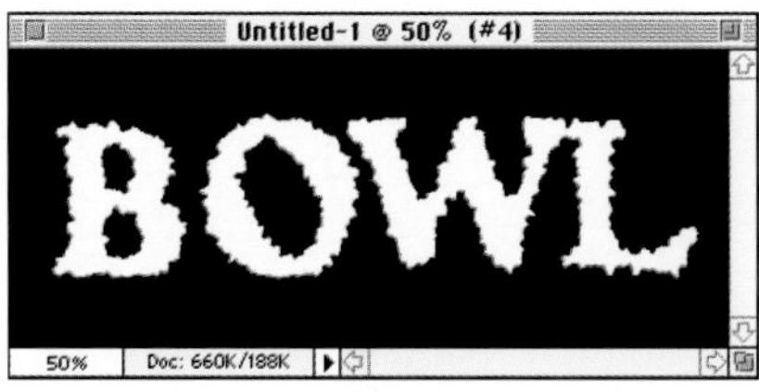


**3** Choose Filter➞Pixelate➞Crystallize (Cell Size: 10), and Image➞Adjust➞Threshold (255).

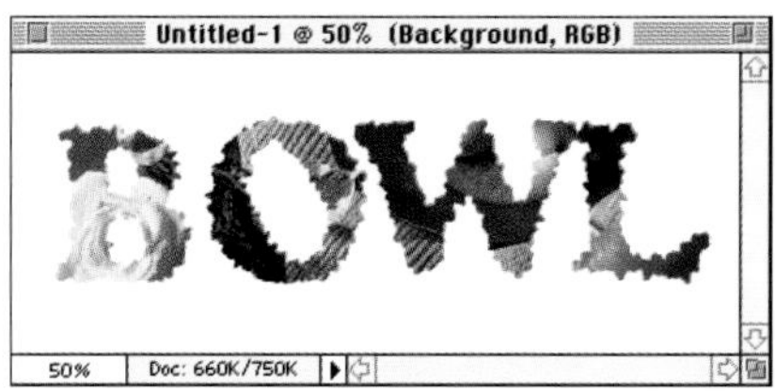


**4** Return to the composite channel, load the selection Channel #4, and choose Edit➞Paste Into. Choose Layer➞Merge Down to bring everything back to the Background layer.

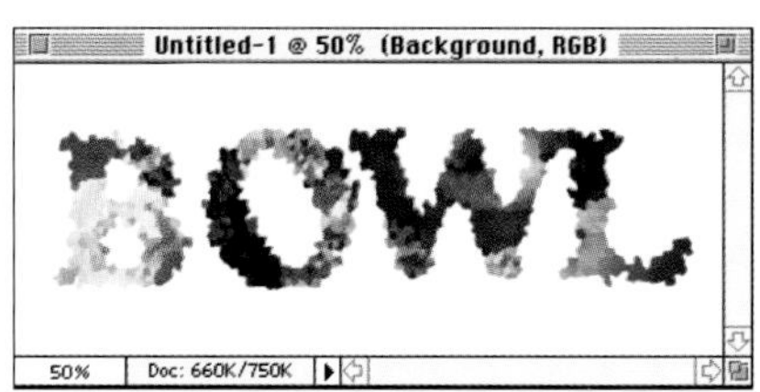


**5** Break up the image again by choosing Filter➞Pixelate➞Crystallize (Cell Size: 10).

**6** Select the entire image, and copy it. Then create a new channel, and paste in the image. Deselect the selection.

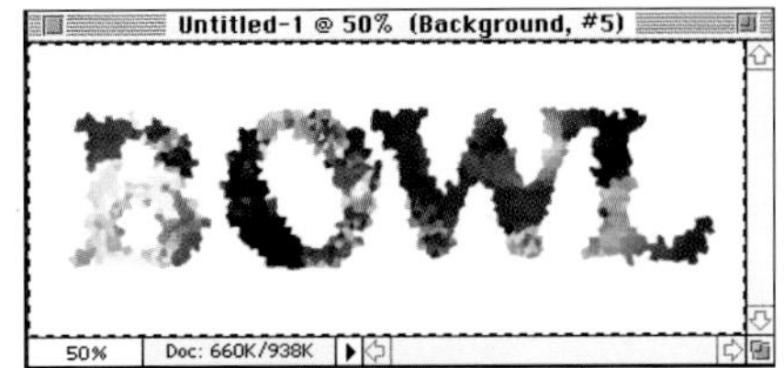


**7** Now, complete Steps 6 and 7. Then press Command-I [Control-I] to invert the channel. Here is what I have now.

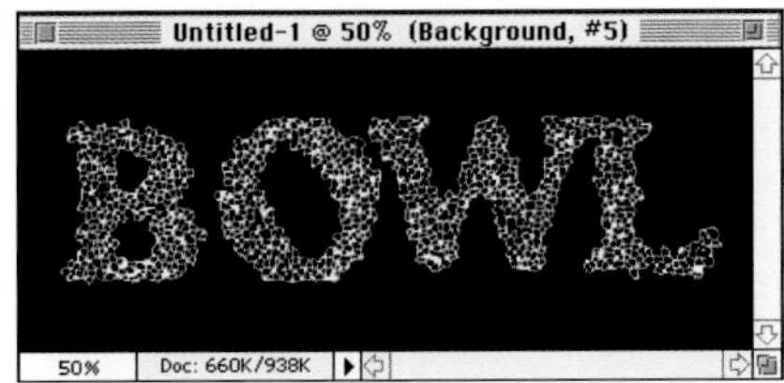


**8** Duplicate this channel to create Channel #5 copy.

**9** Choose Filter➝Blur➝Gaussian Blur (Radius: 1 pixel).

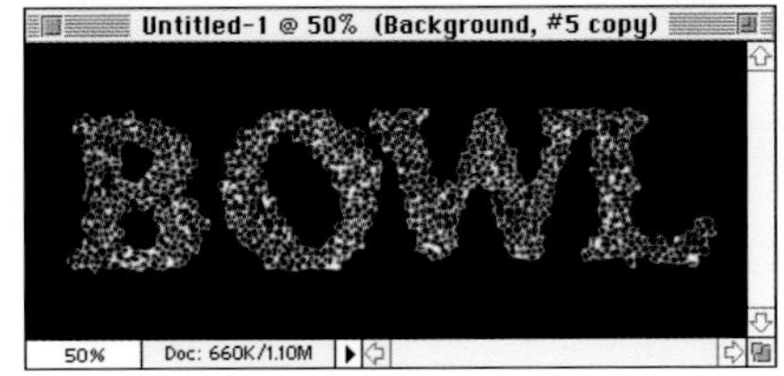


**10** Now we are ready to finish it. Return to the composite channel, load the selection Channel #5, and fill it with white.

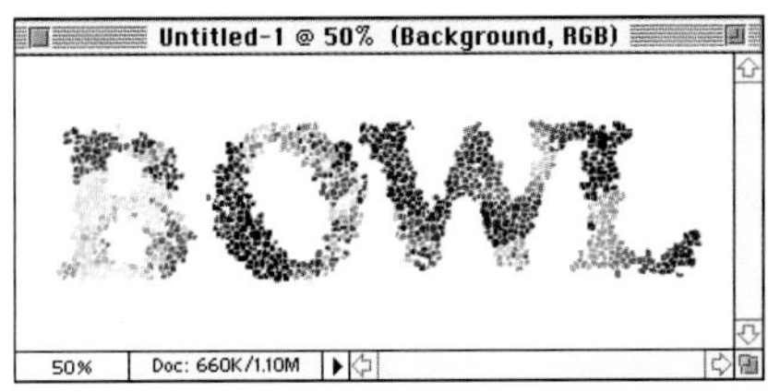


**11** Keep the selection active, and choose Filter➝Render➝Lighting Effects. Then select the Mosaic preset from the Style pop-up menu, or match the settings you see here. Make sure that Channel #5 copy is the texture channel.

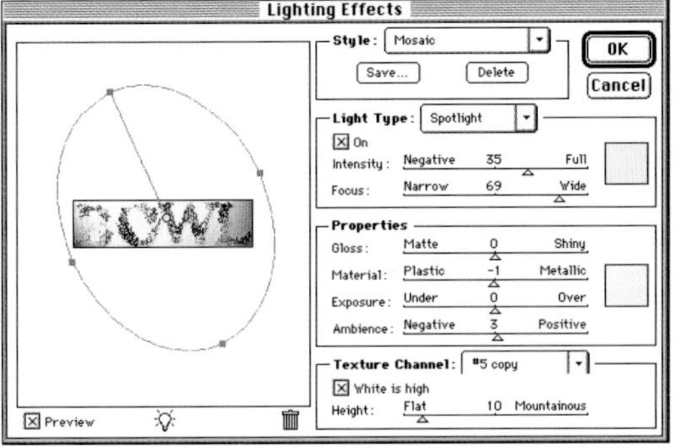

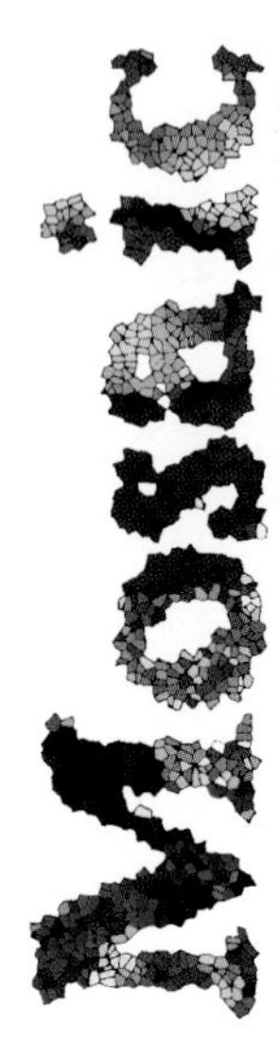


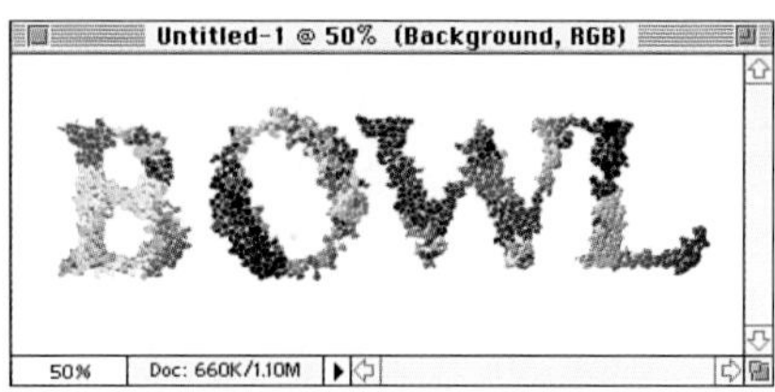


**12** Beautiful mosaic type.

**13** If you turn off the White is High checkbox in the Lighting Effects filter dialog box, then you will get this. ■

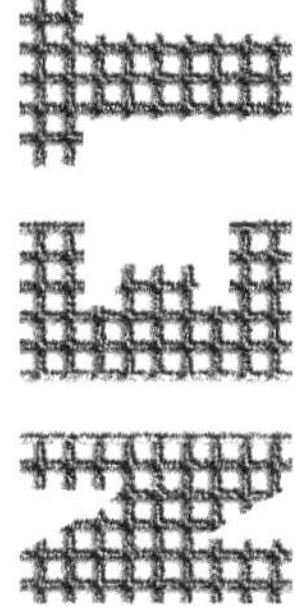

The Tiles filter breaks up type into a grid. Then some texture is added with the Wind filter. Finally, the Lighting Effects filter brings everything together.

**1** Create a new file. I created an oversized file (5" wide x 3" tall) because in Step 7 we will need room to rotate the text. Create a new channel (#4), and use the Type tool to enter the text. This is another effect that needs a thick, hefty font. Poplar at 120 points was used for this example.

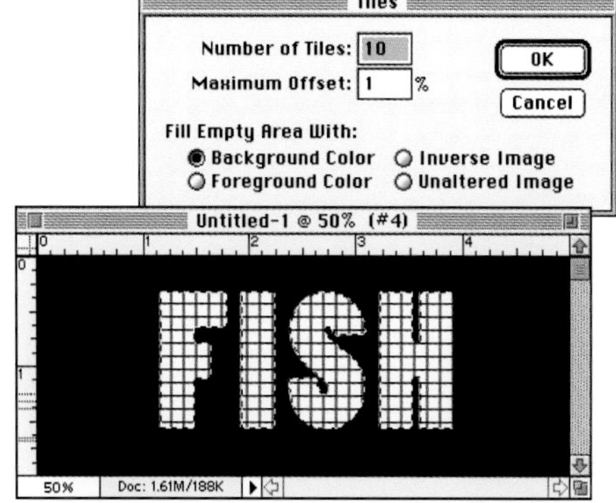


**2** Choose Filter➸Stylize➸Tiles. This filter does most of the work by establishing the grid. Find a Number of Tiles that looks good in the type. I used 10. Keep the Offset percentage set at 1.

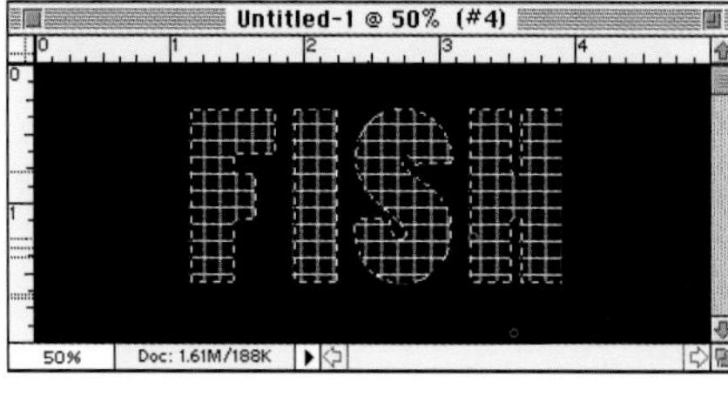


**3** Choose Image➸Adjust➸Invert.



TOOLBOX

Net (Lighting Style Preset)

**4** If you hide the selection edges (Command-H) [Control-H], you can see that there are thin lines on some of the edges of the corners. To get rid of them, choose Select➭Modify➭Contract (1 pixel), and Select➭Inverse. Next fill the selection with black.

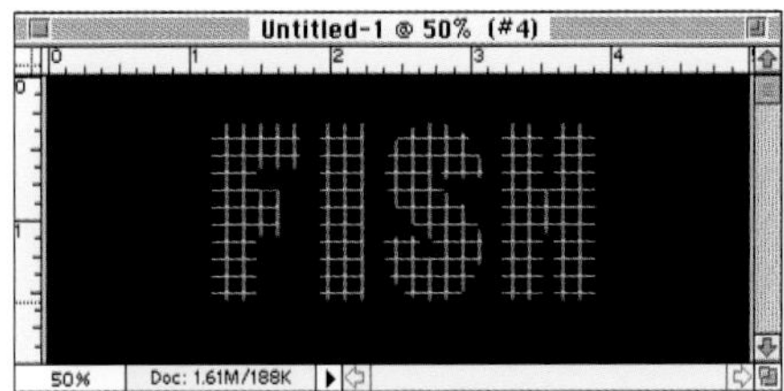

**To get rid of any leftover strange edges, choose Select➭Inverse again. Then set the foreground color to black and use the paintbrush to paint away the edges. If you choose Select➭Inverse to perform this Tip, then skip that part of the next step.**

**5** Choose Select➭Inverse again. Then choose Filter➭Other➭Maximum (Radius: 1). This thickens the lines of the grid. These lines become the ropes in the net: the thicker the lines, the thicker the ropes.

**6** Then, choose Filter➭Noise➭Median (Radius: 1 or 2) to round out the intersections. Deselect the grid.

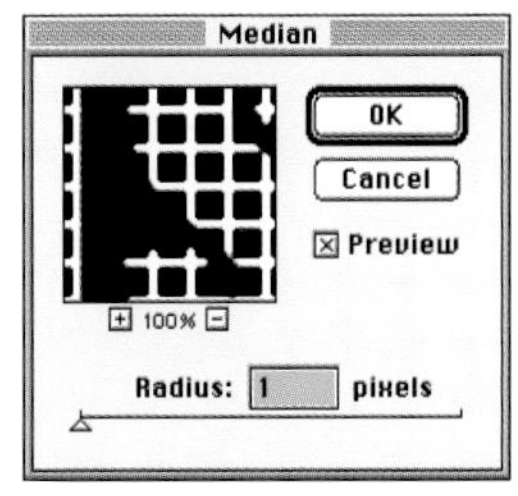

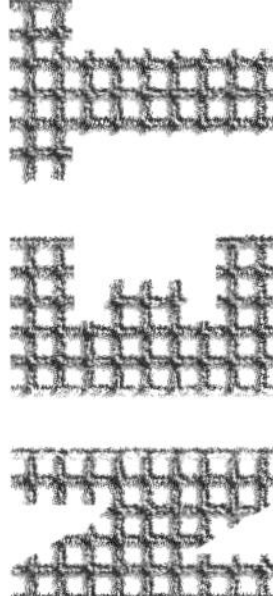


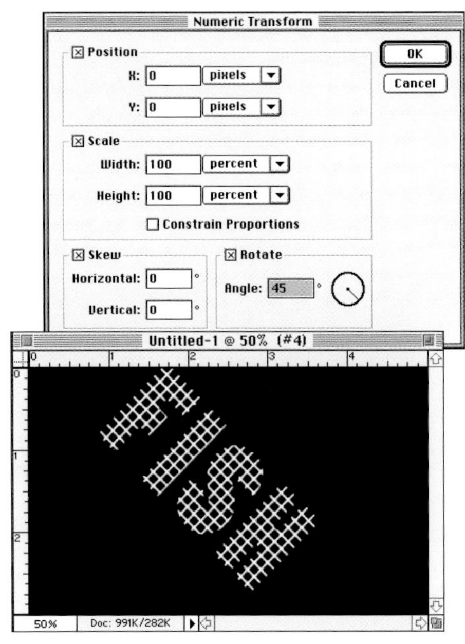


**7** Now for the texture. First, make sure that the background color is black. Then, rotate the entire image 45° by choosing Layer➔Transform➔Numeric (Angle: 45°). After the image rotates, make sure that all of the type is still visible.

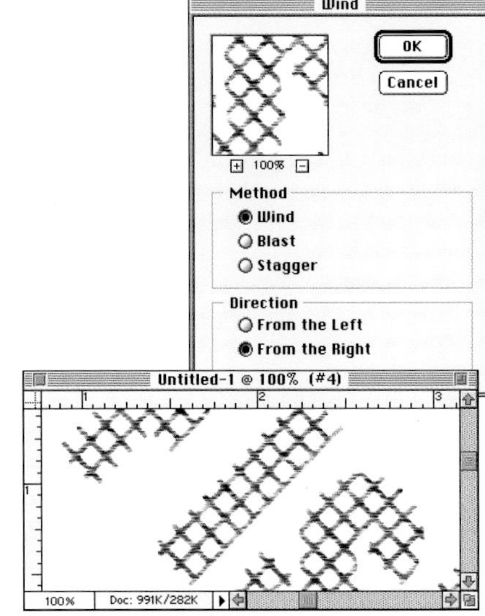


**8** Invert the entire image (Command-I) [Control-I]. Next, apply the Wind filter twice. Once to the left and once to the right by choosing Filter➔Stylize➔Wind (Wind, Left) and Filter➔Stylize➔Wind (Wind, Right).

**9** Invert the image again (Command-I) [Control-I]. Then rotate it back to its horizontal position by choosing Layer➵Transform➵Numeric (Angle: -45°).

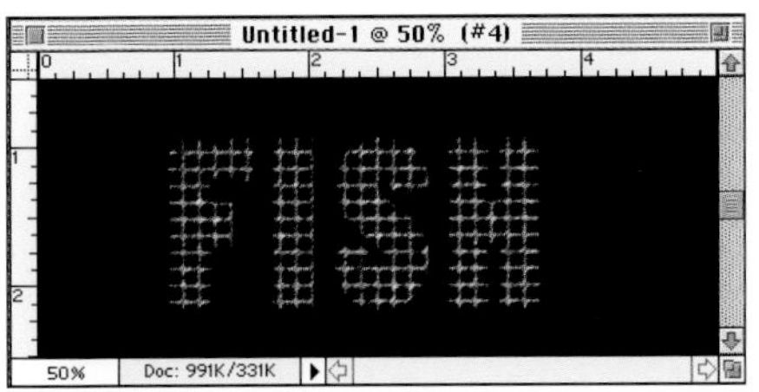


**10** Return to the composite channel. Load the selection Channel #4. Choose Filter➵Render➵Lighting Effects and select Net from the Style pop-up menu or match the settings seen here. Make sure that Channel #4 is selected as the texture channel. The color of the light will become the color of the net.

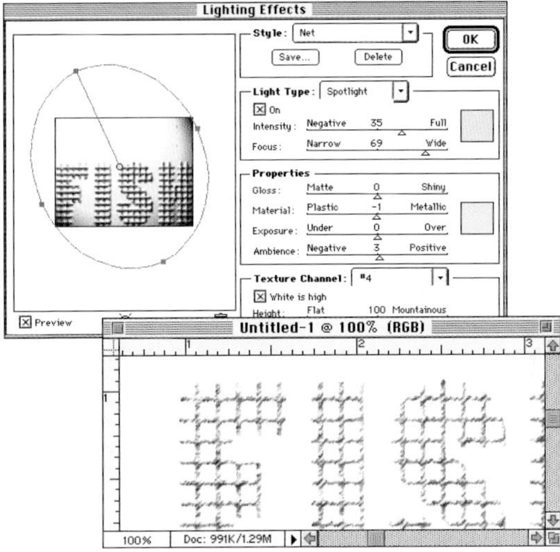


**11** For this example, the Lighting Effects filter was applied a second time by pressing Command-F [Control-F].

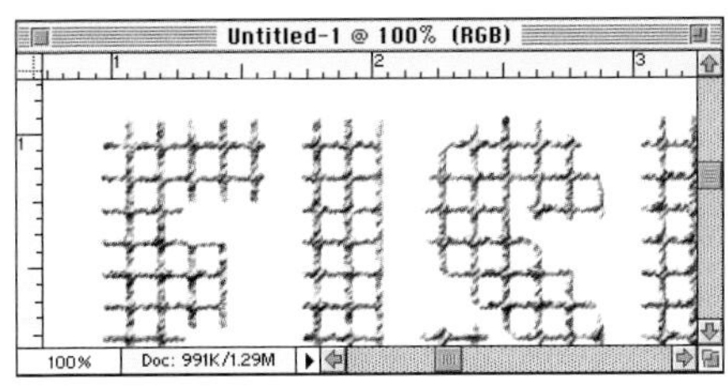


**12** And finally everything was made a little darker using the Levels dialog box.

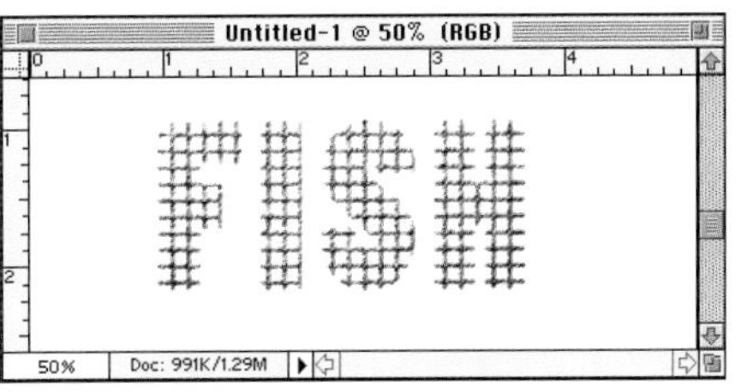

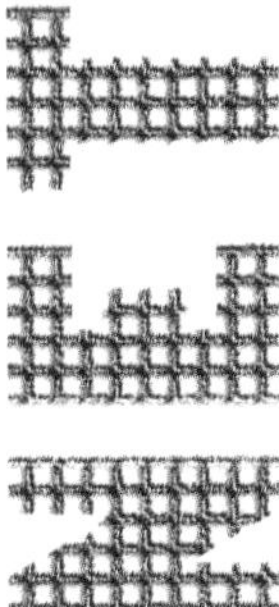

## A Rougher Rope

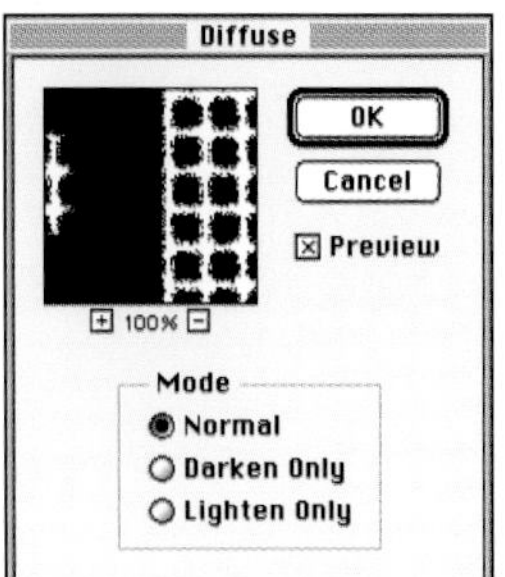


1 Perform Steps 1 through 6 previously listed. Then choose Filter➻Stylize➻Diffuse (Normal).

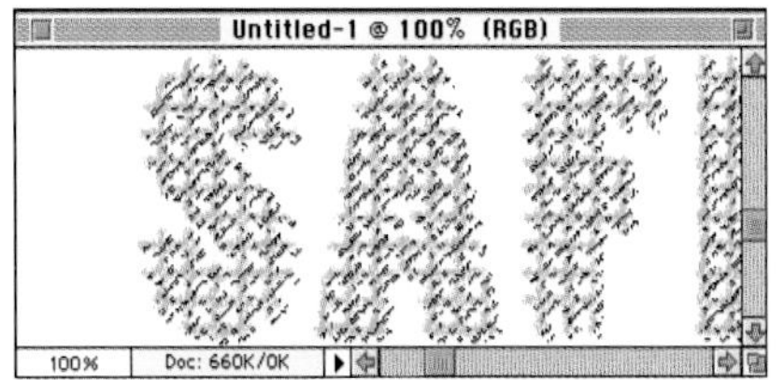


2 Return to the composite channel, and load the selection Channel #4. Choose a foreground color and fill the selection. I used these CMYK values: 17, 24, 74, 4.

3 Now, select the Marquee tool and press the down arrow and right arrow keys three times each to move the selection.

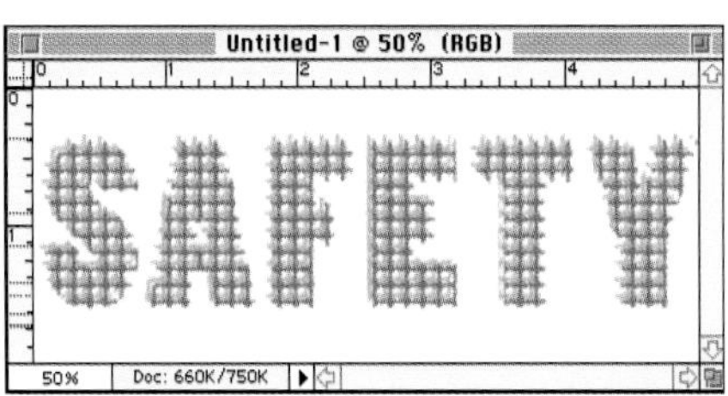


4 Choose another foreground color (I used these CMYK values: 30, 55, 100, 42), and fill the selection.

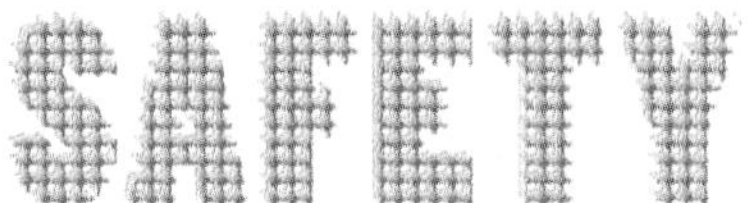

5 Again, with the Marquee tool selected, press the up arrow and left arrow keys two times each. Then, select the Move tool and press the up arrow and left arrow keys one time each. ■

Creating this effect is very similar to creating the Foil effect. Try the subtle changes offered in the Variations section. They improve the look of the paper quite a bit.

**1** Create a new file. It must be an RGB file so that you can use the Lighting Effects filter. Create a new channel (#4).

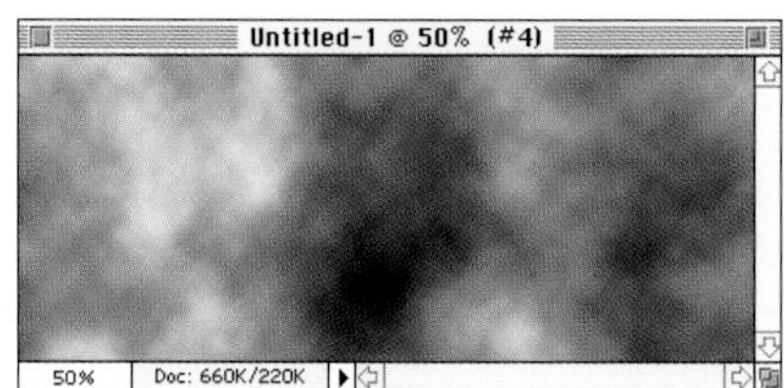


**2** To start creating the paper texture, choose Filter➛Render➛Clouds. Channel #4 should look like this.

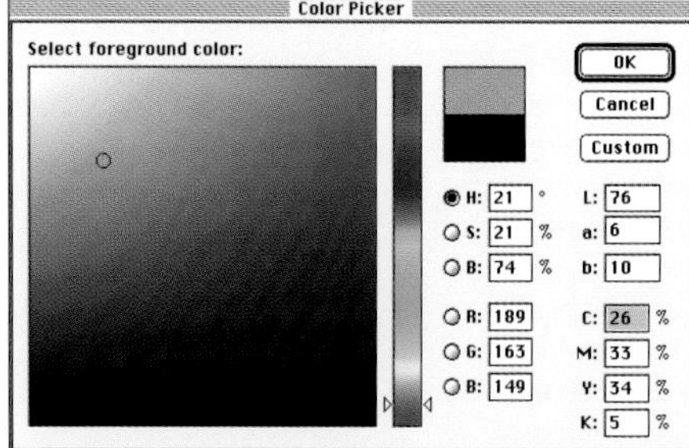


**3** Now go back to the Composite channel (Command-~) [Control-~] and choose a brown paper color for the foreground color. The CMYK values 26, 33, 34, 5 worked well for this effect.

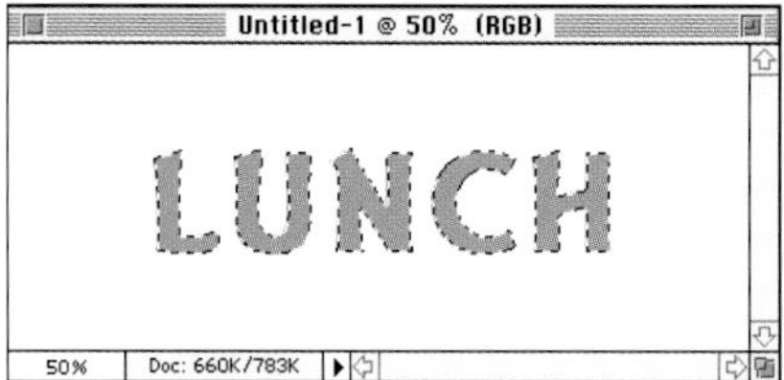


**4** Use the Type Mask tool to enter the text. BadgerBold at 70 points was used for this example. Move the type selection into place, and then fill it with the foreground color. Do not deselect the text.



**TOOLBOX**

Brown Paper Bag (Lighting Style Preset)

**5** So, we've got brown—but we need paper. Choose Filter➛Render➛Lighting Effects and choose BrownPaperBag from the Style menu, or match the settings as seen in this figure.

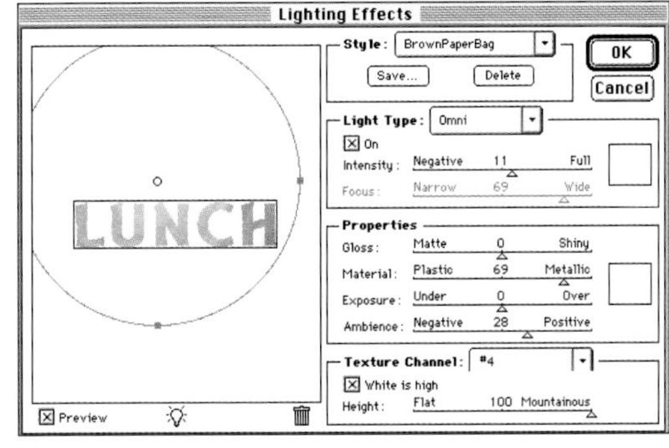


**6** Click OK, deselect the selection, and you are ready for lunch.

# Variations

Giving the letters rough edges adds to the paper effect. After entering the text in Step 4, press Q to switch to the Quick Mask mode. Next, choose Filter➛Pixellate➛Crystallize (Cell Size: 5). Then choose Image➛Adjust➛Threshold (Level: 9). Press Q again to exit the Quick Mask mode. Finish Step 4 and the remainder of the steps. I also chose Image➛Adjust➛Brightness/Contrast and increased the contrast to +40 for this variation. Finally, add a shadow to give the effect of floating paper letters.

# LUNCH

Darker edges can help define the paper's edges. With the type still selected—after applying the Lighting Effects filter in Step 5—save the selection. Next choose Select➛Modify➛Border. Use a Width appropriate for your type. I chose 5 pixels. Then choose Image➛Adjust➛Brightness/Contrast (Brightness: -31; Contrast: 25). You can get rid of the fuzz created around the letters by loading the type selection you just saved, and choosing Select➛Inverse to invert the selection. Hit Delete to fill the selection with white. ■

# Pinched

Here's a quick and easy one that takes advantage of one of Photoshop's distort filters. You guessed it: Pinch.

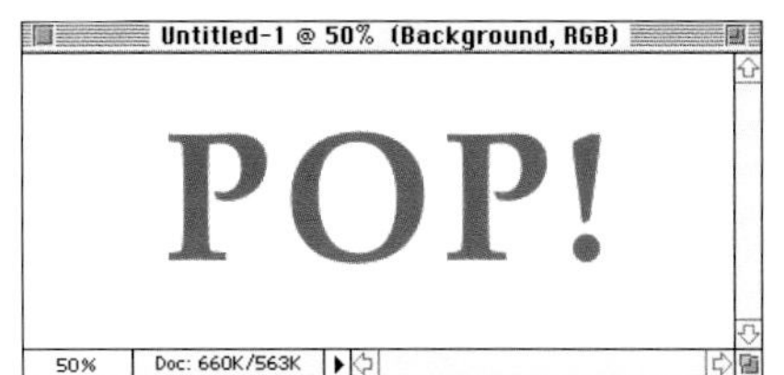


**1** Create a new file. Choose a color for the type and use the Type tool to enter the text (Palatino Bold, 90 points). Choose Layer➛Merge Down to put the type back on the Background layer.

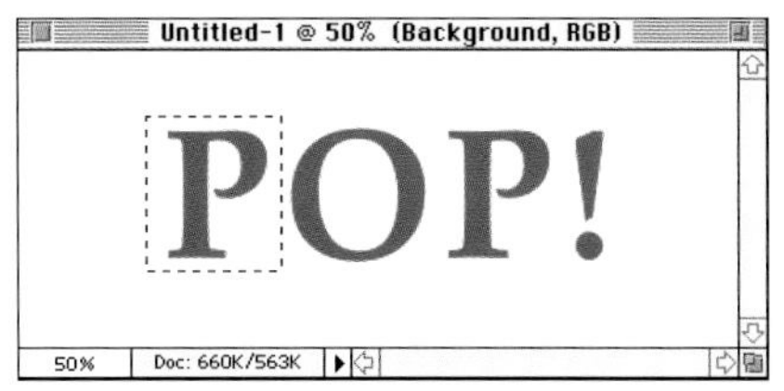


**2** The key to getting the most from your pinches is the selection you make. Use the rectangular Marquee tool and drag a rectangle around the first letter, like this.

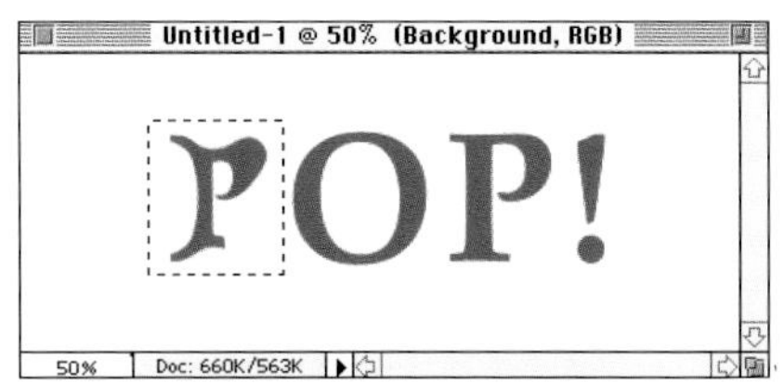


**3** Next, choose Filter➛Distort➛ Pinch (Amount: 100). Play with the slider and watch the effect on the preview. Click OK and you should see something like this.

**4** Repeat Steps 2 and 3 for all the letters in the word. Experiment with the selections you make. Here are the selections I made for the rest of the letters.

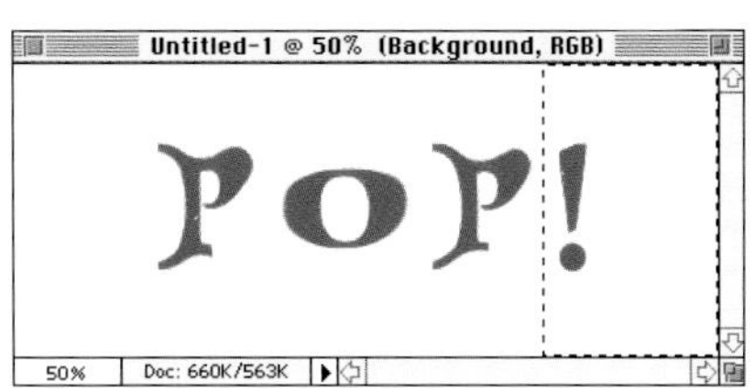

**TIP** **Remember you can use Command-Option-F (Control-Alt-F) to recall the dialog box from the last filter used. So, make your selection, press Command-Option-F, slide, and click OK.**

**5** And here's what you get.

**6** But you don't have to stop there. After pinching the individual letters, I selected the entire image and pinched it.

**7** Then select just the "O", and choose Filter➾Distort➾Twirl (Amount: 999%). Keep experimenting.

## Variations

For this variation, I selected a rectangle around half of the text at a time. With the left half selected, I chose Layer➾Transform➾Perspective to distort the text. Then I used the Pinch filter (Filter➾Distort➾Pinch) with a positive setting. I treated the right half of the text the same, except I used a negative setting in the Pinch filter dialog box. ■

This effect works by combining four Photoshop filters (Fragment, Mosaic, Tile, and Facet) that can be used in various combinations to make different plaids. I found that the following method works the best.

**1** First, create a new file. Choose a foreground color for the color of the type, then use the Type Mask tool to enter the text into a layer. I used 90 point Berliner-Plain type. Fill it with the foreground color.

**2** Keep the selection active and choose Filter➞Stylize➞Tile (Number of Tiles: 10; Maximum Offset: 1%). The Number of Tiles controls the number of vertical tiles that will be in your tallest letter. You can change the number of tiles, but keep the maximum offset at 1% so the grid's lines are straight.

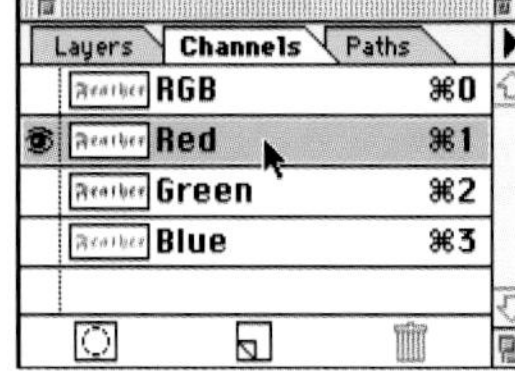


**3** Now, go to the Channels palette and click on one of the color channels to make it the only active channel. (I made the Red channel the active channel). The tiled type looks gray, since you are only viewing one color channel.



**TOOLBOX**

Plaid (Lighting Style Preset)

**TIP** **By choosing a different color channel in Step 3, you will see different colors when you return to the composite channel in Step 5. You can also make two color channels active.**

**4** Choose Filter➛Pixellate➛ Fragment. There are no settings for this filter; the type will divide into even smaller segments.

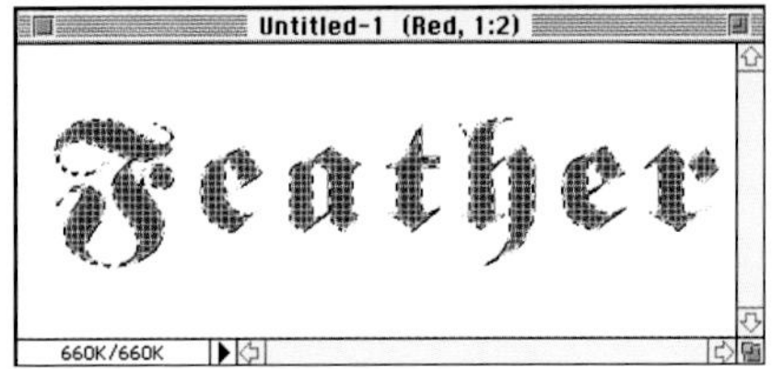


**5** Now, for the magic. Press Command-~ [Control-~] to return to the composite channel. Instant plaid waiting for you. Using the Fragment filter to shift the pixels of only one color channel produces new segments and colors.

**6** To change the colors of the plaid, choose Image➛Adjust➛ Hue/Saturation and use the Hue slider to run through a closet full of plaids.

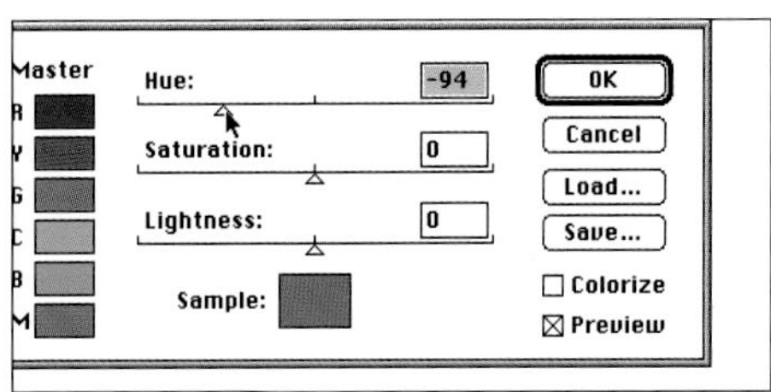


**7** Here's the final type.

## VARIATIONS

The possibilities are endless. Here is a selection of plaids I made by applying just one more filter to the previous above:

Select the Red channel and choose Filter➔Other➔Maximum (Radius: 2).

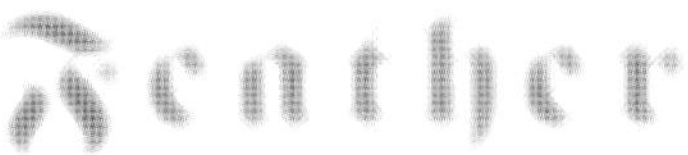

Or, try choosing Filter➔Pixellate➔Fragment. Keep applying the filter until the plaid glows.

Try Filter➔Pixelate➔Facet, and reapply the filter (Command-F) [Control-F] a few times.

Filter➔Stylize➔Find Edges applied several times.

Or, choose only one color channel. (I chose the Green channel.) Choose Filter➔Stylize➔Find Edges, and apply the filter a second time (Command-F) [Control-F].

### Add Some Texture

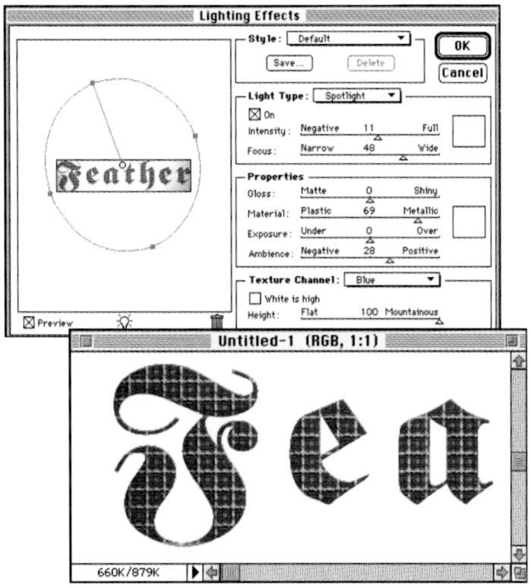

Keep the type selection active and choose Filter➔Render➔Lighting Effects. Use the settings shown here, or choose the Plaid preset from the Style pop-up menu. The most important setting is the texture channel. Choose one of the RGB channels. After you hit OK, the plaid will look like it has some texture.

## Monochrome Plaid

For a monochrome plaid with thick and thin cross lines, complete Steps 1 and 2; then choose Filter➸Pixellate➸Mosaic. Watch the preview to find a Cell Size that gives you the desired effect. A Cell Size of 4 worked for me.

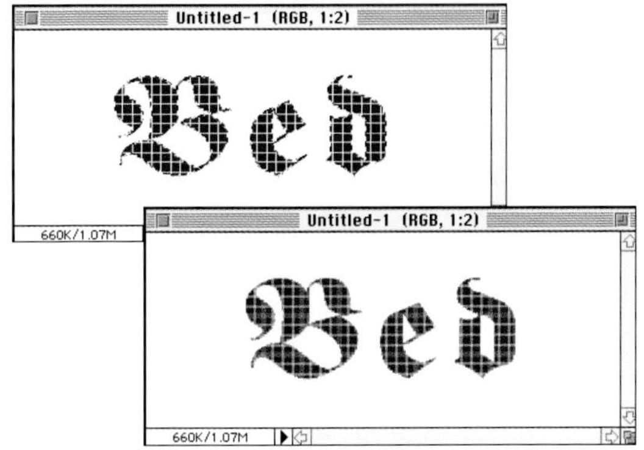


## One More Road to Plaid

Complete Steps 1 through 3. Then, choose Filter➸Pixellate➸Mosaic (Cell Size: 6). ■

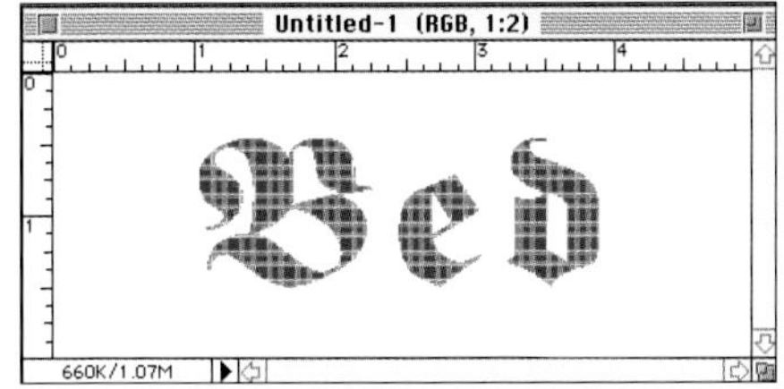

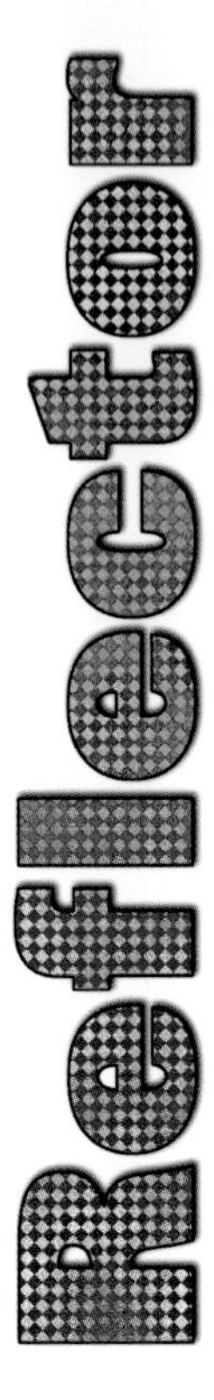


To set up the diamond pattern, this effect borrows a few steps from the Checkered effect (page 44), and then color is added at the end.

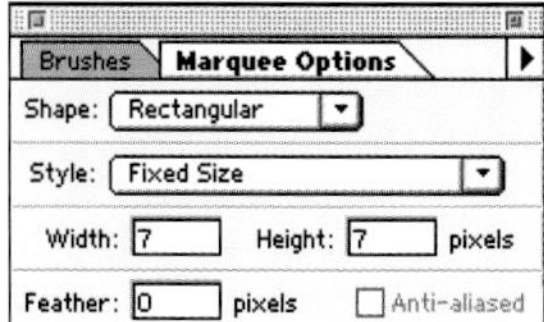


**1** Create a new file. Double-click the Marquee tool to select it and bring the Marquee Options floating palette to the front. Change the Style to Fixed Size. The values you enter for the Width and Height determine the size of the diamonds. It is important that you use the same values for both. I used 7.

**2** Zoom in to an area of the blank image and click with the Marquee tool to make a square selection. Fill the selection with black.

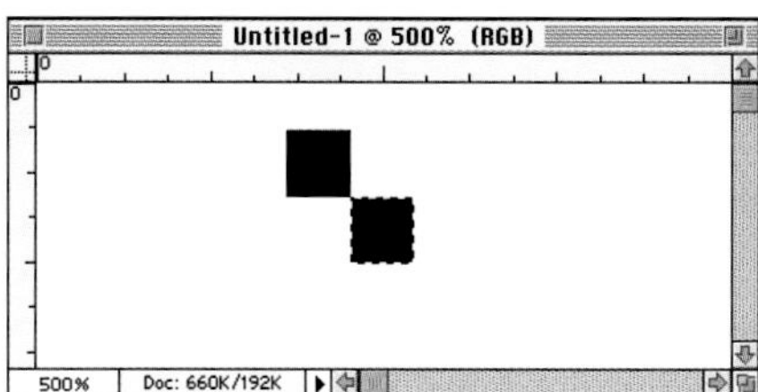


**3** Then move the selection to line up opposite corners of the selection and the black square. Fill the selection.

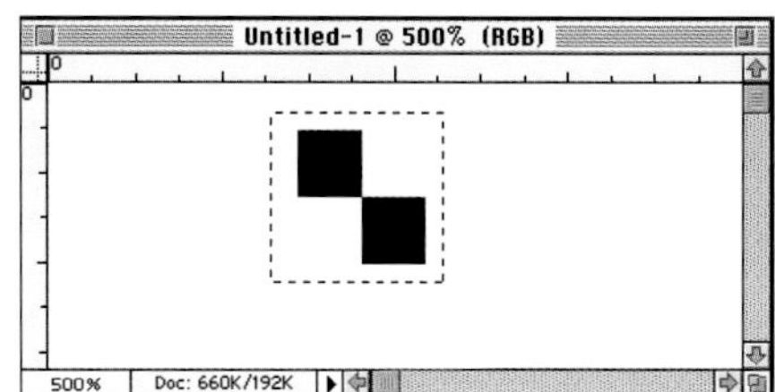


**4** Next, change the Marquee tool Style to Normal, and make a selection that encompasses both of the black squares.

**5** Choose Layer➾Transform➾ Numeric, and turn off all the options except for the Rotate option. Set the Rotate value at 45°. Deselect the selection. You should have something like this:

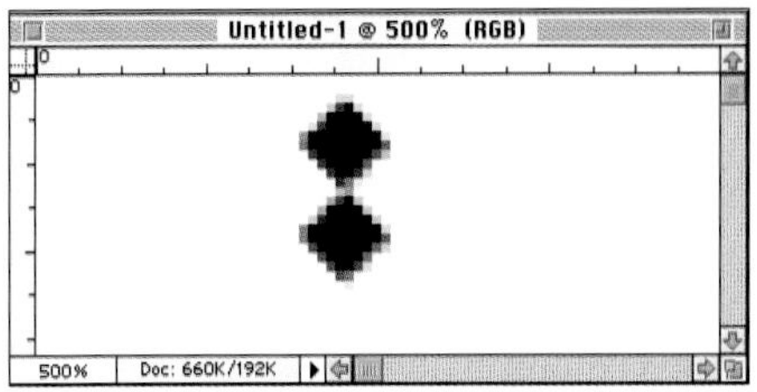


**6** Change the Marquee tool Style to Constrain Aspect Ratio. Leave the Width and Height values at 1. Then click and drag a selection like this:

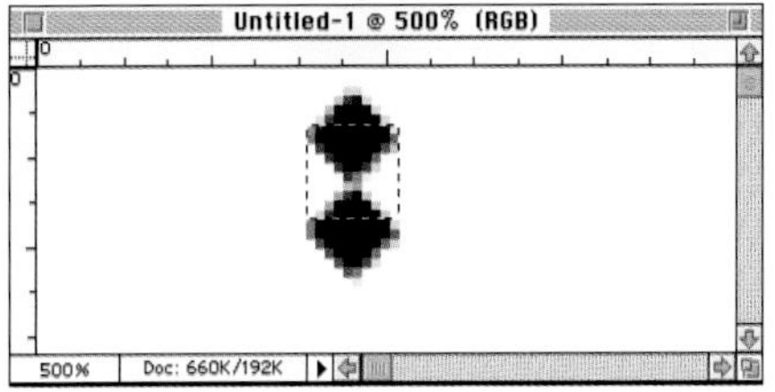


**7** Choose Edit➾Define Pattern to save the selection as a pattern.

**8** Then choose Select➾All and Edit➾Fill. Change the Contents option to Pattern. Here is the full image area:

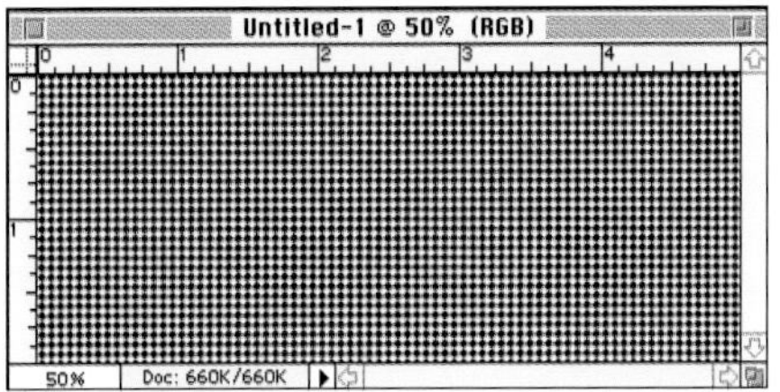


**9** Use the Type Mask tool to enter the text. I used East Bloc at 100 points, a font big enough to show off the effect.

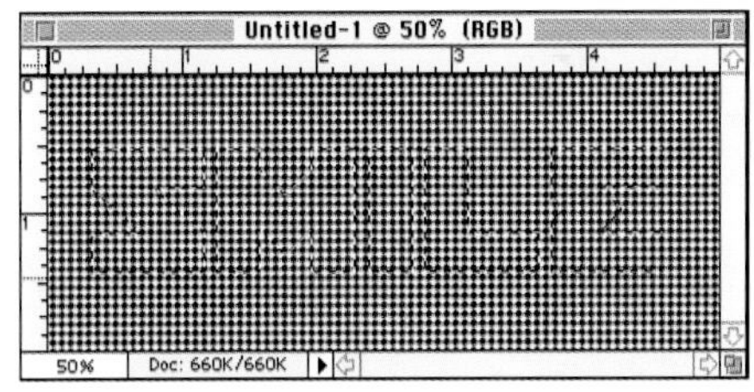


**10** Choose Select➾Inverse, and press Delete.

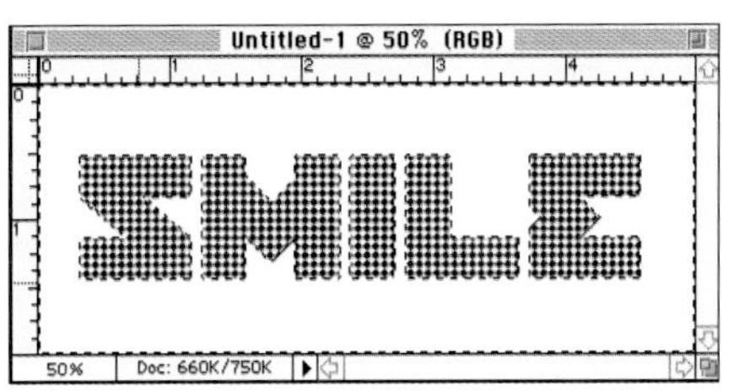

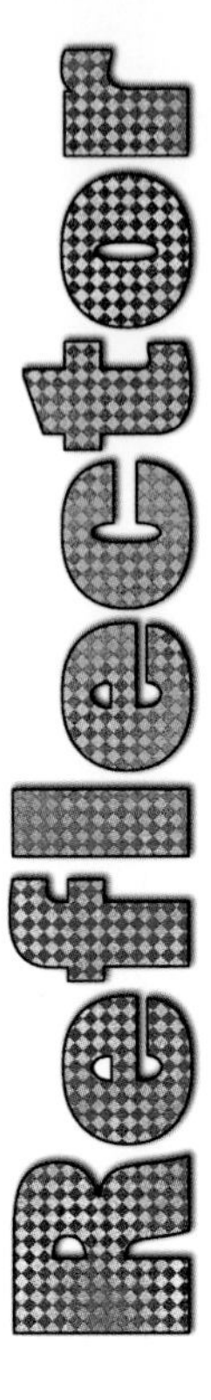




11 Choose Select➛Inverse again. Make a new layer (Layer 1).

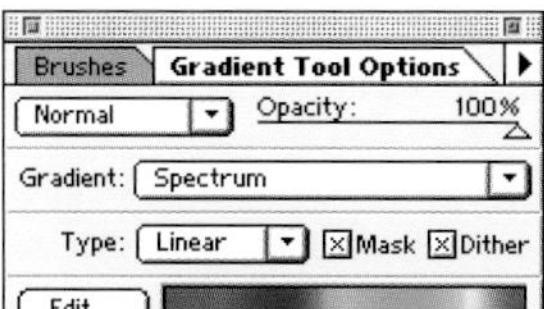


12 Double-click the Gradient tool to select it and bring to the front the Gradient Options floating palette. Choose the Spectrum preset gradient, and set the Type to Linear.

13 Drag the Gradient tool diagonally across the type selection, like this:

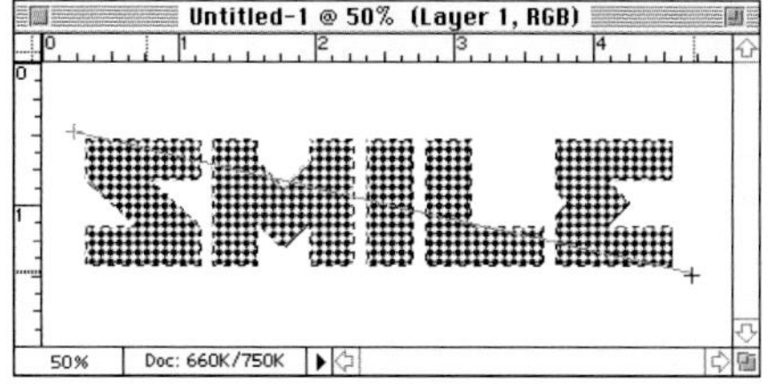


The selection will fill with the gradient.

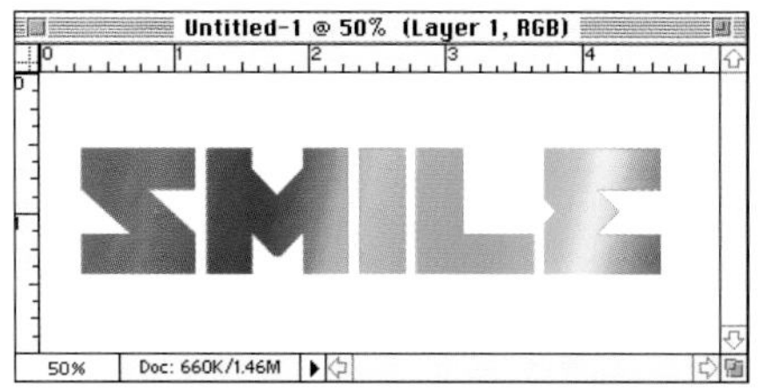


14 Change the Layer 1 blending mode to Color. The diamonds reappear.

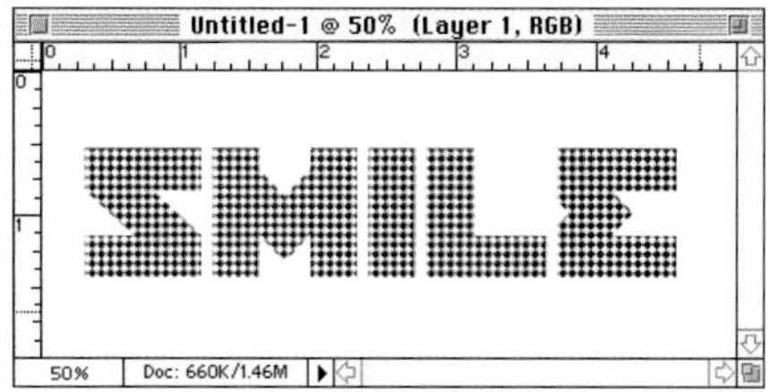


15 Keep the selection active and make the Background layer the active layer.

16 Choose Filter➛Render➛ Difference Clouds to complete the effect.

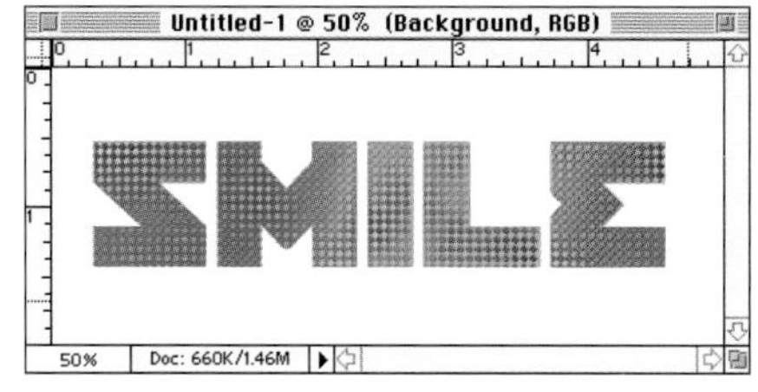

## VARIATIONS

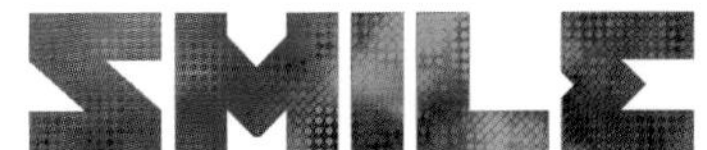

After Step 16, you can reapply the Difference Clouds filter as many times as you like to create more variation in the values of the diamonds. Choose the foreground color before you apply the filter and watch the different effects. If the image gets too dark or has too much contrast, then use the Hue/Saturation dialog box to adjust the values of Layer 1 (Image→Adjust→Hue/Saturation).

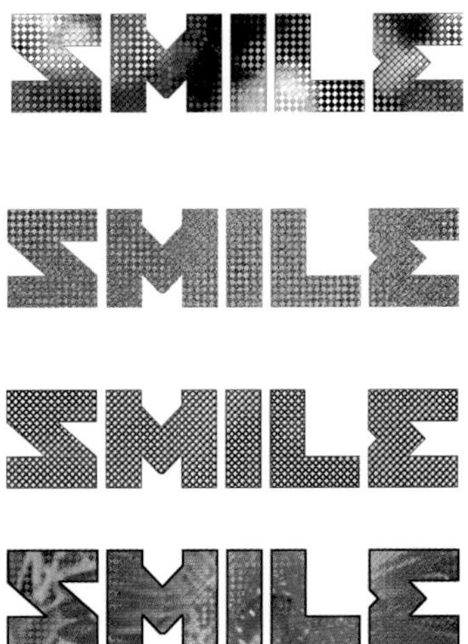

Or, you can choose Image→Adjust→Brightness/Contrast and raise the Contrast (+78) and Brightness (+48) sliders.

Or, you can apply Filter→Noise→Add Noise (Amount: 80).

Or, you can choose Filter→Stylize→Find Edges.

For this one, keep the type selection active, and make a new layer (Layer 2). Then open the Flower file from Photoshop's Tutorial files and choose Edit→Paste Into to paste it into the text selection. Then, change the Layer 2 blending mode to Difference. I also added a 3-pixel black stroke. ■

Rip it up and put it back together again. After letting the Crystallize and Glowing Edges filters tear up the type, the Wand tool will come in handy for scattering them around the image.

**1** Create a new file. Change the foreground color to black. Use the Type tool to enter the text. (I used Playbill at 90 points.) The text will be automatically placed in a new layer (Layer 1).

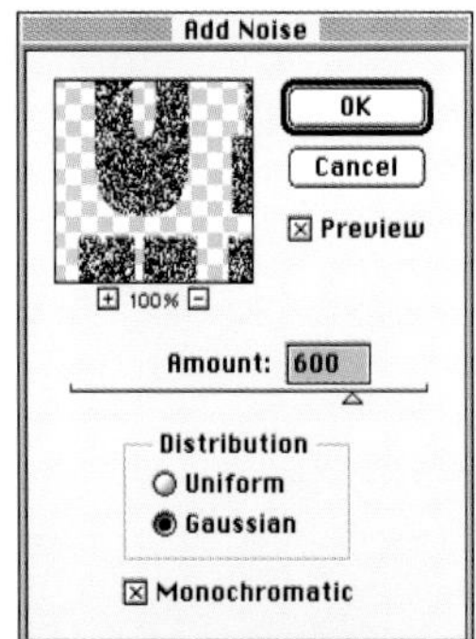


**2** Choose Filter➞Noise➞Add Noise. Set the amount to about 600, and check the Monochromatic box.

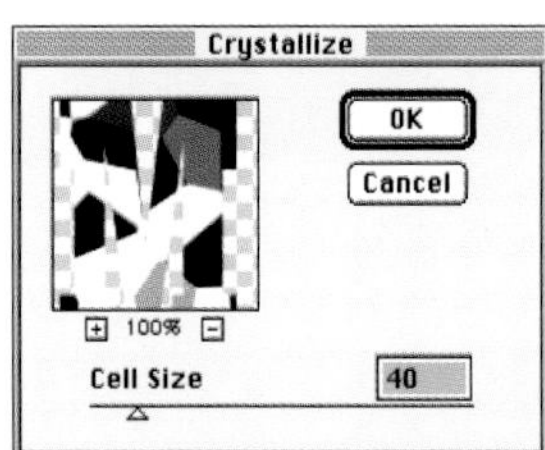


**3** Filter➞Pixelate➞Crystallize. Use a large Cell Size relative to your type. I chose 40.

Your type should look something like this now.

TIP **You can see how the type is split into pieces. If you don't like how the pieces are arranged, then press Command-Z [Control-Z] to undo the filter, and Command-F [Control-F] to redo the filter. The pieces will be randomly redistributed.**

**4** Choose Filter➛Stylize➛Glowing Edges. This new Photoshop 4.0 filter saves a couple of steps. Use these settings: Edge Width: 1, Edge Brightness: 20, and Smoothness: 1.

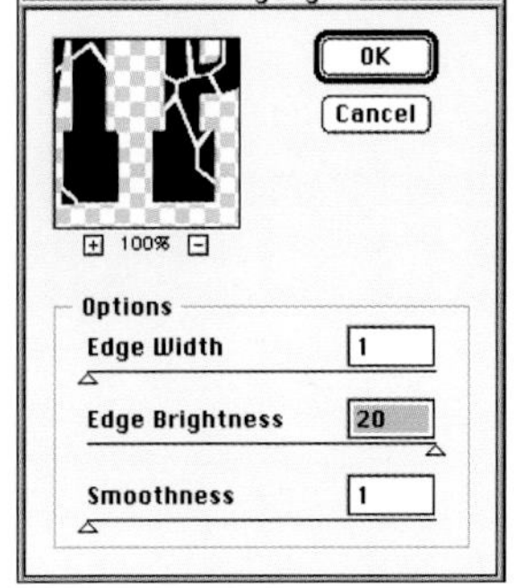


Now the type should be split into pieces.

**5** Choose Select➛Color Range. Using the left eyedropper tool in the dialog box, click one of the pieces of your type. Set the Fuzziness to 200, and turn on the Invert option.

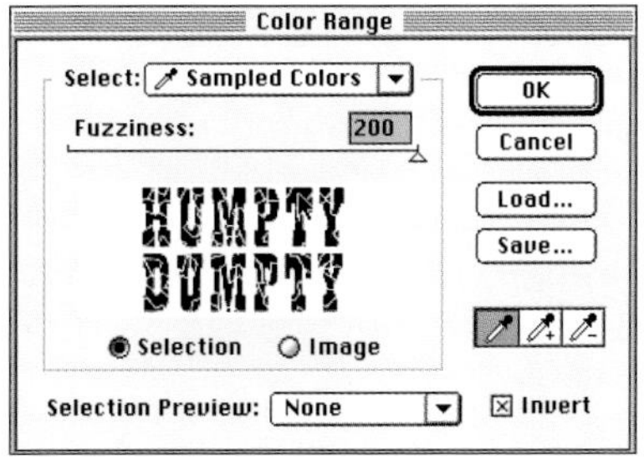

Everything but pieces should be selected. The selection should look like this.

6 Make sure that the Preserve Transparency is turned off. Press Delete. Not much will change, but the white lines between the black pieces are now gone.

7 Deselect the pieces, and turn on Preserve Transparency for Layer 1. Choose a foreground color for the type, and fill the selection with the color.

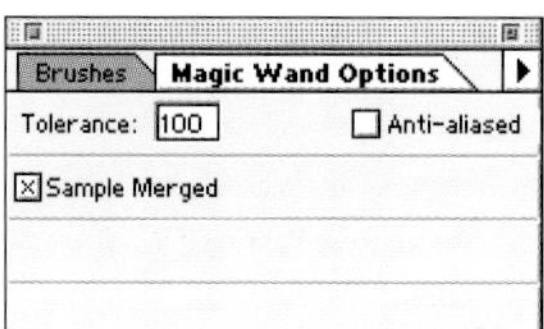


8 Double-click the Wand tool to select it and bring the Magic Wand Options floating palette to the front. Change the tolerance to 100, and turn on the Sample Merged option.

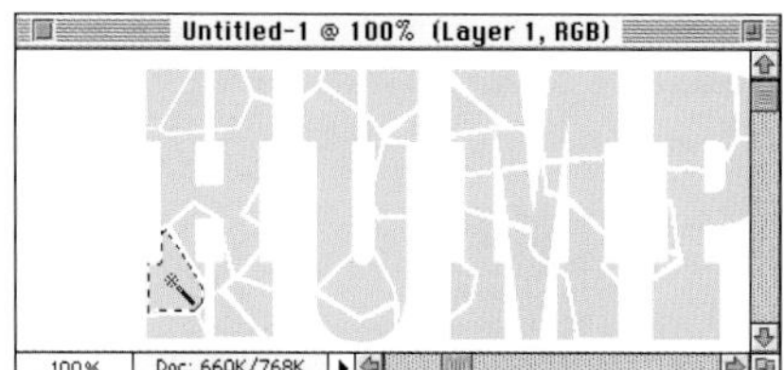


Using the Wand tool, click on one of the colored pieces to select it. Then follow Step 9 to move the colored piece. Next, select another piece with the Wand tool, and then do Step 9 again, and so on....Continue doing this until all the pieces are properly scattered.

**9** Select the Move tool. You can now use the arrow keys or the mouse to shift the pieces. Also try using the Rotate feature (Layer➛Transform➛Rotate) on some of the pieces. Generally, I moved the pieces closer to each other, and tried to make their placement look more scattered. You might also try deleting some of the tinier pieces.

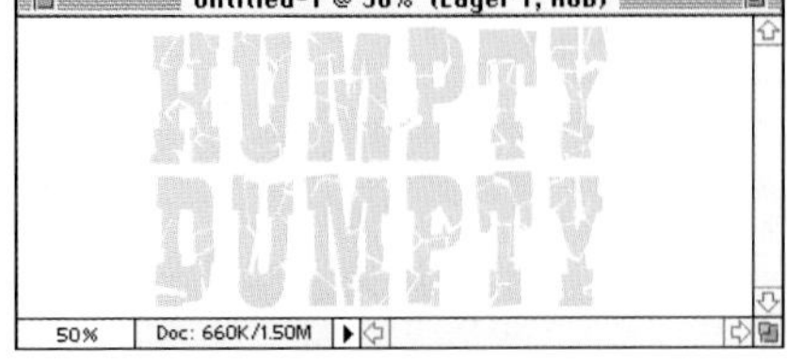


**10** Load the transparency selection of Layer 1 to select all of the pieces.

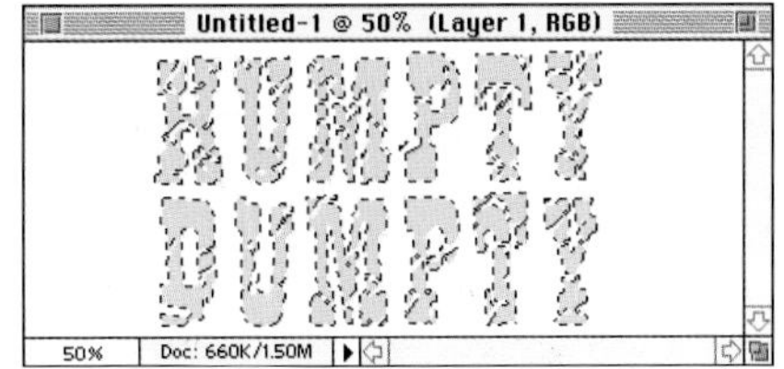


**11** Make a new layer (Layer 2) and move it below Layer 1.

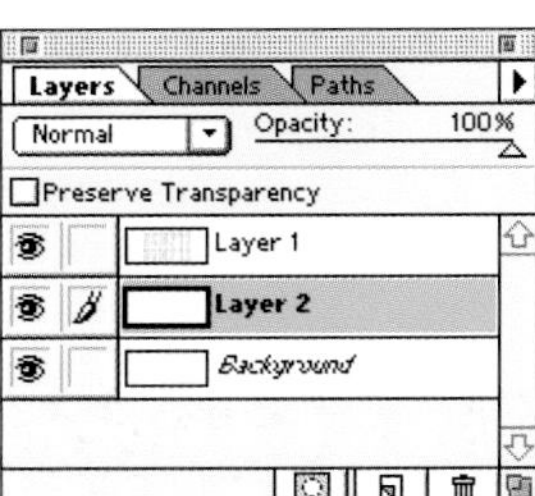


**12** Choose Select➛Feather, and feather the selection a small amount. I chose 1 pixel.

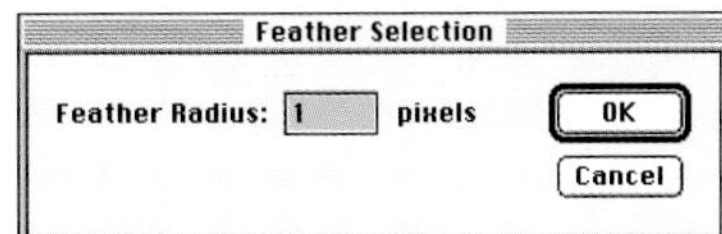


**13** Layer 2 is for the shadow. However, I want the scrap pieces to look like they are floating a little. Press Q to enter Quick Mask mode. The area around the selection will probably turn red (unless you have changed the default settings).

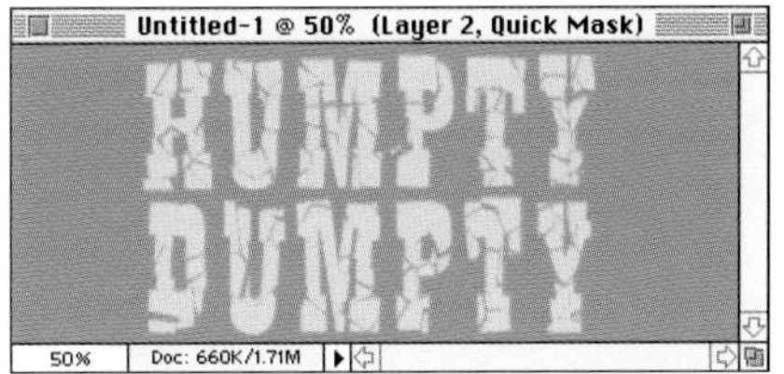

**14** Choose Filter➛Distort➛Wave. Use the settings shown in this figure (Number: 1, Wavelength: 1/45, Amplitude: 1/2, Horizontal Scale: 75%, Vertical Scale: 75%, Type: Sine, Undefined Areas: Repeat edge pixels). You are actually waving the selection, not the type.

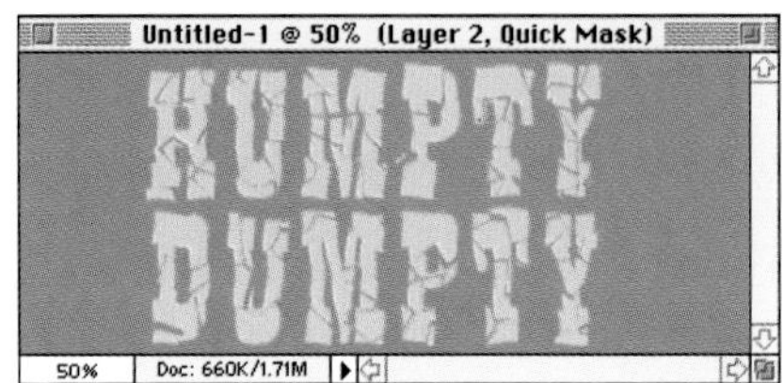


The image window will not look much different. There should be a few white specks around the edges of the letters.

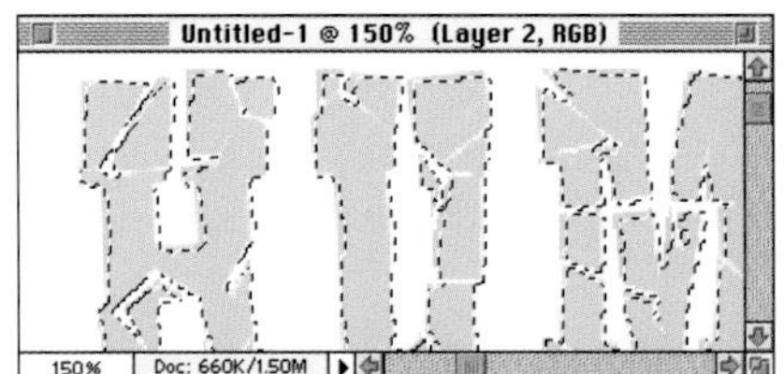


**15** Press Q to exit Quick Mask mode. To shift the shadow, select the Marquee tool. Move the selection one keystroke to the right and one keystroke down.

**16** Change the foreground color to black (or another color for the shadow), fill the selection, and you're finished.

## Variation

To add some curvature to the pieces, choose Filter➛Distort➛Wave before Step 10. Use the same settings as in Step 14. This step puts just a little bend in the pieces.

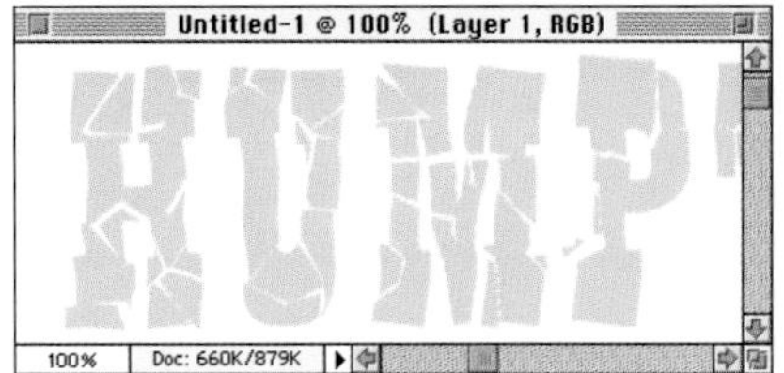

The finished type should look like this. ■

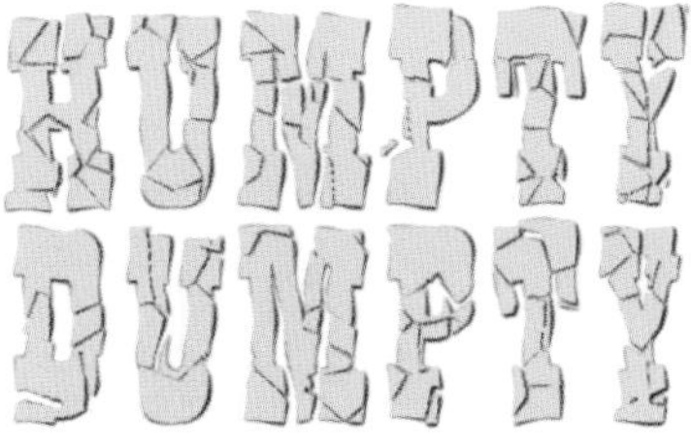

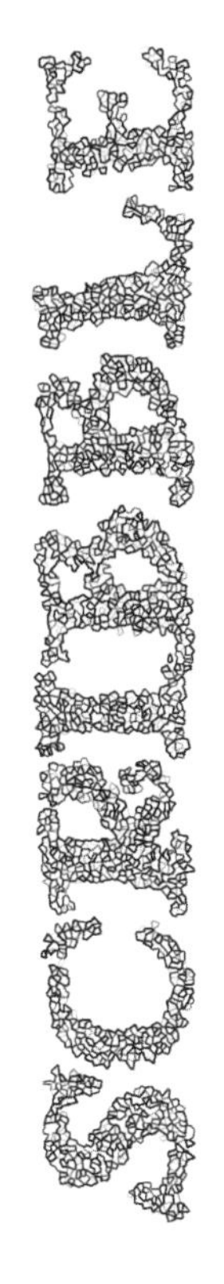

The Noise and Crystallize filters set up the Find Edges filter to create this quick effect. You will have plenty of time to check out the variations.

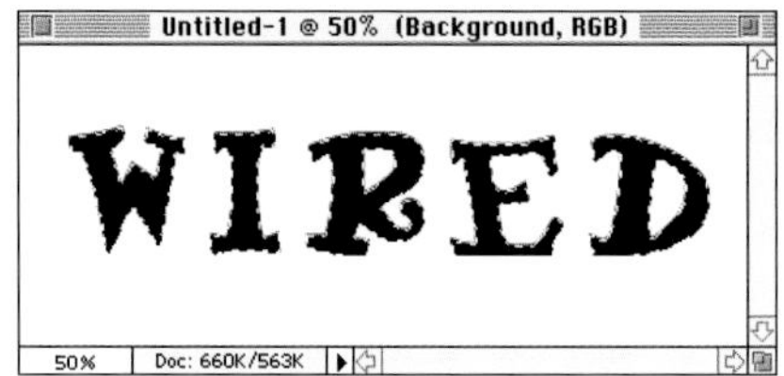


1 Create a new file. Set the foreground color to black and the background color to white (press D). Use the Type Mask tool to enter the text. For this example, I used 100-point Gadzoox. Move the text selection into place, and fill it with black.

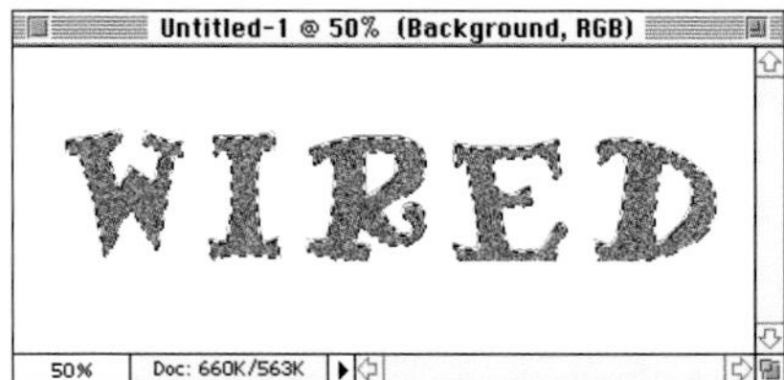


2 Choose Filter➛Noise➛Add Noise (Gaussian, do not turn on Monochromatic). Slide the marker to the right—to about 600.

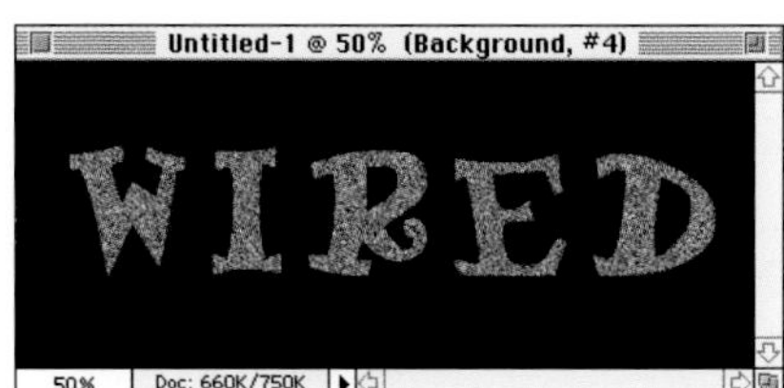


3 Copy the noisy type, create a new channel (#4), and paste in the noise, which will now be gray. (Channels cannot show color.) Deselect the text.

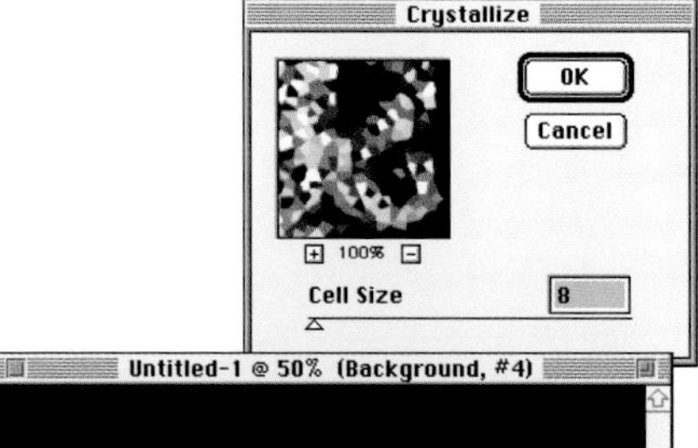


4 Choose Filter➛Pixelate➛Crystallize. The Cell Size here is going to determine the density of the scribbles. I chose a cell size of 8. You can look ahead to Step 7 to see how the scribbles turned out.

TOOLBOX

Spaghetti (Lighting Style Preset)

5 Now, choose Filter➛Stylize➛ Find Edges. The scribbling begins.

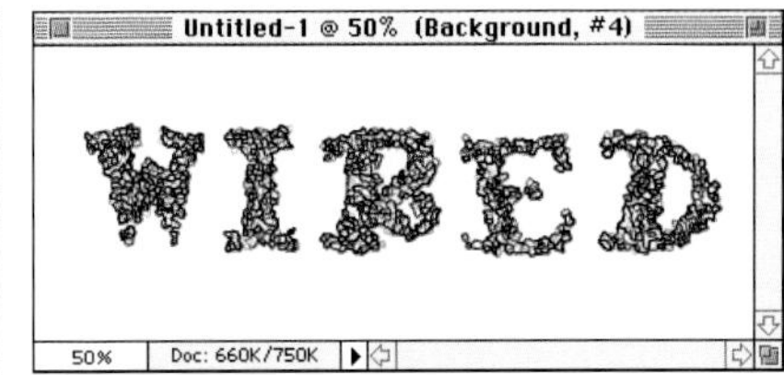


6 Invert the channel (Command-I) [Control-I]. Return to the Composite channel. Select the entire image (Command-A) [Control-A] and press Delete to clear the image area.

7 The foreground color should still be black. Load the selection Channel #4, and fill it with black.

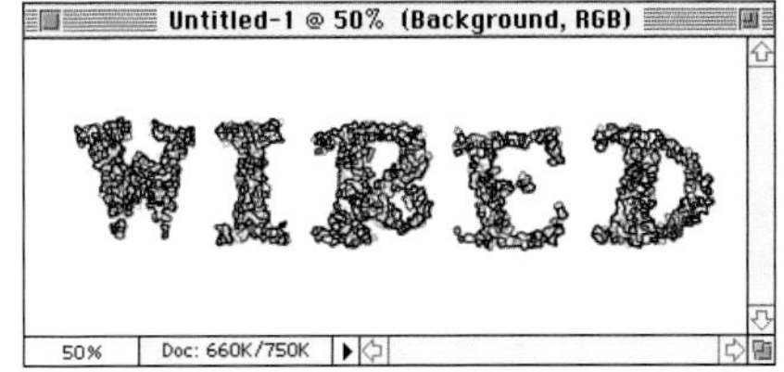


## Variations

I had a lot of fun with this one. There are many simple things you can do with this technique.

If you perform Steps 1 and 2, skip Step 3, deselect the text, use a Cell Size of 5 in Step 4, and stop after Step 5, you get this effect:

Spaghetti, anyone? Perform all the previous steps except Step 7. Then go to the Channels palette and duplicate Channel #4 to create Channel #4 copy. Choose Filter➛Blur➛Gaussian Blur (Radius: .5). Return to the Composite channel and load the selection Channel #4. Choose Select➛ Modify➛Expand (1 pixel). Change the foreground color to the CMYK

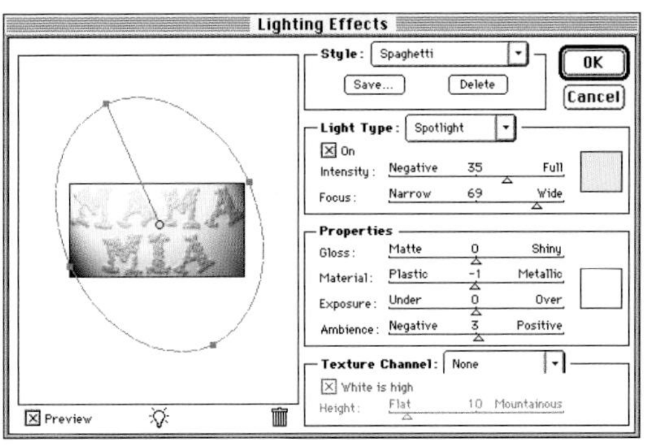

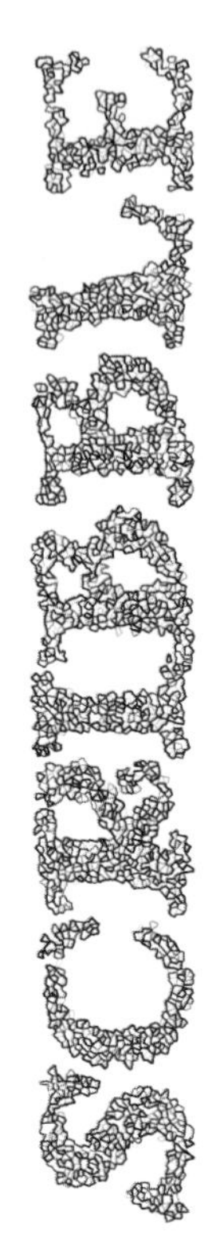

values: 0, 12, 15, 25. Fill the selection. Apply Filter➛Render➛Lighting Effects. Click on the Style pop-up menu and find the Spaghetti preset, or match the settings seen on the previous page. Make sure Channel #4 copy is the texture channel. Finally, to thin down the spaghetti, choose Select➛Inverse and press Delete to fill the selection with white.

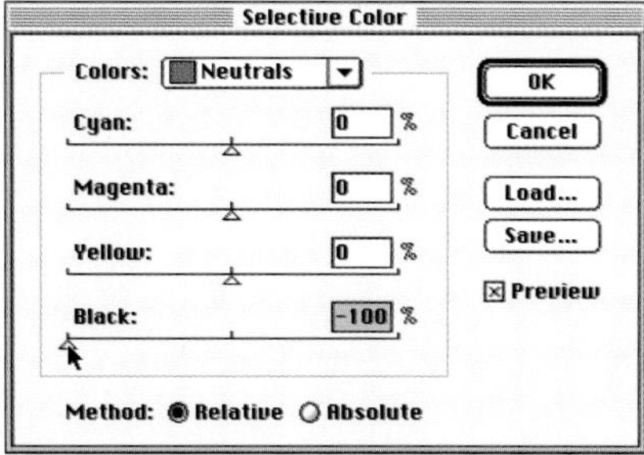


Perform Steps 1 and 2. Skip Step 3. Deselect the text. Use a Cell Size of 5 in Step 4 and do Step 5 as described. Then choose Image➛Adjust➛Hue/Saturation and type -100 in the Saturation box. Next choose Image➛Adjust➛Selective Color. Choose Neutrals from the pop-up menu and slide the black marker all the way to the left (-100%). Do the same for the Whites. You should get this effect.

OK, so I have strayed a little from scribbling. Why stop now? Do Steps 1 and 2. Deselect the text. Choose Filter➛Noise➛Median (Radius: 5). ■

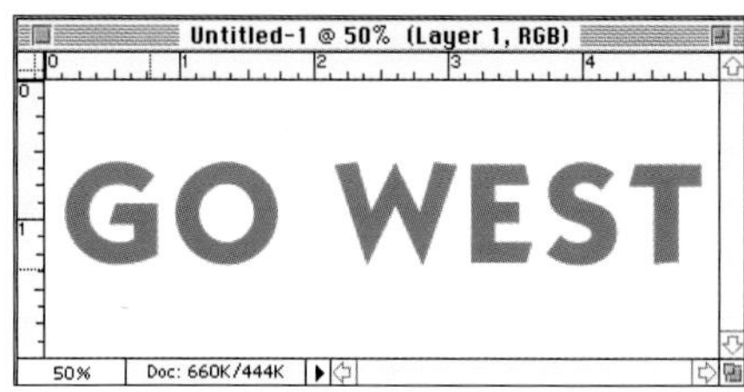


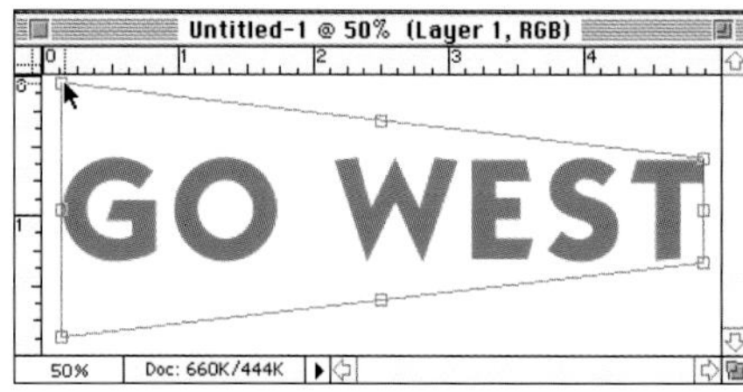

Photoshop does not have true 3D capabilities, but you can perform a few tricks with the Transform feature that will make your type look like it is sitting on a 3D surface.

**1** Create a new file, and use the Type tool to enter the text. This font is Kabel at 75 points. The type will be placed automatically into a new layer.

## The Simple Receding Surface

Method 1. Choose Layer➸Transform➸Perspective. Grab a corner point and drag it toward one of its adjacent corners. The type pinches to look like it recedes. You also can drag in the opposite direction to stretch the text at one end. When finished, press the Return [Enter] key to accept the changes, or Command-. [Control-.] to cancel the changes. It may take you a few minutes to get used to the way the box reacts when you drag one of the corners, but it's really pretty simple.

**TIP** **The Undo command still works while you are distorting the type; it will undo only the last distortion, however.**



TOOLBOX

KPT Planar Tiling Filter

Method 2. Choose Layer➛Free Transform. The transform feature can distort the text in many ways. The advantage to using this feature is that you can change the size of the type at the same time that you pinch or stretch it. To activate the Perspective feature while using the Free Transform feature, hold the Command, Option, and Shift [Control, Alt, and Shift] keys while dragging a corner. To change the size of the type, click and drag on one of the side points.

TIP **All of the Effects tools work the same way. To make a change, click one of the corner tabs and drag it. You can continue to alter the text in this manner. Then, when you are finished, press Return [Enter] to accept the changes. To cancel the changes, press Command-. [Control-.].**

**3** What if you want to put type across the bend of two walls? Use the Perspective feature as you did above, but select only the part of the text that will be on the receding surface.

All of these samples were created with the Perspective feature using one of the previous methods.

**4** And, what if you want to put the text on a receding corner? This effect is a bit more complicated, but it is still just a matter of making the proper selection and using the Transform tools. It is the order in which you do these tasks that makes the difference.

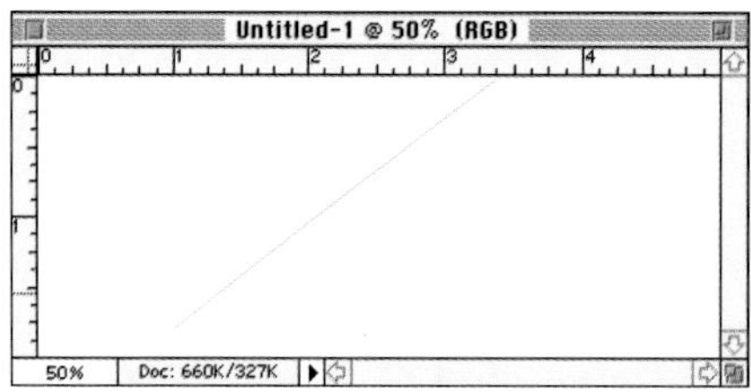


**5** First (in a new file) draw a simple line with the Line tool. Just choose a foreground color for the lines, select the Line tool and click and drag.

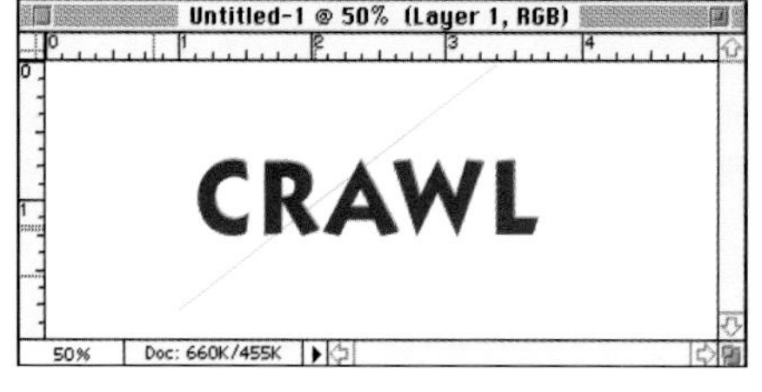


**6** Do Step 1, except use the Type Mask tool instead of the Type tool. Then save the text selection to create Channel #4.

**7** Use the rectangular Marquee tool to select the top half of the type.

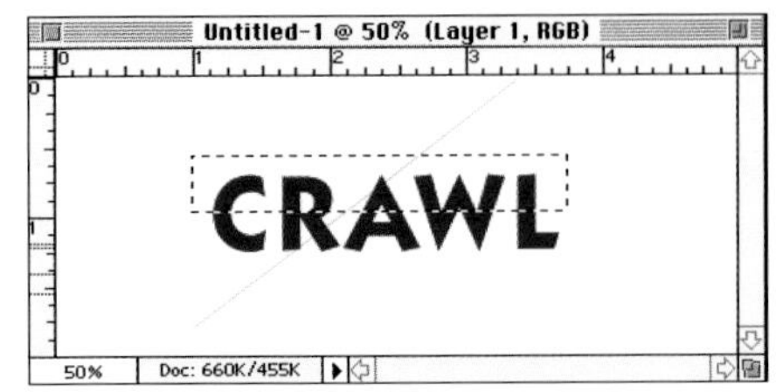


**8** Choose Layer→Transform→Skew. Hold the Option [Alt] key and drag one of the top points to the left—about as far as shown in the figure (approximately 45°). Then press the Return [Enter] key, and deselect the text.

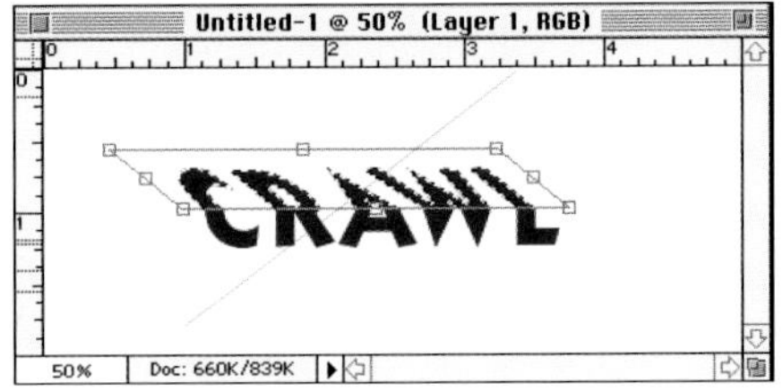


**9** Select the bottom half of the text.

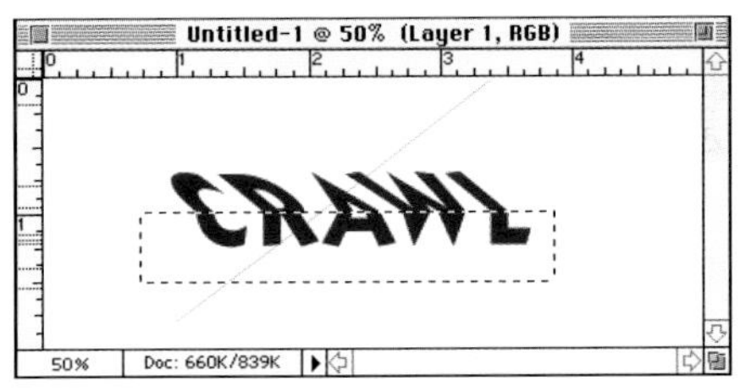


**10** Choose Layer→Transform→Skew again, and pull the box back the same distance.

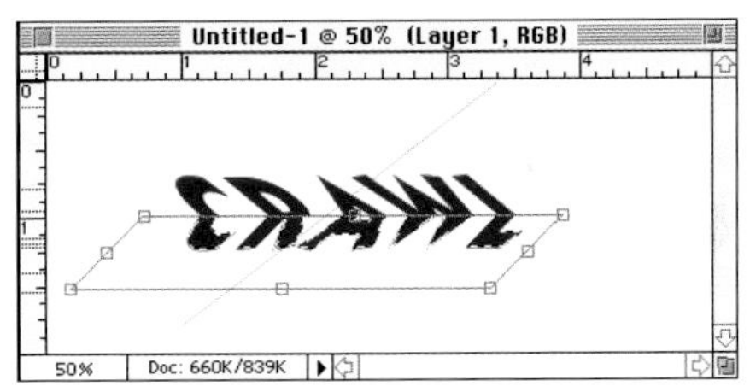


The type should look like this now.

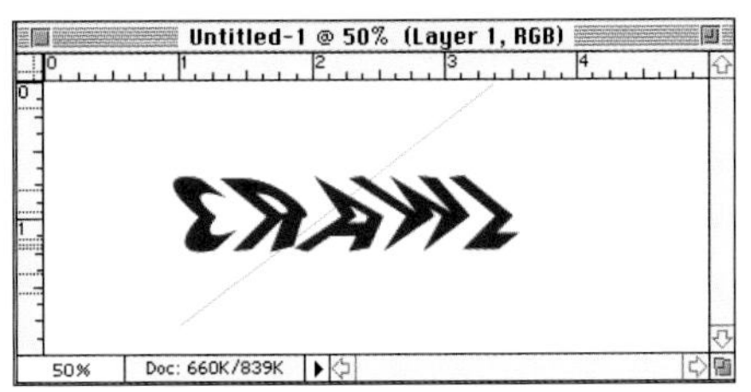

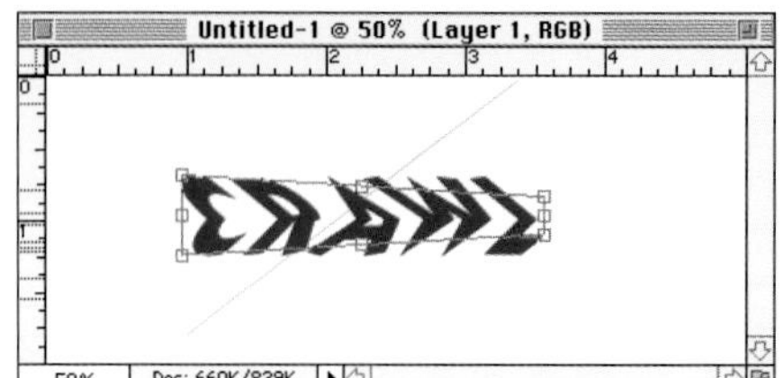


**11** Deselect the text, and choose Layer➙Free Transform. Click on the top-right corner point, hold the Command, Option, and Shift [Control, Alt, and Shift] keys, and drag it down about one fourth of the height of the text.

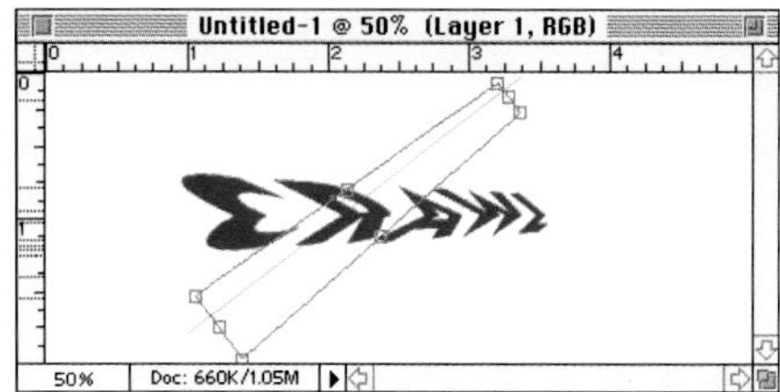


**12** Now move the pointer outside of the distortion box. It will turn into a corner icon with two arrows. Click and drag to rotate the text.

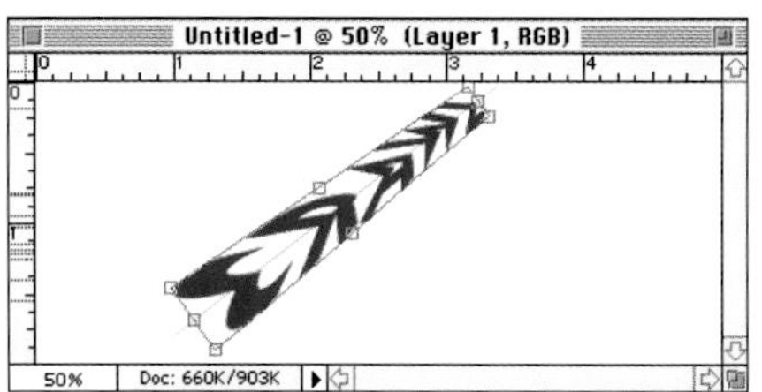


**13** Move the pointer inside the text box until it turns into a solid black arrow. Click and drag to move the type into place over the receding line.

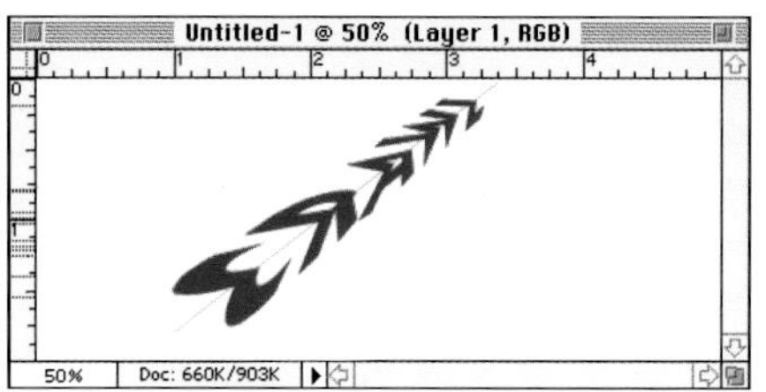


**14** Press the Return [Enter] key to accept the changes.

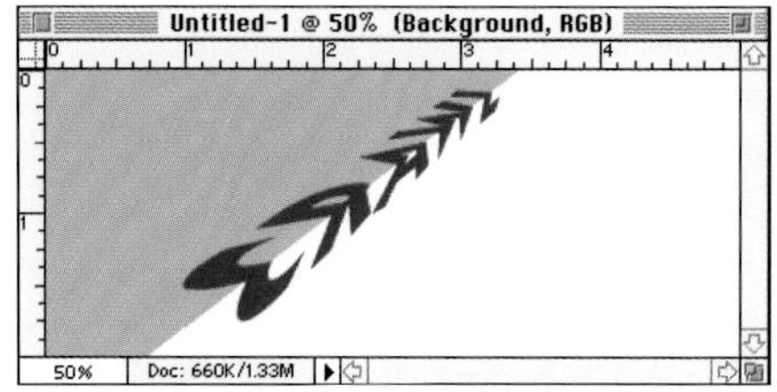


**15** I drew a darker plane to represent the top surface of the receding corner.

## Other Surfaces

On page 20, you can find out how to put type on a ball.

### KPT Planar Tiling

KPT 3.0 contains a filter that will tile your text onto a receding plane. Use the Type tool to enter the text. Choose Layer➛Transform➛Scale and stretch the text until it fills the image window.

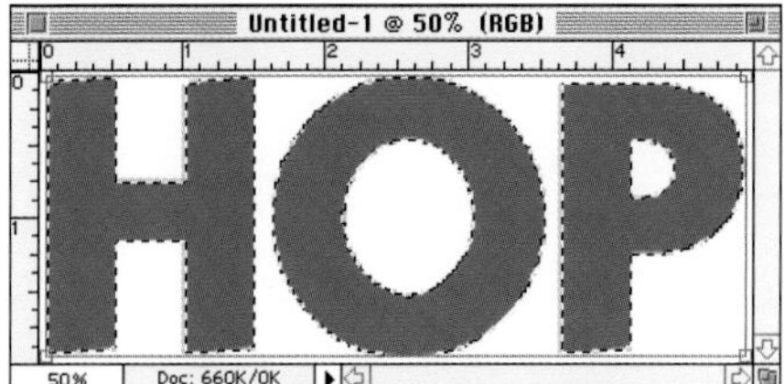


Deselect the text. Choose Filter➛KPT 3.0➛KPT Planar Tiling 3.0. From the Mode menu choose Perspective tiling. Then click on the preview and drag the pointer around. The Height and Shear will adjust as you drag. When you find the desired effect, click the green button. ■

# Shimmering

A simple effect brought to you by the under-used Maximum filter. This filter spreads the white areas of the type into shimmering blocks of light.

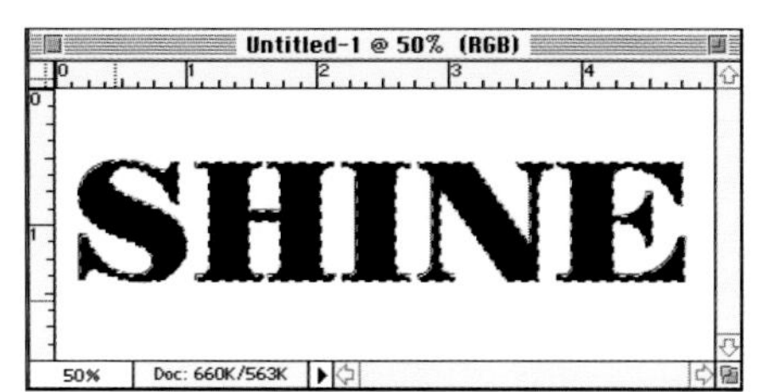


1 Create a new file. Use the Type Mask tool to enter the text. Century Black at 90 points was used for this example. Fill the text with black.

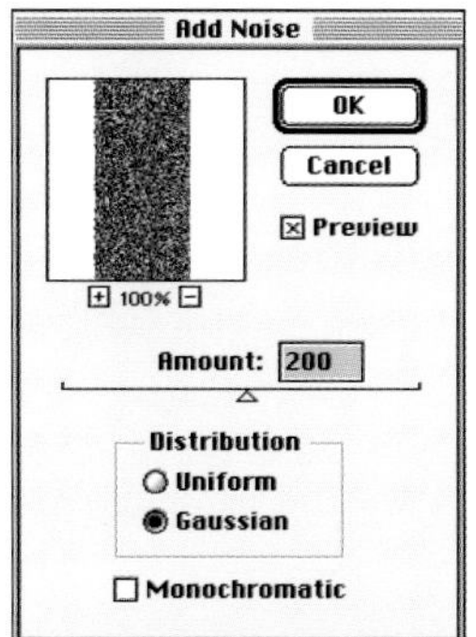


2 To break up the text, add some noise by choosing Filter→Noise→Add Noise. I set the Amount to 200.

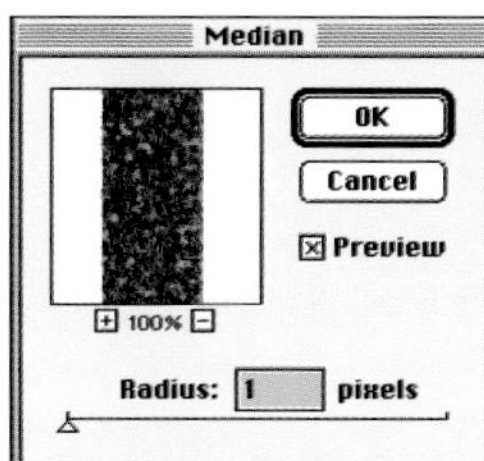


3 Then choose Filter→Noise→Median. Try different settings, but keep it low. I used the minimum: 1 pixel. Deselect the text.

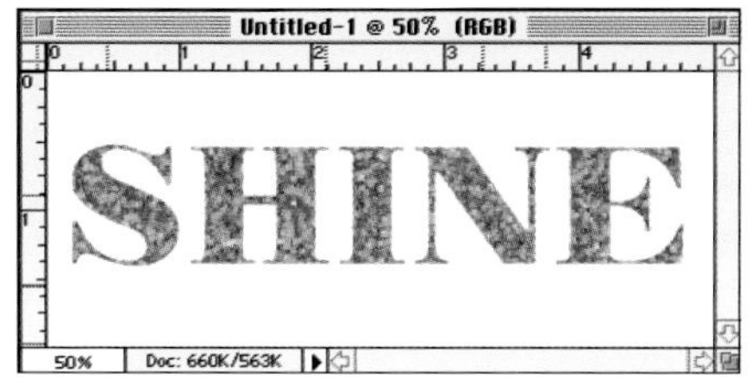


4 Choose Filter→Other→Maximum. Again, use a low setting. I used a Radius of 2.

# Variations

Variations abound for this simple effect.

For brighter text, try the following settings in Steps 2 through 4: Noise: 500; Median: 2; Maximum: 2.

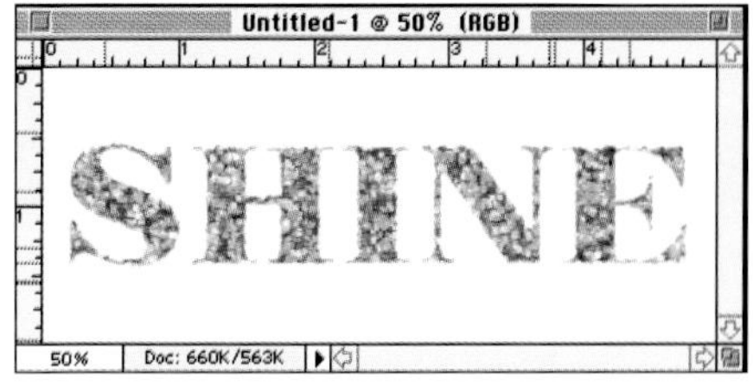


To narrow the color range, fill the text with a color other than black in Step 1. The CMYK values for the color I used are: 0, 72, 72, 0.

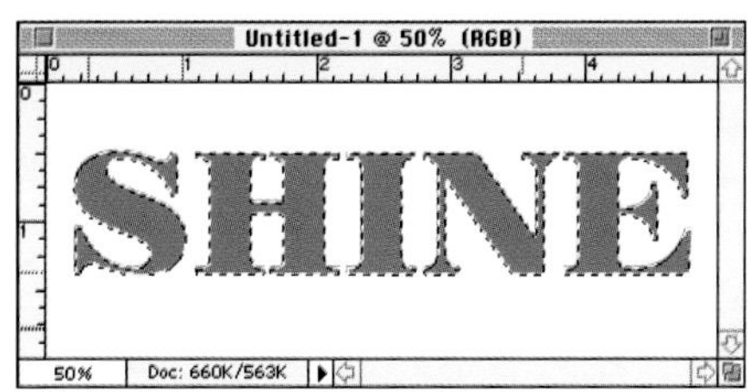


In Step 2, set the Noise amount low. I used 50.

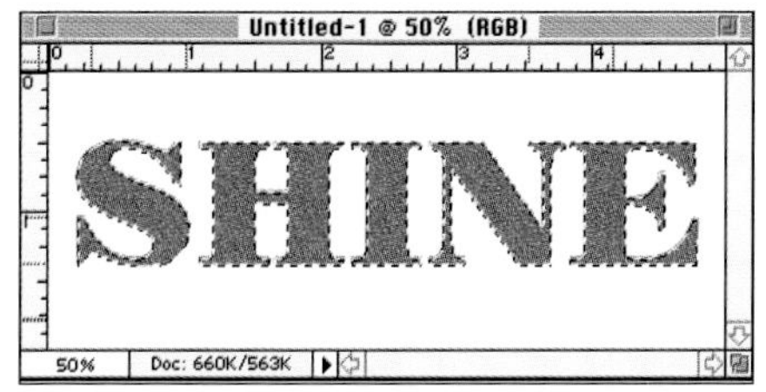


Do Steps 3 and 4 as described.

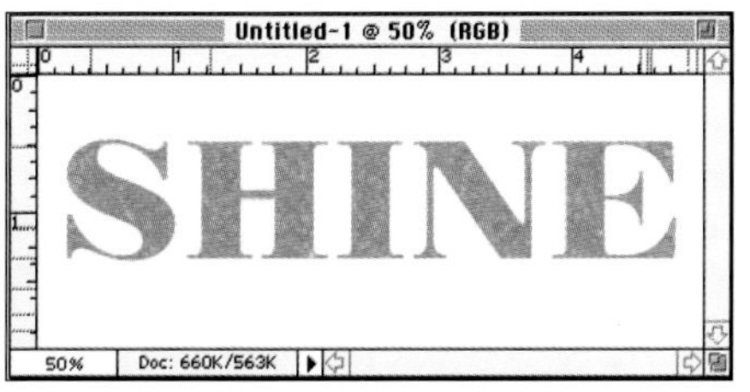

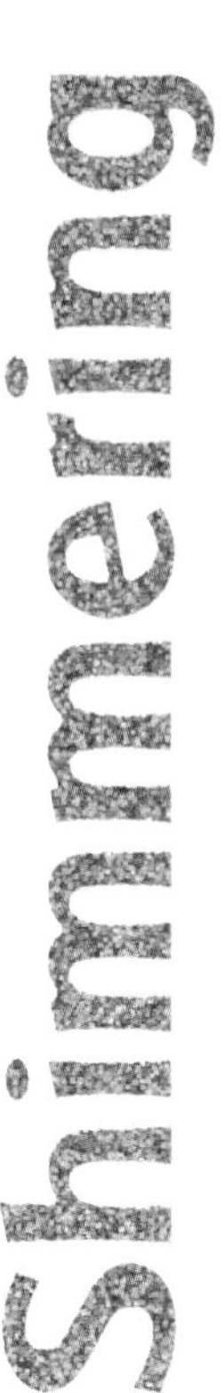


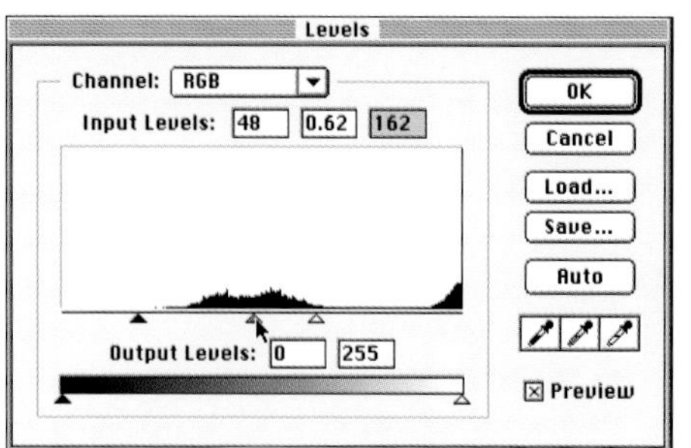


Since the color is a little on the pale side, choose Image➔Adjust➔Levels. Move the black and the white sliders closer to the center.

After Step 4, try applying Filter➔Stylize➔Find Edges to turn the colored areas into colored lines.

Adding more white to the type will make it look more like its shining. Choose Filter➔Other➔Maximum (Radius: 1).

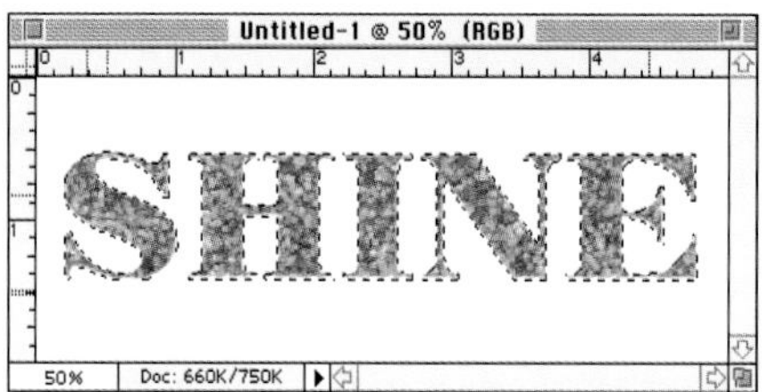


In Step 3, save the selection (to create Channel #4) before deselecting the text. Then after Step 4, load the selection Channel #4.

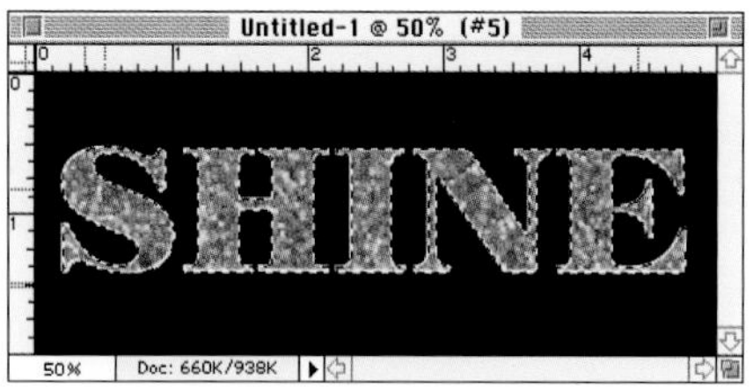


Copy the shimmering text and create a new channel (Channel #5). The selection should still be active. Paste in the type, which will now be black-and-white.

Choose Image➛Adjust➛Levels, and slide the middle (gray) marker to the left until the Input Level box reads 0.25. The channel should look like this:

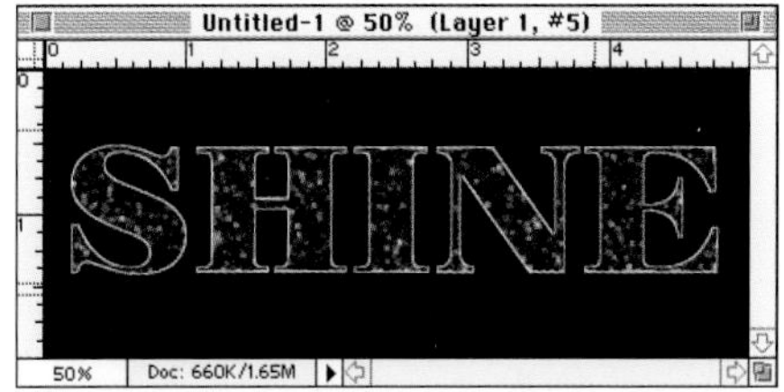


Return to the composite channel, and make a new layer (Layer 1). Then load the selection Channel #5.

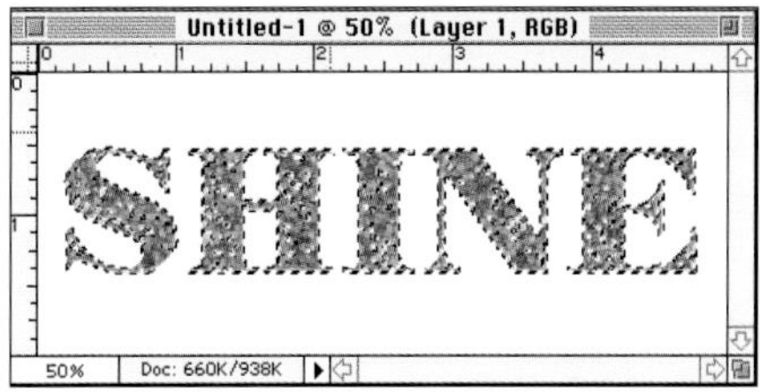


Change the foreground color to a color for the text. I used the CMYK values: 100, 75, 0, 0. Fill the selection.

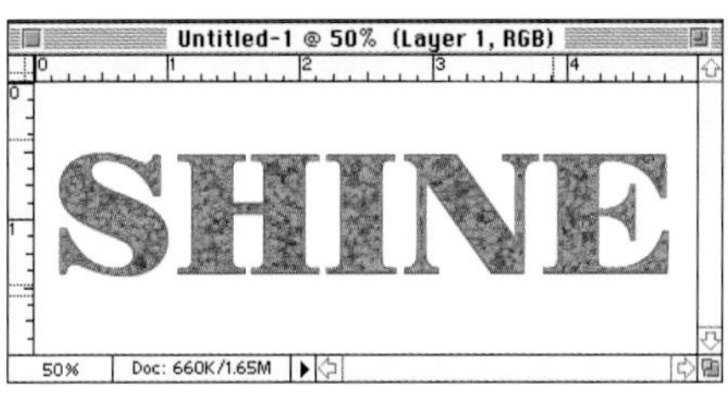


Now, play around with the layer mode settings for unique effects. For this image I chose Dissolve, and set the Layer 1 Opacity at 80%. ■

**1** If you want an image to show through the glass type, then open it now. Otherwise, create a new file.

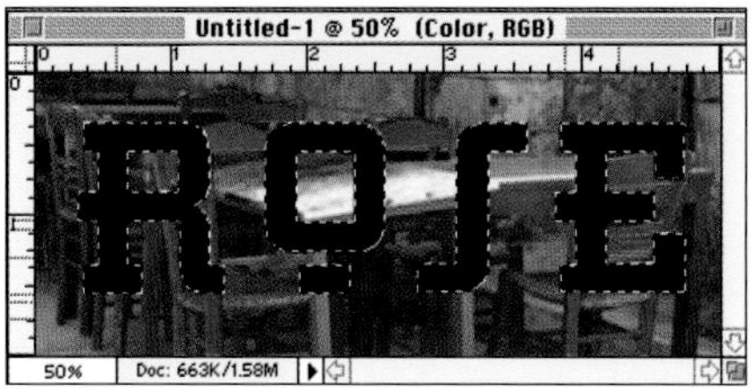

**2** Make a new layer and name it Color. Change the foreground color to black (press D), and use the Type Mask tool to enter the text. A heavy typeface will give you plenty of room to divide the letters into smaller sections of glass. This font is Knomen at 180 points. Fill the text with black. Save the type selection to create Channel #4.

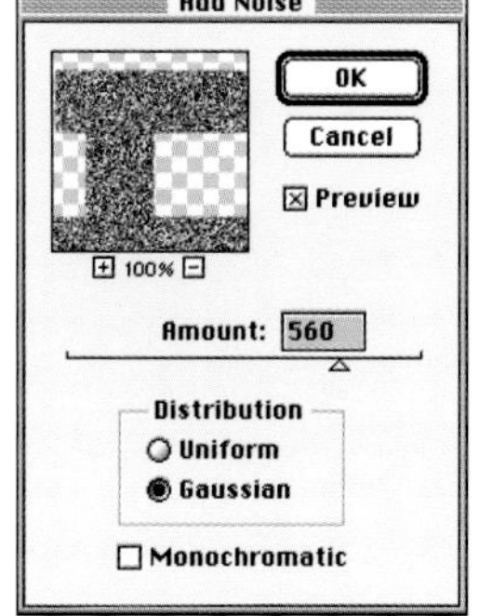


**3** Back in the Color layer, choose Filter➛Noise➛Add Noise (Amount: 560). The Noise filter breaks up the type and adds the color to the glass.

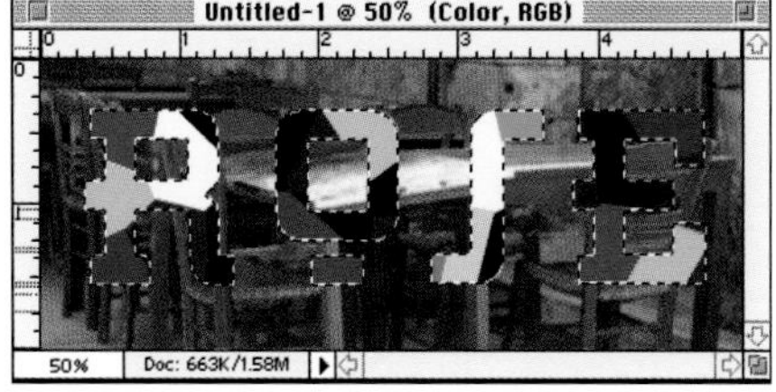


**4** Then choose Filter➛Pixelate➛ Crystallize. This filter establishes the shapes of the glass divisions. Watch the preview, and choose a Cell Size that is right for your text. I chose 100.



## TOOLBOX

Glass (Lighting Style Preset)

Trim (Lighting Style Preset)

**5** Choose Layer➛New➛Layer Via Copy. A new layer is created. Change its name to Trim.

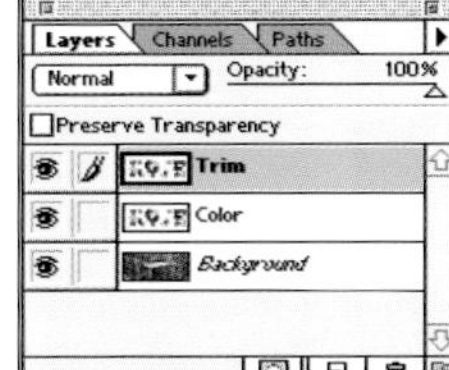


**6** Choose Filter➛Stylize➛Find Edges, and then Image➛Adjust➛ Threshold (255). You can now see the beginnings of the trim.

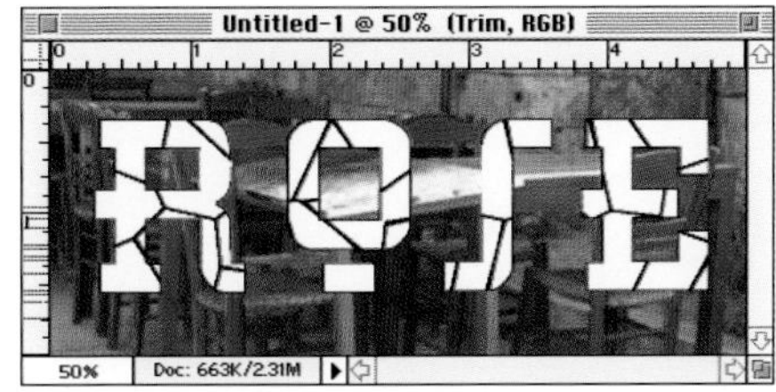


**7** Select the Magic Wand tool, and set the tolerance in its floating palette to 1. Click the wand in a white area of the type.

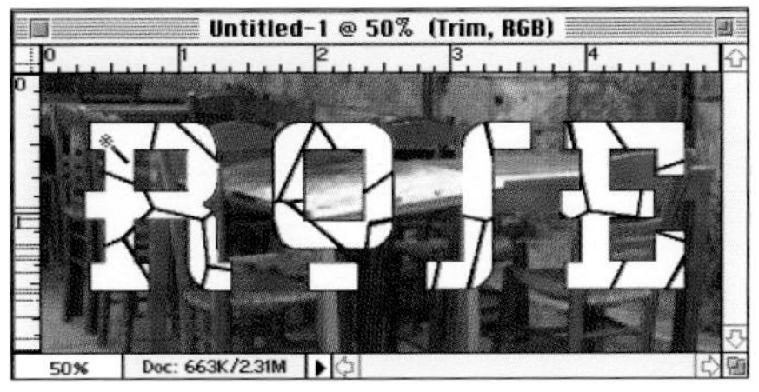


Then choose Select➛Similar.

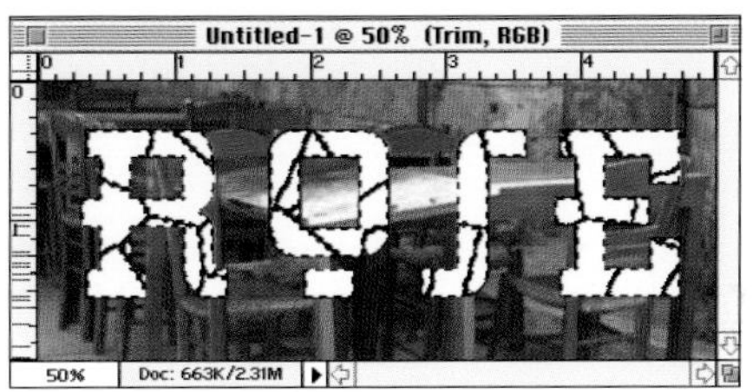


**8** Press Delete to leave only the black lines in the Trim layer. You will see the colors in the Color layer pop through.

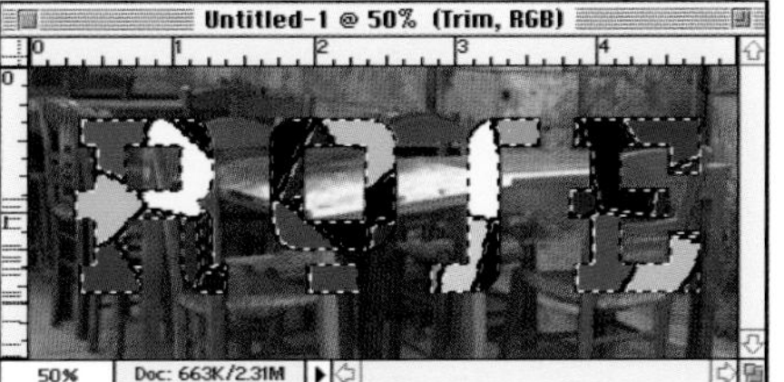

**9** Save the active selection to create Channel #5, and then make Channel #5 the active channel. Deselect the selection.

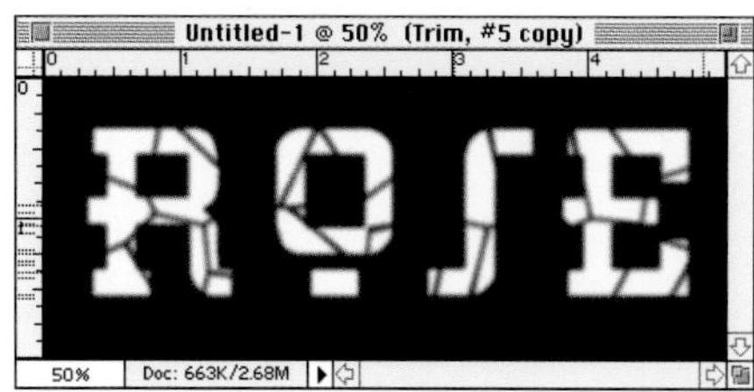


**10** Make a copy of this channel to create Channel #5 copy. While in Channel #5 copy, choose Filter➛Blur➛Gaussian Blur (Radius: 2.5).

**11** Make a copy of this channel to create Channel #5 copy 2. Take a look at the Channels palette in the figure and make sure that you have all of these channels.

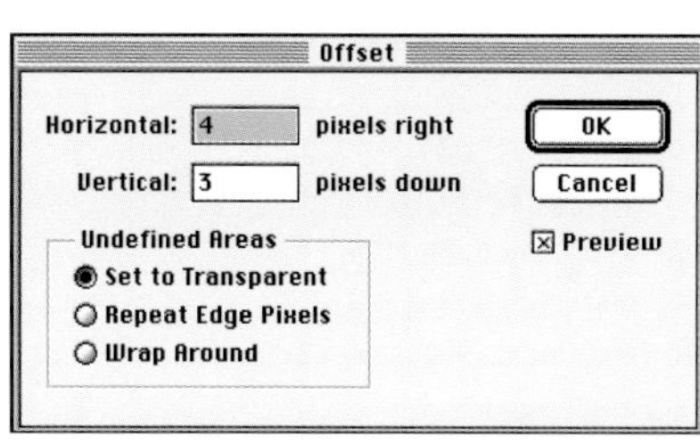


**12** Then choose Filter➛Other➛Offset (Horizontal: -4; Vertical: -3).

**13** Choose Image➞Calculations. Here is the dialog box you will see. Match the settings on your screen to the ones you see here.

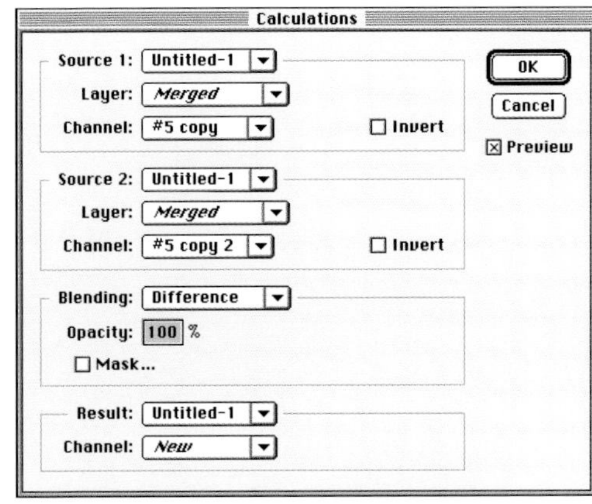


A new channel (#8) is created that should look like this.

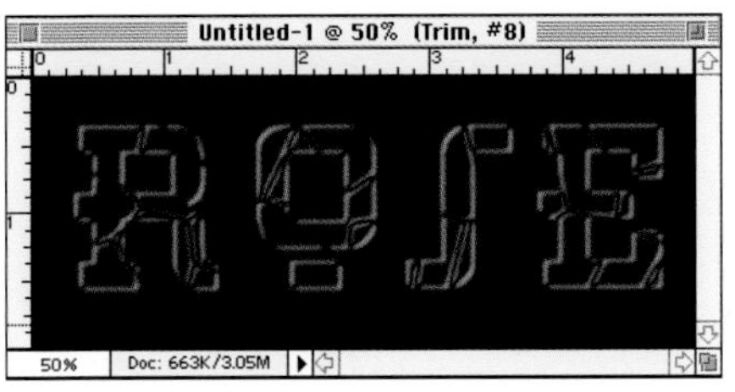


**14** Press Command-I [Control-I] to invert the channel, and then choose Image➞Adjust➞Auto Levels. The contrast in this channel will increase.

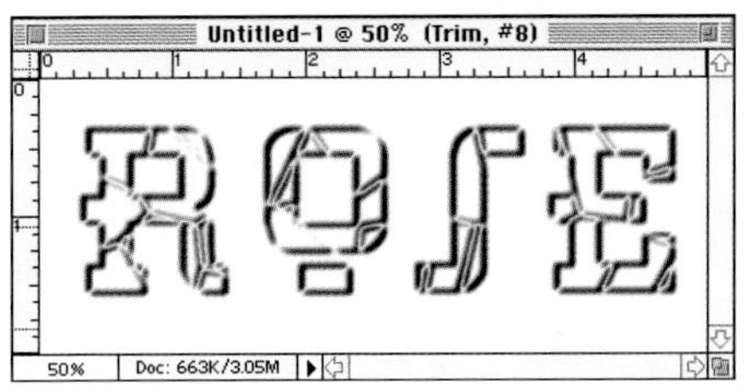


**15** Okay, back to the layers. Return to the composite channel. Everything here is still the same.

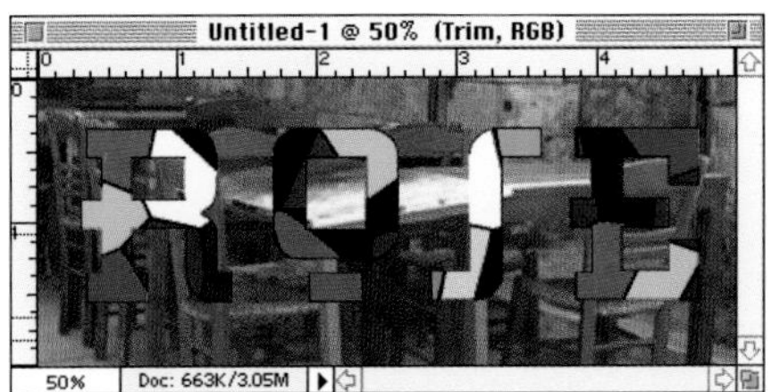

**16** Make the Background layer the active layer and the only visible layer.

**17** Load the selection Channel #5, and choose Filter➞Render➞ Lighting Effects. Match your settings to this dialog box, or choose Glass from the pop-up Style menu. Change the Texture channel to Channel #8.

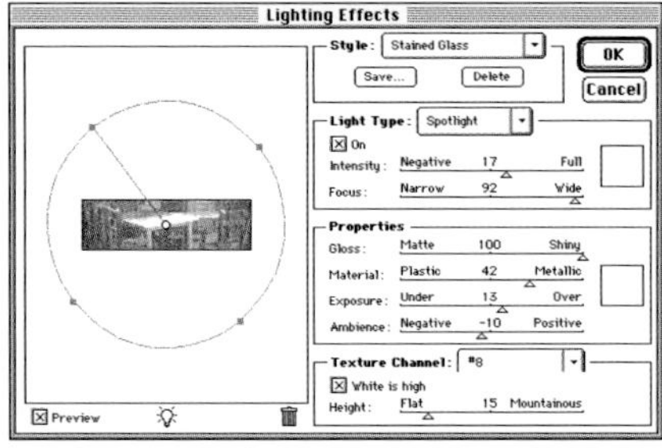


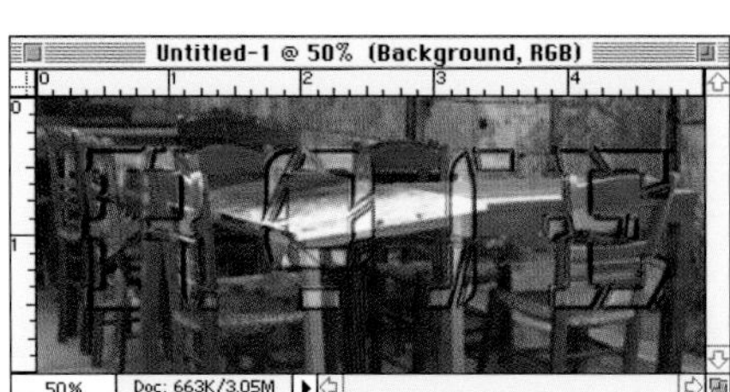


**18** Now, make all of the layers visible and make the Color layer the active layer. Change the mode of the Color layer to Color. That's our stained glass. Now, let's fix the trim.

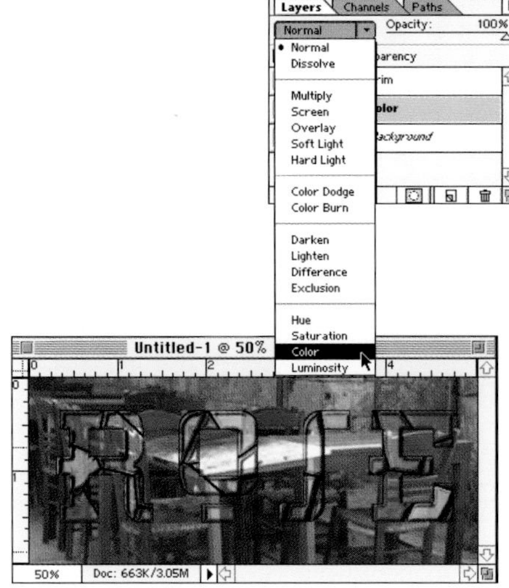

**19** Make the Trim layer the active layer and load the selection Channel #4 (the original text outlines). Choose Edit⇒Stroke. Match the settings here.

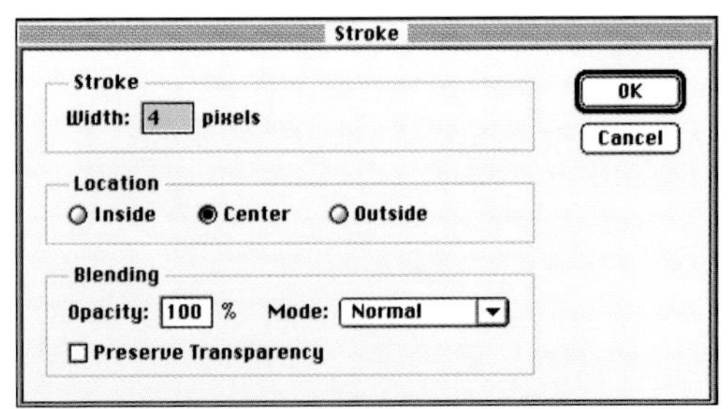


**20** Load the selection of the Trim Layer Transparency to select the trim lines. Change foreground color to a color for the trim. I just used 50% gray. Fill the selection.

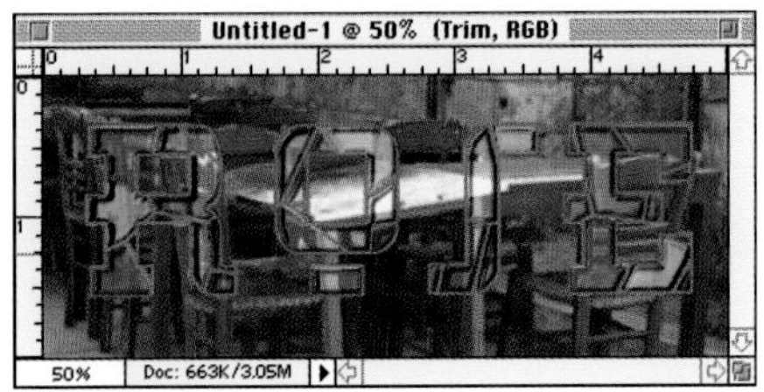


**21** Save the selection to create Channel #9. Make Channel #9 the active channel, and choose Filter⇒Stylize⇒Emboss (Angle: 144, Height: 3, and Amount: 125%). This channel will help the Lighting Effects filter—in the next step—add some dimension to the trim between the colored panes.

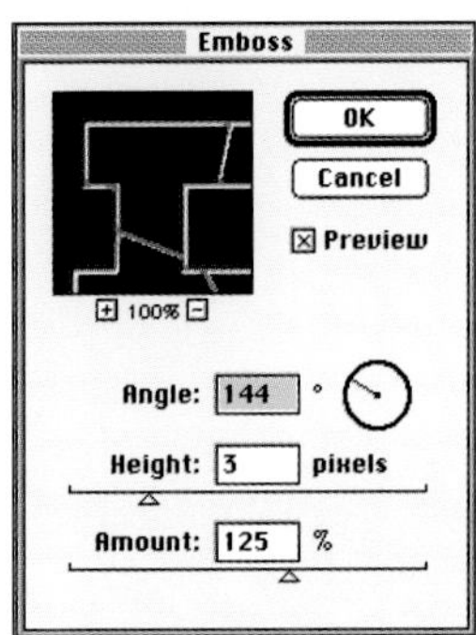


**22** Return to the composite channel and the Trim layer. The selection should still be active. Choose Filter⇒Render⇒Lighting Effects. Choose Trim from the Style pop-up menu, or match these settings.

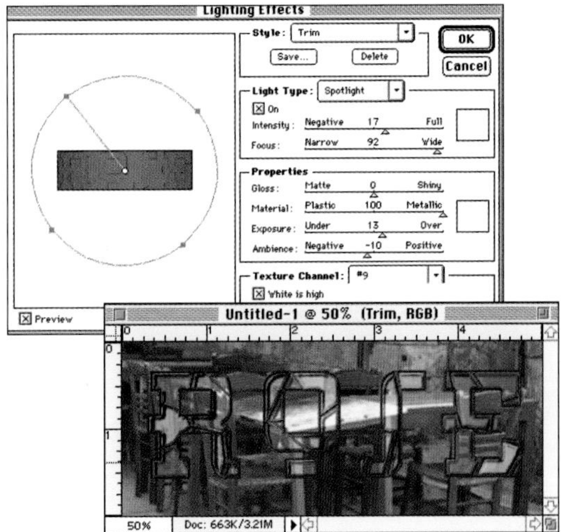

**23** Now, that's better. However, what if you still don't like the colors? Follow me. Make the Color layer the active layer. Select the Magic Wand tool and click on any glass pane.

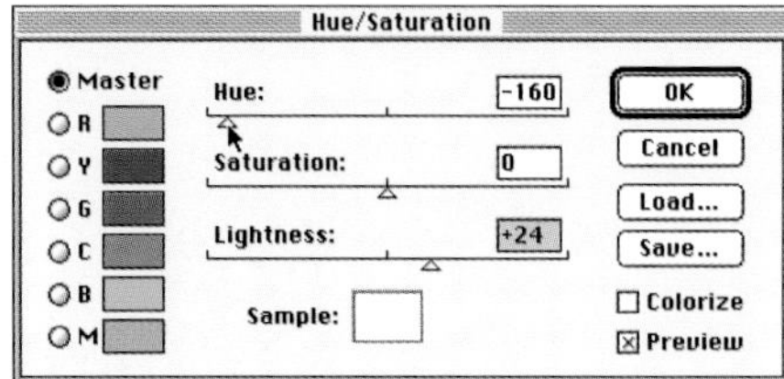


**24** You now can use any of Photoshop's color adjusting features to change the color of this pane. The simplest way is to choose Image⇒Adjust⇒Hue/Saturation. Use the sliders to find a color.

**TIP** **You almost always will have a couple of black glass panes that you will want to change. This happens because the Noise filter you applied earlier in Step 3 includes some black.**

**25** Keep repeating Steps 23 and 24 until all the colors meet your demanding standards.

## Variations

If you want to get rid of the background, then follow these steps. Flatten the image. Load the selection Channel #4 (the original text selection). Choose Select⇒Modify⇒Expand (1 pixel). Choose Select⇒Inverse. Change the background color to white, and then press Delete. ■

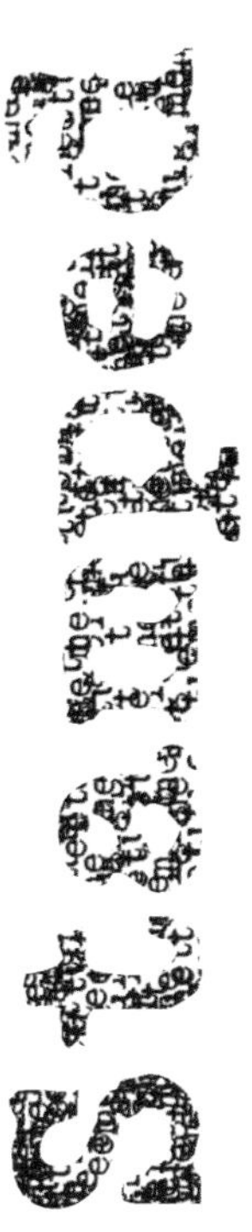


This technique shows you how to make type stamps that you can use to build words or patterns.

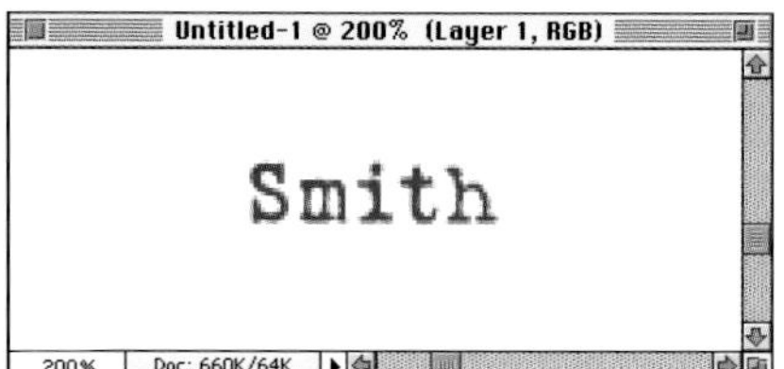


1 Create a new file. Use the Type tool to enter the text. Use a small point size. The type that was used here is Love Letter Typewriter at 10 points. Press Command-E [Control-E] to merge the new layer created by the Type tool back into the Background.

**TIP** **When using small point sizes, you may prefer to turn off the anti-aliasing option in the Type dialog box. If you don't, then the type may be blurred.**

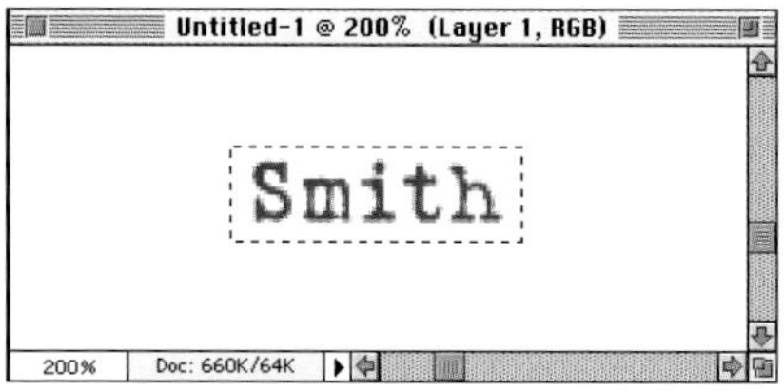

2 Zoom in on the type. Then select the Marquee tool and drag a rectangular selection around the type.

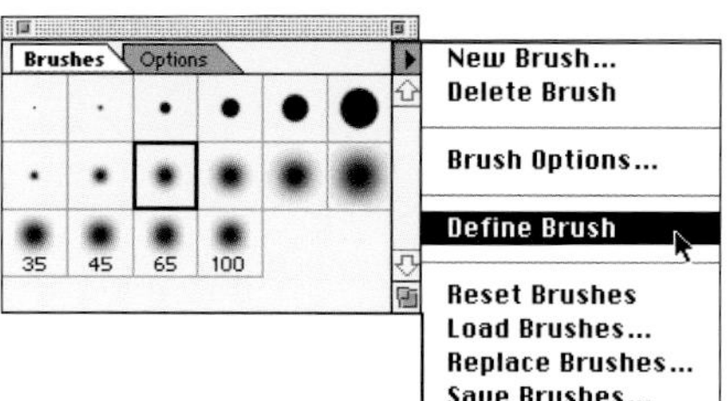


3 Double-click the Paintbrush tool to select it and to bring to the front the Paintbrush Options floating palette. Click on the Brushes tab to bring it to the front. Choose Define brush from the pull-down menu.

4 The text you selected in Step 2 can now be used as a paintbrush. Press Delete to get rid of the original text. Deselect the rectangle. Next, with the Paintbrush tool still active and the new brush selected, click once in Layer 1. Keep clicking one stamp at a time to build your type.

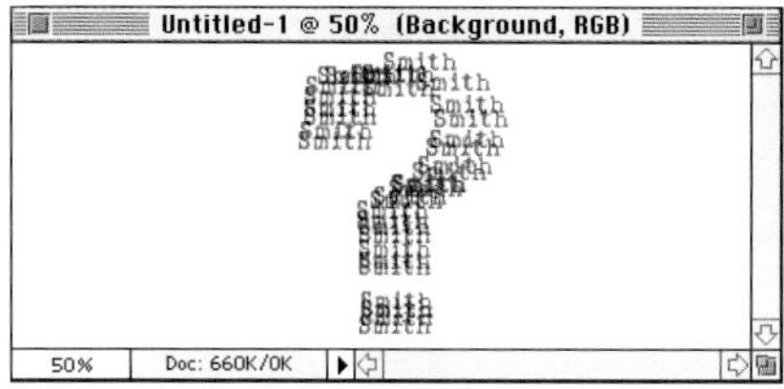

**TIP** **Just like all other Paintbrushes, the stamp will be applied in the current foreground color.**

**5** You also can click and drag the word, but it probably will not be readable because the letters will blur together. To fix that problem, double-click the brush you created (on the Brushes floating palette).

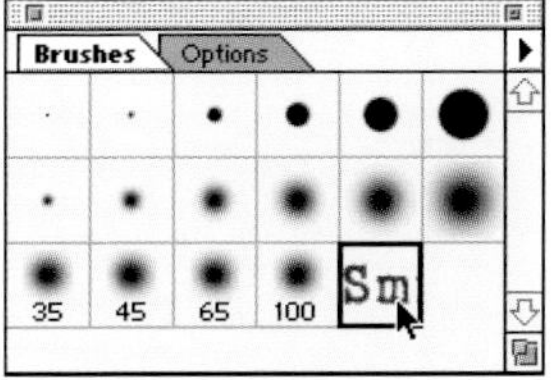


**6** A dialog box will appear that will enable you to change the brush Spacing. The Spacing is the distance the brush will move, relative to the vertical height of the brush (the text), before placing another stamp. Change the Spacing to 100%.

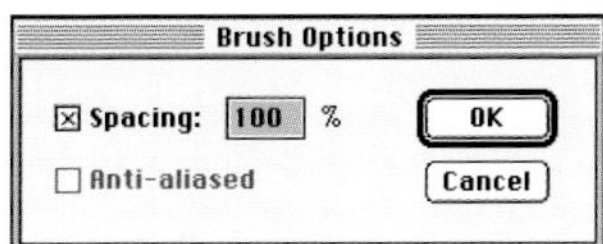


**7** Now try painting with the same brush. See how you can make textures by simply dragging the type brush and overlapping the words.

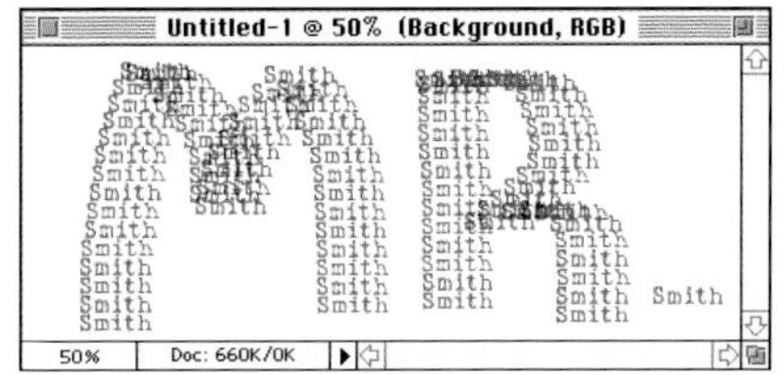


**8** Click on the Paintbrush Options tab to bring it to the front. Check the Fade box to turn it on. Type a number in the Fade box (I used 15), and set the steps to to Transparent.

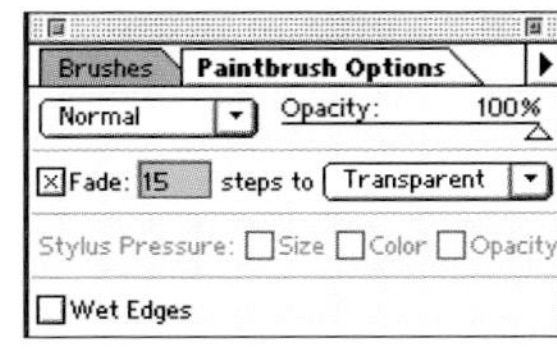


Then drag the same brush around. After dragging the brush, I changed the foreground color to red and clicked on top of one of the names.

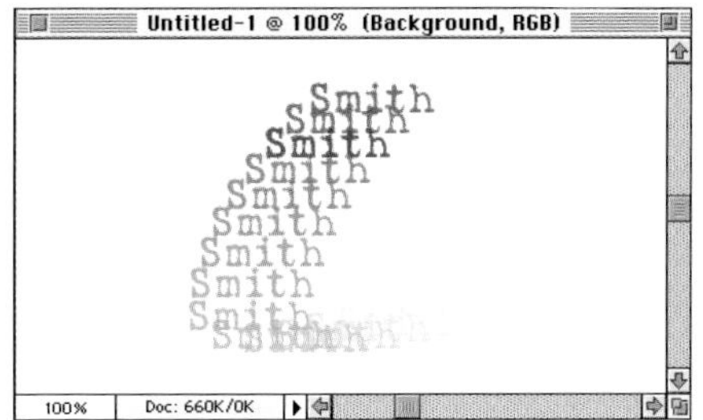

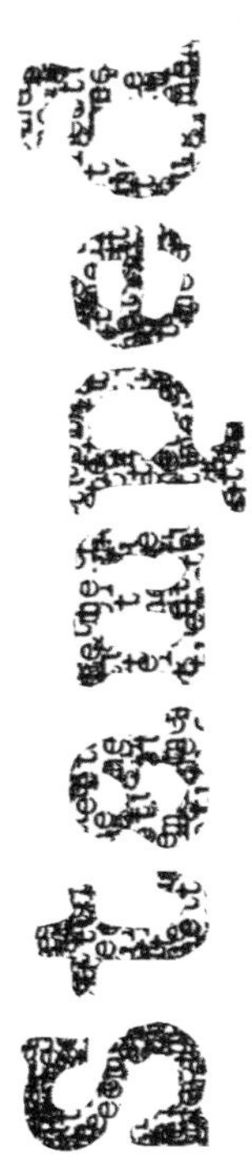

**9** Try this. Open a file that has an image in it, like this one taken from the Photoshop Tutorial folder (Follow this path to find the Leaf image: Adobe Photoshop 4.0➻Tutorial➻Leaf). Flatten the image to place it on a white background.

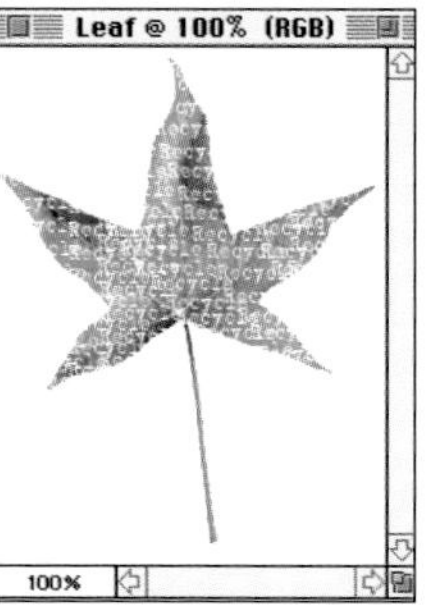


**10** Change the foreground color to white, and paint the type over the photo to "mask" the image.

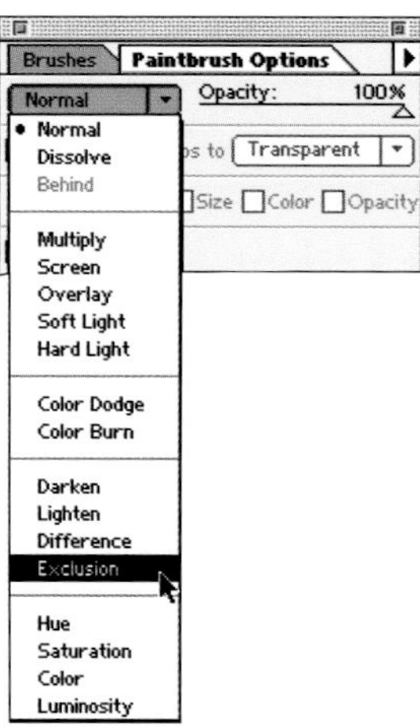


**11** If it is not already active, click on the Paintbrush Options tab to bring it to the front. Then choose Exclusion from the pop-up menu.

**12** Choose a color for the foreground color (other than white). I used a red from Photoshop's default swatches.

**13** Next, click and drag the brush across the image.

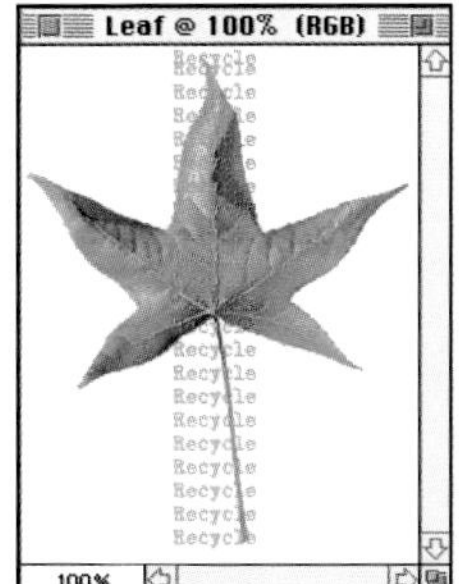


**14** You could build type one letter at a time for a variation on the Binary effect (page 24). Do all the steps above as indicated, except select only one letter of the type in Step 2, and then do Step 3.

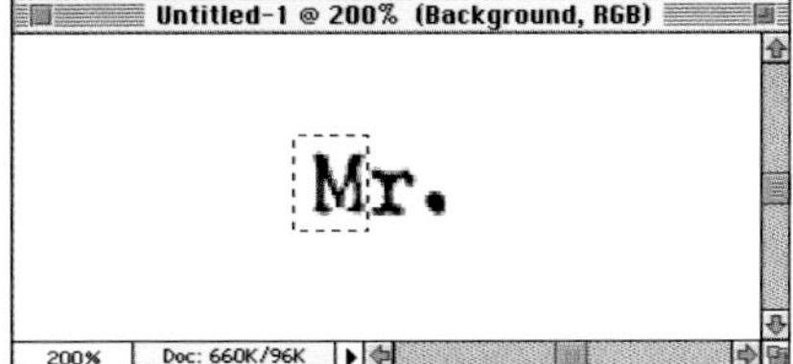


**15** Repeat Step 14 until you have created a brush for each letter of the word.

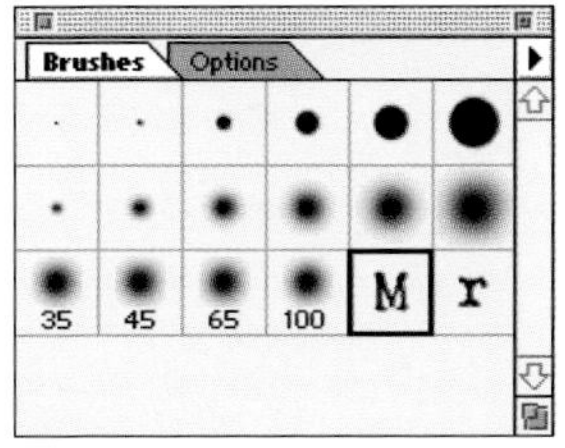


**16** Then use the brushes you have created to rebuild the word you typed.

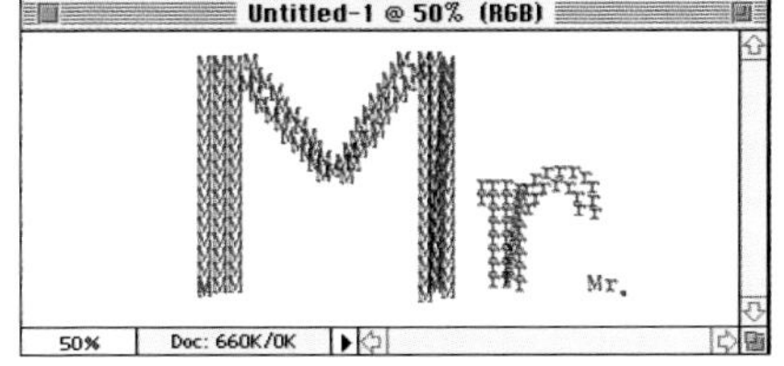


## VARIATIONS

For this variation, type in several lines of type and then use the Marquee tool to select only a portion of the text.

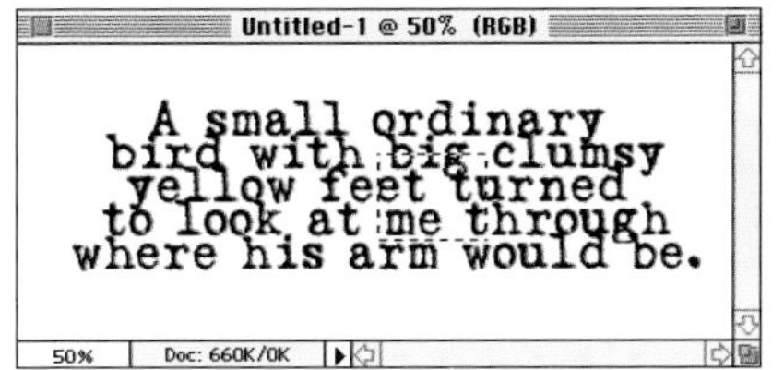

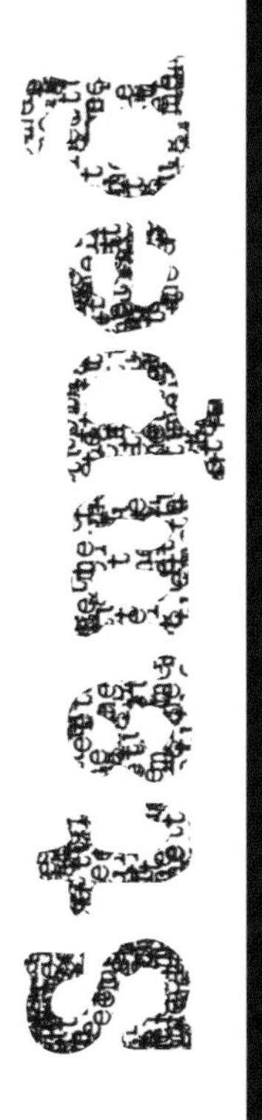

Define that selection as a brush, and change the brush spacing to 100% (as you did in Steps 5 and 6). Delete all the text. Then use the Type Mask tool to enter the text.

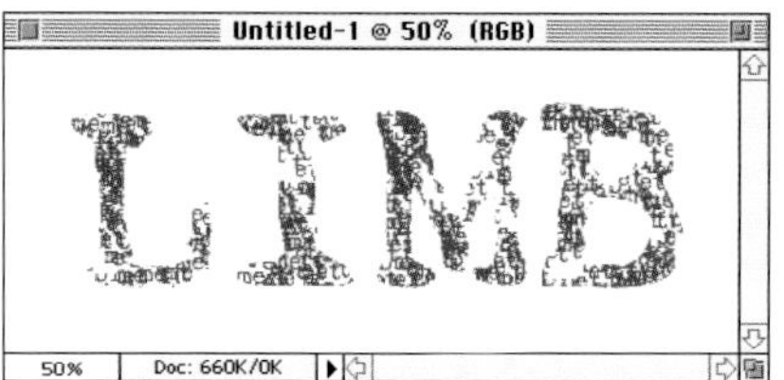


Change the foreground color to a color for the type. Select the Paintbrush tool again, and paint into the blank selection.

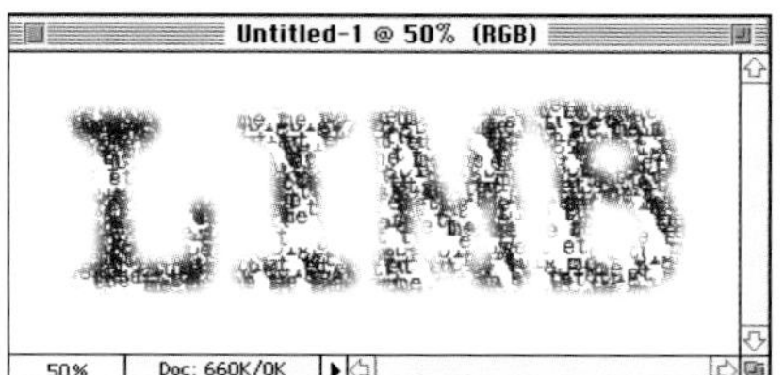


If you feather the selection above by choosing Select➼Feather (10 pixels) before you paint in the text, then you will get something like this.

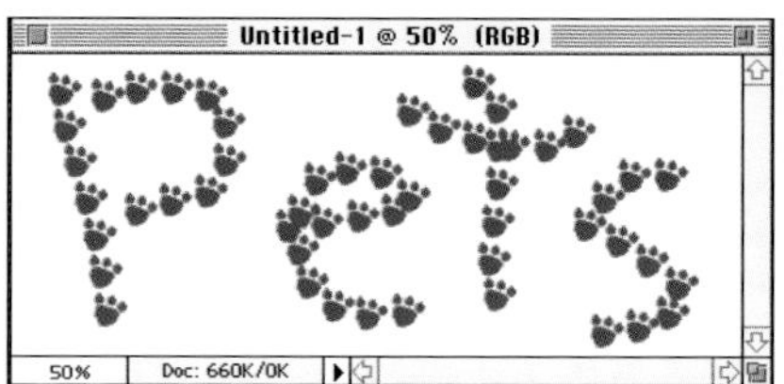


Try making other brushes for painting type. I painted a paw, defined it as a brush, changed its spacing to 105%, and then painted this text.

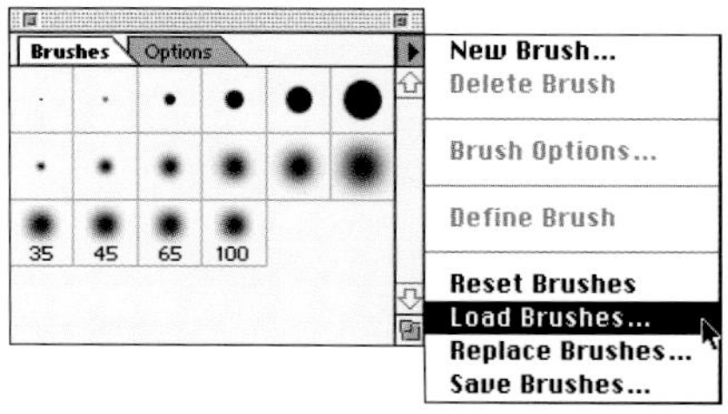


Try using one of the built-in brushes in Photoshop. From the Brushes floating palette arrow menu choose Load Brushes.

Find the Assorted Brushes file on your hard disk: Adobe Photoshop 4.0➠Goodies➠Brushes & Patterns➠Assorted Brushes. Open this file. You can use any of these brushes to paint your type. Don't forget that you can adjust the spacing for any of these brushes.

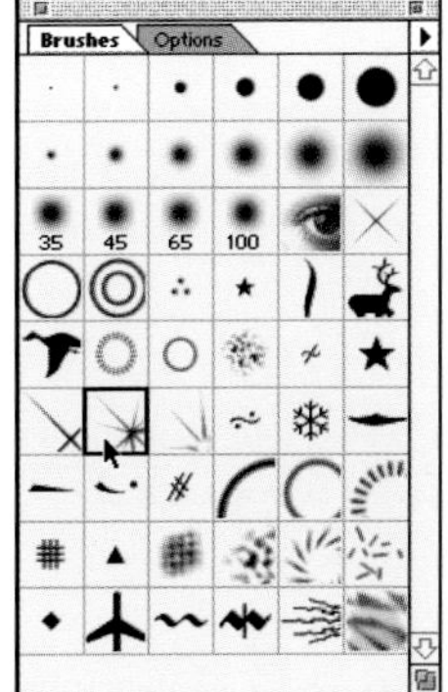


I made this image with the brush that was selected in the previous figure. ■

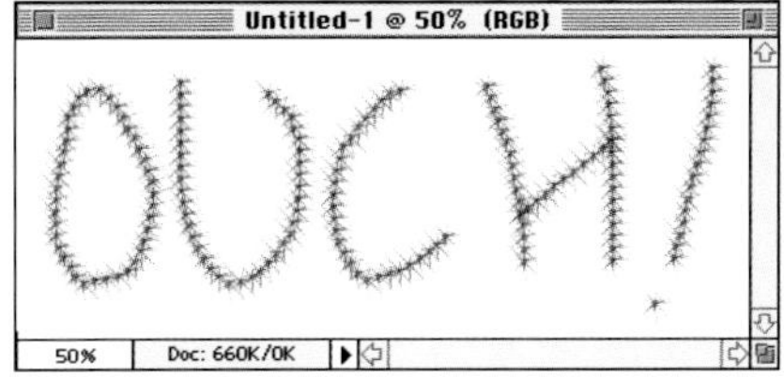

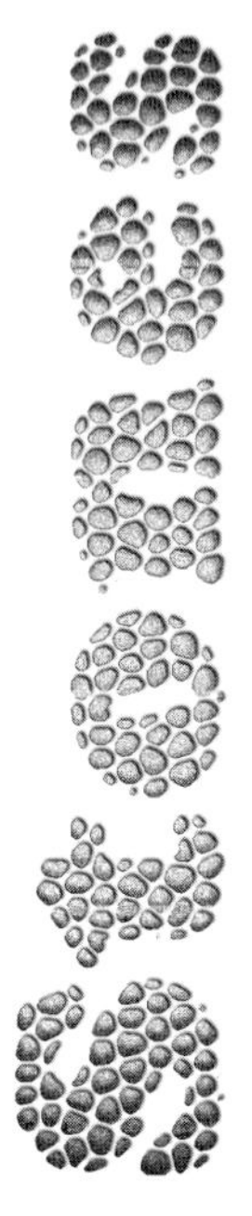

TOOLBOX

Stones (Lighting Style Preset)

The new Stained Glass filter gets the Stones effect started by dividing up the letters. From there a little selection manipulation takes you to the Lighting Effects filter, which rounds out the stones and the effect.

**1** Create a new file. Use the Type tool to enter the text. I used a thick font named Cooper Black at 100 points. The type will be placed automatically on a new layer (Layer 1).

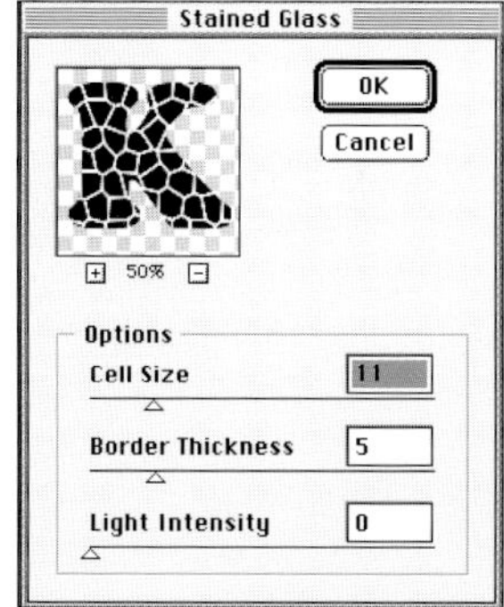


**2** Change the foreground color to white. Then choose Filter➺Texture➺Stained Glass. Watch the preview to see the approximate sizes of the stones. Adjust the Border Thickness slider for spacing between the stones, and set the Light Intensity to 0. These settings...

...will yield this.

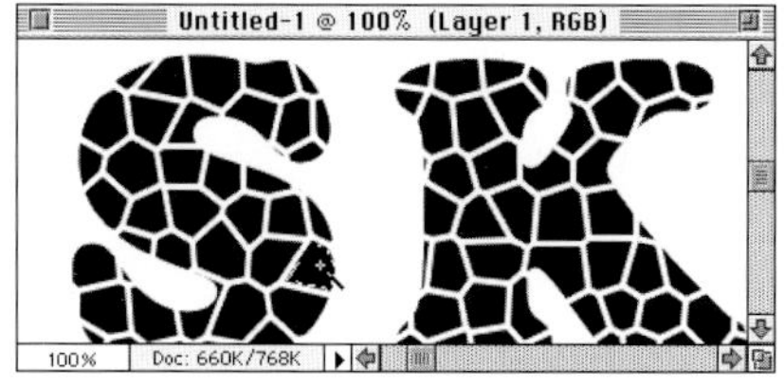


**3** Select the Wand tool and click the wand inside one of the black spots.

**4** Choose Select➔Similar. Save this selection to create Channel #4. Then choose Select➔Modify➔ Smooth. Smooth the selection about 3 pixels.

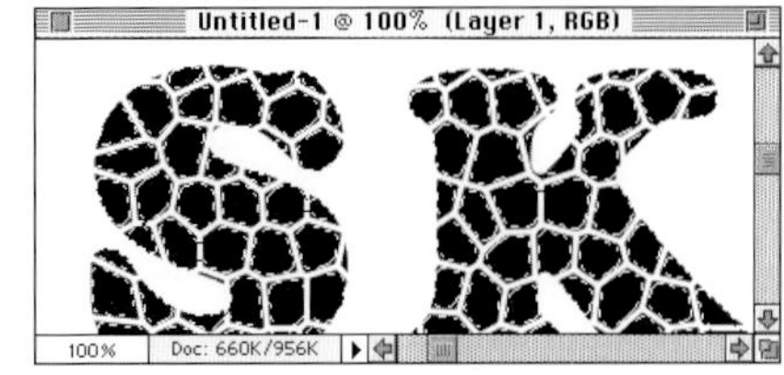


**5** Press Command-J [Control-J] to float the smoothed selection into a new layer (Layer 2). Make Layer 1 invisible.

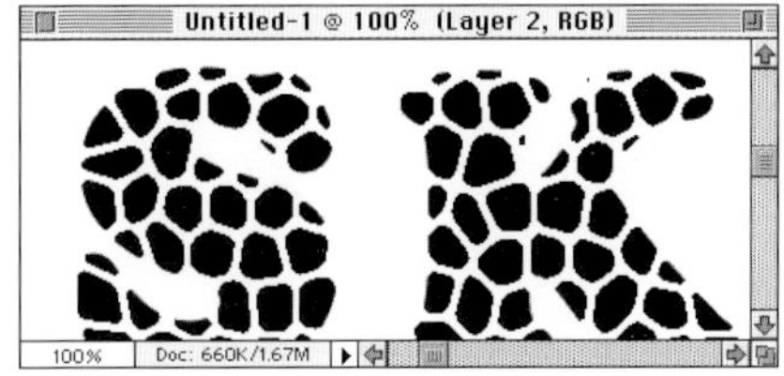


**6** Turn on the Preserve Transparency option for Layer 2 on the Layers floating palette. Change the foreground color to black, and press the Option-Delete [Alt-Delete] keys to fill the layer with black. Then turn off the Preserve Transparency option. A few stones still may be attached to each other.

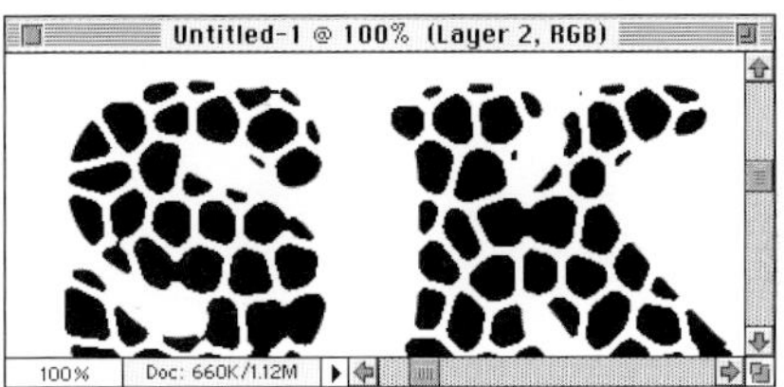


**7** To get rid of these connections, load the selection Channel #4. Choose Select➔Inverse and press Delete.

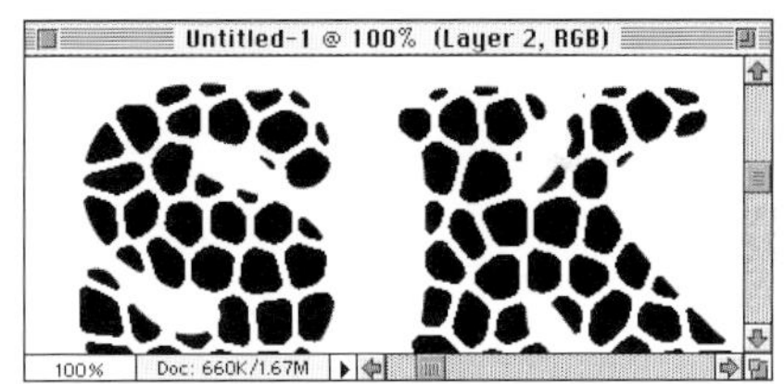


**8** Next, duplicate Layer 2 to create Layer 2 copy. Then make Layer 2 the active layer again.

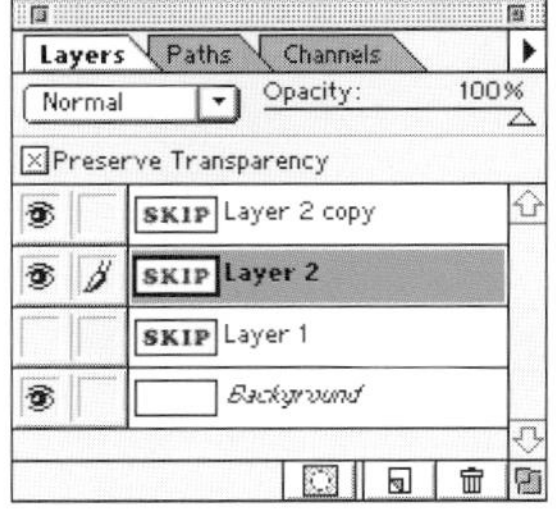

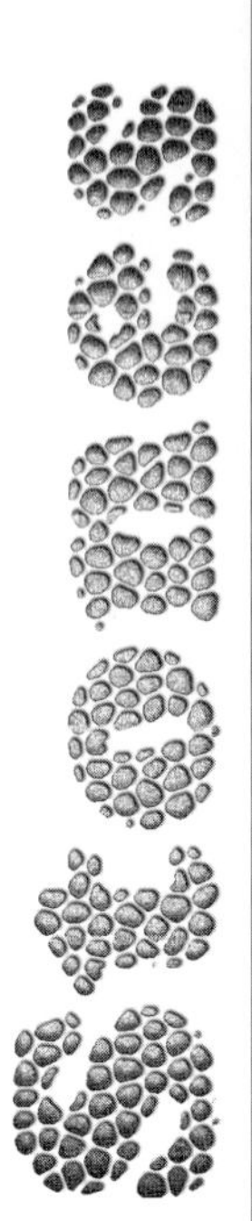

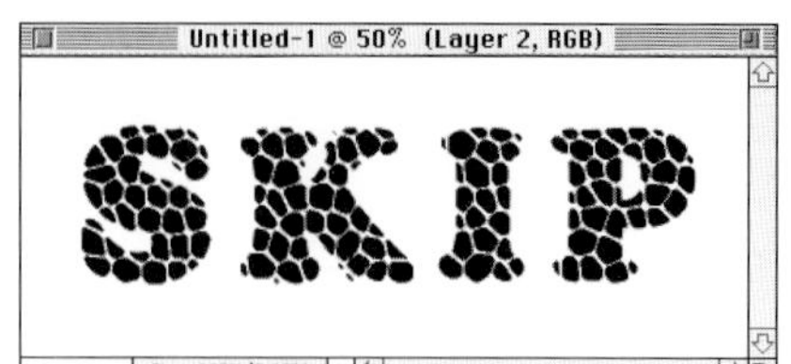


**9** Select the Move tool and use the arrow keys to move this layer, which will be the shadow. I moved it two keystrokes to the right and two keystrokes down. It will look like the type is spreading in the direction you move it.

**10** Then load the transparency selection for Layer 2 copy. Press Delete. You shouldn't see anything change, except for traces of white around the lower left of the stones.

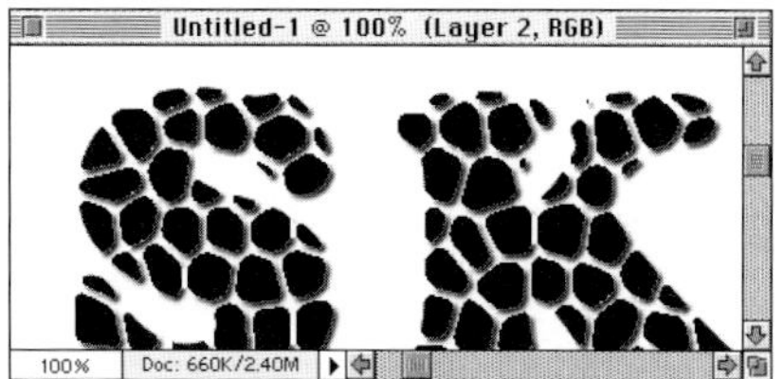


**11** Deselect the selection, and choose Filter➛Blur➛Gaussian Blur. Blur the shadow just a little, about 1 pixel.

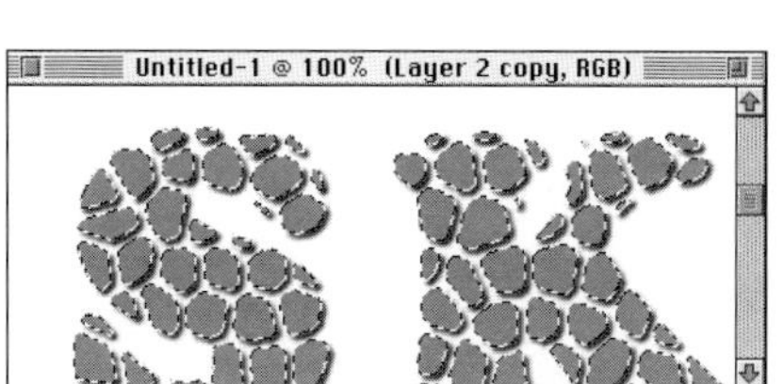


**12** Make Layer 2 copy active and load the transparency selection for this layer. Change the foreground color to 40% gray and fill the selection.

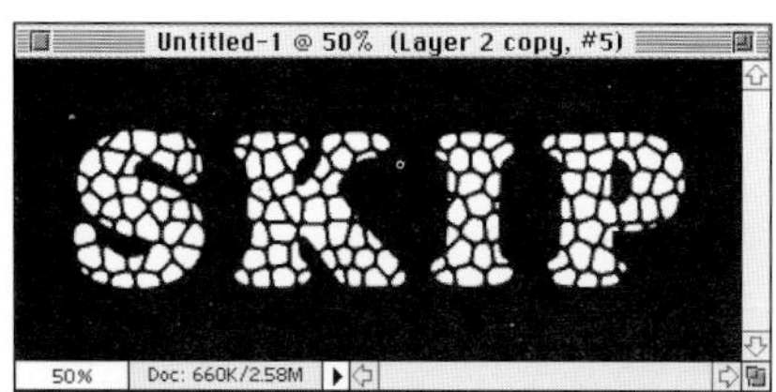


**13** Save the selection to create Channel #5. Make Channel #5 active.

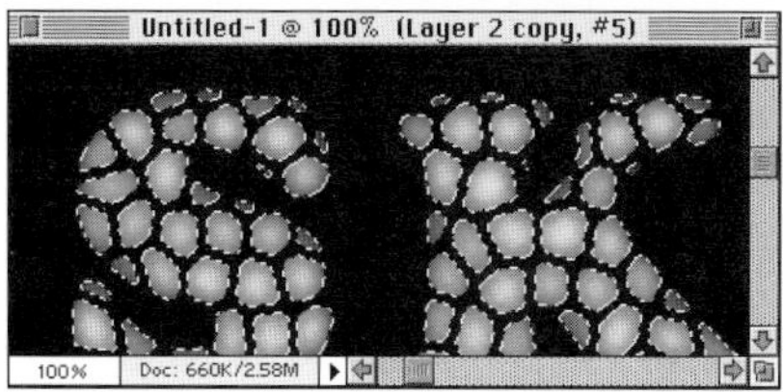


**14** While the selection is still active, choose Filter➛Blur➛Gaussian Blur. Raise the radius to about 6. Since the selection is active, there will be blurring only inside the white areas.

**15** Return to the composite channel, and make Layer 2 copy the active layer.

**16** Next, choose Filter➛Render➛Lighting Effects. You can select the Stones preset from the pop-up menu or match these settings (which are very similar to the default settings). Move the light in the Preview box if necessary.

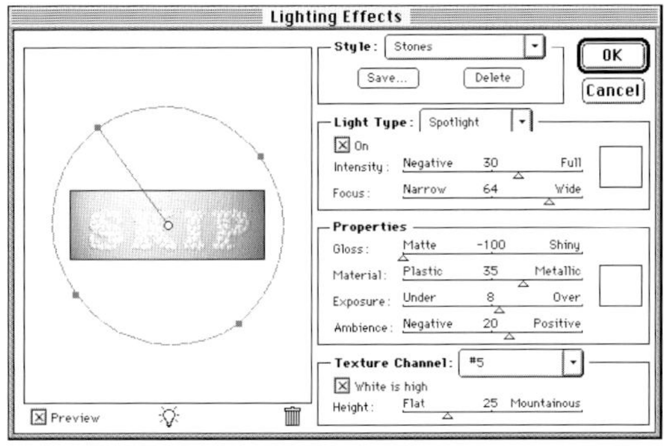


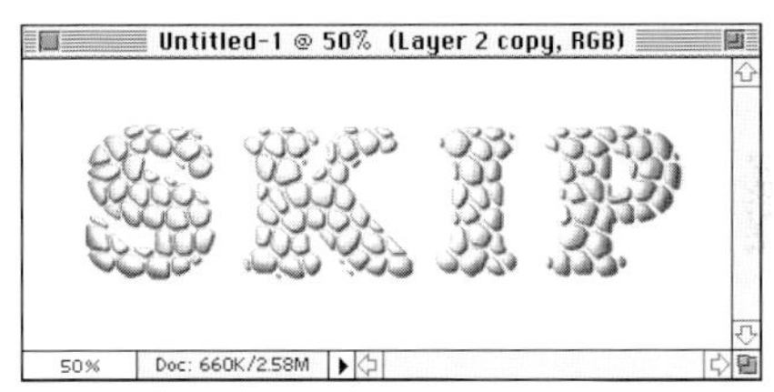


**17** For the final touch, choose Filter➛Noise➛Add Noise. Adjust the Amount to your liking. I set it at 25, and turned on the Gaussian option. Turn the Monochromatic option on as well. ■

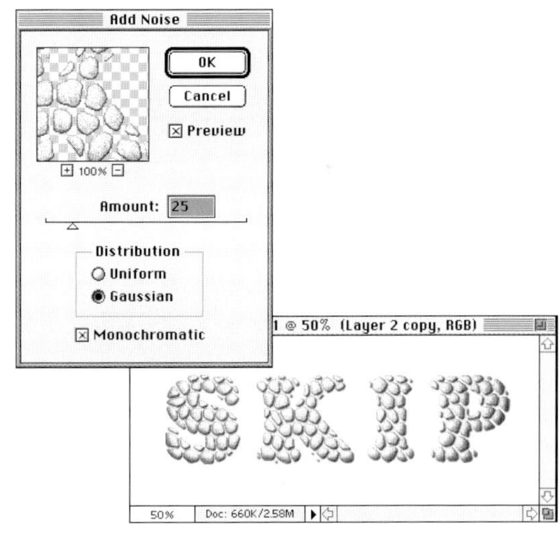

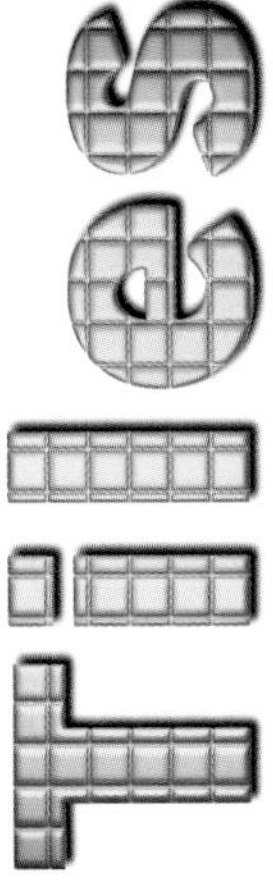

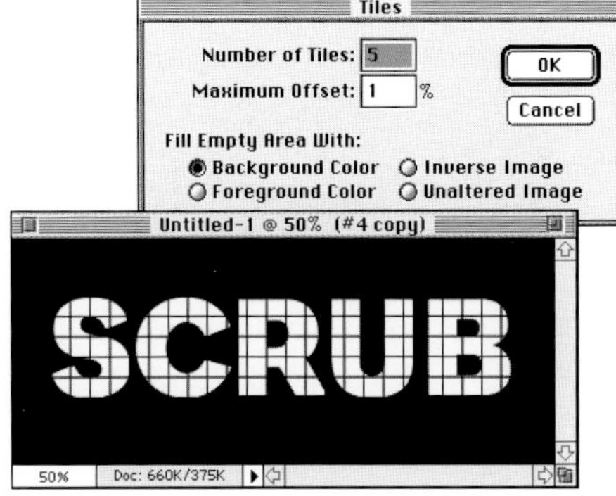

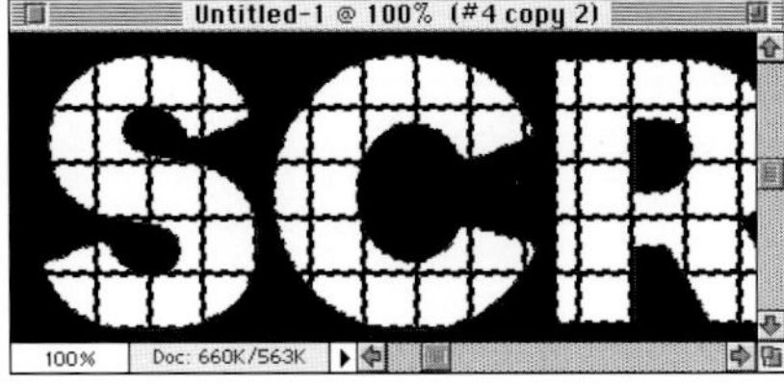


For this effect, I will show you two ways to create raised tiles. Some extra channel manipulation is needed to create tiles with hard, beveled edges, but first here's the easy way.

**1** Create a new file, and a new channel (#4). Use the Type tool to enter the text. Use a wide font because narrow letter pieces will turn into awkward tile shapes. I used Eagle Book at 90 points.

**2** Duplicate Channel #4 to create Channel #4 copy.

**3** While the selection is still active, choose Filter➝Stylize➝Tiles. The Number of Tiles setting is self-explanatory—choose a number that is appropriate for your type. Keep the Offset percentage at 1%.

**4** Duplicate Channel #4 copy to create Channel #4 copy 2.

**5** Load the selection of the same channel (Channel #4 copy 2).

## TOOLBOX

Tile (Lighting Style Preset)

**6** Choose Filter➛Blur➛Gaussian Blur. Blur the tiles just a little—about 2.5 pixels.

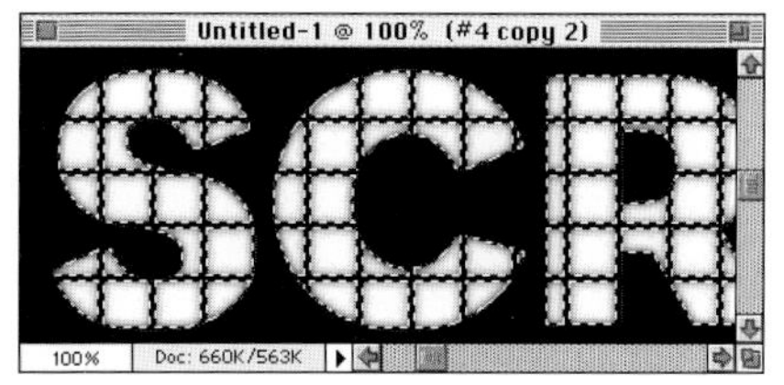


**7** Next, choose Select➛Inverse. Then load the selection of Channel #4 with the Intersect with Selection option turned on. The grout should now be selected.

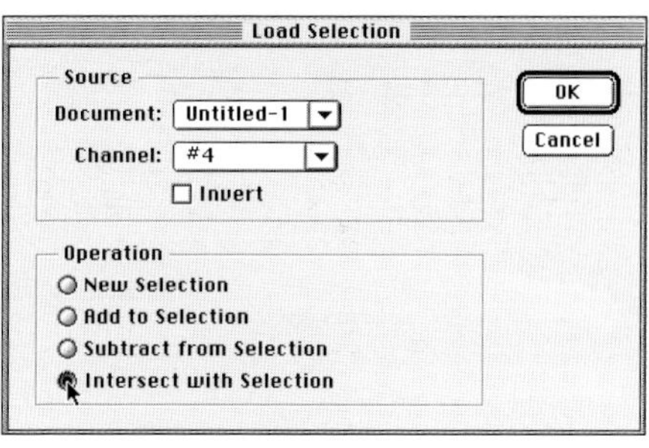


**8** Blur the grout by choosing Filter➛Gaussian Blur. Use a smaller Radius than that used in Step 6. I set the Radius to 1.5.

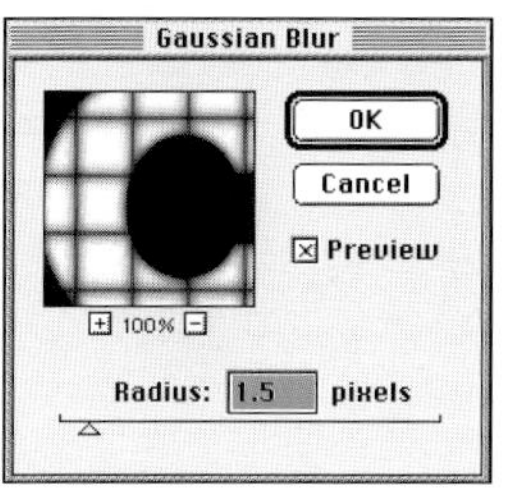


**9** Return to the composite channel, and load the selection Channel #4. Change the foreground color to a color for the type, and then fill the selection with the color. I used the CMYK values 50, 0, 0, 0.

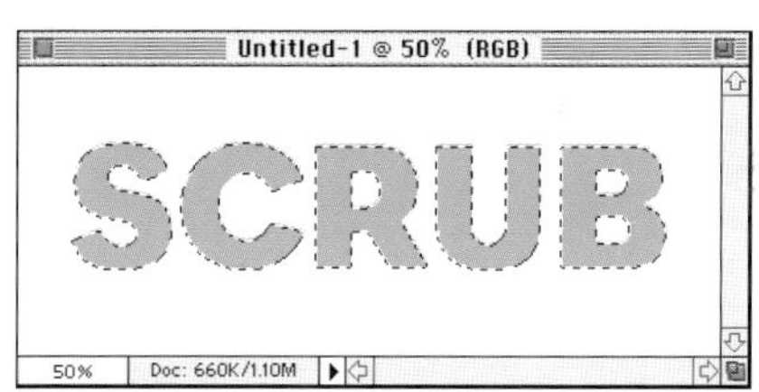


**10** Choose Filter➛Render➛Lighting Effects. From the Style pop-up menu choose Tiles, or match the settings you see here.

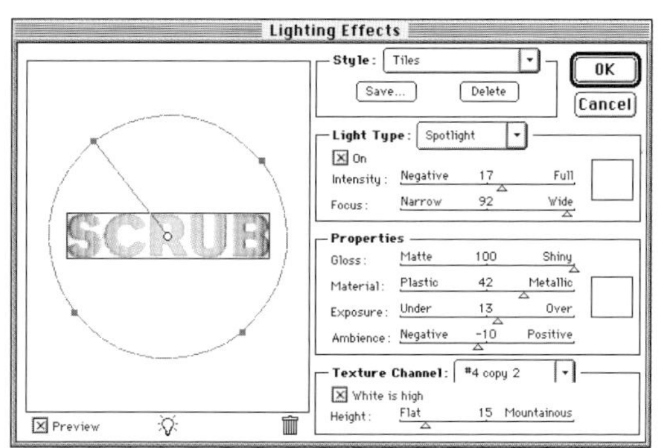

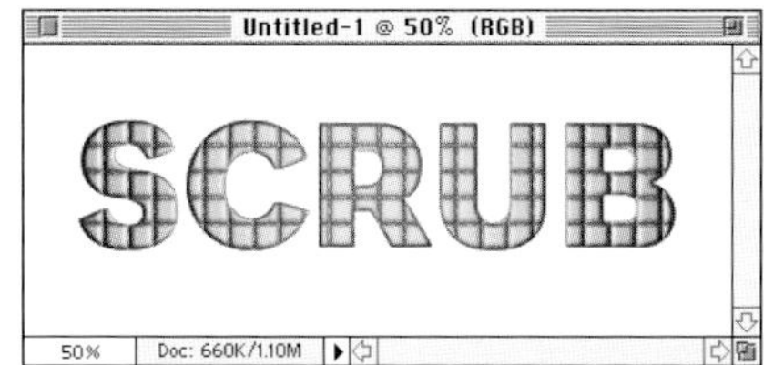


Easy tiles.

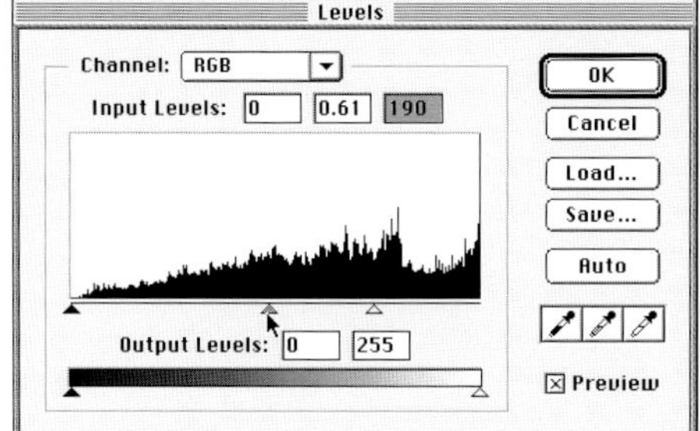


**11** If you want to adjust the surface coverage of the color, then choose Image➛Adjust➛Levels. Use the Input Levels sliders to reduce or increase coverage and contrast. These adjustments...

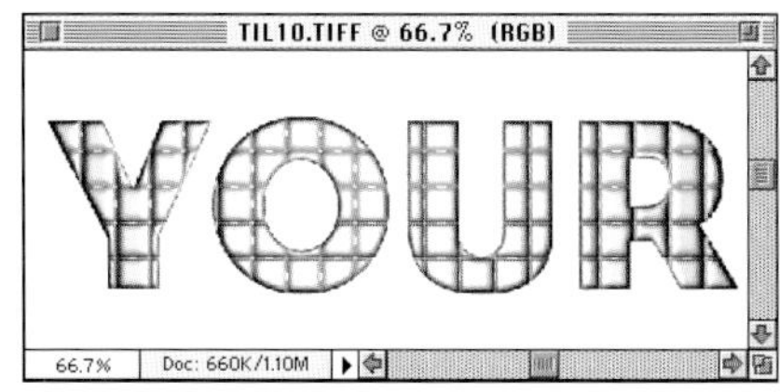


...yielded this type.

## VARIATION

If you want harder edges, then follow these steps.

**1** Perform Steps 1 through 4, and then deselect the text.

**2** Choose Filter➛Blur➛Gaussian Blur and blur the channel about 1 pixel.

**3** Duplicate Channel #4 copy 2 to create Channel #4 copy 3.

**4** Then select the Move tool and nudge the channel one keystroke to the right and one keystroke down. Make Channel #4 copy 2 the active channel and nudge it one keystroke to the left and one keystroke up. This slight nudging sets up the next step.

**5** Choose Image➻Calculations. Match your settings to the ones shown in this figure. This feature will create a new channel that is the result of combining Channel #4 copy 2 and Channel #4 copy 3. Because the channels are slightly offset, you get an interesting effect that helps create highlights on the tiles.

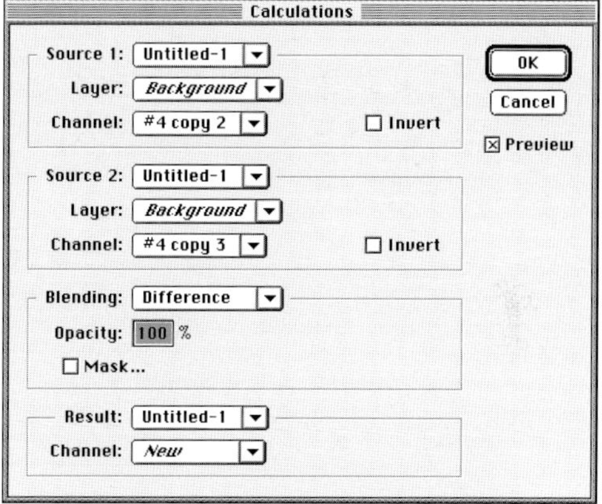


Click OK. The new channel (#8) should look like this.

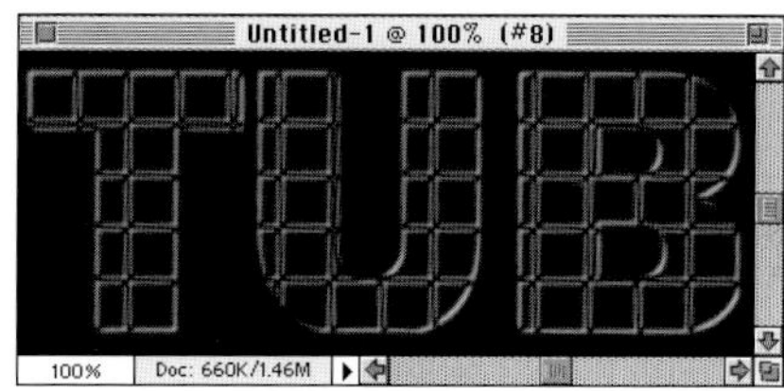


**6** Choose Image➻Adjust➻Invert, and then Image➻Adjust➻Auto Levels. There should be more contrast in the type now.

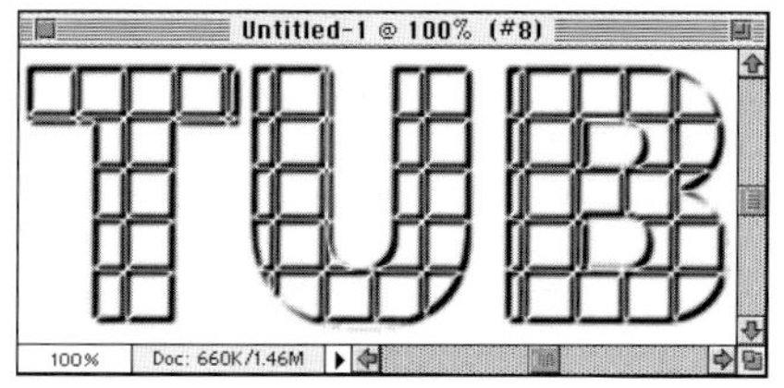

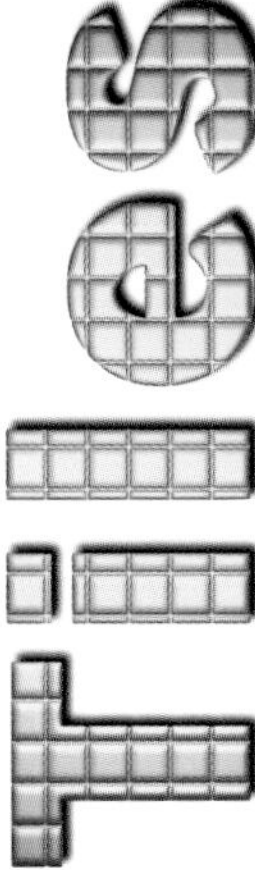


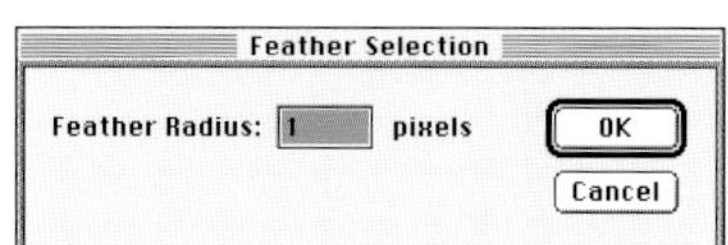


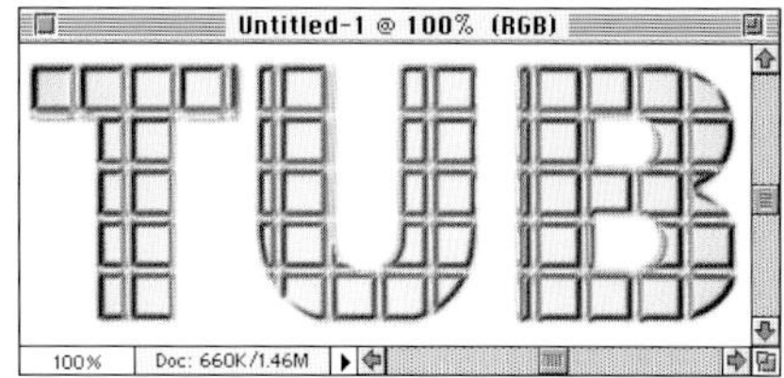

**7** Return to the Composite channel, and load the selection (Channel #4 copy). Choose Select➛Feather (1 pixel).

**8** Change the foreground color to a color for the tiles and fill the selection. Then choose Filter➛Render➛Lighting Effects. From the Style pop-up menu choose Tiles, or match the settings on page 191. Be sure to change the Texture Channel to Channel #8 in the Lighting Effects dialog box.

**9** To add color to the grout, load the selection (Channel #4 copy), choose Select➛Inverse, and load the selection (Channel #4) with the Intersect with Selection option turned on. Choose a foreground color for the grout and fill the selection. I used the same color for the grout as I did for the tiles. ■

# Tire Tracks

A custom paintbrush makes this effect a snap.

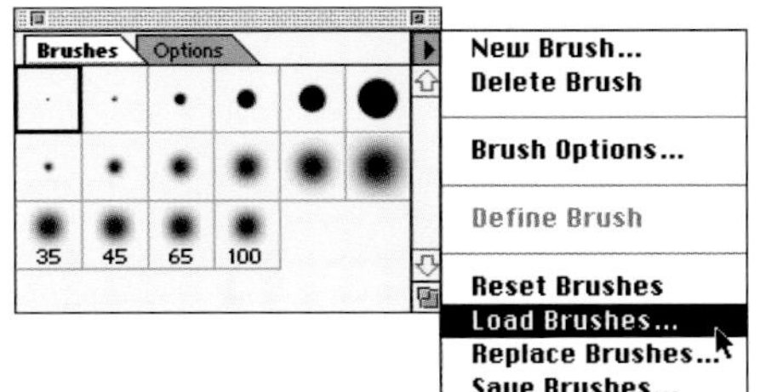


**1** Create a new file. Double-click the Paintbrush tool to select and bring the Paintbrush Options floating palette to the front. Click the Brushes tab to make it active. Then, from the Brushes arrow menu, choose Load Brushes.

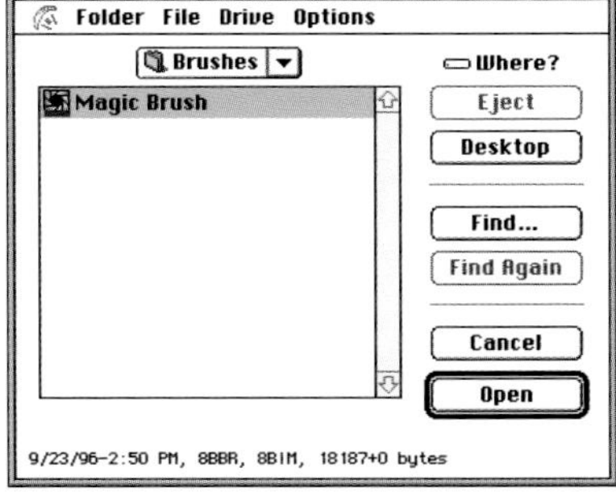


**2** Find the Magic Brush file on the CD that came with this book. Follow this path to find the file: Photoshop Type Magic 2➛Type Magic Presets➛Magic Brush.

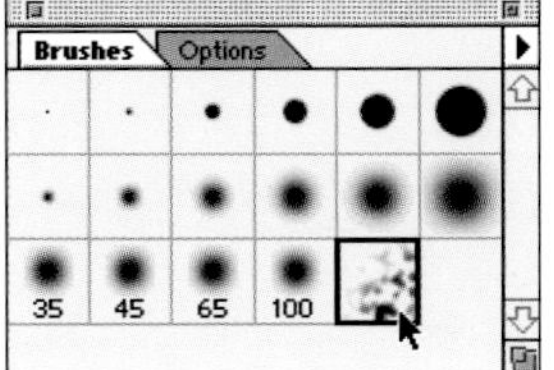


**3** A new brush will appear at the end of the Brushes palette. I made this brush by modifying a brush from Photoshop's Assorted Brushes file. Select the new brush.

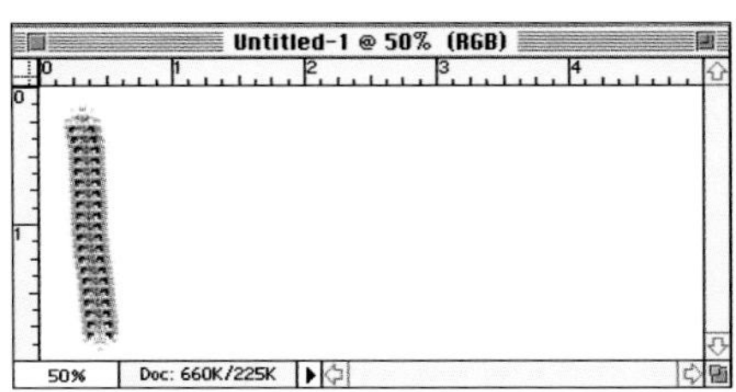


**4** With the Paintbrush tool click and drag in the image window.

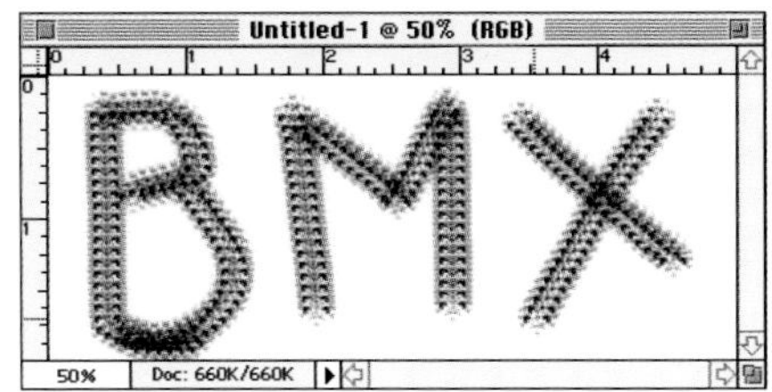


**5** Simply draw your letters with the mouse.

## TOOLBOX

Magic Brush

Tire Tracks (Lighting Style Preset)

## VARIATIONS

If your hand is a little unsteady, or just want straighter lines, then try these steps.

Follow the instructions in Steps 1 through 3 above. Then select the Pen tool and use it to draw the center lines for the type. Like this:

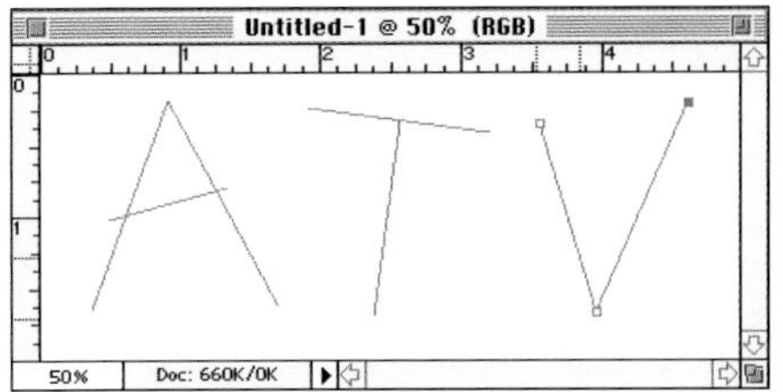


**TIP** **Turning on the Rubber Band option on the Pen Tool Options floating palette helps you see what you're doing as you create the letters.**

Now, from the Paths floating palette arrow menu, choose Stroke Path.

When the dialog box pops up, choose Paintbrush.

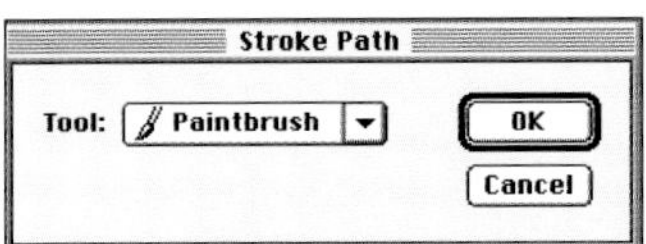


Click OK, and you have automatic tire tracks.

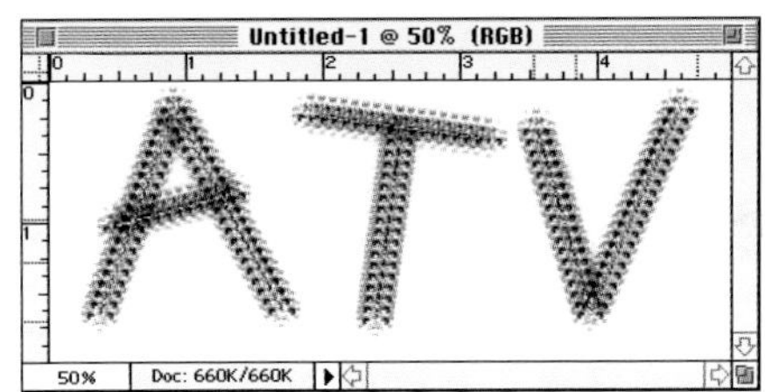




To add some depth to the tracks, follow these steps.

Double-click the new brush (the one that you selected in Step 3) to open the Brush Options dialog box. Set the Spacing at 35%.

Brush Options

Spacing: 35 %

Anti-aliased

OK

Cancel

Create a new channel (#4), and draw the letters (as described above) in the channel.

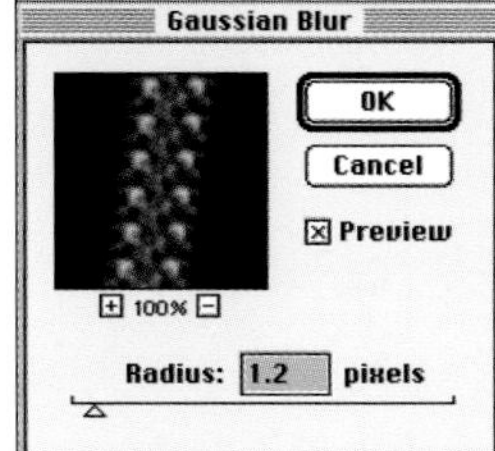


Apply Filter➭Blur➭Gaussian Blur (Radius: 1.2 pixels).

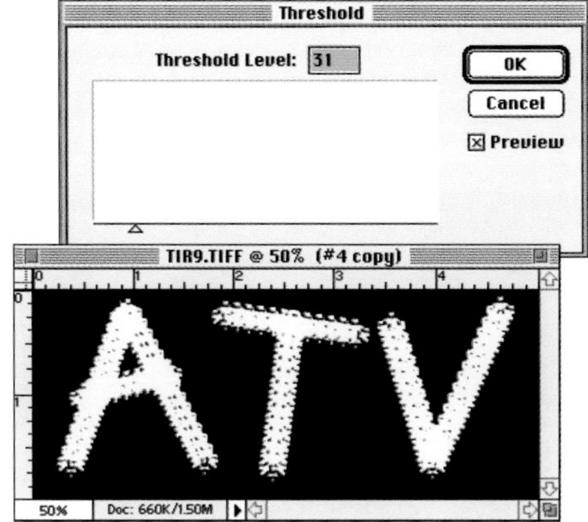


Duplicate Channel #4 to create Channel #4 copy. In the new channel, choose Image➭Adjust➭Threshold. Lower the level until most of the text is white. I set the level at 30.

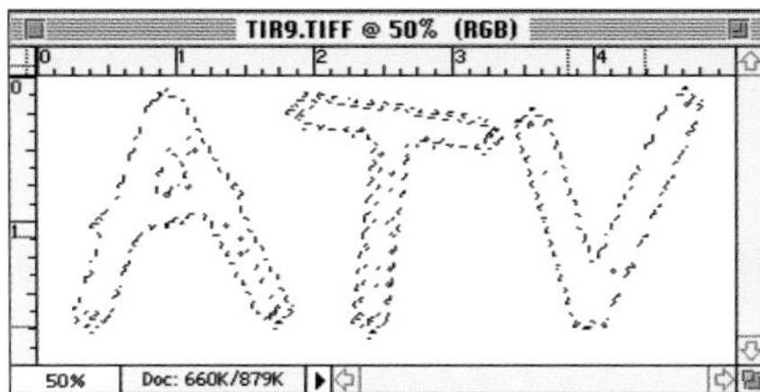


Return to the composite channel, and load the selection of Channel #4 copy. Choose Select➭Feather (1 pixel) to soften the edges.

Change the foreground color to a color for the tracks and fill the selection. The CMYK values for this color are 30, 59, 87, and 44.

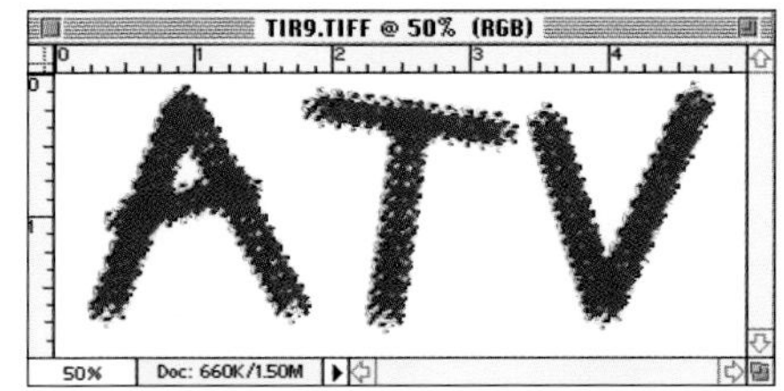


Choose Filter➝Render➝Lighting Effects. Use the Tire Tracks preset file or match these settings. ■

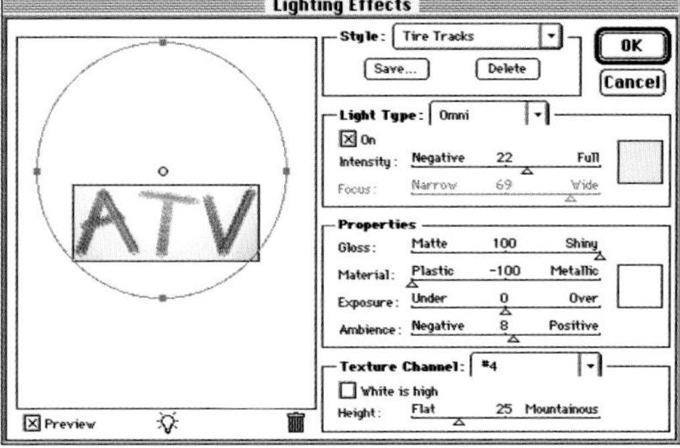

The type treatment for the frustrated. This technique is very easy, so don't let the number of steps intimidate you.

**1** Create a new file, and a new channel (#4). Use the Type tool to enter the text. Something with a little weight will work best since part of the edges will diffuse into the tears. I used Bauhaus at 90 points.

**2** Save the selection to create Channel #5.

**3** Choose Select➛Modify➛Contract. Contract the selection enough to create a good solid edge between the selection and the edge of the type. I chose 6 pixels.

**4** Save the selection to create Channel #6. While still in Channel #4, load the selection Channel #4 to select the type. Then load the selection Channel #6 with Subtract from Selection option turned on. This is the selection you should now have.

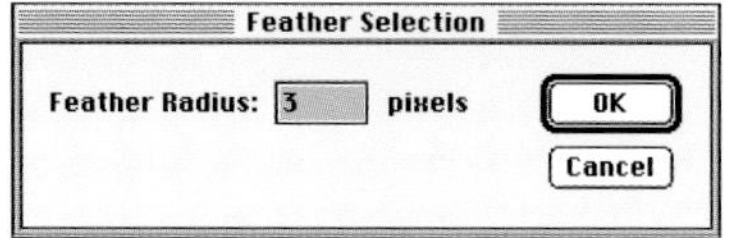


**5** Choose Select➛Feather and "feather" just a little. I chose 3 pixels.

**6** Choose Filter➵Pixelate➵ Crystallize. Pick a medium Cell Size that ruffles the edge of the type similar to what you see in this figure. I chose 5 for my type.

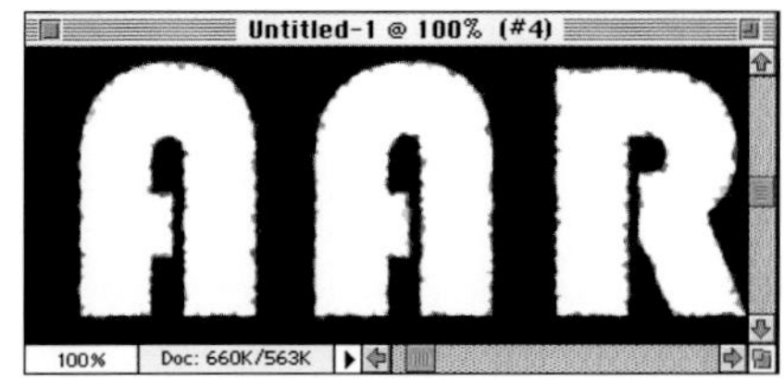


**7** Next, choose Filter➵Noise➵Add Noise Set the Amount near 140. The edges will look like they are beginning to disintegrate.

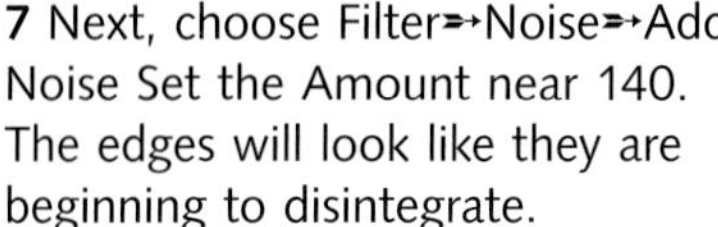

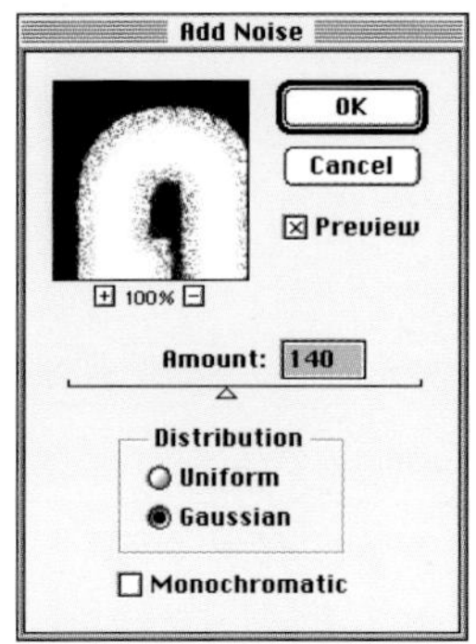


**8** Now choose Filter➵Noise➵ Median (1).

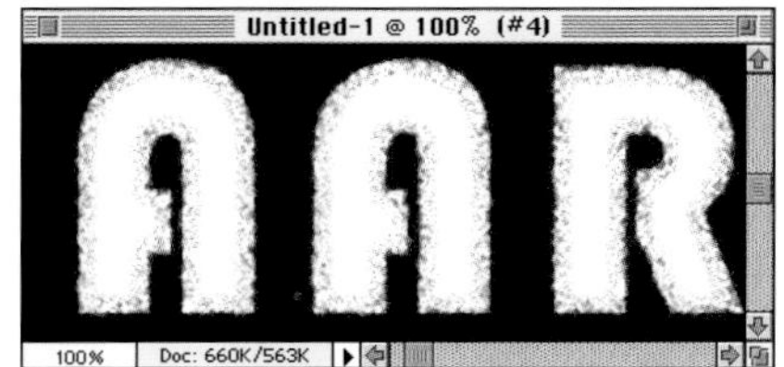


**9** If you want rougher edges, keep the selection active and repeat Steps 6 (use Cell Size of 3) through 8 again. Otherwise, move on.

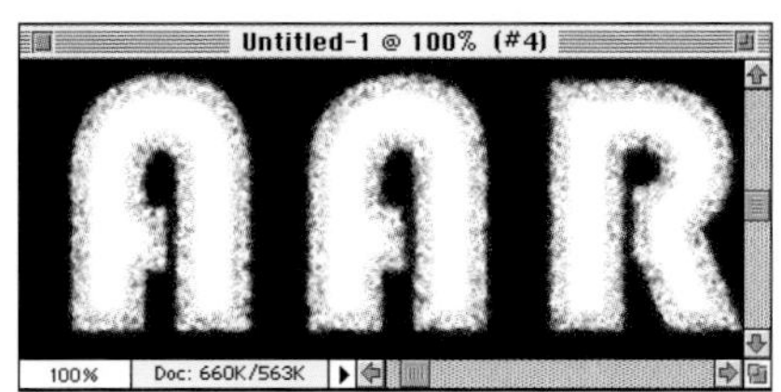


**10** Choose Filter➵Noise➵Add Noise. Again, add just a small amount–about 40 pixels.

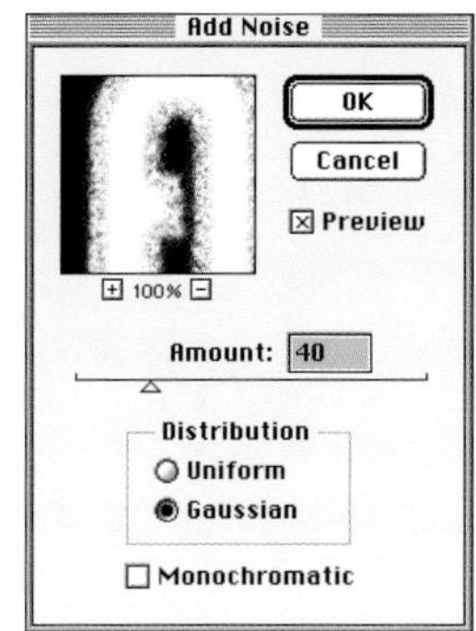

**11** Deselect the type, and make Channel #5 active. Choose Filter➡Pixelate➡Crystallize. Choose a Cell Size similar to the Cell Size you used in Step 6. I chose 5.

**12** Choose Image➡Adjust➡Threshold, and slide the marker to the middle. I set the Threshold Level at 255.

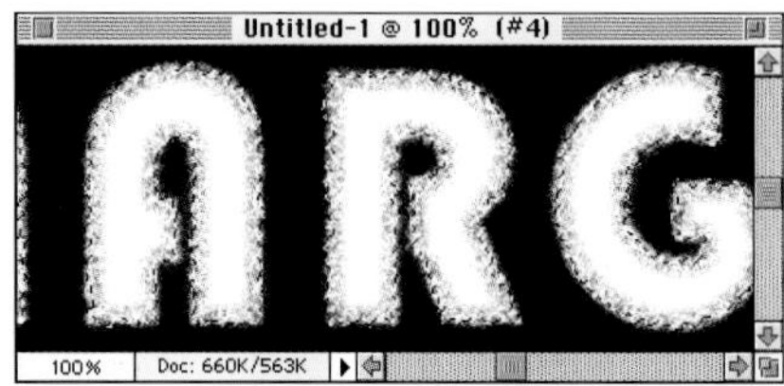


**13** Make Channel #4 the active channel, then load the selection (Channel #5).

**14** Choose Select➡Inverse, and fill the selection with black to harden the edges.

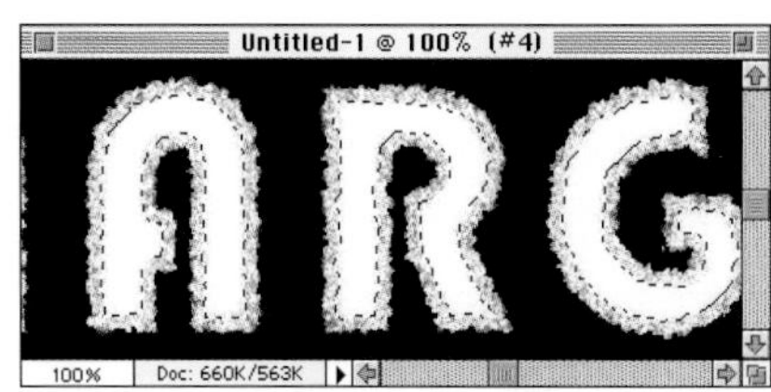


**15** Choose Select➡Inverse again, and then choose Select➡Modify➡Contract. Contract the selection the same amount as you did in Step 3.

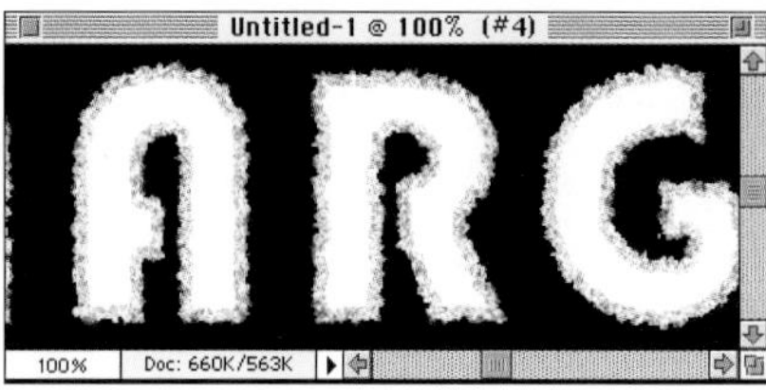


**16** Fill this selection with white to harden the inside edges.

**17** Return to the composite channel, and make a new layer (Layer 1). Load the selection Channel #4.

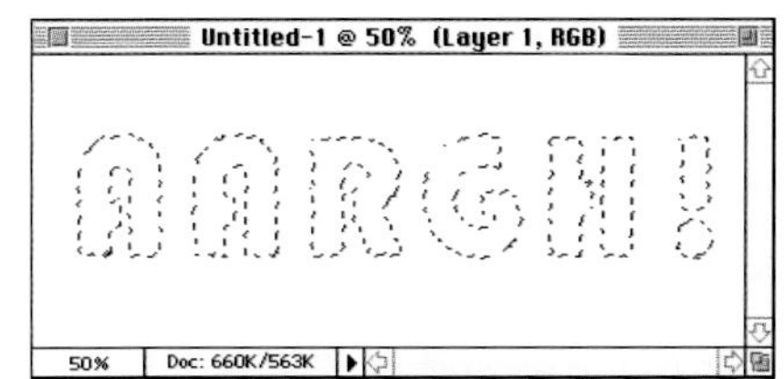


**18** Fill the selection with white. Nothing should happen in the image window because right now you have white on white.

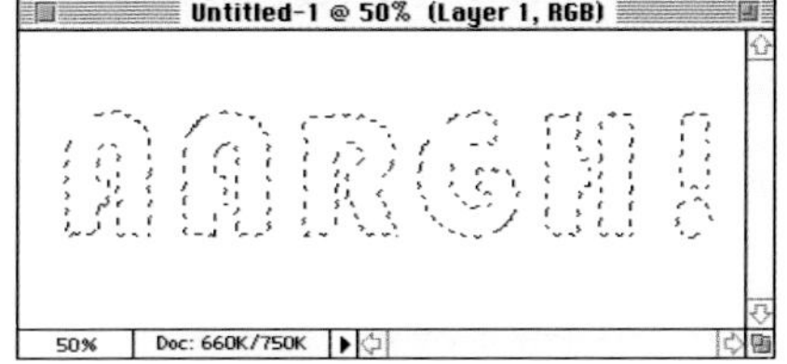


**19** Make another layer (Layer 2), then move that layer below Layer 1.

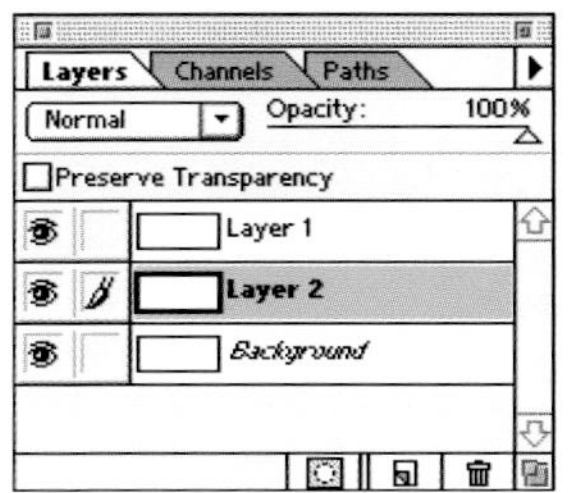


**20** The selection should still be active. Change the foreground color to black. Choose Select➛Feather and feather the selection just one pixel.

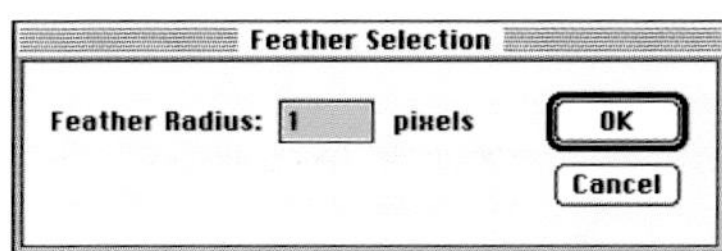


**21** Fill the selection with black.

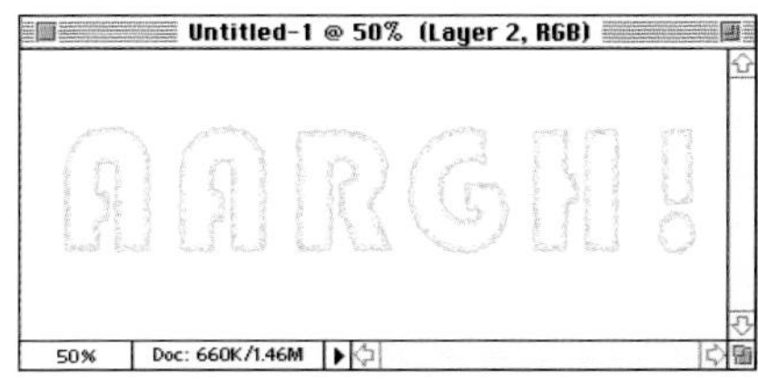


**22** Select the Move tool and use the arrow keys to move the selection one or two keystrokes to the right and one or two keystrokes down.

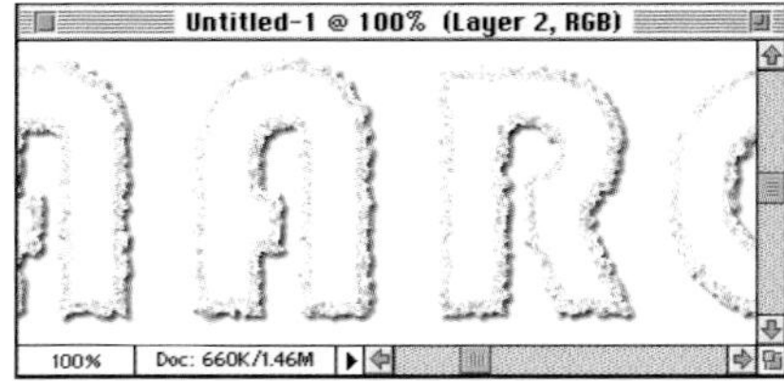

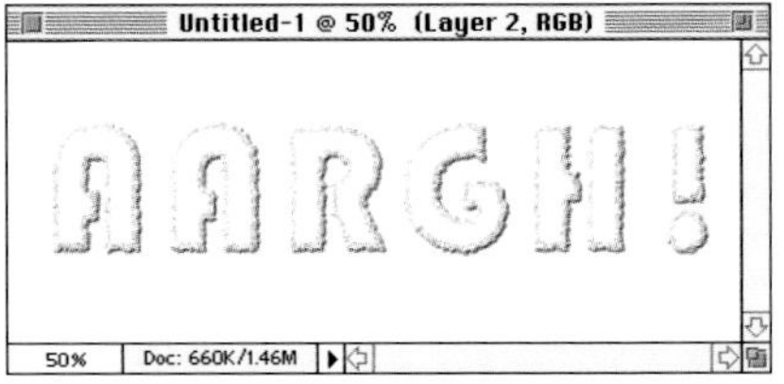


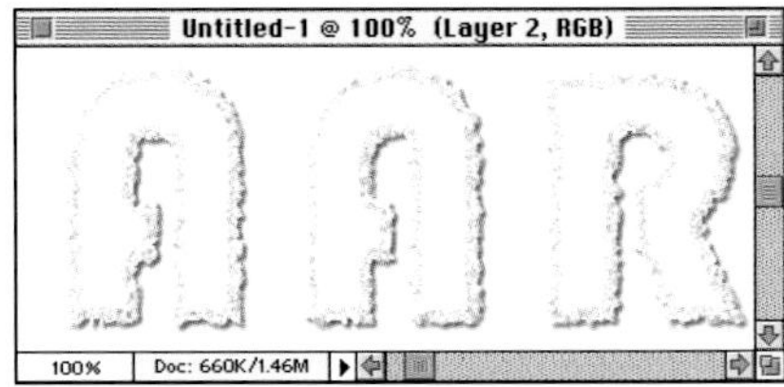


**23** That's the type.

TIP **If you want to soften the contrast, use the Opacity slider on the Layers palette for Layer 2.** ■

A few fancy selections serve up this delicious effect.

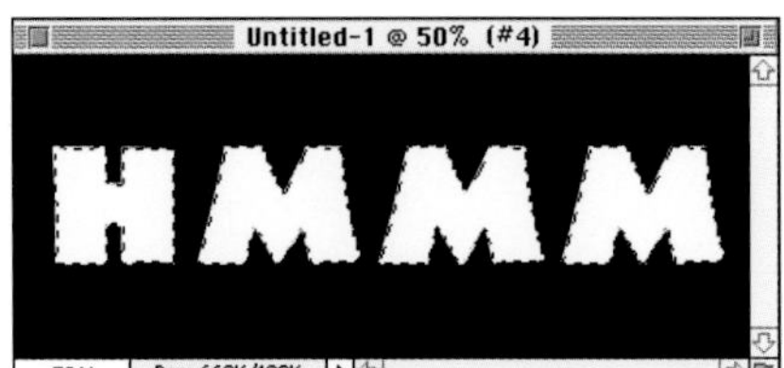


1 Create a new file, and a new channel (#4). Use the Type tool to enter text into the new channel: the bigger the font, the bigger the waffle. The fattest font I had was Informal Black (80 points).

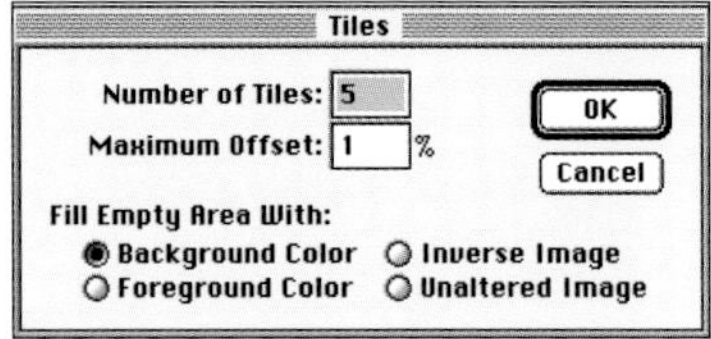


2 Make a copy of Channel #4 to create Channel #4 copy. Choose Filter➛Stylize➛Tiles. The first setting in this filter will determine scale of the pancake grid. I set the Number of Tiles to 5. Keep the Maximum offset percentage at 1 to keep everything in line.

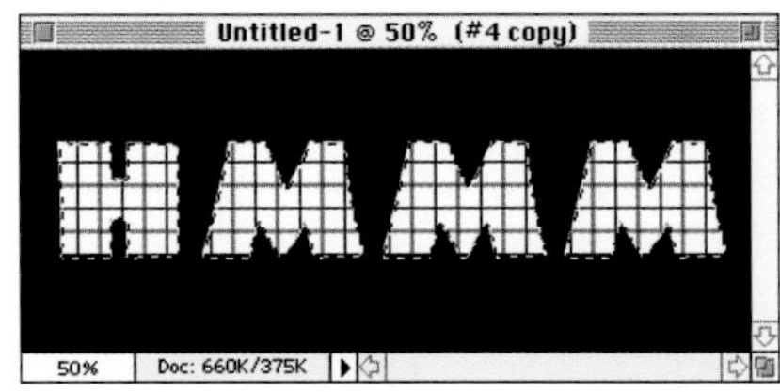


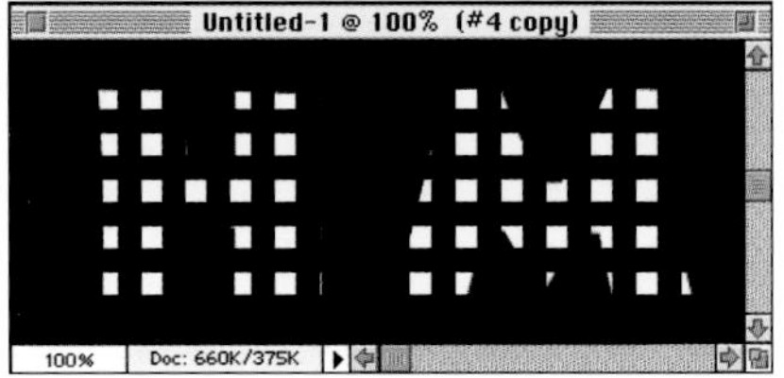


3 Choose Select➛Modify➛Expand (1 pixel). Apply Filter➛Other➛Minimum (Radius: 5). These commands build the hollows. Deselect the text.

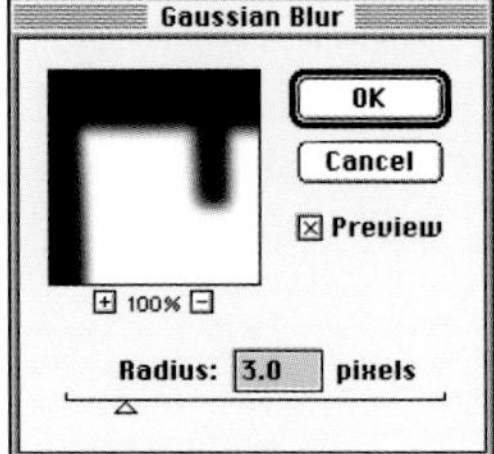


4 Make another copy of Channel #4. You should now be in Channel #4 copy 2. Choose Filter➛Blur➛Gaussian Blur (Radius: 3).

TOOLBOX

Waffle (Lighting Style Preset)

**5** Load the selection Channel #4 copy, and choose Select➸Modify➸Smooth (1 pixel). Then Select➸Feather (2 pixels). Change the foreground color to a medium gray. Fill the selection, and then deselect it.

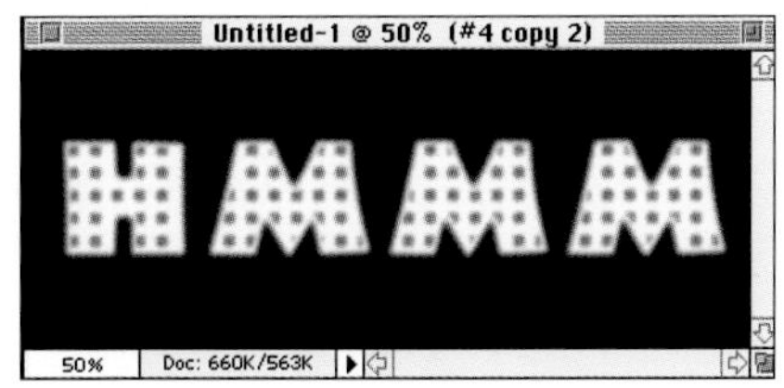


**6** Return to the composite channel, and load the selection Channel #4. Choose Select➸Modify➸Expand (1 pixel), and Select➸Modify➸Smooth (1 pixel).

**7** Change the foreground color to the CMYK values 11, 15, 70, 2. Fill the selection with this color.

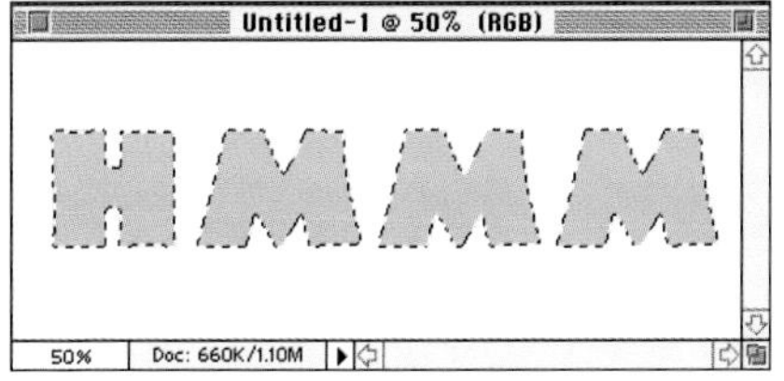


**8** Choose Filter➸Render➸Lighting Effects. Click on the Style pop-up menu and find the Waffle preset. If you haven't loaded the presets from the CD, then you can match the settings you see here. Don't forget the Texture channel.

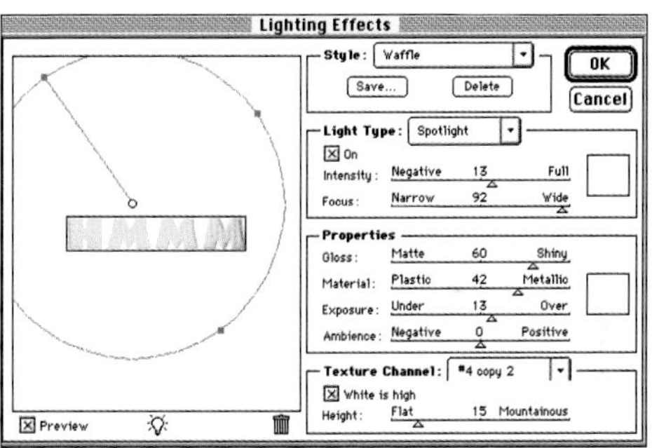


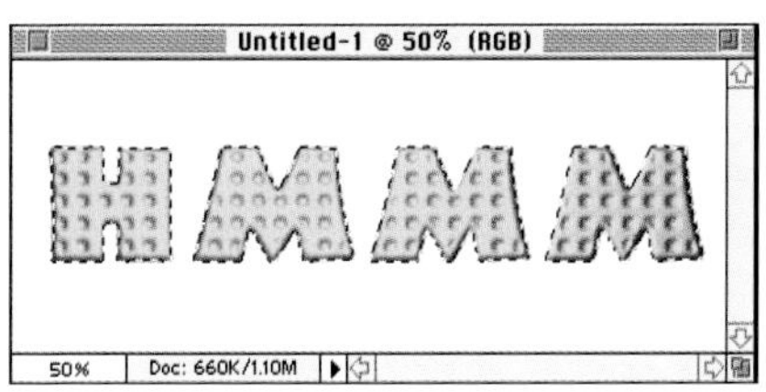

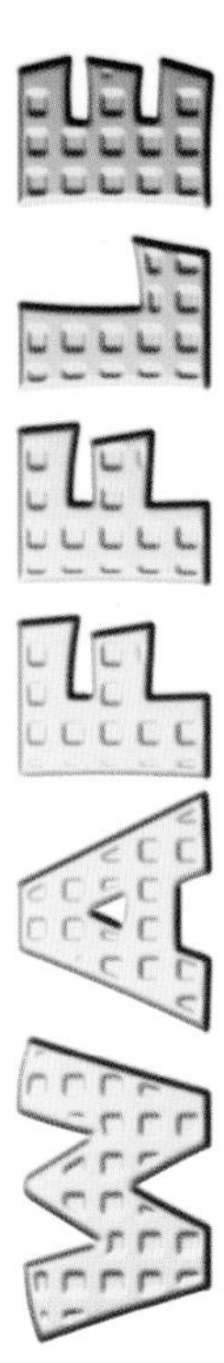


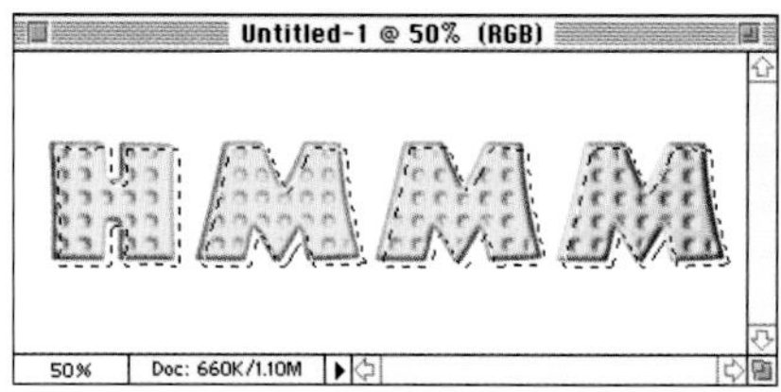


**9** Put down that fork, there is still one more touch. Keep the selection active, and select the Marquee tool. Move the selection using the arrow keys. Press the right arrow and down arrow keys two times each. I am setting up a selection for a shadow.

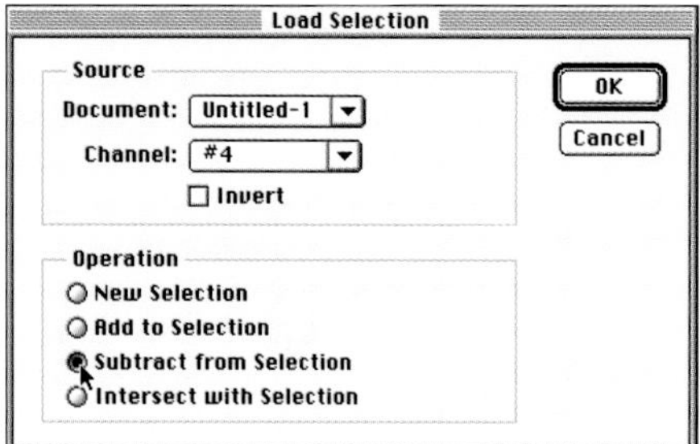


**10** Load the selection Channel #4 (the original text channel), but choose the Subtract from Selection option in the Load Selection dialog box. The part of the selection that was on top of the letters is cut out.

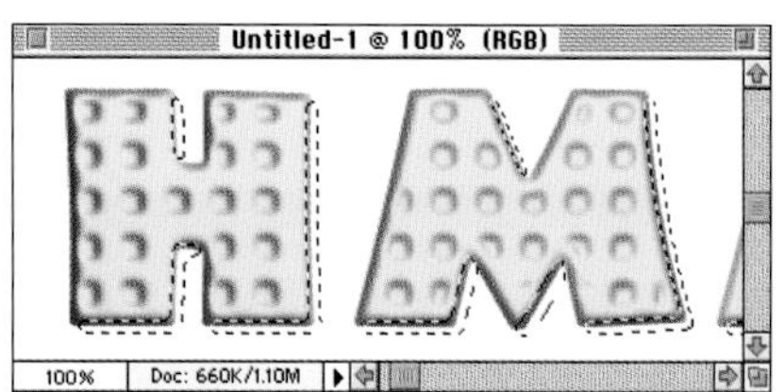


**11** Next, choose Select➝Feather (2 pixels). Again, use the arrow keys to move the selection. Up one keystroke and left one keystroke.

**12** Change the foreground color to 70% gray, and fill the selection. Deselect the text, and pour on the syrup.

## Variations

Okay, so you probably wouldn't eat these. Load the selection Channel #4 copy, and choose Image➸Adjust➸Hue/Saturation. Turn on the Colorize option and use the markers to change the color of the hollows. Then load the selection Channel #4 copy 2, and change the color of the rest of the type in the same way.

Follow the variation above, but choose Filter➸Stylize➸Find Edges, rather than changing the colors in the selections.

To make lead waffles, load the selection Channel #4, and choose Filter➸Other➸High Pass. I set the Radius in this example to 12 pixels. ■

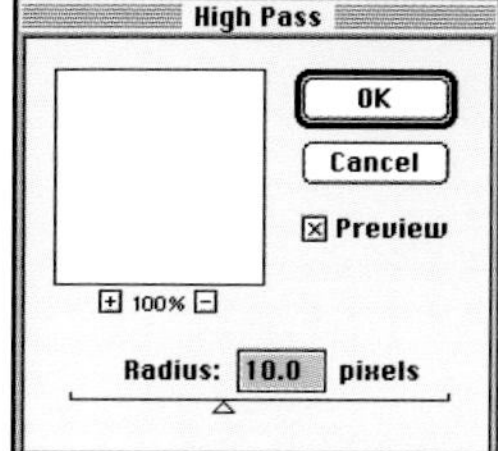

The new Grid feature in Photoshop 4.0 helps make a "seamless" pattern to fill this text.

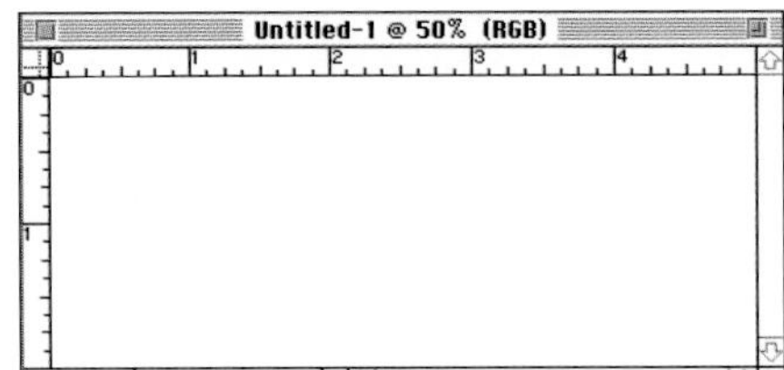


**1** Create a new file. Change the foreground color to a color for the background. Fill the Background layer with this color. I left it white.

**2** Make a new layer (Layer 1).

**3** You can draw any image you want for the wallpaper pattern. I loaded the Assorted Brushes file into the Brushes palette and used the eye paintbrush.

**Don't forget that you can define your own brush using an image that you have created. See your Photoshop user manual to find out how to define a brush.**

**4** Change the Foreground color to 80% black, and click in the image area with the eye paintbrush.

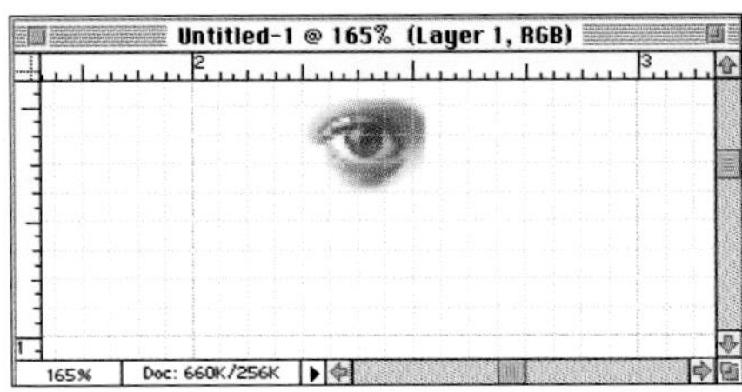


**5** Choose View➛Show Grid, and then choose File➛Preferences➛Guides and Grid. Change the Subdivisions amount to something that divides your image into four or five boxes in either direction. The grid will change as you try different Subdivision values. I set it at 16. After clicking OK, choose View➛Snap to Grid.

**6** Select the Move tool and move the image until the upper-left part of the image locks into a corner of the grid.

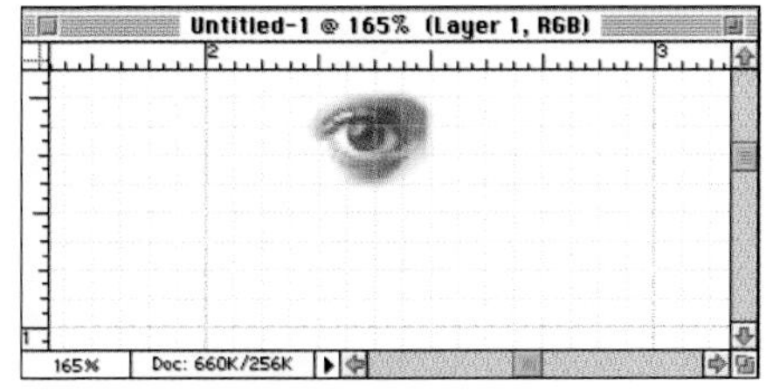


**7** Duplicate Layer 1 (Layer 1 copy). Use the Move tool and move the image to the right and down any distance that you like. As you move the image, let it bounce from gridline to gridline. Keep track of the number of lines you move the image. I moved this image four lines to the right and two down.

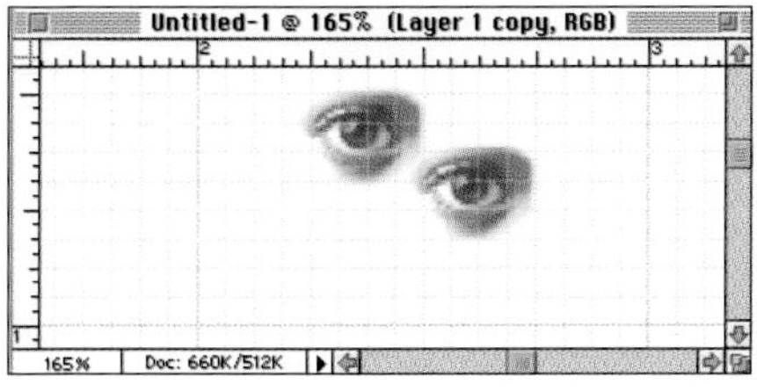


**8** Choose Layer→Merge Down to press the two eyes together into Layer 1. Layer 1 copy will merge into Layer 1, so you can duplicate Layer 1 again to create a new Layer 1 copy.

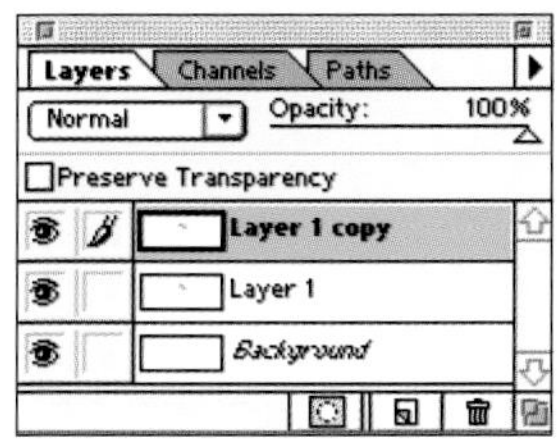


**9** Use the Move tool and move the image the same number of gridlines down as in Step 7. Also, move the image the same number of gridlines to the left as you moved it to the right in Step 7. Choose Layer→Merge Down.

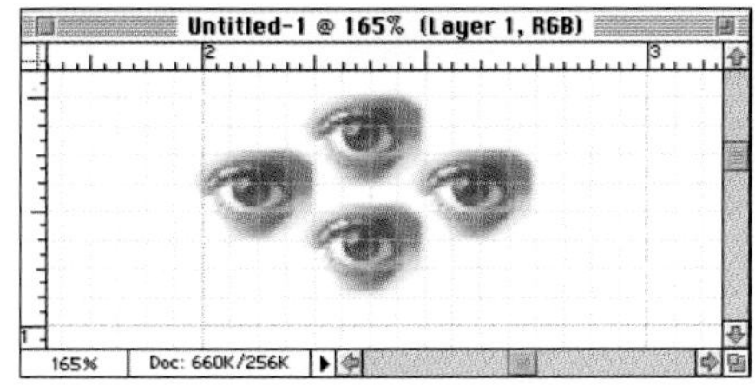

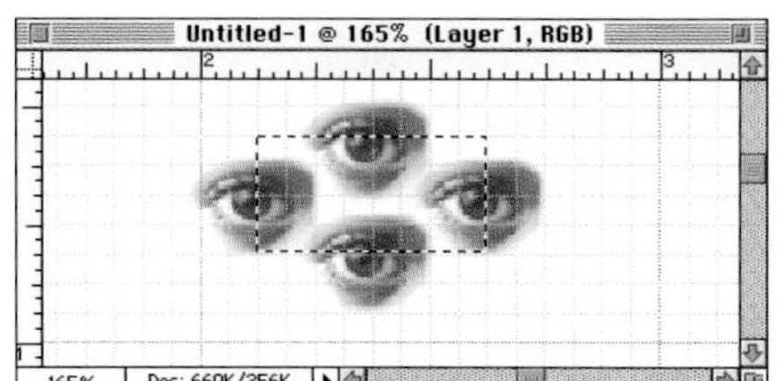


**10** Choose View➞Snap to Grid to turn off the grid snap. Select the Marquee tool and drag a selection like the one shown in the figure. It is very important that the top of the selection runs through the top image in the same place as the bottom of the selection runs through the bottom image. Treat the left and right edges of the selection in the same way.

**11** Choose Edit➞Define Pattern to set this selection as the wallpaper pattern. Deselect the selection.

**12** Delete Layer 1. Fill the Background layer with white (if it isn't already). Turn off the grid by choosing View➞Hide Grid.

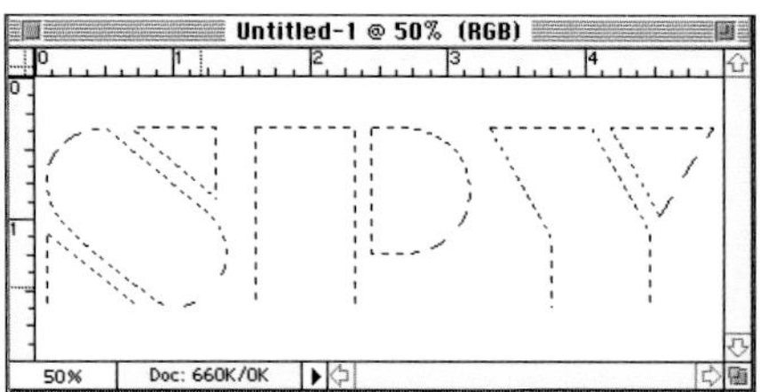


**13** Then use the Type Mask tool to enter the text. Use something like Braggadocio that has a lot of room for the pattern (120 points).

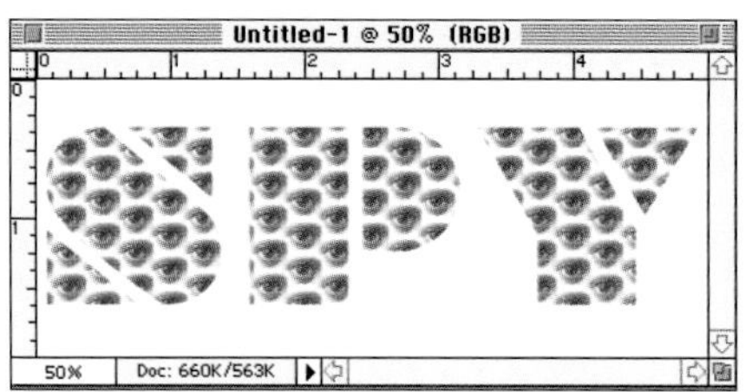


**14** Choose Edit➞Fill, and then choose Pattern from the Contents pop-up menu.

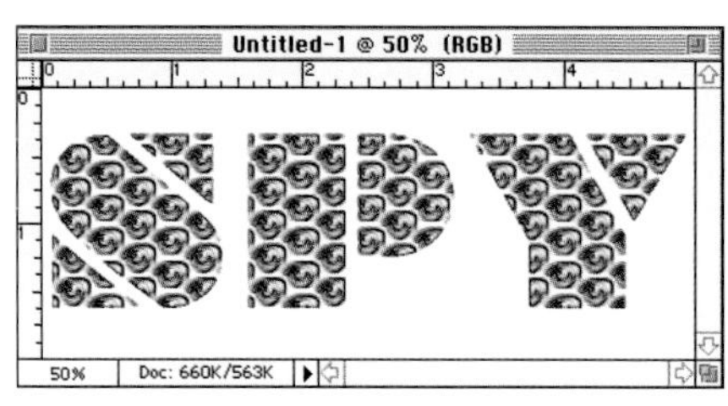


**15** I couldn't resist a filter. I applied Filter➞Stylize➞Find Edges.

## VARIATIONS

You also can make an arrangement of images, like this...

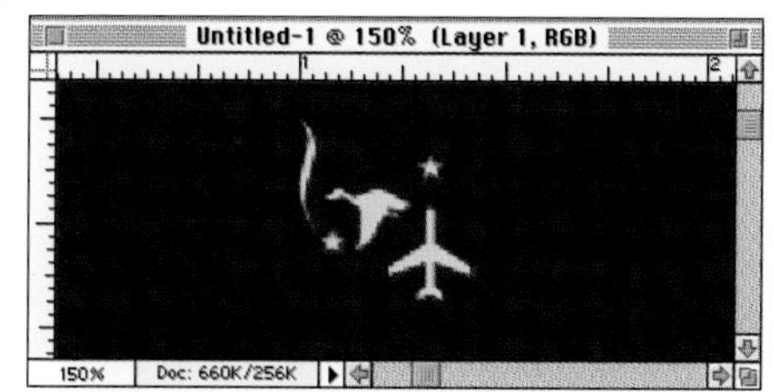


...into a pattern using the same steps listed previously. Just treat the arrangement as if it were a single image.

If you make the Background layer invisible before Step 11, then you can define a pattern with a transparent background. This enables you to place a pattern over type you have already created—like this type that already has a texture.

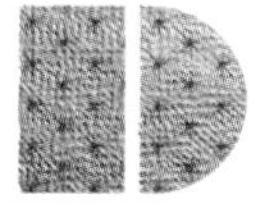
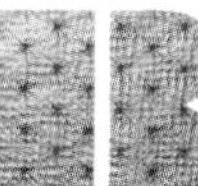

Photoshop contains a set of seamless patterns that you can use to make wallpaper. Follow this path to find the PostScript Patterns folder: Adobe Photoshop 4.0➪Goodies➪Brushes and Patterns➪Postcript Patterns.Choose one of the patterns to open. I opened the Mali primitive file.If the Rasterize Generic EPS Format dialog box opens, click OK to accept the values it provides for the settings.

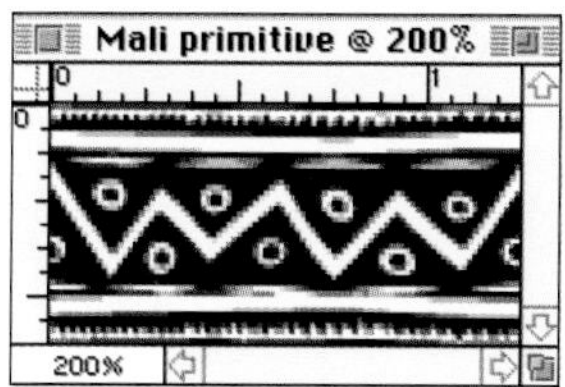


Choose Select➪All, and then choose Edit➪Define Pattern. Close the file, create a new file and follow the instruction in Steps 13 and 14. I also colorized the image (Image➪Adjust➪Hue /Saturation). ■

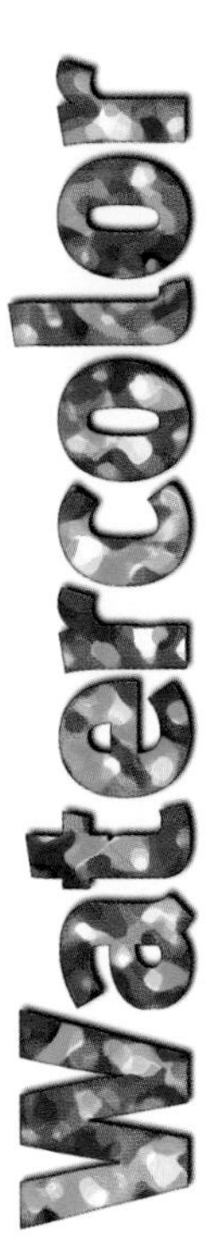


This effect uses the Median filter to blur colored areas together. It works much better in an RGB file than a CMYK file because of the brighter RGB gamut.

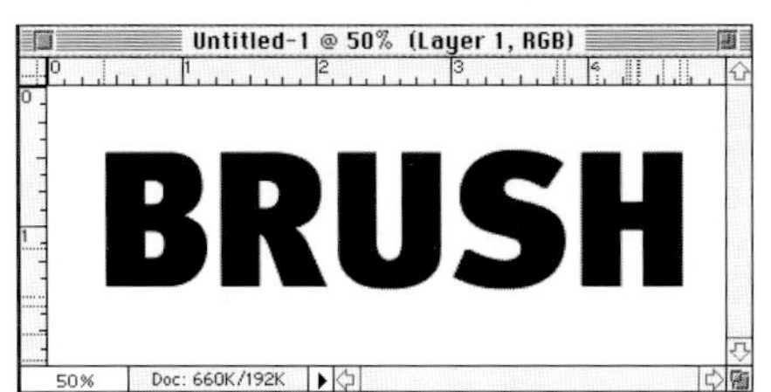


**1** Create a new file. Use the Type tool to enter the text. MetaPlus-Black at 100 points was used for this effect. The type will be placed automatically on a new layer (Layer 1).

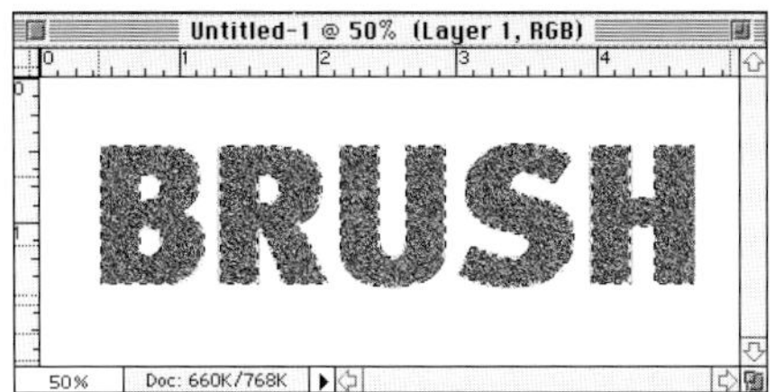


**2** Load the selection Layer 1 Transparency. To break up the flat color and to add some new colors, choose Filter➛Noise➛Add Noise. I set the Amount at 600.

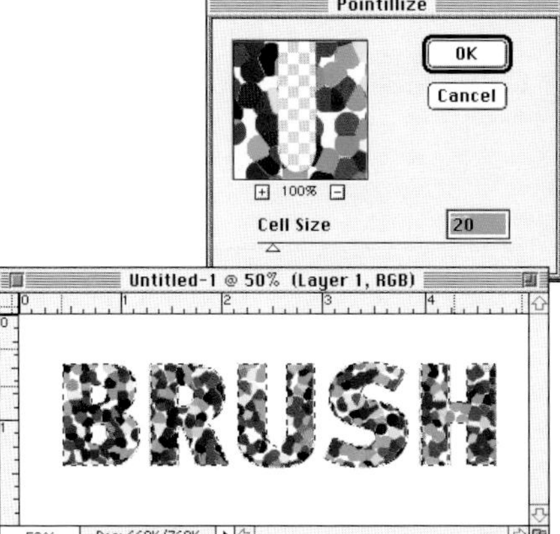


**3** Choose Filter➛Pixelate➛Pointillize. Choose a medium-to-large Cell Size. I used 20. Find a Cell Size that fits your type like this.

**4** The black areas in the type will take away from the watercolor look. To get rid of them, choose Image➛Adjust➛Replace Color. Now get the eyedropper in the dialog box and click a black dot in the image window.

**5** Use the Fuzziness slider to control how much of the other blacks are selected. If the Selection button is on, then the white areas represent the areas that will be affected by changing the sliders below. If you set the Fuzziness to high, then when you change the black in the next step you may also change some of the other colors. So, set the Fuzziness high enough to select as much black as possible without affecting the other colors very much.

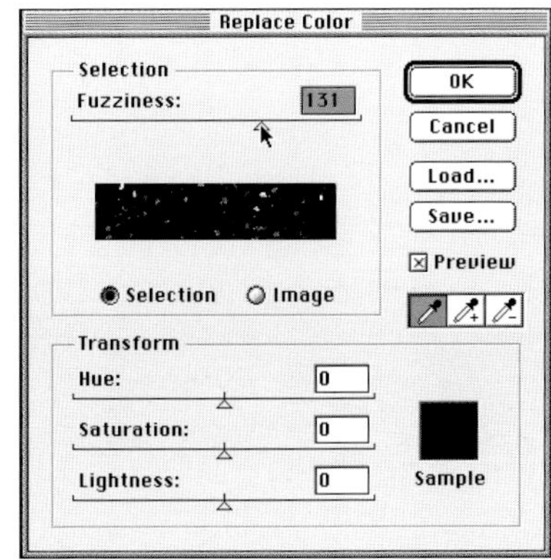

**You will still be able to adjust the Fuzziness setting after moving the markers in the next step.**

**6** To change the blacks to another color, slide the Saturation marker all the way to the right. Then use the Hue and Lightness markers to find a new color.

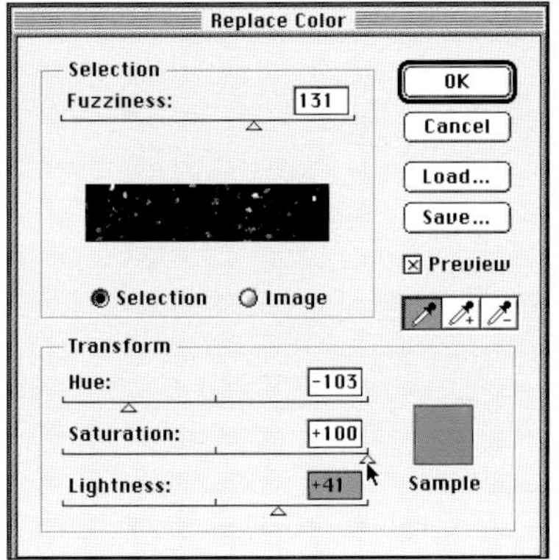


**7** Choose Filter➛Noise➛Median. This filter is going to blend and overlap the dots made with the Pointillize filter. Play with the setting. This image was made by setting the Radius to 14.

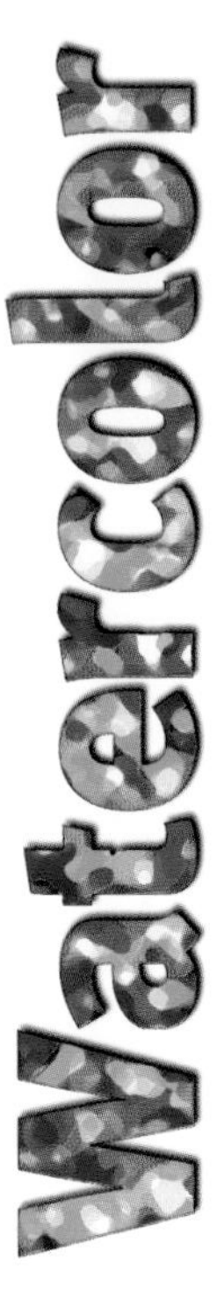


## VARIATIONS

Variations abound for this effect. Here are two minor variations that you may prefer to the hard-edged type above.

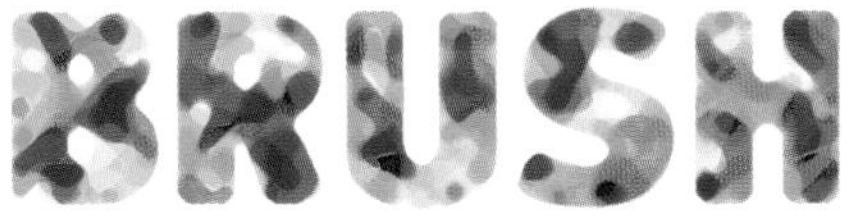


**1** Complete all of the steps above, then choose Layer➞Merge Down. Deselect the text. Choose Filter➞Noise➞Median again and use a low setting to smooth the edges of the type. I used a Radius of 6 for this image.

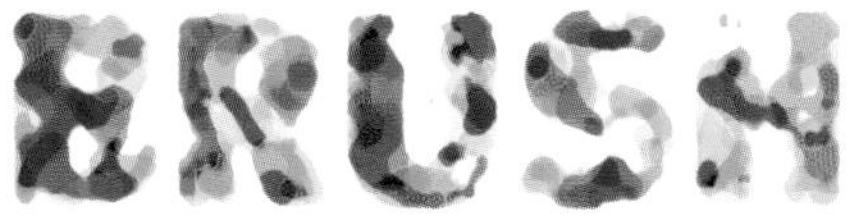


**2** After Step 3, choose Layer➞Merge Down. After you complete the rest of the steps, your type will look something like this.

Here are some other variations that are take-offs from the steps above.

**3** Do Steps 1 through 7. Then choose Filter➞Stylize➞Find Edges to turn the seeping-color spots into lines.

Then choose Filter➞Other➞Minimum. You probably will not want to use a Radius higher than 1 or 2. If you do then the lines will blur together as they become dark and thick.

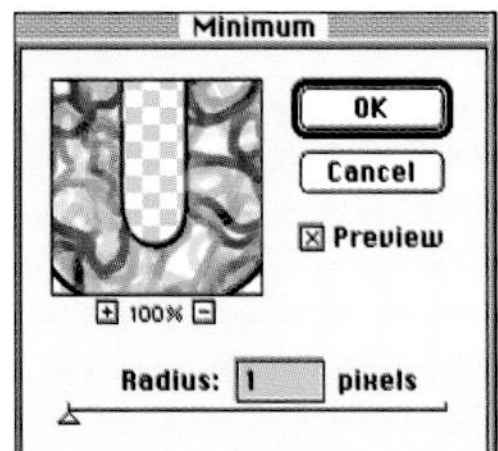


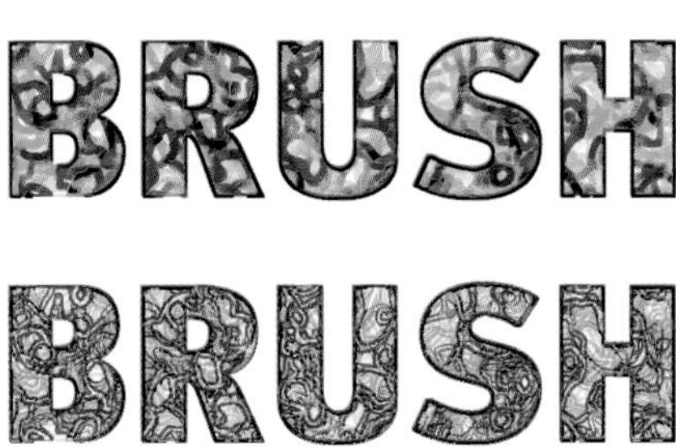


**4** Keep going. Again, choose Filter➞Stylize➞Find Edges to build patterns into the type.

**5** For a variation of that variation, choose Layer➜Merge Down after Step 7, and deselect the text. Then do the steps for Variations 3 and 4.

**6** Do the steps for Variations 3 and 4 and try this: choose Filter➜Pixelate➜Fragment to get some funky patterns.

**7** Instead of applying the Fragment filter above, choose Merge➜Down. Then choose our friend Filter➜Noise➜Median. For this image I used a Radius of 6.

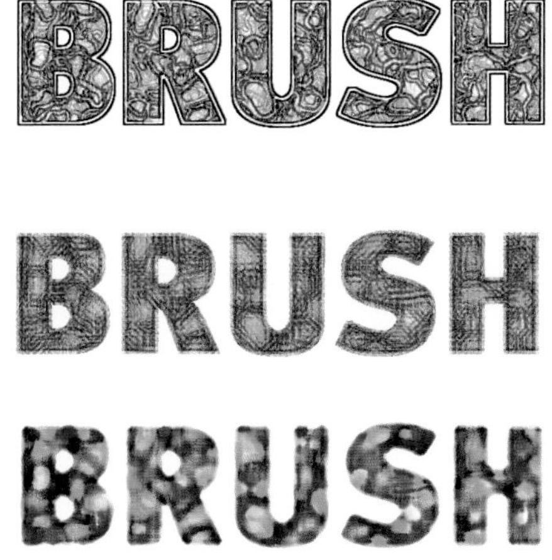

**8** If you use colored type in Step 1 and choose a low noise value such as 50 in Step 2, then completing the rest of the steps will give you something like this. ■

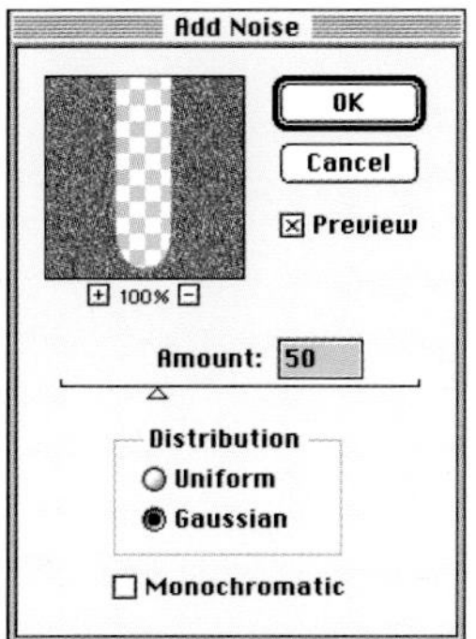

For this woven effect, you need to create the texture first, and then turn it into type.

**1** Create a new file. Double-click the Marquee tool to select it and make the Marquee Options floating palette active. Make sure that you have selected the rectangular Marquee tool.

**2** Change the Style to Fixed Size. The Width and Height dimensions determine the size of the weave. Enter the same number for both dimensions. I used 15 pixels.

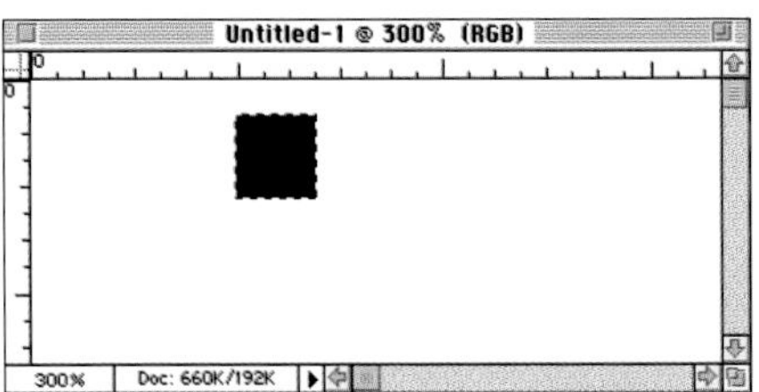


**3** Zoom in to any area of the blank image area. I zoomed in to 300%. With the Marquee tool click once in the image area. Fill the square selection with black.

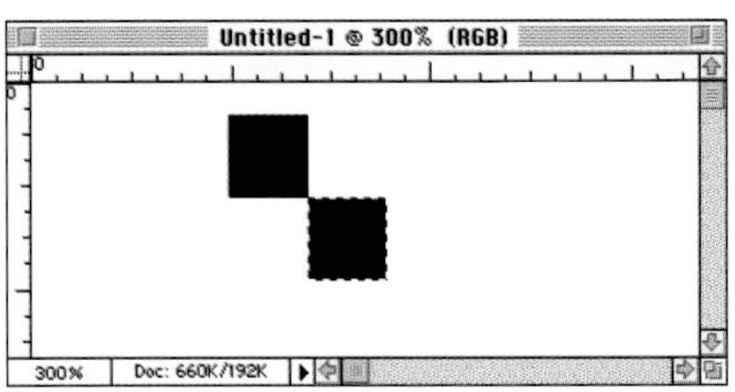


**4** Then move the selection, with the Marquee tool, until the upper-left corner of the selection meets the lower-right corner of the black square. Fill the selection with black.

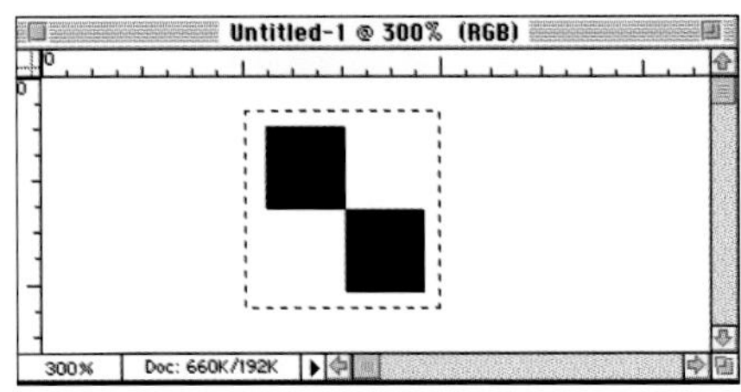


**5** Find the Marquee Options floating palette again and change the Style back to Normal. Drag a selection to encompass both black squares.

**6** Then choose Layer➼Transform➼ Numeric and enter 45° in the Rotate box. Turn off the Position, Scale, and Skew options.

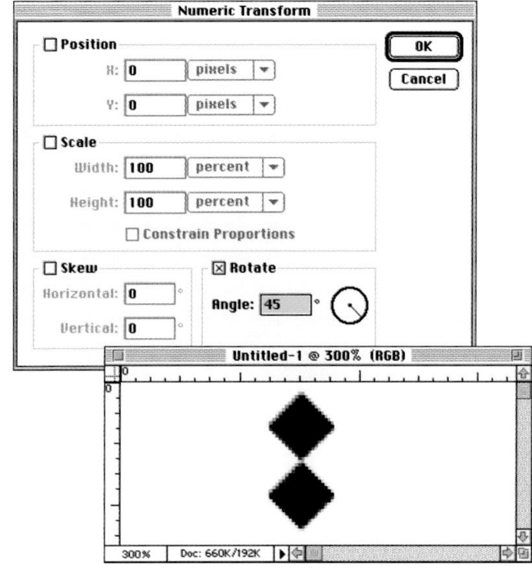


**7** One more time, find the Marquee Options floating palette. Change the Style to Constrain Aspect Ratio. Leave the Width and Height values at 1.

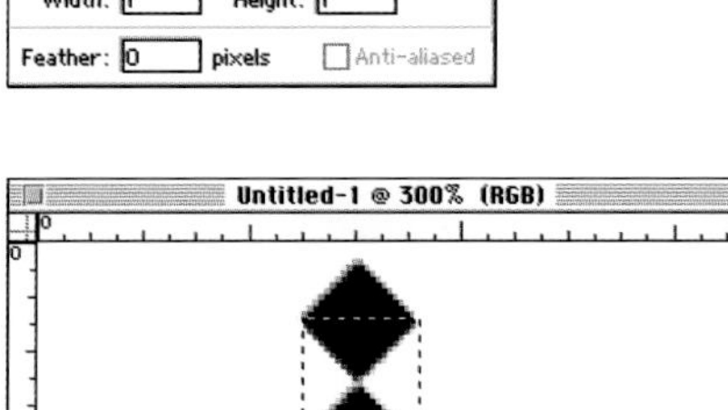


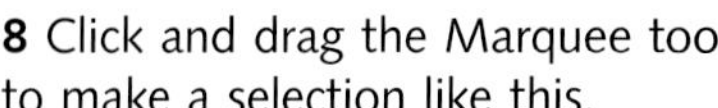

**8** Click and drag the Marquee tool to make a selection like this.

**9** Choose Edit➼Define Pattern. Nothing happens, but the active selection has been saved as a pattern.

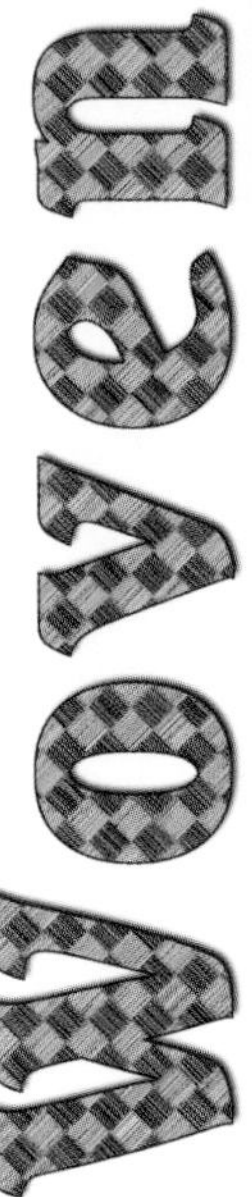


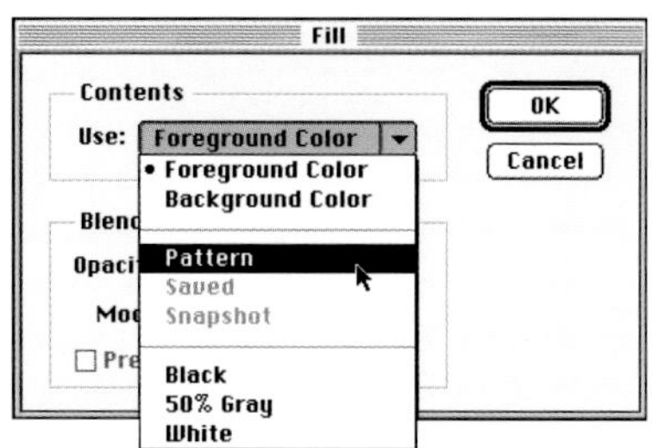


10 Choose Select➛All, and then choose Edit➛Fill. Change the Contents option to Pattern. Deselect the selection.

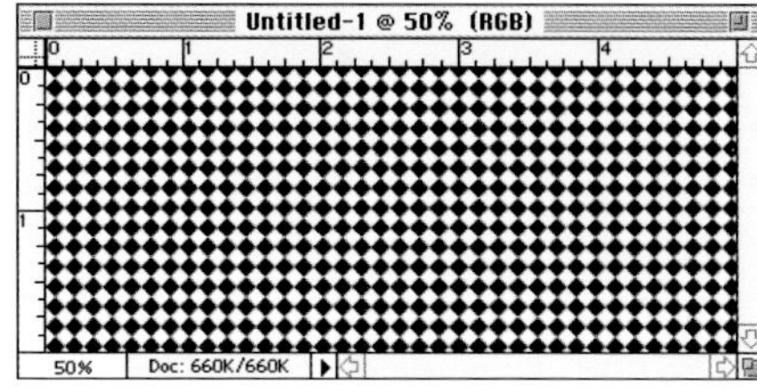


Click OK.

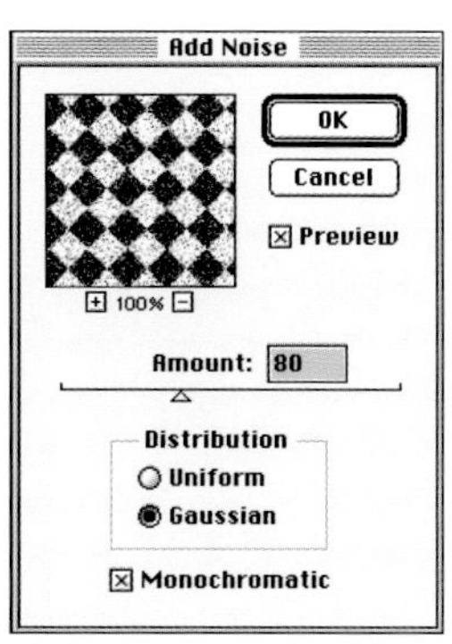


11 Add a little noise to the checkers by choosing Filter➛Noise➛Add Noise. I set the Amount at 80. Turn on the Monochromatic option. The noise helps the next filter do its job.

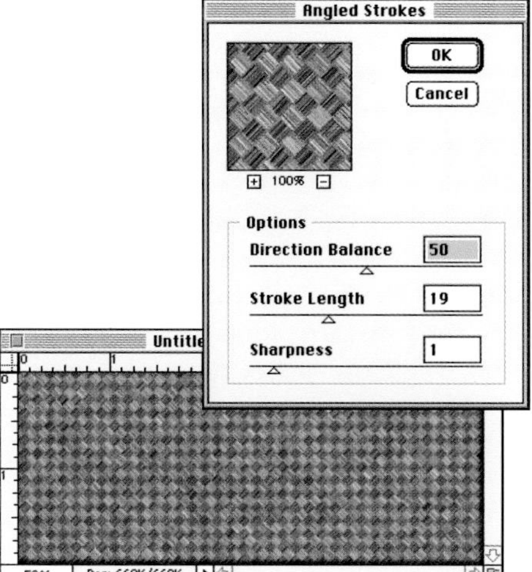


12 Apply Filter➛Brush Strokes➛Angled Strokes. Use these settings: Direction Balance, 50; Stroke Length, 19; and Sharpness, 1.

**13** Now, we need some type. Use the Type Mask tool to enter the text. This font is Seagull Heavy at 100 points.

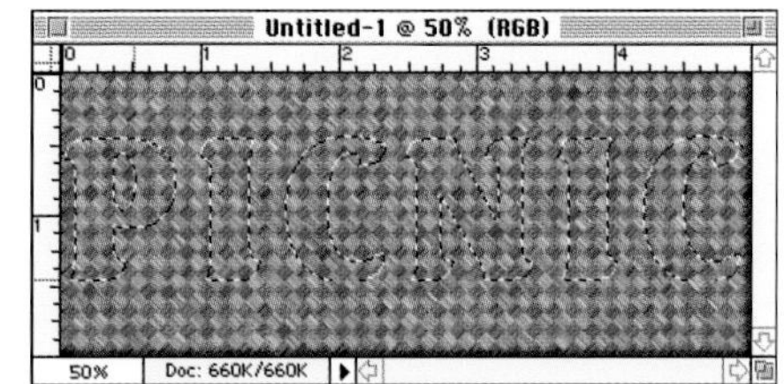


**14** Choose Select=›Inverse and press Delete.Then choose Select=› Inverse again to select the type.

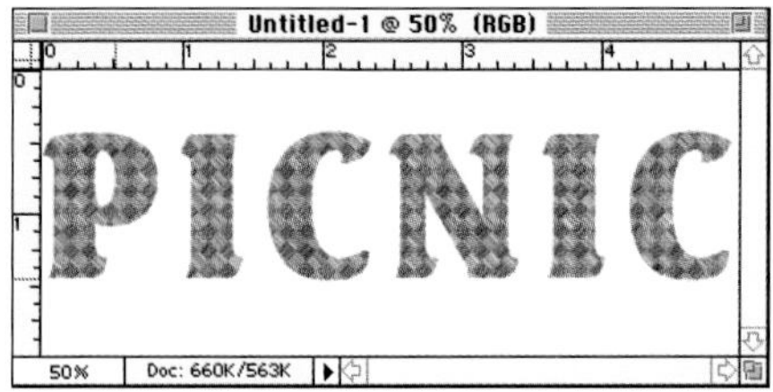


**15** To add some color, choose Image=›Adjust=›Hue/Saturation. Now turn on the Colorize option and find a color for the texture.

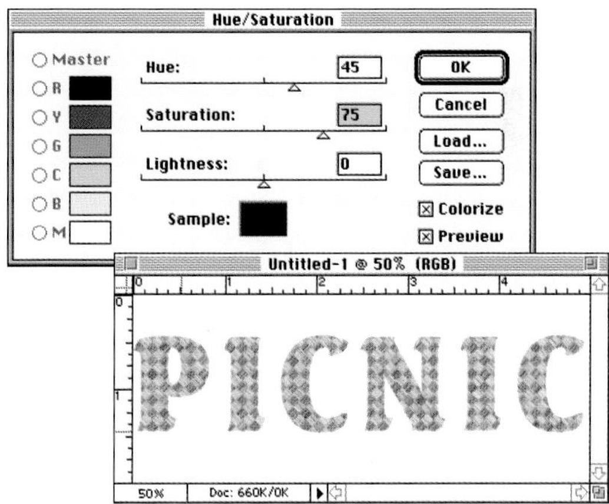


**16** For some fine-tuning, choose Image=›Adjust=›Levels. Use the Input markers to adjust the values in the weave. I set the Input markers at 21, 0.88, and 255. For extra contrast, click the Auto button. ■

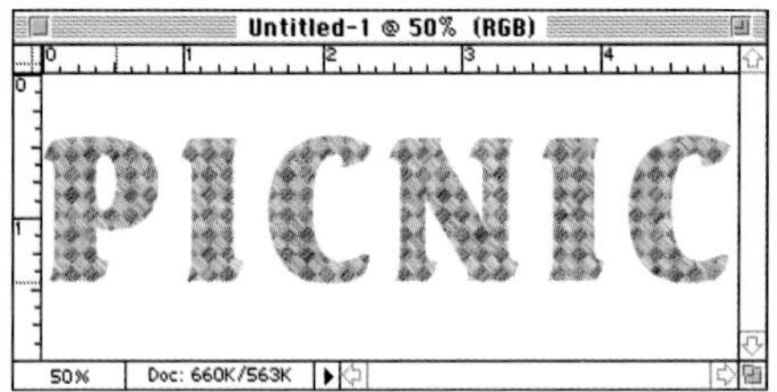

# Appendix A

## Contributor's Listing

The following companies have provided the software, filters, and stock photography for the CD-ROM that is included with this book. For more information on their products, use the contact information listed here.

### Filters

**Alien Skin Software**

2522 Clark Avenue

Raleigh, NC 27607

voice: 919/832-4124

fax: 919/832-4065

email: alienskin@aol.com

On the CD: Cutout filter demo

**Andromeda Software**

699 Hampshire Road, Suite 109

Westlake Village

Thousand Oaks, CA 91361

voice: 805/379-4109, 800/547-0055

fax: 805/379-5253

email: andromeda@aol.com

On the CD: Series 1-4 filters demo

**MetaTools, Inc.**

6303 Carpinteria Avenue

Carpinteria, CA 93013

voice: 805/566-6200

fax: 805/566-6385

web: http://www.metatools.com

On the CD: KPT filter hub demo

**Xaos Tools, Inc.**

600 Townsend Street, Suite 270 East

San Francisco, CA 94103

voice: 415/487-7000, 800/289-9267

fax: 415/558-9886

email: macinfo@xaostools.com

On the CD: Terrazo, Paint Alchemy, Typecaster demos

## Software

**Adobe Systems Incorporated**

345 Park Avenue

San Jose, CA 95110-2704

voice: 408/536-6000

fax: 408/537-6000

web: http://www.adobe.com

On the CD: Acrobat Reader, After Effects, Dimensions, Illustrator, Photoshop, Premiere, Streamline, TextureMaker demos

**Affinity Microsystems Ltd.**

934 Pearl Street, Suite H

Boulder, CO 80302

voice: 800/367-6771

fax: 303/442-4999

On the CD: TempoEZ demo

**Equilibrium**

475 Gate Five Road, Suite 225

Sausalito, CA 94965

voice: 800/524-8651, 415/332-4343

fax: 415/332-4433

On the CD: DeBabelizer lite (full working version), DeBabelizer demo

**Jawai Interactive**

501 E. Fourth Street, #511

Austin, TX 78701

voice: 512/469-0502

email: jawai@aol.com

On the CD: Screen Caffeine Pro demo, Java Beat demo

**Macromedia, Incorporated**

600 Townsend Street

San Francisco, CA 94103

voice: 415/252-2000

fax: 415/626-0554

web: http://macromedia.com

On the CD: Director, Fontographer, xRes demos

**MicroFrontier**

P.O. Box 71190

Des Moines, IA 50322

voice: 515/270-8109, 800/388-8109

fax: 515/278-6828

email: Mfrontier@aol.com

On the CD: ColorIt demo, plus patterns



**Specular**

479 West Street

Amherst, MA 01002

voice: 413/253-3100, 800/433-7732

fax: 413/253-0540

email: specular@applelink.apple.com

web: http://www.specular.com

On the CD: InifiD, LogoMotion, TextureScape demos

## Images

**PhotoDisc Inc.**

2013 Fourth Avenue

Fourth Floor

Seattle, WA 98121

voice: 206/441-9355, 800/528-3472

fax: 206/441-9379

web: http://www.photodisc.com

**Image Club Graphics**

729 Twenty-Fourth Avenue, SE

Calgary, AB CANADA

T2G 5K8

voice: 403/262-8008, 800/661-9410

fax: 403/261-7013

web: http://www.adobe.com/imageclub

Used with express permission.

Adobe® and Image Club Graphics™

are trademarks of Adobe Systems

Incorporated.



**Digital Stock**

400 S. Sierra Avenue, Suite 100

Solana Beach, CA 92075-2262

voice: 619/794-4040, 800/545-4514

fax: 619/794-4041

web: http://www.digitalstock.com

**D'Pix**

Division of Amber Productions

414 W. Fourth Avenue

Columbus, OH 43201

voice: 614/299-7192

fax: 614/294-0002

# Appendix B

## What's on the CD-ROM

The CD-ROM included with this book is full of filters, images, and software applications for you to try. It is also where you will find the special preset files to be used with the effects described in this book.

The CD-ROM that comes with this book is both Macintosh and Windows CD-ROM compatible. Please note: There are several demos and tryouts available for Macintosh users that are not available for Windows users, and vice versa. This means one of two things: either the product has not been created for that platform, or a version of the product is being created but is not yet completed.

I suggest that you refer to the READ ME and other information files which are included in the demo software program's folder. Also, visit the corporate Web sites; the URLs are noted in the Contributors Listing (Appendix A). There are often demos of new software available for downloading and tryout.

The contents of the CD-ROM are divided into four folders: Type Magic Presets, Filters, Software, and Images. The following is a brief description of the folder contents.

### Type Magic Presets

Inside the Type Magic Presets folder you will find another folder named Lighting Presets. This folder contains 22 Lighting Style presets to be used with Photoshop's Lighting Effects filter. Proper installation of these files is critical. In order to use these files, they must be copied from the CD-ROM into the Lighting Styles folder within the Adobe Photoshop folder on your hard drive. Follow this path to find the proper folder: Adobe Photoshop 4.0➡Plug-ins➡Filters➡Lighting FX➡Lighting Styles. After copying these files, the next time you start Photoshop they will appear in the Style list in the Lighting Effects dialog box.

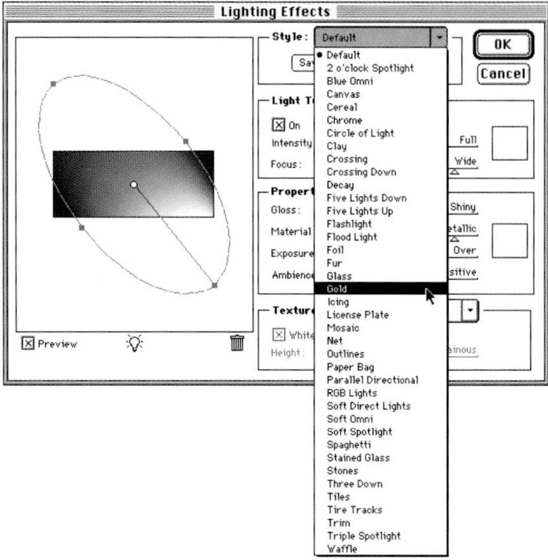


There is one more file in the Type Magic Presets folder. This file, Magic Brush, contains a custom paintbrush to be used in the Canvas and Tire Tracks effects. If you want, you can leave this file on the CD and simply access it when needed. You also can copy it to the folder that contains the Photoshop brushes files. Follow this path to find the folder: Adobe Photoshop 4.0➙Goodies➙Brushes and Patterns. Copy the file to the Brushes and Patterns folder.

## Filters

Inside the Filters folder are four folders. Each of these folders, named for the software companies that created the filters, contain demo filters that you can test on your type and other images. To use any of these filters, they need to be copied into the Plug-ins folder inside the Adobe Photoshop 4.0 folder on your hard drive. Follow this path to copy the files: Adobe Photoshop 4.0➙Plug-ins. The next time you start Photoshop, these third-party filter demos will appear at the bottom of the Filter menu. For example:



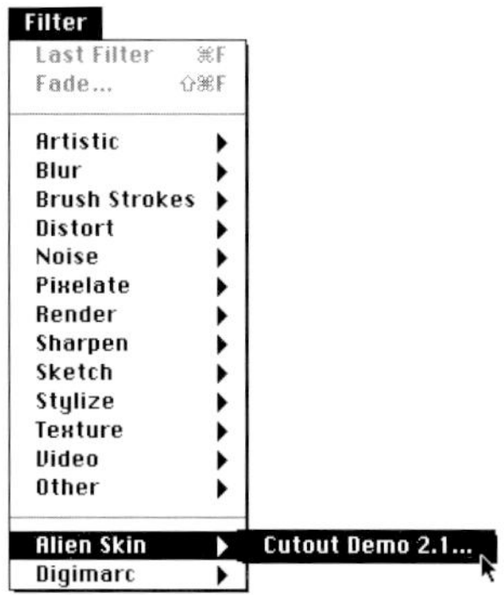

These filters appear on the CD:

KPT Filter Hub, Full demo

Black Box Cutout filter demo

Andromeda Series 1-4 demo

Terrazo demo

Paint Alchemy demo

Typecaster demo

## Software

Inside this folder are demo versions of popular software applications that you can try. For detailed information about how to install and run these applications, consult the READ ME files that are contained within the individual folders. Each folder contains an installation file that walks you through the installation of the software.

These applications appear on the CD:

Adobe Acrobat Reader

Adobe After Effects

Adobe Dimensions

Adobe Illustrator

Adobe Photoshop

Adobe Premiere

Adobe Streamline

ColorIt

InfiniD

LogoMotion

TextureScape

DeBabelizer

DeBabelizer Lite (full working versions)

Director

Fontographer

FreeHand

xRes

Power/Pac 1

Sample output from Adobe TextureMaker

TempoEZ

## Images

Inside the Images folder are four folders that contain a variety of low, medium, and high resolution stock photography images. Many of the images contain textures and backgrounds that can be used to make great-looking type. Most likely you will decide to keep these images on the CD, where you can access them at will—without having them eat up memory on your hard drive. (If you wish, they also may be moved to your hard drive.) All of these images can be opened with the Open command in Adobe Photoshop.

These companies have provided images for the CD:

Digital Stock

D'Pix

Image Club Graphics

PhotoDisc

# Gallery

*page 18*

*page 24*

**Camouflage**

*page 28*

**Canvas**

*page 32*

**CARPET**

*page 38*

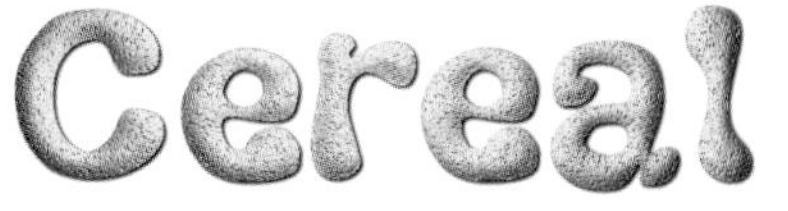


*page 40*

**Checkered**

*page 44*

*page 50*

*page 54*

*page 58*

*page 60*

*page 66*

Decayed

*page 72*

*page 74*

*page 78*

*page 84*

page 88

page 102

FONTS
page 90


page 106

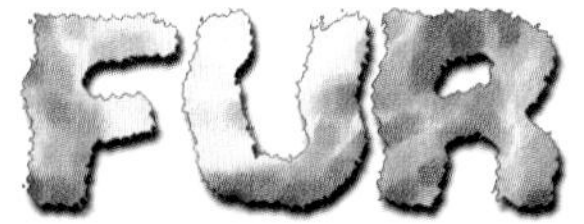

page 96

page 112

page 100

page 114

MARBLE

page 120

page 122

Mosaic

page 126

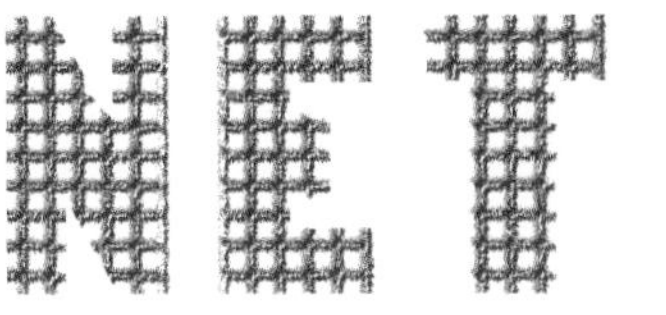


page 132

PAPER BAG

page 138

page 142

page 144

page 148

page 152

page 158

page 162

Shimmering

page 168

STAINED GLASS

page 172

page 180

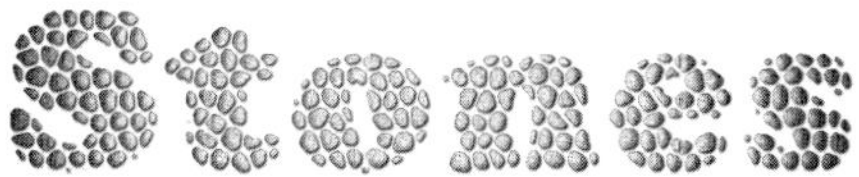


page 186

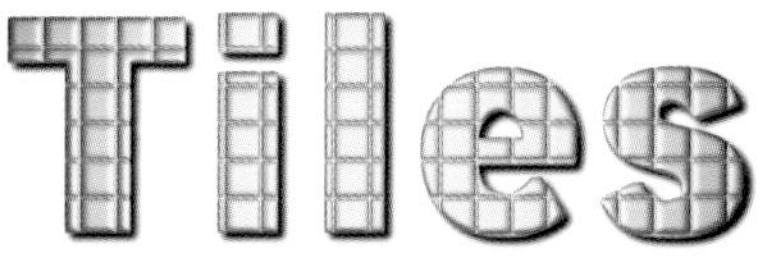


page 190

TIRE TRACKS

page 196

TORN PAPER

page 200

page 206

WALLPAPER

page 210

Watercolor

page 214

Woven

page 218

# Other DESIGN/GRAPHICS Titles

**Designing Business**

Provides the design/business communities with a new way of thinking about how the right design can be a strategic business advantage. It is the definitive guide to presenting a business identity through the use of traditional media vehicles and emerging technologies.

- CD-ROM (dual-platform) exhibits interactive prototypes of multimedia brochures, interactive television, and Web sites as developed by Clement Mok Designs Inc., one of the most sought after interactive design agencies in the world
- Shows how effective communication is one way to out-think, out-plan, and out-perform the competition

*Clement Mok*
1-56830-282-7 ■ $60.00 USA/$81.95 CDN
264 pp., 8 x 10, Covers PC and Macintosh, New - Expert
*Available Now*

**Adobe Persuasion: Classroom in a Book**
1-56830-316-5 ■ $40.00 USA/$56.95 CDN
*Available Now*

**Learning Adobe FrameMaker**
1-56830-290-8 ■ $60.00 USA/$81.95 CDN
*Available Now*

**Adobe Illustrator for Windows: Classroom in a Book**
1-56830-053-0 ■ $44.95 USA/$59.99 CDN
*Available Now*

**Adobe Pagemaker for Windows: Classroom in a Book**
1-56830-184-7 ■ $45.00 USA/$61.95 CDN
*Available Now*

**Adobe Photoshop: Classroom in a Book**
1-56830-317-3 ■ $45.00 USA/$63.95 CDN
*Available Now*

**Advanced Adobe PageMaker for Windows 95: Classroom in a Book**
1-56830-262-2 ■ $50.00 USA/$68.95 CDN
*Available Now*

**Advanced Adobe Photoshop for Windows: Classroom in a Book**
1-56830-116-2 ■ $50.00 USA/$68.95 CDN
*Available Now*

**The Amazing PhotoDeluxe Book for Windows**
1-56830-286-X ■ $30.00 USA/$40.95 CDN
*Available Now*

**Branding with Type**
1-56830-248-7 ■ $18.00 USA/$24.95 CDN
*Available Now*

**The Complete Guide to Trapping, Second Edition**
1-56830-098-0 ■ $30.00 USA/$40.95 CDN
*Available Now*

**Design Essentials, Second Edition**
1-56830-093-X ■ $40.00 USA/$54.95 CDN
*Available Now*

**Digital Type Design Guide**
1-56830-190-1 ■ $45.00 USA/$61.95 CDN
*Available Now*

**Fractal Design Painter Creative Techniques**
1-56830-283-5 ■ $40.00 USA/$56.95 CDN
*Available Now*

**Photoshop Type Magic 1**
1-56830-220-7 ■ $35.00 USA/$47.95 CDN
*Available Now*

**Photoshop Web Magic**
1-56830-314-9 ■ $45.00 USA/$63.95 CDN
*Available November 1996*

**Adobe Photoshop Complete**
1-56830-323-8 ■ $45.00 USA/$61.95 CDN
*Available Now*

**Production Essentials**
1-56830-124-3 ■ $40.00 USA/$54.95 CDN
*Available Now*

**Stop Stealing Sheep & find out how type works**
0-672-48543-5 ■ $19.95 USA/$26.99 CDN
*Available Now*

Copyright © 1996, Macmillan Computer Publishing USA. A Simon & Schuster Company.
The Publishing Operation of Viacom, Inc.

**Visit your fine local bookstore, or for more information visit us at http//:www.mcp.com/hayden**

## Other INTERNET Titles

### Creating Killer Web Sites

The book has an accompanying Web site, where visitors can see the pages in action, download the code for their favorite designs, see tutorials and examples not found in the book, and interact with the author. An estimated 100,000 Web site designers are hungry for this information; by August of 1996, their number was expected to double.

- Conferences about designing for the Internet are selling out, and designers are challenged as they make the transition from print to new media design
- Written by one of today's most noted Web designers
- The first book to teach the art as well as the craft of site design

*David Siegel*
1-56830-289-4 ■ $45.00 USA/$63.95 CDN
272 pp., 8 x 10, Covers PC and Macintosh, Accomplished - Expert
*Available Now*

**Advertising on the Web: Planning & Design Strategies**
1-56830-310-6 ■ $40.00 USA/$56.95 CDN
*Available October 1996*

**Macromedia Shockwave for Director**
1-56830-275-4 ■ $30.00 USA/$40.95 CDN
*Available Now*

**Photoshop Web Magic**
1-56830-314-9 ■ $45.00 USA/$63.95 CDN
*Available November 1996*

**Virtus VRML Toolkit**
1-56830-247-9 ■ $40.00 USA/$54.95 CDN
*Available Now*

**Designer's Guide to the Internet**
1-56830-229-0 ■ $30.00 USA/$40.95 CDN
*Available Now*

**Internet Starter Kit for Windows 95**
1-56830-260-6 ■ $35.00 USA/$47.95 CDN
*Available Now*

**Internet Starter Kit for Windows, Second Edition**
1-56830-177-4 ■ $30.00 USA/$40.95 CDN
*Available Now*

**The Adobe PageMill 2.0 Handbook**
1-56830-313-0 ■ $40.00 USA/$56.95 CDN
*Available Now*

**Designing Multimedia Web Sites**
1-56830-308-4 ■ $50.00 USA/$70.95 CDN
*Available Now*

**Designing Animation for the Web**
1-56830-309-2 ■ $40.00 USA/$56.95 CDN
*Available Now*

**Designing Interactivity for the Web: How to Keep People Coming Back**
1-56830-311-4 ■ $50.00 USA/$70.95 CDN
*Available Now*

**Internet Publishing with Adobe Acrobat**
1-56830-300-9 ■ $40.00 USA/$56.95 CDN
*Available Now*

**Kids do the Web**
1-56830-315-7 ■ $25.00 USA/$35.95 CDN
*Available Now*

**Style Sheets for the Web**
1-56830-306-8 ■ $35.00 USA/$49.95 CDN
*Available Now*

**Web Page Scripting Techniques: JavaScript, VBScript, and Advanced HTML**
1-56830-307-6 ■ $50.00 USA/$70.95 CDN
*Available Now*

**World Wide Web Design Guide**
1-56830-171-5 ■ $40.00 USA/$54.95 CDN
*Available Now*

**Adobe PageMill 2.0: Classroom in a Book**
1-56830-319-X ■ $40.00 USA/$56.95 CDN
*Available Now*

**Visit your fine local bookstore, or for more information visit us at http//:www.mcp.com/hayden**

Copyright © 1996, Macmillan Computer Publishing USA. A Simon & Schuster Company.
The Publishing Operation of Viacom, Inc.

*PLUG YOURSELF INTO...*

# THE MACMILLAN INFORMATION SUPERLIBRARY™

**Free information and vast computer resources from the world's leading computer book publisher—online!**

*FIND THE BOOKS THAT ARE RIGHT FOR YOU!*

A complete online catalog, plus sample chapters and tables of contents!

- STAY INFORMED with the latest computer industry news through our online newsletter, press releases, and customized Information SuperLibrary Reports.
- GET FAST ANSWERS to your questions about Hayden books.
- VISIT our online bookstore for the latest information and editions!
- COMMUNICATE with our expert authors through email and conferences.
- DOWNLOAD SOFTWARE from the immense Macmillan Computer Publishing library:
    - Source code, shareware, freeware, and demos.
- DISCOVER HOT SPOTS on other parts of the Internet.
- WIN BOOKS in on-going contests and giveaways!

**TO PLUG INTO HAYDEN:**

WORLD WIDE WEB: **http://www.mcp.com/hayden**

FTP: ftp.mcp.com

# WANT MORE INFORMATION?

## CHECK OUT THESE RELATED TOPICS OR SEE YOUR LOCAL BOOKSTORE

**Adobe Press**

Published by Hayden Books, the Adobe Press Library reveals the art and technology of communication. Designed and written by designers for designers, best-selling titles include the Classroom in a Book (CIAB) series for both *Macintosh* and *Windows* (*Adobe Photoshop CIAB, Advanced Adobe Photoshop CIAB, Adobe PageMaker CIAB, Advanced Adobe PageMaker CIAB, Adobe Illustrator CIAB, and Adobe Premiere CIAB*), the Professional Studio Techniques series (*Production Essentials, Imaging Essentials, and Design Essentials, 2E*), and *Interactivity by Design.*

**Design and Desktop Publishing**

Hayden Books is expanding its reach to the design market by publishing its own mix of cutting-edge titles for designers, artists, and desktop publishers. With many more to come, these must-have books include *Designer's Guide to the Internet, Adobe Illustrator Creative Techniques, Digital Type Design Guide*, and *The Complete Guide to Trapping, 2E.*

**Internet and Communications**

By answering the questions of what the Internet is, how you get connected, and how you can use it, *Internet Starter Kit for Macintosh* (now in 3rd Ed.) and *Internet Starter Kit for Windows* (now in 2nd Ed.) have proven to be Hayden's most successful titles ever, with over 500,000 Starter Kits in print. Hayden continues to be in the forefront by meeting your ever-popular demand for more Internet information with additional titles, including *Simply Amazing Internet for Macintosh, Create Your Own Home Page for Macintosh, Publishing on the World Wide Web, World Wide Web Design Guide, World Wide Web Starter Kit, net.speak: The Internet Dictionary*, and *Get on the Internet in 5 Minutes for Windows and Macintosh.*

**Multimedia**

As you embrace the new technologies shaping of multimedia, Hayden Books will be publishing titles that help you understand and create your own multimedia projects. Books written for a wide range of audience levels include *Multimedia Starter Kit for Macintosh, 3D Starter Kit for Macintosh, QuickTime: The Official Guide for Macintosh Users, Virtual Playhouse, Macromedia Director Design Guide,* and *Macromedia Director Lingo Workshop.*

**High-Tech**

Hayden Books addresses your need for advanced technology tutorials and references by publishing the most comprehensive and dynamic titles possible, including *Programming Starter Kit for Macintosh, Tricks of the Mac Game Programming Gurus, Power Macintosh Programming Starter Kit, FoxPro Machete: Hacking FoxPro for Macintosh, 2E,* and *The Tao of AppleScript: BMUG's Guide to Macintosh Scripting, 2E.*

**Orders/Customer Service** **800-763-7438** **Source Code** **HAYB**

**Hayden Books** 201 West 103rd Street ◆ Indianapolis, Indiana 46290 USA

Visit our Web page at `http://WWW.MCp.com/hayden/`

# REGISTRATION CARD

## Photoshop Type Magic 2

Name ______________________________ Title ______________

Company______________________________Type of business ______________

Address ______________________________________________

City/State/ZIP ______________________________________________

Have you used these types of books before? ☐ yes ☐ no

If yes, which ones? ______________________________________________

______________________________________________

How many computer books do you purchase each year? ☐ 1–5 ☐ 6 or more

How did you learn about this book? ______________________________

☐ recommended by a friend
☐ received ad in mail
☐ recommended by store personnel
☐ read book review
☐ saw in catalog
☐ saw on bookshelf

Where did you purchase this book? ______________________________

Which applications do you currently use? ______________________________

Which computer magazines do you subscribe to? ______________________________

What trade shows do you attend? ______________________________

Please number the top three factors which most influenced your decision for this book purchase.

☐ cover
☐ price
☐ approach to content
☐ author's reputation
☐ logo
☐ publisher's reputation
☐ layout/design
☐ other ______________

Would you like to be placed on our preferred mailing list? ☐ yes ☐ no e-mail address ______________

☐ **I would like to see my name in print!** You may use my name and quote me in future Hayden products and promotions. My daytime phone number is: ______________________

Comments ______________________________________________

______________________________________________

______________________________________________


**Hayden Books** Attn: Product Marketing ◆ 201 West 103rd Street ◆ Indianapolis, Indiana 46290 USA

Fax to **317-581-3576** Visit out Web Page **http://WWW.MCP.com/hayden/**

Fold Here

NO POSTAGE
NECESSARY
IF MAILED
IN THE
UNITED STATES

# BUSINESS REPLY MAIL

POSTAGE WILL BE PAID BY THE ADDRESSEE

HAYDEN BOOKS
Attn: Product Marketing
201 W 103RD ST
INDIANAPOLIS IN 46290-9058

# Support:

If you need assistance with the information in this book or with a CD/Disk accompanying the book, please access the Knowledge Base on our Web site at **http://www.superlibrary.com/general/support**. Our most Frequently Asked Questions are answered there. If you do not find the answer to your questions on our Web site, you may contact Macmillan Technical Support **(317) 581-3833** or e-mail us at **support@mcp.com**.

# Photoshop Textures Magic

Stanger
Stet · Fortuna · Domus

# Photoshop Textures Magic

BY SHERRY LONDON

## Photoshop Textures Magic

©1997 Hayden Books

All rights reserved. Printed in the United States of America. No part of this book may be used or reproduced in any form or by any means, or stored in a database or retrieval system, without prior written permission of the publisher except in the case of brief quotations embodied in critical articles and reviews. Making copies of any part of this book for any purpose other than your own personal use is a violation of United States copyright laws. For information, address Hayden Books, 201 W. 103rd Street, Indianapolis, Indiana 46290.

Library of Congress Catalog Number: 96-80333

ISBN: 1-56830-368-8

Copyright © 1997 Hayden Books

Printed in the United States of America 1 2 3 4 5 6 7 8 9 0

## Warning and Disclaimer

This book is sold as is, without warranty of any kind, either express or implied. While every precaution has been taken in the preparation of this book, the author and Hayden Books assume no responsibility for errors or omissions. Neither is any liability assumed for damages resulting from the use of the information or instructions contained herein. It is further stated that the publisher and authors are not responsible for any damage or loss to your data or your equipment that results directly or indirectly from your use of this book.

## Trademark Acknowledgments

All terms mentioned in this book that are known to be trademarks or service marks have been appropriately capitalized. Hayden Books cannot attest to the accuracy of this information. Use of a term in this book should not be regarded as affecting the validity of any trademark or service mark. Photoshop is a trademark of Adobe Systems, Inc.

**Publisher** Richard Swadley

**Associate Publisher** John Pierce

**Publishing Manager** Laurie Petrycki

**Managing Editor** Lisa Wilson

**Marketing Editor** Kelli Spencer

### The Photoshop Textures Magic Team

**Acquisitions Editor**
Rachel Byers

**Development Editor**
Beth Millett

**Production Editor**
Terrie Deemer

**Copy Editor**
Jeff Durham

**Technical Editor**
Kate Binder

**Publishing Coordinator**
Karen Flowers

**Cover Designer**
Aren Howell

**Book Designer**
Gary Adair

**Manufacturing Coordinator**
Brook Farling

**Production Team Supervisors**
Laurie Casey
Joe Millay

**Production Team**
Trina Brown
Dan Caparo
Diana Groth
Laure Robinson
Pamela Woolf

Composed in *Bembo* and *GillSans*

## About the Author

Sherry London is a principal of London Computing: PhotoFX, a design and consulting company, and a Contributing Editor for *Computer Artist* magazine. She is the author of *Photoshop 3.0 Special Effects How-To* (Waite Group Press, 1995) and *Photoshop 4.0—An Interactive Course* (Waite Group Press, 1997). She is a contributor to *MacWeek* and *MacUser* magazines, and a sysop on the Adobe Forum on CompuServe. She has lectured at the Thunder Lizard Photoshop Conference and at the Professional Photographers of America conventions. She teaches Photoshop and Pre-press for the Desktop Publishing Certification Program at Moore College of Art and Design in Philadelphia, PA.

## Dedication

To my ninth grade art teacher (wherever she may be). She convinced me that I had no art ability, but she also gave me a gift of great value. She taught me how to look at the textures of the natural world and to notice the beauty in the reflection of the sun in a garbage pail.

## Acknowledgments

Beth Millett, Rachel Byers, Terrie Deemer, and Kate Binder for making this book the most fun I have ever had on a project. Thanks also to my husband, Norm—as always—for putting up with me for so long and for tolerating a house that is chaotic at best.

Special thanks to Phyllis London for contributing images to the "Bouclé," "Cane," "Stucco," "Thumbprint," and "Wash" techniques; and to Ellen Zucker for contributing images to the "Parched" technique. Thanks to Dave Tiech of Mind of the Machine for the octopus image used in the "Pearls" technique.

## Hayden Books

The staff of Hayden Books is committed to bringing you the best computer books. What our readers think of Hayden is important to our ability to serve our customers. If you have any comments, no matter how great or how small, we'd appreciate your taking the time to send us a note.

You can reach Hayden Books at the following:

Hayden Books
201 West 103rd Street
Indianapolis, IN 46290
317-581-3833

Email addresses:

America Online: Hayden Bks
Internet: hayden@hayden.com

Visit the Hayden Books Web site at
`http://www.mcp.com/hayden/`

# Contents

# Introduction

I am a fiber artist and fabric designer by training. I cannot remember a time when I did not have some type of needlework or knitting project in hand. Through my love of fiber, I developed a love of pattern and texture.

The basic understanding that you need in order to create these textures is the understanding of how something repeats or generates a "seamless" pattern. I have tried to provide that understanding for you through a variety of seamless tiling techniques listed in the Basics section, and by giving you a large variety of patterns and textures with which to play.

Please enjoy these and try them out. I had a marvelous time writing this book. I hope you take pleasure from working with the techniques as much I relished creating them.

—Sherry

# Before You Start

## Welcome

Welcome to another volume in the series for creating magic with Photoshop. Like its sisters, *Photoshop Type Magic*, *Photoshop Web Magic*, and *Photoshop Effects Magic*, this book is more than a how-to manual—this book is a what-to guide. The steps in this book tell you exactly what you need to do in order to create exactly what you want. Flip through the thumbtabs to find the texture you want to create and follow the concise, explanatory steps. Or thumb through to discover a texture you never imagined and learn what to do to create it. If you need a little extra help, flip to the Photoshop Basics section. But before you jump in, allow me tell you a little about how this book works. A quick read now will maximize your time later.

## System Setup

Here are the system recommendations for creating these effects.

MacOS users: The Adobe Photoshop 4.0 Info box suggests a memory allocation of 21 megabytes (MB) of RAM to run Photoshop. And your system software may need as much as 10MB of RAM. That's a full bowl of soup, but if you've got the memory, then I would recommend setting the Preferred memory size even higher than 21MB. If you don't have 21MB to spare, then just quit all other applications and give it everything you've got.

Windows users: Adobe suggests 32MB of RAM for Photoshop on any 386 or faster processor running Windows 3.1, Windows 95, or Windows NT, but 40MB is better. Quit any application you can before starting Photoshop to maximize the running of the application. Photoshop runs 32-bit native on both Windows 95 and Windows NT operating systems.

It is not crucial, but it will help if you have a CD-ROM drive. A number of the effects in this book use files that are contained on the CD that comes bundled with this book. (See Appendix B, "What's on the CD-ROM," for information on accessing those files.) However, even if you don't have a CD-ROM drive, you still can perform all of the effects described in the book.



## Adobe Photoshop 4.0

All of the techniques in this book were created with Adobe Photoshop 4.0, and that's the version I recommend you use. If you're attempting to duplicate these techniques using an earlier version of Photoshop, your results may differ slightly or significantly compared to mine. If you're working with version 3.0, then you still will be able to create all of the textures in the book. However, keep in mind you will need to adjust the instructions for the differences between the two versions. You will see that even some of the old Photoshop features work differently in Photoshop 4.0. Many of the textures in this book use features that were not available in earlier versions of Photoshop.

## Conventions

Every image in this book was created initially as an RGB file. You can make your effects in any appropriate color mode, but you should be aware of the variations this will cause as you proceed through the steps. For example, the first new channel created in an RGB file is automatically named Channel #4. But the first new channel created in a CMYK file is named Channel #5. You also should be aware of the differences in the color ranges of the various color modes. Some colors that look great in RGB mode may look like mud after you convert the file's color mode to CMYK. The Lighting Effects filter, for example, will not work in a CMYK or grayscale file.

If you'd like more detailed information about the different color modes, refer to a good general Photoshop book such as *Photoshop 4 Complete*, or to your Photoshop user manuals.

Also, every image was created as a 150-dpi resolution file. (The thumbtab images were created as 300 dpi files.) If you are going to work in a resolution other than 150 dpi, remember that some of the filters and commands will require different settings than the settings I used. Because there are fewer pixels in a 72 dpi image, a Gaussian Blur radius of 5 pixels will blur the image more than if it were a 150 dpi image. Just keep an eye on the figures next to the steps and match the outcome as close as you can.

### The Blue Type

As you work through the steps, you will see phrases that are colored a light blue. These phrases are listed in alphabetical order in the Photoshop Basics section. If the phrase in blue asks you to perform a task that you are unfamiliar with, then you can find that phrase in the Photoshop Basics section and follow the instructions on how to perform that task.

### Menu Commands

You also will see instructions that look like this:

Filter➡Blur➡Gaussian Blur (2 pixels)

This example asks you to apply the Gaussian Blur filter. To perform this command, click on the Filter menu at the top of the screen and drag down to Blur. When Blur is highlighted a new menu opens to the right, from which you can choose Gaussian Blur.

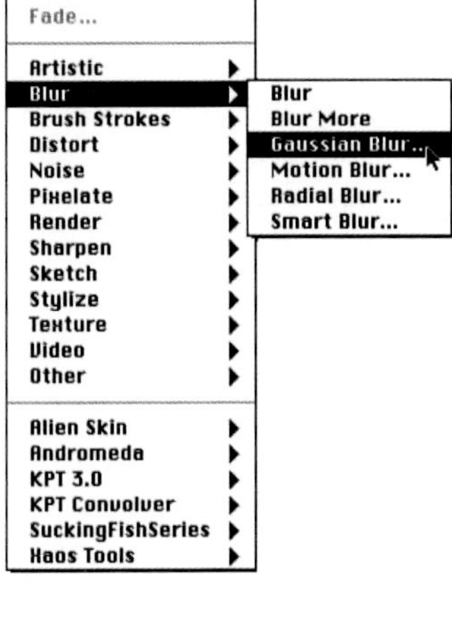


In this example, a dialog box appears asking you for more information. All of the settings that you need to perform each task appear in the text of the step. The previous example tells you to enter 2 pixels as the Radius.

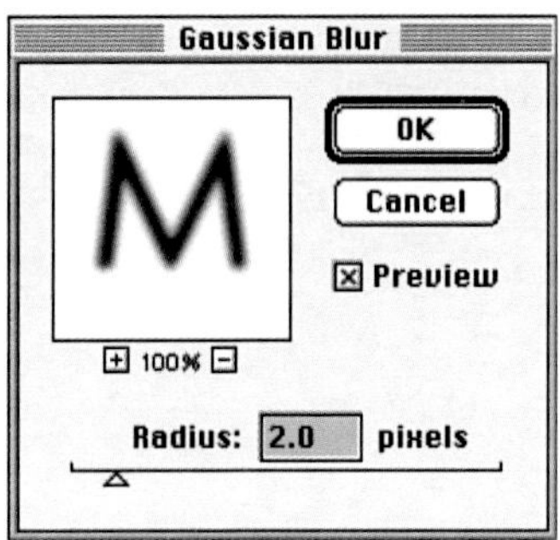


Click OK to blur the image.

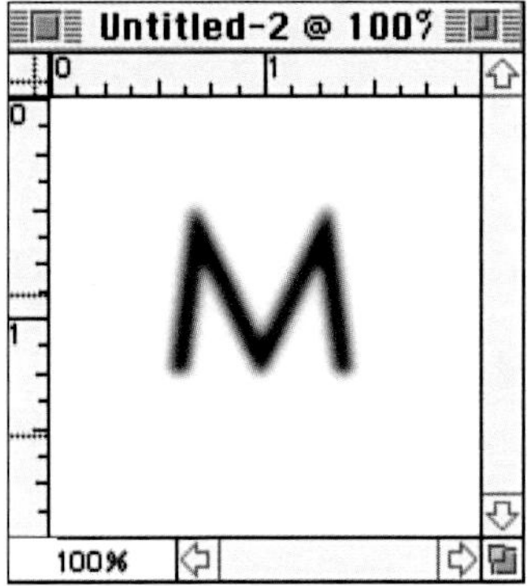

## Settings

Following each action in the steps, you will find the settings for that feature. These recommended settings are meant to act as guides; the best settings for your effect may vary. As a rule, it is best to match the outcomes that you see in the figures as you progress through the technique. The greatest differences occur when the resolution of your file is significantly different from what I used. The following two images demonstrate the importance of adjusting for resolution differences. A 6-pixel Radius Gaussian Blur was applied to both images.

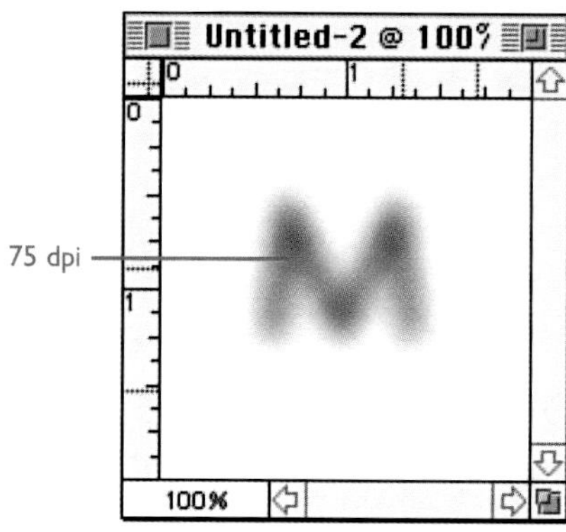


75 dpi

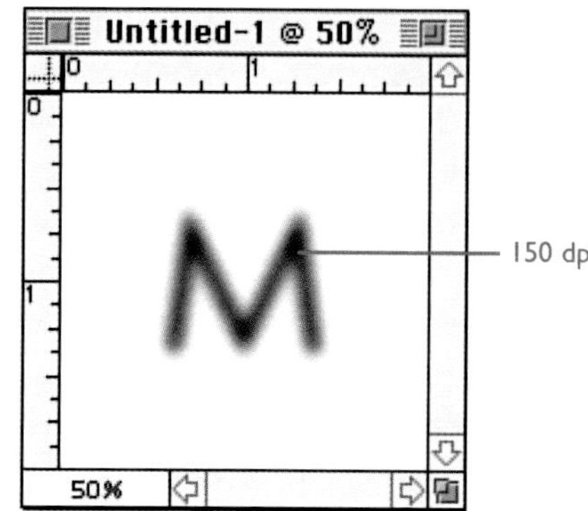


150 dpi

## Tips

Throughout the book, you will find additional bits of information that can help you make the most of Photoshop. These tips provide information beyond the basic steps of each lesson.

# Photoshop Basics

The goal of this section is to help new and novice users of Photoshop with the simple, basic tasks required to create the effects described and illustrated in this book. Each of the basic tasks described in this section corresponds to the blue highlighted text in the chapters that follow. Here, users can easily find the instructions they need for performing a particular Photoshop task.

This chapter proceeds on two assumptions: that you're creating these textures in Photoshop 4.0; and that you're keeping the Toolbox, and the Brushes, Options, and Layer/Channel/Path palettes open. If one or more of these palettes are closed when you refer to this chapter, you can reopen them by name using the Window menu at the top of the screen. If you're using an earlier version of Photoshop, you can refer to the Photoshop manual for instructions on how to perform these tasks.

## Images and Resolution

When you create your own textures, you need to know where you are going to use them. If you are planning to use the texture in a multimedia presentation or on the Web, you only need to work at 72 ppi—this is screen resolution. What you see onscreen is what you are going to see when you display the final texture. If you are going to print the texture, you are in a different ball game. Printing typically needs a 300 ppi resolution. If you have a 50-pixel square file, the image that would be larger than one-half inch onscreen will now be only one-sixth of an inch. Fine detail—especially from the Add Noise filter—will be lost.

Although I generally think it is a bad idea to greatly enlarge your images, it will not hurt many of the textures—especially the "noisy" ones. If you want to preserve as much of the noise as you can, use the Nearest Neighbor interpolation when you scale up the image. This keeps your file from anti-aliasing as it is enlarged. It will look pixellated onscreen, but should print so that it looks like the texture before you enlarged it (assuming that you do not enlarge a texture more than 300%).



## The Toolbox

If you're not familiar with Photoshop's Toolbox, there's no reason to panic. With a bit of experimentation, it doesn't take long to learn each tool's individual functions. This representation of the Toolbox will help both beginners and experts find the tools they need.

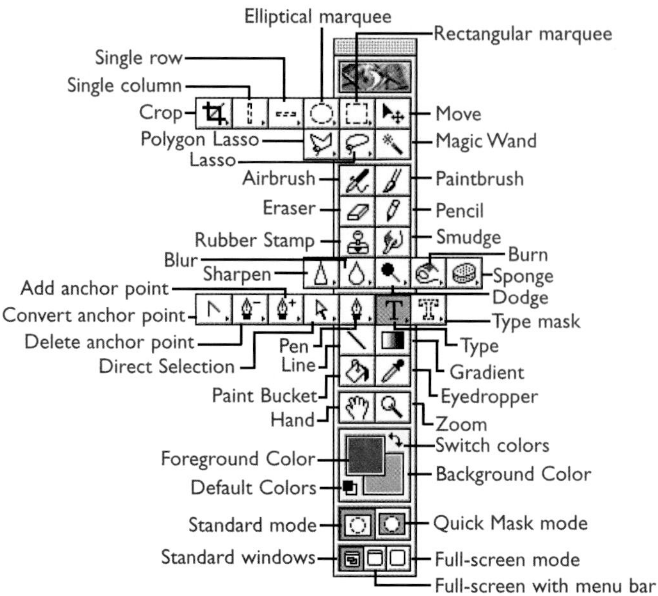


# Basic Photoshop Tasks

## Add a Horizontal or Vertical Guide

Turn on the Rulers (Command-R)[Control-R]. Place your cursor on the horizontal or vertical ruler. Press the mouse button, and drag a guide into the image.

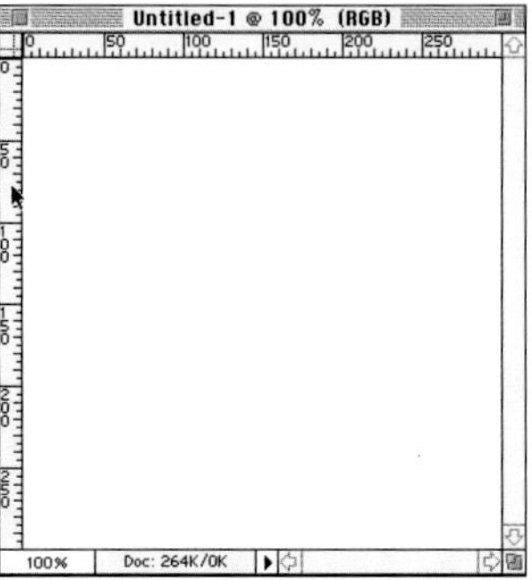


## Choose a Foreground or Background Color

**Shortcut:** Press D to change colors to their defaults: black for the foreground, and white for the background. (Note: If you are working on a layer mask or in a channel, pressing D will give you white foreground and black background.)

Press X to switch the foreground color with the background color.

To change the foreground or background color, click on either the Foreground icon or the Background icon.

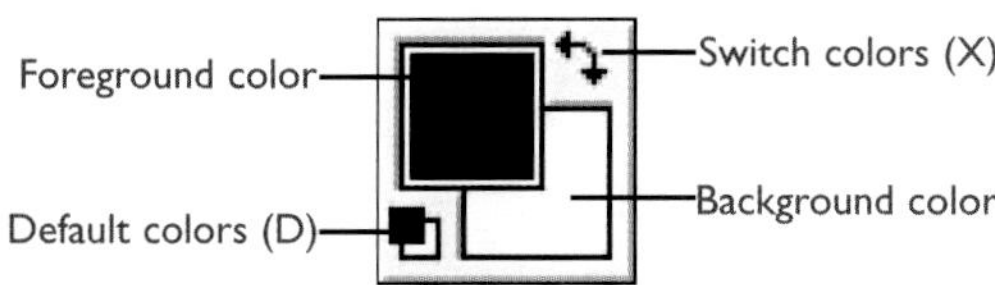


The Color Picker dialog box appears, which enables you to choose a new foreground or background color by moving and clicking the cursor (now a circle) along the spectrum box, or by changing specific RGB, CMYK, or other percentage values. Note that the Foreground and Background icons on the Toolbox now reflect your color choices.

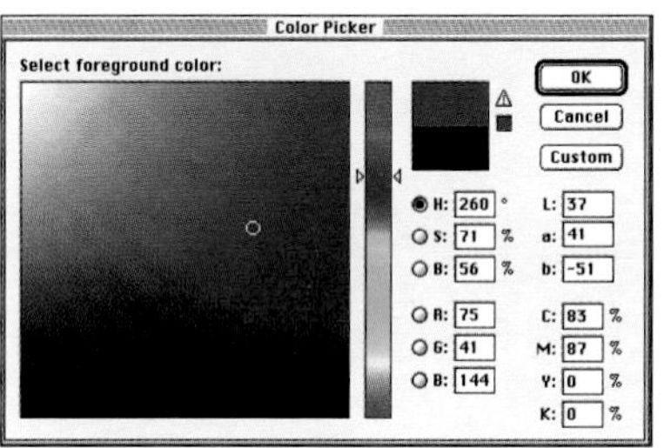


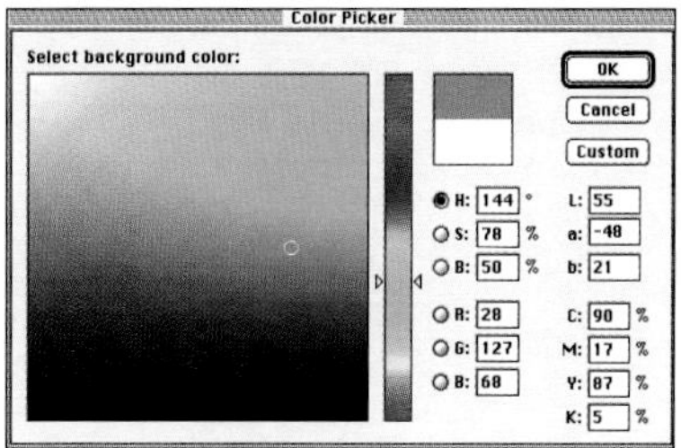

## Change the Blending Mode

In many techniques you will be instructed to change from Normal to another blending mode. This may refer to the Options palette for some tools, or the Layers palette, or the Fade dialog box. Blending mode influences how the pixels from two sources will combine.

To change from Normal mode to any of 16 alternatives, first click the pop-up menu, and then drag to your choice of mode. Consult your Photoshop User Guide for details on how each blending mode works.

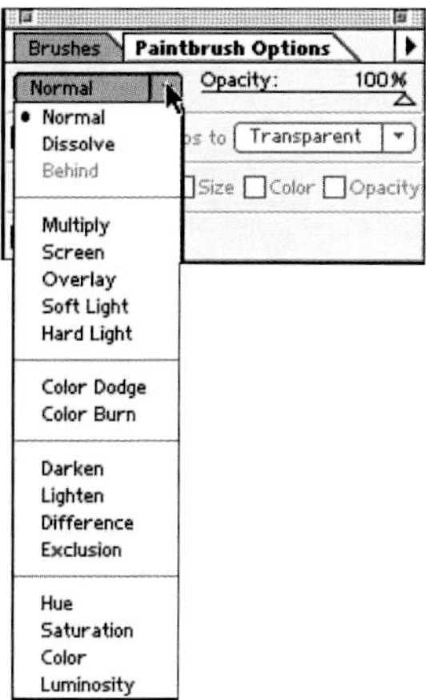

## Convert to a New Mode

To convert from one color mode to another, click on the Image menu at the top of the screen and scroll down to the Mode command. You then can scroll down to select the mode of your preference. If you want to switch from CMYK mode to multichannel mode, for example, you choose Image➥Mode➥Multichannel. The check mark to the left of CMYK will move down to Multichannel, indicating that you are now in multichannel mode.

**Remember that there is a different range of colors available for each color mode. No matter what color mode the file is in onscreen, for example, your printer (if it prints in color) is going to print your work in CMYK. Because the color ranges for RGB and CMYK are different, you should convert your RGB image to CMYK before printing. Otherwise, you may be in for a big surprise when your bright green prints as a dull tan.**

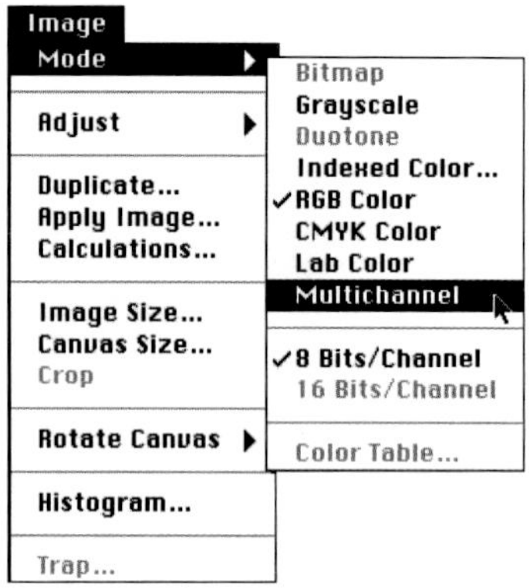


## Create a Layer Mask

To create a layer mask, click the Layer Mask icon at the bottom of the Layers palette. A layer mask is used to mask out (or hide) parts of a layer. Painting with black hides an area, and painting with white reveals it. Dragging a layer mask to the trash icon at the bottom of the Layers palette enables you to make its effects permanent or delete it. Here the layer mask is active, indicated by the black border around it and the mask icon in the active layer.

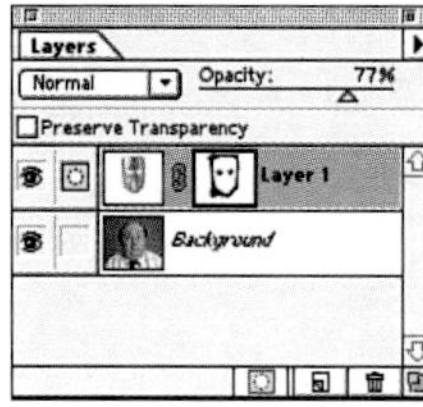


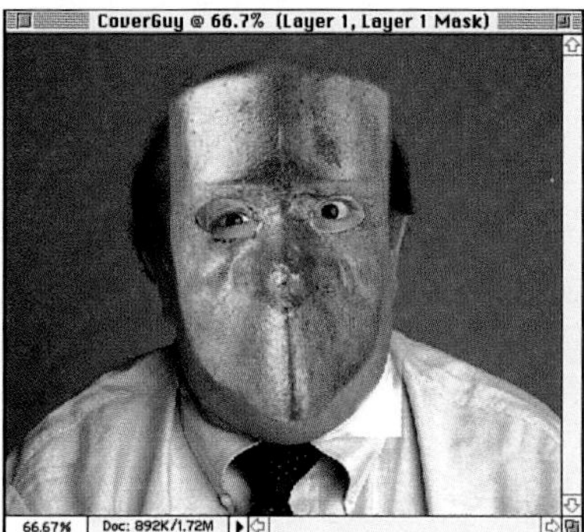

## Create an Adjustment Layer

**Shortcut:** Press the (Command)[Control] key and click on the New Layer icon at the bottom right of the Layers palette.

Select Layer palette menu➡New Adjustment Layer.

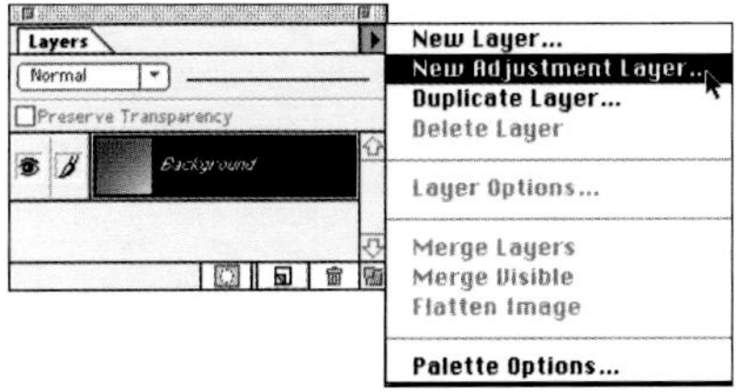


The resulting dialog box enables you to select the type of adjustment layer—Levels and Hue/Saturation are the ones most often used here. You can also change the blending mode of the adjustment layer at the same time.

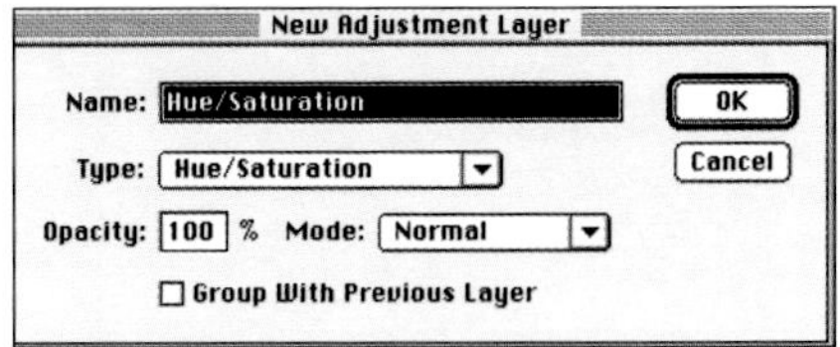


## Create a New Background Layer

This works in an image only if it does not contain a Background layer. Press the (Option)[Alt] key and click on the New Layer icon. This opens up a dialog box. In the blending mode list, scroll down to the very last entry in the menu. It will say "Background." Select this as the mode and it creates a new Background layer.

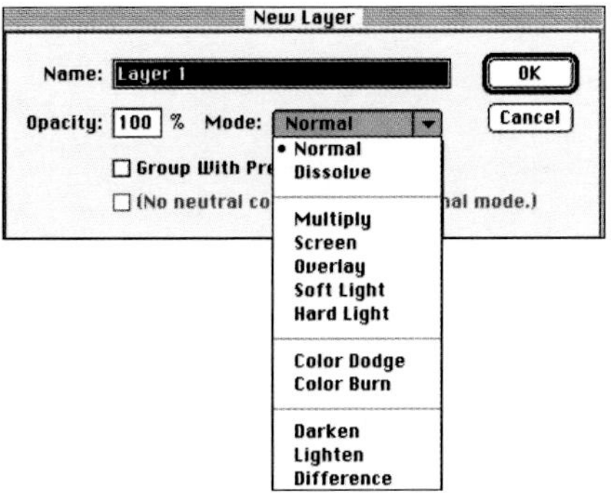

## Create a New Channel

**Shortcut:** Click the New Channel icon on the Channels palette.

To create a new channel, choose New Channel from the Channels palette pop-up menu. You will not see the Options dialog box if you use the shortcut.

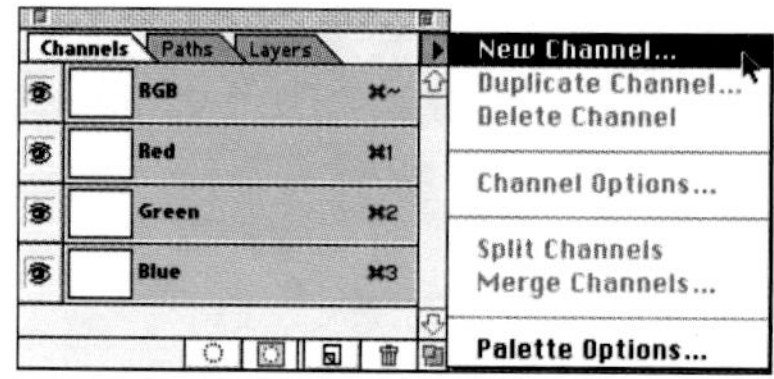


Use the Channel Options dialog box to establish your settings. Unless noted otherwise, we used the default settings when creating a new channel. This figure shows Photoshop's default settings.

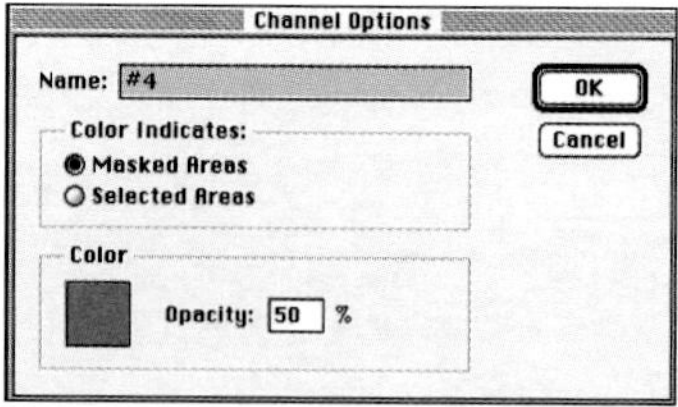


## Create a New File

**Shortcut:** Press (Command-N)[Control-N].

To create a new file, choose File➡New. The New dialog box appears, which is where you name your new file and establish other settings. See the "Before You Start" section for information on the conventions that were used when creating new files for the type effects in this book.



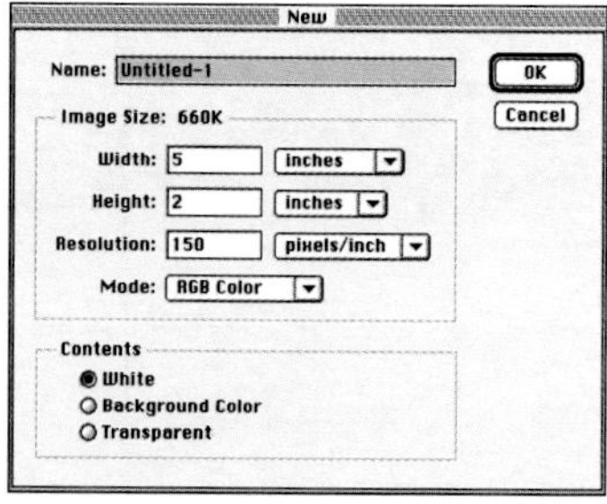


## Create a New Layer

**Shortcut:** Click the New Layer icon on the Layers palette. You will not see the Options dialog box if you use the shortcut unless you press the (Option)[Alt] key as you click on the New Layer icon.

To create a new layer, choose New Layer from the Layer palette pop-up menu, or choose Layer➡New➡Layer.

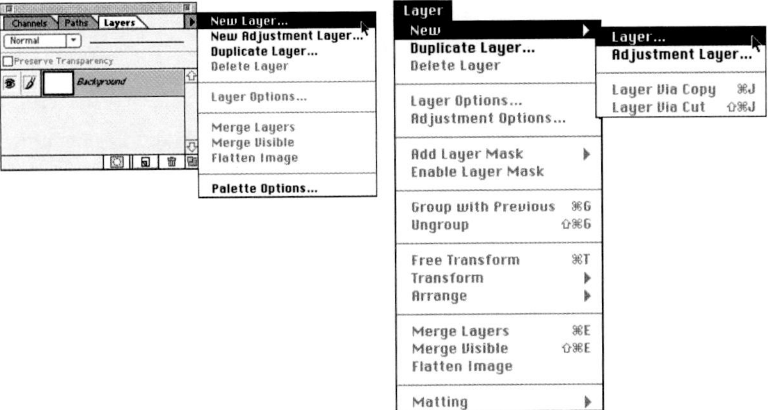


The New Layer dialog box opens, which is where you name the new layer and establish other settings.

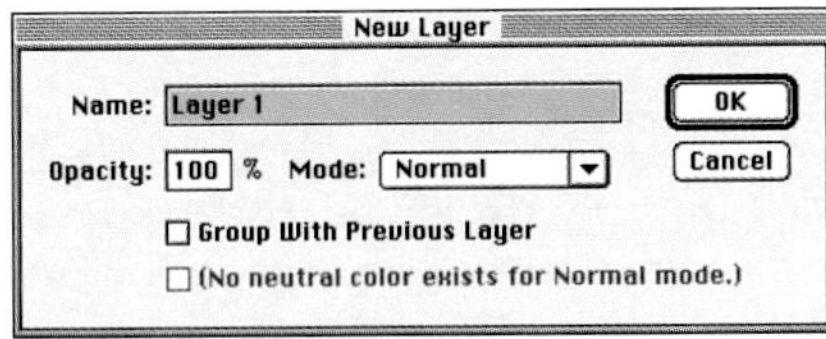


## Create Layer 0

Double-click the Background layer of an image. In the dialog box, press (Return)[Enter] and the layer is automatically named Layer 0. This action "detaches" the layer from the background (you no longer have a Background layer) and allows the layer to contain transparency (though it does not add any transparency to an image that is already in the layer).

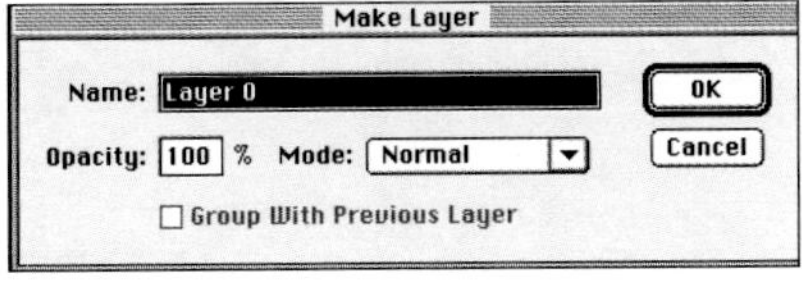


## Define a Clone Source

Select the Rubber Stamp tool. Place the cursor at the location from which you wish to start copying. Press the (Option)[Alt] key and click the mouse. This defines the start of the cloning operation. Move the cursor to another location and press the mouse to paint.

## Define a Pattern

Select➡All (or create a selection using the rectangular Marquee tool). Select Edit➡Define Pattern. Now you can fill with this pattern.

## Delete a Channel

To delete a channel, go to the Channels palette and select the channel you want to delete; drag it to the Trash icon at the lower-right corner (just like dragging an icon to the Recycling Bin in Windows 95 or to the Trash in the MacOS Finder). You also can select the channel you want to delete, and choose Delete Channel from the Channels palette menu.

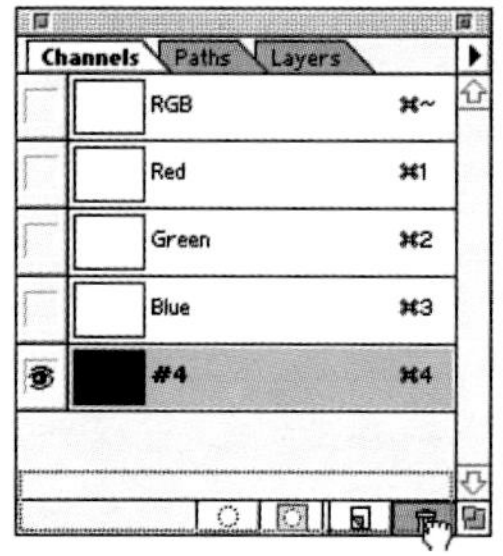


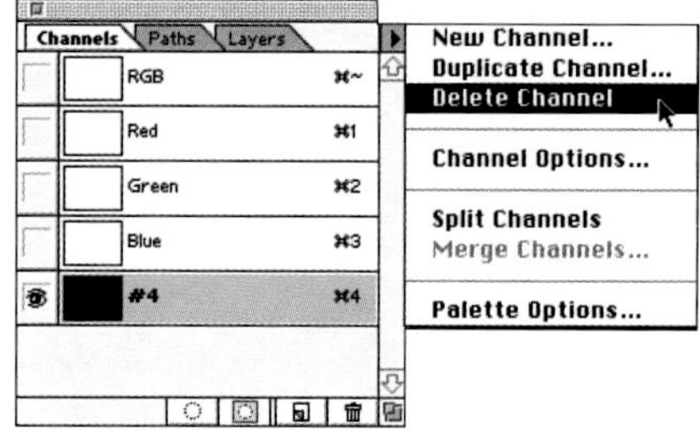


## Delete a Layer

To delete a layer, go to the Layers palette and select the layer you want to delete; drag it to the Trash icon at the lower-right corner (just like dragging an icon to the Recycling Bin in Windows 95 or to the Trash in the Mac OS Finder). You also can select the layer you want to delete, and choose Delete Layer from the Layers palette menu or from the Layers menu.

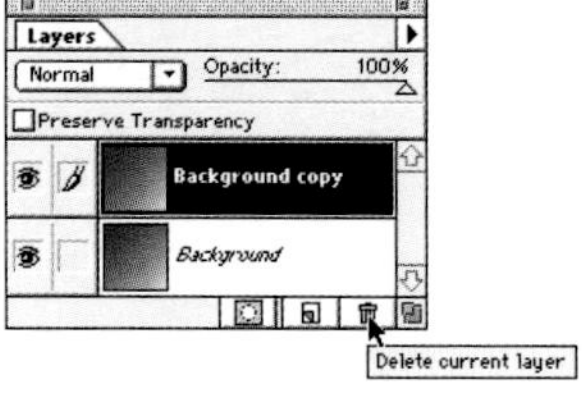


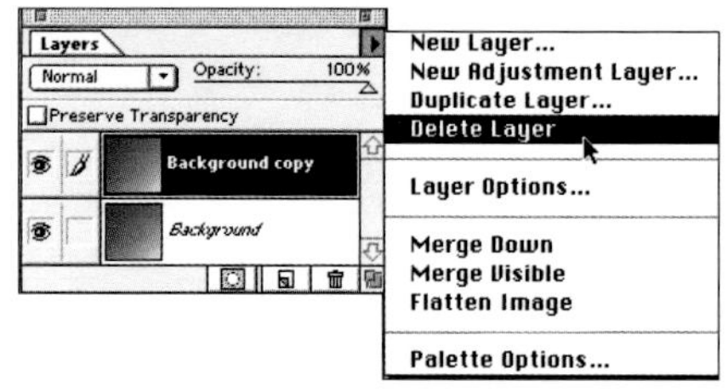


## Deselect a Selection

**Shortcut:** Press (Command-D)[Control-D].

To deselect a selection, choose Select➡None. The marquee disappears.

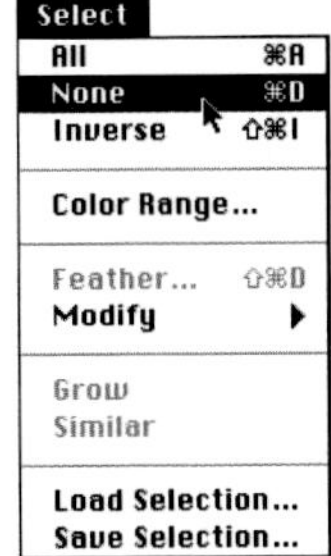


## Drag and Drop

This technique *is* a shortcut. It eliminates copying to and pasting from the clipboard. With two images open, select an area from the source image and drag it over to the destination image, using the Move tool. A new layer is created automatically.

**Shortcut:** Press (Command)[Control] to access the Move tool.

## Drag and Drop Centered

Before you drag the selection from one image to another, press the Shift key and keep it pressed until the selection is in its new home. This works whether you drag the selection from the image itself or you drag the layer from the Layers palette. For this to consistently work correctly, the two images must be the same size.

## Drag the Marquee

There are many places in the book where you are asked to create a rectangular marquee of a fixed size. The instruction, drag the marquee, requires you to place your cursor in the image, press the mouse button, and move the marquee to the instructed place in the image *without* letting go of the mouse button. If you learn to place and drag the marquee in one movement, you can easily get the fixed size marquee into any corner of the image without fear of dragging off of the image. If you create the marquee in this manner, it cannot be dragged outside of the image boundaries. Should you let go of the mouse button before the marquee is in its desired location, you will not be able to position it accurately. If this happens, deselect and try it again.



## Duplicate a Channel or Layer

**Shortcut:** Click the channel or layer you want to duplicate, and drag it on top of the New Channel or New Layer icon. This keeps the layer or channel within the *same* document as the original. Unless the menu command below is explicitly stated, you should use the shortcut.

To create a duplicate of a channel or layer, make it active and then select Duplicate Channel or Duplicate Layer from the appropriate palette menu. This enables you to duplicate the layer or channel and place it, if you want, into another existing image or into a new image of its own. You will always see explicit instructions (written Layer➥Duplicate Layer or Channels palette menu➥Duplicate Channel) when you are asked to create a duplicate layer or channel in this manner. The reason to use this method is to copy the layer or channel into a new document.

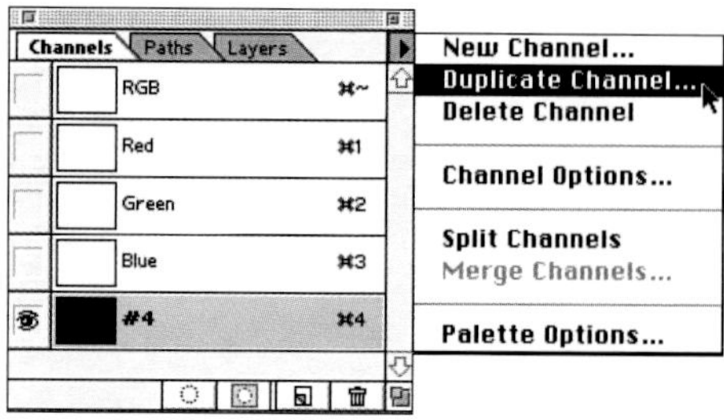


A new copy of the channel you selected for duplication is created automatically, and the Duplicate Channel dialog box appears.

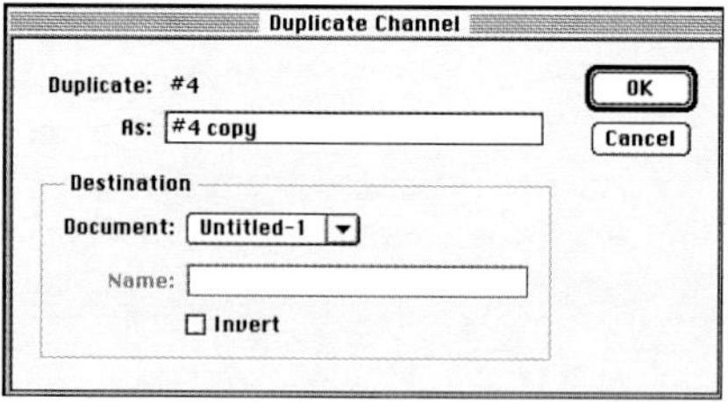


## Duplicate the Image

Select Image➥Duplicate. You usually are not asked to name the new image, though you certainly may if you want. Sometimes, you will be told to select Image➥Duplicate (Merged layers only). Click the checkbox in the dialog box. This flattens the layers in the image as it copies it.

## Enter/Exit Quick Mask

**Shortcut:** Press Q to enter and exit the Quick Mask mode.

Click the Quick Mask icon to switch to Quick Mask mode; conversely, click the Standard mode icon to return to Standard mode.

Essentially, a Quick Mask is a temporary channel. When you're in Quick Mask mode, you can use any of the Photoshop tools and functions to change the selection without changing the image. When you switch back to Standard mode, you'll have a new selection.

## Enter the Text

Before entering the text using the standard Type tool, make sure that the foreground color is set to your desired text color. If you are entering text into a layer, the standard Type tool will create a new layer for the type.

To enter the text, select the Type tool, and then click anywhere in the image to open the Type Tool dialog box. Type the text in the large box at the bottom of the dialog box, and make your attribute choices from the options. Unless noted otherwise in the instructions, always make sure that you have the Anti-Aliased box checked.

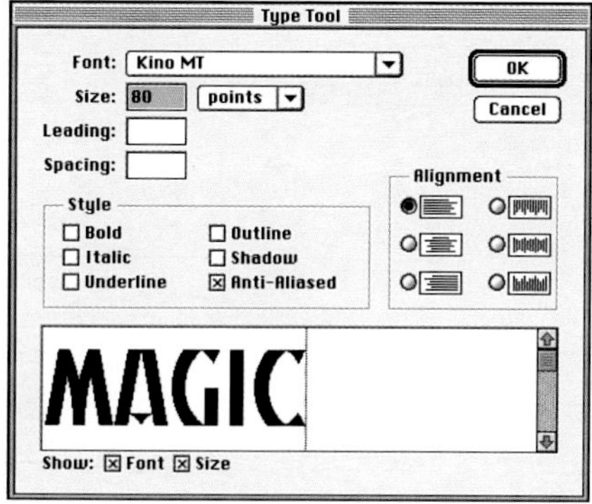


After clicking OK, move the type into position with the Move tool.



## Fade the Effect

**Shortcut:** (Shift-Command-F)[Shift-Control-F] opens a dialog box for fading the last filter or Image➡Adjust command used and changing its blending mode.

To fade the last filter applied, or some other effects such as Invert, choose Filter➡Fade. The Fade slider acts like a partial undo for the last effect you applied. The Blending Mode pop-up menu enables you to determine how the pixels of the before and after versions of the image are combined.

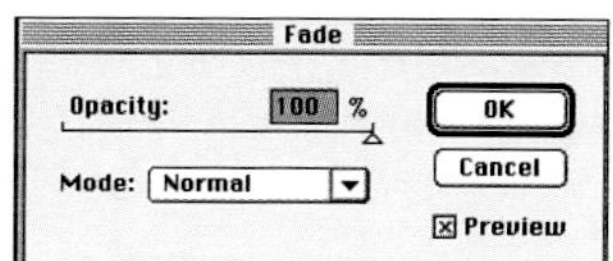

## Fill a Selection with Foreground or Background Color

First, choose a foreground or background color you want to use (see page 8 in this section for instructions). Keep the selection active and press (Option-Delete) [Alt-Backspace] to fill the selection with the foreground color. If you are in the Background layer, then you can press (Delete)[Backspace] to fill the selection with the background color. To fill a transparent area with the background color, first turn off Preserve Transparency for that layer, then press (Command-Delete)[Control-Backspace].

You also can fill in your selections by choosing Edit➥Fill, or press (Shift-Delete) [Shift-Backspace] to open the Fill dialog box.

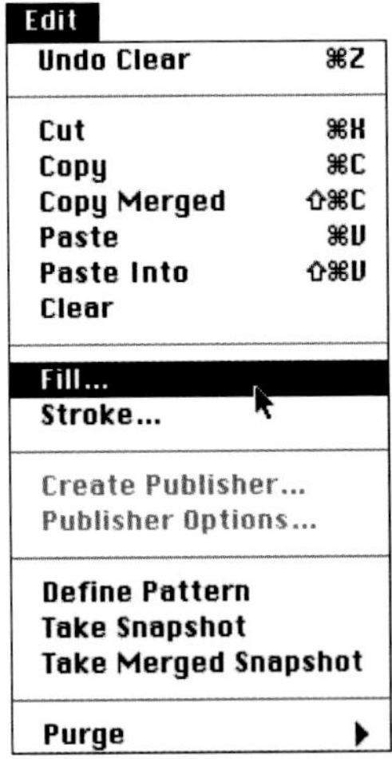


This causes the Fill dialog box to appear, enabling you to establish the Contents option, the Opacity, and the Blending Mode you want to use.

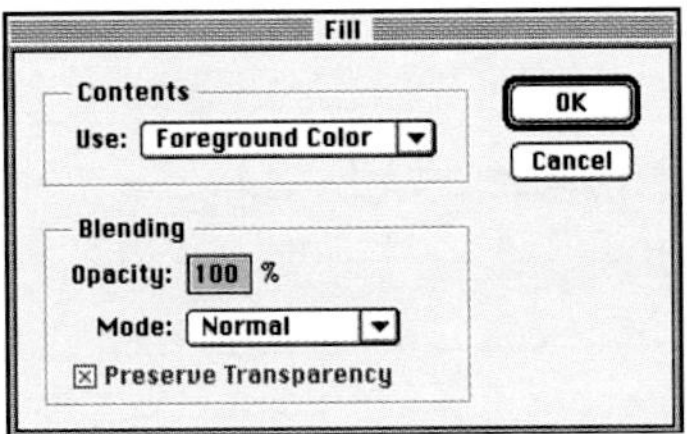


**TIP** **If a selection is empty (a transparent area of a layer) and the Preserve Transparency option is turned on for that layer, then you will not be able to fill the selection. To fill the selection, simply turn off the Preserve Transparency option before filling it.**

**If you want to fill only the areas of a layer that contain non-transparent pixels, you can either turn on Preserve Transparency, or press the Shift key along with the other keystrokes (depending upon whether you are trying to fill with foreground or background color).**

## Fill a Selection with Pattern

With a pattern defined, press (Shift-Delete)[Shift-Backspace]. You also can fill your selections by choosing Edit➡Fill.

This causes the Fill dialog box to appear, allowing you to change the Contents option to Pattern, and set the Opacity and the blending mode.

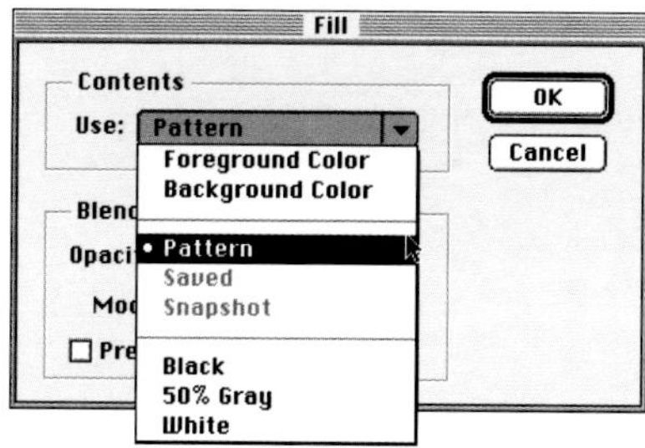


## Flatten an Image

To flatten an image (merge all the layers into a single layer), choose Flatten Image from the Layers palette menu, or choose Layer➡Flatten Image.

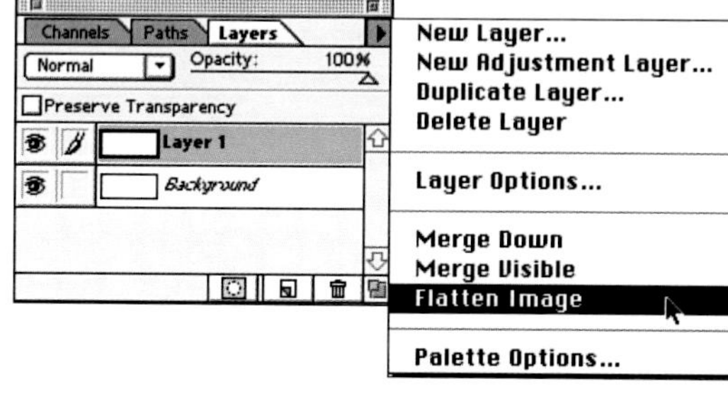

## Load Brushes

To load another library of brushes, choose Load Brushes in the Brush palette pop-up menu. You can choose whether to "append" additional brushes to the default library or replace the defaults. I recommend you append the Assorted Brushes that come with Photoshop. I've also included a few custom brushes in the Presets folder on the CD-ROM that comes with this book.

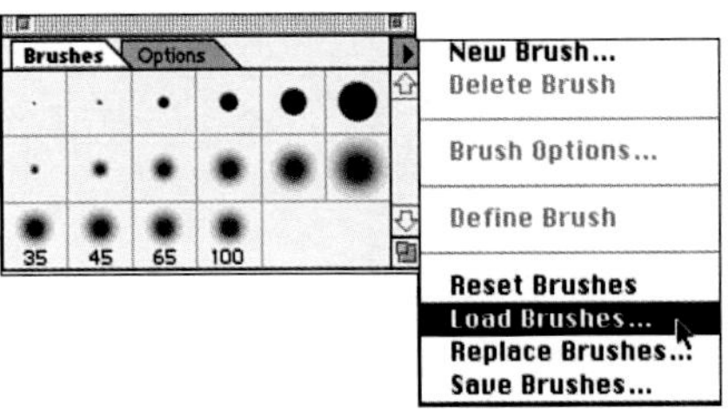


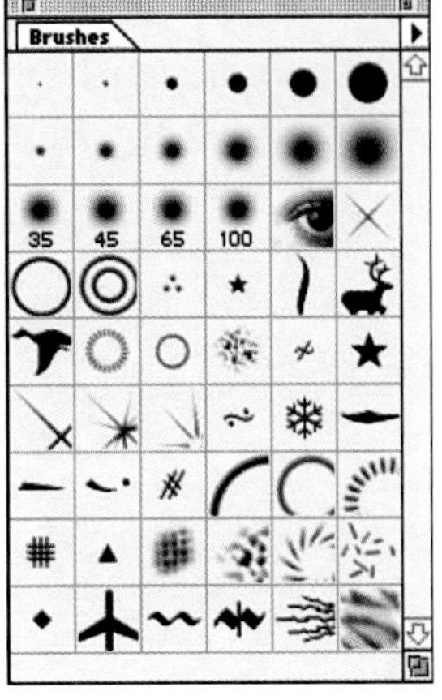


## Load a Selection

**Shortcut:** Hold down the (Command)[Control] key and click the channel (on the Channels palette) that contains the selection you want to load.

To load a selection, choose Select➡Load Selection. This brings up the Load Selection dialog box, in which you can establish document, channel, and operation variables.

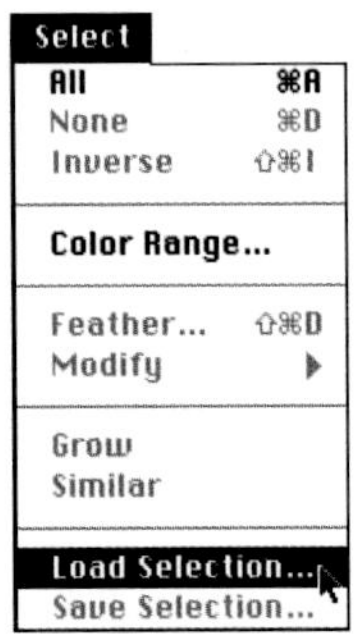


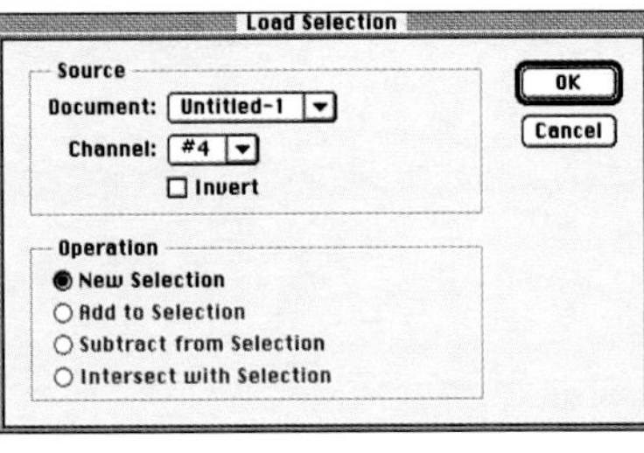

## Make a Channel Active

To make a channel active for editing or modification, click on its thumbnail or name on the Channels palette.

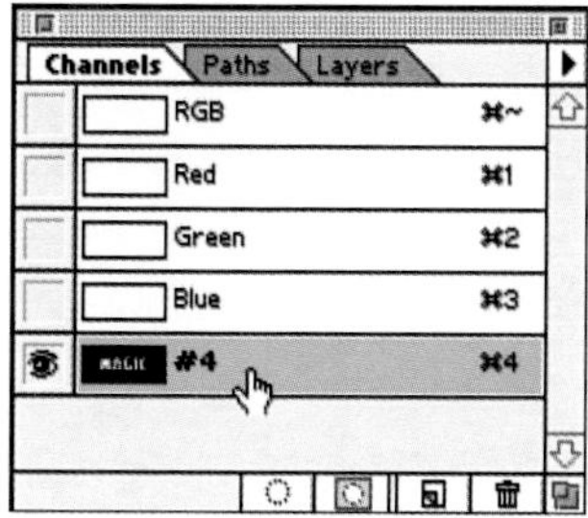


You can tell the channel is active if it is highlighted with a color.

## Make a Layer Active

To make a layer active, click on its thumbnail or name in the Layers palette.

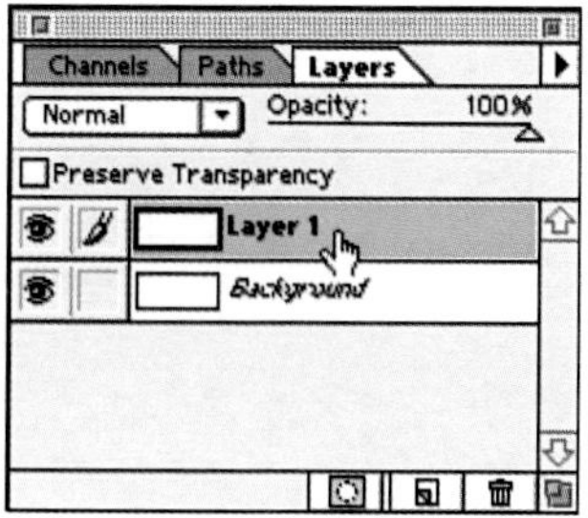


You can tell the layer is active if it is highlighted with a color.

## Make a Layer Visible/Invisible

To make a layer visible or invisible, click in the left-most column in the Layers palette. If an eye appears, then the layer is visible. If the column is empty, then that layer is hidden (invisible).

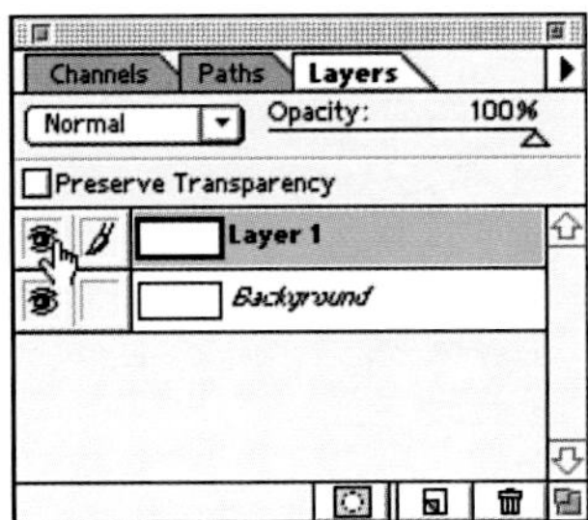


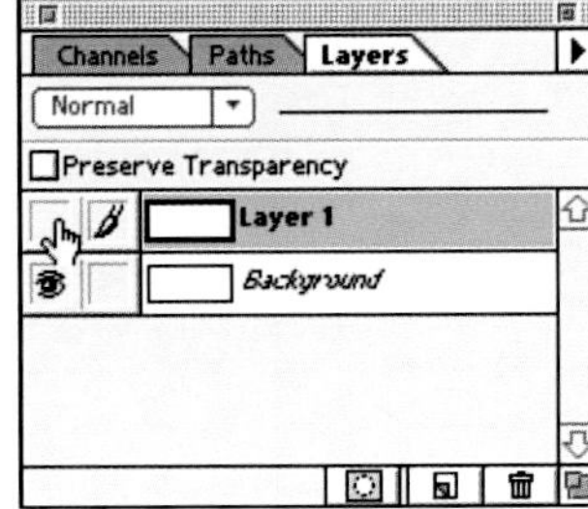


## Make an Image Seamless

**Center Cross Method:** Select the Lasso tool. Select Filter➥Other➥Offset (Wrap Around). Make the Horizontal and Vertical distances one-half of the image dimensions. Draw a selection in the shape of a fat cross around the area where the Offset filter joined the original corners of the image. Choose Select➥Feather, and pick a large feather. Reapply the Offset filter to the selection.

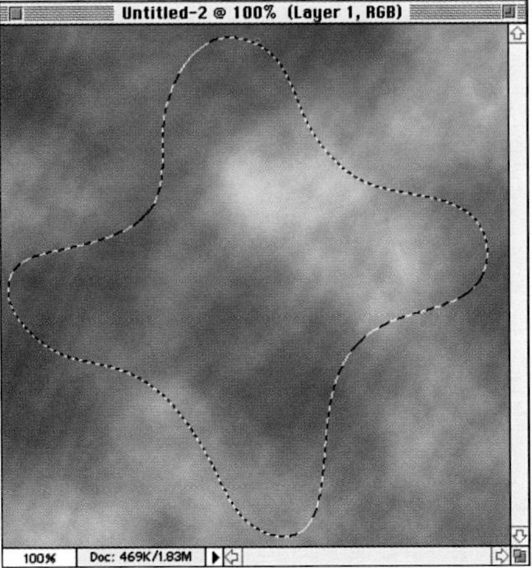


**Masked Offset Method:** Use the finished tile. Duplicate the Background layer. Select Filter➥Other➥Offset (Wrap Around). Set the Horizontal and Vertical distances to one-half of the image dimensions. Create a layer mask. Use black, the Paintbrush tool, and a large, soft brush. Brush out the center seam line by painting over the area on the layer mask.

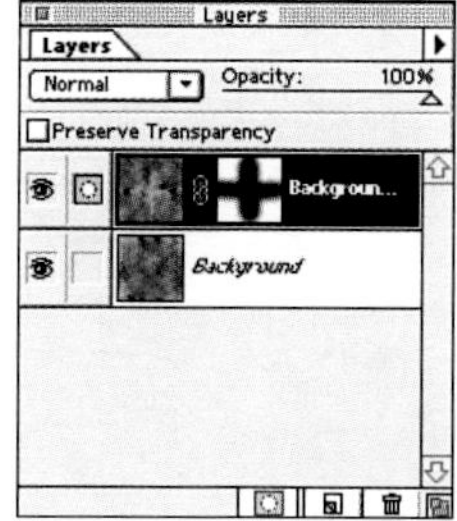


Create a new layer. (Option)[Alt] Merge Visible to a new layer. Select Filter➥Other➥Offset (Wrap Around). Create a layer mask. Use black, the Paintbrush tool, and the soft brush. Brush out the seam line near the edges by painting over the area on the layer mask.

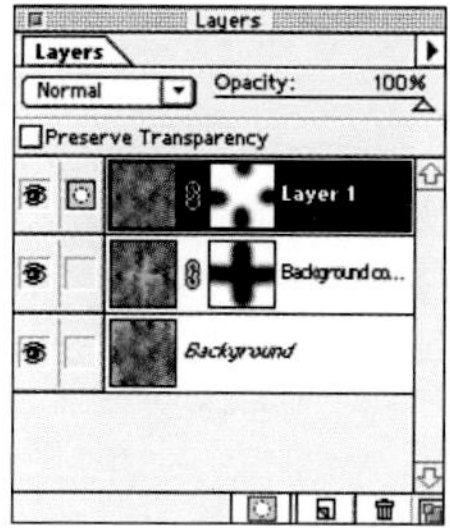


Create a new layer. (Option)[Alt] Merge Visible to a new layer. Select Filter➥Other➥Offset (Wrap Around). Check to make sure that your image is seamless. It should be. Touch-up using the layer mask if it is not.

**Mosaic Method:** Double-click the rectangular Marquee and set the fixed size to the current size of your tile. If the tile is in the Background layer, double-click the Background layer in the Layers palette to "raise" the layer to Layer 0. Press (Enter)[Return] in the dialog box—the layer is automatically named Layer 0. Select Image➥Canvas Size and double the image dimensions either numerically or by selecting 200% for each dimension. Place the anchor in the top-left square. Click OK. Drag the Marquee to the top-left square and copy it to the clipboard (Command-C)[Control-C]. Drag the Marquee into the top-right corner of the image. Edit➥Paste. You will get a new layer. Select Layer➥Transform➥Flip Horizontal. Drag the Marquee into the bottom-left corner. Edit➥Paste. Select Layer➥Transform➥Flip Vertical. Drag the Marquee into the bottom-right corner. Edit➥Paste. Select Layer➥Transform➥Flip Vertical. Select Layer➥Transform➥Flip Horizontal. You have a perfectly seamless tile.

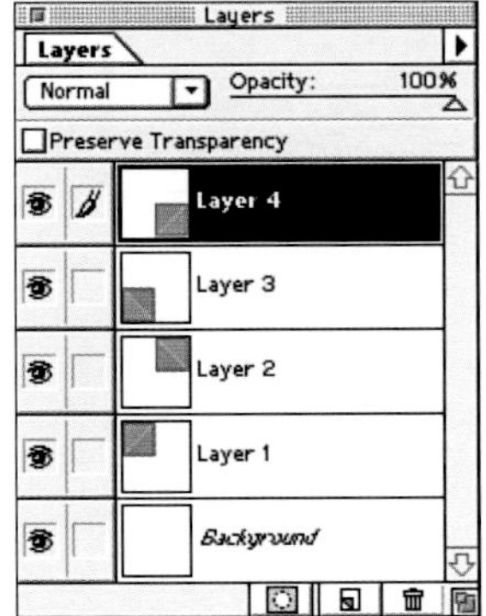


**Rubber Stamp Method:** After you have offset the image, define a clone source that is not on a seam line. Use the Rubber Stamp tool to cover over the seam line with bits and pieces of other parts of the pattern.

## Name/Rename a Layer

To change the name of a layer, double-click its name in the Layers palette and type the new name in the Layer Options dialog box.

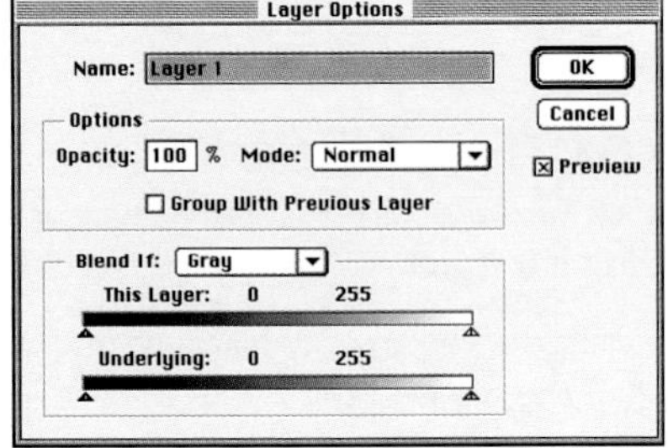




## (Option)[Alt] Merge Visible

**Shortcut:** Press (Shift-Command-Option-E)[Shift-Control-Alt-E].

This command creates a combined picture of all of the visible layers in your image and places it in the active layer. You are usually asked to create a new layer before this command is given, as you must have an empty layer for this to work properly. Press the (Option)[Alt] key and select Layer➡Merge Visible from either the Layers menu or the Layers palette menu. The advantage to this command is that it enables you to keep all of the layers but still have one combined layer that can be manipulated as a single entity. This is one of the most useful and least documented features in Photoshop.

## Place an Image

Use File➡Place to bring an EPS (Encapsulated PostScript) image into an open Photoshop document. The image will appear in a bounding box that can be manipulated before anchoring with a click of the (Return)[Enter] key. A new layer is created automatically with the name of the EPS file.

## Position a Layer

To move a layer's position in the Layers palette list, click on the layer you want to move in the Layers palette and drag it up or down the list of layers to the place you want to move it. As you drag the layer, the lines between the layers will darken to indicate where the layer will fall if you let go.

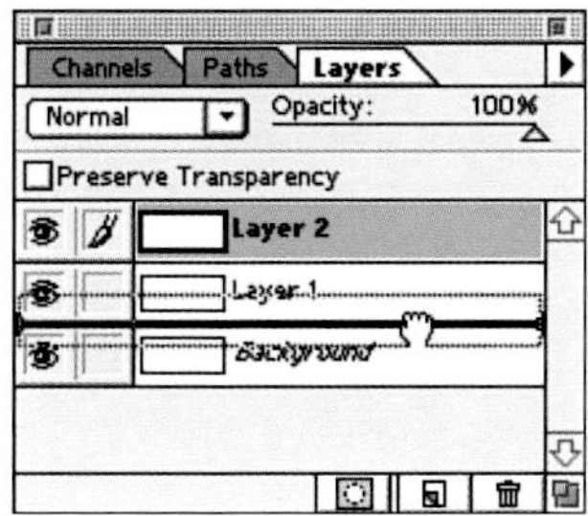


## Reduce a Layer's Opacity

Drag the Opacity slider in the Layers palette toward the left. If you need to increase the opacity, drag it toward the right.

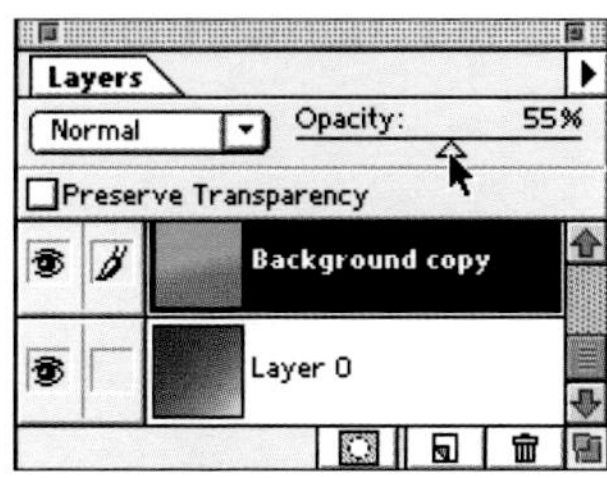


## Return to the Composite Channel

**Shortcut:** Press (Command-~)[Control-~].

If you want to return to the composite channel, click on its thumbnail or title (RGB, CMYK, Lab). The composite channel always will be the first one in the list.

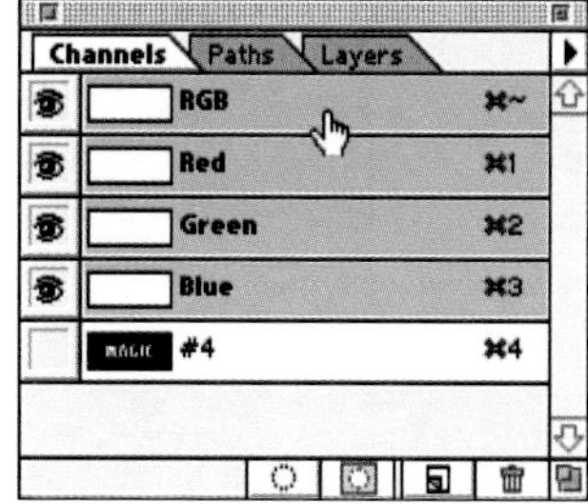


If you are in an RGB file, then Channels 0 through 3 should now be active because each of the R, G, and B channels are individual parts of the RGB image.

## Save a File

To save a file, choose File➡Save As. This displays the Save As dialog box, in which you name your new file and choose a format in which to save it.

File format selection depends on what you have in your file, what you want to keep when you save it, and what you're going to do with the file after it is saved. Consult a detailed Photoshop book, such as *Photoshop 4 Complete*, for more guidance on which file format is best for your needs.

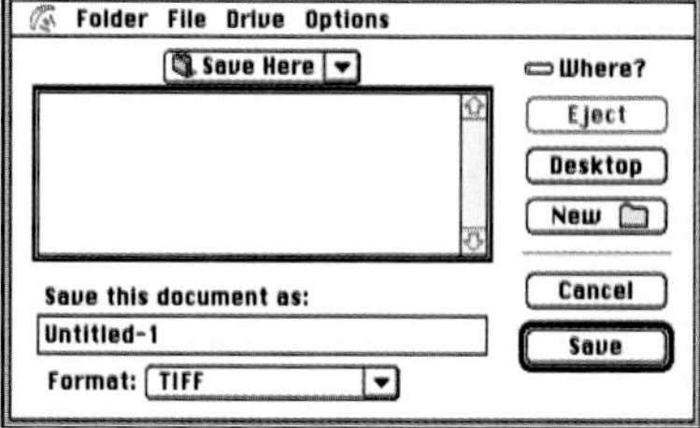


## Save a Selection

**Shortcut:** Click the Save Selection icon on the Channels palette.

To save a selection, choose Select➡Save Selection.

The Save Selection dialog box opens. Choose your options and click OK to save the selection.

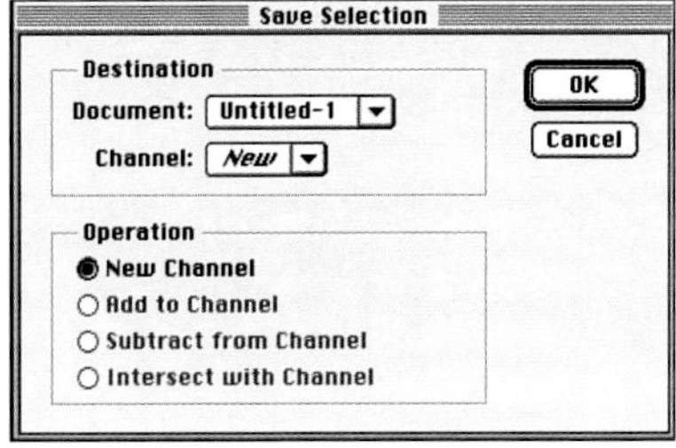


## Scale Up

Select Image➡Image Size. Check the Resample Image box at the bottom of the Image Size dialog box. Increase the number of pixels in the image. This instruction will usually tell you to change the Interpolation Method to Nearest Neighbor as well.

### Switch Foreground/Background Colors

**Shortcut:** Press X to switch the foreground and background colors.

To switch the foreground and background colors, click on the Switch Colors icon. This flips the two colors shown in this icon only, and does not affect the rest of the image.

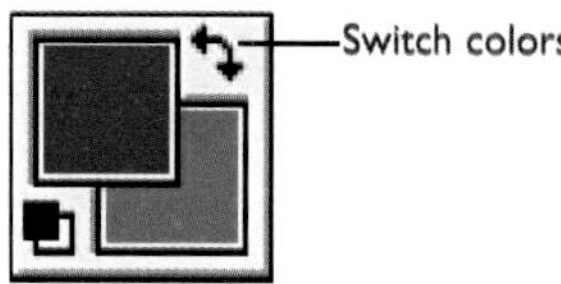


### Switch to Default Colors

**Shortcut:** Press D to switch to the default foreground and background colors.

To change the foreground and background colors to black and white respectively, click on the Default Colors icon.

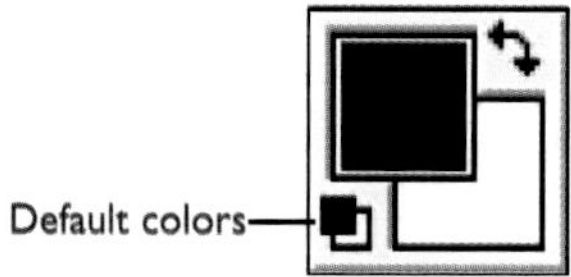


### Turn On/Off Preserve Transparency

To turn on or off the Preserve Transparency option for a particular layer, first make that layer the active layer. Then, click the Preserve Transparency checkbox on the Layers palette. This option is not available for the Background layer.

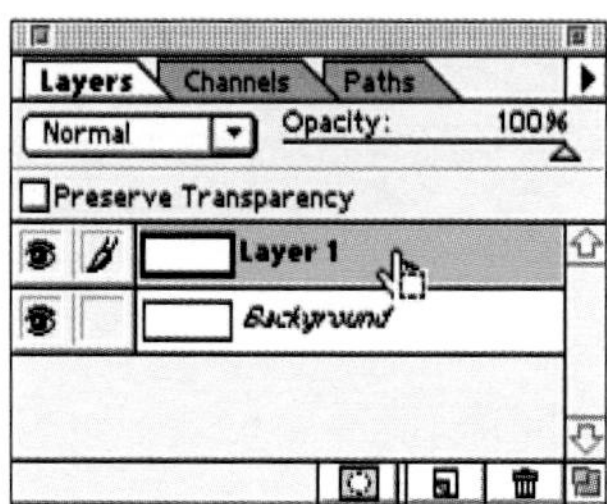


### Vary Pressure

If you are using a graphics tablet and pressure-sensitive stylus you can vary the brush size, color, or opacity as you paint by varying your pen pressure; check the appropriate boxes in the Options palette for a tool to vary any or all of these three characteristics.

If you are using a mouse, you can specify a number of steps in the Fade field to make a stroke that feathers out. The higher the number of steps, the slower the fade.

Changing the value on the Opacity slider is effective for both mouse and tablet users.

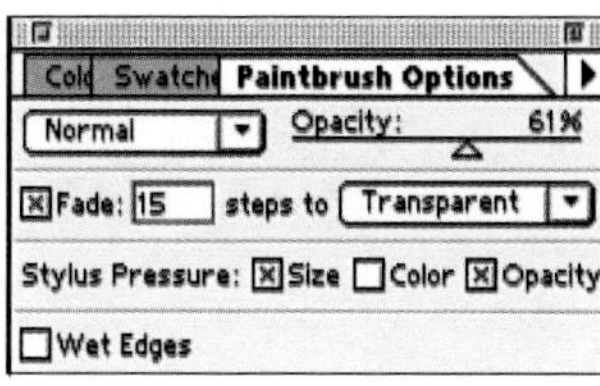

A bouclé is fabric woven from thick, fuzzy, textured yarns. This effect creates a heavy texture that makes wonderful fabric. I'd love to have this fabric in a winter coat! You can make this texture seamless with a bit of extra work.

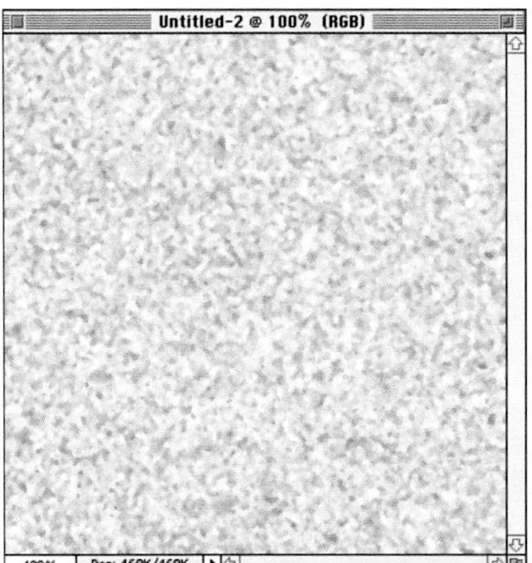


**1** Create a new file. I used one at 400×400 pixels. Choose Filter➡Texture➡Grain (Intensity: 100, Contrast: 50, Grain Type: Clumped).

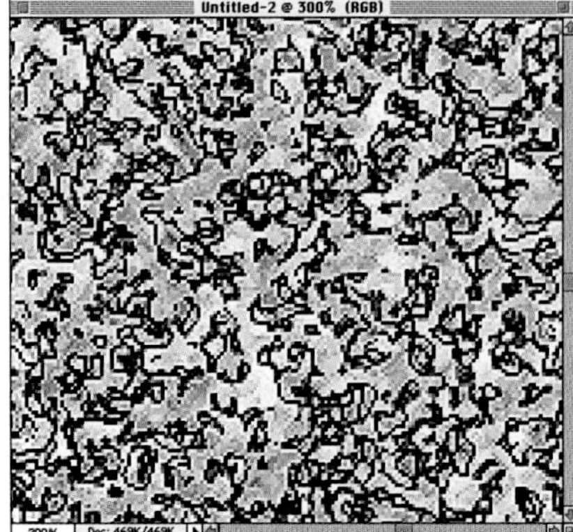


**2** Select Filter➡Brush Strokes➡Ink Outlines (Stroke Length: 4, Dark Intensity: 20, Light Intensity: 10).

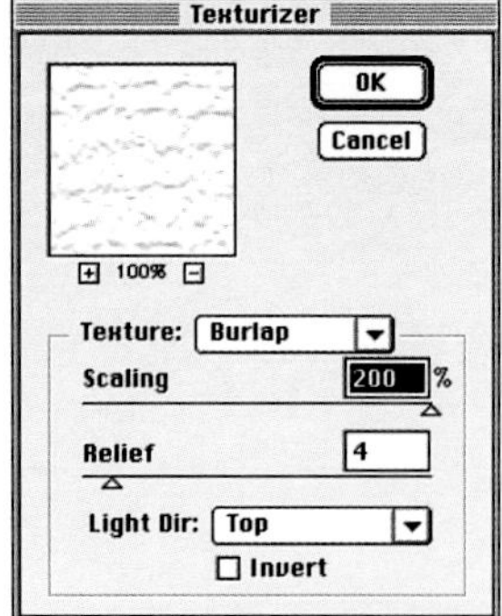


**3** Create a new layer (Layer 1) by holding down the (Option)[Alt] key and clicking on the New Layer icon. In the dialog box, change the blending mode to Multiply and check the box marked Fill with Multiply—neutral color (white). Choose Filter➡Texture➡Texturizer (Texture: Burlap, Scaling: 200, Relief: 4, Light Direction: Top).

**4** The filter does not show up. Choose Image➥Adjust➥Levels (Command-L)[Control-L]. Drag the black Input slider until it is under the place where the black pixels on the graph start to increase. I chose 220 for my image.

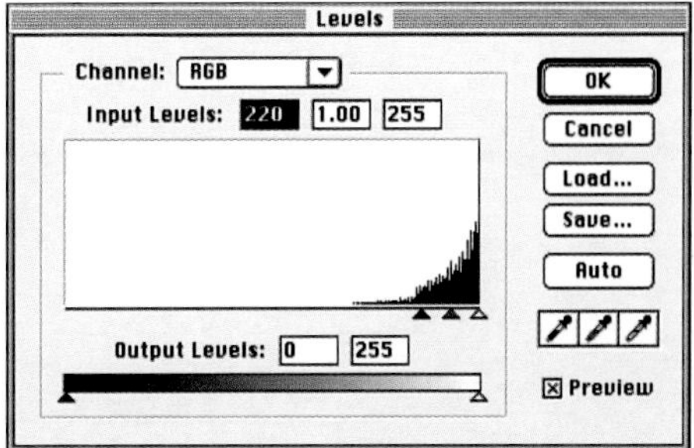


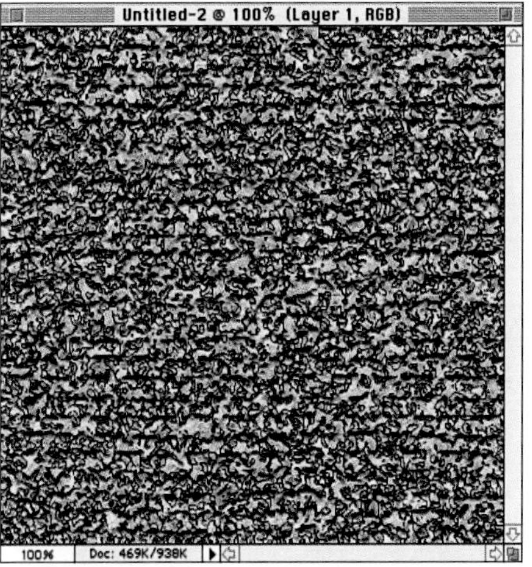


**5** Create a new layer (Layer 2). Merge the visible layers to this blank layer (Shift-Command-Option-E)[Shift-Alt-Control-E]. This is a way to have your cake and eat it too. You can add a filter to the combined layer, but you don't lose your originals. Select Filter➥Brush Strokes➥Angled Strokes (Direction Balance: 50, Stroke Length: 50, Sharpness: 3).

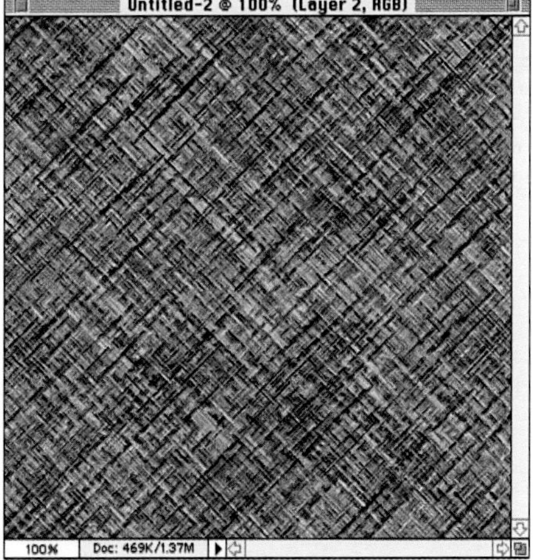

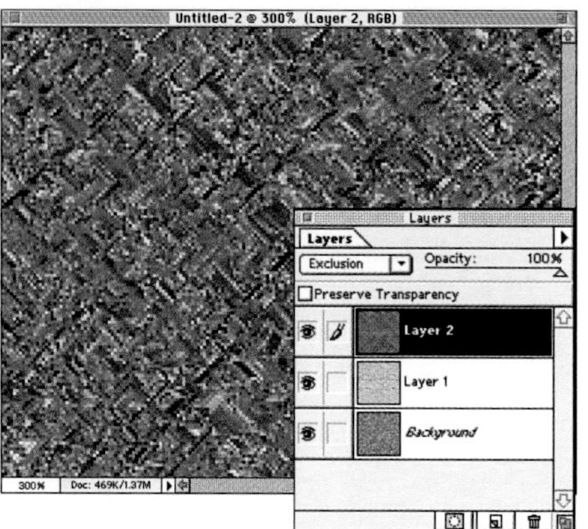


6 Change the blending mode to Exclusion.

## VARIATIONS

If you want to make the image into a seamless pattern, select Filter➡Other➡Offset (Wrap Around) and set the distances to half of your image size. For my 400×400 pixel image, I offset 200 pixels to the right and 200 pixels down. Make the pattern seamless using the Rubber Stamp method. In most cases, you will have little or nothing to touch up. Select➡All. Define the pattern. Create a new file at the desired size. Fill with pattern.

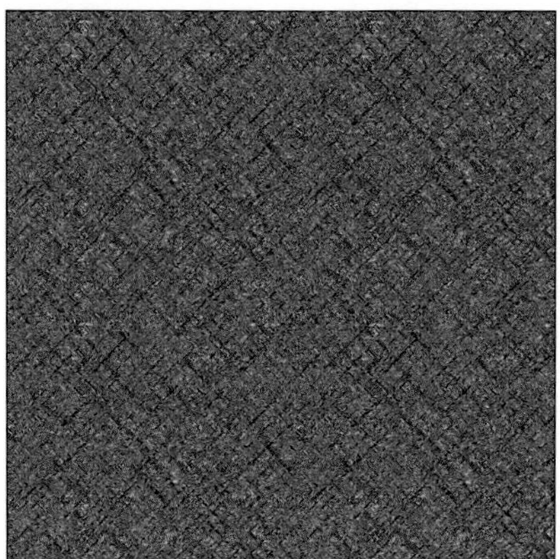

To make a darker texture with bright highlights, use Difference mode in Step 6 instead of Exclusion mode.

To get a texture that is fuzzy, but does not look woven, stop after Step 4 and change the blending mode to Exclusion.

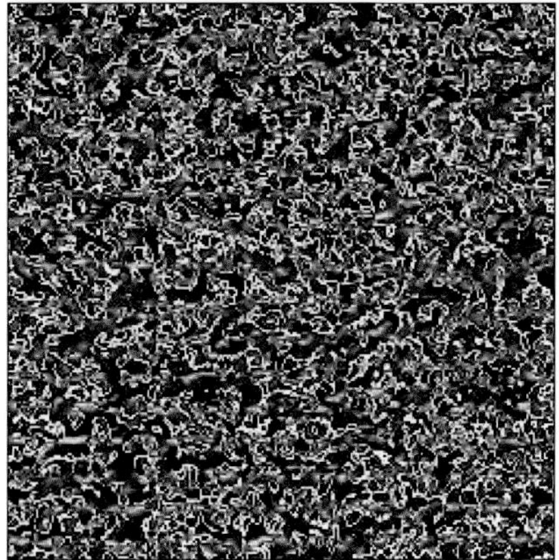

Try making a fabric with darker flecks of yarn. In Step 3, choose Filter➥Pixelate➥Crystalize with a Cell size of 10. Omit Step 4. ■

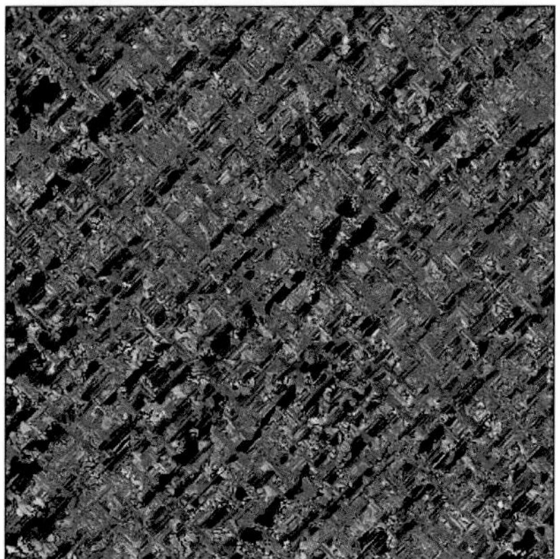

Bricks are another deceptively simple texture. You can draw an accurate rendition of a brick—which is simply a rectangle—and repeat it quite quickly, but it will probably not look real. Bricks that are too perfect practically scream "computer-generated." Here's how to make bricks that could almost fool the wolf.

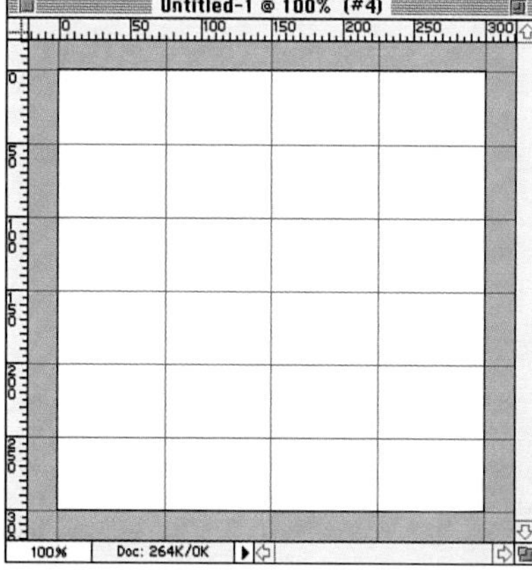


**1** Create a new file. Mine is 300×300 pixels. This is the template in which you will create the outlines of the bricks. Luckily for you, you really only have to build it once—as long as you don't create your bricks inside of it, you can reuse it for any size project. Turn on the Rulers (Command-R)[Control-R]. Create a new channel. Invert the channel (Command-I)[ Control-I] so that it is white. Add vertical guides at the 0, 75, 150, 225, and 300 pixels marks on the top ruler. Add a horizontal guide every 50 pixels on the side ruler (including the 0 and the 300 pixel position). The guides divide the file into 24 pieces.

**2** Resize the window so that it is a little bit larger than the image. Double-click the Line tool. Set the Line width to the relative thickness that you want between the bricks. I used a Line width of 6 pixels. Switch the foreground color to black. Channel #4 is active. Select View➡Snap to Guides. Cover all of the horizontal guides with the Line tool (press the Shift key to keep the line straight). You get a more reliable line if you start dragging the cursor from outside of the image on the guide and release the mouse button only after you are clear of the image on the other side. If you don't do this, you risk leaving some needed pixels white.



**TOOLBOX**

Bricks

Act color swatches

**3** Double-click the rectangular Marquee tool. Make certain that Feather is set to 0. Set a fixed size to 300 pixels wide × 50 pixels high. Drag the Marquee to select the top 1/6 of the image. Because Snap to Guides is on, the Marquee will snap to the exact locations needed after you drag it into the vicinity. Hold down the Shift key and drag the Marquee to select the third and fifth sections of the image as well.

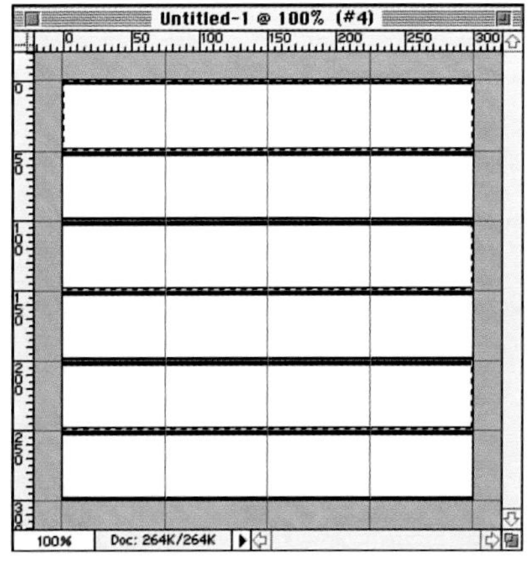


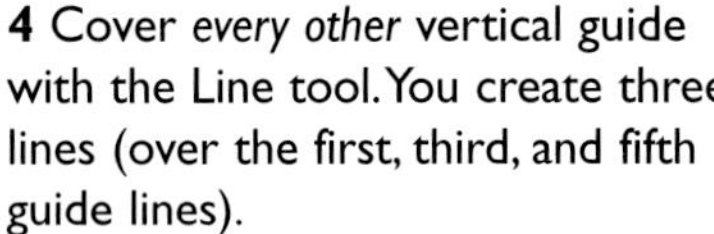

**4** Cover *every other* vertical guide with the Line tool. You create three lines (over the first, third, and fifth guide lines).

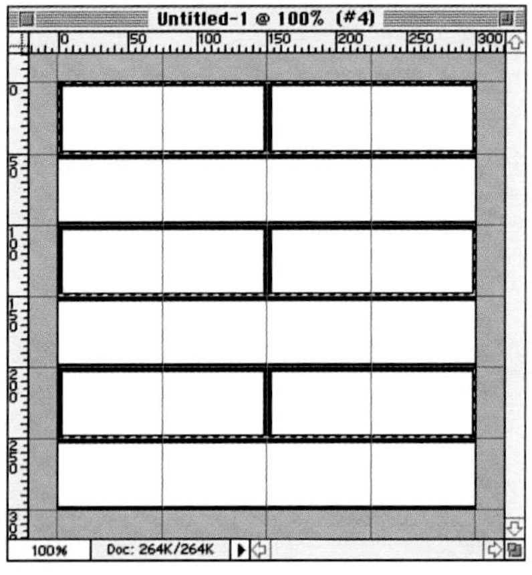


**5** Reverse the selection (Select➡ Inverse). Draw straight lines over the remaining two uncolored guide lines. Deselect. Turn off the guides (Command-;)[Control-;].

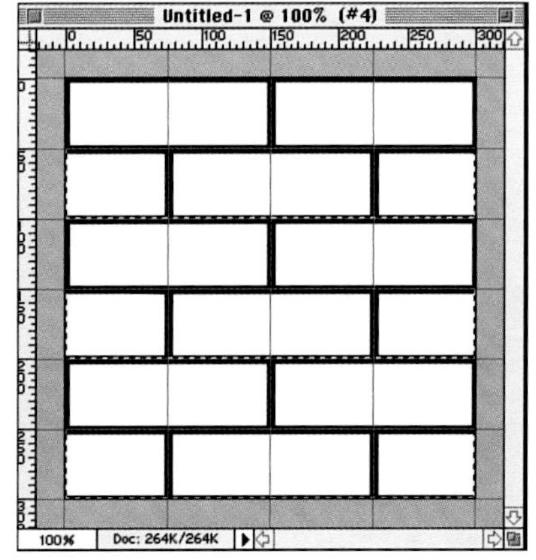

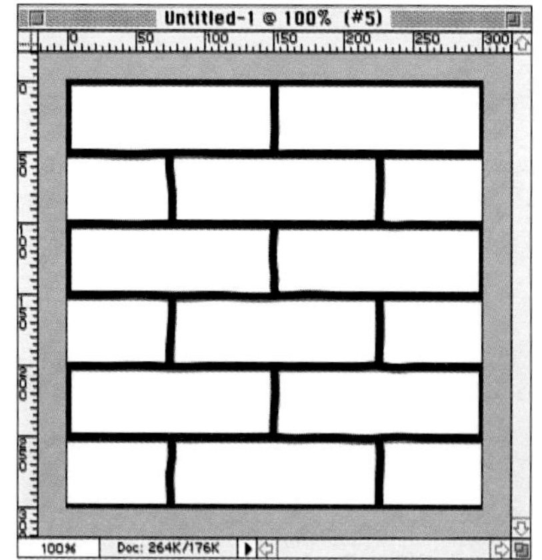


**6** You now have a perfect grid block for creating bricks. Nature is not perfect, however, so if you want to add some realism, you need to distress the outline. Duplicate Channel #4 (Channel #5). This allows you to keep one unadulterated copy for future needs. Double-click the rectangular Marquee tool. Change the Style to Normal. Select an area in Channel #5 that is centered on a vertical line. Apply Filter➥Distort➥Twirl. Keep the setting somewhere between + or – 16. You want to subtly move the line off of the perpendicular. The key word here, though, is *subtly*. Use too high a setting and your bricks will look decidedly odd. Continue to make selections and apply the Twirl filter with a variety of low settings. You can press (Command-Option-F) [Control-Alt-F] to reapply the same filter with new settings.

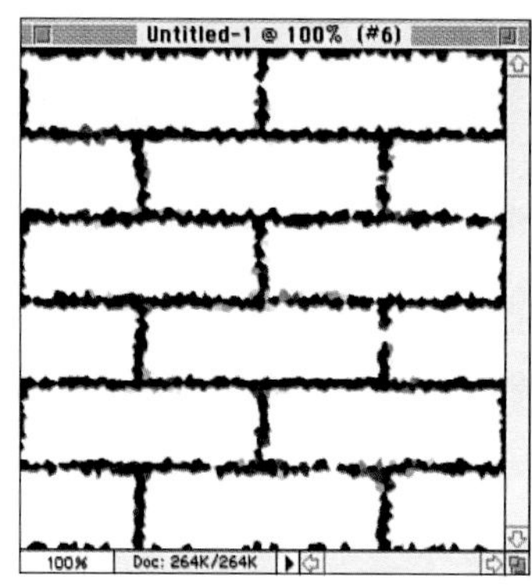


**7** Duplicate Channel #5 (Channel #6). This way, you can play with additional changes to the mortaring for the bricks and not have to redo the Twirl filter. Select Filter➥Pixelate➥Crystallize. Select a cell size smaller than 11. I used a cell size of 6.

**8** Reapply the Crystallize filter (Command-Option-F)[Control-Alt-F] and change the cell size to something smaller. I used a cell size of 3. The outlines of the bricks are nicely irregular.

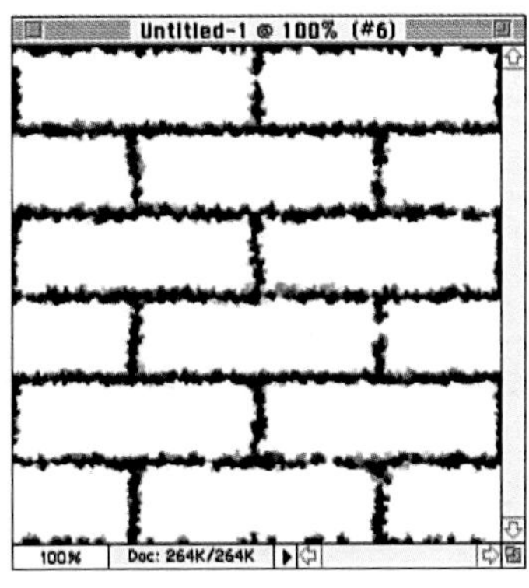


**9** Select Filter➥Blur➥Gaussian Blur. I used a Radius of 2.0. Keep the setting between about 1.0 and 3.0.

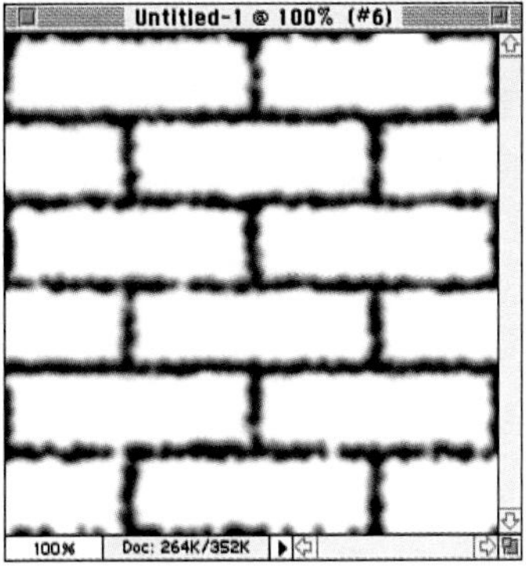


**10** This step is optional. Look at the blurred lines. If you see areas where the line is very thin or not there, that means that you will have no mortaring on your bricks in that location. Although the mortar can get thin, it should always be present. Also, areas that are too dissimilar cause the viewer's eye to notice the repeat—which is something that you really want to avoid. Now—with that buildup…with Channel #6 active, load the selection in Channel #4. Reverse the selection (Select➥Inverse). Choose Select➥Modify➥Contract. I contracted the selection by 2 pixels. Fill with black. The only purpose of this step is to make sure that there is some part of a mortar line all along the bricks. Deselect.

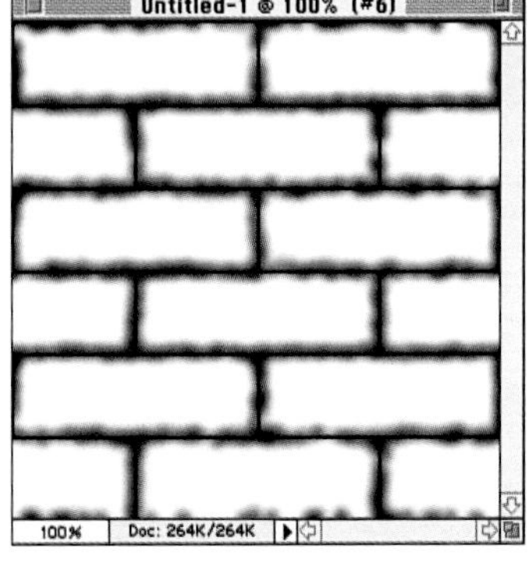

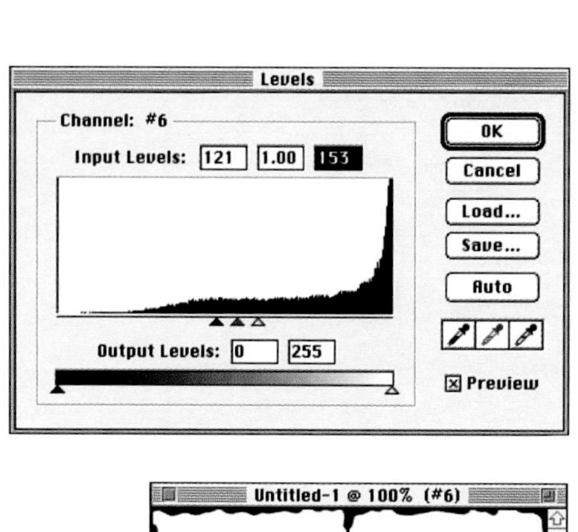


**11** Select Image➥Adjust➥Levels. Drag the right and left Input sliders until they are quite close to each other. This sharpens the blur that you applied by forcing many of the gray levels to white or black. You can control the thickness of the line by the location of the three sliders. The closer that three sliders are to the right, the thicker the line will be. If all three sliders are toward the left, the mortar will be very thin. I kept the sliders a bit to the left of center. Save the template file.

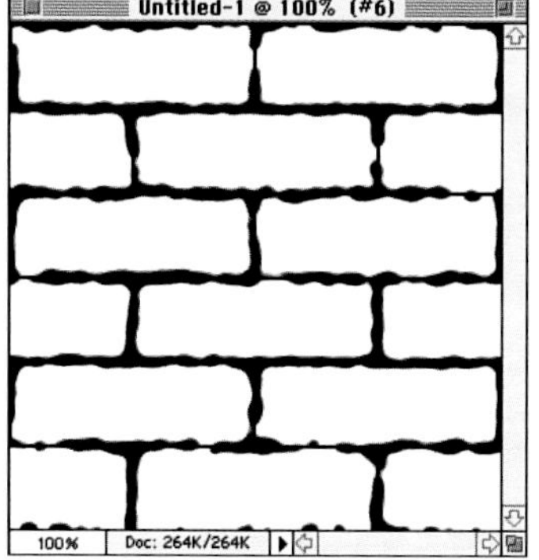


**12** It's time to build the brick surface. Create a new file the same size as the template file (300×300). Change the foreground color to a brick color. I used RGB: 100, 36, 30. You can also load the Brick.Act color swatches from the *Photoshop Textures Magic* CD-ROM. This palette is taken from a photograph of real bricks and includes a variety of brick colors. Fill the new image with foreground color.

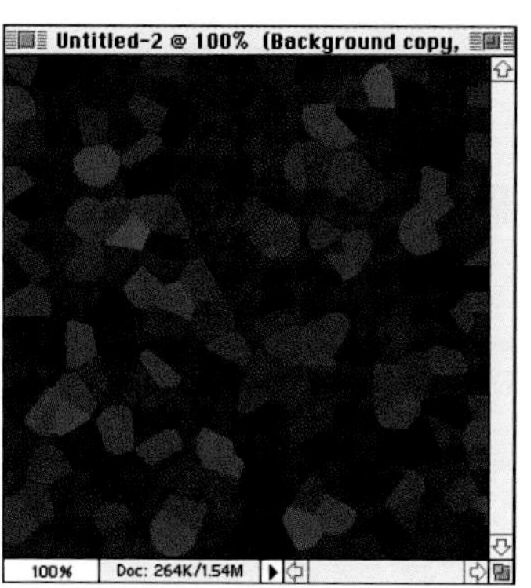


**13** You need to add a variety of colors to this tile to simulate the range of colors in real brick. There are many ways to do this. For now, switch foreground/background colors and then select Filter➥Pixellate➥Pointillize. I used a cell size of 30. Any number from 12 to 40 is fine.

**14** Choose Filter➥Blur➥Motion Blur (Angle: 81°, Distance 118). The Angle is just a little bit off of 90°. The Distance is long enough to get a run of color without wiping out the color differences. Select Filter➥Blur➥Gaussian Blur. I used a Radius of 6.8. The larger the cell size that you used in Step 13, the larger of a blur Radius you will need to use here. The idea is to create a range of colors that blend softly.

**15** Now you are ready to create surface texture on the brick. The surface texture is a mix of two Hard Light maps. Create a new layer. Switch to default colors. Choose Filter➥Render➥Clouds. Select Image➥Adjust➥Posterize and choose 5 levels.

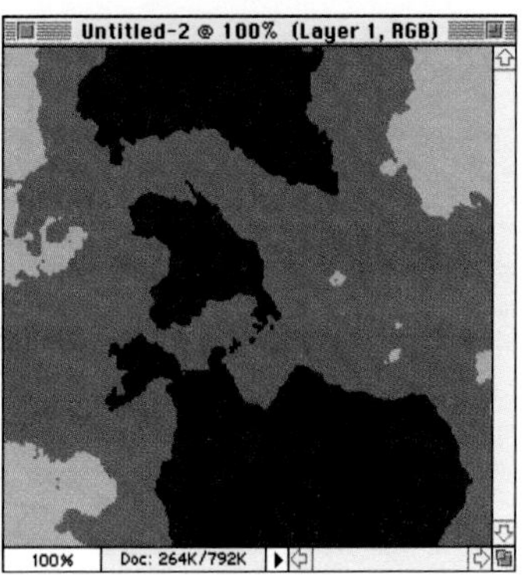


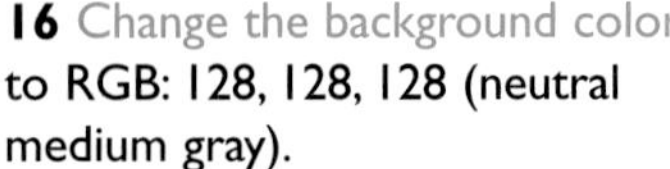

**16** Change the background color to RGB: 128, 128, 128 (neutral medium gray).

**17** Apply these filters *exactly*. Choose Filter➥Stylize➥Emboss (Angle: 136°, Height: 4 pixels, Amount: 100). Select Filter➥Stylize➥Find Edges. Select Filter➥Blur➥Gaussian Blur (0.6). Choose Filter➥Pixelate➥Pointillize (3). Select Image➥Adjust➥Desaturate. Select Filter➥Noise➥Add Noise (Amount: 42, Distribution: Gaussian, Monochromatic). Select Filter➥Blur➥Gaussian Blur (0.6) Choose Filter➥Stylize➥Emboss (Angle: 136°, Height: 2 pixels, Amount: 100). Select Filter➥Blur➥Gaussian Blur (0.3). This series of filters produces the pitted surface texture on the bricks.

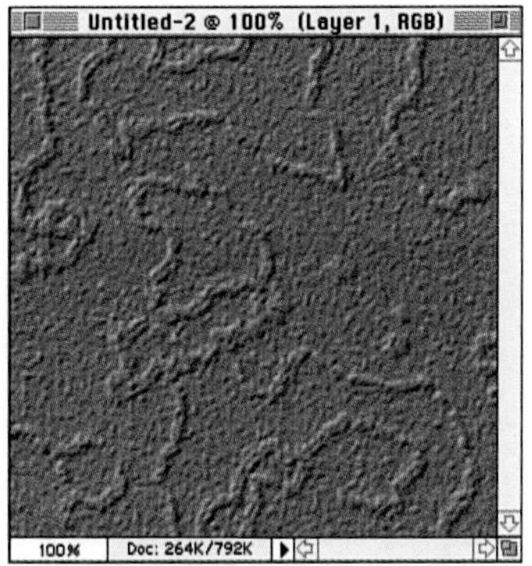

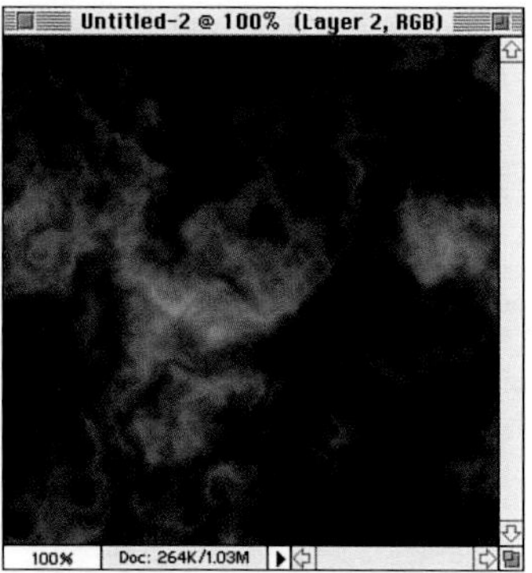


**18** Change the blending mode to Hard Light. Switch to default colors. Create a new layer. Choose Filter➥Render➥Clouds. Select Filter➥Render➥Difference Clouds. Apply the Difference Clouds filter approximately 20 times. This increases the internal complexity of the cloud structure.

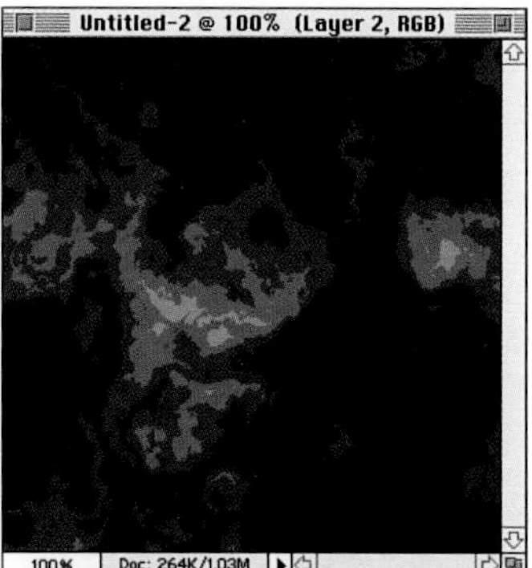


**19** Select Image➥Adjust➥ Posterize. (7 levels). This is a much more complex structure than the one produced in Step 15.

**20** Choose Filter➥Stylize➥Emboss (Angle: 136°, Height: 3 pixels, Amount: 100). Change the blending mode to Hard Light.

**21** Your image will probably have a bit more shine than brick usually contains. Make Layer 2 active (if it is not already). Select Image➡Adjust➡Curves. Use the Pencil in the Curves dialog to match the setting shown. Your surface texture is complete.

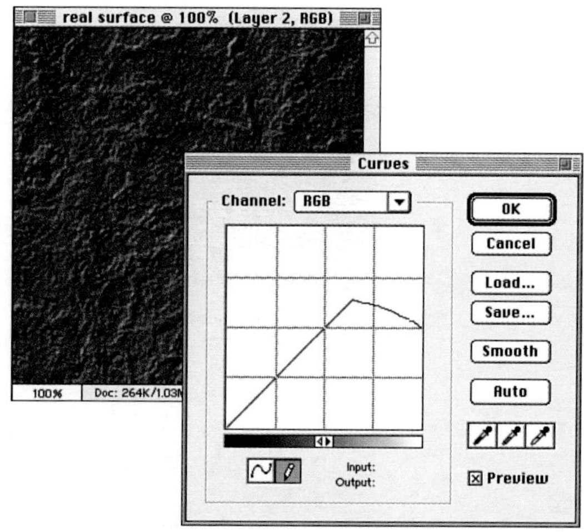


**22** Finally—it is time to create the bricks. Make the saved Brick Template document active. Select Image➡Duplicate➡OK. Work in the duplicate. Choose Image➡Apply Image. Select the brick surface image as the Source (mine is called Untitled-2). Use the Merged layers, RGB channel as shown.

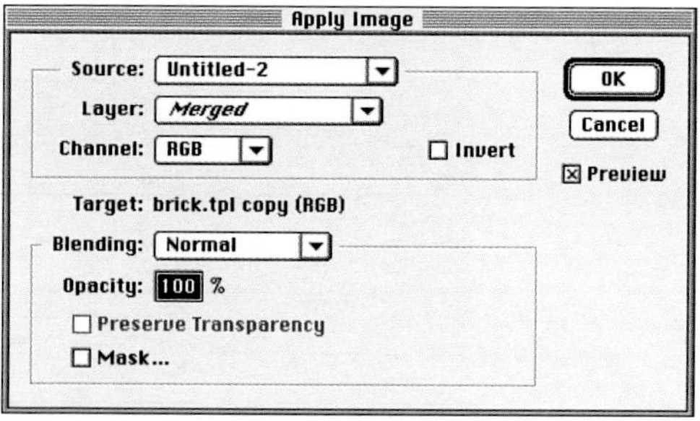


**23** Switch the foreground color to a good mortar color. I chose RGB: 182, 162, 148, which is a warm blush gray. Create a new layer. Load the selection in Channel #6 (Command-Option-6)[Control-Alt-6]. Invert the selection (Select➡Inverse). Fill with foreground color.

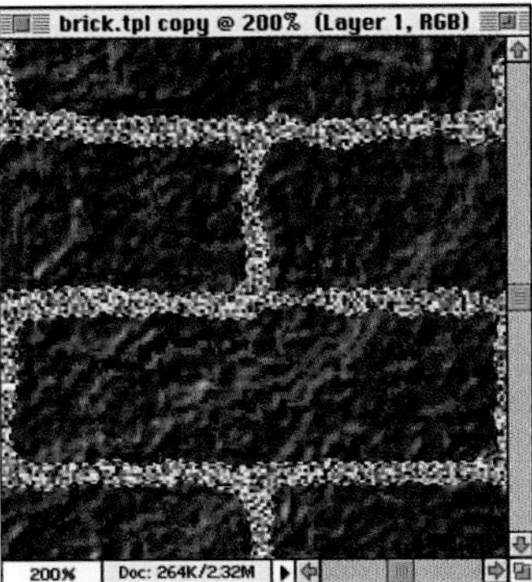


**24** Select Filter➡Noise➡Add Noise (Distribution: Gaussian, Monochromatic). I used an Amount of 76.

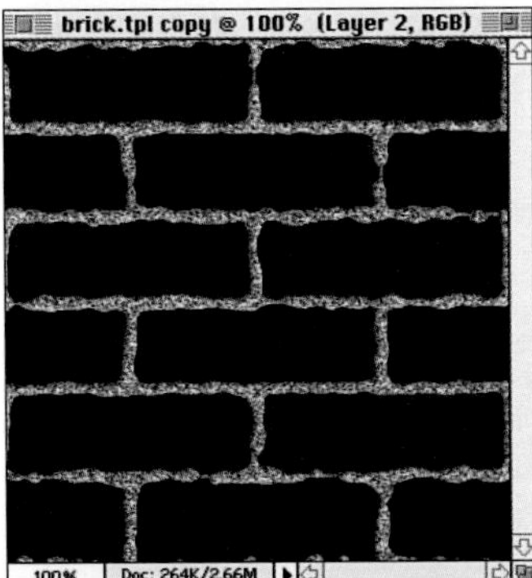


**25** Create a new layer. Invert the selection (Select➡Inverse). Switch to default colors. Fill with foreground color. Deselect. This creates the basis for raising the bricks away from the mortar.

**26** Choose Filter➡Stylize➡Emboss (Angle: 136°, Height: 5 pixels, Amount: 100). Select Filter➡Blur➡Gaussian Blur (2.0). You see gray bricks with a slight highlight and shadow. Change the blending mode to Hard Light. Now the gray disappears and only the highlight and shadow are left.

**27** The bricks are fairly close to being finished, but the brick is so realistic that it seems a pity not to make the mortar a little more natural as well. Create a new layer. Load the selection in Channel #6 (Command-Option-6)[Control-Alt-6]. Invert the selection (Select➡ Inverse). Select Filter➡Render➡ Clouds. Select Filter➡Noise➡Add Noise (Distribution: Gaussian, Monochromatic). I used an Amount of 76. The Clouds filter gives a random shading to the mortar and the noise adopts that shading. Reduce the layer opacity to about 60%.

**28** The mortar from Step 27 needs to gain some color. Duplicate Layer 1 (the original mortar) and position the layer at the top of the Layers list. Change the blending mode to Color.

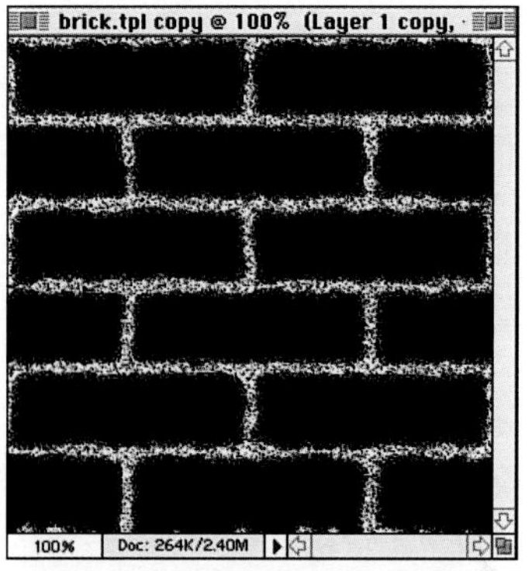


**29** If you want a final touch of realism—for use in an onscreen presentation or on the Web (this will not survive the printing process as effectively), in the Channels palette, duplicate Channel #6 (Channel #7). Invert the channel (Command I) [Control-I]. Load the selection in Channel #7. Choose Select➡ Modify➡Expand (3 pixels). Choose Select➡Feather (3 pixels). Select Filter➡Noise➡Add Noise (Distribution: Gaussian, Monochromatic). I used an Amount of 200.

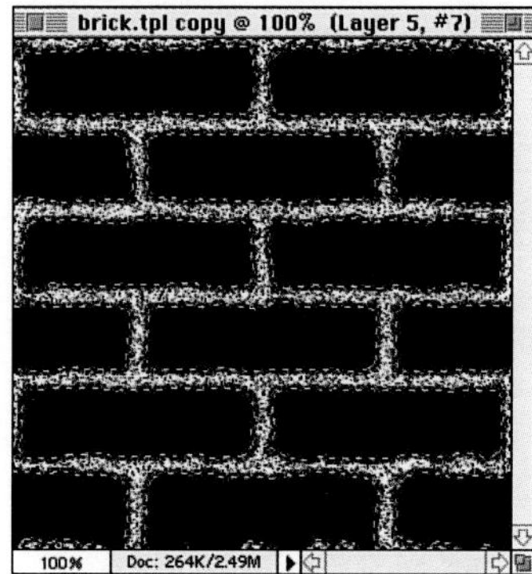

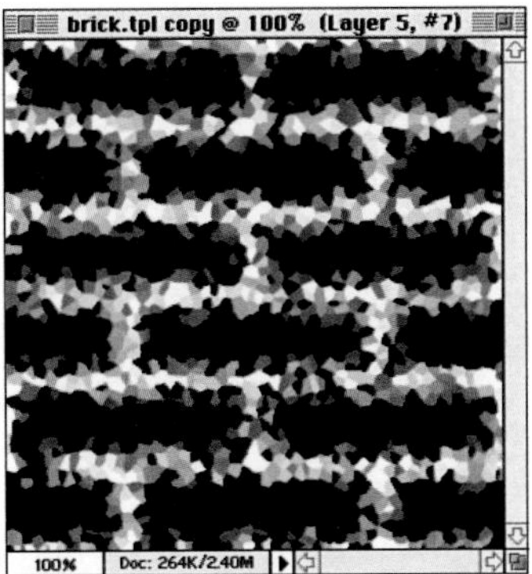


**30** Deselect. Choose Filter➡Pixelate➡Crystallize. I used a cell size of 9. You need a fairly small cell size to leave values of gray "outside the lines"—as if a messy bricklayer splattered mortar around a bit. Choose Image➡Adjust➡Equalize.

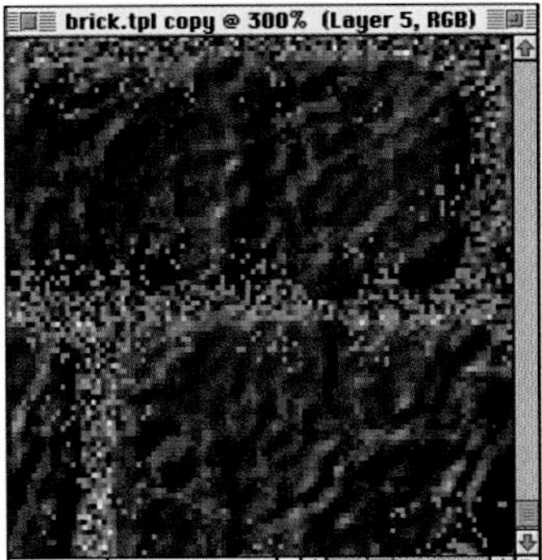


**31** Return to the composite channel. Create a new layer. Load the selection in Channel #7. Double-click the Airbrush tool and change the mode for the Airbrush to Dissolve. Set the Pressure to about 6%. Switch the foreground color to the mortar color that you used. Hide the marching ants (Command-H)[Control-H]. Quickly brush over the image leaving bits of mortar outside the mortar lines. The image shows a close-up of noise on the bricks.

**32** You can now build the final pattern tile. Select Image➡Duplicate➡Merged Layers only. Duplicate the Background layer. Select Image➡Canvas Size. Double the width of the image (600 pixels) and anchor the image in the top-left. Select Filter➡Other➡Offset (Horizontal: 300, Vertical: 200, Wrap Around). This setting keeps the pattern accurate as you offset. By offsetting the image, you more thoroughly randomize the bricks and make it harder to see the repeat.

**33** Select➡All. Define the pattern. Create a new file of the desired dimensions. Fill with pattern.

## VARIATIONS

If you want a different brick pattern, you can use the file Flemish.Psd on the *Photoshop Textures Magic* CD-ROM. Follow the original instructions starting with Step 6. This pattern is called a Flemish Bond by bricklayers.

To add other colors to the brick, airbrush the brick color map rather than generating it using the Pointillize filter. I used the colors in the Bricks.Act file on the *Photoshop Textures Magic* CD-ROM. ■

Brocades are two-toned fabrics in which the pattern and toning occur in the weave structure rather than in the color of the threads used. Brocades are elegant and change depending upon the play of light. Here is a computer-generated technique that retains the optical magic of a woven brocade.

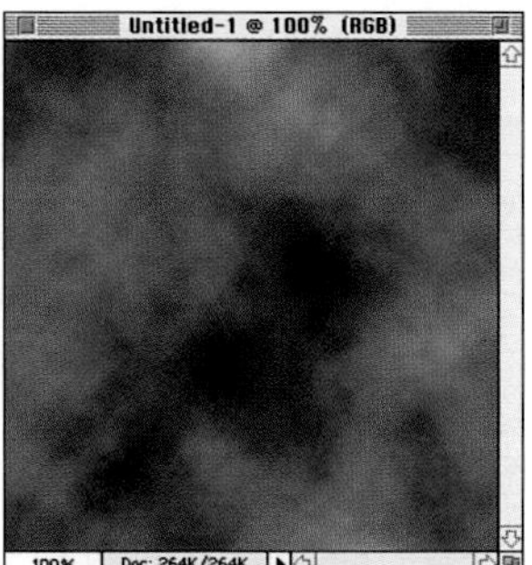


**1** Create a new file. Mine is 300×300 pixels. Switch to default colors. Select Filter➡Render➡Clouds. You can press (Command-F) [Control-F] to repeat the filter until you like the general mix of black-and-white.

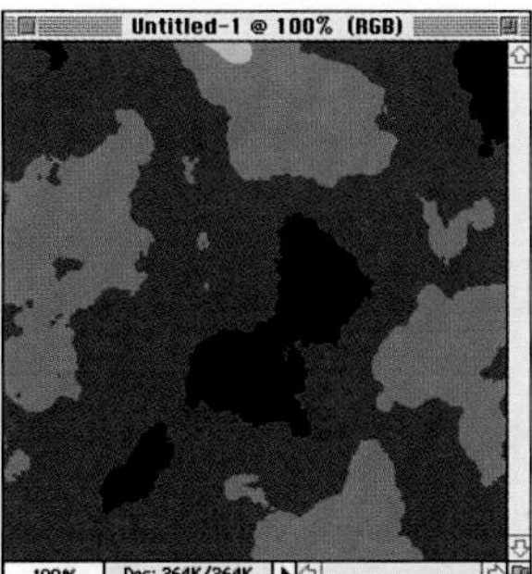


**2** Select Image➡Adjust➡Posterize. The number of levels should be an even number from 4–10. I chose 6 levels because that seemed most attractive when I tried out a variety of levels on this texture.

**3** To remove the jagged edges (to get spots or dots), you need to apply Filter➡Blur➡Gaussian Blur. I used a Radius of 5. Blur the image until you almost cannot distinguish the separate colors.

**4** Select Image➡Adjust➡Posterize again. Use the same number of Levels as before. Notice how much rounder the shapes have become.

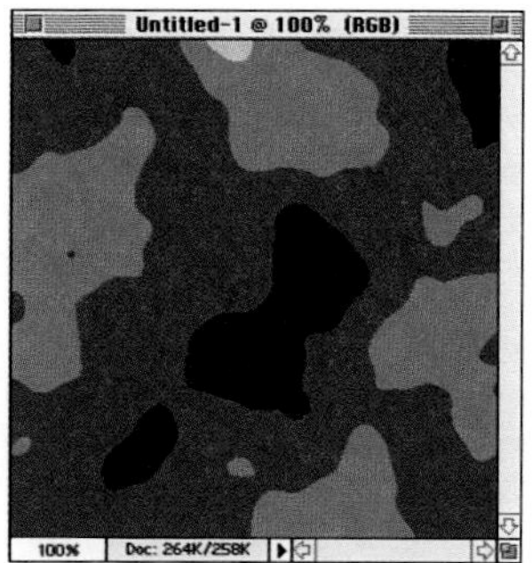


**5** Double-click the Magic Wand tool and set the Tolerance to 0. Turn Anti-aliased on. Click in the darkest spot in the image. Choose Select➡Similar. Fill the selection with foreground color (black).

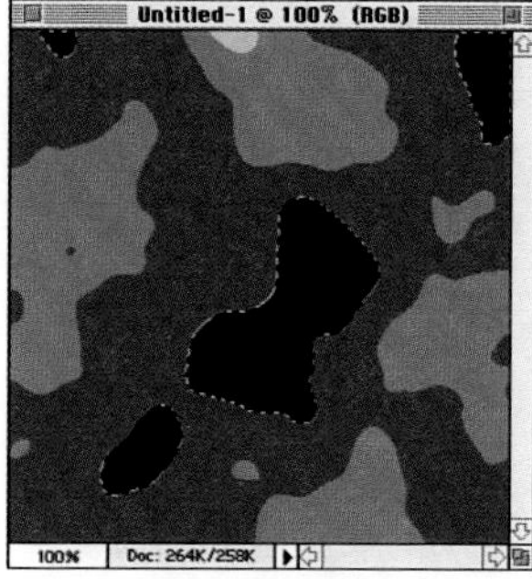


**6** Click inside of the next-darkest area (it should surround your last selection). Choose Select➡Similar. Fill the selection with background color (white).

**7** Repeat Steps 5 and 6 for all of the remaining values in the image. There may not be six values even if you selected six levels, so it is difficult to predict how many times you need to do this. The object of this is to make the image black-and-white but still preserve the dots and spots. Deselect.

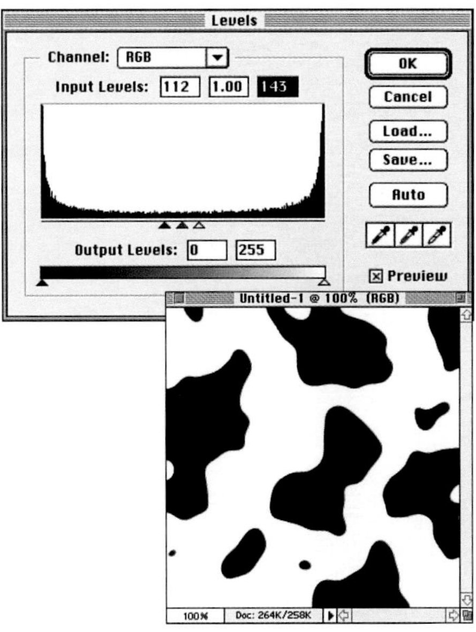


**8** Select Filter➥Blur➥Gaussian Blur. I used a Radius of 3.5. Anything from 2–5 should be okay as long as you can see the image detail when the image is blurred. You do need to use a Radius of at least 1 in order to smooth the edges of the shapes. Select Image➥Adjust➥Levels, and drag the black and white Input sliders toward the center of the histogram. They should line up close to one another at a position where the shape edges are smooth.

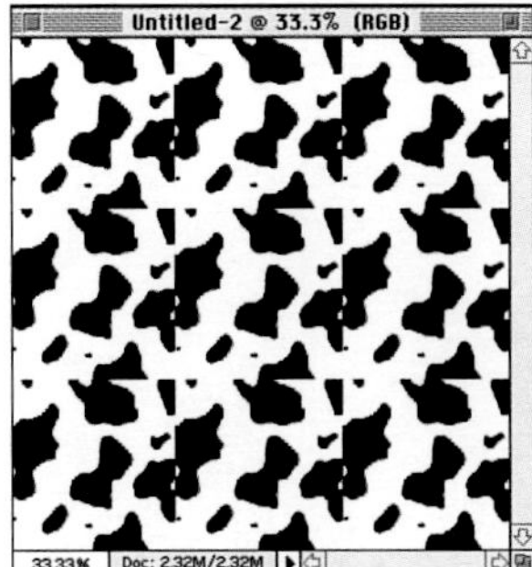


**9** Select➥All. Define the pattern. Create a new file that is three times the size of the original. Fill with pattern. This image is not seamless, but because it is black-and-white (and will remain two-toned), it does not matter. The straight edges will actually look good.

**10** Make the Channels palette active. Create a new channel (Channel #4). Fill with pattern. This is the same pattern that is in the RGB channel.

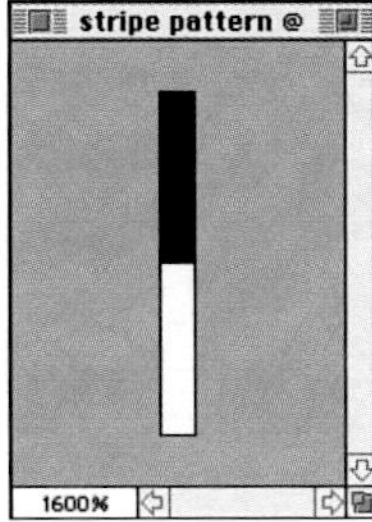


**11** To create the pattern that produces the brocade, create a new file 1 pixel wide × 10 pixels high. Using the Pencil tool and the 1-pixel brush, color the first five pixels of the file black.

**12** Select➡All. Define the pattern. Make the large, pattern-filled brocade image active. Return to the composite channel. Load the selection in Channel #4. Fill with pattern. Do not deselect.

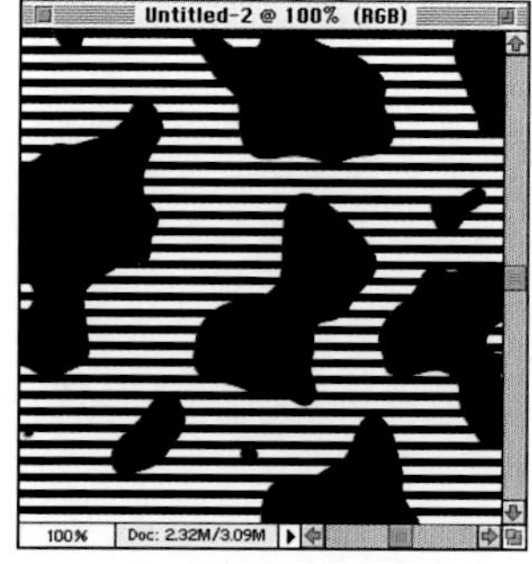


**13** Make the stripe pattern file active. Select Image➡Rotate Canvas➡90° CW. Select➡All. Define the pattern. Make the large brocade image active. Reverse the selection (Select➡Inverse). Fill with pattern. Drop the selection.

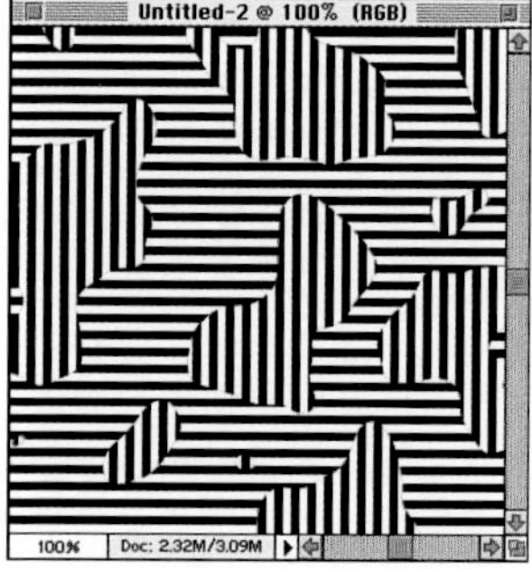


**14** Select Filter➡Blur➡Gaussian Blur. I used a Radius of 2. You just need to blur the pattern a little bit before you emboss it.

**15** Choose Filter➡Stylize➡Emboss (Angle: 136°, Height: 3 pixels, Amount: 100).

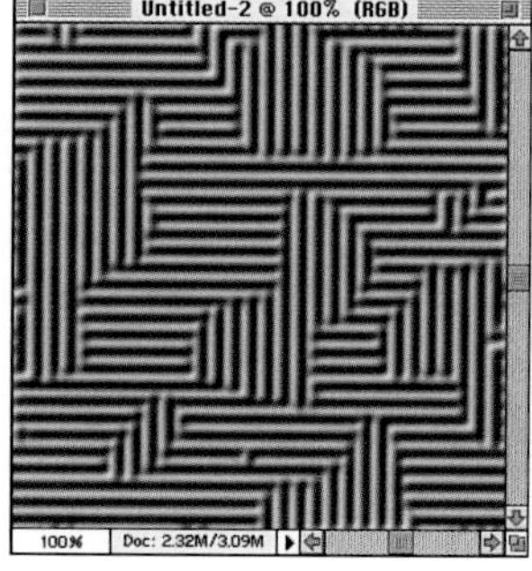

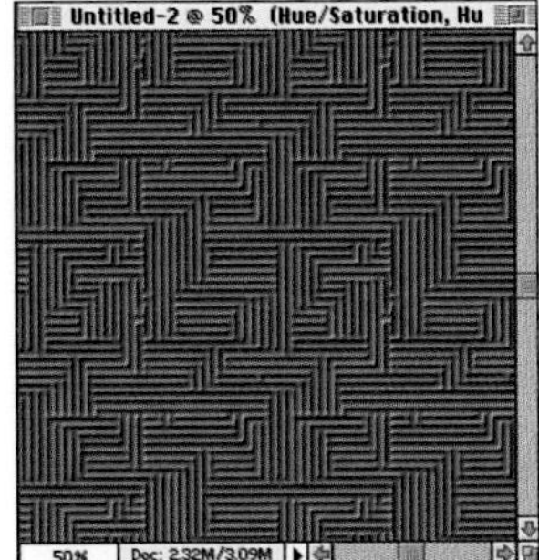

**16** You can now color the texture. Create an adjustment layer for Hue/Saturation. Click the Colorize button and pick any color that you like. I used settings of –131 for Hue, 37 for Saturation, and –12 for Lightness.

**17** Double-click the rectangular Marquee and set a fixed size to the size of the original image (mine is 300×300 pixels). Drag the Marquee into the center of the image. It does not need to be exactly the center but it does need to be close to the center. Make the Background layer active. Define the pattern. Create a new file of the desired size (or simply crop the pattern image and save the tile for later use). If you create a new file, fill with pattern. The 300-pixel selection is seamless—which it would not have been, because of the embossing, if you had built it all in the original 300-pixel square image.

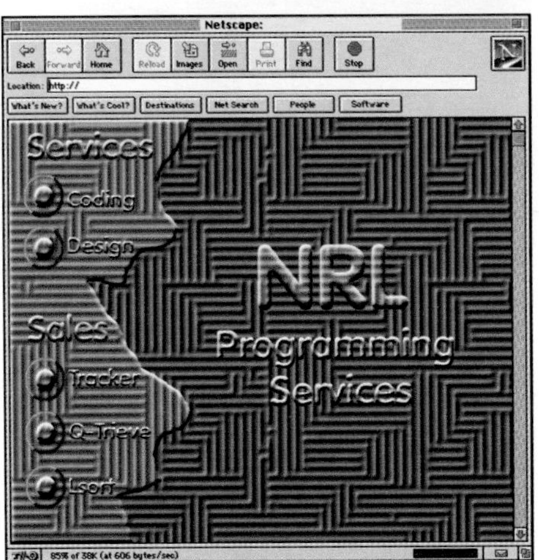

## Variations

If you want a pattern that is seamless before you add the brocade, after Step 9, select Filter➡Other➡Offset (Wrap Around). Make the Horizontal and Vertical distances one-half of the image dimensions. Select Filter➡Blur➡Gaussian Blur. Apply as large a blur as you can without losing any shapes. I used a Radius of 7. Select Image➡Adjust➡Levels and adjust the histogram exactly as you did in Step 8. Select and define a center tile as you did in Step 17. Deselect. Fill with pattern. This time, it is seamless. You can proceed with the original instructions—or create a Dalmatian, or a spotted cow.

To add an actual tone on tone after Step 16, make the Background layer active. Load the selection in Channel #4. Create an adjustment layer for Levels (this one will use the selection). Drag the gamma Input slider to the right or left to make the selection darker or lighter. Proceed with Step 17. ■

# Bumpy

A bumpy texture almost sounds redundant. You need to remember, however, that "smooth" is also a texture. A "bumpy" texture is the basic building block for using textures in Photoshop. In its simplest form, you can create a bumpy surface by applying the Add Noise filter to an empty image, embossing the image, and then blurring it a tiny bit.

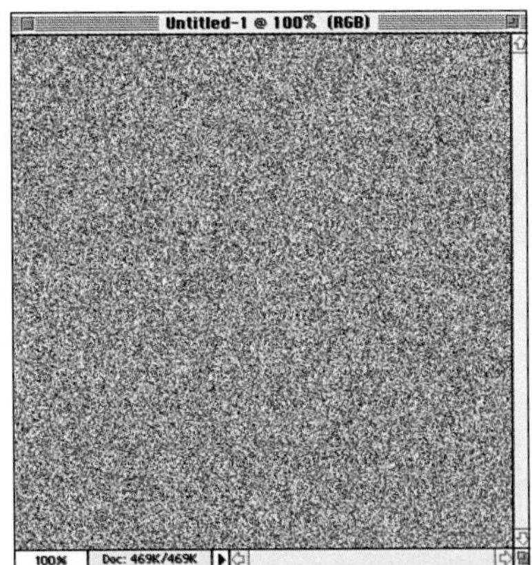


**1** Create a new file. Mine is 400×400 pixels. Select Filter➡Noise➡Add Noise. Add Noise is one of the few filters that works in a totally white image. You can use any settings you want. I used an Amount of 300, a Gaussian distribution, and Monochromatic off. A larger setting results in stronger texture, whereas a lower setting can produce a slight texture. The amount of noise needed depends on the resolution of your finished image. An image that is to be printed at a 150-line screen needs more noise than a 72 dpi image of the same dimensions in inches.

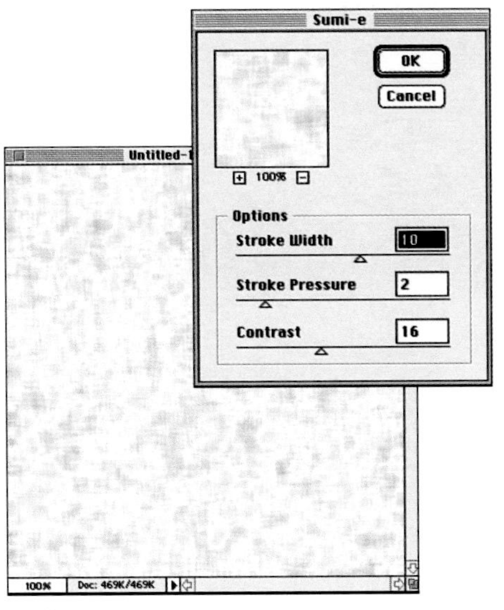


**2** Apply Filter➡Brush Strokes➡Sumi-e with a Stroke Width of 10, a Stroke Pressure of 2, and a Contrast of 16. Most of the filters from the Artistic, Brush Strokes, or Sketch categories will also produce interesting textures using this effect.

**3** Choose Filter➡Stylize➡Emboss. I used an Angle of 130°, a Height of 2 pixels, and an Amount of 100. Select Image➡Adjust➡Desaturate to remove the "odd" colors left by the Emboss filter. If the embossed surface looks too harsh, apply Filter➡Blur➡Gaussian Blur. Use a low setting of 0.3 to 1.5. You can always blur your image more—if you over-blur, the only way to fix it is to apply the Emboss filter again.

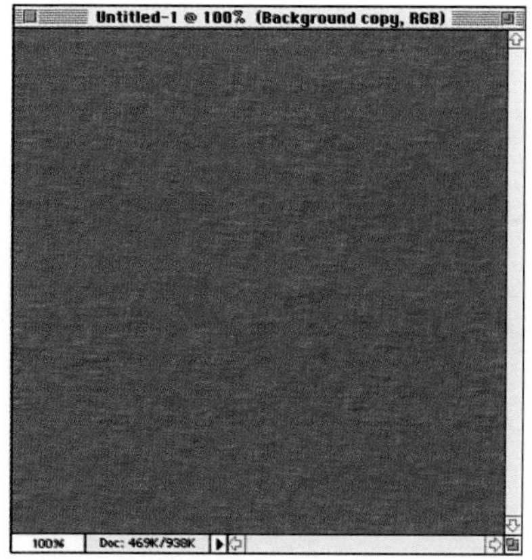


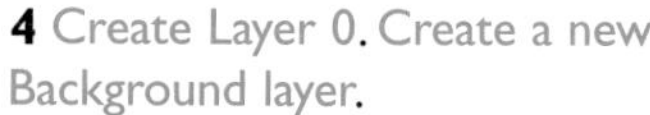

**4** Create Layer 0. Create a new Background layer.

**5** Switch the foreground color to whichever color you want to use for the base. I selected a medium blue. Fill the Background layer with the foreground color.

**6** Make Layer 0 active. Change the blending mode to Hard Light.

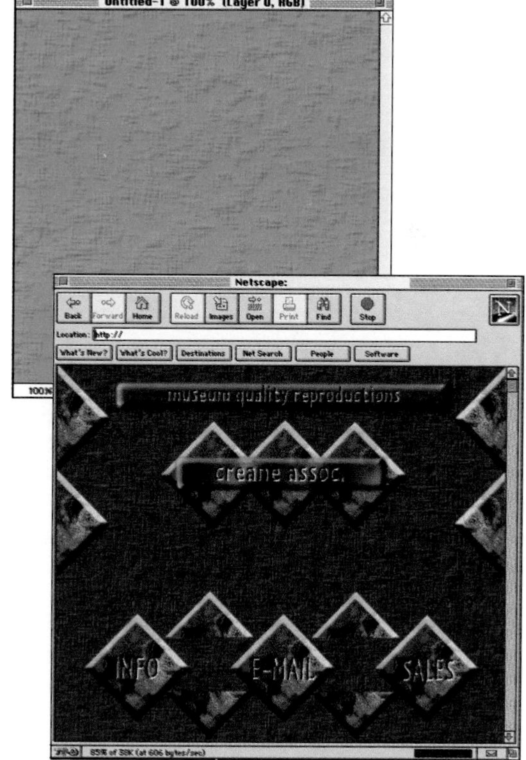

## Variations

### Texture Variations

If you want a deeper image, change the blending mode to Color Burn.

Or change the blending mode to Multiply.

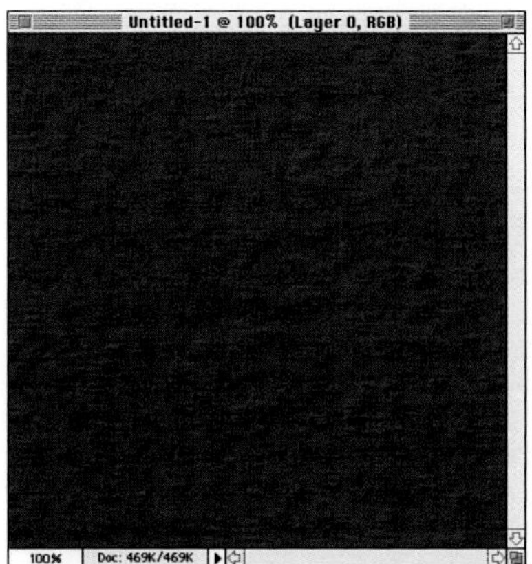


To add softness, make Layer 0 active. Choose Image➡Adjust➡Auto Levels. Select Filter➡Blur➡Gaussian Blur. I used a Radius of 3.2.

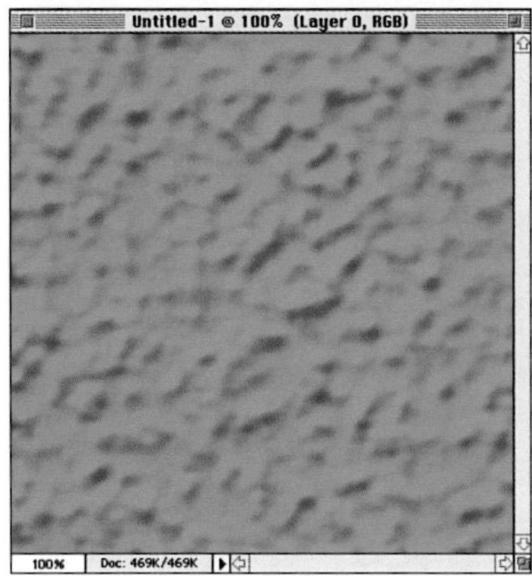

Then, you can make a double texture. Make the Background layer active. Select Filter➡Noise➡Add Noise. I used an Amount of 40.

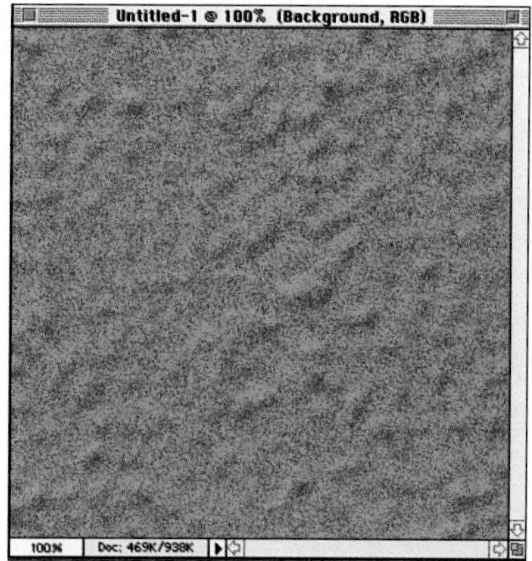


Try applying a filter to the Background layer. I used Filter➡Brush Strokes➡Ink Outlines with a Stroke Length of 4, a Dark Intensity of 20, and a Light Intensity of 10.

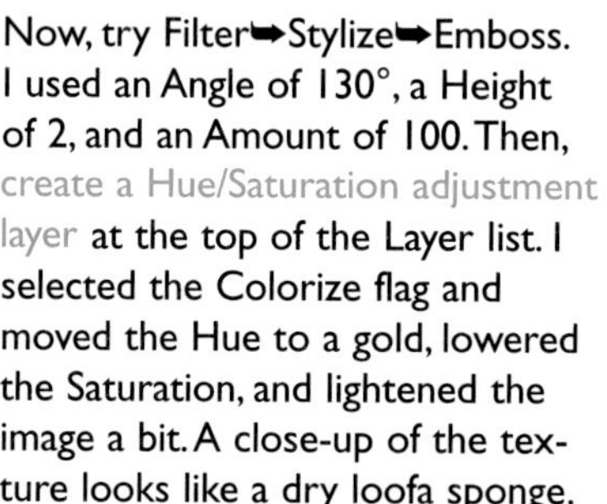

Now, try Filter➡Stylize➡Emboss. I used an Angle of 130°, a Height of 2, and an Amount of 100. Then, create a Hue/Saturation adjustment layer at the top of the Layer list. I selected the Colorize flag and moved the Hue to a gold, lowered the Saturation, and lightened the image a bit. A close-up of the texture looks like a dry loofa sponge.

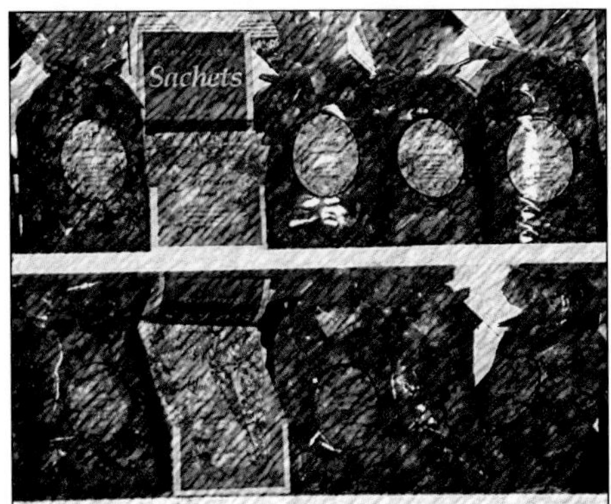


Try varying the type of noise (Filter➡Artistic➡Film Grain and Filter➡Texture➡Grain make wonderful noisy textures), and vary the amount of noise as well.

## Textured Photos

You can add wonderful textures to photographs using this effect. Open the photo that you want to texture. Create a new file that is the same size as the photo. In the new file, complete Steps 1, 2, and 3 from the original instructions. Make the photo active. Drag and drop the photo centered into the texture image. Change the blending mode to Hard Light. You could instead drag the texture on top of the photo. If you do, select Overlay or Soft Light as the blending mode.

You get a slightly different application of texture if you use a layer mask for the texture. In the photo, create Layer 0. Create a new Background layer. Make Layer 0 active. Create a layer mask. Complete Steps 1 through 3 of the original instructions in this layer mask. Select Image➡Adjust➡Levels and move the Gamma slider until you are satisfied with the amount of texture in the image. Making the layer mask darker will remove more of the original image from view, whereas making it lighter will keep more of the original image. ■

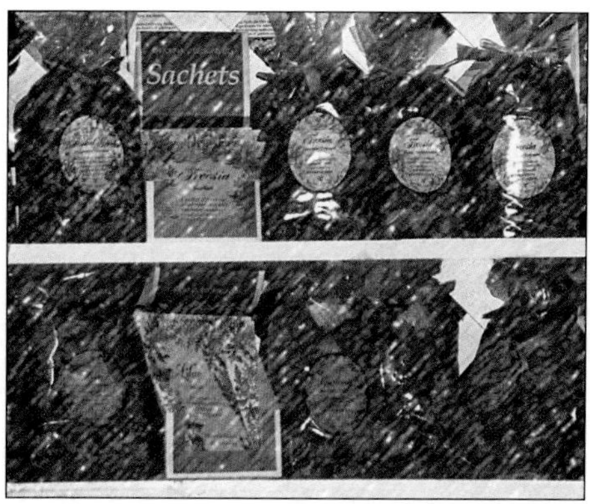

Did you ever sit on a cane chair as a child and press your hand into the open spaces of the weave? If you pressed hard enough, you picked up a lovely pattern. The interlacing always fascinated me, but I never had the patience to construct my own chair seats. Now, neither of us needs patience—just these instructions.

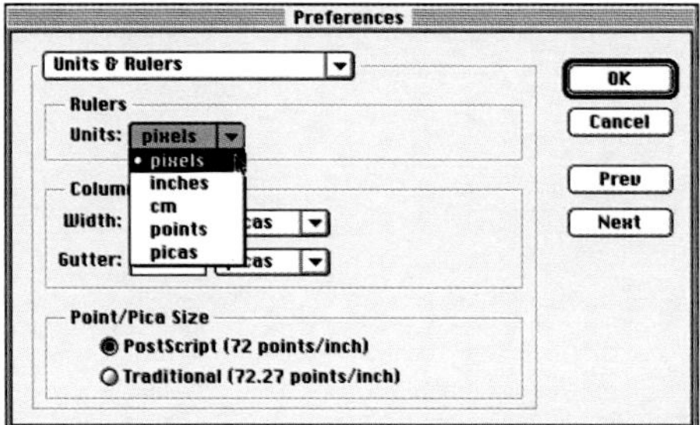


**1** When a craftsperson creates a chair, every portion of the seat needs to be woven. On the computer, you only need to create one "intersection." Create a new file 60×60 pixels. View the image at 500% (or the largest amount that will fit on your screen) by dragging the slider on the Navigator palette. Make the window a little bit larger than the image. Turn on the Rulers (Command-R)[Control-R]. To make the ruler units appear in pixels, double-click on one of the rulers. The Units & Rulers Preferences dialog appears. Change the units to pixels.

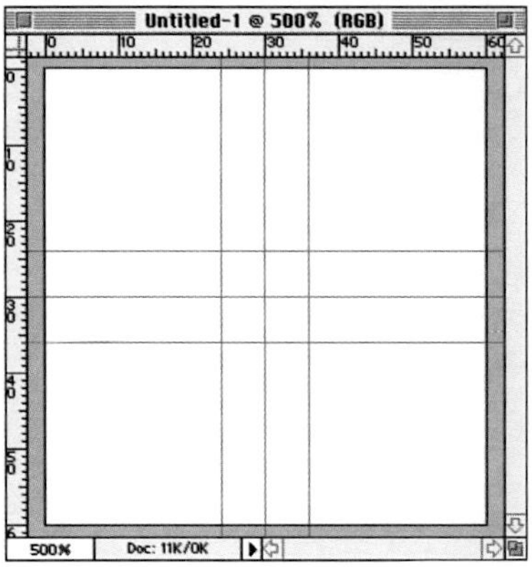

**2** Add a vertical and horizontal guide at the center mark on both rulers (30 pixels). This guide is for reference only. The next set of guides determines where the cane "fibers" will be. They need to be created at the center of the lines that you will draw. Add vertical and horizontal guides at 24 and 36 pixels on both rulers.

**3** Switch to default colors. Double-click the Line tool. Set the Mode to Normal, Opacity to 100%, Line width to 8, and Anti-aliased off. Do not select Arrowheads. Create a new layer. Place the cursor on the 24-pixel vertical guide *above* the image, and drag a line along the guide to a point *below* the image (this ensures that the line traverses the entire image). Press the Shift key as you drag to constrain the line vertically.

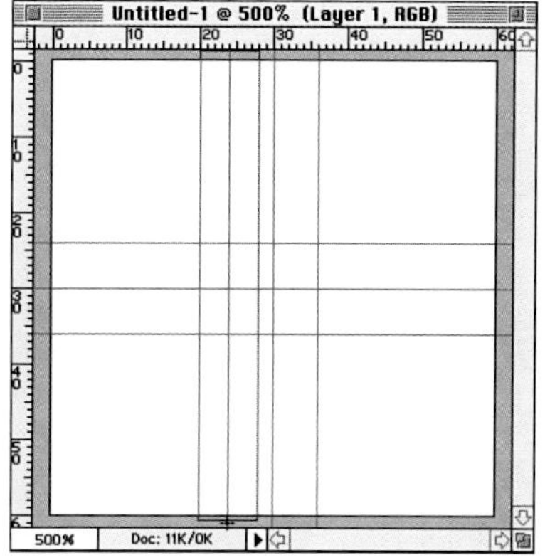


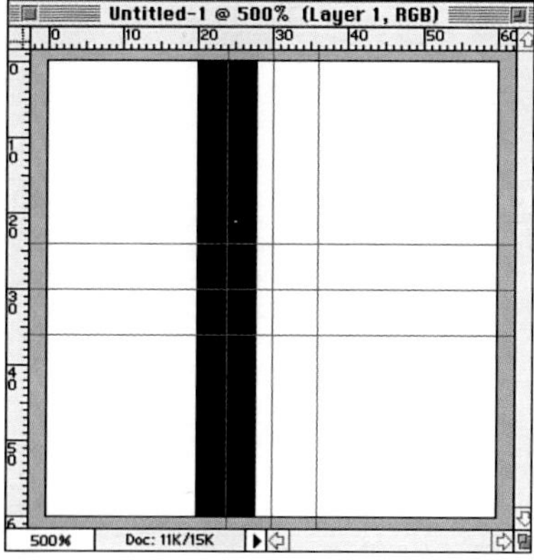


**4** Select Filter➥Stylize➥Find Edges. This step allows you to color the cane later.

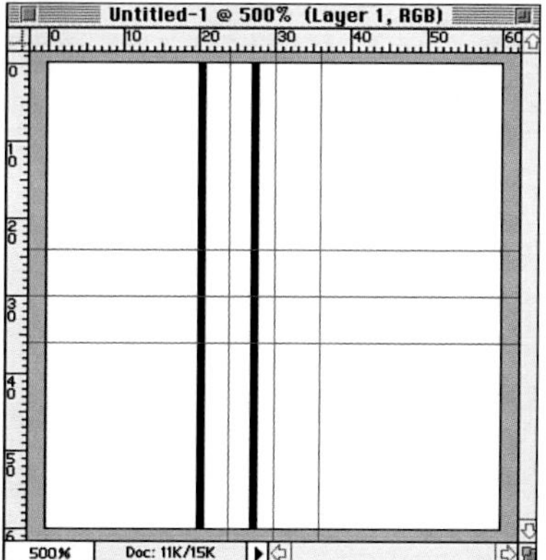

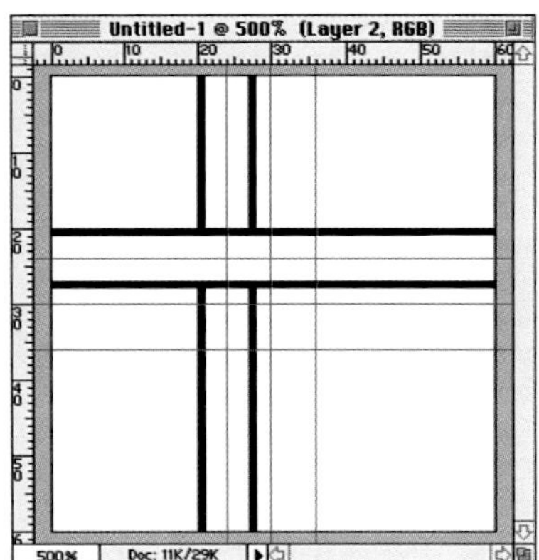


**5** Create a new layer. Place your cursor on the 24-pixel horizontal guide at the left outside the image and drag a line to the right along the guide. Press the Shift key as you drag to constrain the line horizontally. Select Filter➡Stylize➡Find Edges.

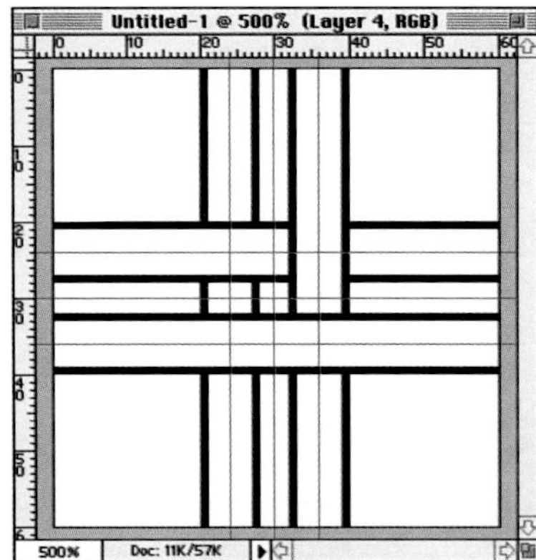


**6** Create a new layer. Place your cursor on the 36-pixel vertical guide at the top outside the image and drag a line to the bottom along the guide. Press the Shift key as you drag to constrain the line vertically. Select Filter➡Stylize➡Find Edges. Create a new layer. Draw a line along the 36-pixel horizontal guide. Select Filter➡Stylize➡Find Edges.

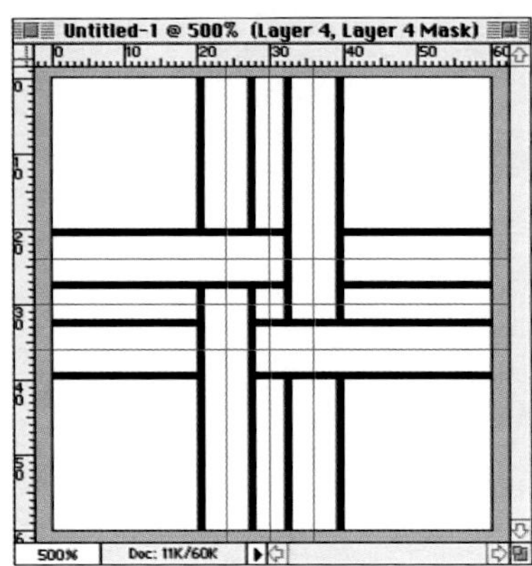


**7** Whoops! Weaving is supposed to go over-and-under, and this last line goes over and over. Not to worry. Create a layer mask. Your foreground color should still be black. Switch the foreground color to black if it is not. Place the cursor on the 24-pixel vertical guide line and drag a line on the mask so that it covers the horizontal line that crosses it. The cane line looks as though it has been woven "under." Turn off the Rulers (Command-R) [Control-R].

**8** This is the cane repeat unit. Click on the thumbnail for Layer 4 so that the mask is no longer active. Make the Background layer invisible. Select➥All. Define the pattern.

**9** Create a new file 360×360 pixels. (I know that is an unusual file size—however, it is an *even* multiple of the repeat tile size of 60 pixels.) Create a new layer. Fill the new image with the pattern. Notice, please, that I have been careful to have you create the pattern so that it preserves transparency. By turning off the Background layer, you have a pattern that can layer over other images. By filling a *layer* in the new image, you continue to keep open the pattern options.

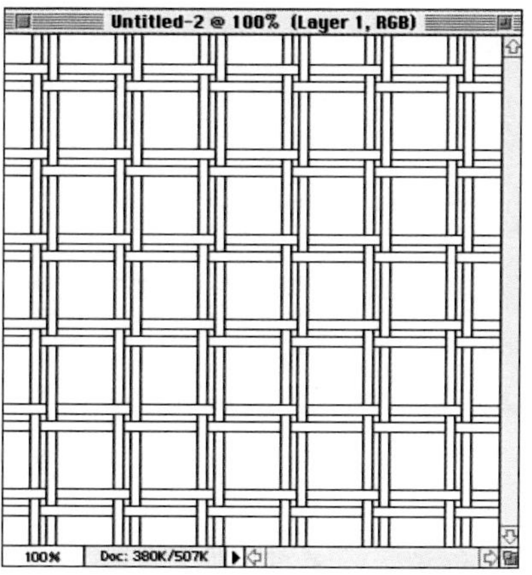


**10** The image is useful as it is now, but the beauty of caning is that there is a diagonal element as well. Duplicate Layer 1. Select Layer➥Transform➥Numeric (Shift-Command-T)[Shift-Control-T]. Set the Angle to 45°.

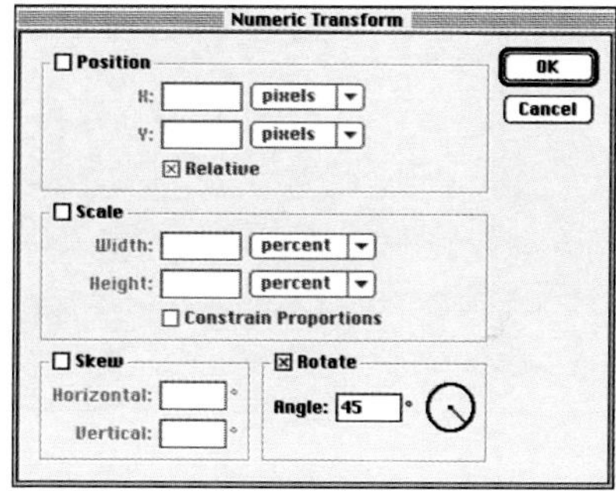


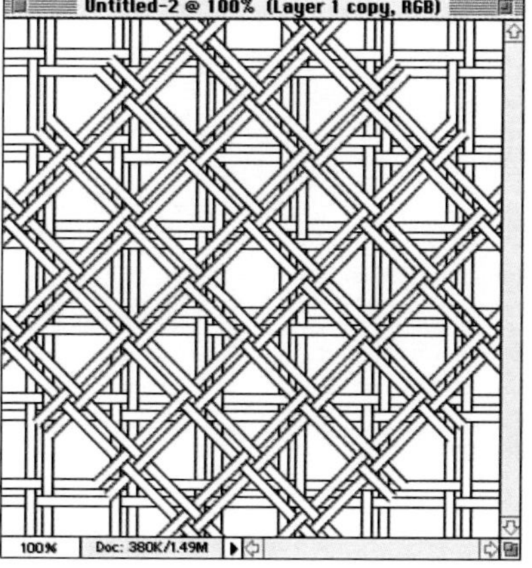

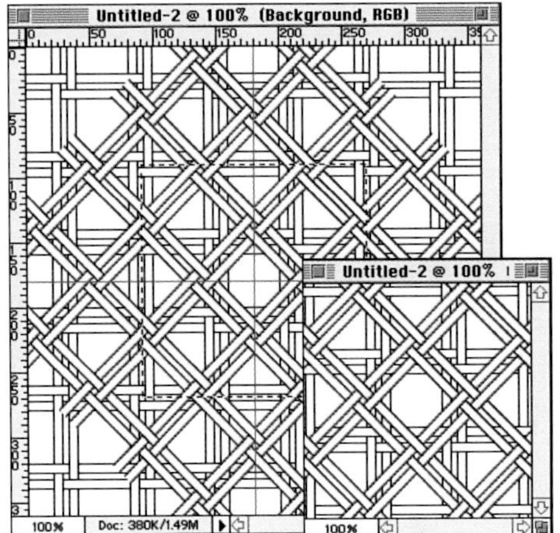


**11** That is much more interesting. You need to define a new repeat pattern from this. Double-click the rectangular Marquee tool. Set a fixed size to 180×180 pixels (three times the size of the original tile). Turn on the Rulers (Command-R) [Control-R]. Add a vertical and horizontal guide at the 180 pixel mark on both rulers (this is the exact center of the image). Place your cursor at the intersection of the two guides, press the (Option)[Alt] key and click the mouse button. The fixed size selection rectangle is perfectly centered. Select Image➡Crop to crop to the dimensions of the Marquee.

**12** Now you can color the weave. "Natural" cane chairs are usually some brownish color. Switch the foreground color to your "cane" color. I selected RGB: 181, 99, 50. Make Layer 1 active. Duplicate Layer 1 (Layer 1 copy 2). Turn on Preserve Transparency. Fill with foreground color. Position the layer below Layer 1. Make Layer 1 active. Change the blending mode to Multiply. Now you can see the black outlines around the weave.

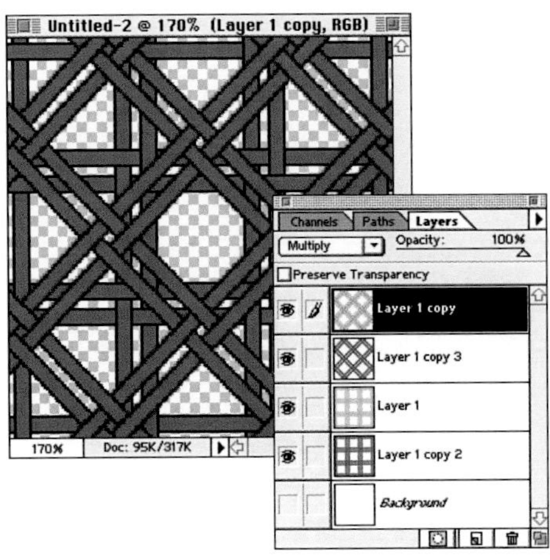


**13** Make Layer 1 copy active. Duplicate Layer 1 copy (Layer 1 copy 3). Turn on Preserve Transparency. Fill with foreground color. Position the layer below Layer 1 copy. Make Layer 1 copy active. Change the blending mode to Multiply.

**14** Make the Background layer invisible. Select➡All. Define the pattern. Create a new file. Mine is 750 pixels square. Create a new layer. Fill with pattern. You have created a complex (though technically impossible) weave. However, only a weaver with very good eyesight would realize that the weave structure on this does not work.

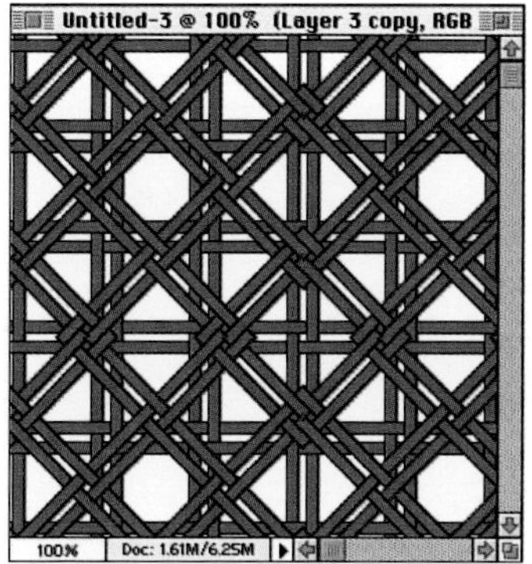


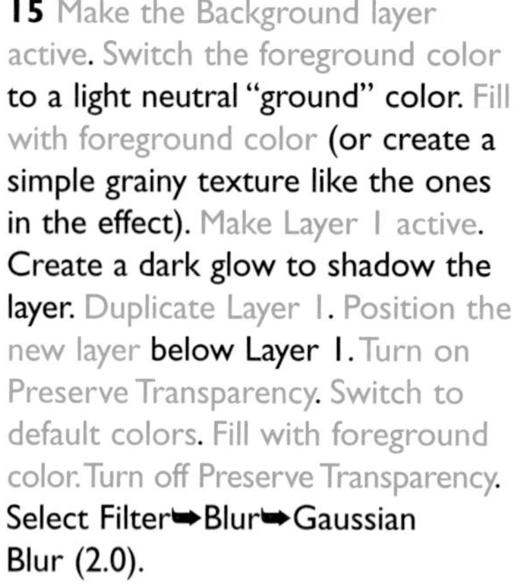

**15** Make the Background layer active. Switch the foreground color to a light neutral "ground" color. Fill with foreground color (or create a simple grainy texture like the ones in the effect). Make Layer 1 active. Create a dark glow to shadow the layer. Duplicate Layer 1. Position the new layer below Layer 1. Turn on Preserve Transparency. Switch to default colors. Fill with foreground color. Turn off Preserve Transparency. Select Filter➡Blur➡Gaussian Blur (2.0).

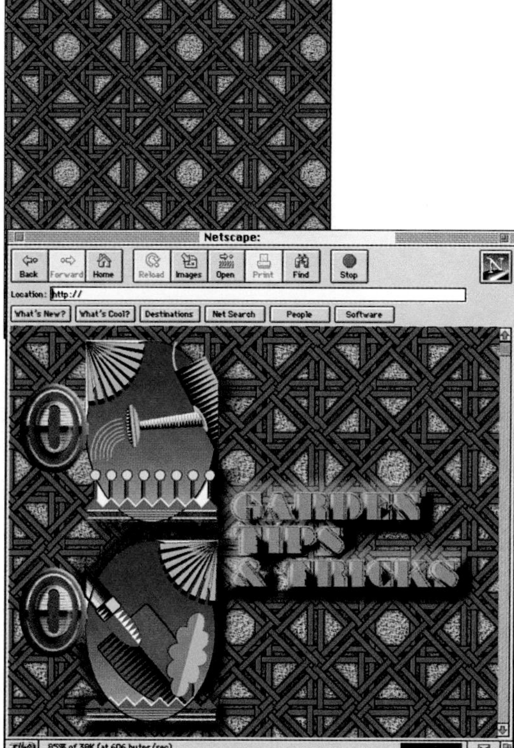

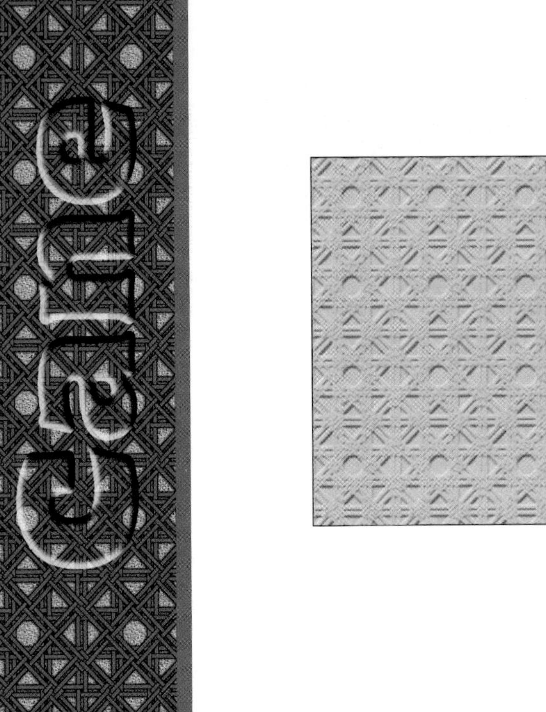

## VARIATIONS

This effect makes a wonderful embossed texture. Complete the original instructions through Step 14. Make the Background layer active. Change the foreground color to your desired color. I used RGB: 219, 201, 166. Fill with foreground color. Make Layer 1 active. Choose Filter➡Stylize➡Emboss (Angle: 118°, Height: 3 pixels, Amount: 100). Select Image➡Adjust➡Desaturate (Shift-Command-U)[Shift-Control-U]. Change the blending mode to Hard Light. Select Filter➡Blur➡Gaussian Blur. I used a Radius of 2.0, but you can increase the Radius to soften the effect (or use a smaller Radius if you like a sharper image).

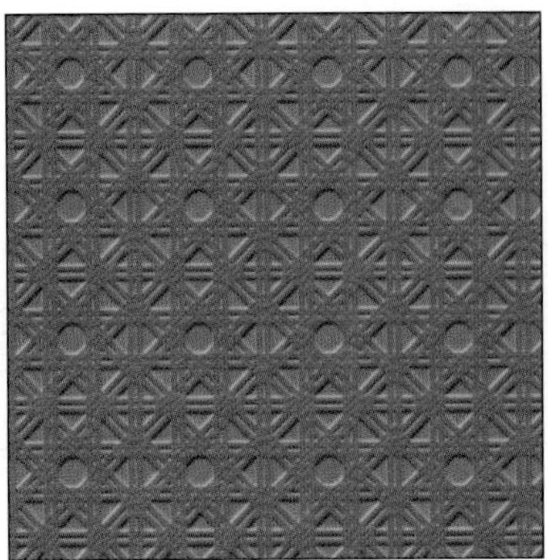

To add a two-toned look to the embossing you just did, redefine (if it is not the current pattern) the cane tile as a pattern as you did in Step 14. Create a new layer in the embossed image. Position the layer below the Hard Light layer. Fill with pattern. Turn on Preserve Transparency. Switch the foreground color to the desired color. I used RGB: 214, 31, 24. Fill with foreground color. Reduce the layer opacity as desired. I set it to 23%.

Then, if you want embossing that sets the cane into the background rather than out of the background, make the Hard Light layer active. Invert the image (Command-I) [Control-I]. (You could also emboss the layer at an Angle of –67° if you were starting over). Shown here is the image with the second color layer (created in Variation 2) turned off. ■

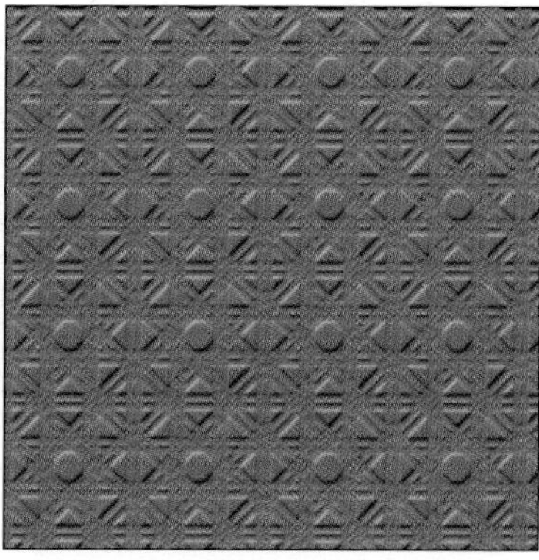

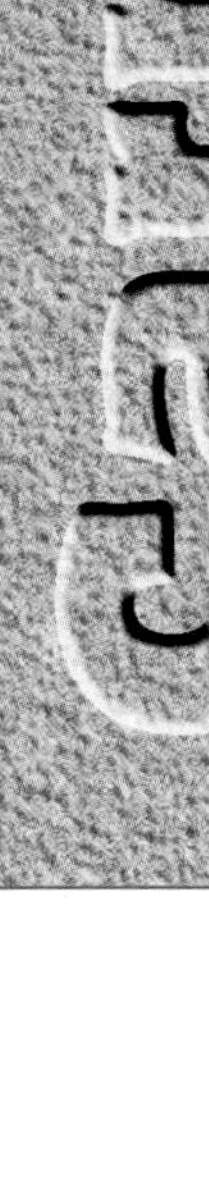


I've always loved the way carpet squishes beneath my feet. The play of light on carpet fibers is fascinating. There is hidden complexity in the very simplest of structures if you take the time to notice it. This effect recreates a slightly shaggy rug—almost a cut Berber texture. It's a comfortable carpet—you'd notice spilled wine, but pretzel crumbs just sink right in.

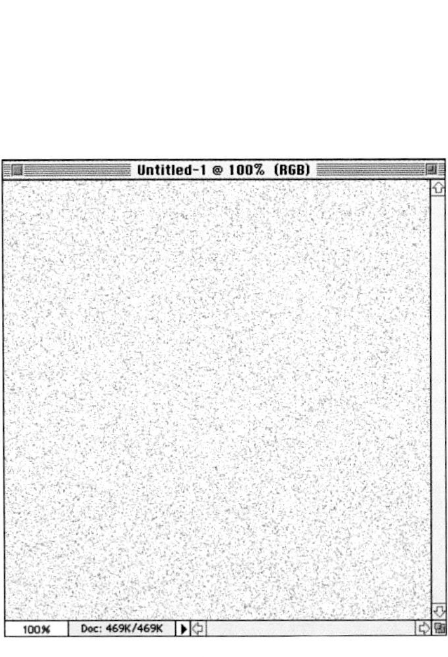


**1** Create a new file. Mine is 400×400 pixels. Select Filter➡Noise➡Add Noise (Distribution: Gaussian, Monochromatic Off). I used an Amount of 43. The noise needs to be kept fairly light for the effect to work properly.

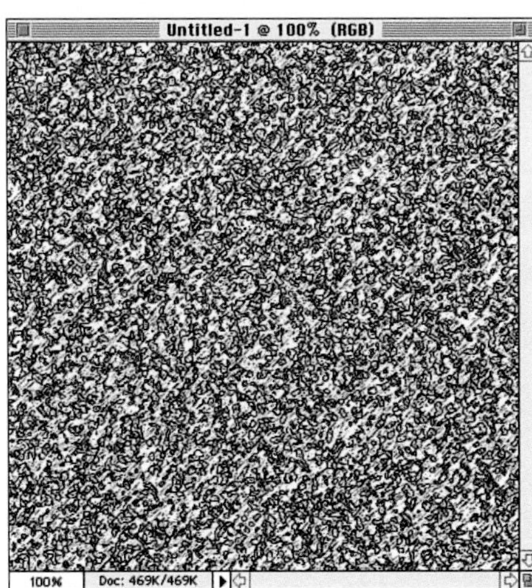


**2** Select Filter➡Brush Strokes➡Ink Outlines. I used a Stroke Length of 4, a Dark Intensity of 20, and a Light Intensity of 10. The Stroke Length setting is the important one. Longer should be okay, but too short a Stroke Length makes the texture too dense and black.

**3** Choose Image➥Adjust➥Curves (Command-M)[Control-M]. Make scribbles with the Pencil tool in two or more of the image's color channels. The colors do not matter. What matters is the shape of the texture that appears. You need to create a texture with interesting areas in it, but one which still contains a lot of white space. I drew in the Red and Green channels and left the Blue channel alone. Click OK when you have finished playing with the Curves and return to the main image. Save the file as Cmap.Psd.

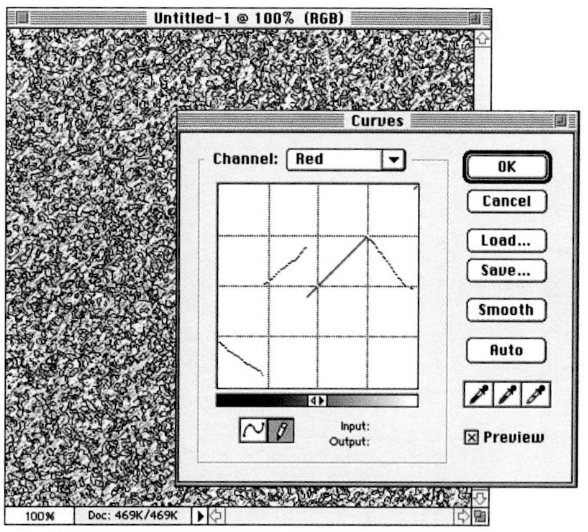


**4** Create a new file the same size as the first. Change the foreground color to neutral gray (RGB: 128, 128, 128). Fill with foreground color. Select Filter➥Pixelate➥Pointillize (8). This is the start of the surface map.

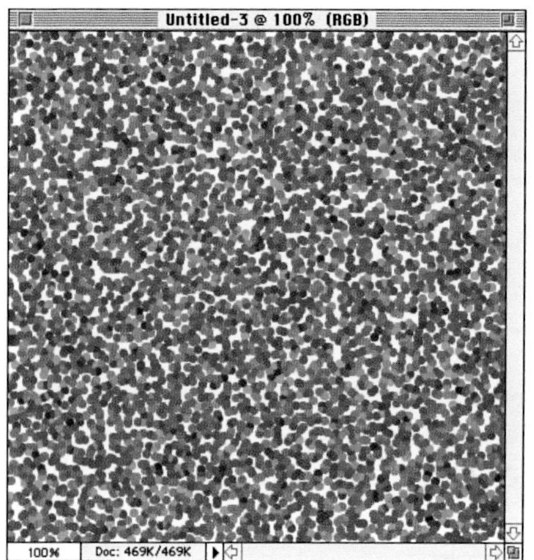

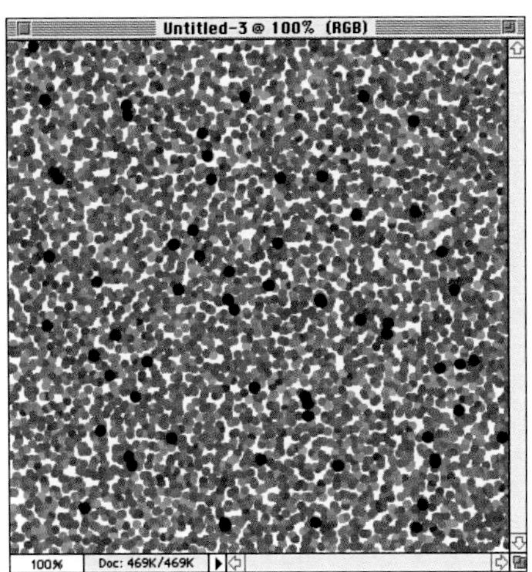


**5** Switch to default colors. Double-click the Paintbrush tool. The Mode should be Normal and the opacity 100%. Select a small hard brush (the fourth one of the top row is a good size match to the result of the Pointillize filter). Spatter approximately 50 drops of "paint" all over the image (for a 400-pixel image). Make sure that they are not evenly distributed. Add some additional spots near ones that are already in the image (perhaps another 10). These spots will become the areas of highlight and shadow that give the carpet some interest.

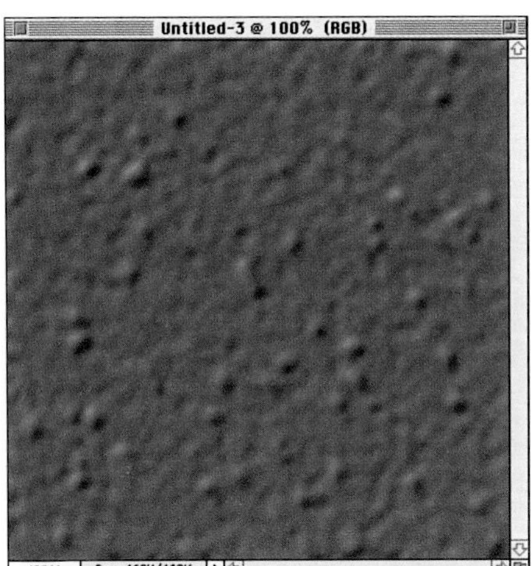


**6** Select Filter➡Blur➡Gaussian Blur (4.1). Choose Filter➡Stylize➡Emboss (Angle: 130°, Height: 3 pixels). Use an Amount of 80–130. I chose an Amount of 116. Select Image➡Adjust➡Desaturate (Shift-Command-U)[Shift-Control-U]. The Desaturate command removes the color from the image so that it does not detract from the embossing that you just did.

**7** Select Filter➡Blur➡Gaussian Blur (4.1) again. The surface map should look very shiny and almost smooth except for the larger bumps where you painted on the Pointillize filter.

**8** Create a Hue/Saturation adjustment layer. Click the Colorize button. Set the Hue to something "natural"—in the earth tones—and turn the saturation way down. The image should be fairly light.

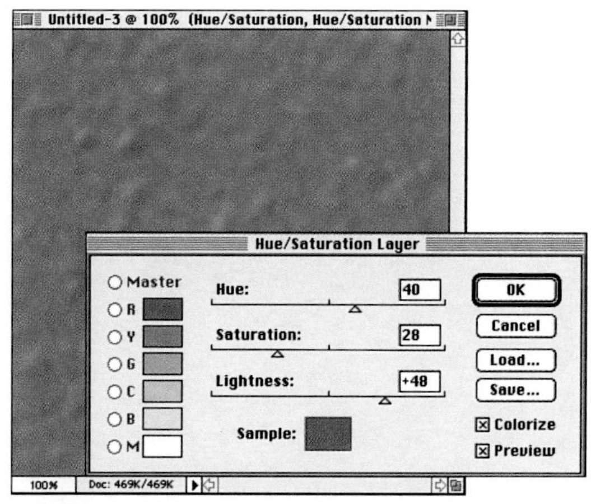


**9** Drag and drop centered the Cmap.Psd image into the surface map image. It should be the top layer. Change the blending mode to Color Burn and reduce the layer opacity to approximately 60%.

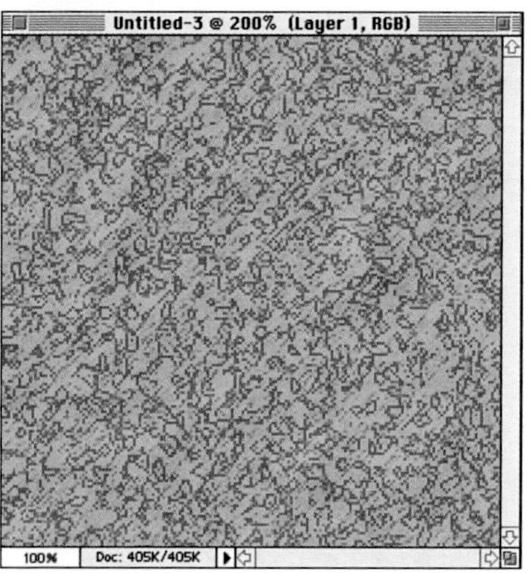


**10** Make the Background layer active. Duplicate the Background layer. Position the duplicate layer at the top of the Layers list. Change the blending mode to Hard Light.

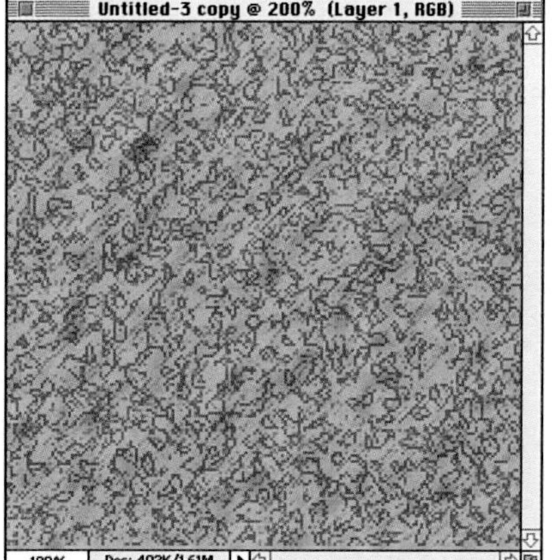

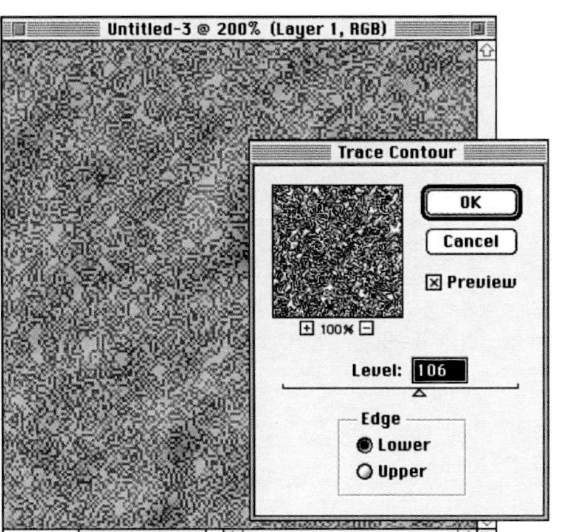


**11** Make Layer 1 active. Select Filter➥Stylize➥Trace Contour. I used a lower edge of 106. This filter adds back some of the detail bleached out by the Hard Light and Color Burn modes. This image will become the "fuzz" on the carpet.

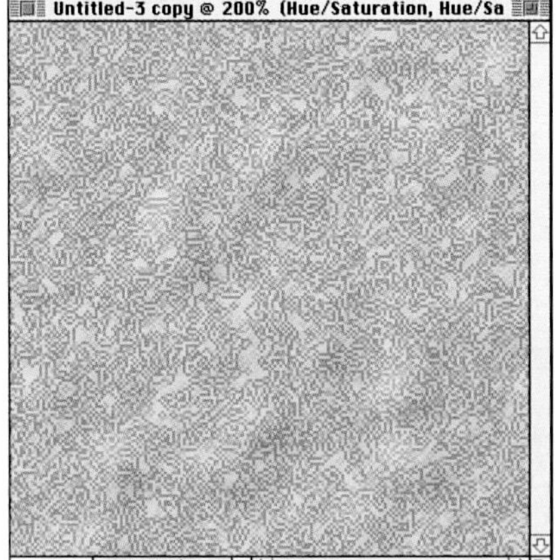


**12** Flatten the image (or select Image➥Duplicate (Merged Layers only) if you want to keep a copy of your work editable). Create a Hue/Saturation adjustment layer. Click the Colorize button. Select the color that you want your carpet to be. I stayed with the neutral earth tones.

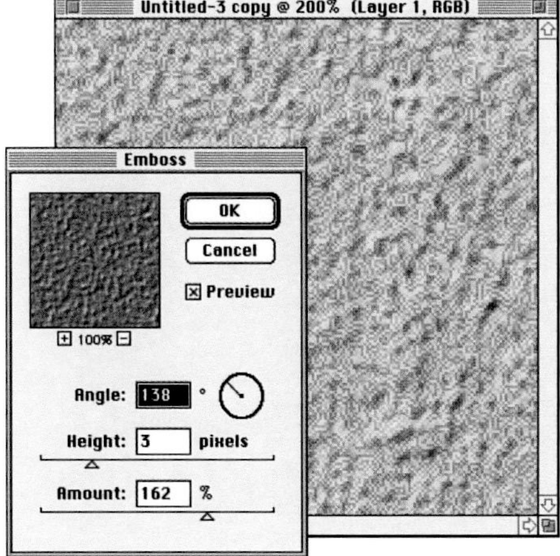


**13** Create a new layer. Change the foreground color to neutral gray (RGB: 128, 128, 128). Fill the image with the foreground color. Select Filter➥Noise➥Add Noise (Distribution: Gaussian, Monochromatic). I used an Amount of 42. Select Filter➥Blur➥Gaussian Blur (0.9). Choose Filter➥Stylize➥Emboss (Angle: 138°, Height: 3 pixels, Amount: 162). Change the blending mode to Hard Light. Select Filter➥Blur➥Gaussian Blur (0.7) if the shag is too sharp.

## VARIATIONS

If you want to add a little bit more color interest, double-click the Hue/Saturation adjustment layer (if you did not flatten the image and you have more than one, use the highest one) and remove the Colorize flag. Move the Hue slider until you find a combination that you like. I used Hue: +32, Saturation: –34: and Lightness: +46. Of course, your results depend upon your starting colors.

To create a two-toned carpet, create a Curves adjustment layer below the Hue/Saturation adjustment layer. Reverse some of the channel values or draw in the channel grid. Shown is the only change that I made to the Curves. Depending upon the colors in your image, you may need to make more substantial changes to the image Curves.

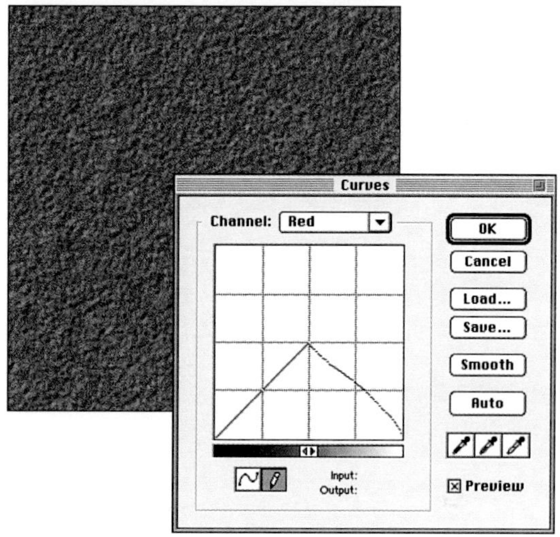


You can also make a mostly seamless repeat from this texture with no extra work. Generally, the pattern only leaves the type of seams that you would see from a vacuum cleaner. ■

Creating ceramic tiles can really spark your creativity. It is easy and breezy, and works because of a trick—you develop little, diagonally colored blocks that can be arranged in a myriad of ways.

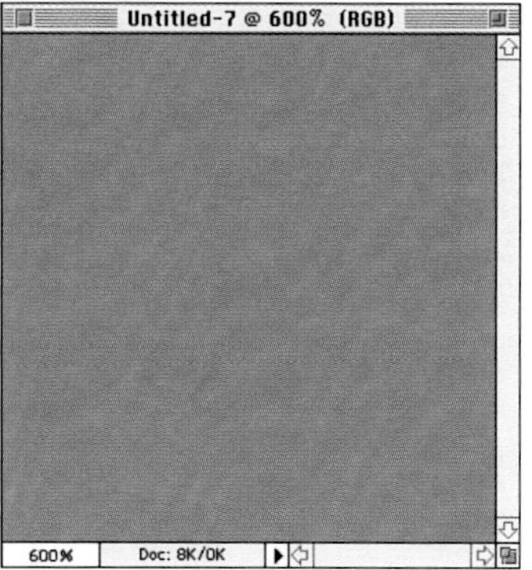


**1** Create a new file. The file size can be any size, but for right now, it should be a perfect square. Mine is 50×50 pixels (so the result will print at approximately six to the inch). You need to select two colors—one for the tile grout and one to "influence" the color of the tile. Switch the foreground color to your grout color. Switch the background color to the influence color. I selected a light gray for the grout, and a soft lilac for the influence. Fill with background color.

**2** Apply Filter➥Texture➥Grain (Grain Type: Clumped). I used an Intensity of 40 and a Contrast of 50.

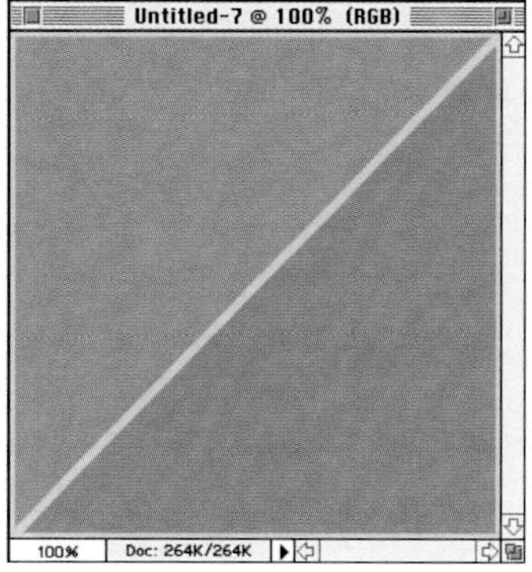


**3** Select Filter➥Texture➥Stained Glass (Cell Size: 50, Light Intensity: 0). I used a Border Thickness of 4. You must use a cell size of 50 (the maximum) in order for this trick to work. I recommend a light intensity of 0, as the lighting play from this filter is not very attractive at the settings used here. Notice how the original influence color has changed. The color results from the Stained Glass filter are not totally predictable, but they are based on the colors found in the image. The border thickness uses the foreground color to set the grout.

**4** Next, you need to make the tile look beveled. Select➡All. Select➡Modify➡Border. The amount of the border that you should select depends on your image size. For the 50-pixel image, I selected a border of 8 pixels (64 pixels is the maximum possible).

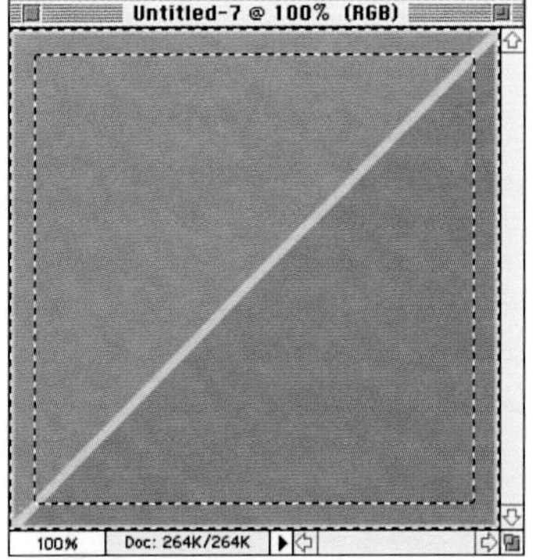


**5** Switch to default colors. Create a new layer. Fill the border selection with foreground color. Deselect. Reduce the layer opacity. I used an opacity of 43%. You can define this tile as a pattern and use it as is, but there is a lot more that you can do in addition to just repeating it.

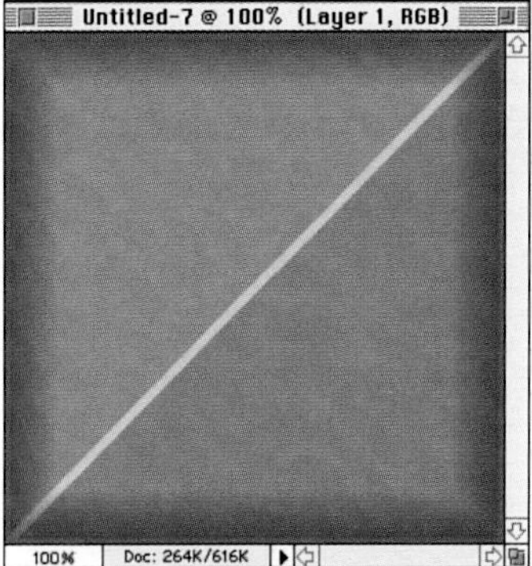


**6** Flatten the image. Select➡All and copy the image to the clipboard. Create a new file that is twice the dimensions of the copy on the clipboard. Make the tile seamless using the Mosaic method.

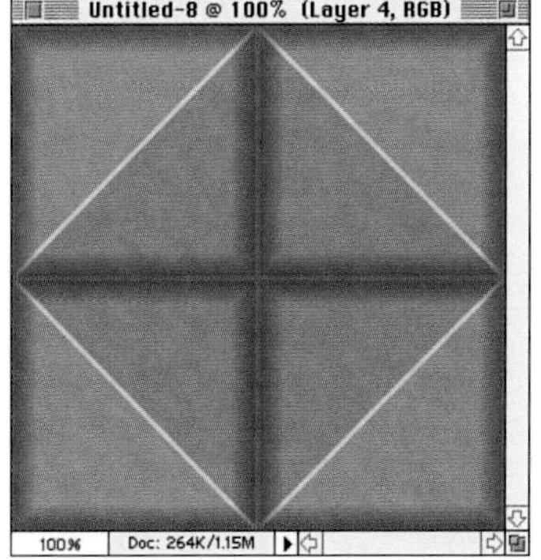

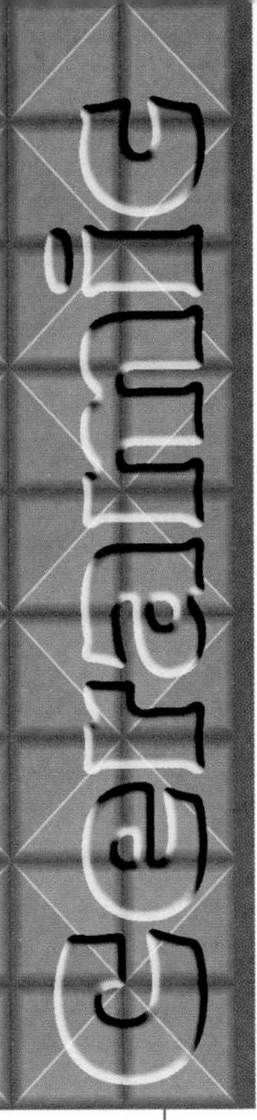

**7** Select➥All. Define the pattern. Create a new file. Mine is 750×750 pixels. Fill with pattern.

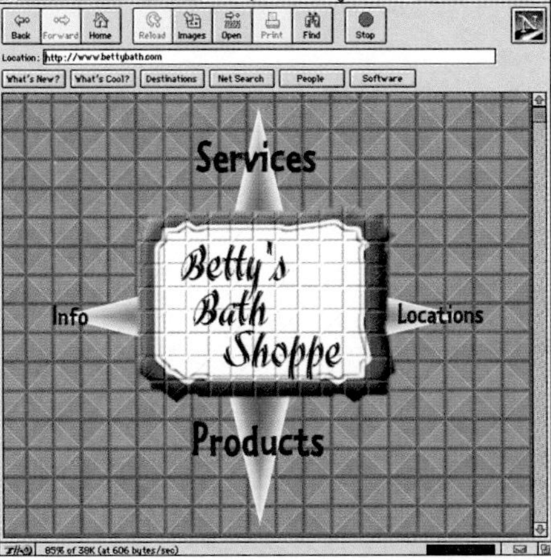


## VARIATIONS

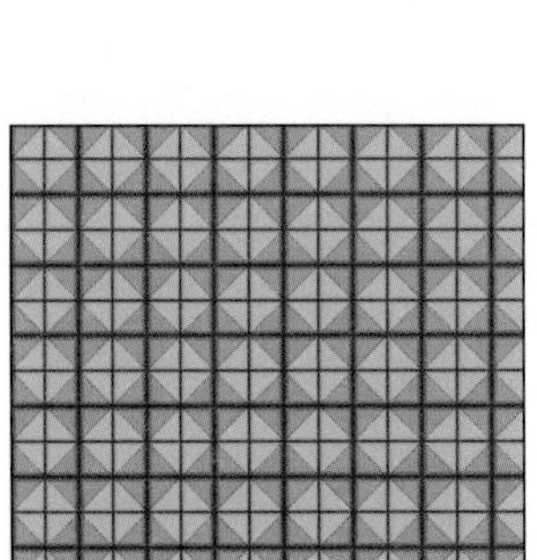

If you want a two-toned tile with more contrast in the halves, use the Add Noise filter in Step 2 instead of the Grain filter. The more noise that you add, the greater the variation possible in the two halves of the tile. This image used RGB: 174, 201, 97 and a noise amount of 29…

…and this one used a noise amount of 300.

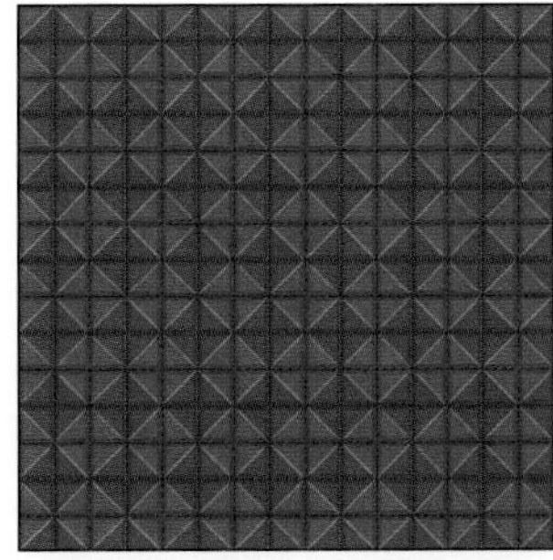

To vary the repeat a bit, you can use a pinwheel method of making the image seamless. Create a new file twice the dimensions of the original. Make the pattern seamless using the Mosaic method with these exceptions: Copy the upper-left tile to the upper-right corner, and instead of flipping it horizontally, select Layer➡Transform➡Rotate 90° CCW. Copy this rotated image (using the fixed size Marquee) and paste it into the bottom-right corner. Select Layer➡Transform➡Rotate 90° CCW. Copy this and paste it into the bottom-left corner. Select Layer➡Transform➡Rotate 90° CCW. Select➡All. Define the pattern. Create a new file. Fill with pattern.

You can mix and match tiles that were created separately using the Mosaic or Pinwheel repeat method.

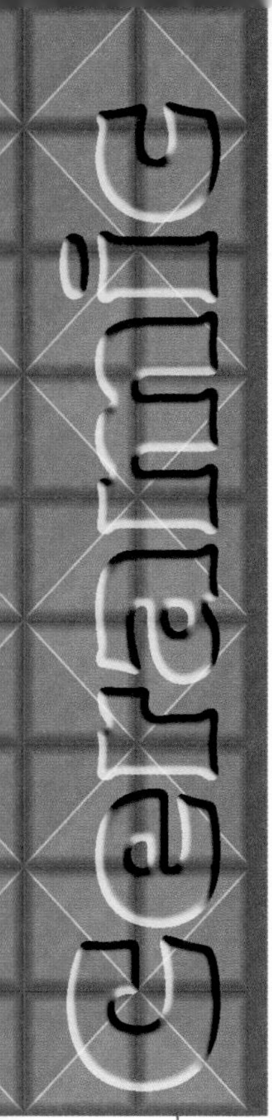


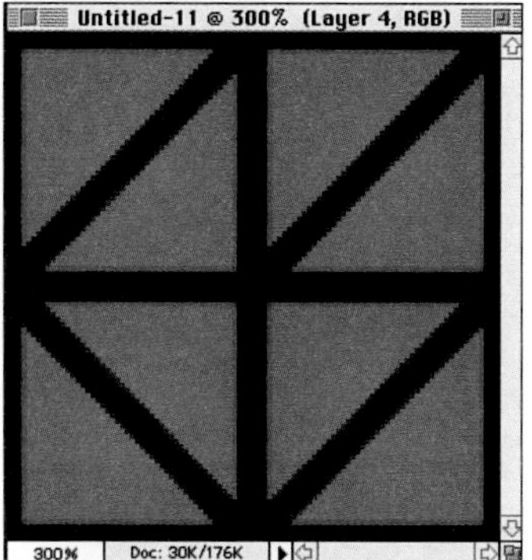


To create a tile with no color variation, do not add a noise filter in Step 2. You must use a Border Thickness greater than 1 if you want a decent result. You also need to use a color that contrasts with your fill as the foreground color. I used a Border Thickness of 8 and a Light Intensity of 1 (just a gentle light for the sake of variation). I also used the Mosaic method to make the pattern seamless, but I left the upper-right corner as a repeat of the upper-left corner. This breaks the pattern and creates even more interest.

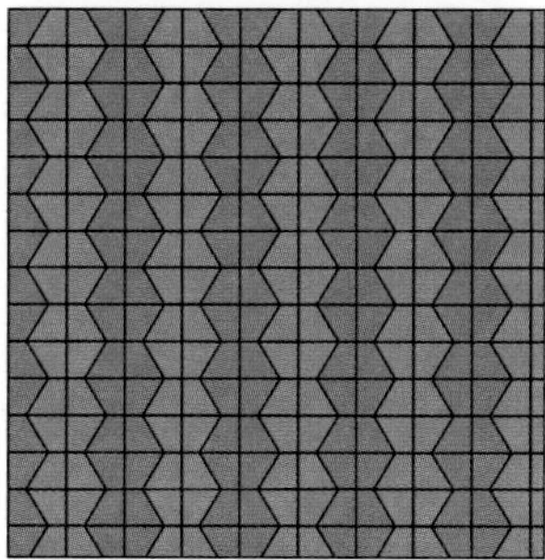

You can also create rectangular tiles that form hexagonal shapes. Create a new file 81 pixels wide × 50 pixels high. Complete the original steps. Make the pattern seamless using the Mosaic method.

If you want to mix sizes of tiles, follow the original steps for each size. The sizes should be multiples of one another. Here, I used a 150-pixel tile surrounded by 50-pixel tiles. ■

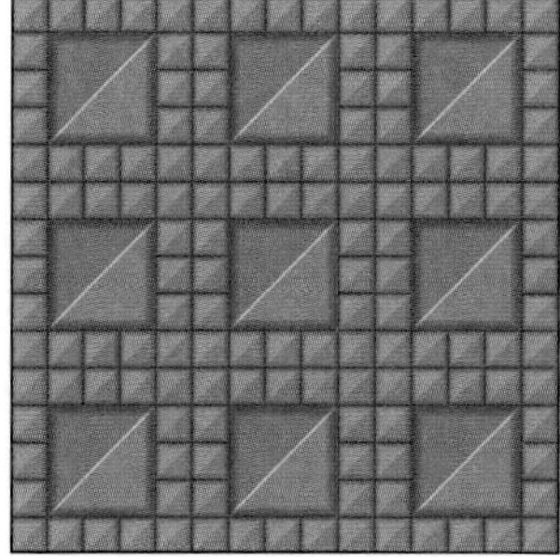

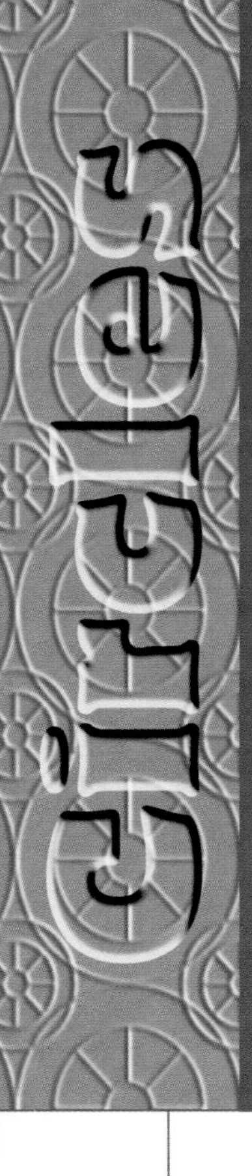


Whether you see a circle as a geometric object or a metaphor for life, you see circles everywhere. They have been used as symbols since prehistoric times. This pattern uses circles within circles to create an embossed repeat, suitable for a background or a texture wrap of a three-dimensional object. It can be as subtle or as flashy as you want.

**1** Create a new file. Use an even number of pixels. Mine is 300×300 pixels. Create a new layer. Switch to default colors. Turn on the Rulers (Command-R)[Control-R]. Add a vertical guide in the center of the image. Add a horizontal guide at the mid-point of the side ruler.

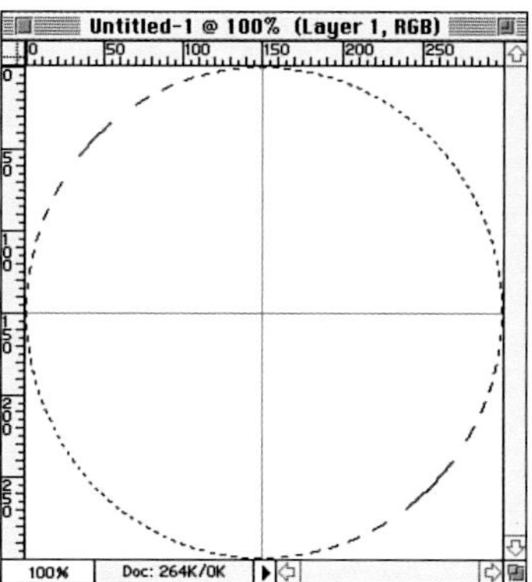


**2** Double-click the Marquee tool to open the Marquee Options dialog box. Select elliptical as the Shape. Set a fixed size for the Marquee tool of 300×300 pixels (or the size of your image). Place the cursor at the intersection of the horizontal and vertical guides. Press the (Option)[Alt] key and click with the mouse. This leaves a perfect circle selected at the exact center of the image.

**3** Select Edit➥Stroke. Set the Stroke width to 3 pixels and the Location to Inside. Make sure that the opacity is 100% and the Mode is Normal. Deselect.

**4** Set a fixed size for the elliptical Marquee tool of 200×200 pixels (or the same general fraction of your image). Place the cursor at the intersection of the horizontal and vertical guides. Press the (Option) [Alt] key and click with the mouse.

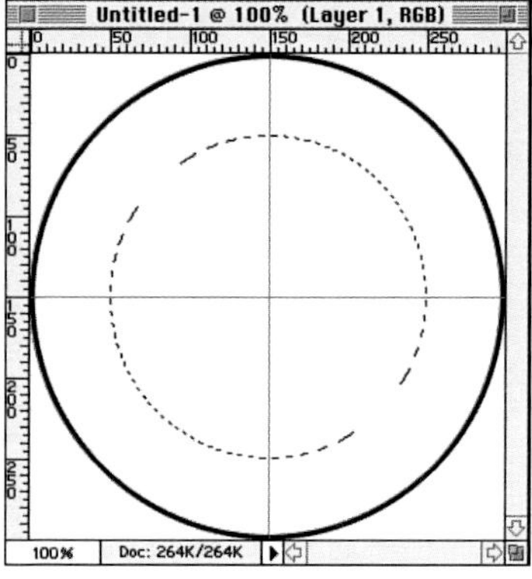


**5** Choose Edit➥Stroke with the same settings used in Step 3. Deselect.

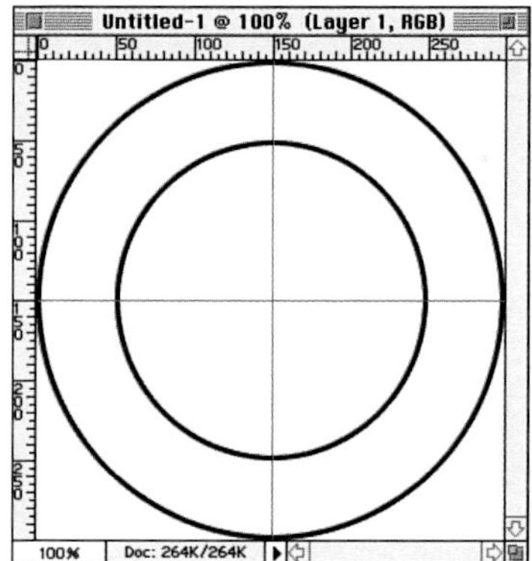

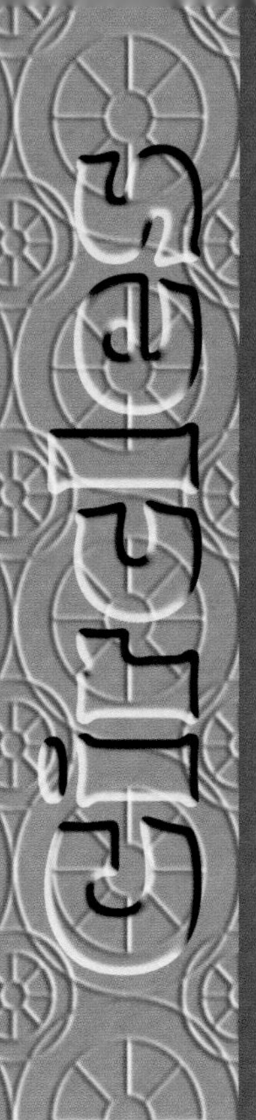


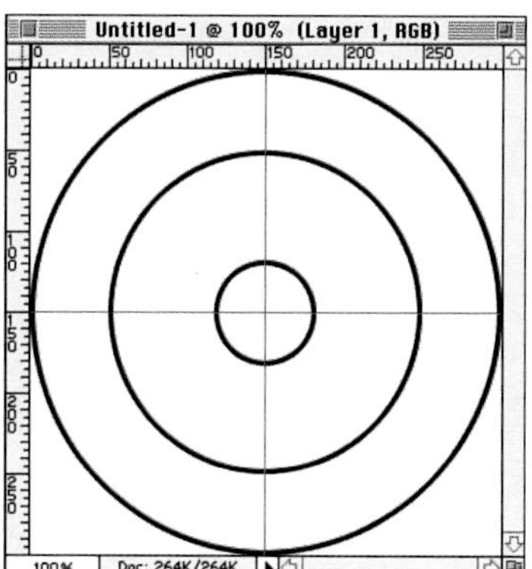


**6** Set a fixed size for the elliptical Marquee tool of 65×65 pixels (or the same general fraction of your image). Place the cursor at the intersection of the horizontal and vertical guides. Press the (Option) [Alt] key and click with the mouse. Choose Edit➡Stroke with the same settings as before. Deselect.

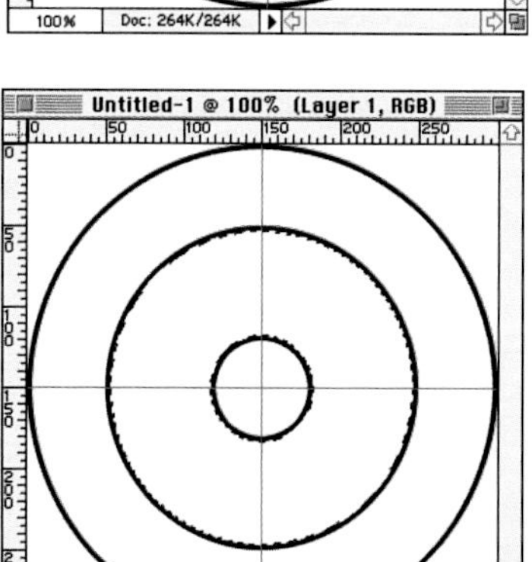


**7** Double-click the Magic Wand tool and set the Tolerance to 10 and Anti-aliased on. Click inside of the middle circle to select it.

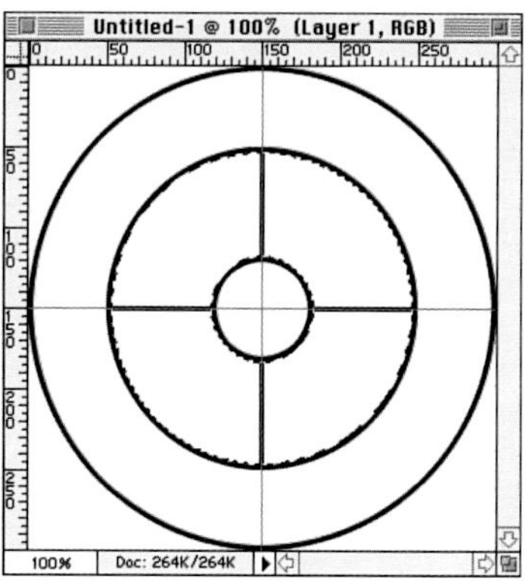


**8** Double-click the Line tool. Set the Line Width to 3 and Anti-aliased on. Do not use arrowheads. Place the cursor at the intersection of the two guidelines, and draw a straight line up to the top of the image. Because of the selection Marquee, the line is only drawn in the middle circle. Repeat for straight lines going down, left, and right from the center.

**9** You next need to draw lines going diagonally. Again, place your cursor at the center of the image. This time, because you have no diagonal guides to follow, press the Shift key as you drag a line diagonally from the center. The Shift key will constrain it to a 45° angle. Place all four diagonal lines. It is critical that you start from the exact center of the image. You will know that the cursor is correctly positioned when it turns a different color as it is situated over the intersection of the guides. Turn off the Rulers (Command-R)[Control-R]. Hide the guides (Command-;)[Control-;]. Deselect.

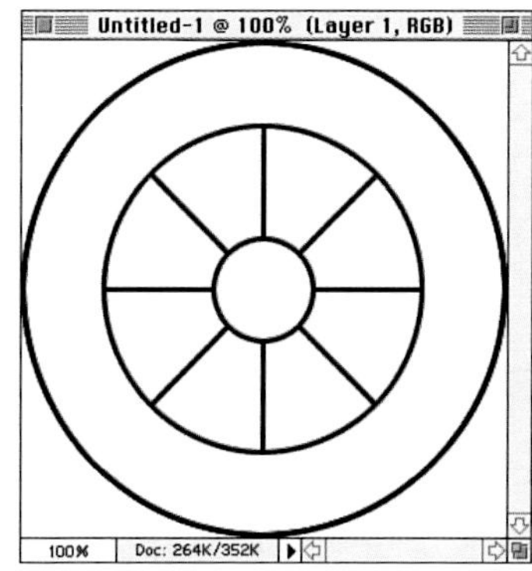


**10** Duplicate Layer 1. Select Filter➡Other➡Offset (Wrap Around). Make the Horizontal and Vertical distances one-half of the image dimensions (150 pixels in each direction).

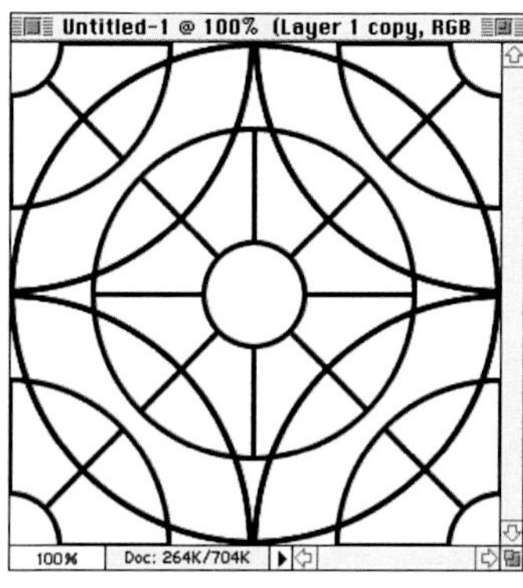


**11** Make Layer 1 active. Select Layer➡Free Transform (Command-T) [Control-T]. Press the Shift and (Option)[Alt] key and drag the upper-right corner point until it touches the lower portion of the diagonal line in the upper-right of the image (as shown in the figure). Press the (Return)[Enter] key to execute the transformation.

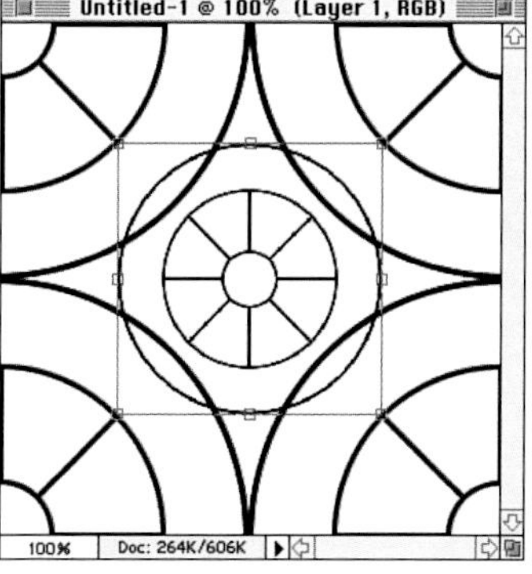

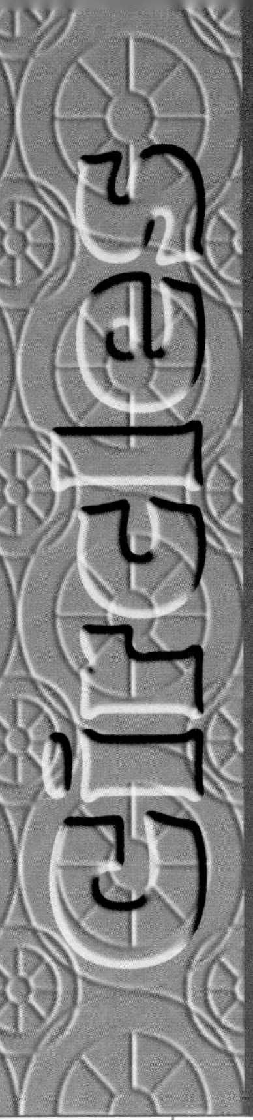

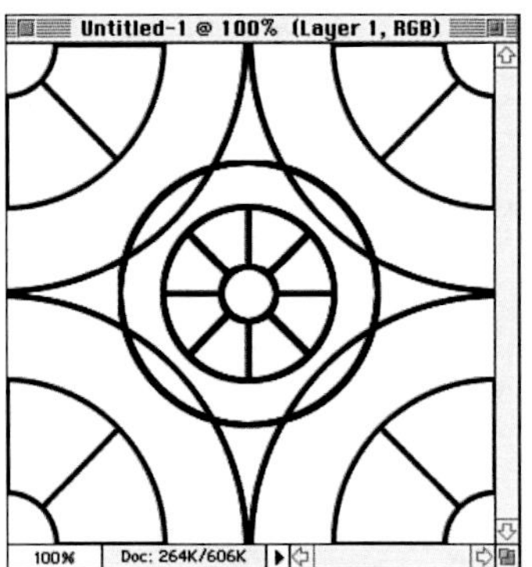


**12** Load the transparency selection of Layer 1. Select Edit➥Stroke, 2 pixels, Center. This thickens the lines that were scaled. Deselect.

**13** Flatten the image. Select Filter➥Blur➥Gaussian Blur (2.5).

**14** Choose Filter➥Stylize➥Emboss (Angle: –67°, Height: 3 pixels, Amount: 100). If you change these settings, watch the preview carefully. At a number of different angles, some of the straight or diagonal lines are completely lost.

**15** Create an adjustment layer for Hue/Saturation. Click Colorize. Change to the desired color. I set a Hue of –68, Saturation of 28, and lightness of +41.

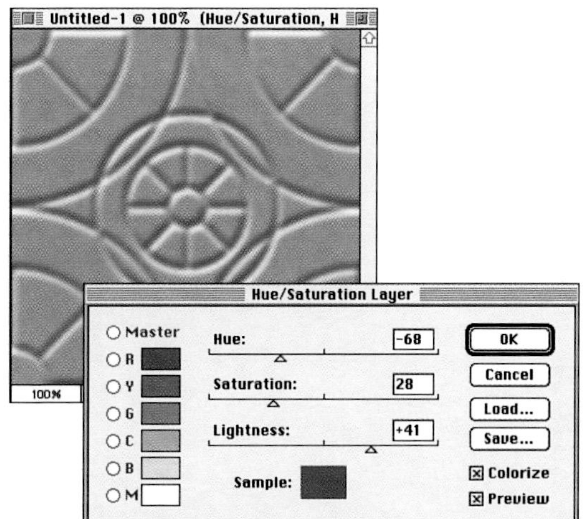


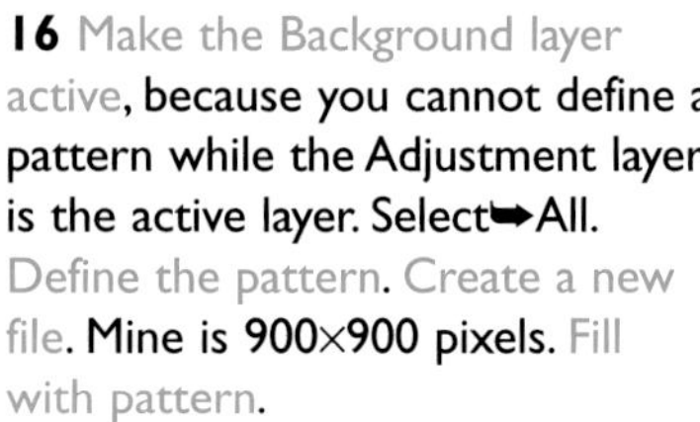

**16** Make the Background layer active, because you cannot define a pattern while the Adjustment layer is the active layer. Select➡All. Define the pattern. Create a new file. Mine is 900×900 pixels. Fill with pattern.

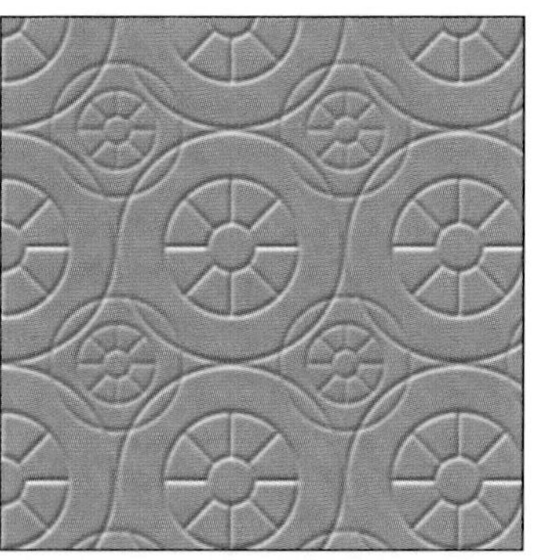

## VARIATIONS

If you want the texture to be raised rather than indented, make the Background layer active. Invert (Command-I)[Control-I].

To create a much softer embossing, at the end of Step 15, make the Background layer active. Select Filter➥Blur➥Gaussian Blur, and soften as much as you want. I used a Radius of 6.0.

You can also use a multi-colored image on top of the embossed layer. Omit Step 15. Complete Step 16 to give you an image of the desired size. Create a new layer. Switch the foreground and background colors to your desired colors. I used a light yellow and a light lavender. Apply Filter➥Render➥Clouds. Change the blending mode to Overlay. Apply Filter➥Render➥Difference Clouds several times. I applied the filter three times. ■

Listen carefully. Can you hear the clip-clop of horses' hooves as they trot down this cobblestone road?

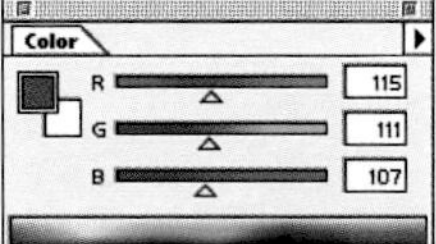


**1** Create a new file. Mine is 600×400 pixels. Switch the foreground color to a medium gray or whatever color you want to use for the mortar that holds the cobblestones in place. (The original mortar was probably a light color, but the cobblestone streets in Olde Philadelphia are certainly not light anymore!) I used RGB: 115, 111, 107. Fill with foreground color.

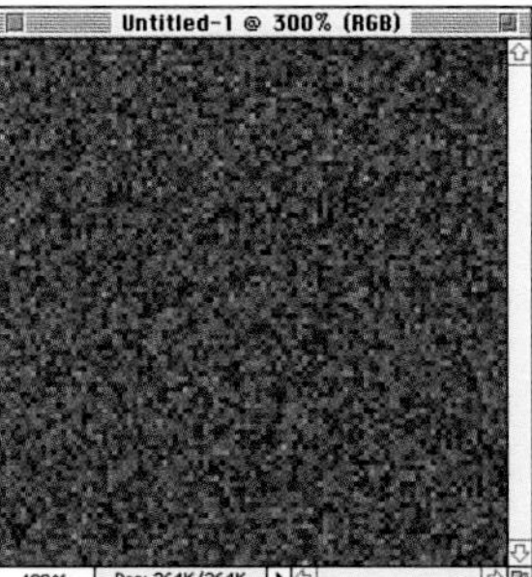


**2** Select Filter➡Noise➡Add Noise (Amount: 20, Distribution: Gaussian, Monochromatic). The Amount needs to be low enough so that you do not create white pixels. Use my settings this time before you start experimenting with this one.

**3** Create a new layer. The cobblestones are created with the Pointillize filter. This filter uses the Background color as the background for the filter, but it uses the colors already in the image to tone to color blobs. Therefore, you need to first select two colors to apply to the layer. I used an olive (RGB: 119, 116, 72) and a brown (RGB: 92, 57, 41).



**TOOLBOX**

Cobblestones Lighting Effects preset

**4** Select Filter➥Render➥Clouds. This varies the tone of the image for the Pointillize filter's color blobs.

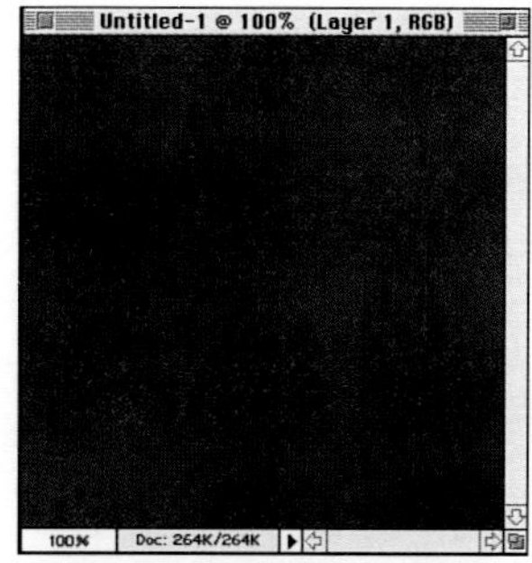


**5** Switch the background color to a darker gray. I used RGB: 52, 62, 72. This color will be used to add overall background tone to the cobblestones. Select Filter➥Pixelate➥Pointillize. I used a cell size of 34. The cell size to choose really depends on where you will use the final result. If you are going to print, you need a larger cell size than you would if you are going to display the image at 72 dpi.

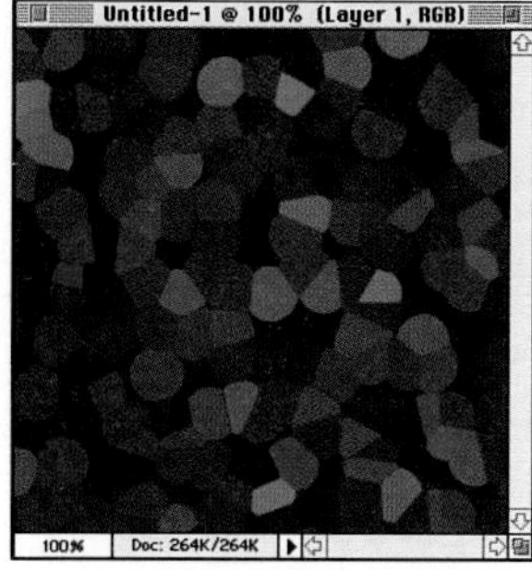


**6** Duplicate Layer 1 and rename the layer Mortar Map. Make the Mortar Map layer invisible and make Layer 1 active. Rename Layer 1 color map. Change the blending mode to Color Burn and reduce the layer opacity to 40%.

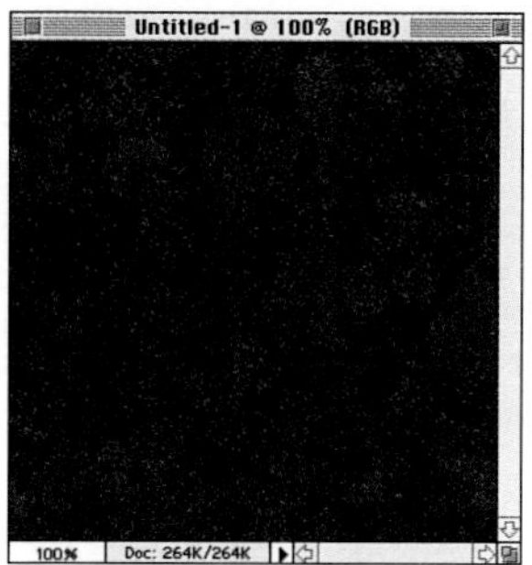


**7** Make the Background layer active. Duplicate the Background layer. Rename the Background copy layer Texture Map. Position the layer above the Color Map layer and below the Mortar Map layer.

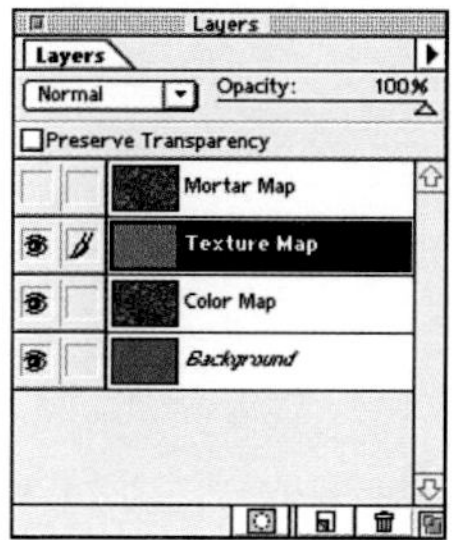

**8** With the Texture Map layer active, choose Filter➡Other➡Minimum (2 pixels). This filter selects the darker pixels and is a way to increase the size of the noise. Choose Image➡Adjust➡Auto Levels.

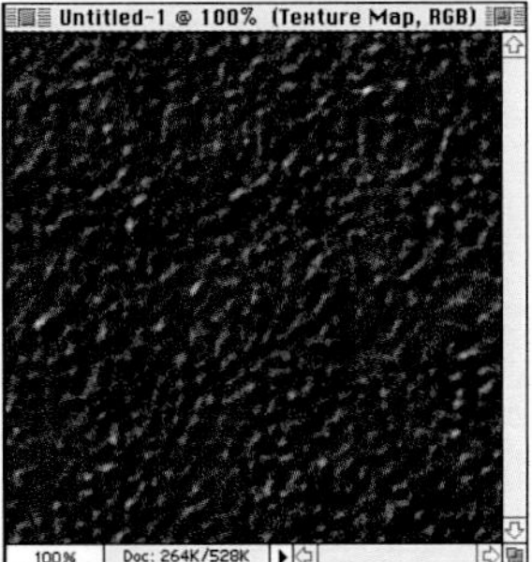


**9** Select Filter➡Blur➡Gaussian Blur (1.5) to soften the noise. Choose Filter➡Stylize➡Emboss. I used an Angle of 125°, a Height of 3, and an Amount of 100. Change the blending mode to Hard Light.

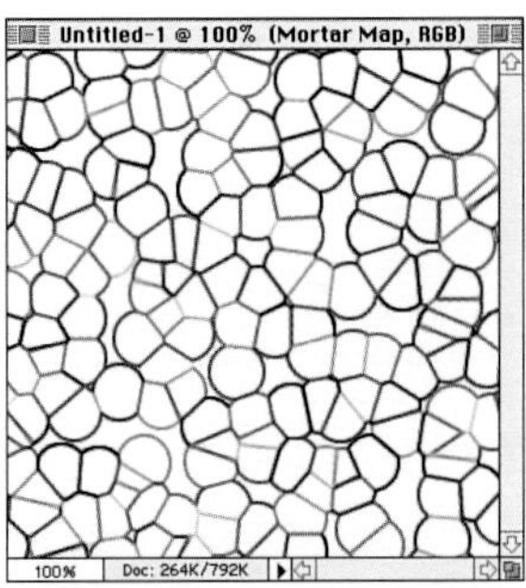


**10** Make the Mortar Map layer active. Choose Filter➡Stylize➡Find Edges and then select Image➡Adjust➡Desaturate. Apply Image➡Adjust Auto Levels.

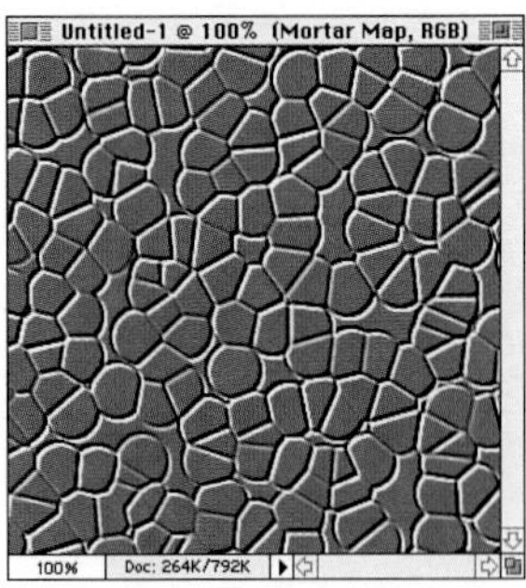


**11** Change the blending mode to Hard Light. Apply Filter➡Stylize➡Emboss. You need to set the angle so that the embossing sinks into the cobblestones. I used the following: Angle: –47°; Height: 3; Amount: 100.

**12** The cracks are much too sharp. Apply Filter➡Blur➡Gaussian Blur. You can fiddle with the setting, but somewhere around 1.1 should work.

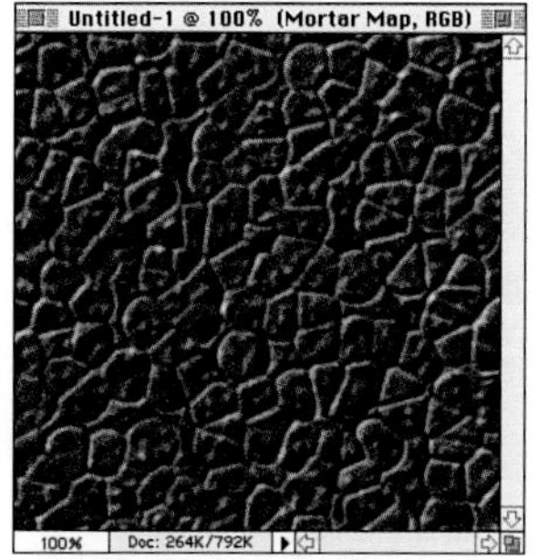


**13** The color is still too strong—unless you like colorful cobblestones. Make the Color Map layer active. Create a Hue/Saturation adjustment layer. Change the settings as you prefer. I decreased the Saturation to –42 and the Lightness to –16.

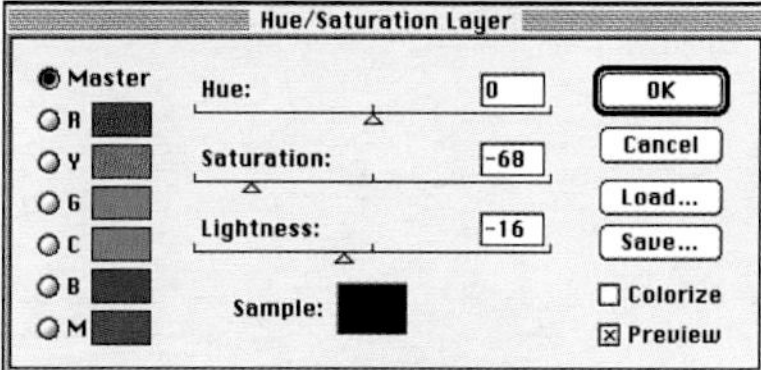


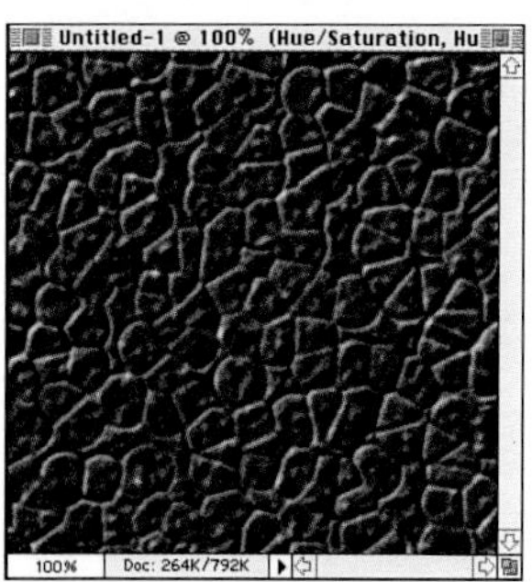


**14** Now that you've set the color of the cobblestones, you may want to tweak the Texture Map and Mortar Map layers again. I applied another 1.1 Gaussian Blur to the Mortar Map layer. If you think there is too much shine on the cobblestones, choose Image➡Adjust Levels and bring the white Output slider to the left until you have removed as much of the highlighting as you want.

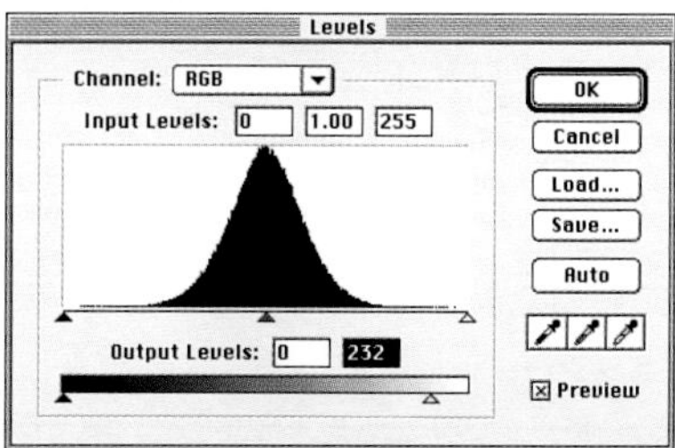


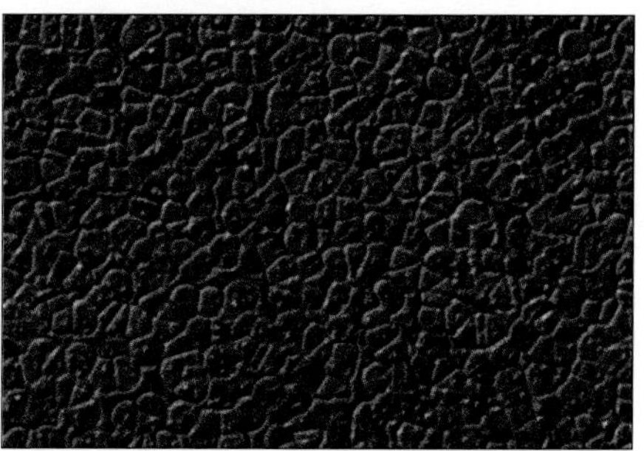

# VARIATIONS

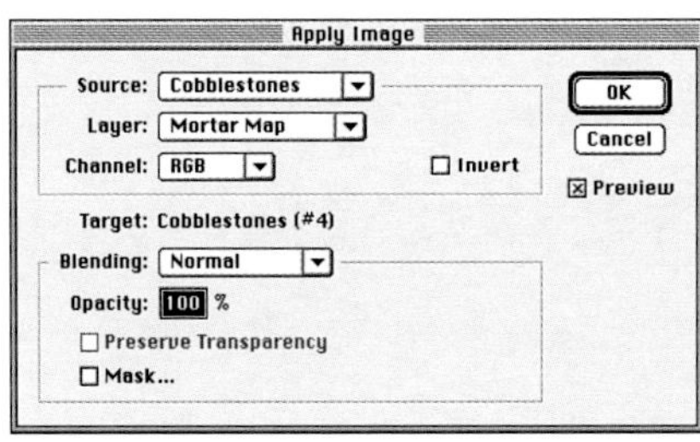


If you want a more deeply etched texture, you can apply the Lighting Effects filter to the image. Create a new channel (Channel #4). Select Image➥Apply Image (Source: your image, Layer: Mortar Map, Channel: RGB, Blending: Normal, Opacity: 100%).

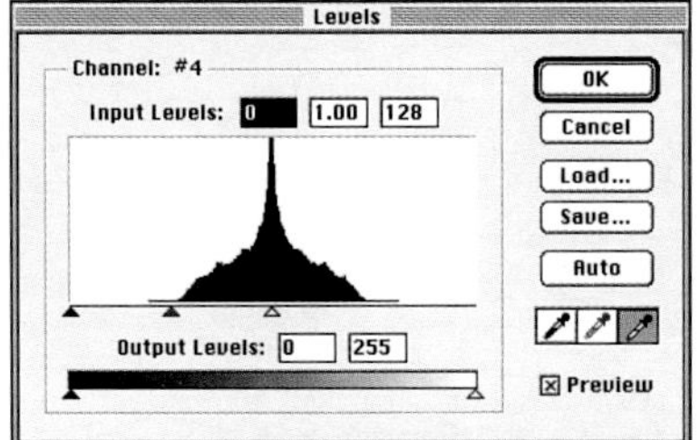


Select Image➥Adjust➥Levels. Click to pick up the white point Eye-dropper (the one on the right). Click on one of the areas of neutral gray in the channel. The gray areas turn white.

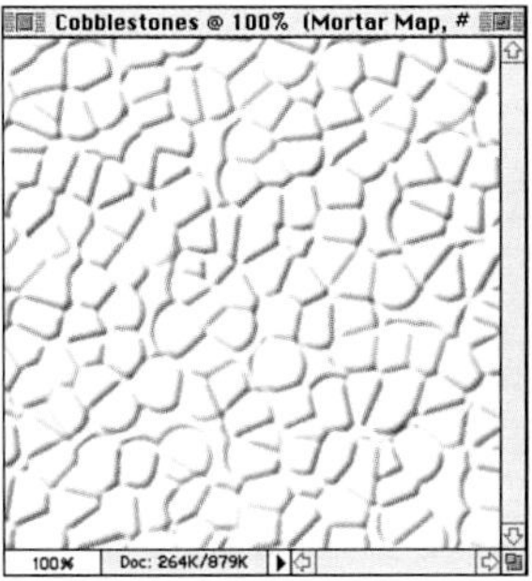


This enables the cobblestones to come forward and the cracks to recede when you apply the Lighting Effects filter.

Return to the composite channel. Flatten the image. Choose Filter➥Render➥Lighting Effects. Use the settings shown, or select the Cobblestones preset in the Lighting folder on the *Photoshop Textures Magic* CD-ROM. ■

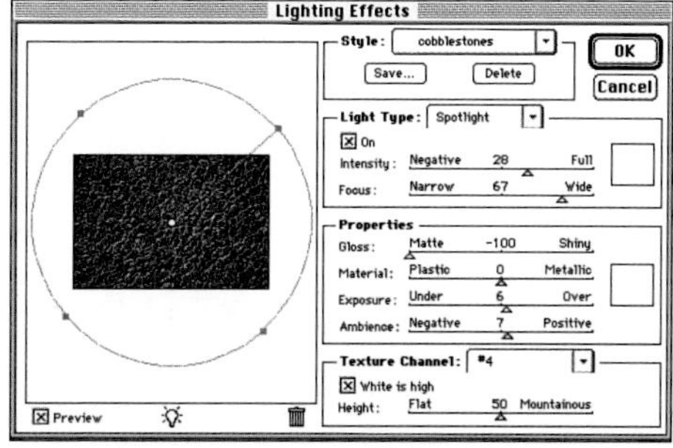

This texture looks like a major celebration in process. It is wonderful for any RGB output even if it looks a bit anemic on the printed page. The strong magentas and blues that come from the applied RGB noise do not translate well to print, but this makes a terrific background for a Web page. So grab a bottle of champagne and your party hat!

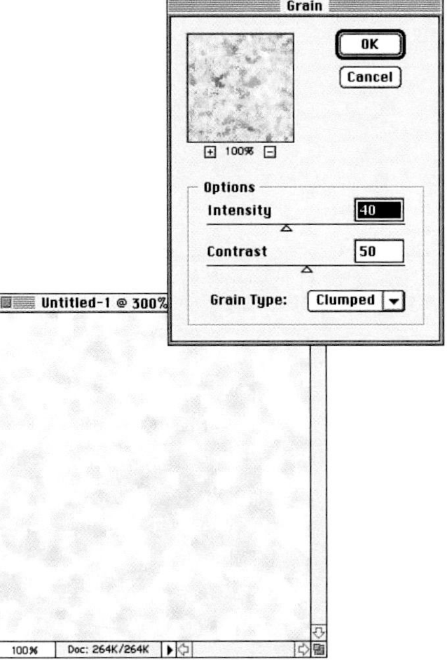


**1** Create a new file. Any size file will work—I started with a file that is 600×400 pixels. Choose Filter➡Texture➡Grain. Select Clumped as the Grain Type. I use an Intensity setting of 40 and a Contrast of 50.



## TOOLBOX

Diamond Texture Lighting Filter preset

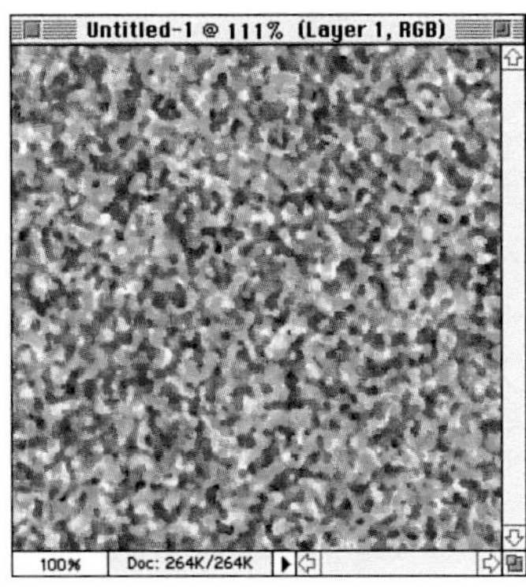


**2** Choose Image➡Adjust➡Auto Levels.

**3** This is much too dark. Select Filter➥Fade Auto Levels. Decrease the opacity to about 44% and select Hard Light blending mode.

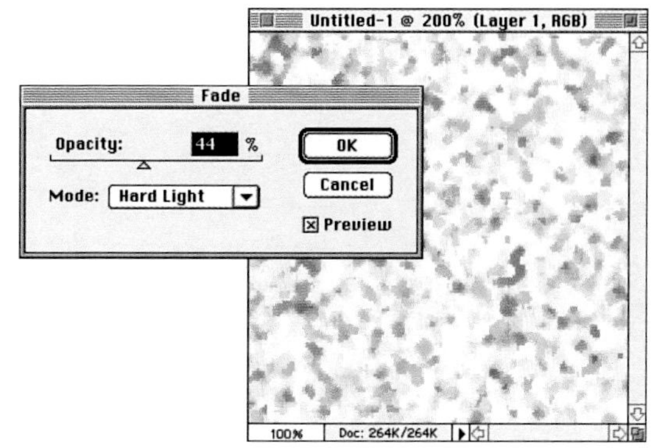


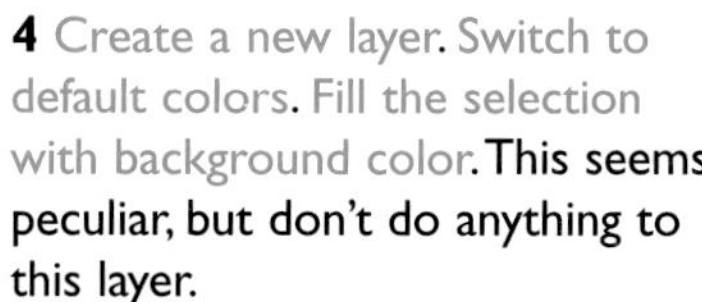

**4** Create a new layer. Switch to default colors. Fill the selection with background color. This seems peculiar, but don't do anything to this layer.

**5** Duplicate the Background layer. Position the layer at the top of the layer list in the Layers palette.

**6** Make the Background copy layer active. Choose Filter➥Blur➥ Gaussian Blur (8.5 pixels). The data in the image becomes so light as to be almost invisible. That's fine—it is still there.

**7** Choose Filter➥Stylize➥Find Edges. The data is still too light to see.

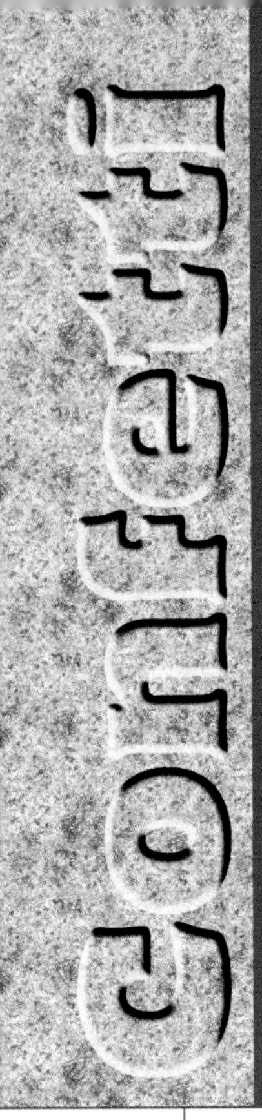


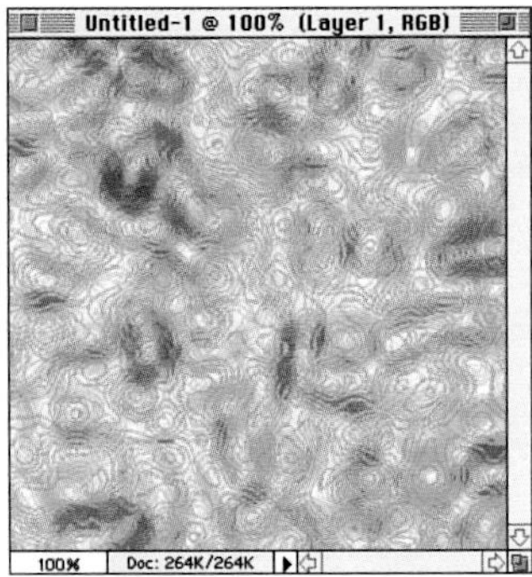


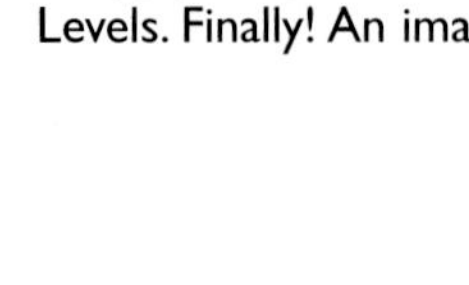
**8** Apply Image➡Adjust➡Auto Levels. Finally! An image appears.

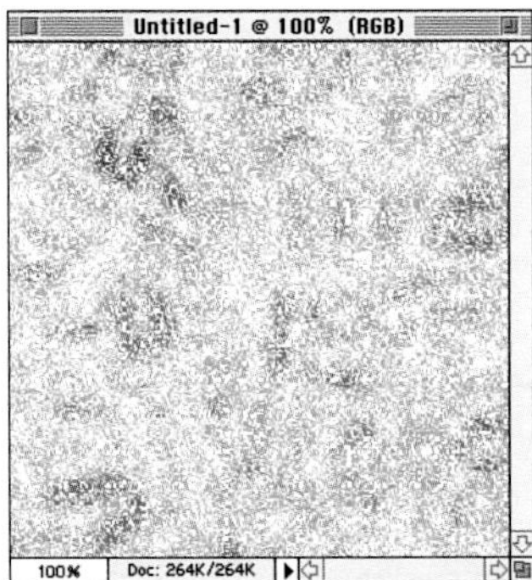


**9** Change the blending mode to Dissolve and reduce the layer's opacity until the image looks spattered onto the blank layer beneath. I used an opacity of 60%.

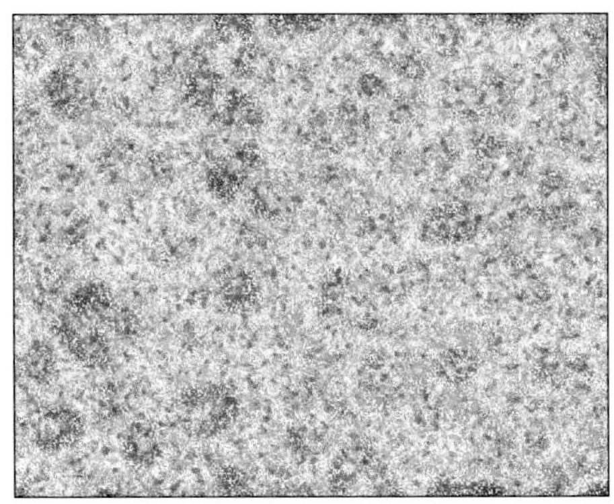

**10** Merge Down (Command-E) [Control-E]. Now change the blending mode to Multiply. This keeps the "spots" created by using Dissolve mode, and enables you to change the blending mode as well.

## VARIATIONS

### Web Patterns

If you want to make a seamless tile for the Web, you need to first decide how big the tile can be. I started with a tile 50×50 pixels. Set the rectangular Marquee to a fixed size of whatever you want your tile size to be. Drag the Marquee around the original image (use the Marquee tool, not the Move tool to drag) until you find a spot that you like. Copy the selected area to the clipboard. Create a new file. Paste the image in from the clipboard. Do not flatten. Select➥All. Define a Pattern. Create a new file at least as large as your Web page to test the pattern. I used 640×480. Fill the selection with pattern. Most areas of the original will tile seamlessly without doing anything to them. If necessary, make the image seamless using the Rubber Stamp method. When you like the results, convert the image to Indexed Color mode, using the Web Palette option. Save the file in GIF format.

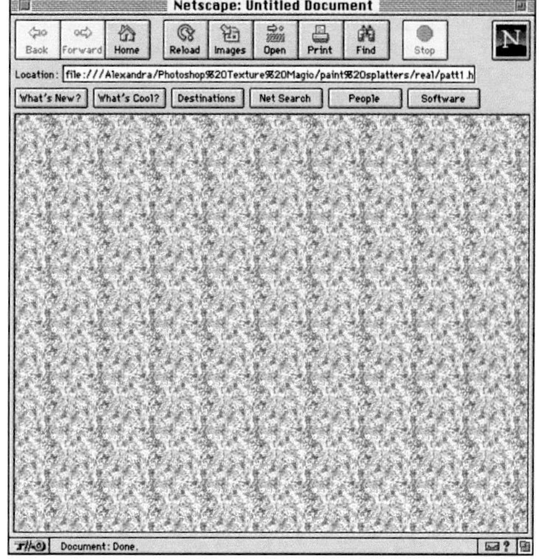


To add some interest to the pattern, use a brick repeat rather than a simple rectangular repeat. Repeat the instructions for the first Web pattern until you have pasted the small pattern into its own file. Again, do not flatten. Choose Image➥Canvas Size. Anchor the image in the upper-center square, and double the original height (I doubled the 50-pixel height to 100 pixels). Duplicate layer 1. Choose Filter➥Other➥Offset. Offset the layer by half of the current height and width of the image (I used an offset of 50 pixels down and 25 pixels right). Wrap around. Select all. Define the pattern. Fill a new selection with the pattern.

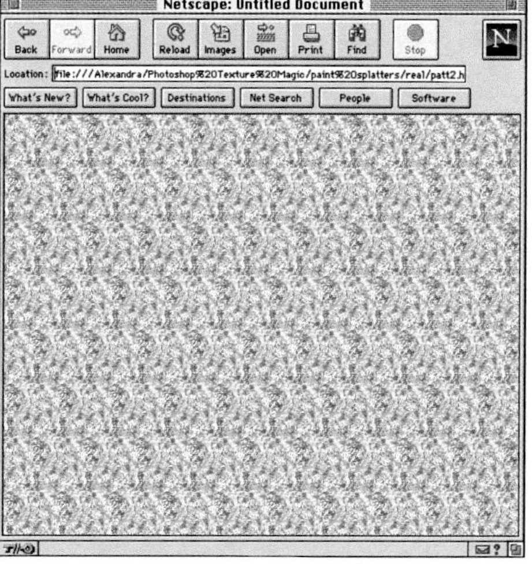

## A Stronger Celebration

If you want to create a darker version of the original texture, complete Steps 1–10. Create a new layer. Fill with white. Choose Filter➡Texture➡Grain. Select Clumped as the Grain Type. I used an Intensity setting of 40 and a Contrast of 50. Apply Filter➡Stylize➡Find Edges and then apply Filter➡Blur➡Gaussian Blur. Blur the image until the colors merge. I used a Radius of 4.9. Choose Image➡Adjust➡Levels. Move the black Input slider to the left until it reaches the spot where the values in the graph start to sharply increase. Click OK. Change the blending mode to Difference.

## A Persian Cloisonné

To produce a delicate texture similar in feel to a Persian garden, repeat the instructions for the previous variation. Instead of creating a blank layer, and filling it with grain, duplicate the Background layer, and apply the Gaussian Blur filter. You do not need to adjust the levels on this variation after you blur it.

## Sequined Splendor

You can also get a completely different look by applying the Lighting Effects filter to the original texture through a pattern and doubling it back on itself. Start with the finished image from the original instructions. Flatten the image. Create a new channel. This channel should be solid black. Open the file Diamonds.Psd, choose Select➡All, and define the pattern. Click the original texture image to make it active, and fill the blank channel with pattern. Return to the composite channel. Choose Filter➡Render➡Lighting Effects. Select the Diamond Texture Lights preset that came from the *Photoshop Textures Magic* CD-ROM. Duplicate the Background layer. Choose Layer➡Transform➡Flip Horizontal. Change the blending mode to Multiply. This texture may be too dark and too busy to be a successful Web pattern, but it certainly lights up a night on the town. ■

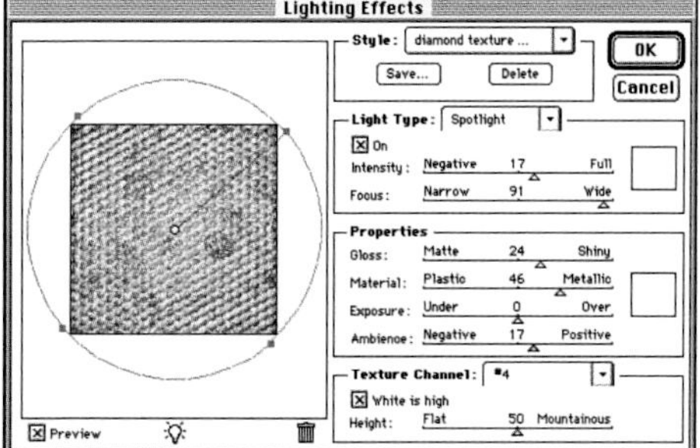

Have you ever stared at a cracker before you ate it? I mean, really looked hard at the texture? It's wonderful! It's lumpy and nicely browned. You can easily create a Saltine-type cracker, or a water-based cracker on the computer. For a large cracker such as a piece of matzo, you can make this seamless using the Brushed Mask method shown in the Photoshop Basics section.

**1** Create a new file. Mine is 300×300 pixels. Switch the foreground color to a light cracker-background color. I used RGB: 230, 230, 231. Add the color to your Swatches palette by moving to the first empty spot at the end of the palette. Fill your image with the foreground color.

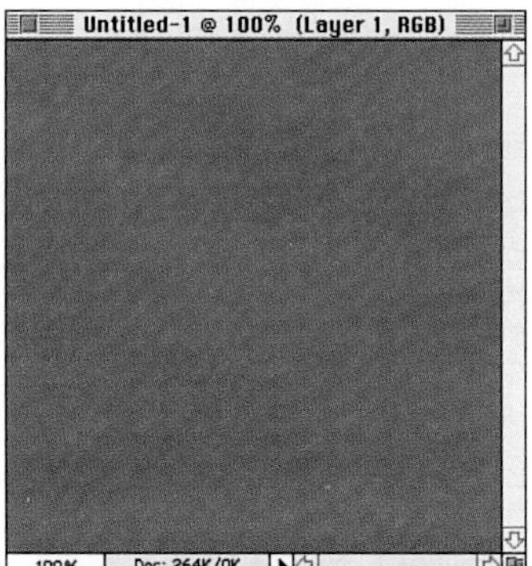


**2** Create a new layer (Layer 1). Switch the foreground color to a color suitable for the browned portions of the cracker. I chose RGB: 177, 131, 85. Fill the layer with the foreground color.

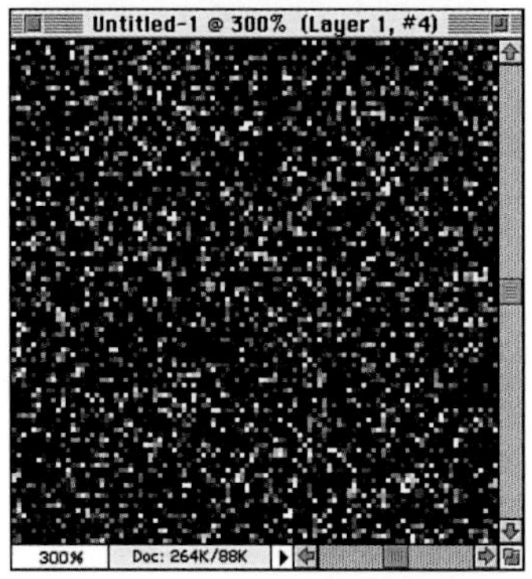


**3** Create a new channel (#4). The channel is probably filled with black. This is okay. Apply Filter➡Noise➡Add Noise (Gaussian). In a channel, the noise already is Monochromatic. I used an Amount of 135.

**4** Select Filter➥Pixelate➥ Crystallize (10). The filter is used to help produce the little lumpies in the cracker.

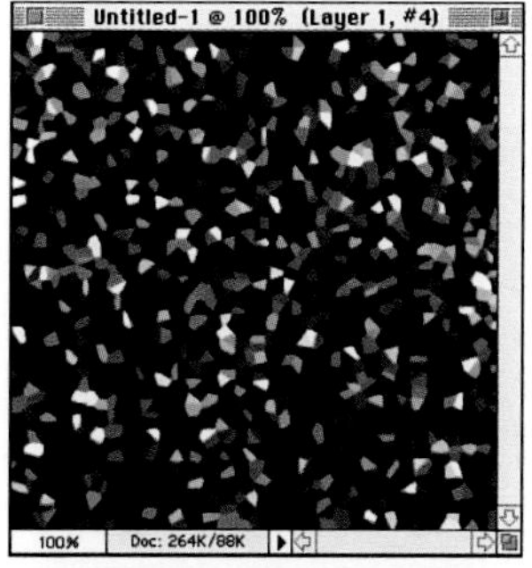


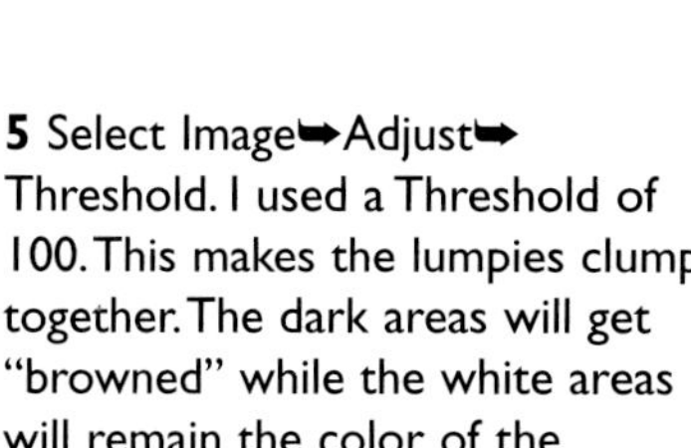

**5** Select Image➥Adjust➥ Threshold. I used a Threshold of 100. This makes the lumpies clump together. The dark areas will get "browned" while the white areas will remain the color of the Background layer.

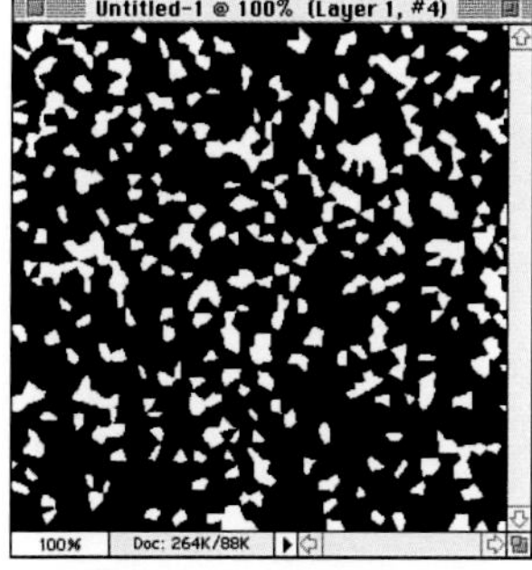


**6** Choose Filter➥Blur➥Gaussian Blur. I used a Radius of 5.0. Softening the channel keeps the color from being applied too sharply.

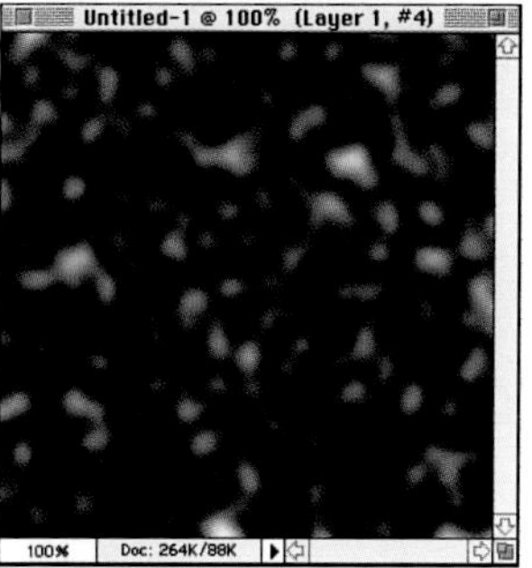


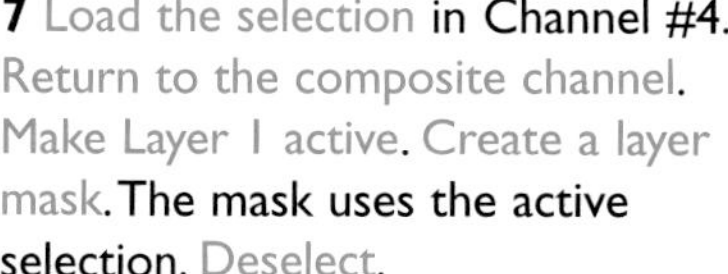

**7** Load the selection in Channel #4. Return to the composite channel. Make Layer 1 active. Create a layer mask. The mask uses the active selection. Deselect.

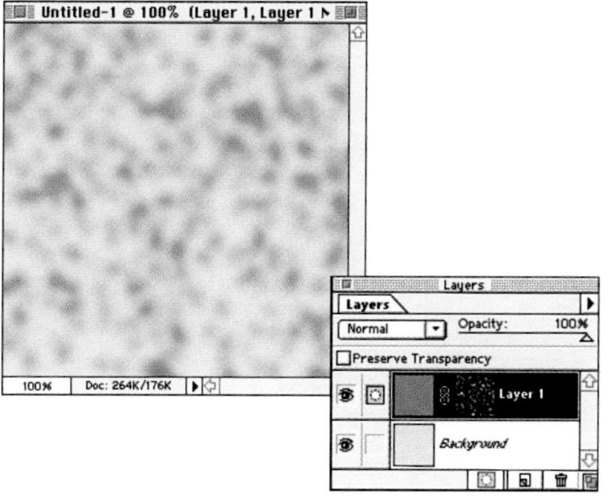

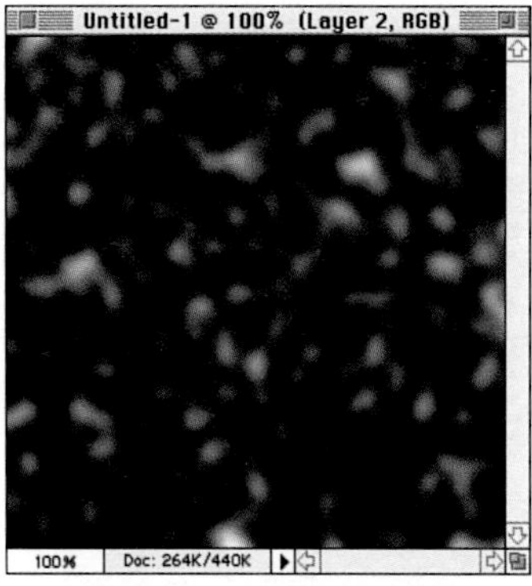


**8** So far, you just have a two-toned flat wafer. You need to add some dimension to it. Create a new layer (Layer 2). Select Image➥Apply Image (Channel: #4, Opacity: 100%, Blending: either Normal or Multiply).

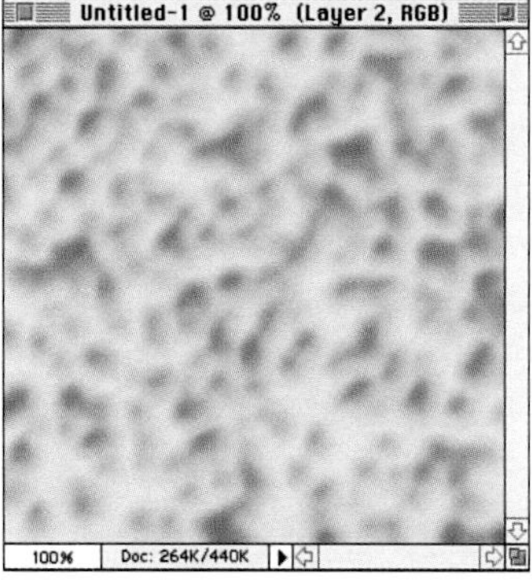


**9** Change the blending mode of Layer 2 to Hard Light. Choose Filter➥Stylize➥Emboss (Angle: 127°, Height: 3 pixels, Amount: 64).

**10** Switch the foreground color to a darker or different "browned" color. Duplicate Layer 1. Select➡ All. Press the Delete key. This leaves an empty layer that is protected by a layer mask. Select the Airbrush tool with a large brush and a low pressure. Spray a little bit of one or more contrasting colors on this layer. Crunch!

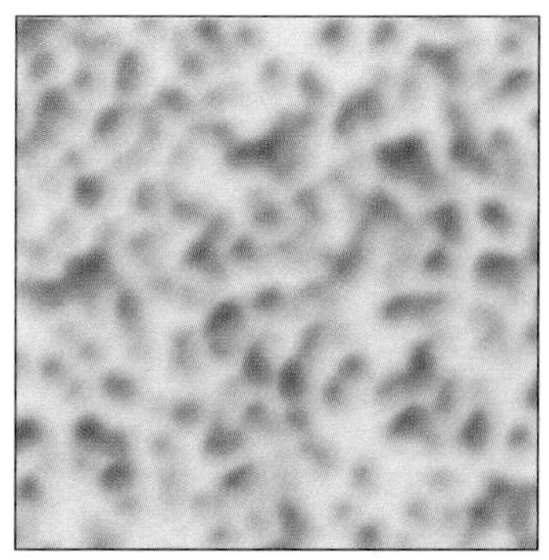

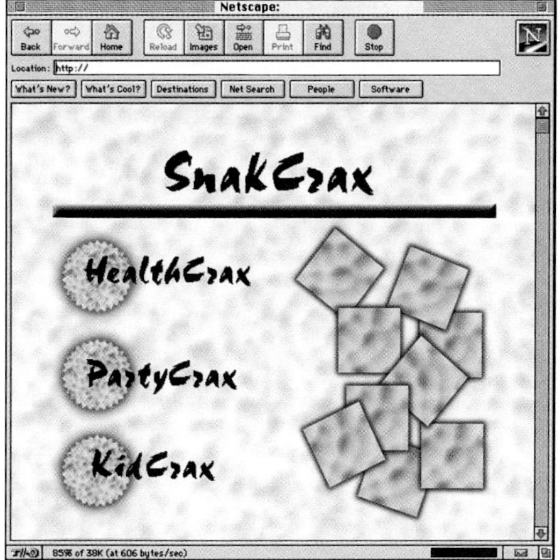

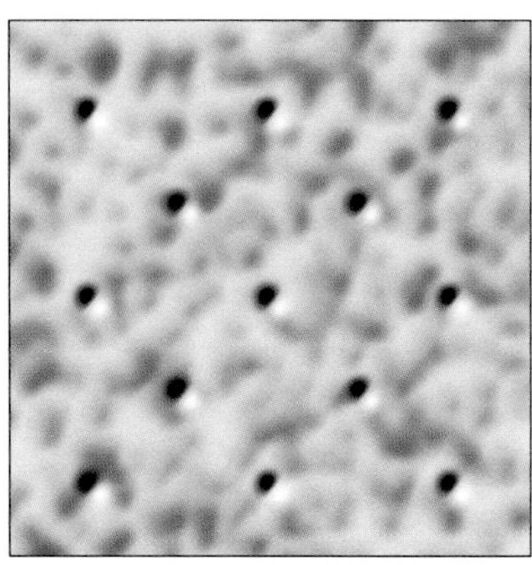

## VARIATIONS

If you want to add holes to turn the cracker into a Saltine, turn on the Rulers (Command-R)[Control-R]. Add 3 vertical guides at even intervals. In the 300-pixel square image, I added them at 50, 150, and 250 pixels. Add 3 horizontal guides at the same coordinates on the horizontal axis. Create a new layer (Layer 3). Switch to default colors. Fill Layer 3 with the background color (white). Select the Paintbrush and the 9-pixel hard brush (third from the right in the default Brushes palette). Stamp a brushstroke down on each grid intersection. Select View➥Clear Guides. Add 2 horizontal guides evenly spaced, and add 2 vertical guides at the same location on the vertical ruler. I added these guides at 100 and 200 pixels. Stamp a brushstroke on these intersections as well. Select Filter➥Blur➥Gaussian Blur (1.3). Change the blending mode to Hard Light. Choose Filter➥Stylize➥Emboss (Angle: –27°, Height: 4 pixels, Amount: 126). You might want to soften the embossing by applying Filter➥Blur➥Gaussian Blur (2.0). You can emboss again at an Angle of 127° if you want to leave light on both sides of the cracker holes.

To add salt to the cracker, create a new channel (#5). It should automatically be filled with black. Select Filter➥Noise➥Add Noise (Distribution: Gaussian, Monochromatic). I used an Amount of 135. Choose Filter➥Pixelate➥Crystallize (3). Select Image➥Adjust Levels and move the Gamma slider (the center one) toward the right until the Gamma point is about 0.53 or the spot at which there is only a small amount of bright white. Load the selection Channel #5. Make the Composite channel active. Make Layer 3 invisible (if you have added holes to the cracker). Make any visible layer active. Merge the visible layers (Shift-Command-E)[Shift-Control-E]. Make Layer 3 visible again. Switch to default colors. Press the Delete key to add a layer of "salt." Deselect. ■

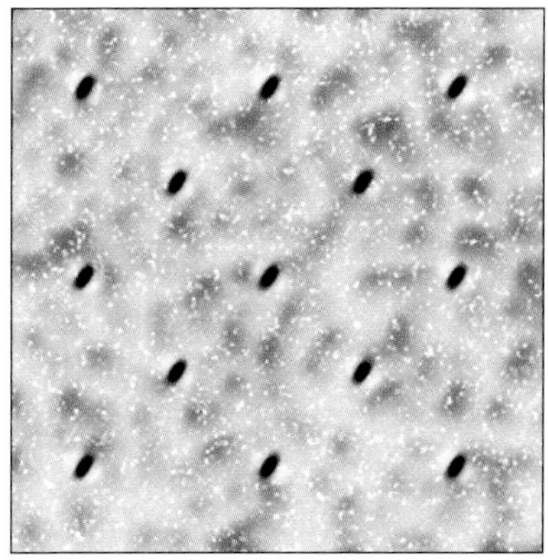

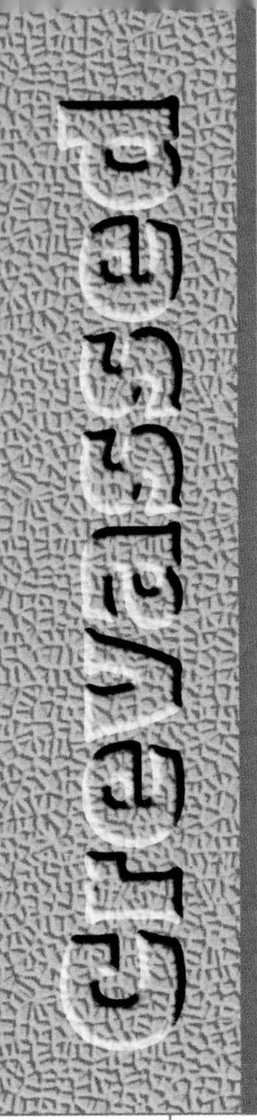


Creased, crumbled, cracked, *crevassed.* This effect fractures your image into organic bits. It makes an effective, soft Web page background when created with a solid color or a muted gradient. This effect also adds a wonderful craquelure accent to an image—in a much more natural manner than the Craquelure filter, and it is excellent as a texture wrap on a 3-D model.

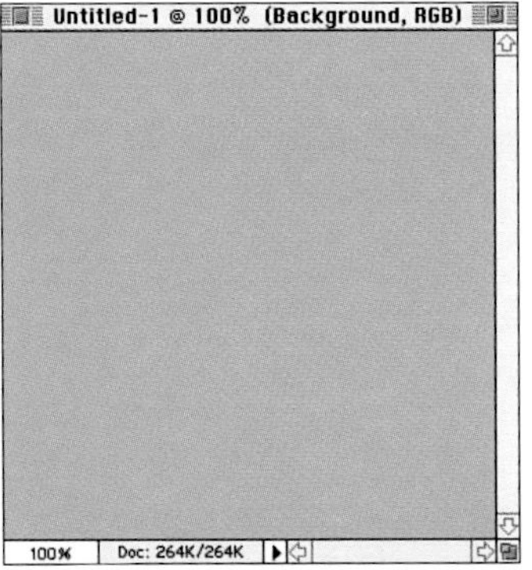


**1** Create a new file. Mine is 300×300 pixels. Switch the foreground color to your desired texture color. I selected a light mint-green. Fill with foreground color.

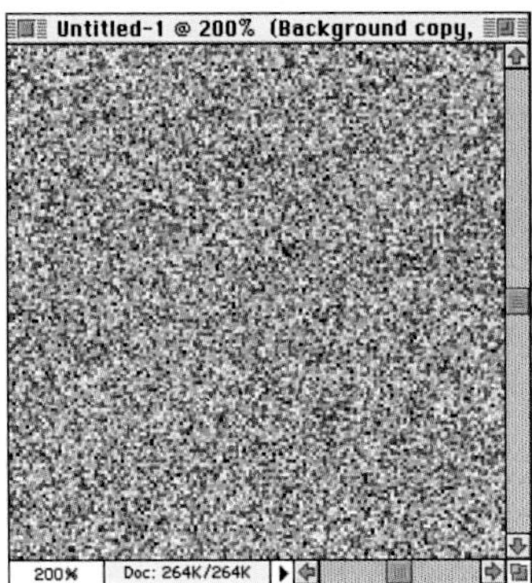


**2** Duplicate the Background layer. Select Filter➡Noise➡Add Noise (Distribution: Gaussian, Monochromatic Off). I used an Amount of 135.

**3** Apply Filter➥Pixelate➥ Cyrstallize. I used a cell size of 11. Cell sizes of 8 to 14 give good results. Larger cell sizes produce the networks seen in "Cobblestones" (page 86).

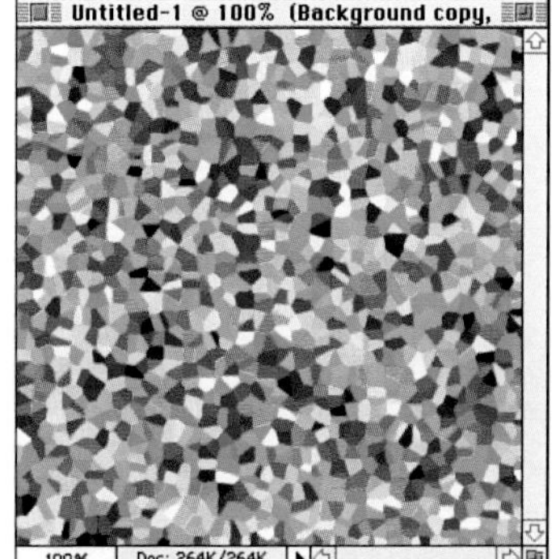


**4** Choose Filter➥Stylize➥Find Edges. These edges form the shadows in the cracks.

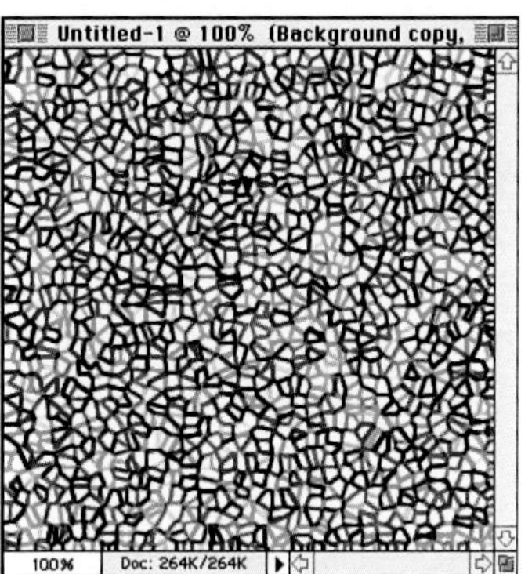


**5** Select Image➥Adjust➥ Desaturate (Shift-Command-U) [Shift-Control-U]. This removes the odd colors in the image.

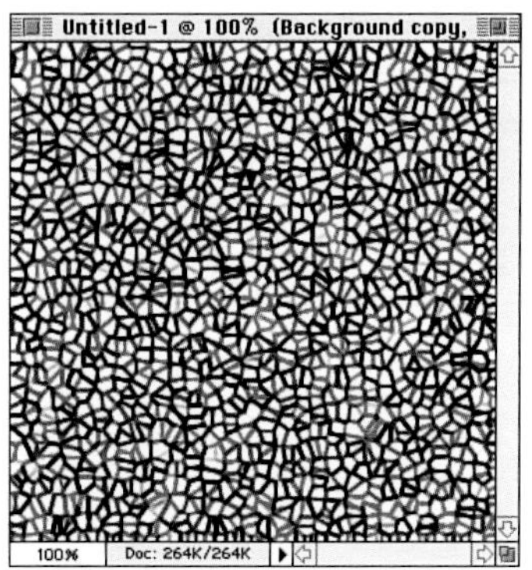

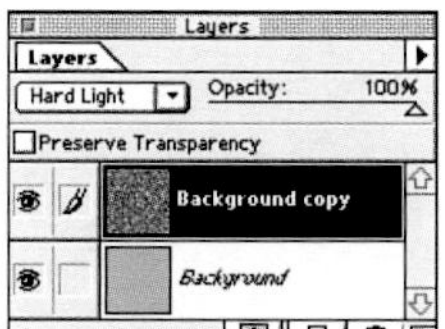


6 Change the blending mode to Hard Light. Now you will be able to evaluate the Emboss filter as you apply it.

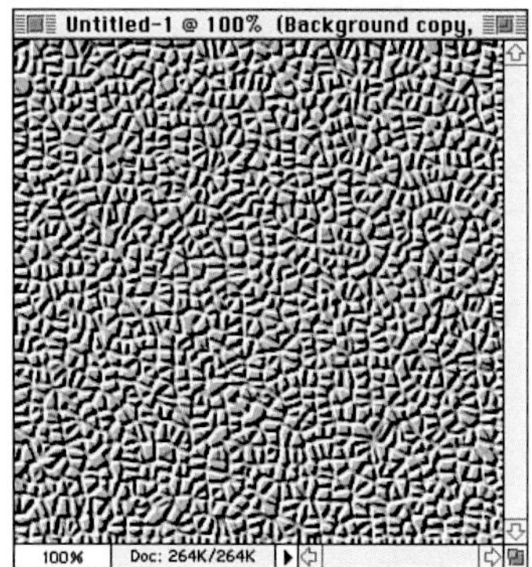


7 Choose Filter➡Stylize➡Emboss (Height: 3 pixels, Amount: 100). I used an Angle of –47° so that the crevasses sink into the texture rather than standing up.

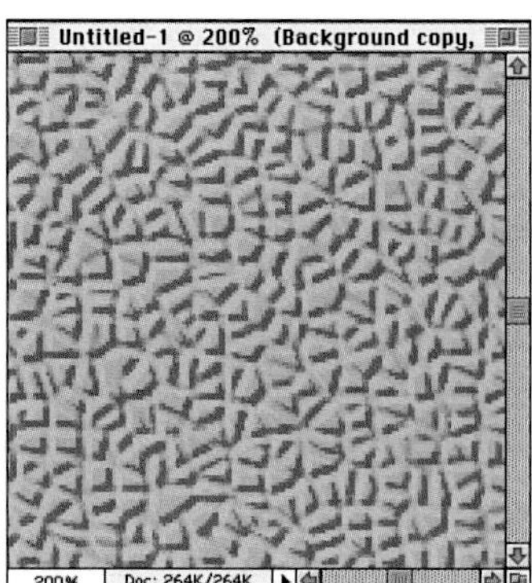


8 The Hard Light mode produces an effect that is much too strong. Reduce the top layer's opacity until you are satisfied with the effect. I used an opacity of 35% because I wanted it to show up in print. If you are using this on a Web page, you can reduce the layer's opacity to as little as 5% and still have a textured background tile.

**9** Now, you need to create a seamless tile. Change the blending mode on the Background copy layer back to Normal and set the opacity at 100%. Duplicate the Background copy layer. Make the pattern seamless using the Masked Offset method. Select Layer➥Merge Down (Command-E) [Control-E]. Change the blending mode to Hard Light and reduce the layer opacity back to your desired amount. Select➥All. Define the pattern. Fill an image of the desired size with the pattern (or save the tile as .GIF and use it in a Web page).

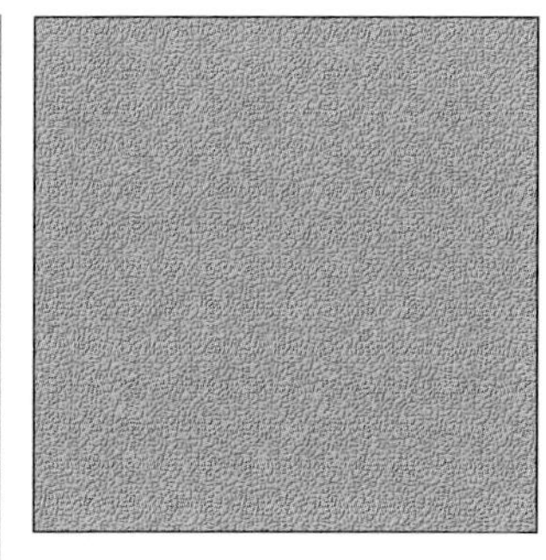

## VARIATIONS

If you want to texture a photograph, use the photograph as the Background layer. Create an empty layer filled with white in Step 2 instead of duplicating the Background layer. Complete all of the remaining steps until Step 9. This photograph is from the Vivid Details Sampler on the *Photoshop Textures Magic* CD-ROM.

To add a more varied texture to the photograph, duplicate the photograph in Step 2 of the original instructions. Do not apply the Add Noise filter. The texture is not as uniformly crevassed, but the craquelure lines hug the image better. This photograph is also from the Vivid Details Sampler on the *Photoshop Textures Magic* CD-ROM. ■

# Fish Scales



## TOOLBOX

Fishscale gradient preset

GoldGrad gradient preset

Fish scales is one of the classic "building block" patterns that has been used since antiquity. It is a simple geometric form to construct, but can be used as a decoration, texture, or realistic material if you happen to be modeling fish.

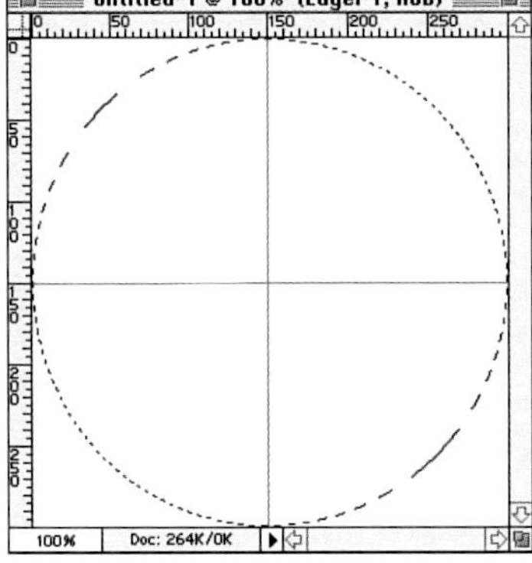


**1** Create a new file 300 pixels square. You are not limited to that size, but the image does need to be square. Create a new layer (Layer 1). Turn on the Rulers (Command-R) [Control-R]. Add a horizontal and vertical guide at the center point along both rulers. Double-click the Marquee tool. Set the Style to Elliptical and the fixed size to 300×300 pixels (or the size of your image). Place the cursor at the intersection of the two guides. Press the (Option)[Alt] key to create a perfect circle centered in the image.

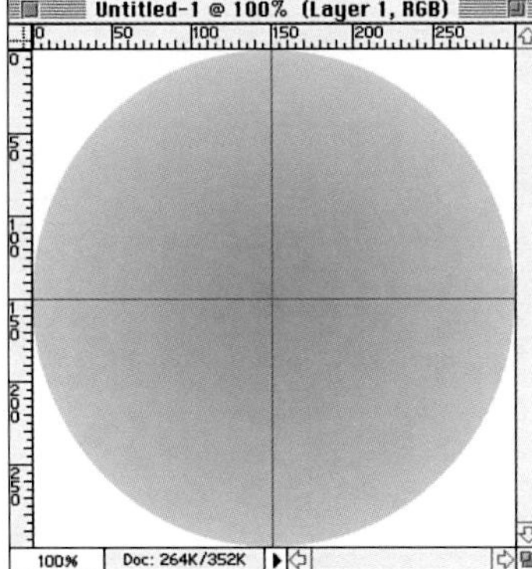


**2** Switch the foreground color to the inside color for the fish scale pattern. I used a yellow-green—RGB: 78, 163, 32. Switch the background color to a contrasting color. I used RGB: 202, 215, 65. Double-click the Gradient tool, select the Foreground to Background gradient, and set Dither off. Choose a Radial gradient Type. Place the Gradient cursor at the intersection of the two guides, press the Shift key and the mouse button, and drag the cursor to the edge of the circular selection. Release the mouse button.

**3** Select Image➥Adjust➥Posterize. Select 40 levels. This is enough to see real banding in the gradient—which is actually what you are trying to achieve. The banded fish scale pattern is an ancient one in Chinese art.

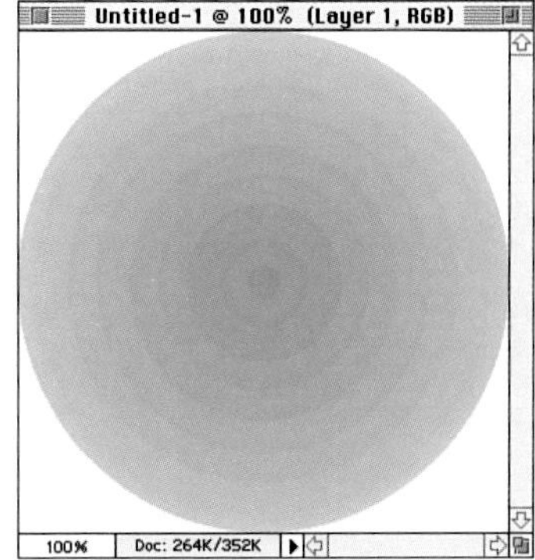


**4** Duplicate Layer 1. Deselect. Select Filter➥Other➥Offset (Wrap Around). Make the Horizontal and Vertical distances one-half of the image dimensions (150 pixels for both dimensions in this example).

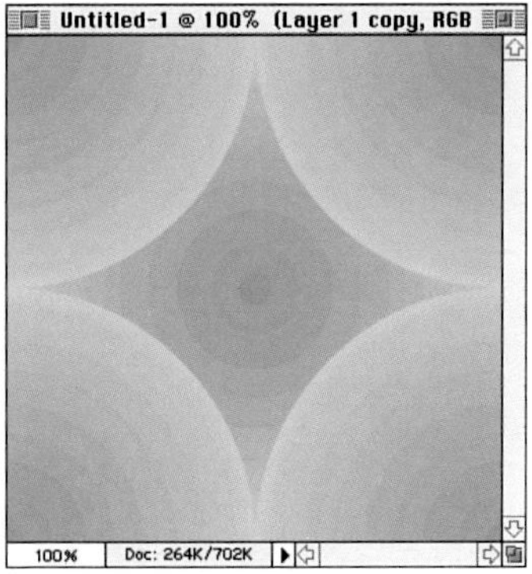


**5** Select the rectangular Marquee and set the fixed size to 300 pixels wide × 150 pixels high (or the full width of your image and one-half of the length). In order to create the fish scale illusion, you need to separate the top and bottom halves of Layer 1 copy. Drag the Marquee to select the top half of the image. Select Layer➥New➥Layer Via Cut (Shift-Command-J)[Shift-Control-J]. Position the layer below Layer 1.

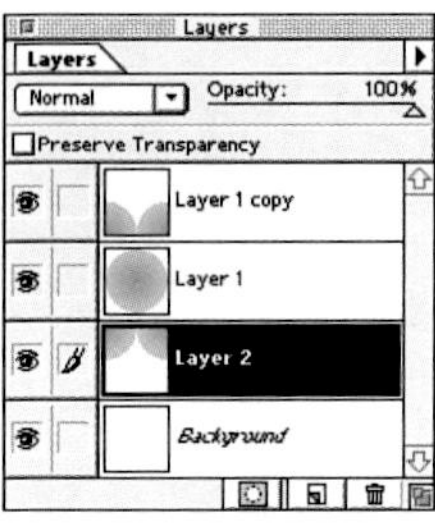


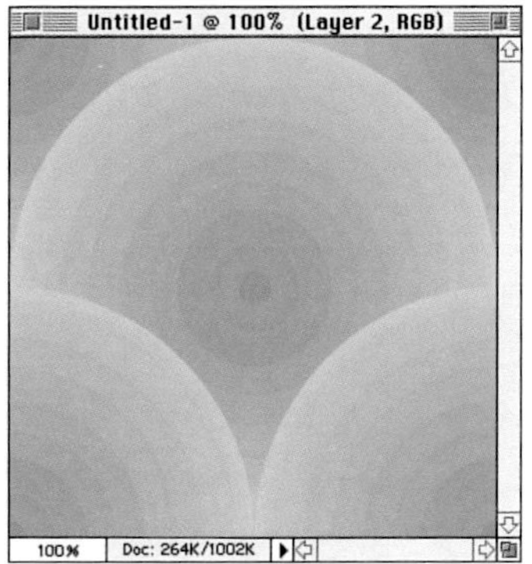

**6** Select➡All. Define the pattern. Create a new file that is the desired size. Fill the selection with pattern.

## VARIATIONS

An infinite number of variations are possible. If you want shadows under the fish scales, you can use a work-around that is fairly easy. A real shadow is difficult to make seamless in this pattern. Complete the example through Step 5. Make Layer 2 invisible, and make Layer 1 active. Load the transparency selection of Layer 1. Create a new layer (Layer 3). Switch to default colors. Fill the selection with background color. Turn on preserve transparency. Choose Select➡Modify➡Border and set a border size of about 26 pixels. Fill the selection with foreground color. This will create the area of darkness at the edges of the fish scale. Duplicate Layer 3. Repeat Steps 4 and 5 with the new layer. Drag each shadow layer above the layer that looks like it. You can see the "shadow" layers in the layers palette—they are Layer 4, Layer 3, and Layer 3 copy. You will not see Layer 4 in the actual image because it is completely covered over.

Change the blending mode to Multiply for each of the shadow layers. Reduce the layer opacity if you want. Continue with Step 6.

You can create a metallic fish scale effect. In Step 2, select the GoldGrad from the *Photoshop Textures Magic* CD-ROM. Fill the circle with a linear gradient dragged across the image from left to right. Choose Select➥Modify➥Contract (10 pixels). Apply the linear gradient, again dragging the cursor from the top of the image to the bottom. Omit Step 3, and proceed with the rest of the original instructions.

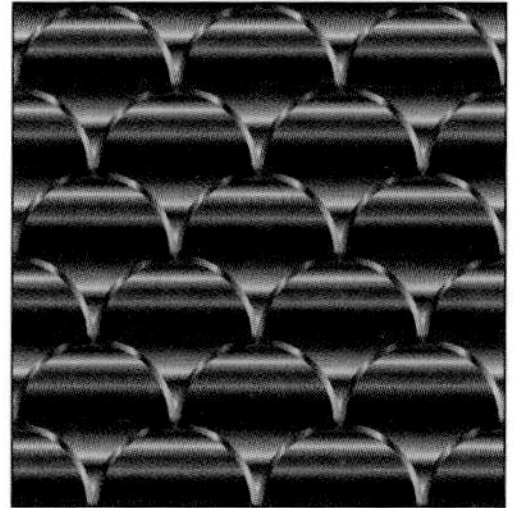

If you are unhappy with the way the Posterize command works in Step 3, use a radial gradient that only contains shades of gray. Switch the foreground color to RGB: 64, 64, 64 and switch the background color to RGB: 192, 192, 192. Use the Fishscale Gradient preset on the *Photoshop Textures Magic* CD-ROM. In Step 4, posterize the circle into 6 levels. The grays will posterize correctly. Work Steps 4 and 5. Select the Paintbrush tool. Pick up the color at the center of each layer (the darkest gray) and paint out the other colors at the bottom of the fish scale. You only need to do this on Layers 1 and 2. Create an adjustment layer for Hue/ Saturation. I changed the Hue to –34, the Saturation to 35, and the Lightness to 23. Work Step 6.

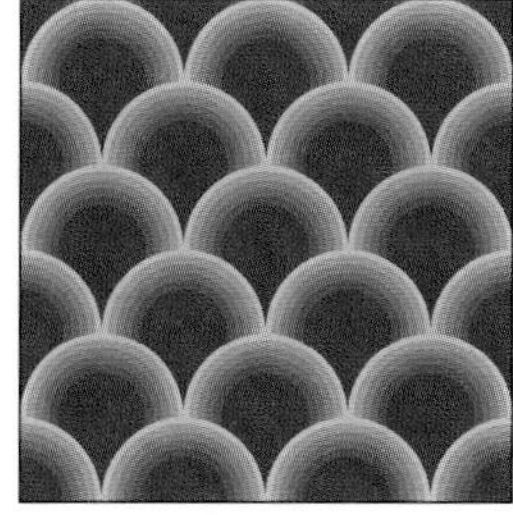

You can also work the original instructions using the Fishscale Gradient preset. If you omit Step 4 and do not posterize, you get a lovely, soft blend. ■

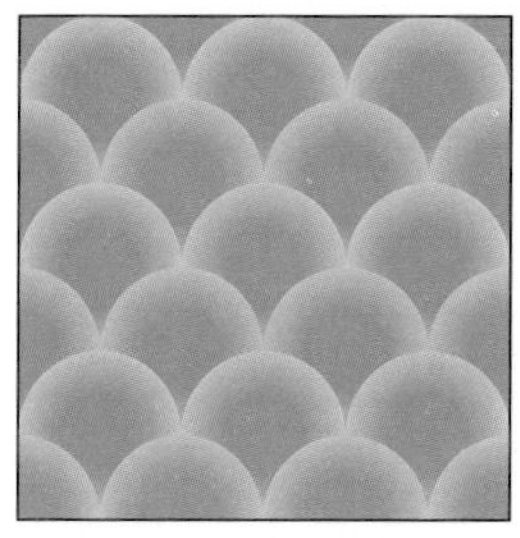

Grass is a challenging texture to design. It has a large number of variables. Do you want to look at the grass up close and personal or from a distance? And what kind of grass—(no, not *that* kind)—do you want to see: grass on a golf course, or the mixture of grass and weeds on an ordinary front lawn (like mine)? The instructions in this effect can work in all situations. This texture will hold its character in print or in multimedia. You just need to decide on the shade of green.

**1** Create a new file. You can talk this texture into tiling, so your file can be either full-size or tile-size. Mine is 400×400 pixels. Switch the foreground color to the desired shade of green. I used RGB: 0, 112, 54. Fill with foreground color. Select Filter➥Noise➥Add Noise (Distribution: Gaussian, Monochromatic). I used an Amount of 29. You need to keep the Amount low enough to not place white pixels in the image.

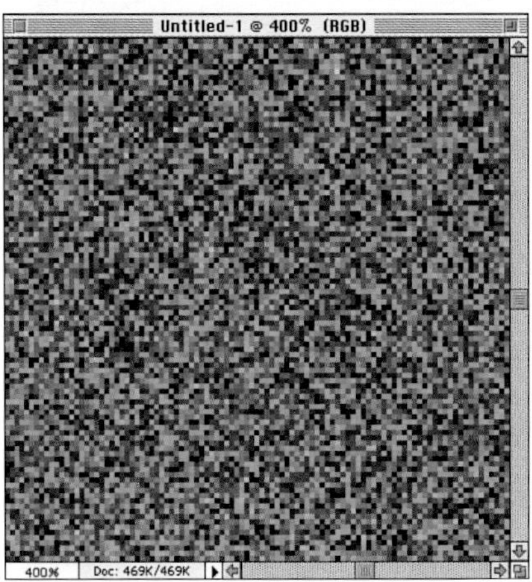


**2** Apply Filter➥Texture➥Grain (Grain Type: Regular). I used an Intensity of 40 and a Contrast of 50. This adds a small amount of contrasting (but related) pixels—not the RGB "primary" noise of the Add Noise filter.

**3** Apply Filter➡Texture➡Grain (Grain Type: Clumped). I used an Intensity of 40 and a Contrast of 50. This further helps to create a "grassy" base.

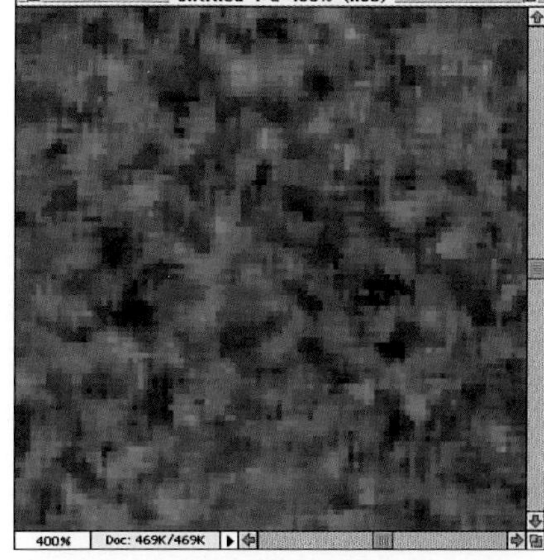


**4** Select Filter➡Brush Strokes➡Spatter. I used a Spray Radius of 10 and a Smoothness of 5. This makes a very paint-like grass texture.

**5** Duplicate the Background layer.

**6** Choose Filter➡Blur➡Motion Blur. Pick an Angle that is just a little bit away from 90° and a short Distance. I used an Angle of –74° and a Distance of 8 pixels. This motion blur actually forms the grass blades.

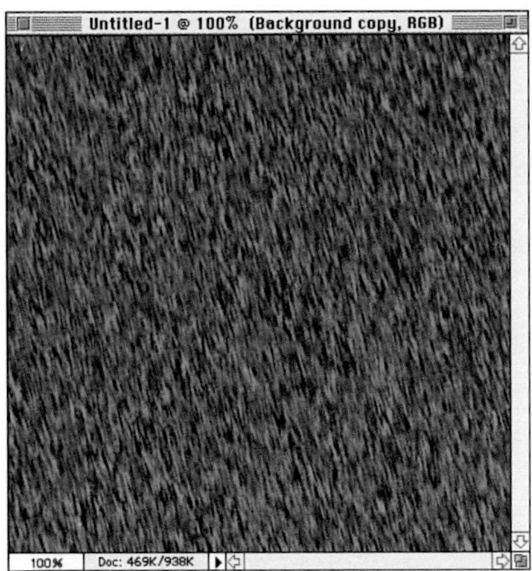


**7** The grass needs to be further defined. Select Filter➡Sharpen➡ Unsharp Mask (Amount: 450, Radius: 1.5, Threshold: 0). As in so many of these effects, I chose settings that work for the textures, but are preposterous for prepress use.

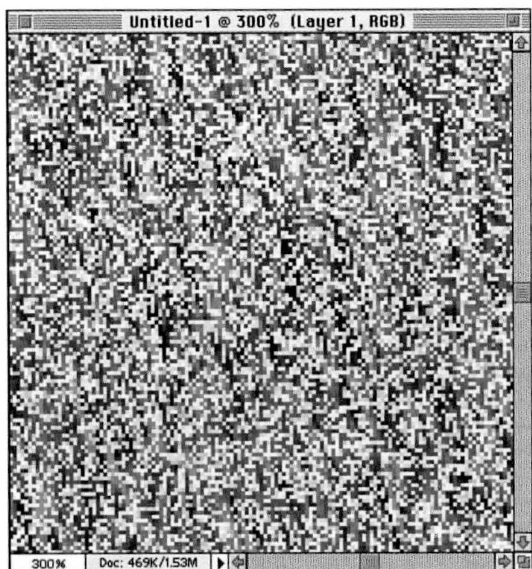


**8** Most lawns contain some brown—if not dead spots, then old crabgrass, thatch, or just plain dirt as an underpainting. Create a new layer. Switch the background color to white. Fill with background color. Select Filter➡Noise➡Add Noise (Distribution: Gaussian, Monochromatic). I used an Amount of 29. Double-click the Magic Wand tool and set the Tolerance to 0, Anti-alias off, and no feather. Magnify the layer so that you can see to click on a white pixel. Select➡Similar. Press the Delete key. This leaves only the noise that was on the layer.

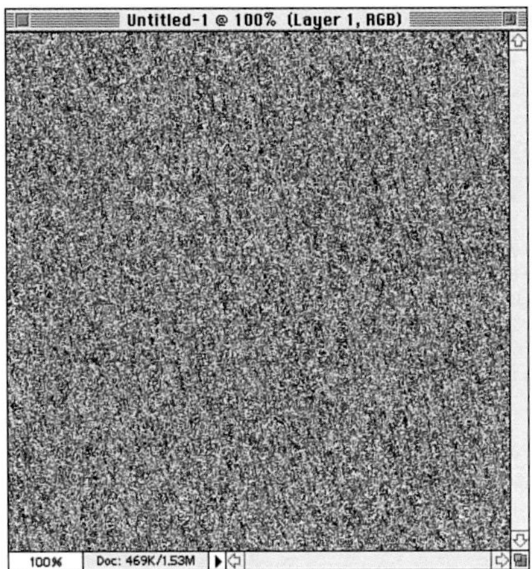


**9** Turn on Preserve Transparency. Switch the foreground color to a brown dirt color. I used RGB: 154, 105, 22. Press Shift-Delete to show the Fill dialog box. Fill the layer with foreground color at 100% Opacity in Color mode. Color mode keeps the variation in the value of the noise that is in the layer.

**10** Turn off Preserve Transparency. Choose Filter➡Blur➡Motion Blur. Use the same settings as before, or vary the angle a little bit.

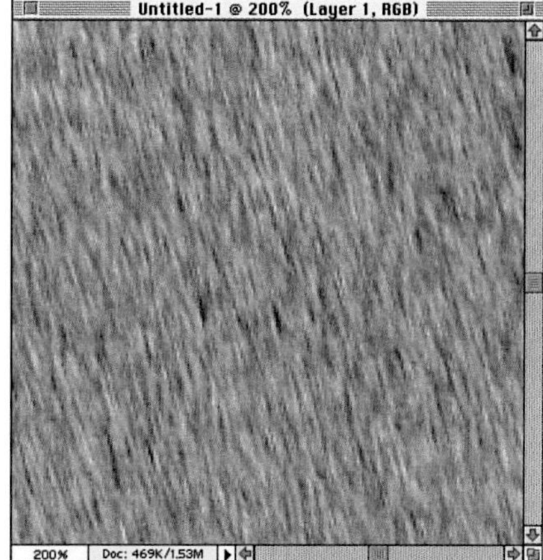


**11** Select Image➡Adjust➡Auto Levels.

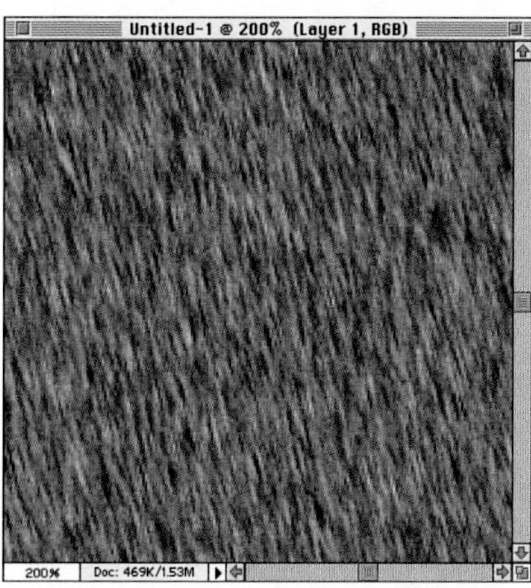


**12** You can remove some of the levels adjustment that you just added if the image is too dark. Choose Filter➡Fade➡Auto Levels. I set the Opacity at 70%.

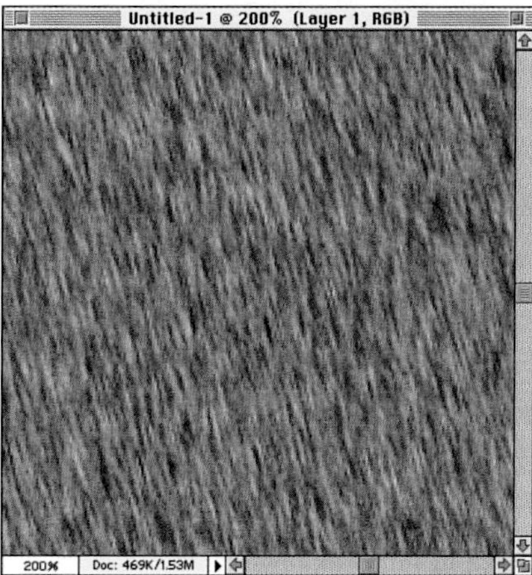

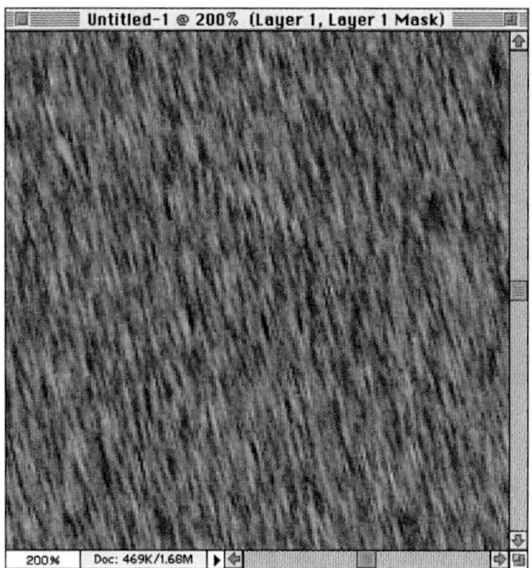


**13** Create a layer mask. Select Image➡Apply Image (Source: Layer 1, Mode: Normal, Opacity: 100%). The layer mask uses the values in the layer to filter out some of the darker brown grass.

**14** For further control over the color, you can select Image➡Adjust➡Auto Levels. By changing the values in the layer mask, you make less of the layer visible. I used the Fade command (Filter➡Fade➡Auto Levels) to set the Opacity of the Auto Levels adjustment to 34%, thereby undoing a large part of it.

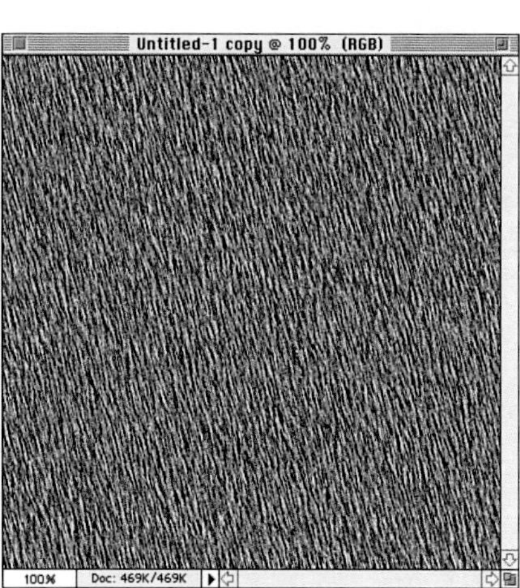


**15** Select Image➡Duplicate (Merged Layers only), or you could flatten the image. I prefer to duplicate the image—it allows me to keep the texture editable. The grass is okay the way it is, but it could be better. Choose Filter➡Sharpen➡Unsharp Mask (Amount: 450, Radius: 1.5, Threshold: 0). The image becomes almost painfully sharp.

**16** Select Filter➥Fade➥Unsharp Mask. I set the Opacity to 55%.

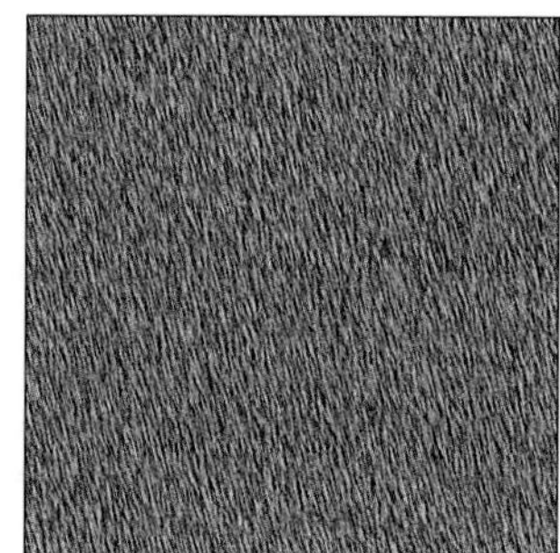

## Variations

If you want to vary the colors in the grass, you can change the blending mode for Layer 1 to something other than Normal. The example shown here uses Hard Light mode, but Overlay, Multiply, Soft Light, Darken, and Luminosity modes also work well. The changes may be subtle.

To add a more drastic change to the color of the grass, change the Mode in Step 16 when you fade the Unsharp Mask filter. Almost every mode except Difference and Exclusion gives you a good result. Shown here is the grass with Darken mode selected in the Fade Unsharp Mask dialog box, and an Opacity of 100%.

To get this image, select Filter➥Fade➥Unsharp Mask and set the Opacity to 20%, and the Mode to Multiply.

To create a more stylized, decorative grass, in Step 15 select Filter➥Artistic➥Poster Edges. I used an Edge Thickness of 0, an Edge Intensity of 1, and a Posterization of 0.

Try making the grass texture seamless. After you have your finished texture, select Image➥Duplicate (Merged Layers only). Duplicate the Background layer. Select Filter➥Other➥Offset (Wrap Around). Make the Horizontal and Vertical distances one-half of the image dimensions. Create a layer mask. Use a soft 100-pixel paintbrush and black. Paint out the center area of the image in the layer mask leaving only the area around the rim. Try not to fog the tile. Select➥All. Define the pattern. Create a new file to the desired size. Fill with pattern.

Now, try making a grass that has a pebbly quality to it. After you have your finished texture, select Image➡Duplicate (Merged Layers only). Duplicate the Background layer. Turn off the Eye icon for the top layer and make the Background layer active. Select Filter➡Brush Strokes➡Ink Outlines (Stroke Length: 0, Dark Intensity: 20, Light Intensity: 10). Make the background layer copy active. Change the blending mode to Color Dodge and reduce the Opacity to around 46%. ■

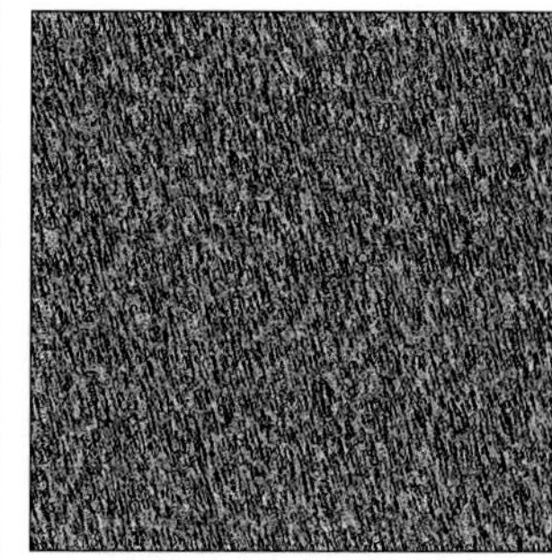

You can make very convincing leather or cowhide easily using the Clouds, Noise, and Emboss filters.

**1** Create a new file 640×480 pixels, RGB. Change the foreground color to the color that you want to use for the duller leather accent color. I used RGB 185, 170, 150 (a dull beige). Change the background color to white.

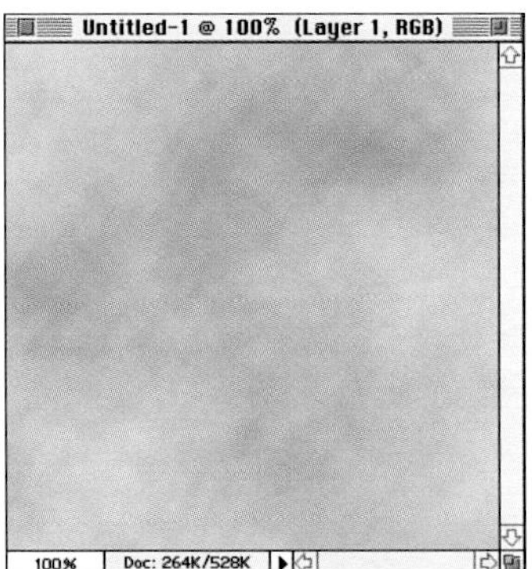


**2** Create a new layer. Select Filter➥Render➥Clouds. Clouds is the only native Photoshop filter that works on a totally transparent layer. Reduce the layer opacity to 50%.

**3** Change the foreground color to the color that you want to use for the brighter leather accent color. I used RGB 236, 144, 31 (a medium-strong orange). Change the background color to white.

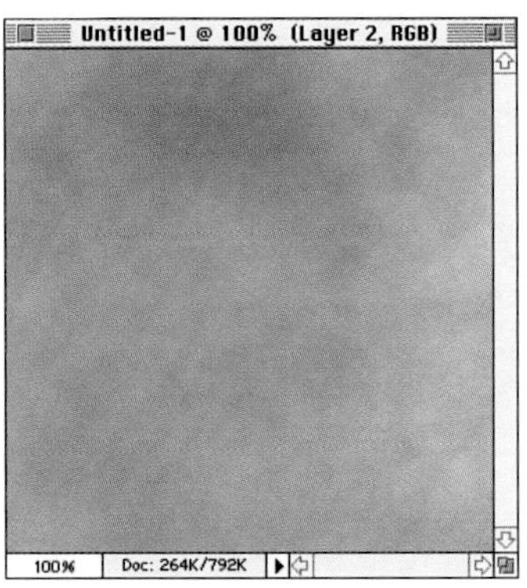


**4** Create a new layer. Apply Filter➥Render➥Clouds. Change the blending mode to Multiply and reduce the layer opacity to 68%.

**5** Make the Background layer active. Create a new layer. Double-click on the Layer name and change its name to "Texture layer." Fill with background color (white).

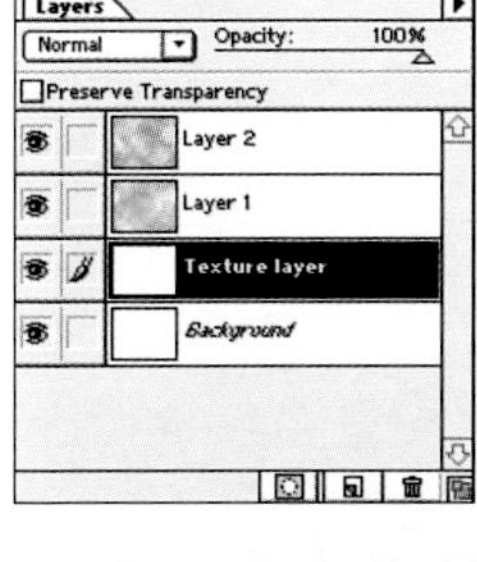


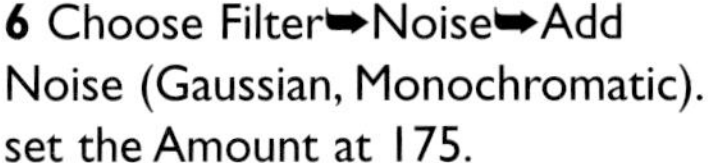

**6** Choose Filter➡Noise➡Add Noise (Gaussian, Monochromatic). I set the Amount at 175.

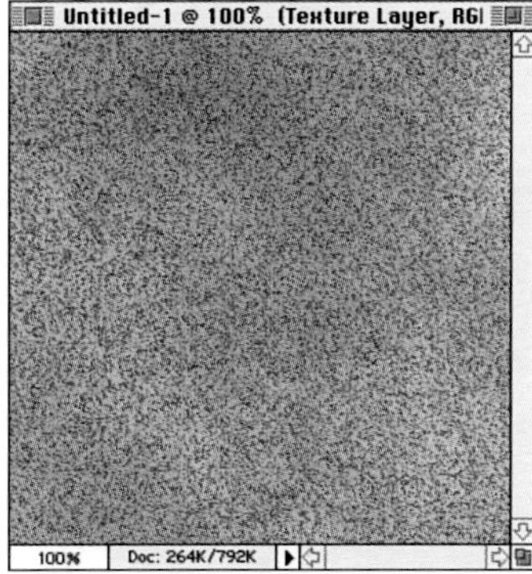


**7** Select Filter➡Stylize➡Emboss. Typically, Angles of 37° or 137° look best. I used a 37° Angle, a Height of 3, and an Amount of 100%.

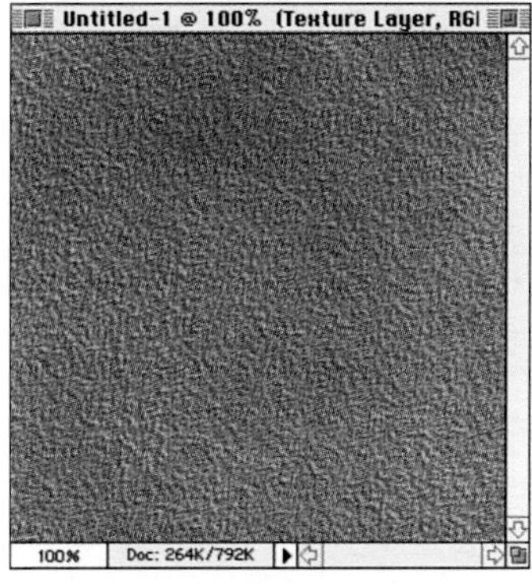


**8** Select Filter➡Blur➡Gaussian Blur. The Amount of blur determines the smoothness of the leather. I used a Radius of 0.9.

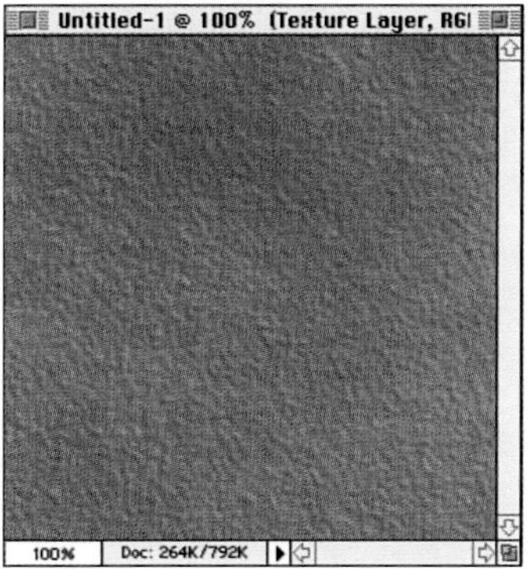

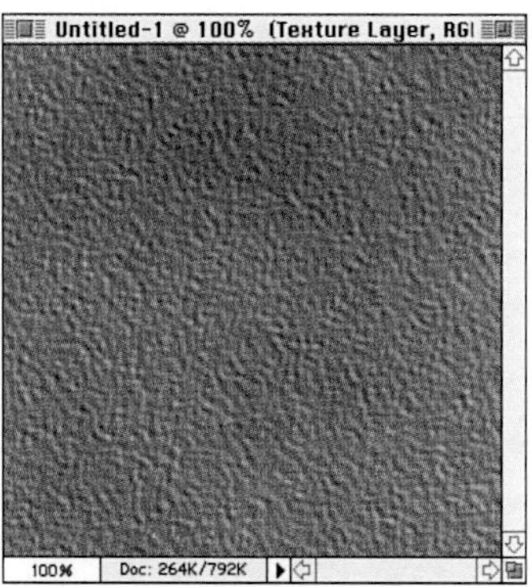


**9** One could stop here, but I prefer a bit more pronounced texture. Choose Filter➥Stylize➥Emboss. Leave the Angle alone but vary the Amount or the Height. I used a Height of 4.

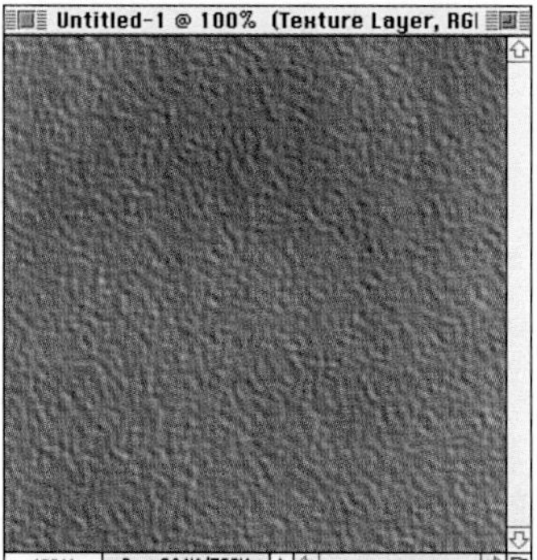


**10** Choose Filter➥Blur➥Gaussian Blur. This time, I used a Radius of 0.5. You may continue the Emboss and Blur cycle until you are satisfied with the resulting leather.

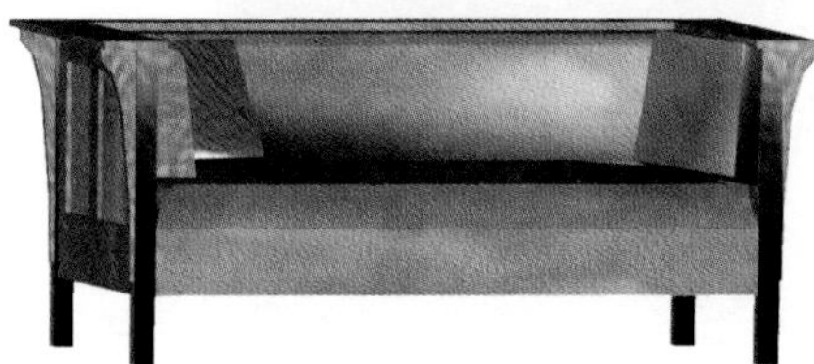

## Variations

You can vary the texture created by changing the type of noise used. Variations of the Grain filter (Filter ➥Texture➥Grain) work very well.

**1** Complete the original example through Step 5. Choose Filter➥ Texture➥Grain. I used a Clumped Type with an Intensity of 49 and a Contrast of 26. Many other combinations are possible.

**2** Choose the Threshold command (Image➡Adjust➡Threshold). I picked a Threshold Level about midpoint in the available range (186).

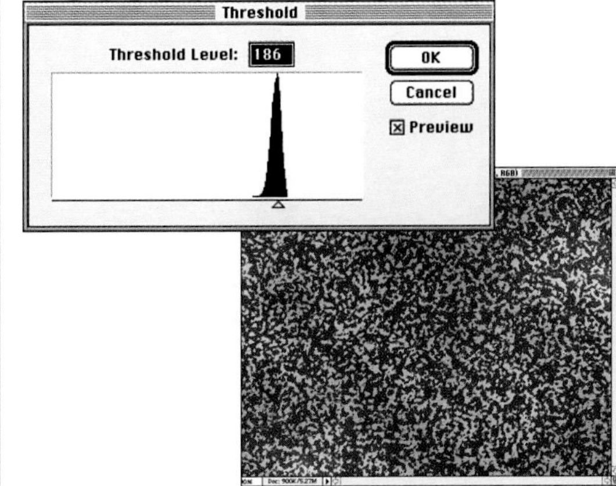


**3** Choose Filter➡Blur➡Gaussian Blur. I used a Radius of 2.1.

**4** Select Filter➡Stylize➡Emboss. I used an Angle of 37°, a Height of 3, and an Amount of 100%.

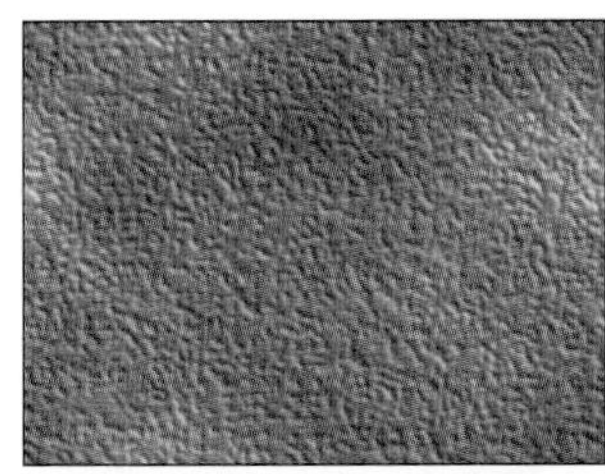

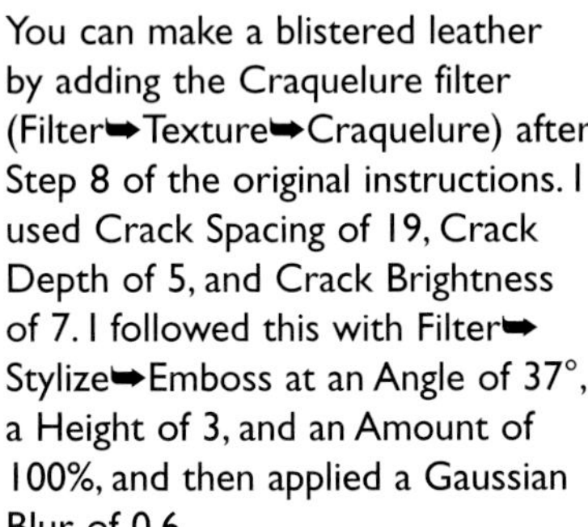

You can make a blistered leather by adding the Craquelure filter (Filter➡Texture➡Craquelure) after Step 8 of the original instructions. I used Crack Spacing of 19, Crack Depth of 5, and Crack Brightness of 7. I followed this with Filter➡Stylize➡Emboss at an Angle of 37°, a Height of 3, and an Amount of 100%, and then applied a Gaussian Blur of 0.6.

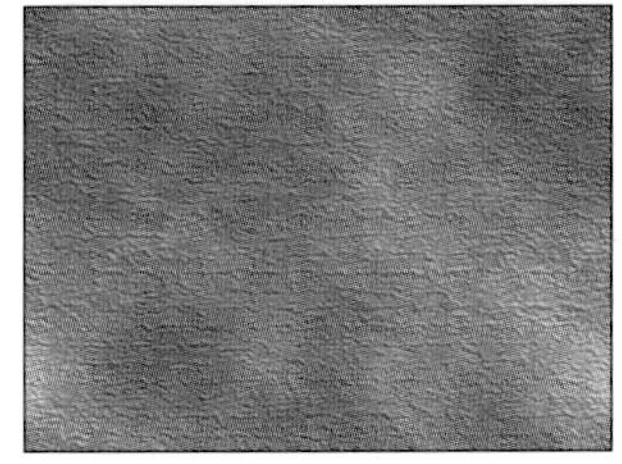

You can make a truly pitted leather by applying the Craquelure filter a second time. I did not blur the filter afterward. ■

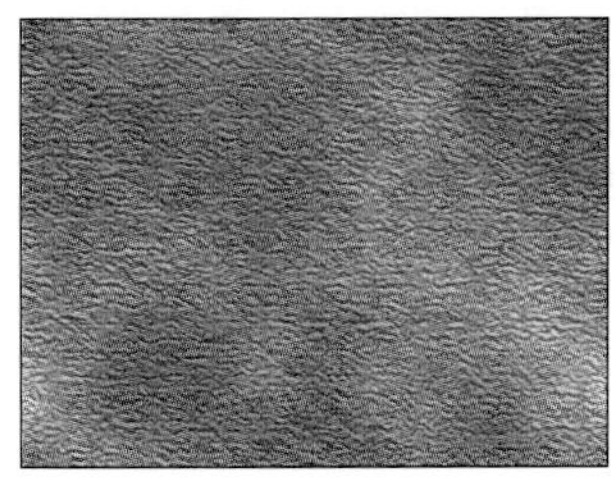

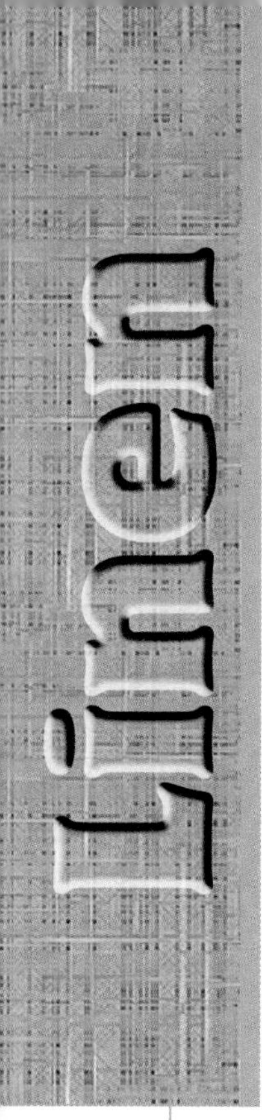

# Linen

You've heard the fairy tale about the girl the who spun straw into gold. This effect turns gold into linen (of course, you first have to create the gold).

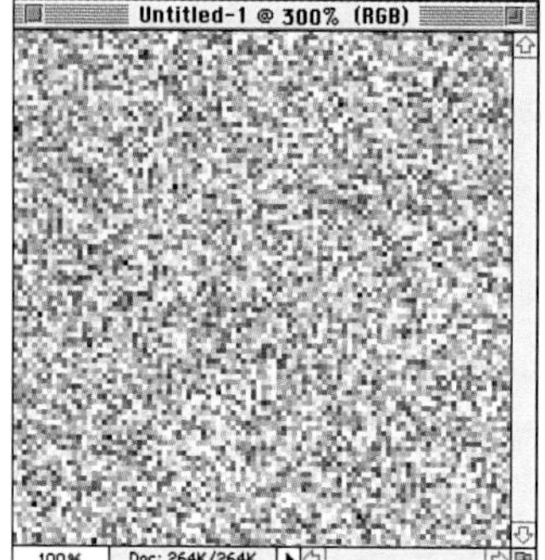


**1** Create a new file. I used a tile size of 300×300 pixels. Choose Filter➥Noise➥Add Noise (Gaussian, do not check Monochromatic). I used an Amount of 135.

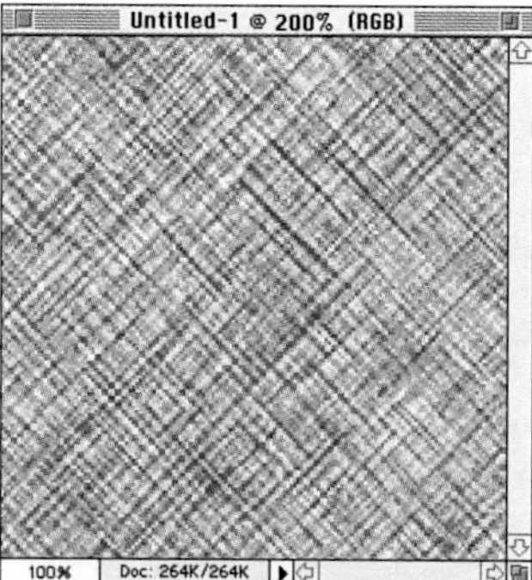


**2** Select Filter➥Brush Strokes➥Crosshatch. I used a Stroke Length of 21, Sharpness of 2, and Strength of 1. Choose Image➥Adjust➥Auto Levels to darken the effect.

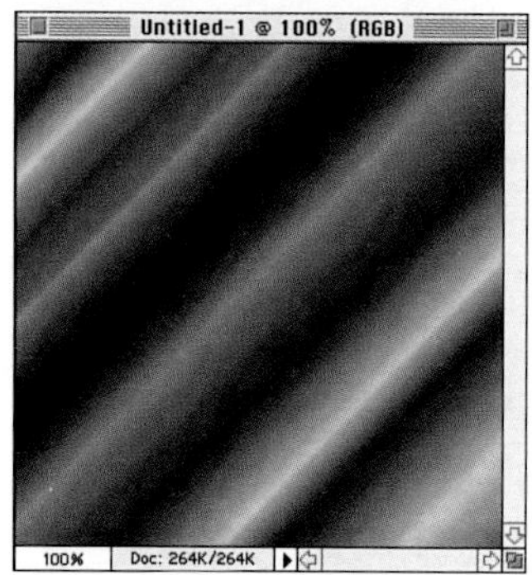


**3** Create a new layer. Double-click the Gradient tool. Choose the Goldgrad gradient from the Gradients presets on the *Photoshop Textures Magic* CD-ROM. Use a Linear gradient. Drag the gradient from the upper-left corner to the lower-right corner of the image.

## TOOLBOX

Goldgrad gradient preset

**4** Choose Filter➥Distort➥Wave. The effect needs a Square Type. I used 23 Generators, Min. Wavelength of 4 and Max. Wavelength of 999, a Min. Amplitude of 23, and a Max. Amplitude of 174. I left the Horizontal and Vertical Scale at 100%, and set the Undefined Areas to Wrap Around.

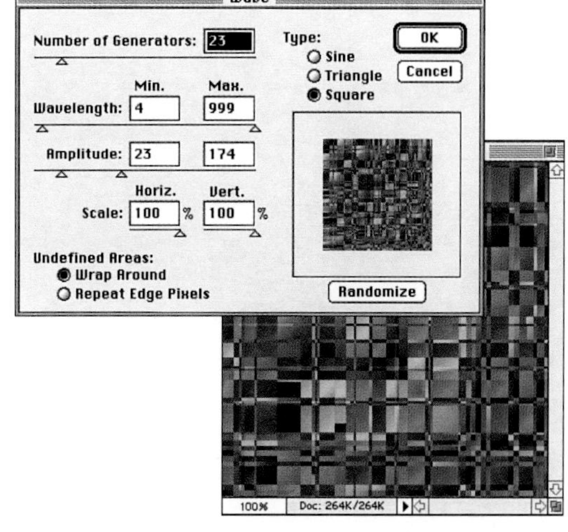


**5** Choose Image➥Adjust➥ Hue/Saturation. Set the Saturation to +100. This causes only a small—but noticeable—difference.

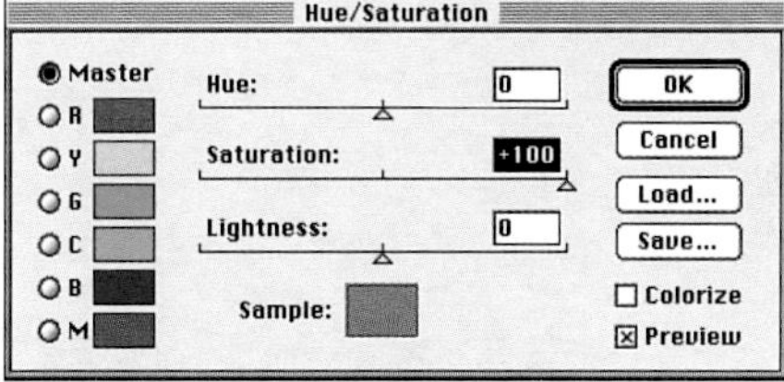


**6** Change the blending mode to Color.

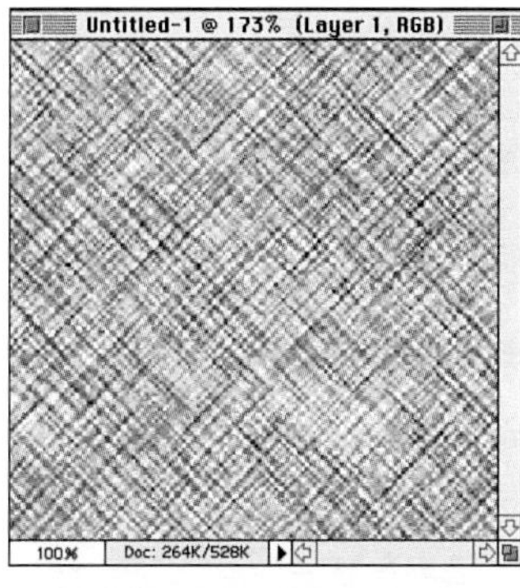


**7** Duplicate Layer 1. Leave the Layer 1 copy at the top of the layer list. Make Layer 1 active. Change the blending mode to Hard Light.

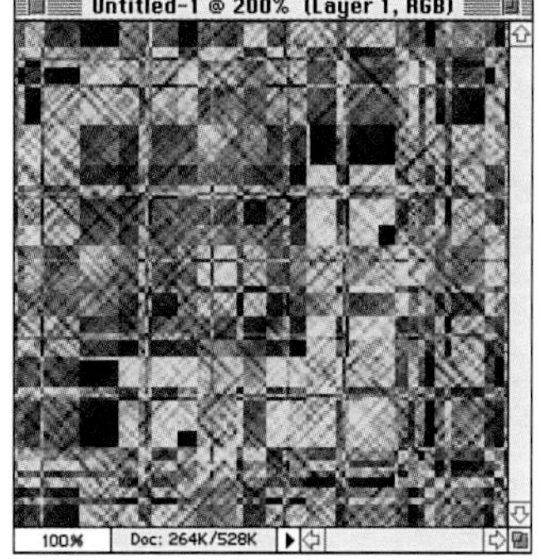

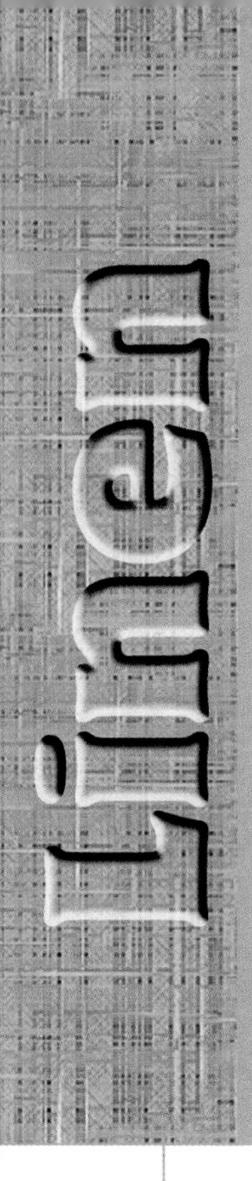


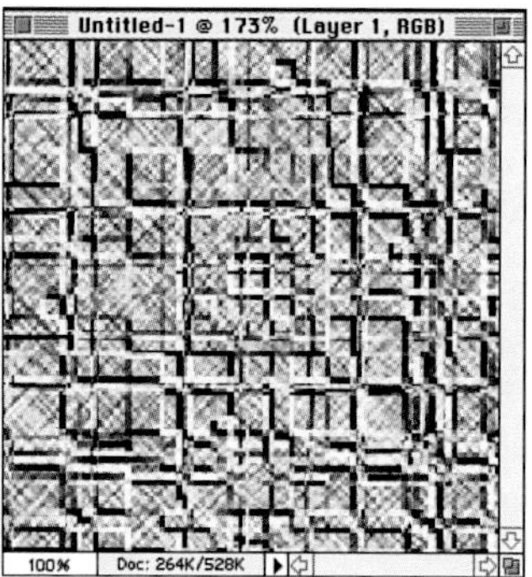


**8** Choose Filter➥Stylize➥Emboss (Angle: 37°, Height: 3). There is room to play with the Amount, however. I used an Amount of 167%. Because the layer is already in Hard Light mode, you can easily judge the effect that the Embossing filter creates.

**9** Choose Image➥Duplicate. Check the Merged Layers Only box. You can certainly use the texture as it is now, if you like it, but it is just getting ready to become linen. Create the linen texture in the new, merged image.

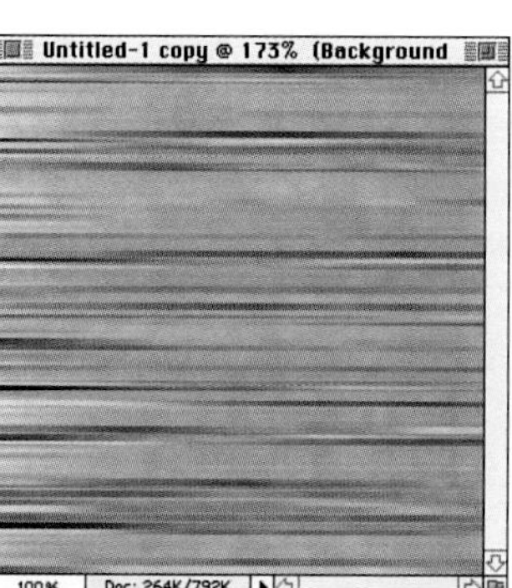


**10** Duplicate the Background layer. Select Filter➥Blur➥Motion Blur (Angle: 0°). Set the Distance until you can barely see the vertical lines in the image. I used a Distance of 110.

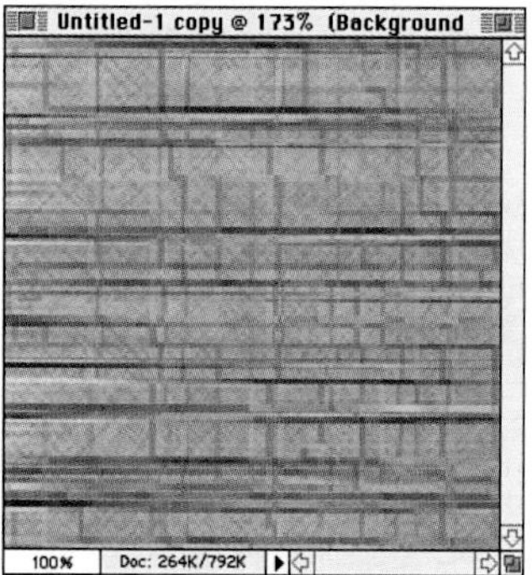


**11** Reduce the layer's opacity so that you can see a bit of the original texture showing through. I set the opacity at 84%.

**12** Duplicate the Background copy layer. Choose Layer➥Transform➥Rotate➥90° CW. Change the blending mode to Lighten. If you want a seamless pattern, make the pattern seamless using the Mosaic method. If you are going to print the texture, you should apply the Unsharp Mask filter (Filter➥Sharpen➥Unsharp Mask). I used a Radius of 1.4, an Amount of 140, and a Threshold of 0. The Threshold of 0 is reasonable because of this specific texture.

## Variations

If you want a darker linen, you can add another step between Steps 7 and 8. Duplicate Layer 1. This creates Layer 1 copy 2, which is already in Hard Light blending mode. Apply the Emboss filter in Step 8 to this layer.

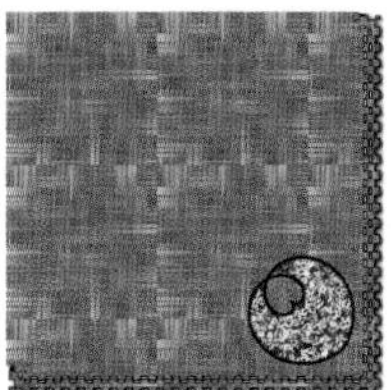

You can completely change the color of the linen if you want. After Step 12, create an adjustment layer. Make it a Hue/Saturation layer. I moved the Hue to –29, the Saturation to –59, and the Lightness to –26.

You can make an evenly woven fabric by using a large Distance on the Motion Blur in Step 10. I used a Distance of 590. I left the opacity at 100% by not completing Step 11. ■

Many cultures throughout time have been fascinated by the design possibilities to be realized by dragging a stick through a bath of wet paint. Marbling has been practiced in Japan, China, Turkey, Persia, and throughout Europe. Today, marbled designs are being used in items as varied as book endpapers and children's sneakers. It is a much sought-after look. You can purchase stock photos of marbled papers for use on the computer, but you can also make some of your own. Here's a way to capture the beauty of marbling without the mess.

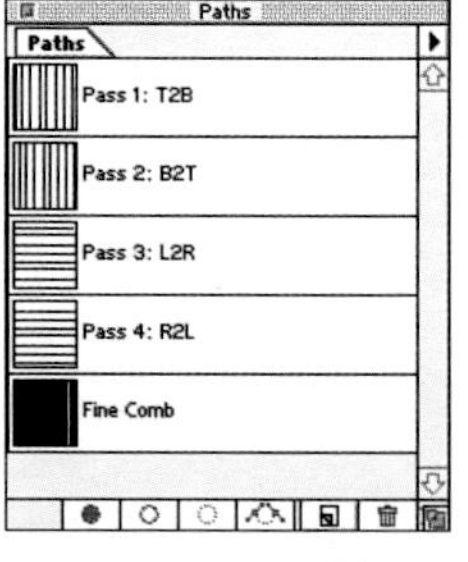


**1** This effect uses the Photoshop Paths tool to create its magic. Open the file Marbled.Psd on the *Photoshop Textures Magic* CD-ROM. This file contains the paths that you need to get started.

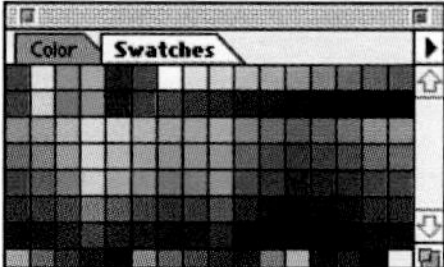


**2** Select your palette. You need three to six harmonious colors. I used the Grape.Aco Swatches document in the Swatches folder on the *Photoshop Textures Magic* CD-ROM. To place the color table into the Swatches palette, select Load Swatches from the Colors palette menu. The last five colors on the Swatches palette are the new ones.

**3** Switch the foreground color to one of the new colors. I used the lightest green. Select Image➥Duplicate to make a copy of the Marbled.Psd file. Fill the selection with foreground color.



## TOOLBOX

Marbled.Psd

Grape.Aco color palette document

**4** Select the Paintbrush tool and the 100-pixel soft brush. Switch the foreground color to one of the other palette colors. Stamp circles of the color onto your image. Use all of the colors in your chosen palette in random or designed placement in the image. This acts as the base for the marbling process. I made a fairly regular distribution of the colors.

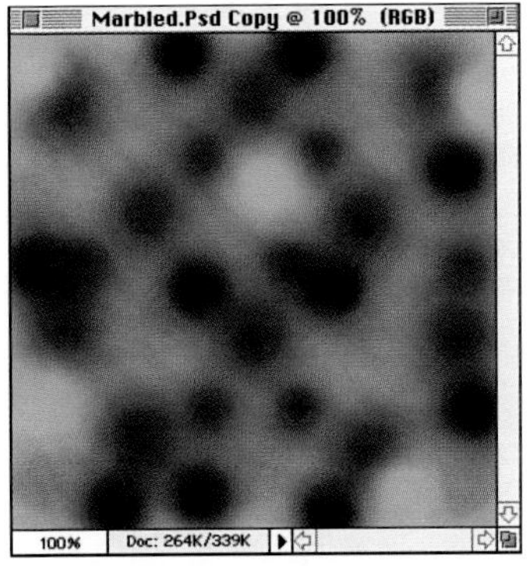


**5** Double-click the Smudge tool. Set the Mode to Normal and the Pressure to 80%. Make sure that the Finger Painting box is *not* checked. Select the 21-pixel soft-edged brush (second from the right on row 2 of the default Brushes palette). Show the Paths palette. Click the path labeled Pass 1:T2B to make it active.

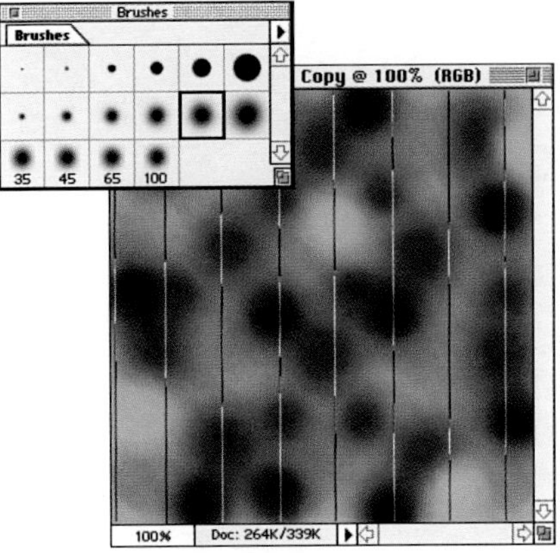


**6** Click the second icon at the bottom of the Paths palette to stroke the path. Even though it says "Strokes path with foreground color," because you have the Smudge tool selected, the Paths will be smudged, not stroked. The Pressure of 80% causes the Smudge tool to pull the colors in the image along the path.

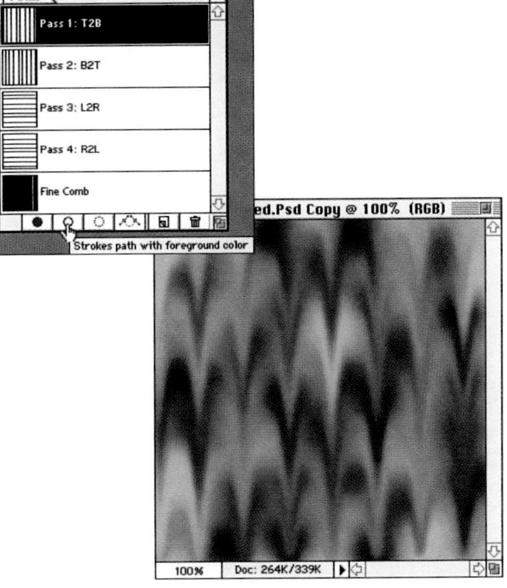

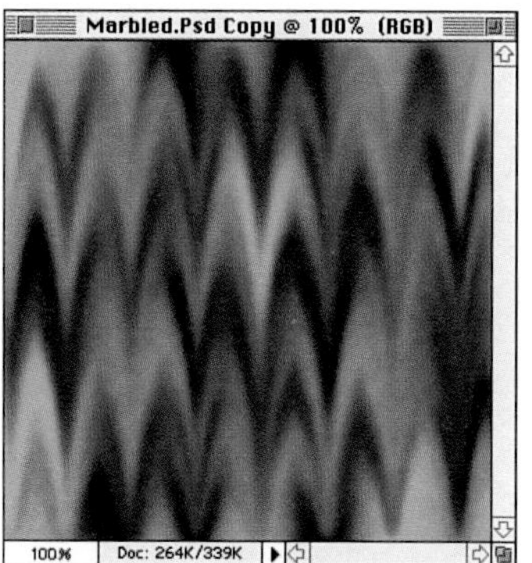


**7** Change the Pressure setting on the Smudge Tools Options palette to 60%. Click the Pass 2: B2T path. Stroke the path as you did in Step 6.

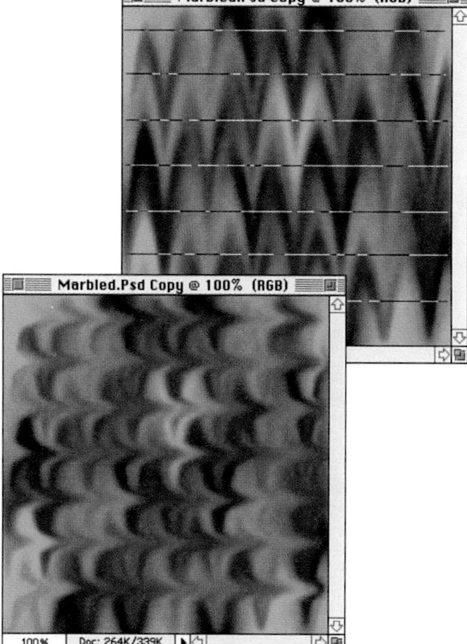


**8** Click the Pass 3: L2R path. This path moves across the combed image from left to right. Stroke the path.

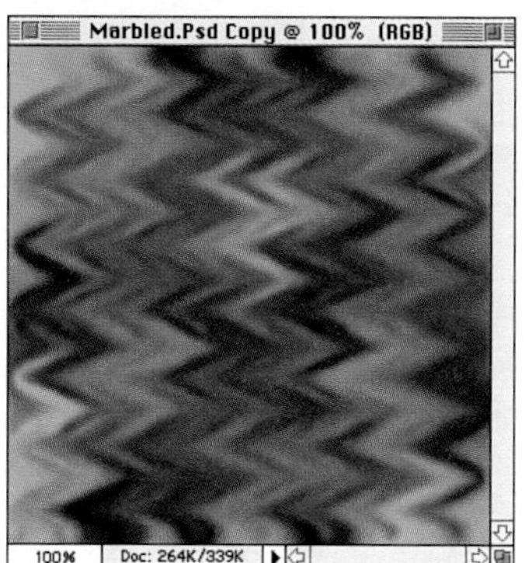


**9** Click the Pass 4: R2L path. Stroke the path. This finishes the "traditional" combing process of the marble bath. Of course, you do not need to mix your colors this well if you prefer.

**10** The last combing step gives the image its finished design. I chose to create a one-step "fine tooth comb" for this final path. Set the Pressure back to 80% in the Smudge Tools Options palette. Select a tiny brush (the 9-pixel brush that is second from the left on the second row of the default Brushes palette works well). Stroke the fine-tooth comb path.

## VARIATIONS

### Seamless Marble

If you want, you can easily make the marbled image seamless. This is a variation on the Center Cross method of creating a seamless pattern that is described in the "Photoshop Basics" section.

**1** Use the finished marble tile. Duplicate the Background layer. Select Filter➥Other➥Offset (Wrap Around). Set the Horizontal and Vertical distances to one-half of the image dimensions. Create a layer mask. Use black, the Paintbrush tool, and the 100-pixel soft brush. Brush out the center seam line by painting over the area on the layer mask.

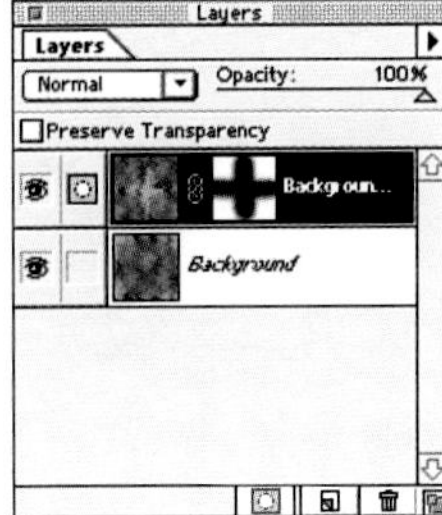


**2** Create a new layer. (Option)[Alt] Merge Visible to a new layer. Select Filter➥Other➥Offset (Wrap Around). Create a layer mask. Use black, the Paintbrush tool, and the 100-pixel soft brush. Brush out the seam line near the edges by painting over the area on the layer mask.

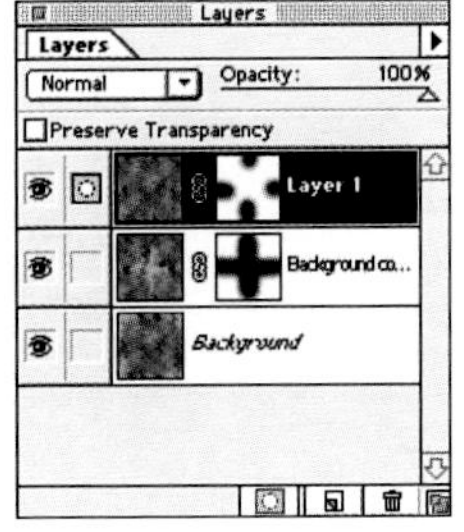

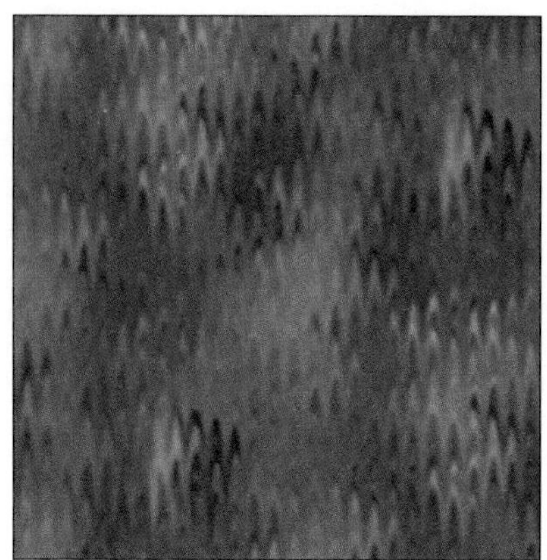

**3** Create a new layer. (Option)[Alt] Merge Visible to a new layer. Select Filter➥Other➥Offset (Wrap Around). Check to make sure that your image is seamless. It should be. Touch-up using the layer mask if it is not.

## Fancy Finish

You can use or create additional paths and finishing shapes. There are several more finishes in the Paths.Psd image on the *Photoshop Textures Magic* CD-ROM. The easiest way to create additional paths is to Select➥All. Choose Paths Palette menu➥Make Work Path. Copy this path and paste it into Adobe Illustrator. Fill the path in Illustrator and lock it. Draw the paths for the finished shape that you want. Duplicate it as many times as you need. Select all of the unlocked paths and copy them back into Photoshop. Paste as paths.

Complete Steps 1 through 7 of the original effect, using the colors of your choice. Open the Paths.Psd image. Drag the Wings2 path into your marbled image (make sure that no other path is selected at the same time). Click Wings2 to make it active. Stroke with the Smudge tool at 80% pressure and the 21-pixel soft brush. Make it seamless if you want. ■

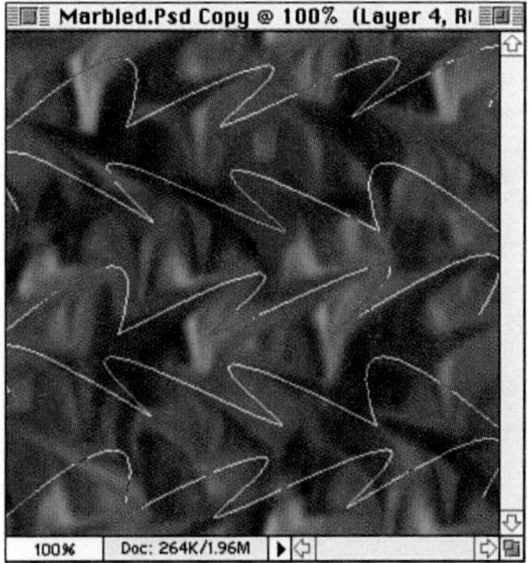


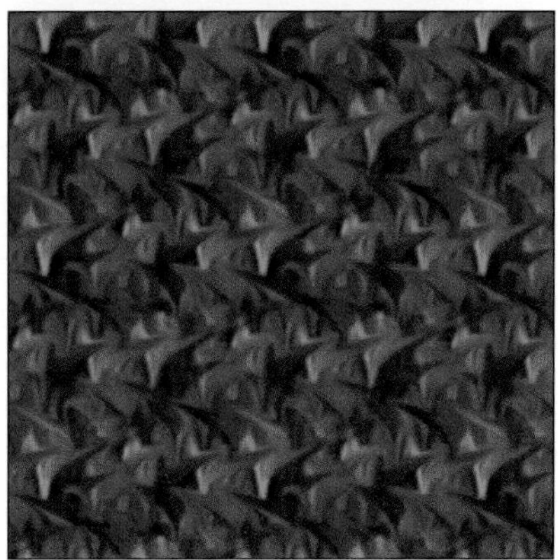

Brushed metal is an easy texture to create. If you manufacture enough, you can easily cover three-dimensional objects and various aliens with it.

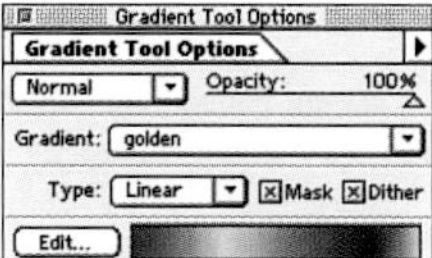


**1** Create a new file. I used one 400×400 pixels. Double-click the Gradient tool. Select the Golden preset that came from the *Photoshop Textures Magic* CD-ROM.

**2** Drag the Gradient cursor from the top-left corner of the image to the bottom-right corner.

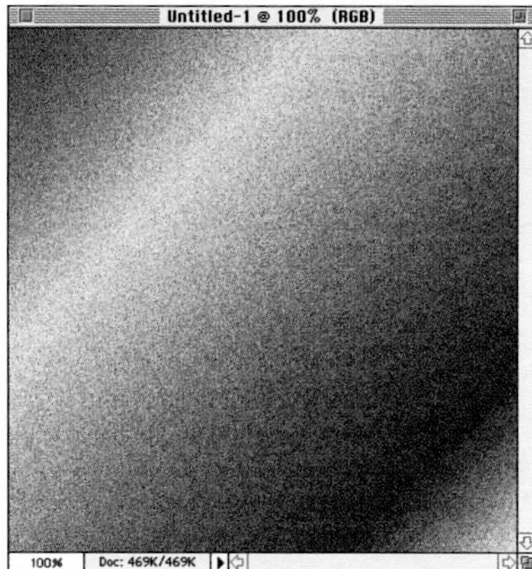


**3** Apply Filter➥Noise➥Add Noise (Amount: 23, Gaussian, Monochromatic). You can fiddle with the Amount, but it needs to be low enough not to overwhelm the image.

**TOOLBOX**

Golden gradient preset

Silver gradient preset

4 Choose Filter➥Blur➥Motion Blur. I used an Angle of –47°, and a Distance of 37. These settings can be changed as you prefer.

5 Duplicate the Background layer. Change the blending mode to Lighten.

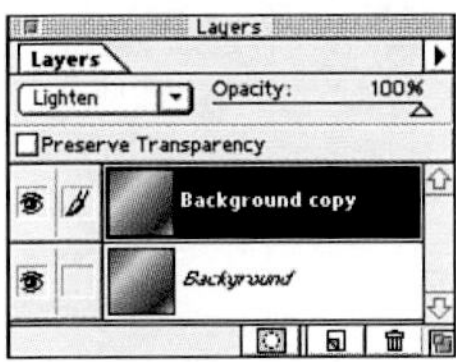


6 Apply Filter➥Blur➥Gaussian Blur. I used a Radius of 5. You will want to lighten the effect of the blurred noise on the metal, but it should still be visible.

7 Create a new layer (Layer 1) by pressing the (Option)[Alt] key before you click the New Layer icon. In the dialog box, change the blending mode to Multiply and check Fill with Multiply—neutral color (white).

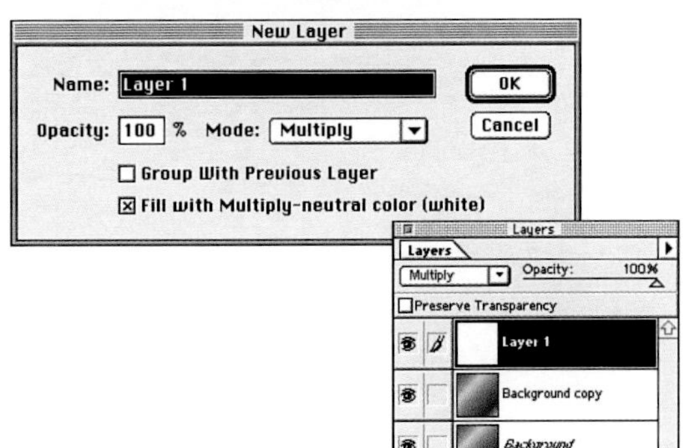

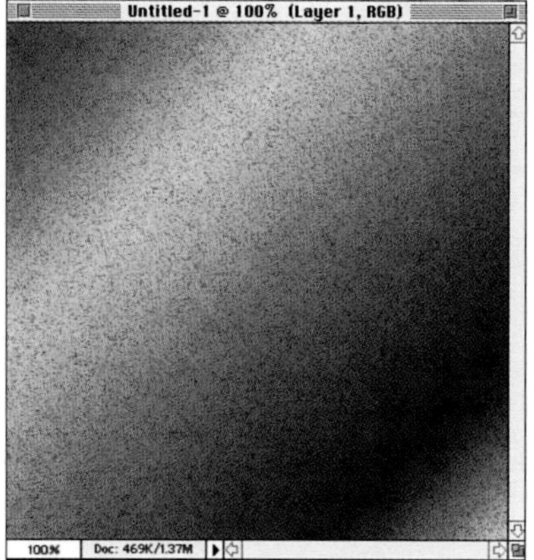


**8** Apply Filter➡Noise➡Add Noise. Use a slightly higher Amount than before. This noise is on its own layer so that it can be manipulated separately, and so the opacity of the layer can be fine-tuned. I used an Amount of 45.

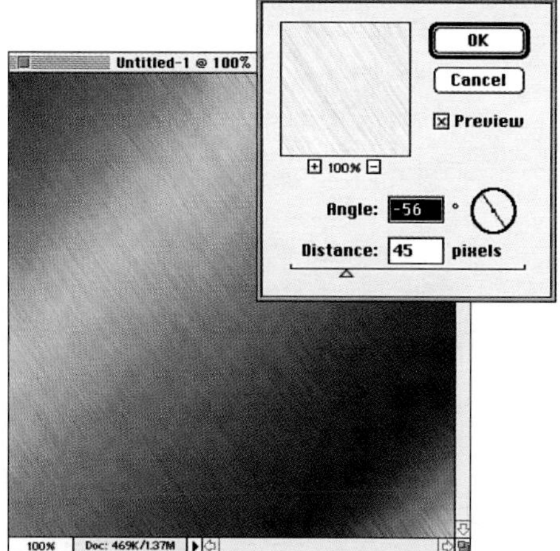


**9** Choose Filter➡Blur➡Motion Blur. Use an Angle and a Distance that vary slightly from your first application of the filter. I used an Angle of –56° and a Distance of 45. Adjust the opacity of the layer if you want.

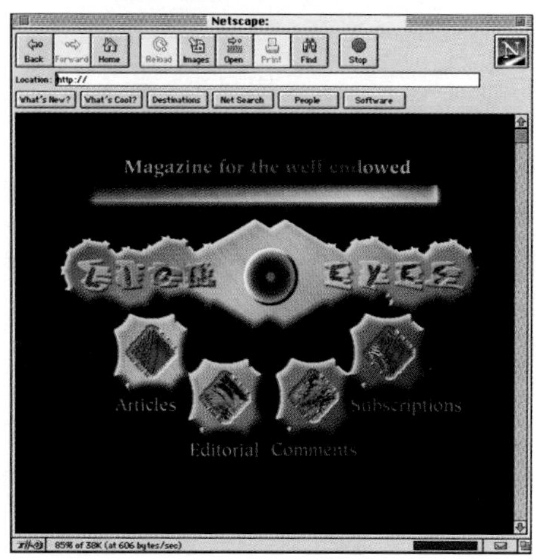

## VARIATIONS

The same technique works on other precious metals as well. You can try the Copper Gradient preset...

...or the Silver Gradient preset from the *Photoshop Textures Magic* CD-ROM.

You could also use the Chrome preset, but it requires special handling. The Motion Blur in Step 4 needs to have a greater Distance to obliterate the color change line on the Chrome Gradient. I used an Angle of –62°, and a Distance of 640. In Step 8, I used a Noise amount of 110, and in Step 9, I used a Motion Blur angle of –47° (a decidedly different angle from the first blur) and a Distance of 640. These changes almost make the chrome surface look pitted. ■

If you have art in your soul, you have sometimes marveled at the colors in a piece of mother-of-pearl. Now you can create an electronic version. You could start with one of the "Opals" textures (page 146), or with a totally blank canvas. I'm going to show you how to begin from scratch.

**1** Create a new file. Mine is 400 × 400 pixels. Switch the foreground color to medium gray. I used RGB: 89, 89, 89. Fill with foreground color. Select Filter➥Noise➥Add Noise (Distribution: Gaussian, Monochromatic: Off). I used an Amount of 100.

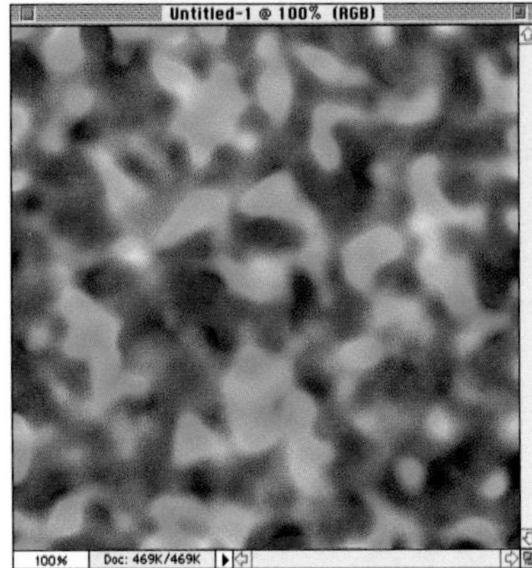


**2** Choose Filter➥Blur➥Gaussian Blur (6.0). Select Image➥Adjust➥Auto Levels. The color blobs should be bigger. Repeat the Gaussian Blur and Auto Levels to make the blobs the right size



**TOOLBOX**

Mother-Of-Pearl lighting effects preset

**3** Duplicate the Background layer. Switch the foreground color to a darker gray. I used RGB: 69, 69, 69. Load the values of the layer (Command-Option-~)[Alt-Control-~]. Fill the selection with foreground color. Deselect. Change the blending mode to Multiply. When you load the values of the layer, you convert the values in the composite channel into a selection. The lighter values in the original accept more of the foreground color fill than do the darker values.

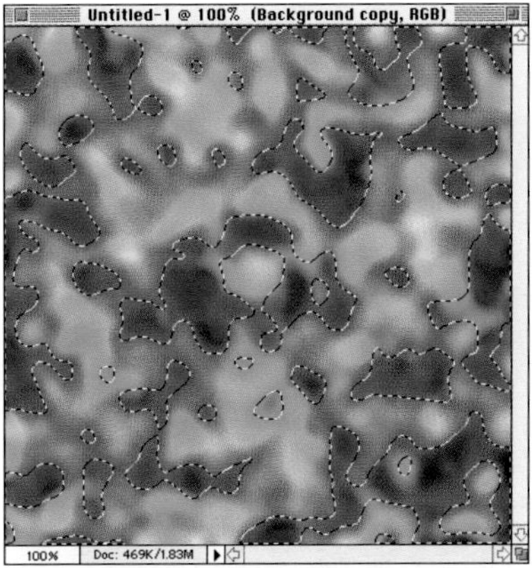


**4** Create a new layer. (Layer 1) (Option)[Alt] Merge Visible to a new layer. Apply Filter➥Blur➥ Gaussian Blur (7.0). Change the blending mode to Darken.

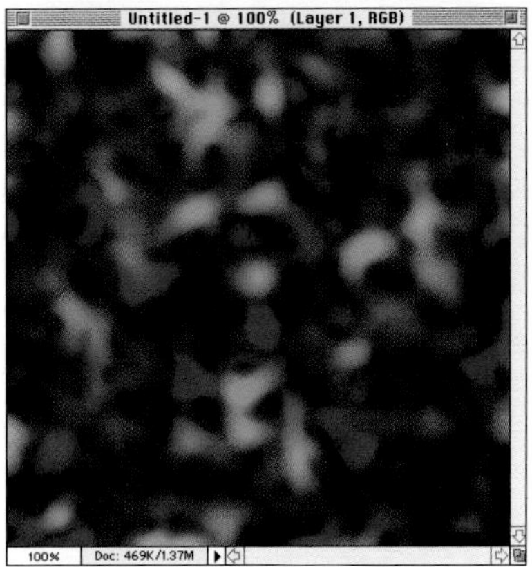

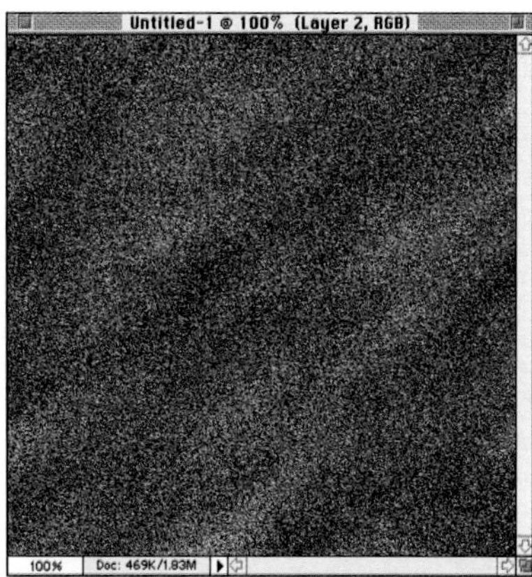

**5** Create a new layer (Layer 2). (Option)[Alt] Merge Visible to a new layer. Select Filter➡Blur➡Motion Blur. I used an Angle of 38°, and a Distance of 100 pixels. In this example, texture needs more lines. Select Filter➡Noise➡Add Noise (Distribution: Gaussian, Monochromatic: Off). I used an Amount of 100.

**6** Choose Filter➡Blur➡Motion Blur. Reuse the last settings. The noise that you just added now helps to create the fine lines.

**7** Create a Levels adjustment layer. Change the blending mode to Screen. Do not change the Levels histogram at all.

**8** Duplicate the adjustment layer several times until the texture loses color (Screen mode makes the image lighter; with enough adjustment layers, you will end up with solid white). I created a total of three adjustment layers. I also set the layer opacity on the final adjustment layer to 80%.

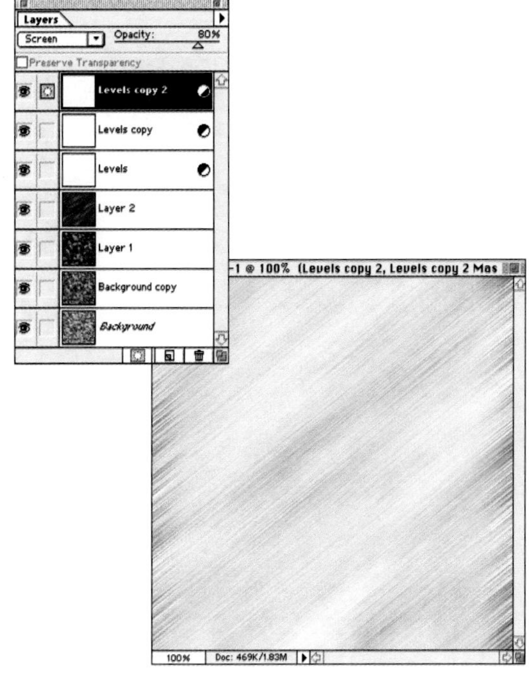


**9** Make Layer 2 active. Apply Filter➡Blur➡Gaussian Blur. Apply just enough of a blur to smooth the rough lines from the image. I used a Radius of 2.8.

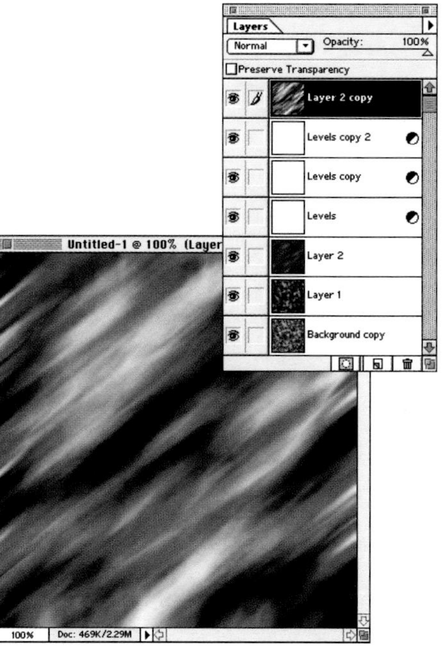


**10** Mother-of-pearl is usually smooth, but not necessarily flat. You need to add texture and depth to your flat image. Duplicate Layer 2. Position the new layer at the top of the Layers palette list. Select Image➥Adjust➥Equalize and then Image➥Adjust➥Desaturate.

**11** Select Filter➥Stylize➥Emboss (Angle: 29°, Height: 3, Amount: 100). This adds some streaky details. Change the blending mode of Layer 2 copy to Hard Light.

**12** This step is optional. If you want to smooth out the texture a bit more, select Filter➡Blur➡Gaussian Blur. Apply just enough of a blur to smooth the rough lines from the image. I used a Radius of 2.8 again.

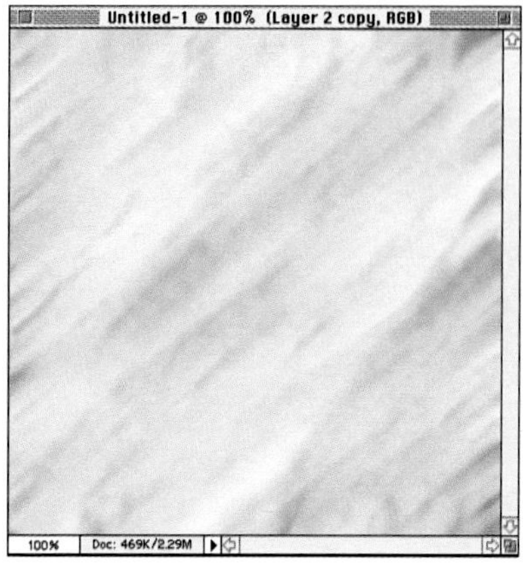


**13** Create a new layer. (Option) [Alt] Merge Visible to a new layer. Choose Filter➡Render➡Lighting Effects. Use the settings shown, or select the mother-of-pearl preset from the *Photoshop Textures Magic* CD-ROM. You may want to search for the best channel to use for the texture channel. You want the lighting to be just a bit too bright, but if it's much too bright, turn down the Ambiance setting just a notch.

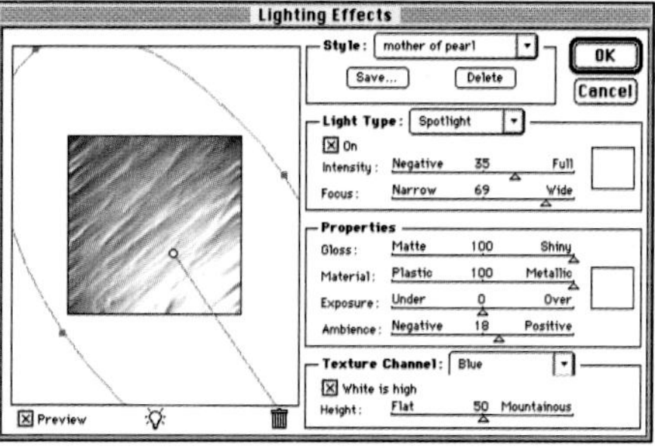


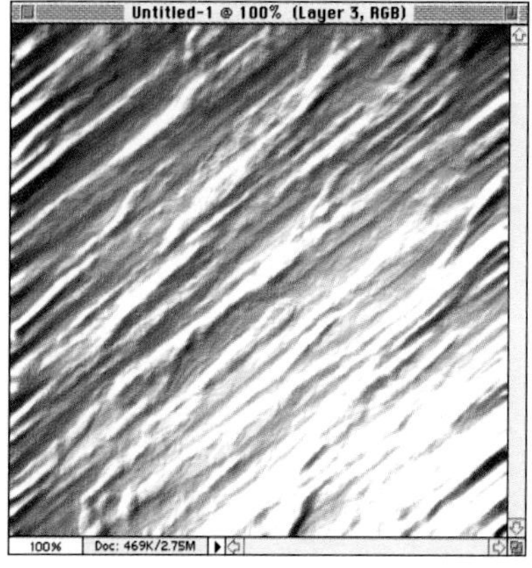

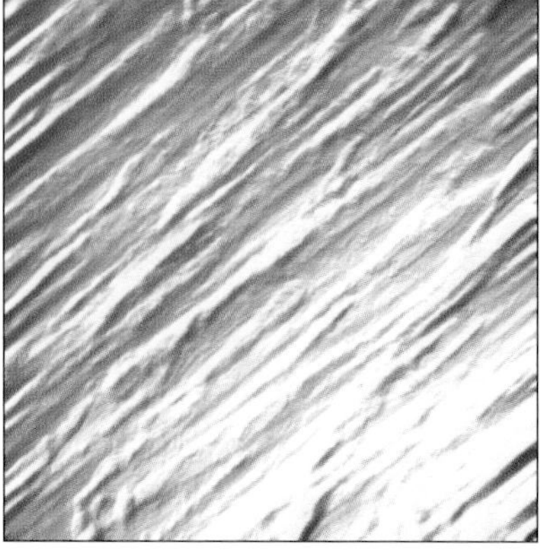

**14** Select Filter➡Fade Lighting Effects. I set the opacity to 75%. Flatten the image.

## VARIATIONS

If you want a rougher texture, omit Step 9. Create a new channel (Channel 4). You can emphasize the fine lines by using the Apply Image command to copy Layer 2 to Channel 4. Make Channel 4 active. Select Image➡Adjust➡Auto Levels. Use Channel 4 in the Lighting Effects filter as the Texture channel instead of the Red channel.

If you want to start from the opal texture, apply Filter➡Blur➡Smart Blur (Threshold: 26, Radius: 21, Quality: High, Method: Normal). If you are using a high-contrast image, you can set both the Threshold and the Radius as high as they go. Select Filter➡Blur➡Motion Blur (Angle: 38°, Distance: 36). Create a new layer. Fill with white. Change the blending mode to Overlay. Create a new layer. Position the layer at the top of the layer list. (Option)[Alt] Merge Visible to the new layer. Change the blending mode to Screen. I set the layer opacity to 74%. ■

For as long as I can remember, I have been fascinated with the fiery color in the depths of the opal. The Opal effect will help you to re-create some of the fire of that most special of stones.

**1** Create a new file. Mine is 400×400 pixels. Change the fore-ground color to neutral gray (RGB: 128, 128, 128). Fill with foreground color. Select Filter➡Noise➡Add Noise (Amount: 45, Gaussian, Monochromatic).

**2** Choose Filter➡Pixellate➡Cyrstallize. I used a cell size of 38. The Gaussian Noise gives the Crystallize filter something to process. The result is a crystal net-work of gray shapes.

**3** Select Image➡Adjust➡Auto Levels. Select Image➡Adjust➡Posterize. Each level that remains in the image becomes a group of opal shapes. I left 5 levels. Decide upon the number of levels by watching the dialog box's preview. The different gray values in the image are reduced into fewer when you Posterize the image. Start by previewing 3 levels and look at the image at 4 to 8 levels as well. Pick the number that makes the most pleasing arrangement of gray values. Anywhere from 3 to 8 levels are manageable.

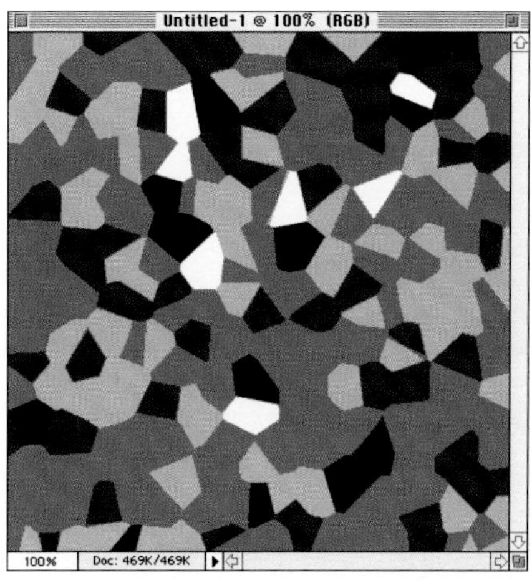


**4** Double-click the Magic Wand tool. Set the Tolerance to 0, Anti-aliased on, and Sample Merged off. Click a white shape. Select➡Similar. Change the foreground color to white (to match the color that you clicked). Create a new layer (Layer 1). Fill the selection with foreground color. Deselect. Turn on Preserve Transparency.

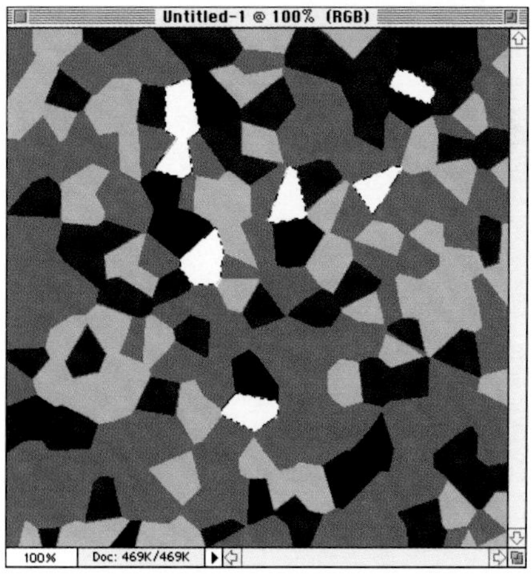


**5** Choose Filter➡Noise➡Add Noise (Amount: 45, Distribution: Gaussian, Monochromatic: Off). If you choose Monochromatic noise, you will get no opal. Select Filter➡Blur➡Gaussian Blur (4.0). Select Image➡Adjust➡Auto Levels. Opals begin to emerge. Steps 4 and 5 are the basic "create opal" steps. They are repeated (with some variations) for every level of gray that you selected when you posterized the image (which is why I suggest that you keep the number of levels fairly low).

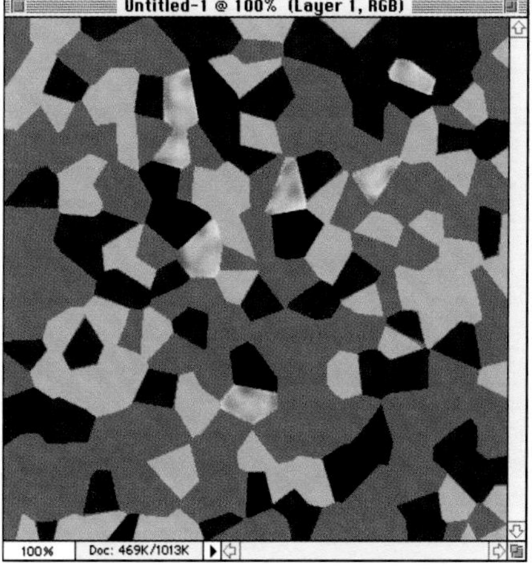

6 Make the Background layer active. Choose the Magic Wand tool and click the lightest gray in the Background. Select➡Similar. Choose the Eyedropper tool, and click inside the selected gray area to pick up a new foreground color. Create a new layer (Layer 2). Fill with foreground color. Deselect. Turn on Preserve Transparency.

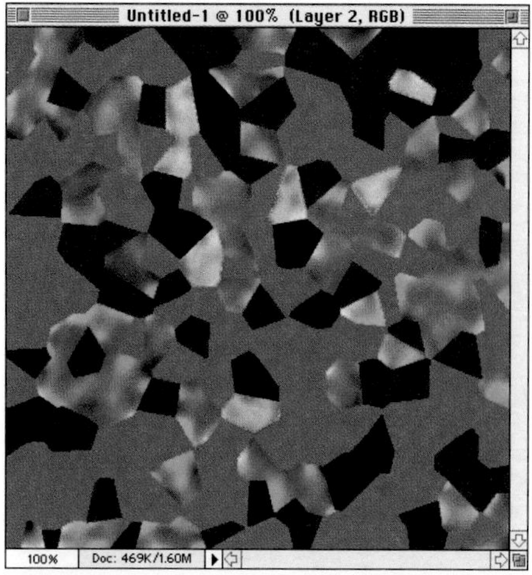


7 Choose Filter➡Noise➡Add Noise (Amount: 45, Distribution: Gaussian, Monochromatic: Off). Select Filter➡Blur➡Gaussian Blur (6.0). Next, select Image➡Adjust➡Auto Levels.

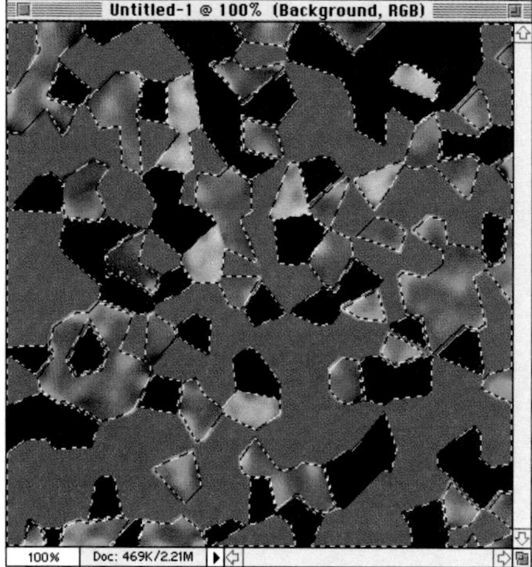


8 Make the Background layer active. Choose the Magic Wand tool and click another gray in the Background. Select➡Similar. Choose the Eyedropper tool, and click inside the selected gray area to pick up a new foreground color. Create a new layer (Layer 3). Fill the selection with foreground color. Deselect. Turn on Preserve Transparency.

**9** Choose Filter➡Noise➡Add Noise (Amount: 90, Distribution: Gaussian, Monochromatic: Off). Select Filter➡Blur➡Gaussian Blur (5.0). Next, select Image➡Adjust➡Auto Levels. The texture is more interesting if the opals are different in each layer. Choose Filter➡Fade➡Auto Levels. Change the Opacity to 42%, and the Mode to Color Burn.

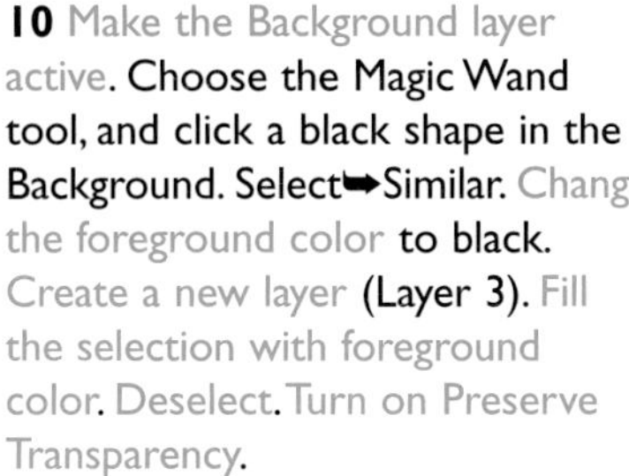

**10** Make the Background layer active. Choose the Magic Wand tool, and click a black shape in the Background. Select➡Similar. Change the foreground color to black. Create a new layer (Layer 3). Fill the selection with foreground color. Deselect. Turn on Preserve Transparency.

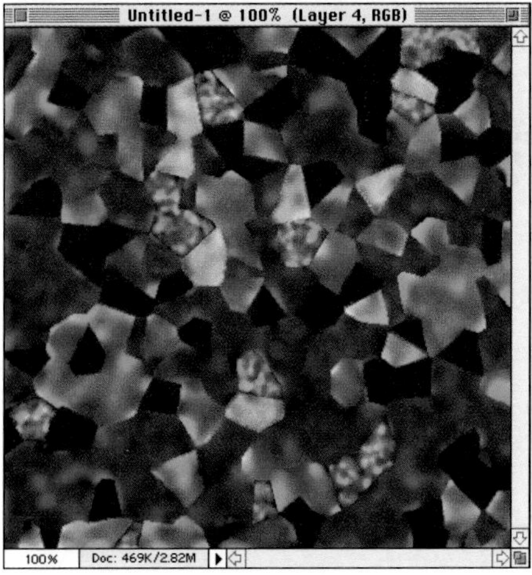


**11** Choose Filter➡Noise➡Add Noise (Amount: 45, Distribution: Gaussian, Monochromatic: Off). Select Filter➡Blur➡Gaussian Blur (2.0).Next, select Image➡Adjust➡Auto Levels.

**12** If there are any more gray levels, repeat Steps 6 and 7 until you have created opal layers for each color level in the Background layer.

**13** You could be finished...but maybe you'd like your opal to have a bit more drama. Make the Background layer the only visible layer by holding down the (Option)[Alt] key while clicking the eye icon in the Layers palette. Type (Command-Option-~)[Control-Alt-~]. This function loads the values in the Background layer as a selection. Change the foreground color to a medium-dark gray. I used RGB: 63, 63, 63. Turn on all of the layers again by holding down the (Option)[Alt] key and clicking the eye icon next to the Background layer in the Layers palette. Create a new layer. Position the layer at the top of the Layers palette list. Fill with foreground color. This places a range of gray shades over the other layers.

**14** Now you can have fun with the layers. You might want to turn down the opacity of the top layer. I set it at 58%. I also changed the blending mode of Layer 5 to Hard Light, and reduce the layer opacity to 43%. This setting made the color stand out more.

## VARIATIONS

If you change the blending mode on the top layer, you can create other interesting variations. Make the top layer active. Change the blending mode to Screen...

...or Overlay mode.

To change the texture from opal to abalone, select Image➥Duplicate (Merged Layers only). Change the foreground color to a shade of deep green. I used RGB: 73, 164, 65. Create a new layer. Fill with foreground color. Change the blending mode to Color Burn, and reduce the layer opacity to about 42%. Make the Background layer active. Apply Filter➥Pixellate➥Fragment several times. In my example, I used it three times. Finally, select Image➥Sharpen➥Unsharp Mask (Amount: 103%, Radius: 4.2, Threshold: 0). ■

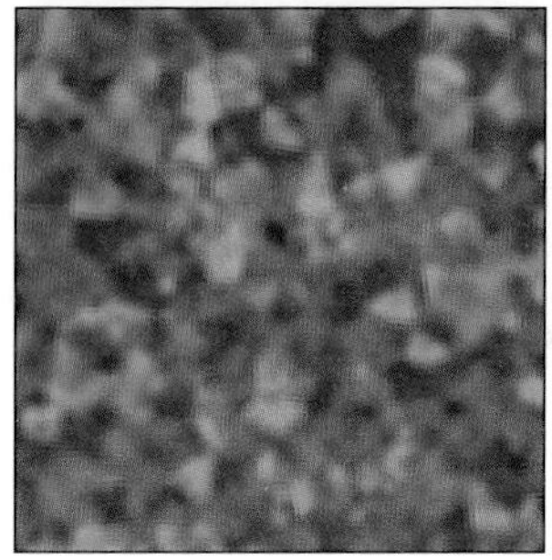

# Parched

Want to create miles of cracked, mistreated earth? Here's how. Create it to size, though, as this texture is not happy as a repeat.

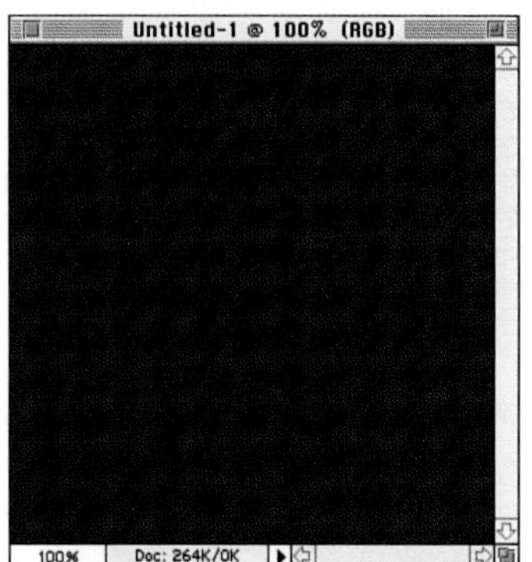


**1** Create a new file. Switch the foreground color to a deep brown or whatever earth color you prefer. I used RGB: 79, 58, 38. Fill the selection with foreground color.

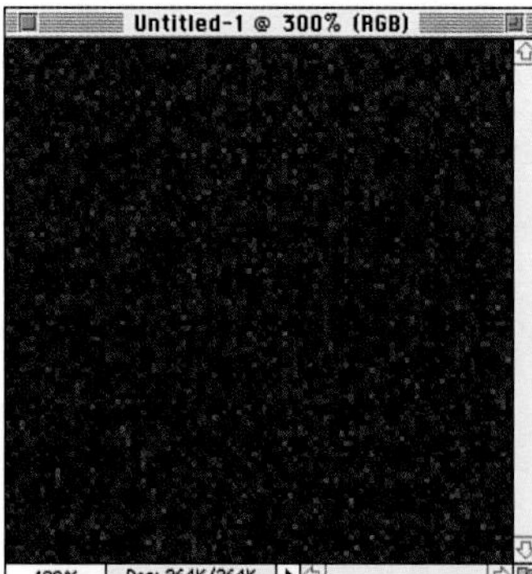


**2** Select Filter➥Noise➥Add Noise (Amount: 20, Distribution: Gaussian, Monochromatic). The Amount needs to be low enough so that you do not create white pixels. Use my settings first before you start experimenting with this one.

**3** The parched earth effect is fairly easy to create, but it needs to be constructed in pieces. It will be easier to follow along if you name things the same way that I do—at least your first time through. Save the file as Parched.Psd (I'll just refer to it as "parched" for short).

Duplicate Layer

Duplicate: Background
As: Background
Destination
Document: New
Name: texture
OK
Cancel

**4** Select Layers➥Duplicate Layer to place the Background layer into a new document that you should call "texture."

**5** Choose Filter➥Other➥Minimum (2 pixels). This filter works on the darker pixels and is a way to increase the size of the noise.

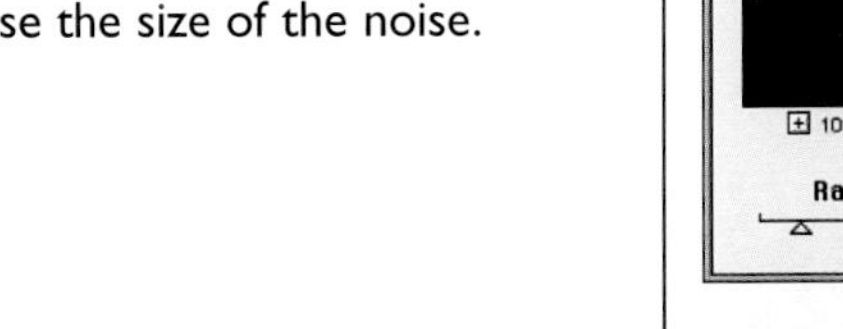


**6** Choose Image➥Adjust➥Auto Levels.

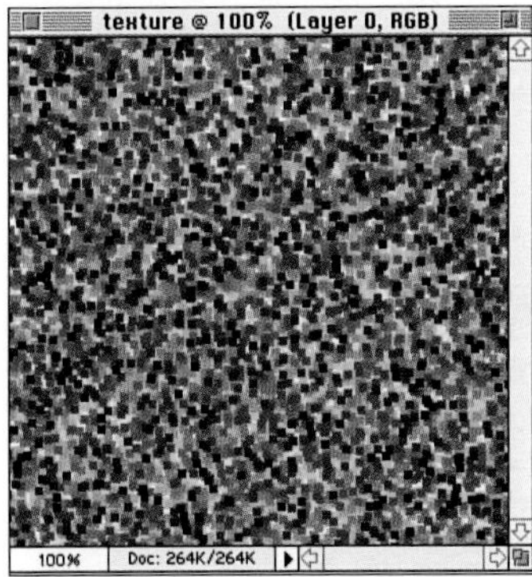


**7** Select Filter➥Blur➥Gaussian Blur (1.5).

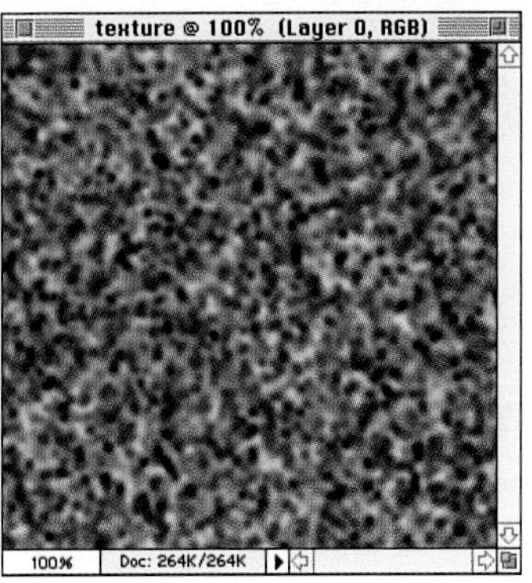


**8** Let's emboss this without using the Emboss filter. Duplicate the Background layer (Background copy). Invert the copy (Command-I) [Control-I]. Reduce the layer opacity to 50%. The image turns a totally neutral gray.

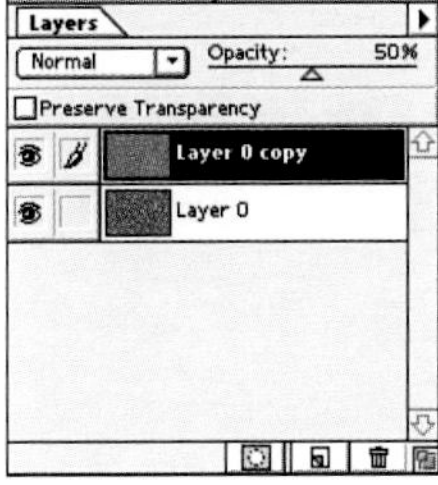

texture @ 100% (Layer 0 copy, RGB)

100% Doc: 264K/528K

**9** Press the (Command)[Control] key to access the Move tool, and use the arrow keys to move the top layer to the right and down several pixels. I moved the image two pixels right and two pixels down. This leaves a slight flaw at the left and top edges that you may want to trim off later.

parched.psd @ 200% (Layer 1, RGB)

100% Doc: 264K/792K

**10** Flatten the image. Drag and drop centered into the Parched image (Layer 1). Double-click on the name Layer 1 in the Layers palette, and change the layer name to Texture. Change the blending mode to Hard Light.

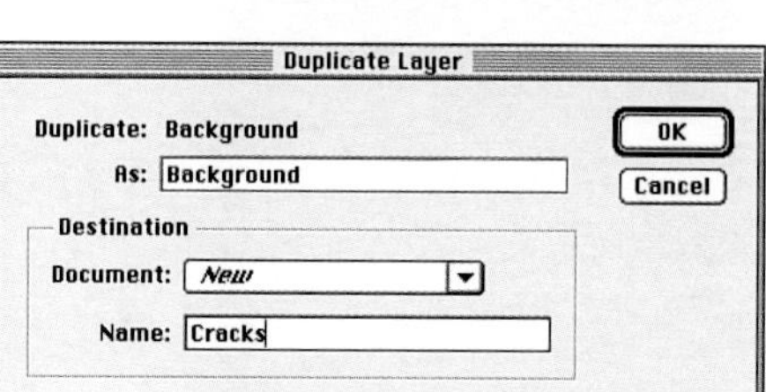


**11** Make the Background layer active. Select Layer➥Duplicate Layer. Send the duplicate to a new image. Name the image Cracks.

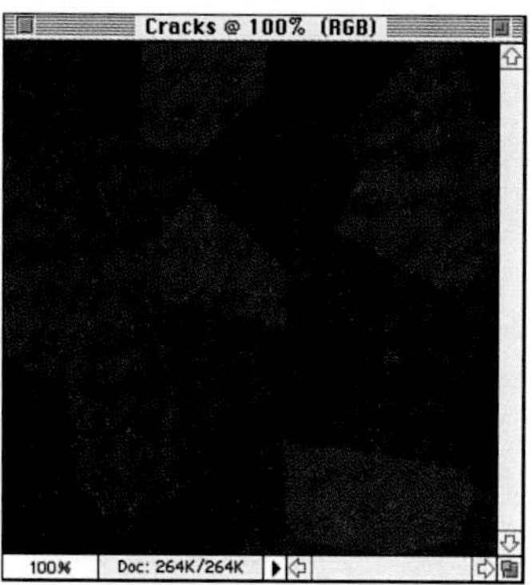


**12** Select Filter➥Pixelate➥Crystalize. Choose a fairly large cell size. I used a cell size of 99. If you do not like the shapes that appear, select Undo, and reapply the filter. It will be slightly different at each application. We need to create two different images from this one.

**13** Choose Filter➥Stylize➥Find Edges.

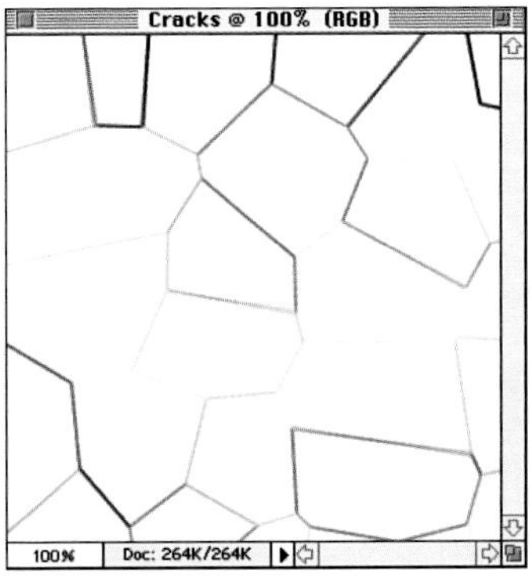

**14** Select the Eraser tool and remove the lines that you do not like. Edit your "crack map" until it looks suitably cracked.

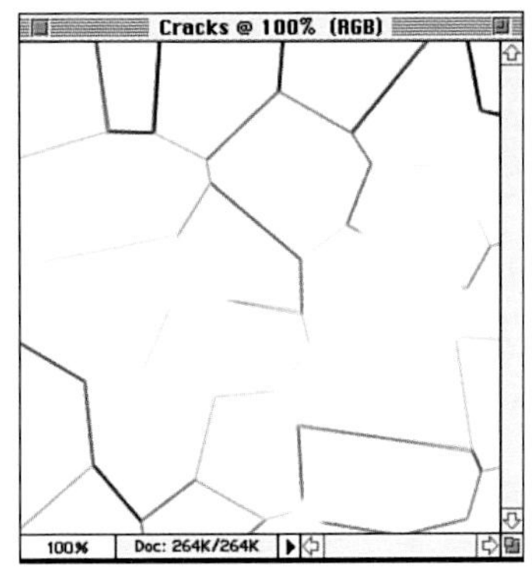


**15** Drag and drop centered into the Parched image. It needs to be the layer above the Background layer (Layer 1). Double-click on the name Layer 1 in the Layers palette and name the layer Shadows. Change the blending mode to Multiply. The cracks are almost too light to see. Select Image➥Adjust➥Levels. Drag the left Input slider until the cracks become as dark as you want.

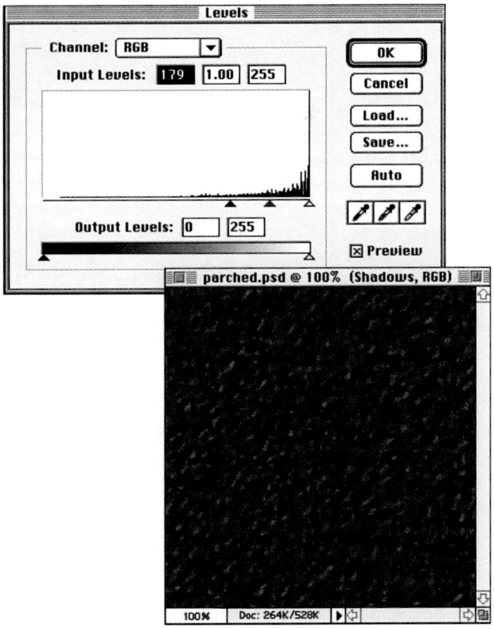

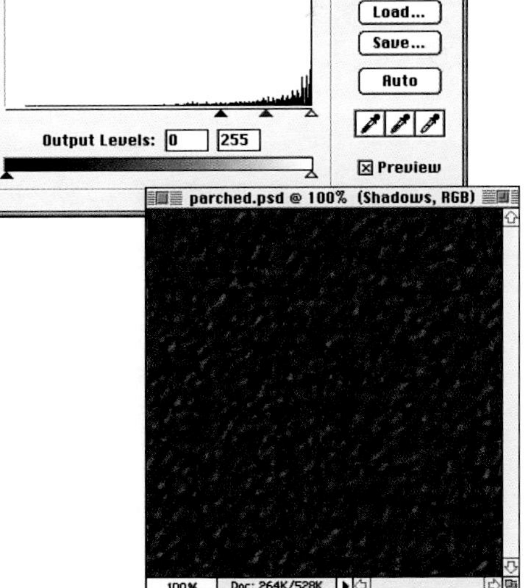

**16** Apply Filter➥Blur➥Gaussian Blur (2.9) to soften the crack lines so that they begin to look like shadows.

**17** Now we need to create the crack embossing. Click on the Cracks image to make it active. Duplicate the Background layer. Change the blending mode to Multiply. Apply Filter➥Pixelate➥Crystallize (Cell size: 24). The cracks that you generated originally with the Crystallize filter at size 99 aren't very natural. By adding more shapes on top of these, you can make a much more organic-looking set of cracks.

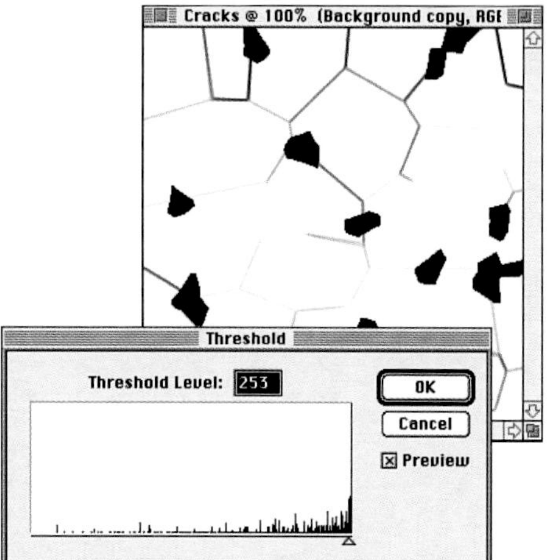


**18** You need to make the new shapes black so that the final embossing works properly. Choose Image➥Adjust➥Threshold and move the slider to the right until all of the shapes turn black.

**19** The shapes created are a bit too sparse. You really need to have most of the straight lines forming the original cracks covered with irregular shapes. Make the Background layer active. Duplicate the Background layer. Change the blending mode to Multiply. Apply Filter➥Pixelate➥Crystallize again with a new setting (Command-Option-F)[Alt-Control-F]. This time, use a cell size of about 17. The smaller shapes fill in quite nicely.

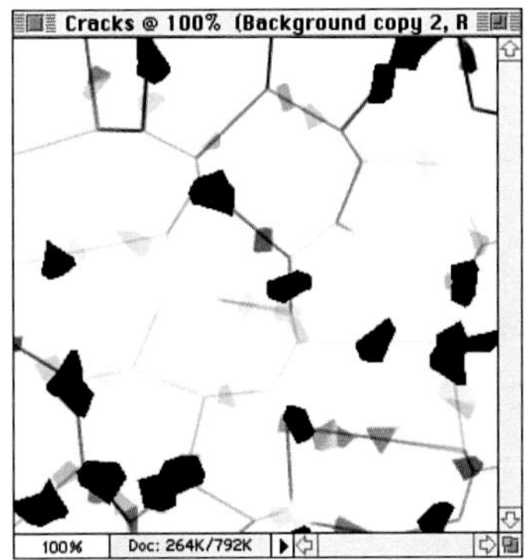


**20** You also need to turn these shapes to black—or mostly black. This time, select Image➥Adjust➥Levels. Although you could use the Threshold command again, using Levels enables you to keep some of the shapes a lighter color. Drag the left Input slider almost all the way toward the right. As you can see, not all the shapes turn solid black this time.

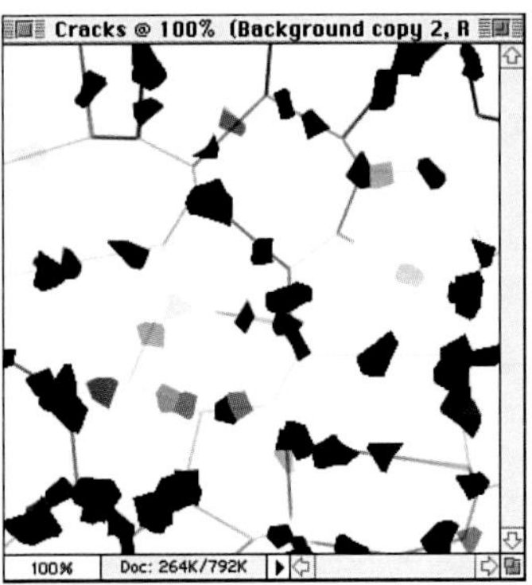


**21** You are almost ready to create the embossed crack map. You need to make the Background layer a bit darker so that some of the straight crack lines show up in the in the final embossing. Duplicate the Background layer (Background copy 3). Select Image➥Adjust➥Levels (Command-L)[Control-L]. Move the left Input slider until it is close to the right edge.

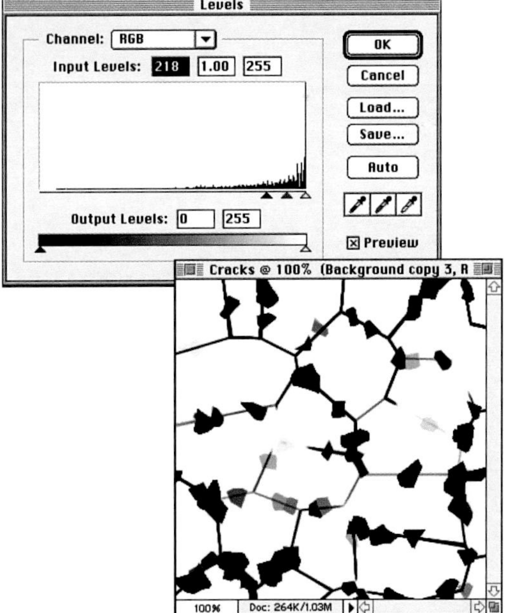

**22** You now have a choice, and a decision to make. If you are *sure* that you like the cracks that have developed, you can flatten the image. If you want to give yourself the option to change your mind (without starting the example from scratch), (Option)[Alt] Merge Visible to a new layer. (That's what I usually prefer to do.)

**TIP** **You may be wondering why I didn't just leave the levels of the two crystallize layers and the Background layer alone and make them darker at this point—now that all three layers have been merged. You certainly can do that. You have more flexibility, however, doing it the other way (even if it is a bit more complex).**

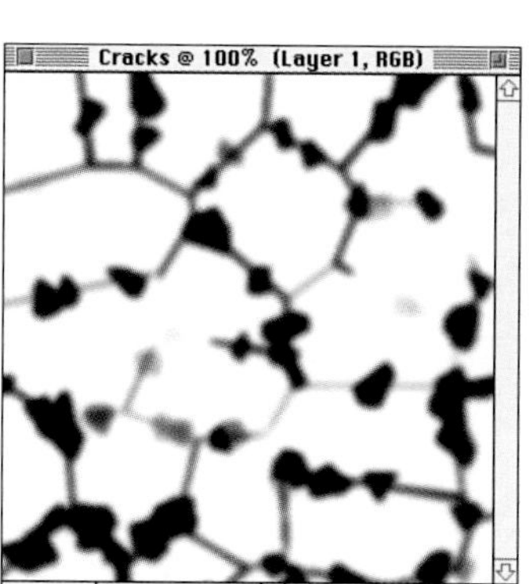


**23** If you emboss the combined image now, you still get a jagged crack map. You need to blur the image before you emboss it to exaggerate its organic qualities and smooth out the rough edges. Select Filter➡Blur➡Gaussian Blur (2.3). But you're not done…

**24** Select Image➥Adjust➥Levels (Command-L)[Control-L]. You need to move the left and right Input sliders closer together. As you do, the image will sharpen focus. If the three sliders are more toward the right, the image sharpens and fattens. If the sliders are more toward the left, the image still sharpens, but the shapes get thinner. I prefer something more centered but toward the right as you can see in the settings here. (One reason I advocate the "keep the other layers" approach is that if you don't like the embossing when you finally get to do it, it is easy to (Option) [Alt] Merge Visible the layers again and try it again.)

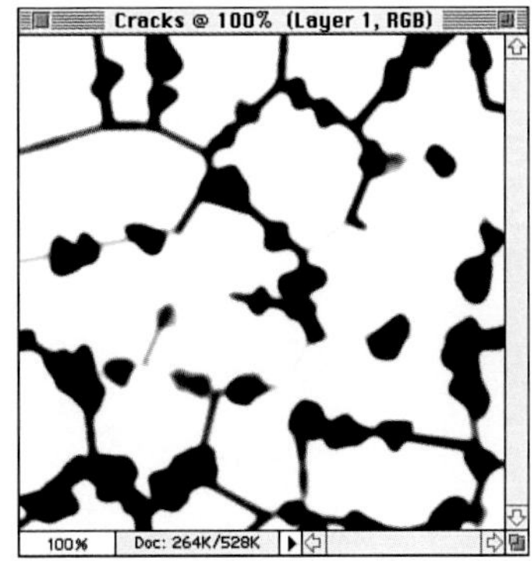


**25** Finally…now you can apply Filter➥Stylize➥Emboss (Height: 2, Amount: 100%). I used an Angle of –43° so that the cracks would sink *in* to the ground and not come out of it.

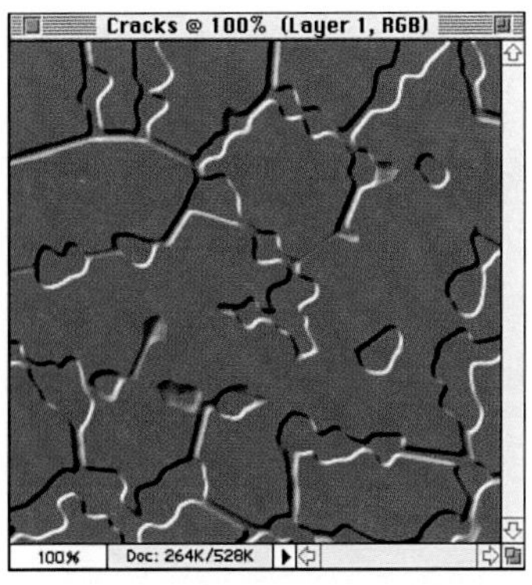


**26** Drag and drop centered the newly embossed layer into the Parched image. Move the layer to the top of the Layers palette. Double-click on the layer name in the Layers palette and change the name to Embossed Cracks. Change the blending mode to Hard Light.

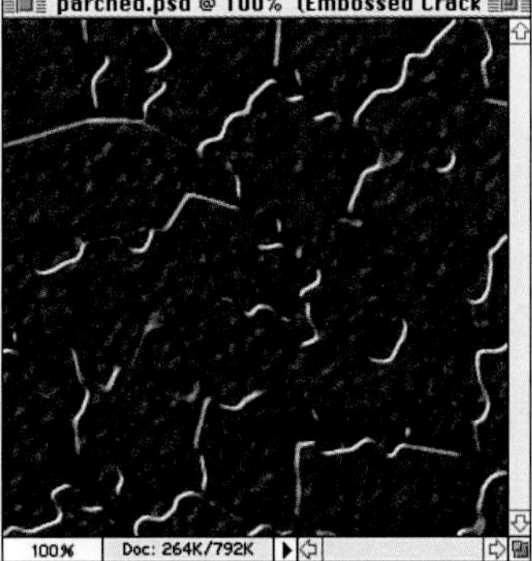

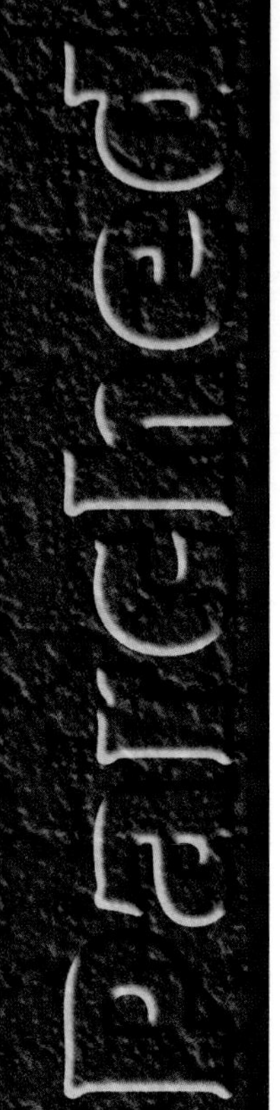

**27** The image certainly looks interesting, but I've never seen ground with sharp white highlights! You need to tone down the Embossed Cracks layer. Select Filter➥Blur➥Gaussian Blur. A Radius of 2.3 is a good choice, although you could go higher or lower as you prefer.

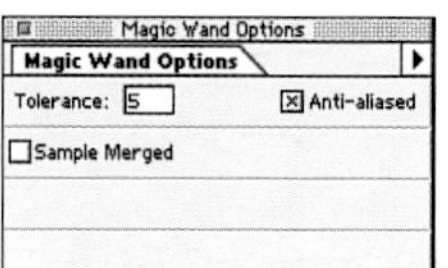


**28** There is still a bit too much highlight to my taste. Parched earth shouldn't look like wet cobblestones. Change the blending mode to Normal so that you can see the layer as it actually is. Double-click the Magic Wand tool and set the Tolerance to 5, Anti-aliased on, and Sample Merged off.

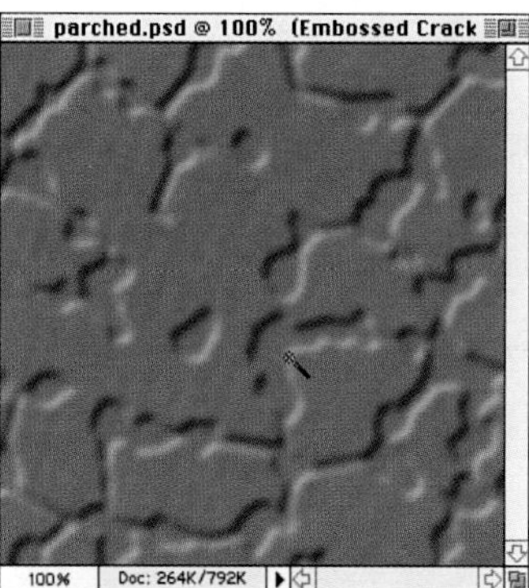


**29** Click one of the highlight edges and then choose Select➥Similar.

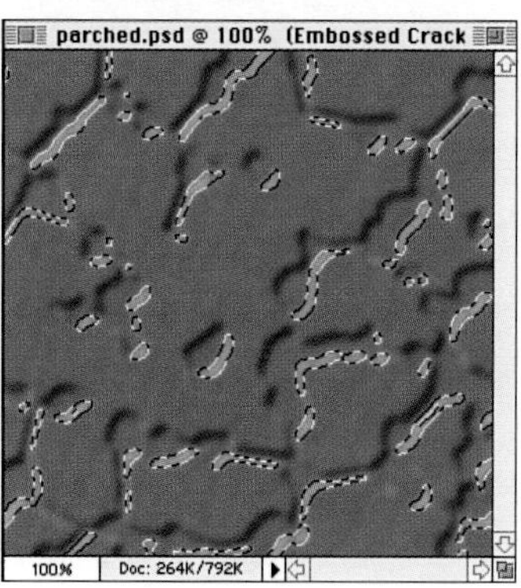

**30** Change the blending mode to Hard Light. Hide the marching ants (Command-H)[Control-H]. Now you can see what happens as you select Image➡Adjust➡Levels (Command-L)[Control-L]. Drag the Gamma slider (the center slider) to the left edge of the values in the selection. Deselect.

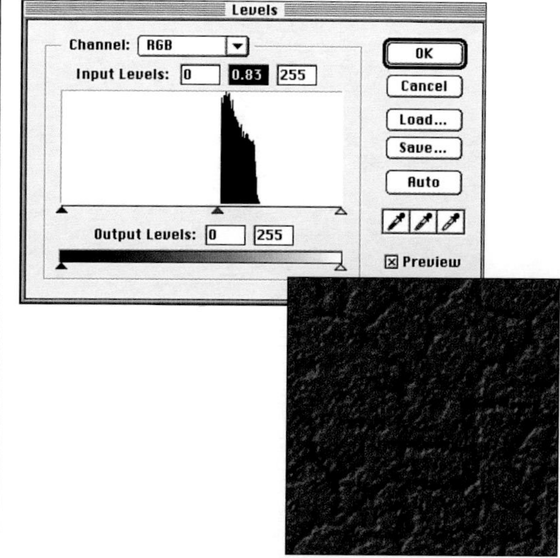


**31** Select Image➡Canvas Size and reduce the dimensions by the amount of the "bad edges" from the hand embossing in Step 9. Anchor the image to the lower-right corner. I trimmed off two pixels on the top and left edge. Now all you need to do is to decide where to use your parched earth. ■

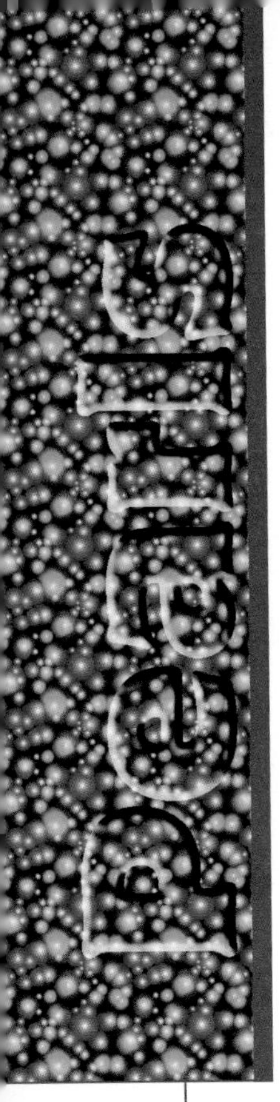


This technique creates small pearls that repeat seamlessly across an image. Variations can create effects that range from wild to caviar.

**1** Create a new file. The file I used is 300×300 pixels. Switch to default colors.

Gradient Tool Options
Darken | Opacity: 100%
Gradient: Foreground to Background
Type: Radial | ☒ Mask ☒ Dither
Edit...

**2** Double-click the Gradient tool to bring up the Gradient Options. Set the Gradient to Foreground to Background, and the Type to Radial. Set the Apply mode to Darken, and the Opacity to 100%. Check Dither and Mask.

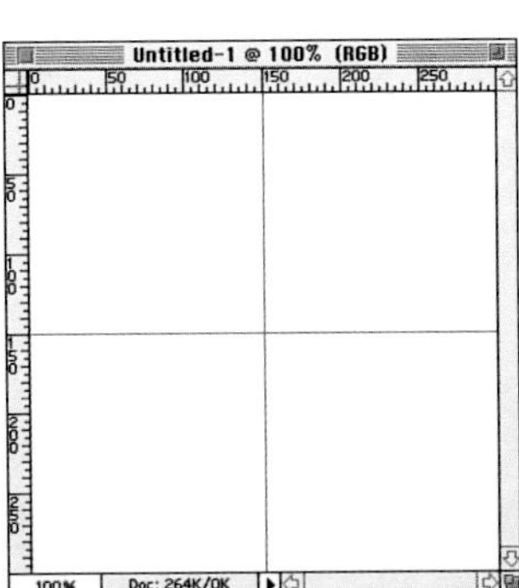


**3** Turn on Rulers (Command-R) [Control-R]. Add a horizontal and vertical guide to the 150-pixel line along each ruler. The guides will cross in the exact center of the image.

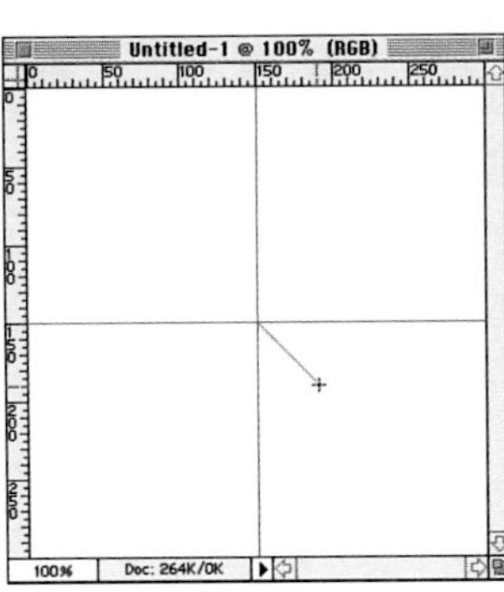


**4** Place the cursor in the center of the image, drag it to the 180, 180 pixel marker to the bottom-right, and release. You will see one gradient circle.

**5** Start the next circle a small distance away, and drag the rubberband Gradient cursor so that it just overlaps the first circle. Release it. Because of the Darken mode, the circles seem to fuse where they touch.

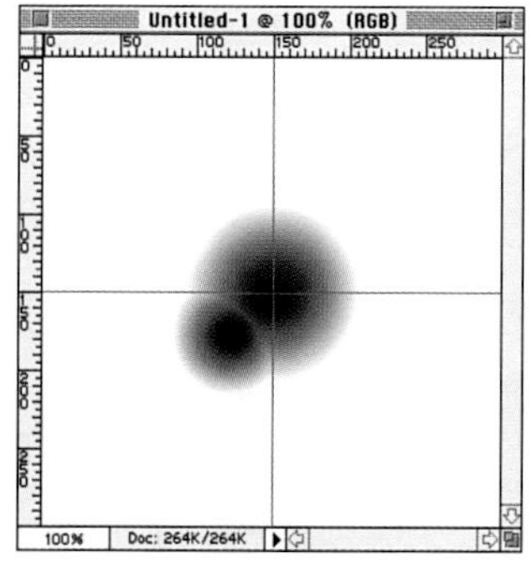


**6** In order to make this pattern seamless, you need to place the circles carefully along the guidelines. Don't try to make them stay in a straight line—that looks awful when it is done. Fill in the image, only around the area that follows the lines. As you get near any of the sides, you need to make a circle that touches the side but does not get cut off by it. You may need to Undo your side circles a few times until you get them close enough without getting too close.

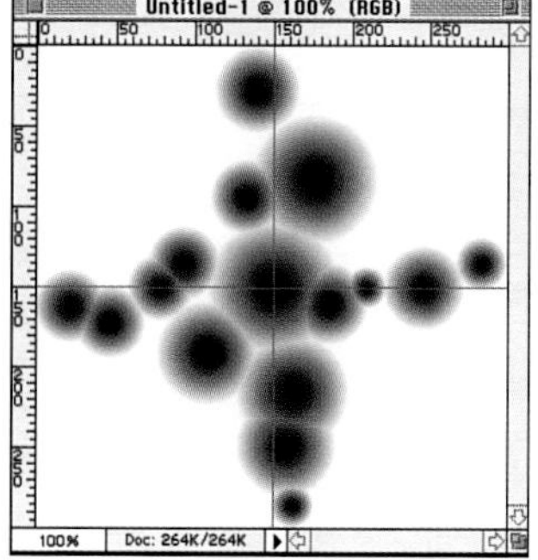


**7** Choose Filter➥Other➥Offset (Right: 150, Down: 150, Wrap Around).

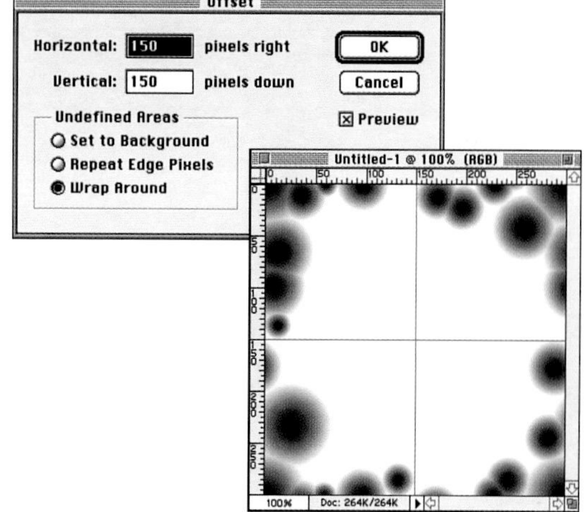

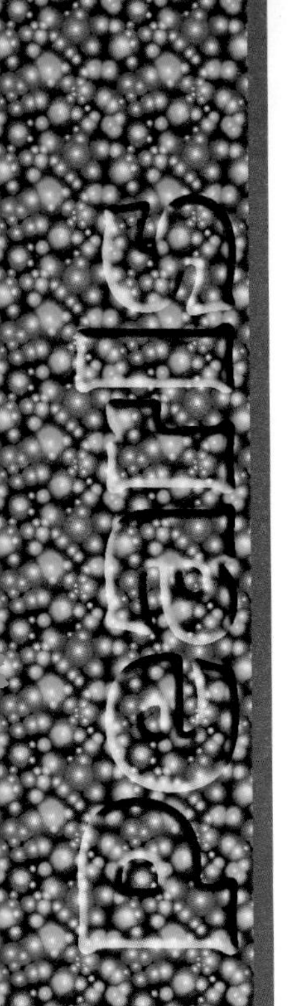


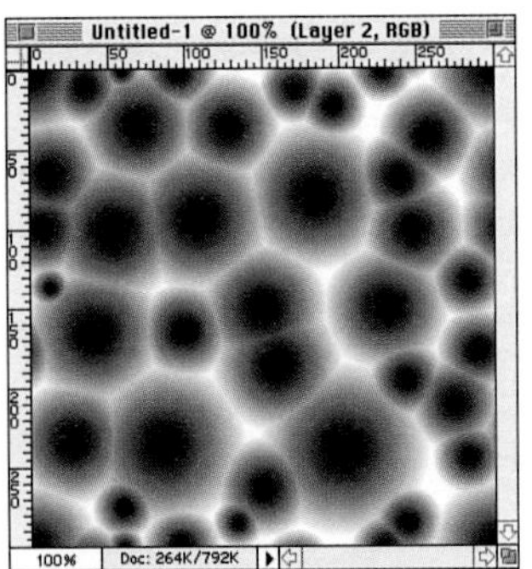


**8** Now you have a tile that will definitely tile seamlessly, so you can fill in the rest of the image with more circles without having to worry about the way it wraps. Finish the image, but keep the size of the circles in synch with the sizes you have used so far.

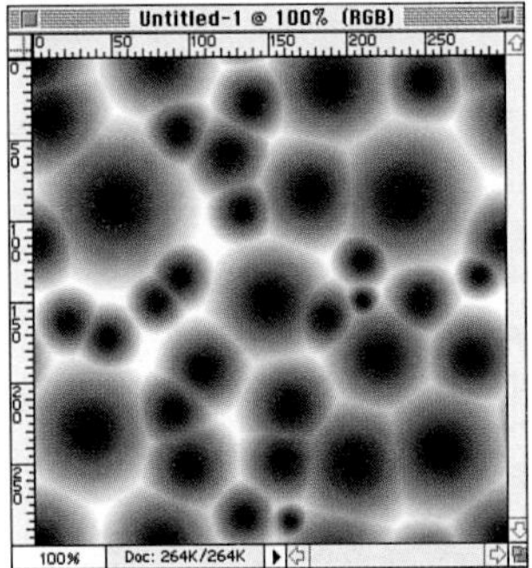


**9** Reapply the Offset filter (Command-F)[Control-F]. Look carefully at the image. If you see any hard, sharp lines on the seam line, then cover them over gently with another circle. Make sure that your pattern is seamless.

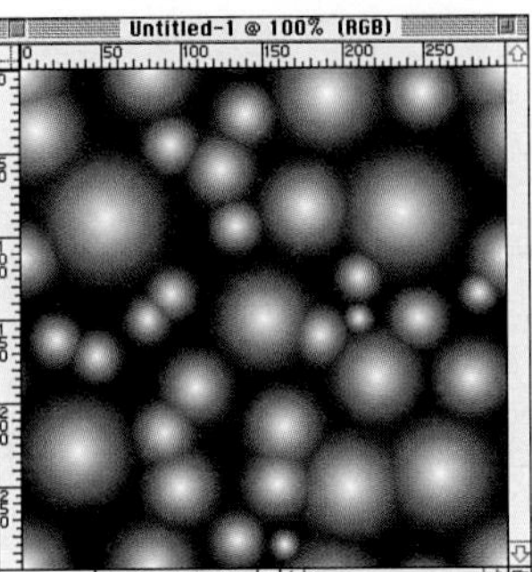


**10** Invert the image (Command-I) [Control-I]. Wow! Pearls!

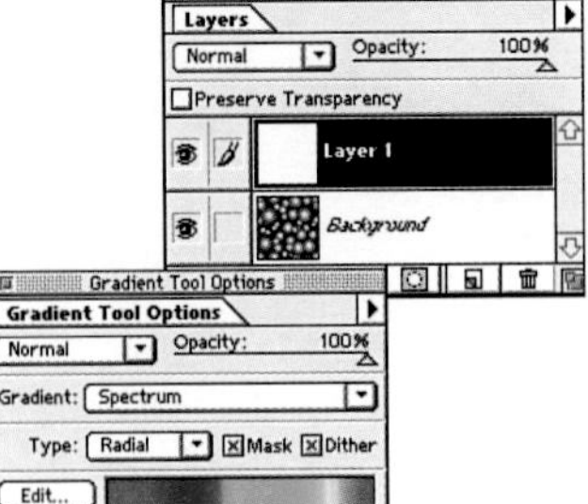


**11** The next step is to add color. Create a new layer. Change the Gradient to Spectrum, and change the blending mode for the Gradient to Normal; however, keep it as a Radial gradient.

**12** Turn on Rulers if they are off (Command-R)[Control-R]. Add a horizontal and vertical guide to the 250-pixel position on both rulers (there should already be guides at the 150-pixel center of the image. If you have removed them, re-create them, too). Place your cursor in the center of the image, and drag the rubber-band Gradient cursor to the intersection of the 250-pixel guide lines. Release the mouse.

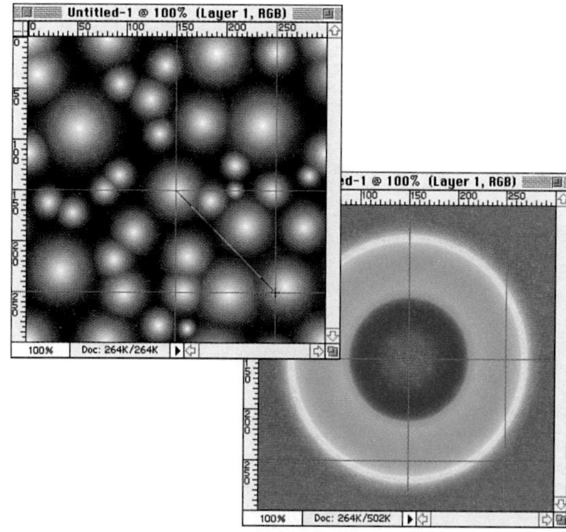


**13** Change the blending mode to Color.

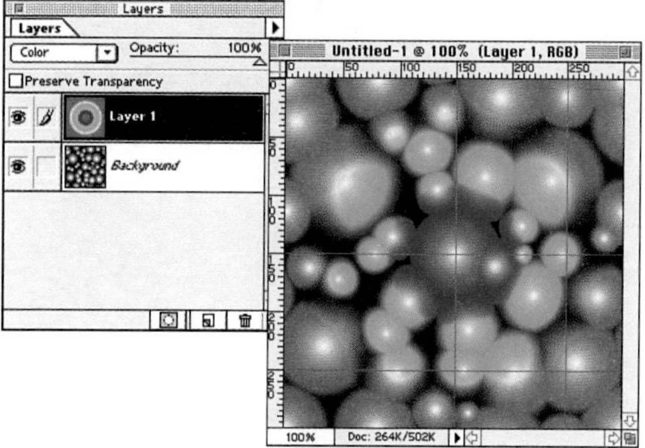


**14** Duplicate Layer 1. The blending mode is already set to Color. Reapply the Offset filter (Command-F)[Control-F].

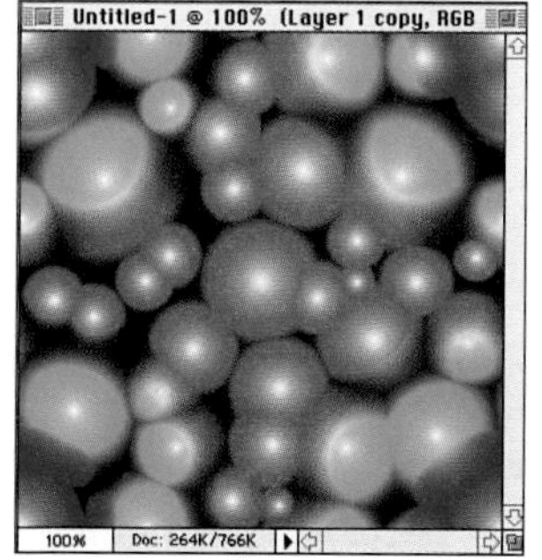

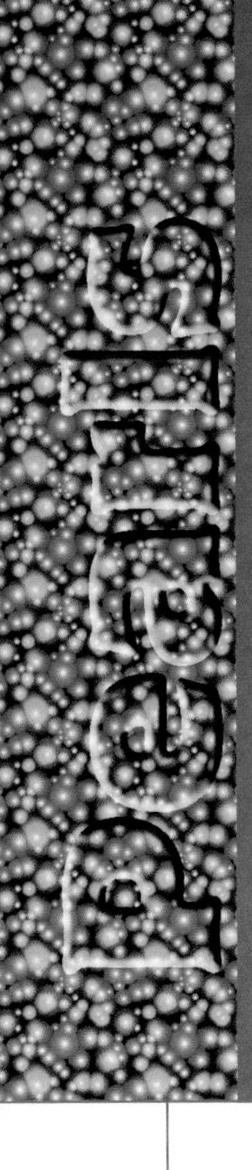


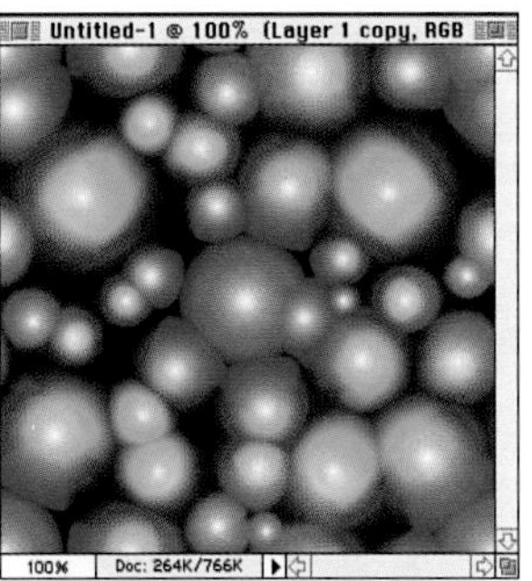


**15** Reduce the layer opacity to 50%.

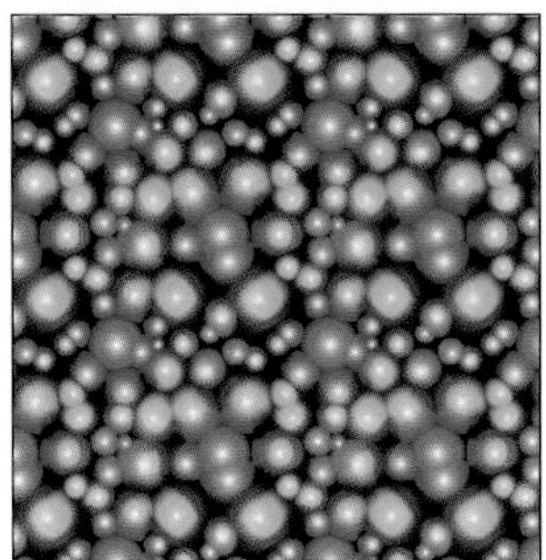

**16** Select➡All. Define the pattern. Create a new file 1000×1000 pixels. Fill with pattern.

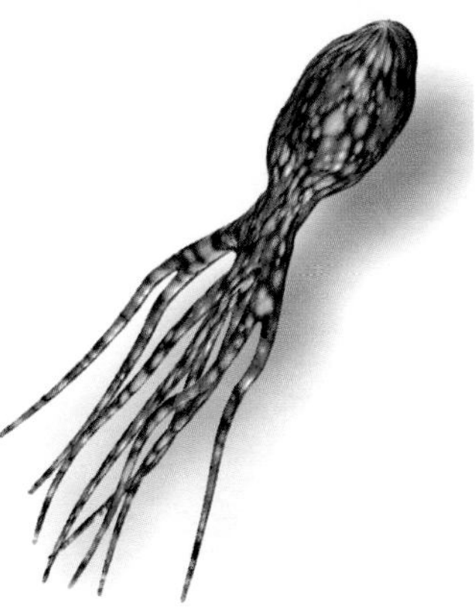

## Variations

One thing you can do that is immediately interesting is to invert the image again. Now you have amoebas swimming in a test tube!

To create a festive image, click the pattern-filled image to make it active. Duplicate the Background layer. Rotate the top Layer 90° (Layer➥Transform➥Rotate 90° CW). Change the blending mode to Exclusion.

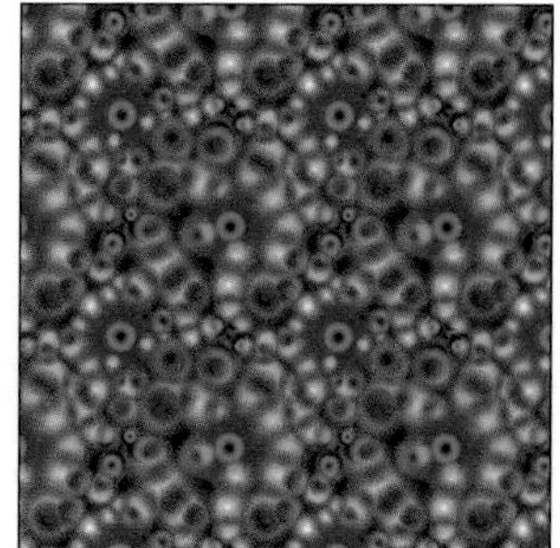

You can also try the following. Click the original pattern image to make it active. Choose Image➥Duplicate➥OK, Merged Layers only. Duplicate the Background layer in this new image. Choose Layer➥Transform➥Rotate 90° CW. Change the blending mode to Difference. This makes a fractured texture with a black hole in the center (where the two layers were the same).

To fix the black hole, select Filter➥Other➥Offset (Wrap Around). Play with the offset amounts until you no longer see the hole. I used 25 pixels right and 170 pixels down. The colors will change dramatically depending upon your offset amounts. Select all. Define a pattern. Create a new file 1000×1000 pixels. Fill the selection with pattern. ■

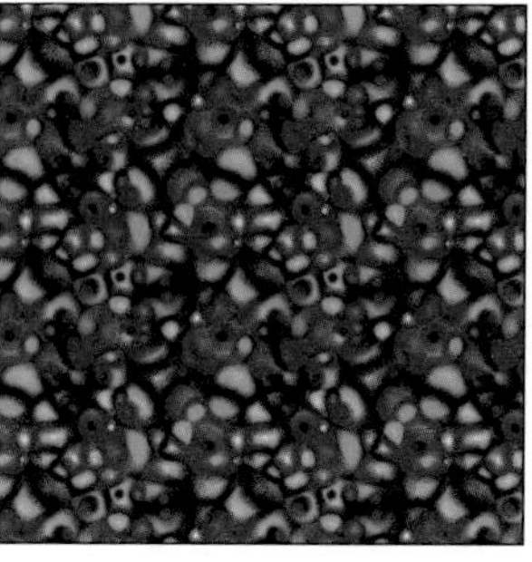

A riddle for you—"When is randomness not random?" The answer: when it is placed in repeat. Chaos theory is based on the order inherent at the heart of randomness—or is it the randomness at the heart of order? This effect takes you on a magic carpet ride through both kingdoms, and allows you to ponder the conundrum of order versus chaos at your own pace.

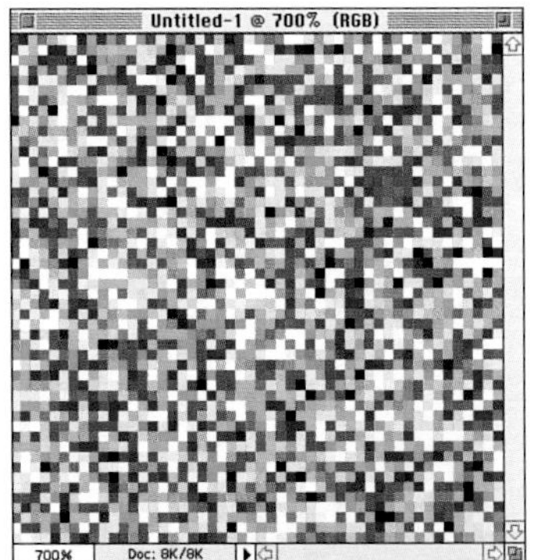


**1** Create a new file. Because this is to be a tile, a small file works well. Mine is 50×50 pixels. Select Filter➡Noise➡Add Noise (Distribution: Gaussian, Monochromatic: Off). Use an Amount large enough to cover much of the white in the image. I used an Amount of 300. The tile is most definitely random.

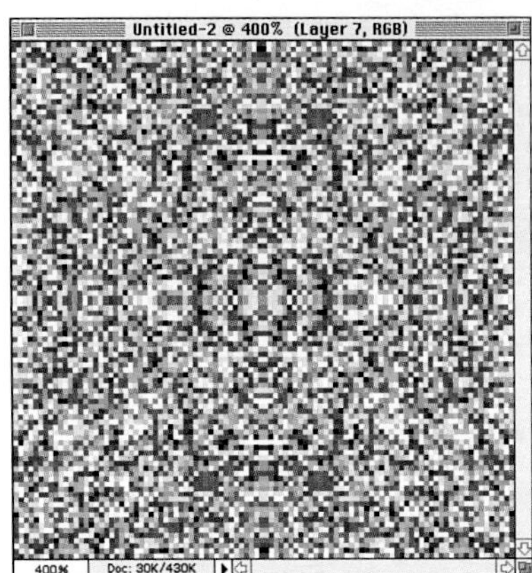


**2** Create a new file that is twice the dimensions of the original tile. Mine is 100×100 pixels. Make the image seamless using the Mosaic method. This still looks random, but there is order emerging from the center of the tile along the seam lines.

**3** Select➡All. Define the pattern. Create a new file. Mine is 430×680. To make a magic carpet, you need a file that is flying carpet-shaped. Fill the selection with pattern. It's not random now!

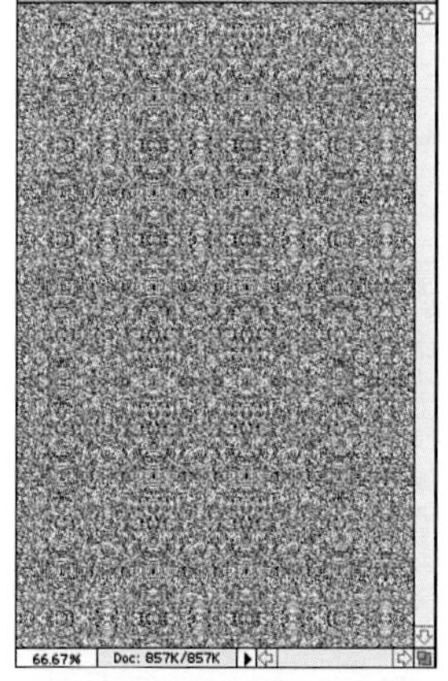


**4** Choose two colors to be a border. Switch the foreground color to your deeper color. Switch the background color to the brighter color. I selected a royal blue and a burgundy. Choose Image➡Canvas Size. Increase the dimensions of the file by the same amount in each direction. Anchor in the center. I added 50 pixels to both dimensions. The image is now bordered by a 25-pixel swath of the brighter background color on all four sides.

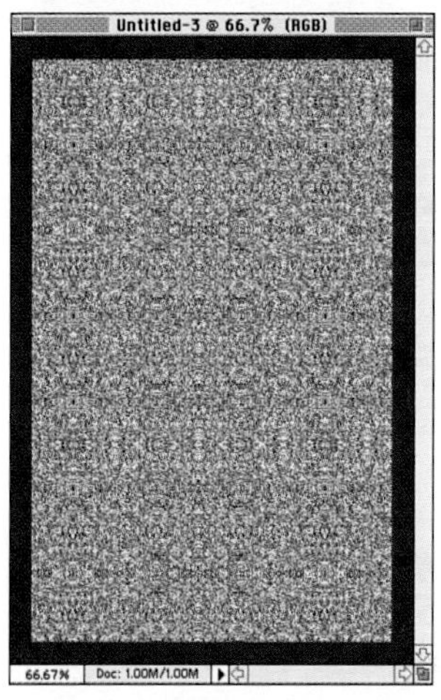


**5** Switch foreground/background colors. Choose Image➡Canvas Size. Increase the dimensions of the file by the same amount in each direction. Anchor in the center. I added 30 pixels to both dimensions. The image is now bordered by a 15-pixel swath of the darker background color on all four sides.

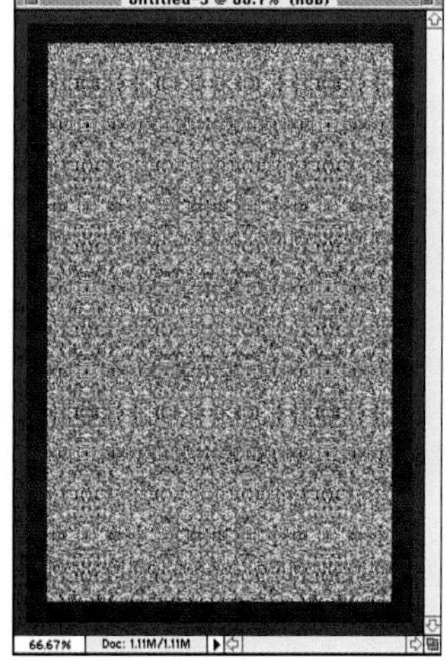

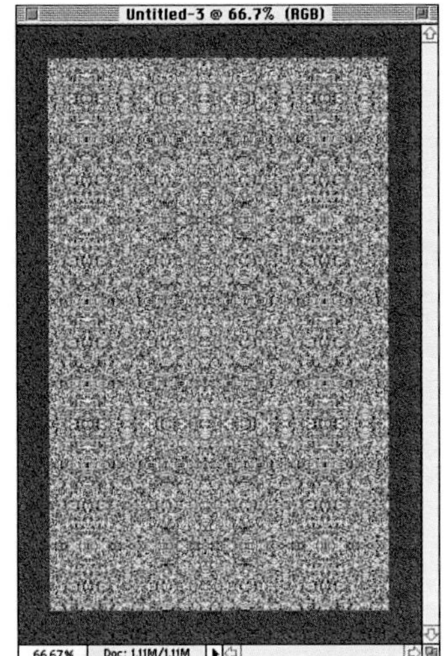


6 Double-click the Magic Wand tool. Set the Tolerance to 0 and Anti-aliased off. Click to select the inner border. Hold down the Shift key, and click to select the outer border. Fill the selection with pattern at 20–50% opacity. I used a 30% fill.

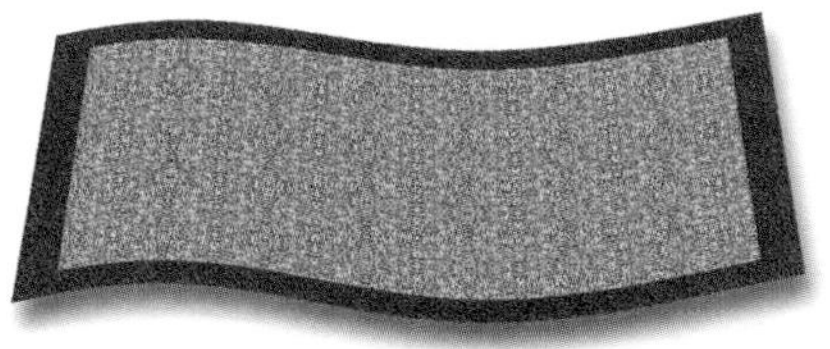

## VARIATIONS

If you want a somewhat more practical use for this effect, it makes a wonderful bump or texture map. Complete Steps 1 and 2. Flatten the image. Convert the image to grayscale mode. Select Filter➡Blur➡Gaussian Blur (.06). Select➡All. Define the pattern. Create a new file of the desired size. Switch the foreground color to your desired pattern color. Fill the selection with foreground color. Create a new layer. Change the blending mode to Hard Light. Fill the selection with pattern.

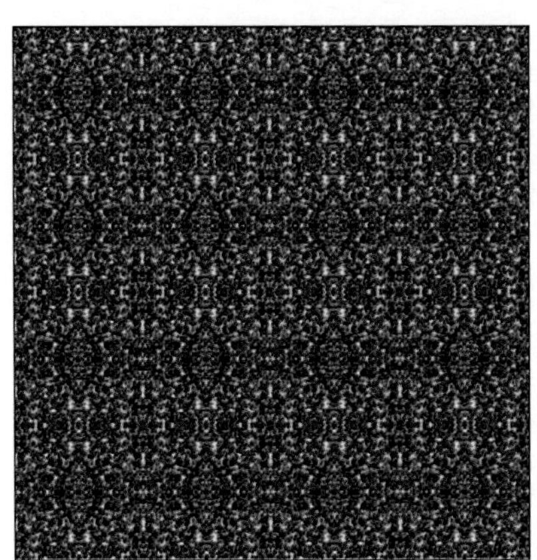

To add an embossed texture to this, select Image➥Adjust➥Threshold. Select a Threshold Value near the center. I chose a value of 128. Select Filter➥Blur➥Gaussian Blur. I used a Radius of 0.9 to just add back in a touch of gray. Choose Filter➥Stylize➥Emboss. I used an Angle of 120°, Height: 2 pixels, and Amount: 63.

A softly blurred tile looks good too. Take the tile at the end of Step 2, select Image➥Duplicate (Merged Layers only). Select Filter➥Blur➥Gaussian Blur (.09). Select➥All. Define the pattern. Create a new file of the desired size. Fill the selection with pattern.

To get a slightly different look—one that is a bit glazed—create a new layer. Make the original unblurred image active. Select➥All. Define the pattern. Make the image with the new layer active. Fill with pattern. Change the blending mode to Darken. Apply Filter➥Blur➥Gaussian Blur to the Background layer again if you want. The higher the blur, the more pronounced the glaze (until you blur the image so much that you can no longer distinguish any image at all). ■

# Rice Paper

Japanese rice paper is truly a thing of beauty. Tiny flecks of color thread their way through the sometimes lumpy texture of the paper. You can create an electronic version of rice paper and emboss and color it with no mess, and little fuss. Unlike real paper, it's immediately dry and ready to go!

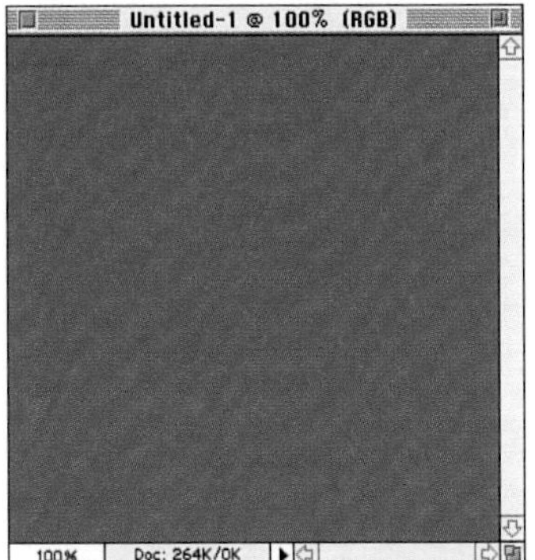


**1** Create a new file. I used one 300×300 pixels. Switch the background color to RGB: 98, 106, 191. Other colors can certainly be used, but you will get different results. Colors that are less saturated and medium-dark seem to work best—which is why I used a gray-blue as my starting color. Fill with background color.

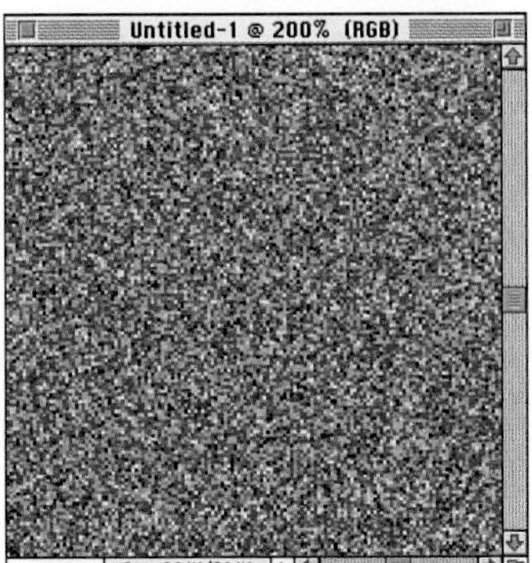


**2** Select Filter➡Noise➡Add Noise (Distribution: Gaussian, Monochromatic Off). I used an Amount of 135.

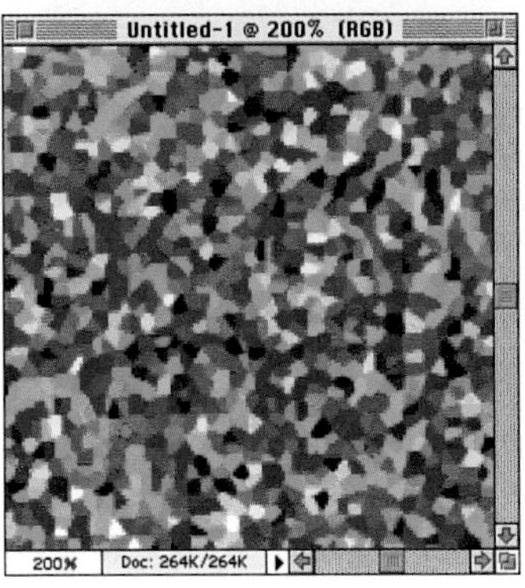


**3** Choose Filter➡Pixelate➡Pointillize. I chose a Cell Size of 6. Smaller sizes produce lighter and somewhat more delicate results. Much larger sizes become unusable for this effect. The background becomes the color between the "dots" created by the filter.

**4** Select Filter➥Noise➥Median (3). This creates a watercolor-like base for the effect.

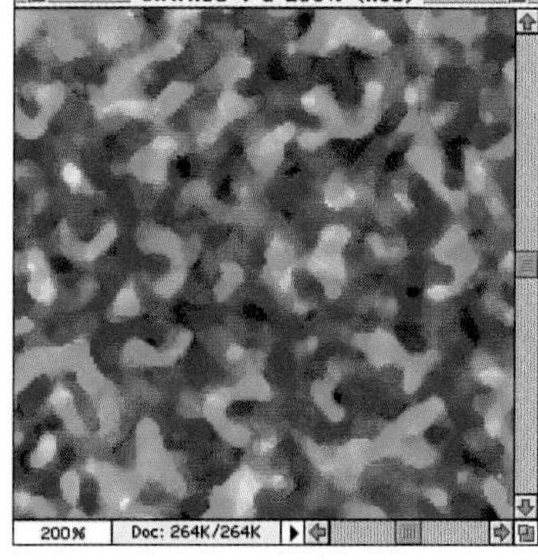


**5** Duplicate the Background layer twice. Change the blending mode of the top layer to Darken.

**6** If Background Copy 2 isn't the top layer, move it to the top of the Layers palette. Make the top layer invisible. Make the center layer (Background copy) active. Apply Filter➥Blur➥Motion Blur (Angle: 45°, Distance: 33 pixels). This streaks the image but does not obliterate it.

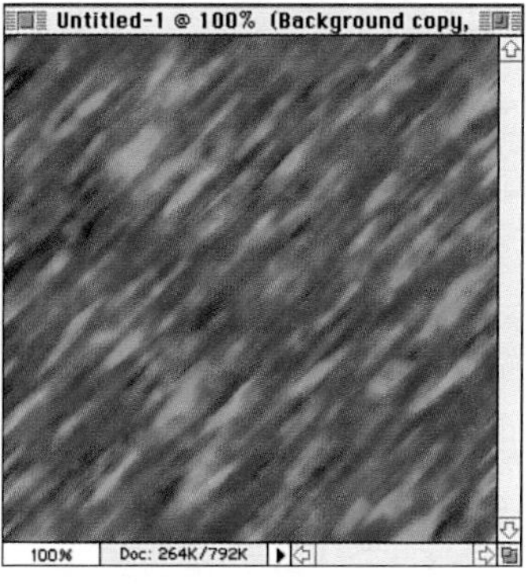


**7** Make the top layer active. (It will become visible again as soon as you make it active.) Apply Filter➥Blur➥Motion Blur (Angle: –45°, Distance: 33 pixels). This produces a criss-cross effect (because of the Darken mode), similar to the Crosshatch filter, but it's more controllable.

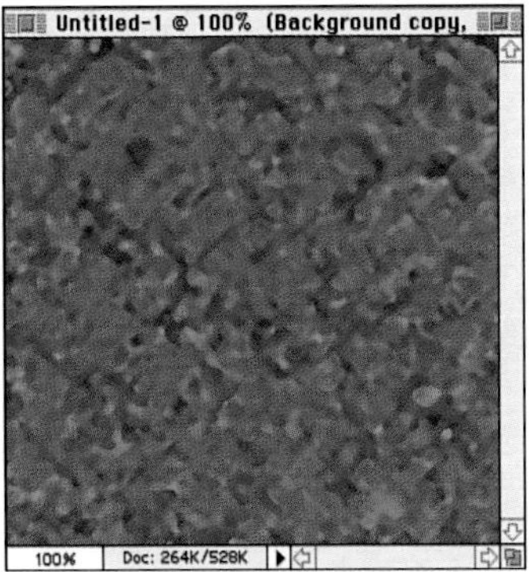


**8** Select Layer➡Merge Down (Command-E)[Control-E]. Change the blending mode to Exclusion. The background areas of the image gray out, leaving threads of bright color. Here's why it's important to choose less saturated or medium-dark colors to start with—not all colors gray out this way in Exclusion mode.

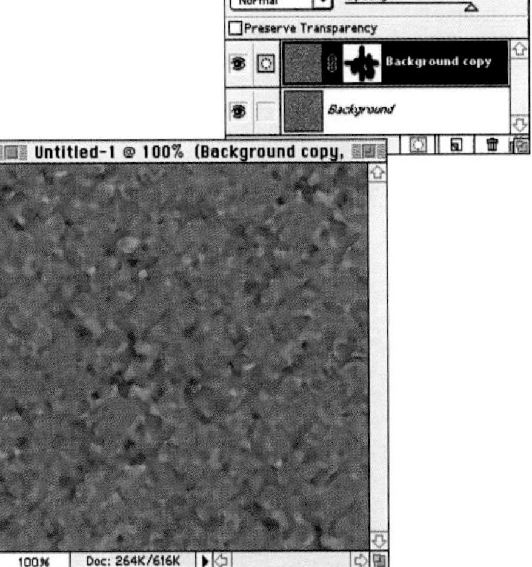


**9** Flatten the image. Make the pattern seamless using the Masked Offset method.

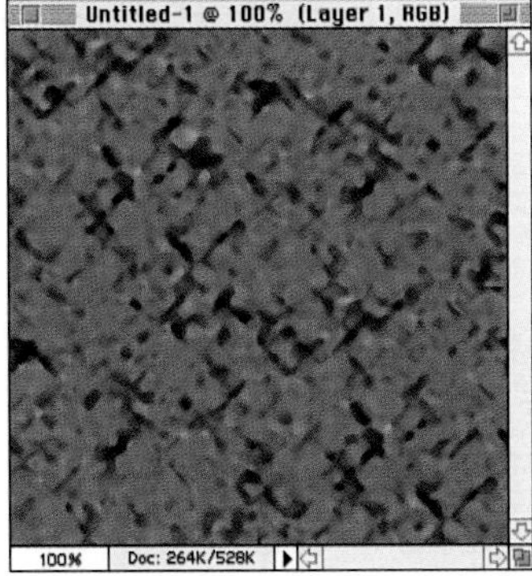


**10** Flatten the image. Create a new layer. Select Image➡Apply Image (Channel: Green, Opacity: 100%, blending mode: Normal). Although you could use any of the color channels, the Green channel has the most consistently "good" (that is, clear and crisp rendering) image.

**11** Change the blending mode to Hard Light. Choose Filter➡Stylize➡Emboss. I used an Angle of –47°, a Height of 3 pixels, and an Amount of 100. The embossing gives a nice texture to the image.

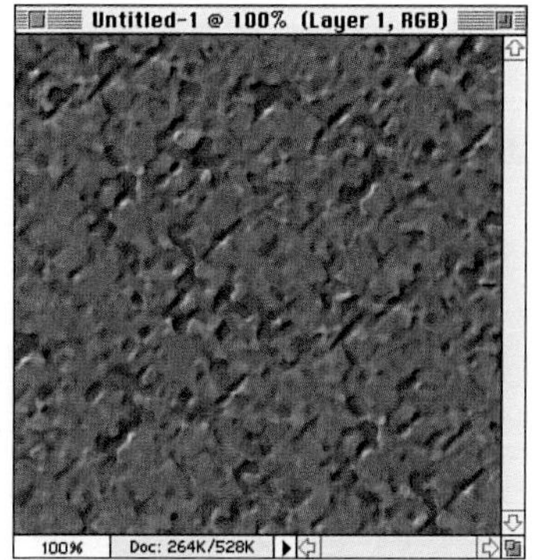


**12** Select➡All. Define the pattern. Create a new file that is the desired size. Fill with pattern. I placed a layer of white over the pattern and then reduced the opacity to lighten the image.

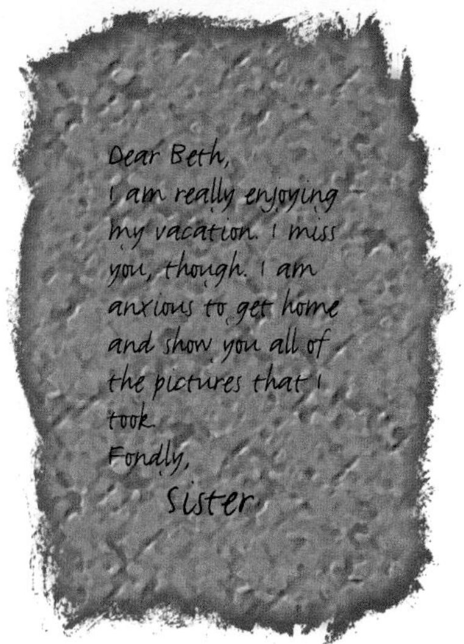


## VARIATIONS

If you want monotoned rice paper, work the original instructions through Step 11. Create a new layer. Switch the foreground color to your "stationery" color. Fill with foreground color. Change the blending mode to Color. ■

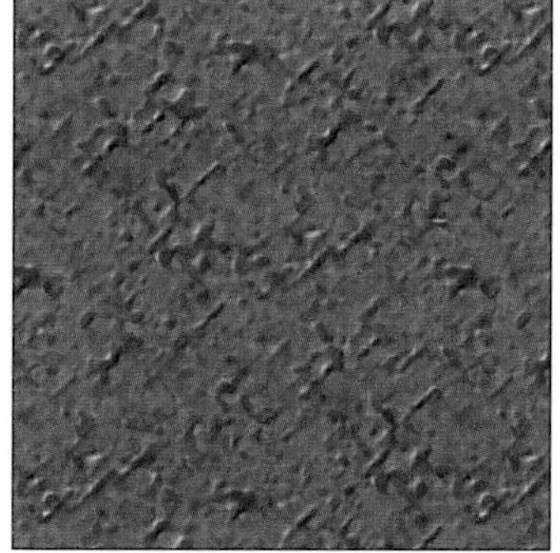

When I was young, my pockets were always filled with rocks. Their patterns and colors are endlessly fascinating. There are so many possibilities as you create this effect, that you may not want to stop! If you really want to model a specific type of rock, you can, but you can also create your own varieties.

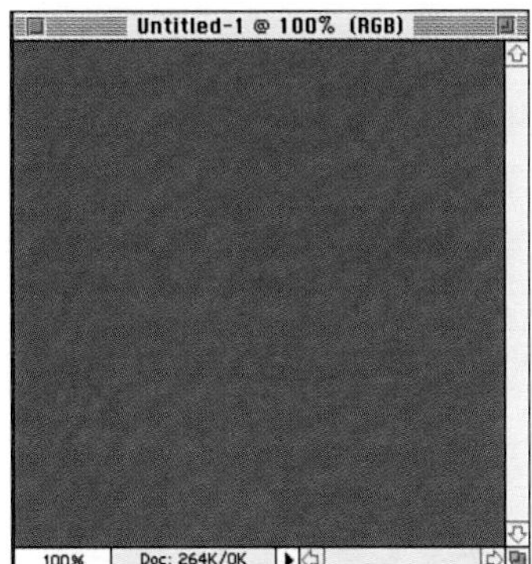


**1** Create a new file. This texture can be tiled, but real rock never repeats itself. I created a file 300×300 pixels. Switch the foreground color to your base "tone." I used RGB: 96, 121, 31—a grayed yellow-green. The color is not extremely critical as you can easily change it afterward. Fill the image with the foreground color.

**2** Create a new layer. Switch the foreground color to the second most used color in your palette. I used RGB: 255, 174, 111, which is a peach color. Fill the layer with foreground color.

**3** Create a layer mask. This effect—which is similar in construction to Water—is actually built in the layer "mask." Switch to default colors (your colors should already be showing black and white when the layer mask is selected). Select Filter➥Texture➥Grain (Clumped). I used an Intensity of 40 and a Contrast of 50. Then apply Filter➥Noise➥Add Noise. I used an Amount of 65 to keep the noise from removing all traces of the Grain filter.

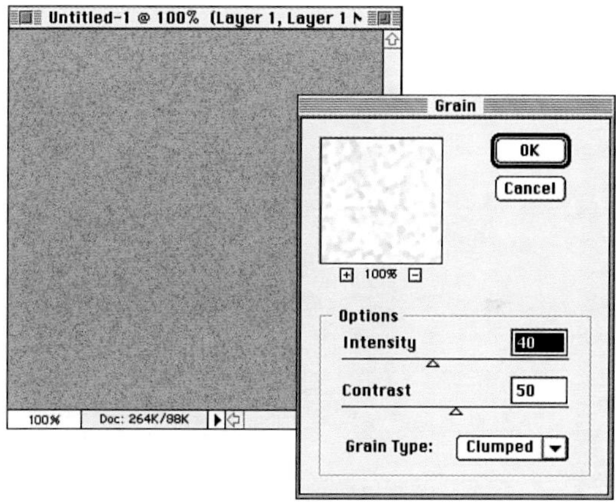


**4** Select Filter➥Render➥Difference Clouds. Reapply this filter (Command-F)[Control-F] about 10 times to build up complexity.

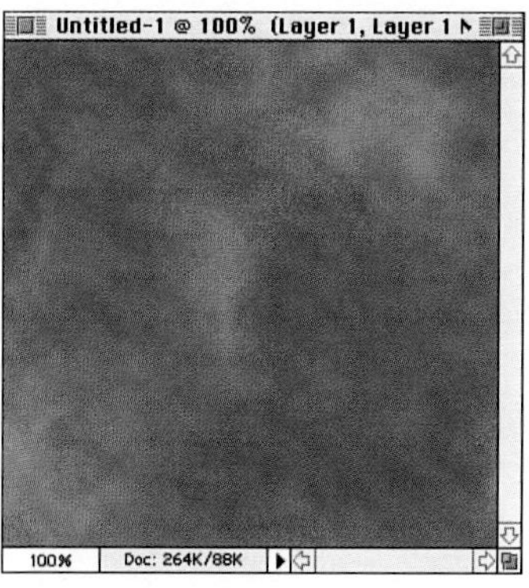


**5** You are still working in the Layer mask for this entire Step. Choose Filter➥Stylize➥Find Edges. The rock sample is supposed to be green with clumps of peach. If your image is too peach (and it almost certainly will be), select Image➥Adjust➥Invert (Command-I)[Control-I]. Then, select Image➥Adjust➥Auto Levels.

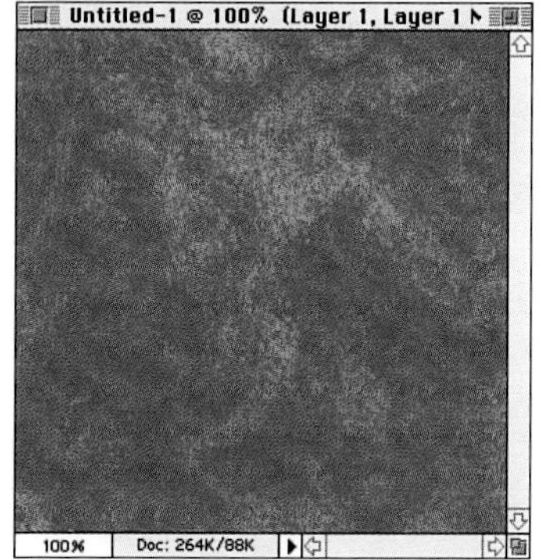

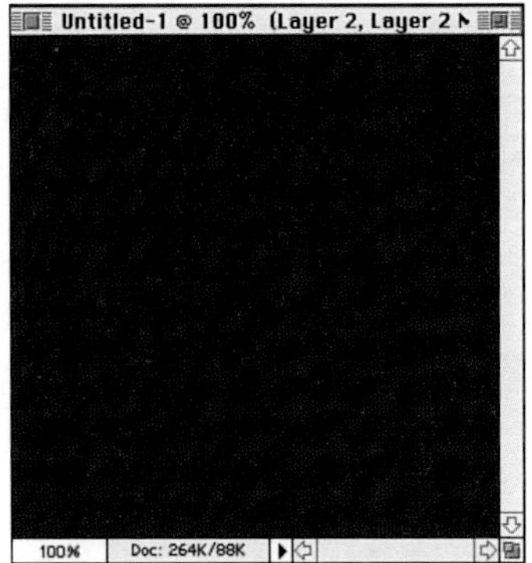


**6** Create a new layer. Switch the foreground color to the third color in your palette. I used RGB: 56, 66, 31. Fill with foreground color. Create a layer mask.

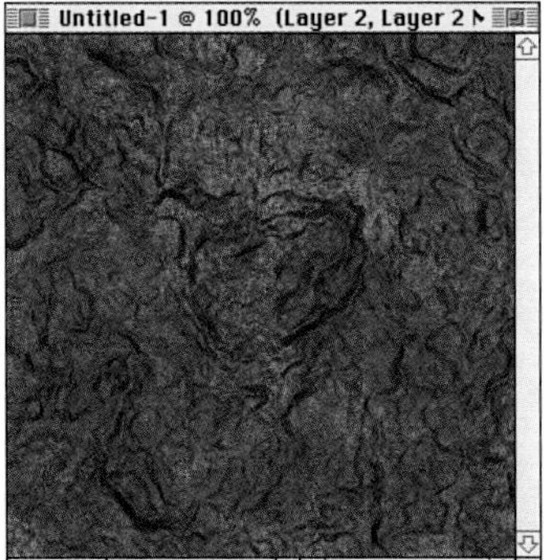


**7** With the layer mask active, select Filter➥Render➥Clouds. Then apply Filter➥Render➥Difference Clouds—approximately 24 times (Command-F)[Control-F]. Choose Filter➥Stylize➥Find Edges. Select Image➥Adjust➥Auto Levels. The image will probably be mostly dark green. Select Image➥Adjust➥Invert (Command-I)[Control-I].

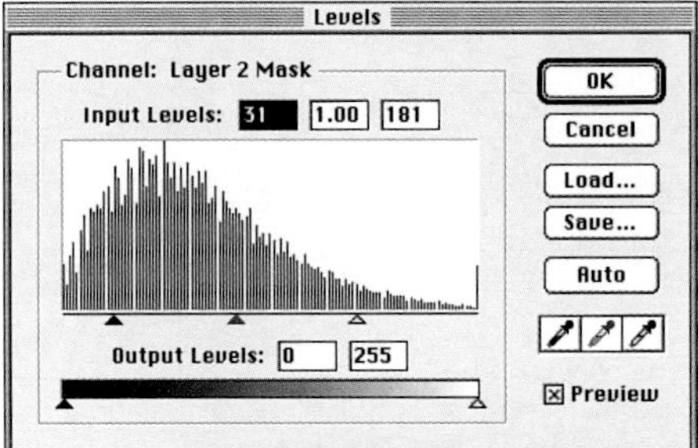


**8** Choose Image➥Adjust➥Levels (Command-L)[Control-L]. Move the right and left Input sliders closer together as shown. This removes some of the layer mask detail and darkens what remains.

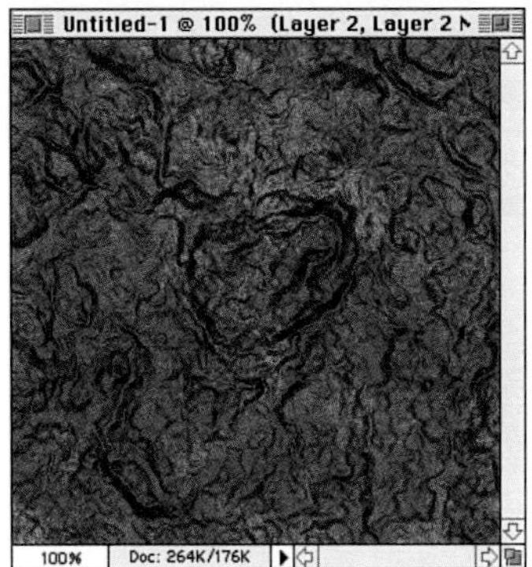

**9** Repeat Step 6 with a fourth color. I used RGB: 96, 0, 31—a strong wine tone. With the layer mask active, select Filter➥Render ➥Clouds. Then apply Filter➥Render ➥Difference Clouds once. Choose Filter➥Stylize➥Find Edges. The image will probably be mostly dark red. Select Image➥Adjust➥Invert (Command-I)[Control-I]. Select Image➥Adjust➥ Levels. Move the right Input slider to the start of the data. Move the left Input slider almost next to it as shown. The object is to leave only streaks of red in the image.

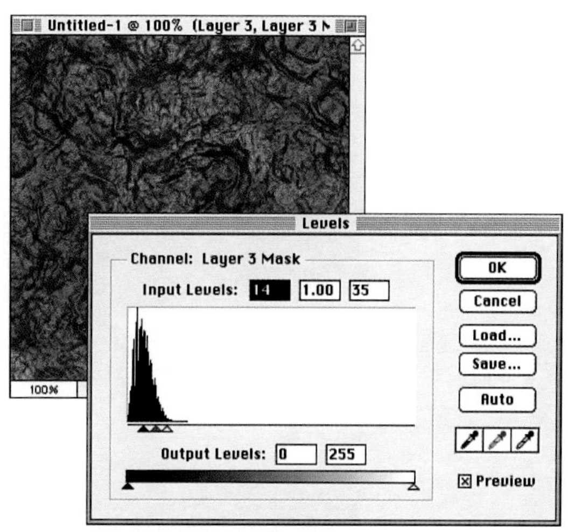


**10** Duplicate Layer 1, which is the peach layer. Position the layer at the top of the Layers list. Make the layer mask active. Select Filter➥ Blur➥Gaussian Blur. I used a Radius of 2.0. You need a fairly small Radius for this to work well. Apply Filter➥ Stylize➥Find Edges. Select Image➥ Adjust➥Invert (Command-I) [Control-I]. Select Image➥Adjust➥ Auto Levels.

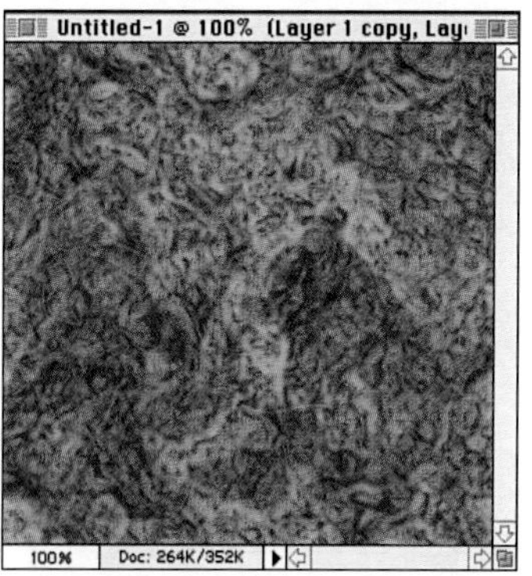


**11** Select Image➥Adjust➥Levels. Drag the left Input slider part way toward the right to darken the peach streaks.

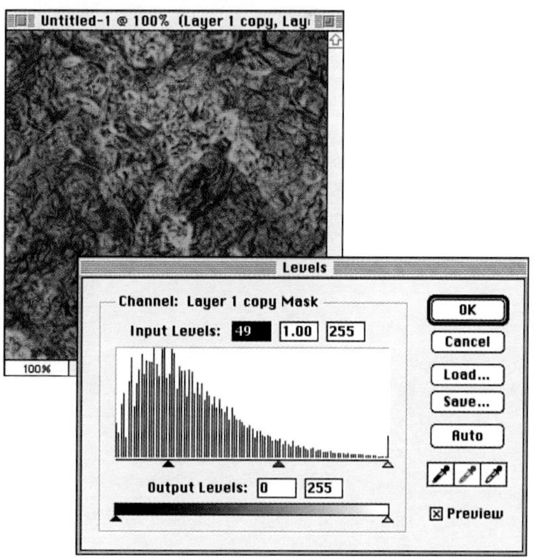

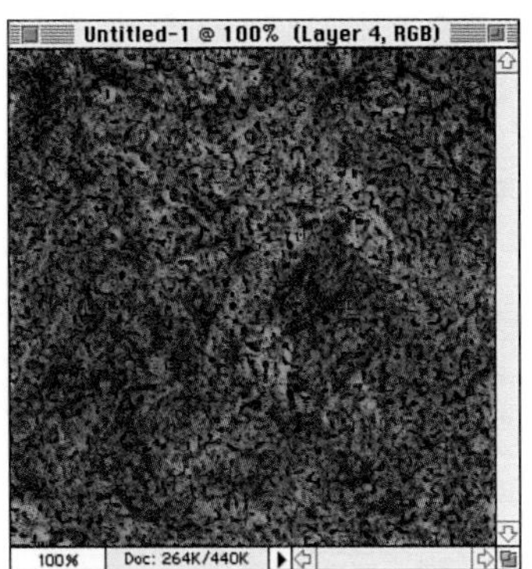


**12** Repeat Step 6 with a fifth color. I selected RGB: 31, 46, 28—a very dark grayed-green. After you create the layer mask, switch foreground/background colors so that black is your background color. With the layer mask active, select Filter➡Pixelate➡Pointillize (5). Apply Filter➡Stylize➡Find Edges two times.

**13** Create a new layer. Select Image➡Apply Image. Make Layer 3 the source Layer and the Layer Mask the Channel.

**14** Change the blending mode to Hard Light. Choose Filter➡Stylize➡Emboss (Angle: 132°, Height: 2 pixels, Amount: 77).

**15** Temporarily change the blending mode to Normal. Load the selection from Layer 5 (Command-Option-~) [Control-Alt-~]. Select Image➥ Adjust➥Levels (Command-L) [Control-L]. Move the white Output slider to about 225 to cut down on some of the embossed highlights. Change the blending mode back to Hard Light.

**16** Create a new layer. Switch to default colors. Select Filter➥ Render➥Clouds. Then select Filter➥Noise➥Add Noise (Distribution: Gaussian, Monochromatic). I used an Amount of 65. Choose Filter➥Sketch➥Plaster (Image Balance: 20, Smoothness: 2. Light Position: Top). This makes another rough surface. Apply Image➥ Adjust➥Threshold and leave the balance near the center. Change the blending mode to Hard Light. Choose Filter➥Stylize➥Emboss (Angle: 130°, Height: 2 pixels, Amount: 100). Select Filter➥Blur➥ Gaussian Blur (0.6) to smooth the embossing a little bit. ■

The Displace filter can be used in conjunction with the Darken blending mode to create interlaced patterns of seemingly great complexity. Here I use it to create a metallic rosette pattern.

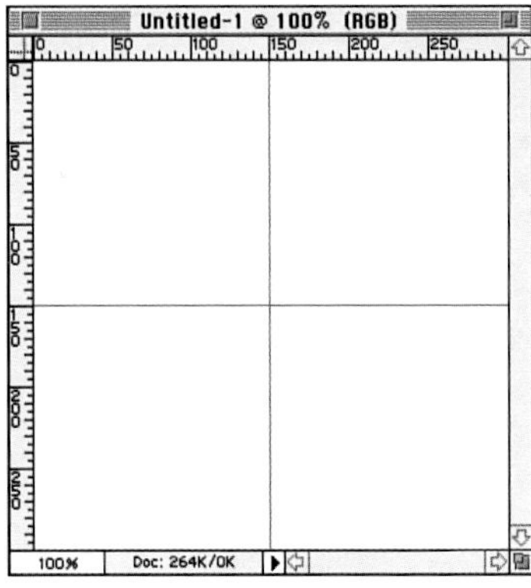


**1** Create a new file 300×300 pixels. Turn on the rulers (Command-R) [Control-R]. Add a horizontal guide at the 150-pixel mark. Add a vertical guide at the 150-pixel mark.

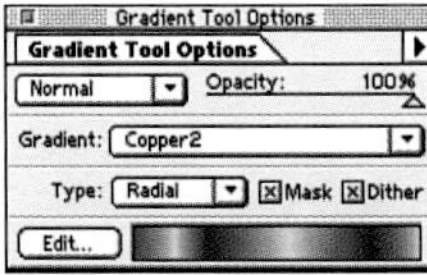


**2** Double-click the Gradient tool. Use the Copper2 preset from the *Photoshop Textures Magic* CD-ROM and change the Gradient Type to Radial.

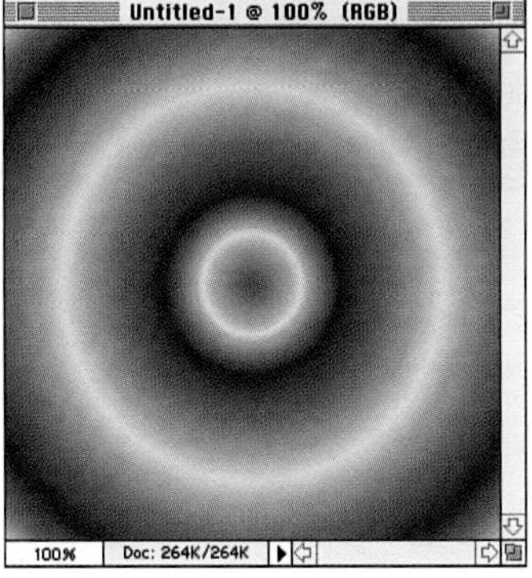


**3** Place your cursor in the center of the image and drag it to the upper-right corner to create a radial Gradient. Hide the guides (Command-;)[Control-;] and turn off the rulers (Command-R) [Control-R].

**TOOLBOX**

Copper2 gradient preset

**4** We need to create a displacement map—an image that the Displace filter uses to move the pixels in the image being filtered. Black and white pixels in the displacement map create the most movement. Create a new file 300×300 pixels, grayscale mode. Select the rectangular Marquee tool and set a fixed size to 300 pixels wide × 50 pixels high. Drag the marquee to the top of the image. Switch to default colors. Fill with foreground color.

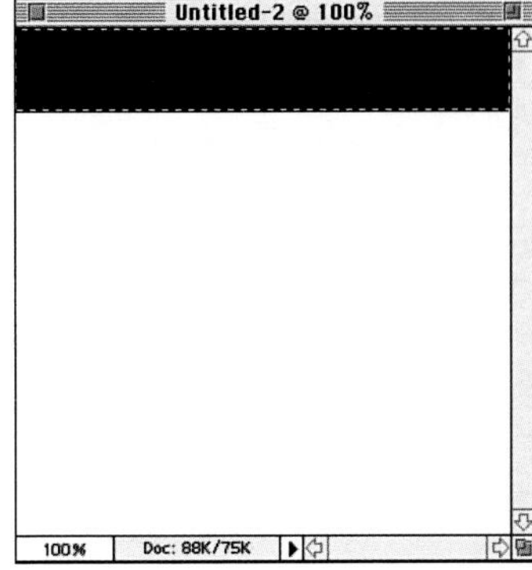


**5** Set the fixed size of the rectangular Marquee to 300 pixels wide × 100 pixels high. Drag the marquee to the top of the image (it will select 50 black and 50 white pixels).

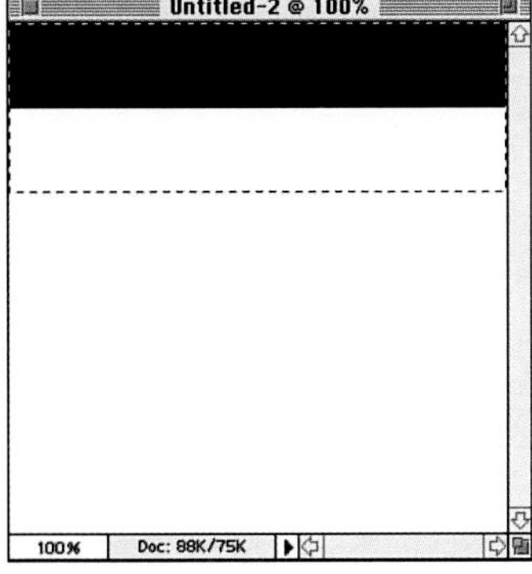


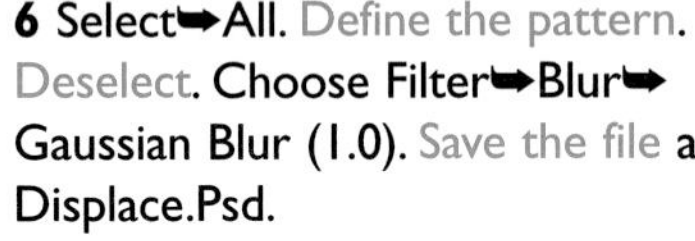

**6** Select➡All. Define the pattern. Deselect. Choose Filter➡Blur➡Gaussian Blur (1.0). Save the file as Displace.Psd.

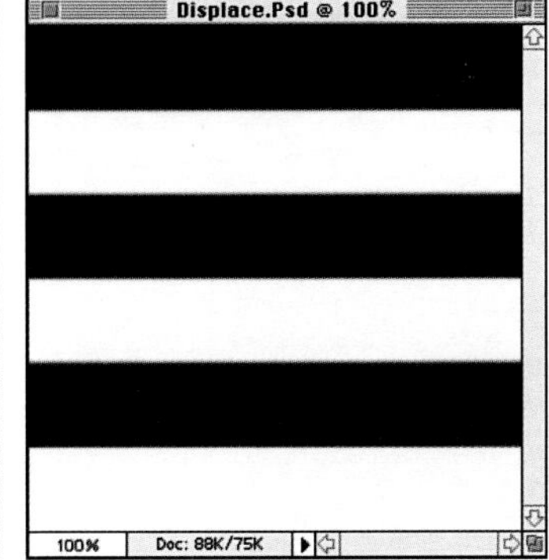

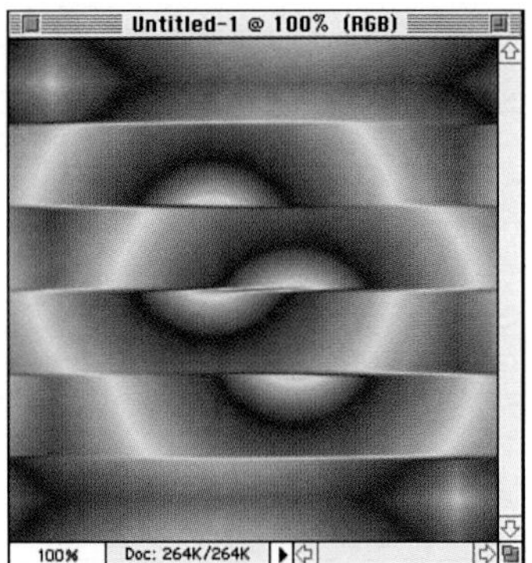


**7** Click on the gradient image to make it active. Choose Filter➡Distort➡Displace. I made the Horizontal and Vertical Scales both 20%, and set the Displacement Map to Stretch to Fit and the Undefined Areas to Wrap Around. Click OK. When you are prompted for the name of the file to use as a displacement map, select the Displace.Psd that you just created.

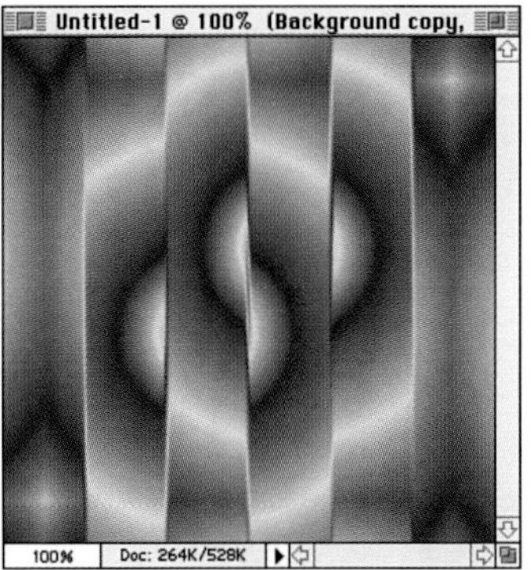


**8** Duplicate the Background layer (Background copy). Select Layer➡Transform➡Rotate 90° Clockwise.

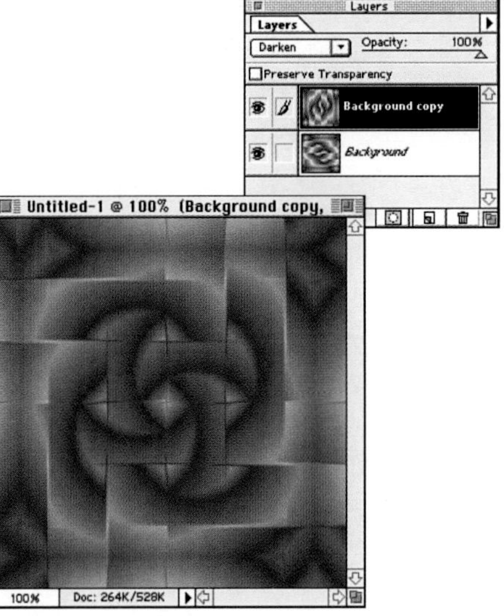


**9** Change the blending mode to Darken. This is the basic pattern unit, but it needs to be made seamless before you use it.

**10** Make the pattern seamless using the Mosaic method.

## VARIATIONS

If you want an even stronger rosette in the center of the pattern, after you have displaced the image in Step 7, apply Filter➡Distort➡Displace again using a Scale factor of –10%, both horizontally and vertically. Set the Displacement Map to Stretch to Fit and the Undefined Areas to Wrap Around. Use the Displace.Psd map that you created. Make the pattern seamless using the simple method.

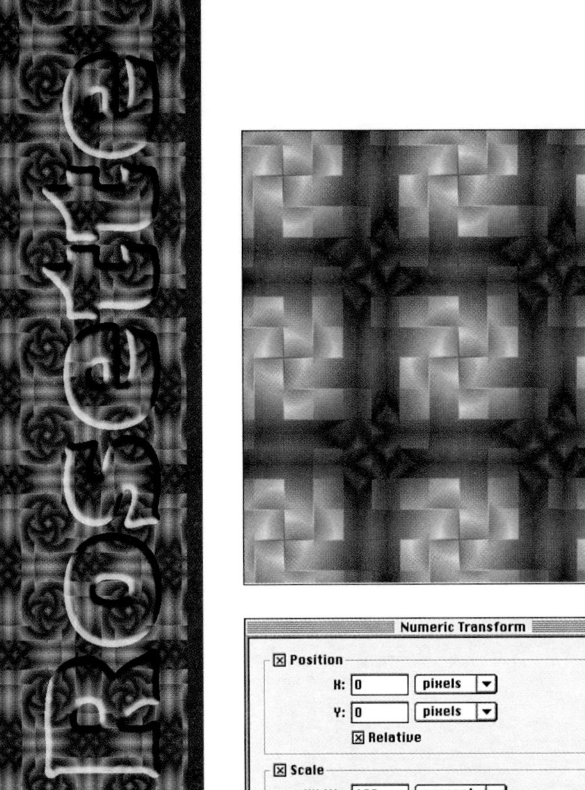

To create a pattern that does not have a strong center, you can use the Copper gradient preset that comes with Photoshop 4.0. Follow all of the original instructions, but choose the Copper gradient instead of the one provided on the *Photoshop Textures Magic* CD-ROM.



You can get an interlaced effect with a little bit more work. I used the Copper gradient as the starting point because that enhances the interlaced effect. Complete the original instructions through Step 7 (except for the choice of the gradient). Duplicate the Background layer. Use the Numeric Transform command (Shift-Command-T)[Shift-Control-T] to rotate the layer 60°. Duplicate the background layer again. Use the Numeric Transform command again to rotate the layer –60°. Make the Background copy layer active. Change the blending mode to Darken. Define the pattern. Fill any desired selection with the pattern.

Finally, you can get a hexagonal interlaced effect. Use the same instructions as used in the interlaced effect. When you duplicate the Background layer a second time, use the Numeric Transform command (Shift-Command-T) [Shift-Control-T] to rotate the layer 120°.

You can use this hexagonal effect (or any of the others) as a bump map rather than as a pattern. Create a new file of the desired size. Switch the foreground color to the color that you want your texture to be. I chose RGB: 154, 161, 204. Fill with foreground color. Create a new layer. Fill with one of the pattern variations. Select Image➥Adjust➥Desaturate (Shift-Command-U)[Shift-Control-U]. Choose Filter➥Stylize➥Emboss (Angle: 147°, Height: 3 pixels, Amount: 100). Change the blending mode to Hard Light. ■

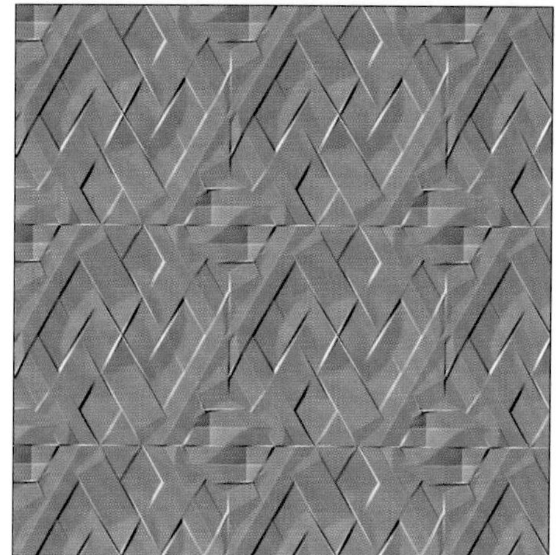

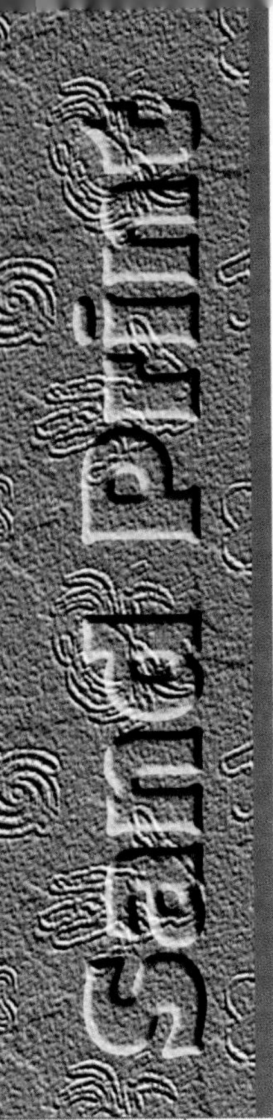


I have always lived about an hour away from the New Jersey shore, and my summers growing up were spent, in part, by the sea (or "down the shore" as the Philadelphiaism goes). I remember spending hours drawing in the wet sand as the tide receded. I used my finger, a convenient seashell, or a left-over popsicle stick from the Good Humor man. This texture pays fond tribute to those idyllic long-gone days.

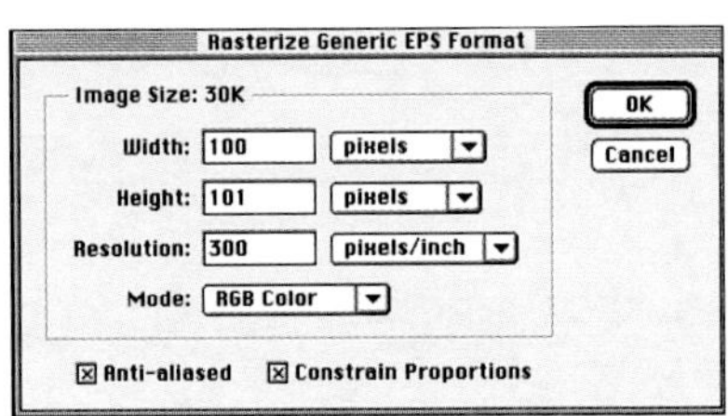


**1** Open the file 03N31.eps from the *Photoshop Textures Magic* CD-ROM. Because it is a vector file, you are asked to select a size for it within Photoshop. Set the width to 100 pixels, constrain the proportions, and check the Anti-aliased box.

**2** Select Image➡Canvas Size and change the size to 300×300 pixels. Leave the Anchor in the center. This gives your pattern more room and centers it all at the same time. Create a new Background layer.

**3** Duplicate Layer 1. Choose Layer➡Transform➡Flip Horizontal. This adds variety to the pattern-to-be. Select Filter➡Other➡Offset (Wrap Around). Make the Horizontal and Vertical distances one-half of the image dimensions (in this case, 150 pixels right and 150 pixels down).

4 Open the file 01K29.eps. Rasterize it at 100 pixels wide, Constrain Proportions, and select Anti-aliased. Drag and drop centered into the pattern file. Choose Layer➡Free Transform (Command-T) [Control-T]. Place the cursor outside of the bounding box and rotate the crab slightly. (The figure shown here has the lower two image layers made invisible for clarity). Press (Enter)[Return] to execute the transformation.

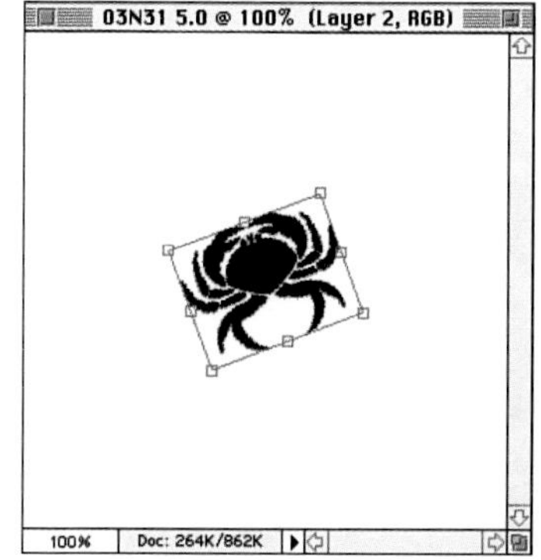


5 Select Filter➡Other➡Offset (Wrap Around). Make the Horizontal distance one-half of the image dimensions (150) and the Vertical distance 0.

6 Duplicate Layer 2. Reapply the Offset filter (Command-F) [Control-F]. This puts the new layer back into the center. Select Layer➡Transform➡Flip Horizontal. Select Filter➡Other➡Offset (Wrap Around). Make the Horizontal distance 0 this time, and the Vertical distance one-half of the image dimensions (150 pixels). This sends the crab to the top and bottom of the image.

**7** You now have a completely seamless pattern, but there is still a lot of white space. Open the files 03N31.eps (Hand), 06A11.eps (Arrow), 08B33.eps (Heart), and 07D04.eps (Spiral). Rasterize these at 50 pixels wide, Constrain Proportions, Anti-aliased on.

**8** Drag and drop the star into the white space on the upper-left. Do not try to center it in the space—the result is more interesting if you preserve some randomness. Drag and drop the spiral into the upper-right white space, the heart into the lower-left, and the arrow into the lower-right. If you want, rotate the arrow slightly so that it does not seem so artificial.

**9** Select➥All. Define the pattern. Create a new file that is three times the tile size (900×900 pixels). Fill with pattern. You need to work the remaining steps inside of a repeated pattern so that you have a 300 pixel square seamless repeat at the end. The Find Edges filter and the Emboss filter that you will use leave artifacts along the image edges. If you were to continue working in the 300-pixel tile, your final tile would not be seamless.

**10** Choose Filter➥Stylize➥Find Edges. This looks nice just as it is (and could make a good background for an ad)!

**11** Choose Filter➥Stylize➥Emboss (Angle: 151°, Height: 2 pixels, Amount: 100). When you finish all of the embossing to be done (a total of three times), the lines will look as if they are drawn in the sand. For this to work, you need to raise the embossing, not sink it into the texture—so keep the angle positive.

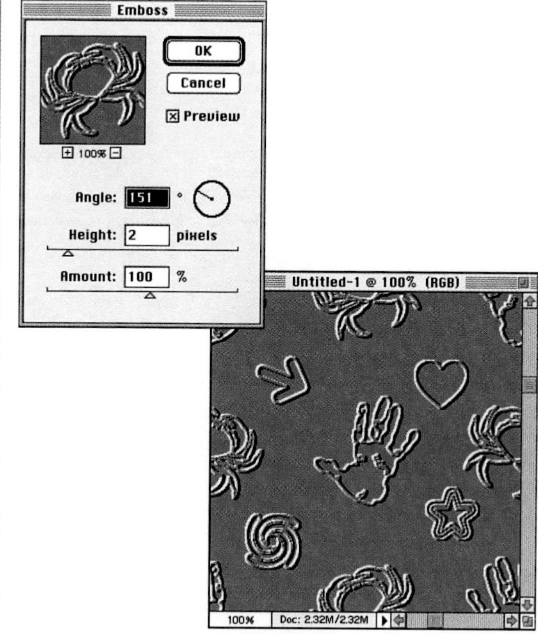


**12** Emboss the image again (Command-F)[Control-F].

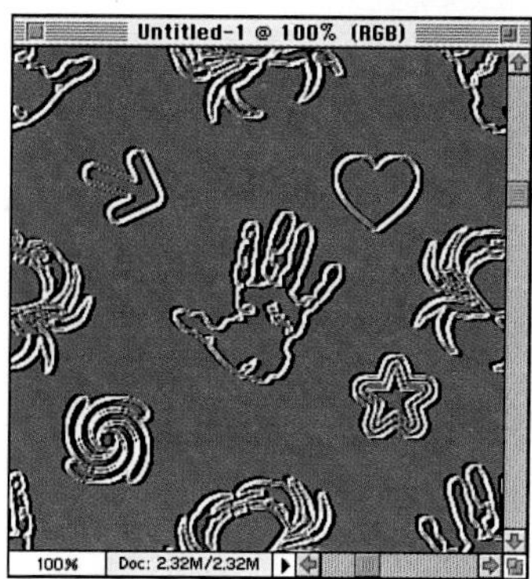


**13** Select Filter➥Noise➥Add Noise (Distribution: Gaussian, Monochromatic). I used an Amount of 42. You don't want the noise to overwhelm the image. Select Filter➥Blur➥Gaussian Blur (0.5). Use a very small blur here. Choose Filter➥Stylize➥Emboss (Angle: 151°, Height: 2 pixels, Amount: 100). Reuse the settings from the previous steps. Your artwork is now etched in sand.

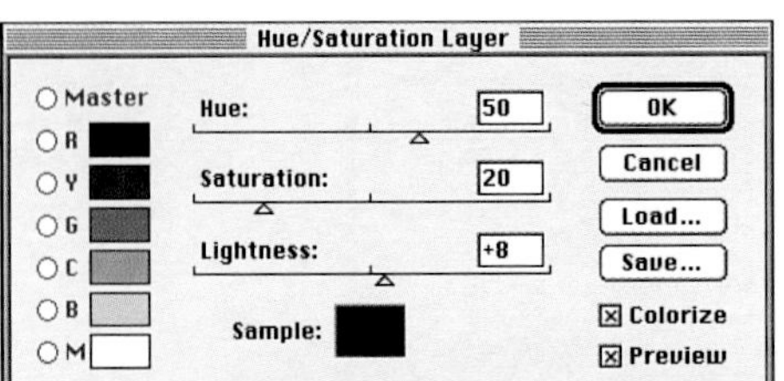


**14** Gray sand is not particularly appealing. Create an adjustment layer for Hue/Saturation. Click Colorize. I moved the Hue to 50, the Saturation to 20 and the Lightness to +8. You can pick your favorite "sand" color.

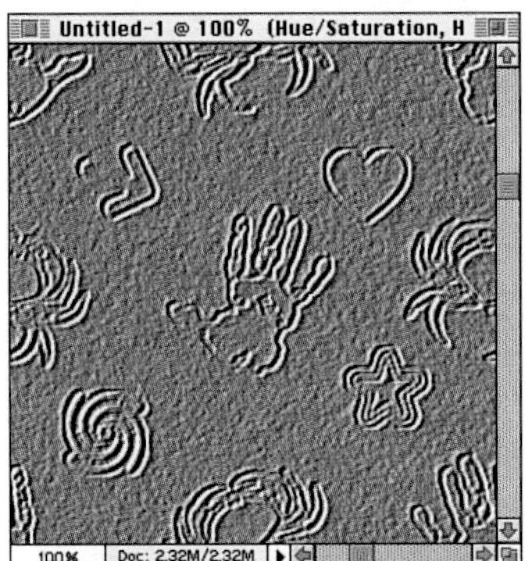


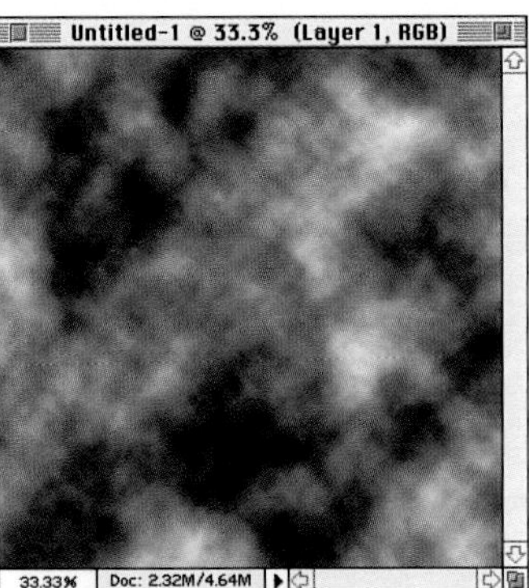


**15** The sand in tidal areas is not flat. In addition to the sand texture, you can see where the waves lapped against the beach and then receded. You can simulate that play of waves. Create a new layer at the top of the Layers list. Switch to default colors. Choose Filter➥ Render➥Clouds.

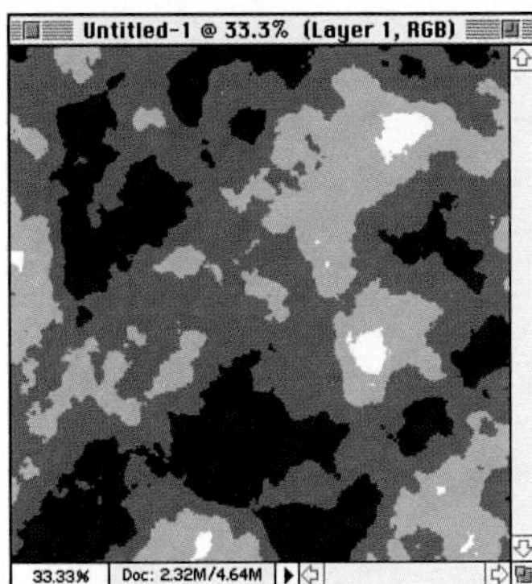


**16** Select Image➥Adjust➥ Posterize. I used 5 levels, but this depends on the clouds formation in your image. Pick a number of levels that looks good to you, but keep it relatively simple.

**17** Select Filter➥Noise➥Add Noise (Distribution: Gaussian, Monochromatic). I used an Amount of 42. Select Filter➥Blur➥Gaussian Blur. Use the same settings as before (0.5). Emboss the image with the same settings used in Step 11. Change the blending mode to Hard Light. You now have an instant trip to the shore.

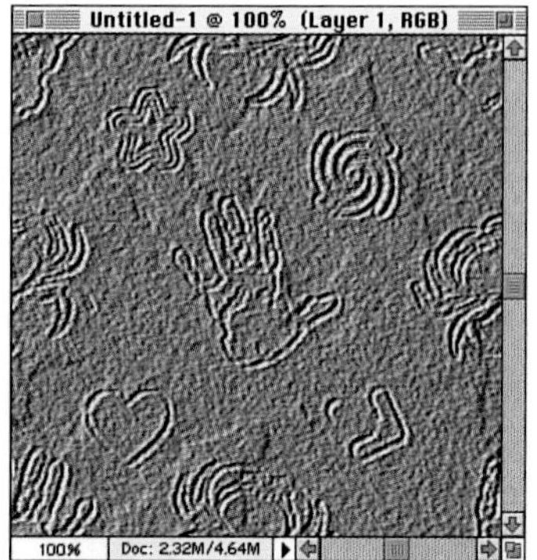


**18** Select the rectangular Marquee and set a fixed size to 300×300 pixels (or the size of your original tile). Drag the Marquee into the center of the image. It need not be exactly the center, but it needs to be near the center. Define the pattern. Create a new file of the desired size for your intended use. Fill with pattern. Once you are sure that your repeat is seamless, you can crop (Image➥Crop) the 900×900 pixels image down to the single repeat tile.

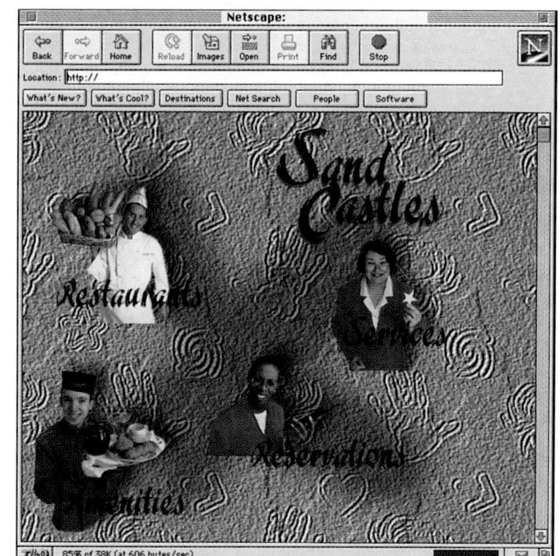

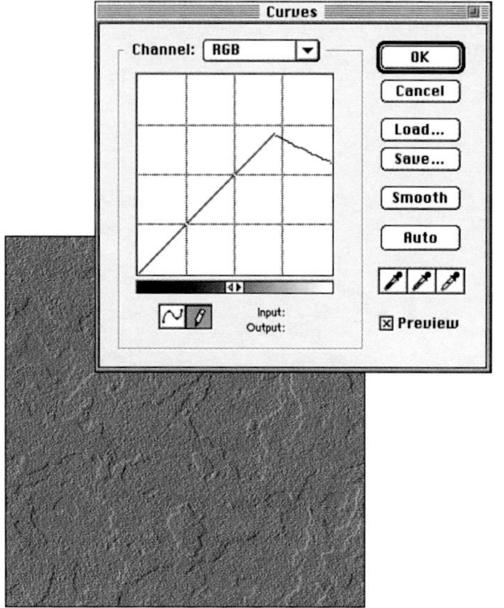

## VARIATIONS

If you want just the sand texture and no pattern, start your image from Step 15. When you have constructed the sand, Create an adjustment layer for Hue/Saturation above the sand. You can make a repeat pattern from sand, but it is more natural if you create it at the needed size. If the highlights are too strong from the embossing, choose Image➥Adjust➥Curves, and use the Pencil tool in the Curves dialog box as shown to cut off some of the highlights.

## Slate

To create slate, create a new file at the final size for your texture (slate doesn't repeat well either). Change the foreground color to a deep charcoal gray. Fill the image with the foreground color. Select Filter➥Noise➥Add Noise (Distribution: Gaussian, Monochromatic Off). I used an Amount of 56. Choose Filter➥Pixelate➥Crystallize. I used a cell size of 24 but almost any amount is okay. Select Filter➥Fade Crystallize. Change the blending mode to Multiply and reduce the opacity to 50%. Select Filter➥Blur➥Motion Blur (Angle: 0° or something near to that). Set the distance to something that does not destroy the range of colors. I used 120. Select Image➥Adjust➥Desaturate. Then select Filter➥Fade Desaturate. Change the blending mode to Dissolve and reduce the Opacity to 50%. Create a new layer. In this layer, complete Steps 15 and 16 from the original instructions. Double-click the rectangular Marquee tool. Make sure the Feather is set to 0 and the Style is Normal. Select the left 1/5 of the image (across the full height of the image, but only about 1/5 of the width). You need to stretch the posterized clouds to elongate them in a manner similar to slate. Choose Layer➡Free Transform (Command-T)[Control-T]. Drag the middle handle on the right side of the selection until it reaches the right side of the image. Press (Enter)[Return] to execute the transformation. Proceed with Step 17. For added highlights, duplicate Layer 1.

You can also use only the offset technique from Steps 1 through 9 to create a comic-book like wrapping paper effect. If you use a single application of the Emboss filter and a subdued setting on the Hue/Saturation layer, you create a well-bred wrapping paper…

…or, you can use all primary colors and apply Filter➡Pixelate➡Color Halftone to the clip art, and create a very wild wrapping paper. Both of these images use the animals from the Art Parts clip art collection from FontHaus. ■

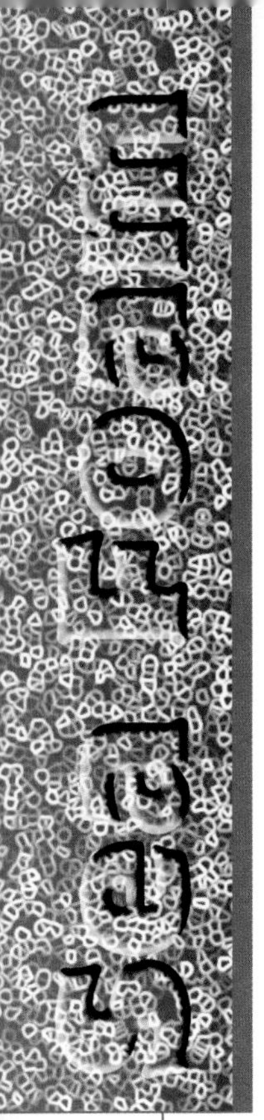

Picture waves breaking at the shore, and the sea foam boiling as the tide crashes up against dry land. This effect will never win a photographic look-alike competition, but it is a good artistic substitute. Besides, you never know when you might want to draw a fish tank. Sea foam can also be sized correctly for printing—it looks even more realistic when viewed at lower than 1:1 ratio on your screen.

**1** Create a new file. Mine is 600×400 pixels. This version is not seamless, so make the file as large as you want your texture to be. Switch the foreground color to a medium sea green. I used RGB: 16, 141, 119. Switch the background color to a deep sea green/blue. I used RGB: 39, 71, 61.

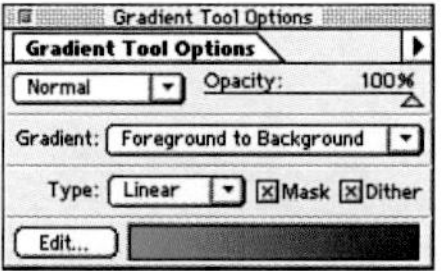


**2** Double-click the Gradient tool and change the Gradient to Foreground to Background, set the opacity to 100%, and set the Type to linear. Drag the Gradient cursor from the top-left corner of the image to the bottom-right.

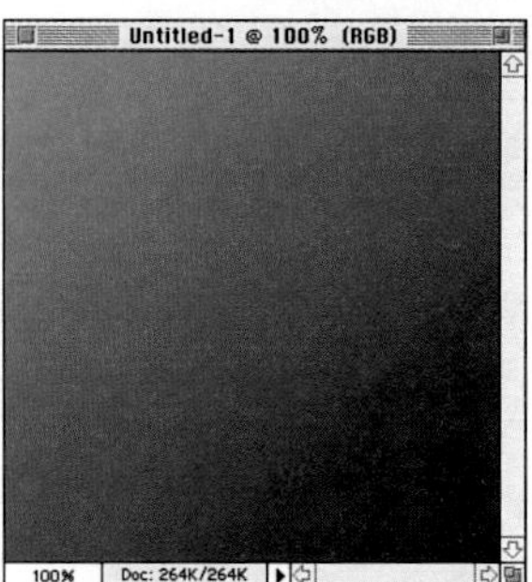


**3** Change the opacity of the Gradient tool to 30%. Place the Gradient cursor in the center of the image and drag on a straight line to the bottom of the image. This adds another subtle dimension to the Gradient.

**4** Switch the background color to a dark navy blue. I used RGB: 0, 42, 99. Set the Gradient opacity to 10%. Create a new layer. Drag the Gradient cursor from the top to the bottom of the new layer. Add two additional gradients to this layer. Both should move on the diagonal. Place one from top-left to bottom-right, and the other from top-right to bottom-left. Let both of these gradients start and end about 1/4 of the distance from the edge of the image.

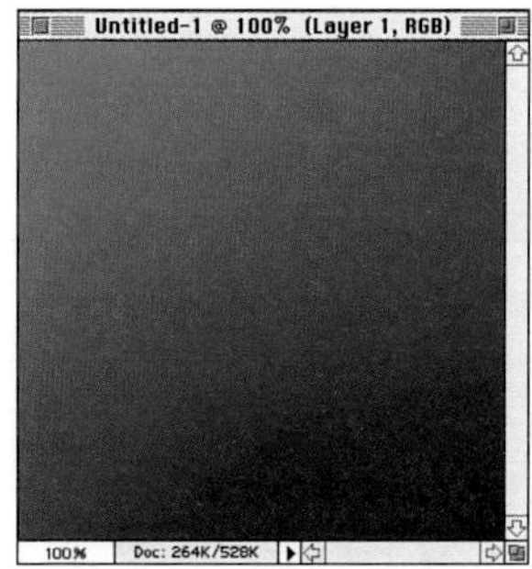


**5** Create a new layer. Switch the foreground color to a greener sea green. I used RGB: 0,124.94. Switch the background color to a gold or rust. I used RGB: 130, 100, 23.

**6** Change the Gradient tool opacity to 60%. Drag the Gradient cursor from about 1/8 of the way from the top to about 1/8 of the distance from the bottom. These three layers are your background "sea." If you are not happy with the color, you can adjust it now, or do it later (because there is no pressing need to flatten the layers).

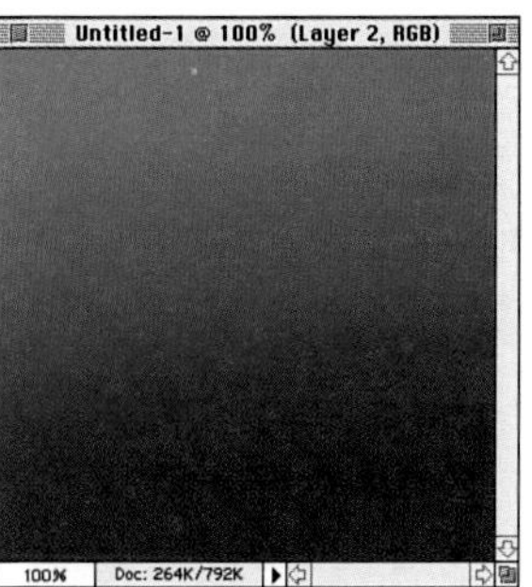


**7** Create a new layer. Switch to default colors. Fill the layer with the background color. Select Filter➥ Pixelate➥Pointillize. I used a cell size of 9, though you might want a smaller one if you are going to use this texture at 72 dpi. The Pointillize filter uses your background color as the background behind the dots that it creates. For this effect to work, the background color selected in the toolbox must be white.

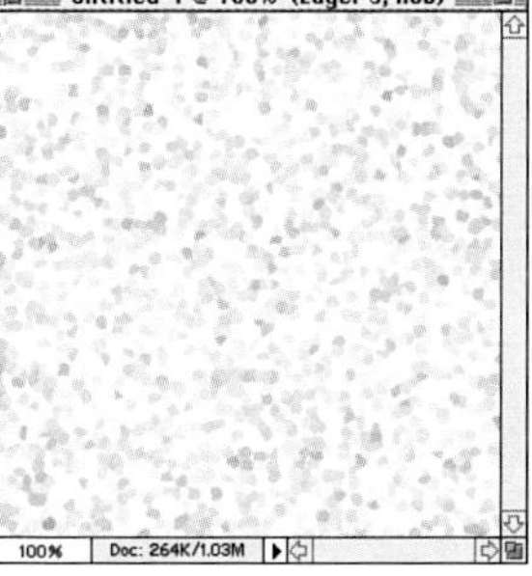

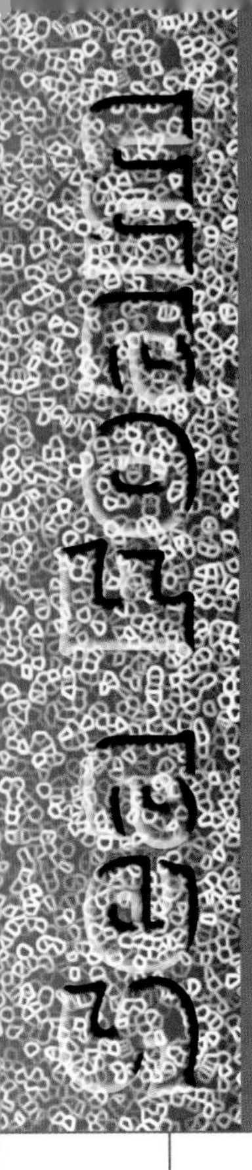

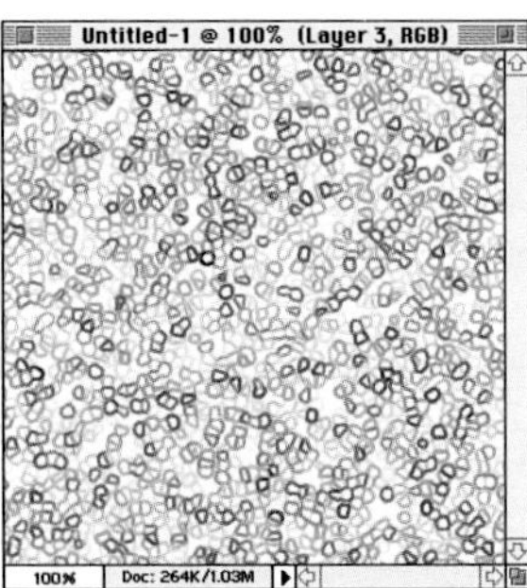


**8** Select Filter➡Stylize➡Find Edges. Choose Image➡Adjust➡Auto Levels to make the edge colors sharper.

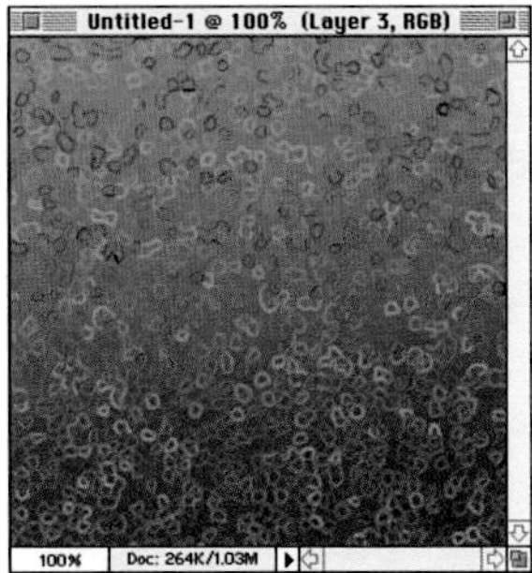


**9** Here's where it gets tricky. Show the Channels palette. Load the selection in the Composite channel by (Command)[Control]-clicking the RGB channel name in the Channels palette. This creates a selection from the values in the RGB channel. Pixels that are white are totally selected; darker pixels are proportionally less selected. Press the Delete key. *Do not deselect.*

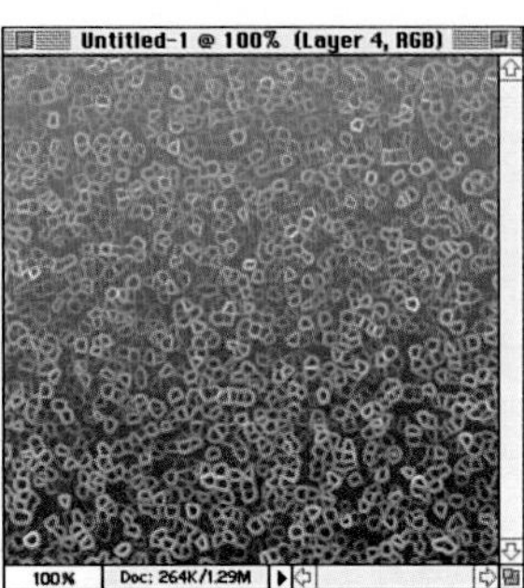


**10** At this point, you have a wonderful background for water in a fish tank. Create a new layer. Reverse the selection (Select➡Inverse). Fill with your background color (white). *Do not deselect.*



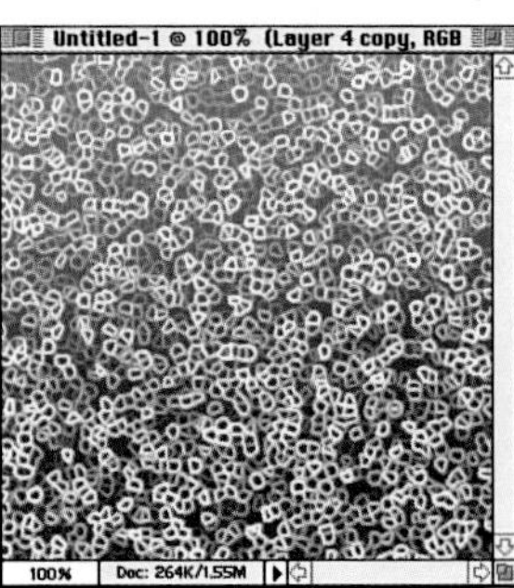


**11** Duplicate Layer 4 (Layer 4 copy). Fill with the background color (white). You may need to fill this layer several times—because the selection is partially transparent, it will become whiter each time you fill it.

**12** Duplicate Layer 4 copy. Select Layer➡Transform➡Flip Horizontal. Deselect. This just mixes the foam up a bit more.

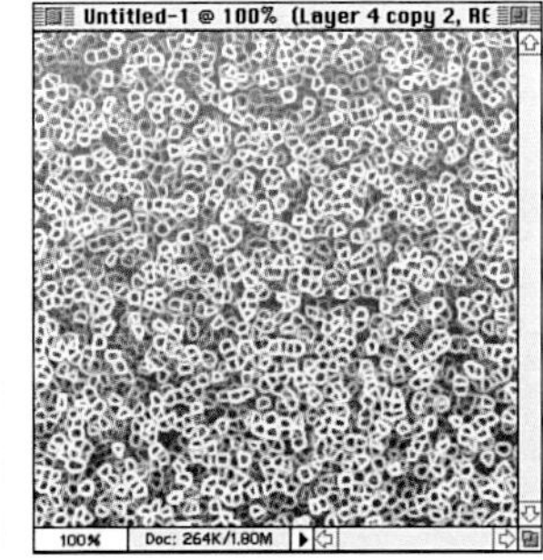


## VARIATIONS

If you want to make the foam look like it is cresting a wave, choose Image➡Rotate Canvas➡90° CW after you have finished the texture. (You really *do* want to rotate the image rather than the layer.) Now, apply Filter➡Distort➡Shear. You rotated the canvas just to apply this filter. Drag the center point of the line to the second line to the left on the graph as you see in the settings here. Click OK. Select Image➡Rotate Canvas➡90°CCW, which puts the image back into its original orientation. Now it looks as if the wave is just breaking. ■

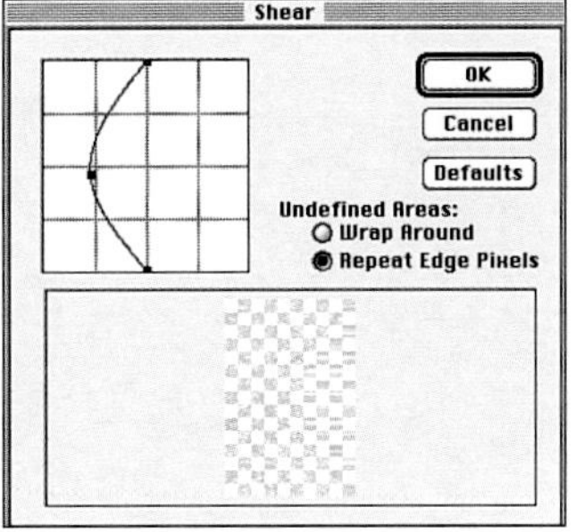


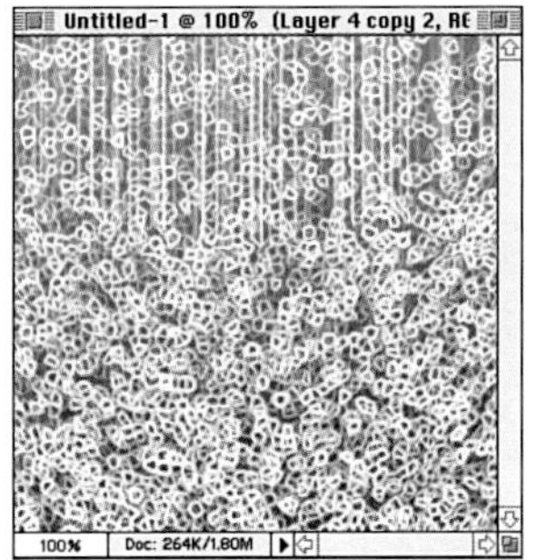

Snakes are not usually the most favorite things to contemplate. Most folks find reptiles to be so...reptilian! But snakeskin is a prized fabric, and the range of patterns possible on snakes is breathtaking. In this simulation, you will generate an organic (that is, random but naturalistic) shape for the snakeskin pattern. It may not resemble a real breed, but it will be both individual and unique—your own species of snake—as flamboyant or subtle as you prefer.

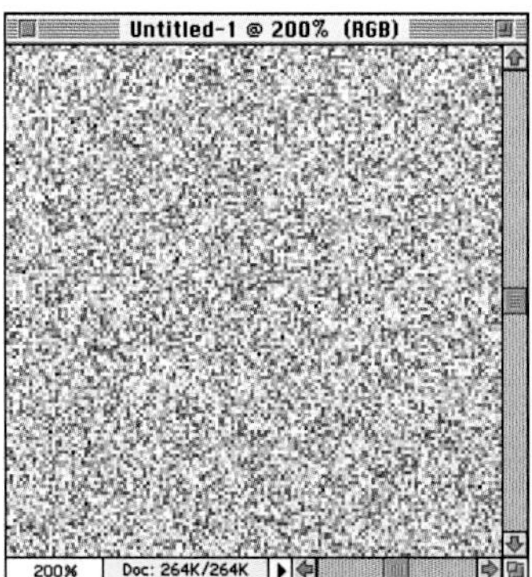


**1** Create a new file. Mine is 300×300 pixels. In this file, you will create the basic snakeskin repeat. The scales will come later. Switch to default colors. Select Filter➥Noise➥Add Noise (Distribution: Gaussian, Monochromatic Off). I used an Amount of 135.

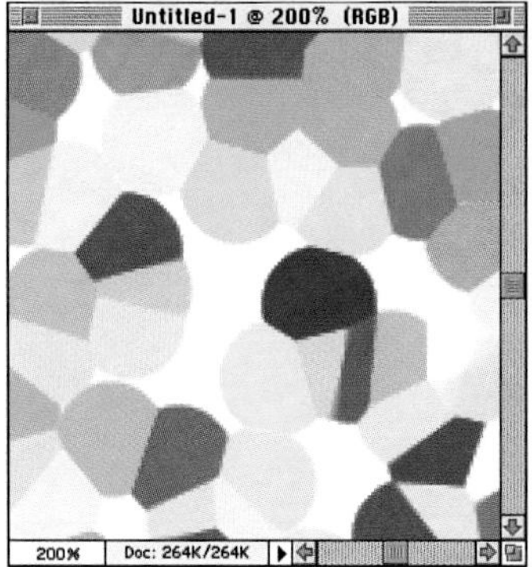


**2** Apply Filter➥Pixelate➥Pointillize. I used a cell size of 35, but the size is not really critical.

**3** Select Filter➥Blur➥Gaussian Blur (60). It is important that a very large blur be used in order to generate a few possible lines that become the snakeskin pattern. Choose Image➥Adjust➥Auto Levels.

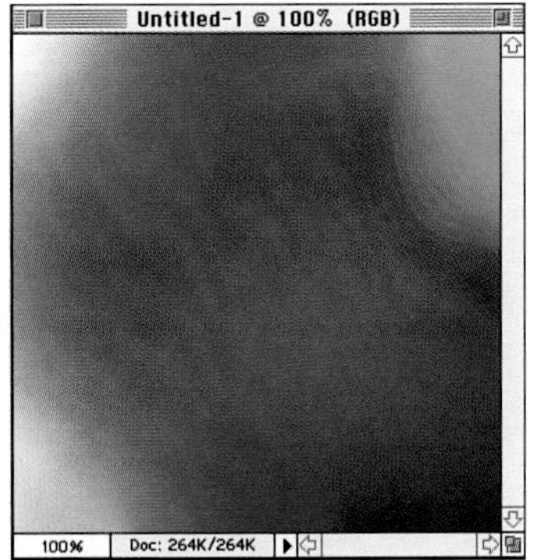


**4** Select Filter➥Stylize➥Trace Contour. I used a Level of 101 with an Upper Edge. When you apply this filter, you see curved, organic lines. Choose the setting that gives you an interesting line or shape in any of the three colors that it shows. Later the shapes will be filled with a series of radial gradients to create the snakeskin background, so it is important that you like the curves.

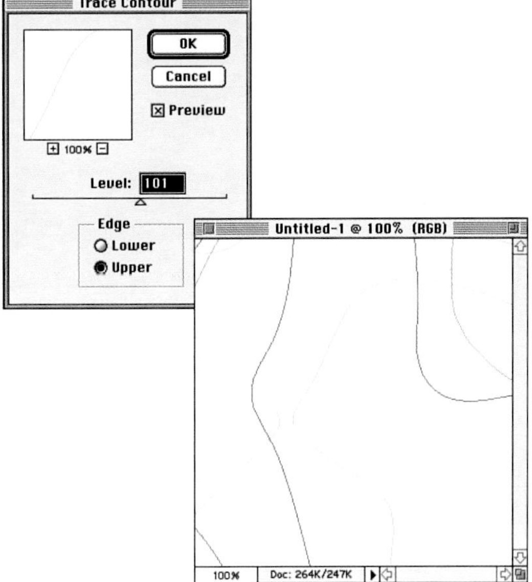

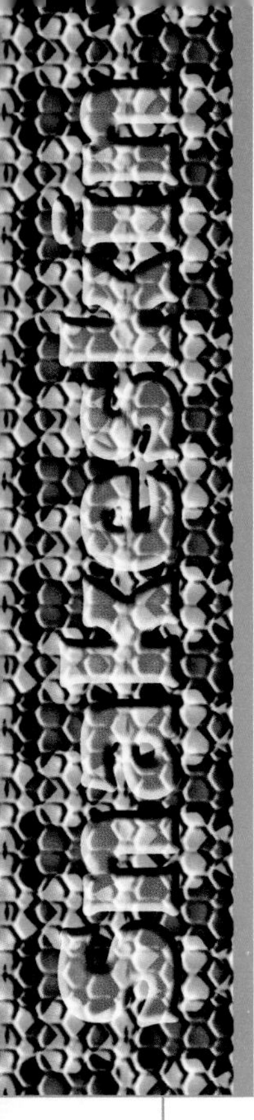


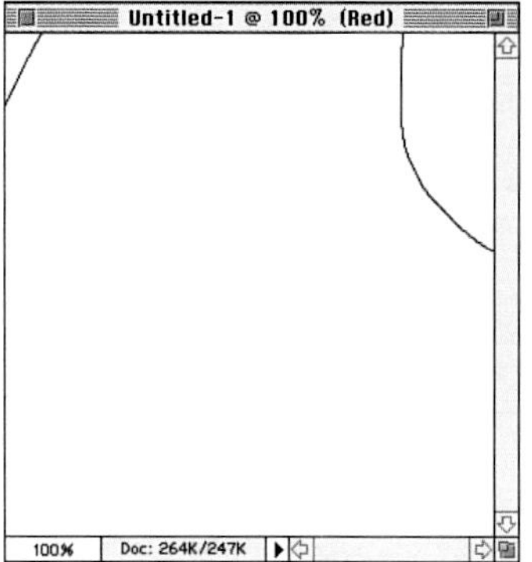


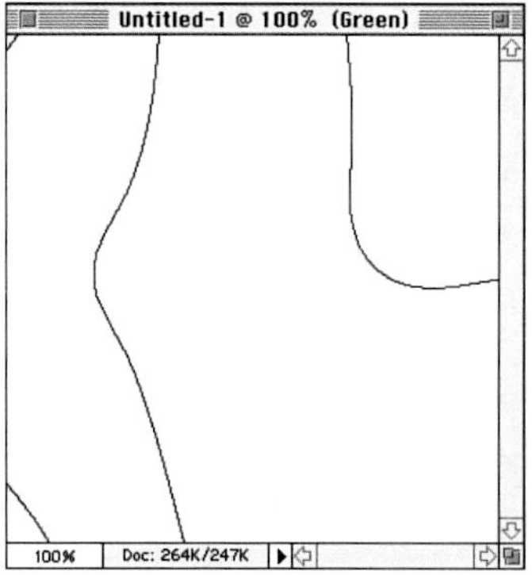


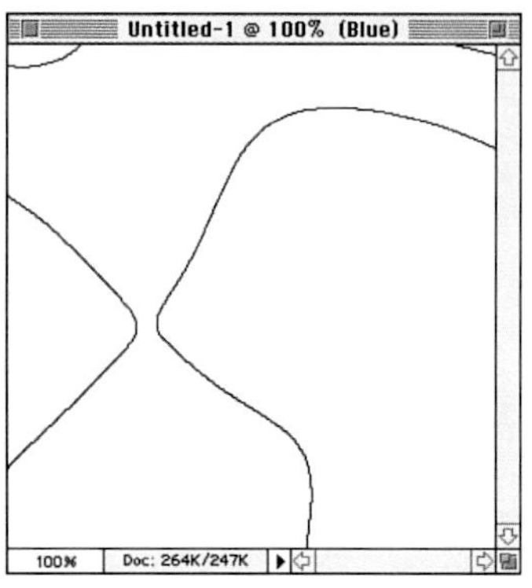


**5** Make the Channels palette active. Make each channel active, one by one, to see which one has the most interesting shape. I like the Blue channel best.

**6** Duplicate the channel to a new document (Untitled-2). Convert the image to Grayscale mode. Convert the image to RGB mode. (You cannot go directly from Multichannel—the image mode that was duplicated—to RGB.)

**7** Double-click the Magic Wand tool and set the Tolerance to 10 with Anti-aliased on. Click inside of one of the shapes to select it. Choose Select➡Modify➡Expand (1 pixel). This allows you to cover the line.

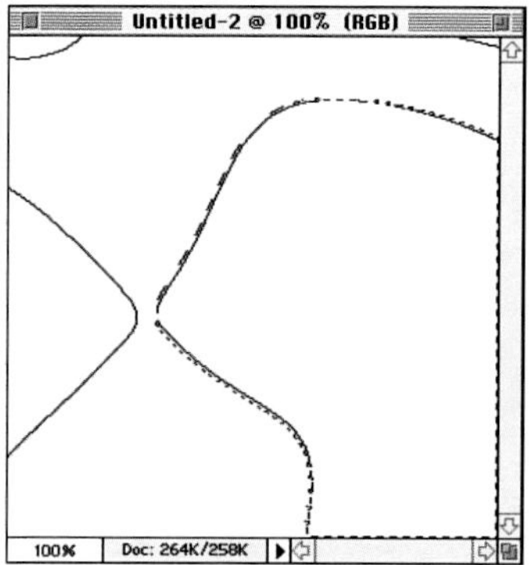


**8** Switch the foreground color to the starting color for one gradient. Switch the background color to the ending color for the gradient. I used red and black. Double-click the Gradient tool and select a Foreground to Background radial gradient (or build your own, more complex one if you prefer). The center of the gradient leaves an "eye," so you need to determine where you want it to be. Place the cursor at the desired center location in the selection and drag to create the gradient.

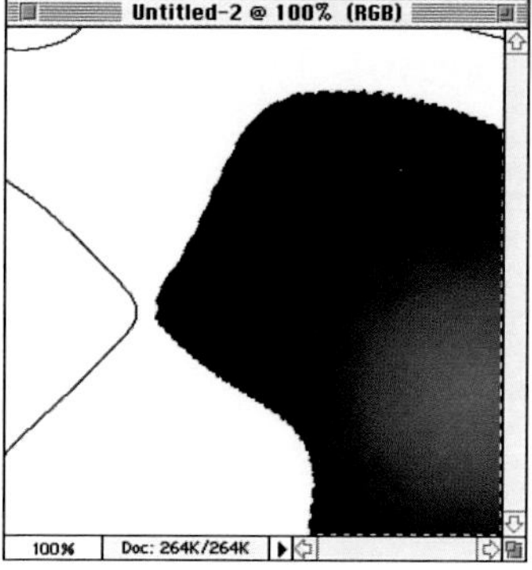


**9** Select and color any additional areas in which you want to use the same gradient.

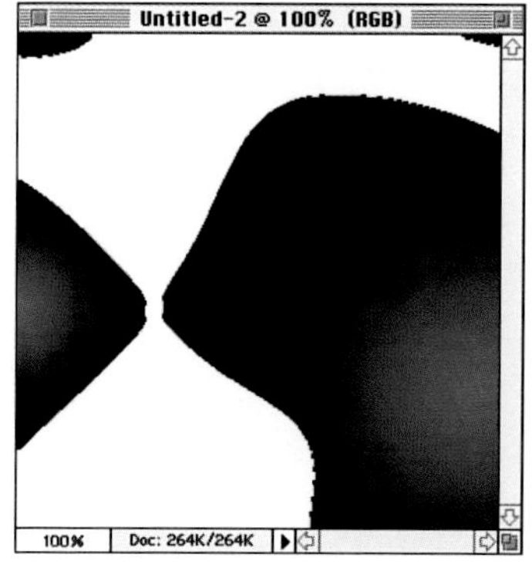

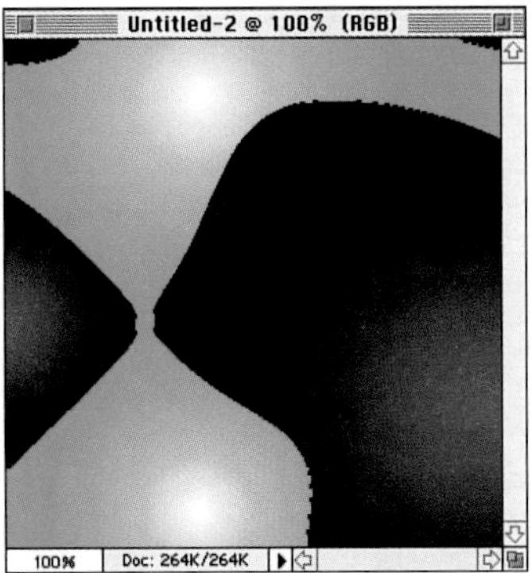


**10** Select one or more areas with a new set of gradient colors. I chose a green-to-white gradient.

**11** Smooth out any rough areas between the gradients using the Blur tool at 100% pressure.

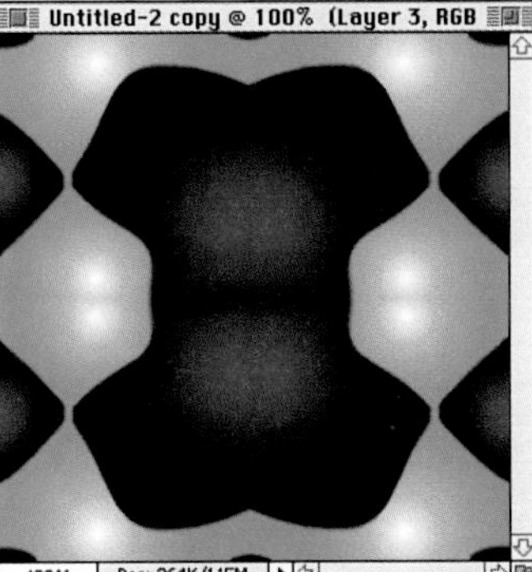


**12** You now have the base repeat unit for the snakeskin. The pattern, however, is probably too large. Save it for future reference. Select Image→Duplicate. Choose Image→Image Size and reduce the image to 50%.

**13** Create Layer 0. Select Image→Canvas Size. Anchor the image to the top-left corner and double the image dimensions. Make the pattern seamless using the Mosaic method. Select Layer→Merge Visible. You will still have a layer (the image should not be flattened).

**14** Select Image➥Image Size and reduce the pattern to your desired width. I set a size of 100×100 pixels to give me a tile that is 1/3 inch in print. Choose Image➥Canvas Size, double the height, and anchor the image in the top center.

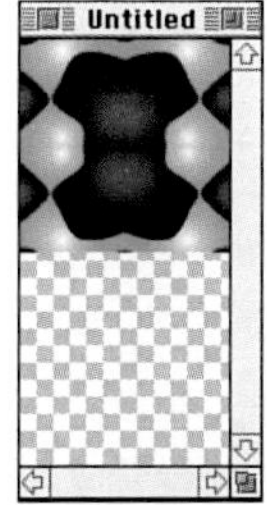


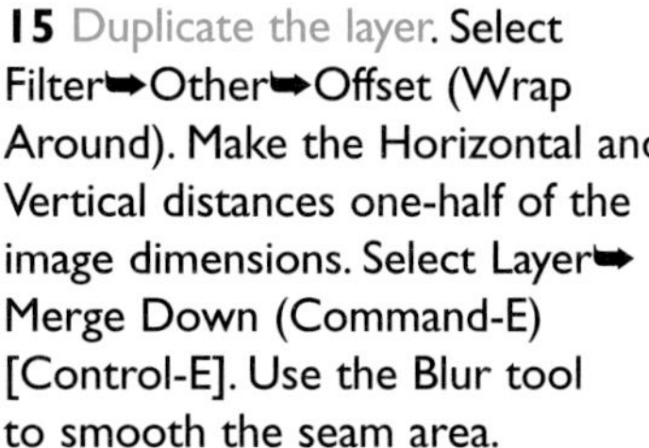

**15** Duplicate the layer. Select Filter➥Other➥Offset (Wrap Around). Make the Horizontal and Vertical distances one-half of the image dimensions. Select Layer➥Merge Down (Command-E) [Control-E]. Use the Blur tool to smooth the seam area.

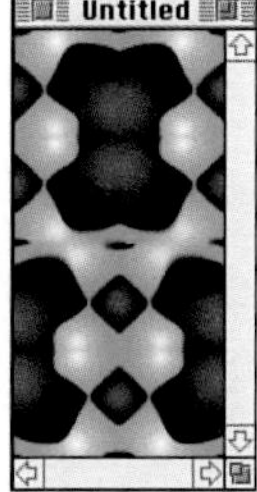


**16** Select Filter➥Other➥Offset, again using the same settings (Command-F)[Control-F]. Make the new seam area smooth using the Blur tool. The tile is now seamless. Select➥All. Define the pattern. Create a new file size that you want for your finished snakeskin. Mine is 900×900 pixels. Fill with pattern. If the texture looks too hard or sharp, soften it by selecting Filter➥Blur➥Gaussian Blur, and setting a Radius of about 1.0.

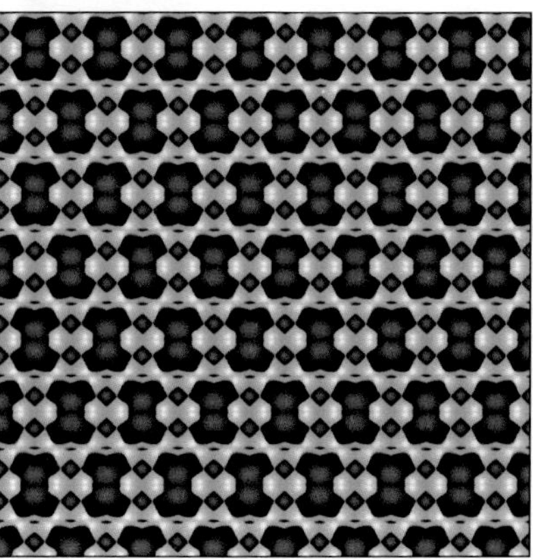

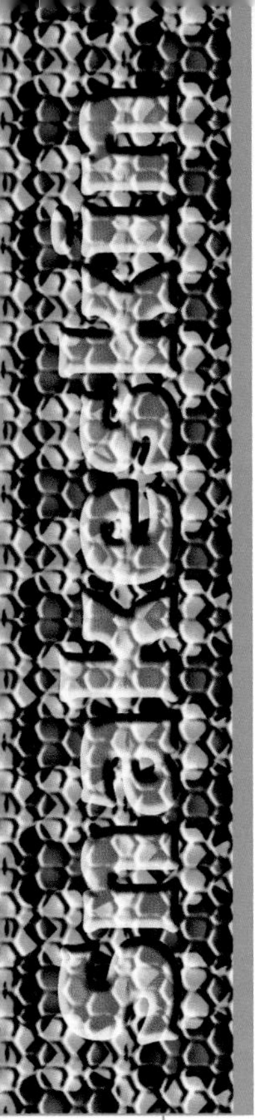

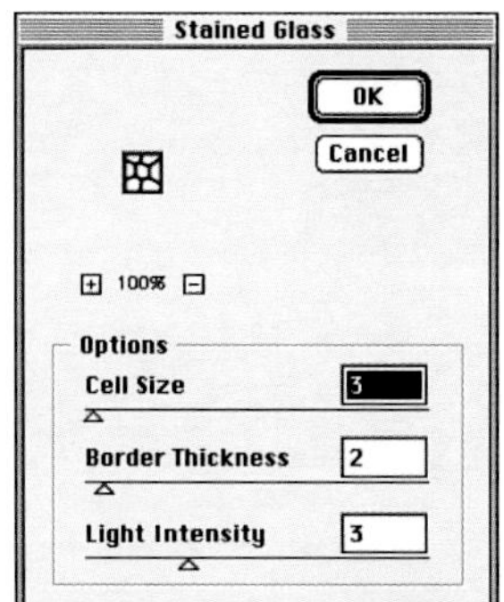


**17** You still need to create the scales. A snake's scales are vaguely hexagonal and honeycombed, but give the impression of occurring in a straight line. The method to create the scales works only at the exact sizes and settings that I used. You can enlarge the result, however, with little difficulty. Create a new file 20 pixels square. Switch to default colors. Select Filter➥Texture➥Stained Glass (Cell Size: 3, Border Thickness: 2, Light Intensity: 3).

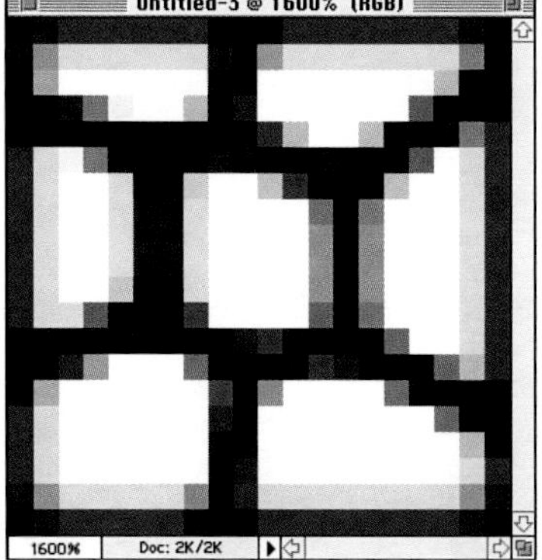


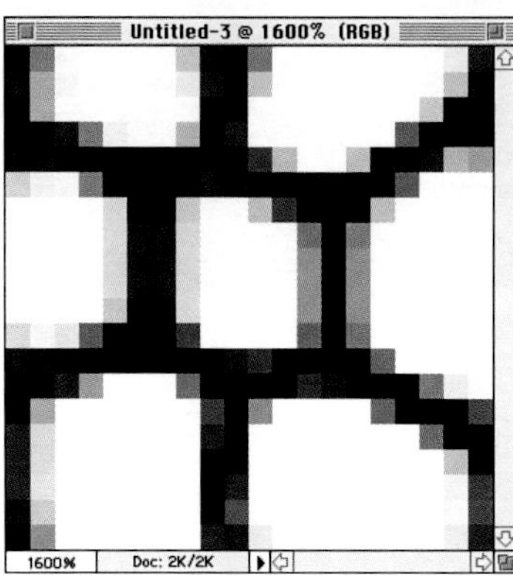


**18** Magnify the image to 1600%. Switch the foreground/background colors. Use a small Paintbrush and remove the border areas of the image, leaving the honeycomb alone.

**19** Select Filter➥Other➥Offset (Wrap Around, Horizontal: 10, Vertical: 10). Touch up the seams where needed. Select Image➥Image Size, and increase the image size to 40×40 pixels.

**20** Select➥All. Define the pattern. Make the snakeskin background image active. Create a new layer. Fill with pattern. Select Filter➥Blur➥Gaussian Blur. I used a Radius of 1.2.

**21** Change the blending mode to Hard Light. Choose Filter➥Stylize➥Emboss (Angle: –67°, Height: 3 pixels, Amount: 100). Now, depending on your partiality to snakes, you can create either a slithering beastie—or a piece of luggage! ■

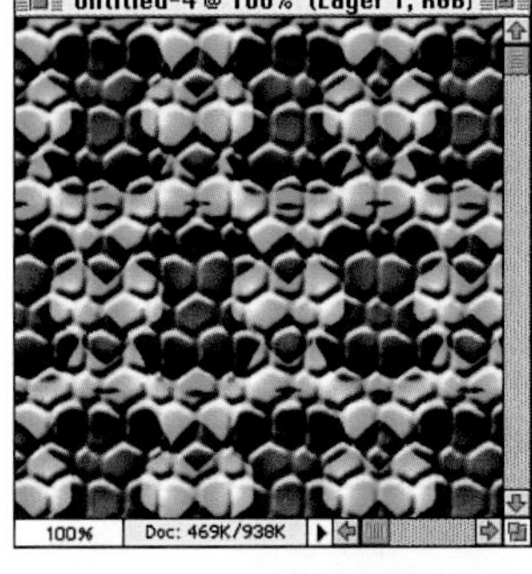


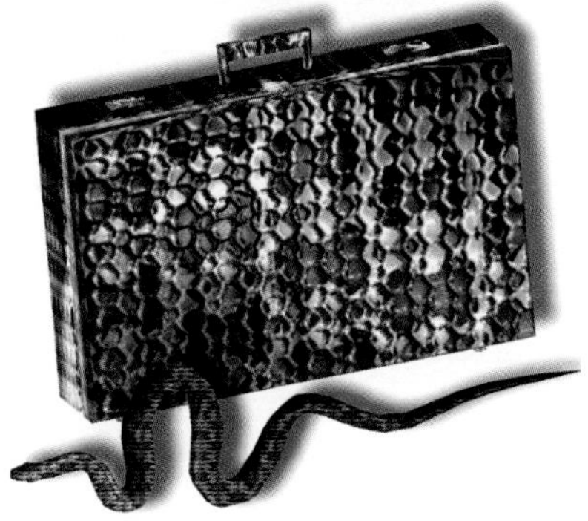

Striped patterns provide a good base for design. You can combine them in infinite ways and make them into plaids or diamond patterns for even more variety.

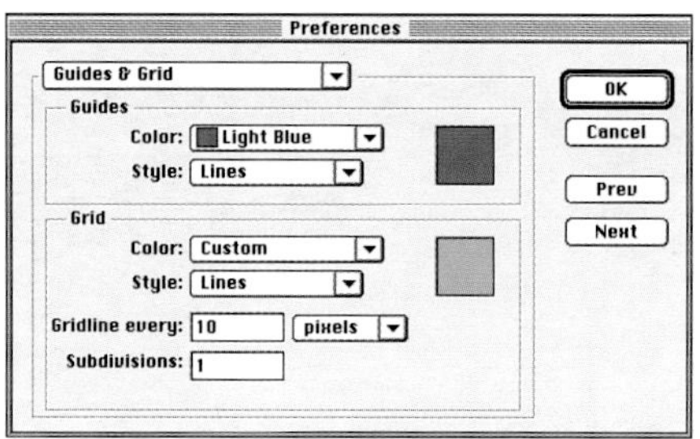


**1** Create a new file 10 pixels wide × 100 pixels high. Select File➡Preferences➡Guides & Grid. Set the Gridlines every 10 pixels with 1 subdivision. Turn on the Grid (Command-")[Control-"]. Turn on Snap to Grid (Shift-Command-") [Shift-Control-"].

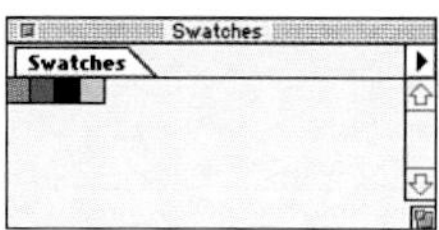


**2** Create a palette of 4 colors. I selected light gray, gold, medium blue, and deep rust. Switch the foreground color to the lightest color (light gray).

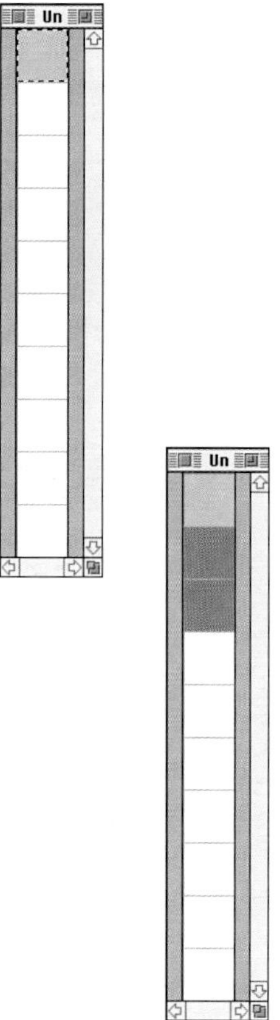


**3** Select the rectangular Marquee and set the fixed size to 10 pixels wide × 10 pixels high. Drag the Marquee to the top of the image. Fill the selection with the foreground color.

**4** Switch the foreground color to your second color (I used gold). Select the next 2 grid squares (after making first selection, press the Shift key and select the next square). Fill with the foreground color.

**5** Follow the chart to complete the rest of the stripe:

Next 3 grid squares: medium blue

Next I grid square: rust

Next I grid square: light gray

Next I grid square: gold

Next I grid square: medium blue

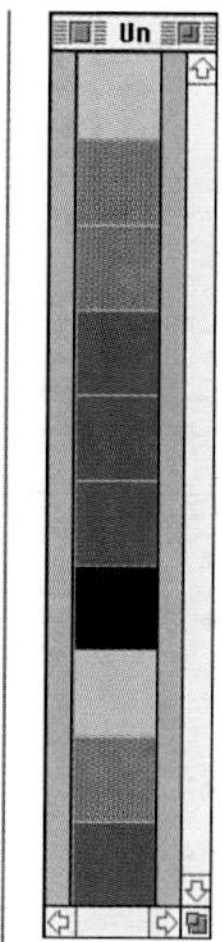

**6** Hide the grid (Command-") [Control-"]. Create Layer 0. Select Image➥Canvas Size (10 pixels wide, 190 pixels high, Anchor: top center square).

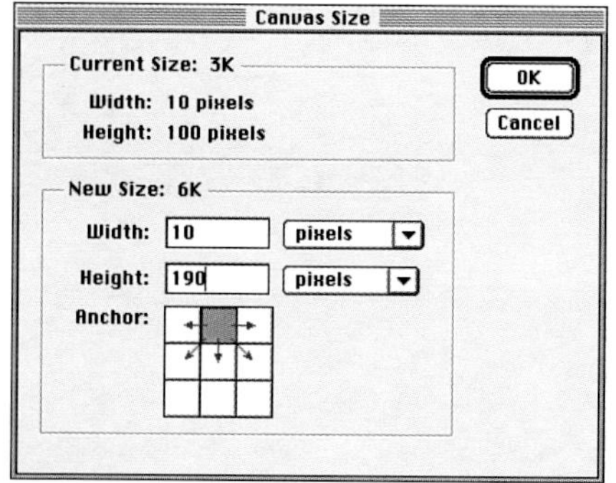


**7** Duplicate Layer 0. Select Layer➥Transform➥Flip Vertical. Select Filter➥Other➥Offset (Horizontal: 0, Vertical: 90, Wrap around). Flatten the image. You have a stripe that is symmetrical from the center.

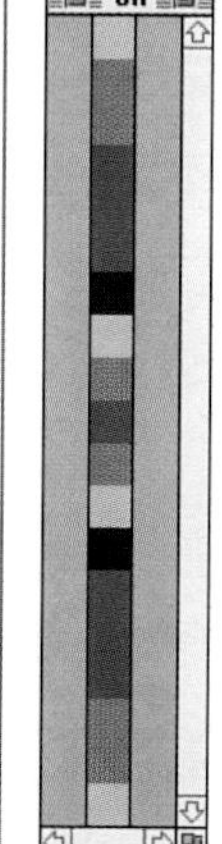

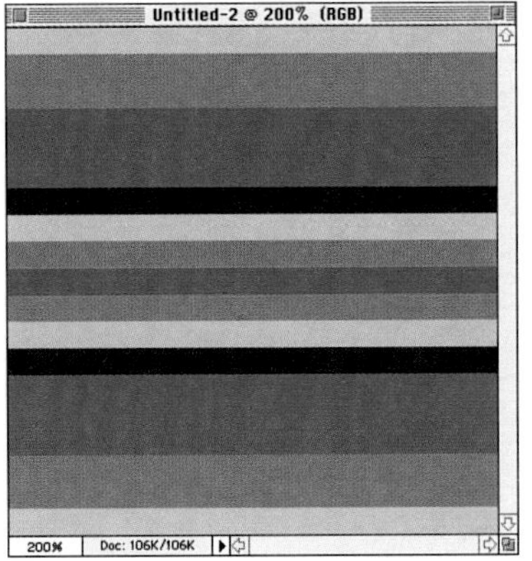


**8** Choose Image➡Image Size. Uncheck Constrain Proportions. Check Resample Image. Change the Interpolation Method to Nearest Neighbor. Change the width to 190 pixels and leave the height at 190 pixels. Press OK.

**9** Select➡All. Define the pattern. Create a new file at the desired size. Fill with pattern.

## VARIATIONS

### Basic Faux Plaid

If you want to create a false plaid, duplicate the Background layer of the image in Step 9. Select Layer➡Transform➡Rotate 90° CW. Change the blending mode to Overlay…

…or Color Burn…

…or Difference.

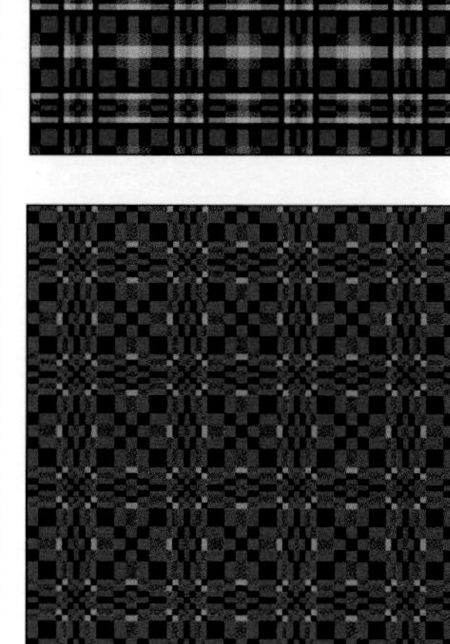

Experiment with all of the blending modes.

## Diamonds

You can create interlocked diamonds from your finished stripe.

**1** Select Image➥Duplicate. Convert the image to a new mode—Indexed Color mode (Exact palette). This enables you to create a diagonal stripe that does not anti-alias. Select Image➥Rotate Canvas➥Arbitrary (45°).

**2** Show the rulers (Command-R) [Control-R]. Add a horizontal and vertical guide in the center of the image. If you magnify the image to 500%, you can see to place the guides on the exact pixel.

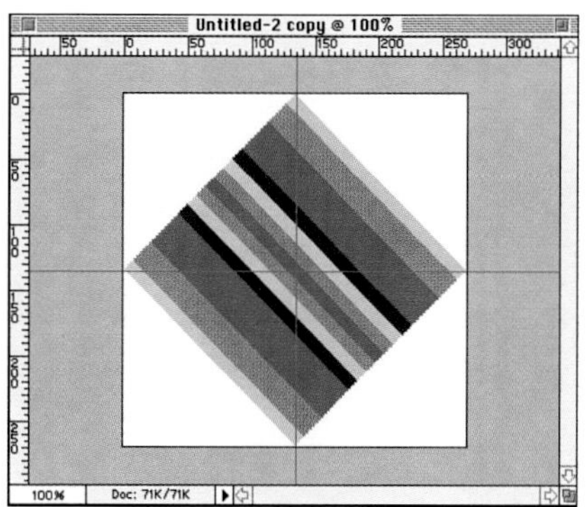

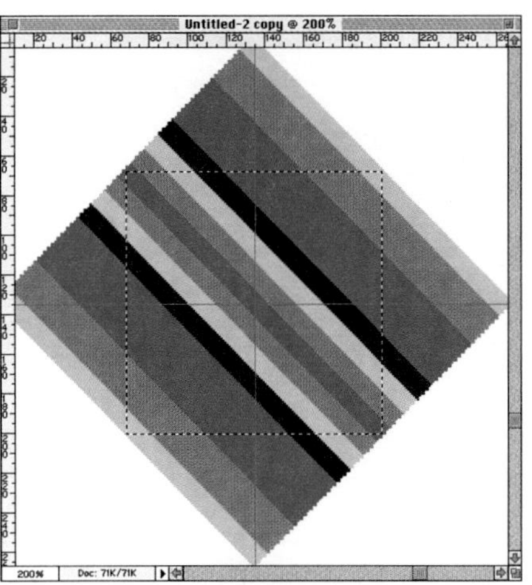


**3** Double-click the rectangular Marquee tool and set the Style to Normal with a Feather of 0. Hold the (Shift-Option)[Shift-Alt] keys and place the cursor at the intersection of the two guides. Click and drag out a square marquee that is as large as possible but only contains the stripes (no background).

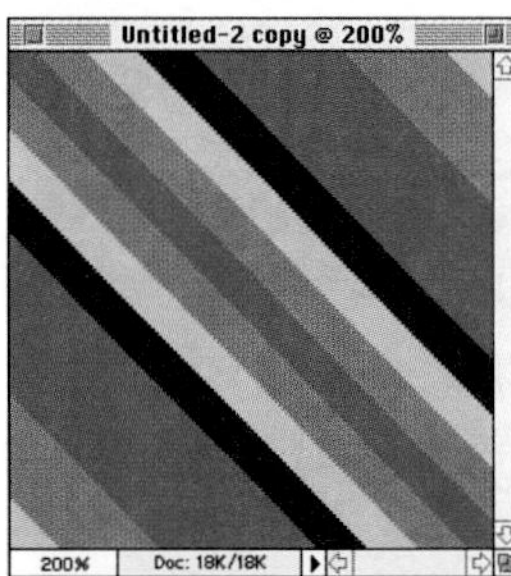


**4** Select Image➥Crop.

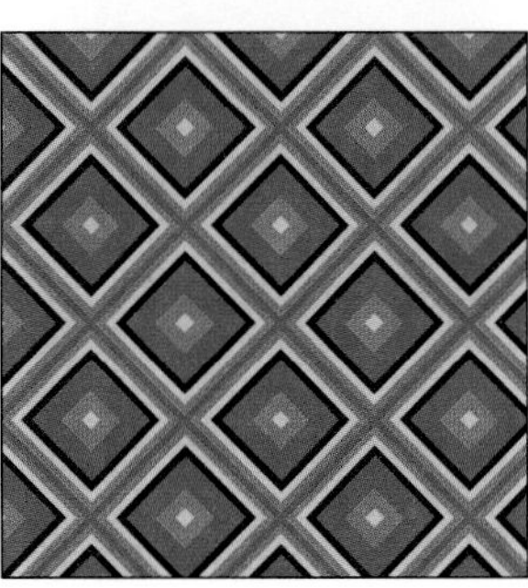

**5** Convert the image to RGB mode. Make the tile seamless using the Mosaic method. Select➥All. Define the pattern. Create a new file of the desired size. Fill with pattern.

Try adding some embossing and depth to the diamond repeat. Create a new channel (Channel 4). Fill with the diamond pattern. Choose Image➡Adjust➡Auto Levels. Return to the composite channel. Select Filter➡Render➡ Lighting Effects and use the Stripe Lights preset from the *Photoshop Textures Magic* CD-ROM or duplicate the settings shown.

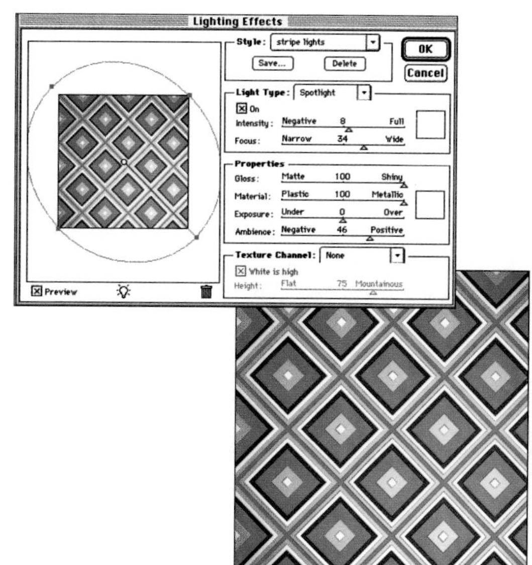


TIP **You may not remember the Fibonacci series from high school math, but it is the secret to successful stripes. Stripes that use the numbers in the progression will always be pleasing. The Fibonacci series starts with the numbers 1 and 2. Each of the following numbers is equal to the sum of the preceding two numbers (1, 2, 3, 5, 8, 13, 21, and so on). If you create your stripes so that they use these proportions, they will always work. You can start with 1 pixel, 1 inch, or one foot—the principle remains the same.** ■

Stucco has so many uses—it can be applied to houses, walls, and Web pages. Although most noisy, embossed, and blurred textures are called stuccos, this effect actually creates one type of plaster pattern that you might see on a neighbor's house. You can vary it in an almost infinite number of ways.

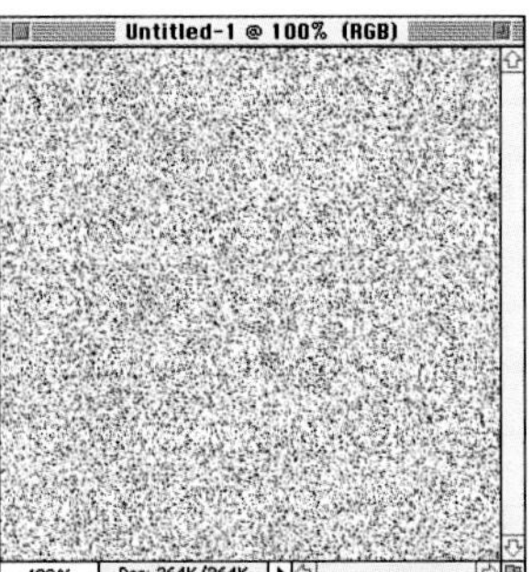


**1** Create a new file. This pattern tiles, so you really only need a file as large as one tile. Mine is 300 pixels square so that my tile is one inch when printed. Select Filter➥Noise➥Add Noise (Distribution: Gaussian, Monochromatic). I used an Amount of 100.

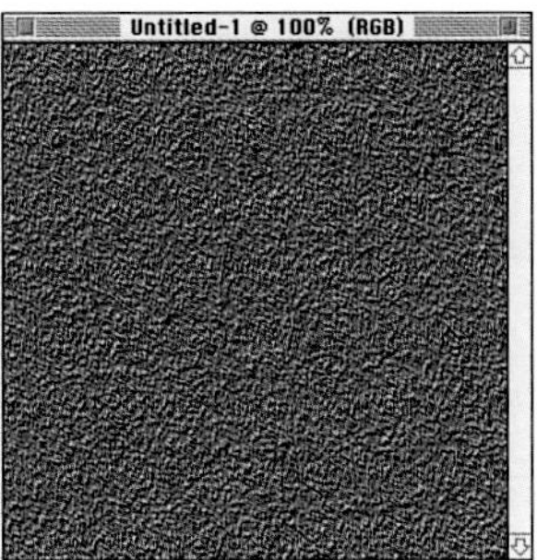


**2** Choose Filter➥Stylize➥Emboss (Angle: 130°, Height: 2 pixels, Amount: 100).

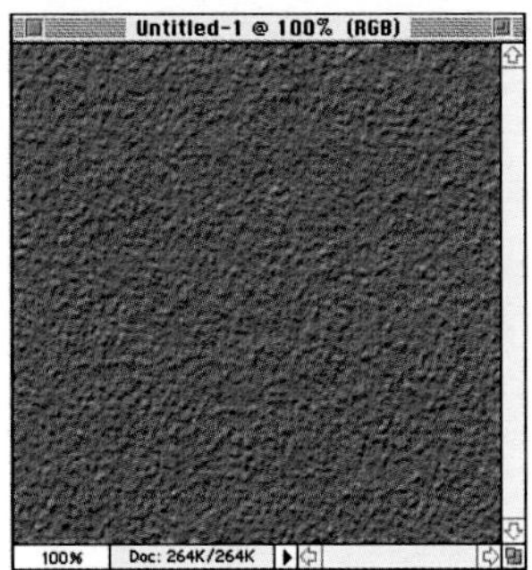


**3** Select Filter➥Blur➥Gaussian Blur. I used a Radius of 0.9. The purpose is simply to remove the hard edges—not to blur the texture beyond recognition.

**4** Select Image➥Adjust➥Auto Levels.

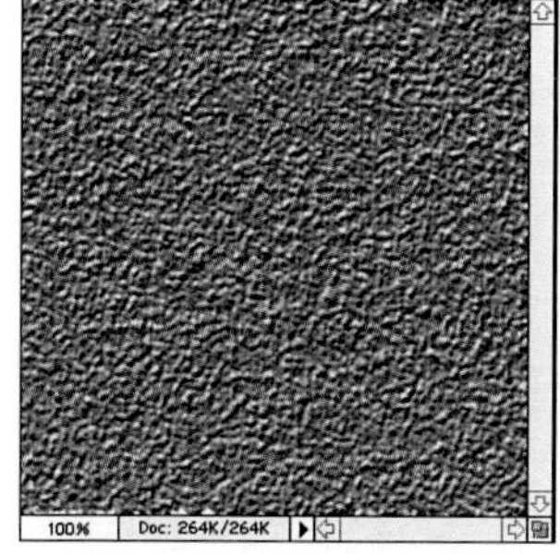


**5** Choose Filter➥Fade➥Auto Levels. Did you know that you can Fade any of the Image➥Adjust commands? Leave the opacity at 100%, but change the Mode to Color Burn. This leaves a wonderful texture that almost resembles coal.

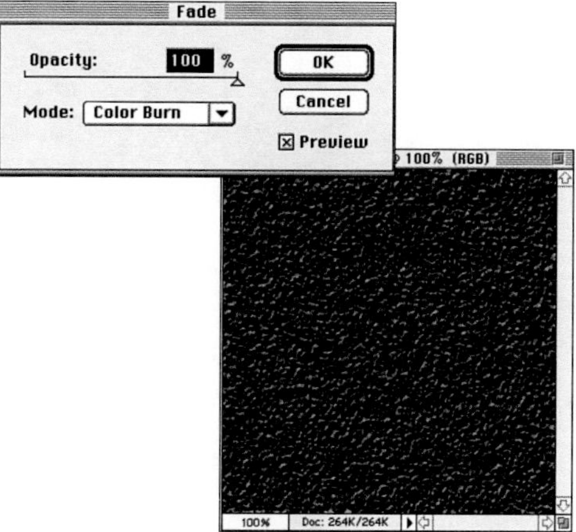


**6** Select Filter➥Stylize➥Emboss. Change the Angle to –45° but leave the other settings alone.

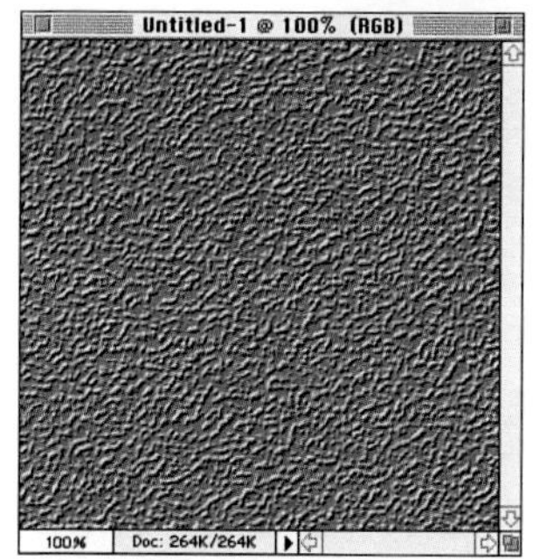

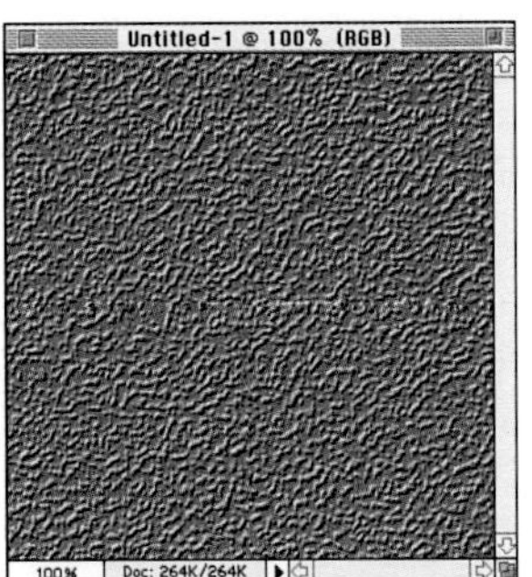


7 Now, you need to add the swirl of the brush to this texture. Select Filter➥Other➥Offset (Wrap Around). Make the Horizontal and Vertical distances one-half of image dimensions. As an added bonus, it makes the texture seamless, although it was practically seamless anyway.

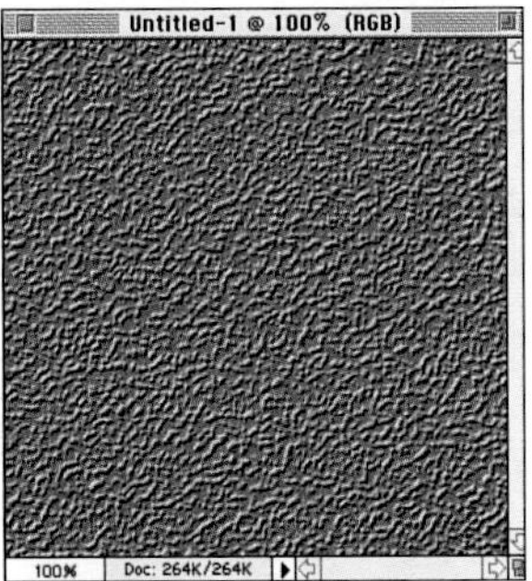


8 Choose Filter➥Distort➥Twirl. I used an Angle of 50°. This is gentle enough to swirl the texture without mangling it.

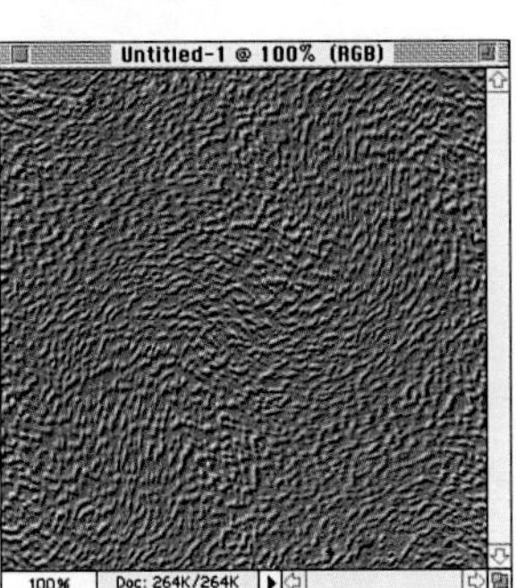


9 Select Filter➥Other➥Offset (Wrap Around). Reuse the last settings. Choose Filter➥Distort➥Twirl, and use the same settings again. This twirls both seam lines in the image, gives good texture, and keeps the tile seamless.

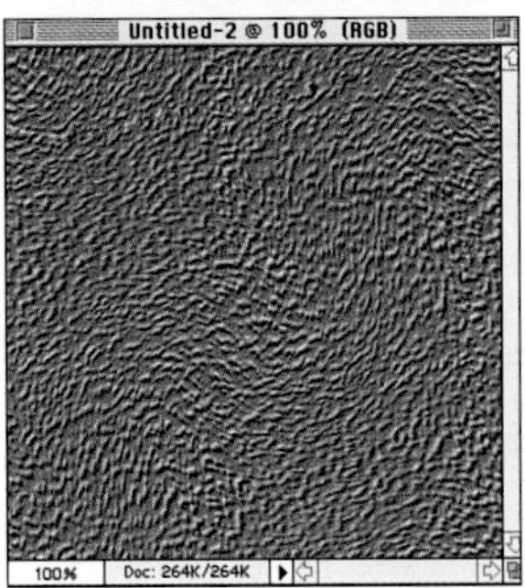


10 In order to keep this texture seamless, you need to finish it in repeat (so that the edges of the texture do not get compromised when the other filters are applied). Select➥All. Define the pattern. Create a new file three times your tile size. Mine is 900×900 pixels for my 300-pixel tile. Fill with pattern.

**11** Select Filter➡Sketch➡Graphic Pen (Light/Dark Balance: 50). I used a Stroke Length of 15 and a Direction of Right Diagonal. This makes a wonderful criss-crossed light and dark texture.

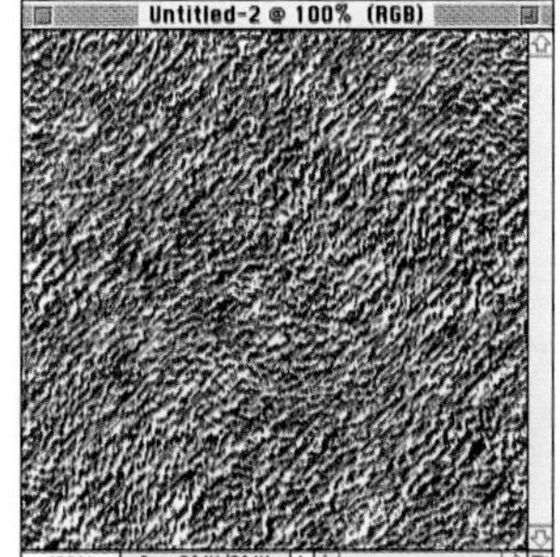


**12** Choose Filter➡Stylize➡Emboss (Angle: 138°, Height: 2 pixels, Amount: 100).

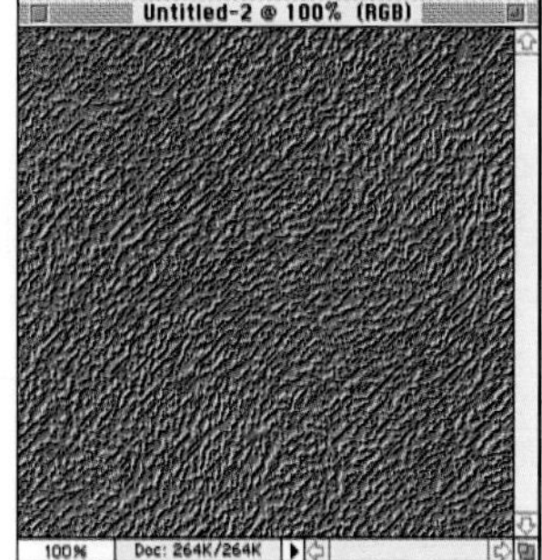


**13** Select Filter➡Blur➡Gaussian Blur. I used a Radius of 0.9. Again, this is just to soften the hard edge.

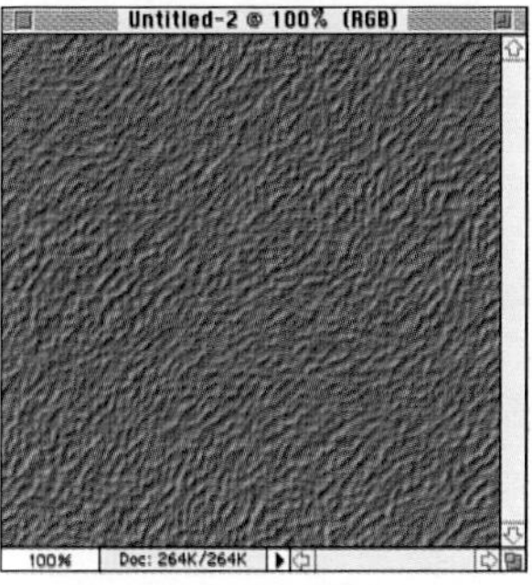


**14** Double-click the rectangular Marquee. Set the fixed size to the same dimensions as your original tile. Drag the Marquee near the center of the image. Define the pattern.

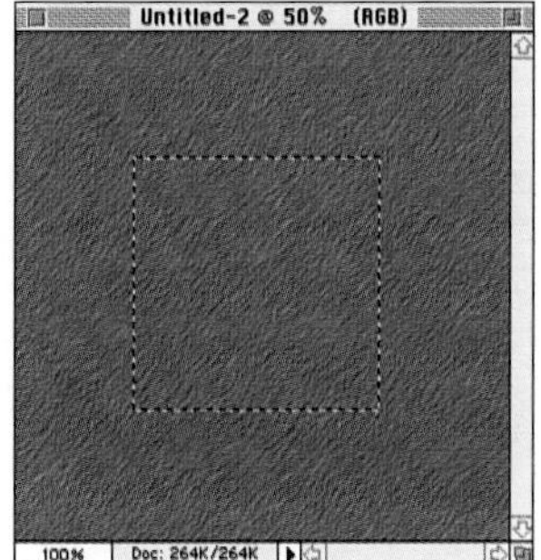

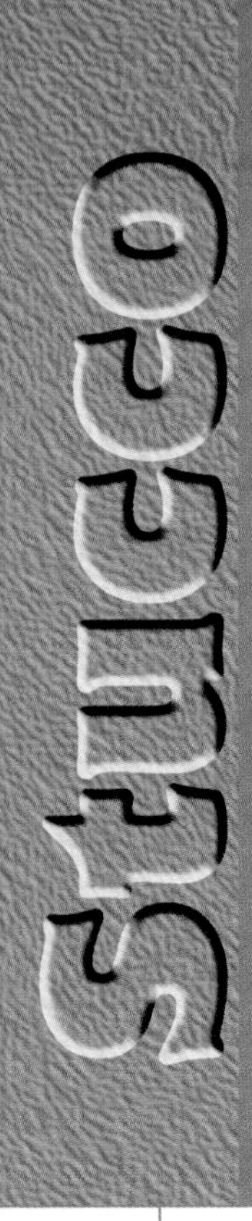


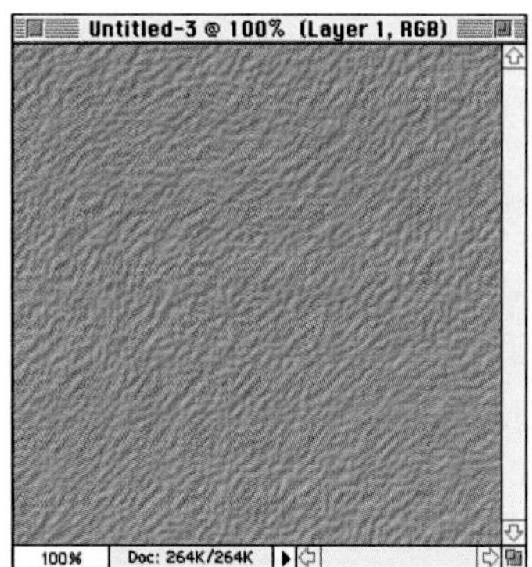


**15** Create a new file the same size as your original tile. Decide upon a base color for the stucco. I chose a light peach. Switch the foreground color to the desired color. Fill with foreground color. Create a new layer. Fill the selection with pattern. Change the blending mode to Luminosity. Reduce the layer opacity to about 50%.

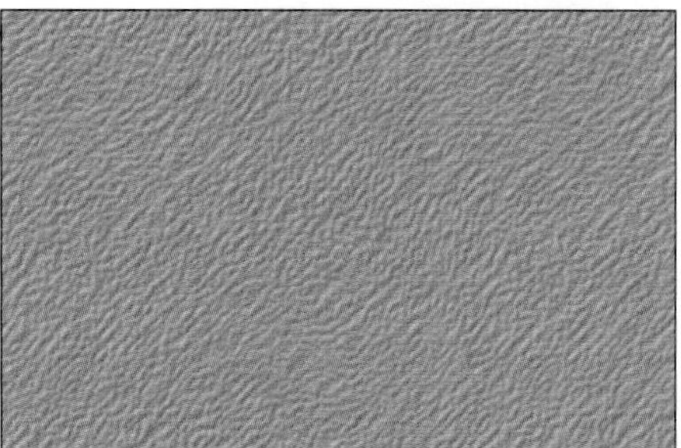

**16** Select➡All. Define the pattern. Create a new file to the finished size needed. Fill with pattern.

## VARIATIONS

If you want a different color stucco, switch the foreground color to whatever color you want. Make the Background layer active for your finished tile. Fill with foreground color. Complete as in Step 16.

To add stronger highlights and shadows, select Image➥Adjust➥Levels. Move the left and right Input sliders to the start of the values on the histogram. If you want to make the texture a bit shinier, move the Gamma (midpoint) slider to the right. If you want to make the texture look as if it is in brighter sunlight, move the Gamma slider to the left.

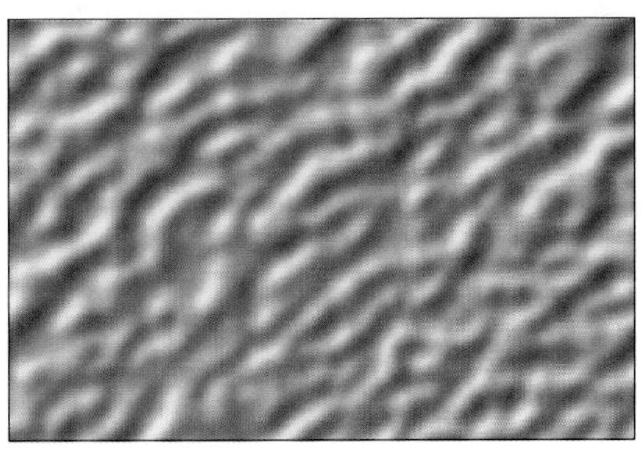

Try making a tile that is more angular and somewhat sharper. In Step 11, select Filter➥Artistic➥Poster Edges. I used an Edge Thickness of 2, an Edge Intensity of 1, and a Posterization of 2. Omit Step 13. ■

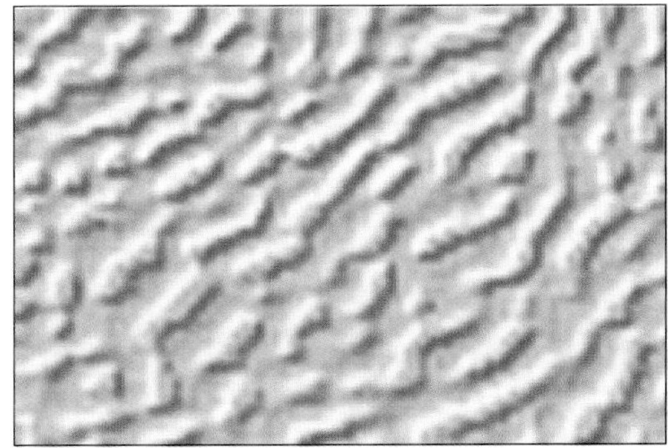

# Thumbprint

If you are tired of seeing endless "noise" patterns or loud repeats that obscure the text you are trying to read on the Web, here is a no-fail method of generating a seamless tile that is always soft enough to read through. It works with any source image that you can give it—a piece of stock photography or color that you have blobbed onto a file. Let's try it using an image donated by Vivid Details for the *Photoshop Textures Magic* CD-ROM. Best of all, it is never the same twice—it is as individual as your thumbprint.

**1** Open the file MM_0248.TIF in the Vivid Details folder on the *Photoshop Textures Magic* CD-ROM, or you can use your own example if you prefer. The starting photo can have an influence on the colors of the final image, but the subject matter of the image is of no importance at all and will not be seen.

**2** Double-click the rectangular Marquee tool and set the fixed size to your desired tile size. I used 300×300 pixels.

**3** Drag the Marquee into the image anywhere you want. Select Image➡Crop. Save the file under a new name.

**4** Switch to default colors. Fill with background color (white).

**5** Double-click the Rubber Stamp tool. Select the Impressionist option, and adjust the other settings as you see them here. Select the 100-pixel soft brush.

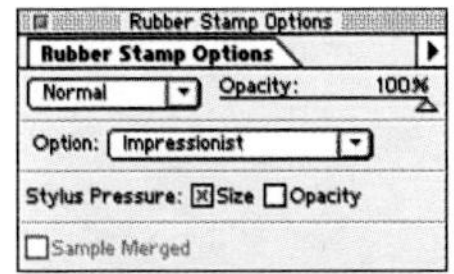


**6** The Impressionist version of the Rubber Stamp tool pulls color out of your saved file. It does not pull detail—especially using such a large brush size. Brush the saved color all over your image. You have some control over the color that appears—each time you start and stop, the color changes. Brush with short, choppy strokes.

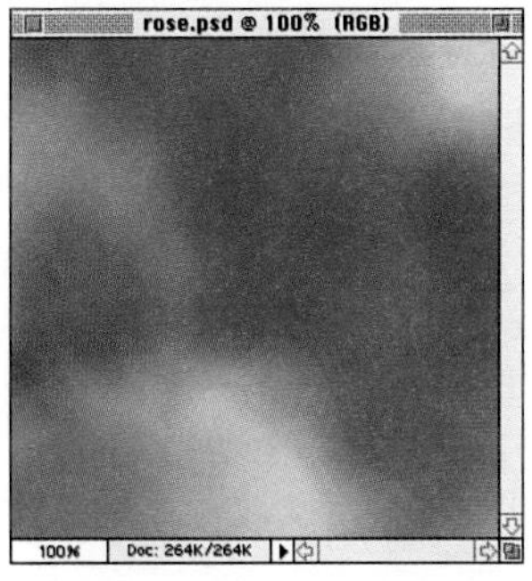


**7** For this effect to work, you need to make the tile seamless. Select Filter➥Other➥Offset (Wrap Around), and make the settings approximately one-third of the tile size. I offset the image by 100 pixels in each direction. This is different from the "normal" seamless wrap.

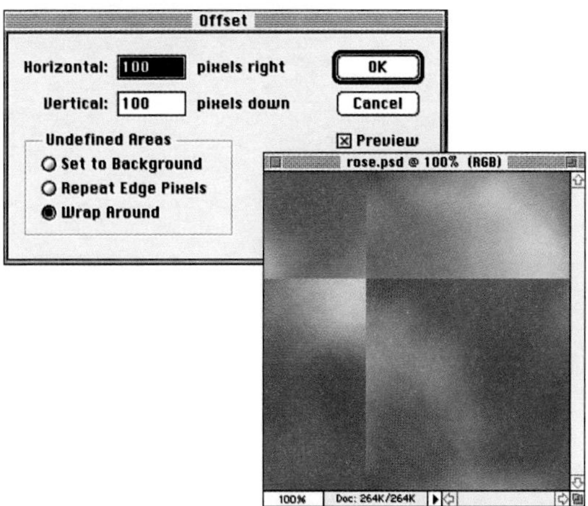

**8** You need to cover the hard edge. Don't worry if you have to go to the edges of the image. Continue to use the Impressionist Rubber Stamp tool and the 100-pixel brush (you will need to decrease the size of the brush if your image is smaller). Because you have offset the image, different colors will appear as you brush over the seams. This is good—it helps to move the colors around a bit.

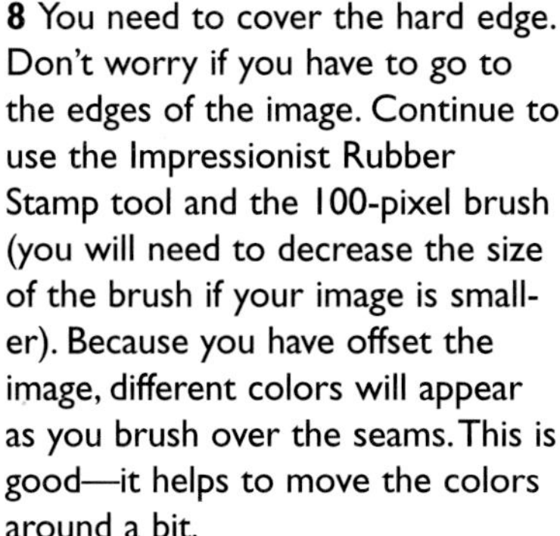

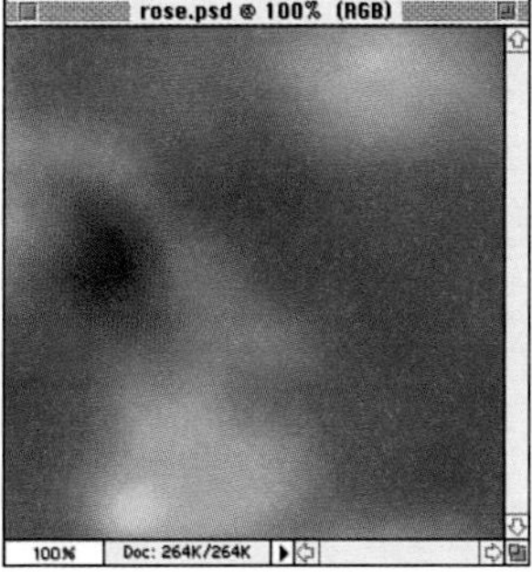

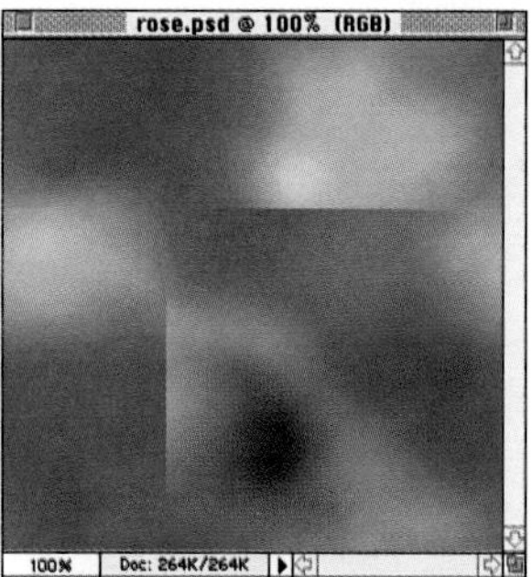


**9** Select Filter➡Other➡Offset again with the same settings (Command-F)[Control-F]. Look carefully at this image. This time, the seam line is not quite as sharp and is much less noticeable at the edges.

**10** Repair the seam line as you did in Step 8. Only brush over the seam line. Try not to get any closer to the edges than you absolutely must in order to repair the hard edge. Reapply the Offset filter (Command-F)[Control-F]. Continue this cycle of repair and offset until you no longer see a seam line when the image is offset. It takes between 3 and 5 applications of the repair-and-offset cycle to get a totally seamless tile.

**11** Select➡All. Define the pattern.

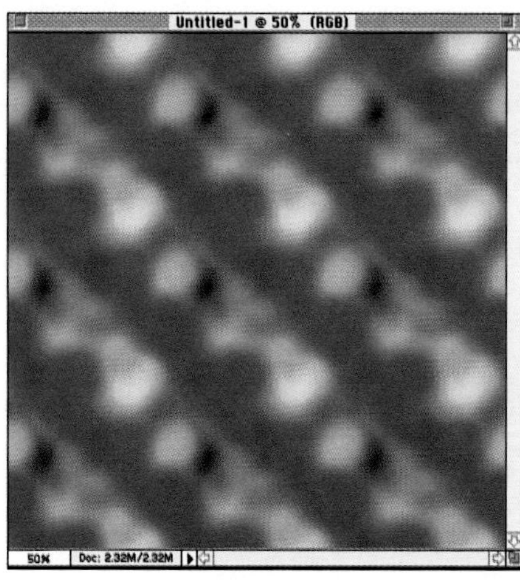


**12** Next comes the magic! In order to get a totally seamless tile in the end, you need to create a file that is *three times* your current file size. Create a new file. I created one that is 900×900 pixels (300 pixels × 3). Fill with pattern.

**13** Choose Filter➡Stylize➡Find Edges.

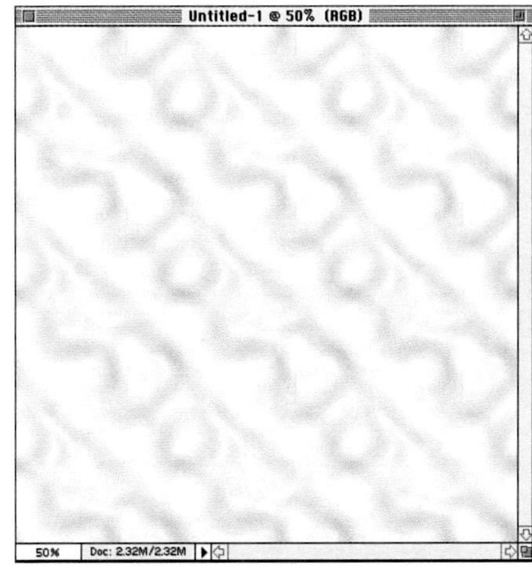


**14** Choose Filter➡Blur➡Gaussian Blur. You need to set the Radius high enough for the image to almost completely blur out. You should still be able, however, to see slight variations in color. I used a Radius of 30, but some images have required a Gaussian Blur Radius as high as 63. The size that you select for the Radius determines the amount of detail in the final image.

**15** Select Filter➡Stylize➡Find Edges. The image will look blank.

**16** Choose Image➡Adjust➡Auto Levels. A fine line pattern appears—and it *is* a pattern. Because you developed this from a seamless tile, the center of the image contains an area that can form a seamless repeat.

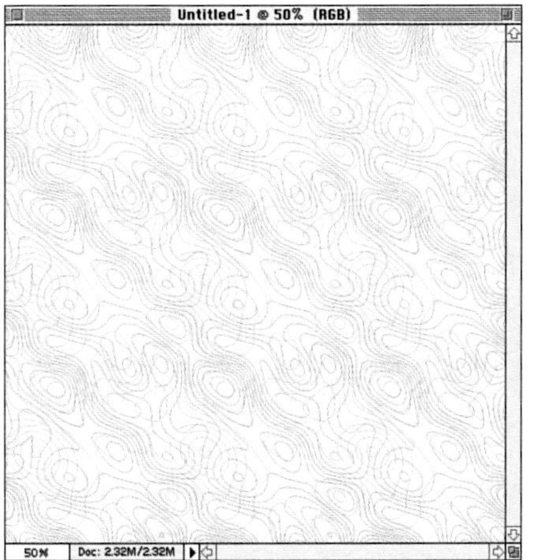

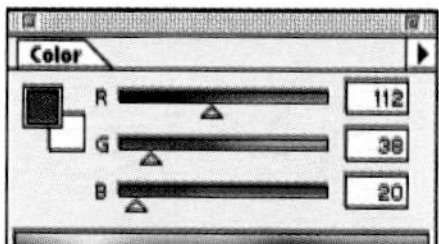


**17** Switch the foreground color to whatever color tone you would like your finished pattern to be. Select a color that is at least a middle value or darker. I chose a dark orange-brown.

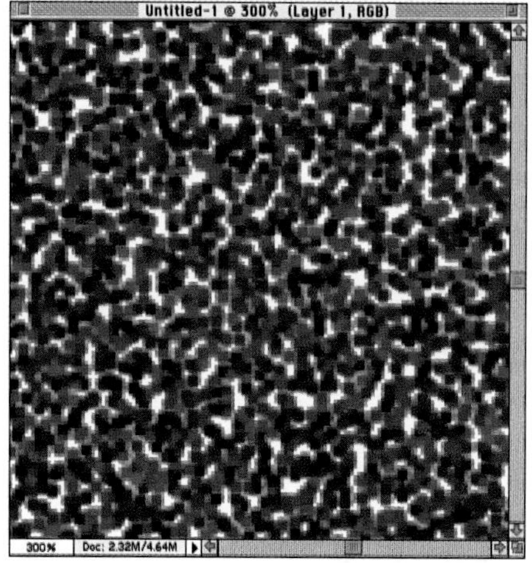


**18** Create a new layer (Layer 1). Fill with foreground color. Choose Filter➥Pixelate➥Pointillize. I selected a Cell size of 5. The size that you select has a major impact on the final tile.

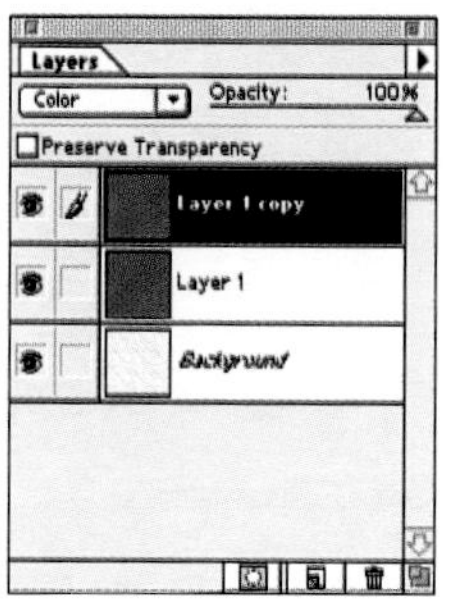


**19** Duplicate Layer 1. Change the blending mode to Color.

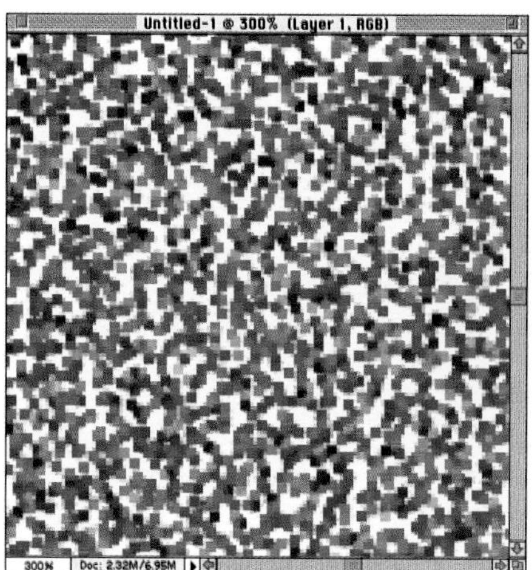


**20** Make Layer 1 active. Change the blending mode to Hard Light.

**21** Select Filter➥Stylize➥Emboss. The settings that I used here make a good place to start. You are more likely to want to decrease the Height and Amount than you are to increase them.

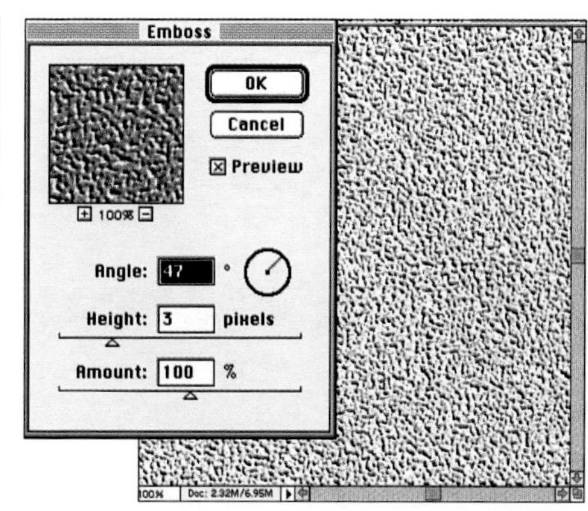


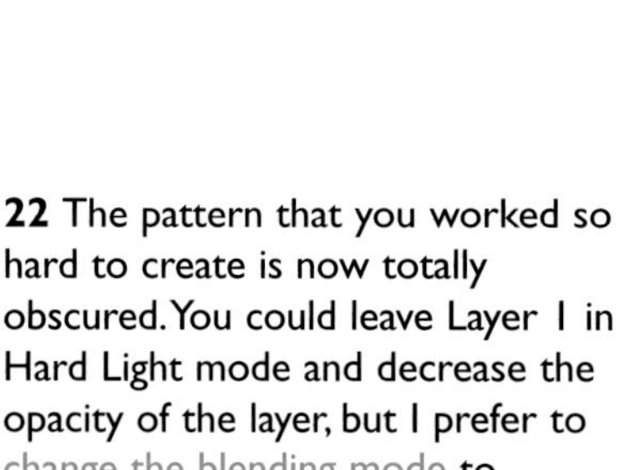

**22** The pattern that you worked so hard to create is now totally obscured. You could leave Layer 1 in Hard Light mode and decrease the opacity of the layer, but I prefer to change the blending mode to Multiply at this point and reduce the layer opacity to about 30%.

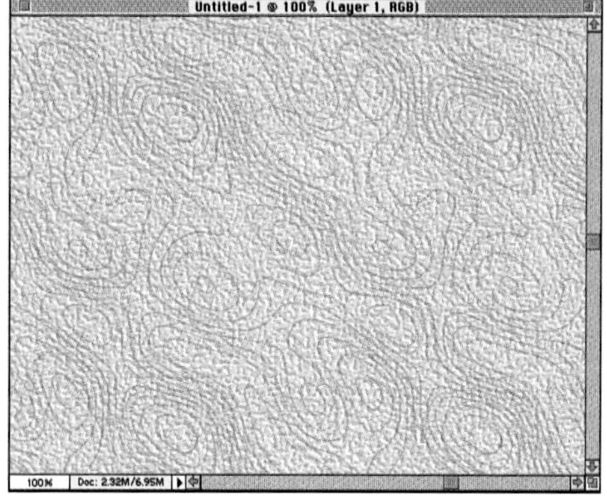


**23** You might also want to reduce the opacity of the Layer 1 copy—a setting of 85% is usually enough to remove the "funny" colors produced by the Color blending mode.

**24** Finally, drag the fixed-size rectangular Marquee near the center of the image. It does not need to be exact, but it does need to be in the center area.

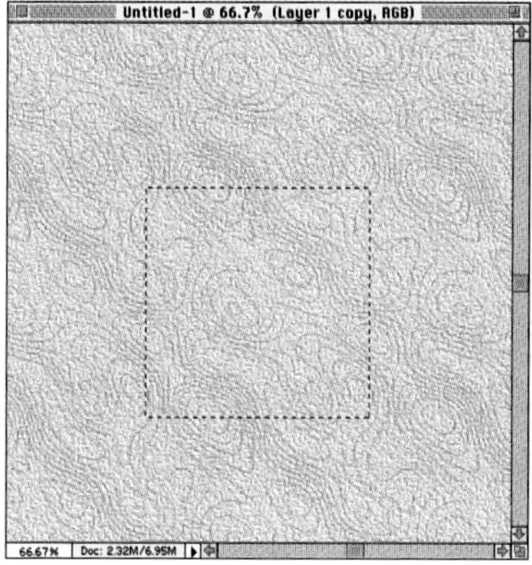

**25** Select Image➥Crop. Flatten the image. Convert the image to a new mode—the Indexed Color mode (Web, 216 colors, Diffusion Dither). Save the file as a GIF. The pattern is totally seamless and can be used as a Web background pattern (or for whatever other use you may find). If you want to make the tile smaller, reduce the image size (Image➥Image Size) *before* you change it to Indexed Color mode.

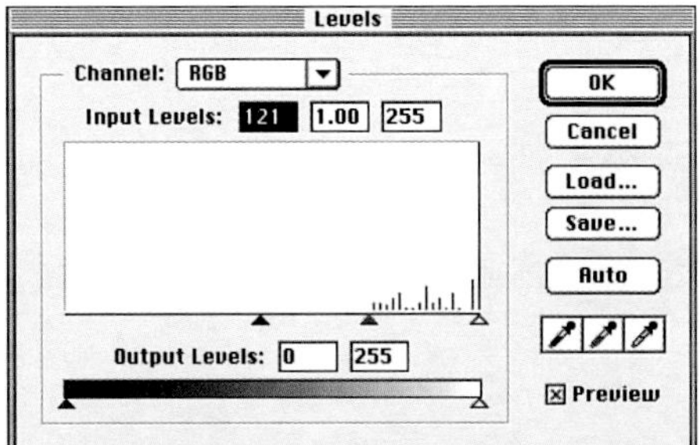


## Variations

If you want the fine edges to be stronger and more noticeable, after Step 23, make the Background layer active. Select Image➥Adjust➥Levels and move the left Input slider to the right until you like the new image. I prefer to move it only until the Gamma slider (the middle slider) reaches image data, as you can see in the dialog box here.

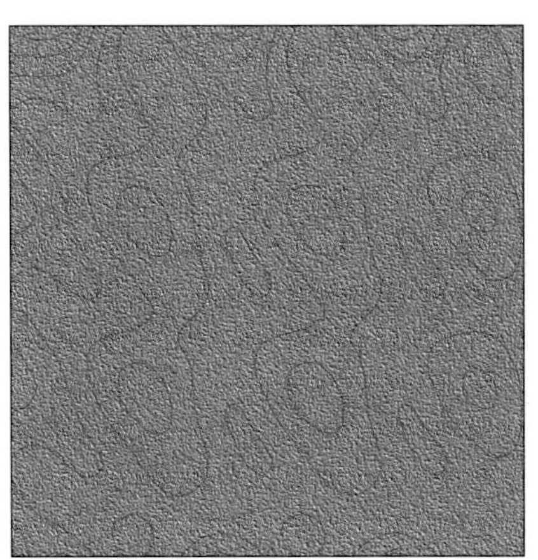

A larger Gaussian Blur makes the pattern much larger. Here, I used a Gaussian Blur of 63 in Step 14. The base tile was the same.

Here it is with a Gaussian blur of 45. The pattern is larger than the original, but not nearly as simple and large as the blur of 63 produces.

**TIP** **You can experiment easily with a number of different settings by duplicating the Background layer a few times and using different Gaussian blur settings. Complete Steps 15 and 16 for each layer. If you then complete Steps 17–23 at the top of the layer list, you have a file that you can play with and hide and show layers, change opacities and blending modes, and so on. Here's the way I structured mine.**

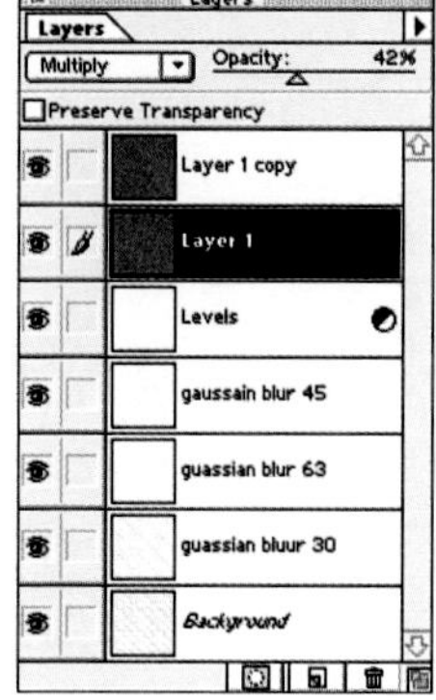


You could make the original photo extract tile seamless using the Rubber Stamp method. This cuts out Steps 4 through 10. However, even at a Gaussian blur of 63 in Step 14, the resulting pattern may be too detailed. This method is faster, but you may want to repeat Steps 13 and 14 twice (Find Edges and Gaussian Blur), using a different setting for Step 14.

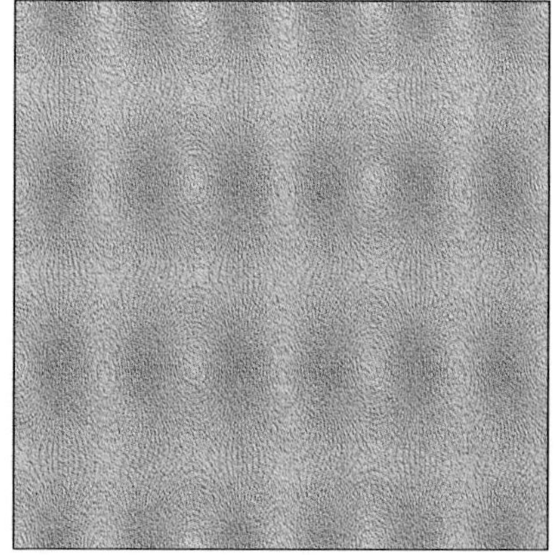

A pattern based on a watercolor wash makes a lovely and unusual Web background. This technique is amazingly simple—but it has many uses and can be varied endlessly by merely changing the colors used.

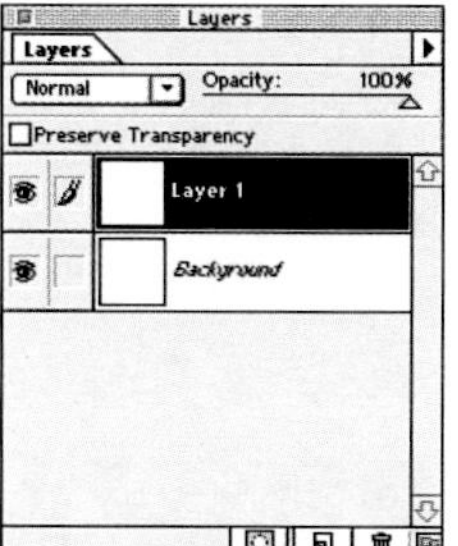


**1** Create a new file. Mine is 400×400 pixels. Switch to default colors. Create a new layer (Layer 1). Switch the foreground color to any dark color that you want. I chose a medium-dark blue.

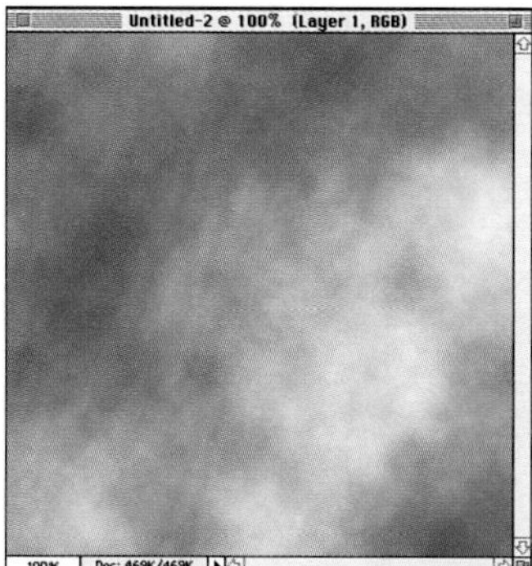


**2** Apply Filter➥Render➥Clouds. Clouds is the only native Photoshop filter that works in a totally blank and transparent image. Reduce the layer opacity to about 90%.

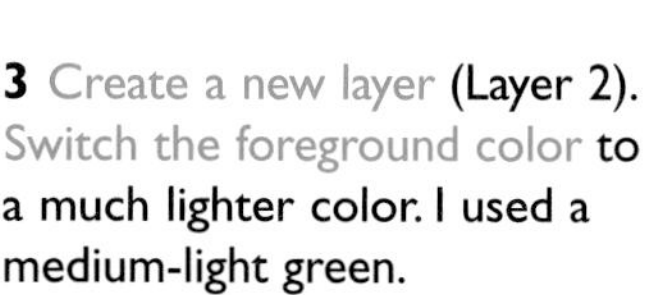

**3** Create a new layer (Layer 2). Switch the foreground color to a much lighter color. I used a medium-light green.

**4** Reapply the Clouds filter (Command-F)[Control-F]. Reduce the layer opacity to 50%.

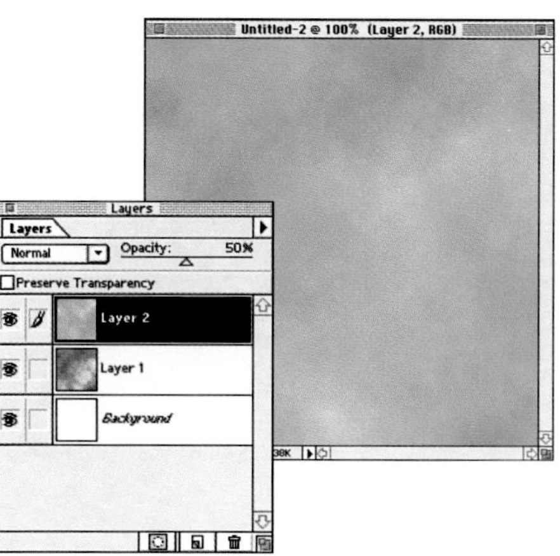

**5** Create a new layer (Layer 3). Switch the foreground color to a strong color that is not already in the image. I used a strong red. Switch the background color to another dark color—a color that is almost the complement of the foreground color seems to work best. I chose a deep, dull green.

**6** Reapply the Clouds filter (Command-F)[Control-F]. Change the blending mode of the layer to Overlay.

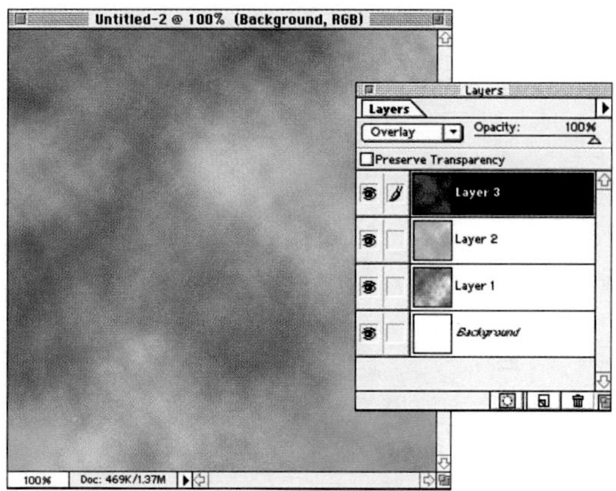


**7** Make the Background layer active. Choose Filter➡Noise➡Add Noise (Gaussian, do not check Monochromatic). Use a large amount—until you can see it through the other textures. I used an Amount of 700.

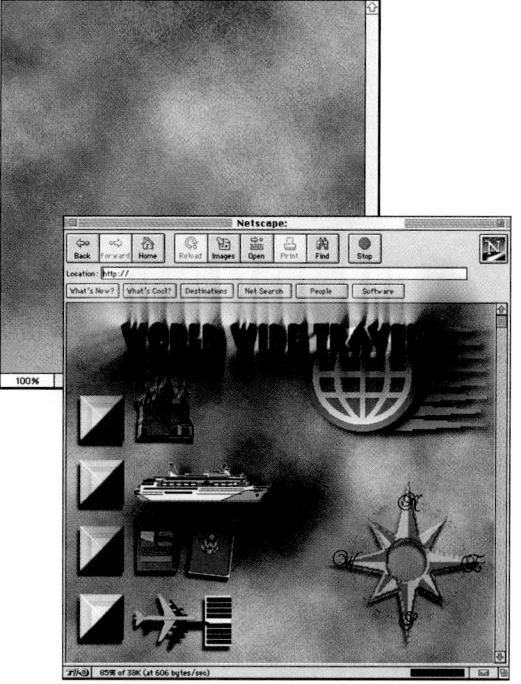

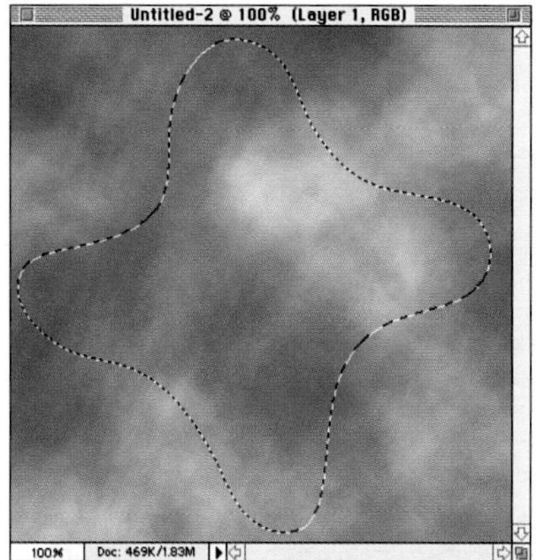


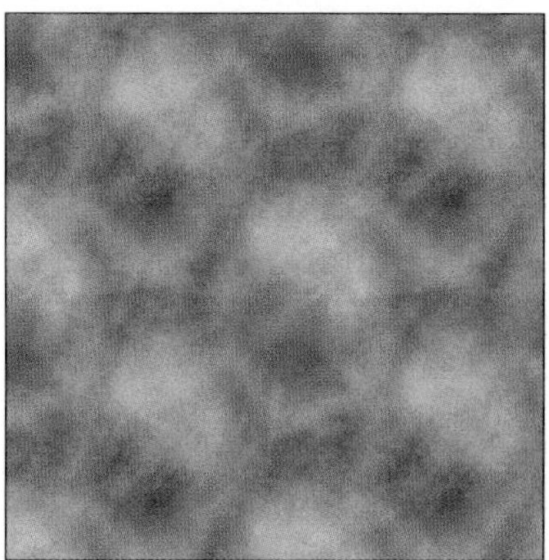

## VARIATIONS

If you want to make the texture seamless, you need to make each layer seamless after you apply the Clouds filter—and before you change the layer opacity or change the blending mode. Each time that you apply the Clouds filter, make the pattern seamless using the Rubber Stamp method. This is only partially successful because it is hard to use the Rubber Stamp tool on the Clouds filter. After you do the best job that you can—especially on the areas at the edges of the image, select the Lasso tool. Draw a selection in the shape of a fat cross around the area where the Offset filter joined the original corners of the image. Choose Select➥Feather, and pick a large feather. I used 15 pixels. Reapply the Clouds filter to the selection. It will blend perfectly. You do not need to make the Background layer seamless. When all three clouds layers are seamless, define the pattern, and use it to fill a new image with pattern.

To create a different color range, you can select Image➥Duplicate (Merged Layers Only) and then invert the result (Command-I) [Control-I].

You can also change the opacities of the layers to change the look of the watercolor wash. I changed Layer 1 to 82% opacity and Layer 2 to 14% opacity.

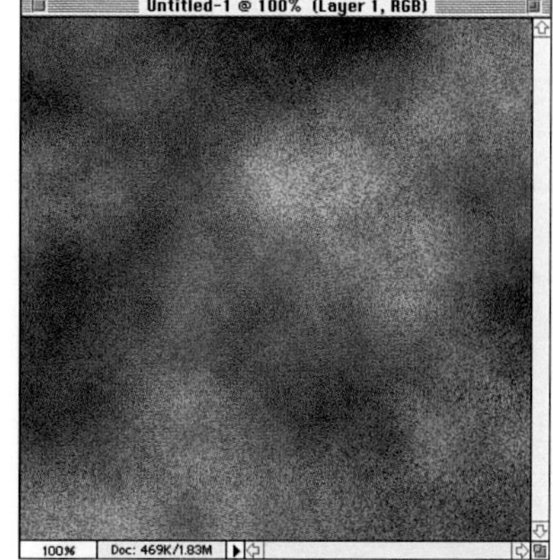


You can change the blending mode on Layer 3. I set it to Luminosity mode.

Of course, you can try a totally different color scheme as well. I used a light yellow for Layer 1, a deeper red for Layer 2, and a very dark blue and maroon for Layer 3.

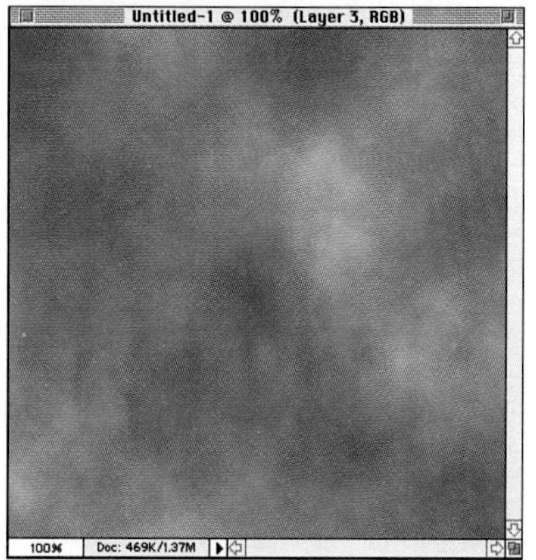


If you want more, the "Leather" effect (page 120) shows you another technique using the Clouds filter. ■

Still water may run deep, but turbulent water is more fun to design. This effect allows you to play creator to ponds and rivers and streams—in sun or in storm.

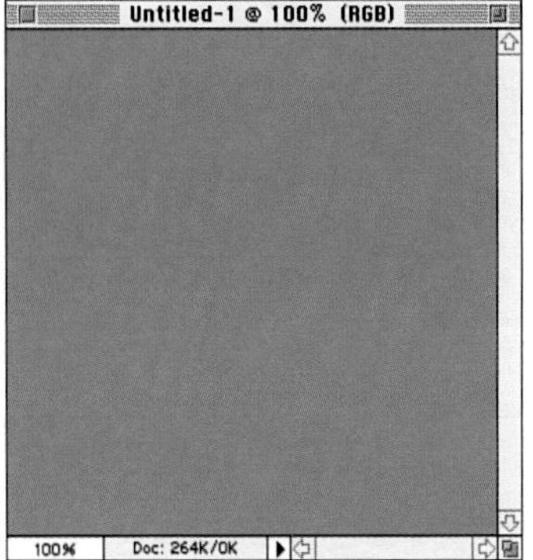


**1** Create a new file. You will be able to tile this, but you should use a tile size as large as practicality allows to give the water the maximum variety. My file is 300×300 pixels—but you will be happier with the results if you use a tile of at least 400×600 pixels. Switch the foreground color to a "watery" blue. I used RGB: 0, 138, 183. The color is not extremely critical because you can easily change it afterwards. Fill the image with foreground color.

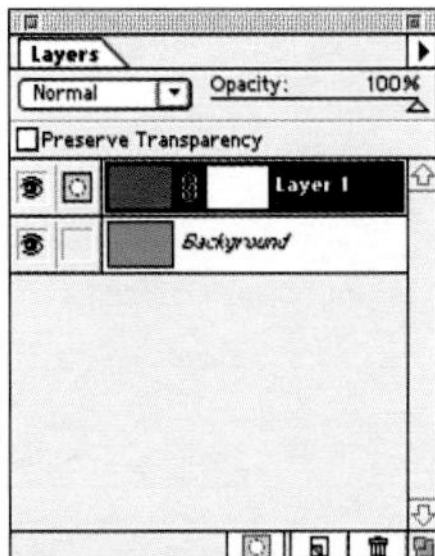


**2** Create a new layer (Layer 1). Switch the foreground color to a deeper sea blue. I used RGB: 0, 92, 120. Fill Layer 1 with the foreground color. Create a layer mask.

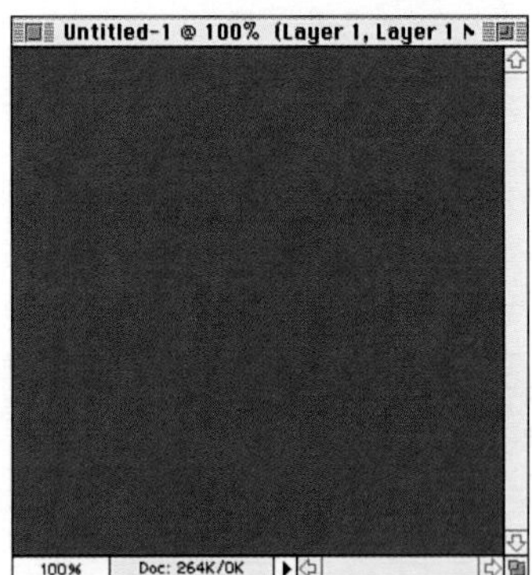

**3** Gee, that looks boring! So far, we have one color on top of another and a layer mask that does nothing. Never fear...the effect is actually built in the layer mask. Switch to default colors (your colors should already be showing black and white while the layer mask is selected). Choose Filter➡Render➡Clouds. Finally, you can see something happening other than a solid color!

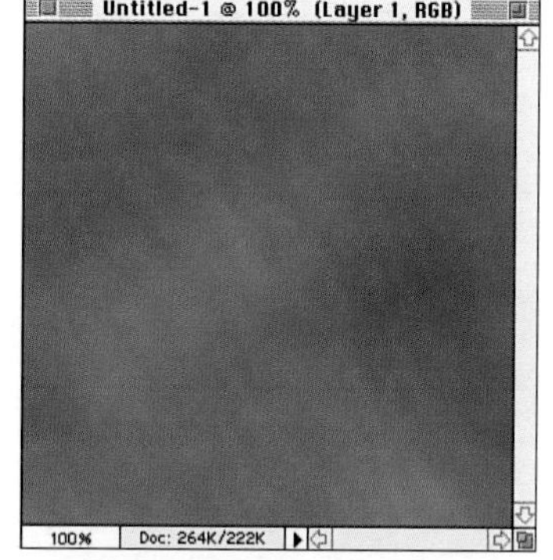


**4** Select Filter➡Render➡Difference Clouds. Reapply this filter (Command-F)[Control-F] several times (2 or 3 is enough). Each time you reapply the Difference Clouds filter, you are adding internal complexity to the clouds—even if the difference is not visible onscreen. Shown here is just the layer mask (which, of course, is grayscale).

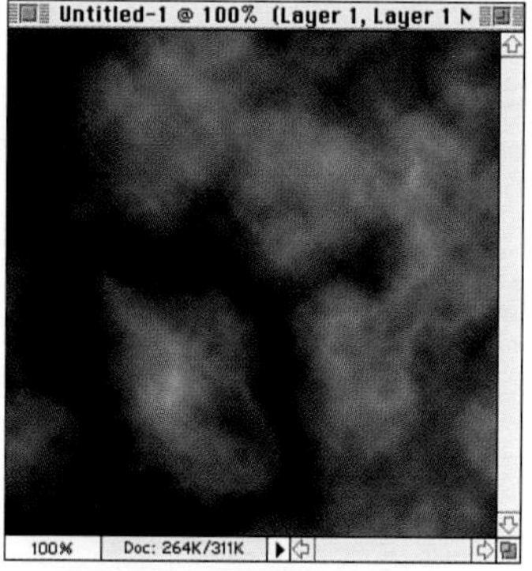


**5** Choose Filter➡Stylize➡Find Edges. Invert the image (Command-I)[Control-I]. The layer mask is pictured here because the effect is still too light to be printable. (Your screen will show the effect rather than the layer mask.)

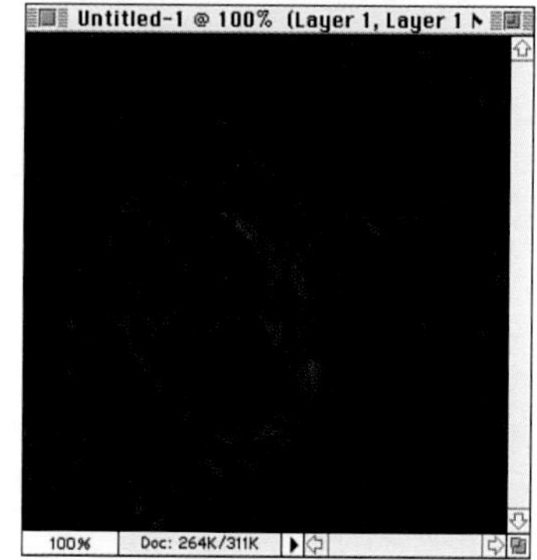

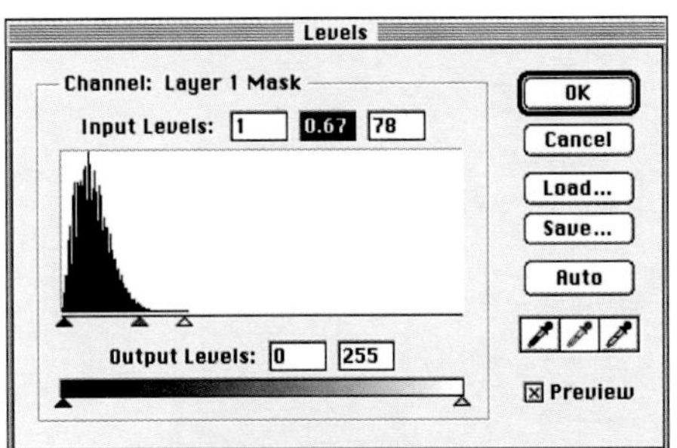


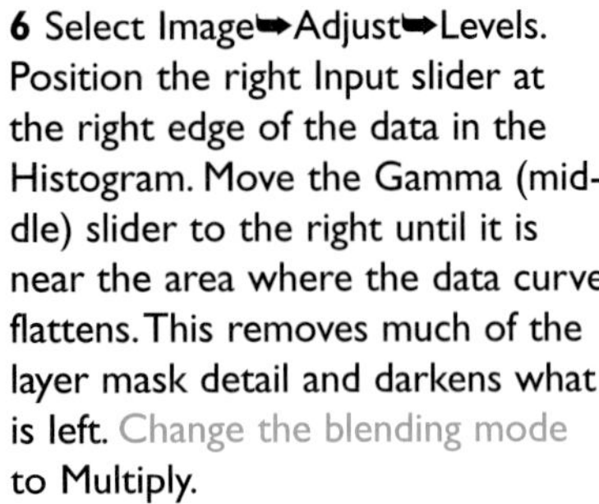
**6** Select Image➡Adjust➡Levels. Position the right Input slider at the right edge of the data in the Histogram. Move the Gamma (middle) slider to the right until it is near the area where the data curve flattens. This removes much of the layer mask detail and darkens what is left. Change the blending mode to Multiply.

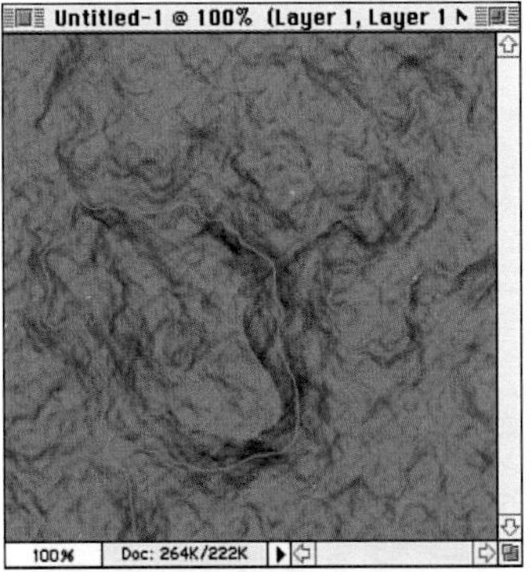


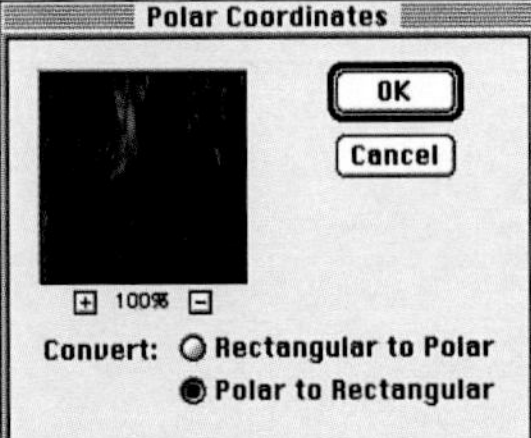


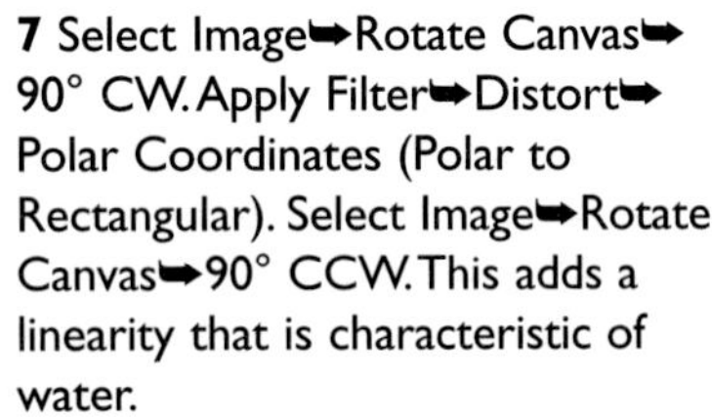
**7** Select Image➡Rotate Canvas➡90° CW. Apply Filter➡Distort➡Polar Coordinates (Polar to Rectangular). Select Image➡Rotate Canvas➡90° CCW. This adds a linearity that is characteristic of water.

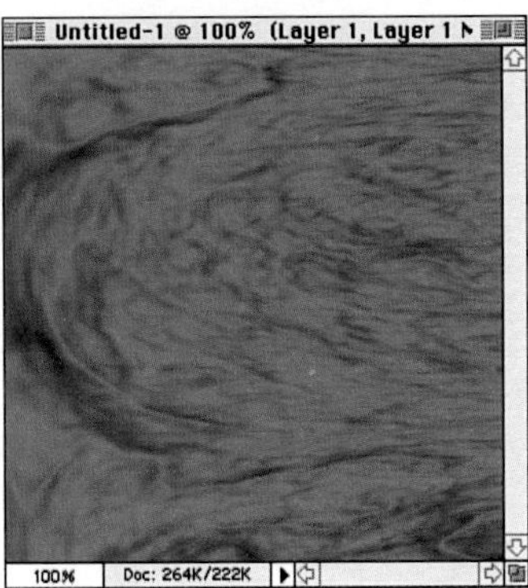

**8** The Polar Coordinates filter always leaves some curved shapes and lines on the left side of the image (if you rotated the image as I did). This needs to be removed if the image is to resemble water. Double-click the rectangular Marquee tool and set the Style to Normal and the Feather to 0. Select the entire area to the right of the curved stuff. Choose Layer➥Transform➥Free Transform (Command-T)[Control-T]. Place your cursor on the center control point on the left edge of the selected area and drag the point to the left edge of the image. This stretches the "good" part of the layer mask over the entire image. Double-click inside of the selection to execute the transformation. Deselect.

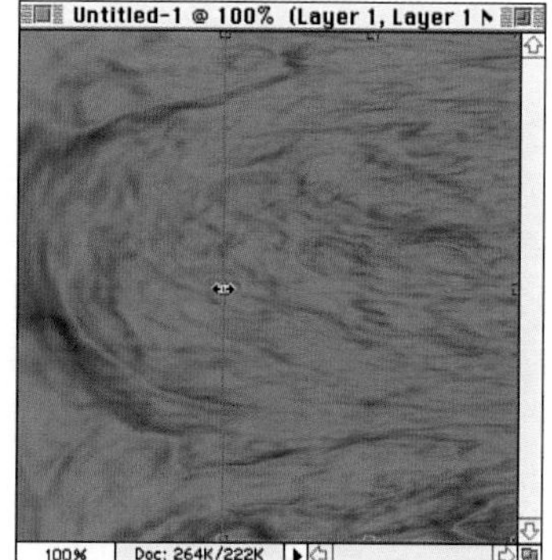


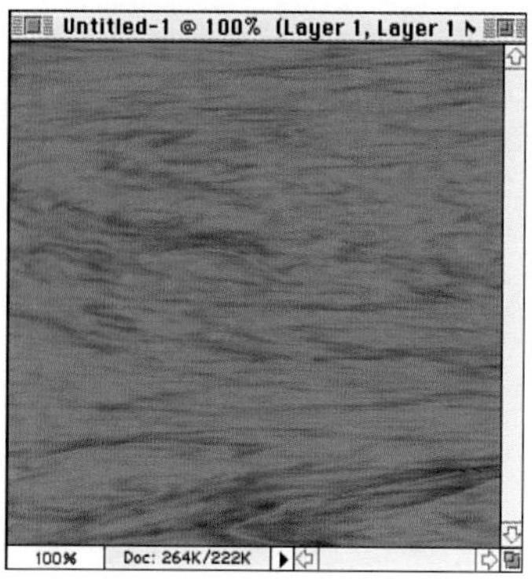


**9** This looks much more like water, but it may still be too light. The easy way to darken the image is to use the Levels command and move the right Input slider to the left. That is a permanent move, however, and cannot be changed later. I prefer maximum editability. Therefore, load the layer mask of Layer 1 by pressing the (Command)[Control] key and clicking on the layer mask thumbnail in the Layers palette. Create a Levels adjustment layer with a blending mode of Multiply. Click OK in the Levels dialog box without making any changes. If it is still not dark enough, you can always duplicate the adjustment layer.

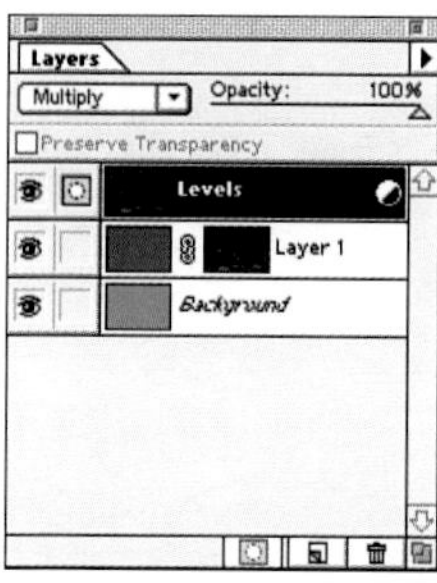

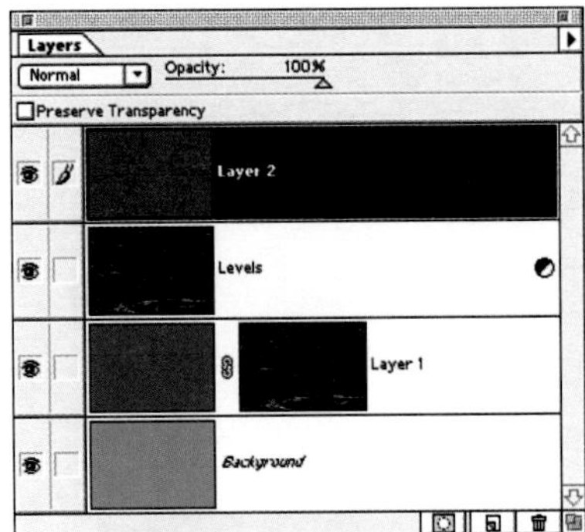


**10** The water needs highlights. Create a new layer (Layer 2). Switch the foreground color to a contrasting color for highlights. I used a strong green—RGB: 30, 85, 31. Fill with foreground color. Now the image is solid green. But not for long…

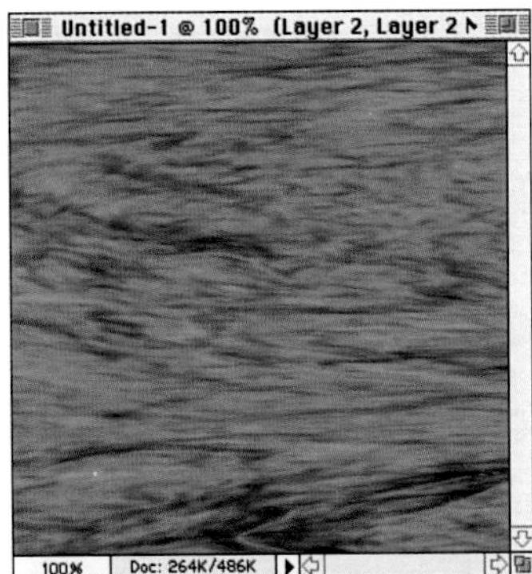


**11** Create a layer mask. Repeat Steps 3 through 8 in the Layer 2 layer mask. A slightly different pattern will form. When you repeat Step 6, select Screen mode rather than Multiply.

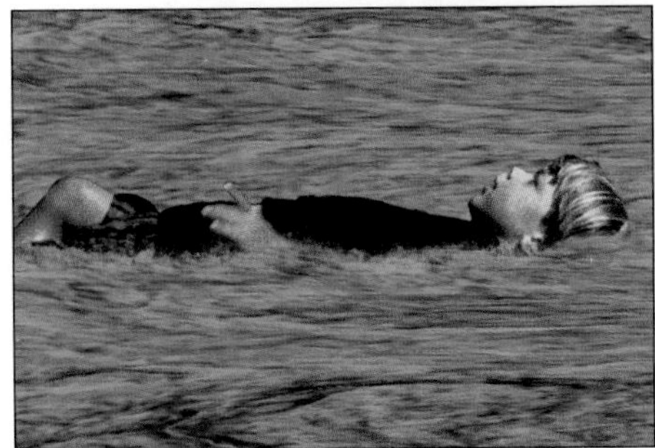

**12** Load the layer mask of Layer 2 by pressing the (Command) [Control] key and clicking on the layer mask thumbnail in the Layers palette. Create a Levels adjustment layer with a blending mode of Screen. Click OK in the Levels dialog box without making any changes.

## VARIATIONS

If you want to see the green streaks in the water, duplicate Layer 2. Position the layer at the top of the Layers list. Make the layer mask active. You can redo Steps 3 through 8 to create a different layer mask, or you can take the easy way out and select Layer➡Transform➡Flip Horizontal to simply reposition the layer mask to let the original Layer 2 show through. Leave the Blending mode in Normal. Load the layer mask of Layer 2 copy by pressing the (Command)[Control] key and clicking on the layer mask thumbnail in the Layers palette. Create a Levels Adjustment layer. Leave the Mode in Normal and move the Input sliders where you want them to bring out the values in the image.

To create the ocean on a cloudy—almost stormy—day, make the background layer active in the finished image. Switch the foreground color to a gray. I used RGB: 142, 142, 142. Fill the Background layer with the foreground color. You can leave the other layers alone or adjust or recolor them as well. You can also create additional layers to bring in streaks of other colors (following Steps 2 through 9 to do so).

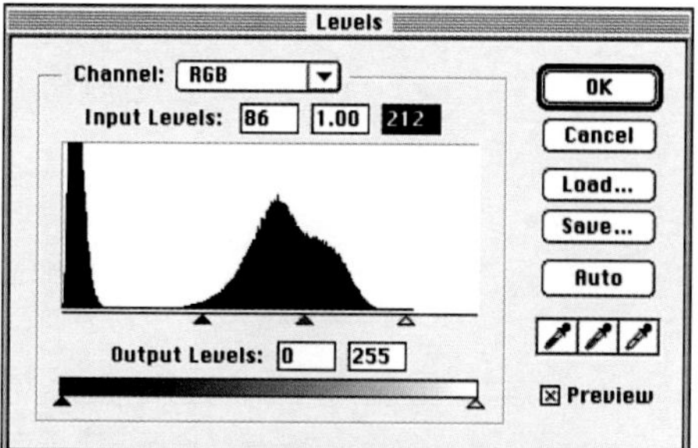


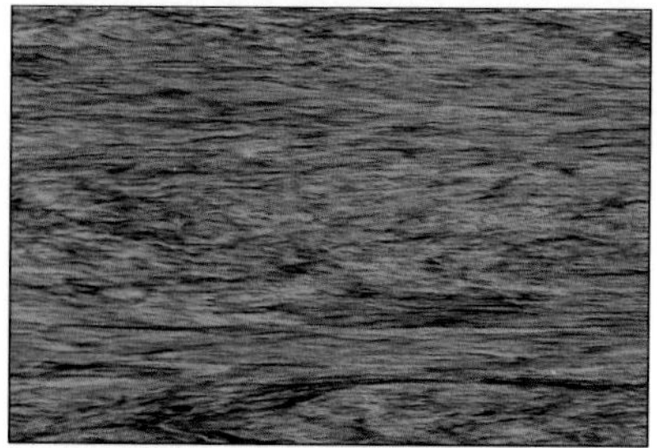

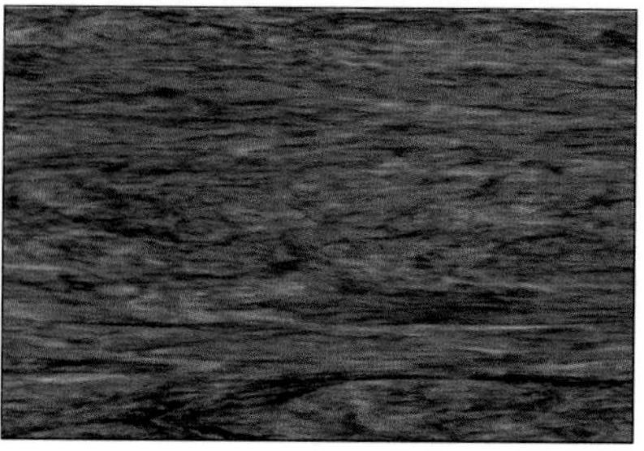

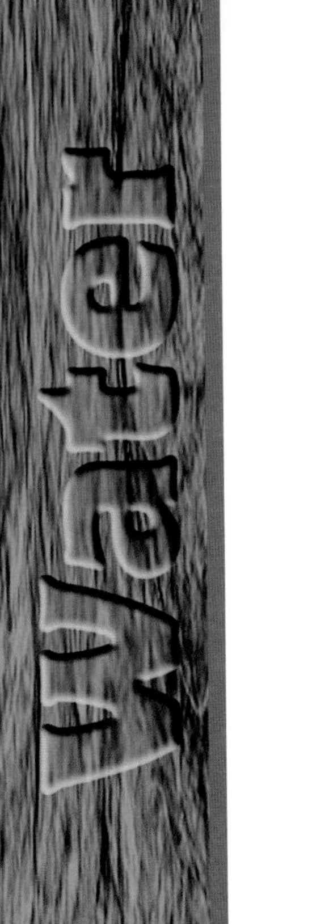


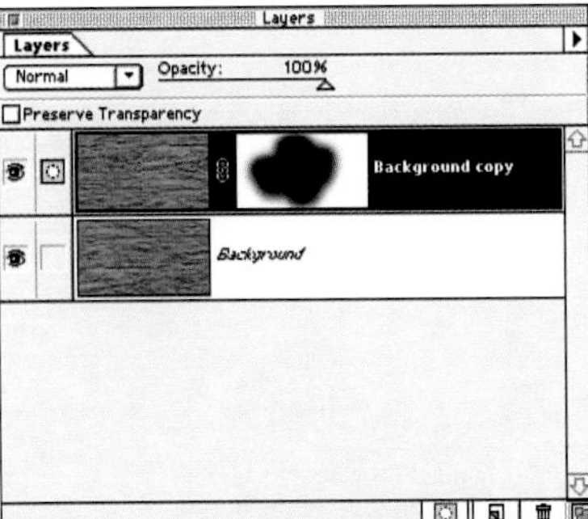


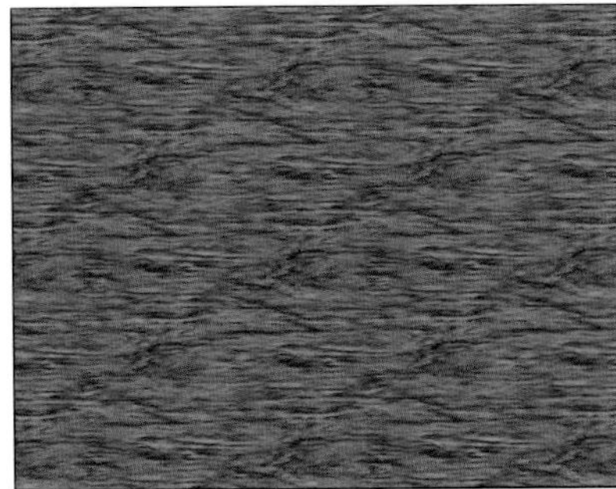

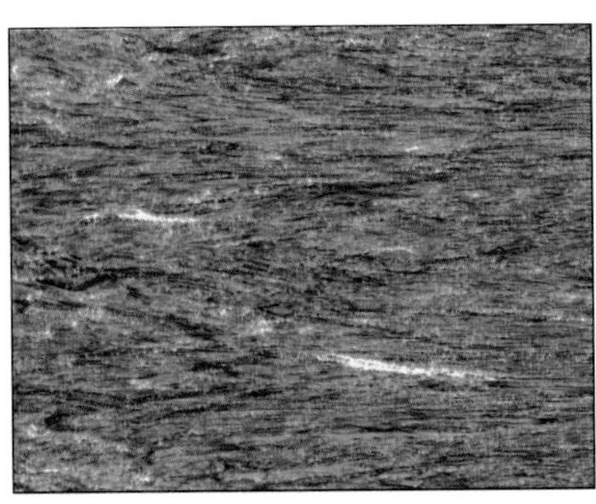

You can make the water tile seamlessly. After you have your finished tile, select Image➡Duplicate (Merged Layers only). Duplicate the Background layer. Select Filter➡Other➡Offset (Wrap Around). Make the Horizontal and Vertical distances one-half of image dimensions. Create a layer mask. Use a hard 100-pixel paintbrush and black. Paint out the center area of the image in the layer mask leaving only the area around the rim. Try not to fog the tile (that is why I recommend a fairly hard brush). Select➡All. Make sure that the layer—*not* the layer mask—is active. Define the pattern. Create a new file to the desired size. Fill with pattern. You will get the best results using a rectangular rather than a square tile, and using a fairly large tile size. Water is supposed to be completely random. If you notice the same formations multiple times, the incongruity becomes distracting. You can use the layer mask to also help remove the most obvious sections of the repeat. Simply paint on the layer mask to pick up detail from the other image. It may take a few tries to get it right.

Try making sparkling highlights in the water. Create a new layer at the top of the Layers list. Fill with white. Repeat Steps 2 through 8 to create a new layer mask texture. In Step 6, leave the blending mode at Normal. When you are finished, set the levels as you want and change the blending mode to Dissolve. This sprinkles tiny, too-sharp dots on the water. Create a new layer. Position the layer below the sparkles highlights layer. Make the sparkles layer active. Merge down

(Command-E)[Control-E]. This keeps the Dissolve mode dots in a Normal mode layer (in other words, this layer now just contains the sparkles, some transparency, and no layer mask). Select Filter➡Blur➡Gaussian Blur (0.9 or other small amount).

Now, try changing the water into tree bark. Select Image➡Rotate Canvas 90° CW. Make the Background layer active. Switch the foreground color to a shade of "tree" brown. I used RGB: 79, 59, 42. Fill the Background layer with foreground color. The green layer needs to be changed as well (Layer 2, in the original example). Change it to a shade of orange/brown (I used RGB: 135, 66, 11). Change the blending mode to Overlay. For additional realism, (Option) [Alt] Merge Visible to a new layer. Select Image➡Adjust➡Desaturate (Shift-Command-U)[Shift-Control-U]. Choose Image➡Adjust➡Auto Levels. Change the blending mode to Hard Light. Choose Filter➡Stylize➡Emboss (Angle: 127°, Height: 4 pixels, Amount: 50). If the embossing looks too "perfect," select Layer➡Transform➡Flip Horizontal (or Vertical or Rotate 180°) to move the embossing. If you want, Select Filter➡Blur➡Gaussian Blur (0.9 or less) to soften the embossing.

If you want more textures that you can create in a layer mask, try "Rocks" (page 176). ■

You probably did not expect a Photoshop book to introduce you to Basket Weaving 101. Wicker and other types of natural-fiber basket weaves, however, have a long and honorable history. The textures that they create have been copied and imitated in many different media—why not the electronic one? Besides, with the wonder of Photoshop, you only have to create a tiny piece of the basket.

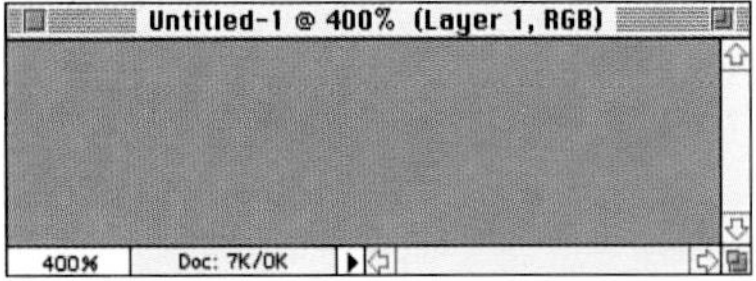


**1** Create a new file 86 pixels wide × 24 pixels high. This file is for the wicker fiber. Magnify the image to 500%. Switch the foreground color to a medium earth tone. I selected RGB: 185, 161, 87. Create a new layer. Fill with foreground color.

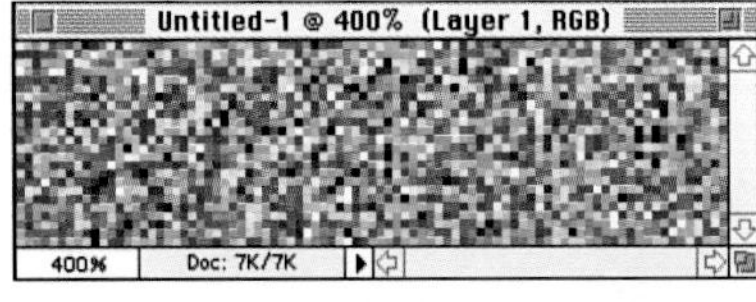


**2** Select Filter➥Noise➥Add Noise (Distribution: Gaussian, Monochromatic Off). I used an Amount of 135.

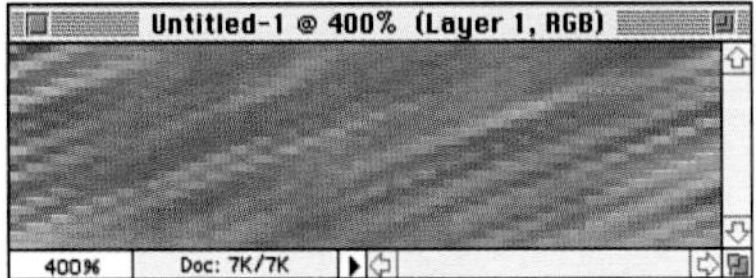


**3** Apply Filter➥Blur➥Motion Blur. I used an Angle of 20° and a Distance of 33. You are creating the "twist" in the fiber, and the bits of noise from Step 2 are the range of colors that are twisted into the fiber.



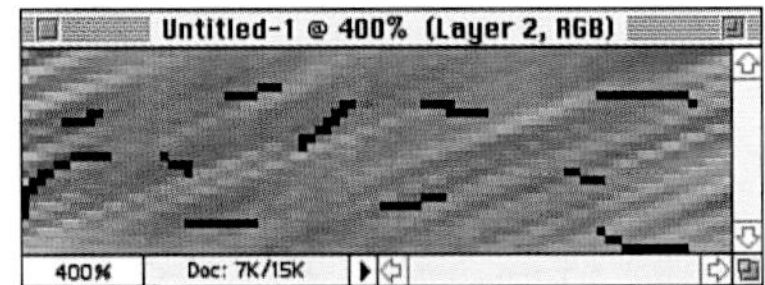


**4** Create a new layer. Choose the Pencil tool and the 1-pixel brush. Switch foreground/background colors so that you can keep the wicker color in the toolbox. Switch the foreground color to black. Paint some random short lines on the image.

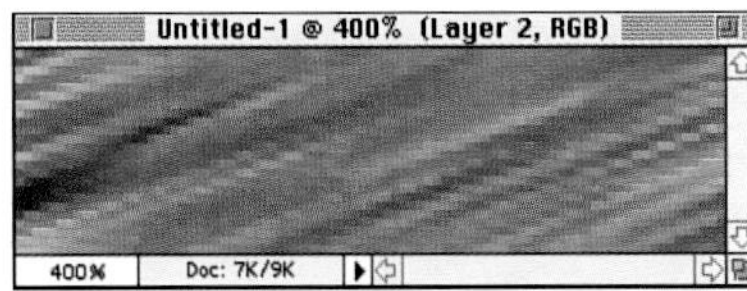


**5** Reapply Filter➥Blur➥Motion Blur (Command-F)[Control-F]. This puts a little bit of shadow detail into the fiber.

## TOOLBOX

Center High gradient preset

Center White gradient preset

**6** Create a new layer. Fill with background color. Reduce the layer opacity to about 35%. You just want to influence the color of the fiber a bit—not obliterate all of the work you just put into it.

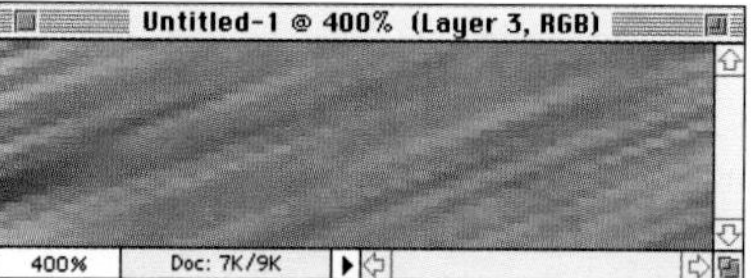

**7** Create a new layer. Double-click on the Gradient tool and select the Center High gradient preset from the *Photoshop Textures Magic* CD-ROM. Change the Type to Linear. Drag the Gradient cursor from the top of the image to the bottom, and press the Shift key to constrain the direction. Wicker material is round, and you have just added that roundness to your image.

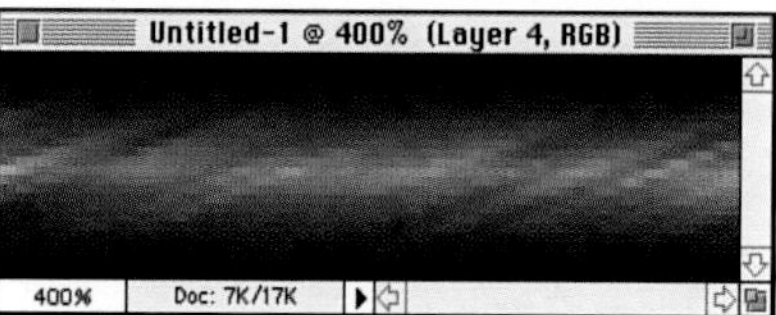

**8** This next step is tricky. The two horizontal ends of the image are going to "virtually" sink under the vertical strands of fiber to either side. Therefore, the ends need to be darker than the center of the file. However, if you make the ends too dark, the illusion of roundness disappears. Change the Gradient to Foreground to Transparent. Create a new layer. Turn on the Rulers (Command-R)[Control-R]. Add a Horizontal guide at the 12-pixel mark on the side ruler (the half-way point). Place the Gradient cursor in the upper-left corner of the image, press the Shift key, and drag the cursor diagonally until it reaches the guide. Then place the Gradient cursor in the lower-right corner of the image, press the Shift key, and drag the cursor diagonally until it reaches the guide. Now, the two corners are gently shadowed. If you want a slightly stronger shadow, reapply the Gradient to the top-left corner (over the first one).

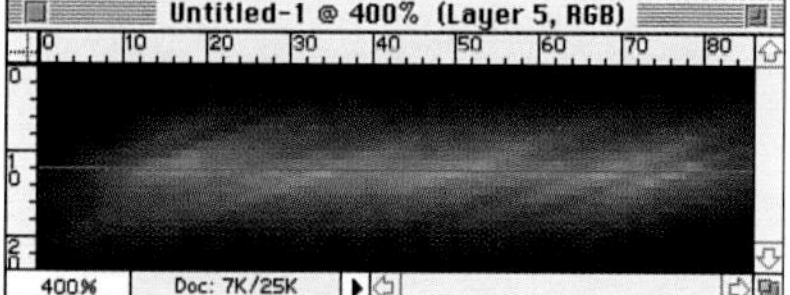

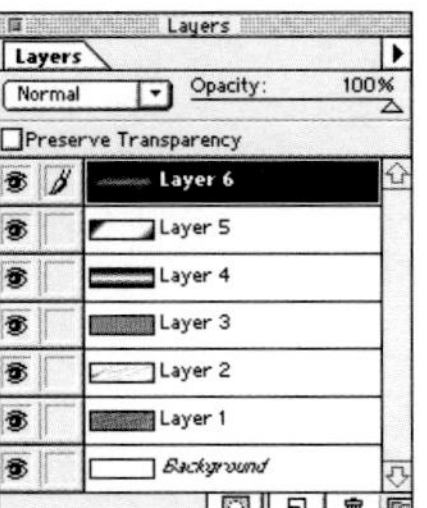


**9** Create a new layer (Layer 6). (Option)[Alt] Merge Visible to the new layer (which should be at the top of the Layers list). Select➥All. Copy.

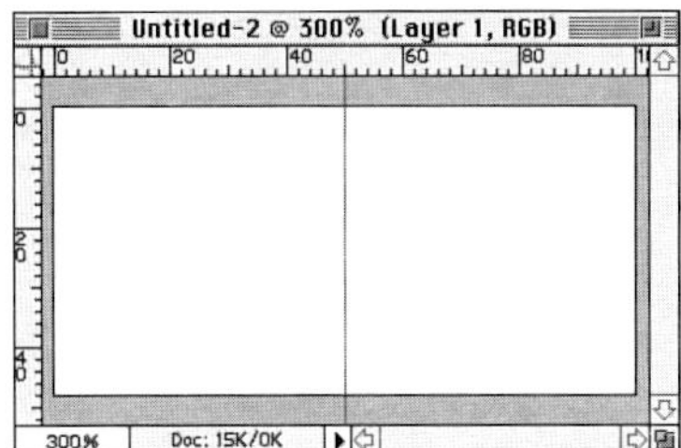


**10** Create a new file 100 pixels wide × 48 pixels high. There actually is a logic behind this file size. It needs to be twice the height of the fiber image (24×2=48), and the width of the fiber image plus the width of the vertical fiber that needs to be drawn (86 plus a warp width of 14 pixels=100 pixels). Create a new layer. Turn on the Rulers (Command-R)[Control-R]. Add a Vertical guide at the 50-pixel mark on the top ruler. Enlarge the window so that it is a little bit bigger than the image.

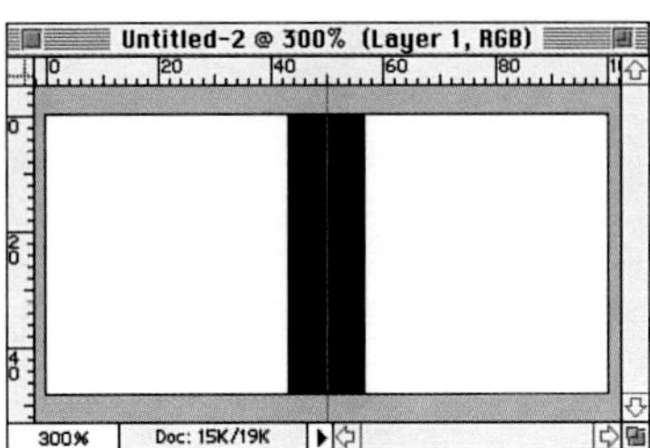


**11** Double-click the Line tool. Set the Line Width to 14 pixels and Anti-aliased off. Do not use arrowheads. Place your cursor on the guideline at the bottom of the window outside of the image. Press the Shift key and drag the line vertically up the guide. Release when it is outside of the image again. This ensures that the line covers the entire image.

**12** Switch to default colors. Double-click the Gradient tool. Choose the Center white Gradient preset from the *Photoshop Textures Magic* CD-ROM. Set the Gradient opacity to 30% and the mode to Normal. Turn on Preserve Transparency. Position the Gradient cursor exactly at the left edge of the line and drag it exactly to the right edge of the line. Press the Shift key as you drag to create a perfectly straight Gradient. This gives depth and roundness to the vertical wicker fiber.

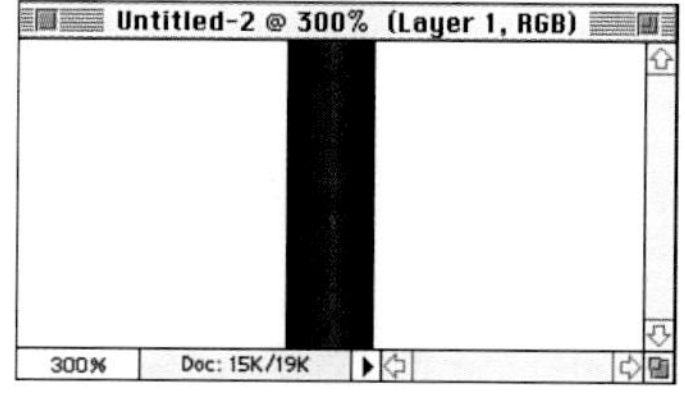


**13** Paste the fiber swatch that you copied in Step 9 into the new image. As long as you have nothing selected in the image, the horizontal fiber will paste in the exact center of the file. Select Layer➥Merge Down (Command-E)[Control-E]. This makes one row of wicker weaving.

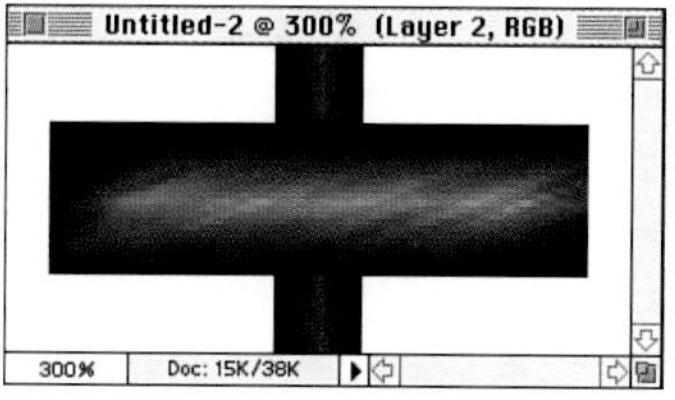


**14** Duplicate Layer 1. Select Filter➥Other➥Offset (Horizontal: 50, Vertical: 24, Wrap Around). These distances are one-half of image dimensions. This gives you a perfect staggered repeat, and simulates a true under-and-over weave.

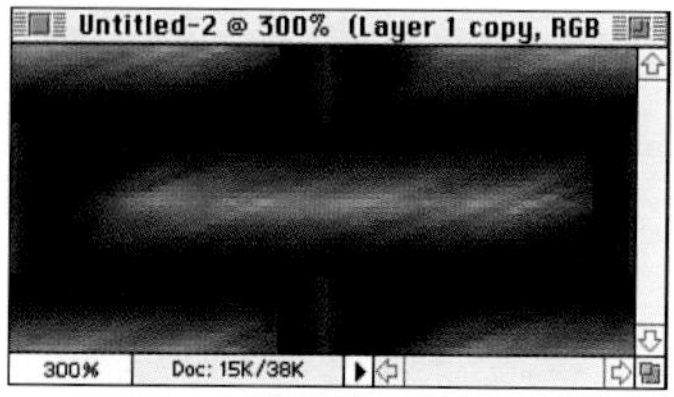


**15** Select➥All. Define the pattern. Create a new file of the desired dimensions. Mine is 750×750 pixels. Fill the new image with pattern.

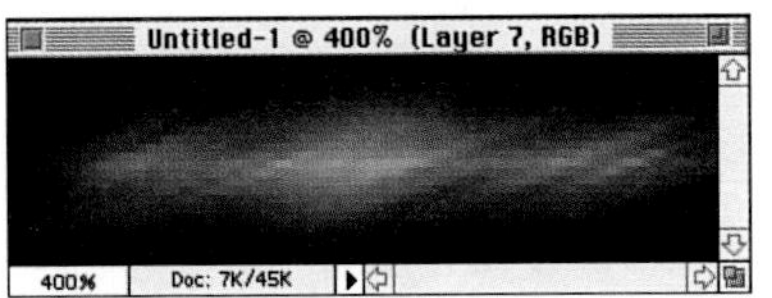


## VARIATIONS

### Highlighted Wicker

If you want the wicker to look as if it is bending a little as it goes over the vertical fiber, you need to highlight the center of the weft fiber and shadow the ends more deeply. To do this, you need to add some new steps after Step 8. Press the (Option)[Alt] key as you create a new layer. In the Layer Options dialog box, select Soft Light mode and check the Fill with Soft-Light-neutral color (50% gray) box. Double-click the Toning tool and select the Dodge tool at 12% exposure. Select Midtones as the mode. Use a soft, fairly large brush and lighten the center of the fiber in a somewhat diagonal direction that follows the angle of the fiber "twist."

To add additional shadowing, create a new layer. Double-click the Gradient tool. Change the Gradient to Foreground to Transparent. Set the Gradient opacity to 30%. Place the Gradient cursor in the upper-left corner of the image, press the Shift key, and drag the cursor diagonally until it reaches the bottom of the image. Repeat two more times. Then, place the Gradient cursor in the lower-right corner of the image, press the Shift key, and drag the cursor diagonally until it reaches the top of the image. Do this a total of three times. Your fiber now has almost a lozenge shape. From this point, follow Steps 9 to the end of the original instructions.

## Curved Wicker

To add a real curve to the wicker fiber, make these changes after Step 13. Turn off Preserve Transparency. Choose Image➡Rotate Canvas➡ 90° CW. Apply Filter➡Distort➡ Shear and create a center curve similar to the one shown.

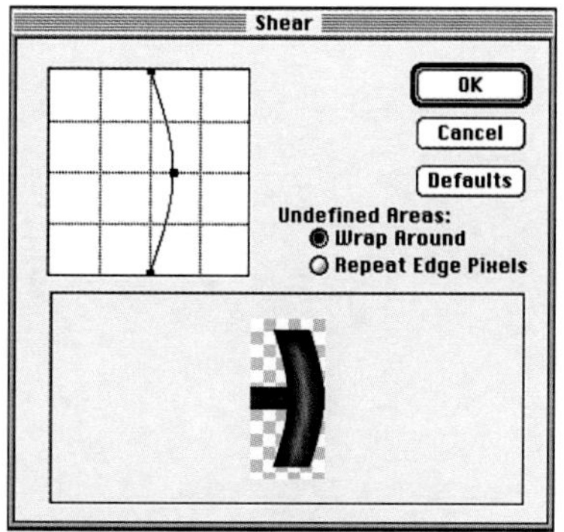


Then complete Step 14. However, the points that you can see here...

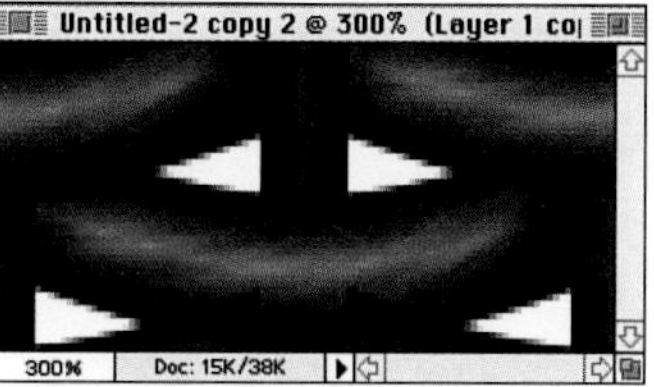


...need to be "tucked behind" the fiber on the row above. Create a layer mask. Use black and a soft brush and brush out the points. Return to the composite channel or you will not be able to define the pattern.

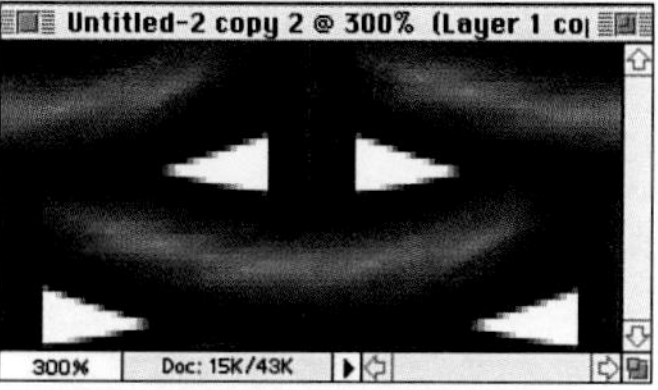


Then finish according to the original instructions. This makes a very open wicker texture. ■

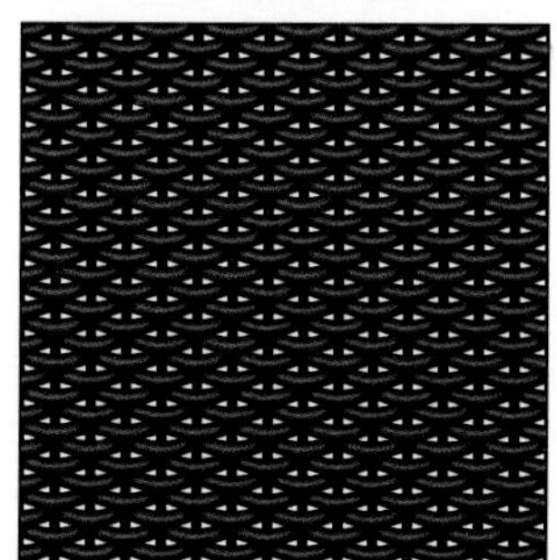

Woodgrain is a very useful texture for backgrounds, three-dimensional work, and as paneling. This wood technique creates a grainy wood that is characteristic of walnut. It is also a seamless pattern. It is much easier to make if you don't worry about tiling it, but it looks great tiled!

**1** Create a new file. I used one 300×300 pixels. If you need this texture for printed work, create it at 72 dpi and scale up to 300 dpi later using nearest neighbor interpolation. Switch the foreground color to a deep brown (I used RGB: 75, 30, 14). Switch the background color to a lighter brown (I used RGB: 132, 86, 50). Fill with background color.

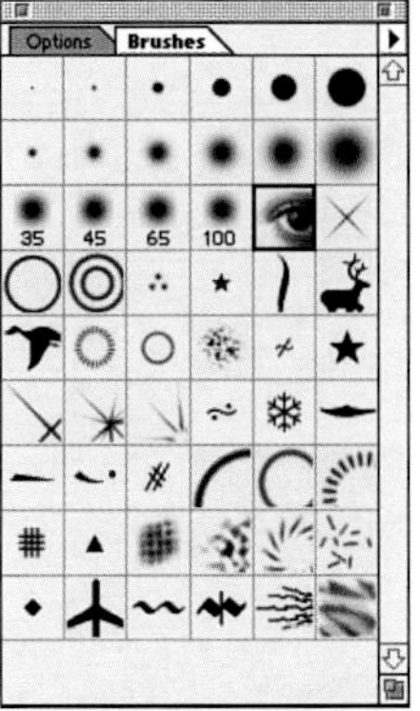


**2** Load the Assorted Brushes into the Brushes palette. They are located inside of the (Photoshop/ Goodies/Brushes & Patterns folder) [Photoshop/Brushes directory]. Select the brush that looks like an eye.

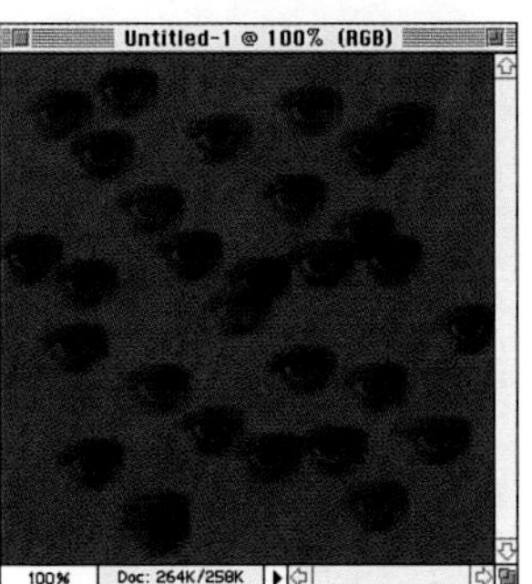


**3** Choose the Paintbrush tool and stamp the brush in a random manner all over your image.

**4** Choose Filter➡Blur➡Motion Blur. I used an Angle of –18° and a Distance of 44 pixels.

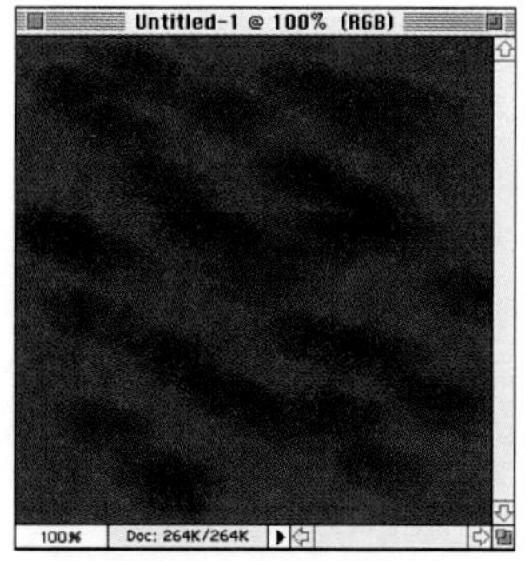


**5** We need to make the background seamless. Choose Filter➡Other➡Offset set at half of your file size in each direction, Wrap Around.

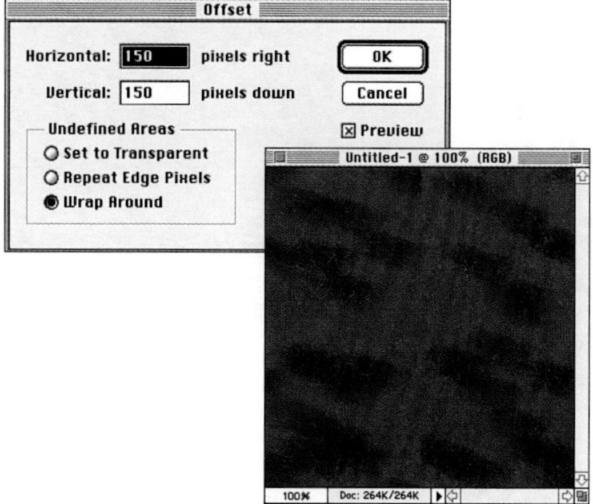


**6** Dab some additional "eyes" on the areas that seem to need it. Repeat Step 4.

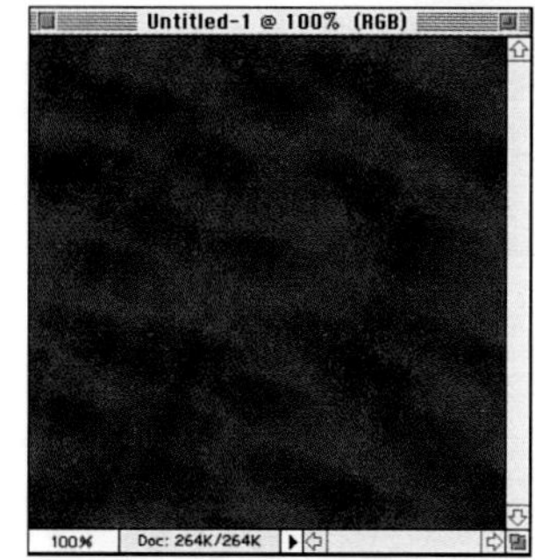

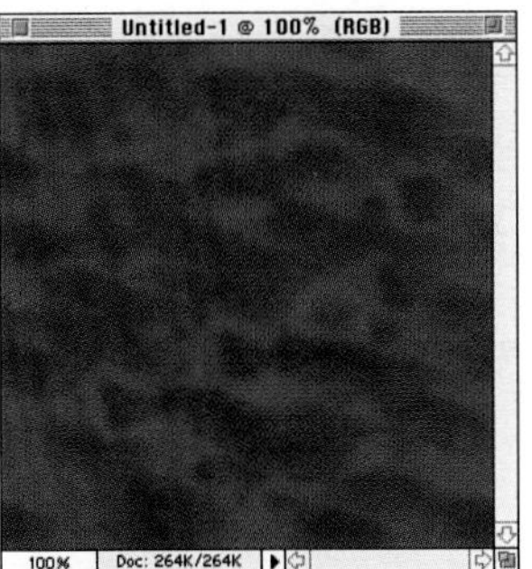


**7** Apply Filter➥Other➥Offset at the same settings as before to put the background into its original position. You will probably see a slight line across the center. Make the pattern seamless using the Rubber Stamp method. You can really mix up the color areas as you work. Just be careful not to get too close to the sides of the image.

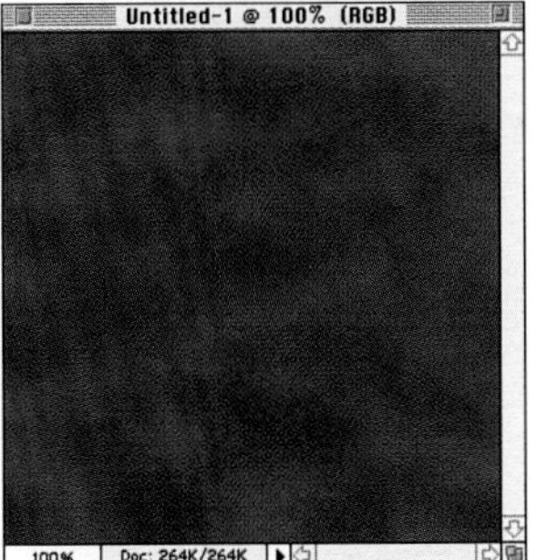


**8** Choose Filter➥Blur➥Gaussian Blur. Smooth out the Background. I used a Radius of 5.4. Don't over-smooth it—if you don't smooth it enough, you can fix it later.

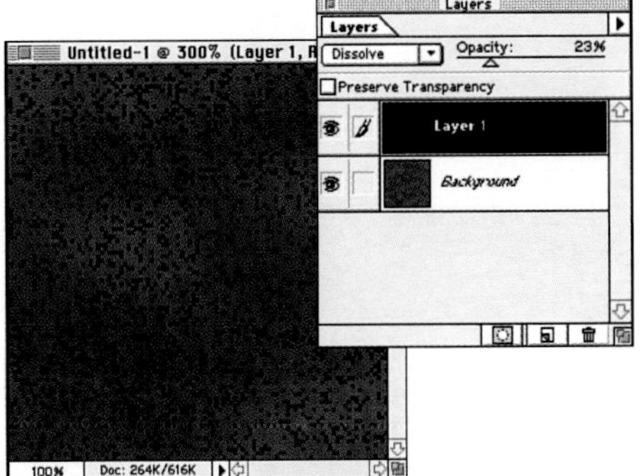


**9** Wood generally has grain and noise in it. Let's add some noise that uses the colors in our image. Create a new layer. Fill with foreground color. Change the blending mode to Dissolve, and reduce the layer opacity until you like the amount of noise. I used 23%.

**10** Now it's time to create the wood grain. Create a new layer. The grain needs to be seamless, so select the rectangular Marquee and set the fixed size to 250 pixels wide × 275 pixels high. Drag the Marquee into the center of the image. This way, it is easier not to draw woodgrain on the entire layer.

**11** Choose the Paintbrush tool and a small, soft brush. This is a good place to vary pressure if you have a pressure-sensitive tablet. Draw any shaped woodgrain lines that you like. Many types of wood tend to have narrow rings horizontally whereas the vertical spaces are more generous.

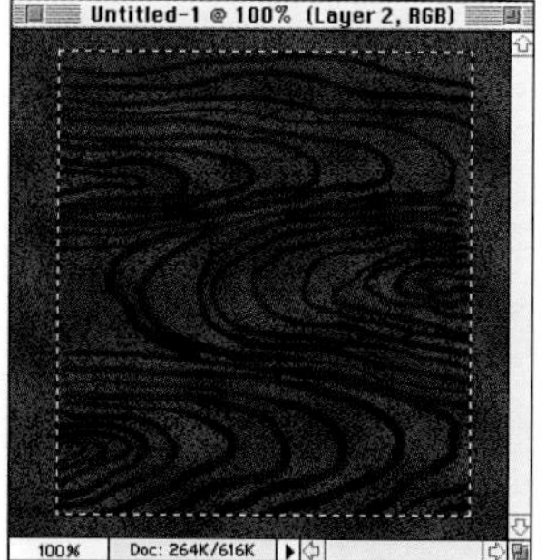


**12** Deselect. Apply Filter➡Other➡Offset. Continue to use the same settings as before. You can clearly see where it is necessary to join the lines.

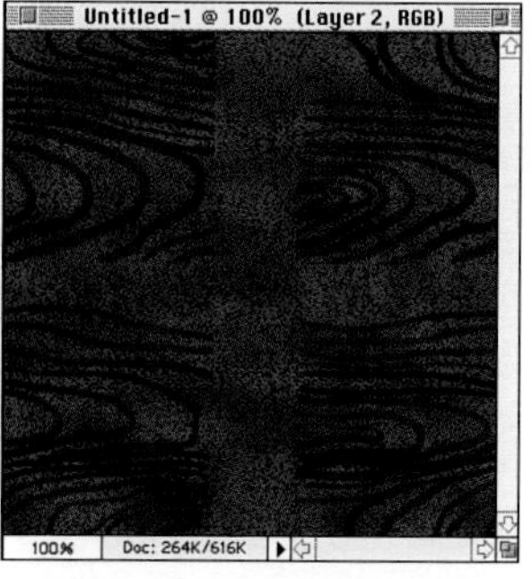


**13** Connect the lines as best you can. Sometimes, you may want to use the Eraser tool if you cannot get an area to join.

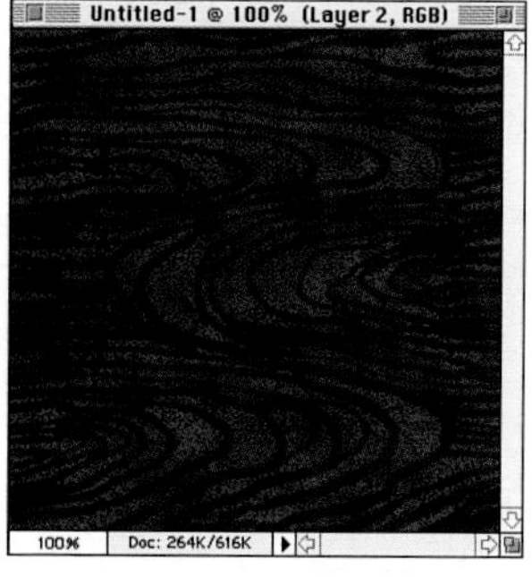


**14** Here's how to narrow the distance between the growth rings. Turn on the rulers (Command-R) [Control-R]. Add a Horizontal guide from the top ruler to the halfway mark on the vertical rule (I placed mine at the 150 pixel mark).

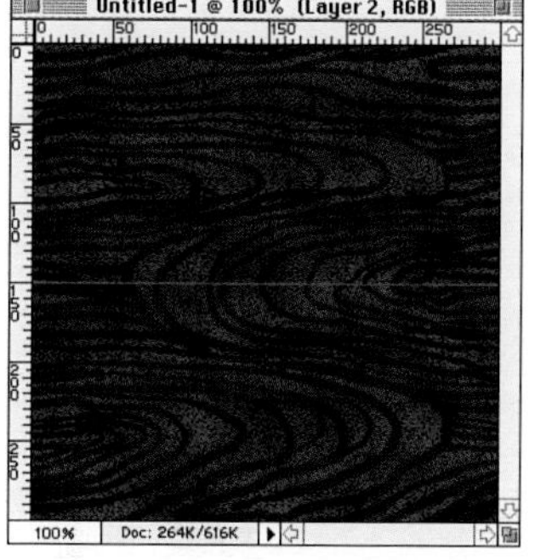

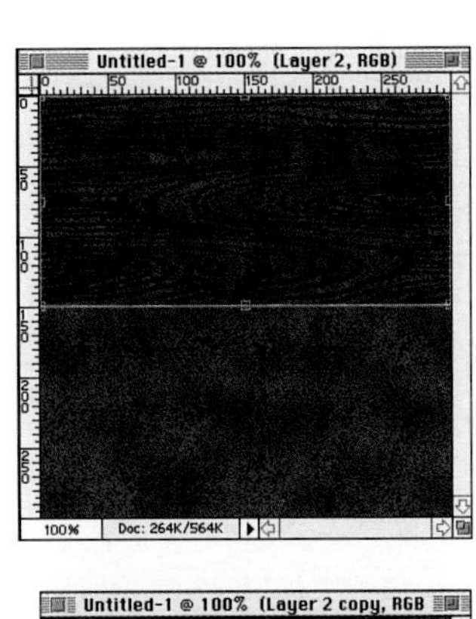


**15** Use the Free Transform command (Command-T)[Control-T] to scale the image by bringing the center-bottom point up to the guide. Double-click inside the shape to execute the scaling function.

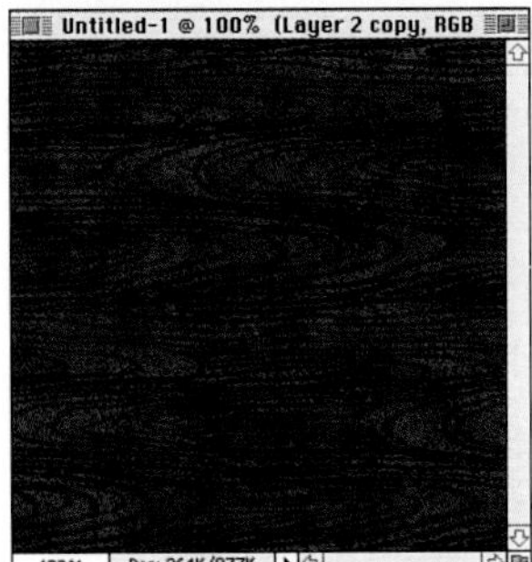


**16** Duplicate Layer 3. Apply Filter➡Other➡Offset. By using the same settings, you move the copied layer down to the other half of the image and wrap it from side to side as well. The pattern should still be seamless. Merge Down (Command-E)[Control-E]. Touch up as needed to make the image seamless if there is a matching problem. You might also want to try using the Masked Offset method of making an image seamless if you cannot get the wood to join any other way.

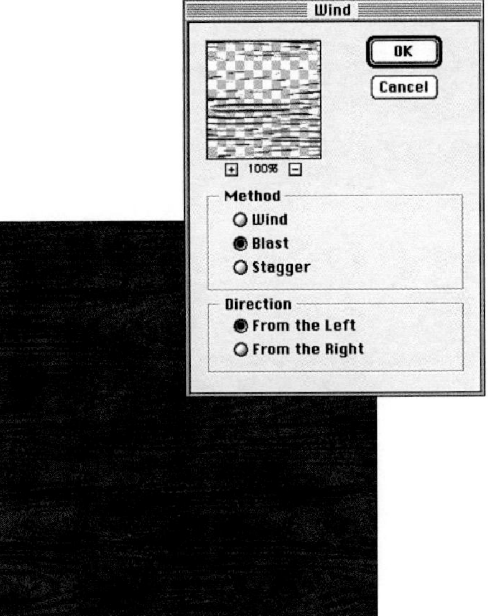


**17** Duplicate Layer 2. Choose Filter➡Stylize➡Wind (Blast, From the Left). Make Layer 2 active. Reduce the layer opacity so that the Wind filter changes can appear but you can still see some of the original grain. I used an opacity of 34%.

**18** When you have finished, tweak the opacity of the Dissolve layer (Layer 1) to control the amount of grain, or the opacities of Layer 2 and Layer 2 copy to fine-tune the effect.

## VARIATIONS

### A Quick, Non-Repeating Method

If you want a quick wood texture with a stronger grain, you can create a new file and fill with background color (your lighter color). Create a new layer. Fill with foreground color. Change the blending mode to Dissolve, and reduce the layer's opacity as you did in Step 9. Create a new layer and draw your woodgrain lines. Flatten the image. Duplicate the Background layer. Choose Filter➡Blur➡Gaussian Blur and increase the Radius until the image loses focus but is not obliterated. I used a Radius of 2.4. Change the blending mode to Darken. (This gives a subtle glow to the image—like polished wood.) Duplicate the Background layer again. Position the layer at the top of the layer list. Select Filter➡Stylize➡Wind (Blast, From the Left). Reduce the opacity of the layer until you like the results. I used an opacity of 90%.

## Weather-Beaten Wood

To create weathered wood, follow the Quick, Non-Repeating method instructions. Change the blending mode for the top layer to Exclusion. I used foreground color RGB: 81, 50, 16, and background color RGB: 163, 125, 23 in the example.

## Distressed Wood

You can add dark grain to any finished wood texture very easily. Create a new layer (Layer 1) by holding the (Option)[Alt] key and clicking on the New Layer icon. In the dialog box, change the blending mode to Multiply and check the box marked Fill with Multiply—neutral color (white). Choose Filter➡Noise➡Add Noise (Gaussian, Monochromatic). I used an Amount of 130. Select Filter➡Stylize➡Diffuse (Normal). Reapply this filter as many times as you want until you create clumps of noise (Command-F)[Control-F].

## Colorized Wood

Try changing the color of the wood. After your texture is complete (or at a preliminary stage if you want), create an adjustment layer using Hue/Saturation. You can click the Colorize button to make your wood more monochromatic, or not (the "not" option cycles the colors around the color wheel). ■

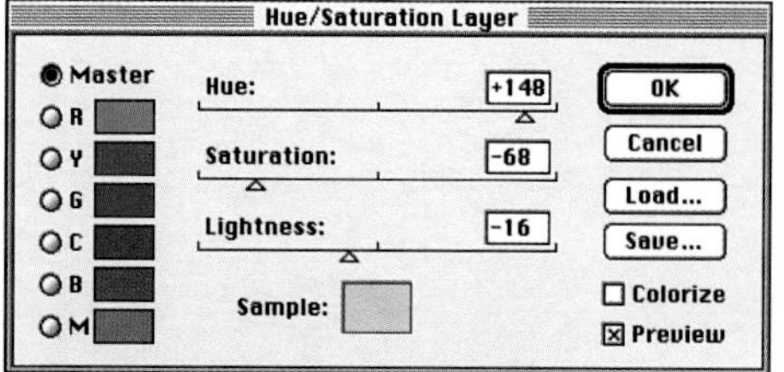

# Appendix A

## Listing of Contributors

### Software and Filters

**Adobe Systems, Inc.**
345 Park Avenue
San Jose, CA 95110-6000
Phone: 408-536-6000
Fax: 408-537-6000
`http://www.adobe.com`

Acrobat Reader™ 3.0 (Mac and PC)
Photoshop™ 3.0.5 Tryout (Mac and PC)
After Effects™ 3.0 Tryout (Mac only)
Streamline™ 3.1 Tryout (Mac and PC)
Dimensions™ 2.0 Tryout (Mac only)
Illustrator® 6.0 Tryout (Mac only)

**Alien Skin Software**
1100 Wake Forest Rd. Suite 101
Raleigh, NC 27604
Phone: 919-832-4124
Fax: 919-832-4065

Eye Candy 3.0 Demo (Mac and PC)

**Andromeda Software, Inc.**
699 Hampshire Rd. Suite 109
Thousand Oaks, CA 91361
Phone: 800-547-0055 or 805-379-4109
Fax: 805-379-5253
`orders@andromeda.com`

Series 1,2, 3, & 4 Demos (Mac and PC)

**AutoFX**
15 North Main Street Suite 8
Wolfeboro, NH 03894
Phone: 603-569-8800
Fax: 603-569-9702
`http://www.autofx.com`

Sample Edge, Page Effects (Mac and PC)
Sample Patterns and Textures (PC)

**Cochenille**
P.O. Box 4276
Encinitas, CA 92023
Phone: 619-259-1698
Fax: 619-259-3746
info@cochenille.com

StitchPainter (Mac and PC)

**Digital Frontiers**
1019 Asbury Ave.
Evanston, IL 60202
Phone: 827-328-0880
Fax: 827-869-2053
http://www/digfrontiers.com

HVS Color (Mac and PC)
HVS Photo JPEG (PC)

**Extensis**
1800 SW First Ave. Suite 500
Portland, OR 97201-5322
Phone: 503-274-2020
Fax: 503-274-0530
http://www.extensis.com

Intellihance (Mac and PC)
PhotoTools (Mac and PC)

**Fractal Design, Inc.**
5550 Scotts Valley Drive
Scotts Valley, CA 95066
Phone: 408-688-5300
http://www.fractal.com

Detailer (Mac and PC)



**Fortune Hill, Inc.**
814 Glendover Cove
Lexington, KY 40502
Phone: 606-269-0933
samoore@best.com

Wild River SSK Demo (Mac only)

**MetaTools, Inc.**
6303 Carpinteria Ave.
Carpinteria, CA 93013
Phone: 805-566-6200
metasales@aol.com

KPT 3.0 Demo (Mac and PC)

| | |
|---|---|
| **Specular, International**<br>7 Pomeroy Lane<br>Amherst, MA 01002<br>Phone: 800-433-SPEC<br>Fax: 413-253-0540 | Infini-D™ Demo (Mac and PC)<br>Collage 2.0 Demo (Mac only)<br>LogoMotion Demo (Mac only)<br>TextureScape™ Demo (Mac only) |
| **Three-D Graphics**<br>1801 Avenue of the Stars<br>Suite 600<br>Los Angeles, CA 90067-5908<br>Voice: 310-553-3313<br>Fax: 310-788-8975<br>`http://www.threedgraphics.com` | Texture Creator (Mac and PC) |
| **Vertigo**<br>Phone: 1-888-4-VERTIGO<br>Fax: 604-684-2108<br>`http://www.vertigo3d.com` | 3D Dizzy (Mac only) |
| **Xaos Tools, Inc.**<br>55 Hawthorn Suite 1000<br>San Francisco, CA 94105<br>Phone: 1-800-BUY-XAOS | Paint Alchemy 2™ Demo (Mac only)<br>Terrazo 2™ Demo (Mac only)<br>TypeCaster™ Demo (Mac only) |

## Stock Images

| | |
|---|---|
| **Artis**<br>Edvard Hartmann Platz 3M12<br>Laxenburg, Austria<br>Phone: 43-2236-73570<br>Fax: 43-2236-73661<br>`http://www.artis.com` | Sample images created with Texture Magic™ (Mac) |
| **DigitalShowbiz**<br>`http://www.dsb.com` | Sample images from Ruff Stuff (Mac and PC) |
| **MetaTools, Inc.**<br>6303 Carpinteria Ave.<br>Carpinteria, CA 93013<br>Phone: 805-566-6200<br>`metasales@aol.com` | |

**Ultimate Symbol Collection**

31 Wilderness Drive

Stony Point, NY 10980-3447

Phone: 800-611-4761

Fax: 914-942-0004

**Vivid Details**

8228 Sulphur Mtn. Rd.

Ojai, CA 93023

Phone: 805-646-0021

http://www.vividdetails.com

# Appendix B

## What's on the CD-ROM

The CD-ROM that comes with this book is both Macintosh and Windows compatible. Please note that there are several demos and tryouts available for Macintosh users that are not available for Windows users, and vice versa. This means that either the product does not exist for that platform, or a version is being created but was not available at the time of publication.

It is suggested that you refer to the READ ME and other information files included in the demo software program's folder. Also, visit the corporate Web sites for updates and more information. (The URLs are noted in Appendix A.) There are often demos of new software available for downloading and tryout.

The CD-ROM is divided into four folders.

## Contents

### Filters

This folder contains lots of different filters you can use to manipulate your images. You can do a variety of things with filters, one of the most powerful features of Photoshop. These filters are all commercial demos.

### Images

Some of the techniques in *Photoshop Textures Magic* begin with stock art provided by commercial stock photo companies. You'll find them here.

### Presets

Here's where you'll find the "pieces" referred to in the Toolbox section at the start of many of the techniques. These include the Lighting Styles presets, Gradient presets, and a variety of Curves and Color sets, as well as some templates to use to create marbled patterns.

### Software

This folder contains demos of commercial software, including Adobe products and Fractal Design products.

## Installation

For detailed instructions on how to install and use the resources I've included on the CD-ROM, please consult the READ ME and ABOUT files in the individual Software, Filters, Presets, and Images folders. General installation information follows:

### Filters

Filters should be copied into the Plug-Ins folder, located in the same place as your Adobe Photoshop application. Then, relaunch Photoshop, and find the filters in the Filter menu. You can now access and apply these third-party filters the same way you use Photoshop's filters.

### Preset Files

The Lighting Styles presets should be copied into the Lighting FX folder in the Plugins/Filters folder inside of the Photoshop folder or directory.

You can load the other presets through their specific menus (example: the Gradients presets can be loaded into the Gradients list by selecting the Edit button on the Gradient Options palette and then choosing Load... from the Edit dialog box). The files suffixed by .act or .alt are color tables and can be opened either by the Custom option in the Image➡Mode➡Color Table command or by the Load or Replace command in the Swatches palette menu. These files are in the CLUTS subfolder.

.Acv files can be opened by the Levels or Curves commands. .Ahu files may be opened by the Hue/Saturation command. These files are found in the Maps subfolder.

The Images subfolder contains the files that are specifically referred to by the effects in the book. They are all .PSD files (native Photoshop format).

All of the files in all of the subfolders here may be copied to your hard disk if you want.

### Stock Imagery and Textures

The stock photos and textures located in the Images folder do not need to be copied to your hard drive. For most files, you can double-click on them to open them in Photoshop. If they do not open, try opening Photoshop first, then select File➡Open. Then choose the file you would like to open. If you particularly like a certain image and would like to access it quickly, by all means copy it to your hard drive.

# Gallery

*page 30*

*page 34*

*page 46*

*page 52*

*page 58*

*page 66*

page 72

page 78

page 86

*page 92*

*page 98*

*page 104*

page 108

page 112

page 120

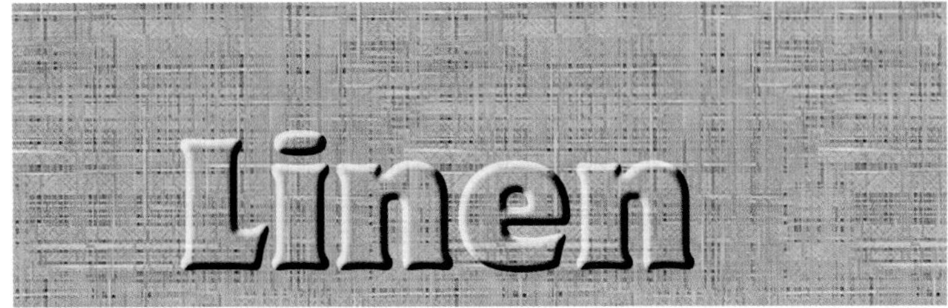


*page 124*

*page 128*

*page 134*

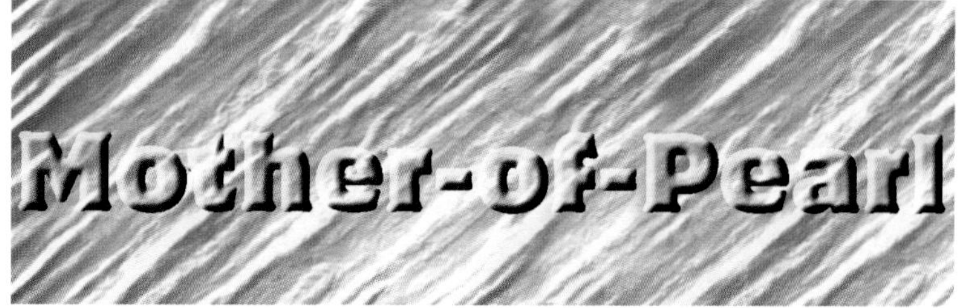


*page 138*

*page 146*

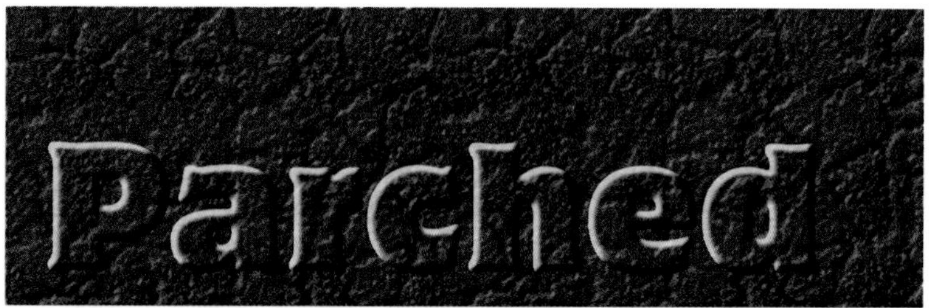


*page 152*

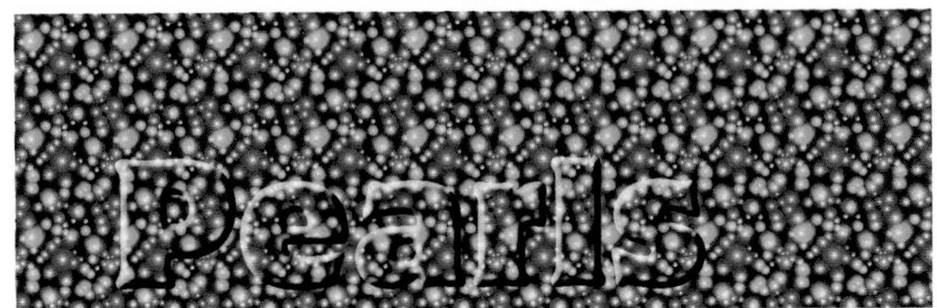


page 162

page 168

page 172

*page 176*

*page 182*

*page 188*

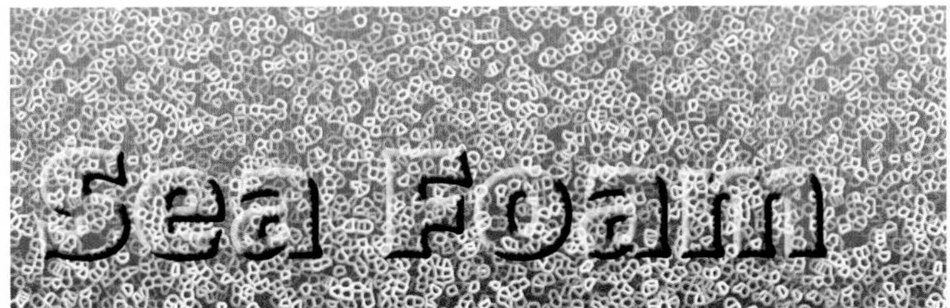


page 196

page 200

page 208

*page 214*

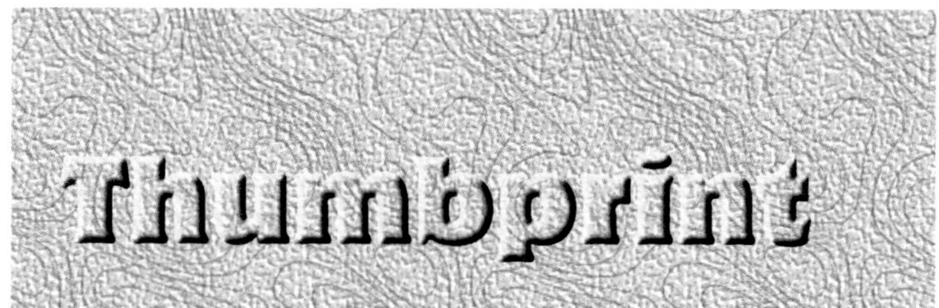


*page 220*

*page 228*

page 232

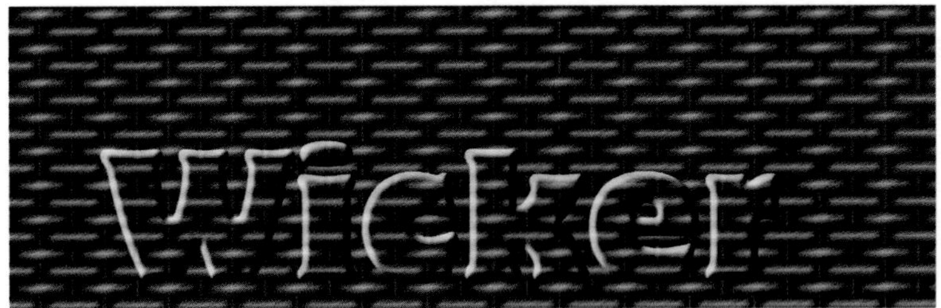


page 240

page 246

# Other DESIGN/GRAPHICS Titles

**Designing Business**

Provides the design/business communities with a new way of thinking about how the right design can be a strategic business advantage. It is the definitive guide to presenting a business identity through the use of traditional media vehicles and emerging technologies.

- CD-ROM (dual-platform) exhibits interactive prototypes of multimedia brochures, interactive television, and Web sites as developed by Clement Mok Designs Inc., one of the most sought after interactive design agencies in the world
- Shows how effective communication is one way to out-think, out-plan, and out-perform the competition

*Clement Mok*
1-56830-282-7 ■ $60.00 USA/$81.95 CDN
264 pp., 8 x 10, Covers PC and Macintosh, New - Expert
*Available Now*

**Adobe Persuasion: Classroom in a Book**
1-56830-316-5 ■ $40.00 USA/$56.95 CDN
*Available Now*

**Learning Adobe FrameMaker**
1-56830-290-8 ■ $60.00 USA/$81.95 CDN
*Available Now*

**Adobe Illustrator for Windows: Classroom in a Book**
1-56830-053-0 ■ $44.95 USA/$59.99 CDN
*Available Now*

**Adobe PageMaker for Windows: Classroom in a Book**
1-56830-184-7 ■ $45.00 USA/$61.95 CDN
*Available Now*

**Adobe Photoshop: Classroom in a Book**
1-56830-317-3 ■ $45.00 USA/$63.95 CDN
*Available Now*

**Advanced Adobe PageMaker for Windows 95: Classroom in a Book**
1-56830-262-2 ■ $50.00 USA/$68.95 CDN
*Available Now*

**Advanced Adobe Photoshop for Windows: Classroom in a Book**
1-56830-116-2 ■ $50.00 USA/$68.95 CDN
*Available Now*

**The Amazing PhotoDeluxe Book for Windows**
1-56830-286-X ■ $30.00 USA/$40.95 CDN
*Available Now*

**Branding with Type**
1-56830-248-7 ■ $18.00 USA/$24.95 CDN
*Available Now*

**Digital Type Design Guide**
1-56830-190-1 ■ $45.00 USA/$61.95 CDN
*Available Now*

**Fractal Design Painter Creative Techniques**
1-56830-283-5 ■ $45.00 USA/$56.95 CDN
*Available Now*

**Photoshop 4 Type Magic 1**
1-56830-380-7 ■ $39.99 USA/$47.95 CDN
*Available Now*

**Photoshop Web Magic**
1-56830-314-9 ■ $45.00 USA/$63.95 CDN
*Available Now*

**Adobe Photoshop Complete**
1-56830-323-8 ■ $49.99 USA/$61.95 CDN
*Available Now*

**Stop Stealing Sheep & Find Out How Type Works**
0-672-48543-5 ■ $19.95 USA/$26.99 CDN
*Available Now*

Copyright © 1997, Macmillan Computer Publishing USA. A Simon & Schuster Company. The Publishing Operation of Viacom, Inc.

**Visit your fine local bookstore, or for more information visit us at http//:www.mcp.com/hayden/**

# PLUG YOURSELF INTO...

# THE MACMILLAN INFORMATION SUPERLIBRARY™

**Free information and vast computer resources from the world's leading computer book publisher—online!**

FIND THE BOOKS THAT ARE RIGHT FOR YOU!
A complete online catalog, plus sample chapters and tables of contents!

- STAY INFORMED with the latest computer industry news through our online newsletter, press releases, and customized Information SuperLibrary Reports.
- GET FAST ANSWERS to your questions about Hayden books.
- VISIT our online bookstore for the latest information and editions!
- COMMUNICATE with our expert authors through email and conferences.
- DOWNLOAD SOFTWARE from the immence Macmillan Computer Publishing library:
  - Source code, shareware, freeware, and demos.
- DISCOVER HOT SPOTS on other parts of the Internet.
- WIN BOOKS in ongoing contests and giveaways!

**TO PLUG INTO HAYDEN:**

WORLD WIDE WEB: **http://www.mcp.com/hayden/**

FTP: ftp.mcp.com

# REGISTRATION CARD

## Photoshop Textures Magic

Name ______________________________ Title ______________

Company ______________________________ Type of business ______________

Address ______________________________________________

City/State/ZIP ______________________________________________

Have you used these types of books before? ☐ yes ☐ no

If yes, which ones? ______________________________________________

______________________________________________

How many computer books do you purchase each year? ☐ 1–5 ☐ 6 or more

How did you learn about this book? ______________________________

- ☐ recommended by a friend
- ☐ recommended by store personnel
- ☐ saw in catalog
- ☐ received ad in mail
- ☐ read book review
- ☐ saw on bookshelf

Where did you purchase this book? ______________________________

Which applications do you currently use? ______________________________

Which computer magazines do you subscribe to? ______________________________

What trade shows do you attend? ______________________________

Please number the top three factors which most influenced your decision for this book purchase.

- ☐ cover
- ☐ approach to content
- ☐ logo
- ☐ layout/design
- ☐ price
- ☐ author's reputation
- ☐ publisher's reputation
- ☐ other ____________

Would you like to be placed on our preferred mailing list? ☐ yes ☐ no email address ____________

☐ **I would like to see my name in print!** You may use my name and quote me in future Hayden products and promotions. My daytime phone number is: ______________________

Comments ______________________________________________

______________________________________________

______________________________________________

**Hayden Books** Attn: Product Marketing ◆ 201 West 103rd Street ◆ Indianapolis, Indiana 46290 USA

Fax to **317-581-3576** Visit our Web Page **http://www.mcp.com/hayden/**

Fold Here

NO POSTAGE
NECESSARY
IF MAILED
IN THE
UNITED STATES

**BUSINESS REPLY MAIL**

**FIRST-CLASS MAIL PERMIT NO. 9918 INDIANAPOLIS IN**

**POSTAGE WILL BE PAID BY THE ADDRESSEE**

**HAYDEN BOOKS**
**Attn: Product Marketing**
**201 W 103RD ST**
**INDIANAPOLIS IN 46290-9058**

# Technical Support:

If you cannot get the CD-ROM/Disk to install properly, or you need assistance with a particular situation in the book, please feel free to check out the Knowledge Base on our Web site at **http://www.superlibrary.com/general/support**. We have answers to our most Frequently Asked Questions listed there. If you do not find your specific question answered, please contact Macmillan Technical Support at **(317) 581-3833**. We can also be reached by email at **support@mcp.com**.

# Photoshop 4 Type Magic 1

Stanger
Stet · Fortuna · Domus

# Photoshop 4 Type Magic 1

BY DAVID LAI AND GREG SIMSIC

# Photoshop 4 Type Magic 1

©1997 David Lai and Greg Simsic

All rights reserved. Printed in the United States of America. No part of this book may be used or reproduced in any form or by any means, or stored in a database or retrieval system, without prior written permission of the publisher except in the case of brief quotations embodied in critical articles and reviews. Making copies of any part of this book for any purpose other than your own personal use is a violation of United States copyright laws. For information, address Hayden Books, 201 W. 103rd Street, Indianapolis, Indiana 46290.

Library of Congress Catalog Number: 97-071008
ISBN: 1-56830-380-7

Copyright © 1997 Hayden Books

Printed in the United States of America 3 4 5 6 7 8 9 0

## Warning and Disclaimer

This book is sold as is, without warranty of any kind, either express or implied. While every precaution has been taken in the preparation of this book, the authors and Hayden Books assume no responsibility for errors or omissions. Neither is any liability assumed for damages resulting from the use of the information or instructions contained herein. It is further stated that the publisher and authors are not responsible for any damage or loss to your data or your equipment that results directly or indirectly from your use of this book.

## Trademark Acknowledgments

All terms mentioned in this book that are known to be trademarks or services marks have been appropriately capitalized. Hayden Books cannot attest to the accuracy of this information. Use of a term in this book should not be regarded as affecting the validity of any trademark or service mark. Photoshop is a trademark of Adobe Systems, Inc.

# The Photoshop 4 Type Magic 1 Team

**President**
Richard Swadley

**Associate Publisher**
John Pierce

**Publishing Manager**
Laurie Petrycki

**Managing Editor**
Lisa Wilson

**Marketing Manager**
Stacey Oldham

**Acquisitions Editor**
Rachel Byers

**Development Editors**
Beth Millett

**Copy/Production Editor**
Kevin Laseau

**Technical Editors**
Kate Binder, Rick Wallace

**Publishing Coordinator**
Karen Flowers

**Cover Designer**
Aren Howell

**Book Designer**
Gary Adair

**Manufacturing Coordinator**
Brook Farling

**Production Team Supervisors**
Laurie Casey, Joe Millay

**Production Team**
Dan Caparo, Diana Groth, Mary Hunt,
Billy Huys, Pamela Woolf

Composed in *Bembo* and *GillSans*

Some thumbtab imagery provided by CMCD, Digital Stock,
D'Pix, FotoSets, Image Club Graphics, and PhotoDisc, 1997.

## About the Authors

David Lai is the author of *Icons for the Masses* published by Peachpit Press and owner of Lai Design.

Greg Simsic, currently a student of sculpture at Herron School of Art in Indianapolis, is the author of *Photoshop Type Magic 2*, published by Hayden Books.

## Hayden Books

The staff of Hayden Books is committed to bringing you the best computer books. What our readers think of Hayden is important to our ability to serve our customers. If you have any comments, no matter how great or how small, we'd appreciate your taking the time to send us a note.

You can reach Hayden Books at the following:

Hayden Books
201 West 103rd Street
Indianapolis, IN 46290
317-581-3833

Email addresses:

America Online: Hayden Bks
Internet: hayden@hayden.com

Visit the Hayden Books Web site at `http://www.hayden.com`

# Contents

# About This Book

## Welcome

Welcome to this collection of special type techniques for Adobe Photoshop users. More than a how-to manual, this book is a what-to guide. The steps in this book tell you what you need to do in order to create exactly what you want. Flip through the alphabetized thumbtabs to find the type effect you want to create and follow the concise, explanatory steps. If you need a little extra help, flip to the Photoshop Basics section. But, before you jump into the type treatments, let me tell you a little about how this book works. A quick read now will maximize your time later.

## System Setup

Here are the system recommendations for creating these type treatments.

Mac users: The Adobe Photoshop 4 Info box suggests a memory allocation of 21 megabytes (MB) of RAM to run Photoshop, and your system software may need as much as 10MB of RAM. That's a full bowl of soup, but if you've got the memory, then we would recommend setting the Preferred memory size even higher than 21MB. If you don't have 21MB to spare, then just quit all other applications and give it everything you've got.

PC users: Adobe suggests 32MB of RAM for Photoshop on any 386 or faster processor running Windows 3.1, Windows 95, or Windows NT, but 40MB is better. Quit any application you can before starting Photoshop to maximize the running of the application. Photoshop runs 32-bit native on both Windows 95 and Windows NT operating systems.

It is not crucial, but it will help if you have a CD-ROM drive. A number of the effects in this book use files that are contained on the CD-ROM that comes bundled with this book. (See Appendix A, "What's On the CD-ROM," for information on accessing those files.) If you don't have a CD-ROM drive, however, you still can perform all of the effects described in the book.



## Adobe Photoshop 4

All of the techniques in this book were created with Adobe Photoshop 4, and that's the version we recommend you use. If you're attempting to duplicate these techniques using an earlier version of Photoshop, your results may differ slightly or significantly compared to ours. If you're working with version 3, then you still will be able to create all of the effects in the book. Keep in mind, however, that you will need to adjust the instructions for the differences between the two versions. You will see that even some of the old Photoshop features work differently in Photoshop 4. Most of the effects in this book use features that were not available in earlier versions of Photoshop.

## Conventions

Every image in this book was created initially as a RGB file. You can make your effects in any appropriate color mode, but you should be aware of the variations this will cause as you proceed through the steps. The first new channel created in an RGB file, for example, is automatically named Channel #4. But the first new channel created in a CMYK file is named Channel #5. You also should be aware of the differences in the color ranges of the various color modes. Some colors that look great in RGB mode may look like mud after you convert the file color mode to CMYK. **Note:** Quite a few techniques in this book use the Lighting Effects filter. This filter will not work in a CMYK or Grayscale file.

If you'd like more detailed information about the different color modes, refer to a good general Photoshop book such as *Photoshop 4 Complete* or to your Photoshop user manuals.

Also, every type image was created as a 5×2-inch, 150-dpi resolution file. (The thumbtab images were created as 300 dpi files.) If you are going to work in a resolution other than 150 dpi, remember that some of the filters and commands will require different settings than the settings I used. Because there are fewer pixels in a 72 dpi image, a Gaussian Blur radius of 5 pixels blurs the image more than if it were a 150 dpi image. Just keep an eye on the figures next to the steps and match the outcome as closely as you can.

## The Toolbox

For some of the effects, I used a third-party filter or a specially prepared preset file. Any of these extra tools that are not included with the standard Photoshop software are listed in the Toolbox in the lower-left corner of the first page of each technique. The Toolbox lists everything that you'll need to create each type effect and any of its variations. The CD-ROM that comes with this book contains all of the files needed to perform all of the basic techniques. For information on accessing and installing these files, turn to Appendix A, "What's On the CD-ROM."



## The Blue Type

As you work through the steps, you will see phrases colored blue. These same phrases are listed in alphabetical order in the Photoshop Basics section (pages 5–21). If the phrase in blue asks you to perform a task unfamiliar to you, then you can find that phrase in the Photoshop Basics section and follow the instructions on how to perform that task.

## Menu Commands

You also will see instructions that look like this:

Filter➡Blur➡Gaussian Blur (2 pixels)

This example asks you to apply the Gaussian Blur filter. To perform this command, click the Filter menu at the top of the screen and drag down to Blur. When Blur is highlighted a new menu opens to the right, from which you can choose Gaussian Blur.

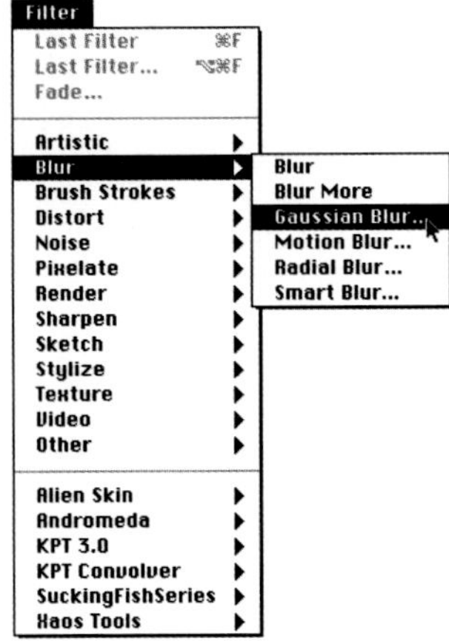


In this example, a dialog box appears asking you for more information. All of the settings that you need to perform each task appear in the text of the step. The previous example tells you to enter 2 pixels as the Radius.

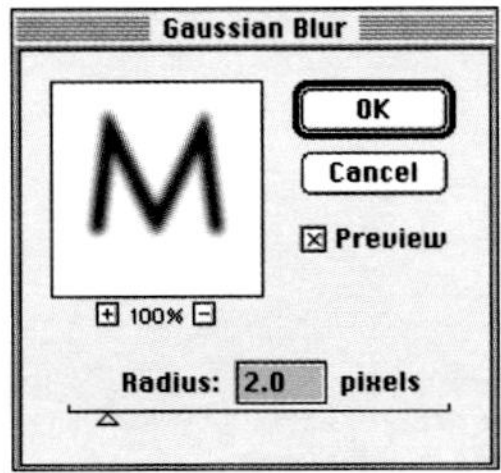


Click OK to blur the type.

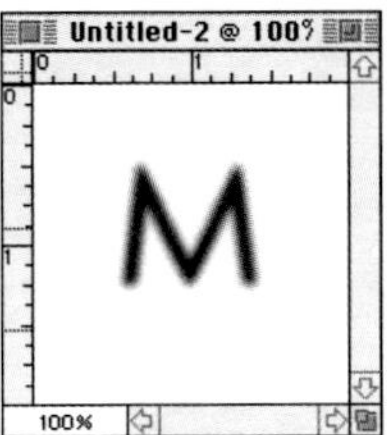

## Settings

Following each action in the steps, you will find the settings for that feature. These recommended settings are meant to act as guides; the best settings for your type effect may vary depending on variables such as your font, color, background, or size. As a rule of thumb, it is best to match the outcomes that you see in the figures as you progress through the technique. The greatest differences occur when the resolution of your file or the point size of your type are significantly different from what we used. The following two images demonstrate the importance of adjusting for resolution differences. A 6-pixel Radius Gaussian Blur was applied to both images.

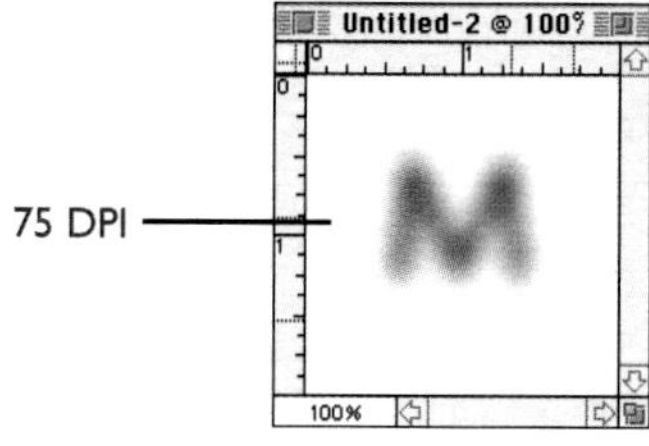


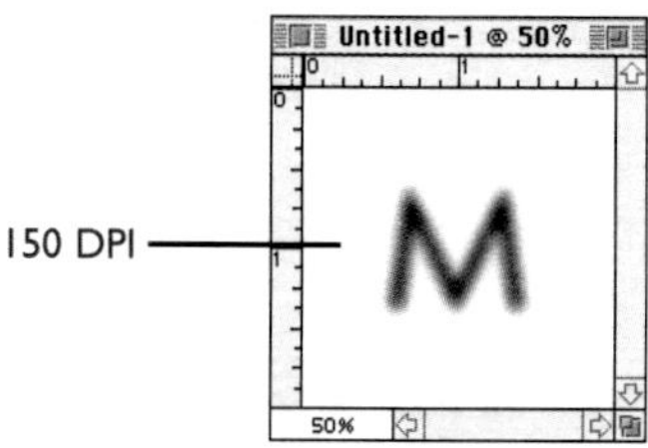


## Tips

Throughout the book, you will find additional bits of information that can help you render a better type effect. These tips provide information beyond the basic steps of each lesson. ■

# Photoshop Basics

The goal of this section is to help novice users of Photoshop with the simple, basic tasks required to create the type effects described and illustrated in this book. Each of the basic tasks described in this section corresponds to the blue text in the chapters that follow. Here, users can easily find the instructions they need for performing a particular Photoshop task.

This chapter proceeds on two assumptions: that you're creating our type effects in Photoshop 4; and that you're keeping the Tool and Layer/Channel/Path palettes open. If one or both of the Tool and Layer/Channel/Path palettes are closed when you refer to this chapter, you can reopen them by name by using the Window menu at the top of the screen. If you're using an earlier version of Photoshop, you can refer to the Photoshop manual for instructions on how to perform these tasks. Also, keep in mind that Photoshop 2.5 does not offer the capability to work in layers.

## The Toolbox

If you're not familiar with Photoshop's Toolbox, there's no reason to panic. With a bit of experimentation, it doesn't take long to learn each tool's individual functions. To help the beginning Photoshop user along the way, here is a representation of the toolbars from both Photoshop 3 and 4. This will also help advanced users find the rearranged tools.

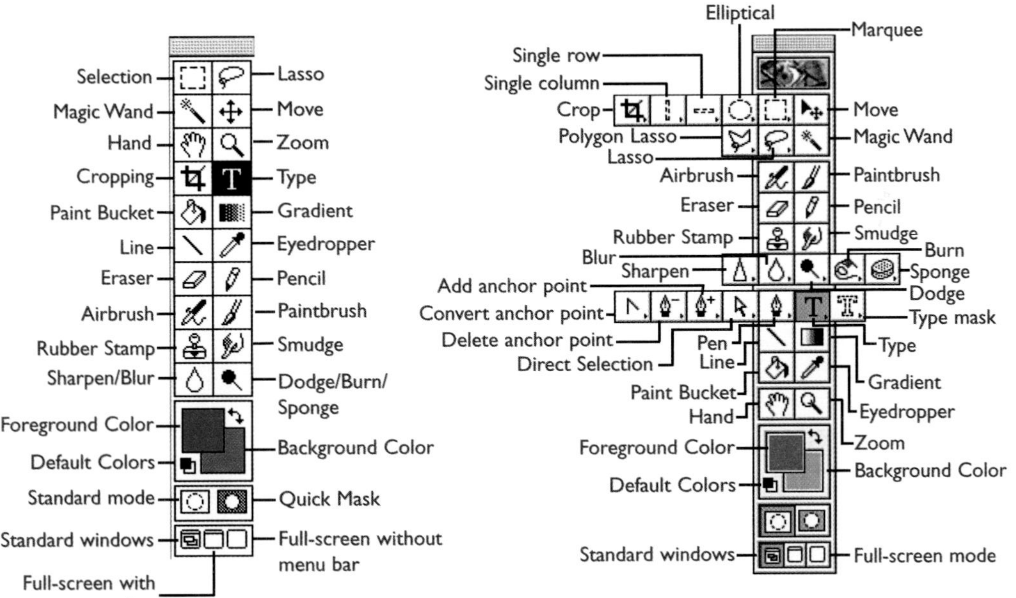

## Choose a Foreground or Background Color

**Shortcut**: Press D to change colors to their defaults: black for the foreground, and white for the background if you're working on a layer, and the other way around in a channel or on a layer mask or adjustment layer.

Press X to switch the foreground color with the the background color.

To change the foreground or background color click either the Foreground icon or the Background icon.

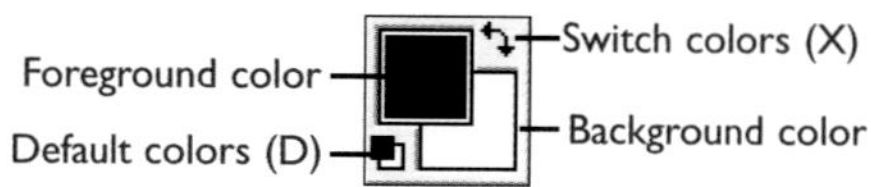


The Color Picker dialog box appears, which enables you to choose a new foreground or background color by moving and clicking the cursor (now a circle) along the spectrum box, or by changing specific RGB, CMYK, or other percentage values. Note that the Foreground and Background color icons on the Toolbox now reflect your color choices.

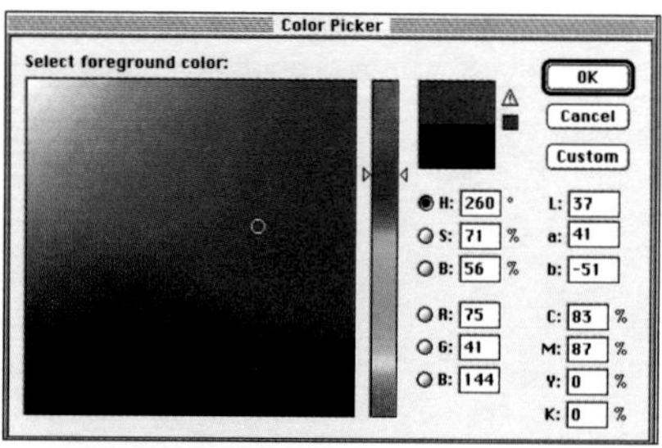


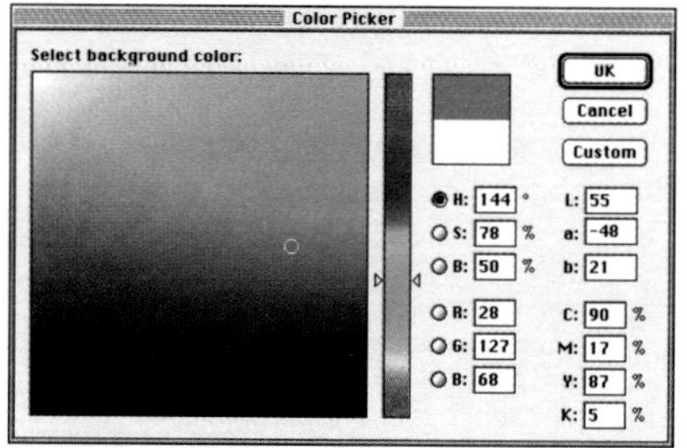

## Convert to a New Mode

To convert from one color mode to another, click the Image menu at the top of the screen and scroll down to the Mode selection. You then can scroll down to select the mode of your preference. If, for example, you want to switch from CMYK mode to Multichannel mode, you choose Image➡Mode➡Multichannel. The check mark to the left of CMYK moves down to Multichannel, indicating that you are now in Multichannel mode.

**TIP** **Remember that there is a different range of colors available for each color mode. No matter what color mode the file is in onscreen, for example, your printer (if it prints in color) is going to print your work in CMYK. Because the color ranges for RGB and CMYK are different, you should convert your RGB image to CMYK before printing. Otherwise, you may be in for a big surprise when your bright green prints as a dull tan.**

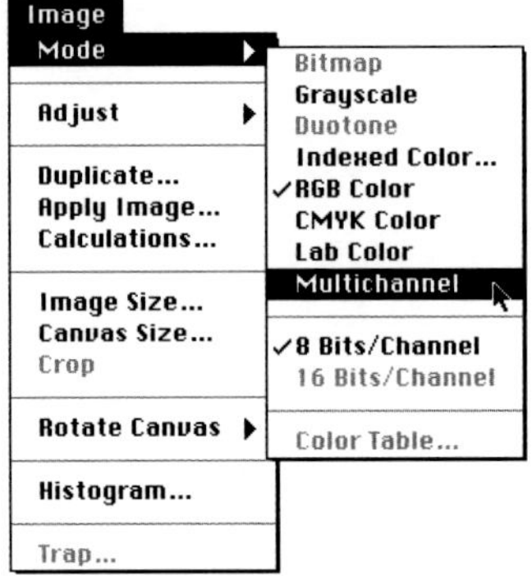


## Create a Layer Mask

**Shortcuts:** Click the Add Layer Mask icon on the Layers palette.

To create a layer mask, choose Layer➡Add Layer Mask, and choose either Reveal All (white) or Hide All (black). For the purposes of the effects in this book, always choose Reveal All. A layer mask is used to mask out (or hide) specified parts of a layer.

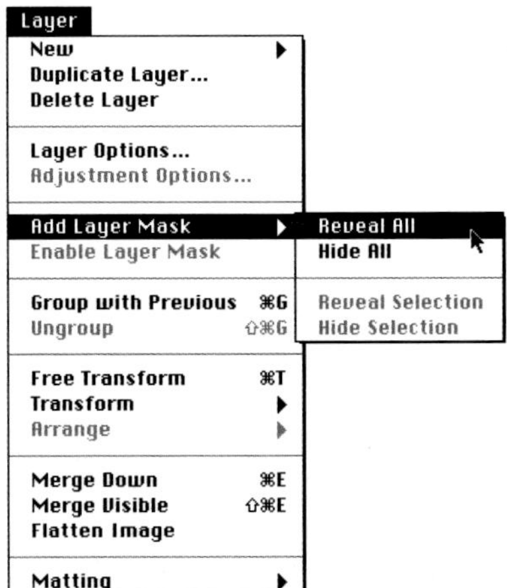

## Create a New Channel

**Shortcuts**: Click the New Channel icon on the Channels palette.

To create a new channel, choose New Channel from the Channels palette pop-up menu.

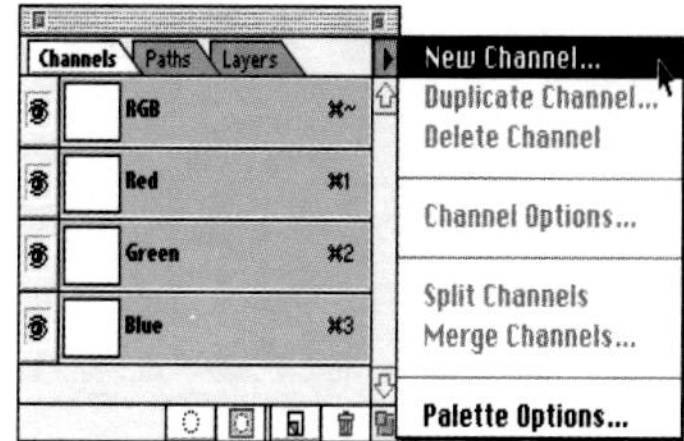


Use the Channel Options dialog box to establish your settings. Unless noted otherwise, we used the default settings when creating a new channel. This figure shows Photoshop's default settings.

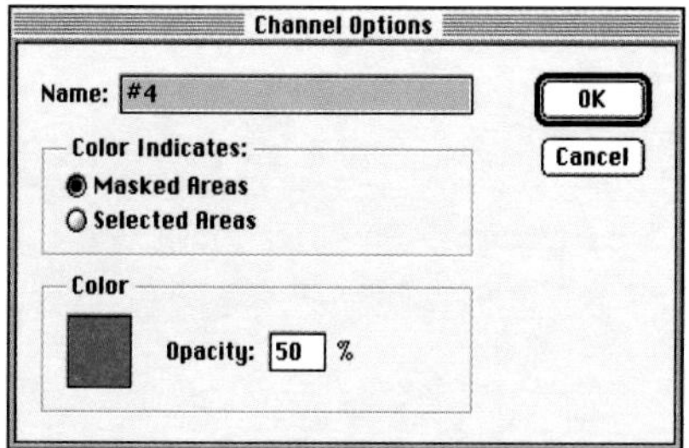


## Create a New File

**Shortcuts**: Press (Command-N) [Control-N].

To create a new file, choose File➡New. The New dialog box appears, which is where you name your new file and establish other settings. See "About This Book" for information on the conventions that were used when creating new files for the type effects in this book.

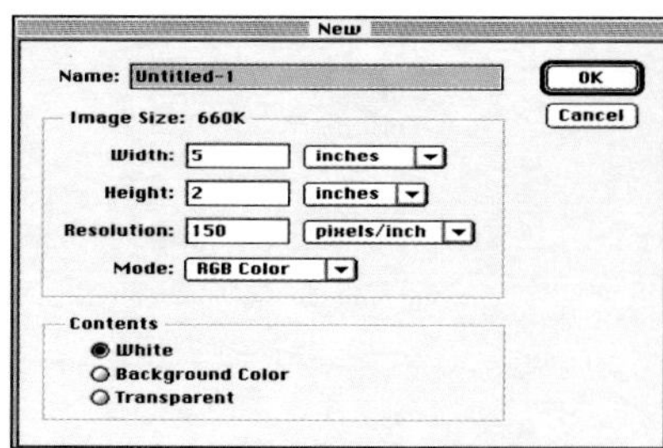

## Create a New Layer

**Shortcuts**: Click the New Layer icon on the Layers palette.

To create a new layer, choose New Layer from the Layer palette pop-up menu, or choose Layer➡New➡Layer.

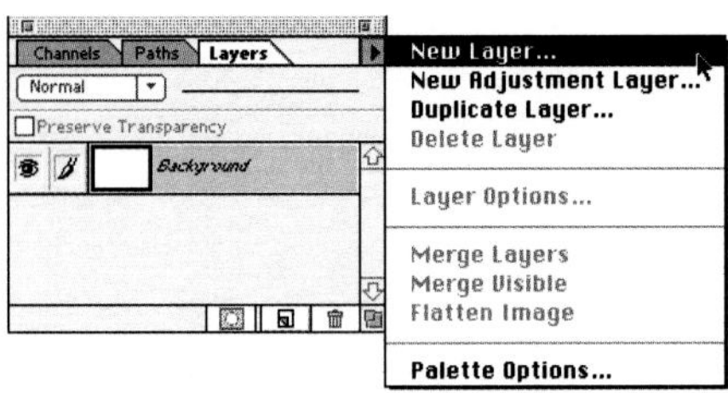


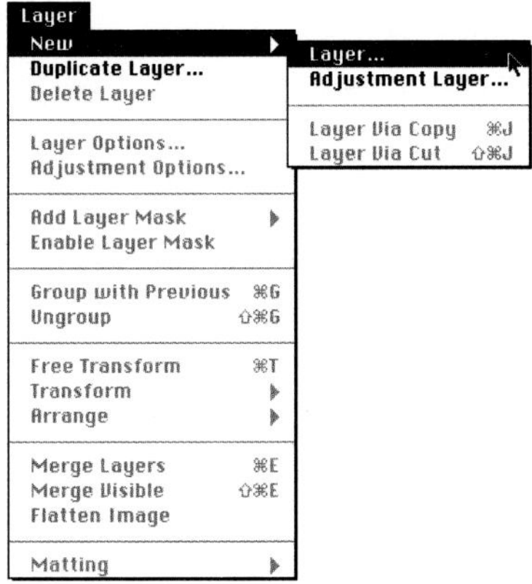


The New Layer dialog box opens, which is where you name the new layer and establish other settings.

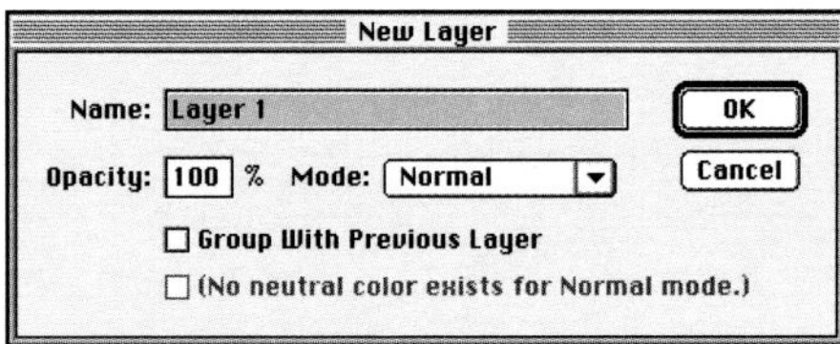

## Delete a Channel

To delete a channel, go to the Channels palette and select the channel you want to delete; drag it to the Trash icon at the lower-right corner. You also can select the channel you want to delete, and choose Delete Channel from the Channels palette menu.

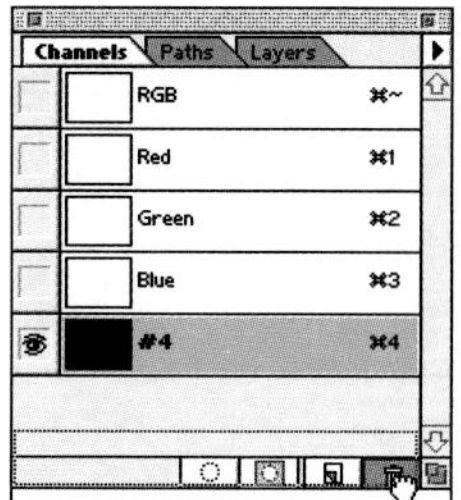


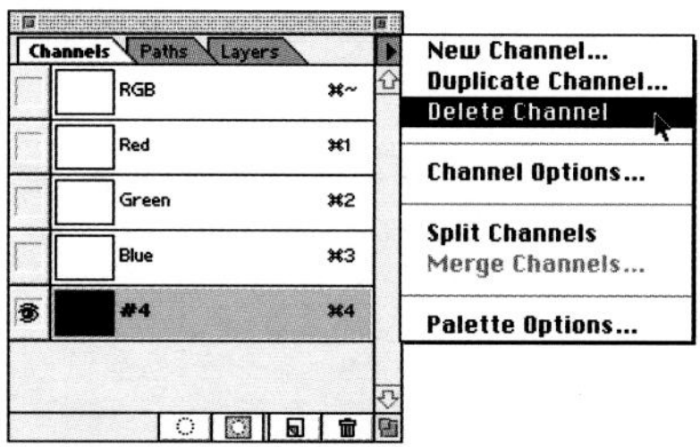


## Deselect a Selection

**Shortcut**: Press (Command-D) [Control]-D.

To deselect a selection, choose Select➡None. The marquee disappears.

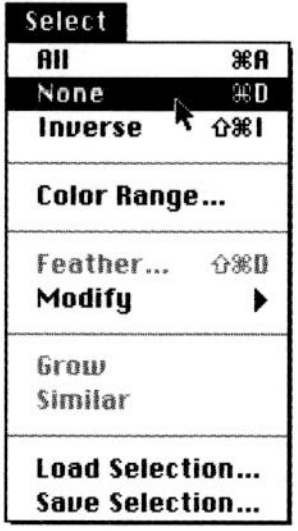


## Duplicate a Channel

**Shortcut**: Click the channel you want to duplicate, and drag it on top of the New Channel icon.

To create a duplicate of a channel, make the channel active and then select Duplicate Channel from the Channels palette menu.

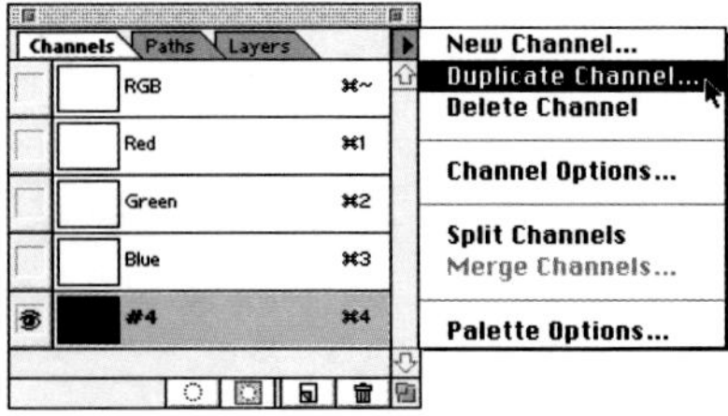


A new copy of the channel you selected for duplication is created automatically, and the Duplicate Channel dialog box appears.

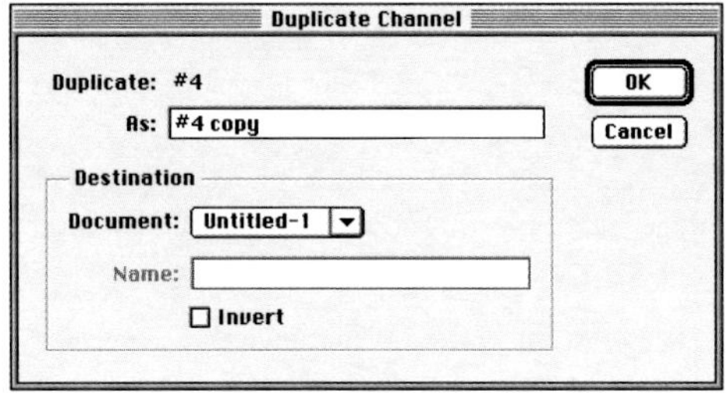


## Enter/Exit Quick Mask

**Shortcuts**: Press Q to enter and exit the Quick Mask mode.

Click the Quick Mask icon to switch to Quick Mask mode; conversely, click the Standard mode icon to return to Standard mode.

Essentially a Quick Mask is a temporary channel. When you're in Quick Mask mode you can use any of the Photoshop tools and functions to change the selection without changing the image. When you switch back to Standard mode you'll have a new selection.

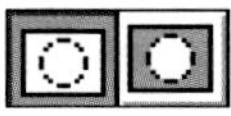

## Enter the Text

There are two type tools in Photoshop 4; the standard Type tool and the Type Mask tool. Each effect in this book specifies which type tool to use.

Before entering the text using the standard Type tool, make sure that the foreground color is set to your desired text color. Often, the instructions in this book ask you to enter text into a channel. Unless noted otherwise, it is assumed that you are entering white text onto the black background of the channel. If you are entering text into a layer, then the standard Type tool creates a new layer for the type.

The Type Mask tool creates selection outlines of the text you enter without filling the outlines with a new color, and without creating a new layer.

To enter the text, select the type tool that you want to use, and then click anywhere in the image to open the Type Tool dialog box. Type the text in the large box at the bottom of the dialog box, and make your attribute choices from the options (listed previously). Unless noted otherwise in the instructions, always make sure that you have the Anti-Aliased box checked.

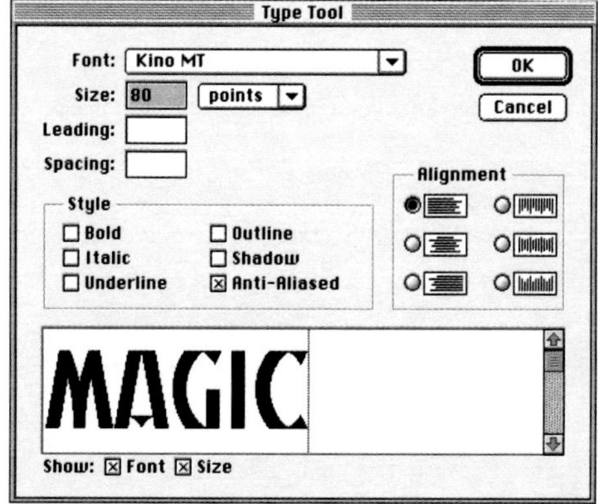


After clicking OK, move the type into position with the Move tool (if you entered your text with the standard Type tool) or Marquee tool (if you used the Type Mask tool).

## Fill a Selection with Foreground or Background Color

First, select the foreground or background color you want to use (see page 6 in this section for instructions). Keep the selection active and press the (Option-Delete) [Alt-Delete] keys to fill the selection with the foreground color. If you are in the Background layer or any layer that has the Preserve Transparency option turned on, then you can press Delete to fill in the selection with the background color.

You also can fill in your selections by choosing Edit➡Fill, or press (Shift-Delete) [Shift-Backspace] to bring up the Fill dialog box.

Edit
Undo Clear ⌘Z
Cut ⌘X
Copy ⌘C
Copy Merged ⇧⌘C
Paste ⌘V
Paste Into ⇧⌘V
Clear
Fill...
Stroke...
Create Publisher...
Publisher Options...
Define Pattern
Take Snapshot
Take Merged Snapshot
Purge

This causes the Fill dialog box to appear, enabling you to establish the Contents option you want to use, the Opacity, and the Blending Mode.

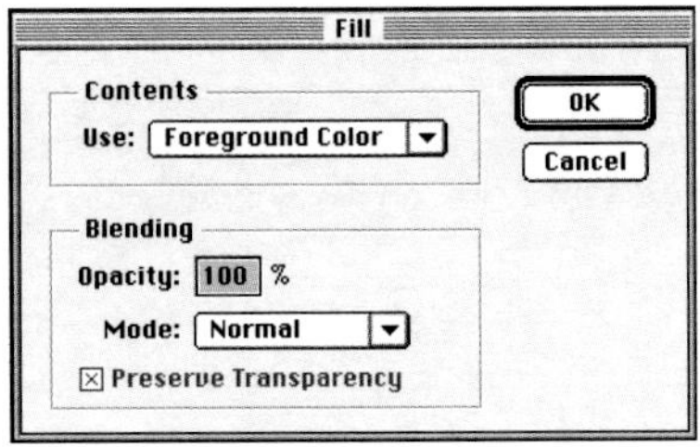


**TIP** **If a selection is empty (a transparent area of a layer) and the Preserve Transparency option is turned on for that layer, then you will not be able to fill the selection. To fill the selection, simply turn off the Preserve Transparency option before filling it.**

## Flatten an Image

To flatten an image (merge all the layers into a single layer), choose Flatten Image from the Layers palette menu, or choose Layer➡Flatten Image.

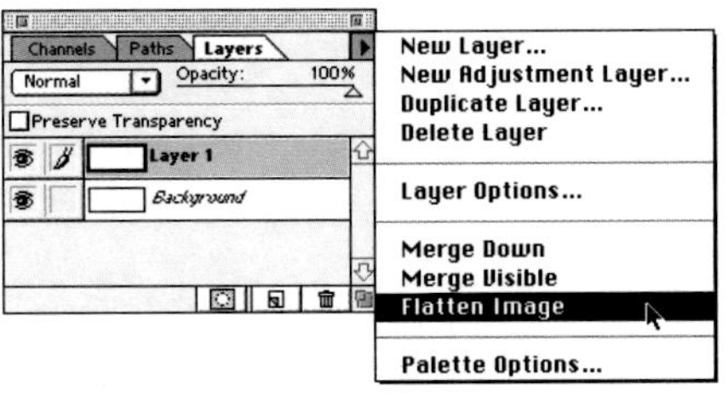

## Load a Selection

**Shortcut**: Hold down the (Command) [Control] key and click the channel (on the Channels palette) that contains the selection you want to load.

To load a selection, choose Select➡Load Selection. This brings up the Load Selection dialog box, where you can establish document, channel, and operation variables.

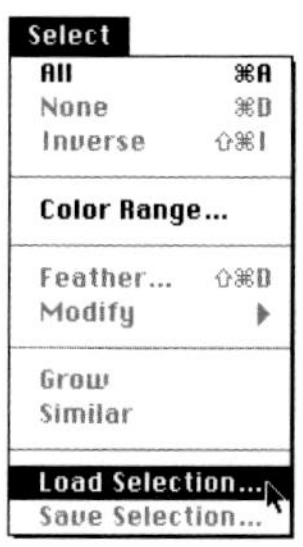


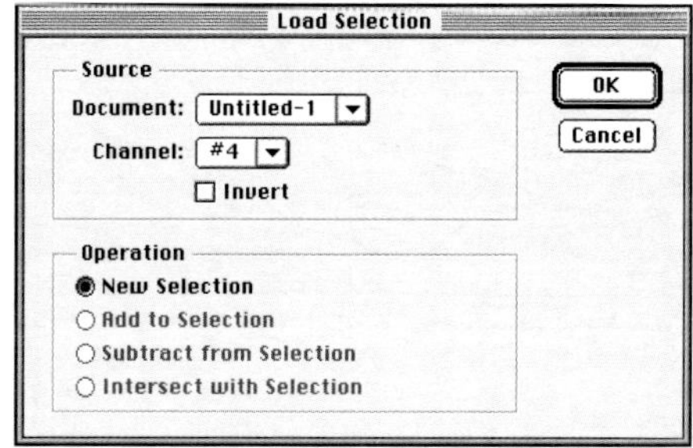

## Load the Transparency Mask (of a Layer)

To load the transparency selection of a layer, hold down the (Command) [Control] key and click the layer (on the Layers palette) that contains the transparency selection you want to load.

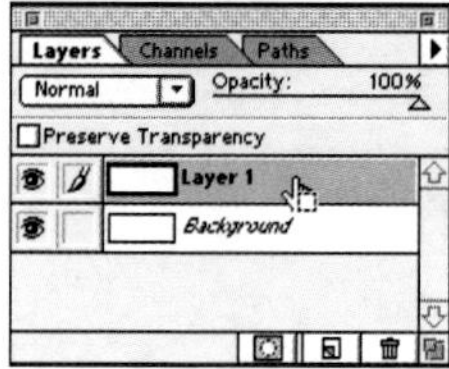


## Make a Channel Active

To make a channel active for editing or modification, click its thumbnail or title on the Channels palette.

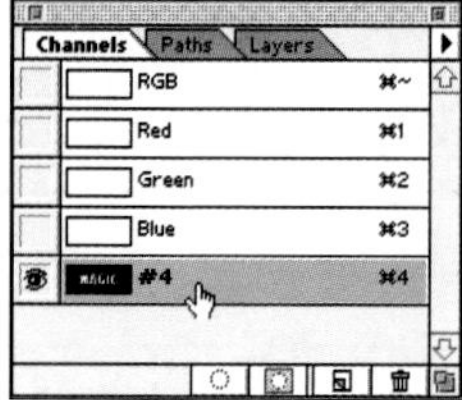


You can tell the channel is active if it is highlighted with a color.

## Make a Layer Active

To make a layer active, click its thumbnail or title in the Layers palette.

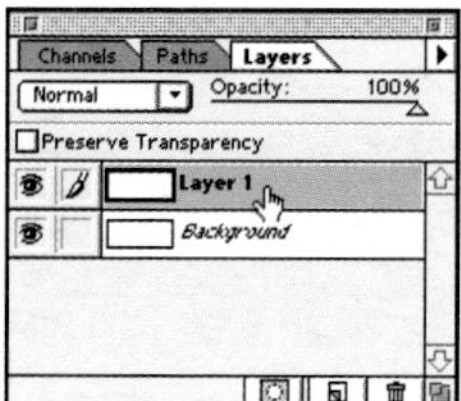


You can tell the layer is active if it is highlighted with a color.

## Make a Layer Visible/Invisible

To make a layer visible, click in the left-most column in the Layers palette. If the Eye icon appears, then the layer is visible. If the column is empty, then that layer is hidden (invisible).

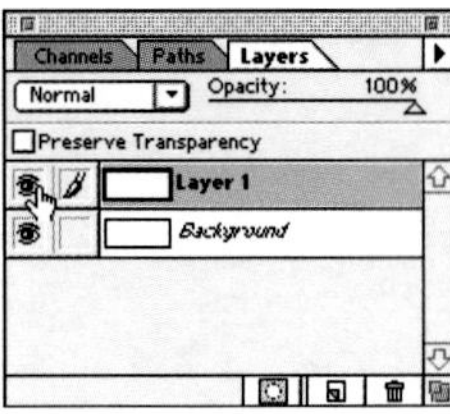


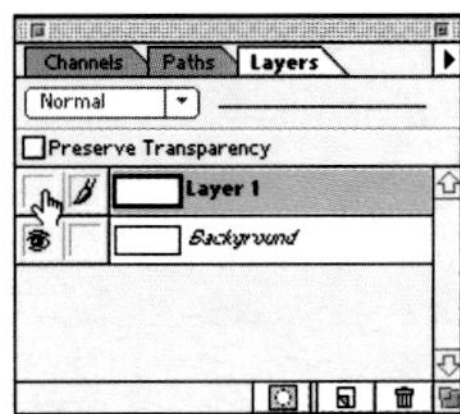


## Move a Layer

To change the stacking order of a layer, click the layer you want to move in the Layers palette and drag it up or down the list of layers to the place you want to move it. As you drag the layer, the lines between the layers darken to indicate where the layer will fall if you let go.

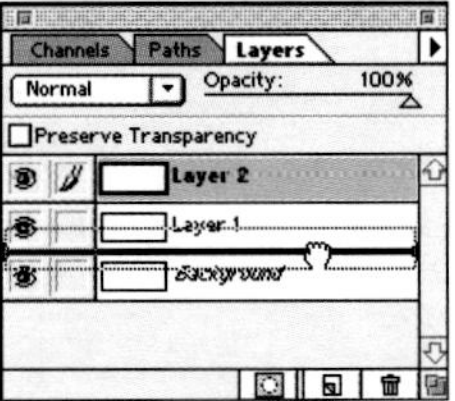


The layer you moved appears between layers.

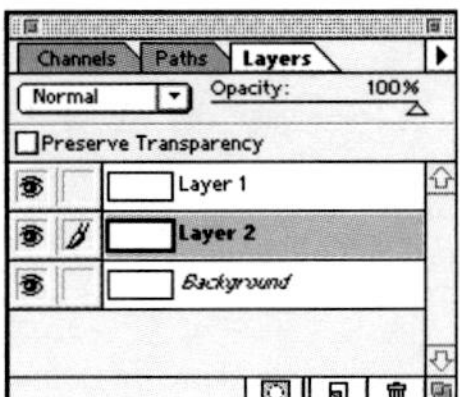

## Rename a Layer or Channel

**Shortcuts:** Double-click the layer or channel name to bring up the options dialog box. You can change the name in this dialog box.

To rename a layer or channel, chose Layer Options or Channel Options from the Layer or Channel palette's pop-up menu. This will bring up an options dialog box where you can edit the name.

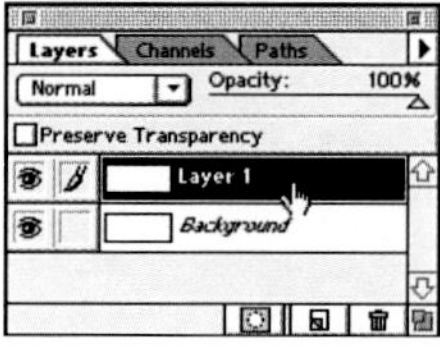


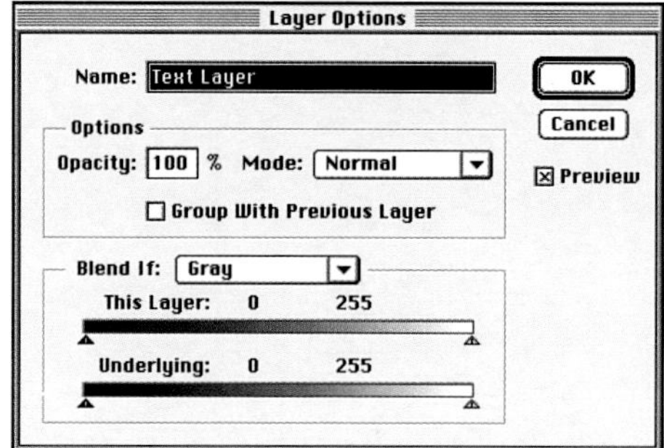


## Return to the Composite Channel

**Shortcut**: Press (Command-~) [Control-~].

If you want to return to the composite channel, click its thumbnail or title (RGB, CMYK, Lab). The composite channel will always be the one with (Command-~) [Control-~] after its title.



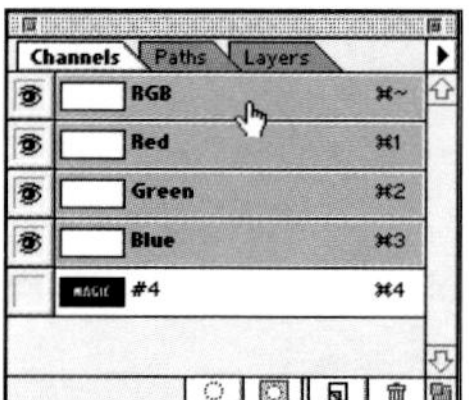


If you are in an RGB file, then Channels 0 through 3 should now be active because each of the R, G, and B channels are individual parts of the RGB channel.

## Save a File

**Shortcut:** Press (Shift-Command-S) [Shift-Control-S] to bring up the Save As dialog box.

To save a file, choose File➡Save As. This displays the Save As dialog box, where you name your new file and choose a format in which to save it.

File format selection depends on what you have in your file, what you want to keep when you save it, and what you're going to do with the file after it is saved. Consult a detailed Photoshop book, such as *Photoshop 4 Complete*, for more guidance on which file format is best for your needs.

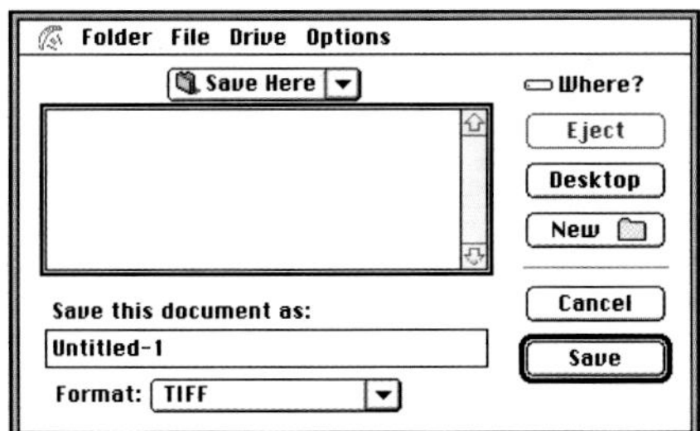


## Save a Selection

**Shortcut**: Click the Save Selection icon on the Channels palette.

To save a selection, choose Select➡Save Selection.

The Save Selection dialog box opens. Choose your options and click OK to save the selection.

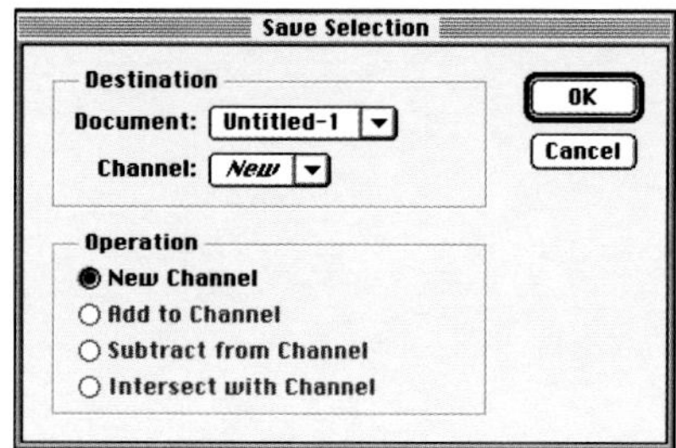


## Switch Foreground/Background Colors

**Shortcut**: Press X to switch the foreground and background colors.

To switch the foreground and background colors, click the Switch Colors icon. This flips the two colors shown in this icon only, and does not affect the rest of the image.

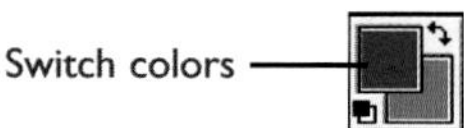




## Switch to Default Colors

**Shortcut**: Press D to switch to the default foreground and background colors.

To change the foreground and background colors to black and white respectively (if you're on a layer), click the Default Colors icon. If you're working in a channel or on a layer mask or adjustment layer, clicking the Default Colors icon changes the foreground colors to white and black, respectively.

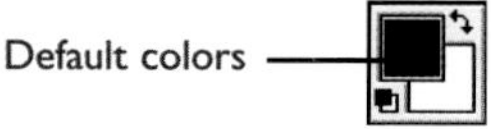

## Turn On/Off Preserve Transparency

To turn on or off the Preserve Transparency option for a particular layer, first make that layer the active layer. Then, click the Preserve Transparency checkbox on the Layers palette. This option is not available for the Background layer. ■

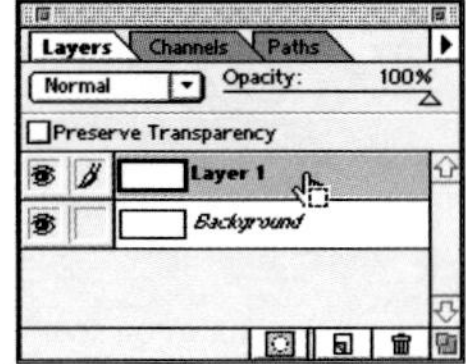

These steps provide some tips and tricks on how to work through the assembly process. Remember, though, that every assemblage project is going to present its own problems that require unique solutions.

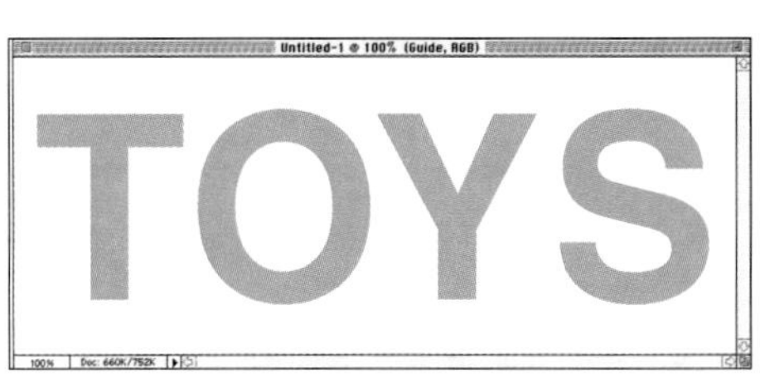


**1** Create a new file. Use the Type tool to enter the text that serves as a guide for the assembled type. I used a simple sans serif font, Helvetica, at 125 point with a spacing of 5 between the letters. This gave us more room to work. Note that Photoshop 4.0 creates a new layer with the type on it. Name this layer "Guide."

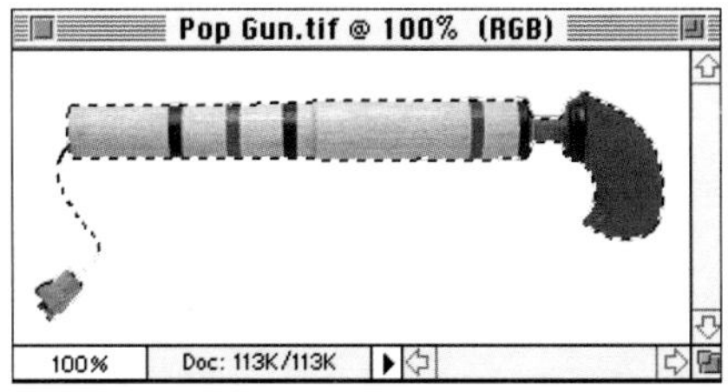


©Image Club Graphics 1995

**2** Next, open the file containing the art you are using to assemble the type. I opened a stock photo from Image Club Graphics. Use the Selection tools to select the item you want to use for assembling the type. Linear shapes are obviously the easiest to work with when creating type. Draw a path around irregular shapes and then convert it into a selection. After selecting the item, copy it to the clipboard (Command-C) [Control-C].

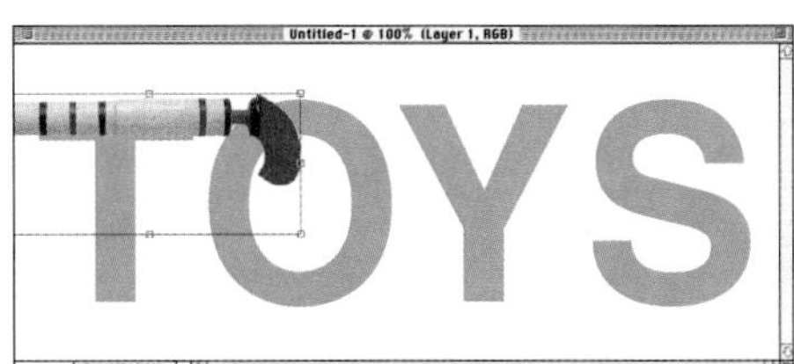


**3** Return to your text file and paste from the clipboard (Command-V) [Control-V]. Again, Photoshop 4.0 automatically places the item in a new layer. I moved and scaled the pop gun (Layer➡Transform➡Scale) into position as the horizontal member of the letter T.

Then use the selection tools to crop the T. Remember to use the background type as your guide.

**4** To make the vertical component of the T, paste the picture of the pop gun from the clipboard again (Command-V) [Control-V]. If you haven't already noticed, every time you paste in a new item, Photoshop 4.0 places it in a new layer. Rotate (Layer➡Transform➡Rotate 90° CCW), scale (Layer➡Transform➡ Scale), and move (use the Move tool) the pop gun into position to finish the T.

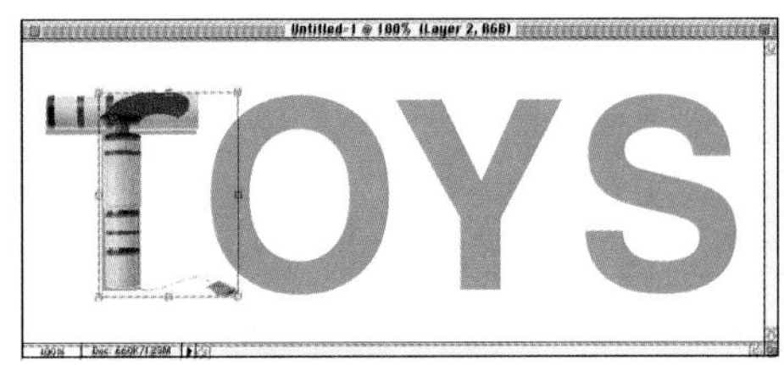


**5** I then opened an image of a banana and copied it into the clipboard (Command-C) [Control-C]. Return to your working file and paste it from the clipboard (Command-V) [Control-V]. Then move and scale the banana (Layer➡Transform➡Scale) into position.

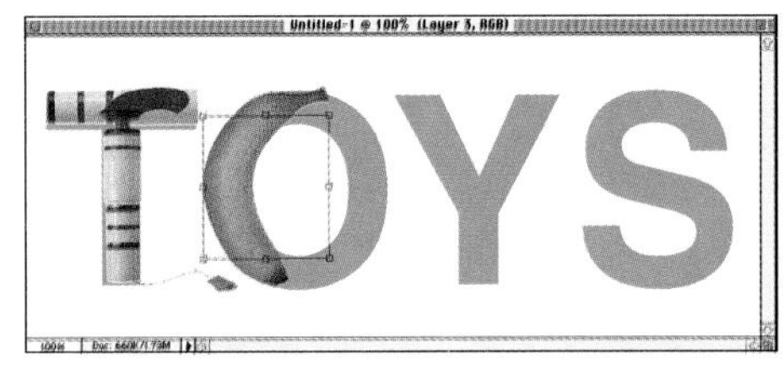


Then distort the banana (Layer➡ Transform➡Distort) for a better fit.

**6** To complete the other side of the letter O, load the selection and copy it to the clipboard (Command-C) [Control-C]. Paste in the image (Command-V) [Control-V] and rotate the banana (Layer➡Transform➡Rotate 180°). Use the Move tool to position the banana into place.

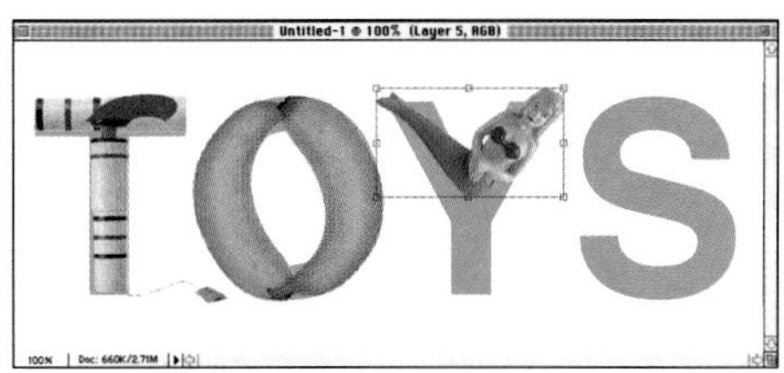


7 Look for images that most closely resemble parts of the letter you are trying to create. I copied an image of a mermaid into the clipboard (Command-C) [Control-C]. Return to your working file and paste it from the clipboard (Command-V) [Control-V]. Then move and scale the mermaid (Layer➥Transform➥Scale) over the upper portion of the Y.

8 To complete the Y, I used an image of an aviator that was opened and copied into the clipboard (Command-C) [Control-C]. Paste it from the clipboard (Command-V)[Control-V] into your file. Then move and scale it (Layer➥Transform➥Scale) into position.

**Press the V key to quickly activate the Move tool. Use the arrow keys for precise control when aligning your images.**

9 Next I opened and copied an image of an alligator into the clipboard (Command-C) [Control-C]. Again, note how I chose an object that most closely represented the shape of the S. Paste it from the clipboard (Command-V) [Control-V] into your file. Then move it over the S with the Move tool.

**10** Unfortunately, the shape of the alligator is not close enough to an S, so you need to use the Shear filter to help. Choose Filter➡ Distort➡ Shear. You have to adjust the settings to get the shape closest to an S.

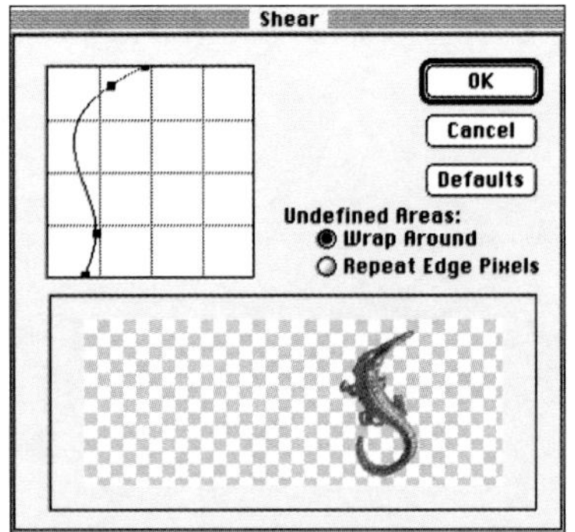


You should get something that looks like this.

**11** Now you need to distort the alligator some more (Layer➡ Transform➡Distort). The guide is there to help you, but it is not critical that you follow it exactly. In this case, it is still pretty obvious that the alligator forms an S.

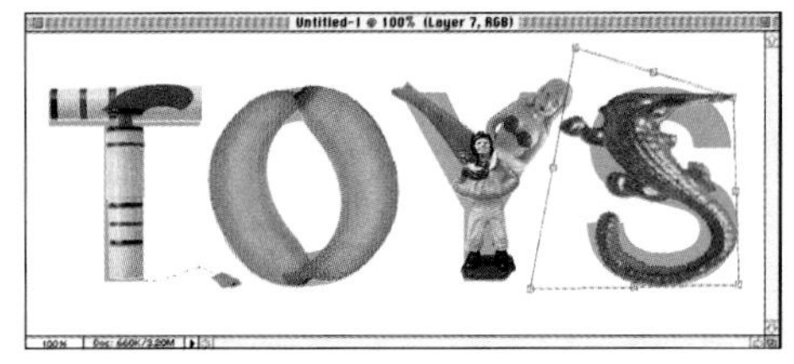

TIP **Use the Smudge tool to help you when you need to quickly blend together two objects. This is especially useful if you are working with organic shapes.**

**12** To finalize the image, I deleted the Guide layer and flattened the image. That's all there is to it!

Photo credits for this chapter: Image Club Graphics, PhotoDisc, CMCD, D'Pix, Digital Stock, 1995.

Need some cheap subliminal advertising? Here are two quick ways to create a background filled with text.

1 Create a new file with the dimensions of the background you want to fill. Use the Type tool to enter the text you want repeated in the background. In the Type dialog box, type the text twice in the same row. We used Weideman Black at 17 points. After setting the type, we copied it, pasted it, and then offset the second copy. Flatten the image.

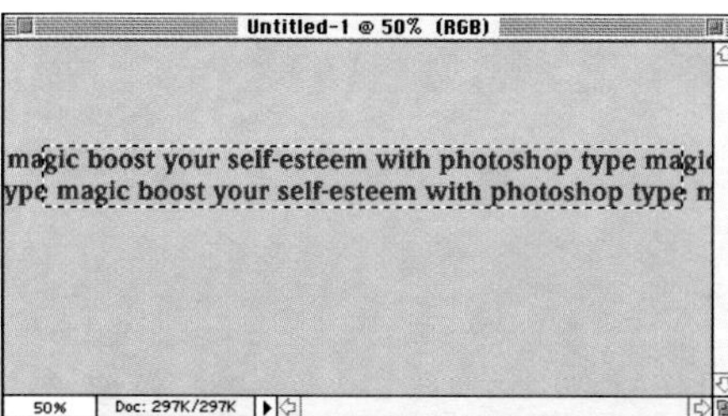


2 This is the most difficult step for this technique. You have to be careful what you select if you want to get the pattern to repeat correctly. Use the rectangular Marquee tool to draw a box around the portion of the text used as a pattern for the entire background. It's okay to cut the selection through the middle of a letter as long as the other end of the selection cuts through the same letter in the same place. You can control the spacing between lines in the final pattern by including more or less space in the selection rectangle above or below the text.

**TIP** **Make the area you want to use for your pattern as large on the screen as you can. You can zoom in by holding down the (Command) [Control] key and Spacebar and clicking in the image, no matter which tool is currently active. To zoom back out, click within the image while holding down the (Option) [Alt] key and Spacebar.**

**3** Now choose Edit➥Define Pattern. Then Select➥All (Command-A) [ Control-A] and choose Edit➥Fill (Pattern, Opacity: 100%, Normal).

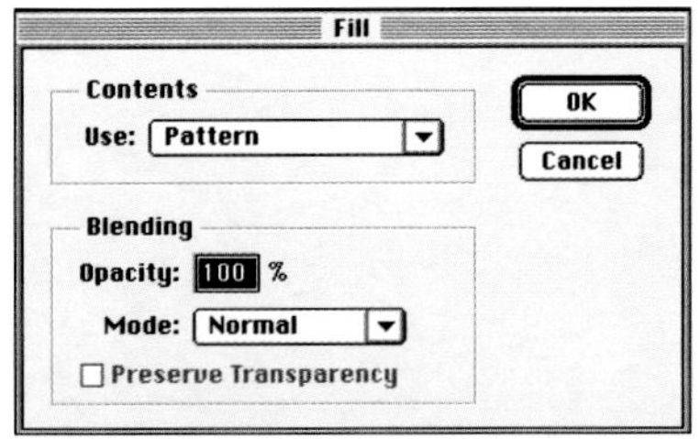


You now have a very simple background and can work on the rest of the image by creating new layers above it. Or try the following variations.

## VARIATIONS

Apply Photoshop's Emboss filter…

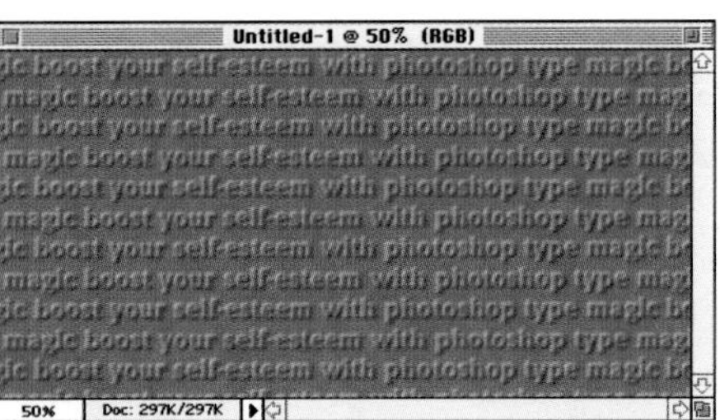


…or maybe use the Offset filter on one channel and then combine it with a photograph, such as this one from Digital Stock…

©Digital Stock 1995

...or maybe apply the Offset filter to only one channel...

...then add the Wave filter...

...then apply the Shear filter to only one channel.

## Background 2

Another way to create a background filled with text is to use the Wave filter.

**1** In a separate file create the type you want to use for the background tile. Select the text with the rectangular Marquee and copy it to the clipboard (Command-C) [Control-C].

**2** Now, create a new file with the dimensions of the background you want to fill. Paste the text from the first file into this background file (Command-V) [Control-V]. Place the text in the middle of the background image.

**3** Choose Filter➥Distort➥Wave. Start with these values: Generators: 5; Wavelength: 500 & 660; Amplitude: 10 & 925; Horizontal: 100%; Vertical: 100%. Choose the Wrap Around option. Of course, this is only one of the countless possibilities for this filter. Use the Randomize button to see other options, or adjust the sliders until you see something you like. You could also apply the filter again for more variations. Simply choose Filter➥Wave (Command-F) [Control-F]. Here are some of the variations we came up with. ■

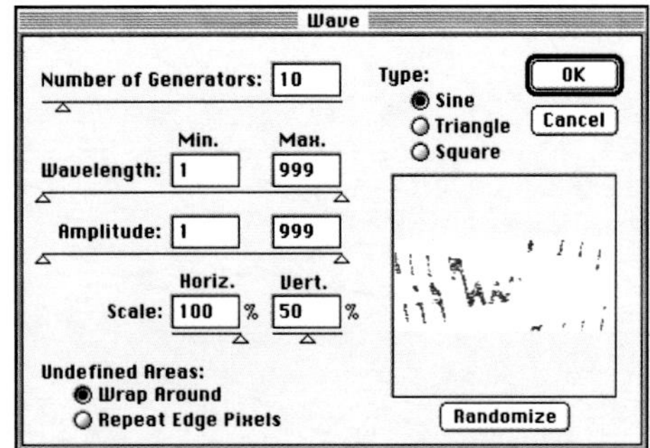


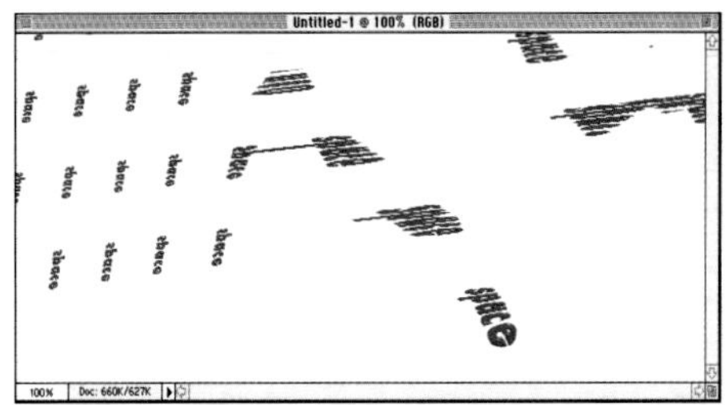


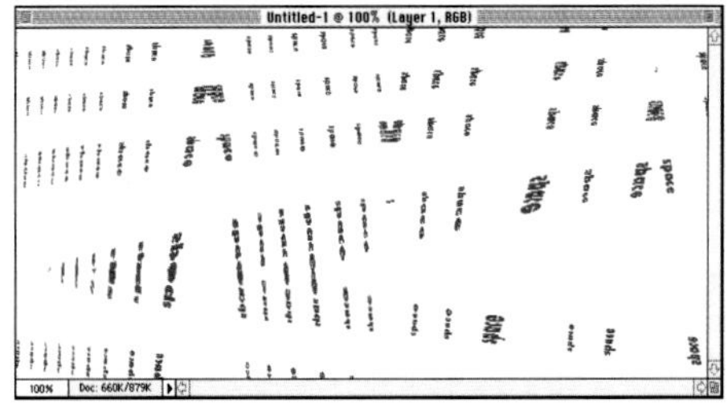


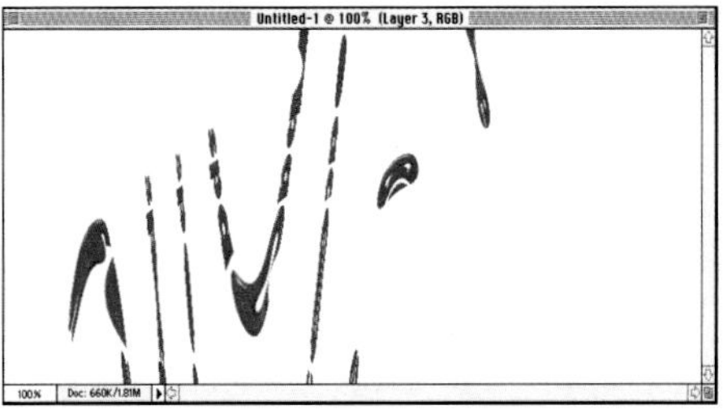


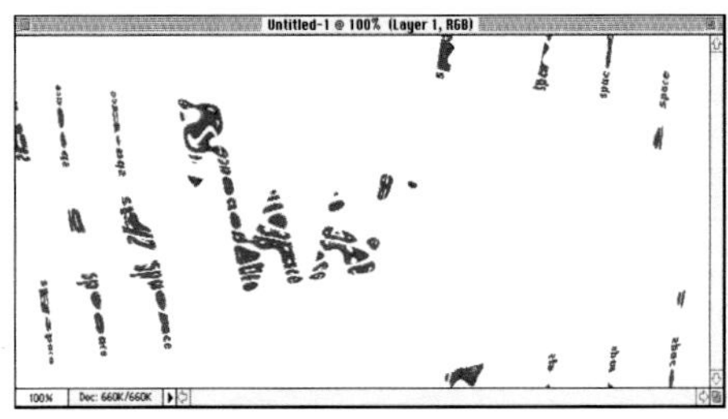

Sometimes it's best to let Adobe's other software do some of the dirty work for you—and if it's beveled text you're looking for, then Adobe Dimensions gets the honor. A demo version of Dimensions 2.0 (Mac only) is included on the CD-ROM so you can try it for yourself. If you don't have Dimensions, skip to the Photoshop Bevel section, where you can learn how to create a bevel with Photoshop's Lighting Effects filter.

## Dimensions Bevel

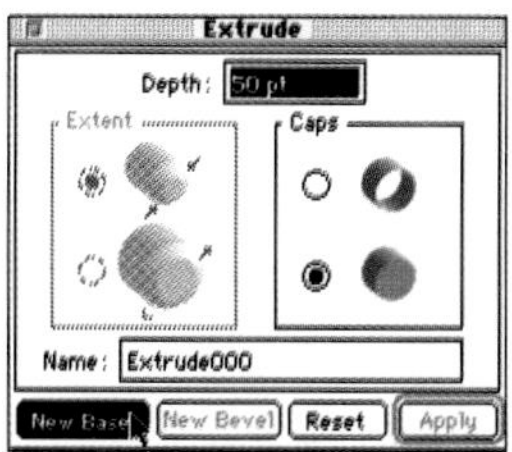


**1** Open Adobe Dimensions 2.0. A new document window automatically opens. Press (Command-E) to make sure that you are working in Edit Mode, where everything runs faster. Then choose Operations➡Extrude (Command-Shift-E). The Extrude floating palette appears onscreen. Click the New Base button on the palette.

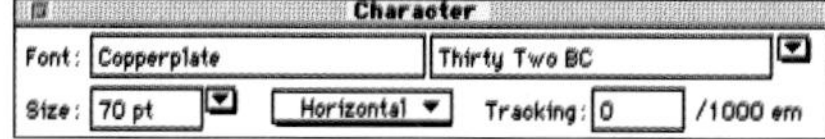


**2** A new untitled window opens, and the icons in the toolbar change. Double-click the Type tool to select it and open the Character floating palette. Make your selections in the Character palette. We used 70-point Copperplate 32BC.

**3** With the Type tool, click in the Extrude window that opened in Step 2. Type in the text. If you plan on having the bevels extend outward from the text, then make sure you increase the letter spacing by entering a positive value in the Tracking box. This gives them some room to spread. First, select the text by dragging the Type tool insertion bar over it. We set the tracking at 150.

### TOOLBOX

Adobe Dimensions (Mac only)

Alien Skin's Inner Bevel filter

Alien Skin's Outer Bevel filter

**TIP** **If you don't like what you see, make changes to the text by selecting the text as described earlier and making new selections in the Character palette. The text changes automatically.**

**4** Now click the New Bevel button on the Extrude floating palette. Move through the directories to locate the Bevel Library within the Adobe Dimensions 2.0 folder on your hard drive. Adobe provides 22 preset bevels for you to use. We chose the Classic Normal bevel. Watch the preview window and click Import when you're done.

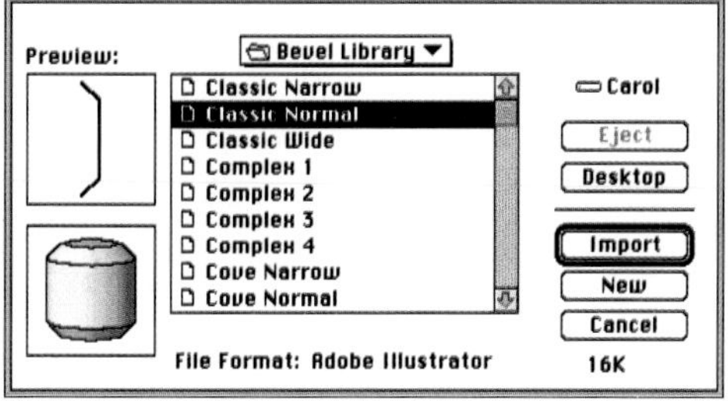


**5** Another new window opens showing the contour of the bevel. Find the Extrude floating palette again. Enter, in points, the depth you want the text to extrude. Our text is going to be facing front so we entered an arbitrary medium depth of 20 points. We also chose an outer bevel and end caps.

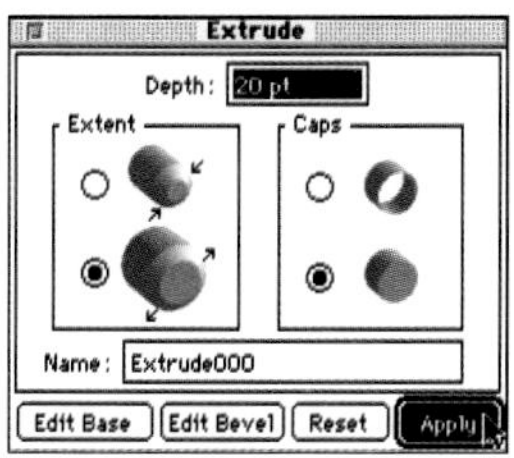


Click the Apply button on the Extrude floating palette.

**6** If you can't see the original window that opened when you opened Dimensions, choose Window➡ Untitled-1. Now you can see that the text has been extruded and beveled.

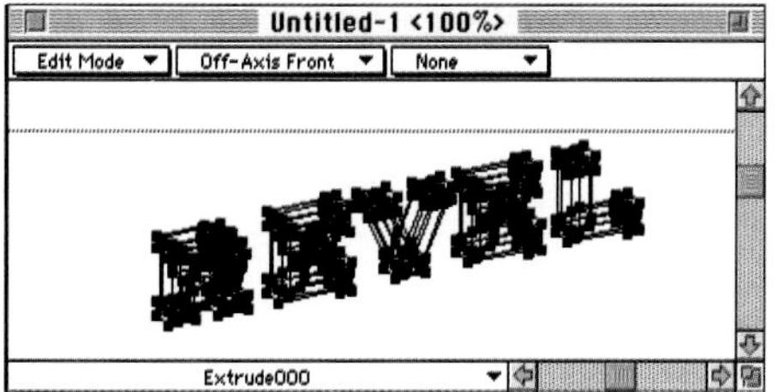

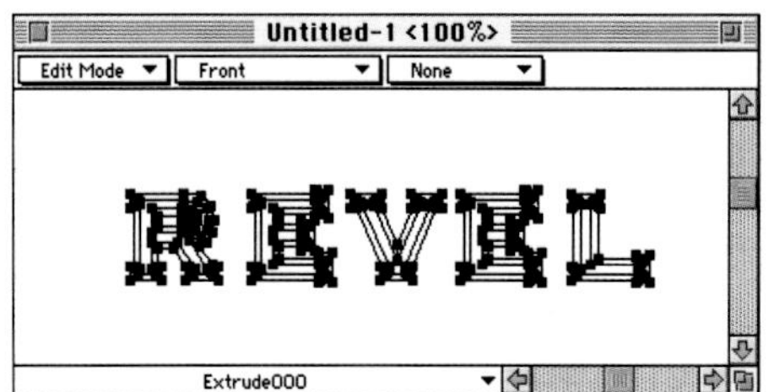


**7** Choose View➥View Angles➥Front. Now, all you need to do is edit the surface properties of the text and render it.

**TIP** **If you want to change the direction of the light source, choose Appearance➥Lighting, and make your selections in the Lighting floating palette.**

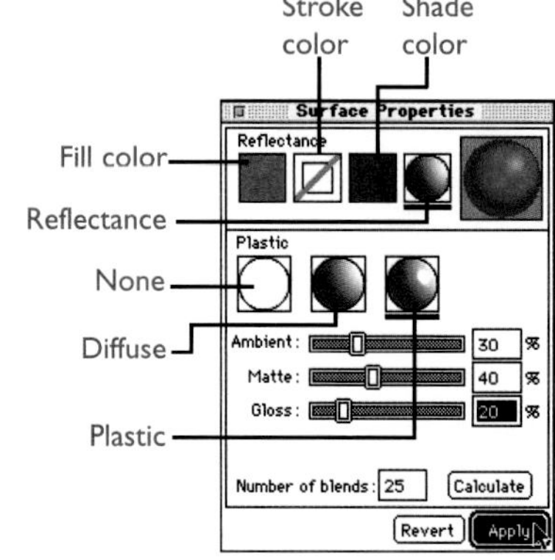


**8** Choose Appearance➥Surface Properties. A floating palette appears. The figure here explains its features. For the Fill (text) color, we used these CMYK values: 0/100/100/0. For the Shade (shadow) color, CMYK: 100/100/0/60. We left the Stroke (edge) color at none. Click the Reflectance icon, then the Plastic icon, and use the values shown in the figure. Click the Apply button when you're finished.

**TIP** **Make sure that the number of blends is at least 25 to avoid banding. If your text has a lot of curves, you probably want to increase it.**

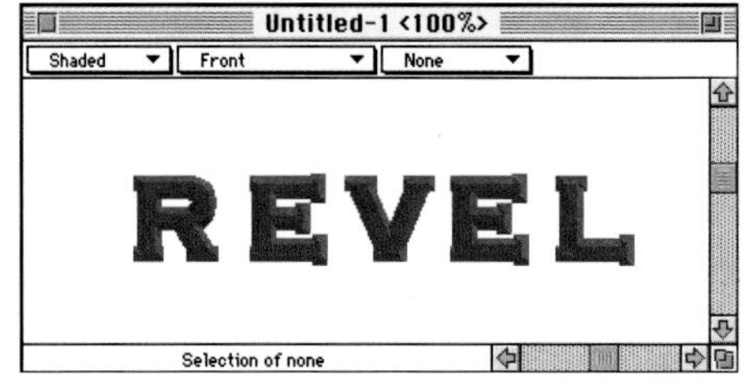


**9** You won't see any changes in the text because you're not in a render mode yet. Choose View➥Shaded Render. (Complex text may take some time to render. Be patient.) If you don't like what you see, use the Surface Properties palette to make appearance changes or go back to the Extrude palette and use the Edit buttons to alter the text.

**10** When you're satisfied, deselect the type (Command-Shift-A) [Control-Shift-A], and choose File➡Export. In the Export dialog box, choose Color Macintosh and Adobe Illustrator from the pop-up menus. Quit Dimensions (Command-Q) [Control-Q]. No need to save changes—you already exported what you wanted.

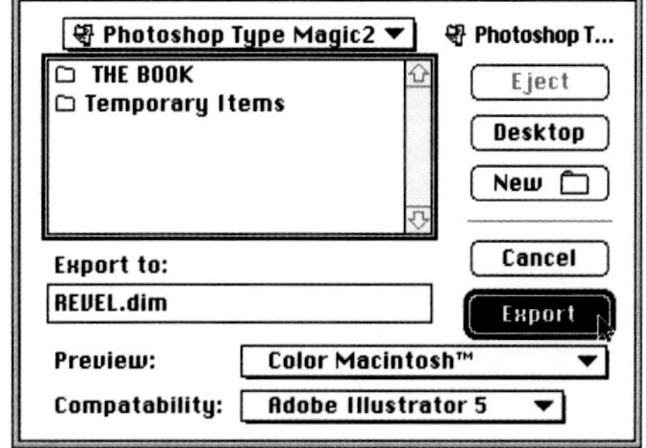


**11** Open Photoshop, and open the file you just exported from Adobe Dimensions. Here are the settings we used in the Rasterize box:

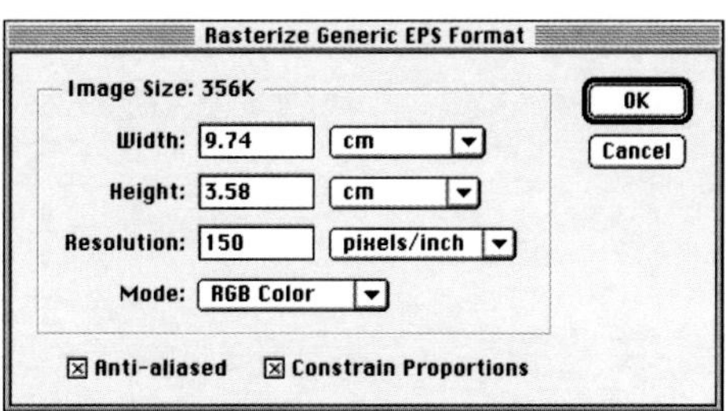


**12** The text opens into Layer 1 and there is no background layer.

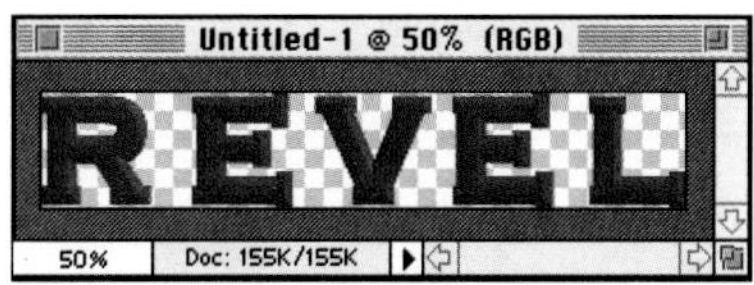


**13** If you simply want a white background, choose Flatten Image from the Layers palette menu. If not, take a look at the Variations section.

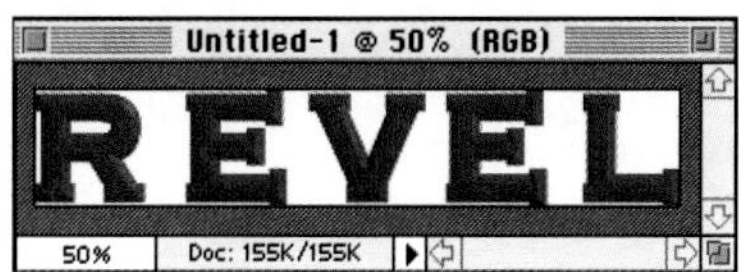


## VARIATIONS

If you want to make modifications to the text, don't flatten the image. (Command-clicking) [Control-clicking] the layer in the Layers palette selects the text. Now you can use any of Photoshop's tools to alter the text.

To change the color of the text, choose Image➥Adjust➥Hue/Saturation, check the Colorize option, and use the Hue slider to find or modify the color.

To add a background, create a new layer (Layer 2), and move the layer in the Layers palette below Layer 1. The new layer is the active one. Fill the background with a color or paste in an image.

To get this transparent bevel, we put the same beveled text on a background and double-clicked Layer 1 (the beveled text layer) in the Layers palette to bring up the Layers Options dialog box. The settings we used are shown in this figure.

For this variation we used KPT 3 Gradient Designer to fill the selection with the Metal Sweep Cymbal II + a gradient. We chose Procedural Blend from the Options menu. After applying the blend, we raised the contrast using the Levels (Command-L) [Control-L] dialog box.

## Photoshop Bevel

**1** Create a new file (it must be in RGB mode). Create a new channel (#4), and use the Type tool to enter the text. We used Frutiger Bold at 70 points.

**2** Duplicate Channel #4 to create Channel #5. Deselect the text (Command-D) [Control-D]. Choose Filter➡Blur➡Gaussian blur (5 pixels). The blurring creates the area for the bevel.

**3** Load the original text channel selection (#4). Choose Select➡Modify➡Contract (3 pixels). Fill the selection with white so the bevel has hard edges.

**4** Return to the composite channel. Load the selection Channel #4. Fill the selection with a color for the type.

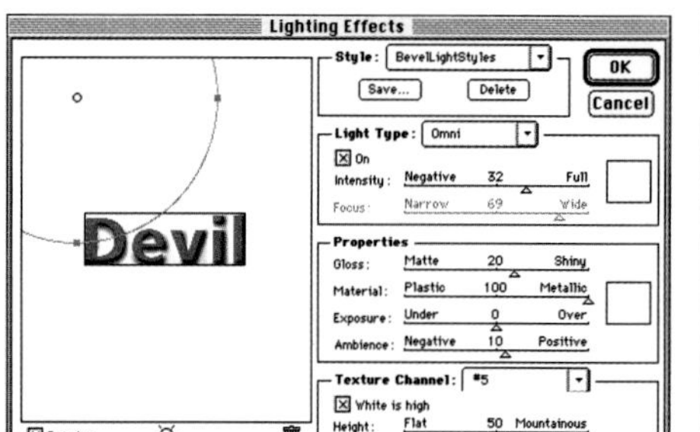


**5** Choose Filter➡Render➡Lighting Effects. From the pop-up menu choose BevelLightStyles, or match the settings shown in this figure. Make sure you specify the Texture Channel (#5) when you apply this filter.

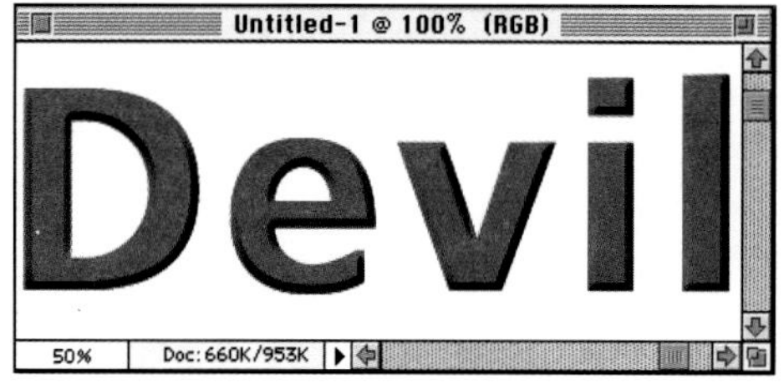


Click OK and you've got beveled text.

©D'Pix 1995

## More Variations

To bevel a surface, before Step 1 copy the surface into the clipboard. Then, in Step 4, instead of filling the text with a color, choose Edit➡Paste Into. Also, to automatically add a drop shadow we chose Select➡None at the end of Step 4.

Alien Skin's Outer Bevel 2.0 and Inner Bevel 2.0 filters make beveling a breeze. If you use the outer bevel, remember that the filter uses the color outside the text selection for the color of the beveled edges. If you want the bevels to be the same color as the text then the text should be placed on a background of the same color. For this variation, we placed white text on a stock photo from PhotoDisc. ■

©PhotoDisc 1995

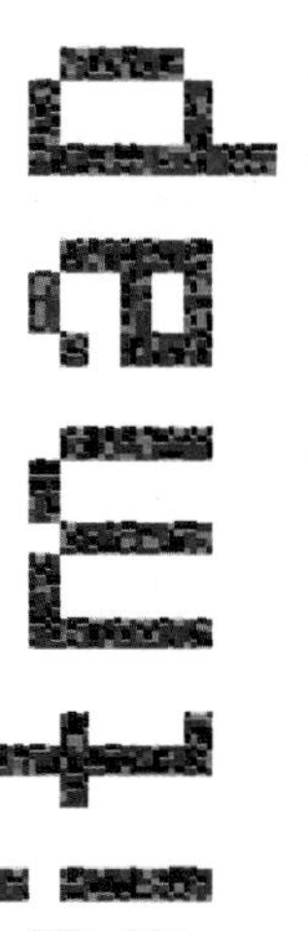


This technique is especially useful if you are trying to quickly get the bitmapped, computer look.

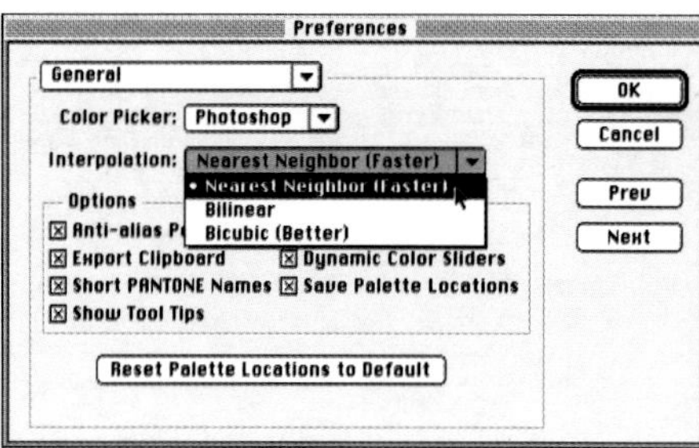


**1** In the File➥Preferences➥General (Command-K) [Control-K] menu, choose Nearest Neighbor (Faster) for the Interpolation Method. When this method is used, Photoshop duplicates the neighboring pixels when a selection is enlarged rather than averaging them. Remember to change your preferences back after applying this technique; otherwise you'll start seeing all your graphics as big, blocky bitmaps.

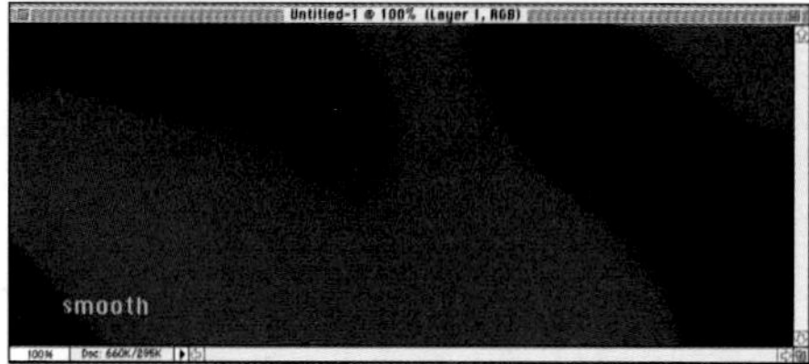


**2** Create a new file. In this example, we created a background first using a KPT filter. Choose the Type tool and enter the text. In the Type tool dialog box, choose a small point size. We used Chicago at 10 points. This enables your text to be very bitmapped when enlarged. Be sure that Anti-Aliased is not checked. Type your text and click OK.

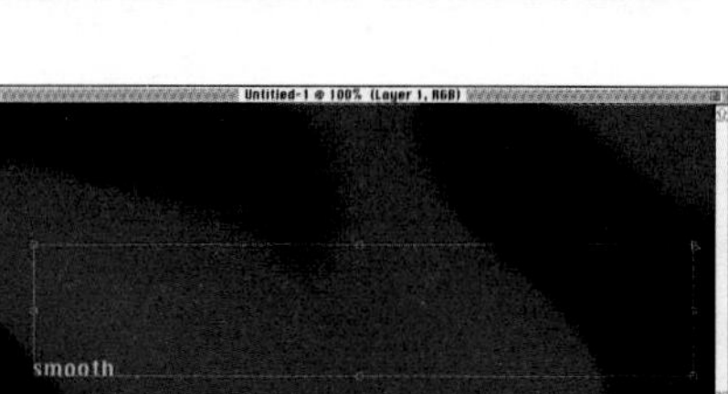


**3** (Command-click) [Control-click] the type layer in the Layers palette to select the type, and choose Layer➥Transform➥Scale from the menu bar and enlarge the text. Holding down the Shift key keeps the selection in proportion.

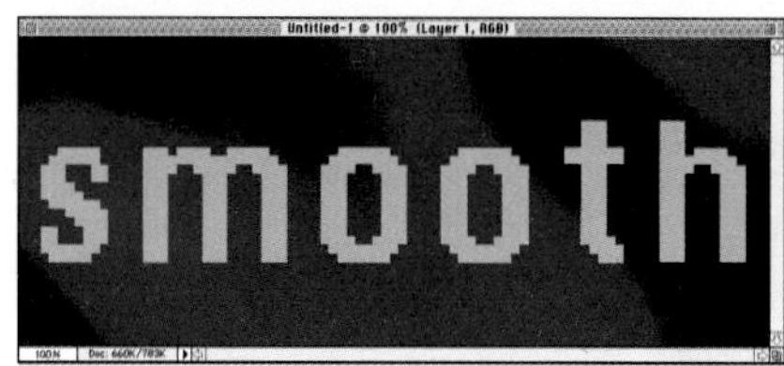


Because the Nearest Neighbor interpolation method was chosen in Step 1, the enlarged selection gets blocky.

That's all there is to it!

## TOOLBOX

Sucking Fish
MidnightsTV filter

## VARIATIONS

Add smooth text to contrast the "jaggies" for a nice effect.

Bit
Boyeez

You can get an outline around your text by using Edit➥Stroke. This command strokes the selection with the foreground color, so be sure it's not the same color as your text!

Mint
Chocolate
Chunk

After enlarging the text a little (about 25%), choose Filter➥Noise➥Add Noise. Then enlarge the text even more. The noisy pixels inside the text enlarge along with the text, complementing the bitmappy look.

Blaring

Or, instead of using Filter➥Noise, try Filter➥MidnightsTV (from the Sucking Fish Series of filters). ■

TTFN

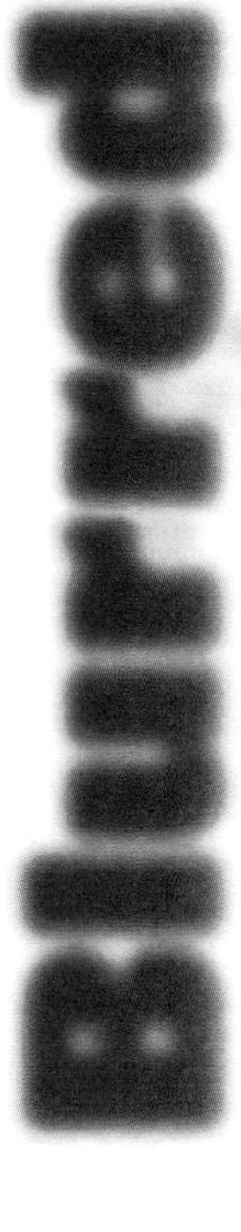


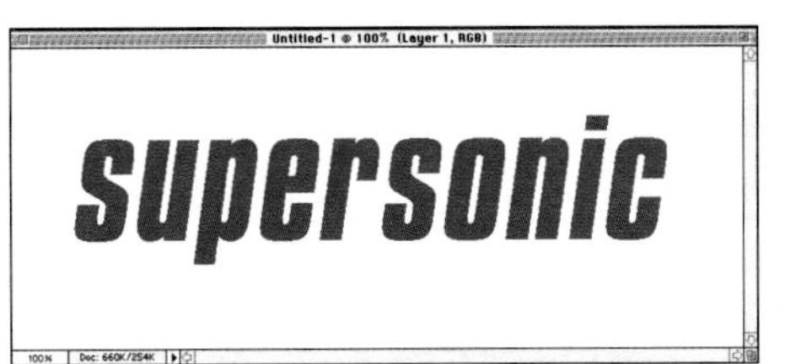


**1** Create a new file. Use the Type tool to enter the text you want to blur. I used Compact Bold Italic at 80 points in this example.

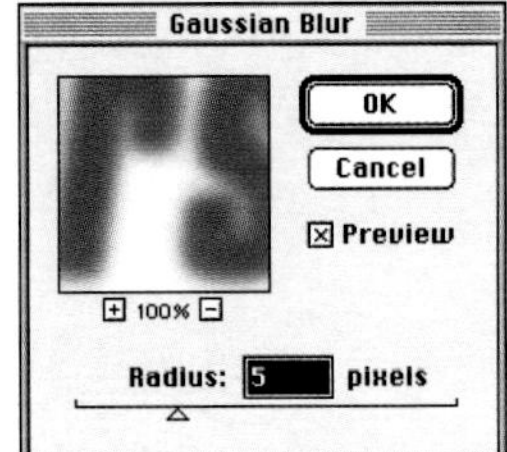


**2** Flatten the image. Then apply Filter➥Blur➥Gaussian Blur. I used a radius of 5 pixels.

You should get something like this.

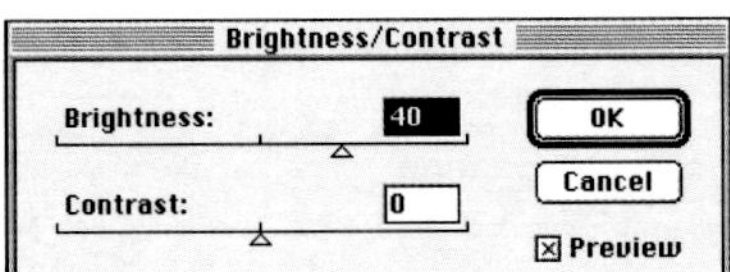


**3** In order to lighten the type, choose Image➥Adjust➥ Brightness/Contrast (Brightness: +40). This adds some haziness to the image.

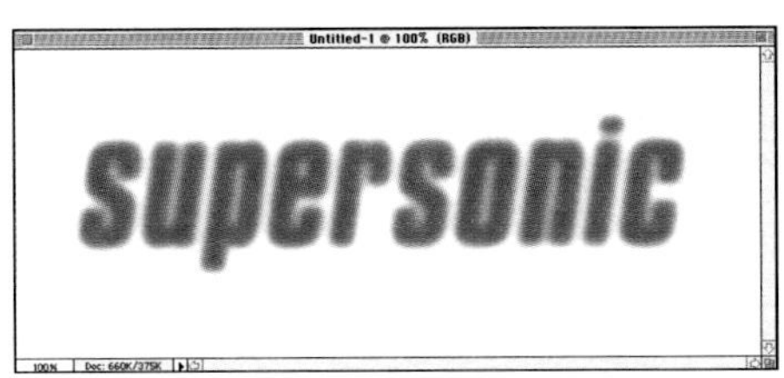


Your type should now look something like this.

## VARIATIONS

Blurred text looks particularly good when contrasted against unblurred text.

After applying Photoshop's Gaussian Blur filter, choose Filter➥Other➥Minimum to beef up the blur. The higher the setting, the wider the blur. A setting of 5 pixels was used here.

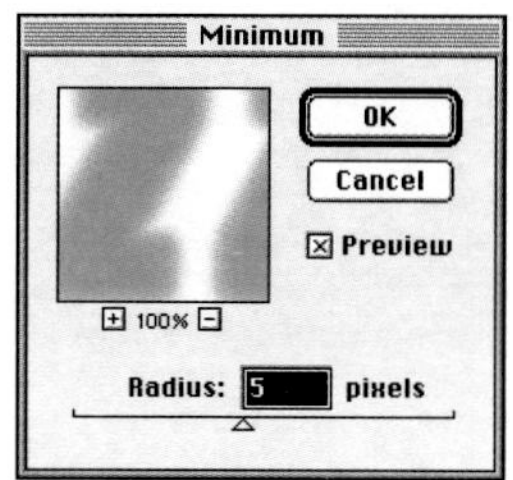


The result is a more robust blur.

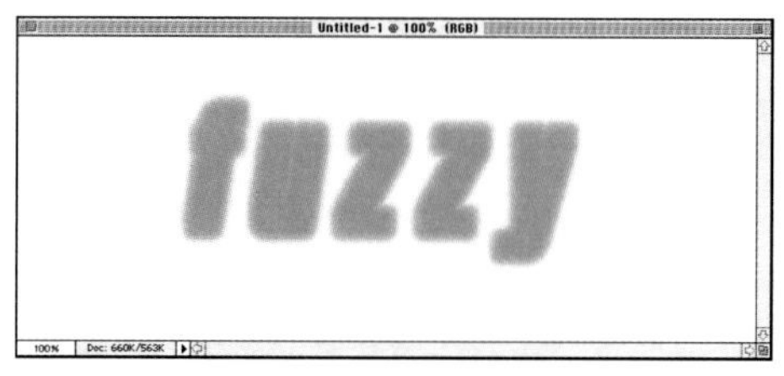


You could also use Filter➥Other➥Maximum to thin down the type. A setting of 7 pixels was used here.

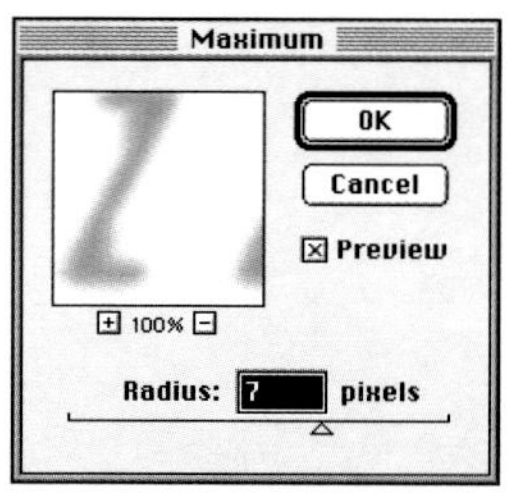


Some interesting residue is left between the letters.

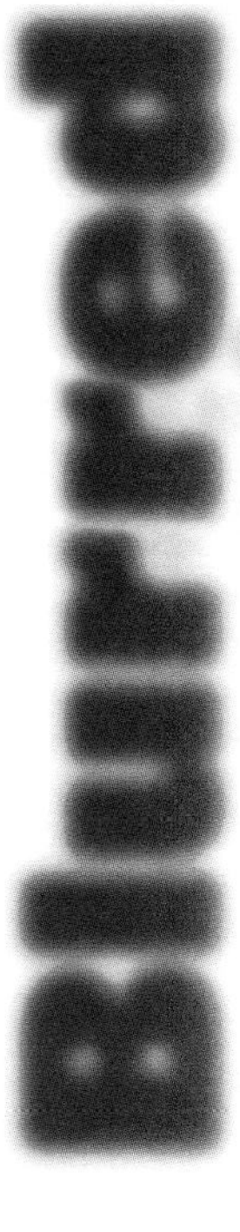


## Clouds

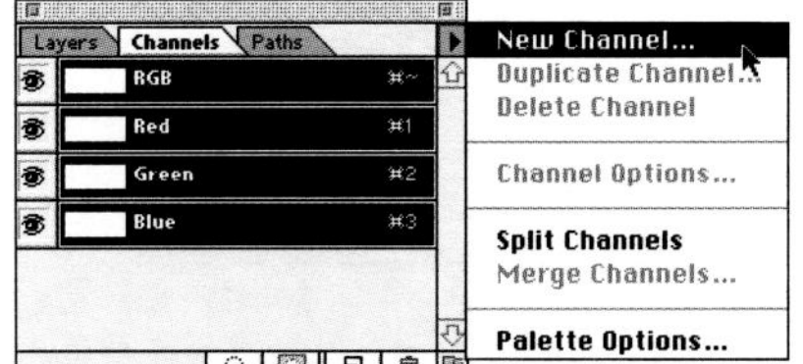


**1** Create a new file, and create a new channel (Channel #4).

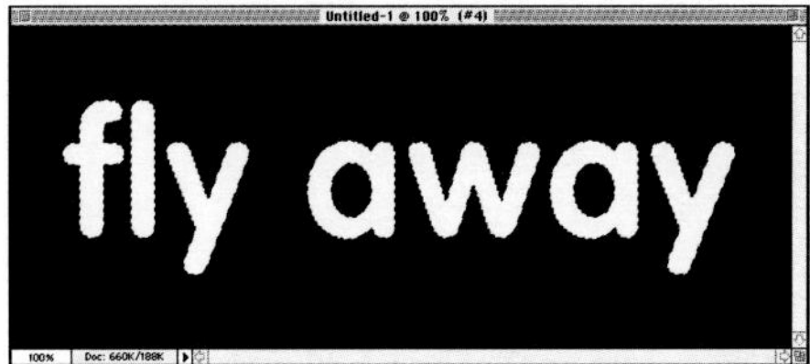


**2** Set the foreground color to white. Enter your text into Channel #4. A round-edged font such as VAG Rounded, which I used here at 80 points, works best.

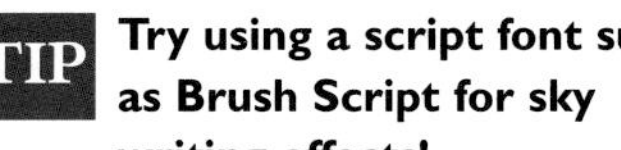

TIP **Try using a script font such as Brush Script for sky writing effects!**

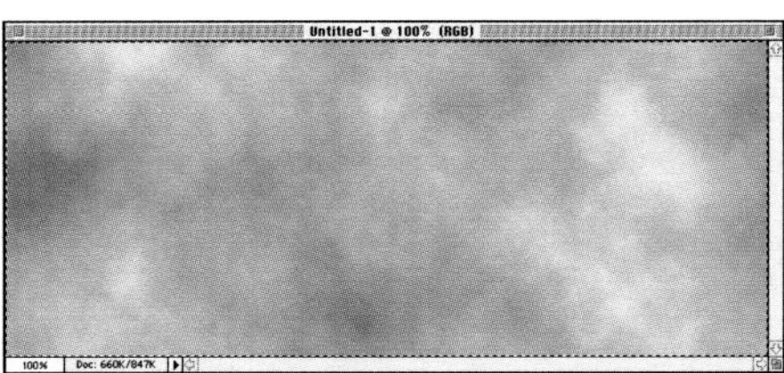

**3** Return to the composite channel (Command-~) [Control-~] and Select➡All. Change the background color to a sky blue. Select Filter➡Render➡Clouds.

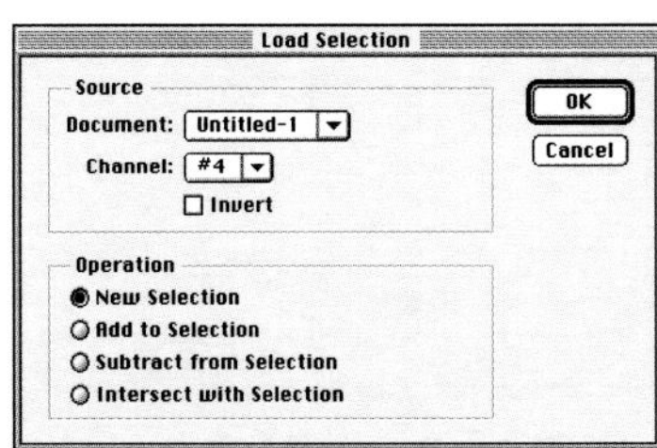


**4** Load the selection Channel #4.

**5** Now choose Select➡Feather and use a setting of 7 pixels.

**If you increase the Feather settings, you increase the radius of the feather. Similarly, by decreasing the settings, you decrease the radius of the feather.**

**6** Press (Option-Delete) [Alt-Delete] to fill the selection with white. ■

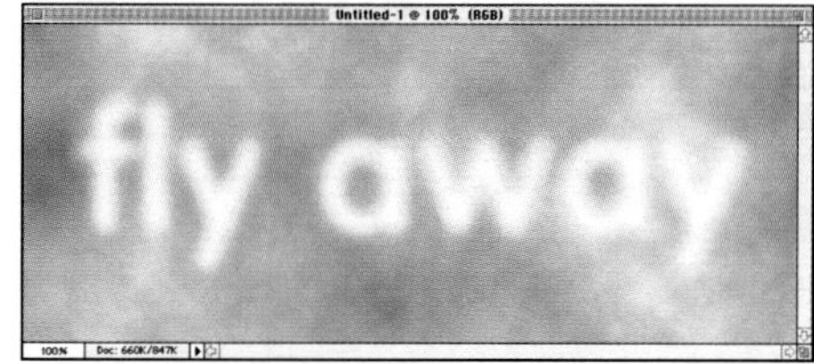

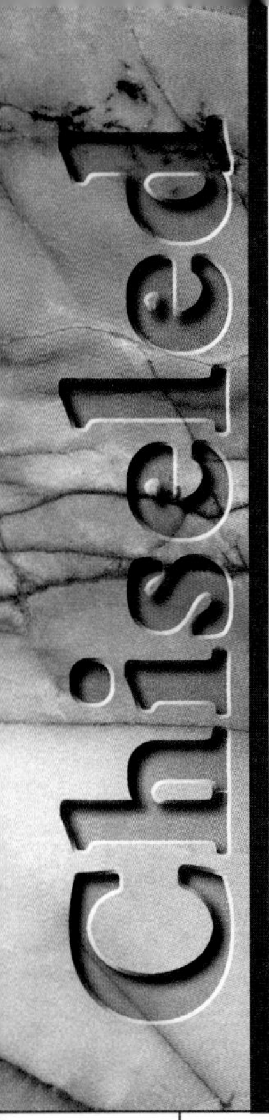


©D'Pix 1995

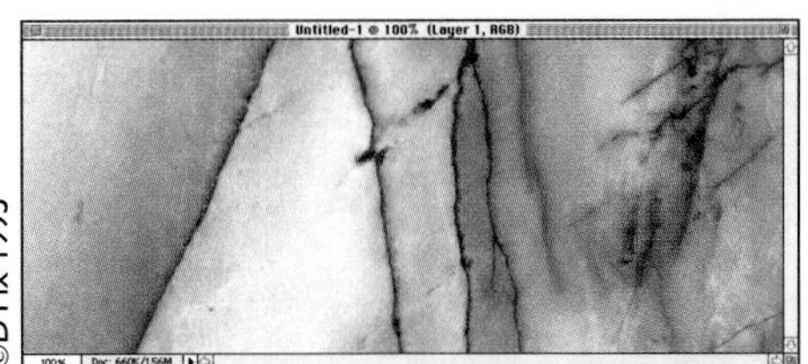


**1** Open a file containing the background you want to chisel. Obviously, a marble or stone texture works best for this effect. We used a stock photo of a piece of rosetta marble from D'Pix for this example.

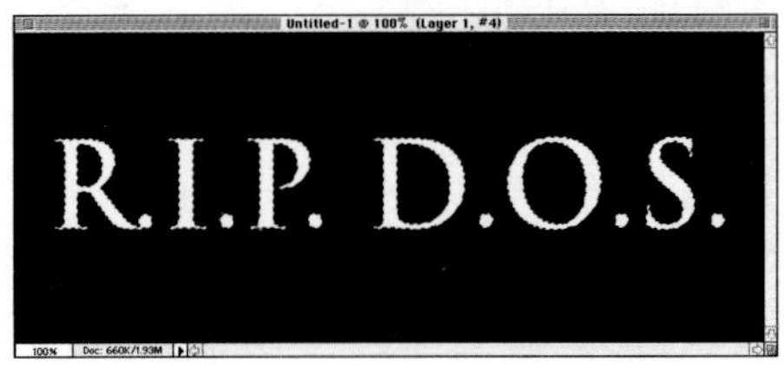


**2** Create a new channel (Channel #4), and change the foreground color to white. Use the Type tool to enter the text in the new channel. This epitaph appears in Trajan Bold at 55 points.

**3** Create another new channel (Channel #5). Choose Edit➡Stroke (3 pixels, Outside, 100%, Normal). Choose Select➡None (Command-D) [Control-D] and Image➡Adjust➡Invert (Command-I) [Control-I].

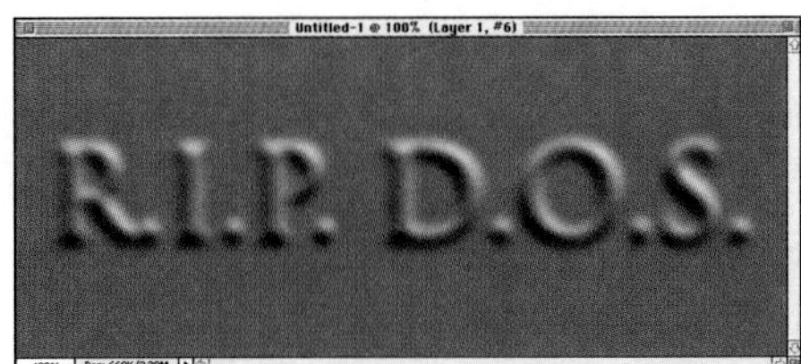


**4** Make Channel #4 active and duplicate it to create Channel #6. Choose Filter➡Blur➡Gaussian Blur (6 pixels). Choose Filter➡Stylize➡Emboss (240°, 3 pixels, 200%).

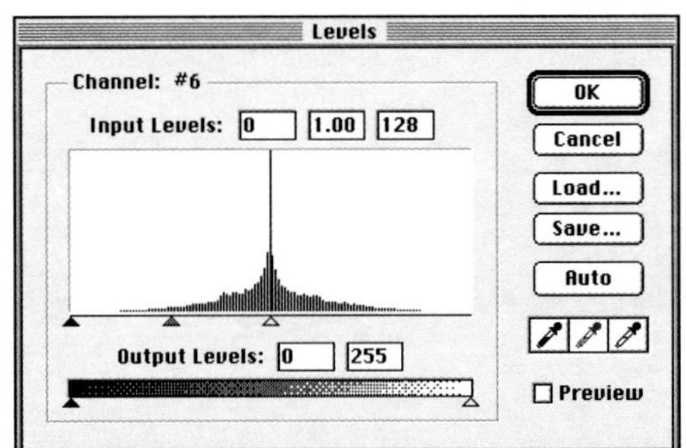


**5** Select➡All (Command-A) [Control-A] and Copy (Command-C) [Control-C] the image to the clipboard. Choose Image➡Adjust➡Levels (Input Levels: 0, 1, 128).

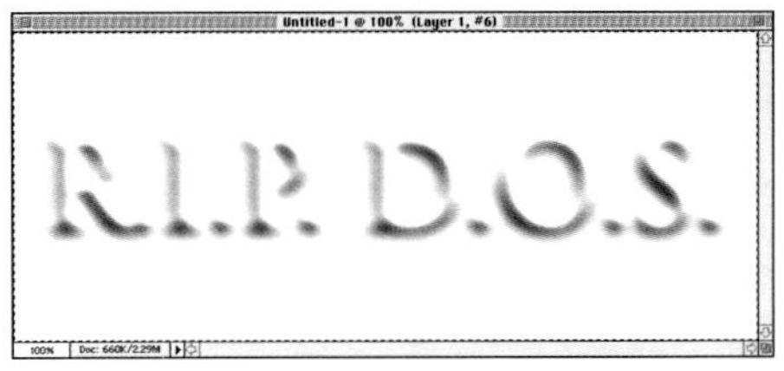

**6** Load the selection Channel #5. Press (Option-Delete) [Alt-Delete] to fill the background with white. Deselect the text. Choose Image➥Adjust➥Invert (Command-I) [Control-I].

**7** Create a new channel (#7) and paste (Command-V) [Control-V] in the clipboard. Choose Image➥Adjust➥Invert (Command-I) [Control-I], then Image➥Adjust➥Levels (Input Levels: 0, 1, 128).

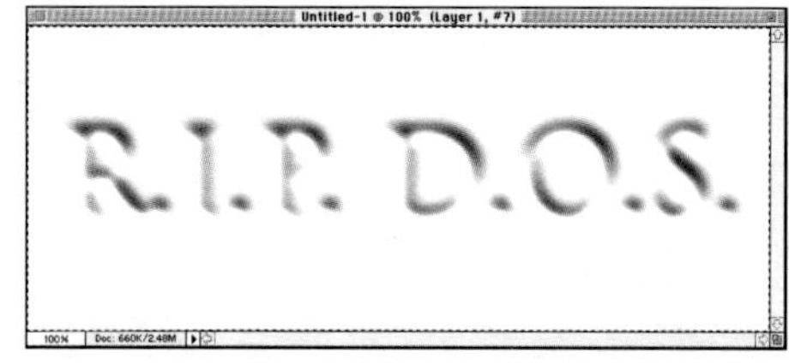

**8** Load the selection Channel #5. Press (Option-Delete) [Alt-Delete] to fill the background with white. Deselect the text. Choose Image➥Adjust➥Invert (Command-I) [Control-I].

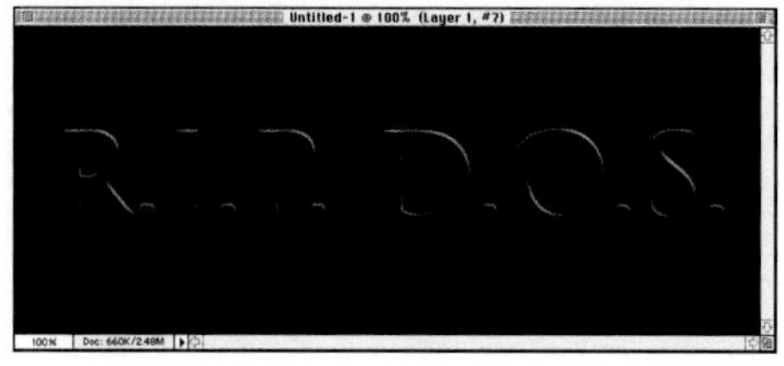

**9** Make Channel #4 active and duplicate it to create Channel #8. Choose Image➥Adjust➥Invert (Command-I) [Control-I]. Apply Filter➥Blur➥Gaussian Blur (3 pixels). Change the background color to white. Select➥All (Command-A) [Control-A] and press the left arrow key and down arrow key four times to offset the image.

**10** Load the selection Channel #4. Choose Select➥Inverse. Change the foreground color to black and press (Option-Delete) [Alt-Delete] to fill the selection.

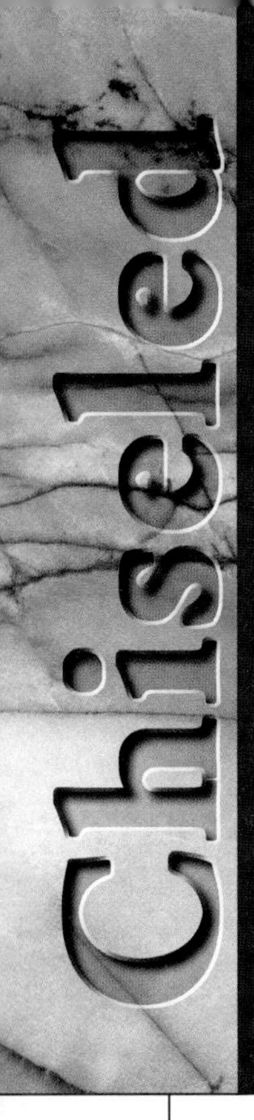


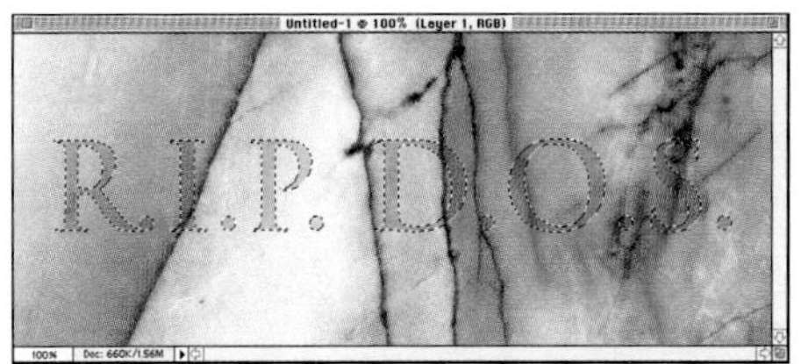


**11** Return to the composite channel. Make sure the foreground color is black. Choose Select➥Load Selection (Channel #4) and Edit➥Fill (Foreground Color, 15%, Normal).

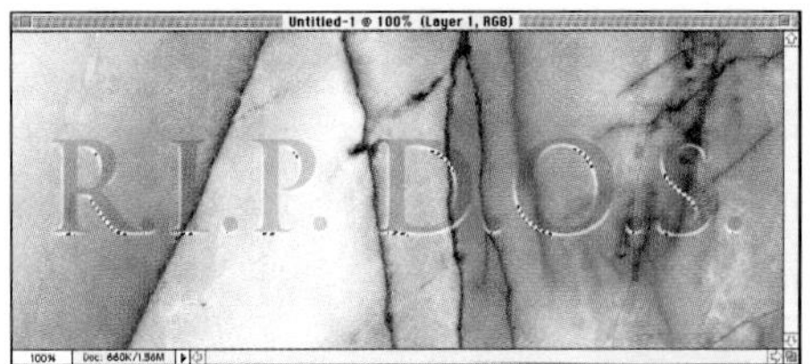


**12** Load the selection Channel #6 and change the foreground color to white. Press (Option-Delete) [Alt-Delete] twice to fill the selection twice.

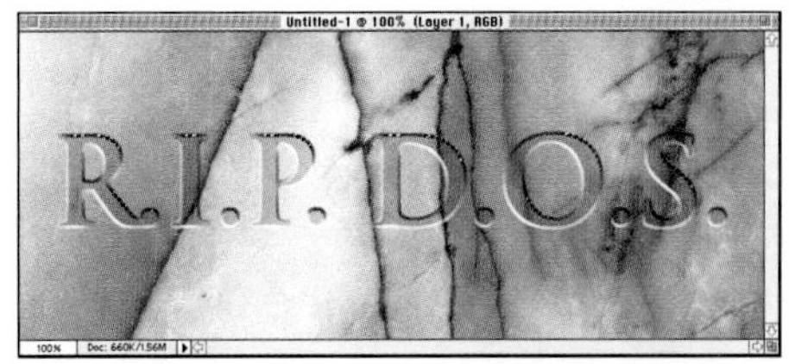


**13** Load the selection Channel #7 and change the foreground color to black. Press (Option-Delete) [Alt-Delete] twice to fill the selection twice.

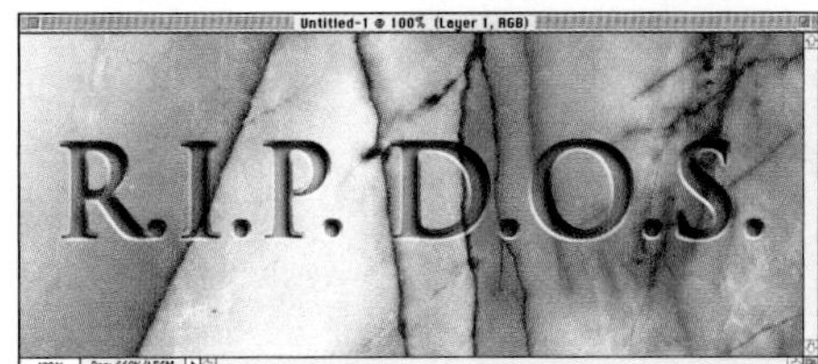


**14** Load the selection Channel #8 then Edit➥Fill (Foreground Color, 85%, Normal). You might want to make adjustments to the Opacity setting to get the desired effect since this may vary from image to image. ■

CHROME



**TOOLBOX**

MagicCurve preset file

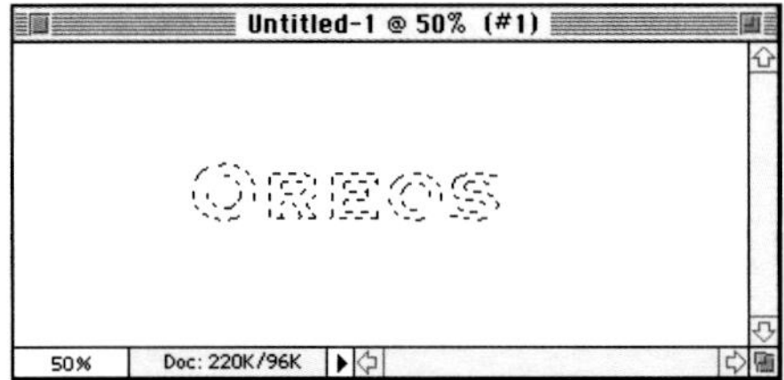


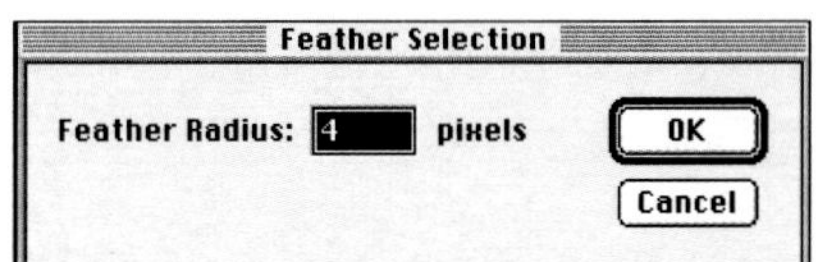


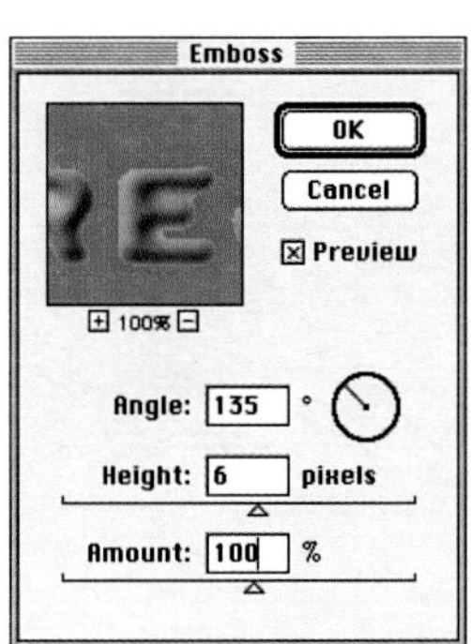

**1** Create a new file, selecting the Grayscale mode in the New File dialog box. In the new file, choose Mode➥Multichannel. Create a new channel (#2). You should now see a blank, black image area.

**2** Make sure that the foreground color is white. Click the Type tool, choose the font you wish to use (in this example, we used Copperplate 33BC, 50 point), and enter the text you want to work with in the new channel.

**3** Choose black as the foreground color and white for the background color.

**4** Make Channel #1 active. You should still be able to see the active selection. If you don't, then load the selection Channel #2 to make the area inside the type active.

**5** Now, choose Select➥Feather and set the amount to 4 pixels. You may find that varying this number produces a better effect—it depends on the typeface you choose. Choose Edit➥Fill (Foreground Color, Opacity: 100%, Normal). Choose Select➥None (Command-D) [Control-D].

**6** Apply Filter➥Stylize➥Emboss (Angle: 135°, Height: 6, Amount: 100%) to raise the text. The angle setting determines the direction of the primary source of light.

**7** Load the selection Channel #2 (Invert selection). Click the foreground color and change it to 50% gray by changing the B setting of the HSB to 50%.

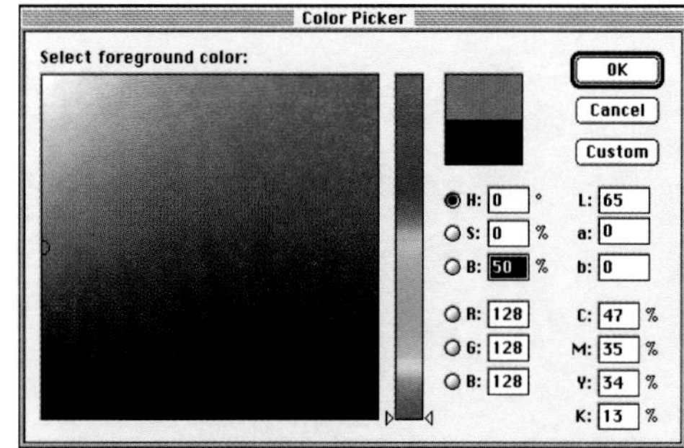


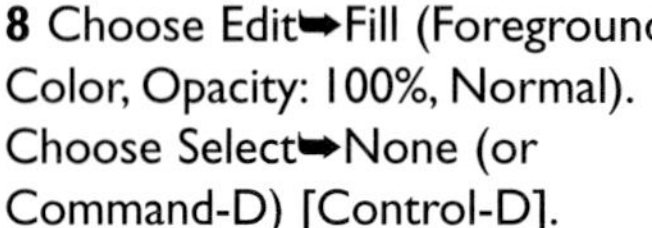

**8** Choose Edit➥Fill (Foreground Color, Opacity: 100%, Normal). Choose Select➥None (or Command-D) [Control-D].

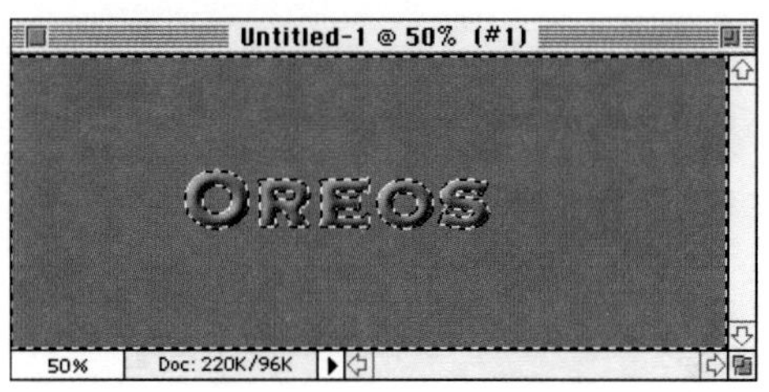


**9** This is the magical step. Go to Image➥Adjust➥Curves (Command-M) [Control-M]. Click the Load button and find the MagicCurve file, or re-create the curve you see here. The more precise it is, the better it works. Click OK.

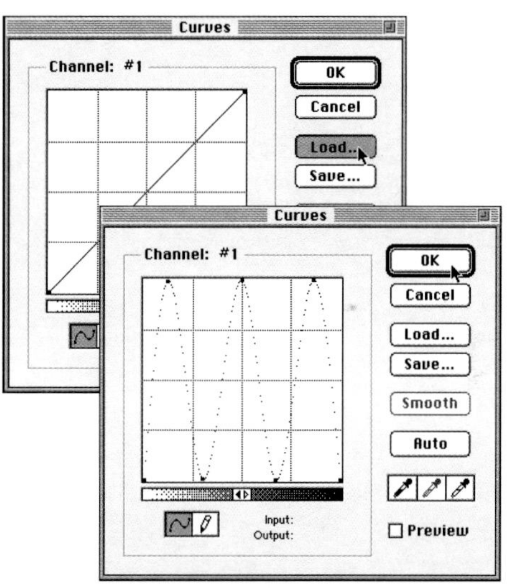

Do you see this?

**10** Load the selection Channel #2. Then choose Image➥Adjust➥ Invert (Command-I) [Control-I].

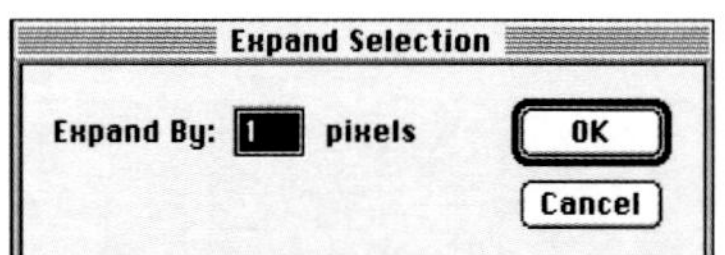


**11** Choose Select➥Modify➥ Expand (1 pixel). Choose Select➥Inverse. Choose white as the foreground color (press X) and press (Option-Delete) [Alt-Delete] to make the background white.

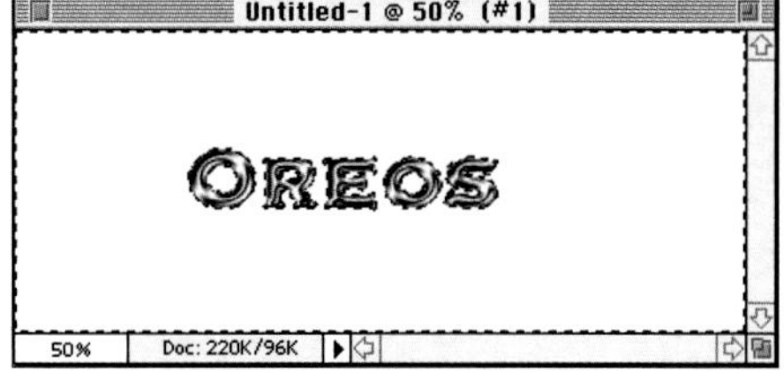


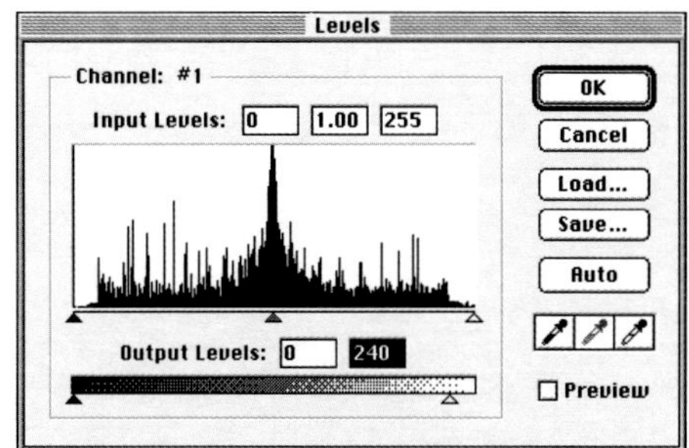


**12** Go to Select➥Inverse, then Image➥Adjust➥Levels (Command-L) [Control-L]. In this dialog box, change the Output Levels white point (the lower-right box) from 255 to 240 and click OK.

**TIP** **You can use the Input Levels in the Levels dialog box to fine-tune the greys in the chrome. Moving the middle (gray) slider to the left will brighten things up.**

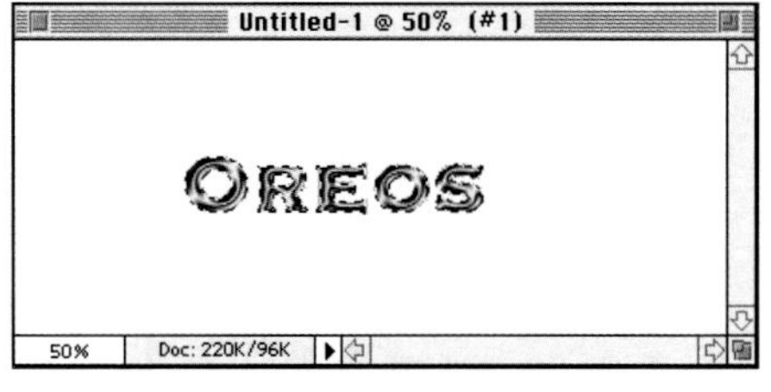


**13** Add a background and experiment with adding a bit of color to your type.

## Chrome 2

Follow the steps for creating Plastic type (page 174) with the following exceptions:

**4** Do not deselect the selection.

**5** Return to the composite channel.

**6** Deselect the text (Command-D) after this step.

**7** Skip this step.

Now, choose Filter➥Stylize➥ Find Edges. You may prefer using Find Edges & Invert. Choose Edit➥ Select All, then copy (Command-C) [Control-C] the image. Go to the RGB channel (Command-0) [Control-0], and paste the text into this composite channel. That's it.

## VARIATIONS

Adding a little color to the chrome might be the final touch it needs. You need to convert the file to a color mode first. I chose CMYK (choose Mode➥CMYK). Choose Image➥Adjust➥Curves (Command-M) [Control-M]. Best results come from working in the color channels one at a time. In these two variations, I bent the Cyan curve up a little, then down a little. You may find it easier to use the Hue/Saturation (Command-U) [Control-U] dialog box, in which you can slide the Hue slider to the left and right to produce subtle color changes.

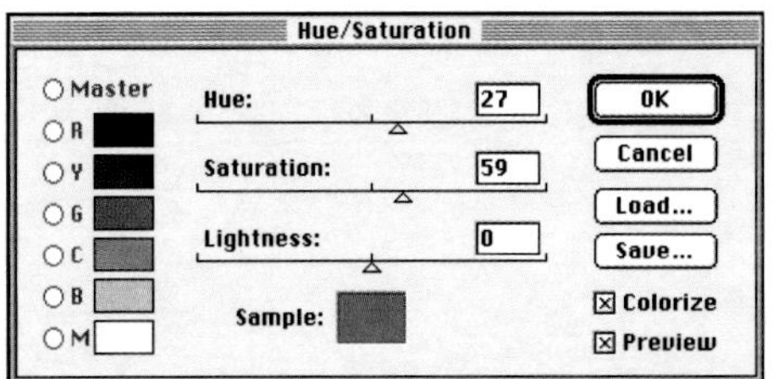

Adding a lot of color can change your chrome to something that looks more like gold. Choose Image➡Adjust➡Hue/Saturation (Command-U) [Control-U]. Make sure the preview box is checked so you can see what you're doing. Click the Colorize checkbox in the lower right, and try these values: Hue: 27, Saturation: 59, Lightness: 0. ■

**1** Open the picture you want to use as your credit card background or create a new file. This stock photo comes from Digital Stock.

**2** Use the Type tool to enter the text and move it to where you want it to fall on the image. We used the OCR-A font at 30 points to achieve a more realistic look. Change this layer name to "Text" and leave all other settings at their default.

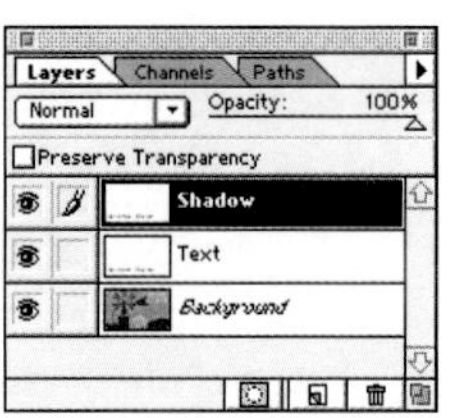


**3** Choose Duplicate Layer from the Layer palette menu and name it "Shadow." You should now have a total of three layers in your file.

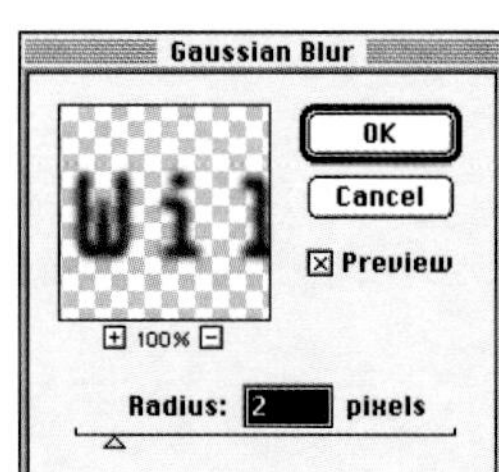


**4** Make the Text layer the active layer. For ease, you might also want to make it the only visible layer, too. Make sure Preserve Transparency is not checked, and apply Filter➡Blur➡Gaussian Blur. A setting of 2 pixels was used for this image. If your type is considerably larger, use a higher pixel setting.

**5** Apply Filter➥Stylize➥Find Edges to the text layer. This is the beginning of the raised effect.

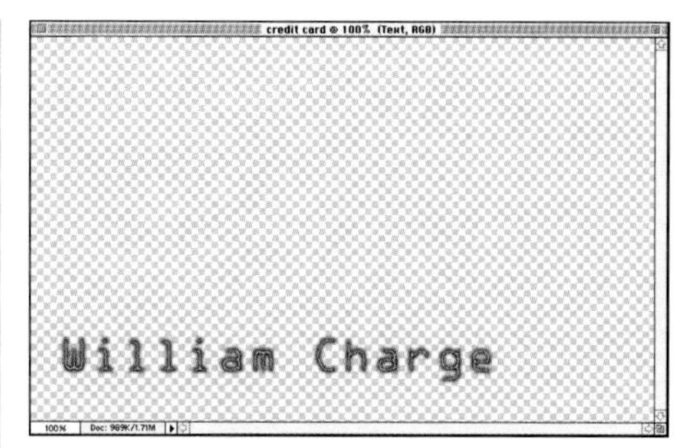


**6** Next, apply Filter➥Other➥Offset to the text layer. For this example, we used settings of 3 pixels right and 2 pixels down. This filter moves the text slightly so that the Shadow layer shows on the top and left sides.

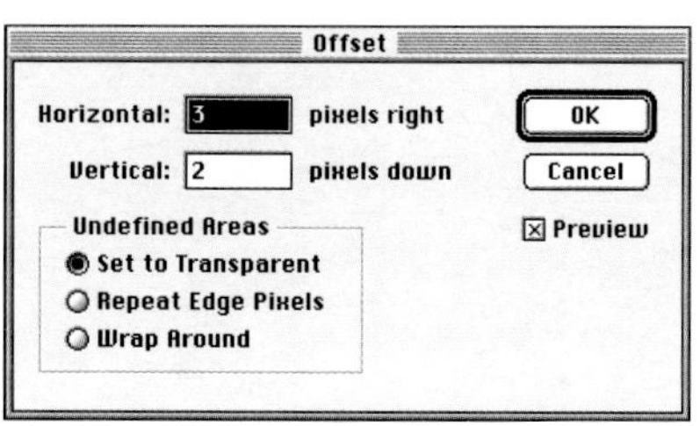


**7** Make the Shadow layer the active layer. Apply Filter➥Blur➥Gaussian Blur. Use a setting of 2, as you did in Step 4.

**8** Make the Text layer visible and keep the Shadow layer active, so you can see what you're doing.

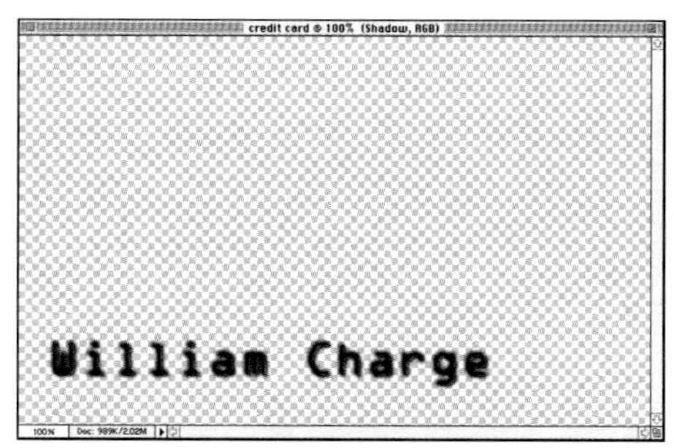


Use Filter➥Other➥Maximum to thin down the text on the Shadow layer. This text is the shadow side of the letters. A setting of 2 pixels was used here.

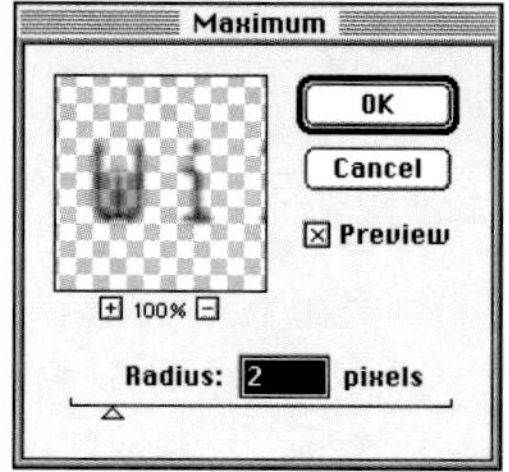

**9** Make all three layers visible. Move the Shadow layer to make it the layer directly below the Text layer. This puts the Shadow layer behind the Text layer so it doesn't obscure the words.

**10** Make the Text layer active. Adjust the Opacity level to 70%. This lets the background image show through and reduces the harshness of the shadows.

If you like the way the image shows through the text, you can flatten the image and stop now. But if you want the look of ink printed onto the "raised" letters, keep going.

**11** To add the ink, make the Shadow layer active and duplicate it by choosing Duplicate Layer from the Layers palette menu. Name the layer "Ink." Move the Ink layer above the other layers in the Layers palette.

Use Filter➡Other➡Offset to move this layer the same amount that you moved the Text layer in Step 6. The Offset dialog box has the same settings you used the last time the effect was applied, so all you need to do is click OK.

Use Filter➥Other➥Maximum with a setting of 1 pixel to thin the text even more. At higher settings, the letters may start to fill in, so do some experimenting first!

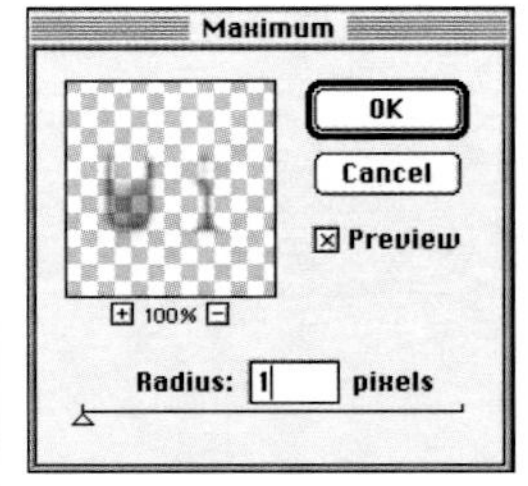


**12** Choose Image➥Adjust➥Invert (Command-I)[Control-I] to make the text white.

## VARIATION

To colorize the type, choose Image➥Adjust➥Hue/Saturation. Be sure to check the Colorize checkbox first to give you the appropriate sliders to work with. Adjust the sliders until you get the color you want. You can also try different backgrounds before you flatten your image. When you're done, flatten the image and charge it! ■

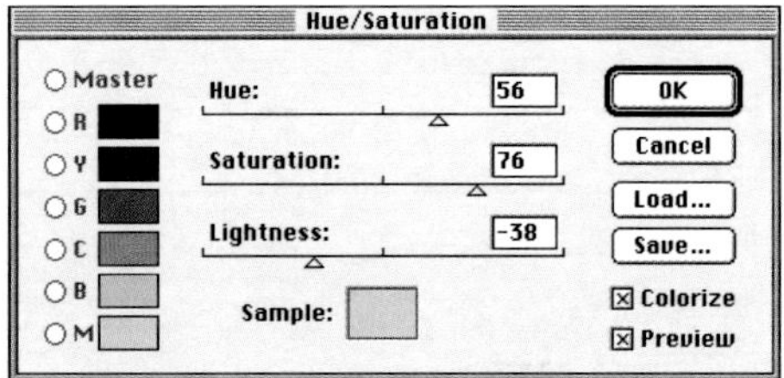

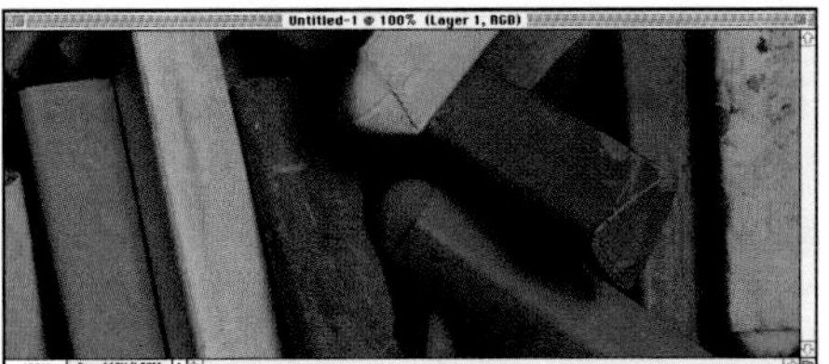

**1** Open a new file or a file with an image you want to cut the text from.

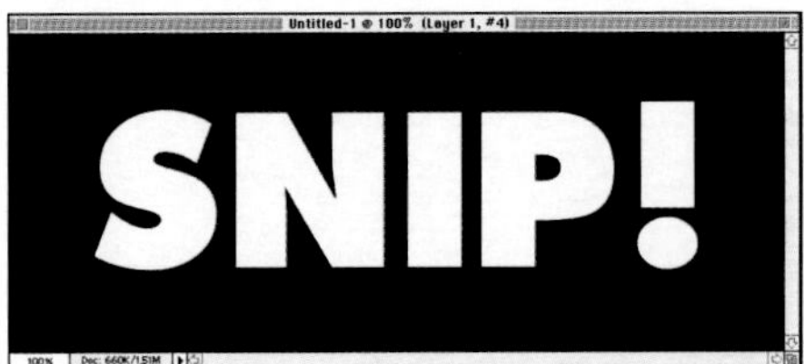


**2** Create a new channel (Channel #4). Choose white as the foreground color and use the Type tool to enter the text. While the text selection is still active, save the selection (Channel #5).

Deselect the text (Command-D) [Control-D].

Offset

Horizontal: 10 pixels right

Vertical: 10 pixels down

OK

Cancel

☒ Preview

Undefined Areas

○ Set to Transparent

● Repeat Edge Pixels

○ Wrap Around

**3** Now, apply Filter➥Blur➥Gaussian Blur (3.5 pixels). Then choose Filter➥Other ➥Offset (10 pixels right, 10 pixels down, and make sure to choose the Repeat Edge Pixels option). This channel is the shadow that appears behind the text.

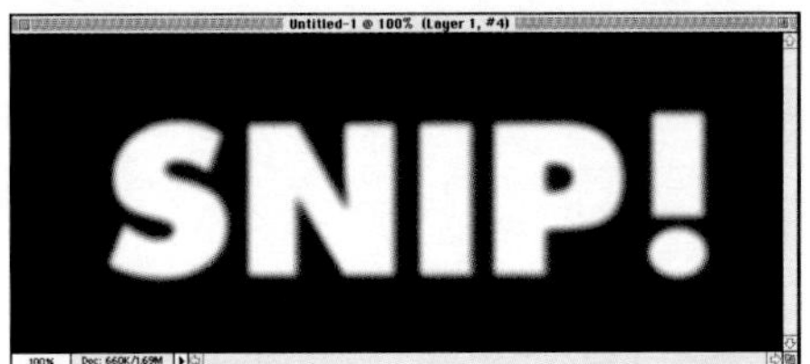

**4** Return to the composite channel (Command-~) [Control-~], and create a new layer (Layer 1).

**5** Load the selection you saved in Step 2 (Channel #5) and fill it with black, or any other color you want to use for the shadow.

**6** Keep the selection active. Now, choose Select➡Load Selection, activate the shadow channel (#4), and choose the Intersect with Selection option.

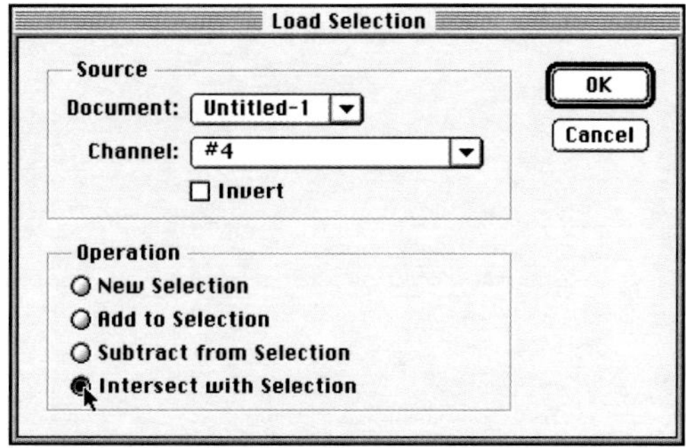


The active selection should look like this.

**7** Change the foreground color to the color you want to make the background. Press (Option-Delete) [Alt-Delete] to fill the selection, deselect it (Command-D) [Control-D] and you're done. No cuts, no bleeding, no errors.

**If you want to fine tune the shadow (brighten, soften, change its color), then load the selection Channel #5. Now load the selection Channel #4, selecting the Subtract from Selection option. The shadow is now selected.**

## VARIATIONS

If you want to cut through one image to see another underneath, before opening the file containing the foreground image in Step 1, open the file containing the background image. Copy the part of the image you want to use as the background. Complete all the steps above except Step 7. Instead choose Edit➥Paste Into. Presto! If you need to move the background image, drag it around using the Move tool—but only if you didn't deselect it first.

In Step 1 create a new file with a white image area and do the entire exercise. In Step 7, choose white as the foreground color. The type needs a soft outline to separate the foreground from the white background, so load the selection #5 you saved in Step 2, and choose Edit➥Stroke (1 pixel, Center, 10% Opacity, Normal).

You can apply this technique to anything you put in a channel. Try using a hard-edged paintbrush and adding text or art into the channel, like the steam curls in this image. ■

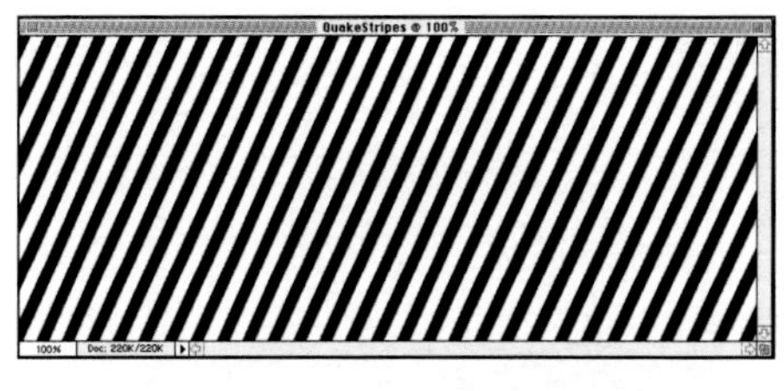


**1** Open the QuakeStripes preset file included on the CD-ROM, choose Select➥All and copy the image to the clipboard (Command-C) [Control-C]. Close the file (Command-W) [Control-W].

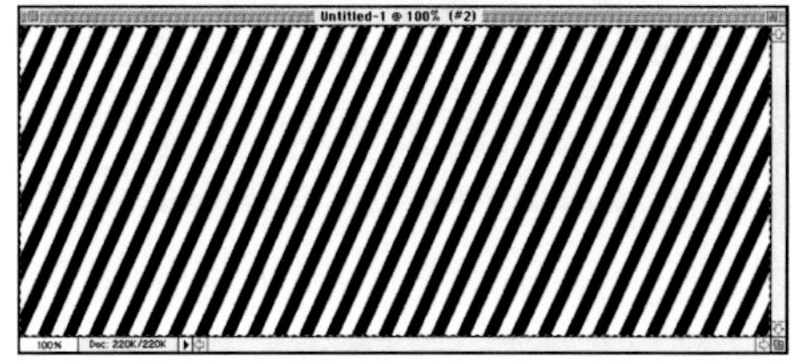


**2** Create a new file. (Be sure to select RGB mode.) Create a new channel (Channel #4). Paste the clipboard into this new channel (Command-V) [Control-V]. Use Layer➥Transform➥Scale to fill the channel with the stripes if it does not fit properly.

**The width of the stripes in this file may not be a good width for the text size you want to distort. If the stripes are too small, then use the Scale command to make them larger. If they are too big, then scale them down, copy them, paste the copy back into the channel, and move the copy so it continues the striped pattern. Repeat if necessary.**



**TOOLBOX**

QuakeStripes preset file

**3** Return to the composite channel (Command-~) [Control-~]. Change the foreground color to a color for the text. Use the Type tool to enter the text. We used Helvetica Bold Oblique at 65 points for this example. If you do not choose an oblique font, then check the Italic style option. It is also important to give the letters some room to move. We increased the spacing to 10.

**4** Load the transparency selection for the new layer containing the type (Layer 2), and save the selection (Channel #5). Flatten the image before you continue.

**5** Move the letters in pieces by using the two channels to select only certain parts of the letters. To select the first part, choose Select➡Load Selection and choose Channel #4 with the Subtract from Selection option checked.

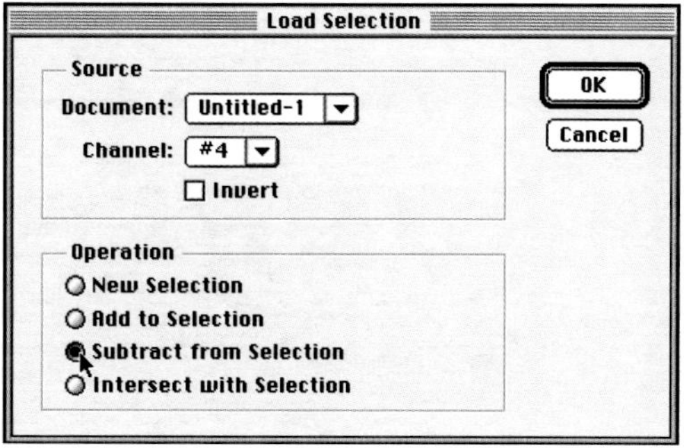


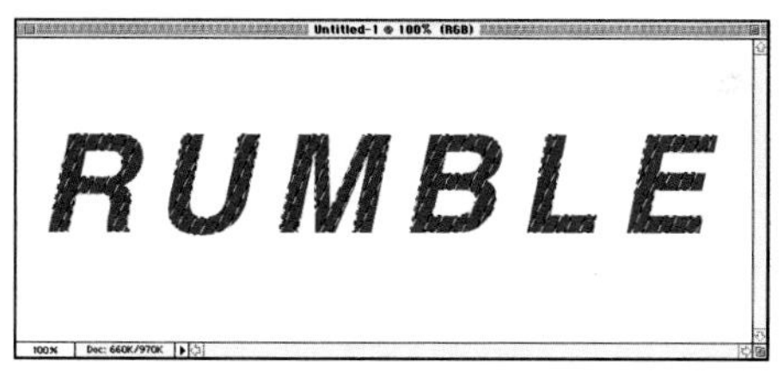


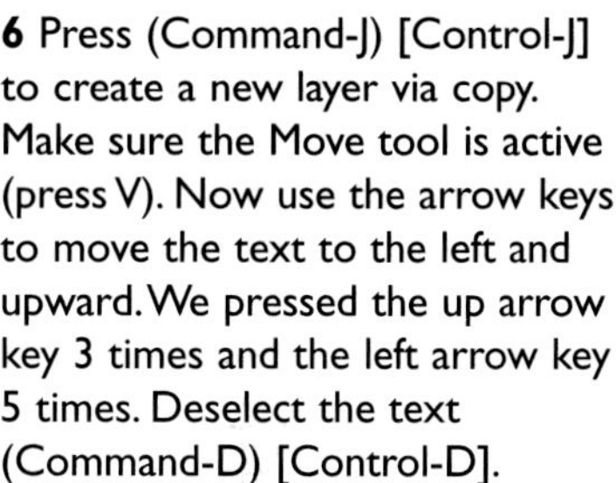

**6** Press (Command-J) [Control-J] to create a new layer via copy. Make sure the Move tool is active (press V). Now use the arrow keys to move the text to the left and upward. We pressed the up arrow key 3 times and the left arrow key 5 times. Deselect the text (Command-D) [Control-D].

**7** Make the Background layer active. Load the text selection (Channel #5), then load the stripes selection (Channel #4) with the Intersect with Selection option checked.

Load Selection

Source
Document: Untitled-1
Channel: #4
Invert
OK
Cancel
Operation
New Selection
Add to Selection
Subtract from Selection
Intersect with Selection

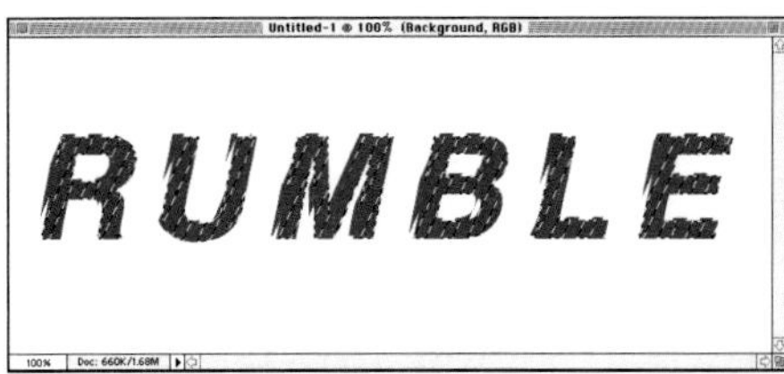


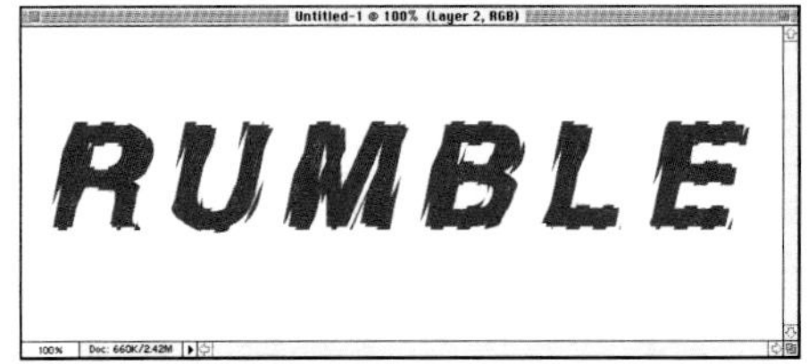


**8** Press (Command-J) [Control-J] to create a new layer via copy. Make sure the Move tool is active (press V). Again, use the arrow keys to move the text. This time move the selection to the right and down. We pressed the down arrow key 3 time and the right arrow key 5 times. Deselect the text (Command-D) [Control-D].

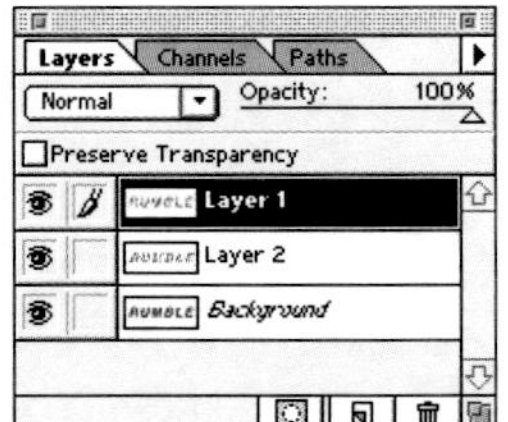


**9** You can stop at Step 8 but if you want to add some more realism, try adding some motion blurs. First, note that Photoshop 4 has created some new layers in the process of creating this image. Activate each of those layers and apply Filter➥Blur➥Motion Blur (we used a setting of 5). Remember, don't be afraid to experiment!

## VARIATIONS

Two extra steps make this variation. Before Step 5, and after loading the text selection in Step 7, choose Select➥Modify➥Border (7 pixels).

Add color. After copying the text selection onto a new layer in Steps 6 and 8, change the foreground color and press (Option-Delete) [Alt-Delete] to fill the slices with the new color. ■

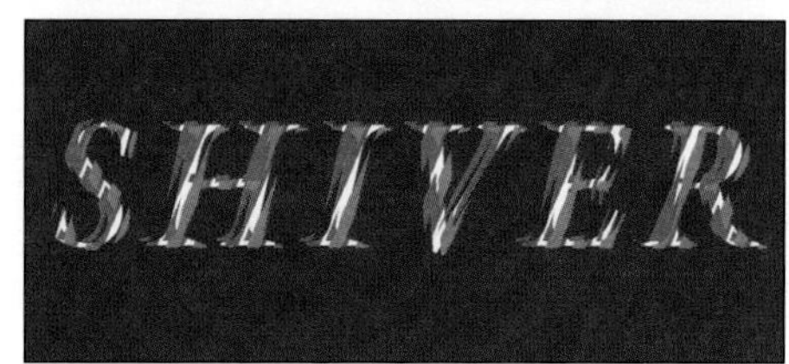

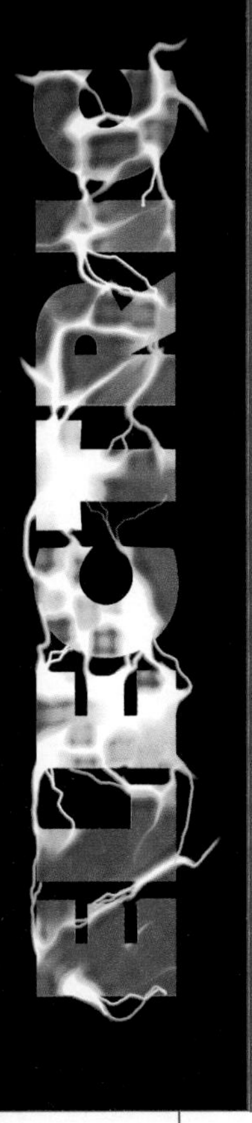

**1** Open a marble image. Choose Select➡All and Copy the image to the clipboard. Close the file.

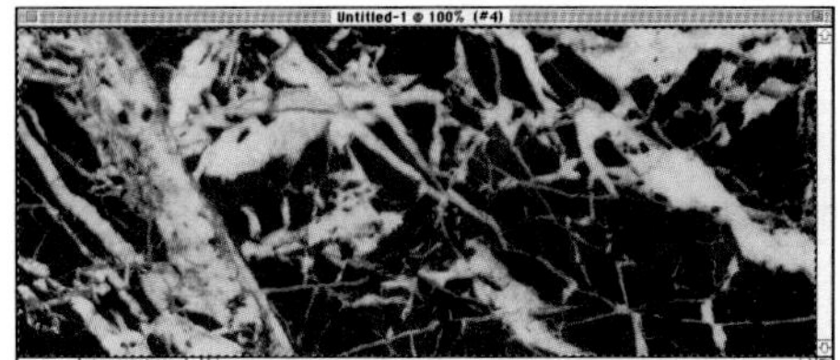

**2** Create a new file for your final image, choosing white for the Background color in the New File dialog. Create a new channel (#4), and paste in the marble image from the clipboard. Move it around so a fair amount of white streaks are in view.

**3** Apply Filter➡Blur➡Gaussian Blur (10 pixels).

**4** Apply Filter➡Other➡Minimum (10 pixels). This step creates the bright bolts.

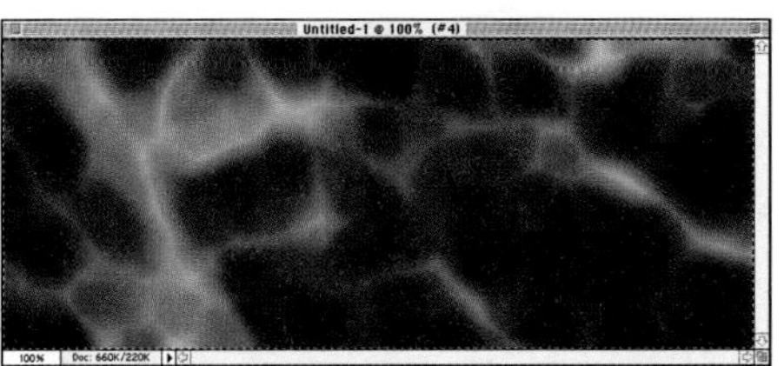

You should now have something similar to this.

## TOOLBOX

Alien Skin's Glow filter

**5** Apply Filter➥Sharpen➥Unsharp Mask (344%, 9.1 pixels, 9 levels).

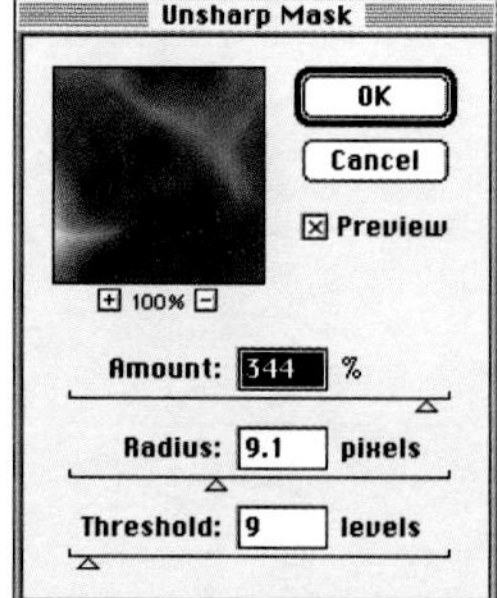


You should have something like this.

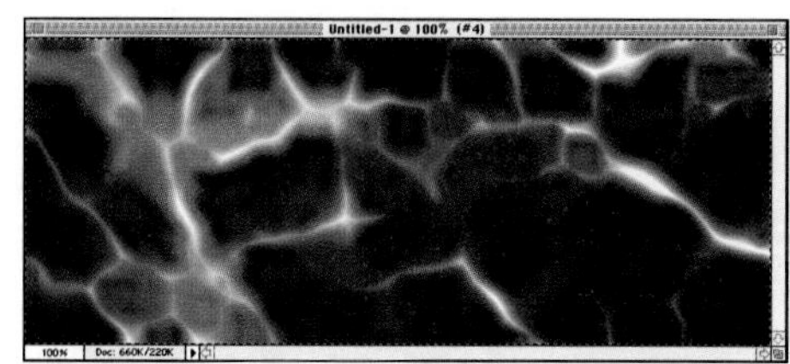

**6** Create a new channel (#5). Choose white as the foreground color and use the Type tool to enter the text. We used Fortuna Bold at 75 points.

**7** Return to the composite channel (Command-~) [Control-~]. With the type selection still active, load the selection Channel #4. Be sure the Subtract from Selection option is on.

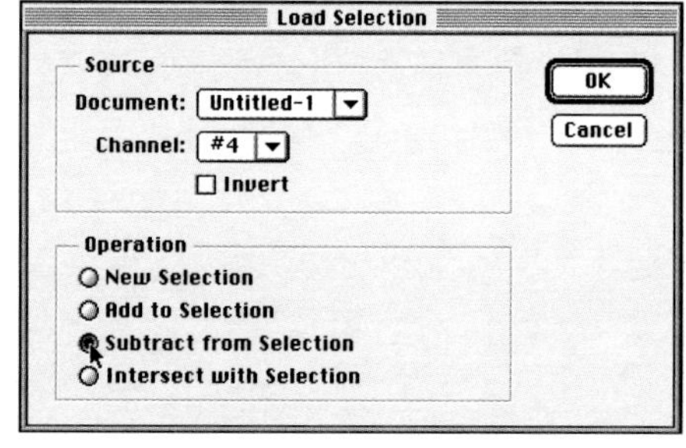


**8** Choose black as the foreground color and press (Option-Delete) [Alt-Delete] to fill the selection. You should get some arcs like this.

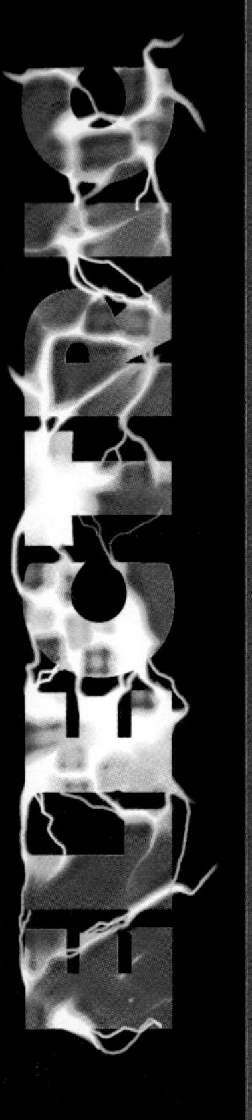

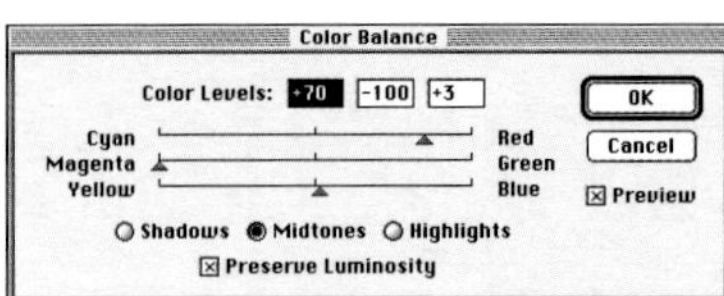


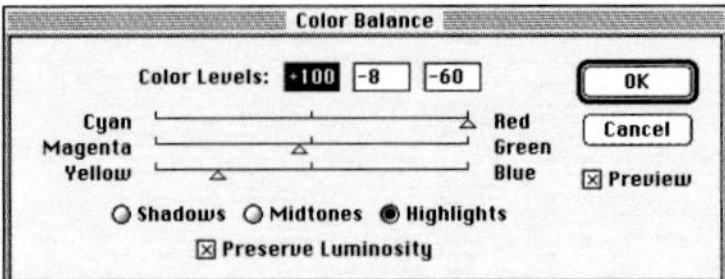


**9** With the selection still active, choose Image➡Adjust➡Color Balance. We used the following settings for this example (Midtones: +70,–100,+3 Highlights: +100, –8, –60) to get a red set of bolts. Use (Midtones: –80,–100,+90, Highlights: –85, 0, +50) for blue bolts. You can experiment here to find different color choices. Also, this effect looks best if you are creating RGB artwork because it can retain more vibrant colors than in CMYK mode.

**10** Load the type selection (Channel #5) and choose Select➡Inverse. Press (Option-Delete) [Alt-Delete] to fill in the background with black. Deselect the selection (Command-D) [Control-D].

**11** Now use the Smudge tool with a fairly small brush size to extend some of the electric bolts.

**12** When you are satisfied, switch to the Airbrush tool. Choose an appropriate brush size and click in a region you are about to airbrush while temporarily holding down the (Option) [Alt] key (to switch to the Eyedropper tool). This chooses a foreground color that is close to the area you are about to paint. Then carefully airbrush in some bolts.

Vary the airbrush size to get some more realistic effects.

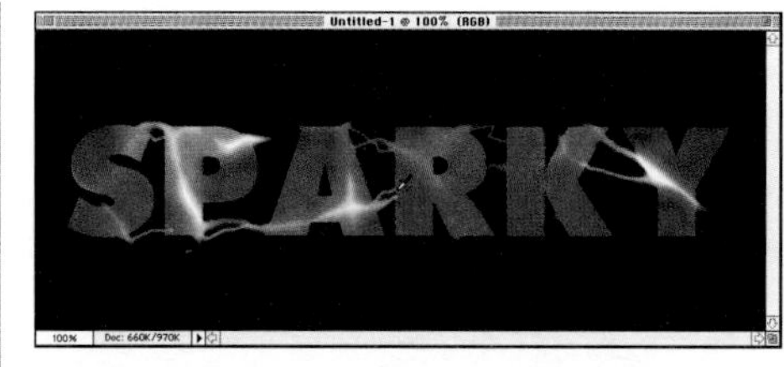


**13** Choose Image➡Adjust➡ Brightness/Contrast (Contrast: 25).

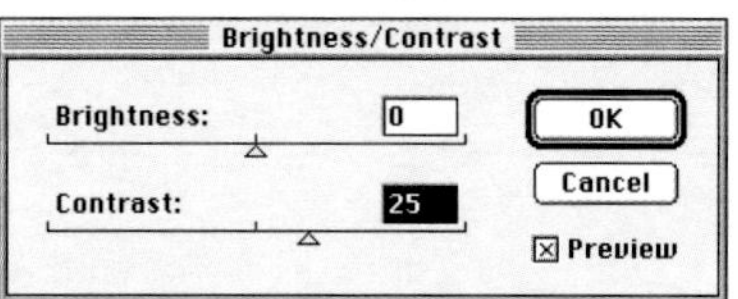


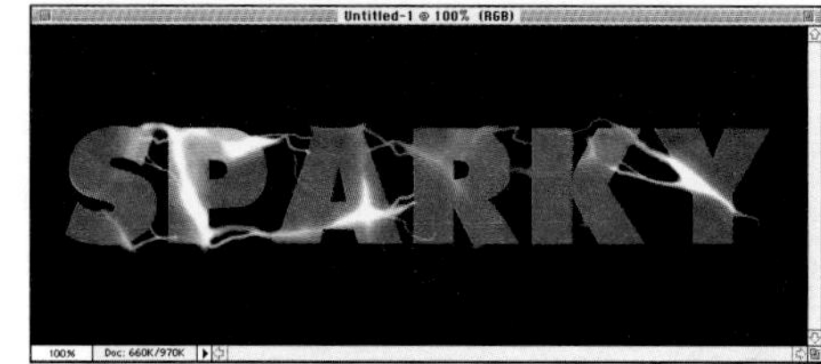


## Variation

After you are finished, try adding a glow and some text. This glow was added very quickly using Alien Skin's Glow filter. ■

There are a number of ways to raise text in Photoshop. The first method shown here is a shortcut to embossing type. The Lighting Effects filter relieves you from having to find the highlights and shadows. The second method is the traditional (Can you use that word when you're talking about Photoshop?) method that uses separate channels for the highlights and shadows, enabling you to edit and re-edit those areas of the type.

## Embossed 1

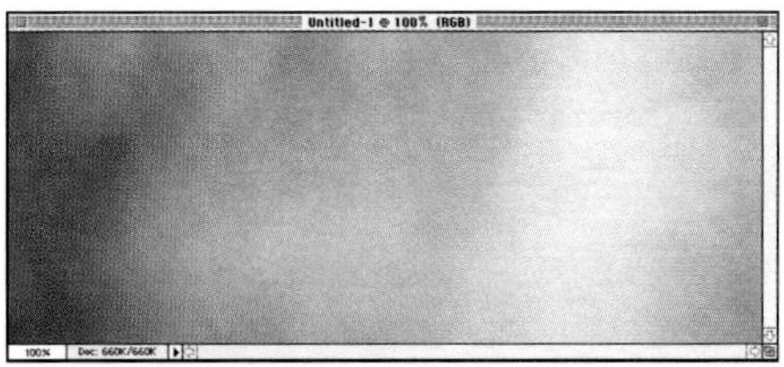

1 Create a new RGB file or open a file containing the surface you want to emboss. Whichever you choose, the file must be in RGB mode because the Lighting Effects filter only works in RGB mode.

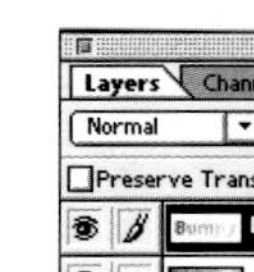


2 Create a new channel, and use the Type Mask tool to enter the text. We used Myriad Bold at 100 points. Fill the text with white. Keep the selection active, and choose Filter➡Blur➡Gaussian Blur (4 pixels) to blur only the inside of the type. The lower the pixel radius you use when blurring, the softer and slighter the edges of the text will be. Make the Background layer active. Now choose Layer➡New➡Layer Via Copy (Command-J) [Control-J]. This creates the text on a separate layer.



### TOOLBOX

Alien Skin's Inner Bevel

EmbossLightStyles file

**3** Choose Filter➡Render➡Lighting Effects. Either choose the Emboss-LightStyles preset from the pop-up menu or adjust the settings as you see them here. If it doesn't show up in the list, see page 242 to find out how to load it from the CD-ROM. Make sure that you position the light far enough away from the text that the letters aren't completely washed out. Click OK and you're finished.

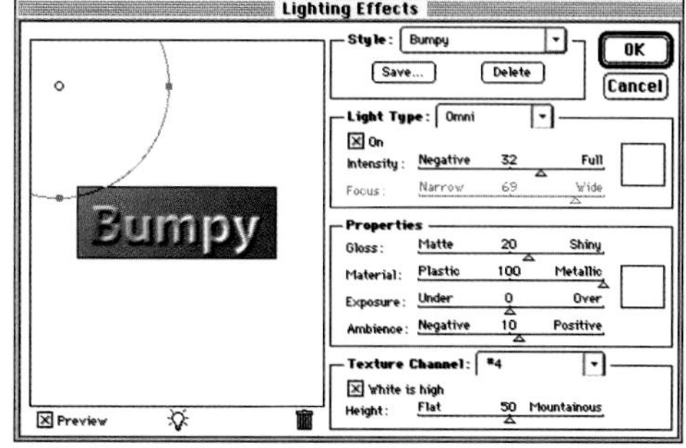

TIP **If you want the same lighting effects on your background, make that layer active and apply the same lighting effect settings. Another way to try this technique is to load the texture channel in the Lighting Effects filter with the type channel you created in Step 2 (Channel #4).**

## Embossed 2

Created by Craig Swanson

**1** Create a new file or open a file containing the surface you want to emboss. We filled this background image with blue.

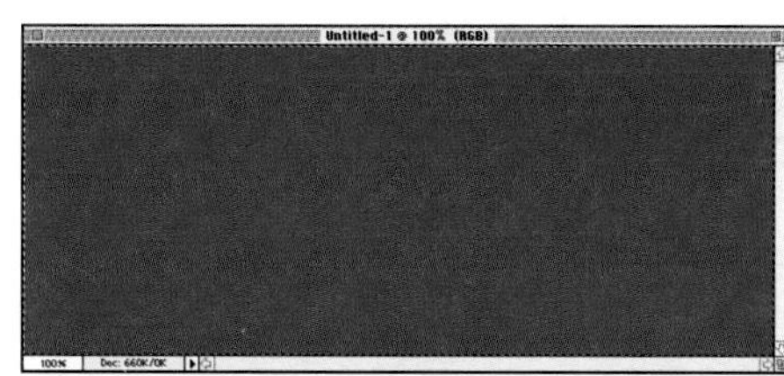

**2** Create a new channel (Channel #4). Use the Type tool to enter the text you want to apply the effect to in the new channel. Again, we used Myriad Bold at 100 points. Deselect the text (Command-D) [Control-D].

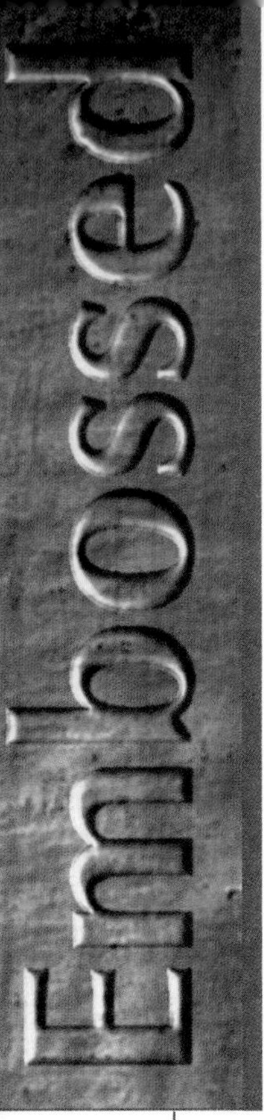


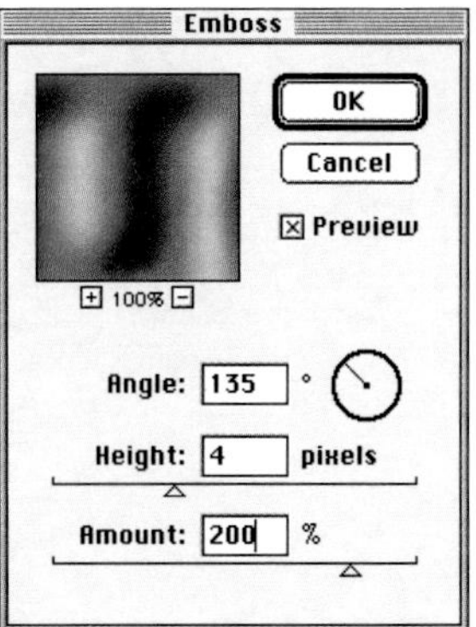


**3** Duplicate Channel #4 to create Channel #5. To soften the edges, apply Filter➥Blur➥Gaussian Blur (8 pixels). Apply Filter➥Stylize➥ Emboss (135°, 4 pixels, 200%). The type should now look like this.

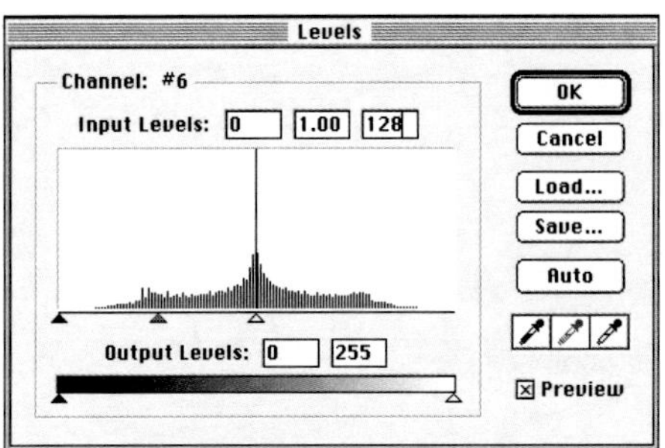


**4** Duplicate Channel #5 to create Channel #6. To isolate the shadow areas in this channel, choose Image➥Adjust➥Levels (Input Levels: 0, 1, 128).

**5** Load the selection Channel #4. Check the Invert checkbox. Choose white as the background color and press Delete. Deselect the background (Command-D) [Control-D] and invert the image (Image➡Adjust➡ Invert). This channel is used as the selection for the shadows.

**6** To make the channel for the highlights, make Channel #5 active. Choose Image➡Adjust➡Invert and then Image➡Adjust➡Levels (Input Levels: 0, 1, 128).

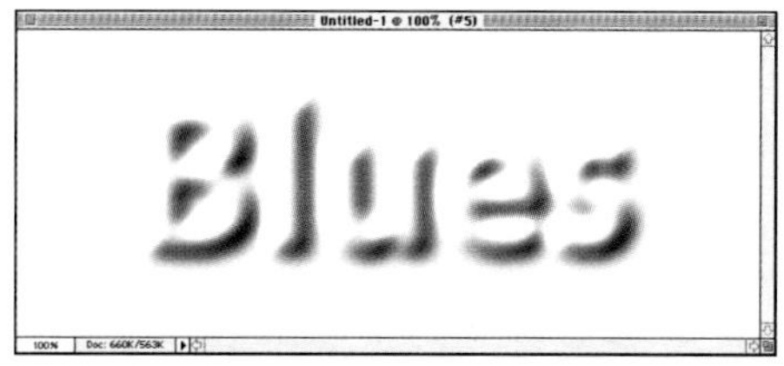

**7** Load the selection Channel #4. Check the Invert checkbox. Choose white as the background color and press Delete. Deselect the background (Command-D) [Control-D]. Choose Image➡ Adjust➡Invert. Now you have a selection channel for the highlights.

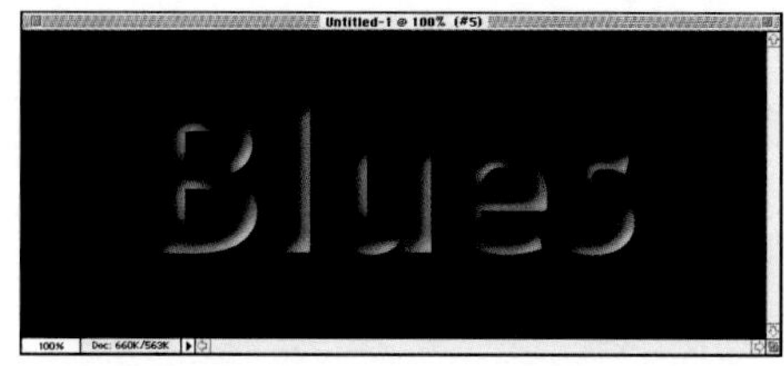

**8** Return to the composite channel (Command-~) [Control-~], and load the selection Channel #6. Choose black as the foreground color. Now press (Option-Delete) [Alt-Delete] to fill in the shadows, and then a second time if you want a stronger edge.

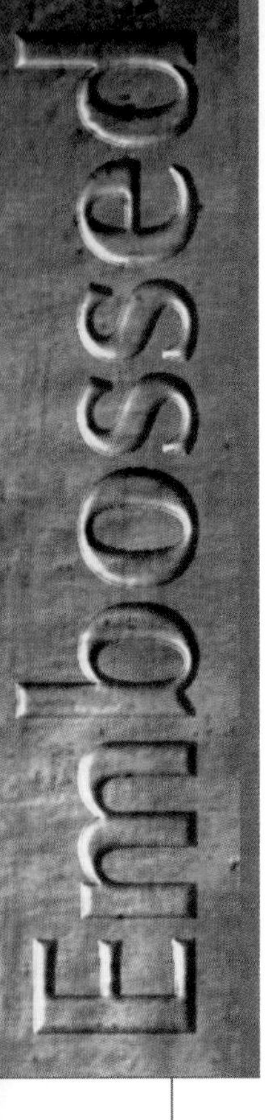

9 Finally, load the selection Channel #5 and choose white as the foreground color. Now press (Option-Delete) [Alt-Delete] to fill in the highlights. If you want a stronger edge, press (Option-Delete) [Alt-Delete] a second time.

**The advantage to Emboss 2 is that you can load the highlight and shadow selections again if you want to make alterations.**

## Variation

Another quick way to create embossed type is with the Inner Bevel filter—part of Alien Skin's Eye Candy (formerly called Black Box) collection of filters.

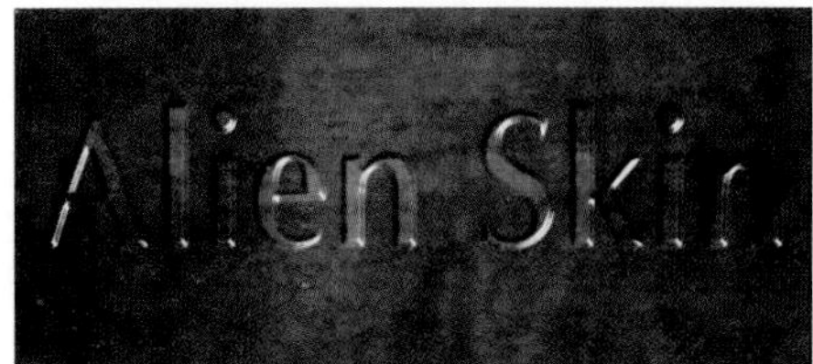


Create a new file. Use the Type tool to enter the text you want to apply the effect to in the new channel. Keep the selection active as you return to the composite channel (Command-~) [Control-~]. Apply Filter➡Alien Skin➡Inner Bevel 2.1. Experiment with the settings. Here's what we came up with after loading the selection again and raising the contrast inside the text. ■

1 Create a new file. Set the foreground color to black (press D). Use the Type tool to enter the text. We used City Medium at 70 points for this example. Flatten the Image.

**TIP** **The point size and thickness of the font are important in this technique because the Wind filter can really blow small or thin type away. If you want smaller type, we still suggest you use 70 points and choose Image➥Effects➥Scale to reduce the type when you're finished.**

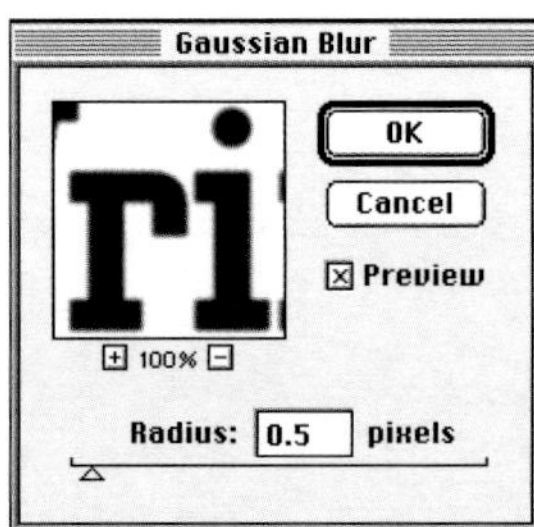


**2** Choose Filter➥Blur➥Gaussian Blur (0.5 pixels). The thicker the font, the higher the pixel radius should be.

**3** Choose Filter➥Stylize➥Wind (Wind, Left). Press (Command-Option-F) [Control-Alt-F] to bring back the last filter dialog box, and switch the Wind direction to Right.

**4** Choose Image➡Adjust➡Invert (Command-I) [Control-I].

**5** Choose Duplicate Layer from the Layers palette menu to create the Background copy layer. Click OK to accept the defaults.

**6** Double-click the Magic Wand tool. Find the Magic Wand Tool Options palette (it's hiding somewhere on your screen) and change the Tolerance setting to 25. With the Magic Wand, click in the black area of the image. You also need to select the enclosed areas within letters such as "e" and "o" by holding the Shift key and clicking within these areas. Press Delete.

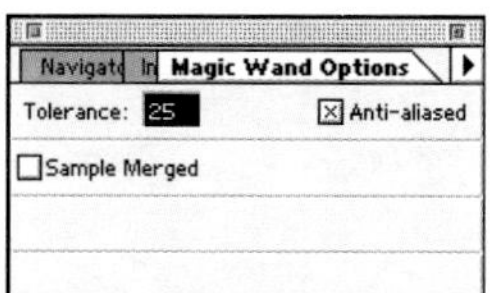

**7** Deselect the text (Command-D) [Control-D], and choose Filter➡Stylize➡Emboss (135°, 5 pixels, 100%).

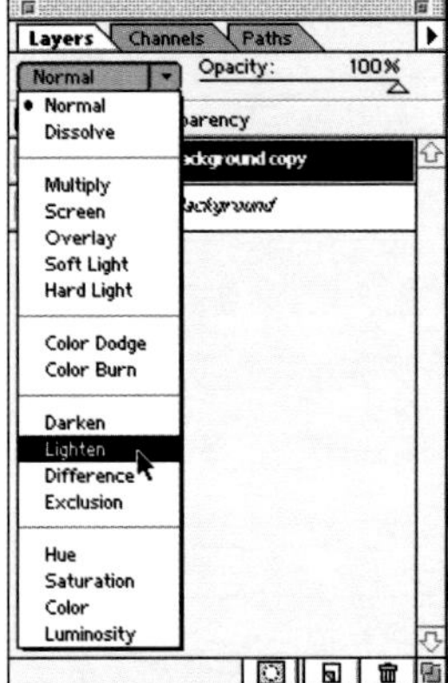


**8** In the Layers palette click the Blending Modes pop-up menu and choose Lighten. Leave the opacity at 100%.

**9** Flatten the image.

**TIP** **To copy the type onto another background, use the Magic Wand tool again to select the black area around the type and in the middle of letters (as in Step 6). Choose Select➡Inverse, then copy the type (Command-C) [Control-C]. Go to the file you want to paste the text into, and paste it in (Command-V) [Control-V].**

## VARIATIONS

Add subtle color to the thread. Use the Magic Wand tool to select the area around the type (as in Step 6). Choose Select➡Inverse. Then choose Image➡Adjust➡ Hue/ Saturation, and click the Colorize checkbox. Use the Hue slider to find the color you're looking for, and drop the Saturation slider to control the brightness of the color. For this variation we set the Saturation at 20.

Change the color of the thread. Before entering the text in Step 1, fill the background with a dark version of a color near the complement of the thread color you want to use (for example, a dark blue if you are using orange thread). Don't use black for the foreground color. Instead, choose as the foreground color a light version of the color of the thread you want. Complete the rest of the steps and you're finished. ■

Created by Sal Gilberto
Revision by David Lai

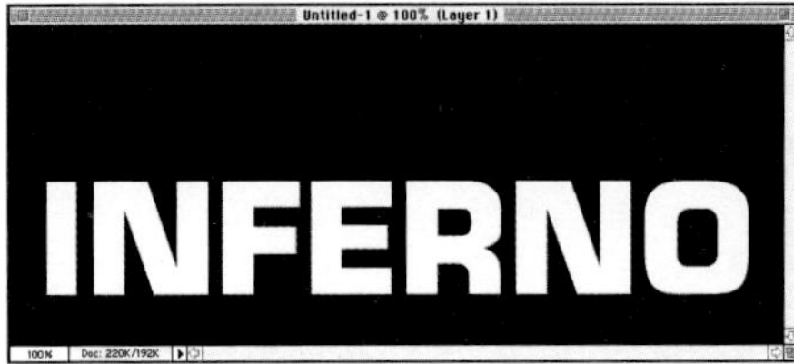


**1** Create a new file. Choose Image➡Mode➡Grayscale and press D to set the foreground color to black. Press (Option-Delete) [Alt-Delete] to fill the image with black.

**2** Choose white as the foreground color (press X) and use the Type tool to enter the text. For best results, use a large sans serif font (in this example, we used Micro-Technic at 65 points). Set the text toward the bottom of the window so there is enough room for the flames.

**3** Choose Select➡Load Selection (Layer 1 Transparency), and with the text selection still active, save the current selection (Channel #2). Switch to the Layers palette and flatten the image.

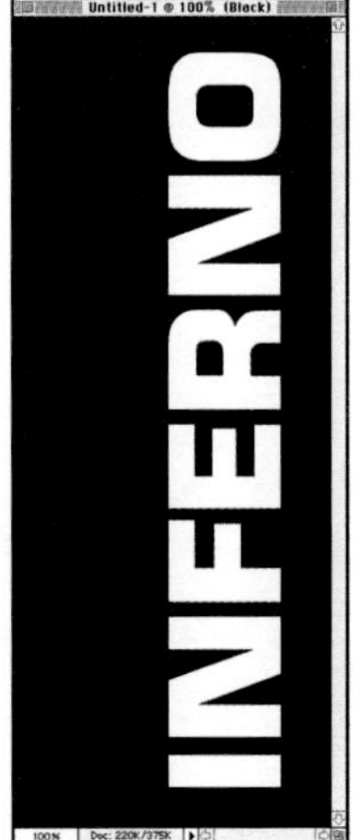


**4** Deselect the text (Command-D) [Control-D], and rotate the image 90 degrees counterclockwise (Image➡Rotate Canvas➡90° CCW).

TOOLBOX

Natural Gas Palette

**5** Apply Filter➥Stylize➥Wind (Blast, Left). The larger your text, the more wind it needs. If you are using a smaller point size, Wind might do the job. Larger text might need the Blast applied twice. You should see something like this.

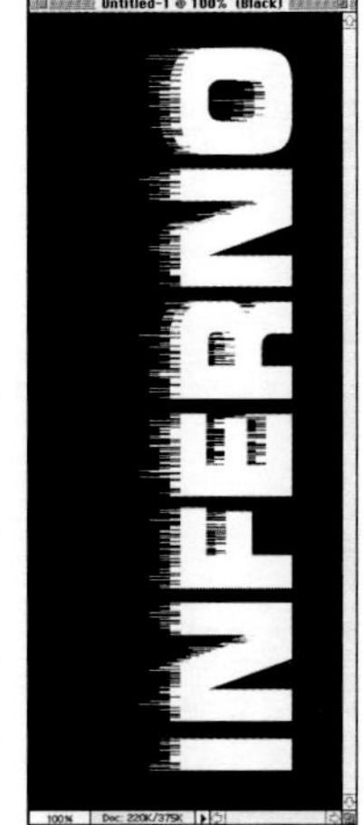


**6** Return the image to its original orientation by rotating it 90 degrees clockwise (Image➥Rotate Canvas➥90° CW).

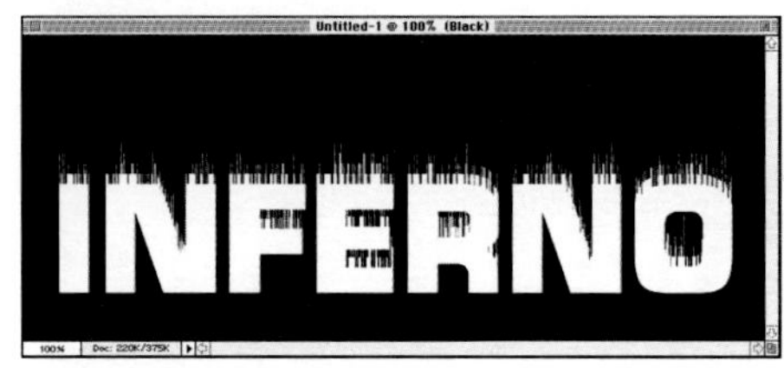


**7** Apply Filter➥Stylize➥Diffuse (Normal).

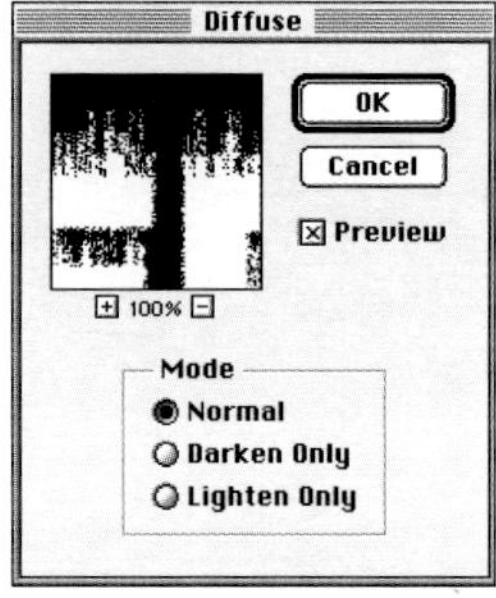


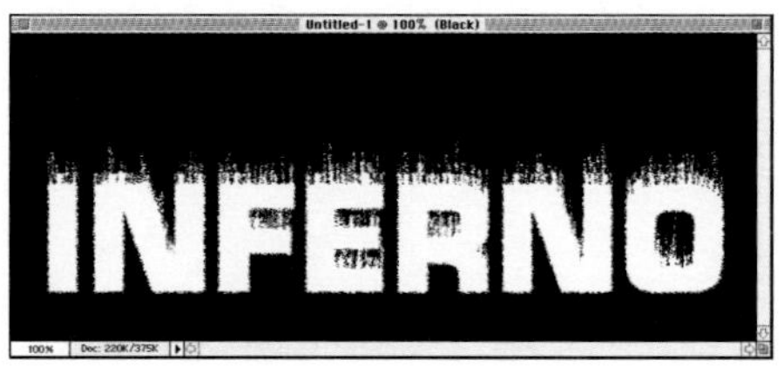

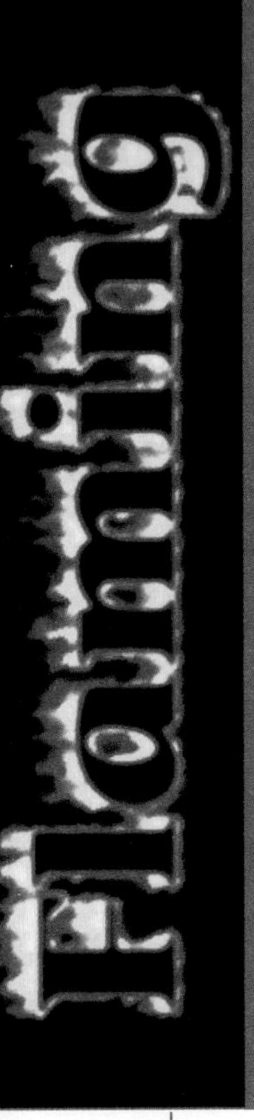


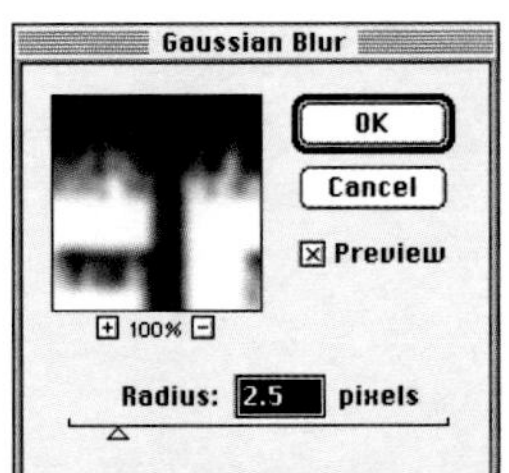


**8** Apply Filter➥Blur➥Gaussian Blur (Radius: 2.5).

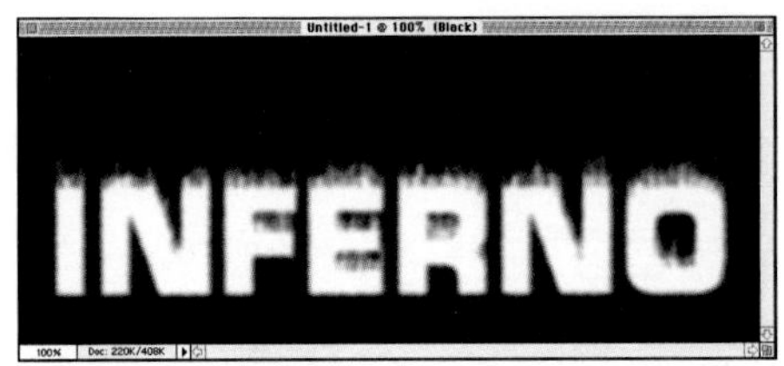


The image should now look like this.

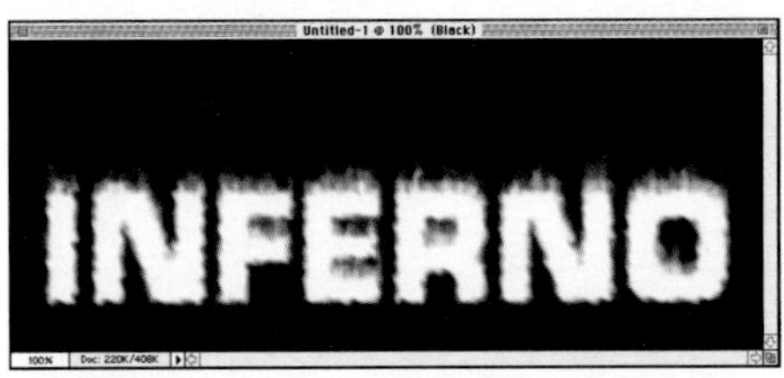


**9** Apply Filter➥Distort➥Ripple. Use the default settings (100, Medium).

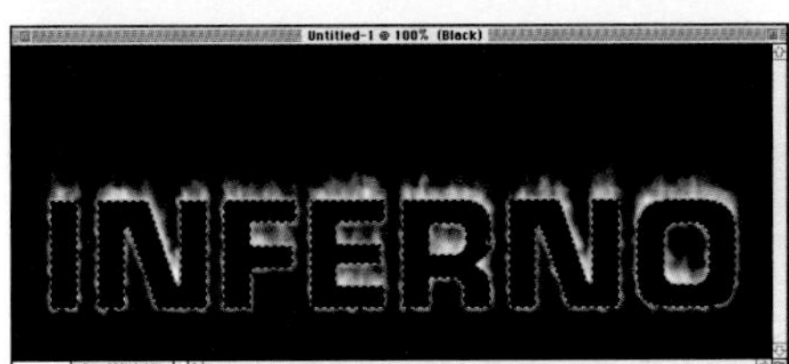


**10** Load the selection Channel #2. Choose Select➥Modify➥Contract (2 pixels) and Select➥Feather (1 pixel). Choose black as the foreground color (press D) and press (Option-Delete) [Alt-Delete] to fill the selection. Deselect the selection. (Command-D) [Control-D].

**If you want a lighter, more realistic-looking flame, adjust the gray values before converting the image to color. Choose Image➥Adjust➥Levels (Command-L). Try these settings for the Input Levels values: 0, 3.46, 190.**

**11** Convert the image to Indexed Color mode (Image➡Mode➡ Indexed Color). Choose Image➡ Mode➡Color Table and choose Black Body from the pop-up menu.

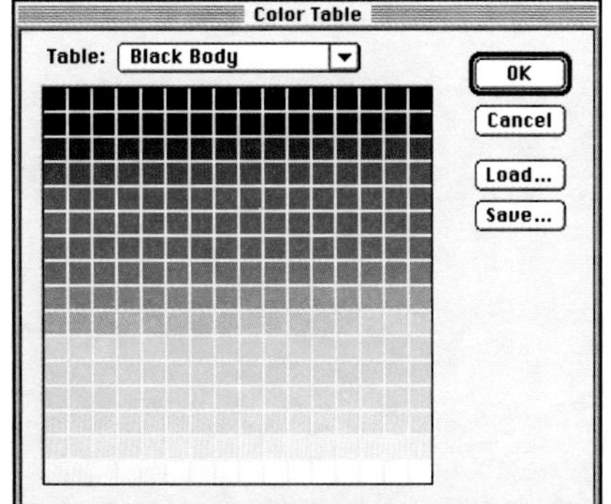


After changing color tables, your type should look like it's on fire.

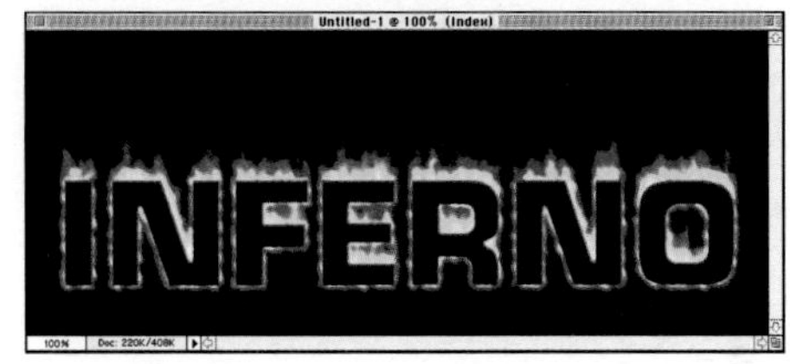


**TIP** **You can use the Levels dialog box to adjust the color and height of the flames. Choose Image➡ Adjust➡ Levels (Command-L) [Control-L]. It helps to work in the Red and Green channels separately.**

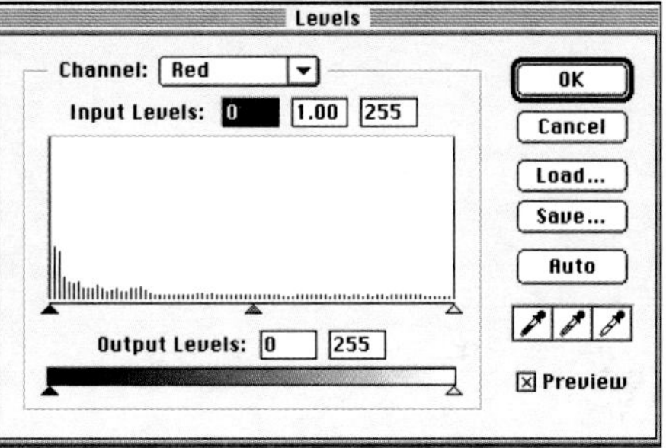

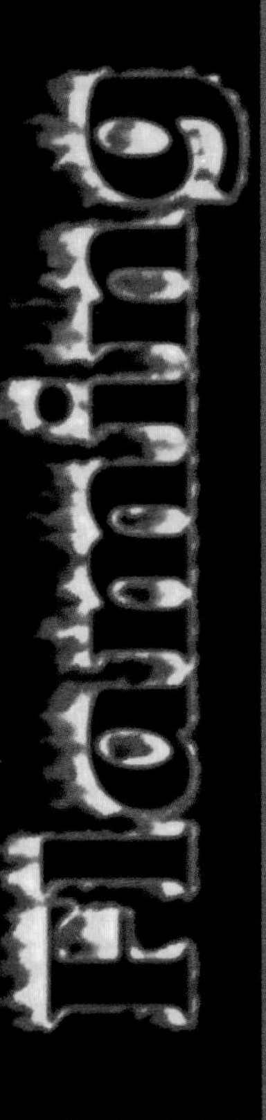


## VARIATIONS

For this variation, we used black text on a white background. Use all the same steps except skip Step 10.

After Step 10, adjust the Output Levels (Command-L) [Control-L] white point to 240. In Step 11, use the Natural Gas palette (included on the CD-ROM accompanying this book) instead of the Black Body palette, then convert the image to RGB and apply Filter➥Blur➥Blur.

Now don't light any matches.

Create a flaming shadow by choosing Image➥Adjust➥Invert ((Command-I) [Control-I]) right before doing Step 11.

In a grayscale file, create a new channel (#2) and enter the text in that channel. Make the Black channel active. Load the selection Channel #2. Fill it with black. Deselect the text. Apply the Gaussian Blur filter (5 pixels). Load the selection Channel #2. Fill it with black. Choose Filter➥Render➥Difference Clouds. Deselect the text, and choose Filter➥Render➥Difference Clouds. Do Step 11. ■

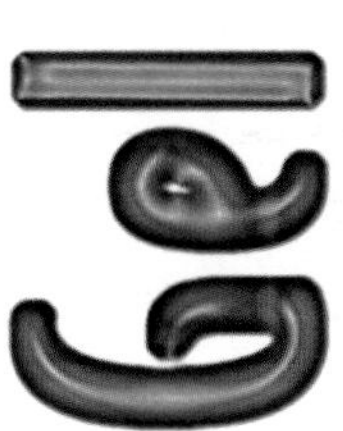

**1** Create a new file. Fill the image area with black.

**2** Create a new channel (#4) and use the Type Mask tool to enter the text. We used Tekton Bold at 75 points. This technique works with both simple and complicated fonts, but keep in mind that you have to play with the settings to get it right.

**If the font you choose has hard edges, choose Select➡Modify➡Smooth (5 pixels). If that doesn't round your selection enough, then smooth it again until it has a good round contour.**

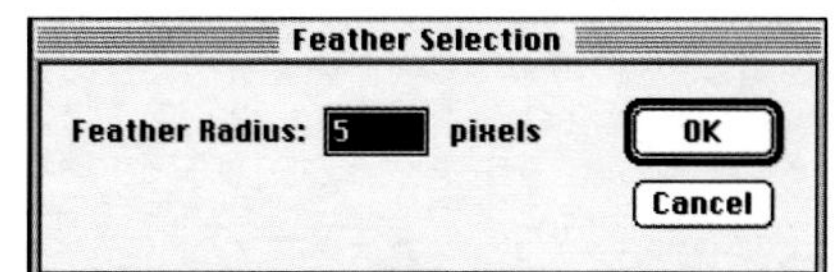


**3** Fill the type selection with white, then return to the composite channel (Command-~) [Control-~]. The text selection should still be active. Choose Select➡Feather (5 pixels).

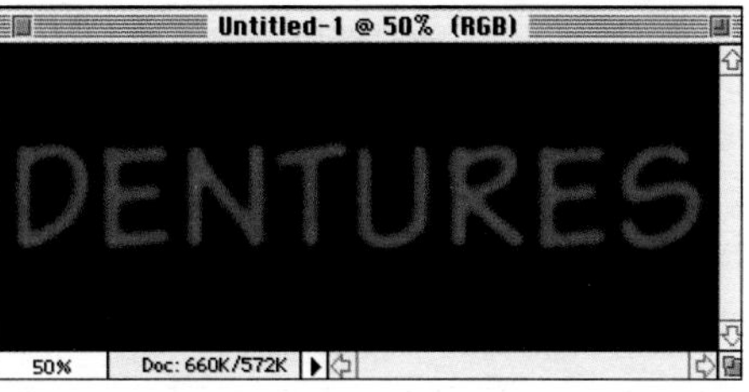


**4** Choose a foreground color for the gel. We used 100% Magenta. Press (Option-Delete) [Alt-Delete] to fill the text selection. Deselect the text (Command-D) [Control-D].



**TOOLBOX**

KPT 3 Gradient Designer

**5** To add a gloss to the text, use the Plastic Wrap filter. This filter produces very different results depending upon the size of the area selected. Therefore, apply the filter to each letter one at a time. First, load the text selection Channel #4.

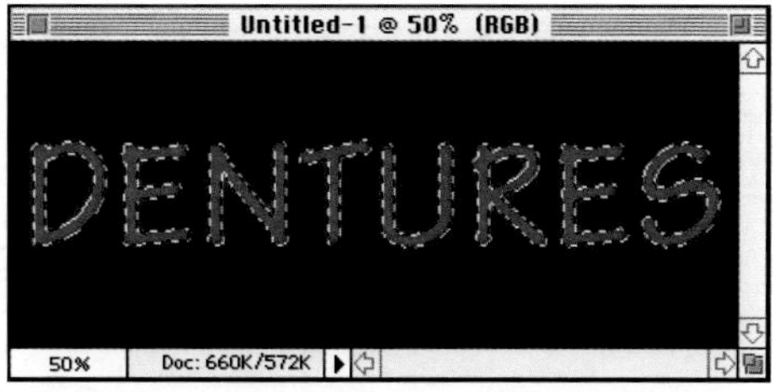


**6** Choose the Lasso tool, and hold down the (Option) [Alt] and Shift key while you draw around the letter you want to select. The selection you draw can be as sloppy as you want as long as you don't run over any of the other selection lines. After you complete the loop around the letter and let go of the mouse button, only that letter is selected.

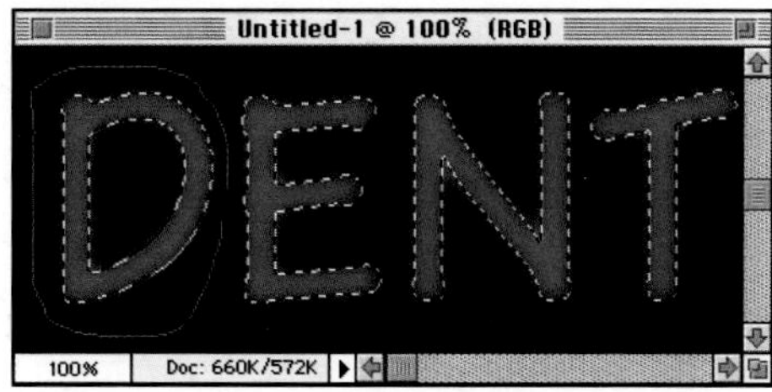

**7** Now, choose Filter➡Artistic➡ Plastic Wrap. Use these settings: Highlight Strength: 15, Detail: 9, Smoothness: 7. Use the preview to test the best settings for your text and to find something that looks like this figure. You may need to use different settings for each letter to get the best results.

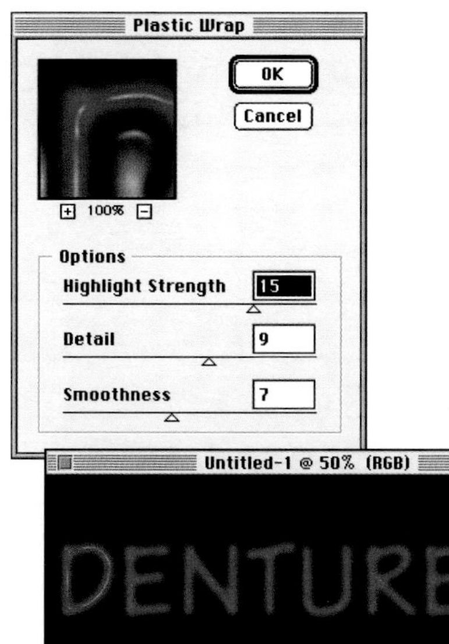

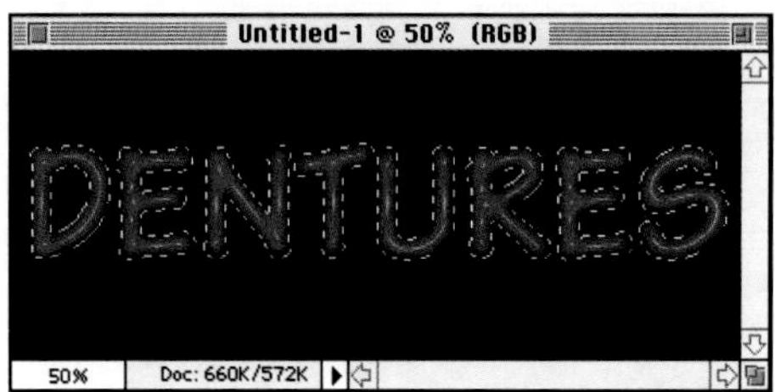

**8** For each letter, load the text selection Channel #4, then repeat Step 6. After each new letter is selected, press (Command-F) [Control-F] to apply the Plastic Wrap filter with the same settings.

**9** To make a selection for the text, load the text selection Channel #4. Then choose Select➥Modify➥ Expand. Start with an expansion of 1 pixel. You want to expand the selection so that it includes almost all of the blurred color.

**10** With this selection, you can copy the text and paste onto any background you want. We applied a 2 pixel stroke around the text to give it more definition.

## VARIATIONS

### Outlines

If you want to create an outline gel text, you can insert these steps after Step 2 to change the solid text to outlines. It is difficult to get this technique to work if you choose a narrow or complicated font, so keep it simple and let the effect carry your message.

Choose Select➡Modify➡ Contract (8 pixels). We used 8 pixels, but use whatever works for your text to create an outline like the one shown in this figure. Fill the selection with black. Then simply complete the rest of the steps.

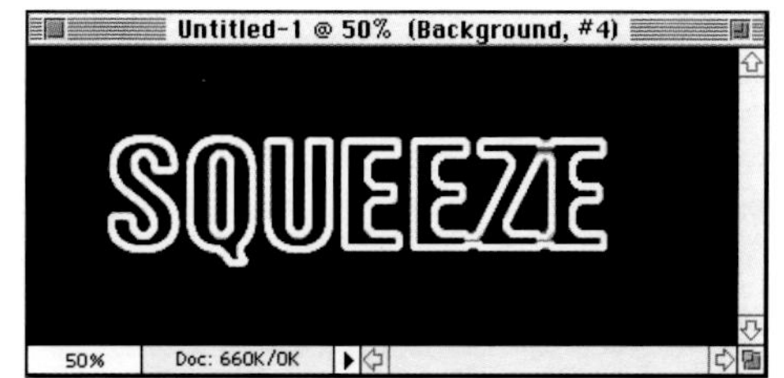


Or try this: After finishing the steps above, copy your image and do whatever you want to it. In this example, we copied the text to a yellow background, smudged the edges of the text, and applied Filter➡Sharpen➡Unsharp Mask (55%, 3 pixels, 0 levels). Smudging the text helps incorporate the edges with the background.

## KPT 3 Gradient Designer

We used the Shelley Andante font for this variation. After completing the steps, we created a new layer, loaded the text selection Channel #4 into the new layer, and filled it with white. With the selection still active, we applied Filter➡KPT 3.0➡KPT Gradient Designer 3.0. We used the Tacky Wacky preset, then customized it. Finally, I chose Color from the Layers palette menu. ■

This effect turns your dull, boring text into a shiny piece of see-through type. The smudging in Steps 7 through 12 makes it look ultra-realistic.

1 Open the image you want to use as a background. We used this photo from Digital Stock for this example.

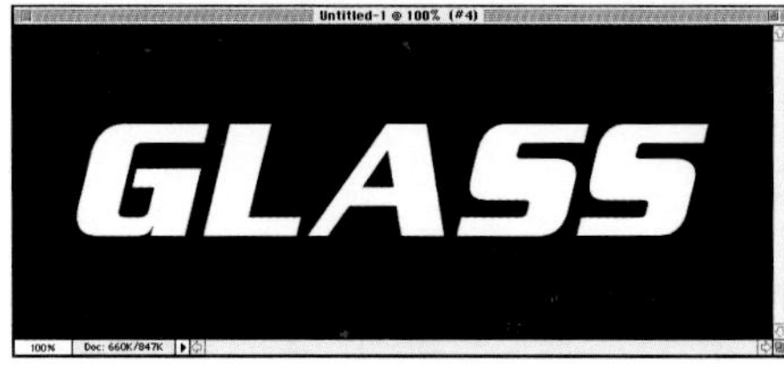


**2** Create a new channel (Channel #4) and use the Type tool enter your text into it. We used Serpentine Bold Oblique at 80 points for this example. Select➡None (Command-D) [Control-D] so you have no active selection.

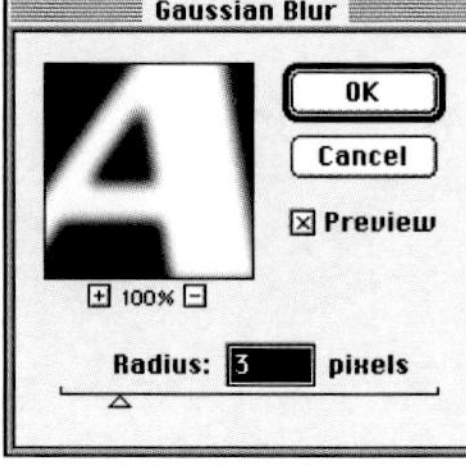


**3** Duplicate Channel #4 and rename it Blur #1 (to make remembering what the channel is easier). To the Blur #1 channel, apply Filter➡Blur➡Gaussian Blur with a setting of 3 pixels.

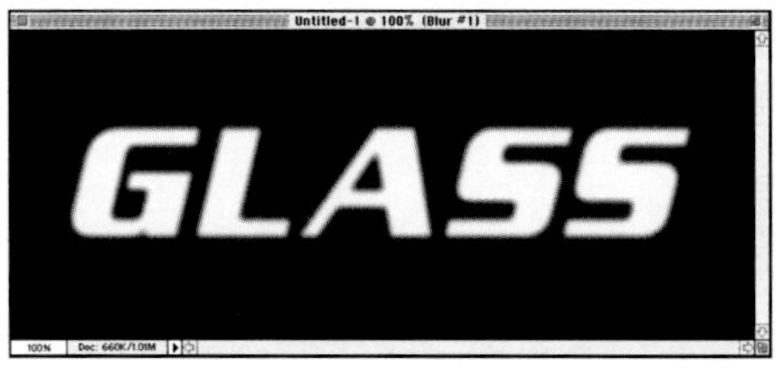


**TOOLBOX**

GlassLightingStyles file

**4** Duplicate Channel Blur #1 and rename it Blur #2. Apply Filter→Other→Offset with a setting of –4 pixels right and –3 pixels down.

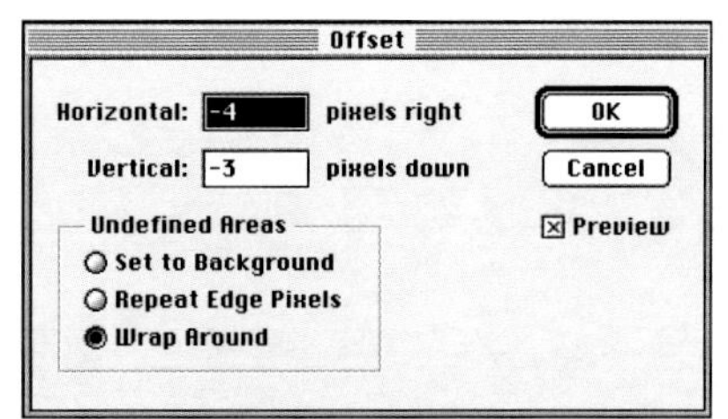


**5** Now apply Image→Calculations. Both Source options and the Result option should be set to the name of your current document (they probably are, by default). In Source 1, set Layer: Background and Channel: Blur #1. For Source 2, set Layer: Background, Channel: Blur #2. Set the Blending mode to Difference and the Opacity to 100%. Leave the Invert and Mask boxes unchecked.

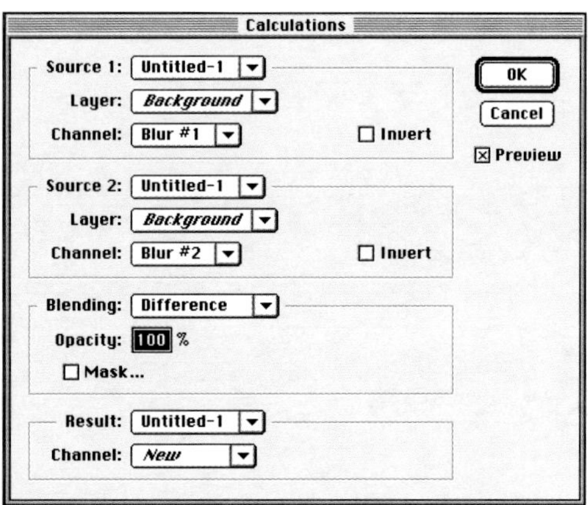


You should get something like this.

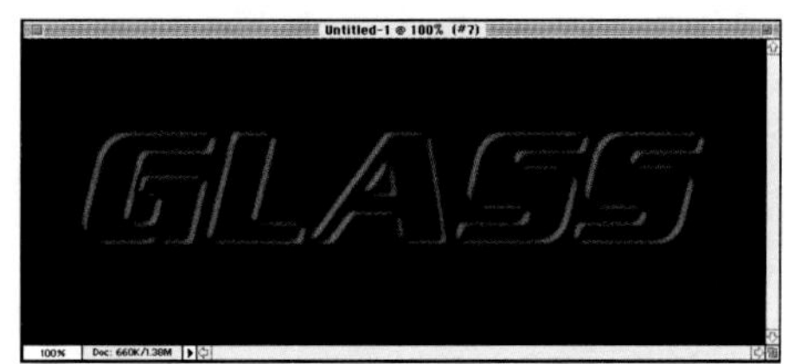


**6** Choose Image→Adjust→Invert to invert the new channel (Channel #7), and apply Image→Adjust→Levels (Command-L) [Control-L]. Click the Auto button to adjust the levels automatically.

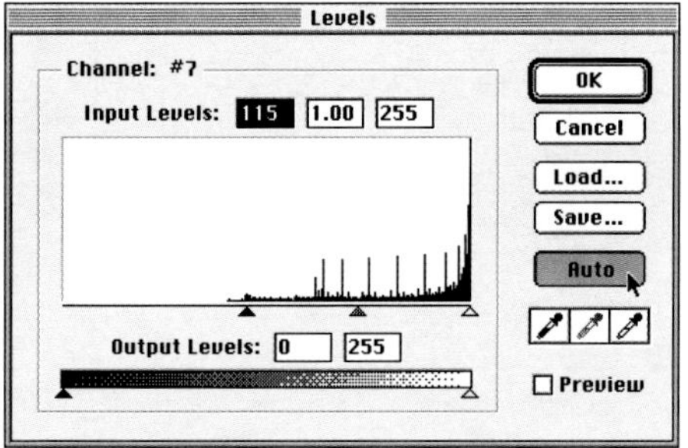

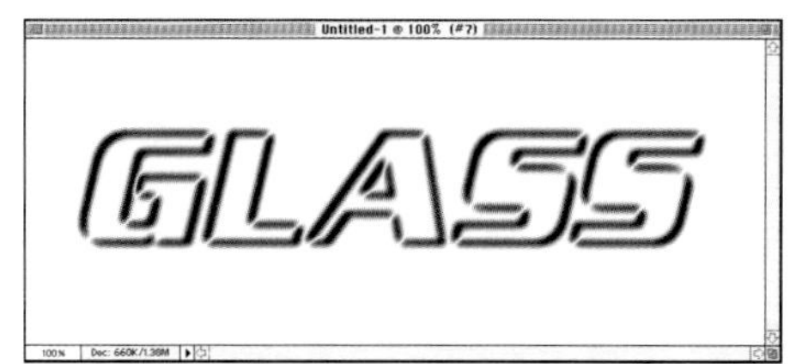


The result should be an image with more contrast.

**7** Now return to the composite channel (Command-~) [Control-~] and get ready for some fun! Load the selection Channel #4 (the channel with the original, unblurred text). Choose Make Work Path from the Paths palette menu.

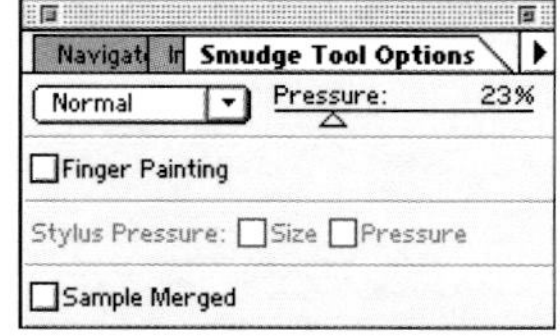


**8** Choose the Smudge tool and choose a large soft-edged brush from the Brushes palette. In the Smudge Tool Options palette, set the pressure of the Smudge tool to 23%.

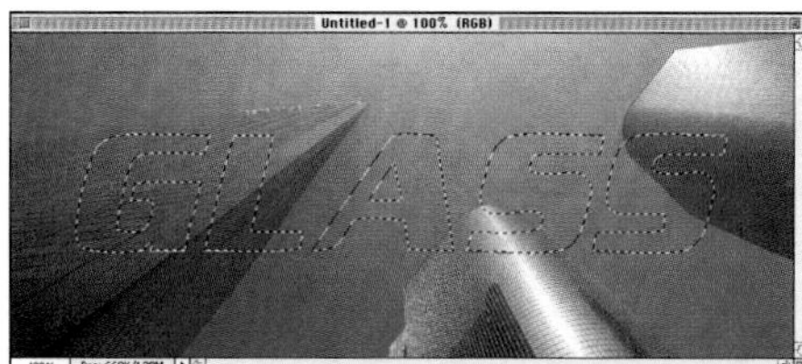

**9** Load the selection Channel #4 again. Onscreen you'll see the path and the selection active. If not, bring the Paths palette to the front, click the path in the palette, then choose Make Selection.

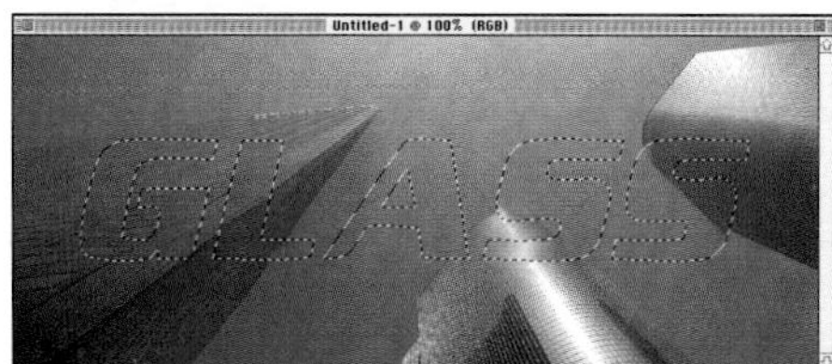

**10** Choose Stroke Path from the Paths palette menu, and make sure the Smudge tool is active in the Tool palette. After a few moments, the image inside the selection will be smudged somewhat. Because the selection from Channel #4 was loaded, the blurring only took place inside the selection, not outside.

**11** Because glass distorts images more at the outer edges, a little more smudging needs to be done, but closer to the edges. With both the path and Channel #4 still active and the Smudge tool selected, choose a medium-sized feathered brush. Bump the pressure up to 40%.

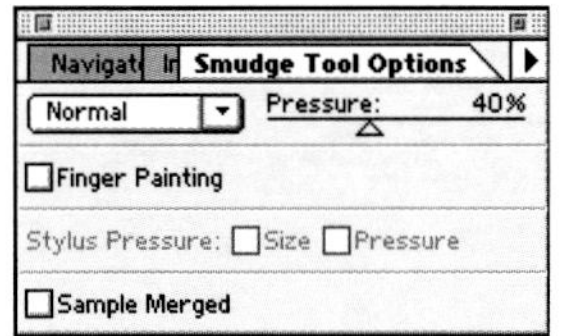


**12** Once again, stroke the path (choose Stroke Path from the Paths palette) with the Smudge tool.

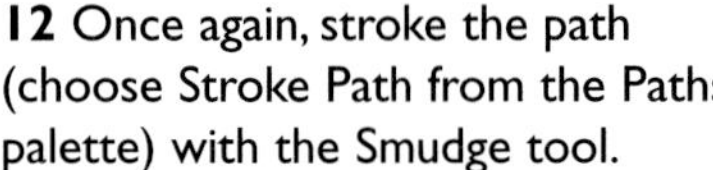

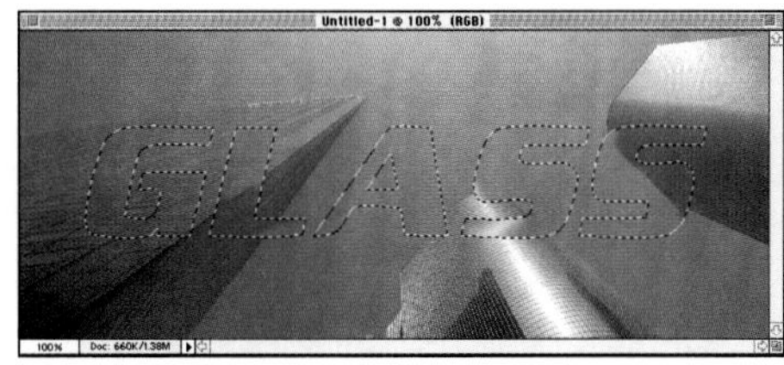


**13** You're finished with the path, so it can be turned off. Simply shift-click its name in the Paths palette. Keep Channel #4 an active selection, however.

**14** Now comes the fun part—making it shiny. Bring up the Filter➡Render➡Lighting Effects dialog box. If you loaded the GlassLightingStyles file from the CD ROM, choose it from the preset pop-up menu. If it's not there, just look at the figure to get the settings. Also, be sure that the Texture Channel option is set to Channel #7 (or whatever channel was created when the two blurred channels were combined).

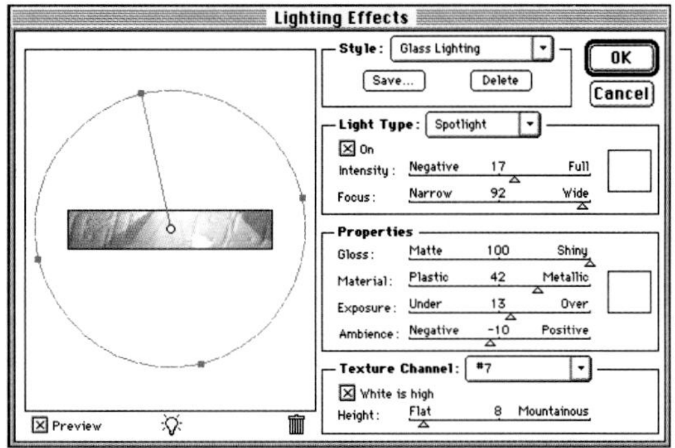

**15** If the preset settings don't give you the ideal result, then tweak any of the settings in the Light Type or Properties sections of the dialog box. Try playing with the light direction and size, too. You can also adjust the Height slider to make the text appear bumpier or flatter. Don't, however, change the Texture Channel setting. It should be set to the channel that resulted when the two blurred channels were combined. This channel is used to determine where the highlights and shadows occur on the text. If you change it to a different channel, your text probably appears really flat with very few highlights, if any! After clicking OK, you should get some nice, bright text.

Unsharp Mask
OK
Cancel
Preview
100%
Amount: 61 %
Radius: 2.3 pixels
Threshold: 0 levels

**16** To add an extra gloss to the text, make sure that Channel #4 (the regular text channel) is still loaded. Apply Filter➥Sharpen➥Unsharp Mask with the settings Amount: 61%, Radius: 2.3 pixels, and Threshold: 0 levels.

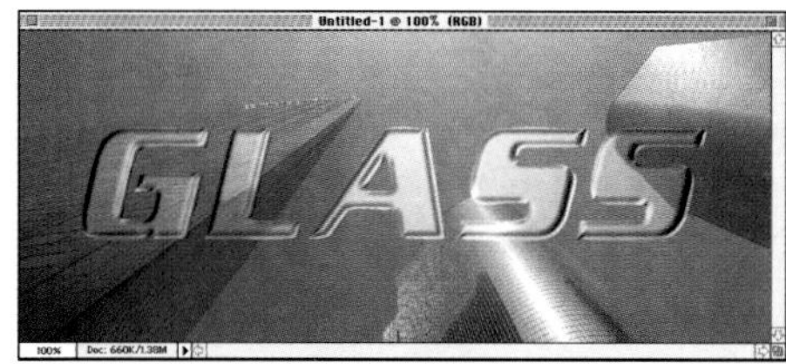


This sharpens the image inside the text and nudges the contrast up a smidgen. Be sure to note how the smudging done earlier really adds to the believability factor! ■

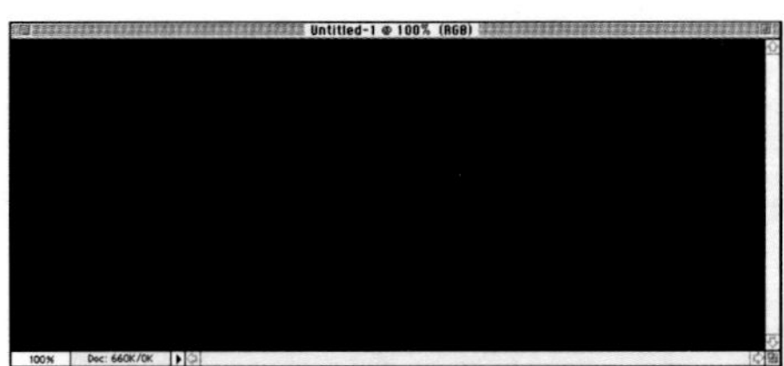

**1** Create a new file. Choose black as the background color. Select➡All and press Delete to fill the image with black. Select➡None (Command-D) [Control-D].

**2** Create a new channel (Channel #4). Choose white as the foreground color. With the Type tool, enter the text you want to apply the effect to in the new channel. We used FontHead Design's BlueMoon at 80 points for this example.

**3** Return to the composite channel. (Command-~) [Control-~]. Your text should still be the active selection. If it's not, then load the selection Channel #4.

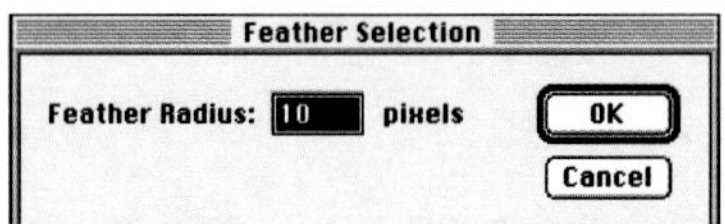


**4** Choose Select➡Feather and use a setting of 10 pixels. Don't worry if it looks like part of your letters disappear, particularly the skinny lines. They're still there, but the feathering decreased their strength, so Photoshop doesn't show them inside the area of active selection.

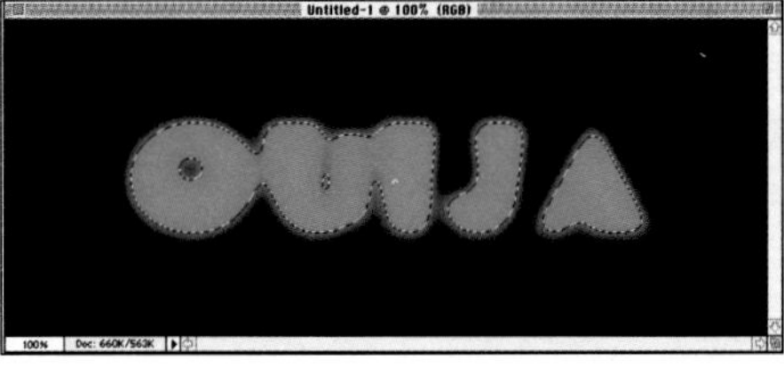


**5** Choose a glow color for the foreground color. We used bright green. Press (Option-Delete) [Alt-Delete] to fill the selection with the foreground color. You should get something like this.

## TOOLBOX

KPT 3 Gradient Designer

Alien Skin's Glow filter

**6** Once again, choose Select➥Feather and use a setting of 10 pixels. This feathers the already feathered selection, creating a really diffused look. Press (Option-Delete) [Alt-Delete] to fill the selection.

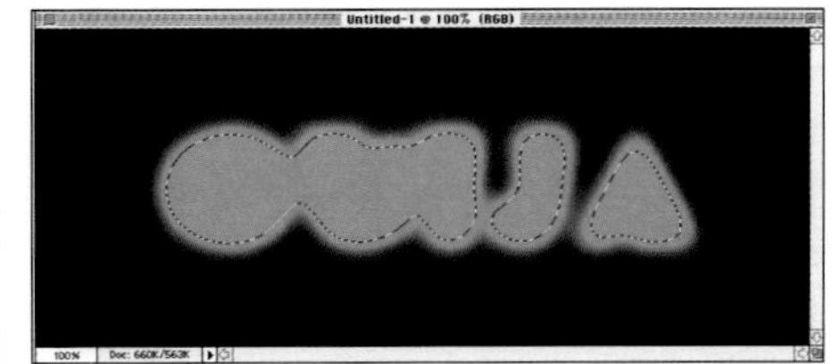

**If you try combining the two feathering steps by using a setting of 20 pixels for one feathering, the result will be a much less vibrant glow. By using two separate steps, you achieve a more neon-like effect.**

**7** Now load the selection Channel #4.

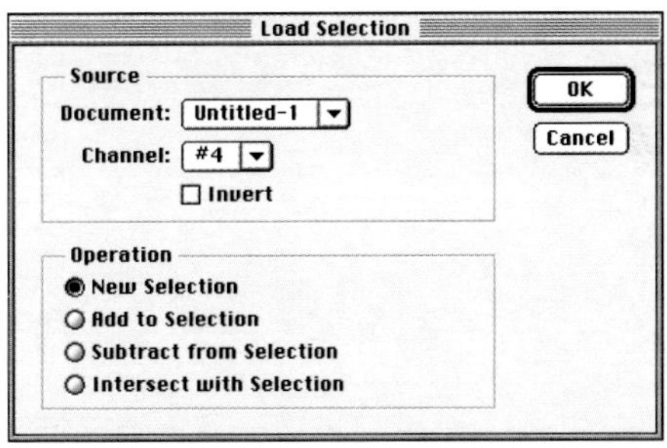


**8** Choose black as the foreground color and press (Option-Delete) [Alt-Delete] to fill the selection. Select➥None (Command-D) [Control-D].

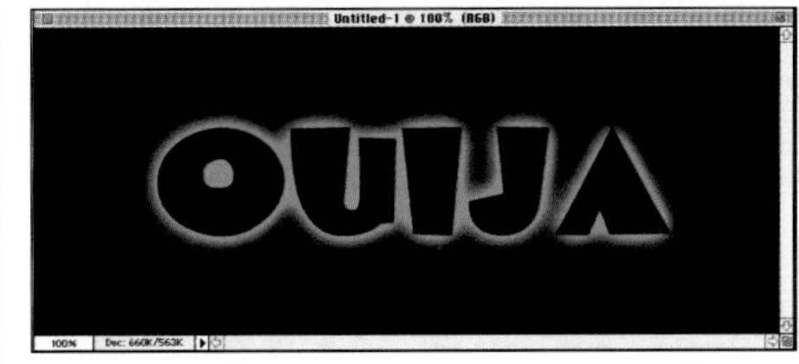


## VARIATIONS

## Blinding Glow

**1** Follow Steps 1 through 7 listed previously. Choose Select➥Feather, and feather the selection just a little—3 pixels.

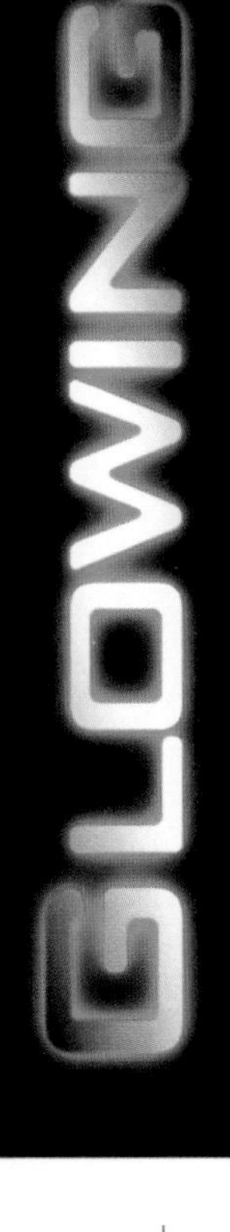

**2** Choose white as the foreground color. Press (Option-Delete) [Alt-Delete] to fill the selection with white. Wow!

## Filled Glow

**1** Follow Steps 1 through 7 listed previously.

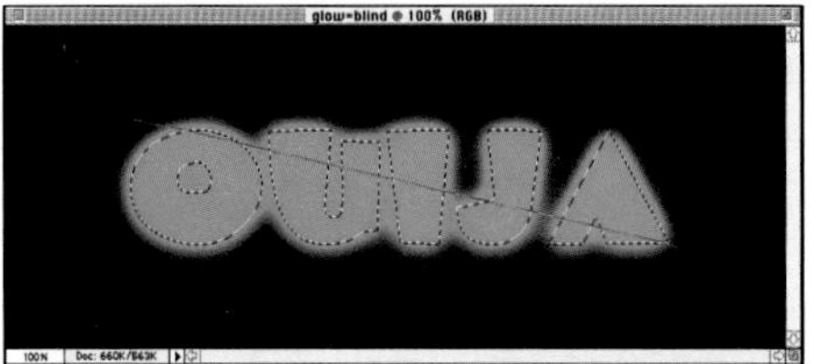

**2** Choose white as the foreground color and black for the background color. Use the Gradient Fill tool (choose Foreground to Background from the Gradient pop-up menu in the Gradient Tool Options palette) and drag from the upper-left corner of the word to the lower-right corner.

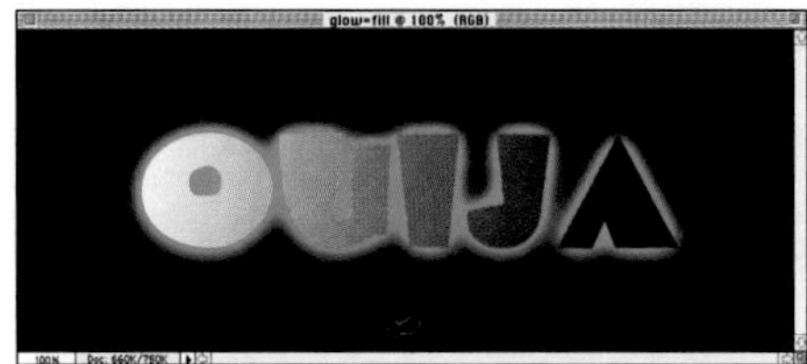

**3** Select➥None (Command-D) [Control-D]. You should end up with something like this.

## Filled Glow with KPT 3 Gradient Designer

This variation is another way you can fill your type. Follow all the same steps for the Filled Glow above, except change Step 2 to:

**2** Choose Filter➥KPT 3.0➥KPT Gradient Designer 3.0. Choose Blue Green Metal Cone from the submenu and set the mode to Linear Blend. Set the repeat option to Triangle A➥B➥A and click OK. (You can use any KPT setting you want.)

And here's what you get.

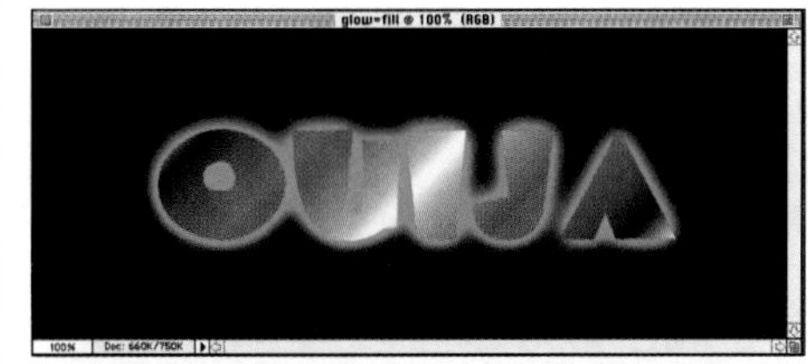


## Ghosting

By using a second layer for the text, you can put type with a ghosted effect over an existing photo.

**1** Create a new file with the image you want to use for the background. Create a new layer. Keep both layers visible, so you can see what you're doing, but make sure that Layer 1 is the active layer!

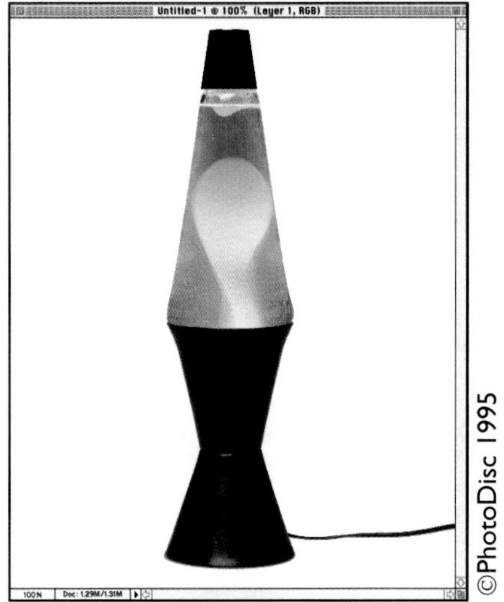


©PhotoDisc 1995

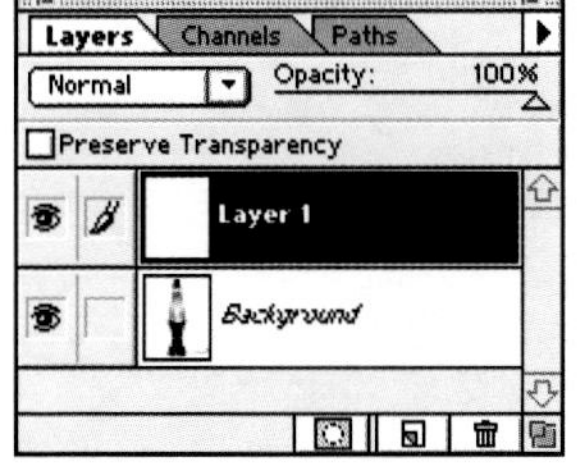

**2** Create a new channel (Channel #4) and enter in your text with the Type tool. We used FontHead Design's Bonkers at 80 points here. Select➡None (Command-D) [Control-D].

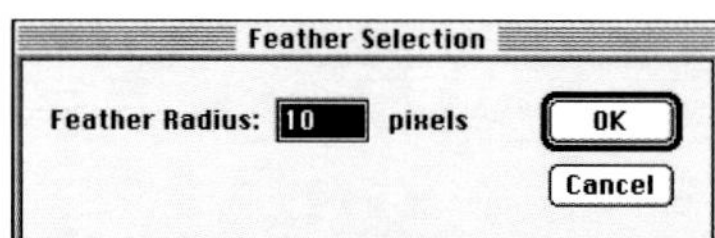


**3** Return to the composite channel and make Layer 1 the active layer. Load the selection Channel #4. Choose Select➡Feather and use a radius of 10 pixels.

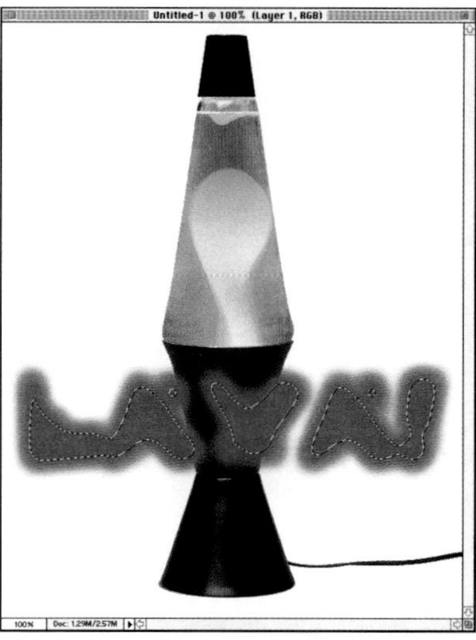


**4** Choose for the foreground color the color you want to use for the blur. We used a bright red. Press (Option-Delete) [Alt-Delete] to fill the selection with the foreground color. Press (Option-Delete) [Alt-Delete] again to intensify the color. Select➡None (Command-D) [Control-D].

**5** If you want to remove color from the selection, then load the selection Channel #4 and choose Edit➡Clear.

## Aura

**1** Create a new file or create a new file with a white background.

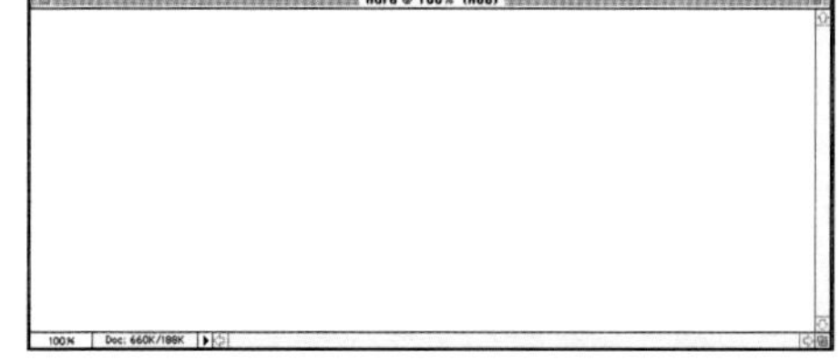


**2** Create a new channel and enter the text with the Type tool.

**3** Return to the composite channel. Choose Select➡Feather using a setting of 15 pixels.

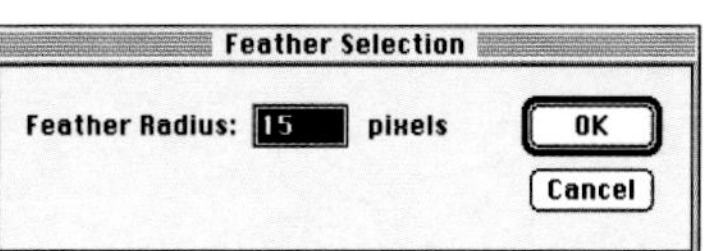


**4** Choose a medium blue for the foreground color. Press (Option-Delete) [Alt-Delete] to fill the selection with the foreground color.

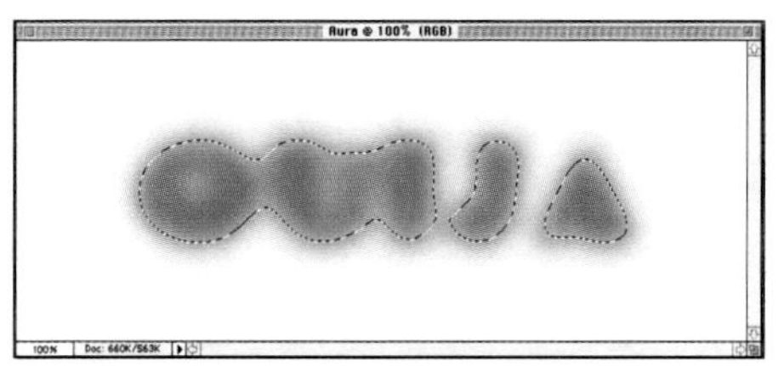

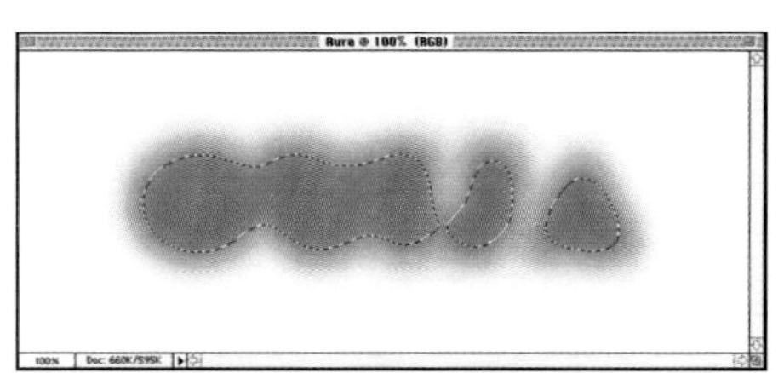

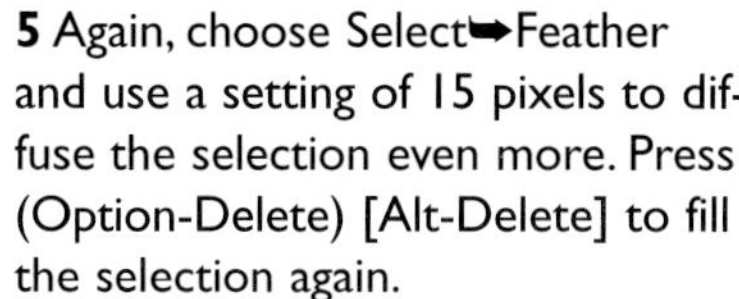
**5** Again, choose Select➡Feather and use a setting of 15 pixels to diffuse the selection even more. Press (Option-Delete) [Alt-Delete] to fill the selection again.

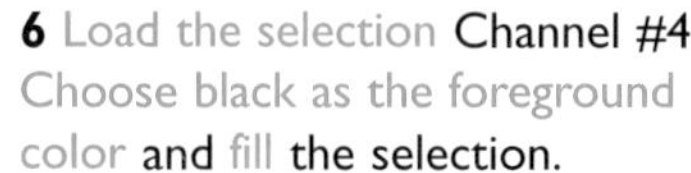
**6** Load the selection Channel #4. Choose black as the foreground color and fill the selection.

## VARIATIONS

### Alien Skin's Glow Filter

Here's another easy way to create a glow around your type.

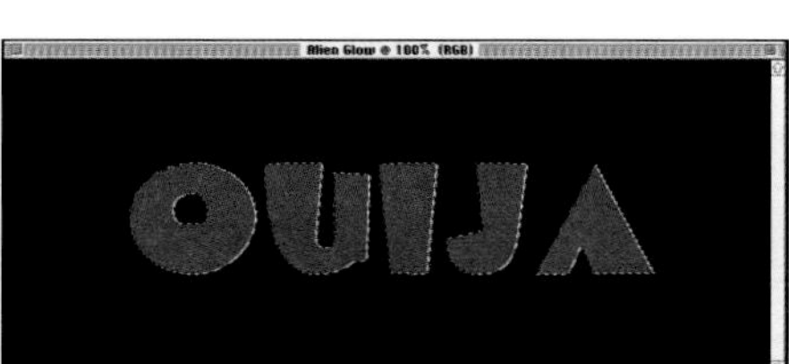


**1** Create a new file. We used a black background to make the glow stand out (press D, then (Option-Delete) [Alt-Delete]). Choose as the foreground color a color for the text. Enter the text with the Type Mask tool. Fill the text selection with the foreground color.

**2** Choose as the foreground color a color for the glow. We used a light blue for a misty look.

**3** Choose Filter➥Alien Skin➥ Glow. Set the Glow Color to Foreground. You can vary the settings for the Width (pixels) and the Opacity (%) of the glow. We used 40 pixels of Width and 80% Opacity. Set Opacity Dropoff to Thin. This makes the glow look thin and hazy. If you want a more intense glow, try the Fat option.

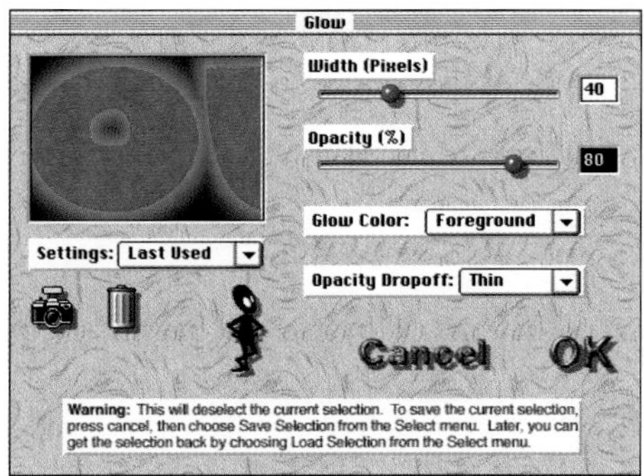


**4** Click OK and presto—a super easy glow! ■

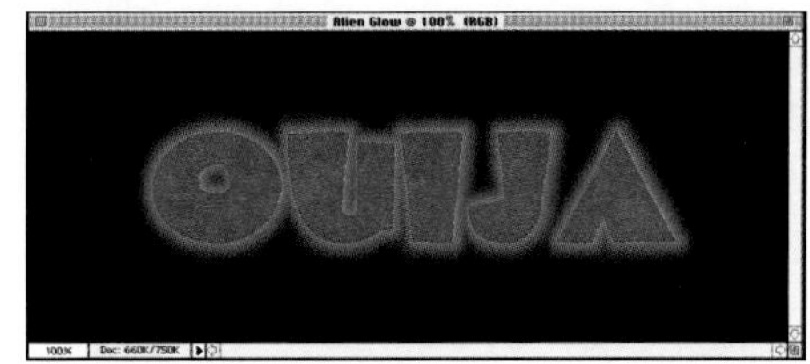

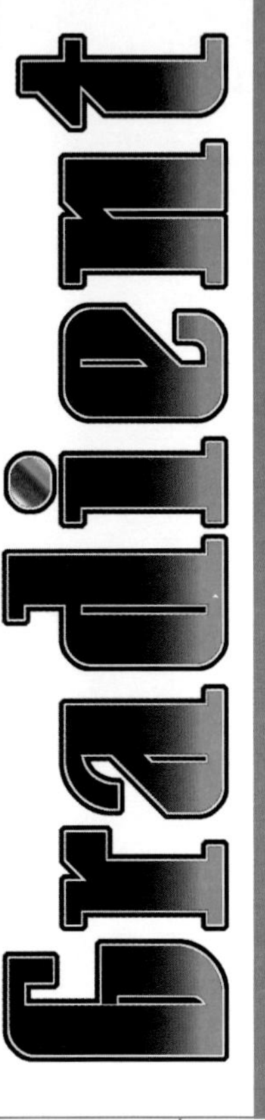


Filling text with a gradient is a very simple task, but it can produce great effects. As soon as you get to know your way around with masks, the possibilities will seem endless.

## Setup

As always, the first steps: create a new file, then create a new channel (Channel #4), and use the Type tool to enter the text in the new channel (white text on a black background). After entering the text, return to the composite channel (Command-~) [Control-~].

**TIP** **To access the Gradient Tool Options palette, double-click the Gradient tool. Unless otherwise noted, we are assuming that the options are set to the defaults. You can revert to the defaults by choosing Reset Tool from the Gradient Tool Options palette menu.**

## Basic Gradient

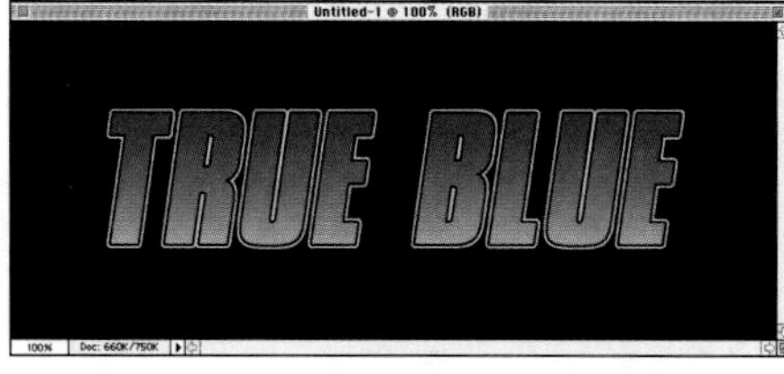


Here's the basic gradient fill. The Gradient tool creates a blend between the foreground color and the background color. Choose the colors, then load the text selection (Channel #4). Now, use the Gradient tool, click where you want to start the gradient, and drag to the point where you want it to end. We also gave the text a white stroke to set it apart from the background (Edit➥Stroke (2 pixels, Outside, 100% Opacity, Normal Mode)).





KPT 3 Gradient Designer

## Spectrum

The Gradient Tool Options palette offers some very useful variables. If you want a blend to include all of the colors that lie between the foreground color and the background color on the color spectrum, choose one of the spectrum options from the Style pop-up menu.

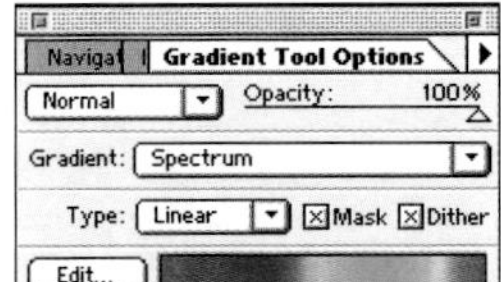

## Transparency

Grading from a color to transparency is magic for your text. This option enables you to fade type into a background.

## KPT 3 Gradient Designer

Use KPT 3 Gradient Designer for a more complex, but no more difficult, gradient. Sifting through the possibilities could consume hours, but don't forget to come back and read the rest of this section.

## KPT 3 Procedural Blend

We used KPT 3 Gradient Designer for this one, too. We rendered the type using the Marquee method (page 124), then chose the Procedural Blend option in KPT 3 Gradient Designer. This option grades the color according to the values already in the type.

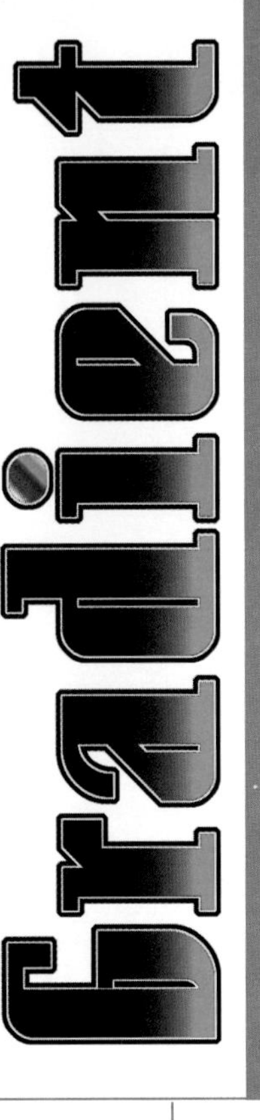


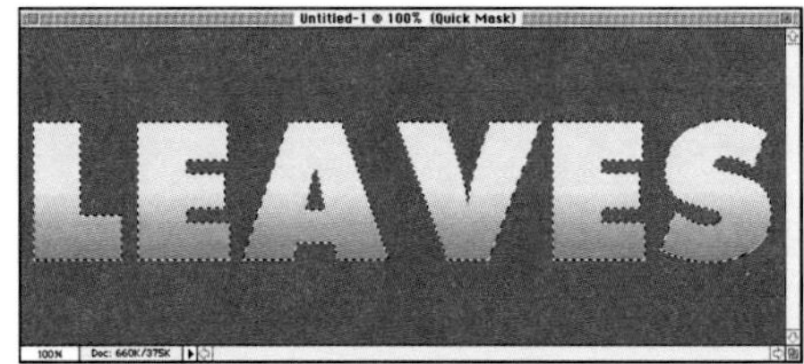


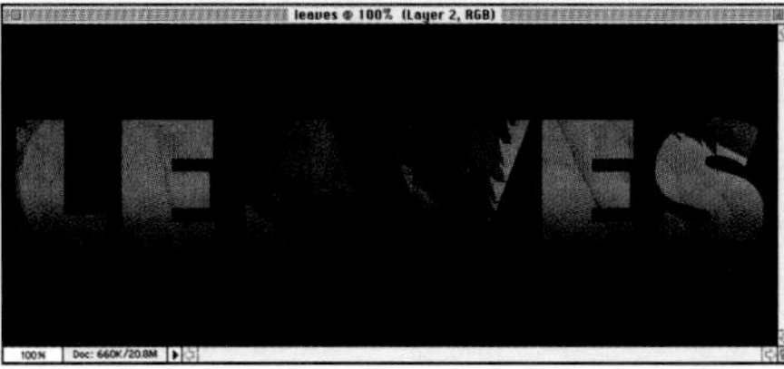


## Graded Selections

Photographs and other images can be graded into a text selection. First copy an image from another file into the clipboard. Return to the empty file, load the text selection, then enter Quick Mask mode. Now use the Gradient tool as you did earlier, only choose Foreground to Transparent from the Gradient pop-up menu. The non-red areas in this window represent the areas where the photograph will be seen at full strength. Where there is solid red, the photograph will be completely masked or hidden. Areas in between will gradually fade the photograph. Press Q to exit the Quick Mask mode, and choose Edit➡Paste Into.

## Blending Images

You can also use Quick Masks to blend two photographs together into a type selection.

Copy the first image from a separate file into the clipboard. Then, return to the file that contains your type, return to the composite channel (Command-~) [Control-~], and load the type selection. Press Q to enter Quick Mask mode. Use the Gradient tool, as described earlier (with Foreground to Transparent chosen from the Gradient pop-up menu), and drag from just above the bottom of the text to just below the top of the text. You should see something like this.

Exit Quick Mask mode (press Q), and choose Edit➡Paste Into to paste in the first image.

Now, copy the second image from a separate file into the clipboard. Again, return to the file that contains your type, return to the composite channel, and load the type selection. Press Q to enter Quick Mask mode. Use the Gradient tool and drag from just below the top of the text to just above the bottom of the text.

Exit Quick Mask mode (press Q), and choose Edit➡Paste Into to paste in the second image. That's it. We added a couple of strokes to the text selection to separate the text from the background.

## Putting It All Together

This image combines several gradient techniques in a composite of several layered steps.

**1** The background image is copied to the clipboard, then pasted into a graded mask.

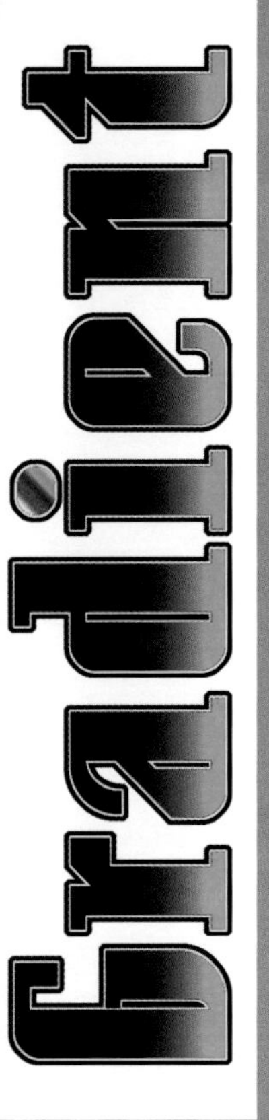

**2** A violet to transparent blend inside the type selection...

**3** A cyan to transparent gradient inside the type selection...

**4** A 2 pixel stroke is added to separate the type from the black background.

The final image. ■

**1** Create a new file. Enter the text with the Type tool that you want to use. We used Myriad Bold for this example. Here we used two different colors.

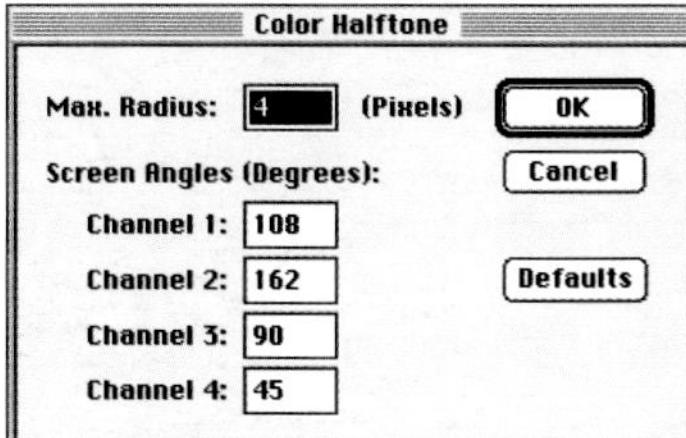


**2** Choose Layer➥Flatten Image, then apply Filter➥Pixelate➥Color Halftone. Change the Max. Radius to 4 pixels and leave the Screen Angles at their defaults.

You should get something that looks like this.

## VARIATIONS

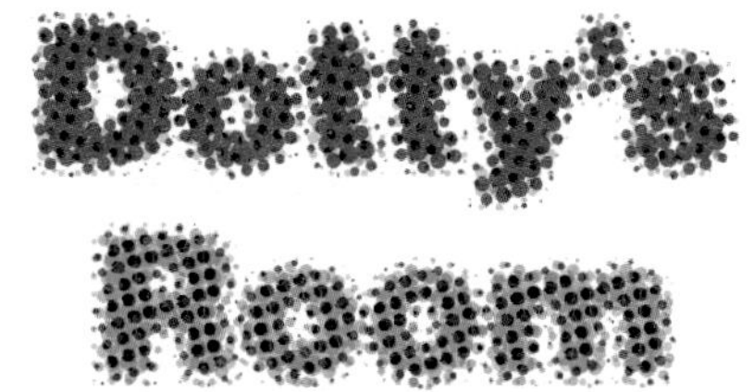


For larger dots, change the Max. Radius in the Color Halftone dialog box. Here a setting of 8 pixels was used.

For something more abstract, go crazy with the Max. Radius! Try 20 pixels!

You can also create different effects by varying the Screen Angles in the Color Halftone dialog box. Here, all Screen angles were set to 0 (the Max. Radius was set to 6 pixels).

A bit of a wavy effect can be achieved by using Screen Angles of 0, 15, 30, 45. Again, Max. Radius was set to 6 pixels.

## Keeping A Defined Edge

**1** If you want to keep a solid edge on the text, create a new channel and enter the text with the Type tool.

**2** Return to the composite channel, load the selection Channel #4 and fill with your choice of colors. Don't lose the selection yet!

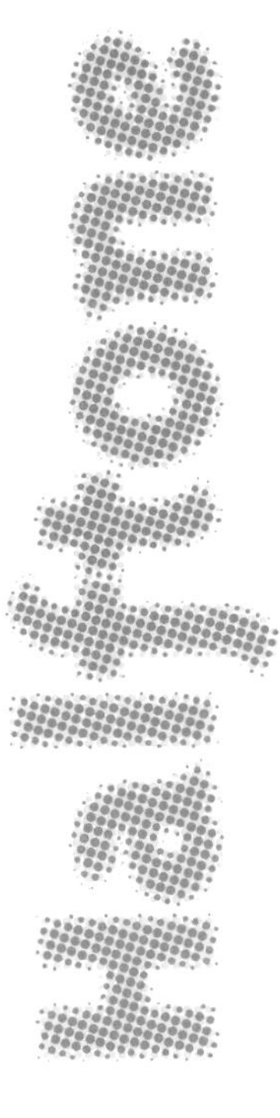

3 Choose Layer➥Flatten Image, then apply Filter➥Pixelate➥Color Halftone. We used 6 pixels for the Max. Radius and the default Screen Angles.

## Black-and-White Halftone

You can also halftone black-and-white images.

**1** Create a new grayscale file. Enter the text with the Type tool using different values of gray.

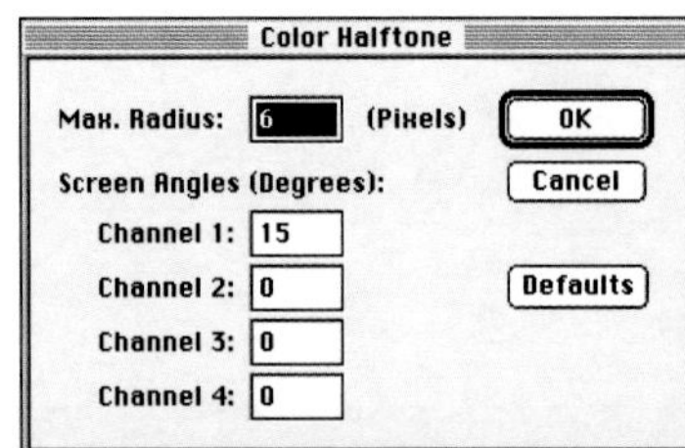


**2** Choose Filter➥Pixelate➥Color Halftone. Use 6 pixels for the Max. Radius and 15 degrees for Channel 1's Screen Angle. Because this is a grayscale file, there is only one channel. The other values are ignored.

Your final image should look like this.

## Fun with Channels

**1** Create a new image and choose a foreground color for the type (we used green). Then enter the text.

**2** Use Image➥Duplicate twice to make two copies of the image in separate files.

**3** With one of the duplicate images, convert to grayscale (Image➥Mode➥Grayscale).

**4** Next, use Image➥Mode➥Bitmap to convert the grayscale image to a bitmap. Photoshop will ask if you want to flatten the image's layer's—click OK. In the Bitmap dialog box, be sure the Output Resolution matches the Input Resolution. For Method, choose Halftone Screen.

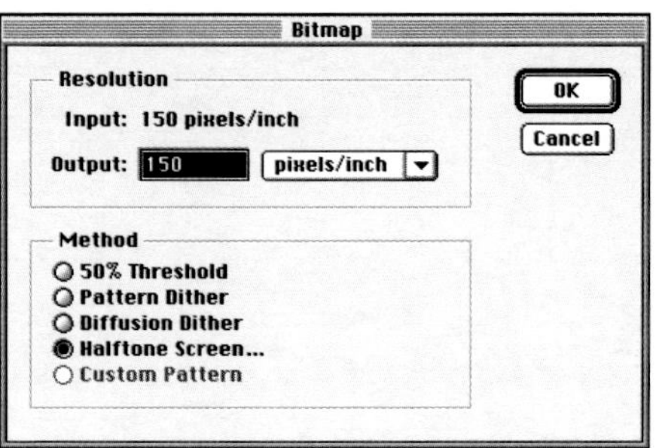


In the Halftone Screen dialog box, use a setting of 20 lines/inch for the Frequency, 30 degrees for the Angle, and Round for the Shape.

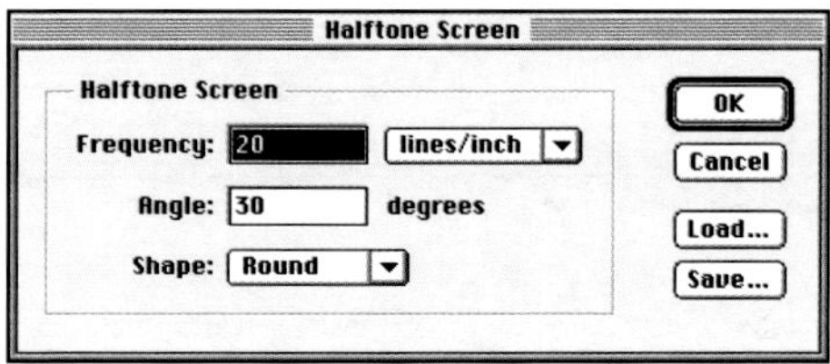


The image should now look something like this.

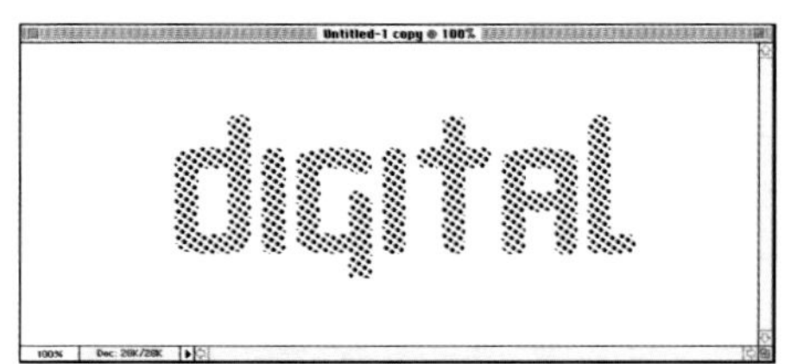

5 Select➡All and copy the image. Return to the original image and make the Red channel active. Paste the clipboard image into this channel, replacing what was already there. Return to the composite channel. You should have something like this.

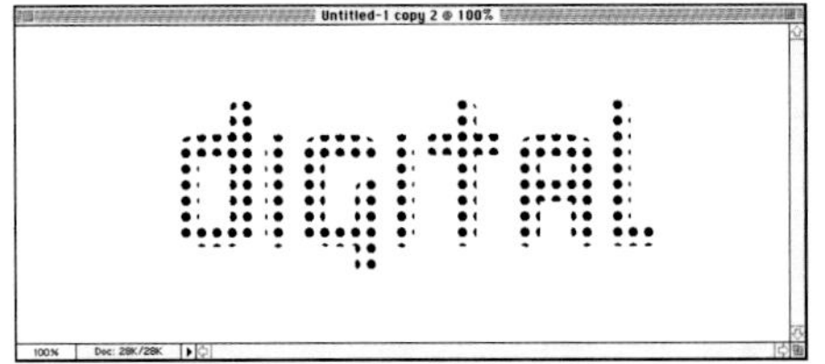


6 Convert the other duplicate to grayscale. Then convert it to bitmap, but use the following settings. Frequency: 10 lines/inch, Angle: 0, Shape: Round. First, though, Photoshop will ask if you want to flatten the image's layer's—click OK. You should end up with something like what you see in this figure. Choose Select➡All to copy the image.

7 In the original image, paste the clipboard image into the Blue channel. Your final image should look like this.

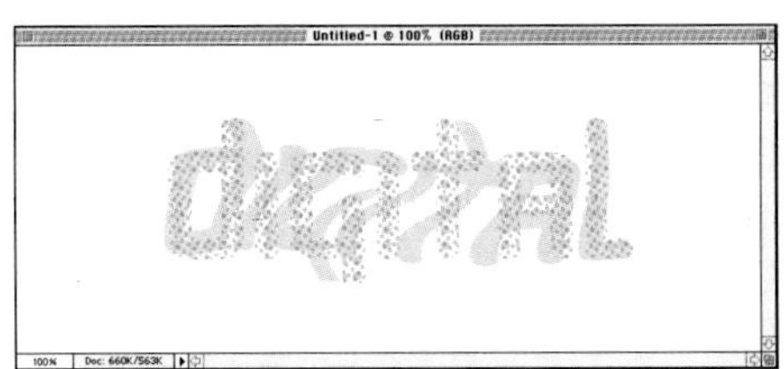


8 For some added excitement, try distorting one of the channels. Here we used Filter➡Distort➡Twirl with a setting of 56° on the Green channel.

## Custom Patterns

You can also use a custom pattern for halftoning.

**1** Before converting the mode to Bitmap, open a custom pattern. Keep in mind that smaller sizes tend to work better. Here we used the Deco pattern supplied in Photoshop. (Mac users will find it in Photoshop 4.0/Goodies/Brushes and Patterns/PostScript Patterns; Windows users should look in the Patterns directory inside the Photoshop directory.)

**2** Select➡All and Edit➡Define Pattern to define the pattern.

**3** Use Image➡Duplicate to make a copy of your original image. Then convert the mode of the duplicate to Grayscale (Image➡Mode➡Grayscale).

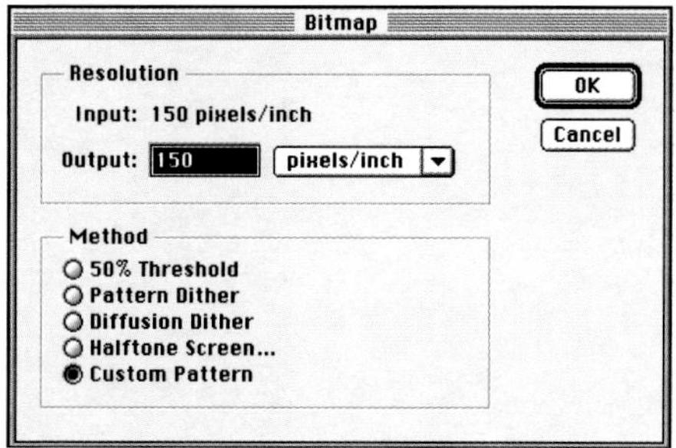


**4** Choose Image➡Mode➡Bitmap and make sure both Input and Output numbers are the same. Choose Custom Pattern from the Method choices.

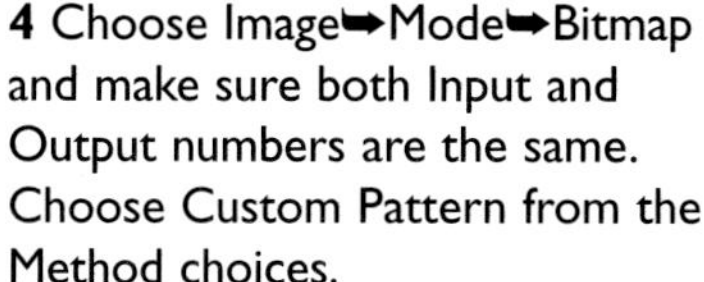

This uses your defined pattern for the dot size. The size of the pattern defines the frequency.

**5** Copy the image and paste it into a channel in your original file. We pasted into the Green channel for this example. ■

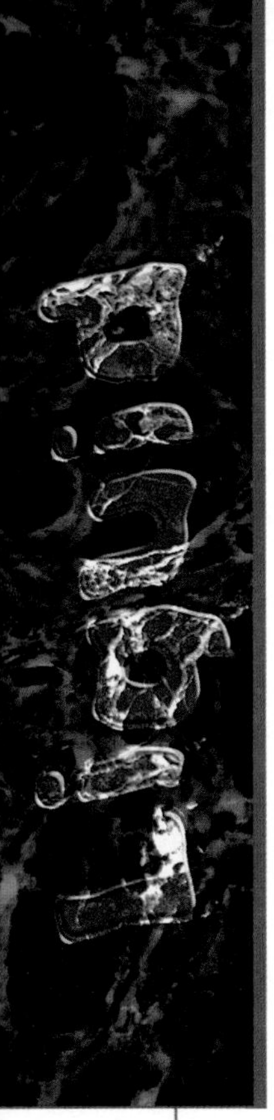

1 Create a new file (it must be an RGB file) or open an existing image. We used an image from D'Pix for this example. We changed the resolution to 150 dpi and cropped it down.

Hey man, use a coaster!

2 Create a new channel (#4), choose white as the foreground color, and use the Type tool to enter the text into Channel #4. This example uses Helvetica Condensed Black at 60 points. Choose Select➡None (Command-D) [Control-D].

3 You may be somewhat familiar with this step and the next few that follow it—they're very similar to the beginning steps of Melting text, just in a slightly different order. Use Image➡Rotate Canvas➡90° CW to rotate the image.

## TOOLBOX

LiquidCurve file

LiquidLighting file

**4** Apply Filter➥Stylize➥Wind with a setting of Wind and Left. Do this twice (press (Command-F) [Control-F]) to get a good amount of streakage.

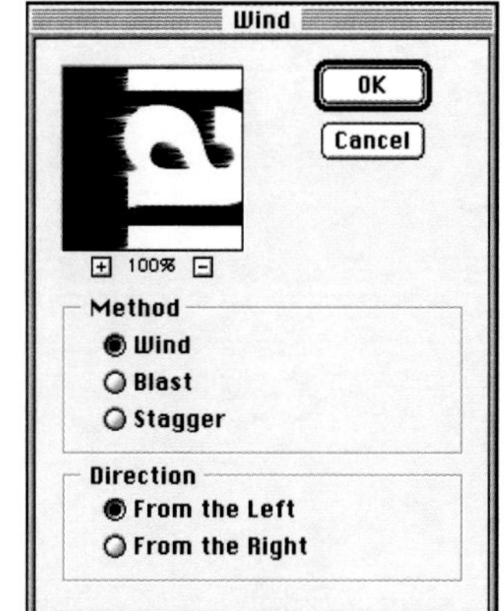


You should have something like this.

**5** You can now rotate the image back to right side up using Image➥Rotate Canvas➥90° CCW.

**6** Apply Filter➥Brush Strokes➥ Spatter. Use settings of around 19 for the Radius and 15 for Smoothness. This adds some rough undulation to the text (don't worry—it'll be smoothed out in the next step).

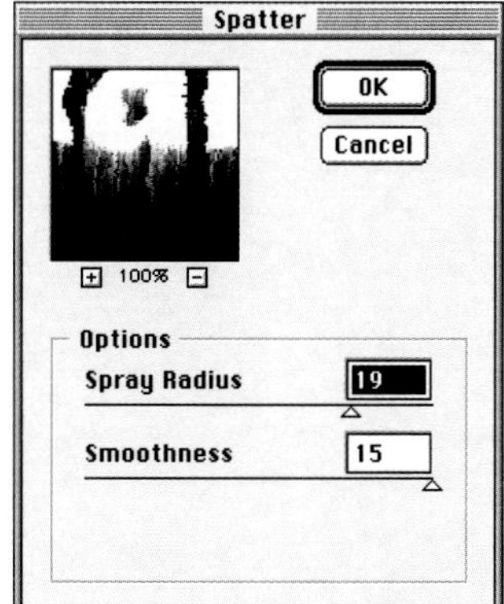

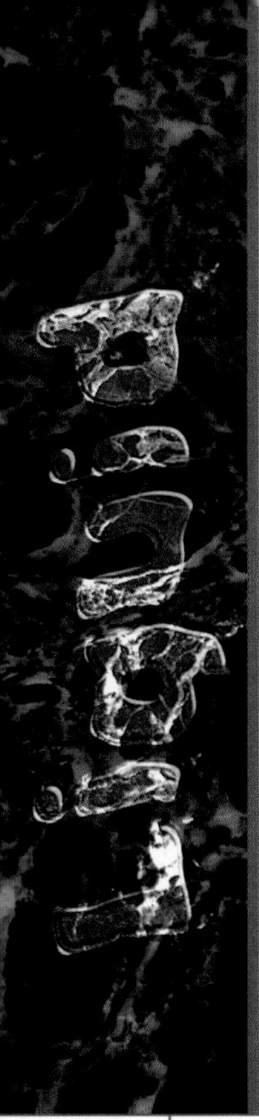

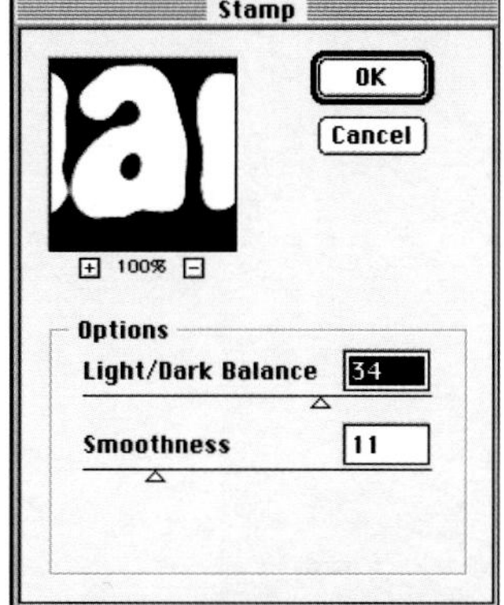


**7** To smooth out the edges, apply Filter➥Sketch➥Stamp with the setting at 34 for Light/Dark Balance and 11 for Smoothness.

You should end up with something like this.

**8** For more variation in the type, use Filter➥Distort➥Wave with the following settings: Generators: 5; Wavelength: 42, 170; Amplitude: 9, 26; Horiz.: 28; Vert.: 21; Type: Sine). Click the Randomize button a few times until the preview looks like what you're aiming for.

You should now have some nice, moderately wavy text.

9 Duplicate Channel #4 and rename the new channel "Texture" because that's what it's going to be. In the Texture channel, load the selection Channel #4 and apply Filter➥Blur➥ Gaussian Blur (6 pixels). Because the selection is loaded, the blur only occurs on the inside of the text.

10 Bring up the Image➥Adjust➥ Curves dialog box, click the Load button, and find the LiquidCurve file.

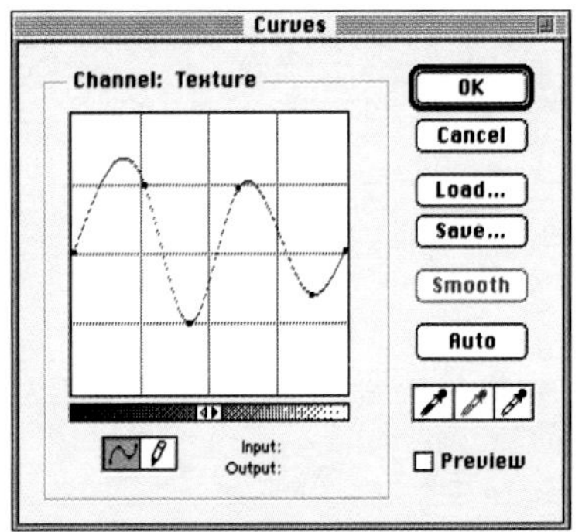

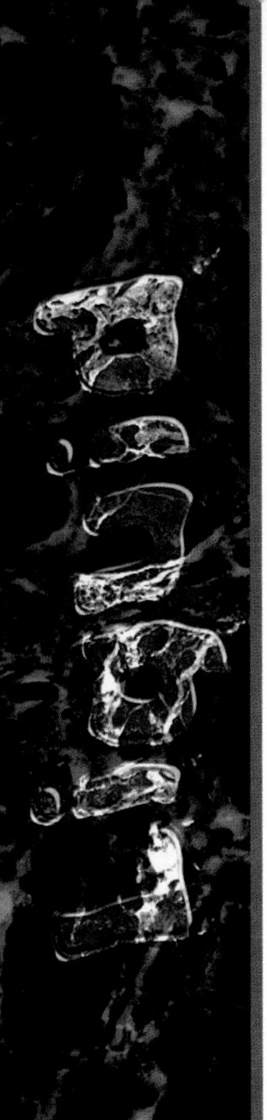

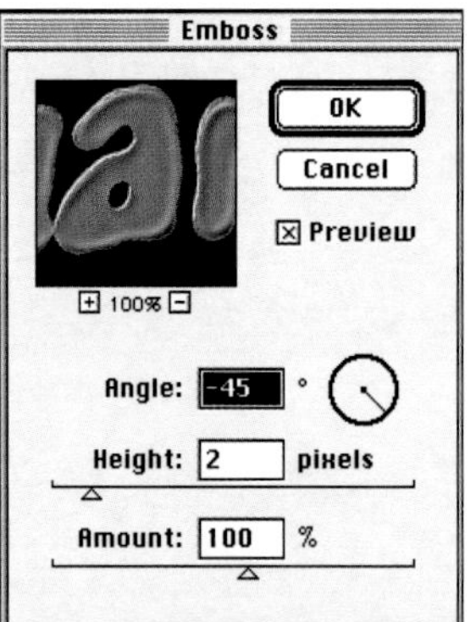


**11** Still working in the Texture channel, but with the selection from Channel #4 still loaded, apply Filter➥Stylize➥Emboss. Use settings of Angle: –45°, Height: 2 pixels, and Amount: 100%. Your text should now look like it has a bit of a ridge around the outside of the letters.

**12** Select➥None (Command-D) [Control-D] and apply Filter➥ Blur➥ Gaussian Blur with a radius of 2 pixels to smooth out any jaggies.

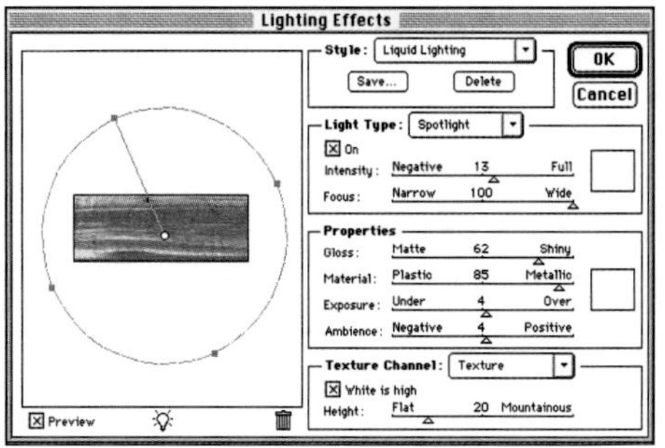


**13** Now it's time to liquefy the text. Return to the composite channel and load the selection Channel #4 (the original text channel). Apply Filter➥Render➥ Lighting Effects and choose the LiquidLightStyles preset from the Style pop-up menu, with the Texture channel you created chosen in the Texture Channel pop-up menu. If you haven't installed it from the CD-ROM accompanying this book, simply copy these settings here.

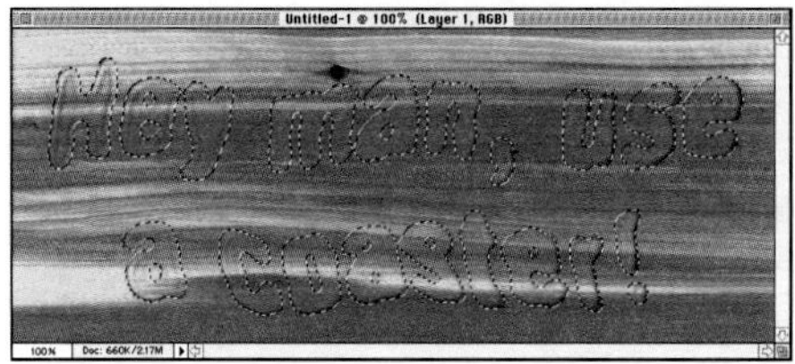

This preset uses the Texture channel you created as, well, a texture. This results in highlights and shadows from the various levels of gray in the channel.

**14** With Channel #4 still loaded, apply Filter➡Sharpen➡Unsharp Mask with a setting of Amount: 55%, Radius: 3.0 pixels, and Threshold: 0 levels. This brings up the contrast just a bit to give the illusion of looking through a liquid.

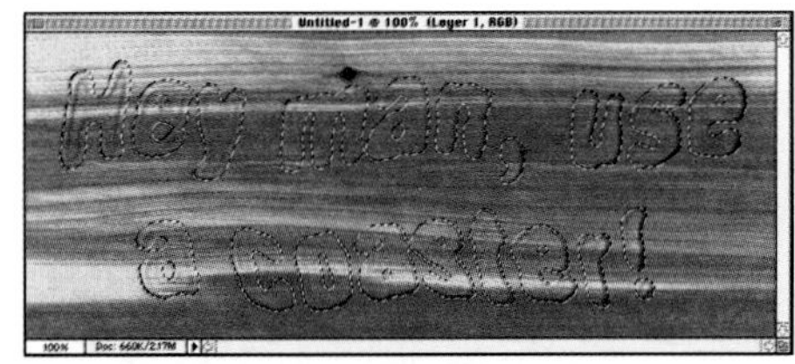


**15** It may look good, but the highlights still need to be added. In the Texture channel, load the selection Channel #4, and copy the channel (Command-C) [Control-C]. Return to the composite channel and create a new layer (Layer 1). Paste the copied image onto this layer and Select➡None (Command-D) [Control-D]. You should now have something like this.

**16** To pull out some highlights, use Image➡Adjust-Brightness/Contrast with settings of Brightness: –13 and Contrast: +87.

**17** Double-click Layer 1 (the one you just created) in the Layers palette. This brings up the Layer Options dialog box. Set the Mode to Luminosity and adjust the This Layer slider until the numbers read 130 and 235/255 (you can split the arrows by holding down the (Option) [Alt] key and moving just half of the slider triangle).

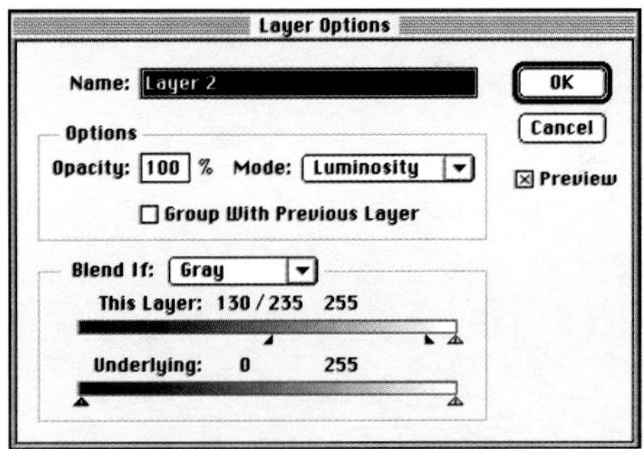


Adjusting this slider determines which values of gray are being used to increase the luminosity. By moving the arrows around you can allow different grays to affect the underlying image.

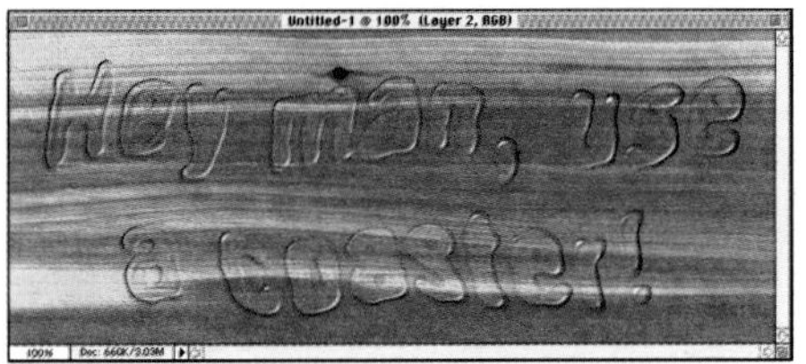

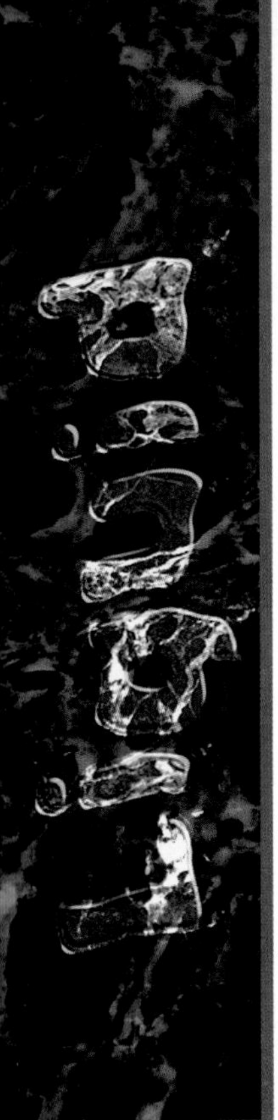

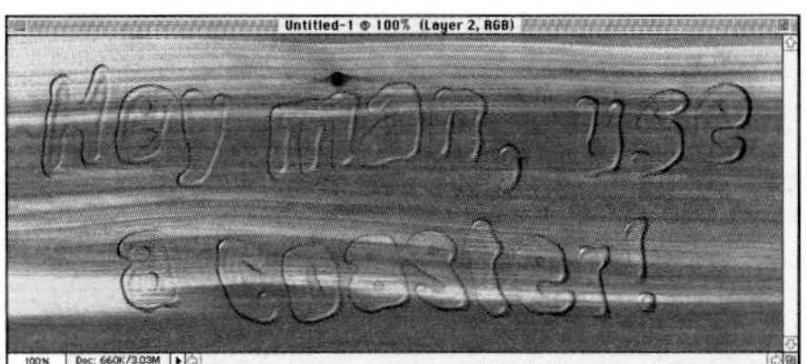

**18** Finally, take down the opacity of Layer 1 to around 80%. This softens the intensity of the highlights a bit.

## VARIATIONS

If you're looking for something other than clear liquid, try changing the light color in the Light Type section of the Lighting Styles dialog box in Step 13. Here, a medium green colored light was used. To change the light color, click the colored box at the right side of the Lighting Styles dialog box and choose a new color from the Color Picker.

If you're looking for an opaque substance, move the Materials slider in the Lighting Effect dialog box from Metallic all the way down to Plastic when you render the text. When you get to Step 16, where you adjust the Brightness and Contrast of Layer 1, use values of 100 for Brightness and 25 for Contrast. For Step 17, change the mode of Layer 1 to Luminosity, but skip the rest of that step. For Step 18, adjust the opacity of Layer 1 until the background is just barely visible. We used 76% for this variation. ■

# MARQUEE

It doesn't get any easier than this. The Lighting Effects filter that comes with Photoshop (combined with the PlasticLightStyles preset file supplied on the *Type Magic* CD-ROM) does almost all the work for you.

**1** Create a new file. Change the foreground and background colors to their default settings (press D). Create a new channel (#4). Use the Type tool to enter the text. We used Futura CondExtraBold at 50 points.

**2** With the selection still active, choose Filter➡Blur➡Gaussian Blur (4 pixels).

**3** Return to the composite channel (Command-~) [Command-~]. Choose as the foreground color a color for the marquee letters. Press (Option-Delete)[Alt-Delete] to fill the text with the foreground color.

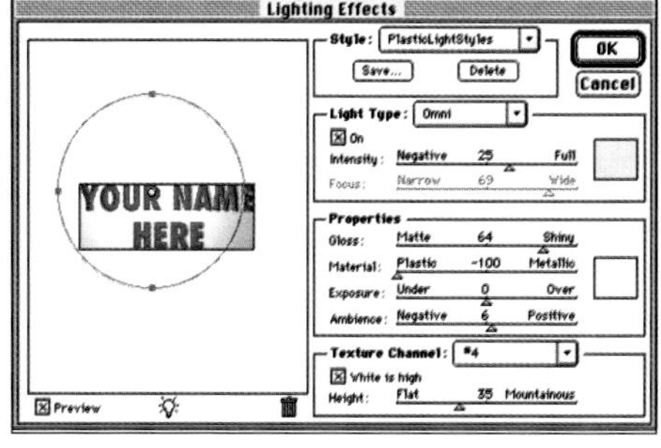


**4** Keep that selection active. Choose Filter➡Render➡Lighting Effects. Choose PlasticLightStyles (included on the CD) from the pop-up menu. If it doesn't show up in the list, see page 242 to find out how to load it from the CD. You might need to increase the Height setting to get the type as full as you want it.



TOOLBOX

PlasticLight-Styles file

**The text selection should still be active, which means you could copy the text right to the clipboard or use the selection to make a path if you need to drop out the background.**

## VARIATIONS

If you are going to include this text in a composition, you can use the controls in the Lighting Effects dialog box to make the marquee letters appear as if they are being lit by the same light source as other objects in your composition. For this variation, we chose the Soft Direct Lights preset from the pop-up menu.

We manipulated the Five Lights Down preset to get this image.

If you deselect the text before applying the Lighting Effects filter, then the light affects the background, too. This text looks a little more like it belongs with its background.

Flip to page 174 to find out out how to create more Plastic text. ■

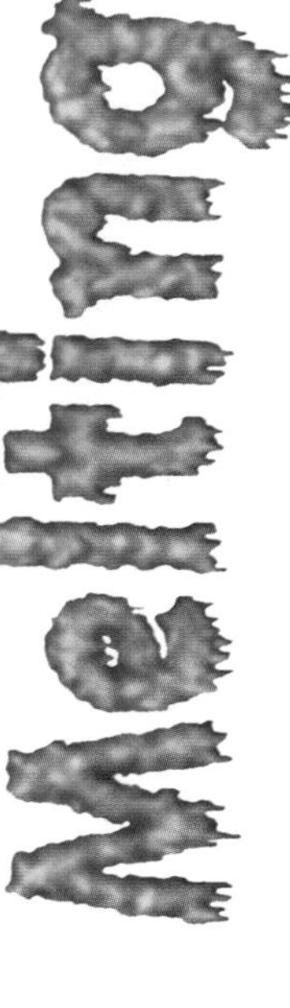

**1** Create a new file, and create a new channel (#4). Use the Type tool to enter the text into the new channel. This example uses Triplex Extra Bold at 100 points.

**2** Use Layer→Tranform→Distort to give your text some dimension. If you don't want much dimension, at least stretch the letters vertically—if your letters are too short, they may turn out to be unrecognizable blobs.

**3** Choose Select→None (Command-D) [Control-D], then Image→Adjust→Invert (Command-I) [Control-I].

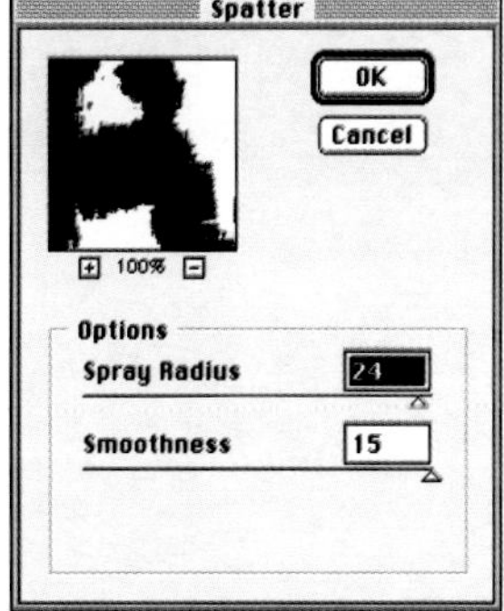


**4** Apply Filter→Brush Strokes→Spatter. Crank the settings up to 24 for the Radius and 15 for the Smoothness.

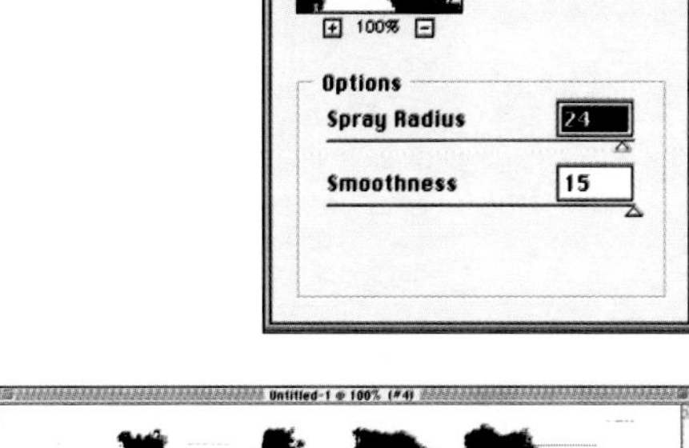


Your type looks pretty rough.

**5** Image➡Rotate Canvas➡90° CW and Image➡Adjust➡Invert. Apply Filter➡Stylize➡Wind, with the settings at Wind and From the Left, twice.

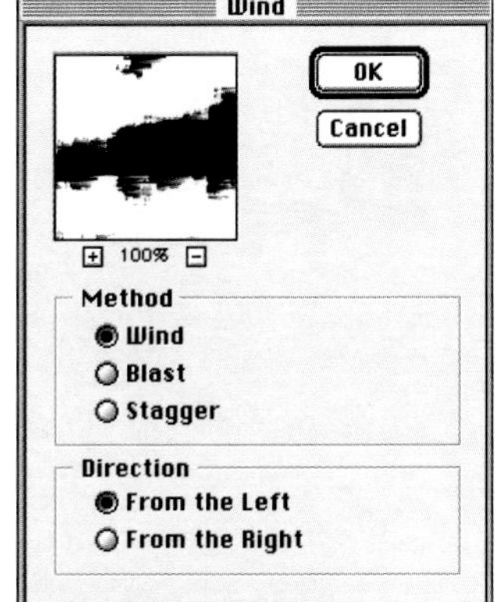


Your image looks like this.

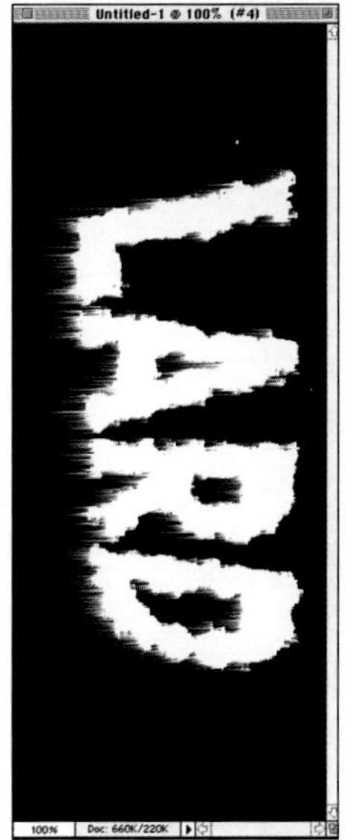


**6** Image➡Adjust➡Invert (Command-I) [Control-I] and Image➡Rotate Canvas➡90° CCW to get the text back to being right-side-up.

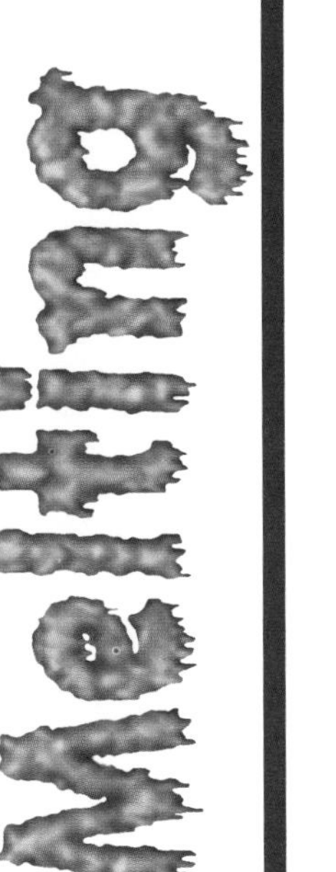


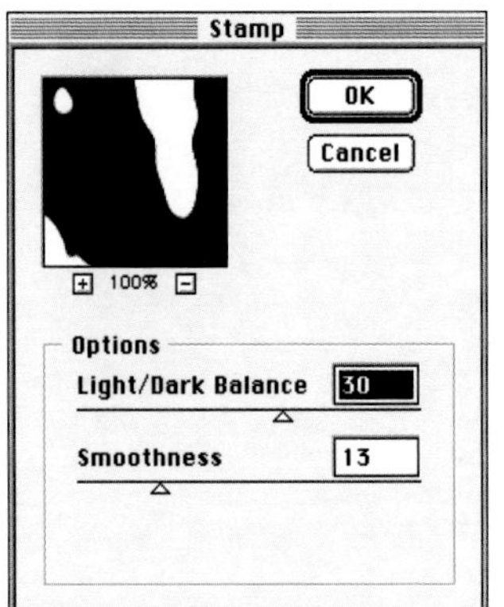


7 Apply Filter➡Sketch➡Stamp. Set the Light/Dark Balance at 30 and the Smoothness at 13.

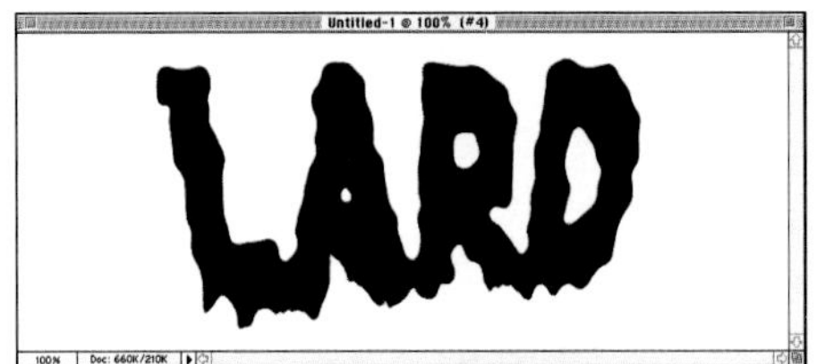


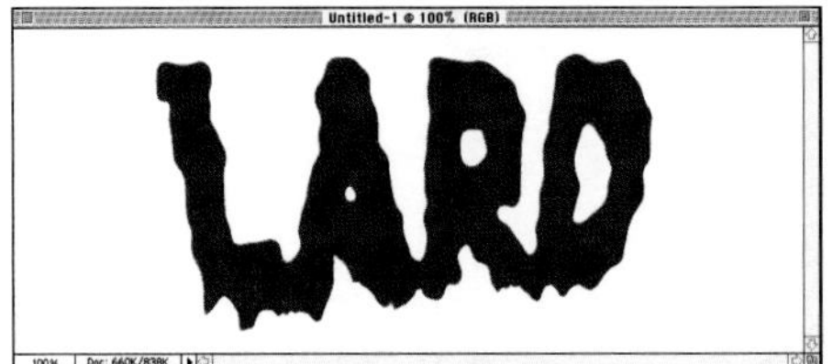


8 Choose Image➡Adjust➡Invert (Command-I) [Control-I], then return to the composite channel (Command-~) [Control-~]. Choose for the foreground color a dark brown. Load the selection Channel #4. Press (Option-Delete) [Alt-Delete] to fill the selection with the foreground color. Select➡None (Command-D) [Control-D].

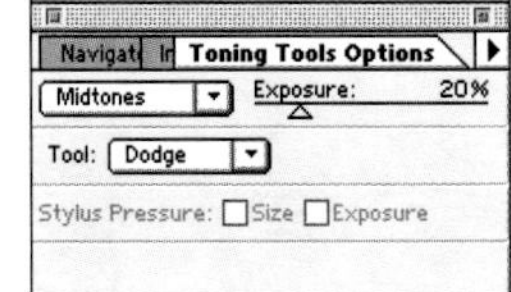


9 To give the type a more oozy quality, use the Dodge and Burn tools to add highlights and shadows. The Dodge tool adds highlights by "under-exposing" what's painted with its tool. Burn does the opposite: It adds shadows by painting with "over-exposure." Keeping the Exposure level low (in the Burn Tool Options palette) gives greater control over the application. We used a setting of 20% here with the tone values set to Midtone. The same goes for the Burn tool.

**10** To create a blobby effect, apply the Dodge tool several times in the same spot, move a short distance, and repeat. Use varying brush sizes. For this image, the brush size ranged from 25 and 45 pixels. Add shadows with the Burn tool in the same manner. A few streaks of dodging were used to connect the blobs.

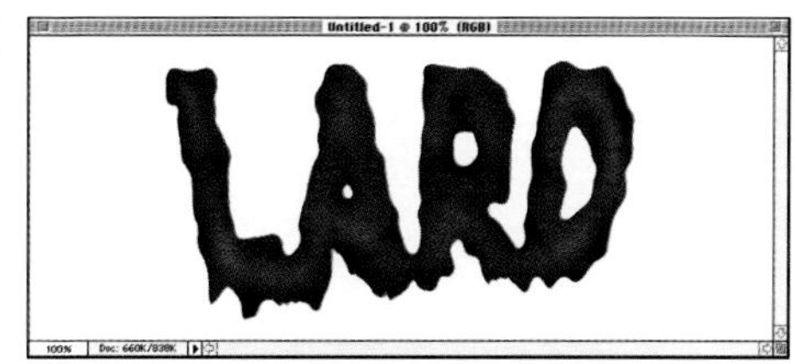

**11** Finally, use the Smudge tool, sparingly, to blur the blobs together a bit. That's it, and you didn't even need an oven!

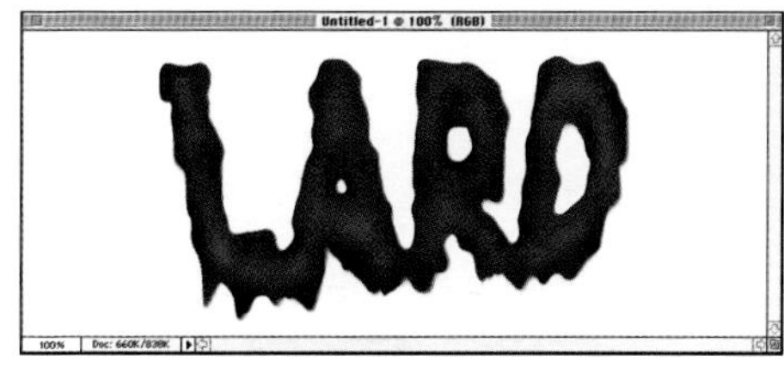

## VARIATIONS

Want more or less drippiness? Try varying the settings in Step 7. Here are some different results:

Molasses on a picnic table: Use Light/Dark Balance: 40 and Smoothness: 25.

Ice milk in your hands: Use Light/Dark Balance: 25 and Smoothness: 10.

Snowman in Florida: Use Light/Dark Balance: 20 and Smoothness: 5. ■

You can produce this effect using a variety of combinations of the steps that follow.

**1** Create a new file. Choose for the foreground color the color you want for the type. Use the Type tool to enter the text you want to use (we used Myriad Black Oblique at 50 points for this example). If you do not use an oblique font, make sure the Italic checkbox is checked. Click OK. When placing the text in the image area, be sure to leave some room to the left (or right depending on the direction you want the text to be moving). Flatten the image.

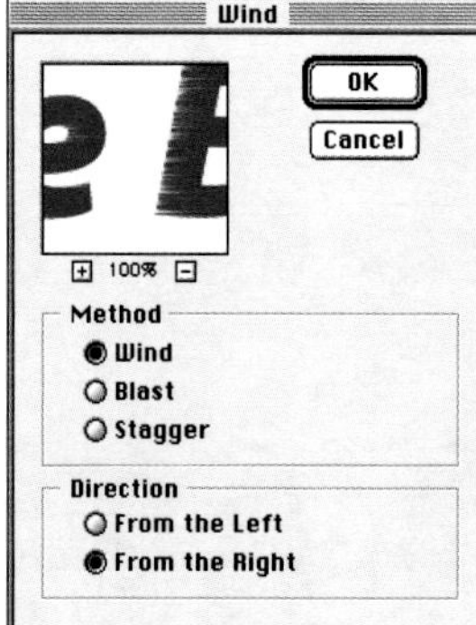


**2** Apply Filter➡Stylize➡Wind (Wind, Right).

**TIP** **To improve the dynamic of the movement use the Smudge tool to lengthen the streaks. This is not necessary, but a few touches can greatly improve this effect. Set the Smudge tool pressure to 50% and use a feathered brush.**

## TOOLBOX

Andromeda's Velocity filter

**3** Now apply Filter➥Blur➥Motion Blur (10 pixels). You could raise this setting some, but if you go too crazy, Herbie is going to look like he's just standing there shaking.

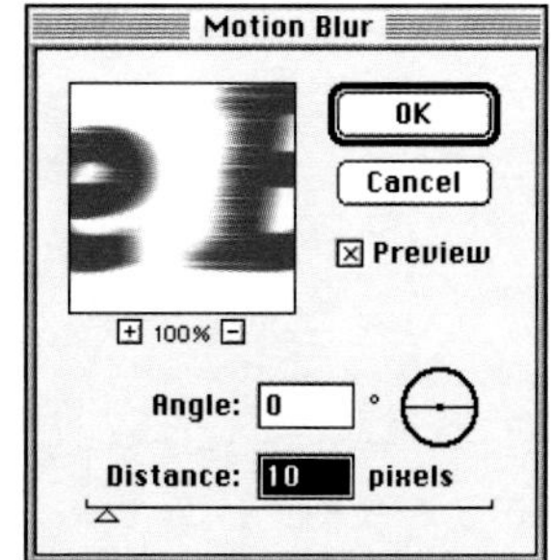

**4** One more time, apply Filter➥Stylize➥Wind (Wind, Right).

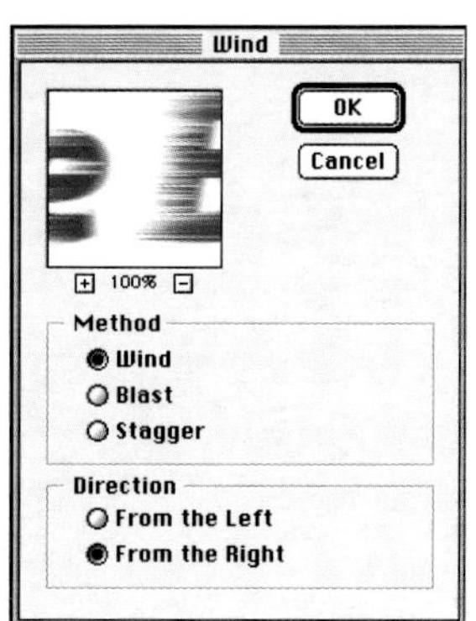


**5** Apply Filter➥Sharpen➥Unsharp Mask (50, 3.5, 2) to sharpen the edges.

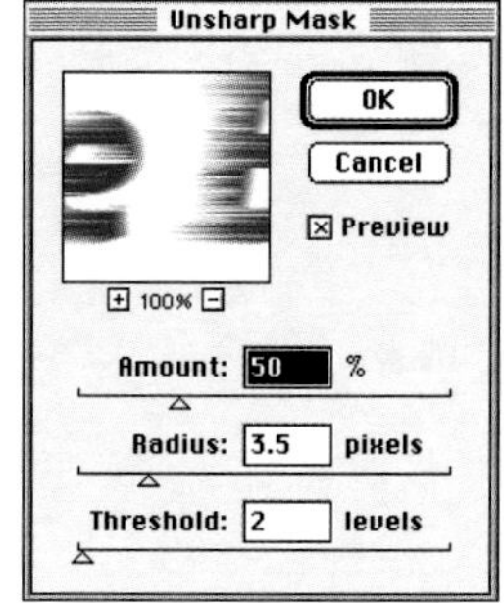

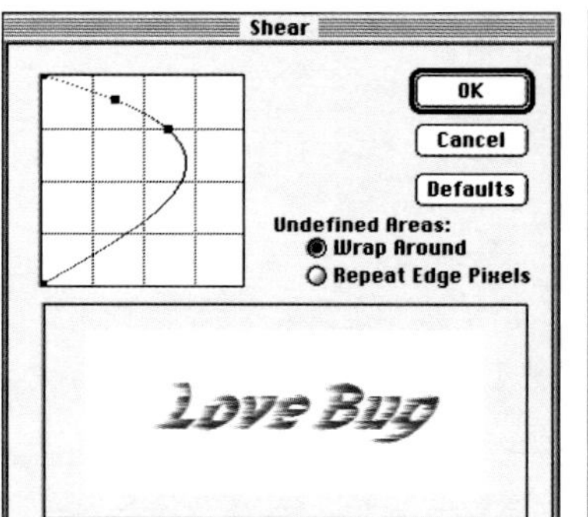


6 Next, choose Filter➥Distort➥Shear. You can grab the line in the grid at any point and drag to make it bend. We added one point, then pulled the top and bottom points all the way to the left. Finally, we added another point on the curve to get just the bend we were looking for.

**TIP** **Here's another good place to use the Smudge tool to lengthen and smooth the streaks.**

7 Finally, choose Filter➥Distort➥Spherize. We set the amount to 55.

There are many possible combinations of these steps that yield good results. You might have decided a few steps ago that you had what you were looking for.

## VARIATIONS

If you're just trying to put a quick swerve in your type, then enter the text. Remember that Photoshop 4 creates the type on a separate layer, so flatten the image before you continue. Choose Filter➥Distort➥Shear. Use the mouse to pull the center of the line out and drag the top and bottom back.

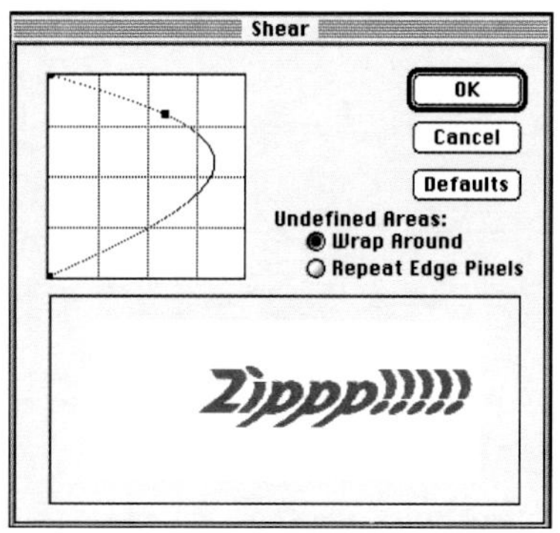


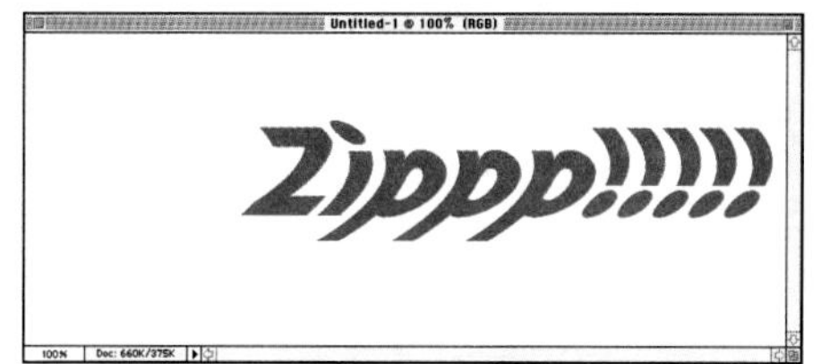


## Velocity Filter

The easy way: Andromeda Software's Velocity filter was used for this effect (One-way smear, Intensity: 50, Angle: 0, Height: 50, Width: 90). ■

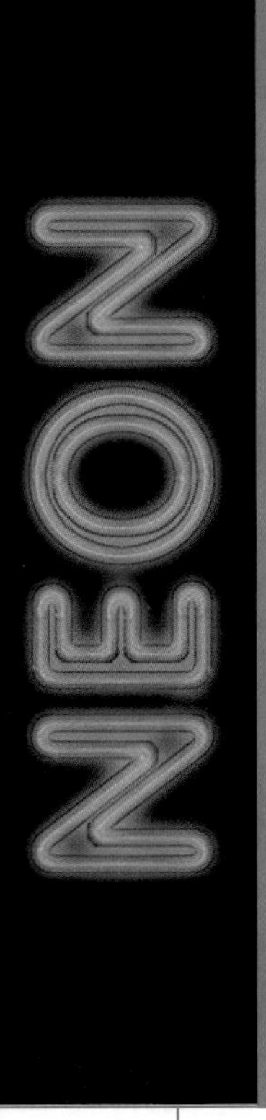


There are a number of ways to create neon using simple blurring and feathering techniques.

## Quick Neon

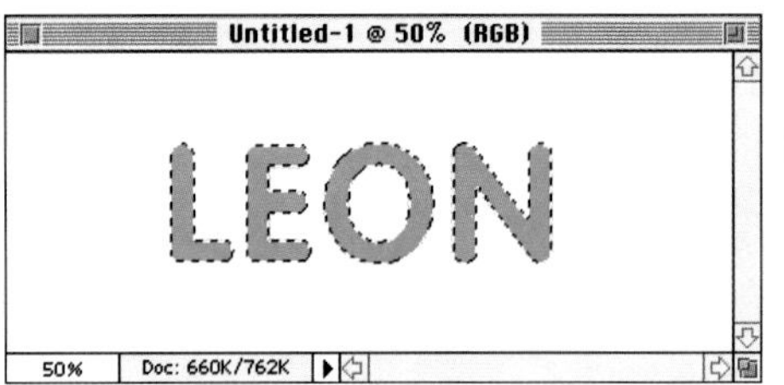


**1** Create a new file. Choose for the foreground color a bright color. Use the Type tool to enter the text. A round-edged font such as VAG Rounded Bold (80 points) works best for this effect. Flatten the image.

**2** Use the Magic Wand tool to select the background, then Select➡Feather (6 pixels).

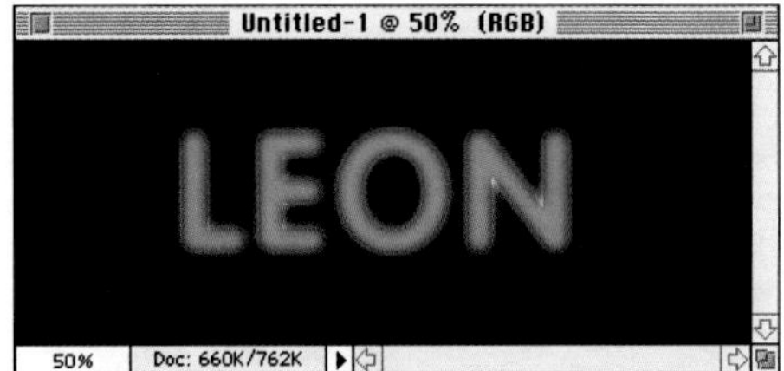


**3** Choose black as the foreground color (press D). Press (Option-Delete) [Alt-Delete] to fill the background. That's it—short and simple.

## Variations

This quick technique works well for creating handwritten neon. Create a new channel (Channel #4), then use a hard-edged brush to paint white text on a black background. Return to the composite channel (Command-~) [Control-~], and load the painted text selection (Channel #4). Fill with a color for the neon and do Steps 2 and 3.

### Toolbox

KPT 3 Gradient Designer

## CMYK

If you are producing an RGB image, the text may look bright enough already. But if your CMYK neon looks a little dull, try this. After Step 1 save the selection. After Step 4, load the selection and choose Select➡Modify➡Contract (6 pixels, or until the selection has moved away from the edges of the text). Choose Select➡Feather (1 pixel). Now, choose Image➡Adjust➡Curves and bend the center of the curve upward slightly, like this. This should help brighten the text.

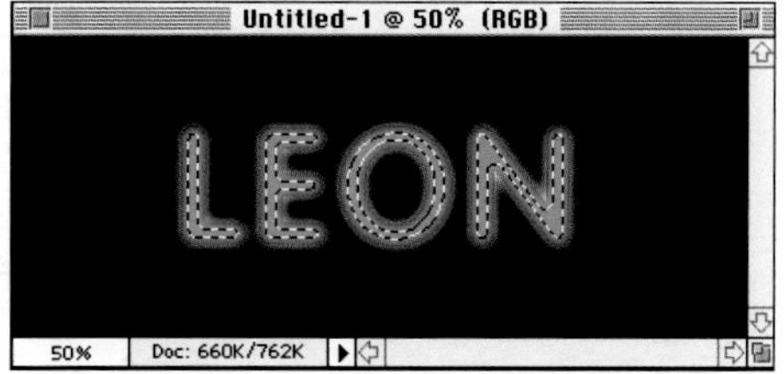


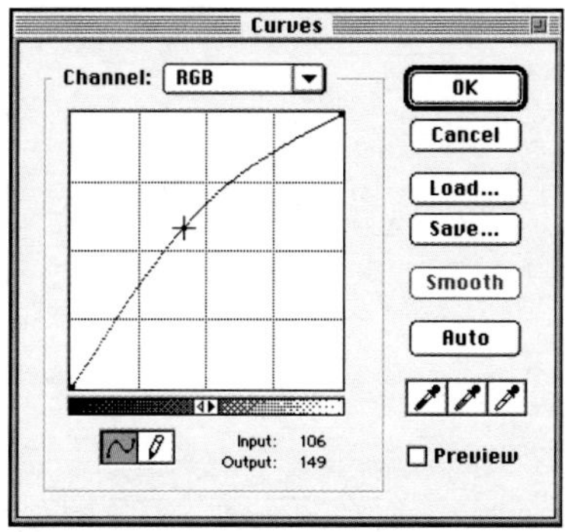


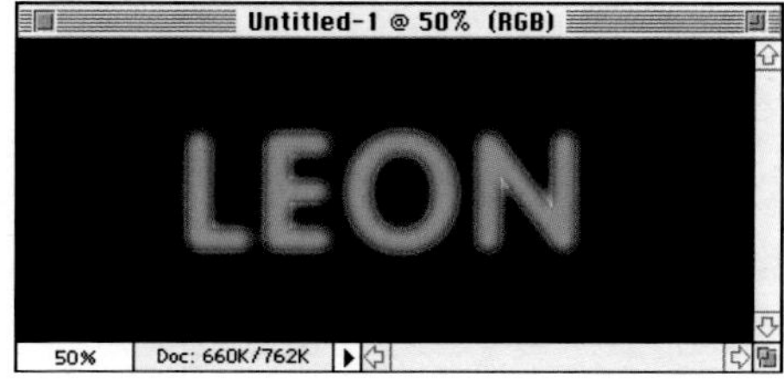


## Detailed Neon

1 Create a new file. (We used a 300 dpi file for this effect.) Set the colors to the defaults (press D). Use the Type tool to enter the text. Again, we started with Vag Rounded Bold at 65 points. (Command-click) [Control-click] on the name of the new text layer to load the text selection, then save the text selection (Channel #4).

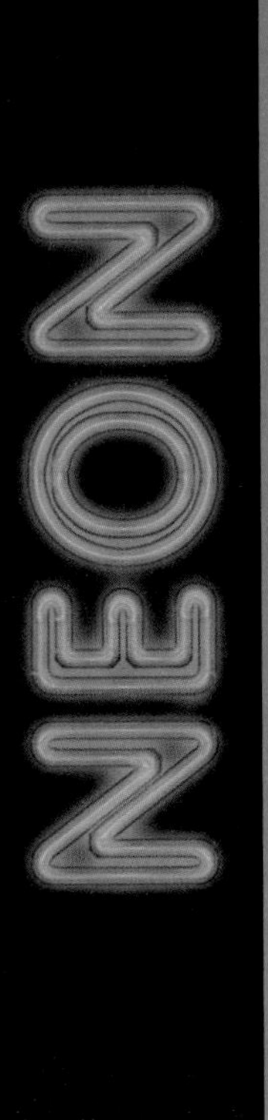

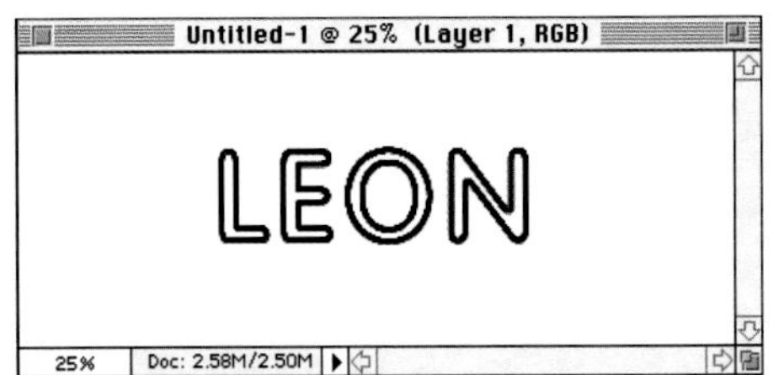


2 Choose Select➡Modify➡Contract (12 pixels). You want a thin selection running all the way through the text. Save this selection (Channel #5). Press delete and deselect the text (Command-D) [Control-D].

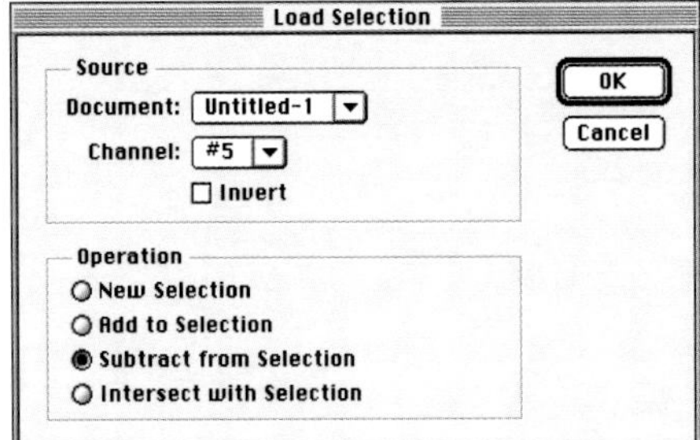


3 Load the original text selection (Channel #4). Now, load the channel saved in Step 3 (Channel #5), and check Subtract from the Selection option. Save this new selection to Channel #6. This saves the selection of what your text looks like now. Deselect the tubes (Command-D) [Control-D].

4 Choose Image➡Map➡Invert.

5 Choose Filter➡Blur➡Gaussian Blur (5 pixels). This establishes the extent of the glow.

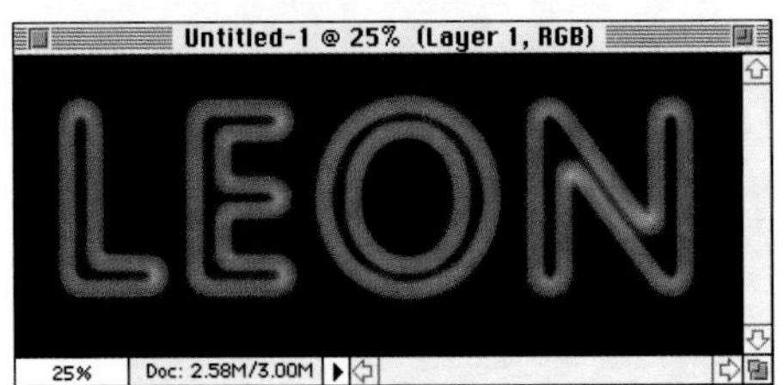


6 Load the selection saved in Step 4 (Channel #6), then choose Filter➡Blur➡Gaussian Blur. Choose an amount that matches the effect you see here. We used 8 pixels.

**7** Choose Image➥Adjust➥ Brightness/Contrast (Brightness: –5, Contrast +10). The settings for your text are probably different. Find something that looks like our end result. Choose Select➥None.

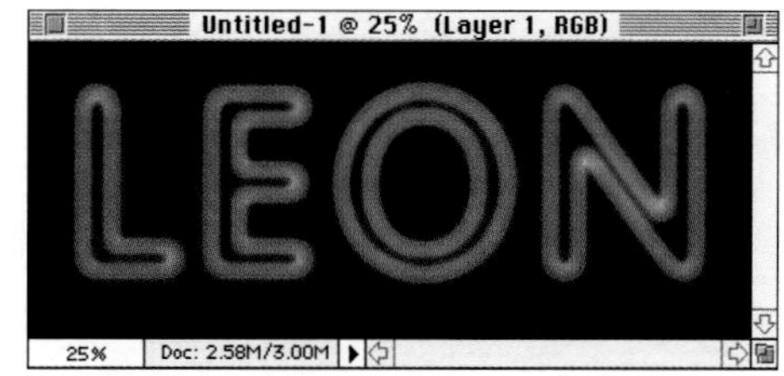


TIP **If you plan on printing this file and need a CMYK image, it's a good idea to either convert to CMYK mode or choose View➥ CMYK Preview now. The RGB mode produces the brightest neon, but you are setting yourself up for a big disappointment when you switch to CMYK mode later.**

**8** Choose Image➥Adjust➥ Hue/Saturation. Click the Colorize checkbox. The preview immediately glows bright red. Use the Hue and Saturation sliders to find a color for the neon. Try to strike a balance (with the Saturation slider) between the most intense color and the greatest amount of detail. You want a nice even color in the middle of the tubes. These are the values we used: Hue: 166, Saturation: 60, Lightness: 0.

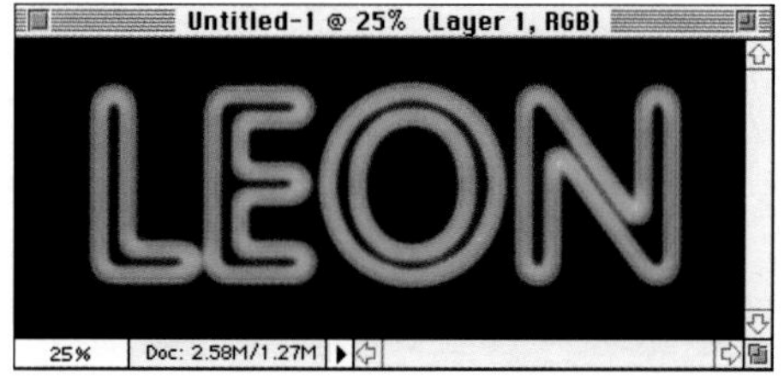


**9** Load the tubes selection (Channel #6). Then choose Select➥ Modify➥Contract (4 pixels) to select a narrow line within the tubes. Choose Select➥Feather (1 pixel).

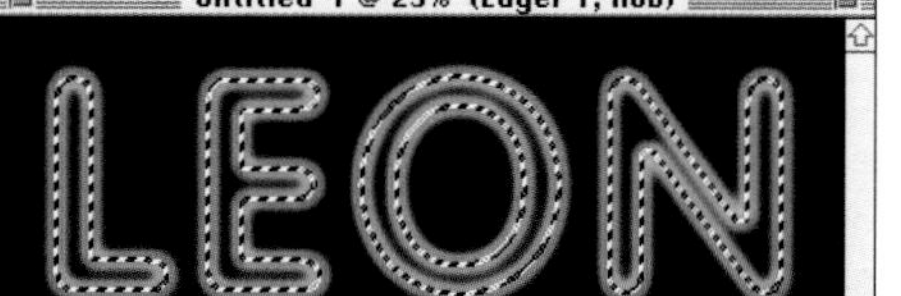

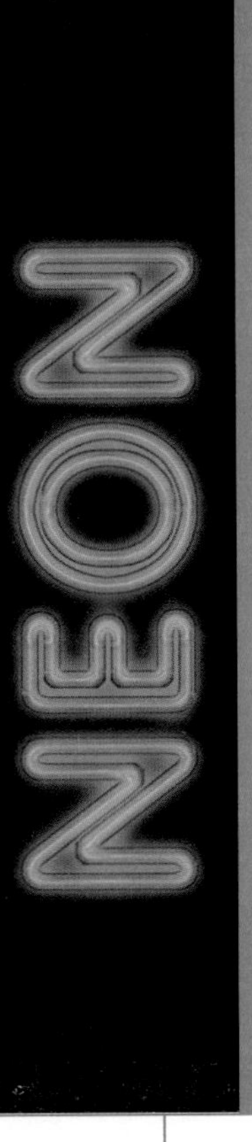


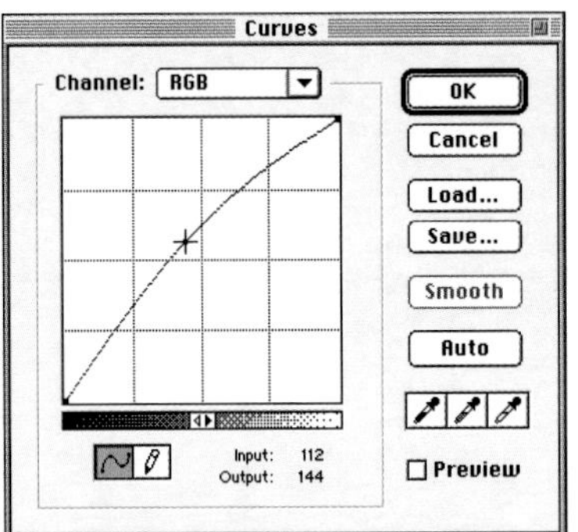


**10** Choose Image➡Adjust➡Curves, and bend the composite curve up slightly from the center, like in this figure.

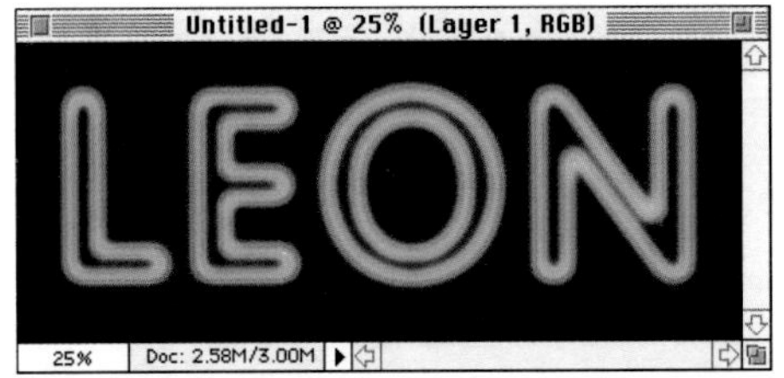

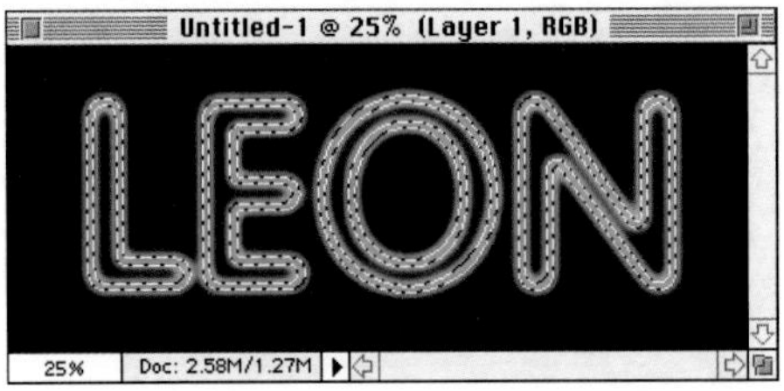

**11** Now choose Select➡Modify➡Contract (2 pixels) to select an even narrower line within the tubes. Choose Select➡Feather (1 pixel).



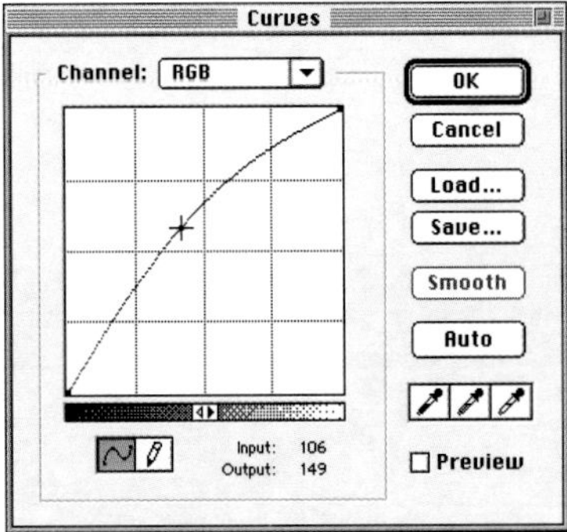


**12** Choose Image➡Adjust➡Curves. Bend the composite curve up a little more this time.

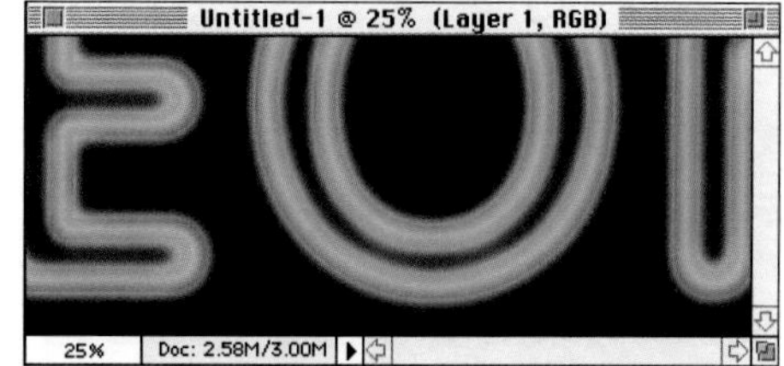


**13** Load the tubes selection (Channel #6), then choose Select➡Modify➡Expand (4 pixels). The selection should now contains almost all of the glow. Save this selection (Channel #7).

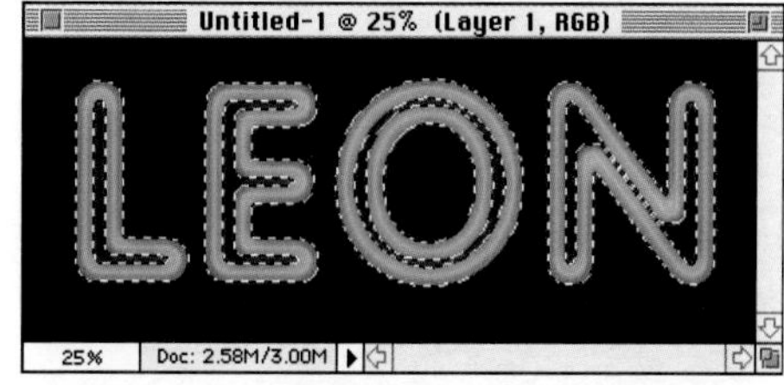


**14** Cut the type (Command-X) [Control-X], then fill this layer with black. Create a new layer, load the selection Channel #7 and paste it back in on the new layer.

**15** Make the background layer active. The Channel #7 selection should still be active. Choose Select➡Feather (12 pixels). Choose a foreground color near the color of your text. Fill the selection. We feathered and filled the selection again in this example.

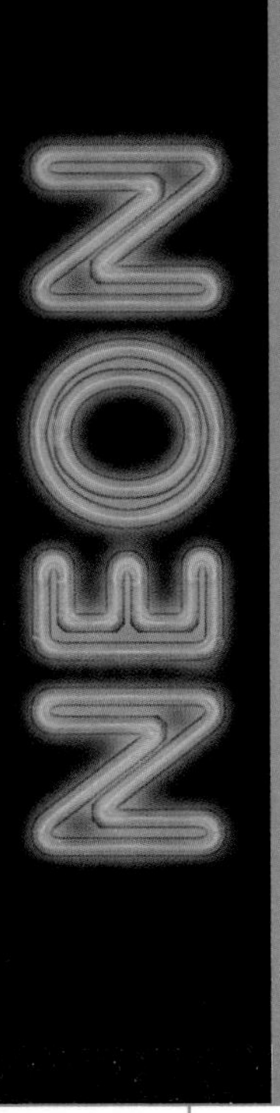

**16** Add highlights to the tubes by applying the Plastic Wrap filter. Load the tubes selection (Channel #6), and choose Filter➡Artistic➡ Plastic Wrap (Highlight Strength: 6, Detail: 15, Smoothness: 10).

## More Variations

Filters can make a quick neon easy.

### KPT 3 Gradient Designer

Use the Type Mask tool to enter your type, then choose Select➡ Feather (3 pixels). Then, apply Filter➡KPT 3.0➡KPT Gradient Designer 3.0. We used one of the preset gradients for this example: True Blue Tube. Try creating your own.

## Photoshop's Neon Glow Filter

Press D, then X to make the foreground color white and background color black. Choose a foreground color for the neon. Use the Type tool to enter the text. (Command-click) [Control-click] on the new layer in the Layers palette to load the type selection. Save the selection (Channel #4), then deselect the text (Command-D) [Control-D] and flatten the image. Press X. The foreground color should now be black and the background color should be the color of the text. Choose Filter➥Artistic➥Neon Glow. Finally, we loaded the text selection Channel #4, feathered it, and filled it with the neon color again. ■

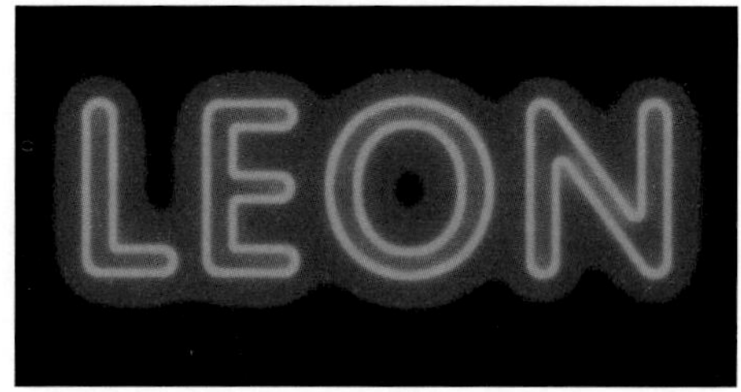

# OVERGROWN

**1** Create a new file. Choose a foreground color for the text. Enter the text with the Type tool, leaving enough room below the type for the overgrowth to hang down. Note that Photoshop 4 automatically creates the type in a new layer (Layer 1). Any font works well for this simple effect, but something with serifs gives the overgrowth some extra limbs to hang from. We used Cheltenham Bold at 50 points.

**2** While still in the type layer (Layer 1), load the transparency selection and then immediately save the text selection to create Channel #4. Deselect the text (Command-D) [Control-D] and go to Channel #4. Duplicate Channel #4 and name the new channel Short Growth. Choose Image➡Adjust➡Invert (Command-I) [Control-I] to invert this new channel (Short Growth).

**3** Then rotate the entire image 90° clockwise (Image➡Rotate Canvas➡90° CW).

**TOOLBOX**

KPT 3 Fractal Explorer

KPT 3 Gradient Designer

**4** Apply Filter➥Stylize➥Wind (Wind, Right), then press (Command-Option-F) [Control-Alt-F] to bring the Wind filter dialog box back. Switch the direction to Left and click OK to apply it again.

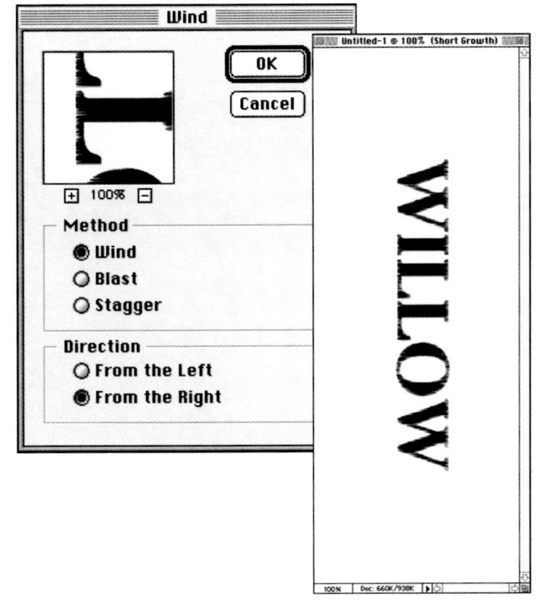


**5** Press (Command-I) [Control-I] to invert the Short Growth channel. Then duplicate the Short Growth channel and rename the new channel Long Growth.

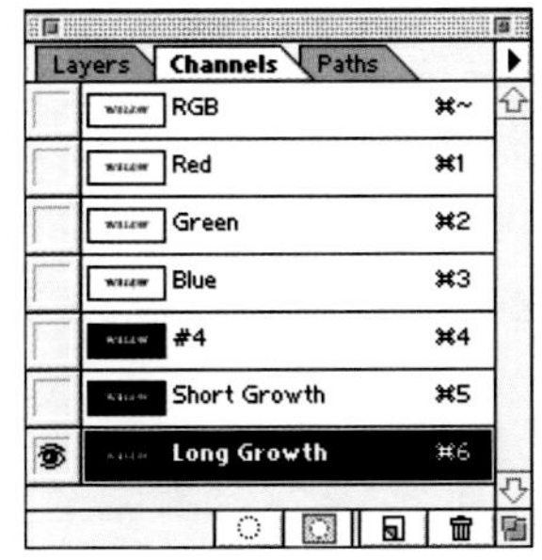


**TIP** **You can press (Command-F) [Control-F] to apply the last filter you used with exactly the same settings. If you want to apply the filter again, but with different settings, press (Command-Option-F) [Control-Alt-F] and the dialog box from the last filter used comes up.**

6 Press (Command-I) [Control-I] to invert the Long Growth channel. To build the overgrowth, apply the Wind filter 3 times and invert the channel again after each application. So, the dance goes like this: (Command-F) [Control-F], (Command-I) [Control-I], (Command-F) [Control-F], (Command-I) [Control-I], (Command-F) [Control-F], (Command-I) [Control-I]. Hopefully, you get something like this.

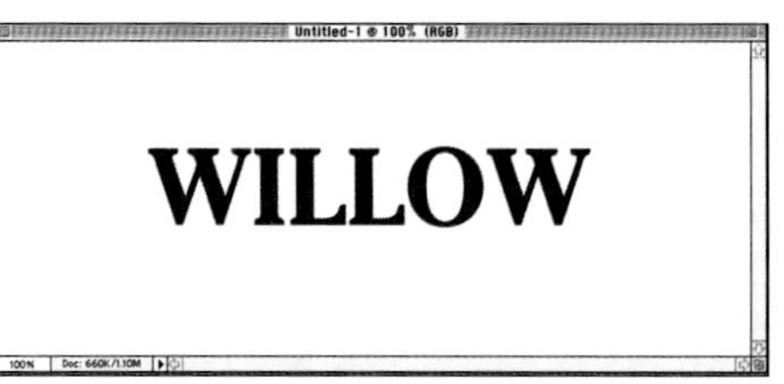


7 Choose Image➡Rotate Canvas➡90° CCW to rotate the entire image back to its original orientation. Then return to the composite channel (Command-~) [Control-~].

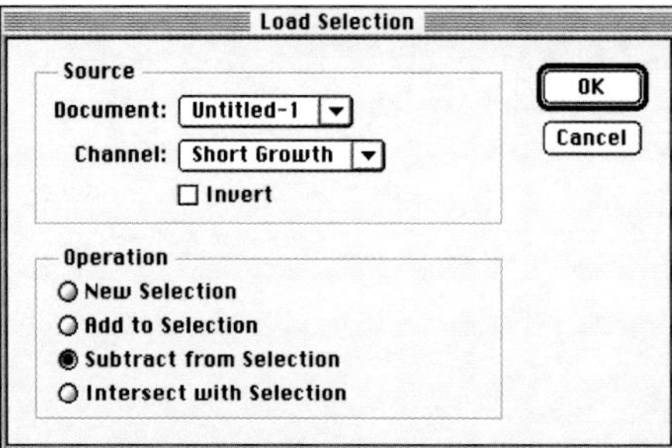


8 First, choose for the foreground color a color for the overgrowth. Then load the selection Channel #4. While this selection is still active, choose Select➡Load Selection, choose Short Growth from the Channel pop-up menu, and click the Subtract from Selection option.

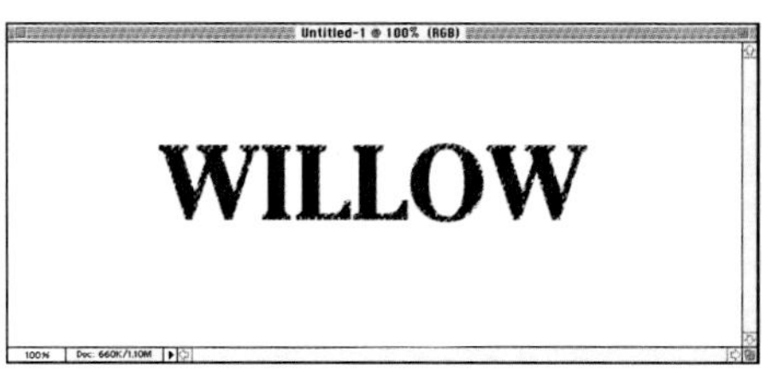


Make sure Preserve Transparency is not checked for the Type layer, and press (Option-Delete) [Alt-Delete] to fill the new selection with the foreground color.

**9** Now, load the Long Growth channel selection, and press (Option-Delete) [Alt-Delete] again to fill the new selection with the same color.

**10** Deselect the active selection (Command-D) [Control-D]. To add some final touches to the drooping overgrowth, first use the rectangular Marquee tool to draw a rectangle around the extra growth beneath the text.

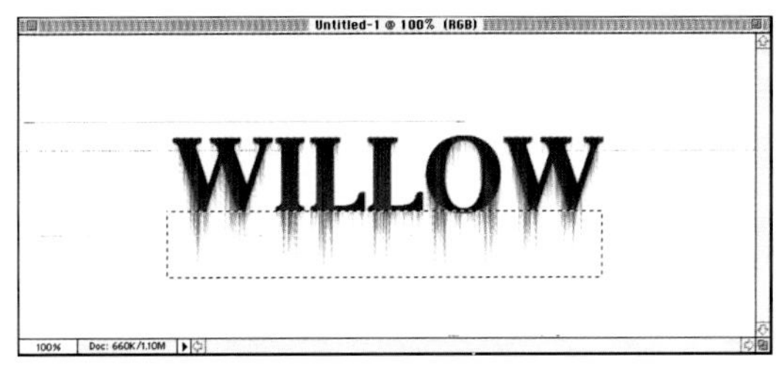


**11** Apply Filter➡Distort➡Ripple (100, Medium).

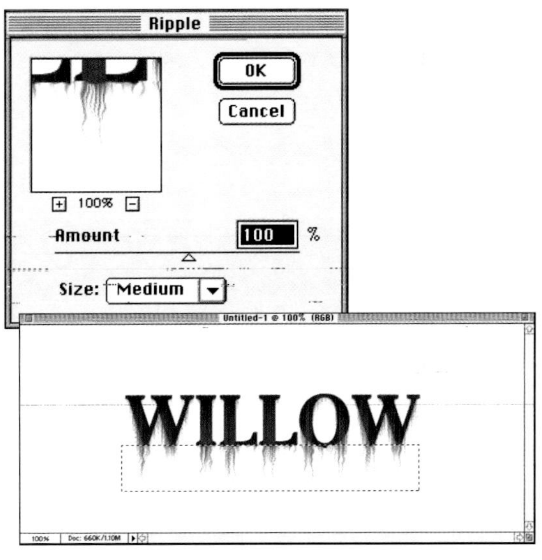


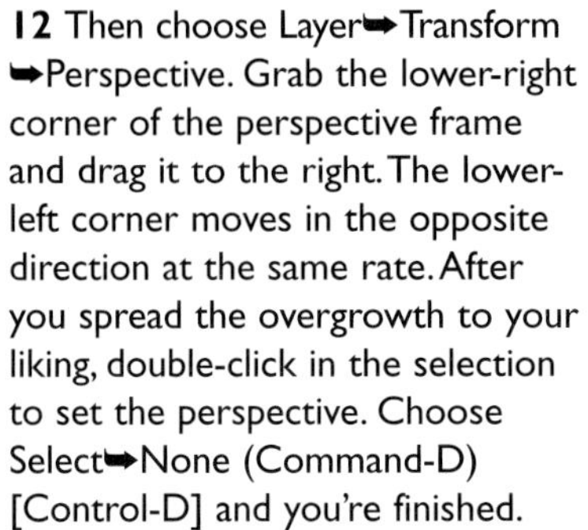

**12** Then choose Layer➡Transform ➡Perspective. Grab the lower-right corner of the perspective frame and drag it to the right. The lower-left corner moves in the opposite direction at the same rate. After you spread the overgrowth to your liking, double-click in the selection to set the perspective. Choose Select➡None (Command-D) [Control-D] and you're finished.

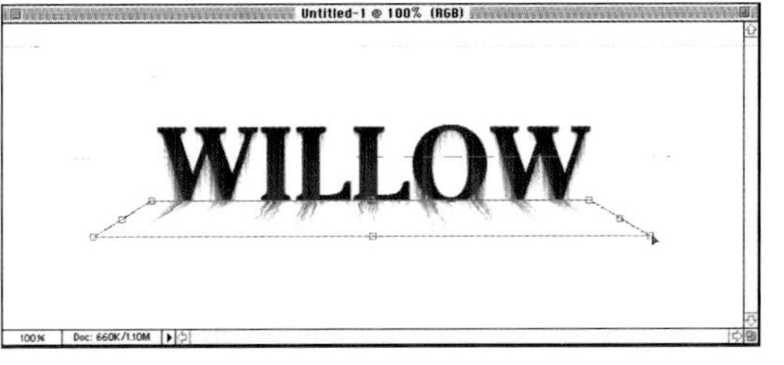

## VARIATIONS

For our tribute to peace, love, and hair we used KPT 3 Gradient Designer and Fractal Explorer 3.0 to fill the text selection. In Step 2, after saving the selection but before deselecting the text, choose Filter➥KPT 3.0➥KPT Gradient Designer 3.0. Also, after we filled the Long Growth selection in Step 9, we shifted the selection to the right (hold down the (Option) [Alt] and (Command) [Control] keys and press the right arrow) and filled it with a different color.

You can make steam with this effect, too. We started with black text on a black background. In Step 3, we rotated the image 90° CCW instead of 90° CW. (And made sure to rotate back 90° CW in Step 7.) Then in Step 6 we applied Filter➥Stylize➥Diffuse (Normal) and Filter➥Distort➥Ripple (100, Medium). In Steps 8 and 9, we chose white as the foreground color for filling the selections. Finally, we converted the image to Grayscale mode (Image➥Mode➥Grayscale), then Duotone mode (Image➥Mode➥Duotone). The two colors I used were black and Trumatch 38-a5. ■

These techniques show you how to create text that takes on the characteristics of the surface it's painted on. The same techniques enable you to create other cool effects, too.

## Painted Type

**1** Create a new file, or open a file containing the background you want to put your text on.

**2** Choose Select➡Select All, and copy it to the clipboard. Create a new channel (Channel #4), then paste in the clipboard.

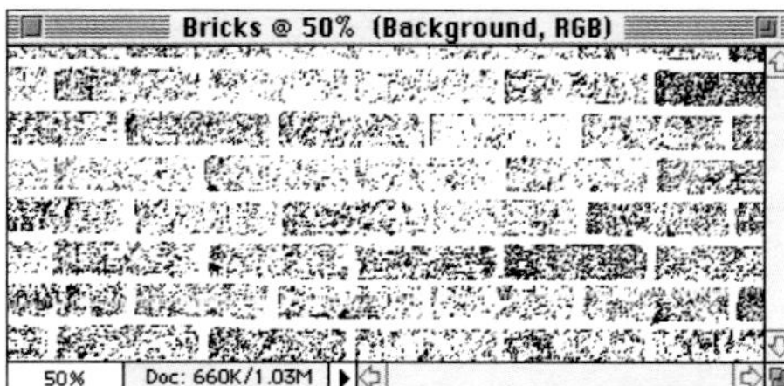


**3** The light areas of this channel represent the areas of the surface that will accept the most paint. You probably need to increase the amount of white in this channel. Choose Image➡Adjust➡Levels. Grab the right (white) Input slider and drag it to the left until the image has a good amount of white in it. Take a look at what we came up with.

**4** Create another new channel (Channel #5), and use the Type tool to enter the text into this channel. We chose the Eraser Dust font (50 points). Deselect the text (Command-D) [Control-D].

**5** Return to the composite channel (Command-~) [Control-~] containing your background. Make a new layer (Layer 1). Load the text channel selection (Channel #5). Then choose Select➡Load Selection, and choose the bricks channel (#4). Be sure to check the Intersect with Selection option.

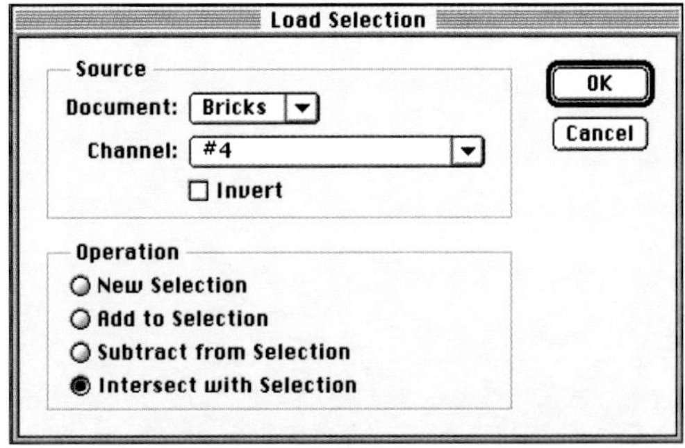


**6** Choose Select➡Feather (1 pixel). Choose a foreground color for the text, and press (Option-Delete) [Alt-Delete] to fill the text. To bring out more of the bricks lower the opacity of the new layer to 95%. Presto! Fresh paint without the mess.

**TIP** **If the paint is too faint, you didn't give the texture channel enough white in Step 3. If it's too saturated, you gave it too much.**

## Painting the Paint

If you want to paint this painted text, skip Steps 4 through 6. Instead, return to the composite channel (Command-~) [Control-~], make a new layer, and load the selection Channel #4. Choose Select➡Feather (1 pixel), and press (Command-H) [Control-H] to hide the selection edges. Lower the opacity of the new layer to around 95% before you begin painting. Choose a foreground color for the paint, and then choose the Airbrush tool (use a feathered brush with about 50% opacity). Now you can paint on the surface without completely obliterating it.

Any texture works.

## Underpainting

The Texturizer filter (formerly part of the Gallery Effects package) is now included with Photoshop 4.0. This filter contains four textures you can paint on. We used the burlap texture for this example.

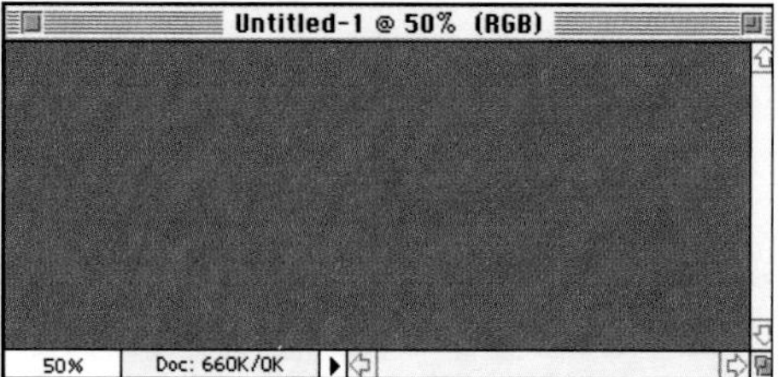


1 Create a new file and choose a foreground color for the burlap. Fill the image area with the foreground color.

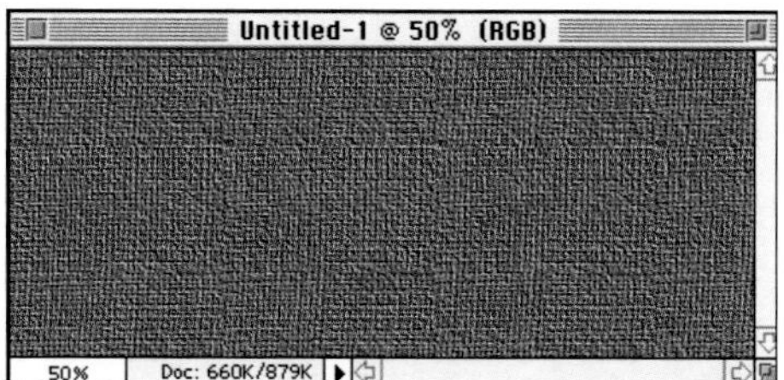


2 Choose Filter➥Texture➥Texturizer and choose Burlap from the Type pop-up menu. Set the scaling to 175% and the Relief to 10.

TIP **If you want to paint the text yourself using the Airbrush tool, skip Steps 3 and 4, create a new layer, paint the text, and the rest of us will meet you at Step 5.**

3 Create a new channel (Channel #4), and use the Type tool to enter the text into this channel. We used Brush Stroke Fast at 70 pts for this example.

4 Return to the composite channel (Command-~) [Control-~] containing the burlap background. Load the text selection Channel #4 and choose Select➥Feather (2 pixels). Choose a foreground color for the text, and press (Option-Delete) [Alt-Delete] to fill the text.

**5** Keep the text selection active, and reapply the Underpainting filter (Command-Option-F) [Control-Alt-F] to get the texture to show through. To exaggerate the texture, we applied the Texturizer filter again.

### Note Paper

We created a texture using the Note Paper filter for this example and used the painting method described earlier.

## Painting with Photographs

The same techniques already discussed can be used to "paint" text with a photograph. Here are three ways to do this.

**1** The first step is the same for all three. Open the file containing the photograph you want to paint with.

### Use the Type Tool to Enter the Type.

**2** Create a new channel (Channel #4), and use the Type tool to enter the text in the new channel. Choose Filter➥Blur➥Gaussian Blur (3 pixels) so the text has soft edges.

**3** Return to the composite channel (Command-~) [Control-~], and paste in an image for the background you will paint over, or fill the image area with a color.

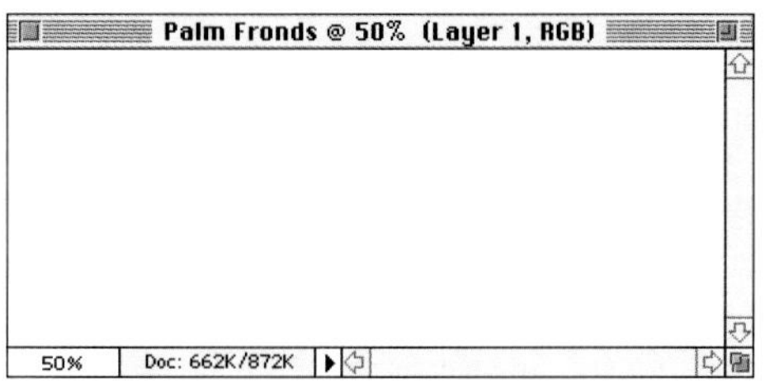

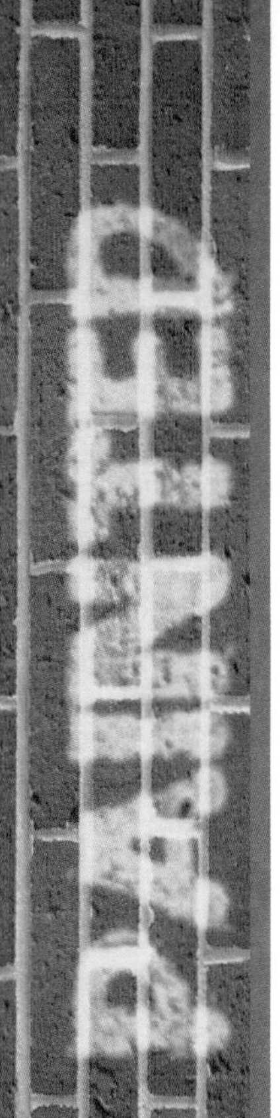

**4** Load the selection Channel #4. Press Delete to reveal the photograph.

### Use the Type Tool to Create Boundaries for Painting:

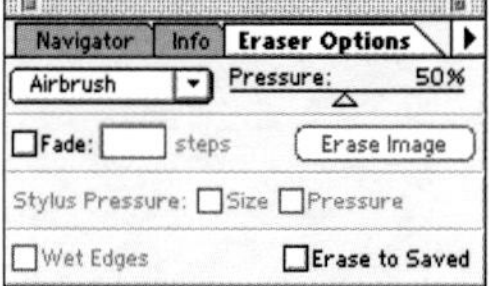


Do Steps 1 through 3. Double-click the Eraser tool to activate it and to open the Eraser Tool Options palette. Choose a soft brush and use the Airbrush option from the pop-up menu. (Use the Opacity slider to vary the intensity of the paint.) Load the text channel selection (Channel #4), and hide the selection edges (Command-H) [Control-H]. Start "painting" within the text. There is no need to be careful because although the selection is active, you can only affect the area within it.

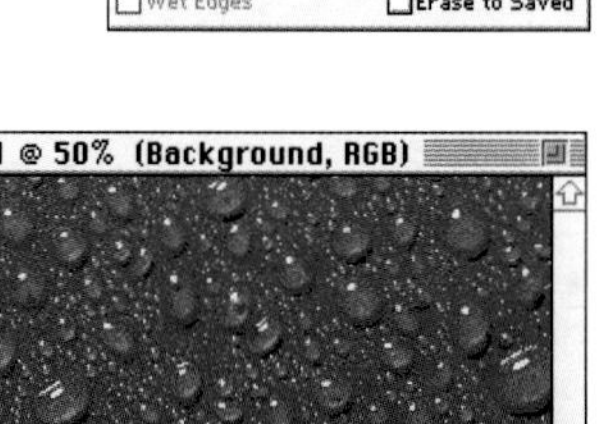


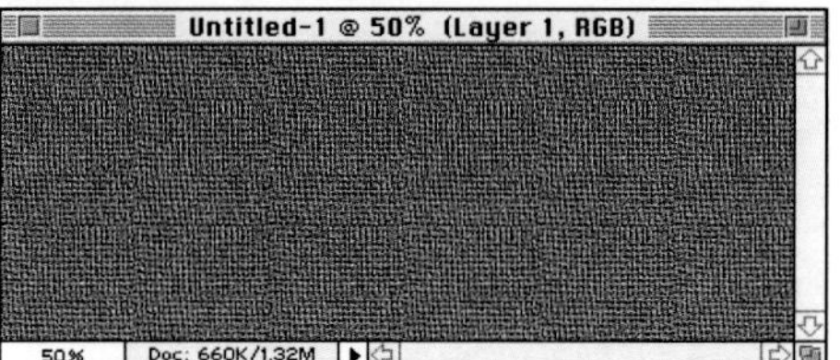

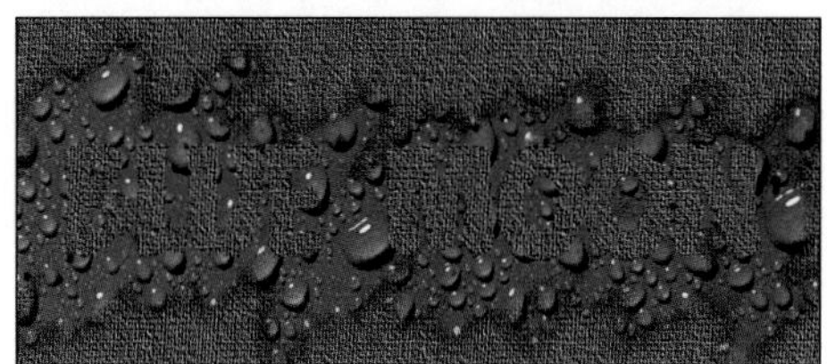

If you want to mask the type inside the brush strokes, choose Select➡Inverse after loading the text selection. Now you can only paint outside the text selection.

Try filling the top layer with white.

## Use the Airbrush Tool to Paint the Type

Do Steps 1 and 3 on page 151. Double-click the Eraser tool to activate it and to open the Eraser Tool Options palette. Choose the Airbrush option from the pop-up menu. We raised the opacity to around 75%. Now just click and paint.

## VARIATIONS

If you want to add texture to the painted photograph, copy the texture and paste it into a new channel (#4). Make sure there is plenty of white in this channel. Use the Levels (Command-L) [Control-L] dialog box if you need to add white. Return to the composite channel and make Layer 1 active. Load the selection Channel #4. Hide the edges of the selection (Command-H) [Control-H], and paint away with the Eraser tool. ■

Where can you find some really amazing patterns and textures? Just about everywhere! Check out the stock photo collections on the CD-ROM accompanying this book for some examples. There are also several commercial filters included that let you control the creation of your own textures and patterns—we've used them on the next few pages. After you create a pattern or texture you like, you can use it within your type, or even cut your type out of it. There's no limit to what you can do with these images and filters in Photoshop!

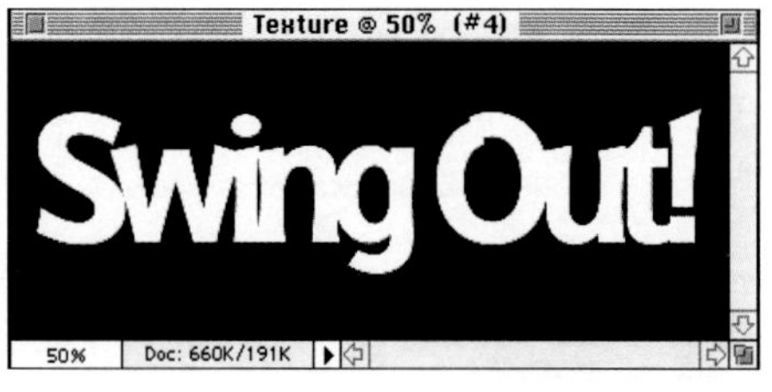


**1** Create a new file. Create a new channel (#4). Enter the text, using the Type tool. We used the font Badger at 92 points with spacing of –10 for this example.

**2** Open the pattern you want to fill the type with. Here we've used a custom pattern we call the Disco Frog Pattern. Select➡All and use Edit➡Define Pattern to make the entire picture into a pattern.

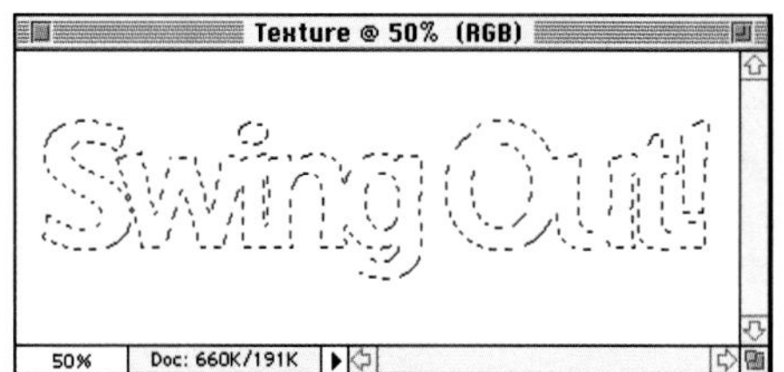


**3** Go back into your new file, return to the composite channel, and load the selection Channel #4. Your text should be selected.

## TOOLBOX

KPT 3 Gradient Designer

Adobe's TextureMaker (Mac only)

MicroFrontier's Pattern Workshop

Specular's TextureScape (Mac only)

Virtus' Alien Skin Textureshop (Mac only)

**4** Choose Edit➥Fill and use the settings of Pattern, 100%, and Normal. This fills your text with the pattern defined in Step 3.

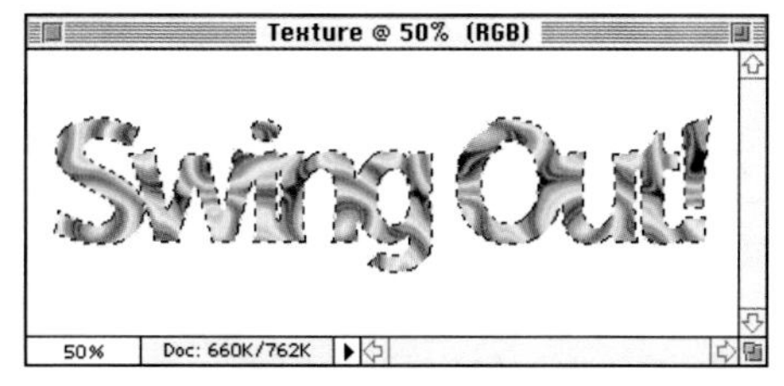


**5** If you want a border around your text, choose a foreground color. We chose an obnoxious red for this example. Use Edit➥Stroke... with a setting of 3 pixels, Outside, 100%, and Normal. This puts a stroke 3 pixels wide on the outside of your selection at 100% opacity.

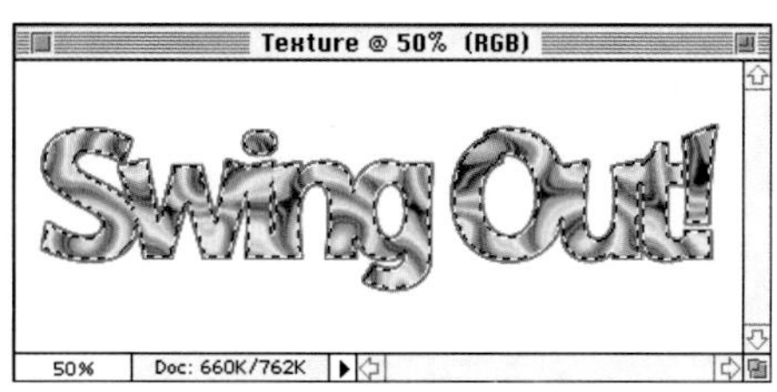


**6** To stroke on the inside of the text, choose a different foreground color. We used yellow here. Again, choose Edit➥Stroke..., but use settings of 2 pixels wide, Inside, 100%, and Normal. This puts a yellow line on the inside of your selection. Voilà!

## Variations

### Bubbles

To create a texture that looks like the Lawrence Welk bubble machine just exploded, try this variation. Apply Filter➥Xaos Tools➥Paint Alchemy and use the Bubbles Grid saved style.

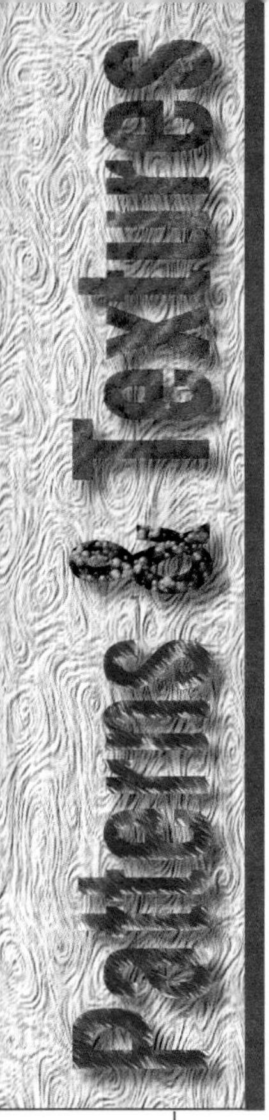


Swing Out!

## Just Plain Weird

To create really unusual textures, try Virtus' Alien Skin Textureshop. With this filter you can randomly mutate various parameters to different degrees. The results are truly wild!

To further "funkify" your text, try Filter➡Alien Skin➡Inner Bevel 2.0 along with Filter➡Alien Skin➡Glow 2.0.

Following are some filters and programs that help you create your own textures.

### TextureScape

TextureScape comes from Specular, the makers of Collage and Infini-D. This is a stand-alone application, rather than a plug-in. Its sole purpose is for creating textures and patterns...and it does so very well! If you can't find just the right texture on a stock photo CD-ROM, take a look at TextureScape!

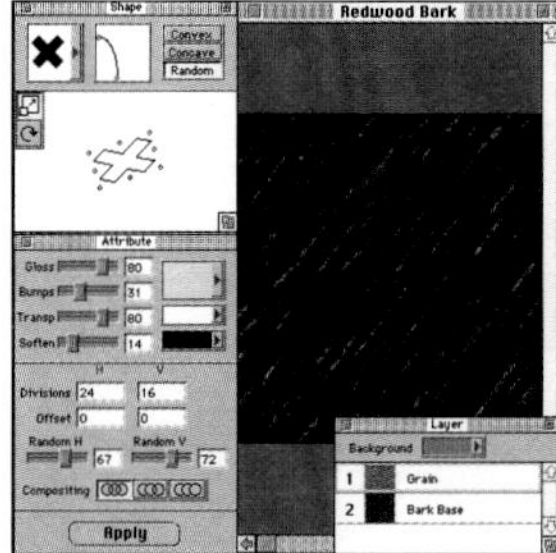

Here, TextureScape was used to render the bark pattern, which was then imported into Photoshop for editing.

## Kai's Power Tools

MetaTools offers several KPT 3 filters for creating textures. First, you could use the Gradient Designer for some pretty wild effects.

Texture Explorer is also one of the most useful tools for developing textures.

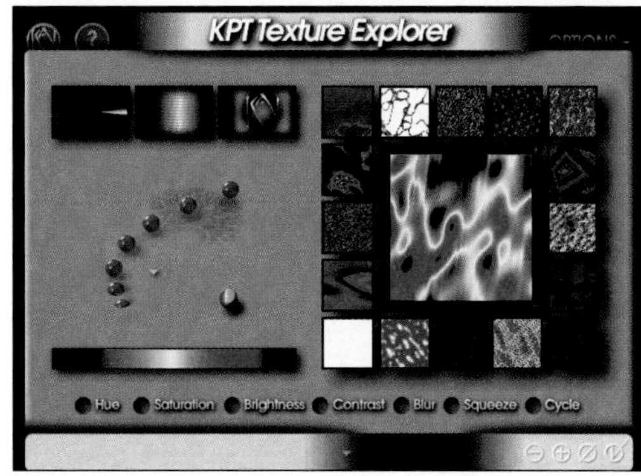


## Terrazzo

This commercial filter from Xaos Tools was specifically designed to make patterns. The super simple interface makes creating patterns a snap—you can even preview the patterns as you move your cursor around the image!

We started out with this stock photo from Digital Stock.

©Digital Stock 1995

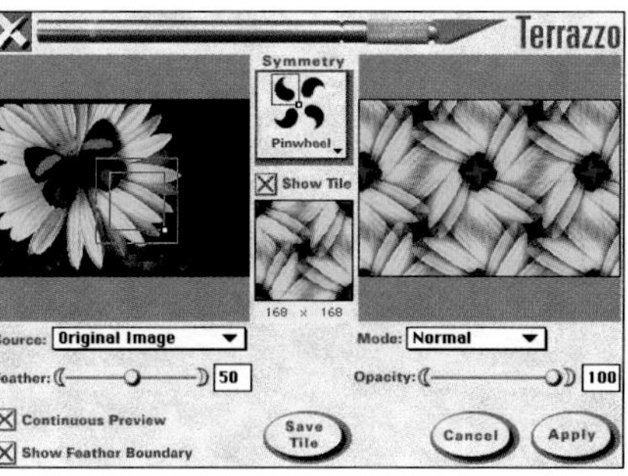


Dragging the tile around the image instantly updates the pattern preview.

By changing the symmetry, you can create all kinds of patterns.

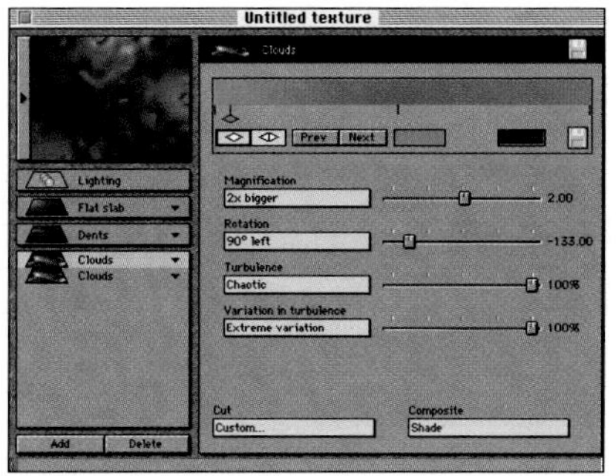


## Adobe TextureMaker

From the architects of Photoshop comes Adobe TextureMaker, another stand-alone program designed for creating custom textures. Being able to control several lighting effects is fantastic!

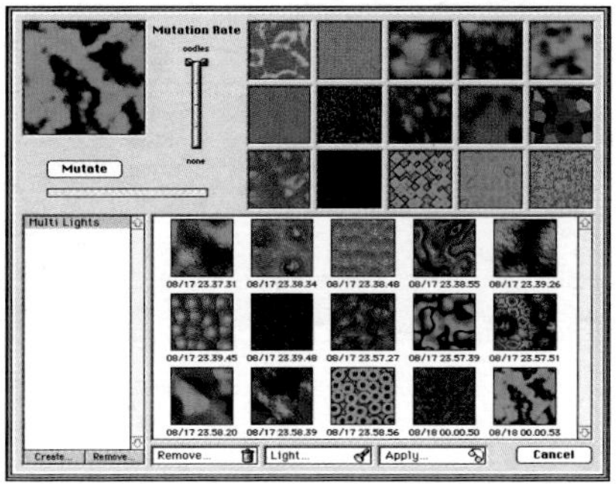


## Virtus Alien Skin Textureshop

This program has two flavors: a stand-alone application as well as a Photoshop plug-in. By working with the sliders under the Light ...and Apply...drawer, you can create some really exciting textures.

## MicroFrontier's Pattern Workshop

If you like instant gratification, this is the filter for you! Pattern Workshop lets you choose from a series of premade textures in its library. This is a great plug-in if you need a texture in a hurry.

It also comes with a companion filter that lets you edit the patterns. ■

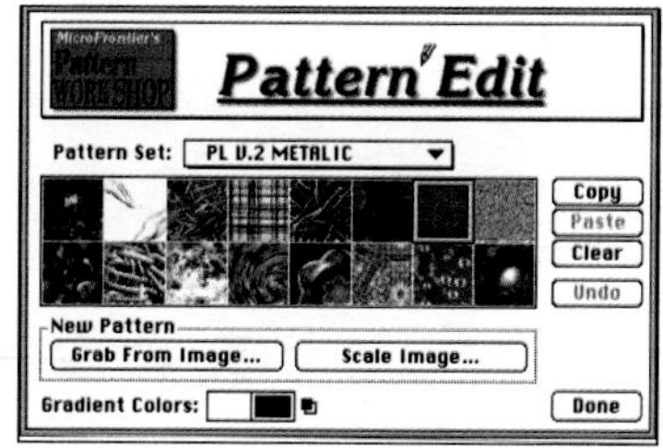

# Peel-Away



**TOOLBOX**

KPT 3 Page Curl

The KPT Page Curl 3.0 filter makes great curls, but it also has some limitations. The success of this technique is based almost entirely on making the right selections. So, this technique spends some time talking about selection tools. If you follow these tips, you can get the Page Curl filter to do great work for you.

**1** Create a new file, and use the Type tool to enter the text. We used Cheltenham Bold at 70 points for this example. Save the selection (Channel #4). You may not need the selection, but it's better to have it on hand just in case.

**2** The KPT Page Curl filter uses the foreground color as the color it places underneath the peel-away type. So choose as the foreground color a color for the surface. (Note: The color fills in the entire area within the selection and to the right of the curl.)

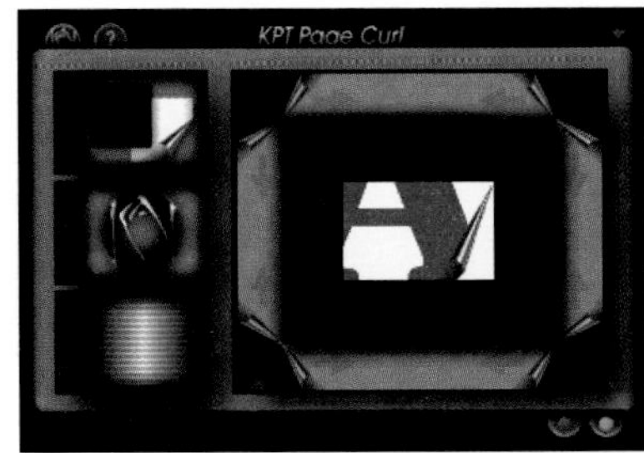


## The Easy Way

To use this filter you must first make a selection. In most cases, you want to make simple rectangular selections. Inside a rectangular selection, the KPT Page Curl filter peels the type away from the bottom right (unless you change the settings).

The angle of the top of the flap follows an imaginary line from the top-right corner to the bottom-left corner of the selection rectangle. This selection (made with the rectangular Marquee tool) yields this result after applying Filter➥KPT 3.0➥Page Curl 3.0.

This is not what you want because it looks like the background is peeling up, too. The top right corner needs to be on the right edge of the text, so make a selection such as this…

…to get this.

Now you can select the Paintbrush tool and paint over the leftover pieces of text.

This figure shows the selection we made for the P.

You could render the entire text with the method above (which is what we did to create this figure), but if you want more control, check out what we did next.

## More Control

To get more control you have to make some irregular selections. Use the rectangular Marquee tool to make this selection.

If you have a selection active and hold down the (Option) [Alt] key while making a second selection, the new selection area is subtracted from the active one. Select the Lasso tool. Start outside the active selection and cut into it along the contour of the text, like this.

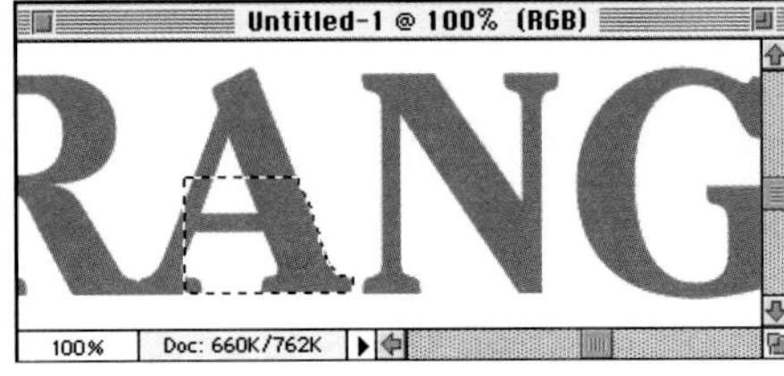

Now, apply Filter➡KPT 3.0➡Page Curl 3.0 to get this.

The only problem is the funny edge on the top of the curl. Press (Command-Z) [Control-Z] to undo the curl. Again hold down the (Option) [Alt] key, and draw a ring to clip off the corner of the selection, like this.

Apply Filter➡KPT 3.0➡Page Curl 3.0 again to get this.

If you took too much of the selection away and came up with this...

...you can hold down the Shift key instead of the Option key to add a new selection to the active selection to get this.

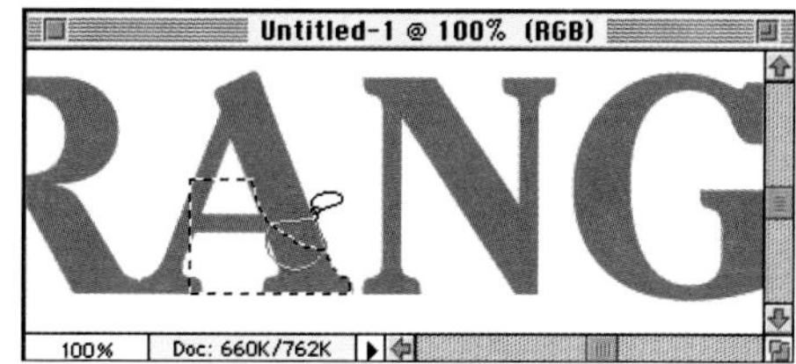


Then apply Filter➡KPT 3.0➡Page Curl 3.0 to get this.

TIP **If you want the tops of all the peels to come up to the same point, turn on the Rulers (Command-R) [Control-R] and pull down a guide from ruler at the top of the window to the point where the tops of your selections should be.**

ORANGES

So, build the type one curl at a time. First, make the selection, then apply Filter➥KPT 3.0➥Page Curl 3.0. It's really very simple after you get used to what the KPT Page Curl filter is going to do with your selection. You don't have to be satisfied with one peel per letter, either. Here is the final type.

## VARIATIONS

### Darken the Peel

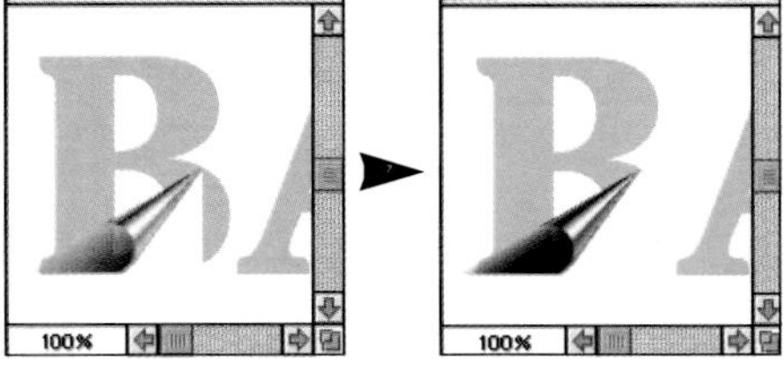


If you want to darken the curl and make it more opaque, then reapply the filter and adjust the opacity setting in the KPT Page Curl dialog box. You can get something to look like this.

### Torn Peels

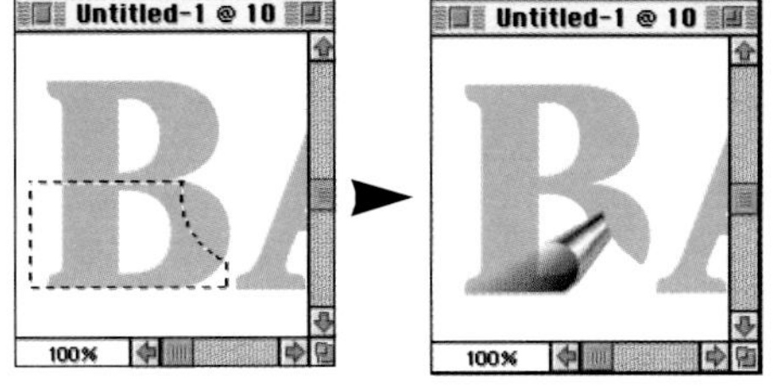


You can use the selection technique described in the previous section, "More Control," to make the text look like it's been torn. When you use the Lasso tool, cut further down into the text.

### More Peels

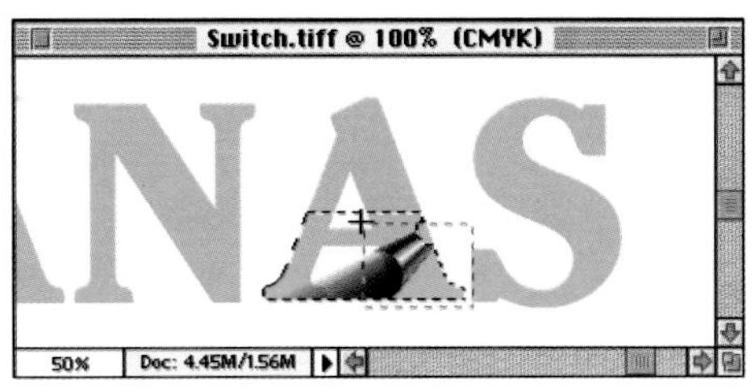


First, choose the same foreground color as the type color. Then, after applying the Page Curl filter, keep the selection active, and select the rectangular Marquee tool. Hold down the (Option) [Alt] and Shift keys while drawing a box starting from the lower-right and moving to the upper-left. Stop before you draw the box over the entire original selection.

Use the Lasso tool as described in "More Control" to subtract any parts of the selection, and apply Filter➥ KPT 3.0➥Page Curl 3.0. Before making the last peel, choose the same foreground color as the color of the image's background (white in this case).

## Switch Directions

If you want the text to peel up from another direction, just click and drag on the arrows in the KPT Page Curl filter to choose your direction.

## Color Underneath

If you want the Page Curl filter to insert a color under the areas of the letters that were lifted, first choose that color as the foreground color. Next, load the type selection Channel #4 (saved in Step 1). Then hold down the (Option) [Alt] and Shift keys and draw a selection with the Lasso tool around one of the letters. Now only that letter is selected. Use the Marquee tool as described in the "More Control" section to make the proper selection for the letter. You probably need to subtract the top half of the letter from the selection. In the case of a letter such as an A, you need to add to the selection the space between the legs of the A so the filter has some space to put the curl. ■

# Perspective

Photoshop's Layer➡Transform features can be used by themselves to quickly add dimension to your type, or they can be a useful aid in layering type onto preexisting surfaces.

**1** Here's the way the perspective feature works. Create a new file, and use the Type Mask tool to enter the text. We began with Cheltenham Bold at 50 points.

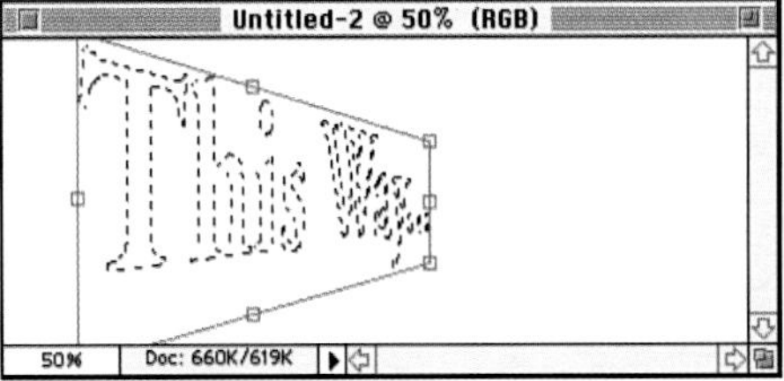


**2** While the text selection is still active, choose Layer➡Transform➡Perspective. A box appears around the type. You can use the square tabs on the corners of the box to reshape the box. When you move one of the tabs, another tab (the one that's along the same line as the direction of your movement) moves at the same rate and along the same line but in the opposite direction. It sounds a little confusing, but as soon as you try it you'll understand. The result is that the text is either compressed or expanded at one end, creating the illusion that it's receding in space.

**3** Press (Return) [Enter] key to set the text as you see it, or press Escape to cancel the perspective transformation. This is what you end up with if you press (Return) [Enter] and then fill the selection with purple.

**4** You can have the perspective move in any direction you want.

## Placing Text On a Receding Surface

**1** We opened a stock photo of a mailbox from CMCD for this example. Using the perspective feature helped put Santa's name on the box.

©CMCD 1995

**2** Use the Type tool to enter the text (15-point Cheltenham Bold). Remember, font size is important to make this look authentic. Also, we used the Eyedropper tool to select a color for the type from the mailbox flag. The type is on a new layer (Layer 1). This enables us to make changes to the type without affecting the background image of the mailbox.

**3** The quickest way to lay type on a flat, receding surface such as this mailbox is not to use the Perspective feature, but rather the Skew feature. Position the type so that the first letter is in place, as in the previous figure, then choose Layer➥Transform➥Skew. A box appears identical to the box used in the Perspective feature.

**4** If you move one of the corner tabs, the tab you move toward moves away in the same direction, creating a parallelogram. After you release the tab for the first time, however, the tabs act independently of all the others. So, first we grabbed the tab on the upper right and moved it upward until the top line of the Skew box was in line with the lines near it on the mailbox.

**5** Then we moved the lower-right tab upward to compress the text and make it appear as if it was receding. Press (Return) [Enter] when you're finished.

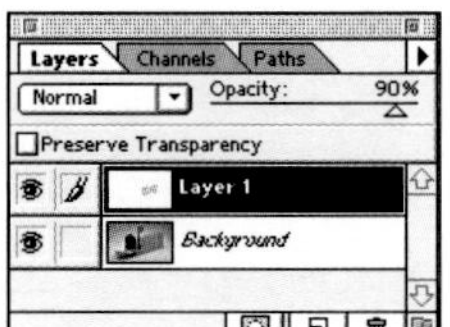


**6** The next two steps help blend the text into the side of the mailbox. First, find the Opacity slider on the Layers palette and lower the opacity in Layer 1 (the type layer) to 90% to allow some of the mailbox to blend with the colored type.

**7** Next, create a layer mask for Layer 1. In the layer mask, choose Filter➡Noise➡Add Noise (Uniform). Before pressing Return you can watch the type in the image window change as you adjust the noise Amount, which we set at 80. Click OK, flatten the image, and you're finished.

## VARIATIONS

The perspective feature was used to create this type, before adding the drop shadow. See page 199 to find out how to create the shadow.

■

# Pillow

Here is a soft 3-D look with a crimp around the edges.

**1** Open a new file, and create a new channel (#4). Choose black as the foreground color and white as the background color. Use the Type Mask tool to enter the text in the new channel. We used Futura Bold at 100 points in this example.

**2** We began with a typeface that had hard edges, so we chose Select➡Modify➡Smooth (5 pixels) to round the edges. If you choose a nice rounded typeface to begin with, you can skip this step.

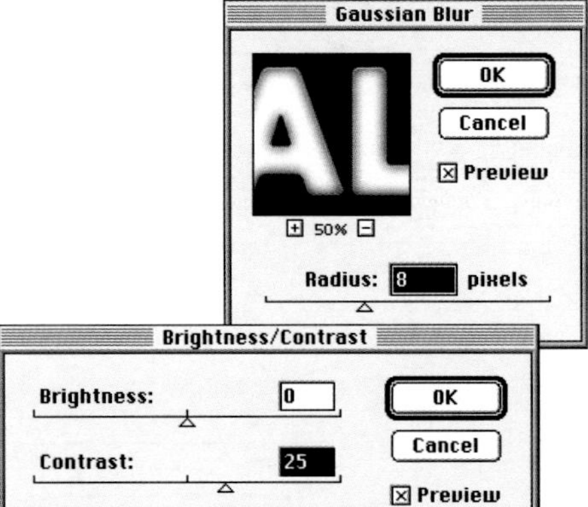

**3** Press X to switch the foreground and background colors. Choose Edit➡Stroke (2 pixels, Outside, 50% Opacity, Normal). Press (Option-Delete) [Alt-Delete] to fill the selection with white.

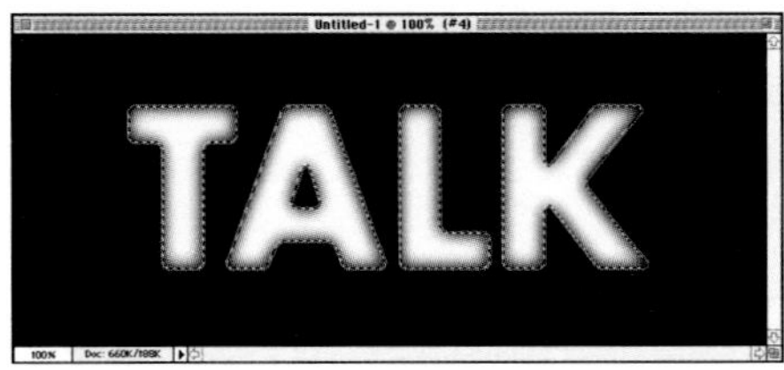

**4** Choose Filter➡Blur➡Gaussian Blur. The amount depends on the thickness of your text. We chose 8 pixels. Then choose Image➡Adjust➡Brightness/Contrast and raise the contrast until you see some black move in around the edges. We raised the contrast to 25.

**5** Choose Image➡Adjust➡Levels (Command-L) [Control-L], and slide the Output Levels right (white) slider to the left until the box above it reads about 200.

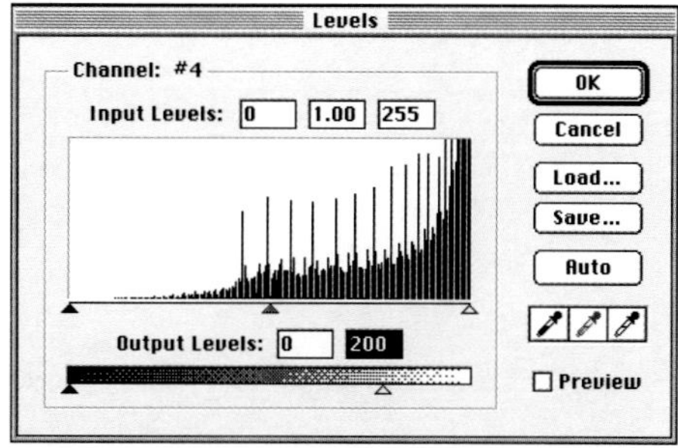


**6** Now, to fluff the pillow. Choose Filter➡Stylize➡Find Edges. If the text is too contrasty after applying the Find Edges filter, then you probably raised the contrast too high in Step 4. You can use the Levels dialog box (Image➡Adjust➡Levels) to adjust the values in the text.

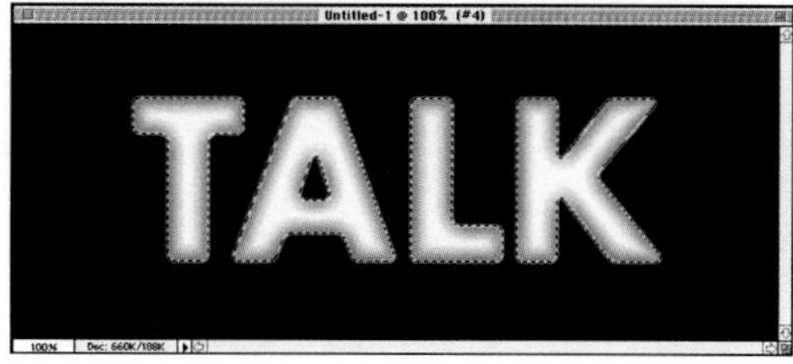


**7** Return to the composite channel (Command-~) [Control-~]. We filled the background with black to get the shiny text to stand out. Load the selection Channel #4.

**8** Choose the foreground color for the text. Press (Option-Delete) [Alt-Delete] to fill the text.

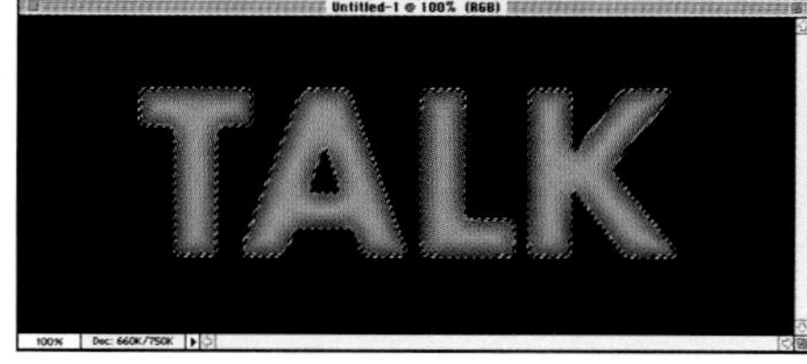

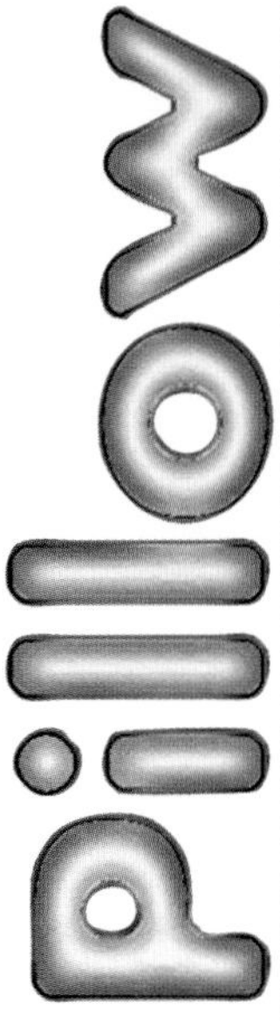

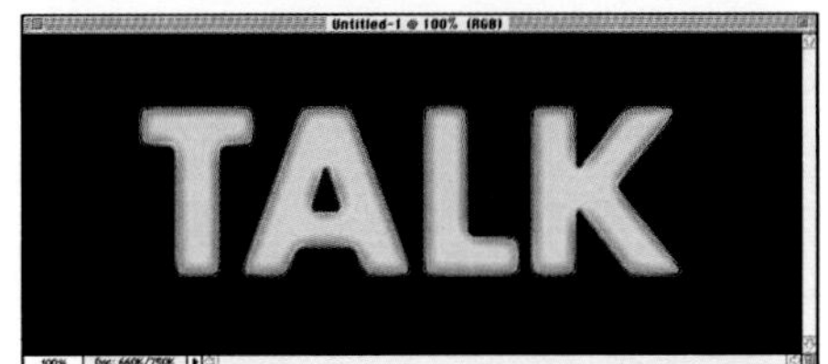


**9** You may think the text looks a little dull. Choose Image➥Adjust➥ Variations and use the previews to monitor your alterations.

Then choose Image➥Adjust➥ Brightness/Contrast and bump the contrast up again to 25. You may need to experiment with the settings. You could also fill the text twice by pressing (Option-Delete) [Alt-Delete] a second time in Step 8.

TIP **Don't forget that hiding the active selection gives you a better, unobstructed view of what your text really looks like. Press (Command-H) [Control-H] to hide the selection marching ants, and press it a second time to make them reappear.**

## Variations

To add a slight glow and softness to the text, after Step 9, with the selection still active, choose Edit➥Stroke (2 pixels, outside, 50% opacity, normal).

To add some texture to the text, choose Filter➥Stylize➥Wind (Wind, Left). Then apply the same filter (Command-Option-F) [Control-Alt-F], but change the settings to Wind and Right.

For this variation, we created a new layer and loaded the selection Channel #4 and pasted a colorful image into the selection. Then we chose Color from the blending mode pop-up menu. ■

This task takes advantage of Photoshop's Lighting Effects filter. Included on the CD-ROM is a lighting styles file that contains the presets for this effect. If you want to use this preset file, consult Appendix A, "What's On the CD-ROM," to find out where to put it on your hard drive.

**1** Create a new RGB file. (It must be an RGB file in order for the Lighting Effects filter to work.) Create a new channel. Change the foreground color to black and the background color to white. Use the Type Mask tool to enter your text. We used OCR-B at 50 points in this example.

**2** If you want to give your text some smoother corners choose Select➡Modify➡Smooth (3 pixels).

**3** Fill the text with white by pressing Delete. Deselect the text (Command-D) [Control-D]. Choose Filter➡Blur➡Gaussian Blur (3.5 pixels).

**TOOLBOX**

PlasticLightStyles file

**4** Load the selection of the same channel you are working in (Channel #4). Choose Filter➡ Blur➡ Gaussian Blur. Blur the text until you get something resembling what you see in this figure. You should be able to see highlights and dark areas. Deselect the text (Command-D) [Control-D].

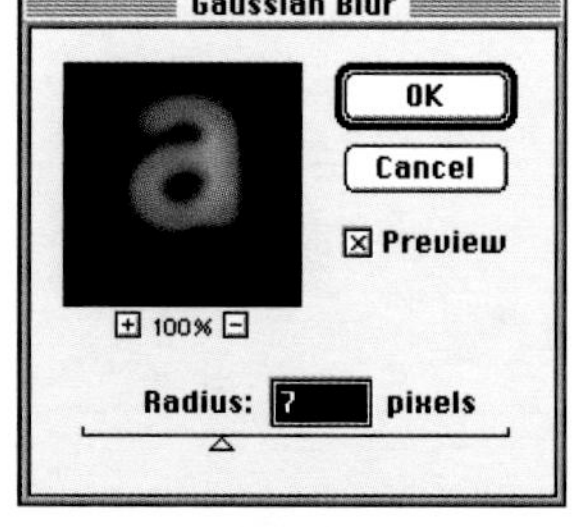

**5** Return to the RGB window (Command-~) [Control-~]. Select a foreground color near the complement of the color you want the text to be. We used a blue for the red-orange text we wanted to make. Fill the image with this color (Option-Delete) [Alt-Delete].

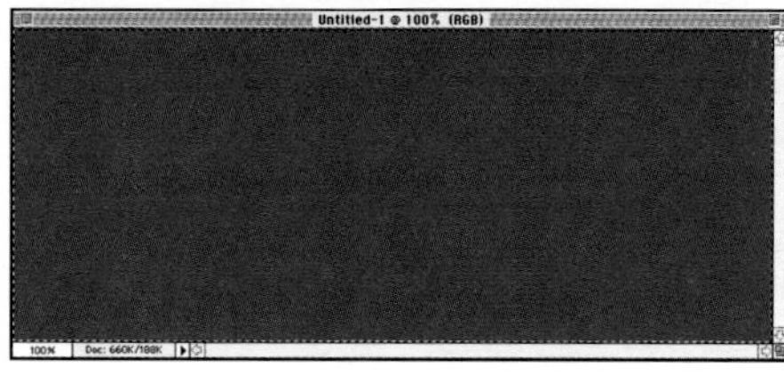

**6** Choose Filter➡Render➡Lighting Effects, and choose PlasticLight-Styles from the pop-up menu or match the settings seen in this figure. The circular ring surrounding the light source should encompass your text. Click and hold on one of its handles and drag to resize it.

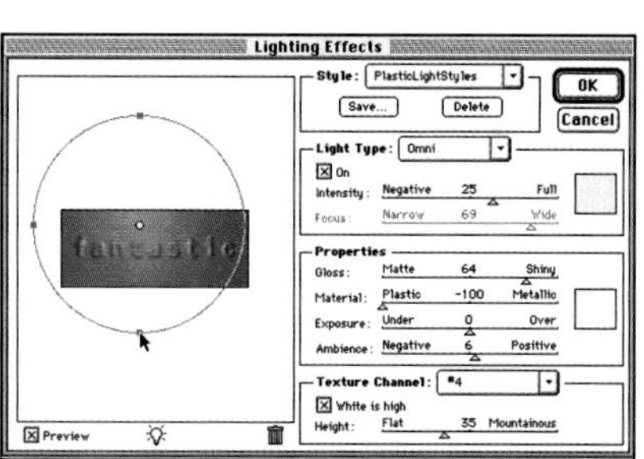

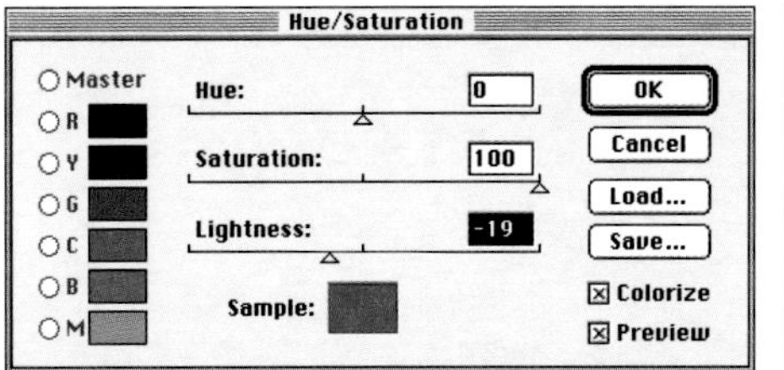


**7** Load the same selection you did in Step 4 (Channel #4). Choose Image➥Adjust➥Hue/Saturation (Command-U) [Control-U], click the Colorize checkbox, and use the Hue slider to choose the color of your text. We also slid the Lightness slider to –19. Depending on your color choices you also might want to lower the Saturation.

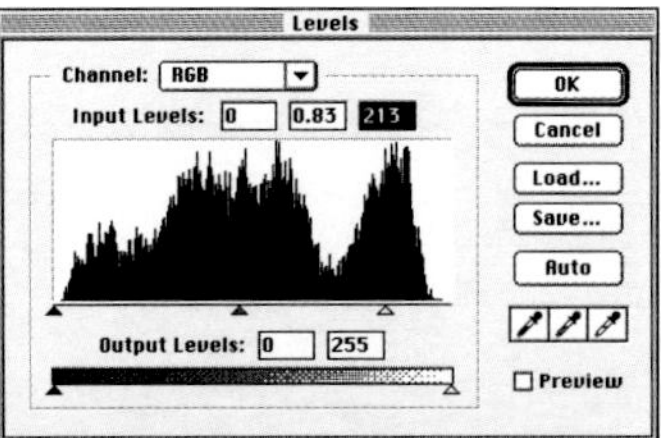


**8** You might also want to open the Levels dialog box now (Command-L) [Control-L] and adjust the Input Levels to fine tune the plastic. Moving the right (white) and middle (gray) sliders to the left helps brighten the image.

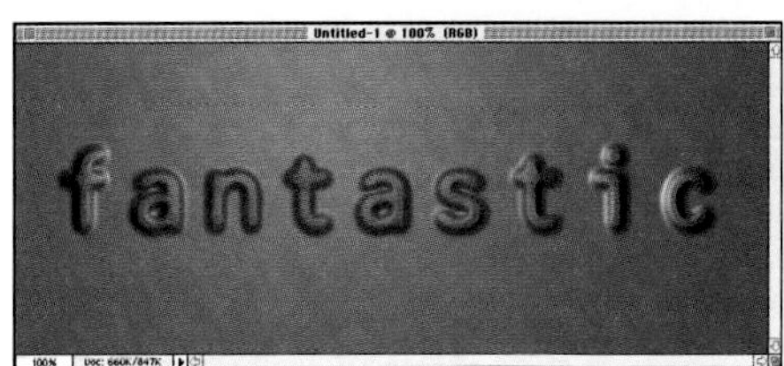

**To select the letters without the background, load the selection Channel #4. Choose Select➥Modify➥Expand. The amount depends upon the typeface you are using. We used 6 pixels in this example.**

## Variations

To bring out more ridges in the plastic (like you see in the "Plastic" thumb tab), before deselecting the text in Step 4, choose Image➥ Adjust➥Brightness/Contrast, and try these settings: Brightness –33, Contrast +13. You are trying to bring out some light and dark areas within the text selection. Continue with the rest of the steps above. We also increased the saturation as a final step.

For a quick embossed plastic, you can skip Step 4 and stop after Step 6. We opened a stock photo from Digital Stock for this example and also skipped everything in Step 5, except returning to the composite channel.

© Digital Stock 1995

The Chrome section contains a variation that uses the steps above to create a chrome look like this. See page 48 for details on creating Chrome type. ■

# Pop-Up

©Photo 24 1995

This type effect is great for making your type look as though it pops out of the background. It's a really quick and dirty technique!

**1** Create a new file or open up an existing image. We used a stock photo from Photo 24 (cropped, obviously) from the CD.

**2** Create a new layer (Layer 1) for the text. Use the Type Mask tool to enter the text. Be sure that you're in the text layer (Layer 1), not the background layer. We used the font Hobo at 100 points for this example.

**3** Save the selection (#4).

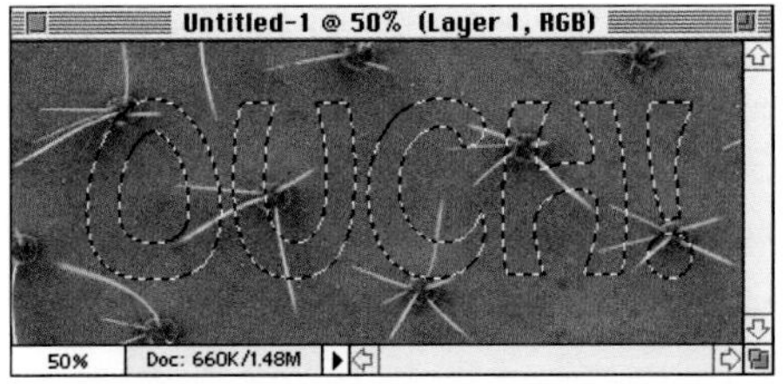


**4** Select➡Feather and use a setting of 3 pixels. Change the foreground color to black. Change to the Gradient tool and set the options to Transparent to Foreground, Linear, and 100% opacity. Drag the Gradient tool, top to bottom, about [1/3] of the way down the selection. You should get something such as this.

**5** Now load the saved selection (#4). Using the Marquee tool, move the selection up and to the right with the arrow keys until there's a thin line of black on the bottom and left sides of the selection.

**6** Press Delete to remove what's in the selection and Select➥None. If you need to reposition the shadow, simply use the Move tool. The underlying background is not affected.

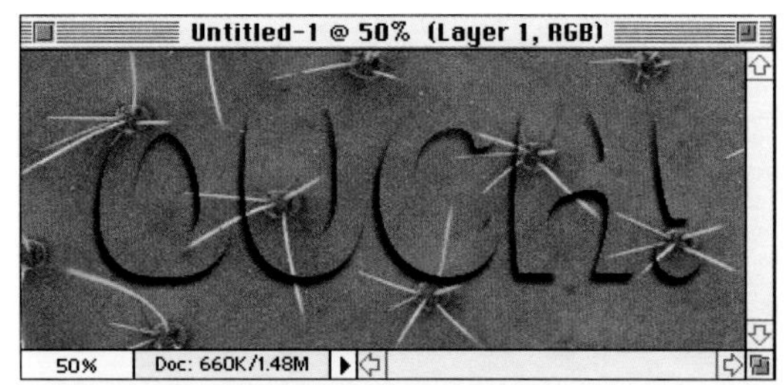


To make the text look like it's popping up even more, after Step 4, use the Layer➥Transform➥Skew command and skew the shadow's bottom to the left. Continue with Step 5. ■

©Digital Stock 1995

**1** Open the file containing the image onto which you want to reflect your type.

**2** Use the Type tool to enter the text. The text is placed on a new layer (Layer 1). Move the type into position with the Move tool (press V, and then use the arrow keys).

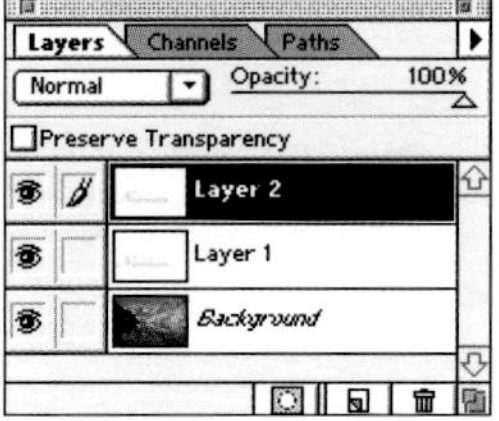


**3** Click the text layer (Layer 1) and drag it to the New Layer icon in the Layers palette. This creates a new layer (Layer 2) for the reflection.

**4** Choose Select➡All (Command-A) [Control-A]. Choose Layer➡Transform➡Flip Vertical, then drag the flipped type down (while holding the Shift key to make sure it moves straight down) until the bottoms of the letters touch each other.

**TOOLBOX**

Andromeda's Reflection filter

**5** Choose Layer➥Transform➥Scale and pull the bottom of the scale box up to squeeze the text vertically. Press Return to set the scaling. Load the reflection layer's transparency selection and save this selection (Channel #4), then deselect the type (Command-D) [Control-D].

**6** On the Layers palette, slide the Opacity down to around 45%. This number varies depending on how dark your text is and how dark the surface is. It's that simple to make the reflection. The rest of the steps are for fine tuning.

TIP **You may find that switching to either Soft Light mode or Overlay mode works better for your text. If you do switch to one of these modes, keep the Opacity higher.**

**7** Choose Layer➥Add Layer Mask➥Reveal All. The Layers palette should now look like this.

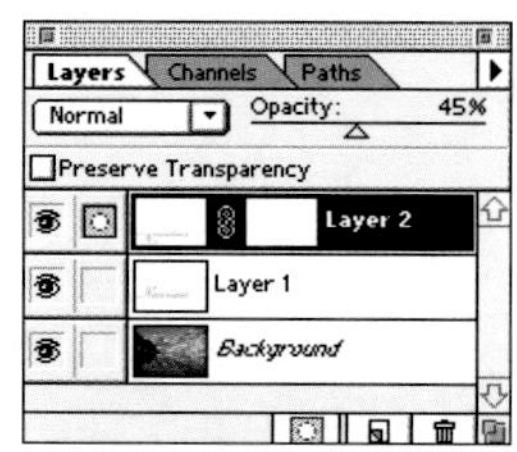


**8** Now use the rectangular Marquee tool to select the reflected type and a small area around it.

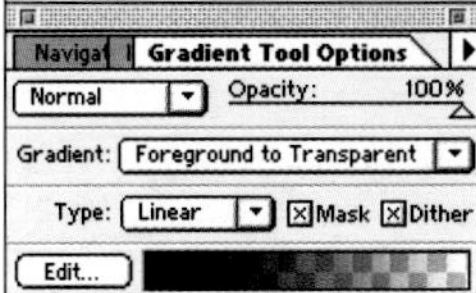


**9** Double-click the Gradient tool to select it and to open the Gradient Tool Options palette. Choose the Foreground to Transparent option from the style pop-up menu. The gradient Type should be set to Linear. Choose black as the foreground color (press D then X).

**10** After you make the gradient, the bottom of the reflection fades into the surface. Click near the bottom of the rectangular selection and drag toward the top, about two thirds the height of the word. You should now see something like this.

Layers Channels Paths
Normal
Opacity: 45%
Preserve Transparency
Layer 2
Layer 1
Background

New Layer...
New Adjustment Layer...
Duplicate Layer...
Delete Layer
Layer Options...
Merge Down
Merge Visible
Flatten Image
Palette Options...

**11** Make Layer 2 active. Now, choose New Layer from the Layers palette menu and keep the selection active.

**12** Make sure the foreground color is set to black (or another dark color). Use the Gradient tool with the same options as you set up in Step 9. Click near the middle of the original text and drag (while holding the Shift key) a short way into the reflected text to create a shadow.

**13** To distort the text, because ours was underwater, we hid all layers except Layers 2 and 3 and chose Merge Visible from the Layers palette menu. After the layers were merged, only Layer 2 remained, with a Blending mode of Normal (rather than the Soft Light or Overlay mode you may have changed it to after Step 6).

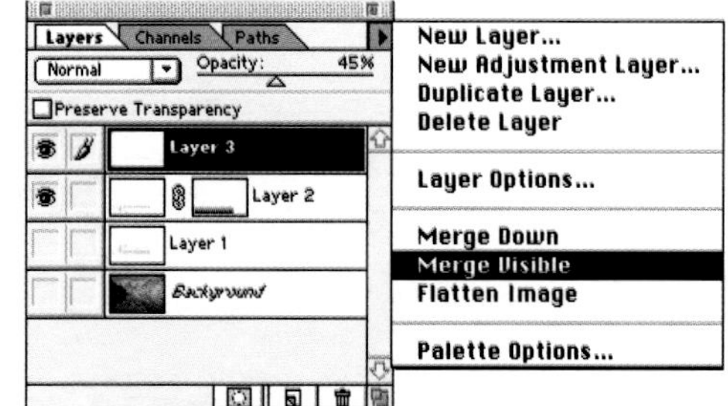


**14** With the rectangular selection around the reflected type still active, apply Filter➥Distort➥Ripple (100, Large) to supply the final touch.

## VARIATIONS

Andromeda's filters contain a Reflection filter that makes reflections much easier, but only in certain situations because the area surrounding the type is also reflected. (If you select the type only, then the filter has no area in which to place the reflection.) The Filter➥Andromeda➥Reflection dialog box enables you to control 5 characteristics of the reflected type, and gives you a preview.

Wonderland

This checkerboard stock photo from Fotosets already had a slight reflection. We added the type (from the Chrome section, see page 48) and made its reflection match the already existing one. ■

Background: © Fotosets 1995

There are countless Photoshop and third-party filters that can be used by themselves or in combinations to add rough edges to your text. The following pages contain demonstrations of what some of the third-party filters can do. But first, here are a few combinations we came up with by using only Photoshop's built-in set of filters.

## Set-Up

Create a new file, and use the Type tool to enter the text. You could also use any type that you rendered with another technique and want to embellish. This type is Frutiger Bold at 45 points.

## Photoshop Filters

Mosaic

Apply Filter➥Distort➥Ripple (100, Large), then apply Filter➥Distort➥ Ripple (500, Small).

Mosaic

Apply Filter➥Pixelate➥Mosaic (6 pixels).

Mosaic

Apply Filter➥Pixelate➥Fragment.

Mosaic

Apply Filter➥Pixelate➥Fragment, then Filter➥Distort➥Ripple (100, Medium).



**TOOLBOX**

Xaos Tools' Paint Alchemy (Mac only)

Apply Filter➥Pixelate➥Fragment, Filter➥Distort➥Ripple (100, Medium), and Filter➥Stylize➥Find Edges.

Apply Filter➥Pixelate➥Mosaic (6 pixels), Filter➥Stylize➥Find Edges, and Image➥Adjust➥ Threshold (255).

Apply Filter➥Distort➥Ripple (300, Medium), and Image➥Adjust➥ Brightness/Contrast (Contrast: +50).

Apply Filter➥Distort➥Wave (Type: Triangle; 1 generator; Wavelength: 2, 40; Amplitude: 10, 10; Scale: 100, 100; Wrap Around).

Apply Filter➥Distort➥Wave (Type: Square; 1 generator; Wavelength: 2, 20; Amplitude: 10, 10; Scale: 50, 50; Wrap Around), and Filter➥ Distort➥ Ripple (200, medium).

## Displace Filter

Inside the Adobe Photoshop➥ Plug-ins folder is a folder named Displacement Maps. In this folder, Adobe has supplied some ready-made displacement maps. Test them all if you have the time, or consult your Photoshop manual to see how you can make your own.

Deselect the text (Command-D) [Control-D], and apply Filter➥ Distort➥Displace (Horiz.: 7, Vert.: 7, Tile, Repeat Edge Pixels).

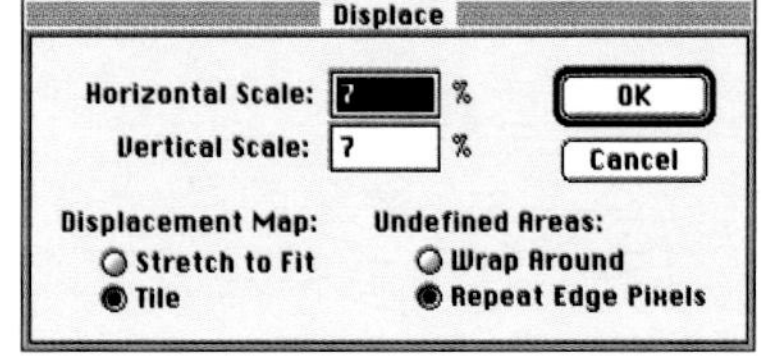

Mosaic

A dialog box appears and asks you to find a displacement map. Find the Displacement Maps folder mentioned above. We chose the Crumbles file for this example. You can use the same technique to create all the type variations on this page.

In the Displace dialog box, we entered 10 for both the Horizontal and Vertical settings, and switched to the Stretch to Fit option. Then we chose the Mezzo effect displacement map.

Mosaic

To the last figure we applied Filter➥Stylize➥Diffuse (Darken) three times for this result.

Mosaic

The Horizontal and Vertical settings were both set to 7 (Stretch to Fit), and we used the Rectangular tiles (10%) displacement map.

Mosaic

We (Command-clicked) [Control-clicked] the new type layer in the Layers palette to select the type. Then we changed the Horizontal and Vertical settings in the Displace dialog both to 5. Finally, we used the Schnable Effect displacement map.

Photoshop 4 comes with a set of filters full of features to help you roughen the edges of the text. These used to be called Aldus's Gallery Effects filters.

Here is the Spatter in action.

Here is Ripple.

Rough Pastels with Canvas chosen as the texture.

Water Paper and some hairy extensions.

A slight fuzz provided by Conte Crayon.

## Paint Alchemy

Xaos Tools' Paint Alchemy is a perfect Photoshop plug-in for roughening the edges of text. There is a working version of Paint Alchemy 1.0 on the CD-ROM, and a demo version of Paint Alchemy 2.0. We used version 1.0 to create these type treatments. Here is what the interface for Paint Alchemy 1.0 looks like.

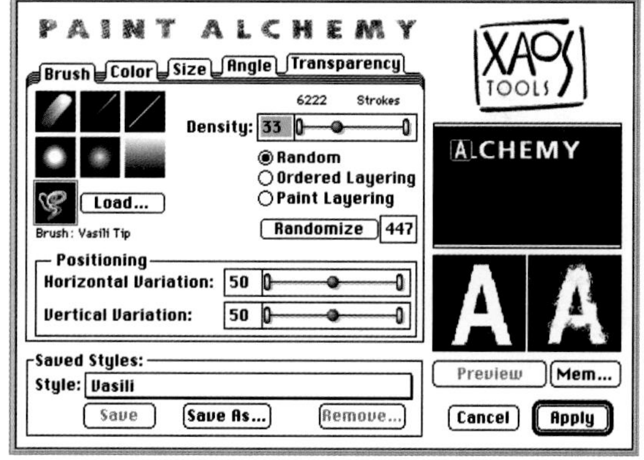

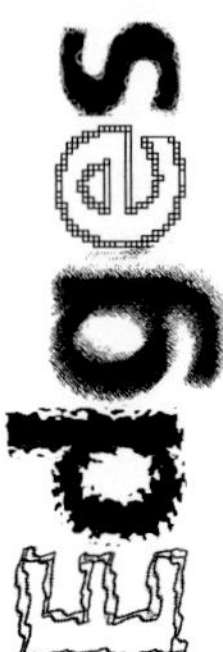


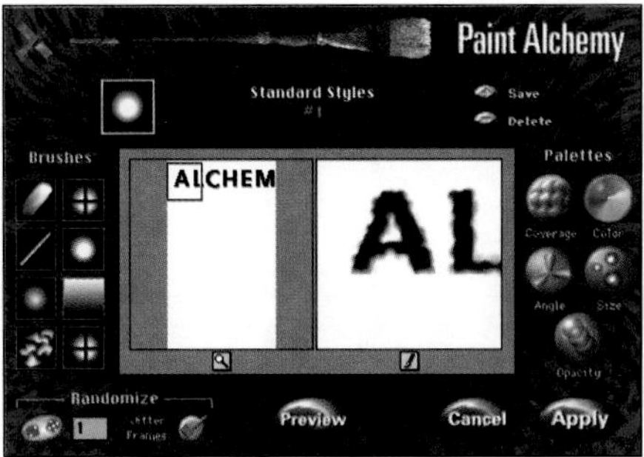


And this is the Paint Alchemy 2.0 interface:

Use the Type tool to enter the text, then deselect it (Command-D) [Control-D], and choose Filter➥ Xaos Tools➥Paint Alchemy 1.0 (or Paint Alchemy 2.0). Your options in this interface are endless. If you use the preset styles, you probably need to make adjustments so that only the edges of your text are affected. After you find an effect you like, click the Randomize button then the Preview button to see variations of the same settings. Here are some treatments we discovered.

Mosaic

For this one, we chose the preset Vasili from the Abstract Styles submenu in the Paint Alchemy dialog, then adjusted the settings to affect only the edges.

Mosaic

This one began with the Cotton Ball preset from the Misc. Styles submenu in the Paint Alchemy dialog.

To create this one we started with the Pointillist preset from the Misc. Styles submenu in the Paint Alchemy dialog box. Then we used Image➥Adjust➥Brightness/Contrast to increase the contrast.

For the last one here we began with the Screen Mosaic preset from the Misc. Styles submenu in the Paint Alchemy dialog box. ■

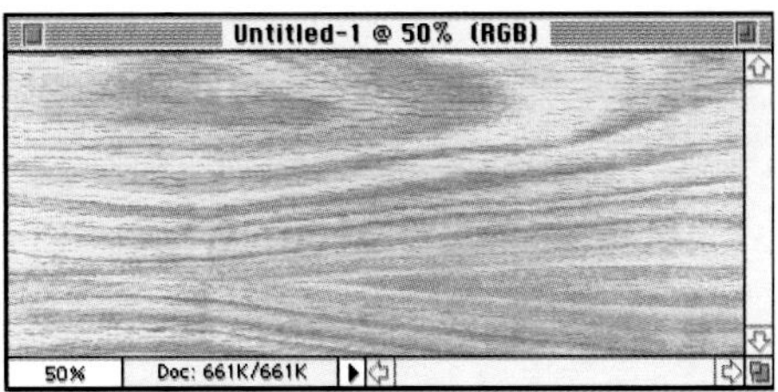


**1** Create a new file or open an existing image. We opened a stock photo from D'Pix to use as our background. Create a new channel (Channel #4) and choose white as the foreground color. Press (Option-Delete) [Alt-Delete] to fill the image area with white.

**2** Using the Type Mask tool, enter the text in the new channel. We used Stencil at 50 points.

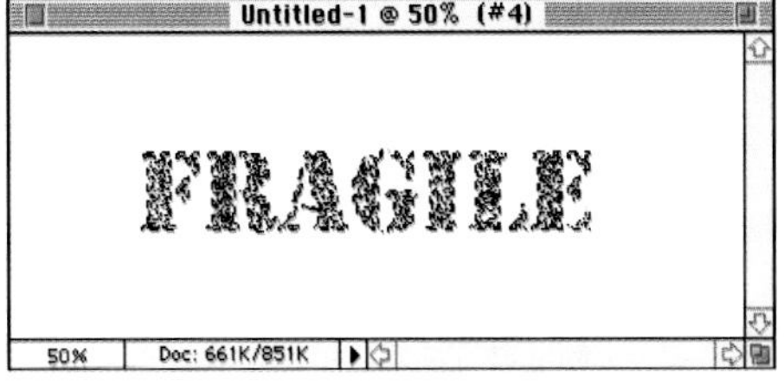


**3** While the selection is still active choose Filter➡Noise➡Add Noise (999, Gaussian, Monochromatic).

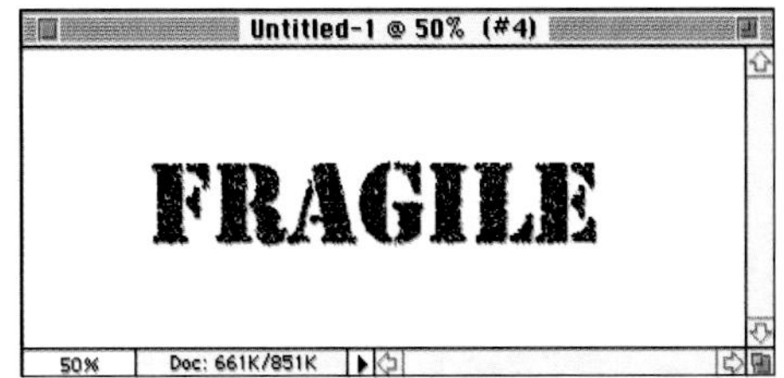


**4** Now apply Filter➡Stylize➡ Diffuse (Darken Only). Choose Select➡None and reapply the diffuse filter (Command-F) [Control-F].

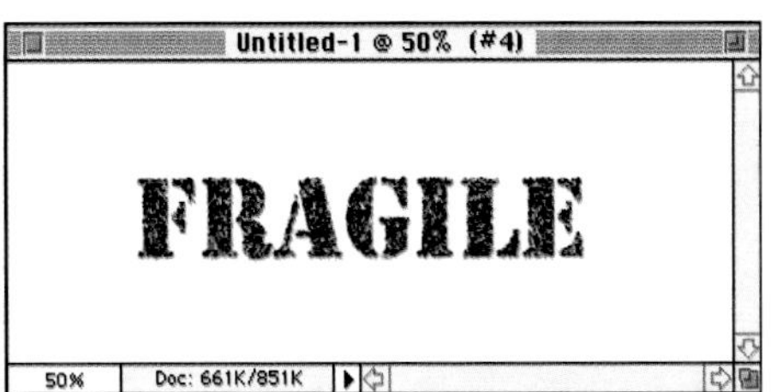


**5** Apply Filter➡Blur➡Blur, then choose Image➡Adjust➡ Levels (Input Levels settings: 0, 2.05, 239).

**TOOLBOX**

Rubber Stamp curve file

**6** Now choose Image➡Adjust➡Curves (Command-M) [Control-M]. Click the Load button and find the Rubber Stamp curve, or bend the curve up just like you see it here. Press (Command-I) [Control-I] to invert the channel.

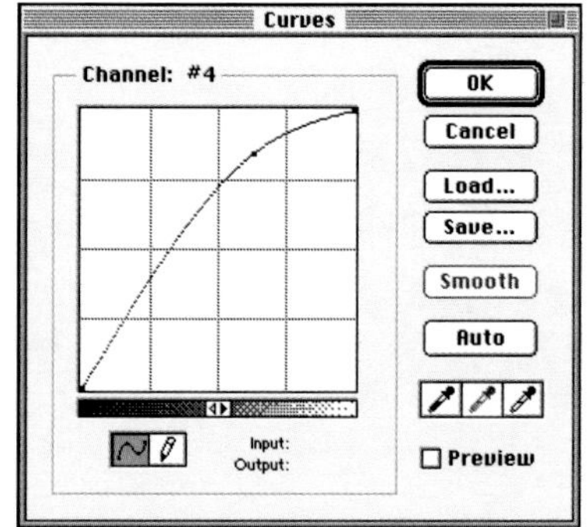

**7** Return to the composite channel and load the selection Channel #4. Choose red as the foreground color and press (Option-Delete) [Alt-Delete] to fill the selection. Fill it a second time for stronger ink. You can experiment with the Opacity slider for a more realistic effect.

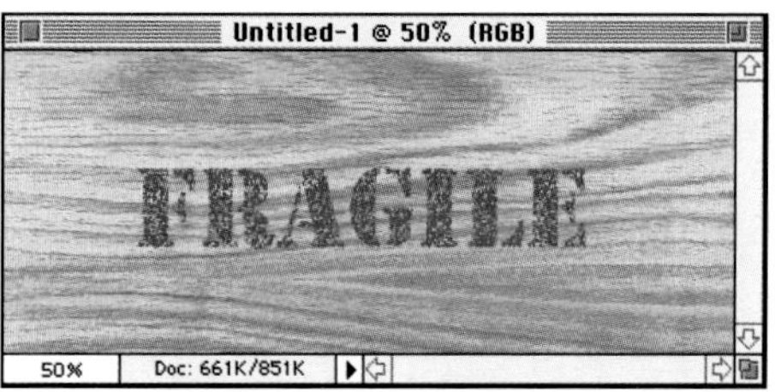


**8** Now deselect the text (Command-D) [Control-D], rotate the type selection (Layer➡Transform➡Rotate), and it's ready to ship.

## VARIATIONS

Here's another ink-stamped effect, that is more heavily stamped as if someone had used too much ink on the pad. Complete all the preceding steps, with these exceptions:

**4** Skip this step.

**5** After blurring the text, choose Filter➥Noise➥Median (3 pixels). Finish this step, and all the others, too.

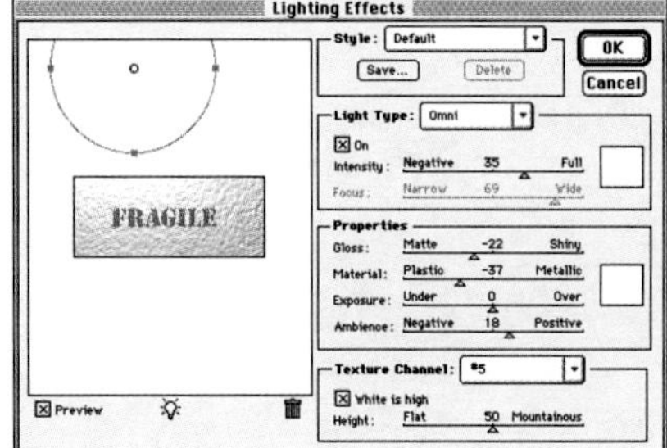


To incorporate a paper texture with the ink, we first built the text (using all the steps except Step 8) in a new file. Then we applied the Note Paper filter (Filter➥Sketch➥Note Paper) to an empty white channel (#5), returned to the composite channel, and chose Filter➥Render➥Lighting Effects. We chose the Note Paper channel (Channel #5 for us) as the Texture Channel and set the Height to 50. We used a white Omni light and moved it far enough away that it wouldn't shine too harshly on the paper surface.

Now see what happens when you apply the Note Paper filter to the final image with these settings: Image Balance: 25; Graininess: 10; Relief: 13. ■

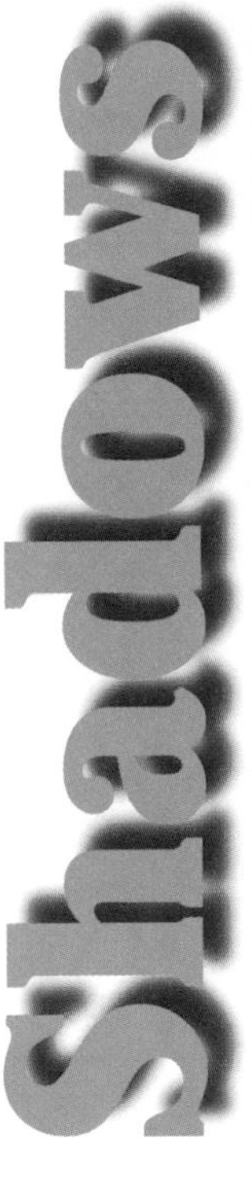


## Basic Drop Shadow

**1** Create a new file, choosing white for the background color in the New File dialog box, or open a file containing a background for your type.

**2** Choose a foreground color for your type, and use the Type tool to enter the text. We made this groundhog with 50-point Cheltenham Bold type. Rename this layer Type. Load the type selection by (Command-clicking) [Control-clicking] the Type layer.

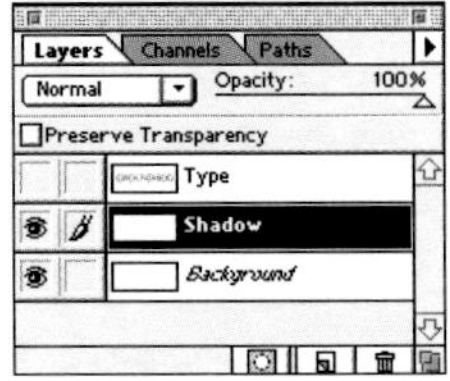


**3** Create a new layer, name it Shadow, and drag the layer so it becomes the layer directly below the Type layer. Make the Type layer invisible so you can see the Shadow layer—just a blank white screen in our case.

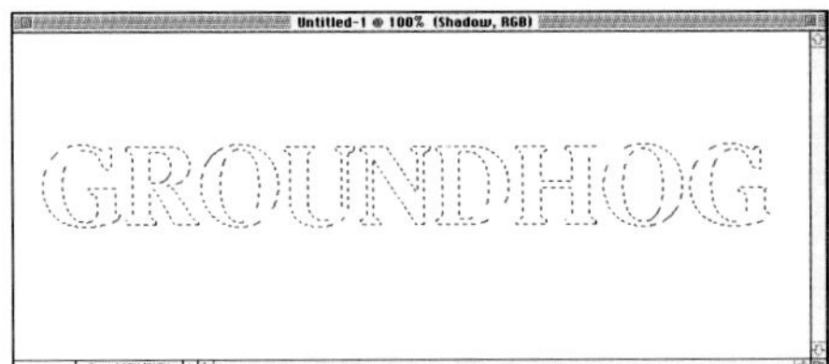




**4** The text selection should still be active. Choose Select➡Feather (7 pixels). The higher the feather radius, the more diffused the shadow. Choose a foreground color for the shadow color, and fill the selection. Deselect the shadow selection (Command-D) [Control-D].

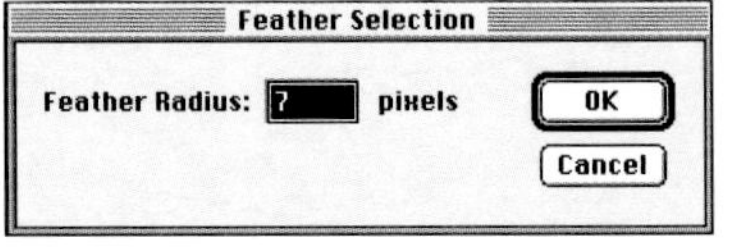

**TOOLBOX**

Alien Skin's Drop Shadow filter

KPT 3 Gradient Designer

TIP **Black is the most common color for shadows, but choosing black doesn't mean that the shadow won't have any color. If the shadow is black and you lower the opacity of the layer, the color from the background will show through the shadow.**

**5** Make the Type layer visible again, but keep the Shadow layer as the active one. The Layers palette will look like this.

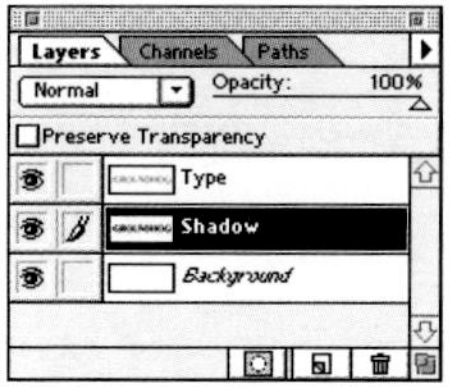


**6** Use the Move tool to move the shadow out from underneath the text. Then use the Opacity slider on the Layers palette to control how strongly the shadow covers the background. The Shadow layer opacity in this example is 90%. Now you have a basic drop shadow.

## Shadows on Images

If you are placing the text on top of an image and want a more realistic shadow that takes the background image into account, then do Steps 1 and 2 and continue with these steps:

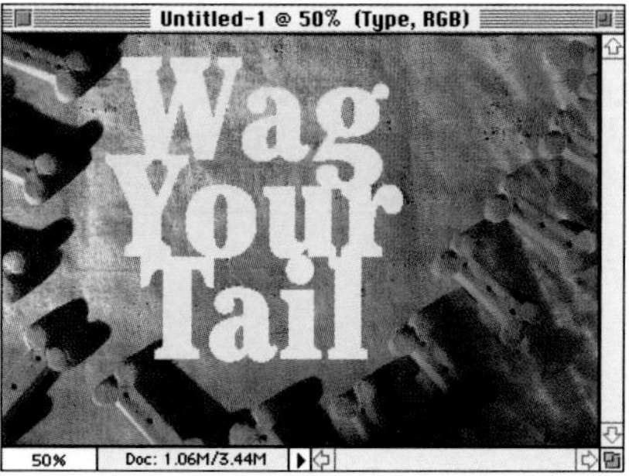

**3** Select the Marquee tool and drag the selection slightly away from the type. The selection will move, but your type should stay where it is. Choose Select➥Feather (7 pixels).

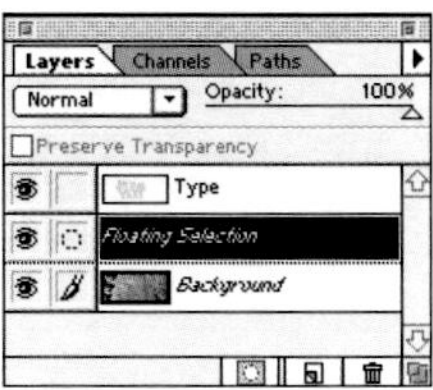


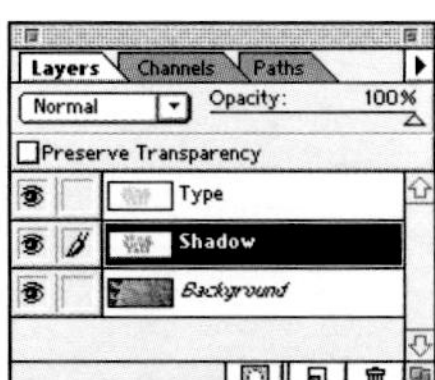


**4** Now, make the Background layer active. Press Command-J to create a layer by copying the selected area of the background. The floating selection will become this new layer. Rename this new layer Shadow.

**5** Now that you have the background copied into the Shadow, you can alter it with any of Photoshop's tools. For this example, we chose Image ➥Adjust ➥Hue/Saturation (Hue: –115, Saturation: –65, Brightness: –49), and set the Shadow layer mode to Multiply. For a soft shadow set the mode of the Shadow layer to Multiply in the Blending Mode pop-up menu on the Layers palette. Or try colorizing the shadow with the Image➥Adjust➥Hue/Saturation Colorize option.

## Variations

### Adding a Glow

Make the Shadow layer the active layer. (Command-click) [Control-click] the Shadow layer to select the shadow. Make a new layer. Drag the new layer so that it becomes the layer directly below the Shadow layer. Choose Select➡Modify➡Border (15 pixels, Outside). Choose a foreground color for the glow, and press Option-Delete to fill the selection. Press Option-Delete two or three more times to intensify the glow.

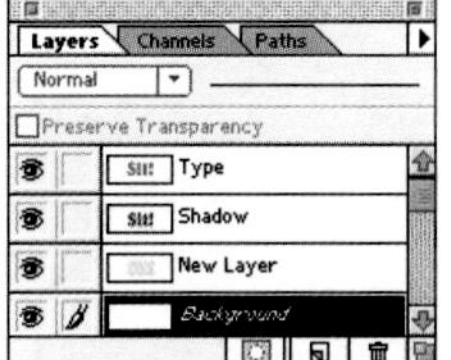

### KPT 3 Gradient Designer

This multicolored drop shadow was created using KPT 3 Gradient Designer to fill in the shadow in Step 4 of the Basic Drop Shadow technique.

Roll Over!

### Alien Skin Drop Shadow 2.0 Filter

A much easier way to create a drop shadow is to use the Drop Shadow filter from Alien Skin's Eye Candy collection, formerly called Black Box (included on the CD). Just enter the text in the composite channel. Choose the foreground color you want to use for the drop shadow. Load the selection, choose Filter➡Alien Skin➡Drop Shadow 2.0.

## Perspective Shadows

Creating a perspective shadow is virtually the same as creating a drop shadow. You only need to distort the shadow so that it looks like it's falling back on a surface. Complete Steps 1 through 3 of the Basic Drop Shadow section (except don't hide the Type layer), then continue with these steps:

**4** Fill the selection with white. (You won't see any change when you fill the selection because the Type layer is on top of the Shadow layer.)

**5** Since our shadow is coming forward we first had to flip it, and then align it. Choose Layer➥Transform ➥ Flip➥Vertical, then drag the flipped text down until the bottoms touch.

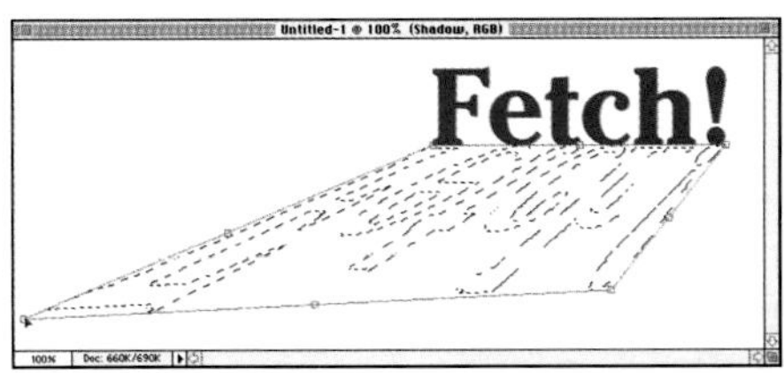


**6** Photoshop has several distortion tools useful for creating the right form for the shadow, but the most versatile is the Distort command. Choose Layer➥Transform➥ Distort. You can now drag the four corners of the selection in any direction you want. We dragged the bottom two corners down and to the left. Press the Return [Enter] key when you're satisfied.

**7** Now we have the shape for the shadow, but before filling it we're going to fade the near edges of the text. Press Q to enter Quick Mask mode. Double-click the Gradient tool to select it and open the Gradient Tool floating palette. Make the settings as you see them in this figure, and choose black as the foreground color.

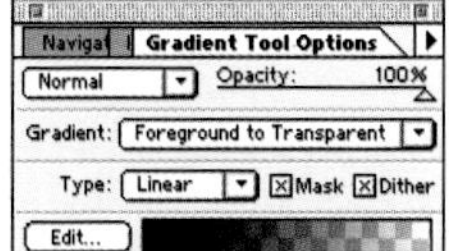


**8** Click the bottom of the shadow with the Gradient tool and drag straight up about one-third of the way through the shadow. You should see something like this in Quick Mask mode.

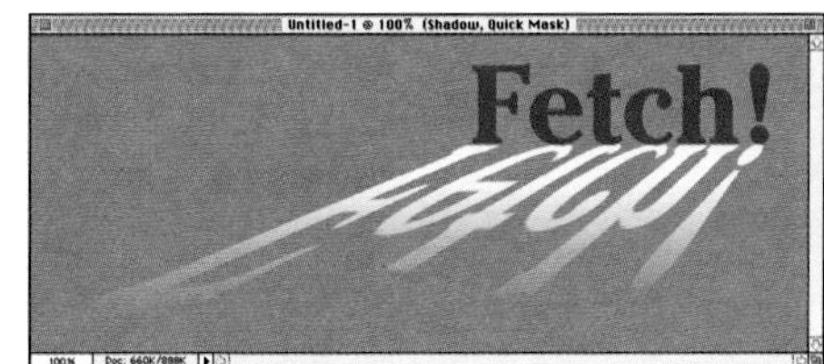


TIP **Holding the Shift key while dragging the Gradient tool keeps the gradient straight.**

**9** Press Q to exit Quick Mask mode. Choose Select➡Feather (2 pixels) to soften the selection. Choose a foreground color for the shadow. Press Option-Delete to fill the shadow.

To create this floating type, the original text was distorted with the Image➡Effects➡Distort transformation (as described in the Perspective Shadow steps above), then we followed the Basic Drop Shadow steps on page 194. ■

This is your one-step guide to shattered type. For this effect, I've done all the work for you.

**1** Create a new file, and use the Type tool to enter the text. We used Lydian at 60 point. You may want to increase the letter spacing in the Type dialog box to give the letters some room for splintering. If you want a more concentrated shattering effect, leave the spacing alone. Flatten the image.

**2** Use the rectangular Marquee tool to select an area surrounding the type. Grab some of the surrounding area, but not too much.

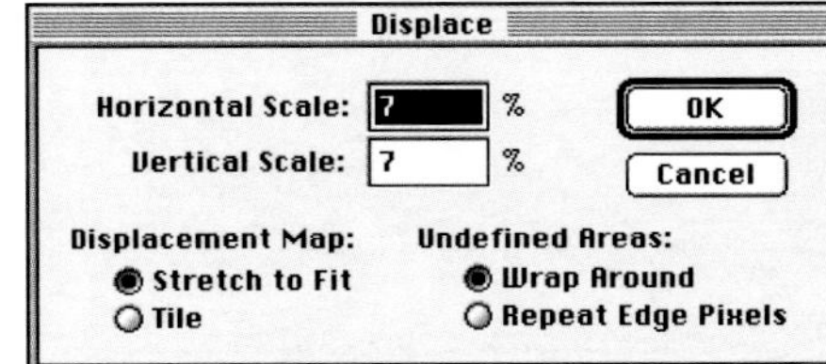


**3** Choose Filter➡Distort➡Displace. Use these settings: Horizontal Scale 7, Vertical Scale 7, Stretch to fit, Wrap Around. Click OK.

**4** A dialog box appears asking you to choose a displacement map. Find the ShatterMap preset file from the CD-ROM. This file is a grayscale displacement map that we created. It shifts parts of the image (or text) according to the lightness or darkness in areas of the displacement map. Although you won't see this figure, we wanted to show you what the displacement map looks like.

**TOOLBOX**

ShatterMap file

**5** Click OK, and that's it. If the displacement map distorts your text too much or too little, either adjust the size of the area you select around the text in Step 2 or adjust the values in Step 3.

## VARIATIONS

For this variation, we applied the Displace filter a second time with the same displacement map and the same settings.

Before flattening the image in Step 1, load the transparency selection of the type layer. We opened a stock photo from D'Pix, copied it, returned to our text file, and chose Edit➡Paste into.

First, we rendered the type using the Marquee effect on page 124, then followed Steps 2 through 4 to create this type. ■

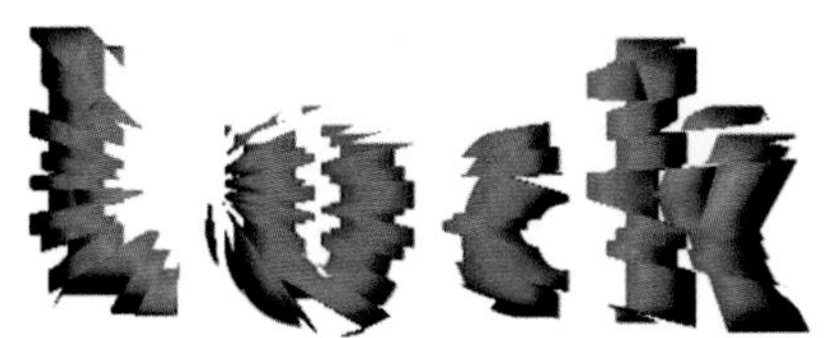

Depending on how you use this effect, it can also look like fog.

©Digital Stock 1995

**1** Create a new file or open a file containing the image you want to place the foggy or smoky text over.

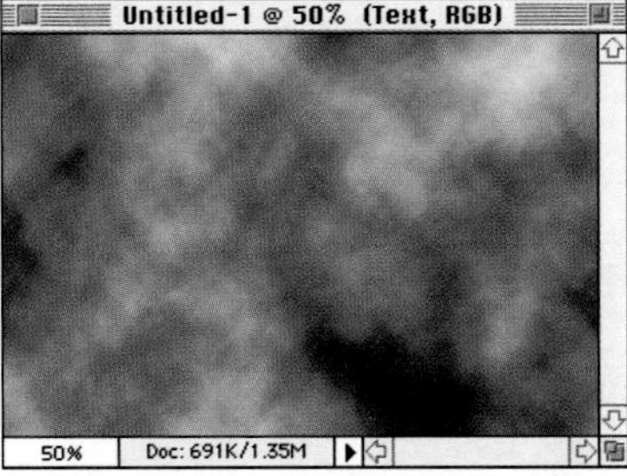


**2** Create a new layer, and rename it "Text". Make the Text layer active, then choose Filter➡Render➡ Clouds.

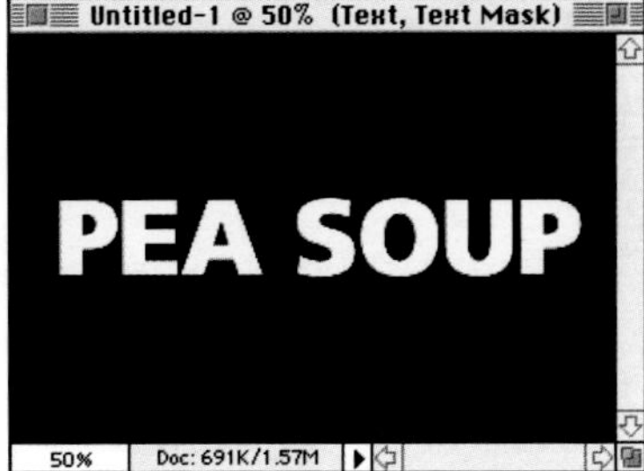


**3** Create a layer mask for this layer. Hold the (Option) [Alt] key and click on the layer mask, so only the mask is visible. Fill the mask with black and enter the text in white with the Type tool. We used Frutiger Black at 50 points, with bold applied.

**TOOLBOX**

KPT 3
Gaussian f/x

**4** Choose Image➡Rotate Canvas➡90° CW, then Filter➡Stylize➡Wind (Wind, Right). Reapply the filter (Command-F) [Control-F].

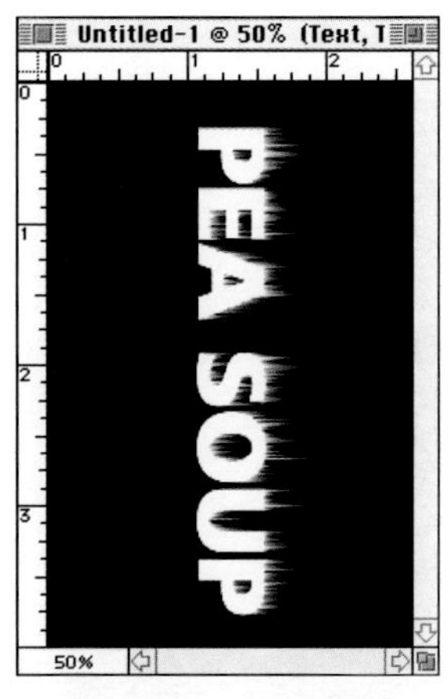


**5** Choose Image➡Map➡Invert (Command-I) [Control-I]. Apply the Wind filter two more times (Command-F, Command-F) [Control-F, Control-F], and invert the image again (Command-I) [Control-I]. Rotate the image back (Image➡Rotate Canvas➡90° CCW).

**6** Now apply these filters: Filter➡Distort➡Ripple (–50, Large), Filter➡Blur➡Motion Blur (20°, 10 pixels), Filter➡KPT 3.0➡KPT 3.0 Gaussian f/x. You may also use the KPT 2.1 Gaussian Electrify filter instead. You may want to apply the Gaussian filter two or three times.

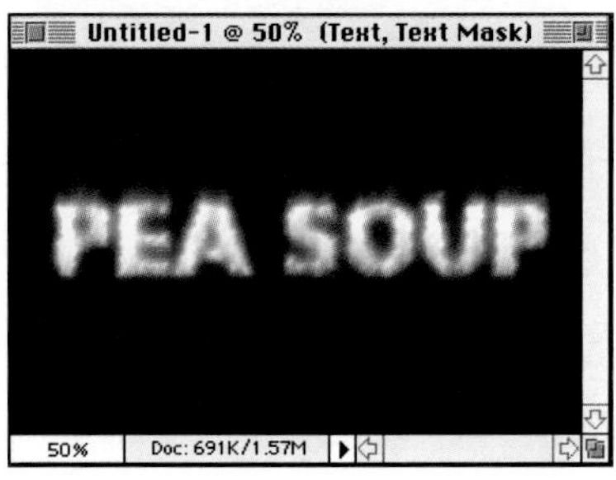


TIP **If you (Option-click) [Alt-click] again on the Text layer mask to make everything visible, you can see that you now have a smoky text. A shortcut to a whiter foggy text is to choose Image➡Adjust➡Brightness/Contrast and raise both the Contrast and the Brightness. For more subtle variations, follow the rest of the steps.**

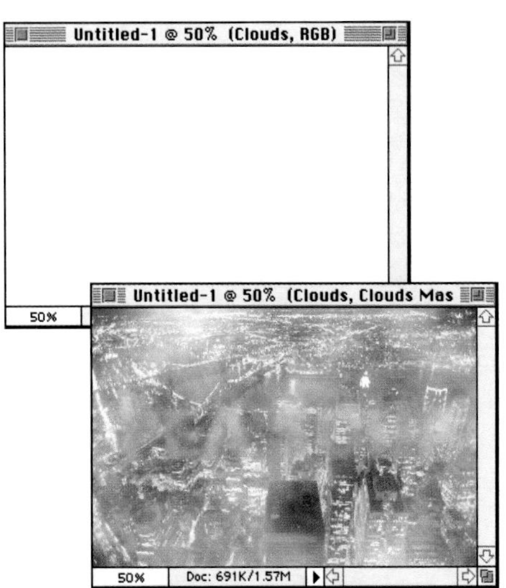


**7** Create a new layer (rename it "Clouds"). Then create a layer mask for this layer, and choose Filter➥Render➥Clouds.

**8** Hold down the (Option) [Alt] key and use the mouse to position the hand icon over the line that separates the Text layer from the Clouds layer. When the hand turns into an icon that looks like INSERT fog.mask.icon, click on the line. This makes the Text layer act as a mask for the Clouds layer.

## Variations

These variations give you some minor adjustments you can use to make your type look a little better.

Use the Smudge tool to improve the look of the smoke or fog. If you click on the layer mask for the Text layer to make it active, you can use the Smudge tool on the text while viewing the results to the entire image without affecting the other layers. Set the Smudge tool Pressure to 50%.

If you want to strengthen the text, then make the Clouds layer mask active and choose Image➡Adjust➡ Brightness/Contrast and raise the Contrast. You can also do this to the Text layer window. If raising the Contrast is too harsh, then try adjusting the Levels (Command-L) [Control-L].

You probably noticed that after Step 7 and before Step 8, clouds were floating in front of the entire image. If you like that effect, but want the text to stand out more, then stop after Step 7 and choose Image➡Adjust➡Brightness/ Contrast. Raise the Contrast all the way to 100, and slide the Brightness slider either all the way up or all the way down.

Add some color to the text by selecting a foreground color after creating the new layer in Step 2, or filling the Clouds layer with a solid color instead of white. ■

This effect uses the extremely powerful Lighting Effects filter. Included on the CD-ROM are several preset LightingStyles files to be used with this filter. To find out what you need to do to load these files, turn to page 241 in Appendix A, "What's On the CD-ROM."

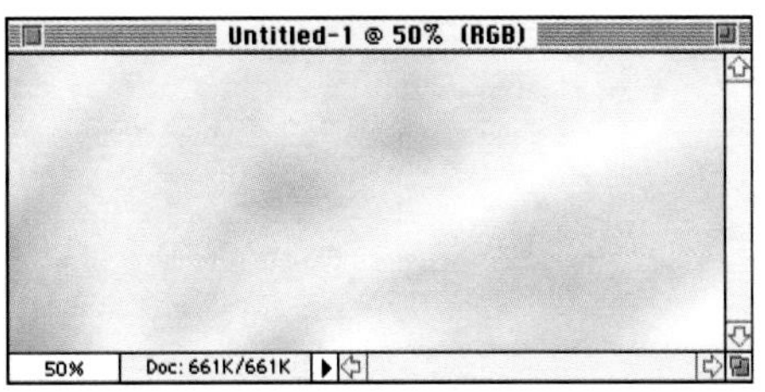


**1** Create a new file, or open a file containing the background that you want to stitch. Whatever you use, it must be an RGB file in order for the Lighting Effects filter to work.

**2** Create a new channel (Channel #4). Use the Type tool to enter the text in the new channel. This effect was created with a script font, such as Shelley Andante (which we used here at 70 points), in mind. Save the type selection in another new channel (Channel #5).

**3** Return to Channel #4 (if necessary), and choose Filter➥Blur➥Gaussian Blur (3 pixels) to blur the inside of the text selection only.

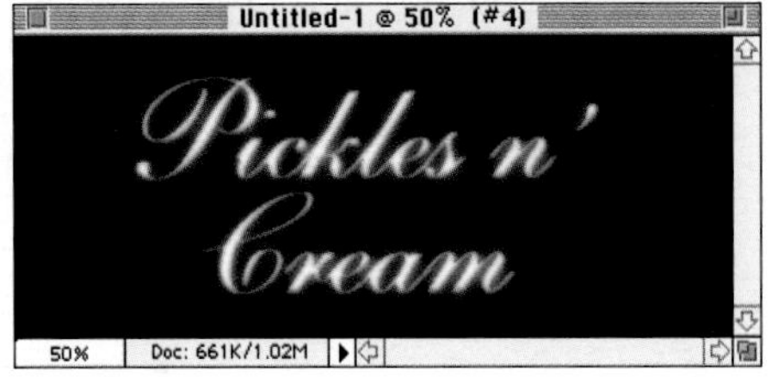


**4** Choose Select➥Inverse, then Filter➥Blur➥Gaussian Blur (5.5 pixels) to blur only the outside of the text selection. Now, you can get rid of that annoying active selection (press Command-D or Control-D).

**TOOLBOX**

EmbossLighting Styles file

Adobe Illustrator

**5** Choose Filter➥Stylize➥Find Edges.

**6** You are building a grayscale texture channel to be used with the Lighting Effects filter. Right now, things are a bit too harsh for a stitched-on-silk look. Choose Image➥Adjust➥Brightness/Contrast and use settings near these: Brightness 22, Contrast –46.

**7** For a final softening choose Filter➥Blur➥Gaussian Blur (1 pixel).

**8** Return to the composite channel (Command-~) [Control-~] where the innocent silk awaits your cruel puncturing. Choose Filter➥Render➥Lighting Effects. If you loaded the LightingStyles files, choose EmbossLightStyles from the styles pop-up menu. If you haven't loaded it, then use the settings you see in this figure.

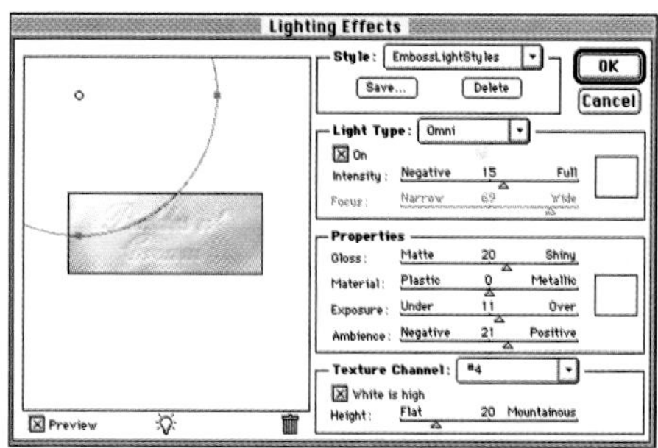


You should see something like this.

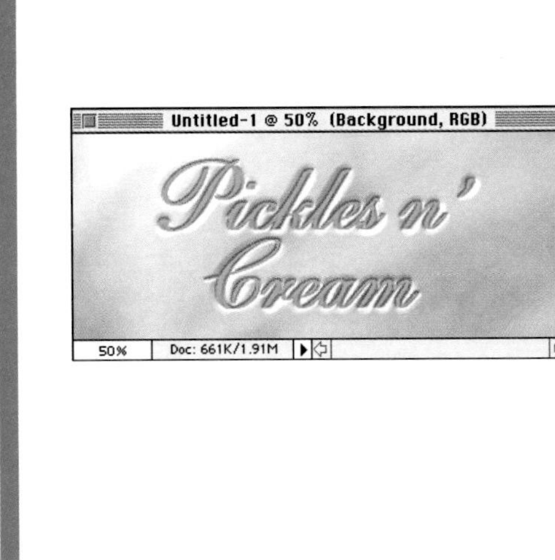


9 To change the color of the type, load the selection Channel #5 (the original type selection), and choose Image➡Adjust➡Hue/Saturation. You may or may not want to check the Colorize checkbox. If you don't, then the Hue slider is only going to affect the darker areas of the type. Use the sliders to find the color you want. Here are the settings we used for this example: Hue: 95, Saturation: 74, Lightness: –42.

## VARIATIONS

### Adding Stitches

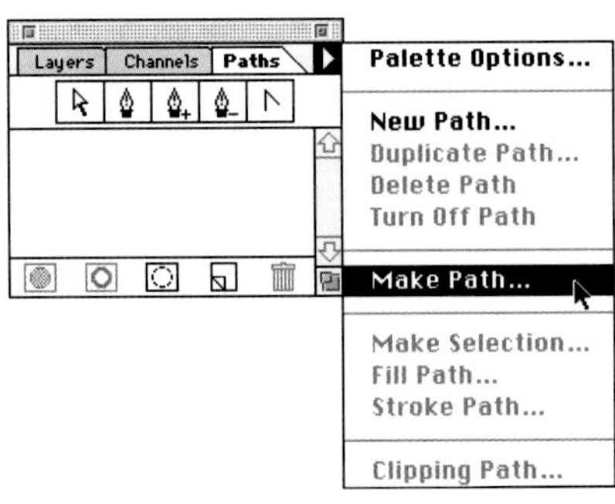


1 We used Adobe Illustrator to create the stitches. Open Adobe Illustrator, and open a new file. Return to Photoshop while Illustrator runs in the background. Load the selection Channel #5, and choose Make Work Path (1 pixel) from the Path palette menu.

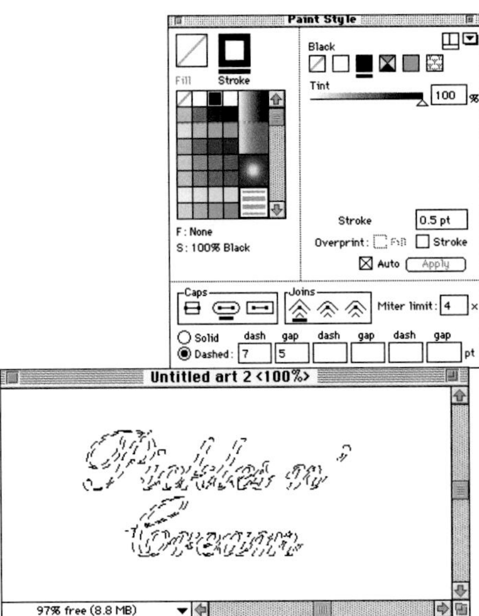


2 Copy the path to the Clipboard and switch to Adobe Illustrator. On the empty page, paste in the path from the Clipboard. The path appears in Illustrator. Do not lose the selection. In the Paint Styles palette, choose black for the stroke color. Make the stroke weight 0.5 points. Switch the line style to Dashed with a 7 pt. dash and a 5 pt. gap. Make the ends round. Your settings should match what you see in this figure.

And the text path should look like this (press (Command-Shift-H) [Control-Shift-H] to hide the blue guides).

**3** Copy the path to the Clipboard (Command-C) [Control-C]. Return to Photoshop. Choose Turn off Path from the Paths palette menu. Load the selection Channel #5, and paste in the Clipboard (Command-V) [Control-V]. A dialog box appears; choose Paste as Pixels (anti-aliased) and click OK.

**4** Press (Command-H) [Control-H] to hide the edges. You can see the stitches are black now. If you want to change their color or soften them, Choose Image➥Adjust➥Hue/Saturation. We checked the Colorize box for this example and used these settings: Hue: 180, Saturation: 100, Lightness: +16.

## More Stitches

If you want to make the stitches look more raised, after Step 7 complete Steps 1 through 3 of Adding Stitches with one exception: choose white as the stroke color in Step 2. Deselect the stitches (Command-D) [Control-D] and finish Steps 8 and 9. The image should now include a row of indentations that gives the impression of stitches.

To add color to More Stitches, load the stitches selection Channel #6. Hold down the (Command and Option) [Control and Alt] keys and press the up arrow and left arrow once. Then choose Select➥Feather (1 pixel). Choose Image➥Adjust➥Hue/Saturation. We used these settings: Hue: –25, Saturation: 100, Lightness: 0. ■

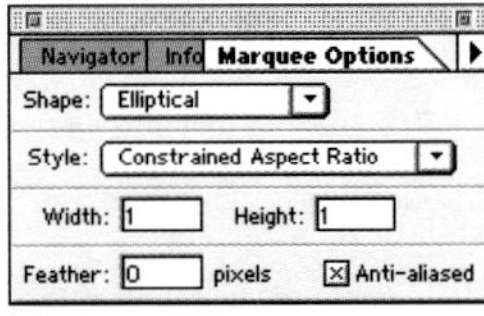


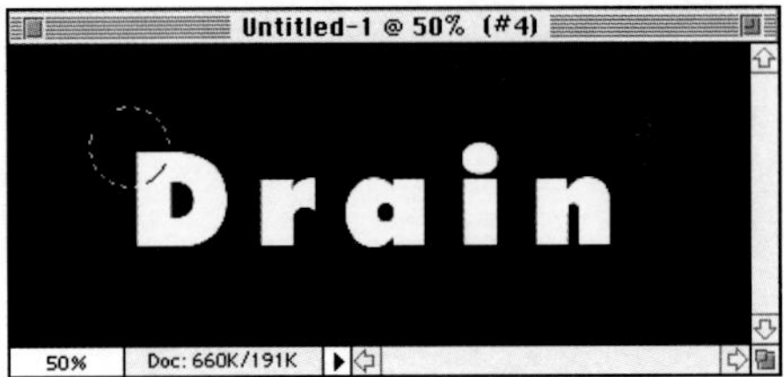


This effect will take some patience—and a lot of trial and error. Save often and get friendly with the Undo command!

**1** Create a new file, and create a new channel. Choose white as the foreground color and black for the background color. Use the Type tool to enter your text into the new channel. We used Futura Extra Bold at 60 points for this example, with the spacing set at 12 to provide some extra room between the letters.

**2** Change the Marquee tool shape to Elliptical and the Style to a Constrained Aspect Ratio with Width: 1 and Height: 1. This gives you a perfect circle.

**3** Select a part of one of the letters, keeping the body of the letter less than halfway through the circle. If part of the letter goes over halfway through the circle, the result is the background bleeding into the letter rather than a spike coming out of the letter (just try it…you'll see what we mean). If you need to move the marquee, but don't want to change the size, just drag the selection. Only the marquee moves—not what's in it!



## TOOLBOX

Alien Skin's Swirl filter

KPT 3 Gradient Designer

**4** Choose Filter➥Distort➥Twirl. Move the slider until you like what you see in the preview window. If you can't get what you want, cancel and move the selection a bit or try using a different size selection. Both of these changes can have profound effects on the filter.

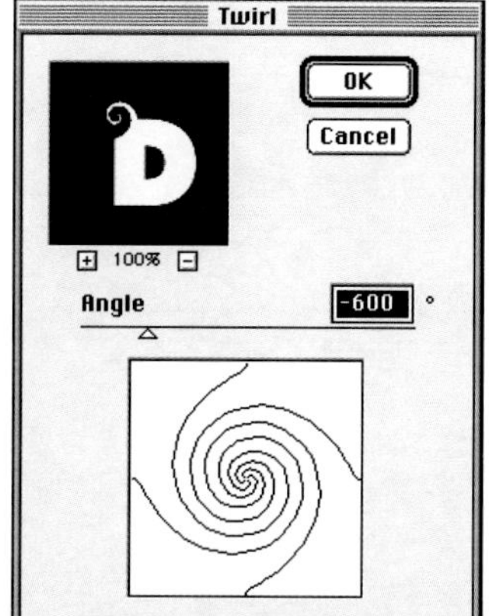


Now you have the first one.

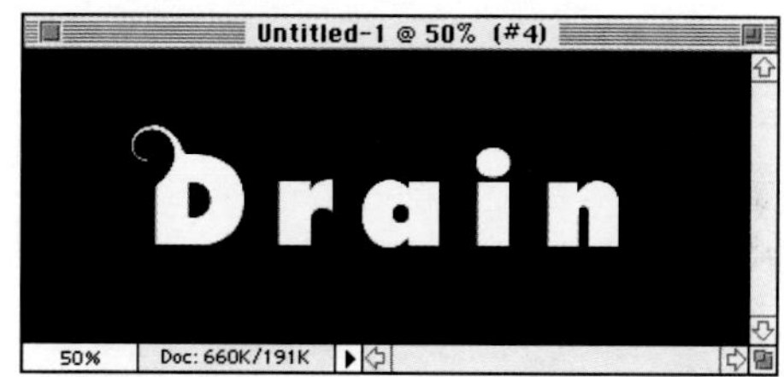


**5** Move the selection or make a new one and continue swirling until you have a finished product.

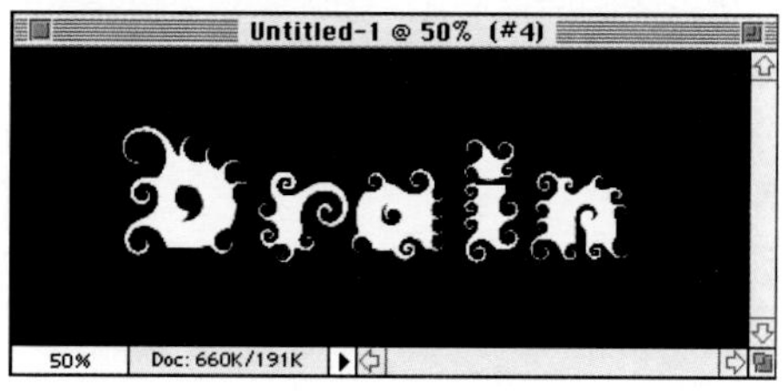


**6** Return to the composite channel ((Command-~) [Control-~]) and fill the area with any color or texture you want to appear in your type. We used a texture from Kai's Power Tools and applied Filter➥Alien Skin➥Swirl 2.0 (Spacing: 22, Length:7, Twist: 90, and Detail: 100). (Warp and Smooth were checked too.)

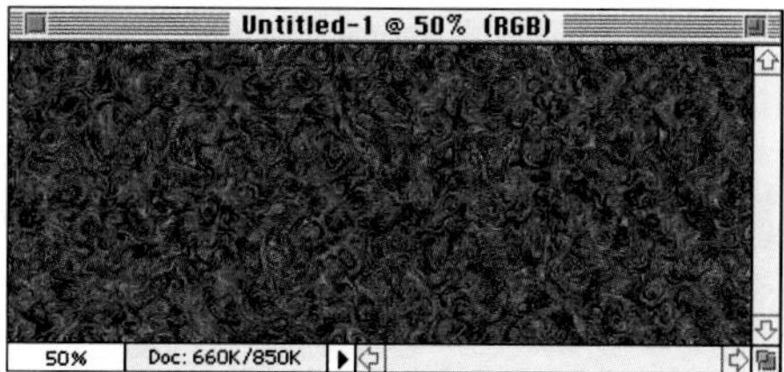

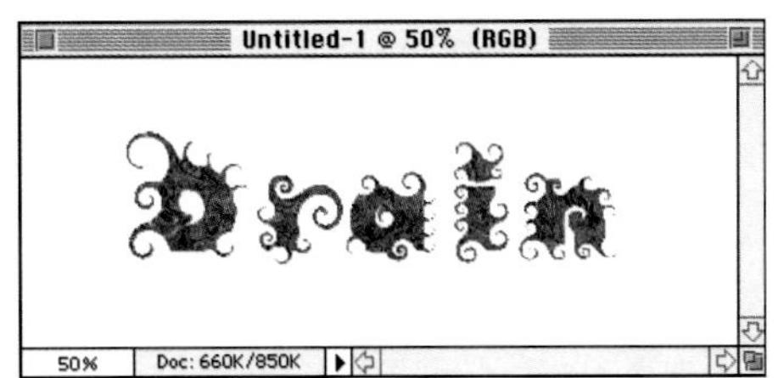

**7** Load the selection. Channel #4 and Select➡Inverse (or you could have clicked the Invert box in the Load Selection dialog box.) Press Delete to fill the selection with white. You're left with the letters filled with a pattern!

## VARIATIONS

You can treat your swirled type just as you could anything typed with the Type tool, meaning you can apply a barrage of other effects from this book. Try some Neon, for instance (page 134) we feathered the selection 3 pixels, then used KPT Gradient Designer's Gradient on Paths option with a custom gradient.

Or try Flaming (page 80). A few extra swirls really add to that "hot" effect, don't they? ■

Although it is possible to create type that looks three-dimensional within Photoshop, there are several other applications that make this task a lot easier. On the CD are demo versions of a few of these three-dimensional rendering applications, including: Adobe Dimensions, Infini-D, and StrataType 3d. There is also a demo version of Andromeda Software's 3-D Photoshop filter. This technique uses Dimensions to model some 3-D type, then uses Photoshop to dress it up.

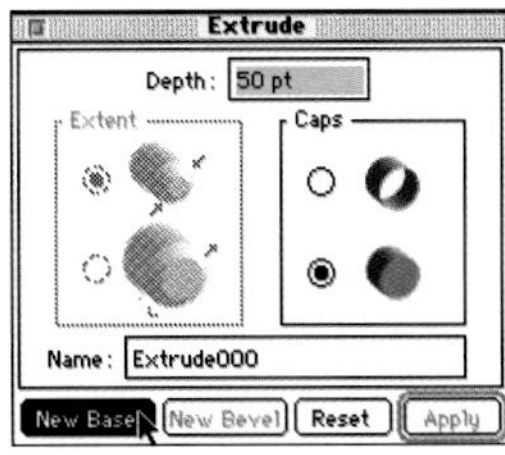


**1** Open Adobe Dimensions 2.0. A new document window opens. Press (Command-E) [Control-E] to make sure that you are working in Edit mode, where everything runs faster. Then choose Operations➡Extrude (Command-Shift-E) [Control-Shift-E]. The Extrude floating palette appears onscreen. Click the New Base button on the palette.

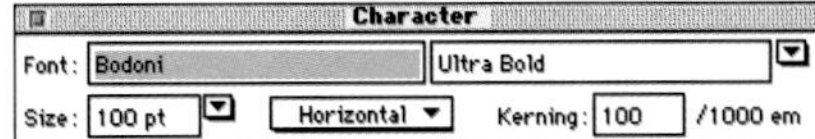


**2** A new untitled window appears onscreen, and the icons in the toolbar change. Double-click the Type tool to select it and open the Character palette. Make your selections in the Character palette. We used 100-point Bodoni Ultra Bold for this example.

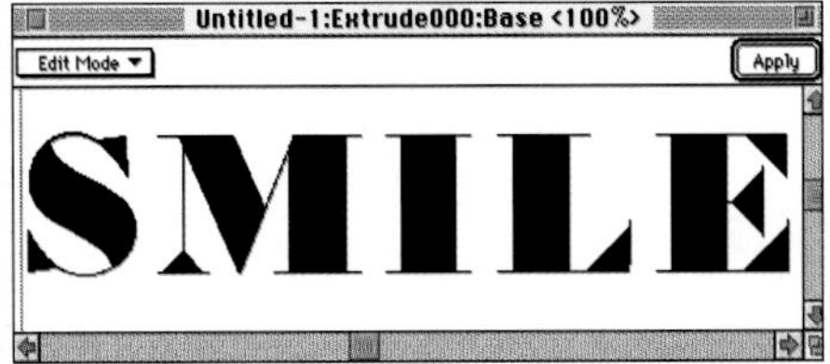


**3** With the Type tool, click in the Extrude window that opened in Step 2. A cursor appears. Type in the text.

## TOOLBOX

Adobe Dimensions (Mac only)

KPT 3 Texture Explorer

**TIP** **If you want beveled type, then see Steps 3, 4, and 5 in the Beveled type section on page 30, then skip to Step 5 of this section.**

**4** Find the Extrude floating palette. Enter, in points, the depth you want the text to extrude. We used a value of 25 points. We also chose the end caps option. Click the Apply button on the Extrude floating palette.

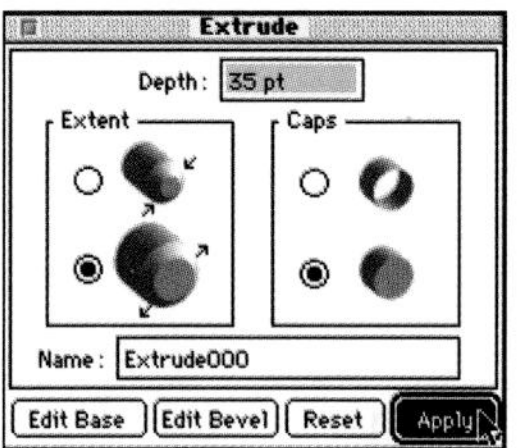


**5** To go back to the original image window choose Window➡Untitled-1. Now you can see that the text has been extruded. What you see is actually a wireframe model of the type. Before rendering the final image, you need to set its color.

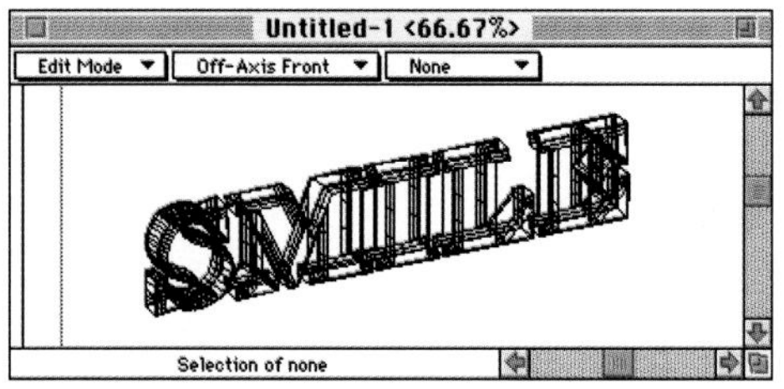


**6** Choose Appearance➡Surface Properties. A floating palette appears. The figure here explains its features. For the Fill (text) color, we used these CMYK values: 0/95/80/0. For the Shade (shadow) color, we used black. We left the Stroke (edge) color at none. Click the Reflectance icon, then the Plastic icon, and use the values shown in the figure. Click the Apply button when you're finished.

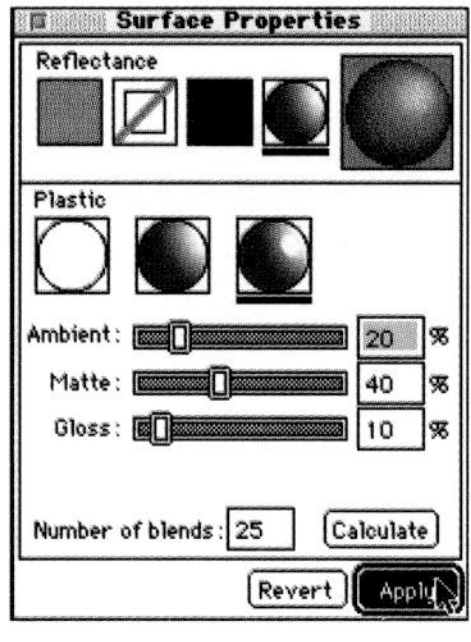

**7** To show off more of the perspective of the type, we selected View➡Custom Perspective and set the angle to 115°. Then we moved the type straight down so the perspective would affect the type even more.

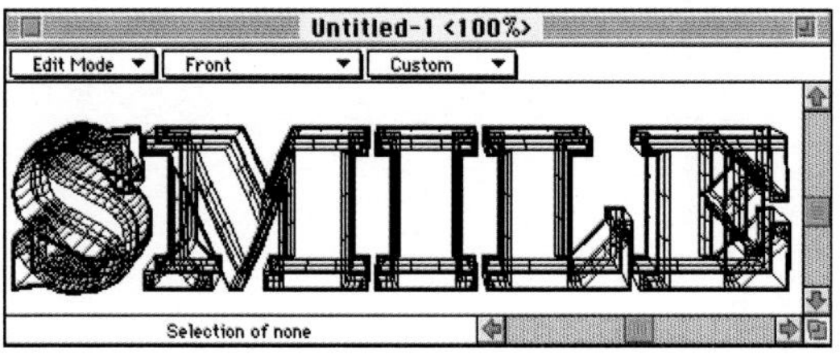

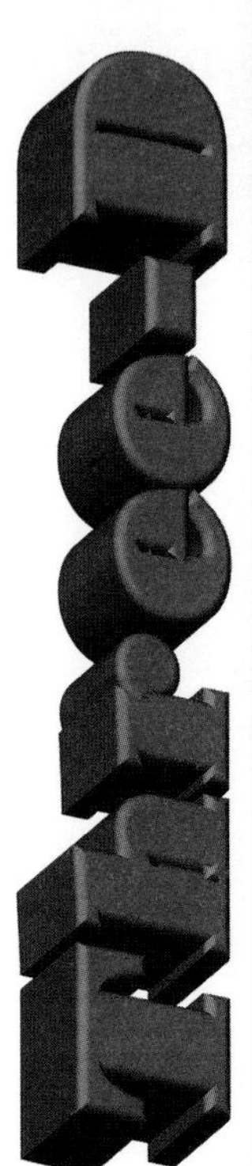


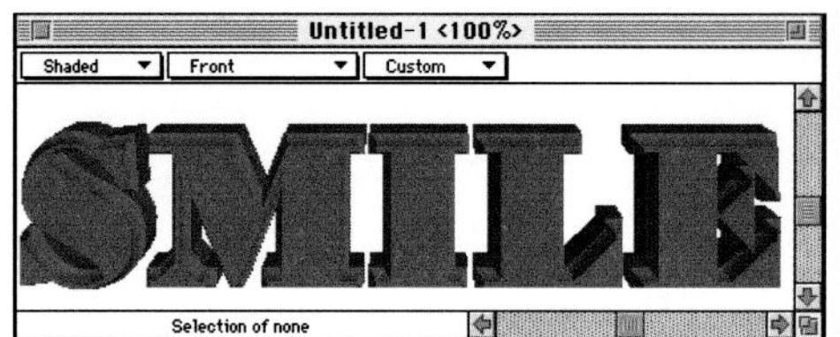


**8** You won't see any changes in the text because you're not in a render mode yet. Choose View➡Shaded Render. (Complex type may take some time to render, depending on your system configuration.) If you don't like what you see, you can simply use the Surface Properties palette to make appearance changes, or go back to the Extrude palette and use the Edit buttons to alter the text. Remember, it's always quicker to work in Edit mode (View➡Edit Mode).

Art for Chapters
Photoshop T...
3d.1
3D.2
3D.3
3D.4
3D.5
Eject
Desktop
New
Export to:
SMILE
Cancel
Export
Preview: Color Macintosh™
Compatability: Adobe Illustrator 5

**9** When you are satisfied with the type, deselect the type (Command-Shift-A) [Control-Shift-A], and choose File➡Export. Choose Color Macintosh and Adobe Illustrator 5 from the pop-up menus in the Export dialog box. Quit Dimensions. No need to save changes—you already exported what you wanted.

Rasterize Generic EPS Format
Image Size: 21K
Width: 1.24 cm
Height: 1.227 cm
Resolution: 150 pixels/inch
Mode: CMYK Color
OK
Cancel
☒ Anti-aliased ☒ Constrain Proportions

**10** Open Photoshop, and open the file you just exported from Adobe Dimensions. Here are the settings we used in the Rasterizer box.

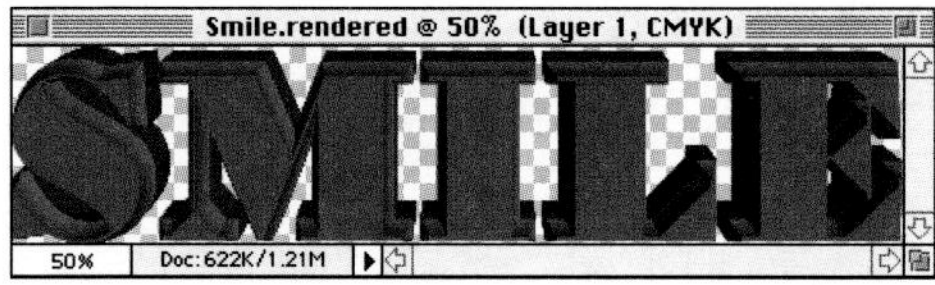


**11** The text opens into Layer 1 and there isn't a background layer. The image is complete and ready for you to embellish with Photoshop.

**12** The rest of the steps demonstrate how to map a pattern onto the 3-D type. First duplicate Layer 1 to make Layer 1 copy. Then, choose Luminosity from the Layers palette blending mode pull-down menu.

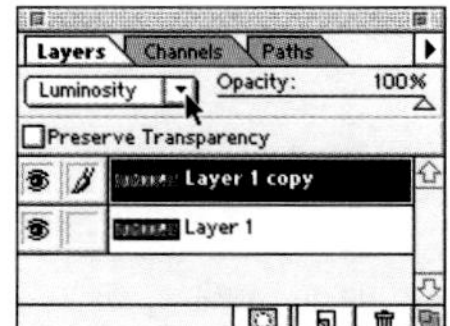


**13** Make Layer 1 active, and Select➡Load Selection (Layer 1 Transparency) to select the outline of the type. While the selection is active, fill the selection with white.

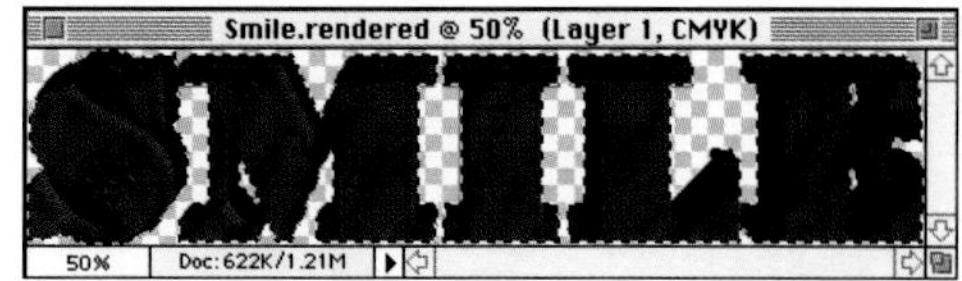


**14** Add a texture to jazz up the type, if you want; we used KPT Texture Explorer. Then flatten the image.

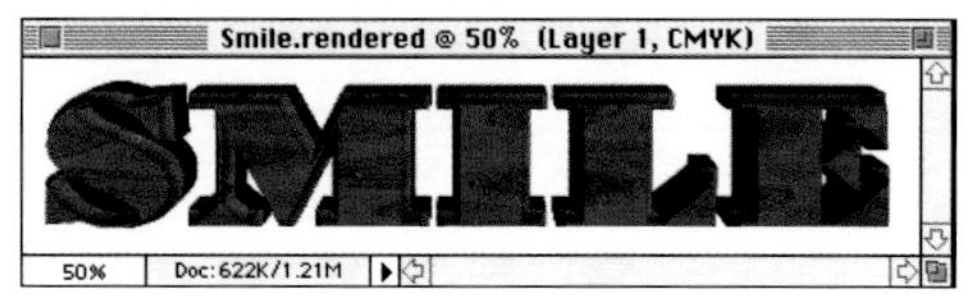

**To map a stock photo texture onto the type, open the photo, select the area you want to use, copy it to the Clipboard (Command-C) [Control-C], and close the file. In Step 13, instead of filling the text with white, choose Edit➡Paste Into.**

## Type on a 3-D Surface

Adobe Dimensions is also a valuable tool for placing flat type on a three-dimensional surface.

**1** Again, open Adobe Dimensions 2.0. A new window appears. The toolbar includes tools to create boxes, spheres, cones, and cylinders. We decided to put our type on a sphere. Click the Sphere tool on the Tool palette to select it, then use the crosshairs to draw a box in the Untitled-1 window area. To make a perfectly round sphere, hold the Shift key to keep all the dimensions the same.

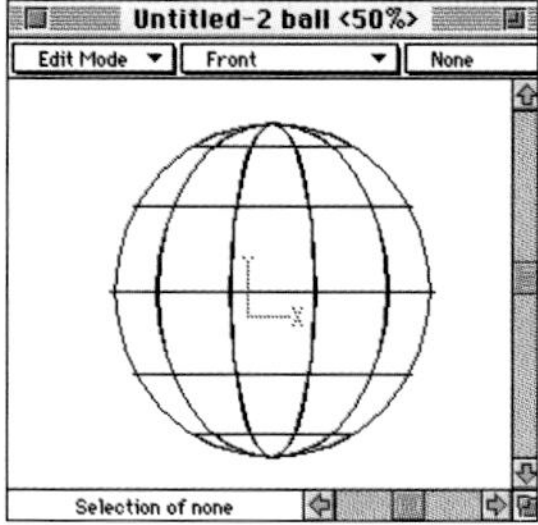

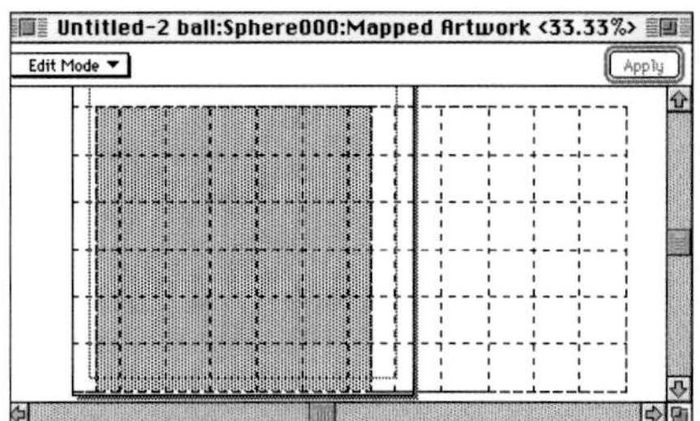


2 Choose Appearance➡Map Artwork (Command-Option-M). A new window opens and the tools in the toolbar change. The grid in the new window is a "map" of the sphere. The gray areas are the areas of the sphere hidden from view in the Untitled-1 window.

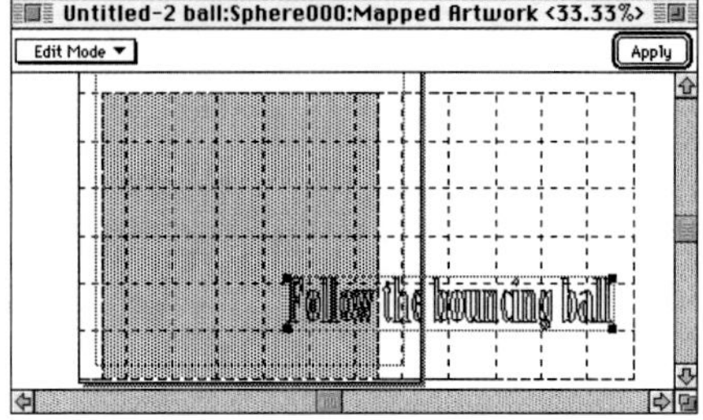


3 Double-click the Type tool to select it and open the Character floating dialog box. Type in the text, press Return, then move the text where you want it on the map.

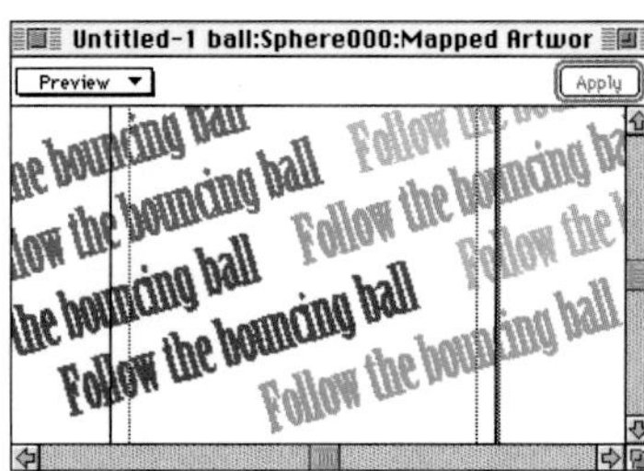


4 Press (Command-Y) to see a preview of the text only. To change the fill or stroke color of the text, press (Command-I) to open the Surface Properties floating dialog box.

TIP **If you want to edit the type while still in the Map Artwork window, go back to the Edit mode (Command-E) and use the Type tool to select the text and the floating Character dialog box to make any changes.**

**5** Click the Apply button in the upper-right corner of the Map Artwork window, then choose Window➡Untitled-1 to see the type mapped onto the sphere.

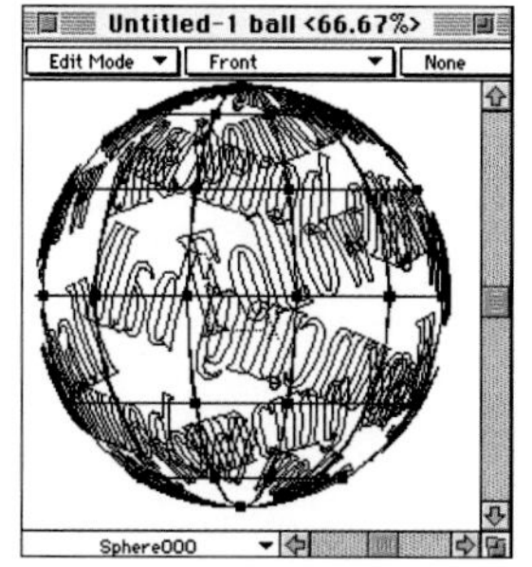


**6** Now, because you don't want to see the sphere, but only the type, you have to make sure the Surface Properties of the sphere are set to none. Press (Command-I) to open the Surface Properties dialog box and set the Fill and Stroke colors to None. Be sure to click the Apply button to activate your changes.

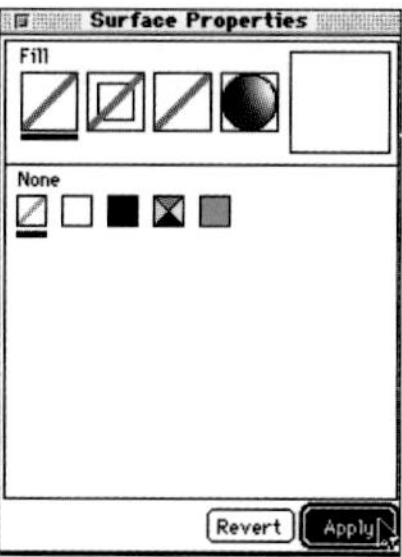


**7** Now choose View➡Shaded Render (Command-Shift-Y) to render the type. That's it.

**You can import this type for use in a Photoshop file by following Steps 9 and 10 listed previously.** ■

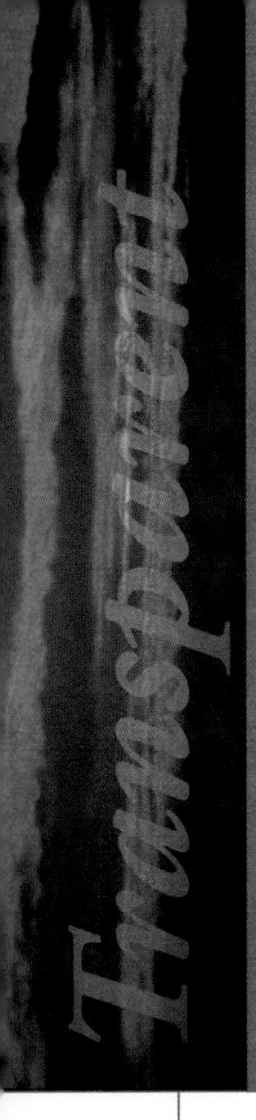


Photoshop's layer features make this one a breeze. By placing the type on a layer on top of the background images, we can adjust the opacity and experiment with many different effects without actually affecting either layer permanently.

©Digital Stock 1995

**1** Open the file containing the background you want to lay the type over. We used a stock photo from Digital Stock here.

**2** Choose white as the foreground color. Use the Type tool to enter the text.

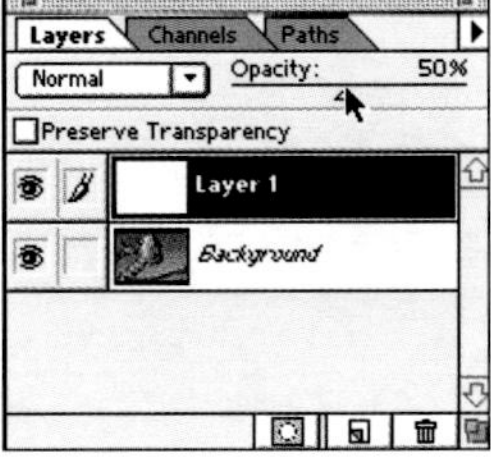


**3** To make this type transparent, all you have to do is lower the opacity of this new layer.

Grab the Opacity slider in the Layers palette and slide it to the left.

## VARIATIONS

This technique is so simple it gives you lots of time to experiment.

To make the text a little brighter in this image, we chose Overlay from the Layers palette blending mode pop-up menu.

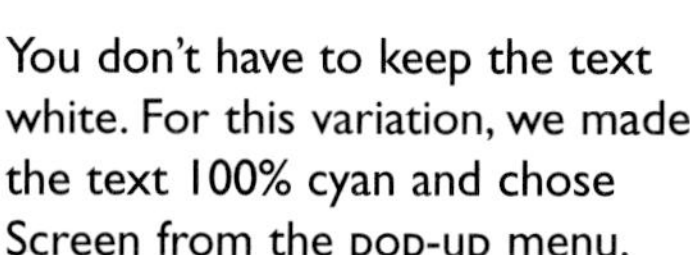

You don't have to keep the text white. For this variation, we made the text 100% cyan and chose Screen from the pop-up menu.

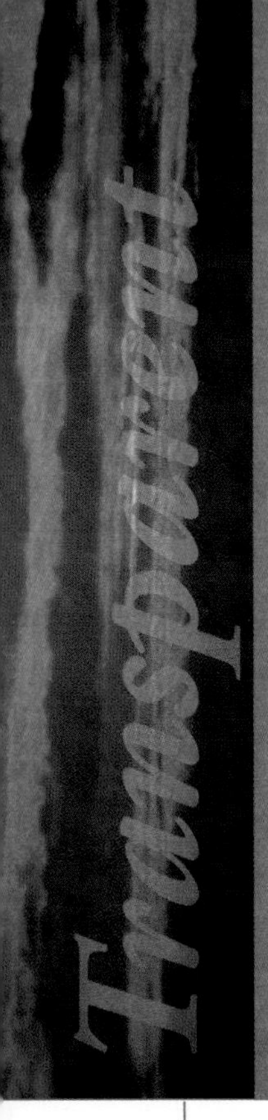

Another quick way to work with this effect is to create a new channel (#4) and type the text into it. Then return to the composite channel and load the selection Channel #4. You can now manipulate the selection any way you like. In this variation, we chose Image➡Adjust➡Brightness/Contrast, and bumped the brightness all the way up to 100. Use the Levels sliders (Image➡Adjust➡Levels) for more control.

You can also knock words out of a transparent overlay. First, in a new layer above the background photo, we filled a box with white and lowered its opacity. Then after creating each word with the Type Mask tool, we pressed Delete.

If you want a foggy or smoky transparency, flip to page 202 and take a look at the Smoke technique. ■

**1** Create a new file, and create a new channel (Channel #4).

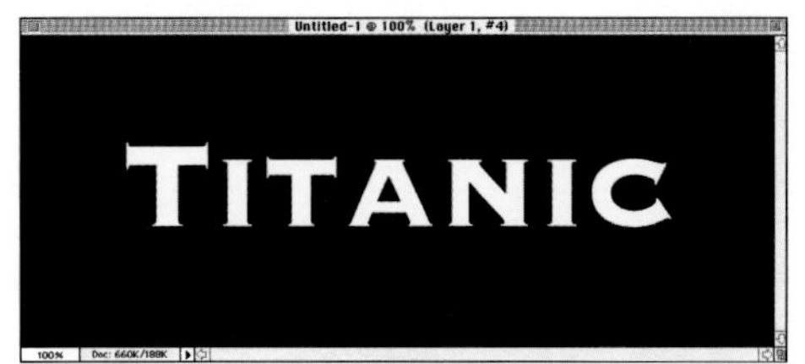


**2** Use the Type tool to enter the text in the new channel. We used Copperplate 33 BC at 70 points in this example.

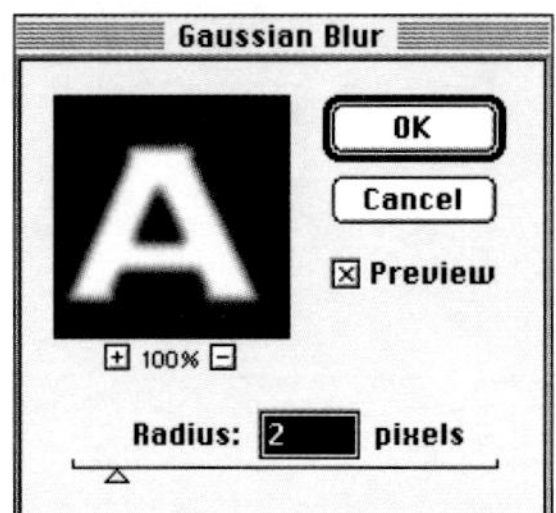


**3** Use Filter➥Blur➥Gaussian Blur (2 pixels) to soften the edges of the text.

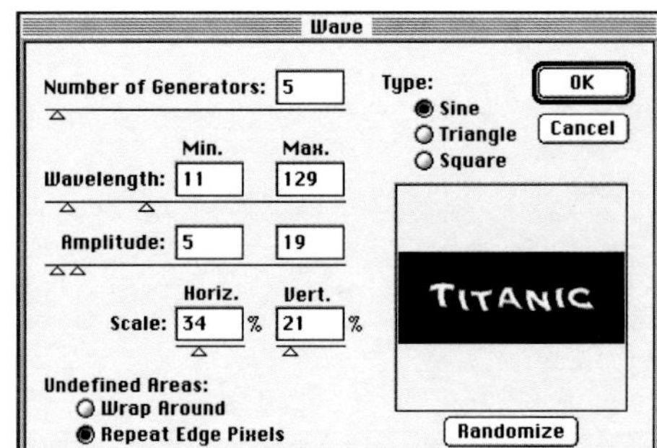


**4** Apply Filter➥Distort➥Wave (Type: Sine; Generators: 5; Wavelength: 11, 129; Amplitude: 5,19; Horiz.: 34%; Vert.: 21%).

Click the Randomize button a few times until the thumbnail has a watery look to it (this randomizes settings based on the values you entered). Your text should look something like this.

**5** To make the shadow, duplicate Channel #4. In the new channel (#5) select the text with the rectangular Marquee tool. Use Layer➥Transform➥Distort to offset and warp the text a little more (remember, this will be a shadow so you may want to move the layer around a little).

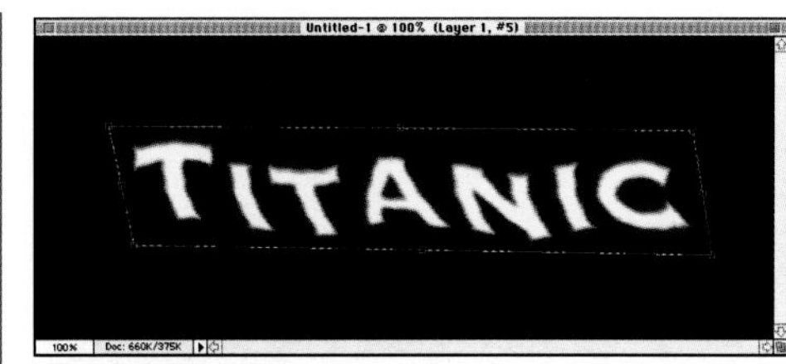


**6** Use Filter➥Blur➥Gaussian Blur (6 pixels) to blur the shadow channel. Drop the selection ((Command-D) [Control-D]).

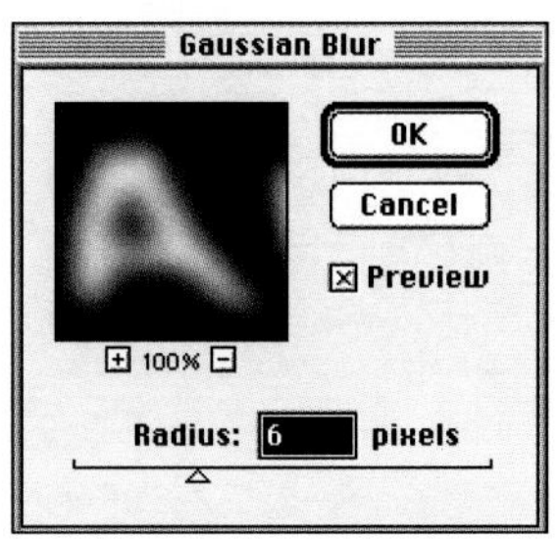


**7** For the water, create a new channel (Channel #6). Apply Filter➥Pixelate➥Mezzotint using the Medium strokes option. Repeat this two more times (press (Command-F) [Control-F] twice).

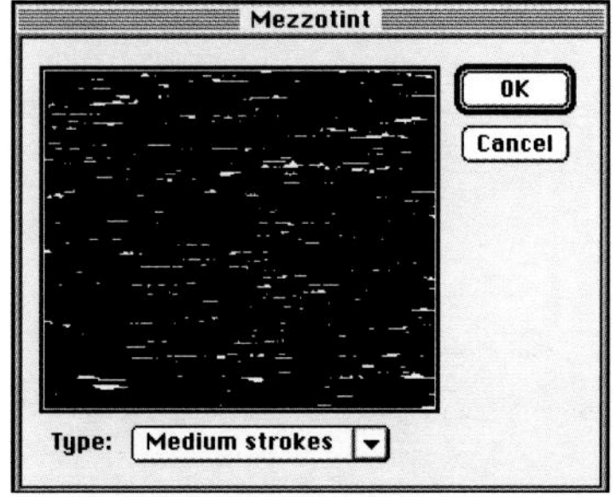


Channel #6 should now look something like this.

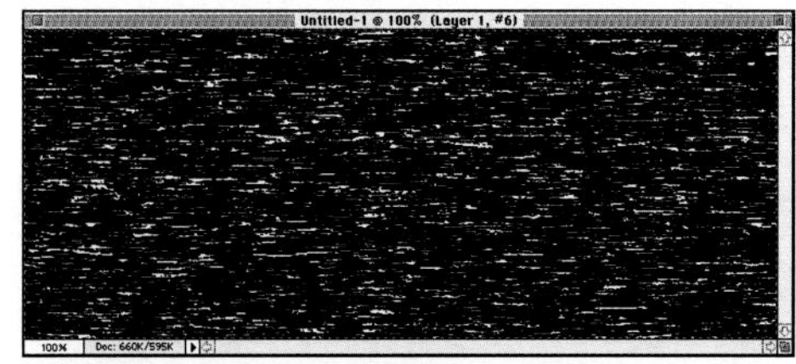

**8** Apply Filter➥Blur➥Gaussian Blur (4 pixels).

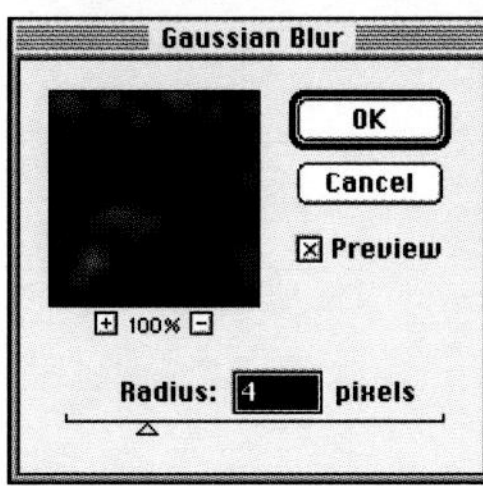

**9** Apply Filter➥Other➥Minimum (3 pixels.) This creates the spider-web look for sunlight shimmering on the water.

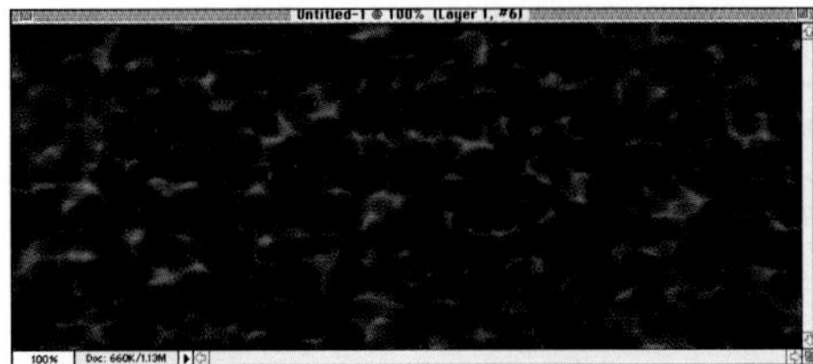

**10** Choose Image➥Adjust➥ Brightness/Contrast and adjust the settings to get something like this.

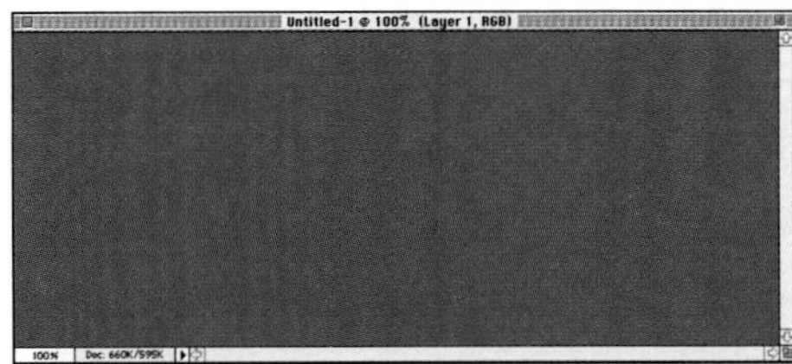

**11** Now it's time to create the visible image. Return to the composite Channel. Choose a foreground color for the water. We used a medium cyan color here. Press (Option-Delete) [Alt-Delete] to fill the entire image with the chosen color.

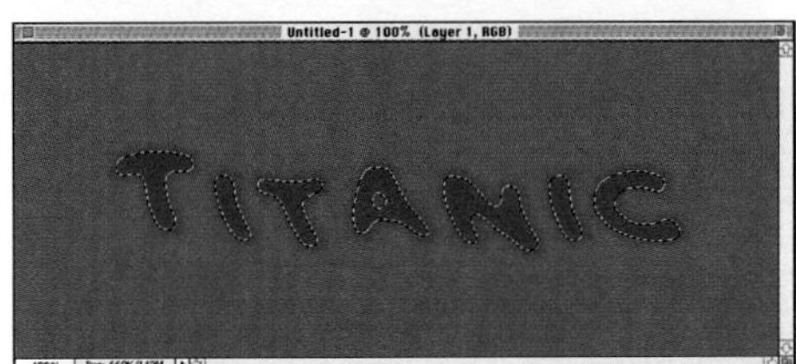

**12** Load the selection Channel #5 (the shadow channel). Choose for the foreground color a medium blue color for the shadow. Press (Option-Delete) [Alt-Delete] to fill the selection.

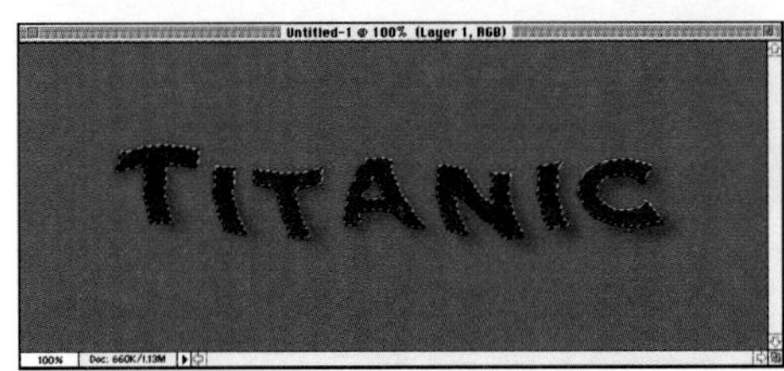

**13** Use Select➥Load Selection to load Channel #4 (the text channel). Set the foreground color to the color you want the text to be. Here we used a forest green. Press (Option-Delete) [Alt-Delete] to fill the selection.

**14** Load the selection Channel #6 (the highlight channel). Choose white as the background color and press Delete to fill the selection. Don't lose the selection yet!

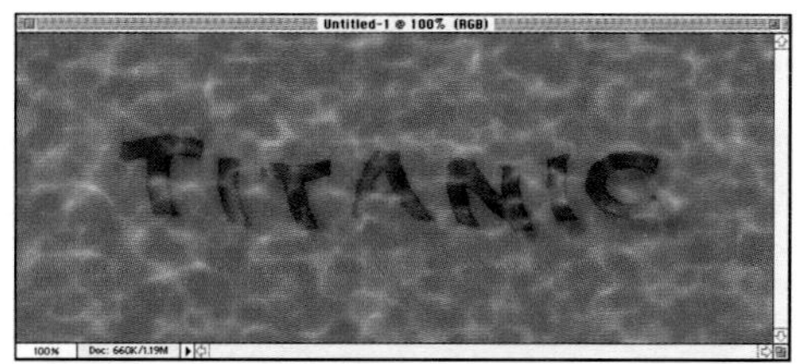

**15** To add a few more highlights, apply Filter➡Artistic➡Plastic Wrap with the settings Highlight Strength: 20, Detail: 13, Smoothness: 15. Don't worry what the preview looks like—it doesn't take into account the various levels of your selection.

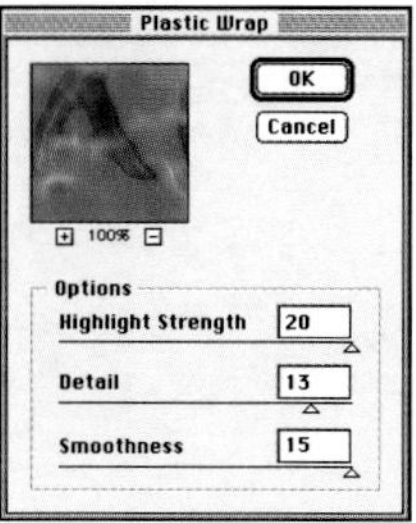


Presto! Don't forget to breathe!

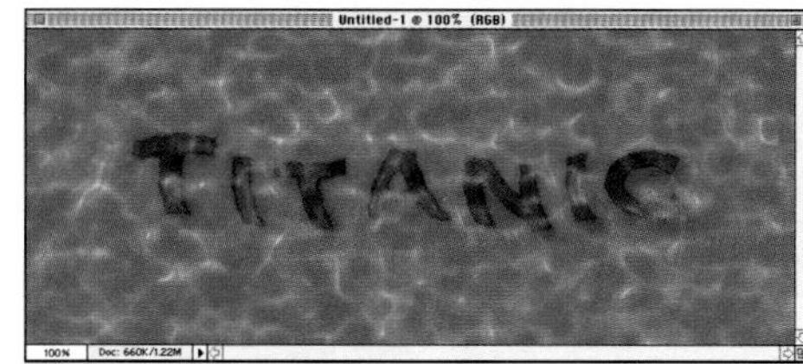

## VARIATIONS

To create the watery text without the background, follow Steps 1 to 10. Then,

**11** Load the selection Channel #5 to load the shadow channel. Choose for the foreground color a color for the shadow. Here we used cyan. Press (Option-Delete) [Alt-Delete] to fill the selection. If the shadow isn't dark enough, press (Option-Delete) [Alt-Delete] again as we did here.

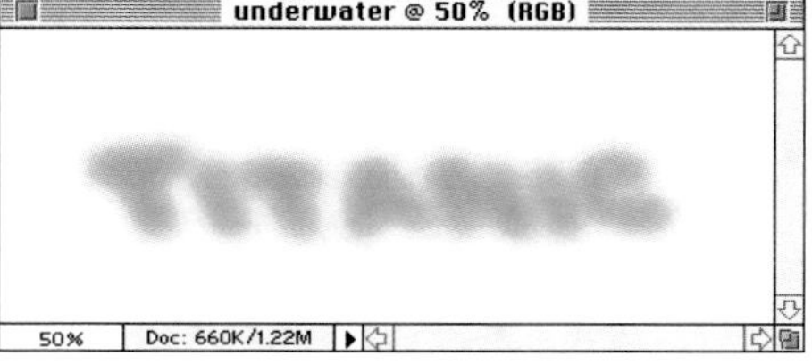

**12** Load the selection Channel #4 to load the text channel. Choose a foreground color for the text be. We used a dark blue color. Press (Option-Delete) [Alt-Delete] to fill the selection.

**13** Load the selection Channel #6 to load the highlight channel. Choose white as the background color. Press Delete to fill the selection. If you want the highlights brighter, press Delete again. (Using the Plastic Wrap filter causes some dark streaks in the large white areas of the image which are much more noticeable on white than on a colored background.) ■

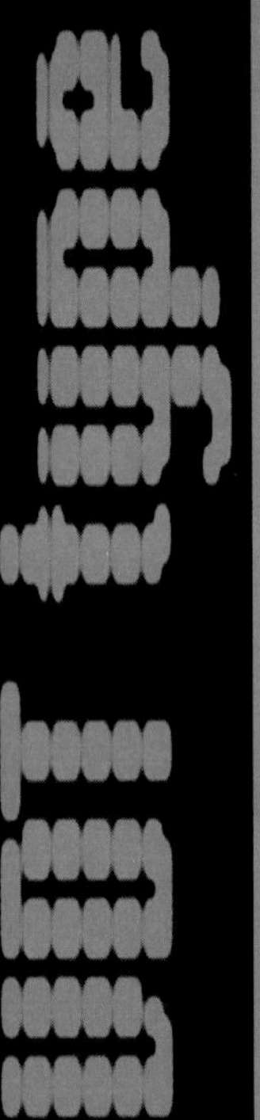

This effect works best if you intend to use it for onscreen display. In other words, if you are going to use it as an RGB image. You just can't get that glowing green color in a CMYK image.

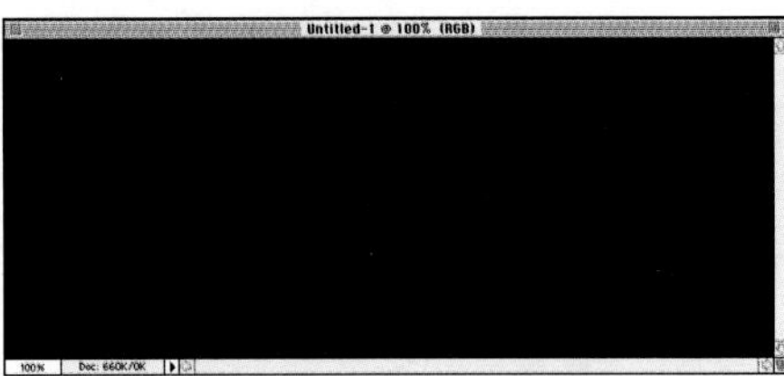

**1** Create a new file. Choose black as the foreground color (press D), and press (Option-Delete) [Alt-Delete] to fill the image with black.

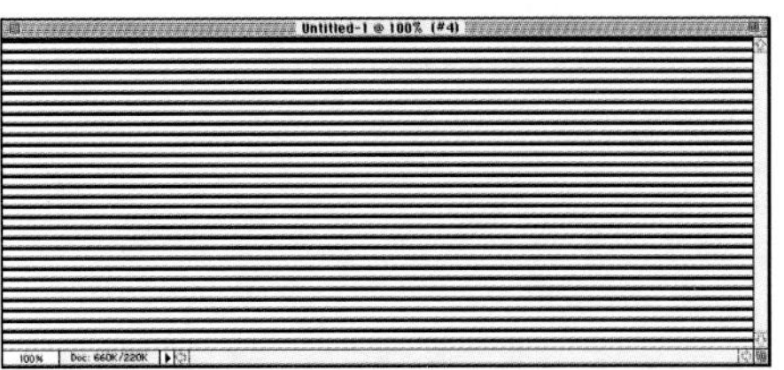

**2** Create a new channel (#4), choose Filter➡Render➡Texture Fill, and load the StripesForVDT file from the *Type Magic* CD-ROM. Or, create the stripes yourself: First, use the rectangular Marquee tool to select the left half of the new channel, and fill the selection with white. Then choose Filter➡Distort➡Wave (Type: square; Generators: 1; Wavelength: 1, 50; Amplitude: 999,999; Horiz.: 100; Vert.: 0). Be sure to choose the Repeat Edge Pixels option. Choose Filter➡Other➡Maximum (amount: 1) to fatten the white stripes and thin down the black stripes.

**Use the upper-limit value of the Wavelength in the Wave filter to control the thickness of the lines if you are using a different size type. If you increase this value, then slightly increase the value used when applying the Maximum filter to this channel.**



## TOOLBOX

Xaos Tools' Paint Alchemy (Mac only)

StripesForVDT file

3 Create another new channel (#5) and use the Type Mask tool to enter the text you want to use. We used 90-point Compacta Bold for this effect.

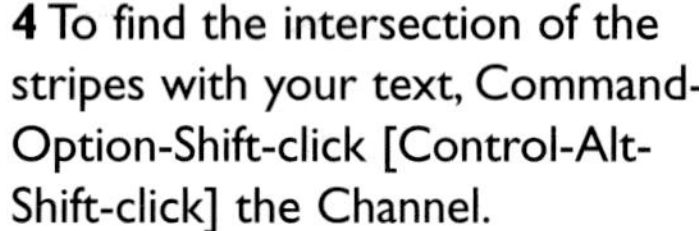
4 To find the intersection of the stripes with your text, Command-Option-Shift-click [Control-Alt-Shift-click] the Channel.

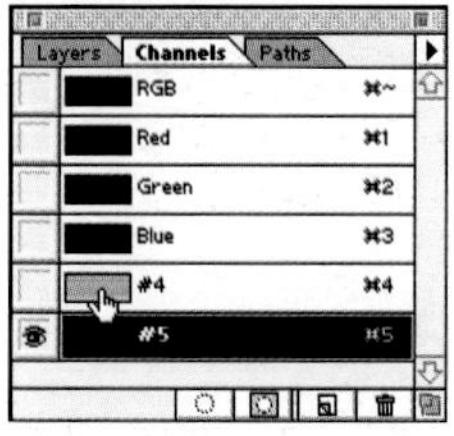

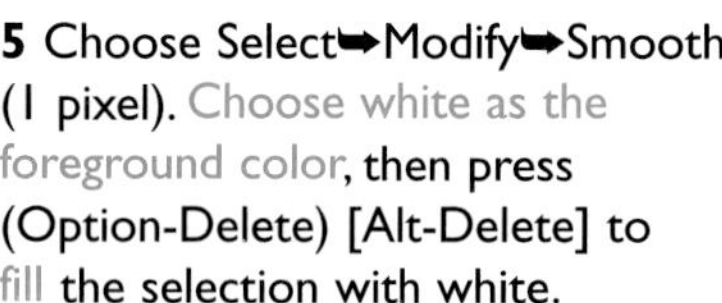
5 Choose Select➥Modify➥Smooth (1 pixel). Choose white as the foreground color, then press (Option-Delete) [Alt-Delete] to fill the selection with white.

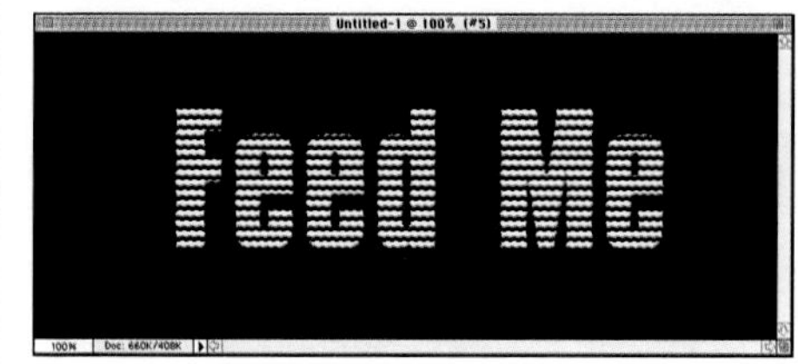

6 Choose Filter➥Blur➥Gaussian Blur (5 pixels). Deselect the type (Command-D) [Control-D].

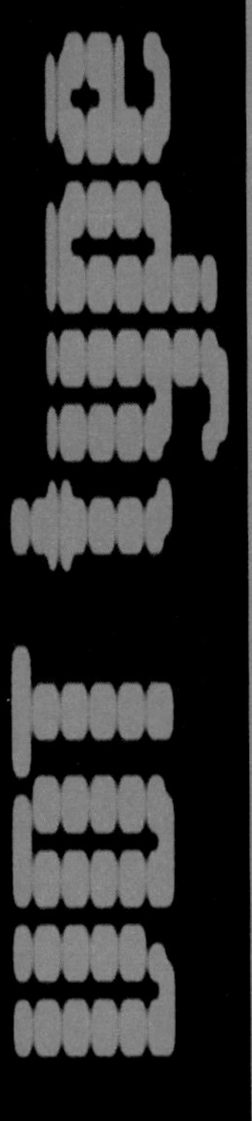

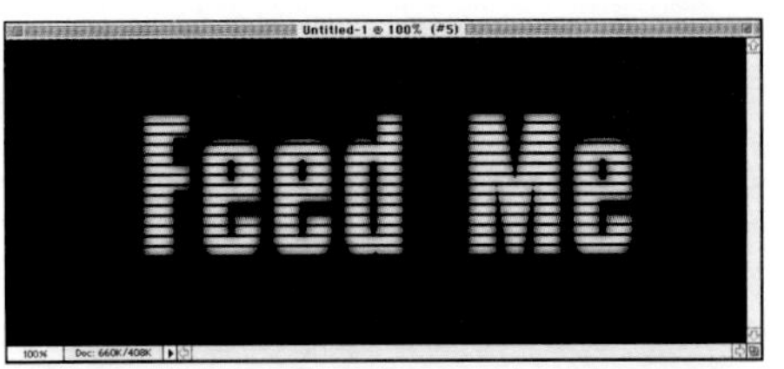


**7** Choose Image➡Adjust➡Brightness/Contrast and raise the contrast to 25.

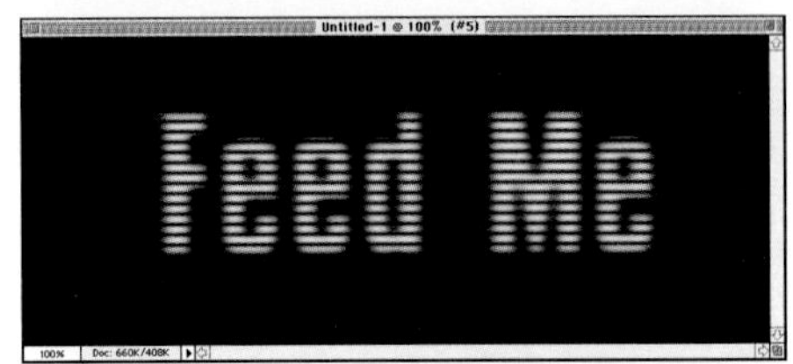


**8** Choose Filter➡Blur➡Motion Blur (Angle: 0; Distance: 10). Choose Filter➡Blur➡Gaussian Blur (1 pixel).

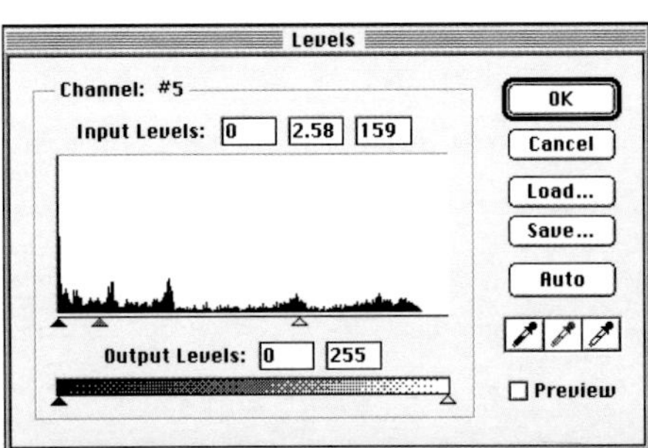


**9** Choose Image➡Adjust➡Levels (settings: 0, 2.58, 159).

**10** (Command-~) [Control-~], and choose a foreground color. Here, we used R: 0, G: 255, B: 0. Load the selection Channel #5 (the blurred text). Press (Option-Delete) [Alt-Delete] two or three times to fill the selection to the desired brightness.

TIP **If you plan on using this text as a CMYK file, you should convert to CMYK mode (Mode➥CMYK Mode) before selecting the foreground color. That way you won't be shocked when you convert to CMYK mode and find all the brightness stripped from your otherwise-glorious VDT text.**

**11** Press (Command-D) [Control-D] to deselect the text. A final blurring finishes it off. Choose Filter➥Blur➥ Gaussian Blur (1 pixel).

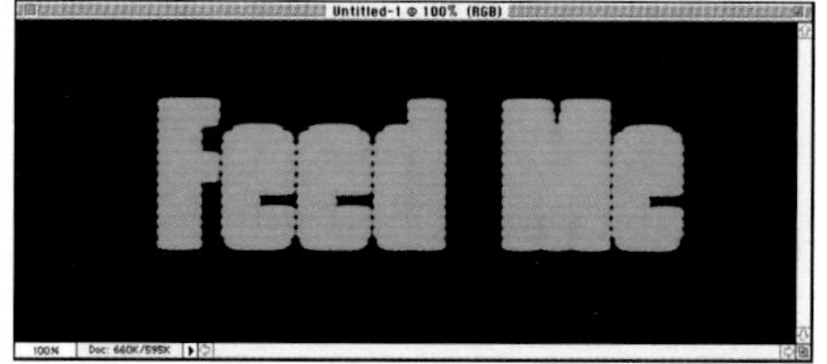

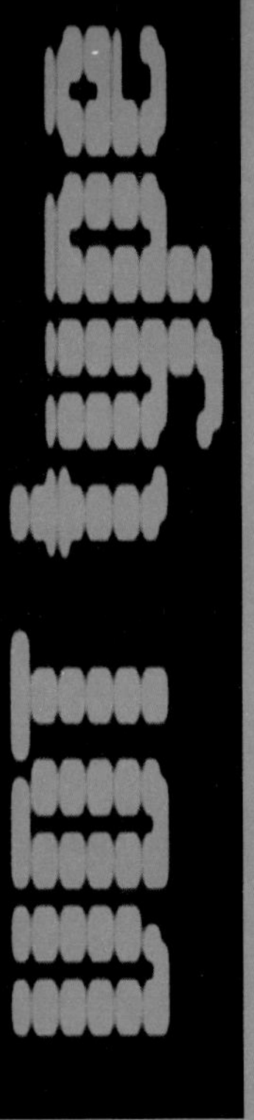

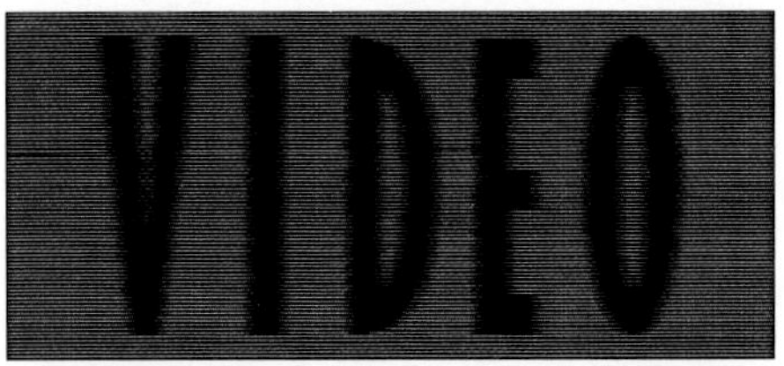

## Variations

Apply Filter➥Xaos Tools➥Paint Alchemy (Video Styles➥Blue Video). The Gilded CD font was used for these examples.

If green is your favorite color, color the type black and apply Filter➥ Xaos Tools➥Paint Alchemy (Video Styles➥Green Video). That's all there is to it. ■

**1** Open a file containing a cement background. The file must be in RGB format because this effect uses the Lighting Effects filter. We used a stock photo of stucco which you can find in the D'Pix folder.

**2** Create a new channel (#4). Use the Type tool to enter the text. Use a font that looks like it has been handwritten or distort the text to make it look handwritten. Deselect the text (Command-D) [Control-D].

**3** Duplicate Channel #4 (#5). In the new channel, choose Filter➥ Stylize➥ Diffuse (Lighten Only). Press (Command-F) [Control-F] four or five times to re-apply the filter.

**TOOLBOX**

PlasticLightStyles file

**4** Load the selection Channel #4 (the text selection). Choose Filter➥Blur➥Gaussian Blur (4 pixels).

**5** Press (Command-I) [Control-I] to invert the area within the selection. Choose Brightness/Contrast and raise the Brightness to about 55 and the Contrast to 20. Deselect the text (Command-D)[Control-D].

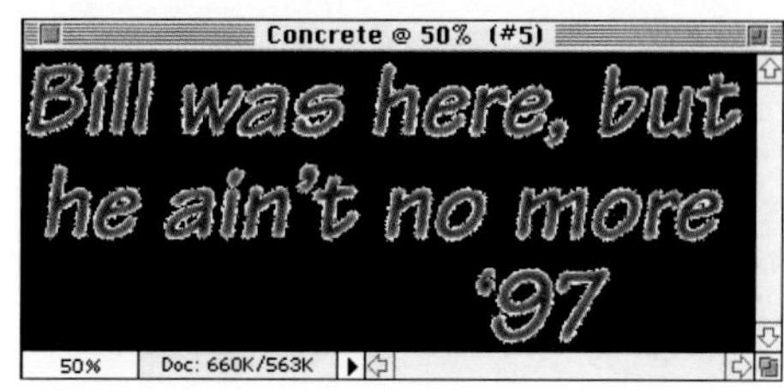


**6** Return to the composite channel. Choose Filter➥Render➥Lighting Effects. Choose the PlasticLight-Styles from the pop-up menu. Choose Channel #5 for the texture channel, change the Height to about 45. To move the light so it doesn't wash out the type, click it in the preview and drag it to its new location.

TIP **If the PlasticLightStyles does not appear in the menu, then you need to load it into your Adobe Photoshop folder. See Appendix A, "What's On the CD-ROM", on page 241 for more info.**

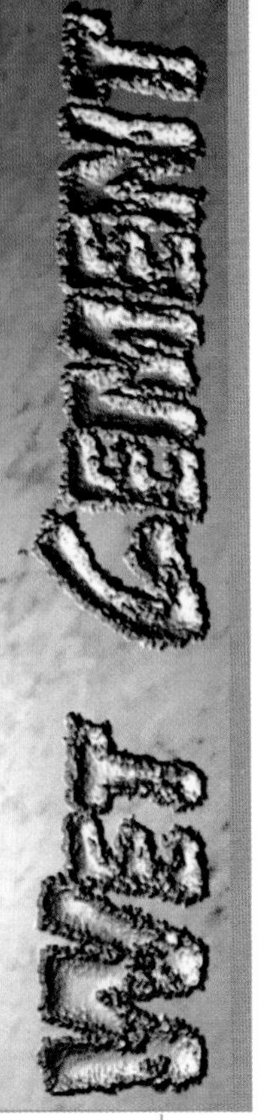

## VARIATIONS

To make the text look more hand-written, use the Paintbrush tool to draw the letters. Choose a hard-edged brush and follow the rest of the steps.

Try using a rougher font such as Brush Stroke Fast. Before deselecting the text in Step 5, choose Filter➡Stylize➡Diffuse (Lighten Only). Reapply the filter (Command-F) [Control-F], deselect the text (Command-D) [Control-D], do Step 6, and you're done.

If you want to make a mess, before deselecting the text in Step 5, choose Filter➥Stylize➥Find Edges. Follow Step 6. Make Channel #5 active, set the Magic Wand tool Tolerance to 10, and use it to click in the white area surrounding the text (also, hold the Shift key and click in white areas in the middle of letters such as O and Q). Return to the composite channel. Choose white as the foreground color and press (Option-Delete) [Alt-Delete] to fill the selection with white. ■

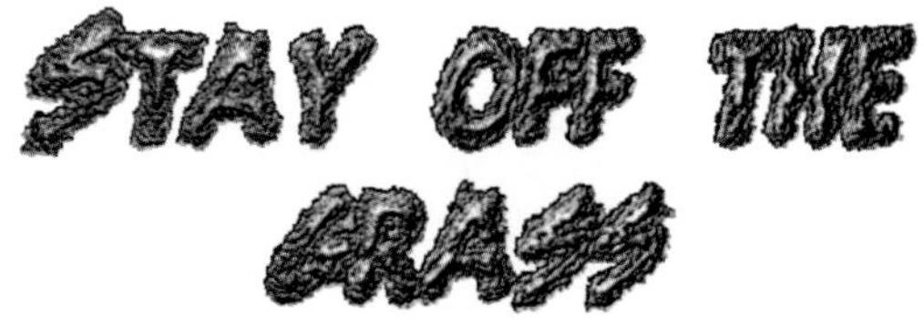

# Appendix A

## What's On the CD-ROM

The CD-ROM that comes with this book is both Macintosh and Windows compatible. Please note that there are several demos and tryouts available for Macintosh users that are not available for Windows users, and vice versa. This means that either the product does not exist for that platform, or a version is being created but was not available at the time of publication.

We suggest that you refer to the READ ME and other information files included in the demo software program's folder. Also, visit the corporate Web sites for updates and more information. (The URLs are noted in Appendix B.) There are often demos of new software available for downloading and tryout.

The CD-ROM is divided into six folders. Macintosh folder names are in parentheses, and Windows folders are in brackets.

### Contents

#### (Type Effect Preset Files) [TEPF]

This is a collection of ready-to-use files listed in the Toolbox section of techniques in the book. You'll need to install and refer to these files when creating certain type effects.

#### (Effects) [EFFECTS]

This is a collection of effects for manipulating images in Photoshop. Featured is a sampler of edge effects from AutoF/X.

#### (Filters)

This folder contains lots of different filters you can use to manipulate your images. You can do a variety of things with filters, one of the most powerful features of Photoshop. Some of these filters are freeware, some are shareware, and some are commercial demos.

#### (Fonts) [FONTS]

Here you will find an excellent selection of shareware fonts to use in the various type effects.

#### (Images) [IMAGES]

You'll need some high-quality images to use as backdrops for some of the type effects described in the book. This collection of images from various commercial stock photo companies will give you plenty to play with.

#### (Software) [SOFTWARE]

This folder contains demos of commerical software, including Adobe products, Specular LogoMotion and Equilibrium DeBabelizer—plus much much more.

# Photoshop 4 Type Magic 1

## Installation

For detailed instructions on how to install and use the resources we've included on the CD-ROM, please consult the READ ME or ABOUT files in the individual software, filter, effects, and imagery folders. General installation information follows:

### Filters

Filters should be copied into the Plug-Ins folder, located in the same place as your Adobe Photoshop application. Then, restart your computer, relaunch Photoshop, and find the filters in the Filter menu. You can now access and apply these third-party filters the same way you use Photoshop's filters.

### Preset Files

Before installing the type effects preset files, we recommend you first create a new folder to hold all the presets *except the lighting styles files*. It is *extremely* important that you remember to put the lighting styles files (all named with "LightingStyles" after the effect's name) in the Photoshop➡Plug-Ins➡Filters➡Lighting Effects➡Lighting Styles folder with the other Photoshop lighting styles, otherwise they will not work.

The other preset files we have provided can be opened via the Select a Document dialog box. To bring up this box, you can either choose File➡Open or wait till Photoshop automatically opens it for you, as in the Liquid effect when you choose Load Settings in the Curve dialog box to load LiquidCurve. In either situation, you'll open the Photoshop folder on your hard drive, find the preset folder you created at the start and select the preset file you'd like.

### Fonts (Macintosh)

Fonts should go in the Fonts folder, located in your System Folder. If you would like to try out a specific font, drag it to your closed System Folder. You should see a message stating that the fonts will be moved to the Fonts folder In the case of Type I fonts, you might need to drag multiple files to your System Folder.



### Fonts (Windows)

Fonts should be installed by means of the Fonts Control Panel. Under Windows 95 or Windows NT 4.0 open Start Menu➡Settings➡Control Panel➡Fonts. Then select File➡ Install New Font...from the File menu and select the font from the CD-ROM which you want to install. The fonts can all be found within the Fonts directory on the CD-ROM.

### Stock imagery and textures

The stock photos and textures located in the Images folder do not need to be copied to your hard drive. Because many of them are very large, you'll want to open them from the CD-ROM so they do not take up all the space on your hard drive. For most files, you can double-click on them to open them in Photoshop. If they do not, try opening Photoshop first, then select File➡Open. Then choose the file you would like to open. If you particularly like a certain image and would like to access it quickly, by all means copy it to your hard drive.

## A Note about Shareware

If you use any shareware items beyond an initial trial period, you are obligated to follow the guidelines set forth by the author; this is usually in the form of a reasonable shareware payment. Your purchase of this book and the accompanying CD-ROM does not release you from this obligation. Refer to the READ ME and other information files that accompany each of the programs for specifics.

# Appendix B

## Contributor's Listing

### Fonts

**Fonthead Design (Mac and PC)**

1872-B Darryl Drive
Tallahassee, FL 32301-6017
ethan@fonthead.com
http://www.fonthead.com

**Snyder Shareware Fonts (Mac and PC)**

1797 Ross Inlet Road
Coos Bay, OR 97420
http://www.coos.or.us/~snyderrp/
snyderrp@mailF.coos.or.us rps82@aol.com 76307.2431@compuserve.com

**Synstelien Design (Mac and PC)**

1338 North 120th Plaza Apt. # 9
Omaha, NE 68154
Phone: (402) 491-3065
http://www.synfonts.com
dsynstftrel@aol.com

**Vintage Type (Mac and PC**

5662 Calle Real #146
Goleta, CA 93117-2317
http://www.vintagetype.com/
sales@vintagetype.com



### Effects

**AutoFX Sample Edge Effects (Mac and PC)**

15 North Main Street Suite 8
Wolfeboro, NH 03894
Phone: (603) 569-8800
Fax: (603) 569-9702
http://www.autofx.com
sales@autofx.com

## Software & Filters

### Adobe Systems, Inc.

345 Park Avenue
San Jose, CA 95110-6000
Phone: (408) 536-6000
Fax: (408) 537-6000
sales@adobe.com
http://www.adobe.com
On the CD-ROM:
Acrobat Reader 3.0 (Mac and PC)
Photoshop 3.0.5 Tryout (Mac and PC)
After Effects 3.0 Tryout (Mac only)
Streamline 3.1 Tryout (Mac and PC)
Dimensions 2.0 Tryout (Mac only)
Illustrator 6.0 Tryout (Mac only)

### Alien Skin Software

1100 Wake Forest Rd. Suite 101
Raleigh, NC 27604
Phone: (919) 832-4124
Fax: (919) 832-4065
alien-skinfo@alienskin.com
http://www.alienskin.com
On the CD-ROM:
Eye Candy 3.0 Demo (Mac and PC)

### Andromeda Software, Inc.

699 Hampshire Rd. Suite 109
Thousand Oaks, CA 91361
Phone: (800) 547-0055 or (805) 379-4109
Fax: (805) 379-5253
orders@andromeda.com
http://www.andromeda.com
On the CD-ROM:
Series 1,2, & 3 Demos (Mac and PC)

### Chris Cox

110 Oakland Circle
Madison, AL 35758-8663
ccox@teleport.com|
http://www.teleport.com/~ccox
On the CD-ROM:
Chris's Filters 3.0 (Mac only)

### DataStream Imaging Systems, Inc.

P.O. Box 2148
Lexington, KY 40595-2148
(800) 889-7781 (Orders Only)
Phone: (606) 264-0302
Fax: (606) 263-0183
http://www.datastrem.com
ftp.datastrem.com
On the CD-ROM:
Wild River SSK Demo (Mac only)

### Equilibrium

3 Harbor Drive Suite 111
Sausalito, CA 94965
Phone: (415) 332-4433
Fax: (415) 332-4433
BBS: (415) 332-6152
sales@equilibrium.com
http://www.equilibrium.com
On the CD-ROM:
DeBabelizer Pro Demo (Windows only)
DeBabelizer Lite LE (Mac only)
DeBabelizer 1.6.5 Demo (Mac only)

### Jawai Interactive, Inc.

401 East Fourth Street Suite 443
Austin, TX 78701-3745
Phone: (800) 600-6706 or (512) 469-0502
Fax: (512) 469-7850
info@jawai.com
http://www.jawai.com
On the CD-ROM:
ScreenCaffeine Demo (Mac and PC)

### MetaTools, Inc.

6303 Carpinteria Ave.
Carpinteria, CA 93013
(805) 566-6200
metasales@aol.com
http://www.metatools.com
Neil Schulman
nwcs@usit.net
On the CD-ROM:
KPT 3.0 Demo (Mac and PC)
Frosty Filter (Mac only)

**Specular, International**

7 Pomeroy Lane
Amherst, MA 01002
Phone: (800) 433-SPEC
Fax: (413) 253-0540
sales@specular.com
http://www.specular.com
On the CD-ROM:
Infini-D Demo (Mac and PC)
Collage 2.0 Demo (Mac only)
LogoMotion Demo (Mac only)
TextureScape Demo (Mac only)

**Xaos Tools, Inc.**

55 Hawthorn Suite 1000
San Francisco, CA 94105
Phone: (800) BUY-XAOS
macinfo@xaostools.com
http://www.xaostools.com
On the CD-ROM:
Paint Alchemy 2 Demo (Mac only)
Terrazo 2 Demo (Mac only)
TypeCaster Demo (Mac only)

## Stock Images

**Digital Stock**

400 S. Sierra Ave., Suite 100
Solana Beach, CA 92075
Phone: (619) 794-4040 or (800) 545-4514
Fax: (619) 794-4041
http://www.digitalstock.com
sales@digitalstock.com

**D'Pix Division of Amber Productions, Inc.**

414 W. Fourth Ave.
Columbus, OH 43201
Phone: (614) 299-7192
Fax: (614) 294-0002

**FotoSets**

4104 24th St., #425
San Francisco, CA 94114
Phone: (415) 621-2061
Fax: (415) 621-2917

**Image Club Graphics**

729 24th Ave. SE
Calgary, AB Canada
T2G 5K8
Phone: (403) 262-8008 or (800) 661-9410
Fax: (403)261-7013
http://www.adobe.com/imageclub

**Photo24 Texture Resource**

7948 Faust Ave.
West Hills, CA 91304
Phone: (818) 999-4184 or (800) 582-9492 (outside CA)
Fax: (818) 999-5704
http://www.photo24.com

**PhotoDisc/CMCD**

2013 Fourth Ave., 4th Floor
Seattle, WA 98121
Phone: (206) 441-9355 or (800) 528-3472
http://www.photodisc.com

# Gallery

Background



Beveled



Bitmap



Blurred

Credit Card

Earthquake



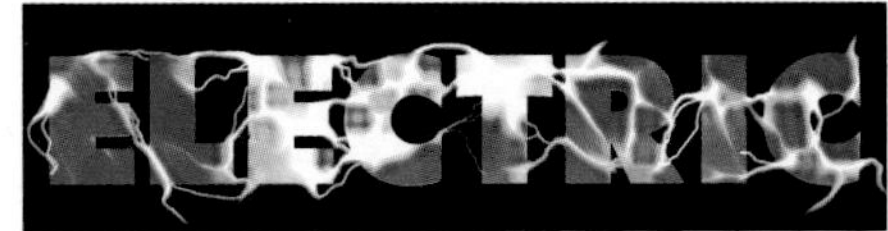

Gel

*page 86*

*page 90*

*page 96*

*page 104*

*page 110*

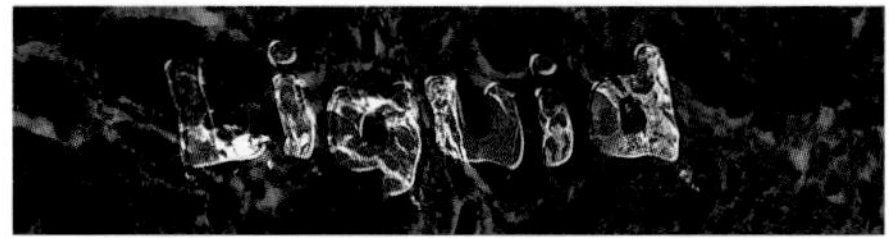


*page 116*

MARQUEE

*page 124*

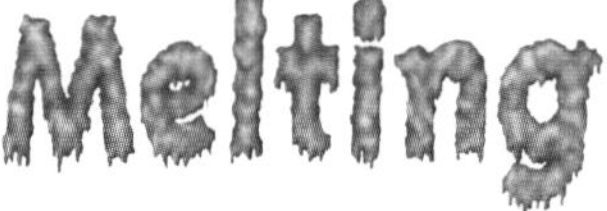


*page 126*

*page 130*

*page 134*

OVERGROWN

*page 142*

*page 148*

*page 154*

Peel-Away

*page 160*

*page 166*

*page 170*

## Photoshop 4 Type Magic 1

Plastic

*page 174*

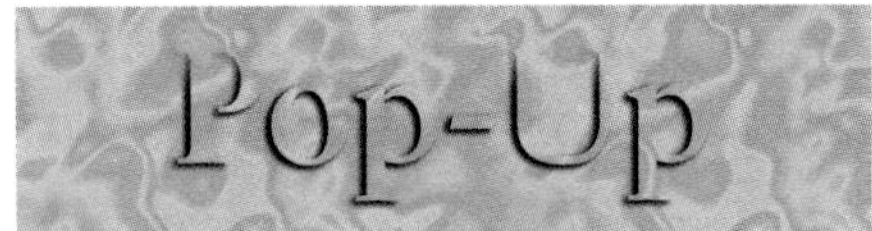


*page 178*

*page 180*

Rough Edges

*page 184*

*page 190*

*page 194*

*page 200*

*page 202*

*page 206*

*page 210*

*page 214*

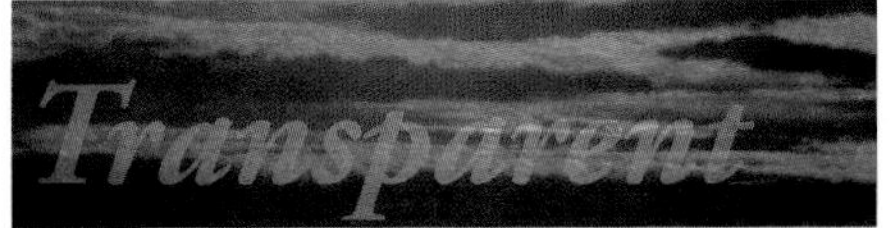


*page 220*

UNDERWATER

*page 224*

*page 230*

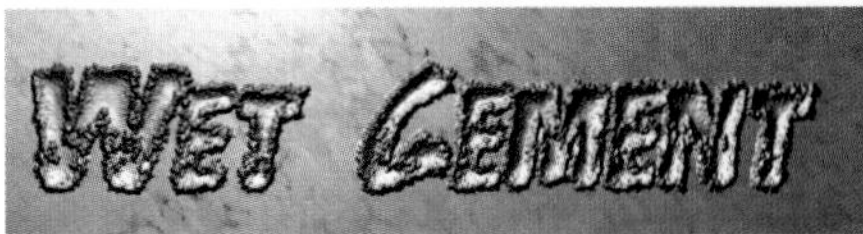


*page 236*

# Technical Support:

If you cannot get the CD/Disk to install properly, or you need assistance with a particular situation in the book, please feel free to check out the Knowledge Base on our Web site at **http://www.superlibrary.com/general/support**. We have answers to our most Frequently Asked Questions listed there. If you do not find your specific question answered, please contact Macmillan Technical Support at **(317) 581-3833**. We can also be reached by email at **support@mcp.com**.

# Photoshop 5 Type Magic

Stanger
Stet · Fortuna · Domus

# Photoshop 5 Type Magic

BY GREG SIMSIC

# Photoshop 5 Type Magic

©1998 New Riders Publishing

All rights reserved. No part of this book shall be reproduced, stored in a retrieval system, or transmitted by any means, electronic, mechanical, photocopying, recording, or otherwise, without written permission from the publisher. No patent liability is assumed with respect to the use of the information contained herein. Although every precaution has been taken in the preparation of this book, the publisher and author assume no responsibility for errors or omissions. Neither is any liability assumed for damages resulting from the use of the information contained herein.

International Standard Book Number: 156830-465-x

Library of Congress Catalog Card Number: 98-84021

Printed in the United States of America

First Printing: June, 1998

00 99 98 4 3 2 1

Interpretation of the printing code: the rightmost double-digit number is the year of the book's printing; the rightmost single-digit number is the number of the book's printing. For example, a printing code of 95-1 shows that the first printing of the book occurred in 1995.

This book was produced digitally by Macmillan Computer Publishing and manufactured using computer-to-plate technology (a film-less process) by GAC/Shepard Poorman, Indianapolis, Indiana.

## Trademarks

All terms mentioned in this book that are known to be trademarks or service marks have been appropriately capitalized. New Riders Publishing cannot attest to the accuracy of this information. Use of a term in this book should not be regarded as affecting the validity of any trademark or service mark.

Photoshop is a trademark of Adobe Systems, Inc.



**Publisher**
Jordan Gold

**Executive and Development Editor**
Beth Millett

**Managing Editor**
Brice Gosnell

**Software Development Specialist**
Adam Swetnam

**Project Editor**
Kevin Laseau

**Copy Editor**
San Dee Phillips

**Technical Editor**
Kate Binder

**Cover Designer**
Aren Howell

**Book Designer**
Gary Adair

**Production**
Marcia Deboy
Michael Dietsch
Jennifer Earhart
Cynthia Fields
Maureen West

# About the Authors

## Greg Simsic

*Photoshop 5 Type Magic* is Greg's third Photoshop type effects book. Greg has traveled the world designing type effects for the rich and poor, young and old, beautiful and ugly alike. He is driven by the belief that everyone should have some "magic" in their lives even if they don't really deserve it. Despite his busy schedule, he always makes time to come home and spend quality time with his pet yak, Camille. "She grounds me," says Greg. Those who were lucky enough to attend the 65th annual Pixies, the Oscars of the flaming logo world, will keep close to their hearts his overheard words, "I dunno, blur it some."

# Acknowledgements

## Special Thanks to...

I would like to thank all of the little people for making me seem taller.

I would also like to thank Beth, Kevin, Adam, Kate and all others who transformed my meanders into a book. Those of you who also fit into the first category please take a second bow.

# Contents at a Glance

# Contents

# Introduction

You might as well face it. Every time Adobe puts out a new version of Photoshop, you will see another *Type Magic* book in the bookstores. But there is good reason to celebrate with a new book this time because Adobe Photoshop 5.0 contains several great new features, including built-in effects such as drop shadows, glows and bevels, editable text layers, aviind a new History palette that allows for multiple undos. These new features make it easier to get to where you're headed—assuming you know where that is. So, I've gone back through some of the old techniques and brought them back in this book—new and improved. Of course, you won't see some of the old effects because the new features are good enough to have made them obsolete. I skipped over these to bring you a whole new batch of never-seen-before-world-premiere-what-will-they-think-of-next-when-would-I-ever-use-that effects. To top it off, the CD-ROM that they told me they would put in the back of this book includes actions that enable you to apply some of the effects in the book at the touch of a button.

Thanks for stopping by, and I hope you enjoy the book.

Greg Simsic

# Before You Start

## Welcome

Welcome to this third volume of special type techniques for Adobe Photoshop users. More than a how-to manual, this book is a what-to guide. The steps in this book tell you exactly what you need to do in order to create exactly what you want. Flip through the alphabetized thumbtabs to find the type effect you want to create and follow the concise, explanatory steps. If you need a little extra help, flip to the Photoshop Basics section. But, before you jump into the type treatments, let me tell you a little about how this book works. A quick read now will maximize your time later.

## System Setup

Most machines now have plenty of power to run Photoshop. With each new Photoshop upgrade, there is an increase in the amount of memory that it takes to run it, but with so many computers equipped for multimedia these days, the basic requirements seem easy to meet. All of the effects in this book were quickly created on a 132Mhz machine with 72 megabytes of RAM and no special graphics acceleration.

When setting up your system, remember that you can never have too much RAM. Adobe recommends 24 to 32MB to run Photoshop. Allocate as much memory to Photoshop as you possibly can to get the most out of your machine.

It is not crucial, but it will help if you have a CD-ROM drive. A number of the effects in this book use files contained on the CD-ROM bundled with this book. (See Appendix B, "What's on the CD-ROM," for information on accessing those files.) However, even if you don't have a CD-ROM drive, you still can perform most of the effects described in the book.

## Adobe Photoshop 5.0

All of the techniques in this book were created with Adobe Photoshop 5.0, and that's the version I recommend you use. If you're attempting to duplicate these techniques using an earlier version of Photoshop, your results might differ slightly or significantly compared to mine. If you work with version 4.0, the biggest deficiency you face is the lack of the new Layer Effects features. I used these features in the book when they made things easier. If you know your way around Photoshop, you can work around most of these situations. Almost all the effects can be created by version 3.0 also, but again beware of the missing Layer Effects. In short, if you have an older version of Photoshop, you can use the techniques in this book as guidelines, but you might not be able to follow them verbatim. Most of the effects in this book use features that were not available in versions of Photoshop earlier than 3.0.

## What's New in Adobe Photoshop 5.0

The latest version of Photoshop has many new changes. Some are minor and some are major. Two major new features change the way that you work through these techniques: Layer effects and the History palette. The History palette is Photoshop's name for multiple undos. With the History palette, you can move backward and forward through up to your last 100 steps. Each of the steps appears on the History palette in the order that you performed them. This feature is invaluable when you work through step-by-step techniques such as those provided in this book. To return to a previous stage in the technique, all you have to do is click on the name of the command in the History palette. Or press (Command-Option-Z) [Control-Alt-Z] to move backward through the steps. To move forward again, press (Command-Shift-Z) [Control-Shift-Z].

Layer effects are features that enable you to apply built-in special effects to individual layers. Drop shadows, glows, and bevels are all covered by the layer effects. The interface for these effects is well-designed, making some of the techniques from my previous books obsolete. You can apply more than one effect to a single layer and even apply them to special type layers, also new to Photoshop 5.0, and still have editable text. It is important to remember that these effects are only applied to the layers. The information in the layer has not changed; the effects can be turned on and off at any time. These effects have been used in this book to save time and effort.

## Conventions

Almost all the type effects in this book were created as RGB files. Many techniques in this book use filters that will not work in CMYK or Grayscale mode files. You can make your effects in any appropriate color mode, but you should be aware of the differences in the color ranges of the various color modes. Some colors that look great in RGB mode might look like mud after you convert the file color mode to CMYK. If you intend to print your files, it is a good rule to work in the RGB mode (in order to take advantage of all Photoshop's features) and turn on the CMYK preview (in order to keep track of what the colors will look like when turn into a CMYK image). To turn on the CMYK preview, choose View➡CMYK Preview.

If you want more detailed information about the different color modes, refer to a good general Photoshop book such as *Inside Adobe Photoshop 5* or to your Photoshop user manuals.

The type images were also created as 5-inch-by-2-inch, 150dpi resolution files. If you are going to work in a resolution other than 150dpi, remember that some of the filters and commands require different settings than the settings I used. Because a 72dpi image has few pixels, a Gaussian Blur radius of 5 pixels blurs the image more than if it were a 150dpi image. Just keep an eye on the figures next to the steps and match the outcome as close as you can.

### The Toolbox

For some of the effects, I used specially prepared preset files. Any of these extras files not included with the standard Photoshop software are listed in the Toolbox in the lower-left corner of the first page of each technique. The Toolbox lists everything that you need to create each type effect and any of its variations. The CD-ROM that comes with this book contains all the files needed to perform all the basic techniques. For information on accessing these files, turn to Appendix B, "What's on the CD-ROM."

## The Blue Type

As you work through the steps, you see phrases colored a light blue. These same phrases appear in alphabetical order in the Photoshop Basics section. If the phrase in blue asks you to perform a task that you are unfamiliar with, you can find that phrase in the Photoshop Basics section and follow the instructions on how to perform that task. Advanced users can perform the task as they normally would.

## Menu Commands

You also will see instructions that look like this:

Filter➡Blur➡Gaussian Blur (2 pixels)

This example asks you to apply the Gaussian Blur filter. To perform this command, click on the Filter menu at the top of the screen and drag down to Blur. When Blur appears highlighted, a new menu opens to the right, from which you can choose Gaussian Blur.

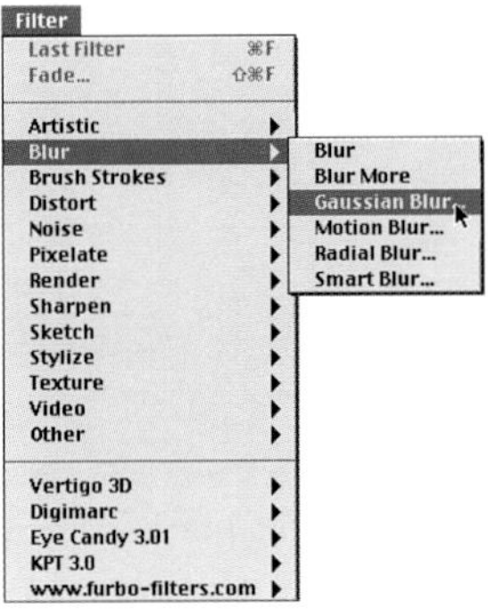


In this example, a dialog box appears asking you for more information. All the settings that you need to perform each task appear in the text of the step. The preceding example tells you to enter 2 pixels as the Radius.

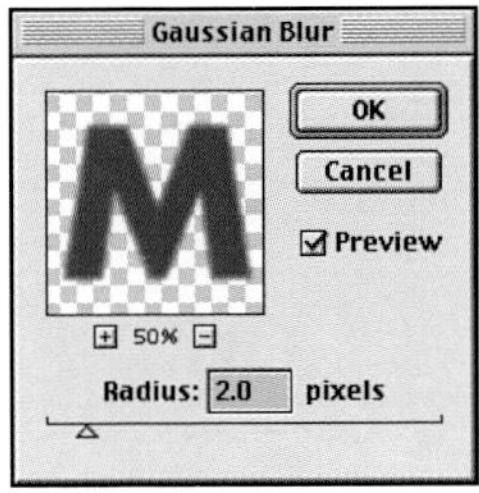

Click OK to blur the type.

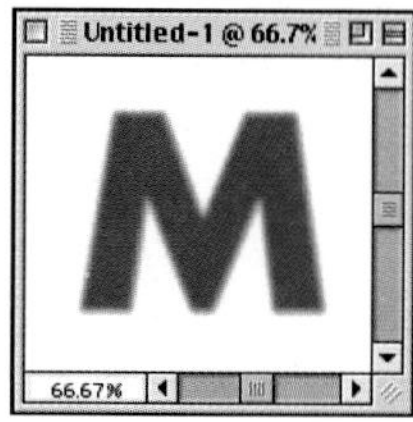


## Settings

Following each action in the steps, you will find the settings for that feature. These recommended settings are meant to act as guides; the best settings for your type effect might vary. As a rule of thumb, it is best to match the outcomes that you see in the figures as you progress through the technique. The greatest differences occur when the resolution of your file and/or the point-size of your type are significantly different from what I used. The following two images demonstrate the importance of adjusting for resolution differences. A 6-pixel radius Gaussian Blur was applied to both images.

75 dpi

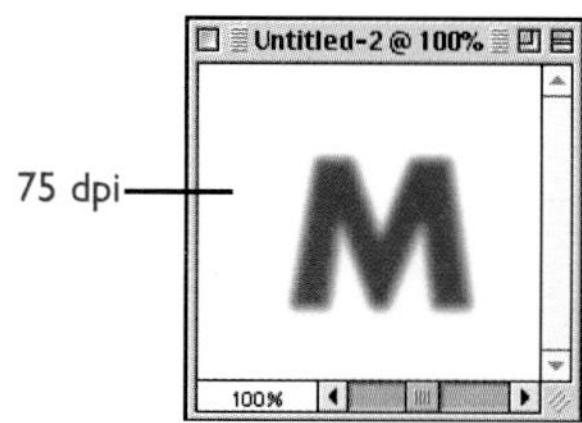


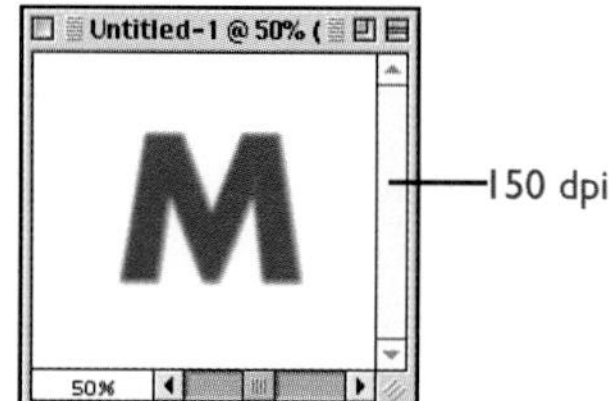


150 dpi

## Tips

Throughout the book, you will find additional bits of information that can help you render a better type effect. These tips provide information beyond the basic steps of each technique. ●

# Photoshop Basics

The goal of this section is to help new and novice users of Photoshop with the basic tasks required to create the type effects illustrated in this book. Each of the basic tasks in this section corresponds to the blue highlighted text in the chapters that follow. Here you can easily find the instructions you need for performing a particular Photoshop task.

This chapter proceeds on two assumptions: that you create our type effects in Photoshop 5.0, and that you keep the Tool and Layer/Channel/Path palettes open. If one or both of the Tool and Layer/Channel/Path palettes are closed when you refer to this chapter, you can reopen them by name by using the Window menu at the top of the screen. If you use an earlier version of Photoshop, you can refer to the Photoshop manual for instructions on how to perform these tasks. Keep in mind that these instructions are for Photoshop 5.0 and instructions for earlier versions might differ.

## The Toolbox

If you're not familiar with Photoshop's Toolbox, don't panic. With a bit of experimentation, it doesn't take long to learn each tool's individual functions. To help the beginning Photoshop user along the way, here is a representation of the Toolbox. This also helps advanced users find the rearranged tools.

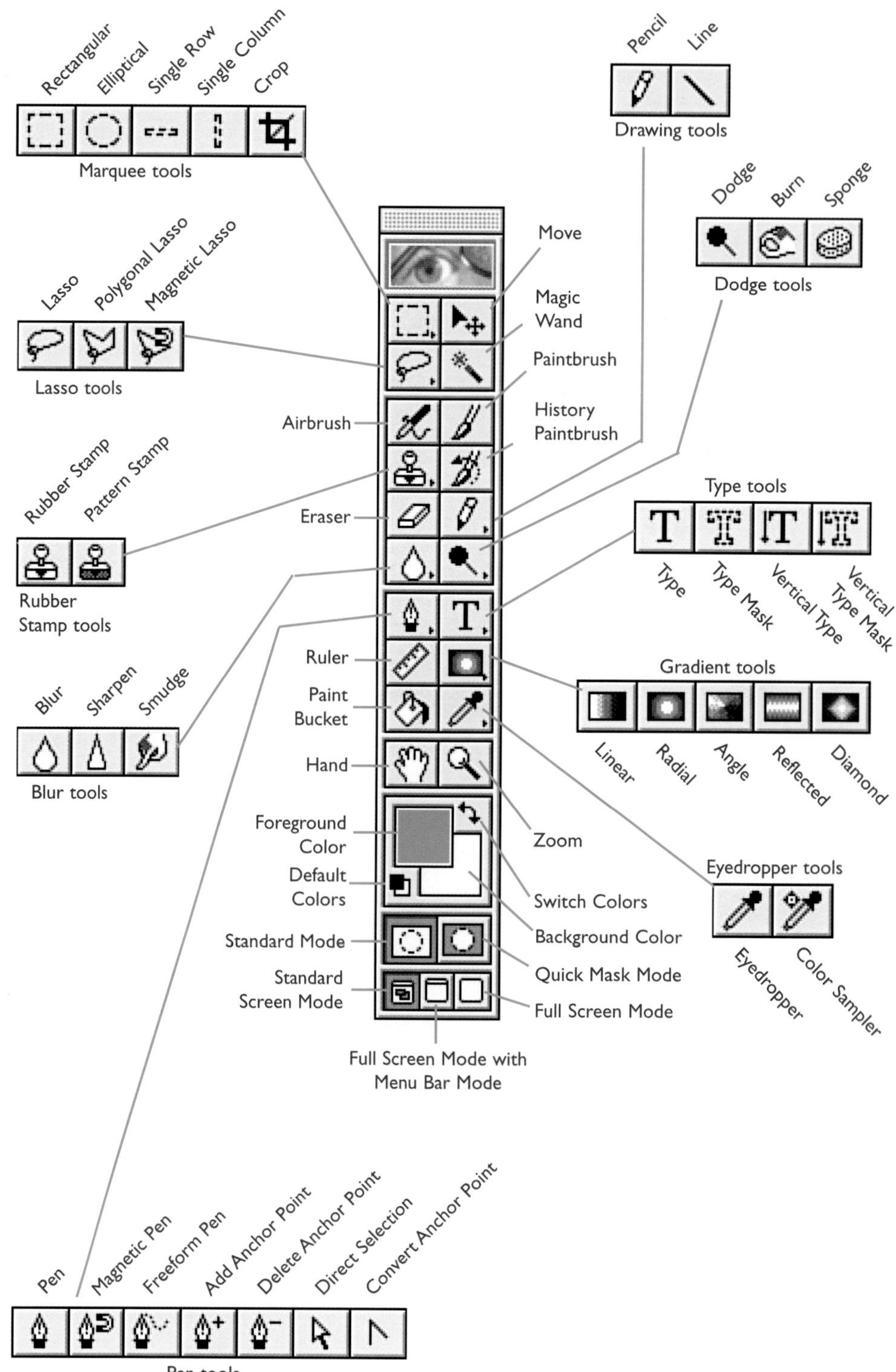
Rectangular
Elliptical
Single Row
Single Column
Crop
Marquee tools
Pencil
Line
Drawing tools
Dodge
Burn
Sponge
Dodge tools
Lasso
Polygonal Lasso
Magnetic Lasso
Lasso tools
Move
Magic Wand
Paintbrush
Airbrush
History Paintbrush
Rubber Stamp
Pattern Stamp
Rubber Stamp tools
Eraser
Type tools
Type
Type Mask
Vertical Type
Vertical Type Mask
Ruler
Gradient tools
Paint Bucket
Blur
Sharpen
Smudge
Blur tools
Hand
Linear
Radial
Angle
Reflected
Diamond
Foreground Color
Zoom
Default Colors
Eyedropper tools
Switch Colors
Background Color
Eyedropper
Color Sampler
Standard Mode
Quick Mask Mode
Standard Screen Mode
Full Screen Mode
Full Screen Mode with Menu Bar Mode
Pen
Magnetic Pen
Freeform Pen
Add Anchor Point
Delete Anchor Point
Direct Selection
Convert Anchor Point
Pen tools

# Basic Photoshop Tasks

## Choose a Foreground or Background Color

**Shortcuts:** Press D to change colors to their defaults: black for the foreground and white for the background.

Press X to switch the foreground color with the background color.

You can choose a foreground color from two palettes. Choose a foreground color from the Swatch palette by clicking on one of the swatches. To choose a background color from the Swatches palette, hold the (Option) [Alt] key while clicking on the swatch. Or choose a color from the Color palette by either using the sliders or entering numeric values. To enter the values using a specific color model such as CMYK, choose that model from the Color palette menu.

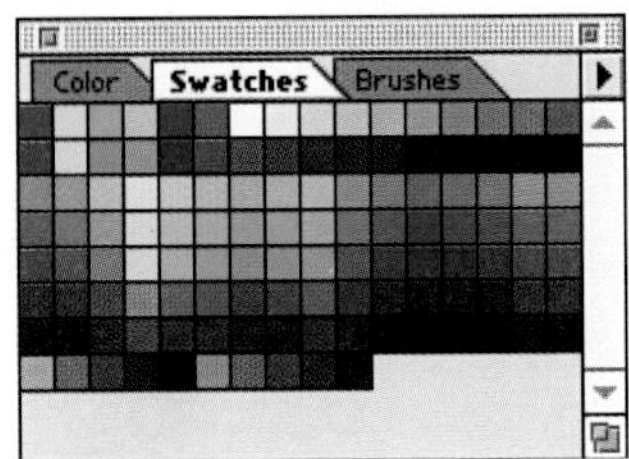


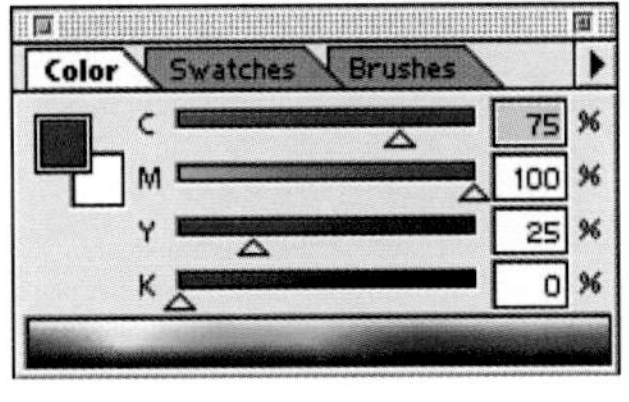


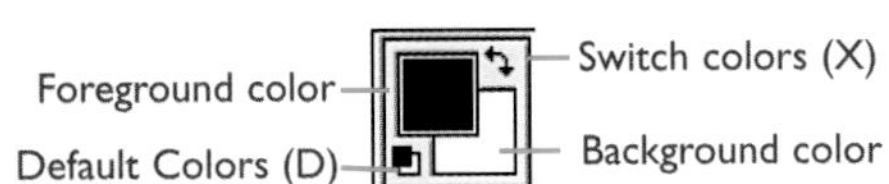


To choose a foreground or background color, click on either the Foreground color icon or the Background color icon on the Toolbox.

The Color Picker dialog box appears offering two methods for choosing a color. To change the color that appears in the large area on the left, use the sliders on either side of the vertical spectrum. To select a color, click in the area on the left. You can also choose a color by entering numeric values. All of the colors I used in these techniques have been specified by their CMYK values. Enter these values as percentages in the appropriate input boxes in the lower right. Note that the Foreground and Background icons on the Toolbox now reflect your color choices.

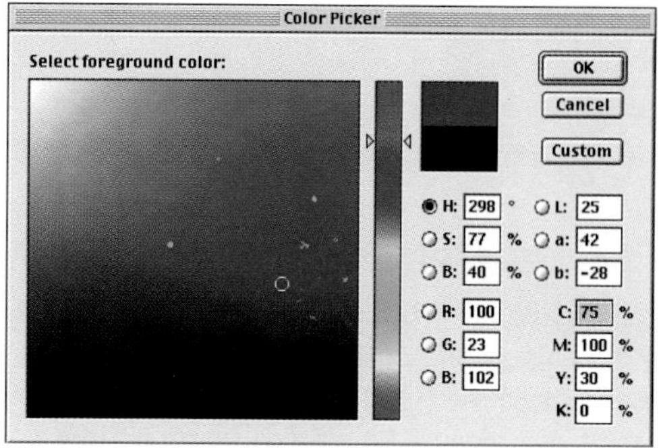

## Create a New Channel

**Shortcuts:** Click the New Channel icon on the Channels palette. Hold the (Option) [Alt] key while clicking the New Channel icon to create a new channel and open the New Channel dialog box.

To create a new channel, choose New Channel from the Channels palette pop-up menu.

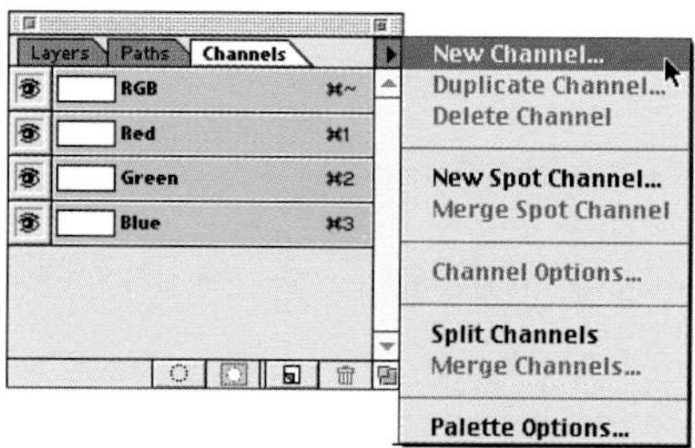


Use the New Channel dialog box to establish your settings. Unless noted otherwise, I used the default settings when creating a new channel. This figure shows Photoshop's default settings.

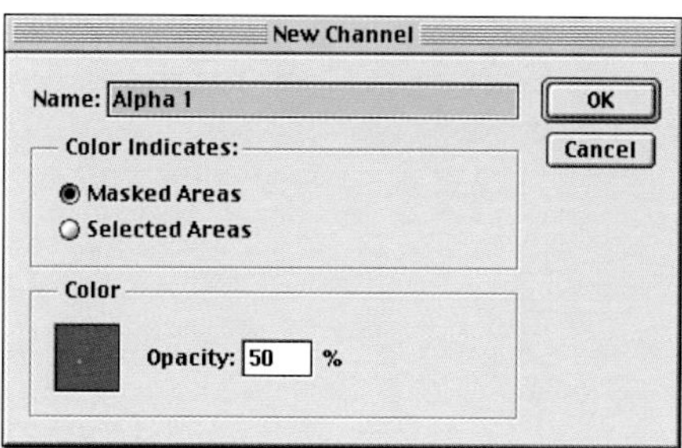

## Create a New File

**Shortcuts:** Press (Command-N) [Control-N].

To create a new file, choose File➡New. The New dialog box appears, which is where you name your new file and establish other settings. Almost all images in this book were begun by creating a file with these settings: Width: 5 inches, Height: 2 inches, Resolution: 150 pixels/inch, Mode: RGB Color, Contents: White.

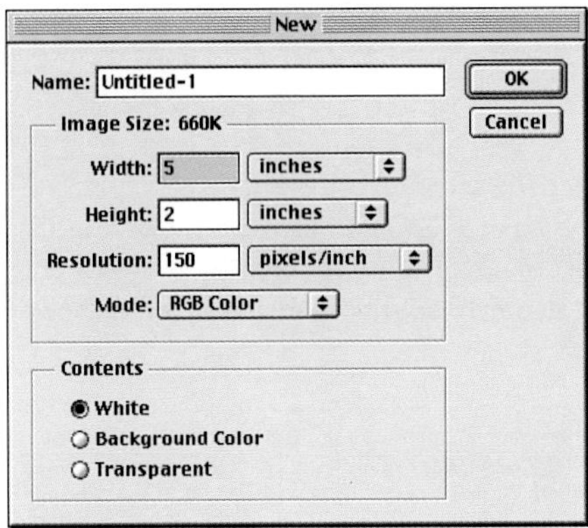


## Create a New Layer

**Shortcuts:** Click the New Layer icon on the Layers palette. Hold the (Option) [Alt] key while clicking the New Layer icon to create a new layer and open the New Layer dialog box.

To create a new layer, choose New Layer from the Layer palette pop-up menu, or choose Layer➡New➡Layer. Or you can press (Command-Shift-N) [Control-Shift-N].

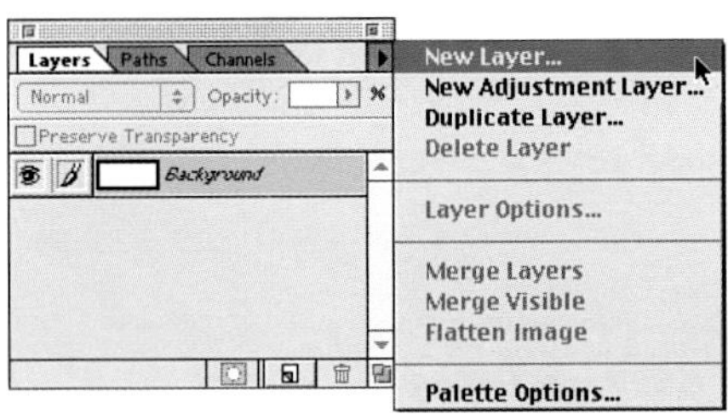


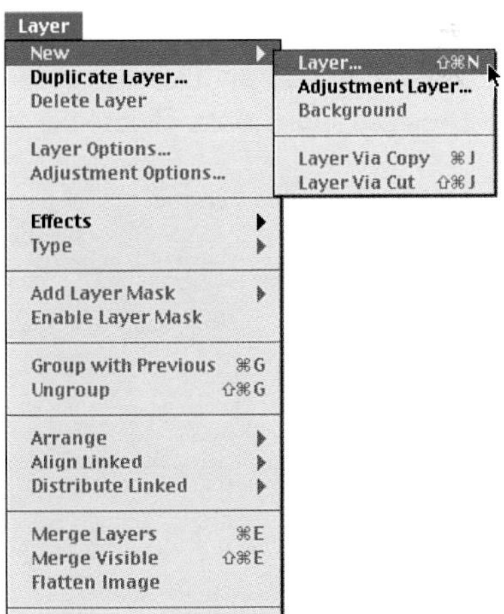

The New Layer dialog box opens, which is where you name the new layer and establish other settings.

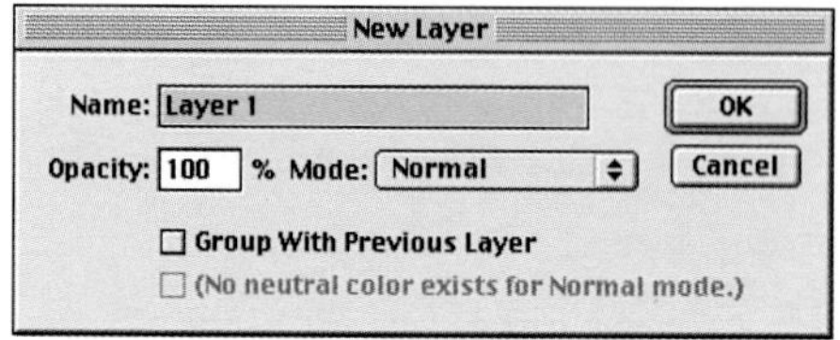


## Delete a Channel

To delete a channel, select the channel on the Channels palette and click on the Trash icon at the bottom of the palette. You can also drag it to the Trash icon (just like you would to get rid of a document on the Desktop by dragging it to the Trash or the Recycle Bin). Finally, you also can select the channel and choose Delete Channel from the Channels palette menu.

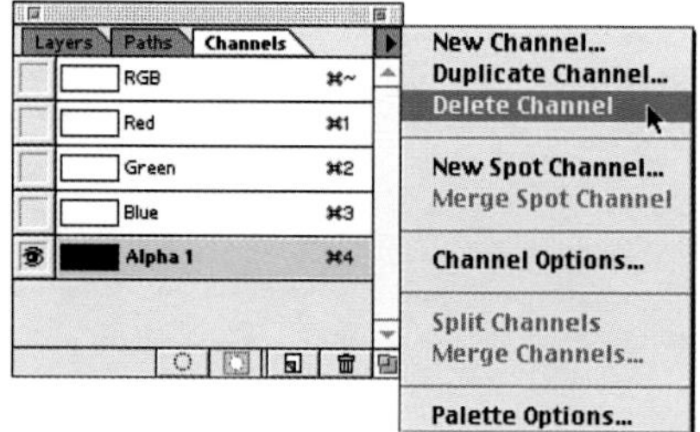


## Delete a Layer

To delete a layer, select the layer on the Layers palette and click on the Trash icon at the bottom of the palette. You can also drag it to the Trash icon (just like you would to get rid of a document on the Desktop by dragging it to the Trash). Finally, you also can select the layer and choose Delete Layer from the Layers palette menu.



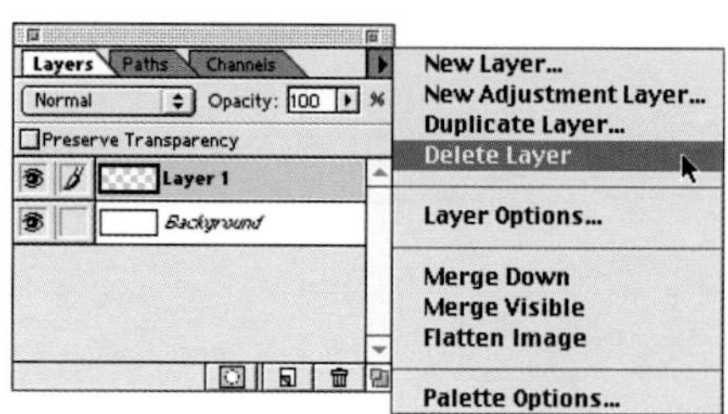

## Deselect the Selection

**Shortcut:** Press (Command-D) [Control-D].

To deselect a selection, choose Select➡Deselect. The marquee disappears. If you have accidentally deselected a selection, you can choose Select➡Reselect to bring back the last active selection.

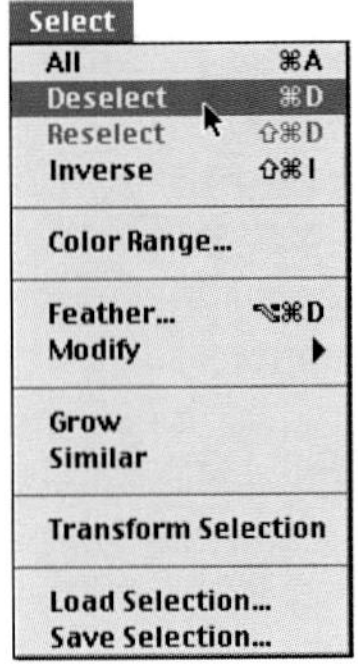


## Duplicate a Channel

**Shortcut:** On the Channels palette, select the channel you want to duplicate and drag it on top of the New Channel icon. Hold the (Option) [Alt] key while dragging the channel to the New Channel icon to create a new channel and open the Duplicate Channel dialog box.

To create a duplicate of a channel, make the channel active and then select Duplicate Channel from the Channels palette menu.

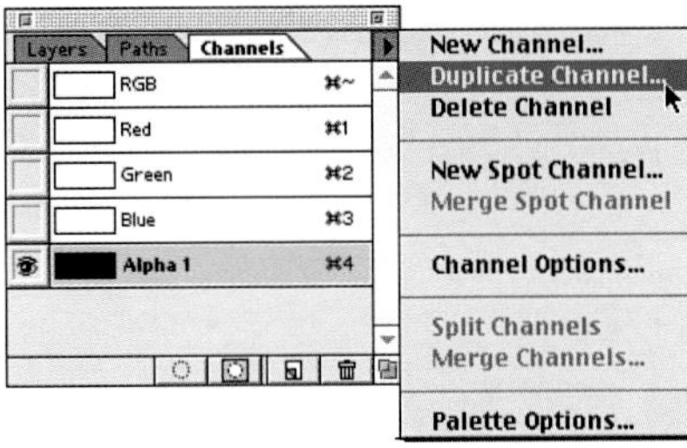


A new copy of the channel you selected for duplication is created automatically, and the Duplicate Channel dialog box appears.

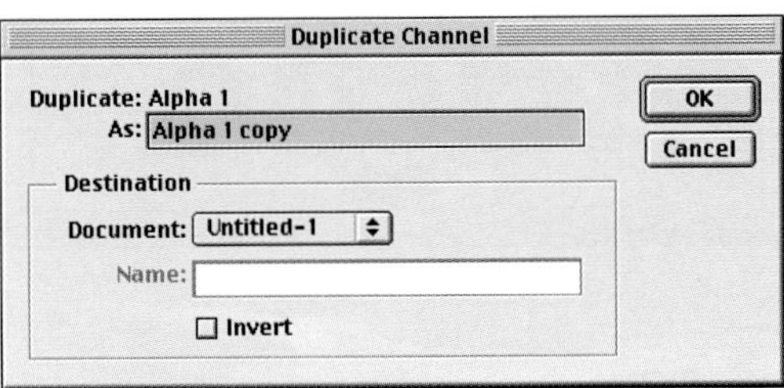

## Enter the Text

Photoshop 5.0 has four type tools. There is a standard Type tool and a Type Mask tool, and each of these tools has a counterpart tool that allows them to place type in vertical columns. In this book, I used only the standard Type tool and the Type Mask tool. Each effect in this book specifies which type tool to use.

The standard Type tool enters the type into a new layer. The color of the type defaults to the foreground color, but you can also select the color by clicking on the color swatch in the Type dialog box. This new layer is marked in the Layers palette by a "T" next to the layer preview on the Layers palette. If you want to edit the text, double-click the "T" to reopen the Type dialog box. These editable type layers can have layer effects (accessible from the Layers menu) applied to them and you can use the Transform tools on them, but you cannot use all of Photoshop's features to manipulate these layers. In order to do so, you must render the layer by choosing Layer➡Type➡Render Layer. After you apply this command, the "T" disappears from the Layers palette and you can no longer edit the type. The instructions direct you to apply this command when necessary.

The Type Mask tool creates selection outlines of the text you enter without filling the outlines with a color, and without creating a new layer.

In some effects, the instructions in this book ask you to enter text into a channel. Unless noted otherwise, it is assumed that you are entering white text onto the black background of the channel.

To enter the text, select the type tool specified in the instructions, and then click anywhere in the image to open the Type Tool dialog box. Type the text in the large box at the bottom of the dialog box, and make your attribute choices from the preceding options. Because many of the effects in this book apply effects that spread the type, you might find it desirable to increase the spacing between the letters of the words. To do this, enter a positive amount in the Tracking input box. Unless noted otherwise in the instructions, always make sure that you have the Anti-Aliased box checked.

After clicking OK, move the type into position with the Move (standard Type tool) or Marquee (Type Mask tool) tool.

## Fill

In this book, fill normally means to fill the selection with a color. To fill a selection with the foreground color, press (Option-Delete) [Alt-Delete]. To fill the selection with the background color, press (Command-Delete) [Control-Delete]. If you are in the Background layer or any layer that has the Preserve Transparency option turned on, you can press Delete to fill in the selection with the Background color.

You also can fill a selection by choosing Edit➡Fill or pressing Shift-Delete.

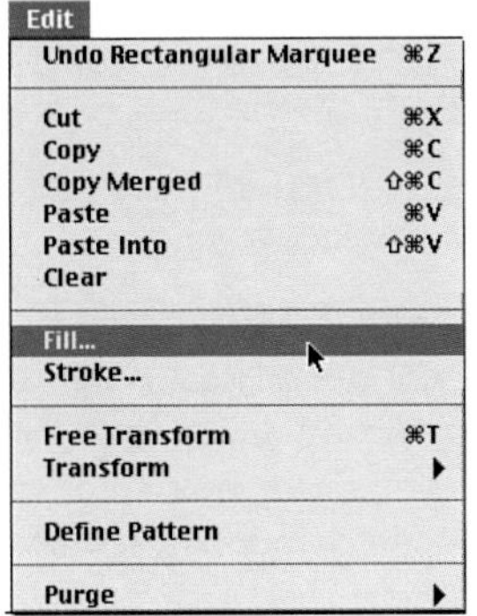


The Fill dialog box opens, allowing you several fill Contents choices as well as the ability to set the Blending Opacity and Mode.

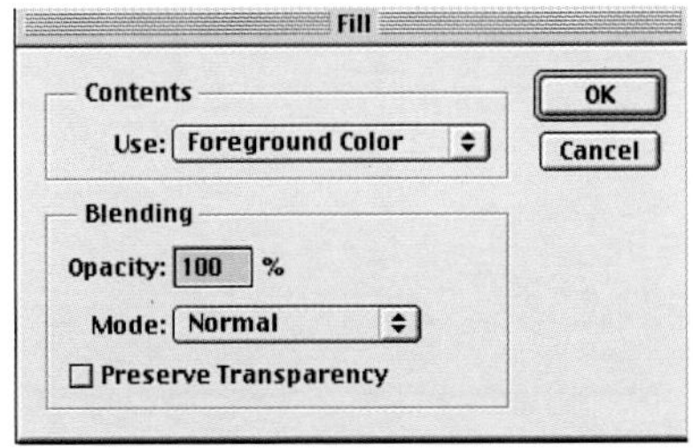


If the Preserve Transparency option is turned on for a layer, using any fill method only fills the areas of that layer already filled—transparent areas remain transparent. If a selection is empty (contains a transparent area of a layer) and the Preserve Transparency option is turned on for that layer, then you cannot fill the selection. To fill the selection, simply turn off the Preserve Transparency option before filling it.

## Group/Ungroup a Layer

**Shortcut:** Select the layer on top and press (Command-G) [Control-G] to group it with the layer below. Press Shift and (Command-G) [Control-G] to ungroup it.

To group one layer with another, hold the (Option) [Alt] key and click on the line that divides the two layers. Or select the layer on top and choose Layer➡Group with Previous. The solid line between the layers will be replaced with a dotted line. To ungroup the layers, (Option) [Alt] click on the dotted line, or choose Layer➡Ungroup.

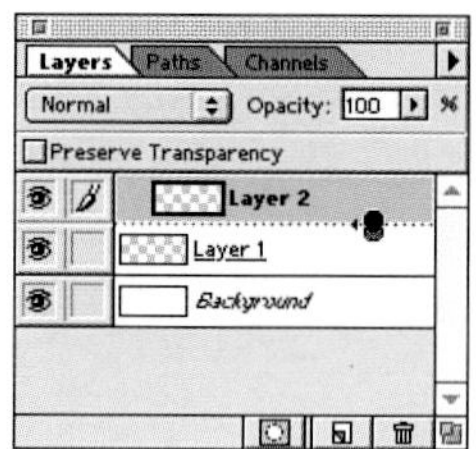


## Intersect the Selection

**Shortcut:** Hold down the Shift and (Option) [Alt] keys and click on the channel or layer that contains the selection to be intersected with the current selection.

Intersecting one selection with another selection results in a new selection that contains only areas that were part of both of the original selections. To do this, one selection needs to be active. Then either perform the previous shortcut or choose Select➡Load Selection to open the Load Selection dialog box. Choose the channel as the source and turn on the Intersect with Selection operation at the bottom. If you click on a layer as described in the shortcut method, the current selection intersects with the layer's transparency selection.

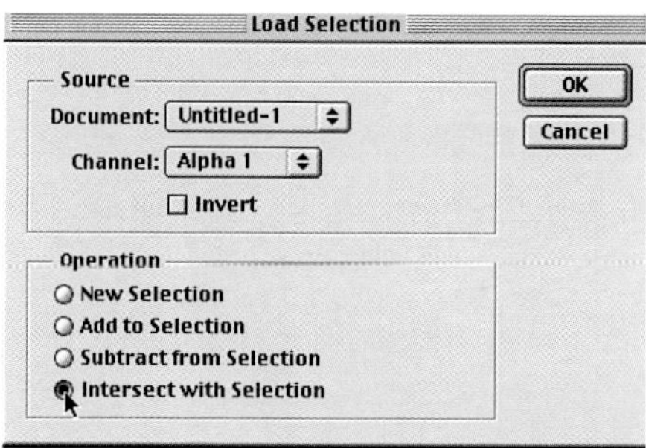


## Link/Unlink a Layer

To link one layer with another, make one of the layers active and click in the box that is just to the left of the other layer's preview. A small chain link icon appears in the box. To unlink the layer, click on the Chain Link icon.

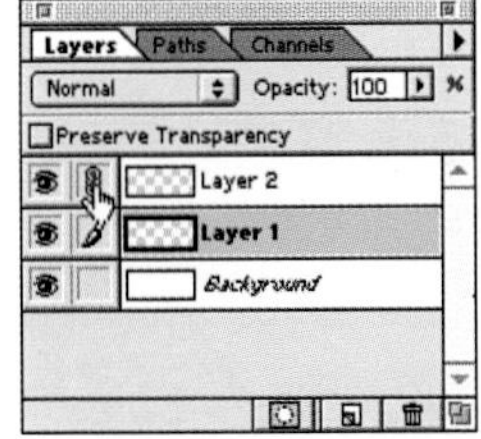


## Load a Selection

**Shortcut:** Hold down the (Command) [Control] key and click on the channel (on the Channels palette) that contains the selection you want to load. Or hold down (Command) [Control] and type the number of the channels whose selection you want to load.

To load a selection, choose Select➡Load Selection. This opens the Load Selection dialog box where you can establish document, channel, and operation variables.

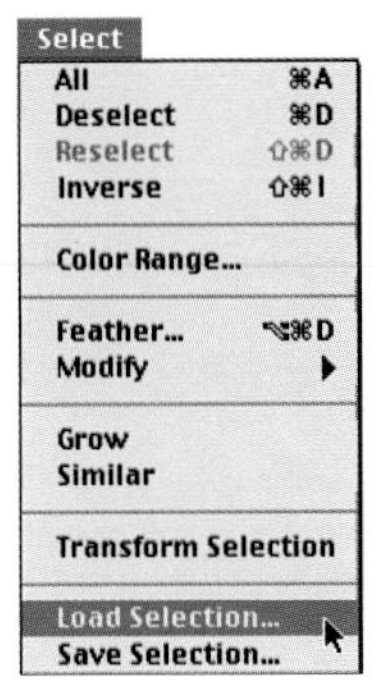


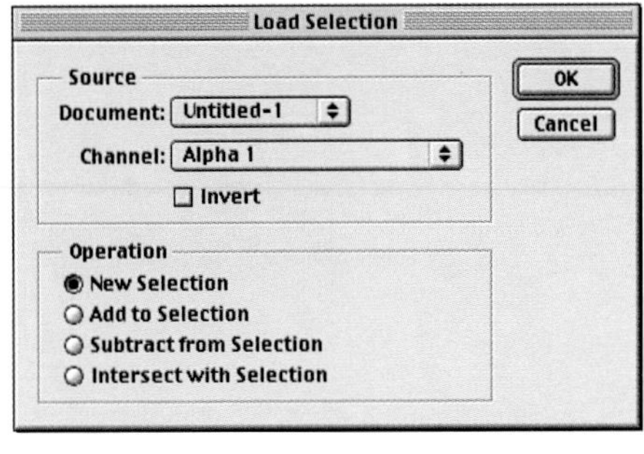


## Load the Transparency Selection (of a Layer)

To load the transparency selection of a layer, hold down the (Command) [Control] key and click on the layer (on the Layers palette) that contains the transparency selection you want to load. The selection encompasses all nontransparent areas of that layer.

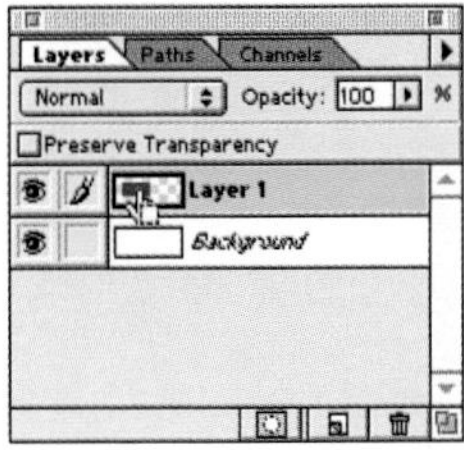


## Make a Channel Active

To make a channel active for editing or modification, click on its thumbnail or name on the Channels palette. If you make the RGB channel (referred to as the composite channel in this book) active, all the color channels (Red, Green, and Blue) become active.

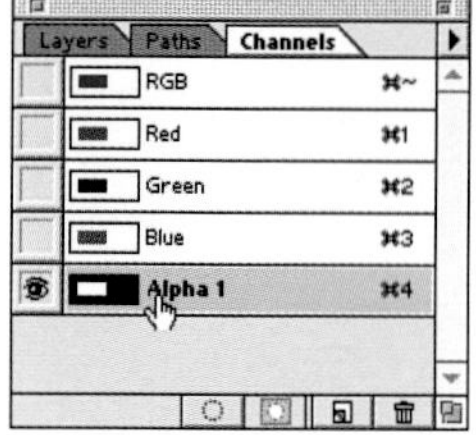


You can tell the channel is active if it is highlighted with a color.

## Make a Channel Visible/Invisible

If you see an eye in the left-most column next to a channel, that channel is visible. To make a channel visible, click in that column to turn on the Eye icon. Click on the eye to remove it and make the channel invisible. If you make the RGB channel (referred to as the composite channel in this book) visible or invisible, all the color channels (Red, Green, and Blue) become visible or invisible.

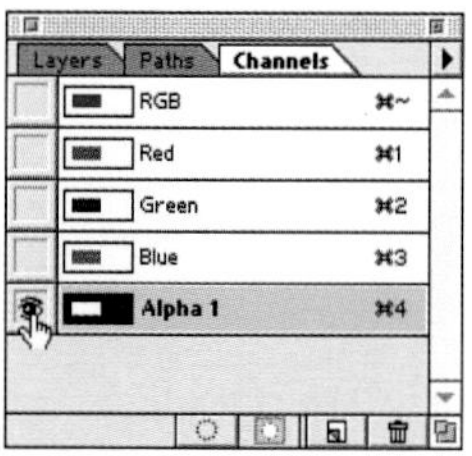


## Make a Layer Active

To make a layer active, click on its thumbnail or title in the Layers palette.

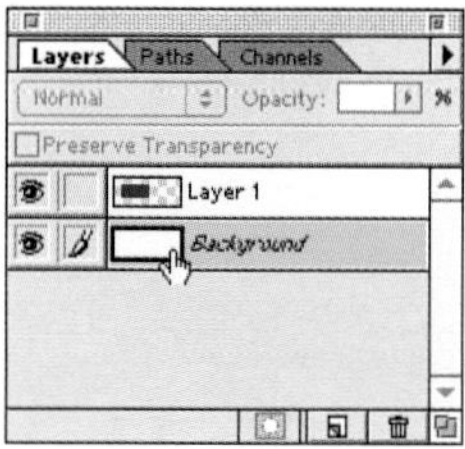


You can tell the layer is active if it is highlighted with a color.

## Make a Layer Visible/Invisible

If you see an eye in the left-most column next to a layer, that layer is visible. To make a layer visible, click in that column to turn on the Eye icon. Click on the eye to remove it and make the layer invisible.

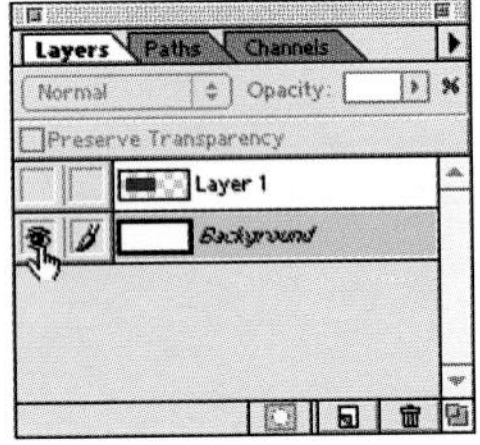


## Move a Layer

To move a Layer, click on the layer you want to move in the Layers palette and drag it up or down the list of layers to the place you want to move it. As you drag the layer, the lines between the layers darken to indicate where the layer will fall if you let go. You can also use the keyboard to move layers. Press (Command-Option-]) [Control-Alt-]] to move the layer up one layer. Press (Command-Option-[) [Control-Alt-[] to move the layer down one layer.

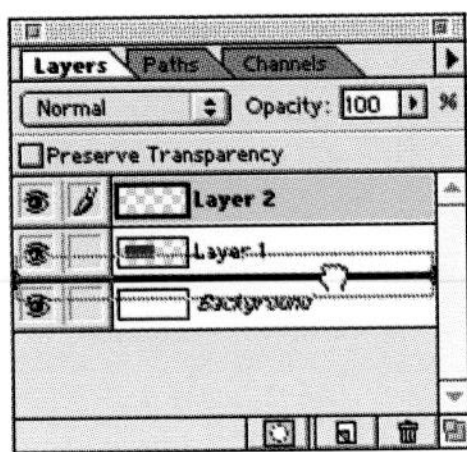


The layer you moved appears between layers, numerically "out of order."

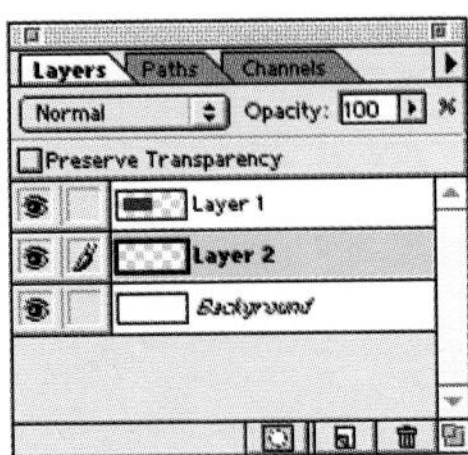


## Return to the Composite Channel

**Shortcut:** Press (Command-~) [Control-~].

If you want to return to the composite channel, click on its thumbnail or title (RGB, CMYK, Lab). The composite channel is always the one with (Command-~) [Control-~] after its title.

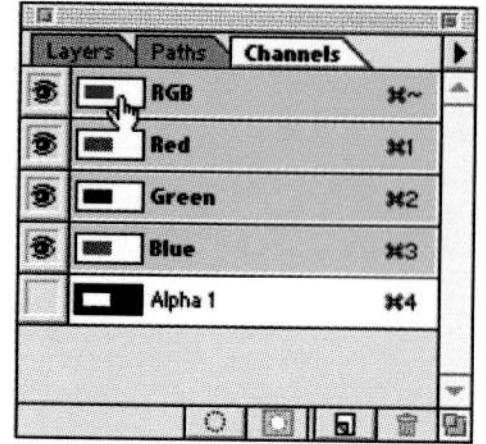


If you are in an RGB file, channels 0 through 3 are now active because each of the R, G, and B channels are individual parts of the RGB channel.

## Save a File

**Shortcut:** Press (Command-Shift-S) [Control-Shift-S] to save a file with a new name, or press (Command-S) [Control-S] to save changes to the current file.

To save a file with a new name, choose File➥Save As. The Save As dialog box opens, in which you can name your new file and choose a format. To save changes to the current file, choose File➥Save.

File format selection depends on what you have in your file, what you want to keep when you save it, and what you're going to do with the file after it is saved. Consult a detailed Photoshop book, such as *Inside Adobe Photoshop 5*, for more guidance on which file format is best for your needs.

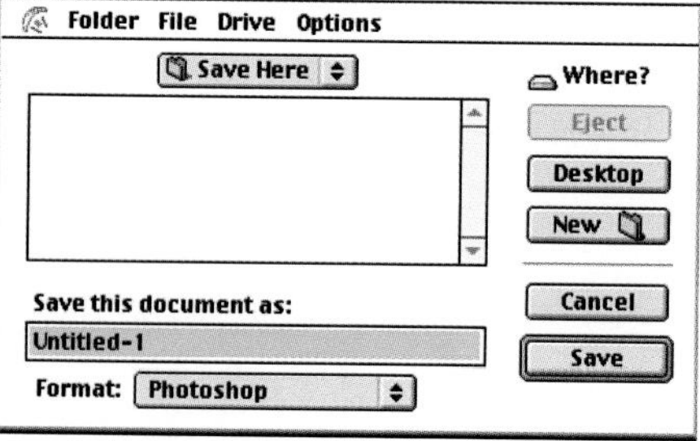


## Save a Selection

**Shortcut:** Click the Save Selection icon on the Channels palette.

To save a selection, choose Select➥Save Selection.

Select
All ⌘A
Deselect ⌘D
Reselect ⇧⌘D
Inverse ⇧⌘I
Color Range...
Feather... ⌥⌘D
Modify ▶
Grow
Similar
Transform Selection
Load Selection...
Save Selection...

The Save Selection dialog box opens. Choose your options and click OK to save the selection.

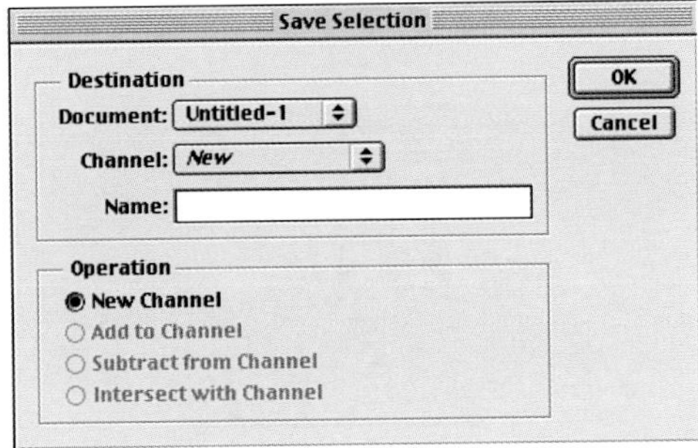


## Subtract from the Selection

**Shortcut:** Hold down the (Option) [Alt] key and click on the channel or layer that contains the selection to be subtracted from the current selection.

Subtracting one selection from another selection results in a new selection that contains all areas of the original selection that are not part of the second selection. To do this, first make a selection. Then either perform the previous shortcut or choose Select➡Load Selection to open the Load Selection dialog box. Choose the channel as the source and turn on the Subtract from Selection operation at the bottom. If you click on a layer as described in the shortcut method, the layer's transparency selection will be subtracted from the current selection.

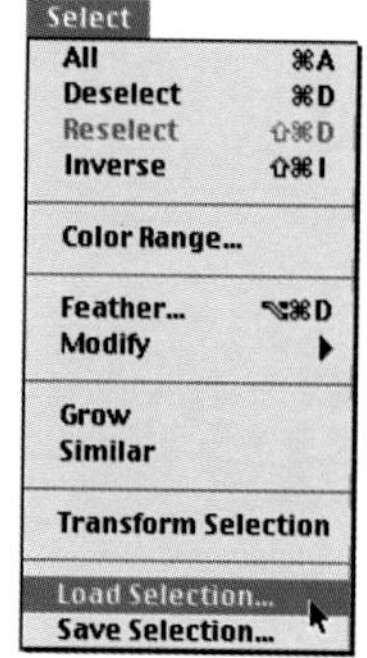


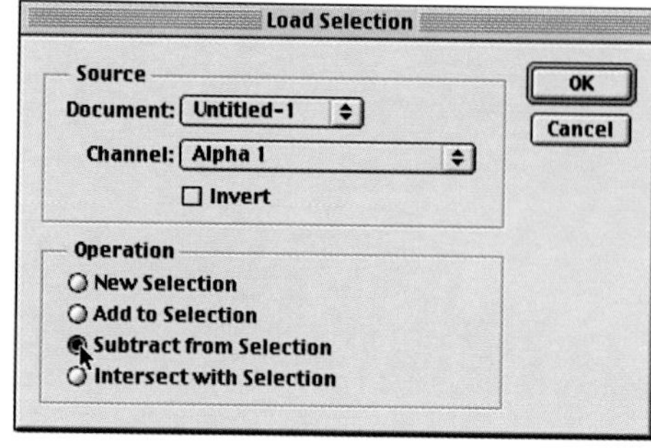


## Turn on/off Preserve Transparency

To turn on or off the Preserve Transparency option for a particular layer, first make that layer the active layer. Then click the Preserve Transparency check box on the Layers palette. This option is not available for the Background layer. ●

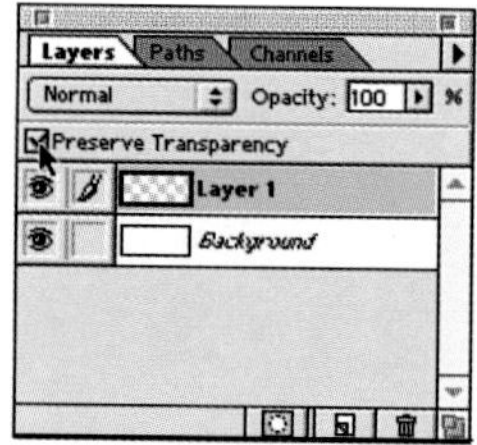

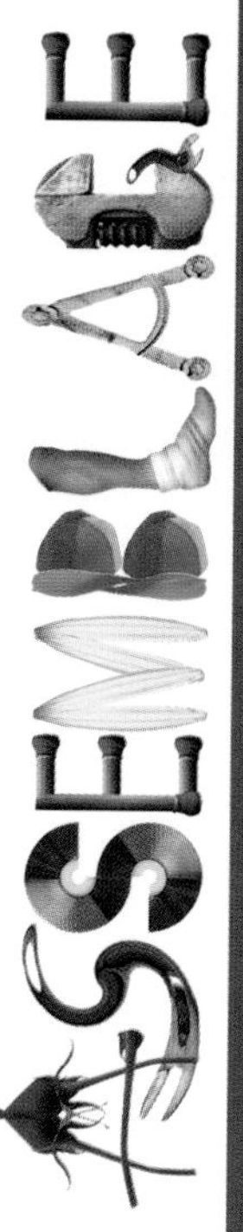


This effect demonstrates several methods for manipulating stock images that can be pasted together to form words. Each new word that you "assemble" requires its own unique solutions, but this example presents some useful techniques.

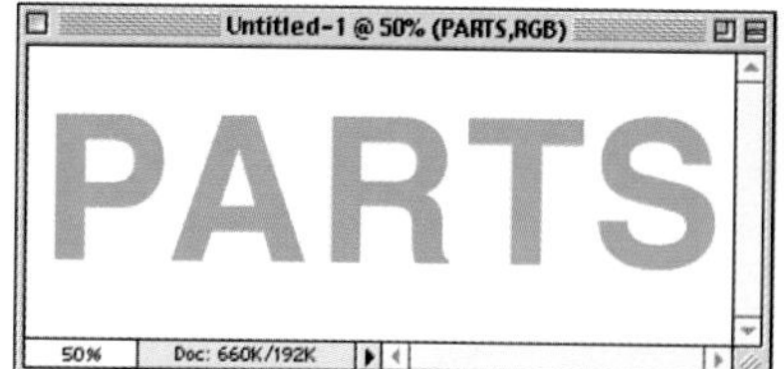


**1** Create a new file, and use the Type tool to enter the text (Helvetica Bold at 100 points). This type layer will be used as a guide when pasting together the various images. Use a simple sans serif typeface such as Helvetica. It is also wise to enter a positive Tracking value (I used +50) in order to spread the letters apart.

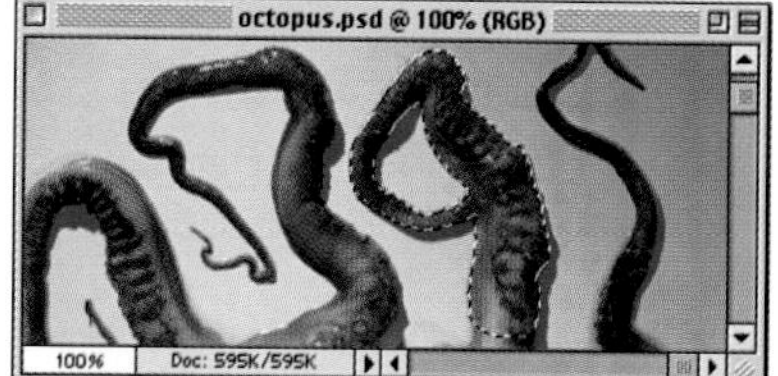


**2** Next open a file that contains an image to be used as a part of one of the letters. One of the tentacles in this octopus image (Octopus.psd from PhotoDisc) forms a perfect "P." All five images used for this effect came from PhotoDisc files on the P5TM CD (P5TM➥Images➥PhotoDisc).

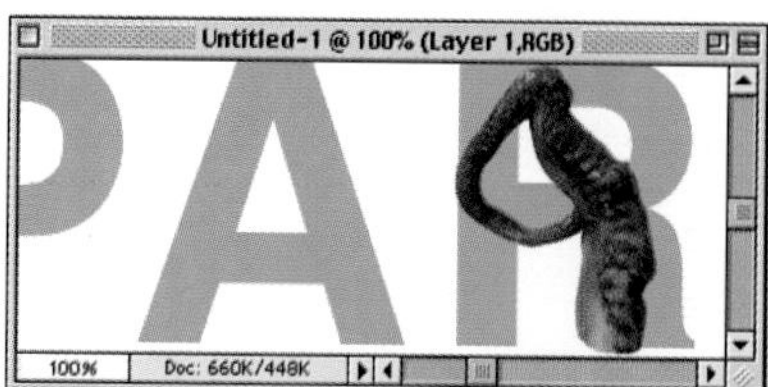


**3** Use the selection tools to select the part of the image you want to use, copy it, and close the file. Paste the image into the file containing the type.

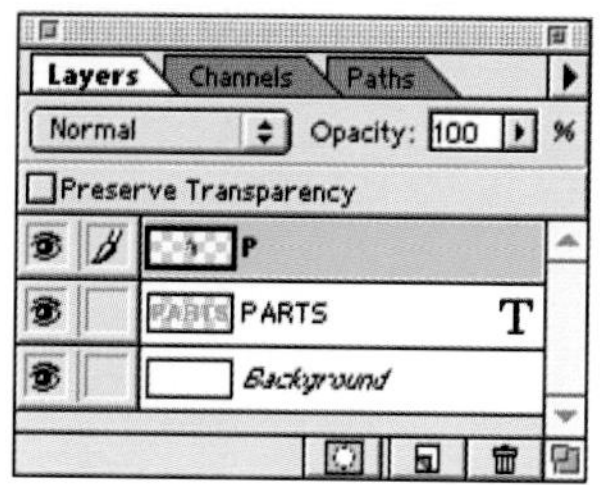


**4** Each time you use the Paste command, the image is conveniently placed onto a new layer. This is very helpful in keeping all of the letters and images organized. After the new layer is created, double-click on the layer name and change the name of the layer to the letter that it will contain.

**5** Use the Move tool to shift the piece into place. The tentacle needs to be flipped. Choose Edit➡Transform➡Flip Horizontal. Then press (Command-T) [Control-T] so that you can use the Transform handles to shape the image and rotate it slightly counterclockwise. The tentacle needs to be scaled to fit the size of the letters in the guide. Press (Return) [Enter] to accept the changes.

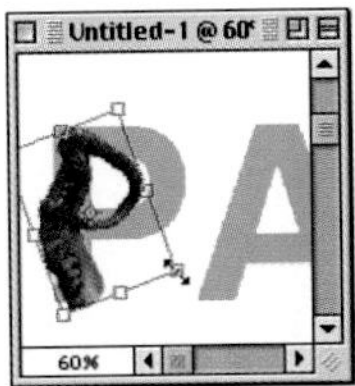


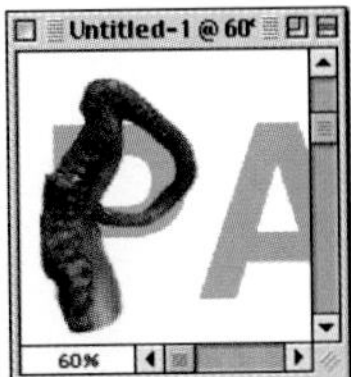


**6** For the "A," copy this coat hanger from another PhotoDisc image (OS05021.TIF) and cut off the metal hook. Paste it into the image file; press (Command-T) [Control-T] and use the Transform handles to squeeze the ends together and stretch its height slightly.

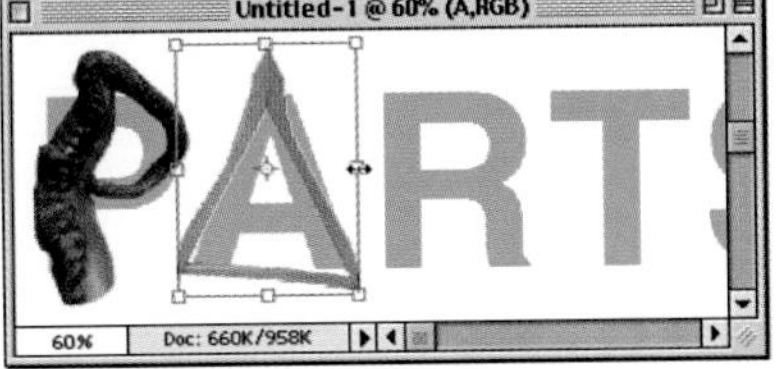


**7** Press (Return) [Enter] to accept the changes and then use the Lasso tool to select the crossbar only. Choose Layer➡New➡Layer Via Cut. Move the new layer (renamed "A2") below the original "A" layer and use the Move tool to shift it into place.

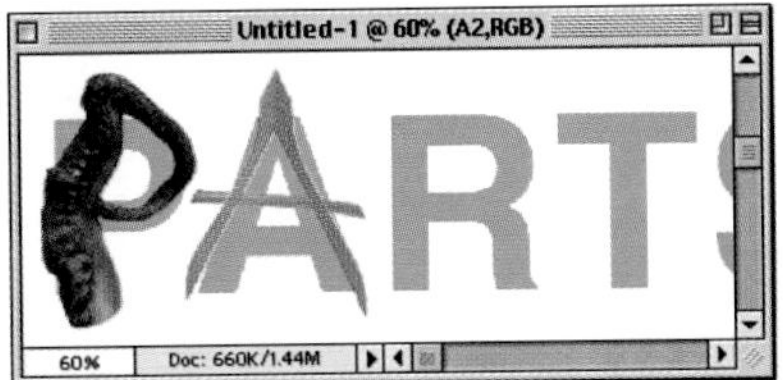

**If you want to blend two parts of a letter together, merge those two layers by making the top layer active and choose Merge Down from the Layers palette. Then use the Smudge tool to blur the images together.**

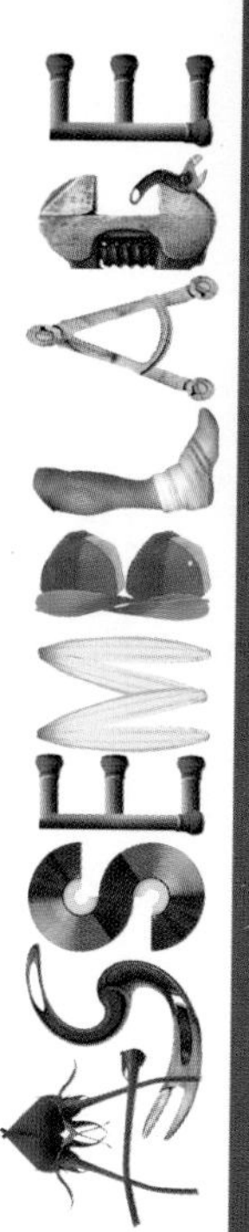

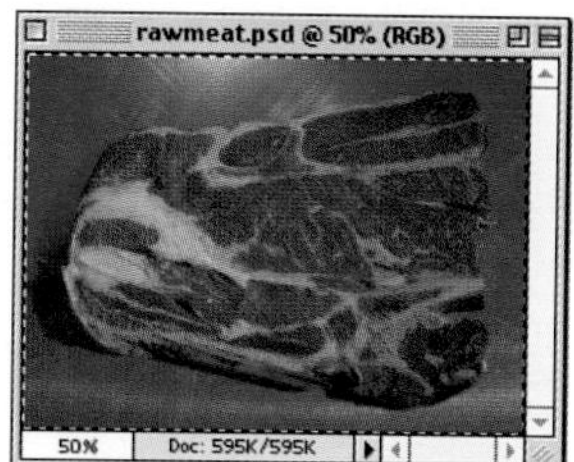


**8** I used a different strategy to make the "R." I opened a file that contained an image of a piece of raw beef (rawmeat.psd from PhotoDisc), chose Select➡All, copied it, and closed the file.

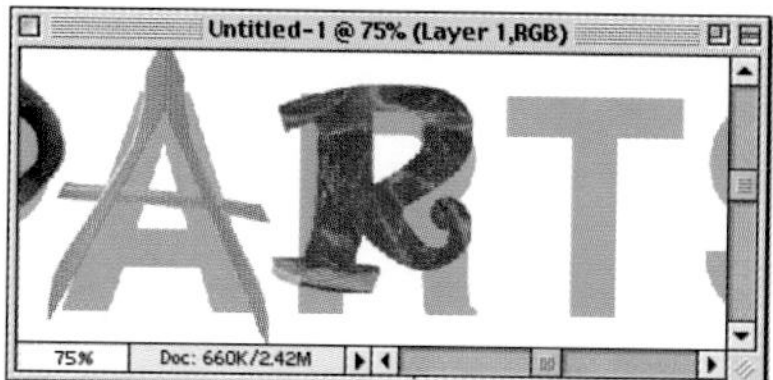


**9** Use the Type Mask tool to enter the letter "R." Then choose Edit➡Paste Into to paste the raw meat image into the type selection. A layer mask is created for this layer. Drag the layer mask to the trash icon at the bottom of the Layers palette and click "Apply" in the dialog box that asks if you want to do so.

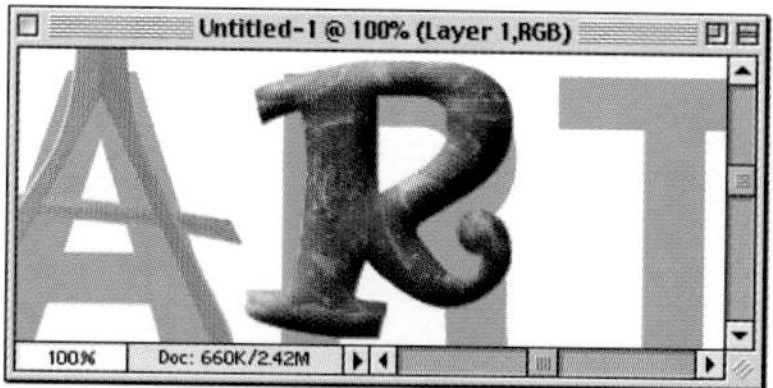


**10** To give the meat a little dimension, choose Layer➡Effects➡Bevel and Emboss. Choose the Inner Bevel style, raise the Depth to 15 pixels, and raise the Blur amount enough so that the letter appears rounded (15 pixels).

**11** The "T" was created much like the "A," but there was no need to distort the shape of the ruler (OS05035.TIF from PhotoDisc).

**12** I copied this pipe from the OS05041.TIF PhotoDisc image and pasted it into a new layer over the "S." Use the Free Transform command again (Command-T) [Control-T] to scale and rotate the pipe. I also chose Edit➡ Transform➡ Flip Horizontal to flip the image.

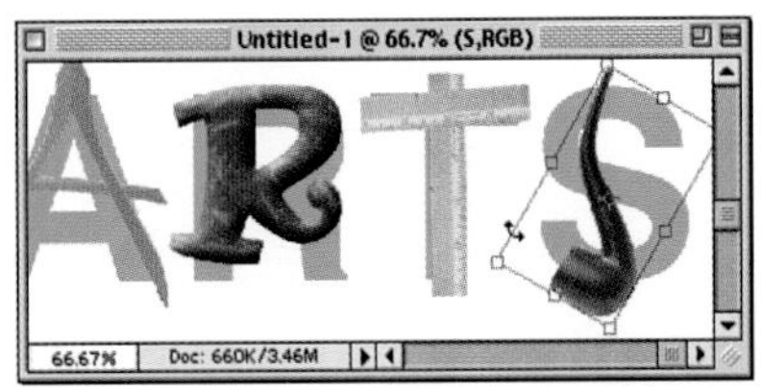


**13** Press (Return) [Enter] to accept the changes; select the Rectangular Marquee tool and select a rectangle around the pipe. The Shear filter used in the next step distorts the pipe within the boundaries set by the marquee selection.

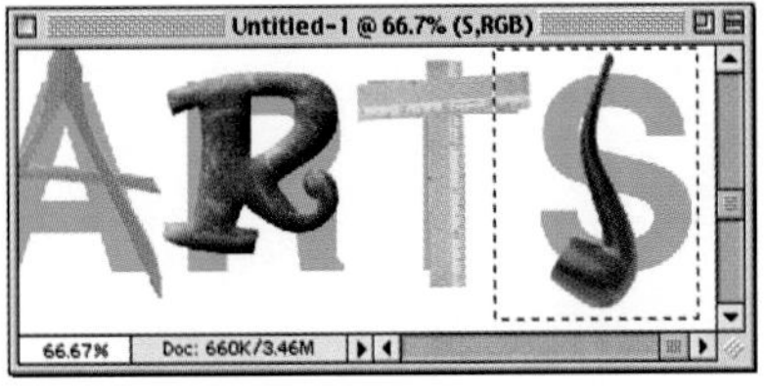


**14** Choose Filter➡Distort➡Shear to open the Shear dialog box. This filter is great at getting curves out of linear shapes. Click and drag points on the graph to shape the pipe.

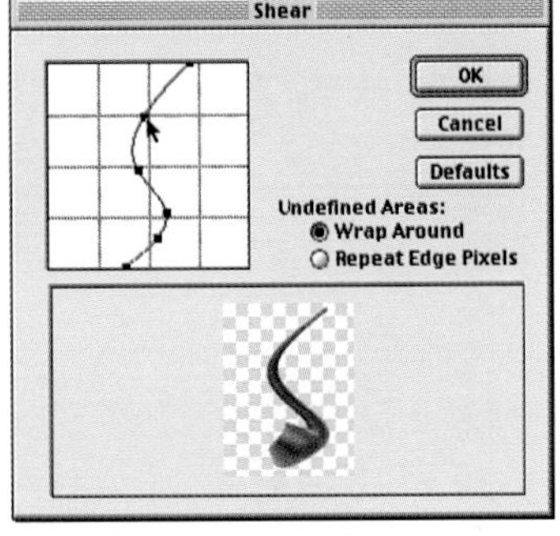


TIP **The filters in the Filter➡Distort submenu are the most useful filters for manipulating the shapes of images into the letters. Try Pinch, Spherize, Shear, Twirl, Polar Coordinates, and Wave.**

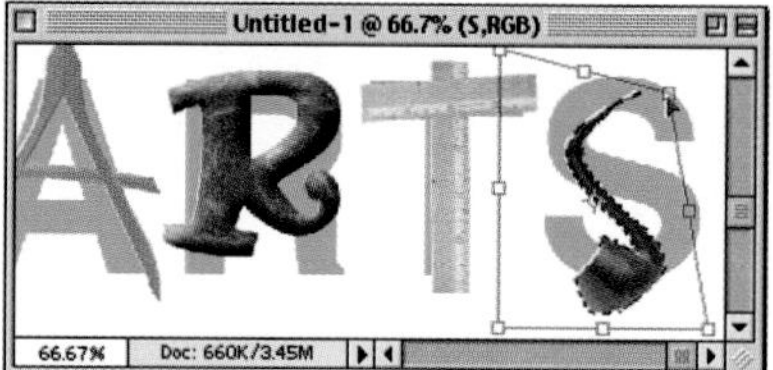


**15** Press (Command-T) [Control-T] again and hold the (Command) [Control] key while dragging the top-right corner in toward the center of the pipe. Use the Transform handles to make any other changes and press (Return) [Enter] to accept the changes.

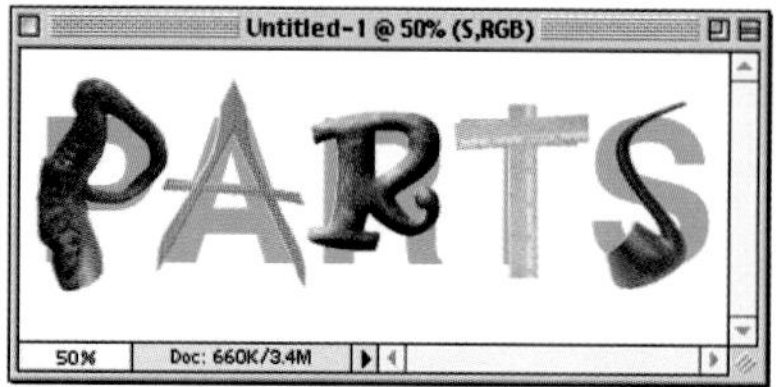


**16** Here's what I have so far.

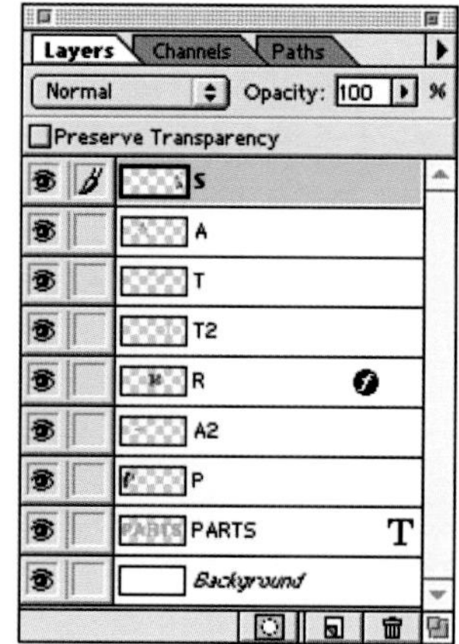


And here is what the Layers palette looks like.

**17** Use the Drop Shadow feature to apply a shadow to one layer and then choose Layer➡Effects➡Copy Effects. Link all of the other layers (by clicking in the box to the right of the eye on the Layers palette) that contain the letters and choose Layer➡Effects➡Paste Effects to Linked to apply the Drop Shadow to all layers. The shadow looks great on letters such as the "A" and "T" in which one part overlaps another.

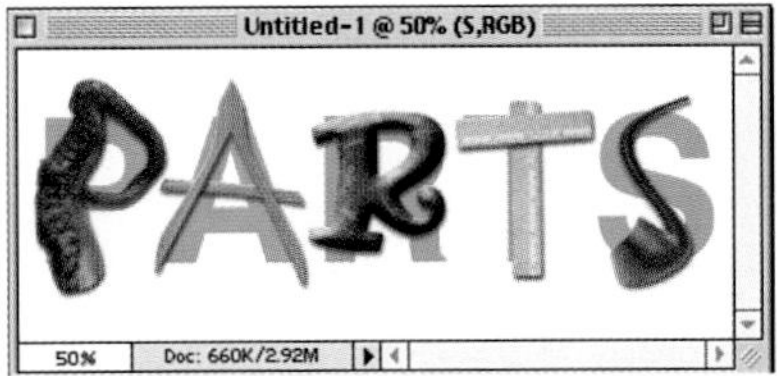


**18** Delete the original type layer to let the images stand on their own. After seeing the type without the type guide behind it, you may want make adjustments. I used the Transform feature once again to increase the size of the "R" and to rotate it back a little. ●

Follow the bouncing balls, or rather the numbered steps, to create a shaded sphere onto which you can lay type. This effect relies on a custom gradient for the Radial Gradient tool and the new 3D Transform filter that seems custom made for laying the type onto the balls.

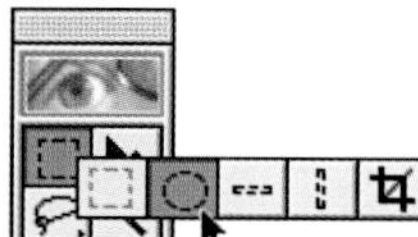

**1** Create a new file and create a new layer (Layer 1). Click and hold the pointer on the Marquee tool. Scroll through the different Marquee tools and select the Elliptical Marquee tool.

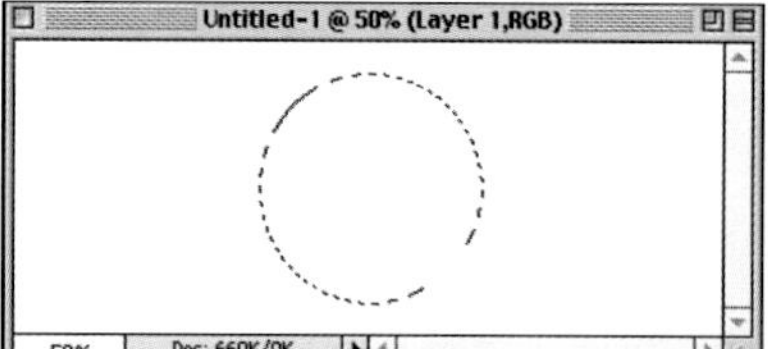


**2** With the Elliptical Marquee tool, draw a circle. If you hold down the Shift key while dragging, the selection will be constrained to a perfect circle.

**3** Change the foreground color to a color for the ball, and change the background color to the color for the shadow. For the ball, I used a yellow (CMYK: 4, 1, 51, 0), and for the shadow, I used black (CMYK: 60, 60, 60, 100).

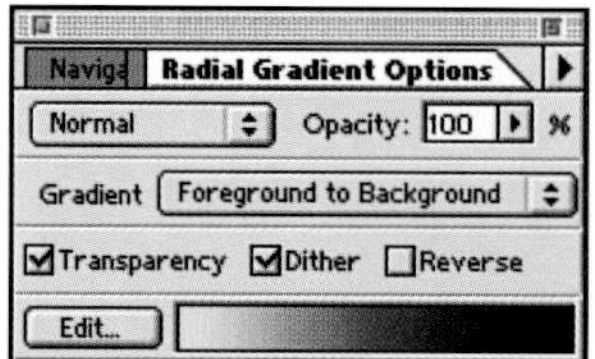


**4** Double-click the Radial Gradient tool to select it and to display the Radial Gradient Options palette. Choose Foreground to Background from the Gradient pop-up menu.

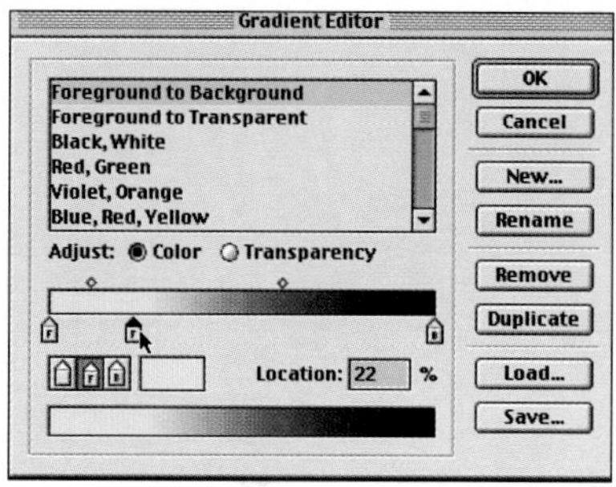


**5** Click the Edit button on the Radial Gradient Options palette. A new dialog box appears. Click the tab in the lower left that has an "F" inside it. "F" stands for foreground color. Then click just below the colored gradient. The color at the location of the pointer is the

foreground color. Drag the new "F" marker until the Location field reads 22%.

**6** Grab the diamond above the colored gradient that is to the right of the marker you just placed. Drag it to the right until the Location field reads 62%. Click OK to save your changes to the Foreground to Background gradient.

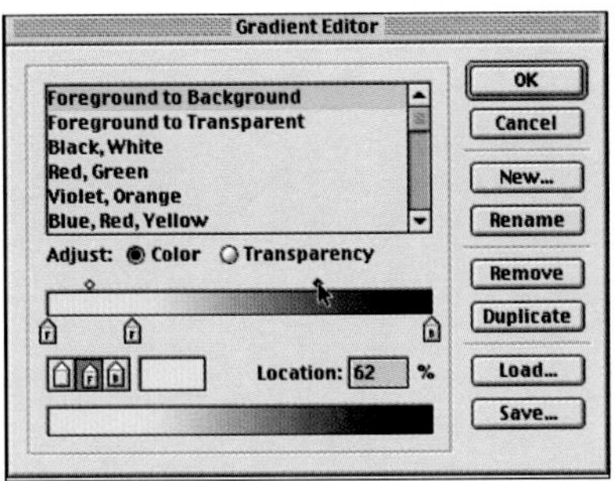


**7** Now, back to the circle selection. Click and drag the Radial Gradient tool from the upper-left part of the active selection to the lower-right part of the selection as shown here.

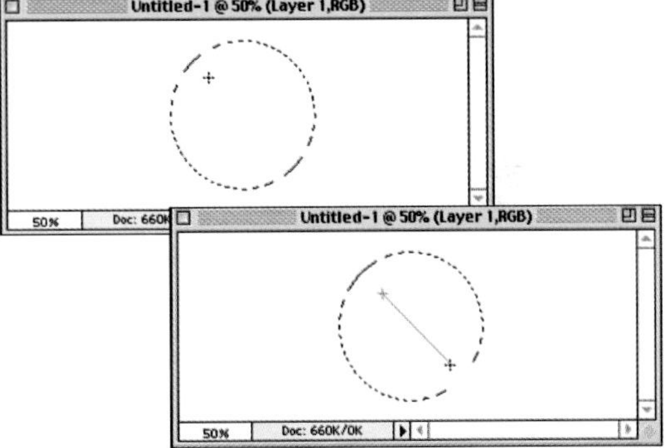


Here's what I got. If you don't like what you get, press (Command-Z) [Control-Z] and repeat this step.

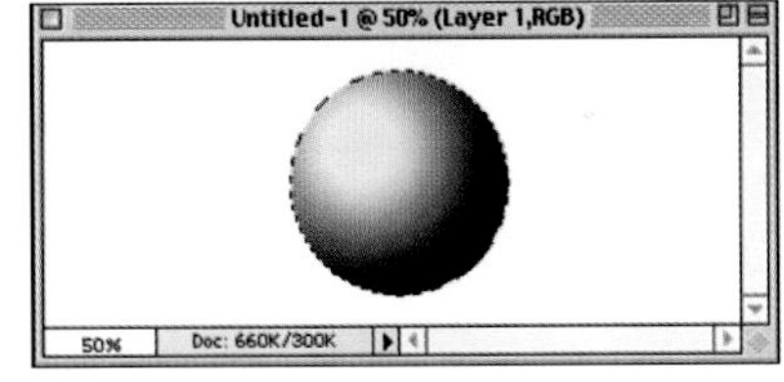


**8** Change the foreground color to a color for the type. I used black. Then use the Type tool to enter the text for the ball. I used 80-point Matrix Bold. The type drops automatically into a new layer. Use the Move tool to position the type in the center of the sphere, and choose Layer➥Type➥Render Layer.

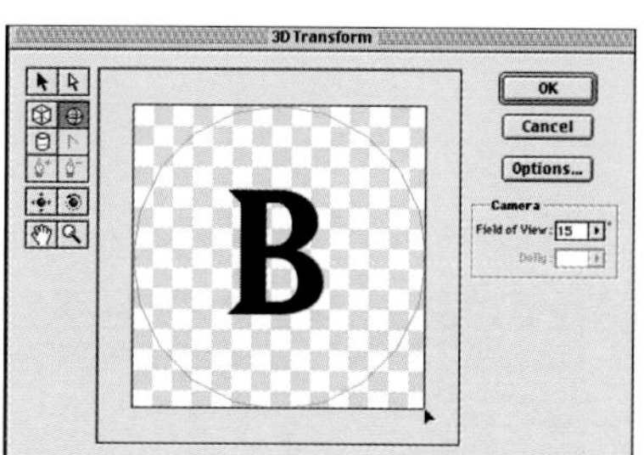


**9** Load the transparency selection of Layer 1, but keep the type layer the active layer. Choose Filter➥Render➥3D Transform. This dialog box has its own set of tools. Select the Sphere tool. Then click the pointer on the upper-left corner of the preview box. Then drag the pointer to the right on top of the bottom-right corner of the preview. This creates a sphere that is the same size as the selection you made in Step 2. (Note: The sphere looks like a circle until you rotate it in the next step.)

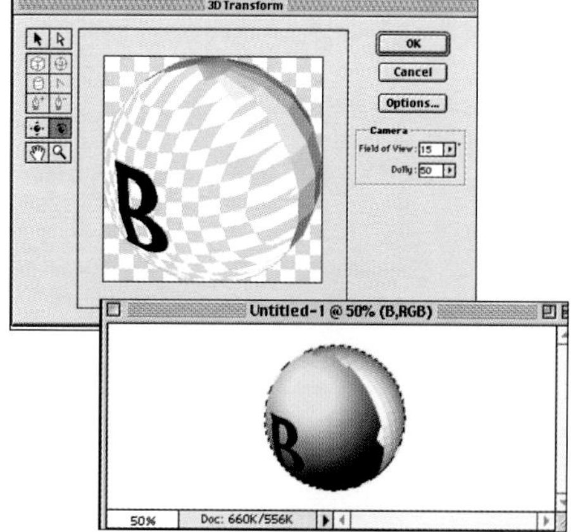


**10** Select the Trackball tool on the Tool palette (highlighted in the figure). Then click the pointer inside the circle and drag it to rotate the sphere and type. Use this tool to position the type as you want.

**TIP** **If, as you rotate the sphere, part of the sphere moves out of the preview window, use the Pan Camera tool to center it again inside the preview window. The Pan Camera tool is the tool to the left of the Trackball tool.**

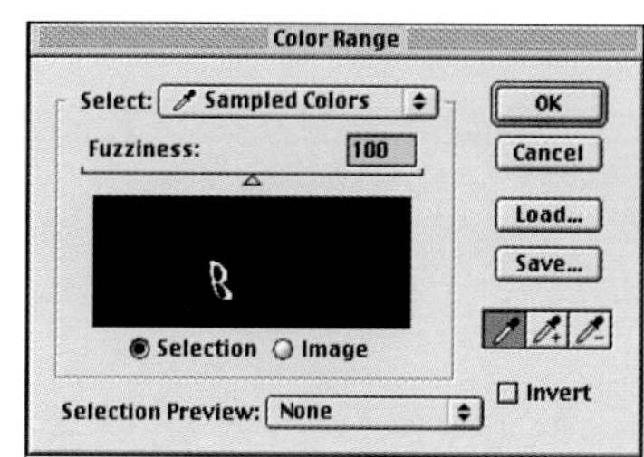


**11** Click OK and deselect the selection. This filter renders some undesirable grayscale shading on the backside of the sphere that has peeked around at the edge. The foreground color should still be the same as the color of the type. Make sure that it is, make Layer 1 invisible, and choose Select➥Color Range. The type will automatically be selected. Set the Fuzziness so that only the type is selected (100).

Click OK and choose Select➡ Inverse. Press Delete to get rid of the shading. Deselect the selection.

**If deleting the Color Range selection gets rid of some of your type, press (Command-Z) [Control-Z] to undo the Delete command. Deselect the selection and use the Lasso tool to draw a new selection around the type. Then do Step 11 to delete the shading.**

**12** Make Layer 1 visible again to see the final image.

# VARIATIONS

## Highlight

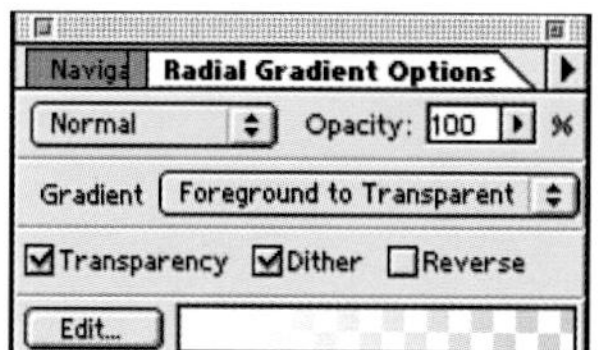


Change the Foreground color to white. Double-click the Radial Gradient tool and use the settings that you see here.

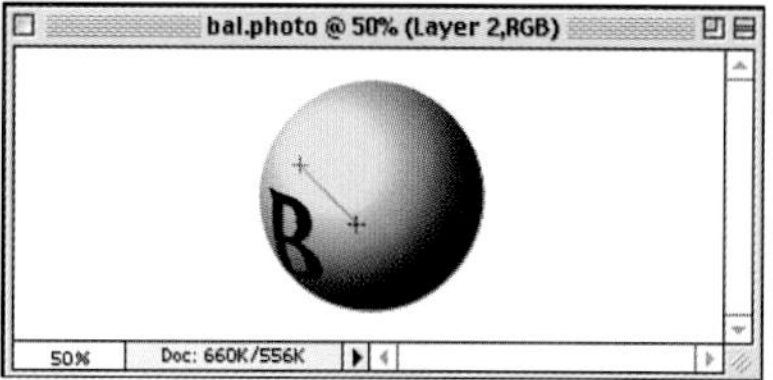


Create a new layer (Layer 2), and drag the Radial Gradient tool from the center of the highlight outward just a short distance.

Here is the highlight.

## Glossy

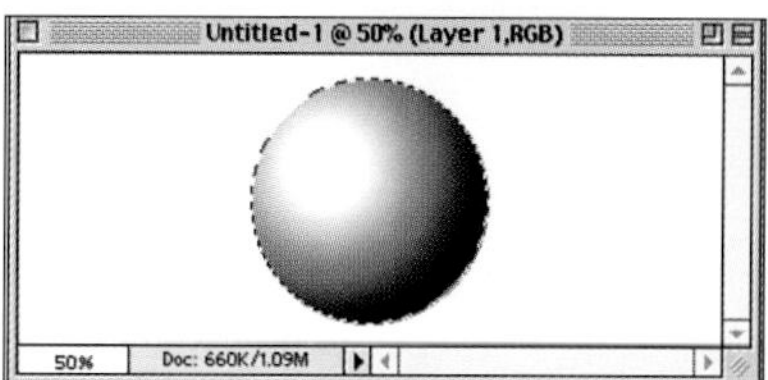


To make glossier balls, perform previous Steps 1 through 3, except in Step 3, choose white for the foreground color and black for the background color. You can do this by pressing D and then X. The circle selection should still be active. Perform Steps 4 through 7.

Then make a new layer and name it Color. Keep the selection active. Choose a foreground color for the color of the ball, and fill the selection. The gradation disappears. From the pop-up menu on the Layers palette, change the layer blending mode to Color. There is your shiny ball. Complete Steps 8 through 12 to add the text.

## Billiard Balls

To turn that ball into a billiard ball, use preceding the Glossy method. After finishing Step 7, create a new layer and select the Elliptical Marquee tool again. Deselect the selection. Then click and drag a perfect circle on top of the ball. Change the foreground color to white and fill the selection.

After Step 8, choose Merge Down from the Layers palette menu to merge the type layer with the white circle. Perform Steps 8 through 10. You probably cannot use Color Range in Step 11. You'd be better off to use the Lasso tool to select and delete the shading. Here is how the type turned out. ●

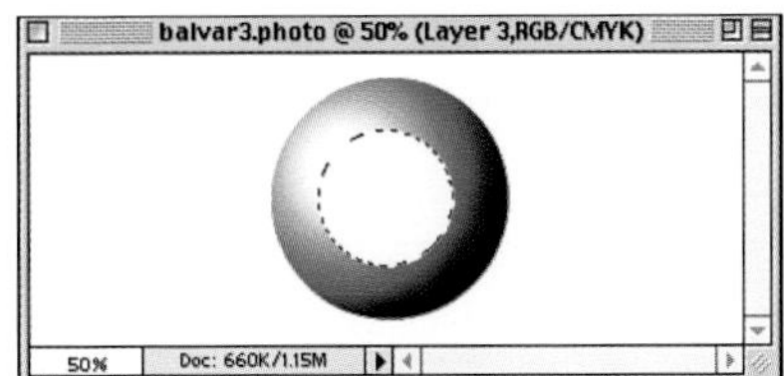

Converting a type selection into a path allows you to use the Stroke Paths command to "paint" borders around the edges of the type.

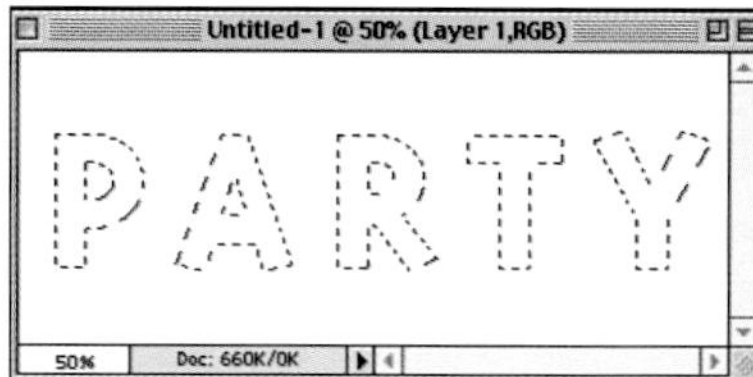


**1** Create a new file and create a new layer (Layer 1). Then use the Type Mask tool to enter the text (Triplex Ultra Bold at 110 points). The Stroke Paths command strokes the path right along its center; it affects the areas just inside and just outside of the path. Tight letterspacing can therefore cause problems. Increase the Tracking amount to spread the letters. I set it at 250.

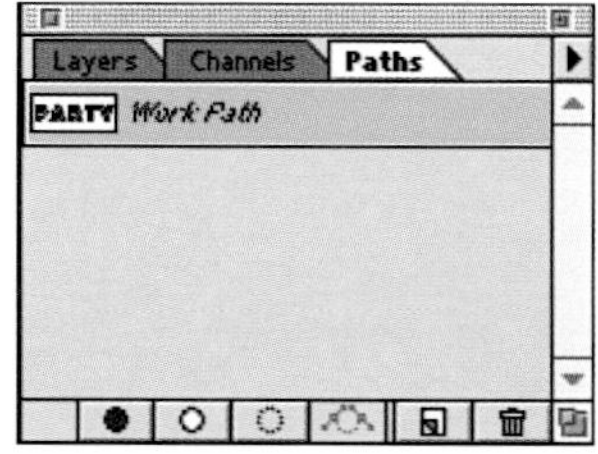


**2** Find the Paths palette and choose Make Work Path (Tolerance: 1 pixel) from the Paths palette menu to turn the selection into a path.

**TOOLBOX**

Diamond Brush

**3** Select the Paintbrush tool. The Stroke Subpaths command used in Step 7 can stroke the path with a variety of tools. The default tool is the currently selected tool (as long as that tool is one of the possible options). This list displays all the tools that the Stroke Paths command can use.

**4** Find the Brushes palette and choose Load Brushes from the Brushes palette menu. On the P5TM CD-ROM find the Diamond Brush file (P5TM➡P5TM Files➡Brushes➡Diamond Brush). You can create borders with any brush. For this effect, I created this diamond brush. Select the diamond brush added at the bottom of the Brushes palette.

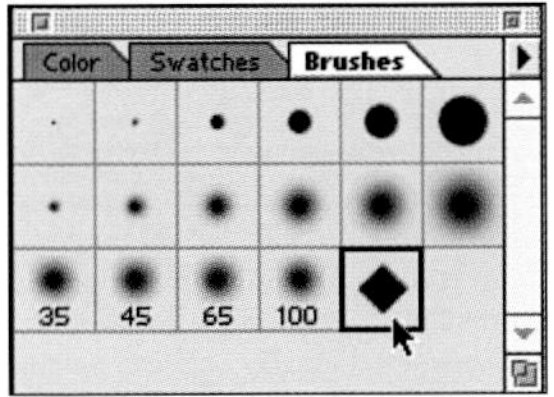


**5** Choose a foreground color for the diamond. (I used CMYK: 72, 0, 72, 0.) The Stroke Paths command pushes the Paintbrush along the path using the diamond brush and "paints" with the foreground color.

**6** Double-click on the diamond brush to open the Brush Options dialog box. Set the Spacing to 100%. As the Stroke Path command pushes the brush along the path, it uses this Spacing percentage to determine how far it moves before placing another diamond.

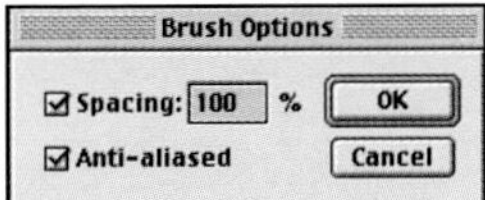


**7** Click on the Stroke Path icon on the bottom of the Paths palette or choose Stroke Path from the Paths palette menu.

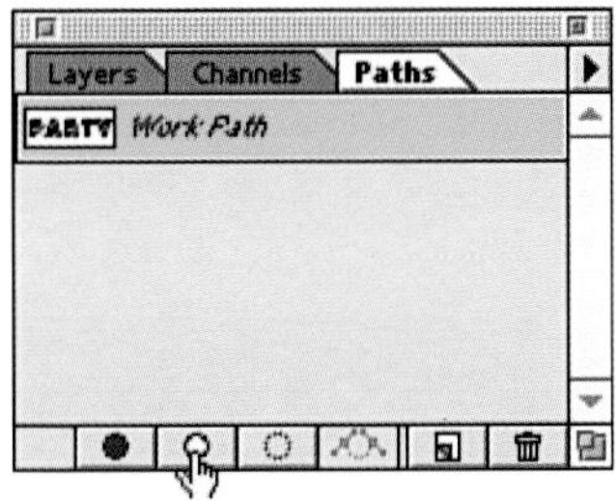

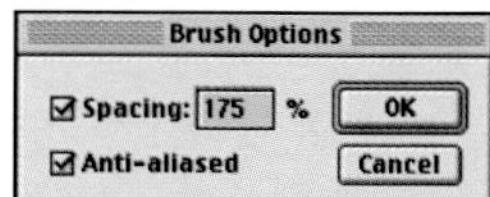


**8** Choose another foreground color (CMYK: 100, 50, 0, 0) and then double-click on the diamond brush again. Set the Spacing to 175%.

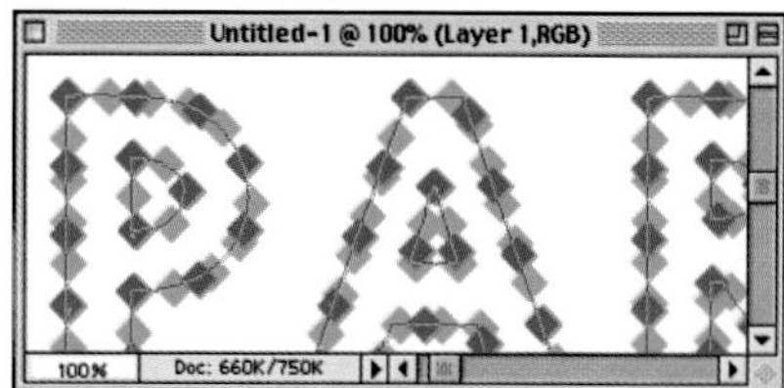


**9** Click on the Stroke Path icon again.

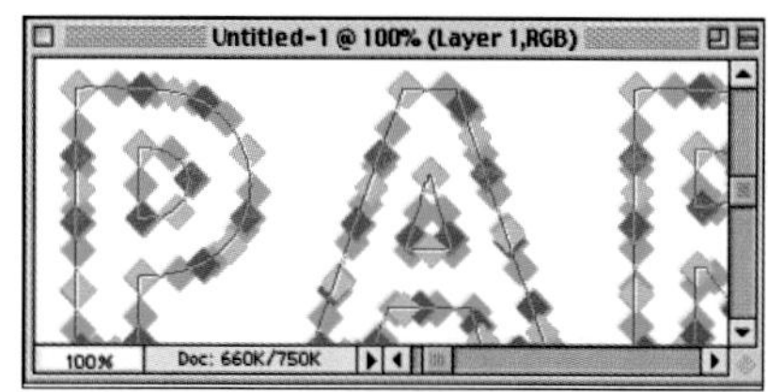


**10** Repeat Steps 8 and 9 using a new color (CMYK: 50, 0, 0, 0) and a new brush spacing (250%).

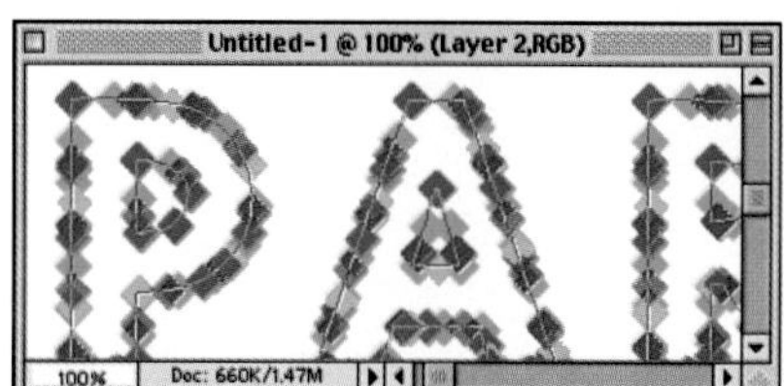


**11** Create a new layer (Layer 2) and change the layer blending mode to Difference. Then Repeat Steps 8 and 9 again (CMYK: 0, 75, 100, 0; Brush Spacing: 150%). Changing the blending mode to Difference produces new colors in the diamonds by partially inverting some of the colors in Layer 1. The diamonds look like they intersect rather than just overlap.

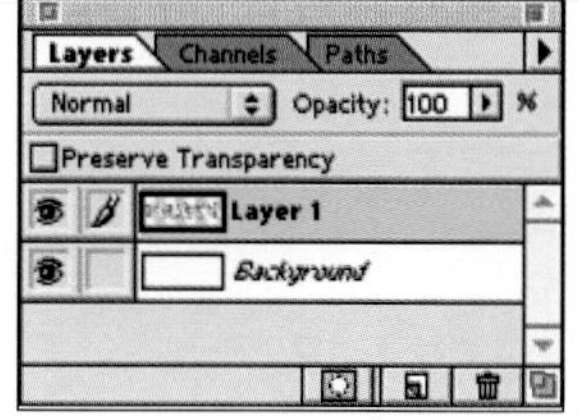


**12** Choose Turn Off Path from the Paths palette menu and Merge Down from the Layers palette menu.

**13** Then choose Filter➡Distort➡Ripple (Amount: 200%, Size: Medium). Finish the type off with a drop shadow. Adjust the Amount as necessary to distort the diamonds without obliterating them.

## Designing Borders

You might think that by stroking the path more than once and using different brushes and colors you can create patterns to run along the borders of type. But this is difficult, if not impossible, because it is hard to match the spacing of different size and shape brushes. However, you can use one closely spaced brush to create a background texture and then use another sparsely spaced brush to run an image on top of the border.

**1** Do previous Steps 1 through 3. Then in Step 4, load the Assorted Brushes file included in Photoshop 5.0 (Adobe Photoshop➡Goodies➡Brushes & Patterns➡Assorted Brushes). A variety of new brushes appear in the Brushes palette. Select the large star brush shown here.

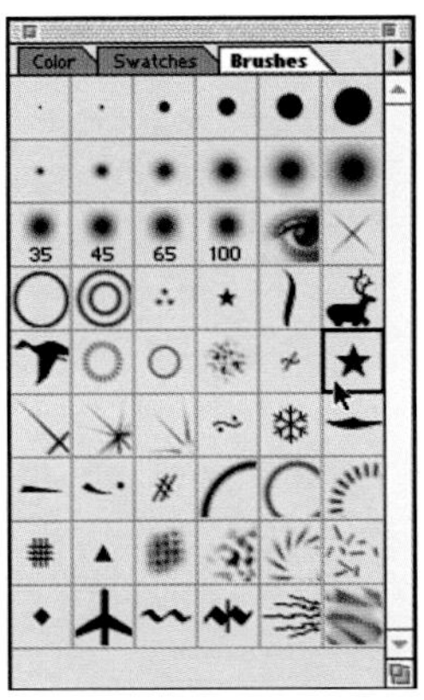


**2** Here is the foreground color I used in Step 5: CMYK: 100, 50, 0, 40. I left the Brush Spacing at the default (25%) in Step 6. Do Step 7 to stroke the path.

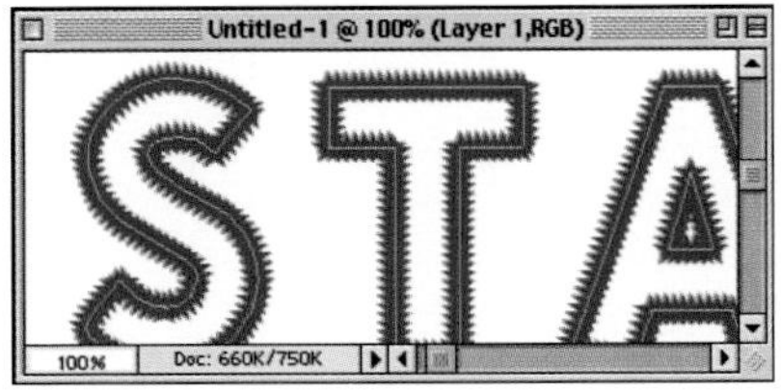

# STARS

3 Double-click on the smaller star brush to select it and open the Brush Options dialog box. Set the Spacing to 100%. Choose a new foreground color (CMYK: 0, 0, 100, 0) and click on the Stroke Path icon again.

## Masks

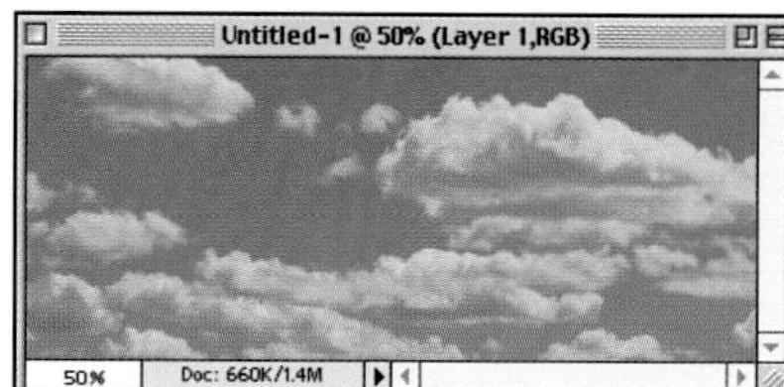


1 Open a file containing the image that you want to mask. I opened an image provided in the Photoshop 5.0 Samples folder (Adobe Photoshop 5.0➥Sample➥Big sky). Copy the image and close the file. Create a new file and paste in the image. It will be placed into a new layer (Layer 1).

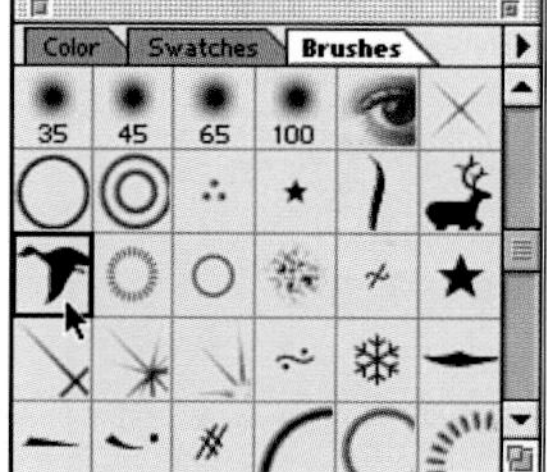


2 Then choose Layer➥Add Layer Mask➥Hide All. The image disappears. The layer mask becomes the active channel. Select the Paintbrush tool and choose white for the foreground color. Double-click on this Duck brush to open the Brush Options dialog box. Set the Spacing at 75%.

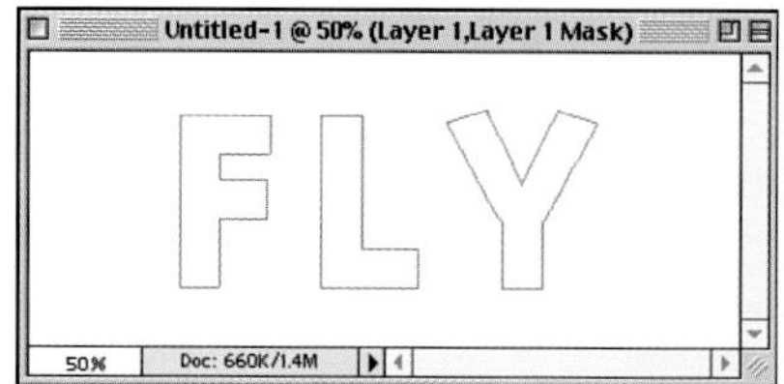


3 Use the Type Mask tool to enter the text (Triplex Ultra Bold at 140 points, Tracking: 250) and then choose Make Work Path from the Paths palette menu (Tolerance: 1 pixel).

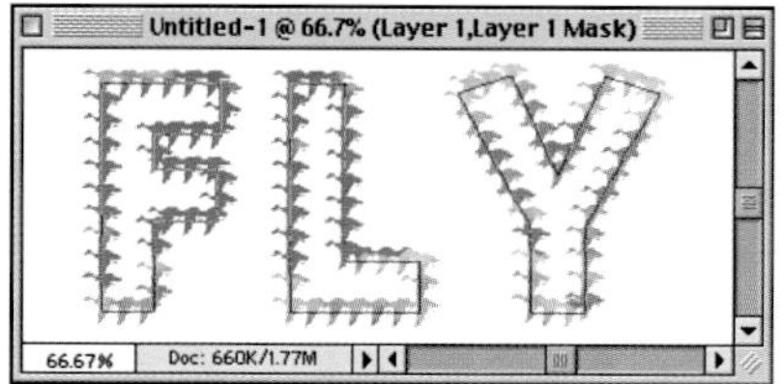


4 Select the Paintbrush tool and click on the Stroke Path icon on the Paths palette. The image is revealed beneath the ducks.

**5** Finally, I add an Inner Bevel and a Drop Shadow to Layer 1.

## VARIATIONS

### Something Simple

After creating a border for the type with a simple round brush (Spacing: 100%), I used the Inner Bevel layer effect to make the circles look like balls. A drop shadow finished the image.

### Something Not

You can apply other effects in the book to the type borders. I used the same round brush to create a border and then used the Chrome effect on page 50 to make this image.

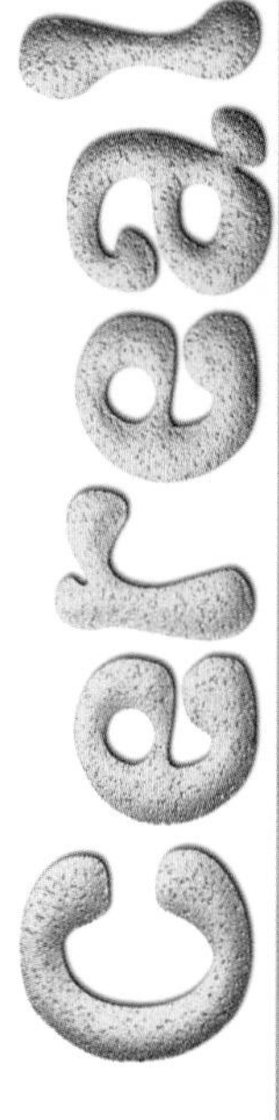


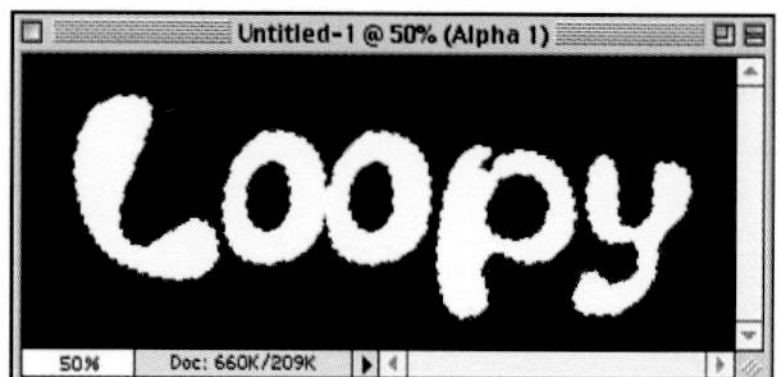


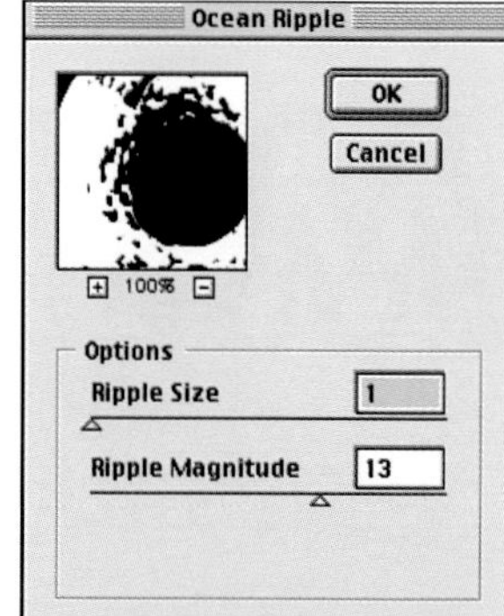


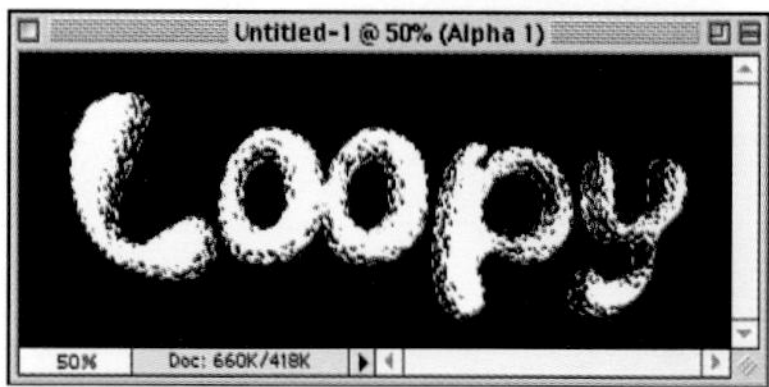


The unlikely Ocean Ripple filter works with the Lighting Effects filter to round out these crunchy letters.

**1** Create a new file, and a new channel (Alpha 1). Use the Type tool to enter the text. Font choice for this effect is important. I used Thickhead (110 points) because the shapes of the letters look like bulbous Cheerios.

**2** Save the selection to create the Alpha 2 channel, which will be identical to Alpha 1. Keep the text selection active.

**3** Choose Filter➥Distort➥Ocean Ripple. This filter distorts the type around the edges by spreading the background into the selection. Try these settings to distort just parts of the type: Ripple Size: 1; Ripple Magnitude: 13.

TIP **This filter is somewhat unpredictable, and if the word you typed is too long, the Ocean Ripple filter might distort some of the letters too much. If this happens, try selecting only a few of the letters at a time and apply the filter. Continue until the Ocean Ripple filter has been applied to all the letters. Then load the selection from the Alpha 2 channel to select all the letters again.**

**4** Next, choose Filter➡Blur➡Gaussian Blur. Blur the text enough to smooth out the distortion created by the Ocean Ripple filter. I set the Radius at 8.8.

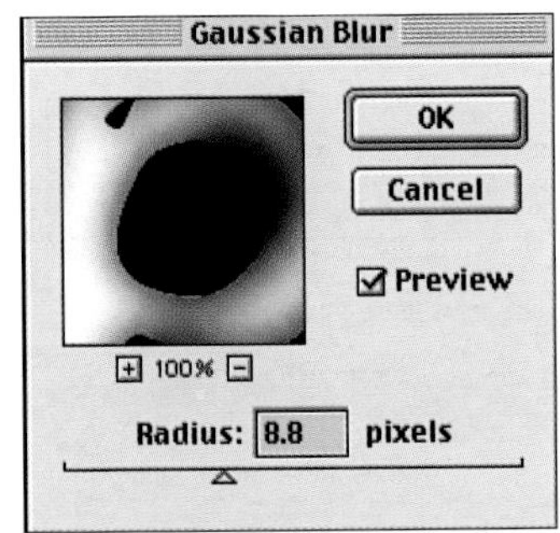


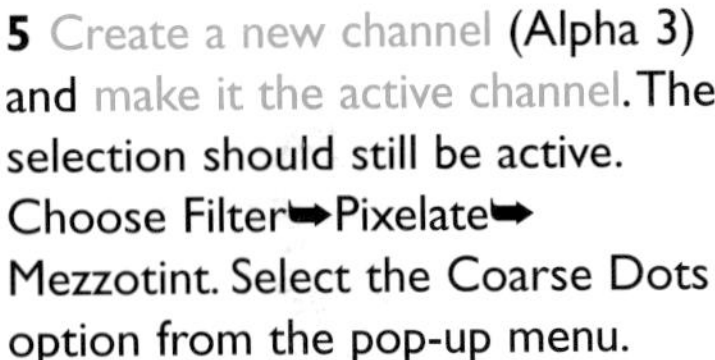

**5** Create a new channel (Alpha 3) and make it the active channel. The selection should still be active. Choose Filter➡Pixelate➡Mezzotint. Select the Coarse Dots option from the pop-up menu.

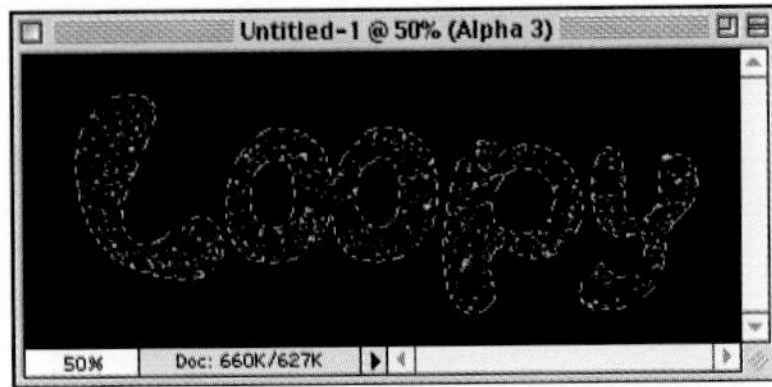


**6** Make the Alpha 1 channel active and then load the Alpha 3 channel selection.

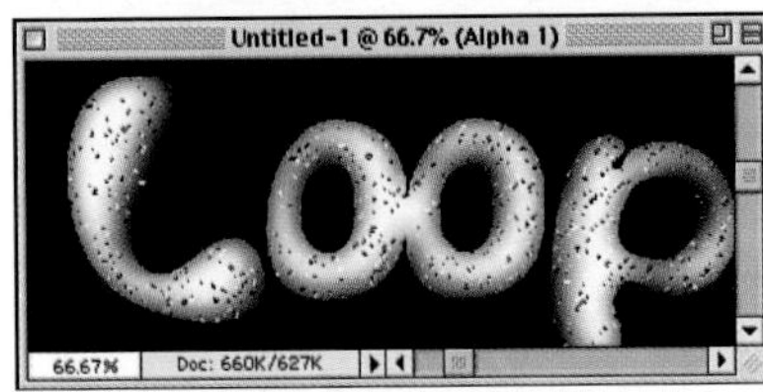


**7** Choose Image➡Adjust➡Brightness/Contrast. Lower the Brightness value to about -35. The dark areas created will aid the Lighting Effects filter in adding the pock marks to the surface of the cereal. Deselect the selection.

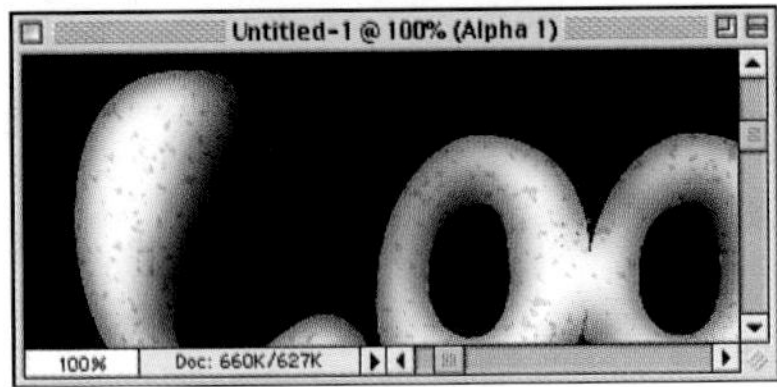


**8** Load the Alpha 2 channel selection. Choose Filter➡Noise➡Add Noise. Set the Amount to approximately 4 (Distribution: Gaussian). The noise helps create some shallower bumps in the cereal letters but keep it low. You will barely see a change in the image but have faith. It will make a difference in the final image.

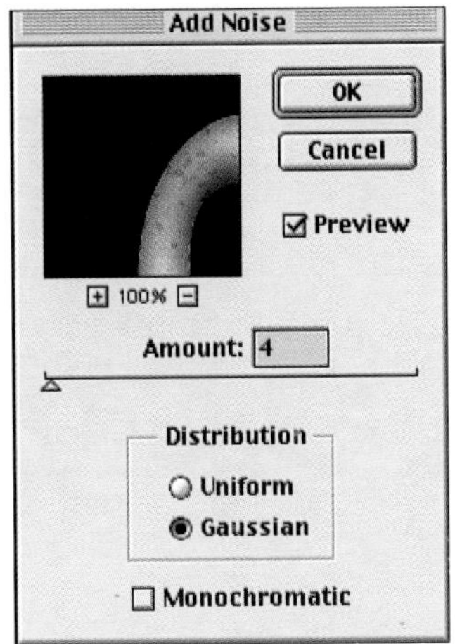

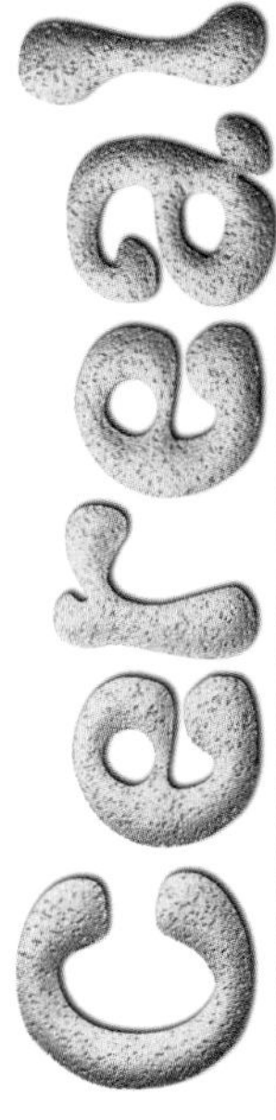

9 Return to the composite channel. Keep the selection active. Make sure that you are in a layer with a flat white background, not a new transparent layer.

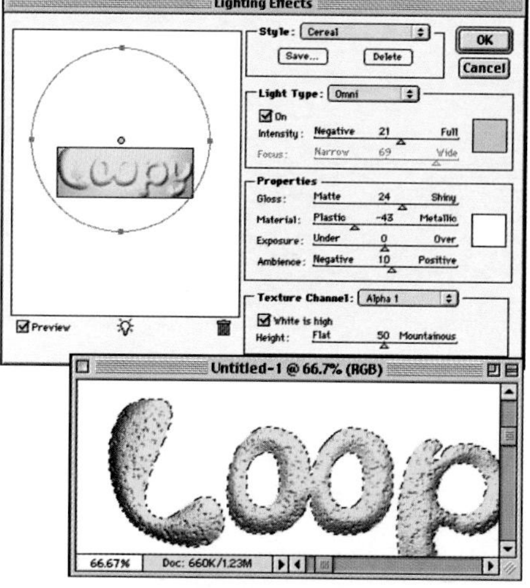


10 Choose Filter➥Render➥Lighting Effects. Choose the Cereal preset from the Style pop-up menu, or match the settings in this figure. Use the Texture Channel Height to adjust the fullness of the letters.

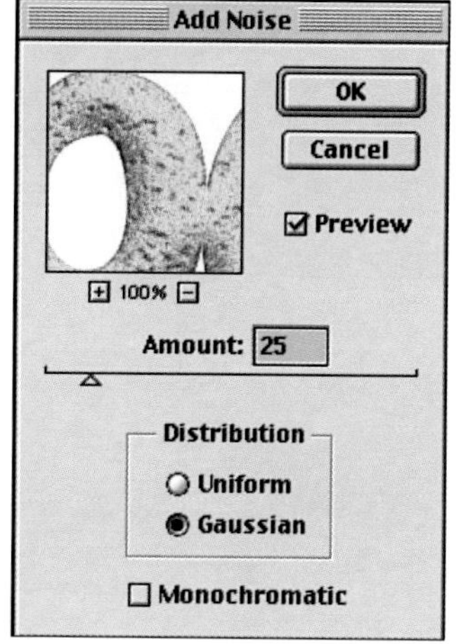


11 As a final touch, I chose Filter➥Noise➥Add Noise and adjusted the Amount to 25. This noise gives the cereal texture a little graininess, and we all know how important grain is to our diets.

## VARIATIONS

I just couldn't resist adding this milky background and a shadow.

If you have a hard-edged font that you want to round off for this effect, follow these steps.

In Step 1, use the Type Mask tool instead of the Type tool. This font is Impact at 100 points.

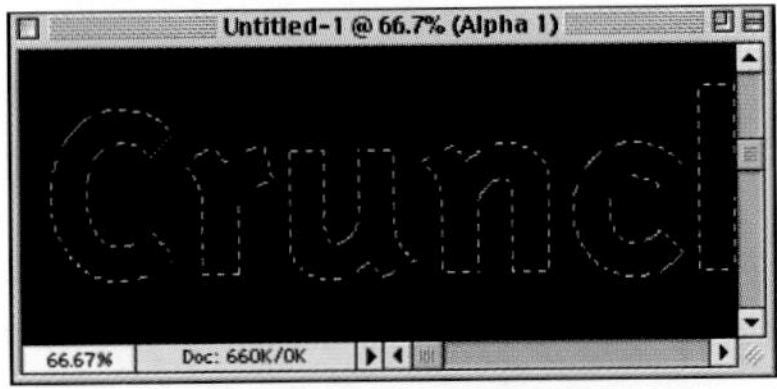


Then choose Select➡Modify➡ Smooth. You might have to try different settings before you get the one you want. I smoothed the selection 10 pixels.

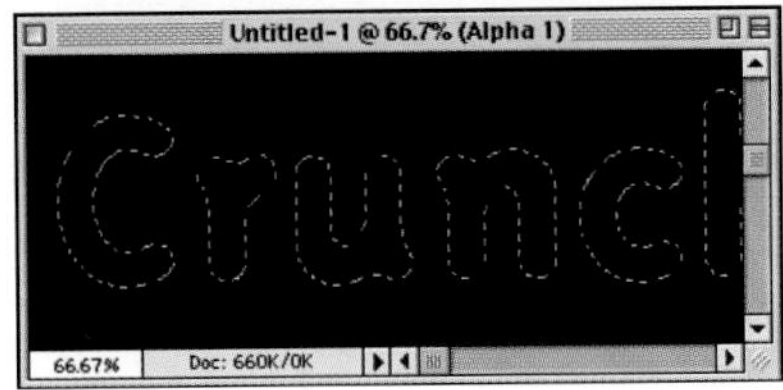


Fill the selection with white and finish the steps preceding (Steps 2 through 11).

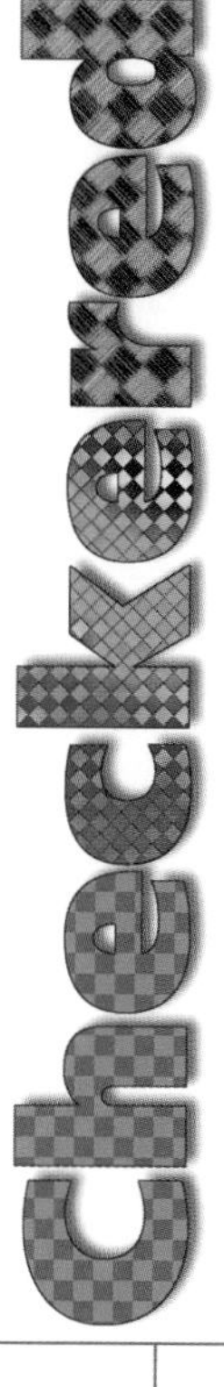


Making a checkered pattern takes only a few steps. After you learn the steps, you can use Photoshop's filters to make some unique effects including Reflector and Woven type.

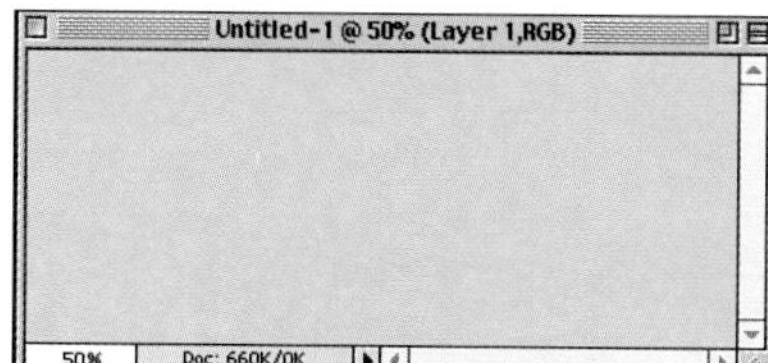


1 Create a new file, and create a new layer (Layer 1). Change the foreground color to one of the colors you want to use for the checkers and fill the entire layer with the color. I used the CMYK values 10, 8, 100, and 0.

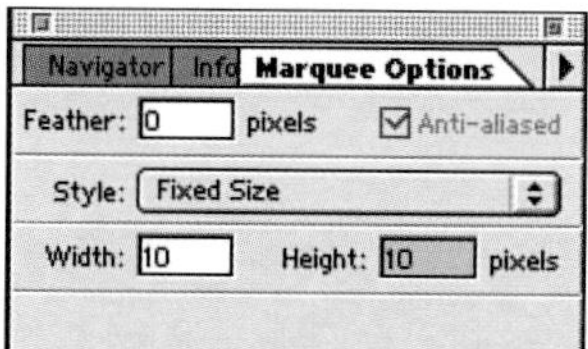


2 Double-click the Marquee tool to select it and to bring the Marquee Options floating palette to the front. Change the style to Fixed Size, and set the Width and Height to 10 pixels. These dimensions determine the size of the squares in the checkered pattern—adjust it to your liking, but make sure you always keep the Width and Height the same.

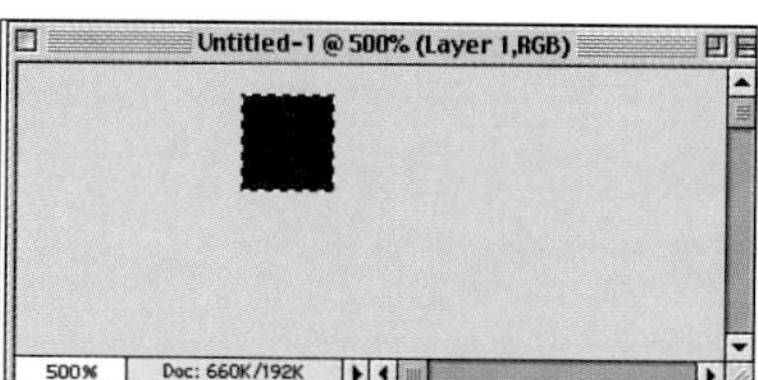


3 Next, click in the image area once with the Marquee tool. A square selection appears. Change the foreground color to the second color for the checkers. I used the CMYK values 90, 60, 30, and 60. Fill the selection with this color.

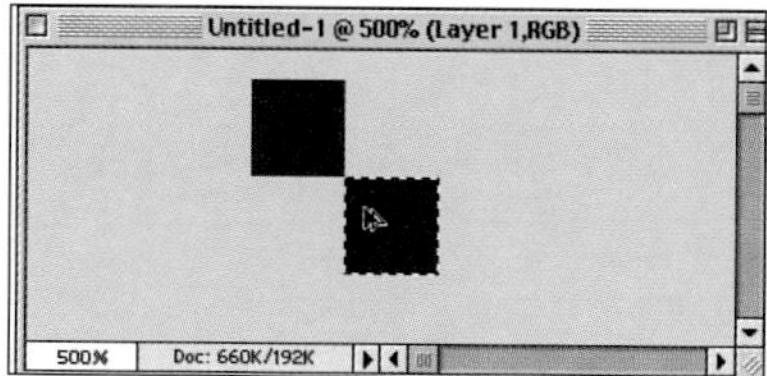


4 Grab the Move tool and hold the (Option) [Alt] key as you drag the selection so that the upper-left corner of the selection meets the lower-right corner of the original colored square. This creates a copy of the original selection in the new position.

**5** Again, select the Marquee tool and find the Marquee Options floating palette. Keep the Style set at Fixed Size and double the Width and Height sizes (20 pixels for me).

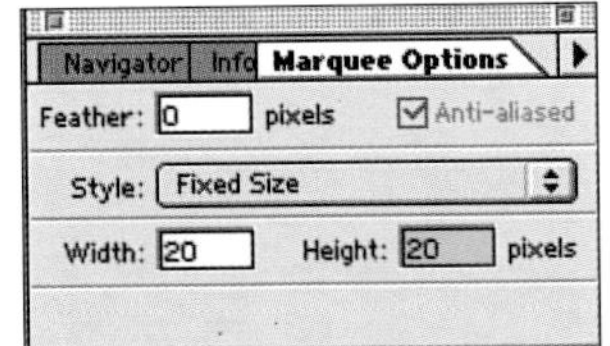


**6** Use the Marquee tool to click in the image area. Drag the new, larger, square selection so that it includes both of the colored squares. It should be a perfect match.

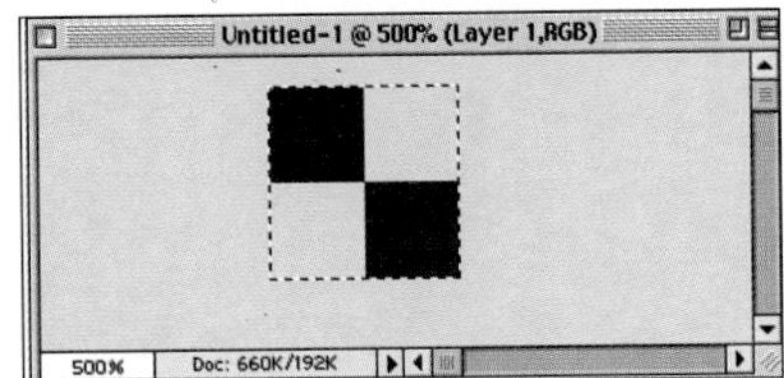


**7** Choose Edit➡Define Pattern. There is no dialog box here. Photoshop uses the checks as the pattern for the Fill command used in Step 9. Choose Select➡All, and press Delete to clear the image window. Deselect the selection.

**8** Use the Type Mask tool to enter the text. I used Frutiger Ultra Black at 80 points.

**9** Choose Edit➡Fill. In the dialog box, change the Contents option to Pattern (Opacity: 100%, Mode: Normal). Click OK, and you have checkers.

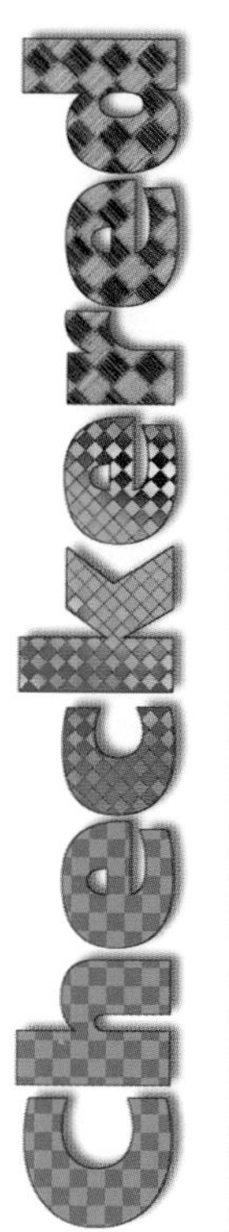

## Reflector

If you make a few alterations to the steps, you can make a diagonal checkered pattern that I used to make this Reflector effect.

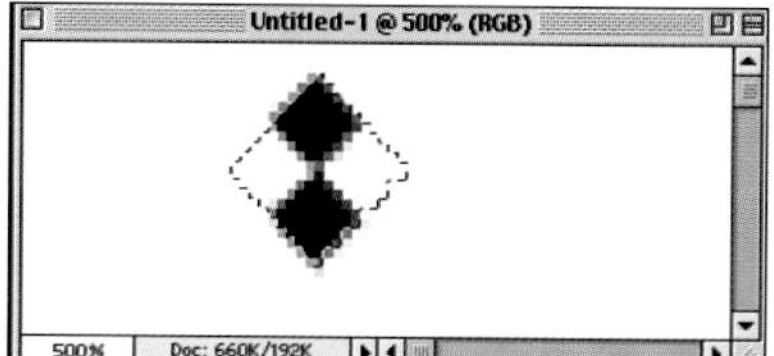


**1** Do the previous Steps 1 through 6 to create a four-square pattern. In Step 2, I set the Width and Height to 7 pixels and in Step 5, I used 14 pixels. After completing Step 6, choose Edit➡Transform➡Numeric. Check only the Rotate box and set the angle to 45°. The diamonds will look jagged.

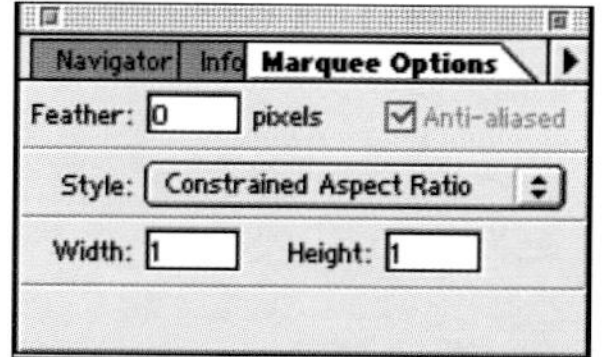


**2** Again, find the Marquee Options floating palette. Change the Style to Constrained Aspect Ratio and make sure that the Width and Height settings are changed to 1. This option keeps the selection a perfect square. Drag the Marquee to make a selection like this:

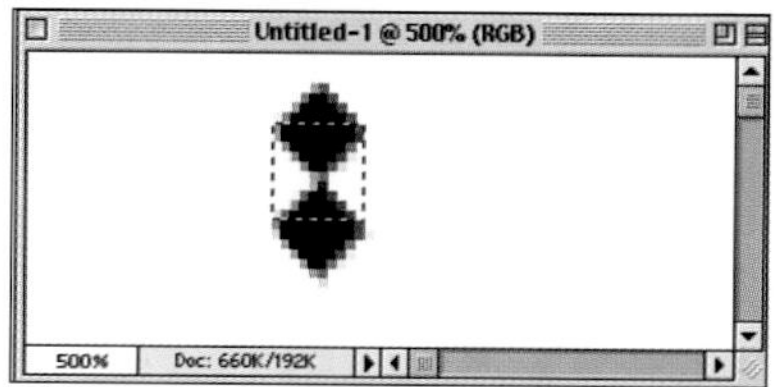


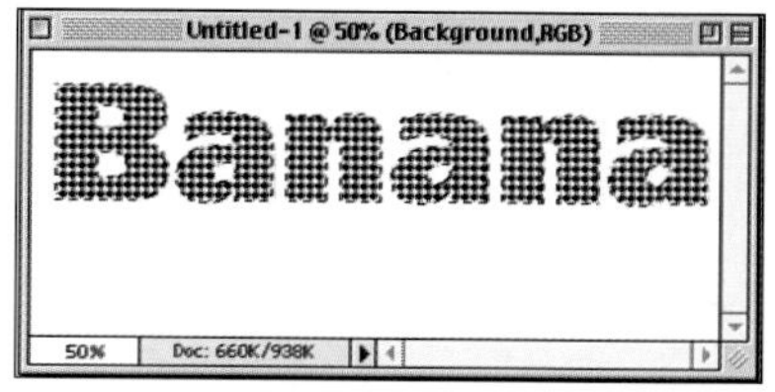


**3** Do Steps 7 through 9 of the Checkered instructions to define the diagonal pattern, create the type, and fill it with the pattern.

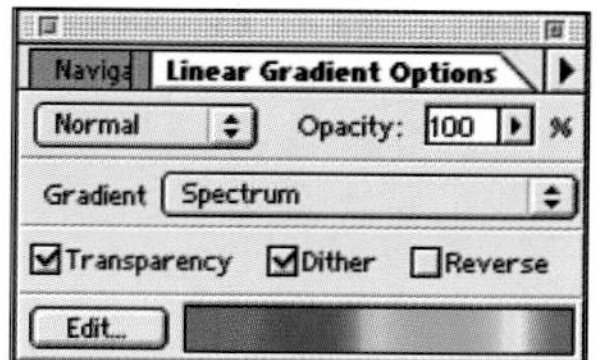


**4** Make a new layer (Layer 2). Double-click the Linear Gradient tool to select it and bring to the front the Linear Gradient Options floating palette. Choose the Spectrum preset gradient.

**5** Drag the Gradient tool diagonally across the type selection.

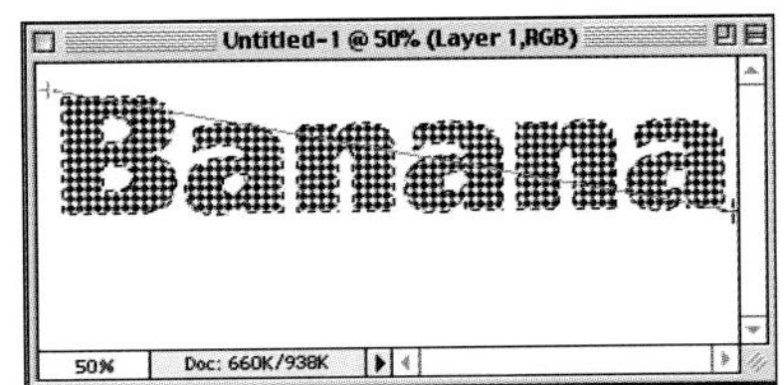


The selection fills with the gradient.

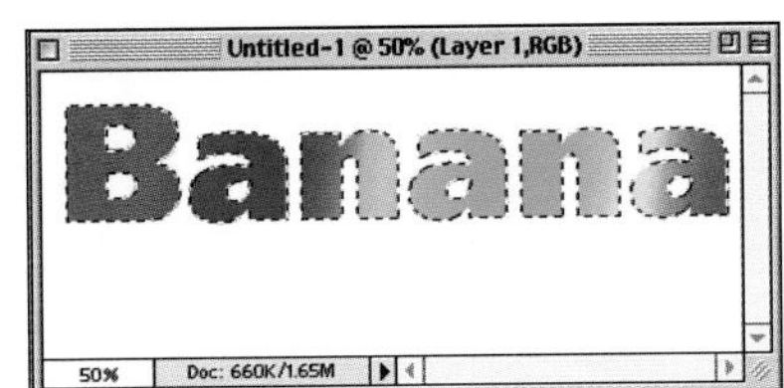


**6** Change the Layer 2 blending mode to Color. The diamonds reappear.

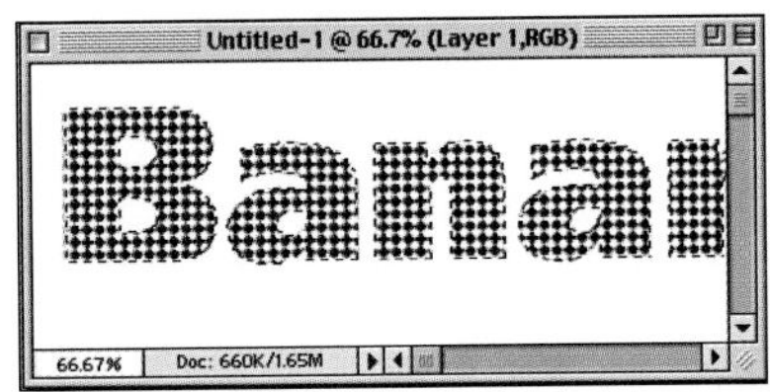


**7** Keep the selection active and make Layer 1 the active layer.

**8** Choose Filter➥Render➥Difference Clouds to complete the effect.



## Woven

**1** Do Steps 1 and 2 of the Reflector instructions. (I set the Width and Height to 15 pixels for the first square and 30 pixels to select the four-square pattern.) Then choose Edit➥Define Pattern. Choose Select➥All and Edit➥Fill (Use: Pattern, Opacity: 100%, Mode: Normal) to fill the layer with the diamond pattern. Deselect the selection and choose Flatten Image from the Layers palette menu.

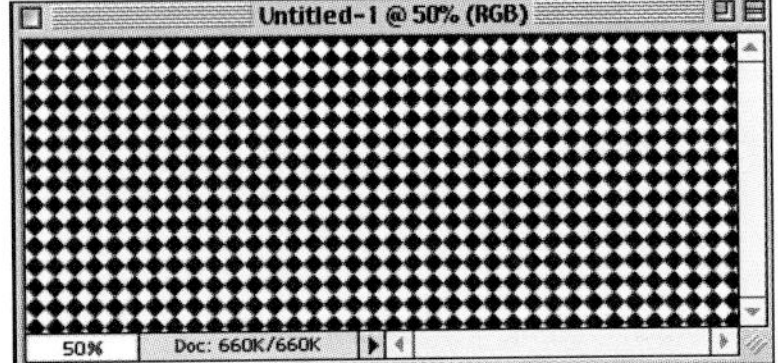

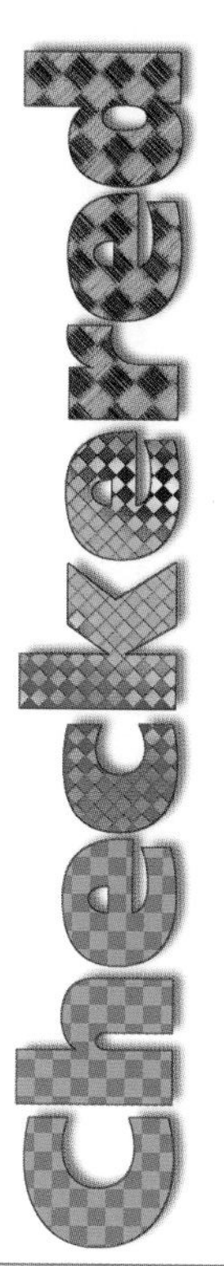


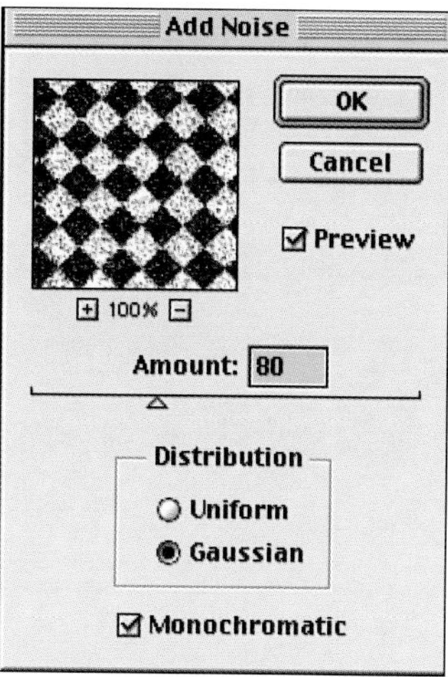


2 Add a little noise to the checks by choosing Filter➡Noise➡Add Noise. I set the Amount to 80 (Gaussian). Turn on the Monochromatic option. The noise helps the next filter do its job.

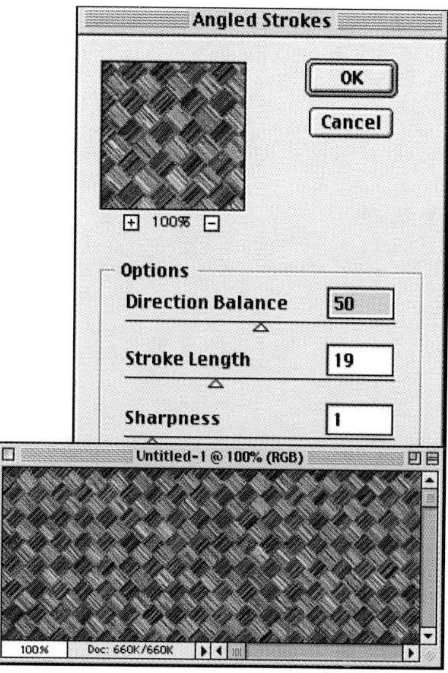


3 Apply Filter➡Brush Strokes➡Angled Strokes. Use these settings: Direction Balance, 50; Stroke Length, 19; and Sharpness, 1. Adjust the settings if necessary. You want to see some good streaks through the checks, but be careful not to obliterate them.

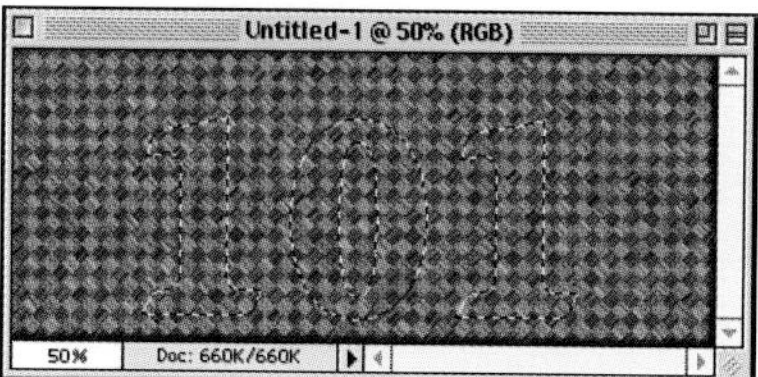


4 Now, we need some type. Use the Type Mask tool to enter the text. This font is Seagull Heavy at 135 points.

**5** Choose Select➡Inverse, make sure the foreground color is white, and press Option-Delete. Then choose Select➡Inverse again to select the type.

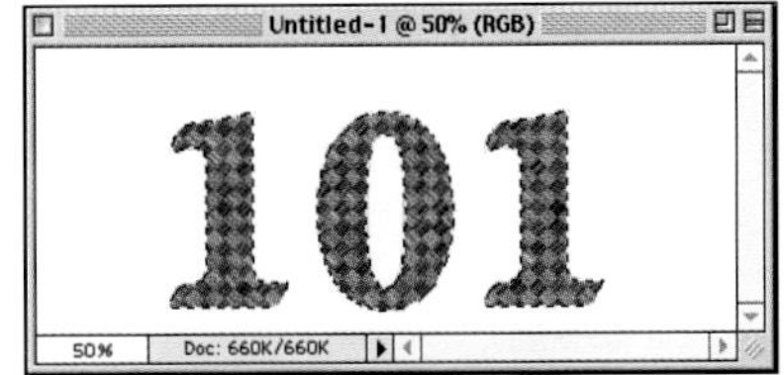


**6** And we need some color. Choose Image➡Adjust➡Hue/Saturation. Now turn on the Colorize option and find a color for the texture.

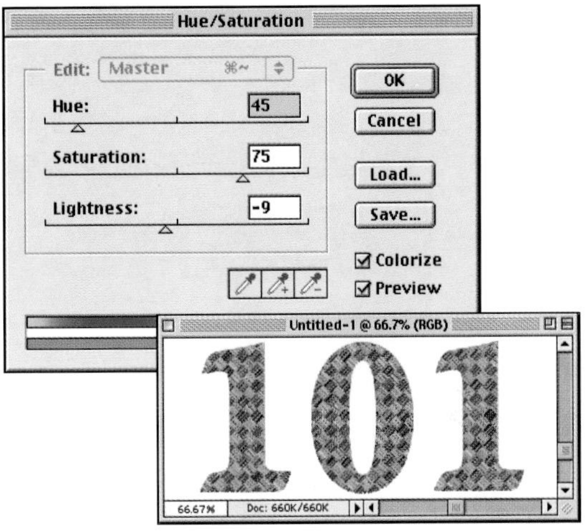


**7** For some fine-tuning, choose Image➡Adjust➡Levels. Use the Input markers to adjust the values in the weave. I set the Input markers at 21, 0.88, and 255. For a darker, more contrasty pattern, click the Auto button. ●

TOOLBOX

Chrome Curves, Chrome (Lighting Effects Style)

Following are three methods for creating shiny metallic type. The first combines Photoshop 5.0's Inner Bevel layer effect with some "magic" Curves. The second uses a channel and the Lighting Effects filter and the third is an airbrushed chrome look that uses the Gradient tool.

## Layer Effects Chrome

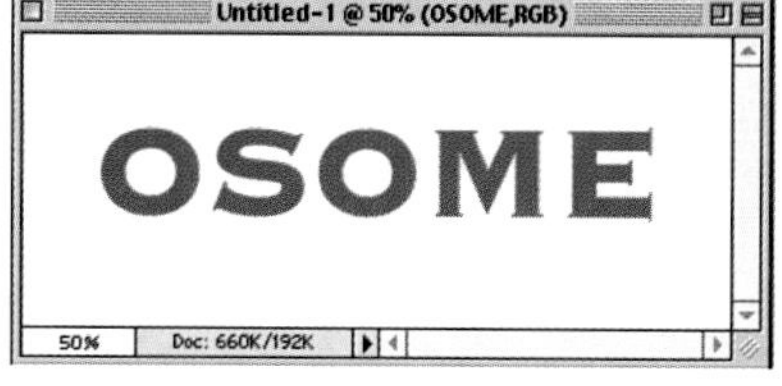


1 Create a new file, choose 50% gray for the foreground color, and use the Type tool to enter the text. (I used Copperplate Gothic Thirty Three BC at 95 points.) This technique works better with thin typefaces. Don't use anything too heavy and blocky. Choose Layer➡Type➡Render Layer.

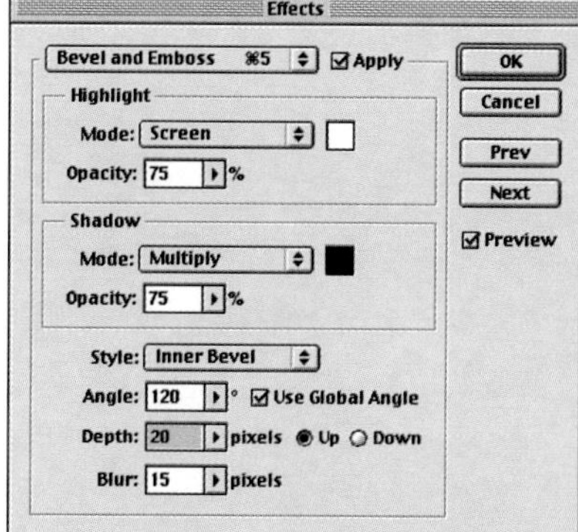


2 Choose Layer➡Effects➡Bevel and Emboss. Select the Inner Bevel style, raise the Depth to 20 pixels, and then raise the Blur amount until the type looks rounded (15 pixels).

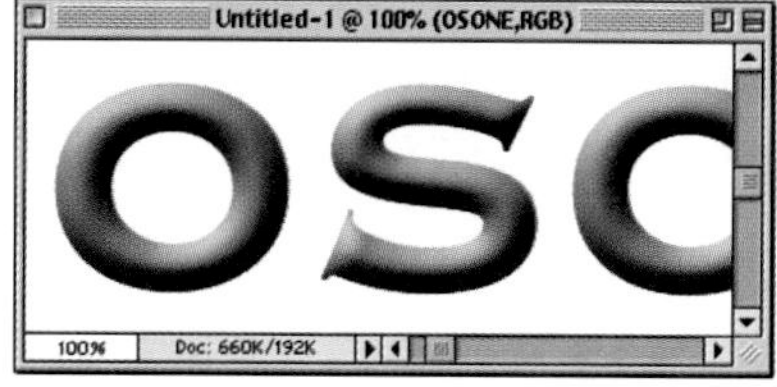

**3** Choose Layer➡Effects➡Create Layers. Two layers will be added to the Layers palette—one for the bevel highlights and one for the shadows. From the Layers palette menu, choose Merge Group. The two new layers will be merged back into the original layer.

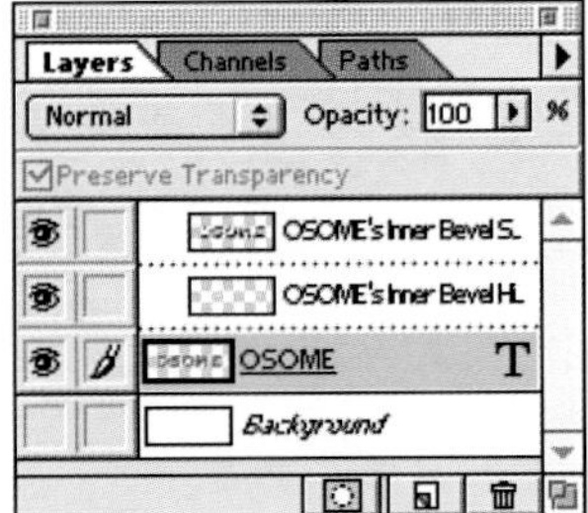


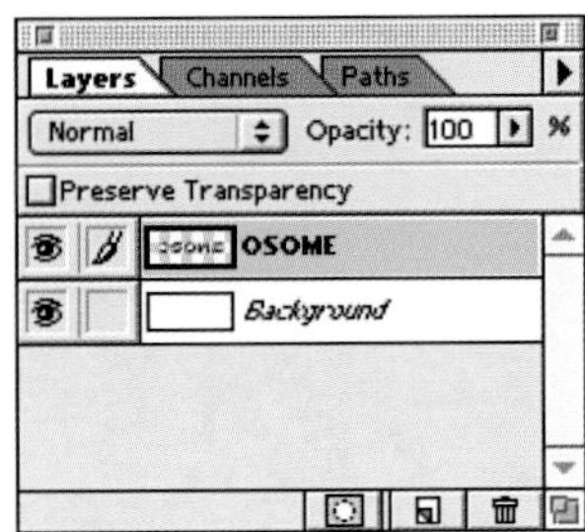


**4** Choose Image➡Adjust➡ Curves, click the Load button, and find the Chrome Curves file on the P5TM CD-ROM (P5TM➡P5TM Files➡Curves➡ Chrome Curves).

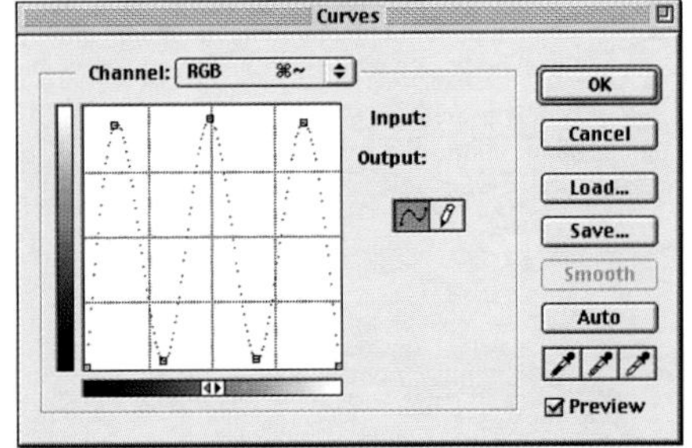


Click OK to get something like this.

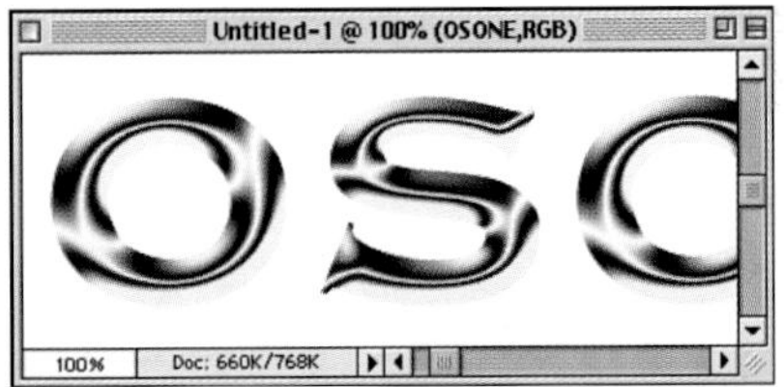

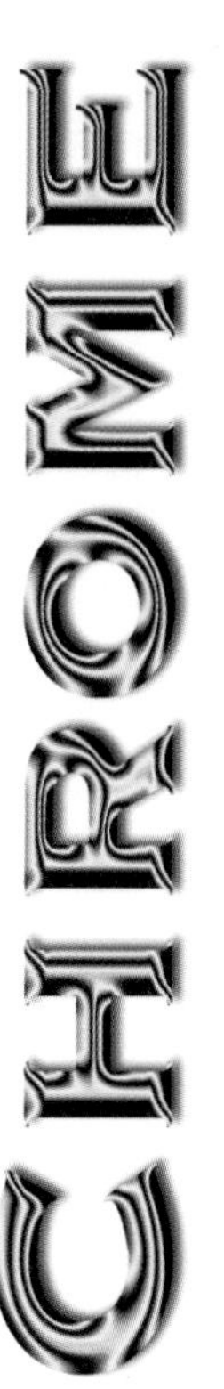


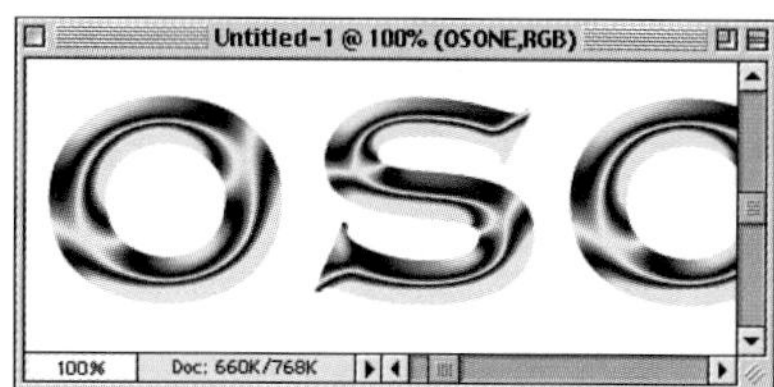


5 Choose Image➡Adjust➡Curves again. The Curves dialog box is an excellent tool for adding some subtle color to the type. From the menu at the top, select only one of the color channels. (I used Blue.) Grab the line on the graph in the center and bend toward the upper-left corner to add a blue tint to the type and bend it toward the lower-right corner to make a warmer chrome. Selecting and adjusting other color channels will result in different effects.

6 A drop shadow finishes off the effect and brings out the lighter colors in the lower-right parts of the letters.

## Color Variations

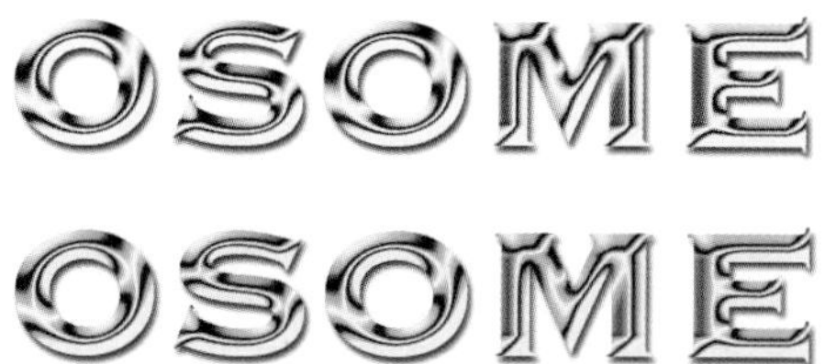


For more drastic color changes, choose Image➡Adjust➡Hue/Saturation and use all three sliders to change the color. Here are two examples.



## Lighting Effects Chrome

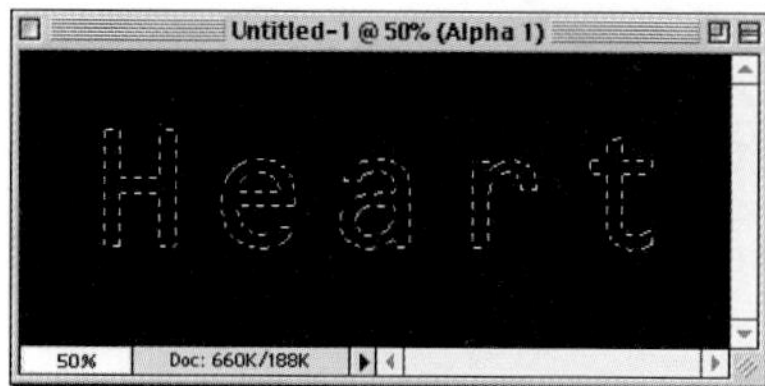


1 Create a new file and create a new channel (Alpha 1). Use the Type Mask tool to enter the text (OCR-B at 85 points). Save the selection to create the Alpha 2 channel.

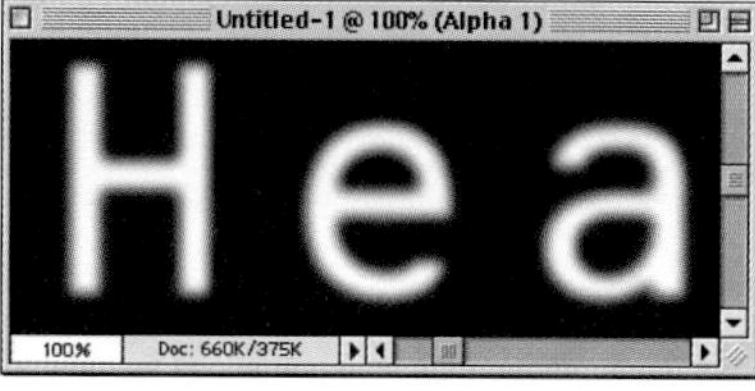


2 Fill the text selection with white and deselect the selection. Choose Filter➡Blur➡Gaussian Blur (3.5 pixels).

**3** Load the selection of the active channel and choose Filter➡Blur➡Gaussian Blur. Set the Radius to at least twice as high as in the last step (9 pixels).

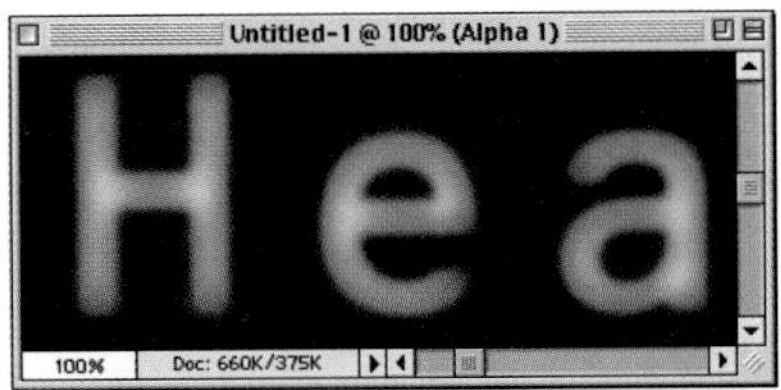


**4** Return to the composite channel and keep the selection active. Choose Filter➡Render➡Lighting Effects. Select the Chrome style from the menu or match the settings in this figure. Make sure that there is plenty of gray in the preview. If your type appears washed out, the light is too strong. Lower the Intensity to fix this problem.

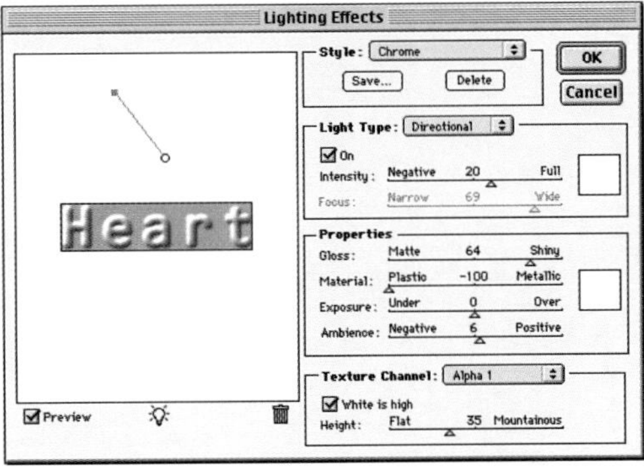


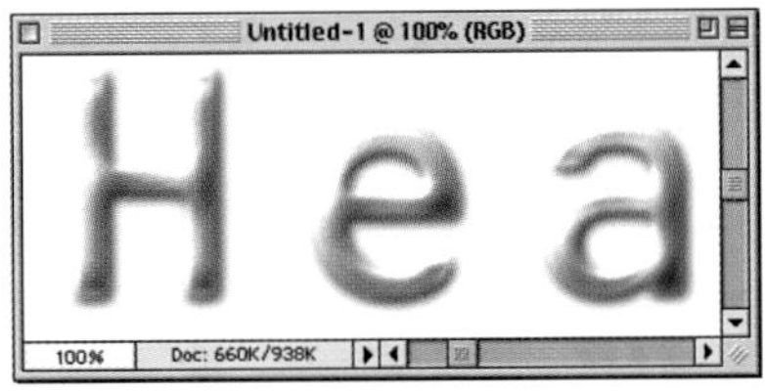


**5** Deselect the selection and choose Filter➡Stylize➡Find Edges. This filter produces good contrasty highlights and shadows.

**6** Choose Image➡Adjust➡ Curves. The Curves dialog box can be used to add subtle color to the chrome. From the menu at the top, select only one of the color channels (Blue). Then grab the line on the graph in the center and bend toward the upper-left corner to add a blue tint to the type and bend it toward the lower-right corner to make a warmer chrome.

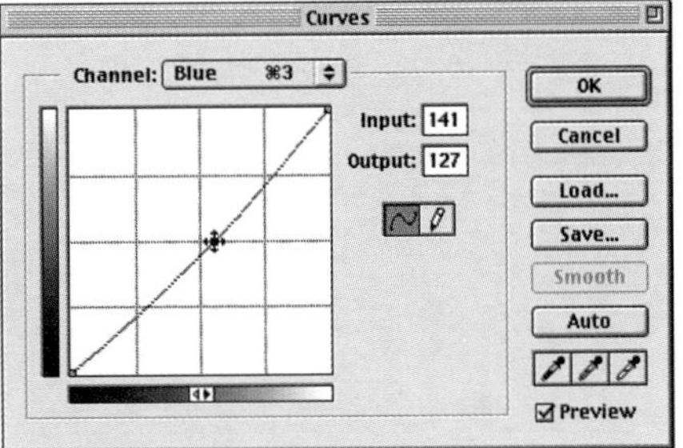

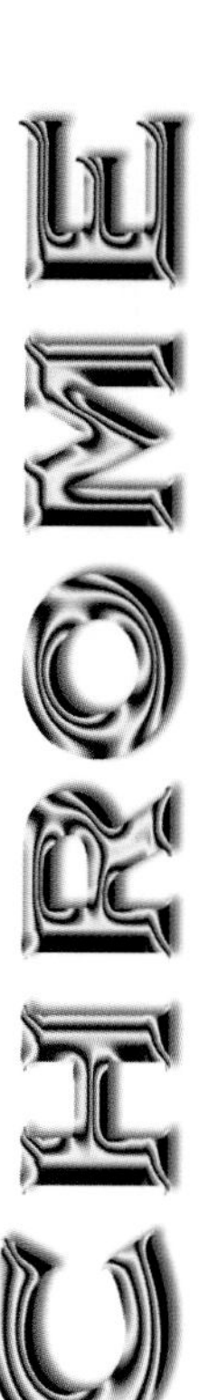

The final type with a drop shadow.

**If you want to pick this type off the Background layer, load the Alpha 2 selection and choose Select➡Modify➡Expand. Expand the selection enough to include most of the shadow areas to the lower right of the type (4 pixels). Choose Layer➡New➡Layer Via Cut to lift the type selection into a new layer.**

## Gradient Chrome

**1** Create a new file, create a new layer (Layer 1), and use the Type Mask tool to enter the text. (I used Poppl-Laudatio Bold Condensed at 110 points.) Save the selection to create the Alpha 1 channel.

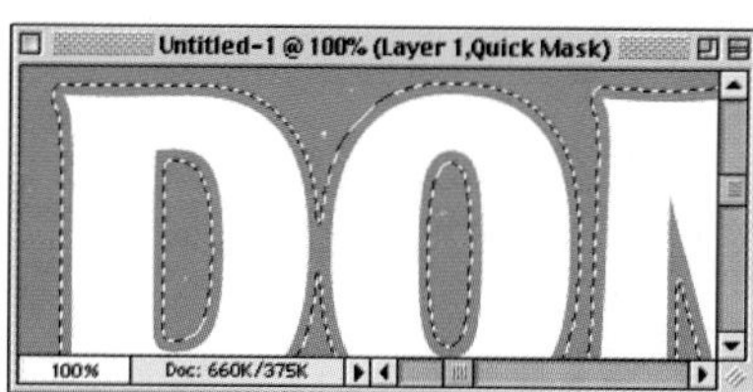


**2** Press Q to enter Quick Mask mode. Load the selection of the Quick Mask channel that has been temporarily added to the Channels palette. Then choose Select➡Modify➡Expand (6 pixels). The expand amount will be the thickness of the rim around the edge of the type.

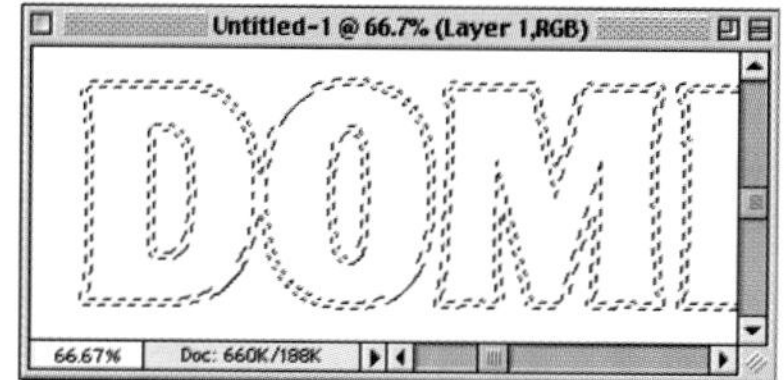


**3** Choose Image➡Adjust➡Invert. Press Q to exit Quick Mask mode. Only a thin border around the type will be selected.

**4** Choose 50% gray for the foreground color and fill the selection. Deselect the selection and then do Steps 2 through 5 on page ?? to turn the rim into chrome.

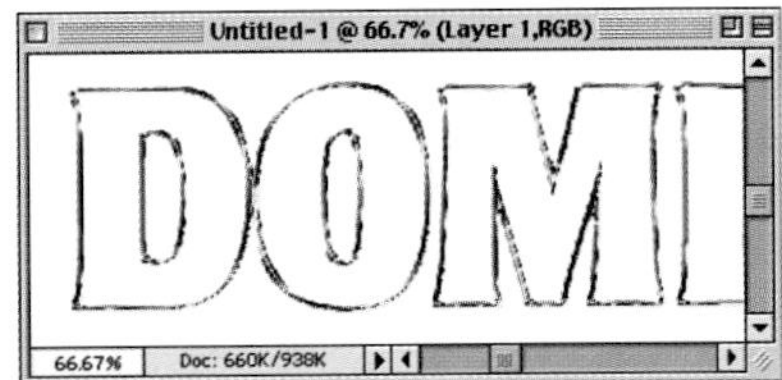

**5** Load the Alpha 1 selection and double-click on the Linear Gradient tool. From the Gradient pop-up menu on the Linear Gradient Options palette select Chrome.

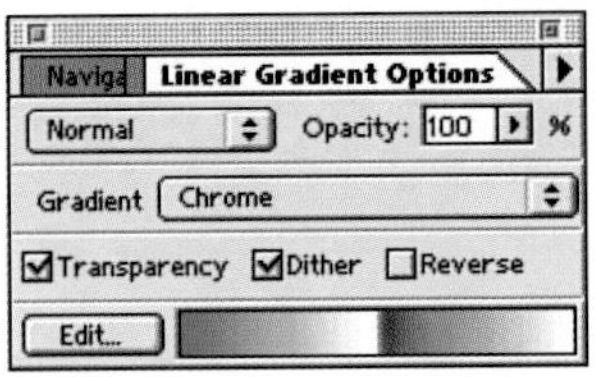


**6** Hold the Shift key as you drag from the top of the type to the bottom of the type.

**7** To finish I added a drop shadow and a couple of highlights (see page 102).

## Variations

After selecting the Chrome gradient in Step 5, click the Edit button on the Linear Gradient Options palette. In the Gradient Editor dialog box that opens, you can change the colors in the gradient. ●

Another texture effect, clay, is created by manipulating the lights and darks in a channel used by the Lighting Effects filter as a texture map.

**1** Create a new file, and create a new channel (Alpha 1). Use the Type tool to enter the text. The type in this example is Lithos Black at 80 points.

**2** Save the selection to create the Alpha 2 channel. Deselect the type.

**3** Then choose Filter➡Render➡ Difference Clouds to fill the channel (Alpha 1).

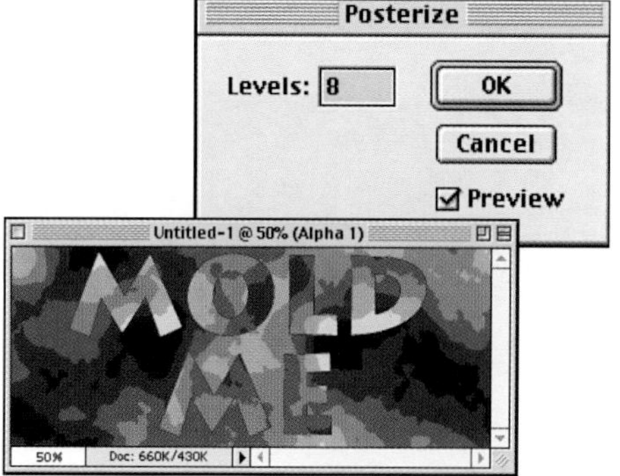


**4** Choose Image➡Adjust➡ Posterize. Keep the setting low. I used 8 levels. This step flattens the cloud gradation into flat areas that look like scraped clay.



**TOOLBOX**

Clay (Lighting Effects Style)

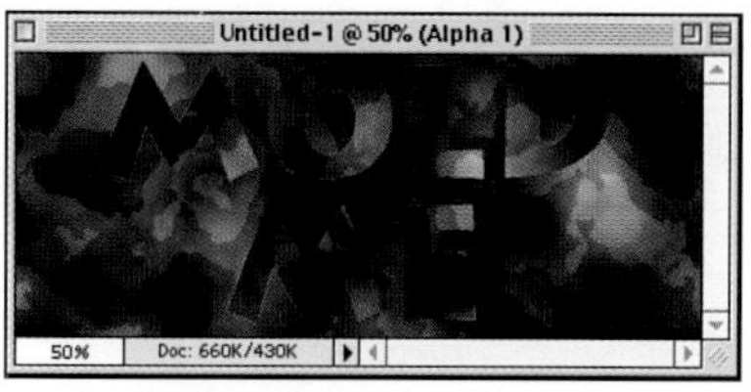


**5** Then choose Filter➡Render➡ Difference Clouds again. This is the channel that will be used for the clay texture.

Expand Selection

Expand By: 2 pixels

OK

Cancel

**6** Return to the composite channel, and load the selection from the Alpha 2 channel. Choose Select➡ Modify➡Expand (2 pixels). Expanding the selection eventually gives the type its lip.

**7** Choose Filter➡Render➡Lighting Effects. You can choose Clay from the Style menu or match the settings in this figure. Make sure to select Alpha 1 in the Texture Channel.

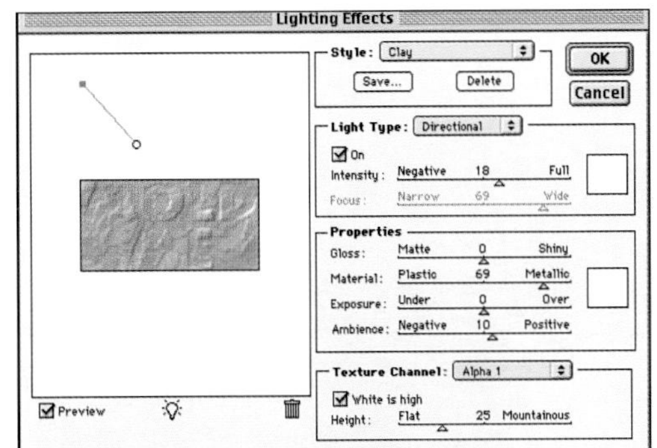

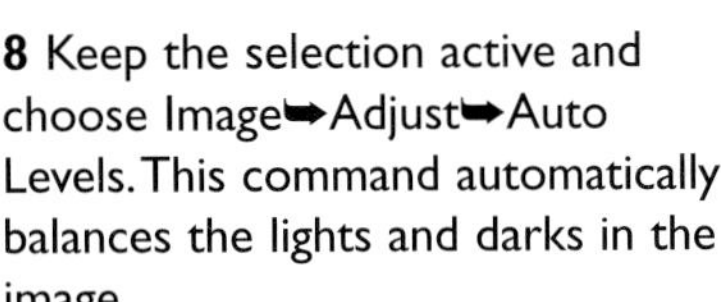

**8** Keep the selection active and choose Image➡Adjust➡Auto Levels. This command automatically balances the lights and darks in the image.

**9** Then choose Image➡Adjust➡Hue/Saturation. Check the Colorize box and try these settings.

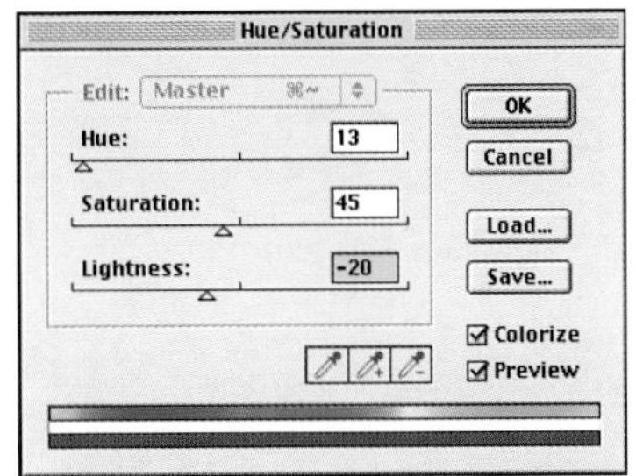


Deselect the text and dig in.

**TIP** **If you want to put this type into its own layer, choose Layer➡New➡Layer Via Cut after Step 9.**

Photoshop 5.0's new built-in drop shadow feature makes this effect simpler than ever. The second version here takes advantage of another of the new layer effects, Inner Bevel, to create cutout type with beveled edges.

**1** Open a file with an image in it. This is a good time to take advantage of the stock photography included on the *Type Magic* CD-ROM. I opened the MM_0353.TIF image from the Vivid Details collection and cropped a part of it to fit into this 5-inch by 2-inch image.

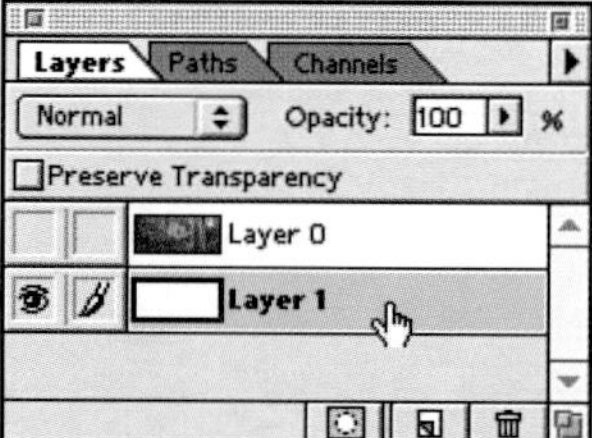


**2** Double-click on the Background layer (the layer that contains the image) to open the Make Layer dialog box. The name defaults to Layer 0. Click OK. The background layer becomes Layer 0, which enables you to create a new layer (Layer 1), and move it below Layer 0.

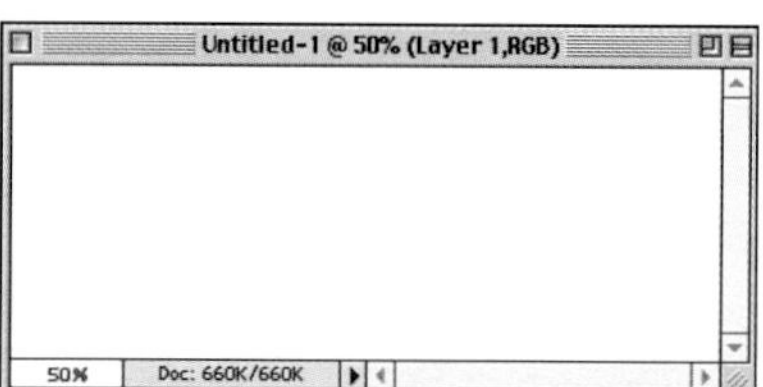


**3** Make Layer 0 invisible, choose a foreground color (I used white) for the underlying layer and fill Layer 1 with the color.

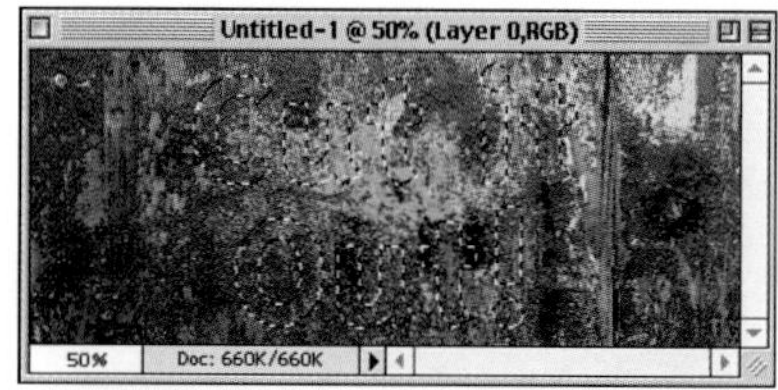


**4** Make Layer 0 visible and make it the active layer. Use the Type Mask tool to enter the text. This is Triplex at 85 points.

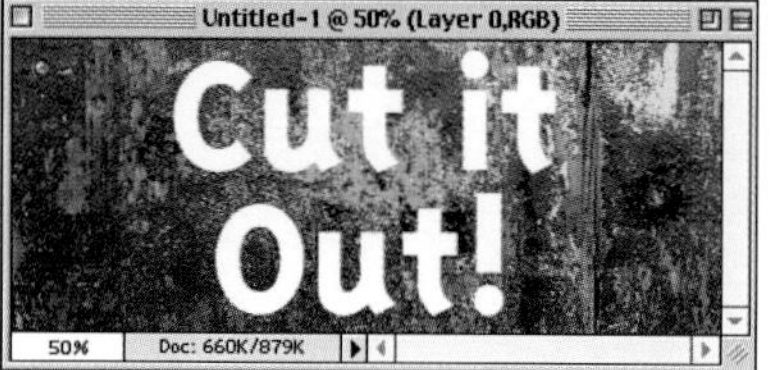


**5** Press Delete to clear the image from the type selection and reveal the contents of Layer 1.

6 All there is left to do is to use Photoshop's Layer Effect's Drop Shadow feature. Choose Layer➡Effects➡Drop Shadow. Use any settings that suit you, keeping an eye on the image to check the results.

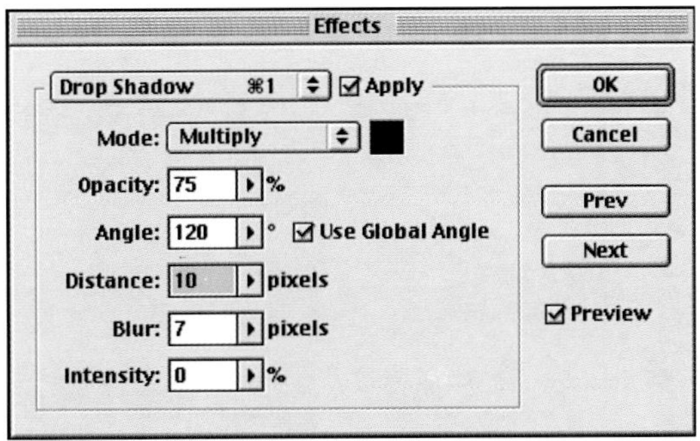

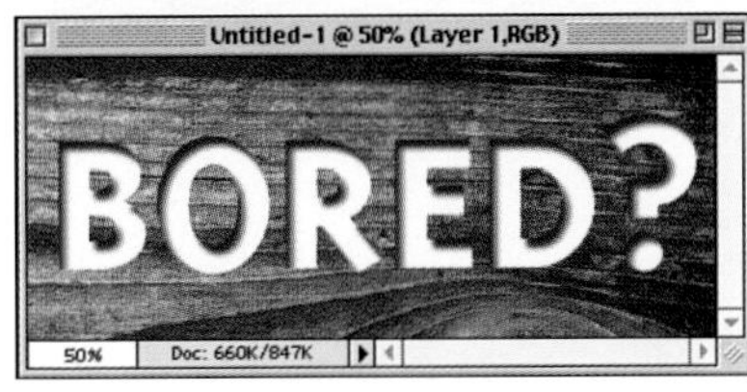


## Beveled Cutout

Complete all previous steps. I cropped part of the MM_0004.TIF image from the P5TM CD-ROM to use with this effect.

1 Create a new layer (Layer 2) and move the new layer above Layer 0, and load the transparency selection from Layer 0. Choose Select➡Inverse and Select➡Modify➡Expand (5 pixels).

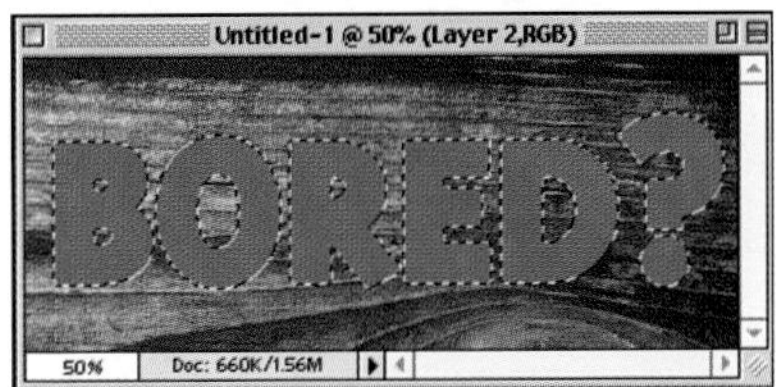


2 Choose 50% gray for the foreground color and fill the selection. Deselect the selection.

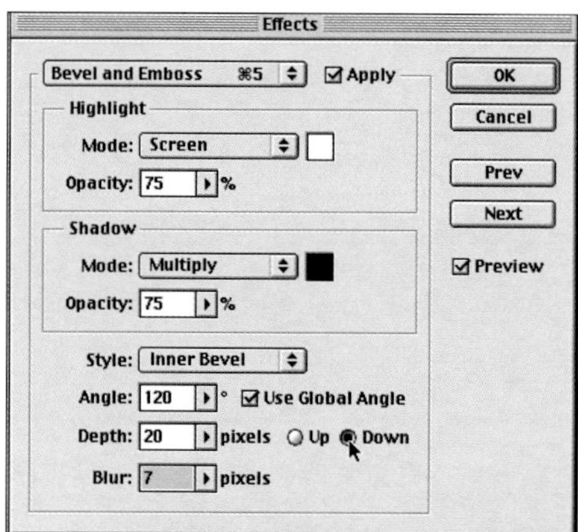


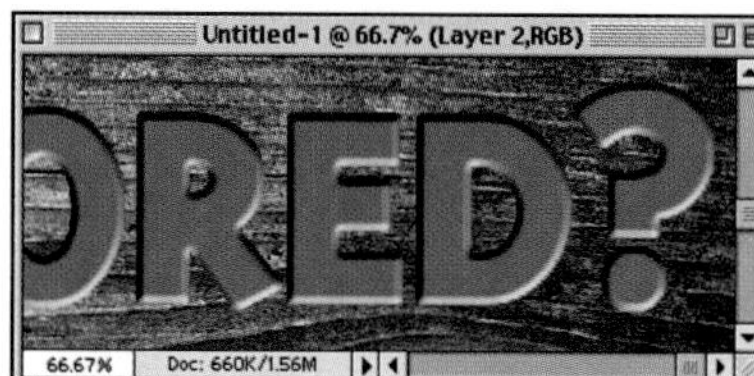


3 Choose Layer➡Effects➡Bevel and Emboss. Choose Inner Bevel, set the Angle so that it comes from the upper left (120°), and set the Depth to the maximum number of pixels (20) and Down. Set the Blur to 7 pixels.

**TIP** **Balancing the Expand amount in Step 1 and the Blur amount in Step 3 is the most crucial element of this technique. If the Expand amount is too high relative to the Blur amount, the image will look as if the beveled surface ends before it reached the inner edge of the letters. If it is too low, there will be some odd light and dark areas around the inner edge of the bevel that will ruin the cutout illusion. Keep the settings near the 5 to 7 ratio used in this example.**

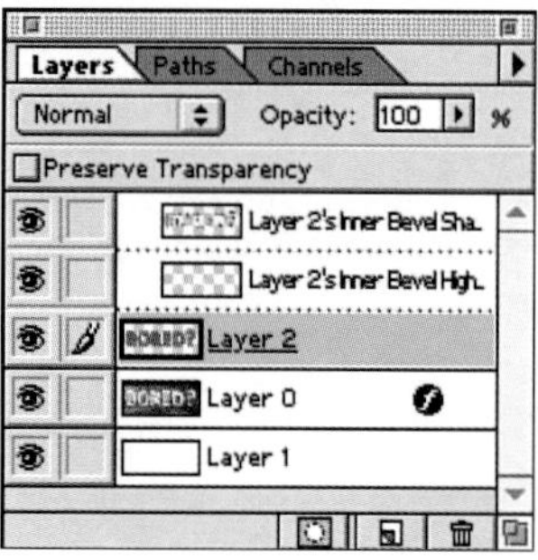


4 Choose Layer➡Effects➡Create Layers. Two new layers show up in the Layers palette above Layer 2: one for the bevel shadows and one for the bevel highlights.

**5** Make Layer 2 invisible, and then hold the (Option) [Alt] key and click on the dotted line just above Layer 2.

The bevel should now be in place.

**If you need to clean up the edges, load the transparency selection from Layer 0, and choose Select➡Inverse. Make the Layer 2's Inner Bevel Highlights layer active and press Delete. Do the same for the Layer 2's Inner Bevel Shadows layer.**

## VARIATIONS

You can float the cutout type on top of itself by making these alterations to the steps that begin on page 59. Instead of Steps 2 and 3, duplicate the Background layer to create the Background copy layer and make this new layer the active layer for Steps 4 through 6.

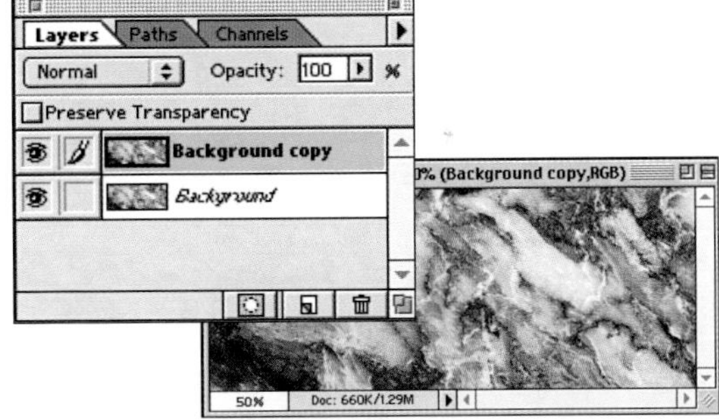


After Step 6, make the Background layer the active layer and choose Image➡Adjust➡Brightness/Contrast. Lower the Brightness (-20) to help set the Background layer back. ●

# Distressed

Photoshop contains a virtual arsenal of features that you can use to distress type. This technique does some fancy selection manipulations using the Quick Mask feature to distress type without using any channels.

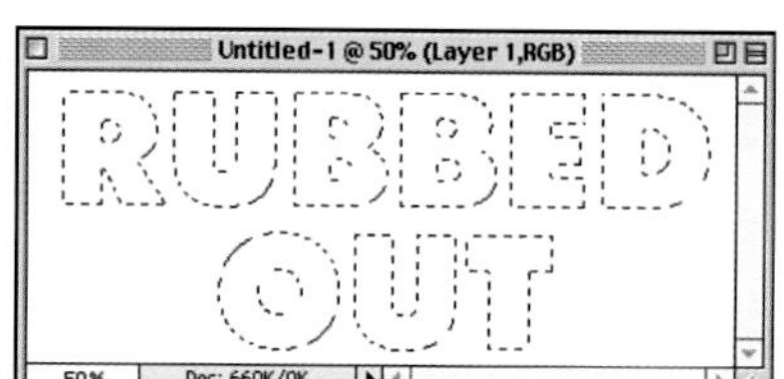


**1** Create a new file and create a new layer (Layer 1). Use the Type Mask tool to enter the text (Futura Extra Bold at 75 points).

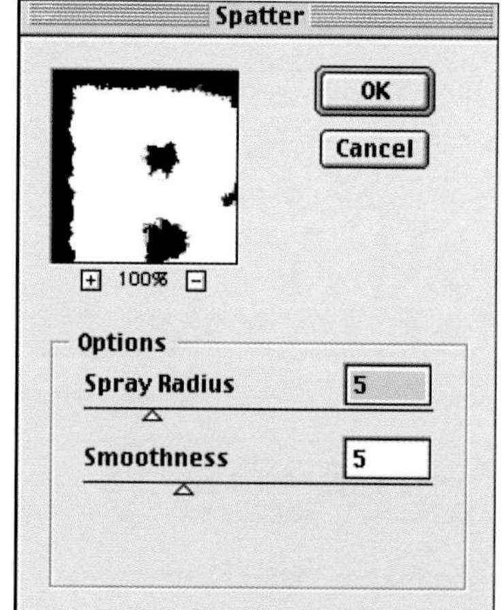


**2** Press Q to enter Quick Mask mode. The area outside of the type selection turns red. Quick Mask mode creates a temporary channel that can be used to manipulate a selection. Choose Filter➡Brush Strokes➡Spatter. This filter distorts the edges of the type. In the preview, you can see the results of the settings you use. I set the Spray Radius and the Smoothness both at 5.

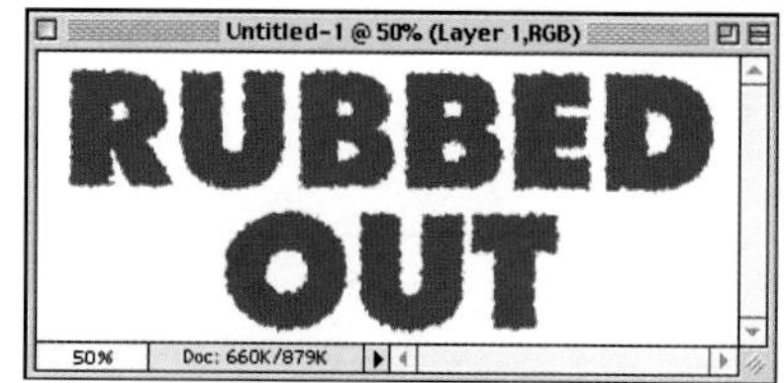


**3** Press Q again to exit Quick Mask mode. The marching ants appear again, but now run around the rough edges created by the Spatter filter. Choose a foreground color for the type and fill the selection. Deselect the selection.

**4** We're not done with the type or the Quick Mask mode. Press Q again. Then choose Filter➡Render➡Clouds. The lighter areas seen here will end up being the areas that are rubbed out. If you don't like what the Clouds filter came up with, undo it and press (Command-F) [Control-F] to reapply the Clouds filter. I also made Layer 1 invisible in order to see the Quick Mask channel better.

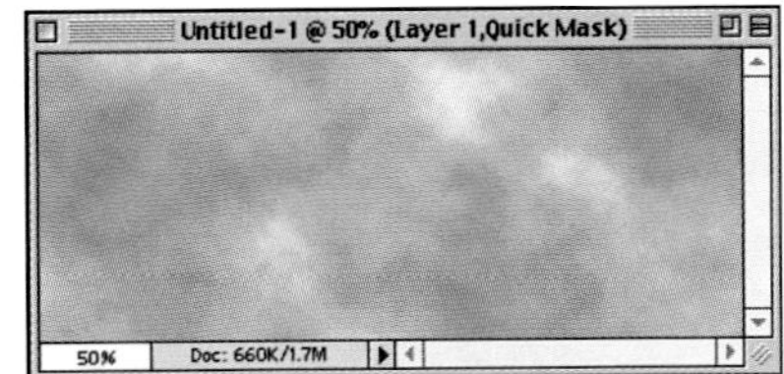


**5** Choose Filter➡Noise➡Add Noise (50, Gaussian). Add a medium amount of noise. Don't obliterate what the Clouds filter did, but the noise should be very visible.

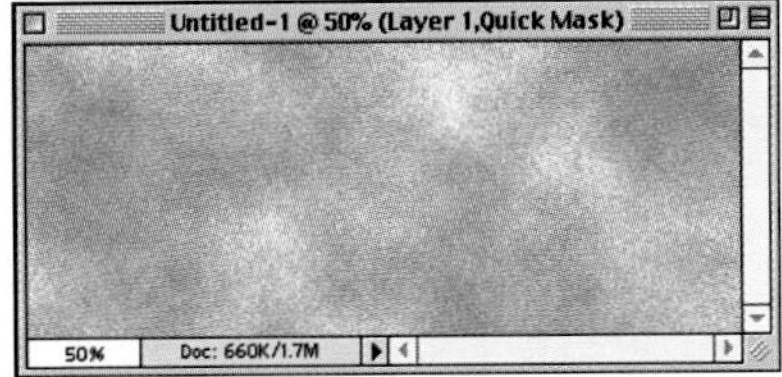


**6** Choose Filter➡Pixelate➡Pointillize and keep the Cell size low (3 pixels).

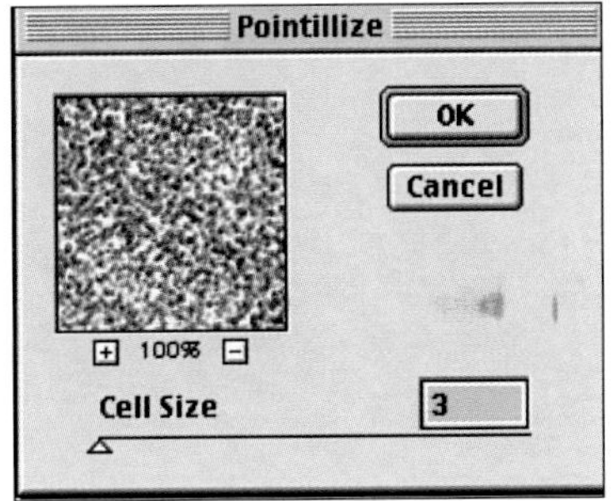


It appears as though the graininess from the Noise filter has been bloated.

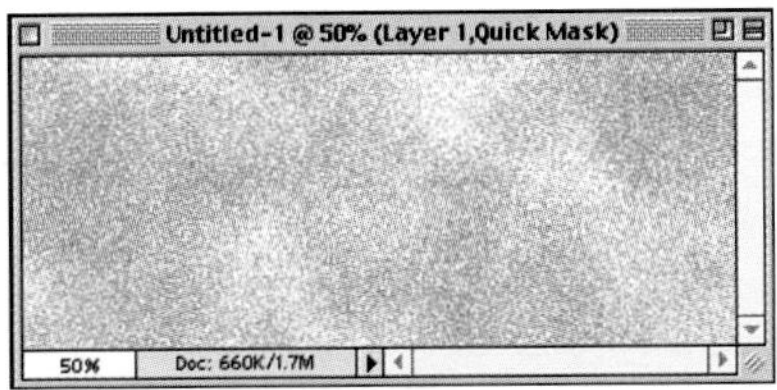


**7** Choose Filter➡Pixelate➡Fragment. A pattern will be created in the texture.

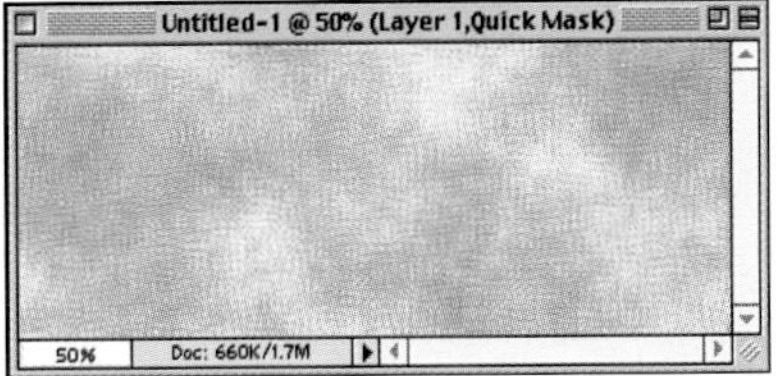

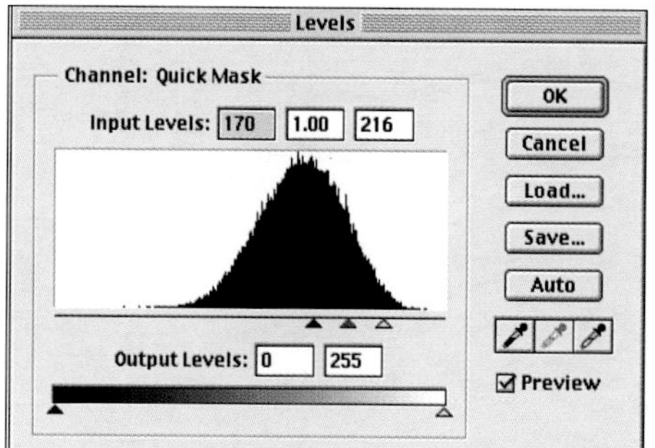


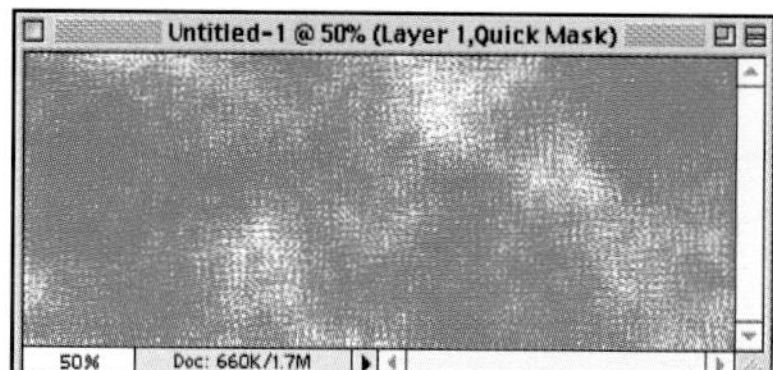

**8** Then choose Image➡Adjust➡Levels. As mentioned in Step 4, the light areas of the Quick Mask channel are the areas where the type will be rubbed out. In order to reduce the white areas, slide the black slider to the right, the white slider to the left, and then adjust the gray slider for fine-tuning. Adjusting these sliders gives you greater control over the white areas of the mask.

Click OK when you're satisfied.

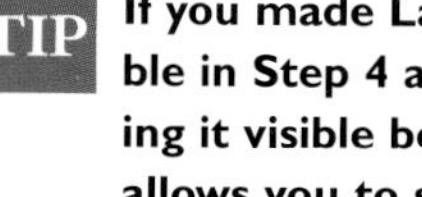


**If you made Layer 1 invisible in Step 4 as I did, making it visible before Step 8 allows you to see exactly what will be "rubbed out" and what will not. The areas where there is no red will be deleted.**

**9** Press Q again to exit Quick Mask mode, and make Layer 1 visible if it is not. Press Delete to distress the type. Deselect the selection.

## Variations

You can vary this technique at almost any stage to create unique distressing effects. The first variation creates two more selections using the Quick Mask feature in order to add two more colors to the distressed type.

## Multicolor

After completing all the preceding steps, repeat Steps 4 through 8. Press Q to exit Quick Mask mode, and choose Image➥Adjust➥Hue/Saturation. Use one or all the sliders to adjust the color of the selection. Here are the three stages of this type.

## Texture

Use Photoshop 5.0's new Inner Bevel layer effect to add some texture to this effect. After completing the Multicolor variation, choose Layer➥Effects➥Bevel and Emboss and match the setting seen here...

Effects

Bevel and Emboss ⌘5 ☑ Apply | OK | Cancel | Prev | Next | ☑ Preview

Highlight
Mode: Screen
Opacity: 75 %

Shadow
Mode: Multiply
Opacity: 75 %

Style: Inner Bevel
Angle: 120 ° ☑ Use Global Angle
Depth: 10 pixels ◉ Up ○ Down
Blur: 5 pixels

...to get here. ●

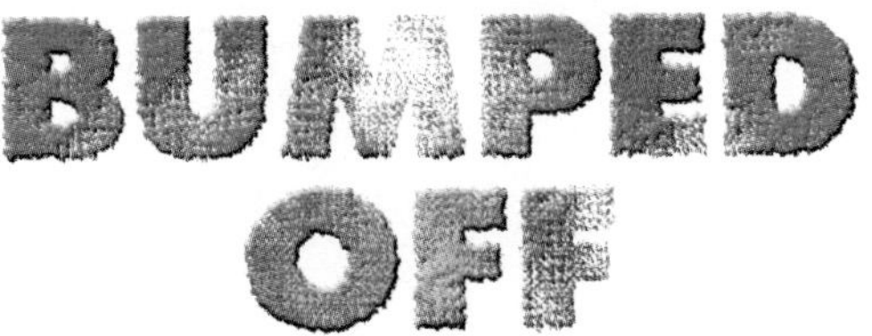

# ELEPHANT SKIN

ELEPHANT

This technique demonstrates how to use an image (found on the P5TM CD-ROM) to help create a unique texture.

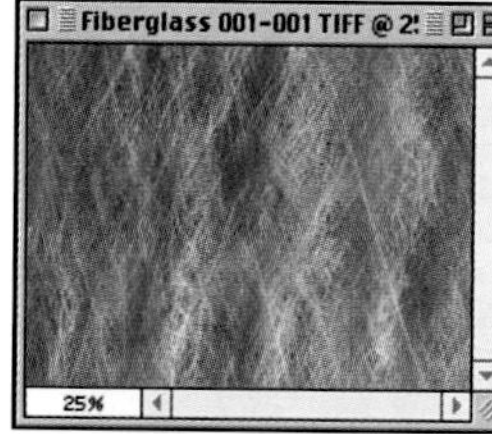


1 Choose File→Open. Find the Fiberglass image in the D'pix collection on the P5TM CD-ROM (P5TM→Images→D'Pix→Medium Resolution→Fiberglass). When the Fiberglass image is open, choose Select→All. Copy the image and close the file.

2 In a new file, create a new channel (Alpha 1), and paste the image into the channel. Because the image has been pasted into a channel, the color will be stripped away leaving a grayscale image. Choose Filter→Sharpen→Sharpen and deselect the selection.

3 Then choose Filter→Other→High Pass. This filter flattens the image. The lower the Radius value, the less detail is retained. I used a radius value of 1.5 pixels for this effect. Deselect the selection.

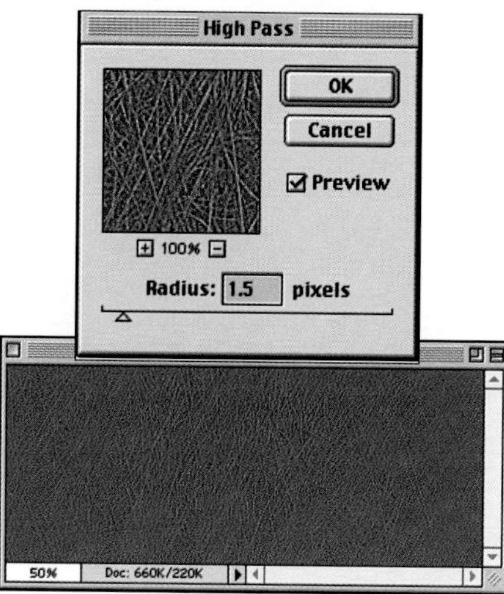


4 Return to the composite channel and use the Type Mask tool to enter the text. (I used Compacta at 90 points.) Choose Select→Feather (2 pixels). Feathering the selection causes the texture to appear to fade into the background.



## TOOLBOX

Fiberglass (D'Pix Image)

**5** Then intersect the text selection with the selection from the Alpha 1 channel. Fill the selection with black and deselect the selection.

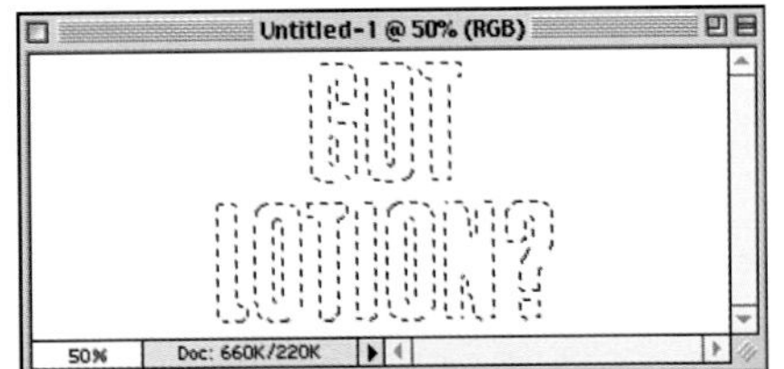


**6** To enhance the texture, choose Image➡Adjust➡Levels. You can play around with these settings, but I found that Input Levels of: 0, .70, 189 worked well for this effect.

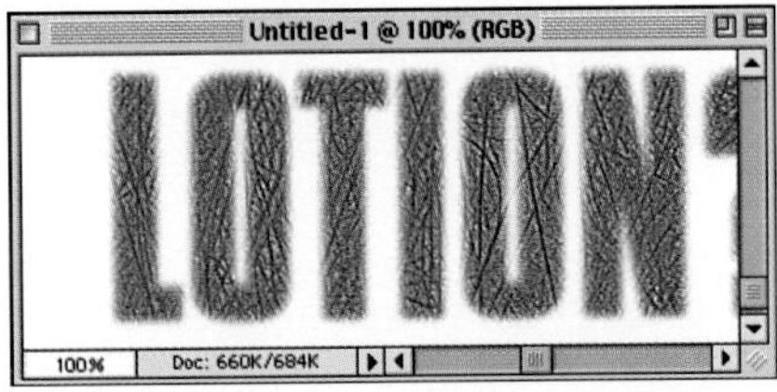


**7** To add a bit of color, but not too much, I converted the image to Grayscale (Image➡Mode➡Grayscale) and then to a duotone (Image➡Mode➡Duotone), using PANTONE Coated 441 as ink 1 and PANTONE Coated 411 as ink 2.

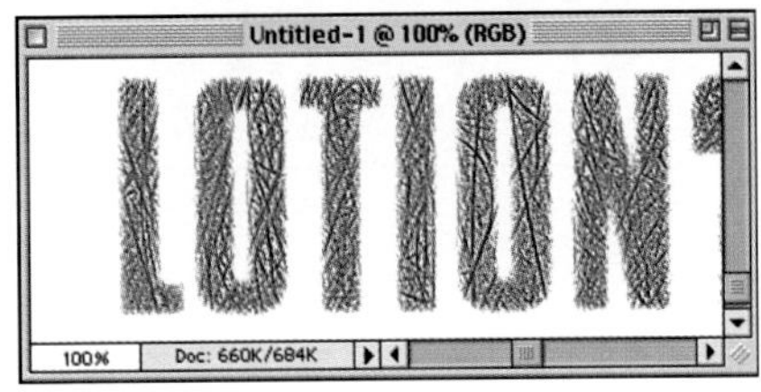


## Variations

After pasting the fiberglass image into the Alpha 1 channel, choose Filter➡Brush Strokes➡Accent Edges. Enter an Edge Width of 1, an Edge Brightness of 50, and a Smoothness of 15. Skip to Step 4 and continue. Instead of doing Step 7, choose Image➡Adjust➡Hue/Saturation and check the Colorize box (Hue: 51, Saturation: 49, Lightness: 0).

For more variations, try applying different filters to the Alpha 1 channel, as in the previous variation. For this effect, I chose Filter➡Pixelate➡Fragment. ●

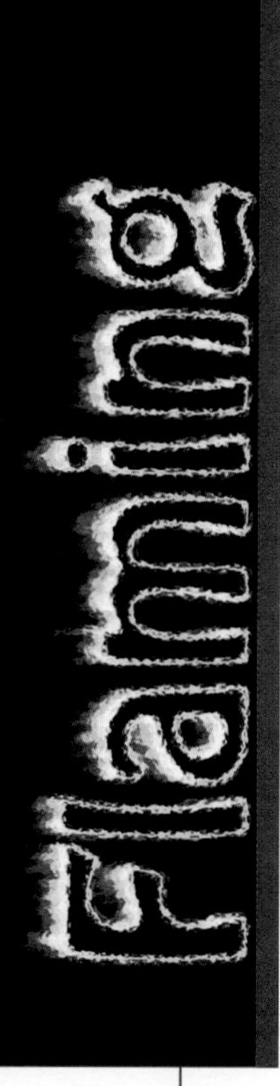


This classic effect builds the flames in a grayscale file and converts the image to a color mode that uses a special palette.

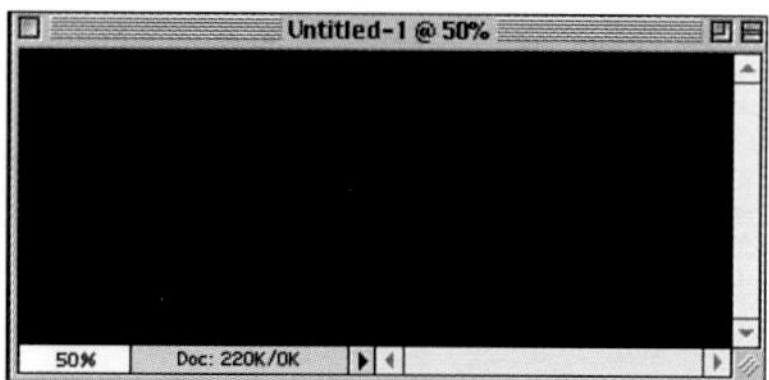


**1** Create a new grayscale file. Choose black for the foreground color and fill the image with black.

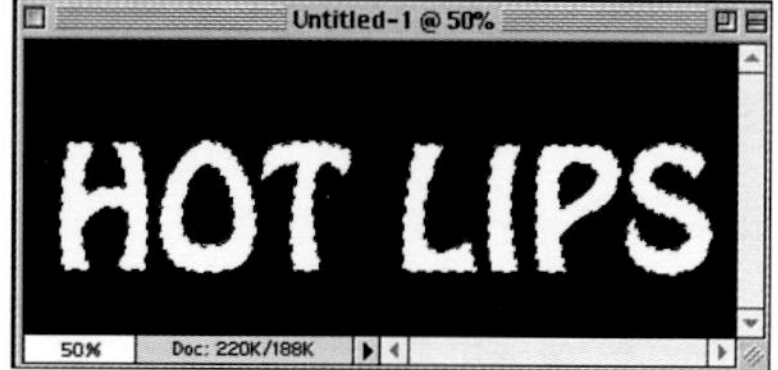


**2** Choose white as the foreground color and use the Type Mask tool to enter the text. For best results, use a heavy typeface (I used Hobo at 75 points). Move the type selection near the bottom of the image so there is room for flames to grow upward. Fill the type selection with white.

**3** Save the selection to create the Alpha 1 channel, and deselect the selection.

**4** Choose Image➡Rotate Canvas➡90° CCW. This temporary rotation is necessary in order to pull the flames upward. The image needs to be rotated because the Wind filter used in the next step only works horizontally.



**TOOLBOX**

Blue Flame (Color Table)

**5** Choose Filter➥Stylize➥Wind (Blast, From the Left). This filter pulls white streaks to the left of the type. The Method setting depends on the size of your type. Smaller type may need only Wind, whereas larger type may require the Blast feature applied twice.

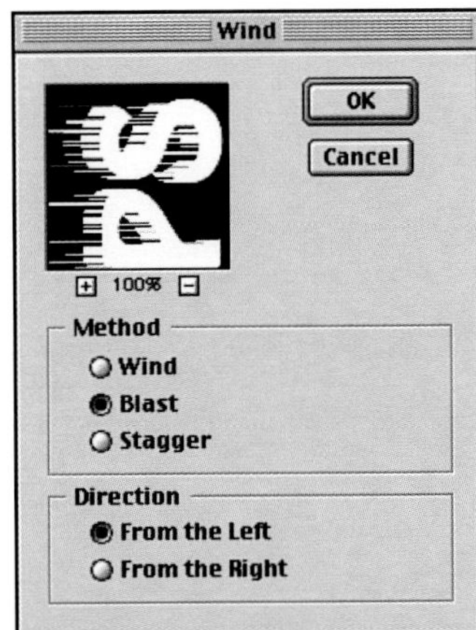


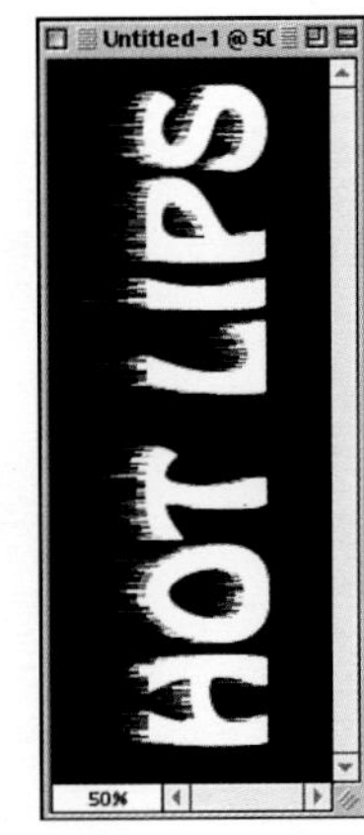


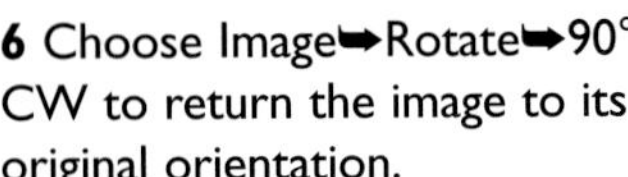
**6** Choose Image➥Rotate➥90° CW to return the image to its original orientation.

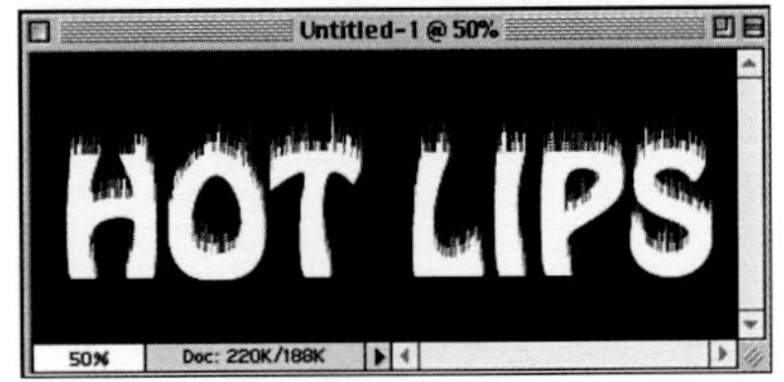


**7** Choose Filter➥Stylize➥Diffuse (Normal) in order to break the lines created by the Wind filter.

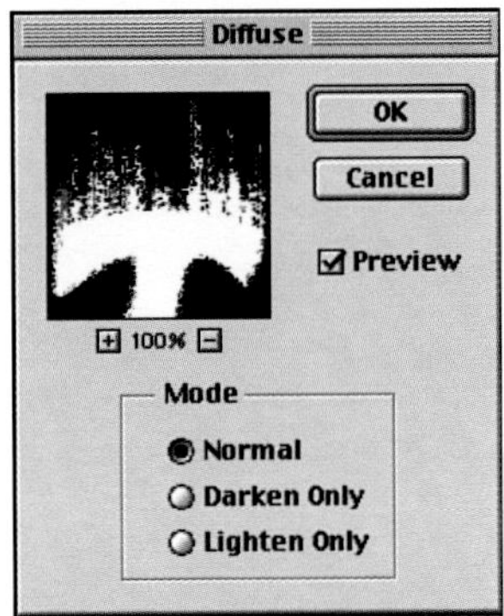


**8** Choose Filter➥Blur➥Gaussian Blur (2.5 pixels). Set the Radius just high enough to smooth out the flames.

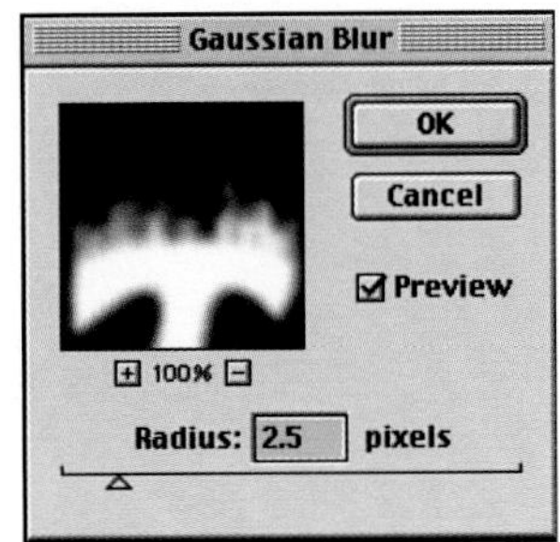

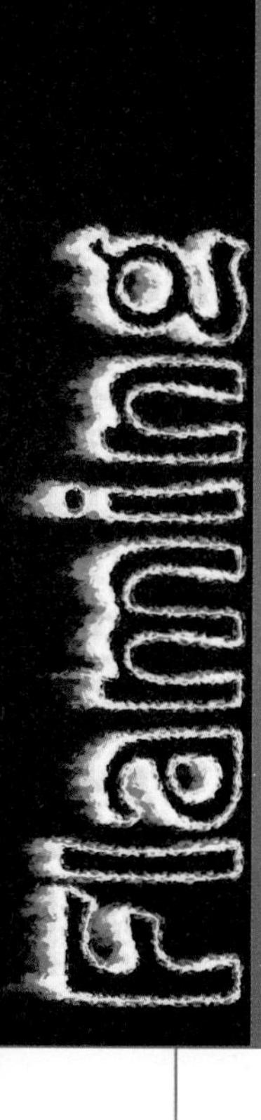


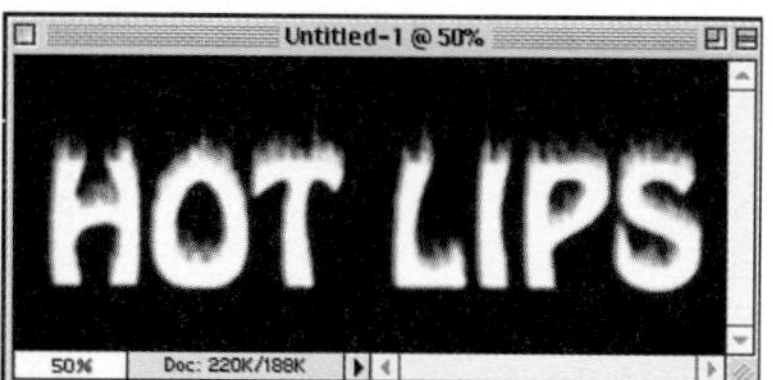


The type image should now look like this.

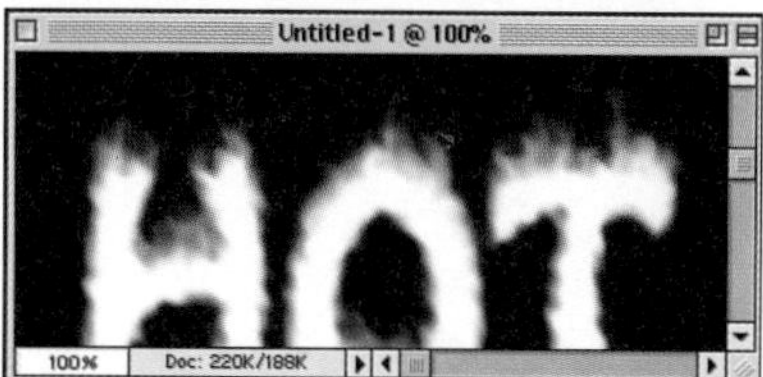


**9** Choose Filter➥Distort➥Ripple (100, Medium) to add a little waviness to the type and flames.

**10** Load the selection of the Alpha 1 channel, and choose Select➥Modify➥Contract (3 pixels). Adjust the Contract amount so that the interior of the type is selected and a thin wavy border is not selected. Choose Select➥Feather (1 pixel) to soften the selection. Then choose black as the foreground color and fill the selection. Deselect the selection.

**TIP** **If you want the interior outlines of the type to also appear wavy (as in the "Flaming" thumbtab image), do Step 10 before Step 9.**

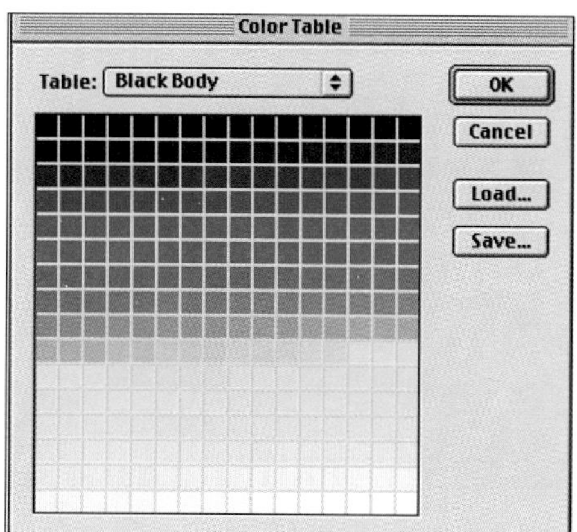


**11** Choose Image➥Mode➥Indexed Color to convert the grayscale file to indexed color, choose Image➥Mode➥Color Table, and choose Black Body from the Table menu.

Just like the title of the book says: Magic!

**TIP** **You can adjust the Input Levels in the Levels dialog box to fine-tune the color and height of the flames. Choose Image➥Adjust➥ Levels.**

## VARIATIONS

The variations for this effect are countless. Here are a few I have gathered.

### Blue Flames

Before Step 11, choose Image➥ Adjust➥Levels and set the Output Levels white slider to 190. Then choose Image➥Adjust➥Invert. In the Color Table dialog box in Step 11, click the Load button and find the Blue Flame color table on the P5TM CD-ROM (P5TM➥P5TM Files➥Miscellaneous➥Blue Flame).

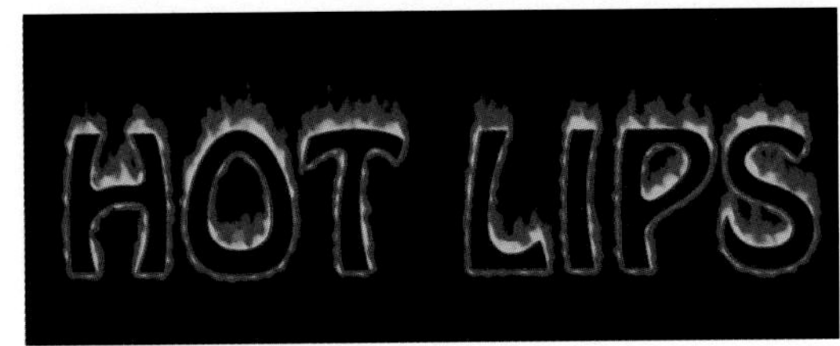


### Glass Texture

After completing Step 10, choose Filter➥Distort➥Glass. Set the Texture to Frosted (100% Scaling). You don't want to distort the type beyond recognition. Try some moderate settings such as Distortion: 2, Smoothness: 3.

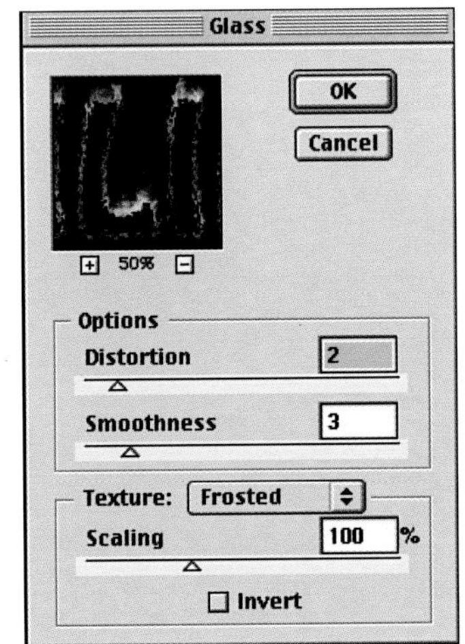

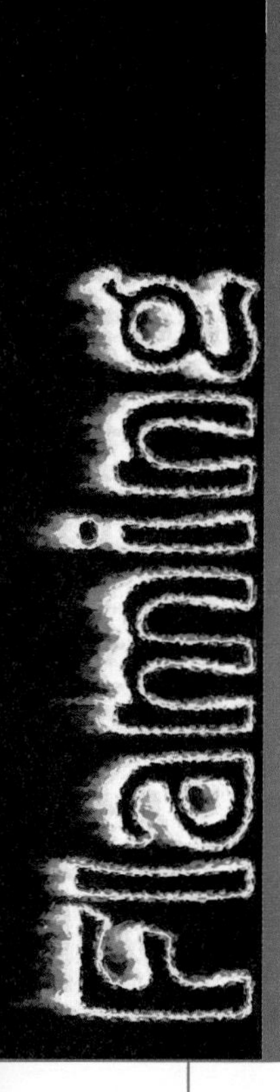

Do Step 11 to finish it off.

## Fiery Clouds

In a new grayscale file (white background), choose black as the foreground color and use the Type Mask tool to enter the text. Fill the selection, and save the selection (Alpha 1). Deselect the text and choose Filter➥Blur➥Gaussian Blur (5 pixels). Load the Alpha 1 selection and fill it with black. Deselect the text, and choose Filter➥Render➥Difference Clouds. Do Step 11 to complete the effect.

## Adding Swirls

Before Step 11, select the Elliptical Marquee tool and make a small selection around the flames of one letter.

Choose Filter➥Distort➥Twirl and adjust the Twirl amount to add swirls to the flames.

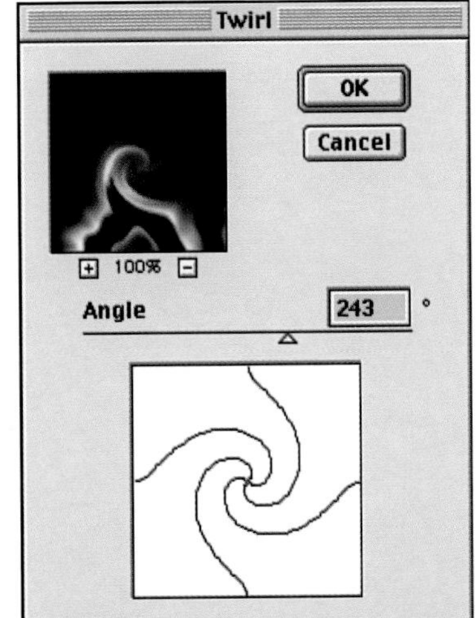


Continue selecting and twirling. ●

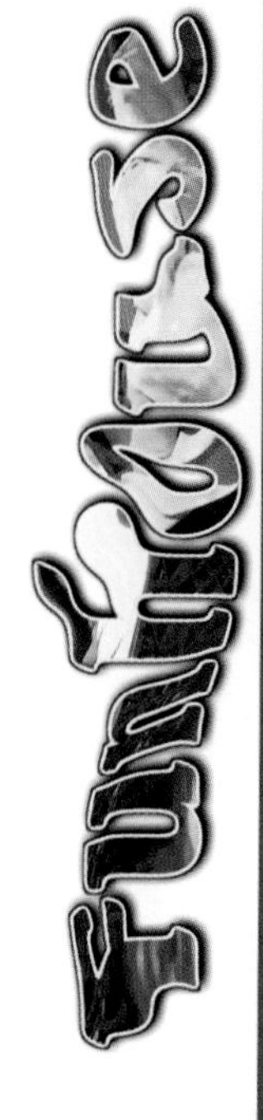

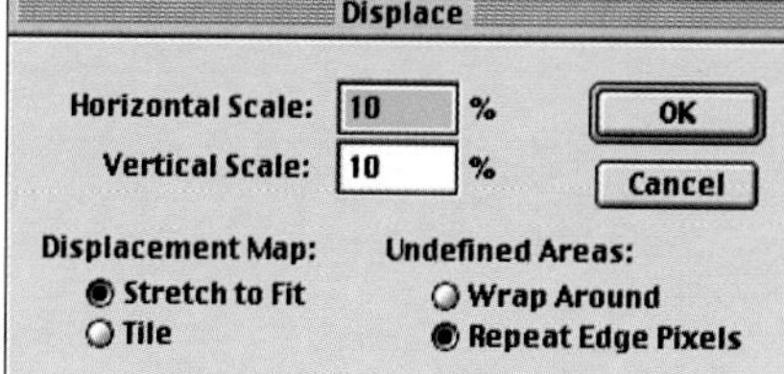

**TOOLBOX**

Waving Line

Offset Blurred Circles

X Polar B Displace

Displacement maps can seem confusing to the new user, but this effect makes simple use of them for some fun distortions. A displacement map is a second Photoshop file that is used to distort an image according to the gray values in the displacement map. You will never see the actual map when applying the Distort filter—Photoshop does all the work behind the scenes. However, for the following effects, I provide some peeks into the custom displacement maps that have been created for this effect. This effect is also easy to use on other effects.

**1** Use the Type tool to enter the text, or place a type image in a layer. Make sure to leave some room around the edges of the type because some of these distortions significantly move the type in all directions. I used Seagull Heavy at 50 points. Choose Layer➡Type➡Render Layer.

**2** Deselect any active selections and choose Filter➡Distort➡Displace. The dialog box enables you to control the intensity of the distortions. For this example, I set both Scale values to 10% (Stretch to Fit, Repeat Edge Pixels).

**You can also use negative values to inverse the distortions.**

**3** Another dialog box appears asking you to select a displacement map. Included on the P5TM CD-ROM are several displacement maps that I have created for this effect. I chose Waving Line for this example (P5TM CD➡P5TM Files➡Funhouse Displacement Maps➡Waving Line).

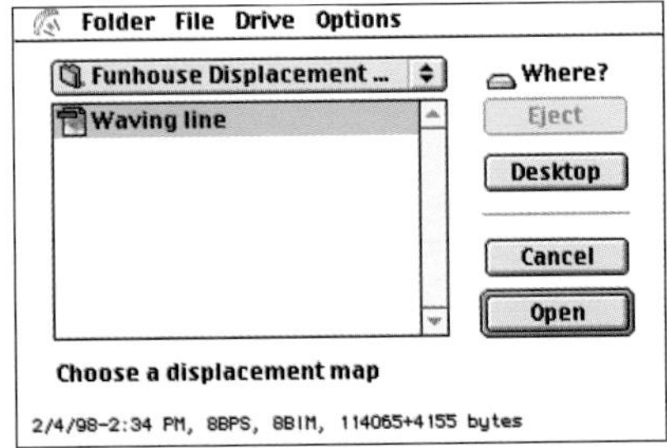


Here's the distorted type…

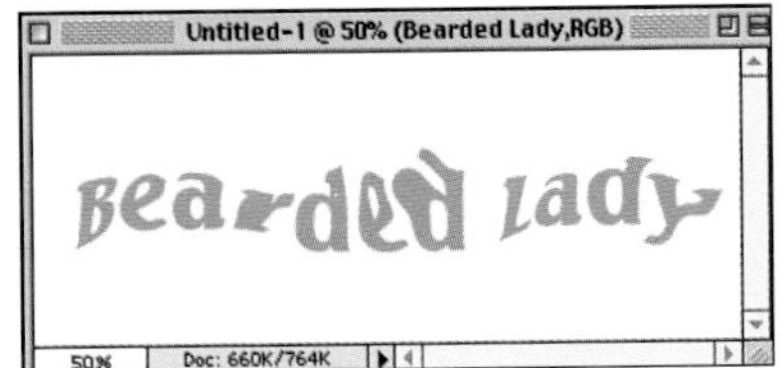


…and here she is after a couple of modifications.

TIP **You can create your own displacement maps to use with the displace filter. Open the files in the Funhouse Displacement Maps folder on the CD-ROM to look at the ones used for these effects. Any Photoshop file can be used as a displacement map, but keeping them simple is your best bet. Here is the displacement map (Waving Line) used on the Bearded Lady.**

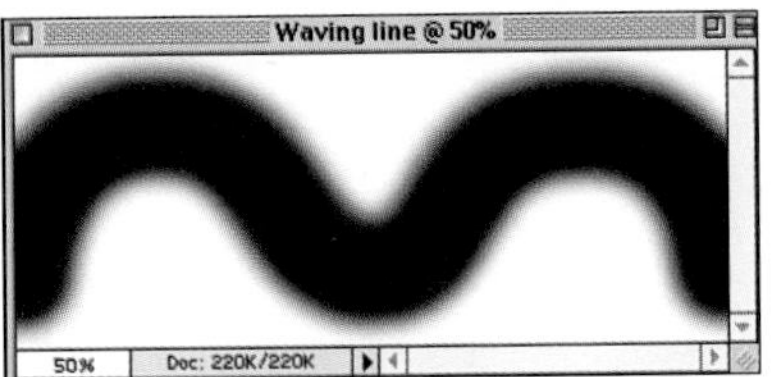

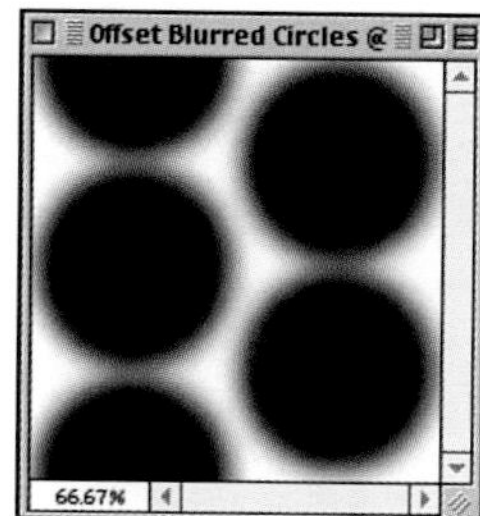

## VARIATIONS

Here are a few more images indicating the displacement map (found on the P5TM CD-ROM) and settings used.

Offset Blurred Circles (Horizontal Scale: 10%, Vertical Scale: 18%)

X Polar B Displace (Horizontal Scale: 15%, Vertical Scale: 10%)

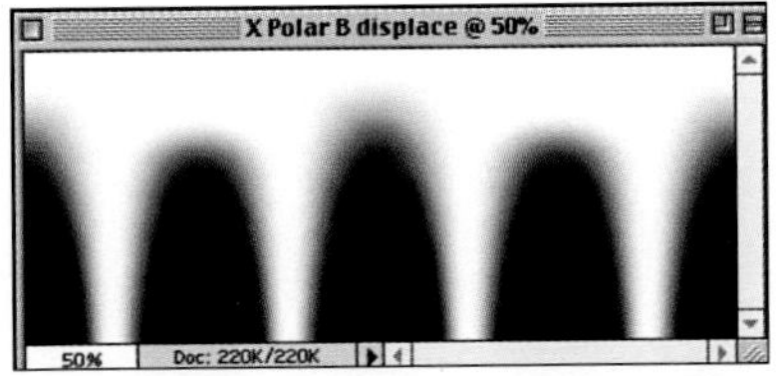

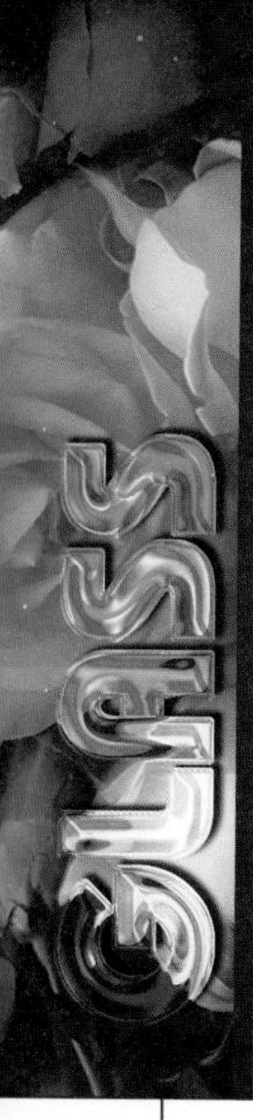

The Glass filter used in this technique does a great job of creating realistic distortions if properly set up. The highlights are created through the aid of layer effects and the Curves feature.

**1** Open a file that contains an image to be used as the background. I opened this file from the P5TM CD-ROM (P5TM➥Images➥Vivid Details➥MM_0266.TIF). Choose Select➥All, copy the image, and deselect the selection.

**2** Create a new channel (Alpha 1) and use the Type tool to enter the text. (I used Bauhaus at 95 points.) Use the Move tool to position the type and save the selection to create the Alpha 2 channel.

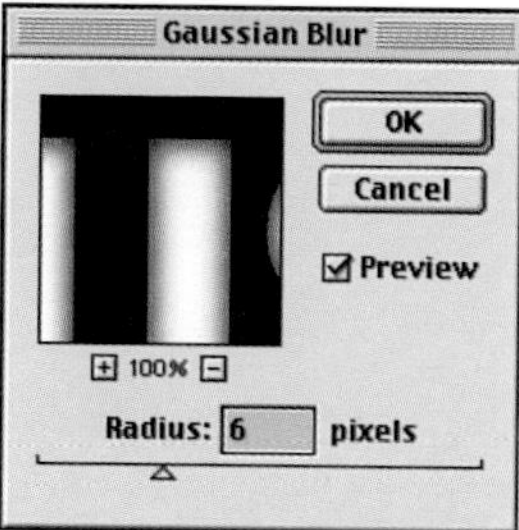


**3** Keep the selection active and choose Filter➥Blur➥Gaussian Blur (6 pixels). Blur the inside of the type enough to appear slightly rounded.

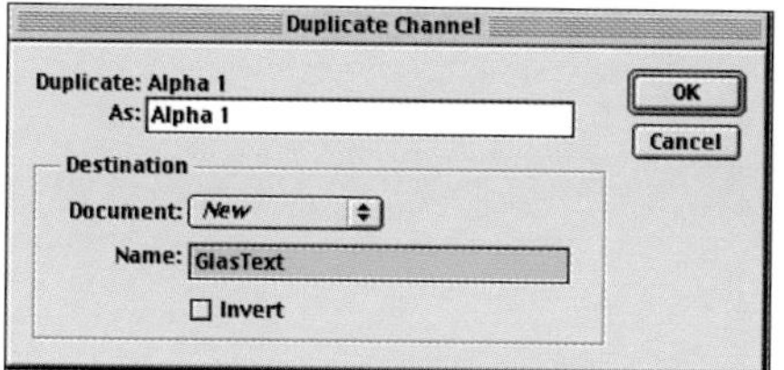


**4** From the Channels palette menu, choose Duplicate Channel. In the dialog box that opens, select New from the Document menu and name the file (GlasText).

**5** The channel opens as a new file. Save the file (Photoshop format) and close it.



TOOLBOX

Chrome Curves

**6** Return to the composite channel, deselect the selection, and choose Filter➡Distort➡Glass. From the Texture menu, choose Load Texture and find the file that was saved in Step 4 (GlasText). Keep the settings close to what I used (Distortion: 7, Smoothness: 5), although you can vary them if you want a little less or more distortion.

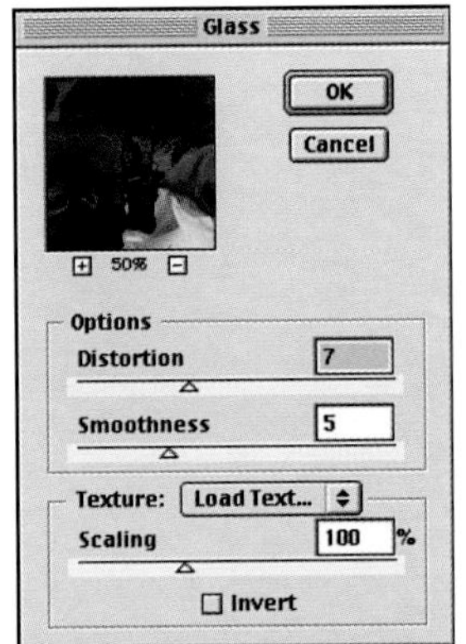


This is one of the filters that does a great job of producing what it promises.

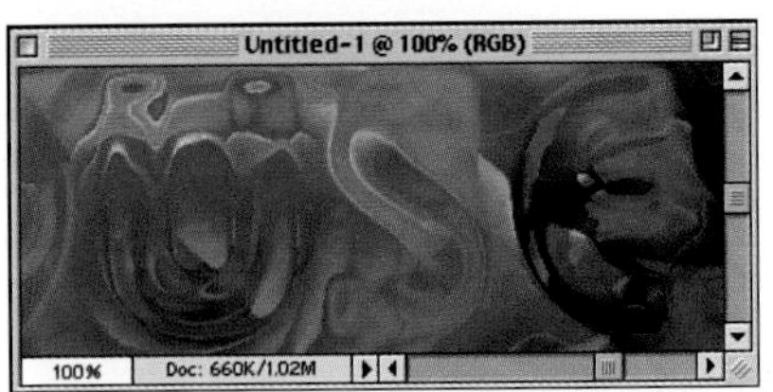


**7** Load the Alpha 2 selection and choose Layer➡New➡Layer Via Copy to raise a copy of the distorted areas into a new layer (Layer 1). Make the Background layer active, choose Select➡All, and paste in the original image. Choose Merge Down from the Layers palette menu, and make Layer 1 the active layer again.

**8** Choose Layer➡Effects➡Drop Shadow. Adding a shadow helps separate the glass from the background, but if you don't want it, skip this step and go on. I used the default settings, raised the Distance to 10, the Blur to 8, and the Intensity to 10%.

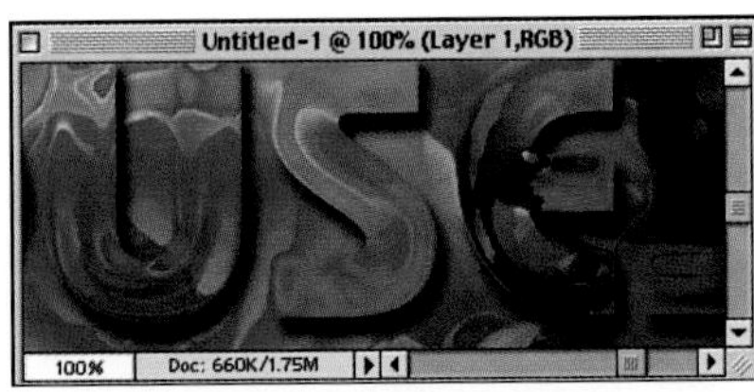


**9** Create a new layer (Layer 2) and load the Alpha 2 selection. Choose 50% gray for the foreground color and fill the selection. Deselect the selection.

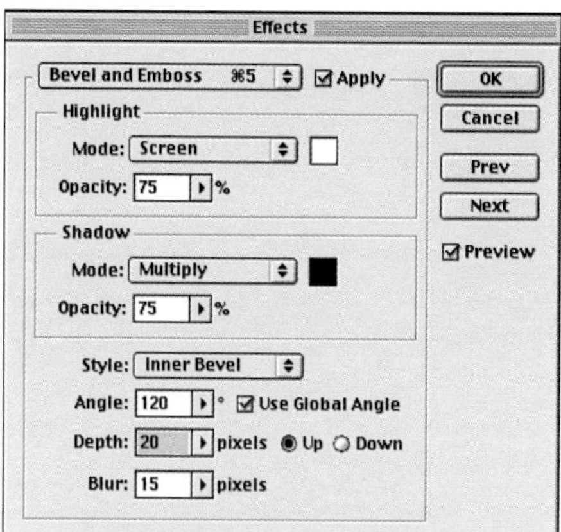


**10** Choose Layer➡Effects➡Bevel and Emboss. Select Inner Bevel from the Style menu and raise the Depth to the maximum—20 pixels. Raise the Blur amount until the text appears rounded (15 pixels).

**11** Choose Layer➡Effects➡Create Layers. Two new layers are added above Layer 2—one for the bevel highlights and one for the shadows. Choose Merge Group from the Layers palette menu to merge the beveled type back into a single layer (Layer 2).

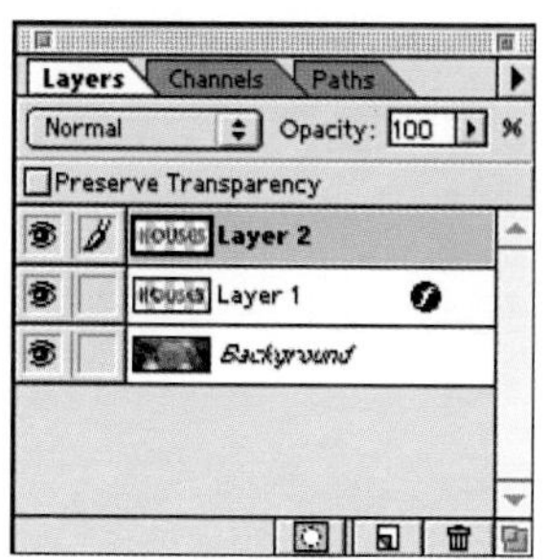

**12** Choose Image➡Adjust➡Curves and click on the Load button. Find the Chrome Curves file on the P5TM CD-ROM (P5TM➡P5TM Files➡Curves➡Chrome Curves). A wavy line is loaded into the graph that produces some wavy patterns inside the type.

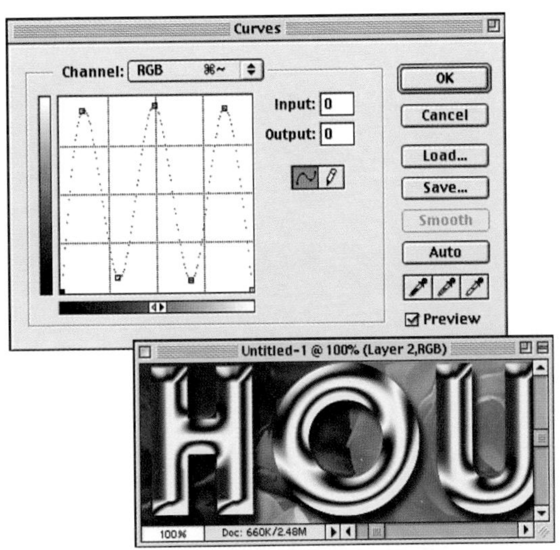


**13** Change the Layer 2 blending mode to Overlay and double-click on the Layer 2 name to open the Layer Options dialog box. Slide the black slider below the This Layer gradient bar to the right—to about 25. Then hold the (Option) [Alt] key and click on the same slider. The slider will split in half. Drag the right half to the right. Watch the preview as the dark areas disappear from the type. I set this marker at 150.

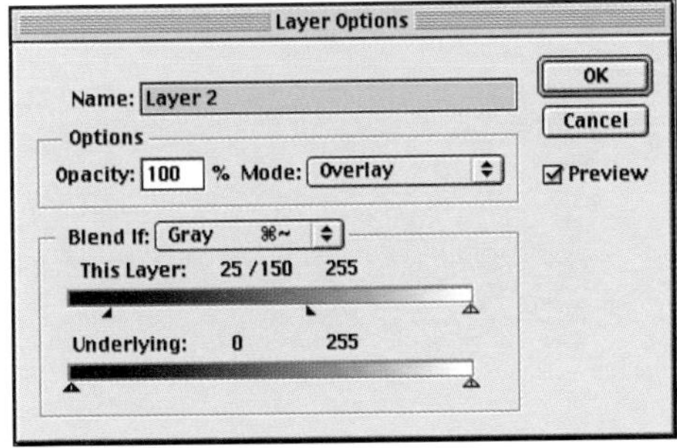


Getting rid of the dark areas greatly helps the glass highlights.

**TIP** **Depending on the colors in the underlying image, the glass type may look better if you invert Layer 2. Choose Image➡Adjust➡Invert.**

**14** To add just a touch of color to the glass, choose Image➡Adjust➡Curves, select Blue from the Channel pop-up menu, and bend the line on the graph toward the upper-left corner. You can skip this step, but I find that it helps to separate the glass from the background.

# Variations

## Ridge

If you don't like the way the type meets the background and want to add a ridge around the letters, add these steps. If you've already gone through all of the steps, use the History palette to revert back through the effect.

In Step 7, after loading the selection, choose Select➡Modify➡Expand (4 pixels). Set the Expand amount to the desired thickness of the edge that runs around the letters. Finish Step 7 and Steps 8 through 11; then add these steps.

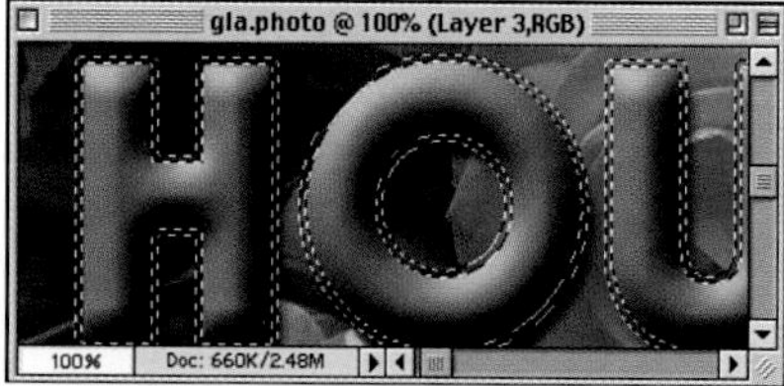


Create a new layer (Layer 3) and load the selection of the Alpha 2 channel. Choose Select➡Modify➡Expand. Set the Expand amount to same amount that you used before. Then subtract from the selection the selection of the Alpha 2 channel. There should now be a thin selection that surrounds all of the letters.

Choose 50% gray for the foreground color and fill the selection. Then choose Layer➡Effects➡Bevel and Emboss. Select the Inner Bevel style and adjust the Depth (5 pixels) and Blur (5 pixels) to round the gray border. The default settings worked well here.

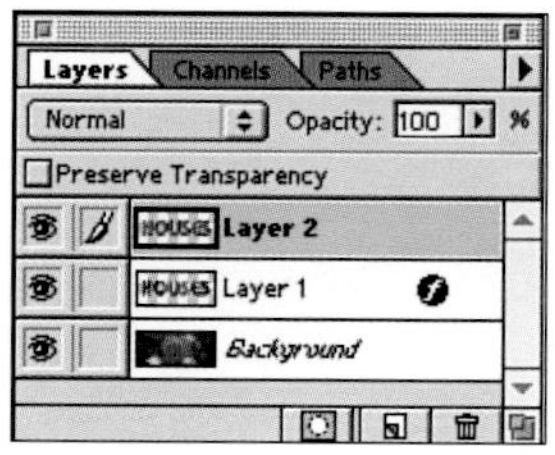


Perform the Step 11 commands on this layer and choose Merge Down to merge Layers 2 and 3.

Deselect the selection and complete Steps 12 through 14.

## Colored Glass

Create a new layer and move the layer above all other layers. Load the Alpha 2 selection. If you added the ridge to the glass, choose Select➡Modify➡Expand and expand the selection the same amount as you did in the first step of the Ridge variation. Choose a foreground color for the color of the glass (CMYK: 75, 0, 100, 0) and fill the selection. Bright colors work best. Change the layer blending mode to Color. ●

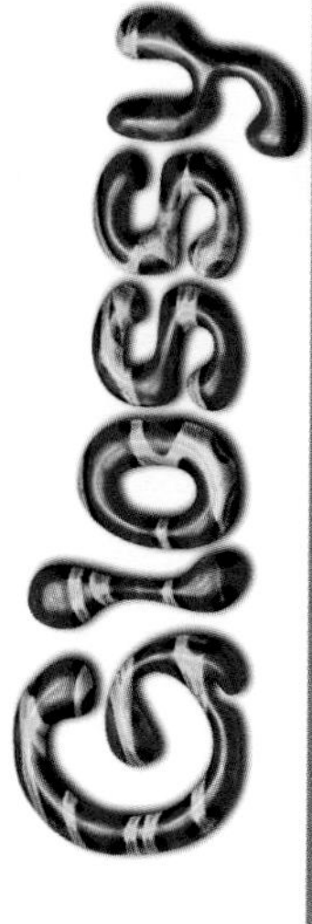



TOOLBOX

Glossy (Lighting Effects Style)

Here are two quick ways to make great-looking glossy type. The first uses a displacement map to help make the textured type look rounded, and the second adds a glossy effect to solid-colored type.

**1** Texture is used in this effect because it emphasizes the roundness of the type as the texture wraps around it. The first step is to find a texture to use. I used KPT Texture Explorer plug-in to generate a texture, but you might simply place an image inside a type mask. If you're going to use an image, open the file now and choose Select➡All. Copy the image and close the file. Several images are located on the CD-ROM that you might use. Follow this path to find them: P5TM CD-ROM➡P5TM Files➡Textures. If you're not using an image, begin with Step 2.

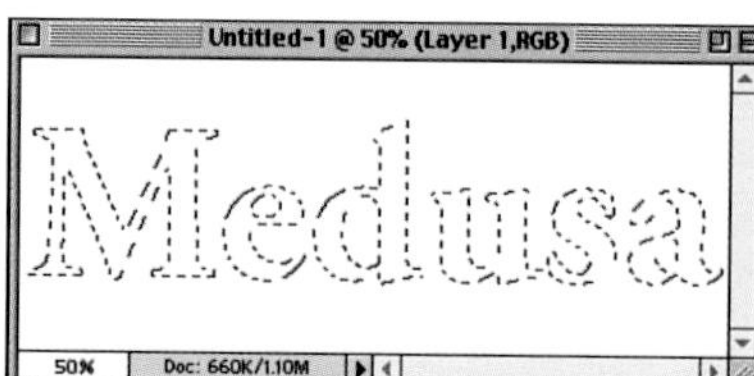


**2** Create a new layer (Layer 1), and use the Type Mask tool to enter the text. This is Adobe Garamond Bold at 110 points.

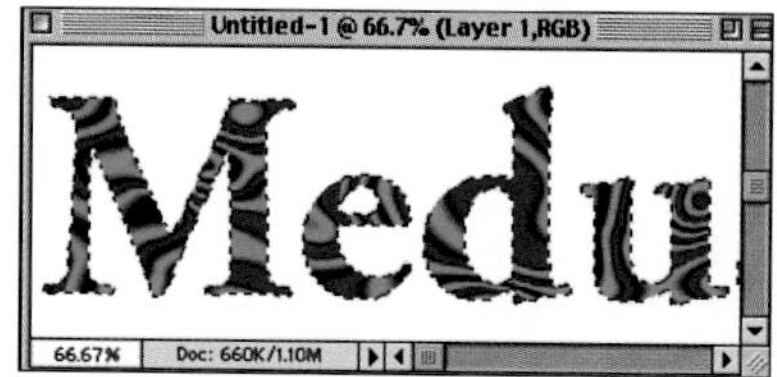


**3** The next step is to fill the type with a texture, pattern, or image. If you use an image, choose Edit➡Paste Into and go on to Step 3. I used a texture provided by the KPT Texture Explorer (Filters➡KPT➡KPT Texture Explorer).

**4** Save the selection as a new channel (Alpha 1). Duplicate the channel to create the Alpha 1 copy channel. Make Alpha 1 copy the active channel.

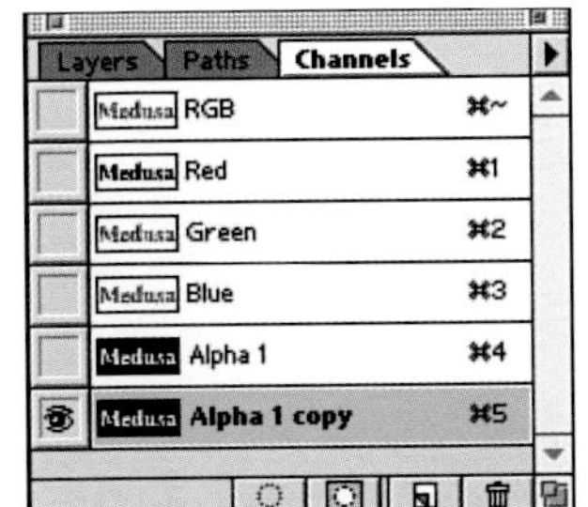


**5** Keep the selection active and choose Filter➡Blur➡Gaussian Blur. The amount that you blur the type is the most crucial step in this effect. The blur will eventually affect the way that the Lighting Effects filter works in Step 9. Set the radius so that your type looks something like what I created here. (I used 6 pixels.) If you blur the letters too much, the edges will look beveled rather than rounded. The blur should be smoothly applied inside the letters.

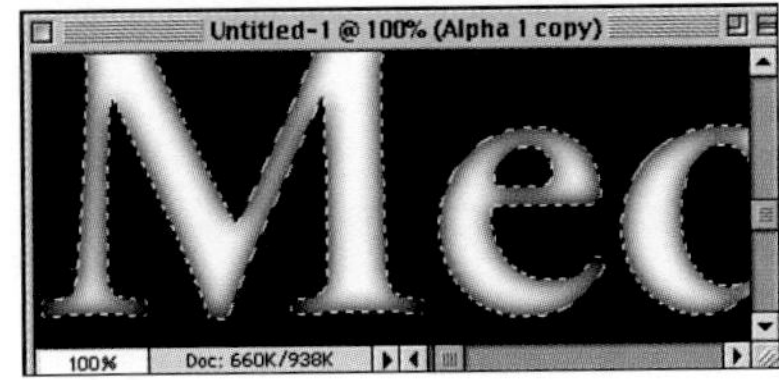


**6** Choose Duplicate Channel from the Channels palette menu. Select new from the Document menu, name the file (Medusa Displace), and click OK. When the new file opens, save it and close it. This new file becomes the displacement map used in Step 7 that tells Photoshop how to distort the image.

**7** Return to the composite channel, choose Select➡All, and Filter➡Distort➡Displace. Adjust the Scale percentages to control the roundness of the letters. I set them both at 5%. If you choose values too high, the effect won't work, so keep it low.

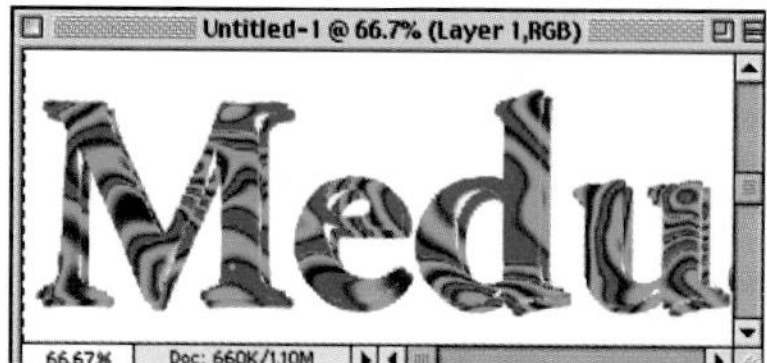


**8** A new dialog box opens asking you to find a displacement map. Find the file that you saved in Step 7 (Medusa Displace) and click Open. The distortion is subtle, but it's enough to aid in getting the type to appear rounded.

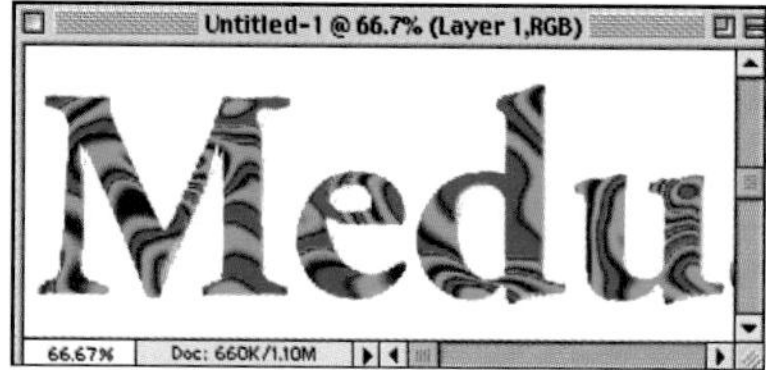


**9** To get rid of the underlying copy of the type that the Displace filter created, load the selection from the Alpha 1 channel, and choose Select➥Inverse and press Delete.

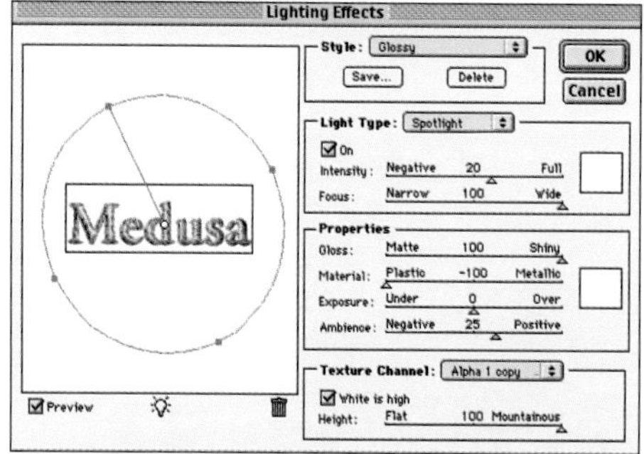


**10** Deselect the selection, choose Filter➥Render➥Lighting Effects, and either select the Glossy preset, match the settings seen here, or choose your own.

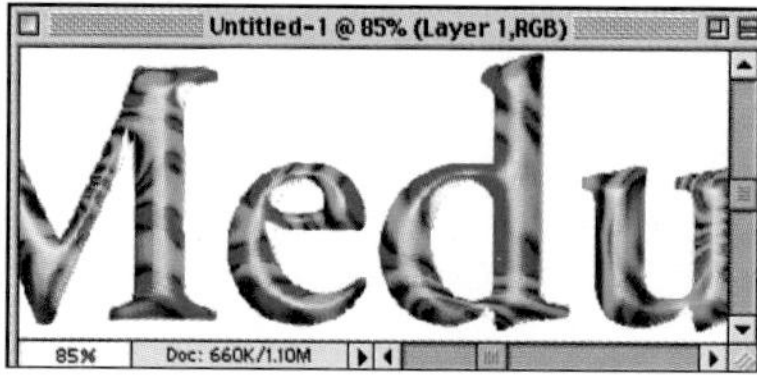


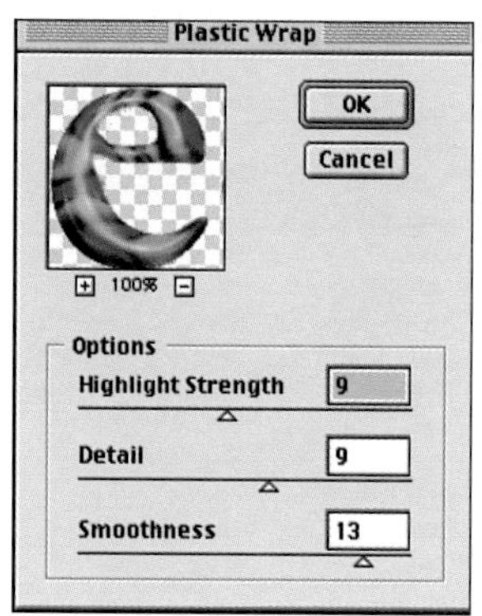


**11** Finally, choose Filter➥Artistic➥Plastic Wrap. You might need to experiment to find the right settings, but try these first: Highlight Strength: 10, Detail: 15, Smoothness: 15.

The Plastic Wrap filter does a nice job of polishing off the glossy finish.

Medusa

**TIP** **The Plastic Wrap filter produces very different results depending upon the size of the area selected. If you don't like the results you got from Step 10, try selecting only one or a few letters at a time and applying the filter. This technique is used in the following Solid Color Glossy section.**

## Solid Color Glossy

**1** Create a new layer, set the foreground color to black, and use the Type Mask tool to enter the text (Thickhead at 125 points). Fill the type selection with black. Save the selection as a new channel (Alpha 1).

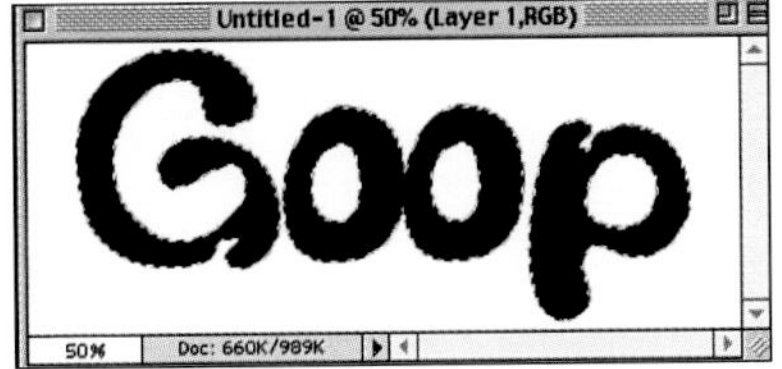


**2** Choose Select➡Feather and set the amount to approximately 5 pixels. The corners of the "running ants" adjust only slightly.

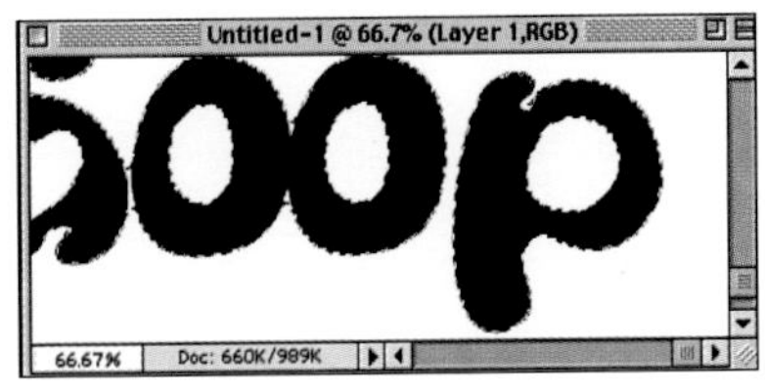


**3** Set the foreground color to a color for the type (I used CMYK: 75, 0, 100, 0), and fill the feathered selection. This two-color fill tricks the Plastic Wrap filter into finding the highlights that you want.

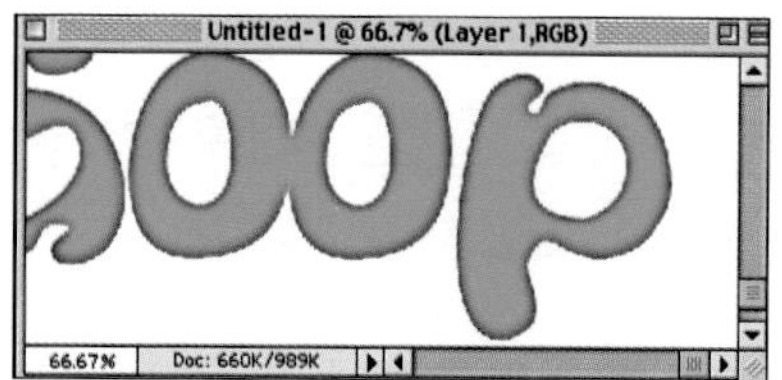


**4** To get rid of the extra color outside the selection, load the selection of the Alpha 1 channel, choose Select➡Inverse, and press Delete. Deselect the selection.

**5** Use the Rectangular Marquee tool or the Lasso tool to select only one of the letters. The Plastic Wrap filter provides drastically different effects depending on how much area is selected. I have found that selecting only one letter at a time gives me just the right highlights when trying to make that glossy look.

**6** Choose Filter➥Artistic➥Plastic Wrap. For solid colors, this filter does all of the work to create the glossy effect. Play with the settings, but try these first: Highlight Strength: 9, Detail: 9, Smoothness: 13.

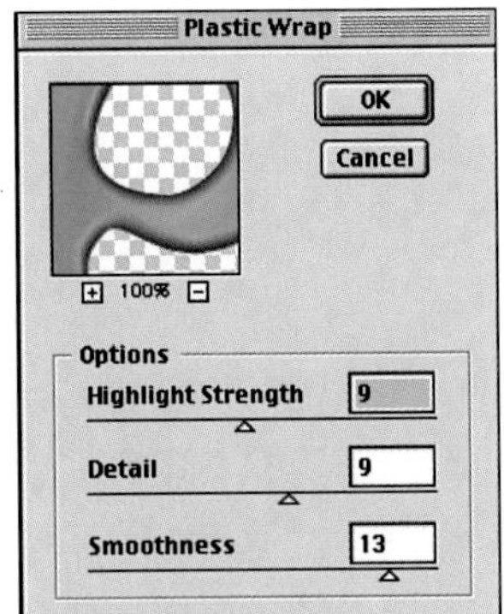


**7** Repeat Steps 5 and 6 for each letter. ●

The Gradient tool can do so much more than fill a type selection with a preset gradient. Following are several techniques that show you how to get a little more out of this powerful tool.

## Basic Gradient

Use the layer blending modes to map a gradient onto existing type.

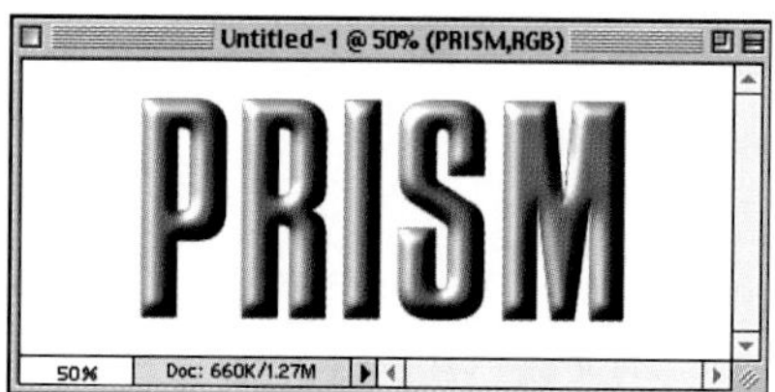



**1** To create this type, choose 50% gray for the foreground color and use the Plastic effect from the Raised section (page 146).

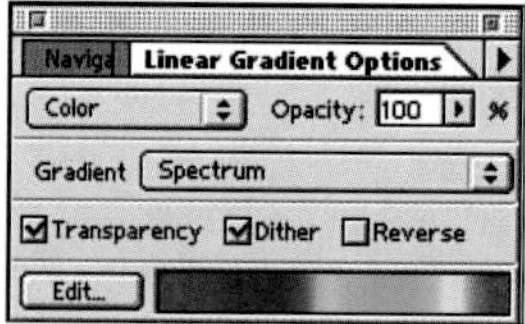



**2** Select any Gradient tool. Find the Gradient Options palette and select a preset gradient from the pop-up menu. Set the blending mode to Color.

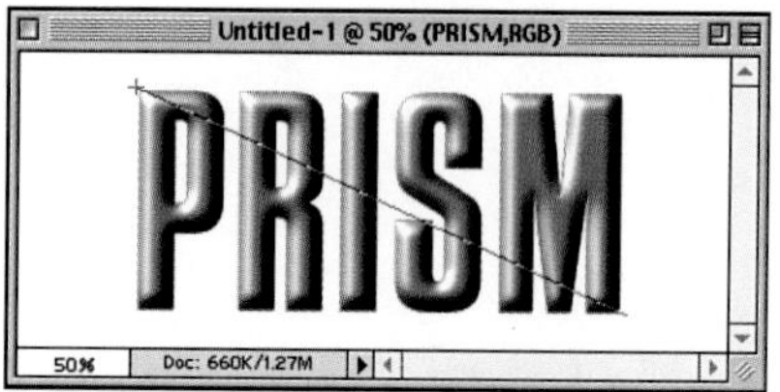



**3** Click and drag the Gradient tool across the type.

The gradient colors blend right over the raised type.

**If you have applied the Spectrum gradient to a type selection and want to shift all the colors along the gradient, choose Image➡Adjust➡Hue/Saturation. As you slide the Hue slider, the spectrum magically rotates.**

## Layering Gradients

By stacking two layers filled with gradients, you can create new gradients using the layer blending modes.

**1** Use the Type tool to enter the text. (I used Informal Black at 110 points.) Choose Layer➡Type➡Render Layer and turn on the Preserve Transparency option.

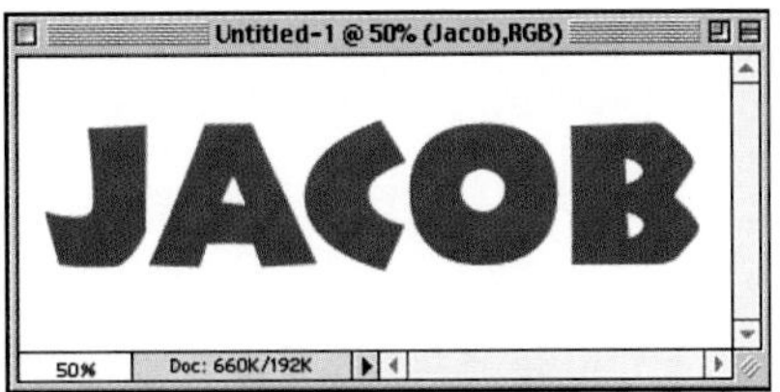


**2** Select the Linear Gradient tool and find the Linear Gradient Options palette. Select a multicolored gradient from the pop-up menu or create your own. I chose the Spectrum gradient.

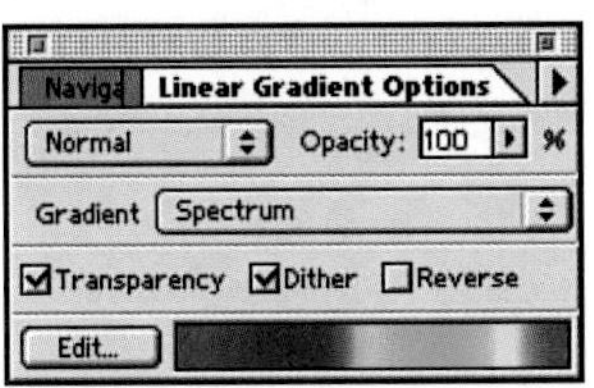


**3** Click and drag the gradient across the type.

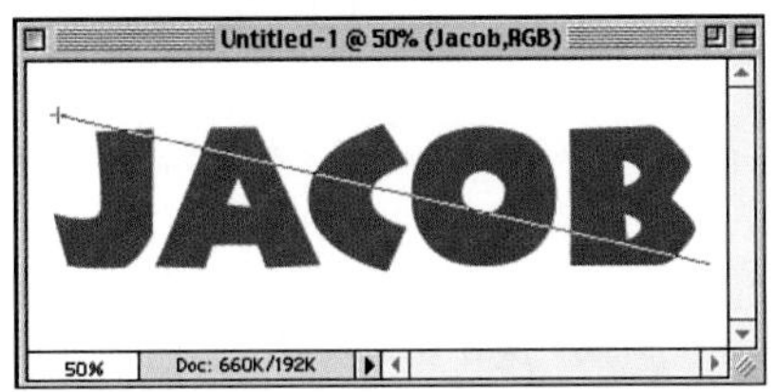


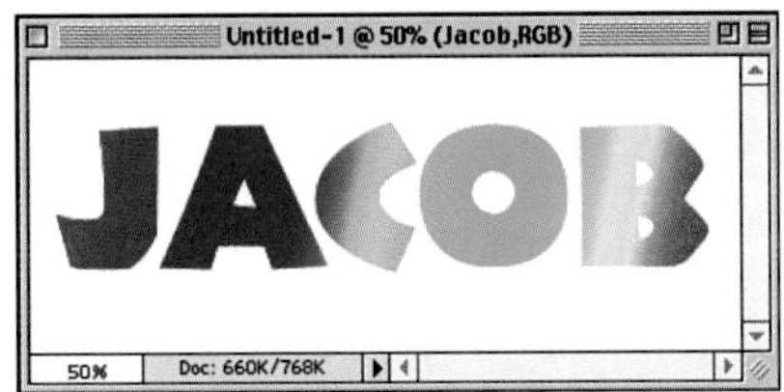


**4** Duplicate the type layer and turn on the Preserve Transparency option for this layer, too. Also, set the layer blending mode to Difference. The type turns black.

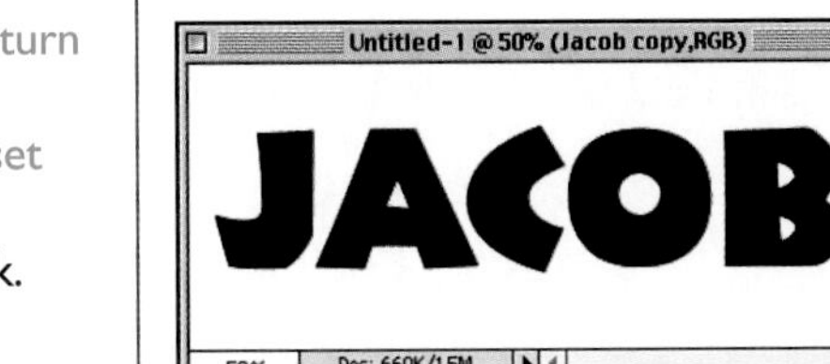

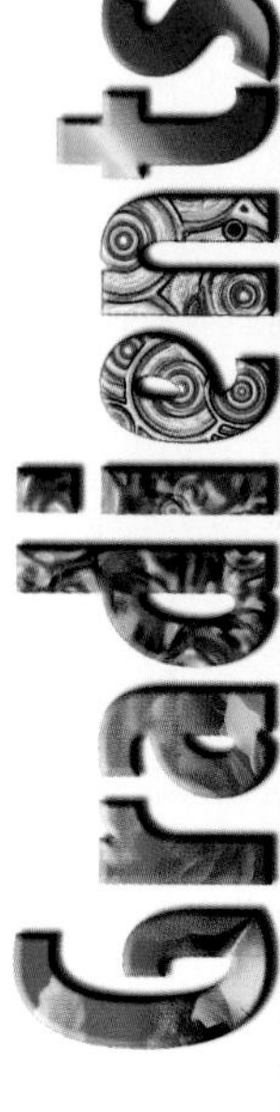


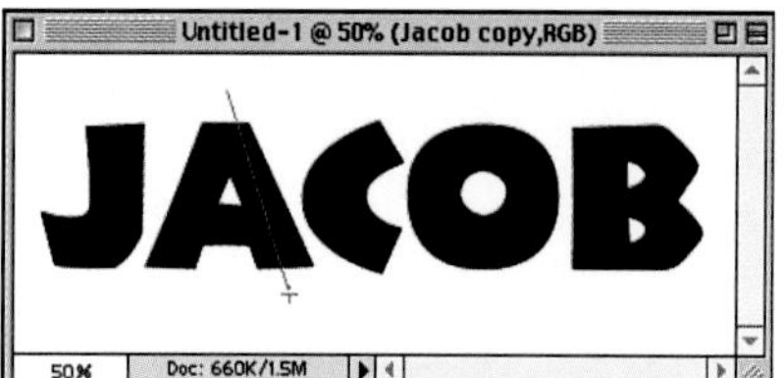


**5** Use the Linear Gradient tool and drag it across the type in a different direction.

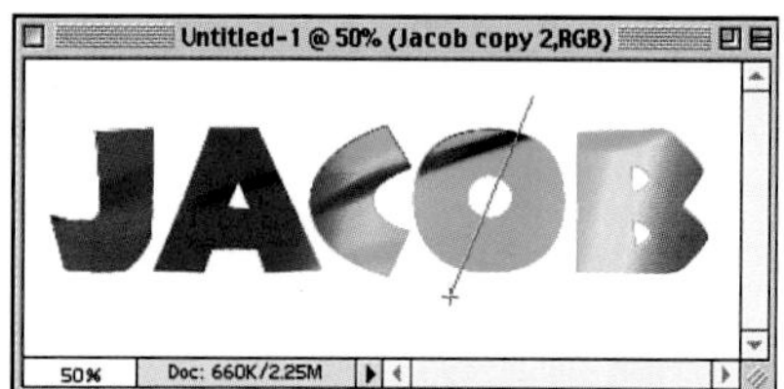


**6** Repeat Steps 4 and 5 to create a third layer. Be sure to drag the gradient in a new direction from Step 5.

**7** I applied an Outer Bevel to finish the type.

## VARIATIONS

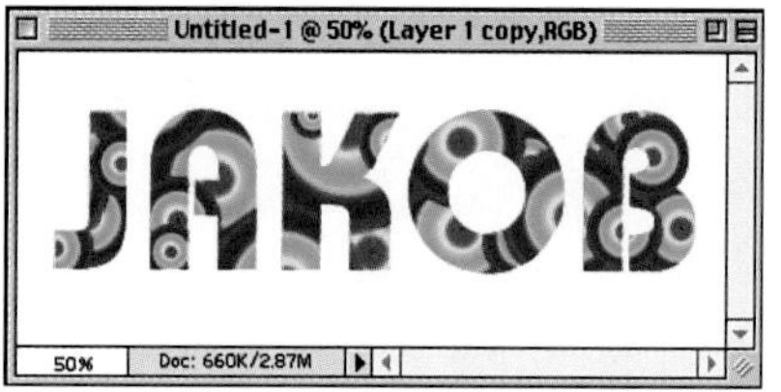


Perform Step 1, create a new layer (Layer 1), select the Radial Gradient tool, and then select Transparent Rainbow gradient. Click and drag many gradients to cover the type. Set the Layer 1 blending mode to Overlay. Group this layer with the type layer.

Then duplicate Layer 1 (Layer 1 copy) and choose Filter➥Other➥Offset (Horizontal: 20 pixels, Vertical: 20 pixels). Set the Layer 1 copy blending mode to Color. Then duplicate Layer 1 again (Layer 1 copy 2) and choose Filter➥Other➥Offset (Horizontal: -20 pixels, Vertical: -20 pixels). Set the Layer 1 copy 2 blending mode to Difference. Finally, group all the gradient layers with the type layer.

**A shortcut to creating your own gradients: Select and use one of Photoshop 5.0's built-in gradients and then choose Image➥Adjust➥Hue/Saturation. Use the Hue slider to run through a store of new gradients.**

## Graded Selections

You can also use the Gradient tool to make graded selections enabling you to blend images together. Try this technique for blending two photographs into a type selection.

**1** Create a new file and use the Type Mask tool to enter the text (Triplex Extra Bold at 110 points). I also chose Select➥Transform Selection and used the handles to stretch the type selection to fill the document window. Save the selection (Alpha 1).

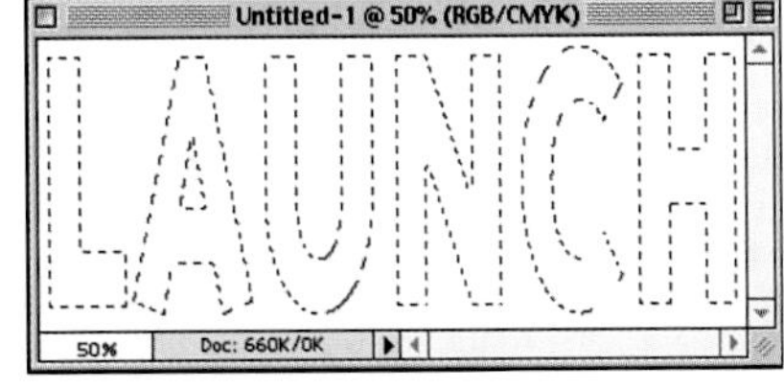


**2** Open a file containing the image to be placed in the top half of the type (Adobe Photoshop 5.0➥Extras➥Samples➥Big Sky). Choose Select➥All, copy the selection, and close the file.

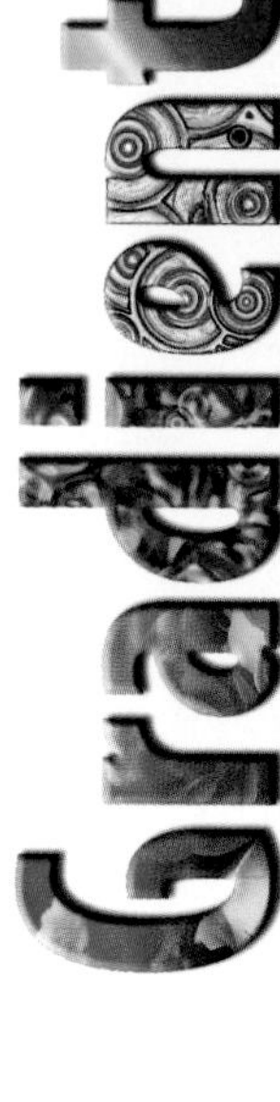

**3** Return to the file that contains the active selection and choose Edit➡Paste Into. The image will be pasted into a new layer (Layer 1) and the type selection will be turned into a layer mask. Use the Move tool to move the image around if desired.

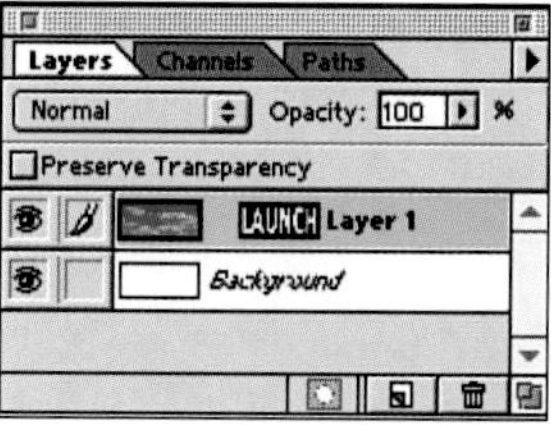


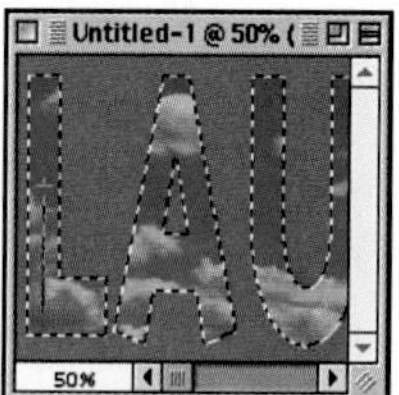


**4** Load the Alpha 1 selection and then press Q to enter Quick Mask mode. Select the Linear Gradient tool and find the Linear Gradient Options palette. Choose the Black, White gradient from the pop-up menu.

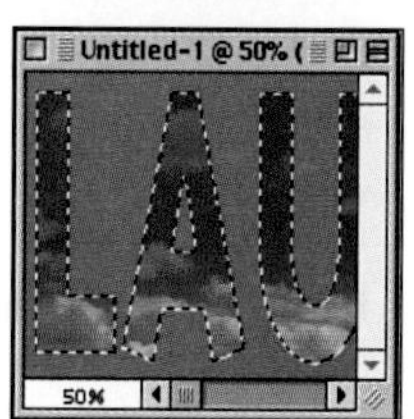


**5** Load the selection of the Layer 1 Quick Mask (temporarily placed in the Channels palette). Then hold the Shift key and click and drag the Gradient tool from just above the center of the type to just above the bottom of the type. This blended quick mask represents the graded selection that you will have after exiting Quick Mask mode.

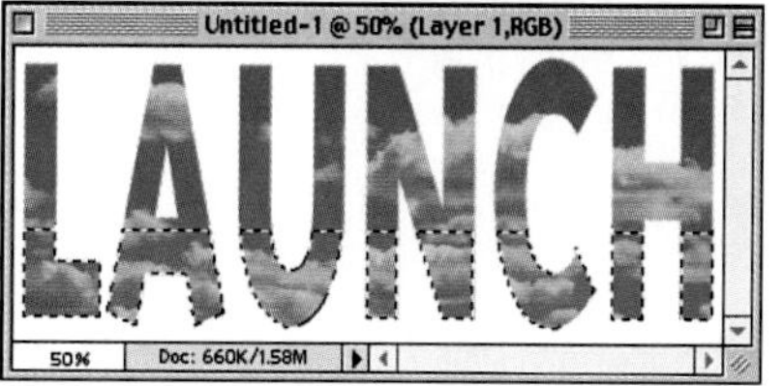


**6** Press Q to exit Quick Mask mode. It will appear as if only half of the type is selected.

7 Again, open a file containing the image that you want to paste into the bottom of the type selection (MM_0266.TIF from Vivid Details). Choose Select➡All, copy it, and close the file.

8 Return to the type file and choose Edit➡Paste Into to paste the image into the graded selection. Again the image is pasted into a new layer (Layer 2) and the graded selection becomes the layer mask. Use the Move tool to position the image.

9 I used the Outer Bevel layer effect to finish the type.

## Variations

After Step 8, deselect any selections. Click on the Layer 2 layer mask (on the Layers palette) to make it active and select the Linear Gradient tool (Black, White gradient). Click and drag the Gradient tool from the center of the type to just above the bottom of the type.

## Piling up the Gradients

If you want to pile up several gradients in a single layer, you must make sure that the ends of the gradients are transparent.

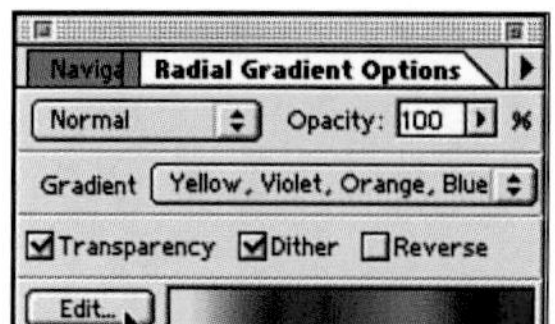


**1** Select one of the gradients from the Gradient Options palette pop-up menu and click on the Edit button.

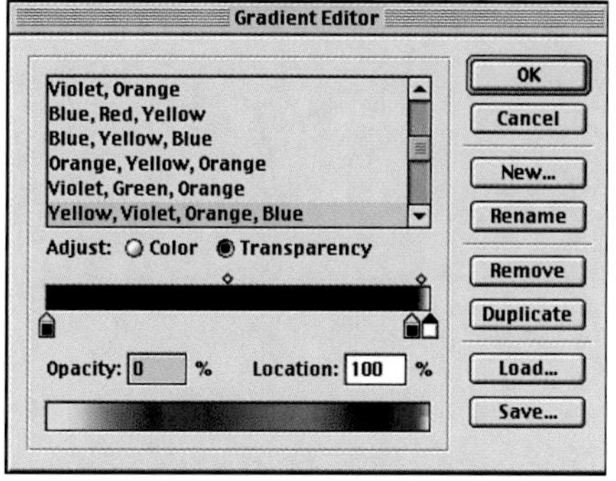


**2** Then click on the Transparency radio button. Click just below the bar to create a new black slider. Position it a little to the left of the slider on the right (Location: 95%). Then click on the slider at the extreme right end of the bar. Change the Opacity to 0%. Click OK.

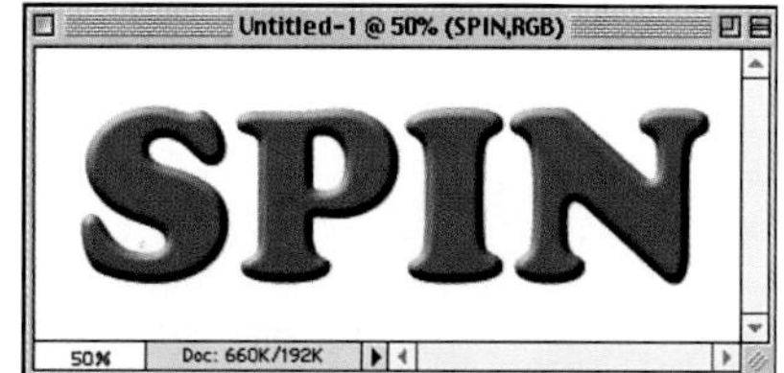


**3** To try out this gradient, use the Type tool to enter the text (Cooper Black at 120 points). Choose Layer➥Type➥Render Layer. Choose Layer➥Effects➥Bevel and Emboss. Select the Inner Bevel style, and set the Depth to 10 and the Blur to 10.

**4** Turn on the Preserve Transparency option for the type layer. Select the Radial Gradient tool and go nuts—keep clicking and dragging to overlap many gradients of varying diameters.

### More Variations

Press D to set the colors to their defaults; then choose Filter➡Render➡Difference Clouds. Choose Image➡Adjust➡Invert. To fine-tune the colors, I used the Levels dialog box to increase the contrast and the Hue/Saturation dialog box to adjust the colors.

Just one more step: Filter➡Stylize➡Find Edges. ●

Creating halftoned type is a simple one-step technique, but you can create many great patterns by starting with the Hafltone filter and then applying various other Photoshop filters. Here are some examples:

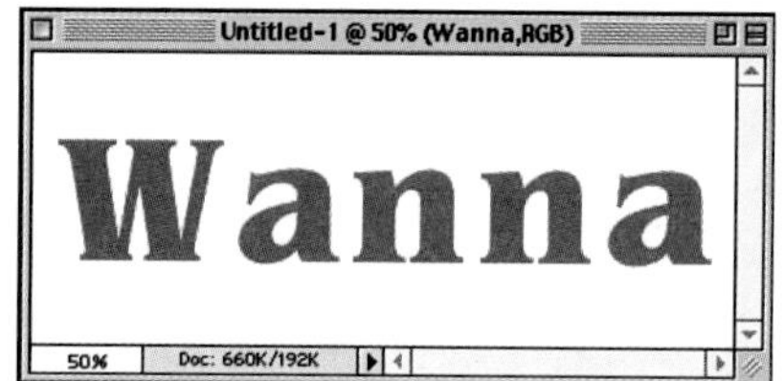


**1** Create a new file and use the Type tool to enter the text. (I used Benguiat at 90 points.) I set the color swatch in the Type tool dialog box to CMYK: 0, 75, 100, 0. Choose Layer➡Type➡Render Layer.

**TIP** **The color that you choose for the type will make a big difference in the results, but the only way to find out what the Color Halftone filter will do with it is to try it out.**

Color Halftone
Max. Radius: 8 (Pixels) OK
Screen Angles (Degrees): Cancel
Channel 1: 108
Channel 2: 162 Defaults
Channel 3: 90
Channel 4: 45

**2** Choose Filter➡Pixelate➡Color Halftone. The channel settings in this dialog box correspond to the red, green, and blue channels of your file. Because only three channels are in an RGB file, the fourth angle setting is ignored. The Max. Radius limits the size of the circles that the filter creates. Try the default angles and set the Max. Radius to 8, a little above the minimum Max. setting.

That's the basic halftoned type.

Wanna

**After applying the Color Halftone filter, choose Image➥Adjust➥Hue/Saturation and use the Hue slider to run through some other color choices.**

## VARIATIONS

### Large Circles

Perform Steps 1 and 2. In Step 2, set the Max. Radius to 40.

Do Steps 1 and 2 and then choose Filter➥Render➥Difference Clouds. Then make only one of the color channels active (Green) and choose Filter➥Stylize➥Find Edges. Make the RGB channel active again and choose Filter➥Render➥Difference Clouds. Press (Command-F) [Control-F] to reapply the Difference Clouds filter. I also applied an Inner Bevel and a Drop Shadow.

### Rippled

Perform Steps 1 and 2 and then choose Filter➥Distort➥Ripple (150, Medium).

Polka?

Polka?

### Clouds

Do Steps 1 and 2; then choose Filter➥Noise➥Dust and Scratches (Radius: 8, Threshold: 168). Choose Filter➥Render➥Difference Clouds. Press (Command-F) [Control-F] to reapply the filter.

### Clouds II

Complete the Clouds variation; then make a copy of the type layer and choose Layer➥Effects➥Clear Effects to clear the effects from the new layer. Choose Filter➥Render➥ Difference Clouds and change the layer blending mode to Difference.

## Spilled-Over Dots

If you don't want to keep the edges contained within the type, choose Flatten Image from the Layers palette menu after Step 1. Complete Step 2.

## Just Dots

Start with the Spilled-Over Dots variation; then load the selection of one of the color channels (Green). Choose Select➡Inverse. Create a new layer, choose a foreground color, and fill the selection. Delete the original type layer. I also applied an Inner Bevel and a Drop Shadow to the new layer. ●

# Highlights

Here are four ways to add a sparkle to your type. Two of them use filters, one uses a custom paint-brush, and the last uses the Gradient tool. Choose your weapon.

## The Custom Paintbrush

**1** Open the file containing the type to which you want to add high-lights. This type was created with the Gradient Chrome effect on page 54.

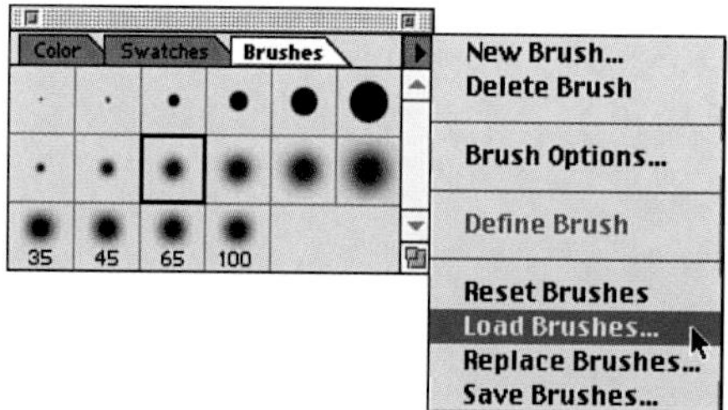


**2** Find the Brushes palette and choose Load Brushes from the palette menu.

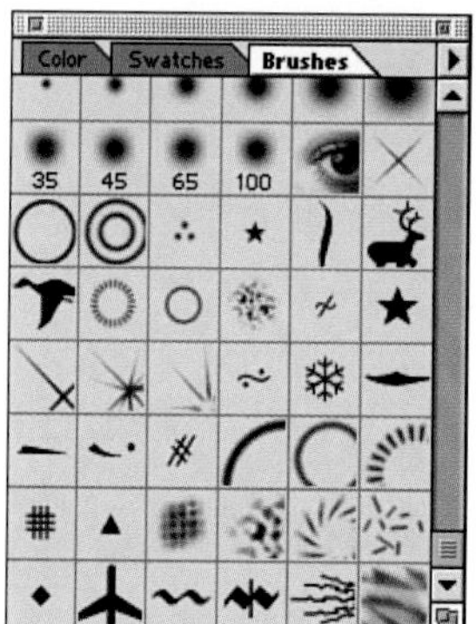


**3** Follow this path to open the Assorted Brushes file: Adobe Photoshop 5.0➡Goodies➡Brushes & Patterns➡Assorted Brushes. A range of new brushes appear in the Brushes palette.

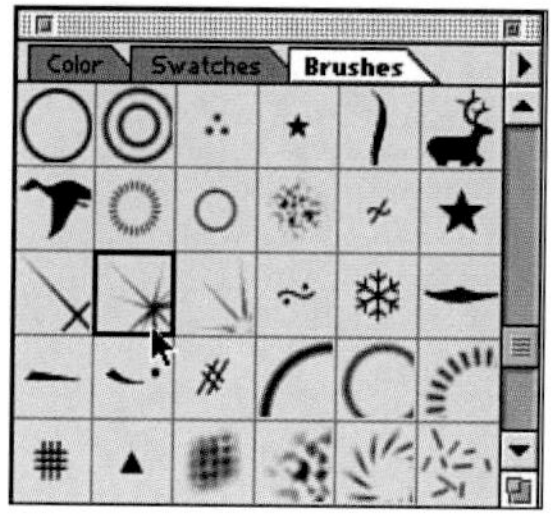


**4** Scroll to the bottom of the palette and select this brush:

**You can use the brush on either side of the brush I recommended for slightly different sparkles.**

**5** Choose white (or another bright color) for the foreground color.

**6** To add sparkles to the type, use the Paintbrush tool to click on the type where you want the sparkle. Don't drag the brush or you will smear the sparkle.

Sparkles, sparkles, sparkles.

**To intensify a sparkle, click twice on the same spot, or make a small circling motion with the sparkle brush to spread and blur it.**

## The Lens Flare

**1** For this method, I started with this type created using the Reflector effect (page 46).

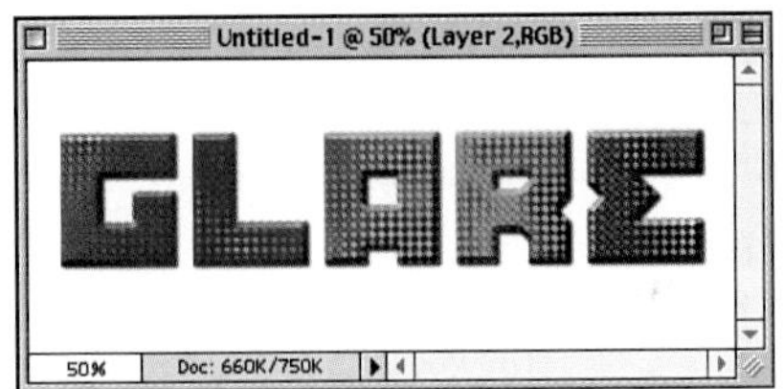


**2** Choose Filter➡Render➡Lens Flare. In the dialog box preview, drag the flare to a spot on the type. I set the Brightness at 150%. Make sure that the Brightness percentage is not so high that you have all highlight and no type.

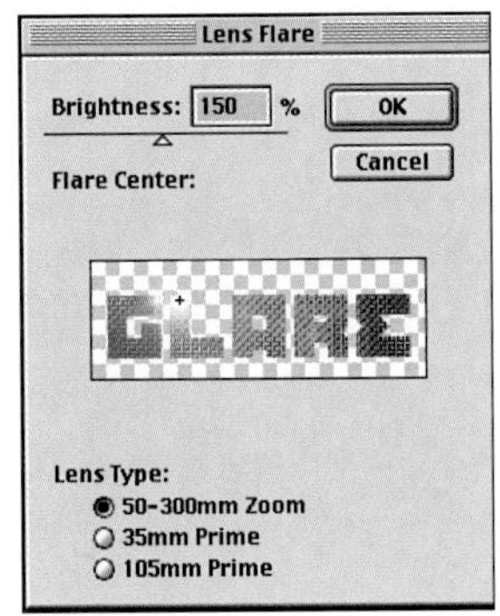

Click OK and you're finished.

## The Gradient Highlight

**1** This type was created using the Plastic effect on page 146.

**2** Choose white for the foreground color or another color for the highlight.

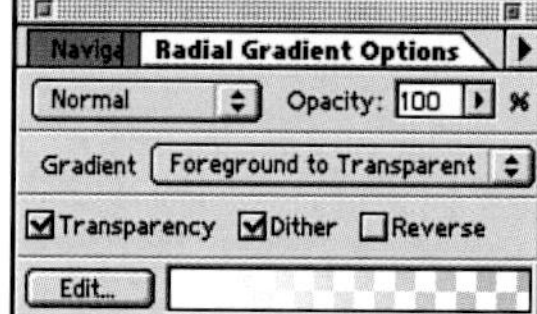


**3** Double-click the Radial Gradient tool to select it and to open the Radial Gradient Options palette. Change the Gradient type to Foreground to Transparent.

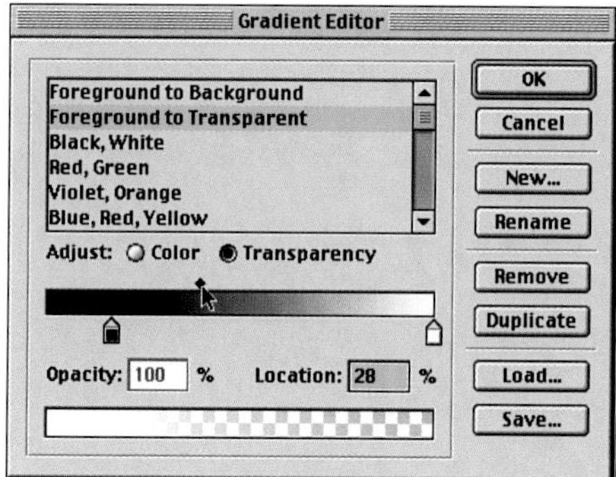


**4** Click on the Edit button. Then click on the Transparency button. The black bar represents the transparency, or opacity, of the gradient at each point along its transition. The gradient is 100% opaque if the bar is black. Grab the black marker and slide it to the right a little. This will slightly extend the completely opaque part of the radial gradient—near the center. Then grab the diamond on top and slide it to the left a little. This will make the gradient fade from opaque to transparent a little quicker. Click OK.

**5** Create a new layer (Layer 1) and change the Layer 1 blending mode to Overlay. Click and drag with the Gradient tool from the point for the center of the highlight. Drag the Gradient line until it reaches as far as you want the highlight to spread. In this example, I dragged the Gradient tool from the center of the word to the end of the word.

## Lighting Effects Filter

In this technique, the highlights are actually added, using the Lighting Effects filter, to a new layer above the type. Then the layer is blended with the type layer.

**1** I made some Plastic type for this filter (page 146).

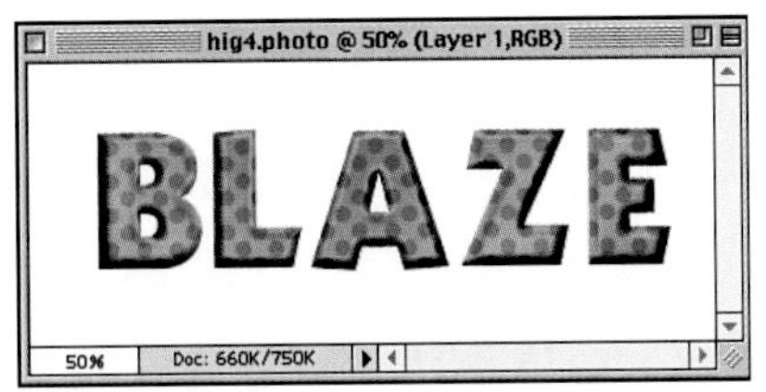


**2** Create a new layer above the layer containing the type and fill the layer with 50% gray or a lighter color. Then choose Filter➡Render➡Lighting Effects. Add lights to the preview where you want highlights. I added just two lights in this example. Raise the Ambience slider enough to make sure that the gray away from the highlights remains relatively close to 50% gray.

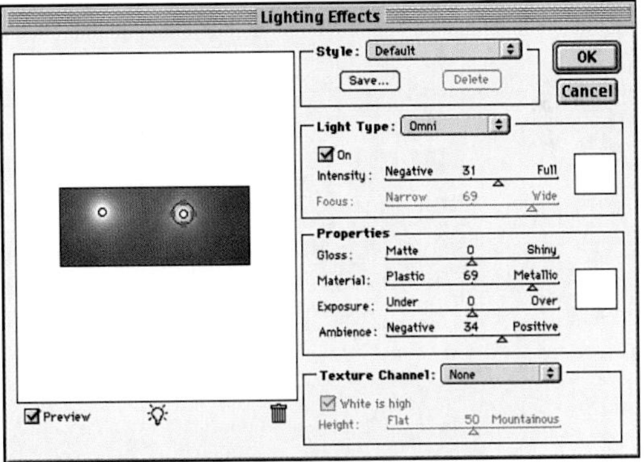


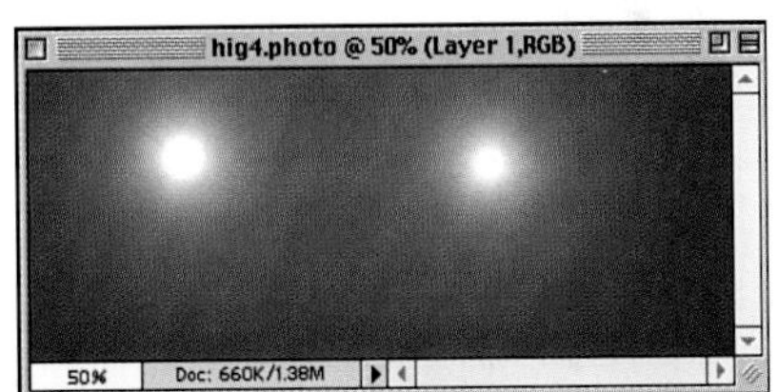


**3** Change the layer blending mode to Overlay for the new layer. The highlights spill right onto the type. ●

The Clouds filter, plus two others, help create this realistic marble from scratch.

**1** Create a new file. Use the Type Mask tool to enter the text onto a white background. Marble looks good in a blocky font such as Machine (135 points).

**2** Keep the selection active. Make sure that the foreground color is set to black and choose Filter➡Render➡Difference Clouds.

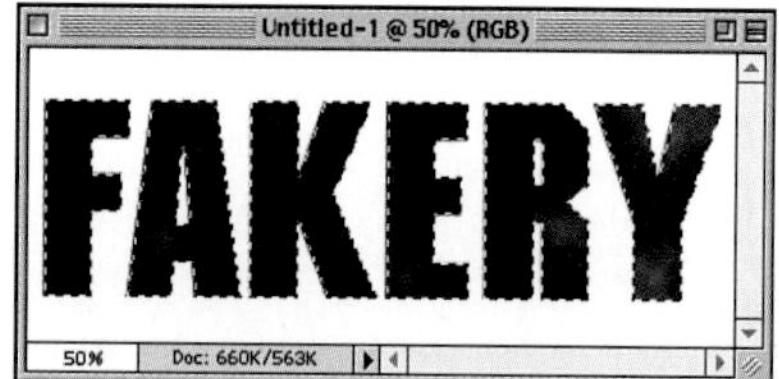


**3** Reapply this filter a few times. The more times you apply the filter, the more the veins of the marble break up. I applied the Difference Clouds filter two times. Here is what my type looked like.

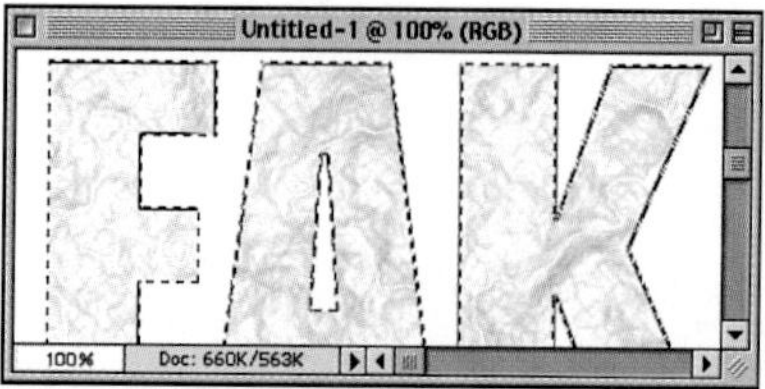


**4** Choose Filter➡Stylize➡Find Edges. This filter pulls the veins out of the clouds.

**5** Choose Image➡Adjust➡Invert.

**6** Next, choose Image➡Adjust➡Levels. Grab the white Input marker and slide it to the left until it sits under the beginning of the steep slope in the previous graph. Then nudge the gray input marker to the right. Watch the preview and use these two sliders to adjust the marbling.

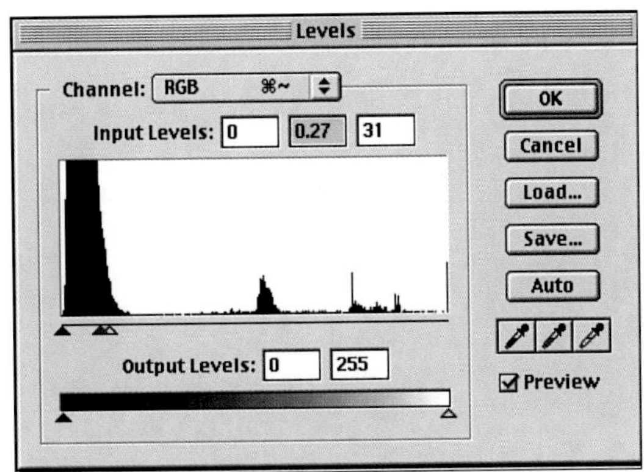

**7** Choose Image➡Adjust➡Hue/Saturation. Turn on the Colorize option. Then adjust the Saturation marker so that the color comes through but isn't too bright. I set it right in the middle, at 50. Use the Hue slider to find a color for the marble. For more color, nudge the Lightness up just a little.

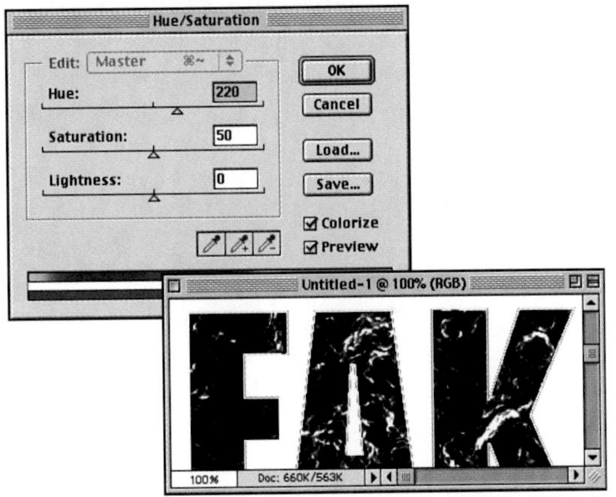


**8** The Find Edges filter leaves a funny edge on the type. Choose Select➡Modify➡Contract. Contract the selection 1 or 2 pixels—just enough so that the selection is inside the marble. I chose 2 pixels. Choose Select➡Inverse and press Delete to fill the background with white. ●

This technique uses some of Photoshop's most basic filters to create a simple, effective, and oh so speedy type treatment.

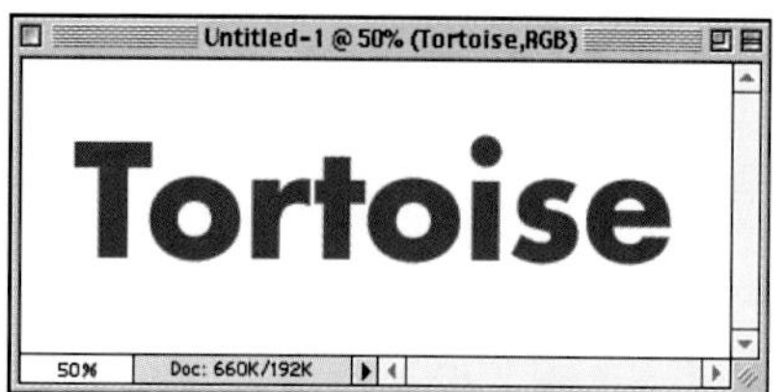


**1** Create a new file, and choose a foreground color for the type (CMYK: 100, 0, 100, 40). Use the Type tool to enter the text (Futura Bold at 75 points). Use a typeface that is heavy enough that it won't be obliterated by the Wind filter used in Step 4. Choose Layer➡Type➡Render Layer. This is another effect that you can apply to any type image as long as it is merged into a single layer.

**2** Choose Filter➡Stylize➡Wind (Wind, From the Right). The filter will not create prominent streaks, but the streaks will be enough to give the Motion Blur filter something to work with.

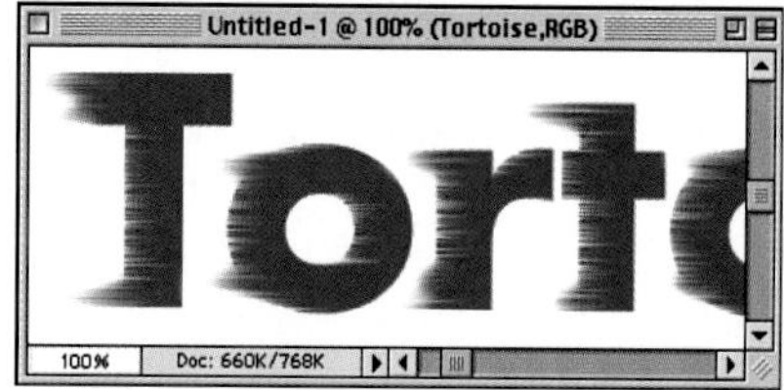


**3** To improve the illusion of movement, use the Smudge tool to lengthen some of the streaks. You can skip this step if you want to, but a few smudges can greatly improve the effect. Double-click the Smudge tool to select it and bring the Smudge Options palette to the front. Set the Pressure to 50% (Normal). Choose a soft-edged brush from the Brushes palette, and drag on the back edges of the type. Hold Shift while dragging to keep the smudging perfectly horizontal.

**4** Choose Filter➥Blur➥Motion Blur (10 pixels). Set the angle to 0° so the blur remains absolutely horizontal. You can raise the Distance setting, but don't go too crazy or the tortoise will look like he's just standing there shaking.

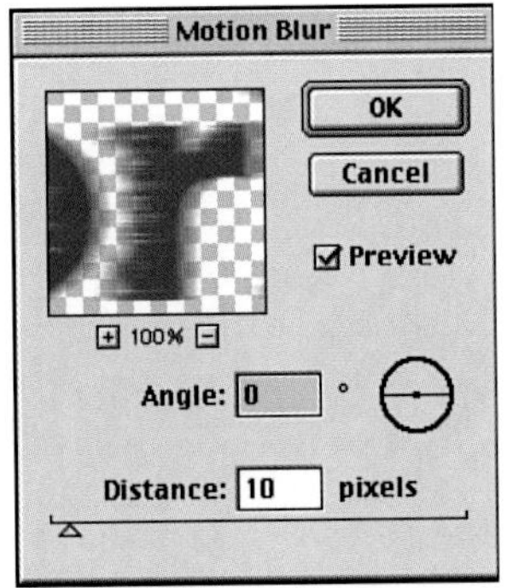


**5** Choose Filter➥Stylize➥Wind (Wind, From the Right) again. After smudging and blurring, applying this filter a second time has a greater impact.

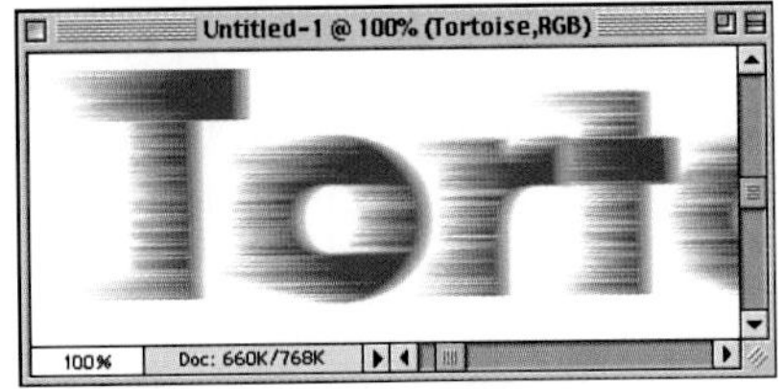


**TIP** **If applying the Wind filter in Step 5 washes away too much of the type, choose Filter➥Fade Wind and lower the percentage. I did that here and set the percentage at 75%.**

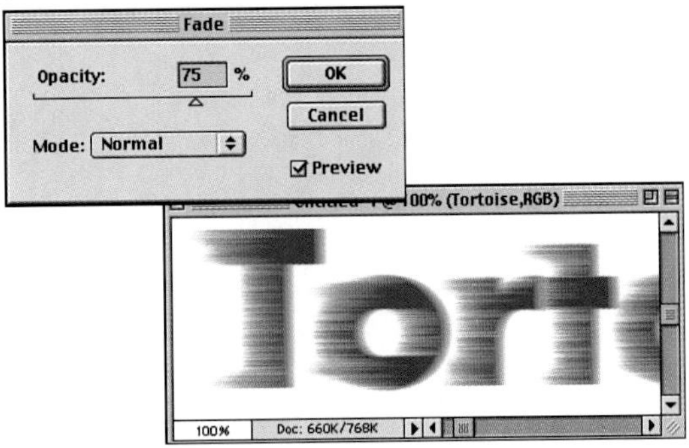


**6** Choose Filter➥Sharpen➥ Unsharp Mask (Amount: 75, Radius: 4, Threshold: 3) to sharpen the edges that became a little too blurry after applying the Motion Blur filter.

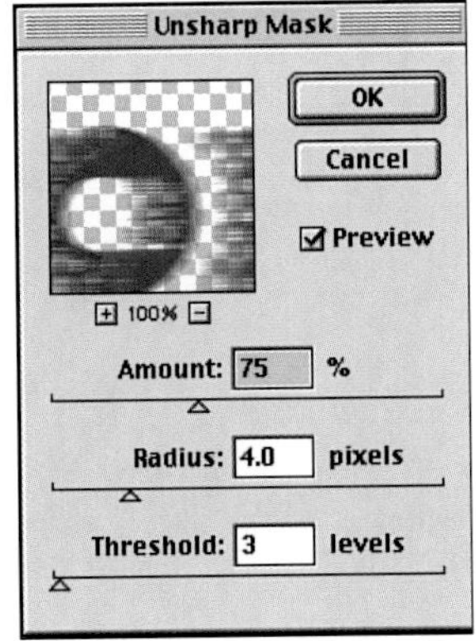

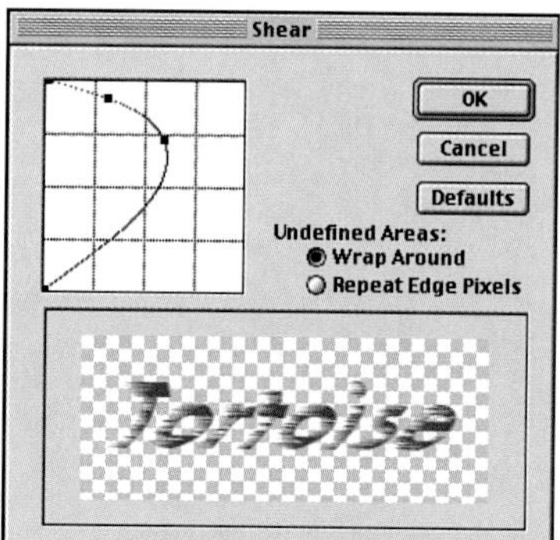


**7** Choose Filter➥Distort➥Shear. This filter distorts the type according to how you distort the line in the 4 × 4 grid. Grab the line in the middle to add a point to it and drag it up to the position of the lower point in this figure. Then pull both of the top and bottom points all the way to the left. Finally, I added another point higher up on the curve to fine-tune the bend.

**TIP** **Here is another good place to use the Smudge tool to lengthen and smooth the streaks.**

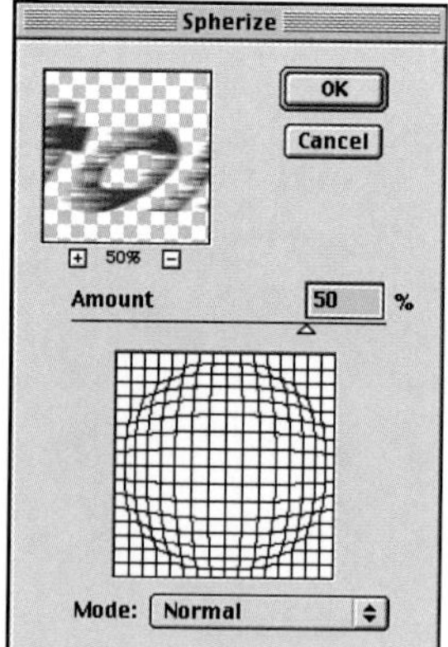


**8** Choose Filter➥Distort➥Spherize. This final distortion bloats the type in the center, making it look a little like it is rounding a corner. I set the Amount to 50% (Normal).

The settings used for all the filters used in this effect might be varied in order to create slightly different effects.

## VARIATIONS

### Quick Fix

If all you want to do is put a quick swerve in your type, use the Shear filter. Do Step 1 and then Step 7. Here is the Shear filter dialog box.

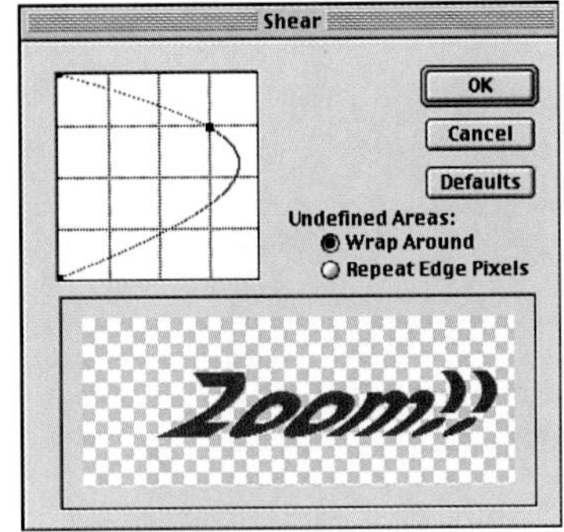


And here is the result.

### Shadow

To add a shadow beneath the type, choose Layer➡Effects➡Drop Shadow (Mode: Multiply, Opacity: 50%, Angle: 0°, Distance: 20 pixels, Blur: 20 pixels, Intensity: 0%). Then choose Layer➡Effects➡Create Layer. A new layer that contains the shadow will be created below the type layer. Make the new layer active. Choose Edit➡Transform➡Scale; grab the top center handle while holding the Shift key and pull it straight down to condense the shadow.

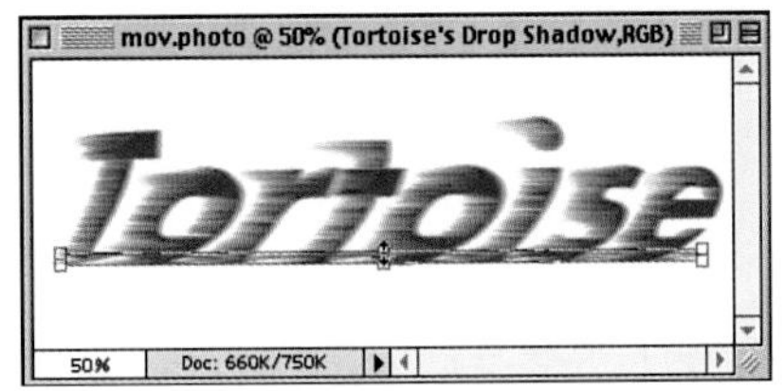


Press (Return) [Enter] to accept the transformation, and use the Move tool to shift the shadow down and to the left of the type. Then choose Filter➡Blur➡Gaussian Blur (1 pixel) to smooth the shadow out a little. ●

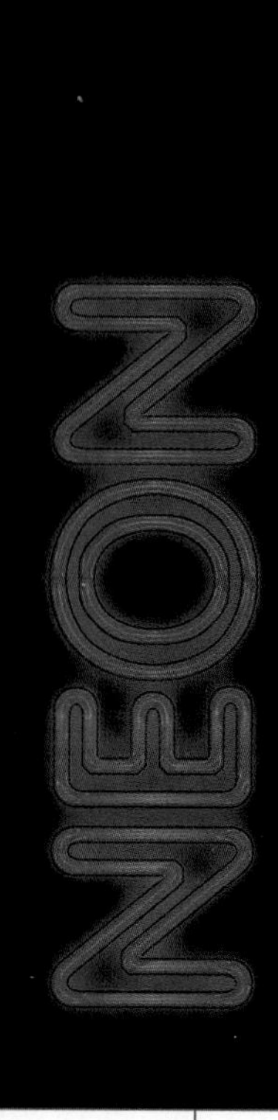


Those fantastic glowing tubes are created with some fancy selections, a couple of color fills, the new Outer Glow layer effect, and the Plastic Wrap filter. A couple of quick methods are shown in the Variations.

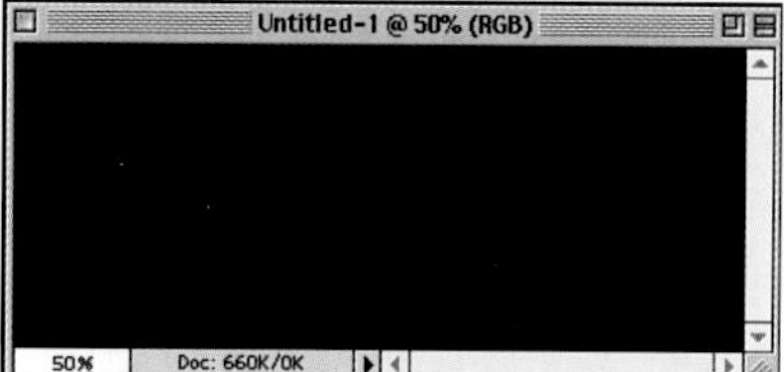


**1** Create a new file; then choose black for the foreground color and fill the Background layer with black. The only way to achieve that radiant neon glow is to contrast the bright color of the type against a dark background color. You don't have to use black, but make sure that the color you choose is significantly darker than the color of the type.

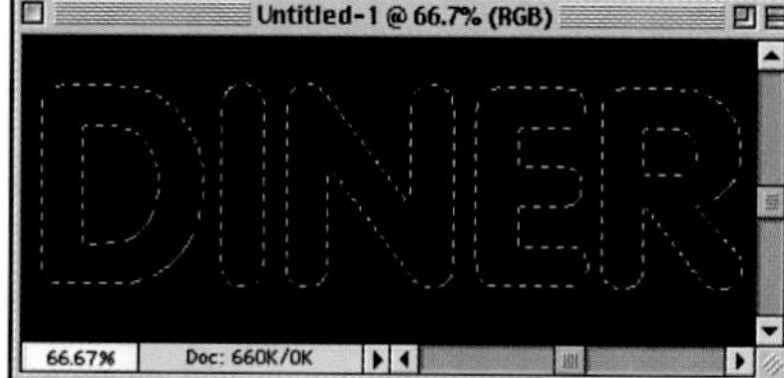


**2** Use the Type Mask tool to enter the text. (I used VAG Rounded at 100 points.) If you have the VAG Rounded typeface, use it; the roundness of this typeface makes creating the tubes a little easier. If you don't, choose a heavy block typeface, choose Select➡Modify➡Smooth, and set the Radius high enough to round the corners of the type.

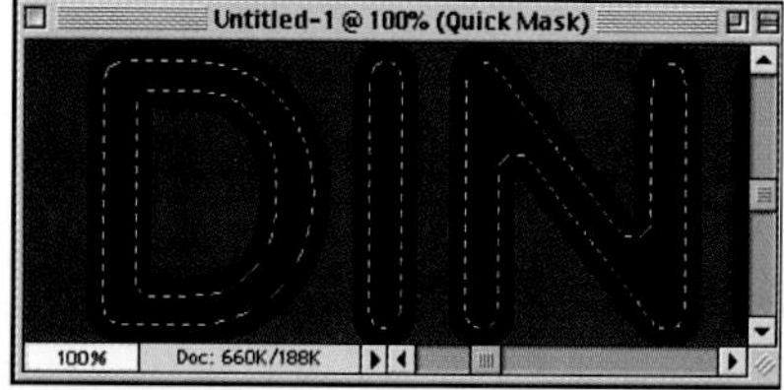


**3** Press Q to enter Quick Mask mode. Here the type selection can quickly be changed into tubes. Load the selection of the Quick Mask (this channel has been temporarily placed in the Channels palette) and choose Select➡Modify➡Contract (8 pixels). Contract the selection enough so that you can see a good black border all the way around the outside of the selection.

4 Fill the contracted selection with black (it will actually fill with red because you're in Quick Mask mode, but use black as the foreground color), and deselect the selection. You can now see the tubes running all the way around the type.

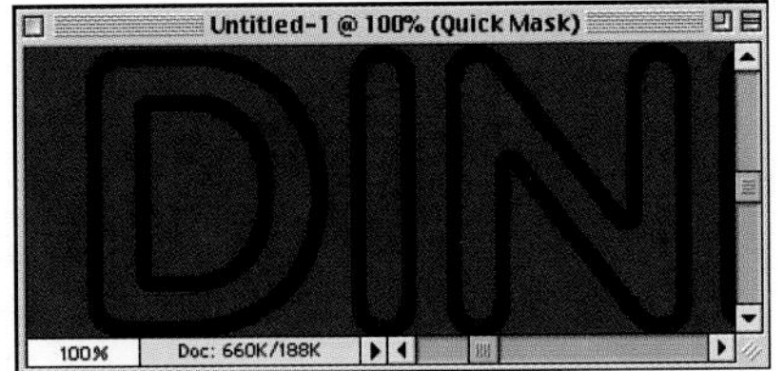


5 Press Q again to exit Quick Mask mode. Choose a foreground color that is somewhat darker than the color you want to use for the neon (CMYK: 0, 75, 100, 40). The selection will be filled again in the next step with a brighter color. Fill the selection and save the selection (Alpha 1).

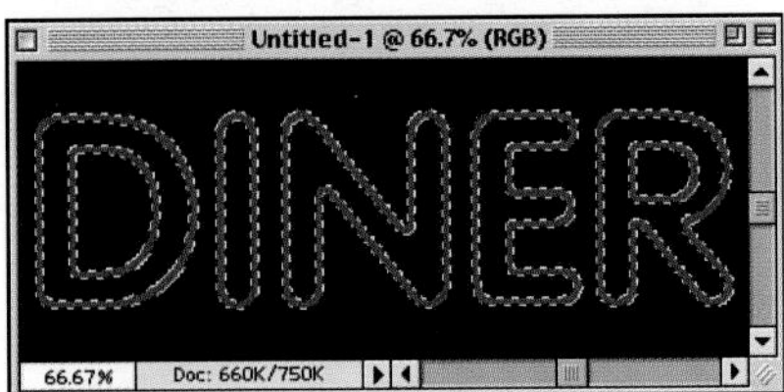


6 Choose Select➡Feather (3 pixels), choose a foreground color that is a brighter variation of the color used in the Step 4 (CMYK: 0, 0, 72, 0), and fill the selection.

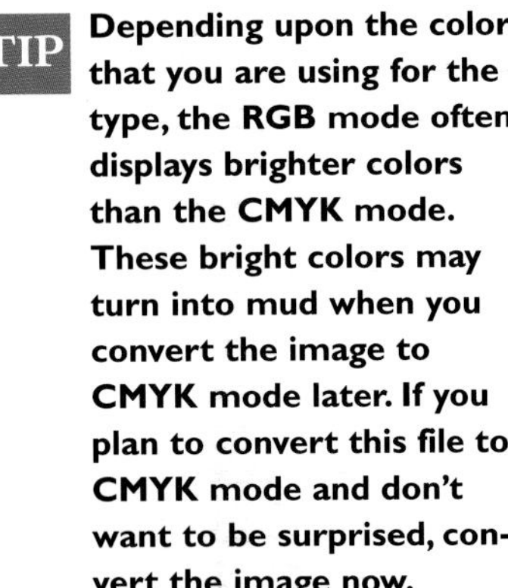

TIP **Depending upon the colors that you are using for the type, the RGB mode often displays brighter colors than the CMYK mode. These bright colors may turn into mud when you convert the image to CMYK mode later. If you plan to convert this file to CMYK mode and don't want to be surprised, convert the image now.**

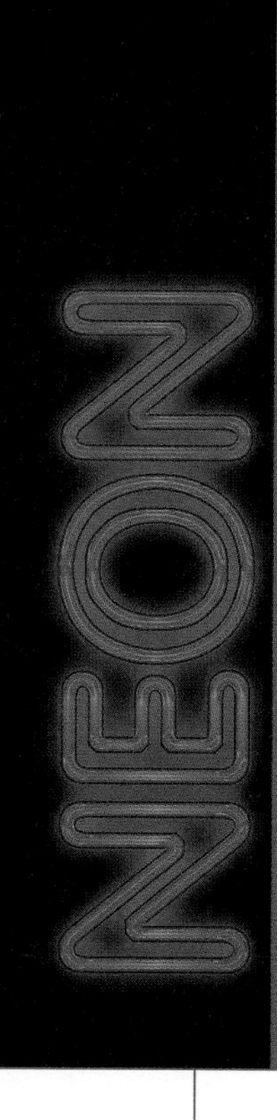


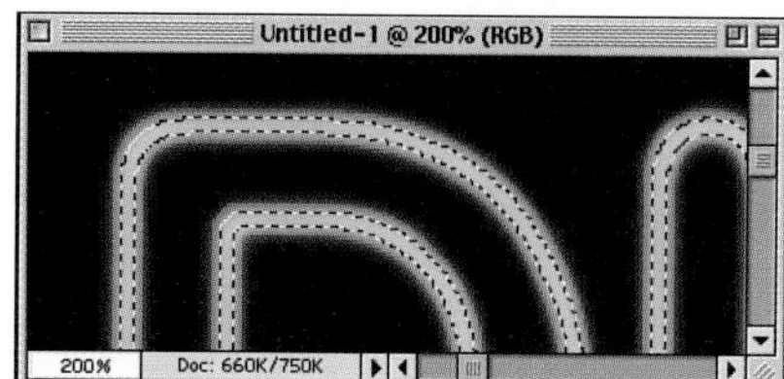


**7** Load the selection of the Alpha 1 channel and choose Select➡Modify➡Contract (2 pixels). After contracting the selection, the selection remains continuous throughout the letters. Choose Select➡Feather (1 pixel) to soften the selection just a bit.

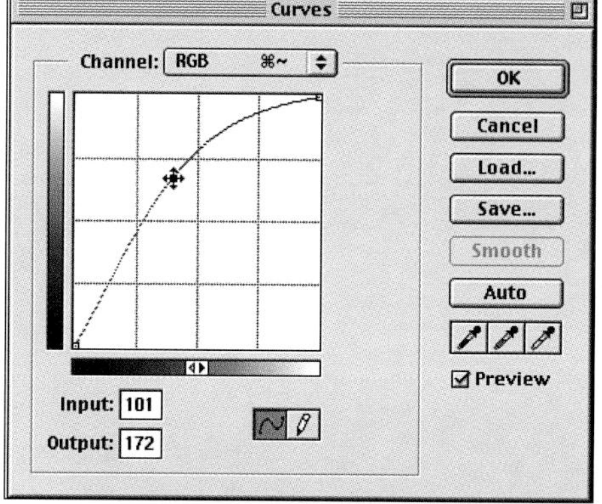


**8** Choose Image➡Adjust➡Curves. Grab the center of the line in the graph and bend it up and to the left. Watch the image. The interior of the letters brighten and improve the look of the glow.

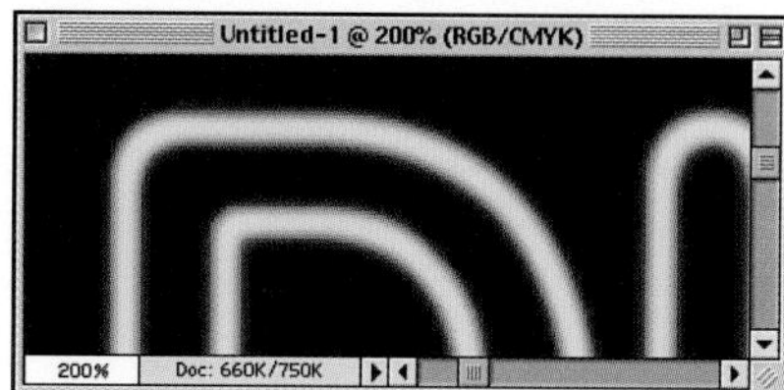


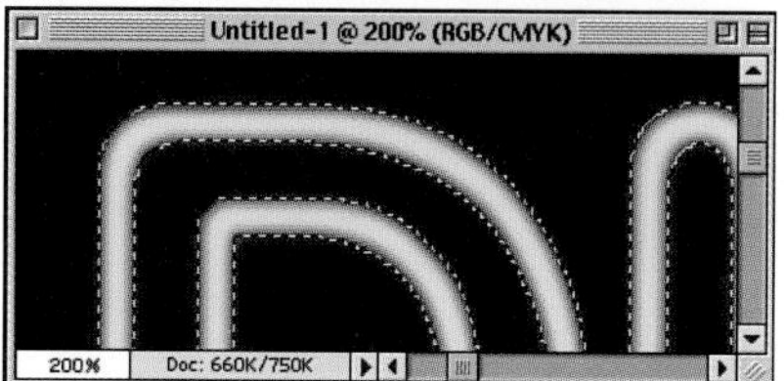


**9** Load the selection of the Alpha 1 channel again; then choose Select➡Modify➡Expand (1 pixel). Expanding the selection just a little will pick up some of the darkness from the black background.

**10** Choose Layer➡New➡Layer Via Cut to create a new layer (Layer 1) that includes only the tubes. Cutting the selection into a new layer leaves a "hole" in the Background layer. Removing the black from this part of the background helps to brighten the glow added in the next step.

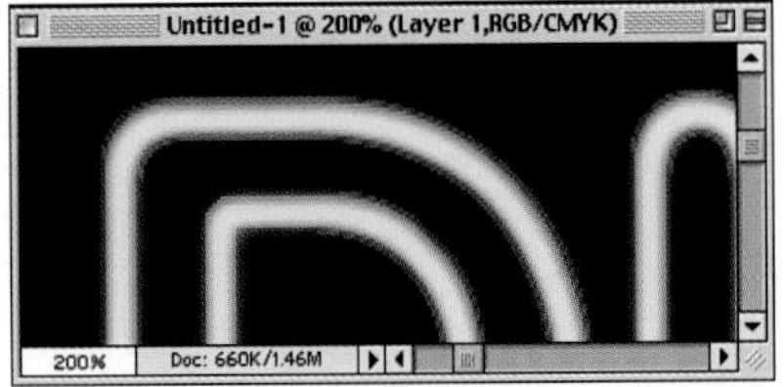


**11** Choose Layer➡Effects➡Outer Glow. Choose a glow color that is close to the bright color chosen in Step 6 (CMYK: 0, 0, 72, 0). Set the Opacity to 100%; raise the Blur to about 20 pixels and the Intensity to around 10%. These settings should work well for you, but adjust them if necessary.

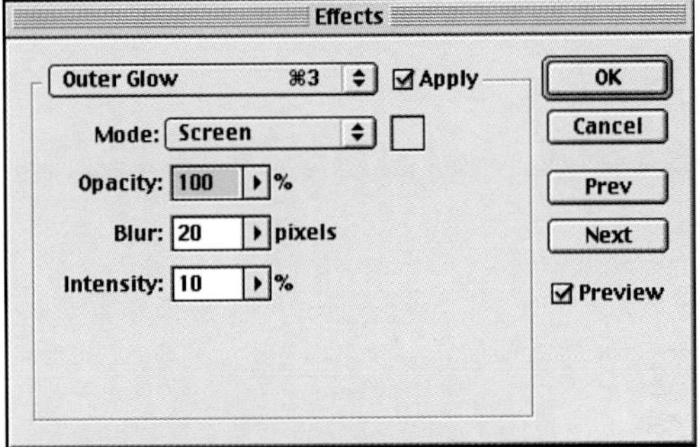


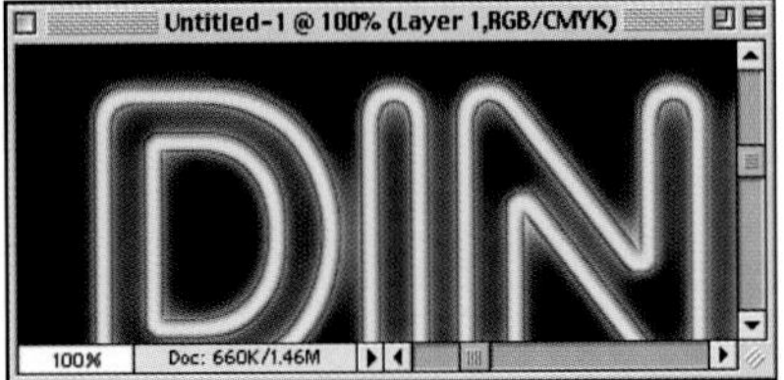

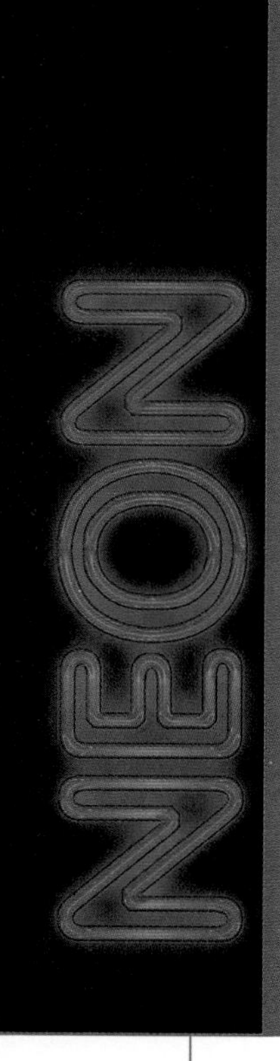

**12** Choose Filter➡Artistic➡Plastic Wrap. This filter places some highlights that follow the shape of the tubes. Try these settings: Highlight Strength: 15, Detail: 9, Smoothness: 7. Because this filter can produce drastically different results depending on the image that is used, you will probably need to experiment with the settings to find the right highlights.

## Variations

### Quick Neon

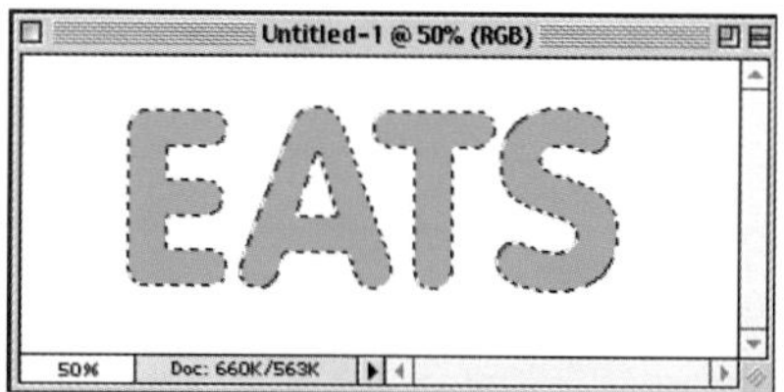


Choose a bright foreground color for the neon text (CMYK: 72, 0, 36, 0), and use the Type tool to enter the text (VAG Rounded at 120 points). Load the transparency selection of the new type layer; then choose Flatten Image from the Layers palette menu.

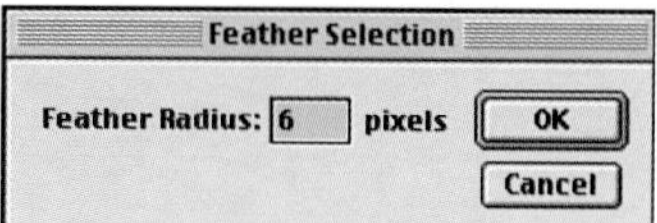


Choose Select➡Inverse and Select➡Feather (6 pixels). The Feather amount determines the softness and extent of the glow.

Choose black (or another dark color) for the foreground color and fill the selection to complete the effect.

## The Neon Glow Filter

Do Steps 2 through 4 on page 112 pand press Q to exit Quick Mask mode. Save the selection (Alpha 1). Choose black for the background color and choose a foreground color for the neon (CMYK: 72, 0, 36, 0). Fill the selection and then deselect the selection. Press X to switch the foreground and background colors; then choose Filter➡Artistic➡Neon Glow. Click on the color swatch to pick a color for the neon glow (CMYK: 100, 80, 0, 0) and adjust the settings to control the glow (Size: 17, Brightness: 35). Finally, load the selection of the Alpha 1 channel, choose Select➡Feather (1 pixel), and feather the selection a small amount. Press X again and fill the selection to complete the effect. ●

This technique uses information from a background image to control the texture of the type that is "painted" on top. The Paint Strokes variation adds a nice finishing touch to this effect.

**1** Begin this effect with a textured background image like this image that was cropped and resized from the Photo 24 020 wall image on the P5TM CD-ROM (P5TM➡Images➡Photo 24➡Walls➡020). Some images work better than others. An image that is almost monochromatic and has an even distribution of texture, like this one, works well. Check out the variations to see what to do if the image is darker.

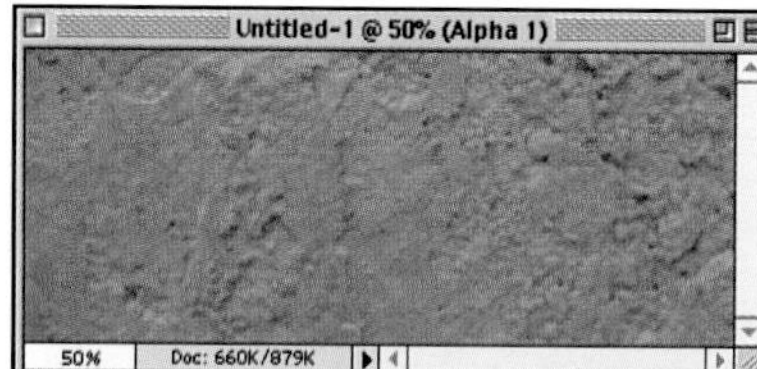


**2** Choose Select➡All to select the entire background image, and copy it. Create a new channel (Alpha 1) and paste in the image. Deselect the selection.

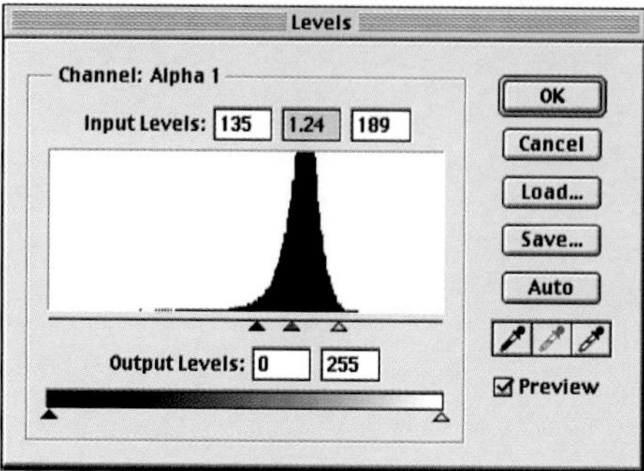


**3** Choose Image➡Adjust➡Levels. In the Levels dialog box, use the Input Levels sliders to adjust the darks and lights in this channel. The values in this channel act as a map for the painted type. Where this channel is light, the type will show through, and where this channel is dark, the background image will show through. You are looking for something that has some of each. Generally, you want to bring the two outside sliders (black and white) in toward the center. If you click the Auto button, it gets you close to what you're looking for. Then adjust the middle (gray) slider so that the image has a good dose of middle grays.

A good gray image such as the one seen here works great.

4 Choose Filter➡Noise➡Add Noise. Keep the setting low; add just enough noise so there is faint texture to the channel (20, Gaussian).

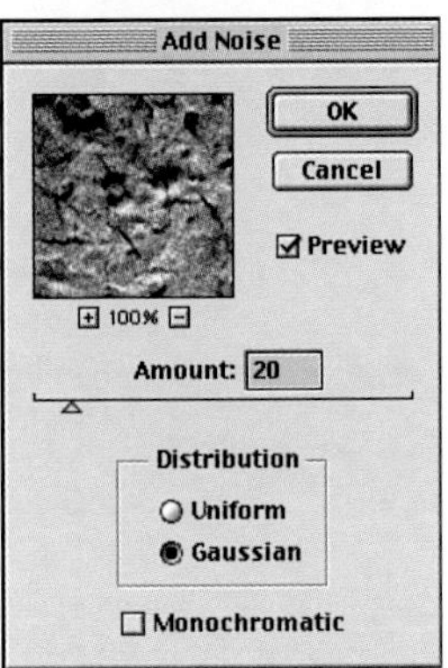


5 Return to the composite channel, create a new layer (Layer 1), and use the Type Mask tool to enter the text. I used AG Book Stencil at 105 points.

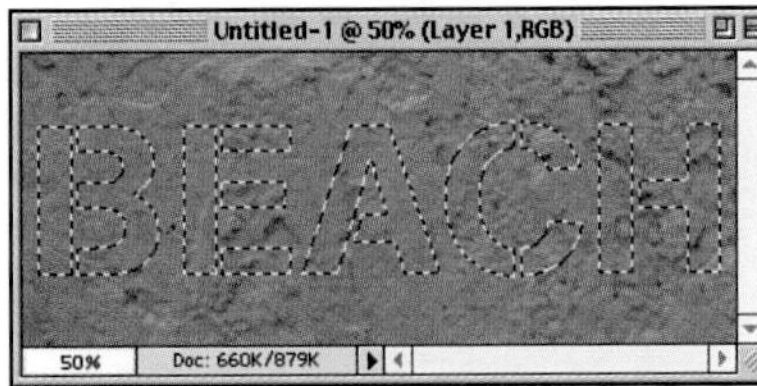


6 Intersect the type selection with the selection of the Alpha 1 channel. Then choose an approximate foreground color (CMYK: 0, 100, 75, 0) for the type and fill the selection. Deselect the selection.

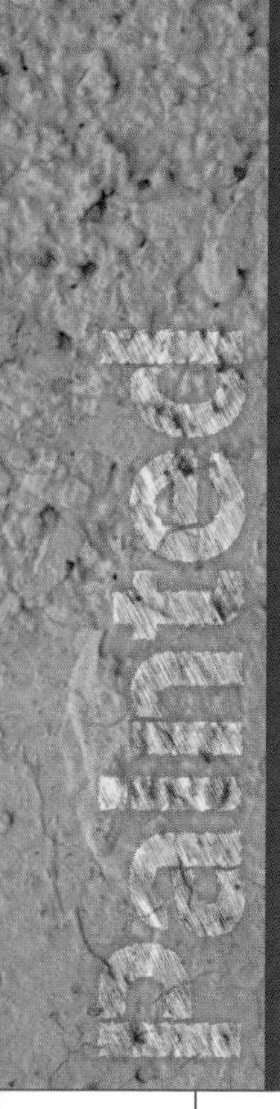

**7** Change the Layer blending mode to Overlay. You might not need to change the Layer blending mode. For some images, Normal works better than Overlay (as in the last image on page 119). It depends upon the color of the type and the color or colors of the background. Try both and pick the one that works best. Don't worry too much about the color right now; it will be adjusted in the next step and again in Step 10.

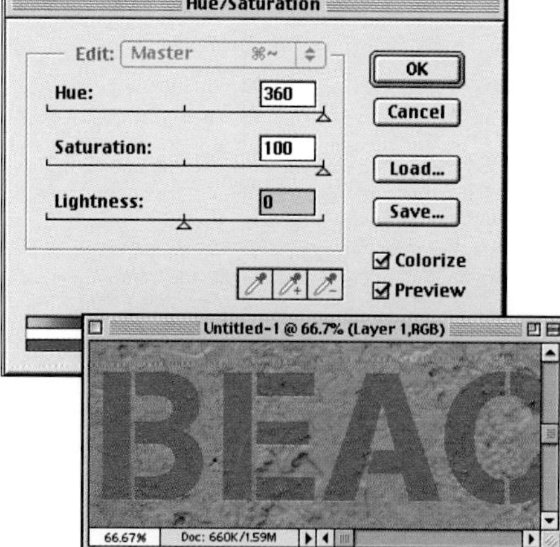


**8** Choose Image➡Adjust➡Hue➡Saturation. Check the Colorize option to turn it on, and watch the preview as you adjust the sliders to find the right color. You will probably need to raise the Saturation level quite a bit (I ended up with 100). If you can't get the type as dark as you want it, don't worry—we will darken it in Step 10.

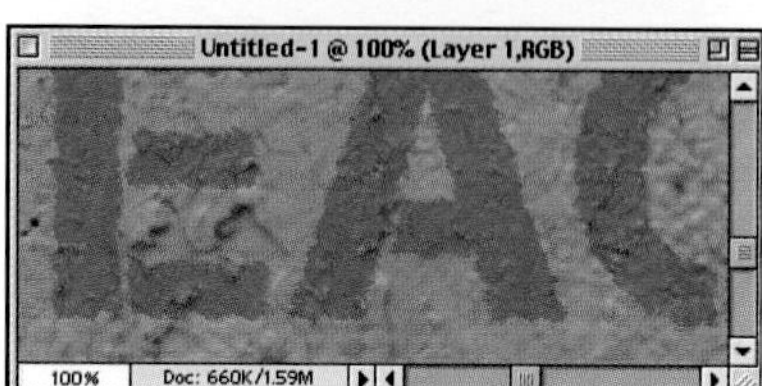


**9** Choose Filter➡Stylize➡Diffuse (Normal) and Filter➡Distort➡Ripple (Amount: 135%, Size: Small). These filters roughen the type, especially at the edges.

**10** Duplicate Layer 1 and move the new layer (Layer 1 copy) below Layer 1. Choose Image➡Adjust➡Levels. After Step 9, the type should have become brighter. To darken and strengthen the type while still letting the background texture show through, adjust the Input sliders. For this image, I brought the black slider almost all the way to the right.

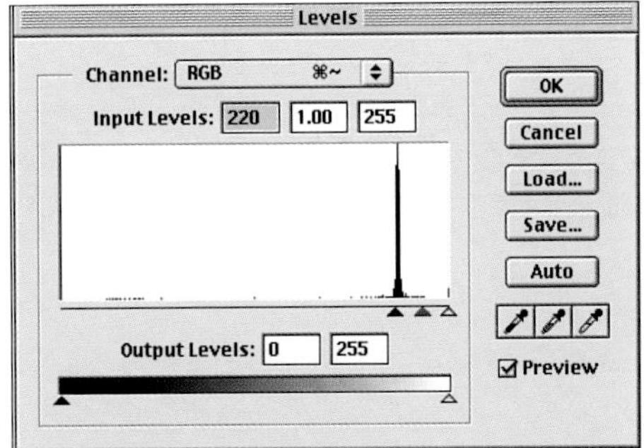


Click OK and you're done.

## VARIATIONS

### Paint Strokes

After completing all of the preceding steps, create a new layer (Layer 2) and move it above Layer 1. Load the transparency selection of Layer 1, choose black for the foreground color, and fill the selection. Then fill it two more times to darken it. Choose Filter➡Noise➡Add Noise (999, Gaussian, Monochromatic). Deselect the selection and choose Filter➡Blur➡Motion Blur. The angle set here will be the angle that the strokes run across the type. I set the Angle to -27°. Adjust the amount so that there are good streaks through the noise (26). Be careful not to set it too high or the blurring will wash everything out.

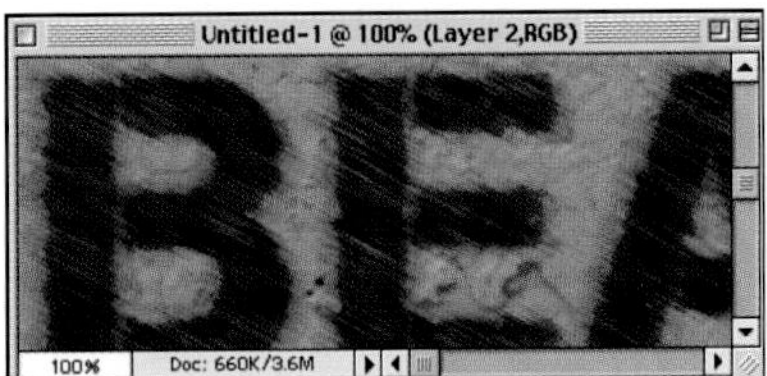

Set the Layer 2 blending mode to Luminosity—instant paint streaks. If the streaks are not subtle enough, lower the Opacity for Layer 2.

**TIP** **If you don't like the dark glow that this variation created around the type, load the transparency selection of Layer 1, choose Select➡Inverse, and press Delete to get rid of it.**

## A Darker Background

As mentioned in Step 7, you might need to make adjustments to this technique for each unique combination of type color and background color. For this example, I used the TEXTR_27.PCT (Image Club) image from the P5TM CD-ROM (P5TM➡Images➡Image Club➡Textures➡TEXTR_27.PCT) and followed all of the previous steps, except that I left the Layer 1 blending mode set at Normal, and I moved Layer 2 on top of Layer 1 and set its blending mode to Overlay.

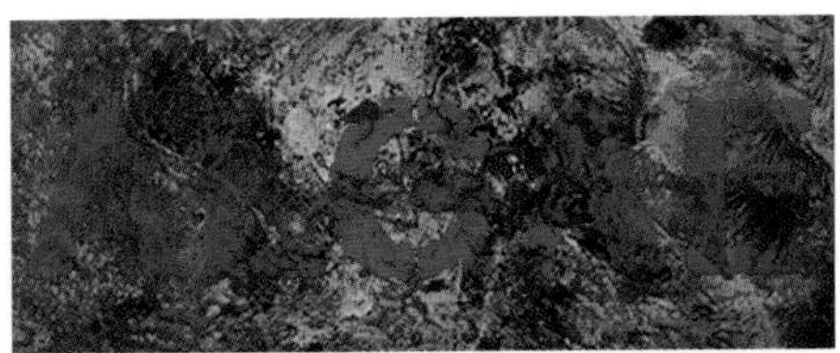

**If you want to add a little thickness to the paint, as in the thumbtab image, deselect any selections, make Layer 1 copy active, and nudge it one keystroke down and one keystroke to the right.** ●

# PAPER BAG

This technique demonstrates a quick-and-easy way to use the Clouds and Lighting Effects filters to create a brown paper bag texture. A quick change of color turns the texture into aluminum foil.

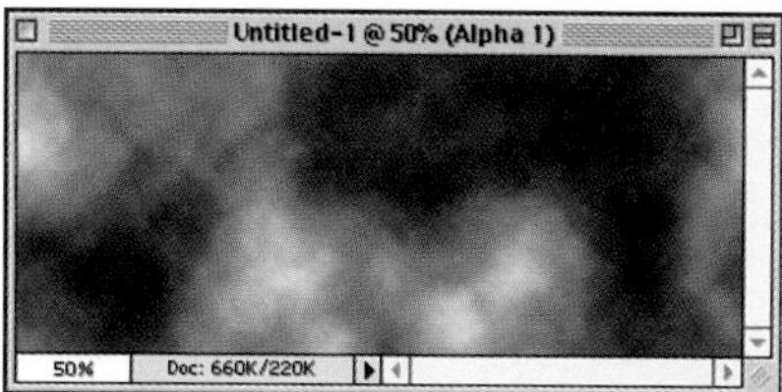


**1** Create a new file. It must be an RGB file so that you can use the Lighting Effects filter. Create a new channel to hold the texture (Alpha 1), and choose Filter➡Render➡Clouds. The Alpha 1 channel should look like this.

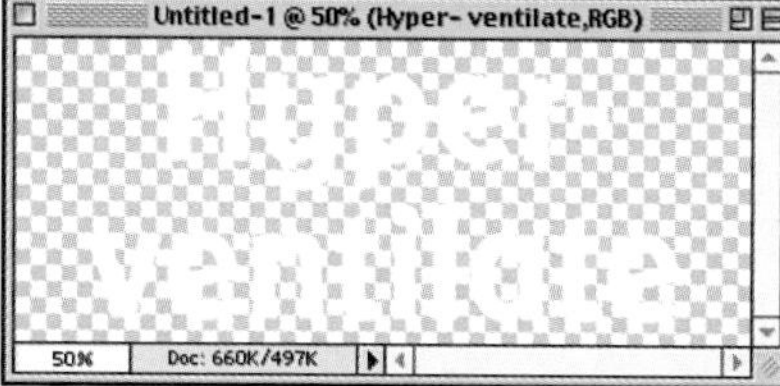


**2** Return to the composite channel, set the foreground color to white, and use the Type tool to enter the text. I used BadgerBold at 80 points. Choose Layer➡Type➡Render Layer. I made the background layer invisible so you can see the white type, barely.

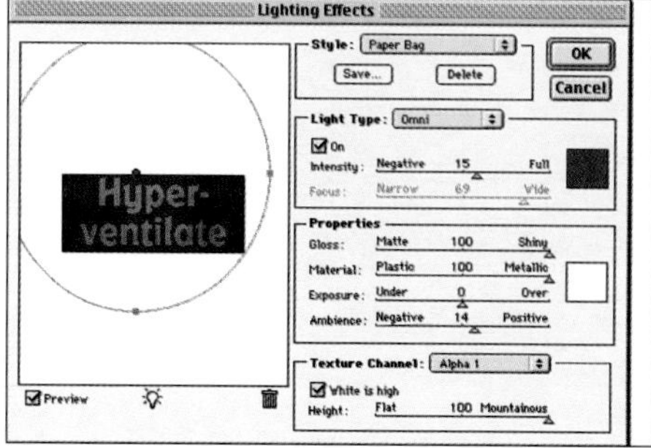


**3** Now, here's the magic step. Choose Filter➡Render➡Lighting Effects and choose Paper Bag from the Style menu, or match the settings as seen in this figure.

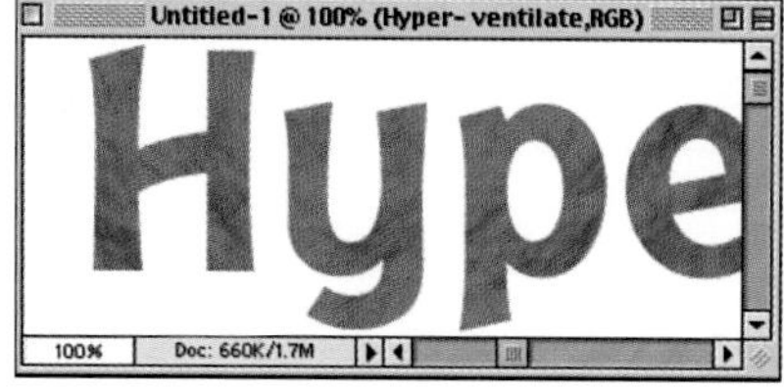


Click OK, and you are ready for lunch.



**TOOLBOX**

Paper Bag (Lighting Effects Style)

**4** Okay, maybe not before a little fine-tuning. Choose Image➡Adjust➡Levels. Bring the black and white sliders to the edges of the Input histogram (as shown). Then slide the white Output slider to the left just enough to take the sheen off of the texture.

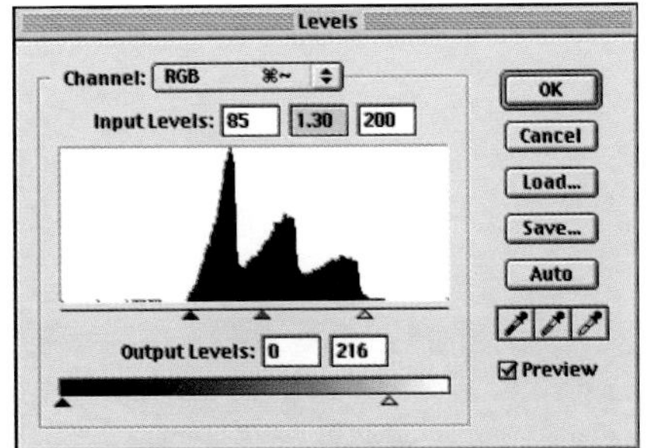


A shadow helped to set off the final image from the background.

Hyper-
ventilate

## Foil

By changing the color of the light in the Lighting Effects filter, you can use this same technique to create foil. Click on the Light Color box and set the values to CMYK: 27, 12, 15, 1.

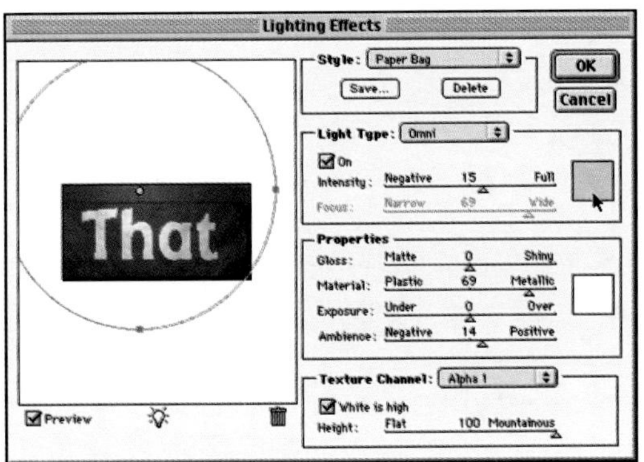

**To fine tune the Foil, choose Image➡Adjust➡Brightness/Contrast and raise the Contrast to about 40.** ●

This technique demonstrates how to create patterns by duplicating layers and using the Offset filter. You can use the pattern to fill any selection, including—what do you know!—type selections.

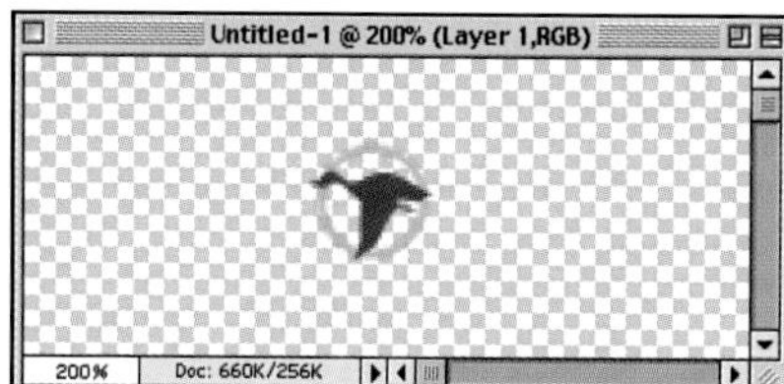


**1** Create a new file and create a new layer (Layer 1). Make the Background layer invisible. In the new layer, create a tile for the pattern. I used two of Photoshop 5.0's Assorted Brushes to create this tile. This tile is on the P5TM CD-ROM for you to use if you want. Open the file (P5TM➡P5TM files➡Patterns➡Duck Pattern), choose Select➡All, copy it, close the file, and paste in to Layer 1.

**TIP** **Making the Background layer invisible in Step 1 gives the pattern a transparent background. If you want the pattern to contain a background color, fill the Background layer with a color and keep it visible.**

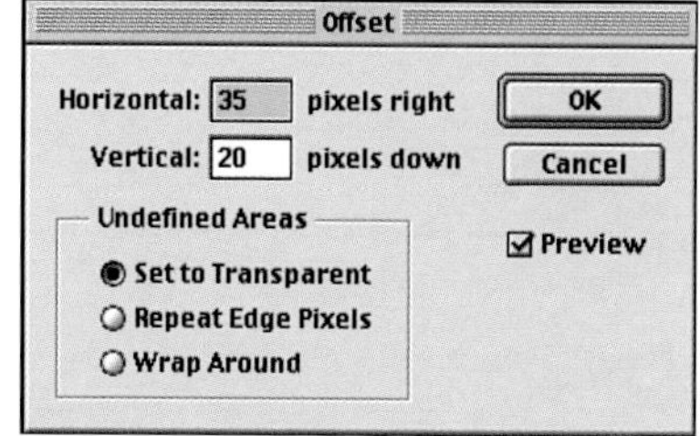


**2** Duplicate Layer 1 and choose Filter➡Other➡Offset. Make sure that the Preview is turned on and set the Horizontal (35 pixels) and Vertical (20 pixels) values so that the copied tile moves down and to the right of the original. Make sure that the Vertical value is high enough to move the second tile down a distance equal to or greater than half the height of the tile.

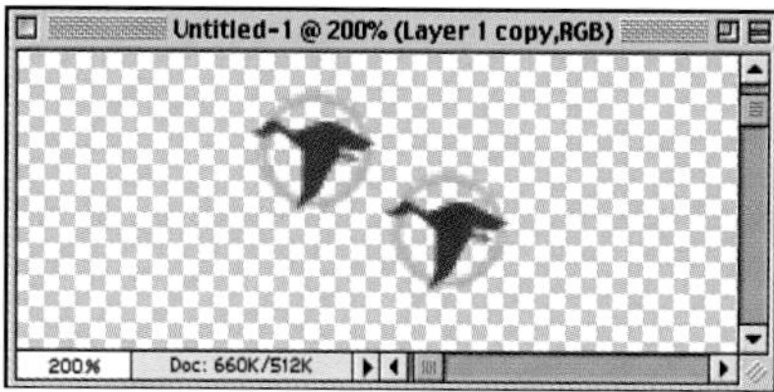




**TOOLBOX**

Duck Pattern

3 From the Layers palette menu, choose Merge Down. Then duplicate the merged layer.

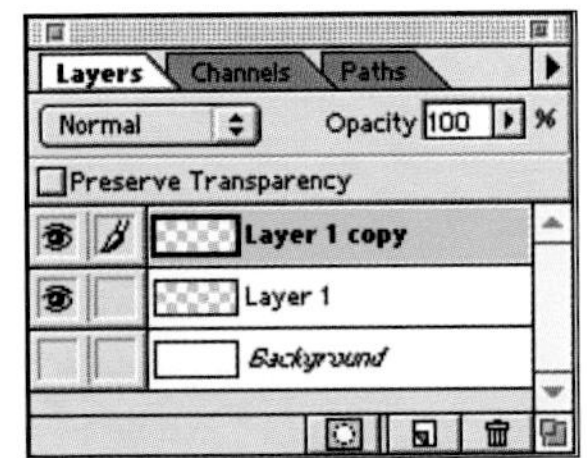


4 Press (Command-Option-F) [Control-Alt-F] to bring back the Offset filter dialog box. Set the Horizontal value to 0. Double the Vertical value.

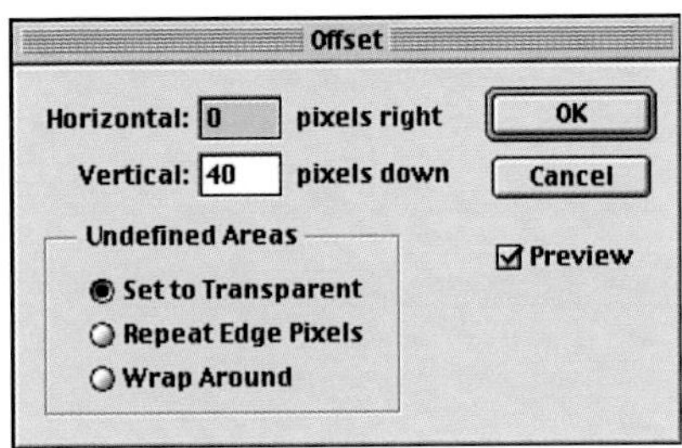


Watch the preview to make sure that the spacing looks good. Here's my design.

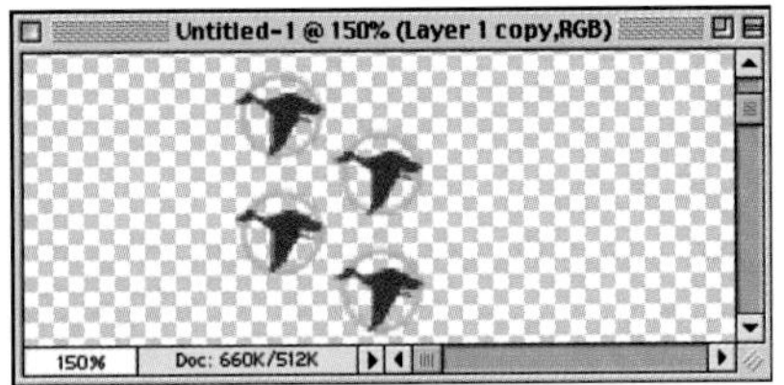


5 Double-click the Rectangular Marquee tool to select it and bring the Marquee Options palette to the front. On the palette, select the Fixed Size option and set the Width value to double the value used for the Horizontal Offset in Step 2. Set the Height to double the Vertical value used in Step 2.

Navigator Info Marquee Options
Feather: 0 pixels Anti-aliased
Style: Fixed Size
Width: 70 Height: 40 pixels

6 Click the Marquee tool once in the image area to place the fixed selection. Drag the selection into place so that the horizontal dimension extends to the outside of the two columns of tile images. Vertically, the top of selection should start somewhere just below the center of the original tile image.

Untitled-1 @ 200% (Layer 1 copy,RGB)
200%
Doc: 660K/512K

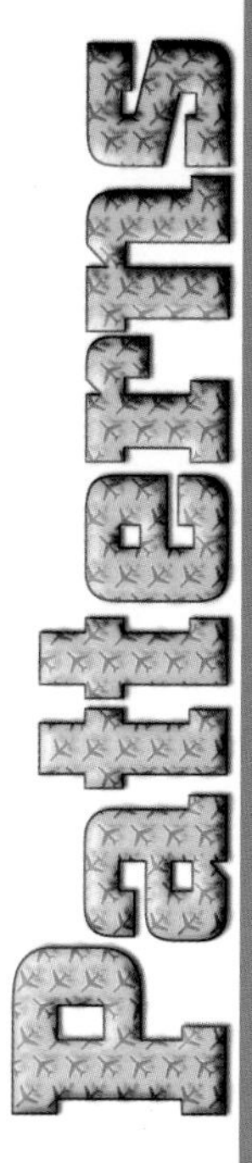

**7** Choose Edit➡Define Pattern. The pattern is now ready for use. Delete all layers except the Background layer. Deselect the selection.

**8** Choose a foreground color (CMYK: 25, 0, 50, 0) for the tile background, and use the Type tool to enter the text (Berthold City at 130 points). Choose Layer➡Type➡Render Layer.

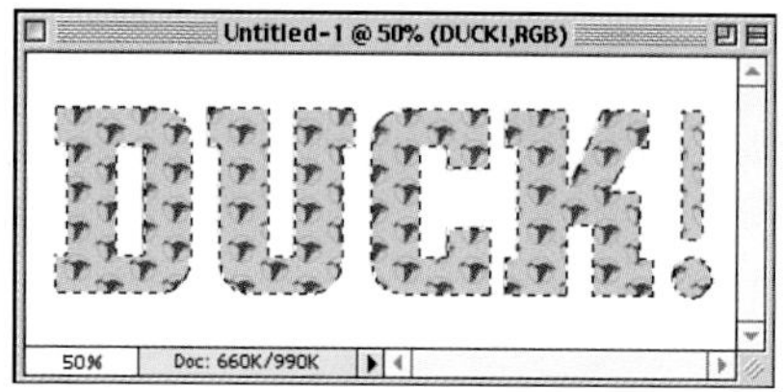


**9** Load the transparency selection of the type layer. Choose Edit➡Fill. Select Pattern from the Use pop-up menu (100%, Normal).

**10** I added a stroke (Edit➡Stroke) and a shadow (Layer➡Effects➡Drop Shadow) to finish the effect.

## VARIATIONS

### Floating Patterns

Do Steps 1 through 8 to define a pattern. If you want to use the pattern I used, open the Plane Pattern file from the CD-ROM (P5TM➡P5TM Files➡Patterns➡Plane Patterns). Then choose Select➡All and Edit➡Define Pattern before closing the file. Create a new file and do Step 8, then continue with the rest of the Floating Pattern steps.

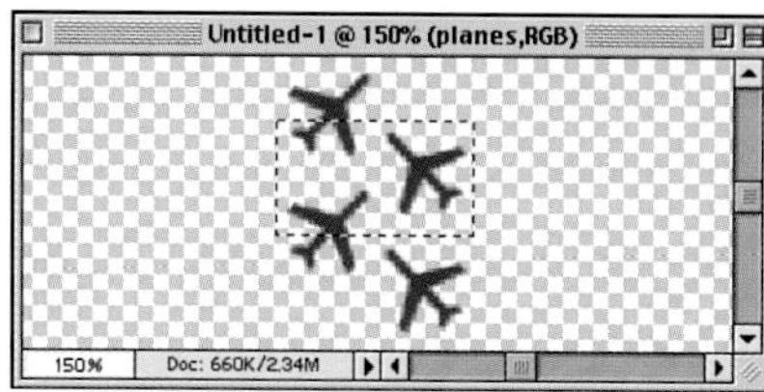


Before Step 9, create a new layer (Layer 1). Complete Step 9.

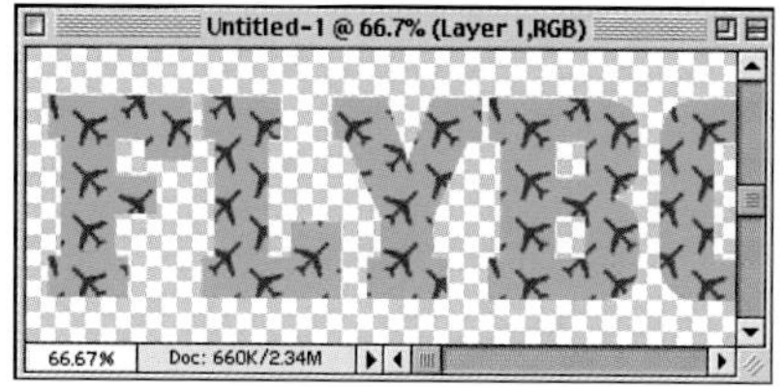

Photoshop's built-in Drop Shadow feature will not work here because the shadow needs to be contained within the type outlines. Create a new layer (Layer 2), move it beneath Layer 1, and load the transparency selection of Layer 1. Choose Select➡Feather (3 pixels) to soften the selection for the shadow. Choose a foreground color for the shadow (CMYK: 100, 100, 0, 60) and fill the selection. Then use the Move tool to nudge the shadow layer down and to the right.

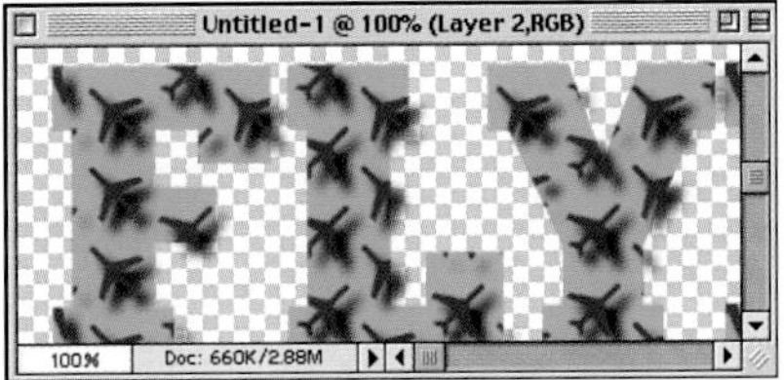


Load the transparency selection from the type layer, choose Select➡Inverse, and press Delete to get rid of the shadow areas that extended outside the borders of the type.

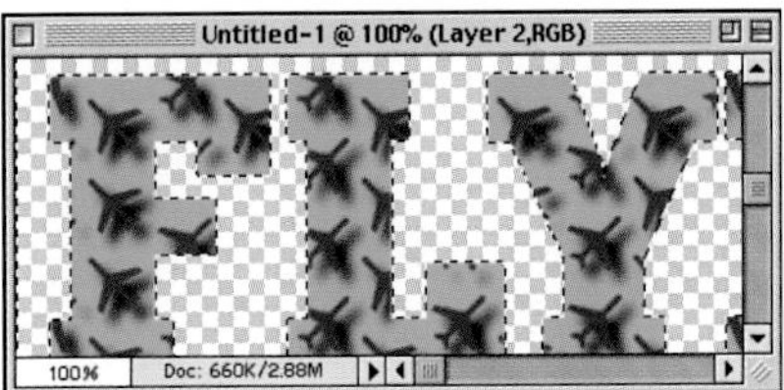


I added the stroke in Layer 1, but applied the drop shadow to the type layer.

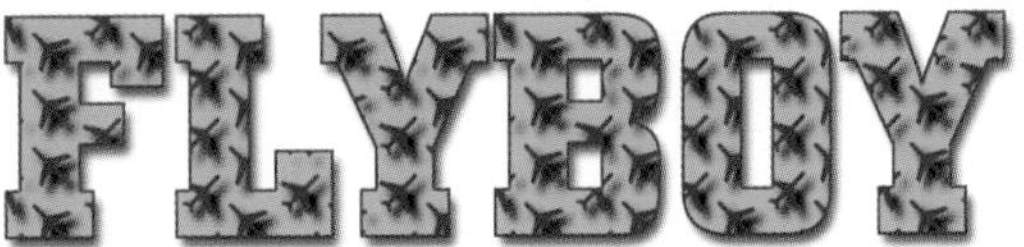


## Photoshop Patterns

There are a number of pattern tiles included with Photoshop 5.0. To use these patterns, open one of them (Photoshop 5.0➡Goodies➡Brushes and Patterns➡Postscript Patterns). Choose Select➡All and Edit➡Define Pattern. Then do Steps 8 through 10. These files create seamless patterns. I opened the Weave-Y pattern...

...and used it to fill this type.

# Peel-Away



**TOOLBOX**

KPT Page Curl 3.0

This is the only effect in the book that completely relies on a third-party plug-in—the KPT Page Curl 3.0 filter from MetaCreations. This technique will not work for all type, but it can be a nice addition in the right cases. Here are some guidelines for using this filter with type:

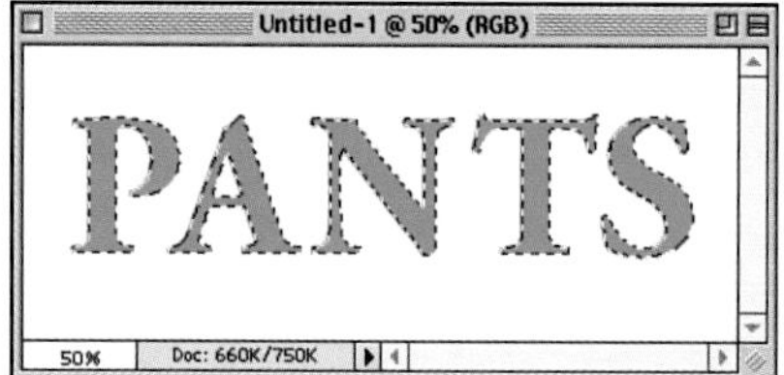


**1** Create a new file and use the Type Mask tool to enter the text (Adobe Garamond Bold at 100 points). Choose a foreground color for the type (CMYK: 100, 0, 50, 0) and fill the selection. Then save the selection (Alpha 1).

**2** Choose a background color to be placed beneath the upturned corners (CMYK: 0, 0, 100, 40). Choose the same color as the background if you don't want any color to appear below the corner.

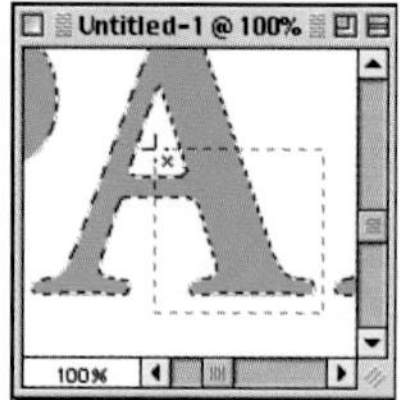

**3** If the type is not already selected, load the Alpha 1 channel selection and then select the Rectangular Marquee tool. The filter does all the work for you in this effect, but you need to make the right selection to get the results that you want. Hold the (Option) [Alt] and Shift keys, and drag the Rectangular Marquee tool to make a selection that is as tall as you want the curl to be and includes the part of the letter that the curl will extend over. Make a selection like this. Holding the (Option) [Alt] and Shift keys intersects the new selection with the existing selection.

**4** The top of the curl will be in the upper-right corner of the selection. Or depending on the selection that you make, in the imaginary top right corner—where the right most and uppermost edges of the selection meet. And the filter curls about one-fourth of the horizontal dimension of the selection.

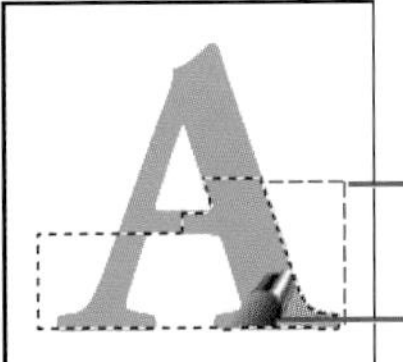

Imaginary top right corner

One-fourth of the horizontal dimension of the selection

**5** Hold the Shift key and drag a rectangle to include any part of the area to the left of the curl that you want to include. Adding this selection gives the Page Curl filter somewhere to place the shadow cast by the curl. It also affects the horizontal dimension of the curl—the further this selection extends to the left, the further the curl will extend to the left.

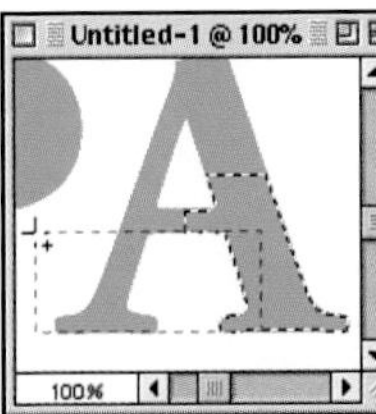


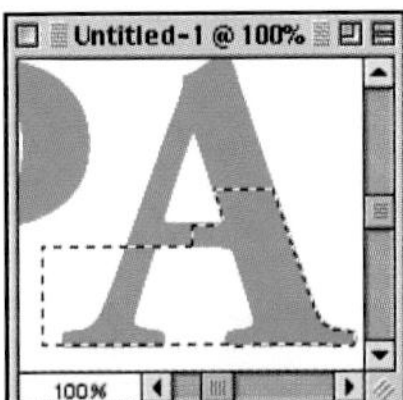


**6** Choose Filter➡KPT 3.0➡KPTPage Curl 3.0. Press (Command-E) [Control-E] to change all the settings to their defaults. There are various settings that you can play with here, but I am going to stick to the basics.

**7** Press (Return) [Enter] to apply the filter.

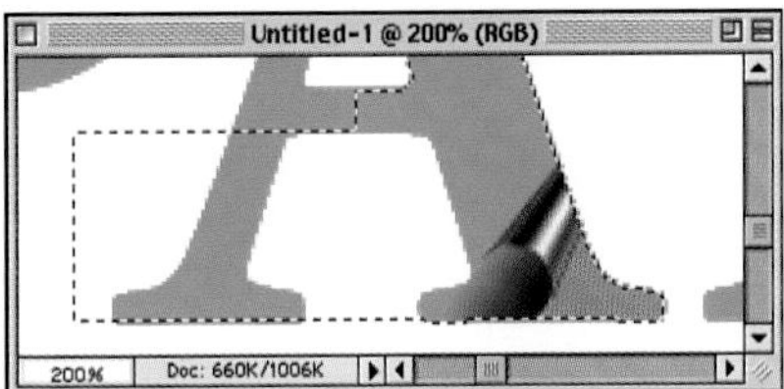

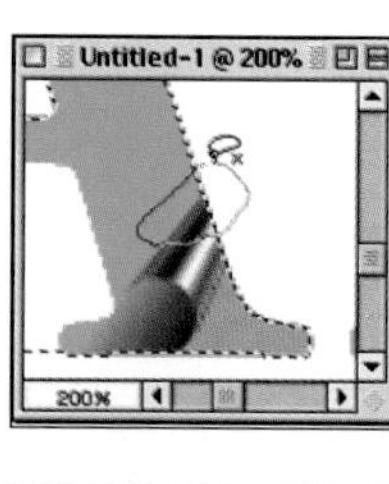


**8** If you don't like the way that the curl lines up with the right edge of the letter, select the Lasso tool and hold the (Option) [Alt] and Shift keys while circling the area that you do not want to be part of the curl, like this:

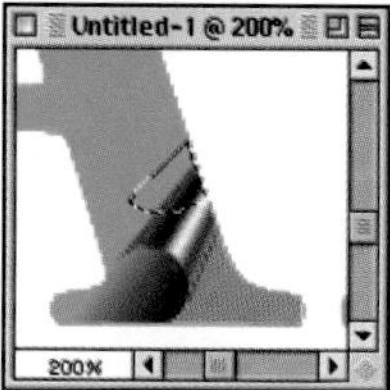


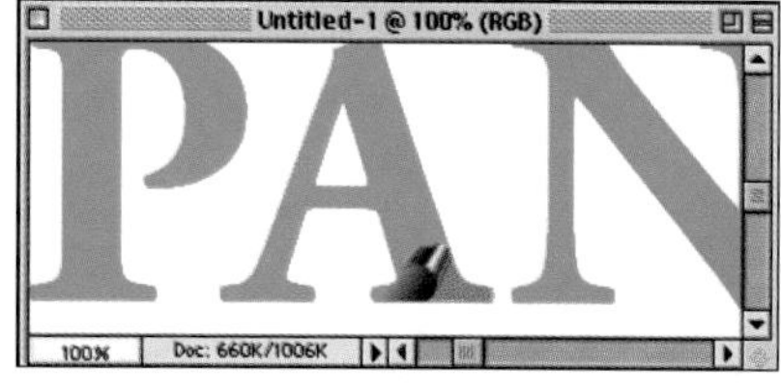


**9** Then fill the selection with the color of the type. With proper selecting, you can make the curl look like the shape of the serif.

PANTS

**10** Repeat Steps 3 through 9 to peel the corners of all the letters.

## VARIATIONS

### Darken

After Step 7, press (Command-F) [Control-F] to reapply the filter and make a darker curl and shadow.

A

### Colorize

Load the Alpha 1 channel selection, and choose 50% gray for the foreground color. Choose Select➡Color Range and use the Fuzziness slider to select as much of the curls as you can without selecting the type. A Fuzziness setting of 80 worked well for this example.

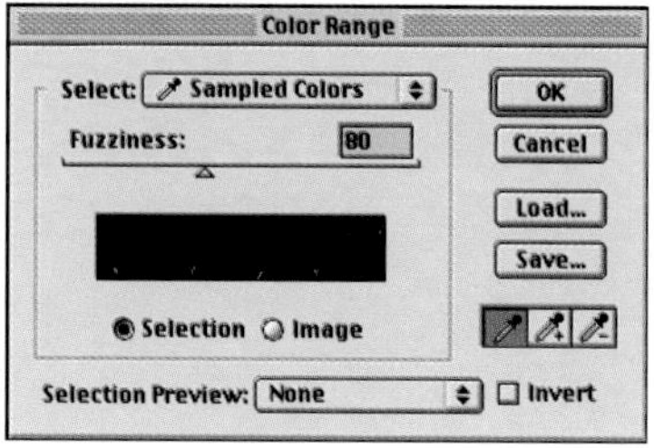

Choose Image➡Adjust➡Hue/Saturation, check the Colorize box, raise the Saturation to 100, and use the Hue slider to find a color.

## Top Curls

The Page Curl filter enables you to make curls in any direction. Make a selection.

Then after changing the filter settings to their defaults in Step 6, click on one of the curls around the border of the preview to choose an alternate direction. ●

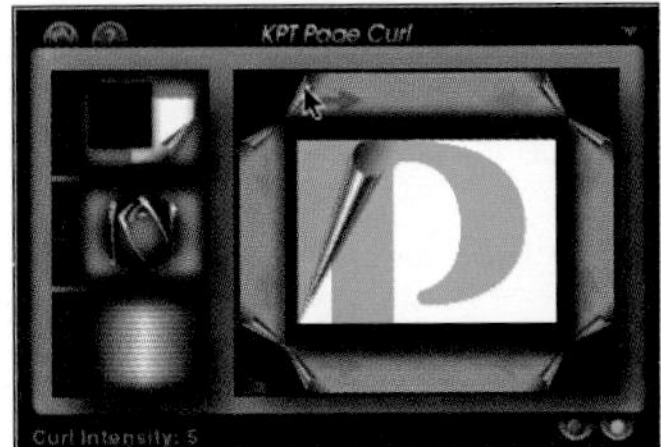

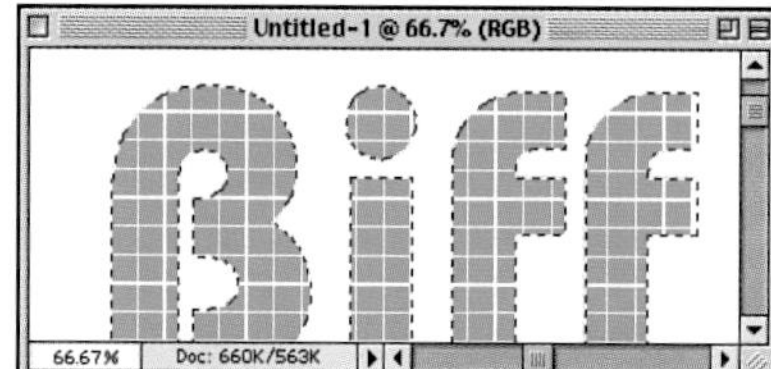


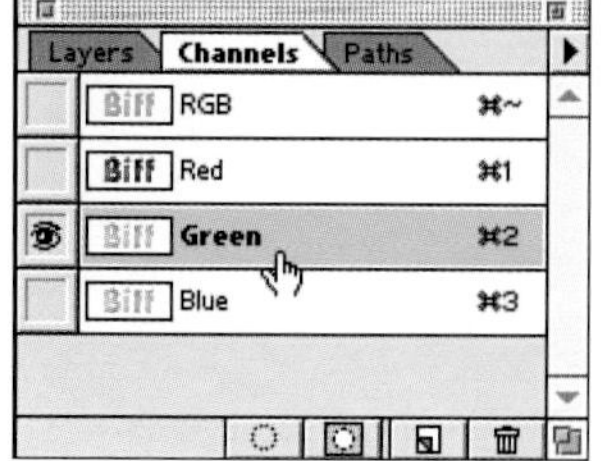


This effect works by combining four Photoshop filters (Fragment, Mosaic, Tile, and Facet) to make different plaids. I found that the following method works the best.

**1** First, create a new file. Choose a foreground color for the color of the type, and then use the Type Mask tool to enter the text into a layer. I used 90-point Bauhaus type. Fill it with the foreground color.

**2** Keep the selection active and choose Filter➡Stylize➡Tiles (Number of Tiles: 10; Maximum Offset: 1%). The Number of Tiles controls the number of vertical tiles that will be in your tallest letter. You can change the number of tiles, but keep the maximum offset at 1% so the grids lines are straight.

**3** Now, go to the Channels palette, and click on one of the color channels to make it the only active channel. I made the Green channel the active channel. The tiled type looks gray because you are only viewing one color channel.

TIP **You can choose any color channel. Each produces the same effect but displays different colors. You can also make two color channels active. The effect still works the same but again produces different colors.**

**4** Choose Filter➡Pixelate➡ Fragment. This filter divides the type into smaller segments. Because the information in all three color channels (Red, Green, and Blue) is mixed together to determine the colors that you see in the composite image, altering one of the color channels affects the color in the composite image. The Fragment filter does this by shifting the white areas (created by the Tiles filter) of only one of the channels (the Green channel in this case).

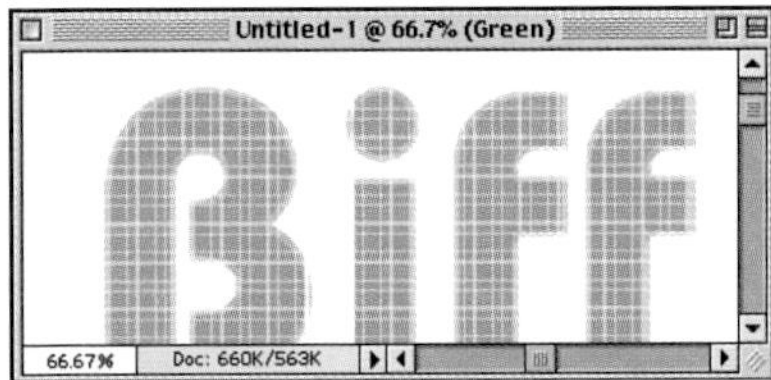


**5** Now, for the magic. Press (Command-~) [Control-~] to return to the composite channel—instant plaid waits for you. Using the Fragment filter to shift the pixels of only one color channel produced new colors in the composite image.

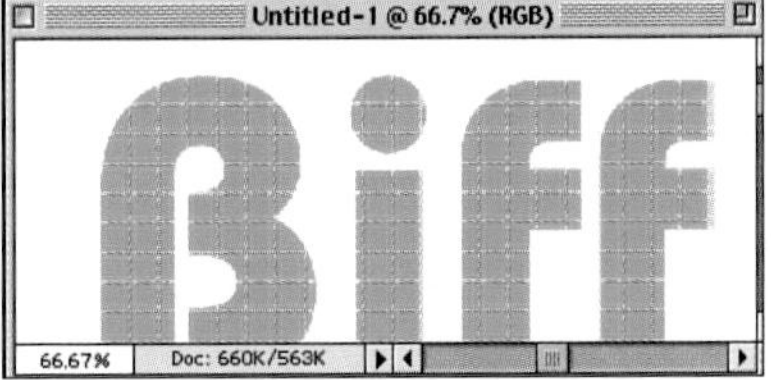


**6** To change the colors of the plaid, choose Image➡Adjust➡ Hue/Saturation and use the Hue slider to run through a closet full of plaids.

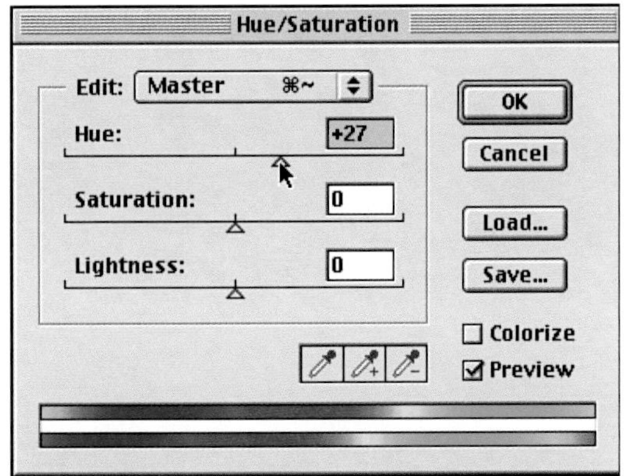


Here's the final type.

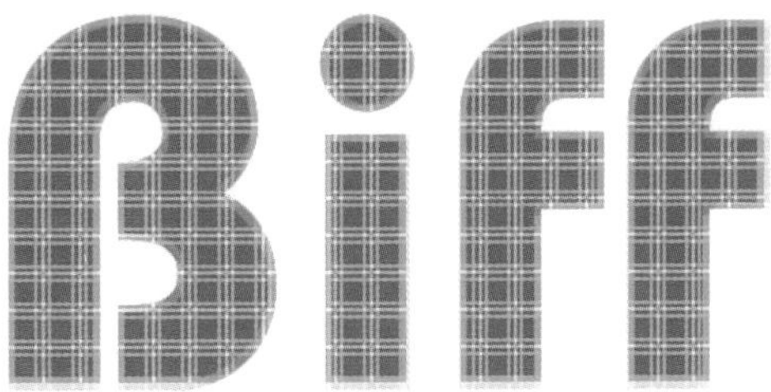

Muffy

Chip

Buffy

Theodore

Jock

## VARIATIONS

The possibilities are endless. Here is a selection of plaids I made by applying just one more filter after completing Step 6:

Select the Red channel and choose Filter➥Other➥Maximum (Radius: 2).

Or, try choosing Filter➥Pixelate➥Fragment. Keep applying the filter until the plaid glows.

Try Filter➥Pixelate➥Facet, and reapply the filter (Command-F) [Control-F] a few times.

Here's what happens with Filter➥Stylize➥Find Edges applied several times.

Or choose only one color channel. (I chose the Green channel.) Choose Filter➥Stylize➥Find Edges, and apply the filter a second time (Command-F) [Control-F].

## Add Some Texture

Keep the type selection active and choose Filter➡Render➡Lighting Effects. Use the settings shown here, or choose the Plaid preset from the Style pop-up menu. The most important setting is the texture channel. Choose one of the RGB channels. After you press OK, the plaid looks like it has some texture.

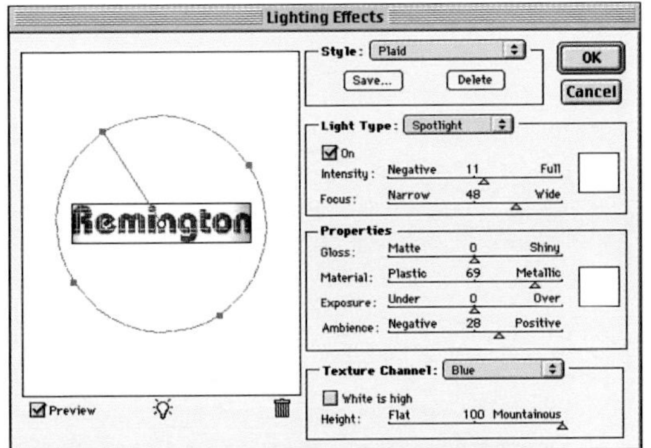


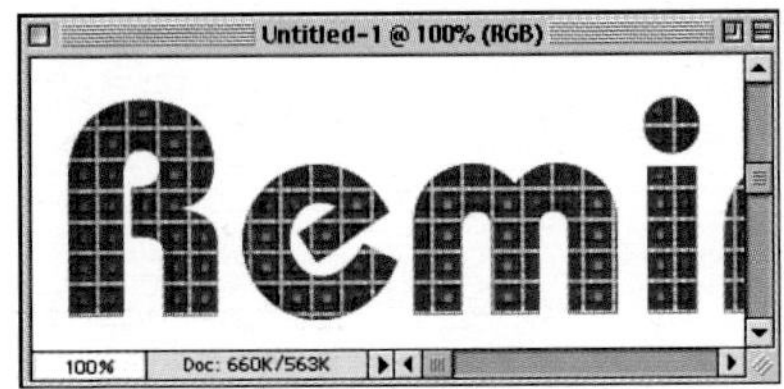


## Monochrome Plaid

For a monochrome plaid with thick and thin cross lines, complete Steps 1 and 2; then choose Filter➡Pixelate➡Mosaic. Watch the preview to find a Cell Size that gives you the desired effect. A Cell Size of 4 worked for me.

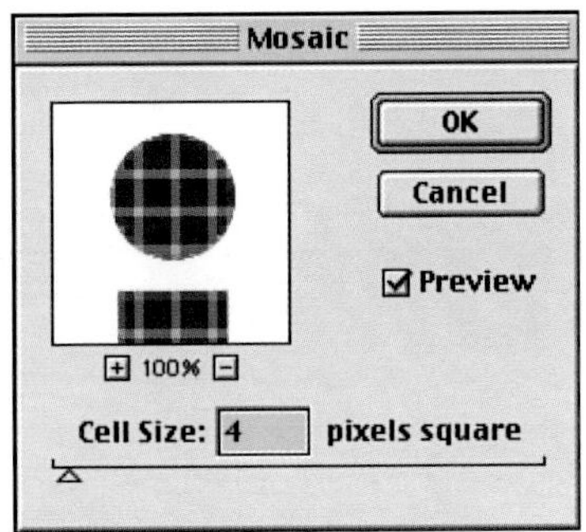


## One More Road to Plaid

Complete Steps 1 through 3. Then choose Filter➡Pixelate➡Mosaic (Cell Size: 6). Return to the composite channel to see something like this. ●

Several software companies produce great plug-ins that you can add to Photoshop's Filter menu. This means that you, the type magician, can produce sophisticated effects by simply adjusting a few sliders. The following pages demonstrate the capabilities of some of the most popular and powerful plug-ins.

## Eye Candy 3.0

There are 21 filters in this set from Alien Skin Software (`http://www.alienskin.com`), formerly known as the Black Box, ranging from shadows and glows to glass and fire. The interface contains a generous preview and all the controls to adjust almost every aspect of each effect. Here is the interface for the Glass filter.

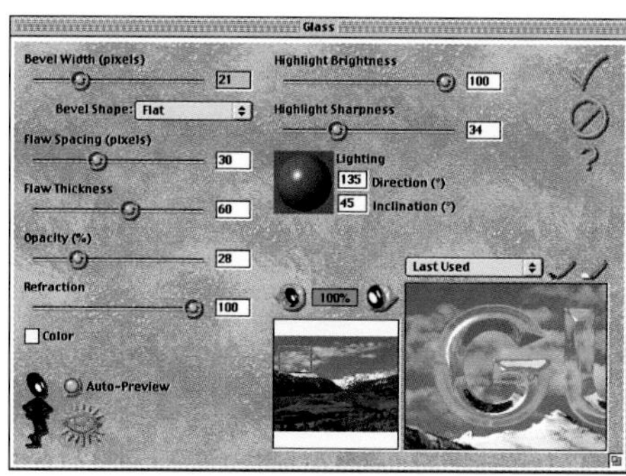


And a few effects.

GUMMY

### Inner Bevel

### Glass

GUMMY

### Fur

### Fire

## HotTEXT

This plug-in from Vertigo Technology (`http://www.vertigo3d.com`) is a fully featured 3D text machine. Not only can you create 3D text, but this plug-in enables you to also place the text on a path, choose lighting options, and map images onto the surface. It is powerful, but be forewarned that it will take some RAM to run it and some practice to master it. Here is the interface.

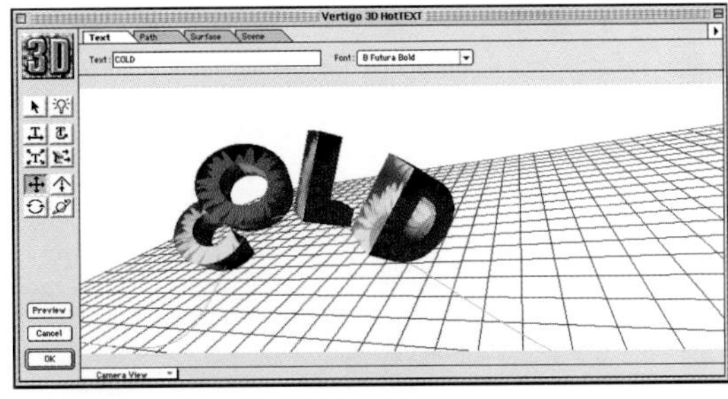


And a few examples.

## Kai's Power Tools (KPT)

This set of plug-ins from MetaCreations (`http://www.metatools.com`) has been around for awhile for good reason. You can create an endless variety of textures and gradients through an interface that is intuitive and friendly. The Page Curl filter was already demonstrated in the Peel-Away effect. Besides the effects shown here, KPT 3.0 includes a number of filters for less exotic effects that improve the standard Photoshop tools. Here is the Texture Explorer interface...

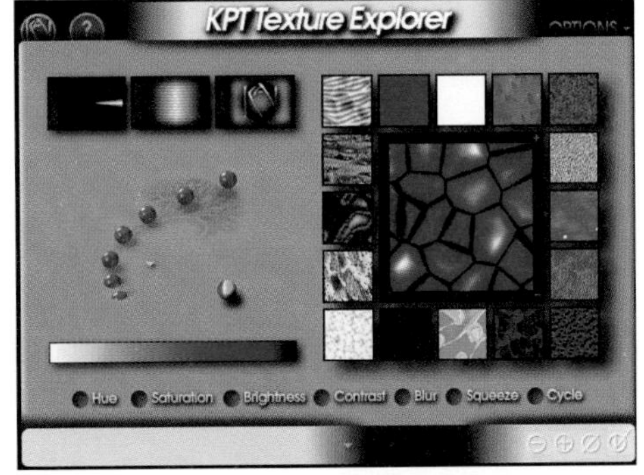

...and some of the effects from that and from other plug-ins in the set.

Texture Explorer

Gradient Designer

Spheroid Designer
(Text rendered using the Balls technique (See Page 28) with an Outer Beveled layer effect applied.)

## Andromeda Series Filters

Six plug-in packages are available from Andromeda Software (`http://www.andromeda.com`). Each concentrates on a different aspect of image creation and manipulation. Series I contains a variety of imaging effects such as the Star filter that provides one more way to add highlights to your type.

The Techtures Filter (Series 4) does more than apply textures. It can map its library of textures to your type and contains other environment effects such as smoke and lightning. This set offers a great variety of textures. Here is the interface.

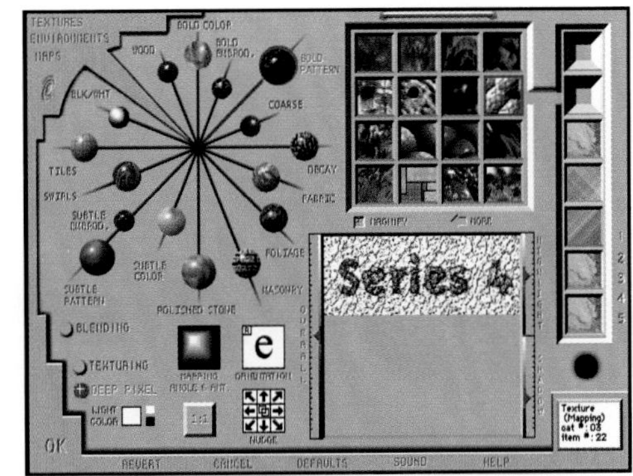


And here's a type image with a texture mapped to its surface.

The Andromeda Shadow Filter is a filter for—surprise!—creating shadows. It does a great job with casting perspective shadows because it enables you to control every aspect of the shadow. It even gradually increases the blur of the shadow as it recedes. ●

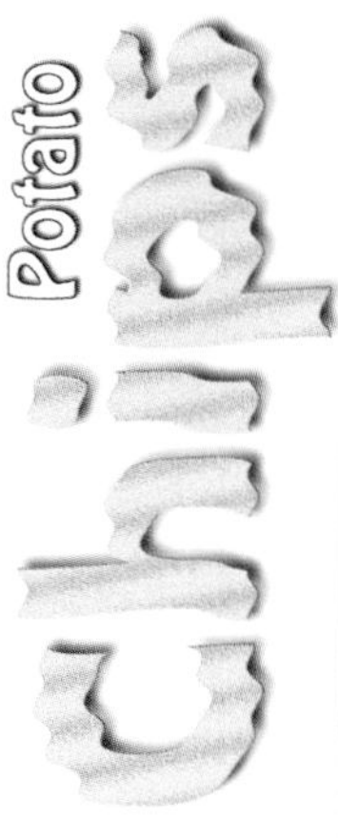


Use a displacement map to make the waves, the Lighting Effects filter to create the texture, and the Curves dialog box to add the shadows and you have a tasty midafternoon snack.

1 Open the Chipsmap.dis file from the P5TM CD (P5TM CD-ROM➥P5TM Files➥Displacement Maps➥Chipsmap.dis).

2 Choose Select➥All, copy the image, and close the file.

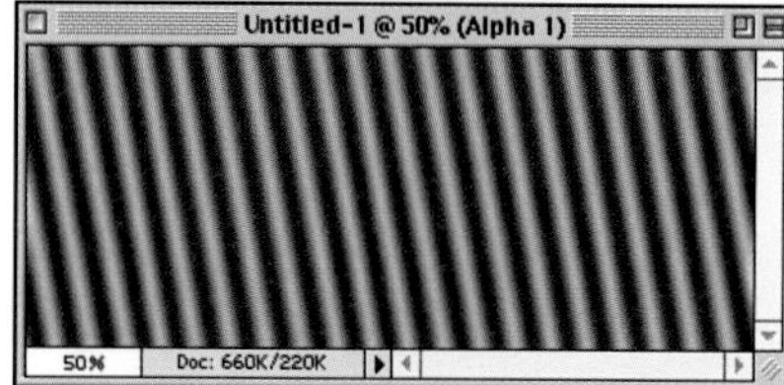


3 Create a new RGB file, create a new channel (Alpha 1), and paste in the image. Deselect the selection.

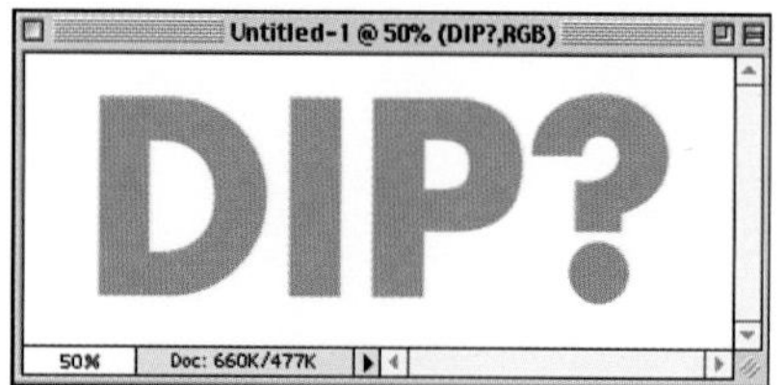


4 Return to the composite channel and set the foreground color to CMYK: 0, 0, 100, 40. Then use the Type tool to enter the text into a new layer (Futura Bold at 130 points). Choose Layer➥Type➥Render Layer.

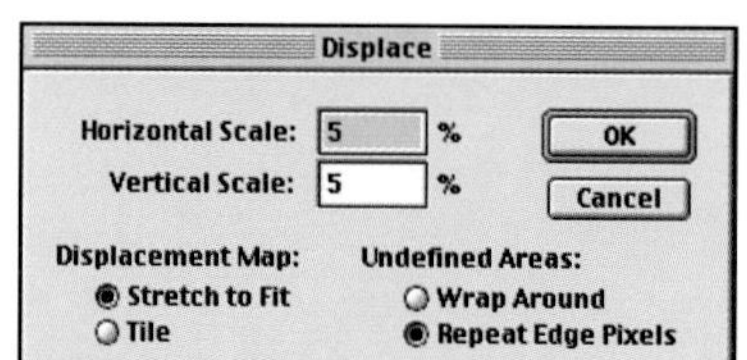


5 Choose Filter➥Distort➥Displace (Horizontal Scale: 5%, Vertical Scale 5%, Stretch to Fit, Repeat Edge Pixels). Click OK.

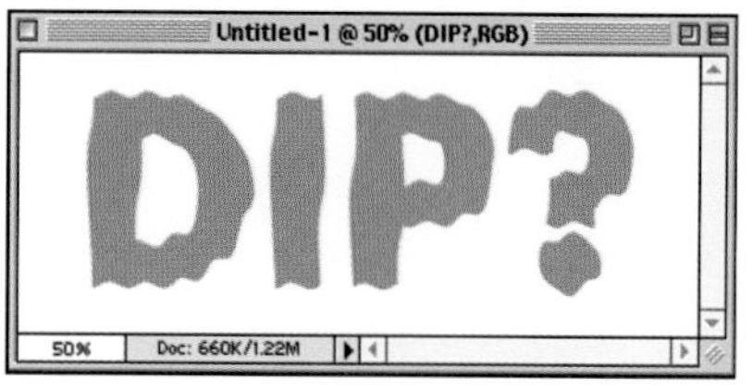


Another dialog box opens asking you to find a displacement map. Find P5TM CD-ROM➥P5TM Files➥Displacement Maps➥Chipsmap.dis and click Open. This filter creates the waves around the edges of the type.

## TOOLBOX

Chipsmap.dis (displacement map)

Chips (Lighting Effects Style)

**6** To add shadows to the ridges, load the selection from the Alpha 1 channel and choose Image➥Adjust➥Curves. Grab the center of the diagonal line in the grid and bend the curve upward about this far.

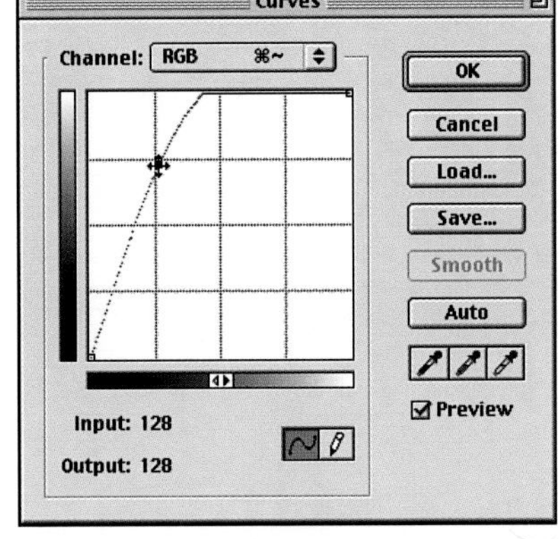


Click OK and deselect the selection to get this effect.

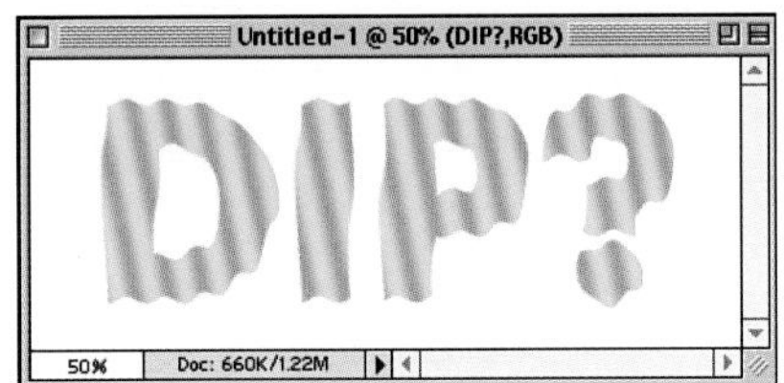


**7** Create a new layer (Layer 1) for the shadow and move the layer below the type layer.

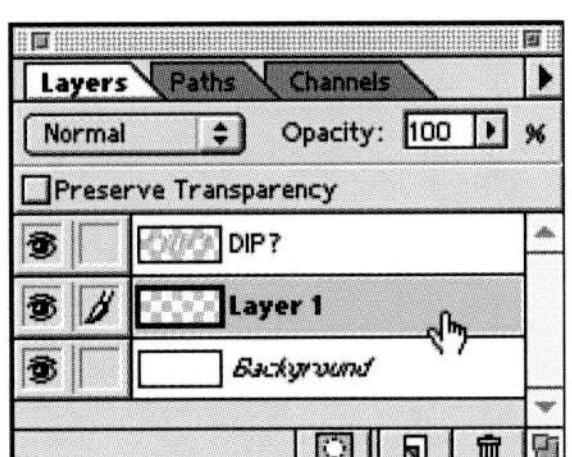


**8** Load the transparency selection from the type layer; then subtract from that selection the selection from the Alpha 1 channel. Choose Select➥Feather (5 pixels). Set the foreground color to black and fill the selection to create a shadow that accentuates the ridges by varying the lights and darks.

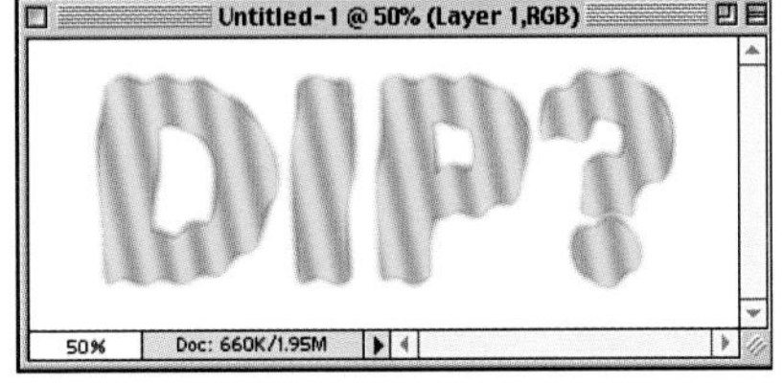


**9** Deselect the selection. Select the Move tool and nudge the shadow down and to the right by using the arrow keys. I pressed each key three times.

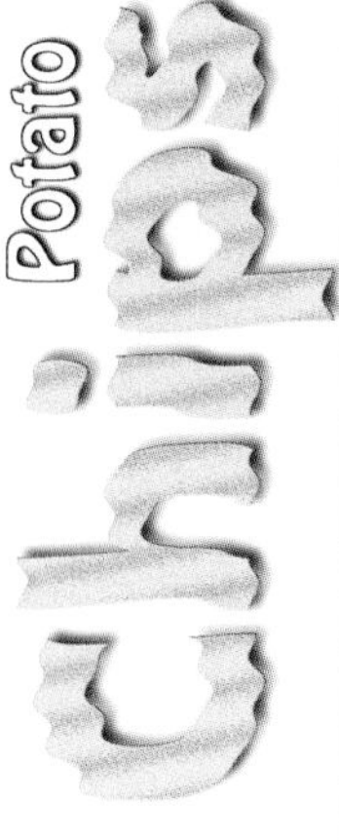


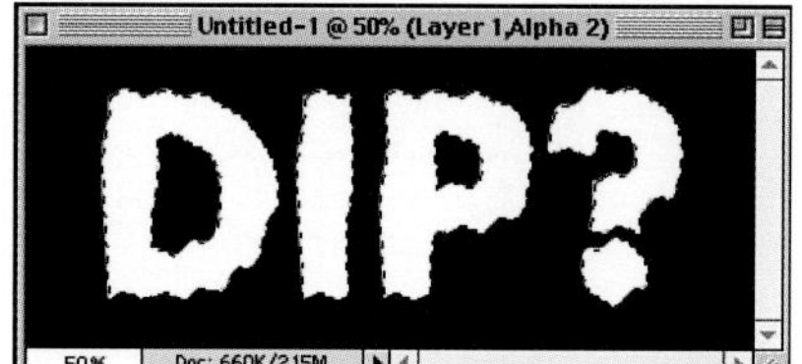


**10** Load the transparency selection of the type layer and save it as a new channel (Alpha 2). Make the new channel (Alpha 2) the active channel.

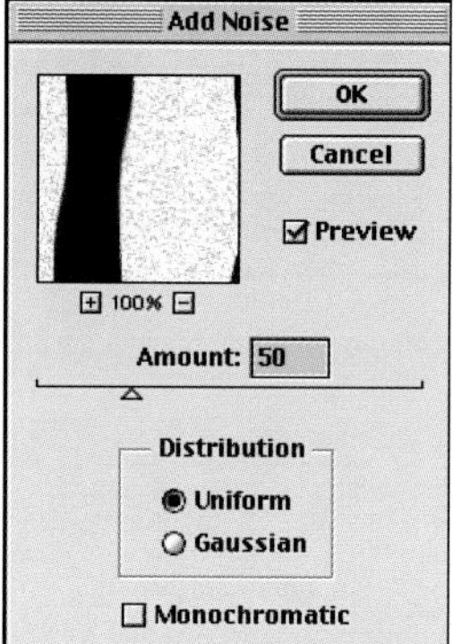


**11** Choose Filter➥Noise➥Add Noise. Try these settings to add a small amount of noise that the Lighting Effects filter can use to create some texture on the surface of the chips (Amount: 35, Uniform).

**12** Deselect the selection, return to the composite channel, and make the type layer the active layer. This is the layer that was created in Step 4 by the Type tool.

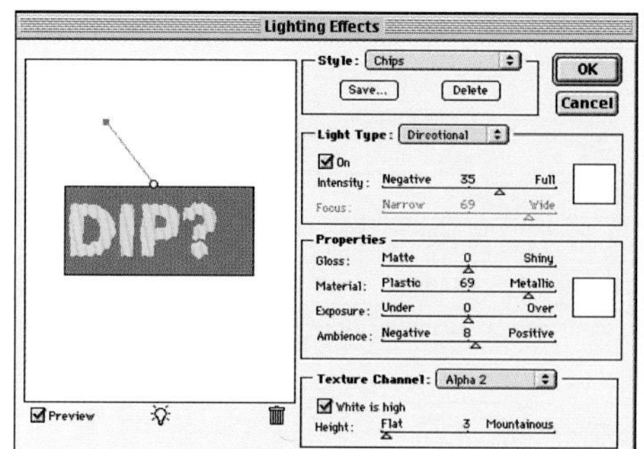


**13** Choose Filter➥Render➥Lighting Effects. Select the Chips preset style or match the settings seen here. Keep the texture amount low so this filter creates just a little roughness on the surface—not moon craters.

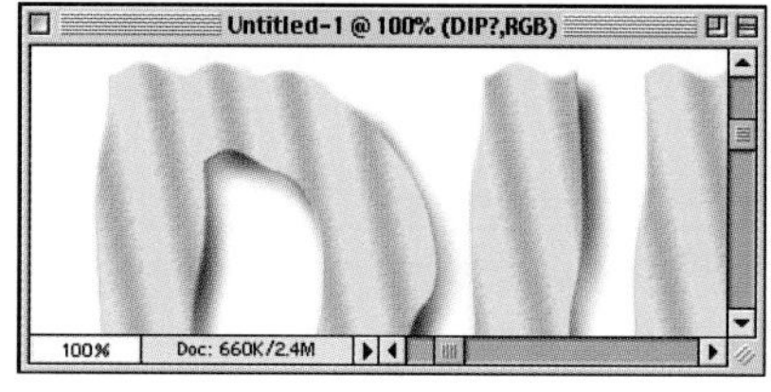

**14** Finally, add a little noise to roughen the surface a little more. Choose Filter➡Noise➡Add Noise (Amount: 25, Uniform, Monochromatic).

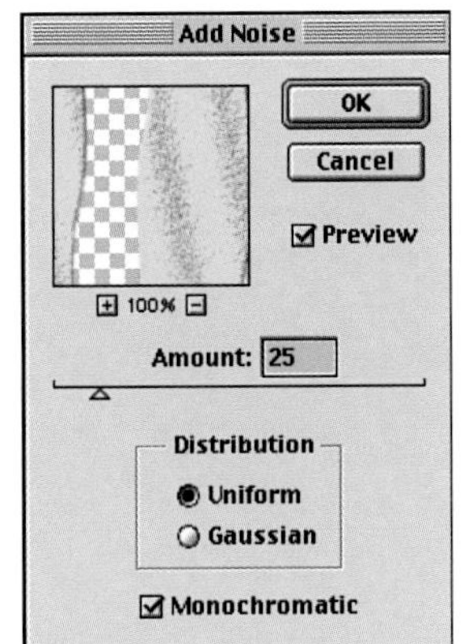

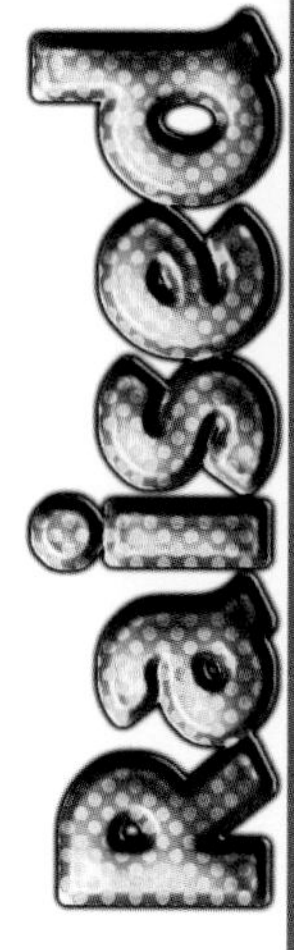

You can now create great embossed and beveled type with Photoshop 5.0's new layer effects features, and you can edit it! But if you want more dramatic raised type effects, try these techniques that use the Lighting Effects filter. For credit-cardlike type, see page ?? for an effect that modifies the built-in Emboss layer effect.

## Plastic

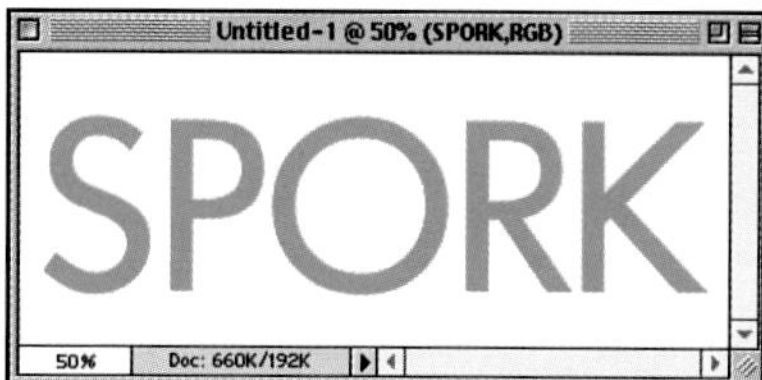


**1** Create a new file and choose a foreground color for the type (CMYK: 50, 0, 100, 0). Then use the Type tool to enter the text. I used Donata at 120 points. It will automatically be placed on a new layer. Choose Layer➡Type➡Render Layer.

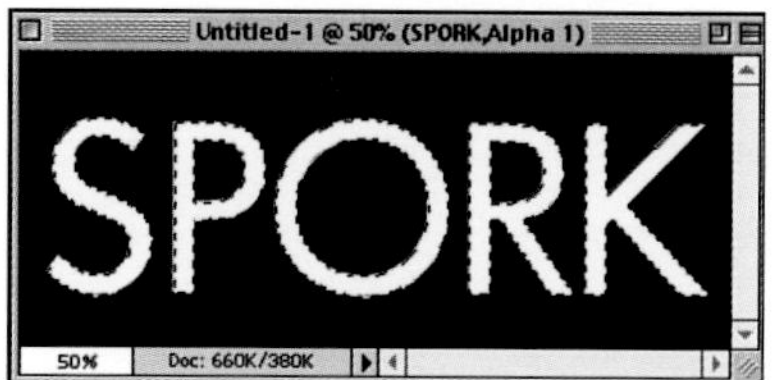


**2** Load the transparency selection of the new layer, create a new channel (Alpha 1), and fill the selection with white.

**3** Keep the selection active and choose Filter➡Blur➡Gaussian Blur. The blur causes the type to be rounded when used as a texture channel with the Lighting Effects filter. The amount of blur affects the shape of the type. All you want is a little gray around the edges. Try 5 pixels.

**TOOLBOX**

Plastic (Lighting Effects Style)

License Plate (Lighting Effects Style)

**4** Return to the composite channel and deselect the selection. Choose Filter➥Render➥Lighting Effects. This filter does the work. Select the Plastic preset style or match the settings seen in this figure. The texture channel should be the channel created in Step 2 (Alpha 1).

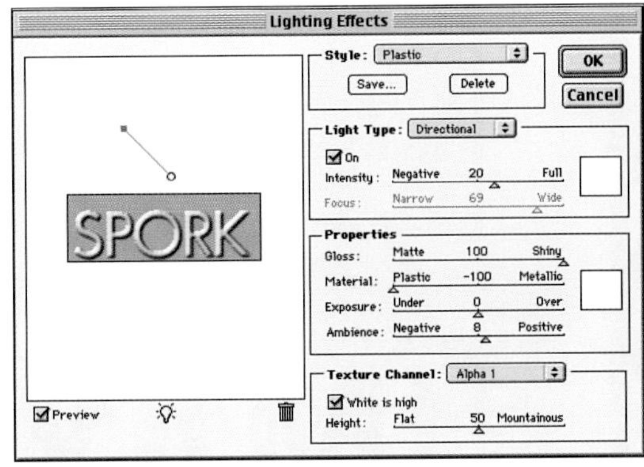


And the result.

**Pay attention to the settings in the Lighting Effects dialog box. This effect looks plastic because of the settings used. Vary the settings in the Properties box to adjust the character of the raised type.**

## License Plate

Here is a slight variation that has some fun with the basic Plastic technique.

**1** Begin this effect on a white layer and use the Type Mask tool to enter the text (Helvetica Condensed Bold at 85 points). Save the selection as the Alpha 1 channel.

**2** While the selection is still active, choose Select➥Modify➥Contract (1 pixel), Select➥Modify➥Smooth (2 pixels), and Select➥Feather (1 pixel). This softens the edges of the colored portion of the type.

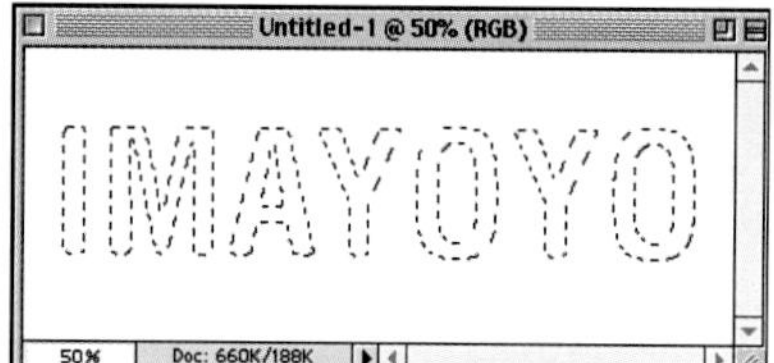


**3** It seems like they never quite get the paint to sit directly on top of the raised metal letters. To replicate this effect, select the Marquee tool and use the arrow keys to nudge the selection slightly (two keystrokes to the left, and one keystroke up).

**4** Choose a foreground color for the type (CMYK: 0, 100, 100, 40) and fill the selection. Deselect the selection.

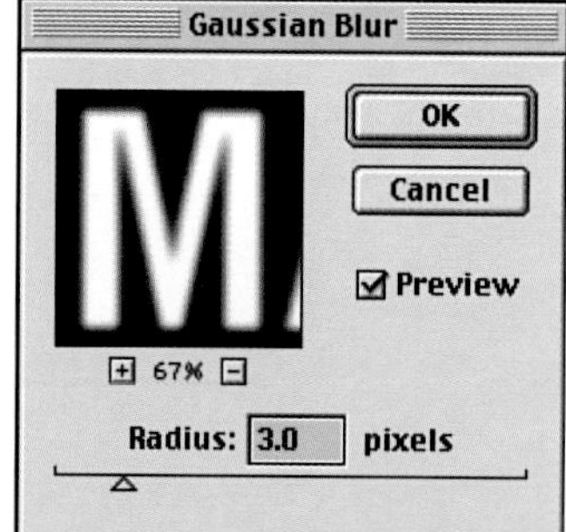


**5** Make the Alpha 1 channel active. Choose Filter➡Blur➡Gaussian Blur and set the Gaussian Blur Radius to 3 pixels.

**6** Then load the selection of the Alpha 1 channel (the same channel that is active). Press (Command-Option-F) [Control-Alt-F] to bring back the Gaussian Blur dialog box. Slide the Radius marker up until dark patches appear near the tips of the letters. I set the Radius at 9 pixels.

**7** While the selection is still active, choose Image➡Adjust➡Invert to invert the type.

**8** Then choose Image➥Adjust➥Brightness/Contrast and slide the Brightness slider up until your type looks something like what you see in the figure. I raised the Brightness all the way to +100, chose Image➥Adjust➥Brightness/Contrast again, and set the Brightness at +25. All this channel fuss produces a raised type that has a slight indentation in the center of the letters.

**9** Return to the composite channel and deselect the selection. Choose Filter➥Render➥Lighting Effects. Use the License Plate preset style or match the settings in this figure.

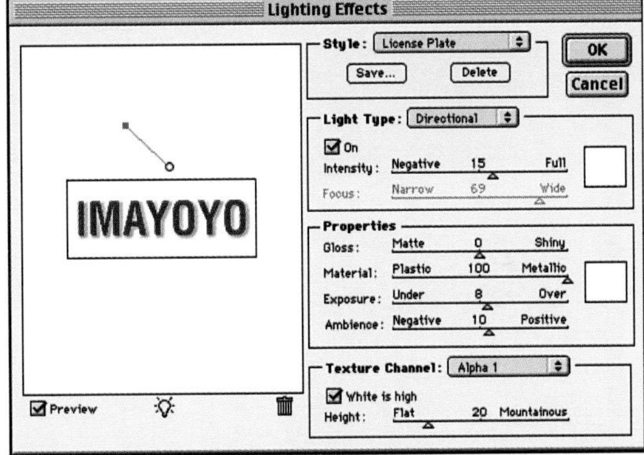


The final type.

# Credit Card

**1** Start this one with a background image for the credit card. I opened the 072 Plant image from the Photo 24 collection on the CD-ROM (P5TM➥Images➥Photo 24➥Plants➥072), copied it, and pasted it into a new image file.

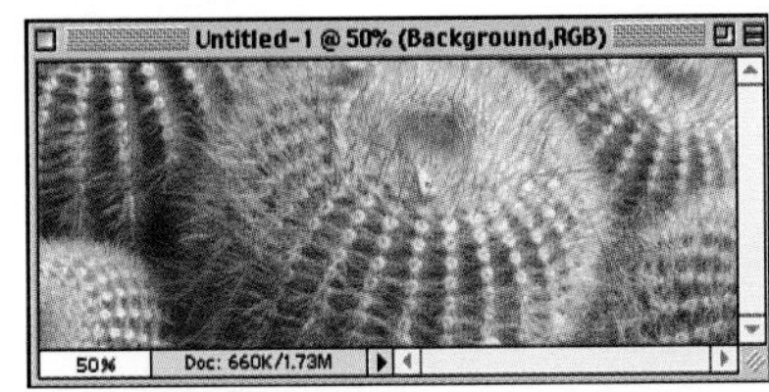


**2** Choose a foreground color that is darker than the color you will use for the type (CMYK: 50, 0, 100, 40). Then use the Type tool to enter the text. The typeface is important for this one; OCR-B is a perfect credit card typeface. I set it at 36 points. Choose Layer➥Type➥Render Layer.

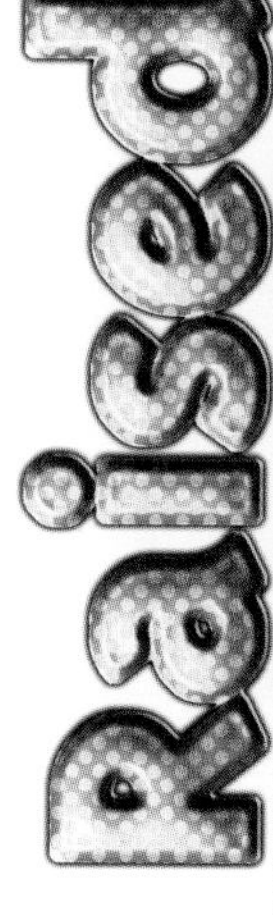

**3** Create a new layer (Layer 1) and load the selection of the type layer. Choose Select➥Modify➥Contract. If your type is as small as mine, you can probably only contract the type 1 pixel before you start to lose the letters. Then choose Select➥Feather (1 pixel). Choose a foreground color for the type and fill the selection.

**4** Deselect the selection and make the original type layer the active layer. Choose Layer➥Effects➥Bevel and Emboss. Set the Style to Outer Bevel and raise the Depth all the way to 20 pixels.

**If you link the two top layers together by making one of them active and clicking in the box to the left of the other on the Layers palette, you can move the raised type around the background and the bevel automatically adjusts to its new position.**

## VARIATIONS

SPORK

For slightly more complex highlights and shadows, complete the Plastic version on page 146 and then choose Layer➥Effects➥Bevel and Emboss. Select the Inner Bevel option and change the Shadow mode to Overlay (Angle: 120°, Depth: 10 pixels, Down, Blur: 5 pixels).

The most crucial element of all the raised type effects is creating the channel used by the Lighting Effects filter as a texture map. Try this one.

In a new file, create a new channel (Alpha 1). Use the Type Mask tool to enter the text. I used Triplex at 150 points. Save the selection to create the Alpha 2 channel. Fill the selection with white and deselect the selection. Choose Filter➥Blur➥Gaussian Blur (5 pixels), load the selection of the Alpha 1 channel, and press (Command-Option-F) [Control-Alt-F] to bring back the Gaussian Blur dialog box. Raise the Radius to approximately 25 pixels. Here is the channel.

Return to the composite channel, choose a foreground color for the type (CMYK: 0, 75, 100, 0), and fill the layer. Choose Filter➥Render➥Lighting Effects (Plastic). Raise the Height to 100.

**To select only the type, load the selection of the Alpha 2 channel and choose Select➥Modify➥Expand. Choose a value high enough to encompass the text (10 pixels) and choose Select➥Modify➥Smooth. Set the Smooth value just enough so the selection is slightly rounded at the edges (3 pixels).** ●

This effect is completed without the aid of channels. Instead, several layers are blended together to create a composite reflection.

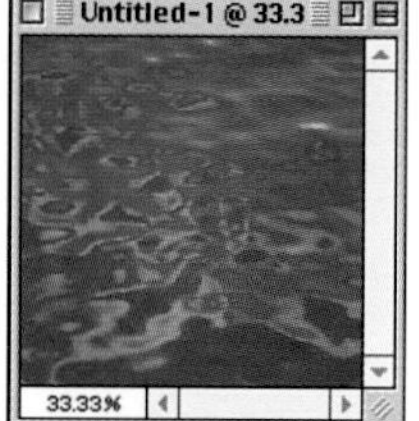


**1** Begin this effect with an image that contains a reflective surface such as this water image from the P5TM CD-ROM (P5TM CD-ROM➡Images➡D'Pix➡Ripples.JPG). The image was cropped and resized for this effect.

**2** Choose a foreground color for the type (CMYK: 0, 50, 100, 0). Use the Type tool to enter the text (Triple Extra Bold at 100 points). It will automatically be placed on a new layer. Choose Layer➡Type➡Render Layer.

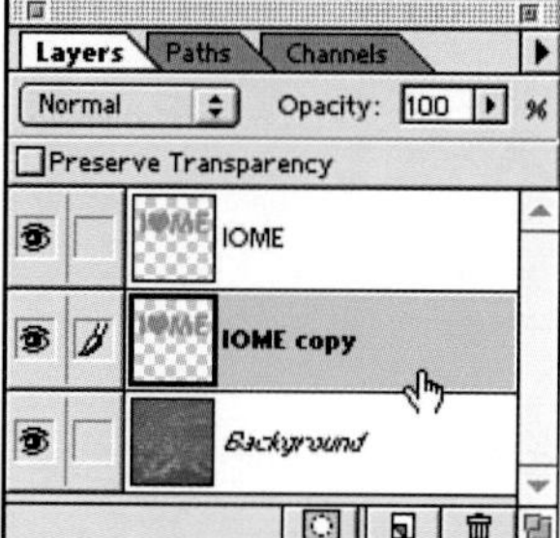


**3** Duplicate the type layer and move the new layer below the type layer.

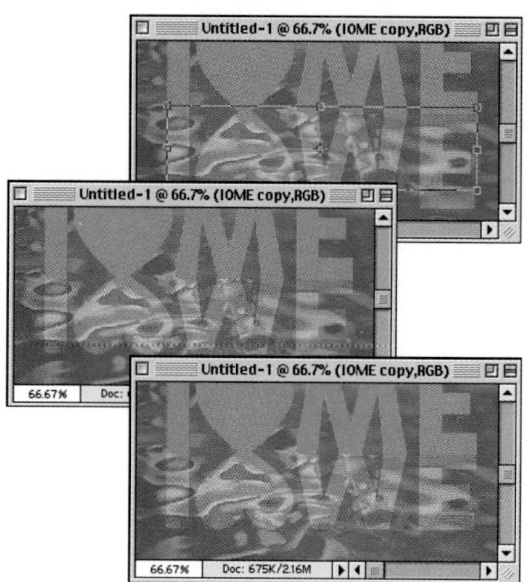


**4** Choose Edit➡Transform➡Flip Vertical. Then use the Move tool to position the flipped type into place below the original type. Change the layer blending mode to Overlay.

**5** Choose Edit➡Transform➡Scale, and hold the Shift key while dragging the bottom center tab upward. The objective is to compress the height of the reflection but don't go too far. Something like this would be great. Press Return to accept the transformation.

**6** Choose Layer➥Add Layer Mask➥Reveal All. The layer mask will be used to fade the reflection into the water. Load the transparency selection of this layer.

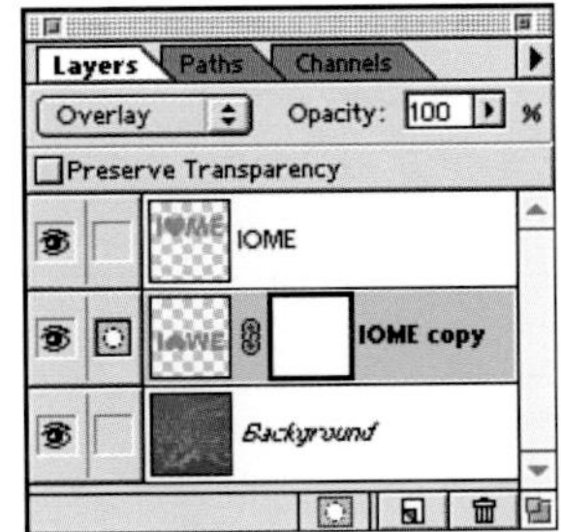


**7** Choose black for the foreground color and double-click on the Linear Gradient tool to select it and bring the Linear Gradient Options palette to the front. Select the Foreground to Transparent Gradient.

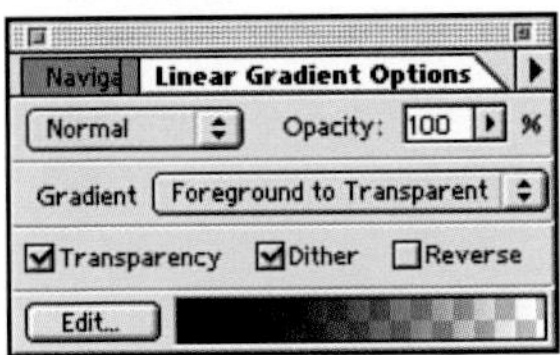


**8** Drag the Gradient tool (while holding the Shift key) from the bottom of the reflected type to a point about two-thirds of the way up the height of the reflection. This fades the reflection into the water.

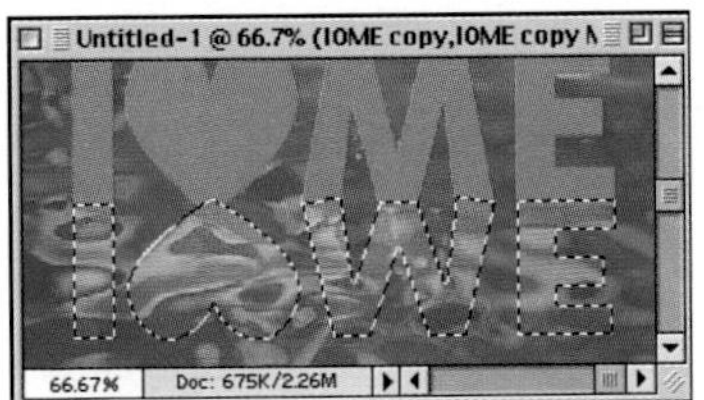


**9** Drag the Gradient tool a second time from near the bottom of the original type to a short distance "below the surface." This second gradient helps the original type stand apart from the reflected type.

**10** Create a new layer (Layer 1) and move it just below the original type layer. This layer holds a gradient that darkens the reflection near the surface of the water.

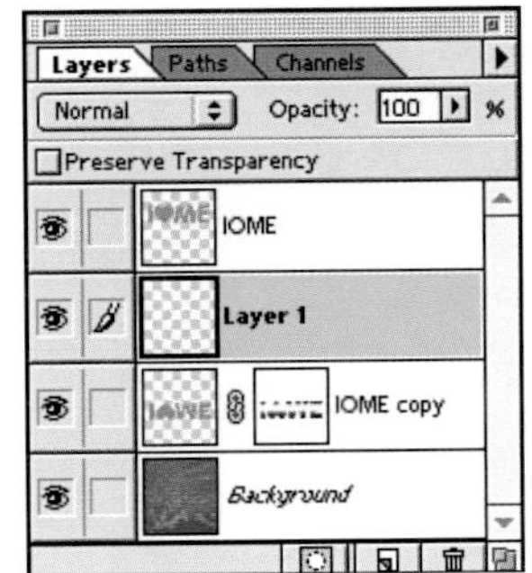

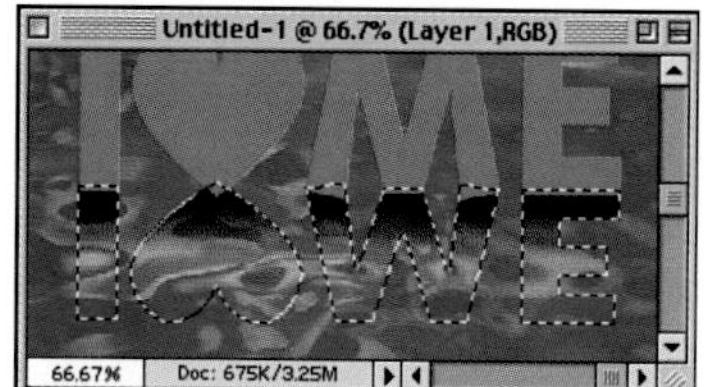


**11** Keep the selection active, and select the Linear Gradient tool again. Keep the same settings chosen in Step 7. Drag the Gradient tool from a point near the bottom of the original type to a point about one-half of the way along the depth of the reflected type.

**12** Change the layer Opacity to about 50%—and that's the basic reflection. The variations include a great addition to this effect.

## VARIATIONS

Deselect any active selections, make the layer containing the water image active, and make all other layers invisible. Choose Select➡Color Range. Use the Eyedropper to select a highlight area of the water.

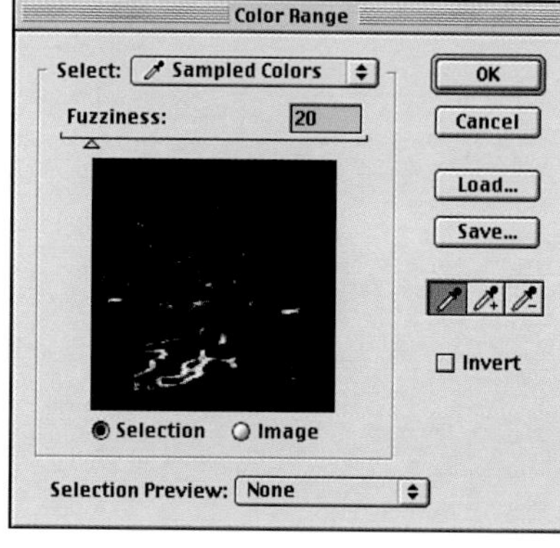

Then use the Fuzziness slider to control the selection so that only the lightest areas of the water are selected. The selected areas should be small.

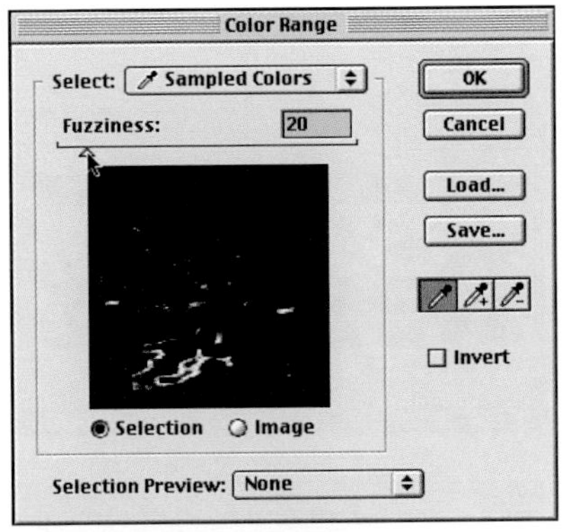


Make all layers visible and select the Lasso tool. Hold the (Option) [Alt] and Shift keys and circle an area of the water that includes all of the reflection and some of the surrounding water. There's no need to be precise. The purpose of the lassoing is to limit the selected areas.

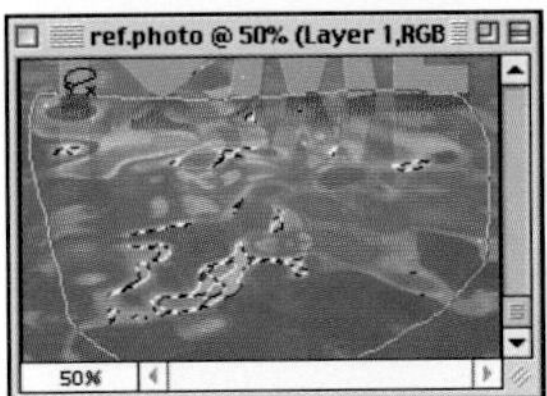


Choose the same foreground color as you used for the type in Step 2. Fill the selection to add a few orange reflections to the surface of the water. If you have too much or too little orange, use the History palette to go back and reselect a new Color Range. Or if the orange is too strong, choose Filter➡Fade Fill and adjust the Opacity percentage to find the right strength. ●

**TOOLBOX**

Magic Brush

Here a custom paintbrush is used to create a texture for adding some 3D texture to the type.

**1** Create a new file, choose a foreground color for your type (CMYK: 9, 75, 100, 40), and use the Type tool to enter the text (Weidemann at 95 points). Choose Layer➡Type➡Render Layer.

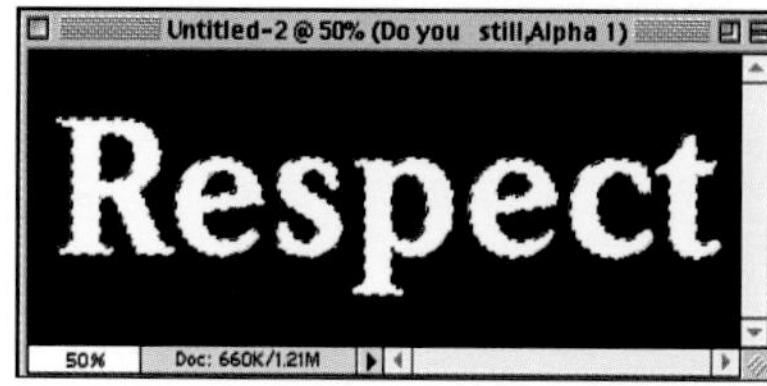


**2** Load the transparency selection of the type layer and save the selection as a new channel (Alpha 1). Make Alpha 1 the active channel.

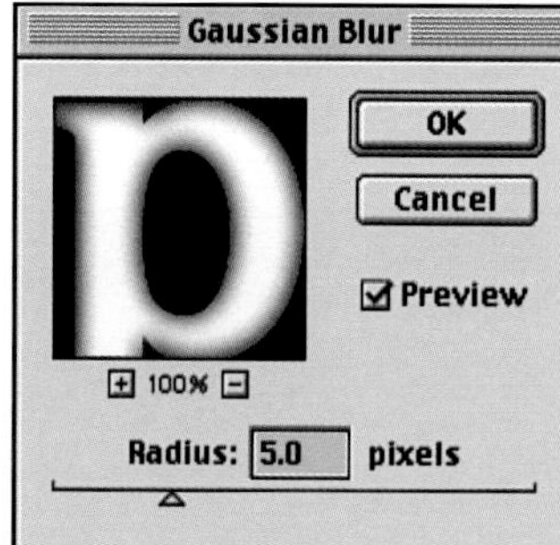


**3** Keep the selection active and choose Filter➡Blur➡Gaussian Blur. Set the Radius to approximately 5 pixels. The blur causes the type to raise when applying the Lighting Effects filter in Step 11. Deselect the selection.

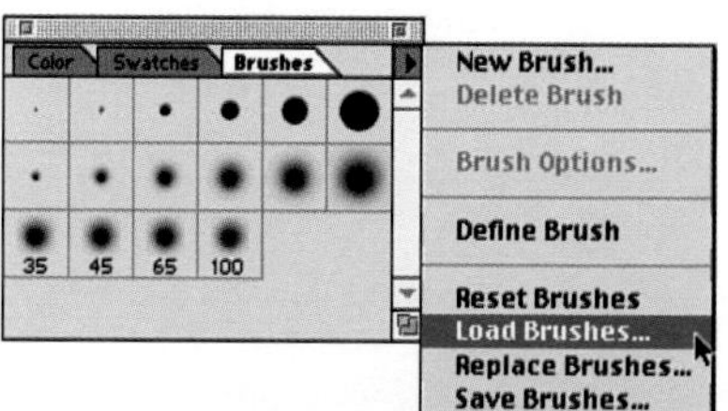


**4** Create a new channel (Alpha 2). Find the Brushes palette, choose Load Brushes from the palette menu, and load the Magic Brush file from the P5TM CD-ROM (P5TM CD-ROM➡P5TM Files➡Brushes➡Magic Brushes).

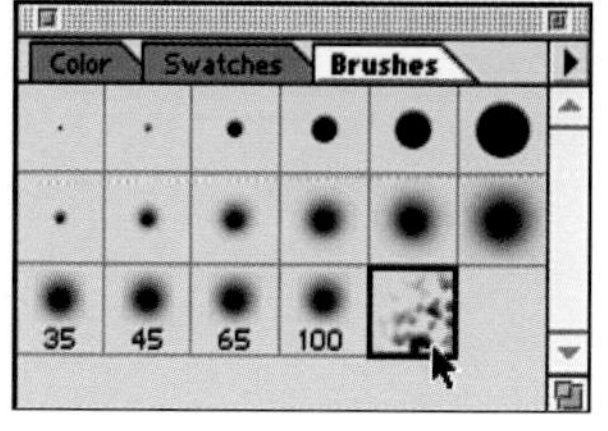


**5** One new brush appears as the last brush in the palette. Select the new brush, which was custom made by altering one of the brushes from Photoshop's Assorted Brushes collection.

**6** Make the Alpha 1 channel visible so that you can see the type without altering it.

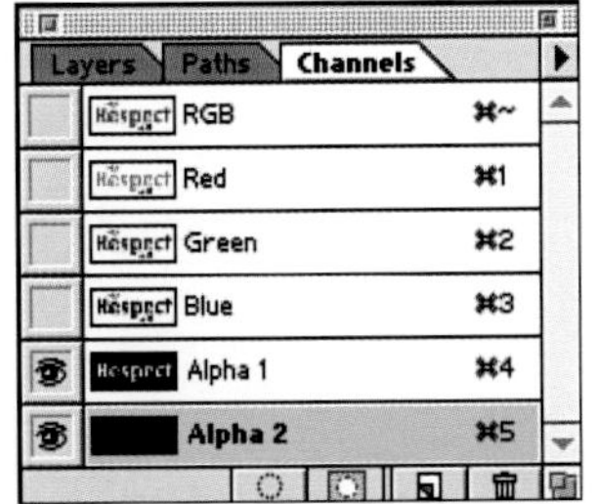


**7** Make sure that the foreground color is white; select the Paintbrush tool and use it to drag two lines across the type (but in the empty Alpha 2 channel) like this.

**8** Now to put the two channels together. Make Alpha 1 the active channel, make the Alpha 1 channel invisible, and load the selection from the Alpha 2 channel. Make sure the background color is black and press Delete to set the tracks into the type.

**9** Return to the RGB channel and the Background layer. Load the selection of the Alpha 2 channel, set the foreground color to black and press (Option-Delete) [Alt-Backspace] to fill the tracks. Deselect the selection.

**10** Choose Image➡Adjust➡Hue/Saturation. Turn on the Colorize option, raise the Saturation and use the Hue slider to choose a color for the tracks. Here are the values I came up with: Hue: 32, Saturation: 50, Lightness: 0.

Lighting Effects
Style: Run Over
Save... Delete
OK
Cancel
Light Type: Directional
On
Intensity: Negative 30 Full
Focus: Narrow 69 Wide
Properties
Gloss: Matte 11 Shiny
Material: Plastic -15 Metallic
Exposure: Under 0 Over
Ambience: Negative 8 Positive
Texture Channel: Alpha 1
White is high
Height: Flat 50 Mountainous
Preview

**11** Make the type layer active and choose Filter➥Render➥Lighting Effects. Choose Trampled from the Style menu or match the settings you see here.

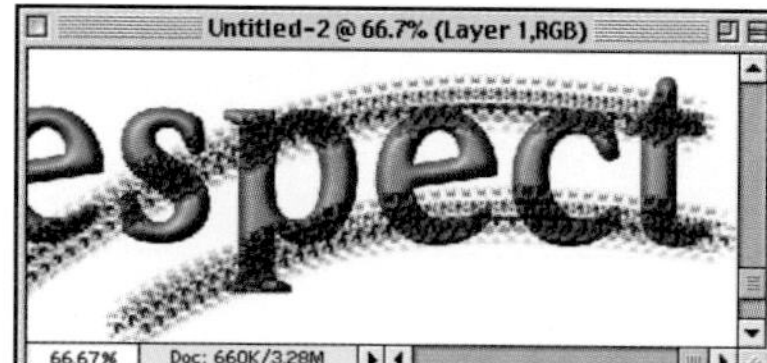


**12** Depending upon the colors you have chosen, you might need to darken the areas where the tracks run over the letters. If so, create a new layer (Layer 1), load the transparency selection of the type layer, and then intersect that selection with the selection from the Alpha 2 channel. Ignore the warning message that will most likely pop up, and press (Option-Delete) [Alt-Backspace] to fill the selection with black. Change the layer blending mode to Overlay and lower the Opacity until the darkness is just right (50%).

**13** Finally, I created some drop shadows and put everything together.

## VARIATIONS

Now that you have the Magic Brush (Step 5), you can use it by itself to make tiretrack type. Just set the foreground color; then click and drag. ●

This effect shows you what you can do by combining techniques of texturing and patterning. A custom scales pattern is included on the P5TM CD-ROM for use with this effect.

**1** Before beginning, open the Scale Pattern file from the CD-ROM (P5TM➥P5TM files➥Scales Pattern). Select All (Command-A) [Control-A], and choose Edit➥Define Pattern. Close the file.

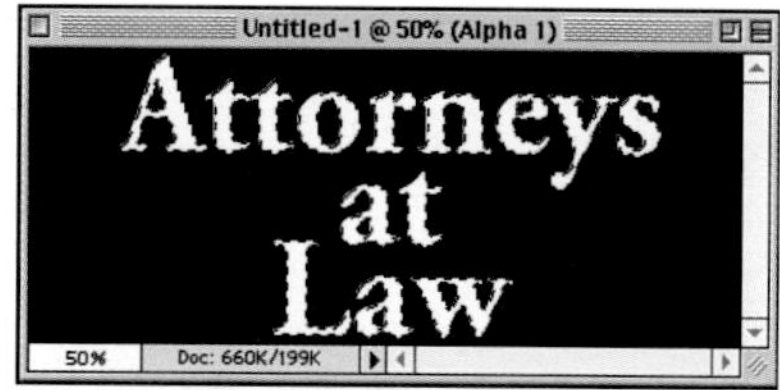


**2** Open the file to contain the type and create a new channel (Alpha 1). Use the Type tool to enter the text. (I used Bodega Sans Black at 70 points.)

**3** Duplicate the channel to create Alpha 1 copy. While the selection is still active, choose Filter➥Blur➥Gaussian Blur. Use just enough to add a little gray around the edges. I set the Radius to 4.0 pixels.

## TOOLBOX

Scale Pattern

Scales (Lighting Effects Style)

Magic Curves

**4** The blur adds some roundness to the letters. Now you can use the Edit➡Fill command to blend the blur with the pattern defined in Step 1. Choose Edit➡Fill (Use: Pattern, Opacity: 100%, Mode: Multiply).

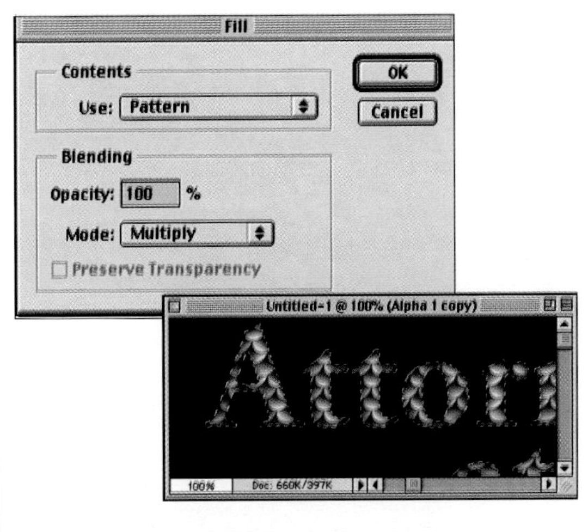


In the result, you can see that the edges of the pattern-filled type are slightly dark and a little blurry.

**5** Return to the composite channel and create a new layer (Layer 1). The selection should remain active. Choose a foreground color and fill the type with the color. Here is the green that I used (CMYK: 75,0,100,0).

**6** Choose Filter➡Render➡Lighting Effects. From the pop-up menu, choose Scales. (If it does not appear in the menu, you can match the settings that you see here, or flip to page 248 in the "What's on the CD-ROM" section to find out how to install the lighting effects that are on the CD.)

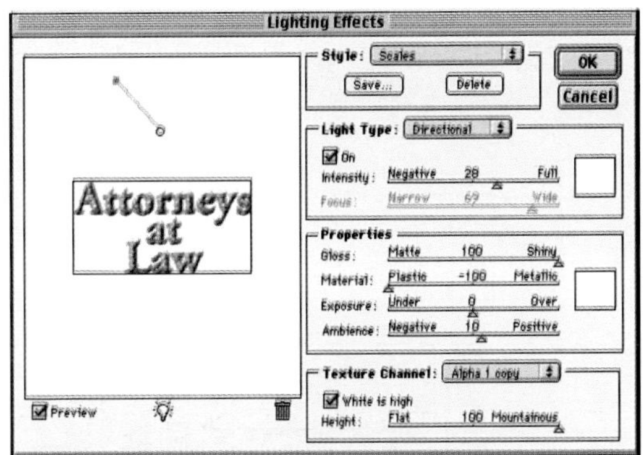

SCALESss...

Attorneys
at
Law

Click OK to see this new slimy type. Check out the variations for ideas on enhancing the scales.

## VARIATIONS

Attorneys
at
Law

### Gloss

After completing Step 6 choose Filter➡Artistic➡Plastic Wrap. Try these settings: Highlight Strength: 15, Detail: 9, Smoothness: 15.

Image Size

Pixel Dimensions: 1K (was 1K)

Width: 50 percent

Height: 11 pixels

OK

Cancel

Auto...

Print Size:

Width: 0.077 inches

Height: 0.073 inches

Resolution: 150 pixels/inch

☑ Constrain Proportions

☑ Resample Image: Bicubic

### Small and Slick

If the scales' scaling doesn't quite fit your type, you can resize them. After opening the Scales Pattern file in Step 1, choose Image➡Image Size. In this example, I set the Width percentage to 50% to create smaller scales. If you make this file any smaller, the scales begin to lose their definition; try using larger type instead.

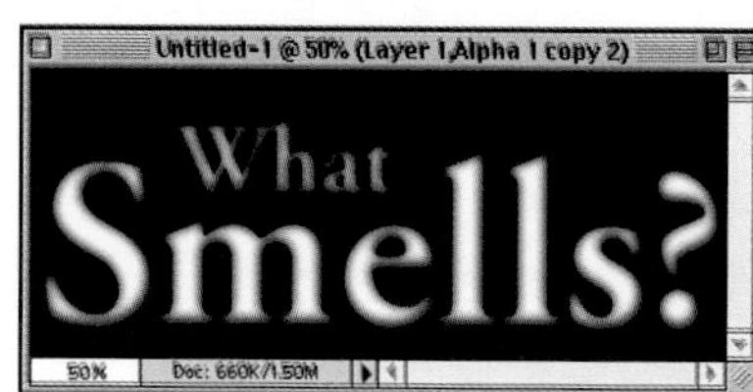


To create this slicker, less bumpy effect, finish the rest of the steps and then duplicate the Alpha 1 channel again to create Alpha 1 copy 2. The selection should still be active. Choose Filter➡Blur➡Gaussian Blur. Raise the Radius slightly. I used 6 pixels.

Return to the composite channel and choose Filter➥Render➥Lighting Effects. Select the Scale preset from the pop-up menu. Then change the Texture Channel to Alpha 1 copy 2.

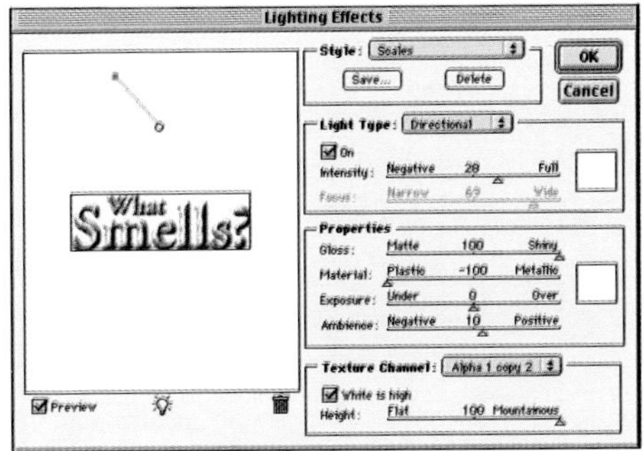


Kind of fishy.

### What's That?

To create this texture, first use the resizing technique from Small and Slick to make the pattern 200% of its original size. Then, in Step 3, do not apply the Gaussian Blur. Instead of Step 4, choose Edit➥Fill (Use: Pattern, Opacity: 100%, Mode: Normal).

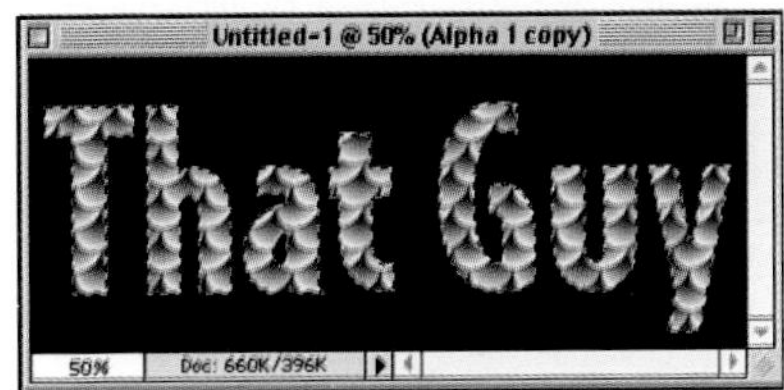

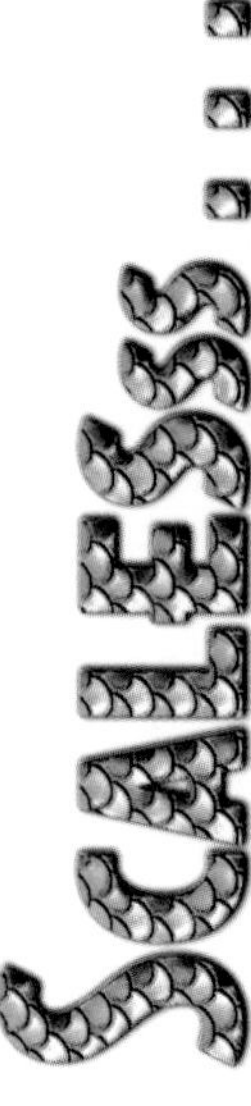


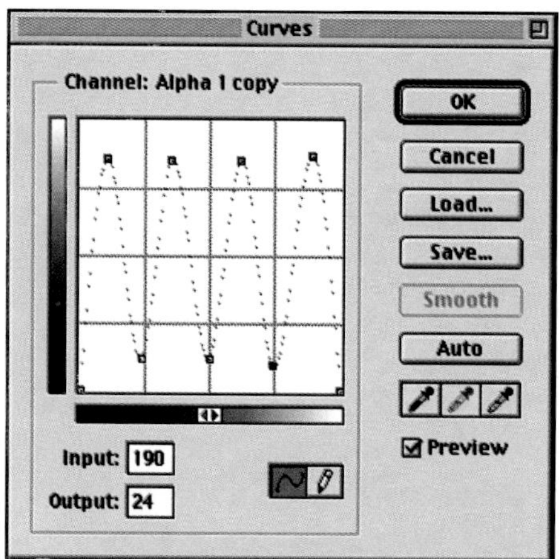


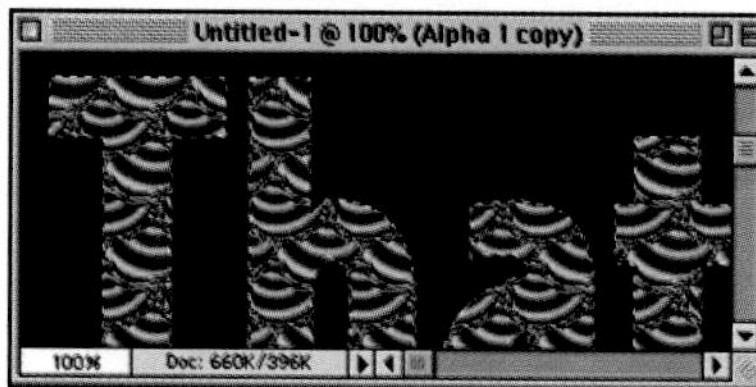


Then choose Image➥Adjust➥ Curves and either load the Magic Curves file from the CD (P5TM CD➥P5TM Files➥Magic Curves) or re-create the wave seen here. This wave radically alters the values in the channel. A wild pattern is produced that will be used by the Lighting Effects filter to make the texture you see in the final image.

In Step 5, fill the type selection with white. In Step 6, select the Scales preset; then change the exposure setting to -25 and Texture Height to 50.

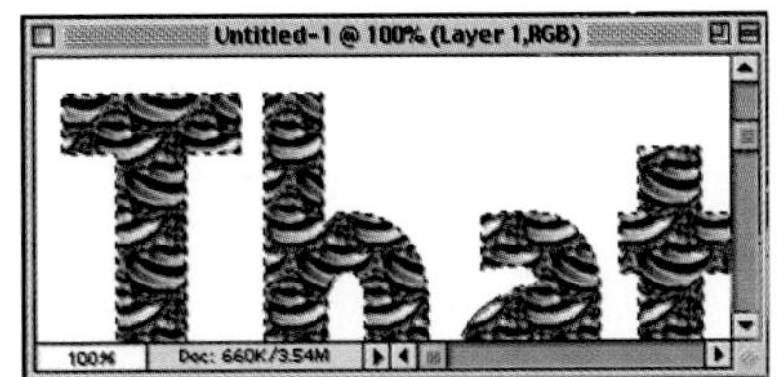


Finally, while the selection is still active, create a new layer (Layer 2) above Layer 1 and paste in a colorful image. Change the layer blending mode to Color. ●

Photoshop 5.0's new Drop Shadow Layer Effect is an excellent new feature that can take care of most of your shadow needs, but it takes the Transform feature to make this perspective shadow. The Transform feature and the Drop Shadow feature are used to make the floating shadows at the end of this chapter.

## Perspective Shadows

**1** Create a new file and use the Type tool to enter the text (Utopia Black at 45 points). Then use the Move tool to position the text in the upper portion of the image window.

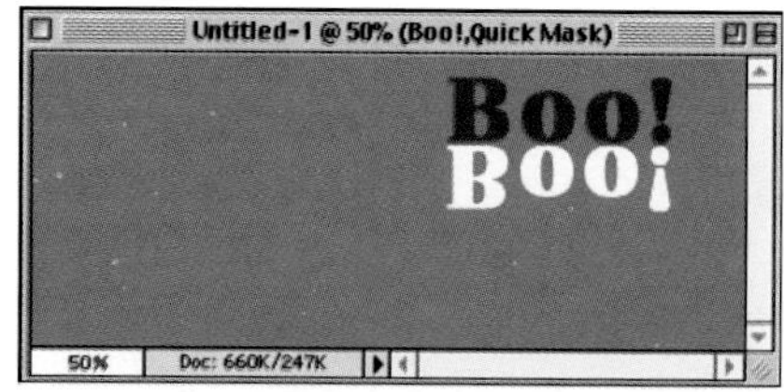


**2** Load the transparency selection of the type layer and press Q to enter Quick Mask mode. Most of the shaping of the shadow will be done here. Choose Edit➥Transform➥Flip Vertical and then use the Move tool to move the flipped type back up to meet the bottom edge of the original type.

**3** Choose Edit➥Free Transform. Hold the (Command) [Control] key and drag the bottom center handle of the transform box down and away from the original type. Holding the (Command) [Control] key enables you to move the bottom of the transform box from side to side, creating a parallelogram.

**4** After slanting and stretching the flipped type, you can fine-tune the shadow by holding the (Command) [Control] key and adjusting the two bottom corner handles. Holding the (Command) [Control] key here enables you to move each handle independently. Watch out for the top of the shadow where it meets the bottom of the type. The distorted shadow type will have a tendency to shift to one side of the original type. Don't move these handles too much.

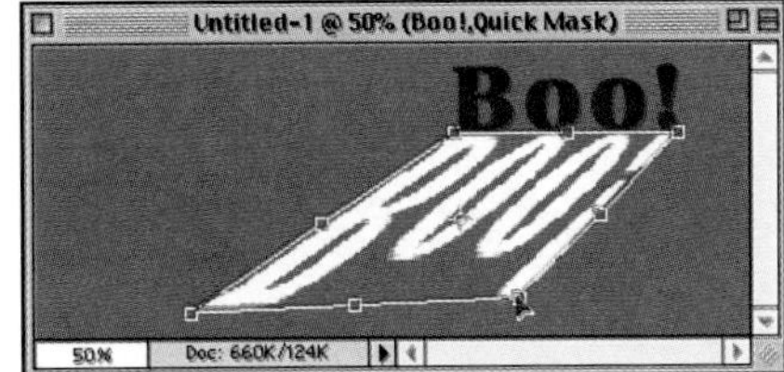


**5** Press (Return) [Enter] to accept the changes. Then double-click the Linear Gradient tool to select it and bring the Linear Gradient Options palette to the front. Set the Gradient to Foreground to Transparent (Normal, Opacity: 100%) and make sure that the foreground color is black.

**6** Click and drag the Linear Gradient tool upward from the bottom of the shadow. Hold the Shift key as you drag to keep the gradient perfectly straight.

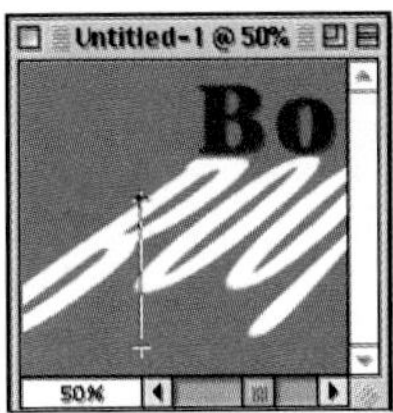

**7** Choose Filter➡Blur➡Gaussian Blur. Blur the Quick Mask just enough to take the hardness off the edges of the shadow. I set the Radius to 1 pixel.

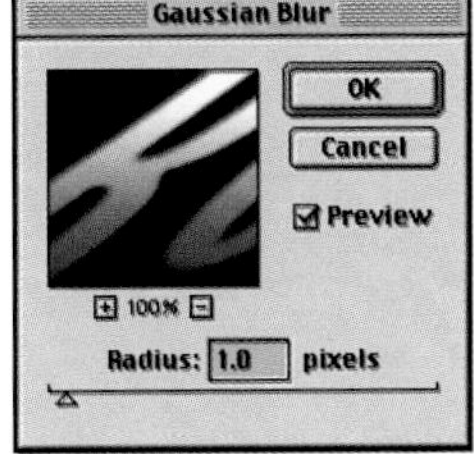

**8** Press Q to exit Quick Mask mode. Choose a foreground color for the shadow (I used black), make the Background layer the active layer and fill the shadow selection. Deselect the selection.

## Floating Shadows

After entering the type, choose Layer➥Type➥Render Layer. Then choose Edit➥Free Transform. Press (Command-Shift-Option) [Control-Shift-Alt] and grab one of the top corner tabs. Drag the corner toward the center of the text. Press (Return) [Enter] to accept the changes. Finally, choose Layer➥Effects➥Drop Shadow. The key to making the type looking like it floats is a high Distance setting—60 pixels in this example.

This alternate floating shadow was started by choosing Layer➡Effects➡Drop Shadow to create a drop shadow. Then choose Layer➡Effects➡Create Layer. A new layer is created that contains the drop shadow. Make the Drop Shadow layer the active layer, and choose Edit➡Free Transform. Click in the center of the transform box to move the shadow down and away from the type. Grab the top center tab, hold the Shift key, and compress the shadow almost completely—until the top and bottom tabs are stacked directly on top of each other. Press (Return) [Enter] to accept the changes. Choose Filter➡Blur➡Motion Blur (Angle: 0°, Distance: 20 pixels) and then Filter➡Blur➡Gaussian Blur (2 pixels).

Boo Hoo

In this technique, the Displace filter is used to break the type apart and scatter the shards. There is a custom displacement map on the CD-ROM that can be loaded and resized to fit your type.

**1** You can shatter anything with this type, including type created by other techniques in this book. To do this make sure that the type image is flattened into a single layer and make that layer active. This type was created with the Reflector technique on page 46. Or use the Type tool to enter the text.

**2** Open the ShatterMap file from the P5TM CD-ROM (P5TM➥P5TM Files➥Displacement Maps➥ShatterMap).

**3** Choose Select➥All and copy the image. Close the file and return to the type image. Create a new channel (Alpha 1) and paste in the ShatterMap image. Make the composite channel visible and keep the selection active.



**TOOLBOX**

ShatterMap (displacement map)

**4** Choose Edit➡Transform➡Scale. Scale the ShatterMap so that it covers all the type. You can see in this view where the type will be shattered. Resizing this image will allow the shattering that takes place in Steps 7 and 8 to align with the selections that are made in Steps 9 and 10.

**5** Deselect the selection, make the composite channel invisible, and choose Duplicate channel from the Channels palette menu. Set the Destination to New and name the file (DreamShat). Click OK. When the new file opens, save it (Photoshop format) and close it.

**6** Next, duplicate the Alpha 1 channel and make the new channel (Alpha 1 copy) active. Choose Filter➡Stylize➡Find Edges and Image➡Adjust➡Invert. The Find Edges filter turns the ShatterMap into a web of sharp lines.

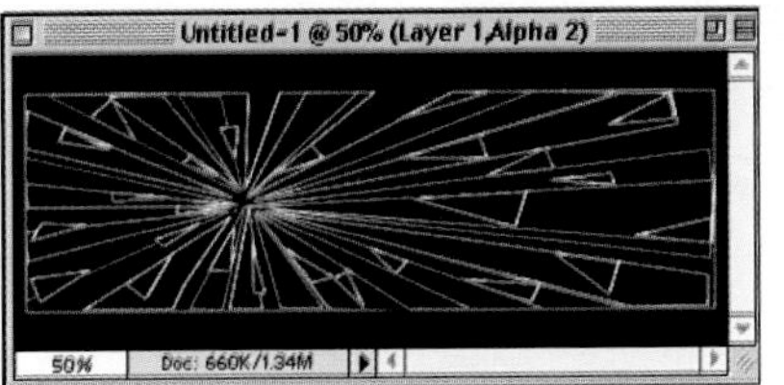


**7** Return to the composite channel, and choose Filter➡Distort➡ Displace. Set the Horizontal and Vertical Scale percentages to 7 (Stretch to Fit, Wrap Around). Click OK.

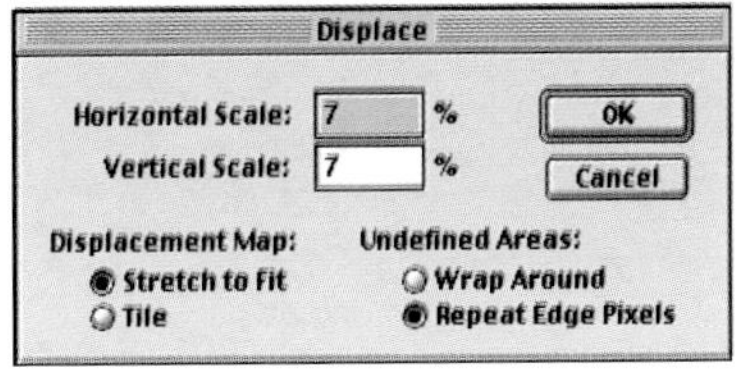

8 A dialog box appears asking you to find a Displacement Map. Find the file that you saved in Step 4 (DreamShat). The Displace filter shifts areas of the original image (the type in this case) according to the values in the chosen displacement map.

TIP **If the Displace filter distorted the type too much, go back to Step 6 (by using the History palette) and use lower settings for the Scale percentages.**

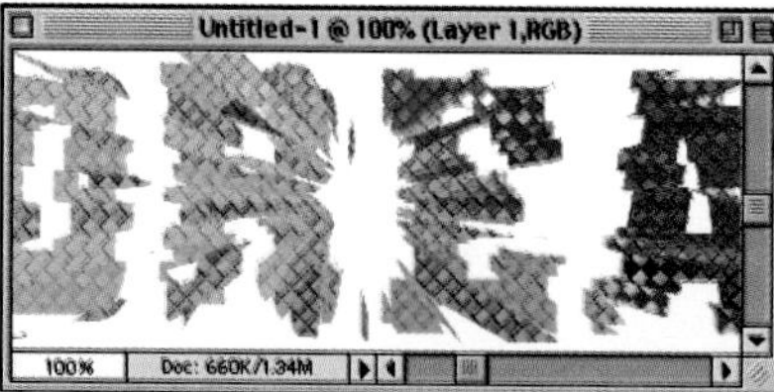


9 Load the selection of the Alpha 1 channel. Then choose Image➡Adjust➡Brightness/Contrast. Raise both the Brightness (+80) and Contrast (+30) so the individual shards of type are distinguishable.

**10** Next, load the selection of the Alpha 1 copy channel and press Delete. This separates the shards by clearing thin lines between them. Deselect the selection.

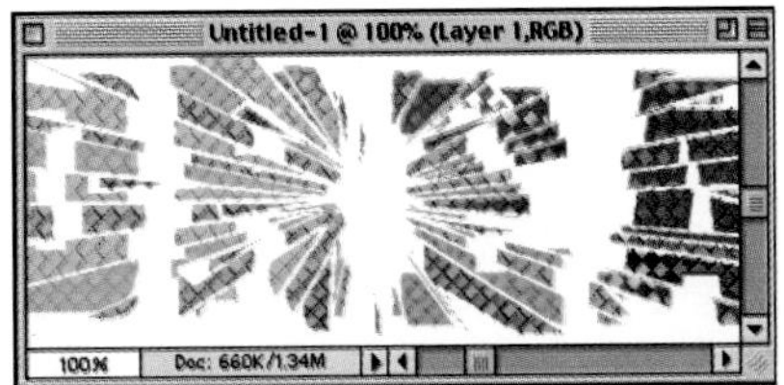


**11** To define the edges, choose a foreground color to use as a stroke color (CMYK: 100, 75, 0, 40). Then load the transparency selection of the type layer, and choose Edit➡Stroke (1 pixel, 100%, Normal, Outside). I also used the Drop Shadow layer effect to finish off the type. ●

There are numerous methods in Photoshop to create multicolored textures. Here is one that gives great results, using the Radial Gradient tool and the Glass filter.

**1** Create a new layer (Layer 1) and use the Type tool to enter the text. (I used Copperplate Bold at 100 points.) Choose Layer➥Type➥Render Layer. Turn on the Preserve Transparency option for the type layer. This causes the gradients to stay within the boundaries of the type when you use the Gradient tool in Step 3.

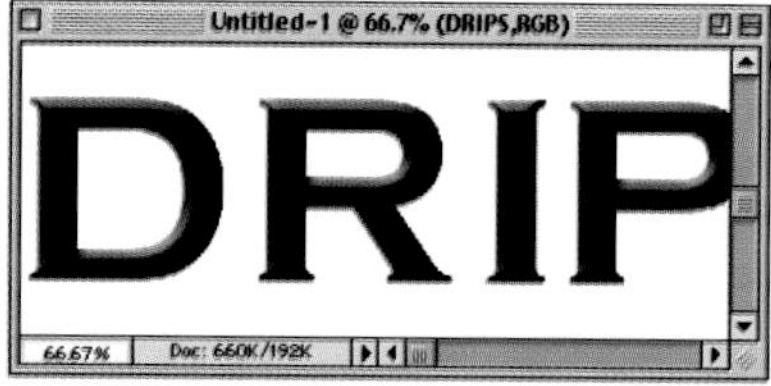


**2** Choose Layer➥Effects➥Bevel and Emboss. This colored texture looks great on raised type. Select the Inner Bevel style (Depth: 20, Blur: 10).

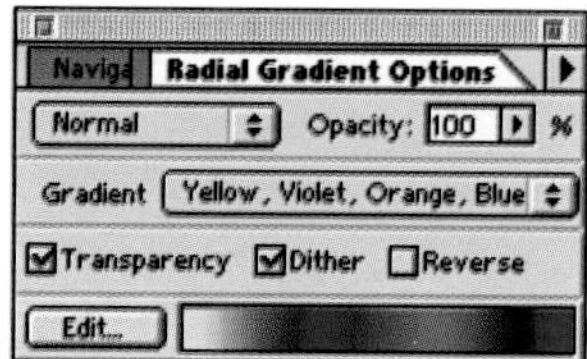


**3** Double-click on the Radial Gradient tool to select it and bring the Radial Gradient Options palette to the front. Select a gradient from the list (or create one of your own) that has at least four colors in it. If you're not creating your own, the presets limit you to the Yellow, Violet, Orange, Blue gradient—which is what I chose. Don't be too concerned with the colors in the gradient. They affect the final colors, but we are going to alter them anyway. The surprises this effect produces are part of the magic.

4 Click the Edit button to open the Gradient Editor; then click the Transparency radio button. You see a black bar with one slider at each end. At the bottom of the dialog box is a preview of the gradient. Click once below the bar to create a new slider. Move it to the 95% Location.

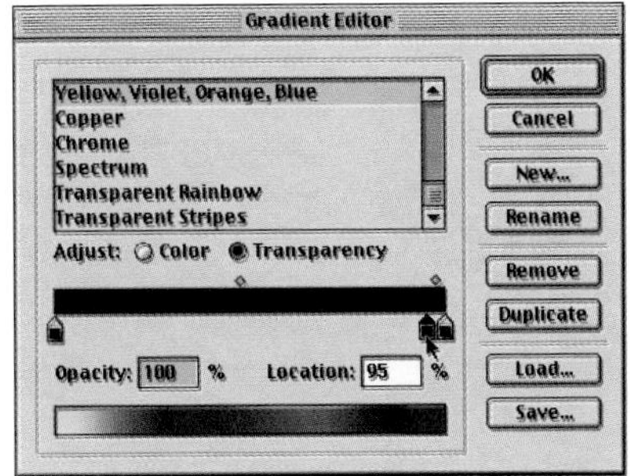


5 Then click on the far right slider and change the Opacity to 0%. Click OK to confirm the changes you made.

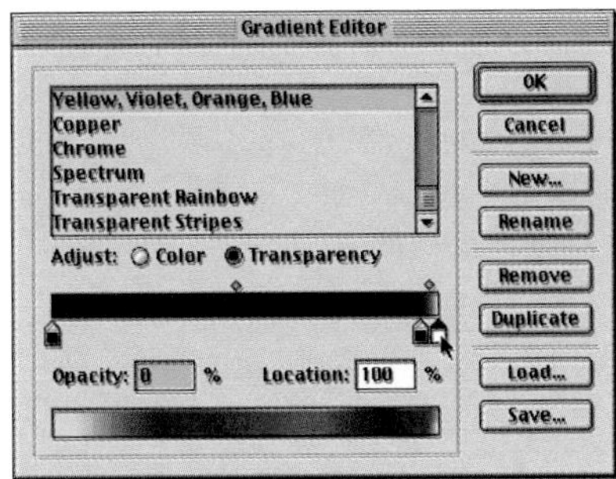


6 Now use the Radial Gradient tool to click and drag many gradients across the type. Making many small gradients helps to break up the colors. Here is the type covered with gradients. The colors stays inside the type outlines and your type remains beveled. Make sure to cover all the type with gradients—don't leave any of the original type color (black) showing.

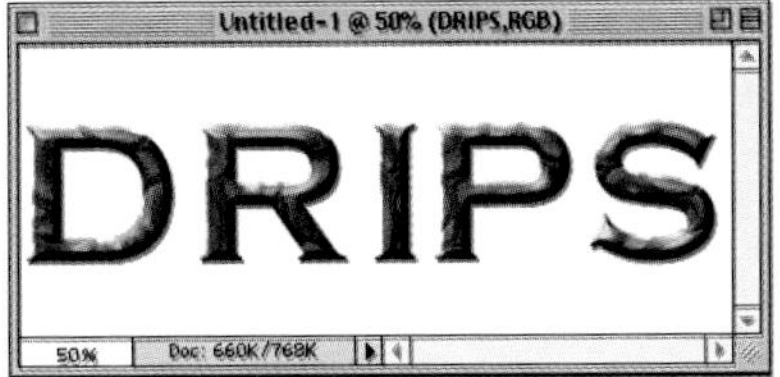

**7** The Clouds and Difference Clouds filters use the foreground and background colors to create their clouds. You will not see these colors when using the Difference Clouds filter in this step, but they do matter. For the purposes of this technique, it is important to know that the difference between the colors affects the final type. Choosing two colors far apart produces the greatest variety of colors and choosing colors near to each other produces the smallest variety of colors. I pressed D to set the colors at their defaults (black and white). After selecting colors, choose Filter➡Render➡Difference Clouds.

**8** Then select Image➡Adjust➡Invert. After applying the Difference Clouds filter, the colors turned dark. Because I wanted brighter colors I inverted them. This step is optional.

**9** Choose Image➥Adjust➥Levels. Now, there is too much white. Grab the black Input slider and move it to the right to increase the amount of dark colors. I also nudged the gray slider slightly to the right.

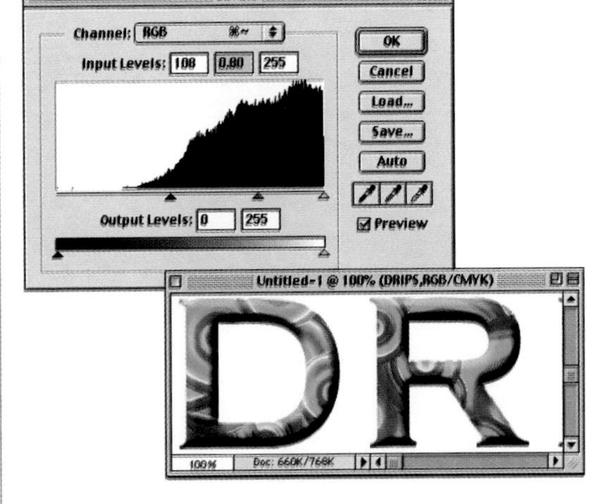


**10** Choose Image➥Adjust➥ Hue/Saturation. Raising the Saturation (+100) sharpens the contrast between bordering colors and makes all the colors brighter at the same time. You can also take this opportunity to use the Hue slider to choose a different set of colors.

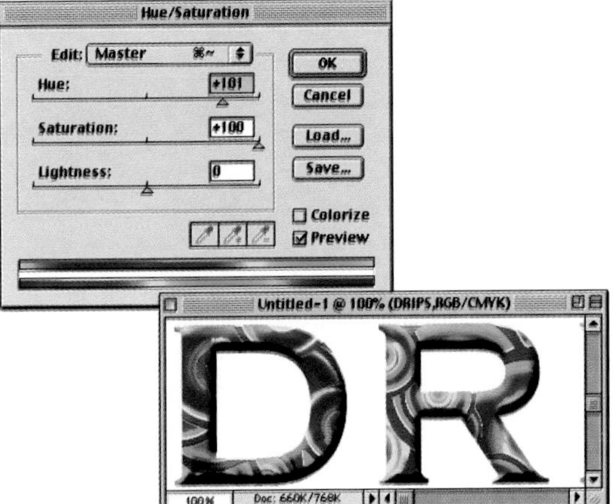

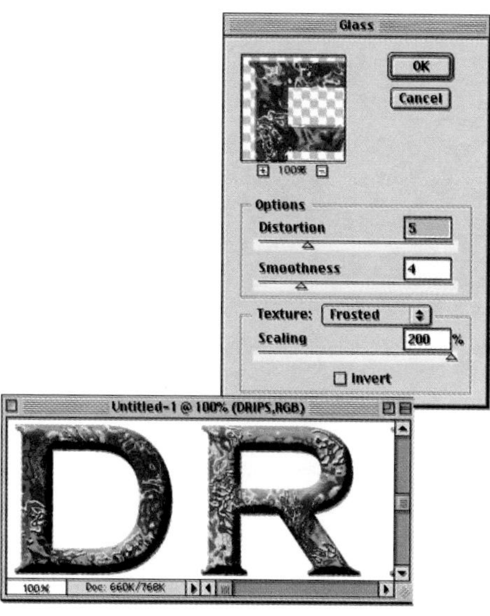


**11** Finally, the Glass filter produces the texture. This filter reveals a background color in some areas when it distorts the colors. Choose a background color that fits into the color scheme already in the type. I chose a blue color (CMYK: 100, 50, 0, 0). Then choose Filter➡Distort➡Glass. Set the Distortion to 5, the Smoothness to 4, the Texture to Frosted, and the Scaling to 200%.

DRIPS

**12** I added a drop shadow to the final image.

## Variations

After Step 12, apply Filter➡Sharpen➡Sharpen More five times.

DRIPS

### Monochrome

This technique can also create a nice monochromatic texture. After completing all of the previous Steps, choose Image➡Adjust➡Hue/Saturation. Click on the Colorize option, raise the Saturation, and use the Hue slider to find a color. I also chose Image➡Adjust➡Auto Levels for a better distribution of darks and lights.

DRIPS

### Texture

Apply these two filters after Step 11 for another texture: Filter➡Pixelate➡Fragment and Filter➡Artistic➡Paint Daubs (Brush Size: 9, Sharpness: 24, Brush Type: Simple).

DRIPS

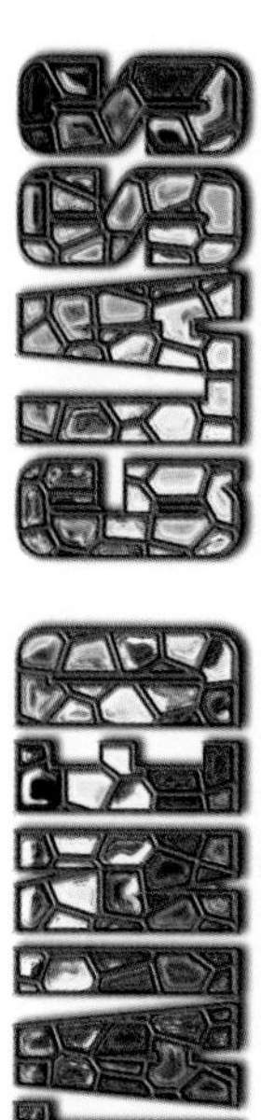

This colored glass effect breaks the type into small pieces and adds distortion, color, and some lead trim. The variations provide some useful adjustments to the basic effect.

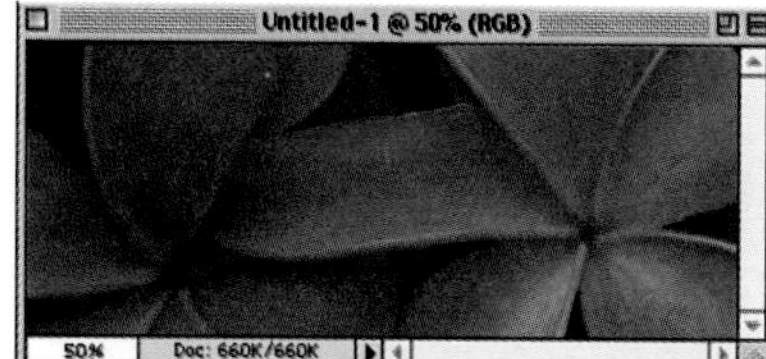


**1** Open the file that contains the background image that you want to place the stained glass type on top of. I opened this file from the P5TM CD-ROM (P5TM➥Images➥Photo 24➥Plants➥024).

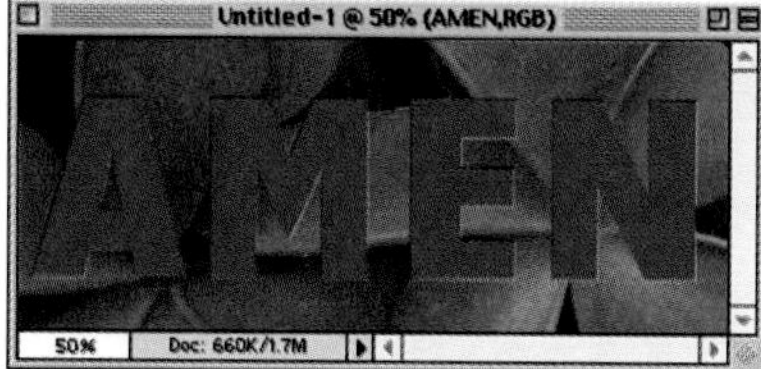


**2** Choose 50% gray for the foreground color and use the Type tool to enter the text (Humanist 521 Extra Bold Condensed at 130 points). Be sure to use a heavy typeface that has plenty of room for dividing the interior into the smaller shapes seen in the thumbtab image.

**3** Load the transparency selection of the new layer and save the selection to create the Alpha 1 channel. Choose Layer➥Type➥Render Layer. Make the Background layer invisible so you can see only the type.



TOOLBOX

Magic Curves

4 While the selection is still active, choose Filter➡Noise➡Add Noise (Amount: 50, Gaussian, Monochromatic). The Amount is not very critical as long as there is enough noise that you can see it easily.

5 Choose a bright color for the foreground color. (I used CMYK: 0, 100, 100, 0.) The Stained Glass filter will divide the type into pieces, using this color to separate the shapes. Using a bright color will make it easy to select the borders in Step 6. Deselect the selection, and choose Filter➡Texture➡ Stained Glass (Cell Size: 25, Border Thickness: 8, Light Intensity: 1). The Cell Size determines the size of the panes of glass within the letters and the Border Thickness determines the thickness of the lead that runs between the glass panes.

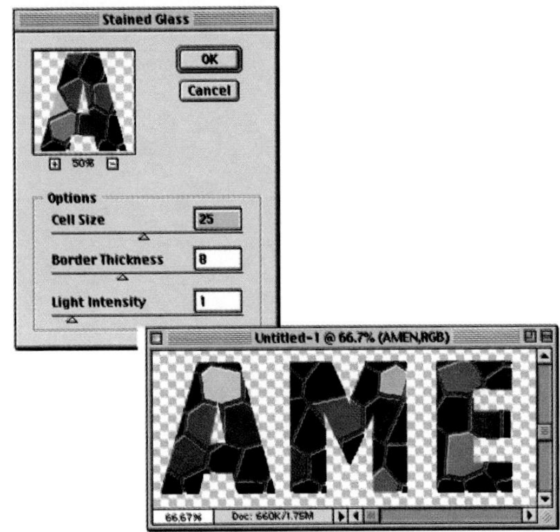

6 Choose Select➡Color Range. Because the foreground color is still the same bright color selected in Step 4, the Color Range automatically selects that color from the image. If necessary, adjust the Fuzziness slider so that all of the red is selected. Click OK to make the selection.

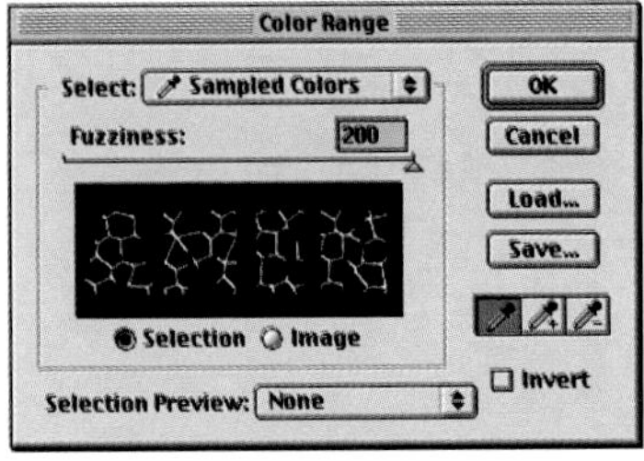

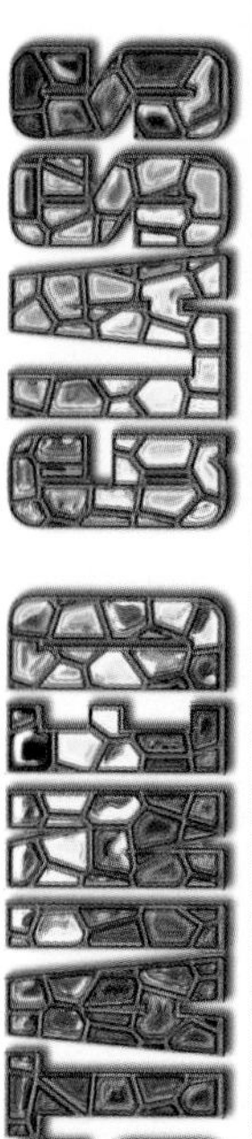

**7** Choose Select➡Inverse and press Delete. Only the red borders should remain. Load the selection of the Alpha 1 channel; then choose Select➡Modify➡Expand (6 pixels). The Expand amount determines the thickness of the lead that runs around the perimeter of the letters. Subtract the selection of the Alpha 1 channel from the current selection. A thin border should now be selected around the perimeter of the letters. Fill the selection and deselect the selection.

**8** Choose 50% gray for the foreground color again, turn on the Preserve Transparency option for the current layer, and fill the layer.

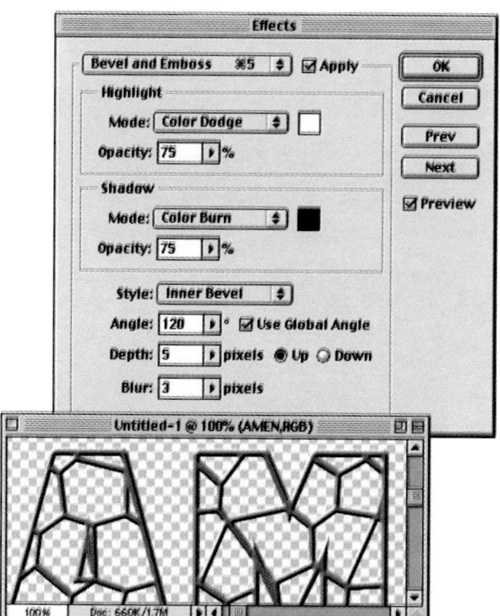


**9** Choose Layer➡Effects➡Bevel and Emboss. Choose the Inner Bevel Style, set the Angle as you want (120°, Up), the Depth to 5 pixels, and the Blur to 3 pixels. Set the Highlight Mode to Color Dodge (Opacity: 75%) and the Shadow Mode to Color Burn (Opacity: 75%).

**10** Load the transparency selection of the current layer; choose Select➡Inverse and intersect the selection with the selection of the Alpha 1 channel. All of the transparent areas within the type should now be selected. Save the selection to create the Alpha 2 channel and make the Alpha 2 channel the active channel.

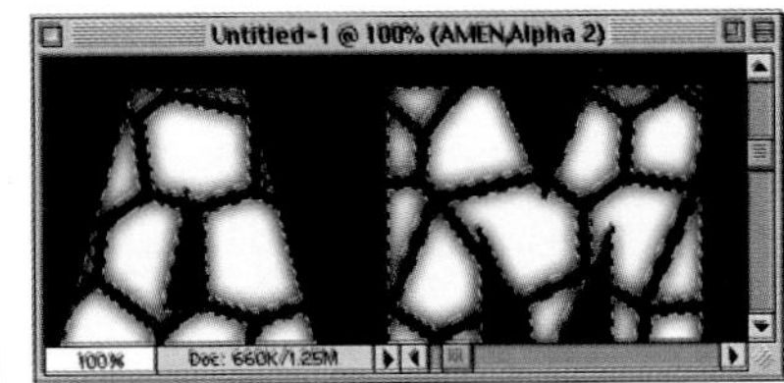


**11** Keep the selection active and choose Filter➡Blur➡Gaussian Blur (5 pixels). Blur the selection enough to add some good gray edges to the interior of the shapes.

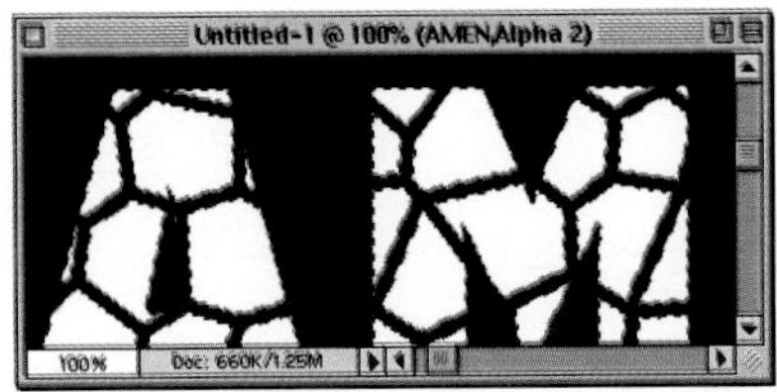


**12** Duplicate the Alpha 2 channel to create the Alpha 3 channel. Then choose Image➡Adjust➡Curves and click the Load button. Find the Magic Curves file on the P5TM CD-ROM (P5TM➡P5TM Files➡Miscellaneous➡Magic Curves) or draw the curve that you see in this figure.

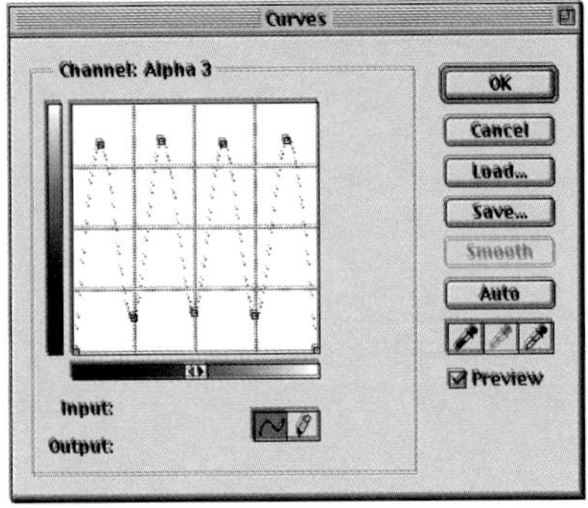


Click OK to accept the changes. Deselect the selection.

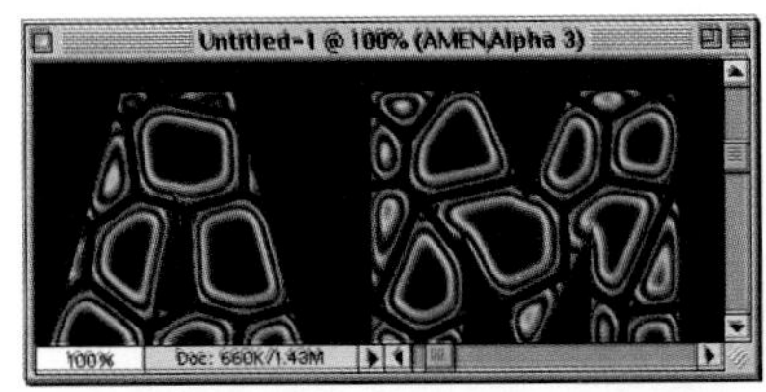


**13** Make the Alpha 2 channel the active channel again. Choose Duplicate Channel from the Channels palette menu. Select New for the Destination Document and name the new document (StainTex).

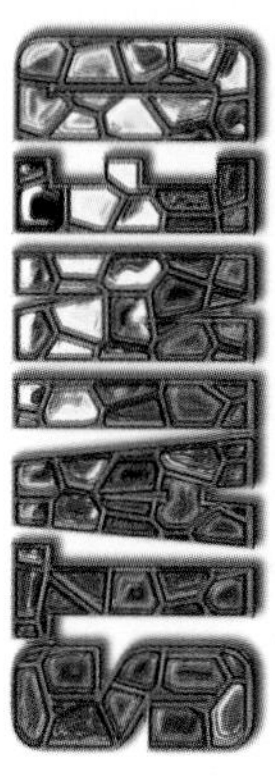

**14** A new image window opens. Save the file (Photoshop format) and close it.

**15** Return to the composite channel, and make the Background layer active. Choose Filter➡Distort➡Glass. Select the Load Texture option from the Texture menu. Find the StainTex file that was saved in Step 13 and open it. Adjust the settings to increase or decrease the amount of the distortion.

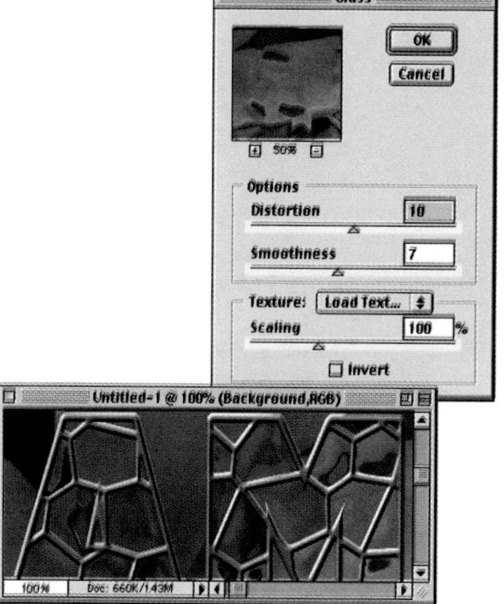


**16** Load the selection of the Alpha 3 channel and choose Image➡Adjust➡Curves. Grab the line on the graph and bend the line up toward the upper-left corner to lighten the selected areas.

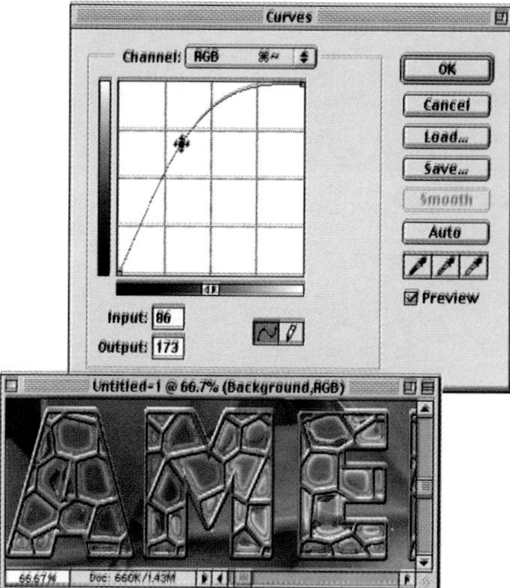

**17** Deselect the selection, create a new layer (Layer 1), and set the layer blending mode to Color (75% Opacity).

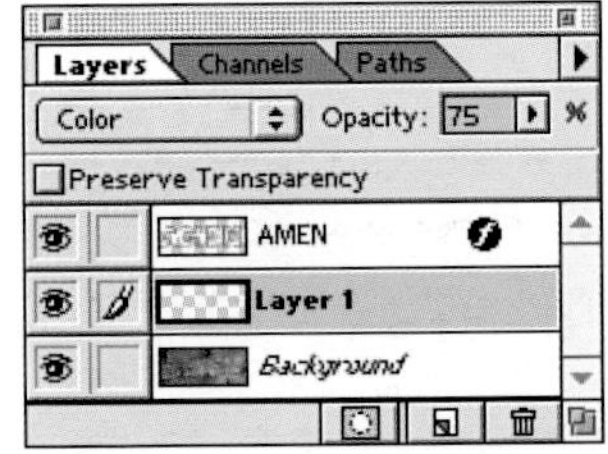


**18** Make the layer containing the lead border the active layer. Double-click the Magic Wand tool to select it and bring the Magic Wand options palette to the front. Set the Tolerance to 1. You can now use the Magic Wand tool to select the individual areas within the lead borders. Click once with the Magic Wand inside one of the transparent areas.

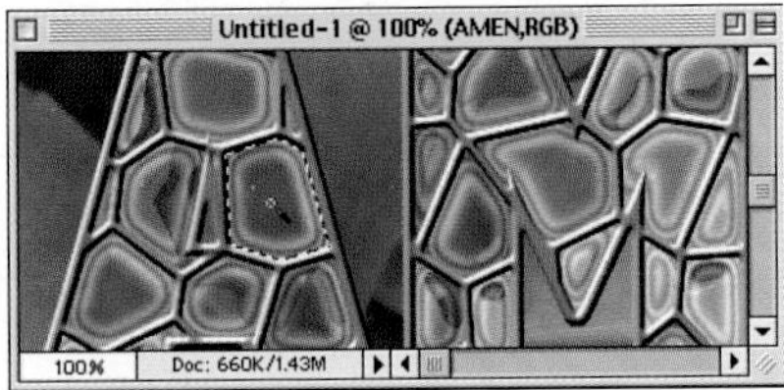


**19** Make Layer 1 the active layer, and choose a foreground color for the piece of glass (CMYK: 100, 0, 100, 40). Dark colors will work best. Fill the selection to color it.

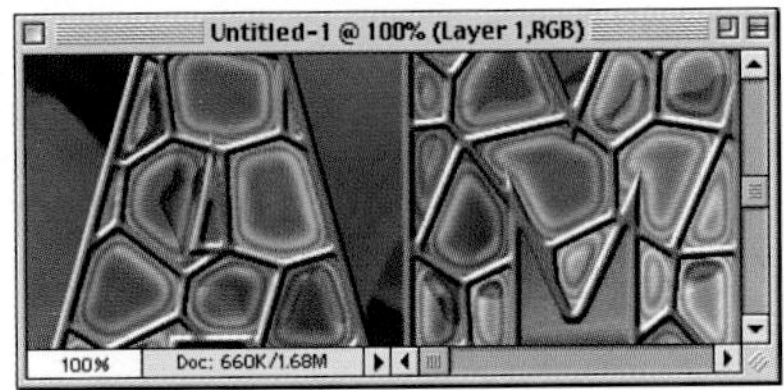


**20** Keep repeating Steps 17 and 18 to fill all of the pieces within the letters. Make sure that you switch back and forth between the layer containing the lead and the color layer. (You don't need to double-click the Magic Wand tool and set the Tolerance each time you repeat the steps.)

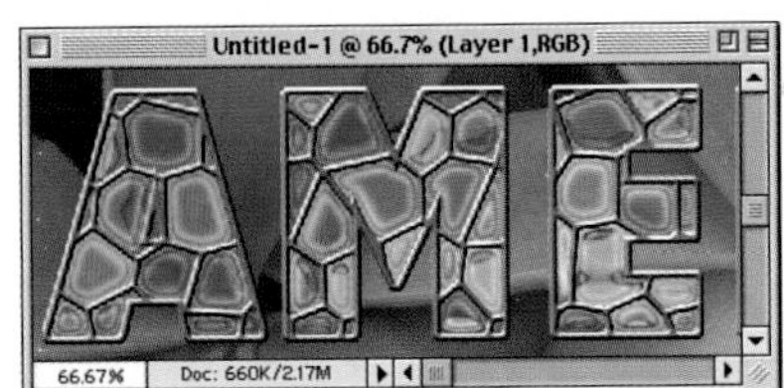

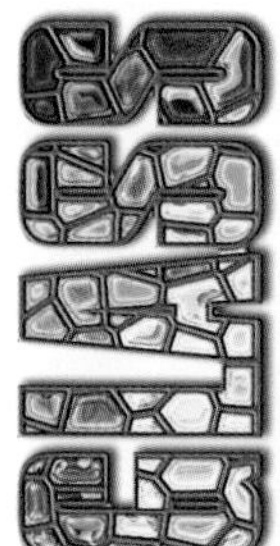

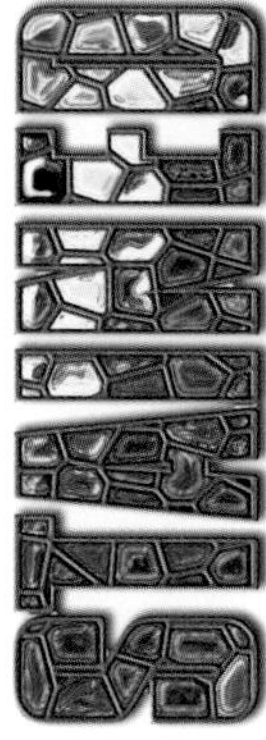

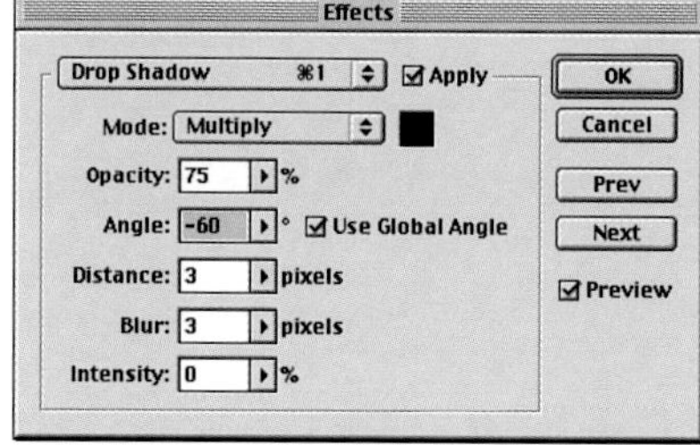

**21** Make the lead layer the active layer and choose Filter➥Noise➥ Add Noise (20, Uniform, Monochromatic) to add some texture to the lead.

# VARIATIONS

## Lead Adjustments

To make the lead and glass panes appear like they are on the same level, double-click on the "f" that appears in the Layers palette next to the text layer name. Choose Bevel and Emboss from the pop-up menu and change the Angle to -60°, Down. Then choose Drop Shadow from the pop-up menu and click on the Apply box. Try these settings to add a small shadow to the glass panes: Angle: -60°, Distance: 3 pixels, Blur: 3 pixels.

## Raised Glass

To make the glass panes pop up from the lead, use the previous variation with these changes: Inner Bevel Angle: 120°, Down; Drop Shadow Angle: 120°.

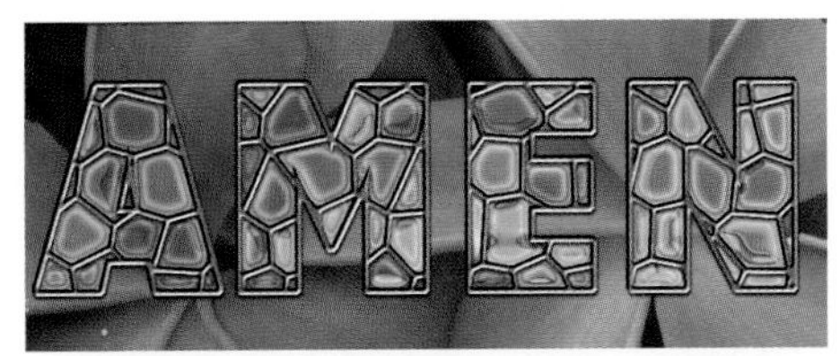



## No background

To get rid of the background around the type, load the selection of the Alpha 1 channel and choose Select➡Modify➡Expand. Expand the selection the same amount as in Step 7. Choose Select➡Inverse, make the Background layer the active layer, and fill the selection with white.

## Jewels

Make these two changes to make a studded jewel effect. In Step 5, set the Border Thickness in the Stained Glass filter to 16. Then in Step 7, expand the selection by 12 pixels. Finish the rest of the steps. ●

This technique shows you how to make type stamps that you can use to build words or fill type outlines.

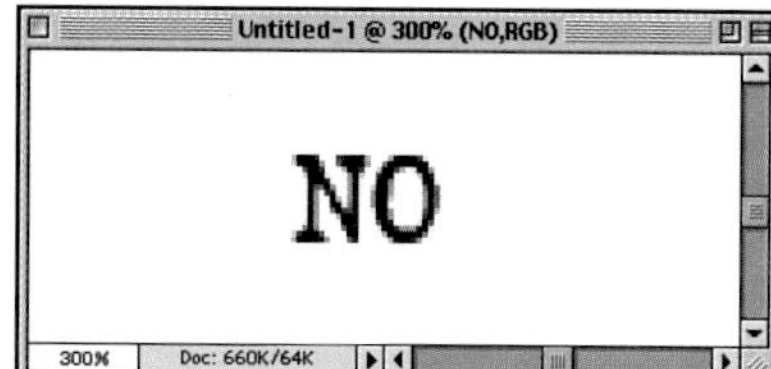


**1** Create a new file and set the foreground color to black (which will ensure the hardness of the type when used as a brush). Use the Type tool to enter the text. Use a small point size. The type that was used here is Love Letter Typewriter at 10 points. Choose Layer➡Type➡Render Layer.

**TIP** **When using small point sizes, you might prefer to turn off the antialiasing option in the Type dialog box. If you don't, the type might be blurred. Make the same adjustment in the Brush Options dialog box in Step 4.**

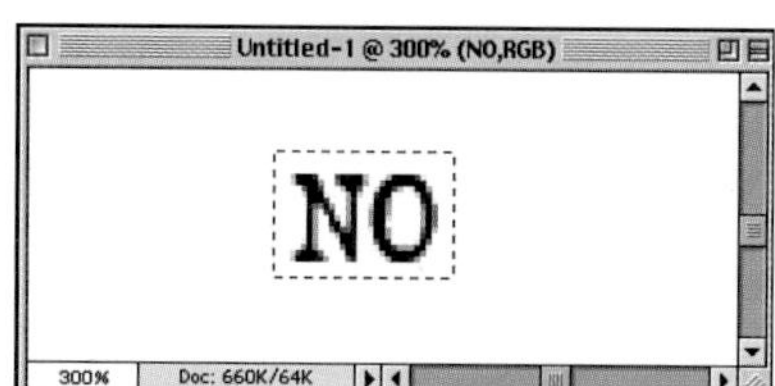


**2** Zoom in on the type. Then select the Marquee tool and drag a rectangular selection around the type.

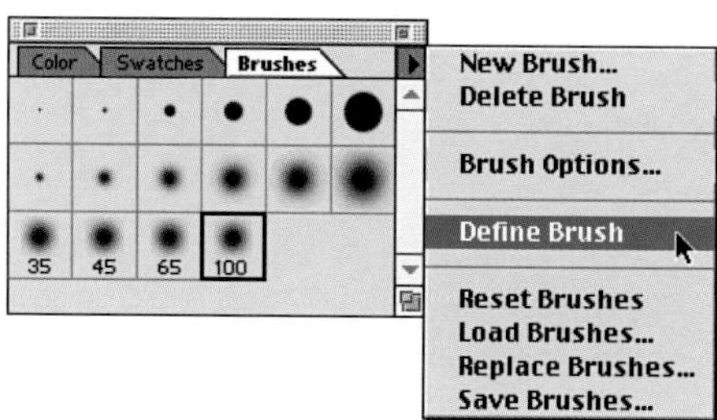


**3** Double-click the Paintbrush tool to select it. Then find the Brushes palette, and choose Define Brush from the palette menu.

**4** If you clicked and dragged the word, now all the letters would blur together and the stamped word would be illegible. To fix that problem, double-click the brush you created (on the Brushes floating palette).

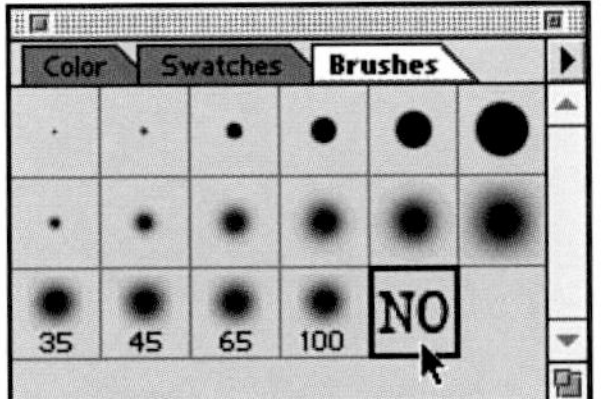


A dialog box appears that will enable you to change the Brush Spacing. The Spacing is the distance the brush will move, relative to the vertical height of the brush (the text), before placing another stamp. Change the Spacing to 100%.

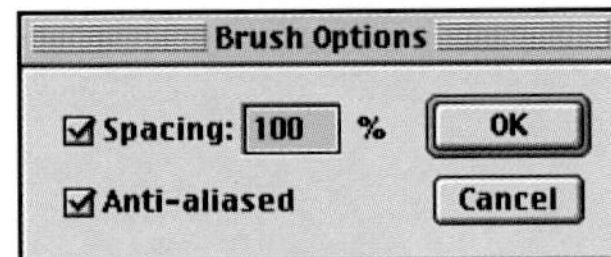


**5** The selection should still be active. Press Delete to clear it and deselect the selection. Double-click the Zoom tool to return to 100% view; then set the foreground color to a color for the stamp (CMYK: 0, 75, 100, 0), and simply "paint" the type.

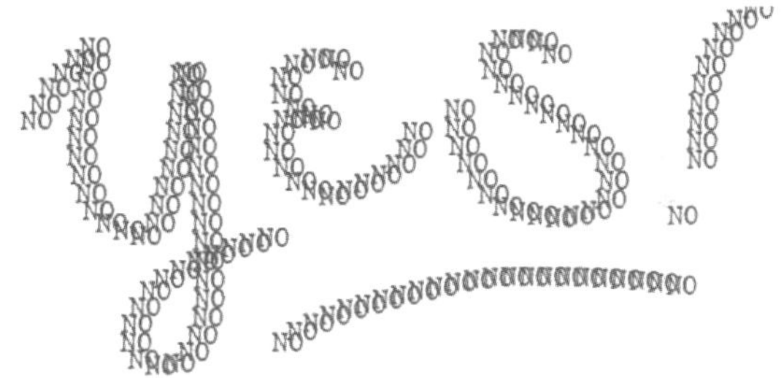

**TIP** **Another useful setting on the Paintbrush Options palette is the Fade amount. Type a number in the Fade box (I used 120 for the "yes" and 10 for the exclamation mark), and set the "Fade to" to Transparent. The type will now fade away as you drag the stamp.**

## Variations

**1** Try using the stamp with a image. Open a file that has an image in it. These apples were clipped from a sample image packaged with Adobe Photoshop 4 (Adobe Photoshop 4➥Samples➥Fruit).

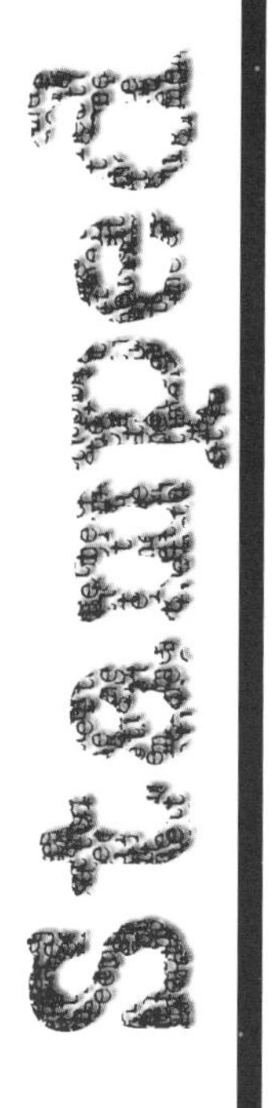

**2** Create a new layer (Layer 2). Change the layer blending mode to Color Dodge, and paint the type over the photo.

For the second apple, I created a new layer (Layer 3) and set the layer blending mode to Color Burn.

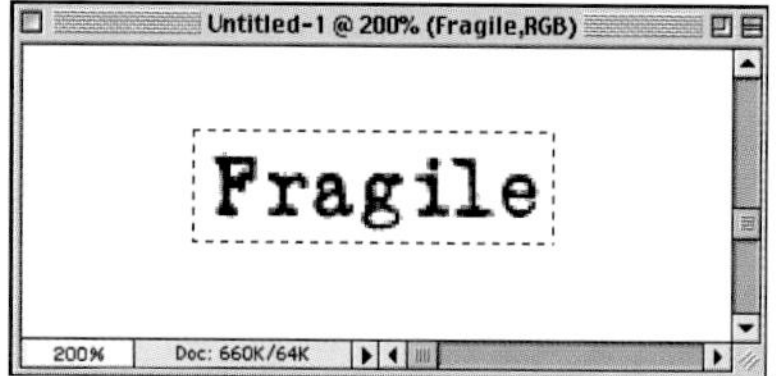


For this variation, I painted with a stamp inside a type selection. Here is the stamp I used.

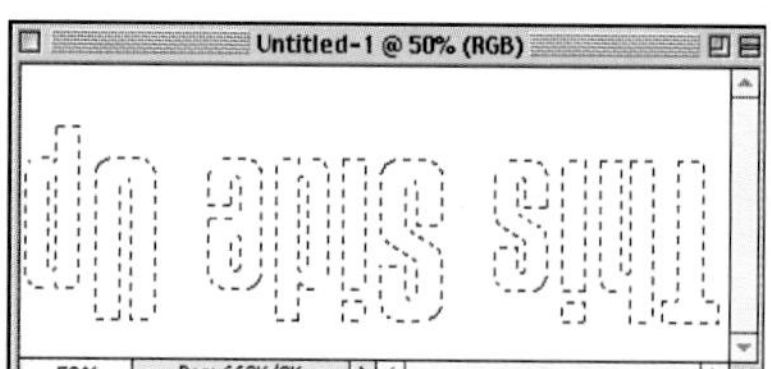


Next, use the Type Mask tool to enter the text (Compacta at 150 points).

Change the foreground color to a color for the type. Select the Paintbrush tool again, and paint into the selection.

If you feather the selection above by choosing Select➡Feather (5 pixels) before you paint in the text, you will get something like this.

Try making other brushes for painting type. I painted a paw, defined it as a brush, changed its spacing to 105%, and then painted this text.

Try using one of the built-in brushes in Photoshop. From the Brushes floating palette arrow menu, choose Load Brushes. Find the Assorted Brushes file on your hard disk: Adobe Photoshop 5.0➥Goodies➥Brushes & Patterns➥Assorted Brushes. Open this file. You can use any of these brushes to paint your type. Don't forget that you can adjust the spacing for any of these brushes.

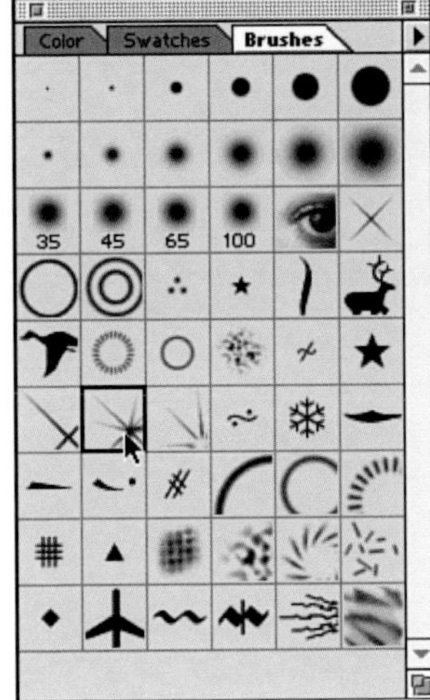


I made this image with the brush that was selected in the previous figure.

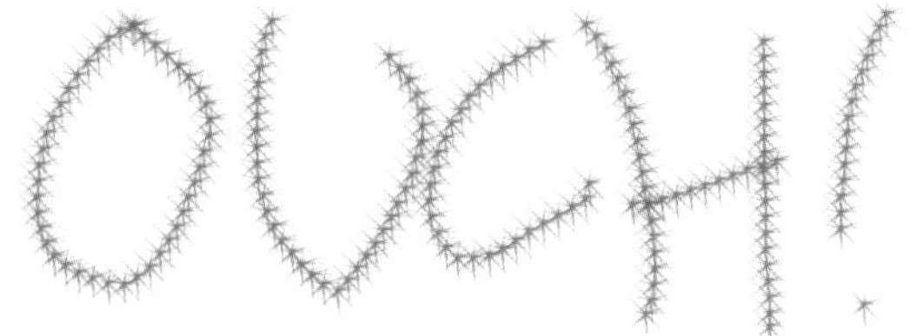

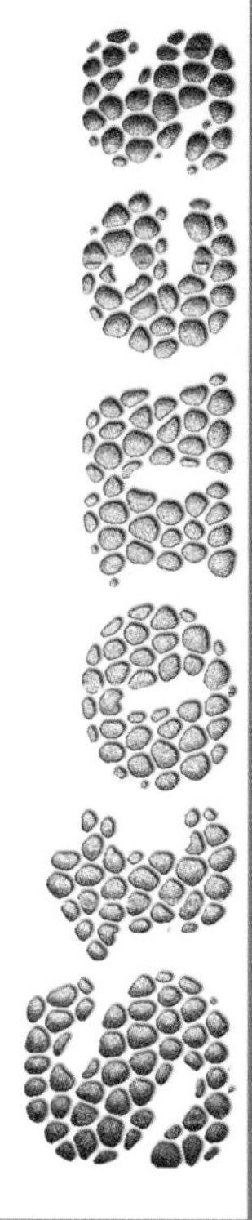

The Stained Glass filter starts the Stones effect by dividing up the letters. From there, a little selection manipulation takes you to the Lighting Effects filter, which rounds out the stones and the effect.

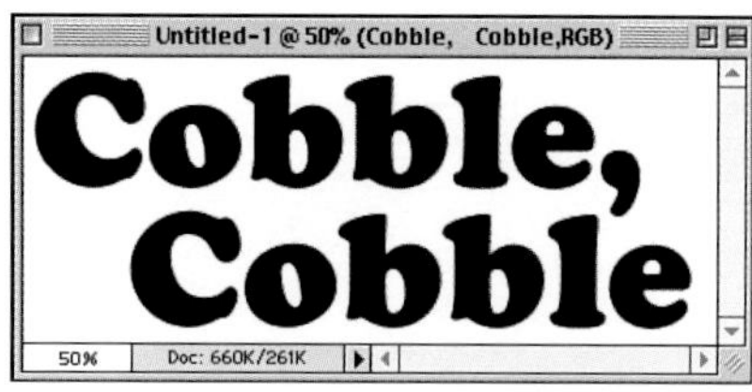


**1** Create a new file. Use the Type tool to enter the text. I used a thick font named Cooper Black at 80 points. The type will be placed automatically on a new layer. Choose Layer➡Type➡Render Layer.

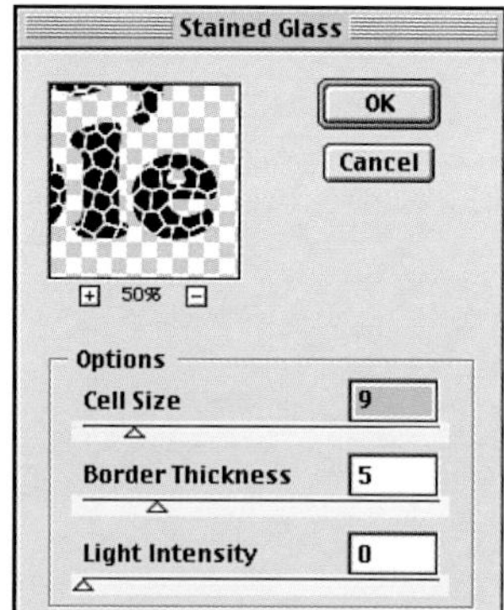


**2** Choose white for the foreground color. Then choose Filter➡Texture➡Stained Glass. Watch the preview to see the approximate sizes of the stones. Adjust the Border Thickness slider for spacing between the stones, and set the Light Intensity to 0. These settings…

…will yield this picture:

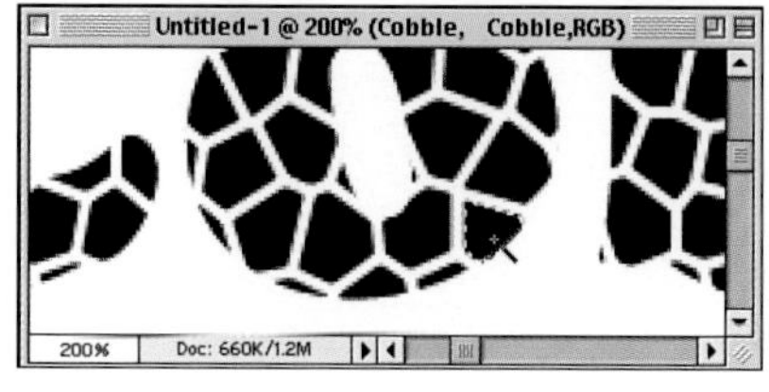


**3** Select the Magic Wand tool and click the wand inside one of the black spots.

4 Choose Select➡Similar. Save this selection to create the Alpha 1 channel. Then choose Select➡Modify➡Smooth. Smooth the selection approximately 3 pixels.

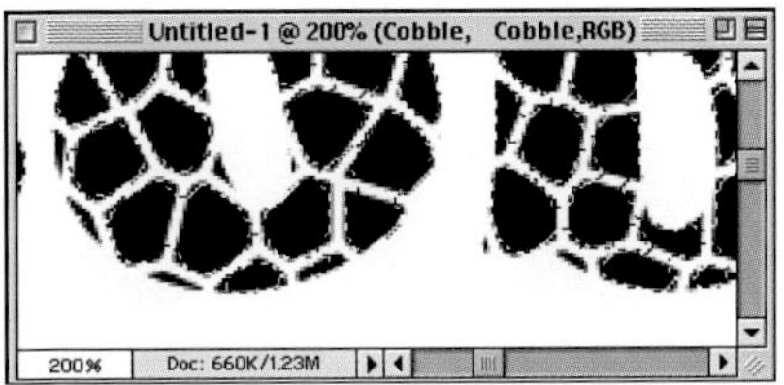


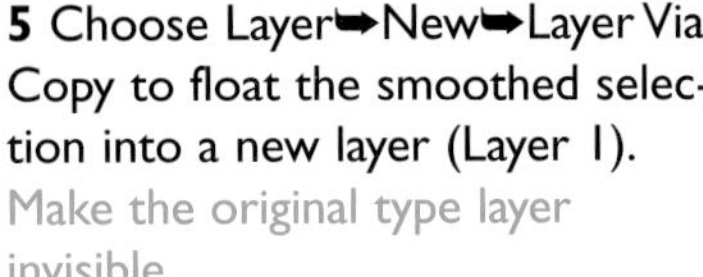

5 Choose Layer➡New➡Layer Via Copy to float the smoothed selection into a new layer (Layer 1). Make the original type layer invisible.

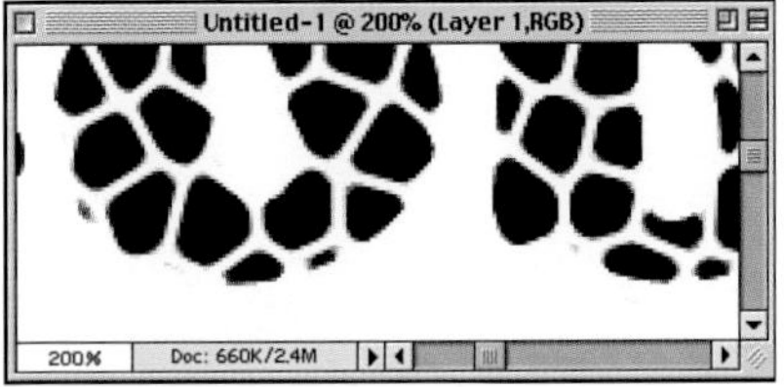


6 Turn on the Preserve Transparency option for Layer 1 on the Layers floating palette. Change the foreground color to black, and press the (Option-Delete) [Alt-Delete] keys to fill the layer with black. Then turn off the Preserve Transparency option. A few stones still might be attached to each other.

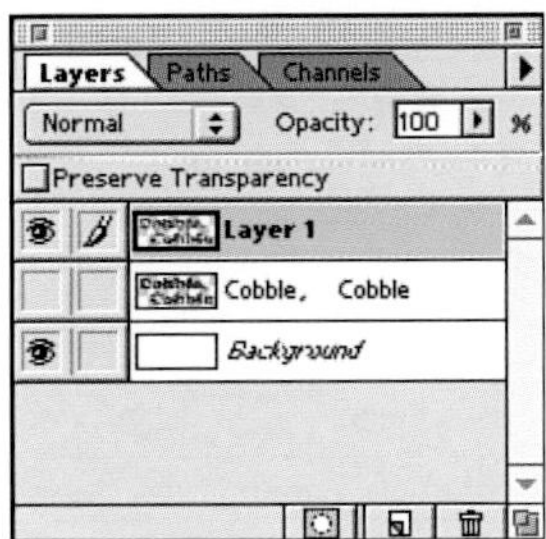


7 To get rid of these connections, load the Alpha 1 channel selection. Choose Select➡Inverse and press Delete. Deselect the selection.

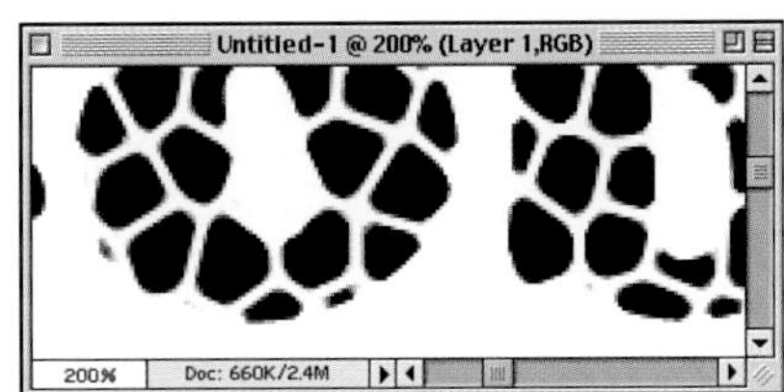


8 Next, duplicate Layer 1 to create Layer 1 copy. Then make Layer 1 the active layer again.

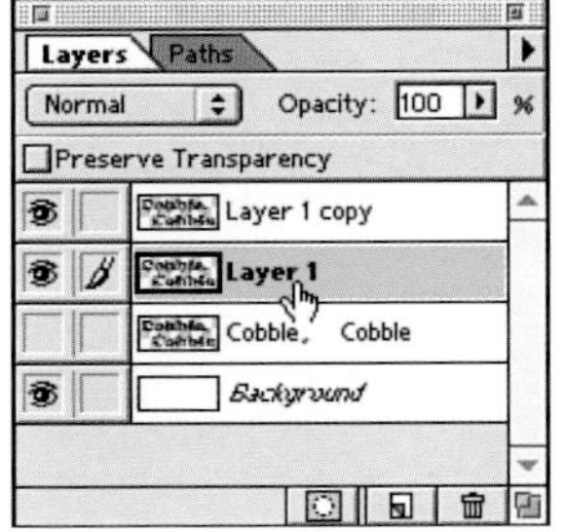

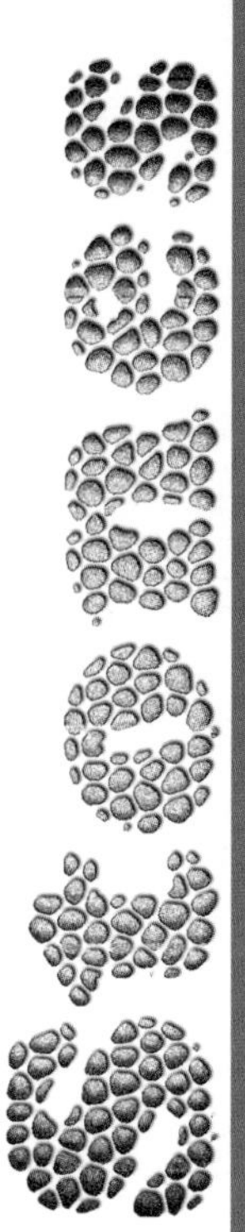

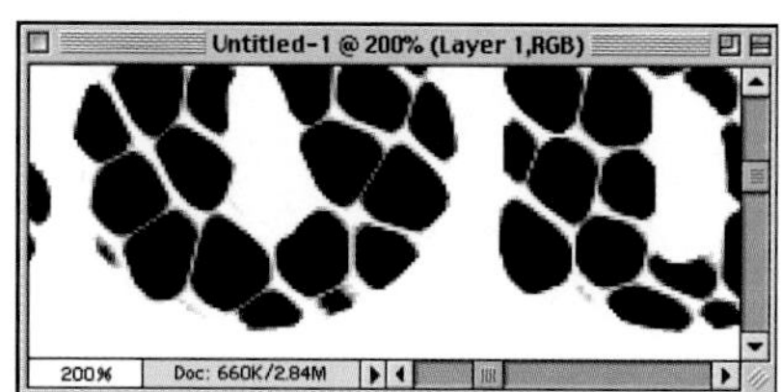


**9** Select the Move tool and use the arrow keys to move this layer, which will be the shadow. I moved it two keystrokes to the right and two keystrokes down. It looks like the type is spreading in the direction you move it.

**10** Then load the transparency selection for Layer 1 copy. Press Delete. You shouldn't see anything change, except for traces of white around the lower right of the stones.

**11** Deselect the selection, and choose Filter➥Blur➥Guassian Blur. Blur the shadow just a little, about 1 pixel. The lightness of the shadow near the edge of the stones makes this homemade shadow work out better for this effect than Photoshop's built-in drop shadow feature.

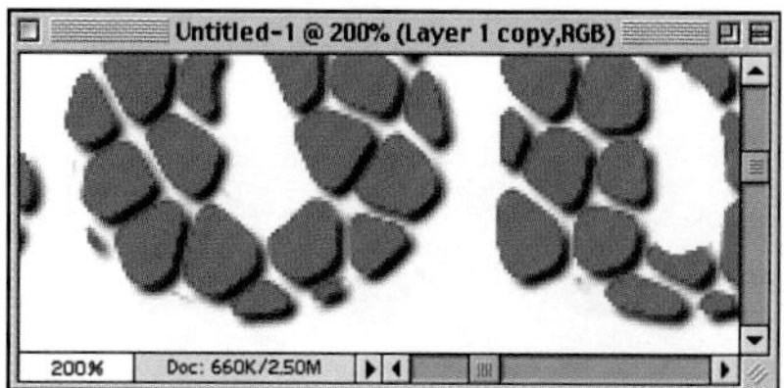


**12** Make Layer 1 copy active and load the transparency selection for this layer. Choose 40% gray for the foreground color and fill the selection.

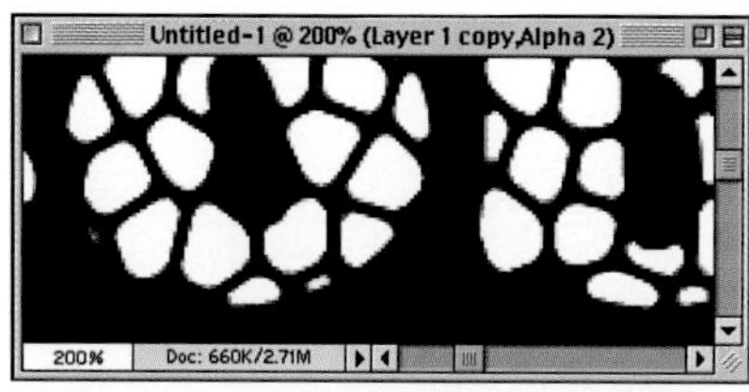


**13** Save the selection to create the Alpha 2 channel. Make the Alpha 2 channel active.

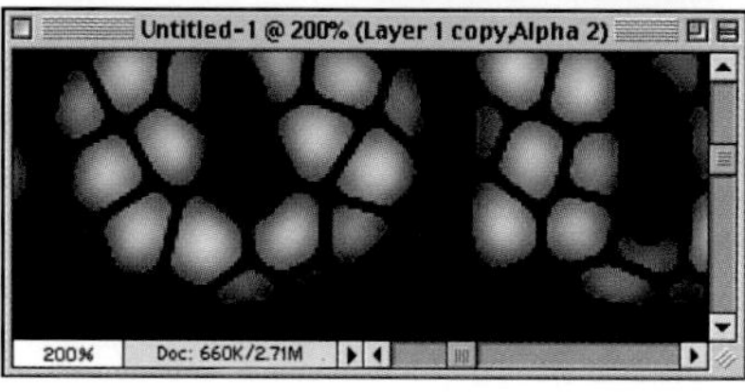


**14** While the selection is still active, choose Filter➥Blur➥ Gaussian Blur. Raise the radius to about 4.5 pixels. Because the selection is active, blurring appears only inside the white areas.

**15** Return to the composite channel, and make Layer 1 copy the active layer.

**16** Next, choose Filter➡Render➡ Lighting Effects. You can select the Stones preset from the pop-up menu or match these settings (which are very similar to the Default settings). Move the light in the Preview box if necessary.

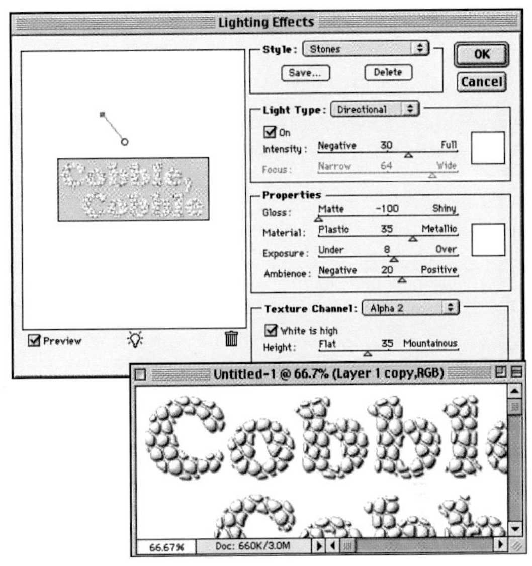


**17** For the final touch, choose Filter➡Noise➡Add Noise. Adjust the Amount to your liking. I set it at 25, and turned on the Gaussian option. Turn the Monochromatic option on as well. ●

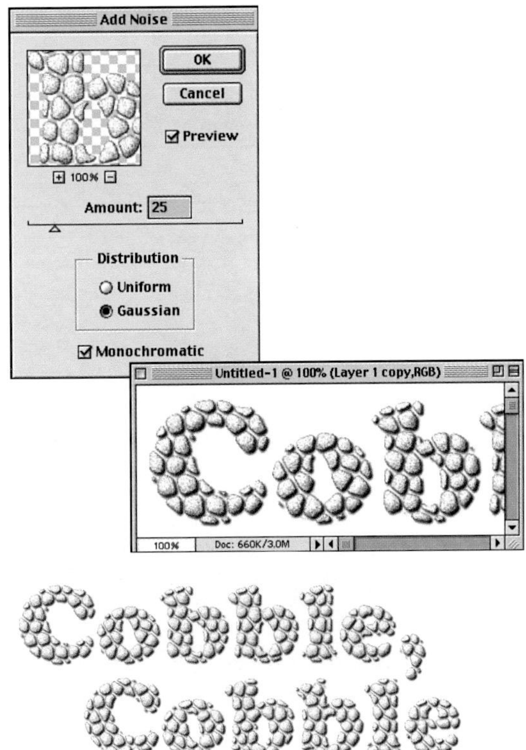

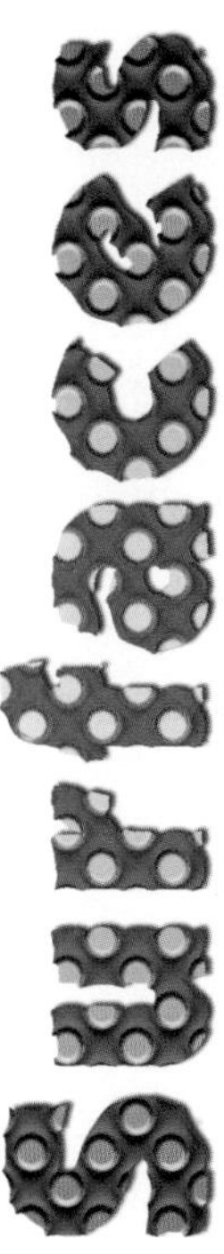

## TOOLBOX

Circle Pattern

Circle Pattern Small

Surface (Lighting Effects Style)

In this technique, the Displace and Lighting Effects filters are used in tandem to create type that appears to be mapped onto an irregular surface. You can create your own surfaces or use the ones that I have created. First I'll show you the method; then I'll show you some of the ways you can use it.

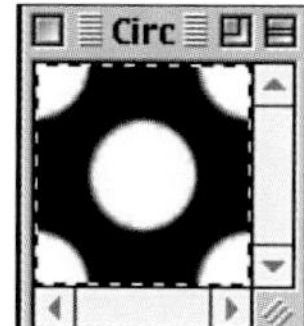

1 Creating surface maps is done in a channel. The best strategy is to fill the channel with a pattern and then use various filters to manipulate the pattern. To produce the first example here, open the Circle Pattern file from the P5TM CD-ROM (P5TM➡P5TM Files➡Patterns➡Circle Pattern). Choose Select➡All and Edit➡Define Pattern. Close the file.

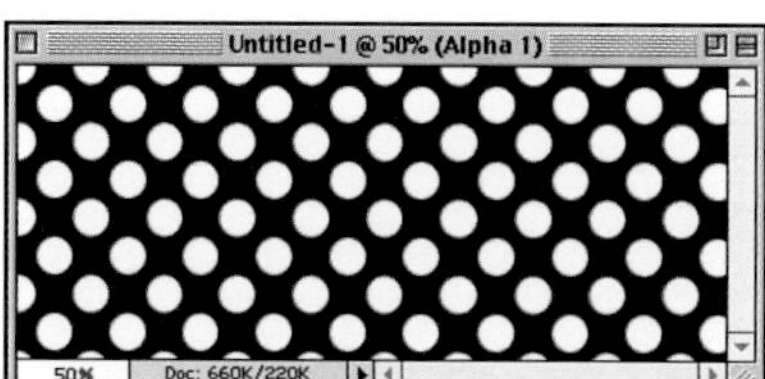


2 In a new file, create a new channel (Alpha 1) and choose Edit➡Fill (Use: Pattern, 100%, Normal).

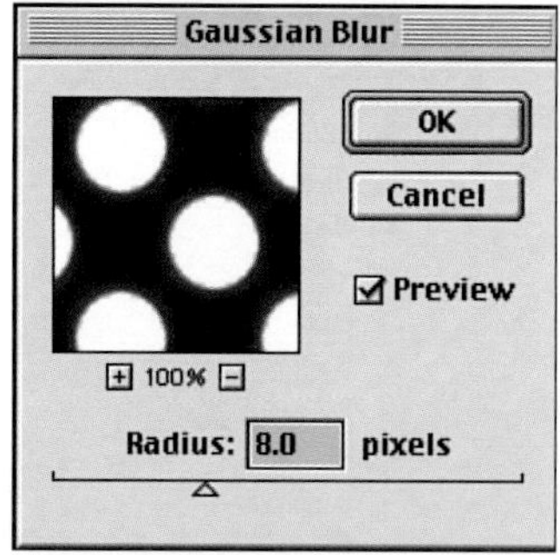


3 Duplicate the channel to make the Alpha 2 channel. Load the selection of the Alpha 1 channel; choose Select➡Inverse and Filter➡Blur➡Gaussian Blur. Blur the selection just enough to bring out some gray around the edges of the circles (8 pixels).

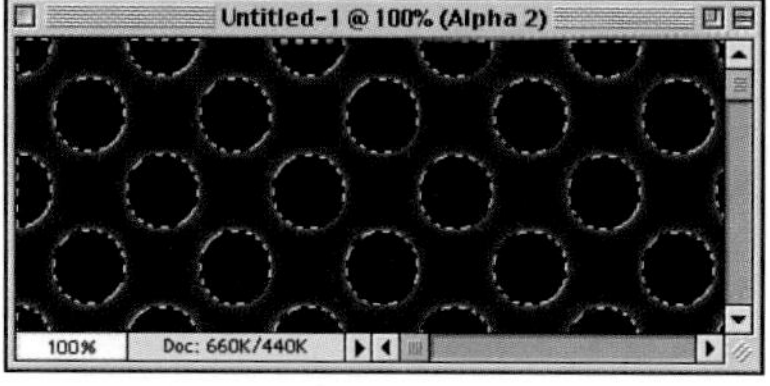


4 Choose Select➡Inverse again and choose Image➡Adjust➡Invert.

**5** Deselect the selection and bring back the Gaussian Blur filter dialog box (Command-Option-F) [Control-Option-F]. Lower the Blur Radius to approximately 3 pixels. This channel will be the surface map for the type.

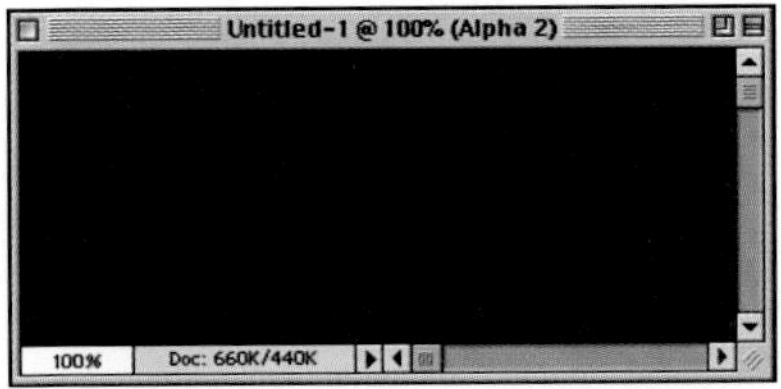


**6** Choose Duplicate Channel from the Channels palette menu, select New from the Document menu, and name the file (Blurred Circles). When the new file opens, save it (Photoshop format) and close it.

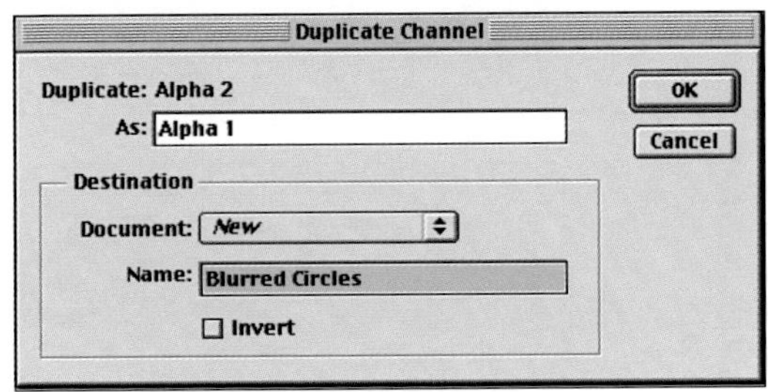


**7** Return to the composite channel, choose a foreground color for the type (CMYK: 54, 0, 72, 0), and use the Type tool to enter the text. I used Kabel Ultra at 85 points. Choose Layer➡Type➡Render Layer.

**8** Choose Select➡All and choose Filter➡Distort➡Displace. Set the Horizontal and Vertical values low and equal to each other. I set them both at 5%. It is important to select the entire layer before using the Displace filter. Otherwise the distorted shape of the type will not align with the highlights and shadows created by the Lighting Effects filter.

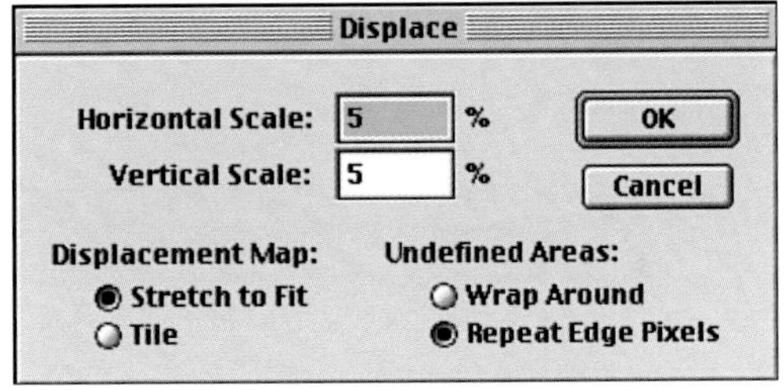


**9** Click OK and a dialog box opens asking you to find a displacement map to use. Find the file that you saved in Step 6 (Blurred Circles), and click Open. The edges of the type will react to the distortion, but there should not be any changes inside the type.

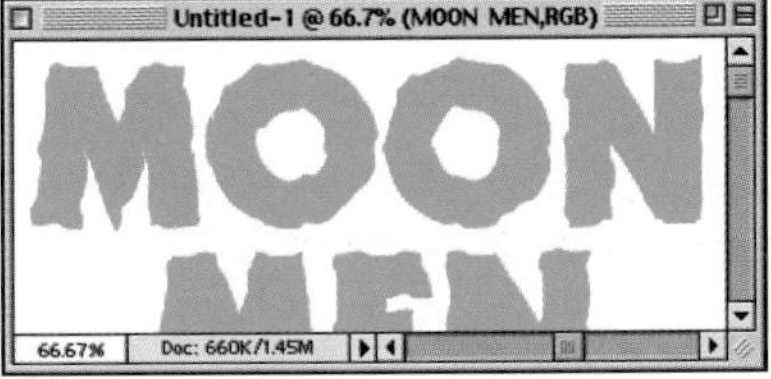

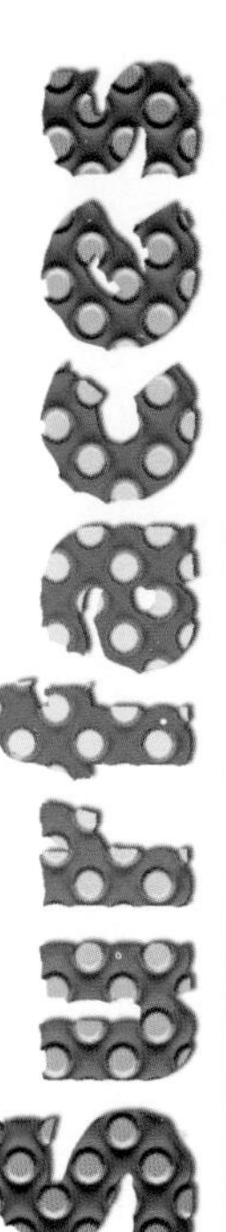


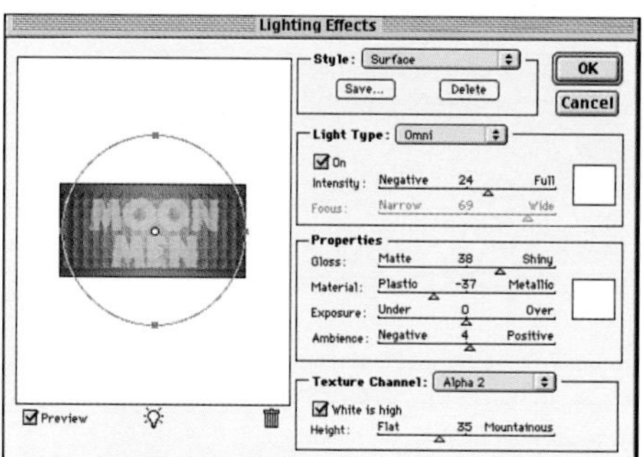

**10** The type has been shaped. To add the highlights and shadows, choose Filter➥Render➥Lighting Effects. Either select the Surface preset or match the settings seen here. The texture map should be the channel that was duplicated in Step 6 (Alpha 2), and the Height should be kept low.

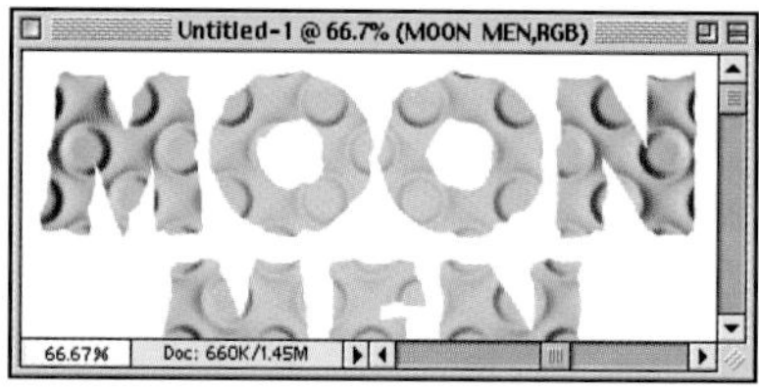

The distortions made by the Displace filter and the highlights and shadows created by the Lighting Effects filter should appear to fit each other.

**11** Adding a drop shadow enhances the three-dimensional nature of this effect. Use the built-in drop shadow feature (Layer➥Effects➥Drop Shadow) with the default settings.

## VARIATIONS

### Holy Perforated Surfaces!

For this variation, I opened the Circle Pattern Small file in Step 1 (P5TM➥P5TM Files➥Patterns➥ Circle Pattern Small). This file is identical to the Circle pattern file but it has been compressed into a smaller size. Repeat Steps 1 through 5. Here is what the Alpha 1 copy channel looks like after Step 5.

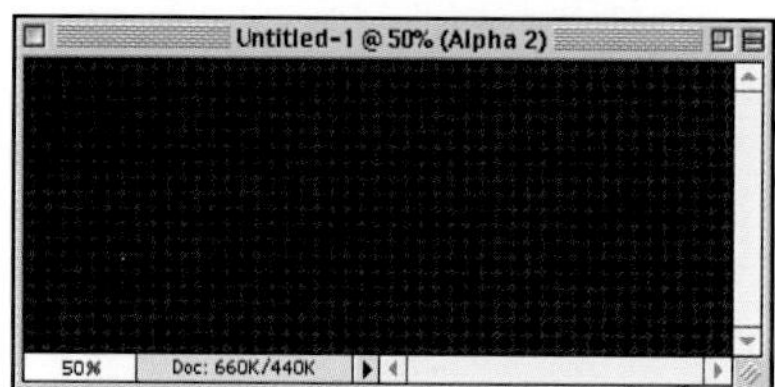

Repeat Steps 6 through 10 (Kabel at 82 points; CMYK: 0, 54, 72, 0).

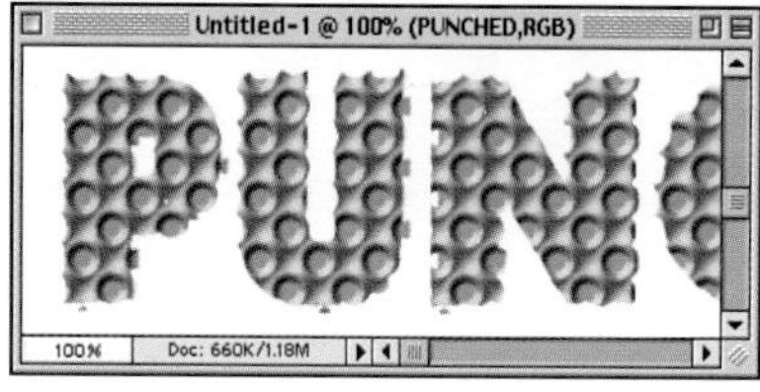

Then load the selection of the Alpha 1 channel and press Delete. Then follow Step 11 to create something like this.

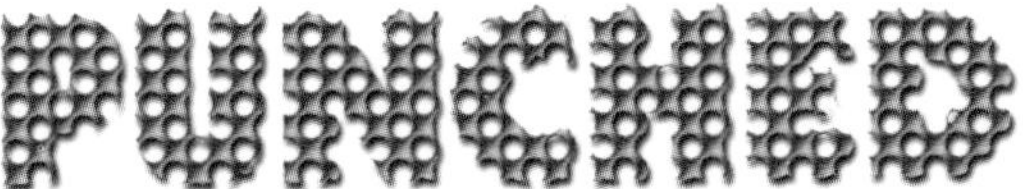


## Photoshop PostScript Patterns

There are a number of patterns included with Photoshop 5.0. You can use these patterns with this technique.

In Step 1, open the Herringbone 2 file (Photoshop 5.0➥Goodies➥Brushes & Patterns➥PostScript Patterns➥Herringbone 2). Choose Image➥Adjust➥Invert; then Select➥All and Edit➥Define Pattern. Close the file but don't save the changes.

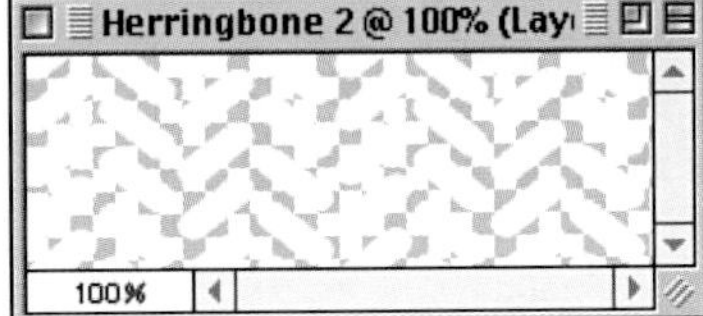


Follow Step 2; then load the selection of the Alpha 1 copy channel. Choose Filter➥Blur➥Gaussian Blur and set the Radius so that the white areas begin to look rounded (2.5 pixels). Then deselect the selection and choose Filter➥Blur➥Gaussian Blur again. Lower the Radius to about 1 pixel. That completes the texture channel.

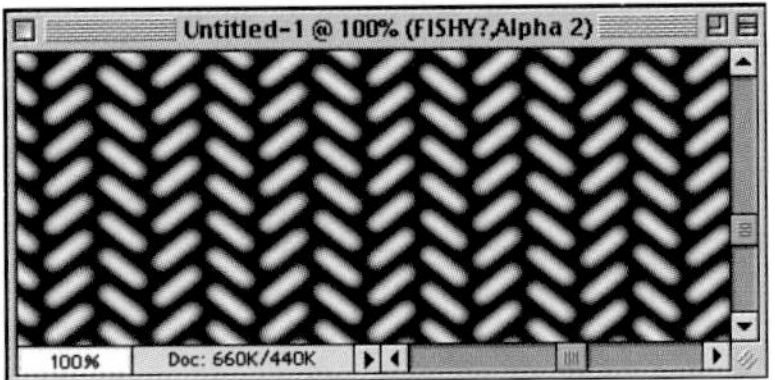


Complete the rest of the steps.

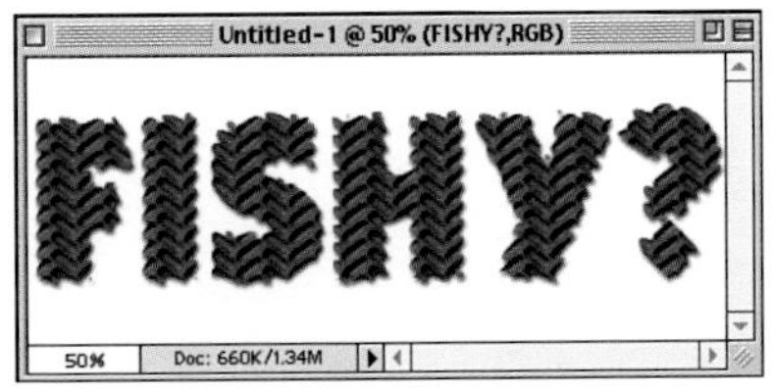


To make this a two-color image, load the selection from the Alpha 1 channel; then choose Image➥Adjust➥Hue/Saturation. Use the Hue slider to find a second color and use the Saturation and Lightness sliders for fine-tuning.

## Type on Type

The last variation maps type across words raised from the background.

Choose a foreground color for the type (CMYK: 0, 100, 75, 25) and use the Type Mask tool to enter the text (Kabel Ultra at 115 points). This type will be the colored type that is mapped onto the textured type.

If you want to rotate the type as I have done here, choose Select➡Transform Selection and use the handles to manipulate the type. When satisfied, press (Return) [Enter] and fill the selection with the foreground color. Deselect the selection.

Create a new channel (Alpha 1) and use the Type Mask tool to enter the text (Kabel Ultra at 115 points). Again choose Select➡Transform Selection if you want to rotate the type. Fill the selection with white.

Keep the selection active and choose Filter➡Blur➡Gaussian Blur. Adjust the Radius so that type begins to look rounded. I set it at 8 pixels.

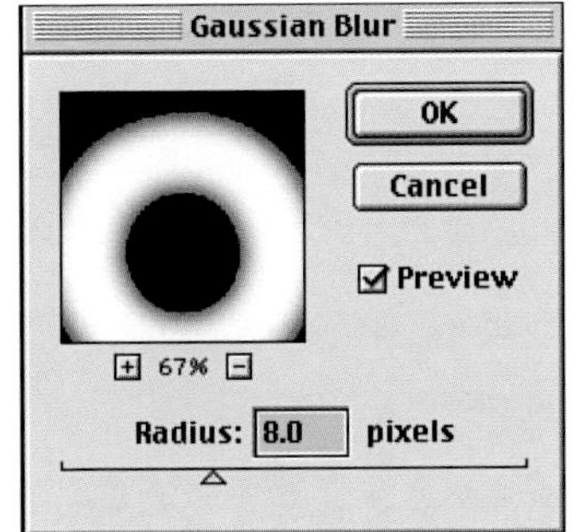


Perform Step 6, return to the composite channel, and then complete Steps 8 through 10. In Step 8, I set the Displace percentages both to 3%. ●

It's time to get in touch with your peelings. Create stripes using paths and the Stroke Subpath command. Then use the Lighting Effects filter to set them apart from each other.

**1** Choose a foreground color for the type (CMYK: 20, 100, 100, 0) and use the Type tool to enter the text. I used Meta Plus Black at 90 points. Choose Layer➡Type➡Render Layer.

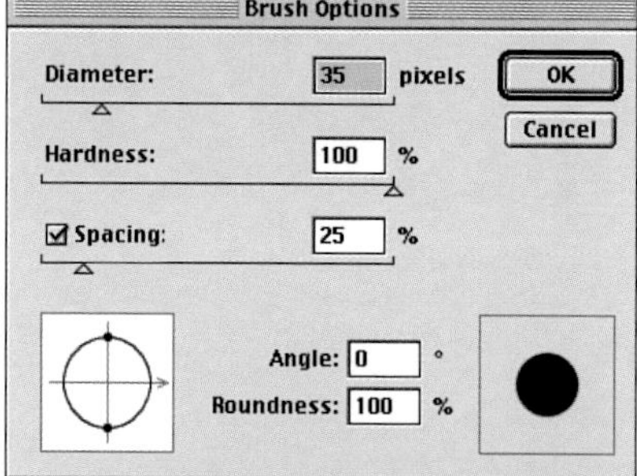


**2** Open the Brushes palette and double-click on any round brush to open the Brush Options dialog box. The Diameter determines the width of the stripes running through the type. I set it at 35 pixels. (Hardness: 100%, Spacing: 25%, Angle: 0°, Roundness: 100%).

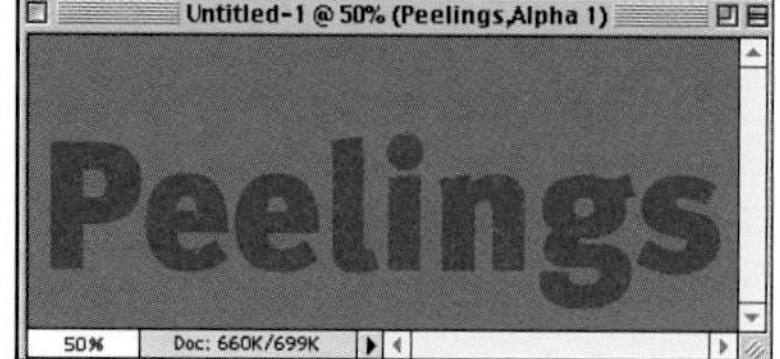


**3** Create a new channel (Alpha 1), and make the RGB channels visible. You should see the type created in Step 1 appear within a red haze. The red haze lets you know that more than one channel is visible, but don't worry—the channel that is highlighted in the channels palette (Alpha 1) is the only channel that will be affected.

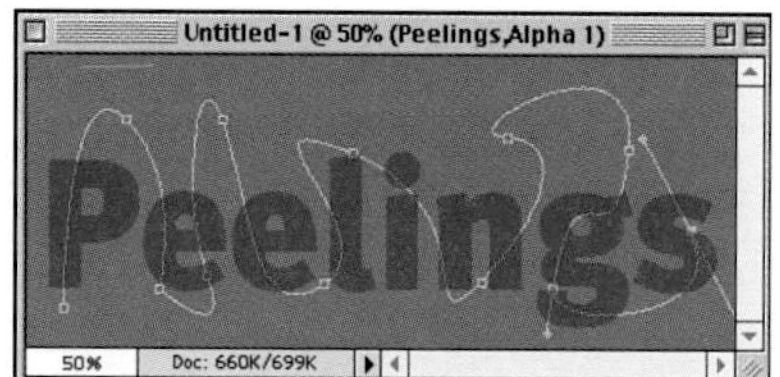


**4** Select the Freeform Pen tool and drag it across the type to create a new path.

TOOLBOX

Torn (Lighting Effects Style)

**5** Make sure that the Foreground color is white, and double-click on the Paintbrush tool to bring the Paintbrush Options palette to the front. Choose Reset Tool from the palette menu. This sets up the Paintbrush for use by the Stroke SubPath command. Find the Paths palette and click on the Stroke SubPath icon at the bottom of the palette.

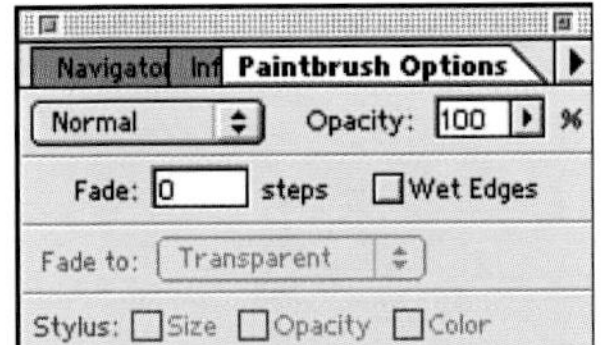


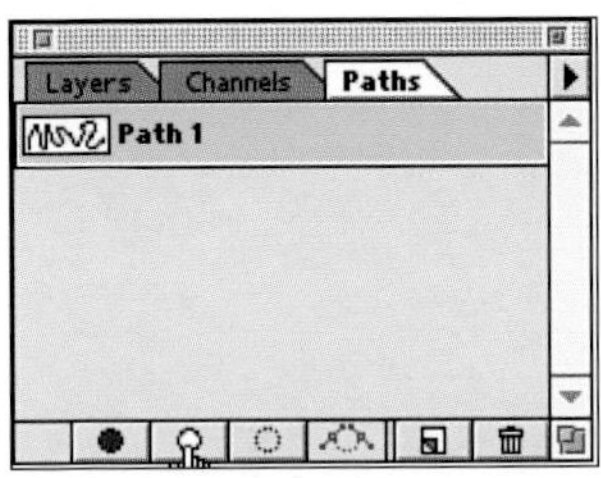


Choose Turn Off Path from the Path palette menu. You should now have a stripe through the type.

**TIP** **It makes no difference whether or not you make one path or many paths. To make more than one path, simply keep repeating Steps 4 and 5.**

**6** Duplicate the channel to create Alpha 1 copy. Load the selection for that channel, and choose Select➡Inverse, and Filter➡Blur➡Gaussian Blur. Set the Radius to approximately 25.

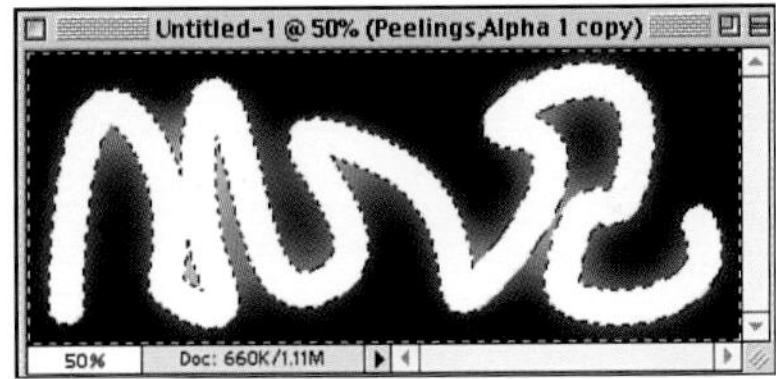


**7** Choose Select➡Inverse and Filter➡Blur➡Gaussian➡Blur again but use a slightly smaller radius this time. Try 8. This is what you're looking for.

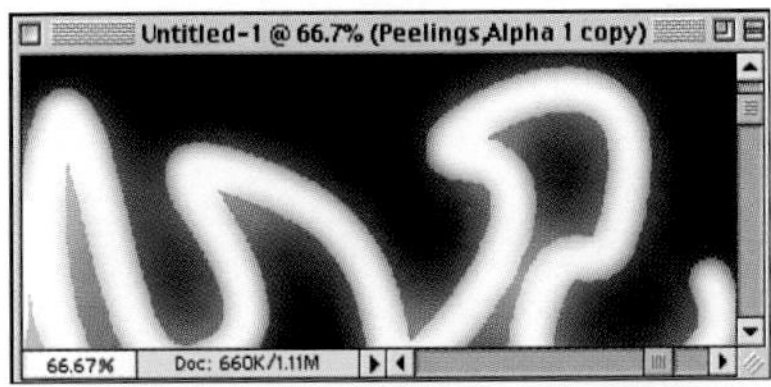


**8** Choose Image➡Adjust➡Invert to invert the stripes.

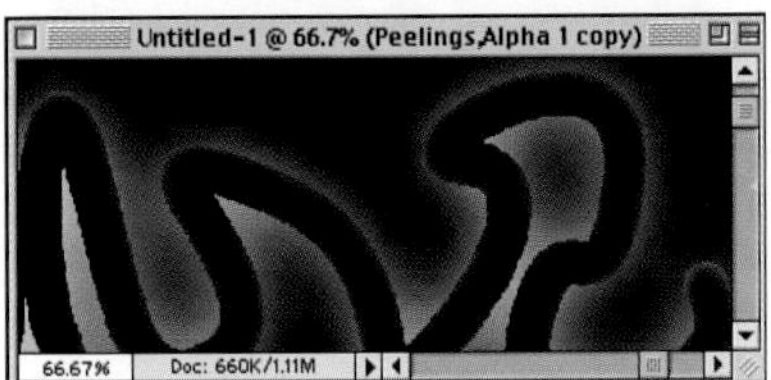

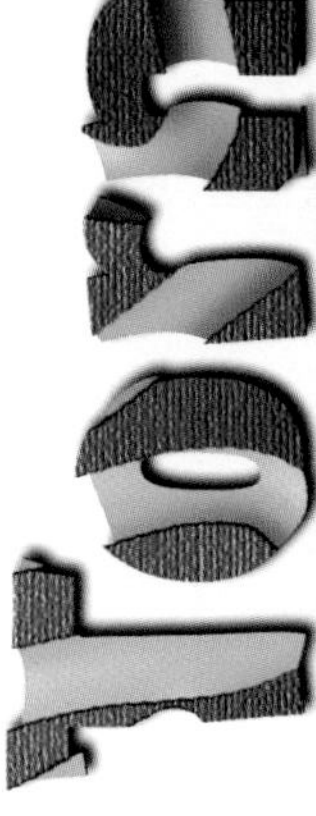

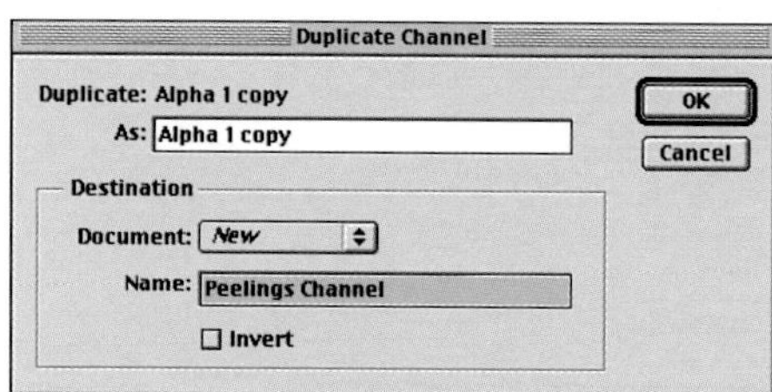


**9** Choose Duplicate Channel from the Channels palette menu. Choose New for the Document, name the new file (Peelings Channel), and click OK.

**10** Save the new file that opened; then close it. This file will be used as a displacement map in Step 12. The blurred, gray edges causes the edges of the stripes to be distorted.

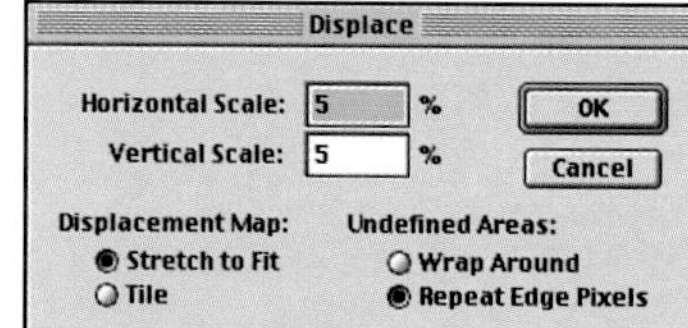


**11** Return to the type layer (Peelings). Select➡All and choose Filter➡Distort➡Displace. Set the Horizontal and Vertical Scale percentages both to 5 (Stretch to Fit, Repeat Edge Pixels).

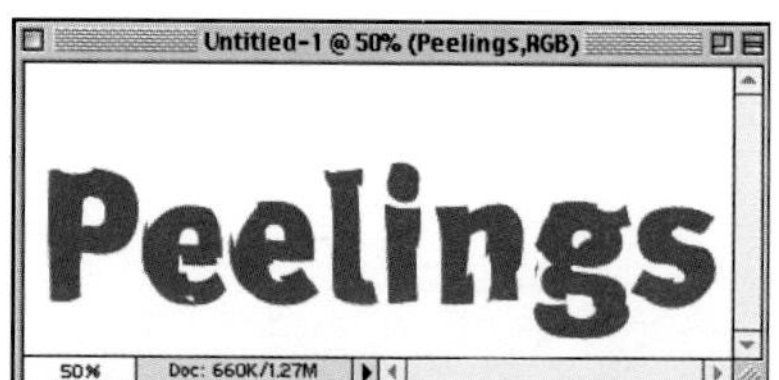


**12** A new dialog box opens asking you to find a displacement map. Locate the file saved in Step 10 (Peelings Channel) and click Open. You see small distortions in the type. Deselect the selection.

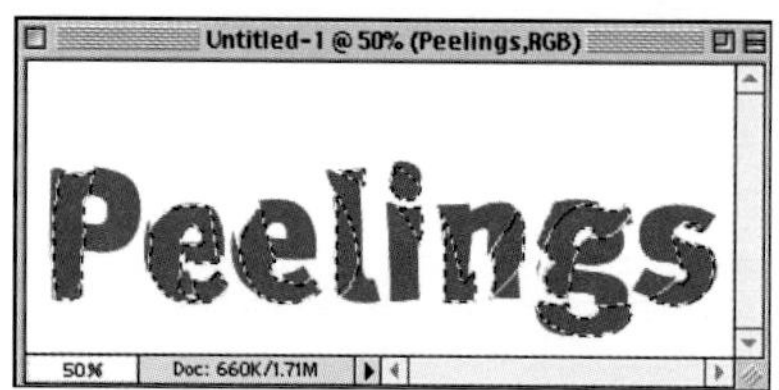


**13** Load the transparency selection from the type (Peelings) layer; then intersect that selection with the selection from the Alpha 1 channel.

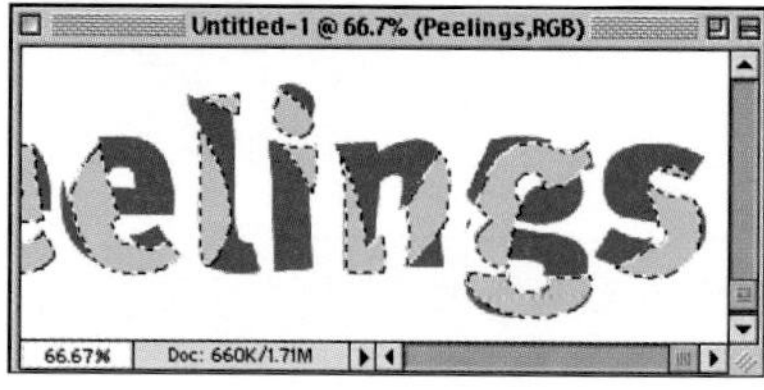


**14** Choose a second foreground color (CMYK: 20, 10, 70, 0) for the type and fill the selection. Deselect the selection.

**15** Next, choose Filter➡Render➡ Lighting Effects. Select the Torn preset from the pop-up menu or match the settings seen here.

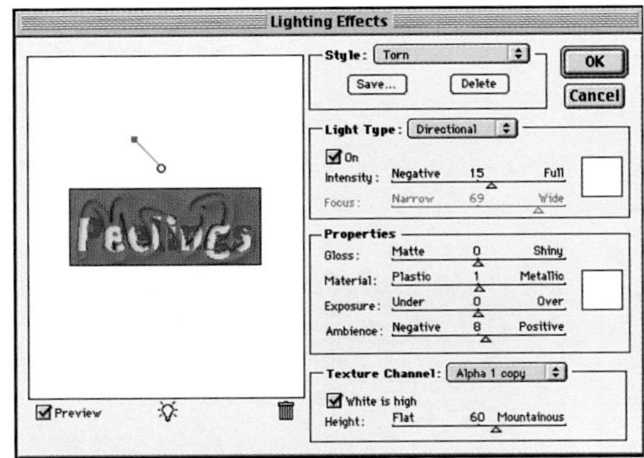


Click OK to see the effect.

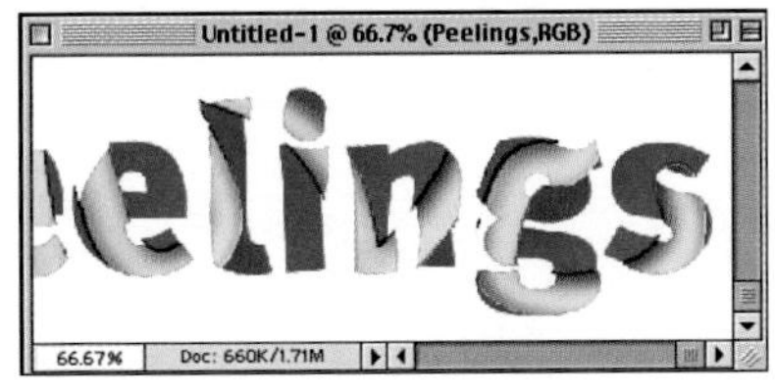


**16** And there you have it. To fine-tune the lighter color, I redid Step 13 to make a selection, added a little noise (Filter➡Noise➡Add Noise), and adjusted the color (Image➡Adjust➡Hue/Saturation). Always the shadow.

## VARIATIONS

Adding texture to one of the colors helps separate the two parts (Meta Plus Black at 130 points). Load the transparency selection from the type layer and then subtract the selection from the Alpha 1 channel.

Choose Filter➡Texture➡ Texturizer. Use these settings: Canvas, Scaling: 135%, Relief: 10, Light: Top. ●

This classic effect has been made even easier with the new layer effects, and the technique described here gives you great control over the transparent box even after it has been created.

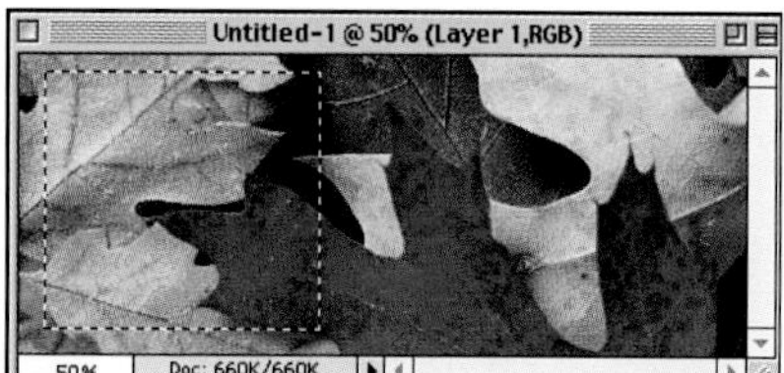


**1** Open a file containing an image for the background. I used this one from Vivid Details (P5TM➥Images➥Vivid Details➥MM_0028.TIF). Create a new layer (Layer 1) and use one of the selection tools to make a selection for the shape of the box.

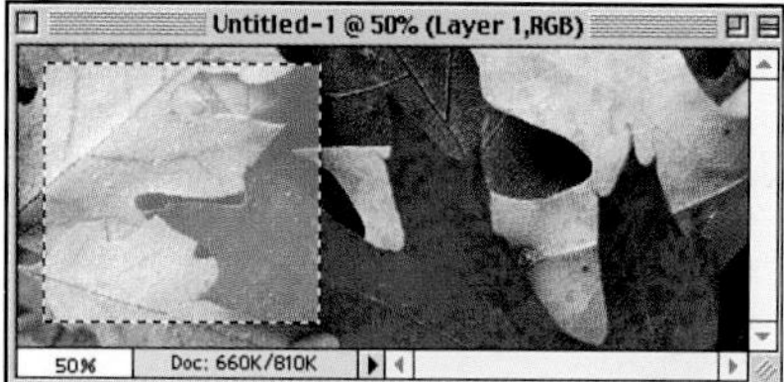


**2** Choose white for the foreground color and fill the selection. Then lower the Layer 1 Opacity to 50%. You might set the Opacity to any percentage that works—as long as it is light enough for the type to be read.

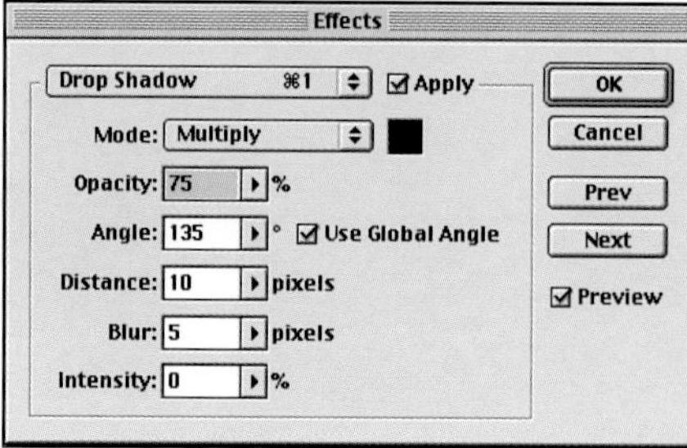


**3** Choose Layer➥Effects➥Drop Shadow and choose settings for the shadow. Here is what I used.

And here is the result.

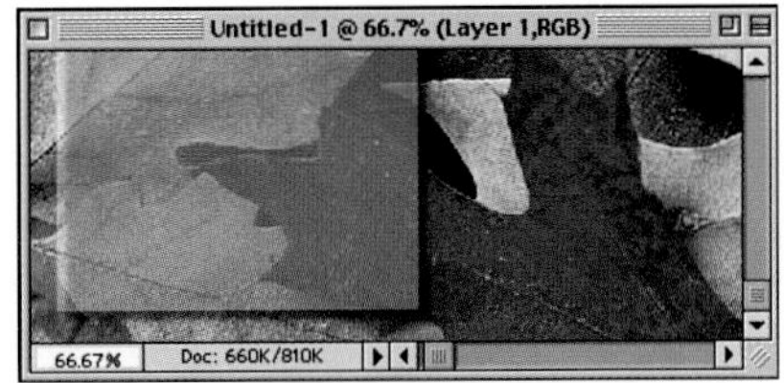


**4** Choose Layer➡Effects➡Create Layer to put the drop shadow into a new layer below the white box.

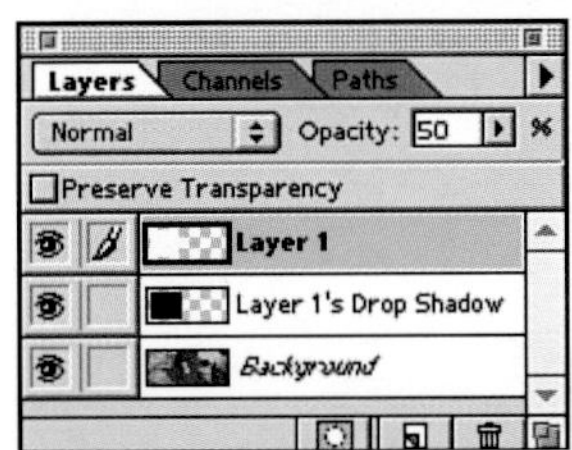


**5** Make the drop shadow layer active. The selection should still be active. Press Delete to clear the shadow away from underneath the white box. Deselect the selection.

**6** Link the two new layers by clicking in the box to the right of the eye next to the Layer 1 preview in the Layers palette. You can now use the Move tool to move the box around the image.

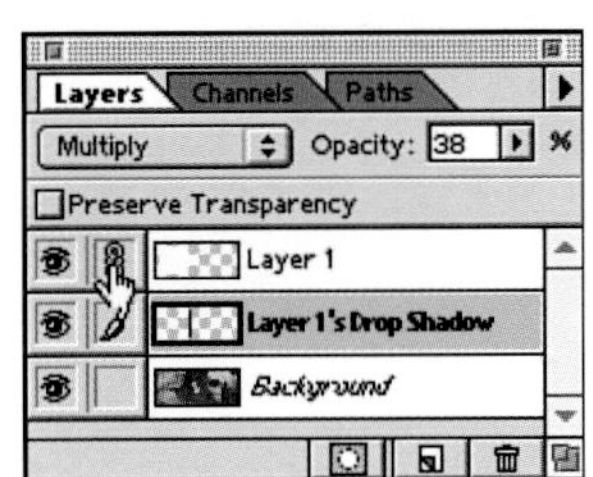


**7** Of course, we need to add type. Make Layer 1 active and use the Type tool to enter the text (Adobe Garamond Regular at 12 points).

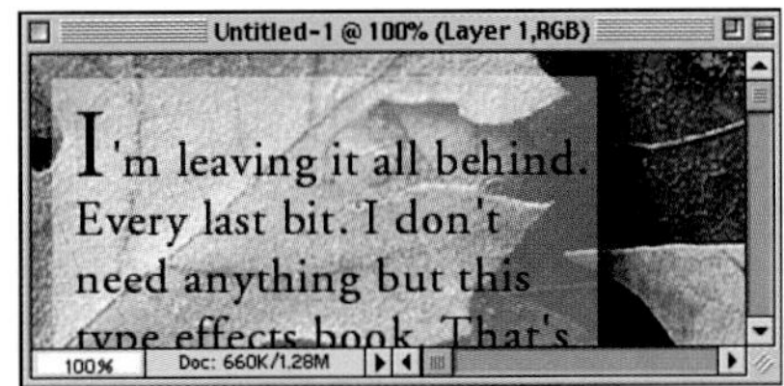

**8** Also, you can adjust the whiteness of the box by using the Layer 1 Opacity slider. And you can darken or lighten the shadow by using the Opacity slider for the shadow layer. Here is the image after adjustments.

## VARIATIONS

### Color

For this variation, I filled the selection in Step 2 with a color (CMYK: 50, 25, 0, 0) instead of white and I used white type. I also added a drop shadow to the type layer after completing Step 8.

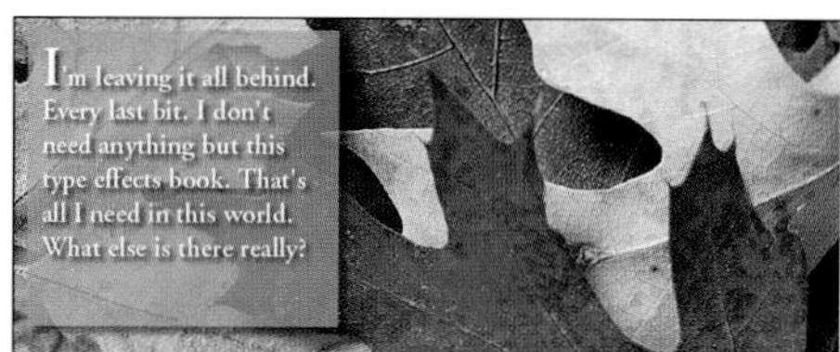

### Transparent Type

Instead of making a box in Step 1, use the Type Mask tool to enter the text (Matrix Bold at 65 points). Complete the rest of the steps. This Vivid Details image is also on the CD-ROM (P5TM➥Images➥Vivid Details➥MM_0122.TIF).

### Cut Out

After Step 2, deselect the selection and use the Type Mask tool to enter the text (Matrix at 65 points). Press Delete to clear the type from the box; then load the transparency selection of the current layer before finishing the rest of the steps.

Applying filters to individual color channels makes these halftone dots vibrate.

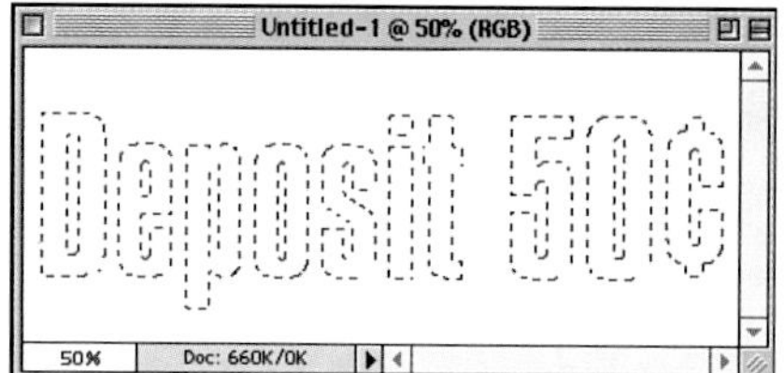


**1** Create a new file and then use the Type Mask tool to enter the text. (I used Compacta at 120 points.)

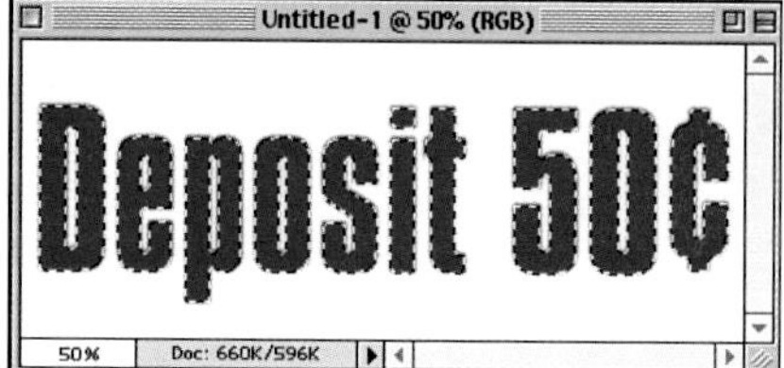


**2** Choose Select➥Feather and enter a value of 1.5 pixels. Choose a foreground color for the type. Color choice for this effect is important. A color that is a mixture of red, green, and blue works best because each of the color channels contain information that can be "vibrated." Purple is a good choice because there is red, green, and blue in it. I have used RGB values of 86, 66, and 129. Fill the type selection with the foreground color.

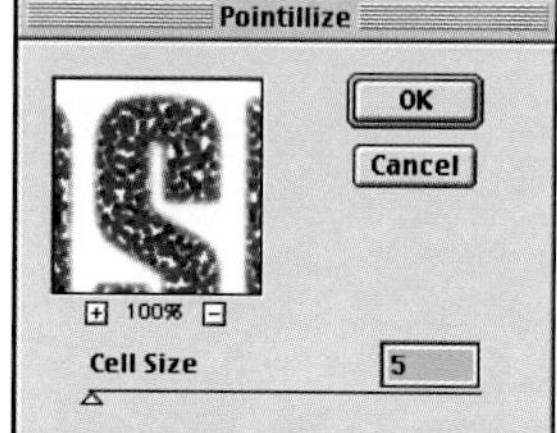


**3** While the type selection is still active, choose Filter➥Pixelate➥ Pointillize. This filter makes your image look like a pointillist painting. Enter a Cell size of 5 pixels.

**4** Deselect the type and choose Filter➥Pixelate➥Color Halftone. Click on the Defaults button and enter a Max. Radius of 4 pixels.

**5** Make only the Red channel active, and choose Filter➡Pixelate➡Mosaic. Enter a cell size of 2 pixels. Then choose Filter➡Blur➡Gaussian Blur and enter a blur Radius of 0.5 pixels.

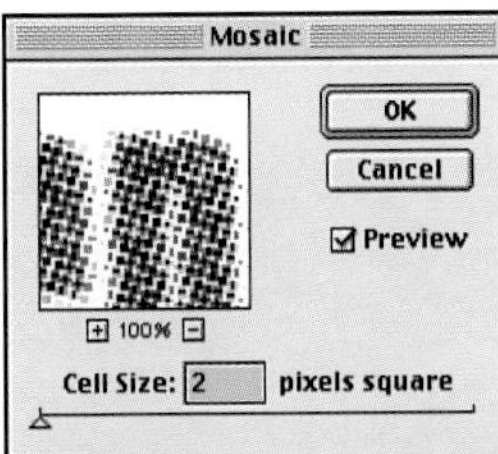

**6** Make only the Green channel active and reapply the same filters used in Step 5, changing the Blur radius to 1.0 pixel.

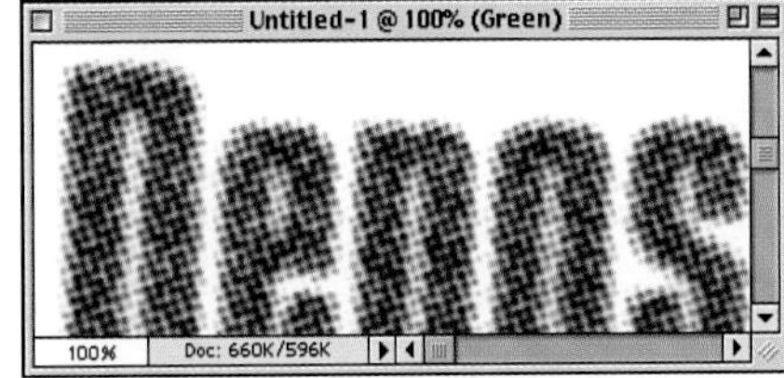


**7** Finally, make only the Blue channel active and choose Filter➡Pixelate➡Fragment.

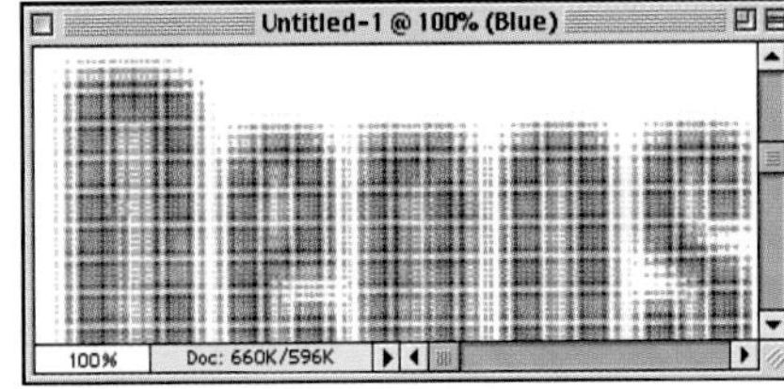


**8** Return to the composite channel to view the finished type.

## VARIATIONS

Instead of applying filters to each channel, try moving the channels independently. In Steps 5, 6, and 7, choose Filter➥Other➥Offset instead of applying the Mosaic, Blur, and Fragment filters. Enter a different distance value each time you offset a channel. For this example, I set the Offset values for the Red channel to -8 for both the Vertical and Horizontal values. I skipped the Green channel, and set both values to 8 for the Blue channel.

For this effect, the Find Edges filter was applied to the Red and Blue channels only after completing Steps 1 through 4. Do Step 8 to complete the effect.

Try applying different filters to the color channels. After step 5, with only the Red channel active, choose Filter➡Noise➡Dust & Scratches and enter a Radius value of 10 and a Threshold value of 100. Repeat for the Blue and Green channels. ●

# Water Droplets



TOOLBOX

Water Droplets (Lighting Effects Style)

For the klutz in all of us, this basic effect is simple, but the enhancements are worth the extra steps.

**1** Use the Type Mask tool to enter the text. I used Seagull Heavy at 65 points. Choose a foreground color for the type and fill the type. Because the type is only in the background for this effect, you can use any type (such as something created by another effect in this book) as long as the type image is merged into a single layer and has a nontransparent background.

**2** Deselect the selection; then use the Elliptical Marquee tool to select a few oval shapes like you see here. These shapes will become the water droplets. The effect works best if you select ovals that run across the edge of the type. To select multiple areas as shown, simply hold down the Shift key as you drag each new selection. Save the selection as a new channel (Alpha 1).

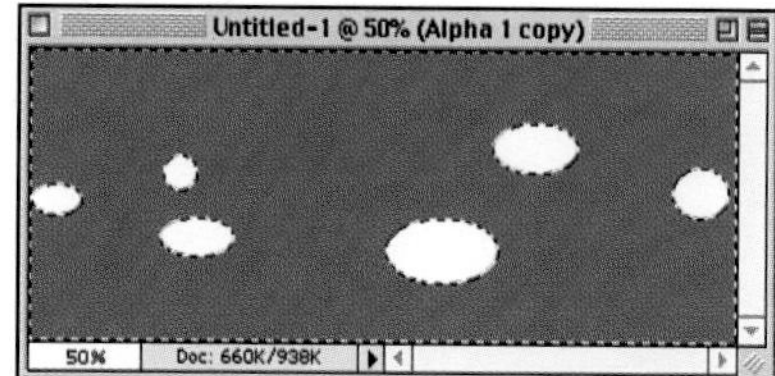

**3** Duplicate the Alpha 1 channel and make the new channel (Alpha 1 copy) the active channel. Choose Select➥Inverse to select the black area outside the white ovals. Change the foreground color to 50% gray and fill the selection.

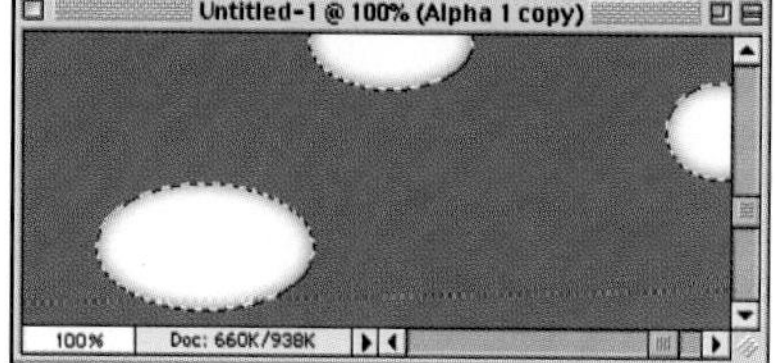


**4** Choose Select➥Inverse again to reselect the ovals. Choose Filter➥Blur➥Gaussian Blur. Blur the ovals slightly to add a little gray inside the edges. I set the radius at 5 pixels. Deselect the selection.

**5** From the Channels palette menu, choose Duplicate Channel. Choose new from the Document pop-up menu and give the file a name (Water Droplet Displace).

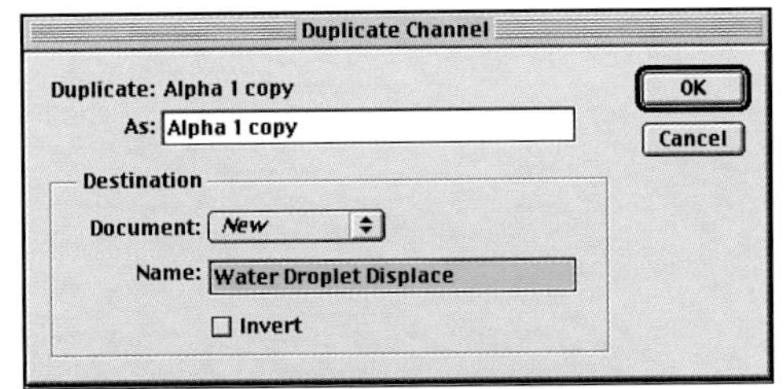


**6** A new file will pop up onscreen that is identical to the Alpha 1 channel. Save the file (Photoshop format) and close it.

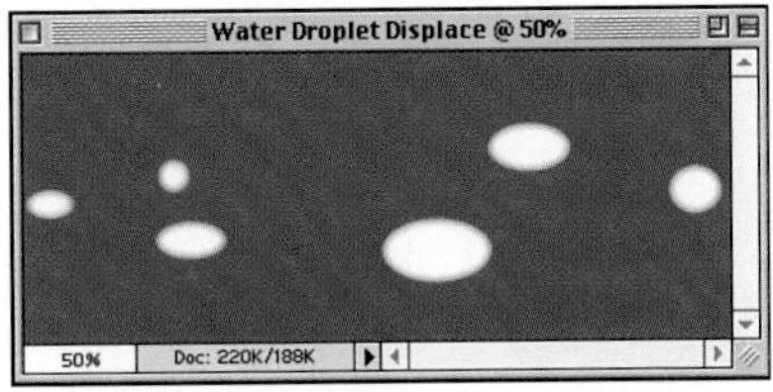


**7** Return to the composite channel and the type layer. Choose Filter➥Distort➥Displace. Use the settings shown here (Horizontal: 5%, Vertical: 5%, Stretch to Fit, Repeat Edge Pixels).

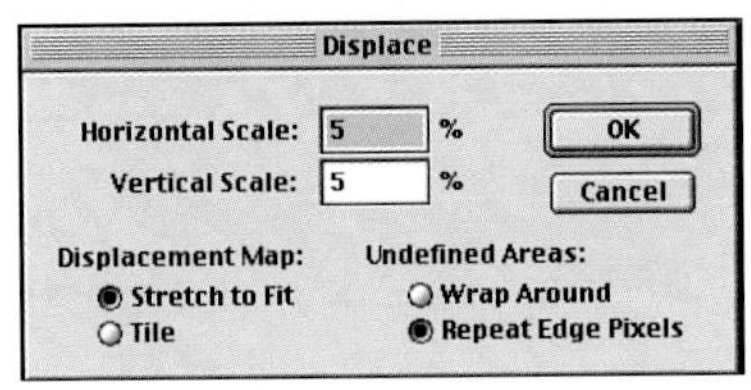


After you click OK, a dialog box asks you to find a file to use as a displacement map. Find and select the file that you saved in Step 6. Click Open to displace the water drops. You should see a slight distortion of the letters in the areas where you made the oval selections.

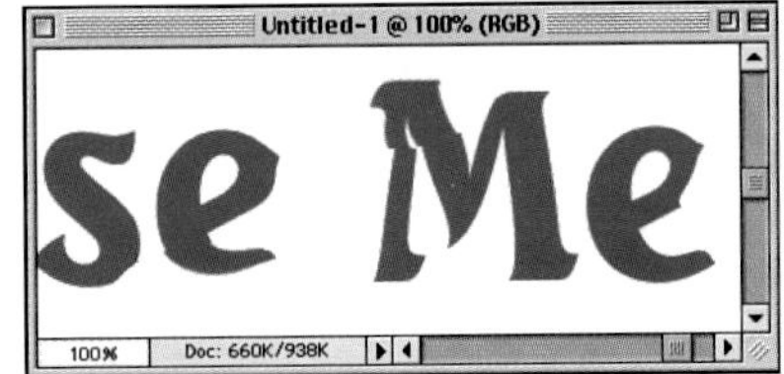


TIP **If you want the type under the drops to be brighter than the rest of the type, load the selection from the Alpha 1 channel now.**

8 Choose Filter➡Render➡Lighting Effects. Load the Water Droplets preset or match the settings seen here.

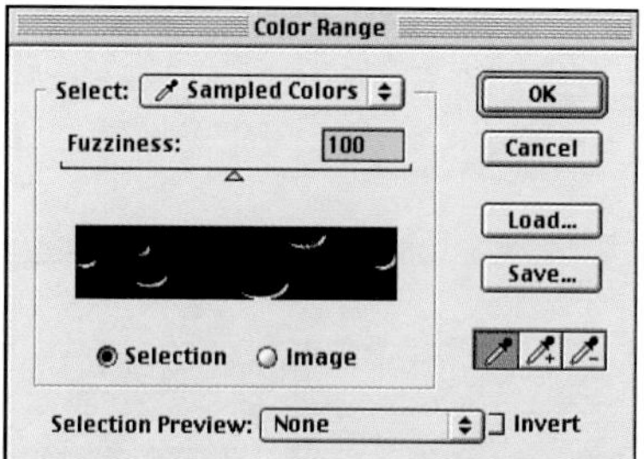


9 Load the selection of the Alpha 1 channel; then choose Select➡Color Range. With the Eyedropper tool, click in the shadow area of one of the drops. Then use the Fuzziness slider to adjust the white areas in the preview so that most, but not all, of the shadows are selected. The Preview should look like this.

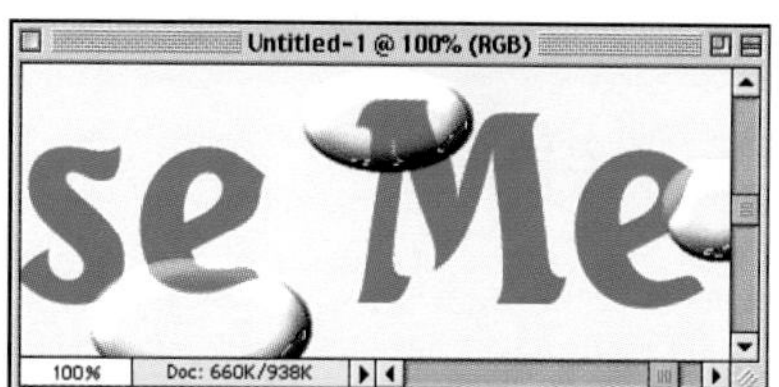


10 Choose Select➡Feather (2 pixels) to soften the selection. You will see the selection areas shrink slightly.

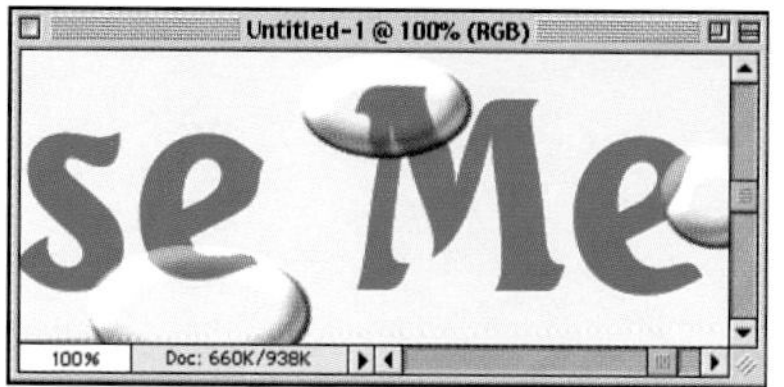


11 Change the foreground color to a light blue (CMYK: 30, 0, 0, 0). Fill the selection with the color to add a reflective highlight in the shadow areas.

**12** Create a new layer (Layer 1), and load the selection from the Alpha 1 channel. Choose a foreground color for the drops (CMYK: 47, 0, 10, 0) and fill the selection with the color. Then change the layer blending mode to Multiply and lower the Opacity to around 90%. This adds color to the drops—but too much.

Choose Layer Options from the Layer palette pop-up menu. Hold the (Option) [Alt] key and drag the left half of the white marker underneath the Underlying bar to the left just slightly so that the light areas of the drops lighten.

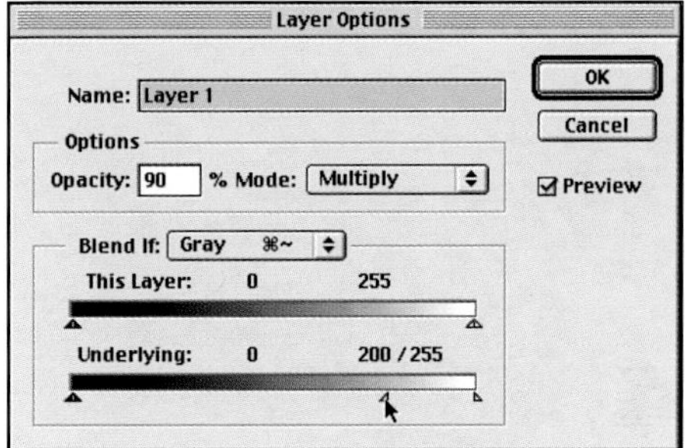

Bufflehead!

Wanna Dance?

## Variations

### A Ripple

After Step 11, load the selection from the Alpha 1 channel, choose Select➥Modify➥Contract (4 pixels) Select➥Feather (3 pixels) to shrink and smooth the selection. Choose Filter➥Distort➥Ripple (Amount: 103%, Large). Vary the amount for the right effect.

### Add Some Gloss

After Step 11, load the selection from the Alpha 1 channel, and choose Filter➥Artistic➥Plastic Wrap (8, 13, 11).

### And a Reflection

Open an image file and copy the image. Close the file.

Create a new layer below Layer 1, and load the selection from the Alpha 1 channel. Paste the image into the selection, and choose Overlay from the layer blending mode menu. ●

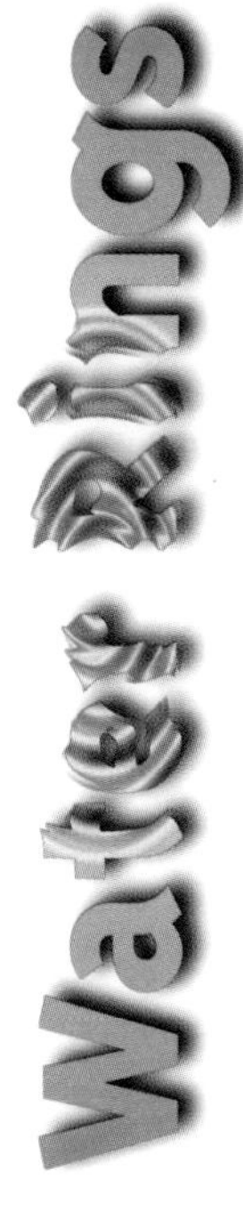


Here's another effect that uses a displacement map and Lighting Effects filter in a one-two punch. In this effect, you load a file included on the CD-ROM, customize it for your type, and then use it for the distortions.

**1** Use the Type tool to enter the text into a new layer (I used Triplex at 135 points). Choose Layer➡Type➡Render Layer.

**2** Open the water rings displacement map file from the P5TM CD-ROM. Follow this path: P5TM➡P5TM Files➡Displacement Maps➡Ring Displace.

**3** Choose Select➡All and copy the image. Close the file.

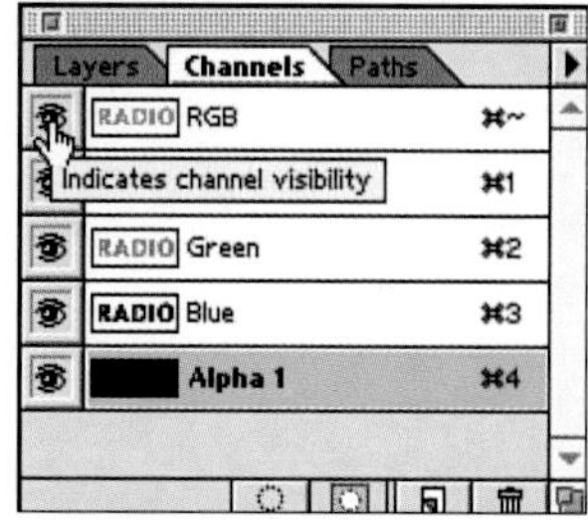


**4** Create a new channel (Alpha 1) in your type file, make it the active channel, and make the RGB channel visible.

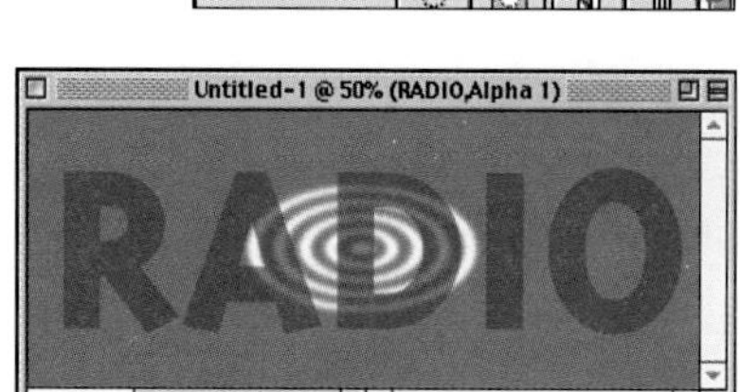


**5** Paste in the image just copied.



**TOOLBOX**

Ring Displace (Displacement Map)

Water Rings (Lighting Effects Style)

**6** Now the rings must be resized to fit the type. Choose Edit➡Transform➡Scale, and drag the box handles to resize the rings so they cover the area of the type that you want to be affected. This effect works best if the rings extend off of the type in the vertical direction as shown here. Press Return when satisfied.

**7** Choose Duplicate Channel from the Channels palette menu. Select New from the Document menu and name the file (Radio Rings). Click OK to open the channel into a new image. Save the new file and close it.

**8** Return to the composite channel, make the Alpha 1 channel invisible, and deselect the selection.

**9** Choose Filter➡Distort➡Displace. Set both of the Scale percentages to 5 (Stretch to Fit, Repeat Edge Pixels).

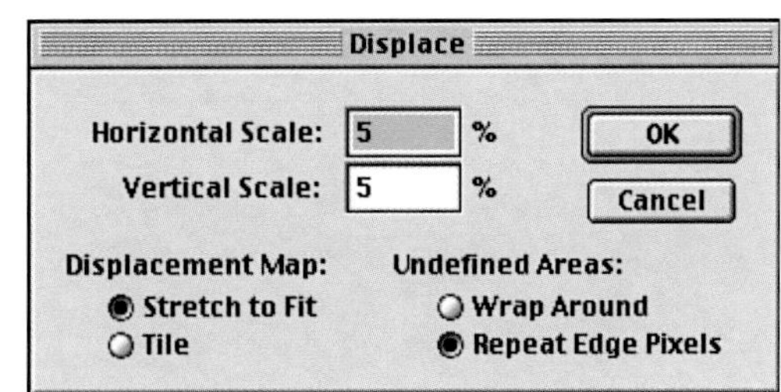


A dialog box opens asking you to find a displacement map. Find the file that you saved in Step 7 (Radio Rings). Click Open to distort the type.

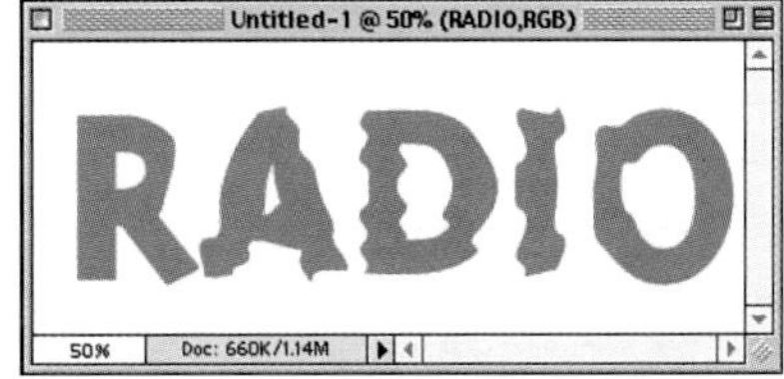

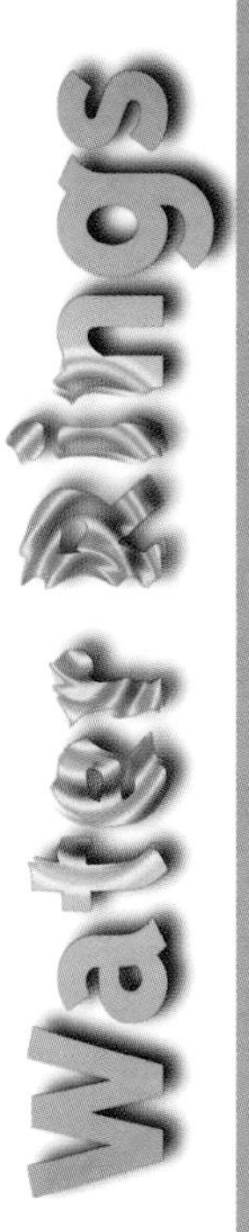


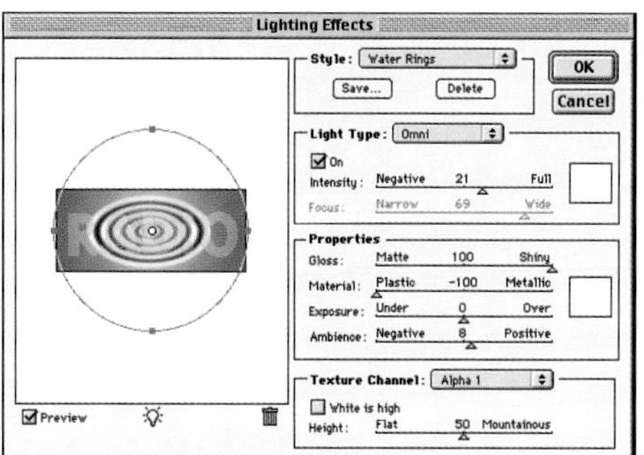


**10** Choose Filter➥Render➥ Lighting Effects. Select Water Rings from the pop-up menu or match the settings seen here. You may need to adjust the Intensity so that the light doesn't wash out the color in your type. Also, make sure that the ring defining the light in the preview covers all of the type.

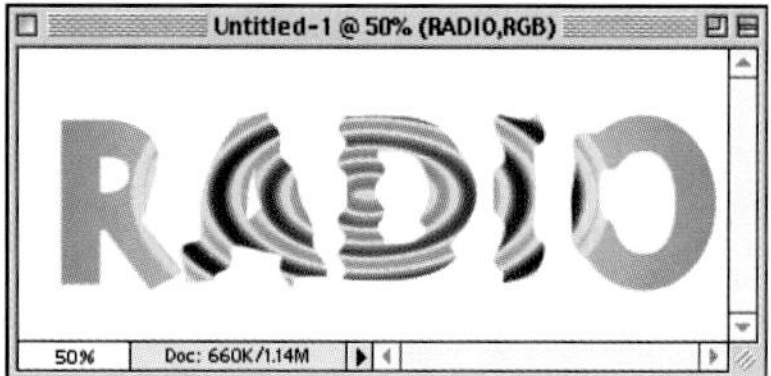


**11** Now load the selection from the Alpha 1 channel and repeat Step 9.

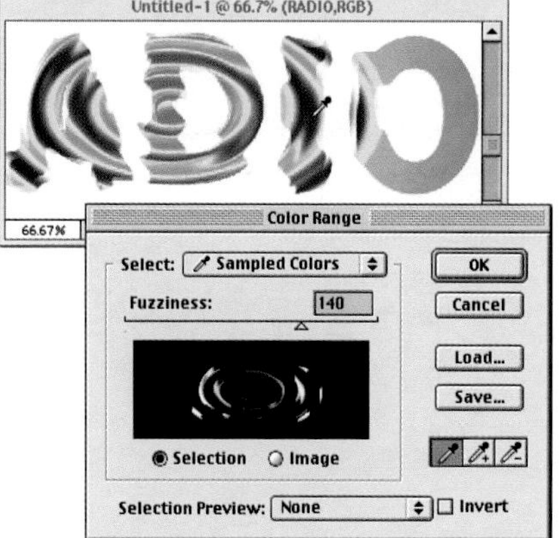


**12** Deselect the selection and choose Select➥Color Range. Use the Eyedropper tool and click it in one of the shadow areas of the rings. Use the Fuzziness slider to adjust the selection (depicted by the white areas in the preview window) so that most, but not all, of the shadow areas are selected.

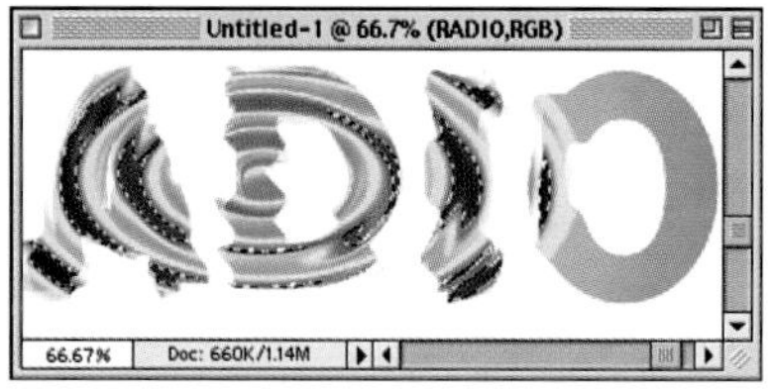

**13** Choose Select➡Feather (4 pixels), and press Delete to reveal the layer below (just a white background for now).

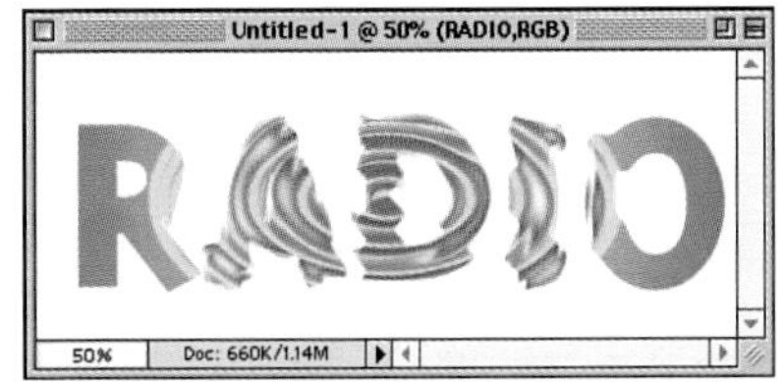


**14** This effect needs a shadow to complete it. Choose Layer➡Effects➡Drop Shadow and try these settings: Multiply, Shadow Color: (CMYK: 95, 87, 28, 50), Opacity: 100%, Angle: 120°, Distance: 15, Blur: 16, Intensity: 0%.

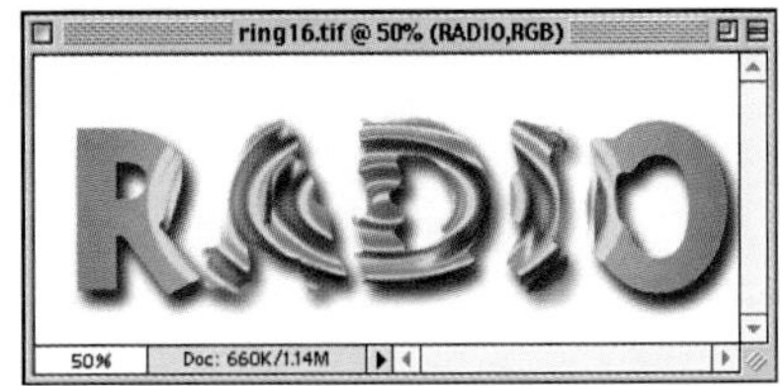


**15** To fine-tune the coloring, deselect the selection and choose Image➡Adjust➡Replace Color. Use the Eyedropper tool and the Fuzziness Slider as in Step 12 to select the areas of color you want to fix. I clicked the eyedropper on the outside edge of the "R." Here is the preview of the selection and the settings that I used to make the color more uniform throughout the image.

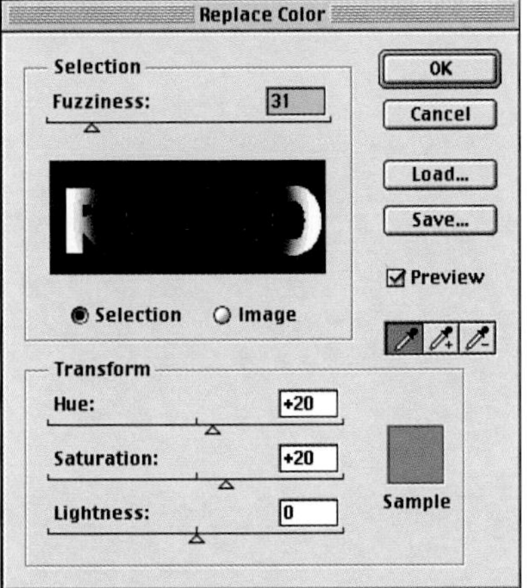


And the result.

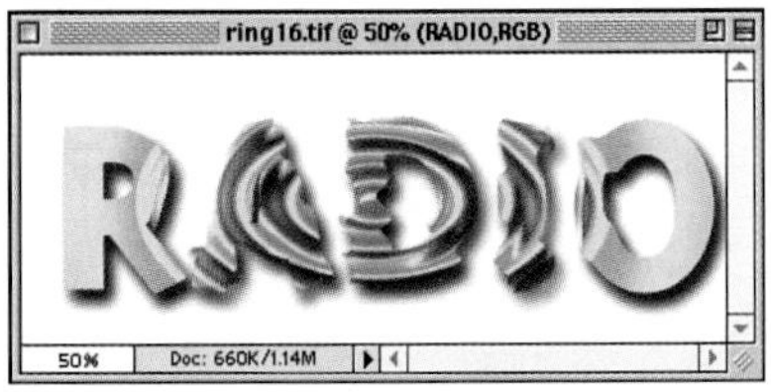


**16** Finally, I added an outline to make the type edges a little more distinct. Create a new layer and move it below the type layer. Then load the transparency selection of the type layer. Choose a Foreground color that is close to the color of the type. Choose Edit➡Stroke (Centered, 2 pixels). ●

# WAX SEAL



**TOOLBOX**

Blank Seal

Wax Seal (Lighting Effects Style)

Create a seal and a blob of wax, and smash them together using the Lighting Effects and Plastic Wrap filters to create the look of a wax-seal impression.

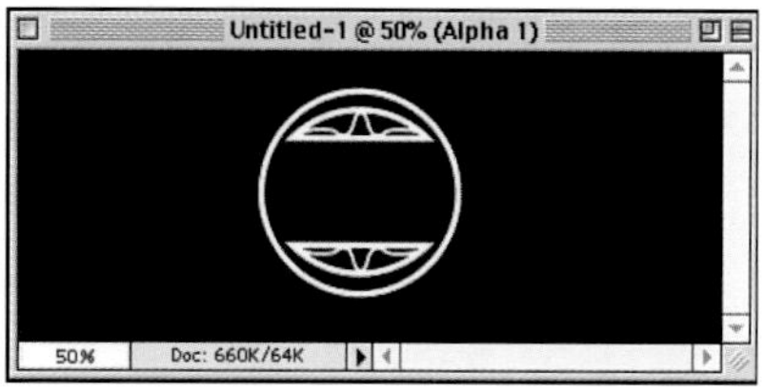

**1** Creating the seal is the first step. It must be a black-and-white image that can be placed into a channel. I used Adobe Illustrator to make the generic image you see here. (It's on the CD-ROM if you want to use it: P5TM➡P5TM Files➡Blank Seal). In Step 2 type will be added. Copy the image and paste it into a new channel (Alpha 1) in a new RGB Photoshop file. Of course, you do not need to use an outline. You can simply use text if you want.

**2** While in the Alpha 1 channel, use the Type tool to enter the text. This is Kabel at 25 points. If you are combining the type with an image, move the type into place within the image.

**3** Create a new channel (Alpha 2), make it the active channel, and make the Alpha 1 channel visible. Use the Lasso tool to draw a blob that will define the shape of the wax. Choose Select➡Modify➡Smooth (2 pixels) to smooth the selection drawn by that shaky hand of yours. Fill the selection with white.

**4** Duplicate the Alpha 2 channel (Alpha 2 copy). Then load the selection from the Alpha 1 channel and press delete to fill it with black.

5 Load the selection of the active channel (Alpha 2 copy), and choose Filter➡Blur➡Gaussian Blur. Keep the blur setting low—all you want is a little grayness around the edges of the white areas. I set the Radius at 3 pixels.

6 Return to the composite channel and make a new layer (Layer 1). Load the selection from the Alpha 2 channel, set the foreground color to a color for the wax (CMYK: 0, 100, 100, 0), and fill the selection with the color.

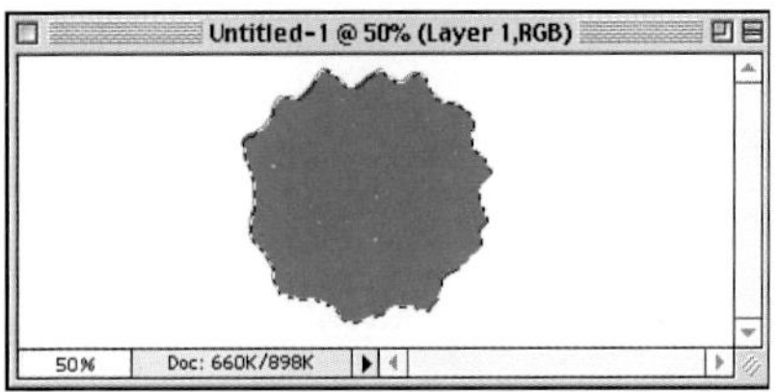


7 Next, choose Filter➡Render➡ Lighting Effects. Select the Wax Seal preset from the Style menu or match the settings seen in this figure.

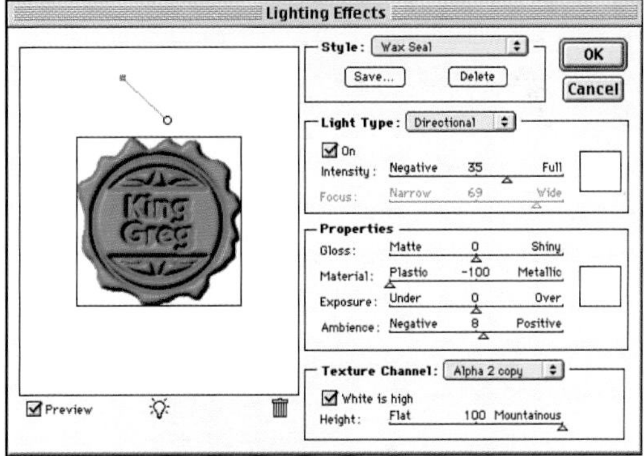


The wax raises.

8 Create a new layer (Layer 2) and move it below Layer 1. Make Layer 1 invisible.

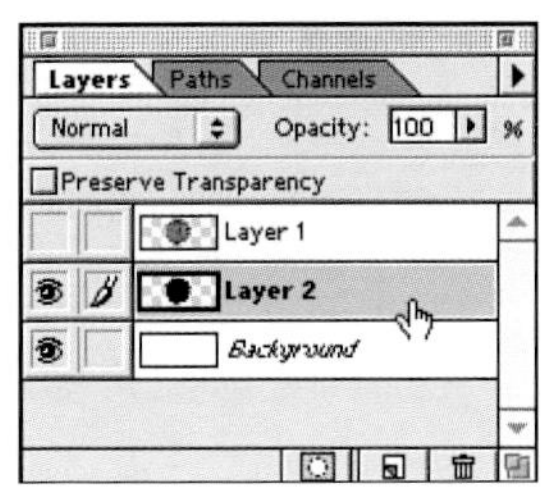

WAX SEAL

9 The selection should still be active. Fill it with black.

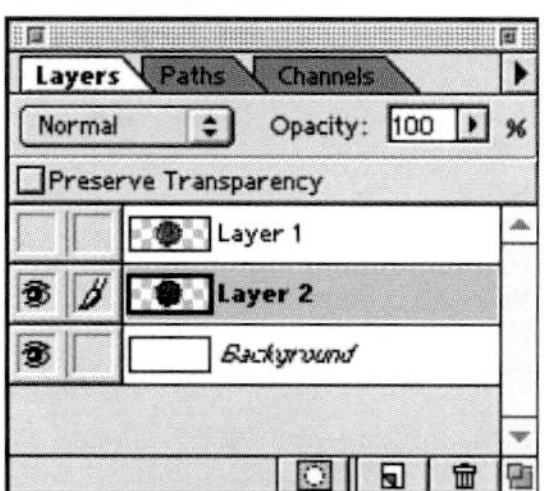

10 Next, make Layer 1 the active layer, load the selection from the Alpha 1 channel, and cut the selection.

11 Make Layer 2 the active layer, make Layer 1 invisible, and paste in the selection just copied. A new layer (Layer 3) has been created. Choose Merge Down from the Layers palette to merge Layer 3 into Layer 2.

12 Choose Filter➡Blur➡Gaussian Blur. Set the Radius to about 2 pixels.

**TIP** **If there are wide areas within the seal imprint, you might want to offset Layer 2. Make Layer 1 visible again, and grab the Move tool. Use the arrow keys to shift Layer 2 down and to the right a little.**

13 Make Layer 1 visible again.

**14** Make Layer 1 the active layer. Choose Filter➡Artistic➡Plastic Wrap. This filter adds a gloss to give the wax the right surface. Try these settings: Highlight Strength: 9, Detail: 9, Smoothness: 7. ●

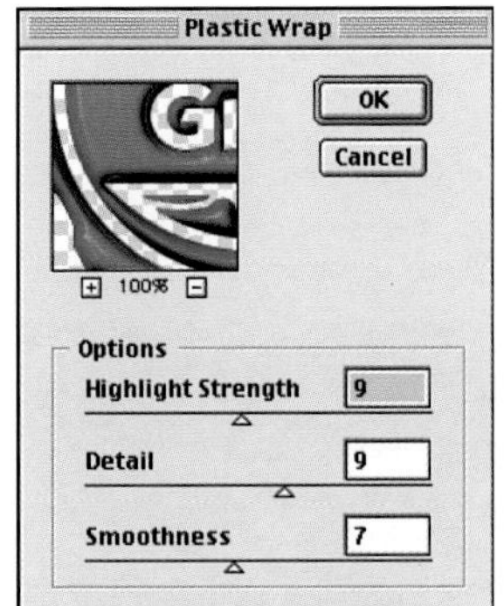

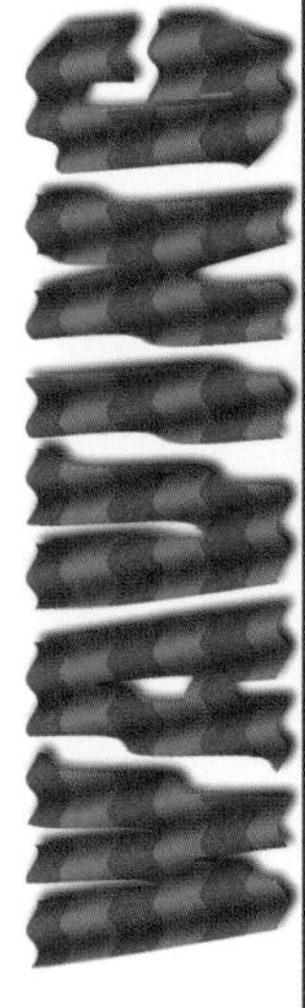

This effect is the very close cousin of the Potato Chips effect. The following technique uses the same displacement map to distort the shape of the edges.

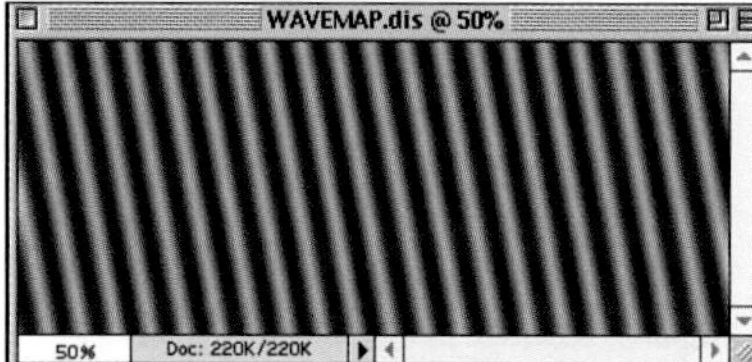


**1** Open the WAVEMAP.dis file from the P5TM CD-ROM (P5TM➡P5TM Files➡Displacement Maps➡WAVEMAP.dis).

**2** Choose Select➡All, copy the image, and close the file.

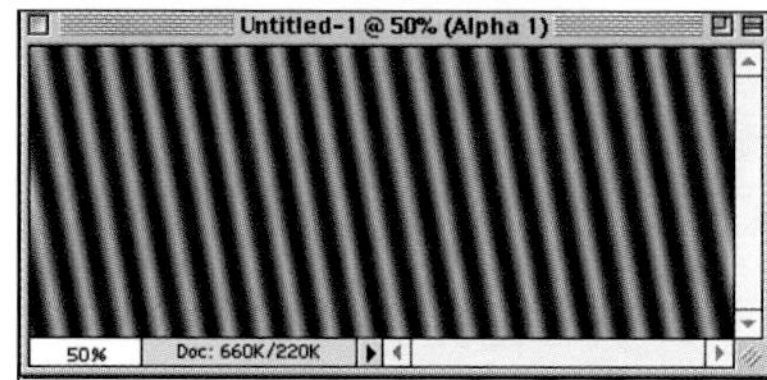


**3** Create a new RGB file and create a new channel (Alpha 1). Paste in the image and deselect the selection.

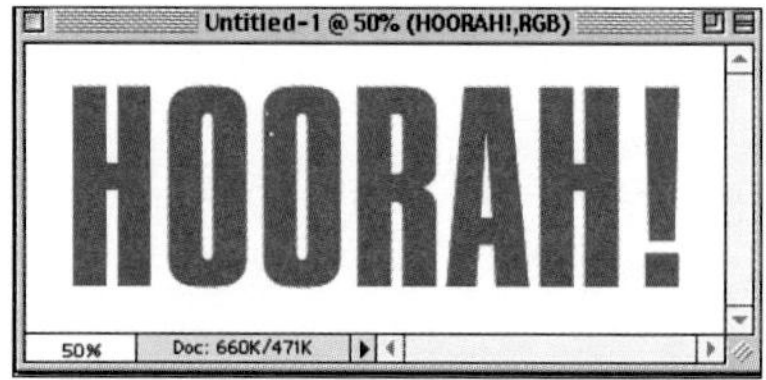


**4** Return to the composite channel and choose a foreground color for the waving type (CMYK: 0, 75, 100, 0). Then use the Type tool to enter the text (Compacta at 150 points). Choose Layer➡Type➡Render Layer.

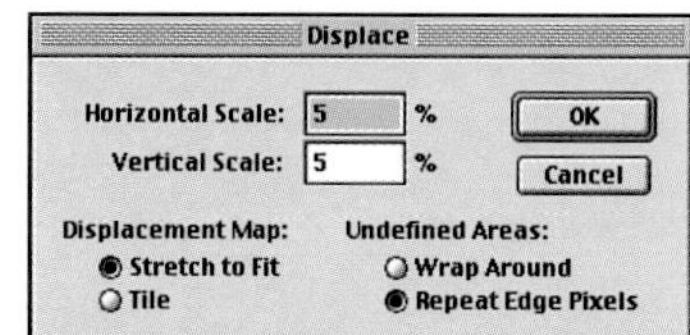


**5** Choose Filter➡Distort➡Displacement Map (Horizontal Scale: 5%, Vertical Scale 5%, Stretch to Fit, Repeat edge pixels). Click OK.

Another dialog box opens asking you to find a displacement map. Find the file that you opened in Step 1 and click Open (P5TM CD-ROM➡P5TM Files➡Displacement Maps➡WAVEMAP.dis). This filter creates the waves around the edges of the type.

**TOOLBOX**

WAVEMAP.dis (displacement map)

**6** Load the selection from the Alpha 1 channel. This selection will be used to add highlights to the crests of the waving type. Choose New Adjustment Layer from the Layers palette menu. Turn on the Group With Previous Layer option, select Curves from the Type pop-up menu, and click OK to open the Curves dialog box. Grab the center of the diagonal line in the grid and bend the curve upward about this far.

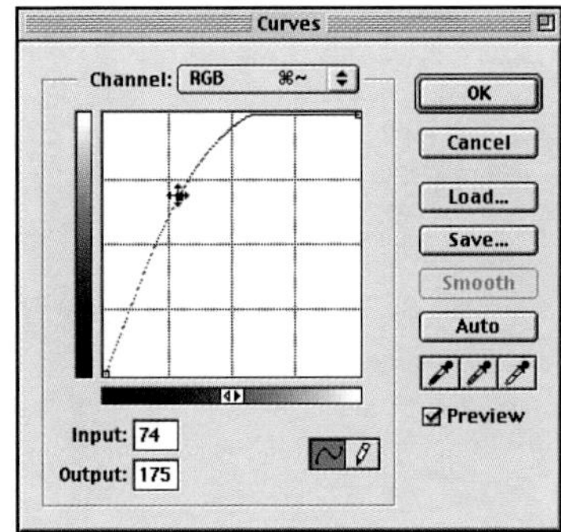


Click OK to get this effect.

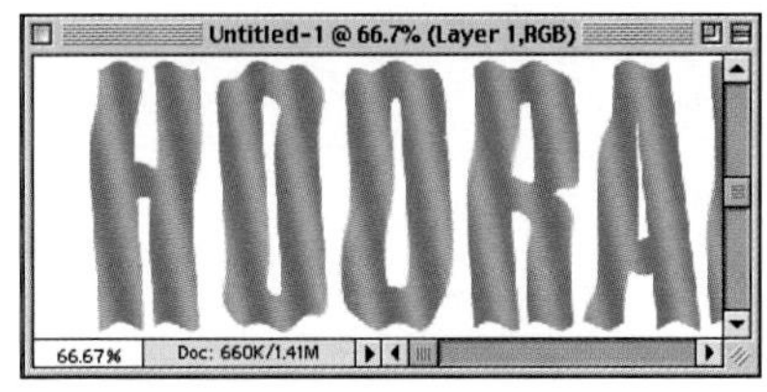


**7** Create a new layer (Layer 1) for the shadow and move it below the type layer. The Layers palette should now look like this.

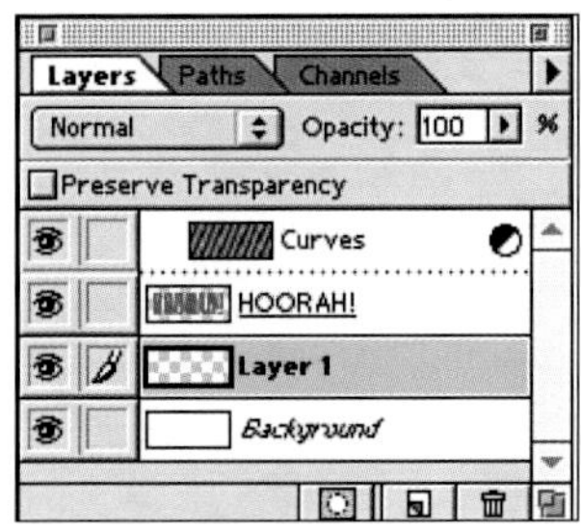


**8** Load the transparency selection from the type layer; then subtract from that selection the selection from the Alpha 1 channel. Choose Select➡Feather (3 pixels). Choose black (or another color for the shadow) for the foreground color and fill the selection to create a shadow that turns darker as the wavy type dips down and lighter where it raises up. If you want to see it, temporarily make the type layer invisible. There's a little more work to do on the shadow.

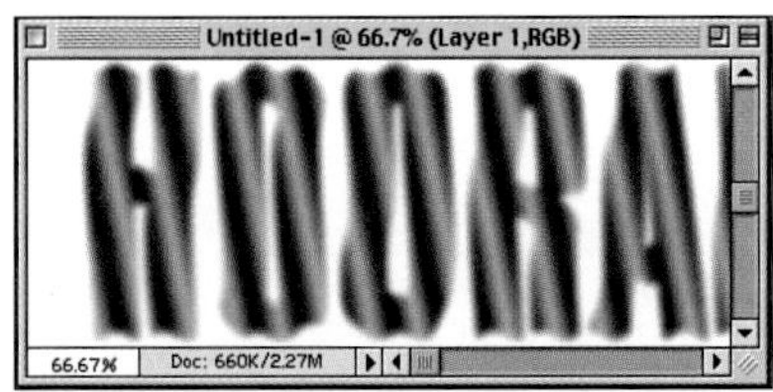

**9** Load the transparency selection of the type layer, choose Select➡Feather (3 pixels), and feather the selection the same amount as in Step 8. Fill the selection with black; then choose Filter➡Fade Fill and lower the Opacity to 25%. Again, I temporarily made the type layer invisible to show you the shadow.

**10** Deselect the selection. Select the Move tool and nudge the shadow down and to the right by using the arrow keys. I pressed each key three times.

## VARIATIONS

### Stripes

If you want to add stripes to the type, insert these three steps after Step 4.

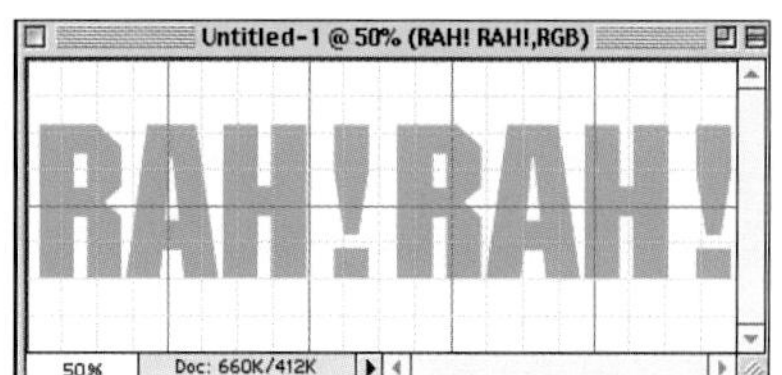


**1** Choose View➡Show Grid and make sure that the Snap to Grid option is turned on (View➡Snap to Grid). Choose File➡Preferences➡Guides & Grid. The grid spacing determines the spacing of the stripes. I set the Gridline Every at one inch and the Subdivisions at 4.

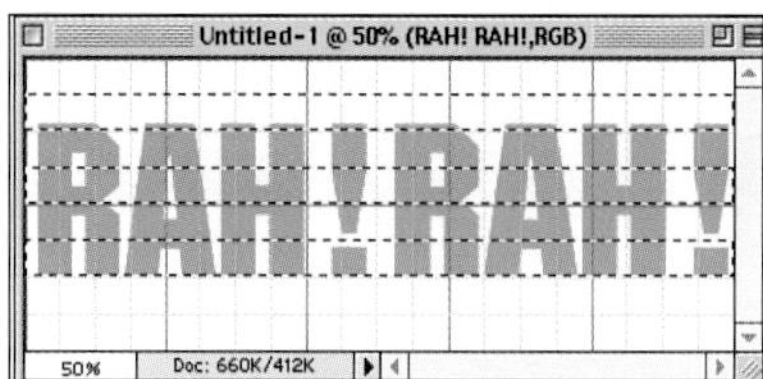


**2** Use the Rectangular Marquee tool to select one row in the grid. Drag the selection across the type; be careful to overlap both ends. Hold down the Shift key and make selections for every other row.

**3** Choose a foreground color for the stripes (CMYK: 100, 75, 0, 0) and choose (Shift-Option-Delete) [Shift-Alt-Backspace] to fill the selection while preserving the layer transparency.

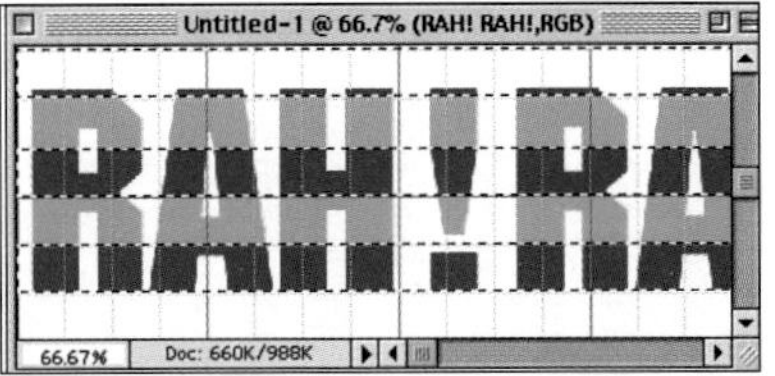


**4** Deselect the selection and complete the rest of the steps (5 through 10).

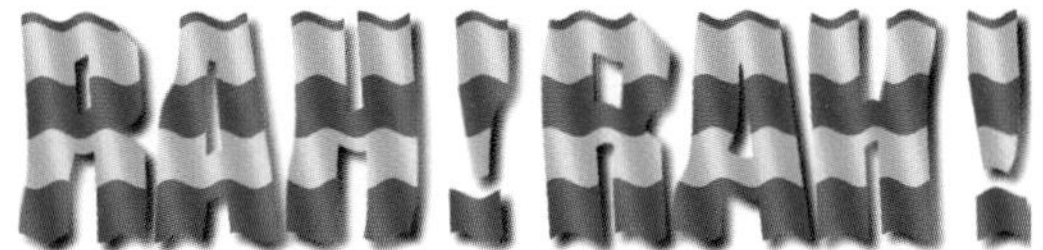

## Making Waves

If you want larger or smaller waves or have odd-sized type that won't work well with the displacement map on the CD-ROM, follow these steps to create your own displacement map.

**1** Create a new file and create a new channel (Alpha 1). Choose View➡Show Grid and make sure that the Snap to Grid option is turned on (View➡Snap to Grid). Choose File➡Preferences➡Guides & Grid. The grid spacing determines the spacing of the stripes. I set the Gridline Every at one inch and the Subdivisions at 4. Here is the grid in the channel.

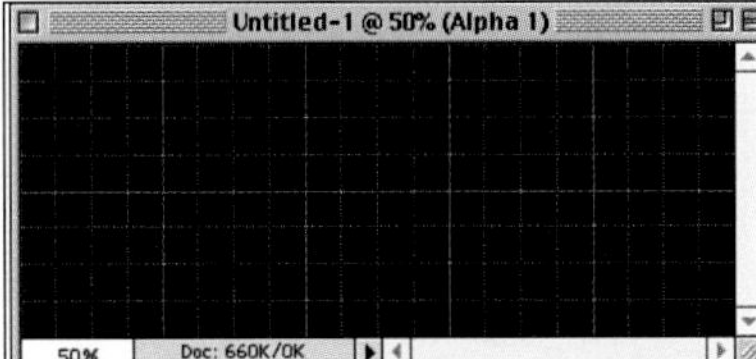

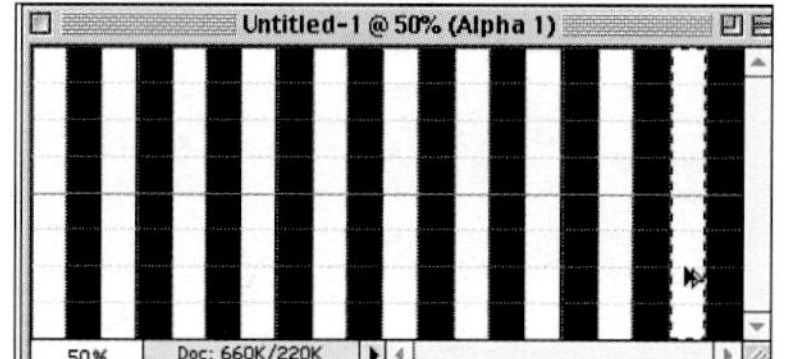


**2** Use the Rectangular Marquee tool to select the first column. Choose white for the foreground color and fill the selection. Hold down (Command and Option) [Control and Alt]. Click on the selected column and drag it two columns to the right. Let go of the copied selection and repeat the copying until the entire channel is filled with stripes.

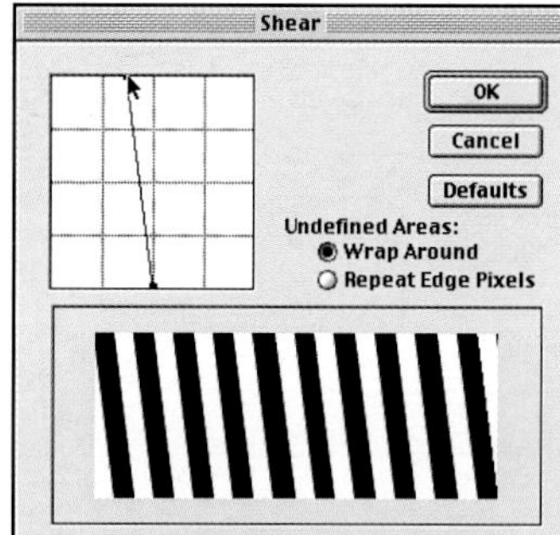


**3** Deselect the selection and choose Filter➡Distort➡Shear. Turn on the Wrap Around option. Then grab the handle at the top of the line on the graph and move it to the left about as far as you see in this figure.

**4** Click OK and choose Filter➥Blur➥Gaussian Blur (10 pixels). Blur the channel just enough so that the white in the stripes is no longer a strong white.

**5** Choose Duplicate Channel from the Channels palette menu. In the dialog box that opens, choose New from the Document menu and name the new channel. The channel opens into a new file. Save the file (Photoshop format) and close it.

**6** Proceed from Step 4 on page 228. In Step 5, use the file you just saved as the displacement map. ●

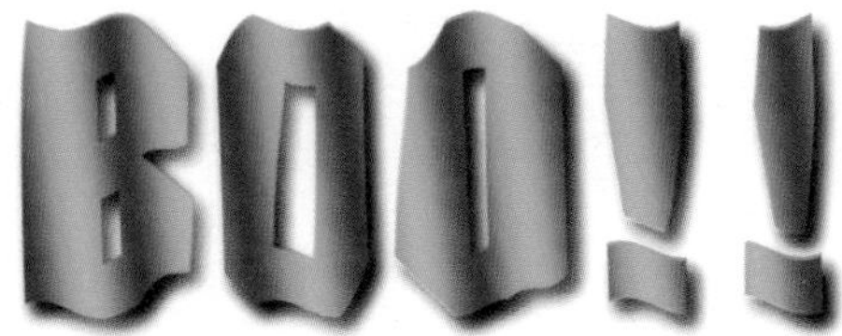

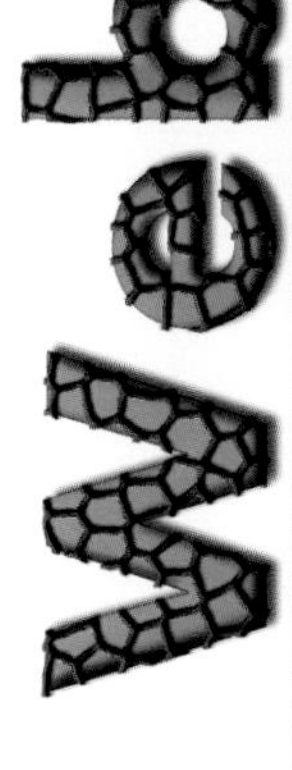


The new layer effects available in Photoshop 5.0 can help make some great effects like this one, which uses the Inner Bevel effect to add some dimension to a web that is spun by the Stained Glass filter.

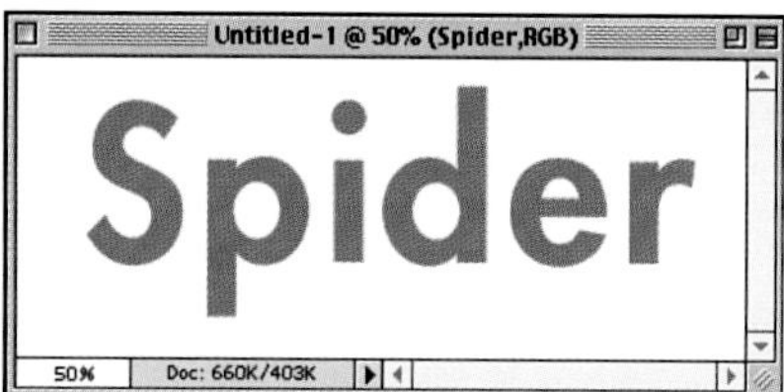


**1** Create a new file and use the Type tool to enter the text. (I used Futura Heavy at 100 points.)

**2** Choose Layer➡Effects➡Bevel and Emboss. Select Inner Bevel as the Style, set the Depth to about 20 pixels, and raise the Blur amount enough to keep the type rounded (15 pixels).

**3** Create a new layer (Layer 1) and load the transparency selection of the type layer. Choose Select➡Modify➡Expand (1 pixel). Expanding this selection causes the lines of the web to stretch a little beyond the edges of the type, making it appear as if they wrap around the type.

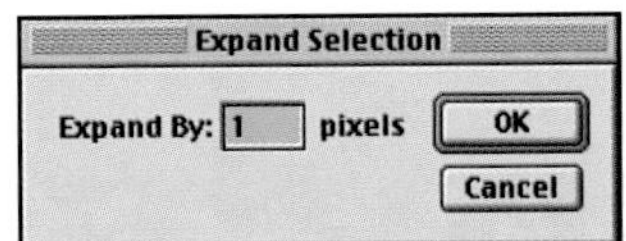


**4** Choose white for the foreground color and fill the selection. Then press X to switch the foreground and background colors and choose a foreground color that will become the color of the web (CMYK: 0,100, 100, 40).

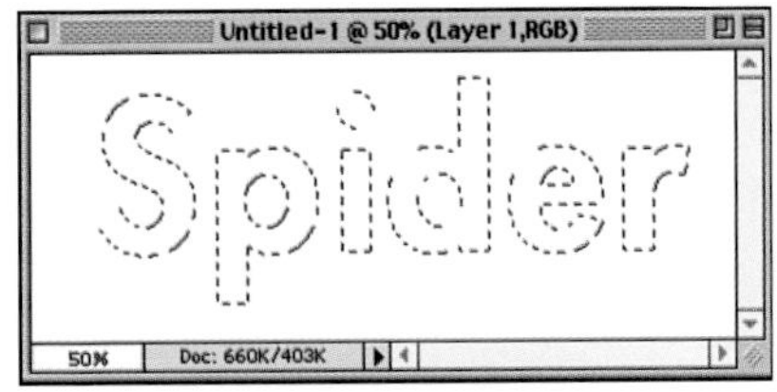


**5** Choose Filter➡Texture➡Stained Glass. The Cell Size (10) determines the spacing in the web. The Border Thickness (4) determines the thickness of the lines. Set the Light Intensity to 0. Watch the preview to determine the best settings for your type.

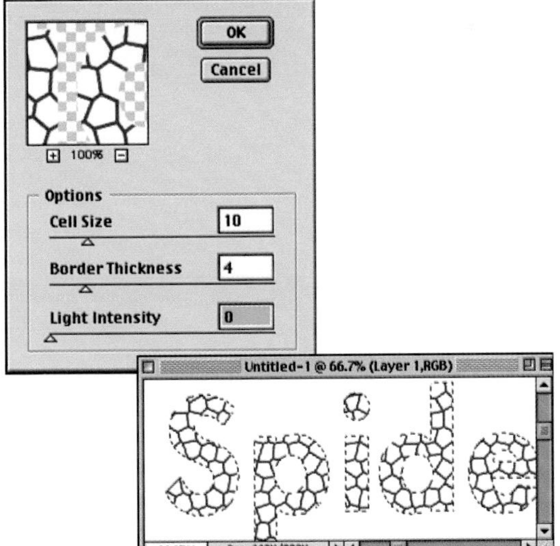


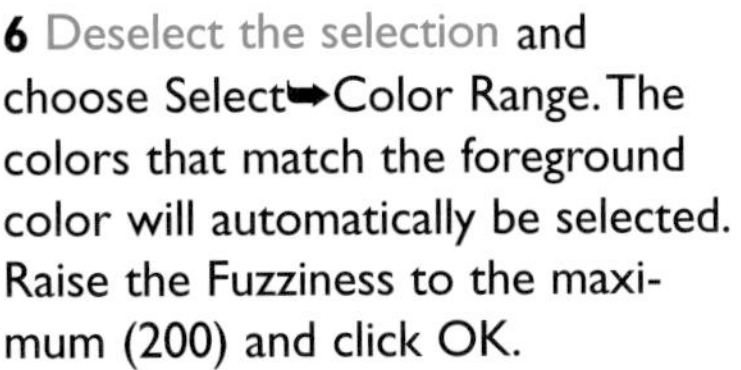

**6** Deselect the selection and choose Select➡Color Range. The colors that match the foreground color will automatically be selected. Raise the Fuzziness to the maximum (200) and click OK.

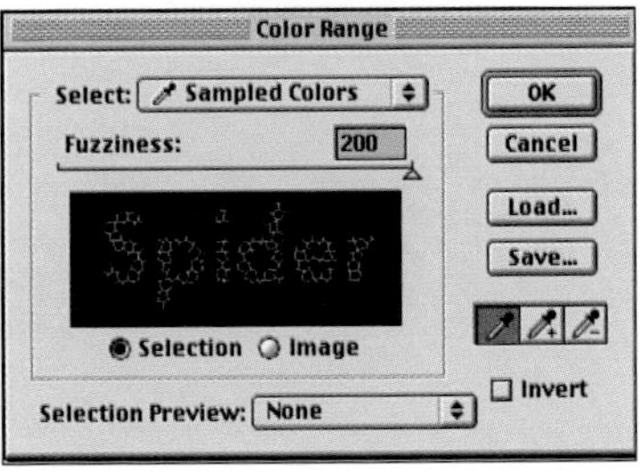

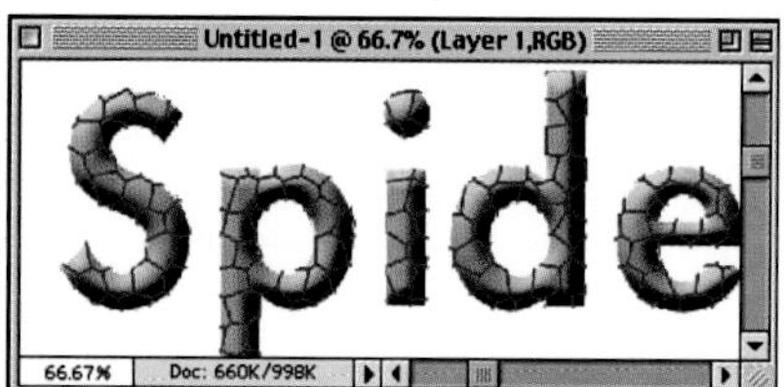


**7** Choose Select➡Inverse and press Delete. Deselect the selection. Only the colored web lines should remain in this layer and you can see the underlying type again.

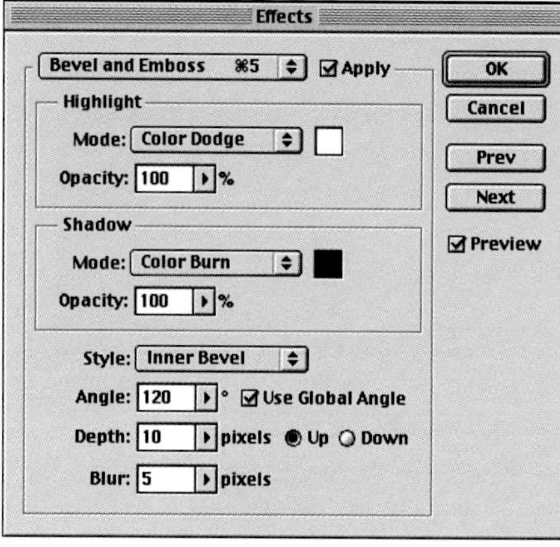


**8** Choose Layer➡Effects➡Bevel and Emboss, and select the Inner Bevel style. Raise the Depth to about 10 pixels and set the Blur at 5 pixels. I also set the Opacity percentages for the shadows and highlights at 100% to raise the contrast in the raised web lines.

**TIP** **If the lines of the web do not appear to raise as they do in the figures here, the blur value may be too high.**

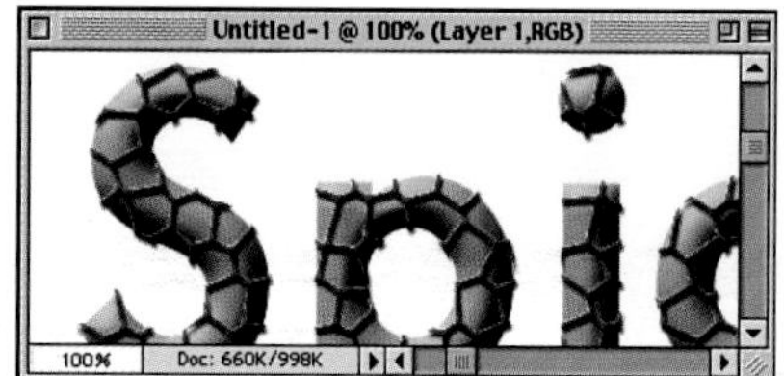


**9** After adjusting the Bevel settings, go to the top of the dialog box and select Drop Shadow from the pop-up menu. Check the Apply box at the top. Create a slight shadow. I set the Distance and Blur both at 2 pixels. Click OK to apply the effects.

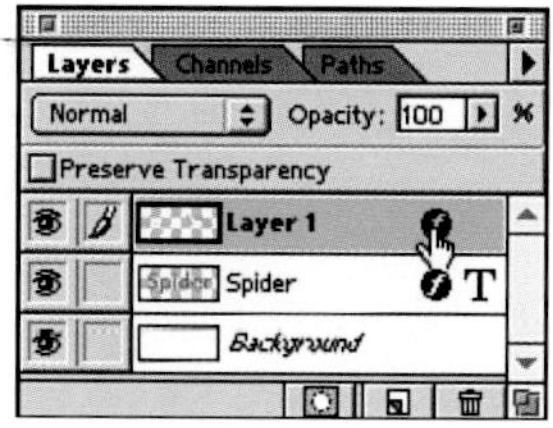


**TIP** **The benefit of using the layer effects to create special effects is that they are editable. To alter any of the settings, double-click on the "f" that appears next to the layer name in the Layers palette. The Effects dialog box opens.**

**10** Finally, I used the Move tool to nudge the web layer up and to the left one keystroke each. I also added a drop shadow to the type layer.

## VARIATIONS

### Multiple Colors

Repeat Steps 3 through 8 to create another layer of webs. I repeated the steps once more to create a third layer of webs.

### Sloppy Web

After Step 9, choose Filter➡Distort➡Ripple (150%, Medium) to create some sloppy lines.

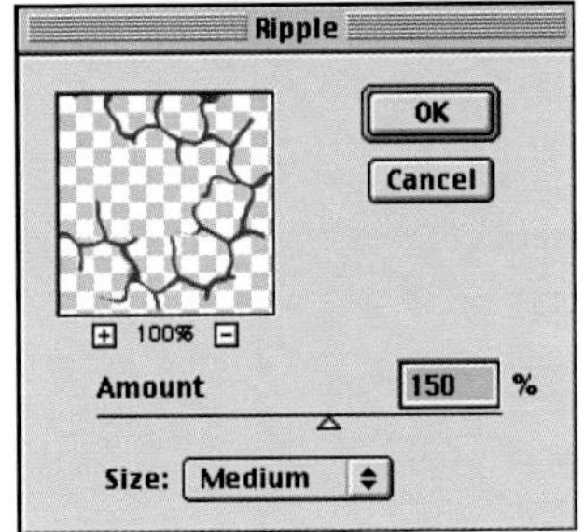

### Silly String

Simply delete the type layer for this web only effect. There are four layers of webs in this example and they have all been rippled using slightly different settings. ●

**TOOLBOX**

Wet Cement (Lighting Effects Style)

In this effect, some surprising results are quickly produced by using the Diffuse filter to set up a texture channel for the Lighting Effects filter.

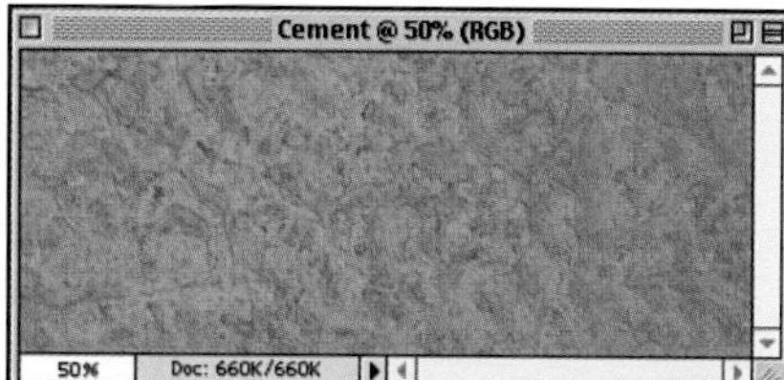


**1** To begin this effect, a background image that looks something like cement is needed. Find your own or use the one provided on the P5TM CD-ROM (P5TM➥P5TM Files➥Images➥Cement).

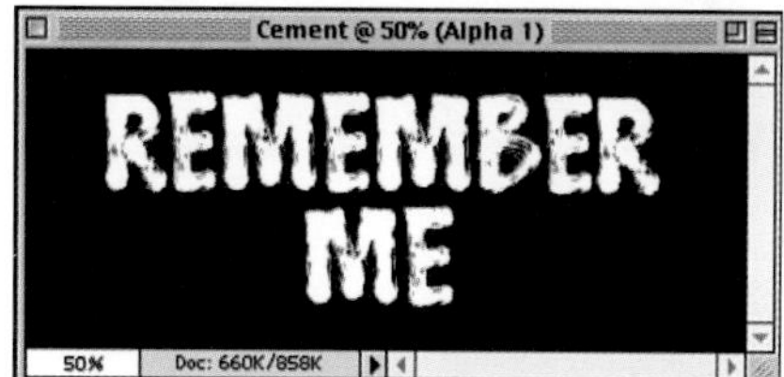


**2** Create a new channel (Alpha 1) and use the Type tool to enter the text. A handwritten typeface looks best, but anything works. I used Brush Stroke Fast at 55 points. Save the selection to create the Alpha 2 channel; then deselect the selection.

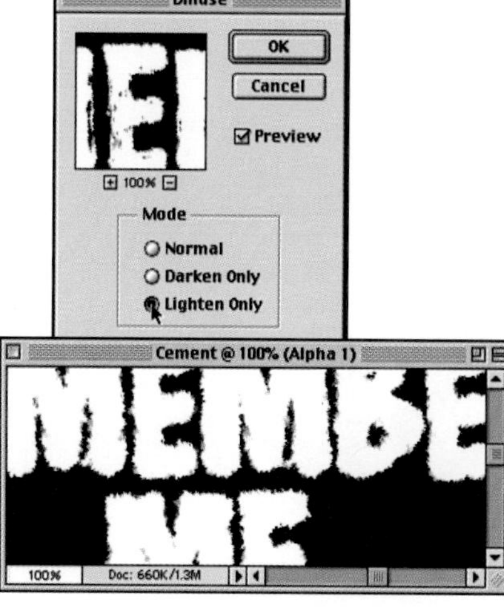


**3** While still in the Alpha 1 channel, choose Filter➥Stylize➥Diffuse. Turn on the Lighten Only mode and click OK. Reapply this filter (Command-F) [Control-F] four or five times. The diffused edges grow a little more each time the filter is applied.

4 Load the selection of the Alpha 2 channel and choose Filter➥Blur➥Gaussian Blur. I set the Radius at 5 pixels—just enough to lighten the inside edges of the type.

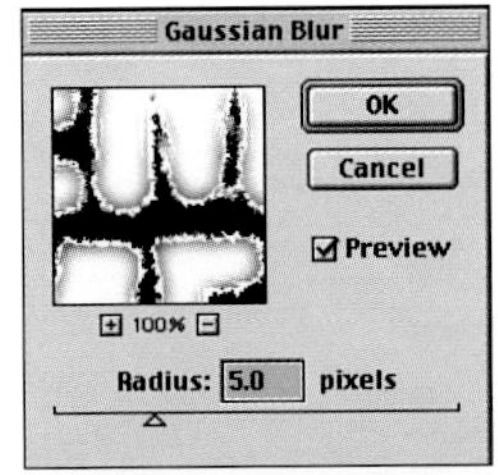


5 Choose Image➥Adjust➥Invert to invert the selection; then choose Image➥Adjust➥Brightness/Contrast. Raise the Brightness to about 55 and the Contrast to 20.

6 Keep the selection active and add just a little bit of noise (Filter➥Noise➥Add Noise; Amount: 5, Gaussian, Monochromatic). The noise will add a little texture inside the type. Deselect the selection.

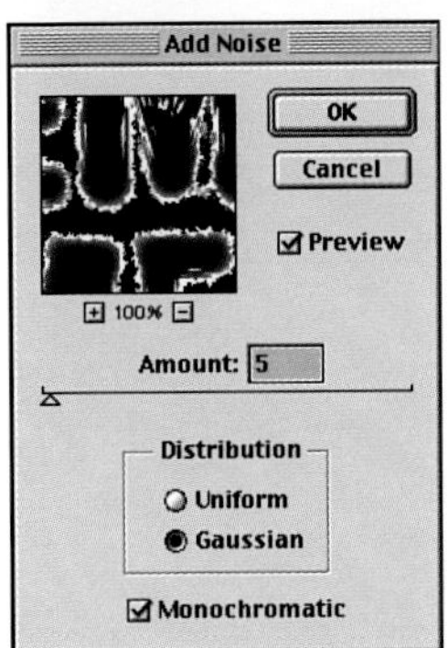

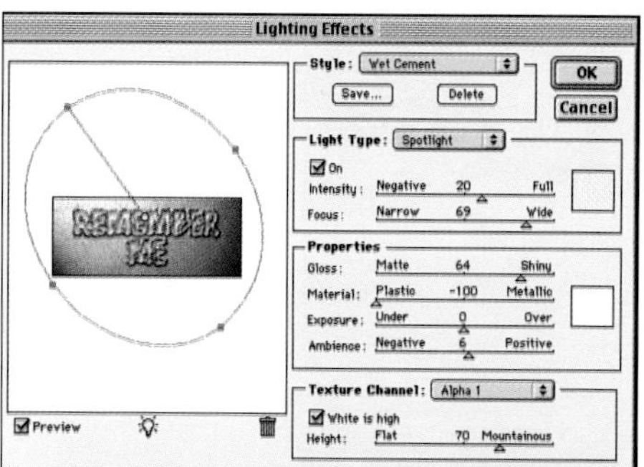

**7** Return to the composite channel and choose Filter➡Render➡ Lighting Effects. Select the Wet Cement preset from the Style menu or match the settings seen here. The colored light that I included in this preset results in a good color for the cement, but if you don't like it, just click on the light color swatch to change it.

## VARIATIONS

To get rid of the background, follow all of the preceding steps and then make the Alpha 1 channel active. Double-click on the Magic Wand tool to select it and bring the Magic Wand Options floating palette to the front. Set the tolerance to 1; then click the Magic Wand in the black area that surrounds the type. Choose Select➡Similar to make sure that all of the black areas are included in the selection. Return to the composite channel, and choose Select➡Modfiy➡Contract (2 pixels). Contract the selection enough so that the raised edges of the type are not included in the selection. Delete the selection and then deselect the selection. Finally, I added a drop shadow. ●

REMEMBER WHO?

# Appendix A

## Contributors Listing

### Filters

**Alien Skin Software**
1100 Wake Forest Rd. Suite 101
Raleigh, NC 27604
Phone: 919-832-4124
Fax: 919-832-4065

**Black Box demo**
**Eye Candy 3.1 demo**
**Eye Candy for After Effects demo**

**Andromeda Software**
699 Hampshire Rd. Suite 109
Thousand Oaks, CA 91361
Phone: 800-547-0055 or 805-379-4109
Fax: 805-379-5253
Orders@andromeda.com

**3D Filter**
**Circular Multiple Images**
**Screens**
**Techture**
**Velociraptor**

**AutoFX**
15 North Main Street. Suite 8
Wolfeboro, NH 03894
Phone: 603-569-8800
Fax: 603-569-9702

**Photo/Graphic Edges demo**
**Photo/Graphic Patterns demo**
**Typo/Graphic Edges demo**
**Ultimate Texture Collection**

**MetaTools, Inc.**
6303 Carpinteria Ave.
Carpinteria, CA 93013
805-566-6200
metasales@aol.com

**Kai's Power Tools demo**

### Fonts

**Delve Media Arts**
P.O. Box 641053
San Francisco, CA 94164-1053
Phone: 415-474-0702
http:www.delvemediaarts.com

**(PC only)**

**Fonthead Design**
20942 Estada Lana
Bola Raton, FL 33433
http://www.fonthead.com
Fax: 561-482-3630

**Foundry Group**
Jon Armstrong
C/O FoundryGroup/Saiph Corporation
250 West 57th Street
New York, NY 10107
Phone: 718-384-2583
Jon@saiph.com

**Garage Fonts**
P.O. Box 3101
Del Mar, CA 92014
Phone: 619-755-3913
Fax: 619-755-4761
Info@garagefonts.com
http://www.garagefonts.com

**Ingrimayne Type**
Robert Schenk
P.O. Box 404
Rensselaer, IN 47979
Bobs@kagi.com
http://ingrimayne.saintjoe.edu/

**Omnibus Typographi**
Box 135
S-135 23 Tyreso
Sweden
Phone: +46 8 742 8336
Fax: +46 8 712 3993

**P22 Type Foundry**
P.O. Box 770 West Side Station
Buffalo, NY 14213-0070
Phone: 716-885-4490
Fax: 716-885-4482
P22@p22.com
http://www.p22.com

**Snyder Shareware Fonts**
1797 Ross Inlet Road
Coos Bay, OR 97420
Snyderrp@mail.coos.or.us

**Synstelien Design**
1338 North 120th Plaza, Apt# 9
Omaha, NE 68154
Phone: 402-491-3065
http://www.synfonts.com

**Three Islands Press**
P.O. Box 442
Rockland, ME 04841-0442
Phone: 207-596-6768
Fax: 207-596-7403
Info@3ip.com
http://www.3ip.com

**Vintage Type**
5662 Calle Real. #146
Goleta, CA 93117-2317

**Vitatype Digital Fonts** **(PC only)**
5204 Hadley Court. #1
Overland Park, KS 66202
Phone: 913-677-2533
Jeff@vitatype.com
http://www.primenet/~jeffib

## Images

**D'Pix Division of Amber Productions, Inc.**
41 W. Fourth Ave.
Columbus, OH 43201
Phone: 614-299-7192
Fax: 614-294-0002

**Digital Stock**
400 S. Sierra Ave. Suite 100
Solana Beach, CA 92075
Phone: 619-794-4040 or 800-545-4514
Fax: 619-794-4041

**FotoSets**
4104 24th Street. #425
San Francisco, CA 94114
Phone: 415-621-2061
Fax: 415-621-2917

**Image Club Graphics**
729 24th Ave. SE
Calgary, AB, Canada
T2G 5K8
Phone: 403-262-8008 or 800-661-9410
Fax: 403-261-7013
http://www.adobe.com/imageclub

**Jawai Interactive**
501 E. Fourth St. #511
Austin, TX 78701
Phone: 512-469-0502
Jawai@aol.com

**Photo24 Texture Resource**
7948 Faust Ave.
West Hills, CA 91304
Phone: 818-999-4184 or 800-582-9492
Fax: 818-999-5704
http://www.photo24.com

**PhotoDisc/CMCD**
2013 Fourth Ave. 4th Floor
Seattle, WA 98121
Phone: 206-441-9355 or 800-528-3472
http://www.photodisc.com

## Software

**Adobe Systems, Inc.**
345 Park Avenue
San Jose, CA 95110-6000
Phone: 408-563-6000
Fax: 408-537-6000

**Acrobat Reader 3.0 demo**
**After Effects 3.1 demo**
**Dimensions 3.0 demo**
**Illustrator 7.0 demo**
**Streamline 4.0 demo**

**Earthlink**
Earthlink ISP
3100 New York Drive
Pasadena, CA 91107
Phone: 626-296-2400
Sales@earthlink.net

**Macromedia**
600 Townsend
San Francisco, CA 94103
Phone: 415-252-2000
http://www.macromedia.com

**Shockwave r10**
**Fontographer 4.1 demo**
**FreeHand 8.0 demo**
**XRes 2.0 demo**

**Netscape**
Phone: 650/937-3777
http://www.netscape.com

**Navigator 4.04**

# Appendix B

## What's on the CD-ROM

The CD-ROM included with this book contains many files that can help you create great type effects with stock images for you to use, demo versions of Photoshop plug-ins, and popular software applications. You can also find many of the type images that are on the pages of this book. Some of the techniques in this book use specially prepared files. All these files are on the CD-ROM.

Finally, on the CD-ROM are actions that you can load into the Photoshop Actions palette and use to create some of the same effects that you see in this book with a click of the mouse.

The CD-ROM is readable on both Macintosh and Windows platforms.

The CD-ROM includes six folders: Filters, Fonts, Images, P5TM Files, and Software. The following is a brief description of the folder contents.

### Filters

Inside the Filters folder are four folders that contain different filters for use with Adobe Photoshop. Each folder represents a different company with varying numbers of filters from each. To use any of these plug-ins, they need to be copied into the Plug-ins folder inside the Adobe Photoshop 5.0 folder on your hard drive. Follow this path to copy the files: Adobe Photoshop 5.0➥Plug-ins. The next time you start Photoshop, these third-party plug-in demos appear at the bottom of the Filter menu, as shown in this figure.

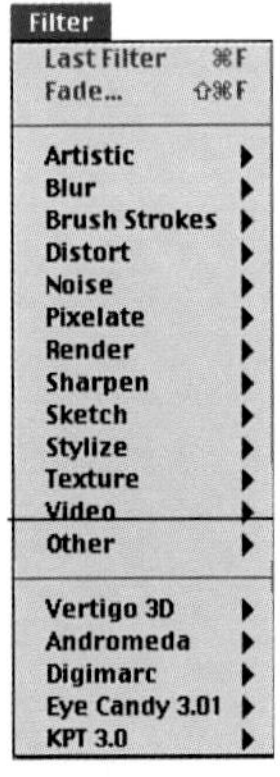


### Fonts

The CD-ROM offers fourteen different folders within the Fonts folder, each from a company supplying the fonts, including over 30 different fonts and several different formats. Please note the instructions provided with each company's product for information on shareware conditions, installation, and purchasing.

## Images

Inside the Images folder are seven folders that contain a variety of low, medium, and high-resolution stock photography images. Many of the images contain textures and backgrounds that you can use to make great-looking type. Most likely, you will decide to keep these images on the CD-ROM where you can access them at will—without having them eat up memory on your hard drive. (If you want, you can also move them to your hard drive.) You can open all these images with the Open command in Adobe Photoshop.

## P5TM Files

There are several folders within this folder. With one exception (the Lighting Styles folder), all of the files within these folders can be left on the CD-ROM and accessed when directed in the instruction steps. If you want, you can also place them in any folder on your hard drive that you don't plan on forgetting about.

### Lighting Styles

There are 21 Lighting Style presets that you can use with Photoshop's Lighting Effects filter. These are the only files within the P5TM Files folder that must be copied to your hard drive in order to be useable. Proper installation of these files is critical. In order to use these files, they must be copied from the CD-ROM into the Lighting Styles folder within the Adobe Photoshop folder on your hard drive. Follow this path to find the proper folder: Adobe Photoshop 5.0➥Plug-ins➥Filters➥Lighting FX➥Lighting Styles. After copying these files, the next time you start Photoshop, they will appear in the Style list in the Lighting Effects dialog box.

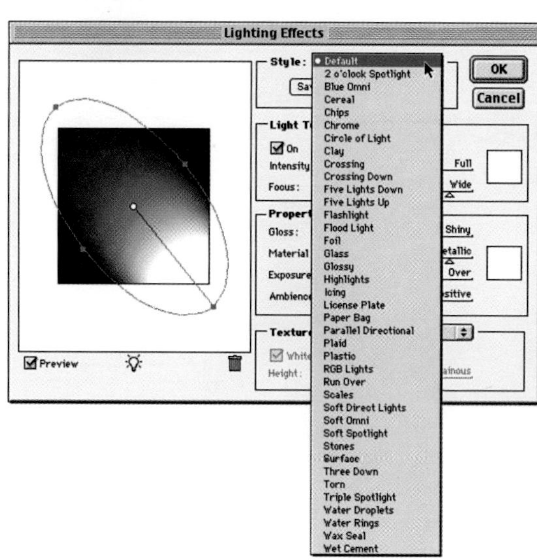

### Actions

There are 31 actions in the action set that enable you to create some of the same effects in this book with a click of a button. To load the actions into the Actions palette, choose Load Actions from the Actions palette menu. Follow this path to find the P5TM Actions file: P5TM➥P5TM Files➥Actions➥P5TM Actions.

The actions are divided into two groups. In order to run the first group, you must first use the Type Mask tool to enter the text; then click on the name of the effect you want to apply and choose Play from the Actions palette menu. To use the actions in the second group, use the Type tool to enter the text before playing the action.

These actions were optimized for 150dpi files. Results might vary depending on the specific characteristics of the files you use. After you load these actions, you can alter them to suit you needs. To learn more about actions and how to modify them, consult your Photoshop 5.0 User's Manual.

## Software

Inside this folder are demo versions of popular software applications that you can try. For detailed information about how to install and run these applications, consult the READ ME files contained within the individual folders. Each folder contains an installation file that walks you through the installation of the software.

# Gallery

page 22

page 28

BORDERS

page 34

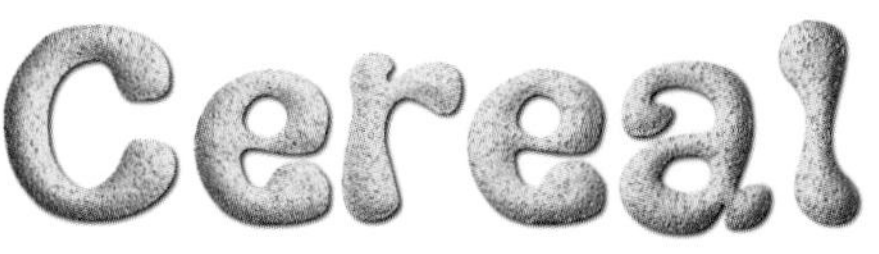


page 40

page 44

page 50

page 56

page 58

Highlights

*page 102*

MARBLE

*page 106*

*page 108*

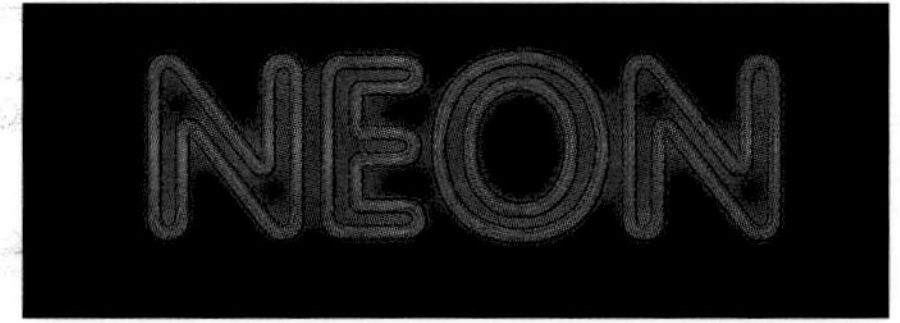


*page 112*

*page 118*

PAPER BAG

*page 106*

*page 126*

Peel-Away

*130*

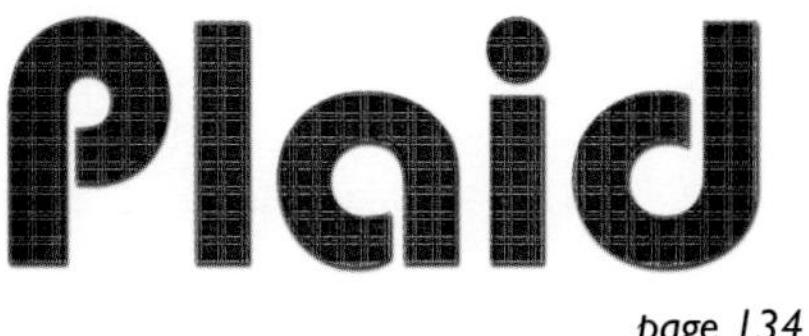


page 134

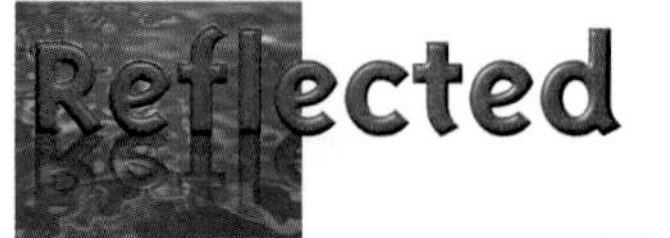


page 152

page 138

page 156

page 142

page 160

page 146

page 166

*page 170*

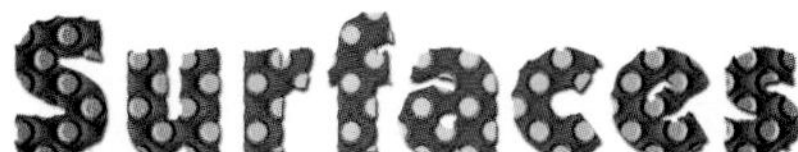


*page 174*

*page 180*

*page 188*

*page 192*



*page 196*

*page 202*

*page 206*

VIBRATION

page 210

page 228

page 214

page 234

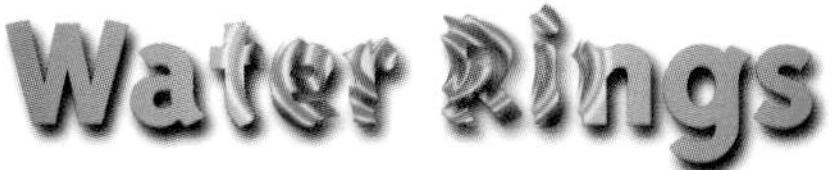


page 220

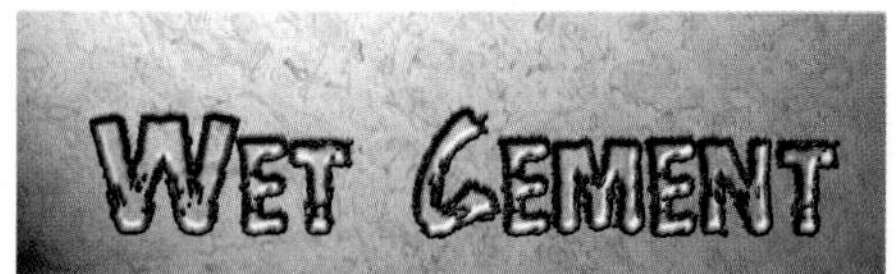


page 238

page 224

# Photoshop Effects Magic

Stanger
Stet · Fortuna · Domus

# Photoshop Effects Magic

by Rhoda Grossman

---

## Photoshop Effects Magic

©1997 Hayden Books

All rights reserved. Printed in the United States of America. No part of this book may be used or reproduced in any form or by any means, or stored in a database or retrieval system, without prior written permission of the publisher except in the case of brief quotations embodied in critical articles and reviews. Making copies of any part of this book for any purpose other than your own personal use is a violation of United States copyright laws. For information, address Hayden Books, 201 W. 103rd Street, Indianapolis, Indiana 46290.

Library of Congress Catalog Number: 96-78986
ISBN: 1-56830-344-0

Copyright © 1997 Hayden Books

Printed in the United States of America 3 4 5 6 7 8 9 0

### Warning and Disclaimer

This book is sold as is, without warranty of any kind, either express or implied. While every precaution has been taken in the preparation of this book, the authors and Hayden Books assume no responsibility for errors or omissions. Neither is any liability assumed for damages resulting from the use of the information or instructions contained herein. It is further stated that the publisher and authors are not responsible for any damage or loss to your data or your equipment that results directly or indirectly from your use of this book.

# Trademark Acknowledgments

All terms mentioned in this book that are known to be trademarks or services marks have been appropriately capitalized. Hayden Books cannot attest to the accuracy of this information. Use of a term in this book should not be regarded as affecting the validity of any trademark or service mark. Apple, Mac, Macintosh, and Power Macintosh are registered trademarks and AppleScript is a trademark of Apple Computer, Inc. Microsoft and Windows are registered trademarks and Windows NT is a trademark of Microsoft Corporation in the USA and other countries. Images provided courtesy of PhotoDisc, Inc. © Copyright 1997 PhotoDisc, Inc. All rights reserved.

**Publisher** Jordan Gold
**Executive Editor** Beth Millet

## The Photoshop Effects Magic Team

**Acquisitions Editor**
Jawahara Saidullah

**Development Editor**
Beth Millett

**Copy/Production Editor**
Terrie Deemer

**Technical Editor**
Kate Binder

**Publishing Coordinator**
Karen Flowers

**Cover Designer**
Aren Howell

**Book Designer**
Gary Adair

**Manufacturing Coordinator**
Brook Farling

**Production Team Supervisors**
Laurie Casey, Joe Millay

**Production Team**
Trina Brown, Dan Caparo, Billy Huys, Christopher Morris, Scott Tullis, Megan Wade

# Hayden Books

The staff of Hayden Books is committed to bringing you the best computer books. What our readers think of Hayden is important to our ability to serve our customers. If you have any comments, no matter how great or how small, we'd appreciate your taking the time to send us a note.

You can reach Hayden Books at the following:

Hayden Books
201 West 103rd Street
Indianapolis, IN 46290

Visit the Hayden Books Web site at `http://www.mcp.com`

# About the Author

**Rhoda Grossman**

Rhoda is a freelance illustrator and cartoonist whose work has appeared in numerous publications on digital art, including Hayden Books' *Photoshop Creative Techniques* and *Fractal Design Painter Creative Techniques*.

Whether in her Sausalito studio or teaching or doing caricature demonstrations as Rhoda Draws A Crowd, she combines hi-tech and lo-tech art and refers to herself as "bi-tech."

She finds time to work for artists' rights and is the founder of AAARGH, Artists Against Arbitrary Regulations and Government Harassment.

Rhoda has a 4-year-old computer, an 11-year-old car and a 28-year-old daughter, all working. You can find her at: `http://www.digitalpainting.com`.

# Dedication

For Sherry London, who led me down the garden path.

***Special Thanks to…***

Sharron Evans for teaching me cool techniques.

Marc Schmid, Barbara Pollack, and Liz Beatrice for contributing artwork, even if it has to wait for Volume 2.

Roy Gordet for his generous gifts of time and legal advice.

Diane Fenster and Helen Golden, for being my role models.

Melanie Rigney, who made me an offer I couldn't refuse, Beth Millett for knowing whether to crack the whip or the joke, and the rest of the Hayden Team.

My mother, Ida, whose jello made the "Saturation" technique possible…and whose love made me possible

The folks at Adobe who have created the software that if I were marooned on a desert island and could only have one graphics application I would pick if only I could answer the question, "where do I plug this in?"

# Contents at a Glance

# Contents

# Introduction

Photoshop users at all levels will find this book a tasty reference. There are easy-to-use recipes for producing all the looks you see as you thumb through these pages. You'll find techniques for working with photos and with line art…and quite a few ways to create something from nothing. The CD-ROM that accompanies this book contains an assortment of photos, drawings and other tidbits. These can serve as ingredients for the recipes, but you are encouraged to find and create your own as well.

So, this isn't just a cookbook, though you could use it that way. It's more like a 42-course dinner. You could eat your way through until you're stuffed, and still come back for seconds. Or you could just nibble and pick.

There's a tempting smorgasbord of effects for digital illustrators, designers and fine artists. Don't worry, I haven't forgotten the "Sunday Painters" though I guess I'd better call them "Weekend Digitizers."

Whatever your reasons for using Photoshop—commercial assignments, personal creativity, or simply "because it's there," put down that knife and fork, and pick up your mouse or stylus. Now, dig in!

Rhoda Grossman

# Before You Start

## Welcome

Welcome to another volume in the series for creating "Magic" with Photoshop. Like its sisters, *Photoshop Type Magic* and *Photoshop Web Magic*, this book is more than a how-to manual—this book is a what-to guide. The steps in this book tell you exactly what you need to do in order to create exactly what you want. Flip through the thumbtabs to find the effect you want to create and follow the concise, explanatory steps. Or thumb through to discover an effect you never imagined and learn what to do to create it. If you need a little extra help, flip to the Photoshop Basics section. But, before you jump in, let me tell you a little about how this book works. A quick read now will maximize your time later.

## System Setup

Here are the system recommendations for creating these effects.

MacOS users: The Adobe Photoshop 4.0 Info box suggests a memory allocation of 21 megabytes (MB) of RAM to run Photoshop. And your system software may need as much as 10MB of RAM. That's a full bowl of soup, but if you've got the memory, then I would recommend setting the Preferred memory size even higher than 21MB. If you don't have 21MB to spare, quit all other applications and give it everything you've got.

Windows users: Adobe suggests 32MB of RAM for Photoshop on any 386 or faster processor running Windows 3.1, Windows 95, or Windows NT, but 40MB is better. Quit any application you can before starting Photoshop to maximize the running of the application. Photoshop runs 32-bit native on both Windows 95 and Windows NT operating systems.

It is not crucial, but it will help if you have a CD-ROM drive. A number of the effects in this book use files contained on the CD-ROM that comes bundled with this book. (See Appendix B, "What's on the CD-ROM," for information on accessing those files.) However, even if you don't have a CD-ROM drive, you still can perform all of the effects described in the book.



## Adobe Photoshop 4.0

All of the techniques in this book were created with Adobe Photoshop 4.0, and that's the version I recommend you use. If you're attempting to duplicate these techniques using an earlier version of Photoshop, your results may differ slightly or significantly compared to mine. If you're working with version 3.0, you still will be able to create all of the effects in the book. Keep in mind, however, you will need to adjust the instructions for the differences between the two versions. You will see that even some of the old Photoshop features work differently in Photoshop 4.0. Many of the effects in this book use features not available in earlier versions of Photoshop.

## Conventions

Every image in this book was created initially as an RGB file. You can make your effects in any appropriate color mode, but you should be aware of the variations this will cause as you proceed through the steps. The first new channel created in an RGB file, for example, is automatically named Channel #4. But the first new channel created in a CMYK file is named Channel #5. You also should be aware of the differences in the color ranges of the various color modes. Some colors that look great in RGB mode may look like mud after you convert the file's color mode to CMYK. The Lighting Effects filter, for example, will not work on a CMYK or grayscale file.

If you'd like more detailed information about the different color modes, refer to a good general Photoshop book such as *Photoshop 4 Complete* or to your Photoshop user manuals.

Also, every image was created as a 150-dpi resolution file. (The thumbtab images were created as 300 dpi files.) If you are going to work in a resolution other than 150 dpi, remember that some of the filters and commands will require different settings than the settings I used. Because there are fewer pixels in a 72 dpi image, a Gaussian Blur radius of 5 pixels will blur the image more than if it were a 150 dpi image. Just keep an eye on the figures next to the steps and match the outcome as close as you can.

I used a pressure-sensitive digitizer tablet and stylus to create all the images, but a mouse works fine for most of them. A tablet is suggested for best results with the "Impressionism," "Cloning," "Burning Type," "Bristle Brush," "Quick Color," "Rough Sketch," and "Textured Brush" techniques.

### The Blue Type

As you work through the steps, you will see phrases colored a light blue. These same phrases are listed in alphabetical order in the Photoshop Basics section. If the phrase in blue asks you to perform a task you are unfamiliar with, you can find that phrase in the Photoshop Basics section and follow the instructions on how to perform that task.



### Menu Commands

You also will see instructions that look like this:

Filter➡Blur➡Gaussian Blur (2 pixels)

This example asks you to apply the Gaussian Blur filter. To perform this command, click on the Filter menu at the top of the screen and drag down to Blur. When Blur is highlighted a new menu opens to the right, from which you can choose Gaussian Blur.

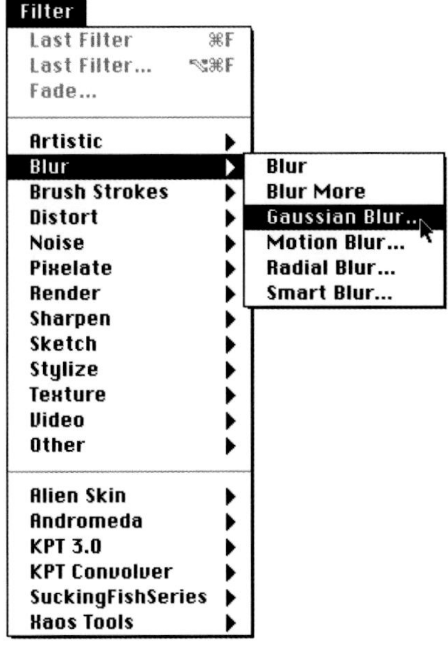


In this example, a dialog box appears asking you for more information. All of the settings you need to perform each task appear in the text of the step. The previous example tells you to enter 2 pixels as the Radius.

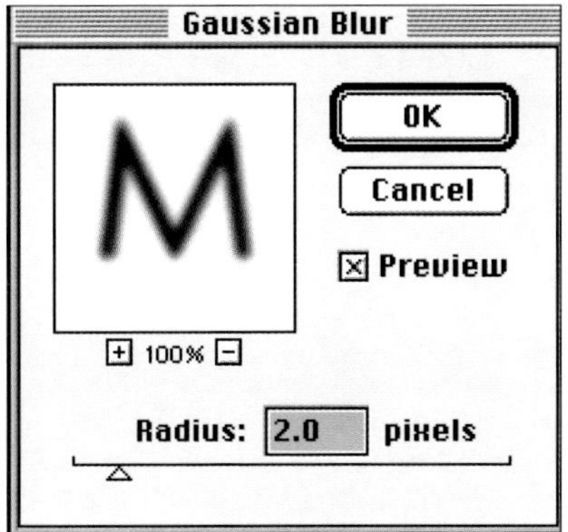


Click OK to blur the image.

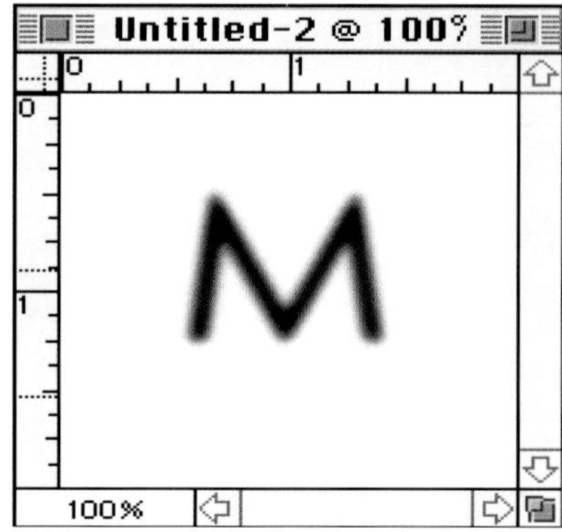


## Settings

Following each action in the steps, you will find the settings for that feature. These recommended settings are meant to act as guides; the best settings for your effect may vary. As a rule, it is best to match the outcomes that you see in the figures as you progress through the technique. The greatest differences occur when the resolution of your file is significantly different from what I used. The following two images demonstrate the importance of adjusting for resolution differences. A 6-pixel radius Gaussian Blur was applied to both images.

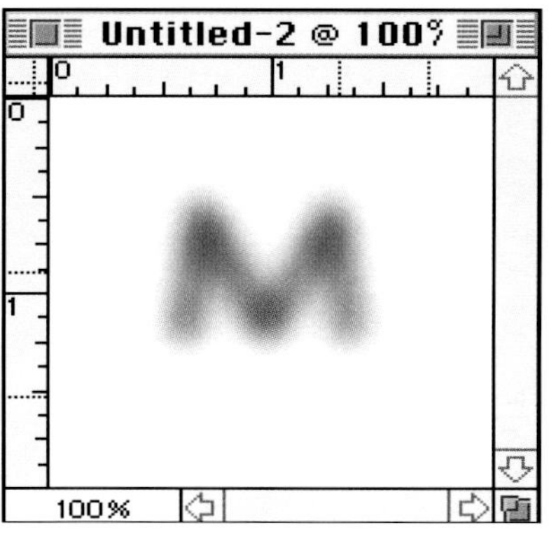


75 dpi

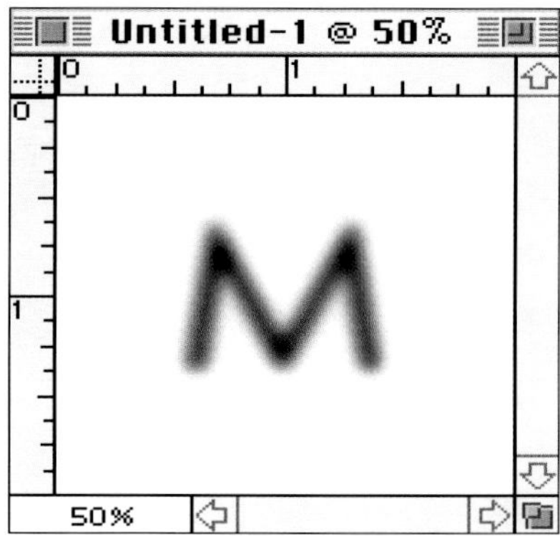


150 dpi

## Tips

Throughout the book, you will find additional bits of information that can help you make the most of Photoshop. These tips provide information beyond the basic steps of each lesson.

# Photoshop Basics

The goal of this section is to help new and novice users of Photoshop with the simple, basic tasks required to create the effects described and illustrated in this book. Each of the basic tasks described in this section corresponds to the blue highlighted text in the chapters that follow. Here, users can easily find the instructions they need for performing a particular Photoshop task.

This chapter proceeds on two assumptions: that you're creating my effects in Photoshop 4.0; and that you're keeping the Toolbox, and the Brushes, Options and Layer/Channel/Path palettes open. If one or more of these palettes are closed when you refer to this chapter, you can reopen them by name by using the Window menu at the top of the screen. If you're using an earlier version of Photoshop, you can refer to the Photoshop manual for instructions on how to perform these tasks.

## The Toolbox

If you're not familiar with Photoshop's toolbox, there's no reason to panic. With a bit of experimentation, it doesn't take long to learn each tool's individual functions. This representation of the toolbox will help beginners and experts alike find the tools they need.

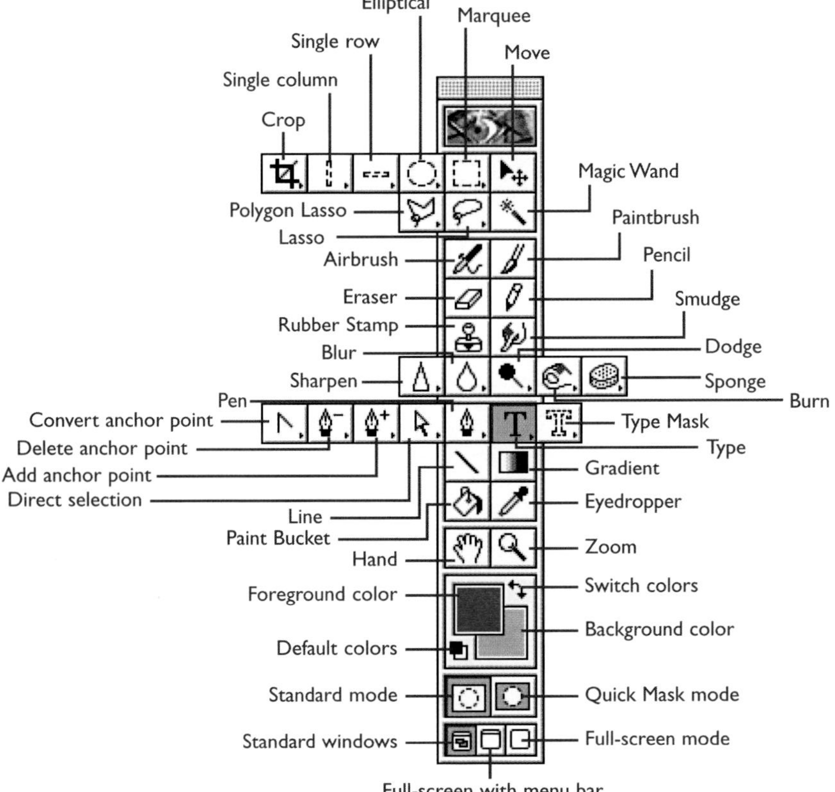

# Basic Photoshop Tasks

## Choose a Foreground or Background Color

**Shortcut**: Press D to change colors to their defaults: black for the foreground, and white for the background.(Note: if you are working on a layer mask, pressing D will give you white foreground and black background.)

Press X to switch the foreground color with the background color.

To change the foreground or background color click on either the Foreground icon or the Background icon.

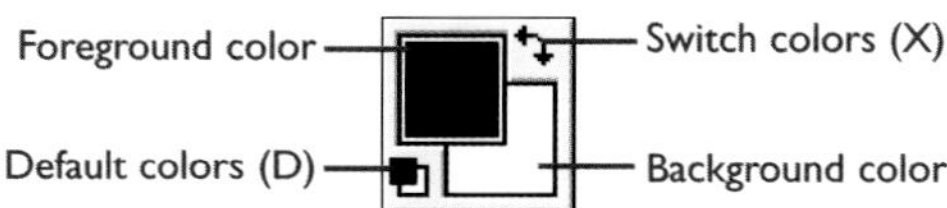


The Color Picker dialog box appears, which enables you to choose a new foreground or background color by moving and clicking the cursor (now a circle) along the spectrum box, or by changing specific RGB, CMYK, or other percentage values. Note that the Foreground and Background icons on the Toolbox now reflect your color choices.

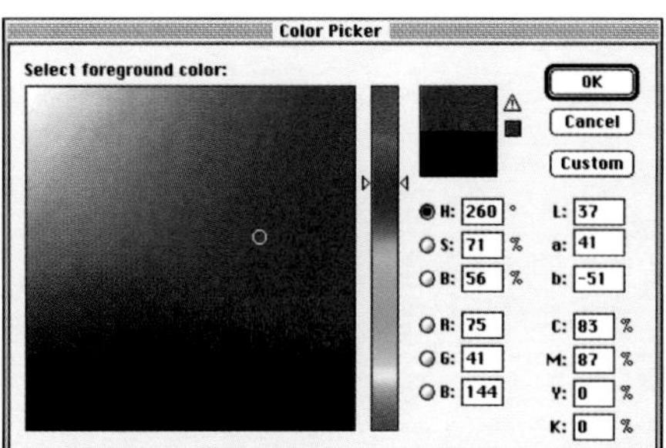


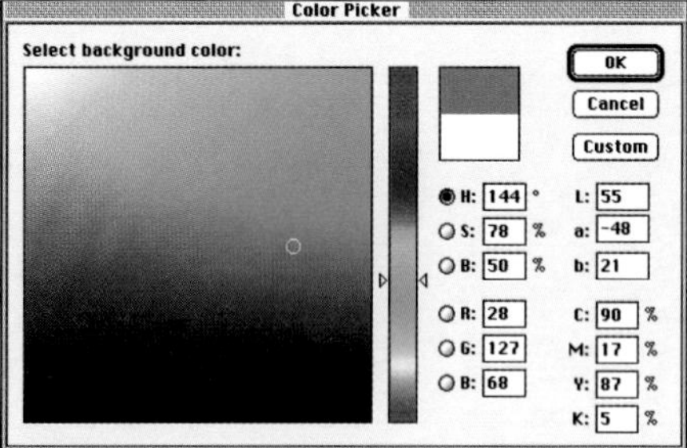


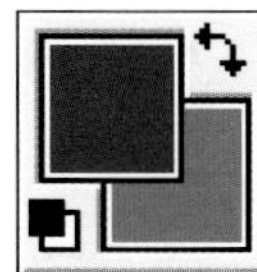

## Convert to a New Mode

To convert from one color mode to another, click on the Image menu at the top of the screen and scroll down to the Mode command. You then can scroll down to select the mode of your preference. If you want to switch from CMYK mode to multichannel mode, for example, you choose Image➡Mode➡Multichannel. The check mark to the left of CMYK will move down to Multichannel, indicating that you are now in multichannel mode.

**TIP** **Remember that there is a different range of colors available for each color mode. No matter what color mode the file is in onscreen, for example, your printer (if it prints in color) is going to print your work in CMYK. Because the color ranges for RGB and CMYK are different, you should convert your RGB image to CMYK before printing. Otherwise, you may be in for a big surprise when your bright green prints as a dull tan.**

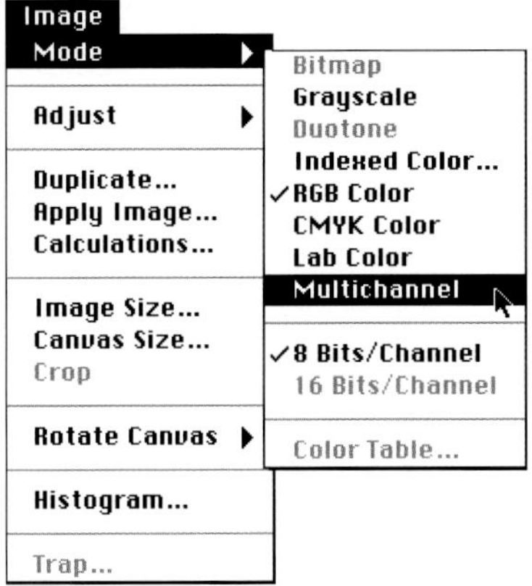


## Create a Layer Mask

To create a layer mask, click the Layer Mask icon at the bottom of the Layers palette. A layer mask is used to mask out (or hide) parts of a layer. Painting with black hides an area, and painting with white reveals it. Dragging a layer mask to the trash icon at the bottom of the Layers palette allows you to apply it or delete it. Here the layer mask is active, indicated by the black border around it and the mask icon in the active layer.

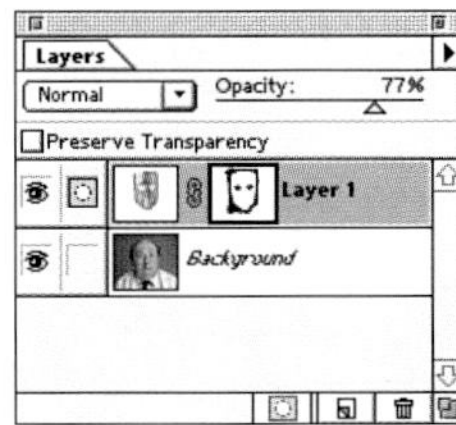


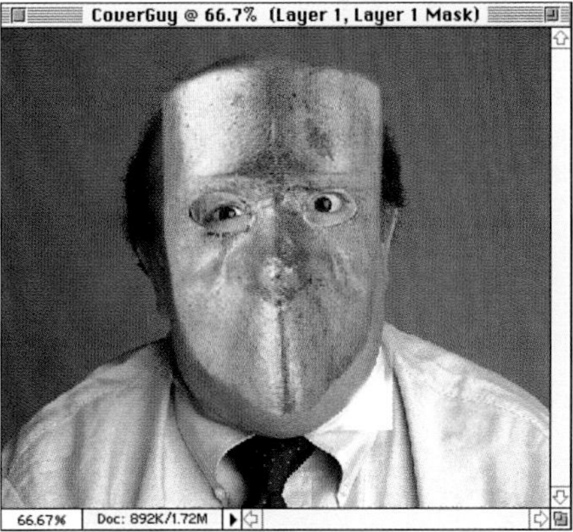

## Create a New Channel

**Shortcut**: Click the New Channel icon on the Channels palette.

To create a new channel, choose New Channel from the Channels palette pop-up menu.

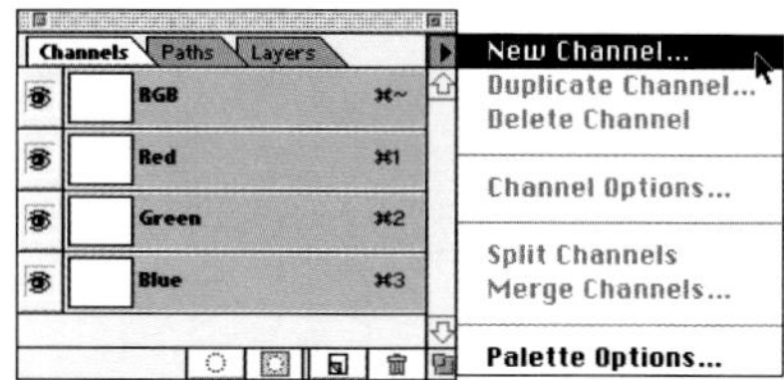


Use the Channel Options dialog box to establish your settings. Unless noted otherwise, we used the default settings when creating a new channel. This figure shows Photoshop's default settings.

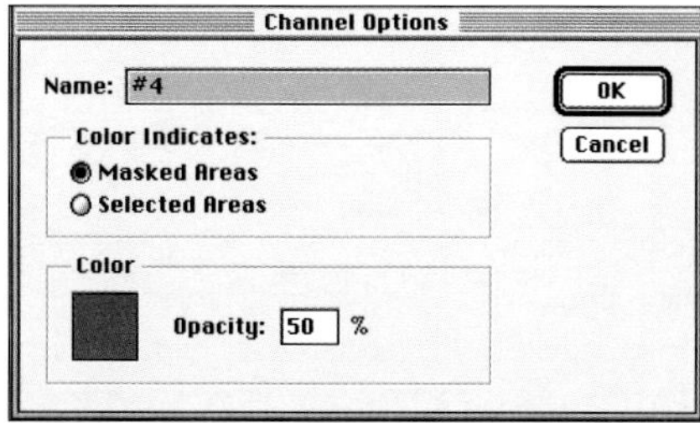


## Create a New File

**Shortcuts**: Press (Command-N)[Control-N].

To create a new file, choose File➥New. The New dialog box appears, which is where you name your new file and establish other settings. See Part I, "Before You Start" for information on the conventions that were used when creating new files for the type effects in this book.



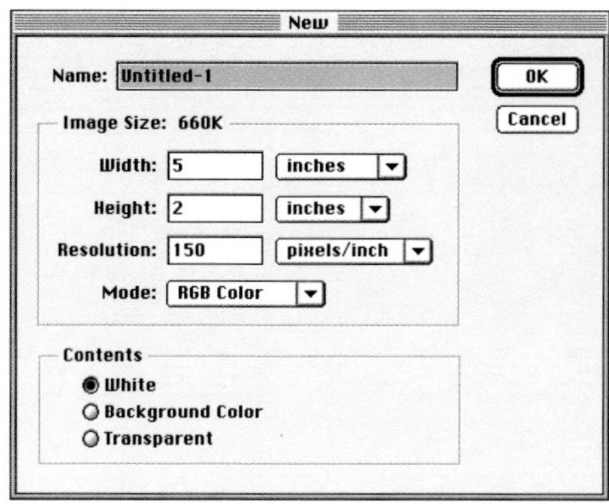

## Create a New Layer

**Shortcut**: Click the New Layer icon on the Layers palette.

To create a new layer, choose New Layer from the Layer palette pop-up menu, or choose Layer➡New➡Layer.

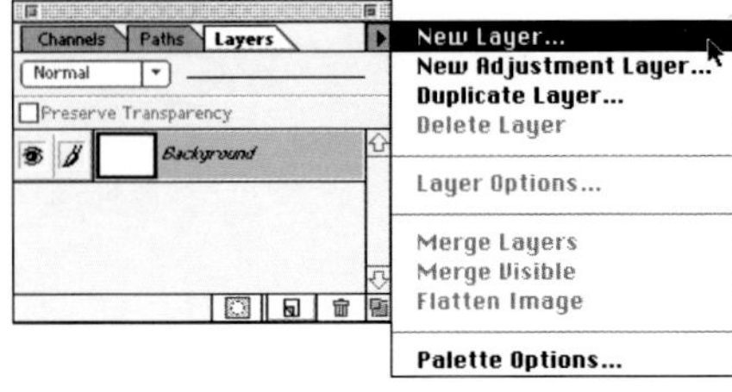


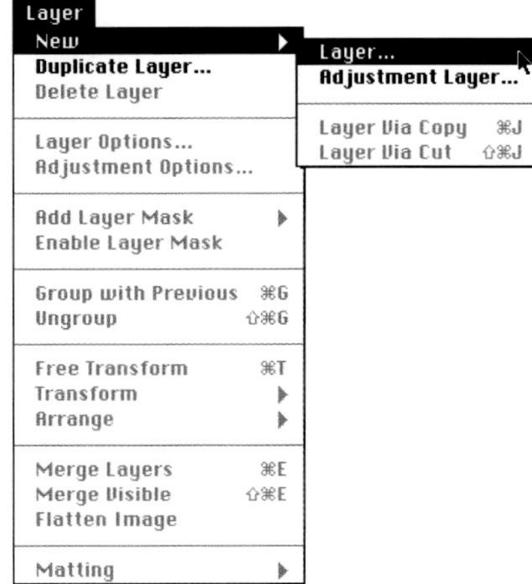


The New Layer dialog box opens, which is where you name the new layer and establish other settings.

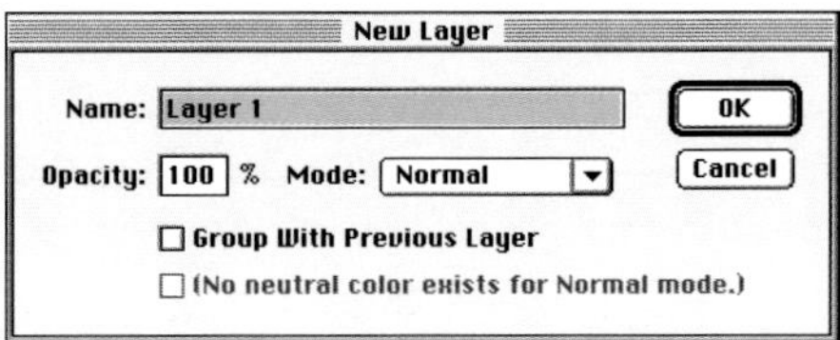


## Delete a Channel

To delete a channel, go to the Channels palette and select the channel you want to delete; drag it to the Trash icon at the lower-right corner (just like you would to get rid of a document on the Desktop for Mac users). You also can select the channel you want to delete, and choose Delete Channel from the Channels palette arrow menu.

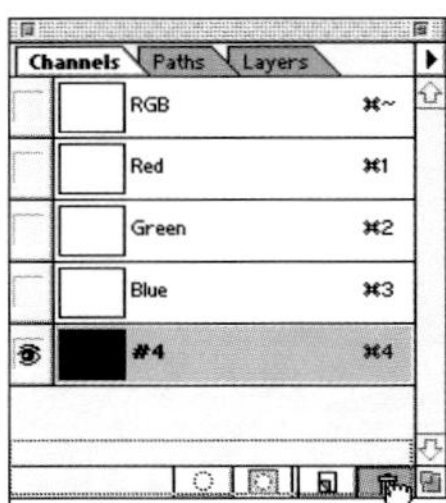


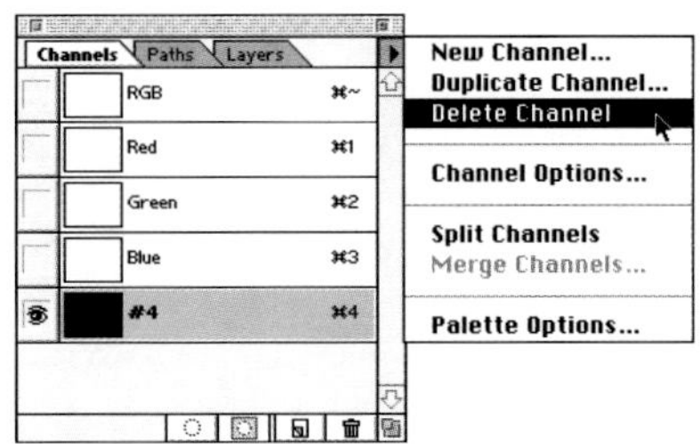

## Deselect a Selection

**Shortcut**: Press (Command-D)[Control-D].

To deselect a selection, choose Select➡None. The marquee disappears.

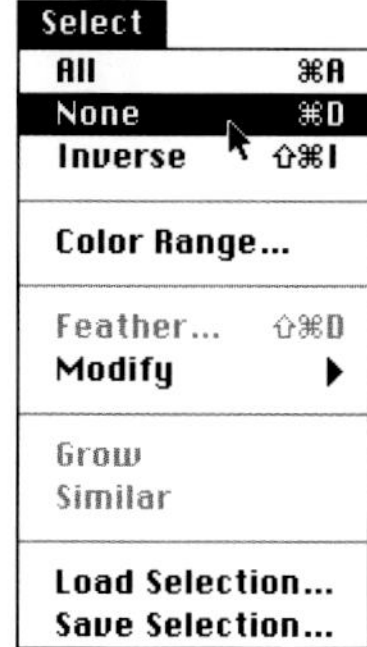


## Drag and Drop

This technique *is* a shortcut. It eliminates copying to and pasting from the clipboard. With two images open, select an area from the source image and drag it over to the destination image, using the Move tool. A new layer is created automatically.

**Shortcut**: Press (Command)[Control] to access the Move tool.

## Duplicate a Channel or Layer

**Shortcut**: Click the channel or layer you want to duplicate, and drag it on top of the New Channel or New Layer icon.

To create a duplicate of a channel or Layer, make it active and then select Duplicate Channel or Duplicate Layer from the appropriate palette pop-up menu.

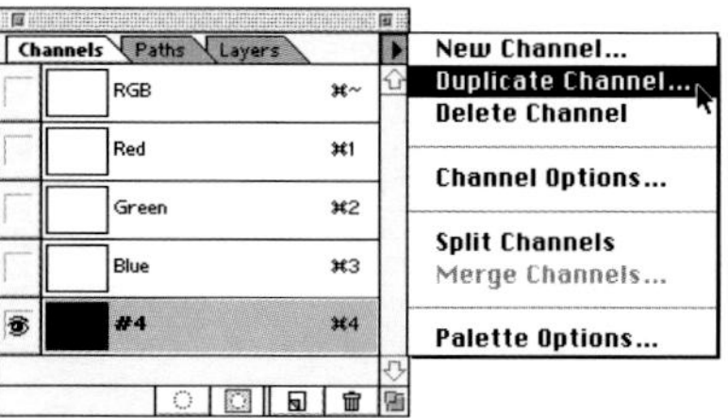


A new copy of the channel you selected for duplication is created automatically, and the Duplicate Channel dialog box appears.

Duplicate Channel
Duplicate: #4
As: #4 copy
OK
Cancel
Destination
Document: Untitled-1
Name:
Invert

## Enter/Exit Quick Mask

**Shortcuts**: Press Q to enter and exit the Quick Mask mode.

Click the Quick Mask icon to switch to Quick Mask mode; conversely, click the Standard mode icon to return to Standard mode.

Essentially a Quick Mask is a temporary channel. When you're in Quick Mask mode you can use any of the Photoshop tools and functions to change the selection without changing the image. When you switch back to Standard mode you'll have a new selection.

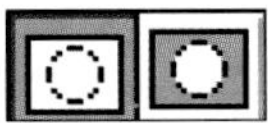

## Enter the Text

Before entering the text using the standard Type tool, make sure that the foreground color is set to your desired text color. If you are entering text into a layer, then the standard Type tool will create a new layer for the type.

To enter the text, select the Type tool, and then click anywhere in the image to open the Type Tool dialog box. Type the text in the large box at the bottom of the dialog box, and make your attribute choices from the options (listed previously). Unless noted otherwise in the instructions, always make sure that you have the Anti-Aliased box checked.



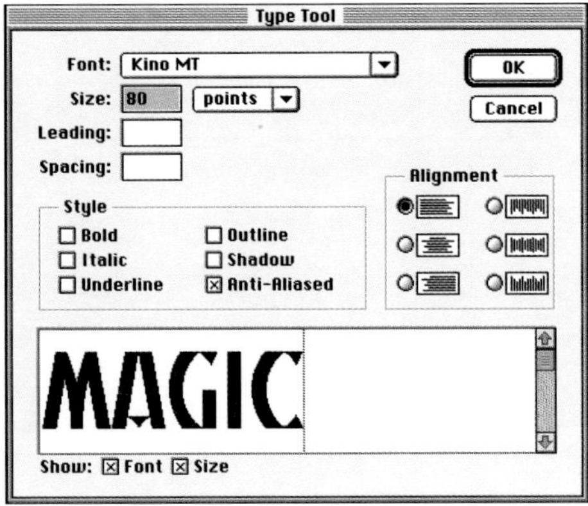

After clicking OK, move the type into position with the Move tool.

## Fade the Effect

**Shortcut:** (Shift-Command-F)[Shift-Control-F] opens a dialog box for fading the last filter used and changing its blending mode.

To fade the last Filter applied, or some other effects such as Invert, choose Filter➡Fade. The Fade slider acts like a partial undo for the last effect you applied. The Blending Mode pop-up menu enables you to determine how the pixels of the before and after versions of the image are combined.

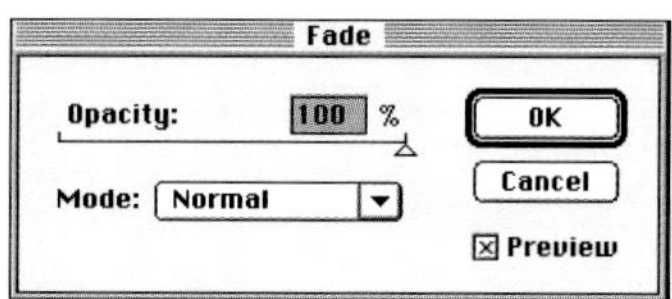


## Fill a Selection with Foreground or Background Color

First, select the foreground or background color you want to use (see page 18 in this section for instructions). Keep the selection active and press the (Option-Delete) [Alt-Backspace] keys to fill the selection with the foreground color. If you are in the Background layer or any layer that has the Preserve Transparency option turned on, then you can press (Delete)[Backspace] to fill in the selection with the background color.

You also can fill in your selections by choosing Edit➡Fill, or press (Shift-Delete) [Shift-Backspace] to open the Fill dialog box.

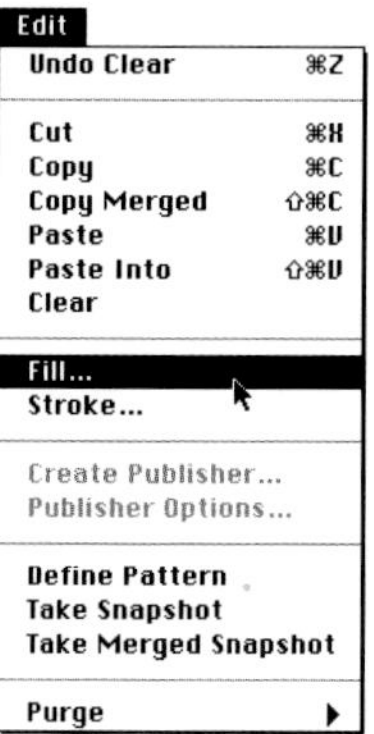


This causes the Fill dialog box to appear, enabling you to establish the Contents option you want to use, the Opacity, and the Blending Mode.

**If a selection is empty (a transparent area of a layer) and the Preserve Transparency option is turned on for that layer, then you will not be able to fill the selection. To fill the selection, simply turn off the Preserve Transparency option before filling it.**

## Flatten an Image

To flatten an image (merge all the layers into a single layer), choose Flatten Image from the Layers palette arrow menu, or choose Layer➡Flatten Image.

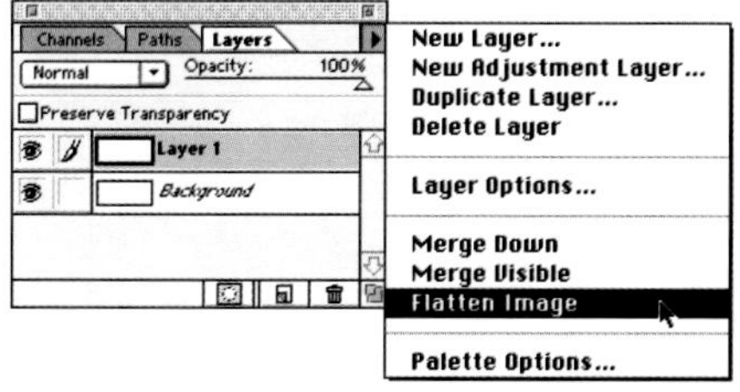


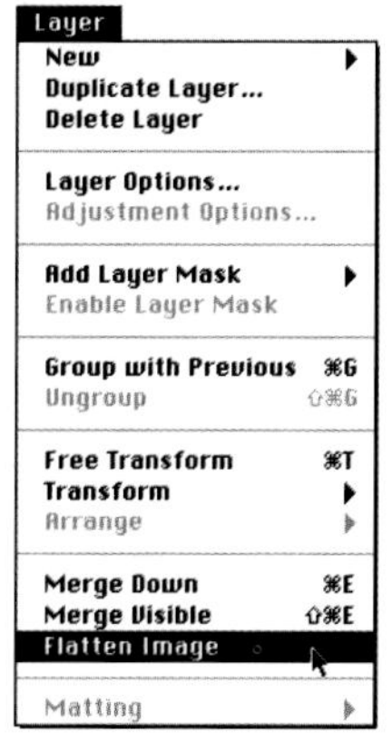


## Load Brushes

To load another library of brushes, choose Load Brushes in the Brush palette pop-up menu. You can choose whether to "append" additional brushes to the default library or replace the defaults. I recommend you append the Assorted Brushes that come with Photoshop. I've also included a few custom brushes in the Presets folder on the CD-ROM that comes with this book.

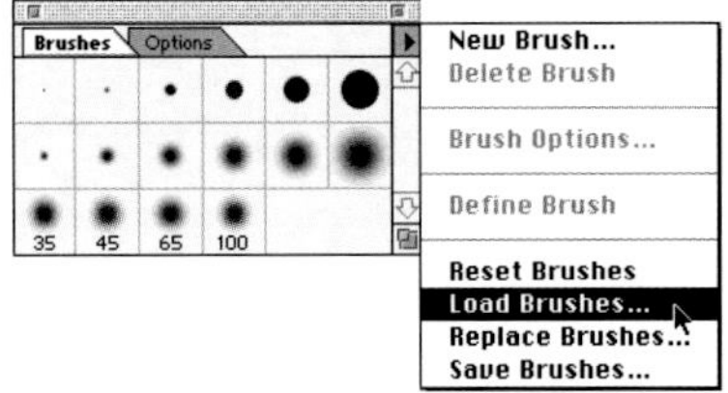


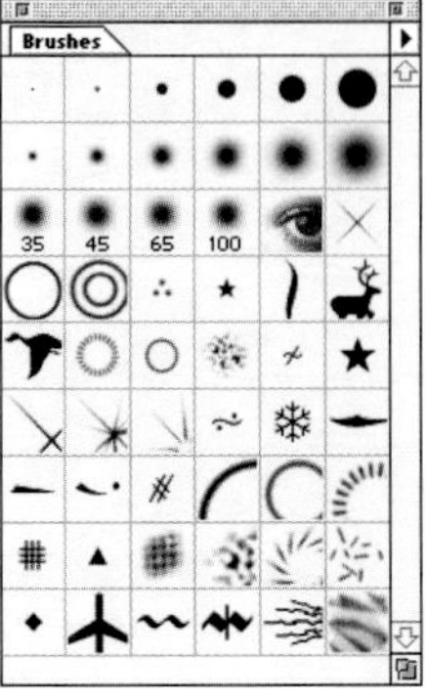


## Load a Selection

**Shortcut**: Hold down the (Command)[Control] key and click the channel (on the Channels palette) that contains the selection you want to load.

To load a selection, choose Select➡Load Selection. This brings up the Load Selection dialog box, where you can establish document, channel, and operation variables.

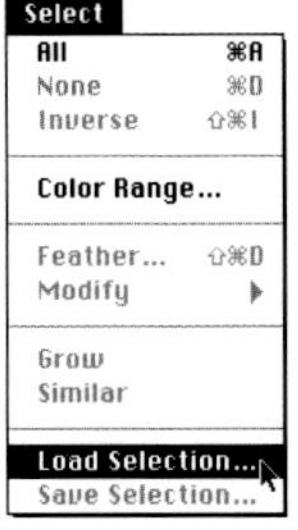


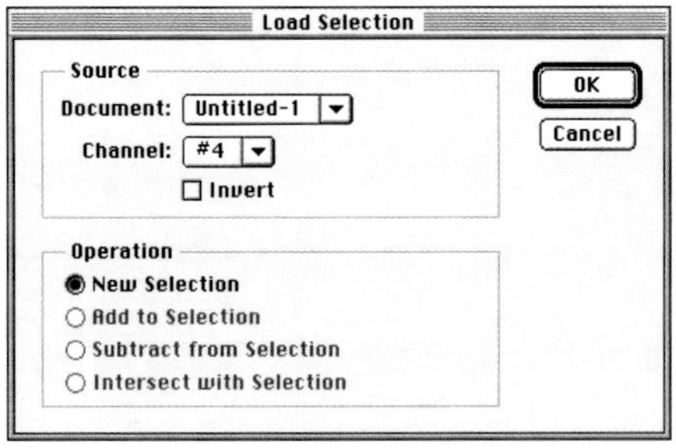


## Make a Channel Active

To make a channel active for editing or modification, click on its thumbnail or name on the Channels palette.

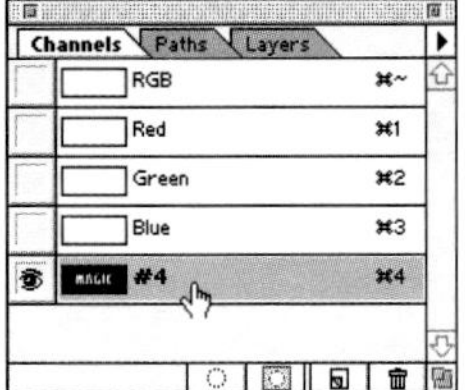


You can tell the channel is active if it is highlighted with a color.

## Make a Layer Active

To make a layer active, click on its thumbnail or name in the Layers palette.

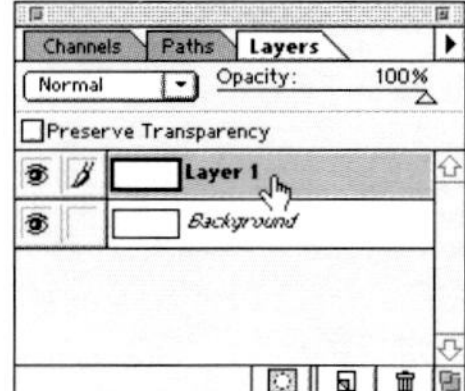


You can tell the layer is active if it is highlighted with a color.

## Make a Layer Visible/Invisible

To make a Layer visible or invisible, click in the left-most column in the Layers palette. If an eye appears, then the layer is visible. If the column is empty, then that layer is hidden (invisible).

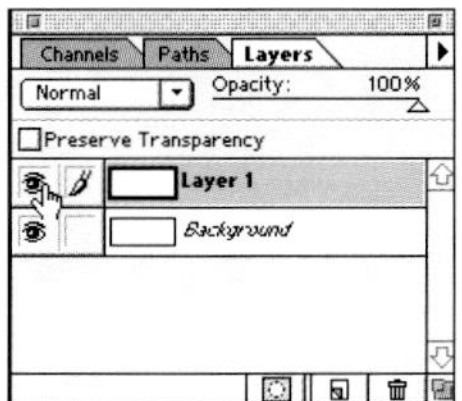


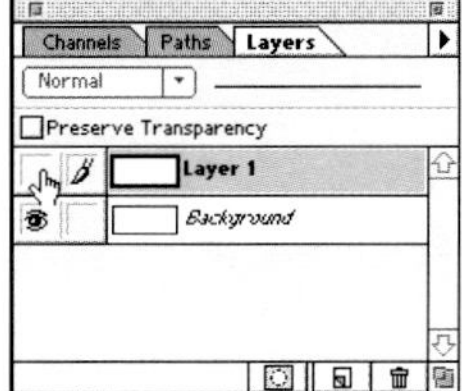


## Move a Layer

To move a layer's position in the list, click on the layer you want to move in the Layers palette and drag it up or down the list of layers to the place you want to move it. As you drag the layer, the lines between the layers will darken to indicate where the layer will fall if you let go.



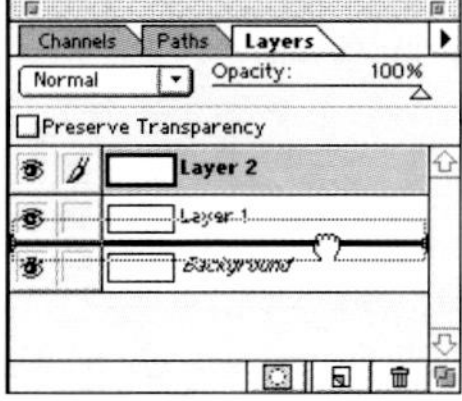


## Name/Rename a Layer

To change the name of a layer double-click its name in the Layers palette and type the new name in the Layer Options dialog box.

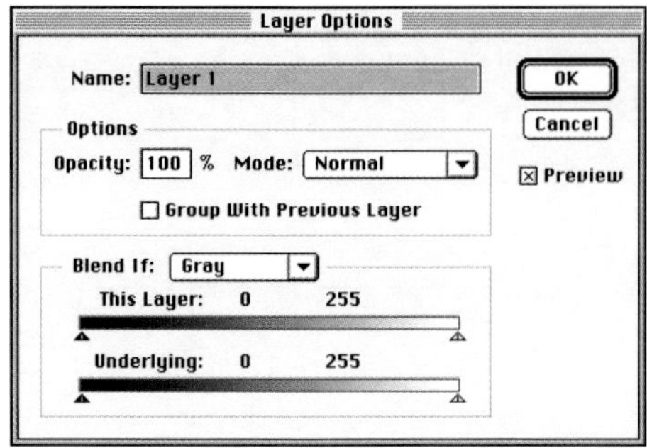


## Place an Image

Use File➥Place to bring an EPS (Encapsulated PostScript) image into an open Photoshop document. The image will appear in a bounding box which can be manipulated before anchoring with a click of the (Return)[Enter] key. A new layer is created automatically with the name of the EPS file.

## Return to the Composite Channel

**Shortcut**: Press (Command-~)[Control-~].

If you want to return to the composite channel, click on its thumbnail or title (RGB, CMYK, Lab). The composite channel always will be the one with (Command-~) [Control-~] after its title.

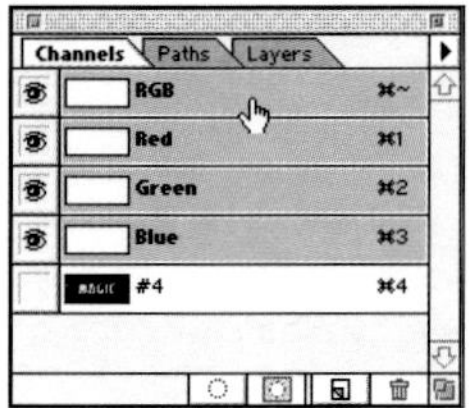


If you are in an RGB file, then Channels 0 through 3 should now be active because each of the R, G, and B channels are individual parts of the RGB image.

## Save a File

To save a file, choose File➥Save As. This displays the Save As dialog box, where you name your new file and choose a format in which to save it.

File format selection depends on what you have in your file, what you want to keep when you save it, and what you're going to do with the file after it is saved. Consult a detailed Photoshop book, such as *Photoshop 4 Complete*, for more guidance on which file format is best for your needs.

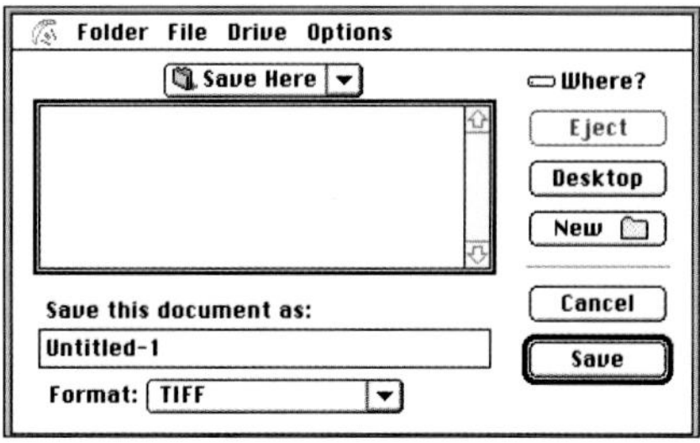


## Save a Selection

**Shortcut**: Click the Save Selection icon on the Channels palette.

To save a selection, choose Select➡Save Selection.

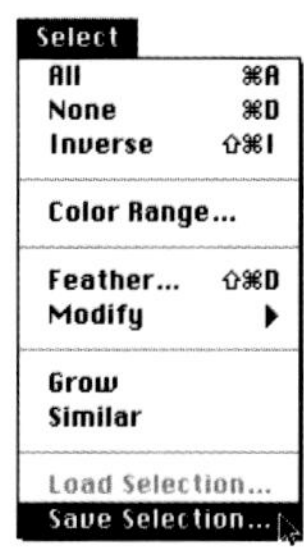


The Save Selection dialog box opens. Choose your options and click OK to save the selection.

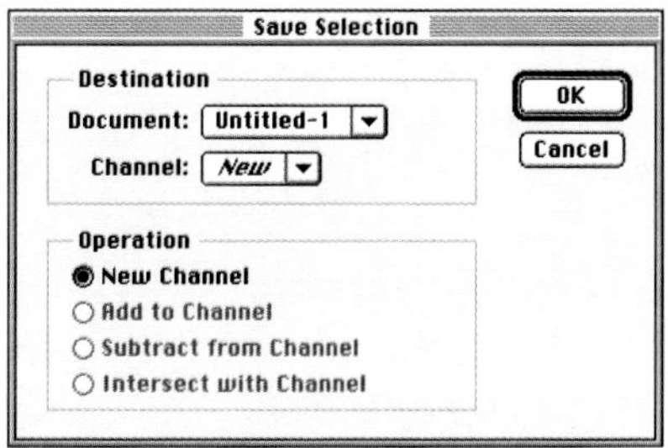


## Switch Blending Mode

In many techniques you will be instructed to change from Normal to another blending mode. This may refer to the Options palette for some tools, or the Layers palette, or the Fade dialog box. Blending mode influences how the pixels from two sources will combine.

To change from Normal mode to any of 16 alternatives, first click the pop-up menu and then drag to your choice of mode. Consult your Photoshop User Guide for details on how each blending mode works.

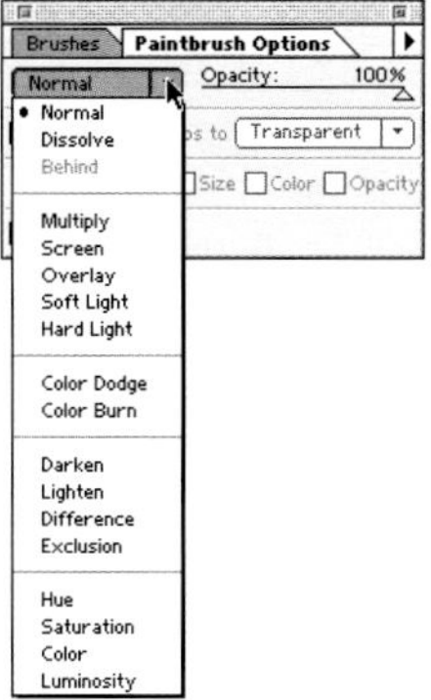


## Switch Foreground/Background Colors

**Shortcut**: Press X to switch the foreground and background colors.

To switch the foreground and background colors, click on the Switch Colors icon. This flips the two colors shown in this icon only, and does not affect the rest of the image.

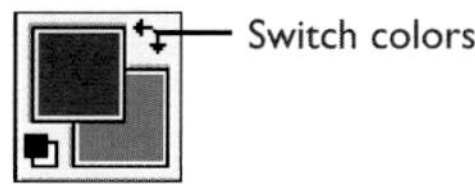


## Switch to Default Colors

**Shortcut**: Press D to switch to the default foreground and background colors.

To change the foreground and background colors to black and white respectively, click on the Default Colors icon.

## Turn On/Off Preserve Transparency

To turn on or off the Preserve Transparency option for a particular layer, first make that layer the active layer. Then, click the Preserve Transparency checkbox on the Layers palette. This option is not available for the Background layer.

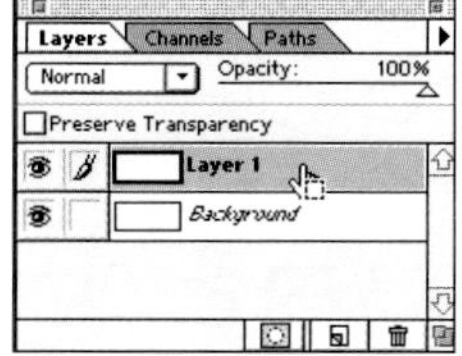


## Vary Pressure

If you are using a graphics tablet and pressure-sensitive stylus you can vary the brush size, color, or opacity as you paint by varying your pen pressure; check the appropriate boxes in the Options palette for a tool to vary any or all of these three characteristics.

If you are using a mouse, you can specify a number of steps in the Fade field to make a stroke that feathers out. The higher the number of steps, the slower the fade.

Changing the value on the Opacity slider is effective for both mouse and tablet users.

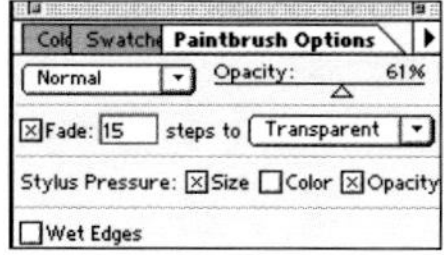

# PART I

## Working with Photos

Why can you no longer use photographs as evidence in court? Why can't you believe the pictures you see in the tabloids? Photoshop is why.

You'll find techniques here for enhancing reality, combining two or more realities and distorting reality beyond all recognition. You'll learn how to add color, reduce color, and alter color in a wide variety of ways. You'll see how to create artistic effects, old-fashioned styles, and some truly terrifying looks I wasn't sure what to call.

The "Impressionism" and "Cloning" techniques work much better if you have a graphics tablet.

Source photos are provided on the CD-ROM. Use your own photos if you prefer. In fact, why not scan family portraits, take digital snapshots at the office party…you begin to see the possibilities?

Photoshop's Layer Mask feature enables you to create a gradual transition between two or more images. First we will compose some simple fades, and then build to a thrilling climax with "Chainlink Symphony." All images used in this section are in the Digital Stock➥Urban Textures folder of your *Photoshop Effects Magic* CD-ROM.

**1** Open the images "Hirise" and "Cans."

**2** In "Cans," Select➥All, then copy and paste the image into "Hirise" where it becomes Layer 1. Hirise is now the background.

By reducing the opacity of Layer 1 to 50% you achieve the simplest kind of blend.

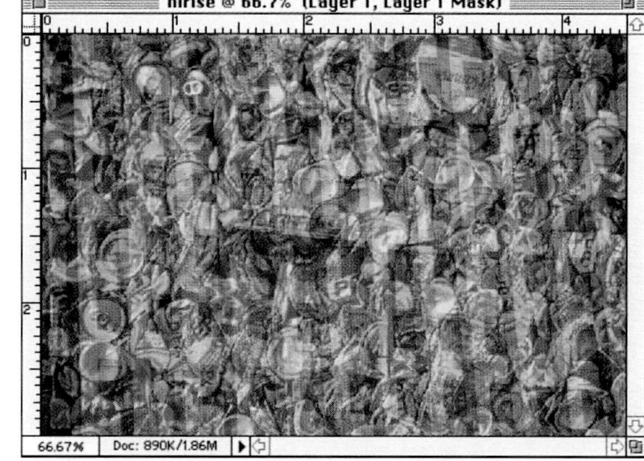


**3** Create a layer mask for Layer 1 ("Cans"). You'll use it to create more complex blends.

**4** Double-click the Gradient icon and use these settings in the Gradient Tool Options palette.

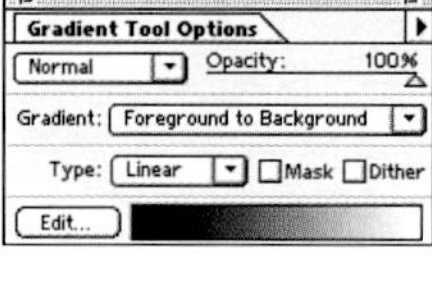


**5** Switch to default colors. Drag the Gradient tool vertically from the top of the image to the bottom. Your Layers palette will show a white-to-black gradient in the Layer Mask.

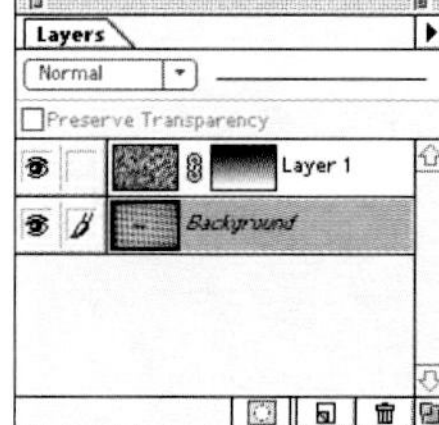

At 100% opacity and in Normal mode the composite image looks like this.

What a compelling image! Recycling cans into building materials...or, modern cities being buried in garbage—it's your choice.

## VARIATIONS

### Horizontal Blend

For this variation, I copied the Railing image into the Door image, and created the layer mask in Layer 1 as done previously.

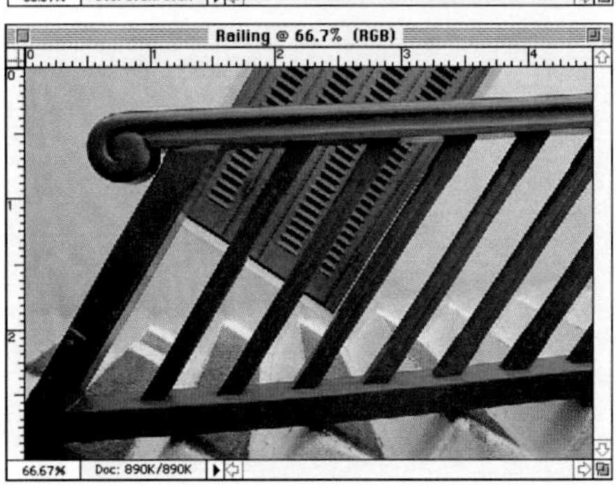

Gradient Tool Options are the same as before. To make the images fade from right to left, drag the Gradient tool horizontally in Step 5. To make the railing fully visible on the left and fading out to the right, the layer mask needs to have black on the right and white on the left.

**Remember "black conceals and white reveals."**

## Radial Blend

For this variation, I copied the Chainlink R (red) image into the Chainlink Y (yellow) image, and created the layer mask in Layer 1 as done previously.

In the Gradient Tool Options palette, I set the type of fill to radial and dragged the gradient from the center to the edge.

Let's create a new layer and add it to the radial blend of red and yellow.

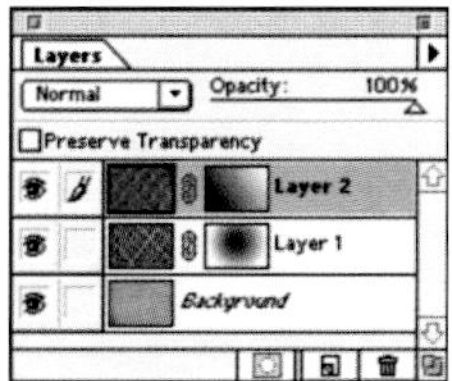


Open "Chainlink B" (blue) and Copy it to the red and yellow composite, where it becomes Layer 2. Create a layer mask and drag a linear gradient diagonally from the lower-left corner to the upper-right corner.

How would the composite look if we changed the blue layer to a radial blend and the red layer to a diagonal linear blend? Layer masks make it easy to try multiple variations before making up your mind.

**1** Drag each of the layer masks to the Trash icon in the Layers palette. Choose "discard" when you are asked whether to apply the masks.

**2** Create another layer mask for the blue layer. Apply the gradient as in Step 5 of the Radial Blend variation.

**3** Repeat Step 8 for the red layer.

I reduced the opacity of the blue layer to 76%, and liked the result. ■

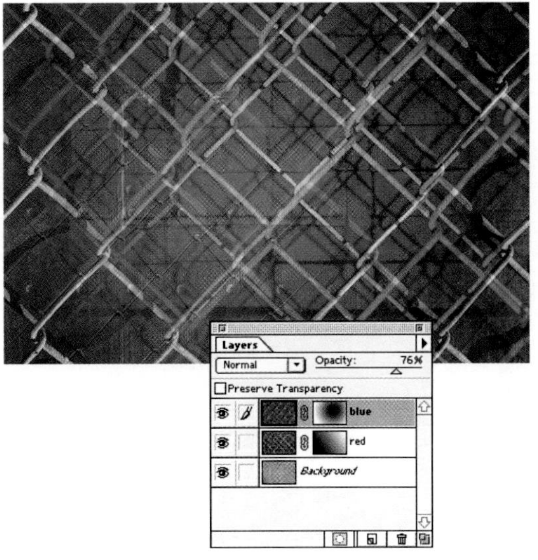

A border or decorative edge can be the finishing touch to your photo or artwork. The Border command in the Select➥Modify pop-up menu is only one of the ways to get the edge. Many variations result from your selection choices, stroke and fill options, feathering, filtering, and colors.

## Flat Borders

The simplest kind of border is a solid stroke or fill.

**1** Open the image you want to work with. I'm using "Houses" from the Urban Textures collection in the Digital Stock folder on the *Photoshop Effects Magic* CD-ROM.

**2** Choose a background color for your border. I picked up the light tan color from the window trim with the Eyedropper tool (CMYK 19, 23, 39, 2). Use Image➥Canvas Size to add space around the artwork. This space fills with the background color.

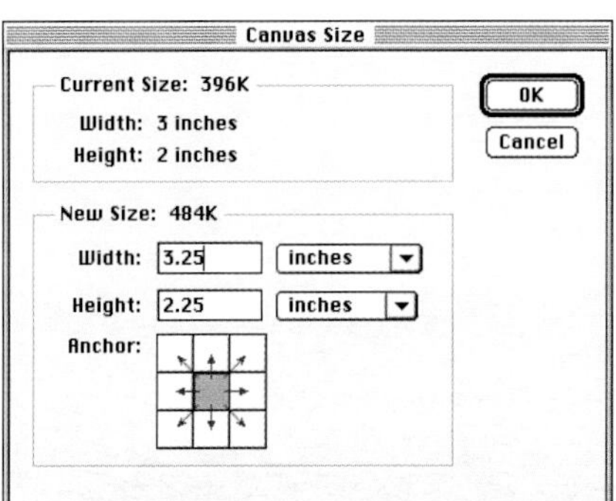

**3** To add a contrasting stroke, choose a foreground color. I picked up orange from the image with the Eyedropper tool. Make a rectangular selection where you want the stroke and use Edit➡Stroke. Choose the width and placement of the line. Mine is 4 pixels and drawn outside the selection.

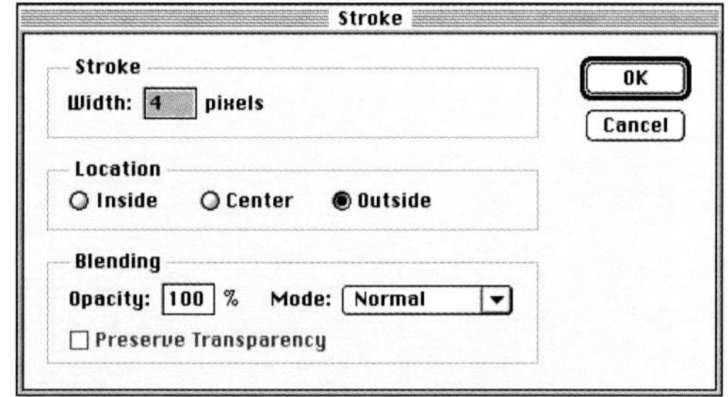

**TIP** **To assure accurate positioning of the stroke, select the image inside the border and use Select➡Modify➡Expand. Enter the number of pixels for enlarging the marquee. Your new selection is perfectly centered. View➡Show Rulers and View➡Show Grids may be helpful too. File➡Preferences gives you options for units of measure and grid spacing.**

## Feathered Borders

Make a selection and use Select➡Modify➡Border. Specify how many pixels wide, and Photoshop automatically feathers both sides of the selection. I began with Select ➡All to eliminate the outer feathering, creating a kind of vignette. For more examples, see "Vignette" (page 108).

The Border command also works on elliptical and free-form selections. Here's "lollipop" from the Digital Stock folder on the CD-ROM.

1 Make a freehand selection with the Lasso tool.

**2** Choose a background color. Use Select➥Inverse to make the area outside the "marching ants" active. Press Delete to fill the selection with background color.

**3** Choose a foreground color. I picked up the golden yellow of the lollipop with the Eyedropper tool. Use Select➥Inverse again.

**4** Use Select➥Modify➥Border and specify width in pixels. I used 24. Fill the selection with the foreground color.

## Fancy Borders

**1** Open the image you want to work with. I'm using "Cameras" from the Image Club folder on the CD-ROM.

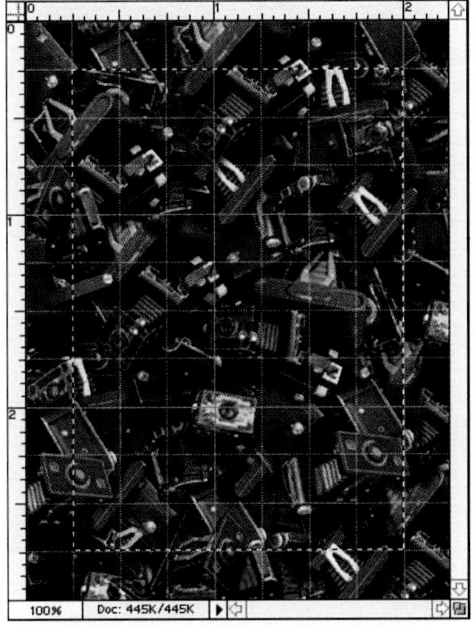


**2** Drag the rectangular Marquee to select the area you want to be inside the border. I'm using a grid to help make my border symmetrical. Feather the selection. I used 24 pixels. The rounded edges of the "marching ants" marquee indicates feathering.

**3** Use Select➡Inverse to make the area outside the "marching ants" active.

**4** Apply a filter effect to the selection.

I used Filter➥Stylize➥Find Edges for this result.

Filter➥Pixellate➥Crystallize applied in Step 4 gives us this rather subtle effect.

As another variation, skip Step 3 and eliminate feathering. Apply a filter to the inside area.

After a Gaussian Blur (15) the original image is recognizable only as the border.

That blurry rectangle seems like a great place for type. ■

As a caricaturist I never met a face I didn't want to distort. Here's a fun drag-and-drop way to make faces.

**1** First we need a blank face. I started with the "Cross-eyed" guy from the Digital Stock folder on *Photoshop Effects Magic* CD-ROM. Use the Eyedropper tool to pick up face color and use a fat Airbrush to cover his features.

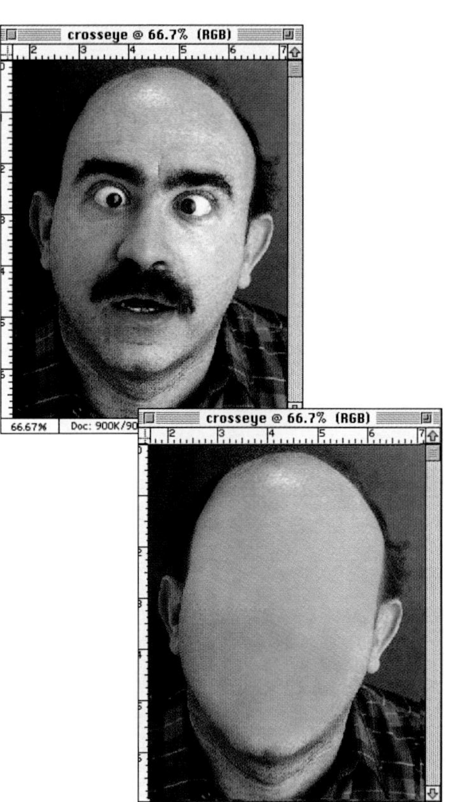


For the remaining steps you may use the ready-to-drag face parts in the ArtStart folder on the CD-ROM. Any other source images are fine.

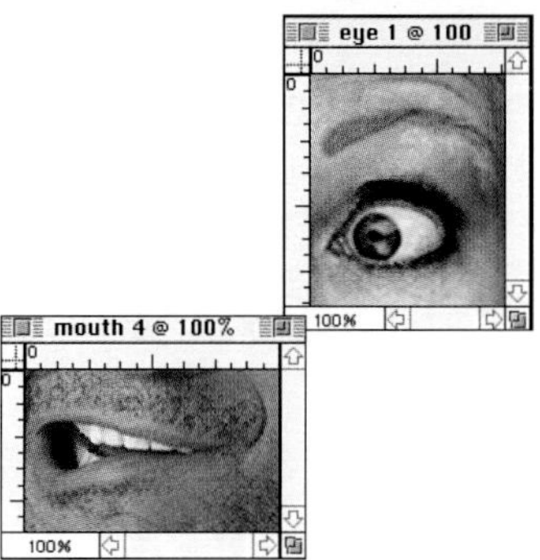

**2** Drag and drop some features onto this blank expression.

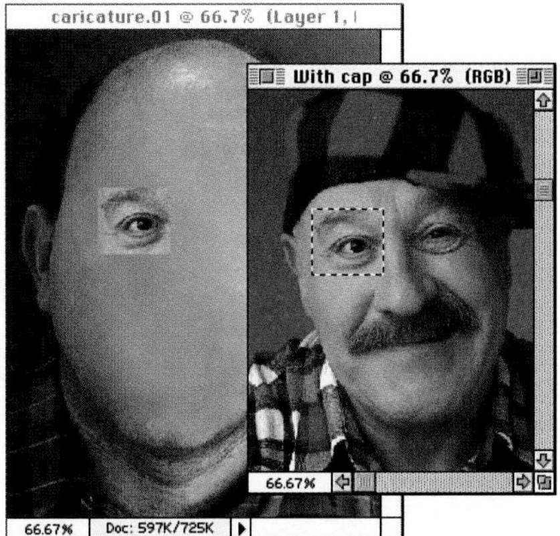


Each feature will have its own layer. Double-click a layer name and type in a descriptive label to avoid confusion.

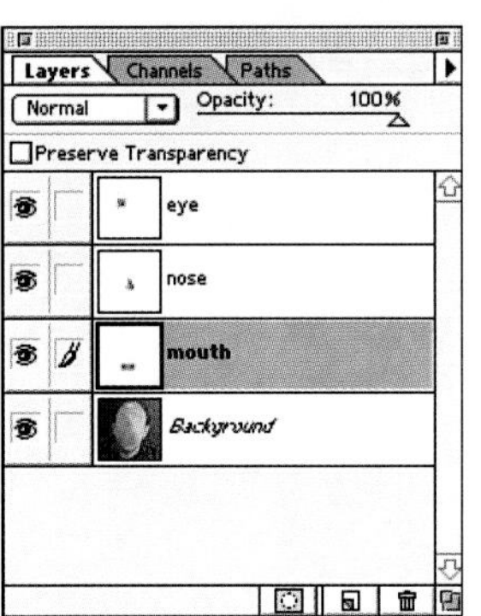


**3** Use Layer➡Transform commands to alter size and position of the face parts. Try several combinations. I covered one mouth with another, enlarged the nose and flipped it horizontally, added another eye, and made the first eye invisible.

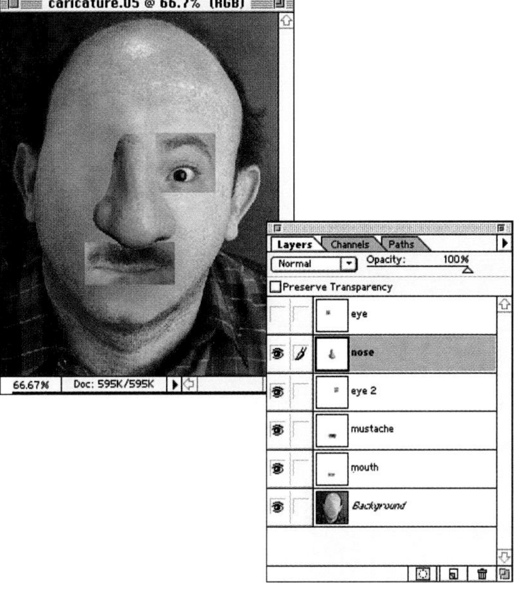

4 Create a layer mask for each of the face parts that you want to blend into the background. Use the Airbrush tool and choose a foreground color of black, then spray gently around the edges of the added pieces. Because you're working on the layer mask, this will fade out the obvious edges, and if you make a mistake, switch the foreground color to white and repaint.

The Layers palette at this stage shows that the outer edges of both eyes and the nose have been masked out. The mustache layer mask is currently active, as you can see from the highlight color on the layer, the mask icon showing, and the black border around the layer mask.

It's not realistic enough to fool anybody, and that's okay. To create more seamless face composites, read on.

## VARIATIONS

Suppose you want to combine expressions or facial features from two or more photographs realistically. You can do a seamless graft. All you need is the right donor.

**1** Open the images you want to work with. I'm using "Surprised" and "Delighted," in the Digital Stock folder on the CD-ROM.

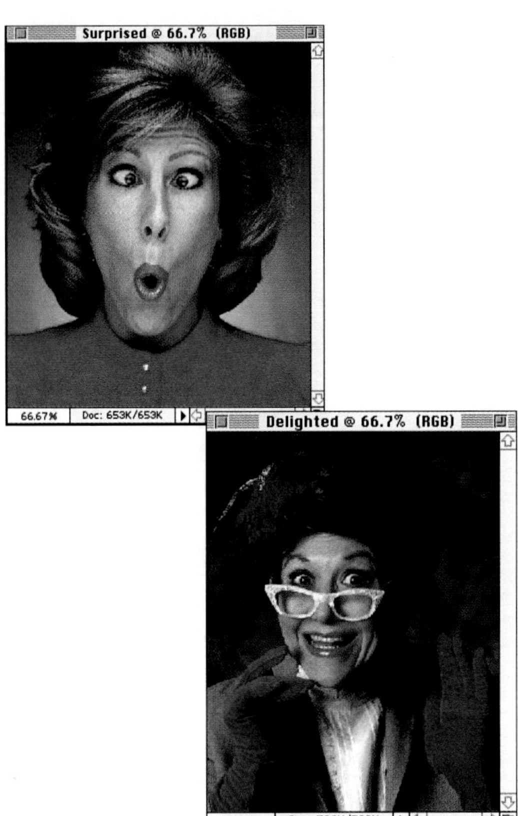


**2** Double-click the Lasso tool to open the Lasso Options palette and set the feathering to 12. Draw a selection around the "Surprised" mouth with the Lasso tool, including a generous amount of extra skin.

**3** Drag and drop the donor mouth onto the recipient image. A new layer (Layer 1) for the mouth is created automatically.

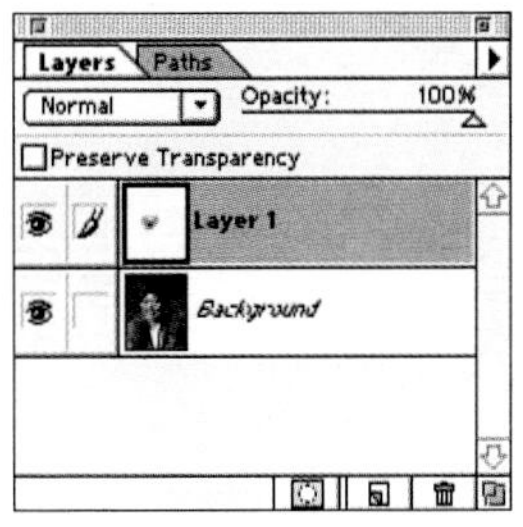

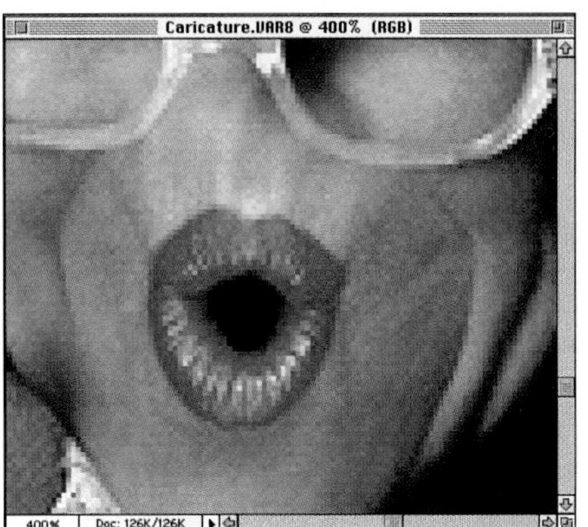


**4** Make sure Layer 1 is active and select Layer➡Transform➡Scale. Drag a corner handle of the bounding box to adjust the size of the new mouth. Press (Return)[Enter] to accept the change.

**5** Create a layer mask for the mouth layer. Now you can eliminate unwanted facial pixels safely.

**6** Choose a foreground color of black. With the Airbrush at low pressure (I used 16%) gently stroke away enough to reveal the nose in the background image. If you remove too much, switch to white and paint the pixels back in.

**7** I now saw that the new mouth wasn't lined up correctly with the recipient nose. I used Layer➡Transform➡Rotate and turned the mouth layer a few degrees counterclockwise. Press (Return)[Enter] to accept changes.

**8** Flatten the image and you're done.

## Tweaking and Tuning

You may want to do one or more of the following after the layers are merged.

I used a circular selection and applied the pinch filter (30%) to make the mouth a bit smaller. The grid in the Pinch preview box shows that the shrinking effect is applied gradually and is strongest in the center of the selection.

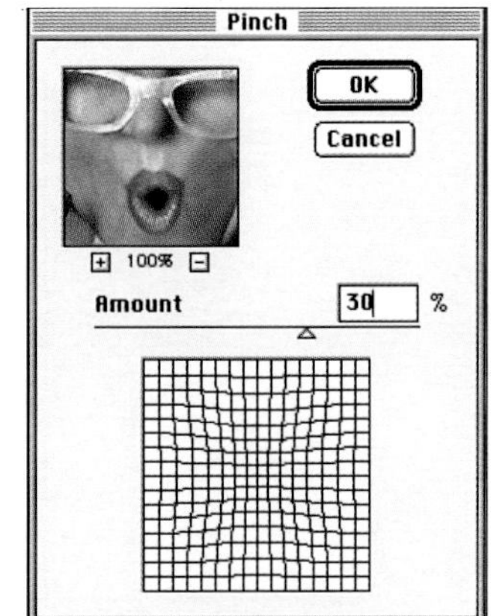


I tried to smooth away any remaining signs of the surgery. I used the Blur tool at 100% pressure to soften and blend some tell-tale edges but then, some of the skin around the mouth looked too smooth! I threw a feathered Lasso around these areas and used Filter➡Noise➡Add Noise (7, Uniform) to re-establish skin texture quickly.

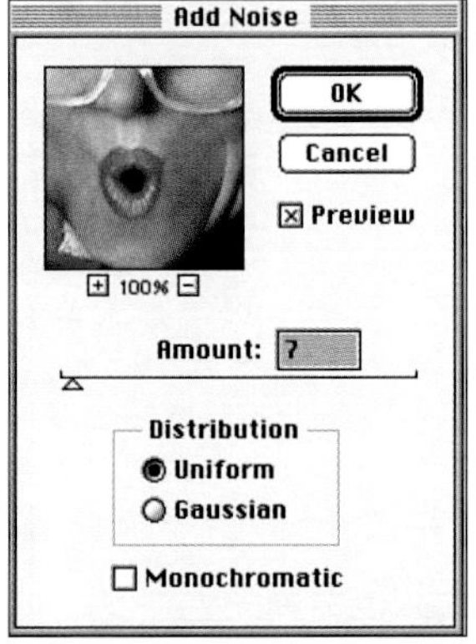


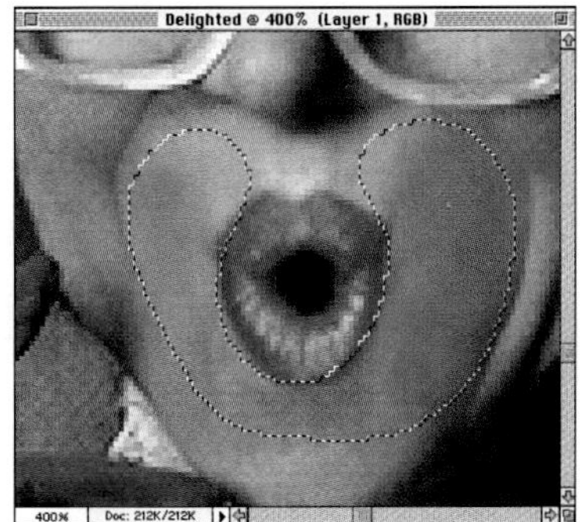

Another way to create quick caricature in Photoshop is with a few simple distortions. Here's an image called "Redhead" in the Digital Stock folder of your CD-ROM.

1 Select➡All and use Layer➡Transform➡Perspective to make the head bigger in proportion to the body, like this. When you pull one of the corner handles out (or in) the adjacent handle moves automatically to create perspective. It may take a moment for you to get a feel for manipulating the handles to get the effect you want.

**2** Now you'll prepare to apply a distortion filter to her head. Use the elliptical Marquee and select the woman's face and hair. Select➡Feather (12 pixels).

**3** Apply Filter➡Distort➡Spherize (100%, Normal).

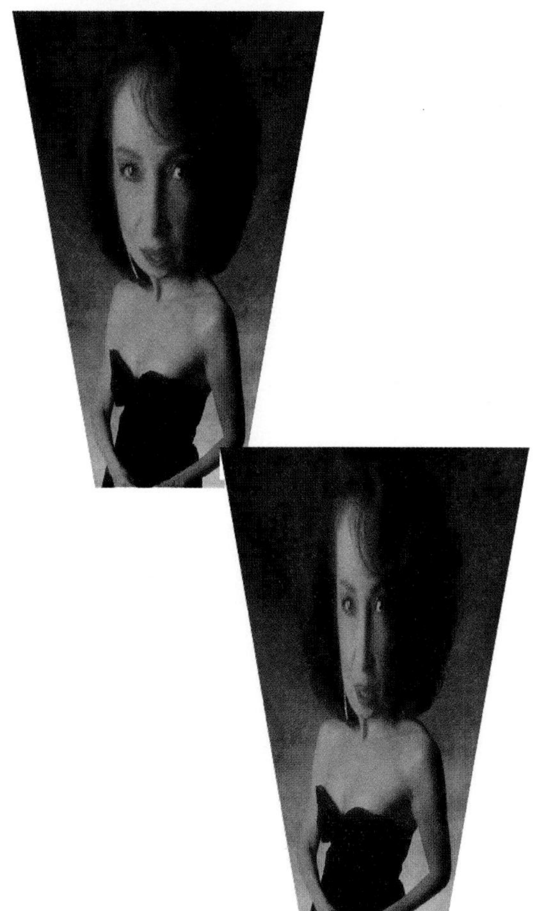

In Step 3, use Vertical only Mode instead of Normal, and you get something like this. Just imagine what you can do with photos of your family! ■

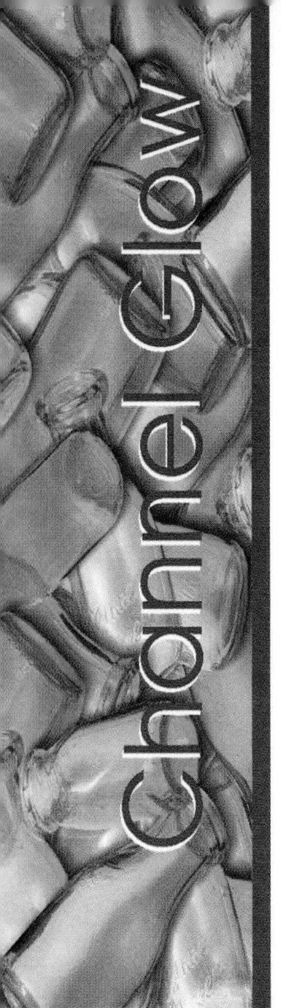


This technique shows how to create color by changing the relative positions of some of the pixels in each of the RGB channels.

If you have grayscale source images, but you're creating a color document, here's a great way to add vibrant color accents. You can shift an entire channel a few pixels for a neon glow, but be careful! Tell your prepress professional what you have in mind so she doesn't try to "fix" the registration for you.

**1** Open the image you want to manipulate. I used "Earring" in the ArtStart folder on the *Photoshop Effects Magic* CD-ROM. Convert to RGB mode and save the image. I am going to select the earring and manipulate it differently in each channel.

Steps 2 through 7 show how to make an exact selection of the earring. Keep the Paths palette open for this sequence.

**2** Choose the Pen tool and click the outside left edge of the earring. Then drag down and left.

Layers | Channels | Paths
RGB ⌘~
Red ⌘1
Green ⌘2
Blue ⌘3

**3** Make your second click on the opposite side of the earring. This time, drag up and to the right.

**4** Close the shape by clicking the first point. You have just created a path using Bézier curves. Don't worry if your curve doesn't match the contour of the earring exactly.

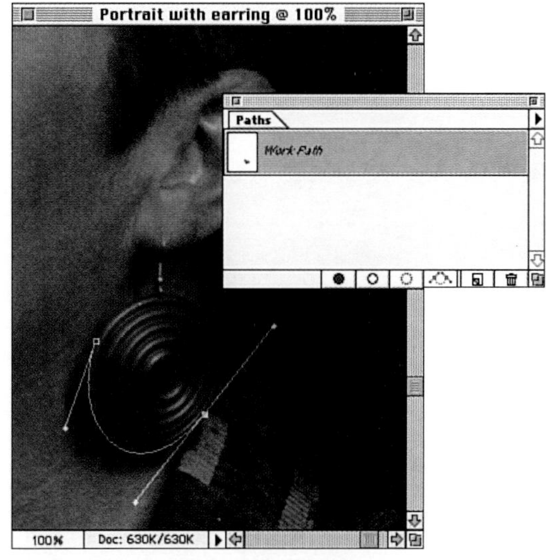


**5** Choose the Direct Selection tool, in the Pen tool group. Use it to match the shape of the earring by moving anchor points or changing the length and angle of direction lines. This might take a few tries.

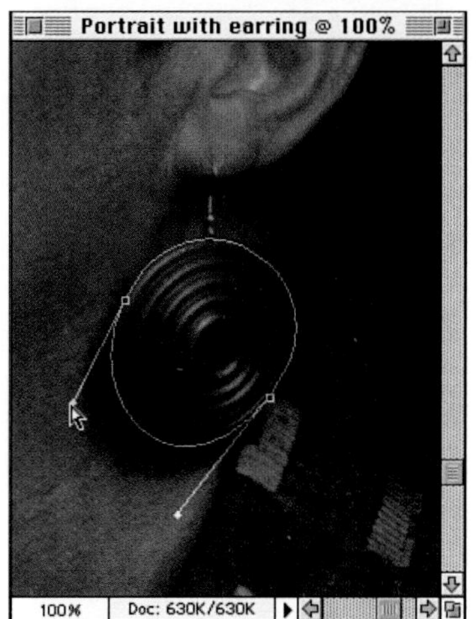


**6** Use the Save Path command in the Paths palette's arrow menu and then choose Make Selection. Name the path "earring," and turn off the path.

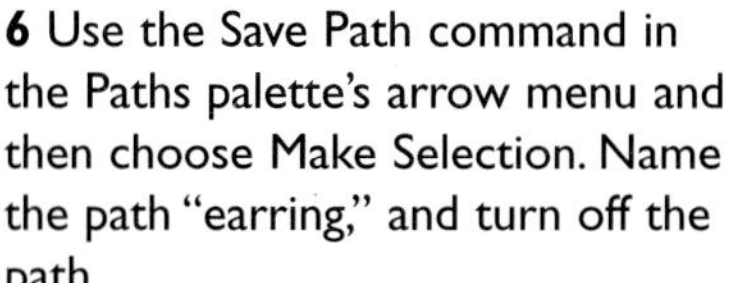

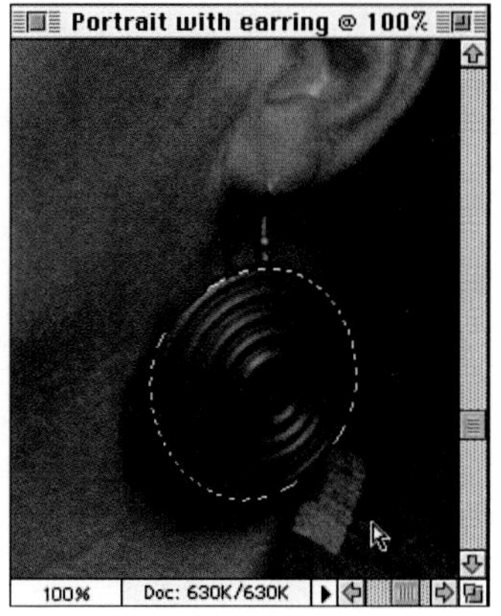

TIP **If you've got a steady hand, you might prefer to select the earring with the Lasso tool and make adjustments as follows. To add to the selection, hold the Shift key down while dragging the Lasso around the pixels you missed. To subtract from the selection, hold down the (Command)[Control] key while you lasso the unwanted areas.**

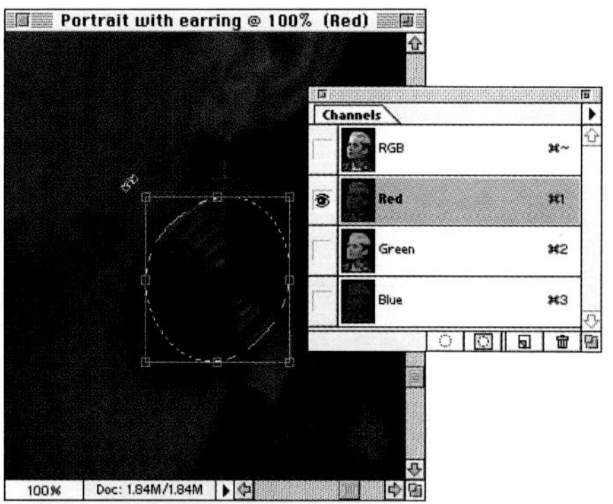


**7** Switch to default colors. Make the Red channel active and choose Layer➡Transform➡Rotate. The selection will have a bounding box. Drag one of the corner handles a few degrees clockwise. This rotates the selection in the Red channel only.

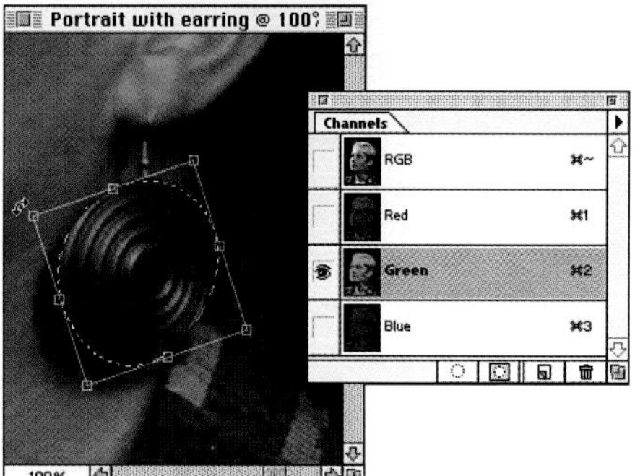


**8** Repeat Step 7 for the Green channel, but use a counterclockwise rotation. You don't need to change any pixels in the Blue channel.

Return to the composite channel to see your results. I created a neon color glow to the earring by offsetting pixels in each channel. The effect will be dramatic or subtle depending on the amount of offset or the techniques used to make changes.

**9** I cleaned things up by eliminating the neon "spill" on the edges with the Eraser tool set at Erase to Saved.

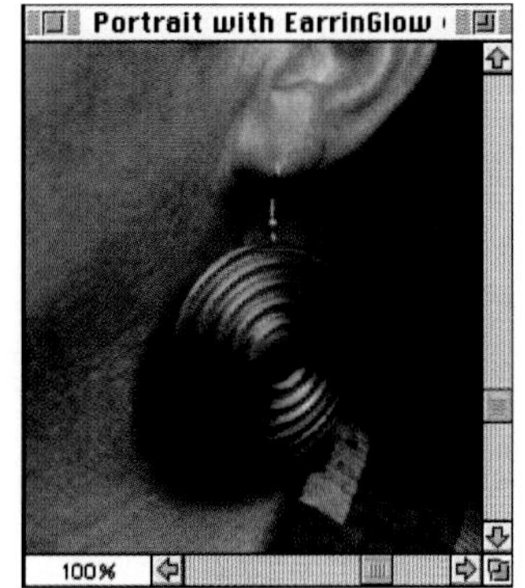


## VARIATIONS

You can start with a color image instead of grayscale. Using a color image gives you a wider range of color combinations when you offset pixels. Try this with "Gold Beetle" in the Image Club folder on the book's CD-ROM.

**1** Using the Elliptical Marquee tool, select an oval area on the beetle's body. Feather the selection (12 pixels).

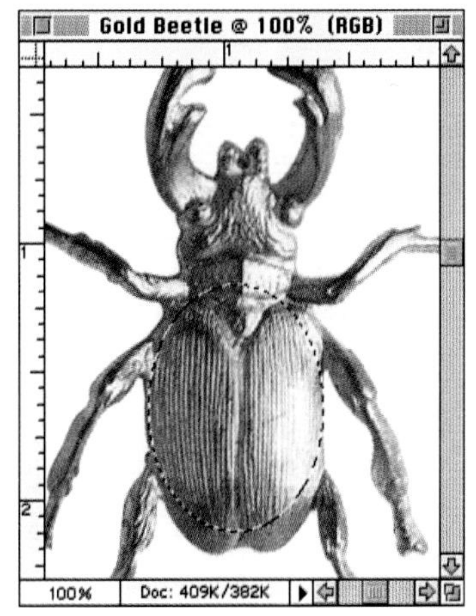


**2** Make the Red channel active. Use Layer➥Transform➥Numeric Transform and type in 90% for both vertical and horizontal scaling.

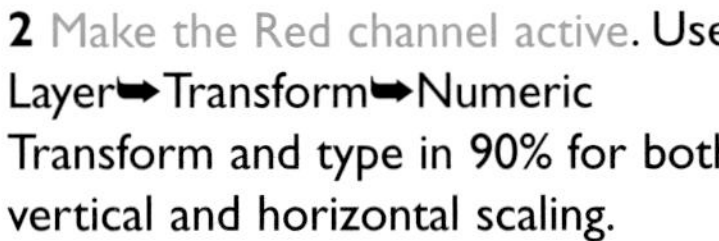

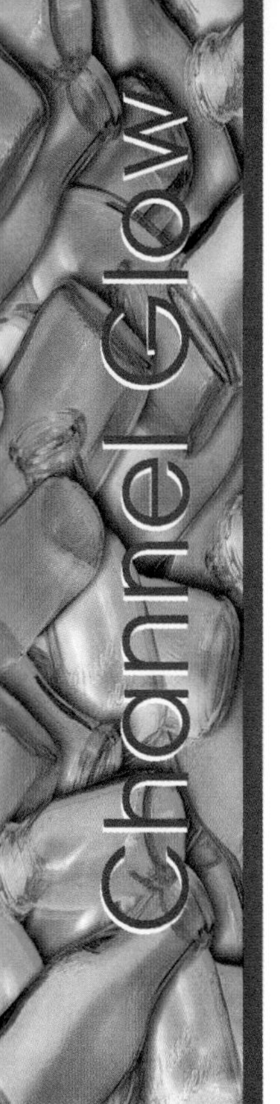


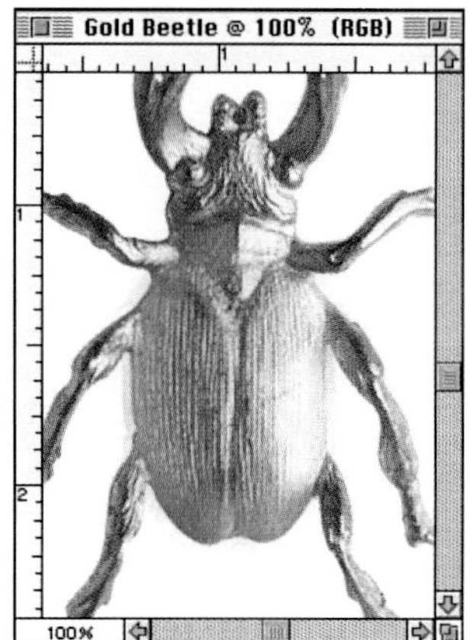


**3** Make the Green channel active. Repeat the Numeric Transform using 110%.

The composite image has an iridescent quality. You can eliminate the pinkish halo with the Erase to Saved function of the Eraser tool.

If that effect is too subtle, you can offset an entire channel rather than just a small element.

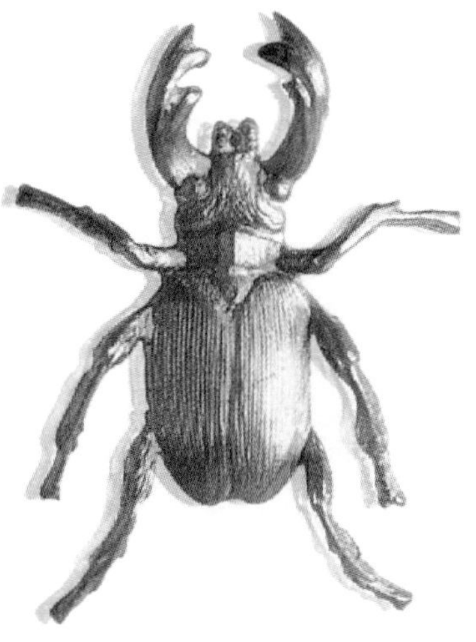

**1** Select➡All. Make the Red channel active.

**2** Hold down the (Command) [Control] key while clicking keyboard arrows. I moved the Red channel about 10 pixels to the left. Return to the composite channel to see your results.

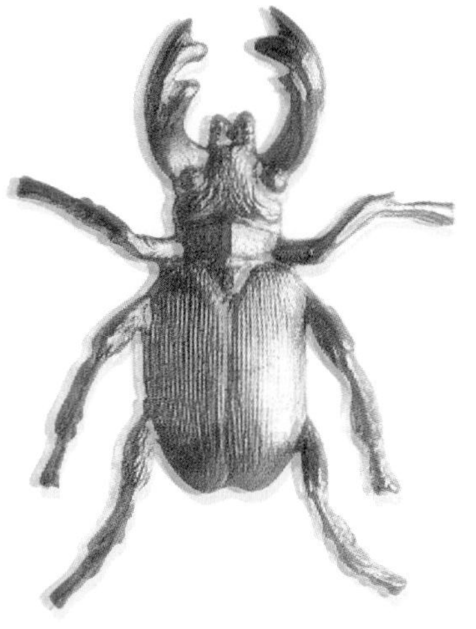

**3** Repeat Step 2 for one of the other channels. I moved the Blue channel about 10 pixels down to produce this glowing beetle.

Another way to offset pixels is to apply different filter effects to each channel.

I opened the grayscale image called "Mask" from the Image Club folder on the CD-ROM. This time I converted to CMYK mode so I'd have an extra channel to play with.

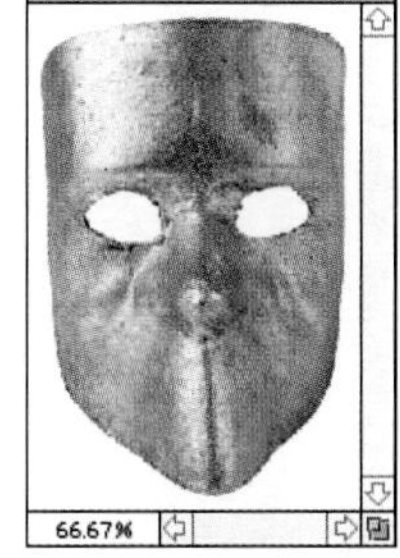


Here are the filter effects I applied to each channel:

Cyan: Artistic➡Fresco

Magenta: Artistic➡Poster Edges.

Yellow: Brush Strokes➡Dark Strokes

Black: no change ■

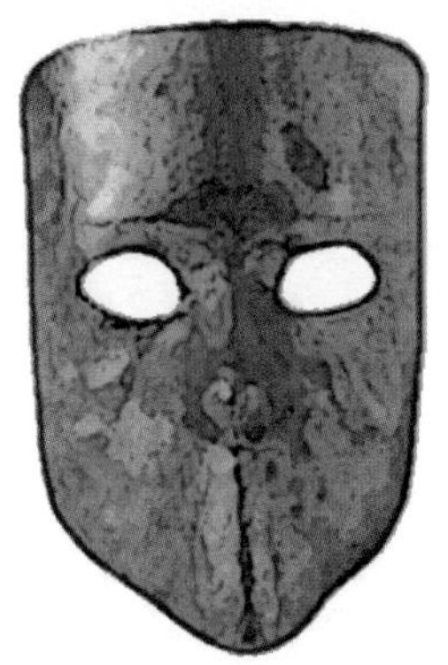

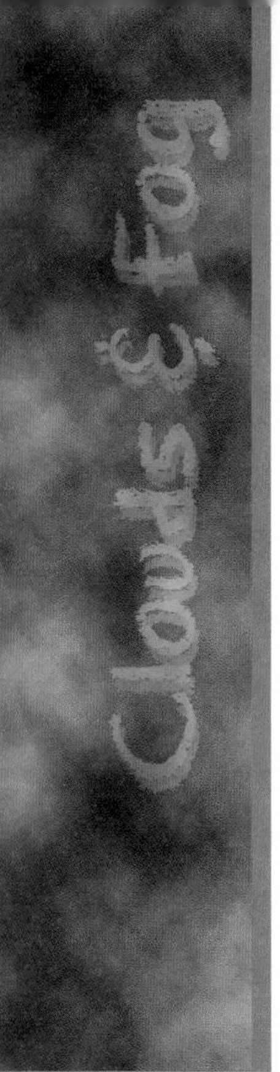


The Render➡Clouds filter can produce all kinds of weather, depending on your choice of colors and apply modes. Thanks to Patrick Lichty's excellent atmosphere effects for encouraging us to reach for the sky.

**1** Open the image to which you would like to add clouds. I used "Brownstone," which is in the Digital Stock➡Urban Textures folder of your *Photoshop Effects Magic* CD-ROM.

**2** Select the background building. I used the Lasso tool while holding down the (Option)[Alt] key. This enabled me to make straight line segments with clicks as I traced the left edge of the Brownstone building. Click the lower-left and the upper-right corner, then click your starting point to complete the selection. Press the Delete key to delete the background; keep the selection active.

**TIP** **If you save the selection now, you can avoid having to repeat Step 2 if you lose the selection. Load the selection if you accidentally deselect the area in which you are creating the clouds.**

**3** Switch to default colors. Select Filter➥Render➥Clouds to fill the background with gray cloud formations. Due to the random nature of the Clouds filter, repeat it until you like the results.

**Use (Command-F) [Control-F] to reapply the Filter.**

To see your image without the "marching ants" use View➥Hide Edges (Command-H)[Control-H].

**4** I noticed a rim of pixels around the building that should have been deleted. That's easy to fix. I used Select➥Modify➥Expand (2 pixels). My next fill fit snugly against the building.

## VARIATIONS

You need to choose the foreground and background colors to make clouds before you apply the filter. Use blue instead of black for a sunny sky. I chose CMYK values of 47, 21, 0, 0 for this Cloud fill. With the selection still active, I used Image➥Adjust Brightness/Contrast and set Brightness to +14.

To create a smokey look, do the following after Step 3. First, be sure the sky is selected. Choose a foreground color of blue and choose a background color of white, and then apply another cloud fill over the black-and-white one. Access the fade control near the top of the Filter menu. Don't fade the effect, just choose Overlay mode, and you get something like this.

This threatening alien sky was made by choosing the foreground color red (0, 86, 73, 0) and choosing the background color purple (85, 94, 0, 0). The building would look pinker in this setting, wouldn't it? I selected the building, using the Select➥Inverse command. Then I used Edit➥Fill (20–30%) in Color mode to retain the contrast and detail.

To simulate fog, decrease the contrast and detail. After Step 3, deselect the sky and apply Clouds to the entire image. Now select Filter➡Fade. I faded the effect to 85%, and we might as well be in London…or San Francisco. ■

Collage is one of the most popular and effective uses for Photoshop. Image elements are put on separate layers, so they can be viewed in various combinations. Each item's size, position and opacity can be manipulated independently.

**1** Open the image you want to use as a background. I used "Postcards" from Image Club, which you can find in the Image Club folder on the *Photoshop Effects Magic* CD-ROM.

**2** Open the "Boots" image from the same folder.

Magic Wand Options

Tolerance: 5 ☒ Anti-aliased

☐ Sample Merged

**3** Select the white area around the boots by clicking anywhere in it with the Magic Wand tool. If there are some unselected white pixels around the boots, increase the Tolerance in the Magic Wand Options palette. I used 5.

**4** Select➥Inverse selects the boot and not the background. That's what we had in mind all along.

**5** Drag and drop the boots to the "postcards" image. Boots automatically creates a new layer. Double-click "Layer 1" and rename it "Boots."

Repeat Steps 2 through 5 for the Baby Shoes and Brooch layers. It doesn't matter what position they are in temporarily, as long as they each occupy their own layer. As you did for the Boots layer, rename them descriptively to avoid confusion.

**6** Hide the Brooch layer and make the Baby Shoes layer active. Use the Move tool to drag the baby shoes down to the foreground of the image.

7 Choose Layer➡Transform➡Flip Horizontal to make the baby shoes face the same direction as the boots. Select Layer➡Transform➡ Scale to reduce the size of the baby shoes to about half, or until they look proportional to the adult boots.

8 Make the Boots layer active. Move the image to the left and slightly down

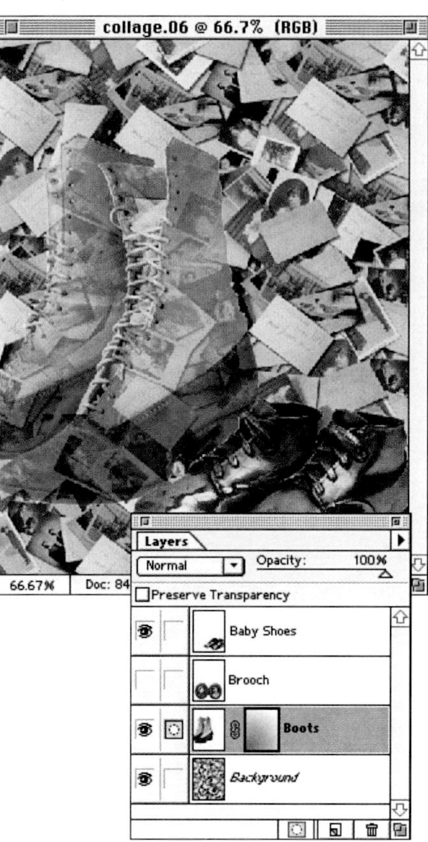


9 Create a layer mask for the boots. Use the Gradient tool to blend the boots into the background.

I experimented with several blending modes for the bronze Baby Shoes layer, finally deciding on Hard Light at 100% opacity.

I also wanted to fade them a bit on the left. Here's how:

10 Create a layer mask for the baby shoes.

**11** Use the Airbrush tool at low pressure (I used 14%) to gently "black-out" some of the shoe. I've hidden all the other layers so you can see only the baby shoes.

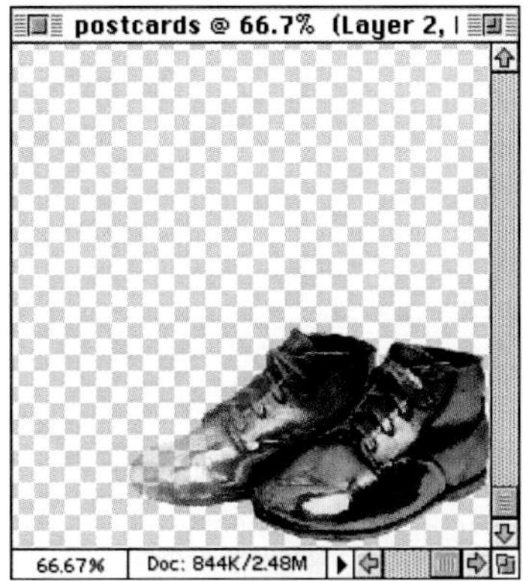


Remember the brooch? We haven't seen it since Step 6. Make the Brooch layer active and hide the Background layer and the Baby Shoes layer. This makes it easier to concentrate on the relationship between the brooch and the boots.

**12** Choose Layer➡Free Transform to resize and rotate the image as shown.

**13** Select Layer➥Transform➥ Distort to apply some perspective to the brooch.

**TIP** **The Distort command enables you to move each corner handle independently, giving you more control than the Perspective command.**

Make all the layers visible to see how the elements fit together. I'd still like to fade the brooch into the boot but everything else looks good.

**14** Double-click the Eraser tool and use Airbrush mode at 50% pressure. Gently brush out enough of the brooch so it blends into the boot. I thought I was close enough to completion that I didn't have to worry about changing my mind, so I didn't use a Layer Mask to produce this little fade.

**15** Drag each Layer Mask to the Trash icon on the Layers palette. You'll be asked if you want to Apply it or delete it. Choose Apply.

**TIP** **It's a good idea to save a version in Photoshop format with all the layers and masks intact, just in case you or your client wants a last-minute change.**

## VARIATIONS

There are many variations possible simply by changing the blending mode of the layers before you flatten them.

We start by altering the background.

**1** Make the Background layer active. (Command-I)[Control-I] inverts the color of the image. I faded the inversion to 75%.

**2** This new background suggested changes for the other collage items. I used Normal mode at 60% opacity for the Baby Shoes layer, Hard Light mode at 80% for the Brooch layer, and Multiply mode at 100% for the Boots layer.

Here's a version with the Baby Shoes layer in Luminosity mode and the Brooch layer in Color Burn mode. The boots have their colors inverted and use Difference mode. All layers are at 100% opacity.

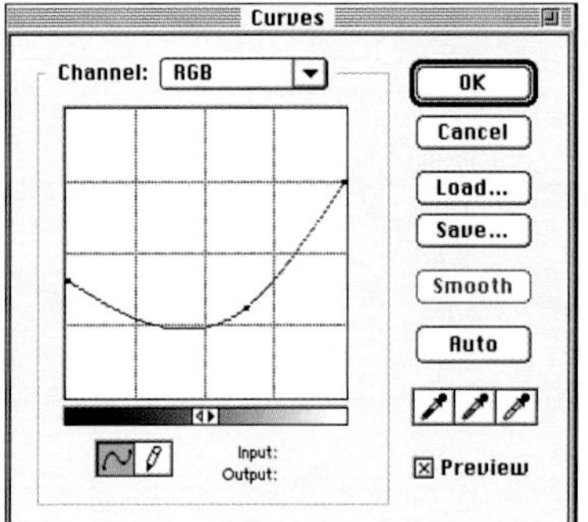


For the next variation, Gaussian Blur (radius: 15 pixels) is applied to the background, and the Fade command is used to change the mode to Lighten. The brooch has a color inversion and Exclusion mode. I altered the Boots layer with Image➥Adjust➥Curves and switched to Multiply mode.

The baby shoes have Filter➥Artistic➥Plastic Wrap applied. Fade the effect to 60% and change the mode to Exclusion. ■

The displacement maps might be hard to find at first, but once you have found them never let them go. These enchanted effects look like they took an entire evening to create, but all you need is a filter, a little fade, and your choice of blending mode.

It's easy to create a displacement map. It's a bit tougher to predict how they will behave. Any image in Photoshop format can function as a displacement map. An RGB image uses only the red and green channels to determine displacement. Essentially, the map influences how pixels in the target image will be distorted, based on color values. You can create a displacement map to produce a specific effect, once you get the hang of it, or just experiment.

**1** Open the image you want to work with. I'm using "Smoker," in the Digital Stock folder on the *Photoshop Effects Magic* CD-ROM.

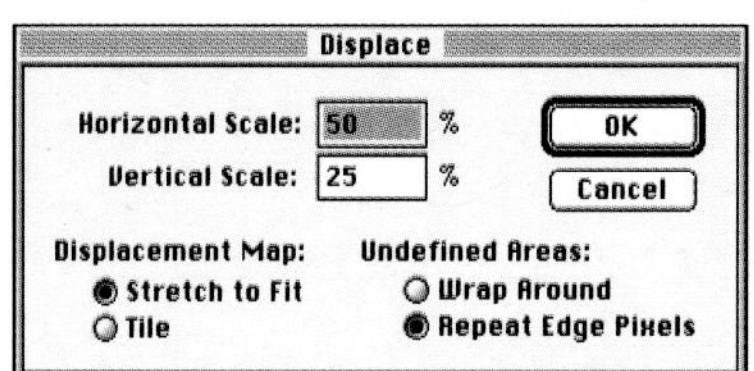


**2** Select Filter➡Distort➡ Displacement. I used 50% horizontal and 25% vertical, for no particular reason, accepting the other default settings.

**3** Click OK and you'll be prompted to choose a displacement map. Navigate through your Photoshop folders to find them in the Plug-ins folder [dispmaps folder for Windows]. I chose Twirl.

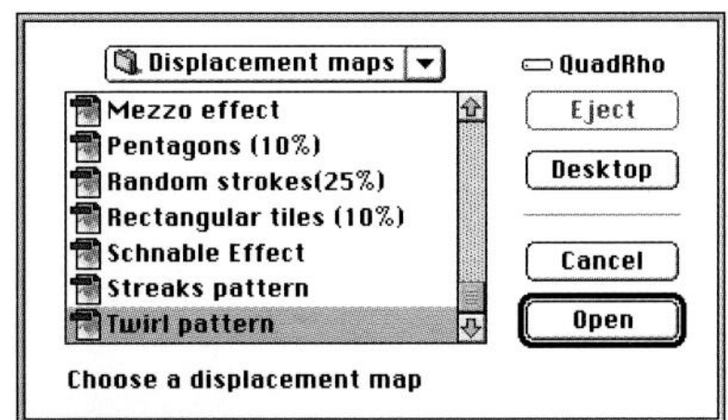


Here's the twirl displacement map.

And this is the effect it has on our smoker.

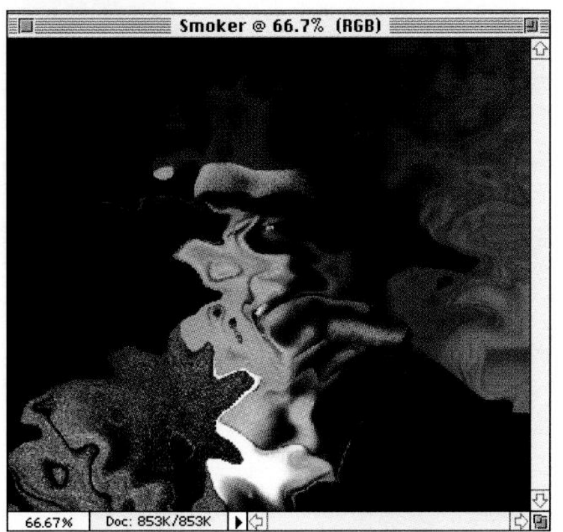


**4** Select Filter➡Fade (50%). In Normal mode, the 50% fade gives us equal parts of the original and the distorted image.

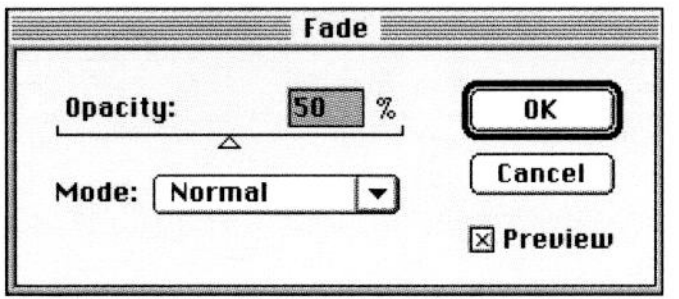

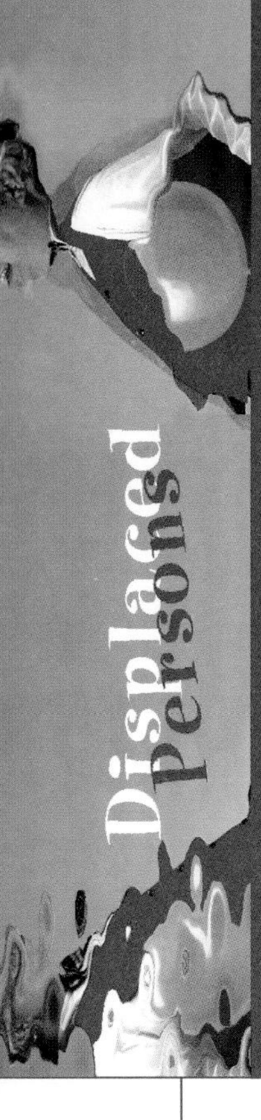


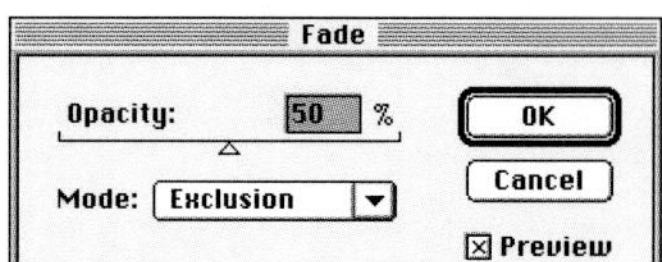


Switching to Exclusion mode makes for some excellent cigar smoke.

**5** If you're going for realism, get rid of those lumpy shapes on the left of his hat with the Eraser tool in "Erase to Saved" mode.

**To repeat the last filter, use (Command-F)[Control-F] To change the settings for the last filter, use (Option-Command-F)[Alt-Control-F] and to fade last filter, use (Shift-Command-F)[Shift-Control-F].**

## VARIATIONS

If realism leaves you cold, displacement maps are your friends. Here's "Smiling Woman" and what I did to her with the Crumbles displacement map (50% vertical and 50% horizontal).

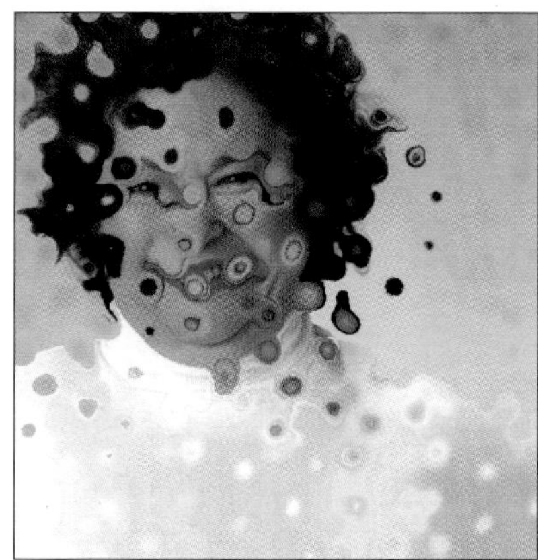

I faded the displacement to 70% and switched to Difference mode, getting this result.

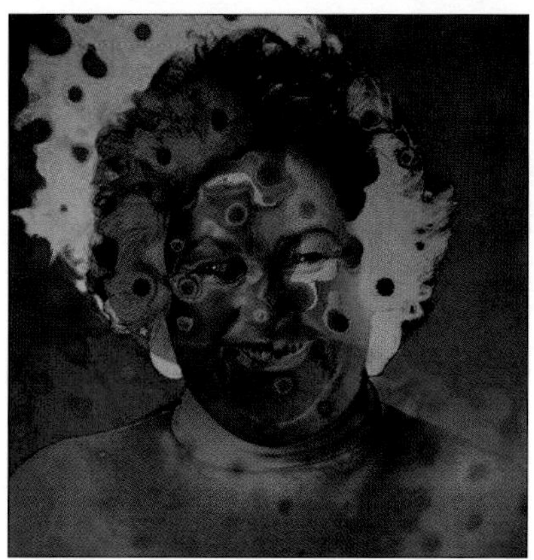

The colors are great. The shapes and movement are an exciting surprise, but I wanted to soften some of the blotches on her skin and hair. I used the Rubber Stamp tool with the Impressionist option and one of the bristle brushes. See "Cloning" (page 96) and "Bristle Brush" (page 172) for details on this.

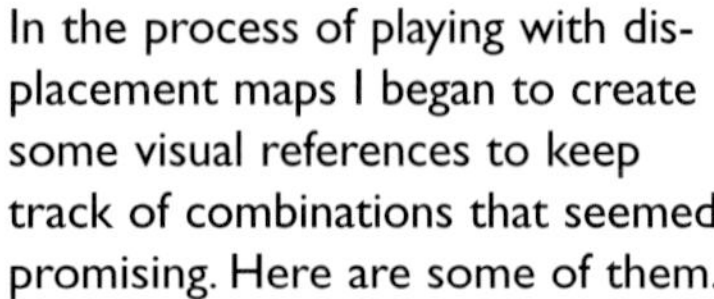

In the process of playing with displacement maps I began to create some visual references to keep track of combinations that seemed promising. Here are some of them.

©Copyright 1997 PhotoDisc,Inc.

Starting with a miniature version of PhotoDisc's Apple, this is Random Strokes (15% ).

This is the Streaks Pattern (15% for both horizontal and vertical).

Here's the result of using the map called "Twirl pattern" at 40% in Darken mode.

This candy comes from PhotoDisc, too.

©Copyright 1997 PhotoDisc,Inc.

Here's the candy using the Crumbly displacement map (15%) in Multiply mode.

I used the Mezzotint map at 15% in Lighten mode for this variation.

Finally, here's an eye chart you're not likely to find in a doctor's office. 10% displacement was applied to each of these. From left to right: Pentagons, Rectangular Tiles, Honeycomb.

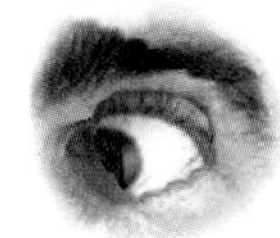

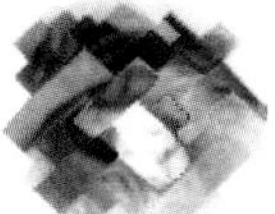

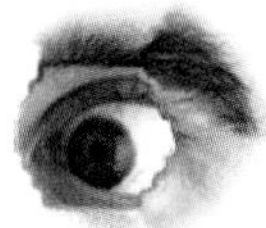

There are a few custom displacement maps included in the Presets folder on your CD-ROM. ■

Here are some great techniques for adding a wet or glistening quality to a photographic image. They all involve using the Chrome filter and a choice of blending mode.

© Copyright 1997 PhotoDisc, Inc.

**1** Open the image you'd like to "juice up." I'm using "Orange" in the PhotoDisc folder on the *Photoshop Effects Magic* CD-ROM.

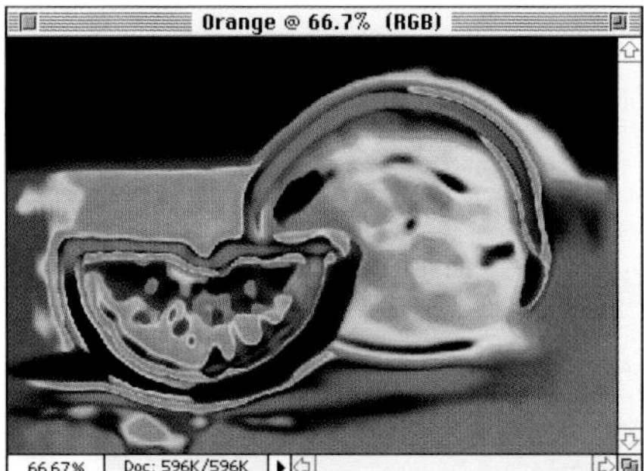


**2** Apply Filter➡Sketch➡ Chrome. The Chrome filter creates a grayscale image that may make the original nearly unrecognizable. It may make an image look chrome-plated. But if you bring back some color, it's as if a thick layer of shiny goo has been poured over the image. The next step will bring back color.

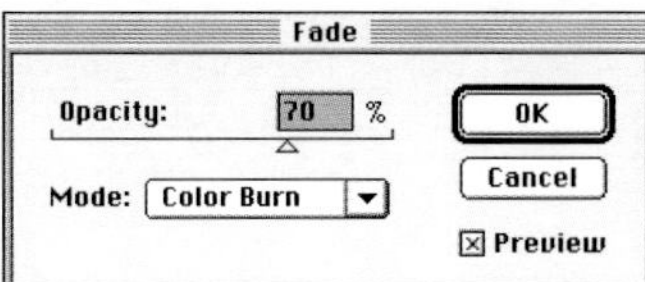


**3** Use Filter➡Fade to change the blending mode to Color Burn. I also faded the effect to 70%.

The Orange slice looks luscious and juicy, but I want to eliminate some of the reddish blotches on the orange rind.

**4** Double-click the Eraser tool and check Erase to Saved. I used the Airbrush type and lowered opacity to have better control. I gently stroked in the original skin of the orange and some of the foreground. I cropped the photo to focus even more on that mouth-watering slice.

## VARIATIONS

This candy, also from PhotoDisc, looks yummy without any special effects. But it's tempting to try.

© Copyright 1997 PhotoDisc, Inc.

After applying the Chrome filter I used Filter➡Fade to change the blending mode to Soft Light (100%). This will melt in your mouth and in your hand.

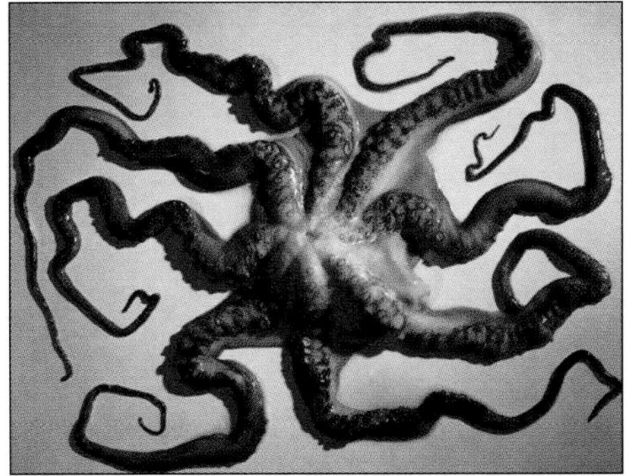

© Copyright 1997 PhotoDisc, Inc.

Not only can you use this technique to make things look more delicious, but you can make them look more disgusting! Here's "Octopus" from PhotoDisc.

This is the slimy green thing I got after applying the Chrome filter and switching to Difference mode in the Filter➡Fade dialog box. Blecchhh. ■

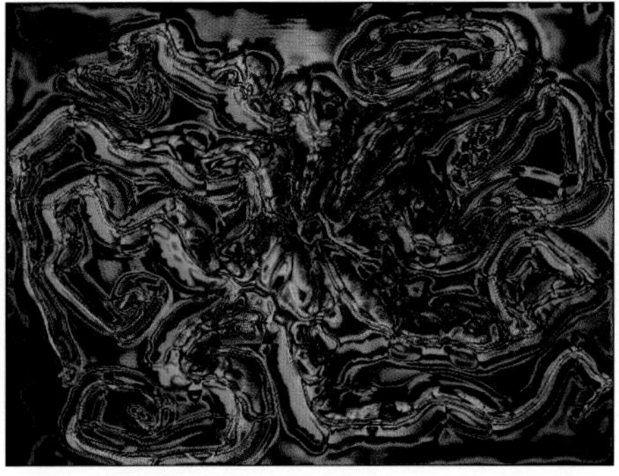

You can change shades of gray to shades of the foreground color by painting in Color mode.This technique shows how to create the look of handpainted crockery.Color mode is also used to imitate hand-tinted photographs on page 74.

**1** Open the image "Fruit Tea Pot grays." You can find it in the Image Club folder on the *Photoshop Effects Magic* CD-ROM.

**2** Convert the image to RGB mode. The image looks the same, but now it is a 3-channel image, and it is ready to accept color.

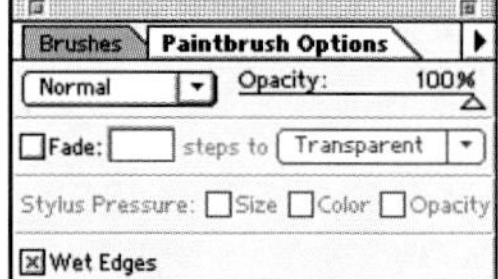


**3** Double-click the Paintbrush tool to open the Paintbrush Options palette and change from Normal mode to Color. I used 100% opacity. To imitate the strokes made by conventional brushes, turn Wet Edges on. This will produce a slight pooling of pigment on the edges of each stroke.

**4** Select a brush size big enough to fill an area with the minimum number of strokes and small enough to give you control. Use CMYK values 67, 59, 15, 17 for purple.

**5** Paint the grapes on both sides of the teapot. Your image should look something like this

Repeat Steps 4 and 5 for the apple. I used CMYK values of 25, 77, 69, 11.

**6** The apple looked too saturated (the color is too strong) in spots, so I used the Sponge tool in desaturate mode (23%) to absorb excess color.

This took out too much color, so I switched to saturate mode (11%) to paint some back in.

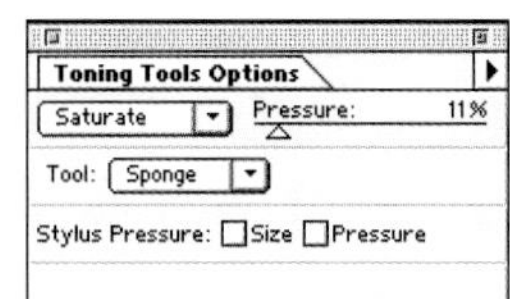


I colored the pear with CMYK values 19, 31, 87, 6. Again I chose to desaturate some of the lighter areas with the Sponge tool.

**7** The strawberries were a bit more involved. They appear to be painted with red and touches of yellow. I used the same red that I used for the apple, and added some strokes of the same yellow used on the pear. Now the image looks like this:

TIP **When altering hue in Color mode, it's not necessary to remove the original color. There is no "buildup." Just paint over an area as often as you want. The transparency remains the same.**

Continue colorizing all parts of the teapot, touching up as needed with the Sponge.

Paint the leaves using these CMYK values 51, 27, 65, 25.

Brown CYMK Values 38, 45, 67, 29 are recommended for the handles and spout.

I used a light tan for the teapot with CYMK values 20, 20, 29, 1. That turnip or whatever it is to the upper-left of the apple is nearly the same color, with a bit of yellow added at low opacity.

You are finished. Now boil some water and sit back with a relaxing cup of tea. ■

# hand-tinted

Before the popularity of color photography, artists were employed to apply color to sepia-tone or grayscale photos. Skin tone, eye color, rosy cheeks, and so on were added by hand with transparent pigment. This can be an effective way to imitate a retro look. A quick way to create transparent color is with the Fill command in Color mode.

A similar technique for hand-painted china is on page 70. In that one you want your brush strokes to show. In this one you don't.

© Copyright 1997 PhotoDisc, Inc.

**1** Open the grayscale image "typist" in the PhotoDisc folder on the *Photoshop Effects Magic* CD-ROM. Convert to RGB mode so it can accept color.

**2** Select➡All. Choose a foreground color with these CMYK values: 44, 48, 63, 37 and select Edit➡Fill. Use these settings in the Fill dialog box to create a sepia tone. Save the image.

**3** Double-click the Lasso tool and type in a feather value in the Options palette. I used 4. Draw around the woman's dress with the Lasso. Don't worry about getting your selection precise. Slight imperfections add charm.

**4** Choose a foreground color for the dress. I used CMYK values of 70, 29, 40, 27 and filled the selection at 50% opacity.

**5** Repeat Steps 4 and 5 for the hair. I used CMYK values of 11, 48, 49, 1 at 40% to give the hair an auburn tone.

6 I switched to the Paintbrush in Color mode and used the same foreground color for the skin (40%) and lips (100%). Zoom in to control the application of lipstick. If you get lipstick on her teeth, use the Erase To Saved function of the Eraser Tool for a touch-up.

7 Finally, use the Airbrush tool to apply blush to her cheeks. I set the opacity at 3%. ■

When is a lighting effect not a lighting effect? When it's a transparent gradient!

The Transparent Stripes preset is put through its paces in my "Kaleidoscope" technique (page 194). Here I used it to make a variety of checkerboard patterns.

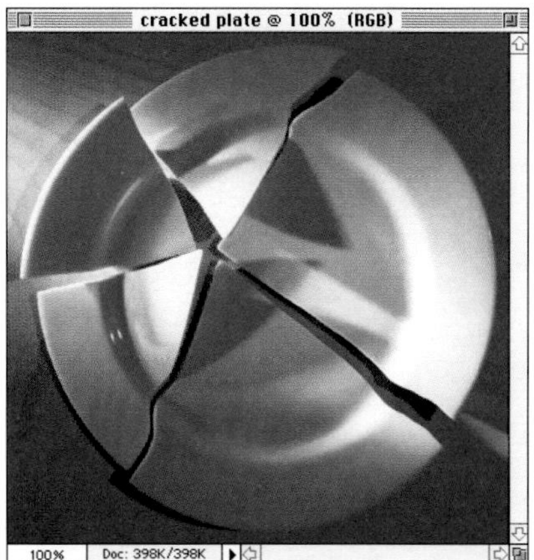


**1** Open the image you want to work with. I started with a photograph that already has some exciting lighting. It's "Plate" from the PhotoDisc folder on the *Photoshop Effects Magic* CD-ROM.

**2** Create a new layer (Layer 1).

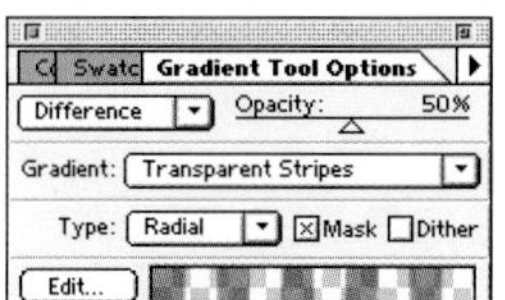


**3** Double-click the Gradient tool and use these settings. The foreground color I'm using is burnt sienna (CMYK values 24, 89, 100, 11).

**4** With Layer 1 still active, drag the Gradient tool from the upper-left corner of the image to the lower-right corner.

**5** With the same gradient settings, drag another diagonal from the lower-left to the upper-right of the image.

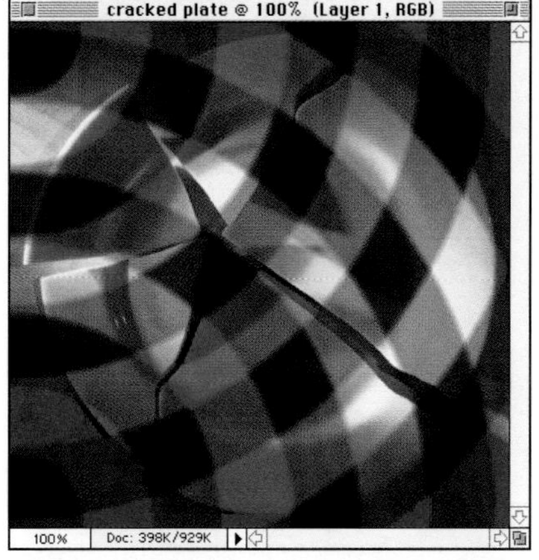


**6** Switch the blending mode in the Layers palette to Difference. There's your "blue plate special."

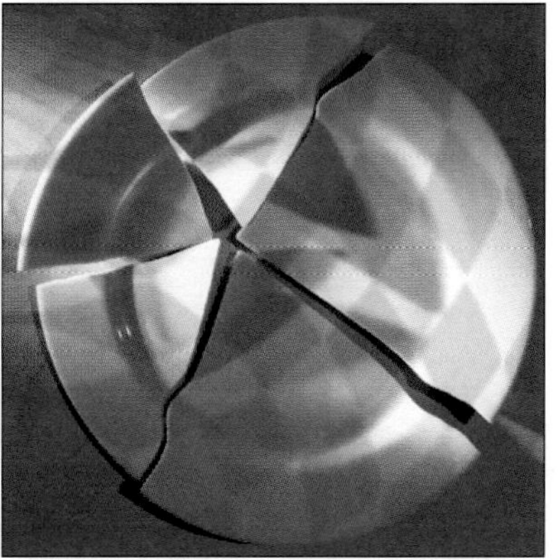

# VARIATIONS

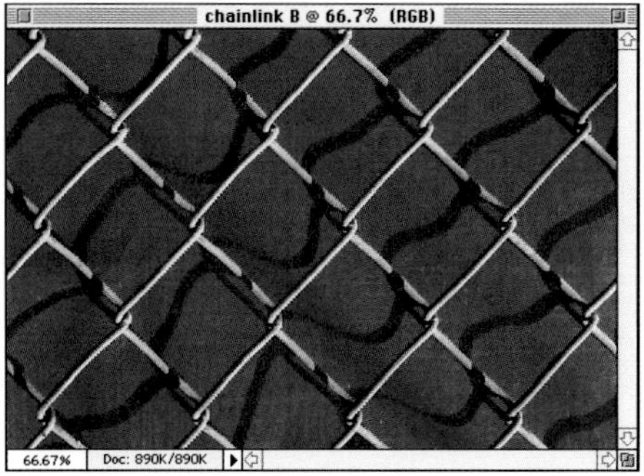


This chainlink image from Digital Stock's Urban Textures collection inspired another diamond design. You'll find this photo in the Urb/Tex file on the CD-ROM.

I switched the gradient type to Linear, leaving the blending mode on Difference and the Opacity at about 50% as before. My foreground color was olive green (CMYK 51, 22, 79, 17) for the first diagonal drag and mustard yellow (CMYK 25, 11, 97, 20) for the second drag.

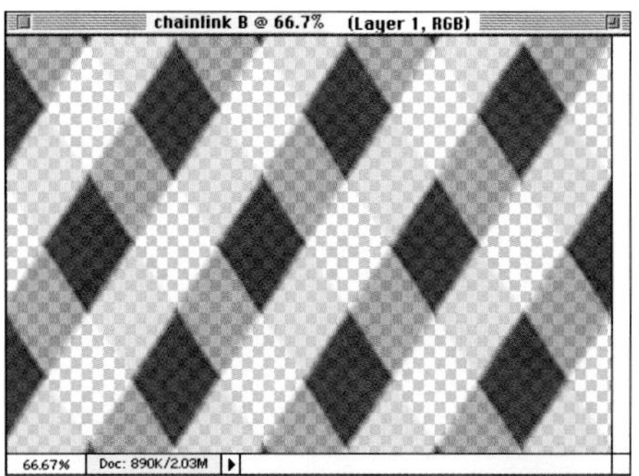


Here's how Layer 1 looks with the background image invisible.

The composite image, with Layer 1 in Difference mode, looks like a patterned fabric has been placed behind the fence.

This tablecloth for an Italian restaurant doesn't require a photo or an additional layer. I created a new white square and used Red at 50% for each diagonal. Gradient type was linear and blending mode was Normal. ■

You can imitate some of the old masterpieces of the Impressionist or Post-Impressionist school by turning a photo into a glorious painting. I recommend using a pressure-sensitive tablet if you have one.

**1** Open the image you want to work with. I'm using "Fruit" in the PhotoDisc folder on the *Photoshop Effects Magic* CD-ROM. Fill the selection with background color medium gray. I used CMYK values 45, 32, 31, 9.

Those realistic colors will have to go. Black shadows? I don't think so.

© Copyright 1997 PhotoDisc, Inc.

**2** Apply the Yellow-Orange-Yellow Gradient using these settings. Drag vertically from top to bottom (or the reverse).

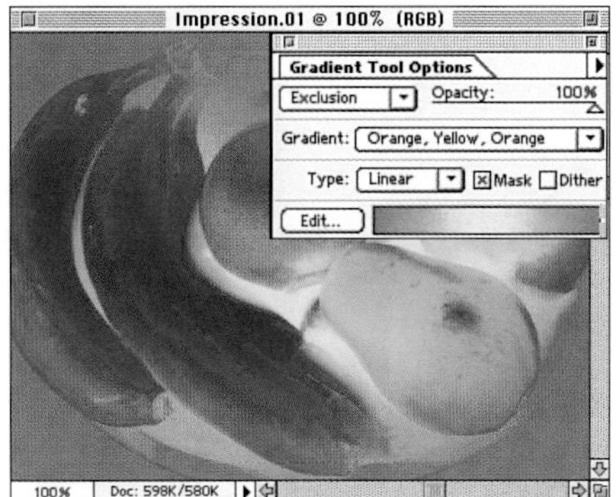


**3** Select Image➡Adjust➡Invert to get something like this:

**4** Load the Assorted Brushes. I've indicated my favorites for adding brush strokes and texture. Do most of your "painting" with the Smudge tool at 100% and one or more assorted brush tips.

Bristle brush

Brushes

Rice grains

Large bristle brush

Big rough

Thunderbolts

3-dot sketchy

**5** Use a variety of strokes to smudge out detail and blend edges. Strokes that follow the contours of the shapes are most effective.

**TIP** **Long scribbly strokes are fun, but they may take a while to appear. If you hate waiting as much as I do, try shorter strokes.**

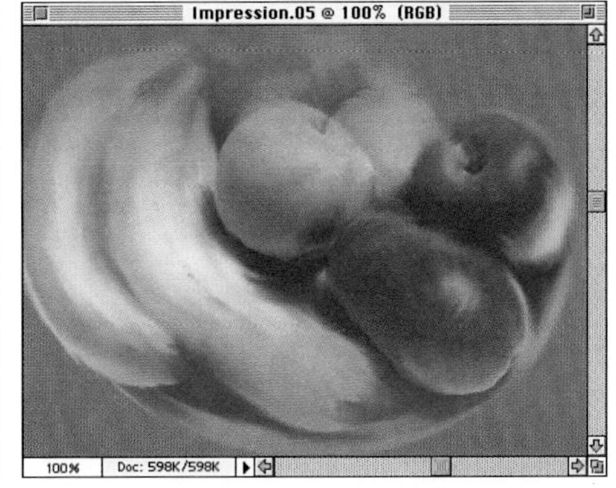


**6** Add a more painterly background by sampling colors from the image with the Eyedropper and using low or medium opacity paintbrush strokes. I used the "Rice-grains" brush to add color and "Thunder-bolts" to blend it with the Smudge tool.

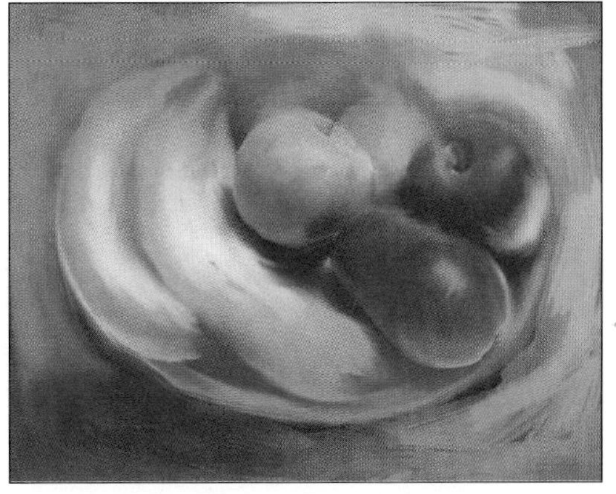

## VARIATIONS

Admirers of George Seurat may continue, adding a Pointillist effect. Apply Filter➥Pixellate➥Pointillize (Cell size: 3).

To get finer dots and no white spots, use the Add Noise Filter to create the Pointillist effect. I used these settings and then the Fade command to reduce the noise to about 60% in Dissolve mode.

Add Noise
OK
Cancel
☒ Preview
100%
Amount: 90
Distribution
◉ Uniform
○ Gaussian
☐ Monochromatic

Fade
Opacity: 60 %
OK
Cancel
Mode: Dissolve
☒ Preview

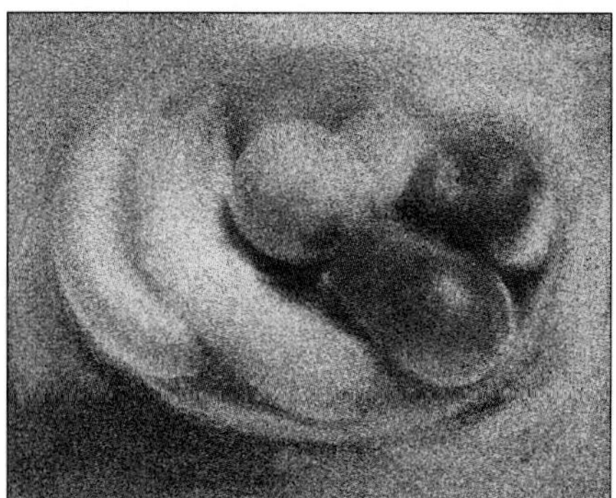

Fat, geometric dots enable you to jump ahead several decades to the Pop Art or Op Art style. After Step 6, apply Filter➡Pixelate➡Color Halftone. I used a Max. Radius of 6 and the default values for screen angles. ■

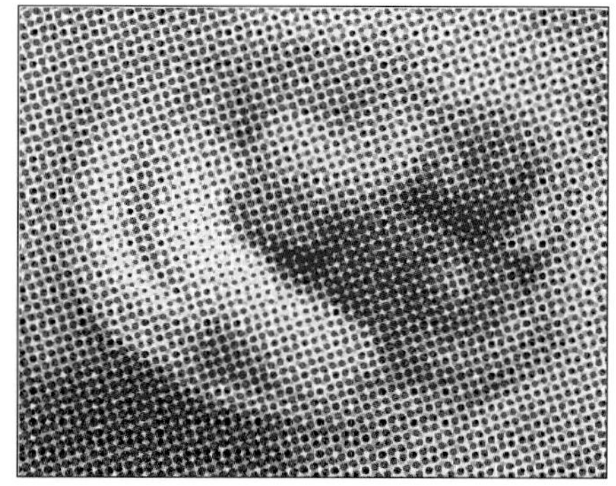

Photoshop 4.0 has a vast array of filters for applying traditional graphic effects. We'll layer and combine some of the effects from the Artistic category to create the look of pastel chalks.

Duplicating an image as additional layers is the first step to a wide variety of blend effects. See "Woodcut" on (page 116) for another example.

**1** Open the "Sourpuss" image in the Digital Stock folder on the *Photoshop Effects Magic* CD-ROM.

**2** Duplicate the layer. Name the layer "cutout." Apply Filter➡Artistic➡Cutout, using these settings.

The portrait has been turned into a silkscreen print.

**3** Duplicate the background layer again. Name this third layer "pencil." Select Filter➥Artistic➥Colored Pencil. I used these values: Width 4, Pressure 8, Brightness 25. The pencil layer looks like this:

**4** You guessed it…duplicate the original layer again, and name it "Fresco." Apply Filter➥Artistic➥ Fresco. I accepted the default values for Size 2, Detail 8, and Texture 1. Here's the result.

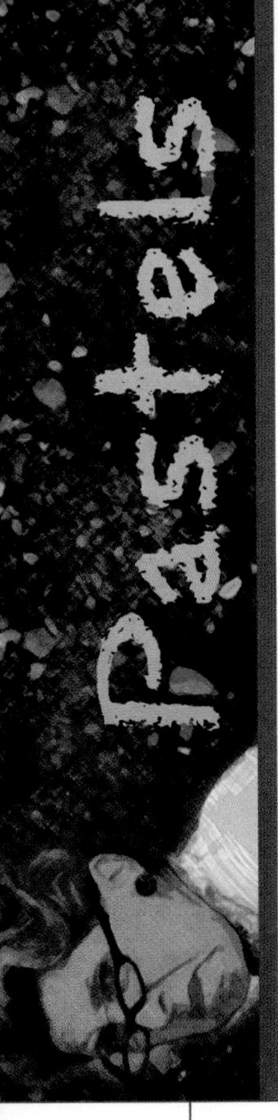

I reduced the opacity of the Fresco layer to 35%, and lowered the opacity of the pencil layer to 50%. Leaving the Cutout layer at 100% completely covers the original image, so I deleted the background layer.

## VARIATIONS

This time I used filters from the Sketch category.

Traditional artists often begin by laying out the areas of light and shadow, and adding details later. The Torn Edges filter gives you a black-and-white simplification of the forms. I softened the harsh black-and-white to light and dark gray by using Image➥Adjust➥Brightness/Contrast (Brightness: +50, Contrast: -60).

I used the Conte Crayon filter for the detail layer. Here's how the combination looks with Conte Crayon in Multiply mode at 100% opacity. The canvas texture is a welcome addition.

I added one more layer and applied the Chrome filter, not a traditional look by itself.

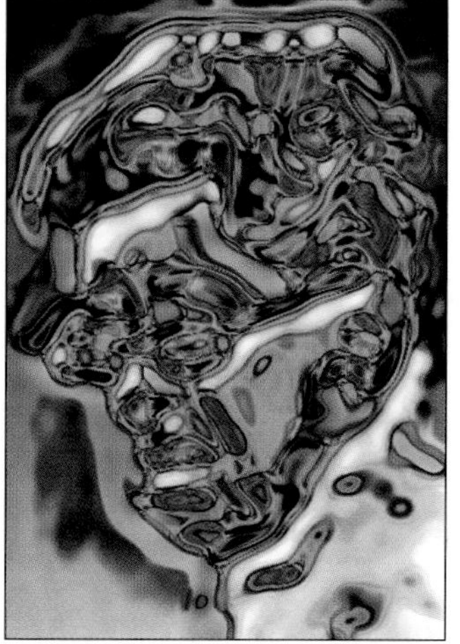

In combination with the other two layers and at 30% opacity, though, I got an interesting wet-on-wet character in some areas.

This kind of experimentation is finished whenever you say so. ■

One of my favorite filters is "Pinch." It's great for distortion effects. And it's handy for making seamless gradual size reductions of a part of your image after you have merged layers.

**1** Open the image you want to pinch. Here I used the "Sourpuss" image, which is included in the Digital Stock folder on the book's CD-ROM. This lady looks like something is already pinching her.

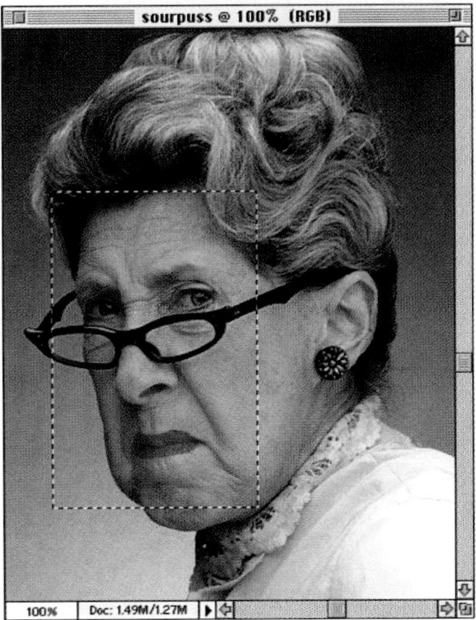


**2** Use the rectangular Marquee selection tool and select the area you want to pinch. No feathering is needed, because the Pinch effect will fade out at the edges of the selection automatically.

**3** Apply Filter➥Distort➥Pinch. Notice the changes in the preview window as you drag the Amount slider. Increasing the percentage reduces the size of her features and brings them closer to the center of her face. I used 58%.

I know that woman! She was my faculty advisor in high school.

Notice the problem with her eyeglasses. They now appear to be in reverse perspective but that won't take long to fix.

To adjust the eyeglasses:

**1** Make a rectangular selection as shown.

**2** Use Layer➡Transform➡Distort and reshape the selection by dragging on the handles of the bounding box.

**3** Now patch up that white space with a gradient fill. Use the Eyedropper tool to pick up the foreground color from a brown pixel just above the white space. The background color should match the lighter brown just below the white space.

**TIP** **Hold the Option key down when you want the Eyedropper to choose a background color.**

If you're a perfectionist, you may want to use the Add Noise filter to match the photo's graininess. This is close enough for one of those supermarket tabloids with a headline such as: "Woman eats 5-pound lemon and lives!"

## VARIATIONS

Open "Smiling Woman" in the Digital Stock folder on the book's CD-ROM.

The Pinch filter has a range that includes negative values. As you might expect, the larger the negative number, the more the selection bulges out. I applied a –42 Pinch to the mouth of the "Smiling Woman" with the selection off-center, resulting in a slightly lopsided smile.

You might as well polish her teeth while you're at it, using the Dodge tool (Midtones, 50% pressure).

Making her squint was accomplished with a circular selection and 100% pinch for each eye.

You can use a shortcut to duplicate the effect on the second eye: move the selection over and press (Command-F)[Control-F] to repeat the last filter.

The finishing touch was a long ellipse enclosing both eyes, and the Pinch filter at 35%. This brought the eyes slightly closer together.

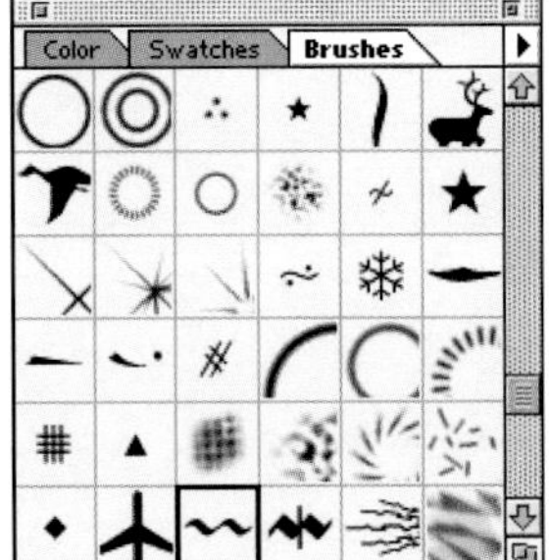


There are lots more uses for the pinch filter than just caricature.

Use it to create a crimp design for a pattern fill. I used the Brush shown, from the Assorted Brushes group.

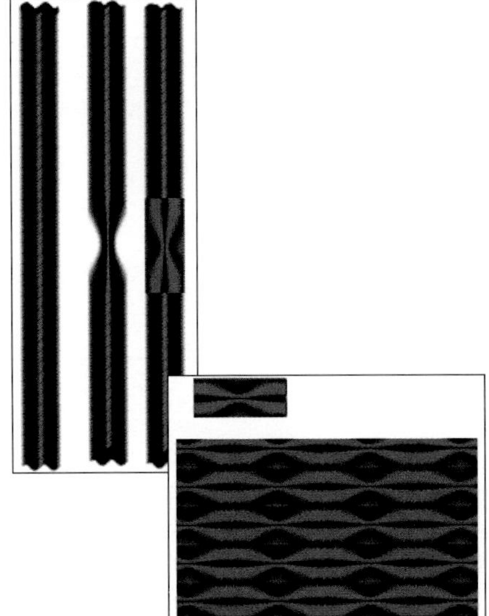

I made a straight stroke by holding the Shift key down as I painted. Then I selected and pinched a portion of the line a few times, colored it and flipped it 90 degrees. Then I used Edit➡Define Pattern followed by Edit➡Fill (Pattern) to pour this design into a new selection.

Pinch some type. Here's Benguiat Book in 36 points. I made a rectangular selection just fitting around the word and set the Pinch filter to 40.

Pinch

I made the pinch more extreme by repeating the effect (Command-F) [Control-F].

Pinch

Give type some punch with the Pinch filter in a negative value. Here's the same type with the Pinch value –55 ■

Punch

There are many ways of combining two or more images in Photoshop. See "Collage" (page 52) and "Blends" (page 22). This one is a favorite of mine because it is so direct and immediate. You don't need to use masks for this technique, but a tablet and stylus is recommended for complete control of the brush strokes.

The Rubber Stamp tool offers a powerful array of techniques for cloning images or parts of images into other images.

One exciting way to combine two photographs is to use one of them as the canvas and the other as the paintbrush. You need two photos for this recipe, one the source and the other the destination.

**1** Open the two images you want to work with. I'm using "Clocks" and "SnuffBox" found in the Image Club folder on the *Photoshop Effects Magic* CD-ROM.

**2** Select a rectangular area on the snuffbox like this. Selecting Edit➡Define Pattern makes the turquoise mosaic a source for the next step.

**3** Double-click the Rubber Stamp tool and choose the Pattern (non-aligned) option. Activate the Clock image and paint a few strokes over the clock faces. I used 50% opacity with a fairly fat brush and varied the blending modes. Some strokes use Normal mode, some use Difference mode. A few of the strokes were in Color Burn or Hard Light mode. Your image might look something like this.

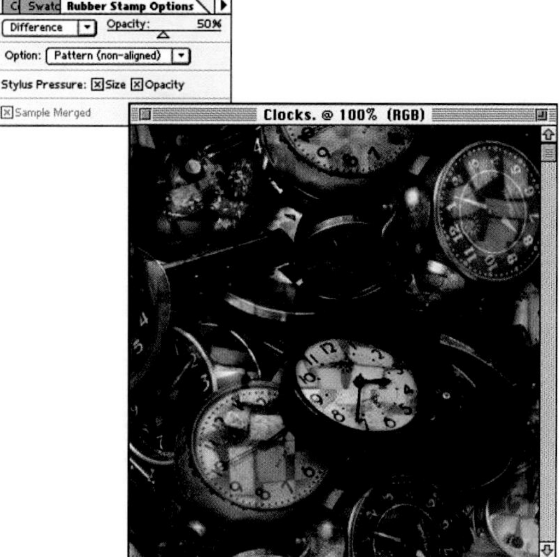


**4** You can add a painterly edge to the image. Be sure white is the background color, then select Image➡Canvas Size to add a white border about ¼-inch wide.

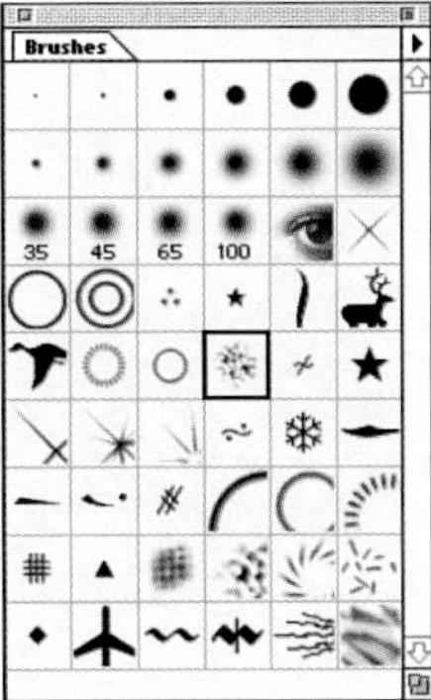


**5** Change to the Impressionist mode in the Rubber Stamp Options palette. Load Assorted Brushes if necessary and use the brush shown here. At 100% pressure and Normal mode, drag short strokes from inside the edges of the Clocks image into the white border.

Continue applying short, curved strokes here and there throughout the image. The effect is to reduce detail and create bristly brush strokes.

If you obliterate too much detail in spots, you can bring back the original pixels by switching to the From Saved option. This is very similar to the Erase to Saved option of the Eraser tool.

## VARIATIONS

This time Clocks is the source and SnuffBox will be altered with the Rubber Stamp tool.

**1** (Option-click)[Alt-click] the Clock image to establish the starting point for cloning.

**2** Activate the SnuffBox image and paint. I used Difference mode at about 60% and the Clone (non-aligned) option.

Try using "Teapot" as the source image. (It's in the Image Club folder on the book's CD-ROM.)

(Option-click)[Alt-click] the center of the teapot. Use Clone (aligned) this time.

For the background, select most of the teapot, excluding handle, spout, and cover. Edit➡Define Pattern and paint the background with one of the bristle brush tips. This one was done using Pattern (aligned) and Exclusion mode. ■

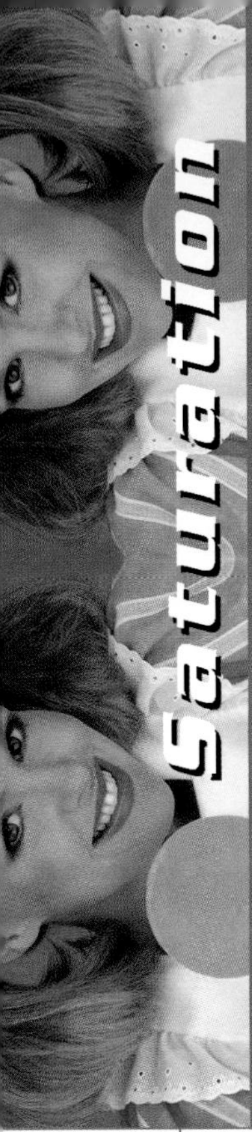


"Hand-Tinted" (page 70) shows how to add color to a grayscale image. Here you learn how to remove or minimize color, and add it back selectively to create emphasis.

**1** Open the image "IdaJello" in the ArtStart folder on the *Photoshop Effects Magic* CD-ROM.

**2** Select➡All. Select Image➡Adjust➡Desaturate to remove all color in the image. Do not save, because you need to be able to restore part of the color image.

**3** Double-click the Eraser tool and select Erase to Saved in the Eraser Options palette. Use the settings shown here.

**4** Erase over the jello and fruit. This will bring back the color at full strength in the areas you stroke.

**5** I accidentally colored Ida's thumbs. No problem. If that happens to you, choose the Sponge tool. Select Desaturate mode at 100% pressure in the Toning Tools Options palette. Now paint over the areas you want to return to grayscale.

# VARIATIONS

You don't have to eliminate color completely. You can reduce the intensity of color to any level. Then "paint" back more intense color where you want it.

"Rooster" is a colorful image in Image Club➥Objects folder on the CD-ROM.

I used Image➥Adjust➥Hue/Saturation and moved the Saturation slider down to –65 to achieve this washed-out look.

Using the Erase to Saved function of the Eraser tool I brought back the color in the rooster's comb and wattles. ■

A traditional commercial art style that is becoming popular again is stippling—black-and-white art consisting of tiny dots. The old-fashioned way is tedious and time-consuming, one dot at a time, but with Photoshop it's a snap.

© Copyright 1997 PhotoDisc, Inc.

The method works best with photographs that have good contrast and lots of texture or detail. I'll use "Orange" from the PhotoDisc folder on the *Photoshop Effects Magic* CD-ROM.

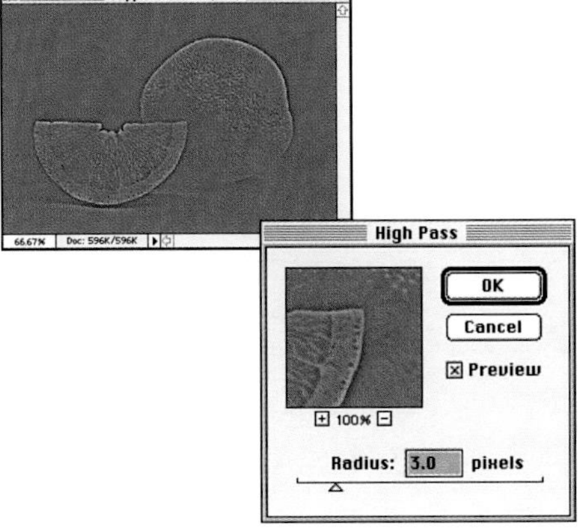


**1** Apply Filter➡Other➡High Pass to the entire image. This produces a medium gray except for the areas of greatest contrast. A low setting (1 to 3) is recommended. The lower the setting the stronger the effect.

**2** Use Image➡Adjust➡Threshold to turn the mostly gray image into black-and-white. Move the Threshold slider, or type the number you want. Most of the pixels are in the medium gray area, so small changes near the center of the threshold curve will produce large effects.

Here's the image with a threshold of 129. There is a great deal of black, especially in the background.

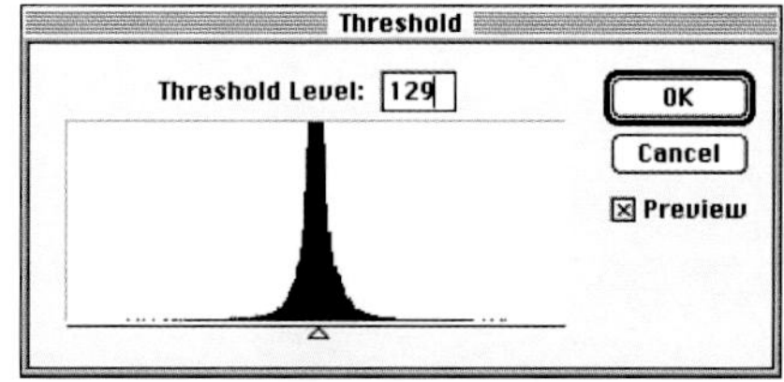


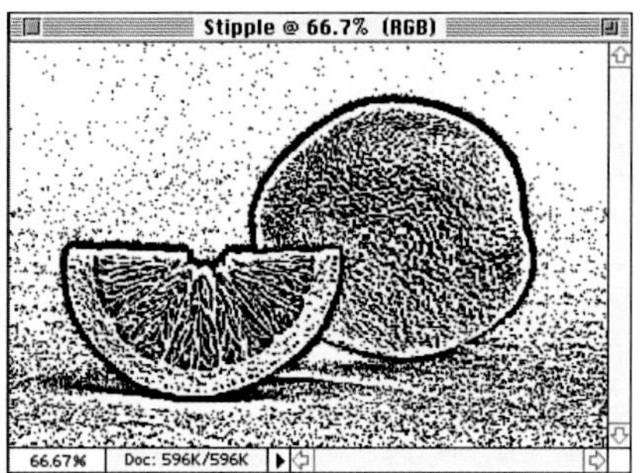


Move the threshold down to 120 and some of the detail is lost, but we can still identify the subject easily.

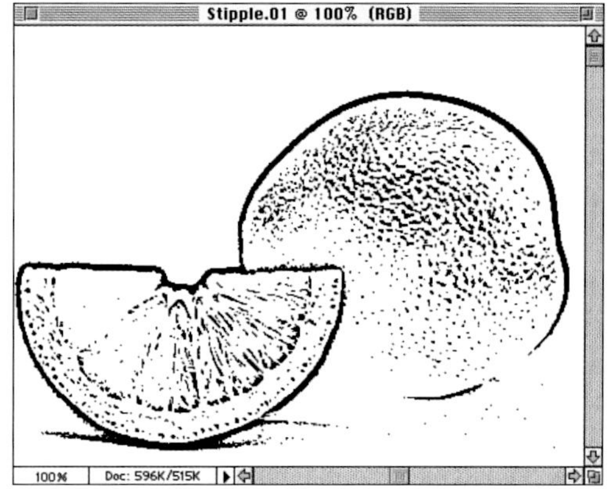


## Variations

We'll add color back to the lightly stippled orange.

**1** Use the Save As command on your stippled image. Open the original photo again.

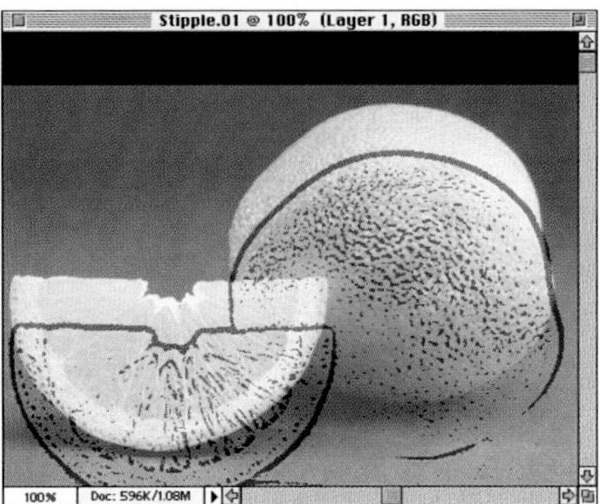


**2** Select➡All of the stippled version. Drag and drop it to the original color photo where it becomes Layer 1. Reduce opacity of Layer 1 so you can move it into position exactly over the color (background) layer.

Adjust the opacity of Layer 1 if needed to get a delicate watercolor wash effect. This is at 60%.

When your intention is to use the original photo as a color source, begin by using the Duplicate Layer command in the Layers palette menu. Then the stippling effect is applied to this "Background copy" layer. Of course, the two layers are perfectly aligned.

Sherry London's "Woodcut" was the inspiration for this recipe. You can find it on page 116.

# VIGNETTE

A vignette is an image, usually small, which fades out at the edges. It's often used by conventional portrait photographers, but any subject is fair game. Here's a classic vignette.

**1** Open the file you want to vignette. I used the "Glamour" image in the Digital Stock folder on the *Photoshop Effects Magic* CD-ROM.

**2** Use the Elliptical Marquee tool and make an oval selection like this.

**TIP** **Hold down the (Option) [Alt] key and drag from the center for more control.**

**3** Choose Select➡Feather (16 pixels). The larger the number, the more gradual the fade-out will be.

**4** Use Select➡Inverse to select everything outside the oval.

**5** Press D to switch to default colors. Press the Delete key and the background fills with white, fading out toward the portrait.

Notice the upper part of the vignette has a hard edge. There wasn't enough space in the image above her hair to allow for the feathering. Let's start again and fix that problem.

**6** Choose File➡Revert to return to the original image.

**7** Choose Image➡Canvas Size and use the settings shown. Click OK and more space is added to the top of the image. It is white space, so fill it with black, using the Paint Bucket tool.

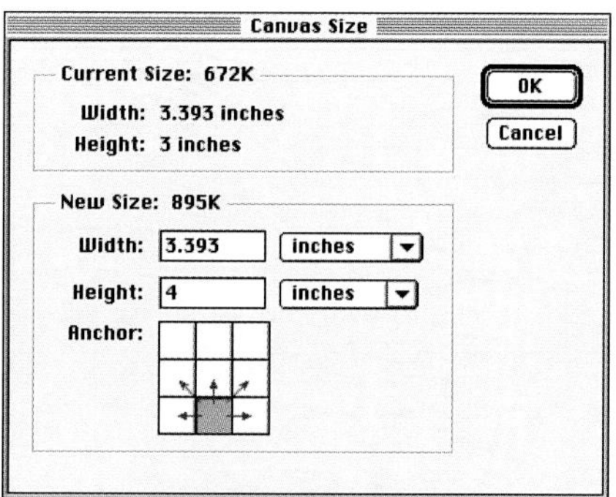


Repeat Steps 2 through 5. This time there is plenty of room at the top for a perfect vignette.

## VARIATIONS

A vignette can be any shape and fade to any color. These variations show some of the possibilities.

Use the "Toasting" image from the Digital Stock folder on the book's CD-ROM. Draw a selection with the Lasso tool, roughly corresponding to the group of figures, including the upraised glasses.

Do Steps 3 and 4, but choose a background color before you press the Delete key. I used CMYK values of 30, 87, 100, 29 for this reddish brown.

This variation uses a filter effect for a gradual fade to gray that allows some of the original image to remain.

You can find the "Camelot" image in the Digital Stock folder of the book's CD-ROM.

Make an oval selection of the queen's head. I used a large feather radius (45 pixels). Select➥Inverse to select everything except the queen's head. Apply Filter➥Other ➥High Pass to the selection, using a radius of 0.4 pixels. The High Pass filter reduces everything to medium gray except areas of high contrast.

This resulted in a fade-out where the filigree design on the King's jacket and some other lines remain visible. ■

If you've ever wondered how to make fancy wallpaper out of fish heads look no further. You can crop an element from any complex image and make it into a tile for a repeating pattern.

© Copyright 1997 PhotoDisc, Inc.

**1** Open the file that contains the image you want on your wallpaper. I used "fish," which is in the PhotoDisc folder on the *Photoshop Effects Magic* CD-ROM. Make a rectangular selection as shown.

**2** Choose Edit➡Define Pattern to store the fish head as a pattern tile.

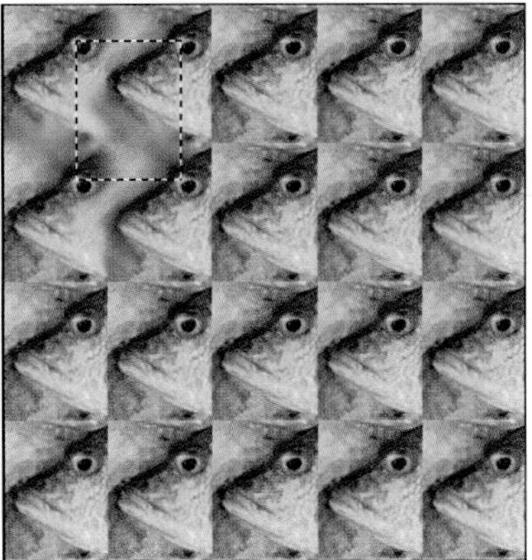

**3** Create a new file about 3 square inches to test the fish head pattern. Select Edit➡Fill and choose Pattern for Contents.

The fish heads do not form a seamless fill, and that's not surprising. It's easy to get a perfect pattern when the image element is "floating" in a solid color background. However, this technique requires a bit of trial-and-error.

**4** Select a new rectangle for a repeating tile, using the fish eyes as guides. Use the Smear tool to blend the area that showed the seam. Select Edit➡Define Pattern to replace the original fish head with this new tile and test it by using Edit➡Fill again.

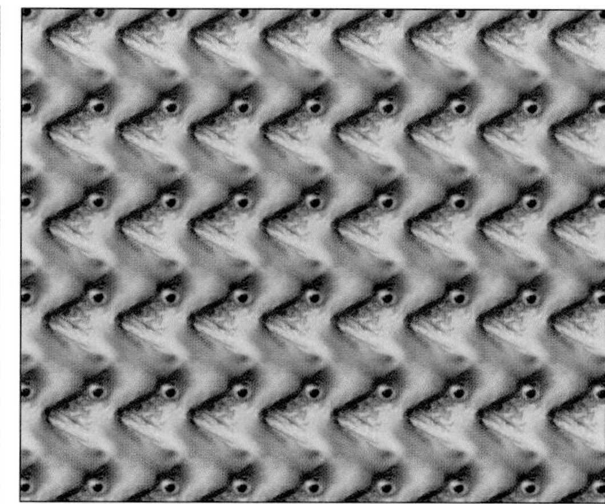

## VARIATIONS

Here's a striped wallpaper that was easy to make. The tile element is the same fish head we used in Step 1 and a chunk of beef (you can find "rawmeat" in the PhotoDisc folder on the CD-ROM).

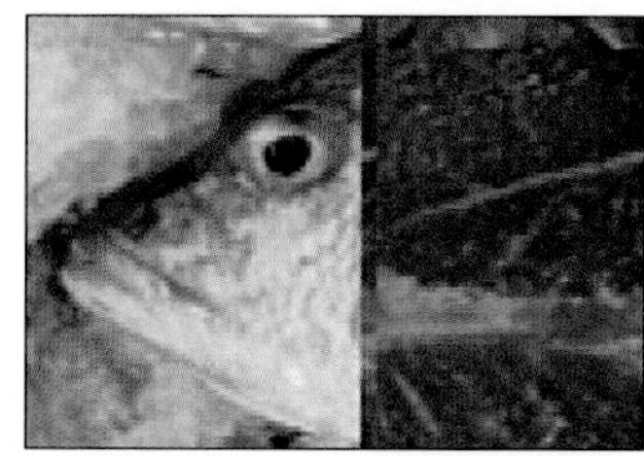

It's not quite seamless, but the tiling doesn't intrude that much. I call it "Surf and Turf."

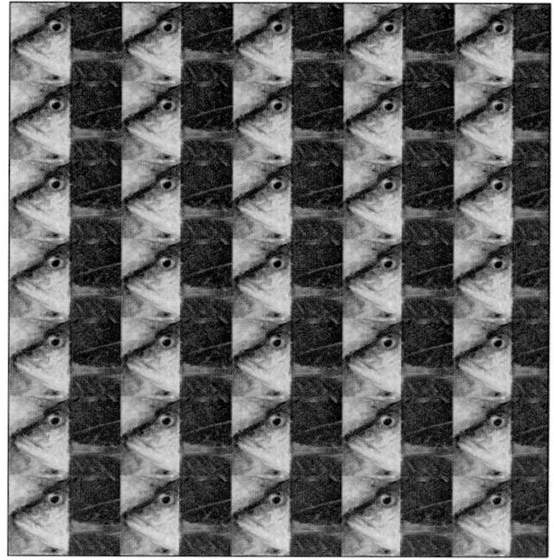

© Copyright 1997 PhotoDisc, Inc.

For the vegetarians, I recommend using the "Squash" image in the PhotoDisc folder on the CD-ROM. Select an area such as this one and copy it to the clipboard.

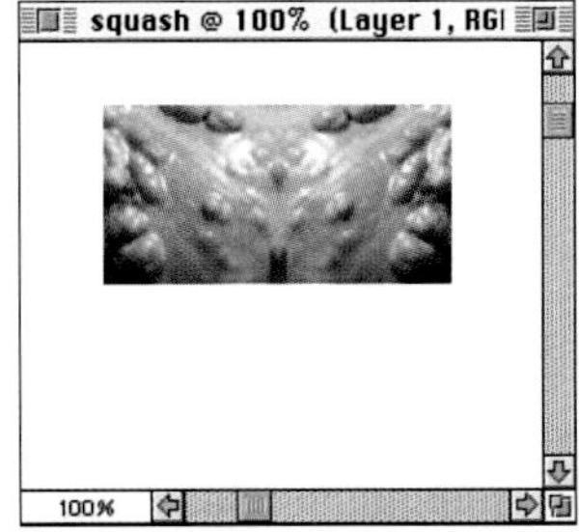


Paste it into a new file about 4 inches wide by 2.5 inches high. Paste again and choose Layer➡Transform➡Flip Horizontally. Choose Layer➡Merge Layers.

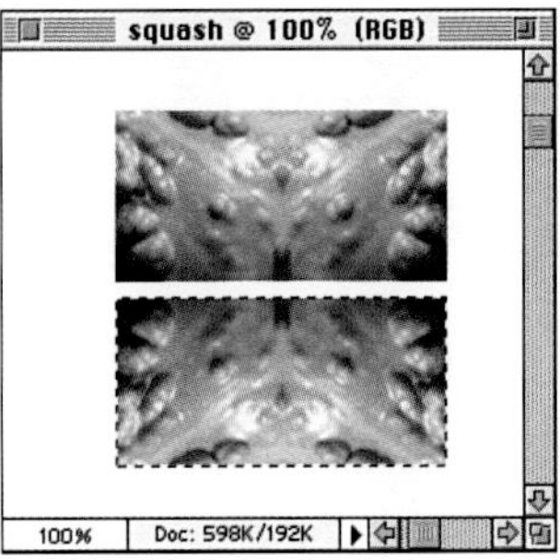


Copy the new double image and then flip it vertically. Move it into place to create a 4-way mirror image. Touch up any seams with the Smudge tool.

This image is the pattern tile for a more elaborate-looking fill. Crop it carefully before you use Edit➥ Define Pattern. Your fill may look something like this. ■

Sherry London's "Woodcut" technique is one of many ways to create effects beginning with two identical layers.

You can imitate the look of a woodblock print by changing the top layer into black-and-white detail and making the white areas transparent. This creates a bold, rough-textured graphic similar to traditional relief prints.

**1** Open the file you'd like to use. I am working with "Alphabet Blocks," which is in the Image Club folder on the *Photoshop Effects Magic* CD-ROM. The ideal image for this technique has a wide range of shapes, good contrast, and is not too dark.

**2** Duplicate the background layer. Steps 3 to 6 are applied to this "Background copy" layer.

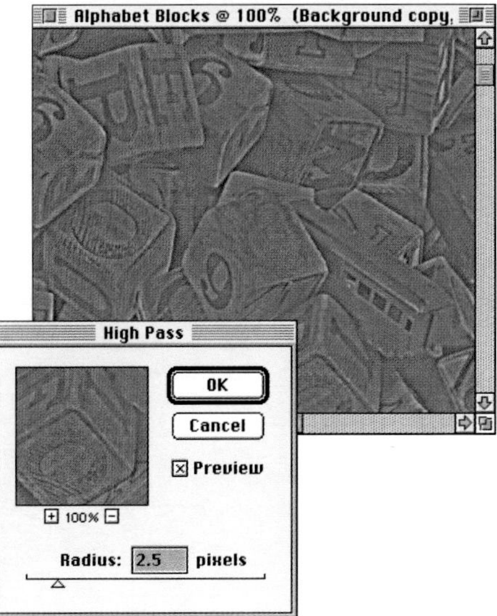


**3** Apply Filter➥Other➥High Pass (2.5). The High Pass filter produces medium gray except in areas of highest contrast. The lower the value, the stronger the effect.

**4** Choosing Image➡Adjust➡ Desaturate will remove what little color remains. Your image should look something like this:

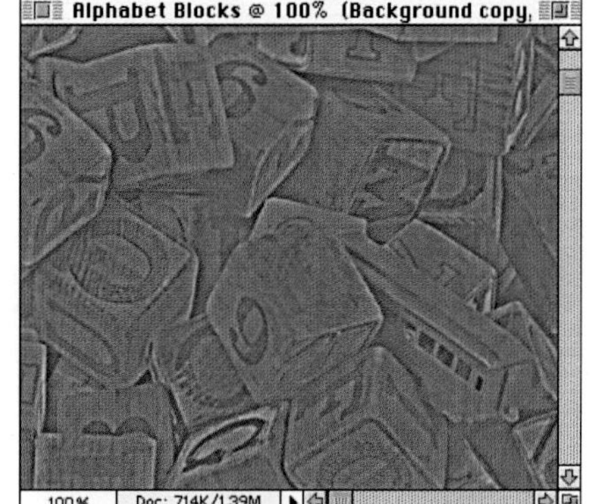


**5** Select Image➡Adjust➡Posterize (2). Using 2 levels makes all the pixels on this layer either black or white. Remember that we will make the white areas transparent.

**6** Switch the blending mode of the layer to Multiply. The white areas of the layer become transparent, so the original colors of the background can show through.

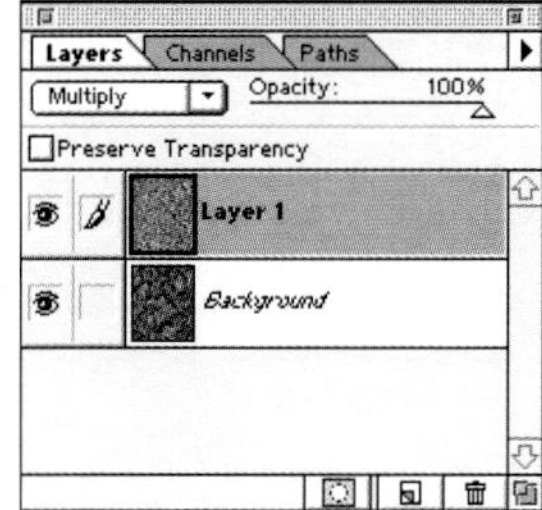

Here's the finished "block print" image.

## VARIATIONS

To get a wet-on-wet watercolor look in the color layer, do this last. Make the background layer active and apply Filter➥Blur➥Gaussian Blur (7 pixels).

You can control the ratio of white to black in Step 5 by using Image➥Adjust➥Threshold instead of Posterize.

If you want the look of sticky, heavily applied black ink, move the Threshold slider to the right to make more pixels black. Here's the complete image when I moved the Threshold right to 137.

Another adjustment or two and we'll get the look of a "crayon scratchboard" image.

**1** Flatten the image.

**2** Increase both Brightness and Contrast (I used +25).

**3** Select All and use Image➡Adjust➡Hue/Saturation. I moved the Saturation slider up to 70 for hot color to show through the "scratches." ■

# PART II

## Using Line Art

Anything strictly black-and-white meets my definition of line art. So, that covers cartoons, lots of clip art and type. Even EPS or vector art can be manipulated in Photoshop. When you have placed such an item in a Photoshop document, it becomes a bit-map or raster image, and it can be manipulated with any of Photoshop's tools. I've also included the paths made with Photoshop's Pen tool in this category.

This section covers several ways for applying color to line art, distorting clip art, a couple of dandy Type effects, and a great way to prepare artwork for two-color printing. The two-color technique as well as Burning Type and Quick Color work much better if you are using a graphics tablet. Have I mentioned that it would be a good idea to get one?

© Cartoon City



Sharron Evans asks, "How do you apply color to a black-and-white drawing and not worry about covering up the black lines or filling in the open/white areas and then having to correct a white halo between the black lines and the color due to dithering or anti-aliased lines?" We've all asked ourselves that question from time to time, haven't we?

Sharron suggests managing your colorizing problems by creating a second layer for color and placing it under the black-and-white layer. Because nothing can go under the background this takes a few steps.

**1** Open your black-and-white line art. I'm using "Vrtual66" in the ArtStart folder on the *Photoshop Effects Magic* CD-ROM. Convert the image to RGB mode.

**2** Duplicate the Background layer. It will be called "Background copy" automatically.

**3** Create a new layer and name it "color." Drag the color layer below the Background copy layer in the Layers palette. Rename the Background copy layer "line art" to avoid confusion.

**4** The original Background layer is no longer needed, so delete it. Your Layers palette looks like this.

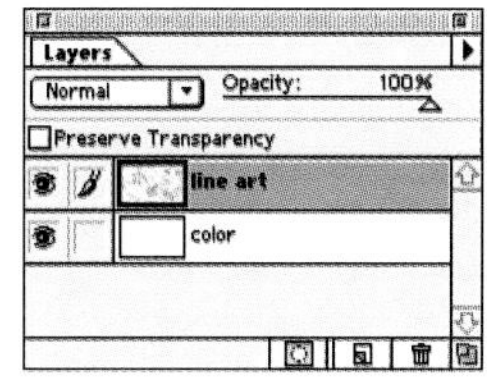


**5** Make the line art layer active and choose Darken in the blending mode menu. Darken mode will protect anything darker than the color you are using to paint with. Because black is the darkest possible color, you can paint without fear of harming any of the line-work. Now make the color layer active.

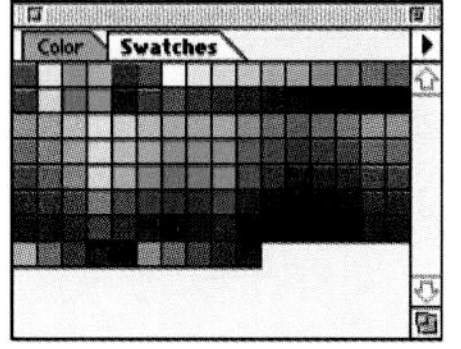


TIP **Keep the Swatches palette open for quick access to a reasonable variety of colors. You can add extra colors by choosing them in the color picker and clicking the empty area in the Swatches palette. To choose a background color from the Swatches palette, hold down the (Option) [Alt] key.**

Painting large areas with flat color can get tedious. What about filling them with the paint bucket or gradient tool?

At this stage my color work includes the rider's hands and neck painted with a fleshtone, and the same color bucket fill for his face. I selected the computer and keyboard with several Magic Wand selections, holding down the Shift key, so they could be added together and filled with a single click. Some gaps still need to be painted in "by hand."

The following steps show how to manipulate selections efficiently and maneuver between layers.

**1** Make the line art layer active and use the Magic Wand to select the areas you want to fill.

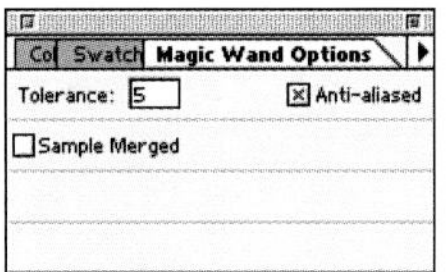


**2** Adjust the pixel tolerance in the Magic Wand Options palette.

The default value for Magic Wand tolerance is 32. When I used that amount and clicked on the front fender, the selection included the front tire because of a small line gap. Rather than altering the line layer (and possibly spoiling the spontaneous quality of the cartoon) I deselected and lowered the tolerance to 5. Now the tire was not included in the selection.

**3** Shift-click all the areas you want to fill with the same color.

**4** Make the color layer active and the same areas will be selected.

**5** Use Edit➡Fill if you want to control opacity. Otherwise just click with the paint bucket in any part of a selection and all selections will be filled.

**6** Hide the "marching ants" (Command-H)[Control -H] so you can see how well the areas were filled.

Using a tolerance of 5 leaves a "halo" of pixels, but you don't have to go all the way back to Step 2 to fix that. You don't even have to undo the fill if it was 100% opacity.

**7** Choose Select➥Modify➥Expand to increase the selection border by one or two pixels and repeat the fill. You still may need to touch up some edges with the paintbrush.

A gradient fill of the cartoon computer screen shows a "halo" at 300% magnification.

Expanding the selection area and redoing the fill solves the problem.

**8** Select the grass in the foreground with the Magic Wand tool at a tolerance of 5. It's hard to tell what's included, so do a test fill. Remember to make the color layer active before you use the Paint Bucket. I used a yellow-green with CMYK values 32, 0, 76, 0. The pine tree and the distant mountains are filled but the building is untouched.

**9** Use the Lasso tool to subtract the mountains from the selection. Hold down the (Option)[Alt] key and drag a closed loop around the area you want to deselect. I decided to use a gradient fill using a darker green (CMYK 75, 0, 100, 0) for the background color, dragging from the bottom to the top of the selection.

At some point it may be more efficient simply to merge layers and use Darken mode for the painting and filling tools, like when you keep forgetting to switch layers (as I do), or you become confident enough in your skills to rely on Erase to Saved as your safety net. See "Quick Color" (page 154) for some pointers on painting with Darken mode.

## Filling with Patterns

I used a pattern fill for the snazzy fabric on his suit.

**1** Open a postscript pattern. This is Herringbone 1.

**2** Select➡All and use the Edit➡ Define Pattern command.

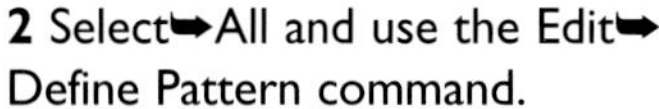

**3** Select the areas of the cartoon you want to fill with the pattern. Edit➡Fill and use Pattern for Contents. I reduced opacity to 50%. To color the pattern, choose a foreground color then apply Edit➡Fill to the same selection at 25% opacity.

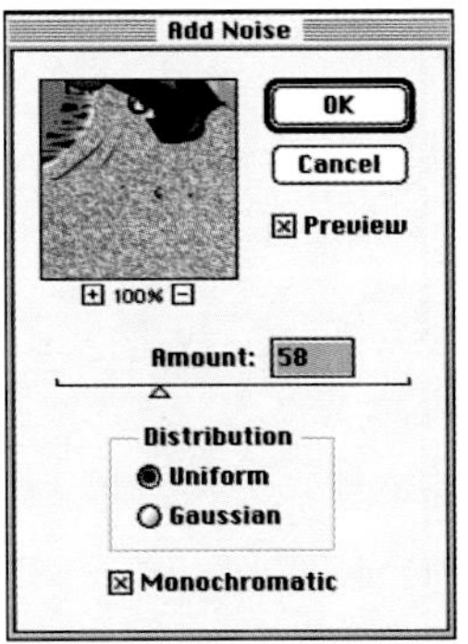


The asphalt highway was a combination of gradients and the Add Noise filter with these settings.

Some glaring gaps remain after the roadway was paved.

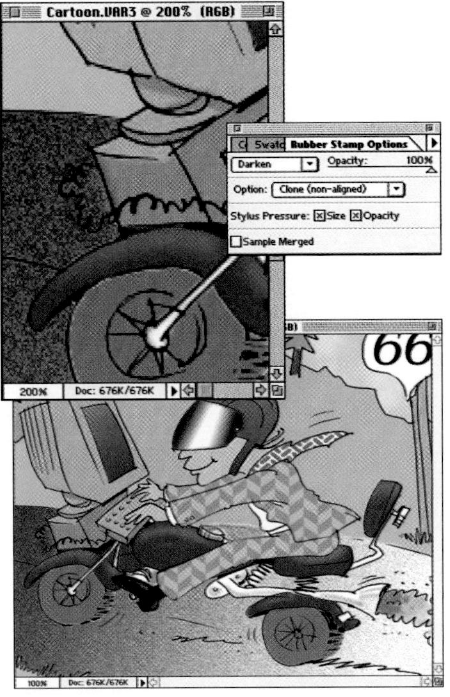


Repair them with the Rubber Stamp tool in Darken mode.

Well, this turned into quite a project, involving a lot more Photoshop skills than meet the eye. After some airbrush work on the tires, a few tiny eraser strokes to show off the wheel spokes…hmm, what if we showed reflections of the environment on his helmet visor? ■

Graphic designers and illustrators can get plenty of mileage from this technique. It shows how to create an image for two-color printing. No, we're not talkin' duotones; that's something completely different.

This method involves working in CMYK and making the contents of two of the color channels disappear. Make sure you discuss this with your prepress person, who may have some additional guidelines.

**1** Create a new file (grayscale, 200 dpi).

**2** Paste or place any line art you want to work with. I'm using the EPS images "Cupcake" and Cake," which you'll find in Image Club➡Sketches on the *Photoshop Effects Magic* CD-ROM. Each item creates its own layer. Use the Layer➡Transform commands and the Move tool to arrange and size them like this. You'll have to erase a bit of the cake plate that shows through the cupcake frosting.

**3** Flatten the image. Convert to CMYK mode.

Let's say some shade of red will be used as the second color for printing. The exact color doesn't matter. We'll work in the Magenta channel because it is the one most similar to red and will give us the best visual approximation to the final printed piece.

**4** Make the Yellow channel active. Select➡All and delete. Repeat this with the Cyan channel.

**5** Make the Black channel active and make the composite channel visible. Your channels palette should look something like this.

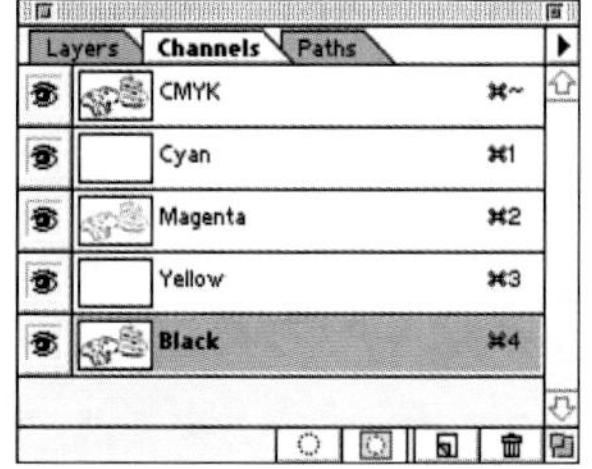


**6** With the Eraser tool, remove all the areas you want to print in shades of red. You can select areas and delete them or fill them with white, or paint them with white; whatever it takes to get rid of them. Here's how mine looks at this stage:

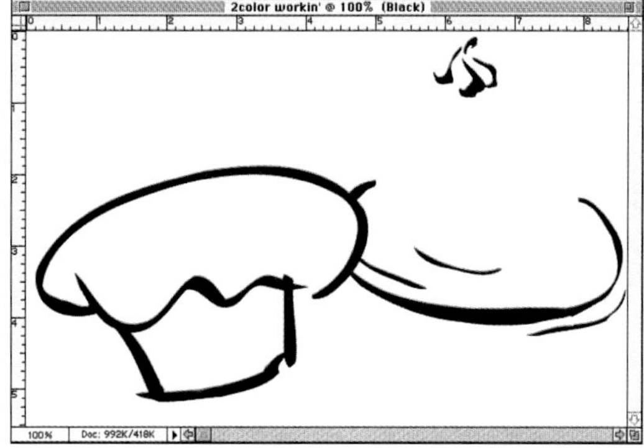


TIP **If you want to see each channel in the appropriate color instead of grayscale go to File➥Preferences➥ Display and Cursors. Check the Color Channels in Color checkbox.**

**7** Make the Magenta channel active and erase everything you want to print in black or shades of gray. You may prefer to have the Black channel invisible so you can see more clearly what is being eliminated.

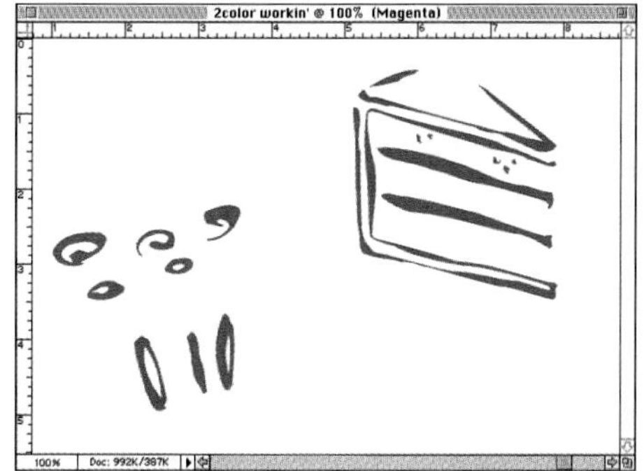

**Print a screenshot of each channel for a good look at stray pixels that escaped your notice. My Magenta and Black channels both show some stray pixels to be eliminated.**

To create different percentages of color in either channel, use shades of gray to paint or fill any area.

**8** In the Black channel I selected the "body" of the cupcake with a click of the Magic Wand. Then I used the Edit➡Fill command and chose 50% gray for the content.

**9** With both channels visible and the Magenta channel active, I made a freehand selection of the cupcake frosting with the Lasso tool. I feathered it (12) and used the 50% gray fill to get pink frosting.

**10** With Magenta still the target channel, I selected the area of the cake slice inside the frosting and used Edit➡Fill with 50% gray at 50% opacity to get a 25% shade of pink.

**TIP** **Use the Lasso tool's polygon function to make the selection. Hold down the (Option)[Alt] key while you click corner points.**

## VARIATIONS

You can start with a blank CMYK file. I made the Cyan channel active and chose a foreground color of medium gray. Filter➡Render➡Clouds produced this blue sky.

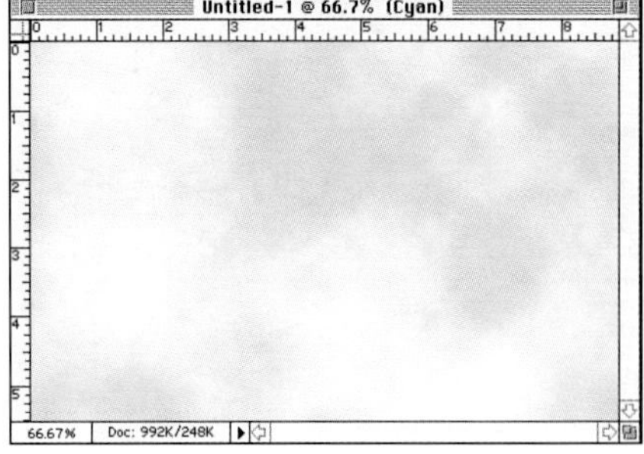

With the composite channel active, place some EPS clip art and it goes to the black channel automatically. I'm using "Bird" from the Image Club➥Woodcuts folder on the book's CD-ROM.

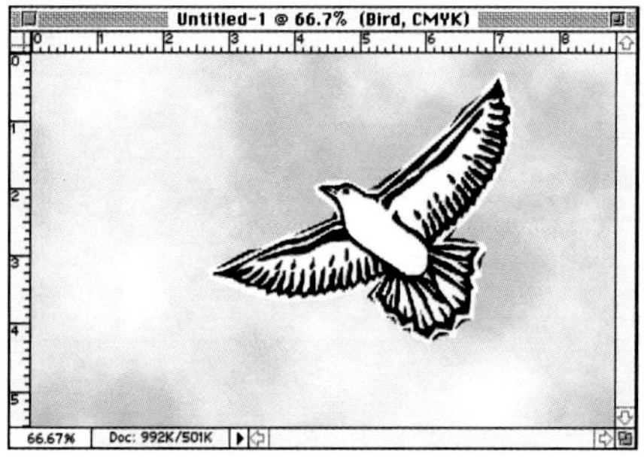


With the Black channel active, I selected the white areas of the bird with the Magic Wand. Switching to the Cyan channel, I painted over the bird with rapid strokes and small brushes. Here's what the Cyan channel looked like with the Black channel invisible.

Say you want to use two "spot" colors in addition to basic black. I added the EPS image "Butterfly" and colored it in the Magenta channel. I kept the Black channel visible to use as a guide, but I didn't make any selections. Here's the Magenta channel, showing a variety of shades.

Here's the Final Image. ■

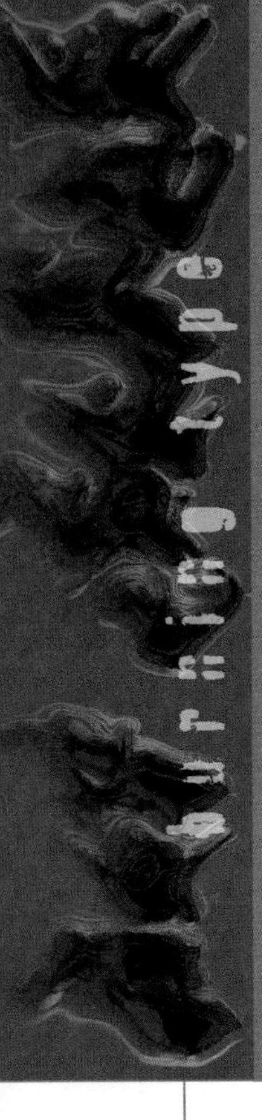


Use any font you want to try this technique for setting fire to type. I've included the text "Hot Coffee" in the ArtStart folder on the *Photoshop Effects Magic* CD-ROM. Appropriately enough, this effect makes excellent use of the Color Burn blending mode!

**1** Create a new file the appropriate size for your type. Fill it with golden yellow (CMYK: 11, 29, 90, 2).

**2** Enter the text in a rich brown (CMYK: 37, 69, 53, 56). Move the type to the lower part of the image, leaving plenty of room at the top for smoke and flames. Flatten the image.

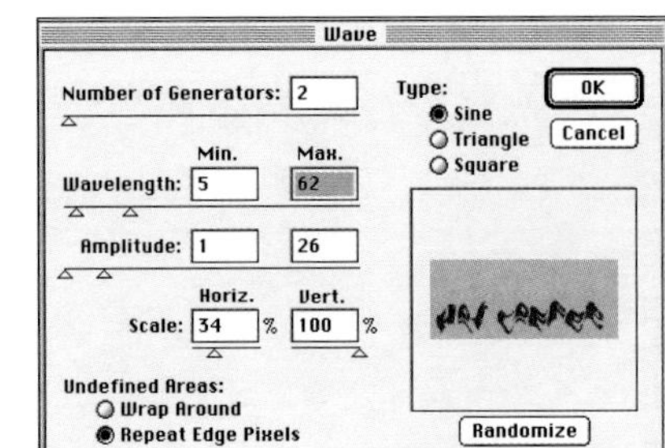


**3** Apply Filter➡Distort➡Wave. Fiddle with the numbers and sliders and radio buttons in the Wave dialog box until you like what you see in the preview. Even if you copy these settings you can get more choices by clicking the Randomize button.

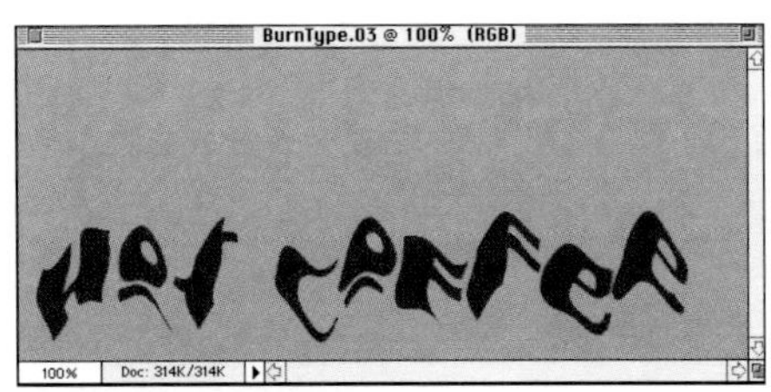

**4** Duplicate the Background layer. Switch the blending mode to Color Burn at 100% opacity.

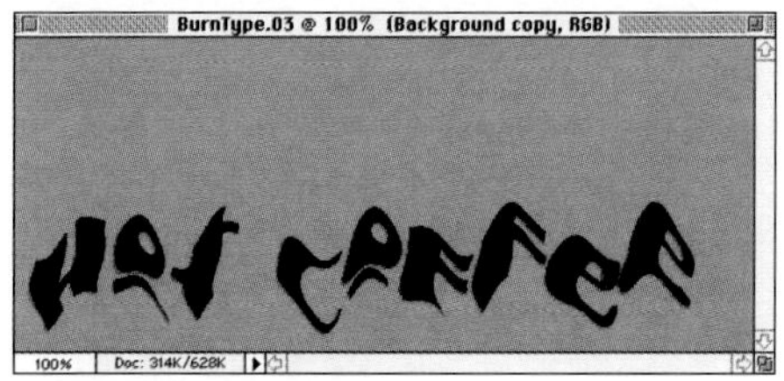


**5** Load Assorted Brushes. Use the "thunderbolt" Brush tip with the Smudge tool to drag smoky streaks through the type on the background layer.

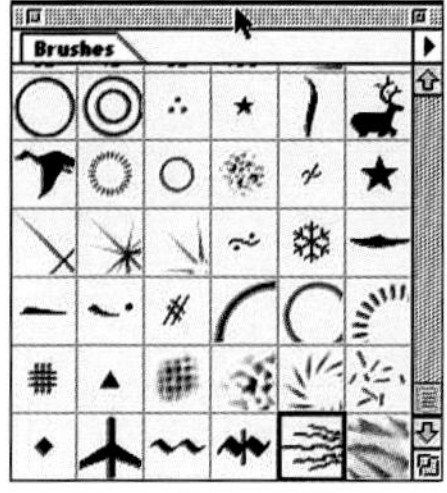


With the Background copy invisible, the Background layer should look something like this during the smudging process.

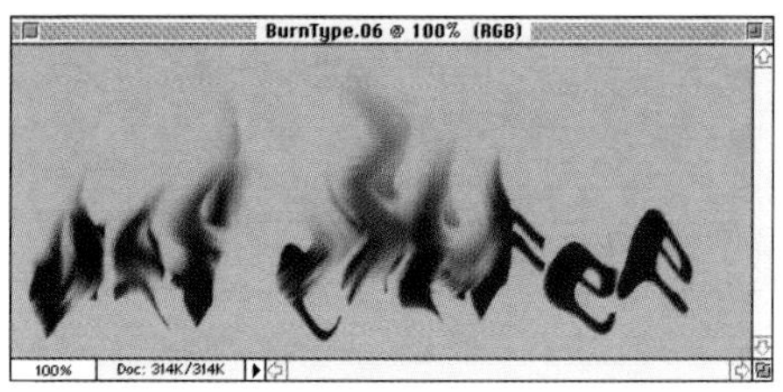


It's more fun to keep the top layer visible.

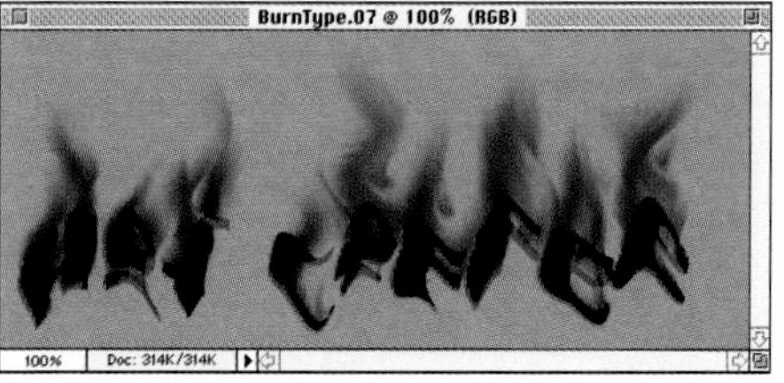

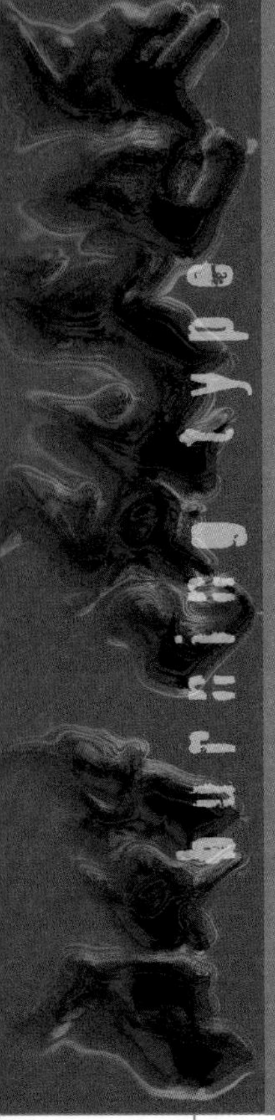


## VARIATIONS

Before you flatten or merge the layers, try some other blending modes. Here's Overlay at 100%.

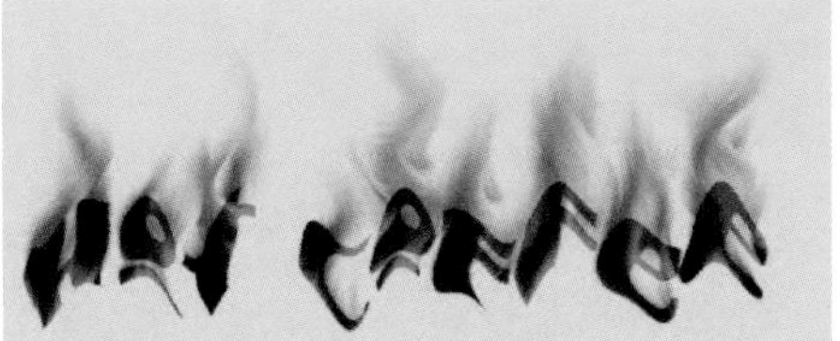

Saturation mode at 100%.

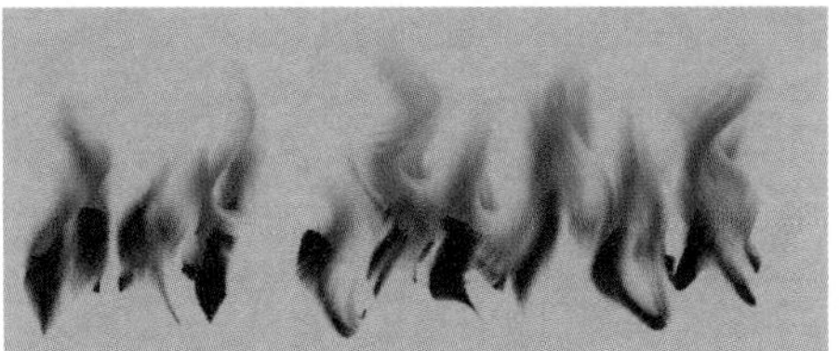

Difference mode at 65%. ■

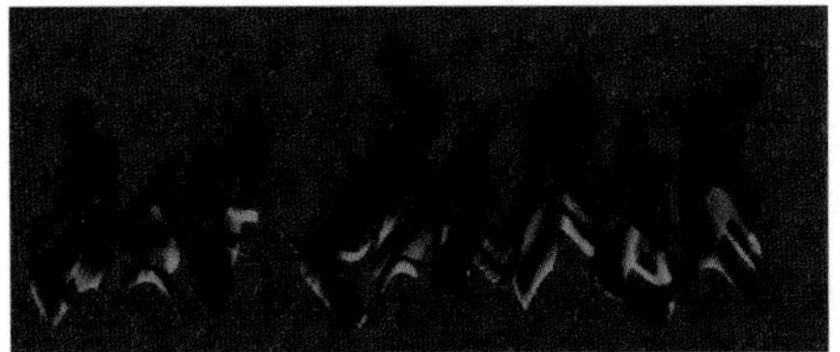

Sharron Evans created an experimental technique that I used to make an effect similar to the Cubist paintings of the early 20th Century. It's the single-pixel-column-and-row-arrow-drag method. We've got to come up with a snappier name than that.

This technique works best with high-contrast images. I'm using the EPS image "Cat," found in the Image Club➡Woodcuts folder on your *Photoshop Effects Magic* CD-ROM. I added color gradients and called the result "Pre-Cubist Cat." It's on the CD-ROM in the ArtStart folder.

**1** Double-click the Marquee tool and choose Single Column for the shape. Hold down the Shift key and click the image several times to establish an irregular array of vertical selection lines.

**2** Now hold down the (Option)[Alt] and (Command)[Control] keys while you click the keyboard's Right arrow 10 to 15 times. It may take a few seconds for your computer to complete this action.

**3** Change to the single row Marquee tool and Shift-click several horizontal selection lines.

**4** Repeat Step 2, this time clicking the Up or Down arrow to alter the image further. Your cat may look something like this.

## VARIATIONS

Wondering how to do the maneuver with diagonal lines? Rotate the canvas. Here's "Dog" from the Image Club➡Woodcuts folder on your Effects Magic CD-ROM.

I used Image➡Rotate Canvas➡ Arbitrary and typed in 45°. I chose clockwise arbitrarily because I'll rotate it back in the opposite direction when I'm finished.

I repeated the single-pixel drag technique for rows and columns, exactly as I did for "Cat." Then I returned the image to horizontal with the Rotate Canvas command. Rotating results in a lot of white space around the image, so I cropped it.

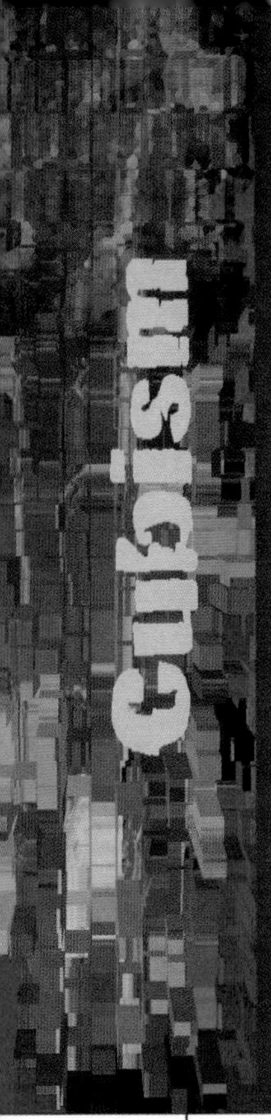


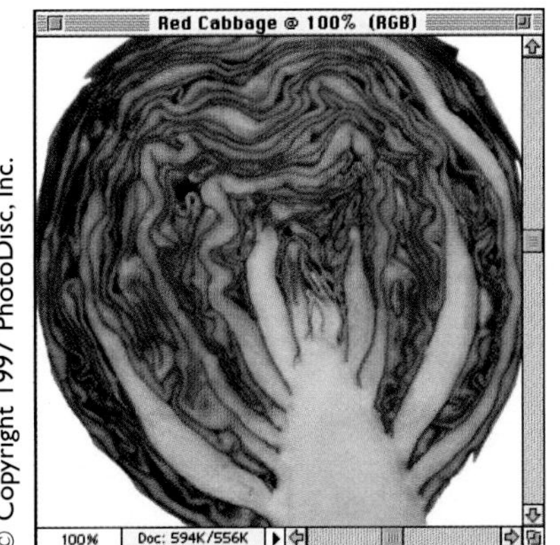


© Copyright 1997 PhotoDisc, Inc.

The larger the spaces between the rows or columns, and the greater the number of clicks on the arrow keys, the more abstract the image becomes.

I'm using a photograph this time. "Cabbage" is on the book's CD-ROM in the PhotoDisc folder. The image has intriguing organic shapes.

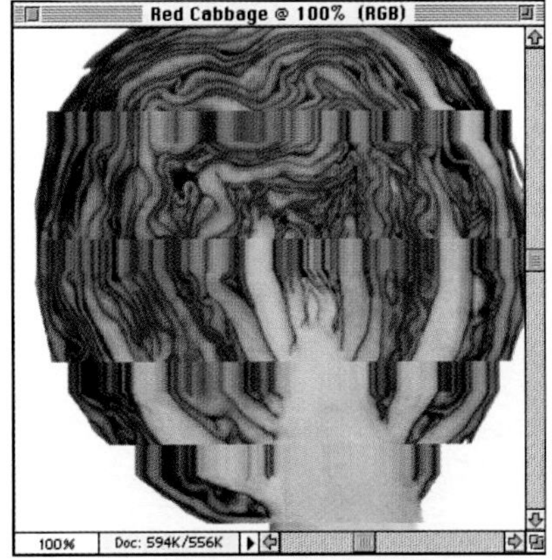


I used only four rows of selection lines and I moved them about 30 pixels.

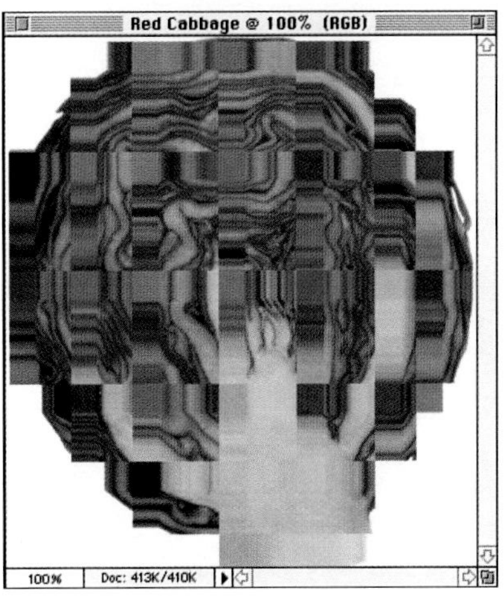


Then I used seven vertical colums and dragged them 30 pixels. The combination of geometric and organic shapes is intriguing.

To add some illusion of 3-D I used Filter➡Stylize➡Extrude, with the settings shown. ■

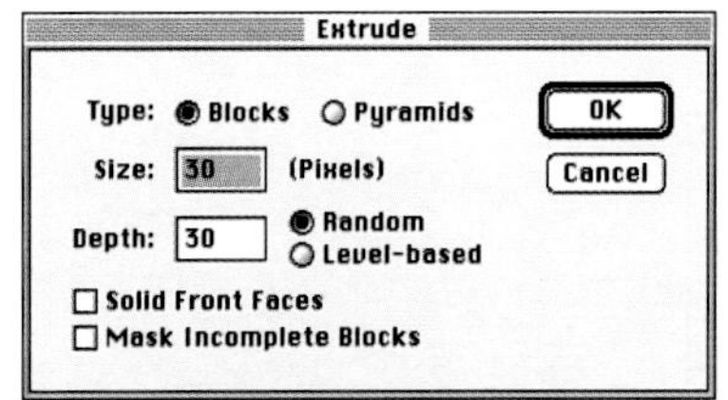

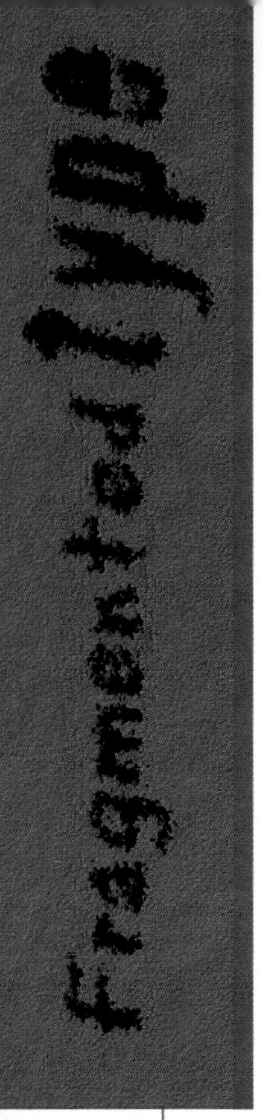


I wasn't sure what to name this section. "Grainy, Flaky, and Crumbly" sounded too much like a law firm.

These techniques work best with fonts that are already somewhat fragmented. Image Club's Fragile and Fajita are crumbly and flaky right out of the box, so I had a head start. I like the idea of pushing or exaggerating what's already there. If you want proof of that, see "Caricature" (page 34).

**1** Create a new file about 5×2 inches and fill it with a fairly dark color. I used a burgundy with CMYK values 51, 88, 12, 15.

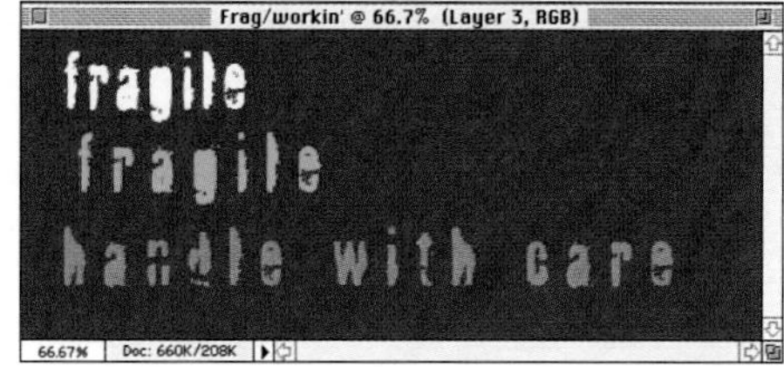


**2** Switch the foreground and background colors to make white the foreground color. Select the Type tool icon and click anywhere on your image to access the Type Tool dialog box. Select a font and point size. Type your text and click OK.

Repeat Step 2, using a light color such as this green (CMYK 45, 0, 45, 0). Increase the letter spacing. I used 8 points.

For the third line choose a foreground color of white and keep the same letter-spacing. Reduce the opacity of the layer to 50%.

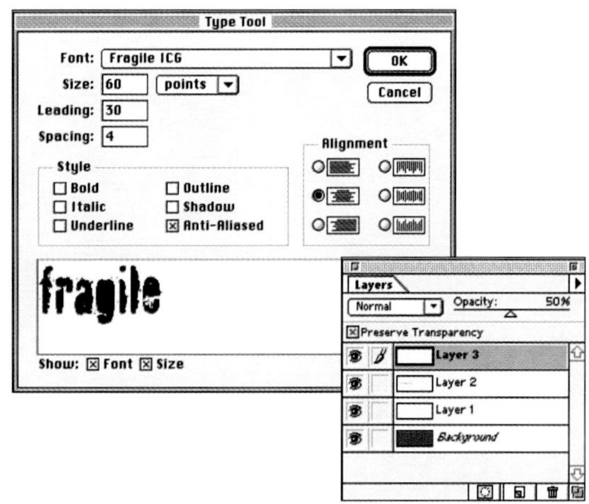


**3** Each line of type exists on its own layer. Use Layer➡Transform commands to resize, rotate, and reposition them. Flatten the image.

**TIP** **Use Free Transform to make more than one change on a given layer, or use the keyboard shortcut (Command-T)[Control-T].**

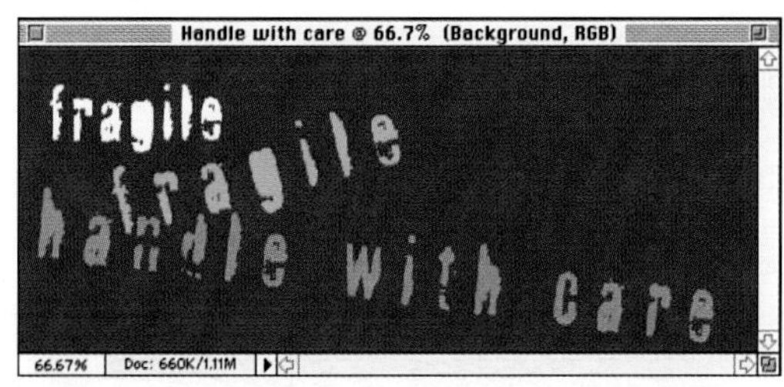


**4** Apply Filter➡Brush Strokes➡ Spatter (Radius 14, Smoothness 5). This will scatter pixels in the type, making the words practically illegible.

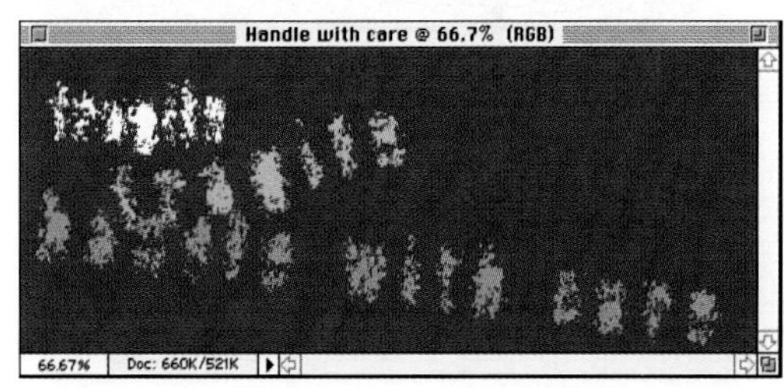


**5** Choose Filter➡Fade to fade the effect to about 50%. Save the image in preparation for the next step.

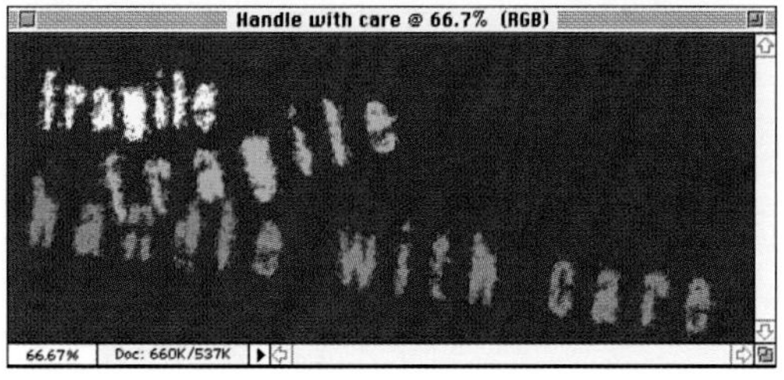

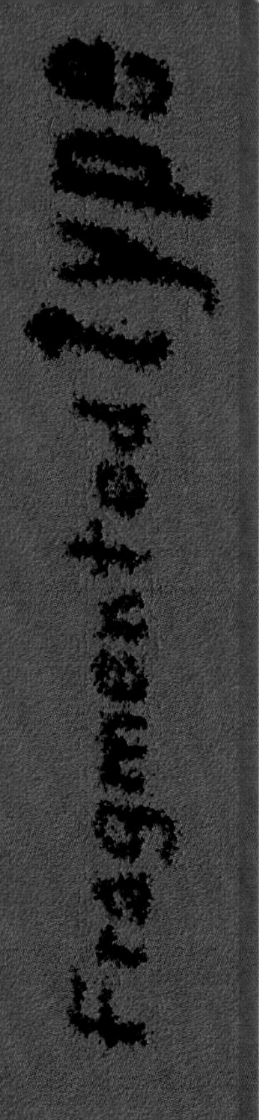


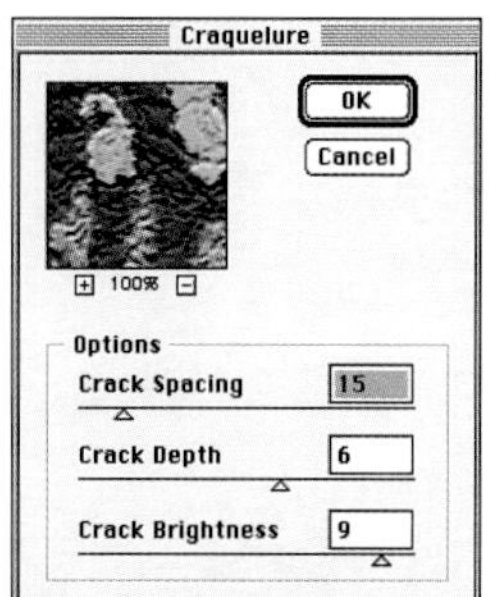


6 Apply Filter➥Texture➥Craquelure, using these settings. This creates a crumbly look with depth resulting from shadows and highlights.

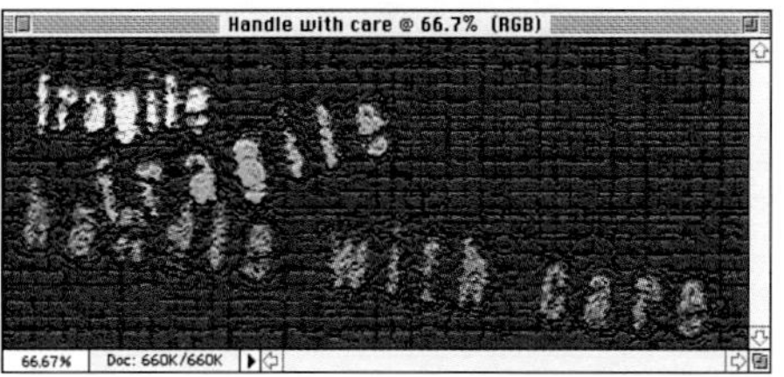


7 The effect will be more dramatic if you eliminate or tone down most of the cracks in the "wall" around the type. Use the Eraser tool with Erase to Saved checked, and vary the pressure as you restore smoothness to parts of the wall.

Eraser Options
Paintbrush
Opacity: 75%
Fade: steps
Erase Image
Stylus Pressure: Size Opacity
Wet Edges
Erase to Saved

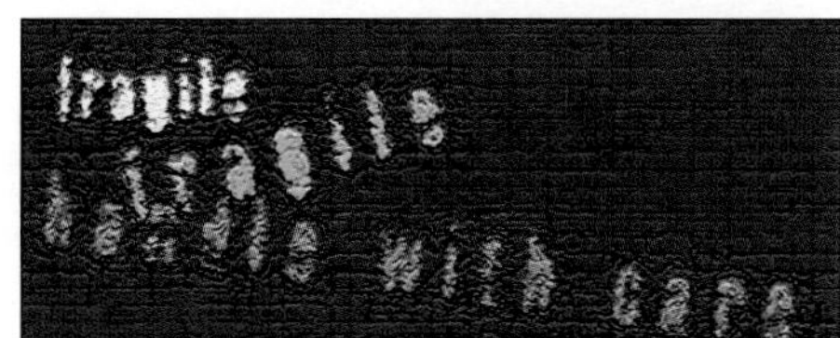

## VARIATIONS

Combining Film Grain and Spatter filters can make type look like sand. Open "Beach" in the ArtStart folder on the CD-ROM, or create it yourself.

**1** Create a new file about 3×1.5 inches. Fill with a sunny yellow with CMYK values 9, 6, 99, 1.

**2** Choose for the foreground color a dark brown such as CMYK 31, 59, 88, 43. Enter the text in Fajita font.

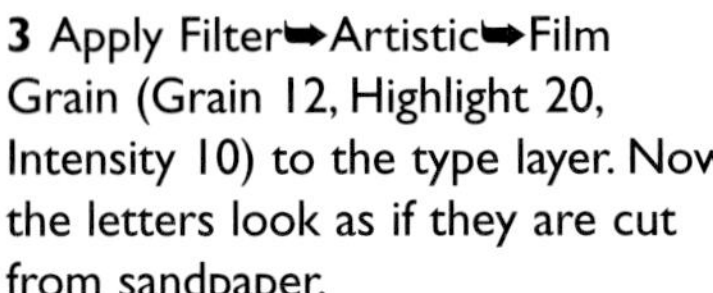

**3** Apply Filter➥Artistic➥Film Grain (Grain 12, Highlight 20, Intensity 10) to the type layer. Now the letters look as if they are cut from sandpaper.

**4** Flatten the image. Apply Filter➥Brush Strokes➥Spatter (Radius 12, Smoothness 4). Select Filter➥Fade to fade the Spatter effect until the type is legible, using Dissolve mode to enhance the graininess.

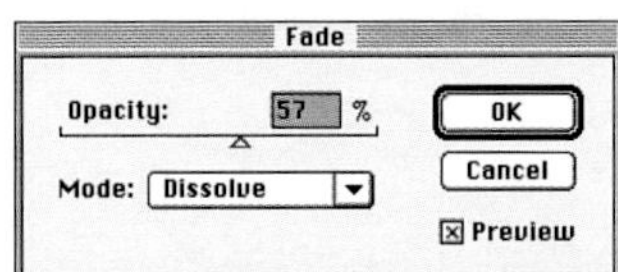

Adding a blast of wind produces a sandstorm.

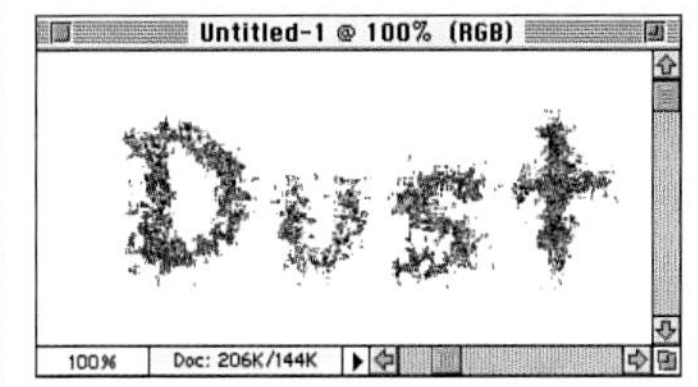


Apply Filter➥Stylize➥Wind (Blast), using either direction. Fade to taste, using Dissolve mode. ■

Here's how to add color to clip art and create the illusion of speedy movement using a combination of Photoshop techniques.

**1** Create a new file. Mine is 7×5 inches at 72 dpi.

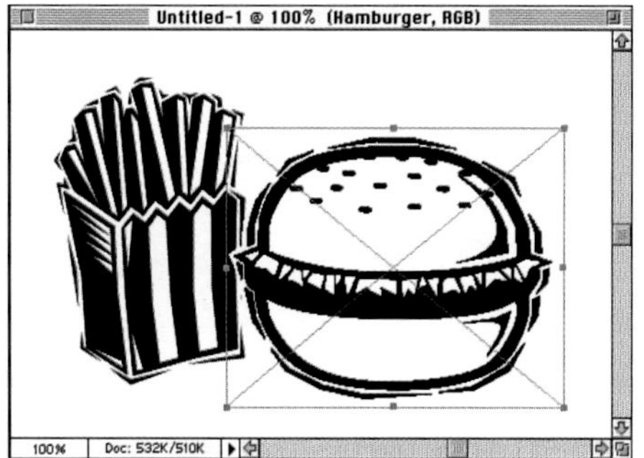


**2** Open or Place the images you want to work with. I am using the EPS images "Fries" and "Burger." You'll find them in the Image Club folder on the *Photoshop Effects Magic* CD-ROM.

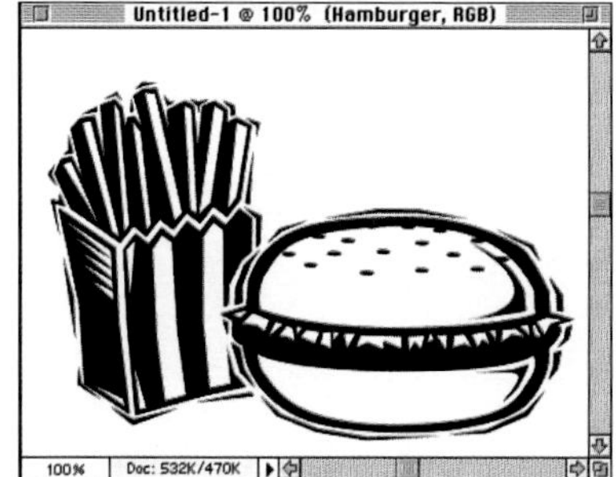


**3** Make the Hamburger layer active. Select Layer➡Free Transform. This puts a bounding box with handles around the burger. Move the top-center handle down to reduce the vertical size of the hamburger.

**4** Make the French Fries layer active. If it is not already behind the hamburger, use Layer➡Arrange to send it backward.

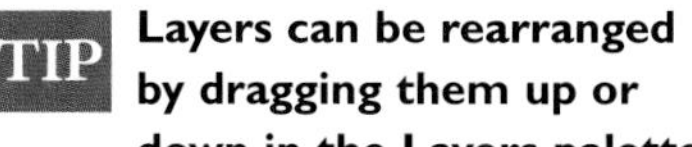

**TIP** **Layers can be rearranged by dragging them up or down in the Layers palette.**

**5** Transform the fries to make them a little more cartoon-like and active. Use Layer➥Transform➥Perspective to get a higher camera angle and Layer➥Transform➥Rotate to make the fries lean to the left. Flatten the image.

**6** Use the Fill Bucket to add flat color. Here are the CMYK values I used: French fries bag: 0, 91, 100, 0; French fries, dark areas: 26, 36, 92, 19; French fries, light areas: 11, 27, 91, 2; burger, beef and outline: 45, 36, 95, 53; lettuce: 73, 0, 96, 0.

**7** Use the Eyedropper to pick up the golden color that was used for the French fries' dark areas. Select the white area of the top half of the bun with the Magic Wand tool. Double-click the Gradient tool to display the Gradient Tool Options floating palette. Use these settings.

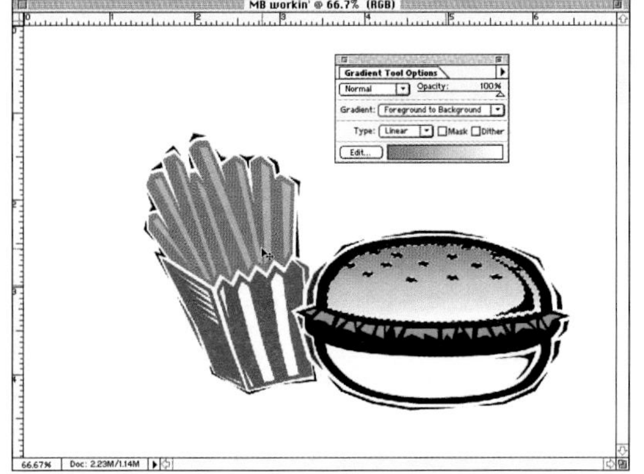

**8** Click the Gradient tool at the top center of the bun and drag straight down to the bottom of the selection. Repeat for the lower half of the bun, but drag upward from the bottom. Here's the image fully colored.

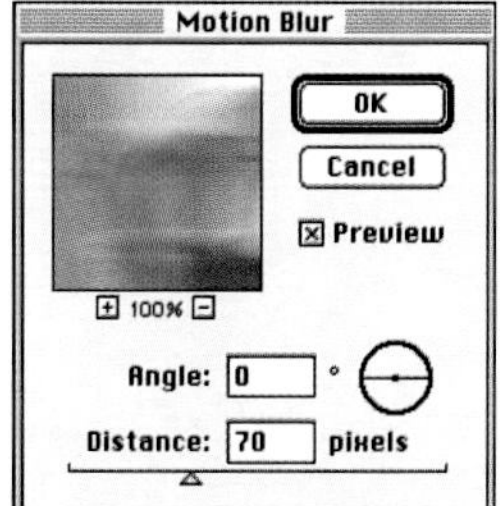


**9** Apply Filter➥Blur➥Motion Blur (Angle: 0, Distance: 70) to the entire image. Do not save.

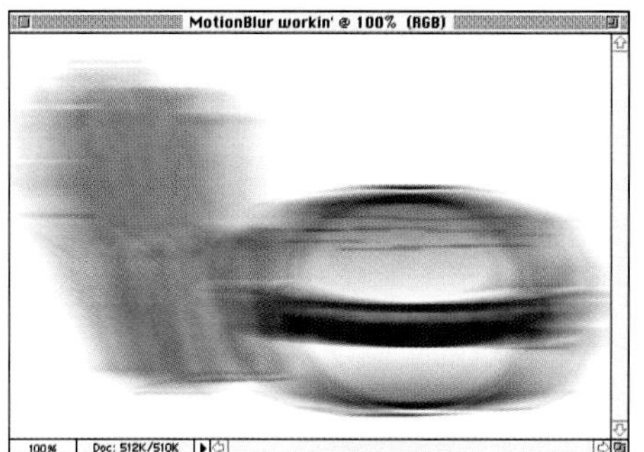


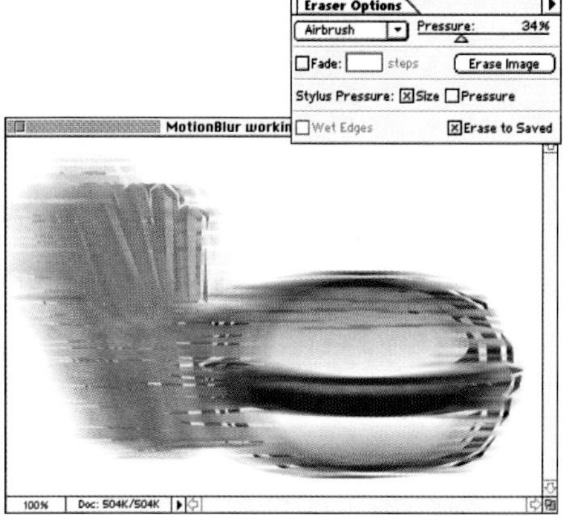


**10** Double-click the Eraser tool to open the Eraser Options palette and set it to Erase to Saved. Use the Eraser to remove portions of the blur. Using Airbrush mode at 25-50% pressure with a large brush enables you to bring back the saved edges on the right side of the French fries and the hamburger softly. Use tiny brush sizes to create streaks of the original across the blur. When you're happy with the effect, save the image.

I need more white space on the left before the next maneuver, so I can add some with the Image➥Canvas Size command.

Canvas Size
Current Size: 504K
Width: 7.167 inches
Height: 4.625 inches
New Size: 608K
Width: 8 inches
Height: 5 inches
Anchor:
OK
Cancel

**11** Select the fries by throwing a loose lasso around them. Include plenty of white space, as shown. Then choose Select➥Feather (12 pixels).

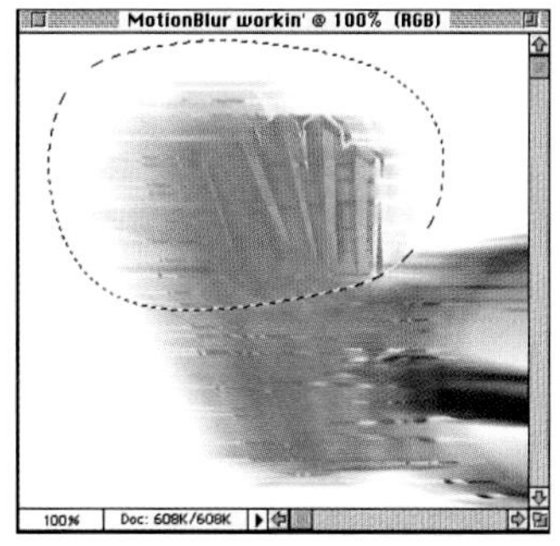


**12** Choose Filter➥Distort➥Shear and adjust the curve to make the fries appear to be "blowing" toward the left.

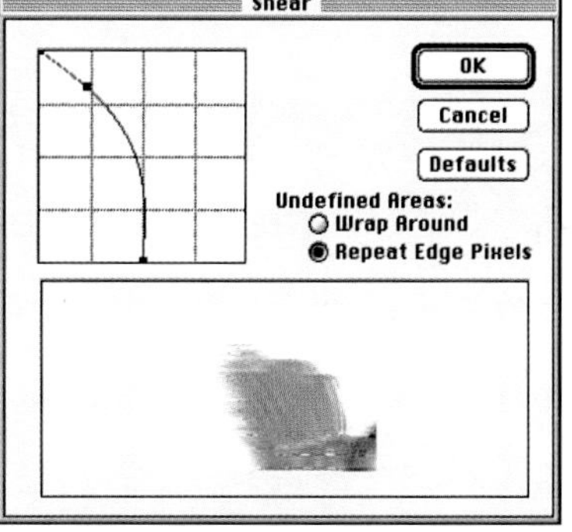

All done. Have some lunch. Maybe the next version of Photoshop will have a cholesterol filter! ■

The Pen tool and the Paths palette are used here to create a tulip garden.

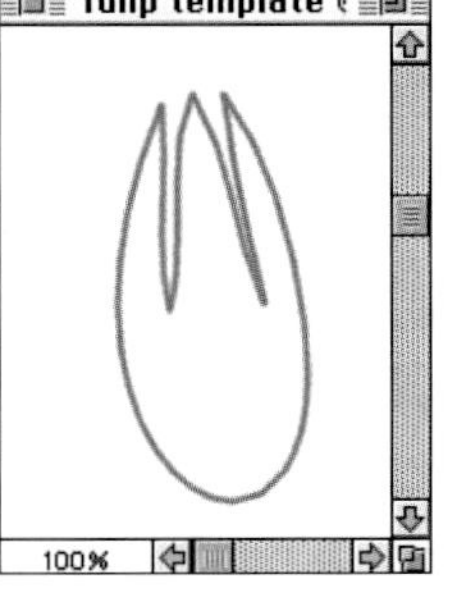


**1** Open "Tulip" in the ArtStart folder on the *Photoshop Effects Magic* CD-ROM.

**2** Use the Pen tool to make a path for the outline of the tulip. Start by clicking on the tip of the left-hand petal and dragging slightly down and to the left. Next click the bottom curve and then drag to the right. Continue around the shape, clicking without dragging, and finish by clicking again on the first point. Don't worry if your path doesn't match the template yet.

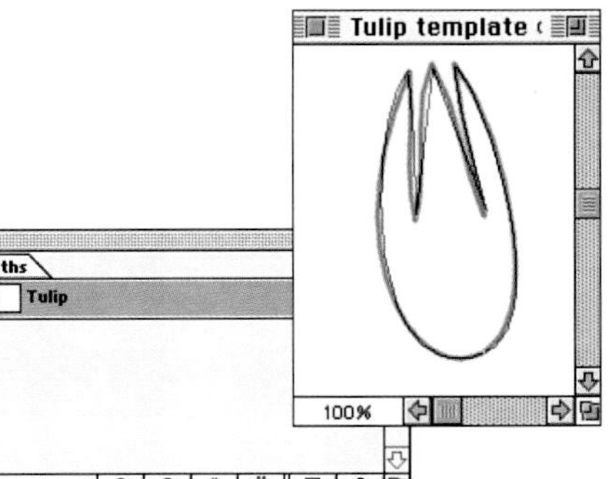


**3** Drag to select the Direct Selection tool in the toolbox. Adjust the curves and points of your path as you want. Use the Save Path command in the Paths palette menu to save the working path as "Tulip."

**4** Create a new file for your tulip garden. Mine is 4×2 inches. Drag and drop Tulip from the Paths palette of the template to the new image window.

**5** Choose bright colors for both the foreground and the background. Red with CMYK values 0, 90, 90, 0, and lavender with CMYK values 34, 60, 0, 0 will do nicely for our first tulip. Choose "fill path" from the Paths pop-up menu. Notice that you can choose to fill with any percentage of the foreground, background, black or white. Use 75% of the foreground color.

To see how the fill looks, turn off the path using the Paths palette menu (but don't delete it!)

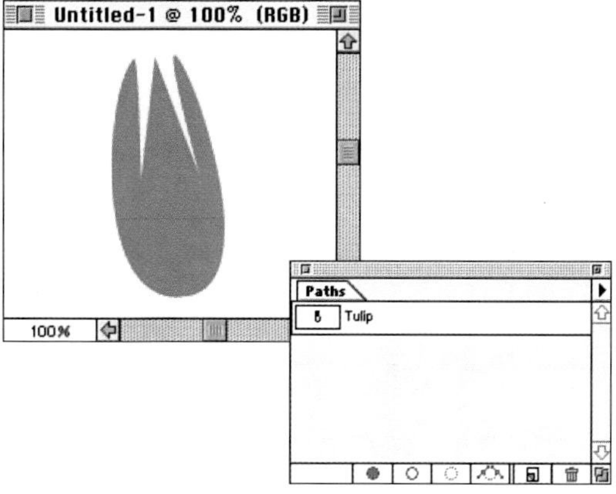


**6** Copy the path to several new locations by selecting it in the Paths palette and clicking on its outline in the image with the Direct Selection tool. Hold down the (Option)[Alt] key as you drag the path.

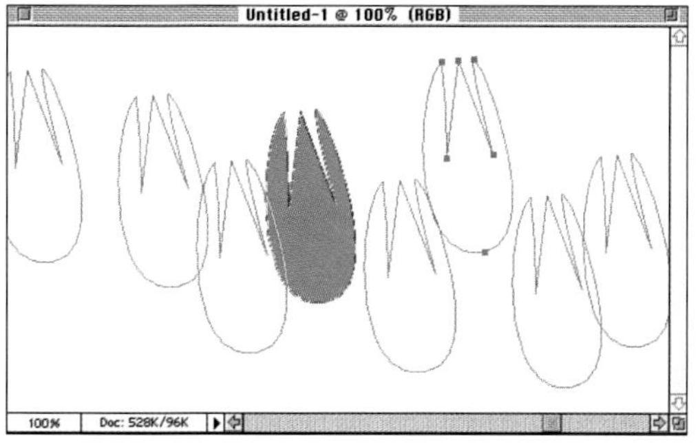

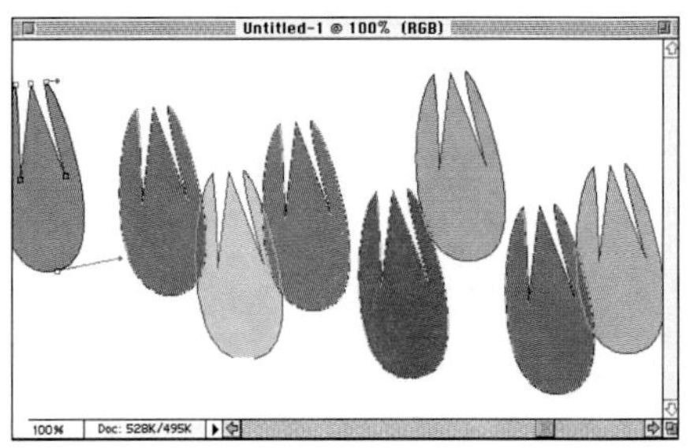


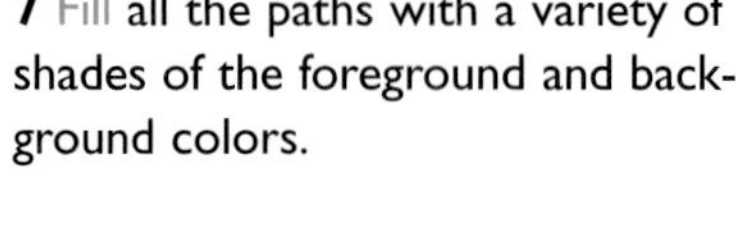

7 Fill all the paths with a variety of shades of the foreground and background colors.

I'll stroke (outline) all the tulips at the same time. First I'll choose a brush tip.

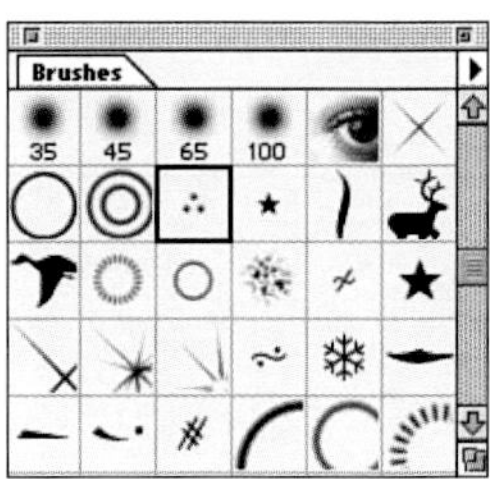


8 Load Assorted Brushes and choose the brush shown here.

9 Select all the paths by dragging a rectangle around them with the Direct Selection tool.

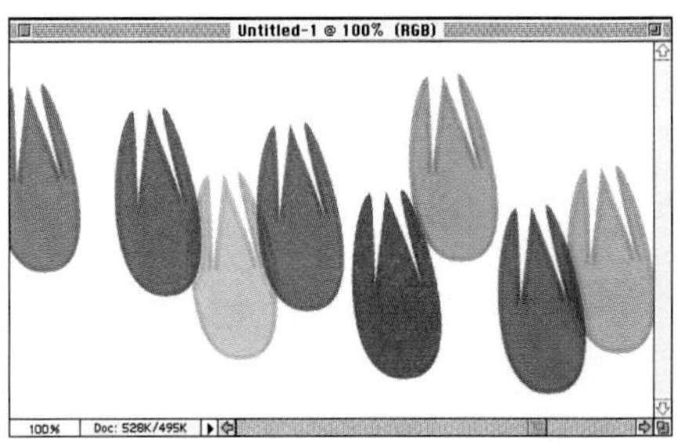


10 Choose the Burn tool from the Stroke Path menu. This results in a slightly darker edge around each tulip.

All you neeed now are stems and leaves.

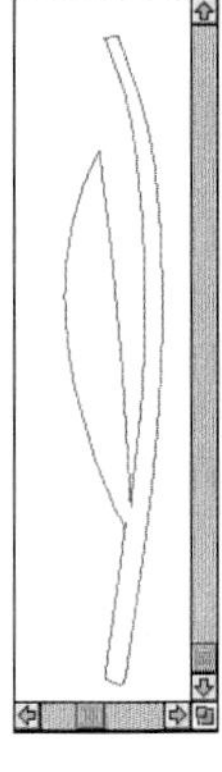


11 Open "Stem & Leaf path" in the ArtStart folder on the CD-ROM.

**12** Drag and Drop the path name from the Paths palette to your tulips image, and make all the copies you need with the (Option-click)[Alt-click] and drag maneuver.

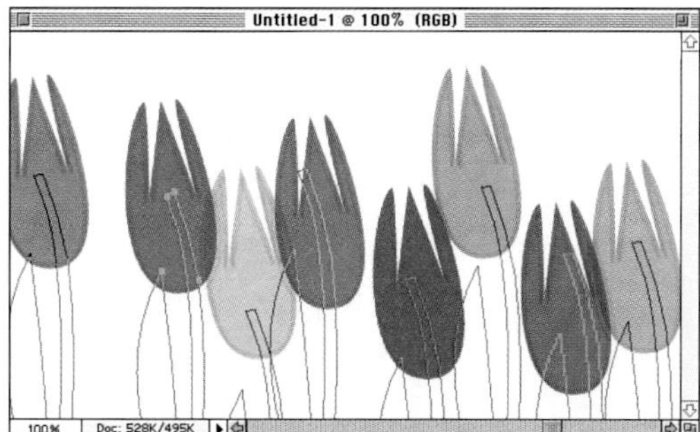


**13** Use the Direct Selection tool to reshape the curves and position the anchor points of each stem and leaf. Notice that you can work with path elements even if they are outside the image's "live" area.

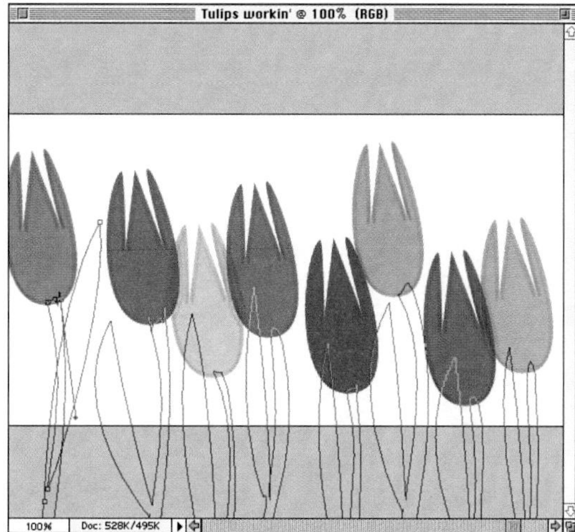


**14** I chose to add another $^1/_2$-inch of canvas to the bottom of the image, using Image➡Canvas Size.

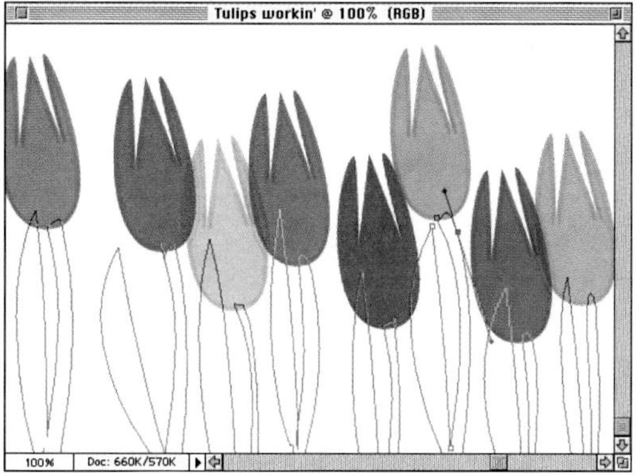

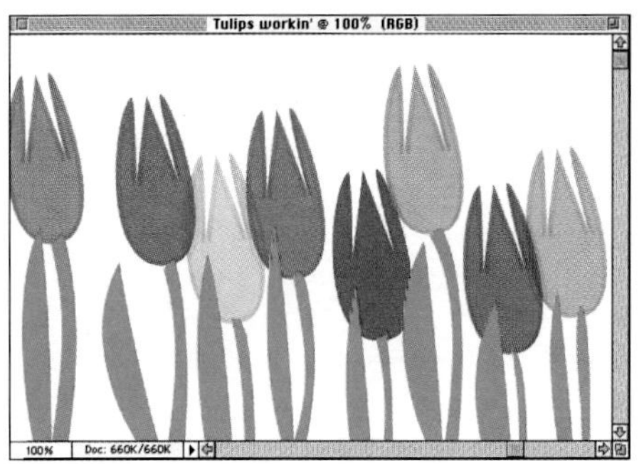


**15** Select the paths by dragging with the Direct Selection tool and fill all the stems and leaves using 100% green with CMYK values 78, 0, 98, 0.

## VARIATIONS

Numerous variations are possible with the same paths you have. Just change the fill and stroke variables.

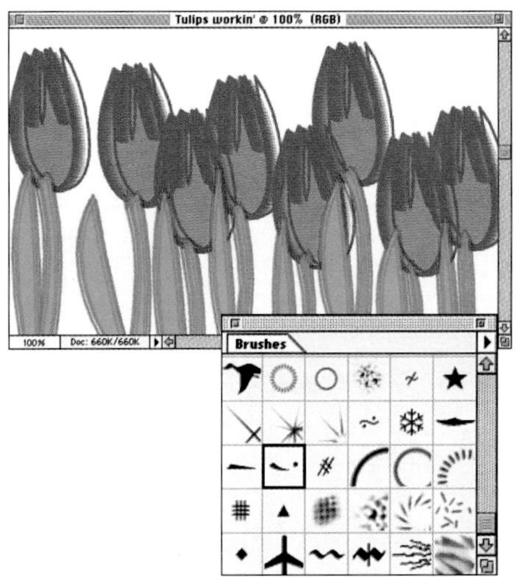


This version has all the tulips filled with 100% pink CMYK values 9, 57, 0, 1. I made the stroke with red after offsetting the paths a few pixels and using the brush shown. I used the "three-dot" brush to stroke the stems and leaves with a darker green than the fill, but I did not offset the paths.

Here's the result of opening up one of the tulips by adding anchor points for the outer petals and converting their tips to smooth points. I copied the open flower several times and filled them with yellow.

I resized one of the new flowers by converting it into a selection so it could be scaled by the Layer➡ Transform command. I pasted this smaller flower into a new path on the same document, where I copied it several times and filled it with orange in Multiply mode. The stems were done quickly with the Line tool at 7 or 9 points wide. ■

If you want to add color to a line art feast, Darken Mode is your friend because it enables you to be sloppy without messing up the line work. This technique is useful for roughs and comps or a spontaneous, casual look in finished art.

**1** Create a new file 4×2 inches.

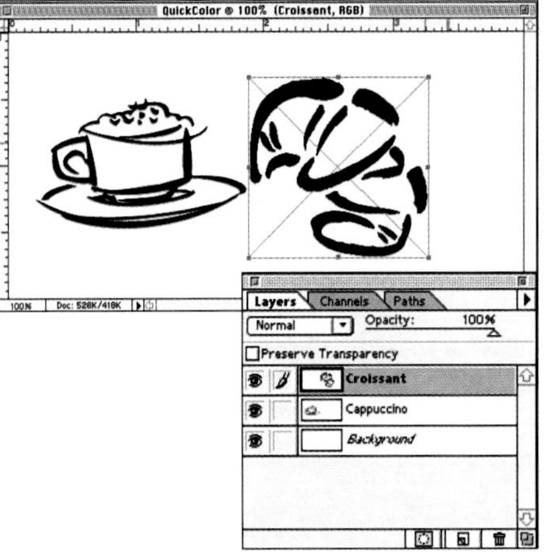


**2** Open or place your line art image. I'm using the EPS clip art "Cappuccino" and "Croissant." You'll find them in the Image Club folder on the *Photoshop Effects Magic* CD-ROM.

**3** Use Layer➡Free Transform to adjust each images size and position. Use the Escape key to cancel a transformation. Press (Return) [Enter] when you are satisfied. It may take a few maneuvers, including rotation and vertical size reduction, to make the croissant look as if it is lying on the table. Now the fun part—applying color!

**4** I chose CMYK 24, 40, 88, 13 for a toasty tan color. Double-click the Airbrush tool to open the Airbrush Options palette and set it for Darken mode, then spray some color on the croissant. Vary your pressure. Notice that the black lines are unaffected because they are already darker than the tone you are adding.

**TIP** **There's no need to be precise with your application of color. The style of the original line art is casual and quick. Use a similar attitude when tossing in some color.**

**5** Airbrush a bit of cinnamon and chocolate onto the foam, using the same color and technique.

**6** Switch to a different color for the cup and saucer. I used a blue composed of these CMYK values: 42, 0, 1, 0. Use a Fat brush and make sure you stay in Darken mode. Paint the cup with vertical strokes that fade out as you go from left to right (and vice versa) to leave a highlight on the cup. Vary pressure to achieve this "casual gradient" effect.

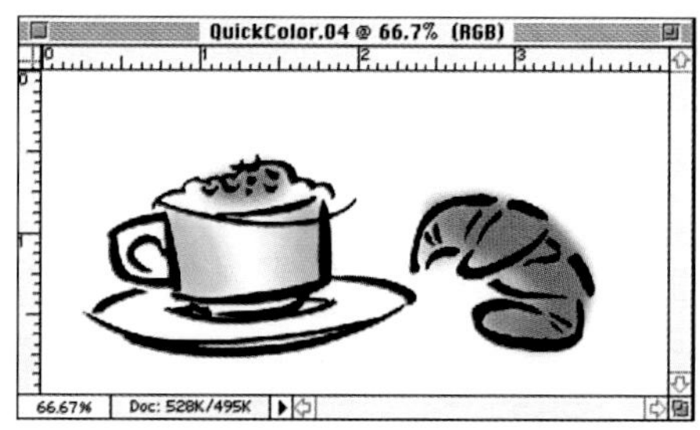

**TIP** **Mouse users may find using the Fade box and typing in a large number of steps the ideal way to achieve the "casual gradient." I used 60 steps. With this method tablet users won't need to change stylus pressure during the stroke.**

**7** The mocha-flavored steam rising from the foam is made with the Smudge tool. I used about 50% pressure in Normal mode and made a few zigzag drags going up and fading out.

## Variations

I added some casual color to the "Spanish Coffee" clip art in the "Sketches on the Town" folder on the CD-ROM.

This time I wanted to color the black areas and leave the white untouched. It's no problem using Lighten mode.

Here's the clip art "Lobster" from Image Club. I applied quick strokes of red with a fat Paintbrush in Darken mode. I also checked the Wet Edges checkbox to get the look of watercolor, with pigment pooling up around the brush strokes.

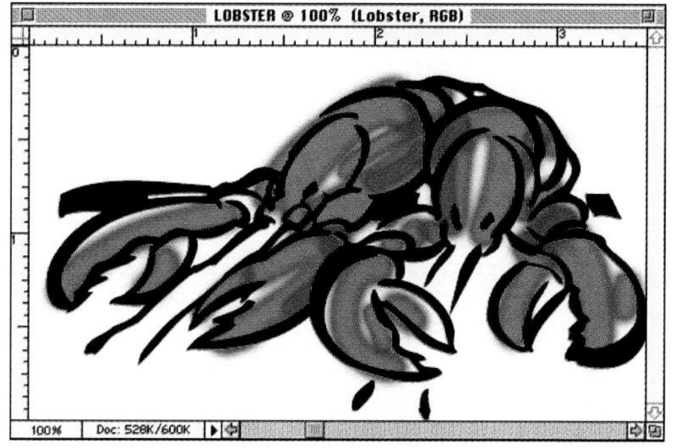


I added some strokes and dabs in light orange and lavender, using Multiply mode. Multiply mode does not disturb the black outlines but does allow light colors to influence darker ones.

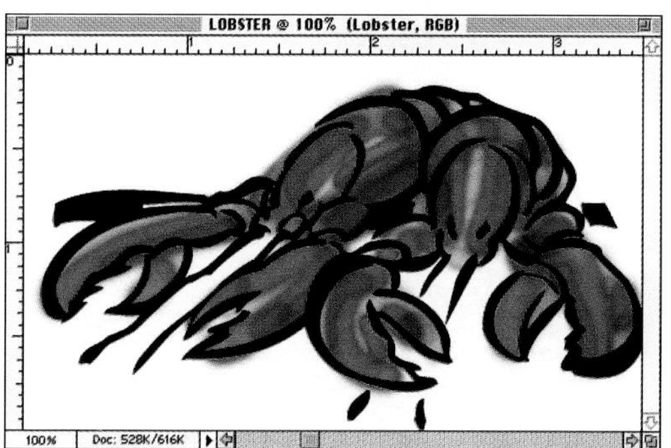

To preserve transparency or not to preserve transparency—that is the question. The answer depends on what you want to do to the image.

With Preserve Transparency turned on, transparent pixels cannot be changed in any way. If you want to change the color of type on a layer, for example, turn Preserve Transparency on to restrict color to the type. If you want to alter the shape of the type, you should turn Preserve Transparency off so that the pixels can change without restriction.

**1** EPS clip art is ideal because the "white" areas are actually transparent. I placed "Big Sandwich" and "Pie" (from the Image Club➡ Sketches folder of your *Photoshop Effects Magic* CD-ROM). Each placed image resides on its own layer, automatically named.

**2** To change the black line art to a color, turn on Preserve Transparency for its layer and fill the layer with the new foreground color. I used green with CMYK values 81, 28, 100, 22 for the Sandwich layer and blue with CMYK values 91, 68, 8, 3 on the Pie layer. Only the lines will be affected because everything else is transparent.

**TIP** **Press (Option-delete)[Alt-delete] to fill the selection with foreground color.**

Want proof that the white areas of the images are transparent? Make the Background layer invisible and the telltale checkerboard appears.

**3** To color transparent areas, you will have to turn off Preserve Transparency. Use the Paint Bucket to fill sections that are completely enclosed. Switch to the Brush tool to paint in areas that have "leaks," such as the pie crust or the lettuce in the middle of the sandwich.

**TIP** **If you are painting with colors that are lighter than the green or blue outlines, use Darken mode. This makes it easier to avoid covering the outlines accidentally. Painting in Darken mode is also a great way to touch up edges that weren't completely filled with the Paint Bucket.**

**4** Enter some text. To change the color of the type without affecting the transparent pixels that make up the rest of the layer, turn on Preserve Transparency. Then use any technique you like for filling or painting the letters.

When you distort type, turn off Preserve Transparency.

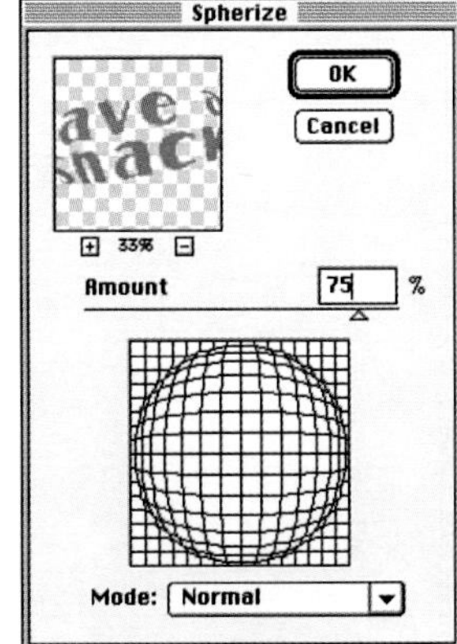


**5** Make a rectangular selection around the type. This will establish the center for the effect and prevent the computer from trying to distort all those transparent pixels! Apply Filter➡Distort➡Spherize (75%, Normal).

**6** Just for fun, repeat Step 5 but turn on Preserve Transparency. The distortion cannot be seen in the transparent areas surrounding the original type.

## Variations

With Preserve Transparency, you can do much more than simply switch colors. You can paint or draw with no fear of going outside the lines. Here's some "plain" type.

This satin finish was created by the Airbrush in some pastel colors dragged across the whole word.

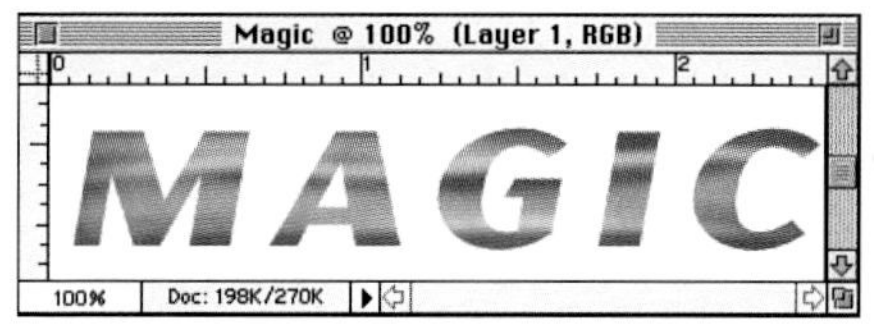


There may be times when you'll deliberately ignore the rule to turn off Preserve Transparency before using a distortion filter. I applied a displacement map to the type with Preserve Transparency on.

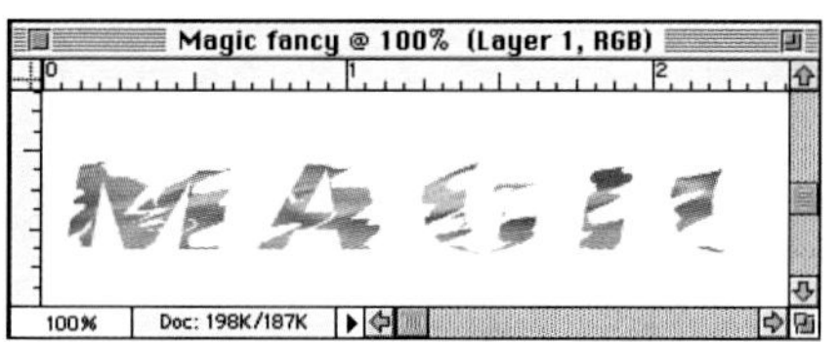


Then I used the Fade command to switch to multiply mode. ■

# Part III

## Starting from Scratch

You don't need to begin with a photo, clip art, or type. You can create amazing effects in Photoshop starting with a blank canvas. Here's where you'll learn how to exploit Photoshop's power as a painting program.

You'll use and create custom brushes and paint with light, gradients, and textures. You'll make patterns and abstract art. You'll even learn to make digital frames for your artwork. Finally, you'll discover a great way to recycle traditional art materials.

Four of these techniques work much better if you have a graphics tablet: "Bristle Brush," "Rough Sketch," "Textured Brush," and "Cobblestones." I hate to nag, but you should really get a tablet already.

Just about anything can serve as raw material for Photoshop art. A scribble. A doodle. Scan some art by a two-year-old (make sure she signs a release form).

Drawing circles is a good way to practice control of your stylus or your mouse. And when you fill an area with circles you have the first stage for colorful abstract art.

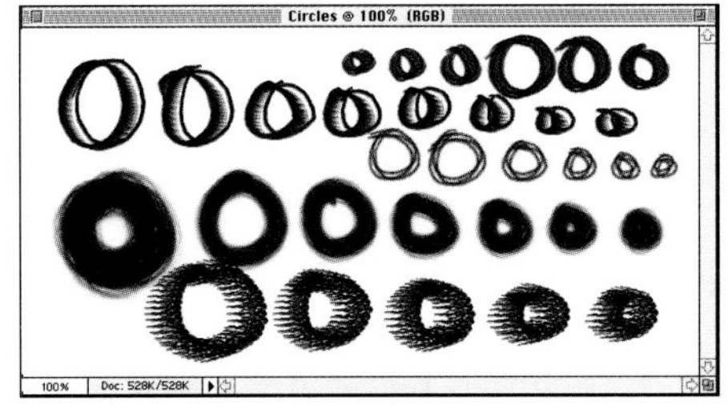


**1** Create a new file and choose a background color of white. Paint some circles in a variety of sizes and with an assortment of brushes. Or open "Circles" in the ArtStart folder on the *Photoshop Effects Magic* CD-ROM.

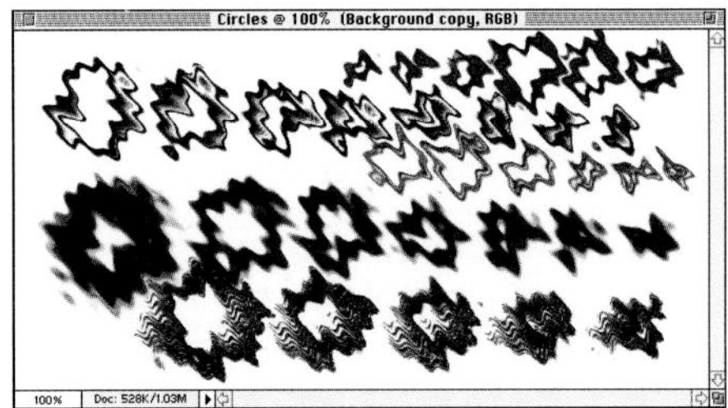


**2** Duplicate the layer and apply a filter effect to this Background Copy. I used Filter➥Distort➥ Ripple (200, Large).

**TIP** **When you expect to be exploring a number of variations of a single source image it's convenient to "stack" them as layers. You can quickly see how any combination of layers looks by controlling the visibility, opacity, and blending modes. Use the Save As command for the versions you want to keep.**

**3** Rename the Background Copy layer "Ripple 200," or whatever describes the effect you used.

**4** Duplicate the original layer again. I'm naming the new layer "Pinch 100" because that's the next effect I plan to use. Here's the Pinch layer at 100% opacity, covering up the original (Background) circle layer. The Ripple layer is invisible for the moment.

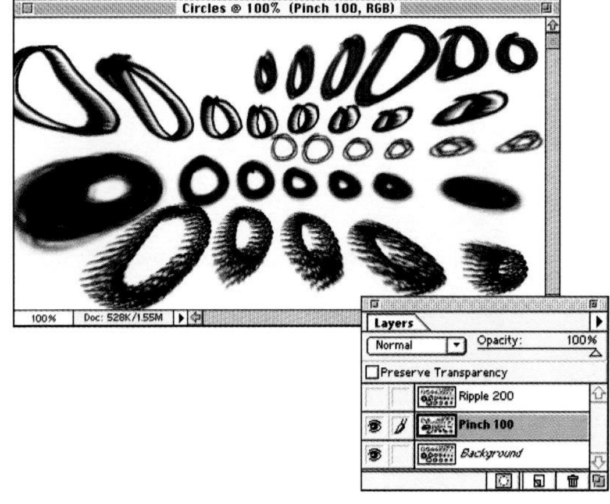


Let's throw in some color.

**5** Make the Ripple layer visible and active. Use the Transparent Rainbow Gradient preset. I used these settings. Darken mode produces rich color without affecting the black areas.

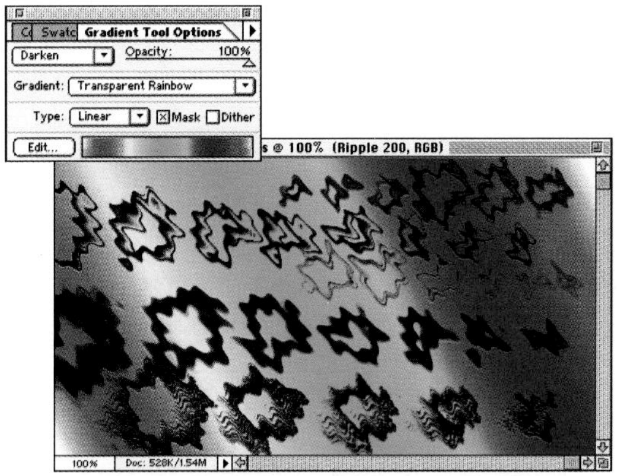


**6** Make the Ripple layer invisible and the Pinch layer active. Change the gradient type to Radial. I dragged from the middle of the image to the edge.

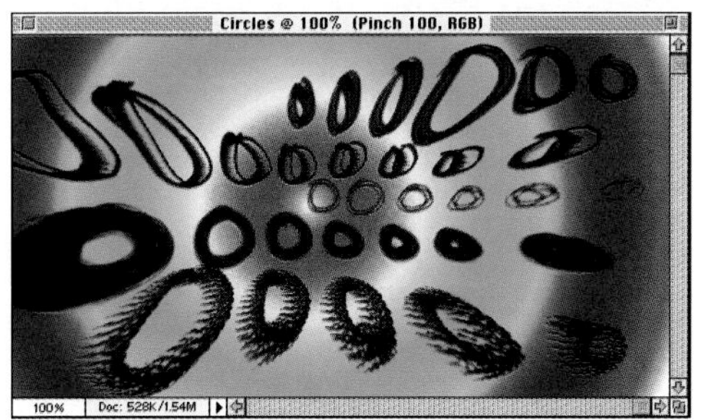

Now you're ready to play around with combinations. I ended up with this for my final image.

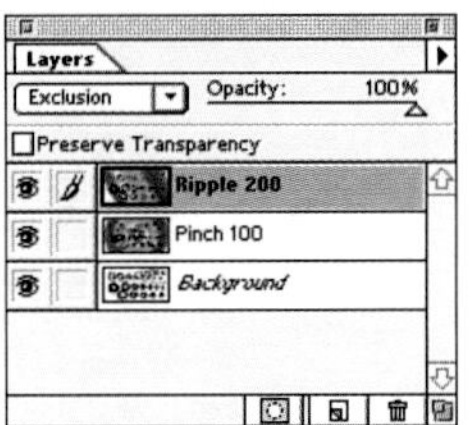


The Layers palette shows Exclusion is the Blending mode for the Ripples layer. I used Difference mode for the Pinch layer.

## VARIATIONS

We'll start with a scribble and turn it into embossed string-art.

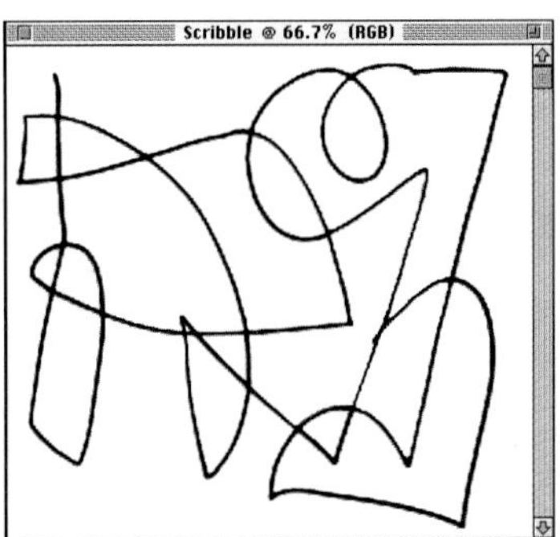


Make a scribble with the Brush tool or use my "Scribble" in the ArtStart folder on the CD-ROM. I used a single stroke with no variation in pressure. Lots of curves and angles crossing each other at several points create a variety of interesting shapes.

Use the Paint Bucket tool to fill all the shapes and the background with various colors. I used a Tolerance of 100 in the Paint Bucket Options.

See "Cartoons" (page 122) for tips on filling line art with flat color.

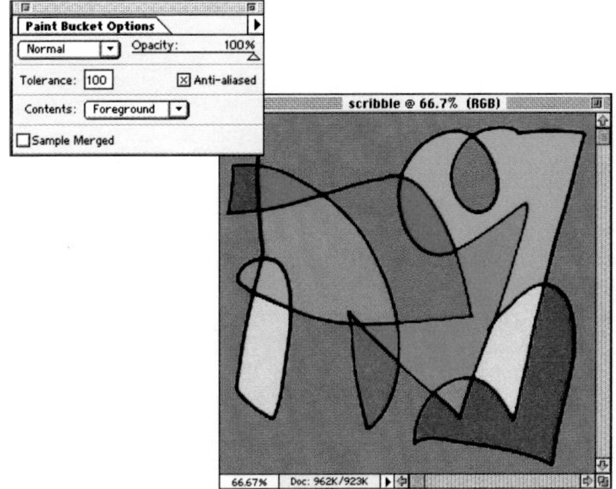


Apply Filter➡Stylize➡Emboss (Angle: 143, Height: 6, Amount: 104). All your fills become gray, but the line stands out in multicolor relief.

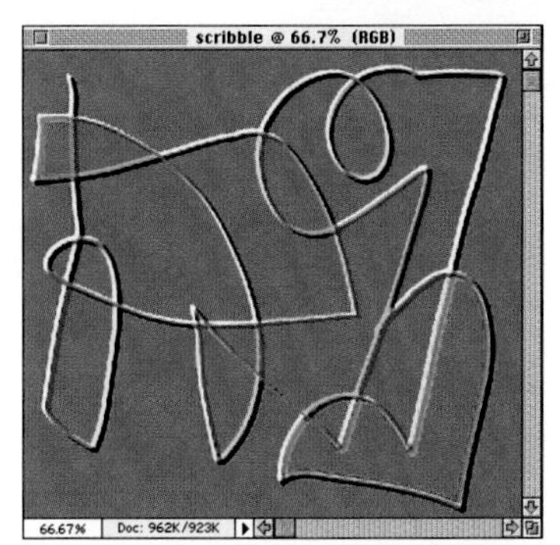


Here's an alternative to the Emboss effect. I applied Filter➡Distort➡ Polar Coordinates (Rectangular to Polar) to the colored scribble.

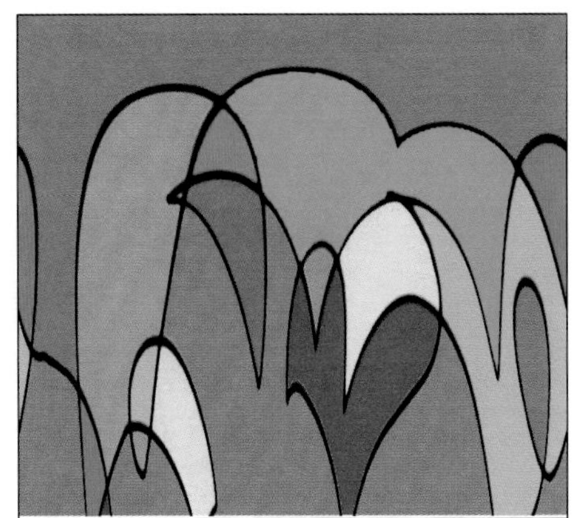

The results are quite different with the Polar to Rectangular conversion.

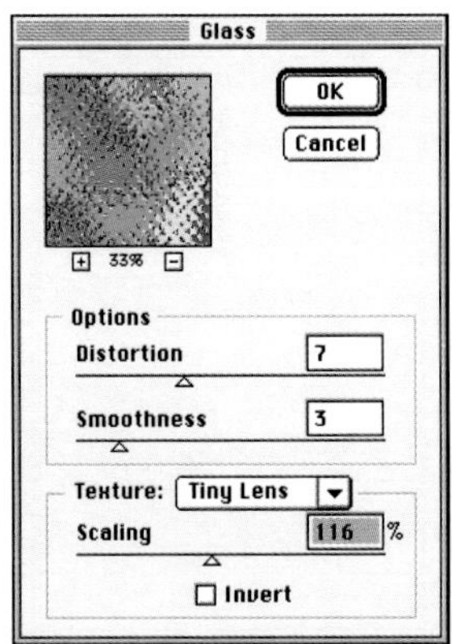


Or, apply Filter➥Distort➥Glass with these settings:

Crop out the excess background to focus on the great optical effects that would make any shower curtain proud!

If you like Polar Coordinates effects, see "Unconventional Tools" (page 210). ■

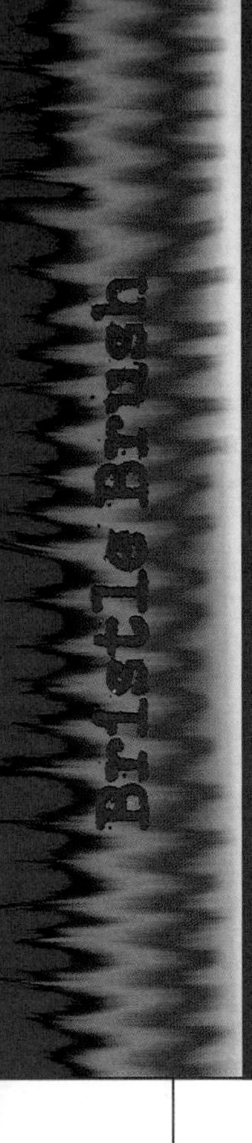


You may already be using some of the alternative brush sets included with Photoshop. If not, this is as good a time as any to try some. And you'll learn how to make custom brushes from scratch. This is especially useful if you don't have Fractal Design Painter, or don't want to switch back and forth between Painter and Photoshop so often. This technique works best with a tablet and stylus.

The default brushes comprise 16 round tips, hard- or soft-edged, in various sizes.

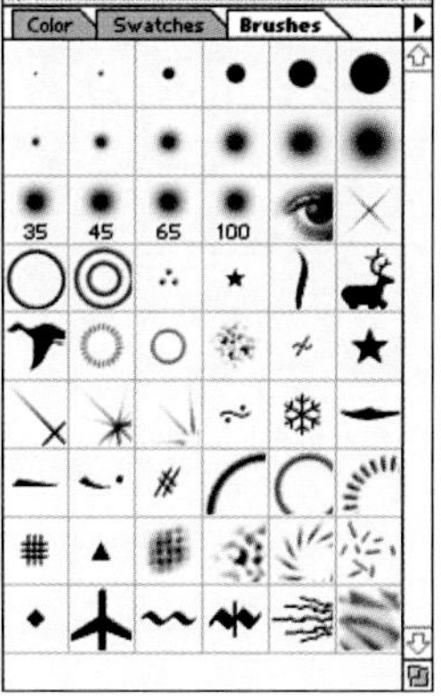


**1** Load Assorted Brushes.

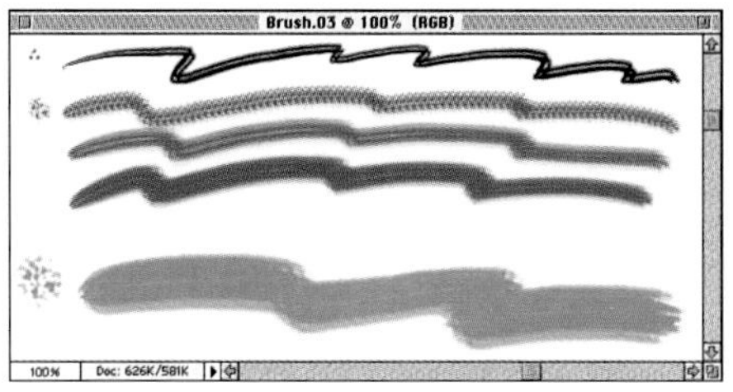


**2** Experiment with some of these brushes. You might not always be able to predict what their strokes will look like just by looking at their "footprints."

The "3-dots" brush makes a sketchy line. You can explore it further in the "Rough Sketch" technique. See page 198.

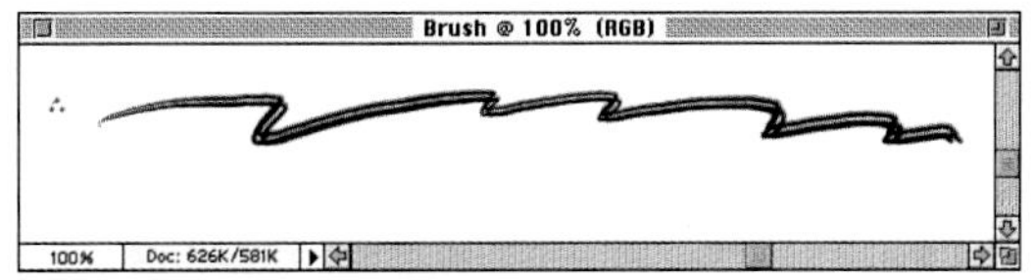


**3** The first stroke in this group was made by the brush I call Medium Bristles, and it looks like tire tracks. We can change that.

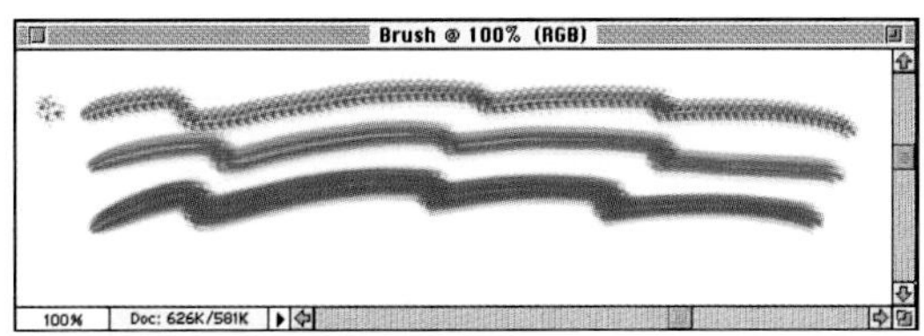


Find Brush Options in the Brushes palette menu. (This is not the same as the Paintbrush Options palette.) Change the default spacing to a lower value. I used 10% for the next stroke, making a dry brush look. Lower the spacing to the minimum 1% to get a smoother stroke, as if the brush is loaded with paint.

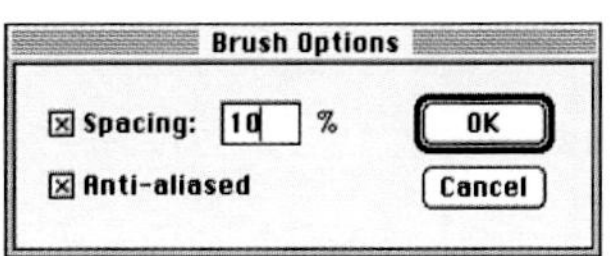


These 2 strokes were made with the "Large Bristle" brush, which is identical to the previous one except for its size. It makes "tire tracks," too, but from a truck. Again, change the spacing to a low enough percentage to get a smooth effect. I used 3% here.

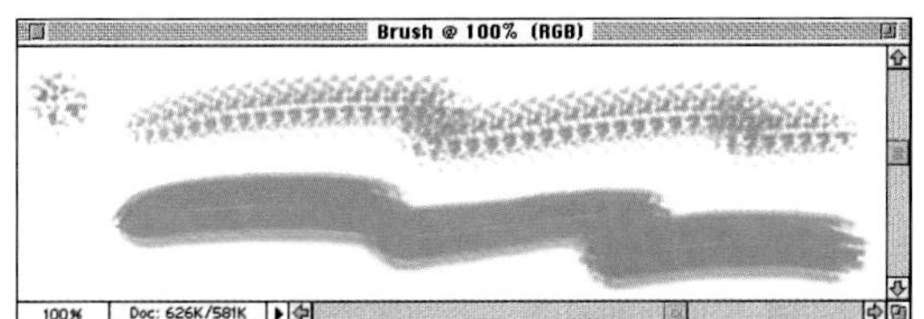


Let's create a new brush.

**1** Open a new grayscale file about 4×4 inches at 72 dpi.

**2** Double-click the Line tool and enter 1 point for line width. Accept the other default variables.

**3** Hold down the Shift key for perfect horizontals and make several short strokes as close together as you can. Make sure you leave a little white space between the strokes. Each of these 1-pixel lines will become a "bristle" in your brush.

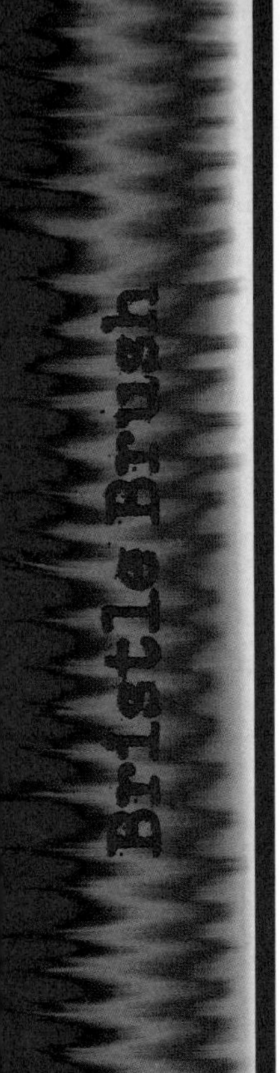


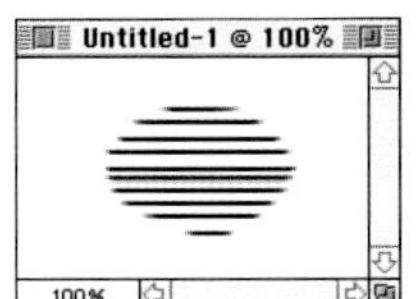


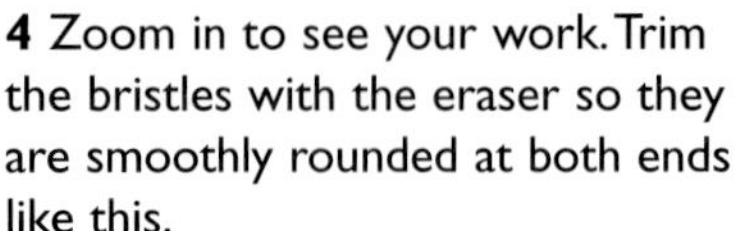

**4** Zoom in to see your work. Trim the bristles with the eraser so they are smoothly rounded at both ends like this.

**5** Drag a selection rectangle around the lines. Choose Define Brush from the arrow menu of the Brushes palette. Voilà! Your new brush occupies a space in the palette.

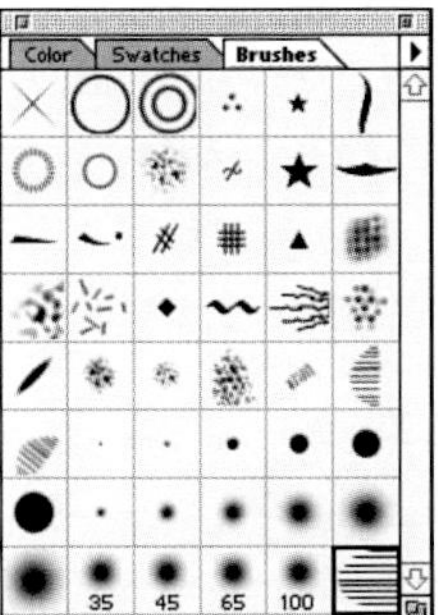


The Brushes palette shown here contains the basic default set plus "Magic Brushes" in the ArtStart folder on the *Photoshop Effects Magic* CD-ROM.

**6** Remember to change the annoying default 25% spacing to a lower number in the Brush Options box.

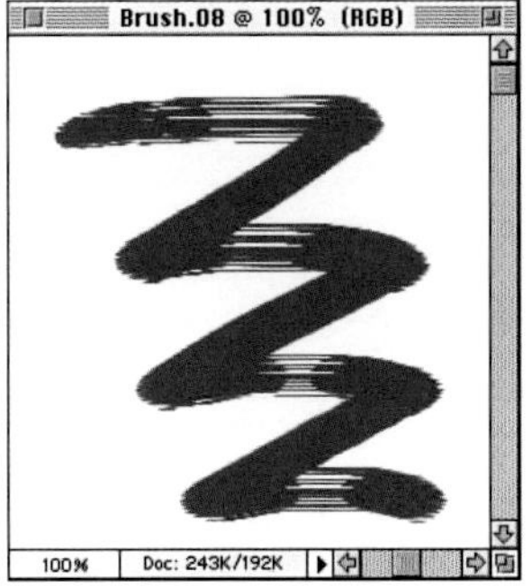


Test your new brush with a zigzag drag. It looks streaky like a "dry" brush when you drag horizontally, but full of paint when you drag in any other direction.

## VARIATIONS

You can probably guess how to make a brush tip that looks streaky when you drag vertically. Go back to step 5. Before you use the Define Brush command, go to Layer➥Transform➥Rotate 90° CW.

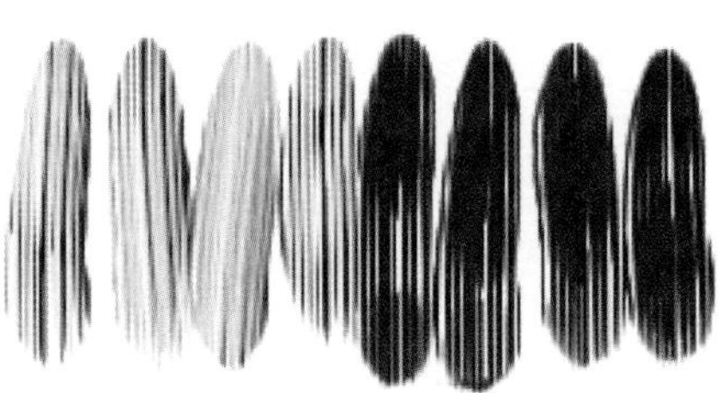

I made eight vertical drags with this new version. Then I switched to the Eraser tool, keeping the same brush, and dragged over the first four strokes.

To make the background design for this section's thumbtab I filled an area with the Yellow, Violet, Orange, Blue gradient and used the Smudge tool (75% pressure) with my new vertical bristle tip. I alternated downward and upward drags through the colors.

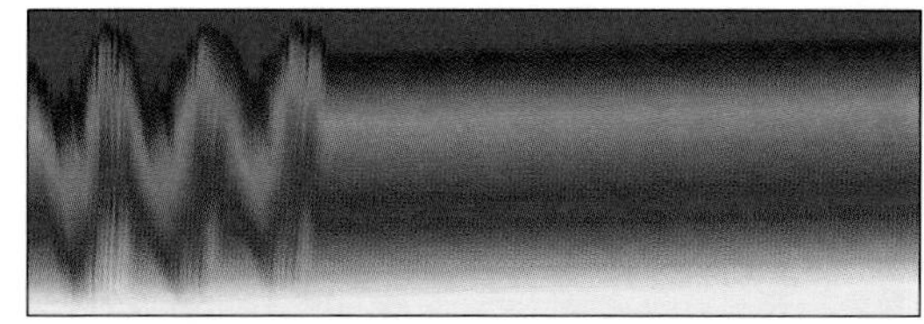

Once you have a horizontal bristle brush it's easy to make motion blur effects just by dragging the Smudge tool across the image. Each stroke should go in the same direction. ■

Didn't you love to pop the bubbles when they came wrapped around something fragile? Don't you still love to? A single circular selection becomes the basic element for a 3-D pattern, and its "op-art" variations.

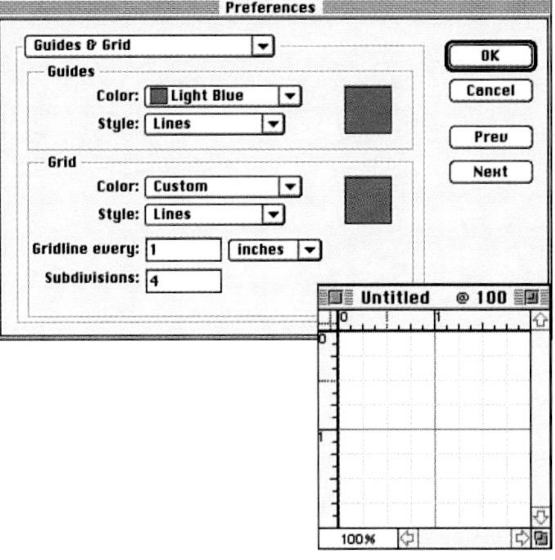


**1** Create a new file 2×2 inches, 72 dpi. Use View➥Show Grid and View➥Snap To Grid. I'm using a gridline every inch, and a subdivision every 1/4 inch. Use File➥Preferences➥Guides & Grid if you need to adjust your grid.

Normally I hate precision, but exactitude will be helpful in creating the pattern tile.

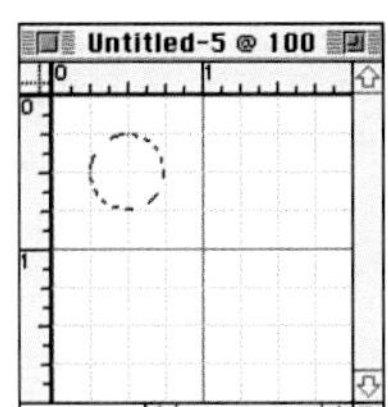


**2** Use the elliptical Marquee. Place your cursor at the center of one of the grid quadrants and hold down the (Option)[Alt] and Shift keys. Drag to make a perfect circle 1/4 inch in diameter.

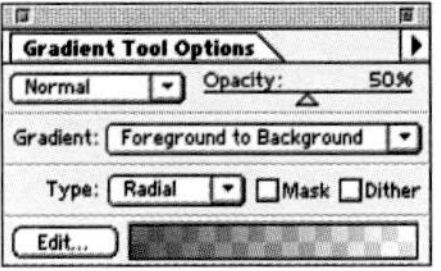


**3** Double-click the Gradient tool to open the Gradient Tool Options palette and choose these settings.

**4** Switch to default colors. Drag the gradient line from the lower-right edge of the circle through the center and finish at the upper-left edge. Your "bubble" is lit from the top-left.

**5** Use Layer➡Transform➡Numeric to increase the size of the circle by 125%.

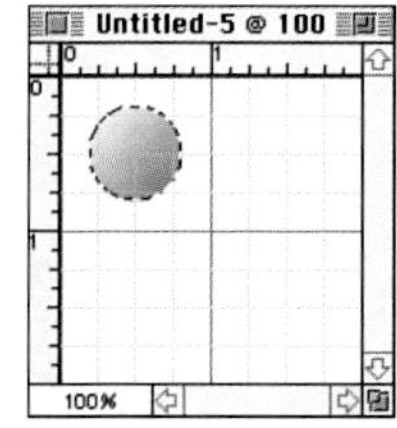


This is the basic element of the pattern. Next you'll prepare the tile for a seamless fill.

**6** Copy the shaded circle into each of the other quadrants by holding down the (Command)[Control] and (Option)[Alt] keys while dragging the circle into place. Drag another copy to the exact center of the image window. The Snap To Grid function will help your accuracy.

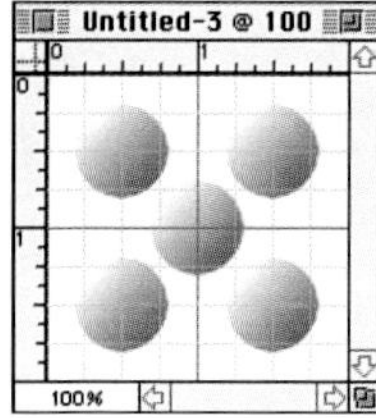


**7** Use the rectangular Marquee to make a selection like this.

**8** Select Edit➡Define Pattern to establish your selection as a pattern fill.

**9** Create a new file and use Edit➡Fill, choosing Pattern for the contents.

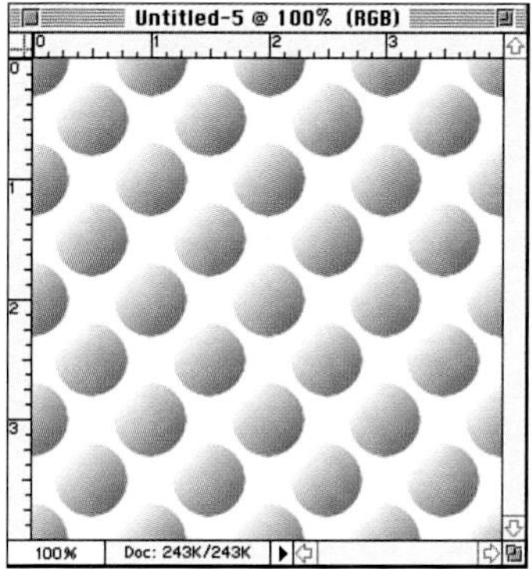

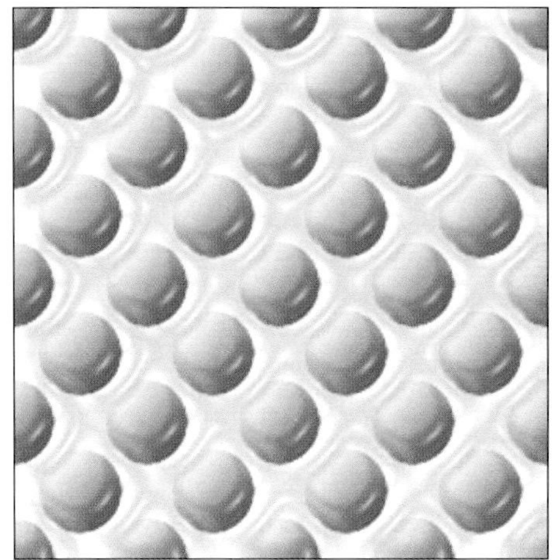

**10** Finally, apply Filter➥Artistic➥ Plastic Wrap (Highlight 11, Detail 6, Smoothness 10).

## VARIATIONS

I used these settings in the Gradient Tool Options palette to add a metallic look.

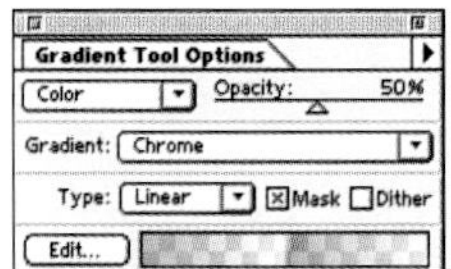


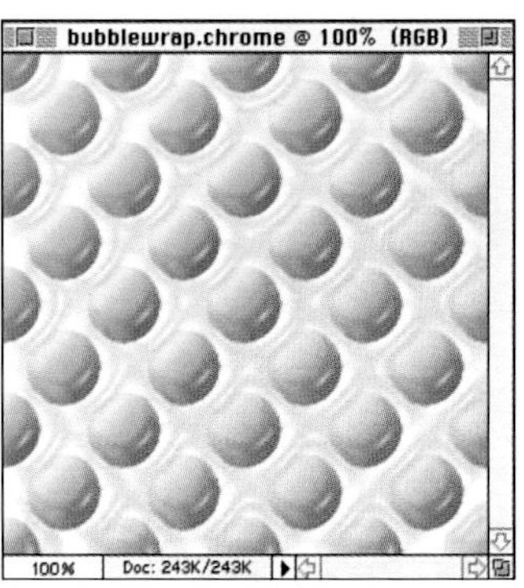

After Step 9, fill with a gradient in Color mode. Then apply Filter➡Distort➡Spherize (100%) and get this op-art design.

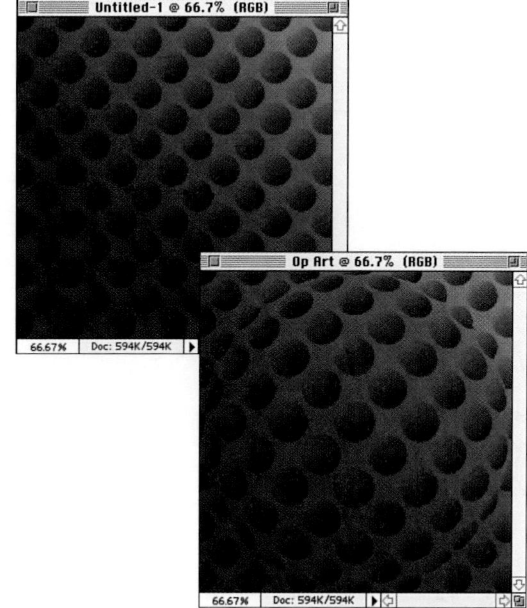


If you omit the center bubble in Step 6, your pattern fill consists of columns and rows. I've also added a solid color fill in Multiply mode.

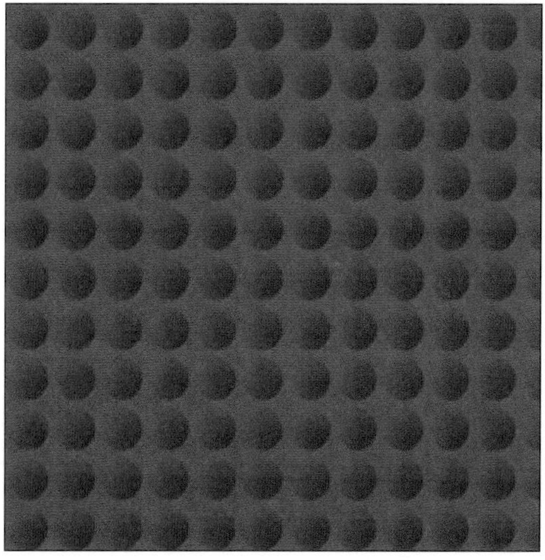

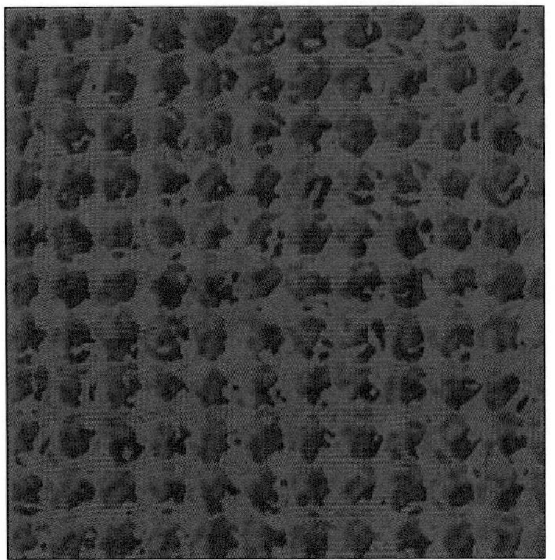

Then I applied Filter➡Distort➡ Ocean Ripple (Size 6, Magnitude 7) to produce this pattern of blobs.

To have more space around each bubble, skip Step 5.

Take this "more space" variation, and fill the columns with color, using a different apply mode for each. I used CMYK values of 58, 0, 15, 0 for the foreground color.

**1** Select the leftmost column with a rectangular marquee. Select Edit➡Fill using Color mode at 50%.

**2** Select the next column and fill using Darken mode at 35%.

**No need to redraw the marquee for each column, just drag the marching ants to the right.**

**3** For the third column, use Lighten mode at 100%.

**4** In the fourth column, apply the Difference mode at 25%.

**5** Finally, fill the last column with Color Burn mode at 75%. ■

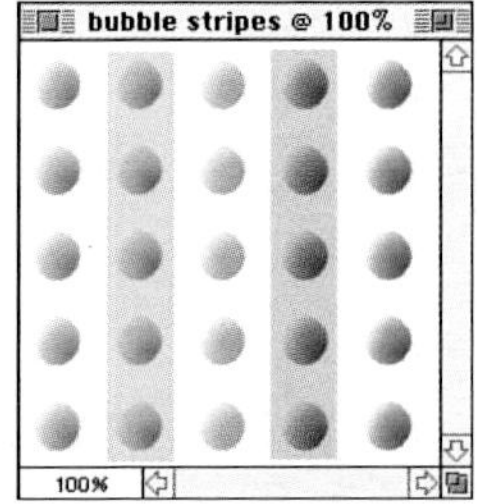

Texture is often added to enhance an image. Here's how to make a "patchwork" where visual interest is created from variety in direction, size, and intensity of the texture alone.

**1** Create a new file. Mine is a strip approximately 1×3 inches at 150 dpi.

Marquee Options
Shape: Rectangular
Style: Fixed Size
Width: 100 Height: 100 pixels
Feather: 0 pixels ☒ Anti-aliased

**2** Double-click the Selection Marquee tool and use these settings in the Marquee Options palette. Each time you click in the document, a perfect 100 pixel square is selected.

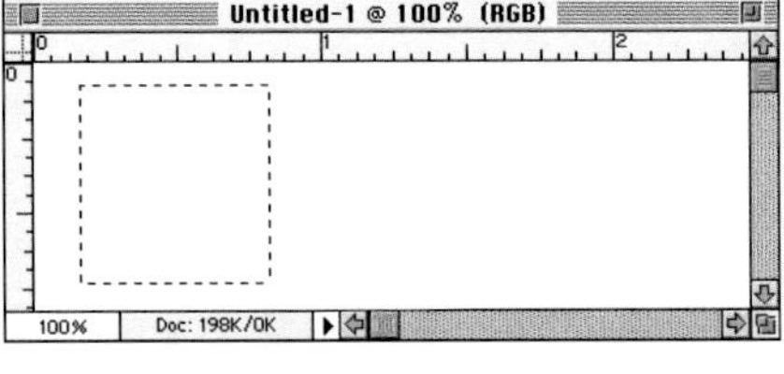


**3** Make your first click.

Texturizer
OK
Cancel
100%
Texture: Burlap
Scaling 100 %
Relief 14
Light Dir: Top Left
☒ Invert

**4** Choose Filter➡Texture➡Texturizer. Use these settings to create your first square.

I made a strip of burlap "swatches," which varied in the scale, direction, and depth of the weave. Make up your own combinations as you go or use my settings.

Burlap remains the choice for the entire sequence. Percentage given refers to size of the texture and numbers from zero to 50 indicate the amount or darkness of the effect. Finally, choice of lighting direction is indicated.

**(Command-Option-F) [Control-Alt-F] opens the Texturizer dialog box again.**

These settings will fill out the first strip:

Square 2: 69%, 9, Top Left

Square 3: 100%, 12, Left

Square 4: 50%, 7, Bottom Right

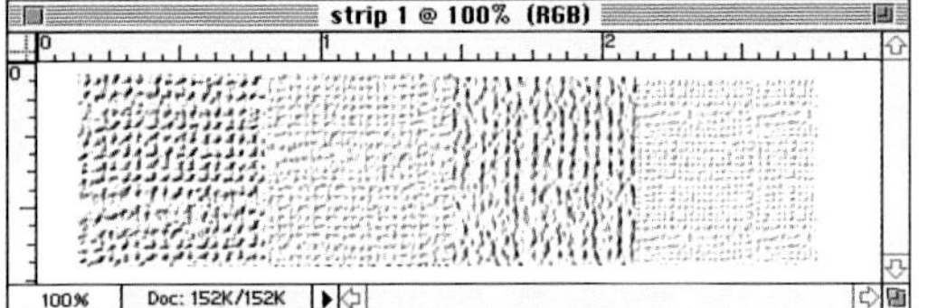


For the second strip use these settings:

Square 1: 108%, 12, Top Left

Square 2: 80%, 21, Left

Square 3: 175%, 13, Bottom

Square 4: 140%, 23, Right

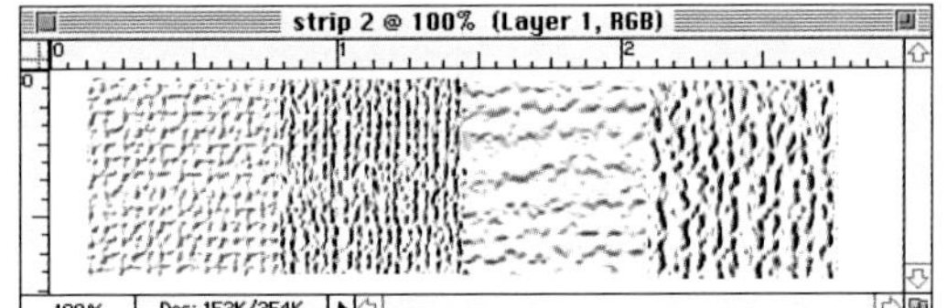


The third strip was created as follows:

Square 1: 93%, 32, Bottom

Square 2: 50%, 16, Top Left

Square 3: 150%, 21, Bottom Right, Invert

Square 4: 69%, 11, Bottom Right

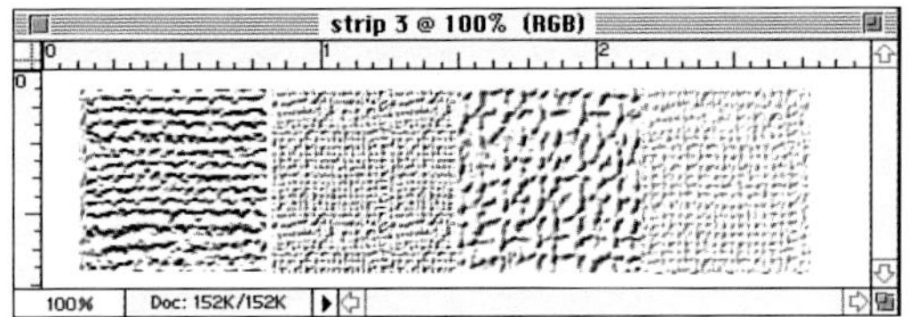

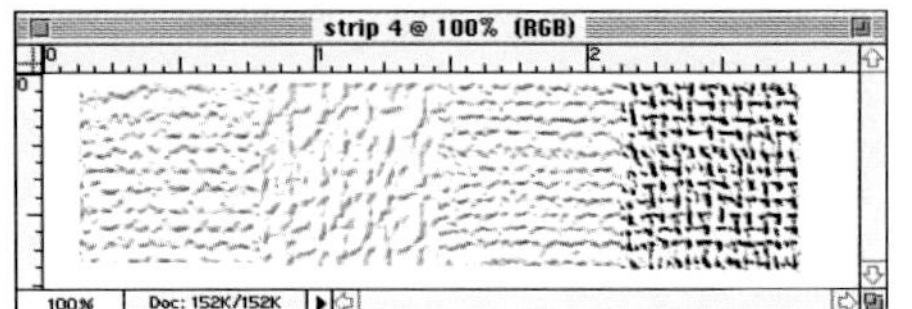

Here's the fourth strip:

Square 1: 140%, 10, Bottom

Square 2: 200%, 10, Top Left

Square 3: 117%, 10, Top

Square 4: 117%, 29, Top Right

To stitch your patchwork quilt together:

**1** Open strip1. Select Image➡ Canvas Size. Increase the vertical dimension to about 3 inches, with the current image at the top as shown. This creates space below the strip.

**2** Drag and drop each of the other strips into place.

## VARIATIONS

You can add color in several ways to your patchwork:

**1** Continue using the 100-pixel square selection marquee. Just click it over the texture swatch you want to color.

**2** I used these CMYK values and selected Edit➡Fill with these blending modes:

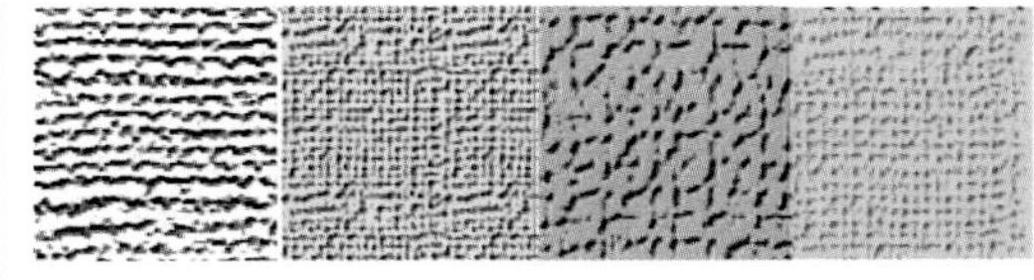

red: 0, 81, 68, 0; Color mode (100%);

purple: 62, 66, 0, 0; Hard Light (50%)

gold: 9, 28, 98, 0; Darken (100%)

blue-green: 56, 0, 25, 0; Darken (50%)

Here is the same strip and the same colors, but this time I used the Paintbrush with the wet edges box checked to get a watercolor look. The blending mode is Normal at 50%.

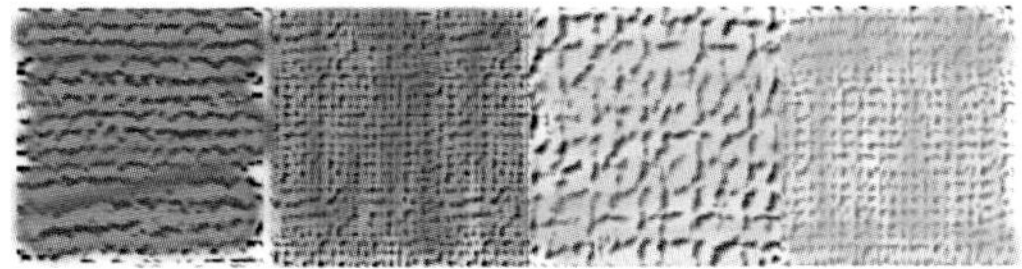

Use the sandstone texture instead of burlap. ■

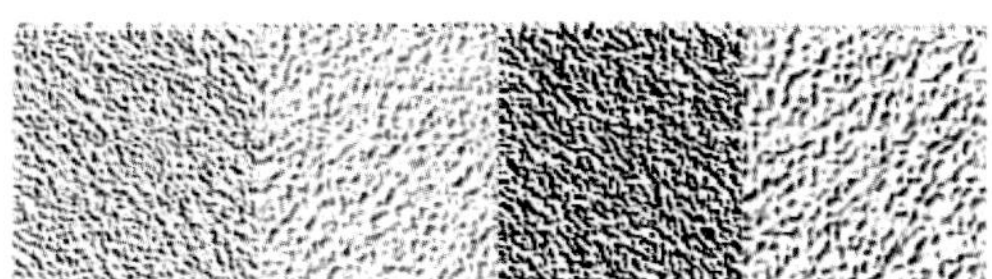

# cobblestones

This technique is useful for anyone who doesn't have time to search for the perfect stone background in their CD-ROM library of Stock images. It's a quick way to create a fill pattern for layouts or comps—or final art if you're going for a hand-drawn look.

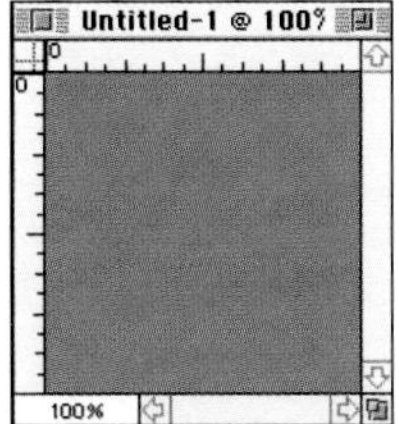


**1** To begin the pattern tile I created a new file in grayscale 1-inch square at 72 dpi and filled it with medium gray.

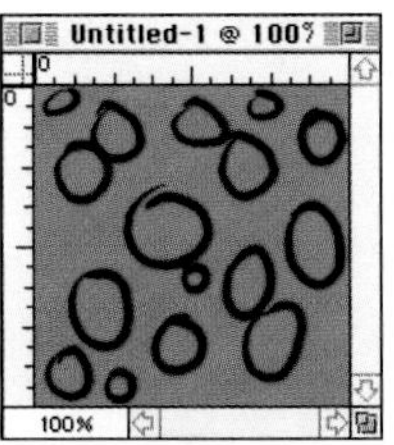


**2** Choose a foreground color of black. With the Brush tool, draw irregular circles of various sizes, randomly arranged.

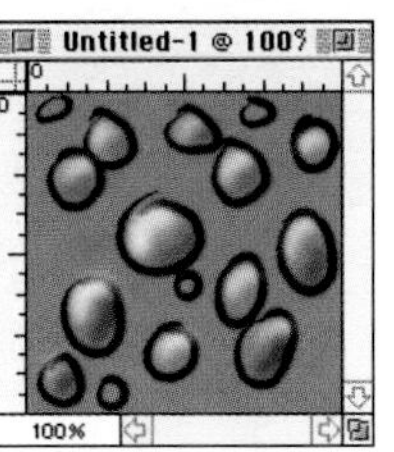


**3** Switch the foreground color to white. With the Airbrush tool at 25–35% pressure, add highlights and shadows to indicate a light source from the upper-left corner.

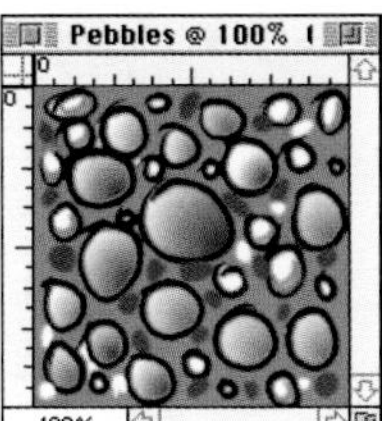


**4** When you're satisfied with the stones it's ready to become a tile for a pattern fill.

**5** Depending on the size and resolution of the image you want to fill, you may want to change the size of the tile. I reduced mine to about 50% size with Layer➡Transform➡Scale.

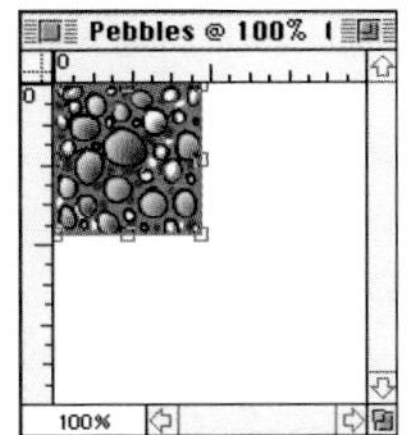


**6** The small tile is still selected. Use Edit➡Define Pattern to make this the element of a pattern fill.

**7** Create a new file or open an image that could use a cobblestone path or wall. I wanted to create a "worm's eye view" for this cartoon of a Medieval knight on a high stone wall. You'll find "Wallguy" in the ArtStart folder on the *Photoshop Effects Magic* CD-ROM.

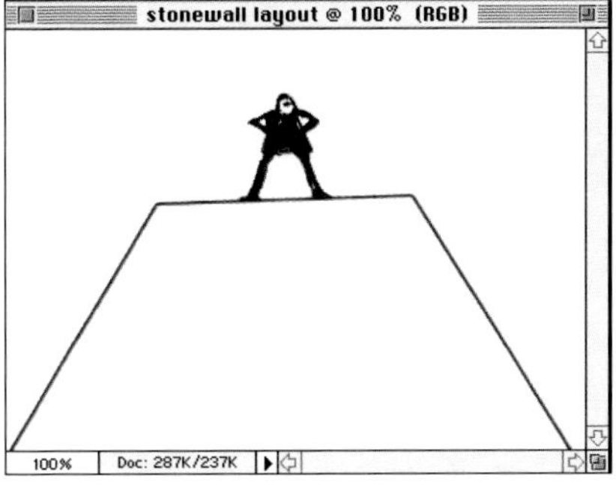


**8** Create a new layer (Layer 1) for the pattern. Make a selection in Layer 1 and fill it with the pattern. I dragged a rectangular Marquee approximately the height and width of the stone wall in my layout.

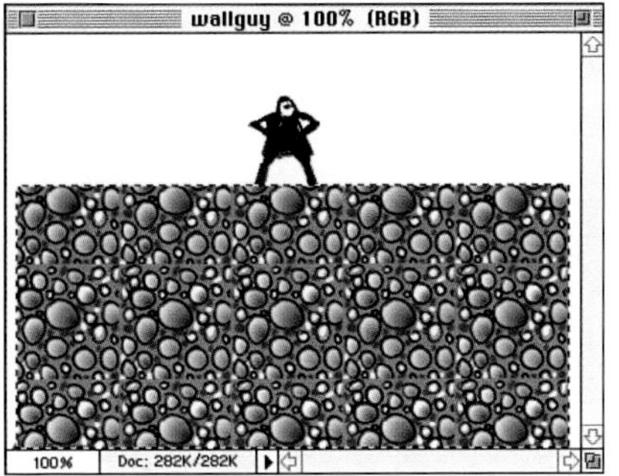

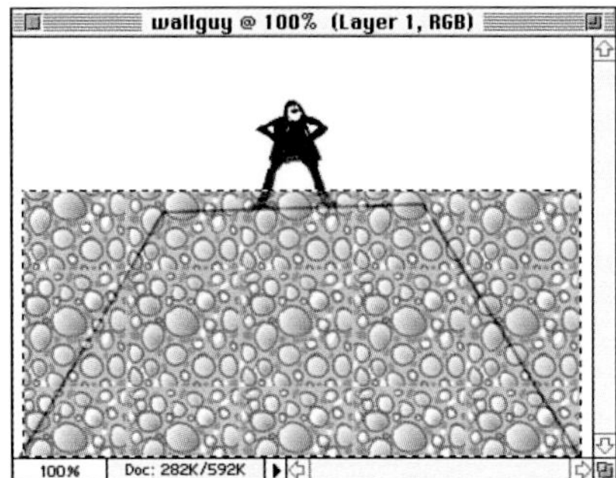

**9** I reduced the opacity of Layer 1 so I could see the outline of the wall. I used Layer➡Transform➡ Distort to create the illusion of perspective.

**TIP** **There is a Perspective option in the Transform commands but it does not enable you to manipulate the handles on the image independently. The Distort option does just that, giving you more control in one step.** ■

# Cobblestones

Create a variety of electronic frames for your Photoshop art. The Border command is your digital mitre box!

**1** Create a new file 3×2 inches. Choose a foreground color and fill the file with a dark color. I used reddish brown with CMYK values 0, 100, 0, 40.

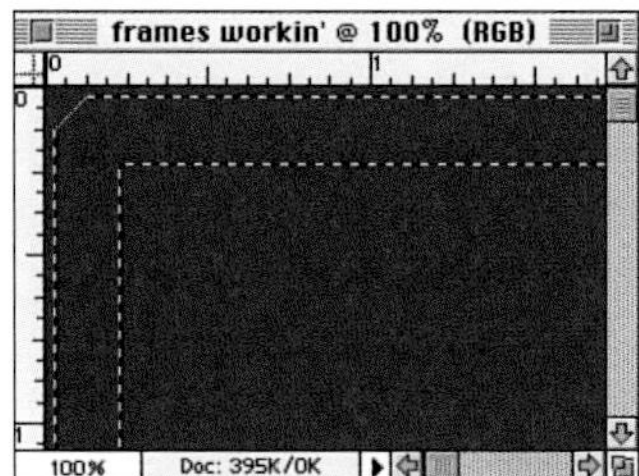


**2** Make the rulers visible with (Command-R)[Control-R]. Drag a rectangular selection marquee about ⅛ inch from the edges of the window. Select➡Modify➡Border (35 pixels). This creates a frame-like selection border with mitred corners and a preset gradient that will show up when you fill the selection with a color.

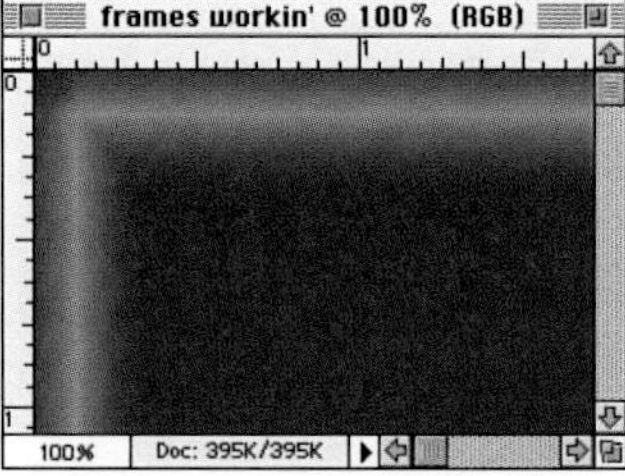


**3** Choose a foreground color for your fill. Mine is light tan (CMYK 0, 25, 50, 25). Select Edit➡Fill at 100% normal.

© Copyright 1997 PhotoDisc, Inc.

**4** Switch to default colors. Select the interior of the frame and insert some artwork with the Paste Into command, like this tropical sunset from PhotoDisc. I also cropped the frame just enough to enhance the mitred corner effect.

## VARIATIONS

This "bleached oak" look resulted from increasing the brightness (+35) and decreasing contrast (–44) after Step 3. I also trimmed off more of the outer frame and I added a bevel-cut mat.

Here's how to make a textured mat in a wide strip inside the frame.

**1** Select the area and apply Filter➡Texture➡Texturizer. I used Canvas.

**2** Choose a foreground color of light cream or pink and use Edit➡Fill in Color mode, so the white remains but the nubby texture has more realism. I used 50% opacity.

**3** Drag a rectangular Marquee around the inside edge of the mat and use Edit➡Stroke to create the beveled edge of the mat.

Multiple borders and strokes can create some complex traditional frames. After Step 3 I added a narrower border just inside the first one.

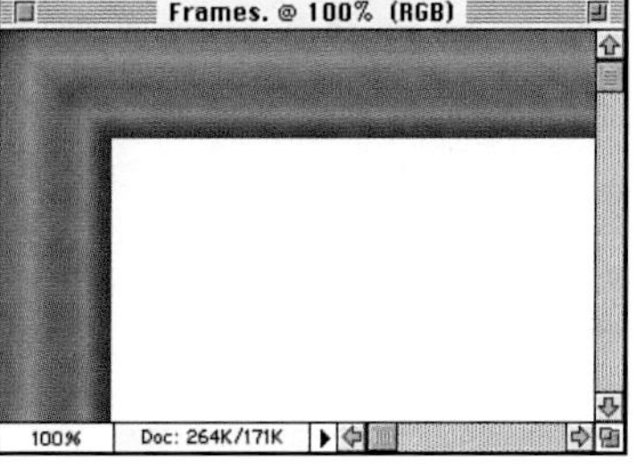

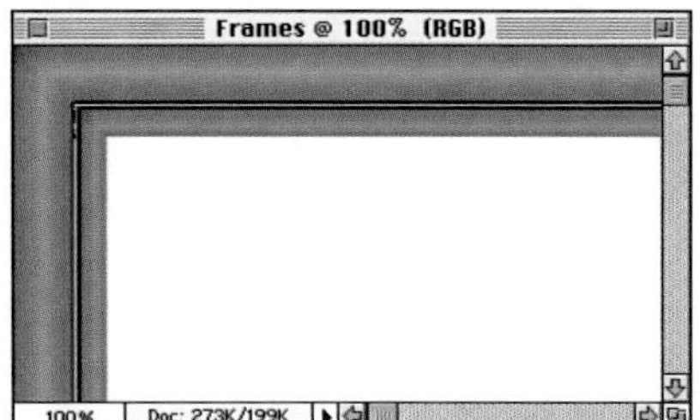


Drag a selection rectangle at the juncture between borders. Edit➥Stroke using Center location with any foreground color and line weight.

**TIP** **Those double-strokes come out perfectly when you use an odd number of pixels (such as 5 or 7) and a single pixel in a contrasting color for the second stroke. Multiple fills will be perfectly centered if you use the Select➥Modify➥Expand (or ➥Contract) commands.**

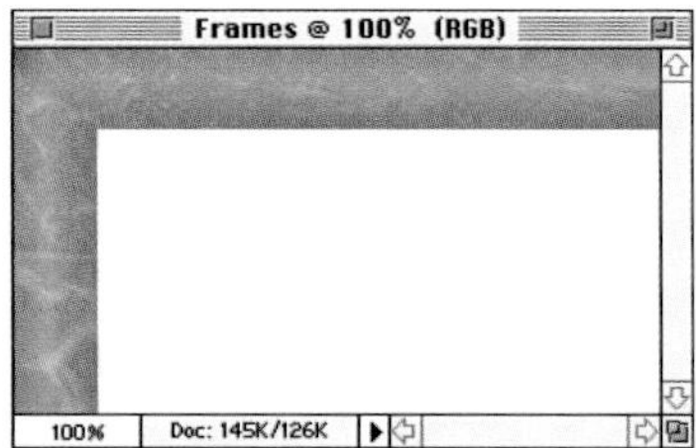


There are plenty of ways to add a wood-grain or other texture to your frame. This marbleized look comes from cutting a slab of "rawmeat" from the PhotoDisc file by that name. It's on the *Photoshop Effects Magic* CD-ROM. Just drag and drop it onto the "bleached oak" frame. I reduced the opacity of the Meat layer to about 20% and used Luminosity mode to eliminate the red color.

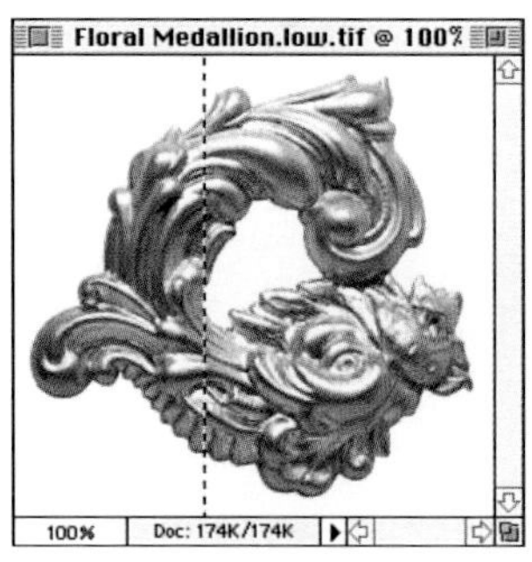


For the museum quality ornate gold I started with the Floral Medallion in the Image Club➥Objects folder on the CD-ROM.

I used the Single Column option of the selection Marquee to "extrude" the top of the frame by clicking on the right arrow of the keyboard while holding down the (Option-Command)[Alt-Control] keys. Yes, it takes lots and lots of clicks.

Floral Medallion.low.tif @ 100%

100% Doc: 174K/174K

The corners consist of the original gold medallion, or parts of it blended together.

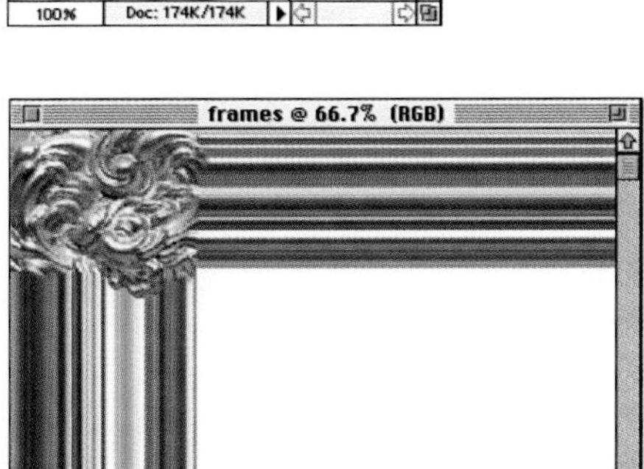


**TIP** **Begin a file of virtual moldings. Crop out all but a 1- or 2-inch corner of the frame. It can be used to piece together a whole frame of any size. Better still, use File Info to enter descriptions or formulas for recreating each design.** ■

File Info

Section: Caption

Caption:

Foreground: 0, 25, 50, 25
Background: 0, 100, 0, 40
Border: 35 pixels
Brightness: +35
Contrast: -44

Caption Writer:

Headline:

BLEACHED OAK

Special Instructions:

OK
Cancel
Prev
Next
Load
Save
Append

You don't need any fancy plug-ins to get these spectacular kaleidoscopic effects. They were all done with the Gradient tool. Begin with a radial fill and use Difference mode for additional fills. Incredible variety results from your choice of colors, the direction and length of the drag and the number of multiple fills. Opacity is another variable.

I used a 2-inch square for each of the designs. The recipes give you colors and dragging movements.

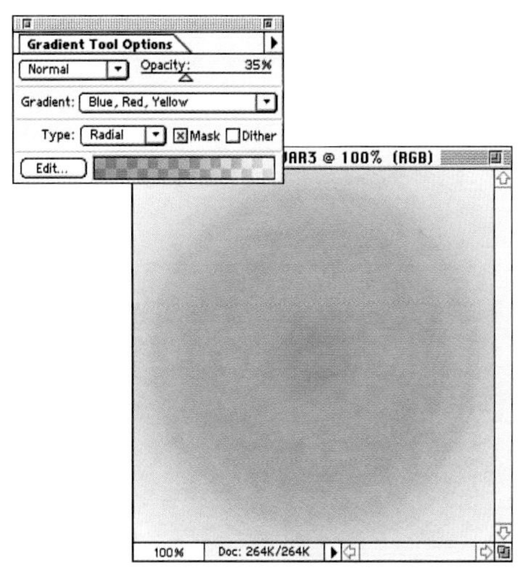


**1** Use the Blue, Red, Yellow gradient at 35% opacity, dragging from the center to any corner.

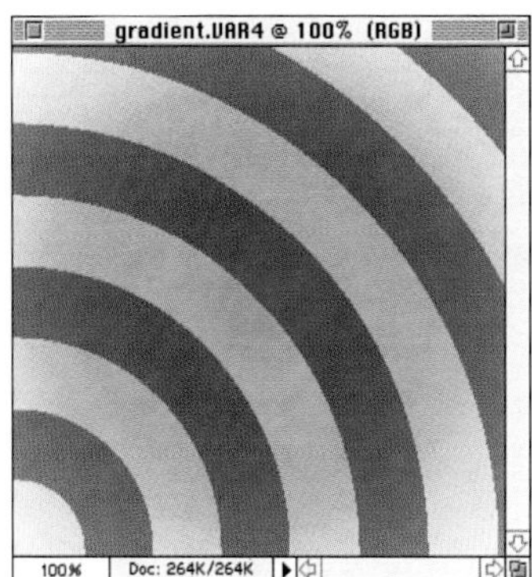


**2** Switch to default colors and use the Transparent Stripes gradient. Choose Difference mode in the Gradient Options palette. I kept opacity at 35%. Make a diagonal drag from one corner to the opposite corner of the image. Here's how my image looks after dragging from the lower-left to the upper-right corner.

**3** Repeat for each of the other three corners of the image.

Here is the final image after all four diagonal fills have been applied.

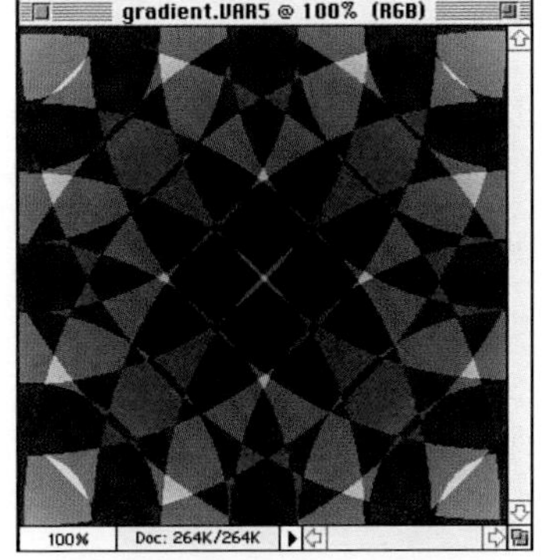


## Pastel Kaleidoscope

A delicate pastel-tinted design is the surprising result after a series of steps that cause increasingly darker images.

**1** Use the Yellow, Violet, Orange, Blue gradient in Normal mode at 100% opacity. Drag diagonally from the upper-left corner to the opposite corner.

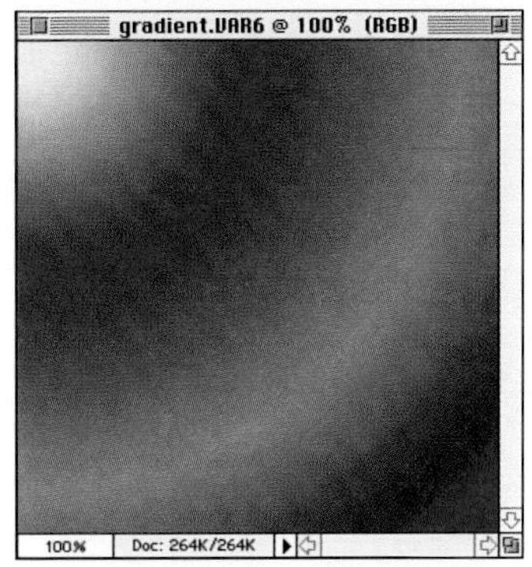


**2** Use the Transparent Stripes gradient at 50% opacity. Remember to change to Difference mode. Drag from the center to any corner.

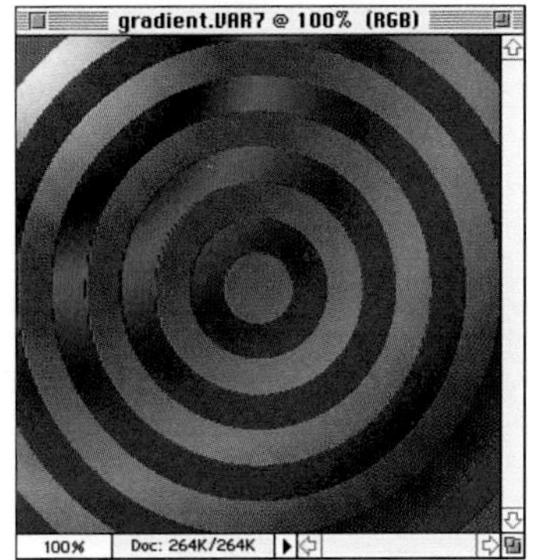

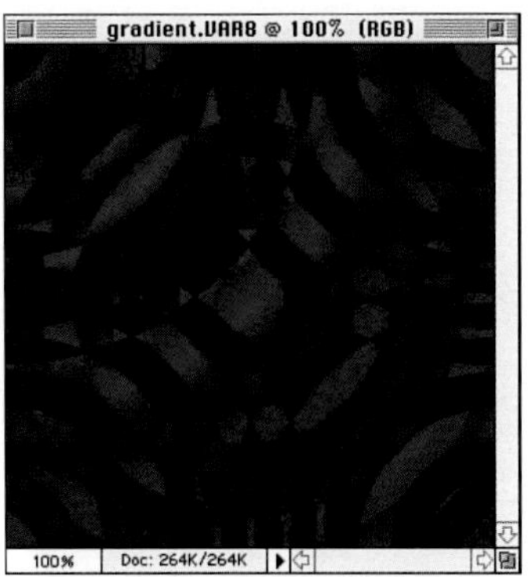


**3** Using the same settings, drag from one of the corners to the center. Repeat for the other three corners. Each successive drag makes the image darker.

To get the look of delicate watercolor washes, use Image➡Adjust➡Invert to invert the colors (Command-I)[Control-I].

## VARIATIONS

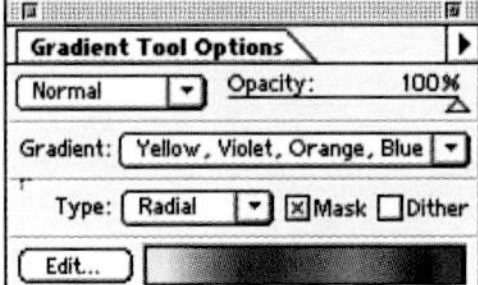


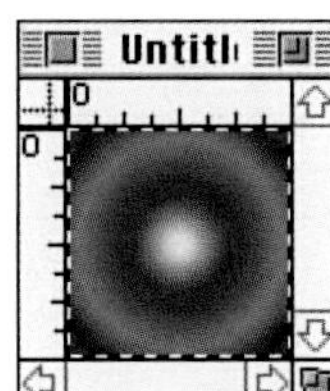


Make a seamless pattern tile with an abbreviated version of the kaleidoscope technique. Start with a radial fill in a 1×1-inch white square document. I'm using the Yellow, Violet, Orange, Blue gradient and dragging from the center to a corner.

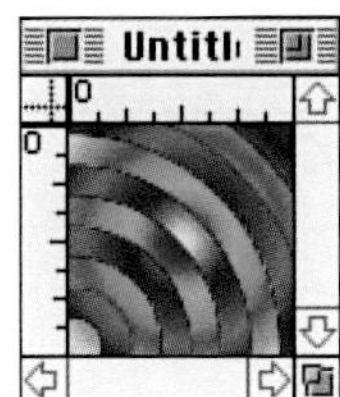


When I used the radial fill with transparent stripes I used Difference mode again, but I switched the foreground color to white. I have no reason for that other than to add a little more variety. I made a diagonal drag from the lower-left to the upper-right corner.

My second drag went from the upper-right to the lower-left corner. This is the completed tile. Select➡All and use Edit➡Define Pattern.

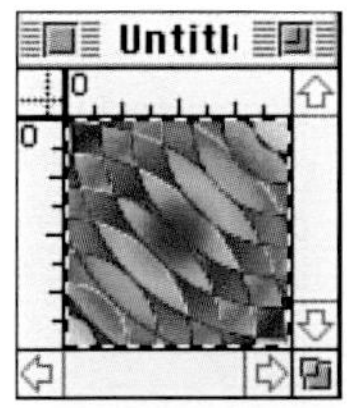


Use Edit➡Fill with Pattern at 100% Normal in a larger document. ■

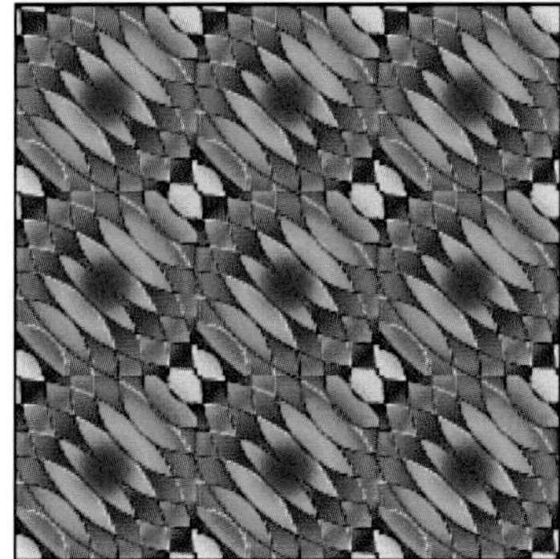

You can imitate the look of conventional art materials, such as bristle brushes (see page 172) and the scribbly pencil I'll use for this technique. Several Brush variables can be manipulated. The most important of these is the Brush tip.

**1** Load the Assorted Brushes. These new brush tips will appear below the default group as you scroll through the brushes.

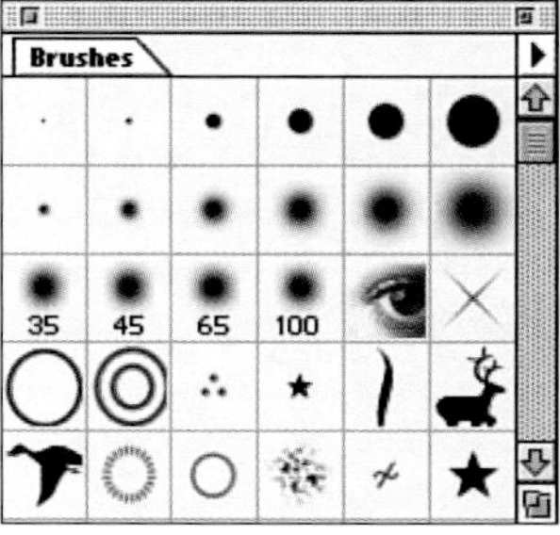


**2** Choose the brush tip that is made up of three dots arranged in a triangle.

Doodle with this new brush to get a feel for its sketchy quality. The three distinct points on the brush make lines that look as if they have been drawn over a couple of times, perhaps by an artist who was in too much of a hurry to erase. I recommend you use a rapid, loose style to take advantage of this rough quality in the tool. I made this series of squiggles using different settings in the Paintbrush Options palette.

The top squiggle was made with all of the boxes unchecked. I used my pressure-sensitive tablet for the rest. The next one used a fade of 150 steps. The third had Size as a function of pressure and the fourth had the Opacity box checked. In the next stroke, both Size and Opacity were a function of pressure.

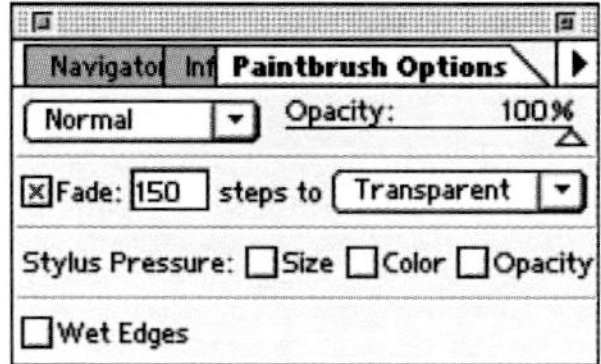


For the last two squiggles, I switched the background color to a bright red and had the Color box checked. This results in firm pressure producing the foreground (black) while lighter pressure fades to the background color.

**3** Roughly sketch a still life with this 3-dot brush. I used green with CMYK values 74, 0, 98, 0 to do this quick sketch of fruit. Normal mode at 100% opacity and only the Size box checked enables variation in stylus pressure to control the thickness of the stroke. My sketch is available in the ArtStart folder on the *Photoshop Effects Magic* CD-ROM.

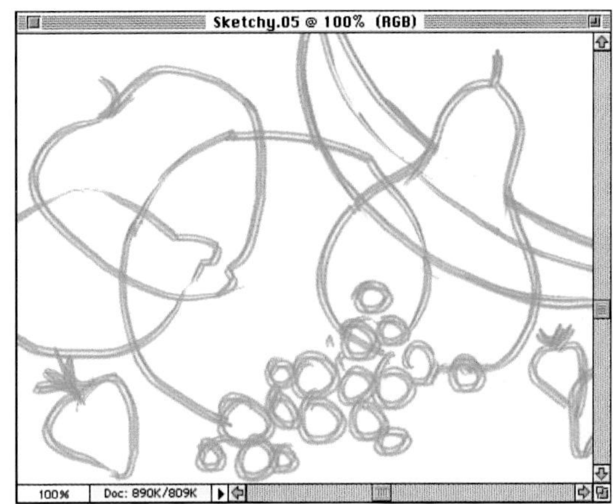


**4** Add color and form using nothing but the 3-dot brush.

I roughed in color with quick strokes that followed the contours of the forms, more or less. The overlapping lines create additional shapes that can have different color fills for more visual interest. I purposely avoided solid fills, enabling the spaces between "bristles" to give the work spontaneity. Rather than undoing strokes, I sketched over them with different colors, which resulted in some nicely layered areas.

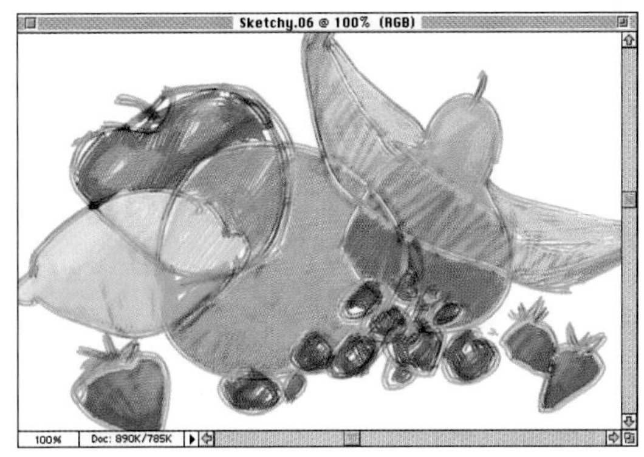


## VARIATIONS

Use the three-dot sketchy brush to work in Quick Mask mode. Draw from scratch or find an image to use as a template for tracing. I'm working with the "Fruit" image in the PhotoDisc folder on the CD-ROM.

**1** Enter Quick Mask mode. Roughly trace the outlines of the image.

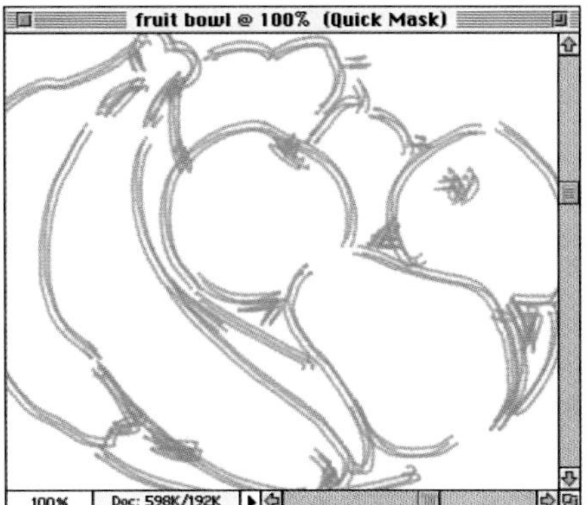


**2** Return to the composite channel. Select➥All and delete the image. Only the mask remains.

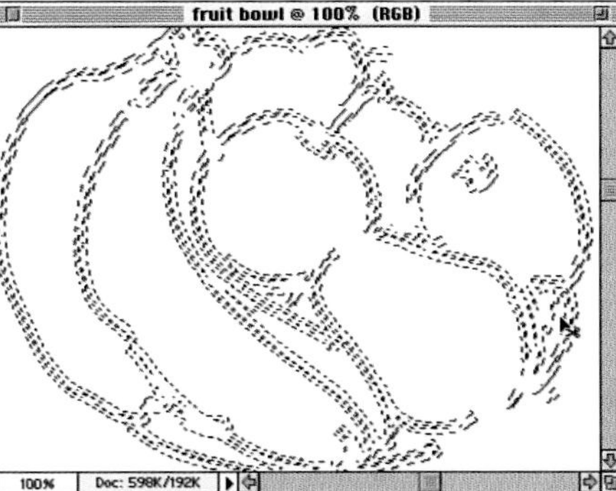


**3** Exit Quick Mask mode and the mask become a selection.

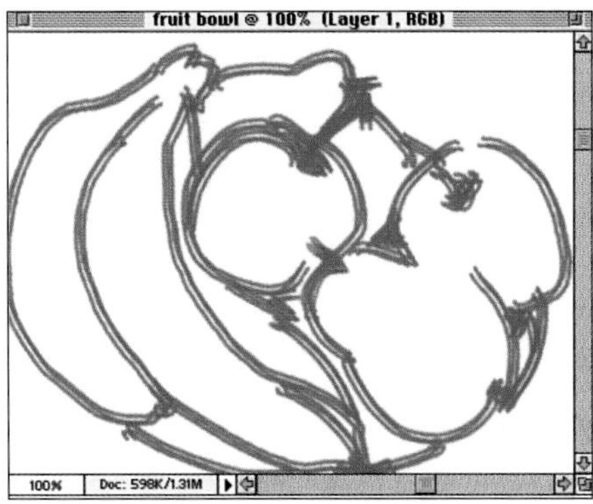


**4** The mask protects the outlines by default, so use Select➥Inverse to protect everything but the outlines. Use Edit➥Fill with a dark color. My choice is purple with CMYK values of 57, 58, 0, 0.

**5** Use Select➥Inverse again and the lines will be protected. Now you can get sloppy and energetic in your application of color and the lines won't be disturbed. ■

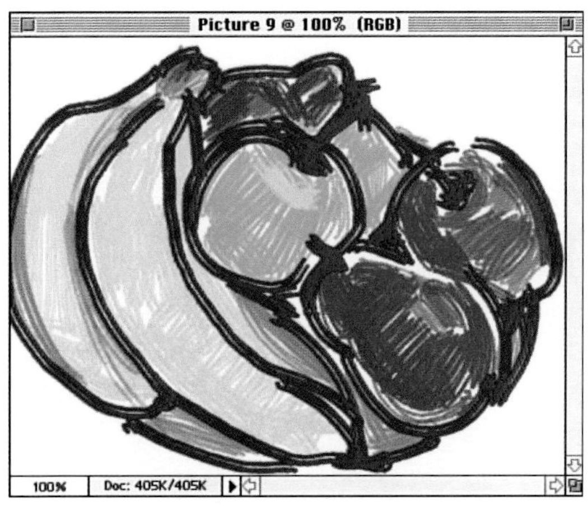

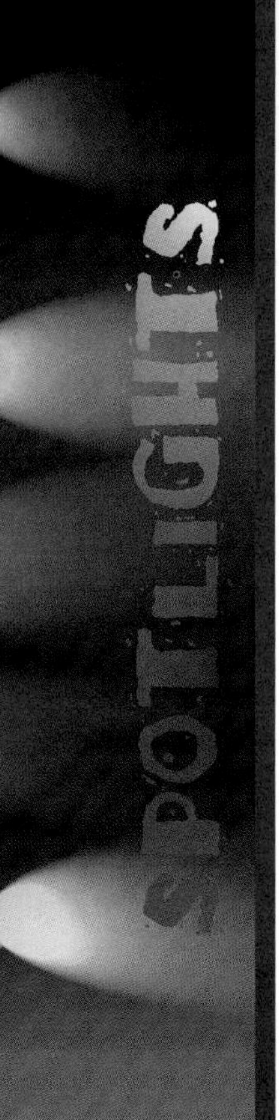


The Lighting Effects Filter provides controls for enhancing an image with a limitless combination of color, exposure, direction and placement of light sources, but you don't need to start with an image. Lights themselves can be all you need to create an image.

**1** Create a new file in RGB mode about 4 inches×3 inches and fill it with a linear gradient, dragging from the upper-left corner to the lower-right. I used CMYK values 5, 90, 0, 1 for the foreground color and CMYK values 61, 0, 22, 0 for the background color.

**2** Apply Filter➡Render➡Lighting Effects. Choose the "Circle of Light" style, accepting all default settings.

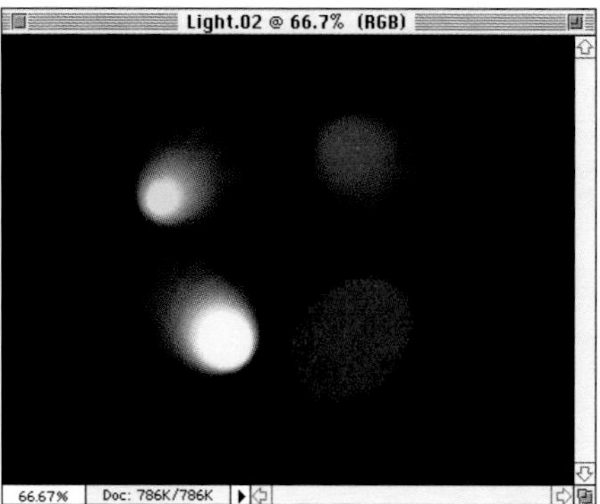

3 Choose Filter➡Fade and fade the effect to 60% with the Luminosity blending mode.

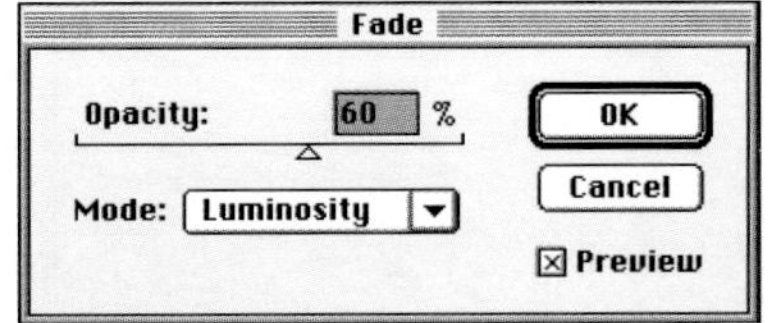


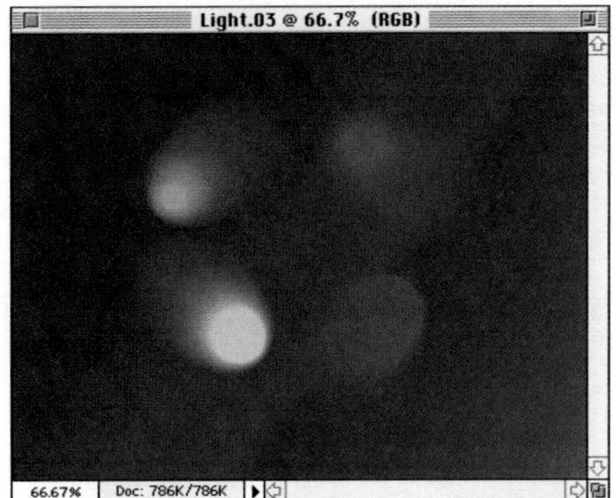


**4** Select Filter➡Render➡Lighting Effects again to open the Lighting Effects dialog box. Because it was the last filter you had open, you can use the keyboard shortcut (Option-Command-F)[Alt-Control-F].

**5** Choose the "Five Lights Down" style. You can move a light by clicking its source and then dragging it (the white spot in the preview image). Arrange three or four of the lights a bit more randomly.

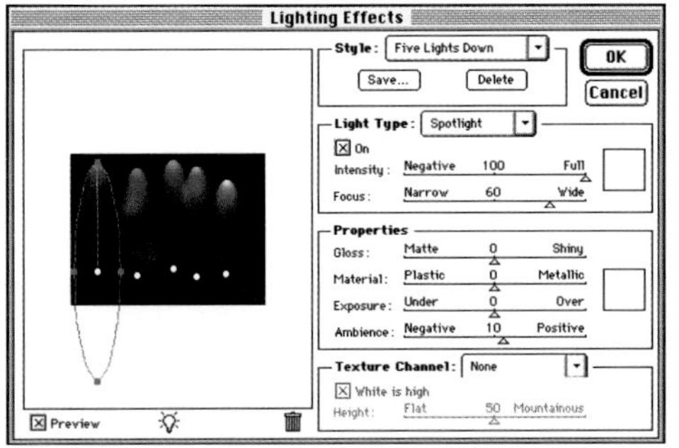

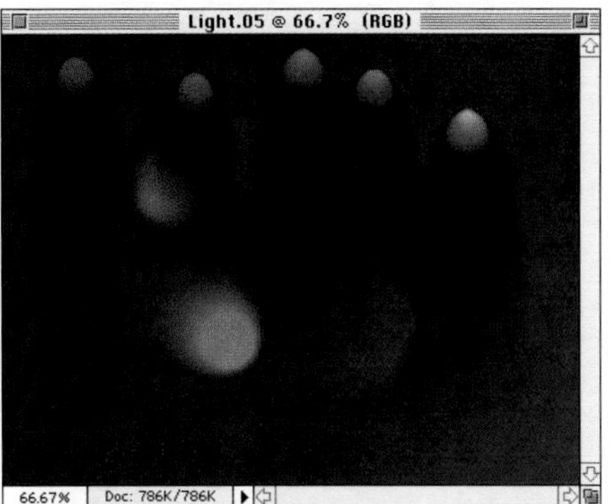


**6** Choose Filter➥Fade and switch the blending mode to Difference at 100% opacity.

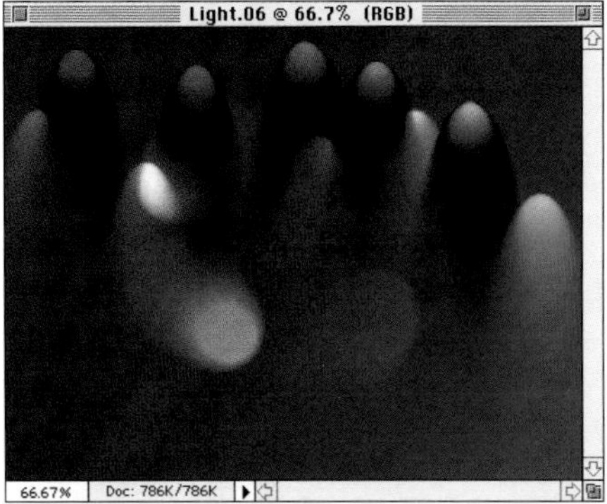


The five lights look like hooded figures, don't they? Repeat Step 5, arranging the lights below the first row. Use the Fade command at 100% opacity to apply the Screen mode. This keeps the image from becoming too dark.

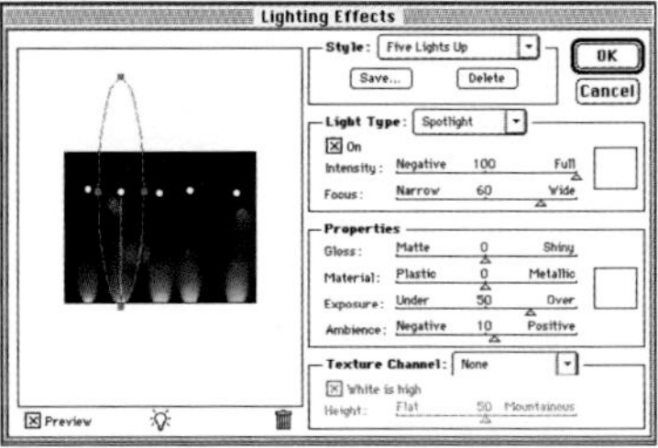


**7** Repeat Step 4 and choose the "Five Lights Up" style. Move the white dots in the preview down slightly to arrange the lights at the lower edge of the image, like this:

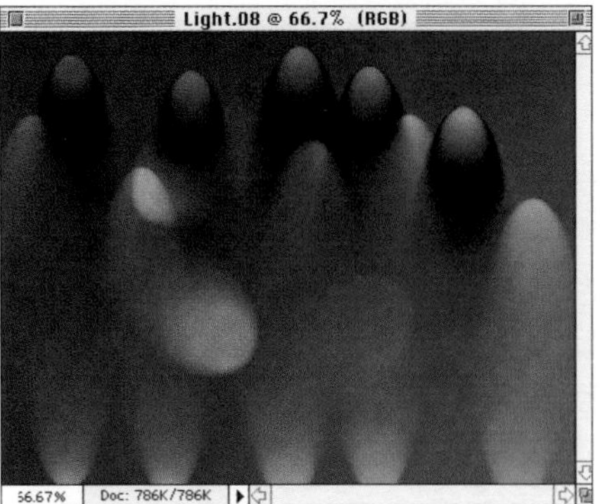


**8** Again, use the Fade command to find a blending mode that will reveal the previous stage. I used Exclusion at 75%.

**9** My final lighting effect is the "Soft Omni" style in Lighten mode. I also cropped away some of the lower part, to keep attention focused on the "figures."

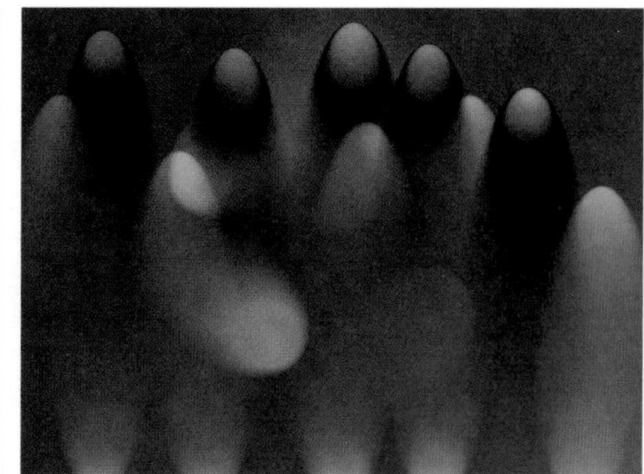

## VARIATIONS

The hardest part about experimental light-painting is knowing when you're done.

Here's a similar image, where I have added the "Triple Spotlight" to all the previous effects, using Screen mode in the Fade dialog box.

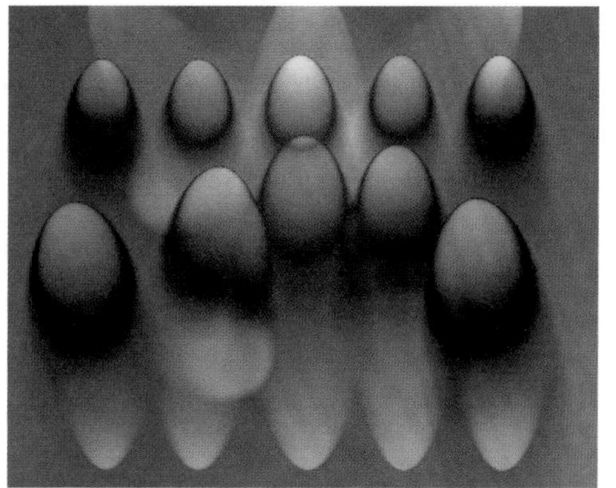

Filter➡Render➡Lens Flare (Brightness: 100, Lens Type: 50-300mm Zoom) makes the previous image look like this. I'll call that the finishing touch. ■

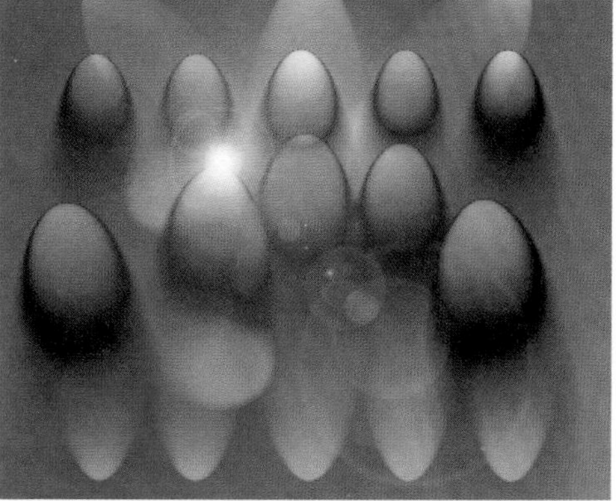

textured Brush

Sharron Evans created this technique for painting with color and texture in the same stroke. The method relies on Sharron's clever use of channels.

First, create a hand-made texture. Here's how I made one:

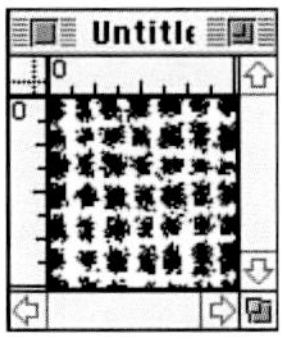

**1** Create a new file, a 1-inch square at 72 dpi.

**2** Fill the square with black.

**3** Switch the foreground color to white and make several vertical and horizontal strokes with the Brush tool in Dissolve mode. I used the brush size in the first column of the second row on the Brush palette.

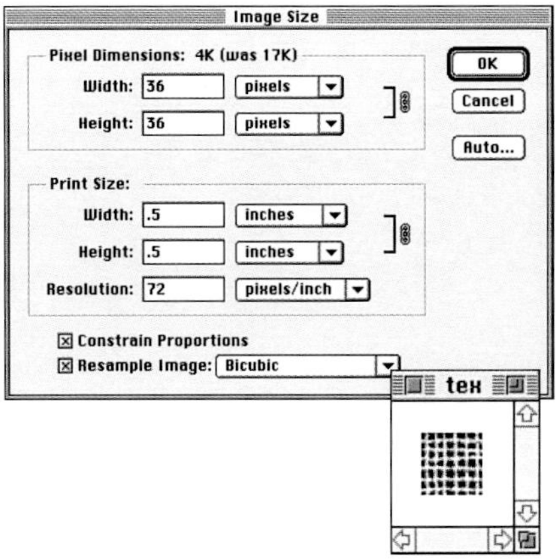

**4** Choose Image➥Image Size (Height: .5 inches, Width: .5 inches). Reducing the texture swatch to a ½-inch square makes a finer weave.

**5** Choose Select➥All then Edit➥Define Pattern to establish your texture as the fill pattern. It will remain available until you use Define Pattern on another selection.

**6** Create a new file 2X4 inches.

**7** Create a new channel (#4). Select Edit➡Fill using the pattern as content. You now have a texture mask.

Fill
Contents
Use: Pattern
OK
Cancel
Blending
Opacity: 100 %
Mode: Normal
Preserve Transparency

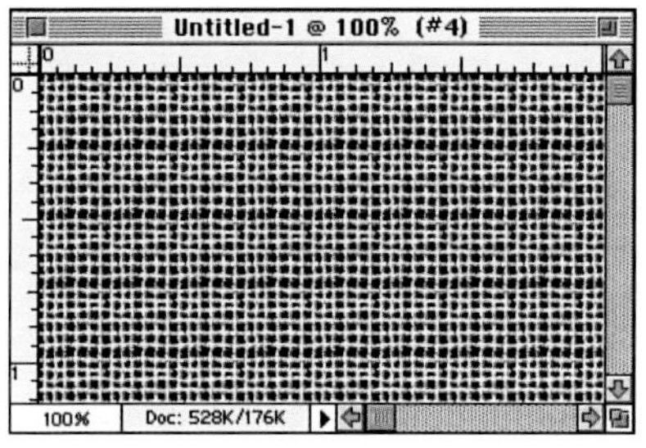


I could see the "tiling" of the repeating pattern, but it wasn't too bad. If you get serious tiling or breaks in the pattern, repeat Steps 2 through 7 until you're satisfied. Here's a good example, or rather a bad example, of a pattern element that needs to be redone.

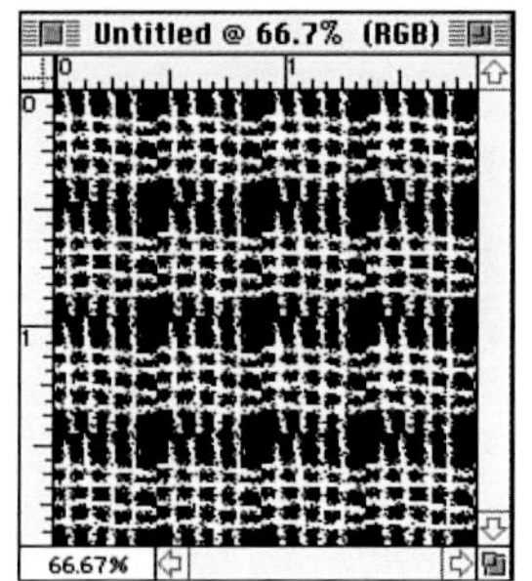


**8** Load the selection Channel #4. Click OK and your pattern is filled with marching ants. Press (Command-H)[Control-H] to hide the marching ants without deselecting anything.



**9** Return to the composite channel. Choose a foreground color and a painting tool and make your mark. I used the calligraphy brush tip shown here, with the Brush tool in Dissolve mode to enhance the grainy quality.

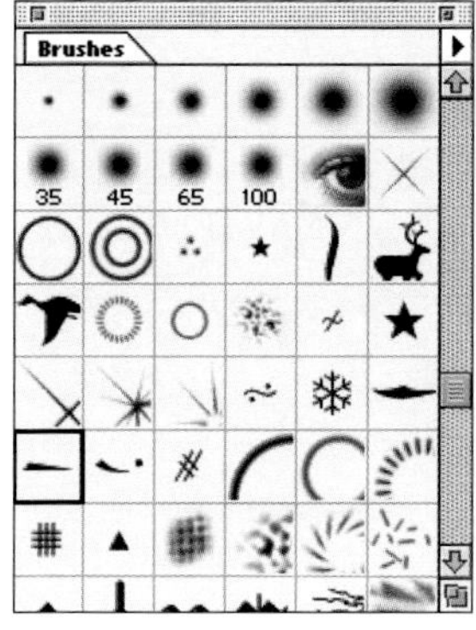

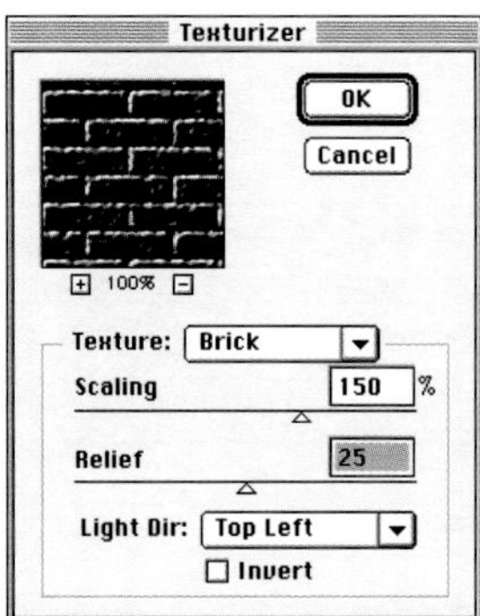


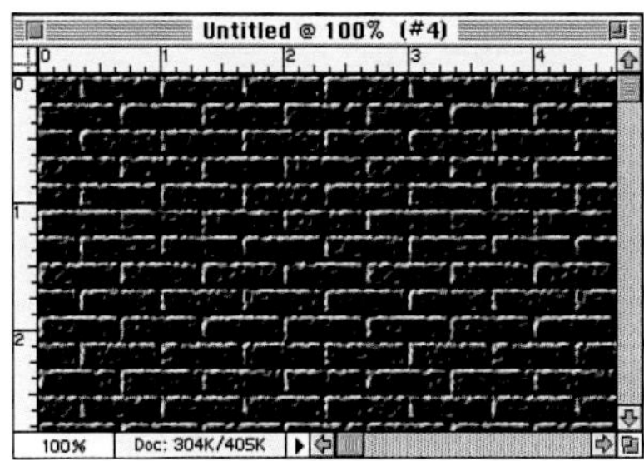




**TIP** **Remember that this works only as long as the pattern in Channel #4 remains the active selection. If you want to make corrections in your work, use the Eraser rather than a select-and-delete maneuver.**

## VARIATIONS

You don't need to make a texture from scratch. You can use the textures available in Photoshop 4.0's Texturizer menu.

**1** Create a new file 4X3 inches. Create a new channel for the texture mask.

**2** Selecting Filter➥Texture➥Texturizer opens a dialog box for texture fills. Choose Brick for this example. Use my values for scale, relief, and light direction or try your own settings. The new channel is filled with a black-and-white brick pattern.

**3** Repeat Step 5, mentioned earlier. This time check the Invert box in the Load Selection dialog box before you click OK.

**4** Return to the composite channel. The image window is now white. Fill the selection with foreground color. I used CMYK values 32, 76, 60, 29 for a brick-red.

**5** Go ahead, scrawl some graffiti, too. I chose black as the foreground color and used a medium-sized Pencil. ■

I still use conventional art materials, but I have to dust them off. If you've made a transition from traditional to digital art, you may wonder what to do with all your pens, pencils, markers, crayons, brushes, pastels, paint tubes, erasers, and so forth. You can still use them in your art, but they become the art rather than the method for creating it. I have scanned in my traditional tools to create an image that I can skew, filter, and modify. You can do the same, or use the image "Tools" in the ArtStart folder on the *Photoshop Effects Magic* CD-ROM.

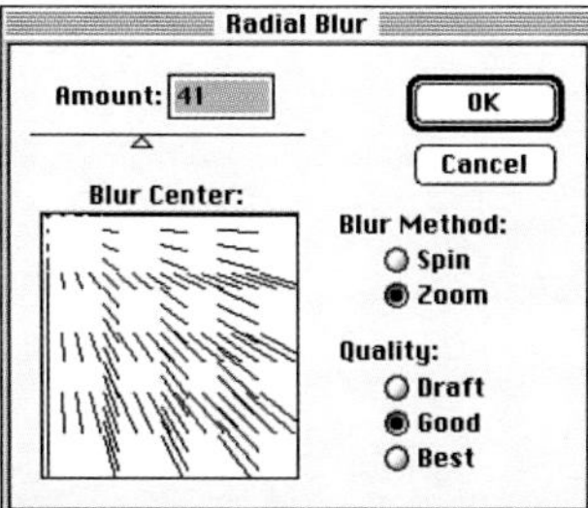


**1** Apply Filter➥Blur➥Radial Blur. Use these settings and move the center of the blur to the upper-left corner.

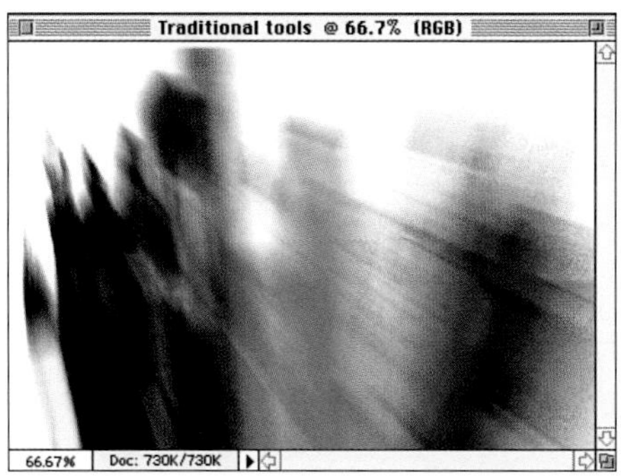

**2** Choose Filter➡Fade, leaving the effect at 100% and switching to Difference mode. The blur creates a mysterious back-lighting.

## VARIATIONS

Here's a completely different series of effects using the Polar Coordinates filter.

**1** Apply Filter➡Distort➡Polar Coordinates (Rectangular to Polar) to the original scan. Crop the image as shown.

There's something about the way all the tools arch their points toward the center that suggests a menacing intent (or is it just me?) They seem to be "looking" for a victim…so, I provided one. He's the "Cross-eyed" guy in the Digital Stock folder of the CD-ROM.

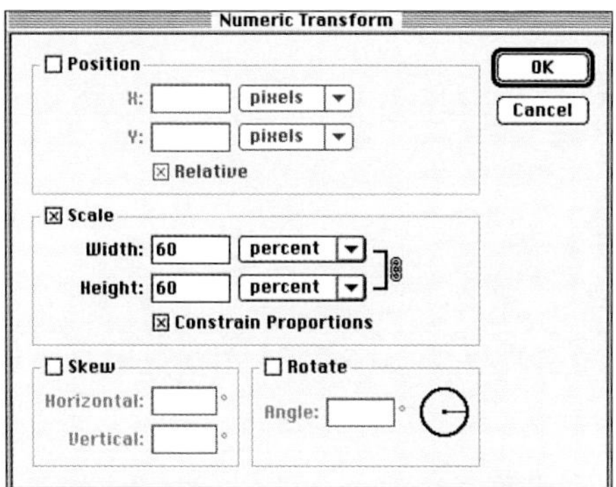


**2** Drag and drop the victim to the Tools image, and turn the opacity of this new layer down to about 50% so you can see both layers. Reduce the victim's size to 60%, using Layer➡Transform➡Numeric.

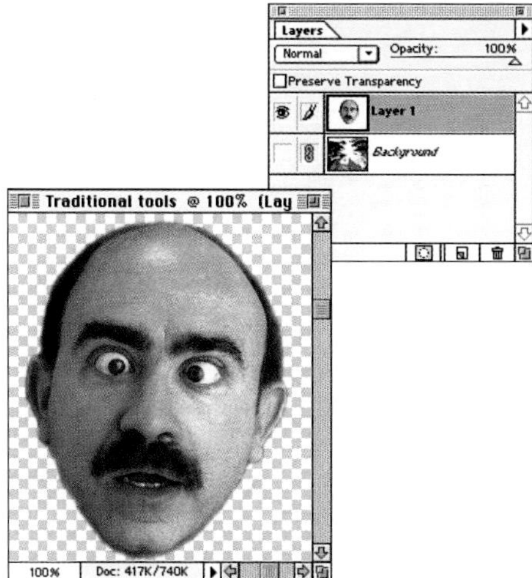


**3** Make the Background layer invisible and erase everything on Layer 1 (the "victim" layer) except his face.

**4** Image➡Adjust➡Invert the colors of the layer to create a negative. The victim looks normal again in Step 5 (though he didn't look very normal to begin with).

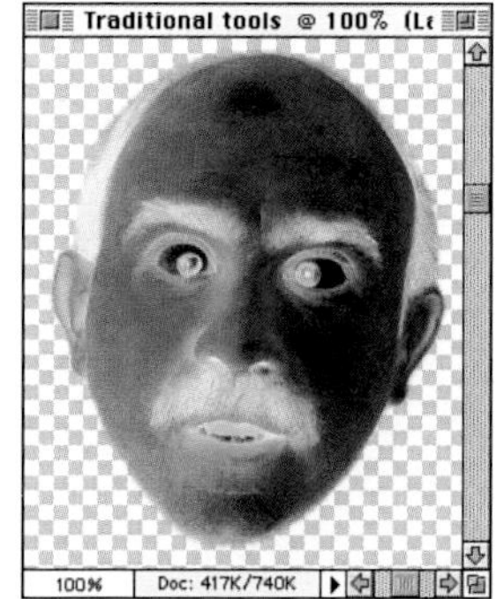


**5** Finally, make the background layer visible and switch the "victim" layer (Layer 1) to Difference mode. This will make the inverted colors of the face go back to normal except where they are overlapped by the tools. ■

Here's a way to make the basic element of quilted upholstery. Use gradients and the Straight Line tool to construct the tile for a pattern fill.

**1** Switch to Default colors. Create a new file at 72 dpi. Mine is 4-inches square.

**2** Double-click the Line tool to open the Line Tool Options palette and match these settings. Hold down the Shift key to draw two perfect diagonals from corner to corner. The CMYK values for my salmon pink are 0, 62, 42, 0.

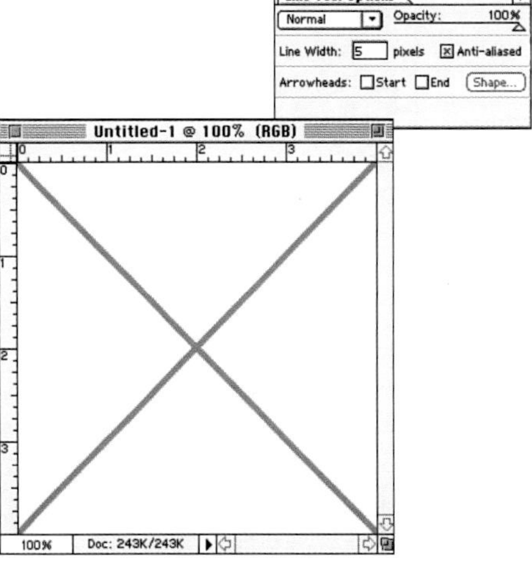


**3** Switch the foreground and background colors so that white is now the foreground and pink is the background.

**4** With the Magic Wand tool, click inside the left-hand white triangle to select it.

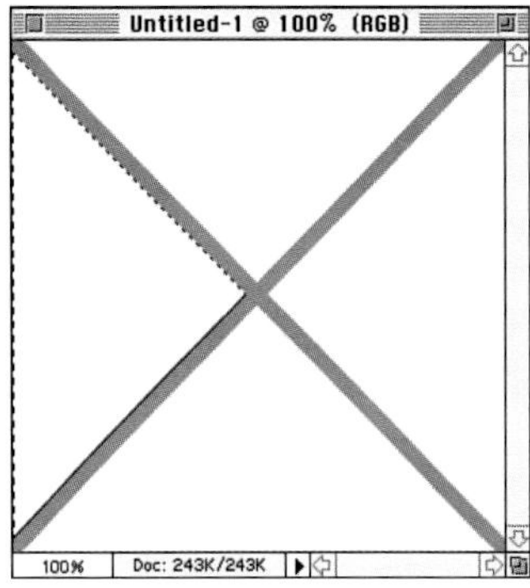

**5** Double-click the Gradient tool to open the Gradient Tool Options palette and match the settings shown here.

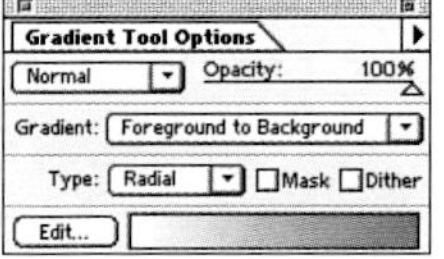


**6** Drag horizontally from the outside edge of the triangle to the center as accurately as you can.

**Use the rulers to help make perfect fills that will result in a seamless pattern. (Command-R) [Control-R] toggles the rulers along the top and left side of the image. Begin your fill exactly at the 2-inch mark and hold down the Shift key for a perfect horizontal as you drag to the center.**

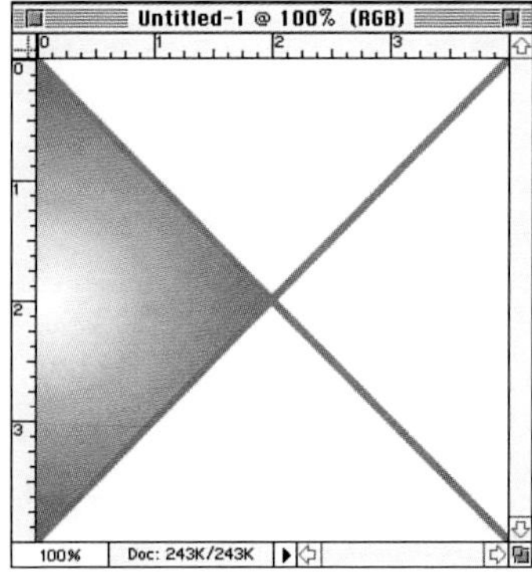


Repeat for each of the other triangles, blending from the middle of the outside edge to the center point. Your image should look like this:

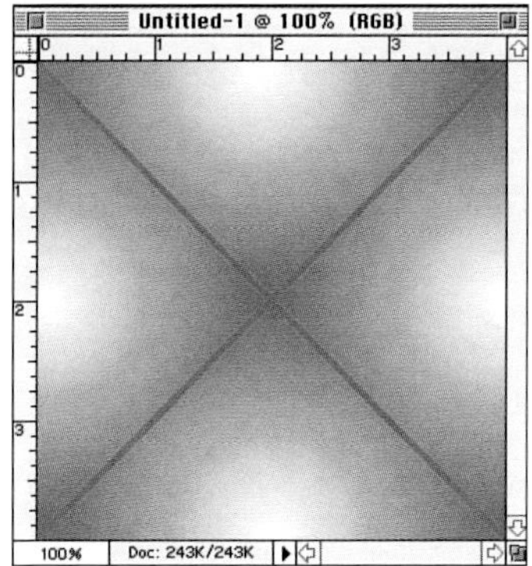

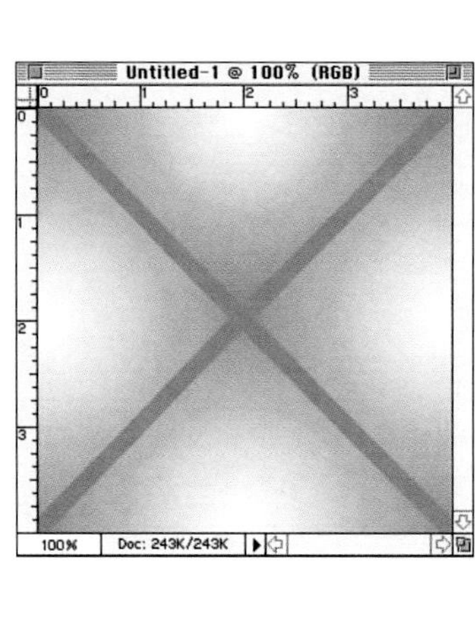


**7** I decided to strengthen the diagonal lines. It isn't necessary to redraw them. Just use the Magic Wand with a tolerance of 1 and click anywhere on the line. Both diagonals are selected. Select➡Modify➡Expand by 1 pixel. If salmon pink is still your background color, press the Delete key and the pink lines become a bit fatter.

Now we want to create the button at the intersection of the diagonal lines. It is helpful to show the Grid and turn on Snap To Grid in the View menu.

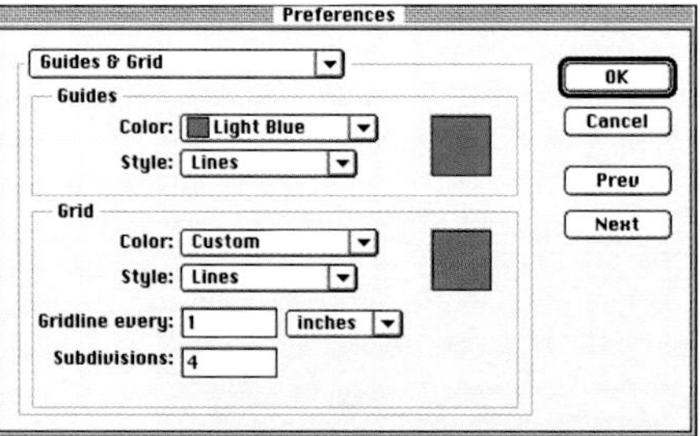


**TIP** **Use File➡Preferences➡Guides & Grid to adjust grid units. My grid is set to show a gridline every inch and a subdivision every 1/4 inch.**

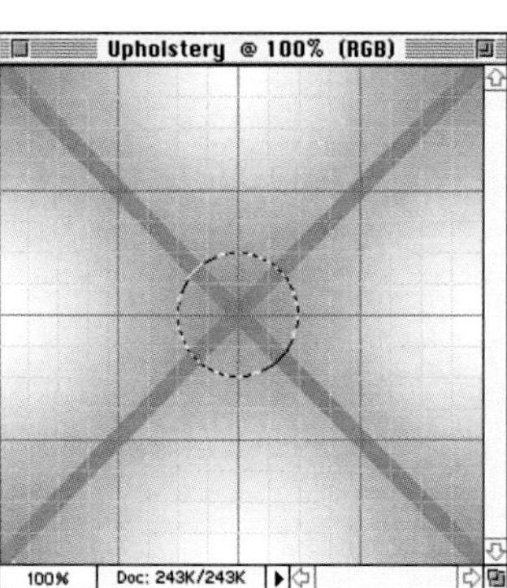


**8** Choose the elliptical Marquee tool. Place your cursor at the center of the image where the lines cross. Hold down the (Option-Shift)[Alt-Shift] keys while you drag outwards. You'll have a perfect circle perfectly centered.

**9** In the Gradient Tool Options palette, change the gradient type from Radial to Linear. Fill the circle with a gradient, using salmon pink as foreground color and white as background color. Drag the gradient from the lower-right to the upper-left of the circle. I dragged a little past the edge of the selection to get more pink and less white. This "button" should remain selected for the next Step.

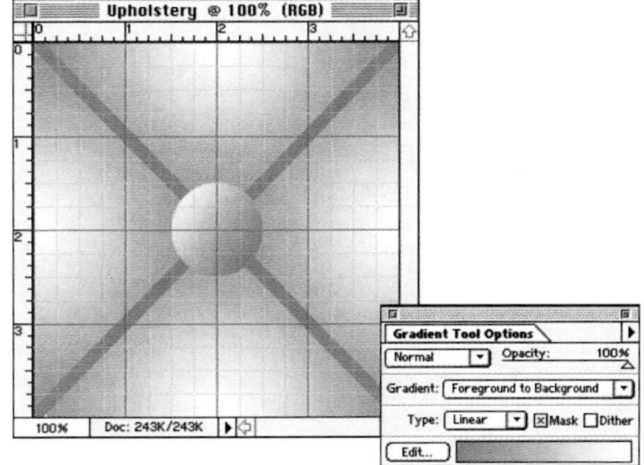


**10** Use the Move tool and the Option key to drag a copy of the button to each corner of the image. You want only a quadrant of the button to show. To make a seamless pattern, it's important to be accurate in placing these corner buttons.

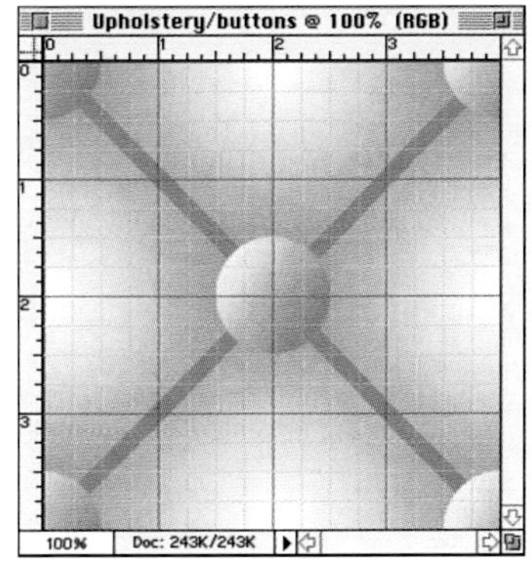


**11** Select Image➥Image Size Turn on Constrain proportions and Resample and change the 4-inch dimension to 2-inches.

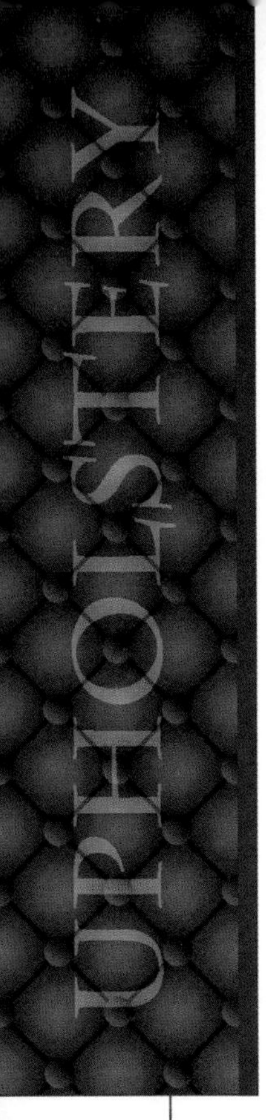

**12** Select all and choose Edit➥Define Pattern. Now you can fill any selected area with your upholstery pattern by using Edit➥Fill.

TIP **Every time you use "Define Pattern" the previous pattern is replaced. Save the tile element from Step 11 as a separate file in case you need it again.**

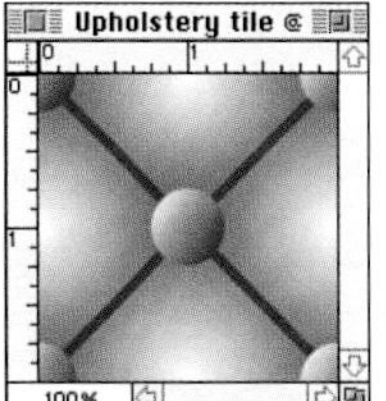


## VARIATIONS

To make a rich velvet look, take the pattern tile in Step 11 and convert to Grayscale mode. Choose Image➥Adjust➥Brightness/Contrast (Brightness: -23, Contrast: +45). Do Step 12 to establish this as your current pattern.

Create a new file. Fill the image with red. I used CMYK values 2, 90, 32, 0. Repeat Step 9. Edit➡Fill using the new pattern element in Multiply mode, to allow the rich red virtual velvet to show through. How Victorian. ■

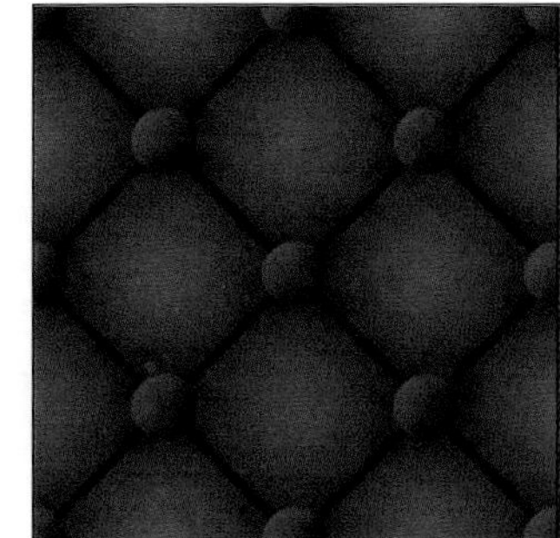

You can create beautiful effects without any raw material but your own ability to draw a straight line. If you are one of those people who "can't draw a straight line," Photoshop can do that for you, too.

**1** Create a new file. Mine is 4×2 inches.

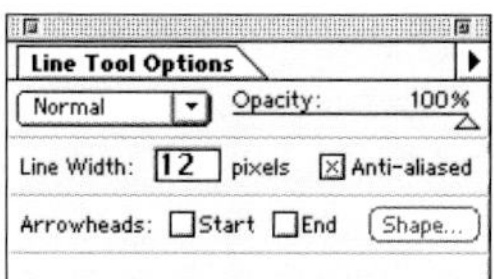


**2** Double-click the Line tool to open the Line Tool Options palette and use these settings.

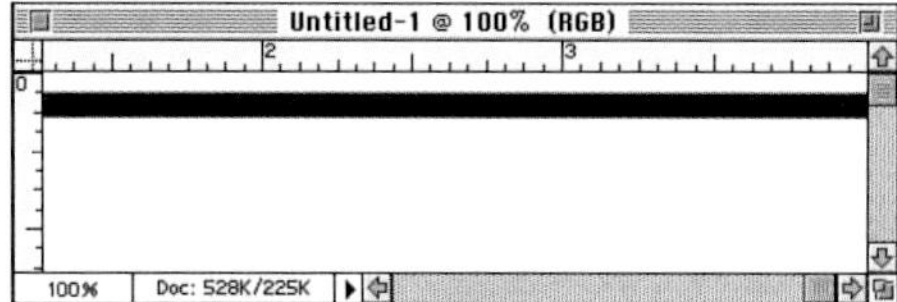


**3** Start near one of the upper corners of the image window and hold down the Shift key while you drag the line horizontally. This creates a perfectly horizontal black line with a thickness of 12 points.

Untitled-1 (RGB, 1:1)

573K/573K

**4** Reduce the Line Width setting by 1 point, and begin drawing it below the first line, leaving enough space for a white stripe. Continue to reduce the thickness of stripes by 1 point until your image looks something like this.



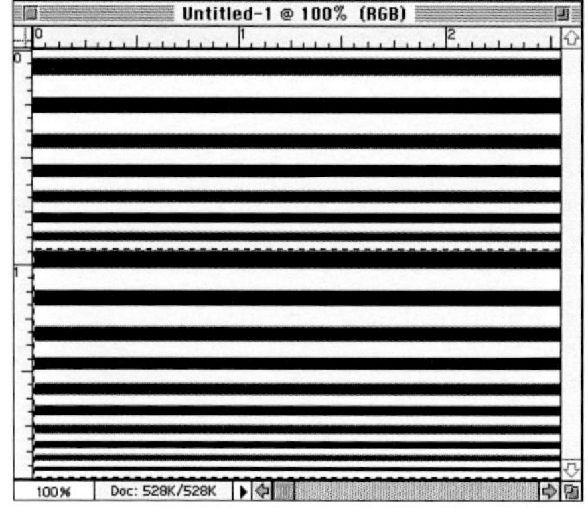


**5** Drag a rectangular Marquee to select the stripes. Press and hold (Option-Command)[Alt-Control] and drag a copy of the stripes to the lower part of the image window. Allow this copy to remain a floating selection.

**6** Apply Layer➡Transform➡Flip Vertical to the floating selection to get a mirror image. You may have to move the floating section into position with a few clicks on the keyboard arrows to get a perfect match. It's OK if a couple of the thinnest lines get "swallowed up" in the process. Then deselect.

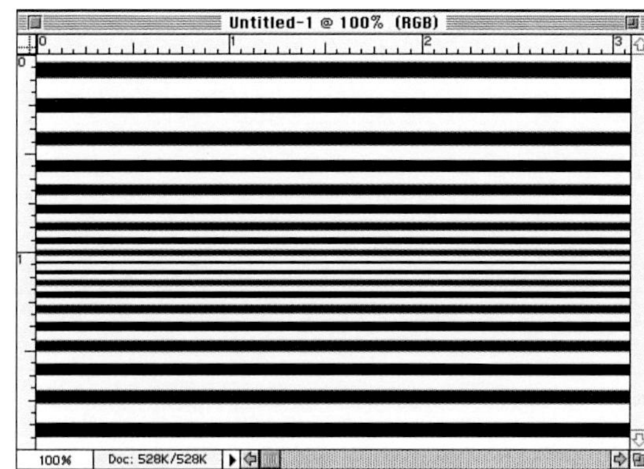


**7** Apply Filter➡Distort➡Twirl (180).

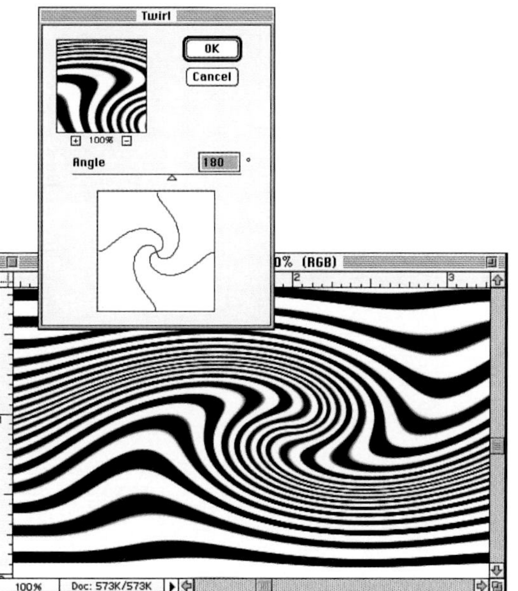


**8** I liked the results but I wanted to have even more twirl, so I applied the same distortion again, using the (Command-F)[Control-F] shortcut. This is the same as applying a 360 degree twirl in Step 7.

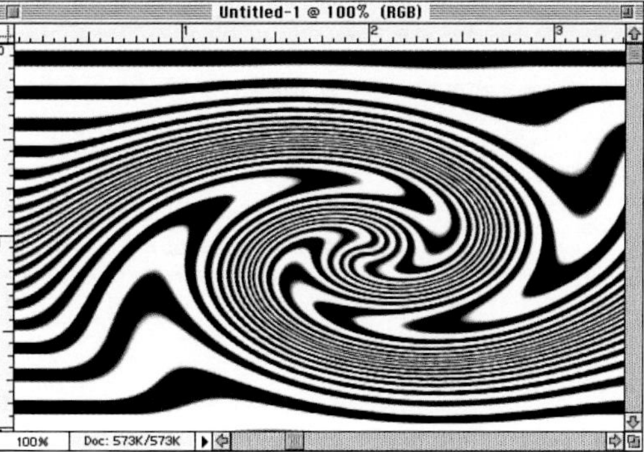

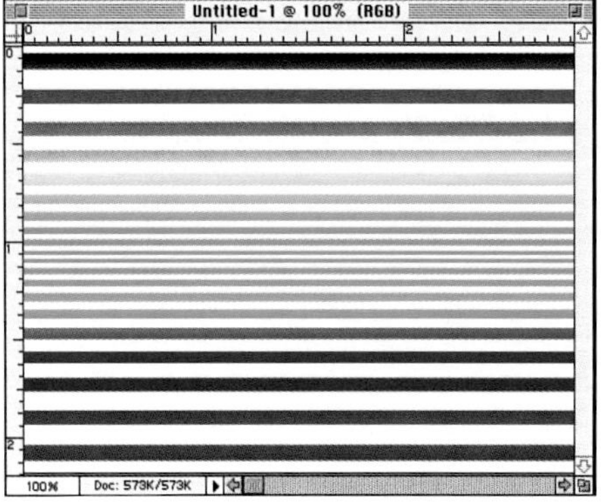


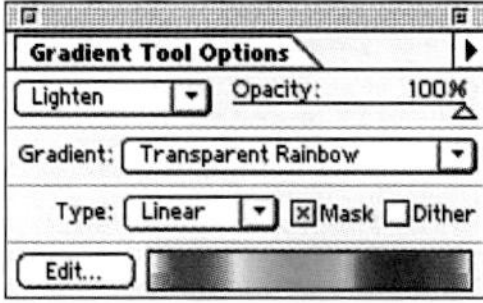

## VARIATIONS

Add color without affecting the white stripes by using Lighten mode with any of the painting tools or fill options.

Double-click the Gradient tool to open the Gradient Tool Options palette and use these settings to prepare for a multi-color fill that colors only the black pixels. Drag the gradient from top to bottom.

Here's a variation that began with the black stripes getting fatter toward the center of the image instead of thinner. Then I inverted the image to make white lines against a black background. The gradient style is radial this time, and the Darken mode was selected to pour color only into the white areas.

Throw caution to the wind and try drawing the lines freehand with the brush tool. I started with the brush in the first column of the second row in the Brushes palette, and for each successive line I selected the next larger size. Then I reversed the process to draw the bottom half of the image with the stripes getting thinner.

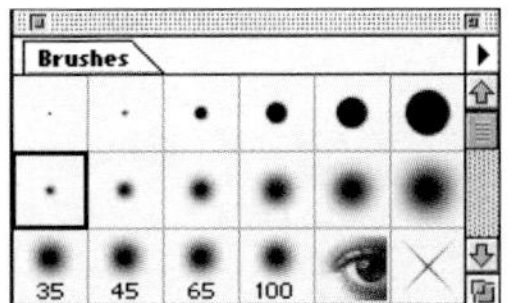


Even with a fairly steady hand, your lines will have a certain "organic" irregularity.

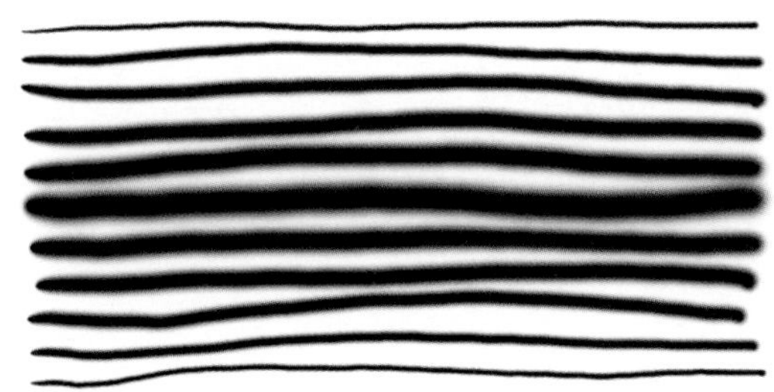

To colorize this variation, I used the violet, green, orange gradient, dragging from top to bottom. But this time I used Difference mode. A wonderful fuzzy glow results from the anti-aliased edges.

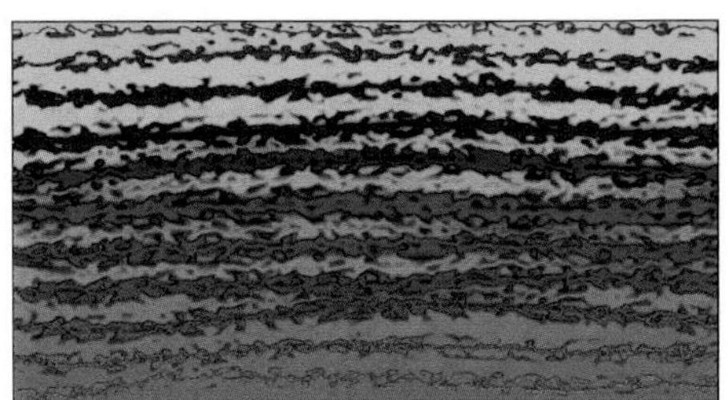

I applied Filter➡Distort➡Ocean Ripple (Size 7, Magnitude 7) to the previous image and got this psychedelic seaweed thing. The possibilities are endless, so try the rest of the distort filters, and more! ■

# Appendix A

## Contributor Listing

### Fonts

**Fonthead Design** **(Mac and PC)**

1872-B Darryl Drive

Tallahassee, FL 32301-6017

ethan@fonthead.com

**Snyder Shareware Fonts** **(Mac and PC)**

1797 Ross Inlet Road

Coos Bay, OR 97420

snyderrp@mail.coos.or.us rps82@aol.com 76307.2431@compuserve.com

**Synstelien Design** **(Mac and PC)**

1338 North 120th Plaza Apt#9

Omaha, NE 68154

Phone: 402-491-3065

http://www.synfonts.com

**Vintage Type** **(Mac and PC)**

5662 Calle Real #146

Goleta CA 93117-2317

### Effects

**AutoFX** **Sample Edge Effects (Mac and PC)**

15 North Main Street Suite 8

Wolfeboro, NH 03894

Phone: 603-569-8800

Fax: 603-569-9702

## Software & Filters

**Adobe Systems, Inc.**

345 Park Avenue

San Jose, CA 95110-6000

Phone: 408-536-6000

Fax: 408-537-6000

**Acrobat Reader™ 3.0 (Mac and PC)**

**Photoshop™ 3.0.5 Tryout (Mac and PC)**

**After Effects™ 3.0 Tryout (Mac only)**

**Streamline™ 3.1 Tryout (Mac and PC)**

**Dimensions™ 2.0 Tryout (Mac only)**

**Illustrator® 6.0 Tryout (Mac only)**

**Alien Skin Software**

1100 Wake Forest Rd. Suite 101

Raleigh, NC 27604

Phone: 919-832-4124

Fax: 919-832-4065

**Eye Candy 3.0 Demo (Mac and PC)**

**Andromeda Software, Inc.**

699 Hampshire Rd. Suite 109

Thousand Oaks, CA 91361

Phone: 800-547-0055 or 805-379-4109

Fax: 805-379-5253

orders@andromeda.com

**Series 1,2, & 3 Demos (Mac and PC)**

**Chris Cox**

110 Oakland Circle

Madison, AL 35758-8663

http://www.teleport.com/~ccox

**Chris's Filters 3.0 (Mac only)**

**DataStream Imaging Systems, Inc.**

P.O. Box 2148

Lexington, KY 40595-2148

800-889-7781 (Orders Only)

Phone: 606-264-0302

Fax: 606-263-0183

**Wild River SSK Demo (Mac only)**

**Fractal Design Corporation**

P.O. Box 66959

Scotts Valley, CA 95067-6959

Phone: 408-430-4000

`http://www.fractal.com`

**Jawai Interactive, Inc.**

**ScreenCaffeine Demo (Mac and PC)**

401 East Fourth Street Suite 443

Austin, TX 78701-3745

Phone: 800-600-6706 or 512-469-0502

Fax: 512-469-7850

`info@jawai.com`

**MetaTools, Inc.**

**KPT 3.0 Demo (Mac and PC)**

6303 Carpinteria Ave.

Carpinteria, CA 93013

805-566-6200

`metasales@aol.com`

**Neil Schulman**

**Frosty Filter (Mac only)**

**Specular, International**

**Infini-D™ Demo (Mac and PC)**

**Collage 2.0 Demo (Mac only)**

**LogoMotion Demo (Mac only)**

**TextureScape™ Demo (Mac only)**

7 Pomeroy Lane

Amherst, MA 01002

Phone: 800-433-SPEC

Fax: 413-253-0540

**Xaos Tools, Inc**

**Paint Alchemy 2™ Demo (Mac only)**

**Terrazo 2™ Demo (Mac only)**

**TypeCaster™ Demo (Mac only)**

55 Hawthorn Suite 1000

SanFrancisco, CA 94105

Phone: 1-800-BUY-XAOS

## Stock Images

### Digital Stock

400 S. Sierra Ave., Suite 100

Solana Beach, CA 92075

Phone: 619-794-4040 or 800-545-4514

Fax: 619-794-4041

### Image Club Graphics

729 24th Ave. SE

Calgary, AB, Canada

T2G 5K8

Phone: 403-262-8008 or 800-661-9410

Fax: 403-261-7013

http://www.adobe.com/imageclub

### PhotoDisc/CMCD

2013 Fourth Ave., 4th Floor

Seattle, WA 98121

Phone: 206-441-9355 or 800-528-3472

http://www.photodisc.com

# Appendix B

## What's on the CD-ROM

The CD-ROM that comes with this book is both Macintosh and Windows compatible. Please note that there are several demos and tryouts available for Macintosh users that are not available for Windows users, and vice versa. This means that either the product does not exist for that platform, or a version is being created but was not available at the time of publication.

We suggest that you refer to the READ ME and other information files included in the demo software program's folder. Also, visit the corporate Web sites for updates and more information. (The URLs are noted in Appendix A.) There are often demos of new software available for downloading and tryout.

The CD-ROM is divided into six folders. Macintosh folder names are in parentheses, and Windows folders are in brackets.

## Contents

### (Effects)[EFFECTS]

This is a collection of effects for manipulating images in Photoshop. Featured is a sampler of edge effects from AutoF/X.

### (Filters)

This folder contains lots of filters you can use to manipulate your images. You can do a variety of things with filters, one of the most powerful features of Photoshop. Some of these filters are freeware, some are shareware, and some are commercial demos.

### (Fonts)[FONTS]

Here you will find an excellent selection of shareware fonts to use in various effects.

### (Images)[IMAGES]

Many of the techniques in *Photoshop Effects Magic* begin with stock provided by commercial stock photo companies. You'll find them here, along with the ArtStart folder containing images prepared especially for this book.

### (Presets)[PRESETS]

Here's where you'll find the custom Brushes library and some extra displacement maps.

### (Software)[SOFTWARE]

This folder contains demos of commercial software, including Adobe products, and Fractal Design products.

## Installation

For detailed instructions on how to install and use the resources we've included on the CD-ROM, please consult the READ ME or ABOUT files in the individual software, filter, effects, and imagery folders. General installation information follows:

**Filters**

Filters should be copied into the Plug-Ins folder, located in the same place as your Adobe Photoshop application. Then, restart your computer, relaunch Photoshop, and find the filters in the Filter menu. You can now access and apply these third-party filters the same way you use Photoshop's filters.

**Preset Files**

The Magic Brushes library is a tiny file so you should copy it to your hard drive, into the same folder where your other Photoshop brushes are stored. You can access them with the Load Brushes command within Photoshop.

The dispmaps folder also contains a few small files, and they can be copied to the Displacement Maps folder using the same steps for copying Filters. None of these files is required for working a technique in the book.

**Fonts** (Macintosh)

Fonts should go in the Fonts folder, located in your System Folder. If you would like to try out a specific font, drag it to your closed System Folder. You should see a message stating that the fonts will be moved to the Fonts folder In the case of Type 1 fonts, you might need to drag multiple files to your System Folder.

**Fonts** (Windows)

Fonts should be installed by means of the Fonts Control Panel. Under Windows 95 or Windows NT 4.0 open Start menu➡Settings➡Control Panel➡Fonts. Then select File➡Install New Font… from the File menu and select the font from the CD-ROM that you want to install. The fonts can be found within the Fonts directory on the CD-ROM.



**Stock imagery and textures**

The stock photos and textures located in the Images folder do not need to be copied to your hard drive. For most files, you can double-click them to open them in Photoshop. If they do not, try opening Photoshop first, then select File➡Open. Then choose the file you want to open. If you particularly like a certain image and would like to access it quickly, by all means copy it to your hard drive.

## A Note About Shareware

If you use any shareware items beyond an initial trial period, you are obligated to follow the guidelines set forth by the author; this is usually in the form of a reasonable shareware payment. Your purchase of this book and the accompanying CD-ROM does not release you from this obligation. Refer to the READ ME and other information files that accompany each of the programs for specifics.

# Gallery

## Part I

*page 22*

*page 28*

*page 34*

*page 42*

*page 48*

*page 52*

page 60

page 66

page 70

page 74

page 78

page 82

*page 86*

*page 90*

*page 96*

page 100

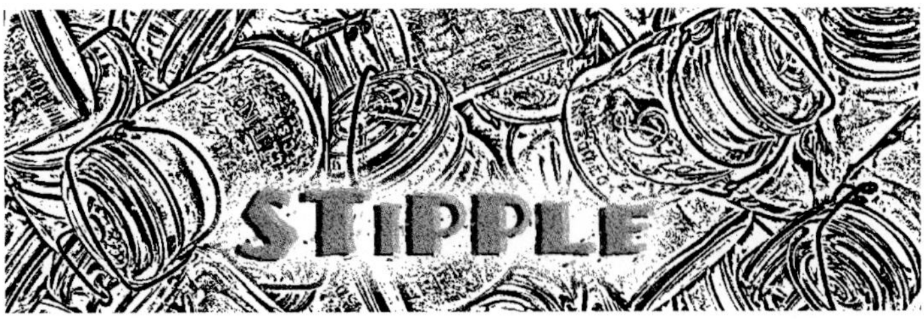


page 104

page 108

*page 112*

*page 116*

## Part II

*page 122*

*page 130*

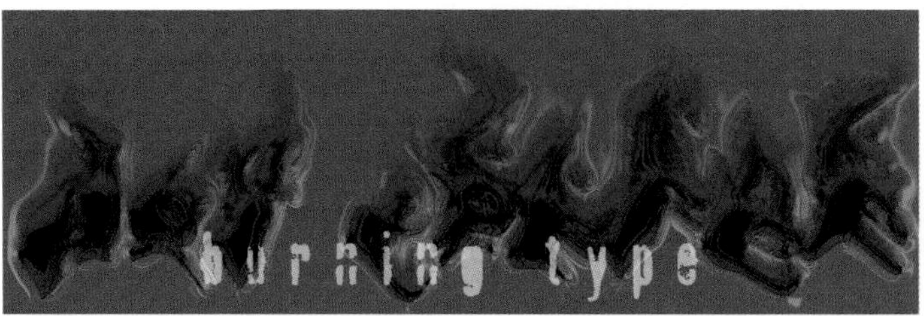


*page 134*

page 138

page 142

page 146

*page 150*

*page 156*

## Part III

*page 160*

*page 166*

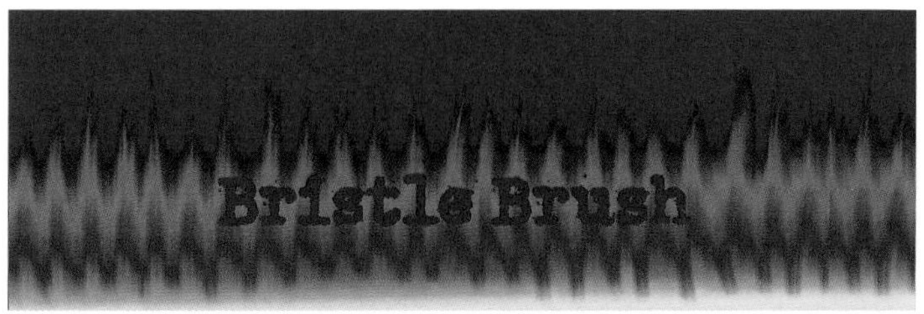


*page 172*

page 176

page 182

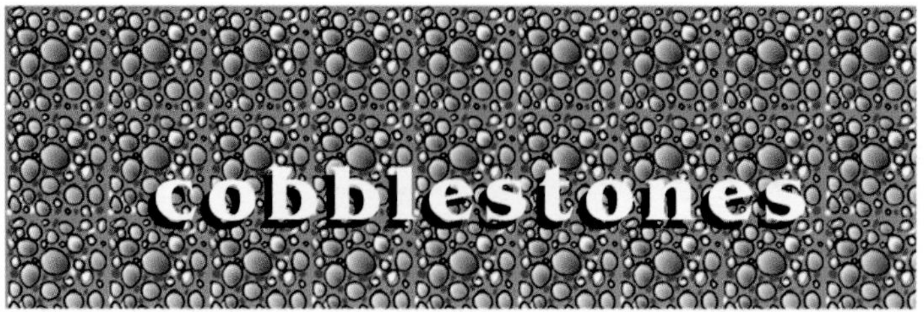


page 186

*page 190*

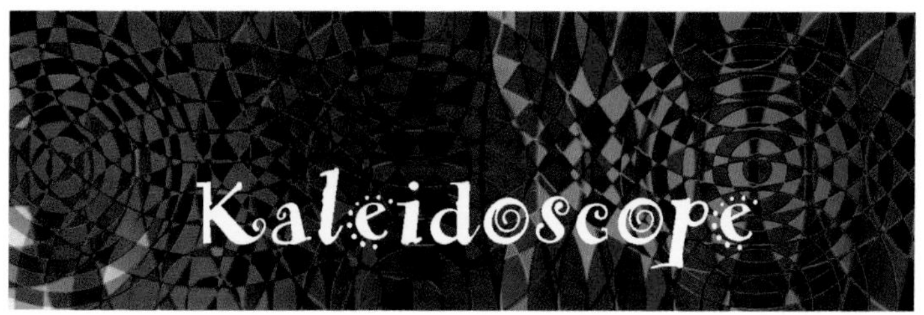


*page 194*

*page 198*

*page 202*

textured Brush

*page 206*

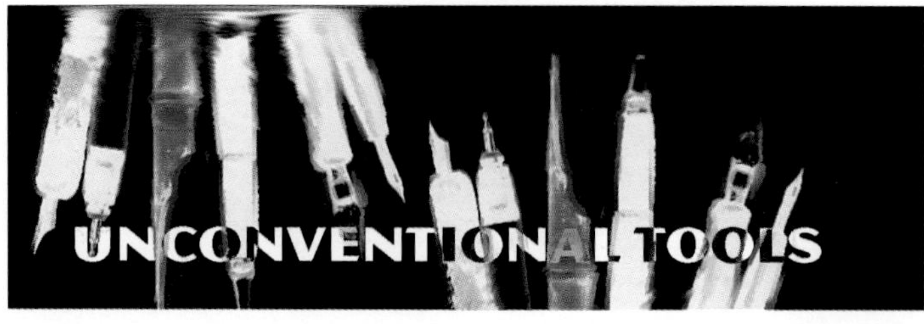


*page 210*

*page 214*

*page 220*

# Other DESIGN/GRAPHICS Titles

**Designing Business**

Provides the design/business communities with a new way of thinking about how the right design can be a strategic business advantage. It is the definitive guide to presenting a business identity through the use of traditional media vehicles and emerging technologies.

- CD-ROM (dual-platform) exhibits interactive prototypes of multimedia brochures, interactive television, and Web sites as developed by Clement Mok designs Inc., one of the most sought after interactive design agencies in the world
- Shows how effective communication is one way to out-think, out-plan, and out-perform the competition

*Clement Mok*
1-56830-282-7 ■ $60.00 USA/$81.95 CDN
264 pp., 8 x 10, Covers PC and Macintosh, New - Expert
*Available Now*

**Adobe Persuasion: Classroom in a Book**
1-56830-316-5 ■ $40.00 USA/$56.95 CDN
*Available November 1996*

**Learning Adobe FrameMaker**
1-56830-290-8 ■ $60.00 USA/$81.95 CDN
*Available Now*

**Adobe Illustrator for Windows: Classroom in a Book**
1-56830-053-0 ■ $44.95 USA/$59.99 CDN
*Available Now*

**Adobe Pagemaker for Windows: Classroom in a Book**
1-56830-184-7 ■ $45.00 USA/$61.95 CDN
*Available Now*

**Adobe Photoshop: Classroom in a Book**
1-56830-317-3 ■ $45.00 USA/$63.95 CDN
*Available October 1996*

**Advanced Adobe PageMaker for Windows 95: Classroom in a Book**
1-56830-262-2 ■ $50.00 USA/$68.95 CDN
*Available Now*

**Advanced Adobe Photoshop for Windows: Classroom in a Book**
1-56830-116-2 ■ $50.00 USA/$68.95 CDN
*Available Now*

**The Amazing PhotoDeluxe Book for Windows**
1-56830-286-X ■ $30.00 USA/$40.95 CDN
*Available Now*

**Branding with Type**
1-56830-248-7 ■ $18.00 USA/$24.95 CDN
*Available Now*

**The Complete Guide to Trapping, Second Edition**
1-56830-098-0 ■ $30.00 USA/$40.95 CDN
*Available Now*

**Design Essentials, Second Edition**
1-56830-093-X ■ $40.00 USA/$54.95 CDN
*Available Now*

**Digital Type Design Guide**
1-56830-190-1 ■ $45.00 USA/$61.95 CDN
*Available Now*

**Fractal Design Painter Creative Techniques**
1-56830-283-5 ■ $40.00 USA/$56.95 CDN
*Available Now*

**Photoshop Type Magic**
1-56830-220-7 ■ $35.00 USA/$47.95 CDN
*Available Now*

**Photoshop Type Magic 2**
1-56830-329-7 ■ $39.99 USA/$56.95 CDN
*Available November 1996*

**Adobe Photoshop Complete**
1-56830-323-8 ■ $45.00 USA/$61.95 CDN
*Available October 1996*

**Production Essentials**
1-56830-124-3 ■ $40.00 USA/$54.95 CDN
*Available Now*

**Stop Stealing Sheep & find out how type works**
0-672-48543-5 ■ $19.95 USA/$26.99 CDN
*Available Now*

Copyright © 1996, Macmillan Computer Publishing USA. A Simon & Schuster Company.
The Publishing Operation of Viacom, Inc.

**Visit your fine local bookstore, or for more information visit us at http//:www.mcp.com**

# REGISTRATION CARD

## Photoshop Effects Magic

Hayden Books

Name ______________________ Title ______________

Company______________________Type of business ______________

Address ______________________

City/State/ZIP ______________________

Have you used these types of books before? ☐ yes ☐ no

If yes, which ones? ______________________

______________________

How many computer books do you purchase each year? ☐ 1–5 ☐ 6 or more

How did you learn about this book? ______________________

- ☐ recommended by a friend
- ☐ recommended by store personnel
- ☐ saw in catalog
- ☐ received ad in mail
- ☐ read book review
- ☐ saw on bookshelf

Where did you purchase this book? ______________________

Which applications do you currently use? ______________________

Which computer magazines do you subscribe to? ______________________

What trade shows do you attend? ______________________

Please number the top three factors which most influenced your decision for this book purchase.

- ☐ cover
- ☐ approach to content
- ☐ logo
- ☐ layout/design
- ☐ price
- ☐ author's reputation
- ☐ publisher's reputation
- ☐ other ______________

Would you like to be placed on our preferred mailing list? ☐ yes ☐ no e-mail address ______________

☐ **I would like to see my name in print!** You may use my name and quote me in future Hayden products and promotions. My daytime phone number is: ______________________

Comments ______________________

______________________

______________________

**Hayden Books** Attn: Product Marketing ◆ 201 West 103rd Street ◆ Indianapolis, Indiana 46290 USA

Fax to **317-581-3576** Visit out Web Page **http://WWW.MCP.com**

Fold Here

NO POSTAGE
NECESSARY
IF MAILED
IN THE
UNITED STATES

**BUSINESS REPLY MAIL**

**FIRST-CLASS MAIL PERMIT NO. 9918 INDIANAPOLIS IN**

**POSTAGE WILL BE PAID BY THE ADDRESSEE**

**HAYDEN BOOKS**
**Attn: Product Marketing**
**201 W 103RD ST**
**INDIANAPOLIS IN 46290-9058**

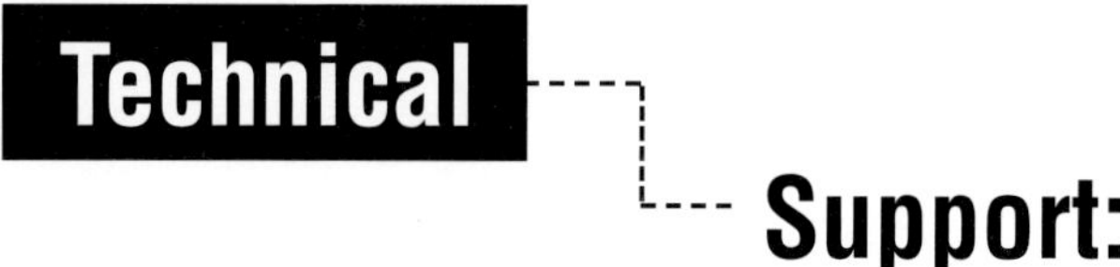


If you need assistance with the information provided by Macmillan Computer Publishing, please access the information available on our web site at **http://www.mcp.com/feedback.** Our most Frequently Asked Questions are answered there. If you do not find the answers to your questions on our web site, you may contact Macmillan User Services at **(317) 581-3833** or email us at **support@mcp.com**.